DIRECTORY OF AMERICAN SCHOLARS

DIRECTORY OF AMERICAN SCHOLARS

TENTH EDITION

VOLUME III

FOREIGN LANGUAGES, LINGUISTICS, & PHILOLOGY

Caryn E. Klebba, Editor

GALE GROUP
THOMSON LEARNING
Detroit • New York • San Diego • San Francisco
Boston • New Haven, Conn. • Waterville, Maine
London • Munich

Caryn E. Klebba, *Editor*

Jason B. Baldwin, *Assistant Editor*

Contributing Editors: Alex Alviar, Claire M. Campana, Eric Hoss, Chris Lopez,
Christine Maurer, Jenai Mynatt, Jaime E. Noce, Kathleen E. Maki Potts, Amanda C. Quick

Lynne Maday, *Contributor*

Erin E. Braun, *Managing Editor*

Ralph Wiazowski, *Programmer/Analyst*
Venus Little, *Manager, Database Applications, Technical Support Services*

Dorothy Maki, *Manufacturing Manager*
Evi Seoud, *Production Manager*
NeKita McKee, *Buyer*

Data Capture Specialists: Nikkita Bankston, Cynthia A. Jones,
Frances L. Monroe

Mike Logusz, *Graphic Artist*

ISBN: 0-7876-5008-0 (Volume 1)
ISBN: 0-7876-5009-9 (Volume 2)
ISBN: 0-7876-5010-2 (Volume 3)
ISBN: 0-7876-5011-0 (Volume 4)
ISBN: 0-7876-5012-9 (Volume 5)
ISBN: 0-7876-5013-7 (Volume 6)
ISBN: 0-7876-5007-2 (set)
ISSN: 0070-5101

Printed in the United States of America
Published in the United States by Gale Group

CONTENTS

PREFACE

First published in 1942 under the auspices of the American Council of Learned Societies, the *Directory of American Scholars* remains the foremost biographical reference to American humanities scholars. With the tenth edition, the Gale Group has added social science scholars, recognizing the close relationship of the social sciences to the humanities.

The directory is arranged for convenient use in five subject volumes: Volume I: History, Archaeology, and Area Studies; Volume II: English, Speech, and Drama; Volume III: Foreign Languages, Linguistics, and Philology; Volume IV: Philosophy, Religion, and Law; Volume V: Psychology, Sociology, and Education. Each volume of biographical listings contains a geographic index. Volume VI contains an alphabetical index, a discipline index, an institutional index and a cumulative geographic index of scholars listed in the first five volumes.

The tenth edition of the *Directory of American Scholars* profiles more than 30,000 United States and Canadian scholars currently active in teaching, research, and/or publishing. The names of entrants were obtained from a variety of sources, including former entrants, academic deans, or citations in professional journals. In most cases, nominees received a questionnaire to complete, and selection for inclusion was made based on the following criteria:

1. Achievement, by reason of experience and training, of a stature in scholarly work equivalent to that associated with the doctoral degree, coupled with current activity in such work;

or

2. Achievement as evidenced by publication of scholarly works;

or

3. Attainment of a position of substantial responsibility by reason of achievement as outlined in (1) and (2).

Enhancements to the tenth edition include the addition of the fifth subject volume, Volume V: Psychology, Sociology, and Education, and the renaming of Volume I to better reflect the disciplines covered within. An outline of the major disciplines within the social sciences and humanities has been added to each volume to assist in locating scholars associated with disciplines related to, but not named outright in the titles of the individual volumes. Please see page ix for this information. Those individuals involved in multiple fields are listed in all appropriate volumes.

The tenth edition of the *Directory of American Scholars* is produced by fully automated methods. Limitations in the printing method have made it necessary to omit most diacritics.

Individual entries can include: place and year of birth, *primary discipline(s), vital statistics, education, honorary degrees, past and present professional experience, concurrent positions, *membership in international, national and regional societies, honors and awards, *research interest, *publications, postal mailing and electronic mailing addresses. Elements preceded by an asterisk are limited as to the number of items included. If an entrant exceeded these limitations, the editors selected the most recent information. Biographies received in the offices of the Gale Group after the editorial deadline were included in an abbreviated manner whenever possible.

The editors have made every effort to include material as accurately and completely as possible within the confines of format and scope. However, the publishers do not assume and hereby disclaim any liability to any party for any loss or damage caused by errors or omissions in the *Directory of American Scholars*, whether such errors or omissions result from negligence, accident, or any other cause.

Thanks are expressed to those who contributed information and submitted nominations for the new edition. Many societies provided membership lists for the research process and published announcements in their journals or newsletters, and their help is appreciated.

Comments and suggestions regarding any aspect of the tenth edition are invited and should be addressed to The Editors, *Directory of American Scholars*, Gale Group, 27500 Drake Road, Farmington Hills, MI 48333-3535.

MAJOR HUMANITIES & SOCIAL SCIENCE DISCIPLINES

Volume I: History, Archaeology, & Area Studies

Aesthetics
Architecture
Archaeology
Area Studies
Art
Art History
Assyriology
Community Studies
Community Planning
Demography
Geography
History
International Studies
Urban Studies
Western Civilization

Volume II: English, Speech, & Drama

Advertising
Audiology
Bibliography
Cinema
Classical Literature
Communications
Composition (Language Arts)
Creative Writing
Drama
English Literature
Film Studies
Journalism
Library Science
Literary Theory
Literature
Marketing
Mass Communication
Media Studies
Music
Music History
Musicology
Performing Arts
Poetry
Rhetoric
Speech Communication
Speech-Language Pathology
Theater Studies

Volume III: Foreign Languages, Linguistics, & Philology

Classical Languages
Comparative Literature
Foreign Languages
Foreign Literature Studies
Linguistics
Modern Languages
Philology
Romance Languages
Translation

Volume IV: Philosophy, Religion, & Law

Accounting
Business Administration
Corrections
Criminal Justice
Criminology
Economics
Epistemology
Ethics
Evangelism
Forensic Sciences
Government
Homiletics
International Relations
Missiology
Philosophy
Political Science
Public Affairs
Religious Studies
Statistics

Volume V: Psychology, Sociology, & Education

Adult Education
Anthropology
Behavioral Sciences
Child Development
Clinical Psychology
Counseling
Culture Studies
Education
Ethnology
Folklore
Gender Studies
Gerontology
Health Studies
Human Development
Language Education
Psychology
Social Work
Sociology
Women's Studies

ABBREVIATIONS

AAAS American Association for the Advancement of Science
AAUP American Association of University Professors
abnorm abnormal
acad academia, academic, academica, academie, academique, academy
accad accademia
acct account, accountant, accounting
acoust acoustical, accounstic(s)
adj adjunct, adjutant
actg acting
activ activities, activity
addn addition(s), additional
AID Agency for International Development
adjust adjust
admin administration, administrative
adminr administrator(s)
admis admissions
adv advisor(s), advisory
advan advance(d), advancement
advert advertisement, advertising
aerodyn aerodynamic(s)
aeronaut aeronautic(s), aeronautical
aesthet aesthetics
affil affiliate(s), affiliation
agr agricultural, agriculture
agt agent
AFB Air Force Base
AHA American Historical Association
akad akademi, akademia
Ala Alabama
Algem algemeen, algemen
allergol allergological, allergology
allgem allgemein, allgemeine, allgemeinen
Alta Alberta
Am America, Americain, American, Americana, Americano, Amerika, Amerikaansch, Amerikaner, Amerikanisch, Amerikansk
anal analysis, analytic, analytical
analog analogue
anat anatomic, anatomical, anatomy
ann annal(s)
anthrop anthropological, anthropology
anthropom anthropometric, anthropometrical, anthropometry
antiq antiquaire(s), antiquarian, antiquary(ies), antiquities
app appoint, appointed, appointment
appl applied
appln application
approx approximate, approximately
Apr April
apt apartment(s)
arbit arbitration
arch archiv, archiva, archive(s), archivio, archivo
archaeol archaeological, archaeology
archaol archaologie, archaologisch
archeol archeological, archeologie, archeologique, archeology
archit architectural, architecture
Arg Argentina, Argentine
Ariz Arizona
Ark Arkansas
asn association
asoc asociacion
assoc(s) associate(s), associated
asst assistant
Assyriol Assyriology
astrodyn astrodynamics
astron astronomical, astronomy
astronaut astronautical, astronautics
astronr astronomer
attend attendant, attending
atty attorney
audiol audiology
Aug August
auth author(s)
AV audiovisual
ave avenue

b born
BC British Columbia
bd board
behav behavior, behavioral, behaviour, behavioural
Bibl Biblical, Biblique
bibliog bibliografia, bibliographic, bibligraphical, bibliography(ies)
bibliogr bibliographer
bibliot biblioteca, bibliotec, bibliotek, bibliotheca, bibliothek, bibliothequeca
biog biographical, biography
biol biological, biology
bk(s) books
bldg building
blvd boulevard
bol boletim, boletin
boll bollettino
bor borough
bot botanical, botany
br branch
Brit Britain, British
Bro(s) Brother(s)
bull bulletin
bur bureau
bus business
BWI British West Indies

c children
Calif California
Can Canada, Canadian, Canadien, Canadienne
cand candidate
cartog cartografic, cartographical, cartography
cartogra cartographer
Cath Catholic, Catholique
CBS Columbia Broadcasting System
cent central
Cent Am Central America
cert certificat, certificate, certified
chap chapter
chem chermical, chemistry
chg charge
chemn chairman
Cie Compagnie
cient cientifica, cientifico
class classical
clin(s) clinic(s)
Co Companies, Company, County
coauth coauth
co-dir co-director
co-ed co-editor
co-educ co-educational
col(s) colegio, college(s), collegiate
collab collaboration, collaborative, collaborating, collaborator
Colo Colorado
Comdr Commander
com commerce, commercial
commun communication(s)
comn(s) commission(s)
comnr commissioner
comp comparative, comparee
compos composition(s)
comput computer, computing
comt committee
conf conference
cong congress
Conn Connecticut

conserv conservacion,conservation, conservatoire, conservatory
consol consolidated, consolidation
const constitution, constitutional
construct construction
consult consultant, consulting
contemp contemporary
contrib contribute, contribution
contribur contributor
conv convention
coop cooperation, cooperative
coord coordinating, coordination
coordr coordinator
corresp corresponding
Corp Corporation
coun council, counsel, counseling
counr councillor, counselor
criminol criminology
Ct Court
ctr center
cult cultra, cultural, culturale, culture
cur curator
curric curriculum
cybernet cybernetics
CZ Canal Zone
Czeck Czechoslovakia

DC District of Columbia
Dec December
Del Delaware
deleg delegate, delegations
demog demographic, demography
demonstr demonstrator
dent dental, dentistry
dep deputy
dept department
Deut Deutsch, Deutschland
develop development
diag diagnosis, diagnostic
dialectol dialectology
dig digest
dipl diploma, diploma, diplomate, diplome
dir director(s), directory directory
Diss Abstr Dissertation Abstracts
dist district
distrib distributive
distribr distributors
div division, divorced
doc document, documentation
Dom Dominion
Dr Doctor, Drive
Drs Doctroandus

e east
ecol ecological, ecology
econ economic(s), economical, economy
ed edicion, edition, editor, editorial, edizione
educ education, educational
educr educator(s)
Egyptol Egyptology
elec electric, electrical, electricity electrical
elem elementary
emer emeriti, emeritus
encour encouragement
encycl encyclopedia
employ employment
Eng England
environ environment, environmental
EPDA Education Professions Development Act
equip equipment
ERIC Educational Resources Information Center
ESEA Elementary & Secondary Education Act

espec especially
estab established, establishment
estud estudante, estudas, estudianet, estudio(s), estudo(s)
ethnog ethnographical, ethnography
ethnol ethnological, ethnology
Europ European
eval evaluation
evangel evangelical
eve evening
exam examination
examr examiner
except exceptional
exec executive(s)
exeg exegesis(es), exegetic, exegetical, exegetics
exhib exhibition(s)
exp experiment, experimental, experimentation
exped expedition(s)
explor exploration(s)
expos exposition
exten extension

fac faculties, faculty
facil facilities, facility
Feb February
fed federal
fedn federation
fel(s) fellow(s), fellowship(s)
filol filologia, filologico
filos filosofia, filosofico
Fla Florida
FLES Foreign Languages in the Elementary Schools
for foreign
forsch forschung, forschungen
found foundation
Fr Francais(s), French
Ft Fort

Ga Georgia
gen general, generale
geneal genealogical, genealogy
genoot genootschap
geod geodesy, geodetic
geog geografia, geografico, geographer(s), geographic,
geographie, geographical, geography
geogr geographer
geol geologic, geological, geology
geophys geophysical
Ger German, Germanic, Germanisch, Germany
Ges gesellschaft
gov governing, governors
govt government
grad graduate
Gr Brit Great Britain
guid guidance
gym gymnasium

handbk(s) handbooks
Hawaii
Hisp Hispanic, Hispanico, Hispano
hist historie, historia, historial, historic, historica,
historical, historique, historische, history
histol histology, histological
Hoshsch Hoshschule
hon honorable, honorary
hosp(s) hospital(s)
hq headquarters
HumRRO Human Resources Research Office
hwy highway

Ill Illinois

illum illuminating, illumination
illus illustrate, illustration
illusr illustrator
imp imperial
improv improvement
Inc Incorporated
incl include, included, includes, including
Ind Indiana
indust(s) industrial, industry(ies)
infor information
inst institut, instritute(s), institution(s), instituto
instnl institutional, institutionalized
instr instruction, instructor(s)
instruct instructional
int internacional, international, internazionale
intel intelligence
introd introduction
invest investigacion, investiganda, investigation,
investigative
investr investigator
ist istituto
Ital Italia, Italian, Italiana, Italiano, Italica, Italien,
Italienisch, Italienne, Italy

J Journal
Jan January
jour journal, journalism
jr junior
jurisp jurisprudence
juv juvenile(s)

Kans Kansas
Koninki koninklijk
Ky Kentucky

La Louisiana
lab laboratorie, laboratorio, laboratorium, laboratory(ies)
lang language(s)
lect lecture(s)
lectr lecturer
legis legislacion, legislatief, legislation, legislative,
legislativo, legislature, legislazione
lett letter(s), lettera, letteraria, letterature, lettere
lib liberal
libr libary(ies), librerio
librn librarian(s)
lic license, lecencia
ling linguistic(s), linguistica, linguistique
lit liteary, literatur, literatura, literature, littera,
literature
Ltd Limited

m married
mach machine(s), machinery
mag magazine
Man Manitoba
Mar March
Mariol Mariological, Mariology
Mass Massachusetts
mat matematica, matematiche, matematico, matematik
math mathematics, mathematical, mathematics, mathematik,
mathematique(s), mathematisch
Md Maryland
mech mechanical
med medical, medicine
Mediter Mediterranean
mem member, memoirs, memorial
ment mental, mentally

metrop metropolitan
Mex Mexican, Mexicano, Mexico
mfg manufacturing
mfr manufacture, manufacturer
mgr manager(s)
mgt management
Mich Michigan
mid middle
mil military
Minn Minnesota
Miss Mississippi
mitt mitteilung
mkt market, marketing
MLA Modern Language Association of America
Mo Missouri
mod modern,moderna, moderne, moderno
monatsh monatsheft(e)
monatsschr monatsschrift
monogr monograph
Mont Montana
morphol morphologica, morphologie, morphology
mt mount, mountain(s)
munic municipal
mus museum(s)
musicol musicological, musicology

n north
nac nacional
NASA National Aeronautics & Space Administration
nat nationaal, national, nationale, nationalis, naturalized
NATO North Atlantic Treaty Organization
naz nazionale
NB New Brunswick
NC North Carolina
MCTE National Council of Teachers of English
NDak North Dakota
NDEA National Defense Education Act
NEA National Education Association
Nebr Nebraska
Ned Nederland, Nederlandsch
Nev Nevada
Neth Netherlands
Nfld Newfoundland
NH New Hampshire
NJ New Jersey
NMex New Mexico
no number
nonres nonresident
norm normal, normale
Norweg Norwegian
Nov November
NS Nova Scotia
NSW New South Wales
NT Northwest Territories
numis numismatic, numismatico, numismatique
NY New York
NZ New Zealand

occas occasional
occup occupation, occupational
Oct October
Ohio
OEEC Organization for European Economic Cooperation
off office, officer(s), official(s)
Okla Oklahoma
Ont Ontario
oper operation(s), operational, operative
ord ordnance
Ore Oregon
orgn organization, organizational
orient oriental, orientale, orientalist, orientalia
ornithol ornithological, ornithology

Pa Pennsylvania
Pac Pacific
paleontol paleontological, paleontology
PanAm Pan American
pedag pedagogia, pedagogic, pedagogical, pedagogico,
pedagogoie, pedagogik, pedagogique, pedagogy
Pei Prince Edward Island
penol penological, penology
phenomenol phenomenological, phenomenologie, phenomenology
philol philologica, philological, philologie, philologisch, philology
philos philosophia, philosophic, philosophical, philosophie,
philosophique, philosophisch, philosophical, philosohpy,
philosozophia
photog photographic, photography
photogr photographer(s)
phys physical
pkwy parkway
pl place
polit politica, political, politicas, politico, politics,
politek, politike, politique, politsch, politisk
polytech polytechnic
pop population
Pontif Pontifical
Port Portugal, Portuguese
postgrad postgraduate
PR Puerto Rico
pract practice
prehist prehistoric
prep preparation, preparatory
pres president
Presby Presbyterian
preserv preservation
prev prevention, preventive
prin principal(s)
prob problem(s)
probtn probation
proc proceding
prod production
prof professional, professor, professorial
prog program(s), programmed, programming
proj project, projective
prom promotion
prov province, provincial
psychiat psychiatria, psychiatric, psychiatrica, psychiatrie,
psychiatrique, psychiatrisch, psychiatry
psychol psychological
pt point
pub pub, publique
publ publication(s), published, publisher(s), publishing
pvt private

qm quartermaster
quad quaderni
qual qualitative, quality
quart quarterly
Que Quebec

rd road
RD Rural Delivery, Rural Free Delivery
Rural Free Delivery
rec record(s), recording
rech recherche
redevelop redevelopment
ref reference
regist register, registered, registration
registr registrar
rehabil rehabilitation
rel(s) relacion, relation(s), relative, relazione
relig religion, religious
rep representative
repub republic
req requirement(s)
res research, reserve
rev review, revised, revista, revue
rhet rhetoric, rhetorical
RI Rhode Island
Rt Right
Rte Route
Russ Russian
rwy railway

s south
SAfrica South Africa
SAm South America, South American
Sask Saskatchewan
SC South Carolina
Scand Scandinavian
sch(s) school(s)
scholar scholarship
sci science(s), scientia, scientific, scientifico, scientifique,
scienza
SDak South Dakota
SEATO Southeast Asia Treaty Organization
sec secondary
sect section
secy secretary
sem seminaire, seminar, seminario, seminary
sen senator, sneatorial
Sept September
ser serial, series
serv service(s)
soc social, sociedad, sociedade, societa, societas, societate,
societe, societet, society(ies)
soc sci social science(s)
sociol sociological, sociology
Span Spanish
spec special
sq square
sr senior
sr sister
St Saint, Street
sta station
statist statistical, statistics
Ste Sainte, Suite
struct structural, structure(s)
subcomt subcommittee
subj subject
substa substa
super superieur, superior, superiore
suppl supplement, supplementary
supt superintendent
supv supervising, supervision
supvr supervisor
supvry supervisory
surg surgical, surgery
surv survey
Swed Swedish
Switz Switzerland
symp symposium
syst system, systematic

tech technic(s), technica, technical, technicky, techniczny,
techniek, technik, technika, technikum, technique, technisch
technol technologic, technological, technologicke,
technologico, technologiczny, technologie, technologika,

technologique, technologisch, technology
tecnol technologia, technologica, technologico
tel telegraph(s), telephone
temp temporary
Tenn Tennessee
Terr Terrace
teol teologia, teologico
Tex Texas
textbk textbook(s)
theol theological, theologie, theologique, theologisch, theology
theoret theoretic(al)
ther therapy
trans transactions
transp transportation
transl translation, translator(s)
treas treasurer, treasury
trop tropical
TV television
twp township

u und
UAR United Arab Republic
UK United Kingdom
UN United Nations
unemploy unemployment
UNESCO United Nations Educational, Scientific & Cultural Organization
UNICEF United Nations Children's Fund
univ(s) universidad, universite, university(ies)
UNRRA United Nations Relief & Rehabilitation Administration
UNRWA United Nations Relief & Works Agency
USA United States of America
US United States
USPHS United States Public Health Service
USSR Union of Soviet Socialist Republics
Utah

Va Virginia
var various
veg vegetable(s), vegetation
ver vereeniging, verein, vereingt, vereinigung
vet veteran, veterinarian, veterinary
VI Virgin Islands
vis visiting
voc vocational
vocab vocabulary
vol(s) volume(s), voluntary, volunteer(s)
vchmn vice chairman
vpres vice president
Vt Vermont

w west
Wash Washington
wetensch wetenschappelijk, wetenschappen
WHO World Health Organization
WI West Indies
wid widow, widowed, widower
Wis Wisconsin
wiss wissenschaft(en), wissenschaftliche(e)
WVa West Virginia
Wyo Wyoming

yearbk yearbook(s)
YMCA Young Men's Christian Association
YMHA Young Men's Hebrew Association
YWCA Young Women's Christian Association
YWHA Young Women's Hebrew Association

z zeitschrift

Biographies

A

AARON, N. GRACE
PERSONAL Born 11/14/1958, Danville, VA **DISCIPLINE** SPANISH **EDUCATION** Col William and Mary, BA, 79; Univ NCar Chapel Hill, MA, 95; PhD, 99. **CAREER** Vis asst prof, Duke Univ, 00; asst prof, Montreat Col, 00-01. **HONORS AND AWARDS** Dana Drake Diss Fel, 98; Teaching Awd, Univ NCar Chapel Hill, 98. **MEMBERSHIPS** MLA, Foreign Lang Assoc of NCar, N Am Christian Foreign Lang Assoc, SAMLA, Conf on Christianity and Lit. **RESEARCH** Peninsular Spanish Literature - Golden Age, San Juan de la Cruz, Christian Mysticism. **SELECTED PUBLICATIONS** Auth, Thought and Poetic Structure in San Juan de la Cruz's Symbol of Night; rev, of Symposium on Fr Luis de Leon and San Juan de la Cruz, Hispanofila, ed Mary Malcolm Gaylord. **CONTACT ADDRESS** 621 Haw Creek Mews Dr, Asheville, NC 28805-1964. **EMAIL** gaaron@montreat.edu

ABBOTT, B.
PERSONAL Born 05/01/1943, Baltimore, MD, m, 1993 **DISCIPLINE** LINGUISTICS **EDUCATION** Univ Calif-Berkeley, PhD, 76. **CAREER** Prof, Ling & Philos, Mich State Univ, 76-. **MEMBERSHIPS** Ling Soc Am; Am Philos Asn; Soc Philos & Psychol; Am Asn Advancement Sci. **RESEARCH** Semantics; pragmatics; philosophy of language. **SELECTED PUBLICATIONS** Auth, Referentiality, Specificity, Strength, and Individual Concepts, WCCFL 12, 94; auth, Thinking without English, Behavior & Philos 23, 95; auth, Doing without Partitive Constraints, in Partitives: Studies on the Syntax and Semantics of Partitive and Related Constructions, Gronigen-Amsterdam Studies in Semantics, Mouton de Gruyter, 96; auth, A Note on the Nature of Water, Mind 106, 97; auth, Models, Truth, and Semantics, Ling & Philos, 97. **CONTACT ADDRESS** Ling & Lang, Michigan State Univ, A-614 Wells Hall, East Lansing, MI 48824-1027. **EMAIL** abbottb@msu.edu

ABBOTT, CARMETA
DISCIPLINE FRENCH LITERATURE **EDUCATION** Ohio State Univ, BA; MA; PhD. **RESEARCH** Seventeenth century theatre; eighteenth century epistolatory novel; contemporary French civilization; second language pedagogy. **SELECTED PUBLICATIONS** Co-ed, Les Jumeaux martirs 1650. **CONTACT ADDRESS** Dept of French, Univ of Waterloo, 200 University Ave W, Waterloo, ON, Canada N2L 3G1. **EMAIL** ceabbott@watarts.uwaterloo.ca

ABBOUD, PETER FOUAD
PERSONAL Born 06/30/1931, Jaffa, Palestine, w, 1952, 1 child **DISCIPLINE** LINGUISTICS, ARABIC STUDIES **EDUCATION** Univ London, BS, 56; Am Univ Cairo, MA, 60; Univ Tex, Austin, PhD, 64. **CAREER** From asst instr to instr English, Am Univ Cairo, 57-61; asst prof, 64-68, assoc prof ling, 68-, prof Arabic, 84, Univ Tex, Austin; visit fac and sch, Georgetown Univ, 63, Univ of Mich, 65, 69, 70, 77, 78, 91, 94, Columbia Univ 66, Princeton Univ, 67, Univ Chicago, 94; dir, sch Arabic, Middlebury Col, 82-90; chmn, dept Mid Eastern Land and Cult, 94-98. **HONORS AND AWARDS** Am Res Ctr is Egypt fel, 71-72; Fulbright fel 75-76. **MEMBERSHIPS** Ling Soc Am; Am Orient Soc; Am Asn Teachers Arabic; Mid E Studies Asn N Am. **RESEARCH** Classical Arabic; Arabic dialectology; and Arabic language teaching. **SELECTED PUBLICATIONS** Coauth, Beginning Cairo Arabic, Univ Tex, 65; Elementary Modern Standard Arabic, Inter-Univ Comt Near Eastern Lang, 68; auth, The Teaching of Arabic in the United States: The State of the Art, ERIC Clearinghouse for Ling, 68; coauth, Modern Standard Arabic: Intermediate Level, Ctr Near Eastern & N African Studies, Mich, 71; auth, Spoken Arabic, In: Current Trends in Linguistics, Vol VI, Mouton, 71; On Ablaut in Cairo Arabic, Afro-Asiatic Ling, 76; auth, The Verb in Northern Najdi Arabic, Bull Sch Oriental and Afr Stu, 79; auth The Classical Arabic Jussive Forms and Their Reflexes in the Modern Arabic Dialects, Zeit Deutsch Morgenlanisch Gesellschaft, 82; auth, Some Grammatical(Morphological and Syntactic-Semantic) Considerations in Arabic-English Bilingual Dictionaries, The Arabic Dictionary to Non-Arabic Speakers, Arab League Education, Cultural, and Scientific Organization, 83; coauth, Computer Assisted Instruction Program for Vocabulary and Reading Comprehension for Modern Standard Arabic, Intermediate Level, 84; auth, "The Hal Construction and the Main Verb in the Sentence," The Fergusonian Impact, Vol I, Mouton, 86; auth, "Speech and Religious Affiliation in Egypt," Studies in Honor of Edgar C. Polome, Mouton, 88; auth, A Methodology for Teaching Grammar Functionally (in Arabic), Al-Arabiyya, 89; coauth, Come Let's Read with the Arabs, Beginning, Intermediate, Advanced Levels, Come Let's Listen with the Arabs, Beginning, Intermediate, Advanced Levels, and Come Let's Speak Fusha, Beginning, Intermediate, Advanced Levels, Sch of Arabic, Middlebury Col, 90; auth, The Teaching of Arabic in the United States: When and Whither, The Teaching of Arabic as a Foreign Language, Issues and Directions, Al-Arabiyya Monograph Series, No 2, 95. **CONTACT ADDRESS** Dept of Middle Eastern Lang and Cult, Univ of Texas, Austin, WMB 5.120, Austin, TX 78712.

ABDELRAHIM-SOBOLEVA, VALENTINA
DISCIPLINE RUSSIAN LINGUISTICS **EDUCATION** Moscow State Univ, MA, 67; Bryn Mawr Col, PhD, 98. **CAREER** Instr, Univ Khartoum, Sudan, 72-92; teach asst, 93-95, 97, instr, summer Russian Lang Inst, 93-98, Bryn Mawr Col; instr, St Joseph's Univ, 95-97; lectr, Lincoln Univ, 98; ASST PROF, LANG & LING, LINCOLN UNIV, 98-. **CONTACT ADDRESS** Dept of Langs and Linguistics, Lincoln Univ, Pennsylvania, 1570 Old Baltimore Pike, PO Box 179, Lincoln University, PA 19352. **EMAIL** vsoboleva@lu.lincoln.edu

ABEL, RICHARD OWEN
PERSONAL Born 08/20/1941, Canton, OH, m, 1970 **DISCIPLINE** CINEMA STUDIES, COMPARATIVE LITERATURE **EDUCATION** Utah State Univ, BA, 63; Univ Southern Calif, MA, 65, PhD(comp lit), 70. **CAREER** Teaching asst comp lit, Univ Southern Calif, 65, teaching asst English, 65-66 & 66-67; instr English, 67-68; from instr to assoc prof, 68-80, prof English, Drake Univ, 80-, dir Cult Studies Prog, 90-93, dir Ctr for the Humanities, 96-00. **HONORS AND AWARDS** Theatre Library Asn Awd for best book on recorded performance, 85, 95; Jay Leyda Prize in Cinema Studies, 89; SCS Katherine Singer Kovacs Awd for best essay in cinema studies, 95-97, 98; NEH Fel for Col Teachers, 83-84; ACLS Res Fel, 86; Nat Humanities Ctr Fel, 88-89; John Simon Guggenheim Memorial Fel, 93-94; Ellis and Nell Levitt Dist Prof of Engl; Special Commendation, 99; KRASZNA-KAUS Moving Image Book Awd. **MEMBERSHIPS** MLA, Soc Cinema Studies, Demtor. **RESEARCH** Early Cinema, French Silent Cinema, American Silent Cinema. **SELECTED PUBLICATIONS** Auth, French Cinema: The First Wave, 1915-1929, Princeton, 84; French Film Theory and Criticism, 1907-1939: A History/Anthology, 2 vols, Princeton, 88; The Cin Goes to Town: French Cinema, 1896-1914, Calif, 94; ed, "Silent Film," in Depth of Field, series, Rutgers, 94; auth, The Red Rooster Scare Making Cinema American, 1900-1910, Calif, 99. **CONTACT ADDRESS** Dept of English, Drake Univ, 2507 University Ave, Des Moines, IA 50311-4505. **EMAIL** richard.abel@drake.edu

ABRAMSON, ARTHUR SEYMOUR
PERSONAL Born 01/26/1925, Jersey City, NJ, m, 1952, 2 children **DISCIPLINE** LINGUISTICS **EDUCATION** Yeshiva Univ, AB, 49; Columbia Univ, AM, 50, PhD, 60. **CAREER** Teacher French & English pub schs, Jersey City, NJ, 50-53; lectr English to foreigners, Columbia Univ, 55-59; men res staff exp phonetics, Haskins Labs, New York, 59-63; assoc prof speech, Queens Col, NY, 63-64, prof, 65-67; head dept ling, 67-74, Prof Ling, Univ Conn, 67-, Fulbright teaching grant, Thailand, 53-55; lectr, NY Univ, 58-59; assoc phonetics, Columbia Univ, 60-63; lectr speech, Hunter Col, 61-63; mem Permanent Coun for Orgn Int Cong Phonetic Sci, 71-; Am Coun Learned Soc & Ford Found fel, Southeast Asia Fel Prog, 73-74; co-ed Lang & Speech, 74-78, ed, 79- **MEMBERSHIPS** AAAS; Ling Soc Am (secy-treas, 74-78, vpres, 82); MLA; fel Acoustical Soc Am; Int Phonetic Asn. **RESEARCH** Experimental Phonetics; Southeast Asian Language. **SELECTED PUBLICATIONS** Auth, The Vowels and Tones of Standard Thai: Acoustical Measurements and Experiments, Bloomington: Indiana U. Res. Center in Anthropology, Folklore, and Linguistics, Pub. 20, 62; auth, A cross-language study of voicing in initial stops: Acoustical measurements, Word 20, (64): 384-422; auth, Laryngeal timing in consonant distinctions, Phonetica 37, (77)J: 259-303; auth, The perception of word-initial consonant length: Pattani Malay, Journal of the International Phonetic Asn 16, (86): 8-16; auth, Tone splits and voicing shifts in Thai: Phonetic plausibility, In Pan Asiatic Linguistics: Proceedings of the Third International Symposium on Language and Linguistics, Vol. 1, Bangkok: Chulalongkorn Univ, (92): 1-16. **CONTACT ADDRESS** Dept of Ling, Univ of Connecticut, Storrs, Storrs, CT 06268. **EMAIL** arthur.abramson@uconn.edu

ABU-ABSI, SAMIR
PERSONAL Born 04/04/1938, Hasbaya, Lebanon, m, 1968, 5 children **DISCIPLINE** LINGUISTICS **EDUCATION** Am Univ Beirut, BA, 63; Ind Univ, Bloomington, MA, 66, PhD(ling), 72. **CAREER** Instr ling, Univ Toledo, 68-72; asst prof, Am Univ, Beirut, 72-73; asst prof, 73-76, from assoc prof to prof Ling, Univ Toledo, 76-87. **MEMBERSHIPS** Ling Soc Am; Am Asn Teachers Arabic. **RESEARCH** Arabic linguistics; English linguistics; applied linguistics. **SELECTED PUBLICATIONS** Coauth, Spoken Chad Arabic, Intensive Lang Training Ctr, Ind Univ, 68; auth, Stubborn structures in Arabic-English, In: Al-Kulliyah, Am Univ Beirut, 73; A method for surveying second language teachers, Ohio Univ working papers, Applied Ling, No 6, 79; Language-in-Education in the Arab Middle East, Ann Rev Applied Ling II, 82; The Western Stereotype of Arab Women, Al-Raida, 94; Stereotypical Images of Arab Women, Phi Beta Delta International Review, 96; Innovative Second Language Education in the Middle East and North Africa, vol 4, Second Language Education, Encyclopedia of Language and Education, Kluwer Publishers, the Netherlands, 97. **CONTACT ADDRESS** English Dept, Univ of Toledo, 2801 W Bancroft St, Toledo, OH 43606-3390. **EMAIL** samir.abu-absi@utoledo.edu

ACHBERGER, KAREN RIPP
PERSONAL Born 04/10/1943, Madison, WI, w, 1975, 2 children **DISCIPLINE** GERMAN LANGUGAGE AND LITERATURE, FILM STUDIES **EDUCATION** Univ Wis-Madison, BS, 67, MA, 68, PhD(Ger lit), 75. **CAREER** Asst prof, Univ Ore, 74-79; Asst Prof to Assoc Prof to Prof of Ger, St Olaf Col, 79-. **HONORS AND AWARDS** NEH, 94-95; ACLS, 84-85; Sr. Fulbright Fel, 81. **MEMBERSHIPS** MLA; Am Asn Teachers Ger; German Studies Assn; Women in Ger; Int Brecht Soc. **RESEARCH** Contemporary German women writers; Ingeborg Bachmann; postwar German Literature 20th Century; Austrian Literature. **SELECTED PUBLICATIONS** Auth, A multi-disciplinary synthesis in teaching German culture and civilization, Pac Northwest Coun Foreign Lang Proc, 76; coauth, Ir-

mtraud Morgner's Gospel of Valeska, New Ger Critique, 78; auth, Ingeborg Bachmann's Homberg Libretto: Kleist between humanism and existentialism, Mod Austrian Lit, 79; GDR women's fiction of the 1970's: The emergence of feminism within socialism, E Cent Europe, 79; Literatur als Libretto: Das deutsche Opernbuch seit 1945 Heidelberg, Winter 80; Bachmann und die Bibel: Gomorrah als weibliche Schopfungsgeschichte, Derdunkle Schatten, Locker, Vienna, 82; co-transl (with Friedrich Achberger), Morgner, White Easter, The Duel Shoes & The Rope, Wolter, I have married again, In: German Feminism, State Univ NY Press, 84; Understanding Ingeborg Bachmann. Understanding Modern European and Latin American Literature, James Hardin, ed, Columbia: U South Carolina Press, 95; Boesartig liebevoll' den Menschen zugetan, Humor in Ingeborg Bachmanns Todesarten-Projekt, Essays zu Ingeborg Bachmanns Todesarten-Projekt, Monika Albrecht and Dirk Gottsche, eds, Munster: Konigshausen & Neumann, 98. **CONTACT ADDRESS** 1520 St Olaf Ave, Northfield, MN 55057-1099. **EMAIL** krach@stolaf.edu

ACKER, ROBERT
PERSONAL Born St. Paul, MN **DISCIPLINE** GERMAN LITERATURE & LINGUISTICS **EDUCATION** St John's Univ, Minn, BA, 68; Univ Tex, Austin, PhD, 74. **CAREER** Asst prof Ger, Univ Mo-Columbia, 74-77 & Wash State Univ, 77-78; asst prof Ger, SDak State Univ, 78-79; asst prof, 79-81, Assoc Prof German, Univ Mont, 82- ; Ed, Selecta: J Pac NW Coun for Lang, 82- . **MEMBERSHIPS** MLA; Am Asn Teachers Ger; Midwest Mod Lang Asn; Westen Asn Ger Studies; Pac Northwest Coun Foreign Lang. **RESEARCH** Twentieth century German literature; German film. **SELECTED PUBLICATIONS CONTACT ADDRESS** Dept of Foreign Lang, Univ of Montana, Missoula, MT 59812-0001.

ACKERMANN, PAUL KURT
PERSONAL Born 09/05/1919, Bremen, Germany, m, 1945, 2 children **DISCIPLINE** GERMAN **EDUCATION** Colgate Univ, AB, 45; Columbia Univ, MA, 47; Harvard Univ, PhD, 54. **CAREER** Instr, Amherst Col, 46-48; asst prof to prof emeritus, Boston Univ, 53-. **MEMBERSHIPS** MLA, Thomas Mann Gesellschaft, Goethe Soc of New Eng. **RESEARCH** Thomas Mann, Bert Brecht, goethe, Gottfried Benn, Franz Kafka. **SELECTED PUBLICATIONS** Auth, Rene Schickele, 53; auth, Thomas Mann: Felix Krull, 58; auth, Friedrich Duerrenmatt: Der Besuch der alten Dame, 60; auth, Max Frishe: Biederman und die Brandstifter, 63; auth, Max Frisch: Home Faber, 63; auth, Bertolt Brecht: Die Dreigroschenoper, 82. **CONTACT ADDRESS** 41 Gibson St, Cambridge, MA 02138-4719. **EMAIL** pkackermann@aol.com

ADAMS, GEORGE ROY
PERSONAL Born 11/23/1928, Lime Springs, IA, m, 1959, 3 children **DISCIPLINE** ENGLISH, LINGUISTICS **EDUCATION** Univ Okla, BA, 52, PhD, 61. **CAREER** Instr English, Boston Univ, 61-63; asst prof, Harpur Col, State Univ NY Binghamton, 63-66; assoc prof, 66-76, prof English, Univ Wis, Whitewater, 76-. **MEMBERSHIPS** MLA; Mediaeval Acad Am. **RESEARCH** Medieval literary esthetic; medieval drama; history of the English language. **SELECTED PUBLICATIONS** Auth, Paul Goodman, Twayne; Chaucer's Shipman's Tale, Explicator, 66; coauth, Good and Bad Fridays and May 3 in Chaucer, English Lang Notes, 66; Chauntecleer's Paradise Lost and Regained, Mediaeval Studies, 67. **CONTACT ADDRESS** Dept of English, Univ of Wisconsin, Whitewater, 800 W Main, Whitewater, WI 53190-1790.

ADAMSON, HUGH DOUGLAS
PERSONAL Born 09/30/1944, Salt Lake City, UT, m, 1970, 2 children **DISCIPLINE** LINGUISTICS **EDUCATION** Univ Calif, Berkeley, AB, 67; San Jose State Univ, MA, 72; Georgetown Univ, PhD, 80. **CAREER** Assoc prof, Univ Ariz, 88-; Dir, Interdisciplinary PhD Prog in Second Lang Acquisition and Teaching, 97-. **HONORS AND AWARDS** Mellon Midcareer Fel, Linguistics Dept Univ Penn, 88. **MEMBERSHIPS** Linguistics Soc of Am, Am Asn of Applied Linguistics. **RESEARCH** Second language acquisition; qualitative sociolinguistics; content-based language instruction. **SELECTED PUBLICATIONS** Auth, Variation Theory and Second Language Acquisition, Georgetown Univ Press (88); auth, Academic Competence: Theory and Classroom Practice, Longman (93). **CONTACT ADDRESS** Dept English, Univ of Arizona, PO Box 210067, Tuscon, AZ 85721-0067.

ADKIN, NEIL
PERSONAL Born 07/04/1954, Hull, England, s **DISCIPLINE** CLASSICS **EDUCATION** Univ Col Oxford, BA, 76 (1st class), MA, 80; Univ Glasgow, PhD, 82. **CAREER** Thesaurus Linguae Latinae fel, Bayerische Akademie der Wissenschaften, 76-79; temporary lect in Medieval Latin, Univ Liverpool, 81-82; Univ Res fel, Univ Liverpool, 83-86; asst through assoc prof of Classics, Univ NE-Lincoln, 86-. **HONORS AND AWARDS** Hertford, De Paravicini, Ireland and Craven Scholarships, 73; Col of Arts and Sciences Awd for Outstanding Teaching, 90. **MEMBERSHIPS** APA. **SELECTED PUBLICATIONS** Author of 142 articles on Patristic, Medieval, and Renaissance Latin, principally Jerome, Walter of Chatillon, and Erasmus. **CONTACT ADDRESS** Dept Classics, Univ of Nebraska, Lincoln, 237 Andrews Hall, PO Box 880337, Lincoln, NE 68588-0337. **EMAIL** nadkin1@unl.edu

ADKINS, ARTHUR WILLIAM HOPE
PERSONAL Born 10/17/1929, Leicester, England, m, 1961, 2 children **DISCIPLINE** CLASSICS; PHILOSOPHY **EDUCATION** Oxford Univ, BA, 52, MA, 55, DPhil, 57. **CAREER** Asst lectr Latin humanities, Univ Glasgow, 54-56; lectr Greek, Bedford Col, Univ London, 56-61; fel class lang & lit, Exeter Col, Oxford, 61-65; prof classics, Univ Reading, 66-74; chmn, Dept Classics, 75-80, prof Greek, philos & early Christian lit, Univ Chicago, 74- ; vis sr fel classics Soc Humanities, Cornell Univ, 69-70. **MEMBERSHIPS** Soc Promotion Hellenic Studies; Class Asn Gt Brit; Am Philol Asn; Am Philos Asn; Asn Ancient Historians. **RESEARCH** Greek philosophy; Greek thought and religion; Greek literature. **SELECTED PUBLICATIONS** Auth, Merit and Responsibility: A Study in Greek Values, Clarendon, Oxford, 60; contribr, Greek religion, In: Historia Religionum Handbook for the History of Religions, Leiden, Brill, 69; auth, From the Many to the One: A Study of Personality and Views of Human Nature in the Context of Ancient Greek Society, Values and Beliefs, Constable, London & Cornell Univ, 70; Moral Values and Political Behavior in Ancient Greece, Chatto & Windus, London & Clark Irwin, Toronto, 72; Paralysis and Akrasia in Eth Nic 1102b16 ff, Am J Philos, Vol 97, 62-64; Polupragmosune and minding one's own business: A study in Greek social and political values, CP, 76; Callinus 1 and Tyrtaeus 10 as poetry, HSCP, 77; Lucretius I, 137 ff and the problems of writing Versus Latini, Phoenix, 77; auth, Poetic Craft in the Early Greek Elegists, Univ Chicago, 85; Ethics with Aristotle, Classical Philol, Vol 0088, 93; rev, Hybris- A Study in the Values of Honor and Shame in Ancient Greece, Class Jour, Vol 0090, 95; rev, Aidos - The Psychology and Ethics of Honor and Shame in Ancient Greek Literature, Class Jour, Vol 0090, 95. **CONTACT ADDRESS** Dept of Classics, Univ of Chicago, 1050 E 59th St, Chicago, IL 60637. **EMAIL** eadkins@midway.chicago.edu

ADLER, SARA MARIA
PERSONAL Born 09/14/1946, Malden, MA, m, 1973, 1 child **DISCIPLINE** ITALIAN LANGUAGE & LITERATURE **EDUCATION** Smith Col, BA, 68; Harvard Univ, MA, 69, PhD(Ital lit), 76. **CAREER** Instr, 74-75, Asst Prof Italian, Scripps Col, 75- . **MEMBERSHIPS** Am Asn Teachers Ital; MLA; Dante Soc; Soc Ital Hist Studies. **RESEARCH** Modern Italian literature. **SELECTED PUBLICATIONS CONTACT ADDRESS** Scripps Col, 1030 Columbia Ave, Claremont, CA 91711-3948.

AFFRON, CHARLES M.
PERSONAL Born 10/16/1935, Brooklyn, NY, m, 1961, 2 children **DISCIPLINE** FRENCH **EDUCATION** Brandeis Univ, BA, 57; Yale Univ, PhD(Balzac), 63. **CAREER** From instr to asst prof French & Ital, Brandeis Univ, 62-65; from asst prof to assoc prof, 65-73, actg chmn dept, 68-69, prof French, NY Univ, 73-. **HONORS AND AWARDS** Fulbright; National Endowment for the Humanitie; French Government, American Council of Learned Societies. **MEMBERSHIPS** MLA. **RESEARCH** U.S. and European cinema, French Romanticism; Narrative and readership, cinema and stylistics, studio system; cultural history. **SELECTED PUBLICATIONS** Auth, Patterns of Failure in La comedie humaine, Yale Univ, 66; A Stage for Poets: Studies in the Theatre of Hugo and Musset, Princeton Univ, 71; Star Acting: Gish, Garbo, Davis, Dutton, 77; auth, "Cinema and Sentiment," Univ of Chicago Press, (82); auth, "Divine Garbo," Ramsay, (85); auth, Fellini's "8 1/2," Rutgers Univ Press, (87); Sets in Motion: Art Direction & Film Narrative, with Minella Jona Affron, (95). **CONTACT ADDRESS** Dept of French, New York Univ, 19 University Pl, New York, NY 10003-4556. **EMAIL** ca1@nyu.edu

AGES, ARNOLD
DISCIPLINE FRENCH LITERATURE **EDUCATION** Univ Carleton, BA; Ohio State Univ, MA; PhD. **RESEARCH** Enlightenment literature. **SELECTED PUBLICATIONS** Auth, The Image of Jews and Judaism in The Prelude to the French Enlightenment; pub(s) in Judeo-French area. **CONTACT ADDRESS** Dept of French, Univ of Waterloo, 200 University Ave W, Waterloo, ON, Canada N2L 3G1. **EMAIL** sages@interlog.com

AGUIRRE, ANGELA M.
PERSONAL Born, Cuba, m, 1987 **DISCIPLINE** SPANISH-SPANISH AMERICAN ROMANTICISM **EDUCATION** CUNY, PhD, 80. **CAREER** Prof. **HONORS AND AWARDS** Certified transl, Amer Transl Asn, ATA. **SELECTED PUBLICATIONS** Auth, Vida y cretica literaria de Enrique Pineyro, New York: Senda Nueva de Ediciones, 81; Latino Caribbean Literature, Multicultural Literature Collection, NJ: Globe Fearon, 94. **CONTACT ADDRESS** Dept of Language and Cultures, William Paterson Col of New Jersey, 300 Pompton Rd., Wayne, NJ 07470. **EMAIL** aguirrea@wpunj.edu

AHEARN, EDWARD J.
PERSONAL Born 10/31/1937, New York, NY, m, 1979, 2 children **DISCIPLINE** COMPARATIVE LITERATURE & FRENCH STUDIES **EDUCATION** Manhattan Col, BA, 59; Yale Univ, PhD, 63. **CAREER** Asst prof French, 63-68, assoc prof, 68-80, Prof, 80-95, Univ Prof, Comp Lit & Fr Studies, Brown Univ, 95-; Fel, Ctr Advan Studies, Univ Ill. **HONORS AND AWARDS** Harbison Awd for Gifted Teaching, Danforth Found, 70. **MEMBERSHIPS** MLA. **RESEARCH** Comparative literature of the 19th & 20th century. **SELECTED PUBLICATIONS** Auth, Rimbaud: Visions of Habitations, Univ Calif, 83; Marx & Modern Fiction, Yale, 91; Visionary Fictions: Apocalyptic Writing from Blake to the Modern Age, Yale, 96. **CONTACT ADDRESS** Dept of Comparative Lit, Brown Univ, Box E, Providence, RI 02912-9127. **EMAIL** Edward_Ahearn@brown.edu

AHRENSDORF, PETER J.
DISCIPLINE CLASSICS **EDUCATION** Yale Univ, BA; Univ Chicago, PhD. **CAREER** Assoc prof pol sci and hum, Davidson Col, 89-. **RESEARCH** Plato and Thucydides; Thomas Pangle; theories of international rel(s) in the hist of polit philos. **SELECTED PUBLICATIONS** Auth, The Death of Socrates and the Life of Philosophy: An Interpretation of Plato's Phaedo, SUNY, 95. **CONTACT ADDRESS** Davidson Col, 102 N Main St, PO Box 1719, Davidson, NC 28036. **EMAIL** peahrensdorf@davidson.edu

AHUMADA, ALFREDO
DISCIPLINE SPANISH LANGUAGE **EDUCATION** CUNY, BA, MA, Mphil, PhD. **CAREER** Eastern Stroudsburg Univ PA **HONORS AND AWARDS** Lane Cooper Dissertation Fel. **RESEARCH** The relationship between Span/Span Am Modernismo and French Symbolism; Avant-garde lit;Pre-Columbian studies. **SELECTED PUBLICATIONS** Area: Span Am lit. **CONTACT ADDRESS** East Stroudsburg Univ of Pennsylvania, 200 Prospect Street, East Stroudsburg, PA 18301-2999.

AIKIN, JUDITH POPOVICH
PERSONAL Born 08/06/1946, Los Angeles, CA, 1 child **DISCIPLINE** GERMAN LITERATURE & LANGUAGE **EDUCATION** Univ OR, BA, 68, MA, 69; Univ CA, Berkeley, PhD, 74. **CAREER** Asst prof, 75-81, assoc prof, 81-88, prof Ger, Univ IA 88, Assoc Dean, Col Lib Arts, 89-92, Dean, Col Lib Arts, 92-97. **HONORS AND AWARDS** Am Coun Learned Soc Fel, 88-89; NEH Summer Res Fel, 88. **MEMBERSHIPS** MLA; Soc Ger Renaissance and Baroque Lit; Lyrica Soc; Lessing Soc. **RESEARCH** Seventeenth-century Ger drama, opera and song. **SELECTED PUBLICATIONS** Auth, The Mission of Rome in the Dramas of Daniel Casper von Lohenstein, Stuttgarter Arbeiten Germanistik, 76; And They Changed Their Lives from That Very Hour: Catharsis and Exemplum in the Baroque Trauerspeil, Daphnis, 81; German Baroque Drama, Twayne World Authors Series, G K Hall, 82; Genre Definition and Genre Confusion in Gryphius Double Bill: Cardenio und Celinde and Herr Peter Squentz, Colloquia Germanica, 83; Romantic comedy as Religious Allegory: The Millennial Kingdom of Caspar Stieler's Die erfreuete Unschuld, Ger Quart, 84; The Audience within the Play: Clues to Intended Audience Reaction in German Baroque Tragedies and Comedies, Daphnis, 84; Happily Ever After: An Alternative Affective Theory of Comedy and Some Plays by Birken, Gryphius and Weise, In: Absurda Comica: Studien zur deutschen Komodie des 16 und 17 Jahrhunderts, Rodopi, 88, Daphnis, 88; The Comedies of Andreas Gryphius and the Two Tpes of European Comedy, Ger Rev, 88; Das klingt sehr tragisch - Lessing's Minna von Barnhelm as Embodiment of the Genre Discussion, Lessing Yearbk, 88; Creating a Language for German Opera: The Struggle to Adapt Madrigal Versification in Seventeenth-Century Germany, Deutsche Vierteljahrsschrift, 88; The Merchant and the Moor of Venice in Lessing's Minna von Barnhelm, Mich Ger Studies, 89; Scaramutza in Germany: The Dramatic Works of Caspar Stieler, Penn State Press, 89; contr, Fertigkeit - A Millenniast Conciet in a Dedicatory Epistle by Stieler, Opitz und sein Welt: Festschrift fur George Shulz-Behrend zum 12 Februar 1988, Rodopi, 90; Narcissus and Echo: A Mythological Subtext in Harsdorffer's Operatic Seelewig (1644), Music and Letters, 91; Baroque, chpt, In: A Concise History of German Literature to 1900, Camden House, 92; Heinrich Schutz and Martin Opitz: A New Basis for German Vocal Music and Poetry, Musica e Storia, 93; Misattributed Melissa, or Let's Give David Elias Heidenreich His Due, Daphnis, 94; The Musical-Dramatic Works of David Schirmer, Daphnis, 97; What Happens When Opera Meets Drama and Vice Versa? J C Hallmann's Experiments and Their Significance, Studien zur Literature des 17 Jahrhunderts: Gedenkschrift fur Gerhard Spellerberg (1937-1996), Rodopi, 97. **CONTACT ADDRESS** Dept of Ger, Univ of Iowa, Iowa City, IA 52242-1409. **EMAIL** judith-aikin@uiowa.edu

AISSEN, JUDITH
DISCIPLINE MAYAN LANGUAGE **EDUCATION** Fordham Univ, BA; Yale Univ, MA; Harvard Univ, PhD, 74. **CAREER** Prof, Ling, Univ Calif, Santa Cruz. **HONORS AND AWARDS** Fel, Center for Advanced Study in Behavioral Sciences, Stanford, Ca, 96-97; Presidential Fellowship in the Humanities, UC Office of the Pres, 96-97. **MEMBERSHIPS** Linguistic Soc of America; Soc for the Study of Indigenous Languages of the Americas. **RESEARCH** Mayan linguistics, optimality theory, morophosyntactic typology. **SELECTED PUBLICATIONS** Auth, The Syntax of Causative Constructions, Garland Publ, 79; Tzotzil Clause Structure, Dordrecht, Netherlands: D Reidel Publ Co, 87; Agreement Controllers and

Tzotzil Comitatives, Language, 89; Toward a Theory of Agreement Controllers, Studies in Relational Grammar 3, Univ Chicago Press, 90; Topic and Focus in Mayan Lang, 92; "Pied piping, abstract agreement, and functional projections in Tzotzil," Natural Language and Linguistic Thoery 14 (96): 447-491; "On the Syntax of Obviation," Language 73 (97): 705-750; "Subject Choice and Markedness in Optimality Theory," Natural Language and Linguistic Theory 17 (99): 673-711; "Inverse and Agent Focus in Tzotzil," Language 75 (99): 451-485. **CONTACT ADDRESS** Dept of Ling, Univ of California, Santa Cruz, 1156 High St, Santa Cruz, CA 95064. **EMAIL** aissen@cats.ucsc.edu

AKEHURST, F. R. P.
DISCIPLINE OLD FRENCH AND THE HISTORY OF FRENCH **EDUCATION** Univ Colo, PhD; Univ Minn, JD. **CAREER** Instr, Univ Minn, Twin Cities. **RESEARCH** Medieval French law. **SELECTED PUBLICATIONS** Ed, Handbook of the Troubadours, Univ Calif Press, 95; transl, "Coutumes de Beauvaisis" of Philippe de Beaumanoir, Univ Pa Press, 92; published on the troubadours, the trouveres, and the fabliaux. **CONTACT ADDRESS** Univ of Minnesota, Twin Cities, 9 Pleasant St. SE, 260 Folwell Hall, Minneapolis, MN 55455.

AL-KASEY, TAMARA
DISCIPLINE SPANISH **EDUCATION** Univ Mass, PhD. **CAREER** Carnegie Mellon Univ. **SELECTED PUBLICATIONS** Auth, L2 acquisition of Spanish factivity, 92; A Return to the initial state in Spanish second language acquisition of Factivity, 92; Why can't Johnny learn Spanish?: A look at Spanish grammar instruction, 92. **CONTACT ADDRESS** Carnegie Mellon Univ, 5000 Forbes Ave, Pittsburgh, PA 15213.

ALBADA-JELGERSMA, JILL ELIZABETH
PERSONAL Born 01/23/1939, Leicester, England, m, 1969, 2 children **DISCIPLINE** SPANISH, SPANISH AM LIT, CRITICAL THEORY **EDUCATION** Univ CA, Davis, PhD, 95. **CAREER** Lect, Univ of the West Indies, 88-89; lect, Univ CA, Davis, 95-97; instr, Sacramento City Col, 97-98. **MEMBERSHIPS** Modern Language Asn; Nat Coalition of Independent Scholars. **RESEARCH** Spanish American literature, poetry, and narrative; critical and culture theory approaches; to Hispanic poetry and art. **SELECTED PUBLICATIONS** Auth, La autocensura y las tecnologias del ser en un poema de Antonio Cisneros, Monologo de la casta Susana, Revista de Critica Literaria Latinoamericana, Univ CA, Berkeley, 96; Antonio Cisneros and Bram Stoker: Continuities and Discontinuities, Chasqui; Revista de Literature Latinoamericana, AZ State Univ, Nov 96; review, Maria Ines Lagos, En tono mayor: relatos de formacion de protagonista femenina en Hispanoamerica, Santiago, Chile, Editorial Cuarto Propio, 96, Bul of Hispanic Studies, Univ Liverpool, UK, 98; Desire as the Abjection of the Maternal Body in the Poem Casa de Cuervos by Peruvian poet, Blanca Varela, Bul of Hispanic Studies, LXXIV 1, Jan 97; Las technologias politicas del ser en los sujetos poeticos de Nancy Morejon y Gioconda Belli, Revista Canadiense de Estudios Hispanicos, Univ Alberta, XX1 3, spring 97; review, Frances R Aparicio and Susana Chavez-Silverman, eds, Tropicalizations: Transcultural Representations of Latinidad, Univ Press of New England, 97, Bul of Hispanic Studies, Univ of Liverpool, UK, 98; review, Ivon Gordon-Vailakis, Colibries en el exilio, Quitor, Ecuador: Editorial El Conejo, 97, Letras Femeninas, 98; review, Elia Geoffrey Kantaris, The Subversive Psyche: Contemporary Women's Narrative from Argentina and Uraguay, Clarendon Press, 95, Bul of Hispanic Studies, 98; La funcion del deseo por la mujer afroantillana en cuatro poemas de Luis Palesm Matos, Hispanic J, spring 98; 31 entries on major Caribbean Figures and Movements, Encyclopedia of Contemporary Latin American Culture, Routledge, 98; entries on Venezuelan writers Laura Antillano and Antonieta Madrid for Feminist Encyclopedia of Latin American Literature, Greenwood Press, in press; Las relaciones del poder en Cronica del Nino de Chilca, de Antonio Cisneros, Confluencia, spring 99. **CONTACT ADDRESS** 1221 Lexington Ct, El Dorado Hills, CA 95762. **EMAIL** je.albadajelgersma@prodigy.net

ALBANESE, RALPH
PERSONAL Born 11/13/1944, New York, NY **DISCIPLINE** FRENCH LITERATURE **EDUCATION** Queens Col, BA, 66; MA, 68; Yale Univ, PhD, 72. **CAREER** Lectr, Queens Col, 66-69; TA, Yale Univ, 70-71; Asst prof, Purdue Univ, 71-73; asst prof, Univ of Southern Calif, 73-74; asst prof, Univ of Mich, 74-78; asst prof to prof, Univ of Nebr Lincoln, 78-90; prof, chair, Univ of Memphis, 90-. **HONORS AND AWARDS** Superior Performance in Univ Res Awd, Univ of Memphis, 95; Univ Distinguished Res Awd, Univ of Memphis, 97. **MEMBERSHIPS** Phi Kappa Phi; AATF; MLA; SSCFL. **RESEARCH** 17th Century French Literature, Sociocriticism, 17th, Century French Theatre; School discourse, History of French Education. **SELECTED PUBLICATIONS** Auth, Le Dynamisme de la peur chez Moliere: Une analyse socioculturelle de Dom Juan, Tartuffe et L'Ecole des Femmes, Romance Monograph Series, Univ Miss, 76; auth, Initiation aux problemes socio-culturels de la France au XVIIeme siecle, Etudes sociocritiques (Montpellier), 77; auth, "La Poetique de l'espace dans Andromaque", Australian j of Fre Studies XXXII.1 (95): 6-18; auth, "Dynamisme social et jeu individuel dans Dom Juan", L'Espirit Createur XXXVI.1 (96): 50-72; auth, "Moliere: Preface", L'Esprit Createur XXXVI.1 (96): 3-6; auth, "National Identity: Writing and Rewriting the Seventeenth Century: Avant-propos", Papers on Fr Seventeenth Century Lit 46, (97): 1-3; auth, "Le Discours scolaire au XIXeme siecle: Le cas La Fontaine", Fr Rev 72, (99): 824-838; auth, "Les Fables de La Fontaine et la pedagogie republicaine de la francite", Cahiers du XVIIeme siecle, (forthcoming); auth, "Britannicus: Une Dramaturgie de Vespace", Papers on French Seventeenth Century Lit, (forthcoming); auth, "La Fontaine and the Teaching of Frenchness", Shape of Change: Essays in Honor of David Lee Rubin, (forthcoming). **CONTACT ADDRESS** Dept For Lang, Univ of Memphis, 375 Winfield Dr, Memphis, TN 38152-0001. **EMAIL** ralbanes@cc.memphis.edu

ALBERT-GALTIER, ALEXANDRE
PERSONAL Born Graveson, France **DISCIPLINE** FRENCH **EDUCATION** BA, 81; MA, 82; Universite Lyon II, PhD, 88. **CAREER** Carge de Cours, Univ Lyon II, 86-88; Visiting Instructor to Visiting Asst Prof, Univ Ore, 90-93; Asst Prof, Mount Holyoke Col, 93-94; Assoc Prof, Univ Ore, 94-96. **HONORS AND AWARDS** Jr Fac Development Grant, 95; New Fac Awd, 95. **MEMBERSHIPS** Societe d'Etudes du XVIIeme Siecle, N Am Asn for Seventeenth-Century French Literature, SE Am Soc for French Seventeenth-Century Studies, Mod Lang Asn of Am, Asn des Amis d'Andre Gide, Asn des Amis de Lancelot Desquais. **SELECTED PUBLICATIONS** Auth, "Un comedien en colere: masques et grimaces de Moliere dans la querelle de 'L'Ecole des femmes'," Cahiers du sixseptieme siecle: an Interdisciplinary Journal, 99; auth, "Derniers embrassements et consommation amoureuse: un aspect des amours masculines chez Cyrano," Papers on French Seventeenth Century Literature, 95; auth, La Connaissance des Corps, Avignon, 94; auth, La Traversee du Pacifique, Avignon, 98; auth, six Poemes. Revue Greges, Montpellier, 99. **CONTACT ADDRESS** Dept Romance Lang, Univ of Oregon, Eugene, OR 97403.

ALEINIKOV, ANDREI G.
PERSONAL Born 03/13/1948, Sverdlovsk, Russia, m, 1970, 1 child **DISCIPLINE** LINGUISTICS **EDUCATION** State Pedagogical Univ, Volgograd, Russia, BA, MA; State Univ, Georgia, PhD. **CAREER** Analyst & sr analyst, Ministry of Defense, Russia, 75-84; asst prof, Military Univ, Moscow, Russia, 84-88, assoc prof, 88-92, post-doctoral fel, 89-92; Int fel, Air War Col, USAF Univ, Maxwell, Ala, 92-93; adjunct indtr, Troy State Univ and Auburn Univ, Montgomery, Ala, 94-; pres, Mega-Innovative Mind Int Inst, Montgomery, Ala, 95-; Dir, Innovative Ed Div, Venturist, Inc, Montgomery, Ala, 96-2000. **HONORS AND AWARDS** Doctor of Sci in Creative Linguistics, Military Univ, Moscow, Russia; Int fel, Air War Col USAF Univ, Maxwell, Ala; President's Excellence Awd, Trot State Univ Montgomery, Ala. **MEMBERSHIPS** Creative Ed Found, Buffalo, NY; Phi Delta Kappa; Int Soc of Eds, Bloomfield, Ind; Int Coun on Innovation in Higher Ed, Toronto, Can. **RESEARCH** Novology, the science of newness and innovation; creative linguistics; creative education: creative pedagogy and metapedagogy (89), generagony, creagogy, innovagogy (98). **SELECTED PUBLICATIONS** Auth, "Super Effective Communication," Ala English (96): 28-31; auth, "Openess. It's That Simple," Teaching for Success (97): 3; auth, "Humane Creativity," in Encyclopedia of Creativity, San Diego: Acacdemic Press (99): 837-844; auth, Mega-Creator: From Creativity to Mega-, Giga-, and Infi-Creativity, Montgomery: MIMII (99). **CONTACT ADDRESS** Dept Arts & Scis, Troy State Univ, Montgomery, PO Box 4419, Montgomery, AL 36103-4419. **EMAIL** aleini13@aol.com

ALLAIRE, GLORIA
PERSONAL Born 02/20/1954, Reedsburg, WI **DISCIPLINE** ITALIAN **EDUCATION** Univ Wisc Madison, BM, 76; MA, 86; PhD, 93. **CAREER** Vis asst prof, Fla State Univ, 93-94; vis asst prof, Ohio Univ, 94-97; vis instr, Purdue Univ, 97-98; vis asst prof, Univ Miami, 98-99; asst prof, Gettysburg Col, 99-01. **HONORS AND AWARDS** Fulbright Dissertation Grant, 90-91; Wisc Alumni Res Found Dissertation Fel, 91-92; Andrew W. Mellon Fel, St Louis Univ, 92; NEH Summer Inst, 93; Am Philos Soc Grant, 96; Medieval Acad of Am Travel Grant, 98; Res and Prof Develop Grants, Gettysburg Col, 99-00. **MEMBERSHIPS** Medieval Acad of Am; Intl Courtly Lit Soc; Societe Rencesvals; MLA: Am Asn of Teachers of Italian; Am Asn for Italian Studies. **RESEARCH** Chivalric literature in Italy, late medieval vernacular literature and book culture, codicology, editing manuscripts. **SELECTED PUBLICATIONS** Auth, "Unknown Exemplars of Andrea da Barberino in the Ashburnham Collection of the Biblioteca medicea Laurenziana," Scriptorium, (94): 151-158; auth, "Tullia d'Aragona's Il Meschino altramente detto il Guerino as Key to a Reappraisal of Her Work," Quaderni d'italianistica, (96): 33-50; auth, Andrea da Barberino and the Language of Chivalry, Gainesville, 97; auth, "Medieval Italian Pilgrims to Santiago de Compostela: New Literary Evidence," J of Medieval Hist, (97): 177-189; auth, "Un frammento di un romanzo sconosciuto di Andrea da Barberino (?)," Cultura Neolatina, (98): 101-120; auth, "Frate Cipolla as Scribe: A Note on Decameron VI, 10," Neophilologus, (98): 393-402; ed, Modern Retellings of Chivalric Texts, Ashgate, 99; auth, "Memory, Commemoration and Lineage in Le Storie Nerbonesi," Italian Culture, (00): 1-14; auth, "Considerations on Huon d'Auvergne/Ugo d'Alvernia," Viator, 01; auth, Il Tristano panciatichiano, Boydell and Brewer, (forthcoming). **CONTACT ADDRESS** Dept Italian Studies, Gettysburg Col, PO Box 394, Gettysburg, PA 17325.

ALLAIRE, JOSEPH LEO
PERSONAL Born 02/23/1929, Detroit, MI, m, 1974, 1 child **DISCIPLINE** FRENCH **EDUCATION** Univ Detroit, AB, 52; Wayne State Univ, MA, 57, PhD(Mod Lang), 66. **CAREER** Teacher French & Latin, pub schs, Mich, 53-62, head dept, 62-67; instr French, Wayne State Univ, 60-67; asst prof, 67-72, assoc chmn Mod Lang, 69-73, assoc prof French, Fla State Univ, 72-. **MEMBERSHIPS** Am Asn Teachers Fr; MLA; S Atlantic MLA; S Cent MLA; AAUP; Asn des Seiziemistes, Renaisance Soc of Am. **RESEARCH** French Renaissance; pre-Reformation lit; late medieval French lit, especially the 15th century. **SELECTED PUBLICATIONS** Ed, Le Miroir de l'Ame Pecheresse de Marguerite de Navarre, Wilhelm Fink, Munich, 72; auth, Foreign languages and the Founding Fathers, S Atlantic Bull, 1/77. **CONTACT ADDRESS** Dept of Mod Lang, Florida State Univ, Tallahassee, FL 32306-1540. **EMAIL** jallaire@mailer.fsu.edu

ALLEN, JOHN
PERSONAL Born 05/20/1932, Wichita, KS, m, 1984, 3 children **DISCIPLINE** SPANISH LANGUAGE & LITERATURE **EDUCATION** Duke Univ, AB, 54; Middlebury Col, MA, 57; Univ Wis, PhD, 60. **CAREER** Asst to full prof, Univ Fla, 60-83; vis Mellon prof, Univ Pitts, 82; prof Span, Univ Ken, 83-99. **HONORS AND AWARDS** NEH fel; Nat Hum Ctr fel Research Triangle, NC, Kirwan Awd Univ Kent. **MEMBERSHIPS** MLA, AIH, AATSP. **RESEARCH** Cervantes, Renaissance playhouses. **SELECTED PUBLICATIONS** Auth, Don Quixote: Hero or Fool?, Univ Fla Press, Part I, (69), Part II, (79); auth, The Reconstruction of a Spanish Golden Age Playhouse, Univ Fla Press, (83); ed, Don Quijote de la Mancha, Madrid Catedra, (77); auth, El Gran Teatro del Mundo, Caderon/Barcelona Critica, (97). **CONTACT ADDRESS** Dept Span & Ital, Univ of Kentucky, 1153 Stirling Dr, Danville, KY 40422. **EMAIL** jjallen@kih.net

ALLEN, ROGER MICHAEL ASHLEY
PERSONAL Born 01/24/1942, Devon, England, m, 1972, 2 children **DISCIPLINE** ARABIC LANGUAGE AND LITERATURE **EDUCATION** Oxford Univ, BA, MA & DPhil, 68. **CAREER** Assoc prof, 73-83, Prof Arabic Lang & Lit, Univ PA, 83-; Nat Proficiency Trainer in Arabic, Am Council for the Teaching of Forrign Langs (ACTFL), 86-; Dir, Huntsman Prog in Int Studies & Business, Univ PA, 93-; ed, Edebiyat, 76-91; book ed, Al-'Arabiyya, 90-95; ed bds: J of Arabic Lit, 91-96, World Lit Today, 91-, Arabic & Middle eastern Lits, 97-. **HONORS AND AWARDS** Lindback Found Award for Distinguished Teaching, Univ PA, 72; Am Res Center in Egypt fels, 70, 71, 75; Univ Helsinki Medal, 94. **MEMBERSHIPS** Am Guild of Organists, 77-; Am Coun for the Teaching of Foreign Langs (ACTFL), 88-. **RESEARCH** Second language teaching techniques, specifically Arabic; Arabic literature; translation from Near Eastern literatures. **SELECTED PUBLICATIONS** Auth, A Study of Hadith Isa ibn Hisham, Al-Muwaylihi's View of Egyptian Society during the British Occupation, State Univ NY, 74; Al-Muwaylihi's Hadith Isa Ibn Hisham, 74, A Period of Time, 2nd rev ed, 92; Egyptian drama and fiction in the 1970s, Edebiyat, 76; contribr, Arabic literature, In: The Study of the Middle East: Research in the Humanities and Social Sciences, Wiley, 76; transl, Nagib Mahfuz, Mirrors, 77 & auth, In the Eye of the Beholder: Tales from Yusuf Idris, 78, Bibliotheca Islamica; The Arabic Novel: An Historical and Critical Survey, Syracuse Univ Press, 82; The Arabic Novel: An Historical and Critical Introduction, 82, 2nd English ed, rev and enlarged, 95; modern Arabic Lit, 87; Let's Learn Arabic, with Adel Allouche, 88; Najib Mahfuz and World Literature, in the Arabic Novel Since 1950, Mundus Arabicus vol 5, 92; The Early Arabic Novel and The Arabic Novel Outside Egypt, Chapters 5 and 6 of Modern Arabic Literature, Cambridge Hist of Arabic Lit, 92; Arabic Poetry, Arabic Poetics, Rhyme (Arabic & Persian), in New Princeton Encyclopedia of Poetry & Poetics, 93; Najib Mahfuz and the Nobel Prize: The Historical Context, in Naguib Mahfouz From Regional Fame to Global Recognition, 93; Critical Perspectives on Yusuf Idris, 94; The Short Story in Arabic and the Status of Women, in Sex and Gender in Modern Arabic Literature, 95; Higher Level Language Skills in Arabic: Parameters and Issues, in The Teaching of Arabic as a Foreign Language: Issues & Directiona, 95; Najib Mahfuz, in African Writers, 97; A Different Voice: the Novels of Ibrahim al-Kawni, in Tradition and Modernity in Arabic Literature, 97; The Development of Fictional Genres: The Novel and Short Story in Arabic, in Humanism, Culture, and Language in the Near East, 97; hadith 'Isa ibn Hisham by al-Muwaylihi, Thirty Years Later, Arab and Islamic Studies in Honor of Marsden Jones, 97; The Arabic Literary Tradition, Cambridge University Press, 98; Introduction to Arabic Literature, Cambridge University Press, 00; many literary articles and several translations in book form. **CONTACT ADDRESS** Dept Asian & Middle Eastern Studies, Univ of Pennsylvania, 847 Williams Hall, Philadelphia, PA 19104-6305. **EMAIL** rallen@ccat.sas.upenn.edu

ALLEN, WENDY
PERSONAL Born, VT **DISCIPLINE** LANGUAGE ACROSS THE CURRICULUM **EDUCATION** CT, BA; IN Univ, MA, PhD. **CAREER** Language, St. Olaf Col. **HONORS AND AWARDS** ACTFL's Nelson Brooks award. **SELECTED PUBLICATIONS** Coauth: Paralleles. **CONTACT ADDRESS** St. Olaf Col, 1520 St Olaf Ave, Northfield, MN 55057.

ALLGOOD, MYRALYN FRIZZELLE
PERSONAL Born 03/02/1939, Atlanta, GA, m, 1964, 1 child **DISCIPLINE** SPANISH **EDUCATION** Howard Col, Samford Univ, BA, 61; St Ala tchr cert, 61; Univ of Ala, MA, 63; PhD, 85. **CAREER** Chair, dept of World Lang & Cult, 82-, prof, 63-, Samford Univ. **HONORS AND AWARDS** Macon Mem Awd for Tchg, Samford Univ, 78; Spec Svc Awd, Rio Grande River Ministry, Babtist Gen Convention of Tex, 81; Samford Univ Res Grant, 83; Capstone Int Opportunity Grant, Univ of Ala, 84; Samford Prof Devel Grant, 87, 89; James Porter & Julia Hanlin Smith Fac Enrich Grant, 90; NEH Grant, 90-91, 92-93, 92-95; Spec Svc Awd, Ala Asn of For Lang Tchrs, 94; Outstanding For Lang Tchr Awd: Post Secondary, Ala Asn of For Lang Tchrs, 95. **MEMBERSHIPS** Phi Kappa Phi; Ala-Guatemala Partners; South Atlantic Mod Lang Asn; MLA; ACTFL; NASILP; Am asn of Tchrs of Span and Port; Ala Asn of For Lang Tchrs; SEastern Women's Studies Asn; S Conf on Lang Tchg; Birmingham Hispanic Conf; Pi Delta Phi; Sigma Delta Pi; Ala Council for Int Progs; Am Asn for the Advancement of Core Curriculum; Asn of Deps of For Langs; Birmingham Area Consortium on Higher Educ. **SELECTED PUBLICATIONS** Auth, "FLES for You?" Alahispania 24 (May 76); auth, "Mexico Honors Rosario Castellanos," Hispania 68, No 1 (March 85); coauth, "Love at Work," Crusader 17, No 4, (Jan 87); auth, Another Way to Be: Selected Works of Rosario Castellanos in English Translation, Univ of Ga Pr (Athens & London), 90; coauth, "Summer Immersion Institutes: A Consortium Approach," in Homenaje a Enrique Ruiz-Fornells (Erie, PA: Asociacion de Licenciados Y Doctores Espanoles en los Estados Unidos, 90); transl, "Cooking Lesson," (transl of Rosario Castellanos/ 'Leccion de cocina') in Short Stories from Mod Mex (KCRW/Friends of the Arts of Mex, 99); auth, "Rosario Castellanos," in Literary Companion to South and Central Am (Brighton, UK: Print Pub Ltd, 93); transl, "A Palm Tree," (transl of Rosario Castellanos' 'Una Palmera') in Twentieth Century Latin American Poetry: A Bilingual Anthology (Austin: Univ of Tex Pr, 96); transl, "A Palm Tree," (transl of Rosario Castellanos' 'Una Palmera') in Poetry in Six Dimensions: Twentieth Century Voices, eds Carol Clark and Norma Fifer (Educators Pub Svc, Inc, 99); transl, "The Luck of Teodoro Mendez Acubal," (transl of Rosario Castellanos' 'La suerte de Teodoro Mendez Acubal,' in Glencoe Litereture Library: Hispanic American Literature (Glencoe/McGraw-Hill, 00). **CONTACT ADDRESS** Dept of World Langs & Cultures, Samford Univ, Birmingham, AL 35229-2298. **EMAIL** mfallgoo@samford.edu

ALLOCATI, IRIS F.
PERSONAL Born 02/04/1942, Buenos Aires, Argentina, m, 1966, 2 children **DISCIPLINE** INTERPRETATION, TRANSLATION, ENGLISH, SPANISH **EDUCATION** MA, Span, Ling, Lit; MA, Clin Psychol. **CAREER** Asst prof, Cal State Univ, LA. **HONORS AND AWARDS** Awd Cert, CSULA. **MEMBERSHIPS** AAISP; CCIA; NAIIT. **RESEARCH** Translation English/Spanish **SELECTED PUBLICATIONS** Auth, Manual for the Medical Interpreter and Translator, English/Spanish. **CONTACT ADDRESS** English and Foreign Languages, Pasadena City Col, 1570 East Colorado Blvd, Pasadena, CA 91106-2003. **EMAIL** ifiorit@calstatela.edu

ALMEIDA, JOSE AGUSIN
PERSONAL Born 08/28/1933, Waco, TX, m, 1964, 1 child **DISCIPLINE** SPANISH LANGUAGE & LITERATURE **EDUCATION** Baylor Univ, BA, 61; Univ Mo, Columbia, MA, 64, PhD, 67. **CAREER** Teaching asst, Univ Mo Columbia, 61-66; instr Span, Baylor Univ, 62-63; from asst prof to assoc prof emeritus, Lit & Span, Univ NC, Greensboro, 66-; vis prof, Elmira Col, 67; consult, Living Lang Method, Hampton Inst, Va, 76 & 78; chmn, Latin Am studies, Univ NC, Greensboro, 79-81. **HONORS AND AWARDS** Hon assoc, The Hispanic Soc of Am, 99; NEH fel, 70; **MEMBERSHIPS** MLA; Am Asn Teachers Span & Port; Asn de Cervantistas; Cervantes Soc Am; Soc Renaissance & Baroque Hisp Poetry. **RESEARCH** Poetics: literary criticism & literature, especially poetry of the Golden Age of Literature in Spain. **SELECTED PUBLICATIONS** Auth, La Critica Literaria de Fernando de Herrera, Ed Gredos, 76; coauth, Descubrir y Crear & Teacher's Guide for Descubrir y Crear, Harper & Row, 76, 3rd ed, 86; auth, Elementos picarescos en la poesia satirica del Siglo de Oro, In: La picaresca, origenes, textos y estructuras, Madrid: Fundacion Universitaria Espanola, 79; El concepto aristotelico de la imitacion en el Renacimiento de las letras espanolas: Sigo XVI, In: Actas del Sexto Congreso Internacional de Hispanistas, Paul Malak & Son, 80; Origen de La tragedia de las equivocaciones de Xavier Villarrutia, National Symposium on Hispanic Theater, April 22-24, 1982, Univ Northern Iowa, 82; La apologia personal y la defensa teoricoliteraria disimuladas en La Dorotea, Homenaje a Alberto Porqueras Mayo, Kassel: Reichenberger, 89; Los momentos finales del primer y ultimo actos en Invitacion a la muerte de Xavier Villaurrutia, Explicacion de Textos Literarios, 90-91. **CONTACT ADDRESS** Dept of Romance Langs, Univ of No Carolina, Greensboro, 1000 Spring Garden, Greensboro, NC 27412-5001. **EMAIL** jalmeida@uncg.edu

ALSTRUM, JAMES
PERSONAL Born 12/18/1946, New Haven, CT, m, 1971, 4 children **DISCIPLINE** SPANISH **EDUCATION** Fairfield Univ, BA, 68; Vanderbilt Univ, MA, 73; PhD, 77. **CAREER** Asst Prof, Univ of Wyoming, 77-79; Asst Prof, Univ of Miss, 79-81; Asst to Assoc Prof, Ill State Univ, 81-. **HONORS AND AWARDS** NDEA Title IV Fel, Vanderbilt Univ, 71-74; Fulbright Scholar, Colombia, 75; Res Grant, Orgn of Am State Grad, 76. **MEMBERSHIPS** Asn of Colombianists. **RESEARCH** Colombian Literature of all periods and genres especially contemporary poetry, Poetry and Prose of Alvaro Mutis. **SELECTED PUBLICATIONS** Auth, "Las 'gotas amargas' de Silva la poesia de Luis Carlos Lopez," in Jose Asuncian Silva, vida y creacion, 85; auth, La satira y antipoesia de Luis Carlos Lopez, El Banco de la Republica (Bogota), 86; auth, "Generacion de 'Golpa de dadas'," in Historia de la poesia colombiana," (Bogota: Casa de Poesta Silva, 91); auth, "Metapoesia e inter textualdad: Las demandas sobra el lector en la obra de Alvaro Mutis," in Tras Las rutas de Magroll el Gaviaro," (Bogota: Colcultura, 93). **CONTACT ADDRESS** Dept For Lang, Illinois State Univ, Campus Box 4300, Normal, IL 61790-0001. **EMAIL** jjalstr@ilstu.edu

ALTER, ROBERT
PERSONAL Born 04/02/1935, Bronx, NY, m, 1961, 4 children **DISCIPLINE** COMPARATIVE LITERATURE **EDUCATION** Columbia Col, BA, 57; Harvard Univ, MA, 58, PhD, 62. **CAREER** From instr to asst prof English, Columbia Univ, 62-67; assoc prof Hebrew & comp lit, 67-69, chm dept comp lit, 70-72, Prof Hebrew & Comp Lit, 69-, Class of 1937 Prof, 89-, Univ Calif, Berkeley. **HONORS AND AWARDS** English Instr Essay Prize, 65; Guggenheim fel, 66-67 & 78-79; Meier Segals vis lectr, Sir George Williams Univ, 68; Roland vis lectr Jewish studies, Stanford Univ, 71; Nat Endowment Humanities sr fel, 71-72; Harry Kaplan scholar in residence, Ohio State Univ, 72; contrib ed, Commentary, 73-89; Buckstein vis lectr, Trent Univ, 76; Gale vis lectr, Univ Tex, Austin, 82; Nat Jewish Book Awd, 82; Speaker's Lectr, Oxford Univ, 95-96; Burnshaw Lectr, Univ Tex, Austin, 97; Rosenzweig Lectr, Yale, 98. **MEMBERSHIPS** Am Comp Lit Asn; Asn Jewish Studies; Assoc of Lit Scholars and Critics. **RESEARCH** Modern Hebrew literature; the novel; Biblical literature. **SELECTED PUBLICATIONS** Auth, Rogue's Progress: Studies in the Picaresque Novel, 64 & Field and the Nature of the Novel, 68, Harvard Univ; After the Tradition, Dutton, 69; Partial Magic: The Novel as a Self-Conscious Genre, Univ Calif, 75; ed, Modern Hebrew Literature, Behrman House, 75; auth, Defenses of the Imagination, Jewish Publ Soc, 78; A Lion for Love: A Critical Biography of Stendhal, 79 & The Art of Biblical Narrative, Basic, 82; auth, The Art of Biblical Poetry, Basic, 85; auth, The Pleasures of Reading in an Ideological Age, Simon & Schuster, 89; auth, Necessary Angels, Harvard, 91; auth, The Work of Biblical Literature, Basic, 92; auth, Hebrew and Modernity, Indiana, 94; auth, Genesis: Translation and Commentary, Norton, 96; auth, The David Story, Norton, 99; auth, Canon and Creativity, Yale, 00. **CONTACT ADDRESS** Dept of Comp Lit, Univ of California, Berkeley, 250 Barrows Hall, Berkeley, CA 94720-1941. **EMAIL** altcos@uclink4.berkeley.edu

ALTISENT, MARTA E.
PERSONAL Born 07/20/1950, Spain, d **DISCIPLINE** SPANISH LITERATURE **CAREER** Assoc prof, Univ Calif Davis, 90-. **MEMBERSHIPS** MLA. **RESEARCH** Comparative, Spanish, Catalan Literature, Critical theory. **SELECTED PUBLICATIONS** Auth, "La aventura equinoccial de Lope de Aguirre: Ramon Sender entre la caricatura y la tragedia", Explicacion de textos literarios 13.2, Calif State Univ, (94-95): 65-83; auth, "La circunstancia mexicana de Max Aug: A proposito de Cuentos mexicanos", Actas XXIX Congreso del Instituto Int de Lit Iberoamericana, Univ of Barcelona, (95): 447-457; auth, "Unamuno y la metafora organicista de la creacion literaria", Letras de Deusto 26.72; Univ of Bilbao, (96): 75-93; auth, "La aventura equinoccial de Lope de Aguirre. Ramond Sender entra la caricatura y la tragedia", Alba de America 14.26-27, (96): 409-427; auth, "El topos del viejo verde en la ficcion breve de Clarin", Bull of Hispanic Studies LXXV, (98): 183-99; auth, "Theatre and Life in A Light Comedy by Eduardo Mendoza", Comparative Literature, Linguistics and Culture: An Iberian Dialogue, Univ of Calif Pr, 99; rev of "Understanding Camilo Jose Cela", by Lucile C. Charlebois, Diacritics, Univ of SC Pr, 00. **CONTACT ADDRESS** Dept Span and Classics, Univ of California, Davis, 1 Shields Ave, 603 Sproul Hall, Davis, CA 95616-5270. **EMAIL** mealtisent@ucdavis.edu

ALTMAN, RICK (CHARLES FREDERICK)
PERSONAL Born 01/09/1945, De Ridder, LA, m, 1967, 1 child **DISCIPLINE** FRENCH LITERATURE; CINEMA **EDUCATION** Duke Univ, AB & MA, 66; Yale Univ, PhD, 71. **CAREER** Fulbright-Hayes fel and lectr, Am studies, Univ Paris X, Nanterre, 70-71; asst prof French and comp lit, Bryn Mawr Col, 71-74; asst prof French, 74-77; assoc prof French and comp lit, 77-82; assoc prof Film, French and Comp Lit, Univ Iowa, 82-86; prof French & Film, 86-99; fel, Cornell Univ Soc for Hum, 74-75; dir, Paris Film Ctr, 80-81; vis prof, Univ Paris III-Censier, 80-81; prof, Cinema & Comp Lit, 99-; vis prof, Univ de Provence, 96; dir, The Living Nickelodion, 99-. **HONORS AND AWARDS** Russell B Nye Prize, Jour Pop Cult, 80; French nat. Decoration, Chevalier de L'Ordre des Palmes Academiques, 84; Soc for Cinema Studies prize, 84; French film critics award for best film book publ. in 1992, 92; NEW Fel, 90-91; Soc for Cinema Studies 2000 Katherine S. Kovacs prize for best film book published in 1999. **MEMBERSHIPS** MLA; SCS; Domitor. **RESEARCH** Narrative; 12th century Western culture; Film. **SELECTED PUBLICATIONS** Auth, "A Semantic/Syntactic Approach to Film Genre," Cenema J 23, no. 3 (Spring 84): 6-18; auth, The American Film Musical, Ind Univ Pr (Bloomington), 87; auth, The Video Connection: Integrating Video into Language Teaching, Houghton Mifflin (Boston), 88; auth, "Dickens, Griffith, and Film Theory Today," South Atlantic Q 88, no 2 (Spring 89): 321-59; ed, Sound Theory/Sound Practice, Routledge/Am Film Inst (NYork), 92; ed, "The State of Sound Studies," ispec issue of IRIS 27 (99); co-ed, "Global Experiments in Early Synchronous Sound," spec issue of Film Hist, 11:4 (99); auth, "Film Sound--All of It," IRIS 27 (99): 31-48; auth, Film/Genre, Ind Univ Pr & British Film Inst (Bloomington & London), 99; co-ed, The Sounds of Early Cinema, Ind Univ Pr (Bloomington), forthcoming. **CONTACT ADDRESS** Dept of Cinema & Comp Lit, Univ of Iowa, Iowa City, IA 52242. **EMAIL** rick-altman@uiowa.edu

ALVARINO, MADELYN L.
PERSONAL Born 12/10/1945, Havana, Cuba, m, 1963, 2 children **DISCIPLINE** SPANISH **EDUCATION** Villanova Univ, BA, 91; MA, 93; SUNY, PhD, 99. **CAREER** Instr, Widener Univ, 91-92; instr, Villanova Univ, 92-93; teaching asst, SUNY Albany, 92-93; instr, Skidmore Col, 94-99; asst prof, Immaculata Col, 99-. **HONORS AND AWARDS** Grad Acad Honors, SUNY; Fel, Villanova Univ; Sigma Delta Pi Hispanic Honor Soc. **MEMBERSHIPS** MLA; ACTFL; AATSP; Asn of Hispanic Feminine Lit; Latin Am Studies; Sigma Delta Pi. **RESEARCH** Latin American literature. **SELECTED PUBLICATIONS** Auth, Guia suplementari y banca de actividades para cursos de immersion, 2nd ed, McGraw-Hill, 95; auth, "La deshumanizacion en Parabola del naufragio," De la letra, (96): 11-18; auth, "La fragmentacion como constante en A hora da estrela," J on Film and Lit, (97): 25-31. **CONTACT ADDRESS** Dept Spanish, Immaculata Col, 636 Hamilton Ct, Collegeville, PA 19426-2253. **EMAIL** malvarino@immaculata.edu

ALZATE, GASTON A.
PERSONAL Born 06/16/1959, Cali, Colombia, m, 1991 **DISCIPLINE** LATIN AMERICAN LITERATURE **EDUCATION** Univ Javeriana, BA, 89; Univ del Rosario, MA, 92; Univ Ariz, PhD, 97. **CAREER** Vis prof, Univ Javeriana, 90-94; TA, Univ Ariz, 94-97; asst prof, Gustavus Adolphus Col, 97-01. **HONORS AND AWARDS** Nat Short Story Awd, Fundacion Alejo Carpentier, 87; Nat Essay Awd, Colombia, 92. **MEMBERSHIPS** MLA, LASA, Asociacion Norteamericana de Colombianistas, Feministas Unidas. **RESEARCH** Latin American Culture and Literature. **SELECTED PUBLICATIONS** Auth, Un aspecto desesperanzado de la literatura. Sofocles, Holderlin y Mutis, Colcultura (Bogota), 94; auth, "Leon De Greiff o la musica de un archilunatico," Universitas Humanisticas 23.38, (94): 56-61; auth, "Resistencia, musica y sicotropicos: comentarios a la novaela 'Que viva la musica' de Andres," Latin Am Lit Rev 24.48 (96): 39-55; auth, "Expaniendo los limites del teatro: Astrid Hadad," Latin Am Theater Rev 30.2, (97): 153-63; auth, "Jesusa rodriguez: cabaret, disidencia y legitimacion en el teatro mexicano contemporaneo," Gestos 28.14, (99): 81-102; auth, "El descentramiento de la palabra: Andres Caicedo Estela," Narrativa y Cultura Colombiana en el, ed Maria Mercedes Jaramillo et al, (00); auth, "Astrid Hadad: un espectaculo no apto para mochos," Chasqui 29.1 (00): 3-18; auth, "Astrid Hadad," Noted Twentieth Century Latin American Women: A Bibliographical Dictionary, ed Cynthia Margarita Tompkins and David William Foster, (01): 130-134. **CONTACT ADDRESS** Gustavus Adolphus Col, 800 W College Ave, Vickner 214, Saint Peter, MN 56082. **EMAIL** galzate@gac.edu

AMADOR, RAYSA E.
PERSONAL Born, Cuba, m, 2 children **DISCIPLINE** SPANISH **EDUCATION** NY Univ, PhD, 78. **CAREER** Lectr, Rutgers Univ, 77-78; asst to assoc prof, Adelphi Univ, 78-. **HONORS AND AWARDS** Phi Theta Kappa, 70; Phi Beta Kappa; Penfield Fel, NY Univ, 76-77; Grant NY Counc for Humanities, 83; Septima Clark Distinguished Fac Awd, Adelphi Univ, 99. **RESEARCH** Latin American Female Writers and Colonial Literature. **SELECTED PUBLICATIONS** Auth, "El mito en El obsceno pajaro de la noche," Estudios de historia literatura y arte, Artes Graficas Benzel (77): 11-24; auth, Una aproximacion historica a Los Comentarios Reales, Editorial pliegos, (Madrid), 85; auth, "Life and Works of Gertrudiz Gomez de Avellaneda," Women Writers of Sp Am: An Annotated Biographical Guide, ed Diana Marting, Greenwood Pr, (Westport, 87); auth, "Legalidad y discursor la Coonica de las Indias," Proceed Rediscovering America 1492-1992, La State Univ, (Baton Rouge, 92): 6-19; auth, "The Papal bulls of the SVI and SVII Century," Hist Dict of the Span Empire, ed James Olson, Greenwood Pr, (Westport, 92): 468-473; auth, "Reconstruction of the Self: the Visual as the Text in Querido Diego," Reading a Woman's Per-

spective, Studies of Gender in Literary Texts, eds Ellen S. Silber, Nora Glickman and Virgina Skord-Waters, US Dept of Educ, (NY, 95): 35-38; auth, "Latina's Self Narrative," Hispanic Women in the World: Accomplishments and Challenges, in press; coauth, The Female Body: Latina Perspectives from Frida Kahlo to Isabel Allende, forthcoming. **CONTACT ADDRESS** Sp and Lat Am Studies, Adelphi Univ, PO Box 276, Garden City, NY 11530. **EMAIL** amador@adlivb.adelphi.edu

AMAR, JOSEPH P.
PERSONAL Born 12/29/1946, Grand Rapids, MI, s **DISCIPLINE** SEMITIC LANGUAGES; HISTORY **EDUCATION** The Catholic Univ of America, PhD, 88. **CAREER** Prof, Univ NortreDane, 88-, Chair, Classics Dept, 97-. **MEMBERSHIPS** North Amer Patristics Soc (NAPS); Middle East Studies Assoc (MESA). **RESEARCH** Cultural/linguistic interplay; Syriac language & lit; medieval Christian Arabic; Islamic history. **CONTACT ADDRESS** Dept of Classics, Univ of Notre Dame, 304 O'Shaughnessy Hall, Notre Dame, IN 46556. **EMAIL** Joseph.P.Amar.1@nd.edu

AMASTAE, JON EDWARD
PERSONAL Born 07/20/1946, Los Angeles, CA **DISCIPLINE** LINGUISTICS **EDUCATION** Univ NMex, BA, 68; Univ Ore, PhD(ling), 75. **CAREER** Asst prof English, Pan Am Univ, 75-79; Fulbright lectr ling, Univ de los Andes, Bogota, Colombia, 79-80; Asst Prof Ling, Univ Texas, El Paso, 80-84, Assoc Prof 84-92, Prof 92-, Actg Dir, Lang & Ling Res Ctr, Pan Am Univ, 76-78; Chemn, Dept of Lang & Ling, UTEP 86-93; Dir, Center for Interamerican & border studies, 98-. **MEMBERSHIPS** Ling Soc Am; Ling Asn Can & US; Soc Caribbean Ling. **RESEARCH** Phonology; Creoles; language contact; linguistic variation. **SELECTED PUBLICATIONS** Co-ed, Contemporary Research in Romance Linguistics, John Benjamis, 95; auth, Variable Spirantization: Constraint Weighting in Three Dialects, Hispanic Ling, 95; The Intersection of S-aspiration/deletion and Spirantization in Honduran Spanish, Lang Variation and Change, 89; Mid-Vowel Raising and its Consequences in Spanish, Ling, 82; A Note on Natural Generative Phonology and Paradigm Leveling, Ling Inquiry, 78; Dominican English Creole Phonology: An Initial Sketch, Anthrop, Ling, 79; Dominican Creole Phonology; Georgetown Univ, Papers in Lang & Ling, 79; co-ed, Spanish in the US: Sociolinguistic Aspects, Cambridge Univ Press, 82. **CONTACT ADDRESS** Dept of Lang & Ling, Univ of Texas, El Paso, 500 W University Ave, El Paso, TX 79968-0001. **EMAIL** jamastae@utep.edu

AMBROSE, Z. PHILIP
PERSONAL Born 06/09/1936, Ponca City, OK, m, 2 children **DISCIPLINE** CLASSICAL LANGUAGES **EDUCATION** Princeton Univ, PhD, 63. **CAREER** Roberts Prof Of Classical Languages And Lit, 62-, Univ Vt **HONORS AND AWARDS** Phi Beta Kappa; CANA Barlow Beach Awd for Dist Serv, 85. **MEMBERSHIPS** CANE; APA; Soc for Ancient Greek Philos. **RESEARCH** Greek drama; classical tradition, J. S. Bach. **SELECTED PUBLICATIONS** Auth, The Homeric Telos, Glotta, 48, 65; auth, The Lehythian and the Anagram of Frogs 1203, AJP 89, 68; auth, Two Textual Notes on the Miks Gloriosus, CJ, 72; auth, The Etymology and Geneology of Palinusus, AJP 101, 80; auth, Weinen, Klagen, Sorgen, Fayen und die antike Redekunst, Bach Sakrbuch, 80; auth, Socrates and Prodieus in the Clouds, Essays in Ancient Greek Philos, vol 2, 83; auth, Did Women Sing in the Thesmophoriazousae?, Didascalia Sup I; transl, The Texts to Johann Sebastian Bach's Church Cantatas, Stuttgart, 84; auth, Euripides Heraclisae, Bryn Mawr, 90; auth, Ganymede in Euripides' Cyclops, N Eng Class J, 96; auth, The Complete Texts to J. S. Bach's Vocal Works, transl and commentary, 98. **CONTACT ADDRESS** Dept of Classics, Univ of Vermont, 481 Main St, Burlington, VT 05405. **EMAIL** zambrose@zoo.uvm.edu

AMER, SAHAR
PERSONAL Born 08/20/1964, Egypt, s **DISCIPLINE** LINGUISTICS, FRENCH, ARABIC **EDUCATION** Bryn Mawr, BA, MA, 86; Boston Univ, MA, 88; Yale Univ, 94. **CAREER** Asst prof, Univ NCar Chapel Hill, 94-00; vis assoc prof, Vanderbilt Univ, 00-01; assoc prof, Univ NCar Chapel Hill, 01-. **HONORS AND AWARDS** UNC Res Fel, 95, 97, 98, 99, 00, 01. **MEMBERSHIPS** MLA; MESA; SEMA. **RESEARCH** Cultural divinity in medieval Europe; Orientalism; sexuality. **SELECTED PUBLICATIONS** Auth, "Le Voile ou la Construction Sociale de la Masculinite Chez Ben Jelloun," Soc Afr 9 (98); auth, Esope au Feminin: Marie de France et la Politique de l'interculturalite, Rodopi Pr, 99; co-ed, Rereading Allegory, Yale UP (New Haven, London), 99. **CONTACT ADDRESS** Romance Lang Dept, Univ of No Carolina, Chapel Hill, Cb 3170, 238 Dey Hall, Chapel Hill, NC 27599-0001. **EMAIL** samer@email.unc.edu

ANADON, JOSE
DISCIPLINE SPANISH LITERATURE **EDUCATION** Albion Col, BA, 68; Univ Mich, MA, 70, PhD, 74. **CAREER** Prof. **RESEARCH** Contemporary narrative of Latin America. **SELECTED PUBLICATIONS** Auth, Pineda y Bascunan, defensor del araucano, 77; La novela colonial de Barrenechea y Albis, 83; Historiografia literaria de America Colonial, 88. **CONTACT ADDRESS** Romance Languages and Literatures Dept, Univ of Notre Dame, Notre Dame, IN 46556.

ANDERLINI-D'ONOFRIO, SERENA
PERSONAL Born 09/12/1954, Rome, Italy, d **DISCIPLINE** ITALIAN STUDIES, ITALIAN CINEMA **EDUCATION** Univ Sassari, Laurea in Lingue, 76; Univ Calif Riverside, MA, 83; PhD, 87. **CAREER** TA to assoc prof, UCR, 81-87; asst prof, Vanderbilt Univ, 88-91; holistic health practioner, North County Healing Arts Center, 95-97; assoc prof, Univ PR, 97-. **HONORS AND AWARDS** Harry Ransom Humanities Res Ctr Fel, 99; Reconocimiento del Presidente, Norman Maldonado, UPR, 00; Seed Money, Univ Puerto Rico, 01. **MEMBERSHIPS** MLA, Europ Assoc for Am Studies, Am Assoc for Ital Studies, Assoc for the Study of Lit and the Environ. **RESEARCH** Italian Cinema, Ecocriticism, Ecofeminism, The Gaia Hypothesis, Science Studies, Controversies in Aids Science. **SELECTED PUBLICATIONS** Auth, The "Weak" Subject on Modernity, Eros, and Women's Playwriting, Associated univ Pr, (London, NJ), 98. **CONTACT ADDRESS** PO Box 1941, Mayaguez, PR 00681-1941. **EMAIL** serena1@centennialpr.net

ANDERSEN, ELAINE
DISCIPLINE LINGUISTICS **EDUCATION** Stanford Univ, PhD, 78. **CAREER** Prof. **RESEARCH** Relationship between language & nonlinguistic cognition. **SELECTED PUBLICATIONS** Auth, Speaking with Style: The Sociolinguistic Skills of Children, London: Routledge, Kagan Paul, 90, rep 92; co-ed, Developing Commuicative Competence in a Second Language, NY: Harper & Rowe, 90, rep 91. **CONTACT ADDRESS** Dept of Linguistics, Univ of So California, University Park Campus, Los Angeles, CA 90089. **EMAIL** elaine@gizmo.usc.edu

ANDERSON, DANNY L.
PERSONAL Born 08/08/1958, Houston, TX, m, 1998 **DISCIPLINE** LATIN AMERICAN LITERATURE **EDUCATION** Univ Kansas, PhD 85, MA 82; Austin Col, BA 80. **CAREER** Univ Texas Austin, asst prof 85-88; Univ Kansas, asst prof, assoc prof, dir LAS, 88-99. **HONORS AND AWARDS** NEH Fel; U of K Diss Fel; ITT Intl Fel. **MEMBERSHIPS** MLA; Midwest MLA; LASA. **RESEARCH** Mexican literature and social history; history of reading; sociology and literature. **SELECTED PUBLICATIONS** Auth, Creating Cultural Prestige: The Case of Editorial Joaquin Moritz, 1962-1992, Latin Amer Res Rev, 96; auth, Cultural Studies and Reading Culture in twentieth Century Mexico, Indiana Jour of Hisp Lit, 95; auth, Difficult Relations Compromising Positions: Telling Involvement in Recent Mexican Narrative, Chasqui, 95; auth, Reading Social Control and the Mexican soul in: Al filo del agua, Mexican studies/Estudios Mexicanos, 95; auth, Profession and Position: Histories of the Spanish American Novel and the Academy in the United States, Siglo XX/20th Century, 94; auth, Toward a History of Post Colonial Reading, rev essay, Col Eng, 94. **CONTACT ADDRESS** Dept of Spanish and Portuguese, Univ of Kansas, Lawrence, Lawrence, KS 66045. **EMAIL** djand@falcon.cc.ukans.edu

ANDERSON, DAVID G.
PERSONAL Born 02/21/1945, Tarboro, NC, m, 1968, 4 children **DISCIPLINE** LINGUISTICS **EDUCATION** Univ of NC at Chapel Hill, AB, 67; Vanderbilt Univ, MA, 74; PhD, 85. **CAREER** Instr, Union Univ, 75-76; instr, Ouachita Baptist Univ, 76-85; asst prof, NE La Univ, 85-87; from asst prof to assoc prof, John Carroll Univ, 87-. **HONORS AND AWARDS** NEH Summer Seminar for Col Teachers, Georgetown Univ, 90; Nat Dir of Latin Americanists, 92; Who's Who in the Midwest, 94-95; George E. Grauel Fac Fel, John Carroll Univ, 97; Phi Beta Kappa, Univ of NC at Chapel Hill. **MEMBERSHIPS** MLA, Am Asn of Teachers of Spanish & Portugese **RESEARCH** Contemporary Latin American poetry, poetry of Pablo Neruda **SELECTED PUBLICATIONS** Auth, "Neruda y la elegia en 1973," Nerudiana 1 (95): 129-135; auth, "La Elegia de Neruda y el "catalogo de difuntos" personal," La Torre: Revista de la Universidad de Puerto Rico 9(34) (95): 167-174; auth, "Haunting the Lyric Voice in Raul Zurita's Anteparaiso," Selected proceedings of the Pennsylvania Foreign Language Confernce 1988-1990 (Pittsburg: Duquesne Univ, 92): 17-21; auth, "Generic Tradition and Innovation in the Odas of Pablo Neruda," Discurso Lit 6 (88): 113-125; auth, "The Non-celebratory Odes of Pablo Neruda," Romance Notes 26 (86): 226-231; auth, On Elevating the Commonplace: A Structuralist Analysis of the Odas of Pablo Neruda, Albatros/Hispanofila (Valencia, Spain), 87. **CONTACT ADDRESS** Dept Mod & Class Lang, John Carroll Univ, 20700 N Park Blvd, Cleveland, OH 44118-4520. **EMAIL** danderson@jcu.edu

ANDERSON, GREG
PERSONAL Born 10/24/1962, Weston Super Mare, England **DISCIPLINE** CLASSICS; HISTORY **EDUCATION** Univ of Newcastle UK, BA, 86; Univ of London UK, MA, 88; Yale Univ PhD, 97. **CAREER** Asst Prof, 97-98, Elmira College; Asst Prof, 98-, Univ of IL, Chicago. **MEMBERSHIPS** APA **RESEARCH** Ancient Grecian to ancient greek political & cultural history, sports history, nationalism. **SELECTED PUBLICATIONS** Auth, The Athenian Experiment: Building a New Kind of Political Community in Ancient Attica, 508-490 B.C.", Ann Arbor, Univ of Mich Press, forthcoming; Alcmeonid Homelands Political Exile and the Unification of Attica, in: Historia, forthcoming; Games for Heros, Greek Athletics and the Invention of the Olympic Tradition, in: Report of the Yale-Smithsonian Annual Seminar on Material Culture, 97. **CONTACT ADDRESS** Dept of History, Univ of Illinois, Chicago, 601 S Morgan St, Chicago, IL 60607-7109. **EMAIL** gregand@uic.edu

ANDERSON, HELENE M.
PERSONAL Born 04/26/1927, New York, NY, m, 1950, 2 children **DISCIPLINE** SPANISH, PORTUGUESE **EDUCATION** Brooklyn Col, BA, 47; Syracuse Univ, MA, 52; PhD, 61. **CAREER** Coordinator, Latin American Poetry on Tape; Library Teaching Asst & Instr, Dept of Romance Languages, Syracuse University, 48-52; Asst, Assoc & Full Prof, Dept of Spanish & Portuguese of NYork Univ 66-; Chair of Department of Spanish & Portuguese, NYU, 83-92; Chair of Faculty Council, NYU, 95-96 & 99-00. **HONORS AND AWARDS** Deans Distinguished Fac Awd, NYU; Golden Dozen Teaching Awd (2x); College of Arts & Science, NYU; Great Teachers Awd of the Alumni Association, NYU, Distinguished Teaching Medal, NYU. **MEMBERSHIPS** Modern Language Assoc; Latin American Studies Assn; International Assoc of Hispanists; Amer Assoc of Univ; Amer Society; Instituto Cervantes. **RESEARCH** Latin Amer Literature, 19-20th Centuries; Women Writers of Mexico; Shaping the literary canon in Mexico's 19th century; Pre-Hispanic Cultures. **SELECTED PUBLICATIONS** Auth, "El mundo Narrativo de Carlos Montemayor; auth, "Tinisima: Imagen y texto en la obra de Elina Poniatowska;" auth, "Rosario Castellanos y las estructuras del poder;" auth, "Luisa Valenzuela: Elyo/ojo en Realidad nacional desde la cama," (forthcoming), with Angel del Rio, Masterpieces of Spanish American Literature, 2 vols, Translation: Gabriela Mistral: The Poet & Her Work, M. Acre de Vazquez. **CONTACT ADDRESS** Dept Spanish & Portuguese, New York Univ, 19 University Place, New York, NY 10003-4556. **EMAIL** hma1@is8.nyu.edu

ANDERSON, JAMES C., JR.
PERSONAL Born 04/15/1951, Malden, MA, m, 1978, 2 children **DISCIPLINE** CLASSICS **EDUCATION** Colo Col, BA, 73; Univ NC, Chapel Hill, MA, 76, PhD, 80. **CAREER** From asst prof to assoc prof to prof, 80-, Univ Ga; Mellon prof in charge, Intercollegiate Ctr Classical Stud, Rome, 93-94; dir, Classical Summer Sch Am Acad, Rome, 92-94. **HONORS AND AWARDS** Josiah Meigs Prof, 99-; Gen S. Beaver Tchg Prof, 96-99; NEH Fel Col Tchrs, 94-95; NEH Summer Stipend, 83; Fel Am Acad Rome, 78-79; Thomas J. Watson Fel, 73-74; Phi Beta Kappa, 73; fel, 78-79, am acad rome; thomas j. watson fel, 73-74, greece, britain; phi beta kappa, 73. **MEMBERSHIPS** Archaeol Inst Am; Soc of Architectureal Historians; Soc Fel Am Acad, Rome; Classical Assoc Middle West and South. **RESEARCH** Roman archaeology; Roman art and architecture; Latin Epigraphy. **SELECTED PUBLICATIONS** Auth, Historical Topography of the Imperial Fora, 84; auth, Roman Brick Stamps: The Thomas Ashby Collection, 91; auth, Roman Architecture and Society, 97. **CONTACT ADDRESS** Dept of Classics, Univ of Georgia, Park Hall, Athens, GA 30602-6203. **EMAIL** janderso@arches.uga.edu

ANDERSON, KIRK
DISCIPLINE SOFTWARE APPLICATIONS FOR LANGUAGE PEDAGOGY, CIVILIZATION, 20TH-CENTURY FRE **EDUCATION** Princeton Univ, PhD. **CAREER** Fr, Wheaton Col. **RESEARCH** Relation of history to literature. **SELECTED PUBLICATIONS** Auth, Actes du colloque international de Paris: L-F Cline, Fr Rev; Literary Generations, A 'Festschrift' in honor of Edward D. Sullivan. **CONTACT ADDRESS** Dept of Fr, Wheaton Col, Massachusetts, 26 East Main St, Norton, MA 02766.

ANDERSON, MICHAEL JOHN
PERSONAL Born 05/30/1967, London, England, m, 1993 **DISCIPLINE** CLASSICAL LANGUAGES; LITERATURE **EDUCATION** Princeton Univ, AB, 89; Univ Oxford, DPhil, 94. **CAREER** Vis asst prof, Univ Oregon, 93/94; Mellon postdoctoral fel in humanities, Columbia Univ 94-96; asst prof, Yale Univ, 97- . **HONORS AND AWARDS** Fulbright Sch for study in Freiburg, GER, 89/90; Marshall Scholarship for study in Oxford, ENG, 90-93. **MEMBERSHIPS** APA **RESEARCH** Greek literature; Greek art. **SELECTED PUBLICATIONS** The Fall of Troy in Early Greek Poetry and Art, 97; The Sophrosyne of Persinna and the Romantic Strategy of Heliodorus' Aethiopica, Classical Philology, 97. **CONTACT ADDRESS** Dept of Classics, Yale Univ, New Haven, CT 06520-8266. **EMAIL** michael.j.anderson@yale.edu

ANDERSON, WILLIAM SCOVIL
PERSONAL Born 09/16/1927, Brookline, MA, m, 1983, 5 children **DISCIPLINE** CLASSICS **EDUCATION** Yale Univ, BA, 50, PhD, 54; Cambridge Univ, BA, 52, MA, 56. **CAREER** Instr classics, Yale Univ, 55-60; from asst prof to assoc prof Latin, 60-65, chmn dept classics, 70-73, Prof Latin & Comp Lit Univ CA, Berkeley, 65-; prof in charge, Intercol Ctr Class Studies, Rome, 67-68; ed Vergilius, 65; res prof, Univ Melbourne, 84; Robson Lectr, Victoria Col, Toronto, 87; Blegen Res Prof, Vassar Col, 89-90; Vis Distinguished Prof, FL State Univ, 95. **HONORS AND AWARDS** Prix de Rome, 54; Morse fel, 59; Am Coun Learned Soc grant to deliver lect at Int Cong

Satire, Rostock, Ger, 65; Nat Endowment Hum sr fel, 73-74; classicist-in-residence, Am Acad, Rome, 73-74. **MEMBERSHIPS** Am Philol Asn (pres, 77); Soc Relig Higher Educ; Philol Asn Pac Coast. **RESEARCH** Roman satire and comedy; Vergil; Ovid. **SELECTED PUBLICATIONS** Auth, The Art of the Aeneid, Prentice-Hall, 69; Ovid's Metamorphoses: Books 6-10, Univ OK, 72, Books 1-5, Univ OK, 96; Ovidius, Metamorphoses, Leipzig: Teubner, 77; Essays on Roman Satire, Princeton Univ, 82; Barbarian Play: Plautus' Roman Comedy, Toronto, 93. **CONTACT ADDRESS** Dept of Class, Univ of California, Berkeley, 7212 Dwinelle Hall, Berkeley, CA 94720-2521. **EMAIL** wsa@socrates.berkeley.edu

ANDO, CLIFFORD

PERSONAL Born 05/03/1969, Philadelphia, PA **DISCIPLINE** CLASSICAL STUDIES **EDUCATION** Univ Mich, PhD, 96. **CAREER** Asst prof, York Univ, 96-98; asst prof, Univ of Southern Calif, 98-. **HONORS AND AWARDS** Fel, Am Coun of Learned Soc. **MEMBERSHIPS** Am Philol Asn; North Am Patristics Soc. **RESEARCH** Roman history; Latin and Greek historiography. **SELECTED PUBLICATIONS** Auth, "Pagan Apologetics and Christian Intolerance in the Ages of Themistius and Augustine" in J of Early Christian Studies, 96; "Tacticus, Annales VI: Beginning and End" in Am J of Philol, 97; auth, "Was Rome a polis?, Classical Antiquity, 99; auth, "Imperial ideology and provincial loyalty in the Roman Empire," Berkeley: Univ of Calif Press, 00; auth, "Signs, idols and the incarnation in Augustinian metaphysics," Representations, 01. **CONTACT ADDRESS** Classics Dept, Univ of So California, Taper Hall 224, Los Angeles, CA 90089-0352. **EMAIL** cando@usc.edu

ANDRE, MARIA CLAUDIA

PERSONAL Born 08/12/1959, Buenos Aires, Argentina, m, 1998, 1 child **DISCIPLINE** LATIN AMERICAN LITERATURE, 20TH CENTURY, GENDER STUDIES **EDUCATION** Univ del Salv, trans, interp, 84; SUNY, PhD, 95. **CAREER** Vis prof, Marist Col, 90-91; vis prof, Bard Col, 91-93; teach asst, SUNY, 92-95; assoc prof, Hope Col, 94-. **HONORS AND AWARDS** Sigma Delta Phi. **MEMBERSHIPS** LASA; MLA. **RESEARCH** Latin American women writer; Latin American politics; gender studies. **SELECTED PUBLICATIONS** Rev of "Intimas suculencias: tratado filoscfico de cocina by Laura Esquivel (Letras Femeninas, Univ Neb-Lin, forthcoming); auth, "Griselda Gambaro: feminismo e influencia en su narrativa," Confluencia J 14 (99); auth, "Entrevista a Luisa Valenzuela," Revista Atenea 476 (98); auth, "Entorno a canones, memorias y recuerdos : conversacion con Tununa Mercado" Alba de Am Inst Lit Cult Hisp16 (98); auth, "Entre el sicoanalisis y Ta literatura: conversaci6n con Liliana Heker," Alba de Am 19 (OO); auth, "Entre los bordes de lo real y el desarrollo de la imaginacion: Entrevista con Liliana Heker," Alba de Am 19 (00); auth, "Entrevista a Luisa Valenzuela," Revista Hisp (00); auth, "Empowering the Feminine/Feminist/Lesbian Subject through the Lens: Representation of Women in Yo, Ta peor de todas," by Maria Luisa Bemberg's, in Tortilleras: Hispanic and Latina Lesbian Expression (Temple Univ Press, forthcoming). **CONTACT ADDRESS** Dept Modern, Classical Language, Hope Col, 137 East 12th St, Holland, MI 49423-3607. **EMAIL** andre@hope.edu

ANDRES, CARLOS M.

PERSONAL Born 03/14/1962, Segovia, Spain, m, 1994, 3 children **DISCIPLINE** SPANISH **EDUCATION** Univ autonoma de Madric, Licenciatura en Filosofia, 86; Ohio State Univ, MA, 89; Univ Wis, PhD, 95. **CAREER** Asst prof, Iowa State Univ, 95-00; asst prof, Calif State Univ Stanislaus, 00-. **MEMBERSHIPS** MLA, Cervantes Soc of Am. **RESEARCH** Golden Age Poetry, Spanish Poetry, Literary Criticism, Philosophy. **SELECTED PUBLICATIONS** Auth, Flor Sin Tallo y Sin Raiz: La Poetica Modernista de Juan Ramon Jimenez; auth, Antiesclavismo e Independentismo en Cecilia Valdes; auth, El Libro de Avellaneda Como Purgante de la Locura Quijotesca; auth, La Poetica del Osaso en rosaura Alvarez; auth, La Experiencia Mistica Como repliegue del Sujeto en Juan de la Cruz. **CONTACT ADDRESS** 1200 Hardwick Ave, Turlock, CA 95382. **EMAIL** candres@stan.csustan.edu

ANDREU, ALICIA GRACIELA

PERSONAL Born 09/07/1940, Lima, Peru, m, 1980, 1 child **DISCIPLINE** SPANISH LITERATURE **EDUCATION** Chapman Col, BA, 65; Univ Wis, MA, 68; Univ Ore, PhD, 78. **CAREER** Chmn, Span & Ital Dept, 80-81, 83-84, 88-91, Prof Span, Middlebury Col, Dean, Spanish School, 84-86; Native instr, Nat Defense Educ Act, summer 64 & 65; Fulbright-Hays res grant, Madrid, Spain, 9/74-6/76; NEH grant, 79 & 81-82, consult, 81-; consult, D C Heath & Co, 80; Am Coun Learned Soc grant, 81; Fel, School Criticism & Theory, Northwestern Univ, summer 81; eval panelist, NEHcol teachers fels, 82-; Prog for Cultural Coop, Ministry of Culture, Spain and U S Univ, res grant, summer 96. **HONORS AND AWARDS** Tuition Scholarship: Chapman Col, CA, 61-65; Fulbright-Hays Research Grant, 74-76; NEH Summer Seminar Fellow: Yale Univ, 79; Fellow: Schl of Criticism and Theory, Northwestern Univ, 81; ACLS Traveling Grant: Santander, Spain, 81; Ada Howe Kent Summer Research Fellowship, Middlebury Col, 90; Research grant, Program for Cultural Cooperation Between Spain's Ministry of Culture and United States' Universities, 96, NEH Fellow for Col Tchrs and Independent Scholars, 99-00. **MEMBERSHIPS** MLA; Asoc Galdosistas; Asoc Int Hisp; Asoc Iberoamericana; Latin Am Indian Lit Asn. **RESEARCH** Nineteenth century Spanish literature; 20th century Spanish & Spanish American literature. **SELECTED PUBLICATIONS** Auth, Relacion intima entre Galdos y la literature popular, Actas del Sequndo Congreso Int Estudios Galdosianos, 78; ed, La Cruz del Olivar de Faustina Saez de Melgar, Anales Galdosianos, 80; auth, Galdos y la literatura popular, SGEL, 82; Arte y consumo Angela Grassi y El Correo de la Moda, Nuevo Hisp, winter 82; El folletin como intertexto en Tormento, AG, 82; El folletin: de Galdos a Manuel Puig, RIA, 4-9/83; Garcilaso y Bernal: Interpretations Interpreted, REH, 84; Pedo Camacho: prestidigitator del lenguaje, MLS, spring 86; Dialogo de voces en Fortunata y Jacinta, Actas del VIII Congreso de la AIH, Brown Univ, 86; Cartas de Benito Perez Galdos a Ricardo Palma, AG, 85; Miau: La escritura del poder o el poder de la escritura, AG, 86; La biblioteca de Benito Perez Galdos, KRQ, 8/88; Penito Perez Galdos: lectura y creacion, in Realismo y naturalismo en Espana en la segunda mitad del s.XIX, Antrhopos, Barcelona, 88; Garcilaso y Bernal: Interpretaciones Interpretadas, Historica, 12/88; Tormento: Un discurso de amantes, Hispania, 5/89; Juanito Santa Cruz en dialogo con el mito de don Juan, RHM, 6/89; Modelos dialogicos en la narrativa de Benito Perez Galdos, Univ de Perdue, Amsterdam, 89; Una nueva aproximacion al lenguaje de las Tradiciones Peruanas de Ricardo Palma, REH, 90; Benito Perez Galdos y el discurso americano, La Torre, 4-6/91; Tristana: El deseo y la produccion de las escritura, RLA, 91; Ramon Perez de Ayala y el mito de don Juan, ALEC, 92; Amor de Madre: Pardigma intertextual en una obra de Ricard Palma, Discurso Literario, spring 93; Maria Guerrero y el teatro de Benio Perez Galdos, in A Sesquecentennial Tribute to Galdos, JDLC, 93; Habla la ciudad: Poetica de la migracion, RCL, 8/93; Cronica de Lima, de Antonio Cisneros, o Hermelinda y la subversion de la historia, in Hispanic Culture on the Pacific Coast of the Americas: From Chilenos to Chicanos, CASU Press, 94; El crimen de la Calle de Fuencarral: Texto y contexto, in Narrativa Decimononica: Creacion Popular y Literatura de Consumo, Rodopi; Legitimidad linguistica y legitimidad socio-economica en un relato de Julio Ramon Ribeyro, RCLL, 94; Una re-lectura de Fabla Salvaje, de Cesar Vallejo, Contratexto, 94; Maria Guerrero: Ficcion y mito, Critica Hispanica, 95; El discurso materno en La Cruz del Olivar, de Faustina Saez de melgar, RCEH, winter 95; La critica feminista y las obras de Benio Perez Galdos y Leopoldo Alas, in Breve Historia Feminista de la literatura espanola; A day in the Bronx (short story), Array Mag, winter 95; El intertexto folletinesco en Tormento, HCLE, 3/95; Maria Guerrero: Texto y contexto en la obra dramatica de Benito Perez Galdos, in Actas del Simposio Galdos y el hispanismo norteamericano (homenaje), 2/95; El discurso matsigenka en El hablador de Mario Vargas Llosa, HJ, 96; Benito Perez Galdos, Higinia Balaguer, y El Crimen de la Calle de Fuencarral, AG, 96/97; La obra de Carmen de Icaza en la difusion de un nuevo concepto de nacion espanola, RHM; Historia y literatura en un texto de Galdos, in Actas del XII C de la AIH, England; El bildungsroman de Andrea en Nada de Carmen Lafotre, RL. **CONTACT ADDRESS** Span & Ital Dept, Middlebury Col, Middlebury, VT 05753-6001. **EMAIL** andreu@panther.middlebury.edu

ANDREWS, LARRY RAY

PERSONAL Born 08/09/1940, Greencastle, IN, m, 1961, 4 children **DISCIPLINE** ENGLISH; COMPARATIVE LITERATURE **EDUCATION** Ohio State Univ, BA, 62; Rutgers Univ, PhD(comp lit), 71. **CAREER** Instr English, Univ SC, 66-69; asst prof, 69-78, Assoc Prof English, Kent State Univ, 78-, Dean, Honors Col, 93-. **MEMBERSHIPS** Col Lang Asn. **RESEARCH** European romanticism; Russian-Western literary relations in 19th century; African American women's fiction. **SELECTED PUBLICATIONS** Auth, D V Venevitinov: A sketch of his life and works, Russ Lit Triquart, 74; Dostevskij and Hugos Le Dernier Jour d'un Condamne, Comp Lit, 77; The Spatial Imagery of Oblomovism, Neophilologus, 88; Black Sisterhood in Gloria Naylor's Novels, CLAS, 89; Hugo's Gilliatt and Leskov's Golovan: Two Eccentric Folk-Epic Heroes, Comp Lit, 94. **CONTACT ADDRESS** Honors Col, Kent State Univ, PO Box 5190, Kent, OH 44242-0001. **EMAIL** landrews@kent.edu

ANDREWS, STEPHEN J.

PERSONAL Born 06/15/1954, Baltimore, MD, m, 1979, 4 children **DISCIPLINE** HEBRAIC AND COGNATE STUDIES **EDUCATION** Carson-Newman Col, BA, 76; Eastern Bapt Theol Sem, M Div, 79; Southeastern Bapt Theol Sem, Th M, 83; Hebrew Union Col, PhD, 95, M Phil, 98. **CAREER** Asst prof, 91-96, assoc prof, 96-98, old testament and Hebrew, Southeastern Bapt Theol Sem; prof, old testament and archaeol, Midwestern Bapt Theol Sem, 98-; dir, Morton Inst of Archaeol, Midwestern Bapt Theol Sem, 98-. **MEMBERSHIPS** Amer Oriental Soc; Inst of Bibl Res; Soc of Bibl Lit. **RESEARCH** Syro-Palestinian archaeology; Biblical Hebrew; Ancient near east. **SELECTED PUBLICATIONS** Article, Duck Tales at Nuzi: A Note on the Trussed-duck Weights Excavated at Yorgan Tepa, Studies on the Civilization and Culture of Nuzi and the Hurrians, vol 8, 241-43, CDL Press, 96; rev, Two Hundred Nuzi Texts from the Oriental Institute of the University of Chicago, Part I, Studies on the Civilization and Culture of Nuzi and The Hurrians, vol 6, Jour of the Amer Oriental Soc, 116, 269-70, 96; article, A Knowledge of Hebrew Possible to All? Old Testament Exposition and the Hebraica Veritas, Faith and Mission, 13/1, 98-114, Fall 95; rev, Analytical Key to the Old Testament, Faith and Mission, 12/1, 97-98, Fall, 94; rev, The Seven Pillories of Wisdom, Faith and Mission, 10/1, 107-110, Fall, 92; rev, An Introduction to Biblical Hebrew Syntax, Faith and Mission, 9/2, 104-6, Spring, 92; rev, The NIV Exhaustive Concordance, Faith and Mission, 9/1, 85-86, Fall, 91; contr, Mercer Dict of the Bible, Mercer Univ Press, 90. **CONTACT ADDRESS** Midwestern Baptist Theol Sem, 5001 N Oak St Trafficway, Kansas City, MO 64118. **EMAIL** archaeology@mbts.edu

ANDRIOPOULOS, STEFAN

PERSONAL Born 10/04/1968, Aschorffemburg, Germany, s **DISCIPLINE** GERMAN **EDUCATION** Univ Regensburg, BA, 90; Univ Hamburg, MA, 94; PhD, 98. **CAREER** Acad res, Univ of Cologne, 99-00; asst prof, Columbia Univ, 00-. **HONORS AND AWARDS** Fel, Bavarian State for Highly Gifted Students, 88-90, 91-94; Fulbright Fel, 90-91; DAAD Fel, 95-96; Fel, Studienstaftung des deutschen Volkes, 96-98. **MEMBERSHIPS** MLA. **RESEARCH** 18th to 20th Century Literary and Cultural History, Weimar Cinema, Media Theories, Intellectual History, History of Science, Occultism. **SELECTED PUBLICATIONS** Auth, Unfall und Verbrechen: Konfiguahonen wischen juristischem und zitcrarischem Dislcuis um 1900, Centautus, (Pfaffemwciler), 96; auth, "The Invisible Hand," ELH 66.3 (99): 739-758; auth, Besesseme Viorper: Hyphose, Korpetschoften und die Erfindung des Kinos, Fink (Munich), 00; ed, Die Adresse des Mediums, Du Mont, (Cologne), 01. **CONTACT ADDRESS** Dept German, Columbia Univ, 319 Hamilton Hall, Mail Code 2812, New York, NY 10027. **EMAIL** sa610@columbia.edu

ANDRIST, DEBRA D.

DISCIPLINE SPANISH **EDUCATION** Fort Hays Kans State Univ, BA, 72; Univ Utah, MA, 79; SUNY, Buffalo, PhD, 85. **CAREER** Teach asst, Univ Utah, 78-79; adm asst, 81-82, teach asst, 79-81, instr, Intensive Eng Lang Inst, 80, 81; dir, Ctr Critical Langs, 80, SUNY, Buffalo; assoc prof, 92-96, asst, 86-92, Baylor Univ; assoc prof, 96-, CHAIR, 97-, PROF SPAN, 98-, UNIV ST THOMAS. **CONTACT ADDRESS** MACL, Univ of St. Thomas, Texas, 3800 Montrose, Houston, TX 77006. **EMAIL** andrist@stthom.edu

ANDRONICA, JOHN LOUIS

PERSONAL Born 10/06/1942, Boston, MA, m, 1966, 2 children **DISCIPLINE** CLASSICAL LANGUAGES **EDUCATION** Col of the Holy Cross, AB, 63; Boston Col, MA, 66; Johns Hopkins Univ, PhD, 69. **CAREER** Asst prof classic lang, 69-72, dir, Wake Forest-in-Venice Prog, 71-72 & 81, assoc prof class lang, Wake Forest Univ, 72-. **MEMBERSHIPS** Am Philol Assn; Class Assn Midwest & South; Vergiliam Soc; Petronian Soc. **RESEARCH** Latin love elegy; Latin epic. **CONTACT ADDRESS** Dept of Class Lang, Wake Forest Univ, PO Box 7343, Winston-Salem, NC 27109-7343. **EMAIL** andy@wfu.edu

ANGELES, JOSE LUIS

PERSONAL Born Valencia, Spain, m, 2001 **DISCIPLINE** SPANISH LITERATURE, LANGUAGE **EDUCATION** Univ Valencia, PhD, 98. **CAREER** Teaching assoc, Brown Univ, 97-98; vis asst prof to asst prof, Univ N Fla, 98-. **HONORS AND AWARDS** Erasmus Grant, 91-92; Univ Fla Travel Grant, 01. **MEMBERSHIPS** MLA; UEPV; CABC; EBC; Lunas Rojas. **RESEARCH** Contemporary Spanish poetry; literary theory; Spanish and Spanish American novels on dictatorships; Spanish epic poetry. **SELECTED PUBLICATIONS** Co-auth, "Las Actitudes Liricas. El Otro y Yo: Jaime Gil de Biedma," in En el Nombre de Jaime Gil de Biedma. Actas de los Primeros Encuentros de Poetica Jaime Gil de Biedma y su Generacion Poetica (Zaragoza: Pr Univ Zaragoza): 389-397; co-auth, "Recepcion Critica de Miguel Hernandez en los Arios 70 y 80," in Miguel Hernandez, Cincuenta Anos (Pr Univ Alicante, 93): 241-251; auth, "Estrategias de tension Ideologica: Dialectica de los Signos en las Escrituras de Juan Goytisolo, Jorge Riechmann y Jenaro Talens," in Mundos de Ficcion: Actas del Congreso Mundos de Ficcion. VI Congreso Internacional de la Asociacion Espanola de Semiotica, eds. J. Ma Pozuelo Yvancos, F. Vicente Gomez (Pr Univ Murcia, 96): 217-226; auth, Poesia y Poder, Ediciones Bajo Cero (Valencia), 97; auth, "Y sin embargo se Mueve, Poesia Espanola en Castellano, 1995-1996: Ejercicio de Zapeo," Diablotext 3 (97): 415-426; auth, "Intorno All'evolozione Narrativa di Juan Goytisolo," Ling Letter 29 (98): 99-116; auth, "La Poesia en Marcha 'Hacia la Desalienacion' Algunas claves de Lectura a la Produccion Poetica de Jenaro Talens," Immagine Segno-Parola (99): 495-516; auth, Hacia una Ideologia de la Produccion Literaria, Ediciones Bajo Cero (Valencia), 00; auth, "La Historia Literaria Como Productora de Patrones Ideologicos: El exempla del Patriarcalismo en el Cantar de mio Cid," Lunas Rojas (01); auth, "La Suprervivencia Ideologica del Cantar de mio Cid," Univ Bologna (forthcoming). **CONTACT ADDRESS** 1746 Nettington Ct, Jacksonville, FL 32246-7698. **EMAIL** jangeles@unf.edu

ANGELIS, PAUL J.
PERSONAL Born 01/28/1941, Scranton, PA, m, 1965, 3 children **DISCIPLINE** LINGUISTICS **EDUCATION** Univ Scranton, AB, 62; Georgetown Univ, PhD(ling), 68. **CAREER** Asst prof English, Col Mil Royal, 69-72; Fulbright lectr ling & English, Univ Rome, 72-73; training dir, Food & Agr Orgn UN, 73-74; from assoc to asst prof ling & English, Tex A&M Univ, 74-77; prog dir lang, Educ Test Serv, 77-81; Assoc Prof & Chmn Ling, Southern Ill Univ, 81-. **MEMBERSHIPS** Teachers English Speakers Other Lang; Nat Asn Foreign Student Affairs; Ling Soc Am. **RESEARCH** Language testing; second language acquisition; English as a foreign language. **SELECTED PUBLICATIONS** Auth, The importance and diversity of aural comprehension, Mod Lang J, 3/73; Listening comprehension and erroranalysis, AILA Proc, 74; coauth, The performance of non-native speakers of English on Toefl and verbal aptitude tests, 78 & Effects of item disclosure of Toefl performance, 12/80, Educ Testing Serv; Psycholinguistics: Two views, In: Language and Communication, Hornbeam Press, 80. **CONTACT ADDRESS** Dept of Ling, So Illinois Univ, Carbondale, Carbondale, IL 62901-4300. **EMAIL** pangelis@siu.edu

ANKROM, JEFFREY
PERSONAL Born New Castle, IN **DISCIPLINE** FRENCH **EDUCATION** Ball State Univ, BA, 78 Northwestern Univ, MA, 83 Purdue Univ. **CAREER** Music Ed, IN Univ Press, 97. **SELECTED PUBLICATIONS** Transl of jour articles. **CONTACT ADDRESS** Univ Press, Indiana Univ, Bloomington, 601 N. Morton St., Bloomington, IN 47404-3797. **EMAIL** jankrom@indiana.edu

ANSART, GUILLAUME
PERSONAL Born 12/10/1960, Paris, France, m, 1986 **DISCIPLINE** FRENCH, ITALIAN **EDUCATION** Univ Paris, DEA, 84; Princeton Univ, PhD, 95. **CAREER** Lectr, Univ NMex, 93-94; Lectr, Ind Univ, 94-95; Asst Prof, Ind Univ, 95-. **MEMBERSHIPS** Mod Lang Asn, Am Asn of Teachers of Fr, Am Soc of Eighteenth-Century Studies, Soc of Utopian Studies. **RESEARCH** Eighteenth-Century French literature, political philosophy, anthropology, aethetics of the novel, utopias. **SELECTED PUBLICATIONS** Auth, Reflexion utopique et pratique romanesque au siecle des lumieres: Prevost, Rousse au, Sade," Lettres Modernes Minard (99). **CONTACT ADDRESS** Dept Lang, Indiana Univ, Bloomington, 1020 E Kirkwood Ave, Bloomington, IN 47405-7103. **EMAIL** gansart@indiana.edu

ANYINEFA, KOFFI
PERSONAL Born 11/20/1959, Badougbe-Adjome, Togo, m, 1990, 1 child **DISCIPLINE** FRENCH LITERATURE, FRANCOPHONE LITERATURES & CULTURES **EDUCATION** Universitat Bayreuth, Germany, PhD, 89. **CAREER** Asst prof, Haverford Coll, 90-96 assoc prof, 96-present. **HONORS AND AWARDS** Alexander von Humboldt-Stiftung Fel, 97-98; NEH Summer Stipend, 97. **MEMBERSHIPS** African Literature Assn; African Studies Assn; Amer Assn of Teachers of French **RESEARCH** Francophone Lit and Culture; French Lit, colonial lit. **SELECTED PUBLICATIONS** Auth, Intertextuality in Dongala's Un fusil dans la main, un poem dans la poche, Research in African Literatures, 93; Hello and Goodbye to Negritude: Senghor, Dadie, Dongala and America, Research in African Literatures, 96; Y a bon banania: L'Afrique et le discours nationaliste dans Tombouctou de Maupassant, forthcoming in The French Review, 97; Postcolonial Postcoloniality in Henri Lopes's Le Pleurer-Rire, Research in African Literature, 98. **CONTACT ADDRESS** French Dept., Haverford Col, 370 Lancas, Haverford, PA 19041-1392. **EMAIL** kanyinef@haverford.edu

AOKI, MICHIKOY
PERSONAL Born, Japan, m, 1964 **DISCIPLINE** JAPANESE **EDUCATION** Syracuse Univ, MA, 63; Columbia Univ, PhD, 70. **CAREER** Asst Prof to Assoc Prof, Clark Univ, 90-. **MEMBERSHIPS** Asiatic soc of Great Britain and Ireland. **RESEARCH** Pre-modern history of Japanese women. **SELECTED PUBLICATIONS** Auth, "Women in Ancient Japan," in Women's roles in ancient civilizations: Reference Guide, Greenwood press, 99; auth, records of Wind and Earth, Asn for Asian Studies, 97. **CONTACT ADDRESS** Dept For Lang, Clark Univ, 950 Main St, Worcester, MA 01610-1400. **EMAIL** maoki@law.harvard.edu

AOUN, JOSEPH
DISCIPLINE SEMITIC LANGUAGES **EDUCATION** MIT, PhD. **CAREER** Prof, Univ Southern Calif. **RESEARCH** Distribution & interpretation of pronominal & definite descriptions. **SELECTED PUBLICATIONS** Coauth, Minimality, Reconstruction and PF- movement, Ling Inquiry 29.4, MIT Press, 98; Resumption and Last Resort to appear in J. Ouhalla and U. Shlonsky Semitic Syntax, Kluwer, 97; Epithets ms USC, 97. **CONTACT ADDRESS** Dept of Linguistics, Univ of So California, 3601 Watt Way, Grace Ford Salvatori 301, Los Angeles, CA 90089-1693. **EMAIL** aoun@usc.edu

ARAUJO, NORMAN
PERSONAL Born 03/22/1933, New Bedford, MA **DISCIPLINE** FRENCH, PORTUGUESE **EDUCATION** Harvard Col, AB, 55; Univ Aix-Marseille, cert, 55-56; Harvard Univ, MA, 57, PhD, 62. **CAREER** Asst prof French & Port, Univ MA, Amherst, 62-64; asst prof mod lang, 64-68, acting chm dept, 69-70, assoc prof Romance Lang, Boston Col, 68-; Gulbenkian Found fel, 70; Cape Verdean Govt fel, 78. **HONORS AND AWARDS** Bartolomeu Dias Prize, Acad Int Cult Portuguesa, 68. **MEMBERSHIPS** MLA; Int Conf Group Mod Port. **RESEARCH** Portuguese and French romanticism; Portuguese-African Literature. **SELECTED PUBLICATIONS** Auth, A study of Cape Verdean literature, 66; Time and Rhythm in Balzac's La Peau de Chagrin, Fr Rev, 70; The Role of Death in Becque's Les Corbeaux, Rev Langues Vivantes, 70; In Search of Eden: Lamartine's Symbols of Despair and Deliverance, Classical Folia Eds, 76; New Directions in Cape Verdean Literature?, The First Numbers of Raizes, Critical Perspectives on Lusophone African Literature, Three Continents Press, Inc, 81; Ferdinand Brunetiere, Critical Survey of Literary Theory, ed Frank Magill, vol 1, 88; Theophile Gautier, Critical Survey of Lit Theory, ed Frank Magill, vol 2, 88; Hippolyte-Adolphe Taine, Critical Survey of Lit Theory, ed Frank Magill, vol 4, 88; The Language of Business and the Business of Language in Becque's Les Corbeaux, French Rev 63, 89; Prosaic Licence and the Use of the Literary Past in Daudet's La Chevre de M. Seguin, Forum for Modern Language Studies 27: 3, 91; Petrus Borel, Dictionary of Lit Biography, ed Catharine Savage Brosman, vol 119: Nineteenth-Century French Fiction Writers: Romanticism and Realism, 1800-1860, 92; auth, Ferdinand Brunetiere, Theophile Gautier, Hippolyte-Adolphe Taine, Encyclopedia of Literary Critics and Criticism, 99. **CONTACT ADDRESS** Dept Romance Lang, Boston Col, Chestnut Hill, 140 Commonwealth Ave, Chestnut Hill, MA 02167-3800. **EMAIL** araujo@bc.edu

ARCHAMBAULT, PAUL JOSEPH
PERSONAL Born 09/17/1937, Webster, MA, m, 1983, 2 children **DISCIPLINE** FRENCH, LATIN **EDUCATION** Assumption Col, AB, 58; Yale Univ, PhD(Romance lang), 63. **CAREER** From instr to asst prof, Amherst Col, 62-68; assoc prof, 68-73, Prof French, Syracuse Univ, 73-, Amherst Col factrustee fel, 65-66; Nat Found on Arts & Hum jr scholar, 69. **MEMBERSHIPS** MLA; Medieval Acad Am. **RESEARCH** Mediaeval French and Latin lit; 20th century French lit. **SELECTED PUBLICATIONS** Auth, Thucydides in France: Commynes, J Hist Ideas, 1/67; Commynes and the Renaissance idea of wisdom, Humanisme et Renaissance, fall 67; Sallust in France: Thomas Basin, Papers on Lang & Lit, summer 68; Camus' Hellenic Sources (Studies in Romance Lang & Lit Ser), Univ NC, 72; Seven French Chroniclers: Witnesses to History, Syracuse Univ, 74; A Monk's Confession, Penn State Press, 96; ed, Syracuse Scholar, 79-82; Medieval romance and language, Symp, spring 81. **CONTACT ADDRESS** Dept of For Lang & Lit, Syracuse Univ, 305 H.B. Crouse Hall, Syracuse, NY 13244-1160. **EMAIL** pjarcham@syr.edu

ARENAS, FERNANDO
DISCIPLINE SPANISH AND PORTUGUESE LITERATURE **EDUCATION** N Ariz Univ, MA, 86; Univ Calif Berkeley, MA, 88; PhD, 94. **RESEARCH** Portuguese, Brazilian and Lusophone African literary and cultural studies; theoretical approaches to the study of literature and culture. **SELECTED PUBLICATIONS** Auth, Entre o lixo e a esperanza: Morangos Mofados de Caio Fernando Abreu, 90. **CONTACT ADDRESS** Spanish and Portuguese Dept, Univ of Minnesota, Twin Cities, 34 Folwell Hall, 9 Pleasant St SE, Minneapolis, MN 55455. **EMAIL** arena002@gold.tc.umn.edu

AREND, JUTTA
DISCIPLINE GERMAN **EDUCATION** Case Western Reserve Univ, MA, 71, PhD, 72. **CAREER** Sr lectr; Ger for lang asst liaison; Ger study abroad adv; contact, Int Summer Courses, Univ Freiburg; Ger dept Fulbright adv for prog in Ger and Austria. **RESEARCH** 20th century literature; women's studies; Postmodernism; Romanticism. **SELECTED PUBLICATIONS** Auth, Man verelendet, So - oder so Patrick Suskinds Sonderlinge und ihr Verhaltnis zum Weiblichen, Ger Stud Rev 19 2, 96; Crazy Horse in Mecklenburg: Indianervisionen in Joochen Laabs Der Schattenfanger, Ger Quart 65, 92 & Dokumentation: Ingeborg Drewitz, Ger Quart 59, 86. **CONTACT ADDRESS** Dept of Modern Languages and Literatures, Col of the Holy Cross, 1 College St, Worcester, MA 01610-2395. **EMAIL** jarend@holycross.edu

ARENS, HILTRUD
PERSONAL Born 12/08/1961, Paderbern, Germany, m, 1991, 1 child **DISCIPLINE** GERMAN LITERATURE **EDUCATION** Univ of Md, MA, 88, PhD, 97. **CAREER** Vis Asst Prof, Univ of Mont, 98-00, Asst prof, Univ of Montana, 00-. **HONORS AND AWARDS** Prahe Awd, Univ of Md, 92; Am Fel, AAUW Ed Found, 95-96. **MEMBERSHIPS** MLA; GSA; AITG; WIG; AAUW. **RESEARCH** Contemp German lit & culture; minority lit. **SELECTED PUBLICATIONS** Auth, "Kulturelle Hybriditat" in der deutschen Minoritatenliteratur der achtziger Jane, Stauffenburg Verlag, 99; Libuse Monikova, Women Writers in German-Speaking Countries, Greenwood Press, 98; Industrial Revolution, Encycl of German Lit, Greenwood Press, 97; Auslandergesetz, Encycl of German Lit, Greenwood Press, 97; Erahlstrategie und Geschlechtskomponente in Bettina von Arnims Die Gunderode und Clemens Brentanos Fruhlingskranze. Ein Vergleich, Internationales Jahrbuch der Bettina-von-Arnim-Gesellschaft, Saint Albin Verlag, 93. **CONTACT ADDRESS** FLL Dept, Univ of Montana, Missoula, MT 59812. **EMAIL** harens@selway.umt.edu

ARENS, KATHERINE M.
PERSONAL Born 11/29/1953, Chicago, IL, s **DISCIPLINE** GERMAN **EDUCATION** Northwestern Univ, BA, 75; Stanford Univ, MA, 76; PhD, 81. **CAREER** Asst prof to prof, Univ of Tex Austin, 80-. **HONORS AND AWARDS** NEH Summer Res Stipend, 82; Outstanding Graduate Teaching, Univ of Rex; Best Article in Unterrichtspraxis, 97. **MEMBERSHIPS** MLA; Am Philos Assoc; Am Assoc ofTeachers of Ger; Ger Studies Assoc. **RESEARCH** European Intellectual history, 1720-, German Literatur, 1750-1900, Austrian Cultural Studies, Romanticism, German Idealism, Literary and Cultural Theory. **SELECTED PUBLICATIONS** Auth, Structures of Knowing: Psychologies of the Nineteenth Century, Boston Studies in the Philos of Sci 113, Reidel, (Dordrecht), 89; coauth, Reading for Meaning: An Integrated Approach to Language Learning, Prentice-Hall, (Englewood Cliffis, NJ), 91; auth, Austria and Other Margins: Reading Culture, Camden House, (Columbia, SC), 96; auth, "On Rereading Paul's Prinzipien der Sprachgeschichte", Multiple Perspectives on the Historical Dimension of Language, ed Kurt R. Jankowsky, Nodus Pub, (Munster, 96): 105-114; auth, "Discourse Analysis as Critical Historiography: A Semanalyse of Mystic Speech", Rethinking Hist 2.1 (98): 23-50; auth, "From Caillois to The Laugh of the Medusa: Vectors of a Diagonal Science", Textual Practice 12.2 (98): 225-250; auth, "The Linguistics of French Feminism: Semanalyse as Critical Discourse Practice", Intertexts 2.2 (98): 171-184; auth, "For Want of a Word: The Case for Germanophone", Unterrichtspraxis/Teaching German 32.2 (99): 130-142; coauth, "Reading Goals and the Standards for Foreign Language Learning", FLAnnals 33.1, (00): 104-122; auth, Empire in Decline: Fitz Mauthner's Critique of Wilhelminian German, Peter Lang, (NY), 00. **CONTACT ADDRESS** Dept Ger, Univ of Texas, Austin, 0 Univ of Tex, Austin, TX 78712-1013. **EMAIL** k.arens@mail.utexas.edu

ARGYROS, ALEX
DISCIPLINE FRENCH LITERATURE **EDUCATION** Cornell Univ, PhD, 77. **CAREER** Prof. **SELECTED PUBLICATIONS** Auth, Crimes of Narration: Camus' La Chute, Editions Paratexte, 85; A Blessed Rage for Order: Deconstruction, Evolution, and Chaos, Univ Mich, 91; Narrative & Chaos, New Lit Hist, 92; Towards a View of Time as Death, Diogenes, 90. **CONTACT ADDRESS** Dept of Literature, Univ of Texas, Dallas, Richardson, TX 75083-0688. **EMAIL** aargyros@utdallas.edu

ARIETI, JAMES ALEXANDER
PERSONAL Born 05/12/1948, New York, NY, m, 1976, 2 children **DISCIPLINE** CLASSICS, HISTORY **EDUCATION** Grinnell Col, BA, 69; Stanford Univ, MA, 72, PhD(classics), 72. **CAREER** Asst prof classics, Stanford Univ, 73-74; asst prof, Pa State Univ, 74-75; asst prof classics & hist, Cornell Col, 75-77; asst prof, 78-81, assoc prof, 81-88, prof classics, Hampden-Sydney Col, 88-95, Thompson Prof Classics, 95-; asst bibliographer ling, MLA, 74-75; NEH fel, classics, 77-78; chemn bd & sr fel, Hesperis Inst for Humanistic Studies, 77-. **HONORS AND AWARDS** Phi Beta Kappa, 69; Woodrow Wilson fel, 69; Mettauer Reseach Award, 86, 97; John Templeton Prize for Science & Religion, 96. **MEMBERSHIPS** Am Philol Asn; Class Asn of Middle West & South; VA Classical Asn. **RESEARCH** Ancient historiography and philosophy; ancient literary criticism; Septuagint. **SELECTED PUBLICATIONS** Auth, The Vocabulary of Septuagint Amos, J Biblical Lit, 74; Nudity in Greek Athletics, Class World, 75; coauth, The Dating of Longinus, Studia Classica, 75; co-ed, MLA Int Bibliography, In; 1974 Vol III, MLA, 76; contrib, Two Studies in Latin Phonology, Studia Ling et Philol, 76; coauth, Love Can Be Found, Harcourt Brace Jovanovich, 77; auth, Empedocles in Rome: Rape and the Roman Ethos, Clio, 81; A Herodotean Source for Rasselas, Note & Queries, 81; coauth, Longinus on the Sublime, Edwin Meller pub, 85; co-ed, Hamartia: The Concept of Error in the Western Tradition, Edwin Mellen Pub, 83; auth, Interpreting Plato: The Dialogues as Drama, Rowman & Littlefield, 91; Discourses on the First Book of Herodotus, Littlefield Adams Books, 95; numerous articles and reviews. **CONTACT ADDRESS** Dept of Classics, Hampden-Sydney Col, Hampden-Sydney, VA 23943. **EMAIL** jarieti@email.hsc.edu

ARLYCK, ELISABETH C.
PERSONAL Born 03/20/1942, Dakar, Senegal, m, 1969, 2 children **DISCIPLINE** FRENCH **EDUCATION** Univ Paris, Sorbonne, Agregation de Leltres classique, 67; Univ Paris, VIII, Doctorat de 3_e cycle, 80. **CAREER** From Asst Prof to Prof, Vassar Col, 74-. **HONORS AND AWARDS** NEH Summer Stipend, 86; Pittsburgh Endowment Humanities, 91; NEH Fel, 95-96. **MEMBERSHIPS** MLA. **RESEARCH** Modern and contemporary French Poetry, French cinema, women's studies.

SELECTED PUBLICATIONS Auth, "Le Metaphore raconte. Pratique de Julien Gracq, Klincksieck (Paris, France), 84; ed, Une Annee dans le Sahel, by Eugune Fromentin, Flammarion (Paris, France), 91; auth, "Women Poets: The Speaking E," in Reconceptions: Reading Mod Fr Poetry (Nottingham: Univ Nottingham Pr, 96), 167-182; auth, "Michel Deguy chez les Mutants," in Michel Deguy (Paris: Belin & La Table ronde, (96), 254-262; auth, "Le Grand Identificateur," in Joe Bousquet et l'ecriture (Paris: L'Harmattan, 99), 171-182; auth, "Articles en tous genres: le composite," L'Eclatement des genres, Presses de la Sorbonne Mouvelle (Paris, France), 00; **CONTACT ADDRESS** Dept Lang, Vassar Col, 124 Raymond Ave, Poughkeepsie, NY 12604-0002. **EMAIL** arlyck@vassar.edu

ARMBRECHT, THOMAS J. D.
PERSONAL Born 04/09/1970, ME **DISCIPLINE** FRENCH STUDIES **EDUCATION** Middlebury Col, BA, 92; Brown Univ, MA, 95; PhD, 99. **CAREER** For asst, Lycee Fenelon, France, 95-96; TA, Brown Univ, 93-99; instr, Antink Lang, Turkey, 99; asst prof, Colby Col, 00; asst prof, Col of William & Mary, 00-. **HONORS AND AWARDS** Phi Beta Kappa, Middlebury Col, 92; Gay Scholar Awd, Johnson and Wales Univ, 95. **MEMBERSHIPS** MLA, Centre de Documentation Professionale Marguerite Yourcenar. **RESEARCH** 20th-century French Literature, French Theatre, Queer Studies, Minority Literature. **SELECTED PUBLICATIONS** Auth, "Paradox and Perversions: the Intersection of Catholicism and Queer Culture," Univ of Mass Pr, forthcoming. **CONTACT ADDRESS** Col of William and Mary, PO Box 1852, Williamsburg, VA 23187-1852. **EMAIL** txarmb@wm.edu

ARMENGOL, ARMANDO
DISCIPLINE SPANISH **EDUCATION** Univ Ill, PhD, 74. **CAREER** Certified Oral Proficiency tester and trainer. **RESEARCH** Latin American literature. **SELECTED PUBLICATIONS** Publ on, Latin Amer Poetry and Novel; co-ed, Palabra Nueva, ser of 3 bks on recent Chicano lit. **CONTACT ADDRESS** Dept of Languages and Linguistics, Univ of Texas, El Paso, 500 W University Ave, El Paso, TX 79968. **EMAIL** armengol@utep.edu

ARNETT, CARLEE
PERSONAL Born 08/13/1964, Trenton, NJ, m, 1991, 2 children **DISCIPLINE** GERMAN STUDIES, SECOND LANGUAGE ACQUISITION **EDUCATION** Mt Holyoke Col, BA, 87; Univ Calif, Berkeley, MA, 91; Univ Mich, PhD, 95. **CAREER** Vis asst prof, coordr, Ohio State Univ, 97-98; asst prof, dir, Univ Ariz, 98-00; asst prof, Univ of Calif, Davis, 00-. **HONORS AND AWARDS** Rackham Dissertation Fel, Frank X. Braun Tchg Prize, Univ Mich, 94. **MEMBERSHIPS** Modern Lang Asn; Soc Germanic Philol; Am Asn Tchrs German. **RESEARCH** German syntax; second language acquisition; older Germanic languages. **SELECTED PUBLICATIONS** Auth, Perfect Auxiliary Selection in the Old Saxon Heliand, 97; auth, German Impersonal Passives, 97; auth, "Perfect Auxiliary Selection in the Old Saxon Heliand," Am J of Germanic Ling and Lit 9 (97); coauth, "The Professionalization of Teaching Assistants: Can it be accomplished?," Unterrichtspraxis/ Teaching German 33 (00); auth, "Cognitive Approach to the Passive in Old Saxon," Am J of Germanic Ling and Lit 12 (00). **CONTACT ADDRESS** Dept of German, Univ of California, Davis, 1 Shields Ave, 622 Sproul Hall, Davis, CA 95616-8606. **EMAIL** clarnett@ucdavis.edu

ARONSON, HOWARD ISAAC
PERSONAL Born 03/05/1936, Chicago, IL **DISCIPLINE** LINGUISTICS **EDUCATION** Univ IL, AB, 56; IN Univ, MA, 58, PhD, 61. **CAREER** Asst prof Slavic lang, Univ Wis, 61-62; from asst prof to assoc prof ling & Slavic lang, 62-73, chmn dept ling, 72-80, Prof Ling & Slavic Lang, Univ Chicago 73-. **MEMBERSHIPS** Am Asn Tchr(s) Slavic & East Europ Lang; Am Asn Advan Slavic Studies; Bulgarian Studies Group; Am Asn Southeast Europ Studies. **RESEARCH** Georgian linguistics; Bulgarian and Russian linguistics; Yiddish linguistics. **SELECTED PUBLICATIONS** Auth, The Grammatical Categories of the Indicative in the Contemporary Bulgarian Literary Language, In: To Honor Roman Jakobson, 67 & Bulgarian Inflectional Morphophonology, 68, Mouton; Towards a Semantic Analysis of Case and Subject in Georgian, Lingua, 70; Grammatical Subject in Old Georgian, Bedi Kartlisa, 76; Interrelationships Between Aspect and Mood in Bulgarian, Folia Slavica, 77; English as an Active Language, Lingua, 77; Georgian: A first-year reading grammar, Slavica, 82; Form, Function, and the 'perfective' in Bulgarian, In: The Scope of Slavic Aspect, Slavica, 85; Modern Georgian, In: The Indigenous Languages of the Caucasus, Caravan, 91. **CONTACT ADDRESS** Dept of Slavic Lang & Lit, Univ of Chicago, 1130 E 59th St, Chicago, IL 60637-1539. **EMAIL** hia5@midway.uchicago.edu

ARREDONDO, ISABEL
PERSONAL Born 05/08/1960, Madrid, Spain, 1 child **DISCIPLINE** SPANISH **EDUCATION** Univ Calif, Berkeley, PhD, 92. **CAREER** Lectr, Saint Mary's Col, Maraga, Calif, 92-93; vis asst prof, Univ Mich, Dearborn, 93-94; asst prof of Spanish, Plattsburgh State Univ, 94-. **HONORS AND AWARDS** Dresser Awd, United Univ Professions, New York, 98-99. **MEMBERSHIPS** Latin Am Studies Asn. **RESEARCH** Film, Latin America, women studies. **SELECTED PUBLICATIONS** Auth, De brujos y naguales: La Guatemala imaginaria de Miguel Angel Asturias, Lewiston, New York: The Edwin Mellon Press (97); auth, "From Transparent to Translucid: Cuban Filmmakers in 1990," Latin Am Literary Rev, no 49 (98): 25-38; auth, "De transparente a Translucida: Directores Cubanos en 1990," Genero y cultura en America latina, Centro de Estudios Sociologicos y Programa Interdisciplinario de Estudios de la mujer, Colegio de Mexico (98); auth, "By Popular Demand: I Will Seed Danzon until I Can't Stand It Any More," J of Commun Inquiry, vol 23:2 (99): 183-196; auth, "Abrochense los cinturones!: el viaje al inconsciente en las leyendas de Miguel Angel Asturias," critical ed of Cuentos y leyendas by Miguel Angel Asturias, ALLCA XX, Univ de Paris: Colecciones Archivos (2000); auth, In Our Own Image, An Oral History of Mexican Women Filmmakers 1989-1994, Univ Tex Press (under review, 2000); auth, Palabra de Mujer: Directoras Mexicanas de cine 1989-1994, Ediciones Catedra, Spain (under review, 2000). **CONTACT ADDRESS** Dept Foreign Lang, SUNY, Col at Plattsburgh, 101 Broad St, Plattsburgh, NY 12901-2637. **EMAIL** isabel.arredondo@plattsburgh.edu

ARRINGTON, MELVIN
PERSONAL Born 07/26/1949, Jackson, MS, m, 1973, 2 children **DISCIPLINE** SPANISH **EDUCATION** Miss Col, BA, 71; Univ Kent, MALS, 72; MA, 74; PhD, 79. **CAREER** Vis asst prof, Western Carolina Uiv, 80-81; asst prof, 79-80 & 81-82, Univ of Tenn at Knoxville; from asst prof to prof, Univ of Miss, 82-. **HONORS AND AWARDS** Fulbright Summer Sem, 83; Miss Comt for the Humanities Grant, 83; Rotary Found Group Exchange Awd, 85; NEH Summer Sem, Yale, 85 & Stony Brook, 95; Mellon Regional Fac Development Sem, Vanderbilt Univ, 86; NEH Summer Inst, Univ of Tex, 89. **MEMBERSHIPS** Am Asn of Teachers of Spanish & Portuguese, Asn of Columbianists, Inst Int de Lit Iberoamericana, Latin Am Studies Asn, Southeastern Coun on Latin Am Studies, Miss For Lang Asn. **RESEARCH** Spanish American literature. **SELECTED PUBLICATIONS** Auth, "Magda Portal, Vanguard Critic," Reinterpreting the Spanish American Essay: Women Writers of the 19th- & 20th-Centaries, Univ of Tex Press, 95; contribur, Encyclopedia of Latin American Literature, Fitzroy Dearborn (London, Engl), 97; transl, I'm Going to Have a Little House: The Second Diary of Carolina Maria De Jesus, Univ of Nebr Press (Lincoln, NE), 97. **CONTACT ADDRESS** Dept Modern Lang, Univ of Mississippi, PO Box 1848, University, MS 38677-1848. **EMAIL** marringt@olemiss.edu

ARROYO, CIRIACO MORON
PERSONAL Born 08/08/1935, Pastrana, Spain, m, 1962, 7 children **DISCIPLINE** HISPANIC STUDIES & COMPARATIVE LITERATURE **EDUCATION** Pontif Univ of Salamanca, BA, 56; MA, 57; Univ of Munich, PhD, 63. **CAREER** Prof, Univ of Pa, 68-71; Emerson Hinchliff Prof, Cornell Univ, 71-. **HONORS AND AWARDS** Guggenheim Fel, 72-73; Doctor Honoris Causa, St Joseph's Univ. **MEMBERSHIPS** Asn Int Hispanistas. **RESEARCH** Theory of the Humanities, Hispanic & European Intellectual History. **SELECTED PUBLICATIONS** Auth, El 'alma de Espana,' Cien anos de inseguridad, 96; auth, Las Humanidades en la Era Tecnologica, 98. **CONTACT ADDRESS** Dept Modern Lang, Cornell Univ, 203 Morrill Hall, Ithaca, NY 14853-4701. **EMAIL** cma6@cornell.edu

ARROYO, JOSSIANA
PERSONAL Born 03/13/1967, Hato Rey, PR **DISCIPLINE** LATIN AMERICAN LITERATURE AND CULTURE **EDUCATION** Univ PR, BA, 92; Univ Calif Berkeley, PhD, 98. **CAREER** Asst prof, Univ Mich Ann Arbor, 98-. **HONORS AND AWARDS** Grant, Univ Calif Berkeley, 93, 95-96; Lesley B Simpson Fel, 96-97; Grant, Univ Mich, 99-00; Univ PR Fel, 99; Ford Fel, NRC, 00. **MEMBERSHIPS** MLA, Latin Am Studies Asn, Brazilian Studies Asn, PR Studies Asn. **RESEARCH** Latin American and Caribbean Literatures and Cultures, Brazilian Literatures and Cultures, Gay and Lesbian Studies, Literary Theory. **SELECTED PUBLICATIONS** Rev, of Diaz Quinones, Arcadio. La memoria rota, Ensayos sobre cultura y politca, Revista de critica latinoamericana XX.40, (94): 383-86; auth, "Manuel Ramos Otero: las narrativas del cuerpo mas alla de Insularismo," Revists de Estudios Hispanicos XXI, (94): 303-24; auth, "La figura del criminal y la ilegalidad del estado en dos novelas del siglo XIX puertoriqueno: La charca y El negocio de Manuel Zeno Gandia," Ariel, (94): 55-85; auth, "El cuerpo del esclavo y la narrativa de la nacion en Casa Grande and Senzala de Gilberto Freyre, Lucero, Jour of Iberian and Latim Am Studies 4, (95): 31-42; auth, Travestismos culturales: literatura y etnografia en Cuba y Brasil, Editorial Iberamericana (forthcoming); auth, "Historias de familia: migraciones y escritura homosexual en la literatura puertoriquena," Revista Canadiense de Estudioos Hispanicos, (forthcoming). **CONTACT ADDRESS** Dept Romance Lang, Univ of Michigan, Ann Arbor, 4108 Mod Lang Bldg, Ann Arbor, MI 48109-1275. **EMAIL** jarroyo@umich.edu

ASCARI, ROSALIA COLOMBO
DISCIPLINE ITALIAN LANGUAGE AND LITERATURE **EDUCATION** Universita Bocconi; PhD. **CAREER** Prof, Sweet Briar Col . **RESEARCH** 19th and 20th century Italian lit; Occhipinti. **SELECTED PUBLICATIONS** Auth, articles and reviews in Annali d'Italianistica; coauth, L'Analyse du texte. **CONTACT ADDRESS** Sweet Briar Col, Sweet Briar, VA 24595. **EMAIL** ascari@sbc.edu

ASHBY, WILLIAM JAMES
PERSONAL Born 09/27/1943, Detroit, MI, m, 1969, 2 children **DISCIPLINE** ROMANCE LINGUISTICS, FRENCH LANGUAGE AND LITERATURE **EDUCATION** Alma Col, BA, 65; Univ MI, MA, 66, PhD(Romance ling), 73. **CAREER** Asst prof, 71-80, Assoc Prof French, Univ CA, Santa Barbara, 80-, Am Coun Learned Socs res fel, 76. **MEMBERSHIPS** Ling Soc Am; MLA; Am Asn Teachers Fr. **RESEARCH** Sociolinguistics; French language. **SELECTED PUBLICATIONS** **CONTACT ADDRESS** Dept of French, Univ of California, Santa Barbara, 552 University Rd, Santa Barbara, CA 93106-0001.

ASHLEY, LEONARD R. N.
PERSONAL Born 12/05/1928, Miami, FL **DISCIPLINE** ENGLISH, LINGUISTICS **EDUCATION** McGill Univ, BA, 49, MA, 50; Princeton Univ, AM, 53, PhD, 56. **CAREER** Instr, 53-55, Univ Utah; instr, 55-56, Royal Can Air Force, London; 2nd asst to air hist, 56-58; instr, 58-61, Univ Rochester; from instr to assoc prof, 61-72, prof, 72-, prof emeritus, 95-, Brooklyn Col; res grants, Univ Utah, 55 & Univ Rochester, 60; lectr, 61-, New Sch Social Res; Brooklyn Col fac res grant, 68; contrib ed, Papertexts, Simon & Schuster & Washington Sq Press; consult, Harper & Row & Oxford Univ Press; exec bd, Amer Name Soc; ed bd, 65-99, reviewer, Bibliotheque d' Humanisme et Renaissance, Geneva; co-ed, 97, 99, 01 Goelinguistics; Pres, Amer Soc of Geolinguistics, 91-. **HONORS AND AWARDS** Shakespeare Gold Medal, 49; hon, LHD, 98. **MEMBERSHIPS** MLA; Am Name Soc (pres, 79, 87); Int Conf Gen Semantics; NY Acad of Sci; Intl Linguistics Assn, secretary 80-82; Amer Soc of Geolinguistics, pres, 85, 91-; Am Dialect Soc. **RESEARCH** English drama; English language, especially onomastics and geolinguistics; English nondramatic literature. **SELECTED PUBLICATIONS** Auth, The Complete Book of Superstition, Prophecy, and Luck, Barricade Bks, 95; auth, The Complete Book of Magic and Witchcraft, Barricade Bks, 95; auth, The Complete Book of Devils and Demons, Barricade Bks, 96; auth, The Complete Book of Devil's Disciples, Barricade Bks, 96; auth, The Complete Book of Spells, Curses and Magical Recipes, Barricade Bks, 97; auth, The Complete Book of Vampires, Barricade Bks, 98; auth, The Complete Book of Ghosts and Poltergeists, 99; auth, George Alfred Henty and the Victorian Mind, Internet Scholar pub, 98; auth, Turkey: Names and Naming Practices, Univ Press of America, 01. **CONTACT ADDRESS** Dept of English, Brooklyn Col, CUNY, Brooklyn, NY 11210.

ASHLIMAN, D. L.
PERSONAL Born 01/01/1938, Idaho Falls, ID, m, 1960, 3 children **DISCIPLINE** GERMAN **EDUCATION** Rutgers, PhD, 69; Univ of UT, BA, 63 **CAREER** Assoc Prof, 77-86, Chair, 94-97, Univ of Pittsburgh; Visit Prof, 92, 96, 97, 98, Univ of Augsburg, Ger **HONORS AND AWARDS** Academ Dean, Semester at Sea, 94 **RESEARCH** Indo-European folktales **SELECTED PUBLICATIONS** Auth, Voices from the Past: The Cycle of Life in Indo-European Folktales, Kendall/ Hunt Publishing Co., 95; A Guide to Folktales in the English Language, Greenwood Press, 87 **CONTACT ADDRESS** German Dept, Univ of Pittsburgh, Pittsburgh, PA 15260. **EMAIL** dash+@pitt.edu

ASMIS, ELIZABETH
DISCIPLINE CLASSICS **EDUCATION** Univ Toronto, BA, 62; Yale Univ, MA, 66, PhD, 70. **CAREER** Lectr, McGill Univ, 63-65; res asst, British Museum, 66-68; asst prof, Cornell Univ, 70-79; Assoc prof, Univ Chicago, 79-94; Prof, Univ Chicago, 94-. **HONORS AND AWARDS** Woodrow Wilson Fel; Phi Beta Kappa Fel; NEH Fel; ed, clas philol. **SELECTED PUBLICATIONS** Auth, Epicurus' Scientific Method, Cornell Univ Press, 84; auth, Asclepiades Rediscovered?, Class Philol, 93; auth, Philodemus on Censorship, Moral Utility, and Formalism in Poetry, Philodemus and Poetry: Poetic THeory and Practice in Lucretius, Philodemus and Horace, 95; auth, Epicurean Semiotics, Knowledge Through Signs, Ancient Semiotic Theoris and Practices, 95; The Stoics on Women, Ancient Philos and Feminism, 96. **CONTACT ADDRESS** Dept of Classics, Univ of Chicago, 1050 E 59th St, Chicago, IL 60637. **EMAIL** e-asmis@uchicago.edu

ASSA, SONIA
PERSONAL Born 01/10/1949, Tanger, Morocco, m, 1979, 2 children **DISCIPLINE** FRENCH LITERATURE **EDUCATION** NY Univ, PhD, 82. **CAREER** Assoc prof, SUNY Old Westbury, 91-. **MEMBERSHIPS** Women in Fr; Conseil Int d'Etudies Francophones. **RESEARCH** Francophone literature, women's writing, surrealism. **SELECTED PUBLICATIONS** Auth, "Rien n'aura en lieu que le lieu: Une lecture du 'coup de Des'", Litterature No 56 (84):119-128; auth, "Ceci est absolument une pipe, ou la poesie que se voulait peinture", Bulletin de la Societe des Professeurs francais en Amerique (85):35-55; auth, "Un ruban autour d'une bombe: Andre Breton lit Frida Kahlo", Bulletin de la Soc des Prof Fr en Am, (89):131-140; auth, "Telle que je me vois en toix: Le mythe de la

femme'enfant dans Arcane 17", Modern Language Studies, XXI.2 (90):28-38; auth, "Of Hairdressers and Kings: Ready-Made Revelations in 'Les Malheurs des Immortels'", the French Review, 64.4 (91):643-658; auth, "Gardens of Delight, or What's Cooking? Leonora Carrington in the Kitchen", Studies in Twentieth Century Literature 15.2, (91):213-227; auth, "M'introduire dans ton histoire: Entree des narrateurs dans L'amour, la fantasia d'Assia Djebar", Etudes Francophones, XII.2 (97):67-80. **CONTACT ADDRESS** Dept Humanities, SUNY, Col at Old Westbury, PO Box 210, Old Westbury, NY 11568-0210. **EMAIL** soniaassa@cs.com

ATHANASSAKIS, APOSTOLOS N.
PERSONAL Born 09/20/1938, Astrochorion, Arta, Greece, d, 2 children **DISCIPLINE** CLASSICAL LINGUISTICS, GREEK POETRY **EDUCATION** Univ Pa, PhD, 65. **CAREER** Prof, Class Ling, Univ Calif, Santa Barbara. **HONORS AND AWARDS** Nat Board of Lecturers for the Bicentennial, 74-76; NEH Fellow, 76-77; Fulbright Professor to Iceland, 77; Guggenheim Fellow, 87-88. **SELECTED PUBLICATIONS** Transl, introd, text, Via Sancti Pachomii, Scholars' Press, 75; Transl, introd, comment, The Homeric Hymns, Johns Hopkins Univ Press, 76; Transl, text, The Orphic Hymns, Scholar's Press, 77; Transl, introd, Hesiod: Theogony, Works and Days, Shield, Johns Hopkins Univ Press, 88; ed, Essays on Hesiod, Vol I, Ramus 21, 92; Essays on Hesiod, Vol II, Ramus 21, 93; auth, The Life of St. George of Choceba, coauth, Tim Vivian, Catholic Scholars Press, 93; auth, The Life of St. Anthony, coauth, Tim Vivian, Catholic Scholars Press, 98. **CONTACT ADDRESS** Dept of Classics, Univ of California, Santa Barbara, Santa Barbara, CA 93106-7150. **EMAIL** gmangold@humanitas.ucsb.edu

ATKINSON, JAMES BLAKELY
PERSONAL Born 11/24/1934, Honolulu, HI, m, 1970, 1 child **DISCIPLINE** ENGLISH & COMPARATIVE LITERATURE **EDUCATION** Swarthmore Col, AB, 56; Columbia Univ, MA, 61, PhD(English & comp lit), 68. **CAREER** Asst prof English, Dartmouth Col, 66-73, fac fel, 71; Asst Prof English, Earlham Col, 73-. **MEMBERSHIPS** MLA; Renaissance Soc Am; AAUP. **RESEARCH** Literature of the Renaissance in Europe and England; the novel. **SELECTED PUBLICATIONS** Transl, Mandrou Duby's A History of French Civilization, Random, 65; auth, Montaigne and Naivete, Romanic Rev, 73; Naivete and Modernity: The French Renaissance Battle for a Literary Vernacular, J Hist Ideas, 74; ed & translr, Machiavelli's The Prince, Bobbs-Merrill, 75; Changing Attitudes to Death, 19th-Century Parlor Songs as Consolation Literature, Can Rev of Am Studies, vol 23, 93; with Anne Wheathill, A 'Handfull of Holesome Through Homelie Hearbs' 1584, The First English Gentlewomans Prayer Book, Sixteenth Century J, vol 27, 96; Machiavellian Rhetoric-From the Counterreformation to Milton, with V. Kahn, Renaissance Quart, vol 50, 97. **CONTACT ADDRESS** 115 S 17th St, Richmond, IN 47374.

ATLAS, JAY DAVID
PERSONAL Born 02/01/1945, Houston, TX **DISCIPLINE** PHILOSOPHY & LINGUISTICS **EDUCATION** Amherst Col, AB, 66; Princeton Univ, PhD, 76. **CAREER** Asst prof, 76-80, assoc prof Philos, 81-88, prof philos, Pomona Col, 89-, Mem common rm, Wolfson Col, Oxford, 78 & 80; vis fel, Princeton Univ, 79; sr assoc, JurEcon, Inc, 81-; res assoc, Inst Advan Study School Hist, Princeton, NJ, 82-84, 86; vis lectr, Dept Philos, Univ Hong Kong, 86; vis prof, Dept Philos, UCLA, 89-95; vis prof, Dept Dutch Ling, Univ Groningen, The Netherlands, spring 95; vis scholar, Max Planck Inst for Psycolinguistics, nijmegen, The Netherlands, 97. **MEMBERSHIPS** Am Philos Asn; Asn Symbolic Logic. **RESEARCH** Philos of lang; metaphysics; linguistics and lit theory. **SELECTED PUBLICATIONS** Auth, Frege's polymorphous concept of presupposition and its role in theory of meaning, Semantikos, 1: 29-44; Presupposition: A sematico-pragmatic account, Pragmatics Microfiche, 1.4, D13-G9, 75; Negation, ambiguity, and presupposition, Ling & Philos, 1: 321-336; On presupposing, Mind, 87: 396-411; Reference, meaning, and translation, Philos Books, 21: 129-140; coauth, It-clefts, informativeness, and logical form: Radical pragmatics, In: Radical Pragmatics, Acad Press, 81; auth, Is not logical?, Proc 11th Int Symposium on Multiple-Valued Logic, Inst Elec & Electronics Engrs, 81; Comparative adjectives and adverbials of degree, Ling & Philos, 84; Whate are negative existence statements about?, Ling & Philos, 88; Philosophy without Ambiguity: A Logico-Linguistic Essay, Clarendon Press, Oxford, 89; Only noun phrases, pseudo-negative generalized quantitatives, negative plarity items, and monotanacity, J Semantics, 96. **CONTACT ADDRESS** Dept Philos, Pomona Col, 333 N College Way, Claremont, CA 91711-6319. **EMAIL** jatlas@pomona.edu

ATTARDO, SALVATORE
DISCIPLINE LINGUISTICS **EDUCATION** Catholic Univ, Milan, PhD, 86; Purdue Univ, PhD, 91. **CAREER** Asst prof, Youngstown State Univ, 92-96, Assoc prof, Youngstown State Univ, 96-. **MEMBERSHIPS** Linguistics Soc Am; Int Pragmatics Asn; Speech Comm Asn; Int Soc Humor Studies; Col Eng Asn. **SELECTED PUBLICATIONS** Auth, Linguistic Theories of Humor, Mouton de Gruyter, 94; Introduction to Theoretical Linguistics: Course notes;York State Univ, Mimeo, 92; Humor, Handbook of Pragmatics, 96; auth, Competition and cooperation: beyond gricean pragmatics, Pragmatics and Cognition, 5:1, (97), 21-50; auth, "Locutionary and Perlocutionary Cooperation: the Perlocutionary Cooperative principle," J of Pragmatics, vol 27, (97), 753-779; auth, "The semantic foundations of cognitve theories of humor," Humr: Int J of Humor Res, 10:4, (97), 395-420; auth, "The analysis of humorous narratives," Humor: Int J of Humor Res, 11:3, (98), 627-636; auth, "Are socio-pragmatics and (Neo-) Gricean pragmnatics incompatible?" J of Pragmatics, 30:5, (98), 627-636; auth, "Irony as relevant Inappropriatenss," J of Pragmatics, 32, (00), 793-826; auth, Humorous Texts: A semantic and pragmatic analysis, Mouton de Gruyter, 01; coauth, Understanding Language Structure, Interactio, and Variation: An Intoroduction to Applied Linguistics and Sociolinguistics for Nonspecialists, Univ of MI Press. **CONTACT ADDRESS** Youngstown State Univ, One University Plaza, Youngstown, OH 44555. **EMAIL** sattardo@cc.ysu.edu

AUBERY, PIERRE
PERSONAL Born 08/08/1920, Mt. St. Aignan, m, 1950, 1 child **DISCIPLINE** FRENCH LANGUAGE & LITERATURE **EDUCATION** Lycee du Havre, BA, 39; Univ Toulouse, LicLet, 44; D Univ, Paris, 55. **CAREER** Journaliste Parlementaire, Paris, 47-52; instr romance lang, Duke Univ, 53-57; asst prof French, Mt Holyoke Col, 57-61; vis prof, Univ Alta, 61-62; assoc prof, 62-67, Prof French to Prof Emer, SUNY, Buffalo, 67-; pres, Buffalo Br, Alliance Francaise, NY, 65-68; civilization ed, Fr Rev, 67-74; consult French lit, Encycl Judaica; rev ed, Comtemp Fr Civilization, 76-. **HONORS AND AWARDS** Guggenheim fel, 64-65. **MEMBERSHIPS** Soc Ecrivains Normands; Am Asn Teachers Fr; Am Soc 18th Century Studies. **RESEARCH** Jewish literature; romantic Religions and social consciousness; a sociological approach to literature and literary criticism. **SELECTED PUBLICATIONS** Auth, Milieux juifs de la France contemporaine, PLON, 62; coauth, Juifs et Canadiens, Ed du Jours, Montreal, 67; auth, Pour une lecture ouvriere de la litterature, Ed Syndicalistes, 69; Mecislas Golbert, Intellectual Biography, Minard, 78. **CONTACT ADDRESS** Dept of Mod Lang and Literature, SUNY, Buffalo, 910 Clemens Hall, N Campus, Buffalo, NY 14260.

AUGER, JULIE
DISCIPLINE FRENCH LITERATURE **EDUCATION** Univ Pa, PhD, 94. **CAREER** Asst prof. **RESEARCH** Sociolinguistics; morphosyntax; Quebec Colloquial French; spoken French in general and other Gallo Romance dialects. **SELECTED PUBLICATIONS** Coed, Explorations du lexique, 97; auth, "Redoublement des clitiques en francais parle: une approche morphologique," Revue quebecoise de linguitique 24 (95): 21-60; auth, "On the history of relative clauses in French and some of its dialects," in H. Andersen ed, Historical Linguisitics 93 (Amsterdam: John Benjamies, 95), 19-32; auth, "Variation data and linguistic theory: Grammatical agreement and subject doubling," in A.D. Green & V. Motapanyane eds, Proceedings of the Thirteenth Eastern States Conference on Linguistics 96 (Ithaca: Cornell Univ, 96), 1-11; auth, "Subject-Clitic inversion in Romance: A morphological analysis," in Aspects of Romance Linguistics, C. Parodi et al, eds (Washington: Georgetown Univ Press, 96), 23-40; auth, "Le redoublement des sujets en francais informel quebecois: une approche variationiste," Canadian Journal of Linguistics 43 (98): 37-63; coauth, "Letting french students hear the diverse voices of francophony," Modern Language Journal 83 (99): 403-412; coauth, "Vowel epenthesis in Vimeu Picard: A preliminary analysis," in A Selection of Papers from NWAVE 27 (University of Pennsylvania, in press). **CONTACT ADDRESS** Dept of French and Italian, Indiana Univ, Bloomington, 300 N Jordan Ave, Bloomington, IN 47405. **EMAIL** jauger@indiana.edu

AULD, LOUIS
DISCIPLINE FRENCH LANGUAGE AND LITERATURE **EDUCATION** Oberlin Col, BA; Univ Calif Los Angeles, MA; Bryn Mawr Col, PhD, 68. **CAREER** Fac, Kenyon Col, Smith Col, and Duke Univ; admstr, Yale Schl Music; dir, Lang Lrng Ctr, Central Conn State Univ. **HONORS AND AWARDS** Founder, LYRICA Soc; ed, Ars LYRICA. **MEMBERSHIPS** LYRICA. **RESEARCH** 17th century French literature, with special emphasis on word-music relations. **SELECTED PUBLICATIONS** Auth, studies of Moliere's comedy-ballets, the literary origins of French opera, early French art song, and the court ballet. **CONTACT ADDRESS** Central Connecticut State Univ, 1615 Stanley St, New Britain, CT 06050.

AUSTIN, J. NORMAN
PERSONAL Born 05/20/1937, Anshun, China, s **DISCIPLINE** CLASSICS **EDUCATION** Univ of Toronto, BA, 58; Univ of Calif, MA, 60, PhD, 65 **CAREER** Lect, 64-65, Oakland Univ MI; Asst Prof, 65-66, Univ S CA; Assoc Prof, 66-76, Univ of CA, Los Angeles; Aurelio Prof, 76-78, Boston Univ; Prof, 78-80, Univ MA Amherst **HONORS AND AWARDS** John S Guggenheim Fel, 74-75; Jnr Fel, Center for Hellenic Studies, 68-69 **MEMBERSHIPS** Am Philol Assoc; Am Assoc of Univ Profs **RESEARCH** Homer; Archaic Greek Culture & Literature; Comparative Literature **SELECTED PUBLICATIONS** Auth, Archery at the Dark of the Moon Poetic Problems in Homer's Odyssey, Univ of CA Press, 75; auth, Meaning and Being in Myth, Penn State Univ Pr, 90; auth, Helen of Troy and her Shameless Phantom, Cornell Univ Pr, 94. **CONTACT ADDRESS** Dept of Classics, Univ of Arizona, 2939 E Third St, Tucson, AZ 85716. **EMAIL** naustin@u.arizona.edu

AUSTIN, PAUL MURRAY
PERSONAL Born 05/17/1941, China, m, 1964, 3 children **DISCIPLINE** RUSSIAN LANGUAGE & LITERATURE **EDUCATION** Univ Toronto, BA, 63, PhD(Russ lit), 70; Cornell Univ, MA, 64. **CAREER** Lectr Russ, Brock Univ, 67-68; lectr, 68-70, asst prof, 70-75, Assoc Prof Russ, McGill Univ, 75-, Chmn Dept, 81-. **MEMBERSHIPS** Can Asn Slavists; Am Asn Advan Slavic Studies; Am Asn Teachers Slavic & E Europ Lang. **RESEARCH** Soviet Karelian, and post-Soviet linguistic policy in Karelia and Russian Romanticism. **SELECTED PUBLICATIONS** Auth, Patrimoine Litteraire Europeen 11a, Renaissances nationales et conscience universelle, 1832-1885, Romantismes Triomphants, Paul M. Odievski; auth, Anthologie en langue francaise sous la direction de Jean-Claude Polet, Belgium, De Boeck Universite, (99): 733-34; auth, "Lenin and the 60s," Letter to the Editor, Times Literary Supplement, no 5068, (00): 17. **CONTACT ADDRESS** Dept of Russ & Slavic Studies, McGill Univ, 688 Sherbrooke St W, Ste 0341, Montreal, QC, Canada H3A 3R1. **EMAIL** pausti1@po-box.mcgill.ca

AUSTIN, TIMOTHY ROBERT
PERSONAL Born 05/22/1952, Tonbridge, England, m, 1996, 4 children **DISCIPLINE** STYLISTICS, LINGUISTICS **EDUCATION** Oxford Univ, England, MA, 73; Univ Mass, PhD, 77. **CAREER** Asst prof Eng, 77-83, dir, interdisciplinary prog ling studies, 81-85, assoc prof, 83-94, prof, 94, dept chemn, 96-, Loyola Univ Chi. **MEMBERSHIPS** MLA; Midwest Mod Lang Assn. **RESEARCH** Linguistic analysis of literary style; English early romantic poets; history of the English language. **SELECTED PUBLICATIONS** Auth, Language Crafted: To Linguistic Theory of Poetic Syntax, Bloomington: Indiana UP, 84; auth, Poetic Voices: Discourse Linguistics and the Poetic Text, Tuocaloosa: University of Alabama Press, 94; auth, Confronting the Ancestral Voices: Some Thoughts on Assessment, ADE Bulletin, 97. **CONTACT ADDRESS** Dept of English, Loyola Univ, Chicago, 6525 N Sheridan Rd, Chicago, IL 60626-5385. **EMAIL** taustin@luc.edu

AVALLE-ARCE, JUAN BAUTISTA
PERSONAL Born 05/13/1927, Argentina, d, 5 children **DISCIPLINE** SPANISH LITERATURE **EDUCATION** Harvard Univ, AB, 51; MA, 52; PhD, 55. **CAREER** Teaching fel, Harvard Univ, 52-55; asst prof to assoc prof, Ohio State Univ, 55-58; prof, Smith Col, 61-65; prof, Univ of NC, 69-84; prof, Univ of Calif Santa Barbara, 84-. **HONORS AND AWARDS** Guggenheim Fel; Commemorative Medal, Kyoto Univ, Japan; Hispanic Soc of Am; Academia Argentina de Lectrae; Barandiavan Prof of Basque Studies, UCSB. **MEMBERSHIPS** Assoc de Cervantistics; Real Soc Vasconqaon de Amigos del Pais; Medieval Acad of Am; Assoc Asiatica de Hispanistas; Assoc Argentina de Hispanistas, Cervantes Soc of Am. **RESEARCH** Spanish literature and colonial Spanish American literature. **SELECTED PUBLICATIONS** Auth, La Epica Colonial, Universidad de Navarra, (Pamplona), 00. **CONTACT ADDRESS** Dept Sp and Port, Univ of California, Santa Barbara, 552 University Rd, Santa Barbara, CA 93106-0002. **EMAIL** jbavalle@humanitas.ucsb.edu

AVELAR, IDELBER
DISCIPLINE SPANISH LITERATURE **EDUCATION** Univ NC, MA; Duke Univ, PhD. **CAREER** Asst prof, Univ Ill Urbana Champaign. **RESEARCH** Latin American literature and intelectual histories; critical theory. **SELECTED PUBLICATIONS** Auth, Alegoria y postdictadura: Notas sobre la memoria del mercado, 97; Marx en inminencia y urgencia (o la hipotesis de una espectrologia deconstructiva), 95; El espectro en la temporalidad de lo mesi¤nico: Derrida y Jameson a proposito de la firma Marx, 95; Conficciones y la retorica del nombre propio: Autobiografia y politica en Juvenilia, de Miguel Can La Torre, 95; A Morta, de Oswald de Andrade: A Emergencia de uma Mimesis Paradoxal no Teatro Brasileiro, Latin Am Theatre Rev, 95; Bares desiertos y calles sin nombre: Literatura y experiencia en tiempos sombrios, Rev de Critica Cult, 94. **CONTACT ADDRESS** Spanish, Italian, and Portuguese Dept, Univ of Illinois, Urbana-Champaign, 52 E Gregory Dr, Champaign, IL 61820. **EMAIL** iavelar@mailhost.tcs.tulane.edu

AVERY, GEORGE COSTAS
PERSONAL Born 07/27/1926, Philadelphia, PA, m, 1951, 2 children **DISCIPLINE** GERMAN LANGUAGE AND LITERATURE **EDUCATION** Univ PA, AB, 51, AM, 55, PhD, 59. **CAREER** From instr to asst prof Ger lang & lit, St Joseph's Col, PA, 55-60; from instr to asst prof, 60-67, assoc prof Ger, 67-71, Prof Ger, Swarthmore Col, 71-, Lectr, Swarthmore Col, 59-60; Fulbright-Hays res grant, Ger, 65-66. **MEMBERSHIPS** MLA; Am Asn Teachers Ger. **RESEARCH** German literature since 1900; Herwarth Walden and Der Sturm; German romanticism. **SELECTED PUBLICATIONS CONTACT ADDRESS** Dept of Language, Swarthmore Col, Swarthmore, PA 19081.

AVERY, HARRY COSTAS
PERSONAL Born 04/09/1930, Philadelphia, PA, m, 1962, 4 children **DISCIPLINE** CLASSICS **EDUCATION** Univ PA, AB, 53; Univ IL, MA, 56; Princeton Univ, PhD, 59. **CAREER** Instr Greek, Bryn Mawr Col, 59-61; from asst prof to assoc prof classics, Univ TX, Austin, 61-67; Prof Classics & Chmn Dept, Univ Pittsburgh, 67-, Jr fel, Ctr Hellenic Studies, 63-64; chmn adv coun, Comt Sch Class Studies, Am Acad Rome, 70-73, trustee, 75-78; vis res prof Greek hist & lit, Am Sch Class Studies Athens, 71-72, mem exec comt, Managing Comt, 72-76. **HONORS AND AWARDS** Bromberg Awd, Univ TX, 66. **MEMBERSHIPS** Am Philol Asn; Soc Promotion Hellenic Studies; Archaeol Inst Am. **RESEARCH** Greek history and literature; Roman history. **SELECTED PUBLICATIONS** Auth, Euripides' Heracleidai, 71 & Herodotus' Picture of Cyrus, 72, Am J Philol; Herodotus 6.112.2, Trans Am Philol Asn, 72; Themes in Thucydides' Account of the Sicilian Expedition, Hermes, 73; Sophocles' Political Career, Historia, 73; The Three Hundred at Thasos, 411 BC, Class Philol, 78; A Lost Episode in Caesar Civil War, Hermes-Zeitschrift Fur Klassische Philologie, Vol 121, 93; Glaucus, A God, 'Iliad' Zeta-128-143 & Homer, Hermes-Zeitschrift Fur Klassische Philologie, Vol 122, 94. **CONTACT ADDRESS** Dept of Classics, Univ of Pittsburgh, Pittsburgh, PA 51260.

AVINS, CAROL JOAN
PERSONAL Born 05/09/1950, New York, NY **DISCIPLINE** RUSSIAN & COMPARATIVE LITERATURE **EDUCATION** Univ PA, BA, 70; Yale Univ, PhD(Slavic lang & lit), 74. **CAREER** Asst prof, 74-80, Assoc Prof Russian Lang & Lit & Comp Lit, Northwestern Univ, 80-00; assoc prof, Rutgers Univ, 00-. **MEMBERSHIPS** MLA; Am Asn Teachers Slavic & East Europ Lang; Am Asn Advan Slavic Studies; AAUP; Am Coun Teachers Russ. **RESEARCH** Twentieth century Russian literature; 20th century comparative literature. **SELECTED PUBLICATIONS** Auth, Border Crossings: The West and Russian Identity in Soviet Literature, 1917-1934, Univ CA Press; Kinship and Concealment in 'Red Cavalry' and Babel 1920 Diary, Slavic Rev, Vol 53, 94. **CONTACT ADDRESS** Comp Lit and Slavic Lang, Rutgers, The State Univ of New Jersey, New Brunswick, 43 College Ave, 227 Scott Hall, New Brunswick, NJ 08901. **EMAIL** avins@rci.rutgers.edu

AVOTINS, IVARS
PERSONAL Born 11/16/1931, Riga, Latvia, m, 1967 **DISCIPLINE** CLASSICS **EDUCATION** Univ Toronto, BA, 59; Harvard Univ, PhD, 68. **CAREER** Lectr, asst prof, Univ W Ontario, 62-66; asst prof, Univ Calif, Berkeley, 68-70; assoc prof, prof, Univ W Ontario, 70- . **RESEARCH** Epicurus and Lucretius; the second Sophistic; Greek legal language in the Roman Empire. **SELECTED PUBLICATIONS** Auth, Index to the Lives of the Sophists of Philostratus, 78; Index in Eunapii, 83; On the Greek of the Code of Justinian, 89; On the Greek of the Novels of Justinian, 92. **CONTACT ADDRESS** Dept of Classical Studies, Univ of Western Ontario, Rm 420, Talbot College, London, ON, Canada N6A 3K7.

AXELROD, MARK R.
PERSONAL Born 03/31/1946, Philadelphia, PA, m, 2 children **DISCIPLINE** COMPARATIVE LITERATURE **EDUCATION** Ind Univ, BA, 69, MA, 77; Univ Minn, PhD, 88. **CAREER** Tutor, Edinburgh Univ, 89-90; asst prof, Chapman Univ, 90-. **HONORS AND AWARDS** Ind Univ Experimental Fiction Writing Awd, 76; Allaince Francaise Nat Lit Essay Awd, 74, 75, 76; Camargo Fel in Fiction Writing, 82, 86; Western Ill Univ Nat Playwriting Awd, 84; Nat Teleplay Awd, Univ Wis Screenwriters Forum, 90; McGinnis Awd, Univ Iowa, Best Short Story 1990, Iowa Review, 90; Bronze Awd for Screenwriting, Festival Int de Video do Algarve, 90; Silver Seal Awd for Screenwriting, London Int Film & Video Festival, 91; Awd in Screenwriting, Scottish Asn Filmmakers, 93; recipient of numerous grants and fellowships. **MEMBERSHIPS** New Novel Asn; MLA; Am Comp Lit Asn; Samuel Beckett Soc; Int Comp Lit Asn. **RESEARCH** Film; Latin American fiction. **SELECTED PUBLICATIONS** Auth, Neville Chamberlain's Chimera or Nine Metaphors of Vision, Membrane Press, 78; auth, The Politics of Style in the Fiction of Balzac, Beckett & Cort zar, Macmillan Publ/St. Martin's Press, 92; auth, Bombay California, Pac Writers Press, 94; auth, Cardboard Castles, Pac Writers Press, 96; auth, Cloud Castles, Pac Writers Press, 98; auth, The Poetics of Novels: Fiction & Its Execution, Macmillan Publ, 98; auth, Capital Castles, 00; auth, Aspects of the Screeplay, Heinemann Publ, 00; auth of numerous articles and other publications. **CONTACT ADDRESS** Dept English, Chapman Univ, Orange, CA 92866.

AXELROD, MELISSA
DISCIPLINE LINGUISTICS **EDUCATION** Univ Colo, PhD. **CAREER** Instr, Univ NMex. **RESEARCH** Native American languages; morphosyntax; semantics; sociolinguistics. **SELECTED PUBLICATIONS** Eds, Jones, E. and M. Axelrod Sitsiy Yugh Noholnik Ts'in. As My Grandfather Told It: Traditional Stories from the Koyukuk. Fairbanks, AK: YKSD and ANLC. 83; auth, Thompson, C., M. Axelrod, and E. Jones. Han Zaadlitlee. Koyukon Language Curriculum, Nenana, AK: YKSD, 83; auth, Axelrod, M. "Incorporation in Koyukon Athabaskan," IJAL 56:179-95, 90; auth, Axelrod, M. The Semantics of Time: Aspectual Categorization in Koyukon Athabaskan, Lincoln: University of Nebraska Press, 93; ed, Arce-Arenales, M., M. Axelrod, and B. Fox, "Active voice and middle diathesis: A cross-linguistic perspective," In B. Fox and P. Hopper Voice: Form and Function, Amsterdam: John Benjamins, 94, Pp. 1-21; ed., Axelrod, M. and J. Gomez de Garcia, "Language Policy and Programs in the Mescalero and Plains Apache Communities," ." In Clifton Pye, Mid-America Linguistics Conference Papers, Lawrence: University of Kansas, Pp. 25-30, 96, Pp. 24-33; auth, Gomez de Garcia, J. and M. Axelrod, "Rhetorical strategies and language learning in Apache," In Mid-America Linguistics Conference Papers, Columbia: University of Missouri, 97; ed, Axelrod, M. "The semantics of classification in Koyukon Athabaskan Syntax and Semantics, Oxford University Press, 99; ed, Axelrod, m. "Lexis, grammar, and grammatical change: The Koyukon classifier prefixes," In Darnell, M. et al Fuctionalism and Formalism in Linguistics, Volume 2: Case Studies in Language Companion Series, 42, Amsterdam: John Benjamins, 99, Pp. 39-58. **CONTACT ADDRESS** Dept of Linguistics, Univ of New Mexico, Albuquerque, Humanities Bldg., Rm. 556, Albuquerque, NM 87131-1196. **EMAIL** axelrod@unm.edu

AYCOCK, WENDELL M.
DISCIPLINE ENGLISH AND COMPARATIVE LITERATURE **EDUCATION** Univ SC, PhD, 69. **CAREER** Prof, chp, dept Eng, TX Tech Univ, 90-97; bibliogr, Stud in Short Fiction; assoc dean of The Graduate School, Tex Tech Univ, 00-. **HONORS AND AWARDS** Two Fulbright grants; NEH grant; Mellon grant. **RESEARCH** Short story. **SELECTED PUBLICATIONS** Ed or co-ed eighteen volumes coming from the Comparative Literature Symposium project at Texas Tech, produced 20th-Century Short Story Explication, New Ser, Vol II. **CONTACT ADDRESS** Texas Tech Univ, Lubbock, TX 79409-5015. **EMAIL** W.Aycock@ttu.edu

AYUNINJAM, FUNWI
PERSONAL Born, Cameroon **DISCIPLINE** LINGUISTICS **EDUCATION** Univ Yaounde I, BA, 83; Georgetown Univ, MS, 87; PhD, 94. **CAREER** Fr Teacher, Holton-Arms Sch, 90-95; Asst Prof, Ky State Univ, 95-. **HONORS AND AWARDS** Who's Who of Outstanding Men and Women Around the World, 98. **MEMBERSHIPS** Ling Soc of Am, African Lang Teachers' Asn. **RESEARCH** Languages and linguistics, African studies, race and ethnic issues (African and African-American). **SELECTED PUBLICATIONS** Auth, A Reference Grammar of Mbili, UP of Am, 98. **CONTACT ADDRESS** Dept Lang, Kentucky State Univ, 400 E Main St, Frankfort, KY 40601-2334.

AZEVEDO, MILTON M.
PERSONAL Born 04/27/1942, Ouro Fino, Brazil **DISCIPLINE** LINGUISTICS **EDUCATION** Cornell Univ, MA, 71, PhD, 73. **CAREER** Lecturer, Univ Ill, Fall 72; Asst Prof, 72-76; Univ Calif, Berkeley, Asst Prof, 76, Assoc Prof, 83, Prof, 90; Vis Prof, Univ Colo, 75-76, Univ Minn, 77-78; Dir, Univ Calif & Univ Ill Barcelona Stud Ctr, 96-98. **MEMBERSHIPS** Am Asn Teachers Span & Port, MLA. **RESEARCH** Literary linguistics; translation theory. **SELECTED PUBLICATIONS** Auth, O Subjuntivo em Portugues: Um Estudo Transformacional, Petropolis, 76; auth, Passive Sentences in English and Portugese, Georgetown Univ Press; 80; auth, A Contrastive Phonology of Portugese and English, Georgetown Univ Press, 81; co-auth, A Practical Guide to Teaching of Spanish, 2nd ed, Nat Textbook Co, 88; Introduccion a la linguistica espanola, Prentice Hall, 92; La parla i el text, Llieda, Spain, 96; Lecturas periodisticas, 5th ed, DC Health, 96; co-ed, Catalan Review, 9:3, 95. **CONTACT ADDRESS** Univ of California, Berkeley, Berkeley, CA 94720. **EMAIL** mazevedo@socrates.berkeley.edu

AZZI, MARIE-DENISE BOROS
PERSONAL Born 11/25/1938, Paris, France, w, 1968, 2 children **DISCIPLINE** FRENCH **EDUCATION** Univ Calif Los Angeles, PhD, 64 **CAREER** Prof, Rutgers Univ **MEMBERSHIPS** AAUP; PMLA; BAAG; Sarte Stud Int; NEMLA. **SELECTED PUBLICATIONS** Auth, La problematique de l'ecriture dans Les Faux-Monnayeurs d'Andre Gide, Les Lettres Modernes, 90; The Immoralist, in Cyclopedia of Literary Characters, Salem Press, 90; The Infernal Machine, in Cyclopedia of Literary Characters, Salem Press, 90; Lafcadio's Adventures, in Cyclopedia of Literary Characters, Salem Press, 90; Vautrin et Protos: une etude intertextuelle, Modern Lang Stud, 93. **CONTACT ADDRESS** 79 Kingsberry Dr, Somerset, NJ 08873. **EMAIL** borosazz@rci.rutgers.edu

B

BAACKMANN, SUSANNE
PERSONAL Born 10/14/1958, Gladbeck, Germany, m, 1993, 1 child **DISCIPLINE** GERMAN STUDIES **EDUCATION** Univ Duisburg, MA; Univ Calif Berkeley, PhD. **CAREER** Assoc prof, Univ NMex, 93-. **HONORS AND AWARDS** Fulbright Fel, 86; Outstanding Teaching Awd, 89. **MEMBERSHIPS** MLA; AATG. **RESEARCH** Contemporary German culture; women's literature. **SELECTED PUBLICATIONS** Auth, Erular Mirliebe Chamburg: Argument, 95; auth, Conquering Women: Women, War and Sexuality in the German Cultural Imagination, Univ Calif Pr, 00. **CONTACT ADDRESS** 4050 Anderson Ave SE, Albuquerque, NM 87108-4309. **EMAIL** theodo@unm.edu

BABBY, LEONARD HARVEY
PERSONAL Born 07/29/1939, New York, NY **DISCIPLINE** SLAVIC & GENERAL LINGUISTICS **EDUCATION** Brooklyn Col, BA, 62; Harvard Univ, MA, 65, PhD, 70. **CAREER** Asst prof Slavic ling, Princeton Univ, 69-71; asst prof, 71-79, Prof Slavic Ling, Cornell Univ, 80-; prof, Princeton. **MEMBERSHIPS** Ling Soc Am. **RESEARCH** Russian syntax and the Russian language in general; Slavic syntax. **SELECTED PUBLICATIONS** Auth, The deep structure of adjectives and the participles in Russian, Language, 73; A note on agreement in Russian, Glossa, 73; Towards a formal theory of parts of speech, Readings in Slavic Transformational Syntax, 74; A Transformational Grammar of Russian Adjectives, Mouton, The Hague, 74; Nominalization, Passivization and Causativization-Evidence from Russian, Welt Der Slaven-Halbjahresschrift Fur Slavistik, Vol 42, 97. **CONTACT ADDRESS** Dept Slavic Lang & Lit, Princeton Univ, Morrill Hall, Ithaca, NY 14850. **EMAIL** babbylh@princeton.edu

BABCOCK, ARTHUR EDWARD
PERSONAL Born 05/15/1946, Chicago, IL, m, 1972 **DISCIPLINE** FRENCH LANGUAGE & LITERATURE **EDUCATION** Univ MI, AB, 68, MA, 69, PhD(French), 74. **CAREER** Asst prof, 74-80, Prof French, Univ Southern CA, 80-. **MEMBERSHIPS** AAUP; Am Asn Teachers French; MLA; Philol Asn Pac Coast. **RESEARCH** Twentieth-century French literature; Andre Gide. **SELECTED PUBLICATIONS CONTACT ADDRESS** Dept of French & Ital, Univ of So California, Los Angeles, CA 90007.

BABCOCK, ROBERT
PERSONAL Born 10/17/1958, Marion, IN, m, 1979, 2 children **DISCIPLINE** CLASSICS **EDUCATION** La State Univ, BA, 78; Duke Univ, MA, 81; PHD, 83. **CAREER** Asst Prof, 84-86, Miss St Univ; Asst Prof, 87, Bucknell Univ; Cur/Lect, 87, Yale Univ **HONORS AND AWARDS** Alexander von Humbolt Fellow, 84; Comite Internationale de Paleographielitve, 98 **MEMBERSHIPS** Am Philolol Assoc; Medieval Acad of Am; Am Soc of Papyrologists **RESEARCH** Classical Transmission **SELECTED PUBLICATIONS** Auth, Reconstructing a Medieval Library, New Haven, 93; coauth, Learning from the Greeks, New Haven, 94; ed, The Rosenthal Collection of Printed Books with Manuscript Annotations, New Haven, 97. **CONTACT ADDRESS** Beinecke Library, PO Box 208240, New Haven, CT 06520-8240. **EMAIL** robert.babcock@yale.edu

BACH, EMMON
DISCIPLINE LINGUISTICS **EDUCATION** Univ Chicago, PhD, 59. **CAREER** Prof emer. **SELECTED PUBLICATIONS** Auth, In Defense of Passive, Ling Philos, 81; On Time, Tense, and Aspect: An Essay in English Metaphysics, Acad, 81; Some Generalizations of Categorial Grammars, Foris, 84; Informal Lectures on Formal Semantics, SUNY, 89; co-ed, The Algebra of Events, Ling Philos, 88. **CONTACT ADDRESS** Linguistics Dept, Univ of Massachusetts, Amherst, S College 133, Amherst, MA 01003. **EMAIL** bach@unbc.edu

BACHMAN, CHARLES ROGER
PERSONAL Born 10/15/1936, Oskaloosa, IA, m, 1983, 3 children **DISCIPLINE** COMPARATIVE LITERATURE **EDUCATION** Baylor Univ, BA, 61; Ind Univ, PhD, 65. **CAREER** From asst prof to assoc prof, 65-78, prof Eng, 78-, State Univ NY Col Buffalo; Lectr drama, Univ Queensland, Australia, 74-76. **HONORS AND AWARDS** State Univ of NY Res Fel, 66. **RESEARCH** Modern and contemporary drama; fiction; Native American Literature. **SELECTED PUBLICATIONS** Art, Communion and conflict in Hardy and Hauptmann, Revue des Langues Vivantes, autumn 68; art, Life into art: Gerhart Hauptmann and Michael Kramer, Ger Quart, 5/69; art, Albee's A Delicate Balance: Parable as nightmare, Revue des Langues Vivantes, spring 70; art, Defusion of menace in the plays of Sam Shepard, Mod Drama, 12/76 & Contemp Lit Criticism, Vol 17, 80. **CONTACT ADDRESS** Dept of English, SUNY, Buffalo, 1300 Elmwood Ave, Buffalo, NY 14222-1095.

BACON, HELEN HAZARD
PERSONAL Born 03/09/1919, Berkeley, CA **DISCIPLINE** CLASSICAL LANGUAGES & LITERATURE **EDUCATION** Bryn Mawr Col, BA, 40, PhD(classics), 55. **CAREER** Instr Greek & English, Bryn Mawr Col, 46-48, instr Greek, 48-49; instr classics, Woman's Col, 51-52; from instr to assoc prof, Smith Col, 53-61; assoc prof, 61-65, Prof Classics, Barnard Col, Columbia Univ, 65-, Mem, Col Bd Latin Comt, 61-64; Am Asn Univ Women Founders fel, 63-64; mem fac, Bread Loaf Sch English, Vt, summers 66, 68, 73 & 75; scholar-in-residence, Am Acad in Rome, 68-69; Blegen Distinguished vis res prof, Vassar, fall 79; consult Latin lang & scholar, Comt Physicians Overseeing Translation of 16th Century Latin Medieval Text,

73-. **HONORS AND AWARDS** DLitt, Middlebury Col, 70. **MEMBERSHIPS** Am Philol Asn; Archaeol Inst Am. **RESEARCH** Greek tragedy; Plato; ancient romances. **SELECTED PUBLICATIONS** Auth, Socrates crowned, Va Quart Rev, 59; Barbarians in Greek Tragedy, Yale Univ, 61; The Shield of Eteocles, Arion, 64; Woman's Two Faces: Sophocles' View of Woman's Relation to the Tragedy of Oedipus and His Family, Sci & Psychoanal, 66; co-transl, Aeschylus' Seven against Thebes, Oxford Univ, 73; auth, In-and Out-door Schoolings Robert Frost and the Classics, Am Scholar, 74; For Girls: From Birches to Wild Grapes, Yale Rev, 77; Aeschylus and Early Tragedy, In: Ancient Writers: Greece, Scribner's, 82; The Chorus in Greek Life and Drama, Arion-A Journal of Humanities and the Classics, Vol 3, 95. **CONTACT ADDRESS** Dept of Greek & Latin, Barnard Col, New York, NY 10027.

BACON, THOMAS IVEY
PERSONAL Born 08/15/1940, Lubbock, TX, m, 1968, 1 child **DISCIPLINE** GERMAN LANGUAGE & LITERATURE, SCHOLARLY & LITERARY TRANSLATIONS **EDUCATION** TX Tech Univ, BA, 63; Univ TX, Austin, MA, 67, PhD(Ger), 70. **CAREER** Asst prof, Furman Univ, 69-74; Assoc Prof Ger & Chmn Dept, TX Tech Univ, 74-. **MEMBERSHIPS** Am Asn Teachers Ger; MLA; Western Asn Ger Studies; Am Literary Translr Asn. **RESEARCH** German theater; German expressionism; Dadaism. **SELECTED PUBLICATIONS** Translr, Gerald Bisiner, Fragmente Zum Ich, 72 & Herbert Heckmann, Ubuville, The City of the Grand Egg, 73, Dimension; auth, Two from Germany, Furman Studies, 74; translr, Gerald Bisinger, Free and Alone and Other Poems, Dimension, 75; auth, Martin Luther and the Drama, Ed Rodopi, Amsterdam, 76; translr, Martin Roda Becher, No Luck with Women, Dimension, 78; Understanding Max Frisch, with W. Koepke, German Studies Rev, Vol 16, 93. **CONTACT ADDRESS** Dept of Class and Mod Lang and Lit, Texas Tech Univ, Lubbock, TX 79409.

BADIAN, ERNST
PERSONAL Born 08/08/1925, Vienna, Austria, m, 1950, 2 children **DISCIPLINE** HISTORY, CLASSICAL STUDIES **EDUCATION** Univ NZ, BA, 45; MA, 46; Oxford Univ, BA, 50; MA, 54; DPhil, 56; Victoria Univ, Wellington, LitD, 62. **CAREER** Jr lectr classics, Victoria Univ Wellington, 47-48; asst lectr classics & ancient hist, Univ Sheffield, 52-54; lectr classics, Univ Durham, 54-65; prof ancient hist, Univ Leeds, 65-69; prof classics & hist, SUNY Buffalo, 69-71; prof hist, Harvard Univ, 71-82; John Moors Cabot Prof Hist, Harvard Univ, 82-98; John Moors Cabot Prof Hist Emer, Harvard Univ, 98-. **HONORS AND AWARDS** Conington Prize, Oxford Univ, 59, for Foreign Clientelae; Fel Brit Acad, Am Acad Arts & Scis, Am Numismatic Soc; corresp mem, Austrian Acad Scis, German Archaeol Inst; for mem, Finnish Acad Scis; hon mem, Soc Prom Roman Studies; hon Fel, Univ Col, Oxford; Austrian Cross of Hon in Sci & Art, 99; fel, Am Coun Learned Socs 72, 82; Leverhulme Fel, 73; Guggenheim Fel, 84; vis mem, Inst Adv Study, Princeton, fall 80, fall 92; fel, Nat Hum Ctr, 88; Hon LitD, Macquarie Univ, 93, Univ Canterbury, 99. **MEMBERSHIPS** Mem, Am Philol Asn, Asn Ancient Historians, Class Asn Can, UK Class Asn, Soc Prom Hellenic Studies, Virgil Soc. **RESEARCH** Alexander the Great; Roman Republic; Achaemenid Persia. **SELECTED PUBLICATIONS** Auth, Foreign Clientelae 264-270 BC, 58; auth, Studies in Greek and Roman History, 64; ed, Polybius, 66; ed, Ancient Society and Institutions, 66; auth, Roman Imperialism in the Late Republic, 67; auth Publicans and Sinners, 72; ed, "Sir Ronald Syme," Roman Papers Vols 1-2 (79); auth, From Plataea to Potidaea, 93; auth, Zoellner und Suender, 97; Ed, Am J Ancient Hist, 76-00. **CONTACT ADDRESS** Dept of Hist, Harvard Univ, Robinson Hall, Cambridge, MA 02138.

BAGBY, LEWIS
PERSONAL Born 07/24/1944, Brooklyn, NY, m, 1978, 2 children **DISCIPLINE** RUSSIAN LITERATURE **EDUCATION** Pomona Col, BA, 66; Stanford Univ, MA, 69; Univ Mich, Ann Arbor, PhD(Slavic lang & lit), 72. **CAREER** From Instr to Assoc Prof, 70-85, Prof Russ Lang & Lit, Univ Wyo, 85-, Dir, Int Programs, 95-, Dir, Wyoming-Saratov Initiative, 91-. **HONORS AND AWARDS** John P. Ellbogen Meritorious Classroom Teaching, 85; Hon Doctorate, Saratov State Univ, 98; recipient of many other contracts and grants. **MEMBERSHIPS** Rocky Mountain Mod Lang Asn; Am Asn of Teachers of Slavic and E Europ Lang; Am Asn for the Advancement of Slavic Studies. **RESEARCH** Prose fiction of Aleksandr Bestuzhev-Marlinjkij; Russian romantic prose fiction; transition from Russian romanticism to realisim. **SELECTED PUBLICATIONS** Auth, Pedagogical Devices in Third Year Russian Composition, Russ Lang J, spring 74; Contribr, Human values, quantification and literary evolution, In: The Architecture of Reading, Ohio State Univ, 76; auth, Narrative Double-Voicing in Lermontov's A Hero of Our Time, Slavic & East Europ J, 78; transl, The Test, Bestuzev-Marlinksij's tale, Russian Romantic Prose: An Anthology, 79; auth, A Concurrence of Psychological and Narrative Structures: Anamnesis in Valentin Rasputin's Upstream, Downstream, Can Slavonic Papers, fall 80; Aleksandr Bestuzev-Marlinskij's Roman i Ol'ga: Generation and degeneration, Slavic & East Europ J, winter 81; Mikhail Bakhtin's Discourse Typologies: Theoretical and Practical Considerations, Slavic Rev, spring 82; Bestuzev-Marlinskij's Mulla Nur: A Muddled Myth to Rekindle Romance, Russ Lit, spring 82; auth, Alexander Bestuzhev-Marlinsky and Russian Byronism, Penn State Univ Press, 95; A Hero of Our Time: An AATSEEL Critical Companion, NW Univ Press, forthcoming 99; author of numerous other journal articles, chapters in books, encyclopedias, and dictionaries. **CONTACT ADDRESS** International Programs, Univ of Wyoming, PO Box 8707, Laramie, WY 82071-3707. **EMAIL** lbagby@uwyo.edu

BAGNALL, ROGER SHALER
PERSONAL Born 08/19/1947, Seattle, WA, m, 1969, 2 children **DISCIPLINE** GREEK PAPYROLOGY, ANCIENT HISTORY **EDUCATION** Yale Univ, BA, 68; Univ Toronto, MA, 69, PHD(class studies), 72. **CAREER** Asst prof classics, Fla State Univ, 72-74; asst prof Greek & Latin, 74-79, assoc prof to prof Classics & Hist, Columbia Univ, 74-; mem bd, Scholars Press, 77-85; pres, Egyptological Sem of NY, 81-83; vis prof, Univ Florence, 81. **HONORS AND AWARDS** Am Coun Learned Soc grant-in-aid, 75; Am Coun Learned Soc study fel, 76-77; Am Philos Soc grant-in-aid, 80; Guggenheim fel, 90-91; Fel, Am Numismatic Soc; Assoc Academie Royale des Sciences; des Lettres et des Beaux-Arts de Relgique; Member, American Academy of Arts and Sciences. **MEMBERSHIPS** Am Soc Papyrologists (secy-treas, 74-79); Am Philol Asn (secy-treas, 79-85); Asn pour les Etudes Grecques; Egypt Exploration Soc; Asn Ancient Historians. **RESEARCH** Greek papyri; social and economic history of the late Roman Egypt; Hellenistic social and economic history. **SELECTED PUBLICATIONS** Coauth, Ostraka in the Royal Ontario Museum (2 vols), Samuel Stevens, Toronto, 71-76; auth, Ptolemaic Foreign Correspondence in Tebtunis Papyrus 8, J Egyptian Archaeol, 75; The Administration of the Ptolemaic Possessions, Brill, Leiden, 76; coauth, Ostraka in Amsterdam Collections, Terra, Zutphen, 76; auth, The Florida Ostraka: Documents from the Roman Army in Upper Egypt, Duke Univ, 76; Bullion Purchases and Landholding in the Fourth Century, Chronique d'Egypt, 77; coauth, The Chronological Systems of Byzantine Egypt, Terra, Zutphen, 78; Columbia Papyri VII, Scholars Press, 78; auth, Egypt in Late Antiquity, Princeton, 93; coauth, Demography of Roman Egypt, Cambridge, 94; auth, Reading Papyri, Writing Ancient History, Routledge, 95. **CONTACT ADDRESS** Columbia Univ, 1130 Amsterdam Ave, Rm 606, New York, NY 10027-6900. **EMAIL** bagnall@atscolumbia.edu

BAGULEY, DAVID
PERSONAL Born 04/28/1940, Leicester, England **DISCIPLINE** FRENCH LITERATURE **EDUCATION** Univ Nottingham, BA, 63; Univ Leicester, MA, 66; Univ Nancy, DUniv, 69. **CAREER** Asst English, Univ Nantes, 66-67; lectr French, Univ Leicester, 67-68; from lectr to assoc prof, 68-77, Prof French, Univ Western Ont, 77-. **MEMBERSHIPS** MLA; Soc Fr Studies. **RESEARCH** French literature of the 19th century; the naturalist novel; literary criticism. **SELECTED PUBLICATIONS** Auth, Fecondite d'Emile Zola: Roman a These, Evangile, Mythe, 73 & Bibliographie de la Critique sur Emile Zola, 1864-1970, 76, Univ Toronto; Emile Zola-An Intellectual in the Dreyfus Affair (French), French Rev, Vol 66, 93; Emile Zola Revisited, with W. J. Berg and L. K. Martin, French Forum, Vol 19, 94; Literature and Rationality-Ideas of Agency in Theory and Fiction, with P. Livingston, French Studies, Vol 49, 95; Emile Zola-'Nana', A Critical Edition (French), C. Becker, ed, Revue d'Histoire Litteraire de la France, Vol 95, 95; Correspondence, Vol 9, October 1897-September 1899 Laffaire Dreyfus (French), with E. Zola and B. H. Bakker, Nineteenth-Century French Studies, Vol 23, 95; Emile Zola-Correspondence, Vol 10-October 1899 to September 1902 (French), with O. Morgan and J. A. Walker, eds, B. H. Bakker, ed dir, H. Mitterand, Lit Advisor, Nineteenth-Century French Studies, Vol 24, 96; Zola-A Life, with F. Brown, French Forum, Vol 21, 96; The Poetics of Maupassant (French), with M. Bury, French rev, Vol 69, 96; Politics and Narratives of Birth-Gynocolonization from Rousseau to Zola, with C. A., Mossman, French Rev, Vol 69, 96; Alexandre Dumas, The 'Vicomte de Bragelonne' (French), with D. Coward, French Studies, Vol 51, 97; Emile Zola Centenary Colloquium 1893-1993, London, 23-25 September 1993, with P. Pollard, Modrn Language Rev, Vol 92, 97. **CONTACT ADDRESS** Dept of French, Univ of Western Ontario, London, ON, Canada N6A 5B8.

BAHR, EHRHARD
PERSONAL Born 08/21/1932, Kiel, Germany **DISCIPLINE** GERMAN LITERATURE **EDUCATION** Univ KS, MS, 58; Univ CA, Berkeley, PhD(Ger), 68. **CAREER** Acting asst prof, 66-68, from asst prof to assoc prof, 68-72, Prof Ger, Univ Calif, Los Angeles, 72-, Chmn Dept Ger Lang, 81-84, 93-98. **HONORS AND AWARDS** UCLA Distinguished Teaching Awd, 70. **MEMBERSHIPS** MLA; Am Asn Teachers Ger; Am Soc 18th Century Studies; Am Lessing Soc; Heinrich Heine Soc. **RESEARCH** Eighteenth century German literature; German classicism; modern German literature. **SELECTED PUBLICATIONS** Auth, Kafka and the Prague spring, Mosaic, summer 70; Georg Lukacs, Colloquium, 71 (also in English & French translr); Die Ironie im Spatwerk Goethese, Erich Schmidt, Berlin, 72; Goethes Wanderjahre as an experimental novel, Mosaic, spring 72; Ernst Bloch, Colloquium, Berlin, 74; ed, Kant, Was ist Aufklarung, Reclam, Stuttgart, 74; auth, The pursuit of happiness in the political writings of Lessing and Kant, In: Studies on Voltaire and the Eighteenth Century, 151: 167-184, 76; Personenwechselung in Goethes Westostlichem Divan, Chronik des Wiener Goethevereins, 73: 117-125; Nelly Sachs, H C Beck, 80; ed, Goethe, Wilhelm Meisters Lehrjahre, Reclam, Stuttgart, 82; Adversaries of Goethe in His Later Years-Writes Associated with the Young-German School, Nationalists, and Orthodox Christians, Goethe Jahrbuch, Vol 112, 95; auth, History of German Literature, 3 vols, 2nd ed, 98-99; auth, The Novel as Archive, 98. **CONTACT ADDRESS** Dept of Germanic Lang, Univ of California, Los Angeles, 405 Hilgard Ave, PO BOX 951539, Los Angeles, CA 90095-1539. **EMAIL** bahr@humnet.ucla.edu

BAILEY, PHILLIP
PERSONAL Born Carbondale, IL, m, 1983, 3 children **DISCIPLINE** FRENCH **EDUCATION** Saint John's Univ, BA, 85; Univ Va, MA, 87, PhD, 93. **CAREER** Assoc prof, Univ Central Ark, 93- . **RESEARCH** Nineteenth and twentieth-century French literature; problems of narrative technic; study of foreign language anxiety and learning styles. **SELECTED PUBLICATIONS** Auth, Proust's Self Reader: The Pursuit of Literature as Privileged Communication, Summa Publ, 97. **CONTACT ADDRESS** Univ of Central Arkansas, 201 Donaghey Ave, Conway, AR 72035-0001. **EMAIL** phillipb@mail.uca.edu

BAILLY, JACQUES A.
PERSONAL Born 01/28/1966, Salt Lake City, UT **DISCIPLINE** CLASSICS **EDUCATION** Brown Univ, BA, 88; Cornell Univ, PhD, 97. **CAREER** Lectr, Colby Col, 96-97; lectr, 97-98, asst prof, 98- , Univ Vermont. **HONORS AND AWARDS** Fulbright award, 88-90; Jakob K Javits Scholarship, 91-95. **MEMBERSHIPS** APA. **RESEARCH** Ancient philosophy; philology. **CONTACT ADDRESS** Dept of Classics, Univ of Vermont, 481 Main St, Burlington, VT 05401. **EMAIL** jbailly@zoo.uvm.edu

BAKER, DEBORAH LESKO
DISCIPLINE FRENCH LITERATURE **EDUCATION** Yale Univ, PhD. **CAREER** Assoc prof, 89-. **RESEARCH** Renaissance literature. **SELECTED PUBLICATIONS** Auth, Narcissus and the Lover, Stanford, 87; The Subject of Desire, Purdue, 96; pubs on Petrarch, Joachim DuBellay, Louise Lab, rhetorical and mythical structures in texts by Flaubert and Marguerite Duras. **CONTACT ADDRESS** French Dept, Georgetown Univ, 37th and O St, Washington, DC 20057.

BAKER, JOSEPH O.
PERSONAL Born 12/26/1938, Murray, UT, m, 1961, 3 children **DISCIPLINE** GERMAN LANGUAGE & LITERATURE **CAREER** Asst prof, 67-73, Assoc Prof Ger, Brigham Young Univ, 73-, Dir Study Abroad, 74-86. **HONORS AND AWARDS** Fulbright Scholar, Germany, Summer, 88. **MEMBERSHIPS** MLA; Rocky Mountain Mod Lang Asn; Heinrich von Kleist Gesellschaft; AATG; ICEE Board of Directors, 83-87. **RESEARCH** Heinrich von Kleist; German poetic realism. **SELECTED PUBLICATIONS** Ethics of Life and Death with H J Kleist; 19th C Women Writers; Im Nonengarten, Anthology of German Women's Writing (1850-1907) w/Michelle Stott; German Cultural History, Multimedia, independent study course. **CONTACT ADDRESS** Brigham Young Univ, 4094 Jkhb, Provo, UT 84602-0002. **EMAIL** Joseph_baker@BYU.edu

BAKER, MARY JORDAN
PERSONAL Born Chicago, IL **DISCIPLINE** FRENCH RENAISSANCE LITERATURE **EDUCATION** Stanford Univ, AB, 61; Univ VA, MA, 64; Harvard Univ, PhD(Romance lang), 69. **CAREER** Instr French, DePauw Univ, 64-65; asst prof, 68-75, Assoc Prof French, Univ TX, Austin, 75-. **MEMBERSHIPS** Am Asn Teachers Fr; Renaissance Soc Am; Mod Humanities Res Asn. **SELECTED PUBLICATIONS** Auth, Didacticism and the Heptameron: the Misinterpretation of the Tenth Tale as an Exemplum, Fr Rev, 12/71; Fiammetta and the Angiosses douloureuses qui procedent d'amours, Symposium, winter 73; France's First Sentimental Novel and Novels of Chivalry, Bibliot Humanisme et Renaissance, 1/74; The sonnets of Louise Labe: a reappraisal, Neophilologus, 76; The Role of the Moral Lesson in Heptameron, Fr Studies, 1/77; coauth, Panache Litteraire, Harper & Row, 78; Metadiegetic Narrative in the 'Heptameron', Studies in the Literary Imagination, Vol 25, 92; The Disnarrated in Les 'Cent Nouvelles Nouvelles' & Events That Do Not Happen But Could Have, Orbis Literarum, Vol 50, 95. **CONTACT ADDRESS** 2301 Windsor Rd, Austin, TX 78703.

BAKER, SUSAN READ
PERSONAL Born 12/15/1942, El Dorado, AR **DISCIPLINE** FRENCH LITERATURE **EDUCATION** Univ TX Austin, BA, 64; Harvard Univ, MA, 65, PhD(French), 70. **CAREER** Asst prof, Harvard Univ, 70-76; Assoc Prof French, Univ FL, 76-. **MEMBERSHIPS** MLA; North Am Soc 17th Century Fr Lit; Am Asn Teaching Fr; Am Soc 18th Century Studies; SAtlantic Mod Lang Asn. **RESEARCH** Comedy in 17th-18th centuries; 17th century French moralists; 17th century philosophy and history of ideas. **SELECTED PUBLICATIONS CONTACT ADDRESS** Dept of Romance Lang & Lit, Univ of Florida, P O Box 117405, Gainesville, FL 32611-7405.

BALASUBRAMANIAN, RADHA
PERSONAL Born 08/16/1950, India, m, 1989, 1 child **DISCIPLINE** RUSSIAN LITERATURE **EDUCATION** Ind Univ, PhD. **CAREER** Assoc prof Russ, Univ Nebr, Lincoln. **RESEARCH** The influences of India on Russian literature and vice-versa. **SELECTED PUBLICATIONS** Published articles on works by Dostoevsky, Korolenko, Sholokhov, Sologub, Bulgakov, Salman Rushdie, Tolstoy, and on teaching Russian to foreigners; Also a book on Korolenko. **CONTACT ADDRESS** Univ of Nebraska, Lincoln, Lincoln, NE 68588-0417. **EMAIL** rbalasubramanian1@unl.edu

BALDERSTON, DANIEL
DISCIPLINE SPANISH **EDUCATION** Univ California-Berkeley, AB, 74; Princeton Univ, MA, 78, PhD, 81. **CAREER** Asst Prof, Earlham Col, 80-82; Asst Prof, Wittenburg Univ, 82-83; Asst/Assoc/Full Prof, Tulane Univ, 83-98; Prof, Univ Iowa 99-. **MEMBERSHIPS** MLA; Instituto Internacional de Literatura Iberoamericana; Am Asn of Teachers of Spanish and Portuguese; Centro de Estudios de la Literatura y Cultura del Rio de la Plata. **SELECTED PUBLICATIONS** Auth, El precursor velado: R. L. Stevenson en la obra de Borges, Editorial Sudamericana, 85; auth, The Literary Universe of Jorge Luis Borges: An Index to References and Allusions to Person, Titles and Places in His Writings, Greenwood Press, 86; auth, The Latin American Short Story: An Annotated Guide to Anthologies and Criticism, Greenwood Press, 92; auth, Out of Context: Historical Reference and the Representation of Reality in Borges, Duke Univ Press, 93; transl, Fuera de contexto? Referencialidad historica y expresion de la realidad en Borges, Beatriz Viterbo Editora, 96; co-ed, Sex and Sexuality in Latin America, New York Univ Press, 97; co-ed, Sexo y sexualidades en America Latina, Paidos, 98; co-auth, Borges, una enciclopedia, Editorial Norma, 99; auth, El deseo: enorme cicatriz luminosa, Ediciones ExCultura, Caracas, 99; auth, Borges, realidades_y simulacros, Biblos, Buenos Aires, 00; co-ed, Encyclopedia of Contemporary Latin American and Caribbean Cultures, Routledge, 00; auth, Sexualidad y nacion en America Latina, Instituto Internacional de Literatura Iberoamericana, Pittsburgh, 00. **CONTACT ADDRESS** Dept of Spanish, The Univ of Iowa, Iowa City, IA 52242. **EMAIL** daniel-balderston@uiowa.edu

BALDWIN, THOMAS PRATT
PERSONAL Born 02/25/1941, Rome, GA, 4 children **DISCIPLINE** GERMAN LITERATURE **EDUCATION** Univ Heidelberg, Zertifikat, 63; Univ Wis-Madison, MA, 67, PhD, 72. **CAREER** From instr to asst prof, 68-74, assoc prof, 74-79, prof Ger, 80-, Western KY Univ; consult, Nat Endowment Humanities, 78-. **HONORS AND AWARDS** NDEA Fellow **MEMBERSHIPS** Am Assn Teachers Ger; Soc for German Am Studies, Ky Coun on Teaching of Foreign Lang **RESEARCH** Austrian literature; pedagogy. **SELECTED PUBLICATIONS** Auth, The Public Image of Germans in Louisville and Jefferson County, Kentucky: 1840-1872, Yearbook of German-American Studies 29, 94. **CONTACT ADDRESS** Dept of Foreign Lang, Western Kentucky Univ, 1 Big Red Way St, Bowling Green, KY 42101-3576. **EMAIL** thomas.baldwin@wku.edu

BALESTRA, ALEJANDRA
PERSONAL Born 10/23/1956, Argentina, m, 1999, 1 child **DISCIPLINE** SPANISH **EDUCATION** Univ Buenos Aires, BA; Univ Houston, MA; PhD. **CAREER** Teaching asst to project coordr, Univ Buenos Aires, 90-96; res asst and project coordr, Univ Houston, 97-. **HONORS AND AWARDS** Kappa Phi Kappa; Sigma Delta Phi; Staff Scholar, Univ Houston, 01; Halpern-Kanellos Scholar, 00, 01; Good Neighbor Scholar, 98. **MEMBERSHIPS** MALCS; MLA Soc of Am Archivists; Am Asn of Teacher of Spanish and Portuguese. **RESEARCH** Historical linguistics; Sociolinguistics; Language contact; Morphosyntactic variation and change in Spanish; Computational linguistics; Women and language; Hispanic women writers in the United States. **SELECTED PUBLICATIONS** Auth, "Lo personal y lo impersonal en la narrativa folklorica de los trabajadores no-docentes de la Facultad de Filosofia y Letras," in Memorias de las Segundas Jornadas de Estudio de la Narrativa Folklorica, (91): 110-121; auth, "Las glosas en Historia de las Indias," in Actas del III Congreso Argentino de Hispanistas, (Buenos Aires, 92), 284-292; auth, "Lecto-escritura: un enfoque constructivista," Jardincito te ensena a leer y a escribir, 94; co-ed, Libro de la Anothomia del Hombre del Doctor Bernardino M. de Monserrate, Madison, 95; auth, "Vocabulario basado en Textos Medicos del los Siglos XIII al XVI (Enfermedades)," in Medicina y Sociedad: curar y sanar en la Espana de los siglos XIII al XVI, Univ Buenos Aires, 96; auth, "Cambio de armas de Luisa Valenzuela: una guerra desde el punto de vista femenino," in The Politics of Written Word in the Americas, Baylor Univ, 99; coordr, Herencia: The Anthology of Hispanic Literature in the United States, Oxford Univ Pres, 01. **CONTACT ADDRESS** Literacy Prog, Univ of Houston, 256 Cullen Performance Hall, Houston, TX 77204-2006. **EMAIL** abalestr@mail.uh.edu

BALL, DAVID
PERSONAL Born 02/27/1937, New York, NY, m, 1967, 2 children **DISCIPLINE** COMPARATIVE LITERATURE **EDUCATION** Brandeis Univl, BA, 59; Licence es lettres, Sorbonne, 65; docteur en lit generale et comparee, Univ de Paris III, Sorbonne, 72. **CAREER** Lectr to full prof, French & Comparative Lit, Smith Col, 69-. **HONORS AND AWARDS** Scaglione prize for literary transl, MLA, 96. **MEMBERSHIPS** ALTA. **RESEARCH** Translation of poetry; Writing under occupation, 1940-44. **SELECTED PUBLICATIONS** Auth, Des Poux et des hommes: La Solution finale dans les quotidiens en 1942, Les Temps Modernes, 97; auth, Acclaiming Adair: Against a Certain Tendency in Translation Theory, Transl Rev, 96; auth, Underground Laughter (1940-1944), Literature and War, Editions Rodopi, 90; co-auth, Moliere's Dom Juan: Form, Meaning, Audience, Mod Philol, 83; rev, Dickens in French, Dickens Studies, fall, 83; article, Is Tenure a Threat to Academic Freedom?, Can Asn of Univ Teachers, 81; auth, On Translating Goethe's Faust, The Ger Rev, 80; auth, Turgenev's Dialectic, The Mass Rev, 79; auth, La Definition ironique, Rev de Lit Comparee, 76; auth, Vers une theorie de l'ironie: perspectives sur Swift, Etudes Anglaises, 76; co-auth, Listening to an Angolan Revolutionary, The New Republic, 62. **CONTACT ADDRESS** Smith Col, Northampton, MA 01063. **EMAIL** dball@sophia.smith.edu

BALL, ROBERT J.
PERSONAL Born 11/04/1941, New York, NY **DISCIPLINE** CLASSICS **EDUCATION** Queens Col, BA, 62; Tufts Univ, MA, 63; Columbia Univ, PhD(class), 71. **CAREER** Asst prof, 71-76, assoc prof, 76-83, prof class, Univ Hawaii, 83-. **HONORS AND AWARDS** Excellence in Teaching Awd, Am Philol Asn; Regents' Medal for Excellence in Teaching, Univ Hawaii. **MEMBERSHIPS** Am Philol Asn. **RESEARCH** Latin poetry; Latin pedagogy; history of classical scholarship. **SELECTED PUBLICATIONS** Auth, Tibullus the Elegist: A Critical Survey, Vandenhoeck & Ruprecht, 83; ed, The Classical Papers of Gilbert Highet, Columbia Univ Press, 83; auth, Reading Classical Latin: A Reasonable Approach (2nd ed), McGraw-Hill, 97; auth, Reading Classical Latin: The Second Year (2nd ed), McGraw-Hill, 98; ed, The Unpublished Lectures of Gilbert Highet, Peter Lang Pub, 98. **CONTACT ADDRESS** Dept Europ Lang & Lit, Univ of Hawaii, Manoa, 1890 E West Rd, Honolulu, HI 96822-2318. **EMAIL** rball@hawaii.edu

BANDERA, CESAREO
DISCIPLINE SPANISH LANGUAGE & LITERATURE **EDUCATION** Univ Sevilla, Lic, 56; Univ Salamanca, Lic, 68; Cornell Univ, MA, 63; PhD, 65. **CAREER** Asst prof, Cornell Univ, 65-68; asst prof, State Univ NYork at Buffalo, 69-85; distinguished univ prof, Univ NC, 85-. **HONORS AND AWARDS** Fulbright Fel; Berkowits Post-Doctoral. **RESEARCH** Spanish Medieval & Golden Age Literature, Theory of Literature. **SELECTED PUBLICATIONS** Auth, El Poema de Mio Cid: Poesia, Historia, Mito, Gredos, 69; auth, Mimesis Conflictiva, Gredos, 74; auth, The Sacred Game. The Role of the Sacred in the Genesis of Modern Literary Fiction, Pa State Univ Press, 96. **CONTACT ADDRESS** Dept Romance Lang, Univ of No Carolina, Chapel Hill, 440 W Franklin St, Chapel Hill, NC 27599-2319.

BANGERTER, LOWELL A.
DISCIPLINE GERMAN **EDUCATION** Univ IL, PhD, 70. **CAREER** Prof; Univ WY, 70-; served as dir, UW Hum Semester, dept grad adv & dept head. **HONORS AND AWARDS** WY Coun for the Hum fel, 78; UW res grant, 80. **RESEARCH** 18th century Ger lit; mod Austrian and East Ger lit. **SELECTED PUBLICATIONS** Auth, 7 bk(s) & numerous articles; publ, Engl transl of several works of 20th-century Austrian lit. **CONTACT ADDRESS** Dept of Mod and Class Lang(s), Univ of Wyoming, PO Box 3964, Laramie, WY 82071-3964. **EMAIL** BANG@UWYO.EDU

BANNON, CYNTHIA J.
DISCIPLINE CLASSICAL STUDIES **EDUCATION** Harvard Univ, AB, 84; Univ Mich, PhD, 91. **CAREER** Asst prof, Intercollegiate Center for Class Studies, Rome, 96-97; asst prof, Ind Univ, Bloomington. **RESEARCH** Roman law; Latin prose style and grammar; rhetoric; history. **SELECTED PUBLICATIONS** Auth, The Brothers of Romulus, Princeton, 97. **CONTACT ADDRESS** Dept of Classical Studies, Indiana Univ, Bloomington, 1020 E Kirkwood Ave, 547 Ballantine Hall, Bloomington, IN 47405. **EMAIL** cbannon@indiana.edu

BANTA, FRANK GRAHAM
PERSONAL Born 05/31/1918, Franklin, IN **DISCIPLINE** GERMAN LINGUISTICS **EDUCATION** IN Univ, AB, 39; Univ MD, MA, 41; Univ Berne, PhD, 51. **CAREER** Instr foreign lang, Univ MD, 39-44; from instr to assoc prof Ger, Univ IL, Urbana, 51-64, chmn dept 55-64; assoc prof, 64-70, Prof Ger Ling, IN Univ, Bloomington, 70-, Dir, Arts & Sci Teaching Resources Ctr, Ind Univ, 75-77. **MEMBERSHIPS** MLA; Ling Soc Am; Am Asn Teachers Ger (vpres, 71-73); Indoger Ges. **RESEARCH** Middle High German; Germanic and Indo-European linguistics. **SELECTED PUBLICATIONS CONTACT ADDRESS** Dept of Ger Lang, Indiana Univ, Bloomington, Bloomington, IN 47401.

BANZIGER, HANS
PERSONAL Born 01/15/1917, Romanshorn, Switzerland, m, 1943, 3 children **DISCIPLINE** GERMAN LITERATURE **EDUCATION** Univ Zurich, Dr Phil(Ger lit), 42. **CAREER** Teacher Ger, County Sch, Trogen, Switz, 43-67; docent Ger lit, Col Indust & Social Educ, St Gallen, Switz, 53-67, pvt docent, 65-67; assoc prof, 67-70, chmn dept, 71-72, prof, 71-82, Emer Prof Ger, Bryn Mawr Col, 71-. **MEMBERSHIPS** MLA; Am Asn Teachers Ger; Int Ger Asn; Swiss Authors Soc; Swiss Pen. **SELECTED PUBLICATIONS** Auth, Frisch und Durrenmatt, 60, 7th ed, 76 & Zwischen Protest & Traditionsbewusstsein: On M Frisch, 75, Francke, Bern; contribr, Glucksfischer und Auswanderer: On Jakob Schaffner, Schweizer Monatshefte, 75; Widerstand gegen Modestromungen: on R Henz, Festschrift Rudolf Henz, 77; Das namenlose Tier und sein Territorium: On Kafka, Deutsche Vierteljahresschrift, 79; Verzweiflung unf Auferstehungen auf dem Todesbett, Deutsche Vierteljahresschrift, 80; Durrenmatt in Ungarn, Schweizer Monatshefte, 81; Schloss-Haus-Bau, Studien zu einem Motivkomplex, Francke, Bern/Munchen, 82; Max Frisch, with W. Koepke, Colloquia Germanica, Vol 25, 92. **CONTACT ADDRESS** Dept of Ger, Bryn Mawr Col, Bryn Mawr, PA 19010.

BARABTARLO, GENE
PERSONAL Born 02/15/1949, Moscow, Soviet Union, m, 1968, 1 child **DISCIPLINE** RUSSIAN LITERATURE & LINGUISTICS **EDUCATION** Univ Moscow, Diploma in Russian Letters (equivalent to MA), 72; Univ Ill, PhD, 85. **CAREER** Sr res fel, 72-75, vice-provost for res, The Pushkin Lit Museum, 76-78; res & teaching asst, Univ Ill, Champaign-Urbana, 80-84; from asst prof to assoc prof, 85-94, prof Russ lit, 94-, Dept Chair, 95-, Univ Mo. **RESEARCH** Pushkin; Nabokov. **SELECTED PUBLICATIONS** Auth, Phantom of Fact: Nabokov's Pnin, Ardis, 89; co-ed, A Small Alpine Form: Nabokov's Short Stories, Garland Publ, 92; auth, Aerial View: Essays on Nabokov's Art and Metaphysics, Peter Lang, 93; ed, What a Pity: Solzhenitsyn's Short Stories, Duckworth, 96. **CONTACT ADDRESS** Dept of German and Russian Studies, Univ of Missouri, Columbia, 451 GCB, Columbia, MO 65211. **EMAIL** Barabtarlo6@missouri.edu

BARAN, HENRYK
DISCIPLINE SLAVIC LANGUAGES & LITERATURES **EDUCATION** Harvard Univ, PhD. **CAREER** Prof, Univ Albany, State Univ NY. **RESEARCH** 19th and 20th Century Russian Literature, with a special emphasis on modernism and the avant-garde; poetics and theory of literature, semiotics, folklore and literature, Polish literature. **SELECTED PUBLICATIONS** Managing ed, Elementa: A Journal of Slavic Studies and Comparative Semiotics, Harwood Acad Publ. **CONTACT ADDRESS** Slavic & Eurasian Studies Dept, SUNY, Albany, Humanities 235, Albany, NY 12222. **EMAIL** hbaran@albany.edu

BARBE, KATHARINA
PERSONAL Born Berlin, Germany, m, 1990, 2 children **DISCIPLINE** LINGUISTICS **EDUCATION** Paedagogische Hochschule Berlin/Technische Universitaet Berlin, 78-80; Univ Houston, BA, 84; Rice Univ, MA, 88; PhD, 89. **CAREER** Instr, 89-90, asst prof, 90-96, assoc prof, 96- , Northern Ill Univ, 89-. **HONORS AND AWARDS** DAAD Scholar, 80-81; NEH, 93. **MEMBERSHIPS** AATG; ICTFL; GFDS. **RESEARCH** Linguistic pragmatics; translation theory; SLA. **SELECTED PUBLICATIONS** Auth, Isn't it Ironic that.., Jour Pragmatics, 93; auth, Begin in German, Teaching Ideas: A Collection of Successful Classroom Strategies, Cherry Hill, 93; auth, Reading in the Intermediate Classroom: Der Rattenfanger von Hameln, Teaching German, 94; auth, The Translation of Loans: Anglicisms in German, Perspectives: Studies in Translatology, 94; auth, The Dichotomy Literal and Free Translation, META: Transl Jour; auth, Dubbing in the Translation Classroom, Perspectives: Studies in Translatology, 96; auth, Bewerbung um eine Praktikantenstelle im Ausland, Unterrichtsmaterialien zur Vorbereitung auf die Prufung Zertifikat Deutsch fur den Beruf, 98; auth, Auf der Bank: Deutsch im Beruf von Anfang an, Schatzkammer, 99; auth, The Dilemma with Dichotomies, Language and Communication, 00; auth, Translation and Textanalysis, in Functional Approaches to Language, Culture, and Cognition, ed. D.G. Lockwood et al., 00; auth, Mit dem Autoschwimmbad in die Verkehrsmarmelade: Learning to use a Bilingual Dictionary Successfully, Unterrichtspraxis, 01; auth, Irony in Context, Number 34 in Pragmatics and Beyond, John Benjamins Publishers (Amsterdam). **CONTACT ADDRESS** Dept of Foreign Langs & Lit, No Illinois Univ, De Kalb, IL 60115. **EMAIL** kbarbe@niu.edu

BARBER, ELIZABETH J. WAYLAND
PERSONAL Born 12/02/1940, Pasadena, CA, m, 1965 **DISCIPLINE** ARCHAEOLOGY, LINGUISTICS **EDUCATION** Bryn Mawr Col, BA, 62; Yale Univ, PhD, 68. **CAREER** Res assoc, Princeton Univ, 68-89; LECTR TO FULL PROF, OCCIDENTAL COL, 70-. **HONORS AND AWARDS** NEH Grants, 72, 74, & 93; J Guggenheim Memorial Fel, 79-80; Wenner-Gren ACLS Haynes grants; book prizes from Amer Hist Asn, 93, Costume Soc, 92, 95 & 00. **MEMBERSHIPS** Archaeol Inst of Am; Linguistic Soc of Am; Textile Soc of Am; Costume Soc of Am; CIETA. **RESEARCH** Prehistoric archaeology and languages of Southern & Eastern Europe; decipherment; ancient textiles, costumes, & rituals. **SELECTED PUBLICATIONS** Auth, The Mummies of Urumchi, W.W. Norton, 99; auth,

Women's Work-The First 20,000 Years, W.W. Norton, 94; auth, Prehistoric Textiles, Princeton Univ Press, 91; auth, Archaeological Decipherment, Princeton Univ Press, 74; auth, On the Origins of the Vily/Rusalki, Varia on the Indo-European Past, 97; auth, Minoan Women and the Challenge of Weaving for Home, Trade, and Shrine, TEXNH: Craftsmen, Craftswomen and Craftsmanship in the Aegean Bronze Age, 97; auth, Textiles of the Neolithic through Iron Ages, The Oxford Encycl of Archaeol in the Near East, 97; auth, On the Antiquity of East European Bridal Clothing, Dress, 94; auth, The Peplos of Athena, Goddess and Polis: The Panathenaic Festival in Ancient Athens, Princeton, 92. **CONTACT ADDRESS** Language Dept, Occidental Col, 1126 N. Chester Ave., Los Angeles, CA 90041. **EMAIL** barber@oxy.edu

BARBER, PAUL THOMAS
PERSONAL Born 07/16/1941, Santa Barbara, CA, m, 1965 **DISCIPLINE** GERMAN **EDUCATION** Univ of Calif at Santa Barbara, BA, 63; Yale Univ, PhD, 68. **CAREER** Instr, 67-68, asst prof, Princeton Univ, 68-70; FOWLER MUSEUM OF CULTURAL HIST, UCLA, RES ASSOC, 90-. **RESEARCH** Folklore; oral literature; rhetoric. **SELECTED PUBLICATIONS** Auth, Vampires, Burial and Death: Folklore and Reality, Yale Univ Press, 88; auth, Staking Claims: Vampires of Folklore and Legend, Skeptical Inquirer, 96; auth, Mummification in the Tarim Basin, J of Indo-European Studies, 95; auth, The Real Vampire, Nat Hist, 95; auth, Cremation, J of Indo-European Studies, 90; auth, Forensic Pathology and the European Vampire, J of Folklore Res, 87. **CONTACT ADDRESS** 1126 N. Chester Ave., Pasadena, CA 91104.

BARBOUR, SARAH E.
PERSONAL Born 12/26/1949, Gainesville, FL **DISCIPLINE** FRENCH **EDUCATION** Maryville Col, BA, 71; Cornell Univ, MA, 78; PhD, 85. **CAREER** Assoc prof, Wake Forest Univ, 85-. **MEMBERSHIPS** MLA, AAUP, AAUW, Col Lang Assoc. **RESEARCH** Modern and contemporary French and Francophone narrative, women writing in French, French and Francophone cinema, translation studies. **SELECTED PUBLICATIONS** Auth, Nathalie Sarraute and the Feminist Reader: Identities in Process, Bucknell Univ Pr, 93. **CONTACT ADDRESS** Wake Forest Univ, Reynolda Stn, PO Box 7566, Winston-Salem, NC 27109. **EMAIL** barbour@wfu.edu

BARCHILON, JACQUES
PERSONAL Born 04/08/1923, Casablanca, Morocco, m, 1998, 2 children **DISCIPLINE** FRENCH LITERATURE **EDUCATION** Univ Rochester, AB, 50; Harvard Univ, AM, 51, PhD, 56. **CAREER** Teaching fel, Harvard Univ, 52-55; instr, Smith Col, 55-56; instr, Brown Univ, 56-69; instr, 59-65, assoc prof, 65-71, Prof French, Univ CO, Boulder, 71-, Chmn, French & Ital Dept, 81-, Res grants, Coun Res & Creative Work, Univ Colo, 61, 63, 64, 76, 77, 79 & 80 & Am Philos Soc, 63, 64, 71 & 80; fac fel, Univ CO, 64; exchange prof French & comp lit, Ctr Univ Savole, Chambery, France, 78-79; Emer, 91-. **MEMBERSHIPS** MLA; Am Asn Teachers French, NAm Soc for 17th Century French Lit, Am Asn Literary Scholars and Critics (ALS). **RESEARCH** French literature, the fairy tale, Charles Perrault, M med'Avlnoy. **SELECTED PUBLICATIONS** Auth & ed, Perrault's Tales of Mother Goose, Peirpont Morgan, 56; co-ed, The Authentic Mother Goose, Swallow, 60; auth, Charles Perrault, Dix-septieme Siecle, 62; Esprit et Humor chez Perrault, Studi Francesi, 67; Le Conte merveilleux francais, Champion, 75; A Concordance to Charles Perrault's Tales, Prose and Verse (2 vols), Norwood, 77-79, chap, In: La Coherence Ingerieure, Hean-Michel Place, 77; Contes de Perrault, Slatkine Reprints, 80; Charles Perrault, A Critical Biography, G K Hall, 81; 20th-Century Renewal of Interest in the 16th-Century 'Roman De Perceforest', Lettres Romanes, Vol 46, 92; auth, Contes de Madamed'Avlnoy, 2 vols, Societe Textes Fzancais Modernes, 97-98. **CONTACT ADDRESS** Dept of French & Ital, Univ of Colorado, Boulder, Boulder, CO 80309.

BARLOW, JOHN DENISON
PERSONAL Born 09/28/1934, Brooklyn, NY, m, 1970, 3 children **DISCIPLINE** GERMAN LITERATURE, FILM, PHILANTHROPY & LITERATURE **EDUCATION** NYork Univ, BA, 58, MA, 61, PhD, 67. **CAREER** Instr Ger, Univ Col, NY Univ, 61-67; asst prof, 67-72, assoc prof Ger, 72-81, prof German, 81-98, dir, 82-84, prof English, 91-98, assoc dean lib arts, 84-87, act dean Lib Arts, 88-98, dean Emeritus, prof Emeritus English & German, 98-, Ind Univ-Purdue Univ, Indianapolis; Ottendorfer mem fel, 66-67; Danforth assoc, 70-. **MEMBERSHIPS** MLA; Am Assn Teachers Ger. **RESEARCH** Twentieth century literature; film. **SELECTED PUBLICATIONS** Auth, German Expressionist Film, Twayne, 82; translator, Jean Amery, On Aging, 94. **CONTACT ADDRESS** Dept of German, Indiana Univ-Purdue Univ, Indianapolis, 1100 W Michigan St, Indianapolis, IN 46202-2880. **EMAIL** jbarlow@iupui.edu

BARNARD, SYLVIA
PERSONAL Born Greenfield, MA, s, 1 child **DISCIPLINE** CLASSICS **EDUCATION** Cambridge Univ, BA, 62; MA, 67; Yale Univ, MA, 63; PhD, 66. **CAREER** Asst prof, Kenyon Col, 66-67; asst to prof, State Univ of NY, 67-. **MEMBERSHIPS** Am Philological Asn, Am Inst of Arch. **RESEARCH** Women in Antiquity. **SELECTED PUBLICATIONS** Auth, "Hellenistic Women Poets," Classical Journal, 78; auth, Ante, Poet of Children and Animals, in Rose di Pieria, 91; auth, "The Matres of Roman Britain," Archaeological Journal, 85; auth, Cornelia and the Women of her Family, 90. **CONTACT ADDRESS** Sept Classics, SUNY at Albany, 1400 Wash Ave, Albany, NY 12222-10000. **EMAIL** sbarnard@csc.albany.edu

BARNES, BETSY
DISCIPLINE FRENCH LINGUISTICS **EDUCATION** Ind Univ, PhD. **CAREER** Instr, Univ Minn, Twin Cities. **SELECTED PUBLICATIONS** Auth, The Pragmatics of Left Detachment in Spoken Standard French, Benjamin's, 85; coauth, Deux Mondes, 2nd ed, McGraw-Hill, 93. **CONTACT ADDRESS** Dept of French and Italian, Univ of Minnesota, Twin Cities, 9 Pleasant St SE, Minneapolis, MN 55455. **EMAIL** bjkerr@umn.edu

BARNES, JIM WEAVER
PERSONAL Born 12/22/1933, Summerfield, OK **DISCIPLINE** COMPARATIVE LITERATURE, CREATIVE WRITING **EDUCATION** Southeast Oklahoma State Univ, BA, 64; Univ Ark, Fayetteville, MA, 66, PhD, 72. **CAREER** Instr English, Northeastern Okla State Univ, 65-68; prof comp lit, 70-, ed, The Chariton Review, Truman State Univ, 76-; Nat Endowment for the Arts creative writing fel, 78; Rockefeller Found Bellagio Fel, 90; Sr Fulbright to Switzerland, 93-94; Akademie Schloss Solitude Fel, 98. **HONORS AND AWARDS** Transl Prize Summons and Sign, Columbia Univ, 80; The Am Book Awd, 98. **MEMBERSHIPS** Coord Coun of Lit Mags; MLA. **RESEARCH** Twentieth century fiction and poetry; creative writing. **SELECTED PUBLICATIONS** Auth, On Native Ground, University of Oklahoma Press, 97; auth, Paris, University of Illinois Press, 97. **CONTACT ADDRESS** Div of Lang & Lit, Truman State Univ, 100 E Normal St, Kirksville, MO 63501-4221. **EMAIL** jbarnes@truman.edu

BARNES, TIMOTHY DAVID
PERSONAL Born 03/13/1942, Yorkshire, England, m, 1965, 3 children **DISCIPLINE** CLASSICS, HISTORY **EDUCATION** Oxford Univ, BA, 64, MA, 67, DPhil, 70. **CAREER** Jr res fel classics, Queen's Col, Oxford, 66-70; from asst prof to assoc prof, Univ Col, Toronto, 70-76; assoc chmn grad studies, 79-83, Prof Classics Univ Toronto, 76-. **HONORS AND AWARDS** Conington Prize, Oxford Univ, 74. **MEMBERSHIPS** Am Philol Asn; Can Class Asn; Am Soc Papyrologists; Am Asn Ancient Historians; Soc Promotion Roman Studies. **RESEARCH** Hist, lit, culture and religions of Roman Empire from Augustus to the sixth century, Theodosian Code, Early Christian Hagiography. **SELECTED PUBLICATIONS** Auth, Athanasius and Constantius, Theology and Politics in the Constantinian Empire, Harvard UP, 93; auth, From Eusebius to Augustine, Selected papers 1982-1993, Aldershot: Varorium Reprints, 94; auth, "The Sources of the Historia Augusta 1967-1992," Historae Augustae Colloquium Maceratense, (95): 1-28; auth, "Statistics and the Conversion of the Roman Aristocracy," Journal of Roman Studies 85, (95): 135-147; auth, "Emperors, Panegyrics, Prefects, Provinces and Palaces," Journal of Roman Archaeology 9, 96; auth, Representation and Reality in Ammianus Marcellinus, book being prepared for submission to Cornell UP. **CONTACT ADDRESS** Dept of Classics, Univ of Toronto, 97 St George St, Toronto, ON, Canada M5S 2E8. **EMAIL** tbarnes@chass.utoronto.ca

BARNOUW, DAGMAR
DISCIPLINE GERMAN **EDUCATION** Yale Univ, PhD. **CAREER** Prof, Univ Southern Calif. **SELECTED PUBLICATIONS** Auth, Weimar Intellectuals & the Threat of Modernity, 88; Visible Spaces: Hannah Arendt & the German-Jewish Experience, 90; Critical Realism: History, Photography & the Work of Siegfried Kracauer, 94; Deutschland 1945: Ansichten von Krieg und Gewalt; Germany 1945: Photography, History and Memory, 96; Anthropologische Dichtungen: Elias Canetti, 96. **CONTACT ADDRESS** Col Letters, Arts & Sciences: German Dept., Univ of So California, University Park Campus, Los Angeles, CA 90089. **EMAIL** barnouw@usc.edu

BARNSTONE, WILLIS
PERSONAL Born 11/13/1927, Lewiston, ME, m, 1949, 3 children **DISCIPLINE** SPANISH & COMPARATIVE LITERATURE **EDUCATION** Bowdoin Col, BA, 48; Columbia Univ, MA, 56; Yale Univ, PhD, 60. **CAREER** Teacher French & English, Anavrita Acad, Greece, 49-50; instr French, Univ MD Overseas Prog, Perigueux, France, 55-56; from instr to asst prof Span, Wesleyan Univ, 58-62; assoc prof Span & comp lit, 62-66, prof Span & Port, 66-68, prof E Asian studies, 73-76, Prof Comp Lit, IN Univ, Bloomington, 66-, Prof Latin Am Studies, 76-, Guggenheim fel, Spain, 61-62; Am Coun Learned Soc Studies fel, 68-69; vis prof, Univ CA, Riverside, 68-69 & Inst Prof, Buenos Aires, 75-; Fulbright teaching fel, Argentina, 75; Nat Endowment for Humanities sr res fel, 79-80. **HONORS AND AWARDS** Cecil Hemley Mem Awd, 68; Lucille Medwick Awd, 78, Poetry Soc Am; Gustav Davidson Mem Awd, 80; dlitt, bowdoin col, 81. **MEMBERSHIPS** MLA. **RESEARCH** Spanish; ancient Greek; English, Greek and Spanish poetry; theory and practice of translation. **SELECTED PUBLICATIONS** Auth, New Faces of China, IN Univ, 73; Egypt: Love, Death and Magic, Rev, 75; My Voice Because of You, State Univ NY, 76; China Poems, Univ MO, 76; Portugal: Poet Kings and the Sea, Sat Evening Post, 77; Real and Imaginary History in Borges and Cavafy, Comp Lit, 77; Billy and Meursault: A Failure of the Senses, Tex Quart, 78; Antonio Machado: a Theory of Method in His Dream, Landscape and Awakening, Revista Hisp Mod, 78; Memoir About a Metaphysical and Mystical Poet & Deciphering the Borges Persona Through the Essays and the Poetry, Critica Hispanica, Vol 15, 93; Translation Theory With a Semiotic Slant, Semiotica, Vol 102, 94; 'Federico in August', Partisan Rev, Vol 61, 94; 'Sunflower', Chicago Rev, Vol 42, 96; 'Into the Sun', Chicago Rev, Vol 42, 96. **CONTACT ADDRESS** Dept of Comp Lit, Indiana Univ, Bloomington, Bloomington, IN 47401.

BAROLINI, TEODOLINDA
PERSONAL Born 12/19/1951, Syracuse, NY, w, 1980, 1 child **DISCIPLINE** ITALIAN LITERATURE **EDUCATION** Sarah Lawrence Col, BA, 72; Columbia Univ, MA, 73, PhD, 78. **CAREER** Asst prof Italian, Univ Calif, Berkeley, 78-83; assoc prof, 83-89, full prof, 89-92, Italian, NY Univ; prof and chemn Dept of Italian, Columbia Univ, 92- ; Lorenzo Da Ponte prof of Italian, 99-. **HONORS AND AWARDS** AAUW fel, 77; ACLS fel, 81; NEH fel, 86; Marraro Prize of MLA, 86; John Nicholas Brown Prize, Medieval Acad, 88; Guggenheim fel, 98; Fel, Medieval Acad, 00. **MEMBERSHIPS** Dante Soc, Pres, 97-03; Medieval Acad; Renaissance Soc of Am; Am Asn of Tchrs of Italian; MLA. **RESEARCH** Medieval and early Renaissance Italian literature, especially lyric tradition through Petrarch; Dante; Petrarch; Boccaccio. **SELECTED PUBLICATIONS** Auth, "The Undivine Comedy: Detheologizing Dante," Princeton: Princeton University Press, (92): 356; auth, "Dante's Poets: Textuality and Truth in the Comedy," Princeton: Princeton University Press, (84): 312; auth, "Guittone's Ora parra, Dante's Doglia me reca, and the Commedia's Anatomy of Desire," In Seminario Dantesco Internazionale/International Dante Seminar 1," ed. Z. Baranski, Pirenze: (Le Lettere97): 3-23; auth, "Dante and Cavalcanti, On Making Distinctions in Matters of Love, Inferno 5 in its Lyric Context, (Dante Studies 00), 31-63; auth, "Dante and Francesca da Rimini: Realpolitik, Romance, Gender," Speculum 75 (00): 1-28; auth, "Medieval Multiculturalism and Dante's Theology of Hell," In The Craft and the Fury: Essays in Honor of Glauco Cambon, ed. Joseph Francese, Bordighera Press, (Italiana 00), 82-102; auth, "Francesca de Ramini," The Dante Encyclopedia, New York and London: Garland Publishing, (00): 409-414; auth, "Hell," The Dante Encyclopedia, New York and London: Garland Publishing, (00): 472-477; auth, "Lyric Poetry (Dante's)," The Dante Encyclopedia, New York and London: Garland Publishing, (00): 578-582; auth, "Ulysses," The Dante Encyclopedia, New York and London: Garland Publishing, (00): 842-847. **CONTACT ADDRESS** Dept of Italian, Columbia Univ, 502 Hamilton Hall, New York, NY 10027. **EMAIL** tb27@columbia.edu

BARON, FRANK
DISCIPLINE GERMAN **EDUCATION** Univ Ill, BA, 58; Ind Univ, MA, 61; Univ Calif, PhD, 66. **CAREER** From Asst Prof to Prof, Univ Kan, 70-. **HONORS AND AWARDS** Alexander von Humbolt Fel, 68-70; Fulbright Fel, 85. **MEMBERSHIPS** AATG, Soc of Ger studies. **RESEARCH** Modern literary history from 1400 to the present. **SELECTED PUBLICATIONS** Auth, Faustus on Trial: The Origins of Johann Spie's Historia in an Age of Witch Hunting, Niemeyer Publ (Tubingen), 92; coauth, Con Ungarn nach Auschwitz Die Verschwiegene Warnung, 94; auth, Albert Bloch: German Poetry in War and Peace: A Dual-Language Anthology, 95; auth, Albert Bloch: Artistic and Literary Perspectives, Prestel (Munich, Germany), 97. **CONTACT ADDRESS** Dept Lang, Univ of Kansas, Lawrence, 1 University of Kansas, Lawrence, KS 66045-0001. **EMAIL** fbaron@ukans.edu

BARON, JAMES
PERSONAL Born 11/21/1942 **DISCIPLINE** CLASSICAL STUDIES **EDUCATION** Catholic Univ Am, AB, 64; Univ Minn, MA, 67, PhD, 72. **CAREER** Tchg asst, 66-69; tchg assoc, 69-70, Univ Minn; asst prof, Macalester Col, St Paul, Minn, 70-71; asst prof, Concordia Col, Moorehead, Minn, 70-71; asst prof, Col William and Mary in Va, 71-76; assoc prof, 76- & ept ch, 83-89 & 91-92. **RESEARCH** Augustan poetry; classical tradition in film; Scandinavian literature. **SELECTED PUBLICATIONS** Auth, Drag Humor in Aristophanes Comedies, Class Asn Mid W and S, 90; Direct Address to the Audience in the Films of Ingmar Bergman: A Classical Device Radically Transformed, Inaugural Meeting Int Soc for the Class Tradition, Boston, 91; The Orpheus Myth in the Early Films of Ingmar Bergman, CAMWS Southern Sect Meeting, Richmond, 92; Horatii Carmina I.37.17-20: Citus Venator: Homo aut Canis, Class Asn Mid W and S, Atlanta Georgia, 94; Bergman's Cries and Whispers, a Masterpiece of Classical Architecture, Soc Advancement for Scand Study, Davenport, 94; Alliteration and Other Sound Effects in Seneca's Tragedies, Class Asn Mid W and S, Southern Section, Chapel Hill, NC, 94; Willa Cather's Alexandra Bergson: Aeneas on the Nebraska Prairie, Class Asn Mid W and S, Omaha, 95 & A Child of Soil Reads Catullus, Horace, and Vergil, Amer Philol Asn, San Diego, 95; rev, Persona: the Transcendent Image, Scand Stud, vol 60, 98. **CONTACT ADDRESS** Dept of Classical Studies, Col of William and Mary, Morton Hall, PO Box 8795, Williamsburg, VA 23187-8795. **EMAIL** jrbaro@facstaff.wm.edu

BARRACK, CHARLES MICHAEL
PERSONAL Born 01/06/1938, Los Angeles, CA, s **DISCIPLINE** GERMANIC LINGUISTICS **EDUCATION** San Diego State Col, BA, 61; Univ WA, MA, 66, PhD(Ger ling), 69. **CAREER** Actg asst prof Ger, 68-69, asst prof, 69-74, assoc Prof Germanics, Univ WA, 74-; Prof, Germanic Linguistics, 99. **MEMBERSHIPS** Ling Soc Am. **RESEARCH** Historical linguistics. **SELECTED PUBLICATIONS** Auth, A diachronic phonology from Proto-Germanic to Old English stressing West-Saxon conditions. Janua Linguaruem, Series Practica, No. 144 (The Hague: Mouton and Co, 75); auth, "Lexical diffiusion and the High German consonant shift," Lingua, Vol 40 (76): 151-175; auth, "The High German consonant shift: polygenetic or monogenetic?" Lingua, Vol 44 (78): 1-48; auth, "Keyser, Kiparsky, O'Neill and Postal versus Sievers," Lingua, Vol 77 (91): 223-296; auth, "PGmc. -VCiV- revisited," Vol 3, No 2 (91): 119-144; auth, Mosaik: Grammatik, Third, completely revised edition, McGraw-Hill, 92; auth, "The putative strengthening of glides in Gothic," Insights in Germanic Linguistics II: Classic and Contemporary, 94; auth, "PGmc. -VCiV-: a response to Murray," Vol 2 (97): 117-178; auth, Sievers' Law in Germanic, Peter Lang Publishing, 98. **CONTACT ADDRESS** Dept of Germanics, Univ of Washington, PO Box 353130, Seattle, WA 98195. **EMAIL** cbarrack@u.washington.edu

BARRETT, TRACY
PERSONAL Born 03/01/1955, Cleveland, OH, m, 1983, 2 children **DISCIPLINE** ITALIAN; WOMEN'S STUDIES **EDUCATION** Brown Univ, ABM 76; Univ Calif-Berkeley, MA, 79; PhD, 88. **CAREER** Teaching asst to assoc, Univ Calif-Berkeley, 78-83; Lectr to sr lectr ital, Vanderbilt Univ, 84- . **HONORS AND AWARDS** Ital-Am Fel, 78; Distinguished Teaching Asst, 82; NEH, 94; Harriett S. Billiam Awd Exc Teaching, 96. **MEMBERSHIPS** Am Assn Teachers Ital; Am Coun Teaching For Lang; Auth Guild Soc Children's Book Writers & Illusr. **RESEARCH** Medieval Women Authors, Children's Literature. **SELECTED PUBLICATIONS** Auth, Growing Up in Colonial America, Millbrook Press, 95; auth, "Album Quilts" Quilt World, (96); auth, "Virginia," Celebrate the States, Benchmark Books, (97); auth "Tennessee," Celebrate the States, Benchmark Books, (98); auth, Kidding Around Nashville, John Muir Publ, 98; auth, "Kentucky," Celebrate the States, Benchmark Books, (99); auth, Anna of Byzantium, Bantam Doubleday Dell, 99. **CONTACT ADDRESS** Dept Fr & Ital, Vanderbilt Univ, 2201 W End Ave, Nashville, TN 37235-0001. **EMAIL** tracy.barrett@vanderbilt.edu

BART, BENJAMIN FRANKLIN
PERSONAL Born 12/21/1917, Chicago, IL, m, 1942, 3 children **DISCIPLINE** FRENCH LITERATURE, LANGUAGE EDUCATION **EDUCATION** Harvard Univ, AB, 38, AM, 46, PhD, 47. **CAREER** Instr Romance lang, Harvard, 47; asst prof, Pomona Col, 47-50; asst prof, Univ MI, 50-56; from assoc prof to prof, Syracuse Univ, 56-67; Prof French, Univ Pittsburgh, 67-, Dir Comp Lit Prog, 74-, Ford Found fel, 52-53; Am Coun Learned Socs grants-in-aid, 60, 61, & 63; Am Philol Soc grant, 74; Camargo Found fel, 81; Nat Endowment for Humanities fel, 81. **MEMBERSHIPS** Am Asn Teachers Fr; MLA. **RESEARCH** French 19th century literature; the teaching of French. **SELECTED PUBLICATIONS CONTACT ADDRESS** Dept of French, Univ of Pittsburgh, Pittsburgh, PA 15260.

BARTSCH, SHADI
PERSONAL Born 03/17/1966, London, England, m, 2000 **DISCIPLINE** LATIN LITERATURE OF THE EARLY EMPIRE, CULTURAL THEORY AND INTERPRETATION, HISTORY OF CLASSICAL RHETORIC, THE ANCIENT NOVEL **EDUCATION** Princeton Univ, BA (summa cum laude), 87; Harvard Univ, in PhD prog, 87-89, then as exchange scholar at the Univ CA, Berkeley, 88-89; Univ CA, Berkeley, MA, Latin, 89, PhD (Classics), 91. **CAREER** Acting asst prof, Classics and Rhetoric, Univ CA, Berkeley, 91-92, asst prof, 92-95, assoc prof, 95-98; vis assoc prof, Classics, Univ Chicago, Jan-June, 98, prof, Classics and the Committee on the History of Culture, Univ Chicago, July 98-; ed bd, Representations, 97-98; ed bd, Classical Philology, 98-; editor-in-chief, Classical Philology, 00-. **HONORS AND AWARDS** Mellon fel in the Humanities, Harvard Univ, 87-89; Berkeley fel, Univ CA, Berkeley, 89-91; Richardson Prize for Trans into Latin, Univ CA, Berkeley, 90; Honorary P S Allen Junior Res fel, Corpus Christi, Oxford, 90; Humanities Res fel, Univ CA, Berkeley, 95-96; George Walsh Memorial Lecturer, Univ Chicago, 98; Jackson Knight Lecturer, Exeter 00; Quantrell Awd, Chicago, 00; ACLS Fellow, 99-00. **MEMBERSHIPS** APA; adv committee for APA 1998; adv committee for ICAN 2000; coordinator, Workshop on Ancient Societies, Univ Chicago, 98-99. **SELECTED PUBLICATIONS** Auth, Decoding the Ancient Novel: The Reader and the Role of Description in Heliodorus and Achilles Tatius, Princeton Univ Press, 89; Actors in the Audience: Theatricality and Doublespeak from Nero to Hadrian, Harvard Univ Press, 94; Ideology in Cold Blood: A Reading of Lubcan's Civil War, Harvard Univ Press, 98; review, V Rudich, Dissidence and Literature under Nero: The Prince of Rhetoricization, in the Times Literary Supp, March 27, 98; Ars and the Man: The Politics of Art in Vergil's Aeneid, Classical Philology, forthcoming 98; The Philosopher as Narcissus: Knowing Oneself in Classical Antiquity, in Robert S Nelson, ed, Seeing as Others Saw: Visuality Before and Beyond the Renaissance, Cambridge Univ Press, 00; ed with Tom Sloan, Oxford Encyclopedia of Rhetoric, Oxford Univ Press, forthcoming; auth, The Cult of the Trope: Hermeneutics and the Classics in the Middle Ages, Princeton Univ Press, forthcoming; The Mirror of Philosophy: Specularity, Sexuality, and Self-Knowledge in the Roman Empire, forthcoming; numerous other articles, reviews, papers, and publications. **CONTACT ADDRESS** Dept of Classics, Univ of Chicago, 1010 E 59th St, Chicago, IL 60637. **EMAIL** sbartsch@midway.uchicago.edu

BASHIRI, IRAJ
PERSONAL Born 07/31/1940, Behbahan, Iran, m, 1968, 3 children **DISCIPLINE** CENTRAL ASIAN AND IRANIAN LANGUAGES, LITERATURES, AND CULTURES **EDUCATION** Pahlavi Univ, BA, 63; Univ Mich, Ann Arbor, MA, 68, PhD, 72. **CAREER** Lectr, Pahlavi Univ & British Coun, Shiraz, Iran, 63-64; instr, Imperial Iranian Air Forces, 65; lectr, Univ of Mich, 67-72; vis asst prof, 72-73, asst prof, 73-78, assoc prof, 78-96, prof, Univ Minn, Minneapolis, 96-, assoc chemn, 81-83, acting chemn, 83-84, 89-91, assoc chemn, 87-89, chemn, 97-98; IREX Res Resident Scholar for Tajikistan, 93-94. **HONORS AND AWARDS** Col of Liberal Arts Distinguished Teacher Awd, 80; honorary doctorate in History and Culture, Tajikistan State Univ, 96; honorary Academician, Acad of Scis of Tajikistan, 97. **MEMBERSHIPS** Soc for Iranian Studies, Middle East Studies Asn of North Am, Asn for the Advancement of Central Asian Res, Asn for Central Asian Studies. **RESEARCH** Central Asian and Iranian languages, literatures and cultures; Islam and communism; identity. **SELECTED PUBLICATIONS** Auth, Persian for Beginners (72); auth, To Be as the Origin of Syntax: A Persian Framework, Bibliotheca Islamica (73); auth, Hedayat's Ivory Tower: Structural Analysis of the Blind Owl, Manor House (74); auth, Hafiz' Shirazi Turk: A Structuralist's Point of View, Muslim World, 7 & 8 (79); auth, "Hafiz and the Sufic Ghazal," Studies in Islam (Jan 79); auth, Persian for Beginners: Pronunciation and Writing (80), Tape Manual with Notes on Grammar (80), Reading Texts (81), Persian Syntax (91), Burgess Pub Co; auth, The Fiction of Sadeq Hedayat, Amir Kabir Inst of Iranian Studies, Mazda Pubs (84); ed and contribur, The Pearl Canon, Mazda Pubs Bilingual Series (86); auth, Firdowsi's Shahname: 1000 Years After, Acad of Scis of Tajikistan, Dunshanbe (94); auth, Kamal Khujandi: Epoch and Its Importance in the History of Central Asian Civilization, Tehran-Dushanbe (96); transl, The History of a National Catastrophe by Rahim Masov (96); auth, The Samanids and the Revival of the Civilization of the Iranian Peoples, Acad of Scis of Tajikistan, Dunshanbe (99). **CONTACT ADDRESS** Dept Slavic & Central Asian Langs & Lits, Univ of Minnesota, Twin Cities, 211 Nolte Center, 315 Pillsbury Dr SE, Minneapolis, MN 55455. **EMAIL** bashi001@maroon.tc.umn.edu

BATES, MARGARET JANE
PERSONAL Born 01/27/1918, New York, NY **DISCIPLINE** SPANISH, PORTUGUESE **EDUCATION** Hunter Col, AB, 38; Columbia Univ, MLA, 40; Cath Univ Am, PhD, 45. **CAREER** Mem interdept comt orgn of libr in Peru & Brazil, US Dept of State, 41-44; from asst prof to assoc prof Romance lang, 44-55; vdir, Inst Ibero-Am studies, 50-55; Prof Romance Lang, Cath Univ Am, 44-, Dir, Inst Ibero-Am Studies, 55-, Ford fac fel, 53-54. **MEMBERSHIPS** MLA, Am Asn Tchrs Span & Port. **RESEARCH** Spanish and Portuguese linguistics and lit; discretion in the works of Cervantes; Gregorio de Mattos, poet of 17th century Brazil. **SELECTED PUBLICATIONS** Ed, Las Poesias Completas de Gabriela Mistral, Aguilar, Madrid, 58, 2nd ed, 62, 3rd ed 66. **CONTACT ADDRESS** 5914 Carlton Lane, Bethesda, MD 20016.

BATES, SCOTT
PERSONAL Born 06/13/1923, Evanston, IL, m, 1948, 4 children **DISCIPLINE** FRENCH, FILM **EDUCATION** Carleton Col, BA, 47; Univ Wis, MA, 48, PhD(French), 54. **CAREER** Asst prof, 54-64, Prof French Lang & Lit, Univ of The South, 64-, Ed, Ecol Papers, 70-72. **RESEARCH** Modern French poetry; modern English and American poetry; Film and Theatre. **SELECTED PUBLICATIONS** Auth, Guillaume Apollinaire, Twayne, 67 Rev. ed., 89; ed, Poems of War Resistance, Grossman, 69; Petit glossaire des mots libres d'Apollinaire, Sewanee, 75; The ABC of Radical Ecology, Highlander, 82; Lupo's Fables, 83; Merry Greenpeace, 95; Songs for the Queen of the Animals, 97; The Zyx of Political Sex, Highlander, 99; Ed, Poems of Protect for the Year, 00, War Resisters League, 00. **CONTACT ADDRESS** Dept of Lang & Lit, Univ of the South, P O Box 1263, Sewanee, TN 37383-1000. **EMAIL** sbates@seraphl.sewanee.edu

BATTS, MICHAEL S.
PERSONAL Born 08/02/1929, Mitcham, England **DISCIPLINE** GERMANIC STUDIES **EDUCATION** Univ London, BA, 53, DLitt, 73; Univ Freiburg, DPhil, 57; Univ Toronto, MLS, 74. **CAREER** PROF EMER GERMANIC STUD, UNIV BRITISH COLUMBIA. **MEMBERSHIPS** Can Asn Univ Tchrs Ger; Mod Hum Res Asn. **SELECTED PUBLICATIONS** Auth, The Bibliography of German Literature: A Historical and Critical Survey, 78; auth, A History of Histories of German Literature: Prolegomena, 87; auth, A History of Histories of German Literature 1835-1914, 93; coauth, Scandinavian Literature in English Translation 1928-77, 78; ed, Echoes and Influences of German Romanticism, 87. **CONTACT ADDRESS** Germanic Stud, Univ of British Columbia, 1873 East Mall, Vancouver, BC, Canada V6T 1Z1. **EMAIL** msb@interchange.ubc.ca

BAUER, KARIN
PERSONAL Born 02/18/1958, Germany, m, 1994, 1 child **DISCIPLINE** GERMAN, LITERATURE **EDUCATION** Univ Ariz, BA, 84; Univ Wash, MA, 86; PhD, 92. **CAREER** Asst prof, Mich State Univ, 92-94; asst prof to assoc prof to chmn, McGill Univ, 94-. **HONORS AND AWARDS** SSHRC Fel. **MEMBERSHIPS** GSA; CAUTG; MLA; AATG. **RESEARCH** Critical theory; Nietzsche; contemporary literature and theory. **SELECTED PUBLICATIONS** Auth, Adono's Nietzschean Narratives, SUNY Pr, 99. **CONTACT ADDRESS** Ger Studies, McGill Univ, 688 Sherbrooke West, Ste 486, Montreal, QC, Canada H3A 3R1. **EMAIL** kbauer@po-box.mcgill.ca

BAUER, OTTO FRANK
PERSONAL Born 12/01/1931, Elgin, IL, m, 1956, 2 children **DISCIPLINE** COMMUNICATION, SEMANTICS **EDUCATION** Northwestern Univ, BS, 53, MA, 55, PhD, 59. **CAREER** From instr to asst prof English, US Air Force Acad, 59-61; from instr to prof speech, 61-71, dir grad admis & fels, 65-69, asst dean grad sch, 67-69, asst vpres, 70-71, Bowling Green State Univ; vchancellor, Univ Wis, Parkside, 71-76, actg chancellor, 74-75, prof commun, 71-79; vchancellor acad affairs, 79-94, prof commun, 78-, vchancellor emeritus, 95, Univ Neb, Omaha; Midwest Forensic Asn res grant, 66-67; Am Coun Educ fel, Univ Calif, Berkeley, 69-70; spec asst to chancellor & vis prof commun arts, Univ Wis, Madison, 76-77. **MEMBERSHIPS** Am Forensic Asn; Speech Commun Asn. **RESEARCH** Semantics; debate; political campaigning. **SELECTED PUBLICATIONS** Auth, Fundamentals of Debate: Theory and Practice, Scott, 66; art, Student trust at Berkeley, Educ Rec, 71; art, Relational Abstracting and the Structural Differential, Research Designs in General Semantics, Gordon & Breach, 72; art, The Early Debates, Commun Asn Pac, 7/77; art, State Government Trust of Higher Education in Wisconsin, fall 79; auth, Lower Moments in Higher Education, Rockbrook Press, 97. **CONTACT ADDRESS** Dept of Communications, 6001 Dodge St, Omaha, NE 68182-0002. **EMAIL** obauer@cwis.unomaha.edu

BAUMGARTEN, JOSEPH M.
PERSONAL Born 09/07/1928, Vienna, Austria, m, 1954, 6 children **DISCIPLINE** ORIENTAL STUDIES **EDUCATION** Brooklyn Col, BA, 50; Mesifta Torah Vodaat, dipl, 50; John Hopkins Univ, PhD(Orient studies), 53. **CAREER** Prof Rabbinc Lit, Baltimore Hebrew Col, 53-, Vis prof, Univ MD, 62-63, 76-77, Towson State Col, 70-71 & Univ of the Negev, Israel, 72-73. **MEMBERSHIPS** Soc Bibl Lit; Am Orient Soc; Rabbinical Coun Am. **RESEARCH** Jewish law and sects in time of the second temple; Qumran (Dead Sea Scrolls) literature. **SELECTED PUBLICATIONS** Jewish Studies; A New Qumran Substitute for the Divine Name and Mishnah-Sukkah 4.5 & A 2nd Temple Variant in a Berakhah Formula From 4Q266, An Investigation of a Disguise or a Substitution, Jewish Quart Rev, Vol 83, 92; Jewish Law From Jesus to the Mishnah, with E. P. Sanders, Jewish Quart Rev, Vol 83, 93; Hoo-Hakol You Are All or AunSIC-Hoo-Hakol & Scribal Error or a Peculiar Variant of the Divine Name Form the Qumran Damascus Document-A Reply to M. Kister, Jewish Quart Rev, Vol 84, 94; Zab-Impurity in Qumran and Rabbinic Law & The Significance of Levitical Purity in the Religious Life of the Jews of the 2nd Temple Period, J of Jewish Studies, Vol 45, 94; The Red Cow Purification Rites in Qumran Texts & An Evaluation of the Significance of the Para-Ritual Tebul-Yom-Fragments in Light of Tannaitic Sources, J of Jewish Studies, Vol 46, 95; Review of Qumran Cave 4, Vol 5, Miqsat-Maase-Ha-Torah, with E. Qimron and J. Strugnell, J of the Am Oriental Soc, Vol 116, 96; Qumran Prayer and Religious Poetry, with B. Nitzan, J of Semitic Studies, Vol 41, 96; The Religious Laws of the Qumran Community, Annales-Histoire Sciences Sociales, Vol 51, 96; The Damascus Document, Qumran Cave 4 XII, Oxford, 96; Halakic Texts, Qumran Cave 4 XXV, Oxford, 99. **CONTACT ADDRESS** Baltimore Hebrew Univ, 3200 Labyrinth Rd, Baltimore, MD 21215. **EMAIL** baumgart@umbc.edu

BAUMGARTNER, INGEBORG HOGH
PERSONAL Born 01/29/1936, Oberstuben, Czechoslovakia, m, 1967, 1 child **DISCIPLINE** GERMAN LITERATURE **EDUCATION** Univ Mich, AB, 58, PhD(Ger), 70; Univ Wis, AM, 59. **CAREER** Instr Ger, Loyola Univ Chicago, 65-66; Prof Ger, Albion Col, 66- **MEMBERSHIPS** MLA; Am Asn Teachers Ger. **RESEARCH** German drama; 19th and 20th century German literature; Thomas Mann. **SELECTED PUBLICATIONS** Auth, Ambiguity in Buchner's Woyzeck, Mich Ger Studies, fall 75; coauth, A one-semester introduction to literary interpretation, Die Unterrichtspraxis, spring 77. **CONTACT ADDRESS** Dept of Foreign Lang, Albion Col, 611 E Porter St, Albion, MI 49224-1831. **EMAIL** ibaumgartner@albion.edu

BAUML, FRANZ H.
PERSONAL Born 06/12/1926, Vienna, Austria, m, 1958 **DISCIPLINE** GERMAN **EDUCATION** Univ Berkeley, BA, 53,

MA, 55, PhD(Ger), 57. **CAREER** From instr to assoc prof, 57-65, Prof Ger, Univ CA, Los Angeles, 65-, Am Coun Learned Soc res grant-in-aid, 59. **HONORS AND AWARDS** Fel, Netherlands Inst for Advan Study, 91-92. **MEMBERSHIPS** MLA; Mediaeval Acad Am. **RESEARCH** Medieval German literature; medieval literacy; gestures. **SELECTED PUBLICATIONS** Auth, Rhetorical Devices and Structure in the Ackermann aus Bohmen, Univ CA, 60; Zur mundlichen Uberlieferung des Nibelungenliedes, Deut Vierteljahrsschrift, 67; Kudrun: Die Handschrift, W de Gruyter Berlin, 69; Medieval Civilization in Germany: 800-1273, Thames & Hudson, London, 69; coauth, Weiteres zur mundlichen Uberlieferung des Nibelungenliedes, Deut Vierteljahrsschrift, 72; A Dictionary of Gestures, Scarecrow, 75; A Concordance to the Nibelungenlied, Maney & Son, Leeds, 76; Varieties and Consequences of Medieval Literacy and Illiteracy, Speculum, 80; Vocalism-Old English Poetry Between Orality and Literacy (German), with U. Schaefer, Poetica-Zeitschrift Fur Sprach-Und Literaturwissenschaft, Vol 27, 95. **CONTACT ADDRESS** Dept of Ger Lang, Univ of California, Los Angeles, Los Angeles, CA 90024.

BAZIN, NANCY TOPPING

PERSONAL Born 11/05/1934, Pittsburgh, PA, m, 1992, 6 children **DISCIPLINE** ENGLISH, FRENCH **EDUCATION** Ohio Wesleyan Univ, BA, 56; Middlebury Grad School of French, MA, 58; Stanford Univ, PhD, 69 **CAREER** Eminent Scholar, Old Dominion Univ, 96-; prof, Old Dominion Univ, 84-; assoc prof, Old Dominion Univ, 78-84; Chair, Dept Eng, Old Dominion Univ, 85-89; dir, Women's Studies, Old Dominion Univ, 78-85 **HONORS AND AWARDS** Winner, 2nd Annual Charles O and Elisabeth C Burgess Faculty Res and Creativity Awd, 96; Resident Fel, Center for the Humanities of the Virginia Foundation for the Humanities and Public Policy, 95; Outstanding Faculty Awd, State Council Higher Education Virginia, 94; Ball Brothers Res Found Fel, 94; Phi Kappa Phi, 88; Sigma Tau Delta, 88; Phi Beta Kappa, 55; Mortar Board, 55; Kappa Delta Pi, 56 **MEMBERSHIPS** Modern Lang Assoc; African Lit Assoc; Ntl Women's Studies Assoc; Virginia Woolf Soc; Doris Lessing Soc **RESEARCH** 20th Century Writers **SELECTED PUBLICATIONS** Auth, Virginia Woolf and the Androgynous Vision, Rutgers, 73; coed, Conversations with Nadine Gordimer, Univ Miss, 90; auth, "Venturing into Feminist Consciousness: Two Protagonists from the Fiction of Buchi Emecheta and Bessie Head," Critical Perspectives on Buchi Emecheta, 96 **CONTACT ADDRESS** 4005 Gosnold Ave, Norfolk, VA 23508-2917. **EMAIL** nbazin@odw.edu

BEARD, LAURA J.

DISCIPLINE SPANISH, LITERATURE, PORTUGUESE **EDUCATION** Carleton Col, BA, 84; Johns Hopkins Univ, MA, 89; PhD, 94. **CAREER** Vis instr to vis asst prof, Univ of Victoria, 93-95; asst to assoc prof, Tex Tech Univ, 95-01. **HONORS AND AWARDS** Fulbright-Hays Sem, 91; Fel, Am Asn of Univ Women Educ Found, 92-93; NEH Fel, 95, 01; Fulbright Scholar, 99-00; Phi Beta Kappa. **MEMBERSHIPS** MLA, Feministas Unidas, Brazilian Studies Assoc, Soc for the Study of Narrative Lit, Am Comp Lit Assoc, Assoc for the Study of Am Indian Lit. **RESEARCH** Women writers of the Americas, feminist theories, narrative theories, Native American and First Nations writers and cultures, autobiographical and testimonial literatures. **SELECTED PUBLICATIONS** Auth, "The Mirrored Self: Helena Parene Cunha's Mulher no Espelho," Col Lit, (95); coed, Intertexts 1.1, Tex Tex Univ Pr, 97; auth, "A is for Alphabet, K is for Kabbalah: The Babelic Metatext of Luisa Futoransky," Intertext, (97); auth, La sujetividad femenina en la metaficcion feminista latinoamericana, Revista iberoamericana, 98; auth, "Transgressive Textualities, Transgressive Sexualities: Nelida Pinon's A Forca do Destino," Brasil/Brazil, (99); auth, "Navigating the Metafictional Text: Julieta Camps' Tiene los cabellos rojizos y se llama Sabina," Hispanofila, (00). **CONTACT ADDRESS** Class & Mod Lang & Lit, Texas Tech Univ, Lubbock, TX 79409-2071. **EMAIL** pvljb@ttacs.ttu.edu

BEARD, ROBERT EARL

PERSONAL Born 02/26/1938, Fayetteville, NC, m, 1960, 2 children **DISCIPLINE** SLAVIC LINGUISTICS **EDUCATION** Univ NC, AB, 59; Univ Mich, MA, 61, PhD(Slavic ling), 66; Moscow State Univ, cert Russ, 69. **CAREER** Lectr Russ lang, Univ Mich, 64-65; asst prof Russ & ling, 65-73, Assoc Prof Russ & Ling, Bucknell Univ, 73-, Dir Prog, 65-, Int Res & Exchanges Bd, exchange scholar, 76; Fulbright exchange scholar, Univ Beograd, Yugoslavia, 76-77. **HONORS AND AWARDS** Sierzega Prof of Linguistics, 83-93, 98-00; AATSEEL Teaching Merit, 97; AATSEEL Best Website, 99. **MEMBERSHIPS** Ling Soc Am; Am Asn Teachers Slavic & East Europ Lang; Am Asn Advan Slavic Studies; Int Ling Asn; Am Asn Southeast Europ Studies. **RESEARCH** Teaching of Russian; generative grammar; lexicology. **SELECTED PUBLICATIONS** Auth, Dynamic glossing, Slavic East Europ J, 19: 49-57; Semantically based model .., Language, 52: 108-20; Once more on ed-adjectives, J Ling, 12: 155-7; Material adjectives, Linguistics, 190: 5-34; On the extent of irregularity, Lingua, 42: 305-41; Derivations within derivations, VIII Int Cong Slavists, Zagreb-Ljubljana, 9/78; The Indo-European Lexicon, North-Holland Publishing Co, 81; auth, Bibliography of Morphology, 88; auth, "On the Separation of Derivation from Morphology: Toward a Lexeme/Morpheme-Based Morphology," Quaderni di semantica 9 (88): 3-59; auth, "The Nature and Origins of Derivational Polysemy," Lingua 81 (90): 101-140; auth, "Number," in Oxford Encyclopedia of Linguistics (Oxford: The Univ Pr, 91); auth, "Simultaneous Dual Derivational Origin," Language 69 (93): 716-741; auth, "Lexeme-Morpheme Based Morphology," in Encyclopedia of Language & Linguistics, (London: Pergamon Pr and Univ of Aberdeen Pr, 93); auth, "The Hist of Moprhology," Encylcopedia of Language & Linguistics (London: Pergamon Pr and Univ Aberdeen Pr, 93); auth, Lexeme-Morpheme Bas Morphology, SUNY, 95; auth, "The Gender-Animacy Hypothesis," J of Slavic Linguistics, 3 (95): 59-96; auth, "Derivation," in Handbook of Morphology, ed. A. Spencer * A. Zwicky (Blackwell, 98). **CONTACT ADDRESS** Bucknell Univ, Lewisburg, PA 17837-2029. **EMAIL** rbeard@yourdictionary.com

BEARDSLEY, THEODORE S., JR.

PERSONAL Born 08/26/1930, East St. Louis, IL, m, 1955, 3 children **DISCIPLINE** SPANISH, FRENCH **EDUCATION** Southern Ill Univ, BS, 52; Wash Univ, MA, 54; Univ Pa, PhD, 61. **CAREER** Asst Prof, Univ Wis, 62-65; dir, Hispanic Soc of Am, 65-95, pres, 95-. **HONORS AND AWARDS** Fulbright Grant, 53-54; Jusserand Travel Fel, 63. **MEMBERSHIPS** Intl Ling Asn; Acad Norteam de la Lengua Espanola. **RESEARCH** Spanish Dialectology in the US; Hispano American Music; Celestina. **SELECTED PUBLICATIONS** Auth, Hispanic Influences in the United States; auth, Tomas Navarro Tomas; auth, Hispano-Classical Translations, 1482-1699. **CONTACT ADDRESS** Hispanic Soc of Am, 613 W 155th St, New York, NY 10032.

BEASLEY, FAITH E.

PERSONAL Born 03/18/1958, Springfield, OH, m, 1994, 1 child **DISCIPLINE** FRENCH **EDUCATION** Mount Holyoke Col, BA, 80; Princeton Univ, MA, PhD, 86. **CAREER** Asst prof, 86-91, assoc prof, 91- , Dartmouth Col; vis assoc prof, Univ Michigan, 95-96; vis assoc prof, Am Grad Sch of Int Mgt, 96-97. **MEMBERSHIPS** MLA; NASSCFL; SE-17. **RESEARCH** Women writers; history and literature, seventeenth century France; memoirs; development of literary criticism; salons. **SELECTED PUBLICATIONS** Auth, Revising Memory: Women's Fiction and Memoirs in Seventeenth-Century France, Rutgers, 90; auth, Un Mariage Critique: Zayde et De L'Origine des Romans, XVIIieme Siecle, 93; auth, The Voices of Shadows: Lafayette's Zayde, in, Goldsmith, ed, Going Public: Women and Publishing in Early Modern France, Cornell, 95; auth, Moliere's Precious Women in Context, in Gaines, ed, Approaches to Teaching Moliere, MLA, 95; co-ed, Approaches to Teaching The Princess of Cleves, MLA, 98; auth, Villedieu and Her Public, in Lalande, ed, A Labor of Love: Critical Reflections on the Writing of Mme de Villedieu, Greenwood, forthcoming; auth, Roger Chartier, in Kritzman, ed, Columbia History of Twentieth-Century French Thought, Columbia, forthcoming; contribur, Sartori, ed, The Feminist Companion to French Literature, Greenwood, forthcoming. **CONTACT ADDRESS** Dept of French and Italian, Dartmouth Col, Hanover, NH 03755. **EMAIL** Faith.Beasley@dartmouth.edu

BEATTY, MICHAEL

DISCIPLINE INTERPERSONAL AND ORGANIZATIONAL COMMUNICATION **EDUCATION** Univ MO, BS; Cent MO State Univ, MA; OH State Univ, PhD. **CAREER** Prof, Communication, Univ Mo-St Louis. **SELECTED PUBLICATIONS** Co-auth, Personality and Communication: Trait Perspectives, Hampton Press, 97; Trait Verbal Aggressiveness and the Appropriateness and Effectiveness of Fathers' Interaction Plans, Commun Quart, 96; auth, Thinking Quantitatively, An Integrated Approach to Communication Theory and Research, Hillsdale, NJ: Erlbaum, 96. **CONTACT ADDRESS** Commun Dept, Univ of Missouri, St. Louis, 8001 Natural Bridge Rd, Saint Louis, MO 63121. **EMAIL** beatty@umsl.edu

BEAUDRY, AGNES PORTER

PERSONAL Born 12/09/1932, Charleston, WV, m, 1973 **DISCIPLINE** FRENCH LITERATURE **EDUCATION** Marshall Univ, AB, 54; Case Western Reserve Univ, MA, 58; Univ Ill, Urbana, PhD(French), 68. **CAREER** Teacher French, Fairfax Hall, Waynesboro, Va, 55-57; teacher, Mansfield High Sch, Ohio, 58-59; instr, Ft Hays State Col, 59-60; instr Muskingum Col, 60-62; asst, Univ Ill, Urbana, 63-65, instr, 65-67; asst prof, Depauw Univ, 67-72, assoc prof, 72-80, Prof French, Depauw Univ, 80-, Prof Emerita, 98-. **MEMBERSHIPS** Am Asn Teachers Fr; Simone de Beauvoir Soc; Women in Fr **RESEARCH** Marcel Proust; 20th-century French memoirs; Marguerite Duras. **SELECTED PUBLICATIONS** Auth, "Proust's Final Montesquiou Pastiche," Marcel Proust, A Critical Panorama, Univ Ill, 73; "The Treatment of Time in Proust's Pastiches," Fr Rev, spring 74; Memoirs in Critical Bibliography of French Literature, XX Century, Syracuse Univ Press, 80; "Detruire, ditellc: Destruction or deconstruction," Int Fiction Rev, 81; auth, "A Neophyte in Literary Semiotics," American Journal of Semiotics, 82; assoc ed, Simone de Beauvoir Studies, 97-98, 98-99, 99-00; book reviews, Fr Rev, 99-00. **CONTACT ADDRESS** Dept of Modern Lang, DePauw Univ, 1503 Sheri Circle, Plainfield, IN 46168. **EMAIL** ajbeaudry@juno.com

BEAUVOIS, MARGARET H.

DISCIPLINE FRENCH **EDUCATION** Univ Tex-Austin, PhD, 92. **CAREER** Asst prof, French, Univ Tenn. **RESEARCH** Computer-mediated communication and writing via a local area network (LAN). **SELECTED PUBLICATIONS** Co-auth, Schemas, 96. **CONTACT ADDRESS** Dept of Mod For Langs & Lits, Univ of Tennessee, Knoxville, 701 McClung Tower, Knoxville, TN 37996. **EMAIL** beauvois@utk.edu

BECK, ROGER L.

PERSONAL Born 01/11/1937, London, England **DISCIPLINE** CLASSICS **EDUCATION** New Col, Oxford Univ, BA, 61; Univ Ill, MA, 63, PhD, 71. **CAREER** Lectr, Univ Man, 63-64; lectr, Univ Col, Univ Toronto, 64-65; asst prof, 68 to prof Classics, Erindale Col, Univ Toronto; prof emer. **MEMBERSHIPS** Class Asn Can (secy 77-79); Am Philol Asn. **RESEARCH** Petronius and the ancient novel; the cult of Mithras. **SELECTED PUBLICATIONS** Auth, "Cosmic models: some uses of hellenistic science in Roman religion", in T.D. Barnes, The Sciences in Greco-Roman Society, (95); coauth, "The mysteries of Mithras", in J.S. Kloppenborg and S.G. Wilson, Voluntary Associtions in the Ancient World, (96); auth, "Myster religions, aretalogy and the ancient novel," in G. Schmeling, The Novel in Antiquity, (96); auth, "Mithras" and "Astrology" in Hornblower and Spawforth, Oxford Classical Dictionary, (96); auth, "The Mysteries of Mithras: a new account of their genesis," Journal of Roman Studies 88, (98): 115-28. **CONTACT ADDRESS** Erindale Col, Univ of Toronto, 97 St. George St, Toronto, ON, Canada M5S 2E8. **EMAIL** rbeck@credit.erin.utoronto.ca

BECK, SIGRID

DISCIPLINE LINGUISTICS **EDUCATION** Univ Tuebingen, PhD. **CAREER** Asst prof, Univ Conn. **RESEARCH** Semantics, syntax-semantics interface. **SELECTED PUBLICATIONS** Auth, Quantified Structures as Barriers for LF-Movement, Natural Lang Semantics 4, 96; coauth, Degree questions, maximal informativeness and exhaustivity, In P. Dekker and M. Stokhof, eds., with Beck, S. and Rullman, Hotze, Proceedings of the 10th Amsterdam Colloquium, (96): 73-92; auth, Negative Islands and Reconstruction In Extraction and Extraposition in German, Amsterdam: John Benjamins, 95. **CONTACT ADDRESS** Dept of Linguistics, Univ of Connecticut, Storrs, 1266 Storrs Rd, Monteith Bldg, Unit 1145, Storrs, CT 06269-1085. **EMAIL** sigrid.beck@uconn.edu

BECKER, ALTON LEWIS

PERSONAL Born 04/06/1932, Monroe, MI, m, 1953, 3 children **DISCIPLINE** LINGUISTICS **EDUCATION** Univ MI, BA, 54, PhD(ling), 66; Univ CT, MA, 56. **CAREER** Instr English, Univ CT, 54-56 & Ripon Col, 56-58; Fulbright teacher, Kambawsa Col, Burma, 58-61; instr, 61-64, instr English & Thai, 64-65, instr English, 65-68, from asst prof to assoc prof ling, 68-74, Prof Ling & Anthrop, Univ MI, Ann Arbor, 74-, Assoc mem exec comt, Ctr S & Southeast Asian Studies, Univ MI, 63-, dir, 72-75; mem Ctr Res on Lang & Lang Behav, 65-; Ford Found vis prof ling, Inst Keguruan dan Ilmu Pendidikan, Malang, Java, 69-71; mem, Inst for Advan Study, Princetown, 81-82. **MEMBERSHIPS** Ling Soc Am; Burma Res Soc. **RESEARCH** Formal description of discourse; history and structure of Southeast Asian languages. **SELECTED PUBLICATIONS** Auth, Journey Through the Night: Some Reflections on Burmese Traditional Theatre Drama Rev, winter 70; coauth, Rhetoric: Discovery and Change, Harcourt, 71; A Linguistic Image of Nature: The Burmese Numerative Classifier System, Int J Sociol of Lang, 75; co-ed, The Imagination of Reality, Ablex, 79; auth, Text-building, Epistemology and Aesthetics in Javanese Shadow Theatre, 79; coauth, Person in Kawi, Oceanic Ling, 176; auth, The Figure a Sentence Makes, Syntax & Semantics, 12/79; On Emerson on Language, Georgetown Univ, 82; On Arnheim on Language, J of Aesthetic Education, Vol 27, 93. **CONTACT ADDRESS** Dept of Ling, Univ of Michigan, Ann Arbor, Ann Arbor, MI 48104.

BECKER, ANDREW S.

PERSONAL Born 09/12/1959, Taungayi, Burma, m, 1987, 3 children **DISCIPLINE** CLASSICS **EDUCATION** Univ Mich, BA, 82; Cambridge Univ, BA, 84; MA, 88; Univ NCar, PhD, 88. **CAREER** Asst to Assoc Prof, Va Tech, 88-. **HONORS AND AWARDS** Cert of Teaching Excellence, VA Tech; Phi Beta Kappa; Phillips Prize; Countess Martmengo Cesaresco Awd; Pogue Fel. **MEMBERSHIPS** Am Philol Asn; Classical Asn of MidWest & S Emerson Soc **RESEARCH** Ancient and Modern Literature and Literary Theories; Epic; Ecphrasis; Pedagogy. **CONTACT ADDRESS** Dept For Lang, Virginia Polytech Inst and State Univ, 100 VA Tech, Blacksburg, VA 24061-0001. **EMAIL** andrew.becker@vt.edu

BECKER, LUCILLE FRACKMAN

PERSONAL Born 02/04/1929, New York, NY, m, 1954, 4 children **DISCIPLINE** FRENCH LANGUAGE & LITERATURE **EDUCATION** Barnard Col, BA, 49; Univ Aix-Marseille, Dipl Etudes Francaises, 50; Columbia Univ, MA, 54, PhD(French), 58. **CAREER** Instr French, Columbia Univ, 54-58 & Rutgers Univ, 58-68; assoc prof, 68-76, Prof French & Chmn Dept, Drew Univ, 77-. **MEMBERSHIPS** MLA; AAUP; Am Asn Teachers Fr. **RESEARCH** Twentieth century

French literature; 19th century French literature; French novel. **SELECTED PUBLICATIONS CONTACT ADDRESS** Dept of French, Drew Univ, Madison, NJ 07940.

BECKER-CANTARINO, BARBARA
PERSONAL m, 3 children **DISCIPLINE** GERMAN **EDUCATION** Univ NC, MA, PhD. **CAREER** Instr, Ind Univ; asst prof to prof, Univ of Tex, 73-85; prof, chair, res prof, Ohio State Univ, 85-. **HONORS AND AWARDS** Guggenheim Fel; NEH; ACLS; Fulbright Senior Res Fel; Alexander von Humboldt Res Prize; Distinguished Scholar Awd, Ohio State Univ. **MEMBERSHIPS** AATG; Goethe Soc; Lessing Soc; German Studies Assoc; MLA; ASECS. **RESEARCH** Early Modern German Literature and Culture; Enlightenment; Romanticism; German Women Authors; Post-1945 Germany. **SELECTED PUBLICATIONS** Auth, Der Lange Weg zur Mundigkeit: Frau und Literatur in Deutschland 1500-1800, Metzler (Stuttgart) , 87; ed, auth," Die Frau von der Reformation zur Romantik. Die Situation der Frau vor dem Hintergrund der Literatur-und Sozialgeschichte", Modern German Studies 7, Bouvier (Bonn), 80; ed, auth, Satire in der Fruhen Neuzeit,Rodopi (Amersterdam), 82; coed, auth, Opitz und seine Welt. Festschrift fur George Schulz-Behrend, Rodopi, (Amsterdam) 90; coed, auth, The Enlightenment and Its Legacy. Essays on German Literature in Honor of Helga Slessarev, Bouvier, (Bonn) 91; coed, auth, Frauenfreundschaft - Mannerfreundschaft. Literarische Diskurse im 18. Jahrhundert, Niemeyer (Tubingen) 92, ed, auth, Berlin in Focus: Cultural Transformations in Modern Germany, Praeger, (Westport, CT), 96; auth, Anna Louisa Karsch. Auserlesene Gedichte (1764), Neue Gedichte (1772), Gedichte (1792), (Frankfurt) 96; auth, Sophie von La roche. Mein Schreibetisch (1799), Briefe uber Mannheim (1791), Tagebuch einer Reise durch Holland und England (1788), Herbsttage (1805), (Frankfurt) 98. **CONTACT ADDRESS** Dept Ger, Ohio State Univ, Columbus, 1841 Millikin Rd, Columbus, OH 43210-1229. **EMAIL** becker-cantarino.1@osu.edu

BECKERS, ASTRID M.
PERSONAL Born 12/30/1964, Duisburg, Germany, m, 1994 **DISCIPLINE** GERMAN, LITERATURE, CULTURE **EDUCATION** Heinrich-Heine Univ, MA, 90; MA, 90; Univ Miss, MA, 92; PhD, 99. **CAREER** Instr, Heinrich-Heine Univ, 88-90; instr to grad asst to instr, Univ Miss, 95-99; asst prof, Univ System Ga, 99-. **HONORS AND AWARDS** Fulbright Scholar, 87-88; Nat Merit Scholar, 90-92; Grad Honors Tuition Fel, 96-99; Outstanding Ling Thesis Award, 90; Cert Excellence, Outstanding Performance/Dedication Teaching, 97; Most Inspirational Prof, 99. **MEMBERSHIPS** TESOL; MLA; DSI; IABD; AATG; SECOL; ACTFL; INFORMS. **RESEARCH** Cross-cultural communication; sociolinguistics; technology assisted foreign language instruction; media bias; marketing/advertising. **SELECTED PUBLICATIONS** Co-auth, "Neural Networks in Business Applications," Int Bus Schs Computing Quart (96); auth, "The Use of Email in the Foreign Language Classroom," J Tech Teacher Educ (99); auth, "Writing Project Increases Computer Skills of Education Students," J Tech Teacher Educ (99); co-auth, "An Educational Application of Group Decision Support Systems," Business/Economic Rev (00); auth, "A Cross-cultural Comparison of Women in Advertisements," Business Res Yearbk (00); co-auth, "Effects of Group Decision Support Systems on Total Quality Management in the Workplace," Business Res Yearbk (00); co-auth, "Selection of Strategic Suppliers in a Manufacturing-Oriented Firm," Business Res Yearbk (01); co-auth, "An Evaluation of the Group Decision Support Systems Technology's Impact on Quality Programs," J Business/Management (01); auth, "The Role of Women in the Workplace as Reflected by the Urban Media," 01. **CONTACT ADDRESS** 1227 Pin Oak Dr, Apt A12, Jackson, MS 39208. **EMAIL** ambeckers@yahoo.com

BEDFORD, DAVID
PERSONAL Born 07/24/1949, Fort Worth, TX, m, 1977, 3 children **DISCIPLINE** SPANISH AND LATIN AMERICAN STUDIES **EDUCATION** Texas Tech Univ, BA, 70; MA, 73, Univ Tex at Austin, PhD, 76; SW Baptist Theol Sem, MA, 94. **CAREER** Linguist, Missionary Orient Center, 75-83; Dir, S Ill Univ at Carbondale, 84-88; Dir, Port Lang School, Brazil, 88-94; Instr, Texas Christian Univ, 96-. **MEMBERSHIPS** AATSP; ACTFL. **RESEARCH** Argentine fantastic literature, contemporary Argentine authors, culture studies. **SELECTED PUBLICATIONS** Auth, "Afro-Brazilian Spritist Christology: the Attraction and challenge of Umbaude", Boletin Teologizo 2 (97):29-95; auth, Myths of Buenos Aires by Alejandro Polina", Hispania 81 (98):519-29. **CONTACT ADDRESS** Dept Spanish, Texas Christian Univ, Fort Worth, TX 76129. **EMAIL** d.bedford@tcu.edu

BEDINI, SILVIO A.
PERSONAL Born 01/17/1917, Ridgefield, CT, m, 1951, 2 children **DISCIPLINE** COMPARATIVE LITERATURE **EDUCATION** Columbia Univ, 35-42; Univ Bridgeport, LLd 70. **CAREER** Smithsonian Inst Nat Museum Hist Tech, curator, 61-65, asst dir, 65-72, dep dir, 72-77; Smithsonian Inst, keeper of the rare books, 77-82, Hist emeritus, 82-. **HONORS AND AWARDS** Abbot Payson Usher Awd; Paul Bunge Awd; J T Fraser Prize of Excellence. **MEMBERSHIPS** APA; SAH; AAS; WAS. **RESEARCH** Historical research in history of horology and history science; scientific instruments; early Amer Science. **SELECTED PUBLICATIONS** Auth, The Pope's Elephant, Manchester Eng, Carcanet Press, 97; The Mace and the Gavel: Symbols of Authority in America, Philadelphia, Amer Philo Soc, 97; Science and Instruments in 17th Century Italy, Alsershot Eng, Ashgate Pub, 94; The Trail of Time: Time Measurement With Incense in East Asia, Cambridge, Cambridge Univ Press, 94; Thomas Jefferson Statesman of Science, NY, Macmillan Pub, 90. **CONTACT ADDRESS** Smithsonian Inst, 4303 47th St N W, Washington, DC 20016-2449. **EMAIL** sbedini@compuserve.com

BEECHER, MAUREEN URSENBACH
PERSONAL Born 03/19/1935, Calgary, AB, Canada **DISCIPLINE** COMPARATIVE LITERATURE, WESTERN HISTORY **EDUCATION** Brigham Young Univ, BSc, 58; Univ UT, MA, 66, PhD(comp lit), 73. **CAREER** Res historian & ed western hist, Church of Jesus Christ Latter-Day Saints, 72-80; Assoc Prof to Prof Emer English & Res Historian, Brigham Young Univ, Provo, UT, 80-. **HONORS AND AWARDS** John Whitmer Hist Asn Awd, 78. **MEMBERSHIPS** AHA; Western Hist Asn; Mormon Hist Asn; Asn for Mormon Lett. **RESEARCH** History of women in America; history of Mormon women; literature of the Mormon movement. **SELECTED PUBLICATIONS** Auth, Three Women and the Life of the Mind, UT Hist Quart, winter 75; Letters From the Frontier: Commerce, Nauvoo and Salt Lake City, J of Mormon Hist, 75; Past and Present: Some Thoughts on Being a Mormon Woman, Sunstone, 76; Under the Sunbonnets: Mormon Women with Faces, BYU Studies, summer 76; contribr, The Oft-crossed Border: Canadians in Utah, In: The Peoples of Utah, Utah State His Soc, 76; contribr, Eliza R Snow, In: Mormon Sisters, Emmeline, 77; auth, The Eliza Enigma: The Life and Legend of Eliza R Snow, Dialogue: J Mormon Thought, reprinted in, Sister Saints, spring 78; contribr, Women in Twentieth Century Utah, In: Utah's History, Brigham Young Univ, 78. **CONTACT ADDRESS** Dept of English, Brigham Young Univ, Provo, UT 84602. **EMAIL** maureen_beecher@byu.edu

BEER, JEANETTE MARY AYRES
PERSONAL Born Wellington, New Zealand, m, 1959, 2 children **DISCIPLINE** MEDIEVAL FRENCH, LINGUISTICS, COMPARATIVE LITERATURE **EDUCATION** Victoria Univ, Wellington, BA, 54, MA, 55; Oxford Univ, BA, 58, MA, 62; Columbia Univ, PhD(French), 67. **CAREER** Asst lectr French, Victoria Univ, Wellington, 56; lectr English & French, Univ Montpellier, 58-59; lectr French, Otago Univ, 62-64; instr, Barnard Col, 66-68; from assoc prof to prof, Fordham Univ, 68-80, dir medieval studies, 72-80, prof French, 77-80; prof, 80-, Purdue Univ & Chmn Dept, 80-83, Actg assoc dean, Thomas More Col, 72-73; Una Goodwin Res Fel, St. Anne's Col, Oxford, 59-60; asst dir, division of fels and seminars, nat endowment for the Humanities, 83-84. **HONORS AND AWARDS** Una Goodwin res fel, St. Anne's Col, Oxford Univ, 59-60; Nat Endowment Humanities prog grant, 75-; mem, Nat Bd Consult, Nat Endowment Humanities, 77-; Nat Endowment Humanities res fel; fel, Ctr for Humanisic Stu; Purdue Res Fnd Res Gra; Phi Kappa Phi; Dean's Incentive Awd; Am Cnl of Learned Soc Travel Gra; Am Philops Soc Gra; post-graduate scholarship in arts, 56-58; Commonwealth fel, Lady Margaret Hall, Oxford Univ, 56. **MEMBERSHIPS** Am Asn of Tchr of French; Anglo-Norman Text Sco; Columbia Univ Medieval Sem; Col Univ Grad Faculties Alumni; Int Arthurian Soc; Int Courtly Lit Soc; Lady Margaret Hall; Medieval Acad of Am; Mod Lang Asn of Am; Sr Mem of Oxford Univ; Soc Guilhem IX; Soc Rencesvals; assoc of sr common room, Lady Margaret Hall, Oxford Univ, 95-. **RESEARCH** Medieval French literature, especially historians; linguistic and stylistic aspects of Old French; comparative literature; theory and practice of translation. **SELECTED PUBLICATIONS** Trans, Master Richard's Bestiary of Love and Response, Penny Royal, 81, 86, 00; auth, "Richard de Fournival's Anonymous Lady: The Character of the Response to the Bestiaire d'amour," Romance Philology 42 (3) (89); auth, Medieval Translators and Their Craft, Medieval Institute, 90; auth, Early Prose in France, Medieval Inst, 92; auth, "Gendered Discourse in Two Medieval Bestiary texts," Jour of the Inst of Romantic Studies 3 (94-95); co-ed, Translation and the Transmission of Culture Between 1300 and 1600, Medieval Inst, 95; co-ed, Romance Languages Annual, Vols III, IV, V, VI, and VII, Purdue Res Fnd, 92-96; auth, "Medieval Translations and the Vernacular Languages," in Medieval Latin: An Introduction and Bibliographical Guide, Catholic Univ of America Press, 96; ed, Translation Theory and Practice in the Middle Ages, Medieval Inst, 97; auth, "Heroic Language and the Eyewitness: The Gesta Francirum and La Chanson D'Antioche," in Echoes of the Epic: Studies in Honor of Gerard J. Brault, Summa Publication, 98. **CONTACT ADDRESS** Dept of Foreign Lang & Lit, Purdue Univ, West Lafayette, West Lafayette, IN 47907-1968. **EMAIL** beer@purdue.edu

BEGNAL, MICHAEL HENRY
DISCIPLINE MODERN ENGLISH & COMPARATIVE LITERATURE **EDUCATION** Univ Conn, BA, 61; Pa State Univ, MA, 63; Univ Wash, PhD, 68. **CAREER** Instr English, Colgate Univ, 63-65; assoc prof, English & comp lit, 68-80, prof Eng & comp lit, 80-, PA State Univ; prof Am lit, Charles Univ Prague, 73-74 & 75-76. **RESEARCH** James Joyce; Irish literature; modern literature; beat generation. **SELECTED PUBLICATIONS** Auth, Joseph Sheridan LeFanu, 71; auth, Narrator and Character in Finnegans Wake, Bucknell Univ, 74; co-ed & contribr, A Conceptual Guide to Finnegans Wake, Pa State Univ, 74; auth, Dreamscheme: Narrative and Voice in Finnegans Wake, Syracuse U Press, 88; auth, On Miracle Ground: Essays on the Fiction of Lawrence Durrell, Bucknell, 90. **CONTACT ADDRESS** Dept of English, Pennsylvania State Univ, Univ Park, 117 Burrowes Bldg, University Park, PA 16802-6200. **EMAIL** mhb3@psu.edu

BEHLER, ERNST
PERSONAL Born 09/04/1928, Essen, West Germany, m, 1967, 1 child **DISCIPLINE** GERMANICS, COMPARATIVE LITERATURE **EDUCATION** Univ Munich, PhD, 51. **CAREER** Docent philos, Univ Bonn, 61-63; assoc prof Germanics, WA Univ, 64-65, prof Ger & comp lit, 65-66; chmn Humanities Coun, 73-78, Prof Ger & Comp Lit, Univ WA, 66-, Co-Dir Humanities Prog & Chmn Comp Lit, 76-, Guggenheim Found fel, 67 & 75-76; Am Coun Learning Soc fel, 70-71. **MEMBERSHIPS** MLA; Comite d'honneur de la Societe des Etudes Staeliennes; hon mem, Ovidianum Societas, Bucharest; Am Comp Lit Asn. **RESEARCH** Romanticism; history of ideas and critism. **SELECTED PUBLICATIONS** Coauth, Critical Edition of F Schlegel's Works (35 vols), 58 & auth, Die Ewigkeit der Welt, 65, Schoeningh, Paderborn; Friedrich Schlegel, Rowohlt, Hamburg, 66; Madame de Stael a Weimar, Studi Francesi, 69; Techniques of Irony in Light of the Romantic Theory, Rice Univ Studies, 72; Klassische Ironie, Romantische Ironie, Tragische Ironie, Wiss Buchgesellschaft, Darmstadt, 72; Die Geschichte des Bewusstseins, Hegel-Studies, 72; Nietzsche's Challenge to Romantic Humanism, Can Rev Comp Lit, 5/78; The Reception of Calderon Among the German Romantics, Studies in Romanticism, 81; Historicism and Sense of Modernity in Herder 'Auch Eine Philosophie Der Geschichte Zur Bildung Der Menschheit', Etudes Germaniques, Vol 49, 94. **CONTACT ADDRESS** Univ of Washington, Seattle, WA 98195.

BEIZER, JANET L.
PERSONAL Born 04/09/1952, New York, NY, 1 child **DISCIPLINE** FRENCH LITERATURE **EDUCATION** Cornell Univ, BA, 74; Yale Univ, PhD(French), 81. **CAREER** Asst prof, 81-88, assoc prof, 88-95, dir, undergrad studies/distinguished majors/study abroad, 89-90, chair, grad studies comm, 92-94, dir grad studies, 94-95, Prof French, Univ VA, 95-. **HONORS AND AWARDS** Phi Beta Kappa, Phi Kappa Phi, 74; Fulbright Fellowship, Paris, 74-75; Univ VA Fac summer research grants, 82, 85, 86, 89, 90, 92, 93, 95, 97; NEH summer research grant, 88, 98; NEH travel grant, 91; MLA Aldo and Jeanne Scaglione Prize for French and Francophone Studies, 95 (for Ventriloquized Bodies); Nat Humanities Center Fellow, 98-99. **MEMBERSHIPS** MLA. **RESEARCH** Nineteenth century narrative, psychoanalysis and literature. **SELECTED PUBLICATIONS** Transl, Maria Paganini, Intertextuality and the Strategy of Desire: Melancolique Villegistare de Madame de Breyues, Yale French Studies, 79; Family Plots: Balzac's Narrative Generations, Yale Univ Press, 86; Reading Women: The Novel in the Text of Hysteria, Compar(a)ison 1, 93; Emma's Daughter: Femininity, Maternity, and 'Mothersickness' in Madame Bovary, in From Exile to Vagrancy: Home and its Dislocations in Nineteenth-Century France, ed Suzanne Nash, SUNY Press, 93; Les Lettres de Flaubert a Louise Colet, Une Physiologie du style, in L'Oeuvre de l'oeuvre: Etudes sur la correspondance de Flaubert, ed Raymonde Debray Genette & Jacques Neefs, Presses Universitaires de Vincennes, 93; Rewriting Ophelia: Fluidity, Madness and Voice in Louise Colet's La Servante, in Embodied Voices: Representing Female Vocality in Western Culture, ed Nancy Jones and Leslie Dunn, Cambridge Univ Press, 94; Ventriloquized Bodies: Narratives of Hysteria in Nineteenth-Century France, Cornell Univ Press, 94; Mirrors and Fatherhood in Le Pere Goriot, in Pere Goriot, Norton Critical Edition, ed Peter Brooks, Norton, 98; Critical Introduction to Rachilde in The Decadent Reader, ed Asti Hustvedt, Zone Books (forthcoming 98); You Can't Judge a Book By It's Cover: Old Goriot and Modernism, in Approaches to Teaching Balzac's Ols Goriot, ed Michal Ginsberg, MLA (forthcoming). **CONTACT ADDRESS** Dept of French, Univ of Virginia, 302 Cabell Hall, Charlottesville, VA 22903-3125. **EMAIL** jlb@virginia.edu

BEJEL, EMILIO
PERSONAL Born, Cuba **DISCIPLINE** SPANISH, SPANISH AMERICAN LITERATURE **EDUCATION** Univ Miami, BA, 67; Flor State Univ, MA, 69; PhD, 70. **CAREER** Asst prof, 71-75, assoc prof, 75-80, prof, 80-82, Fairfield Univ; assoc prof, 82-84, prof, 84-91, Univ Fla; prof, Univ Colo, 91-. **HONORS AND AWARDS** Yale Vis Fel; NEH; Lilly Found Fel; Lit Guild Frst Prize; Phi Delta Pi. **MEMBERSHIPS** MLA; LASA. **RESEARCH** Contemporary Spanish American literature; Cuban literature and culture. **SELECTED PUBLICATIONS** Auth, Buero Vallejo: lo moral, lo social y lo metafisico, Inst de Estudios Superiores (Montevideo), 72; auth, Literatura de Nuestra America: Estudios de literatura cubana e hispanoamericana, Cen Invest Ling Lit Univ Veracruzana (Xalapa), 83; coauth, La subversion de la semiotica: Analisis estructural de textos hispanicos, Hispamerica (Gaithersburg), 88; auth, Jose' Lezama Lima: Poet of the Image, Univ Press Flor (Gainesville), 90; auth, Escribir en Cuba: Entrevistas con escritoires cubanos,

1979-89, Univ Puerto Rico (San Juan), 91. **CONTACT ADDRESS** Dept Spanish, Portuguese, Univ of Colorado, Boulder, PO Box 278, Boulder, CO 80309-0278. **EMAIL** bejel@spot.colorado.edu

BEKKER, HUGO
PERSONAL Born 02/12/1925, Netherlands, m, 1952, 2 children **DISCIPLINE** GERMAN **EDUCATION** Univ Mich, MA, 56, PhD, 58. **CAREER** Asst prof Ger, Univ Ore, 58-61, res grant, 60; assoc prof, 61-66, Prof Ger, Ohio State Univ, 66-, Vis prof, Univ British Columbia, 71. **MEMBERSHIPS** Am Asn Teachers Ger; MLA; Renaissance Soc Am. **RESEARCH** Poetry. **SELECTED PUBLICATIONS** Auth, The Nibelungenlied: A Literary Analysis, Univ Toronto, 71; Andreas Gryphius: Poet Between Epochs, Lang Verlag, Bern, 73; Friedrich von Hausen: Inquiries into His Poetry, Univ NC, 77; The Poetry of Albrecht von Johansdorf, Univ Calif, Davis, 78; Gottfried von Strassburgs Tristan: Journey through the Realm of Eros, Camden House, 87. **CONTACT ADDRESS** Dept of Ger, Ohio State Univ, Columbus, 1841 Millikin Rd, Columbus, OH 43210-1229.

BELIFIORE, ELIZABETH S.
PERSONAL Born 06/21/1944, Austin, TX, m, 1966, 1 child **DISCIPLINE** CLASSICAL STUDIES **EDUCATION** Barnard Col, BA, 66; Univ Calif Los Angeles, MA, 72; PhD, 78. **CAREER** Asst prof, Scripps Col, 79-80; asst prof to prof, Univ Minn, 80-. **HONORS AND AWARDS** Fel, ACLS, 87-88; Fel, NEH, 88. **MEMBERSHIPS** Am Philol Asn; Class Asn of the Mid W and S; Women's Class Caucus; Soc for Ancient Greek Philos **RESEARCH** Ancient Philosophy; Greek tragedy. **SELECTED PUBLICATIONS** Auth, Tragic Pleasures: Aristotle on Plot and Emotion, Princeton Univ Press, 92; auth, "Aristotle and Iphigenia," in Essays on Aristotle's Poetics, (Princeton Univ Press, 92),359-377; auth, "Harming Friends: Reciprocity in Greek Tragedy," in Reciprocity in Ancient Greece, (Oxford Univ Press, 98), 139-158; auth, Murder Among Friends: Violation of Philia in Greek Tragedy, Oxford Univ Press, 00. **CONTACT ADDRESS** Dept Class and Near E Studies, Univ of Minnesota, Twin Cities, 9 Pleasant St SE, 305 Folwell Hall, Minneapolis, MN 55455. **EMAIL** esb@tc.umn.edu

BELKNAP, ROBERT LAMONT
PERSONAL Born 12/23/1929, New York, NY, m, 1997, 3 children **DISCIPLINE** RUSSIAN LITERATURE **EDUCATION** Princeton Univ, AB, 51; Columbia Univ, MA, 54, PhD, 60. **CAREER** From instr to assoc prof Russ lang & lit, 57-69, assoc dean student affairs, Columbia Col, 68-69, chmn dept Slavic lang, 70-76, actg dean, 76-77, dir, Columbia Russ Inst, 77-80, Prof Russ, Columbia Univ, 69-00, Emer, 00-; dir, Univ Seminars, 00. **HONORS AND AWARDS** Inter-Univ Comt Travel Grants study grant, Leningrad, 63; Am Coun Learned Soc & IREX fel study in Moscow, 66-67; NEH, Kennan Inst, Bellagio Ctr, and Guggenheim fels. **MEMBERSHIPS** Am Asn Advan Slavic Studies. **RESEARCH** Nineteenth century Russian novel. **SELECTED PUBLICATIONS** Auth, The Structure of The Brothers Karamazov, Mouton, The Hague, 67, Northwestern, 89, St. Petersburg, Acad Proj, 97; coauth, Tradition and Innovation, General Education and the Reintegration of the University, Columbia, NY, 78; auth, The Genesis of the Brothers Karamazov, Northwestern, 90. **CONTACT ADDRESS** Dept of Slavic Lang, Columbia Univ, 2960 Broadway, New York, NY 10027-6900. **EMAIL** rb12@columbia,edu

BELL, STEVEN
DISCIPLINE MODERN SPANISH AMERICAN LITERATURE **EDUCATION** Univ Kans, BA, 77; Univ Ky, MA, 79; Univ Kans, PhD, 84. **CAREER** English and Lit, Univ Ark. **SELECTED PUBLICATIONS** Ed & coauth, Critical Theory, Cultural Politics, 93. **CONTACT ADDRESS** Univ of Arkansas, Fayetteville, Fayetteville, AR 72701.

BELL-VILLADA, GENE HAROLD
PERSONAL Born 12/05/1941, Port-au-Prince, Haiti, m, 1975 **DISCIPLINE** SPANISH, COMPARITIVE LITERATURE **EDUCATION** Univ Ariz, BA, 63; Univ Calif, Berkeley, MA, 67; Harvard Univ, PhD(Romance lang), 74. **CAREER** Instr Span, State Univ NY, Binghamton, 71-73; lectr, Yale Univ, 73-74; from asst to prof Span, Williams Col, 75-, Nat Endowment for Humanities fel, 7-12/79; Am Philos Soc grant, 82; res dir, Hamilton Col, prog in Madrid, 86-87; chmn Romance Lang, 93-95, 97-00. **MEMBERSHIPS** MLA; Am Asn Teachers Span & Port; Latin Am Studies Asn. **RESEARCH** Spanish-American Comparative literature; Latin-American studies; sociology of literature. **SELECTED PUBLICATIONS** Auth, Borges and His Fiction: A Guide to His Mind and Art, Univ NC Press, 81; Names and narrative pattern, In: One Hundred Years of Solitude, Latin Am Lit Rev, spring-summer 81; Garcia Marquez: The Man and His Work, UNC Press, 90; Art for Art's Sake and Literary Life, Univ of Nebraska Press, 96. **CONTACT ADDRESS** Dept of Romance Lang, Williams Col, 995 Main St, Williamstown, MA 01267-2600. **EMAIL** Gene.H.Bell-Villada@Williams.edu

BELLAMY, JAMES ANDREW
PERSONAL Born 08/12/1925, Evansville, IN **DISCIPLINE** ARABIC **EDUCATION** Centre Col, Ky, AB, 46; Univ Pa, PhD(Orient studies), 56. **CAREER** Interim lectr Arabic, Univ Pa, 56-57; asst prof, Wayne State Univ, 58-59; lectr, 59-60, from asst prof to assoc prof, 60-68, Prof Arabic, Univ Mich, Ann Arbor, 68-, Assoc ed, J Am Orient Soc, 70-75; Am Coun Learned Soc fel. **MEMBERSHIPS** Mid East Inst; MLA; Mid Eastern Stud Asn N Am. **RESEARCH** Arabic literature. **SELECTED PUBLICATIONS CONTACT ADDRESS** Univ of Michigan, Ann Arbor, Ann Arbor, MI 48109.

BELLOS, DAVID M.
PERSONAL Born 06/25/1945, Rochford, United Kingdom, 3 children **DISCIPLINE** FRENCH AND COMPARATIVE LITERATURE **EDUCATION** Oxford Univ, UK, BA, 67, MA, 70, PhD, 71. **CAREER** Fel by Examination, Magdalen Col, Oxford, 69-71; lectr, Univ Edinburgh, Scotland, 72-81; prof, Univ Southampton, UK, 82-85; prof, Univ Manchester, UK, 86-96; prof, Princeton Univ, 96-. **HONORS AND AWARDS** IBM-France Translation Prize, 88; Prix Goncourt de la Biographie, 94. **RESEARCH** French 19th and 20th century fiction; French film; comparative European literature. **SELECTED PUBLICATIONS** Auth, Georges Perec. A Life in Words, London: Harvill (93); ed, Review of Contemporary Fiction, Vol XIII, 1, "Georges Perec," Normal, Ill: Dalkey Archive (93); auth, Georges Perec. Une vie dans les mots, Edition francaise par l'auteur et Francoise Cartano, Paris: Seuil (94); auth, "Jacques Roubaud," Sites, 3.1 (fall 98): 389-392; auth, Jacques Tati. His Life and Art, London: Harvill Press (99); auth, "Tati and America: Jour de fete and the Blum-Byrnes Agreement of 1946," French Cultural Studies, 10:29 (June 99): 145-160; auth, "Ce que Momo veut dire. La memoire de la Shoah dans La vie devant soi de Romain Gary," Perspectives. Revue de l'Universite hebraique de Jerusalem, 6 (99): 55-66; auth, "The 'Third Dimension' of Perec's W ou le souvenir d'enfance," French Studies Bull, 70.1 (spring 99): 1-3. **CONTACT ADDRESS** Dept Romance Langs, Princeton Univ, 201 East Pyne Hall, Princeton, NJ 08544-0001. **EMAIL** dbellos@princeton.edu

BELTRAN, LUIS
PERSONAL Born 09/06/1932, Salmanca, Spain, m, 1962, 2 children **DISCIPLINE** COMPARATIVE LITERATURE **EDUCATION** Univ Salamanca, LLB, 54, lic philos, 56; Univ Mich, MA, 61, PhD(comp lit), 66. **CAREER** From asst prof to assoc prof, 66-77, Prof Comp Lit, Span & Port, Ind Univ, Bloomington, 77- **MEMBERSHIPS** Mediaeval Acad Am; MLA. **RESEARCH** Comparative medieval literature; Spanish poetry. **SELECTED PUBLICATIONS** Auth, Hacia la Tierra Alfaguara, Madrid, 70; The poet, the king and the cardinal virtues in Juan de Mena's Laberinto, Speculum, 71; La Vieille's past, Romanische Forsch, 72; Anaya mi Esperanza, Alfaguara, Madrid, 73; El Fruto de su Vientre, Samo, Mex, 73; Razones de Buen Amor: Oposiones y Convergencias en el Libro del Arcipreste de Hita, Castalia, Madrid, 77. **CONTACT ADDRESS** Dept of Compt Lit, Indiana Univ, Bloomington, Bloomington, IN 47401.

BENALIL, MOUNIA
PERSONAL Born 03/05/1971, Morocco, s **DISCIPLINE** FRENCH **EDUCATION** Univ Hassan, BA, 92; Univ Mohammed, DEA, 93; Univ Brit Colum, MA, 96; PhD, 01. **CAREER** Teaching asst to teacher, Univ Brit Colum, 95-98. **HONORS AND AWARDS** DEA Scholar, 92093; Grad Fel, Univ Brit Colum, 97-01. **MEMBERSHIPS** MLA; Dalhousie Fr Stud; Spirale. **RESEARCH** Literary theory; post-structuralist thought; Francophone literature; Bakhtin and the poetics of the Carnival; Said and Orientalism. **SELECTED PUBLICATIONS** Auth, "Tatouer ou Ecrire la Decolonisation: La Memoire Tatouee d'Abdelkebir Khatibi," Le Maghreb Lit Rev 1 (97): 71-89; auth, "Sade Entre les Ordres Institutionnels et le Miroir de la censure," Dal Fr Study 44 (98): 23-30; auth, "Trajets Ideologiques de la bi-langue khatibienne dans Amour Bilingue," Etudes Franco 13 (98): 93-103; auth, "Espaces Orientaux Dams le Roman Francais du XXe Siecle: Proust a la Croisee du Mythe et de la Realite - Le Temps Retrouve," Dal Fr Study 48 (99): 47-59; auth, "Gerard Etienne et le Carnaval: pour une Esthetique de la Revolte au Teminin," Que Study 27 (99): 24-45; auth, "Ecrire le Corpsparler le Feminin et Volonte de (sur) vie dans Pluie et Vent sur Telumce Miracle de Simone Schwarz-Bart," in Acies du Colloque sur 'Le Marronnage aux Caraibes: Mythe et Realite,' ed. Bernard Delpoche (Montreal: CIDIHCA, 01). **CONTACT ADDRESS** 1180 Du Fort, Apt 807, Montreal, QC, Canada H3H 2B4. **EMAIL** benalil@interchange.ubc.ca

BENARDETE, SETH GABRIEL
PERSONAL Born 04/04/1930, New York, NY, m, 1960, 2 children **DISCIPLINE** CLASSICS **EDUCATION** Univ Chicago, BA, 49, MA, 53, PhD, 55. **CAREER** Teaching intern Greek & humanities, St John's Col, Md, 55-57; jr fel, Harvard Univ, 57-60; asst prof Greek & Latin, Brandeis Univ, 60-65; assoc prof, 65-76, prof classics, NY Univ, 76-, vis lectr philos, Grad Fac, New Sch Social Res, 65-; Nat Endowment for Humanities sr fel, 72. **HONORS AND AWARDS** D Litt, Adelphi, 89. **RESEARCH** Greek poetry and philosophy. **SELECTED PUBLICATIONS** Transl, Aeschylus II,The Persians and The Suppliant Maidens, Univ Chicago, 56; Herodotean Inquiries, M Nijhoff, 69; The Being of the Beautiful, Univ Chicago, 84; The Rhetoric of Morality & Philosophy, Univ Chicago, 91; Socrates Second Sailing, Univ Chicago, 89; The Tradegy & Comedy of Life, Univ Chicago, 93; The Bow & the Lyre, Rauman & Littlefield, 97; Sacred Transgressions, St Augustine's Press, 98; auth, the Argument of the Action, Univ Chicago, 00; auth, Plato's "Laus": The Discovery of Being, Univ Chicago, 00. **CONTACT ADDRESS** Dept of Classics, New York Univ, 25 Waverly Pl, New York, NY 10003-6701. **EMAIL** sb5@isq.nyu.edu

BENARIO, HERBERT W.
PERSONAL Born 07/21/1929, New York, NY, m, 1957, 2 children **DISCIPLINE** CLASSICS **EDUCATION** City Col New York, BA, 48; Columbia Univ, MA, 49; Johns Hopkins Univ, PhD(classics), 51. **CAREER** Instr Greek & Latin, Columbia Univ, 53-58; asst prof classics, Sweet Briar Col, 58-60; from asst prof to assoc prof, 60-67, chmn dept, 68-73 & 76-78, Prof Classics, Emory Univ, 67-, Mem Latin achievement test comt, Col Entrance Exam Bd, 63-66; fel, Southeastern Inst Medieval & Renaissance Stud, 65; consult, Nat Endowment for Humanities, 71 & 72; Am Coun Learned Soc fel, 78. **HONORS AND AWARDS** Ovation from Class Asn Midwest & South, 79. **MEMBERSHIPS** Am Philol Asn; Vergilian Soc Am (pres, 80-82); Class Soc Am Acad Rome (pres, 65); Archaeol Inst Am; Class Asn Midwest & South (pres, 71-72). **RESEARCH** Latin literature; Roman history; Roman monuments and topography. **SELECTED PUBLICATIONS** Auth, Christians and Pagans in Roman Britain, Classical World, Vol 0086, 92; Roman Papers, Vol 6, Vol 7, Classical J, Vol 0087, 92; Tacitus and Commotus in 'Ann 13.56'/, Historia-Zeitschrift Fur Alte Geschichte, Vol 0043, 94; Roman Towns in Britain, Classical World, Vol 0087, 94; Tacitus and Commotus in 'Ann 13.56'/, Historia Zeitschrift Fur Alte Geschichte, Vol 0043, 94; Recent Work on Tacitus 1984-1993, Classical World, Vol 0089, 95; Camws the Classical Assoc of the Middle West andSouth--the 9th Decade, Classical J, Vol 0091, 96; Academic Tributes to 97, Classical J, Vol 0093, 97. **CONTACT ADDRESS** Dept of Classics, Emory Univ, Atlanta, GA 30322.

BENDA, GISELA
PERSONAL Born 10/05/1941, Brandenburg-Havel, Germany **DISCIPLINE** GERMAN LANGUAGE & LITERATURE **EDUCATION** Univ Munster, BA, 62; Marquette Univ, MA, 64; Northwestern Univ, PhD(Ger), 67. **CAREER** Asst prof, 67-72, Assoc Prof Ger, Marquette Univ, 72-. **MEMBERSHIPS** Am Asn Teachers Ger; MLA; AAUP. **RESEARCH** Works of Heinrich Heine, Friedrich Nietzsche, Rainer Maria Rilke and Franz Kafka. **SELECTED PUBLICATIONS CONTACT ADDRESS** Dept of Ger, Marquette Univ, Milwaukee, WI 53233.

BENDER, BYRON WILBUR
PERSONAL Born 08/14/1929, Roaring Spring, PA, m, 1950, 5 children **DISCIPLINE** LINGUISTICS **EDUCATION** Goshen Col, BA, 49; Ind Univ, MA, 50, PhD(ling), 63. **CAREER** Asst prof anthrop & ling, Goshen Col, 59-62; English prog supvr, Trust Territory of Pac Islands, 62-64; assoc prof English Lang Inst, 64-65, assoc prof to prof Ling, 65-99; chm dept Ling, 69-95, Univ Hawaii, Manoa, US Peace Corps grant, Pac & Asian Ling inst for develop pedag materials on Marshallese lang, 66-67; consult Maori educ, NZ Coun Educ Res, 66-69; dir, Ling Inst of Ling Soc Am, 77; Prof Emeritus, 00-. **MEMBERSHIPS** Ling Soc Am; Polynesian Soc. **RESEARCH** Morphology; Micronesian languages; Austronesian linguistics. **SELECTED PUBLICATIONS** Auth, Marshallese Phonology, Oceanic Ling, 68; Spoken Marshallese, Univ Hawaii, 69; contribr, Current Trends in Linguistics: Linguistics in Oceania, Mouton, The Hague, 71; auth, Linguistic factors in Maori education, NZ Coun Educ Res, 71; Parallelisms in the Morphophonemics of Several Micronesian Languages, Oceanic Ling, 73; coauth, A Ulithian Grammar, Australian Nat Univ, 73; Marshallese-English Dictionary, Univ Hawaii, 76; contribr, Studies in Pacific Languages and Cultures in Honour of Bruce Biggs, 81. **CONTACT ADDRESS** Dept of Ling, Univ of Hawaii, Manoa, 1890 E West Rd, Honolulu, HI 96822-2318. **EMAIL** bender@hawaii.edu

BENDER, HENRY V.
PERSONAL Born 05/23/1945, Teaneck, NJ, m, 1973, 3 children **DISCIPLINE** CLASSICS **EDUCATION** Fordham Univ, AB, 67; Pa State Univ, MA, 68; Rutgers Univ, PhD, 87. **CAREER** Dept Chair, St Joseph's Preparatory Sch, 69-98; Adj Prof, St Joseph's Univ, 81-; Adj Prof, Villanova Univ, 85-; Dept Chair, Hill Sch, 98-; Adj Prof, Rutgers Univ, 93-96. **HONORS AND AWARDS** Pres Fel, 63-67; Nat Defense Fel, Bryn Mawr, 68-70; Fulbright Fel, Am Acad Rome, 84; Fel, NEH, 88, 92, 98; Ignatian Awd for Teaching, St Joseph's Preparatory Sch, 88; Adv Placement Teacher Recognition Awd, 94; alumnus of the Year, St Joseph's Preparatory Sch, 97. **MEMBERSHIPS** Class Asn of the Atlantic States; Class Asn of N Eng; Class Asn of the Midwestern States; Am Philol Asn; Philadelphia Class Soc; NJ Class Soc; Pa Class Asn; Nat Asn of Indep Sch; Intl Tour Managers Asn. **RESEARCH** Classical architecture and typography in Renaissance settings; Roman topography and Augustan Age Literature. **SELECTED PUBLICATIONS** Contrib,

The World of Roman Costume, Univ Wis Press, 90; co-auth, Catullus for the AP, Bolchazy-Carducci, 97; auth, A Horace Reader, Focus Press, 98. **CONTACT ADDRESS** Dept Humanities, Hill Sch, 717 E High St, Pottstown, PA 19464. **EMAIL** hbender@thehill.org

BENDER, TODD K.
PERSONAL Born 01/08/1936, Stark County, OH, m, 1958, 2 children **DISCIPLINE** ENGLISH, CLASSICAL LANGUAGES **EDUCATION** Kenyon Col, BA, 58; Stanford Univ, PhD(class lang & English), 62. **CAREER** Instr English, Stanford Univ, 61-62; instr, Dartmouth Col, 62-63; asst prof, Univ Va, 63-65; assoc prof, 65-73, Prof English, Univ Wis, Madison, 73-, Am Coun Learned Soc grant-in-aid, Oxford Univ, 63 & fel, Bibliot Nat, Paris, 65-66; Am Philos Soc grant, Paris, 69; vis prof, World Campus Prog, 73; Fulbright lectr, Univ Athens, Greece, 78-79. **MEMBERSHIPS** MLA. **RESEARCH** Nineteenth century English and European literature; Homeric Greek; computational linguistics. **SELECTED PUBLICATIONS** **CONTACT ADDRESS** Dept of English, Univ of Wisconsin, Madison, Madison, WI 53706.

BENITO-VESSELS, CARMEN
PERSONAL Born 04/30/1955, Salamanca, Spain, m, 2 children **DISCIPLINE** SPANISH **EDUCATION** Univ de Salamanca, Licenciatura in Filologia Romanina, 77; Univ Calif Santa Barbara, PhD, 88. **CAREER** Assoc prof, Univ Md. **HONORS AND AWARDS** Teaching Excellence Awds, Univ Md, 95, 96. **RESEARCH** Medieval Spanish Literature and History, History of Spanish Language. **SELECTED PUBLICATIONS** Auth, Juan Manuel: Escritura y recreaucion de la historia, HSMS, (Madison), 92; coed, Women at Work in Medieval and Early Modern Spain; AUTH, "Hetertopia e imperio sonado en la Gran conquistador Ultramer", Poetice, 99. **CONTACT ADDRESS** Dept Span & Port, Univ of Maryland, Col Park, 2215 Jiminez Hall, College Park, MD 20742-4835. **EMAIL** cb56@umail.umd.edu

BENNET, JOEL F.
DISCIPLINE LAW OFFICE MANAGEMENT **EDUCATION** Brown Univ, AB, 68; Georgetown Univ Law Ctr, JD, 72. **CAREER** Adj fac; trial atty, Fed Trade Commission's Bureau of Consumer Protection; assoc, Stein, Mitchell & Mezines, 75-76; partner, Bennet, Deso, Greenberg & Thomas, 81-84. **SELECTED PUBLICATIONS** Publ on var aspects of, private practice; ed, Flying Solo: A Survival Guide for the Solo Lawyer, 2nd ed, Am Bar Assoc(s) Section on Econ of Law Practice, 94. **CONTACT ADDRESS** School of Law, Univ of District of Columbia, 4200 Connecticut Ave Northwest, Washington, DC 20008.

BENNETT, JANICE L.
PERSONAL Born 01/31/1951, Chicago, IL, m, 1973, 2 children **DISCIPLINE** SPANISH LITERATURE **EDUCATION** N Ill Univ, BA, 73; Metro State Col, BA, 93; Colo Univ Boulder, MA, 97. **CAREER** Graphic designer, Classic Typography/ Charter Graphics, 80-89; instr, Metro State Col, 95-00; pub, ed, auth, Libri de Hispania, 01-. **HONORS AND AWARDS** Phi Sigma Iota Honor Soc; Golden Key Honor Soc; Who's Who Am Col, 93-94; MSCD Outstanding Student, 93-94; Delta Phi Delta Art Honor Soc; Who's Who Am HS, 69; Nat Honor Soc. **MEMBERSHIPS** MLA; AATSP; CES; Sigma Delta Pi; Turin Shroud Ctr. **RESEARCH** Medieval and 18th century Spanish literature; Christian relics of Spain; Spanish and early church history; Spanish and Jewish culture; Biblical passages and hagiography related to the study of relics in Spain; history, development and culture of Spanish pilgrimage sites and Marian Shrines. **SELECTED PUBLICATIONS** Auth, ed, pub, Guia Practica a la Literaura, el Analisis y la Redaccion, Coterie Pr, 98, 99; auth, ed, pub, Scared Blood, Scared Image: The Sudarium of Oviedo, New Evidence for the Authenticity of the Shroud of Turin, Libri de Hisp, 01. **CONTACT ADDRESS** Libri de Hispania, PO Box 270262, Littleton, CO 80127-0005. **EMAIL** acbc@sprintmail.com

BENNETT, ROBERT E.
PERSONAL Born 11/07/1942, Des Moines, IA, p, 1986 **DISCIPLINE** CLASSICS **EDUCATION** Trinity Col, BA, 64; Yale Univ, MA, 65; PhD, 70. **CAREER** Vis instr, Trinity Col, 66; instr to prof, acad dean, assoc prov, Trinity Col, 67-. **HONORS AND AWARDS** Woodrow Wilson Fel, 64-67; Am School Athens, 66; Ford-Mellon Grants, 70, 71, 72; NEH, 75-76; Mellon Grant, 00-01. **MEMBERSHIPS** Assoc of Ancient Hist, Am Philol Assoc, OH Class Conf, Class Assoc of the Middle West and South, Women's Class Caucus, Great Lakes Col Assoc. **RESEARCH** Ancient Religion, Gender in Antiquity, Plutarch, the Cappadocian Fathers. **SELECTED PUBLICATIONS** Auth, "Let His Children Be Waifs and Beggars: On Reading the Psalms," Gambier Jour, (96); auth, "Classical Influence in Mary Shelley's 'Frankenstein,'" Humanitias, (96); auth, "Homosexuality in the Gilded Age," Dict of the Gilded Age, (01); coauth, "Can Men Learn to Float," Men at Church, ed Philip Culburtson, Fortpress Pr, (01). **CONTACT ADDRESS** Dept History, Kenyon Col, Ascension Hall 11, Gambier, OH 43022. **EMAIL** bennett4@kenyon.edu

BENNETT, TINA L.
PERSONAL Born 02/08/1954, La Mesa, CA, m, 1979, 5 children **DISCIPLINE** LINGUISTICS **EDUCATION** Calif Inst Arts, BFA, 73; Univ Southern Calif, AM, 76; PhD, 78. **CAREER** Asst prof to prof, Wichita State Univ, 78-; vis scholar, Inst of Ireland, 95. **HONORS AND AWARDS** Hall Fel, Kans Univ, 87; Univ Res Awds, 79, 82, 88, 91-. **MEMBERSHIPS** Ling Soc of Am, New York Acad of Sci, Am Speech, Lang, and Hearing Asn. **RESEARCH** Language development, bilingualism, discourse analysis, Irish language and literature. **SELECTED PUBLICATIONS** Co-ed, Discourse Across Time and Space, 77; auth, "Noun Phrases and Coherence in Child Narratives," J of Child Lang (83); auth, "The Two Fields of Child Language Research," First Lang (85); auth, "Cohesion and Predication in Children's Narrative," J of Child Lang (86); auth, Analyzing Children's Language Methods and Theories, Basil Blackwell (88); coauth, "Form and Role of the Noun Phrase in Irish Children's Narratives," Proceedings of the XVth International Congress of Linguists (92); contribur, Repetition in Discourse, 94; auth, "Anaphora, Nonanaphora, and the Generic Use of Pronouns by Children," Am Speech (96); auth, "Predications and non-referential cohesion in Irish-speaking Children's Narrative," Functions of Lang (99). **CONTACT ADDRESS** Dept English, Wichita State Univ, 1845 Fairmount St, Wichita, KS 67260-0001. **EMAIL** bennettk@twsuvm.uc.twsu.edu

BENOUIS, MUSTAPHA KEMAL
PERSONAL Born 05/24/1936, Descartes, Algeria, m, 1961, 3 children **DISCIPLINE** FRENCH LANGUAGE & LITERATURE **EDUCATION** Univ Toulouse, CELG, 60, Lic es Lett, 63, Dipl Etudes Super, 64; Univ Ill, Urbana, PhD(French), 71. **CAREER** Prof hist geog, Cours Brossolette, Ain Temouchent, Algeria, 56-57; lectr French, Campbell Col, Belfast, 61-62; prof English, Lycee d'Etat de Mazamet, France, 64-65; teaching asst French, Univ Ill, Urbana, 65-68, instr, 68-69; from instr to asst prof, Univ Tenn, Knoxville, 69-72; asst prof, 72-76, assoc prof & chmn div, 76-81, Prof French & Chmn Europ Lang & Lit, Univ Hawaii, Manoa, 81-, Assoc ed, Fr Contemp Civilization, 75-; Nat Endowment for Humanities fel, Inst Contemporary Fr Cult, 81. **MEMBERSHIPS** Am Asn Teachers Fr. **RESEARCH** French Renaissance; French civilization, stylistics. **SELECTED PUBLICATIONS** Auth, The Thorny Business of Name Genre in Some Special Cases, Fr Rev, Vol 0067, 94. **CONTACT ADDRESS** Dept of European Lang & Lit, Univ of Hawaii, Manoa, 1890 E West Rd, Honolulu, HI 96822-2362. **EMAIL** mustapha@hawaii.edu

BENSKY, ROGER DANIEL
DISCIPLINE FRENCH LITERATURE **EDUCATION** Univ Western Australia, BA, MA; Univ Paris, PhD. **CAREER** Eng Dept, Georgetown Univ **RESEARCH** Modern theater; mysticism. **SELECTED PUBLICATIONS** Auth, pubs on symbolism, thematic of puppetry and contemporary dramatists. **CONTACT ADDRESS** French Dept, Georgetown Univ, 37th and O St, Washington, DC 20057.

BENSON, DOUGLAS KEITH
PERSONAL Born 06/08/1944, Marysville, CA, m, 1965, 2 children **DISCIPLINE** SPANISH LITERATURE & CULTURE **EDUCATION** NMex State Univ, BA, 66; Univ NMex, MA, 68, PhD(Spanish lit), 73. **CAREER** Chmn mod lang, Hastings Col, 69-80; asst prof, 80-82, Assoc Prof Spanish Lang & Lit, Kans State Univ, 82-. **MEMBERSHIPS** Am Asn Teachers of Span & Port. **RESEARCH** Contemporary Spanish poetry (1950-1970); teaching culture in language classrooms; Spanish Amer literature and culture. **SELECTED PUBLICATIONS** **CONTACT ADDRESS** Kansas State Univ, 233 Harvey Dr, Manhattan, KS 66506.

BENSON, MORTON
PERSONAL Born 12/13/1924, Newark, NJ, m, 1955 **DISCIPLINE** RUSSIAN, LEXICOGRAPHY **EDUCATION** NYork Univ, BA, 47; Univ Grenoble, Cert, 48; Univ Pa, PhD(Russ), 54. **CAREER** Asst prof Russ & Ger, Ohio Univ, 54-60; Prof Slavic Lang, Univ PA, 60-, Vis lectr Princeton Univ, 64 & Columbia Univ, 65; mem joint comt East Europ, Am Coun Learned eoc, 71-73. **MEMBERSHIPS** MLA; Am Asn Teachers Slavic & East Europ Lang (pres, 64); Ling Soc Am. **RESEARCH** Russian; Serbocroatian; Slavic linguistics. **SELECTED PUBLICATIONS** Auth, On Russian Names, Russ Ling(s), Vol 0016, 92; A Notes on Russian Orthography, Slavic and E Europ J, Vol 0037, 93; A Supplementary Russian English Dictionary, Slavic and E Europ J, Vol 0037, 93; Encounters With Fugard the 'Blood Knot' in Native of the Karoo, 20th Century Lit, Vol 0039, 93; A Notes on Russian Orthography, Slavic and E Europ J, Vol 0037, 93; Pikes-Peak Vision in the Broadmoor Art Academy, 1919-1945, NMex Hist Rev, Vol 0068, 93; Schoenberg Private Program For the 'String Quartet in D Minor, Op.7', J Musicol, Vol 0011, 93; A Supplementary Russian English Dictionary, Slavic and E Europ J, Vol 0037, 93; Eisenhower, Dwight, D. and the West, J West, Vol 0034, 95; Defining Dictionary of the Russian Language, Slavic and E Europ J, Vol 0039, 95; Defining Dictionary of the Russian Language - Slavic and E Europ J, Vol 0039, 95; Rs-A Concordance to the Dictionaries of Modern Russian, Russ Ling(s), Vol 0019, 95; Art, Hist and Politics in the Former Yugoslavia in An Interview With Benson,Michael, Cineaste, Vol 0022, 96; Retracing Major Long, Stephen ,H. 1820 Expedition in the Itinerary and Botany, Montana-Mag of Western Hist, Vol 0047, 97; Tear Gas and Etiquette A Report on Censorship and Fear at the Seoul Documentary Film and-Video Festival Special Reference to Hinton/Gordon the 'Gate of Heavenly Peace', Sight and Sound, Vol 0007, 97; Market Stalinism Experiences at the 2nd Annual Seoul Documentary Film and Video Festival, Sight and Sound, Vol 0007, 97. **CONTACT ADDRESS** Dept of Slavic Lang, Univ of Pennsylvania, Philadelphia, PA 19104.

BENSON, RENATE
PERSONAL Born, Germany **DISCIPLINE** GERMAN STUDIES **EDUCATION** Univ Cologne, 61-62; Univ Montreal, LL, 65; McGill Univ, PhD, 70. **CAREER** Lectr to Prof, German Studies, Univ Guelph, 67-. **HONORS AND AWARDS** Distinguished Prof Awd, Col Arts, 90. **MEMBERSHIPS** MLA; CAUTG; OATG; Hum Asn. **SELECTED PUBLICATIONS** Auth, Erich Kastner, Studien zu seinem Werk, 73; auth, Aspects of Love in Anne Hebert's Short Stories, in J Can Fiction, 79; auth, German Expressionist Drama: Ernst Toller and Georg Kaiser, 84. **CONTACT ADDRESS** Dept of German Studies, Univ of Guelph, Guelph, ON, Canada N1G 2W1. **EMAIL** rbenson@uoguelph.ca

BENTLEY, ERIC
PERSONAL Born 09/14/1916, England, m, 2 children **DISCIPLINE** DRAMA, COMPARATIVE LITERATURE **EDUCATION** Oxford Univ, BA, 38, BLitt, 39; Yale Univ, PhD, 41. **CAREER** Matthews prof dramatic lit, Columbia Univ, 54-69; Cornell Prof Theatre, State Univ NY Buffalo, 77-82, Guggenheim fel, 48-49 & 67-68; Charles Eliot Norton prof poetry, Harvard Univ, 60-61; ed, Works of Brecht, Grove Press, 60-67; Ford Found artist in residence, Berlin, 64-65. **HONORS AND AWARDS** Longview Awd, 60; George Nathan Prize, 67; Obie, 78; inducted into the Theatre Hall of Fame, New York, 98; dfa, univ wis, 75; dlitt, univ east anglia, uk, 79. **MEMBERSHIPS** Fel Am Acad Arts & Sci; PEN Club; Am Acad of Arts and Letters; **RESEARCH** Literary record albums; poetry and songs. **SELECTED PUBLICATIONS** Auth, The Life of the Drama, 64; The Theatre of Commitment, 67; Theatre of War, 72; The Recantation, 72; Are You Now Or Have You Ever Been, 72; Rallying Cries, Three Plays, New Repub Bks, 77; Lord Alfred's Lover (play), Can Theatre ,Rev, 78; The Brecht Commentaries, Grove Press, 81; auth, The Kleist Variations, 81; auth, Monstrous Martyrdoms, 85; auth, Bentley on Brecht, 98. **CONTACT ADDRESS** 194 Riverside Dr, Ste 4E, New York, NY 10025-7259.

BEREAUD, JACQUES
DISCIPLINE FRENCH **EDUCATION** l'Universite de Lille, PhD, 64. **CAREER** Prof; fac, Cornell Univ, 66-; chemn dept, 81-84 and actg ch, 91-92; dir Educo, Cornell-Duke prog in Paris, 92-93; coordr, Lang Prog, 66-; dir, Undergrad Stud, 84-. **RESEARCH** Pedagogy of foreign language teaching; contemporary French culture and civilization. **SELECTED PUBLICATIONS** Auth, Nouveaux points de vue, by J. Noblitt, DC Heath, 78; Un memoire inedit de Defauconpret Revue du Nord Lille, 65; La traduction en France a l'epoque romantique Comparative Litterature Studies, 71; La chanson francaise depuis mai 1968, Fr Rev, 88; coauth, Appreciations du francais moderne, an advanced integrated French text, Holt, Rinehart and Winston, 72. **CONTACT ADDRESS** Dept of Romance Studies, Cornell Univ, 283 Goldwin Smith Hall, Ithaca, NY 14853. **EMAIL** jb73@cornell.edu

BERG, WILLAIM J.
PERSONAL Born 10/26/1942, Dunkirk, NY, m, 1986, 4 children **DISCIPLINE** FRENCH STUDIES, LANGUAGE, EDUCATION **EDUCATION** Hamilton Col, BA, 64; Princeton Univ, MA, 66; PhD, 69. **CAREER** Asst prof to prof to dept chmn, Univ Wis Madison, 67-. **HONORS AND AWARDS** Vilas Assoc, 91-93; Hon Fel, 94; Malverson Baslom Profshp, 95-00; Excellence Teaching Chancellor's Awd, 95. **MEMBERSHIPS** MLA; ACTFL. **RESEARCH** French literature; literature and painting; technology in teaching. **SELECTED PUBLICATIONS** Co-ed, Poemes, Pieces, Prose, Schofer/ Rice, 73; co-auth, Images, 89; co-auth, Emile Zola Revisited, 92; auth, The Visual Novel, 92; co-auth, Gustave Flaubert, 97; co-auth, Paroles, 99. **CONTACT ADDRESS** For Lang Dept, Univ of Wisconsin, Madison, 750 Van Hise Hall, Madison, WI 53706. **EMAIL** wjberg@facstaff.wisc.edu

BERGEN, JOHN J.
PERSONAL w, 2 children **DISCIPLINE** SPANISH **EDUCATION** St. Bonaventure Univ, BA, 61; Cornell Univ, MA, 63; UCLA, PhD, 71. **CAREER** Teaching Asst to Instructor, Univ Calif, 64-69; Instructor, Nazareth Col, 67-68; Asst Prof to Full Prof, Univ NMex, 69-. **HONORS AND AWARDS** Fel, Cornell Univ, 62. **MEMBERSHIPS** Sigma Delta Phi, Nat Hispanic Honor Soc; Delta Epsilon Sigma, Nat Honor Soc. **RESEARCH** Spanish linguistics (philogy, semantics, sociolinguistics, grammatical theory). **SELECTED PUBLICATIONS** Auth, "The Semantics of Gender Contrasts in Spanish," Hispania, (80): 48-67; ed, Spanish and Portuguese in Social Context, Georgetown Univ Press, 83; auth, "Spanish Language Shift and Maintenance among Albuquerque Police

Officers," in Mexican-American Language: Usage, Attitudes, Maintenance, Instruction and Policy, (Rio Grande, 86), 71-90; auth, "Language Use and Perceived Discrimination: The Case of Spanish speakers at the University of New Mexico," in Mexican-American Spanish in Its Societal and Cultural Contexts, (Rio Grande, 89), 177-188; ed, Spanish in the United States: Sociolinguistic Issues, Georgetown Univ Press, 90. **CONTACT ADDRESS** Dept Spanish & Portuguese, Univ of New Mexico, Albuquerque, 1 Univ Campus, Albuquerque, NM 87131-0001. **EMAIL** jjmbn@unm.edu

BERGEN, ROBERT D.
PERSONAL Born 05/18/1954, Lawrence, KS, m, 1979, 1 child **DISCIPLINE** OLD TESTAMENT, BIBLICAL HEBREW **EDUCATION** Hardin Simmons Univ, BA, 76; Southwestern Baptist Theol Sem, MD, 80, PhD, 86. **CAREER** Assoc Prof of OT and Biblical Lang, 86-98, Hannibal-LaGrange Coll. **MEMBERSHIPS** SBL, ETS, Inst of Biblical Res. **RESEARCH** Discourse Linguistics. **SELECTED PUBLICATIONS** Auth, 1,2 Samuel, New American Commentary, vol 7, 96; 1,2, Samuel, Shepherd's Notes, 98; Ed of Biblical Hebrew and Discourse Linguistics, 94. **CONTACT ADDRESS** Hannibal-LaGrange Col, 2800 Palmyra Rd, Hannibal, MO 63401. **EMAIL** bbergen@hlg.edu

BERGHAHN, KLAUS L.
PERSONAL Born 08/04/1937, Dusseldorf, Germany, m, 1966, 1 child **DISCIPLINE** GERMAN LITERATURE & CULTURE **EDUCATION** Univ Muenster, MA, 63; PhD, 67. **CAREER** From asst prof to prof, Univ Wis at Madison, 67-; dir, Ctr for German and European Studies, 98-. **HONORS AND AWARDS** Dissertation Fel, Stiftung Volkswagen, 65-67; APS, 69 & 73; Inst for Res in the Humanities, 72-73 & 89-94; Romnes Res Fel, 75-80; ZiF, Bielefeld, 80-81; Zinn Fel, 83; Schiller Medal, Jena, 84; ACLS, 85; DAAD Fel, 90 & 99; DAAD/ACLS Coop Grant, 96-97. **MEMBERSHIPS** MLA, AATG, IVG, GSA, Lessing Soc, Herder Soc, Schiller Soc, Goethe Soc, DEGl8J. **RESEARCH** German Literature and Culture Since the Eighteenth-Century, Literary Theory and Criticism Since the Eighteenth-Century, Theory of Genres (drama, poetry), History of Germanistik, Utopian Literature, History of German-Jewish Culture Since the Eighteenth-Century, History of Anti-Semitism. **SELECTED PUBLICATIONS** Auth, The German-Jewish Dialogue--Reconsidered, 96; auth, Grenzen der Toleranz. Juden und Christen in der deutschen Aufklaerung, 00; ed, Fr. Schiller: Ueber die aesthetische Erziehung des Menschen, 00; co-ed, Goethe in German-Jewish Culture, 00. **CONTACT ADDRESS** Dept German, Univ of Wisconsin, Madison, 1220 Linden Dr, 818 Van Hise Hall, Madison, WI 537056-1525. **EMAIL** klbergha@facstaff.wisc.edu

BERGMANN, FRANK
PERSONAL Born 01/20/1941, Markneukirchen, Germany, m, 4 children **DISCIPLINE** AMERICAN & COMPARATIVE LITERATURE **EDUCATION** Univ AR, MA, 66; Eberhard-Karls-Universitaet Tuebingen, GER, DPhil(Am lit), 69. **CAREER** Instr lang, KS Wesleyan Univ, 65-66; Wiss asst Am lit, Am Studies Dept at Tuebingen, WGer, 66-68 & Univ Frankfurt, WGer, 68-69; asst prof English & Ger, 69-73, chm div humanities, 73-76, assoc prof, 73-79, prof English & Ger, Utica Col, Syracuse Univ, 79-, assoc dean for humanities, 91-96, assoc dean for arts and sciences, 96-00, acting dean of the fac, 98; mem, vis comt mod foreign lang & lit, Lehigh Univ, 74-78; member, fac ed comt, Syracuse Univ Press, 94-98; series ed, New York Classics reprints, Syracuse Univ Press, 86-; member, nat screening comt for Fulbright graduate study awards to Germany, 95-96, 99-. **HONORS AND AWARDS** Valedictorian, Neues Gymnasium, Ravensburg, 61; Fulbright scholarship to Hamilton Col, 61-62; Dr Phil, Magna Cum Laude, 69; Distinguished Teaching Awd, Utica Col, 85; Clark Res Awd, Utica Col, 94. **MEMBERSHIPS** ALSC; Cooper Soc; Arthur Miller Soc; MLA; NYSHA. **RESEARCH** American literature 1861-1914; literature of upstate New York; fairy tales and literary fantasy. **SELECTED PUBLICATIONS** Auth, The Worthy Gentleman of Democracy: John William De Forest and the American Dream, Carl Winter Univ, Heidelberg, Ger, 71; Robert Grant, Twayne Publ, 82; ed and auth, Upstate Literature: Essays in Memory of Thomas F O'Donnell, Syracuse Univ Press, 85 (John Ben Snow manuscript prize; certificate of merit, Regional Conference of Hist Agencies, NY State). **CONTACT ADDRESS** Div Arts and Sciences, Utica Col of Syracuse Univ, 1600 Burrstone Rd, Utica, NY 13502-4892. **EMAIL** fbergmann@utica.ucsu.edu

BERGREN, ANN L. T.
DISCIPLINE CLASSICAL PHILOLOGY **EDUCATION** Wellesley Col, BA, 61-65; Univ Iowa, MA, 65-68; Harvard Univ, PhD, 68-73. **CAREER** Tchg fel, Harvard Univ, 71; instr, Wellesley Col, 72; asst prof, Princeton Univ, 72-79; summer vis asst prof, Univ Iowa, 73; vis asst prof, Stanford Univ, 76; vis prof, Harvard Univ, 93; adj prof, South Calif Inst of Arch, 87-; Prof, Class, UCLA, 79-. **HONORS AND AWARDS** Fel(s), Ctr Hellenic Stud, 76-77; Amer Coun of Learned Soc, 84; Chicago Inst for Arch and Urbanism, 89-90; Hum Res Inst, Univ Calif-Irvine, 91; Hon(s) Collegium Fac Recognition award, 86; distinguished tchg award, Univ Calif, LA, 88; award for excellence in the tchg of classics, Amer Philol Assn, 88; ed bd(s), amer philol assn, 80-84; helios, jour of the class assn of the southwestern us, 79-82; univ calif publ in class stud, 83-88. **RESEARCH** Architecture. **SELECTED PUBLICATIONS** Auth, "Letter to Jennifer Bloomer on Architecture and the Feminine," ANY Architecture New York, "Architecture and the Feminine: Mop-Up Work," 94; "The (Re)Marriage of Penelope and Odysseus," Architecture Gender Philosophy, Assemblage, A Critical Jour of Arch and Design Cult 21, 93. **CONTACT ADDRESS** Dept of Classics, Univ of California, Los Angeles, PO Box 951436, Los Angeles, CA 90095-1436.

BERGSTROM, ANNA
PERSONAL Born 03/25/1961, Sweden **DISCIPLINE** FRENCH, FRENCH EDUCATION, SPANISH **EDUCATION** Univ Wis-Madison, BA, 83, MA, 86; Penn State Univ, PhD, 95. **CAREER** Vis lectr, Dept Fr & Ital, Ind Univ, 93-95; ASST PROF, DEPT FOR LANG, LIT, UNIV DEL, 95-. **HONORS AND AWARDS** Mortar Board Outstanding Prof Awd Distinction, 98 **MEMBERSHIPS** Am Asn Appl Ling, Europ Second Lang Acquisition, Am Asn Teachers of Fr, Del Coun on the Teaching of For Lang. **RESEARCH** Appl ling, second lang acquisition, acquisition of temporality. **SELECTED PUBLICATIONS** Auth, L'influence des distinctions aspectuelles sur l'acquisition des temps en francais langue etrangere," Acquisition et Interaction en Langue Etrangere, No. 9; coauth, "Tense and Aspect in SLA and FLL: Learner Narratives in English (SL) and French (FL)," Can Modern Lang Rev, No. 52; review, "Semantique de la temporalite en fracais," The French Reivew, Apr 98. **CONTACT ADDRESS** Dept For Lang & Lit, Univ of Delaware, 326 Smith Hall, Newark, DE 19716. **EMAIL** bergstro@udel.edu

BERKLEY, CONSTANCE E. GRESHAM
PERSONAL Born 11/12/1931, Washington, DC **DISCIPLINE** AFRICAN LITERATURE, ISLAMIC LITERATURE **EDUCATION** Columbia University, BA, 1971, MA, 1972; New York University, Dept of Near Eastern Language & Literature, PhD, 1979. **CAREER** Fordham University, Black Drama, 71-72; Vassar College, literature lecturer, 72-75; Ramapo College, African literature, 76; Fordham Univ, asst prof, African/Afro-American & Islamic literature, starting 79; Vassar College, Studies Program, lecturer of Africana Studies, currently. **HONORS AND AWARDS** One of the founders of the Sudan Studies Assn, 1981; Editor of the SSA Newsletter; Specialist in the literature of the famous Sudanese writer, Tayeb Salih; Invited participant in special tribute to Tayeb Salih at Asilah's 17th Season in Asilah Morocco, 1994; Fulbright Lecturer at Ahfad Univ for Women, Omdurman, Sudan, 1990 **MEMBERSHIPS** Harlem Writer's Guild, 1961-; NEC Dramatists Workshop Affiliate, 1969-; New York State Council of the Arts, lecturer; Intl Poetry Society; Assn Study Afro-American Life & History; Middle Eastern Studies Assn; bd dir, Natl Council of Soviet American Friendship, 1968; African Literature Assn; New York African Studies Assn; contributing editor, American Dialog, 1967; guest lecturer, "Islam in Africa," CBS/NYU Sunrise Semester Program, "1400 Years of Islam," 1980; guest lecturer, New School for Social Research, 1980-81. **SELECTED PUBLICATIONS** Poetry published in several anthologies; auth, Black American Writers Past & Present; auth, Biography of Living Black Writers, Fisk University; numerous articles concerning Sudanese literature. **CONTACT ADDRESS** Program in Africana Studies, Vassar Col, 124 Raymond Ave, Poughkeepsie, NY 12601-6121.

BERKVAM, MICHAEL
DISCIPLINE FRENCH LITERATURE **EDUCATION** Univ Wis, PhD, 73. **CAREER** Assoc prof. **SELECTED PUBLICATIONS** Auth, Correspondence and Collected Papers of Pierre Michel Hennin, 79; pubs on Proust, Sartre; co-auth, Eighteenth-Century Cities: A Panorama. **CONTACT ADDRESS** Dept of French and Italian, Indiana Univ, Bloomington, 1020 E Kirkwood Ave, Ballantine Hall 642, Bloomington, IN 47405. **EMAIL** berkvam@indiana.edu

BERLIN, NETTA
DISCIPLINE LATIN AND GREEK LANGUAGE AND LITERATURE **EDUCATION** Wellesley Col, BA, 84; Univ MI, MA, 88, PhD, 93. **CAREER** Asst prof, 93-, Tulane Univ. **RESEARCH** Epic poetry, mythology, ancient literary criticism. **SELECTED PUBLICATIONS** Auth, War and Remembrance: Aeneid 12.554-60, and Aeneas' Memory of Troy, Amer Jour Philol 119, 98. **CONTACT ADDRESS** Dept of Class Stud, Tulane Univ, 6823 St Charles Ave, New Orleans, LA 70118. **EMAIL** nberlin@mailhost.tcs.tulane.edu

BERNARDO, ALDO SISTO
PERSONAL Born 05/17/1920, Italy, m, 1942, 3 children **DISCIPLINE** ROMANCE PHILOLOGY **EDUCATION** Brown Univ, AM, 47; Harvard Univ, PhD, 50. **CAREER** Instr French and Ital, Triple Cities Col, Syracuse, 49-50; from asst prof to assoc prof Romance lang, State Univ NY Binghamton, 50-58, prof Ital, 58-73, chmn humanities div, 59-73, founder and co-dir ctr medieval and early Renaissance studies, 66-73; pres, Verrazzano Col, 73-75; Prof Ital and Comp Lit, State Univ NY Binghamton, 75-, Fulbright res grant, Rome, 55-56; Am Coun Learned Soc res grant, 58; Guggenheim fel, 64-65; mem nat screening comt, Fulbright-Hays Act, Italy and Greece, 66-67; chmn univ awards comt, Res Found State Univ NY, 68-; sr fel, chair, Int Comm to commemorate 600th anniversary of Petrarcg' death: chaired Petrarch Congress "Petrarch, Citizen of the World," Folger library, Washington, 74, Ctr Medieval and Early Renaissance Studies, State Univ NY Binghamton, 75-; distinguished serv prof, 79-; Nat Endowment for Humanities transl grant, 79-80; Wilber Found translation grant, 84. **HONORS AND AWARDS** Hon Mem of Academia Arcadia, Rome, 74. **MEMBERSHIPS** MLA; Am Asn Teachers Ital; Mediaeval Acad Am; Dante Soc Am. **RESEARCH** Computer-aided translations; Petrarch; mediaeval esthetics. **SELECTED PUBLICATIONS** Auth, Petrarch, Scipio and the "Africa," Johns Hopkins, 62; auth, "Petrarch, Laura and the "Triumphs," SUNY Press, 74; auth, Petrarch, Letters on Familiar Matters, Translation of Bks 1-8, SUNY Press, 75; ed, Petrarch, Citizen of the World, SUNY Press, 81; auth, Petrarch, Letters on Familiar Matters, Trans of Bks 9-16, Johns Hopkins, 82; auth, Petrarch, Letters on Familiar Matters, Trans of Bks 17-24, Johns Hopkins, 92; auth, A Concordance to the "Familiares" of F. Petrarca, 2 vols, Antenore, 94. **CONTACT ADDRESS** Dept of Romance Lang, SUNY, Binghamton, Binghamton, NY 13901. **EMAIL** Bernie@Binghamton.edu

BERND, CLIFFORD ALBRECHT
PERSONAL Born 05/14/1929, Bronxville, NY, m, 1972, 2 children **DISCIPLINE** GERMAN LITERATURE **EDUCATION** NYork Univ, BA, 50; Univ Md, MFS, 52; Univ Heidelberg, PhD , 58. **CAREER** From instr to asst prof Ger, Princeton Univ, 58-64; assoc prof, 64-68, chmn dept, 65-76, Prof Ger, Univ Calif, Davis, 68-, German Foreign Off Exchange fel, 54-56; rev ed, German Quart, 64-68; Ed Bd, German Quart, 88-94; Am Philos Soc Grant, 65; Humanities Inst awards, Univ Calif, 66 and 71; Fulbright res scholar, Kiel, Ger, 68-69; Fritz Thyssen Found fel, 72; vis fel Ger lit, Univ Leicester, 77. **MEMBERSHIPS** MLA; AATG; Grill parzer Ges; Int Fed Mod Lang and Lit; Schiller Ges; Goethe Ges; Kleist Ges; Holderlin Ges; corresp mem Storm Ges. **RESEARCH** German literature of the 17th, 18th and 19th centuries. **SELECTED PUBLICATIONS** Auth, Theodor Storm's Craft of Fiction, Univ NC, 66; ed, T. Storm and P. Heype Correspondence, 3 vols, Schmidt, Berlin, 69-74; auth, German Poetic Realism, Twayne, 81; coed, Goethe Proceedings, Camden House 84; auth, Romanticism and Beyond: Festschrift for John F. Fetzer, Lang, New York; auth, Grillparzer's Der arme Spielmann: New Directions in Criticism, Camden House, 88; auth, Elfriede Stutz Fruhe deutsche Novellenkunst, Kummerle, Goppingen 91; auth, Poetic Realism in Scandinavia and Central Europe 1820-1895, Camden House, Columbia, SC, 95; **CONTACT ADDRESS** Dept of Ger, Univ of California, Davis, Davis, CA 95616-5200.

BERNINGHAUSEN, JOHN
DISCIPLINE CHINESE **EDUCATION** Univ Minn, BA, 65; Stanford Univ, MA, 68, PhD, 80. **CAREER** Charles A. Dana prof & dept chem; spec lang training, Mandarin Training Ctr, Taipei, 63; CIC Far Eastern Lang Inst, Ohio State Univ, 65; Inter-Univ Prog, Taipei, 65-66; CIC Far Eastern Lang Inst, Ind Univ, 69; Inter-Univ Prog, Taipei, 70-71; dean, Middlebury Chinese Sch, 88-94; chem, Div For Lang, Middlebury Col, 91-94; actg dir, Lang Sch, Middlebury Col, 90-91; chem, Div For Lang, Middlebury Col, 81-86; co-founder & 1st chem, interdisciplinary major in East Asian Stud, 79-84; established a Chinese lang prog, Middlebury Col, 76-; dir, Chinese Lang Prog, Univ Vermont, 73-76, founded the UVM Chinese Prog, full-time instr; Engl Lang Tchr, Extramural Prog, Chinese Unive Hong Kong, 71-72. **MEMBERSHIPS** Asn Asian Stud; Chinese Lang Teachers Asn & Nat Asn Scholars. **SELECTED PUBLICATIONS** Auth, A Great Leap Backward, Middlebury Col Mag, 89; Modern Chinese Short Stories, ITEMS, joure Soc Sci Res and Coun, 83; coauth, Chinese Breakthrough, Cheng and Tsui Co, Boston, 95; transl, Literature and Life, Stanford UP, 96; 3 dissident 1979 short stories, Locks, Cats, & Fire, under the title of Three Professors, 84; We Must Still Prepare for a Long and Determined Struggle, A 1949 speech in commemoration of the 30th anniversary of the May Fourth Movement by Mao Dun, in Lit in Revolutionary China, 80. **CONTACT ADDRESS** Dept of Chinese, Middlebury Col, Middlebury, VT 05753.

BERNSTEIN, CAROL L.
PERSONAL Born 02/09/1933, New York, NY, m, 1955, 4 children **DISCIPLINE** ENGLISH, COMPARATIVE LITERATURE **EDUCATION** Swarthmore Col, BA, 54; Yale Univ, MA, 56, PhD(English), 61 **CAREER** Instr English, Hebrew Univ, Israel, 57-58; lectr, Albertus Magnus Col, 65; vis lectr English & Am lit Hebrew Univ, Israel, 65-66; lectr English, Univ Pa, 67-69, asst prof, 69-74; lectr, 74-76, assoc prof, 76-90, Prof English, Bryn Mawr Col, 90-, Prof Comp Lit, 93-. **HONORS AND AWARDS** Phi Beta Kappa; Ford and Pew Found grants; NEH summer stipend; Fairbank Prof Humanitities, 92-97; Mary E Garrett Alumnae Prof English, 97-. **MEMBERSHIPS** MLA; ACLA **RESEARCH** Nineteenth and twentieth century literature; narrative theory; Walter Benjamin and theories of the sublime; psychoanalyic theory and literary criticism; cultural memory. **SELECTED PUBLICATIONS** Auth, Precarious Enchantment: A Reading of Meredith's Poetry, Cath Univ Am Press, 79; The Celebration of Scandal: Toward the Sublime in Victorian Urban Fiction, Penn State Univ Press, 91. **CONTACT ADDRESS** Dept of English, Bryn Mawr Col, 101

N Merion Ave, Bryn Mawr, PA 19010-2899. **EMAIL** cbernste@brynmawr.edu

BERNSTEIN, ECKHARD RICHARD
PERSONAL Born 08/05/1938, Grimma, Germany, m, 1965, 2 children **DISCIPLINE** GERMAN & COMPARATIVE LITERATURE **EDUCATION** Univ Marburg, Staatsexamen, 65, Assessorexamen, 68; Case Western Reserve Univ, PhD(comp lit), 71. **CAREER** Instr English lit, Youngstown Univ, 65-66; instr Ger lit, Lake Erie Col, 66-67; teaching asst English & Latin, Kirchain Sch, Ger, 67-68; from instr to asst prof, 70-74, assoc prof, 74-81, prof Ger Lit, Col of the Holy Cross, 81-. **MEMBERSHIPS** Am Asn Teachers Ger; Renaissance Soc of Am; Pirckheimer Gesellschaft; Gutenberg Gesellschaft. **RESEARCH** German Renaissance and Baroque literature; reception of antiquity; East German literature; German resistance to Hitler. **SELECTED PUBLICATIONS** Auth, Thomas Murner's Latin: Some Notes on the First German Aeneid, Class Folia, 72; Die Erste Deutsche Aeneis, Anton Hain, Meisenhaim, Ger, 74; From Struwwelpeter to Rotfuchs: Suggestions for Using Children's Books in Culture Classes, Unterrichtspraxis, 76; Daniel Symonis Aneis - ubersetzung, Daphnis, 78; Die Literatur des Fruhhumanismus, Metzler Verlag, Stuttgart, 78; German Humanism, Twayne Publ, 83; Ulrich von Hutten, 88; Hans Sachs, 94. **CONTACT ADDRESS** Dept of Mod Langs, Col of the Holy Cross, 1 College St, Worcester, MA 01610-2322. **EMAIL** ebernste@holycross.edu

BERNSTEIN, MARK H.
PERSONAL Born 03/19/1948, New York, NY, s **DISCIPLINE** CLASSICS, PHILOSOPHY **EDUCATION** CUNY, 69; Univ Calif, Santa Barbara, PhD, 82. **CAREER** Cis Asst Prof, Wesleyan Univ, 82-83; From Asst Prof to Prof, Univ Tex, 83-. **HONORS AND AWARDS** 2 NEH Fels, Res Develop Awd. **MEMBERSHIPS** APA, SSPP **RESEARCH** Applied ethics, animal ethics, metaphysics, free will. **SELECTED PUBLICATIONS** Auth, Fatalism, Univ Nebr Pr, 92; auth, On Moral Considerability, Oxford UP, 98. **CONTACT ADDRESS** Dept Classics & Philos, Univ of Texas, San Antonio, 6900 N Loop 1604 W, San Antonio, TX 78249-1130. **EMAIL** markb@10.com

BERROA, REI
PERSONAL Born 03/11/1949, Dominican Republic, s **DISCIPLINE** SPANISH **EDUCATION** Universidad Catolica de Puerto Rico, BA, 70; Middlebury Col, MA, 77; Univ Pittsburgh, MA, 80; PhD, 83. **CAREER** Asst prof to assoc prof, George Mason Univ, 84-. **HONORS AND AWARDS** Leadershp Awd, Fundacion Juan Pablo Duarte, Dominican Republic, 77; Man of the Year, Cambriiiiridge, 93; International Who's Who and Poets' Encyclopaedia, Cambridge, 93; Hispanic of the Month, Washington, 87; summer grant, Revista Iberoamericana, 86. **MEMBERSHIPS** Mod Lang Asn, Instituto Intl de Lit Iberoamericana, Acad Iberoamericana de Poesia, Am Biographical Inst, Teatro de la Luna, N Va Woodburn Center for the Mentally ill, Coun for the Arts Grants on Music and Educ. **RESEARCH** Contemporary European and Latin American discourse, The interrelation of the arts, especially as they connect to poetry, Rhetoric and ideology in modernity and postmodernity, especially in the relationship between history, literature and philosophy. **SELECTED PUBLICATIONS** Auth, Sobre literatura dominicana, Santo Domingo, (forthcoming); auth, "Al tercer dia el poeta subio a los cielos: Garcia Lorca cumple 100 anos," Umbral, (98): 11-18; auth, "Exilio e identidad: entrevista con Rei Berros," Horizonte, (96): 3-5; auth, "Formacion y transformaciondel heroe hernandian," Iin Miguel Hernandez, cincuenta anos despues, , (93): 411-424; auth, "Vivir del cuento (Entrvista)," El Siglo, (92): 17; auth, "Poetry and Painting: Garcia Lorca's Dual Manifestation of Symbol and Metaphor, Lorca's Legacy, (91): 30-50; auth, "La palabra y los demonis poeticos de Fernando Arbelaez," in Texto Critico, (90): 33-44; auth, "Notas y vinetas de mis andanzas," in Isla Abierta, (90): 5-10; auth, Poesia y pintura: La manifestacion dual de simbolo y metafora en la imaginacion lorquiana," Mundaiz, (89): 27-59; auth, auth, "La critica de Fuentes como lectura conflictiva: De Fuentes, a Espana, A Cervantes," Testo Critico, (88): 44-53. **CONTACT ADDRESS** Dept Mod & Classical Lang, George Mason Univ, Fairfax, 4400 Univ Dr, Fairfax, VA 22030-4422. **EMAIL** rberroa@gmu.edu

BERRONG, RICHARD
PERSONAL Born 09/29/1951, Milwaukee, WI, s **DISCIPLINE** FRENCH **EDUCATION** Univ of Va, BA, 73; Stanford Univ, MA, 74; Cornell Univ, PhD, 77. **CAREER** Asst prof, Univ Louisville, 77-81; vis asst prof, Univ Nebr, 84-85; asst prof to prof, Kent State Univ, 85-. **HONORS AND AWARDS** Mellon Fel, Case W Res Univ, 82-84. **MEMBERSHIPS** MLA; NEMCA. **RESEARCH** Francois Rabelais, nineteenth century French literature, sixteenth century French literature, Pierre Loti, French gay literature. **SELECTED PUBLICATIONS** Auth, "Every Man for Himself: Social Order and Its Dissolution in Rabelais", Stanford French and Italian Studies 38, (Saratoga: Anma Libri, 85); auth, Rabelais and Bakhtin: Popular Culture in "Gargantua and Pantagruel", Univ of Nebr Pr, (Lincoln) 86; auth, "Changing Depictions of Popular Revolt in Sixteenth-Century England: The Case of Sidney's Two Arcadias", The Jour of Medieval and Renaissance Studies 19, (89):15-33; auth, "Changing Attitudes Toward Material Wealth in Sidney's Arcadias", Sixteenth Century Jour 22, (91):331-49; auth, The Politics of Opera in Turn-of-the-Century Italy, as seen through the letters of Alfredo Catalani, Edwin Mellen Pr, (Lewiston) 92; auth, "Turandot as Political Fable", the Opera Quarterly 11, (95):65-75; auth, Grammar and Translation for the Italian Libretto, NY Excalibur Pub Inc, 96; auth, "Different Contexts, Different Sexualities: A Gay Reading of Loti's Pecheur d'Islande", Dalhousie French Studies 44, (98):65-80; auth, "Portraying Male Same-Sex Desire in Nineteenth Century French Literature: Pierre Loti's Aziyade", Col Lit 25, (98):91-108. **CONTACT ADDRESS** Dept Mod Class Lang, Kent State Univ, 2452 Victoria Parkway, Hudson, OH 44236. **EMAIL** rberrong@kent.edu

BERRY, MARGARET
PERSONAL Born Greensboro, NC **DISCIPLINE** ENGLISH, SOUTH ASIAN STUDIES **EDUCATION** St Joseph Col, BA, 44; Cath Univ, Am, MA, 50; St Johns Univ, NYork, PhD (English), 56; Univ Pa, MA, 68. **CAREER** From instr to assoc prof English, St Joseph Col, 54-65; Assoc Prof English, John Carroll Univ, 65-, Ford Found Asian studies grant, 63-64; NDEA fel S Asia studies, 67-68; Danforth assoc, 72; vis res scholar, Univ Mysore, fall 73; vis lectr, Univ Madurai, fall 73; fac fel, John Carroll Univ, 73. **MEMBERSHIPS** Asn Asian Studies; AAUP. **RESEARCH** Literary criticism of the English Catholic revival; Indian fiction in English. **SELECTED PUBLICATIONS CONTACT ADDRESS** Dept of English, John Carroll Univ, 20700 N Park Blvd, Cleveland, OH 44118.

BERS, VICTOR
PERSONAL Born 08/30/1944, Providence, RI, m, 1966, 2 children **DISCIPLINE** CLASSICS **EDUCATION** Chicago Univ, AB, 66; Oxford Univ, BA, 68; Harvard Univ, PhD, 72. **CAREER** Lectr to prof, 72-, Yale Univ. **MEMBERSHIPS** APA **RESEARCH** Greek literature, especially tragedy; Greek stylistics. **SELECTED PUBLICATIONS** Auth, Enallage and Greek Style, Leiden, 74; auth, Greek Poetic Syntax in the Classical Age, New Haven, 84; auth, Speech in Speech: Studies in Incorporated Oration Recta in Attic Drama and Oratory, Langham, MD, 97. **CONTACT ADDRESS** Dept of Classics, Yale Univ, Box 8266, New Haven, CT 06520-8266. **EMAIL** victor.bers@yale.edu

BERTHOFF, ANN EVANS
PERSONAL Born 02/13/1924, New York, NY, m, 1949, 2 children **DISCIPLINE** ENGLISH, SEMIOTICS **EDUCATION** Cornell Col, Iowa, AB, 45; Radcliffe Col, AM, 48. **CAREER** Instr English, Bradford Jr Col, 48-51, Bryn Mawr Col, 51-62 and Haverford Col, 63-65; lectr, Swarthmore Col, 65-67; assoc prof, 70-78, Prof English, Univ Mass, Boston, 78-87, prof emer, 88; Mem, NCTE Comn on Compos, 78-81; consult, WNET/Channel 13, 79- and Bread Loaf Sch English, 80; dir, Nat Endowment for Humanities Summer Sem, 80. **HONORS AND AWARDS** Randolph Vis Distinguished Prof, Vassar Col, 89-90; Exemplar CCCC, 98. **MEMBERSHIPS** NCTE; Conf Col Compos and Commun; Col English Asn; New England Col English Asn (pres, 77-78); MLA. **RESEARCH** English pedagogy; philosophy of language; Renaissance poetry. **SELECTED PUBLICATIONS** Auth, The Resolved Soul: A Study of Marvell's Major Poems, Princeton Univ Press, 70; auth, " Remembering Paulo Freire," Journal of Advanced Composition, 17. 87; ed, Richards on Rhetoric, Oxford Univ Press, 91; auth, " Walker Percy's Castaway," Sewanee Rev, Vol 0102, 94; auth, " A Semiotic Journey Across the Field of Geist," Semiotica, 119-3/4, 98; auth, The Mysterious Barricades: Language and Its Limits, Univ of Toronto Press, 99; auth, " Reclaming the Active Mind," College English, Vol61, 99; auth, " Susanne K Langer and 'the odyssey of the mind,' Seminotica, 128-1/2,00. **CONTACT ADDRESS** 14 Thoreau St, Concord, MA 01742.

BERTMAN, STEPHEN
PERSONAL Born 07/20/1937, New York, NY, m, 1968, 2 children **DISCIPLINE** CLASSICS **EDUCATION** NYork Univ, BA, 59; Brandeis Univ, MA, 60; Columbia, PhD, 65. **CAREER** Asst prof, Fla State Univ, 63-67; Prof, Univ Windsor, 67-. **HONORS AND AWARDS** Phi Beta Kappa; Eta Sigma Phi; Alumni Awd Exc, Univ Teaching, Univ Windsor. **MEMBERSHIPS** Amer Philol Asn; Archaeol Inst Amer; Class Asn Mid W & S; World Future Soc; Soc Psychol Study Soc Issues. **RESEARCH** The impact of time and speed on cultural values and memory. **SELECTED PUBLICATIONS** auth, Art and the Romans, 75; The Conflict of Generations in Ancient Greece and Rome, 76; Doorways Through Time: The Romance of Archaeology, 86; Hyperculture: The Human Cost of Speed, 98; Cultural Amnesia: America's Future and the Crisis of Memory, 00. **CONTACT ADDRESS** 5459 Piccadilly Circle N, West Bloomfield, MI 48322.

BERTRAND DE MUNOZ, MARYSE
PERSONAL Born Montreal, PQ, Canada **DISCIPLINE** SPANISH LITERATURE **EDUCATION** MA (litterature espagnole), 59; LL (litterature et langues modernes) 59; Dipl del Inst de Cultura Hispanica, 60; Univ Paris, PhD, 62. **CAREER** PROF TITULAIRE DE LITTERATURE, ESPAGNOLE, UNIV MONTREAL. **MEMBERSHIPS** Asn Can Hispanists (pres, 94-96); Am Asn Tchrs Span Port; Asn Espanola de Semiotica; Asn Int Hispanistas; Asn Int Semiotica; Asn docteurs Univ Paris; Asn diplomes Univ Montreal. **SELECTED PUBLICATIONS** Auth, La guerra civile espagnole et la litterature francaise, 72; auth, La guerra civil espanola en la novela, 82, 87; auth, La comena de Camelo Jose Cela, 89; auth, La novela europea y americana y la guerra civil espanola, 94; auth, La guerra civil espanola y la literatura francesca, 95. **CONTACT ADDRESS** Dept of literature, Univ of Montreal, CP 6128, Succ Centre Ville, Montreal, QC, Canada H3C 3J7. **EMAIL** bertdmun@magellan.umontreal.ca

BERWALD, JEAN-PIERRE
PERSONAL Born 05/10/1935, Antwerp, BEL, Belgium, w, 1958, 2 children **DISCIPLINE** FRENCH LITERATURE **EDUCATION** OH State Univ, PhD. **CAREER** Tchr, Univ MA Amherst. **HONORS AND AWARDS** ACTFL, Nelson Brooks Award for Cultural Teaching, 91; MaFLA, Distinguished Service Award, 97. **MEMBERSHIPS** Am Assoc of Teachers of French, Massachusetss foreign Language Assn; ACTFL. **SELECTED PUBLICATIONS** Auth, Au Courant: Teaching French with the Mass Media. **CONTACT ADDRESS** Dept of French and Italian Studies, Univ of Massachusetts, Amherst, Amherst Mass Ave, Amherst, MA 01003. **EMAIL** berwald@frital.umass.edu

BESSETTE, GERARD
PERSONAL Born 02/25/1920, Sabrevois, Canada **DISCIPLINE** FRENCH **EDUCATION** External Classique St Croix, BA, 41; Univ Montreal, MA, 46, LittD, 50, Univ Ottawa, 82. **CAREER** From instr to asst prof French, Univ Sask, 46-51; asst prof, Duquesne Univ, 51-60; from asst prof to assoc prof, 60-79, Prof French, Queen's Univ, Ont, 79-, Can rep, poetry sect, Olympic Games, 48. **HONORS AND AWARDS** Prix Litteraire de la Prov de Que, 65; Prix du Gov General, 66 and 72; Prix Athanase David, 80. **MEMBERSHIPS** Royal Soc Can; Sov Ecrivains Can. **RESEARCH** French and French Canadian literature. **SELECTED PUBLICATIONS** Auth, The Conversion, Queens Quart, Vol 0100, 93. **CONTACT ADDRESS** Dept of French, Queens Col, CUNY, Kingston, ON, Canada K7L 3N6.

BEST, JANICE
DISCIPLINE FRENCH LITERATURE **EDUCATION** Univ Strasbourg, PhD. **CAREER** French Prof, Acadia, 84-. **HONORS AND AWARDS** Soc Sci and Hum Res Coun of Canada, Grant, SSHRC, Grant. **MEMBERSHIPS** APFUCC **RESEARCH** Nineteenth century literature **SELECTED PUBLICATIONS** Auth, Adaptation et experimentation: essai sur la methode experimentale d'Emile Zola, Jose Corti, 86; Lieux de rencontre et d'intrigue; Moralite, politique et dialogisme. **CONTACT ADDRESS** Acadia Univ, Wolfville, NS, Canada B0P 1XO. **EMAIL** janice.best@acadiau.ca

BEST, OTTO FERDINAND
PERSONAL Born 07/28/1929, Steinheim, Germany, m, 4 children **DISCIPLINE** GERMAN LITERATURE **EDUCATION** Univ Munich, PhD, 63. **CAREER** Asst, Col Hippolyte Fontaine, DiJon, France, 52-53; ed, Insel Verlag, S Fischer Verlag, Verlag Kiepenheuer and Witscher, R Piper and Co, 54-68; lectr Ger philol, Univ Munich, 65-68; prof Ger, Univ NDak, 68-69; assoc prof, 69-71, Prof Ger, Unix MD, College Park, 71-. **MEMBERSHIPS** MLA; AAUP; Am Asn Teachers Ger; Lessing Soc. **RESEARCH** European literature of the 18th century; European literature of the 20th century; European philosophy. **SELECTED PUBLICATIONS** Auth, The Fin De Siecle Culture of Adolescence, J Engl Germ Philol, Vol 0095, 96. **CONTACT ADDRESS** Dept of Ger and Slavic Lang and Lit, Univ of Maryland, Col Park, College Park, MD 20742-0001.

BETHIN, CHRISTINA Y.
DISCIPLINE SLAVIC LINGUISTICS **EDUCATION** Univ Roch, BA, 72; Univ Ill, Urbana-Champaign, MA, 74, PhD, 78. **CAREER** Lectr, Univ Va, 78-79; asst, 79-85, assoc 85-95, chair, dept Ger, Slav langs & lits, 94-97, PROF, 95-, SUNY, STONY BROOK. **HONORS AND AWARDS** NEH Sr Fel, 88-89; 93-94; AATSEEL bk Award, 95, 98; Chancellor's Award for Excellence in Teaching. **RESEARCH** Slavic phonology. **SELECTED PUBLICATIONS** Auth, Polish Syllables, Slavica, 92; auth, "Journal of Slavic Linguistics," 93; auth, "Slavic Prosody," Cambridge, 98; auth, "Die Welt der Slaven," 94. **CONTACT ADDRESS** Dept of Lings, SUNY, Stony Brook, Stony Brook, NY 11794-4376. **EMAIL** christina.bethin@sunysb.edu

BETLYON, JOHN WILSON
PERSONAL Born 05/05/1949, York, PA, m, 9 children **DISCIPLINE** NEAR EASTERN LANGUAGES AND CIVILIZATIONS **EDUCATION** Bucknell Univ, AB (cum laude), 71; Harvard Univ, MTS, 73, PhD, 78. **CAREER** Asst prof, Relig, NC Wesleyan Col, 78-80; Campus minister, Lycoming Col, 80-81; Chaplain & assoc prof, Relig, Smith Col, 81-89; Chaplain, US Army, 89-92; Chaplain & assoc prof, Univ North FL & Jacksonville Univ, 92-95; lect, PA State Univ, 95-. **MEMBERSHIPS** SBL; ASOR. **RESEARCH** Persian Period history and religion. **SELECTED PUBLICATIONS** Auth, Coins, Commerce, and Politics: Coins from the Limes Arabicus Project,

1976-1985, in The Roman Frontier in Central Jordan: Interim Report of the Limes Arabicus Project, 1980-1985, S Thomas Parker, ed, British Archaeological Reports Int Series 340, part ii, Oxford British Archaeological Reports, 87; Archaeological Evidence of Military Operations in Southern Judah during the Early Hellenistic Period, The Biblical Archaeologist, 91; Canaanite Myth and the Early Coinage of the Phonecian City-States, in Ancient Economy in Mythology: East and West, Morris Silver, ed, Rowman & Littlefield, 91; Coinage, in Anchor Bible Dictionary, vol 1, D N Freedman, ed, Doubleday, 92; Money, in HarperCollins Bible Dictionary, rev ed, P J Achtemeier, ed, Harper, 96; many other publications. **CONTACT ADDRESS** 1243 Haymaker Rd, State College, PA 16801. **EMAIL** jwb14@psu.edu

BETT, RICHARD
PERSONAL Born 06/10/1957, London, England, m, 1986 **DISCIPLINE** CLASSICS AND PHILOSOPHY **EDUCATION** Oxford Univ, BA, 80; UC Berkley, PhD, 86. **CAREER** Asst Prof, Univ TX at Arlington, 86-91; Asst Prof, Johns Hopkins Univ, 00; 91-94; Assoc Prof, 94-, Sec Appt in Classics, 96-; Acting Exec Dir, APA, 00; Prof, 00-. **HONORS AND AWARDS** Fel Center for Hellenic Stud, Washington DC 94-95. **MEMBERSHIPS** APA; Soc for Ancient Greek Phil; North Amer Nietzsche Soc **RESEARCH** Ancient Greek philosophy, especially Greek skepticism. **SELECTED PUBLICATIONS** Art, Scepticism and Everyday Attitudes in Ancient and Modern Philosophy, Metaphilosophy, 93; art, What Did Pyrrho Think about the Nature of the Divine and the Good, Phronesis, 94; art, Aristocleson Timon on Pyrrho the Text it Logic and its Credibility, Oxford Stud in Ancient Phil, 94; auth, Sextus Against the Ethicists Scepticism, Relativisim or Both, Apeiron, 94; art, Hellenistic Essays Translated, Papers in Hellenistic Phil, 96; Entries in Encyl of Class Philos, 97; auth, Sextus Empiricus, Against the Ethicists (Adversus Mathematicos XI): Introduction, Translation and Commentary, (Oxford: Clarendon Press, 97); auth, Pyrrho, his Antecedents and his Legacy (Oxford: Clarendon Press) forthcoming. **CONTACT ADDRESS** Dept of Philosophy, Johns Hopkins Univ, Baltimore, Gilman Hall, Baltimore, MD 21218-2890. **EMAIL** bett_r@jhunix.hcf.jhu.edu

BETZ, DOROTHY
DISCIPLINE FRENCH LITERATURE **EDUCATION** Cornell Univ, MA, PhD. **CAREER** Prof. **RESEARCH** Nineteenth century French poetry. **SELECTED PUBLICATIONS** Auth, Chateaubriand's Itineraire and the Profits of Tourism; Vicor Hugo, Juliette Drouet and an Unpublished Anniversary Letter from 1851; Baudelaire, Swinburne and the Legacy of Greece. **CONTACT ADDRESS** French Dept, Georgetown Univ, 37th and O St, Washington, DC 20057.

BETZ, FREDERICK
PERSONAL Born 06/29/1943, New York, NY, m, 1970 **DISCIPLINE** GERMAN LANGUAGE & LITERATURE **EDUCATION** Columbia Univ, BA, 64; Ind Univ, MA, 67, PhD(Ger Comp Lit), 73. **CAREER** Instr Ger, Univ Ill, Chicago Circle, 69-72; asst prof, Univ Maine, Orono, 74-78; asst prof, 78-80, from assoc prof to prof, 80-86 Ger, Southern Ill Univ, Carbondale; dept chmn, 99-. **HONORS AND AWARDS** SIU Library Delta Awd 90 for scholarly contribs to Ger Lit. **MEMBERSHIPS** MLA; Am Asn Teachers Ger; Mencken Society, Sinclair Lewis Society. **RESEARCH** Theodor Fontane; H. L. Mencken; Sinclair Lewis; 19th and 20th century Ger and Am lit and journalism. **SELECTED PUBLICATIONS** Auth, Der Zug nach dem Westen: Aspects of Paul Lindau's Berlin Novel, Sherwood Nottingham, 79; ed, Erlauterumngen und Dokumente zu fontanes Irrungen, Wirrungen, reclam Stuttgart, 79; auth, Fontane Scholarship, Lieterary Sociology, and Trivialliteraturforschung, Internationales Archiv fur Sozialgeschichte dr deutschen Literatur, 83; auth, Zur Rezeption deutscher realisten des 19, Jahrhunderts in den USA, Fontane Blatter, 92; auth, Mencken and the Patrioteers: On the Hist of word, Menckeniana, 92-93; ed, Erlauterungen und Dokumente zu Heinrich Manns "Der Untertan", Reclam Stuttgart, 93; auth, What's in a Name?: Characterization and Caricature in Dorothy Thompson Criticism, Couirer, 96; auth, Sinclair Lewis's Cautionary Tale "It Can't Happen Here" 1935 Against the Socio-Political Background in Ger and the USA in the 1930's, Orbis Litterarum, 97; auth, A German Main Street and More: Heinrich Mann's Der , Untertan 1918 and sinclair Lewis's Satirical Novels of the 1920's, MidAm, 99; auth, Here is the story the Movies Dared not Make: The Contemporary Context and Receptioon strategies of the New York Post's Serialization 1936 of "It can't Happen Here" 1935, Midwestern Miscellany, 01. **CONTACT ADDRESS** Dept of Foreign Lang & Lit, So Illinois Univ, Carbondale, Carbondale, IL 62901. **EMAIL** fbtz@aol.com/fbetz@siu.edu

BEVINGTON, GARY
PERSONAL Born 02/03/1944, Ft Madison, IA, m, 1981, 2 children **DISCIPLINE** LINGUISTICS **EDUCATION** Middlebury Col, AB, 66, MA, 67; Univ Mass, Amherst, PhD, 70. **CAREER** Asst prof, Univ Mass, Amherst, 70-71; asst prof, Northeastern Ill Univ, 71-75, assoc prof, 75-80, prof, 80-99, Prof Emeritus, 99-. **HONORS AND AWARDS** Alexander-von-Humboldt Res Fel, Univ Munich, 75; NEH Summer Fels: Univ Mass, 81, Univ Ill, 89, Newberry Library, 90; Fulbright Sr Lectr, Univ of Jeno, Germany, 91. **MEMBERSHIPS** Scholar-in-residence, The Newberry Library, 94-. **RESEARCH** American Indian linguistics: Maya, Lakota; language and culture; Balkan linguistics: Albanian; Germanic linguistics. **SELECTED PUBLICATIONS** Auth, Maya for Travelers and Students: A Guide Language and Culture in Yucatan, Univ Tex Press (95); auth, Where Do Words Come From? An Introduction to Etymology, Kendall-Hunt (95); auth of articles in The Encyclopedia of the World's Major Languages: Albanian, Maya, H. Holt & Co (2000). **CONTACT ADDRESS** Dept Linguistics, Northeastern Illinois Univ, 5500 N Saint Louis Ave, Chicago, IL 60625-4679. **EMAIL** G-Bevington@neiu.edu

BEYNEN, GIJSBERTUS (BERT) KOOLEMANS
PERSONAL Born 06/12/1935, Surabaya, Indonesia, m, 1982, 6 children **DISCIPLINE** LINGUISTICS **EDUCATION** Candidate Degree in Law and Slavic Languages, 57 and 59, Leiden Univ; State Univ New York Col at Geneseo, MS, 74; Stanford Univ, PhD, 67. **CAREER** Asst Prof, 63-66, Emporia State Univ; Asst Prof, 66-69, Fordham Univ; Asst Prof, 69-73, Univ Rochester, NY; Interviewer, 83, Univ Chicago and Natl Opinion Research Ctr; Visiting Asst Prof, 83, Kent State Univ; Part-time Asst Prof, 85-88, Ohio Wesleyan Univ; Assoc Prof, 74-88, Univ Libraries, Ohio State Univ; Prof and Chr Designate, 88-91, Univ South Africa; Temp Asst Prof, 92-94, Iowa State Univ; Librarian, 97-98, Newton Correctional Facility; Adjunct Faculty Mem, 98-, Mercy Col of Health Sciences. **HONORS AND AWARDS** UNESCO Scholarship at Novi Sad Univ, 59; UNESCO Scholarship at Warsaw Univ, 61; IREX Exchange Fel at LMSU, 71-72; IREX Summer Grant for Study in Bulgaria, 76; Natl Endowment for the Humanities Translation Grant, 81-82; Midwest Universities Consortium for Intl Activities Exchange Scholarship at LMSU, 81-82; Summer Teachers Exchange Scholarship at Lomonosov Moscow State Univ (LMSU). **RESEARCH** Shota Rustaveli; Bantu linguistics; folklore **SELECTED PUBLICATIONS** Auth, The Slavic Oedipus Tales, in American Contributions to the Ninth International Congress of Slavicists, Slavica, 83; auth, The Vampire in Bulgarian Folklore, in Vtori mezhdunaroden kongres po bulgaristika: Dokladi, tom 15, BAN, 88; Animal Language in the Garden of Eden: Folktale Elements in Genesis III, in Signifying Animals: Human Meaning in the Animal World, Unwin Hyman, 89; auth, The Symbolism of the Leopard in the Vepxist'q'aosani, The Annual of the Society for the Study of Caucasia, 90; Vampires, Cannibals, and Foreign Devils: The Structure of Xenophobia in Bulgarian Folklore, The Southern African Journal for Folklore Studies, 91; A Bulgarian Legend in Relation to the Oedipus Tales, Balcanistica, 92; auth, Shota Rustaveli and the Structure of Courtly Love, in The Court and Cultural Diversity: Selected Papers from the Eighth Trienneal Congress of the International Courtly Literature Society, Boydell & Brewer, 97; The National Bibliographies of the Turkic Republics of the Soviet Union, Government Information Quarterly, 98. **CONTACT ADDRESS** 3320 Valdez Dr, Des Moines, IA 50310-4944. **EMAIL** gkbeynen@dmacc.cc.ia.us

BICKERTON, DEREK
PERSONAL Born 03/25/1926, Bebington, England, m, 3 children **DISCIPLINE** LINGUISTICS **EDUCATION** Cambridge Univ, BA, 49, MA, 68, PhD (ling), 76; Univ Leeds, dipl ling, 67. **CAREER** Lectr English, Univ Col Cape Coast, 64-66; sr lectr ling, Univ Guyana, 67-71; lectr, Univ Lancaster, 71-72; assoc prof, 72-76, Prof Ling, Univ Hawaii, Manoa, 76-, Prin investr, Nonstandard Hawaiian English Proj, 73-75 and Origins Creole Syntax Proj, 75-78. **MEMBERSHIPS** Caribbean Ling Soc. **RESEARCH** Linguistic variation; pidgin and Creole languages; language universals. **SELECTED PUBLICATIONS** **CONTACT ADDRESS** Dept of Ling, Univ of Hawaii, Manoa, Honolulu, HI 96822.

BIEDER, MARYELLEN
PERSONAL Born 08/13/1942, Traverse City, MI, m, 1965 **DISCIPLINE** SPANISH LITERATURE **EDUCATION** Lawrence Univ, BA, 64; Ind Univ, MA, 66; Univ Minn, PhD, 73. **CAREER** Asst prof, Syracuse Univ, 73-74; asst prof, SUNY, 74-76; asst prof to prof, Ind Univ, 76-. **HONORS AND AWARDS** Baker Prize, Lawrence Unv, 64; Phi Beta Kappa, 64; Woodrow Wilson Fel, Ind Univ, 64-65; NDEA Fel, 69-70; Fulbright Grants, 84, 85. **MEMBERSHIPS** MLA; AATSP; AIH; AIG; Midwest MLA. **RESEARCH** Spanish Realism and Naturalism, Contemporary Spanish Narrative, Women's Writing in Spain, Contemporary Catalan Narrative, European Realism. **SELECTED PUBLICATIONS** Auth, Narrative Perspective in the Post-Civil War Novels of Francisco Ayala, Chapel Hill, 79; auth, "Between Gender and Genre: Emilia Pardo Bazan and Los pazos de Ulloa", In the Feminine Mode: Essays on Hispanic Women Writers, eds Noel M. Valis and Carol Maier, Bucknell Univ Pr, (90): 131-45; auth, "Concepcion gimeno de Flaquer", Spanish Women Writers: A Bio-bibliographical Sourcebook, ed Linda Levine Greenwood Pr, (93): 93-110; ed, Writing Against the Current, Ind J of Hispanic Lit, 93; auth, "Woman Transfixed: Plotting the Male Gaze in Valle-Inclan's Rosarito", Ramon Maria del Valle-Inclan, ed Carol Maier and Roberta Salper, Bucknell Univ Pr, (94): 154-76; auth, "Gender and Language: The Womanly Woman and Manly Writing", Culture and Gender in 19th-Century Spain, ed Jo Labanyi and Lou Charnon-Deutsch, Oxford Univ Pr, (95): 98-119; auth, "Intertextualizing Genre: Ambiguity as Narrative Strategy in Emilia Pardo Bazan", Intertextual Pursuits: Literary Mediations in Modern Spanish narrative, ed John Kronik and Jeanne Brownlow, Bucknell Univ Pr, (98): 57-75; auth, "Emilia Pardo Bazan y la emergencia del discurso feminists", Beve Historia feminists de la literatura espanol, ed Iris Zavala, Anthropos, (98): 75-110; auth, "Women, Literature, and Society: The Essays of Emilia Pardo Bazan, Spanish Women Writes and the Essay, ed Kathleen Glenn, Miss Pr, (98): 25-54; auth, "Carmen de Burgos: Feminist Reform and Feminine tradition", Recovering Spain's Feminist Tradition, ed Lisa Vollendorf, MLA, 00. **CONTACT ADDRESS** Dept Span and Port, Indiana Univ, Bloomington, 1020 E Kirkwood Ave, Bloomington, IN 47405-7103. **EMAIL** bieder@indiana.edu

BIEN, GLORIA
PERSONAL Born 12/24/1940, Lanehow, China, m, 1979 **DISCIPLINE** CHINESE **EDUCATION** Univ of Calif, Berkeley, BA, 62; MA, 64; Univ Wash, PhD, 73. **CAREER** Asst Prof, Ct Col, 74-80; From Asst Prof to Prof, Colgate Univ, 82-. **HONORS AND AWARDS** NDEA Fels, 65-66; AAUW Mary Laura Bean Fel, 80-81; NEH Summer Seminar Grants, 80, 83; Mellon Grants for Res, 94-99. **MEMBERSHIPS** CLTA, AAS, MLA, ACLA. **RESEARCH** Chinese-French literary relations, computer-assisted language teaching. **SELECTED PUBLICATIONS** Auth, "Baudelaire in China," Comparative Lit Studies XXI, 1 (85): 121-135; auth, "Chenier and China," Studies on Voltaire and the Eighteenth Century, no 242 (86) 363-375; auth, "Segalen's Escapades," in Explorations: Essays in Comparative Lit (Ueda: UP of Am, 86), 134-147; coauth, Global Voices: Contemporary Literature from the Non-Western World, Prentice-Hall (Englewood Cliff, NJ), 95; coauth, Contemporary Literatures of Asia, Prentice-Hall (Englewood Hills, NJ), 96. **CONTACT ADDRESS** Dept Asian Lang & Lit, Colgate Univ, 13 Oak Dr, Hamilton, NY 13346-1338.

BIGGS, HENRY N.
PERSONAL Born 03/09/1964, St. Louis, MO, m, 1991, 3 children **DISCIPLINE** FRENCH LITERATURE, ITALIAN LITERATURE, LINGUISTICS **EDUCATION** Harvard Univ, BA, 86; Univ Calif Los Angeles, MA, 92, PhD, 96. **CAREER** Chair, dept of foreign lang, Houghton Col. **MEMBERSHIPS** MLA **RESEARCH** Linguistics; French & Italian lit. **CONTACT ADDRESS** 8927 Upper St, Rushford, NY 14777. **EMAIL** hbiggs@houghton.edu

BILES, ZACHARY P.
PERSONAL Born 12/15/1968, Philadelphia, PA, m, 1997, 1 child **DISCIPLINE** CLASSICS **EDUCATION** Univ Maryland, BA, 92; Univ Col, MA, 95, PhD, 99. **CAREER** Lectr, Univ Col, 99-00; asst prof, Univ Ore, 00-01; asst prof, Davidson Col, 01-. **HONORS AND AWARDS** Norlin Fel, 98-99. **MEMBERSHIPS** APA; CAMS. **RESEARCH** Aristophanes and Attic comedy; ancient scholarship; Greek culture. **SELECTED PUBLICATIONS** Auth, "Eratosthenes on Plato Comicus: Didaskaliae or Parabasis?," Zeits fur Papyro and Epigra (99). **CONTACT ADDRESS** Dept of Classics, Univ of Oregon, Eugene, OR 97403. **EMAIL** biles@darkwing.uoregon.edu

BILLICK, DAVID JOSEPH
PERSONAL Born 05/19/1947, Toledo, OH, m, 1973 **DISCIPLINE** SPANISH LITERATURE BIBLIOGRAPHY **EDUCATION** Univ Toledo, BA, 69, MA, 71; Univ Iowa, PhD (Span), 76. **CAREER** Instr, Univ Iowa, 76-77; asst prof Span, Rutgers Univ, 77-80; Assoc Ed, Hispania, 76-, Libr Asst, Univ Mich, 81- **MEMBERSHIPS** Am Asn Teachers Span and Port; MLA; Nat Womens Studies Asn; Am Libr Asn. **RESEARCH** Women in Hispanic literature; Jose de Espronceda; 19th century Spanish literature. **SELECTED PUBLICATIONS** Auth, Bibliography of Publications on the Comedia 1991-1992, Bull Comediantes, Vol 0044, 92. **CONTACT ADDRESS** Grad Libr Ref Dept, Univ of Michigan, Ann Arbor, Ann Arbor, MI 48109.

BILLS, GARLAND D.
DISCIPLINE LINGUISTICS **EDUCATION** Univ Tex, Austin, PhD. **CAREER** Prof and ch, Univ NMex. **MEMBERSHIPS** Exec dir, Ling Asn of Southwest. **RESEARCH** Sociolinguistics; syntax-semantics; Spanish ling; Quechua ling; U.S. Southwest Spanish. **SELECTED PUBLICATIONS** Coauth, "The New Mexico-Colorado Spanish Survey: Methodology and technology," 8th International Conference on Dialectology, Victoria, B.C., Canada, 93; coauth, "El atlas linguistico de Nuevo Mexico y el sur de Colorado: Algunos resultados preliminares," 93; coauth, "Spanish in the Southwest: The 1990 census," 94; coauth, "L base historica para la vricion lexica en el espanol de Nuevo Mexico y el sur de Colorado," 95; auth, "The inguistic assimilation of Hispanics in the Southwestern United States," Univ of Helsinki, Finland, 95; auth, "Language myths in a bilingual setting," Conference on Spanish for Native Speakers: New Directions for 21st Century, Las Curces, NM, 95; auth, "Spanish dialects in the Southwest," Chicago, 95; coauth, "The many faces of language maintenance: Spanish language claiming in five southwestern states," in Spanish in four continents; Studies in language contact and bilingualism, ed. Carmen Silva-Corvalan, (Washington, DC: Georgetown Univ Press, 95): 165-183; coauth, "The geography of language shift: Distnce from

the Mexican border and Spanish language claiming in the southwestern U.S." International Journal of the Sociology of Language, 114, (95): 9-27; auth, "Language shift, linguistic variation, and teaching Spanish to native speakers in the United States," in La ensenanza del espanol a hispanohablantes: Praxix y teori, ed. M.C. Colombi and F.X. Alarcon, (Lexington, MA: D.C. Heath, 96). **CONTACT ADDRESS** Univ of New Mexico, Albuquerque, Albuquerque, NM 87131. **EMAIL** gbills@unm.edu

BINGHAM, JOHN L.
PERSONAL Born 09/19/1919, Pineville, KY, s **DISCIPLINE** SPANISH **EDUCATION** Vanderbilt Univ, BA, 41, MA, 47. **CAREER** Taft teaching fel, Univ Cincinnati, 41; asst, Univ Calif, Los Angeles, 47-50; from instr to asst prof Span and French, 50-62, asst dean, Col Arts and Sci, 55-65, assoc dean, 65-80, Assoc Prof Span, Vanderbilt Univ, 62-86; Prof Emer, 86. **HONORS AND AWARDS** Ernest A. Jones Underclass Advisor Awd, 77; Chancellor's Cup, 82. **MEMBERSHIPS** SAtlantic Mod Lang Asn; Conf Acad Deans Southern States. **RESEARCH** Nineteenth and 20th century Spanish literature. **SELECTED PUBLICATIONS** Auth, Thomas,Earl, W.--We Remember, Hisp J Devoted Tchg Span Port, Vol 0076, 93. **CONTACT ADDRESS** Col of Arts and Sci, Vanderbilt Univ, 1305 Gen Gen Patton Rd, Nashville, TN 37221. **EMAIL** john.l.bingham@vanderbilt.edu

BIRCHER, MARTIN
PERSONAL Born 06/03/1938, Zurich, Switzerland **DISCIPLINE** GERMAN LITERATURE **EDUCATION** Univ Zurich, DrPhil, 65. **CAREER** Asst prof, 68-71, Assoc Prof Ger, McGill Univ, 71-, Schweizer Nationalfonds fel, 65-68; lectr, Univ Zurich, 71-; Guggenheim fel, NY, 71-72; fel, Janggen-Pohn-Stiftung, St Gallen, 72-73 and Privatdozenten-Stiftung, Univ Zurich, 72-73; res fel, Alexander von Humboldt Found, 76-77; ed, Wolfenbutteler Barock-Nachrichten, Hamburg, 78-; Res Dir 17th Century, Herzog August Bibliothek Wolfenbuttel, 78- **MEMBERSHIPS** Shakespeare Ges Wes; Int Asn Ger Studies; Swiss-Ger Acad Soc; Int Asn Studies Ger Baroque Lit. **RESEARCH** German literature, 16th to 18th centuries; Swiss Literature; Shakespeare. **SELECTED PUBLICATIONS** Auth, Arcadia in Helvetia, Euphorion Zeitschrift Literaturgeschichte, Vol 0089, 95; Gryphius, Anderas Autographs, Daphnis Zeitschrift Mittlere Deut Lit, Vol 0023, 94. **CONTACT ADDRESS** Dept of German, McGill Univ, Montreal, ON, Canada 101 PQ H3A 2T5.

BIRD, THOMAS E.
PERSONAL Born 03/28/1935, Rome, NY, m, 1958, 2 children **DISCIPLINE** EUROPEAN LANGUAGE AND LITERATURE **EDUCATION** Syracuse Univ, AB; Middlebury Univ, MA; Princeton Univ, AM, PhD. **CAREER** Lectr, Tufts Univ, 58-61; assoc prof, Queens Col, 65-; prog ch, La Salle Univ, 95-. **HONORS AND AWARDS** Pres Teach Awd; Ed, Queens Slavic Papers; Ed, Zapisy Annal; George Arents Lib Awd; Phi Beta Kappa; Woodrow Wilson Fel. **MEMBERSHIPS** MLA; AAASS; AATSEEL; BIAS; PIAS; RASA; Shevchenko Sci Soc. **RESEARCH** Belarusan; Polish; Russian; Ukrainian, literatures. **SELECTED PUBLICATIONS** Co-ed, Hryhory Savyc Skovoroda: An Anthology of Critical Articles, Canadian Inst of Ukrainian Studies Press (Toronto), 94; auth, "Le Lien: Le Decret de Vatican II sur les Eglise catholiques orientales," Patriarchate of Antioch 60 (95): ch 3, 4-23; ch 4-5, 40-48; coauth, "The Dutch," in Encyclopedia of New York City, ed. Kenneth T Jackson (New Haven: Yale UP, 95); auth, "Byelorussian Literature," in Encyclopedia of World Literature in the 20th Century, St. James Press (Farmington Hills: MI), 99; auth, "Yiddish Literature," in Encyclopedia of World Literature in the 20th Century, St. James Press (Farmington Hills: MI), 99; auth, "The USA in the Emigre Journalism," Zapisy/Annals, Belarusan Inst Arts Sci (99); auth, "Nasha Niva," Zapisy/Annals, Belarusan Inst Arts Sci (99): 5-37; auth, "Dutch," in Encyclopedia of Ethnic Sports in the United States, ed. George B Kirsch (Westport, CT: Greenwood Press, 00): 137-139. **CONTACT ADDRESS** Dept European Lang and Lit, Queens Col, CUNY, 6530 Kissena Blvd, Flushing, NY 11367-1575. **EMAIL** thomas_bird@qc.edu

BIRGE, BETTINE
DISCIPLINE EAST ASIAN LANGUAGES AND CULTURES **EDUCATION** Columbia Univ, PhD, 92. **CAREER** Asst prof, Univ Southern Calif. **RESEARCH** Pre-modern Chinese civilization; Chinese thought and cultural history. **SELECTED PUBLICATIONS** Auth, Chu Hsi and Women's Education. **CONTACT ADDRESS** East Asian Studies Center, Univ of So California, University Park Campus, Los Angeles, CA 90089.

BIRKETT, MARY ELLEN
PERSONAL Born 10/10/1946, Buffalo, NY, m, 1991 **DISCIPLINE** FRENCH **EDUCATION** Smith Col, AB, 68; Yale Univ, MPhil, 71; Yale Univ, PhD, 74. **CAREER** Prof, Smith Col, 90-. **HONORS AND AWARDS** Phi Beta Kappa, 67. **MEMBERSHIPS** MLA, AATF, SEDNS, HHS. **RESEARCH** 19th-Century French literature, 19th-Century French-Hawaiian diplomatic relations. **SELECTED PUBLICATIONS** Auth, Lamartine and the Poetics of Landscape, Fr Forum Publ (Lexington, KY), 82; auth, "French Historical Narratives of Hawaii from the 18th and 19th Centuries and their Translations into English: A Selected Bibliography," Hawaiian Hist Soc, Univ Hawaii (96); auth, "The French Perspective on the Laplace Affair," The Hawaiian J of Hist, vol 32 (98): 67-99; auth, "A Romantic Approach to 'The Red and the Black'," in Approaches to Teaching: Stendhal's The Red and the Black (New York: Mod Lang Asn of Am, 99). **CONTACT ADDRESS** Dept Lang, Smith Col, 98 Green St, Northampton, MA 01063-1000.

BIRNBAUM, HENRIK
PERSONAL Born 12/13/1925, Breslau, Germany, m, 1965, 2 children **DISCIPLINE** SLAVIC LANGUAGES AND LITERATURES **EDUCATION** Univ Stockholm, Phil Cand, 49, Phil Mag, 52, Phil Lic, 54, PhD, 58. **CAREER** Asst Slavic lang, Russ Inst, Univ Stockholm, 47-53, asst prof, univ, 58-61; instr Russ, Ger and Swedish, High Schs and Jr Cols, Stockholm, 53-58; assoc Prof Slavic lang, 61-64, dir Ctr Russ and E Europ Studies, 68-78, Prof Slavic Lang, Univ Calif, Los Angeles, 64-, Vis lectr, Harvard Univ, 60; consult, Rand Corp, Santa Monica, 62-66; prof Slavic, Baltic and Balkan ling, Univ Munich, 72-73. **MEMBERSHIPS** Am Asn Advan Slavic Studies; Ling Soc Am; corres mem Swedish Royal Acad Lett; Am Med Acad; Asn Scand Slavists. **RESEARCH** Comparative and historical Slavic linguistics; mediaeval and Renaissance Slavic literature and history. **SELECTED PUBLICATIONS** Auth, The Location of the Moravian State - Revisited, Byzantinoslavica, Vol 0054, 93; The Legacy of Genghis-Khan and Other Essays on Russia Identity, Welt Der Slaven-Halbjahresschrift Fur Slavistik, Vol 0038, 93; Jakobson the Futurist, Russ Rev, Vol 0053, 94; An Introduction to the Morphological Concept on Slavic Accentology, Slavic and E Europ Jour, Vol 0038, 94; An Introduction to the Morphological Concept on Slavic Accentology, Slavic and E Europ J, Vol 0038, 94; The Linguistic Sign Reconsidered in Arbitrariness, Iconicity, Motivation, Elementa-Jour Slavic Studies Comp Cult Semiotics, Vol 0002, 95; Slavic Studies at the 11th International Slavists Congress in Bratislava, Slavic Rev, Vol 0054, 95; The Linguistic Sign Reconsidered - Arbitrariness, Iconicity, Motivation, Elementa-J of Slavic Stud and Comp Cult Semiotics, Vol 0002, 95; On the Widely-Traveled Methodius and the Location of Old Moravia, Hopefully For the Last Time in Critical Observations on a Recent Publication of Kronsteiner, Byzantinoslavica, Vol 0057, 96; Guro, Elena, Sodergran, Edith, and the Karelian Isthmus, Russ Lit, Vol 0040, 1996; 'Molenie Daniila Zatocnika' and Its Genre--The 'Supplication of Daniel the Exile,' Poetic Forms in Old Russian Literature, Zeitschrift Fur Slawistik, Vol 0042, 97; The Dawn of Slavic - An introduction to Slavic Philology, Welt Der Slaven-Halbjahresschrift Fur Slavistik, Vol 0042, 97; Linguistic interrelations in Early Rus, and East Slavs 9th-Century to 11th-Century, Slavic Rev, Vol 0056, 97; The Slavs - Origins of Their Name, History of Migration to Europe and the Beginnings of Russian History From a Historico-Onomastic Perspective, Slavic Rev, Vol 0056, 97. **CONTACT ADDRESS** Dept of Slavic Lang, Univ of California, Los Angeles, Los Angeles, CA 90024.

BIRNER, BETTY
DISCIPLINE LINGUISTICS **EDUCATION** Northwestern Univ, PhD, 92. **CAREER** Postdoctoral fel, Inst Res Cognitive Sci, IRCS, Univ Pa **RESEARCH** The linguistic realization of inferrable information in discourse; general discourse functions served by classes of syntactic constructions; cross-linguistic correlations between syntax and discourse functions. **SELECTED PUBLICATIONS** Coauth, book on the discourse functions of marked syntactic constructions in English, Benjamins. **CONTACT ADDRESS** Dept of Linguistics, Northwestern Univ, 1801 Hinman, Evanston, IL 60208. **EMAIL** betty@linc.cis.upenn.edu

BISHOP, MICHAEL
PERSONAL Born 04/19/1938, London, England **DISCIPLINE** MODERN FRENCH LITERATURE **EDUCATION** Univ Manchester, BA, 59; Univ Man, MA, 68; Univ Kent, PhD(French lit), 77. **CAREER** Asst master mod lang, King's Sch, Cheshire, England, 60-63; chmn mod & class lang, Sisler High Sch, Winnipeg, Can, 63-66 & 67-69; chmn French lit & lang, George Stephenson Sch, Newcastle, England, 69-70; asst prof, 70-79, Assoc Prof French Lit & Lanf, Dalhousie Univ, 80-, Mem, Manitoba Comt Develop Univ Entrance Oral Tests, 67-69; assoc ed, Dalhousie French Studies, Dalhousie Univ, 78-80 & Ethos, 81-; actg ed, Dalhousie French Studies, Dalhousie Univ, 80- **MEMBERSHIPS** Soc Fr Studies; Am Asn Teachers Fr. **RESEARCH** Nineteenth and 20th century French literature; contemporary French literature, especially poetry; French art. **CONTACT ADDRESS** Dept French, Dalhousie Univ, 6209 Univ Ave, Halifax, NS, Canada B3H 3J5. **EMAIL** bishopm@is.dal.ca

BISHOP, THOMAS
PERSONAL Born 02/21/1929, Vienna, Austria, d, 1 child **DISCIPLINE** FRENCH **EDUCATION** NY UNiv, BA, 50; Univ Md, MA, 51; Univ Calif Berkeley, PhD, 57. **CAREER** Lectr, Ecole Superieure de Guerre, 50-51; asst prof, Univ of Calif, Berkeley, 51-55; prof, NYork Univ, 56-. **HONORS AND AWARDS** Fulbright Scholar, France, 65-66; Palmes Academiques, 71; NEH Summer Sem, 77, 79, 82, 85; OBIE Awd, 79; Legion d"Honneur, Chevalier, 81; Grand Prix de l'Academie Francaise, 93. **MEMBERSHIPS** MLA; Samuel Beckett Soc; Assoc for French Cultural Studies. **RESEARCH** 20th Century French theatre and novel, Samuel Beckett, Avant garde theatre. **SELECTED PUBLICATIONS** Auth, Pirandello and the French Theatre, NYU Pr, 60; auth, Huis Clos de Sartre, Hachette, 75; auth, Le Passeur d'ocean. Carnets d'un ami americain, Payot, 89; auth, From the Left Bank: Reflections on the Modern French Theater and Novel, NYU Pr, 97; auth, "Theater and the Everyday in France: Le Theatre du Quotidien", The Art of the Everyday. The Quotidian in Postwar French Culture, ed Lynn Gumpert, NYU Pr, 97; auth, "Francois Mitterand et les Etats-Unis", Francois Mitterand - Paix et developpement, UNESCO 98; auth, "France and the Need for Cultural Exception", Fr-Am News 18.3 (98): 3; auth, "Europeens attention! L'Amerique vous regarde Entretien aved Tom bishop", regards 46, (99): 48; auth, "USA: Education sous hypotheqye", Les Cahiers du radicalisme 2 (99): 237-40. **CONTACT ADDRESS** Dept Fr, New York Univ, 19 University Pl, New York, NY 10003-4556. **EMAIL** tom.bishop@nyu.edu

BITTRICH, LOUIS EDWARD
PERSONAL Born 11/04/1937, Omaha, NE, m, 1961, 2 children **DISCIPLINE** COMPARATIVE LITERATURE, THEATRE **EDUCATION** Gustavus Adolphus Col, BA, 59; Bowling Green State Univ, MA, 60; Univ NCar, PhD, 67; Southwest Tex State Univ, MA, 85. **CAREER** Instr English & dir theatre, Tex Lutheran Col, 60-62; instr English, Gustavus Adolphus Col, 62-63; asst prof, Winthrop Col, 65-66; asst prof, Gustavus Adolphus Col, 66-67; assoc prof, 67-79, prof English, 79-, chmn dept, 67-95, prof theatre, 95-, chmn dept, Texas Lutheran Col. **HONORS AND AWARDS** Ford Found fel, 65; Exchange prof humanities, Winthrop Col, 65-66. **MEMBERSHIPS** MLA. **RESEARCH** Comparative literature and the arts, especially theatre production. **SELECTED PUBLICATIONS** Auth, Alchemy vindicated in our age, Cresset, 4/72. **CONTACT ADDRESS** Dept of Theatre, Texas Lutheran Univ, 1000 W Court St, Seguin, TX 78155-5978. **EMAIL** lbittrich@tlu.edu

BIXLER, JACQUELINE
PERSONAL Born 05/21/1953, Cleveland, OH, m, 1977, 3 children **DISCIPLINE** LATIN AMERICAN LITERATURE, CULTURE & HISTORY **EDUCATION** Oh Univ, BA, 75; Kans Univ, PhD, 80 **CAREER** Prof, 80-, VA Tech **HONORS AND AWARDS** Alumni Tch Awd, 94; Diggs Tch Schol Awd, 92 **MEMBERSHIPS** MLA; AATSP; Sigma Delta Pi **RESEARCH** Latin Am theatre **SELECTED PUBLICATIONS** Auth, Convention and Transgression: The Theatre of Emilio Carballido, Bucknell U niv Press, 97 **CONTACT ADDRESS** Dept of Foreign Lang, Virginia Polytech Inst and State Univ, Blacksburg, VA 24061-0225. **EMAIL** jbixler@vt.edu

BIZZARRO, SALVATORE
PERSONAL Born 04/15/1939, Tunis, m, 1985, 1 child **DISCIPLINE** ITALIAN, SPANISH **EDUCATION** Fordham Univ, BA, 64; Stanford Univ, MA, 65; PhD, 69. **CAREER** Asst prof, Colorado Col, 68; assoc prof, 76; prof, 84-; dept ch, 85-89; dir Mex prog, 84-98; dir Ita prog, 90-. **HONORS AND AWARDS** Phi Beta Kappa; Woodrow Wilson Fel; Woodrow Wilson Diss Fel; NDEA; NEH Fel. **MEMBERSHIPS** AAI; MLA. **RESEARCH** Italian cinema; Latin American affairs; Renaissance studies. **SELECTED PUBLICATIONS** Auth, Historical Dictionary of Chile, Scarecrow Press, 72, 2nd ed, 87, 3rd ed, 01; auth, "Pablo Neruda's Death: An Interview with Matilde Urrutia," FOLIO (76); assoc ed, contrib, "Latin America During Nixon's Second Term," in Am Coll (Paris Press); auth, "Poet of Civic Courage: The Films of Francesco Rosi," Flick Press (Eng, 96); auth, Pablo Nerurda, Scarecrow Press, 96. **CONTACT ADDRESS** Dept Romance Lang, Colo Col, 14 East Cache La Poudre St, Colorado Springs, CO 80903-3243. **EMAIL** sbizzarro@coloradocollege.edu

BJERKE, ROBERT ALAN
PERSONAL Born 12/23/1939, Eau Claire, WI **DISCIPLINE** GERMANIC LANGUAGES **EDUCATION** Univ Wis, BA, 61, MA, 62, PhD(Ger), 66; Univ Minn-Minneapolis, MA, 73. **CAREER** Asst prof Norweg, St Olaf Col, 66-71; Library Dir, Univ Wis Manitowoc, 73-. **RESEARCH** Genealogy; Norwegian language and literature; bibliography. **SELECTED PUBLICATIONS** Auth, A Contrastive Study of Old German and Old Norwegian Kinship Terms, Ind Univ, 69; Fifteen Modern Norwegian Stories: An Intermediate Norwegian Reader, St Olaf Col, 71; Utvandringen fra Nannestad til Amika, In: Nannestad Bygdebok, Vol 4; Manitowoc-skogen: A Biographical and Genealogical Directory of the Residents of Norwegian Birth and Descent in Manitowoc and Kewaunee Counties in Wisconsin from the First Settlement to 1900, Manitowoc WI, Dobbs, 94. **CONTACT ADDRESS** Univ of Wisconsin Ctr, Manitowoc County, 705 Viebahn St, Manitowoc, WI 54220-6699. **EMAIL** rbjerke@uwc.edu

BLACK, MARGARETTA
PERSONAL Born 10/26/1933, Chicago, IL **DISCIPLINE** FRENCH LANGUAGE & LITERATURE **EDUCATION** Marian Col, BA, 61; Case Western Reserve Univ, MA, 66; Univ Wis-Madison, PhD, 72. **CAREER** Elem tchr, Ind, 54-62;

teacher French & hist, 62-65, Acad Immaculate Conception, Oldenburg; instr French, 66-69, asst prof, 71-80, dean acad affairs, 74-87, prof French 82-, chemn dept for lang, 91-, Marian Col, Ind. **MEMBERSHIPS** Am Assn Teachers French, Am Conf on Teaching For Lang, Central States Conf on Teaching For Lang; Ind For Lang Teachers Assn. **RESEARCH** The French novel since 1950; French cultural history--Middle Ages and Renaissance; French film and cinematography, standards in ed and assessment measures, interview. **CONTACT ADDRESS** Dept of For Lang, Marian Col, 3200 Cold Springs Rd, Indianapolis, IN 46222-1997. **EMAIL** marga@marian.edu

BLACK, NANCY BREMILLER

PERSONAL Born 11/12/1941, Norristown, PA, m, 1964, 2 children **DISCIPLINE** ENGLISH; COMPARATIVE LITERATURE **EDUCATION** Vassar Col, BA, 63; Univ Pa, MA, 64; Columbia Univ, PhD(English), 71. **CAREER** Lectr English, City Col New York, 71-72; from instr to Assoc Prof, 72-95, Prof English, Brooklyn Col, 95-. **HONORS AND AWARDS** Shaughnessy scholar, 81-82. **MEMBERSHIPS** MLA; Mediaeval Acad Am. **RESEARCH** Medieval comparative literature. **SELECTED PUBLICATIONS** Co-ed, White on Red: Images of the American Indian, Kennikat, 76; ed and transl, The Perilious Cemetary, Garland, 94; auth, "Woman as Savior: The Virgin Mary and the Empress of Rome in Gautier de Coinci's Miracles, Romanic Review 88.4, (97): 503-17; auth, "The Politics of Romance in Jean Maillart's Roman du Comte d'Anjou," French Studies 51.2 (97): 129-37; auth, "Language of the Illustrations of Chretien de Troyes's Le Chevalier au Lion Yvain," Studies in Iconography 15 (93): 45-75. **CONTACT ADDRESS** Dept of English, Brooklyn Col, CUNY, 2900 Bedford Ave, Brooklyn, NY 11210-2813.

BLACKMORE, JOSHIAH

PERSONAL Born Columbus, OH **DISCIPLINE** PORTUGUESE LITERATURE **EDUCATION** Ohio State Univ, BA, 81; MA, 84; Harvard Univ, PhD, 92. **CAREER** Asst to assoc prof, Univ of Toronto, 92-. **HONORS AND AWARDS** ITT Int Fel, 81-82; Phi Beta Kappa. **MEMBERSHIPS** MLA, Can Assoc of Hispanists, Assoc Int de Lusitanistas. **RESEARCH** Medieval Portuguese and Spanish literature, literature of conquest and discovery, sexuality and gender studies. **SELECTED PUBLICATIONS** Ed, Vida de Eufrosina, Revista Lusitana, 84; coed, Queer Iberia, Duke Univ Pr, 99; auth, "Essa minha devocao complicada," Revista Hispanica Moderna, (00); auth, "Names and Relics in a Reliquia," Romance Notes, (00); auth, The Tragic History of the Sea, Univ of Minn Pr, 01; auth, Manifest Perdition, Univ of Minn Pr, forthcoming. **CONTACT ADDRESS** Univ of Toronto, 73 Queen's Park Cres, Toronto, ON, Canada M5S 1K7. **EMAIL** blackmore@chass.utoronto.ca

BLACKSHIRE-BELAY, C. AISHA

PERSONAL Born 06/11/1951, Detroit, MI, s **DISCIPLINE** GERMANIC LANGUAGES **EDUCATION** Univ Mich, Ann Arbor, BA, 72; Ludwigs-Maximilians Universitat Munchen, Munich, Germany, Masgister Artium, 81; Princeton Univ, MA, 85, PhD, 89. **CAREER** Asst in instruction, Princeton Univ, 86-89; Post-Doctoral Res and Teaching Fel, Univ Pa, 87-89; asst prof, Ohio State Univ, 88-93; Res assoc, Temple Univ, 93-94, assoc prof, 94-96, prof and Chairperson, Dept of African Am Studies, 96-. **HONORS AND AWARDS** Delta Phi Alpha, 87; W. W. Smith Fel, Res and Teaching Fel, Univ Pa, 87-88; Fontaine Fel, Univ Pa, 88-89; Publication Subvention, Ohio State Univ, 90; Nominated Fel, Ctr for Advanced Study in the Behav Scis, Stanford, CA, 91; Phi Bet Delta, 91; Nat Res Coun and Ford Found Res Grant, Sept 92; Res Travel Grant, Temple Univ, April 95; Res Grant, Indiana State Univ, Sept 96; Grant for Instructional Training of Adjunct Instructors, Col of Arts and Scis, Ind State Univ, July 97. **MEMBERSHIPS** Am Asn of Univ Profs, Am Asn of Univ Women, The African Heritage Studies Asn, Am Asn of Teachers of German, The Black Expressive Culture Studies Asn, The Col Lang Asn, Center for Information and Lang Studies, German Studies Asn, Linguistic Soc of Am Modern Lang Asn, Nat Coun for Black Studies, Res Asn of Minority Profs, Soc for Caribbean Linguistics, Soc for Pidgin and Creole Linguistics. **RESEARCH** Morphology and syntax; comparative linguistics; language contact, untutored second language learning and acquisition; foreign worker speech varieties spoken in contemporary German society; minorities in Germany; diversity issues in national and international contexts; historical and contemporary relations between Germany and Africa; African and African American cultural history. **SELECTED PUBLICATIONS** Auth, Current Issues in Second Language Acquisition and Development, ed Univ Press of Am, Lanham, Md (94); auth, "Historical Revelations: The International Scope of Black Germans Today and Beyond," The African-German Experience: Critical Essays, ed Carol A. Blackshire-Belay, Greenwood Pub Group, Inc (96): 89-124; auth, The African-German Experience: Critical Essays, ed Greenwood Pub Group, Inc, Westport, Ct (96); auth, "In Search of Africa in the German World: Transcultural Migrations," Cross Currents: African Americans, Africa, and Germany in the Modern World, ed, Camden House Inc, Columbia, SC (97): 90-129; co-ed, Cross Currents: African Americans, Africa, and Germany in the Modern World, ed, Camden House Inc, Columbia, SC (97); auth, "Under Attack: The Status of Minority Faculty Members in the Academy," ACADEME, Bull of the Am Asn of Univ Profs, Vol 84, No 4 (Aug 98); ed, Political Strategies of Democracy and Health Issues and Concerns, Special issue of the J of Black Studies, Sage Pubs, Inc, Newbury Park, Ca (May 99). **CONTACT ADDRESS** Dept of African and African Am Studies, Indiana State Univ, Terre Haute, IN 47809.

BLACKWELL, MARILYN JOHNS

PERSONAL Born 08/01/1948, Cincinnati, OH, m, 1980 **DISCIPLINE** SCANDINAVIAN LITERATURE, FILM **EDUCATION** Univ Wis, BA, 70; Univ Wash, MA, 73, PhD(Scand lit), 76. **CAREER** Lectr, Univ BC, 75-77; Asst Prof, Univ VA, 77-; Assoc Prof. **HONORS AND AWARDS** Mellon fac fel, Harvard Univ, 81-82. **MEMBERSHIPS** Soc Advan Scand Studies; MLA. **RESEARCH** 19th and 20th century drama and prose; feminist criticism; film. **SELECTED PUBLICATIONS** Auth, Structures of Influence: Comparative Approaches to August Strindberg, 81; auth, C.J.L. Almqvist and Romantic Irony: The Aesthetics of Self-Consciiousness, 83; auth, Persona: The Transcendent Image, 86; auth, Gender and Representation in the films of Ingmar Bergman, 97. **CONTACT ADDRESS** Dept Germanic Languages and Literatures, Ohio State Univ, 1841 Millikin Rd, 320 Cunz Hall, Columbus, OH 43210. **EMAIL** blackwell.4@osu.edu

BLACKWOOD-COLLIER, MARY

DISCIPLINE FRENCH LITERATURE **EDUCATION** Univ de Paris-Sorbonne, PhD, 90. **CAREER** Instr, Ventura Col, 75-78; diction coach, Mus Acad W, 76-84; instr, Santa Barbara Commun Col, 76-84; assoc prof, 81-. **HONORS AND AWARDS** Tchr yr, 92. **SELECTED PUBLICATIONS** Auth, Carmen: Femme fatale or Modern Myth? Merimee's and Bizet's Image of Rebellion, W Va Univ Philol Papers, vol 41, 95; La Carmen essentielle et sa realisation au spectacle, Peter Lang Publ, 94; co-auth, Christian Readings for the Classroom, NAACFLLF Proceedings Jour 1, 91. **CONTACT ADDRESS** Dept of Fr, Westmont Col, 955 La Paz Rd, Santa Barbara, CA 93108-1099.

BLAIN, NANCY MARIE

PERSONAL Born 07/02/1954, Chicago, IL, m, 1994 **DISCIPLINE** LINGUISTICS, SPANISH, FRENCH, LITERATURE **EDUCATION** Univ Fla, BA, 76; Univ S Fla, MA, 84; Fla State Univ, PhD, 95. **CAREER** Grad asst, Univ S Fla, 80-82; Ohio State Univ, 83-85; Fla State Univ, 90-93; adj prof, Ger Comm Col, 87-88; vis prof, George Mason Univ, 94-96; lectr, Barry Univ, 97-99; asst prof, Jacksonville State Univ, 00-. **HONORS AND AWARDS** NHS Phi Kappa Phi, 84. **MEMBERSHIPS** MLA; SAMLA; AATSP; Confluencia. **RESEARCH** Orphane heroine in all genres of Hispanic literature; peninsular studies, all genres, all centuries; Golden Age drama; 19th-century peninsular drama; 18th, 19th, 20th-century French literature. **SELECTED PUBLICATIONS** Auth, "Spleen: An analysis of a poem by Gabriel Celaya," Aleph (92); auth, The Female Orphan in the Hispanic Novels: 'Maria,' by Jorge Issacs; 'Sotileza,' by Jose Maria de Pereda; 'La Regenta,' by Leopoldo Salas; 'Clarin,' and 'Dona Barbara,' by Romulo Gallegos, Fla State Univ, 95. **CONTACT ADDRESS** Hist Dept, Jacksonville State Univ, Jacksonville, AL 36265. **EMAIL** nblain@jsucc.jsu.edu

BLAIR, JOHN T.

DISCIPLINE GERMAN **EDUCATION** Hendrix Col, BA, 81; Univ Ind, MA, 84, PhD, 94. **CAREER** Prof. **MEMBERSHIPS** Goethe Soc N Am; MLA; Asn Tchr German. **RESEARCH** Kafka literary sociology, Freud, Shakespeare, Goethe, Age of Goethe. **SELECTED PUBLICATIONS** Auth, Tracing Subersive Currents in Goethe's Wilhelm Meister's Apprenticeship, Columbia, SC, Camden House, 97. **CONTACT ADDRESS** Dept of Foreign Languages, State Univ of West Georgia, Carrollton, GA 30118. **EMAIL** jblair@westga.edu

BLAKE, NANCY

DISCIPLINE COMPARATIVE LITERATURE **EDUCATION** Univ Paris, PhD, 80. **CAREER** Prof, Univ IL Urbana Champaign. **RESEARCH** 19th and 20th century Europ and Am lit; painting and film; Modernism and Post-Modernism; interdisciplinary research; psychoanalytic theory; women's studies; transl. **SELECTED PUBLICATIONS** Auth, Ezra Pound et l'imagisme; Henry James: Ecriture et absence; Gertrude Stein; John Barth; Emily Dickinson: L'amour de loin; pubs on literature; Lacanian Theory. **CONTACT ADDRESS** Comp Lit Dept, Univ of Illinois, Urbana-Champaign, E Gregory Drive, PO Box 52, Champaign, IL 61820. **EMAIL** n-blake@staff.uiuc.edu

BLANCO, VIRGIL H.

PERSONAL Born Havana, Cuba **DISCIPLINE** SPANISH **EDUCATION** Univ Miami, BA, 67; Fairleigh Dickinson Univ, MAT, 69; Univ Madrid, PhD, 84. **CAREER** Lectr, Fairleigh Dickinson Univ, 87-88; assoc prof, 72-80, prof, Middlesex County Col, 85-88, 89-. **HONORS AND AWARDS** PTA Fel, 68; Fairleigh Dicksinson Univ Grad Fel, 67-69; Grant, NJ Dept of Labor and Industry, 76-77; Fel, Univ of Madrid, 81-82; NJ World Trade Coun Educ Awd, 82; Above and Beyond Awd for Teaching Excellence, 91. **MEMBERSHIPS** AATSP; ACTFL; ADFL; Int Studies Assoc. **RESEARCH** Spanish civilization, Latin American civilization, Contemporary Spanish literature. **SELECTED PUBLICATIONS** Auth, "Community Resources for International Trade", Proceedings Int Studies Assoc, (Washington, DC), 85; auth, "A Socio-Cultural Model of Consumption", J of Marketing Sci Res, 84; auth, "A Network of Colleges, Business and Government for International Trade Education", Marketing Comes of Age, Southern Marketing Assoc, (Boca Raton, FL), 84; auth, "Ballestero, Enrique, Introduccion a la teoria Economica Cap 12, Alianza Editorial, (Madrid), 88; auth, The Service Export Risk Analyzer, 88; auth, The Manufacturer's Export Risk Analyzer, 88; auth, The Competitive Risk Analyzer, 88; auth, Computer Assisted Management Systems, 88. **CONTACT ADDRESS** Dept For Lang, Middlesex County Col, PO Box 3050, Edison, NJ 08818-3050. **EMAIL** vblanco@pilot.njin.net

BLANEY, BENJAMIN

PERSONAL Born 09/06/1940, Newton, MA, m, 1969, 3 children **DISCIPLINE** GERMANIC LINGUISTICS **EDUCATION** Colby Col, AB, 62; Middlebury Col, MA, 64; Univ Colo, Boulder, PhD, 72. **CAREER** Teacher Ger & English, Woodbridge Jr High Sch, NJ, 62-63; instr Ger, Mich Technol Univ, 64-67; asst prof, assoc prof, 83-93, prof Ger, 93-, Miss State Univ, 72-. **HONORS AND AWARDS** Paideia Awd Serv, 89; Burlington N Excellence Tchg Awd, 90; John Grisham Master Tchr Awd, 97; Distinguished Serv Awd, 97; MSU Outstand Advisor Awd, 99; NACADA Excellence in Advising Awd, 00. **MEMBERSHIPS** Am Asn Teachers Ger; Soc Advan Scand Studies; Int Saga Soc; Soc Ger Philol. **RESEARCH** Historical linguistics; medieval Ger literature; Old Norse literature. **SELECTED PUBLICATIONS** Auth Berserkr, Medieval Scandinavia: An Encyclopedia, Garland, 93; Western European Dissertations on Hispanic and Luso-Brasilian Languages and Literatures: A Retrospective Index, Clearing House Lang Lit, 95. **CONTACT ADDRESS** Dept of For Lang, Mississippi State Univ, Drawer Fl, Mississippi State, MS 39762-5720. **EMAIL** bb1@ra.msstate.edu

BLANK, DAVID L.

DISCIPLINE CLASSICS **EDUCATION** Yale Univ, BA, 74; Amer Sch of Class Stud, 74-75; Princeton Univ, MA, 77; Univ Bonn, grad stud, 77-78; Princeton Univ, PhD, 80. **CAREER** Vis asst prof, UCLA, 80-82; asst prof, UCLA, 82-86; lehrauftrag, Freie-Univ Berlin, 89; assoc prof, UCLA, 86-95; Prof, Ch, UCLA, 95-. **HONORS AND AWARDS** ITT-Fulbright fel, Greece, 74-75; Paul Elmer More fel, Princeton, 75-76, 78-79; Deutscher Akademischer Austauschdienst Stipendium, Ger, 77-78; Whiting res fel, Princeton, 79-80; Alexander-von-Humboldt fel, Berlin, 88-89. **SELECTED PUBLICATIONS** Auth, "Analogy, Anomaly, and Apollonius," Companions to Ancient Thought, 3: Philos of Lang, Cambridge 94; "Philodemus on the Technicity of Rhetoric, Philodemus On Poetry," Oxford, 94; "Diogenes of Babylon and the Kritikoi in Philodemus: A Preliminary Suggestion," Cronache Ercolanesi 20, 93; "Stop or Spirant: A Note on the Division of Nonvocal and Semivocal Elements," Glotta 94; Rev, Stefania N. Pieri, Platone. Gorgia, Ancient Philos, 94; Catherine Atherton, The Stoics on Ambiguity, Philos Rev, 94; Ammonius, Commentary on On Interpretation, Vol 1, London, Duckworth, 95. **CONTACT ADDRESS** Univ of California, Los Angeles, PO Box 951436, Los Angeles, CA 90095-1436.

BLAST, ALBERTO

PERSONAL Born 01/21/1931, Buenos Aires, Argentina, s **DISCIPLINE** SPANISH **EDUCATION** Univ de Buenos Aires, Diploma en Letras, 57; Licenciado en Letras, 65; Universidad de La Plata, doctor en Letras, 76. **CAREER** Prof, Universidad de Rosario, 69-74; Vis Writer, Univ Iowa, 74-75; Assoc Prof, to Prof, Brooklyn Col, 75-. **HONORS AND AWARDS** Honorary Fel, Univ Iowa, Boursier de Marque du Gouvernement Francias; Membre correspondant du CELCIRP. **MEMBERSHIPS** Asociacion Internacional de Hispanistas, Association Internationale de Litterature Comparee, PEN Club **RESEARCH** Latin-American Narrative. **SELECTED PUBLICATIONS** Auth, Los Fundadores: Cambaceres, Martel, Sicardi, Buenos Aires, 62; auth, Guiraldes y Larbaud: Una amistad creadora, Buenos Aires, 70; auth, Un novelista argentino del 80: Manuel T Podesta, Buenos Aires, auth, "Feux croises: Valery Larbaud y las letras mexicanas," Nueva Revista de Filologia Hispanica, 89; auth, "Guiraldes: vida y excritura," Don Segundo Sombra, 96. **CONTACT ADDRESS** Dept Mod Lang, Brooklyn Col, CUNY, 2901 Bedford Ave, Brooklyn, NY 11210-2813.

BLAU, HERBERT

PERSONAL Born 05/03/1926, Brooklyn, NY, m, 1981, 4 children **DISCIPLINE** ENGLISH; COMPARATIVE LITERATURE **EDUCATION** NYork Univ, BchE, 47; Stanford Univ, MA, 49, PhD, 54. **CAREER** From asst prof to prof, San Francisco State Univ, 50-65; co-found and co-dir, The Actor's Workshop of San Francisco, 52-65; co-dir, Repertory Theater of Lincoln Ctr, NY, 65-67; prof, City Univ of NY, 67-68; provost and dean, School of Theater and Dance, Calif Inst of the Arts, 68-71; found and artistic dir, KRAKEN theatre, 71-81; prof of the Arts and dir of Inter-Arts Prog, Oberlin Col, 72-74; dean, div of Arts and Hums, Univ of Md, 74-76; prof, Univ of Md, 76-78; prof, Univ of Wis, 78-84; disting. prof, Univ of Wis, 84-00; ed and adv bds, Performing Arts J, Discourse, Theater

J, Assaph, World Encycl of Contemp Theatre, Mod Int Drama, Jour of Beckett Studies, Contemp Dramatists, The Drama Rev, Arts in Soc. **HONORS AND AWARDS** Ford Found fel, 59; President's Disting. Serv Awd, 65; Guggenheim fels, 62, 77; Camargo Found fel, 84; George Nathan Awd for Dramatic Criticism; Sen fel for Independant Study/Res, Nat Endowment for Hums, 84; Nat Endowment for Hums grant, 81, 83, 87, 90; The Kenyon Rev prize for literary excellence, 93. **SELECTED PUBLICATIONS** Auth, The Impossible Theater: A Manifesto, 64; Blooded Thought: Occasions of Theater, 82; Take Up the Bodies: Theater at the Vanishing Point, 82; The Eye of Prey: Subversions of the Postmodern, 87; The Audience, 90; Universals of Performance; or, Amortizing Play, By Means of Performance: Intercult Studies of Theater and Ritual, ed R. Schechner and W. Appel, 90; The Oversight of Ceaseless Eyes, Around the Absurd: Essays on Modern and Postmodern Drama, ed E. Brater and R. Cohn, 91; Quaquaquaqua: The Babel of Beckett, The World of Beckett, ed J. Smith, Psychiatry and Humanities, vol 12, 91; The Surpassing Body, The Drama Rev 35.2, 91; Readymade Desire, Confronting Tennessee Williams? A Streetcar Named Desire: Essays in Critical Pluralism, ed P.C. Kolin, 92; To All Appearances: Ideology and Performance, 92; Nothing in Itself: Complexions of Fashion, 99; Sails of the Herring Fleet: Essays on Beckett, 00; The Prospect Before Us, Discourse 14.2, 92; Ideology, Performance, and the Illusions of Demystification, Crit Theory and Performance, ed J.G. Reinelt and J. Roach, 92; Spacing Out in the American Theater, The Kenyon Rev 14.2, 93; A Valediction: Chills and Fever, Mourning, and the Vanities of the Sublime, Performing Arts Jour 16.1, 94; Rhetorics of the Body: Do You Smell a Fault?, Cult Artifacts and the Production of Meaning: The Page, the Image and the Body, ed. M. Ezell and K. O'Brien O'Keefe, 94; Fantasia and Simulacra: Subtext of a Syllabus for the Arts in America, The Kenyon Rev 16.2, 94; Flat-Out Vision, Fugitive Images: From Photography to Video, ed P. Petro, 95; coed, Performance Issue(s): Happenings, Body, Spectacle, Discourse 14.2, 92. **CONTACT ADDRESS** Dept of English, Univ of Washington, Seattle, WA 98195-3765.

BLEISCH, PAMELA
DISCIPLINE CLASSICAL STUDIES **EDUCATION** Brown Univ, BA, 83; Univ Chicago, MA, 85; Univ Calif, PhD, 94. **CAREER** Asst prof, Univ Georg, 94-99; asst prof, Boston Univ, 99-. **HONORS AND AWARDS** Univ Georg Res Found Grnt, 98; Univ Georg Hum Cen Fel, 95-96; Luckman Dis Fel, 92-93; Connell Fel, 91-92; Chancellor's Fel, 85-86; Grad Div Stip, 84; J. Hatten Col Teach Hon Awd, 97; Lilly Teach Fel, 96-97; Luckman Dist Teach Awd, 91-92. **MEMBERSHIPS** APA; Vergilian Soc; WCC. **RESEARCH** Latin literature; the Augustan Age; Hellenistic poetry; gender in antiquity. **SELECTED PUBLICATIONS** Auth, "The Empty Tomb at Rhoeteum: Deiphobus and the Problem of the Past," Class Ant (99); auth, "Altars Altered: the Alexandrian Tradition of Etymological Wordplay," Am J Philo (98); auth, "On Choosing a Spouse," Am J Philo (96); auth, "Nisus' Choice: Bovillae at Aeneid," Class Qtly (01); auth, "Silence is Golden: Simonides, Callimachus, and Augustan Panegyric at the close of Horace Carm," Quad Urb di Cult Class (01). **CONTACT ADDRESS** Dept Classical Studies, Boston Univ, 745 Commonwealth Ave, Boston, MA 02215.

BLEZNICK, DONALD WILLIAM
PERSONAL Born 12/24/1924, New York, NY, m, 1952, 2 children **DISCIPLINE** SPANISH LANGUAGE & LITERATURE **EDUCATION** City Col New York BA, 46; Nat Univ Mex, MA, 48; Columbia Univ, PhD (Span lit), 54. **CAREER** Instr Romance lang, Ohio State Univ, 49-55; from asst prof to prof, Pa State Univ, 55-67; dept hd, 67-72; Prof, Univ Cincinnati, 67-; assoc ed, Hispania, 63-74; ed, 74-. **HONORS AND AWARDS** Knight's Cross of the Order of Civil Merit, King Juan Carlos I of Spain, 77; Rieveschl Awd, 80; am philos soc grant, 64. **MEMBERSHIPS** MLA; Am Assn Tchr Span & Port; Renaissance Soc Am; Midwest Mod Lang Assn; Comediantes. **RESEARCH** Political theory of Spain's Golden Age and its influence on literature; history of the Spanish essay; Spanish Golden Age literature. **SELECTED PUBLICATIONS CONTACT ADDRESS** Dept Romance Lang, Univ of Cincinnati, Cincinnati, OH 45221.

BLICKLE, PETER
PERSONAL Born 09/26/1961, Ravensburg, Germany, m, 1988 **DISCIPLINE** GERMAN **EDUCATION** W Mich Univ, BA, 87; Univ Mich, MA, 89; PhD, 95. **CAREER** TA to lectr, Univ of Mich, 87-96; asst prof, W Mich Univ, 96-. **HONORS AND AWARDS** President's Awd, W. Mich Univ, 87; Governor's Awd, State of Mich, 87; Frank X Braun Teaching Awd, Univ of Mich, 93; Fel, Univ of Mich, 95; President's Grant, W Mich Univ, 98; FRACASF Grant, W Mich Univ, 00-01. **MEMBERSHIPS** Ger Studies Assoc, MLA, Am Assoc of Teachers of Ger, Women in Ger, Mich Acad of Sci, Arts and Letters, Soc for contemp Am Lit in Ger, Gesellschaft fur interkulturelle Germanistik. **RESEARCH** German literature, culture and language. **SELECTED PUBLICATIONS** Cotransl, of Lost Weddings, by Maria Beig, Persea Books, (NY), 90; auth, Maria Beig und die Kunst der Scheinbaren Kunstlosigkeit, Edition Isele (Eggingen, Ger), 97. **CONTACT ADDRESS** Dept For Lang and Lit, Western Michigan Univ, 1803 Hazel Ave, Kalamazoo, MI 49008-2843. **EMAIL** blickle@wmich.edu

BLIQUEZ, LAWRENCE J.
PERSONAL Born 06/12/1941, Des Moines, IA, m, 1969, 2 children **DISCIPLINE** CLASSICS **EDUCATION** St Mary's Coll Calif, BA, 63; Stanford Univ, MA, 65; PhD, 68. **CAREER** Asst prof, San Francisco State Coll, 66-69; asst prof Univ Wash Seattle, 69-77; assoc prof, 77-85; prof, Univ Wash Seattle, 85-. **HONORS AND AWARDS** Jr Fel, Center for Hellenic Studies, 77-78; Distinguished Teaching Awd, Univ Wash, 77-78. **MEMBERSHIPS** APA; Soc for Ancient Med. **RESEARCH** Greek and Roman Minor Objects, surgical instruments. **SELECTED PUBLICATIONS** Auth, Roman Surgical Instruments and Other Minor Objectsin the Nat Archaeol Museum of Naples, 94. **CONTACT ADDRESS** Dept of Classics, Univ of Washington, Box 353110, Seattle, WA 98195. **EMAIL** lbliquez@u.washington.edu

BLISS, FRANCIS ROYSTER
PERSONAL Born 06/07/1919, Big Stone Gap, VA, m, 1943, 3 children **DISCIPLINE** LATIN, GREEK **EDUCATION** Bowdoin Col, AB, 40; Univ NC, PhD(Latin), 51. **CAREER** From instr to asst prof classics, Colby Col, 48-55; assoc prof, Western Reserve Univ, 55-66; assoc prof classics, Univ VT, 66-70, Prof, 70-79. **MEMBERSHIPS** Class Asn Mid W & S; Class Asn New England; Soc Ancient Greek Philos; Vergilian Soc; Am Philol Asn. **RESEARCH** Literary imitation, cultural history. **SELECTED PUBLICATIONS** Auth, Roman law and Romand citizenship, Law in a Troubled World, W Reserve Univ, 59; The Plancus ode, Trans & Proc Am Philol Assn, 60; A rogues' gallery, Class Outlook, 63; Unity of Odyssey Eight, Bucknell Rev, 68. **CONTACT ADDRESS** RFD 1, Box 240, New Vineyard, ME 04956.

BLOCK, DANIEL I.
PERSONAL Born 05/22/1943, Borden, SK, Canada, m, 1966, 2 children **DISCIPLINE** SEMITICS, CLASSICAL HEBREW **EDUCATION** Univ Liverpool, England, PhD. **CAREER** Prof Old Testament Interp, S Baptist Theol Sem, 95-; prof Old Testament, Bethel Theol Sem, 83-95; prof Old Test, Providence Col, Manitoba, Canada. **HONORS AND AWARDS** DAAD scholar; Canada coun awd, 78-80. **MEMBERSHIPS** Soc Bibl Lit; inst Bibl res; Evangelical Theol Soc. **RESEARCH** Deuteronomy; Judges; Family Issues in Ancient Israel. **SELECTED PUBLICATIONS** Auth, Ezekiel 1-24, Ezekiel 25-28, in New International Commentary on the Old Testament, Eerdmans, 97, 98; auth, "Judges, Ruth," in New Am Commentary, Broadman, 99; rev ed, The Gods of the Nations, Baker, 00. **CONTACT ADDRESS** Dept of Old Testament, So Baptist Theol Sem, 2825 Lexington Rd, Louisville, KY 40280. **EMAIL** diblock@aol.com

BLOCK, HASKELL M.
PERSONAL Born 06/13/1923, Chicago, IL, d, 3 children **DISCIPLINE** COMPARATIVE LITERATURE **EDUCATION** Univ Chicago, AB, 44; Harvard Univ, AM, 47; Univ Paris, D Univ, 49. **CAREER** Tchg Fel, Harvard Univ, 48-49; instr, Queens Col, NY, 49-52; from asst prof to assoc prof comp lit, Univ Wis, 52-61; prof, Brooklyn Col & Grad Sch, City Univ New York, 61-75; prof, State Univ NY Binghamton, 75-; vis prof English, Univ Dusseldorf, 72-73; chmn exec comt, Eastern Comp Lit Conf, 76-; H Fletcher Brown prof comp lit, Univ Del, 77-78; vis prof comp lit, Univ Antwerp, 81and 83; Prof Emeritus, 91-. **HONORS AND AWARDS** Fulbright res scholar, Univ Cologne, 56-57 & Univ Paris, 68-69; fel, Colloquium Comp Lit, NY Univ, 70-; 18th Century European Culture, COLUMBIA UNIV, 70-; mem selection comt, Camargo Found, 70-96; consult ed, random house, ny, 61-; mem selection comt western europe, foreign area fel prog, 65-68; exec officer, doctoral prog comp lit, city univ new york, 68-71; assoc, sem theory of lit, columbia univ, 70-; mem selection comt, camargo found, 71-. **MEMBERSHIPS** Int'l Comp Lit asn (secy, 58-64); Am Comp Lit Asn (secy, 60-65, vpres. 71-74, pres, 74-77); MLA; Dante Soc Am; Soc Fr Studies. **RESEARCH** Modern drama and novel, symbolist movement, the enlightment in France & Germany. **SELECTED PUBLICATIONS** Auth, Masters of Modern Drama, with Robert G. Shedd, Random House, NY, 62; auth, Mallarme and the Symbolist Drama, Wayne State Univ Press, Detroit, 63; auth, Nouvelles tendances en litterature comparee, Nizet, Paris, 70; auth, Naturalistic Triptych, Random House, NY, 70; ed, The Poetry of Paul Celan, Peter Lang, NY, 91. **CONTACT ADDRESS** Dept of Comp Lit, SUNY, Binghamton, Binghamton, NY 13902.

BLODGETT, EDWARD D.
PERSONAL Born 02/26/1935, Philadelphia, PA **DISCIPLINE** COMPARATIVE LITERATURE **EDUCATION** Amherst Col, BA, 56; Univ Minn, MA, 61; Rutgers Univ, PhD, 69. **CAREER** Res master Eng, Girard Col, 58; tchg asst, Univ Minn, 58-61; instr Fre, Inst Am Univ, Aix-en-Provence, 62-63; instr, Eng & classics, Rutgers Univ & Douglas Col, 63-66; asst to assoc prof, 66-74, prof 75-94, chair, comp lit & film stud, 75-85, 91-93, univ prof, Comp Lit, Univ Alta, 94-; vis prof, Univ Sherbrooke, 79; vis prof, Freie Univ Berlin, 88; assoc ed, Can Rev Comp Lit, 74-; exec coun, Calgary Inst Hum, 77-88. **HONORS AND AWARDS** Delta Phi Lambda; Lambda Alpha Phi; fel, Royal Soc Can; Gov Gen Awd Eng lang poetry. **SELECTED PUBLICATIONS** Auth, Taking Away the Names, 75; auth, Sounding, 77; auth, Beast Gate, 80; auth, Configuration, 82; auth, Arche/Elegies, 83; auth, Musical Offering, 86; auth, Alice Munro, 88; auth, Da Capo, 90; auth, Apostrophes: Woman at a Piano, 96; Transfiguration; Editions du Noroit. **CONTACT ADDRESS** Dept of Comp Lit, Univ of Alberta, Edmonton, AB, Canada T6G 2E6.

BLOOMER, W. MARTIN
DISCIPLINE CLASSICS **EDUCATION** BA, 82; MA, 83; MPhil, 84; Yale Univ, PhD, 87. **CAREER** Asst prof, Stanford Univ. **RESEARCH** Latin lit; ancient rhetoric; ancient historiography. **SELECTED PUBLICATIONS** Auth, Valerius Maximus and the Rhetoric of the New Nobility, 92; The Superlative Nomoi of Herodotus's Histories, 93; A Preface to the History of Declamation: Whose Speech? Whose History?, 96; Latinity and Literary Society at Rome, 97. **CONTACT ADDRESS** Stanford Univ, Bldg 20, Main Quad, Stanford, CA 94305.

BLOOMFIELD, ELISABETH M.
PERSONAL Born 10/01/1960, Le Puy, France, m, 1993 **DISCIPLINE** LITERATURE, FRENCH **EDUCATION** Sorbonne Univ, BA, 82; MA, 83; Univ Calif San Diego, PhD, 00. **CAREER** Lectr, John Hopkins Univ, 96-00; asst prof, Univ Ky, 00-. **MEMBERSHIPS** MLA. **RESEARCH** 20th-century literature and criticism; poetry. **SELECTED PUBLICATIONS** Auth, "The Impossible Sacrifice of Poetry, Bataille and the Critiques of Sacrifice," Diac 26 (96): 86-96; auth, "Reminiscence de Proust," MLN 113 (98): 757-779. **CONTACT ADDRESS** 130 University Ave, Lexington, KY 40503-1032. **EMAIL** earno2@pop.uky.edu

BLUE, WILLIAM ROBERT
PERSONAL Born 04/02/1943, Shreveport, LA, m, 1970 **DISCIPLINE** SPANISH LITERATURE **EDUCATION** Univ Calif, Davis, AB, 65, MA, 67; Penn State Univ, PhD(Span), 71. **CAREER** Asst prof, 70-74, Assoc Prof Span, Univ Kans, 74-, Exec Comt 16th and 17th Century Span Drama, MLA, 78-83. **MEMBERSHIPS** MLA; Am Asn Teachers Span & Port; Comediantes. **RESEARCH** Spanish Golden Age theater and literature. **SELECTED PUBLICATIONS CONTACT ADDRESS** Dept of Span & Port, Univ of Kansas, Lawrence, Lawrence, KS 66044.

BLUMBERG, SHERRY H.
DISCIPLINE JEWISH EDUCATION **EDUCATION** Hebrew Union Col, PhD, 91. **CAREER** Assoc prof, Univ Southern Calif. **RESEARCH** Curriculum; teacher training; educating for religious experience. **SELECTED PUBLICATIONS** Auth, electronic publ, Teaching Children about God. **CONTACT ADDRESS** Hebrew Union College-Jewish Institute Of Religion, Univ of So California, University Park Campus, Los Angeles, CA 90089.

BLUMENFELD-KOSINSKI, RENATE
PERSONAL Born Berlin, Germany, m, 1978 **DISCIPLINE** FRENCH, LITERATURE **EDUCATION** Univ Bonn, BA, 74; Rutgers Univ, BA, 75; Princeton Univ, PhD, 80. **CAREER** Mellon Fel, asst prof to assoc prof, Columbia Univ, 81-93; prof, Univ Pitt, 94-. **HONORS AND AWARDS** NEH Fel, 91-92. **MEMBERSHIPS** MLA; MAA; ICLS. **RESEARCH** Medieval French literature and history. **SELECTED PUBLICATIONS** Auth, Not of Women Born: Representations of Caesarean Birth in Medieval and Renaissance Culture, Cornell Univ Pr, 90; coed, Images of Sainthood in Medieval Europe, Cornell Univ Pr, 91; auth, Reading Myth: Classical Mythology and it's Interpretations in Medieval French Literature, Stanford Univ Pr, 97; auth, The Selected Writings of Christine de Pizan, W. W. Norton, 97. **CONTACT ADDRESS** 47 Cherry Brook Dr, Princeton, NJ 08540-7710. **EMAIL** rbk7580@aol.com

BLUMENTHAL, BERNHARDT GEORGE
PERSONAL Born 03/08/1937, Philadelphia, PA, m, 1996, 4 children **DISCIPLINE** GERMAN **EDUCATION** La Salle Col, BA, 59; Northwestern Univ, MA, 61; Princeton Univ, PhD(Ger), 65. **CAREER** Assoc prof, 63-73, prof Ger, La Salle Col, 73-, chemn dept foreign lang & lit, 69- ; Acting Director, MA Program in Control and Esteem European Studies, 99. **MEMBERSHIPS** Am Asn Teachers Ger. **RESEARCH** German and comparative literatures, especially modern. **SELECTED PUBLICATIONS** Auth, Gertrud Kolmar: Love's Service to the Earth, 9/69 & The Play Element in the Poetry of Else Lasker-Schuler, 9/70, Ger Quart; the Poetry Class, Unterrichtspraxis, fall 71; Paula Ludwig's Poetry: Themes of Love and Death, Ger Quart, 11/71; The Writings of Regina Ullmann, Seminar, 3/73; Original German Lyric Poetry in Lyrical Germanica, 9/74 & Ger Am Studies, 5/77; Imagery in Christine Busta's Writing, Seminar, 5/77; Fragen im Herbst, Jeder fur sich allein and Kultursteine, Impressum, vol 8, no 7/8. 94; Fragen im Herbst, Das Boot, vol 32, no 127, 94; Jeder fur sich allein and Kultursteine, Trans-Lit, vol 3, no 2, 94; Culture Stones, Queries in the Fall, and Alone with Ourselves, Int J of Transpersonal Studies, vol 14, nos 1/2, 95; Uriel Birnbaum: Forgotten Angel of the Sun, Modern Austrian Lit, vol 29, no 1, 96; Wenn du gehst, Das Boot, vol 34, no 134, 96; Fragen im Herbst, Wiedergefunden, Wenn du gehst, Trans-Lit, vol 5, no 2, 96; When You Go, Through Sun and Shower, ed Chris Tyler, Owings Mills, MD: Watermark Press, 97; Review of Birgit R

Erdle's Antlitz--Mord--Gesetz: Figuren des Anderen bei Gertrud Kolmar und Emmanuel Levinas, Monashefte, vol 89, no 2, summer 97; Sprich leise, Trans-Lit, vol 7, no 1, 98; Speak Softly, Best Poems of 1998, ed. Howard Ely, Owinjs Mills, MD: Watermark Press, 98. **CONTACT ADDRESS** Dept of Foreign Lang, La Salle Univ, 1900 W Olney Ave, Philadelphia, PA 19141-1199. **EMAIL** blumenth@lasalle.edu

BLUMSTEIN, SHEILA ELLEN
PERSONAL Born 03/10/1944, New York, NY **DISCIPLINE** LINGUISTICS, PSYCHOLINGUISTICS **EDUCATION** Univ Rochester, AB, 65; Harvard Univ, PhD(ling), 70. **CAREER** Asst prof, 70-76, Assoc Prof Ling, Brown Univ, 76-, Res assoc, Aphasia Res Ctr, Sch Med, Boston Univ, 70-; vis scientist, Mass Inst Technol Res Lab Electronics, 74 & 77-78, consult, 74-; fel, Guggenheim Found, 77-78 & Radcliffe Inst, 77-78; mem, Commun Sci Study Sect, NIH, 76-; bd gov, Acad Aphasia, 78- **MEMBERSHIPS** Acad Aphasia; Ling Soc Am; Acoustical Soc Am. **RESEARCH** Aphasia; speech perception. **SELECTED PUBLICATIONS** Auth, A Perspective on the Neurobiology Of Language, Brain And Lang, Vol 0060, 97; The Influence of Language on the Acoustic Properties of Phonetic Features--A Study of the Feature Strident in Ewe and English, Phonetica, Vol 0051, 94; The Foreign Accent Syndrome--A Reconsideration, Brain and Lang, Vol 0054, 96; The Role of Lexical Status on the Phonetic Categorization of Speech in Aphasia, Brain and Language, Vol 0046, 94; Effects of Speaking Rate on the Vowel Length Distinction in Korean, Jour of Phonetics, Vol 0021, 93; Effects of Speaking Rate on Voice-Onset Time in Thai, French, and English, Jour of Phonetics, Vol 0025, 97. **CONTACT ADDRESS** Dept of Ling, Brown Univ, 1 Prospect St, Box E, Providence, RI 02912-9127.

BOATENG, FAUSTINE
DISCIPLINE FRENCH LANGUAGE AND LITERATURE **EDUCATION** Universite de Besancon, BA; Howard Univ, PhD. **CAREER** Asst prof. **MEMBERSHIPS** ALA; CLA. **RESEARCH** French African and Caribbean literature; works by Francophone African women writers. **SELECTED PUBLICATIONS** Auth, Asante--The Heritage Library of African Peoples; Rosen, 96. **CONTACT ADDRESS** Clark Atlanta Univ, 223 James P Brawley Dr, SW, Atlanta, GA 30314. **EMAIL** fboateng@cau.edu

BOATWRIGHT, MARY T.
PERSONAL Born 04/16/1952, VA, m, 1981, 2 children **DISCIPLINE** CLASSICS **EDUCATION** Stanford Univ, BA, 73; Univ per Stranieri Perugia, Laurea voto ottimo, 74; Univ of Mich, MA, 75, PhD, 80. **CAREER** ICCS, grad Asst, 76-77, Duke Univ; A W Mellon Asst Prof, Asst Prof, Assoc Prof, Prof 79-, Chmn dept Classics 79-99, ICCS Rome; A W Mellon Prof in charge, 92-93. **HONORS AND AWARDS** Phi Beta Kappa, Borso di Studio, Duke Endowment Awd Excellence in Teaching, G A & E G Howard Found Fel, NEH Fel. **MEMBERSHIPS** APA, AIA, SPRS, AAH, SFAAR. **RESEARCH** Social & cultural history during the Imperial Roman period, Roman women, Roman cities. **SELECTED PUBLICATIONS** Auth, Hadrian and the Cities of the Roman Empire, Princeton Univ Press, 00; co-ed, The Shapes of City Life in Rome and Pompeii, Essays in Honor of L Richardson Jr on the Occasion of his Retirement, Caratzas, 00; auth, Hadrian and the City of Rome, Princeton Univ Press, 97; auth, Imperial Women of the Early Second Century A C, Amer J of Philology, 91; Hadrian and Italian Cities, Chiron, 89. **CONTACT ADDRESS** Dept of Classical Studies, Duke Univ, Durham, NC 27708-0103. **EMAIL** tboat@duke.edu

BOBIA, ROSA
PERSONAL Born Spartanburg, SC, m **DISCIPLINE** FRENCH FRANCOPHONE LITERATURE AND CULTURE **EDUCATION** North Carolina Cen, BA, 66; Univ Chapel Hill, MA, 72; Vanderbilt Univ, MA, 81; PhD, 84. **CAREER** Prof, Kennesaw State Univ, 84-. **HONORS AND AWARDS** Fulbright Teach Fel; Fulbright Gnt; Fulbright Sum Sem; NEH; Dist Ser Awd; Outstand Fac; Prof of Year Awd. **MEMBERSHIPS** AAFT; Women in French. **RESEARCH** African literature; French language; African culture. **SELECTED PUBLICATIONS** Auth, The Critical Reception of James Baldwin in France, peter Lang, 97 and 98; contr, Biographical Essays: "Jesse Hill," "Alonzo Herndon," Notable Black American Men, Gale Group, 99; cont, "Sara Burke," Notable Black American Women, 91; cont, The French Reception of African-American Writers in France: From the Beginning to 1970 (Greenwood Press, 95). **CONTACT ADDRESS** Dept Foreign Lang, Kennesaw State Univ, 1000 Chastain Rd, Kennesaw, GA 30144-5588. **EMAIL** rbobia@kennesaw.edu

BODEL, JOHN
PERSONAL Born 01/25/1957, Sharon, CT, m, 1979, 2 children **DISCIPLINE** CLASSICS **EDUCATION** Princeton Univ, BA, 78; Univ Mich, MA, 79, PhD, 84. **CAREER** Asst dir, 83, co dir, 91, 95, Am Acad Rome; asst prof to assoc prof, 84-92; Harvard Univ; vist asst prof, Brown Univ, 92-93; dir to assoc prof to chemn to prof, 94-, Rutgers Univ. **HONORS AND AWARDS** NEH Res Fel, 93; Fel, 82-83, trustee, 99-01, Am Acad Rome; Pres, Am Society of Greek and Latin Epigraphy, 98-00; Dir, US Epigraphy Project, 95-. **RESEARCH** Latin epigraphy; Latin literature; Roman history. **SELECTED PUBLICATIONS** Auth, Roman Brick Stamps in the Kelsey Museum, 83; auth, Graveyards and Groves: A Study of the Lex Lucerina, 94; auth, art, Monumental Villas and Villa Monuments, 97; coauth, Greek and Latin Inscriptions in the USA: A Checklist, 97; auth, ed, Epigraphic Evidence: Ancient Hist from Inscriptions, 00. **CONTACT ADDRESS** Dept of Classics, Rutgers, The State Univ of New Jersey, New Brunswick, 131 George St, New Brunswick, NJ 08901-1414. **EMAIL** bodel@rci.rutgers.edu

BODINE, JAY F.
PERSONAL Born 02/15/1943, m, 4 children **DISCIPLINE** GERMAN LITERATURE **EDUCATION** Princeton Univ, PhD. **CAREER** Assoc prof. **HONORS AND AWARDS** Fulbright, 86. **MEMBERSHIPS** AATG, CALICO.GSA. **RESEARCH** Computer applications in language; literary theory; study of socio-political reality in literature. **SELECTED PUBLICATIONS** Auth, pubs on Karl Kraus, Heinrich Heine, Ludwig Wittgenstein, Walter Benjamin, Manes Sperber, and Max Frisch. **CONTACT ADDRESS** Foreign Languages and Literature Dept, Colorado State Univ, Fort Collins, CO 80523. **EMAIL** jaybodine@colostate.edu

BODKIN, ROBIN O.
PERSONAL Born 03/13/1946 **DISCIPLINE** LINGUISTICS **EDUCATION** Duke Univ, BA, 68; Defense Lang Inst, 69-70; Univ Vir, MA, 74; PhD, 81. **HONORS AND AWARDS** French Govt Grnt, 76-77; Col Intl des Traducteurs Lit, 89, 91-95. **MEMBERSHIPS** ATA; ATLAS; MLA; CALIC; NCTA. **RESEARCH** Modernity; literary theory; semiotics; genetic criticism; translation studies; languages of lesser diffusion. **SELECTED PUBLICATIONS** Auth, "Une Saison au Viet-nam," L'Humanite (91); auth, "Jules Valles," in Dictionary of Literary Biography vol 123: Nineteenth-Century French Fiction Writers: Naturalism and Beyond, 1860-1900, ed. Catharine Savage Brosman (Detroit: Gale Res, 92); auth, "Selected Short Stories in French," Trans Lang (93); auth, "Jean Sans Terre and William Carlos Williams," in Vistas: Proceedings of the 35th Annual Conference of the American Translators Association, ed. Peter W. Krawutschke (Medford, NJ: Learned Information, 94); auth, "The Creative Askesis of Jules Valles," in Studies on Themes and Motifs in Literature: Repression and Expression: Literary and Social Coding in Nineteenth-Century France, vol 22, ed. Carrol F. Coates (NY: Peter Lang Pub, 96); co-auth, "Genetic Criticism: A Dialogics of the Text," ATA Chronicle 5 (97); trans, of Lilas Desquiron's Les chemins de Loco-Miroir: "Reflections of Loko Miwa," (UP of Vir, 98); trans, essays on "Guy de Maupassant, Max Jacob, Francis Ponge, Paul Verlaine," in Encycl of Literary Translation, ed. Olive Classe (London: Fitzroy Dearborn Pub, 01); auth, "Mazas," in Cells, ed. Olivia Sears (San Francisco: Two Lines Pub, 01); trans, Semiotique, marketing et communication: sous les signes, les strategies, by Jean-Marie Floch (NY: Martins/Palgrave, 01). **CONTACT ADDRESS** PO Box 591048, San Francisco, CA 94159-1048. **EMAIL** rbodkin@aol.com

BOEGEHOLD, ALAN
PERSONAL Born 03/21/1927, Detroit, MI, m, 1954, 4 children **DISCIPLINE** CLASSICS **EDUCATION** Univ MI, AB, 50; Harvard Univ, AM, 54, PhD, 58. **CAREER** Instr, asst prof dept classics, Champaign-Urbana, 57-60; from asst prof to prof dept classics, Brown Univ, 60; dir summer session Amer Sch Classical Studies Athens, 63, 64, 74, 80, vis prof, 68-69; dir Ancient studies program Brown Univ, 85-91, chmn dept classics, 66-71, acting chmn, 73-74; visiting lectr hist Harvard Univ, 67; visiting prof classics Yale Univ, 71, Univ CA, Berkeley, 78; mem com to evaluate dept classics Swarthmore Coll, 72, Univ VA, 82, 88, coms humanities and hist Yale Univ Coun, 82-87; interim pres, vp and sec Nargansett Soc Archaeol Inst Am; vice chmn mng com Am Sch Classical Studies,85-90, chmn, 90-98. **HONORS AND AWARDS** Thomas Day Seymour fel Amer Sch Classical Studies Athens, 55-56; Rsch fel, 74-75; Rsch fel Agora Excavations, 80-81; Charles Eliot Norton fel Amer Sch Classical Sudies Athens; Howard fel, 56-57; grantee Amer Coun Learned Socs, 80-81. **MEMBERSHIPS** Active ACLU; Amnesty Internat; Providence Athenaeum; Mass Audubon Soc; Common Cause **RESEARCH** Greek History, Literature, and Art. **SELECTED PUBLICATIONS** Ed, Athenian Identity and Civic Ideology, 93; auth, ed, Agora XXVIII, Law Courts at Athens, 95; auth, When A Gesture Was Expected, 99. **CONTACT ADDRESS** Dept of Classics, Brown Univ, 48 College Hill St, Providence, RI 02912-9079.

BOEHNE, PATRICIA JEANNE
PERSONAL Born 02/04/1940, Neuilly, France, m, 1960, 2 children **DISCIPLINE** MEDIEVAL HISPANO-ARABIC & CATALAN LITERATURE **EDUCATION** Ind Univ, Bloomington, BA, 61, MA, 62, PhD, 69. **CAREER** Instr Span & French, Bradley Univ, 63-65; asst prof Span, Franklin & Marshall Col, 68-70; assoc prof Romance lang, 70-75; Prof Romance Lang, Eastern Col, 75-, Chmn Lang Dept, 74-, Humanist evaluator Hisp, Pub Comt for Humanities Pa, 77-. **HONORS AND AWARDS** Phi Sigma Iota; Sigma Delta Pi; Kappa Delta Pi; Am Philos Soc Mellon fel, Vatican microfilm libr; Linbock Awd, 87. **MEMBERSHIPS** NAm Catalan Soc; MLA; Renaissance Soc Am; Am Asn Teachers Span & Port. **RESEARCH** Catalan Neoplatonism. **SELECTED PUBLICATIONS** Auth, Dream and Fantasy in Early Catalan Prose, Hisp, Barcelona, 75; transl, Introduction to Catalan Literature, Ind Univ 77; Catalan Studies, Hispam, Barcelona, 77; J V Foix, Twayne, 80; The Renaissance Catalan Novel, Twayne. **CONTACT ADDRESS** Dept of Lang, Eastern Col, 1300 Eagle Rd, Saint Davids, PA 19087-3696. **EMAIL** pboehne@eastern.edu

BOENING, JOHN
PERSONAL Born 06/15/1942, New York, NY, m, 2 children **DISCIPLINE** COMPARATIVE LITERATURE **EDUCATION** Pace Col, BA, 64; Univ Md, MA, 66; Ind Univ, PhD(-comp lit), 71. **CAREER** Teaching asst English, Univ Md, 64-66; univ fel, Ind Univ, 66-68; from instr to assoc prof, 69-75; Ed, ICLA Bulletin, 79-88; Treasurer, ICLA, 91-97; Dir Comp Lit Prog, Univ Toledo; prof English Comp Lit, 80; Member Exec Committee and Chair, MLA Division on European Literary Relations, 84-86; chmn dept, 91-97; div rep, MLA Delegate Assembly, 80-82, 85-88; CEAO Chairs Caucus, 95-97; vis scholar Univ Saarbruecken, 97. **HONORS AND AWARDS** Univ fel Indiana Univ; Delta Phi Alpha; Phi Kappa Phi; Arts & Sciences Exceptional Merit Awd, Univ Toledo. **MEMBERSHIPS** MLA; Am Soc Aesthet; Am Comp Lit Asn; Am Soc Eighteenth-Century Studies; Am Lit Translators Assn; Am Lit Translators Assn; Int Comp Lit Asn, Am Lit Translators Assn; Int Herder Soc. **RESEARCH** Literature and the visual arts; Anglo-German literary relations; modern poetry. **SELECTED PUBLICATIONS** Auth, Literature, language frontiers, and cultural thanatology, Proc VII Int Cong Aesthet, 73; auth, Some recent theories of reception and influence: Their implications for the study of international literary relations, Prov VIII Cong Int comp Lit Asn, 76; ed, The Reception of Classical German Literature in England, 1760-1860: A Documentary History from Contemporary Periodicals (10 vols), Garland, NY, 77; auth, Too German, and not German enough: Lessing's reputation in England, Lessing Yearbk, 81; The Sezession Movement as a verbal fiction, Proc IX Cong Int Comp Lit Asn, 81; Pioneers and Precedents: The Rise of the Critic and the Reception of German Literature in England, Int Archiv Sozialgeschichte Deutschen Lit, 82; auth, "Herder and the White Man's Burden: The Ideen zur Philosophie der Geschichte and the Shaping of British Colonial Policy," in Johann Gottfried Herder: Language, History and the Enlightenment, ed, Wulf Koepke, Camden House, 90; auth, Comparative Lit, Incommensurability and Cultural Misreading, in Cultural Dialogue and Misreading, ec Mabel Lee and Yue Daiyun, Beijing, Beijing Univ Press and Sydney, Univ of Sydney World Lit Series, 97; More patchwork than Pastiche: Longfellow's Golden Legend and Goethe's Faust, in Parodia, Pastiche, Mimetismo, ed P Mildonian, Rome, Editore Bulzoni, 97, others. **CONTACT ADDRESS** 2801 W Bancroft St, Toledo, OH 43606-3390. **EMAIL** johnboenin@.utoledo.edu

BOERNER, PETER
PERSONAL Born 03/10/1926, Tartu, Estonia, m, 1959, 3 children **DISCIPLINE** COMPARATIVE LITERATURE, GERMAN LITERATURE **EDUCATION** Univ Frankfurt, DrPhil, 54. **CAREER** Prog asst, Radio Frankfurt, 48-49; fel, Col Europe, Bruges, Belgium, 54-55; cur, Goethe Mus, Dusseldorf, 55-58; asst prof Ger, Stanford Univ & res dir, Stanford Overseas Studies Ctr, Beutelsbach, Ger, 58-61; from asst prof to assoc prof Ger, Univ Wis, 61-64; assoc prof, State Univ NY Buffalo, 64-66; prof comp lit, Univ Wis-Madison, 66-71, Prof Comp Lit, Ger & W Europ Studies, Ind Univ, Bloomington, 71-, Vis prof, Univ Mich, 67, Middlebury Col, 68 & Yale Univ, 78; Guggenheim fel, 70-71; fel, Herzog August Bibliothek, Wolfenbuttel, Ger, 76-77; fel, Zentrum fur interdisziplinare Forschung, Bielefeld, Ger, 80-81. **HONORS AND AWARDS** Fel Wissenschaftskolleg, Berling 86-87; National Endowment for the Humanities 93-94. **RESEARCH** International literary relations; 18th century and romanticism. **SELECTED PUBLICATIONS** Auth, Johann Wolfgang von Geothe. Rowohlts Monographien vol. 100. Reinbek: Rowohlt, 64. 33rd rev. ed. 99. 265th-284th thousand. Translations into English, French, Spanish, Chinese, Japanese, Korean, Czech, and Duth; auth, Tagebuch. Sammlung Metzler vol. 85. Stuttgart: Metzler, 69; editions: Goethe, Samtliche Werke. 45 vols. Munchen: Deutscher Taschenbuch Verlag, 61-63; Sensus Communis. Contemporary Trends in Comparative Literature. Tubingen: Gunter Narr, 86; Concepts of National Identity: An Interdisciplinary Dialogue. Baden-Baden: Nomos, 86; Faust through Four Centuries--Vierhundert Jahre Faust. Tubingen: Niemeyer, 89; Caroline von Wolzogen: Gesammelte Schriften. 6 vols. Hildesheim: Olms, 88-89. **CONTACT ADDRESS** Indiana Univ, Bloomington, 1213 E First St, Bloomington, IN 47401.

BOFMAN, THEODORA HELENE
PERSONAL Born 11/19/1947, Chicago, IL, 2 children **DISCIPLINE** SOUTHEAST ASIAN LANGUAGE & LITERATURE **EDUCATION** Univ MI, BA, 69, PhD, 78; Yale Univ, MA, 71. **CAREER** Lectr ling & Eng, Ben Gurion Univ, 78-80; from Instr to Prof Linguistics, Northeastern IL Univ, Chicago, 81. **RESEARCH** Thai lit & linguistics; lang acquisition. **SELECTED PUBLICATIONS** Auth, Poetics of the Ramakian, Northern IL Univ. **CONTACT ADDRESS** Dept Linguistics, Northeastern Illinois Univ, 5500 N St Louis Ave, Chicago, IL 60625-4699. **EMAIL** t-bofman@neiu.edu

BOGEN, JOSEPH E.
PERSONAL Born 07/13/1926, Cincinnati, OH, m, 1955, 2 children **DISCIPLINE** NEUROSURGERY **EDUCATION** Whittier Col, AB, 49; Univ S Calif, MD, 56; **CAREER** Asst surg, Cornell Med Sch, 57; Res fel Neurophysiol, Calif Inst Tech, 58; res assoc Neurophysiol, 59, asst neurology, 63 Loma Linda Univ; asst clin prof neurosurg, Calif coll Med, 64; Consult Neurosurg, Calif Inst Tech, 68-80; Assoc clin prof, Univ S Calif, 73-77, Clin prof, 77- ; adj prof, Univ Calif Los Angeles, 84- ; vis prof, Calif Inst Tech, 95-00. **HONORS AND AWARDS** Natl Res Council fel, 58-59; diplomate, Am Bd of Neurological Surg, 66; fel Am Coll Surg, 68. **MEMBERSHIPS** Sigma Xi; AAAS; So Calif Neurosurg Soc; Am Acad Neurol; Am Assoc Neurol Surg; Am Coll Surgeons; Soc for Neurosci; Behavioral Neurol Soc; Western Pain Soc; Am Pain Soc; Int Neuropsychol Soc; Acad of Aphasia. **RESEARCH** Postural reflexology; cerebral localization; surgery for epilepsy; neuropsychology and behavioral neurology. **SELECTED PUBLICATIONS** Auth, Disconnection Syndrome, in Blackwell Dictionary of Neuropsychology, Blackwell, 96; auth, Does Cognition in the Disconnected Right Hemisphere Require Right Hemisphere Possession of Language?, in Brain and Lang, 97; auth, The Neurosurgeon's Interest in the Corpus Callosum, in A History of Neurosurgery, Am Assoc Neurol Surg, 97; auth, Split-brains: Interhemispheric Exchange as a Source of Creativity, in Encyclopedia of Creativity, 1999; auth, My Developing Understanding of Roger Wolcott Sperry's Philosophy, Neuropsychologia, 1998; coauth, Encyclopedia of Neuroscience, 1999. **CONTACT ADDRESS** PO Box 50566, Pasadena, CA 91115. **EMAIL** jbogen@cns.caltech.edu

BOGLE, EDRA CHARLOTTE
PERSONAL Born 01/04/1934, Des Moines, IA, m **DISCIPLINE** COMPARATIVE LITERATURE **EDUCATION** Univ Northern IA, BA, 56; Columbia Univ, MLS, 57; Univ Southern Calif, PhD, 69. **CAREER** Asst libr, Ore Col, 57-59; asst libr, State Teachers Col, 59-60; educ libr, USC, 60-64; asst libr, Univ of S Calif, 65-68; asst prof to assoc prof, Univ N Tex, 68-. **HONORS AND AWARDS** Michael Lynch Serv Awd; Gay Caucus for the Mod Lang, 91; Serv Awd, Univ N Tex, 91. **MEMBERSHIPS** Sci Fiction Res Assoc; MLA. **RESEARCH** Sci Fiction **SELECTED PUBLICATIONS** Auth, "Boyce House", "Margaret Bell Houston", "Dorothy Belle Flanagan Hughes", in Southwestern Am Lit: A Bibliography, ed John Q Anderson, Swallow Pr, (Chicago, 80): 319-322; coed, A Dictionary of Anonymous and Pseudonymous Publications in the English Language, Vol 1, 1475-1640, Longman (London), 80; auth, "David Gerrold", "Anne McCaffrey", Dict of Lit Biography, Vol 8: Twentieth-Century American Science Fiction Writers, ed David Cowart and Thomas L Wymer, Gale Res, (Detroit), 81; auth, "Thomas Mann", and "St John Perse", The Who's Who of Nobel Prize Winners", ed Barnard S Schlessinger and June H Schlessinger, Oryx Pr, (Phoeniz, 86); auth, "Andre Norton's Key Out of Time", Guide to Literature and Biography for Young Adults, ed Kirk Beetz, 89. **CONTACT ADDRESS** Dept English, Univ of No Texas, PO Box 311307, Denton, TX 76203-1307. **EMAIL** ebogle@unt.edu

BOHN, WILLARD
PERSONAL Born 12/02/1939 **DISCIPLINE** FRENCH, COMPARATIVE LITERATURE **EDUCATION** Univ Calif at Berkeley, BA, 64; MA, 67; PhD, 73. **CAREER** Asst prof, Brandeis Univ, 72-74; lectr, Univ Calif at Santa Cruz, 79-81; from asst prof to prof, Ill State Univ, 81-. **HONORS AND AWARDS** NEH Fel for Col Teachers, Fowler Hamilton Vis Res Fel, Oxford Univ; Fel, Am Philos Soc. **MEMBERSHIPS** MLA, Am Comparative Lit Asn. **RESEARCH** Modern Poetry, the Avant-Garde, Dada, Surrealism, Futurism, Literature and Art, Visual Poetry, Ekphrasis. **SELECTED PUBLICATIONS** Auth, The Aesthetics of Visual Poetry, 86 & 93; auth, Apollinaire and the International Avant-Garde, 97; auth, Modern Visual Poetry, 00. **CONTACT ADDRESS** Dept of For Lang, Illinois State Univ, 1 Campus Box 4300, Normal, IL 61790-0001. **EMAIL** wbohn@ilstu.edu

BOLCHAZY, LADISLAUS J.
PERSONAL Born 06/07/1937, Slovakia, m, 1965, 1 child **DISCIPLINE** CLASSICS AND PHILOSOPHY **EDUCATION** St. Joseph's Col & Sem, NYork, BA, philos, 63; NYork Univ, MA, classics, 67; SUNY Albany, PhD, classics, 73. **CAREER** Latin/eng, Iona Prep, 64-65; Latin/eng, Sacred Heart High Sch, 62-64; instr, Siena Col, 66-67; asst prof, La Salette Col and Sem, 71-75; visiting asst prof, Millersville State Univ, 75-76; visiting asst prof, Loyola Univ of Chicago, 76-77; adjunct prof, Loyola Univ of Chicago, 79-; pres, Bolchazy-Carducci Publ Inc. **HONORS AND AWARDS** NEH summer inst, ancient hist, Univ Mich, 77; NEH summer sem, Sophocles and Thucydides, Cornell Univ, 76; teaching fel, State Univ of NY Albany, 67-71; res grants, Loyola Univ, spring and summer, 77. **MEMBERSHIPS** Amer Philol Asn. **RESEARCH** History of ethical & theological concepts; Stylometric analysis of language. **SELECTED PUBLICATIONS** Auth, Hospitality in Antiquity, Ares Publ, Chicago, 96; auth, A Concordance to Ausonius, George Olms, Hildesheim, 83; auth, The Coin-Iscriptions and Epigraphical Abbreviations of Imperial Rome, Ares Publ, 78; auth, A Concordance to the Utopia of St. Thomas More, Georg Olms, Hildesheim, 78; auth, Hospitality in Early Rome, Ares Publ, Chicago, 77. **CONTACT ADDRESS** Ladislaus J. Bolchazy, PhD, Bolchazy-Carducci Publishers, Inc, 1000 Brown St., No 101, Unit 101, Wauconda, IL 60084. **EMAIL** classics@bolchazy.com

BOND, GERALD ALBERT
PERSONAL Born 03/15/1944, Rochester, NY, m, 1966, 2 children **DISCIPLINE** FRENCH AND GERMAN LANGUAGE, MEDIEVAL HISTORY **EDUCATION** William Col, BA, 65; Tufts Univ, MA, 66; Yale Univ, PhD(Medieval studies), 73. **CAREER** Instr Ger, 70-73, asst prof French & Ger, 73-78, Assoc Prof French & German, 78- **HONORS AND AWARDS** Younger humanist fel, Mellon Found, 76; Camargo Found fel, 77. **MEMBERSHIPS** Medieval Acad; MLA; Int Courtly Lit Soc. **RESEARCH** Medieval lyric poetry; courtly love; game and literature. **SELECTED PUBLICATIONS** Auth, The Game of Love, Troubadour Wordplay, Romance Philol, Vol 0048, 94; The Envy of Angels--Cathedral Schools and Social Ideas in Medieval Europe, Speculum- Jour Medieval Stud, Vol 0071, 96. **CONTACT ADDRESS** Dept of Foreign Lang Lit & Ling, Univ of Rochester, Rochester, NY 14627.

BOND, ZINNY
PERSONAL Born 09/01/1940, Riga, Latvia, d, 2 children **DISCIPLINE** LINGUISTICS **EDUCATION** Univ Akron, BA; MA; Ohio State Univ, PhD. **CAREER** Prof, Univ Alberta, 71-74; prof, Ohio Univ, 75-. **MEMBERSHIPS** Ling Soc of Am, ASA. **RESEARCH** Phonetics, psycholinguistics, Baltic linguistics. **SELECTED PUBLICATIONS** Auth, Slips of the Ear: Errors in perception of casual cnversation. **CONTACT ADDRESS** Dept Ling, Ohio Univ, Athens, OH 45701-2942. **EMAIL** bond@ohio.edu

BONDANELLA, JULIA CONAWAY
DISCIPLINE ITALIAN LITERATURE **EDUCATION** Univ Oregon, PhD, 73. **CAREER** Assoc prof. **HONORS AND AWARDS** Tchg Awd. **MEMBERSHIPS** Am Asn Italian Studies; Nat Collegiate Honors Coun. **RESEARCH** Medieval and Renaissance literature; comparative literature; history of ideas; Petrarchism. **SELECTED PUBLICATIONS** Auth, Petrarch's Visions and Their Renaissance Analogs; The Dictionary of Italian Literature; The Italian Renaissance Reader; Giorgio Vasari's The Lives of the Artists. **CONTACT ADDRESS** Dept of French and Italian, Indiana Univ, Bloomington, 1020 E Kirkwood Ave, Ballantine Hall 642, Bloomington, IN 47405. **EMAIL** bondane@indiana.edu

BONDANELLA, PETER
DISCIPLINE ITALIAN LITERATURE **EDUCATION** Univ Oregon, PhD, 70. **CAREER** Prof. **MEMBERSHIPS** Am Asn Italian Studies. **RESEARCH** Renaissance and contemporary literature; comparative literature and literary theory; Italian cinema. **SELECTED PUBLICATIONS** Auth, Machiavelli and the Art of Renaissance History; Francesco Guicciardini; The Dictionary of Italian Literature; The Eternal City: Images of Rome in the Modern World; Federico Fellini: Essays in Criticism; Italian Cinema: From Neorealism to the Present; Perspectives on Federico Fellini; The Films of Roberto Rossellini; Umberto Eco and the Open Work. **CONTACT ADDRESS** Dept of French and Italian, Indiana Univ, Bloomington, 1020 E Kirkwood Ave, Ballantine Hall 642, Bloomington, IN 47405. **EMAIL** bondanel@indiana.edu

BONEBAKKER, SEEGER A.
PERSONAL Born 09/21/1923, Wisch, Netherlands, m, 1953 **DISCIPLINE** ARABIC LANGUAGE AND LITERATURE **EDUCATION** State Univ Leiden, Drs, 51, PhD (Semitic lang), 56. **CAREER** Mem acad staff, State Univ Leiden, 49-60; from asst prof to assoc prof, Arabic studies, Columbia Univ, 60-69; Prof Arabic, Univ Calif, Los Angeles, 69-, Dir, Concordance et Indices Tradition Musulmane, Union Acad Int, 59-60; Columbia Univ Coun Res Humanities grant, Neth, 63; Nat Found Arts and Humanities sr fel, 67-68; regents fac fel, Univ Calif, 72-73 and 75-76; prin investr, Onomasticon Arabicum Proj, Univ Calif, Los Angeles, 76-; Corresp, Royal Nether Acad Arts and Sci, Amsterdam, 80. **MEMBERSHIPS** Am Orient Soc. **RESEARCH** Medieval Arabic literature and biography; history of medieval Arabic rhetoric and philology. **SELECTED PUBLICATIONS CONTACT ADDRESS** Dept of Near East Lang and Cult, Univ of California, Los Angeles, Los Angeles, CA 90024.

BONFIGLIO, THOMAS
PERSONAL Born Rochester, NY **DISCIPLINE** GERMAN **EDUCATION** Univ Rochester, BS, 72; Univ Toronto, MA, 74; Univ Wisc, MA, 76; Indiana Univ, PhD, 84. **CAREER** Instr to asst prof, Kalamazoo Col, Mich, 82-84; asst prof to assoc prof, Univ Richmond, 84-, coord, German Studies. **HONORS AND AWARDS** Distinguished Ed Awd, Univ Richmond, 89-90; DAAD grant, 91. **MEMBERSHIPS** MLA, German Studies Asn, Am Asn Teachers of German, Int Soc for 18th Century Studies, Linguistic Soc Am. **RESEARCH** Enlightenment, romanticism, psychoanalysis, gender theory, Americam sociolinguistics. **SELECTED PUBLICATIONS** Auth, "Metaphor, Systemic Leveling, and the Primary Process," Proteus, 2/2 (85); auth, "A Tropical view of Irony and Satire in Arnim," Colloquia Germanica, 18/3 (85); auth, "Arnim and Schelling's 'Naturphilosophie'," Euphorian, 81/3 (87); auth, Achim von Arnim's Novellensammlung 1812: Balance and Mediation, Bern: Peter Lang (87); auth, "Androphilic Emlightenment: Reading Kant's Answer to the Question," Studies on Voltaire and the Eighteenth Century (summer 93); auth, "The Patrilineal Discourse of Enlightenment: Reading Foucault Reading Kant," Bull de la Soc de Philos de lang Francaise, 6/1-2 (94); auth, "Ironie und Modernitat bei Arnim," in Achim von Arnim: Grenzgange, ed Michael Andermatt, Bouvier (94); auth, "Reading the Homerotic in Winckelmann's 'Beschreibung eines Torso im Belvedere zu Rom.'," Studies on Voltaire and the Eighteenth Century (summer 97); auth, "Private Reason(s) and Public Spheres: Sexuality and Enlightenment in Kant," The Eighteenth Century: Theory and Interpretation, 38/2 (97); auth, "Winckelmann and the Aesthetics of Eros," The Germanic Rev (spring 98). **CONTACT ADDRESS** Dept Modern Langs, Univ of Richmond, Richmond, VA 23173-0001. **EMAIL** tbonfigl@richmond.edu

BONFINI, MARIE ROSEANNE
PERSONAL Born 11/21/1935, Philadelphia, PA **DISCIPLINE** FRENCH LANGUAGE & LITERATURE, COMPARATIVE LITERATURE **EDUCATION** Immaculata Col, AB, 58; Univ Paris, dipl French studies, 62; Fordham Univ, MA, 64; Univ Rochester, PhD(French/comp lit), 69. **CAREER** Sec teacher, Norfolk Cath High Sch, Va, 62-65; acad dean, 71-78, Prof French, Immaculata Col, 68-; Coordr, Inst Res, 82-92, pres, 92-; Res grant, Univ Rochester in Paris, 67; Fulbright reviewer, State Pa Selection Comt, 74; Nat Endowment for Humanities res grant, 78; Lilly grant medieval studies, 80; Nat Endowment for Humanities grant, Harvard Univ, 83; Harvard Univ Inst for Presidents, 93. **HONORS AND AWARDS** West Catholic High School Hall of Fame, Phila, 98. **MEMBERSHIPS** Am Asn Teachers Fr. **RESEARCH** Middle Ages and French literature; creative leisure; play theory and comparative literature. **CONTACT ADDRESS** Immaculata Col, Immaculata, PA 19345-0654. **EMAIL** rbonfini@immaculata.edu

BONGIE, CHRIS
PERSONAL Born 03/07/1960, Vancouver, BC, Canada **DISCIPLINE** ENGLISH, COMPARATIVE LITERATURE **EDUCATION** Univ Brit Columb, BA, 82; Stanford Univ, AM, 78; PhD, 82. **CAREER** Asst to assoc prof, director, Col of William and Mary, 94-. **HONORS AND AWARDS** Mellon Fel, 93-94; NEH Grant, 01-02. **RESEARCH** 19th and 20th Century French and Francophone literature, cultural studies, Victorian Literature. **SELECTED PUBLICATIONS** Auth, Exotic Memories: Literature, Colonialism, and the Fin de Siecle, Stanford Univ Pr, 91; auth, Islands and Exiles: The Creole Identities of Post/Colonial Literature, Stanford Univ Pr, 98. **CONTACT ADDRESS** Dept English, Col of William and Mary, Williamsburg, VA 23187-8795. **EMAIL** clbong@wm.edu

BONGIE, LAURENCE L.
PERSONAL Born 12/15/1929, Turtleford, Canada, m, 1958, 1 child **DISCIPLINE** FRENCH **EDUCATION** Univ BC, BA, 50; Univ Paris, PhD, 52. **CAREER** Lectr to dept head and prof emeritus, Univ BC, 53-. **HONORS AND AWARDS** Fel, Can Coun, 63-64, 75-76; Fel, Soc Sic and Humanities Fel, 82-83; Killam Sen Fel, 82-83; Sen Killam Res Prize, 87. **MEMBERSHIPS** Intl Soc for Eighteenth Century Studies; Am Soc for Eighteenth Century Studies; Can Soc for Eighteenth Studies. **RESEARCH** Enlightenment studies; Diderot; Hume; Condillac; Sade; Clandestine press. **SELECTED PUBLICATIONS** Auth, The Love of a Prince: Bonnie Prince Charlie in France, 1744-1748, UBC Press, 86; auth, Sade, A Biographical Essay, Univ Chicago Press, 98; auth, David Hume: Prophet of the Counter-Revolution, Liberty Fund, 00. **CONTACT ADDRESS** Dept French, Univ of British Columbia, 4651 Simpson Ave, Vancouver, BC, Canada V6R 1C2. **EMAIL** lbongie@interchange.ubc.ca

BONVILLAIN, NANCY
PERSONAL Born 08/03/1945, Pittsburgh, PA **DISCIPLINE** ANTHROPOLOGY, LINGUISTICS **EDUCATION** Hunter Col, City Univ NY, BA, 66; Columbia Univ, NY, PhD, 72. **CAREER** Asst Prof, Mich State Univ, E Lansing, 71-73; Asst Prof, Livingston Col, Rutgers Univ, 73-74; Asst Prof, Sarah Lawrence Col, Bronxville, NY, 75-76; Adj Asst Prof, York Col, Queens NY, 75-76; Adj Asst Prof, Kingsborough Community Col, Brooklyn NY, 75-76; Asst/Assoc Prof, SUNY Stony Brook, 76-92; Acting Chairperson, Anthrop Dept, SUNY, Stony Brook, 81; Vis Assoc Prof, Columbia Univ NY, 81-82; Adj Prof, New Sch for Soc Res, NYork City, 79-93; Adj Prof, SUNY Purchase, 93, 94; Fac, Simon's Rock Col of Bard, Mass, 96-; Adj, Berkshire Community Col, Mass, 96-; Anthrop, Summer Session, Columbia Univ, 82-. **HONORS AND AWARDS** Phi Beta Kappa, 67; Res Fel, Nat Endowment for the Humanities, 74-75. **MEMBERSHIPS** Am Anthrop Asn, Ling Soc of Am. **RESEARCH** Native American Cultures, Histories and Languages, Mohawk Linguistics. **SELECTED PUBLICATIONS** Auth, Women and Men: cultural constructs of gender, Prentice Hall (Englewood Cliffs, NJ), 93, 97, 01; auth, The Hopi, Chelsea House Publ (NY), 94; auth, Black Hawk, Sac Rebel, Chelsea House Publ (NY), 94; auth, The teton Sioux, Chelsea House Publ (NY), 94; auth, The Haidas, Millbrook Press (Brookfield, CT), 94; auth, The Sac and Fox, Chelsea House Publ (NY), 95; auth, The Navajos, Millbrook Press

(Brookfield, CT), 95; auth, The Zuni, Chelsea House Publ (NY), 95; auth, Native American Religion, Chelsea House Publ (NY), 96; auth, The Cheyenne, Millbrook Press (Brookfield, CT), 96; auth, The Santee Sioux, Chelsea House Publ (NY), 97; auth, Native American Medicine, Chelsea House Publ (NY), 98; auth, Native Nations: cultures and histories of Native North America, Prentice Hall (Upper Saddle River, NJ), in press. **CONTACT ADDRESS** Dept Soc Sci, Simon's Rock Col of Bard, 84 Aford Rd, Great Barrington, MA 01230.

BOON, JEAN-PIERRE
DISCIPLINE FRENCH LITERATURE **EDUCATION** Columbia Univ, PhD. **CAREER** Lectr, Univ of Kans. **RESEARCH** French film. **SELECTED PUBLICATIONS** Publ(s), on Montaigne, Baudelaire. **CONTACT ADDRESS** Dept of French and Italian, Univ of Kansas, Lawrence, Lawrence, KS 66045.

BORCHARDT, FRANK L.
PERSONAL Born 11/16/1938, New York, NY, s **DISCIPLINE** GERMAN **EDUCATION** Saint Peter's Col, AB, 60; The Johns Hopkins Univ, MA, 62, PhD, 65. **CAREER** Asst prof, Northwestern Univ, 65-68; asst prof, Queens Col, The City Univ of NY, 68-71; assoc prof, Duke Univ, 71-91, prof, 91-. **HONORS AND AWARDS** Phi Bata Kappa, 65; ACLS fel, 78-79; advisory prof, The Shanghai Jiao Tong Univ, 99-. **RESEARCH** Renaissance and Reformation, computer assisted language instruction, aesthetics of multimedia. **SELECTED PUBLICATIONS** Auth, "On the History and Aesthetics of Screen design," MultiMedia CALL: Theory and Practice, Keith C. Cameron, ed, Exeter: Elm Bank Pubs (98): 3-10; auth, "Towards an Aesthetics of Multimedia," CALL J: Computer Assisted Lang Learning, Exeter, 12, 1 (99): 3-28. **CONTACT ADDRESS** Dept Germanic Lang & Lit, Duke Univ, PO Box 90256, Durham, NC 27708-0256. **EMAIL** frankbo@duke.edu

BORDEAU, CATHERINE
DISCIPLINE FRENCH **EDUCATION** Univ MI, Ann Arbor, BA, MA, PhD. **CAREER** Asst prof, Lyon Col. **RESEARCH** 19th century French lit; gender studies. **SELECTED PUBLICATIONS** Auth, The Gendering of the Creator, in Jeering Dreamers: Essays on L'Eve Future, Atlanta, 96. **CONTACT ADDRESS** Dept of For Lang, Lyon Col, 300 Highland Rd, PO Box 2317, Batesville, AR 72503. **EMAIL** cbordeau@lyon.edu

BORER, HAGIT
DISCIPLINE SYNTAX, MORPHOLOGY, LANGUAGE ACQUISITION **EDUCATION** MIT, PhD. **CAREER** Prof, Univ Southern Calif. **RESEARCH** Comparative syntax; interaction between syntax & morphology; language acquisition. **SELECTED PUBLICATIONS** Auth, Parametric Syntax: Case Studies in Semitic &Romance Languages, Foris Publ, Dordrecht, 84; Restrictive Relatives in Modern Hebrew, Natural Lang & Ling Theory 2, 84; I-Subjects, Ling Inquiry 17 3, 86; Anaphoric AGR, in The PRO Drop Parameter, Reidel, Dordrecht, 89; The Causative- Alternative: A Case Study in Parallel Morphology, J Ling Rev, 92; The Ups & Downs of Hebrew Verb Movement, Natural Lang and Ling Theory 13, 95; coauth, The Maturation of Syntax, in Parameter Setting, Reidel, Dordrecht, 87. **CONTACT ADDRESS** Dept of Linguistics, Univ of So California, University Park Campus, Los Angeles, CA 90089. **EMAIL** borer@almaak.usc.edu

BORGESON, PAUL A.
DISCIPLINE SPANISH LITERATURE **EDUCATION** Vanderbilt Univ, PhD, 77. **CAREER** Assoc prof, Univ Ill Urbana Champaign. **RESEARCH** Spanish American Literature; poetry of the 1960s to date; ideology and poetics; popular language; aesthetic tradition. **SELECTED PUBLICATIONS** Auth, Hacia el hombre nuevo: Poesia y pensamiento de Ernesto Cardenal, 84; Los talleres del tiempo: Verso escogido, 92; La lucha permanente: Arte y sociedad en La Espiga Amotinada, 94; Lengua viva, 98. **CONTACT ADDRESS** Span, Ital, and Port Dept, Univ of Illinois, Urbana-Champaign, 707 S Mathews Ave, Urbana, IL 61801-3625. **EMAIL** borgeson@uiuc.edu

BORLAND, ISABEL ALVAREZ
DISCIPLINE SPANISH **EDUCATION** Lycoming Col, BA, 70; Middlebury Col, MA, 72; Pa State Univ, PhD, 80. **CAREER** Prof, Span, Col of the Holy Cross. **HONORS AND AWARDS** Res and Publication Grant, Holy Cross, 98; Summer Fac Fel, Holy Cross, 97; chair, MLA Exec Comm of the Division of Ethnic Studies in lang and lit, 98-99; Hewlett Mellon Grant, Holy Cross, 88, 96; Partial Tuition Grant, The School of Criticism and Theory, 88; Holy Cross Special fac fel, 85, 93; elected fac Marshal, 86, 94; summer fac fel, Holy Cross, 82, 86; NEH Summer Seminar, 83; Col of Liberal Arts Res grant, PSU, 80; The Dubois Campus Educational Found grant, PSU, 80. **MEMBERSHIPS** MLA; AATSP; LASA; IEC; NACAE; NECLAS. **RESEARCH** US Latino literature; Cuban and Cuban-Am literature; Spanish Caribbean literature; contemporary Latin American narrative. **SELECTED PUBLICATIONS** Auth, "Interior Texts in El amor en los tiempos del colera," Hisp Rev 58 (91): 175-186; auth, "Versiones literarias: Sarduy y Cabrera Infante," Linden Lane XI (92): 21-22; auth, "The Task of the Historian in El general en su laberinto," Hispania 76 (93): 192-199; auth, "Displacements and Autobiography in Cuban-American Fiction," World Lit Today 68 (94): 43-49; auth, "Cortazar: On Critics and Interpretation," INTI: Revista de literatura hispanica 43-44 (96): 157-167; auth, Cuban-American Narratives of Exile: From Person to Persona, Univ of VA Press (Charlottesville), 98. **CONTACT ADDRESS** Dept of Modern Languages and Literatures, Col of the Holy Cross, 1 College St, PO Box 190A, Worcester, MA 01610-2395. **EMAIL** ialvarez@holycross.edu

BORMANN, DENNIS ROBERT
PERSONAL Born 11/07/1935, Mitchell, SD, m, 1962, 2 children **DISCIPLINE** SPEECH COMMUNICATION, GERMAN **EDUCATION** Univ SDak, 57; Univ Iowa, MA, 59, PhD (speech, drama), 68. **CAREER** Asst prof Speech, Mankato State Col, 64-66; from instr to assoc prof, 66-77, interim chmn speech, 75-77, Prof Speech, Univ Nebr-Lincoln, 77-, Woods fac res fel, Univ Marburg, 73; comn int and intercultural speech commun, Speech Commun As, 77-79. **HONORS AND AWARDS** Fulbright Scholar, 57-58; Wood Fac Res Fel, 72; Maude Hammond Fling Res Fel, 84; George Holmes Res Fel, 89. **MEMBERSHIPS** Nat Commun Asn; AAUP; Phi Beta Kappa; Omicron Delta Kappa; Tau Kappa Alpha; Delta Phi Alpha. **RESEARCH** Rhetorical theory; German rhetoric and poetic; public address. **SELECTED PUBLICATIONS** Auth, "Some Common Sense about Campbell, Hume, and Reid," Quart J Speech 71 (85); auth, "George Campbell's Cura Prima on Eloquence," Quart J Speech, 75 (88); auth, The 6th Canon--Belletristic Rhetorical Theory and Its French Antecedents, Philos Rhet, Vol 0029, 96. **CONTACT ADDRESS** Dept of Speech Cummun, Univ of Nebraska, Lincoln, P O Box 880329, Lincoln, NE 68588-0329. **EMAIL** bormann@unlserve.unl.edu

BORMANSHINOV, ARASH
PERSONAL Born 12/05/1922, Belgrade, Yugoslavia, m, 1959, 5 children **DISCIPLINE** SLAVIC LINGUISTICS **EDUCATION** Univ Pa, AM, 56, PhD, 58. **CAREER** Asst prof Russ and Ger, Rensselaer Polytech Inst, 58-59; asst prof Russ, Rutgers Univ, 59-60; asst prof Slavic lang and lit, Princeton Univ, 60-66; asst prof Slavic ling, NY Univ, 66-68 and City Col New York, 68-80. John Hay Whitney Found fel, 56-57; lectr Russ, Mohawk Educ TV, Albany, NY, 58-59; Am Coun Learned Soc res grants, Uralic and Altaic Lang, 59-63; Inter-Univ Comt travel grant, 60; consult educ TV, NY Univ, 61; Doris Duke travel grant, 62; fac res grant, NY Univ, 67-68; vis prof, New Sch Soc Res, 68; assoc prof Russ, Univ Okla, 69; Vis Prof, Yeshiva Univ, 71-. **MEMBERSHIPS** MLA; Am Orient Soc; Am Asn Teachers Slavic and East Europ Lang; Mongolia Soc; Asn Asian Studies. **RESEARCH** South Slavic linguistics; Yugoslav literature; Kalmyk-Oirat studies. **SELECTED PUBLICATIONS** Auth, A Secret Kalmyk Mission to Tibet in 1904, Cent Asiatic J, Vol 0036, 92. **CONTACT ADDRESS** 6811 Gairlock Pl, Lanham, MD 20801.

BOSKOVIC, ZELJKO
PERSONAL Born 11/27/1964, Tuzla, Bosnia and Herzegovina, s **DISCIPLINE** LINGUISTICS **EDUCATION** Sarajevo Univ, BA, 88; W Va Univ, MA, 91; Univ Conn, MA, 93, PhD, 95. **CAREER** Asst Prof, Univ Conn, 95-. **HONORS AND AWARDS** Roma Jacobson fel, Univ Conn, 91-93; NSF grant, 95-96; Hasan Brkic Awd, Sarajevo Univ, 87, 88. **RESEARCH** Linguistics; syntax **SELECTED PUBLICATIONS** Auth, Categorial Status of Null Operator Relatives and Finite Declarative Complements, Lang Res, 94; D-Structure, Theta-Criterion, and Movement into Theta-Positions, Ling Anal, 94; Case Properties of Clauses and the Greed Principle, Studia Ling, 95; coauth Comprehension of Non-Lexical Categories in Agrammatism, Jour Psycholinguistic Res, 95; auth Participle Movement and Second Position Cliticization in Serbo-Croatian, Lingua, 95; Selection and the Categorial Status of Infinitival Complements, Natural Lang & Linguistic Theory, 96; Coordination, Object Shift, and V-movement, Linguistic Inquiry, 97; Superiority Effects with Multiple Wh-Fronting in Servo-Croatian, Lingua, 97; On Certain Violations of the Superiority Condition, Agro, and Economy of Derivation, Jour Linguistics, 97; Pseudoclefts, Studia Linguistics, 97; The Syntax of Nonfinite Complementation: An Economy Approach, Mit Press, 97; Formal Approaches to Slavic Linguistics: The Connecticut Meeting, Mich Slavic Publ, 97; Scrambling and Last Resort, Linguistic Inquiry, 98. **CONTACT ADDRESS** Linguistics Dept, Univ of Connecticut, Storrs, Storrs, CT 06269. **EMAIL** boskovic@uconnum.uconn.edu

BOTTERILL, STEVEN
PERSONAL Born 02/10/1958, Shoreham, United Kingdom, m, 1992 **DISCIPLINE** ITALIAN, LITERATURE, MEDIEVAL STUDIES **EDUCATION** Cambridge Univ, BA, 80, MA, 84, PhD, 84 **CAREER** Res Fel, 83-86, Queens' Col, Cambridge; Asst Prof, 86-92, Assoc Prof, 92-, UC Berkeley **MEMBERSHIPS** AAIS, AATI, ALSC, NAS **RESEARCH** Dante **SELECTED PUBLICATIONS** Auth, Dante and the Mystical Tradition: Bernard of Clairvaux in the Commedia, Cambridge UP, 94; ed, Dante: "De Vulgari Eloquentia," Cambridge UP, 96; many articles. **CONTACT ADDRESS** Italian Studies, Univ of California, Berkeley, Berkeley, CA 94720-2620. **EMAIL** Stevenb@uclink4.berkeley.edu

BOUDREAU, HAROLD LAVERNE
PERSONAL Born 03/15/1928, Ashkum, IL, m, 1955, 1 child **DISCIPLINE** MODERN SPANISH LITERATURE **EDUCATION** Univ Ill, Champaign, BA, 48, MA, 50; Univ Wis-Madison, PhD (Span), 66. **CAREER** From instr to prof Span, 58-69, chmn dept Span and Port, 71-77, Prof Span, Univ Mass, Amherst, 69-, Consult, Nat Endowment Humanities, 76-78. **MEMBERSHIPS** MLA; Am Asn Teachers Span and Port. **RESEARCH** Modern Spanish novel and poetry; critical theory. **SELECTED PUBLICATIONS CONTACT ADDRESS** Dept of Span and Port, Univ of Massachusetts, Amherst, Amherst, MA 01003.

BOUISSAC, PAUL A.
PERSONAL Born 11/17/1934, Perigueux, France **DISCIPLINE** FRENCH **EDUCATION** Sorbonne, LL, 56, DP, 70. **CAREER** Asst to assoc prof, 65-74, PROF, VICTORIA COL, UNIV TORONTO, 74-; fel, Netherlands Inst Advan Stud, 72-73. **HONORS AND AWARDS** John Simon Guggenheim Found, 73-74; Killam sr fel, 89-91. **SELECTED PUBLICATIONS** Auth, Les Demoiselles, 70; auth, La mesure des gestes, 73; auth, Circus and Culture, 76. **CONTACT ADDRESS** Victoria Col, Univ of Toronto, 73 Queens Park E, Toronto, ON, Canada M5S 1K7. **EMAIL** paul.bouissac@utoronto.ca

BOULTON, MAUREEN
DISCIPLINE FRENCH LITERATURE **EDUCATION** Col of New Rocjelle, BA, 70; Univ Pa, MA, 72, PhD, 76; Oxford Univ, Mlitt, 80. **CAREER** Prof. **RESEARCH** Textual criticism; manuscript studies; relations between lyric poetry and medieval romance. **SELECTED PUBLICATIONS** Auth, The Song in the Story, 93; ed, Old French Evangile de l'Enfance. **CONTACT ADDRESS** Romance Languages and Literatures Dept, Univ of Notre Dame, 221 Decio Hall, Notre Dame, IN 46556. **EMAIL** maureen.b.boulton.1@nd.edu

BOUTIN, AIMEE MARIE-CARMEN
PERSONAL Born 09/28/1970, Ottawa, ON, Canada **DISCIPLINE** FRENCH LITERATURE **EDUCATION** Carleton Univ, BA, 92; Cornell Univ, MA, 95; PhD, 98. **CAREER** TA, Cornell Univ, 93-98; asst prof, Fla State Univ, 98-. **HONORS AND AWARDS** AAUS Summer Publ Grant. **MEMBERSHIPS** MLA, SMLA, Women in Fr, 19th Century Fr Studies, Am Conf on Romanticism. **RESEARCH** French Romantic poetry, Gender Studies, 19th Century novel critical theory. **SELECTED PUBLICATIONS** Auth, Maternal Echoes: The Poetry of Marceline Desbordes-Valmore and Alphonse de Lamartine, Univ of Del Pr, 01. **CONTACT ADDRESS** Dept Mod Lang, Florida State Univ, 362 Diffenbaugh, Tallahassee, FL 32306. **EMAIL** aboutine@mailer.fsu.edu

BOVE, CAROL MASTRANGELO
DISCIPLINE FRENCH LANGUAGE, LITERATURE, AND CULTURE **CAREER** Prof. **RESEARCH** Contemporary literature and theory; film; and women's studies; Julia Kristeva. **SELECTED PUBLICATIONS** Publ, Twentieth Century French fiction, theory, and film; ed, Claude Richard's study of American literature, Univ Pa Press. **CONTACT ADDRESS** Dept of Mod Lang, Westminster Col, Pennsylvania, New Wilmington, PA 16172-0001. **EMAIL** cbove@westminster.edu

BOWDITCH, LOWELL
PERSONAL Born 12/13/1961, New York, NY **DISCIPLINE** CLASSICS **EDUCATION** Univ Calif, BA, 84; Brown Univ, MA, 89; PhD, 92. **CAREER** Asst Prof to Assoc Prof, Univ Ore, 93-. **MEMBERSHIPS** Am Philol Asn. **RESEARCH** Augustan Literature; Classics and Contemporary Poetry. **SELECTED PUBLICATIONS** Auth, Horace and the Gift Economy of Patronage, Univ Calif Press, 01. **CONTACT ADDRESS** Dept Class, Univ of Oregon, Dept Class, Eugene, OR 97403. **EMAIL** bowditch@oregon.uoregon.edu

BOWLES, B.
PERSONAL Born 08/08/1972, Roanoke, VA, s **DISCIPLINE** FRENCH LANGUAGE, HISTORY, CULTURE **EDUCATION** Univ Vir, BA, 92; MA, 94; Penn State Univ, PhD, 98. **CAREER** Asst prof, Iowa State Univ, 98-. **HONORS AND AWARDS** Camargo Found Res Fel, France. **MEMBERSHIPS** MLA; SFHS; WSFH; AATF. **RESEARCH** Cultural history of 1930's and World War II; Colonialism; film; ideology; book history. **SELECTED PUBLICATIONS** Auth, "Poetic Practice and Historical Paradigm: Charles Baudelaires Anti-Semitism," PMLA 115 (00): 195-208. **CONTACT ADDRESS** Dept Foreign Language, Iowa State Univ, 300 Pearson Hall, Ames, IA 50011. **EMAIL** bcbowles@iastate.edu

BOWMAN, FRANK PAUL
PERSONAL Born 06/12/1927, Portland, OR **DISCIPLINE** FRENCH LITERATURE **EDUCATION** Reed Col, BA, 49; Yale Univ, MA, 52, PhD(French), 55. **CAREER** Asst prof French, Univ Calif, 54-62; assoc prof, Reed Col, 62-63; assoc prof, 63-65, Prof French, Univ PA, 65-, Guggenheim fel, 68-69; vis prof French, Univ Paris, 73-75; Nat Endowment Humanities fel, 78-79. **MEMBERSHIPS** MLA; Mod Humanities Res Asn; Int Asn Fr Studies; Soc Etudes Romantiques. **RESEARCH** French romanticism; autobiography. **SELECTED PUBLICATIONS CONTACT ADDRESS** Dept of Romance Lang, Univ of Pennsylvania, Philadelphia, PA 19174.

BOYCE, ELIZABETH
DISCIPLINE SPANISH **CAREER** Prof; Houston Baptist Univ, 7 yrs; sponsor, Span Club; fac assoc, Rex Fleming Readers; Med Prof Interview Comt. **HONORS AND AWARDS** Fac Woman of the Yr, 96 & Opal Goolsby Outstanding tchg awd, 94. **RESEARCH** Spanish literature before 1700. **SELECTED PUBLICATIONS** Coauth, groundbreaking bk poetry written by women in Spain in the 16th and 17th centuries. **CONTACT ADDRESS** Language Dept, Houston Baptist Univ, 7502 Fondren Rd, Houston, TX 77074. **EMAIL** BoyceES@aol.com

BOYD, BARBARA WEIDEN
PERSONAL Born 03/31/1952, Bronx, NY, m, 1980, 1 child **DISCIPLINE** CLASSICAL STUDIES **EDUCATION** Manhattanville Col, BA, 74; Univ Mich, MA, 76. PhD, 80. **CAREER** Asst prof to prof, Bowdoin Col, 80- . **HONORS AND AWARDS** NEH Fel, 87-88. **MEMBERSHIPS** Am Philol Asn; Vergilian Soc; Class Asn of the Midwest & South; Class Assn of New England. **RESEARCH** Latin poetry, Vergil and Ovid; Augustan Rome; Republican Roman literature and society. **SELECTED PUBLICATIONS** Auth, Cydonea mala: Virgilian Word-Play and Allusion, in Harvard Studies in Class Philol, 83; auth, Tarpeia's Tomb: A Note on Propertius 4.4, in Am J of Philol, 84; auth, Parva seges satis est: The Landscape of Tibullan Elegy in 1.1. and 1.10, in Transactions of the Am Philol Asn, 84; auth, the Death of Corinna's Parrot Reconsidered: Poetry and Ovid's Amores, in the Class J, 87; auth, Propertius on the Banks of the Eurotas, in Class Q, 87; auth, Virtus Effeminata and Sallust's Sempronia, in Transactions of the Am Philol Asn, 97; auth, Non Hortamine Longo: An Ovidian "Correction of Virgil, in Am J of Philol, 90; auth, Vergil's Camilla and the Traditions of Catalogue and Ecphrasis, in Am J of Philol, 92; auth, Non enarrabile textum: Ecphrastic Trespass and Narrative Ambiguity in the Aeneid, in Vergilius, 95; auth, Bibliography for Ovid's Amores and Metamorphoses, in Teacher's Guide to Advanced Placement Courses in Latin, 95; auth, Changes in the 1999 Advanced Placement Examinations in Latin (Vergil and Latin Literature), in Class Outlook, 97; auth, Ovid's Literary Loves: Influence and Innovation in the Amores, Univ Michigan Pr, 97; auth, Pallas and Turnus: Selections from Vergil, Aeneid Books 10 and 12, Bolchazy-Carducci, 98. **CONTACT ADDRESS** Dept of Classics, Bowdoin Col, Brunswick, ME 04011. **EMAIL** bboyd@bowdoin.edu

BRADFORD, CAROLE A.
PERSONAL Born 03/14/1937, Hammond, IN **DISCIPLINE** SPANISH; FRENCH **EDUCATION** Univ Tenn, BA, 58, MA, 59; Vanderbilt Univ, PhD, 72. **CAREER** Instr romance lang, Univ Tenn, 59-66; instr, 70-72, Asst Prof Romance Lang, Bowling Green State Univ, 72-. **HONORS AND AWARDS** Fel, Nat Endowment Humanities, NY Univ, 78-79. **MEMBERSHIPS** MLA; Am Asn Teachers Span & Port; Am Asn Univ Prof. **RESEARCH** Spanish 20th century poetry; Spanish 19th century novel. **SELECTED PUBLICATIONS** Auth, Gilalbert, Juan, Voice In Exile, Anales De La Literatura Espanola Contemporanea, 93. **CONTACT ADDRESS** Dept of Romance Lang, Bowling Green State Univ, Bowling Green, OH 43403.

BRADLEY, JAMES ROBERT
PERSONAL Born 03/28/1935, Philadelphia, PA, d, 4 children **DISCIPLINE** CLASSICS **EDUCATION** Trinity Col, CT, BA, 57; Harvard Univ, MA, 59, PhD(class philol), 68. **CAREER** Instr classics, Hobart & William Smith Cols, 60-62; asst prof, Univ NC, 67-70; asst prof classics,Trinity Col, 74-00, assoc prof classics, Trinity Col, CT, 74-. **MEMBERSHIPS** Am Philol Asn; Archaeol Inst Am. **RESEARCH** Greek and Latin literature; classical civilization. **SELECTED PUBLICATIONS** Auth, The Elegies of Sulpicia: An Introduction and Commentary, New Eng Class Newsletter and Jour, XXII, 159-164, May, 95; rev, Apuleius, Cupid and Psyche, New Eng Class Newsletter and Jour, XIX, May, 92; auth, Chinese New Year: Four Centuries Ago, New Eng Class Newsletter and Jour, XIX, 26-27, Dec, 91; auth, The Sources of Cornelius Nepos, Selected Lives, Garland Publ, 91; auth, All the Tea in China, Class Outlook, 68, Fall, 90; auth, Ovid, Ars 1.39-40: Making Tracks - Speed, Ritual or Art, Class World, 83, 100-101, 89; rev, Ars Amatoria I, New Eng Class Newsletter, XIV, Oct, 86; auth, The Sources of Cornelius Nepos: Selected Lives, NY and London, Garland Pub, 91. **CONTACT ADDRESS** Dept Classics, Trinity Col, Connecticut, 808 Main St, South Windsor, CT 06074. **EMAIL** james.bradley@mail.trincoll.edu

BRADLEY, KEITH RICHARD
PERSONAL Born 04/30/1946, Oldswinford, England, m, 1976, 3 children **DISCIPLINE** ANCIENT HISTORY, CLASSICAL LANGUAGES **EDUCATION** Sheffield Univ, BA, 67, MA, 68; Oxford Univ, BLitt, 75; Sheffield Univ, LittD, 97. **CAREER** Asst prof, Johns Hopkins Univ, 72-77; vis asst prof, Stanford Univ, 77-80; Asst Prof Classics & Ancient Hist, Univ Victoria, 80- **HONORS AND AWARDS** Fel, of the Soc of Antiquaries, 93; Canada Council Killam Res Fel, 96-98; Fel, of Royal Soc of Canada, 96. **MEMBERSHIPS** Soc Prom Roman Studies, Am Philol Asn, Class Asn Can, Soc for Libyan Studies. **RESEARCH** Greek and Roman social and cultural history; Roman historiography. **SELECTED PUBLICATIONS** Auth, Suetonius' Life of Nero: An Historical Commentary, Brussels, 78; auth, Slaves and Masters in the Roman Empire, New York & Oxford, 86; auth, Slavery and Rebellion in the Roman World, Bloomington & London, 89, 98; auth, Discovering the Roman Family, New York & Oxford, 91; auth, Slavery and Society at Rome, Cambridge, 94; auth, Slaves And Freedmen in Roman Society Under the Empire--A Selection of Texts With Translations--German, Greek And Latin, vol 0068, 96; Suetonius, 'Lives Of Galba, Otho And Vitellius', Latomus, vol 0055, 96; coed, A Historical Guide to World Slavery, eds, S. Engerman & S. Drescher, New York, 98. **CONTACT ADDRESS** Greek and Roman Studies, Univ of Victoria, PO Box 3045, Victoria, BC, Canada V8W 3P4. **EMAIL** kbradley@uvic.ca

BRADY, PATRICK S.
PERSONAL Born 10/27/1933, Broken Hill, Australia, D **DISCIPLINE** FRENCH LITERATURE & COMPARATIVE LITERATURE, ART, CULTURE **EDUCATION** Sorbonne Univ, DUP, 60. **CAREER** Prof, French, Univ Tenn. **HONORS AND AWARDS** Schumway Chair of Excellence. **MEMBERSHIPS** SCLA, ACLA, ICLA. **RESEARCH** Provost, Zola, The Moceo; Interdiscplinary apparatus to art, literature, culture. **SELECTED PUBLICATIONS** "L'Oeurve d'Emile Zola, roman sur les arts: manifeste, autobiographie, roman a clef, (Geneva, Dorz), 67; Marcel Proust, G.K. Hall, (Boston), 77; Structuralist Perspectives in Criticism of Fiction: Essays on "Manon Lescaut' and "La Vie de Marianne," Bern, (Lang), 78; Le Bouc emissaire chez Emile Zola: Quarte essais sur "Germinal" et "L'Oeuvre" Carl Winter Verlag, (Heidelberg), 81; Rococo Style versus Enlightenment Novel, Slatkine, (Geneva), 84; "From Transactual Analysis to Chaos Theory: New Critical Perspectives," Australian Journal of French Studies, vol XXVI, no 2 (May-August 89): 176-193; Memory and History as Fiction: An Archetypal Approach to the Historical Novel, New Paradigm Press, (Knoxville), 93; Chaos in the Humanities, New Paradigm Pr, (Knoxville), 94; "Does God Play Dice? Deterministic and Stochastic Chance in Proust's Recherche," Michigan Romance Studies, vol XIV, (94): 133-149; Interdisciplinary Interpretation of Art and Literature: The Principle of Convergence, New Paradigm Pr, (Knoxville), 95. **CONTACT ADDRESS** Dept of ModFor Langs & Lits, Univ of Tennessee, Knoxville, 701 McClung Tower & Plaza, Knoxville, TN 37996. **EMAIL** pbrady@utk.edu

BRAESTER, YOMI
PERSONAL Born 06/24/1964, Israel, m, 1998 **DISCIPLINE** COMPARATIVE LITERATURE, EAST ASIAN STUDIES **EDUCATION** Hebrew Univ, BA, 85, MA, 91; Yale Univ, MA, 92, PhD, 97. **CAREER** Post-doc fel, CCS, Univ Calif, Berkeley, 97-98; Asst Prof, Comp Lit, Univ GA, 98-; dir, Chinese Lang Prog, Univ Ga, 98-. **HONORS AND AWARDS** Pacific Cult Fnd Res Grant; China Times Cultural Fnd Awd. **MEMBERSHIPS** MLA, AAS. **RESEARCH** Comparative lit, E Asian stud **SELECTED PUBLICATIONS** Auth, "Shanghai's Economy of the Spectacle: The Shanghai Race Club in Liu Na'ou's and Mu Shiying's Stories," Modern Chinese Lit, 9:1, 95; "The Cruelty in Writing: Lu Xun's 'Diary of a Madman' and Authorial Complicity," Literature and Cruelty: Proceedings of the Sixth Annual Graduate Conference in French Francophone and Comparative Literature, 96; "Modern Identity and Karmic Retribution in Clara Law's Reincarnations of Golden Lotus," Asian Cinema 10, 98. **CONTACT ADDRESS** 133 Ashley Cir, Apt 3, Athens, GA 30605. **EMAIL** yomi@arches.uga.edu

BRAIDOTTI, ERMINIO
PERSONAL Born 01/21/1944, Udine, Italy, m, 1972, 2 children **DISCIPLINE** ITALIAN, SPANISH **EDUCATION** Youngstown State Univ, BA, 70; Middlebury Col, MA, 71; Univ Pa, PhD, 81. **CAREER** Coodr, West Chester Univ, 85-95; Prof, West Chester Univ, 95-. **HONORS AND AWARDS** Fulbright-Hays, 91; Lindback Teaching Awd, 98. **RESEARCH** Cinema, culture, language and literature. **SELECTED PUBLICATIONS** Auth, An Introduction to Latin America (forthcoming). **CONTACT ADDRESS** Dept For Lang, West Chester Univ of Pennsylvania, 700 S High St, West Chester, PA 19383-0003. **EMAIL** ebraidotti@wcupa.edu

BRAULT, GERARD JOSEPH
PERSONAL Born 11/07/1929, Chicopee Falls, MA, m, 1954, 3 children **DISCIPLINE** FRENCH LITERATURE **EDUCATION** Assumption Col, Mass, AB, 50; Laval Univ, AM, 52; Univ Pa, PhD(Romance lang), 58. **CAREER** Teaching fel Univ, Pa. 54-56; instr French, Bowdoin Col, 57-59, asst prof Romance lang, 59-61; assoc prof, Univ Pa, 61-65, vdean grad sch arts & sci, 62-65; head dept, 65-70, Prof French, Pa State Univ, University Park, 65-90, Distinguished prof French and Medieval Studies, 90, Edwin Erle Sparks Prof. French and Medieval Studies, 90-97, Edwin Erle Sparks Prof Emeritus French and Medieval Studies, 98-; Fulbright fel, Strasbourg, France, 56-57 & res scholar, 68-69; NDEA Lang Res Sect res contracts, 60 & 63; Am Coun Learned Soc travel grants, 60, 66, 70, 73, 76 & grant-in-aid, 63; Am Philos Soc grants-in-aid, 60, 66 & 72; Guggenheim fel, 68-69; fel Inst Arts & Humanistic Studies, Pa State Univ, 76-; bd mem, Medieval Ctr, Univ Lille III, 77-; Senior fel Canadian Studies, Quebec City, 84; Camargo Found fel, Cassis, France, 87 and 94. **HONORS AND AWARDS** Ordre des Palmes Acad, 65, Officer, 75; Officer, Ordre Nat du Merite, 80; Ordre Nat des Francophones d'Amerique, 80; Fac Scholar Medal, Pa State Univ, 81; dlitt, assumption col, mass, 76. **MEMBERSHIPS** MLA; Int Arthurian Soc; fel Mediaeval Acad Am; Am Asn Teachers Fr; fel Heraldy Soc London; fel Soc of Antiquaries of London; fel Acadmeie Internationale d'Heraldique; pres, Middle Atlantic Conference Canadian Studies, 81-8; pres, Societe Rencesvals pour l'etude des epopees romanes, 85-88. **RESEARCH** Medieval French literature, especially Song of Roland; medieval heraldic terminology; New England French language and culture. **SELECTED PUBLICATIONS** Auth, Celestine: A Critical Edition of the First French Translation (1527), Wayne State Univ Press, 63; auth, Early Blazon, Clarendon Press, 72, 2nd ed, Boydell Press, 97; auth, Eight Thirteenth Century Rolls of Arms, Pa State Univ Press, 73; auth, The Song of Roland: An Analytical Edition, Pa State Univ Press, 2 vols, 78; auth, La Chanson de Roland: Student Edition, Pa State Univ Press, 84; auth, The French-Canadian Heritage in New England, Univ Press of New England, 86; auth, Rolls of Arms of Edward I, Boydell Press, 2 vols, 97. **CONTACT ADDRESS** Pennsylvania State Univ, Univ Park, 325 Burrowed Bldg, University Park, PA 16802. **EMAIL** GJB2@PSU.EDU

BRAULT, PASCALE-ANNE
PERSONAL Born, France **DISCIPLINE** COMPARATIVE LITERATURE, FRENCH **EDUCATION** Sorbonne Univ; New York Univ, PhD, 90. **CAREER** Asst prof, Bard Col, 90-91; asst prof, 92-97, assoc prof, De Paul Univ, 97-. **HONORS AND AWARDS** Penfield Diss Fel, NYU, '88; Angis Nin Fel, NYU, 90; grants from the French Consulate for pub of literary journal Mille-Feuille, 93-97; Excellence in Teaching Awd, 95; Vincentian Endowment Fund, 96-98; Fac Res and Development Summer Grants, 97, 99. **MEMBERSHIPS** MLA, AATF, Women in French, Societe de Professeurs, Francais and Francophone d'Amerique. **RESEARCH** 20th century French and Francophone literature; Classical Greek literature; translation studies. **SELECTED PUBLICATIONS** Auth, "Tradire au passage," in Le passage des frontieres (a collection of essays on Jacques Derrida), Editions Galilee, Paris (Feb 94): 297-302; auth, "Herve Guibert, ou le corps du delit," in Regards sur la France des annees 80: le roman, Stanford French and Italian Studies (winter 95): 67-74; auth, "The Mise-en-Scene of Translation," in In Other Words, vol 10, London (winter 97): 135-141; auth, "Bernard-Marie Koltes: Theatre et verite," in Romance Notes (fall 97): 103-110; auth, "Translating the Impossible Debt: Paul Auster's 'City of Glass'," in Critique: Studies in Contemporary Fiction, vol 39, no 3 (spring 98): 228-238; co-transl of Jacques Derrida's Resistance to Psychoanalysis, Stanford Univ Press (fall 98); ed, Writing the Mission: Selected Letters of Saint Vincent de Paul, De Paul Univ (fall 98); co-transl of Jean-Francois Lyotard's Trait d'Union, (The Hyphen--Between Judaism and Christianity), Humanity Press (spring 99); co-transl of Jacques Derrida's Adieu, Stanford Univ Press (spring 99); co-ed with Michael Naas, The Politics of Mourning: A Book of Essays by Jacques Derrida, Univ Chicago Press (forthcoming, 2000). **CONTACT ADDRESS** Dept Modern Langs, DePaul Univ, 802 W Beldon Ave, Chicago, IL 60614.

BRAUN, ERNST
PERSONAL Born 12/16/1921, Breslau, Germany, m, 1956, 2 children **DISCIPLINE** GERMAN LITERATURE **EDUCATION** Univ Wis, BA, 47, MA, 48, PhD, 60. **CAREER** Instr German, Univ Tenn, 49-53; asst prof German & comp lit, Queens Col, NC, 55-57, assoc prof & chmn dept foreign lang, 57-59; asst prof German, Bowling Green State Univ, 60-61, chmn dept German & Russian, 61-62; assoc prof German, 62-64, Prof German, Univ Mo-Columbia, 64-, Chmn Dept German & Slavic Studies, 62-68, 76-, **MEMBERSHIPS** MLA; Midwest Mod Lang Asn; Am Asn Teachers Ger. **RESEARCH** German literature; comparative literature. **SELECTED PUBLICATIONS** Auth, Silences Roar, the Life and Drama of Erdman, New Theatre Quarterly, vol 0009, 93. **CONTACT ADDRESS** Dept of Germanic & Slavic Lang, Univ of Missouri, Columbia, Columbia, MO 65201.

BRAUN, THEODORE
PERSONAL Born 04/18/1933, Brooklyn, NY, m, 1965, 1 child **DISCIPLINE** FRENCH **EDUCATION** St. John's Univ, BA, 55; Univ of Calif Berkeley, MA, 61; PhD, 65. **CAREER** From Asst to Assoc Prof, Univ of Wis Milwaukee, 64-70; Prof, Univ of Del, 70-. **HONORS AND AWARDS** Competitive Scholar, St. John's Univ, 51-55; Outstanding Fac Awd for Serv, Col of Arts and Sci, 97; Leland D. Peterson Awd for Serv, E Central Am Soc for 18th Century Studies, 97. **MEMBERSHIPS** ASECS, EC/ASECS, NEASECS, AATF, Rousseau Asn, Diderot Asn, Voltaire Soc. **SELECTED PUBLICATIONS** Auth, Un ennemi de Voltaire: Le Franc de Pompignan - sa vie, ses oeuvres, ses rapports avec Voltaire, Lettres Modernes-Minard (Paris), 72; coauth, "Aeschylus, Voltaire and Le Franc de Pompignan's 'Promethee',"in Studies on Voltaire and the eighteenth century (CLX, 76), 137-226; co-ed, "Teaching the Eighteenth Century," Eighteenth Century Life V-3 (79); co-ed, Man, God and Nature in the Enlightenment, Colleagues Press (E Lansing), 88; auth, "Critical edition of Voltaire's 'Alzire, ou les Americains' tragedie (1736)," in Complete Works of Voltaire (Oxford: Voltaire Found, 89): XIV 1-210; co-ed, Disrupted Patterns: On Chaos and Order in the Enlightenment, Rodopi (Amsterdam), 00. **CONTACT ADDRESS** Dept For Lang &

Lit, Univ of Delaware, 428 Smith Hall, Newark, DE 19711. **EMAIL** braun@udel.edu

BRAUN, WILHELM
PERSONAL Born 06/29/1921, Vienna, Austria, m, 1966, 2 children **DISCIPLINE** GERMAN **EDUCATION** Univ of Toronto, BA, 49; MA, 50; PhD, 53. **CAREER** Asst Prof, Morehouse Col, Atlanta Ga, 53-56; From Asst Prof to Prof, Univ of Rochester, 56-. **HONORS AND AWARDS** Musil Medal of the City Klagenfurt, 89. **MEMBERSHIPS** MLA, AATG. **RESEARCH** Modern Austrian Literature, especially Robert Musil. **CONTACT ADDRESS** Dept Relig & Classics, Univ of Rochester, PO Box 270074, Rochester, NY 14627-0074.

BREE, GERMAINE
PERSONAL Born 10/02/1907, Lasalle, France **DISCIPLINE** FRENCH LITERATURE **EDUCATION** Univ Paris, Lic es Lett, 30, dipl, 31, Agrege, 32. **CAREER** Teacher, Oran, Algeria, 32-36; from lectr to prof French lit, Bryn Mawr Col, 36-52; chmn dept French, Wash Sq Col, NY Univ, 53-60, head dept Romance lang, Grad Sch Arts & Sci, 54-60; Vilas prof French, inst Res Humanities, Univ Wis-Madison, 60-73; Kenan Prof Humanities, Wake Forest Univ, 73-, Vis prof French, Wellesley Col, 59 & Am Univ Cairo, Egypt, 70; Fulbright prof, Univ London, Eng, 65-66; mem Fleming Comn Doctoral Coun, State Educ Dept, State Univ NY, 72, chmn French Rating Comt doctoral prog; mem adv bd, Am Coun Learned Soc & Nat Foun Arts & Humanities. **HONORS AND AWARDS** Chevalier, Legion of Honor, 58; littd, smith col, 60, mt holyoke col, 63, allegheny col, 63, duke univ, 64, oberlin col, 66, dickinson col, 68, rutgers univ, 69, wake forest univ, 69, brown univ, 71, univ wis-milwaukee, 73, ny univ, 75, univ mass, amherst, 76 & kalamazoo col, 77; lhd, w **MEMBERSHIPS** MLA (vpres to pres, 73-75); Am Philos Soc; Am Asn Teachers Fr; AAUP; PEN Club. **RESEARCH** Contemporary French literature. **SELECTED PUBLICATIONS** Auth, from One Period to Another in Poetics of Passage--a Tribute to Tisonbraun, Micheline, Esprit Createur, Vol 0034, 94; Morot-Sir, Edouard and the Literary Text in Theory and the Pleasure of the Text, Romance Notes, Vol 0035, 95; Morot, Sir Edouard and the Literary Text in Theory and the Pleasure of the Text, Romance Notes, Vol 0035, 95; in One's Heart of Hearts and the Crossing of the Century in Sarraute,Nathalie L'usage De La Parole' and 'Tu Ne Taimes Pas', Esprit Createur, Vol 0036, 96; Two Scholars Reflect on their Careers in the Making of a University Professor, USA-1936-84, PMLA Pub(s) MLA Am, Vol 0109, 94. **CONTACT ADDRESS** Dept of French, Wake Forest Univ, Winston-Salem, NC 27109.

BREINES, JOSEPH
PERSONAL Born 03/08/1947, New York City, NY, m, 1978, 2 children **DISCIPLINE** FRENCH **EDUCATION** Yale Univ, PhD, 94. **CAREER** Adj Asst Prof French, Boston Col, 95-. **SELECTED PUBLICATIONS** Auth, Submerging and Drowning the Characters: Zola's Wet Determinism, Romantic Review, November 96, vol. 87 Number 4; auth, A Trial Against Myself: Identity Determinism in Diderots treques le fataliste Romnnic Review, March 99. **CONTACT ADDRESS** Romance Lang & Lits, Boston College, Lyons Hall, 140 Commonwealth Ave., Chestnut Hill, MA 02467-3804. **EMAIL** breinesj@bc.edu

BRENNAN, MARY ALETHEA
PERSONAL Born 06/11/1909, Larksville, PA **DISCIPLINE** PHILOSOPHY, CLASSICS **EDUCATION** Col Mt St Vincent, BA, 30; Cath Univ Am, MA, 44, PhL, 48, PhD(philos), 50; Univ Freiburg & Univ Dublin, 62. **CAREER** Instr chem & math, Cathedral High Sch, New York, NY, 34-35, chem, 35-41, head dept, 41-43; instr chem & Latin, 44-45, asst prof Latin, 45-47, from instr to assoc prof philos, 50-76, Adj Assoc Prof Philos, Col Mt St Vincent, 76- **MEMBERSHIPS** Am Philos Soc; Am Cath Philos Asn; Metaphys Soc Am; Cath Class Asn (pres, 43-44). **RESEARCH** Science, especially chemistry. **SELECTED PUBLICATIONS** Auth, Religion, Law, and Power, the Making of Protestant Ireland, 1660-1760, Albion, Vol 0025, 93; Neither Kingdom Nor Nation in the Irish Quest For Constitutional-Rights, 1698-1800, Albion, Vol 0027, 95. **CONTACT ADDRESS** Dept of Philos, Col of Mount Saint Vincent, Mount View, CA 94039.

BRENNAN, VIRGINIA M.
PERSONAL Born 12/14/1958, Manhasset, NY **DISCIPLINE** LINGUISTICS **EDUCATION** Yale Univ, BA, 80; Columbia Teacher's Col, MA, 85; Univ Ma Amherst, Phd, 93. **CAREER** Swarthmore Col, 90-94; Vanderbilt Univ, 94- . **RESEARCH** Semantics, lang acquisition, pragmatics. **SELECTED PUBLICATIONS** Auth, Specific Situations II, in Proceedings: Formal Grammar Conference at ESSLLI VIII, ESSLI, 96; Quantificational Modals, Linguistic Inquiry, 97; The Relativization of Modals, Proceedings of the Eleventh Amsterdam Colloquium, 97; Conversational Backgrounds and Topics, Cornell Univ Press, 98; rev, Mood at the Interface, GLOT Int, forthcoming. **CONTACT ADDRESS** Vanderbilt Univ, Box 1567-B, Nashville, TN 37235. **EMAIL** virginia.m.brennan.1@vanderbilt.edu

BREVART, FRANCIS B.
PERSONAL Born 10/17/1945, Casablanca, Morocco, m, 1979, 1 child **DISCIPLINE** GERMAN **EDUCATION** McGill Univ, BS, 66, MA, 70, PhD(comp lit), 75. **CAREER** Lectr Ger lang, Loyola Col, Montreal, 70-71; lectr Ger & French lang, Loyola Col, Montreal & Vanier Col, 71-72; asst prof Ger lit Mid Ages, Univ Munich, 75-77 & Univ Munster, 77-81; Asst Prof Ger Lit Mid Ages, Univ PA, 81- **RESEARCH** Astronomical-astrological German literature manuscripts; epigonic heroic German literature: Dietrich epics; the theme of the Enfances. **SELECTED PUBLICATIONS CONTACT ADDRESS** Univ of Pennsylvania, 255 S 36th St, Philadelphia, PA 19104-3805.

BREWER, JOHN T.
PERSONAL Born 03/01/1938, Palo Alto, CA **DISCIPLINE** GERMAN **EDUCATION** Pomona Col, BA, 59; Univ Tex, PhD(Ger lang), 62. **CAREER** From instr to asst prof Ger, Univ Calif, Riverside, 62-67; asst prof, 68-71, Assoc Prof Ger, Wash State Univ, 71-, Publ dir, PNCFL, 77-81. **HONORS AND AWARDS** Phi Beta Kappa; Woodrow Wilson Fel. **MEMBERSHIPS** MLA; Am Asn Teachers Ger; Western Asn Ger Studies. **RESEARCH** 18th century German literature; Romanticism. **SELECTED PUBLICATIONS** Auth, Lessing 'Nathan the Wise' and the Critics--1779-1991, Seminar--J Germanic Stud, Vol 0032, 96. **CONTACT ADDRESS** Dept of Foreign Lang & Lit, Washington State Univ, Pullman, WA 99164. **EMAIL** jtbfl@mail.wsu.edu

BREWER, MARIA MINICH
PERSONAL Born Budapest, Hungary **DISCIPLINE** FRENCH LITERATURE **EDUCATION** Univ Witwatersrand, Johannesburg, BA, 66; State Univ NYork Buffalo, MA, 70; Yale Univ, PhD(French), 77. **CAREER** Instr, Ohio State Univ, 77-78; asst prof, 78-85, assoc prof, Univ Minn, 86-. **MEMBERSHIPS** MLA, MMLA, IAPL **RESEARCH** 20th century French literature, culture, theater; narrative, theater studies, gender, literary and cultural theory **SELECTED PUBLICATIONS CONTACT ADDRESS** Dept of French & Ital, Univ of Minnesota, Twin Cities, 9 Pleasant St S E, Minneapolis, MN 55455-0194. **EMAIL** brewe003@tc.umn.edu

BRIGGS, WARD W.
PERSONAL Born 11/26/1945, Riverside, CA, s **DISCIPLINE** CLASSICS **EDUCATION** Wash & Lee Univ, AB, 67; Univ of NC, MA, 69, PhD, 74. **CAREER** Instr, Univ of SC, 73-74; from asst prof to prof, Univ of SC, 75-; visting scholar, Univ VA, 88; Carolina disting. prof of Classics and L. Fry Scudder prof of hum, 96- ; Mel Hill disting. prof, Hobart & Wm. Smith Colleges, 92-93; Interim Assoc Provost, 96-97. **HONORS AND AWARDS** Phi Beta Kappa; Founders Awd, Confederate Lit Soc, 99. **MEMBERSHIPS** Am Philol Asn; Class Asn of Middle West and South, Am Class League; Instiitute for Advanced Study, Princton, 99-00. **RESEARCH** Hist of Class Scholarship; Latin lit of the Golden Age. **SELECTED PUBLICATIONS** Auth, Narrative and Simile, 79; Concordantia in Varronis Libros De Re Rustica, 83; Concordantia in Catonis Librum De Agri Cultura, 84; Soldier and Scholar: The Southern Papers of Basil Lanneau Gildeersleeve, 88; coed, Basil Lanneau Gildersleeve: An American Classicist, 86; Classical Scholarship: A Biog Encycl, 90; The Roosevelt Lects of Paul Shorey (1913-1914), 98; ed, The Letters of Basil Lanneau Gildersleeve, 87; Selected Classical Papers of Basil Lanneau Gildersleeve, 92; Biog Dictionary of North American Classicists, 94; Greek Authors, Dictionary of Lit Biog, vol 176, 97; Ancient Roman Auths, Dictionary of Lit Biog, 98. **CONTACT ADDRESS** Dept of French and Classics, Univ of So Carolina, Columbia, Columbia, SC 29208. **EMAIL** wardbriggs@sc.edu

BRIGHT, DAVID F.
PERSONAL Born 04/13/1942, Winnipeg, MB, Canada, m, 2 children **DISCIPLINE** CLASSICS **EDUCATION** Univ Manitoba, BA, 62; Univ Cincinnati, MA, 63 PhD, 67. **CAREER** Univ Manitoba, inst, 61-62; Univ Cincinnati, tchg fel, 63-67; Williams Col, asst prof, 67-70; Univ IL asst prof, assoc prof, prof, ch classics, acting dir, sch Hum, chemn dept classics, dir prog comp lit, acting dean, 70-89; Iowa State Univ, prof, dean of coll lib arts & sci, 89-91, Emory Univ, prof, vpres arts & sci, dean Emory col, 91-. **HONORS AND AWARDS** Skuli Johnson Gold Medal, Univ Man Gold medallist, Woodrow Wilson Fel, Can Council Res fel, Semple Trav fell, Univ Cinci res fel, Elected Society of Fel, Amer Acad Rome, Delmas Found Schl, Phi Beta Kappa **MEMBERSHIPS** APA, CAMW&S, Vergilian Soc., AAHE **RESEARCH** Latin poetry; literature of late antiquity and early mediaeval literature. **SELECTED PUBLICATIONS** Auth, Haec mihi fingebam: Tibullus in His World, Leiden: Brill, 78; auth, Elaborate Disarray: The Nature of Statius' Silvae, Meisenheim, 80; auth, Classical Texts and their Traditions, Studies in Honor of C.R. Trahman, ed., D.F. Bright & E.S. Ramage, Chico CA: Scholars Press, 84; auth, The Miniature Epic in Vandal Africa, Norman: Univ Oklahoma Press, 87; Theory and Practice in the Vergilian cento, IL Class Stud, 84; auth, The Chronology of the Poems of Dracontius, Classica et Mediaevalia, forthcoming. **CONTACT ADDRESS** Dept of Classics, Emory Univ, N404 Callaway Center, Atlanta, GA 30322. **EMAIL** dbright@emory.edu

BRIND'AMOUR, LUCIE
DISCIPLINE LATE MEDIEVAL AND 16TH CENTURY, AND QUEBEC LITERATURE **EDUCATION** Univ Sherbrooke, B.A, 73; Univ Montreal, M.A, 75; PhD, 77. **CAREER** Assoc chair, Dept Fr and Italian, May 97-; acting chair, summers 97, 98; asst prof, 78-81; assoc prof, 81-, La State Univ. **HONORS AND AWARDS** Grant from the Professional Devleopment Fund Prog for Res in Quebec, Quebec government, summer 81; grant from the Center for French and Francophone Studies, LSU, summer 86. **SELECTED PUBLICATIONS** Auth, L'Archeologie du signe, Pontifical Isnt of Medieval Studies (Toronto), 83; auth, "Charles VIII a Rouen: l'image, le mot et le sens," in Semiotics Unfolding, ed. Tasso Borbe (Mouten, Berlin, 84), 775-782; auth, "Amour et litterature a la fin du Xve siecle: Michault Taillevent et Guillaume Cretin," Fifteenth Century Studies XII (Stuttgart, Akademisher Verlag, 87), 5-15; auth, "La tradition de l'amour courtois. L'Epoque de la Renaissance 1400-1600, " in A Comparative History of Literatures in European Languages sponsored by the Int Comparative Literature Asn (Budapest, Akademiai Kiado, 88), 446-459; auth, "Le plaidoye de l'amant doloreux: d'une plainte sans fin," Fifteenth Century Studies XIV (Stuttgart, Akademisher Verlag, 88). **CONTACT ADDRESS** Dept of Fr Grad Stud, Louisiana State Univ and A&M Col, Baton Rouge, LA 70803.

BRINNER, WILLIAM MICHAEL
PERSONAL Born 10/06/1924, Alameda, CA, m, 1951, 3 children **DISCIPLINE** PHILOLOGY, ISLAMIC HISTORY **EDUCATION** Univ Calif, Berkeley, AB, 48, MA, 50, PhD, 56. **CAREER** From instr to assoc prof, 56-64, chmn dept & dir Near Eastern Lang & Area Ctr, 65-70, dir Ctr Arabic Studies Abroad, 67-70, Prof Near Eastern Lang, Univ Calif, Berkeley, 64-, Lectr Arabic, Ctr Mid Eastern Studies, Harvard Univ, 61; Visiting Prof, Hebrew Univ of Jerusalem, 70-71; 73-75; Univ of San Francisco, 85; Univ of Washington, 91. Am Coun Learned Soc-Soc Sci Res Coun grant Near Eastern studies, 61-62; mem, Am Res Ctr Egypt, 68-70; consult, US off Educ, 65-68; Guggenheim fel, 65-66; mem joint comt Near & Mid E, Am Coun Learned Soc-Soc Sci Res Coun, 66-70 & chmn, 69-70; mem exec comt, Am inst Iranian Studies, 68; Founder and U.S. Director, Center for Arabic Studies Abroad, Amer Univ in Cairo, 66-70; Fulbright-Hays fac res award, 70-71 & sr consult, Comt int Exchange Persons, 72-73; Member, Evaluation Panels, Natl Endowmen for the Humanities, 78-81; 85-91; dir, Univ Calif Studies Ctr, Jerusalem, 73-75; Visiting Committee, Dept of Near Eastern Langs. And Lit, Harvard Univ, 84-90; Acting Dir, Annenberg Research Institute, Philadelphia, 92-93. **HONORS AND AWARDS** Berkeley Citation for Academic Achievement and Distinguished Service, 91; Hebrew Union College, Los Angeles, Doctor of Human Letters, 92; Honoree, International Interdisciplinary Conference, Bridging the Worlds of Judaism and Islam, Berkeley, 93. **MEMBERSHIPS** Am Orient Soc (pres, 76-77); Mediaeval Acad Am; Mid E Studies Asn (pres, 69-70); Am Asn Teachers Arabic (pres, 68-69); Soc for Judaco -Arabic Studies; Am Acad for Jewish Research; Association for Jewish Studies. **RESEARCH** Arabic and Hebrew language and literature; Islamic and Jewish history. **SELECTED PUBLICATIONS** Auth, "A Chronicle of Damascus, 1389-97 2 vols, Univ of Cal of Press, 63; auth, "Sutro Library Hebraica: A Handlist," Cal State Library, 67; auth, "Readings in Modern Arabic Literature," E.J. Brill, Leiden, 72; auth, "An Elegant Composition Concerning Relief After Adversity," Yak Univ Press, 78-, reprint by Jason Aronson Inc., 96; auth, "Studies in Islamic and Judaic Traditions," vol 1 86, vol 11 89, Atlanta Scholars Press; auth, "Prophets and Patriarchs," History of al-/ Tabari, vol 11, Suny Press, 87; auth, "The Children of Israel," History of al-Tabari, vol 111, Suny Press, 91. **CONTACT ADDRESS** Dept of Near Eastern Studies, Univ of California, Berkeley, 250 Barrows Hall, Berkeley, CA 94720-1940. **EMAIL** zebrin@socrates.berkeley.edu

BRINTON, LAUREL J.
PERSONAL Born 06/18/1953, Woodland, CA, m, 1992, 1 child **DISCIPLINE** ENGLISH LINGUISTICS **EDUCATION** Univ Calif Davis, BA, 75; Univ Calif Berkeley, PhD, 81. **CAREER** TA, Univ Calif Berkeley, 78-81; asst prof to prof, Univ Brit Colum, 81-. **HONORS AND AWARDS** Killam Res Prize, SSRHC, Fel, 86, 91-94. **MEMBERSHIPS** Ling Soc of Am, MLA, Can Ling Assoc, Int Soc for Hist Ling, Societas Linguistica Europeae. **RESEARCH** English historical linguistics, Tense and aspect, Historical pragmatics, Grammaticalization. **SELECTED PUBLICATIONS** Auth, The Development of English Aspectual Systems: Aspectualizers and Post-verbal Particles, Cambridge Univ Pr, 88; auth, Pragmatic Markers in English: Grammaticalization and Discourse Functions, Mouton de Gruyter, 96; ed, Collocational and Idiomatic Aspects of Composite Predicates in the History of English, John Benjamins, 99; auth, The Structure of Modern English: a Linguistic Introduction, John Benjamins, 00; ed, Historical Linguistics 1999, John Benjamins, 01. **CONTACT ADDRESS** Dept English, Univ of British Columbia, Dept of English, Vancouver, BC, Canada V6T 1Z1. **EMAIL** brinton@interchange.ubc.ca

BRISTER, LOUIS EDWIN
PERSONAL Born 07/14/1938, El Dorado, AR, d, 3 children **DISCIPLINE** GERMAN LANGUAGE & LITERATURE **EDUCATION** Miss State Univ, BA, 62; Univ Tex, Austin, MA, 66, PhD, 68. **CAREER** From instr to asst prof Ger, 66-71,

chmn dept mod lang, 71-78, assoc prof, 71-79, Prof Ger, Southwest Tex State Univ, 79-. **HONORS AND AWARDS** Fulbright Landeskunde Seminar in Germany, 90. **MEMBERSHIPS** SWestern Coun Latin Am Studies; Soc Ger-Am Studies; Tex State Hist Asn. **RESEARCH** German-Americana. **SELECTED PUBLICATIONS** Auth, William von Rosenberg's Kritik: A History of the Society for the Protection of German Immigrants in Texas, Southwestern Hist Quart, 81-82; In Mexican Prisons: The Journal of Eduard Harkort, 1832-1834, 86; Witness to Revolution: Herman Ehrenberg's Memoir of the Texas Revolution (forthcoming 01); author of several articles. **CONTACT ADDRESS** Dept of Mod Lang, Southwest Texas State Univ, 601 University Dr, San Marcos, TX 78666-4685. **EMAIL** lb21@swt.edu

BRISTOL, EVELYN C.
PERSONAL Born San Francisco, CA **DISCIPLINE** SLAVIC LANGUAGE, LITERATURE **EDUCATION** Univ Calif Berkeley, BA, 46; MA, 48; PhD, 59. **CAREER** Asst prof, Univ of Wash, 57-58; acting asst prof, Univ of Calif Los Angeles, 58-59; asst prof, Univ of Tex at Austin, 60-65; assoc prof to prof, Univ IL, 65-. **MEMBERSHIPS** Am Assoc for the Advan of Slavic Studies; Assoc of Lit Scholars and Critics; Am Assoc of Teachers of Slavic Lang and Lit. **RESEARCH** Russian literature. **SELECTED PUBLICATIONS** Auth, A History of Russian Poetry, Oxford Univ Pr, (NY, London), 91. **CONTACT ADDRESS** Dept Slavic Lang and Lit, Univ of Illinois, Urbana-Champaign, 707 S Mathews Ave, Urbana, IL 61801-3625. **EMAIL** ebristol@uiuc.edu

BRIZIO-SKOV, FLAVIA
PERSONAL Born 12/17/1953, Savona, Italy **DISCIPLINE** ITALIAN **EDUCATION** Univ Genoa, Italy, Laurea, 76; Univ Wash, MA, 83; PhD, 88. **CAREER** Assoc prof, Univ Tenn. **HONORS AND AWARDS** UTK prof devel awd, 89-90, 93-94, 97-98. **MEMBERSHIPS** Amer Asn of Tchrs of Ital; Amer Asn for Ital Studies; Tenn For Lang Tchg Asn; Soc for Ital Hist Studies; Asn of Women Fac. **RESEARCH** Contemporary Italian literature. **SELECTED PUBLICATIONS** Ayth, "Tempo e strategie narrative ne 'Le strade di polvere' di Rosetta Loy," Quaderni d'Italianistica XIII.1 (92): 71-83; auth, La Scrittura e la memoria: Lalla Romano, Selene Edizioni (Milano), 93; auth, "Dal fantastico al postmoderno: 'Requiem' di Antonio Tabucchi," Italica 17.1 (94): 96-115; auth, "La narrativa postmoderna de Antonio Tabucchi," La Pagina 15.1 (94): 33-52; auth, "Rosetta Loy e Lalla Romano: ritratto di due scrittrici contemporanee," Rivista di Studi Italiani XIV.2 (96): 206-212; auth, 'Sostiene Pereira': the Crisis of the Intellectual between History and Literature," Spunti e Ricerche 12 (96/97): 186-201; auth, "Ultimi sviluppi critici sulla narrativa tabucchiana," Quaderni d'Italianistica XVIII.1 (Primavera, 97): 93-100; auth, "Immagine e scrittura nella narrativa di Lalla Romano," in I segni incrociati-Letteratura italiana del '900 e arte figurativa, ed M Marcello Ciccuto (Lucca: Mauro Baroni Editore, 98), 499-513; auth, "'Sostiene Pereira' di Antonio Tabucci: cultura e dittatura nel Portogallo di Salazar," Storia e memoria, Istituto Ligure per la Storia della Resistenza (Genova, Italy) Anno 9.1 (1mo Semestre 2000): 127-141. **CONTACT ADDRESS** Dept of Mod For Langs & Lits, Univ of Tennessee, Knoxville, 701 McClung Tower & Plaza, Knoxville, TN 37996. **EMAIL** fbrizio@utk.edu

BRODEN, THOMAS F.
PERSONAL Born 11/19/1951, South Bend, IN, m, 1989 **DISCIPLINE** FRENCH LITERATURE AND CULTURE **EDUCATION** Univ Notre Dame, AB, 73; Ind Univ, AM, 76; PhD, 86. **CAREER** English asst, Lycee Henri IV, 78-79 and Lycee Saint Louis, 81-82; English instr, Inst Nat Agronomique (Paris), 81-82, and Inst Nat des Telecommunications (Paris and Evry), 79-80, 81-82; assoc instr, Indiana Univ, 74-78, 79-81, 82-83; lectr, Univ Notre Dame, 84-87; vis asst prof, Tulane Univ, 87-88; asst prof, Univ Nebr, 88-91; asst prof, Purdue Univ, 91-97, assoc prof, 97-. **HONORS AND AWARDS** Rotary Int Fel, 73-74; French Govt Fel, 81-82; Univ Nebr Maude Hammond Fling Fel and Layman Awd, 91-92 (declined); NEH Travel to Collection Grant, 90; Purdue Res Found Fel, 98-2001. **MEMBERSHIPS** Am Asn of Teachers of French, Can Semiotic Soc, Int Simone de Beavoir Soc, Modern Lang Asn, North Am Asn for the Hist of the Lang Scis, Semiotic Soc of Am, Toronto Semiotic Circle. **RESEARCH** Modern and contemporary French literature, Twentieth-century French fiction, French theory, semiotics. **SELECTED PUBLICATIONS** Auth, "Marguerite Duras," in Sartiori and Zimmerman, eds, Fifty French Women Writers: A Bio-Bibliographical Source Book, Westport, Ct: Greenwood Press (91): 161-170; auth, "Squares and Triads, Growth and Narrative: Semiotics, Signs, and Signification," Yearbook in Comparative and General Lit, 41 (93): 99-122; auth, "Marguerite Duras and le temps de l'ennui," in William Thompson, ed, The Contemporary Novel in France, Gainesville: Univ Press of Fla (95): 89-108; auth, "For a Semiotics of Semiosis: Beyond Signifier and Signified," RSSI Recherches Semiotiques/Semiotic Inquiry, 15.1-2 (95): 163-188; auth, "A.J. Greimas (1917-1992): Commemorative Essay," Semiotica, The J of the Int Asn for Semiotic Studies, 105.3-4 (95): 207-242; auth, "The Sign in Paris Semiotics," Semiotica, The J of the Int Asn for Semiotic Studies , 111, 1-2 (July 86): 1-34; auth, "Greimas Between France and Peirce," The Am J of Semiotics (forthcoming). **CONTACT ADDRESS** Dept Foreign Langs, Purdue Univ, West Lafayette, West Lafayette, IN 47907. **EMAIL** broden@purdue.edu

BRODMAN, MARIAN
DISCIPLINE FRENCH **EDUCATION** Rosemont Col, BA, 67; Bryn Mawr Col, MA, 69, PhD, 77. **CAREER** Asst prof, Lehigh Univ; instr, Univ Ark; assoc prof, Univ Central Ark, 86-. **MEMBERSHIPS** Ark Foreign Lang Tchr Asn; AATF (Arkansas Chapter) Awards Comt Chair, Central States Conf Tchg Foreign Lang. **CONTACT ADDRESS** Univ of Central Arkansas, 201 Donaghey Ave, Conway, AR 72035-0001. **EMAIL** marianb@mail.uca.edu

BRODSKY, PATRICIA POLLOCK
PERSONAL Born 06/22/1941, Douds, IA, m, 1968 **DISCIPLINE** COMPARATIVE LITERATURE, GERMAN **EDUCATION** State Univ Iowa, BA, 64; Univ Calif, Berkeley, MA, 66, PhD(comp lit), 72. **CAREER** Asst prof, 74-80, assoc prof, 74-80, Prof Ger & Russ, Univ MO-Kansas City, 86-; Univ Mo-Kans City fac res grants, 75,77, 94; res, travel grants to Ger, Switz, Poland, 79,84,88,93; Fulbright res award, 84; Univ Kans City Trustees Grant, 86; NEH Trav to Collections grant, 88; NEH summer stipen, 92; DAAD summer study grant, 94; Univ Mo Res Board grant, 96; res assoc, Russ & East Europ Ctr, Univ Ill, Urbana, 76-97. **HONORS AND AWARDS** Weldon Spring Hum Fel, 84; N T Veatch Awd Disting Res & Creative Activity, 93. **MEMBERSHIPS** MLA; Am Comp Lit Asn; Int Comp Lit Asn; Am Asn Teachers Slavic & East Europ Lang; Am Asn Teachers Ger; Am Counc Teachers Russ; Rilke-Ges. **RESEARCH** 20th cent literature; antifascism, ethnic stereotyping in literature; borderland cultures; workers' culture, German-Slavic relations; Rainer Maria Rilke. **SELECTED PUBLICATIONS** Auth, review, "Unkenrufe," World Lit Today, Vol 0067, 93; auth, review, "The Last Years of Soviet Russian Literature in Prose Fiction 1975-1991," World Lit Today, Vol 0068, 94; auth, review, "Atomic Ghost Poets Respond to the Nuclear Age," World Lit Today, Vol 0069, 95; auth, "The Black Cook As Mater-Gloriosa. Grass's 'Faust'-Parodies in 'Die Blechtrommel'," Colloquia Germanica, Vol 0029, 96; auth, "Dressed Like a Soldier. WW II in Central-Europe in two GDR Novels," Symp--Quart J in Modern Lit(s), Vol 0049, 96; auth, "A Gold Mine in Germany's Coal Belt," People's Culture New Series 39-40 (97): 9; auth, "Nomen est Omen. Towards a Definition of Cultural Identity," Germano-Slavica 10.1 (97): 3-12; auth, "The Poet as Citizen. A Profile of William Witherup and John Bradley," Poets and Writers 25.6 (97): 54-59; auth, "Germany Report: The Selective War on History," Progressive Clearinghouse Bulletin 5 (98): 13-14; auth, "The Hidden War: Working-Class Resistance During the Third Reich and the Postwar Suppression of its History," Nature, Society, and Thought 11.2 (98): 171-185. **CONTACT ADDRESS** Dept of Foreign Lang, Univ of Missouri, Kansas City, 218 Scofield Hall, Kansas City, MO 64110-2499. **EMAIL** brodskyp@umkc.edu

BRODY, JULES
PERSONAL Born 03/06/1928, New York, NY, m, 1953, 3 children **DISCIPLINE** FRENCH **EDUCATION** Cornell Univ, AB, 48; Columbia Univ, AM, 49, PhD(French), 56. **CAREER** Lectr French, Columbia Univ, 50-53, from instr to assoc prof, 53-63; prof French & chmn dept foreign & comp lit, Univ Rochester, 63-68; prof romance lang & assoc dean fac, Queens Col, NY, 68-75; Prof Romance Lang & Lit, Harvard Univ, 75-, Chmn Dept, 80-, Guggenheim fel & Fulbright res fel, 61-62. **MEMBERSHIPS** Soc Fr Studies; Soc Studies 17th Century; MLA; Am Asn Teachers Fr. **RESEARCH** French literature of the 17th century; classical tradition in France; Montaigne. **SELECTED PUBLICATIONS** Auth, Referential Practice in Language and Lived Space Among the Maya, Lang in Soc, Vol 0022, 93; Itza Maya Texts--With A Grammatical Overview, Colonial Latin Amer Hist Rev, Vol 0004, 95; Ozumacin Chinantec Texts, Lang, Vol 0073, 97. **CONTACT ADDRESS** Dept Geography & Anthropology, Louisiana State Univ and A&M Col, Baton Rouge, LA 70803.

BROOKS, PETER PRESTON
PERSONAL Born 04/19/1938, New York, NY, 3 children **DISCIPLINE** FRENCH & COMPARATIVE LITERATURE **EDUCATION** Harvard Univ, AB, 59, MA, 62, PhD, 65. **CAREER** From instr to assoc prof French, 65-75, dir lit major, 74-80, prof French & comp lit, 75-80, dir Div Humanities Ctr, 79-82, chmn, Dept Fr, 83-88, Chester D Tripp Prof Humanities, Yale Univ, 80-, Dir Whitney Humanities Ctr, 80-91, 97-, Dir, Dept Comp Lit, 91-97, lectr, Law School, spring 89-90, 92-93, 95-96 & 97-98; Morse fell 67-68; Am Coun Learned Soc grant-in-aid, 67 & 72; contrib ed, Partisan Rev, 72-; Guggenheim fel, 73-74; mem adv comt, PMLA, 76-80; Am Counc Learned Soc fel, 79-80; chmn, ed bd, Yale J Criticism, 87-; NEH res fel, 88-89; vis prof, Summer Inst in Lit, Univ Texas, Austin, 78 & 79; Professore a contratto, Universita di Bologna, 5/90; exec coun, MLA, 94-97; School Criticism & Theory, Dartmouth Col, summer 94; ad bd, Stanford Humanities Ctr, 96; Humanities Advisory comt, NY public library, 97-. **HONORS AND AWARDS** Decorated Officier des Palmes Academiques, 86; Am Acad Arts & Sci, 91; Doctor Honoris Causa, Ecole Normale Superieure, Paris, 97; mah, yale univ, 75. **MEMBERSHIPS** MLA; ACLA. **RESEARCH** Romanticism; theory and analysis of narrative; psychoanalysis and literary criticism, Law and Literature. **SELECTED PUBLICATIONS** Auth, The Novel of Worldliness, Princeton Univ, 69; Nouvelle critique et critique nouvelle aux Etats-Unis, Nouvelle Rev Francaise, 9/69; ed, The Child's Part, Beacon, 72; co-ed, Man and His Fictions, Harcourt, 73; auth, The Melodramatic Imagination, Yale Univ, 76, reprint, Columbia Univ, 85; reprint with new intro, Yale Univ, 95; co-ed, Jean Genet: A Collection of Critical Essays, Prentice-Hall, 78; auth, Reading for the Plot, Alfred A Knopf, 84; reprint Vintage Books, 85; reprint Harvard Univ, 92; auth, Body Work, Harvard Univ Press, 93; auth, Psychoanalysis and Storytelling, Blackwell, 94; co-ed, Law's Stories, Yale Univ Press, 96; ed, Honore de Balzac, Pere Goriot, W W Norton, 98; auth, Troubling Confessions, Univ Chicago, 00. **CONTACT ADDRESS** Whitney Humanities Ctr, Yale Univ, P O Box 208298, New Haven, CT 06520-8298. **EMAIL** peter.brooks@yale.edu

BROUGHTON, THOMAS ROBERT SHANNON
PERSONAL Born 02/17/1900, Corbetton, ON, Canada, m, 1931, 2 children **DISCIPLINE** CLASSICS, ANCIENT HISTORY **EDUCATION** Univ Toronto, AB, 21, MA, 22; Johns Hopkins Univ, PhD (Latin), 28. **CAREER** Instr Greek, Amherst Col, 26-27; assoc Latin, Bryn Mawr Col, 28-30, from assoc prof to prof, 30-65; Paddison prof class, 65-70, Emer Prof Classics, Univ NC, Chapel Hill, 70-, Vis prof, Johns Hopkins Univ, 38-40; Guggenheim fel, 45-46; Fulbright res grant, Italy, 51-52; prof in charge, Sch Classical Studies, Am Acad Rome, 59-61; vpres, int Fed Soc Classical Studies, 59-69; mem comt res libr, Am Coun Learned Soc, 67; ann mem, inst Advan Studies, 71-72. **HONORS AND AWARDS** Awd, Am Philol Asn, 53; lld, johns hopkins univ, 69, univ toronto, 71 & univ nc, chapel hill, 74. **MEMBERSHIPS** Am Acad Arts & Sci; AHA; Archaeol inst Am (hon vpres, 53-58); Am Philol Asn (pres, 54); Class Asn Can. **RESEARCH** Economic history of Rome; provinces of the Roman Empire; Roman constitutional history and politics. **SELECTED PUBLICATIONS** Auth, Dionysus and the History of Archaic Rome, Classical J, Vol 0088, 93. **CONTACT ADDRESS** Dept of Classics, Univ of No Carolina, Chapel Hill, Murphey Hall, Chapel Hill, NC 27514.

BROWN, FREDERICK
PERSONAL Born 12/23/1934, New York, NY **DISCIPLINE** FRENCH **EDUCATION** Yale Univ, BA, 56, PhD, 60. **CAREER** Asst instr French, 59-60; from instr to asst prof, Univ Tex, 60-63; asst prof French & gen lit, State Univ NY Binghamton, 63-65; prof off French desk, African-Am inst, 64-65; from asst prof to assoc prof French, 65-72, Prof French, State Univ NY Stony Brook, 72-, Guggenheim fel, 70-71. **MEMBERSHIPS** MLA **RESEARCH** Modern French literature. **SELECTED PUBLICATIONS** Auth, An essay on surrealism, Tex Quart, 62; On Louis Aragon: Silence and history, Southern Rev, 67; An Impersonation of Angels: A Biography of Jean Cacteau, Viking, 68; co-transl, the Essays of Paul Valery, Bollingen Ser, Vol XI, Princeton Univ, 70; auth, Pere-Lachaise: Elysium as Real Estate, Viking, 73. **CONTACT ADDRESS** Dept of Romance Lang, SUNY, Stony Brook, Stony Brook, NY 11790.

BROWN, JAMES LORIN
PERSONAL Born 09/26/1920, Hanford, CA **DISCIPLINE** FRENCH **EDUCATION** Univ Calif, Berkeley, PhD, 52. **CAREER** From asst prof to assoc prof, 63-73, Prof French, Calif State Univ, Chico, 73-. **SELECTED PUBLICATIONS** Auth, Reference to Cunegonde in 1756, Mod Lang Notes, 11/53; Note sur Pataques, 9/54 & Contribution a L'histoire du nom parade, 4/59, Fr Mod. **CONTACT ADDRESS** Dept of Foreign Lang, California State Univ, Chico, First & Normal St, Chico, CA 95926.

BROWN, JANE K.
DISCIPLINE GERMAN, COMPARATIVE LITERATURE **EDUCATION** Harvard Univ, BA, 65; Yale Univ, MPhil, 69; PhD, 71. **CAREER** Teaching Fel, Yale Univ, 68-69; asst prof, Univ of NH, 71-72; asst prof, Mount Holyoke Col, 73-77; assoc prof, Univ of Va, 77-79; assoc prof to prof, Univ of Colo 79-88; prof, Univ of Wash, 88-. **HONORS AND AWARDS** Deutsche Forschungsgemeinschaft, 92; NEH Fel, 94-95. **MEMBERSHIPS** MLA; ASECS; Goethe Soc of N Am; Boethe-Gesellschaft. **RESEARCH** Goethe, History of Drama. **SELECTED PUBLICATIONS** Auth, "Goethe's Cyclical Narratives: The Unterhaltungen deutscher Ausgewanderten and Wilhelm Meisters Wanderjahe", Univ NC Studies in the Ger Lang and Lit 82, Univ NC Pr, 75; auth, Goethe's Faust: The German Tragedy, Cornell Univ Pr, (Ithaca), 86; ed, cotrans, of "Johann Wolfgang von Goethe, Conversations of German Refugees" in Wilhelm Meister's Journeyman Years or the Renunciants, Suhrkamp (NY), 89; auth, Goethe's Faust: Theater of the World, Twayne Pub, (NY), 92; coed, Interpreting Goethe's Faust Today, Camden House (Columbia, SC), 94; coed, Essays on Goethe, Camden House (Columbia, SC), 95; auth, Ironie und Objektivitat: Aufsatze zu Goethe, Konigshausen & Neuman, (Wurzburg), 99. **CONTACT ADDRESS** Dept Germanics, Univ of Washington, PO Box 353130, Seattle, WA 98195-3130. **EMAIL** jkbrown@u.washington.edu

BROWN, JANICE C. L.
PERSONAL Born, WY **DISCIPLINE** JAPANESE LITERATURE **EDUCATION** Univ Brit Colum, BA, 77; MA, 79; PhD,

85. **CAREER** Lectr, Univ Brit Colum, 81-82; asst to assoc prof, Univ Albta, 91-. **HONORS AND AWARDS** Izaak Walton Killam Fel; Univ Brit Colum Grad Fel. **MEMBERSHIPS** MLA, Asn for Asian Studies, Acad Women's Asn, Can Asian Studies Asn. **RESEARCH** Modern Japanese Literature, modern and contemporary fiction and poetry by Japanese women writers, feminist theory and criticism. **SELECTED PUBLICATIONS** Auth, "Hayashi Fumiko: Voice from the Margin," Japan Quart 43.1, (96); auth, "Re-Writing the Maternal: 'Bad' Mothers in the Writings of Hayashi Fumiko," Mothers in Japanese Lit, Univ Brit Colum, (97); rev, of "The Woman's Hand: Gender and Theory in Japanese Women's Writing," Jour of Asian Studies 56.4, (97); auth, Hayashi Fumiko's I Saw a Pale Horse and Selected Poetry from Diary of a Vagabond, Cornell E Asian Series, (Ithaca, NY), 97; auth, "Oba Minako: Telling the Untellable," Japan Quart 45.3 (98); rev, of "Studies in the Comic Spirit in Modern Japanese Fiction," Monumenta Nipponica 53.4, (98); rev, of "Studies in Modern Japanese Literature: Essays in Honor of Edwin McClellan," Jour of the Asn of Teachers of Japanese 33.2, (99); auth, "De-siring the Center: Hayashi Fumiko's Hungry Heroines and the Male Literary Canon," The Father/Daughter Plots: Japanese Literary Women and the Law of the Fathers, (Univ Hi Pr, 01). **CONTACT ADDRESS** Dept E Asian Studies, Univ of Alberta, Room 400 Arts, Edmonton, AB, Canada T6G 0L4. **EMAIL** janice.brown@ualberta.ca

BROWN, JOAN L.
PERSONAL Born 07/15/1952, New York, NY, m, 1976, 2 children **DISCIPLINE** SPANISH **EDUCATION** Vassar Col, AB, 72; Univ Penn, MA, 74; PhD, 76. **CAREER** Assoc Prof to Elias Ahuja Prof, Univ Del, 83-. **HONORS AND AWARDS** Fel, Univ Del, 97-98. **MEMBERSHIPS** MLA, AATSP, NEMLA, 20th Century Spanish Lit Asn. **RESEARCH** Hispanic literary canon/Contemporary Spanish literature/Literature by women. **SELECTED PUBLICATIONS** Co-auth, Conversaciones creadoras, Second Ed, Houghton Mifflin Co, 99; co-auth, Conversaciones creadoras, D.C. Heath, 94; ed, Women Writers of Contemporary Spain: Exiles in the Homeland, Univ Del Press, 91; auth, Secrets From the Back Room: The fiction of Carmen Martin Gaite, Romance Monographs, 87; auth, "Tiempo de silencio and Ritmo lento: Pioneers of the New social Novel in Spain," Hispanic review, (82): 61-73; auth, "Men by Women in the contemporary Spanish Novel," Hispanic Review, (92): 55-70; co-auth, "The contemporary Hispanic Novel: Is There a Canon?," Hispania, (95): 252-261; co-auth, "Required Reading: The Canon in Spanish and Spanish American Literature," Hispania, (98): 1-19; co-auth, "The Gender of Our Canon: Women Writers and their works on Graduate Reading Lists," Revista de Estudios Hispanicos, (98): 465-490. **CONTACT ADDRESS** Dept For Lang, Univ of Delaware, 18 Amstel Ave, Newark, DE 19716-2599. **EMAIL** jlbrown@udel.edu

BROWN, JOHN LACKEY
PERSONAL Born 04/29/1914, Ilion, NY, m, 1941, 2 children **DISCIPLINE** COMPARATIVE LITERATURE, FRENCH **EDUCATION** Hamilton Col, AB, 35; Cath Univ Am, MA, 36, PhD(French, Medieval Latin), 39. **CAREER** Asst prof French, Cath Univ Am, 39-42; asst chief publ sect, Off War Info, 42-43; correspondent Sunday ed, NY Times, Paris, 45-48; cult attache, US Embassies, Paris, Brussels, Rome, Mexico City, 48-68; Prof Comp Lit, Cath Univ Am, 68-. **HONORS AND AWARDS** Awarded Grand Prix de la Critique, 54; mem, Cath Comn on Intellectual & Cult Affairs, 60-; fel, Ctr Advan Studies, Wesleyan Univ, 62-63; vis prof French & English, Univ Louisville, 66-67; prof Am lit & civilization, Inst Anglo-Am Studies, Nat Univ Mex, 66-68; lectr, Cath Inst Paris, 69, Univs Laval, McGill, Montreal & Toronto, 70; dir gen Am Bicentennial Exposition in Paris and Warsaw, 75; vpres, Int Asn Lit Critics, 73-; sr Fulbright prof Am Lit, Univ Lisbon, 79-80; Newstadt Prize, 82; Doctor honoris causa, Univ Queretaro, 84; Am correspondent J des Poetes. **MEMBERSHIPS** MLA; Am Studies Asn; Am Comp Lit Asn; Mediaeval Acad Am; Dante Soc. **RESEARCH** European, especially Franco, American literary relations in the 19th and 20th centuries; Europe avantgarde movements of the 20th century; the problem of expatriation in American literature. **SELECTED PUBLICATIONS** Auth, Panorama de la litterature contemporaine aux Etats-Unis, Paris, Gallimard, 54; auth, The Methodus of Jean Bodin, Washington, Catholic Univ Press, Reprinted, 71; auth, "V. Larbaud et la jeune poesie americaine," in Larbaud et la litterature de son temps, (Paris, Klinck-seik), 78; auth, "Symbolisme belge et poesie moderniste anglo-saxonne, in 150 ansde litterature francophone en Belgique, (Brussels, Academie Royale), 80; auth, Valery Larbaud, Boston, Twaynne, 81; auth, "Larbaud et quelques amis americains," in Larbaud: La Prose du Monde, (Paris, Presses univesiaires), 81. **CONTACT ADDRESS** 3024 Tilden St NW, Washington, DC 20008.

BROWN, MICHAEL G.
PERSONAL Born 03/31/1938, Scranton, PA **DISCIPLINE** HEBREW **EDUCATION** Harvard Col, BA, 60; Columbia Univ, MA, 63; Jewish Theol Sem, MHL, 66, rabbi, 68; State Univ NY Buffalo, PhD, 76. **CAREER** Assoc prof Humanities & Hebrew, York Univ, 68-, dir, Ctr Jewish Stud, 95-; chair Can stud, vis assoc prof, Hebrew Univ (Jerusalem), 80-82; vis assoc prof, Univ Toronto, 83-84; vis assoc prof, Univ Calif San Diego, 85, 88; fel, Am-Holy Land stud proj, 85-87. **HONORS AND AWARDS** DD (Hon), Jewish Theol Sem, 94 **MEMBERSHIPS** Dir, Asn Hebrew Schs; dir, Can Jewish Hist Soc; Can Sem Zionist Thought; Asn Jewish Stud; Rabbinical Assembly; Toronto Bd Rabbis. **SELECTED PUBLICATIONS** Auth, Jew or Juif? Jews, French Canadians, and Anglo-Canadians, 1759-1914, Jewish Publication Soc, 86; ed, Approaches to Antisemitism: Context and Curriculum, 94; auth, The Israeli-American Connection: Its Roots in the Yishuv, 1914-1915, Wayne State Univ Press, 97; auth, "Henrietta Szold," in Jewish Women in America: An Historical Encyclopedia, 97; auth, Creating the Jewish Future, AltaMira Press, 99. **CONTACT ADDRESS** Dept of Humanities, York Univ, 4700 Keele St N, North York, ON, Canada M3J 1P3. **EMAIL** michaelb@yorku.ca

BROWN, PETER D. G.
PERSONAL Born 10/18/1942, Alton, IL, m, 2 children **DISCIPLINE** GERMAN **EDUCATION** Columbia Col, BA, 64; Columbia Univ, MA, 65; PhD, 71. **CAREER** Instr, Barnard Col, 68-71; asst prof to prof, SUNY New Paltz, 71-. **HONORS AND AWARDS** Woodrow Wilson Fel, 64; Carl Schurz Fel, 64-65; DAAD Fel, 65-66; Vera B David Fel, 66-67; SUNY Chancellor's Awd, 93; German Order of Merit, 99; SUNY New Paltz Lib Arts and Sci Teacher of the Year, 00. **MEMBERSHIPS** MLA, Am Assoc of Teachers of Ger, Women in German, German Studies Assoc. **RESEARCH** 19th Century German Drama, Jewish Studies, Women in German, Film Studies. **SELECTED PUBLICATIONS** Auth, How Enduring is the Present German Democracy?, Praeger, (NY), 63; auth, "Oskar Panizza's First and Last Books," Ger Rev, (73); ed, Nuclear Power in the Hudson Valley, Multi-County CDC, (Highland, NY), 76; auth, Oskar Panizza: His Life and Works, Peter Lang, (NY), 83. **CONTACT ADDRESS** Dept Foreign Langs, SUNY, New Paltz, S Manheim Blvd, JFT 414, New Paltz, NY 12561. **EMAIL** brownp@newpaltz.edu

BROWN, ROYAL SCOTT
PERSONAL Born 06/20/1940, Raleigh, NC, m, 1964, 2 children **DISCIPLINE** CONTEMPORARY FRENCH LITERATURE **EDUCATION** Pa State Univ, BA, 62; Middlebury Col, MA, 63; Columbia Univ, PhD(French), 75. **CAREER** Grad assoc French, Ind Univ, 63-64; lectr romance lang, Queens Col, 64-70; dir, City Univ NY, Prog Study Abroad, Nancy, France, 70-72; lectr, 72-75, asst prof, 75-81, Assoc Prof Romance Lang, Queens Col, 82-, vis assoc prof, NY Univ, summers 81 & 82. **MEMBERSHIPS** MLA. **RESEARCH** Interdisciplinary studies; cinema; contemporary French literature. **SELECTED PUBLICATIONS CONTACT ADDRESS** Dept of Romance Lang, Queens Col, 65-30 Kissena Blvd, Flushing, NY 11367.

BROWNE, E. WAYLES
PERSONAL Born 07/19/1941, Washington, DC **DISCIPLINE** LINGUISTICS **EDUCATION** Harvard Univ, AB, 63; Univ Zagreb, PhD, 83. **CAREER** Lect, Yale Univ, 66-68; Lect, Brown Univ, 68-69; Instr, Inst Ling, 69-83; From Asst Prof to Assoc Prof, Cornell Univ, 74-. **MEMBERSHIPS** LSA, AATSEEL, AAAS, AAUP. **RESEARCH** Slavis linguistics, South Slavic languages (Croation, Bosnian, Serbian, Slovenian, Macedonian, Bulgarian), Polish. **SELECTED PUBLICATIONS** Auth, Relative Clauses in Serbo-Croatian, Univ Zagreb Pr, 86; auth, "Some Problems in Teaching Serbo-Croatian as a Foreign Language," Knjizevnost i jezik 37 (90): 258-261; auth, "Email Lists for the Slavic and East European Scholar," AATSEEL Newsletter, 33.5 (91): 8-9; auth, "How to Agree with an Infinitive: A System of Concepts for Describing Agreement in Serbo-Croatian," Medjunarodni Slavisticki Centar (91): 157-163; auth, "Variation in Serbo-Croatian Noun Phrase Constituents: Declinable and Indeclinable Items," Zbornik Matice srpske za filologiji I lingvistiku, 36 (93): 173-179; auth, "Serbo Croatian." in The Slavonic Lang (London: Routledge, 93), 306-387; auth, "Incomplete and Complete: A Pedagogical Note," in Alexander lipson in Memoriam (Columbus: Slavica, 94), 24-28; auth, "Appreciation: Blaze Koneski 1921-1993," LSA Bull no 143, Ling Soc of Am (94); auth, "Poetry from OSIP: Two Bosnian Poets," The Bookpress (94): 6-7; auth, "Slavic Languages," Encycl Britannica, (96-98). **CONTACT ADDRESS** Dept Ling, Cornell Univ, Ithaca, NY 14853. **EMAIL** ewb2@cornell.edu

BROWNING, BARTON W.
PERSONAL Born 08/22/1940, Springfield, IL, m, 1964, 2 children **DISCIPLINE** GERMAN LITERATURE **EDUCATION** Wesleyan Univ, BA, 62; Univ Calif, Berkeley, MA, 65, PhD(-Ger), 70. **CAREER** Asst prof, 69-76, Assoc Prof Ger, PA State Univ, University Park, 76-. **MEMBERSHIPS** Am Asn Teachers Ger; MLA; Am Soc Ger Lit 16th & 17th Centuries; Int Arbeitskreis Deutsche Barock-Lit; fel, Herzog August Bibliot Wolfenbuttel. **RESEARCH** German Baroque literature; 19th century German literature; European Renaissance and Baroque literature. **SELECTED PUBLICATIONS** Auth, Stifter's Nachsommer and the fourth commandment, Colloquia Germanica, 73; Cooper's influence on Stifter: Fact or scholarly fiction?, Mod Lang Notes, 74; Ein Kleiner Hofmannswaldau fund in Pennsylvanien, Wolfenbuttler Barock-Nachrichten, 75; Joseph Roth's Legende vom heiligen Trinker: Essence and Elirir, Protest-Form-Tradition, 79; Grillparzer ein 'Bruderzwist im Hauser Habsburg' and the Historical Braunschweig,Heinrich,Julius,von/, Mod Austrian Lit, Vol 28, 1995; **CONTACT ADDRESS** German Dept, Pennsylvania State Univ, Univ Park, 311 Burrowes, University Park, PA 16802. **EMAIL** bwb2@psu.edu

BRUEGGEMANN, AMINIA M.
DISCIPLINE GERMAN **EDUCATION** Univ Mich, PhD, 93. **CAREER** Languages, Old Dominion Univ. **SELECTED PUBLICATIONS** Auth, Brueggemann, Aminia & Hubert Rast. Assoziationen: Arbeitsbuch. 2nd Year German Language Program, Communicative Approach; Hill, 91; Brueggemann, Aminia. Chronotopos Amerika bei Max Frisch, Peter Handke, Gunter Kunert und Martin Walser, Peter Lang, 96. **CONTACT ADDRESS** Old Dominion Univ, Hampton Blvd, Norfolk, VA 23529. **EMAIL** abruegge@odu.edu

BRULOTTE, GAETAN
PERSONAL Born 04/08/1945, Quebec, PQ, Canada, d **DISCIPLINE** FRENCH LITERATURE **EDUCATION** Sorbonne & Univ of Paris, PhD. **CAREER** Prof French, Univ S Fla, 88-; vis prof, Univ Quebec, 89-90; vis prof, Sorbonne-Paris, 94; vis prof, Univ Grenoble, 93. **HONORS AND AWARDS** Phi Kappa Phi Artist/Scholar of the Year; Ashford Distinguished Scholar, 99. **MEMBERSHIPS** MLA; Fr Writer's Soc; Quebec Writer's Union **RESEARCH** French & Francophone Studies; Creative Writing; Comparative Literature. **SELECTED PUBLICATIONS** Oeuvres de chair, Figures du discours erotique, Presses de l'Universite, 98; Les Cahiers de Limentinus, Lectures fin de siecle, XYZ, 98; Epreuves, Lemeac, 99; L'Univers de Jean Paul Lemieux, Fides, 96; Ce Qui nous tient (1989 Literary Grand Prize of Trois-Rivieres), Lemeac, 88; Le Surveillant, BQ 95; auth, L'Emprise, Lemeac, 88; co-dir, The Encyclopedia of Erotic Literature, Fritzroy-Dearborn, London. **CONTACT ADDRESS** Dept of World Language Edu, Univ of So Florida, 4202 E Fowler Ave, Tampa, FL 33620-5550. **EMAIL** brulotte@chuma1.cas.usf.edu

BRUMFIELD, WILLIAM CRAFT
PERSONAL Born 06/28/1944, Charlotte, NC, s **DISCIPLINE** RUSSIAN LITERATURE & ART HISTORY **EDUCATION** Tulane Univ, BA, 66; Univ Calif, Berkeley, MA, 68, PhD (Slavic lang), 73 **CAREER** Vis lectr Russ lit, Univ Wis-Madison, 73-74; asst prof Russ lit, Harvard Univ, 74-79; Asst Prof Russ Lit, Tulane Univ, 81-, Res dir, ACTR Moscow, 79-80. **HONORS AND AWARDS** Woodrow Wilson fel, 66; IREX sr exchange scholar, Moscow, 83-84; fel, Kennan Inst, Washington, 89; NEH fel, Nat Humanities Ctr, 92-93; "Notable Books of the Year 1993", for A History of Russian Architecture, New York Times Book Rev, 93; fac res award, Tulane Univ, 97; Guggenheim fel, 00-01. **MEMBERSHIPS** Am Asn Advan Slavic Studies; Am Coun Teachers of Russian; Soc Architectural Historians. **RESEARCH** Russian cultural hist; Russian architectural history. **SELECTED PUBLICATIONS** Auth, Gold in Azure: One Thousand Years of Russian Architecture, David Godine (Boston), 83; ed, Reshaping Russian Architecture: Western Technology, Utopian Dreams, Cambridge Univ Pr, Wilson Ctr, 90; ed, Christianity and the Arts in Russia, Cambridge Univ Pr, 91; auth, The Origins of Modernism in Russian Archietecture, Univ Calif, 91; auth, A History of Russian Architecture, Cambridge Univ Pr, 93; ed, Russian Housing in the Modern Age: Design and Social Hist, Cambridge Univ Pr, Wilson Ctr, 93; auth, An Architectural Survey of St. Petersburg, 1840-1916: Building Inventory, Kennan Inst, Woodrow Wilson Ctr, 94; auth, Lost Russia: Photograhping the Ruins of Russian Architecture, Duke Univ Pr, 95; auth, Landmarks of Russian Architecture: A Photographic Survey, Gordon and Breach, 97. **CONTACT ADDRESS** Dept of Ger & Slavic Lang, Tulane Univ, 305 Newcomb Hall, New Orleans, LA 70118. **EMAIL** brumfiel@mailhost.tcs.tulane.edu

BRUNEAU, MARIE FLORINE
PERSONAL Born 05/18/1943, Casablanca, Morocco, m, 1989 **DISCIPLINE** FRENCH **EDUCATION** Univ Calif-Berkeley, BA, 73, MA, 75, PhD, 80. **CAREER** Tchg asst, 73-77, Instr, 79-80, Univ Cal-Berkeley; asst prof French, 80-86, assoc prof French, 86-96, Prof French, 96- , Univ S Calif; vis assoc prof, Univ Chicago, 88. **HONORS AND AWARDS** Taft lectr at Cinc Conf Romance Lang, 91; NEH 89-90; numerous honors, awards, and grants. **MEMBERSHIPS** MLA; 17th Century Fr Lit Soc; Phi Beta Kappa. **RESEARCH** 17th Century literature; Mystical theology; Gender studies. **SELECTED PUBLICATIONS** Auth, Racine, jansenisme et modernite, Jose Corti, 86; Psychoalysis and its Abject: What Lurks Behind the Fear of 'Mother" Studies in Psychoanalytic Theory, 92; L'Amour maternel comme alibi a la production de l'ecriture chez Marie de l'Incarnation, Etudes Litteraires, 94; Female Mystics and the Modern World. Marie de l'Incarnation (1599-1672) Madame Guyon (1648-1717) SUNY Press, 98; Dans les oubliettes de Versailles: Liberte intellectuelle, tolerance et poursuite du bonheur dans la pensee guyonnienne, Le Labyrinthe de Versailles: Parcours critique de Moliere a Malebranche, Rodopi, 98; Guyon, Jeanne Marie Bouvier de la Motte, Encyclo of Women and World Relig, Macmillan, 98. **CONTACT ADDRESS** Dept of French & Italian, Univ of So California, Los Angeles, CA 90089-0359. **EMAIL** marie-florine.bruneau@wanadoo.fr

BRUNER, JEFFREY
PERSONAL Born 03/20/1960, Holdenville, OK **DISCIPLINE** SPANISH LITERATURE AND CULTURE **EDUCATION** OK Baptist Univ, BA, 83; Rutgers Univ, MA, 86, PhD, 90. **CAREER** Asst Prof, Assoc Prof, 90 to 96-, West Virginia Univ; Asst Prof, 88-90, Trenton State College. **MEMBER-**

SHIPS MLA; NMLA; SCLA. **RESEARCH** Historical Novel, Narratology, Lit and other Arts, Cultural Studies. **SELECTED PUBLICATIONS** Auth, El Valle de los Caidos, La historia de Espana seguin Goya Vasari y Rojas, Bogota, Bogota Cen Univ, 98; Pre-Texts and Con-Texts: Poeta en Nueva York Viaje a la luna and the Theater of Federico Garcia Lorca, MIFLC Rev, 94; The Lie that Reveals Truth: Art as/and History in Carlos Rojas' El Valle de loa Caidos, Hispanofila, 94; Glorias y miserias de la dramaturgia de Maria Manuela Reina, Estreno: Cuadernos del Teatro Espanol Contemporaneo, 93; Visual Art as Narrative Discourse: The Ekphrastic Dimension of Carmen Laforet's Nada, Anales de la Literatura Espanola, Contemporanea, 93. **CONTACT ADDRESS** Dept of Foreign Languages, West Virginia Univ, Morgantown, Box 6298, Morgantown, WV 26506-6298. **EMAIL** jbruner@wvu.edu

BRUNER, M. LANE
PERSONAL Born 07/25/1958, Kansas City, MO, m, 1984 **DISCIPLINE** SPEECH COMMUNICATION, RHETORICAL AND CRITICAL THEORY **EDUCATION** CA State Univ, Northridge, BA, 91; Louisiana State Univ, MA, 93; Univ Washington, PhD, 97. **CAREER** Asst prof of communication, Babson Coll. **HONORS AND AWARDS** Wilma Grimes Memorial Teaching Awd in Performance Studies, 94; MacFarlane Scholarship, Outstanding Humanities Graduate Student, 96. **MEMBERSHIPS** International Communication Assn; Natl Communication Assn; The Assn for the Study of Nationalities; Amer Soc for Hist of Rhetoric **RESEARCH** Rhetorical theory; collective identity construction and political memory; political theory; nationalism; critical theory. **SELECTED PUBLICATIONS** Auth, Producing Identities: Gender Problematization and Feminist Argumentation, Argumentation and Advocacy, Spring 96; Towards a Poststructural Rehetorical Critical Praxis: Foucault, Limit Work and Jenninger's Kristallnacht Address, Rhetorica, Spring 96; From Etnic of Nationalism to Strategic Multiculturalism: Shifting Strategies of Remembrance in the Quebecois Secessionist Movement, Javnost, fall 97; Strategies of Remembrance in Pre-Unification West Germany, Quarterly Journal of Speech, 00; auth, Rhetorics of the State: The Public Negotiation of Political Character in Germany, Russia, and Quebec, National Identities, 00. **CONTACT ADDRESS** History & Society Div, Babson Col, Babson Park, MA 02157. **EMAIL** bruner@babson.edu

BRUNNER, KATHLEEN MARIE
PERSONAL Born 11/05/1953, Torrance, CA, s **DISCIPLINE** FRENCH **EDUCATION** Mt San Antonio Col, AA, 77; City Univ, BS, 87; Univ Wash, MA, 92; MA, 94; PhD, 97. **CAREER** Teaching asst, Univ Wash, 94-96; private tutor, 95-; lectr, Alliance Francaise de Seattle, 99-. **HONORS AND AWARDS** Grant, Univ Franche-Comte, 00; Res, Inst of Adv Res, Univ Columbia at Paris, 94-95. **MEMBERSHIPS** Alliance Francaise de Seattle; Am Teachers of French; Le Grand Concours; Wash Asn for Lang Teaching; N Am Sartre Soc. **RESEARCH** 19th and 20th Century French Art, Film, Literature. **SELECTED PUBLICATIONS** Auth, "Versailles: un jardin a la francaise," Le Canard Dechaine, 00; auth, "Le Stage d'ete au Centre de linguistique appliquee de Besancon," Le Canard Dechaine, 00; auth, "Une conference sur 10,000 arbres pour Versailles: replantation du parc du Chateau de Versailles devaste par la tempete le decemre dernier," Le Canard Dehaine, 00; auth, "La verite en peinture: un hommage a Cezanne,' Le Canard Dechaine, 01; auth, "Jacques Prevert dans la classe; tout ce qui est beau, simple et naturel," Le Canard Dechaine, 01; auth, La Chanson franciase et le cours de langue," Le Canard Dechaine, 01. **CONTACT ADDRESS** Alliance Francaise de Seattle, PO Box 95167, Seattle, WA 98145-2167. **EMAIL** brunnerk@lanepowell.com

BRUNSDALE, MITZI MALLARIAN
PERSONAL Born 05/16/1939, Fargo, ND, m, 1961, 3 children **DISCIPLINE** ENGLISH, COMPARATIVE LITERATURE **EDUCATION** NDak State Univ, BS, 59, IMS, 61; Univ NDak, PhD(English), 76. **CAREER** From asst prof to prof, Mayville State Univ, 76-; chair, div of communicaiton arts, publishers weekly, 96-; bk critic, Houston Post, Tex, 70-89; grant rev panelist, Nat Endowment for Humanities, 77-; chair, Humanities Coun, 80-, bk critic, The Armchair Detective, 96-, bk critic, Publishers Weekly, 98-. **RESEARCH** Early 20th century British literature; early 20th century European comparative literature; D H Lawrence. **SELECTED PUBLICATIONS** Auth, Lawrence and the Myth of Brynhild, Western Humanities Rev, autumn 77; The Effect of Mrs Rudolf Dircks' Translation of Schopenhauer's The Metaphysics of Love on D H Lawrence's Early Fiction, Rocky Mountain Rev Lang & Lit, spring 78; D H Lawrence and Raymond Otis: Brothers of Blood, NMex Humanities Rev, winter 78-79; The German Effect on D H Lawrence and his Works, 1885-1912, P L Verlag, Berne, 79; Alexander Solzhenitsy, In: The Encyclopedia of Short Fiction, 81, Boris Pasternak, In: The Encyclopedia of Short Fiction, 81 & D H Lawrence, In: A Critical Survey of Poetry, Salem Press; D H Lawrence's David: Drama as a Vehicle for Religious Prophecy, In: Themes in Drama V, Cambridge Univ Press, 82; Toward the Greater Day: Rilke, Lawrence, and Immortalilty, Comp Lit Sudies, 82; Sigrid Undset: Ch.. of Norway, Oxford: Berg, 88; Dorothy L. Sayers: Solving the Mystery of Wickedness, Oxford: Berg, 90; James Joyce: The Short Fiction, NY: Twayne, 93; James Herriot, NY: Twayne, 96; auth, A Student Companion to George Orwell, Westport, CT: Greenwood, 00. **CONTACT ADDRESS** Mayville State Univ, 330 3rd St NE, Mayville, ND 58257-1299. **EMAIL** Mitzi_brunsdale@mail.masu.nodak.edu

BRUSH, CRAIG BALCOMBE
PERSONAL Born 05/28/1930, Manhattan, NY, s **DISCIPLINE** FRENCH **EDUCATION** Princeton Univ, AB, 51; Columbia Univ, MA, 55, PhD, 63 **CAREER** Instr French, Choate Sch, 51-54; from instr to asst prof, Columbia Univ, 55-66; asst prof, City Col New York, 66-70; assoc prof, 70-73, chmn dept mod lang, 73-79, Prof French, Fordham Univ, 73- **HONORS AND AWARDS** Fubright, Paris, 1959-61. **MEMBERSHIPS** MLA; Soc Amis Montaigne; Renaissance Soc Am **RESEARCH** French literature in the 16th and 18th centuries **SELECTED PUBLICATIONS** Auth, Montaigne and Bayle, Nijhoff, The Hague, 66; coauth, Bayle: Historical and Critical Dictionary, Bobbs, 67; ed, Selected writings of Pierre Gassendi, Johnson Reprint, 73; auth, From The Perspective of the Self: Montaghe's Self-Portrait Fordham UP, 93. **CONTACT ADDRESS** 411 W 115th St, New York, NY 10025. **EMAIL** cbb15@columbia.edu

BRUSHWOOD, JOHN STUBBS
PERSONAL Born 01/23/1920, Glenns, VA, m, 1945, 2 children **DISCIPLINE** SPANISH AMERICAN LITERATURE **EDUCATION** Randolph-Macon Col, BA, 40; Univ Va, MA, 42; Columbia Univ, PhD, 50; DLitt, Randolph-Macon Col, 81. **CAREER** Instr Romance lang, Va Polytech Inst, 42-44; from instr to prof Span, Univ Mo, 46-67, chmn dept Romance lang, 53-57 & 58-59; Roy A Roberts Prof Emer Latin Am Lit, Univ Kans, 67-. **HONORS AND AWARDS** Fund Advan Educ fel, 51-52; Am Philos Soc grant, 57; Am Coun Learned Soc grant, 61; Soc Sci Res Coun grant, 71; Nat Endowment for Humanities, summer 76; Bellagio scholar in residence, 78. **MEMBERSHIPS** Midwest Mod Lang Asn (pres, 62-63); MLA; Am Asn Teachers Span & Port; Inst Int Lit Iberoam. **RESEARCH** Mexican literature; Spanish American novel **SELECTED PUBLICATIONS** Auth, Mexico in Its Novel: A Nation's Search for Identity, Univ Tex, 66; Enrique Gonzales Martinez, Twayne, 69; Los Ricos en la Prosa Mexicans, Diogenes, 70; Mexico en su Novela, Fondo Cult Economics, 73; The Spanish American Novel: A Twentieth Century Survey, Univ Tex, 75; Genteel Barbarism: New Readings of Nineteenth Century Spanish American Novels, Univ Nebr, 81; cotransl, The Precipice (Galindo), Univ Tex, 69; Don Goyo (Aguilera-Malta), Humana, 80. **CONTACT ADDRESS** Dept of Span and Port, Univ of Kansas, Lawrence, 2071 Wescoe Hall, Lawrence, KS 66044. **EMAIL** riopo@eagle.cc.ukans.edu

BUCHANAN, RHONDA L.
PERSONAL Born 10/23/1954, Alexandria, VA, m, 1975 **DISCIPLINE** SPANISH **EDUCATION** Western Md Col, BA, 76; Univ Colo, Boulder, MA, 80, PhD, 82. **CAREER** Full prof, Univ of Louisville, 85-. **HONORS AND AWARDS** Western Md Col, BA, summa cum laude, 76; Distinguished Teaching Prof, Univ of Louisville, 2000. **MEMBERSHIPS** Modern Lang Asn, Am Asn of Teachers of Spanish and Portuguese. **RESEARCH** Contemporary Spanish American narrative fiction. **SELECTED PUBLICATIONS** Critical articles in journals and books on a number of different Latin Am authors; publications appear in US, Spain, Mexico, Argentina and Cuba. **CONTACT ADDRESS** Dept Classical and Modern Lang, Univ of Louisville, Louisville, KY 40292. **EMAIL** rhondabuchanan@louisville.edu

BUCHER, GERARD C.
DISCIPLINE COMPARATIVE LITERATURE **EDUCATION** Ecole des Hautes Etudes, PhD. **CAREER** Prof, SUNY Buffalo. **RESEARCH** The rel between relig and fiction and among anthrop and philos; critical theory; and philos; M. Heidegger; J. Derrida; R. Girard. **SELECTED PUBLICATIONS** Auth, La vision et l'enigme, Elements pour une analytique du logos, ed. du Cerf, 89; Le testament poetique, 94; articles on literature by Bernanos, Mallarme, Rimbaud, Robbe-Grillet; articles on semiotics and religion (Judaism and Christianity). **CONTACT ADDRESS** Dept Comp Lit, SUNY, Buffalo, 639 Clemens Hall, Buffalo, NY 14260.

BUCK, ROBERT J.
PERSONAL Born 07/05/1926, Vermilion, AB, Canada **DISCIPLINE** CLASSICS **EDUCATION** Univ Alta, BA, 49; Univ Kentucky, MA, 50; Univ Cincinnati, PhD, 56. **CAREER** Asst prof, Univ Kentucky, 55-60; assoc prof, 60-66, head dept, 64-72, prof, 66-91, PROF EMER CLASSICS, UNIV ALTA, 91-; mng comt, Am Sch Classical Stud (Athens), 61-83. **HONORS AND AWARDS** Fel, Can Inst Rome, 76. **MEMBERSHIPS** Can Mediter Inst; Can Archaeol Inst Athens; Class Asn Can. **RESEARCH** Greek history; Greek and Roman archaeology. **SELECTED PUBLICATIONS** Auth, A History of Boetia, 79; coauth, The Excavations of San Giovanni di Ruoti, vol I 93, vol II 96. **CONTACT ADDRESS** Dept Hist and Classics, Univ of Alberta, Edmonton, AB, Canada T6G 2E5.

BUCKLEY, CHRISTINA A.
PERSONAL Born 08/27/1969, NY, s **DISCIPLINE** SPANISH LITERATURE AND CINEMA **EDUCATION** Col William & Mary, BA; Tulane Univ, MA; PhD. **CAREER** Teaching asst, Tulane Univ, 92-97; res asst, Tulane Univ, 97-98; asst prof, Furman Univ, 98-00. **HONORS AND AWARDS** Mellon Found Fel, 97. **MEMBERSHIPS** MLA, Chasqui, SCMLA, MMLA, AATSP, Soc for Cinema Studies. **RESEARCH** Spanish and Latin American Film and Popular Culture, Nineteenth- and Twentieth-Century Spanish Literature. **SELECTED PUBLICATIONS** Auth, "Gender Trouble in Neville D'Almeida's Dama do Lotacao," Studies in Popular Latin American Culture Vol 17, 97; auth, "Los Anos Oscuros: Silence Against Micro-/ Macro-Nationalist Ideology," in Cine-Lit III: Essays on Hispanic Film and Fiction, eds. George Cabello Castellet, Jaume Marti-Olivella, & Guy Wood (OR: Portland State Univ, Reed Col, & Ore State Univ, 98), 131-143; rev, "Men with Guns/ Hombres Armados," by John Sayles, Chasqui 27.2 (98); cotransl, "El Paisaje de la Mirada," by Gomez Molina & Juan Jose, Artes Graficas Hono, 98; transl, "The Dialectics of Cuban Homoerotism in Cuban Narrative," by Jose Alvarez, in Chicano/Latino Homoerotic Identities, ed. David William Foster (NY: Garland Publ, 98; auth, "Silence, Dance, and Disease as Spaces of Agency in the Spanish Film Entre Rojas," Romance Lang Annual (99); rev, of "O que e isso, Companheiro? (Four Days in September)," by Bruno Barreto, Chasqui 28.1 (99); rev, "Americanos: Latino Life in the US," by Andy Young and Susan Todd, Chasqui 29.1 (00). **CONTACT ADDRESS** Dept Modern Lang, Furman Univ, 3300 Poinsett Hwy, Greenville, NC 29613-0002. **EMAIL** christina.buckley@furman.edu

BULLER, JEFFREY L.
PERSONAL Born 09/09/1954, Milwaukee, WI, m, 1996, 2 children **DISCIPLINE** CLASSICS **EDUCATION** Univ Notre Dame, BA, 76; Univ Wis, MA, 77; PhD, 81. **CAREER** Asst prof to assoc prof, Loras Col, 81-90; assoc prof to prof, Ga S Univ, 90-97; asst to acting Dean, 90-. **HONORS AND AWARDS** Phi Beta Kappa; Phi Kappa Phi; Fulbright Fel (2). **MEMBERSHIPS** Am Philog Assoc; Classical Assoc of the Middle W and S; Wagner Soc of NY. **RESEARCH** Influence of classical literature on opera. **SELECTED PUBLICATIONS** Auth, "Looking Backwards: Baroque Opera and the Ending of the Orpheus Myth", Int J of the Class Tradition 1.3 ((5): 57-79; auth, "The Thematic Role of Stabreim in Richard Wagner's Der Ring des Nibelungen", Opera Quart 11.4 (95): 59-76; auth, Sleep in the Ring", Opera Quart, 12.2 (95): 3-22; auth, "The Messianic Hero in Wagner's Ring", Opera Quart, 13.2 (96): 21-38; auth, "From Clemtia Caesaris to La Clemenza di Tito", in Qui Miscuit Utile Dulci: Festschrift for Paul MacKendrick, Bolchazy-Charduzzi, (Wauconda, IL, 98), 69-85; auth, "Spectacle in the Ring", Opera Quart 14.4 (98): 41057; auth, "Ellen Faull: A Life in Song", Opera Quart (00). **CONTACT ADDRESS** Dept Hist, Georgia So Univ, PO Box 8054, Statesboro, GA 30460-1000. **EMAIL** jbuller@gasou.edu

BULLIVANT, KEITH
PERSONAL Born 02/11/1941, Derby, England, m, 1965, 2 children **DISCIPLINE** GERMAN STUDIES **EDUCATION** Birmingham Univ, BA, 63; PhD, 68. **CAREER** Asst prof, Birmingham Univ, 65-70; prof, Univ of Warwick, 70-89; prof, chair, Univ of Fla, 89-. **HONORS AND AWARDS** Brit Coun, 80; Dist Vis Prof, NMex State Univ, 89; Gastprofessor, Univ of Paderborn, 91; Ger-Am Acad Coun, 99-01 **MEMBERSHIPS** MLA, SAMLA, Ger Studies Assoc, Am Assoc of Teachers of Ger. **RESEARCH** Modern German Studies. **SELECTED PUBLICATIONS** Coauth, Literature in Upheaval, Manchester UP, 74; coauth, Industrie und deutsche Literature 1830-1914, Deutscher Taschenbuch Verlag, 76; ed, Culture and Society in the Weimar Republic, 77; auth, Between Chaos and Order: The work of Gerd Gaiser, Manchester UP, 80; auth, Realism Today, Heinz, 87; auth, The Future of German Literature, Berg Publ, 94; coed, Dieter Wellershoff, Werke 1-6, Kiepenheur & Witsch, 96-97; ed, Beyond 1989: Re-reading German Literature Since 1945, Bergham Books, 97; coed, Germany and Eastern Europe, Rodopi, 99; coed, Literarisches Krisenbewusstsein, Iudicium, 01. **CONTACT ADDRESS** Univ of Florida, 6237 NW 19th Pl, Gainesville, FL 32605. **EMAIL** kbulli@germslav.ufl.edu

BULMAN, GAIL A.
PERSONAL Born 05/16/1957, Fitchburg, MA, m, 1983, 3 children **DISCIPLINE** SPANISH, PORTUGUESE **EDUCATION** Assumption Col, BA, 79; Boston Col, MA, 83; Syracuse Univ, PhD, 96. **CAREER** Syracuse Univ, 95-. **HONORS AND AWARDS** Nat Endowment for the Humanities, summer stipend, 87, 92; Syracuse Univ Tolley summer res grant, 99. **MEMBERSHIPS** Modern Language Asn; Am Asn Teachers of Foreign Languages; Am Asn Teachers of Spanish and Portuguese; North East Language Asn. **RESEARCH** Latin American literature. **SELECTED PUBLICATIONS** Auth, "El grito infinito: ecos coloniales en La malasangre de Griselda Gambaro," Symposium, Syracuse Univ, 271-276 (winter 95); auth, "Tracion, cuerpos mutilados y casas quemadas: paralelismos en la obra de tres escritoras de diferentes espacios y distintas epocas," in Actas del Congreso Escritura, Individuo y Sociedad en Espana y las Americas de la Universidad de Arecibo, Frankfurt, Germany: La Editorial Iberoamericana de Klaus Dieter Vervuert (forthcoming). **CONTACT ADDRESS** Dept Foreign Lan-

guage, Syracuse Univ, O H B Crouse, Syracuse, NY 13244-1160. **EMAIL** gabulman@syr.edu

BUMP, JEROME FRANCIS ANTHONY
PERSONAL Born 06/13/1943, Pine River, MN, m, 1998, 2 children **DISCIPLINE** ENGLISH LITERATURE, COMPARATIVE STUDIES **EDUCATION** Univ Minn, Minneapolis, BA, 65; Univ Calif, Berkeley, MA, 66, PhD(English), 72 **CAREER** Asst prof, 70-76, assoc prof, 76-85, Prof English, Univ Tex, Austin, 85-. **HONORS AND AWARDS** Nat Endowment for Humanities fel, 74. **MEMBERSHIPS** NCTE; Int Hopkins Asn **RESEARCH** Emotional intelligence; creativity; Victorian literature. **SELECTED PUBLICATIONS** Auth, 1 bk, 1 ed, 34 articles, 10chap, 1 ed letter, 1 bibliogr, 14 rev essays, 25 rev & 87 papers. **CONTACT ADDRESS** Dept of English, Univ of Texas, Austin, Austin, TX 78712-1164. **EMAIL** bump@mail.utexas.edu

BUNGE, WILFRED F.
PERSONAL Born 11/21/1931, Caledonia, MN, m, 1963, 2 children **DISCIPLINE** RELIGION, CLASSICAL LANGUAGES **EDUCATION** Luther Col, BA, 53; Luther Theol Sem, BTh, 58; State Univ Iowa, MA, 55; Harvard Univ, ThD(-New Testament), 66. **CAREER** Instr Relig & Classics, Luther Col, 56-57; instr Greek, Luther Theol Sem, 57-58; asst prof Relig, 62-69, assoc prof Relig, 69-74, registrar, 72-79, prof Relig, Luther Col, 74-, head dept, 79-87; Bk ed, Dialog, 66-70, asst prof, St John's Univ, Minn, 67-68; prof emer, Rel and Classics, 99-. **MEMBERSHIPS** Soc Bibl Lit; Am Asn Col Registr & Admin Off; corresp mem Inst Antiq & Christianity. **RESEARCH** Ecumenical Christian dialogue; Greco-Roman religions; Apuleius. **SELECTED PUBLICATIONS** Auth, Critical method and the New Testament, In: Theological Perspectives, Luther Col, 64; transl, God's righteousness in Paul, the Bultmann School of Biblical interpretation: New directions?, 65 & Paul and Nascent Catholicism, Distinctive Protestant and Catholic themes reconsidered, 67, J Theol & Church, Harper Torchbk; coauth (with John Bale), The word and words: Liberal education of the clergy, Dialog, Spring 80; Warmly Weston: A Luther College Life, Decorah: Luther College Press, 98. **CONTACT ADDRESS** Dept of Classics & Relig, Luther Col, 700 College Dr, Decorah, IA 52101-1045. **EMAIL** bungewil@luther.edu

BURCH, FRANCIS FLOYD
PERSONAL Born 05/15/1932, Baltimore, MD **DISCIPLINE** COMPARATIVE LITERATURE, THEOLOGY **EDUCATION** Fordham Univ, AB, 56, MA, 58; Woodstock Col, PhL, 57, STL, 64; Univ Paris, Dr, 67. **CAREER** Teacher English & French, Gonzaga High Sch, Washington, DC, 57-60; ordained priest, Roman Catholic, 63; from asst prof to assoc prof, 67-76, trustee, 71-76, asst acad dean, 72-74, prof English, St Joseph's Univ, PA, 76-, Scholar-in-residence English, Millersville State Col, 78. **HONORS AND AWARDS** Alpha Epsilon Delta; Alpha Sigma Nu; Merit Awds for teaching SJU, 80, 83. **MEMBERSHIPS** Int Soc Neoplatonic Studies; MLA. **RESEARCH** Ironic, Conversational poetry 1850 to the present, French and Anglo-American; the neoplatonic tradition in literature and religion; Tristan Corbiere. **SELECTED PUBLICATIONS** Auth, Corbiere and Verlaine's Romances sans paroles, Mod Lang Rev, 58; Clement Mansfield Ingleby on Poe's Raven, Am Lit, 63; Soirees bretonnes: The first published verse of Alexis and Edouard Corbiere, Romance Notes, 70; Tristan Corbiere: L'originalite des amours jaunes et leur influence sur T S Eliot, Nizet, Paris, 70; co-ed, Tristan Corbiere: Oeuvres completes, Gallimard, Paris, 70; auth, Sur Tristan Corbiere: Lettres inedites adressees au poete et premieres critiques le concernant, Nizet, Paris, 75; Introd & transl, The Path to Transcendence: From Philosophy to Mysticism in Saint Augustine, Pittsburgh Theol Monogr Series, No 37, 81; The Iconography of Tristan Corbiere, Studies in Comparative Literature, 91; A Letter from Laurence Housman concerning A E Housman's Poetry, Notes and Queries, 92; RH Benson, Dictionary of Literary Biography, 95; auth, "Charles Warren Currier," "Louis William Valentine DuBourg," "Joseph Hunter Guthrie," in Am Nat Biography, 99; auth, "Three Unpublished Letters of Robert Frost," Am Notes and Queries, 00. **CONTACT ADDRESS** Saint Joseph's Univ, 5600 City Ave, Philadelphia, PA 19131-1376. **EMAIL** fburch@sju.edu

BURGESS, JONATHAN
PERSONAL Born 04/17/1960, Baltimore, MD, m, 1988, 2 children **DISCIPLINE** CLASSICS **EDUCATION** Univ Toronto, PhD, 95. **CAREER** Asst prof, classics, Univ Toronto, 95-. **HONORS AND AWARDS** Gov Gen Gold Medal, Univ Toronto, 95. **MEMBERSHIPS** APA; CAC; CAAS. **RESEARCH** Early Greek epic; mythology. **SELECTED PUBLICATIONS** Auth, The Death of Achilles, forthcoming. **CONTACT ADDRESS** Dept of Classics, Univ of Toronto, 97 St George St, Toronto, ON, Canada M5S 1A1. **EMAIL** jburgess@class.utoronto.ca

BURGIN, DIANA LEWIS
PERSONAL Born 08/04/1943, Boston, MA, S **DISCIPLINE** SLAVIC LANGUAGES & LITERATURES **EDUCATION** Swarthmore Col, BA, 65; Harvard Univ, MA, 67, PhD(Slavic), 73. **CAREER** Teaching fel Russ, Harvard Univ, 70-71; from instr to asst prof, Wellesley Col, 75-; Prof Russ, Univ Mass, Boston, 80-, Corresp, Quincy Patriot Ledger, 72-; assoc Russ lit, Russ Res Ctr, Harvard Univ, 73-; vis lectr Russ, Cambridge Ctr Adult Educ, 74-75. **HONORS AND AWARDS** Outstanding Achievement Awd, 95. **MEMBERSHIPS** Am Asn Advan Slavic Studies, Asn of Women Slavic Studies. **RESEARCH** Nineteenth and 20th century Russian literature; Tsvetaera: Silver Age; Women's and Gender Studies. **SELECTED PUBLICATIONS** Contribr, The Mystery of The Queen of Spades: A new interpretation, Mnemozina, 74; auth, The fate of modern man: Ideas of fate, justice and happiness in Solzhenitsyn's Cancer Ward, Soviet Studies, 74; Rzevsky's Solzhenitsyn: Creator and Heroic Deed, Western Humanities Rev, 78; Bulgakov's early tragedy of the scientist-creator: An interpretation of Heart of a Dog, Slavic & East Europ J, 78; co-transl, The Invisible Book, Ardis, 78; Richard Burgin. A Life in Verse, Slavica, 89; Art in the Light of Conscience - 8 Essays on Poetry by Tsvetaeva,Marina - Tsvetaeva,M/, Russ Rev, Vol 53, 1994; Soma Parnok, The Life and Work of Russia's Sappho, NYU Pr, 94; Mother-Nature Versus the Amazons - Tsvetaeva,Marina and Female Same-Sex Love/, J Hist Sexuality, Vol 6, 1995; co-trans, Mikhail Bulgakov's Master and Margarita, Vintage Intl, 96; Marina Tsvetaeva and Transgressive Eros, Ind Pr, (St. Petersburg), 00. **CONTACT ADDRESS** Dept of Modern Foreign Languages, Univ of Massachusetts, Boston, 100 Morrissey Blvd, Boston, MA 02125-3393.

BURKE, JAMES F.
PERSONAL Born 08/26/1939, Little Rock, AR, m, 1964, 2 children **DISCIPLINE** MEDIEVAL SPANISH LANGUAGE & LITERATURE **EDUCATION** Univ Ark, BA, 61; Univ NC, MA, 63, PhD(Span), 66. **CAREER** Instr Span, Univ NC, 65-66; from asst prof to assoc prof, 66-76, Prof Span, Univ Toronto, 76-. **MEMBERSHIPS** Medieval Acad Am, Am Asn Teachers Span & Port, Can Asn Hispanists. **RESEARCH** Medieval Spanish and Medieval European lit. **SELECTED PUBLICATIONS** Auth, History and Vision: Figural Structure of El Caballero Zifar, Tamesis, 72; Four comings of Christ in Berceo's Santa Oria, Speculum, 73; The Estrella De Sevella and saturnine melancholy, Bull Hispanis Tudies, 74; Juan Ruiz, serranas, and the rites of spring, J Medieval & Renaissance Studies, 75; The Insouciant Reader and the Failure of Memory in 'Celestina'/, Critica Hispanica, Vol 15, 93; The 3rd Chronicle of Alfonso-X - La 'Gran Conquista de Ultramar' - Spanish - Gonzalez,C/, Mod Lang Rev, Vol 89, 94; The 'Poema del Cid' and the 'Poema de Fernan Gonzalez' - The Transformation of an Epic Tradition - Bailey,M/, Hisp Rev, Vol 62, 94; auth, Desire Against The Law: The Juxtaposition of Contraries in Medieval Castilian Literature, Stanford, Calif, Stanford Univ Press, 98. **CONTACT ADDRESS** Dept of Spanish & Portuguese, Univ of Toronto, 21 Sussex Ave, Toronto, ON, Canada M5S 1A1. **EMAIL** jburke@chass.utoronto.ca

BURLING, ROBBINS
PERSONAL Born 04/18/1926, Minneapolis, MN, d, 1951, 3 children **DISCIPLINE** ANTHROPOLOGY & LINGUISTICS **EDUCATION** Yale Univ, BA, 50; Harvard Univ, PhD, 58. **CAREER** From instr to asst prof anthrop, Univ Pa, 57-63; assoc prof, 63-67, Prof Anthrop & Ling, Univ Mich, Ann Arbor, 67-; Fulbright Found lectr, Rangoon, Burma, 59-60; fel, Ctr Advan Studies Behav Sci, 63-64; Guggenheim Found fel, 71-72; vis prof, Univ Gothenburg, Sweden, 79-80; Fulbright Found Lectr, Shillong, India, 96-97. **MEMBERSHIPS** Am Anthrop Asn; Ling Soc Am; Asn Asian Studies. **RESEARCH** Anthropology; linguistics. **SELECTED PUBLICATIONS** Auth, Rengsanggri, Family and Kinship in a Garo Village, Univ Pa, 63; Hill Farms and Padi Fields, Prentice-Hall, 65; Man's Many Voices, 70 & English in Black and White, 73, Holt; The Passage of Power, Acad Press, 74; Sounding Right, Newbury House, 82; Learning a Field Language, Univ Mich Press, 84; Patterns of Language, Acad Press, 92; The Strong Women of Modhupur, Dhaka: Univ Press Ltd, 97. **CONTACT ADDRESS** Dept of Anthrop, Univ of Michigan, Ann Arbor, 500 S State St, Ann Arbor, MI 48109-1382. **EMAIL** rburling@umich.edu

BURNETT, ANNE PIPPIN
PERSONAL Born 10/10/1925, Salt Lake City, UT, m, 1960, 2 children **DISCIPLINE** CLASSICS **EDUCATION** Swarthmore Col, BA, 46; Columbia Univ, MA, 47; Univ Calif, Berkeley, PhD(ancient hist & classics), 53. **CAREER** Instr classics, Vassar Col, 57-58; asst prof, 61-66, assoc prof, 67-69, Prof Classics & Chmn Dept, Univ Chicago, 70-, Am Asn Univ Women traveling fel, Am Sch Class Studies Athens, 56-57; fel, Am Acad Rome, 58-59; grant, Am Philos Soc, 59-60; Am Coun Learned Soc fel, 68-69. **RESEARCH** Greek tragedy; Greek lyric poetry; Greek history. **SELECTED PUBLICATIONS** **CONTACT ADDRESS** Dept of Classics Div of Humanities, Univ of Chicago, Chicago, IL 60637.

BURRES, KENNETH LEE
PERSONAL Born 08/12/1934, Topeka, KS, m, 1956, 3 children **DISCIPLINE** BIBLICAL STUDIES, LINGUISTICS **EDUCATION** Baker Univ, AB, 56; Garrett Theol Sem, BD, 60; Northwestern Univ, MA, 61, PhD, 70. **CAREER** Pastor, United Methodist Church, Gary, IN, 64-67; from asst prof to prof religh, Central Methodist Col, 67-; chair, dept of philos & relig, Central Methodist Col, 97-. **MEMBERSHIPS** Soc Bibl Lit; Am Academy of Relig. **RESEARCH** Linguistic analysis of New Testament Greek; New Testament theology; early Christian history. **SELECTED PUBLICATIONS** Auth, Prolegomena to a new biblical lexicography, Soc Bibl Lit Sem Papers, 71; articles in Encyclopedia of the Ancient World, Salem Pr, forthcoming. **CONTACT ADDRESS** Dept of Relig, Central Methodist Col, 411 Central Methodist Sq, Fayette, MO 65248-1198. **EMAIL** ckburres@mcmsys.com

BURTON, JOAN
PERSONAL Born Columbia, MO, m **DISCIPLINE** CLASSICAL STUDIES **EDUCATION** BA, 75, MA, 78, CPhil, 83, PhD, 88, Univ Calif, Berkeley. **CAREER** Actg instr, tchg assoc, classics, Univ Calif, Berkeley, 79-86; actg instr, classics, Univ Calif, Santa Cruz, 88; asst prof, 88-94, assoc prof, 94-, classics, chemn and assoc prof, comp lit, 98-, Trinity Univ. **HONORS AND AWARDS** Phi Beta Kappa, 74; dept citation class lang, 75; chancellor's fel, classics, 77-78, 80-81; John Rogers Fac Fel, 90-92. **MEMBERSHIPS** APA; Byzantine Stud Conf; Women's Class Caucus. **RESEARCH** Greek and Roman literature and culture; women's studies. **SELECTED PUBLICATIONS** Auth, The Function of the Symposium Theme in Theocritus' Idyll, Greek Roman, and Byzantine Stud, 92; auth, Why the Ancient Greeks Were Obsessed with Heroes and the Ancient Egyptians Were Not, Class Bull, 93; auth, Theocritus' Urban Mimes: Mobility, Gender and Patronage, Univ Calif, 95; auth, Women's Commensality in the Ancient Greek World, Greece and Rome, 98; auth, Reviving the Pagan Greek Novel in a Christian World, Greek,, Roman, and Byzantine Stud, 98. **CONTACT ADDRESS** Dept of Classical Studies, Trinity Univ, 715 Stadium Dr, San Antonio, TX 78212-7200.

BUSI, FREDERICK
DISCIPLINE FRENCH LITERATURE **EDUCATION** CT Univ, PhD. **CAREER** Prof, Univ MA Amherst. **RESEARCH** Lit and the hist of ideas in 19th and 20th century France; fantastic lit; anti-Semitic lit. **SELECTED PUBLICATIONS** Auth, pubs on SuarSs, Beckett, Dumont, and La Pens. **CONTACT ADDRESS** Dept of French and Italian Studies, Univ of Massachusetts, Amherst, Mass Ave, Amherst, MA 01003.

BUTLER, GERALD JOSEPH
PERSONAL Born 02/24/1942, San Francisco, CA, m, 1964, 3 children **DISCIPLINE** ENGLISH AND COMPARATIVE LITERATURE **EDUCATION** Univ Calif, Berkeley, AB, 63; Univ Wash, MA, 65, PhD(English), 68. **CAREER** Prof English, San Diego State Univ, 68-, Ed, Recovering Lit, 72-. **RESEARCH** Sex in literature; 18th century fiction; 20th century fiction. **SELECTED PUBLICATIONS** Auth, Arrows of desire, fall & winter, 74, Recovering Lit; Fielding's Unruly Novels; Making Fielding Novels Speak for Law-and-Order + Reply to Richter,David,Henry/, Eighteenth Century-Theory and Interpretation, Vol 37, 1996. **CONTACT ADDRESS** PO Box 805, Alpine, CA 92001. **EMAIL** butler1@mail.sdsu.edu

BUTLER, THOMAS J.
PERSONAL Born 05/15/1929, Detroit, MI, m, 1954, 3 children **DISCIPLINE** SLAVIC LANGUAGES & LITERATURE **EDUCATION** Harvard Univ, AB, 51, MA, 55, PhD(Slavic lang & lit), 63. **CAREER** Teaching fel Russ, Harvard Univ, 58-60; asst prof, Tufts Univ, 62-67; asst prof slavic lang, Univ Wis-Madison, 68-71, assoc prof, 71-79; vis lectr, 79-80, Mem Fac, Russ Res Ctr, Harvard Univ, 80-, Coun Learned Soc res grant, 72; Am Philos Soc travel grant, Yugoslavia, 73; Fulbright fel, Univ Belgrade, 67-68, 81-82 & Univ Sarajevo, 77-78; rev ed, Slavic & E Eruop J, 70-71; mem rev staff, Books Abroad, 71-. **MEMBERSHIPS** Am Asn Teachers Alavic & E Europ Lang; Int Conf Bulgarian Studies; MLA; Am Asn S Slavic Studies (secy-treas, 73-75). **RESEARCH** South Slavic and Russian languages and literatures; Slavic cultural history; preparation of a bilingual anthology of Serbo-Croatian texts. **SELECTED PUBLICATIONS** Auth, The Origins of the War for a Serbian Language and Orthography, Harvard Univ, 70; The linguistic heterogeneity of Njegos's Gorski Vijenac, Proc Pac Northwest Conf Foreign Lang, 72; Njegos's early poem on a Russian theme, Mnemozina, 74; Literary style and poetic function in Mesa Selimovic's The Dervish and Death, Slavonic & E Europ Rev, winter 75 & Savremenik, 5/75; Yugoslavia's Slavic languages: A historical perspective, Rev Nat Lit, spring 75; The language of Serbian and Croatian medieval tales, Slavic Ling & Lang, Teaching Slavica, 76; ed, Bulgaria Past and Present, AAAS, 76; Monumenta Serbocroatica: A Bilingual Anthology of Serbian and Croatian Texts, Mich Slavic Publ, 80; The Bulgarians in the 17th-Century - Slavic Orthodox Society and Culture under Ottoman Rule - Hupchick,DP/, Slavonic and East Europ Rev, Vol 72, 1994. **CONTACT ADDRESS** Slavic Langs and Lit, Harvard Univ, Boylston Hall, Cambridge, MA 02138-3800.

BUXBAUM, MELBA M.
PERSONAL Born 07/02/1937, St Louis, MO, m, 1966, 2 children **DISCIPLINE** LINGUISTICS, LITERATURE, LANGUAGE, SPANISH **EDUCATION** St Louis Univ, BS, 59; PhD, 72. **CAREER** Chmn to dir, Blackburn Col, 72-. **HONORS AND AWARDS** Fulbright Fel, Spain, 60-61; Outstanding Teaching Blackburn Col, 98. **MEMBERSHIPS** MLA; ICTFL.

RESEARCH Spain; women's issues; Mexico; contemporary culture. **CONTACT ADDRESS** Dept Modern Lang, Blackburn Col, Carlinville, IL 62626. **EMAIL** mbuxb@mail.blackburn.edu

BYBEE, JOAN L.
PERSONAL Born 02/11/1945, New Orleans, LA, m, 1 child **DISCIPLINE** LINGUISTICS **EDUCATION** Univ TX, Austin, BA (Spanish & English), 66; San Diego State Univ, MA (linguistics), 70; Univ CA, Los Angeles, PhD (linguistics), 73. **CAREER** Asst prof, 73-78, assoc prof, Linguistics, 78-85, prof Linguistics, SUNY at Buffalo, 85-89; assoc dean, 92-93, prof Linguistics, Univ NM, 89-. **HONORS AND AWARDS** Distinguished Alumni Awd from the Col of arts and Letters of San Diego State Univ, 76; Guggenheim fel, 87-88; Regent's Prof, Univ NM, 96-. **MEMBERSHIPS** Linguistic Soc of Am; Asn for Linguistic Typology. **RESEARCH** Phonology; morphology; grammaticization; language change; language universals. **SELECTED PUBLICATIONS** Coauth, The evolution of grammar: tense, aspect and modality in the language of the world, Chicago; Univ of Chicago Press, 94; co-ed, Modality in grammar and discourse, Amsterdam: John Benjamins, 95; coauth, "Are affixes more natural than stem changes? Linguistics 33, (95): 633-654; auth, "Regular morphology and the lexicon, "Language and Cognitive Precesses," 10, (95): 425-455; co-ed, Essays on Langauge Function and Language Type, Amsterdam: John Benjamins, 97; auth, "A functionalist approach to grammar and its evolution," Evolution of Commun 2, (98): 249-278; auth, "Irrealis" as a grammatical category, Anthropological Linguistics 40, (98): 257-271; coauth, Prosody and Segmental effect: Some paths of evolution for word stress, Studies in Lang 22, (98): 267-314; coauth, "The effect of usage on degrees of constituency the reduction of don't in English, Linguistics 37-4, (99): 575-596; auth, "Use impacts morphological representation, Behavioral and Brain Sciences 22, (99): 1016-1017. **CONTACT ADDRESS** Dept of Linguistics, Univ of New Mexico, Albuquerque, Humanities 554, Albuquerque, NM 87131-1196. **EMAIL** jbybee@unm.edu

BYRE, CALVIN S.
PERSONAL Born 11/22/1947, Appleton, MN, m, 1972 **DISCIPLINE** CLASSICAL LANGUAGES AND LITERATURES **EDUCATION** Univ Minn, BA, 69; Univ Chicago, PhD, 76; Rosary Col, MALS, 85. **CAREER** Asst prof/head of ref, Roosevelt Univ, 86-90; asst prof of bibliog and adjunct asst prof of classics, Univ Okla, 90-96; assoc prof of bibliog and adjunct assoc prof of classics, Univ Okla, 96-. **HONORS AND AWARDS** Phi Beta Kappa; Robert V. Cram Memorial Scholar in Classics, Univ Minn; Ford four-year fel, Univ Chicago. **MEMBERSHIPS** Amer Philol Asn; Classical Asn of the Middle West and South. **RESEARCH** Greek epic; Literary criticism. **SELECTED PUBLICATIONS** Auth, Suspense in the Phaeacian Episode of Apollonius' Argonautica, Ill Class Studes, 22, 65-73, 97; auth, On the Departure from Pagasae and the Passage of the Plactae in Apollonius, Argonautica, Mus Helveticum, 54, 106-114, 97; auth, The Killing of Apsyrtus in Apollonious Rhodius' Argonautica, Phoenix, 50, 3-16, 96; auth, Distant Encounters: The Prometheus and Phaethon Episodes in Apollonius' Argonautica, Amer Jour of Philol, 117, 275-283, 96; auth, The Rhetoric of Description in Odyssey 9.116-41, Odysseus and Goat Island, Class Jour, 89, 357-367, 94; auth, On the Description of the Harbor of Phorkys and the Cave of the Nymphs, Odyssey 13.96-112, Amer Jour of Philol, 115, 1-13, 94; auth, Narration, Description, and Theme in the Shield of Achilles, Class Jour, 88, 33-42, 92; auth, The Narrator's Addresses to the Narratee in Apollonius Rhodius' Argonautica, Transactions of the Amer Philol Asn, 121, 215-227, 91; auth, Penelope and the Suitors before Odysseus: Odyssey 18.158-303, Amer Jour of Philol, 109, 159-173, 88; auth, Per aspera (et arborem) ad astra. Ramifications of the Allegory of Arete in Quintus Smyrnaeus Posthomerica, 5, 49-68, Hermes, 110, 184-195, 82. **CONTACT ADDRESS** 1727 Bryant Cir., Norman, OK 73026. **EMAIL** cbyre@ou.edu

BYRON, KRISTINE ANN
DISCIPLINE HISPANIC STUDIES **EDUCATION** Wash Univ St Louis, BA, 90; Univ Conn, MA, 97; PhD, 01. **CAREER** Instr, Univ Conn, 92-00; asst prof, Mich State Univ, 01-. **HONORS AND AWARDS** Phi Beta Kappa; Edward Victor Grant Fel. **MEMBERSHIPS** MLA; ACIS; LASA. **RESEARCH** Women's studies; Latin American studies; Irish studies. **SELECTED PUBLICATIONS** Auth, "El Extasis de la Comunicacion: La Imagen en Tres Tristes Tigres," Torre de Papel 4 (94): 43-52; auth, "Entre la Luz y el Abismo: Voces al Atardecer de Francisco Rivera," Cinc Romance Rev (97): 127-134; auth, "(De)Constructing Historiography: 'Organic Intellectuals' and the 1933 Revolution in Cuba," Entrecaminos: J Lat Am Aff 4 (99): 43-64; rev, "Brigid," by Jill Blee, Irish Study Rev (01); auth, "Edith Dimo and Amarilis Hidalgo de Jesus," in Narradoras Venezolanas del Siglo, eds. Escritura, Desafio (INTI, 01) auth, "In the Name of the Mother': The Epilogue of Edna O' Brien's Country Girls Trilogy," Women's Study J (02). **CONTACT ADDRESS** Dept Romance Class Lang, Michigan State Univ, 258 Old Horticulture Bldg, East Lansing, MI 48824-1112. **EMAIL** kristine.byron@uconn.edu

C

CABABAS, MIGUEL ANGEL
DISCIPLINE SPANISH, LANGUAGE **EDUCATION** Univ Salanoca, Lic, 91; Univ Conn, MA, 97; PhD, 00. **CAREER** Instr, Univ Conn, 92-99; asst prof, Col Holy Cross, 99-. **HONORS AND AWARDS** Mellon Development Grant, 00. **MEMBERSHIPS** MLA; LASA; SECOLAS. **RESEARCH** Travel literature; Latin American studies; North American literature. **SELECTED PUBLICATIONS** Auth, "San Manuel Bueno, Martir, Budista," Torre de Papel 3 (93): 34-49; rev of, "Against Literature, by John Beverley, INTI (98): 209-212; auth, "Generos al Matadero: Esteban Echeverria y la Cuestion de los Generos," Rev Critica Lit Latino American 48 (98): 133-147; auth, "'Con los Ojos Bien Abiertos': La Picaresca y Tantas Veces Pedro de Alfredo Bryce Echenique," Hispanofila 128 (00): 91-101; auth, "Sarah Bagley," in American Women Prose Writers 1820-1870: Dictionary of Literary Biography Vo 239 (SCar: Broccoli Clark Layman, 01): 24-30; auth, "Domingo Faustino Sarmiento" and " Jose Marti," in The Literature of Travel and Exploration: An Encyclopedia (Fitzroy Dearborn Pub, forthcoming). **CONTACT ADDRESS** Mod Lang Dept, Col of the Holy Cross, 1 College St, PO Box 138A, Worcester, MA 01610-2322. **EMAIL** mcabanas@holycross.edu

CABAN, PEDRO
DISCIPLINE POLITICS AND COMPARATIVE LITERATURE, PUERTO RICAN STUDIES **EDUCATION** City Col NYork, BA; Columbia Univ, PhD. **CAREER** Assoc prof, dir, Puerto Rican and Lat Am Stud Prog, Fordham Univ; assoc prof, Rutgers, State Univ NJ, Livingston Col, 90-; ed bd, Latin Am Res Rev; bd dir, 85-91, chemn, 87-89, Inst for Puerto Rican Policy. **HONORS AND AWARDS** Fel, Ford Found; fel, Rockefeller Found. **MEMBERSHIPS** Lat Am Stud Asn; Puerto Rican Studies Asn. **RESEARCH** The nature of economic change and the role of the state in Puerto Rico during the post World War II era. **SELECTED PUBLICATIONS** Auth, Constructing a Colonial People: Puerto Rico and the United States, 1898-1932, Westview Prerss, 99. **CONTACT ADDRESS** Dept of Puerto Rican & Hisp Carib Stud, Rutgers, The State Univ of New Jersey, Livingston Col, Tillett Hall 237, Livingston, NJ 50011. **EMAIL** caban@rci.rutgers.edu

CABLE, THOMAS MONROE
PERSONAL Born 06/17/1942, Conroe, TX, m, 1 child **DISCIPLINE** ENGLISH LANGUAGE & LINGUISTICS **EDUCATION** Yale Univ, BA, 64; Univ TX, PhD, 69. **CAREER** Asst prof Eng, Univ IL, Urbana-Champaign, 69-72; assoc prof Eng, 72-79, prof eng, Univ TX, Austin, 79, Blumberg Centennial Prof Eng, 84; Am Coun Learned Socs fel, 76-77; Fulbright, France, 80, 92. **HONORS AND AWARDS** TX Excellence Tchg Awd, Col of Lib Arts, 90. **MEMBERSHIPS** MLA; Medieval Acad Am; Ling Soc Am. **RESEARCH** Hist of Eng prosody; hist of the Eng lang; Old and Middle Eng lit. **SELECTED PUBLICATIONS** Auth, The Meter and Melody of Beowulf, Univ Ill, 74; coauth, A History of the English Language, Prentice-Hall, 3rd ed, 78, 4th ed, 93; The English Alliterative Tradition, Univ Penn, 91; A Companion to Baugh and Cable's History of the English Language, 2nd ed, Prentice-Hall, 93. **CONTACT ADDRESS** Dept of Eng, Univ of Texas, Austin, Austin, TX 78712-1164. **EMAIL** tcable@mail.utexas.edu

CACHIA, PIERRE J. E.
PERSONAL Born 04/30/1921, Fayyum, Egypt, m, 1992, 3 children **DISCIPLINE** MODERN ARABIC LITERATURE **EDUCATION** Am Univ Cairo, BA, 42; Univ of Edinburgh, PhD, 51. **CAREER** Tchr, Am Univ Cairo, 46-48; lectr, sen lectr, reader, Univ of Edinburgh, 50-75; prof, Columbia Univ, 75-91. **HONORS AND AWARDS** Woodrow Wilson fel, 91-92. **MEMBERSHIPS** Am Oriental Soc; Middle East Studies Asn; Brit Soc for Middle Eastern Studies; Union Europeenee D'Islamisants Et Arabisants. **RESEARCH** Modern Arab Lit; Egyptian Folk Lit. **SELECTED PUBLICATIONS** Auth, Taha Husayn: His Place in the Egyptian Literary Renaissance, 56; Popular Narrative Ballads of Modern Egypt, 89; An Overview of Modern Arabic Literature, 90; The Arch Rhetorician of the Schemer's Skimmer: a Handbook of late Arabic badi, 98; coauth, History of Islamic Spain, 65, Landlocked Islands, 99, coed, Jour of Arabic Literature and its Supplements, 1970-1996. **CONTACT ADDRESS** Columbia Univ, 602 Kent Hall, New York, NY 10027. **EMAIL** pjc1@columbia.edu

CADELY, JEAN ROBERT JOSEPH
DISCIPLINE LINGUISTICS **EDUCATION** Quebec Univ, PhD. **CAREER** Assoc prof. **MEMBERSHIPS** MLA; Ling Soc Am; Can Ling Asn. **RESEARCH** Haitian Creole and French Phonology; Haitian culture; Pidgins and Creoles. **SELECTED PUBLICATIONS** Auth, "Etudes Phonologiques du Creole haitien," in Travaux de Recherche sur le Creole haitien, vol 2, ed. Claire Lefebvre (Universite due Quebec a Montreal, Montreal, 88): 424-493; auth, "L'opposition /r/et/w/ en Creole haitien: Un paradoxe resolu," Canadian Journal of Linguistics 3(2) (88): 121-142; auth, Representations syllabiques et distribution des diphtongues en creole haitien, 88; auth, "Domaine Prosodique d'une Regle de Sandhi extreme," Working Paper in Linguistics, Universite du Quebec a Montreal, 90; auth, Elision et Agglutination en Creole Haitien: Le cas des Pronoms Personels: Etudes Creoles, 95; auth, "Prosodie et Cliticisation en Creole haitien," Etudes Creoles, Vol XX, no 1 (97): 77-88; coauth, English/Haitian Creole Legal Glossary, Educa Vision Inc. (Coconut Creek, Florida), 00; auth, "Nasality in Haitian Creole," in Recent Developments in Creole Studies, ed. Dany Adone (Niemeyer Verlag, Tubingen, 00); auth, Phonologie du Creole haitien, Edwin Mellen Press (forthcoming); auth, Basic Introduction to Haitian Creole (forthcoming). **CONTACT ADDRESS** Dept of Modern Languages, Florida Intl Univ, 11200 SW 8th St, Miami, FL 33174. **EMAIL** cadelyj@FIU.edu

CALABRESE, ANDREA
DISCIPLINE LINGUISTICS **EDUCATION** Univ of Padova, Dr of Humanities, 75-80; Mass Inst Tech, PhD. **CAREER** Instr, Univ of Konstanz, 81-82; visiting scholar, Mass Institute of Technology, 83-84; instr, Wellesley Col, 84; asst prof, Harvard Univ, 89-94; assoc prof, Harvard Univ, 94-96; vis prof, Univ of Budapest, 96; assoc prof, Univ of Conn, 97; visiting prof, Universita di Siena, 99. **HONORS AND AWARDS** Scholarship, Univ of Warsaw, 78. **RESEARCH** Phonological theory, Romance linguistics, historical linguistics. **SELECTED PUBLICATIONS** Coauth, "Linguistica," in Gli strumenti del sapere contemporaneo, with Andrea Calabrese, Lorenzo Renzi, and Laura Vanelli, Torino: UTET, (85): 426-439; co-ed, "Syllable Structure in Aphasia: A Case Study," in P.M. Bertinetto and M. Loporcaro, Certamen Phonologicum II, with Andrea Calabrese and Cristina Romani, Torino: Rosenberg & Selliers, 91; auth, "Herr Mueller vivra' a Taranto con I suoi amici austriaci': Phonological Investigations on a Fragment of Etalian Phonology," in G. Chollet et al., eds, Speech Processing, Recognition and Artificial Neural Networks, London: Springer, 21-53; ed, "Sievers' Law in Vedic," in H. van der Hulst and N. A. Ritter, The Syllable: View and Facts, Berlin: Mouton de Gruyter, 673-751; coauth, "On the Representation of Geminate Consonants: Evidence from the Phonological Errors of an Aphasic Patient," with Cristina Romani and Andrea Calabrese, in Journal of Neurolinguistics 9.3, (97): 219-235; coauth, "Grimm's and Verner's Law: A new perspective," in C. Melchert, J. Jasanof and L. Oliver, eds, with Andrea Calabrese and Moris Halle, Mir Curad, A Festschrift in honor of Calvert Watkins, (98): 47-62; coauth, "Palatalizations in an Aphasic Patient: Theoretical Consequences of Phonological Distrubances in Aphasia," in T.Hsin and E. Shortt, Papers in Phonloogy, with Andrea Calabrese and Cristina Romani, Univ of Conn Working Papers in Linguistics 9, (98): 73-103; coauth, "Syllabic Constraints in the Phonological Errors of an Aphasic patient," with Cristina Romami and Andrea Calabrese, in Brain and Language 64, (98): 83-121; ed, "Some Remarks on the Latin Case system and its development in Romance," in J. Lema and E. Trevino, eds, Theoretical Advances on Romance Languages, Amsterdam: John Benjamins, (98): 71-126; auth, "Metaphony Revisited," in Rivista di Linguistica 11, (99): 7-69. **CONTACT ADDRESS** Dept of Linguistics, Univ of Connecticut, Storrs, 1266 Storrs Rd, Storrs, CT 06269. **EMAIL** calabres@uconnvm.uconn.edu

CALDER, WILLIAM M., III
PERSONAL Born 09/03/1932, Brooklyn, NY, s **DISCIPLINE** CLASSICS **EDUCATION** Harvard Col, BA, 54, MA, 56; Univ of Chicago, PhD, 58. **CAREER** TA, Harvard Col, 55-56; TA, Univ of Chicago, 57-58; from instr to prof, Columbia Univ, 58-76; prof, Univ of Colorado Boulder, 76-88; prof of classics & comp lit, Univ of Illinois Urbana, 88-. **HONORS AND AWARDS** Erfurt Acad of Sci, Elected For Mem; Ger Acad Sci, Heinrich Schliemann Medallion; Univ of IL Urbana, A. O. Beckman Awd, Neubukow's Heinrich Schliemann Medallion, Alexander von Humbolat Prize Winner. **MEMBERSHIPS** SPHS London, SPRS London, CAE&W, EES, TM Gesell, ICC, ASGLE, AIA, APA, AAH, CAMS, GSA, ANS. **RESEARCH** Classic Greek lit; Greek and Roman pagan; hist of class scholarship; 19th and 20th cent in Eng, Ger, and US. **SELECTED PUBLICATIONS** Co-auth, Philology and Philosophy: The Letters of Hermann Diels to Theodor and Heinrich Gomperz, Hildesheim, 95; Lieber Prinz: Der Breifwefchsel zwischen Hermann Diels und Ulrich von Wilamowitz-Moellendorf ,1869-1921, Hildesheim 95; Sed serviendum officio.. The Correspondence Between Ulrich von Wilamowitz-Moellendorff and Eduard Norden 1892-1931, Hildesheim, 97; Men in their Books: Studies in the Modern History of Classical Scholarship, Hildesheim, 98. **CONTACT ADDRESS** Dept of Classics, Univ of Illinois, Urbana-Champaign, 609 W Delaware Ave, Urbana, IL 61801. **EMAIL** wmcalder@uiuc.edu

CALDWELL, LARRY
DISCIPLINE LINGUISTICS, ENGLISH LANGUAGE **EDUCATION** Univ Nebr, PhD. **CAREER** Former dir, wrtg. **RESEARCH** Norse myth, saga, and legend. **SELECTED PUBLICATIONS** Articles, English Quart; Extrapolation. **CONTACT ADDRESS** Dept of Eng, Univ of Evansville, 1800 Lincoln Ave, Evansville, IN 47714. **EMAIL** lc4@evansville.edu

CALIN, WILLIAM
PERSONAL Born 04/04/1936, Newington, CT **DISCIPLINE** FRENCH LITERATURE **EDUCATION** Yale Univ, AB, 57; PhD, 60. **CAREER** Instr to asst prof, Dartmouth Col, 60-63;

asst prof to assoc prof to prof, Stanford Univ, 64-73; prof, Univ Ore, 73-88; vis prof, Univ Poitiers, 82-84; grad res prof, Univ Fla, 88-. **HONORS AND AWARDS** Guggenheim Found Fel, 63-64; Am PhilolSoc, 70; Canada Fed in Human Grant, 81; Fulbright Awd, 82; NEH Fel, 84-85; NEH Sum Inst, 85; Fulbright Sr Res Grant, 87-88; ACLS Fel, 96-97; Vis Fel, Clare Hall, Cambridge, 84-85; Vis Fel, Inst Advanced Study in Humanities, Univ Edin, 97; Fel, Northrop Frye Cen, Univ Toronto, 00; Gilbert Chinard First Lit Prize, 81. **MEMBERSHIPS** AIFO; IGMS. **RESEARCH** Medieval French literature; French poetry, renaissance to present; modern Occitan and Breton literature; Franco-British literary relations. **SELECTED PUBLICATIONS** Auth, The Old French Epic of Revolt, Droz, 62; auth, Aux Portes du Poeme, Macmillan, 64; auth, The Epic Quest, John Hopkins, 66; auth, La Changon de Roland, Appleton, Century, Crofts, 68; auth, A Poet at the Fountain: Essays on the Narrative Verse of Guillaume de Machaut, 74; auth, Crown, Cross and Fleur-de-lis, Stanford, 77; auth, A Muse for Heroes, 83; auth, In Defense of French Poetry, Penn State, 87; auth, The French Tradition and Literature of Medieval England, 94; auth, Minority Literatures and Modernism: Scots, Breton, and Occitan, 00. **CONTACT ADDRESS** English Dept, Univ of Florida, PO Box 117405, Gainesville, FL 32611-7405. **EMAIL** wcalin@rll.ufl.edu

CALLAGHAN, CATHERINE A.
PERSONAL Born 10/30/1931, Berkeley, CA **DISCIPLINE** LINGUISTICS **EDUCATION** Univ Calif, Berkeley, BA, 54, PhD(ling), 63. **CAREER** Sci linguist, Smithsonia Inst, 62; asst prof ling, Univ Hawaii, 64; asst prof, 65-69, Assoc Prof Ling, Ohio State Univ, 69-, Am Asn Univ Women fel, 64-65; NSF grant res Calif Indian lang, 66-80. **MEMBERSHIPS** AAAS; Ling Soc Am. **RESEARCH** Reconstruction of proto languages; anthropological linguistics; occult. **SELECTED PUBLICATIONS** Auth, Proto-Miwok Numerals, Intl Jour Amer Ling, Vol 0060, 94. **CONTACT ADDRESS** Dept of Ling, Ohio State Univ, Columbus, Columbus, OH 43210.

CALLAN, RICHARD JEROME
PERSONAL Born 01/04/1932, Mt Vernon, NY, m, 1954 **DISCIPLINE** SPANISH **EDUCATION** Iona Col, AB, 57; Fordham Univ, MA, 59; St Louis Univ, PhD(Span), 65. **CAREER** Instr Span, St Michael's Col, Vt, 60-63; assoc prof, St Louis Univ, 65-69; Assoc Prof Span Am Lit, Univ NH, 69- **MEMBERSHIPS** MLA; Am Asn Teachers Span & Port; Inst Int Lit Iberoam; Midwest Mod Lang Asn. **RESEARCH** Spanish American literature; archetypal approach to literature; Meso-American mythology. **SELECTED PUBLICATIONS** Auth, Archetypes in Stories by Arevalomartinez, Rafael, Critica Hispanica, Vol 0017, 95. **CONTACT ADDRESS** Dept of Ancient & Mod Lang, Univ of New Hampshire, Durham, Durham, NH 03824.

CAMERON, ALAN
PERSONAL Born 03/13/1938, Windsor, England, m, 1961, 2 children **DISCIPLINE** CLASSICAL PHILOLOGY, BYZANTINE STUDIES **EDUCATION** Oxford Univ, BA, 61, MA, 64. **CAREER** Lectr Latin, Univ Glasgow, 61-64, Bedord Col, Univ London, 64-71 & Kings Col, 72-76; Anthon Prof Latin, Columbia Univ, 77- **HONORS AND AWARDS** N H Baynes Prize, London Univ, 67; J Conington Prize, Oxford Univ, 68; fel, British Acad, 75. **MEMBERSHIPS** Soc Roman Studies; Am Philol Asn; fel Am Acad Arts & Sci. **RESEARCH** Latin literature; Roman history; Byzantine history and literature. **SELECTED PUBLICATIONS CONTACT ADDRESS** Columbia Univ, 2960 Broadway, New York, NY 10027-6900.

CAMMARATA, JOAN F.
PERSONAL Born 12/22/1950, New York, NY, m, 1975 **DISCIPLINE** SPANISH **EDUCATION** Fordham Univ, BA, 72; Columbia Univ, MA, 74, MPhil, 77, PhD, 82. **CAREER** Preceptor, Columbia Univ, 74-82; adjunct asst prof, Iona Col and Manhattan Col, 82-84; asst prof, 84-90, assoc prof, 90-96, prof of Spanish, Manhattan Col, 96-. **HONORS AND AWARDS** NY Regents Scholar, Fordham Univ, 68-72; BA, summa cum laude, Spanish Awd, Fordham Univ, 72; Columbia Univ: Univ Fel, 72-73, President's Fel, 73-75, Teaching Assistantship, 74-77, Preceptorship, 77-82; NEH Summer Seminar, 87, 88; Andrew W. Mellon Found Humanities Sem for Vis Scholars, 90; Manhattan Col summer grant, 91; Northeast MLA Res Fel grant, 91; NY Univ Fac Resource Network Summer Series, 92, 94, 95; Scholar-in-residence, NY Univ, 91-92, 97-98; Prog for Cultural Cooperation between Spain's Ministry of Educ and Culture and United States' Universities Res grant, 97-98; ed adv bd, Modern Language Studies; Northeast Modern Lang Asn: Pres, 98-99, Vice-Pres, 97-98, Past Pres, 99-2000. **MEMBERSHIPS** Am Asn of Teachers of Spanish and Portuguese, Am Coun on the Teaching of Foreign Langs, Asn Int de Hispanistas, Cervantes Soc of Am, Modern Lang Asn, NY State Asn of Foreign Lang Teachers, Northeast Modern Lang Asn, Renaissance Soc of Am, South Atlantic Modern Lang Asn. **RESEARCH** Renaissance Spain. **SELECTED PUBLICATIONS** Auth, Mythological Themes in the Works of Garcilasco de la Vega, Madrid: Porria (83); REV, Robert Bonfil, Jewish Life in Renaissance Italy, transl Anthony Oldcorn, Berkeley: Univ Calif Press (94), in Cross Currents: Religion and Intellectual life, 46.1 (96): 116-120; auth, "El discurso femenino de Santa Theresa de Avila, defensora de la mujer renacentista," Actas del XI Congresso de la Asociacion Internacional de Hispanistas, ed Juan Villegras, Irvine, Calif: Univ Calif, 2, (94): 58-65; auth, "St Teresa's Language of Love: the Spiritual Erotocism of the Kiss," Semiotica del Testo Mistico, Atti del Congresso Internazionale, ed Guiseppe De Gennaro, L'Aquila, Italy: Edizioni del Gallo Cedrone (95): 111-117; rev, Bruno Damiani, Moralidad y didactismo en el Siglo de Oro (1492-1615), Madrid: Editorial Origenes (92), in Quaderni Ibero-Americani, 78 (95): 91-93; auth, "Introduccion," Filippo Maria Toscano, El universalismo del pensamiento cristiano de Don Luigi Sturzo, Lewiston, NY: Edwin Mellon Press (97); auth, "Como aguq para chocolate: gastronomio erotica, magicorrealismo culinario," Explicacion de textos literarios, 25.1 (96-97): 87-103; auth, "Epistola consolatoria y contemptus mundi: el epistolario de consuelo de Santa Teresa de Avila," Actas del XIII Congreso de la Asociacion Internacional de Hispanistas, Madrid (99); auth, "La actitud cervantina hacia las Americas: tierras de oportunidad o de infortunio?" Hispanica Polonorum (2000); auth, "Nuyorican Theater," Dictionary of Latin American Theater, eds Eladio Cortes and Mirta Barrea-Marlys, Westport, Ct: Greenwood Press (2000). **CONTACT ADDRESS** Dept Foreign Lang, Manhattan Col, 4513 Manhattan Col Pkwy, Bronx, NY 10471-4004. **EMAIL** jcammara@manhattan.edu

CAMPANA, PHILLIP JOSEPH
PERSONAL Born 04/10/1941, Jersey City, NJ, 2 children **DISCIPLINE** GERMAN **CAREER** Assoc prof, 70-74, Prof Ger, Tenn Technol Univ, 74-, Chmn Dept, 70-, Mem evaluation team foreign lang, Southern Asn Cols & Schs, 72-; assoc ed, Schatzkammer, 80-; chmn, Tenn Bd Regents Task Force on Improv Qual in Teacher Educ. **HONORS AND AWARDS** Outstanding Fac Awd, Tenn Technol Univ, 76. **MEMBERSHIPS** MLA; AAUP; Am Coun Teaching Foreign Lang; Am Asn Teachers Ger. **RESEARCH** German Romanticism; Heinrich Boell; German novel. **SELECTED PUBLICATIONS** Auth, Syracuse Language Systems--Tripleplay-Plus-German, Mod Lang Jour, Vol 0080, 96. **CONTACT ADDRESS** Dept of Foreign Lang, Tennessee Tech Univ, Cookeville, TN 38501.

CAMPBELL, DAVID A.
PERSONAL Born 08/14/1927, Killywhan, Scotland, m, 1956, 3 children **DISCIPLINE** CLASSICS **EDUCATION** Glasgow Univ, MA, 48; Oxford Univ, BA, 53, MA, 67. **CAREER** Asst to sr lectr, Univ Bristol, 53-71; vis asst prof, Univ Toronto, 59-60; vis prof, Univ Texas Austin, 69-70; prof, 71-93, ch, 72-77, prof emer, Univ of Victoria, 93-. **MEMBERSHIPS** Am Philol Asn; Class Asn Can; Class Asn Pac NW; Class Asn Can W. **SELECTED PUBLICATIONS** Auth, Greek Lyric Poetry, 67, 2nd ed 82; auth, The Golden Lyre: The Themes of the Greek Lyric Poets, 83; auth, Greek Lyric, vols 1-5, 82-93; contribur, The Cambridge History of Classical Literature, vol 1, 85;Auth, The Fragments of Mimnermus--Text and Commentary, Jour Class Assn Can, Vol 0049, 95. **CONTACT ADDRESS** Dept of Greek and Roman Studies, Univ of Victoria, B409 Clearihue, PO Box 3045, Victoria, BC, Canada V8W 3P4.

CAMPBELL, GWYN E.
PERSONAL Born 03/11/1957, Cambridge, MA **DISCIPLINE** SPANISH **EDUCATION** McMaster Univ, BA, 79; Univ Western Ontario, MA, 80; Princeton Univ, MA, 83; Princeton Univ, PhD, 88. **CAREER** Prof, Wash & Lee Univ, 85-. **MEMBERSHIPS** MLA, AHCT, AEEA. **RESEARCH** 16th and 17th-Century Spanish prose and drama, literary theory, Golden Age Spanish women writers. **SELECTED PUBLICATIONS** Rev, "Breve historia feminista de la literatura espanola (en langua castellana)," Anthropos Pr (Barcelona, Spain), 97; auth, "(En)gendering Fenisa in Maria de Zayas's 'La traicion en la amistad'," Romance Lang Annual X (99); auth, Zayas and Her Sisters: Essays on the novelas by Seventeenth-Century Spanish Women, forthcoming; auth, Zayas and Her Sisters: An Anthology of novelas by Seventeenth-Century Spanish Women, forthcoming; auth, The Voices of Commentary in Leonor de Meneses's "El desdenado mas firme, forthcoming; auth, "Narcissus and the Shadow of Desire in Leonor de Meneses's 'El desdenado mas firme'," Zayas and Her Sisters: Essays on the novelas by Seventeenth-Century Spanish Women (forthcoming). **CONTACT ADDRESS** Dept Lang, Washington and Lee Univ, 116 N Main St, Lexington, VA 24450-2504. **EMAIL** campbellg@wlu.edu

CAMPBELL, J. LEE
PERSONAL Born 05/08/1960, Peoria, IL, m, 1994, 4 children **DISCIPLINE** COMPOSITION, PROFESSIONAL WRITING, AND LINGUISTICS **EDUCATION** Ill State Univ, BA, 81, MA, 83; Purdue Univ, PhD, 90. **CAREER** Asst prof Eng, 95-, adv, Eng to speakers of other lang endorsement, 95-, web site mgr, dept Eng, 97-, ed, fac Handbk, Valdosta State Univ, 95-; asst prof Eng, Henderson State Univ, 92-95; Asst prof Eng, Marquette U niv, 90-92. **MEMBERSHIPS** Nat Coun of Tchr of Eng; Conf on Col Compos and Commun; Mod Lang Asn; S Atlantic Mod Lang Asn; Soc for Tech Commun; Southeastern Conf on Ling; Rhet Soc of Am; Phi Kappa Phi. **RESEARCH** Applied linguistic theory; argumentation and rhetorical theory. **SELECTED PUBLICATIONS** Auth, 'It is as if a green bough were laid across the page': Thoreau on Eloquence, in Rhet Soc Quart, 90; An Applied Relevance Theory of the Making and Understanding of Rhetorical Arguments, in Lang and Commun, 92; Argument,in Encycl of Eng Stud and Lang Arts, 95. **CONTACT ADDRESS** Dept of Eng, Valdosta State Univ, 1500 N. Patterson St, Valdosta, GA 31698. **EMAIL** jlcampbe@valdosta.edu

CAMPION, EDMUND J.
PERSONAL Born 08/28/1949, Bronx, NY, m, 1978, 2 children **DISCIPLINE** FRENCH **EDUCATION** Fordham Univ, BA, 71; Yale Univ, PhD, 76. **CAREER** Prof, Univ Tenn, 77- . **HONORS AND AWARDS** Lindsay Young Awd for Scholar, Univ Tenn, 84; Distinguished Service Awd, Univ Tenn, 99. **MEMBERSHIPS** Am Asn of Tchr of French. **RESEARCH** Erasmus and French Writers of the Sixteenth- and Seventeenth-Centuries. **SELECTED PUBLICATIONS** Auth, Montaigne, Rabelais, and Manotas Reasers of Erasmus, Edwin Mellen Press (Lewiston, NY), 95. **CONTACT ADDRESS** Dept of Mod For Langs & Lits, Univ of Tennessee, Knoxville, 701 McClung Tower & Plaza, Knoxville, TN 37996-0470. **EMAIL** ejcampion@aol.com

CAMPOS, JAVIER F.
DISCIPLINE SPANISH **EDUCATION** Universidad de Concepcion, Pedagogia en Espanol; Univ MN, PhD **CAREER** Fac, Universidad de Concepcion, OH State Univ, CA State Univ Chico, and Marshall Univ; assoc prof, Fairfield Univ, current. **HONORS AND AWARDS** Letras de Oro, Univ Miami and Span govt, 91. **SELECTED PUBLICATIONS** Auth, Las Ultimas Fotografeas, 81; La Ciudad en Llamas, 86' Las Cartas Olvidadas del Astronauta, 92. **CONTACT ADDRESS** Fairfield Univ, 1073 N Benson Rd, Fairfield, CT 06430.

CAMURATI, MIREYA BEATRIZ
PERSONAL Born 08/17/1934, Buenos Aires **DISCIPLINE** SPANISH AMERICAN LITERATURE **EDUCATION** Univ Buenos Aires, Prof en Letras, 59; Univ Pittsburgh, PhD(Span Am lit), 70. **CAREER** Instr Span lang & lit, Univ Buenos Aires, 59-65, asst prof Span Am lit, 65-68; asst prof Span, IN Univ Northwest, 70-73; asst prof, 73-75, assoc prof Span Am lit, 75-80, Prof Spain AM Lit, State Univ NY Buffalo, 80-, prof Span Am lit, Univ Salvador, 64-68. **MEMBERSHIPS** MLA; Am Asn Teachers Span & Port; Inst Int Lit Iberoam; Int Asn Hispanists. **RESEARCH** Spanish American avant garde poetry; Spanish American modernismo; contemporary Spanish American novel. **SELECTED PUBLICATIONS** Auth, Funcion literaria del cuento intercalado en D Segundo Sombra, La voraergine y Cantaclaro, Rev Iberoam, 4-6/71; Blest Gana, Lukacs, y la novela historical Cuadernos Americanos, 11-12/74; Un capitulo de versificacion modernista: El poema de clausulas ritmicas, Bull Hispanique, 9-12/74; Una ojeada a la poesia concreta en Hispanoamerica: Dos precursores, y escasos epigonos, Cuadernos Hispanoamericanos, 2/76; La fabula en Hispanoamerica, Universidad Nacional Autonoma de Mexico, 78; Bifurcacion, multiplicacion, ficcion, Hispanofila, 1/79; Poesia y poetica de Vincente Huidobro, Fernando Garcia Cambeiro, Buenos Aires, 80; Enfoques, D C Heath, 80; Bioy Casares y el alegre trabajo de la inteligencia, Buenos Aires: Corregidor, 90. **CONTACT ADDRESS** Dept of Mod Lang & Lit, SUNY, Buffalo, P O Box 604620, Buffalo, NY 14260-4620.

CANNON, JOANN CHARLENE
DISCIPLINE LINGUISTICS, ITALIAN **EDUCATION** Wellesley Col, BA, 71; Cornell Univ, PhD, 76. **CAREER** Asst prof to assoc prof, Syracuse Univ, 76-89; prof, Univ Calif Davis, 90-. **MEMBERSHIPS** MLA; AATI; AAIS. **RESEARCH** Modern Italian literature; Italian film. **CONTACT ADDRESS** Dept Fr Ital, Univ of California, Davis, 1 Shields Ave, Davis, CA 95616-5270. **EMAIL** jccannon@ucdavis.edu

CAP, JEAN-PIERRE
PERSONAL Born 06/02/1934, Longueil-Ste-Marie, France, m, 1962, 2 children **DISCIPLINE** FRENCH LANGUAGE & LITERATURE **EDUCATION** Temple Univ, BA, 57, MA, 60; Univ Pa, MA, 60; Rutgers Univ, PhD, 66. **CAREER** Instr French, Skidmore Col, 61-62; from instr to asst prof, Univ Md, 62-68; assoc prof, 68-78, prof, 78-94, Oliver Edwin Williams Prof, for Lang & Lit, Lafayette Col, 94-; Assoc ed, Claudel Studies, 67-80, co-ed, 83; Humanities enrichment grant, 73-74; Nat Hist Publ & Records Comn grant, 85. **HONORS AND AWARDS** Palmes Academiques, 80, officer 95. **MEMBERSHIPS** Am Asn Teachers Fr; AAUP; Soc Fr Prof Am; Claudel Soc; Am Comp Lit Asn; AAA Gide;UVAN; Shevchenko Scientific Soc (bd); Am Soc Fr Acad Palms & others. **RESEARCH** The novel; 20th century French literature; literary criticism; European history. **SELECTED PUBLICATIONS** Auth, Techniques et themes dans l'oeuvre de jean Schlumberger, 71; ed, Jacques Riviere-Jean Schlumberger: Corresp 1909-1995, 80; Decadence of Freedom, Jacques Riviere's Perception of Russian mentality, 84; ed, Henri-Gheon-Jacques Riviere: Corresp 1910-1924, 88; co-ed, Charles DuBos-Jacques Riviere: Corresp 1913-1925 & Charles DuBos-Isabelle Riviere: Corresp 1925-1935, 90; ed, Rozenie ou les Moscovites, 93; articles on Alain-Fournier, Claudel, Conrad, Desjardins, Dostoevsky, Gheon, Gide, Lafayette, Martin du Gard, Mistral, Peguy, Proust, Riviere, Schlumberger & others. **CONTACT ADDRESS** Dept of Lang, Lafayette Col, Easton, PA 18042-1798.

CAPE, ROBERT W., JR.
DISCIPLINE CLASSICS **EDUCATION** Uniz Ariz, BA, 83, MA, 85; UCLA, MA, 88, PhD, 91. **CAREER** Vis asst prof, Skidmore Col, 91-94; asst prof, Austin Col, 94-98; assoc prof, Austin Col, 98-. **HONORS AND AWARDS** Dir of Gender Studies, Austin Col, 95-. **MEMBERSHIPS** Am Philol Assoc; Nat Commun Assoc; Am Class League; Int Soc for the Hist of Rhet; Class Assoc of the Mid W & S. **RESEARCH** Cicero; ancient rhetoric; Roman literatukre & society; women in antiquity. **SELECTED PUBLICATIONS** Auth, The Rhetoric of Politics in Cicero's Fourth Catilinarian, Am J of Philol, 116.2, 155-177, 95; auth, Persuasive History: Roman Rhetoric and Historiography, Roman Eloquence: Rhetoric in Society and Literature, Roufledge, 212-228, 97; auth, Roman Women in the History of Rhetoric and Oratory, Listening to Their Voices: The Rhetorical Activities of Historical Women, Univ SC Press, 112-132, 97. **CONTACT ADDRESS** Dept of Class & Mod Lang, Austin Col, Ste 61653, Sherman, TX 75090-4440. **EMAIL** rcape@austinc.edu

CAPELES, MERVIN
DISCIPLINE SPANISH LANGUAGE AND LITERATURE **EDUCATION** SUNY Buffalo, PhD. **CAREER** Asst prof, Clark Atlanta Univ. **MEMBERSHIPS** CLA; MLA. **RESEARCH** Spanish language, literature, civilization and culture; literary criticism. **SELECTED PUBLICATIONS** Auth, El cuento fantastico en Puerto Rico y Cuba, Reichenberg, 95; Mejunje; Bajo la luna erotica del CaribQ. **CONTACT ADDRESS** Dept of Foreign Languages, Clark Atlanta Univ, 223 James P Brawley Dr, SW, Atlanta, GA 30314.

CAPLAN, JAY L.
PERSONAL Born 04/03/1946, Worcester, MA, m, 1982 **DISCIPLINE** FRENCH **EDUCATION** Oberlin Col, BA, 67; Yale Univ, MA, 70; Ecole Pratique des Hautes Etudes, PhD, 72. **CAREER** Asst Prof, Univ Minn, 73-85; Assoc Prof to Prof, Amherst Col, 85-. **HONORS AND AWARDS** Fel, Amherst Col. **MEMBERSHIPS** MLA; ASECS. **RESEARCH** Early modern French literary and cultural history; Critical theory. **SELECTED PUBLICATIONS** Auth, In the King's Wake: Post-Absolutist Culture in France, Univ Chicago Press, 99. **CONTACT ADDRESS** Dept French, Amherst Col, PO Box 5000, Amherst, MA 01002. **EMAIL** jlcaplan@amherst.edu

CAPPELLETTI, SALVATORE
PERSONAL Born 03/13/1945, Italy, s, 1 child **DISCIPLINE** ITALIAN **EDUCATION** RI Jr Col, AS, 66; Providence Col, BA, 68; Univ Wis, MA, 71; Brown Univ, PhD, 78. **CAREER** Vol Teach, Scuola Galieo, 72; teach, Hope HS, 72-74; res teach asst, Brown Univ, 74-78; asst prof, Boston Col, 78-82; asst prof, Providence Col, 82-87; assoc prof, 88-. **HONORS AND AWARDS** NSF Gnt; Doct Schl; CAFR Gnt; Who's Who East. **MEMBERSHIPS** AAUP; AATI; AAIS; RITI; RIFLA; NIAF; FISBU. **RESEARCH** Theories of comedy and acting; eighteenth century Italian theater; Renaissance comedy; origin and development of Italian drama; Italian romanticism (Manzoni) and criticism of same; contemporary Italian narrative. **SELECTED PUBLICATIONS** Auth, "Ferruccio Ulivi," in Dictionary of Literary Biography, Vol 196: Italian Novelists since World War II, 1965-1959, ed. Augusta Pallotta (Detroit, MI: Gale Group, 98); auth, "Il teatro italiano nel Nord America: Dalle origini al Cinquecento (1980-1990)," Esperienze letterarie 18 (93), 49-60. **CONTACT ADDRESS** Dept Modern Languages, Providence Col, 549 River Dr, Providence, RI 02918-7000. **EMAIL** rino@providence.edu

CAPTAIN, YVONNE
PERSONAL 1 child **DISCIPLINE** SPANISH LITERATURE & FILM **EDUCATION** Pitzer Col, BA, 73, Stanford Univ, PhD, 84. **CAREER** Asst prof to assoc prof, George Washington Univ, 84- ; pres, Phi Beta Delta Honors Soc, 97-99. **HONORS AND AWARDS** Dorothy Danforth-Compton Dissertation Fel, 83; Fel, Sch of Criticism & Theory, 86; Post-Doctoral Fel, 87; Phi Beta Delta Recognition Awd, 98. **MEMBERSHIPS** Phi Beta Delta Honors Soc for Int Scholars; Soc for Values in Higher Educ. **SELECTED PUBLICATIONS** Auth, The Culture of Fiction in the Works of Manuel Zapata Olivella, Univ of Mo Press, 93; El espiritu de la risa en el cuento de Ana Lydia Vega, Revista Iberoamericana, 93; Writing for the Future: Afro-Hispanicm in a Global, Critical Contest, Afro-Hispanic Rev, 94; The Poetics of the Quotidian in the Works of Nancy Morejon, in Singular Like a Bird, Howard Univ Press, 99; Manuel Zapata Olivella, in Encarta Africana, 99. **CONTACT ADDRESS** Dept of Romance Lang & Lit, The George Washington Univ, Washington, DC 20052. **EMAIL** ycaptain@gwu.edu

CARDONA, GEORGE
PERSONAL Born 06/03/1936, New York, NY, m, 1958, 2 children **DISCIPLINE** INDOARYAN AND INDO-EUROPEAN LINGUISTICS **EDUCATION** NYork Univ, BA, 56; Yale Univ, MA, 58, PhD, 60. **CAREER** Asst prof Indo-Aryan lang, 60-65, assoc prof ling, 65-67, Prof Ling, Univ PA, 67-, US Off Educ grant, 62-64, publ grant, 65; Am Inst Indian Studies fac res grant, 65-66; vis prof, Orient Inst, Baroda, 1/66; vis lectr, Swarthmore Col, spring 67. **MEMBERSHIPS** Ling Soc Am; Am Orient Soc; Am Philol Asn; Ling Soc Europe. **RESEARCH** Indo-Aryan and Indo-European linguistics. **SELECTED PUBLICATIONS CONTACT ADDRESS** Dept of Ling, Univ of Pennsylvania, 255 S 36th St, Philadelphia, PA 19104-3805.

CARLE, BARBARA
PERSONAL Born 09/02/1958, Pakistan, m, 1989, 1 child **DISCIPLINE** ITALIAN **EDUCATION** Columbia Univ, BA, 81; MA, 82; PhD, 88. **CAREER** Univ Wisc, 88-91; Loyola Univ, 91-94; Tex Women's Univ, 97-98; Prof, Univ N Tex, 94-. **RESEARCH** American and British Poetry; Art History; Contemporary Art; Cinema and Theatre. **SELECTED PUBLICATIONS** Auth, "Natalia Ginzburg's Narrative Voci della sera," Quaderni di italianistica, (94): 239-254; co-auth, "Il carcere dell' identita: il fenomeno della 'political correctness' negli Stati Uniti d'America," in I Quaderni di Gaia, (Univ of Roma, 94), 97-109; auth, "Mario Luzi's Pictorial Poesis: Avvento notturno (1940) and Viaggio terrestre e celeste di Simone Martini (1994)," Italica, (96): 68-82; auth, "Flower Lexicon, Metaphor and Imagery in Antonia Pozzi's Parole," Romance Notes, (97): 79-86; auth, "On Translating: From Antoine Berman to Amelia Rosselli," Polytext, (00): 72-79; auth, "Stanzare le distanze: On the Poetry of Luigi Fontanella," Rivista di studi italiani, 99. **CONTACT ADDRESS** Dept For Lang, Univ of No Texas, PO Box 311127, Denton, TX 76203-1127. **EMAIL** carleb@unt.edu

CARLIN, CLAIRE L.
PERSONAL Born 01/27/1955, CA, m, 1992 **DISCIPLINE** FRENCH, LITERATURE **EDUCATION** San Diego State Univ, AB, 77; Univ Calif Santa Barb, MA, 79; PhD, 84. **CAREER** Asst prof, Wash State Univ, 84-89; assoc prof, Univ Victoria, 89-. **HONORS AND AWARDS** SSHRC Grant, 01-04; CSRS Fac Fel, 02; Univ Calif Fel, 83-84; Provost Fac, Univ Victoria, 00. **MEMBERSHIPS** MLA; Soc d'Etude du XVIIe Siecle; NASSCFL; APFUCC; AATF; WSFH; Women in Fr; SIFSCS; AIEF. **RESEARCH** Seventeenth-century French literature; feminist theory. **SELECTED PUBLICATIONS** Auth, Pierre Corneille Revisited, Twayne (NYork), 98; auth, La Rochefoucauld, Mithridate, Freres et Soeurs: Actes du XXIX Colloque de la NASSCFL, Gunter Narr (Tubingen), 98; auth, Women Reading Corneille, Peter Lang (NYork), 00; auth, "Le Mariage Sous L'Ancien Regime," Dalhousie Fr Studies (01). **CONTACT ADDRESS** Fr Dept, Univ of Victoria, Victoria, BC, Canada V8W 3P4. **EMAIL** ccarlin@uvic.ca

CARLTON, CHARLES MERRITT
PERSONAL Born 12/12/1928, Poultney, VT, m, 1957, 3 children **DISCIPLINE** FRENCH LANGUAGE, ROMANCE LINGUISTICS **EDUCATION** Univ Vt, AB, 50; Middlebury Col, MA, 51; Univ Mich, PhD, 63. **CAREER** Teaching asst French, Univ Mich, 54-58; teaching asst English as foreign lang, English Lang Inst, 57-58; instr French, Mich State Univ, 58-62; asst prof French & gen ling, Univ Mo, 62-66; from asst to assoc prof, 66-77, prof French & Romance Ling, Univ Rochester, 77-; vis prof, NDEA French Inst, Univ Vt, 64; ed, Comp Romance Ling Newslett, 70-71; lectr English as foreign lang, Babes-Bolyai Univ, Cluj, Romania, 71-72; consult, Nat Endowment for Humanities, Title VI, Dept of Educ, 74-; vis prof, Univ Ky, Cluj program, 77; co-ed, Miorita, 77-89. **HONORS AND AWARDS** Nat Sci Found Awd, 65; Nat Defense For Lang Awd, 70; Fulbright-Hays Awds, Romania, 74, 78 & 82, Brazil, 86; Int Res & Exchanges Bd Awd, Romania, 82, 91. **MEMBERSHIPS** AAA; Soc Romanian Studies. **RESEARCH** Romanian language; Romance linguistics. **SELECTED PUBLICATIONS** Auth, What is so Imperative? Revue Roumaine de Linguistique, 92; auth,Romanian and Its Place in "the Romania" Revue Roumaine de Linguistique, 93-95; auth, Romanian Rural Life & Lexical Differentiation: Latin/non-Latin, Romanian Civilization, 95-96; ed, Papers from the Fourth World Congress for Soviet and East European Studies, Harrogate, 1990, London, 96; auth, Romanian Poetry in English Translation: An Annotated Bibliography & Census (1740-1996), Center for Romanian Studies, 97. **CONTACT ADDRESS** 3 Thornfield Way, Fairport, NY 14450. **EMAIL** carlton@ling.rochester.edu

CARMICHAEL, CARL W.
PERSONAL Born 01/11/1940, PA, m, 1999, 3 children **DISCIPLINE** COMMUNICATION, COMMUNICATION ASPECTS OF AGING, SOCIAL LINGUISTICS **EDUCATION** Univ IA, PhD. **CAREER** Instr, CA State Univ. **RESEARCH** Critical thinking. **SELECTED PUBLICATIONS** Wrote a chapter on aging in a bk on Intercultural Commun; auth, Human Comm and the Aging Process. **CONTACT ADDRESS** California State Univ, Fresno, Fresno, CA 93740. **EMAIL** profcarl@aol.com

CARNICKE, SHARON MARIE
DISCIPLINE RUSSIAN, THEATRE ARTS **EDUCATION** Moscow Univ, cert, 70; Barnard Col, AB, 71; NYork Univ, MA, 73; Columbia Univ, MPhil, 77, PhD, 79. **CAREER** Adj asst prof, Sch Visual Arts, 80-83; adj asst prof, 84-86, vis asst prof, NY Univ, 86-87; asst prof, 87-92, ASSOC PROF, 87-99, UNIV SOUTHERN CALIF; Prof, 99-. **SELECTED PUBLICATIONS** Auth, The Theatrical Instinct, Stanislavsky in Focus. **CONTACT ADDRESS** Sch Theatre, Drama Cte, Univ of So California, Los Angeles, CA 90089-0791. **EMAIL** carnicke@usc.edu

CARPENTER, BOGDANA
PERSONAL Born 06/02/1941, Czestochowa, Poland, m, 1963, 2 children **DISCIPLINE** POLISH, COMPARATIVE LITERATURE **EDUCATION** Warsaw Univ, MA, 63; Univ Cal, PhD, 74. **CAREER** asst prof, Univ Wash, 74-83; asst prof, assoc prof, prof, Univ Mich, 83-. **HONORS AND AWARDS** ICT Awd; Gold Cross Merit, Poland; Witter Bynner Prize; CUT Merit Awd. **MEMBERSHIPS** AATSEEL; AAASS. **RESEARCH** Polish Twentieth-Century poetry; Twentieth-Century poetry; literary translation. **SELECTED PUBLICATIONS** Auth, The Poetic Avan-Garde in Poland, 1918-1939, Univ Wash Press (Seattle), 83; auth, Monumenta Polonica: The First Four Centuries of Polish Poetry, Slav Pub (Ann Arbor, MI), 89. **CONTACT ADDRESS** Dept Slavic Languages, Univ of Michigan, Ann Arbor, 812 East Washington St, Ann Arbor, MI 48109-1275. **EMAIL** bogdana@umich.edu

CARR, GERALD FRANCIS
PERSONAL Born 12/29/1930, Pittsburgh, PA, m, 1965, 2 children **DISCIPLINE** LINGUISTICS, GERMAN STUDIES **EDUCATION** Duquesne Univ, B Ed, 58; Univ Wis, MA, 60; PhD, 68. **CAREER** Instr, Duquesne Univ, 60-62; teaching asst, Univ Wis, 62-64, 65-66; asst prof, Duquesne Univ, 64-68; asst prof to assoc prof to prof, Eastern Ill Univ, 68-88; prof, Calif State Univ, 89-. **HONORS AND AWARDS** Univ Wis Fel, 58; Von Schleinitz Fel, 59; Univ Wis Distinguished Teaching Fel, 66; E Ill Univ Outstanding Fac Merit Award, 79; E Ill Univ, Fac Res Award, 75, 76, 79; Kappa Phi Kappa; Delta Phi Alpha. **MEMBERSHIPS** MLA; AATG; IASS; SSA. **RESEARCH** Germanic philogy/linguistics; structure of medieval poetry. **SELECTED PUBLICATIONS** Auth, New Insights in Germanic Linguistics I, II; co-ed, Essays for Irmengard Rauch; auth, Semiotics Around the World; auth, Synthesis in Diversity; auth, Insights in Germanic Linguistics I, II; auth, Methodology in Transition; auth, On Germanic Linguistics; auth, Issues and Methods; auth, The Semiotic; auth, Trends from California; auth, Language Change; auth, The Signifying Animal; auth, The Grammar of Language and Experience; auth, Linguistic Method: Essays in Honor of Herbert Penzl. **CONTACT ADDRESS** 862 Camden Ct, Benicia, CA 94510-3633. **EMAIL** gfcarr@csus.edu

CARR, RICHARD ALAN
PERSONAL Born 07/15/1938, Maplewood, NJ **DISCIPLINE** FRENCH **EDUCATION** Princeton Univ, AB, 60, MA, 63, PhD(French), 69. **CAREER** Instr, 64-69, asst prof, 69-75, ASSOC PROF FRENCH, IN UNIV, 75-. **MEMBERSHIPS** MLA; Am Asn Teachers Fr; Soc Francaise Seiziemistes. **RESEARCH** French Renaissance literature; Renaissance narrative. **SELECTED PUBLICATIONS** Ed, Histoires tragiques, Champion, Paris, 77; auth, Pierre Boaistuau's Histoires Tragiques: A Study of Narrative, Univ NC, 79; V. Habanc, Nouvelles Histoies tant tragiques que comiques, Droz, 89; B. Poissenot, Nouvelles Histoires tragiques, Geneva, Droz, 96; Marconville, De la bonte et mauvaistie des femmes, Paris, Champion, 98. **CONTACT ADDRESS** Dept French & Ital, Indiana Univ, Bloomington, 1020 E Kirkwood Ave, Ballantine Hall 642, Bloomington, IN 47405. **EMAIL** carrr@indiana.edu

CARRE, MARIE-ROSE
DISCIPLINE FRENCH LITERATURE **EDUCATION** Univ Paris, PhD. **CAREER** Prof, Univ MA Amherst. **RESEARCH** 17th century lit and hist of ideas; 20th century surrealism; poetry. **SELECTED PUBLICATIONS** Auth, Le Bourgeois parisien de 1640 peint par lui-meme. **CONTACT ADDRESS** Dept of French and Italian Studies, Univ of Massachusetts, Amherst, Mass Ave, Amherst, MA 01003.

CARRENO, ANTONIO
PERSONAL Born 07/01/1938, Orense, Spain, m, 1962, 2 children **DISCIPLINE** HISPANIC STUDIES **EDUCATION** Escuela Normal Magisterio, BA, 63; Trinity Col, MA, 70; Yale Univ, MPhil, 74; PhD, 75. **CAREER** Acting instr, Yale Univ, 74-75; asst prof, Columbia Univ, 75-78; assoc prof to prof, Univ of IL, 79-85; prof, Brown Univ, 85-. **HONORS AND AWARDS** Ramon Menendez Pidal Prize, 78; W Duncan MacMillan Family Prof in the Humanities, 93. **MEMBERSHIPS** MLA; Int Assoc of Hispanist; Assoc of Teachers of Span and Port. **SELECTED PUBLICATIONS** Auth, "A un rio lo llamban Carlos", La moderna critica literaria hispanica. Antologia, ed Miguel Angel garrido Gallardo, Editorial Mapfre, (Madrid, 96): 31-37; auth, "The Poetics of Closure in Calderon's Plays", The Calderonian Stage: Body and Soul, ed Manuel Delgado Morales, Bucknell Univ Pr, (97): 25-44; auth, "De mi vida, Amarilis, os he escrito / lo que nunca pense. Las biografias liricas de Lope de Vega", Anuario de Lope de Vega, Univ Autonoma de barcelona, (97): 25-44; auth, "Las dulces / amargas prendas en don Ouijote: Eldiscurso de la locura", Cervantes, Gongora y Ouevedo, Univ Nacional de Cuyo (Argentina, 97): 50-71; auth, "Los concertados disparates de don Quijote: sobre el discurso de la locura", En un lugar de la Mancha: estudios cervantinos en honor de Manuel Duran, Salmanda, Ediciones almar (99): 57-75; auth, "Los silencios criticos de una recepcion: Lope de Vega: Del 98 al 98: literatura e historia literaria en el siglo XX hispano, eds Victor Garcia Ruiz, rosa Fernandez Urtasun, David K Herzberger, RILCE 15.1 , (99): 141-155; auth, "Un canto en disfrazado velo: las Angelicas de Lope de

Vega", Dule et decorum est philogican colere: Festchrift fur Dietrich Briesemesiter zu seinment 65 Geburtstag, Domus Editoria europeae (Berlin, 99); 145-165; ed, Lope de Vega, Rimas humanas y otros versos, Editorial Critica, (Barcelona), 98; ed, Lope De Vega, Rimas humanas y divinas de tome de burguillos, Editorial almar (Salmanca), (forthcoming); ed, Lope de Vega, Poesia completa, Ediciones de Castro, (Madrid), (forthcoming). **CONTACT ADDRESS** Dept Hispanic Studies, Brown Univ, 1 Prospect St, Providence, RI 02912-9100. **EMAIL** antonio_carreno@brown.edu

CARRERA, ALESSANDRO
PERSONAL Born 06/23/1954, Lodi, Italy, m **DISCIPLINE** ITALIAN **EDUCATION** Universita Degii Studi, Milan, Italy, Degree in Humanities, 80. **CAREER** Vis prof, Univ of Houston, 87-91; vis prof, McMaster Univ, 92-94; adj prof, NYork Univ, 95-. **HONORS AND AWARDS** Montale Poetry Prize, Italy, 93; Arturo Loria Prize for Short Fiction, Italy, 98. **MEMBERSHIPS** IAPL; AAIS. **RESEARCH** Italian Literature, Hermeneutics, Aesthetics. **SELECTED PUBLICATIONS** Auth, "L'amore al telescopio. Alla sua donna e il platonismo leopardiano", Rivista di Studi Italiani XVI.2 (98):99-123; transl, ed of "The Four Hard Edges of War" by Edizioni Cadmo, Wings Pr, (Houston, 99); auth, A che punto e il Giudizio Universale, Dodici racconti (Faenza: Mobydick, 99); ed, Giacomo Leopardi poeta e filosofo. Atti del convegno dell'Istito italiano di cultura, New York, (Fiesole: Cadmo, 99); coed, La forma del soggetto. Etica, scrittua, raffigurazione, Intersezioni. Rivista di storia delle idee XIX.3 (99):158; auth, Il principe e il giunsta. Giuseppe tomasi di Lampedusa e Salvatore Satta, (Rome: Pieraldo Editore, 00); trans, of The Third Man, the Quiet American, the Honorary Consul by Graham Greene (Milan: Mondadori, 00); auth, L'amore del secolo/Love of the Century (Bologna: Book Editore, 00) 132; auth, Lode all'isterica e altre dichiarazioni d'amore (Faenza: Mobydick, 00), 80; coed, Il dovere della felicita. Saffi fra due sponde, Baldini & Castoldi (Milan) 00. **CONTACT ADDRESS** Dept Italian, New York Univ, 24 W 12th St, New York, NY 10011-8604.

CARROLL, CARLETON WARREN
PERSONAL Born 10/20/1939, Rochester, NY, m, 1963 **DISCIPLINE** FRENCH LANGUAGE **EDUCATION** Ohio State Univ, BA, 61; Univ Wis-Madison, MA, 65, PhD(French), 68. **CAREER** Asst prof French & Ital, Univ Wis-Madison & Univ Wis-Exten, 67-74, chmn dept, 69-74; asst prof, 74-78, assoc prof French, 78-94, Prof of French, Ore State Univ, 94-. **HONORS AND AWARDS** Chevalier de l'Ordre des Palmes Academiques, 92. **MEMBERSHIPS** Am Asn Teachers Fr; Int Arthurian Soc; Soc Rencesvals; AAUP, Int Courtly Lit Soc. **RESEARCH** Medieval French literature; medieval Provencal literature; interlinguistics. **SELECTED PUBLICATIONS** Co-ed, Chretien de Troyes' Yvain, ou le Chevalier au Lion, Appleton, 68; auth, A Comparative Structural Analysis of Arnaut Daniel's Lo ferm voler and Peire Vidal's Mout m'es bon e bel, Neophilologus, 70; coauth, On the Generalization of the Sestina, Delta, 75; auth, Medieval Romance Paleography-a Brief Introduction, In: Medieval Manuscripts and Textual Criticism, Univ NC, 76; co-transl, Chretien de Troyes, Ywain, the Knight of the Lion, Frederick Ungar, 77,92; ed and trans, Chretien de Troyes' Erec et Enide, Garland, 87; co-trans, Chretien de troyes, Arthurian Romances, Penguin, 91; A Reappraisal of the Relationship Between Two Manuscripts of Erec et Enide, Nottingham French Studies 30.2:34-42, autumn 91; Un Fragment inedit d'Erec et Enide et sa place la tradition manuscrite, Scriptorium: Revue Internationale des Etudes Relatives aux Manuscrits/Int review of Manuscript Studies 46.2:242-50 + pl. 20 (photographs), 92; co-trans, Lancelot, In Lancelot-Grail: The Old French Arthurian Vulgate and Post-Vulgate in Translation, Garland, 93, 95; Quelques Observations sur les reflets de la cour d'Henri II dans l'oeuvre de Chretien de Troyes, Cahiers de Civilisation Medievale, 37: 33-39, 94; Cite or Vile? A Lexical Problem in the Lancelot-Grail Cycle, The Lancelot-Grail Cycle: Text and Transformations, 139-51, ed, William W. Kibler, Austin: Univ of Tx Press, 94; Text and Image: The Case of Erec et Enide, Word and Image in Arthurian Literature, ed Keith Busby, New York: Garland Publishing, 96, 58-78; auth, Ed and co-trans, Ooivier de La Marche, Le Chevalier delibere, Arizonia Center fr Medieval and Renaissance Studies, 99; auth, Representations, of Death in Le chevalier delibere (Olivier de La Marche, 1483), Sewanee Medieval Studies, 10 (00): 77-85. **CONTACT ADDRESS** Dept of Foreign Lang & Lit, Oregon State Univ, 210 Kidder Hall, Corvallis, OR 97331-4603. **EMAIL** ccarroll@orst.edu

CARROLL, DAVID
DISCIPLINE FRENCH LANGUAGE **EDUCATION** The Johns Hopkins Univ, PhD. **CAREER** Prpf/Ch, Fr, Univ Calif, Irvine. **SELECTED PUBLICATIONS** Auth, The Subject in Question: The Languages of Theory and the Strategies of Fiction; Paraesthetics: Foucault, Lyotard, Derrida; French Literary Fascism: Nationalism, Anti-Semitism, and the Ideology of Culture; pub(s), and articles on lit theory. **CONTACT ADDRESS** Dept of Fr and Ital, Univ of California, Irvine, Irvine, CA 92697.

CARROLL, LINDA LOUISE
PERSONAL Born 06/10/1949, Seattle, WA, m, 1997 **DISCIPLINE** ITALIAN, LINGUISTICS **EDUCATION** Princeton Univ, AB, 71; Harvard Univ, MA, 72, PhD , 77. **CAREER** Vis instr, 75-76, instr, 76-77, asst prof Ital, Gonzaga Univ, 76-81; Adj asst prof ling, Whitworth Col, 77-79; chmn dept Mod Lang, Gonzaga Univ, 78-81; asst prof, 81-87, assoc prof, 87-92, grad fac, 89-, prof Ital, Tulane Univ, 92-, women's studies fac assoc 94-; adj assoc prof Ital, Syracuse Univ, spring 86; Newcomb fel, 94. **HONORS AND AWARDS** Gonzaga Res Counc res grant, 79; Fulbright Comn res scholar, 84; NEH Travel to Collections award, 85; Delmas Found res fel, 85; Newberry Library Short-Term Resident fel, 86; Am Philos Soc res grant, 89; Gladys Krieble Delmas Found res grant, 90. **MEMBERSHIPS** Am Asn Ital Studies; Am Asn Tchr(s) Ital/Am Asnc Ital Studies; AAUP; Dante Soc Am; Int Soc Dialectology and Geolinguistics; Ling Asnc Canada and U S; MLA; Pacific Northwest Coun Foreign Lang; Philol Asn Pacific Coast; Renaissance Soc Am; Sixteenth Century Soc; Soc for Renaissance Studies; South Central Mod Lang Asn; WA Asn For Lang Tchr(s). **RESEARCH** Italian historical linguistics; Italian Renaissance theater; phonology. **SELECTED PUBLICATIONS** Auth, Language and Dialect in Ruzante and Goldoni, Longo, 81; Linguistic Variation and Social Protest in the Plays of Ruzante, Allegorica, 83; Carnival Themes in the Plays of Ruzante, Ital Culture, 84; Linguistic Correlates of Emotion in Ruzante, In: The Eleventh LACUS Forum 1984 (Robert A Hall Jr, ed), Hornbeam Press, 85; Carnival Rites as Vehicles of Protest in Renaissance Venice, Sixteenth Century Jour, 85; Cycles in Life and in Literature: The Case of Ruzante, Jour Asn Teachers Ital, 86; Authorial Defense in Boccaccio and Ruzante: From Liminal to Liminoid, Romance Quart, 87; Ruzante's Early Adaptations from More and Erasmus, Italica, 89; Who's on Top?: Gender as Societal Power Configuration in Italian Renaissance Drama, Sixteenth Century Jour, 89; Angelo Beolco tra comico e serio, In: Il Convegno Internazionale di Studi sul Ruzante (Giovanni Calendoli and Giuseppe Vellucci, ed), Corbo e Fiore, 89; Angelo Beolco (Il Ruzante), Twayne, 90, incl Twayne's World Authors on CD-ROM, 97; Giorgione's Tempest: Astrology is in the Eyes of the Beholder, In: Reconsidering the Renaissance Papers from the Twenty-First Annual Conference (Mario Di Cesare, ed), Medieval and Renaissance Texts and Studies, 92; The Peasant as Imperialist: An Unpublished Canzone in Ruzantine Style, Italica, 93; Un Paradiso Senza Dio nella Padova del Rinascimento, In: III Convegno Internazionale di Studi sul Ruzante (Giovanni Calendoli, ed), Societa Cooperative Tipografica, 93; A Non-theistic Paradise in Renaissance Padua, Sixteenth Century Jour, 93; Machiavelli's Veronese Prostitute: Venetia Figurata?, In: Gender Rhetorics: Postures of Dominance and Submission in History (Richard C Trexler, ed), Medieval and Renaissance Texts and Studies, 94; The Spirit in the Body: Physical and Psychological Influence on Holy Anorexia in the Case of Maria Janis, American Society of Church History Papers, Theological Res Exchange Network, 95; Holy Anorexia Revisited: The Reputation of Fasting in the Case of Maria Janis, The Psychohistory Rev, 98; transl, How To (and How Not To) Get Married in Sixteenth-Century Venice (Patricia H Labalme and Laura Sanguineti White), Renaissance Quart, 99; Il Contadino e il Filoimperialismo: Una Canzone Inedita in Stile Ruzantiano, In: Angelo Beolco detto Ruzante IV Convegno Internazionale di Studi sul Ruzante (Filippo Crispo, ed), Edizioni Papergraf, 97; Bernardo Dovizi, Il Bibbiena, In: Encyclopedia of the Renaissance (Paul F Grendler, ed), Scribner's. **CONTACT ADDRESS** Dept of Fr & Ital, Tulane Univ, 6823 St Charles Ave, New Orleans, LA 70118-5698. **EMAIL** lincar@mailhost.tcs.tulane.edu

CARRON, JEAN-CLAUDE
PERSONAL Born 06/21/1945, Switzerland, m **DISCIPLINE** FRENCH **EDUCATION** Univ Geneva, Lic es Lettres; Doctorat es Lettres. **CAREER** Lectr, Oxford Univ, 74-77; asst prof to prof and dept chair, UCLA, 79-. **MEMBERSHIPS** MLA; Renaissance Soc of Am; Societe des Seiziemistes. **RESEARCH** French 16th Century literature and culture; Philosophy and literature; Literary genres (poetry, dialogue). **SELECTED PUBLICATIONS** Auth, "Renaissance dialogue: The Seductive Persuasion," in Contending Kingdoms: Historical, Psychological, and Feminist Approaches to the Literature of the Sixteenth Century France and England, (Wayne State Univ Press, 91), 90-108; auth, "Dialogical Argument: scripting rhetoric," in Reason, Reasoning, and Literature in Renaissance France," (93): 20-31; auth, "Introduction," to Francois Rabelais: Critical Assessments, (Johns Hopkins Univ Press, 95), vi-xxi; ed, Francois Rabelais: Critical Assessments, Johns Hopkins Univ Press, 95. **CONTACT ADDRESS** Dept French, Univ of California, Los Angeles, 212 Royce Hall, Box 951550, Los Angeles, CA 90095-1550. **EMAIL** carron@ucla.edu

CARRUBBA, ROBERT W.
DISCIPLINE LATIN LITERATURE, NEO-LATIN STUDIES **EDUCATION** Princeton, PhD. **CAREER** VP, Acad Aff; prof, Fordham Univ. **SELECTED PUBLICATIONS** Auth, The Epodes of Horace: A Study in Poetic Arrangemen, 69; Englebert Kaempfer's Exotic Pleasures: Fascicle III, Curious Scientific and Medical Observations, 96. **CONTACT ADDRESS** Dept of Class Lang and Lit, Fordham Univ, 113 W 60th St, New York, NY 10023.

CARSON, KATHARINE WHITMAN
PERSONAL Born 10/26/1923, Bistol, TN **DISCIPLINE** FRENCH LITERATURE **EDUCATION** Barnard Col, AB, 45; Columbia Univ, MA, 65, PhD(French), 71. **CAREER** Instr French, Rutgers Univ, 68-71 & lectr, 71-72; Asst Prof French, Baruch Col, 73-78; Res Assoc, US Arab Chamber of Commerce, NY, 81-, Consult educ div, Simon & Schuster, 72-73; consult-evaluator, New York Bd Educ, 74-75; consult-evaluator, NY Bd Educ, 74-75; bibliog-consult, H P Kraus Rare Bks, 79-80; vis assoc prof, Yeshiva Univ, 80 & Fairleign Dickinson Univ, 79-81. **MEMBERSHIPS** AAUP; MLA, Am Asn Teachers Fr. **RESEARCH** Eighteenth century French novel. **SELECTED PUBLICATIONS CONTACT ADDRESS** 435 W 119 St, New York, NY 10027.

CARTER, ALBERT HOWARD, II
PERSONAL Born 03/14/1943, Washington, DC, m, 1967, 1 child **DISCIPLINE** COMPARATIVE LITERATURE **EDUCATION** Univ Chicago, BA; Univ Iowa, MA, PhD. **CAREER** Prof. **HONORS AND AWARDS** Distinguished Tchr Awd; NDEA IV Fel, 66-69; Fel, 89-90. **MEMBERSHIPS** Soc Values Higher Edu; Modern Lang Asn; Am Soc Bioethics Humanities. **RESEARCH** Literature and Medicine, Creative non-fiction. **SELECTED PUBLICATIONS** Auth, Italo Calvino: Metamorphoses of Fantasy; First Cut: A Season In The Human Anatomy Lab, Picador, 97. **CONTACT ADDRESS** Eckerd Col, 54th Ave S, PO Box 4200, Saint Petersburg, FL 33711.

CARTER, JOSEPH COLEMAN
PERSONAL Born 12/23/1941, New York, NY, 3 children **DISCIPLINE** CLASSICAL ARCHAEOLOGY, CLASSICS **EDUCATION** Amherst Col, BA, 63; Princeton Univ, MA, 67, PhD, 71. **CAREER** Asst prof, 71-76, prof class & class Archaeol, Univ TX Austin; Class Archaeol, Univ TX, Nat Endowment for Humanities younger humanist fel, 73-74; Am Coun Learned Soc fel, 79; NEH Fellowships, 88-89; Guggenheim Fellowships, 94-95. **HONORS AND AWARDS** James R. Wiseman Book, Awd Archaeological Institute of Am. **MEMBERSHIPS** Soc Promot Hellenic Studies; Archaeol Inst Am; Soc Promotion Roman Studies; Inst per la Storia della Magna Precia; Fellow Soc of An of London, 84. **RESEARCH** Excavation & research of Greek colonies on the Black Sea; Archaeological excavation, survey and research in Greek colonial S Ialy. **SELECTED PUBLICATIONS** Auth, Relief sculpture from the Necropolis of Taranto, 74 & The Tomb of the Sire, 78, Am J Archaeol; The Sculpture of Taras, Philadelphia, 75; auth, The Chora of Metaponto: The Necropoleis, 97. **CONTACT ADDRESS** Dept of Class, Univ of Texas, Austin, Austin, TX 78712-1026. **EMAIL** j.carter@mail.utexas.edu

CARTER, WILLIAM CAUSEY
PERSONAL Born 03/28/1941, Jesup, GA, m, 1967, 3 children **DISCIPLINE** FRENCH LANGUAGE AND LITERATURE **EDUCATION** Univ Ga, BA, 63, MA, 67; Ind Univ, PhD(-French), 71. **CAREER** Asst prof French, Ohio Univ, 71-74; asst prof, 74-78, Prof French, Univ Ala, Birmingham, 78-**MEMBERSHIPS** MLA; SAtlantic Mod Lang Asn. **RESEARCH** Nineteenth and twentieth century French literature. **SELECTED PUBLICATIONS CONTACT ADDRESS** 604 Warwick Rd, Birmingham, AL 35209.

CASA, FRANK PAUL
PERSONAL Born 11/18/1932, San Lucido, Italy, m, 1957, 2 children **DISCIPLINE** SPANISH **EDUCATION** Univ Ill, BA, 55, MA, 56; Univ Mich, PhD(Span), 63. **CAREER** From instr to asst prof Romance lang, Harvard Univ, 63-69; assoc prof, 69-76, Prof Univ Mich, Ann Arbor, 76-, Chmn Dept, 73-, Guggenheim fel, 67-68; chief-reader, Educ Testing Serv, 78-**MEMBERSHIPS** MLA **SELECTED PUBLICATIONS CONTACT ADDRESS** 1410 Hill St, Ann Arbor, MI 48104.

CASADO, PABLO GIL
PERSONAL Born 08/17/1931, Santander, Spain, m, 1969, 2 children **DISCIPLINE** SPANISH **EDUCATION** Escuela Profesional de Cornesco, TM, 51; Univ Interamericana, MA, 60; Univ Wis, PhD, 67. **CAREER** Instr, Univ N Iowa, 60-63; From Asst Prof to Prof, Univ NC, 67-. **HONORS AND AWARDS** Nat Publ Awd, 88. **MEMBERSHIPS** MLA. **RESEARCH** Historography of the Spanish novel, 20th-Century. **SELECTED PUBLICATIONS** Auth, La novela socil espanola 1920-1971, 2nd Ed, Seix Barral Publ (Barcelona, Spain), 73; ed, Ojancano, revista de literatura espanola (Athens, GA), 88; auth, La novella deshumanizada espanola 1958-1988, Anthropos (Barcelona, Spain), 90. **CONTACT ADDRESS** Dept Lang, Univ of No Carolina, Chapel Hill, 440 W Franklin St, Chapel Hill, NC 27599-3170. **EMAIL** casado@email.unc.edu

CASAGRANDE, JEAN
PERSONAL Born 08/19/1938, Oran, Algeria, m, 1963, 2 children **DISCIPLINE** FRENCH LANGUAGE AND LINGUISTICS **EDUCATION** Univ SFla, BA, 63; Ind Univ, MA, 64, PhD(Fr), 68. **CAREER** Lectr French & Ital, Ind Univ, 66-68, asst prof, 68; asst, 68-73, Assoc Prof French & Ling, Univ Fla, 73-, Vis prof, Ling Soc Am Summer Inst, 72 & co-dir, 75; Nat Endowment for Humanities fel, 72-73. **MEMBERSHIPS** Ling Soc Am; Am Asn Teachers Fr; Southeast Conf Ling (pres, 74-

75); Int Soc Phonetic Sci. **RESEARCH** French language, syntax and semantics; linguistic theory. **SELECTED PUBLICATIONS** Auth, The Canon in a Structure Course--The Case of French, Romance Quart, Vol 0041, 94. **CONTACT ADDRESS** 1732 NW Seventh Ave, Gainesville, FL 32603. **EMAIL** jeancas@ufl.edu

CASCARDI, ANTHONY JOSEPH
PERSONAL Born 12/29/1953, New York, NY, m, 1978 **DISCIPLINE** COMPARATIVE LITERATURE **EDUCATION** Princeton Univ, BA, 75; Harvard Univ, MA, 77, PhD(Romance lang), 80. **CAREER** Asst Prof Comp Lit, Univ Calif, Berkeley, 80-, Soc Fel in the Humanities fel, Columbia Univ, 82-. **MEMBERSHIPS** MLA. **RESEARCH** Skepticism and knowledge in the novels of Cervantes, Dostoyevsky and Flaubert. **SELECTED PUBLICATIONS CONTACT ADDRESS** Dept of Comp, Univ of California, Berkeley, Berkeley, CA 94704.

CASE, FREDRICK I.
PERSONAL Born 09/19/1939, Georgetown, Guyana **DISCIPLINE** FRENCH **EDUCATION** Univ Hull, BA, 65; Univ Leicester, MA, 68; Univ Lille, DUn, 70. **CAREER** Sch tchr, Eng & France, 60-68; lectr to assoc prof, 68-80, coordr African stud prog, 78-80, prof French, Univ Toronto, 80-, assoc ch grad stud Fr, 84-85, ch Fr, 85-90, prin, New Col, 91-96, dir, Caribbean stud prog, 95-96. **SELECTED PUBLICATIONS** Auth, Aime Cesaire; Bibliographie, 73; auth, La Cite Ideale dans Travail d'Emile Zola, 74; auth, Racism and National Consciousness, 79; auth, The Crisis of Identity: Studies in the Guadeloupean and Martiniquan Novel, 85; auth, "L'enjeu ontologique de l'intertete," dans Carrefour de Cultures: Melanges offerts a Jacqueline Leiner, Tubingen, Gunter Narr Verlag, (93): 261-272; auth, "Aesthetics, ideology and social commitment in the Prose Fiction of Ousmane Sembene," dans Ousmane Sembene, Dailouges with Critics and Writers, Amherst, Univ of Mass Press, (93): 3-13; auth, "Semiotique du Cinema d'Ousmane Sembene" in Centenaire du Cinema: Trentieme anniversaire du cinema africain, Paris, Presence Africaine, 95; auth, "Ontological Discourse in Ousmane Sembene's Cinema" in Sheila Petty ed., A Call to Action, (Trowbridge, Praeger/Flicks Books, 96): 87-104; auth, "Esthetique et discours ideologique dans l'oeuvre d'Ousmane Sembene et d'Assia Djebar," in Sada Niang ed., (Paris/Montreal, L'Harmattan, 96): 35-48; auth, "L'Esthetique d'A. Memmi", in H. Bouraoui ed., Tunisie Plurielle, Tunis, (L'Or du Temps, 97): 107-114. **CONTACT ADDRESS** Dept of French, Univ of Toronto, 50 St. Joseph St, 2nd Fl, Toronto, ON, Canada M5S 1J4. **EMAIL** case@chass.utoronto.ca

CASE, THOMAS EDWARD
PERSONAL Born 02/27/1934, Minneapolis, MN, m, 1960, 1 child **DISCIPLINE** SPANISH **EDUCATION** Col St Thomas, BA, 56; State Univ Iowa, MA, 58, PhD(Span), 62. **CAREER** Asst, State Univ Iowa, 56-61; from asst prof to assoc prof, 61-69, Prof Span, San Diego State Univ, 69-, Fulbright lect grant, Bogota, 65; resident dir, Calif Univ Int Progs, Univ Madrid, Spain, 74-75. **MEMBERSHIPS** Am Asn Teachers Span & Port; Philol Asn Pac Coast; Pac Coast Coun Latin Am Studies. **RESEARCH** Latin American novel; Golden Age literature. **SELECTED PUBLICATIONS CONTACT ADDRESS** Dept of Span, San Diego State Univ, 5500 Campanile Dr, San Diego, CA 92182-0002.

CASERTA, ERNESTO
PERSONAL Born 03/19/1937, Montenero V.C., Italy, m, 1968, 2 children **DISCIPLINE** ITALIAN LITERATURE **EDUCATION** Ginnasio-Liceo Antonio Genovesi, Dip di Maturita Classica, 57; Gannon, Col, BA, 60; Tulane Univ, MA, 63; Harvard Univ, PhD, 69. **CAREER** Teacher, NW High School, 59-62; instr, Boston Col, 67-70; asst prof to prof, Duke Univ, 89-. **HONORS AND AWARDS** NDEA Summer Inst, 61; Fel, Tulane Univ 62-64; Fel, Harvard Univ, 64-66; Amer Phos Soc Grant 76-77. **MEMBERSHIPS** Dante Soc Am; Am Asn Teachers Ital; Am Asn Ital Schol. **RESEARCH** 19th and 20th Century Italian literature, aesthetics and criticism. **SELECTED PUBLICATIONS** Auth, Manzoni's Christian Realism, Olschki, 77; auth, L'ultimo Leopardi: pensiero e poesia. Documenti e Studi Leopardiana, Bonacci, 80; auth, Croce and Marxism, Morano, 87; auth, Vent'anni di studi crociani negli Stati Uniti, Loffredo, 88; auth, Il folle volo di Leccafondi all'Inferno, proceedings of congress at UCLA, 88, in Forum Italicum Supplement, 90; auth, Croce e la critica contemporanea, Italian Culture, 91; auth, Un angolo di Napoli di Benedetto Croce, Forum Italicum, 92; auth, vedro Singapore? Di Piero Chiara: Struttura e trama del romanzo, Italian Culture, 93; auth, From Machiavelli to Vico: Three Books of R. Montano, in Battle for Humanism, Washington, DC, 94; auth, Motivi dominanti e personaggi in Una spina nel duore di P. Chiara, in Studies for Dante, 1998. **CONTACT ADDRESS** Dept Romantic Lang, Duke Univ, PO Box 90257, Durham, NC 27708-0257.

CASMIR, FRED L.
PERSONAL Born 12/30/1928, Berlin, Germany, m, 1986, 2 children **DISCIPLINE** SPEECH AND COMMUNICATION **EDUCATION** David Lipscomb Col, BA, 50; Ohio State Univ, MA, 55, PhD, 61. **CAREER** Part-time Fac, East Los Angeles Col, 73-74; Part-time Fac to Assoc Prof, San Fernando Valley State Col, 61-73; Instr to Prof Commun, 56-94, dir, International Studies Major, Chmn, Pepperdine Univ, 89-94, 97-99; distinguished prof emer of International Commun Asn, National Commun Asn, Pepperdine Univ, 94-; assoc ed, editorial boards of Journal of Commun, Critical Studies in Mass Commun, 99-01. **HONORS AND AWARDS** Outstanding Teacher, Pepperdine Univ, 73; Second-place winner, national papers contest, Nat Asn Educ Broadcasters, 81; Teacher of the Year, Alumni Asn, Pepperdine Univ, 85; PRSSA, Outstanding Fac Advisor, 86; Outstanding Sr Interculturalist, Soc Intercultural Educ, Training and Res, Int, 87; Assoc, Sears-Roebuck Found Grant and Assoc Project for Asian Studies, Fac Development, Pepperdine Univ, 90-91; Fel, Irvine Found Grant, 93; recipient of several research grants from Pepperdine University and others. **MEMBERSHIPS** Nat Commun Asn; Pi Kappa Delta; Ger Speech Asn; Int Commun Asn; World Commun Asn; Western Speech Commun Asn. **SELECTED PUBLICATIONS** Ed, Building communication theories: A socio-cultural approach, Lawrence Erlbaum Assoc, 94; Communication in Eastern Europe: The role of history, culture and media in contemporary conflict, Lawrence Erlbaum Assoc, 95; auth, Foundations for the study of intercultural communication based on a third culture building model, Int J Intercultural Relations (in press); ed, Ethics in Intercultural and International Communication, Lawrence Erlbaum Assoc (97); auth and ed, of numerous other articles and publications. **CONTACT ADDRESS** Seaver Col, Pepperdine Univ, 24255 Pacific Coast Hwy, Malibu, CA 90263. **EMAIL** fcasmir@hotmail.edu

CASSELL, ANTHONY K.
PERSONAL Born 03/31/1941, Reading, England **DISCIPLINE** ITALIAN & MEDIEVAL LITERATURE **EDUCATION** Univ Toronto, BA, 63; Johns Hopkins Univ, PhD, 69. **CAREER** Asst prof, 71-76, assoc prof Italian, prof Italian & comp literature, 86, Univ IL, Urbana, 76-, assoc ed, Italian Culture & Dante Studies; Dante Soc Am Coun, 80-84, 90-94. **HONORS AND AWARDS** Outstanding Book Awd, Choice, 76; Guggenheim Fel, 85. **MEMBERSHIPS** Am Asn Teachers Ital; Dante Soc Am; Am Boccaccio Asn; MLA; Mediaeval Acad Am; Am Asn Italian Studies; Ren Soc Am. **RESEARCH** Boccaccio; Danta; Petrarca. **SELECTED PUBLICATIONS** Auth, The crow of the fable and the Corbaccio, Mod Lang Notes, 70; The Corbaccio and the secundus tradition, Comp Lit, 73; Boccaccio's Corbaccio, 75; Moral and structural conflict in the Corbaccio, Mod Lang Notes, 75; ed & translr, the Corbaccio, Univ Ill, 75; auth, Pride failure and conversion in Inferno I, Dante Studies, 76; Farinata and the image of the Arca, Yale Ital Studies, 77; The Tomb, the Tower and the Pit, Italica, 79; The Lesson of Ulysses, Dante Studies, 81; Pier della Vigna: History and Iconography, Dante, Petrarch and Others, 82; Ulisseana: A Bibliography on Dante's Ulysses until 1980, Italian Cult, 81; auth, Dante's Fearful Art of Justice, Univ Toronto, 84; ed Diana's Hunt Caccia di Diana: Boccaccio's First Fiction, Univ Pa, 91; Lectura Dantis Americana, Inferno I, Univ Pa, 89; ed, The Corbaccio or the Labyrinth of Love, Pegasus Press, 93. **CONTACT ADDRESS** Dept Spanish, Italian & Portugues, Univ of Illinois, Urbana-Champaign, 707S Mathews Ave, Urbana, IL 61801-3625. **EMAIL** acassell@uiuc.edu

CASSIDAY, JULIE A.
PERSONAL Born 03/02/1964 **DISCIPLINE** RUSSIAN **EDUCATION** Connell College, BA, 86; Stanford Univ, MA, 90; Stanford Univ, PhD, 95. **CAREER** Asst prof, Williams Col, 94-. **HONORS AND AWARDS** ACTR-ACCELS Travel Grant to Moscow, on US Infor Agency, Bureau of Educ & Cult Aff, Reg Scholar Exchange Fel, 96. **RESEARCH** 19th-Century Russian Literature; Russian Theater and Drama; Revolutionary Cultural Studies. **SELECTED PUBLICATIONS** Auth, The Enemy on Trial: Early Soviet Courts on Stage and Screen. **CONTACT ADDRESS** Center for Foreign Languages, Literatures and Cult, Williams Col, Williamstown, MA 01267. **EMAIL** Julie.A.Cassiday@williams.edu

CASSIRER, THOMAS
PERSONAL Born 04/28/1923, Rome, Italy, m, 1948, 1 child **DISCIPLINE** FRENCH AND AFRICAN LITERATURE **EDUCATION** McGill Univ, BA, 45; Yale Univ, PhD(Fr & comp lit), 53. **CAREER** Asst prof French, Smith Col, 60-65; assoc prof, 65-69, Prof French & African Lit, Univ Mass, Amherst, 69-. **MEMBERSHIPS** MLA; Am Asn Teachers Fr; African Studies Asn. **RESEARCH** Eighteenth century French literature; modern African literature. **SELECTED PUBLICATIONS CONTACT ADDRESS** Dept of French & Italian, Univ of Massachusetts, Amherst, Amherst, MA 01002.

CASTEEN, JOHN
PERSONAL Born 12/11/1943, Portsmouth, VA, 1 child **DISCIPLINE** OLD ENGLISH LITERATURE, HISTORY OF THE ENGLISH LANGUAGE **EDUCATION** Univ Va, BA, 65, MA, 66, PhD(English), 70. **CAREER** Asst to dean, Co of Arts & Sci, Univ Va, 69-70; asst prof English, Univ Calif, Berkeley, 70-75; asst prof, 75-77, Assoc Prof English, Univ VA, 77-, Dean of Admis, 75- **RESEARCH** Patristics; early American literature. **SELECTED PUBLICATIONS** Auth, Poem for Mary Magdalene, Shenandoah, Vol 0046, 96. **CONTACT ADDRESS** Dept of English, Univ of Virginia, Charlottesville, VA 22901.

CASTELLANI, VICTOR
PERSONAL Born 02/14/1947, Brooklyn, NY, m, 1976, 2 children **DISCIPLINE** CLASSICS **EDUCATION** Fordham Univ, BA, 68; Princeton Univ, PhD, 71. **CAREER** Adj lectr, classics, Fordham Univ, 70-71; instr, 71-72, asst prof, 72-80, assoc prof, 80- , chemn 81-85, 89-98, Dept of Lang and Lit, Univ Denver. **HONORS AND AWARDS** Horace Acad, 65; Classic Prize, 66; Phi Beta Kappa, 67; Columbia Tchrs Col Book Awd, 67; NDEA, Princton fel, 68; Woodrow Wilson fel, 68; pres, Rocky Mtn MLN, 84; Awd for Outstanding Support, 93. **MEMBERSHIPS** Am Class League; Archaeol Inst Am; APA; Class Asn of Middle West and South; Pacific Ancient and Modern Lang Asn; Pro-Riesling Verein, Trier, Ger; Rocky Mountain MLA. **RESEARCH** Greek and Latin literature, especially epic and drama; ancient religion; comparative literature, especially narrative poetry, Dante, and drama, Ibsen; art and literature. **SELECTED PUBLICATIONS** Auth, Captive Captor Freed: The National Theater of Ancient Rome, Drama: Beitrage zum antiken Drama und seiner Rezeption, 95; auth, Flesh or Fish or What? Euripides' Orestes, Didaskalia: Ancient Theater Today, 95; auth, Athena and Friends: One Among the Greek Religions, in Dillon, ed, Religion in the Ancient World: New Themes and Approaches, Hakkert, 96; auth, Europa, Euripides, and the Differentiation of Europe, Jour of the Int Soc for the Study of European Ideas, 96; auth, Regulated European Wine: A View From Middle America, and, Classics at a Small University, Selected Proceedings of the 5th International Conference on ISSEI, 96; auth, After Stormy Seas Calm Once More I See: Reconciliation and Re-Moralization in Euripides, Jour of the Int Soc for Stud of European Ideas, 97; auth, Melpomene Polias: Athenian Tragedy and Politics in the Later Fifth Century, in Hillard, ed, Ancient History in a Modern University, vol 1, Eerdmans, 98; auth, Ibsen and the Return of Myth, in M. Deppermann, ed, Ibsen im europaischen Spannungsfeld zwischen Naturalismus und Symbolismus: Kongressakten der 8, Internationalen Ibsen-Konferenz, 98; auth, Beginnings of Ancient Greek History and Historiography, rev article, The European Legacy, 98; auth, Insignes Pietate? The Ancient Romans and Their Religious Life, rev article, The European Legacy, 99. **CONTACT ADDRESS** Dept of Languages and Literatures, Univ of Denver, Denver, CO 80208-2662. **EMAIL** vcastell@du.edu

CASTELLANO, CHARLENE
DISCIPLINE RUSSIAN **EDUCATION** Cornell Univ, PhD. **CAREER** Languages, Carnegie Mellon Univ. **SELECTED PUBLICATIONS** Auth, Making Sense of Synesthesia and The Synesthetics of Apocalypse in Andrey Bely's Petersburg, New Rev, 93; The Mystery Play in Andrey Bely's Dramaturgy and Prose, Canadian-American Slavic Studies, 95; Andrey Bely's Memories of Fiction, in Autobiographical Statements in Twentieth-Century Russian Literature, princeton Univ Press, 98. **CONTACT ADDRESS** Carnegie Mellon Univ, 5000 Forbes Ave, Pittsburgh, PA 15213.

CASTELLANOS, ISABEL
DISCIPLINE SPANISH LITERATURE **EDUCATION** Georgetown Univ, PhD. **CAREER** Prof. **RESEARCH** Afro Cuban and Afro Colombian culture; works of Lydia Cabrera; Spanish American sociolinguistics. **SELECTED PUBLICATIONS** Auth, Patak: A Collection of Afro-Cuban Myths, 96; co-auth, Cultura Afrocubana, 94. **CONTACT ADDRESS** Dept of Modern Languages, Florida State Univ, 11200 SW 8th St, Miami, FL 33174. **EMAIL** castella@servms.fiu.edu

CASTELLS, RICARDO
DISCIPLINE SPANISH LITERATURE **EDUCATION** Duke Univ, PhD, 91. **CAREER** Asst prof. **RESEARCH** Renaissance and Baroque Spanish literature. **SELECTED PUBLICATIONS** Auth, El caballero de Olmedo de Lope de Vega: 'Aojado estes', 95; Damas y caballeria: la mujer guerrera y la prensa neoyorquina durante la guerra de independencia cubana, 95; From Crenica to Comedia: Catholic Evangelization and Indigenous Oral Traditions in the Inca Garcilaso and Calderen, 94; The Hidden Intertext in Alejo Carpentier's Los pasos perdidos, 94. **CONTACT ADDRESS** Dept of Modern Languages, Florida State Univ, 11200 SW 8th St, Miami, FL 33174.

CASTILLA, ALBERTO
PERSONAL Born Zaragoza, Spain **DISCIPLINE** SPANISH **EDUCATION** Univ Zaragoza, Licenciatura, 61; PhD, 74. **CAREER** Prof, chemn, Mt Holyoke Col. **RESEARCH** Hispanic theatre **SELECTED PUBLICATIONS** Auth, El Teatro de Luis Riaza, Catedra (Madrid, Spain), 81; auth, Carolina Coronado de Perry, Beramar (Madrid, Spain), 87; ed, Entremeses de Cervantes, AKAL (Madrid, Spain), 97. **CONTACT ADDRESS** Dept Lang, Mount Holyoke Col, 50 College St, South Hadley, MA 01075-1423.

CASTRO, AMANDA
DISCIPLINE SPANISH LITERATURE **EDUCATION** Univ Pittsburgh, PhD, 91. **CAREER** Asst prof. **RESEARCH** Spanish language and linguistics; poetry. **SELECTED PUBLICATIONS** Auth, Celebracion de mujeres, 93. **CONTACT ADDRESS** Foreign Languages and Literature Dept, Colorado State Univ, Fort Collins, CO 80523. **EMAIL** acastro@vines.colostate.edu

CASTRO-KLAREN, SARA
DISCIPLINE SPANISH **EDUCATION** Univ Calif, BA, 62; UCLA, MA, 65; PhD, 68. **CAREER** Instructor, Calif State Univ, 68; Asst Prof, Univ ID, 68-70; Asst Prof to Prof, Dartmouth Col, 70-84; Visiting Prof, Stanford Univ, 82; Visiting lecturer, Johns Hopkins Univ, 84; Adj Prof, Georgetown Univ, 84, 85, 97, 99; Visiting Clarence Robinson Prof, George Mason Univ, 89; Prof, Johns Hopkins Univ, 87-. **HONORS AND AWARDS** NEH Sem, Long Island Univ, 94-95; NEH Inst, 92; Fel, Darmouth Col, 82-83; Woodrow Wilson Fel, 77-78; Anderw Mellon Foundation, Fel. **MEMBERSHIPS** AAUP; MLA; LASA; AACU; Inst of Andean Studies; Brazilian Studies Asn; Intl Asn of Americanistas; Latin-American Subaltern Studies Group. **RESEARCH** Colonial Studies/Postcolonial Theory; Literary Theory; Narrative Discourse in History and Fiction; The novel; Women's Writing; Cultural Studies. **SELECTED PUBLICATIONS** Auth, Understanding Mario Vargas Llosa, Univ SC Press, 90; ed, Latin American Women's Writing, Westview Press, 91; auth, "The Subject, Feminist Theory and Latin American Texts," Studies in 20th Century Literature, (96): 271-302; auth, "The Paradox of Self in the Idea of a University," in John Henry Newman's Idea of a University, (Yale Univ Press, 96), 318-339; auth, "El Cuzco de Garcilaso: El espacio y el lugar del conocimiento," in Asedios a la heterogeneidad cultural, (Philadelphia, 96), 135-153; auth, "Corporizacion Tupi: Lery y el manifiesto antropofago," Revista de Critica Literaria Lationamericana, (97): 193-210; auth, "Las pacarinas y la virginidad 0 de la sexualidad en Guaman Poma," in Nuevas perspectivas en cultura y literaturas andinas, (Stanford Univ Press, 97), 51-65; auth, "Mimicry Revisited: Latin America, Post-colonial Theory and the Location of Knowledge," in Postmodernidad y discurso postcolonial, 99; ed, New Historiography: Women's Writing and Feminist Criticism, Leipzig, 00; auth, "Peru: The Twentieth Century," in Guide to Cultural Studies in Latin America, (Routledge Press, forthcoming); **CONTACT ADDRESS** Dept Romance Lang & Lit, Johns Hopkins Univ, Baltimore, 3400 N Charles St, 216 Gilman Hall, Baltimore, MD 21218-2608. **EMAIL** sck@jhu.edu

CASTRO-PONCE, CLARA E.
PERSONAL Born 01/31/1966, San Juan, Puerto Rico **DISCIPLINE** SPANISH **EDUCATION** Univ de Puerto Rico, BA, 88; Brown Univ, MA, 90; PhD, 00. **CAREER** TA, Brown Univ, 89-94; vis asst prof, North Park Col, 95-97; asst prof, Allegheny Col, 00-. **HONORS AND AWARDS** Golden Key Nat Honor Soc, 88; Jose Marti Awd, Univ of Puerto Rico, 88; Brown Univ Fel, 88; Dorothy Danford-Compton Fel, 88-93, 93, 94; Bernard E. Bruce Awd, Brown Univ, 01; Sigma Delta Pi. **MEMBERSHIPS** MLA, AAUP, Medieval Acad of Am, Asociacion Hispanica Medieval, Asociacion de Literatura Femenina Hispanica. **RESEARCH** Medieval Spanish literature, Spanish Golden Age literature, contemporary Latin American and Puerto Rican literature. **SELECTED PUBLICATIONS** Rev, of "Milagros de neustra senora," by Juan Manuel Caco Blecua, Synopsis, (92); auth, El si de las hermanas: la escritura y lo intelectual en la obra de Teresa de Cartagena y Sor Juana Ines de la Cruz", Cincinnati Romance Rev, 99; auth, Conversa nun or crypto-Jew? The Converso Experience of Teresa de Cartagena, Univ of NMex, forthcoming; auth, Teresa de Cartagena. Arboleda de los enfermos Admiracion Operum Die, Edicion critica, forthcoming. **CONTACT ADDRESS** Allegheny Col, 520 N Main St, Box 121, Meadville, PA 16335. **EMAIL** ccastro@allegheny.edu

CASTRONOVO, DAVID
PERSONAL Born 10/30/1945, Brooklyn, NY **DISCIPLINE** ENGLISH AND COMPARATIVE LITERATURE **EDUCATION** Brooklyn Col, BA, 67; Columbia Univ, MA, 68, PhD, 75. **CAREER** Adjunct asst prof, Brooklyn Col, 72-76; adjunct asst prof, Pace, 76-78, asst prof, 79-86, assoc prof, 86-88, prof of English, Pace Univ, NY, 88-. **HONORS AND AWARDS** Fac fel, Columbia Univ, 67-71; New York Times Notable Book (Edmund Wilson), 85. **MEMBERSHIPS** PEN; MLA. **RESEARCH** 19th and 20th century lit; social hist; literary criticism. **SELECTED PUBLICATIONS** Auth, Edmund Wilson, Frederick Ungar, 84; Thornton Wilder, Frederick Ungar, 86; The English Gentleman, Frederick Ungar, 87; The American Gentleman, Continuum, 91; From the Uncollected Edmund Wilson, ed and introduced with Janet Groth, OH Univ Press, 95; Richard Yates: Am American Realist, with Steven Goldleaf, Twayne/Macmillan, 96; Edmund Wilson Revisited, Twayne/Macmillan, 98; auth, Encyclopedia of American Literature, 99; auth,"Ungar Encyclopedia of Literature in The 20th Century," in Scribner's Encyclopedia of American Lives (00). **CONTACT ADDRESS** Dept of English, Pace Univ, New York, 1 Pace Plaza, New York, NY 10038.

CATEL, MYLENE
DISCIPLINE FRENCH **EDUCATION** Univ de Caen, Maitrise d'anglais, 88; Ind Univ, MA, 89; PhD, 96. **CAREER** Vis instr, Kalamazoo Col, 95-96; vis asst prof, Hope Col, 96-98; asst prof, Minot State Univ, 98-. **HONORS AND AWARDS** The Grace Young Awd, 94; Ctr of Learning and Res Educ Inst, Mich State Univ, 98; The Mirial Poetry Awd, 98; Int Coun for Can Studies, Ottawa, 99. **MEMBERSHIPS** US Delegate for the "Union Mondiale des Poetes," Int Writers and Artist Asn, Women in French, FLAND. **SELECTED PUBLICATIONS** Auth, "Le Stade du Mimoir," Actes du Colloques," La Relation," Univ of Toronto, Can (spring 94); auth, "Le Jongleur Fou," Paris: Editions Caracteres (95); auth, "JC," Paris: Editions Caracteres (95); coauth with Rosemary Lloyd, "Letters of Stuart Merrill," Nineteenth Century French Studies, Vol 25, no 3 & 4 (spring-summer 97): 386-414; auth, "Points D'O," Agessac, Editions CLAPAS (98); auth, "Amphetamines," Les Saisons du Poeme (summer 98); auth, "Jour" in Resurrection (summer 98); auth, "La Bourse du Diable" in Resurrection (Jan 98); auth, "In-edit," Les Saisons du poeme (spring 99); auth, "Au Trop Pur des Passions," Aguessac Editions CLAPAS (99); auth, "Usure-Passion," Paris, France (forthcoming); auth, "Women, Quebec and the Internet," (forthcoming). **CONTACT ADDRESS** Dept Humanities, Minot State Univ, 500 Univ Ave W, Minot, ND 58707-0001. **EMAIL** mcatel@hotmail.com

CATHEY, JAMES E.
DISCIPLINE LINGUISTICS **EDUCATION** Oregon State Univ, BS, 62; Univ Wash, MA, 64, PhD, 67. **CAREER** Prof. **RESEARCH** Germanic synchronic and historical phonology; Finnish phonology. **SELECTED PUBLICATIONS** Auth, "Manner Features and Finnish Gradation," in The Nordic Languages and Modern Linguistics 7, ed. Jonna Louis-Jensen and Johan Hendrik W. Poulssen (Torshavn, 92), 173-181; auth, "Give us this day our daily rad, " J of English and Germanic Philology 94 (95): 157-175; auth, "Die Rhetorik der Weisheit und Beredheit im Heliand," Literaturwissenschaftliches Jahrbuch, N.F. 37 (96): 31-46; auth, "Vom Analphabetentum zum Schreibeifer: Wulfila, di Goten und vergleichbare Entwicklungen," in Verschriftung - Verschriftlichung: Aspekte des medienwechsels in verschiedenen Kulturen und Epochen, ed. Ursula Schaefer (98), 88-98; auth, "Variation and Reduction in Modern Faroese Vowels," in Gedenkschrift fur Otmar Werner, ed. Heinz Klingenberg and Damaris Nubling (98), 91-100; auth, "Interpretatio Christiana Saxonica: redefinition for re-education," in Interdigitations: Essays for Irmengard Rauch, ed. Gerald Carr, et al, (99), 163-172; auth, "When Languages Mesh: Teenage speech in Helsingfors/Helsinki," Interdisciplinary J for Germanic Linguistics and Semiotic Analysis, 00. **CONTACT ADDRESS** Germanic Languages, Univ of Massachusetts, Amherst, Amherst, MA 01003. **EMAIL** cathey@german.umass.edu

CATTO, BONNIE A.
PERSONAL Born 04/19/1951, Boston, MA, m, 1975 **DISCIPLINE** CLASSICS **EDUCATION** Mt Holyoke Col, AB, 73; Univ Penn, MA, 76, PhD, 81. **CAREER** Vis lectr, Univ Mass Amherst, 78; instr, 78-81, asst prof, 81-87, assoc prof, 87-88, Mt Holyoke Col; vis assoc prof, Middlebury Col, 88-89; assoc prof, 89-97, prof, 97-, classics, Assumption Col. **HONORS AND AWARDS** Fully funded sabbatical, Assumption Col, 95-96; Sloan Found grant, 86; Phi Beta Kappa; Mary Lyon Scholar; Sarah Williston scholar. **MEMBERSHIPS** Amer Philol Asn; Archaeol Inst of Amer; Classical Asn of New England; Vergilian Soc; Pioneer Valley Classical Asn; Classical Asn of Mass. **RESEARCH** Lucretius; Ancient science; Vergil; Lyric & Elegiac poetry; Greek tragedy. **SELECTED PUBLICATIONS** Rev, Lucy Hutchinson's Translation of Lucretius: De Rerum Natura, The New England Classical Jour, 98; auth, Lucretius. Selections from De Rerum Natura, Bolchazy-Carducci Publ, 98; auth, Lucretian Light: Bacon's Debt to Lucretius and Epicurus, New England Classical Jour, 98; auth, The Wedding of Peleus and Thetis, Athenaze Newsletter, 97; auth, Selections from Lucretius' De Rerum Natura, The Classical Asn of New England, Short Greek and Latin Texts for Students, 96; rev, Musical Design in Sophoclean Theater, The New England Classical Jour, 96; auth, Duals, Athenaze Newsletter, 94; **CONTACT ADDRESS** Dept of Foreign Languages, Assumption Col, 500 Salisbury St., Worcester, MA 01609-1296. **EMAIL** bcatto@eve.assumption.edu

CAUFIELD, CARLOTA
PERSONAL 1 child **DISCIPLINE** SPANISH **EDUCATION** Univ Havana, Cuba, MA, 79; San Francisco State Univ, MA, 86; Tulane Univ, New Orleans, PhD, 92. **CAREER** Assoc prof; Mills Col, 92-. **RESEARCH** 20th century Spanish and Latin American poetry; contemporary literature of Spain and Latin America; Hispanic cultures; Hispanic writers in the US; feminist critical theories. **SELECTED PUBLICATIONS** Auth, A las puertas del papel con amoroso fuego, Torremozas, Madrid, 96; ed, Literary and Cultural Journeys: Selected Letters to Arturo Torres-Rioseco, Ctr for the Bk, Oakland, 95; Book of XXXIX Steps, a poetry game of discovery and imagination, Hyperbk for the Macintosh, 5 Diskettes, Mobile, Alabama: Intelibks, 95; Estrofas de papel, barro y tinta, Cafe Central, Barcelona, 95; Visual Games for Words & Sounds. Hyperpoems for the Macintosh, Diskette. Intelibks, San Francisco, 93; bk column, Resenas, 92-95, Tiempo Latino; bk rev(s) for, lit mag Lateral, Barcelona, 95-; contribur to anthologies, Diez jovenes poetas que inspiran en espanol, INTI, 90; Looking for Home, Women Writing about Exile, Milkweed Ed(s), 90; Bridges to Cuba, Michigan Quart Rev, 94; These are not Sweet Girls, Poetry by Latin Amer Women, White Pine Press, 94; Poesea cubana: la isla entera, Betania, 95; Poesea hispano-caribena escrita en Estados Unidos, Fundacion Federico Garcea Lorca, 95 & Poeseda, An Anthology of AIDS Poetry from the US, Latin Am and Spain, Ollantay Press, 95; contribur of poetry to, Haight Ashbury Lit J; Luz en arte y literatura; Lyra, Linden Lane Mage; Mich Quart Rev; Poetry San Francisco: Termino Mag; Tex Rev; Visions & Walrus; contribur essays to, ANQ; Poet's Market; Revista Iberoamericana; Middlebury Col Rev; Chasqui; La Torre; Alba de America; El gato tuerto & Bohemia; ed, International online journal Corner. **CONTACT ADDRESS** Dept of Modern Language and Literature, Mills Col, 5000 MacArthur Blvd, Oakland, CA 94613-1301. **EMAIL** amach@mills.edu

CAUJOLLE, CLAUDE
DISCIPLINE FRENCH LINGUISTICS AND PHONOLOGY **EDUCATION** PA State Univ, PhD. **CAREER** Instr, Hollins Col, 72. **RESEARCH** Tchg of French grammar. **SELECTED PUBLICATIONS** Auth, Plaisir de Lire; See Me Read. **CONTACT ADDRESS** PO Box 9692, Roanoke, VA 24020.

CAUVIN, JEAN-PIERRE BERNARD
PERSONAL Born 02/25/1936, Casablanca, Morocco, m, 1963, 2 children **DISCIPLINE** FRENCH LANGUAGE & LITERATURE **EDUCATION** Princeton Univ, BA, 57, PhD, 68. **CAREER** Lectr, Harvard Univ, 63-66; asst prof, Princeton Univ, 66-72; Assoc Prof French, Univ TX Austin, 72-85, Prof 85-, Chmn, 85-94, Consult French lit, Col Entrance Exam Bd, 76-90; Chief reader, AP Program French, 92-96. **HONORS AND AWARDS** Officier de l'ordre des Palmes Academiques, 93. **MEMBERSHIPS** MLA; SCent Mod Lang Asn; Am Asn Tchr(s) Fr; Soc Professeurs Fr Am. **RESEARCH** Nineteenth and twentieth century French poetry; Surrealism. **SELECTED PUBLICATIONS** Auth, Henri Bosco et la Poetique du Sacre, Klincksieck, Paris, 74; contribr, Le reel et l'imaginaire dans l'oeuvre de Henri Bosco, Jose Corti, Paris, 76; Poems of Andre Breton: A Bilingual Anthology (with M.A. Caws), Univ of Tex Press, 82; Co-ed, Panache Litteraire: Textes du monde francophone, 3rd ed, Heinle & Heinle, 94. **CONTACT ADDRESS** Dept of Fr & Ital, Univ of Texas, Austin, Austin, TX 78712-1197. **EMAIL** jpcauvin@mail.utexas.edu

CAVALLARI, HECTOR MARIO
DISCIPLINE HISPANIC STUDIES **EDUCATION** San Francisco State Univ, BA, 69; Univ Calif at Irvine, MA, 72, PhD, 72. **CAREER** Prof; Mills Col, 86-. **RESEARCH** Contemporary Latin American literature; Hispanic cultures; literary criticism; critical theory, Hispanic cinema. **SELECTED PUBLICATIONS** Auth, La practica de la escritura. Concepcion, Chile: Ediciones LAR, 90; Leopoldo Marechal: El espacio de los signos. Xalapa, Mexico: Univ Vercruzana, 82; Antigona Velez: Justicialismo y obra dramatica, Gestos 10 20, 95; coauth, Escritura y desfetichizacion: En torno a El perseguidor, de Julio Cortazar, Revista de Critica Literaria Latinoamericana XXII, 96; bk contrib, Textualidadm modelacion, descentramiento: Notas sobre el proceso critico, In El puente de las palabras, Wash, EUA: Interamer/OEA, 94; Leopoldo marechal: ideologia, escritura, compromiso, In Ensaos de literatura europea e hispanoamericana, San Sebastian: Editorial de la Univ del Pais Vasco, 90; Liliana Heker: (d)enunciar el orden, In Commemorative Ser, Essays in Honor of Seymour Menton, Riverside: Univ Calif, 91; nJulio Cortazar: Todos los juegos el juego, In Los ochenta mundos de Julio Cortazar, Madrid: Edi-6, 87; El agape de la escritura, In Homenaje a Leopoldo marechal, Buenos Aires: Corregidor, Articles: La tramoya de la escritura en La invencion de Morel, de Adolfo Bioy Casares, Bull Hisp Stud, Liverpool, UK 74, 97; La literatura latinoamericana: Busqueda problematica de una voz propia, Alba de Am 14, 96. **CONTACT ADDRESS** Dept of Hispanic Studies, Mills Col, 5000 MacArthur Blvd, Oakland, CA 94613-1301.

CAVALLO, JOANN
PERSONAL Born 05/21/1959, Summit, NJ **DISCIPLINE** ITALIAN **EDUCATION** Rutgers Univ, BA, 81; Yale Univ, MA, 84, PhD, 87. **CAREER** Assoc prof of Ital, Columbia Univ, 93- ; Dir, Columbia Univ Summer Prog In Scandiano (ITALY), 95-. **HONORS AND AWARDS** Nat Ital Am Found Schol, 86; Columbia Univ Coun for Res in the Humanities, 89-90. **MEMBERSHIPS** Renaissance Soc of Am. **RESEARCH** Italian Renaissance lit and hist. **SELECTED PUBLICATIONS** Auth, Boiardo's "Orlando Innamorato": An Ethics of Desire, 93; L'Orlando Furioso nella critica anglo-americana 1986-1991, Lettere italiane, 93; "Purgatorio 24", Dante's Divine Comedy: Introductory Readings II: Purgatorio, 93; Elsa Morante and the Adventures of Caterina, Forum Italicaum, 94; Paradiso 2, Dante's "Paradiso": Introductory Readings, 95; Fortune and Romance: Boiardo in America, 98; L'Orlando Innamorato come speculum principis, Il Boiardo e il mondo Estense nel Quattrocento: Atti del convegno internazionale di studi, Scandiano-Modena-Reggio Emilia-Ferrara, 98; auth, Armida: la funzione della donna-maga nell epica tassiana," in Torquato Tasso e la Cultura Estense, 99; auth, "Tasso's Armida and the Victory of Romance" in Renaissance Transactions: Ariosto and Tasso, 00; auth, "Joking Matters: Politics and Dissimulation in Castiglione's Book of the Courtier," Renaissance Quarterly, 00. **CONTACT ADDRESS** Columbia Univ, 1130 Amsterdam Ave, Hamilton Hall, Rm 514, New York, NY 10027. **EMAIL** jac3@columbia.edu

CAVIGIOLI, RITA C.
PERSONAL Born 01/10/1954, Turin, Italy, s **DISCIPLINE** ITALIAN LITERATURE **EDUCATION** Univ Turin, Laurea, 78; Univ Wash, MA, 80; UCLA, PhD, 93. **CAREER** Tchr,

Univ Wash, 78-80, Italian Leceo, 80-85, 89-96, UCLA, 85-87, 87-88, Univ Mo, 96-99; tchg asst consult, UCLA, 87. **HONORS AND AWARDS** Laurea cum laude, 78; Tchg Fel, 85-88, Res Assistantship Grant, 89, UCLA; British Council Scholar, 93, Univ E Anglia; EEC, 93, Glasgow-Turin. **MEMBERSHIPS** Modern Lang Asn; Am Asn Italian Stud; Am Asn Tchrs Italian; Am Italian Hist Asn; Immigration Hist Res Ctr. **RESEARCH** 19th/20th century literature; Italian language and culture; women's literature; autobiographical writing; pedagogical literature; migration narratives. **SELECTED PUBLICATIONS** Auth, By Airmail. Testo di letture e civilta inglese e americana, 90; auth, art, Introduction to Comic Language in the EFL Classroom. A Resource Pack for Teacher Trainers, 94; auth, La fatica di iniziare il libro. Problemi di autorita nel diario di Sibilla Aleramo, 95; auth, art, L'America va alle elementari. Tra cultura e immaginario, 96; auth, art, Tutto sta che l'insegnante abbia cuore e intelligenza: esercizio letterario ricerca pedagogica e professionalita femminile in un diario scolastico dell'Italia postunitaria, 98. **CONTACT ADDRESS** Dept of Romance Languages, Univ of Missouri, Columbia, Columbia, MO 65211. **EMAIL** langrita@showme.missouri.edu

CAWS, MARY ANN
PERSONAL Born 09/10/1933, Wilmington, NC, m, 1952, 2 children **DISCIPLINE** FRENCH LITERATURE; ENGLISH LITERATURE; COMPARATIVE LITERATURE **EDUCATION** Bryn Mawr Col, BA, 54; Yale Univ, MA, 56; Univ Kans, PhD, 62. **CAREER** Vis asst prof French, Univ Kans, 64; from asst prof to assoc prof, 66-74, Prof Romance Lang, Hunter Col & Grad Ctr, City Univ New York, 74-, Exec Off Comp Lit Phd Prog, 76-, Asst ed, French Rev, 70-; Guggenheim fel, 72-73; Fulbright-Hays sr travel res scholar, 72-73; ed, Dada/Surrealism, 72-; ed, Le Siecle eclate, 74; mem adv bd Western Europe, Fulbright-Hays Res Prog, 77-; Nat Endowment for Humanities fel, 79-80. **HONORS AND AWARDS** Guggenheim Fel, Fulbright Fel; NEH Sr Fel, NEH Summer Seminars; Phi Beta Kappa Vis Scholar; life mem of Clare Hall, Cambridge Univ; Getty Scholar; Rockefeller Found; Officier, Palmes Academiques. **MEMBERSHIPS** MLA, Asn Studies Dada & Surrealism, Am Asn Teachers Fr, Am Comp Lit Asn; Doctor of Humane Letters, Union Col, 83. **RESEARCH** Contemporary poetry; Dada and surrealism; poetics and literary theory translation. **SELECTED PUBLICATIONS** Auth, Robert Motherwell: What Art Holds, Columbia Univ Pr (New York), 95; auth, Carrington and Lytton/Alone Together, Cecil Woolf (London), 96; auth, Andre Breton, Revisited, Twayne (New York), 96; auth, The Surrealist Look: An Erotics of Encounter, MIT Pr (Cambridge), 97; auth, Surrealism and the Art of Display, Wexner Center, 97; auth, Bloomsbury and France: Art and Friends, Oxford Univ Pr, 99; auth, Picasso's Weeping Woman: The Life and Art of Dora Maar, Little Brown/Bulfinch, 00; ed, The Surrealist Painters and Poets, MIT Pr, (Cambridge), 01; ed, Manifesto: A Century of Isms., Univ of Nebr Pr (Lincoln), 01. **CONTACT ADDRESS** Ph.D. Program in French, Graduate Sch and Univ Ctr, CUNY, 365 Fifth Ave, New York, NY 10016. **EMAIL** cawsma@aol.com

CAZENAVE, ODILE
DISCIPLINE FRANCOPHONE LITERATURE **EDUCATION** Strousburg Univ, BA, 82; MA, 83; Pa State Univ, MA, 85; PhD, 88. **CAREER** Adj assoc prof, French, Univ Tenn; vis assoc prof, French, MIT. **HONORS AND AWARDS** Exec Counc, African Lit Asn, 95- . **SELECTED PUBLICATIONS** Auth, "Femmes rebelles: Naissance d'un nouveau roman africain au feminin, L'Harmattwan, 96. **CONTACT ADDRESS** Dept of Mod For Langs & Lits, Univ of Tennessee, Knoxville, 701 McClung Tower & Plaza, Knoxville, TN 37996. **EMAIL** ocazenav@utk.edu; odile@mit.edu

CERE, RONALD
DISCIPLINE INTERNATIONAL STUDIES, SPANISH **EDUCATION** CUNY, City Col, BA, 66; CUNY, Quebec Col, MA, 69; New York Univ, PhD, 74. **CAREER** Teach, Isaac Remsen Sch, 66-70; teach, Law HS, 70-71; adj asst prof, CUNY, 71-75; asst prof, SUNY, 75-77; asst prof, Univ Texas, 77-78; asst prof, Univ Illinois, 78-80; asst prof, Univ Nebraska, 80-83; asst prof, Gettysburg Col, 83-85; prof, East Michigan Univ, 85-. **HONORS AND AWARDS** Int Cult Hon Dip; Who's Who in World, Am, Am Teach; James C Healy Awd; Fac Appre Awd. **MEMBERSHIPS** AATSP; SCLT; ACTFL; MLA; SIETR; ASTD. **RESEARCH** Applied Spanish language; Hispanic literature and culture; Spanish for special purposes, education, law, business, health sciences, international affairs, social work, literature, intercultural communication. **SELECTED PUBLICATIONS** Auth, Exito comercial: Practicas administrativas y contextos culturales, Holt Rhinehart Winston (Ft Worth, TX), 00; auth, Exito comercial: Cuaderno de correspondencia y documentos comerciales, Holt Rhinehart Winston (Ft Worth, TX), 00; auth, "Bridging Differences: Cross-cultural Training Techniques for Working Successfully with Hispanic Employees," McGraw Hill (NY), 96; auth, "Cross-cultural Communication Training," in the American Association of Teachers of Spanish and Portuguese's Training Manual of Spanish and Portuguese for Business and the Professions (Lincolnwood, IL: Nat Textbook Co, 97). **CONTACT ADDRESS** Dept Foreign Language, Eastern Michigan Univ, 219 Alexander Hall, Ypsilanti, MI 48197. **EMAIL** fla_cere@online.emichu.edu

CERF, STEVEN ROY
PERSONAL Born 10/09/1945, New York, NY **DISCIPLINE** GERMAN, COMPARATIVE LITERATURE **EDUCATION** Queens Col, City Univ New York, BA, 66; Yale Univ, MPh, 71, PhD(Ger), 75. **CAREER** Teaching asst Ger, Yale Univ, 69-70, instr, 70-71; Nat Endowment Humanities fel in residence for col teachers, Ind Univ, 78-79; instr, Bowdoin Col, 71-75; asst prof, Bowdoin Col, 75-82; assoc prof, Bowdoin Col, 82-90; Skolfield Prof, Bowdoin Col, 90-. **MEMBERSHIPS** MLA; Am Asn Teachers Ger; Northeast Mod Lang Asn; Arthur Schnitzler Res Asn; Thomas Mann Ges. **RESEARCH** Thomas Mann; Hugo von Hofmannsthal; Georg Brandes. **SELECTED PUBLICATIONS** Auth, In a New Light--Wagner Buhnenweihfestpiel-Wagner, Wieland 1951 Parsifal Introduced the Postwar Bayreuth Style, Opera News, Vol 0059, 95; Against Fascism--Exile-Literature as History, Colloquia Ger, Vol 0027, 94; Hofmannsthal or the Geometry of the Subject--Psychostructural and Iconographic Studies of the Prose Works, Colloquia Ger, Vol 0025, 92; Music and German Literature--Their Relationship Since the Middle-Ages, Colloquia Ger, Vol 0026, 93; Opera and the Culture of Fascism, Opera News, Vol 0061, 97; Wagner, Richard and the Anti-Semitic Imagination, Ger Quart, Vol 0069, 96; Taming Hansel und Gretel for Opera--Background to Humperdinck Composition-Too Grimm for Words, Opera News, Vol 0061, 96; False Dawn--Wagnerian Problemdichtung-How Hans-Sachs Warning at the End of Die 'Meistersinger' Echoes Through German History, Opera News, Vol 0057, 93; The Films of Wenders, Wim--Cinema as Vision and Desire, German Quart, Vol 0067, 94; Against Fascism--Exile-Literature as History, Colloquia Ger, Vol 0027, 94; Rheingold's Curse--Tracing This Wagner Works Troubled Early Performance History, Opera News, Vol 0061, 97; Undertones of Insurrection--Music, Politics, and the Social Sphere in the Modern German Narrative, Jour English and Ger Philol, Vol 0094, 95; The Problematic Bourgeois-20th-Century Criticism on Mann,Thomas Buddenbrooks and The Magic Mountain, Colloquia Ger, Vol 0028, 95. **CONTACT ADDRESS** Dept of Ger, Bowdoin Col, 7700 College Station, Brunswick, ME 04011-8477. **EMAIL** scerf@bowdoin.edu

CHAFFEE-SORACE, DIANE
PERSONAL m, 2 children **DISCIPLINE** SPANISH **EDUCATION** Wells Col, BA, 73; Duke Univ, MA, 75, PhD, 79. **CAREER** Teach asst, Duke Univ, 75-77; lectr, SUNY, Stony Brook, 77- 80; asst prof, Univ Va, 80-82; lectr, Washington Univ, 82-85; asst prof, 86-90, assoc prof, 91-, chair, dept mod langs & lits, 97-, Loyola Col; **HONORS AND AWARDS** Phi Beta Kappa. **MEMBERSHIPS** Modern Lang Asn of Am, South Atlantic Modern Lang Asn of Am, Am Asn of the Teachers of Spanish and Portuguese, Sigma Delta Pi. **RESEARCH** Spanish golden age poetry and prose, visual art in literature, pedagogy. **SELECTED PUBLICATIONS** Auth, "Gongora's Mientras por competir con tu cabello': Further Thoughts on Imitation and Chronology," Studies in Modern and Classical Languages and Literatures 1, Select Proceedins of the Southeastern Conference, ed Fidel Lopez Criado (Madrid: Editorial Origenes, 87), 39-47; auth, Gongora's Poetic Textual Tradition: An Analysis of Selected Variants, Versions and Imitations of His Shorter Poems, London: Tamesis, 88; auth, "Ekphrastic and Theatrical Interior Duplication: Irony and Verisimilitude in Don Qui jote's Adventure with the Basque," Romanische Forschungen, (89): 208-20; auth, " A Poetic Feast: Food Images in Gongora's Satirical and Burlesque Poems," Symposium, (90): 128-39; auth, "Animal Imagery in Lope de Vega's Fuente Ovejuna," Bulletin of the Comediantes, (90): 199-214; auth, Personalities: A Conversational Review Technique Across Languages, coauthored with L.Z. Morgan and C. Savell, Canadian Modern Language Review, (92): 610-13; auth, "Practicing the Subjunctive with Cards," Canadian Modern Language Review , (95): 115-20; auth, "Dresser, the Lamp, and the Oven: An Activity ofr Learning and Practicing House-Related Vocabulary," coauthored with Baiba Abrams, Canadian Modern Language Review, (95): 127-31; auth, "Computer Pen Pals: Writing Activities for Students for Foreign Languages," Canadian Modern Language Review, (99): 351-54; auth, "Gongora's Poetic Textual Tradition: Threee Representative Works," Revista de Estudios Hispanicos, (00): 107-21. **CONTACT ADDRESS** Dept of Mod Langs, Lit, Loyola Col, 4501 N Charles St, Baltimore, MD 21210-2699.

CHAIKA, ELAINE OSTRACH
PERSONAL Born 12/20/1934, Milford, MA, m, 1960, 3 children **DISCIPLINE** LINGUISTICS **EDUCATION** RI Col, BEd, 60; Brown Univ, MAT, 65; PhD, 72 **CAREER** Teacher, Mill Sch, Eastbrook, Maine, 54-55, Veteran's High Sch, Warwick, RI, 60-61 & George S West Jr High Sch, Providence, RI, 61-62; instr English, Bryant Col, 66-67; asst prof, 71-74, assoc prof, 75-78, Prof Ling, Providence Col, 78-. **HONORS AND AWARDS** Nat Endowment for Humanities fel, 82; Who's Who Among Am Tchr, 94; Outstanding Scholar Awd, Am Asn of Univ Prof, 94; Fulbright fel, Norway, 94-95; sabbatical res, Brit's Nat Inst of Psychiat and Broadmoor Hosp, 96; consult linguist, SUNY Stony Brook Div of Psychiat Res; consult linguist, Oxford Univ/Dept of Psychiat. **MEMBERSHIPS** Am Dialect Soc; Ling Soc Am; MLA. **RESEARCH** Schizophrenic language; deviant linguistic productions; sociolinguistics. **SELECTED PUBLICATIONS** Grammars and Teaching, Col English, 78, reprinted, In: Readings in Applied English Linguistics, 82; Response to Bowden, Col English, 40: 370-374; Jargons and Language Change, Anthropological Ling, 2/80; How Shall a discourse be understood, Discourse Proc, 4: 71-87; Review of Zeleman Making Sense of it, Col Commun & Compos, 2/81; Language: The Social Mirror, Newbury House, 10/82; A unified explanation for the deverse structural deviations in the speech of adult schizophrenics, J Commun Disorders, 15: 167-189; auth, Understanding Psychotic Speech: Understanding Psychotic Speech, Chas C. Thomas, 94; auth, Language: the Social Mirror, Heinle & Heinle, 94; auth, On analysing schizophrenic speech: what model should we use?, Speech and Language Disorders in Psychiatry, Gaskell, 94; auth, Intention, attention, and schizophrenic speech, Commun and the Mentally Ill Patient, Jessica Kingsley Pub, 97. **CONTACT ADDRESS** Dept of Ling, Providence Col, 549 River Ave, Providence, RI 02918-0002. **EMAIL** echaika@providence.edu

CHAITIN, GILBERT D.
DISCIPLINE FRENCH LITERATURE **EDUCATION** Princeton Univ, PhD, 69. **CAREER** Prof. **RESEARCH** Psychoanalytic theory of narrative; Lacan's teachings about the relation of subjectivity to language; psychoanalytic notions of identity in relation to language and culture. **SELECTED PUBLICATIONS** Auth, Rhetoric and Culture in Lacan, 96; pubs on Chretien de Troyes, Dostoyevski, Zola, Stendhal, Hugo, Renan, Camus, Lacan, comparative literature, literature and psychoanalysis; co-ed, Romantic Revolutions, 90. **CONTACT ADDRESS** Dept of French and Italian, Indiana Univ, Bloomington, 1020 E Kirkwood Ave, Ballantine Hall 642, Bloomington, IN 47405. **EMAIL** chaitin@indiana.edu

CHAMBERLIN, JOHN
DISCIPLINE PIERS PLOWMAN; ARTS OF DISCOURSE, ANCIENT; MODERN **EDUCATION** Haverford, BA; Toronto, MA, PhD. **CAREER** Asst Prof **SELECTED PUBLICATIONS** Auth, Increase and Multiply: Arts-of-Discourse Procedure in the Preaching of Donne, 76; What Makes Piers Plowman so hard to read?; The Rule of St. Benedict: The Abingdon Copy , 82; International Development Education in the English Classroom. **CONTACT ADDRESS** Dept English, Wilfrid Laurier Univ, 75 University Ave W, Waterloo, ON, Canada N2L 3C5. **EMAIL** jchamber@mach1.wlu.cas

CHAMBERLIN, V. A.
PERSONAL Born 07/18/1924, Topeka, KS, m, 1955, 2 children **DISCIPLINE** SPANISH LITERATURE **EDUCATION** Wasburh Univ Topeka, AB, 49; Univ Kans, MA, 53; PhD, 57. **CAREER** Fredonia High School kans, 49-51; Pembroke Country Day School Kans City, 51-53; instr, Univ Calif Los Angeles, 57-59; asst to assoc prof, Okla State Univ, 59-63; assoc prof, 63-68; prof, Univ Kans, 68-96. **MEMBERSHIPS** MLA; Am Asn of Tchr of Spanish and Portuguese. **RESEARCH** Perez Galdos; 19th Century Spanish Literature; Hispano-Russian literary relations; Color Symbolism; Animal Imagery; Humor. **SELECTED PUBLICATIONS** Auth, Two Character-Creating Servants: Nina in Gomez de la Avellaneda's El Artista barqueeero and Benina in Galdo's Misericordia, in Romance Quart, 94; Erotic Equine Imagery: a Time-Honored Communicative Metaphor in Spanish Literature, in Studies in Honor of Gilberto Paolini, 96; auth, "Horsing Around in Spanish Literature: Women Writers and the Erotic Equine," in Letras Peninsulares, 99; auth, "The Perils of Interpreting Fotunata's Dream," in Anales Galdosianos, 99; auth, "Nicknames as Artistic Technique in 'La Regenta'," in Anales Galdosianos,99. **CONTACT ADDRESS** Dept of Spanish and Portuguese, Univ of Kansas, Lawrence, Lawrence, KS 66045. **EMAIL** vachamb@ukans.edu

CHAMBERS, J. K.
PERSONAL Born 07/12/1938, Grimsby, ON, Canada **DISCIPLINE** LINGUISTICS **EDUCATION** Univ Windsor, BA, 61; Queen's Univ, MA, 63; Univ Alta, PhD, 70. **CAREER** Asst prof, 70-75, assoc prof, 75-82, PROF LINGUISTICS, UNIV TORONTO, 82-; vis fel Univ Reading(Eng), 76-77, 83-84, 90-91; Hong Kong Univ 97. **SELECTED PUBLICATIONS** Auth, Sociolinguistic Theory: Language Variation and Its Social Significance 95; coauth, A Very Small Rebellion 77; Dialectology 80, 2nd ed, 98; ed, Canadian English 75; The Languages of Canada 79; co-ed, Dialects of English 91. **CONTACT ADDRESS** Dept of Linguistics, Univ of Toronto, Toronto, ON, Canada M5S 3H1. **EMAIL** chambers@chass.utoronto.ca

CHAMBERS, MORTIMER HARDIN
PERSONAL Born 01/09/1927, Saginaw, MI, m, 1973, 3 children **DISCIPLINE** CLASSICAL PHILOLOGY **EDUCATION** Harvard, AB, 49, PhD, 54; Oxford, MA, 55. **CAREER** Instr, classics, Harvard, 54-55; asst prof, history and Greek, Univ Chicago, 55-58; asst prof, assoc prof, prof History, UCLA, 58-. **HONORS AND AWARDS** Rhodes Scholarship; Fulbright Scholarship. **MEMBERSHIPS** Am Hist Asn; Am Philol Asn. **RESEARCH** Greek history; history of classical scholarship. **SELECTED PUBLICATIONS** Auth, Aristotle's History of Athenian Democracy, with J Day, Berkeley-Los Angeles, 62; Polybius, selections trans, ed, E Badian, New York, 66; The Western Experience, with four coauthors, New York, 74, ed 7, 98; Aristotelis Athenaion Politeia, Leipzig, 86, ed 2, 94; Georg Busolt, His Career in His Letters, Leiden, 90; Aristot-

le, Staat der Athener, Berlin-Darmstadt, 90; George Grote's History of Greece, in: George Grote Reconsidered, Hildesheim, 96; Athens' Alliance with Egesta in the Year of Antiphon, with R Galluci-P Spanos, Zeitschrift fur Papyrologie und Epigraphik 83, 90; The Reception of Gibbon in the New World, in: Imperium Romanum, Festschrift for Karl Christ, Stuttgart, 98. **CONTACT ADDRESS** Dept of History, Univ of California, Los Angeles, Los Angeles, CA 90024-1473. **EMAIL** chambers@history.ucla.edu

CHAMPAGNE, ROLAND A.
PERSONAL Born 05/19/1946, m, 1 child **DISCIPLINE** FRENCH **EDUCATION** Ohio State Univ, PhD, 74. **CAREER** Asst prof to prof, Univ of Mo Saint Louis, 75-. **HONORS AND AWARDS** NEH stipend, 76; Chancellor's Awd, Univ Mo Saint Louis, 96. **MEMBERSHIPS** Women in French, AATF: AAUP: International Soc for Philso and Lit. **RESEARCH** The interdisciplinary stakes of the ethics, ideologies, and aesthetics of reading culturally embedded texts. **SELECTED PUBLICATIONS** Auth Philippe Sollers, 96; auth, Georges Bataille, 98; auth, "Hannah Arendt," Idealistic Studies (98); auth, The Ethics of Reading According to Emmanuel Levinas, 98; auth, "Barthes the Pianist," Semiotica (99); auth, "On Italo Svevo," Italliana (99). **CONTACT ADDRESS** Dept Foreign Lang, Univ of Missouri, St. Louis, 8001 Natural Bridge Rd, Saint Louis, MO 63121-4401. **EMAIL** rachampagne@msn.com

CHANDOLA, ANOOP C.
PERSONAL Born 12/24/1937, Pauri, India, m, 1963, 1 child **DISCIPLINE** LINGUISTICS **EDUCATION** Univ Allahabad, BA, 54; Univ Lucknow, MA, 56; Univ Cal, Berkeley, MA, 61; Univ Chicago, PhD, 66. **CAREER** Asst prof to prof, Univ Ariz, 63-. **HONORS AND AWARDS** AAFSA Outstand Fac Awd in Humanities. **MEMBERSHIPS** AAA; AAS; LSA; LSI. **RESEARCH** Human contact; ITS science 'contactics" and philosophy "contactism"; South Asian culture; literature and religion; ethno-musicology and folklore. **SELECTED PUBLICATIONS** Some Systems of Musical Scales and Linguistic Principles, Semiotica, 70; A Systematic Translation of Hindi-Urdu into English, Univ Ariz Press, 70; An Evolutionary Approach to Sentence Foramtion, Linguistics, 75; Folk Drumming in the Himalayas, 77 & Situation to Sentence, 79, AMS; The Way to Treu Worship, Univ Press of Am, 91; Contactics, Univ Press of Am, 92. **CONTACT ADDRESS** Dept Asian Studies, Univ of Arizona, Tucson, AZ 85721-0005. **EMAIL** chandola@u.arizonza.edu

CHANG, CECILIA
PERSONAL 1 child **DISCIPLINE** CHINESE **EDUCATION** Fu-jen Catholic Univ, BA; Univ Calif, Angeles, MA; Univ Mass, EDD. **CAREER** Lectr, Williams Col, 89-; vis lectr, Princeton Univ, 87 & Univ Mich, 88; head instr, Middlebury Chinese Summer Sch, 87-93; Princeton in Beijing Chinese Summer Prog, 94. **MEMBERSHIPS** Chinese Language Teaches Assoc. **RESEARCH** Chinese language pedagogy; applied linguistics, psycholiguistics. **SELECTED PUBLICATIONS** Auth, Computer workbook for Intermediate Reader in Modern Chinese, Princeton UP, 96. **CONTACT ADDRESS** Dept of Asian Studies, Williams Col, Williamstown, MA 01267. **EMAIL** CChang@williams.edu

CHANG, CHUN-SHU
PERSONAL Born 04/25/1934, Shantung, China, m, 1959, 3 children **DISCIPLINE** ANCIENT CHINESE HISTORY, CHINESE LANGUAGE **EDUCATION** Taiwan Univ, BA, 56; Harvard Univ, PhD(hist), 64. **CAREER** Res asst hist, Inst Hist & Philol, Acad Sinica, China, 56-57; lectr Chinese hist, Univ Iowa, 64; dir Far Eastern studies, Wis State Univ, 64-66; assoc prof, 66-73, prof, Hist, Univ Mich, 73- . **HONORS AND AWARDS** Am Coun Learned Soc res grant, 65-66; Soc Sci Res Coun res grant, 66-67; fel Acad Sinica, China; Rackham fac res grants, 67, 70-71, 72-73, 76; Warner G Rice Humanities Awd, Univ Mich, 77. **MEMBERSHIPS** AHA; Asn Asian Studies; Soc Ch'ing Studies; Social Studies Pre-Han China; Soc Sung Studies. **RESEARCH** Hist and civil of China, 1600 BC-1800 AD: sociocultural, intellectual-literary, military-diplomatic, historiography, science & technology **SELECTED PUBLICATIONS** Auth, Premodern China: A Bibliographical Introduction, Ann Arbor Publ, 71; coauth, The world of P'u Sungling's Liao-chai Chih-i: Literature and the intelligentsia during the Ming-Ch'ing dynastic transition, J Inst Chinese Studies, 73; auth, Han-tai pien-chiang shih lun-chi, Taipei, 74; The Making of China: Main Themes in Premodern Chinese History, Appleton, 74; coauth, K'ung Shang-jen and his T'ao-hua Shan: A dramatist's reflections on the Ming-Ch'ing Dynastic transition, J Inst Chinese Studies, 77; auth, Understanding China's international behavior: Old traditions and new perspectives, Mich Quart Rev, 77; Social Change and Military Expansion in Early Han China, Ann Arbor Publ, 78; South China in the Twelfth Century, Hong Kong & Ann Arbor, 78. **CONTACT ADDRESS** Dept of Hist, Univ of Michigan, Ann Arbor, 1029 Tisch Hall, 555 S State St, Ann Arbor, MI 48109-1003. **EMAIL** cschang@umich.edu

CHANG, KANG-I S.
PERSONAL Born 02/21/1944, Beijing, China, m, 1968, 1 child **DISCIPLINE** CHINESE LITERATURE **EDUCATION** Tunghai Univ, BA, 66; Rutgers, MLS, 71; SDak State Univ, MA, 72; Princeton Univ, PhD, 78; Yale Univ, MA, 91. **CAREER** Vis asst prof, Tufts Univ, 79-80; curator, Gest Oriental Libr, Princeton Univ, 80-81; asst prof to prof, Yale Univ, 82-. **HONORS AND AWARDS** Ch'en Kuo-Fu Fel, 63; Sun Yet-Sen Fel, 66-68; Whiting Fel, 77-78; Most Distinguished Alumni, Taiwan, 92; Wu Found Conf Grant, 92-93; CCK Found Grant, 92-93; NEH Grant, 92-93; A Whitney Griswold Awd, 93-94; Judge, Int Col Debate, 95; Imp Scholarly Works Awd, 97. **MEMBERSHIPS** AAS, ACLS, MLA, ICLA, Yale-China. **RESEARCH** Literary Theory and Criticism, Canon Formation, Critical Theory in Hermeneutics. **SELECTED PUBLICATIONS** Auth, The Evolution of Chinese Tz'u Poetry, Princeton Univ Pr, 80; auth, Six Dynasties Poetry, Princeton Univ Pr, 86; auth, The late-Ming Poet Ch'en Tzu-Lung, Yale Univ Pr, 91; auth, Articles and Occasional Essays from Qianxue Studio, Yunchen, 94; coed, Writing Women in Late Imperial China, Stanford Univ Pr, 97; auth, Feminist Readings, Classical and Modern Perspectives, Lianhe Wenxue, 98; coed, Women Writers of Traditional China, Stanford Univ Pr, 99; auth, Reflections on Yale, Gender and Culture, Shanghai Wenyi, 00. **CONTACT ADDRESS** East Asian Lang & Lit, Yale Univ, PO Box 208236, New Haven, CT 06520-8236. **EMAIL** kang-I.chang@yale.edu

CHARBRAN, H. RAFAEL
PERSONAL Born 02/02/1947, Monterey, CA **DISCIPLINE** HISTORY OF SCIENCE, HISTORY OF MEDICINE, LATINO STUDIES, SPANISH LITERATURE **CAREER** Asst prof, La State Univ, 83-85; asst prof to prof, Whittier Col, 85-. **HONORS AND AWARDS** Harry Nerhood Teach Excell Awd; Fulbright Fel; NEH; Albert and Elaine Borchard Found. **MEMBERSHIPS** MLA; ATSP; SLS; AHF. **RESEARCH** History of medicine; history of science; life and works of Miguel Unamuno, 1864-1936; life and works of Francisco Hernandez, 1515-1587. **SELECTED PUBLICATIONS** Co-ed, Latino Encyclopedia, 6 vols, Marshall Cavendish (NY), 96; contrib, The World of Dr Francisco Hernandez, Stanford Univ Press, 00. **CONTACT ADDRESS** Dept Modern Lang, Whittier Col, 13406 Philadelphia St, Whittier, CA 90601-4446. **EMAIL** rchabran@whittier.edu

CHARLEBOIS, LUCILE C.
PERSONAL Born Northampton, MA **DISCIPLINE** LANGUAGE, LITERATURE **EDUCATION** Our Lady Elms Col, BA, 69; Middlebury Col, MA, 70; Univ Mass at Amherst, PhD, 82. **CAREER** Asst prof, Univ of Nebr Lincoln, 82-88; tenured assoc prof, Univ of SC, 88-. **HONORS AND AWARDS** Listed in Who's Who Among America's Teachers. **RESEARCH** Peninsular Spanish Literature of the Twentieth-Century (with an emphasis on narrative and theatre), Literary Theory. **SELECTED PUBLICATIONS** Auth, "Camilo Jose Cela ante las candilejas: Maria Sabina y El carro de heno o el inventor de la guillotina," Anales de la Literatura Espanola Contemporanea 19.3 (94): 241-258; auth, Understanding Camilo Jose Cela, Univ of SC Press, 98; contribur, The Image of America, Univ of S Colo (Pueblo, CO), 99. **CONTACT ADDRESS** Dept Span, Ital, & Port, Univ of So Carolina, Columbia, Columbia, SC 29208.

CHARLES, MAY
PERSONAL Born 01/27/1949, Lethbridge, Alberta, Canada, m, 1971, 2 children **DISCIPLINE** COMPARATIVE LITERATURE **EDUCATION** Concordia Univ, Montreal, BA, 72; Univ Alberta, MA, 87; PhD, 94. **CAREER** Asst prof, Wheeling Jesuit Univ, 96-. **HONORS AND AWARDS** Izzak Walton Killam Memorial Doctoral Scholar, 88-89; Univ Alberta Grad Fac Fel, 89-90; SSHRC Doctoral Fel, 89-90; Ralph Steinhauer Awd of Distinction, 89-91; SSHRC Doctoral Fel, 90-91. **MEMBERSHIPS** Modern Lang Asn, Soc for the Study of narrative Lit, Can Semiotics Asn, Int Comparative Lit Asn, Can Comparative Lit Asn, Can Comparative Lit Asn. **RESEARCH** Narrative theory, fictional-world semantics. **SELECTED PUBLICATIONS** Rev of James Phelan, Reading People, Reading Plots. Character, Progression, and the Interpretation of Narrative, Can Rev of Comparative Lit 17.3/4 (Sept/Dec 90): 375-9; auth, "Fictional-World Semantics: the Next Stage," J of Lit Semantics, 22.1 (April 93): 24-44; auth, "A Postmodern Challenge to Reference-World Construction: Gilbert Sorption's Mulligan Stew," Style 29.2 (summer 95): 235-61; auth, "Historical Reality: From Fictional Construct to Actuality Revision," Cardinal Perspectives (96-97): 34-46; auth, "Reassessing Novelistic Realism: the Role of Interpretive Framework," Int Comp Lit Asn XVth Congress Proceedings (97), vol 5 Cultural Memory (forthcoming0. **CONTACT ADDRESS** Dept English & Langs, Wheeling Jesuit Univ, 316 Washington Ave, Wheeling, WV 26003-6243.

CHARNON-DEUTSCH, LOU
PERSONAL Born 07/02/1946, Freeport, IL, m, 1972 **DISCIPLINE** SPANISH STUDIES **EDUCATION** Mount Mary Col, BA, 68; Purdue Univ, MA, 71; Univ Chicago, PhD, 78. **CAREER** Asst prof to prof, SUNY Stony Brook, 80-; Chair 89-91; 99-00. **HONORS AND AWARDS** SUNY Fac Grant, 85; Presidents Awd for Excellence in Teaching, 90; Fac Travel Grant, SUNY, 87, 91, 92, 93; NEH Grant, 91; PDQWL Continuing Fac Awd, 93, 98; Ministry of Culture Res Grant, Spain, 95; Grant, Ministry of Culture, Spain, 99. **MEMBERSHIPS** Am Assoc of Teachers of Span and Port; MLA, Midwest MLA; Feministas Unidas; Teachers for a Democratic Cult; Asociacion Int de Hispanista. **RESEARCH** Spanish culture and literature, feminist theory. **SELECTED PUBLICATIONS** Auth, The Nineteenth-Century Spanish Short Story: Textual Strategies of a Genre in Evolution, Tamesis (Madrid), 85; auth, Gender and Representation: Women in Nineteenth-Century Spanish Realist Fiction, John Benjamins (Amsterdam), 90; ed, Estudios sobre escritoras hispanicas en honor de Georgina Sabat-Rivers, Castalia (Madric), 92; auth, Narratives of Desire: Nineteenth-Century Spanish Fiction by Women, Penn State Univ Pr, 94; coed, Culture and Gender in Nineteenth-Century Spain, Oxford Univ Pr, (London), 95; auth, Fictions of the Feminine in Nineteenth-Century Spanish Press, Penn State Pr, (University Park, 99. **CONTACT ADDRESS** Dept Hispanic Lang and Lit, SUNY, Stony Brook, 100 Nicolls Rd, Stony Brook, NY 11794-0002. **EMAIL** ldeutsch@notes.cc.sunsb.edu

CHATHAM, JAMES RAY
PERSONAL Born 11/11/1931, Caryville, FL, m, 1961, 1 child **DISCIPLINE** SPANISH PHILOLOGY **EDUCATION** Fla State Univ, BA, 53, MA, 56, PhD, 60. **CAREER** Instr mod lang, Miss State Univ, 57-59; assoc prof mod lang, 60-63, assoc prof Romance lang, Univ Ala, 63-64; Prof Foreign Lang & Head Dept, Miss State Univ, 64-, NDEA fel, Univ Tex, 62; mem bd dir, Am Coun Teaching Foreign Lang, 67-68. **MEMBERSHIPS** SAtlantic Mod Lang Asn; Am Asn Teachers Span & Port; Mediaeval Acad Am. **RESEARCH** Mediaeval Spanish language and literature; Golden Age drama. **SELECTED PUBLICATIONS** **CONTACT ADDRESS** Drawer FL, Mississippi State Univ, Mississippi State, MS 39762.

CHAUDERLOT, FABIENNE SOPHIE
PERSONAL Born 08/11/1960, Marseilles, France **DISCIPLINE** FRENCH **EDUCATION** Fac.des Sciences Humaines, MA, 83; Inst d' Administration des Entreprises, MBA, 85; San Diego State Univ, MA, 89; Univ Calif San Diego, PhD, 95. **CAREER** Lectr, Univ Calif, Riverside, 95-96; asst prof, Univ Puerto Rico, 96-97; asst prof, Wayne State Univ, 97-. **HONORS AND AWARDS** Grant, 97-98, Wayne State Univ; instructional excellence award, san diego commun col district, 88-89, 90-91; col of lib arts teaching award, 00. **MEMBERSHIPS** MLA; IAPL. **RESEARCH** 18TH Century French philosophy and literature; post structuralist french philosophy and theory. **CONTACT ADDRESS** Dept of Romance Languages, Wayne State Univ, 487 Manoogian, Detroit, MI 48202. **EMAIL** f.chauderlot@wayne.edu

CHAUDRON, CRAIG
PERSONAL Born 06/30/1946, St Louis, MO, m, 1990, 3 children **DISCIPLINE** APPLIED LINGUISTCS, ESL **EDUCATION** Wabash Col, BA, 68; Univ Toronto, MEd, 77; PhD, 82. **HONORS AND AWARDS** MLA K.S. Mildenberger Awd, 89; Mellon Fel, 90, 97-98. **MEMBERSHIPS** AAAL; TESOL. **RESEARCH** Classroom research, research methodology, psycholinguistics, second language learning. **SELECTED PUBLICATIONS** Auth, Second Language Classrooms, Cambridge Univ Pr, 88; auth, "Academic listening", A Guide for Teaching Second Lanauge, eds D. Mendelsohn and J. Rubin; coauth, "Discourse markedness and structural markedness", Studies in Second Language Acquisition 12.1 (90): 43-64; auth, Listening, Dominie, (San Diego), 95. **CONTACT ADDRESS** Dept English As A Second Lang, Univ of Hawaii, Manoa, 1890 E West Rd, Honolulu, HI 96822-2318. **EMAIL** chaudron@hawaii.edu

CHAVY, PAUL
PERSONAL Born 07/19/1914, Saint-Florent, France, m, 1938, 2 children **DISCIPLINE** FRENCH LANGUAGE AND LITERATURE **EDUCATION** Univ Paris, Agrege des Let, 42. **CAREER** Head dept, 48-69, prof, 48-80, Emer Prof French, Dalhousie Univ, 80-, Officier de l'Instruction Publique, 56; Chevalier, Legion d'Honneur, 65. **MEMBERSHIPS** Can Comp Lit Asn (pres, 71-73). **RESEARCH** History of translations. **SELECTED PUBLICATIONS** Auth, Traducteurs d'autrefois, Moyen Age et Renaissance: dictionnaire des traducteurs et de la littaerature traduite en ancien et moyen francais (842-1600), ; auth, Dictionnaire des Traducteurs et de la Litterature Traduite en Ancien et Moyen Francais 842-1600, 88. **CONTACT ADDRESS** Dept of French Studies, Dalhousie Univ, 6209 Univ Ave, Halifax, NS, Canada B3H 3J5.

CHELKOWSKI, PETER JAN
PERSONAL Born 07/10/1933, Lubliniec, Poland, m, 1961, 2 children **DISCIPLINE** NEAR EASTERN LANGUAGES AND LITERATURES **EDUCATION** Jagiellonian Univ, MA, 58; Univ Tehran, PhD(lit), 68. **CAREER** Assoc prof Near Eastern Lang & Lit, 68-75, prof Persian and Iranian studies & chmn near eastern lang & lit, dir ctr near eastern studies, 75-78, Prof Near Eastern Studies, NY Univ, 78- **MEMBERSHIPS** Mid Eastern Studies Asn; Am Orient Soc; Coun Nat Lit. **RESEARCH** Persian religious drama; Persian literature; theatre, drama and literature in the Near East. **SELECTED PUBLICATIONS** Auth, Community Process and the Performance of Muharram Observances in Trinidad--Tdr-The Drama Review-Jour Performance Stud, Vol 0038, 94. **CONTACT ADDRESS** Kevorkian Ctr for Near Eastern Studies, New York Univ, 50 Washington Sq South, New York, NY 10003.

CHEN, JINGSONG
PERSONAL Born 04/07/1959, Jiangsu, China, m, 1988, 2 children **DISCIPLINE** CHINESE LITERATURE AND LANGUAGE **EDUCATION** The Jangzou Normal Coll China, BA, 81; Acad of China Arts Beijing, MA, 84; Univ Calif Riverside, PhD, 92. **CAREER** Res, The Acad of Chinese Arts, 84-86; CT interpreter, 89-; lectr, Univ Calif Riverside, 92-. **HONORS AND AWARDS** Outstanding Tchg Asst, Univ Calif Riverside, 92; First Prize Chinese Prose Contest Chicago, 97; Interpreter of the Year, New World Lang Service Riverside, 97. **MEMBERSHIPS** Asian Study Asn; Calif Interpreter Asn. **RESEARCH** Comparative Drama; Dramatic Theories and Criticism. **SELECTED PUBLICATIONS** Auth, Qingshan Shaonian Shi, 97; numerous articles in Chinese and English. **CONTACT ADDRESS** Dept of Literature and Languages, Univ of California, Riverside, Riverside, CA 92521. **EMAIL** Jingsong.Chen@ucr.edu

CHEN, LILLY
DISCIPLINE LINGUISTICS, CHINESE LANGUAGE **EDUCATION** Nat Taiwan Univ, BA; Univ IL, Champaign-Urbana, MA, PhD. **CAREER** Hon vis lectr, Hebei Agr Univ, 83, 84; lectr, Rice Univ. **HONORS AND AWARDS** Shu Juan Awd, Nat Taiwan Univ; Fulbright scholar. **RESEARCH** The great Chinese novel Hung-lou meng (Dream of the Red Chamber). **SELECTED PUBLICATIONS** Publ work includes articles in the J of Chinese Ling and the J of Decorative Art, as well as the publ(s) of the Chicago Ling Soc, the Berkeley Ling Soc. **CONTACT ADDRESS** Rice Univ, PO Box 1892, Houston, TX 77251-1892. **EMAIL** lchen@rice.edu

CHEN, ZHIYUAN
PERSONAL Born, China, d **DISCIPLINE** LINGUISTICS **EDUCATION** Beijing For Lang Univ, BA, 66; Nat Cultural Admin Inst, BA, 85; Mexico Nat Anthrop Inst, MA, 82; Univ Minn, MA, 88; PhD, 95. **CAREER** Instr, Lakewood Community Col, 92-95; vis asst prof, Fort Hays State Univ, 95-96; asst prof Appalachian State Univ, 95-. **HONORS AND AWARDS** Grants, Univ of Minn, 87; 90, 92; Grant, Fort Hays State Univ, 96-97; Grants, Appalachian State Univ, 96-97; 98, 99. **MEMBERSHIPS** SECOL; MLA; Minn Educ Assoc; Assoc of Chinese Prof of Soc Sci in the US; Kans For lang Assoc; NEA; Nat Assoc of Anthrop and Ethnology of China; Pacific Computer Ling Sci Assoc; Ling Assoc of Beijing, China. **RESEARCH** Spanish linguistics in concentration of syntax and its relationship with semantics, Second language acquisition theory and methodology of teaching foreign languages, Comparative approaches of linguistic typology, Civilizations y Cultures, Translation theory. **SELECTED PUBLICATIONS** Auth, "Rincon del idioma", China Reconstructs, For Lang Pr, 82-84; auth, Basic Syntactic Structure of Chinese, Mex Nat Inst of Anthrop and Hist Pr, 83; auth, The Mestization of Mexican Culture, Nat Acad of Soc Sci of China, 87; auth, "Teaching Grammar Towards Language Proficiency", Creighton Univ Pr, (Omaha, 97); auth, "Selectional Elements in the Lexical Conceptual Structure", Selection of 1996 Mid-America Ling Conf Papers, Univ of Kans Pr, (97); auth, "Argument Structure of Spanish Psychological Prediction", Selection of 1997 Mid-America Ling Conf, Univ of Miss Pr, (98); auth, Lexical Cognition, Argument Structure and Culture - A Comparative Approach of Relocation Predication in Spanish, Chinese and English", Univ of Duisburg (Germany), 98; auth, "Una teoria caotica de traduccion", Latin-Am Assoc of Ling and Philology, Univ of Santiago, (99); auth, "Improvement of Chinese Language Software by Morphosyntactic and Lexicographic Methods", Pac Int Computer Ling Assoc, (Waterloo, Can), 99; auth, "The Cultural Unconsciousness in Modern China and the Development of 21st Centure", Int Symp on 21st Century China and the Challenge of Sustainable Development, 99. **CONTACT ADDRESS** Dept For Lang, Appalachian State Univ, 1 Appalachian State, Boone, NC 28608-0001. **EMAIL** chenzhi@conrad.appstate.edu

CHENEY, DONALD
PERSONAL Born 07/14/1932, Lowell, MA, m, 1956, 2 children **DISCIPLINE** ENGLISH, COMPARATIVE LITERATURE **EDUCATION** Yale Univ, BA, 54, MA, 57, PhD, 61. **CAREER** From instr to asst prof English, Yale Univ, 60-67; assoc prof, 67-75, Prof English, Univ Mass, Amherst, 75-, Morse fel, Yale Univ, 64-65; corresp ed, Spenser Newslett, 70-78, ed, 74-78; co-ed, Spenser Encycl, 79- **MEMBERSHIPS** MLA; Renaissance Soc Am; Spenser Soc; Milton Soc Am; ACLA. **RESEARCH** Renaissance poetry and drama. **SELECTED PUBLICATIONS** Auth, Gazing on Secret Sights--Spenser, Classical Imitation, and the Decorum of Vision, Jour Eng and Ger Philol, Vol 0092, 93. **CONTACT ADDRESS** Dept of English, Univ of Massachusetts, Amherst, Amherst, MA 01003-0002.

CHENG, CHUNG-YING
PERSONAL Born 09/29/1935, Nanking, China, m, 1964, 4 children **DISCIPLINE** PHILOSOPHY; LINGUISTICS **EDUCATION** Nat Taiwan Univ, BA, 56; Univ Wash, MA, 58; Harvard Univ, PhD, 64. **CAREER** From asst prof to assoc prof, 63-74, prof philos, Univ Hawaii, Manoa, 74-, vis assoc prof, ch dept phil, 70-72, dir grad inst philos, 70-72, Nat Taiwan Univ, fall 65, vis prof, spring 68; prin investigator inquiries into class Chinese logic, Nat Sci Found grant, 65-67; fellow-participant, Summer Inst Ling, Univ Calif, Los Angeles, 66, Summer Inst Philos Sci, Stanford Univ, 67; vis assoc prof, Yale Univ, 68-69; E/W Ctr Commun Inst Sr. Fel, 78-79; pres Far E Inst Advan Studies, 85-92. **HONORS AND AWARDS** Pac Cult Found Grant, 87-88; Jiuli Zhouyi Awd Best Essay Philos, 94; Honoris Doctoris Excellence Study Devel Chinese Philos Inst Far East Stud, 95; guest prof ceremony Wuhan Univ, 96, Jejiang Univ, 96, & Anhui Univ, 96. **MEMBERSHIPS** Eastern Div Am Philos Asn; Am Asn Asian Studies; Am Orient Soc; Soc Asian & Comp Philos (treas-secy, 68-); Charles S Pierce Soc; Int Soc Chinese Philos; Int Soc I Ching; Ctr Advan Studies Chinese Philos; Far E Inst Advanced Studies; Int Found Chines Mgt Contemp Ethics; Int Fed Confucian Studies. **RESEARCH** Chinese philosophy and logic; philosophy of language and logic; contemporary American philosophy and ethics. **SELECTED PUBLICATIONS** Coauth, Ontic commitment and the empty universe, J Philos, 7/65; auth, Classical Chinese logic: A preliminary description, Philos E & W, 65; Requirements for the validity of induction, Philos & Phenomenol Res, 3/68; Peirce's and Lewis' Theories of Induction, Martinus Nijihof, Hague, 69; Tai Chen's Inquiry into Goodness, Orient Soc, Hanover, 69; Chinese Philosophy and Chinese Civilization, 74 & Scientific Knowledge and Human Value, 75, San Min Publ Co, Taipei; The Philosophical Aspects of the Mind-Body Problem, Univ Hawaii, 75; auth C Theory: Yijing Philosophy of Kuanli, Dongda Book, 95; On the Spirits of Philosophy in China and West, E. Publ Ctr, 96; Study on Zhuxi and Neo-Confucianism, Lienking Press; ed Journal of Chinese Philosophy. **CONTACT ADDRESS** Dept Philos, Univ of Hawaii, Manoa, 2530 Dole St, Honolulu, HI 96822-2303. **EMAIL** ccheng@hawaii.edu

CHERNETSKY, VITALY
DISCIPLINE SLAVIC LANGUAGES **EDUCATION** Moscow State Univ, BA, 89; Univ Pa, MA, 93, PhD, 96. **CAREER** Asst prof. **RESEARCH** Twentieth-century Ukrainian, Russian and East European literature; film and visual arts, and sexuality in Slavic and East European Cultures. **SELECTED PUBLICATIONS** Auth, Late Soviet Culture: A Parallax for Postmodernism, 94; Epigonoi, or Transformations of Writing in the Texts of Valerija Narbikova and Nina Iskrenko, 94; Opening the Floodgates: The New Ukrainian Writing, 97; Travels through Heterotopia: The Textual Realms of Patrick Modiano's Rue des Boutiques Obscures and Mikhail Kuraev's Kapitan Dikshtein, 98. **CONTACT ADDRESS** Dept of Slavic Languages, Columbia Col, New York, 2960 Broadway, New York, NY 10027-6902. **EMAIL** vac10@columbia.edu

CHERRY, CHARLES MAURICE
PERSONAL Born 09/16/1944, SC, m, 1973, 2 children **DISCIPLINE** SPANISH GOLDEN-AGE LITERATURE **EDUCATION** Furman Univ, BA, 65; Univ SC, MA, 69; Northwestern Univ, PhD, 80. **CAREER** Teacher Spanish, George Washington High Sch, VA, 65-67 & Camden High Sch, SC, 67-69; instr, Furman Univ, 69-71; teaching asst, Northwestern Univ, 71-73; teacher, Niles North High Sch, IL, 73-74; instr, 74-80, asst prof, 80-84, assoc prof, 84-90, Prof Spanish, Furman Univ, 90-. **HONORS AND AWARDS** Cervantes Awd, NEH Seminar, Election to Phi Sigma Iota, Sigma Delta Pi, Kappa Delta Pi. **MEMBERSHIPS** MLA; Am Coun Teaching Foreign Lang; Am Asn Teachers Spanish & Portuguese; SCOLT (exec bd); South Eastern Coun on Latin Am Studies. **RESEARCH** Spanish drama of the golden age; foreign language pedagogy; twentieth-century Spanish poetry; cross-cultural studies. **SELECTED PUBLICATIONS** Ed, A History of the South Carolina Chapter of the American Association of Teachers of Spanish and Portuguese, Furman Univ, 81; auth, Jose Hierro, Twentieth Century Spanish Poets, vol 108 of Dictionary of Literary Biography, 91; 15 entries on fifteenth- and sixteenth-century Spanish poets and dramatists in Dictionary of Literature of the Iberian Peninsula, 2 vols, London and Westport, CT: Gale, 93; auth, Claudio Rodriguez, Twentieth Century Spanish Poets, vol 134 of Dictionary of Literary Biography, 94; coed, Dimension, 99; ed, Dimension, (Proceedings of the Southern Conference on Language Teaching), 00. **CONTACT ADDRESS** Dept Mod Langs and Lits, Furman Univ, 3300 Poinsett Hwy, Greenville, SC 29613-0002. **EMAIL** maurice.cherry@furman.edu

CHEUNG, DOMINIC C. N.
DISCIPLINE EAST ASIAN LANGUAGES ,COMPARATIVE LITERATURE **EDUCATION** Univ Wash, PhD, 73. **CAREER** Prof, Univ Southern Calif. **RESEARCH** Modern Chinese fiction & poetry; Asian literature. **SELECTED PUBLICATIONS** Auth, From William Shakespeare to Ueda Akinari; The Isle Full of Noises: Modern Chinese Poetry from Taiwan. **CONTACT ADDRESS** East Asian Studies Center, Univ of So California, University Park Campus, Los Angeles, CA 90089.

CHEW, KRISTINA
PERSONAL Born 12/10/1968, Oakland, CA, m, 1995, 1 child **DISCIPLINE** COMPARATIVE LITERATURE **EDUCATION** Yale Univ, PhD, 95. **CAREER** Vis asst prof, Williams Col, 94-95; Vis scholar, St. Louis Univ, 96-98; asst prof, 98-. **MEMBERSHIPS** Am Philol Asn; Class Asn of the Middle West and South; Am Class League; MLA. **RESEARCH** Roman poetry; Greek philosophy; Classical tradition; Translation; Classics and multiculturalism. **SELECTED PUBLICATIONS** Auth, "What Does 'E Pluribus Unum' Mean?: Teaching Classics and Multicultural Literature Together," in The Class J, 97. **CONTACT ADDRESS** Dept of Modern & Classical Languages, Univ of St. Thomas, Minnesota, Mail Drop 4296, Saint Paul, MN 55105.

CHIAMPI, JAMES T.
PERSONAL 2 children **DISCIPLINE** ITALIAN LANGUAGE **EDUCATION** Yale Univ, PhD. **CAREER** Prof, ITAL, Univ Calif, Irvine. **SELECTED PUBLICATIONS** Auth, Shadowy Prefaces: Conversion and Writing in the 'Divine Comedy'; pub(s), articles on Dante and the lit of the Ital Renaissance. **CONTACT ADDRESS** Dept of Fr and Ital, Univ of California, Irvine, Irvine, CA 92697-2925.

CHICK, EDSON MARLAND
PERSONAL Born 05/29/1924, Boston, MA, m, 1953, 4 children **DISCIPLINE** GERMAN **EDUCATION** Brown Univ, AB, 45; Princeton Univ, PhD(Ger), 53. **CAREER** Instr Ger, Princeton Univ, 51; asst prof, Wesleyan Univ, 52-57 & Univ Calif, Riverside, 57-60; assoc prof, State Univ NY, Binghamton, 61-64; from assoc prof to prof, Dartmouth Col, 64-72; Prof Ger, Williams Col, 72-92, Fulbright res grant, Hamburg, 60-61; mem comt examrs, Ger Col Entrance Exam Bd Advan Placement Prog, 71-74; Fulbright res grant, Berlin, 78-79. **MEMBERSHIPS** MLA; Am Asn Tchrs Ger; Mod Hum Res Asn. **RESEARCH** Twentieth century; satire; censorship. **SELECTED PUBLICATIONS** Auth, Ernst Barlach, Twayne, 67; Voices in discord: Some observations on Die Judenbuche, Ger Quart, 69; Dances of Death, Welekind, Brecht, Durrenmatt, and the Satiric Trdition, Camden House, 84. **CONTACT ADDRESS** 2570 Kingdom Rd., Proctorsville, VT 05153.

CHICKERING, ROGER
PERSONAL Born 08/15/1942, San Francisco, CA, m, 1965, 2 children **DISCIPLINE** GERMAN **EDUCATION** Cornell Univ, BA, 64; Stanford Univ, MA, 65; PhD, 68. **CAREER** Instr, Stanford Univ, 67-68; From Asst Prof to Prof, Georgetown Univ, 68-. **HONORS AND AWARDS** NEH Fel; Guggenheim Fel; Fulbright Comn; Fel, Alexander von Humboldt Found; Woodrow Wilson Fel; Jacques Barzun Prize in Cult Hist. **MEMBERSHIPS** AHA. **RESEARCH** German language and literature, European language studies. **SELECTED PUBLICATIONS** Auth, Imperial Germany and a World Without War: The Peace Movement and German Society 1892-1914, Princeton UP (Princeton, NJ), 75; auth, We Men Who Feel Most German: A Cultural Study of the Pan-German League 1886-1914, George Allen & Unwin (London, UK), 84; auth, Karl Lamprecht: A German Academic Life (1856-1915), Humanities Pr Int (Atlantic Highlands, NJ), 93; auth, Imperial Germany: A Historiographical Companion, Greenwood Pr (Westport, CT), 96; auth, Imperial Germany and the Great War 1914-1918, Cambridge UP (Cambridge), 98; coauth, On the Road to Total War: The German and American Experiences 1871-1914, Cambridge UP (Cambridge), 99; coauth, Great War, Total War: Combat and Mobilization on the Western Front, Cambridge UP (Cambridge), 00. **CONTACT ADDRESS** Dept Lang, Georgetown Univ, Washington, DC 20057-1035. **EMAIL** chickerr@attglobal.net

CHINOSOLE, Null
PERSONAL Born 07/14/1942, New York, NY **DISCIPLINE** COMPARATIVE LITERATURE **EDUCATION** Univ Oregon, PhD, 86. **CAREER** San Francisco State Univ, acting dean Third Wld Stud, 70, asst prof 69-70; Nkrumah Teachers' College Zambia, chmn eng dept 71-73; San Franciso State Univ, chmn womens stud 88-90, assoc prof 90-. **HONORS AND AWARDS** Operation Crossroads; res 6th Pan African Congress. **MEMBERSHIPS** Black Women Stirring the Waters. **RESEARCH** African Diaspora Literary Studies; Black Women's Lit. **SELECTED PUBLICATIONS** Auth, African Diaspora and Autobiographics: SKEINS OF SELF AND SKIN, Peter Lang Publishing, Inc., 00, forthcoming; Schooling the Generations in the Politics of Prison, ed, New Earth Press, 95. **CONTACT ADDRESS** Dept of Womens Studies, San Francisco State Univ, 1600 Holloway Ave, San Francisco, CA 94132. **EMAIL** chinosole@athena.sfsu.edu

CHISHOLM, DAVID
PERSONAL Born 08/30/1940, New Rochelle, NY, m, 1971, 2 children **DISCIPLINE** GERMAN LANGUAGE & LITERATURE **EDUCATION** Oberlin Col, BA, 62; Univ Chicago, MA, 65; Ind Univ, PhD, 71. **CAREER** Lectr Ger, Ind Univ, 70-71; postdoctoral fel, Univ Cincinnati, 71-72; asst prof, Univ Ill, Urbana, 72-73; from asst prof to prof German, Univ Ariz, 73-. **HONORS AND AWARDS** Am Coun Learned Societies grant-in-aid, 73-74; Alexander-Von-Humboldt Found res grant, 79-80 & 81-82; Fulbright selection comt, Bonn, Ger, 81; Fulbright travel grant, 81-82; nominated for Innovative Teaching Awd, 97; faculty development grant to integrate CD, laserdisc and DVD technology into General Education course on Music and German Literature, 97; Alexander von Humboldt Grant, Marbach, Berlin and Leipzig, 97; Fulbright Grant, German Stud Sem, 98. **MEMBERSHIPS** MLA; Am Asn Teachers Ger; Asn Lit & Ling Computing. **RESEARCH** German lyric and dramatic verse; linguistic and computational approaches to literature;

German-Scandinavian comparative literature. **SELECTED PUBLICATIONS** Auth, German Cabaret Songs in the Weimar Republic, Dimensions, van Acken, 93; coauth, Base Tag Set for Verse, Guidelines for Electronic Text Encoding and Interchange, Text Encoding Initiative, 94; auth, Lexicality and the Versification of Johann Heinrich Voss: Observations on Prosodic Feature Analysis, Insights in Germanic Linguistics, de Gruyter, 95; coauth, Encoding Verse Texts, Computers and the Hum, 95; auth, Post-Renaissance German: Computer-Aided Approaches, Lit and Ling Computing, 95; auth, Prosodic Aspects of German Hexameter Verse, Poetics Today, 95; auth, Early Literary Cabaret and Modernism in Berlin, Politics in German Literature, Camden House, 98; auth, Die Aufauge des Literarischen Kabaretts, Francke (Berline), 00. **CONTACT ADDRESS** Dept of German Studies, Univ of Arizona, Tucson, AZ 85721-0067.

CHITORAN, IOANAA
DISCIPLINE LINGUISTICS AND FRENCH **EDUCATION** Cornell Univ, PhD, 97. **CAREER** Asst prof, Dartmouth Col. **RESEARCH** Romance linguistics; phonology--the interface between phonology and phonetics, between phonology and morphology. **SELECTED PUBLICATIONS** Auth, Prominence vs. Rhythm: The Predictability of Stress in Romanian Zagona in Grammatical Theory and Romance Languages, John Benjamins, 96; Les langues romanes: deux ou trois genres?, Les langues naeo-latines, 92. **CONTACT ADDRESS** Dartmouth Col, 3529 N Main St, #207, Hanover, NH 03755. **EMAIL** ioana.chitoran@dartmouth.edu

CHITTENDEN, JEAN STAHL
PERSONAL Born 03/30/1924, Davenport, IA, d, 1 child **DISCIPLINE** SPANISH **EDUCATION** Univ Ariz, BA, 44; Univ Ill, MA, 48; Univ Tex, Austin, PhD(romance lang), 64. **CAREER** Instr Span & English, Elmhurst Col, 49-52; instr Span, Univ Tex, Austin, 59-64; from asst prof to assoc prof, 64-74, Prof Span, Trinity Univ, 74-, Chmn Dept Foreign Lang, 70-, Consult, Dallas Independent Sch Dist, 62, Tex Educ Agency, 62 & MLA, 62-64; reader, Advan Placement Exam, Educ Testing Serv, 72, 74, 75, 77, 78 & 79; exec comt, Asn Dept For Lang, 78-80. **MEMBERSHIPS** MLA; Am Asn Teachers Span & Port; Am Coun Teaching Foreign Lang; AAUP; Asn Depts Foreign Lang. **RESEARCH** Golden Age drama; contemporary Spanish novel. **SELECTED PUBLICATIONS CONTACT ADDRESS** Dept of For Lang, Trinity Univ, San Antonio, TX 78284.

CHOMSKY, NOAM
PERSONAL Born 12/07/1928, Philadelphia, PA, m, 1949, 3 children **DISCIPLINE** LINGUISTICS **EDUCATION** Univ Penn, BA 49, MA 51, PhD 55. **CAREER** Mass Inst Tech, asst prof, prof, Ferrin P Ward Prof, inst prof, 55-76. **HONORS AND AWARDS** Kyoto Prize; Dist Sci Cont Awd; Helmholtz Awd. **MEMBERSHIPS** NAS; AAAS. **RESEARCH** Linguistics; Philosophy; Intl Affairs. **SELECTED PUBLICATIONS** Auth, The Minimalist Program, 95; Year 501, 93. **CONTACT ADDRESS** Room E39-219, Massachusetts Inst of Tech, 77 Massachusetts Dr, Cambridge, MA 02139. **EMAIL** chomsky@MIT.edu

CHOPYK, DAN BOHDAN
PERSONAL Born 01/02/1925, Ukraine, m, 1956, 4 children **DISCIPLINE** RUSSIAN LANGUAGE **EDUCATION** Univ Birmingham, BCom, 53; Univ Colo, Boulder, MA, 62; Ukrainian Free Univ, BLaw, 63, PhD(philol), 70. **CAREER** Prof Lang, Univ UT, 69- **MEMBERSHIPS** Am Asn Advan Slavic Studies; Rocky Mountain Asn Slavic Studies (pres, 79-80); Am Popular Cult Asn; Ukrainian Hist Asn. **RESEARCH** Slavic phonology and morphophonemics; 17th and 18th century East Slavic literature; Slavic folklore and civilization. **SELECTED PUBLICATIONS CONTACT ADDRESS** Dept of Lang, Univ of Utah, Salt Lake City, UT 84112.

CHOW, KAI-WING
PERSONAL Born 08/27/1951, Hong Kong, China, m, 1983, 2 children **DISCIPLINE** LANGUAGES & LITERATURE **EDUCATION** Univ Calif, PhD, 88. **CAREER** From asst prof to assoc prof, Univ Ill, Urbana-Champaign, 88-. **HONORS AND AWARDS** NEH Grant, 97. **MEMBERSHIPS** Asn for Asian Studies. **RESEARCH** Chinese thought and cultural studies, history of the book, printing, moral theories, theories of language and knowledge. **SELECTED PUBLICATIONS** Auth, "The Development of Sung Learning in Ch'ing Thought," Chinese Studies (95): 47-76; auth, "Writing for Success: Examinations, Printing and Intellectual Change in Late Ming China," Late Imperial China (96): 120-157; auth, "Imagining Boundaries of Blood: Zhang Binglin and the Invention of the Han 'Race' in Modern China," in The Construction of Racial Indentities in China and Japan (London: Hurst & Co, 97), 34-52; coauth, "Introduction," in Imagining Boundaries of Confucianism: Texts, Doctrines and Practices in Late Imperial China (99), 1-15; auth, "Between Canonicity and Heterodoxy: The Hermeneutical Moments of the Great Learning," Imagining Boundaries of Confucianism: Texts, Doctrines and Practices in Late Imperial China, St Univ NY (99): 147-163; auth, "Ritualism in Chinese Philosophy," Encycl of Chinese Philos (forthcoming). **CONTACT ADDRESS** Dept Lang & Lit, Univ of Illinois, Urbana-Champaign, 707 S Mathews Ave, Urbana, IL 61801. **EMAIL** k-chow1@uiuc.edu

CHRIST, MATTHEW R.
DISCIPLINE CLASSICAL STUDIES **EDUCATION** Carleton Col, BA, 82; Princeton Univ, PhD, 87. **CAREER** Asst prof, Ind Univ, Bloomington. **RESEARCH** Greek Historiography; Athenian rhetoric and law; Athenian social history. **SELECTED PUBLICATIONS** Auth, Liturgy Avoidance and Antidosis in Classical Athens, 90; auth, Herodotean Kings and Historical Inquiry, 94; auth, The Litigious Athenian, Johns Hopkins Univ Press, 98. **CONTACT ADDRESS** Dept of Classical Studies, Indiana Univ, Bloomington, 1020 E Kirkwood Ave, 547 Ballantine Hall, Bloomington, IN 47405. **EMAIL** mrchrist@indiana.edu

CHRISTENSEN, KAREN L.
PERSONAL Born 07/15/1968, Ames, IA **DISCIPLINE** SPANISH **EDUCATION** IA State Univ, BM, 92; Univ Ga, MA, 95; PhD, 99. **CAREER** Teaching Asst, Univ Ga, 93-96; Lecturer, Southern Ore Univ, 96-97; Asst Prof, Mercyhurst Col, 97-. **MEMBERSHIPS** AATSP, ACTFL, Phi Kappa Phi, Phi Sigma Iota, Sigma Delta Pi. **RESEARCH** Pedagogy; Second language acquisition; Applied linguistics; Sociolinguistics. **CONTACT ADDRESS** Dept For Lang, Mercyhurst Col, 501 E 38th St, Erie, PA 16546-0002. **EMAIL** klchristensen@hotmail.com

CHRISTENSEN, KERRY A.
DISCIPLINE CLASSICS **EDUCATION** Swarthmore Col, BA, 81; Princeton Univ, MA, 83; PhD, 93. **CAREER** Classics Dept, Williams Col **RESEARCH** Greek social and political history of the archaic era; Greek and Roman civic identity and models of leadership; ancient historiography; Greek cult and ritual. **SELECTED PUBLICATIONS** Auth, The Theseion: a Slave Refuge at Athens, Amer J Ancient Hist 9, 84; Solon's Mania: Forms of Public Discourse in Archaic Athens, Bryn Mawr Classics Colloquia, Bryn Mawr Col, 87-88; Kleisthenes, Ajax, and the Athenian Incorporation of Salamis, APA/AIA Annual Meeting, Atlanta, 94. **CONTACT ADDRESS** Classics Dept, Williams Col, Stetson Hall D28, Williamstown, MA 01267. **EMAIL** kchriste@williams.edu

CHRISTENSEN, PETER G.
PERSONAL Born 08/15/1952, Mt. Kisco, NY **DISCIPLINE** COMPARATIVE LITERATURE **EDUCATION** Iona Col, BA, 73; SUNY Albany, MLS, 74; SUNY Bing, MA, 75, PhD, 79. **CAREER** Lectr, SUNY, 79-88; lectr, Marquette Univ, 88-93; lectr, Univ WI, 93-; asst prof, Card Stritch, 98-. **HONORS AND AWARDS** NEH Sem Awd, 85, 88, 94; NEH Inst Awd, 90, 92, 94, 96. **MEMBERSHIPS** MLA, ACLA, SAA, NCS, Powsy Soc NA, Simone De Beauvoir Soc, RSA, RAA, SASS, Asn Teach Slavic and E Euro Lang. **RESEARCH** Twentieth C comparative literature, film studies, historical fiction. **SELECTED PUBLICATIONS** Auth "Edward Bond as a Chekhovian Playwright," in Chekhov Then and Now: The Reception of Chekhov in World Culture, ed. J. Douglas Clayton (NY: Peter Lang, 97); auth, "The Representation of the Late Eighteenth Century in the von Baky/Kastner Baron Muenchhausen: The Old Regime and Its Relation to the Third Reich," Ger Life and Let 44 (90): 13-24; auth, "Georg Groddeck's Defense of Homosexuality in Das Buch vom Es," Monatshefte 85 (93): 198-210; auth, "Benjamin Fondane's 'Scenarii Intournables," Dada Surr 15 (86): 72-85; auth, "Utopia and Alienation in Calvino's Invisible Cities," Forum Italicum 20 (86): 16-27; auth, "Erich Fromm's Escape from Freedom: A Reference Point for Osman Lins' Nove, novena," Chasqui 23 (94): 30-38; auth, "Dieu, sa vie, son oeuvre: Jean D'Ormesson's Attack on Apatheia As a Quality of God," Lit and Theol 8 (94): 405-20; auth, "Sibelius, Kullervo, and Fate Tragedy," Scan Can Stud 8 (95): 79-101; auth, "Jensen's Den lange Rejse: A Blochian Approach," Scan Can Stud 68 (96): 51-73; auth, "Lost in Space": The Nostalgic Anti-Heroes of Two Russian-Italian Co-Productions, Tarkovskii's Nostalgia (83) and Mikhalkov's Occhi Neri (87) ," Can Slav Papers 42, 1-2 (00): 149-69. **CONTACT ADDRESS** Eng Dept, Cardinal Stritch Col, 6801 N Yates Rd, Milwaukee, WI 53217. **EMAIL** pchriste@stritch.edu

CHRISTIANSEN, HOPE
DISCIPLINE MODERN SPANISH AMERICAN LITERATURE **EDUCATION** Kans State Univ, BA, 79, MA, 81; Univ Kans, PhD, 90. **CAREER** English and Lit, Univ Ark. **HONORS AND AWARDS** Fulbright Col Master Tchr Awd. **SELECTED PUBLICATIONS** Auth, "The Rhetoric of Self-Deprecation in Montaigne's Essais," Chimeres, 17, #2, 84; auth, "Writing and Vagabondage: Renee Nene nad Emma Bovary," Vol. XLIII, no. 1, Symposium, 94; auth, "Learning to See: Visual Education in," Les Egarements du coeur et de l'esprit, Studies on Voltaire and the Eighteenth Century, No. 319, 94; auth, The Theatre Industry in Nineteenth Century France by F.W. J. Hemmings, in French Rev, vol. II, 94; auth, "Two Simple Hearts: Balzac's Eugene and Flauberts' Felicite in Romance Quarterly 42.2, (95): 195-202; auth, The Theatre Industry in Nineteenth-Century France by F. W. J. Hemmings in Romance Quarterly 42.4, (95): 237-238; auth, Alekis de Tocqueville by Matthew Manchi in French Review 68, (95): 174-175; auth, Literature francaise du XIX Siecle by Arlette Michel, et. al. in French Review 69, (95): 1104-1105. **CONTACT ADDRESS** Univ of Arkansas, Fayetteville, 1402 E. Shadowridge, Fayetteville, AR 72701. **EMAIL** hopec@comp.uark.edu

CHRISTOPH, SIEGFRIED
PERSONAL Born 10/11/1950, Berlin, Germany, m, 1973, 3 children **DISCIPLINE** GERMAN **EDUCATION** Univ IL-Urbana, AB, 72; MA, 75; PhD, 80. **CAREER** Asst prof to prof, Univ of Wis-Parkside, 80-. **HONORS AND AWARDS** Fulbright Senior Scholar, 86. **MEMBERSHIPS** MLA; Am Assoc of Teachers of Ger; Int Courtly Lit Soc; Int Arthurian Soc; Soc for Ger Philol; Wolfram von Eschenbach-Gesellschaft. **RESEARCH** Middle High German, courtly literature, Arthurian literature, Wolfram von Eschenbach. **SELECTED PUBLICATIONS** Auth, "Zur Spruchdichtung des Salutaris Poeta", Mittellateinisches Jahrbuch 22 (87):230-236; auth, "Guenevere's Abduction and Arthur's Fame", Zeitschrift fur Deutsches Altertun und Deutsche Literatur 188 (89):17-33; auth, Lemmatisierter Index zu den Werken des Stricker, Tubingen, 97; auth, "Authority and Text in Wolfram's 'Titurel'", Deutsche Viertel jahrsschrift fur Literaturwissenschaft und Geistesgeschiche 73 (99): 211-227. **CONTACT ADDRESS** Dept Mod Lang, Univ of Wisconsin, Parkside, 900 Wood Road, PO Box 2000, Kenosha, WI 53141-2000. **EMAIL** christop@uwp.edu

CHRISTY, T. CRAIG
PERSONAL Born 05/16/1952, Knoxville, TN, m, 4 children **DISCIPLINE** GERMAN, LINGUISTICS **EDUCATION** Univ Tenn, BA, 73; MA, 75; Princeton Univ, MA, 77; PhD, 80. **CAREER** Princeton Univ, 76-80; Univ Calif, Los Angeles, 80-88; Univ of North Ala, 88-. **HONORS AND AWARDS** Phi Beta Kappa, 72; Phi Kappa Phi, 773; Fulbright Fel, 75-76; Princeton Grad Fel, 76-78; Whiting Found Fel, 78-79; Res and Development Grants, 80-2000. **MEMBERSHIPS** Modern Lang Asn, Am Asn of Teachers of German, Soc d'Histoire et d'Epistomologie des Sciences du Language, Studienkreis Geschichte der Sprachwissenschaft, Am Asn of Univ Profs, North Am Asn of Hist of the Lang Scis, Semiotic Soc of Am, Coun of Cols of Arts and Scis, Nat Col Honors Asn. **RESEARCH** History of ideas, literacy studies, theory of writing, writing systems, media technology, early printing, semiotics, history and historiography of linguistics, Indo-European linguistics etymology, language change, cognition theory, Germanic philology, applied linguistics. **SELECTED PUBLICATIONS** Auth, Uniformitariansim in Linguistics, Studies in the History of Linguistics, Amsterdam: John Benjamins (83); co-ed with Daniel G. Calder, Germania: Comparative Studies in the Old Germanic Languages and Literatures, Cambridge: Boydell & Brewer (88); auth, "Between Intellect and Intuition: Saussure's 'Anagrams' and the calculus of the Auri-(Ora-)cular," in Interdigitations: Essays for Irmengard Rauch, ed by G. F. Carr, W. Harbert, and L. Zhang, NY: Peter Lang (99): 557-568; auth, " Saussure's 'Anagrams' : Blunder or Paralanguage?," in History of Linguistics 1996, Vol 2: From Classical to Contemporary Linguistics, Studies in the History of the Language Sciences, 95, ed by Davis Cram, Andrew Linn, and Elke Novak, Amsterdam: Benjamins (99): 299-306; auth, "Breal and the Semantics of Etymological Development: On the Need to Forget in Order to Remember," Proceedings of the Xith Int Colloquium of the Studienkreis Geschichte der Sprachwissenschaft, Leuven, Belgium: Peeters (2000); auth, "Lazarus, Moritz," and "Steinthal, Heymann," entries in Biographical Dictionary of Western Linguistics, ed by Pierre Swiggers and John Joseph, London: Routledge (2000). **CONTACT ADDRESS** Foreign Lang, Univ of No Alabama, Box 5074, Florence, AL 35632-0001. **EMAIL** cchristy@unanov.una.edu

CHRZANOWSKI, JOSEPH
PERSONAL Born 09/02/1941, Providence, RI, 2 children **DISCIPLINE** SPANISH AND LATIN AMERICAN LITERATURE **EDUCATION** Fairfield Univ, BA, 66; Pa State Univ, MA, 67, PhD(Span), 71. **CAREER** Assoc prof, 69-80, Prof Span, Calif State Univ, Los Angeles, 80- **HONORS AND AWARDS** NDEH Title IV Fel, Pa State Univ, 66-69. **MEMBERSHIPS** Am Asn Teachers Span & Port; Latin Am Studies Asn; Int Inst Latin-Am Lit; MLA; Philol Asn Pac Coast. **RESEARCH** Latin American novel, theatre and short story. **SELECTED PUBLICATIONS** Auth, Gringo Viejo, the Labyrinth of Solitude-Revisited, Intl Fiction Revw, Vol 0019, 92; A Tribute to Earle, Peter,G., Hisp Rev, Vol 0061, 93. **CONTACT ADDRESS** Dept of Foreign Lang & Lit, California State Univ, Los Angeles, 5151 Rancho Castilla, Los Angeles, CA 90032-4202. **EMAIL** jchrzan@calstaela.edu

CHU, CHAUNCEY CHENG-HSI
PERSONAL Born 11/21/1930, Chang-shu, China, m, 1966, 2 children **DISCIPLINE** LINGUISTICS **EDUCATION** Taiwan Normal Univ, BA, 53, MA, 59; Univ TX, Austin, MA, 64, PhD(ling), 70. **CAREER** Instr English, Taiwan Normal Univ, 59-64, asst prof English & ling, 64-67; asst prof ling & Chinese, 69-74, assoc prof Chinese & Ling, 74-84, prof, Univ FL, 85-; dir, prog in Ling, 79-82. **HONORS AND AWARDS** Distinguished Teaching Awd, Univ FL, 75; Teaching Incentive Prog Awd, Univ Fl, 95. **MEMBERSHIPS** Ling Asn Can & US; Ling Soc Am. **RESEARCH** Historical syntax, functional & discourse grammar. **SELECTED PUBLICATIONS** Auth, A Contrastive Phonology of Mandarin Chinese and American English, Taiwan Normal Univ, 65; Linguistics: Theory, Application & Chinese Syntax, 79; A Ref Grammar of Mandarin Chinese for Speakers of English, Peter Lang, 83; Historical Syntax: Theory and Application to Chinese, Crane, 87; A Discourse Grammar of Mandarin Chinese, Peter Lang, 98; auth, A Cogni-

tive-Functional Grammar of Mandarin Chinese, Crane, 99; and over 70 journal articles and book chapters. **CONTACT ADDRESS** Dept of African & Asian Langs, Univ of Florida, 470 Grinter Hall, Gainesville, FL 32611-5565. **EMAIL** chauncey@aall.ufl.edu

CHUNG, SANDRA
DISCIPLINE AUSTRONESIAN LINGUISTICS **EDUCATION** Radcliffe Col, AB; Harvard Univ, PhD, 76. **CAREER** Prof, Ling, Univ Calif, Santa Cruz. **RESEARCH** Chamorro syntax. **SELECTED PUBLICATIONS** "VP's and Verb Movement," Chamorro, Natural Language and Linguistic Theory, 90; "Functional Heads and Proper Government in Chamorro," Lingua, 91; "Wh-Agreement and "'Referentiality'," Chamorro, Linguistic Inquiry, 94. **CONTACT ADDRESS** Dept of Ling, Univ of California, Santa Cruz, 1156 High St, Santa Cruz, CA 95064.

CHVANY, CATHERINE VAKAR
PERSONAL Born 04/26/1927, Paris, France, m, 1948, 3 children **DISCIPLINE** SLAVIC LANGUAGES AND LITERATURES **EDUCATION** Radcliffe Col, BA, 63; Harvard Univ, PhD(Slavic lang & lit), 70. **CAREER** Instr Russ, Wellesley Col, 66-67; instr, 67-70, lectr, 70-71, asst prof, 71-74, assoc prof, 75-82, prof, 83-93, emeritus, 93-, Mass Inst Technol, Fel, Harvard Russ Res Ctr, 79-97; vis prof, Univ of Paris, 91; Univ of Oregon, 99. **HONORS AND AWARDS** Lilly Postdoctoral Teaching Awd fel, Mass Inst Technol, 75-76; IREX travel grants, 77, 79, 96; Medal Sofia, 88; AATSEEL, 91; Distinguished scholarly career award, 97; Best bk in Linguistics, 97; Distinguished service to the profession, 97. **MEMBERSHIPS** Am Asn Teachers Slavic & EEurop Lang. **RESEARCH** Syntax; Russian language teaching; Bulgarian. **SELECTED PUBLICATIONS** Coed, Slavic Transformational Syntax, 74, 77; auth, On the Syntax of BE-Sentences in Russian, Slavica (Cambridge), 75; coed, Morphosyntax in Slavic, 80; coauth, Gertruda Vakar. Stikhotvoreniia, 84; coauth, New Studies in Russian Language and Literature, 87; coauth, Graduated Word-Nest Generator for Intermediate Russian, Exceller (Ithaca), 89; auth, Selected Essays of Catherine V. Chvany, ed. Olga T. Yokoyama and Emily Klenin, Slavica (Columbus), 97; **CONTACT ADDRESS** Dept of Foreign Languages and Literature, Massachusetts Inst of Tech, 77 Massachusetts Ave, Room 14N305, Cambridge, MA 02139. **EMAIL** cvchvany@mit.edu

CICCARELLI, ANDREA
DISCIPLINE ITALIAN LITERATURE **EDUCATION** Columbia Univ, PhD, 90. **CAREER** Assoc prof. **RESEARCH** Nineteenth and twentieth century poetry, narrative and theatre; literary criticism and theory; current Italian literature and culture. **SELECTED PUBLICATIONS** Auth, Manzoni: la coscienza della letteratura; pubs on Romanticism. **CONTACT ADDRESS** Dept of French and Italian, Indiana Univ, Bloomington, 1020 E Kirkwood Ave, Ballantine Hall 642, Bloomington, IN 47405. **EMAIL** aciccare@indiana.edu

CIHOLAS, KARIN NORDENHAUG
PERSONAL Born Roanoke, VA, m, 1962, 2 children **DISCIPLINE** COMPARATIVE LITERATURE, FRENCH **EDUCATION** Univ Richmond, BA, 62; Univ NC, Chapel Hill, MA, 70, PhD, 72. **CAREER** Instr Comp Lit, Univ NC, Chapel Hill, 72-73; Instr Mod Lang, Campbell Col, 72-74; from Asst Prof to Assoc Prof Mod Lang, 74-94, Van Winkle Prof Lang, Centre Col, 94-, Chmn, Hum Div, 79-83, Assoc Dean of Col, 83-92, Dir Int Prog, 89-92, Chmn Humanities Div, 95-98. **HONORS AND AWARDS** Mod Lang Award, Univ Richmond, 62; Phi Beta Kappa, 62; AAUW Dissertation Fel, 71; Mellon Grants, 81, 86; NEH Distinguished Prof, 94; KY Arts Coun Grant, 97; Acorn Award, Outstanding prof in Kentucky by Kentucky Advocates of Higher Education, 99; Grant for short stories Kentucky Found for Women, 01. **MEMBERSHIPS** MLA. **RESEARCH** Andr Gide; Thomas Mann; 20th century lit. **SELECTED PUBLICATIONS** Auth, Gide'a Art of the Fugue: A Thematic Analysis of Les Faux-Monnayeurs, Univ NC Press, 74; author of numerous short stories, plays, and poems. **CONTACT ADDRESS** Centre Col, 600 W Walnut St, Danville, KY 40422-0000. **EMAIL** Ciholas@centre.edu

CINTAS, PIERRE FRANCOIS DIEGO
PERSONAL Born 02/19/1929, Sfax, Tunisia, m, 1966, 2 children **DISCIPLINE** GENERAL & FRENCH LINGUISTICS **EDUCATION** Univ CO, MA, 62; IN Univ, PhD(French ling), 69. **CAREER** Teacher French & Latin, VT Acad, 59-60; teaching asst French, Univ CO, 60-62; lectr phonetics, Univ Grenoble, 62-63; teaching asst French, IN Univ, 63-65; lectr, Harvard Univ, 65-70; asst prof French & ling, Univ VA, 70-76; asst prof French & educ, Dalhousie Univ, 76-78; asst prof French, 78-82, Assoc Prof French, PA State Univ, 82-; Bibliogr ling, Mod Lang Asn Int Bibliog, 69-80; assoc ed, Bibliog of Am Coun Teaching Foreign Lang, 76-82; instr, French Sch, Middlebury Col, 77-86. **HONORS AND AWARDS** Chevalier des Palmes Academiques. **MEMBERSHIPS** Am Asn Teachers Fr; MLA; Am Coun Teaching Foreign Lang; Int Phonetic Asn; Am Assoc for Applied Linguistics. **RESEARCH** French syntax; applied linguistics; lexicology; computer assisted instruction. **SELECTED PUBLICATIONS** Auth, Self Evaluation and a Sense of Responsibility, Fr Rev, 68; Teacher Evaluation, AAUP Bull, 71; Mechant Poete vs Poete Mechant, In: Papers in Linguistics and Phonetics to the Memory of Pierre Delattre, 72; Apprentissage et Maitrise du langage, Bull FIPF, 74; coauth, Aspect in English and German in a Semantically Based Model, Views on Lang, 75; Language Acquisition, 1977 Northeast Conf Reports, 77; auth, Aspect, aktionsart and lexicalization, In: Contrastive Linguistics, Hochschul Verlag, Stuttgart, 78; Sans Bornes, Holt, Rinehart & Winston, 90; Elements of French Grammar, software interactive program, PA State, 96. **CONTACT ADDRESS** Pennsylvania State Univ, Abington-Ogontz, 1600 Woodland Rd, Abington, PA 19001-3990. **EMAIL** pfc1@psu.edu

CIPLIJAUSKAITE, BIRUTE
PERSONAL Born 04/11/1929, Kaunas, Lithuania **DISCIPLINE** SPANISH **EDUCATION** Lycee Lithuanien, Tubingen, Ger, BA, 47; Univ Montreal, MA, 56; Bryn Mawr Col, PhD(Span lit), 60. **CAREER** From instr Span to prof, 60-73, John Bascom Prof Span, Univ Wis-Madison, 73-98, Univ Wis res grants, 62, 65, 69, 71, 741, 91, 92; Guggenheim fel, 67-68; fel, Inst Res Humanities, Madison, 71-72, 74-98; fel Camargo Found, 85, fel Res Inst Siegen, 83, fel Casa del Traductor Tarazona, 99, vice-president Asn Advancement Baltic Studies, 82-84; Restoration Senate VD Un, Kaunas, 89-96. **HONORS AND AWARDS** Lithuanian Writers' Asn priz for translation, 92. **MEMBERSHIPS** Inst Res Humanities; Am Asn Teachers Span & Port; Inst Lithuanian Studies; Asn Int Hispanistas; AABS. **RESEARCH** Spanish poetry, contemporary and Golden Age; 19th and 20th century novel; Lithuanian literature, 19th to 20th centuries. **SELECTED PUBLICATIONS** Auth, La Soledad y la poesia espanola contemporanea, 62, El poeta y la poesia, 66, Baroja, un estilo, 72, Deber de plenitud: La poesia de Jorge Guillen, 73, Los noventayochistas y la historia, 81, La mujer insatisfecha, 84, La nov femenia contemporanca, 70-85, 88, Literaturos eskizai, 92, Designos y significaciones, I: Juegos con a vanguardia, 99, Carmen Martin Gaite, 00. **CONTACT ADDRESS** Inst for Res in the Humanities, Univ of Wisconsin, Madison, Madison, WI 53706.

CISAR, MARY
PERSONAL Born, IL, m, 2 children **DISCIPLINE** EIGHTEENTH-CENTURY FRENCH LITERATURE **EDUCATION** Kalamazoo Col; Brown Univ, MA, PhD. **CAREER** French, St. Olaf Col. **SELECTED PUBLICATIONS** Area: Mennonite women's autobiography. **CONTACT ADDRESS** St. Olaf Col, 1520 St Olaf Ave, Northfield, MN 55057.

CISMARU, ALFRED
PERSONAL Born 10/26/1929, Paris, France, m, 1957, 2 children **DISCIPLINE** FRENCH LITERATURE **EDUCATION** Fordham Univ, BS, 56; NYork Univ, MA, 58, PhD, 60. **HONORS AND AWARDS** MLA; Am Asn Teachers Fr; instr french & span, brooklyn col, 58-59; from assoc prof to prof french, st michael's col (vt), 59-70, chmn dept lang, 59-70, fac res fund awards, 62-68; prof class & romance lang, tex tech univ, 70-. **MEMBERSHIPS** French literature of the 18th century; contemporary French literature. **RESEARCH** Auth, Marguerite Duras, Twayne, 71; Boris Vian, G K Hall, 73; Marivaux and Moliere: A Comparison, Tex Tech Press, 77. **SELECTED PUBLICATIONS** Auth, Anti-Semitism in France, Midwest Quart-Jour Contemp Thought, Vol 0034, 93; What is the Enlightenment--French, Fr Rev, Vol 0067, 94; Kant Philosophy and the Enlightenment, Fr Rev, Vol 0068, 95; The Cultural Origins of the French-Revolution, Fr Rev, Vol 0066, 93; Sagan, Francoise--The Superficial Classic, World Lit Today, Vol 0067, 93. **CONTACT ADDRESS** Texas Tech Univ, Lubbock, TX 79409.

CITTON, YVES
PERSONAL Born 09/30/1962, Geneva, Switzerland, m, 1990 **DISCIPLINE** FRENCH **EDUCATION** Univ Geneva, Licence es Lettres, 85; PhD, 92. **CAREER** Asst prof, Univ of Geneva, 87-92; asst prof to assoc prof, Univ of Pittsburgh, 92-. **HONORS AND AWARDS** Univ of Pittsburgh Chancellor Distinguished Teaching Awd, 98. **MEMBERSHIPS** MLA; ASECS. **RESEARCH** 18th Century Literature and Philosophy in France, History of Economic Thought. **SELECTED PUBLICATIONS** Coauth, Les doctrines orthographiques du XVIe siecle en France, Droz, (Geneva), 89; auth, Impuissances. Defaillances masculines et pouvoir politique de Montaigne a Stendhal, Aubier, (Paris), 94; auth, "Fragile euphorie: la statue de Condillac et les impasses de l'individu", Studies on Voltaire and the 18th Century, 232, (94): 279-321; auth, "La richesse est un crime. (Im)Moralite de l'accumulation de John Locke a Isabelle de Charriere", Etre riche au siecle de Voltaire, eds Jacques Berchtold and Michel Porret, Droz (Geneva, 96): 47-65; auth, "The Economists' (Un)Natural Order", Newsletter of the Center for West Europ Studies of the Univ of Pittsburgh, Dec 97; auth, "Fabrique de l'opinion et folie de la dissidence: Le "complot" dans Rousseau juge de Jean Jacques", Rousseau, Juge de Jean Jacques, eds Phillip Knee and Jean-Pierre Allard, Univ of Ottawa Pr, 98; auth, "Monsieur Jaques chez l'ami des hommes: visite de Rousseau au coeur de l'economisme" Annales de la Societe Jean-Jacques Rousseau, 42 (forthcoming); auth, "Les chagrins du menages: Souci de l'autre et malaise de la subjectivite autour d'Isabelle de Charriere", Dix-Huitieme Siecle (forthcoming); auth, "Rousseau et la Physiocrates: la justice entre produit net et pitie", Etudes Jean-Jacques Rousseau, ed Reinhard Bach (forthcoming). **CONTACT ADDRESS** Dept Fr and Ital, Univ of Pittsburgh, 1328H Cathedral of Learning, Pittsburgh, PA 15260-6299.

CIVIL, MIGUEL
PERSONAL Born 05/07/1926, Sabadell, Spain, d, 2 children **DISCIPLINE** ASSYRIOLOGY, LINGUISTICS **EDUCATION** Univ Paris, PhD, 58. **CAREER** Res assoc Assyriol, Univ Pa, 58-63; from asst prof to assoc prof Near Eastern Lang & civilizations & ling, 63-70, Prof Near Eastern Lang & Civilizations & Ling, Univ Chicago, 70-, Mem ed bd, Chicago Assyrian Dict, 67-; dir d'etudes associe etranger, Sorbonne, 68-70; ed, Materials for the Sumerian Lexicon, 68- **HONORS AND AWARDS** Hon PhD, Univ Barcelona, 00. **MEMBERSHIPS** Am Orient Soc; Am Sch Orient Res. **RESEARCH** Sumerian grammar and literature; anthropology of Mesopotamia; lexicography. **SELECTED PUBLICATIONS** Auth, Prescriptions medicales Sumeriennes, Rev D'Assyriol, 60; The message of Lu-dingirra, J Near Eastern Studies, 64; Notes on Sumerian lexicography, J Cuneiform Studies, 66; coauth, Vol IX, Materials for the Sumerian Lexicon, 67 & auth, Vol XIII-XIV, 71, Pontificio Inst Biblico, Rome. **CONTACT ADDRESS** Oriental Institute Univ, Univ of Chicago, 1155 E 58th St, Chicago, IL 60637-1540. **EMAIL** mcivil@uchicago.edu

CLACK, JERRY
PERSONAL Born 07/22/1926, New York, NY **DISCIPLINE** CLASSICS **EDUCATION** Univ Pittsburgh, PhD 62, MA 58; Princeton Univ, BA 46. **CAREER** Duquesne Univ, prof 68-; The March of Dimes Pittsburgh, dir 53-68; US Delegation to UNESCO, prog officer 46-67. **MEMBERSHIPS** APA; CAAS; PCA; CAP. **RESEARCH** Hellenistic poetry; Augustan literature. **SELECTED PUBLICATIONS** Auth, The Poems of Meleager, 94; The APA and Regional Associations: Transactions of the American Philological Association, 93; auth, Asclepiades of Samos and Leonidas of Tarentum: The Poems, 99. **CONTACT ADDRESS** Dept of Classic, Duquesne Univ, Pittsburgh, PA 15282. **EMAIL** clack@duq.edu

CLADER, LINDA
PERSONAL Born 02/11/1946, Evanston, IL, m, 1991 **DISCIPLINE** CLASSICAL PHILOLOGY; HOMILETICS **EDUCATION** Carleton Col, AB, 68; Harvard Univ, AM, 70, PhD, 73; Church Divinity School of Pacific, M Div, 88. **CAREER** Instr to full prof Classical languages, Carleton Col, 72-90; asst to prof, homiletics, Church Divinity School Pacific, 91-. **HONORS AND AWARDS** Phi Beta Kappa, 68. **MEMBERSHIPS** AAR/SBL; Acad Homiletics; Am Philol Asn. **RESEARCH** Liturgical preaching; Myth; Homer; Metaphor. **SELECTED PUBLICATIONS** Auth, Helen: Evolution from Divine to Heroic in Greek Epic Tradition, Brill, 76; auth, Preaching the Liturgical Narratives: The Easter Vigil and the Language of Myth, Worship, 98. **CONTACT ADDRESS** Church Divinity Sch of the Pacific, 2451 Ridge Rd, Berkeley, CA 94709. **EMAIL** Lclader@cdsp.edu

CLAMURRO, WILLIAM
PERSONAL Born 04/14/1945, San Antonio, TX **DISCIPLINE** SPANISH LITERATURE **EDUCATION** Amherst Col, BA, 67; Univ Wash, MA, 68; PhD, 75. **CAREER** Adj instr, Montclair State Col, 77-78; asst prof, St. Mary's Col of Md, 78-86; assoc prof, 86-92; prof, Denison Univ, 92-97; prof, Emporia State Univ, 97-. **HONORS AND AWARDS** Roe R. Cross Distinguished Prof Awd, Emporia State univ, 00-01. **MEMBERSHIPS** Asn Int Hispanistas; Cervantes Soc Am; AATSP; Asn Int Siglo de Oro; MLA. **RESEARCH** Spanish Renaissance literature. **SELECTED PUBLICATIONS** Auth, Language and Ideology in the Prose of Quevedo, 91; auth, Manuel Puig y la construccion de la lectura postmoderna, Univ Iowa, 94; auth, Madness and Narrative Form in Estragos que causa el vicio, 95; auth, Beneath the Fiction: The Contrary Worlds of Cervantes's Novelas ejemplares, 97. **CONTACT ADDRESS** Div of Foreign Languages, Emporia State Univ, 1200 Commercial St, Emporia, KS 66801-5087. **EMAIL** clamurrw@emporia.edu

CLARK, EVE VIVIENNE
PERSONAL Born 07/26/1942, Camberley, UK, m, 1967, 1 child **DISCIPLINE** LINGUISTICS, PSYCHOLINGUISTICS **EDUCATION** Univ Edinburgh, MA, 65, dipl, 66, PhD(ling), 69. **CAREER** Res assoc lang, 69-71; asst prof ling, 71-77; assoc prof ling 77-83; prof ling 83-; dept head 92-96. **HONORS AND AWARDS** NSF grants 71-75, 75-79, 80-83,84-87,98-01; US-Isralli Binational Sc Fel, 87-91; Spencer Fdn, 79-80; Guggenheim Fel, 83-84. **MEMBERSHIPS** Ling Soc Am; Soc Res Child Develop; Int Asn Study Child Lang; Int'l Pragmatics Asn. **RESEARCH** Lang acquisition, word-formation, lexical semantics, pragmatics. **SELECTED PUBLICATIONS** Auth, Psychology and Language, 77; Outogenesis of Meaning, 79; auth, Acquisition of Romance, 85; The Lexicon in Acquisition, 93. **CONTACT ADDRESS** Dept of Ling, Stanford Univ, Stanford, CA 94305-2150. **EMAIL** eclark@psych.stanford.edu

CLARK, HUGH R.
DISCIPLINE HISTORY AND EAST ASIAN STUDIES **EDUCATION** Univ Pa, PhD. **CAREER** Prof Hist and E Asian Stud, ch, dept Hist, Ursinus Col. **HONORS AND AWARDS** Laughlin Prof Achievement Awd, Ursinus Col; grant, Chiang Ching-kuo Found, NEH, Comt for Scholarly Res in China. **RESEARCH** Middle period Chinese history. **SELECTED PUBLICATIONS** Auth, Community, Trade, and Networks: Southern Fujian Province from the 3rd to the 13th Centuries. **CONTACT ADDRESS** Ursinus Col, Collegeville, PA 19426-1000.

CLARK, JOHN RICHARD
PERSONAL Born 06/11/1947, Dayton, OH, m, 1 child **DISCIPLINE** CLASSICAL LANGUAGES, MEDIEVAL LATIN **EDUCATION** Univ Cincinnati, BA, 69; Cornell Univ, MA, 71, PhD, 74. **CAREER** Asst prof, Univ Pa, 75-79; Asst Prof, 80-86, Assoc Prof Class, Medieval & Palaeography, Fordham Univ, 86-. **MEMBERSHIPS** Am Philol Asn; Medieval Acad Am. **RESEARCH** Marsilio Ficino's De vita(1489); medieval Latin literature; Plautus. **SELECTED PUBLICATIONS** Auth, Structure and symmetry in the Bacchides of Plautus, Transactions of the Am Philol Asn, 76; Two ghost editions of Marsilio Ficino's De vita, Papers of the Bibliog Soc of Am, 79; Teaching Medieval Latin, Class J, 79; Word play in Plautus' Amphitruo, Class Philol, 80; Marsilio Ficino among the alchemists, Class Bull, 83; coauth, Marsilio Ficino: Three Books on Life: A Critical Edition and Translation with Introduction & Notes, SUNY, 89; auth, Platonianus es, non Plautinianus (Jerome Ep. 22.30), CW, 84; The Traditional Figure of Dina and Abeland's First Planctus, Proceeds of PMR Conf, 82; Roger Bacon and the Composition of Marsilio Ficino's De vita longa, J Warburg & Courtauld Inst, 86; Love & Learning in the Metamorphosis Golye Episcopi, MJ, 86. **CONTACT ADDRESS** Dept of Class, Fordham Univ, 441 E Fordham Rd, Bronx, NY 10458-5191. **EMAIL** clark@fordham.edu

CLARK, MARK E.
PERSONAL Born 09/10/1947, PA **DISCIPLINE** CLASSICS **EDUCATION** Univ NC, BA; Universitat Heidelberg, 73-74; Univ Minn, MA, 77; Ind Univ, PhD, 81. **CAREER** Honors Asst Prof to Assoc Prof, Univ southern Miss, 81-. **HONORS AND AWARDS** NEH grants, 94, 92, 88, 84, 82; Teaching Awd, Univ Southern Miss, 95; FIPSE grant, 86-90. **MEMBERSHIPS** Classical Asn of the Middle West and South, am Philol Asn. **RESEARCH** classics; Intellectual history; The classical tradition. **SELECTED PUBLICATIONS** Auth, "Hippocratic Medicine and Aristotelian Science in the Daemonum Investigatio Peripatetica of A. Caesalpino," bulletin of the History of Medicine (95): 527-41. **CONTACT ADDRESS** Dept History, Univ of So Mississippi, PO Box 5038, Hattiesburg, MS 39406-5038.

CLARK, MARY MORRIS
PERSONAL Born 12/28/1941, Tuscaloosa, AL, 3 children **DISCIPLINE** LINGUISTICS, AFRICAN LANGUAGES **EDUCATION** Univ NH, BA, 62; Univ Mass, PhD(ling), 78. **CAREER** Teacher English, math & sci, US Peace Corps, Nigeria, 64-65; instr, Sch for Int Training, 75-78; Asst Prof Ling, English Dept, Univ NH, 78- **MEMBERSHIPS** Ling Soc Am; African Ling Soc; North Eastern Ling Soc; Teachers of English to Speakers of Other Lang; NCTE. **RESEARCH** The use of tone and intonation in languages; the interaction of phonology with other parts of the grammar; applications of linguistics in language teaching. **SELECTED PUBLICATIONS** Auth, Classification of Adults for Family Studies of Developmental Language Disorders, Jour Speech and Hearing Res, Vol 0039, 96; Guilty if Charged--A Response to the Bernstein, Richard Account of the Silva, Donald Case at the University-of-New-Hampshire--An Exchange, NY Rev Bk(s), Vol 0041, 94. **CONTACT ADDRESS** English Dept, Univ of New Hampshire, Durham, 125 Technology Dr, Durham, NH 03824-4724. **EMAIL** mmc@christa.unh.edu

CLARK, RAYMOND JOHN
PERSONAL Born 07/08/1941, Bristol, England, m, 1964, 3 children **DISCIPLINE** CLASSICS **EDUCATION** Univ Exeter, BA, 63, cert educ, 64, PhD(classics), 70. **CAREER** Assoc prof, 69-80, Prof Classics, Mem Univ Nfld, 80-, Can Coun leave fel, 76-77. **MEMBERSHIPS** Class Asn Can (vpres, 80-82); Vergilian Soc Am; Virgil Soc Eng; Am Philol Soc; Brit Class Asn. **RESEARCH** Greek and Latin epic, especially Homeric and Vergilian; classical religion, mythology and folklore, especially mortuary; pre-Socratic philosophy. **SELECTED PUBLICATIONS** Auth, Peter-of-Eboli, De Balneis Puteolanis--Manuscripts from the Aragonese-Scriptorium in Naples, Traditio-Stud in Ancient and Medieval Hist Thought and Rel, Vol 0045, 90; Giles-of-Viterbo on the Phlegraean-Fields--A Vergilian View, Phoenix-Jour Class Assn Can, Vol 0049, 95. **CONTACT ADDRESS** Dept of Classics, Mem Univ of Newfoundland, Saint John's, NF, Canada A1C 5S7. **EMAIL** rjclark@morgan.ucs.mun.ca

CLARK, THOMAS L.
DISCIPLINE ENGLISH LINGUISTICS **EDUCATION** Univ Utah, BA, 64, MA, 66; Ohio Univ, PhD, 70. **CAREER** Prof, Univ Nev, Las Vegas. **HONORS AND AWARDS** William Morris Awd, 87, App Barrick Res Prof, Univ Nev, Las Vegas, 90. **MEMBERSHIPS** Ed bd, NCTE, 80-93; bd of gov, Am Name Soc, 85-88; vice pres, 83-85, pres, Am Dialect Soc, 85-87; exec bd, Am Coun of Learned Soc, 88-92. **SELECTED PUBLICATIONS** Auth, Expanding the Scope: Volume II of DARE is Only Part of the Story, Am Speech, vol 69, 94; Western Lore and Language: A Dictionary for Enthusiasts of the West, Univ Utah Press, 96. **CONTACT ADDRESS** Dept of Eng, Univ of Nevada, Las Vegas, Las Vegas, NV 89154-5011. **EMAIL** tlc@nevada.edu

CLAS, ANDRE
PERSONAL Born 06/01/1933, Laning, France **DISCIPLINE** LINGUISTICS **EDUCATION** Univ Strasbourg, BA, 53; Univ Montreal, MA, 60; Univ Tubingen, DPh, 67. **CAREER** Lectr to assoc prof, 63-76, dept ch, 72-81, Prof Linguistics, Univ Montreal, 76-; ed, META (Translator's J), 68-. **MEMBERSHIPS** Soc de la linguistique romane; Can Ling Soc. **SELECTED PUBLICATIONS** Auth, Phonetique appliquee, 67; auth, Le francais, langue des affaires, 69; auth, Richesses et particularites du francais ecrit au Quebec, 79, 82; auth, Guide de la correspondance, 80; auth, Sons et langage, 83; auth, Visages du francais, Varietes lexicales de l'espace francophone, 90; auth, Compact Worterbuch der exakten Naturwissenschaften und der Technik Band II Deutsch-Franzosisch, Band I Francais-Allemand, 91, 95; auth, L'environnement traductionnel, 92; auth, La Traductique, 93; auth, TATAO: Recherches de pointe et applications immediates, 95; auth, Introduction a la lexicologie explicative et combinatoire, 95. **CONTACT ADDRESS** Dept of Linguistics, Univ of Montreal, CP 6128, Succ Centre-ville, Montreal, QC, Canada H3C 3J7. **EMAIL** andre.clas@umontreal.ca

CLASSEN, ALBRECHT
PERSONAL Born 04/23/1956, Germany, m, 1984, 1 child **DISCIPLINE** GERMAN LITERATURE, GERMAN HISTORY **EDUCATION** Univ Marburg, MA, 82; Univ Va, PhD, 86. **CAREER** From asst prof to assoc prof to prof, 87-, Univ Ariz. **HONORS AND AWARDS** Edgar-Shannon-Awd, 86, Univ Va; El Paso Natural Gas Found Fac Achievement Awd, 95; Univ Tchr Grant, 99, Rotary Int; pres, aatg, 97-98; pres, aatg, 92-98. **MEMBERSHIPS** MLA; SEMA; Oswald von Wolkenstein Gesellschaft; Rocky Mountain MLA; ICLS. **RESEARCH** Medieval and early modern German literature and history. **SELECTED PUBLICATIONS** Auth, The German Volksbuch. A Critical History of a Late-Medieval Genre, 95; auth, Tristania, Vol. XVI, 95; auth, Tristania, Vol. XVII, 96; auth, Diu Klage, Mittelhochdeutsch-neuhochdeutsch. Einleitung Ubersetzung, Kommentar und Anmerkungen, 97; auth, Trisania, Vol. XVII, 98. **CONTACT ADDRESS** 2413 E 4th St, Tucson, AZ 85719. **EMAIL** aclassen@u.arizona.edu

CLAUSING, GERHARD
PERSONAL Born 02/16/1943, Germany, m, 1989 **DISCIPLINE** GERMAN LINGUISTICS **EDUCATION** Univ of Calif at Berkeley, AB, 66, MA, 68, PhD, 74. **CAREER** Instr to asst prof, Univ of Minn, 72-76; Asst Prof 76-79, Assoc Prof, 79-93, Full Prof, 93-, Chair, Univ of Southern Calif, 90-. **HONORS AND AWARDS** Equipment and res grants, Univ of Southern Calif, 89-94; Sigerson Found, 87; IBM Socrates Grant, 86-88; Goethe Inst Grants, 81 & 84. **MEMBERSHIPS** MLA; AATG. **RESEARCH** German and applied linguistics; cultural studies; drama. **SELECTED PUBLICATIONS** Auth, Ubergange. Sprechen-Berichten-Diskutieren. Genre-Based Conversation in German, Heinle and Heinle, 94; Speaking German Naturally (video tape), Donn Sigerson Found, 87; coauth, Interaktion. A Text-Based Intermediate German Course, Houghton Miffline, 90; Deutsch naturlich! A Communication-Oriented First Course, Houghton Mifflin, 86; Zur Situation der deutschen Sprache in Kalifornien, Deutsch als Muttersprache in den Vereinigten Staaten, Teil 2, Steiner, 85. **CONTACT ADDRESS** Dept of German, Univ of So California, Los Angeles, CA 90089-0351. **EMAIL** clausing@usc.edu

CLAUSS, JAMES
PERSONAL Born 09/01/1953, Scranton, OH, m, 1978, 3 children **DISCIPLINE** CLASSICAL STUDIES **EDUCATION** Univ Scranton, BA, 74; Fordham Univ, MA, 76; Univ Calif Berk, PhD, 83. **CAREER** Instr, asst prof, Creighton Univ, 83-84; asst prof, assoc prof, prof, Univ Wash, 84-. **HONORS AND AWARDS** Dist Teach Awd, 96. **MEMBERSHIPS** APA. **RESEARCH** Hellenistic poetry; Augustan poetry; Roman history and historiography; Roman topography; Greek and Roman literature in general. **SELECTED PUBLICATIONS** Auth, "Allusion and Structure in Horace Satire 2.1: the Callimachean Response," Trans Am Philo Asn 115 (85): 197-206; auth; "Lies and Allusions: the Addressee and the Date of Callimachus' Hymn to Zeus," Class Antiq 5 (86): 155-170; auth, "The Episode of the Lucian Farmers in Ovid's Metamorphoses," Harv Stud Class Philo 92 (88): 297-314; auth, "Vergil and the Euphrates Revisited," Am J Philo 109 (88): 309-320; auth, "The Ignoble Consistency of M. Caelius Rufus," Athen 78 (90): 531-540; auth, "An Attic-speaking Crow on the Capitoline: A Literary Emigr from the Hecale," Zeits fur Papyr and Epig 96 (93): 167-173; auth, "A Delicate Foot on the Well-Worn Threshold: Paradoxical Imagery in Catullus 68b," Am J Philo 116 (95): 237-253; auth, "Domestici Hostes: the Nausicaa in Medea, the Catiline in Hannibal," Mater a Disc 39 (97): 165-185; auth, "The Best of the Argonauts," in The Redefinition of the Epic Hero in Book 1 of Apollonius' Argonautica (Univ Calif Press, 93); auth, Medea: Essays on Medea in Myth, Literature, Philosophy, and Art, Princeton UP, 97. **CONTACT ADDRESS** Dept of Classics, Univ of Washington, PO Box 353110, Seattle, WA 98195-3110.

CLAY, JENNY STRAUSS
DISCIPLINE CLASSICAL STUDIES **EDUCATION** Univ Wash, PhD. **CAREER** Prof. **SELECTED PUBLICATIONS** Auth, Wrath of Athena, Princeton, 83; The Politics of Olympus, Princeton, 89; pubs on Greek and Roman poetry. **CONTACT ADDRESS** Dept of Classics, Univ of Virginia, Charlottesville, VA 22903. **EMAIL** jsc2t@virginia.edu

CLAYMAN, DEE LESSER
PERSONAL Born New York **DISCIPLINE** CLASSICAL PHILOLOGY **EDUCATION** Wellesley Col, BA, 67; Univ Pa, MA, 69, PhD(classics), 72. **CAREER** Asst prof classics, Brooklyn Col, 72-77, assoc prof, 78-81, Prof Classics, Brooklyn Col & Grad Ctr, City Univ New York, 82-, Grants-in-aid, Am Philos Soc, 75 & Am Coun Learned Soc, 78. **MEMBERSHIPS** Am Philol Asn; Asn Lit & Ling Computing; Asn Computational Linguistics. **RESEARCH** Greek poetry; computer-assisted stylometry; history of literary criticism. **SELECTED PUBLICATIONS** Auth, Trends and Issues in Quantitative Stylistics, Transactions of the Amer Philol Assn, Vol 0122, 92. **CONTACT ADDRESS** Dept of Classics, Brooklyn Col, CUNY, Brooklyn, NY 11210.

CLAYTON, JOHN DOUGLAS
PERSONAL Born 12/14/1943, Cheshire, England, m, 1968, 2 children **DISCIPLINE** RUSSIAN LITERATURE **EDUCATION** Univ Cambridge, BA, 65; Univ Ill, Urbana, AM, 67, PhD(Russ), 71. **CAREER** Asst prof Slavic studies, 71-76, Assoc Prof Mod Land & Lit, Univ Ottawa, 76-. **MEMBERSHIPS** Can Asn Slavists, Am Asn Teachers Slavic & East Europ Lang, Am Asn Advan Slavic Studies, Asn Can Theatre History. **RESEARCH** Alexander Pushkin; 20th century Russian theatre; Russian Romanticism, Chekhov. **SELECTED PUBLICATIONS** Ed, Poetica Slavica: Studies in Honour of Zbigniew Folejewski, with Gunter Schaarschmidt, Ottawa: Univ of Ottawa Press, 81; auth, Ice and Flame: Aleksandr Pushkin's Eugene Onegin, Toronto: Toronto Univ Press, 85; ed, Issues in Russian Literature before 1917: Selected Papers of the Third World Congress for Soviet and East European Studies, Columbus, Ohio: Slavica Publishers, Inc, 89; auth, Pierrot in Petrograd: Commedia dell'arte/Balagan in Twentieth-Century Russian Theatre and Drama, McGill-Queen's Univ Press, 94; auth, "The Search for Belief: Tolstoj and the Theatrical Sign in Stanislavskij, Evreinov and Meyerhold," Balagan, (95): 1, 2, 32-48; auth, "Prav-I slav-: opyt semanticheskogo analiza Borisa Godunova A.S. Pushkina," Russian Literature, (95): 38, 227-240; auth, "Povesti Belkina' and the Commedia dell'arte: Callot, Hoffman, and Pushkin," Russian Literature, (96): 40, 277-92; auth, "Boris Godunov A.S. Pushkina: semantika govoreniia I mollchaniia," A.B. Muratova I P.E. Buxarkina, eds, Kontseptsiia I smysl: Sbornik statei v chest' 60-letiia professora V.M. Markovicha, (Izdatel'stvo Sankt-Peterburgskogo universiteta, 96): 82-100; ed, Chekhov Then and Now: The Receptioon of Chekhov in World Culture, New York: Peter Lang, 97; auth, "Touching Solitudes; Chekhov in Canada, 1926-1980," In J. Douglas Clayton, ed, Chekhov Then and Now: The Reception of Chekhov in World Culture, (New York: Peter Lang, 97), 151-72. **CONTACT ADDRESS** Dept of Mod Lang & Lit, Univ of Ottawa, PO Box 450 STN A, Ottawa, ON, Canada K1N 6N5. **EMAIL** jdclayt@uottawa.ca

CLEMENTE, ALICE RODRIGUES
PERSONAL Born 07/28/1934, Pawtucket, RI **DISCIPLINE** SPANISH AND PORTUGUESE **EDUCATION** Brown Univ, AB, 56, MA, 59, PhD(Span), 67. **CAREER** Instr Span, Randolph-Macon Woman's Co], 59-61 & Wheaton Col, 64; from instr to asst prof, 64-71, assoc prof, 64-80, Prof Span & Port, Smith Col, 80-. **MEMBERSHIPS** Asoc Int Hispanistas. **RESEARCH** Gil Vicente; Portuguese novel; Jesuits in the Orient. **SELECTED PUBLICATIONS CONTACT ADDRESS** Dept of Hispanic Studies, Smith Col, Northampton, MA 01060.

CLENDENEN, E. RAY
PERSONAL Born 03/09/1949, Dallas, TX, m, 1971, 2 children **DISCIPLINE** TEXTLINGUISTICS **EDUCATION** Rice Univ, BA, 71; Dallas Theol Sem, ThM, 75; Dropsie Univ, MA, 82; Univ Tex at Arlington, PhD, 89. **CAREER** Prof of Old Testament, Criswell Col, 82-96; Executive ed, Bibles and Reference Books, Broadman & Holman Publ, 92- . **MEMBERSHIPS** Soc of Bibl Lit; Evangel Theol Soc; Inst of Bibl Res; Natl Asn of Prof of Hebrew. **RESEARCH** Textlinguistics, Biblical Hebrew. **SELECTED PUBLICATIONS** Auth, The Structure of Malachi: A Textlinguistic Study, Criswell Theol Rev, 87; auth, Discourse Strategies in Jeremiah 10, J of Bibl Lit, 88; auth, Life in God's Land: An Outline of the Theology of Deuteronomy, in Patterson, ed, The Church at the Dawn of the 21st Century, Criswell, 89; auth, articles in Dockery, ed, The Holman Bible Handbook, Broadman, 92; ed, Old Testament, Believer's Study Bible, Nelson, 91; auth, Old Testament Proph-

ets as Hortatory: Examples from Malachi, J of Textlinguistics and Transl, 93; auth, Postholes, Postmodernism, and the Prophets, in Dockery, ed, The Challenges of Postmodernism, Bridgepoint, 94; auth, Religious Background for the Old Testament, in Dockery, ed, Foundations for Biblical Interpretation, Sloan, Broadman, and Holman, 94; auth, Interpreting the Minor Prophets for Preaching, Faith and Mission, 95; auth, The Minor Prophets, in Dockery, ed, The Holman Concise Commentary, 98; gen ed, 24 vols, The New American Commentary, 98; ed, The Holman Christian Standard Bible. **CONTACT ADDRESS** Broadman & Holman Publishers, 127 9th Ave N, MSN 164, Nashville, TN 37234. **EMAIL** rclende@lifeway.com

CLINTON, JEROME WRIGHT
PERSONAL Born 07/14/1937, San Jose, CA, m, 1983, 3 children **DISCIPLINE** PERSIAN LITERATURE **EDUCATION** Stanford Univ, AB, 59; Univ Pa, MA, 62; Univ Mich, MA, 67, PhD(Persian and Arabic lit), 72. **CAREER** Instr Persian lang & lit, Univ Minn, 70-72; dir, Tehran Ctr, Am Inst Iranian Studies, 72-74; Prof Near Eastern Studies, Princeton Univ, 74-, Assoc ed, Iranian Studies, 71-76. **HONORS AND AWARDS** Language fellows (Persian), NDFL, 65-66; Fulbright-Hayes research fellow, 68-69; NEH, curriculum dev grant, 78-79; NEH, trans grant (Persian), 88-89; Princeton 250th Ann Curriculum Dev grant, 98-99. **MEMBERSHIPS** Soc Iranian Studies; Mideast Studies Asn; Am Inst Iranian Studies. **RESEARCH** Classical Persian literature. **SELECTED PUBLICATIONS** Co-auth, Modern Persian: Spoken and Written, Desktop, 71; auth, Divan of Manuchihri, Bibliotheca Islamica (Minneapolis and Chicago), 72; auth, Madness and Cure in the 1001 Nights: the Tale of Shahriyar and Shahrizad, Studia Islamica, 85; auth, Recent Work on Islamic Literature, special issue of Edebiyat: A Journal of Middle Eastern and Comparative Literature, N.S., 87; auth, Court and Poetry at the Beginning of the Classical Period, Persian Literature (NY), Persian Heritage Foundation, 88; auth, Intertextuality and Middle Eastern Texts, special issue of Edebiyat: A Journal of Middle Eastern and Comprative Literature, N.S., 90; Tragedy of Sohrab and Rostam, from the Persian National Epic, the Shahname of Abol Qasem Ferdowsi, 2nd ed, 96; auth, A Sketch of Translation and the Formation of New Persian Literature, Iran and Iranian Studies: Studies in Honor of Iraj Afshar, Zagros Press, 98; auth, Rumi in America, a review article on The Essential Rumi by Coleman Barks, Edebiyat: A Journal of Middle Eastern and Comparative Literature, 99; In the Dragon's Claws The Story of Rostam and Esfandiyar from the Persian Book of Kins, Mage Books, 99. **CONTACT ADDRESS** Princeton Univ, 110 Jones Hall, Princeton, NJ 08540. **EMAIL** jwc@princeton.edu

CLINTON, KEVIN
PERSONAL Born 09/29/1942, New York, NY, m, 1970, 2 children **DISCIPLINE** CLASSICS **EDUCATION** Boston Col, BA, 64; Johns Hopkins Univ, PhD, 69. **CAREER** Asst Prof Classics, St Louis Univ, 69-70; from Asst Prof to Assoc Prof, 70-81, Prof Classics, Cornell Univ, 81, Chmn Dept, 77-83; Vis Prof, Univ Calif-Berkeley, 86; mem, Inst for Advanced Study, 87-88; 99-00. **HONORS AND AWARDS** Am Coun Learned Soc fel, 75; Soc for Humanities fel, Cornell Univ, 76-77; spec res fel, Am Sch Class Studies, Athens, 83-84; Guggenheim Fel, 87-88; corresponding mem, Ger Archaeol Inst; NEH fel, 99-00. **MEMBERSHIPS** Am Philol Asn; Archaeol Inst Am. **RESEARCH** Greek religion, literature and institutions. **SELECTED PUBLICATIONS** Auth, Inscriptions from Eleusis, Arkhaiologike Ephemeris, 71; Apollo, Pan and Zeus, avengers of vultures: Agamemnon, 55-9, Am J Philol, 74; The Sacred Officials of the Eleusinian Mysteries, Am Philos Soc, 74; The Hymn to Zeus, Traditio, 79; A Law in the City Eleusinion Concerning the Mysteries, 80 & The Nature of the Late Fifth-Century Revision of the Athenian Law Code, Suppl 19, 80, Hesperia; Myth and Cult: The Iconography of the Eleusinian Hysterics, Stockholm, 92; The Thesmophorion in Central Athens and the Celebration of the Thesmophoria in Attica, Stockholm, 97. **CONTACT ADDRESS** Dept of Class, Cornell Univ, 120 Goldwin Smith, Ithaca, NY 14853-0001.

CLIVIO, GIANRENZO PIETRO
PERSONAL Born 01/18/1942, Turin, Italy **DISCIPLINE** LINGUISTICS, LITERATURE **EDUCATION** Univ Torino, Italy, BA, 62; Brandeis Univ, MA, 64; Harvard Univ, PhD (ling), 67. **CAREER** From asst prof to assoc prof, 68-77, prof Ital, Univ Toronto, 77-, Pres, Can Ctr Ital Cult & Educ, 77-81; pres, Nat Cong Ital Canadians, Ont Region, 80-; assoc ed, Can J Ital Studies, 81-; ed, Il Forneri, Bull Can Soc Ital Ling, 81- **MEMBERSHIPS** Am Asn Teachers Ital; Ling Asn US & Can; Int Soc Phonetic Sci; Can Soc Ital Ling (pres, 81-). **RESEARCH** Romance linguistics; sociolinguistics; Italian literature; romance philology, lang contact, bilingualism and lang acquisition, as well as dialectology. **SELECTED PUBLICATIONS** Auth, Observations on Poetic Texts by Borelli, Vittorio, Amedeo and On Settecento Piedemontese, Studi Piemontesi, Vol 0023, 94. **CONTACT ADDRESS** Dept of Ital Studies, Univ of Toronto, Toronto, ON, Canada M5S 1A1. **EMAIL** gclivio@chass.utoronto.ca

CLOGAN, PAUL MAURICE
PERSONAL Born 07/09/1934, Boston, MA, s, 3 children **DISCIPLINE** ENGLISH, COMPARATIVE LITERATURE **EDUCATION** Boston Col, AB, 56, MA, 57; St Michael's Col, PhL, 58; Univ Ill, PhD, 61; Pope John XXIII International, M.Div. 99. **CAREER** From instr to asst prof English, Duke Univ, 61-65; assoc prof English & comp lit, Case Western Reserve Univ, 65-72; adj prof, Cleveland State Univ, 71-72; prof English, Univ N TX, 72-99; prof emer English, Univ N Tex, 00. **HONORS AND AWARDS** Duke Found grant, 62-63; Am Coun Learned Soc fels, 62-64 & 71-72; sr Fulbright-Hays res fels, Italy, 65-66, Scuola Vaticana di Paleografia e Diplomatica, 66-67 & France, 78; Fulbright-Hays res fel; vis lectr, Univ Pisa, 65; Am Philos Soc grants, 65-67 & 69-70; US/UK cult exchange vis lectr, Univ Keele, 66; Bollingen Found & Prix de Rome fels, 66-67; fel, Am Acad Rome, 67; ed, Medievalia et Humanistica, 68-; mem steering comt, Asn Ctr Medieval & Renaissance Studies; Nat Endowment for Humanities fel, 70-71; vis mem, Inst Advan Study, NJ, 70 & 77; Univ N Tx; fac res grants, 72-75 & 80-81; vis lectr, Univ Tours, 78; MLA Medieval Exec Comt, 80-86; Deleg Assembly, 81-86; John Nicholas Brown Prize Comt, 81-83; Medieval Acad Am nominating comt, 75-76; U of N Tex Scholar of the Month, 88, 93; Cert of the U of N Tex Forum on Teaching and Learning, 95. **MEMBERSHIPS** MLA; Medieval Acad Am; Mod Humanities Res Asn; Ling Soc Am; Int Asn Univ Prof of English. **RESEARCH** Medieval literature and culture; history of the English language; literary theory. **SELECTED PUBLICATIONS** Auth, New Directions in Twelfth-Century Courtly Narrative, Mediaevistik, 90; auth, The Knight's Tale and the Ideology of the Roman Antique, Medievalia et Humanistica, 91; auth, The Imagery of the City of Thebes in The Knight's Tale, Typology and English Medieval Literature: Studies in Literary Imagination, 92; auth, Lydgate and the Roman Antique, 92; auth, Renaissance and Discovery: Imagination and Exploration, The Mutual Encounter of East and West, 1492-1992, 92; auth, Visions of Thebes in Medieval Literature, Force of Vision, Visions in History, 95; auth, Moral Discourse in the Trivium, Moral and Political Philosophies in the Middle Ages, 95; auth, Reading Statius in the Renaissance, Acta Selecta Octavi Academiae Latinitati Fovendae, 95; auth, Imaging the City of Thebes in Fifteenth-Century England, Acta Conventus Neo-Latini Hafniensis, 94; Neo-Platoinic_Streak in the Statian Commentary of Fulgentius Planciades, Neoplatonisme et Philosophie Medievale, 97; auth, Italian Humanism in the court of King Robert of Anjou, Acta Conventus Neo-Latini Bariensis, 98. **CONTACT ADDRESS** Univ of No Texas, PO Box 2063, Waterville, ME 04903. **EMAIL** pclogan@ibm.net

CLOUSER, ROBIN
PERSONAL Born 06/04/1942, Philadelphia, PA, m, 1972 **DISCIPLINE** GERMAN **EDUCATION** Ursinus col, AB, 63; Univ Penn, AM 65; Univ Kan, PhD, 71. **CAREER** Asst prof to prof, Ursinus Col, 74-. **HONORS AND AWARDS** Nat Endowment for the Humanities res grant, 82; Am Philos Soc res grant, 82; Am Philos Soc res grant, 91; Laughlin Professional Dev Awd, 92. **MEMBERSHIPS** Am Asn of Teachers of Ger, Phi Sigma Iota, CALICO, NEALL, IALL. **RESEARCH** Johann Wolfgang Goethe, Heinrich von Kleist, Gottfried Keller, Gerhart Hauptmann. **SELECTED PUBLICATIONS** Auth, "Goethe's View of Moravianism in Bekenntnisse einer schonen Seele," Unitas Fratrum, (99): 193-205; auth, Love and Social contracts: Goethe's Unterhaltungen deutscher Ausgewanderten, Stanford Univ, 91; auth, "Gerhart Hauptmann, 1862-1946," Research Guide: Drama, (86): 305-314; auth, "The Pilgrim of Consciousness: Hauptmann's Syncretistic Fairy Tale," Hauptmann-Forschung, Neue Beitrage/Hauptmann Research, New Directions, (86): 303-322; auth, "Heroism in Kleist's Das Erdbeben in Chili," The Germanic Review, (83): 129-140; auth, "Ideas of Utopia in Goethe's Novelle," Publications of the English Goethe society, (79): 1-44; auth, "Romeo und Julia auf dem dorfe: Keller's Variations upon Shakespeare," Journal of english and Germanic Philology, (78): 161-182. **CONTACT ADDRESS** Dept Mod Lang, Ursinus Col, 601 E Main St, Collegeville, PA 19426-2562. **EMAIL** rclouser@ursinus.edu

CLOUTIER, CECILE
PERSONAL Born 06/13/1930, Quebec, PQ, Canada, m, 1966, 1 child **DISCIPLINE** FRENCH **EDUCATION** Laval Univ, BA, 51, LL, 53, DES, 54; La Sorbonne, PhD, 62; McMaster Univ, MPH, 81; Univ Toronto, MTH, 82; Univ Tours, DPs, 83. **CAREER** Prof, Univ Ottawa, 58-64; prof, 64-95, Prof Emer French, Univ Toronto, 95-; guest prof, Laval Univ; guest prof, Queen's Univ; guest prof, Univ Napoli. **HONORS AND AWARDS** Gov Gen Awd poetry, 86; res award, Univ Toronto, 87; Univ Peking Medal, 93; Medaille de la Societe des Poetes francais, 94. **MEMBERSHIPS** PEN; Asn des ecrivains de langue francaise; Union des ecrivains; Soc des ecrivains can; Asn lit can et que. **SELECTED PUBLICATIONS** Auth, Mains de sable, 60; auth, Cuivre et soies, 64; auth, Paupieres, 70; auth, Chaleuils, 79; auth, Pres, 83; auth, Perihelie, 90; auth, Ostraka, 94; auth, Bagues, 96. **CONTACT ADDRESS** Dept of French, Univ of Toronto, Toronto, ON, Canada M5S 1A1.

CLUBB, LOUISE GEORGE
PERSONAL Born 07/22/1930, New York, NY, m, 1954 **DISCIPLINE** COMPARATIVE LITERATURE **EDUCATION** George Washington Univ, AB, 52, MA, 54; Columbia Univ, PhD, 63. **CAREER** Instr, Univ Md, Col Park, 56-57, 61-62; asst prof, George Wash Univ, 62-64; vis asst prof, Univ Calif, Berkeley, 64-65; from assoc prof to full prof, Univ Calif, Berkeley, 66-94; prof of Grad Sch, Univ Calif, Berkeley, 94-; dir, Univ Calif Educ Abroad Prog, Ital Center, 80-82; vis prof, Stanford Univ, 83; dir, Villa I Tatti, Harvard Univ Center for Ital Renaissance Studies, Florence, 85-88. **HONORS AND AWARDS** Fisher Fel, Columbia Univ, 57-59; Am Assoc of Univ Women Fel, 59-60; Folger Shakespeare Libr Fel, 64, 65; Guggenheim Fel, 65-66; Am Philos Soc Grant, 72-73; Am Coun of Learned Soc Fel, 77; Humanities Res Fel, Univ Calif, 76-77, 83; Phi Beta Kappa Excellence in Teaching Awd, 92; Berkeley Citation, 94. **MEMBERSHIPS** Dante Soc Am; Renaissance Soc Am; Am Asn Advan Humanities; Am Comp Lit Asn; Am Asn Teacher Ital. **RESEARCH** Chivalric epic; Renaissance literature; Renaissance drama in England, Italy, Spain and France. **SELECTED PUBLICATIONS** Auth, "Commedia erudita?," Lettere Italiane 4 (92): 598-606; auth, "Pre-Rozzi e Pre-Intronati allo Studio," in Umanesimo a Şiena, Letteratura, arti figurative, ed. R. Guerrini (94), 149-170; auth, "Un repertorio illustrato per compagnie teatrali," Lettere Italiane 3 (95): 240-242; auth, "Italian Renaissance Theatre," in The Oxford Illustrated History of Theatre, ed. John Russell Brown (Oxford Univ Press, 95), 107-141; auth, "Theatrical Examples for Aretino, 'da Siena, studiante in libris, venuto a Roma,'" in Pietro Aretino nel cinquecentenario della nascita, ed. E. Malato (Rome: Salerno Editrice, 95), 981-1008; auth, "Intertextualities: Some Questions," in The Italian World of English Renaissance Drama: Cultural Exchange and Intertextuality, ed. Michele Marrapodi (Newark & London: Univ Del & Assoc Univ Presses, 98); auth, Encyclopedia of the Renaissance, Charles Scribner's Sons (New York), 99. **CONTACT ADDRESS** Dept of Comp Lit, Univ of California, Berkeley, Berkeley, CA 94720.

COADY, JAMES MARTIN
PERSONAL Born 08/14/1941, Kokomo, IN, m, 1966, 1 child **DISCIPLINE** LINGUISTICS **EDUCATION** St Meinrad Col, BA, 63; Ind Univ, Bloomington, IN, 67, PhD(ling), 73. **CAREER** Teacher hist, Bennett High Sch, Marion, Ind, 63-64; instr English, Am Univ Beirut, 67-69; Assoc Prof Ling, Ohio Univ, 71-, Chmn Dept, 80- **MEMBERSHIPS** Ling Soc Am; Teacher English to Speakers Other Lang; Int Reading Asn; Am Asn Applied Ling. **RESEARCH** Reading; vocabulary acquisition; teaching English to speakers of other languages. **SELECTED PUBLICATIONS** Auth, Autonomous Learning of Vocabulary through Extensive Reading, Univ Toulouse (France), 94; author of several articles in, and co-editor of: Second-Language Vocabulary Acquisition: A Rationale for Pedagogy, Cambridge Univ Press, 97; auth, The Development of Lexis in Writing, In: Vom Gelenkten zum Freien Schreiben im Fremdsprachen-Unterricht, Peter Lang Press, 97; author of numerous other articles. **CONTACT ADDRESS** Dept of Ling, Ohio Univ, Athens, OH 45701-2979. **EMAIL** coady@ohiou.edu

COATES, CARROL F.
PERSONAL Born 07/22/1930, Oklahoma City, OK, m, 2 children **DISCIPLINE** FRENCH LANGUAGE AND LITERATURE **EDUCATION** Univ OK, BA; MA; Yale Univ, PhD. **CAREER** Fac, SUNY Binghamton. **HONORS AND AWARDS** Ed, Jour Haitian Studies; assoc ed, Callaloo--A Journal of African-American, Caribbean, and African Arts and Letters. **MEMBERSHIPS** Am Asn of Teachers of French; African Lit Asn; Haitian Studies Asn; Am Translators Asn; Am Literary Translators Asn. **RESEARCH** Poetic structuration of metrical discourse (17th and 19th-century French poetry); Francophone lit, with concentration on the literatures and cultures of Haiti and West Africa; Grammatical and stylistic analysis. **SELECTED PUBLICATIONS** Ed, Transl from Francophone Literature of North Africa, West Africa, and the Caribbean in CARAF Bks series, UP VA; transl, Rene' Depestre, The Festival of the Greasy Pole; transl, Jean-Bertrand Aristide, Dignity; transl, Jacques Stephen Alexis, General Sun; transl, Jacques Stephen Alexis, My Brother; transl, Ahmadou Kourouma, Waiting for the Vote of the Wild Animals. **CONTACT ADDRESS** SUNY, Binghamton, PO Box 6000, Binghamton, NY 13902-6000. **EMAIL** ccoates@binghamton.edu

COBB, EULALIA BENEJAM
PERSONAL Born 10/03/1944, Barcelona, Spain, m, 1967, 2 children **DISCIPLINE** FRENCH, SPANISH **EDUCATION** Birmingham-Southern Col, BA, 66; Univ NC, MA, 68; Univ Ala, PhD(Romance lang), 72. **CAREER** Instr French & Span, Univ Ala, 71-72; instr French, Stillman Col, 72-73; inst assoc, Inst Higher Educ, Univ Ala, 73-74; Assoc Prof French, Western MD Col, 74-, Affirmative action officer, Western Md Col, 77-78; writer, 81- **MEMBERSHIPS** AAUP; Southeastern Mod Lang Asn. **RESEARCH** Jean Anouilh; surrealism; French women writers. **SELECTED PUBLICATIONS** Auth, A Necessary Rigor--The Implications of Multiculturalism for Academic-Standards, Proteus, Vol 0010, 93. **CONTACT ADDRESS** Dept of Foreign Lang, Western Maryland Col, Westminster, MD 21157.

COBBS, ALFRED LEON
PERSONAL Born 09/12/1943, Pamplin, VA **DISCIPLINE** GERMAN LANGUAGE & LITERATURE **EDUCATION** Berea Col, BA, 66; Univ Mo, Columbia, MA, 68; Univ Cincinnati, PhD(German), 74. **CAREER** Instr, Univ Cincinnati, 69-73; asst prof, Univ Va, 73-79; asst prof Wayne State Univ, 79-

84; assoc prof, 84-. **HONORS AND AWARDS** Fulbright Summer Seminars, Federal Republic of Germany, 74, 83; President's Awd for Excellence in Teaching, Wayne State Univ, 84. **MEMBERSHIPS** MLA; Am Asn Teachers German. **RESEARCH** German-American literary relations; modern German literature; literature of minorities in Germany; foreign language pedagogy. **SELECTED PUBLICATIONS** Auth, Teaching Kafka's Verwandlung on the intermediate level, Unterrichtspraxis, 80; Image of the Black in German literature, The Harold Jantz Collection, Duke Univ Ctr Int Studies, 81; auth, The Image of America in Postwar German Literature: Reflections and Perceptions, Peter Lang Verlag, 82; Gunter Grass, Survery of Modern Fantasy Literature, 83; Wilhelm Hauff, Supernatural Fiction Writers, 85; Max von der Grun, Dictionary of Literary Biography, 88. **CONTACT ADDRESS** German and Slavic Stud, Wayne State Univ, 451 Manoogian, Detroit, MI 48202-3919. **EMAIL** a.cobbs@wayne.edu

COBLIN, WELDON SOUTH
PERSONAL Born 02/26/1944, Lexington, KY, m, 1970, 2 children **DISCIPLINE** CHINESE AND SINO-TIBETAN LINGUISTICS **EDUCATION** Univ Wash, BA, 67, PhD(-Chinese), 72. **CAREER** Teaching assoc, Univ Wash, 72-73; asst prof, 73-78, Assoc Prof Chinese, Univ Iowa, 78-, Chmn Dept Asian Lang & Lit, 81- **MEMBERSHIPS** Am Orient Soc; Ling Soc Am; Asn Asian Studies, Soc Study Early China. **RESEARCH** Chinese historical linguistics; Tibetan historical linguistics. **SELECTED PUBLICATIONS CONTACT ADDRESS** Dept of Asian Lang & Lit, Univ of Iowa, Iowa City, IA 52240.

COCOZZELLA, PETER
PERSONAL Born 11/20/1937, Monacilioni, Italy, m, 1964, 1 child **DISCIPLINE** SPANISH LANGUAGE AND LITERATURE **EDUCATION** R Regis Col (Colo), AB, 59; St Louis Univ, PhD(Span), 66. **CAREER** Teacher high sch, Colo, 59-60; from instr to asst prof Span, Univ Mo-St Louis, 65-67; asst prof, Dartmouth Col, 67-70; asst prof, 70-73, Assoc Prof Span, State Univ NY, Binghamton, 73- **MEMBERSHIPS** MLA; Am Asn Teachers Span & Port; NAmer Catalan Soc. **RESEARCH** Castilian and Catalan literatures of the 15th century. **SELECTED PUBLICATIONS CONTACT ADDRESS** Dept of Romance Lang, SUNY, Binghamton, Binghamton, NY 13901.

COELHO, CARL
DISCIPLINE NEUROLOGIC BASES OF SPEECH AND LANGUAGE **EDUCATION** Mich State Univ, BA, 74; Univ Ariz, MS, 76; Univ Conn, PhD, 82. **CAREER** Asst prof, Univ Conn. **RESEARCH** Neurologic disorders of speech and language in adults. **SELECTED PUBLICATIONS** Auth, Discourse Deficits Following Traumatic Brain Injury: A Critical Review of the Recent Literature, Aphasiology, 95; coauth, The Assessment of Limb Apraxia: An Investigation of Task Effects and Their Cause, Brain and Cognition, 96; Treatment Efficacy for Cognitive-Communication Disorders Resulting from Traumatic Brain Injury in Adults, J Speech and Hearing Res, 96; Application of Semantic Feature Analysis as a Treatment for Aphasic Dysnomia, Amer J Speech-Lang Pathology, 95; Impairments of Discourse Abilities and Executive Functions in Traumatically Brain Injured Adults, Brain Injury, 95. **CONTACT ADDRESS** Dept of Communication Sci, Univ of Connecticut, Storrs, 850 Bolton Rd, Storrs, CT 06269-1085. **EMAIL** coelho@uconnvm.uconn.edu

COFFEY, JEROME EDWARD
PERSONAL Born 08/04/1940, Elmira, NY, m, 1964, 2 children **DISCIPLINE** ENGLISH LANGUAGE AND LINGUISTICS **EDUCATION** Canisius Col, AB, 62; State Univ NYork, Buffalo, MA, 65, PhD(English lang), 68. **CAREER** Asst prof English, Western Ill Univ, 66-68 & State Univ NY Col, Brockport, 68-72; Assoc Prof English, Mont State Univ, 72-. **MEMBERSHIPS** MLA; Ling Soc Am. **RESEARCH** Oral poetry in Old and Middle English; the Faeroese language and bardic poetry. **SELECTED PUBLICATIONS CONTACT ADDRESS** Dept of English, Montana State Univ, Bozeman, Bozeman, MT 59715.

COFFTA, DAVID J.
DISCIPLINE CLASSICAL PHILOLOGY **EDUCATION** Adjunct assoc prof, Canisius Col. **MEMBERSHIPS** APA; CAMWS. **SELECTED PUBLICATIONS** Auth, Programmatic Synthesis in Horace, Odes 3 13 in Collection Latomus, forthcoming; Programme and Persona in Horace Odes 1 5, in Eranos, forthcoming. **CONTACT ADDRESS** Classics Dept, Canisius Col, 2001 Main St, Buffalo, NY 14208. **EMAIL** cofftad@canisius.edu

COHEN, ALVIN PHILIP
PERSONAL Born 12/12/1937, Los Angeles, CA, m, 1984, 2 children **DISCIPLINE** CHINESE PHILOLOGY & CULTURAL HISTORY **EDUCATION** Univ Calif, Berkeley, BS, 60, MA, 66, PhD(Orient Lang), 71. **CAREER** Lectr Orient Lang, Univ Calif, Davis, 70-71; asst prof, 71-77, assoc prof Chinese, Univ Mass, Amherst 77-83; actg bibliogr Orient Collection, Univ Mass, Amherst, 71-; prof, Chinese Univ Mass, Amherst, 83-; Dept Chair, 91-97. **HONORS AND AWARDS** Fulbright-Hays Fel, 68-69; China and Inner Asia Council of the Assoc for Asian Studies grant, 95-97. **MEMBERSHIPS** Am Orient Soc; Soc Study Chinese Relig; Assn for Asian Studies; Early Medieval China Group; Tang Studies Soc. **RESEARCH** Chinese historiography; Chinese folk religion; Classical Chinese Language. **SELECTED PUBLICATIONS** Auth, Grammar Notes for Introductory Classical Chinese, Chinese Materials Ctr, 75, 2nd ed, 80; Notes on a Chinese workingclass bookshelf, J Am Orient Soc, 76; Coercing the rain deities in ancient China, Hist Relig, 78; ed, Selected Works of Peter A Boodberg, Univ Calif, Berkeley, 79; Legend, Lore and Religion in China, Chinese Materials Ctr, 79; auth, Introduction to Research in Chinese Source Materials, Far Eastern Publications, Yale Univ, 00. **CONTACT ADDRESS** Asian Lang and Lit Dept, Univ of Massachusetts, Amherst, Amherst, MA 01003-9277. **EMAIL** cohen@asianlan.umass.edu

COHEN, L. KEITH
DISCIPLINE COMPARATIVE LITERATURE **EDUCATION** Columbia Univ, BA, 67; Princeton, PhD, 75. **CAREER** Charge de cours, Univ Paris, 70-74; asst prof to prof, Univ Wisconsin-Madison, 74-. **HONORS AND AWARDS** Woodrow Wilson Fel, 58; Nea Grant, 78; Fulbright Sen Lecureship, 81. **MEMBERSHIPS** MLA, SCS. **RESEARCH** Literature and Other Arts, especially cinema; Modern Latin American, French and Anglo-American Literature, Caribbean Poetry. **SELECTED PUBLICATIONS** Auth, Film and Fiction, Yale Univ Press, 79; auth, Natural Settings, Full Court, 80; auth, Writing in a Film Age, Univ Press of Colo, 91. **CONTACT ADDRESS** Comparative Lit, Univ of Wisconsin, Madison, 1220 Linden Dr, Madison, WI 53706-1525.

COHEN, ROBERT
PERSONAL Born Zurich, Switzerland **DISCIPLINE** GERMAN **EDUCATION** NY Univ, MA, 86; PhD, 88. **CAREER** Adj asst prof to adj prof, NY Univ, 92-. **HONORS AND AWARDS** Choice Outstanding Acad Book Award, 94. **MEMBERSHIPS** MLA, Int Brecht Soc, Internationale Peter Weiss Gesellschaft, Soc for Exile Studies, Anna-Seghers-Gesellschaft, Am Asn of Teachers of Ger. **RESEARCH** Weimer modernism and avantgarde, exile literature, literary representations of the Holocaust, Marxist literary theory. **SELECTED PUBLICATIONS** Auth, Versuche uber Weiss 'Asthetik des Widerstands', Peter Lang (NY), 89; auth, "Bio-Bibligraphisches hand-buch zu Peter Weiss 'Asthetik des Widerstands', Argument Verlag (Berlin), 89; auth, Peter Weiss in seiner Zeit, Metzler, (Stuttgart, (92): auth, Understanding Peter Weiss, Univ SCar Pr, 93; auth, "Arnold Zweig's War Novellas of 1914 and their Versions: Litera-ture, Modernity, and the Demands of the Day," War, Violence and the Mod-ern Condition, ed Bernd Hupp-auf, (97): 277-89; auth, Peter Weiss: Marat/Sade, The Investigation, and The Shadow of the Body of the Coachman, Continuum, (NY), 98; auth, "Brechts 'Furcht und Elend des III. Reiches und der Status des Ge-stus," Brecht Yearbook, Vol 24, (99): 192-207. **CONTACT ADDRESS** Ger Lang and Lit, New York Univ, 726 Broadway, 6th Flr, New York, NY 10003. **EMAIL** robert.cohen@nyu.edu

COHEN, WALTER ISAAC
PERSONAL Born 10/21/1949, New York, NY, m, 1971, 3 children **DISCIPLINE** COMPARATIVE LITERATURE **EDUCATION** Stanford Univ, BA, 71; Univ Calif, Berkeley, MA, 74, PhD(comp lit), 80. **CAREER** Prof Comp Lit, Cornell Univ, 92-; dean grad school, Cornell Univ, 93-; vprovost & dean grad school, 98-. **HONORS AND AWARDS** Clark Distinguished Teaching Awd, Cornell, 86; Mellon Professorship In Teaching, 88-90. **MEMBERSHIPS** MLA; Marxist Lit Group. **RESEARCH** History of European Lit. **SELECTED PUBLICATIONS** Auth, Drama of a Nation: Public Theater in Renaissance England and Spain, Cornell Univ Press, 85; ed, The Norton Shakespeare, Norton, 97. **CONTACT ADDRESS** Grad Sch, Cornell Univ, 350 Caldwell Hall, Ithaca, NY 14853-6201. **EMAIL** wic1@cornell.edu

COHN, DORRIT
PERSONAL Born 08/09/1924, Vienna, Austria, 2 children **DISCIPLINE** GERMAN AND COMPARATIVE LITERATURE **EDUCATION** Radcliffe Col, BA, 45, MA, 46; Stanford Univ, PhD(Ger), 64. **CAREER** From asst prof to prof Ger, Ind Univ, Bloomington, 64-71; actg chmn, Ger Dept, 77-78, Prof Ger, Harvard Univ, 71-, Guggenheim Found fel, 70-71; mem adv comt, PMLA, 75-79; chmn div 20th century Ger lit, MLA, 76-77; mem ed adv bd, German Quart, 78-; vis sr fel, Coun of Humanities, Princeton Univ, 82- **MEMBERSHIPS** Am Asn Teachers Ger; Am Comp Lit Asn; MLA; Acad Lit Studies. **RESEARCH** Modern novel; 19th and 20th century German literature; narrative theory. **SELECTED PUBLICATIONS CONTACT ADDRESS** Dept of Germanic Lang, Harvard Univ, Boylston Hall, Cambridge, MA 02138.

COHN, JOEL
PERSONAL Born New York, NY **DISCIPLINE** JAPANESE LITERATURE **EDUCATION** Cornell Univ, AB, 71; Tokyo Univ Foreign Studies, BA, 75; Harvard Univ, MA, 78, PhD, 84. **CAREER** Lectr, Harvard Univ, 84-85; post-doctoral fel, E. D. Reischauer Inst, Harvard Univ, 85-86; technical writer, Prime Computer, Inc, 86-88; asst prof, Univ Haw at Manoa, 88-95, assoc prof, 95-. **HONORS AND AWARDS** Cornell Univ, AB, summa cum laude, 75. **RESEARCH** Modrn Japanese fiction, comic literature. **SELECTED PUBLICATIONS** Auth, Studies in the Comic Spirits in Modern Japanese Fiction, Harvard Univ Asia Center (98). **CONTACT ADDRESS** Dept East Asian Lang & Lit, Univ of Hawaii, Manoa, 1890 East West Rd, Honolulu, HI 96822-2318. **EMAIL** cohn@hawaii.edu

COHN, ROBERT G.
PERSONAL Born 09/05/1921, Richmond, VA, m, 1947, 2 children **DISCIPLINE** FRENCH **EDUCATION** Univ Va, BA, 43; Yale Univ, MA, 47, PhD, 49. **CAREER** Founding ed, Yale French Studies, 48-49, instr French, Yale Univ, 49-50; Fulbright fel, 50-51; asst prof French, Swarthmore Col, 52-54 & Vassar Col, 54-57; assoc prof, 59-64, Prof French, Stanford Univ, 64-; in charge confs French, Univ NY, 54-57; fels, Am Coun Learned Soc & Nat Endowment for Humanities, 69-70; assoc ed, Stanford Fr Rev & Stanford French & Italian Studies. **HONORS AND AWARDS** Guggenheim fel, 56-57, 86-87; **MEMBERSHIPS** ALSC. **RESEARCH** French poetry; 19th and 20th century French literature. **SELECTED PUBLICATIONS** Auth, L'Oeuvre de Mallarme, 51; auth, Mallarme Prolongation--A Reply to Furbank,P.N., NY Rev Bk(s), Vol 0042, 95; Mallarme Wake, New Lit Hist, Vol 0026, 95; auth, The Poetry of Reinbared, 73, 99; auth, Toward the Poems of Mallarme, 51, reprinted expanded 65, 00. **CONTACT ADDRESS** Dept of French & Ital, Stanford Univ, Stanford, CA 94305.

COLANERI, JOHN NUNZIO
PERSONAL Born 01/08/1930, New York, NY, m, 1967, 1 child **DISCIPLINE** ITALIAN **EDUCATION** City Col New York, BA, 52; Columbia Univ, MA, 54, PhD(Ital), 68. **CAREER** Prof Ital & Chmn Dept Mod Lang, Iona Col, 59-, Part-time lectr Ital, Col New Rochelle, 61- **MEMBERSHIPS** Ital Teachers Asn (pres, 69-71); Am Asn Teachers Span & Port. **SELECTED PUBLICATIONS** Auth, Fra Cristoforon and L'innominato: Two of a kind?, J NY State Fed Foreign Lang Teachers, 5/68; transl, Giovannitti, the United Nations silver anniversary, Thought, summer 70; auth, Reflection of a man: Guido Cavalcanti, Paideuma, winter 72; Edition of Lezzioni d'amore, Fink, Munich, 73; co-ed (with G Lipton), Italian English--English Italian Bilingual Dict, 80, 2nd ed, 82; Italian-English/English-Italian Bilingual Dictionary, 89, Barrons, 2nd ed, revised, 98; 501 Italian Verbs, Barrons, 92; auth, The Immigrant Mother, Ital Am Rev, 93. **CONTACT ADDRESS** Dept of Mod Lang, Iona Col, 715 North Ave, New Rochelle, NY 10801-1890.

COLBY-HALL, ALICE MARY
PERSONAL Born 02/25/1932, Portland, ME, w, 1976, 3 children **DISCIPLINE** MEDIEVAL FRENCH LITERATURE **EDUCATION** Colby Col, BA, 53; Middlebury Col, MA, 54; Columbia Univ, PhD, 62. **CAREER** Teacher high sch, Maine, 54-55; teacher French, Gould Acad, Bethel, Maine, 55-57; lectr, Columbia Univ, 59-60; from instr to assoc prof Romance Studies, 62-75, Prof Romance Studies, Cornell Univ, 75-97; prof emer, 97-. **HONORS AND AWARDS** Fulbright grant, 53-54; NEH Fel, 84-85; recipient, Medaille des Amis d'Orange, 85; Chevalier des Arts et Lettres, French Govt, 97. **MEMBERSHIPS** Mediaeval Acad Am; MLA; Soc Rencesvals; Int Arthurian Soc; Acad de Vaucluse; Les Amis d'Orange; Soc Guilhem IX; Asn Internationale d'Etudes Occitanes. **RESEARCH** Chretien de Troyes; the style of medieval French literary texts; William cycle epics. **SELECTED PUBLICATIONS** Auth, The Portrait in 12th Century French Literature: An Example of the Stylistic Originality of Chretien de Troyes, Droz, 65; In Search of the Lost Epics of the Lower Rhone Valley, Olifant, 80/81; Frustration and Fulfillment: The Double Ending of the Bel Inconnu, Yale Fr Studies, 84; William of Orange in the Canso de la Crosada, Magister Regis: Studies in Honor of Robert Earl Kaske, 86; L'Heraldique au service de la linguistique: le cas du cor nier de Guillaume, Au carrefour des routes d'Europe: la chanson de geste, 87; Guillaume d' Orange sur un nouveau sceau medieval de l'abbaye de Saint-Guilhem-le-Desert, Olifant, 90; Guillaume d' Orange, l'abbaye de Gellone et la vache pie de Chateauneuf-de-Gadagne, Etudes sur l' Herault, 93. **CONTACT ADDRESS** Dept of Romance Studies, Cornell Univ, Morrill Hall, Ithaca, NY 14853-4701. **EMAIL** amc12@cornell.edu

COLE, EVE BROWNING
DISCIPLINE ANCIENT GREEK PHILOSOPHY, FEMINIST THEORY, ETHICS, CLASSICAL STUDIES **EDUCATION** Univ Fla, BA, 73; Univ Calif, San Diego, PhD; 79. **CAREER** Instr, Univ Denver; instr, Ohio State Univ; assoc prof, 84-, ch, Environ Stud adv bd, Univ Minn, Duluth. **RESEARCH** Ancient Greek philosophy; ethics. **SELECTED PUBLICATIONS** Auth, Philosophy and Feminist Criticism, Paragon, 93; coed, Explorations in Feminist Ethics: Theory and Practice, Ind UP, 88. **CONTACT ADDRESS** Univ of Minnesota, Duluth, Duluth, MN 55812-2496.

COLE, GEORGE L.
PERSONAL Born 07/26/1974, Mayaguez, Puerto Rico **DISCIPLINE** SPANISH **EDUCATION** Univ Puerto Rico, MA, 98; WSU, MA, 00. **CAREER** TA, WSU, 98-00; TA, WSU, 98-00. **HONORS AND AWARDS** WSU Travel Grant, 98; Lind-

bergh Scholarship, 98. **MEMBERSHIPS** Am Assoc of Teachers of Span and Port, MLA. **RESEARCH** Latin American Theatre, Puerto Rican Theatre, Cuban Theatre, Santeria, Freemasonry. **SELECTED PUBLICATIONS** Auth, Masoneria es verbo, no sustantivo, Acacia, 98; auth, Humilde defensa de la orden masonica, Acacia. **CONTACT ADDRESS** Lang & Lit, Arizona State Univ, Tempe, AZ 85287. **EMAIL** George.Cole@asu.edu

COLE, PETER
PERSONAL Born 08/01/1941, Miami Beach, FL, m, 1958, 2 children **DISCIPLINE** LINGUISTICS, LANGUAGE TEACHING **EDUCATION** Southern Ill Univ, Carbondale, MA, 71; Univ Ill, Urbana, PhD(ling), 73. **CAREER** Instr English, Haifa Univ, Haifa, 67-68 & Southern Ill Univ, Carbondale, 69-73; asst prof, 73-80, assoc prof ling, Univ Ill, Urbana-Champaign, 80-. **MEMBERSHIPS** Linguistic Soc Am. **RESEARCH** Comparative syntax, ling theory, Chinese, Hebrew, Malay, Quechua, reflexives, questions, relative clauses, pronominals, the interface of ling with other cognitive sciences. **SELECTED PUBLICATIONS** Coauth, Head Movement and Long Distance Reflexives, with Li-May Sung, Linguistic Inquiry 25, (94): 355-406; coauth, Is There LF Movement?, with Gabriella Hermon, Linguistic Inquiry 25, (94): 239-262; co-ed, Language in the Andes, with Gabriella Hermon and Mario Daniel Martin, Newark, D.E., Latin Am Studies Progra, Univ of Del, 95; auth, antecedents and Blockers of Long Distance reflexives: the Case of Chinese Ziji, with Chengchi Wang, Ling Inquiry 27, 3, (96); coauth, "Apa Yang" Apa Yang"?, with Gabriella Hermon and Norhaida Bt. Aman), Universiti Sains Malaysia, 97; coauth, The Typology of WH Movement, with Gabriella Hermon, Syntax 1, (98); coauth, An Apparent Typological Anomaly: Long Distance Reflexives in Singapore Malay, with Gabriella Hermon, Ling Typology 2, 1, (98); coauth, Yes/No Question in the Teochew of Singapore, with Cher Leng Lee, Journal of East Asian Ling, 6:2, (97): coauth, Chaozhou Fangyan Zhong San Zhong Fanfu Wenju, Three Types of Yes/No Questions in a Teochew Dialect, with Cher Leng Lee, (97); co-ed, Long Distance Reflexives, with Gabriella Hermon and James Huang, New York: Syntax and Semantics Series, Academic Press, 99. **CONTACT ADDRESS** Dept of Ling, Univ of Delaware, 46 E Delaware Ave, Newark, DE 19716. **EMAIL** pcole@atsudel.edu

COLECCHIA, FRANCESCA
PERSONAL Born Pittsburgh, PA **DISCIPLINE** SPANISH LANGUAGE AND LITERATURE **EDUCATION** Duquesne Univ, BEd, 47; Univ Pittsburgh, MLitt, 49, PhD, 54. **CAREER** Dir lang lab prog, 60-72, Prof Span, Duquesne Univ, 47-, Chmn Mod Lang Dept, 77-, Assoc ed, Estudios, 51-55; V Cicto Int fel, Cent Univ Eduador, 62; Fulbright lectr grant, Colombia, 63-64; vis prof Span novel, Mt Mercy Col, 68; ed, Nalld Sec Sch Dir Pa, 69; guest lectr Latin Am lit, Educ Prof Develop Assistance Inst, ECarolina Univ, 69; grant, US Off Educ Inst, Crisis: Women in Higher Educ, 71; assoc ed, Garcia Lorca Rev, 73-; coordr res prog, Women Ethnicity and Mental Health, 75-77. **HONORS AND AWARDS** Am-Ital Women of Achievement Awd, 69. **MEMBERSHIPS** MLA; Inst Int Lit Iberoam; Am Asn Univ Women; Nat Coun Admin Women Educ; Am Asn Teachers Span & Port. **RESEARCH** Latin American theatre; theatre of Garcia Lorca; contemporary Latin American literature of protest. **SELECTED PUBLICATIONS** Auth, Blood Wedding, Yerma, and the House of Bernarda Alba, Garcialorca Tragic Trilogy, Estreno-Cuadernos del Teatro Espanol Contemporaneo, Vol 0019, 93; The History of the Commedia-Dellarte in Modern Hispanic Literature with Special Attention to the Work of Garcia-Lorca, Estreno-Cuadernos del Teatro Espanol Contemporaneo, Vol 0023, 97; Love Customs in 18th-Century Spain, Critica Hispanica, Vol 0017, 95; The Answer la Respuesta--English, Spanish, Critica Hispanica, Vol 0018, 96; An Introduction to Spanish-Amer Lit 3rd-Edition, Critica Hispanica, Vol 0018, 96; The State of Theater in Spain--Spanish , Estreno-Cuadernos del Teatro Espanol Contemporaneo, Vol 0023, 97; Celestinas Brood, Continuities of the Baroque in Spanish and Latin-American Literatures, Critica Hispanica, Vol 0016, 94; Funeral En Teruel, Modern Evocations of an Ancient Legend--A Compatarive Study Between Tirso-De-Molina, Hartzenbush and Monteshuidobro, Critica Hispanica, Vol 0016, 94; Lorca Drawings and Poem, Critica Hispanica, Vol 0018, 96; A Selected Bibliography of Studies on Garcia Lorca,Federico la Casa de Bernarda Alba 1985-1994, Estreno-Cuadernos del Teatro Espanol Contemporaneo, Vol 0021, 95; Federico--Una Historia Distinta, Estreno-Cuadernos del Teatro Espanol Contemporaneo, Vol 0021, 95; An Introduction to Spanish-Amer Lit 3rd-Edition, Critica Hispanica, Vol 0018, 96; Writing, Private Space--Laforet, Matute, Moix, Tusquets, Riera and Roig by Themselves--Spanish, Critica Hispanica, Vol 0015, 93. **CONTACT ADDRESS** Dept of Mod Lang, Duquesne Univ, Pittsburgh, PA 15219. **EMAIL** colecchia@duq.edu

COLEMAN, JOHN E.
PERSONAL Born 04/23/1940, Vancouver, BC, Canada **DISCIPLINE** CLASSICAL ARCHEOLOGY, GREEK **EDUCATION** Univ BC, BA, 61; Univ Cincinnati, PhD(classics), 67. **CAREER** Asst prof classics, Univ Colo, 67-69; lectr classical archaeol, Bryn Mawr Col, 69-70; asst prof, 70-74, Assoc Prof Classics, Cornell Univ, 74-, prof 81-, Dir, Excavations at Elean Pylos, Greece, 68 & Cornell Excavations at Alambra, Cyprus, 76-84; Haki and East Lokris Proj, Greece, 98-. **MEMBERSHIPS** Archaeol Inst Am; Am Sch Class Studies Athens. **RESEARCH** Classical archaeology; Aegean archaeology; Cypriot archaeology. **SELECTED PUBLICATIONS** Auth, Alambra, 96; auth, "Haki: the 1992-1994 Field Seasons," Hesperia 68 (99). **CONTACT ADDRESS** Dept of Classics, Cornell Univ, 120-A Goldwin Smith, Ithaca, NY 14853-0001. **EMAIL** jec13@cornell.edu

COLEMAN, PATRICK J.
PERSONAL Born 09/17/1950, Waukegan, IL, m, 1977, 1 child **DISCIPLINE** FRENCH **EDUCATION** McGill Univ, BA, 70; Yale Univ, PhD, 76. **CAREER** Acting Asst Prof, Cornell Univ, 74-75; Acting Asst Prof to Prof, UCLA, 75-. **HONORS AND AWARDS** William Andrews Clark Prof, UCLA, 94-95, 2000-2001; Hooker Vis Prof, McMaster Univ, 01. **MEMBERSHIPS** MLA; Am Soc for 18th Cent Studies; Asn for Can Studies in the U.S.; Am Coun for Que Studies; Asn Benjamin Constant; N Am Soc for the Study of J.J. Rousseau. **RESEARCH** 18th Century French literature and thought; Canadian literature in French and English. **SELECTED PUBLICATIONS** Auth, The Limits of Synmpath: Gabrielle Roy's 'The Tin Flute', Droz, 93; ed, Rousseau, 'Discourse on Inequality', ECW, 94; auth, Reparative Realism: Mourning and Modernity in the French Novel 1730-1830, Droz, 98; co-ed, Reconceptualizing Nature, Science, and Aesthetics; contribution a une approche nouvelle des Lumieres helvetiques, Slatkine, 98; ed, Rousseau, 'Confessions', Oxford Univ Press, 00; ed, Representations of the Self from the Renaissance to Romanticism, Cambridge Univ Press, 00; ed, Benjamin Constant, 'Adolphe', Oxford Univ Press, 01. **CONTACT ADDRESS** Dept French, Univ of California, Los Angeles, PO Box 951550, Los Angeles, CA 90095-1550. **EMAIL** coleman@humnet.ucla.edu

COLILLI, PAUL
DISCIPLINE ITALIAN LITERATURE **EDUCATION** Univ Toronto, PhD. **RESEARCH** Renaissance; modern-to-contemporary lit. **SELECTED PUBLICATIONS** Auth, "Trecento and Quattrocento," Rivista di Studi Italiani, 9, (91): 159-166; auth, "Trecento e quattrocento," Rivista di Studi Italiani, 10, (92): 95-106; auth, "Trecento e quattrocento," Rivista di Studi Italiani, 10, (92): 160-173; auth, "Purgatorio XIV," Lectura Dantis: A Forum for Dante research and Interpretation, 12, (93): 201-211; auth, "Trecento e quattrocento," Rivista di Studi Italiani, 11, (93): 159-177; auth, "La poetica dell'aletheia nell'Africa del petrarca, Cosenza, IT: Marra editore, 93; auth, Signs of the hermetic imagination, Toronto, ON: Victoria Col, Univ of Toronto, 93; coauth, "The Italian cultural presence in Sudbury," in The luminous mosiac: Italian cultural organizations in Ontario, ed. By J. Molinaro and M. Kuitunen, (Welland, ON: Editions Soleil, 93): 237-251; auth, "The pleats of destiny: Marino, Deleuze, the fold," in The Sense of Marino, ed. By F. Guardiani, (New York, NY: Legas): 191-201; auth, The idea of a living spirit: poetic logic as a contemporary theory, (Toronto, ON, Univ of Toronto Press, 97): 290. **CONTACT ADDRESS** Dept of Modern Languages, Laurentian Univ, 935 Ramsey Lake Rd, Sudbury, ON, Canada P3E 2C6. **EMAIL** pcolilli@nickel.laurentian.ca

COLINA, SONIA
DISCIPLINE LINGUISTICS, SPANISH, TRANSLATION **EDUCATION** Univ de Santiago de Compostela, Spain, Licenciatura, 87; Southern IL Univ, MA, 89; SUNY MA, 91; Univ IL, PhD, 95. **CAREER** Asst prof, Ind Univ, 95-97; asst prof, Ariz State Univ, 97-. **HONORS AND AWARDS** Scholar, Univ of London, 86; ISEP, Southern IL Univ; Fel, Ind Univ Fac, 96; Grant, Ind Univ Fac, 96. **MEMBERSHIPS** LSA; MLA; ATA. **RESEARCH** Phonological theory, translation studies. **SELECTED PUBLICATIONS** Auth, "Spanish Noun Truncation: The Emergence of the Unmarked", Ling 34.6 (96): 1199-1218; auth, "Teaching Translation to Undergraduates: What Errors Reveal", Transl 3 (97): 245-258; auth, "Contrastive Rhetoric and Text-typological Conventions in Translation Teaching", Target 9.2 (97): 353-371; auth, "Syntax, Discourse Analysis and Translation Studies", Babel 43.2 (97): 126-137; auth, "Epenthesis and Deletion in Galician: An Optimality-Theoretic Approach", Issues in the Phonology and Morphology of the Major Iberian Languages, eds F. Martinez-Gil and A. Morales-Front, Georgetown Univ Pr, (97): 235-267; auth, "Identity Constraints and Spanish Resyllabification", Lingua 103, (97): 1-23; auth, "Alternatives to Level and Cyclic Ordering: A Non-Derivational Account of Onset-Strengthening in Spanish", Perspectives on Spanish Linguistics, eds J Gutierrez-Rexach, and J del Balle, (98): 41-61; auth, "Reexamining Spanish Glides: Analogically conditioned Variation in Vocoid Sequences in Spanish Dialects", Advances in Hispanic Linguistics: Papers from the Second Hispanic Linguistics Symposium, eds, J. Gutierrez-Rexach, F. Martinez-Gil, Cascadilla Pr, 99; auth, "Transfer and Unwarranted Transcoding in the Acquisition of Translational Competence: An Empirical Investigation", Translation and the (Re)location of Meaning, Selected Papers of the CERA Res Sem in Transl Studies, Leuven (99): 375-391. **CONTACT ADDRESS** Dept Lang and Lit, Arizona State Univ, PO Box 870202, Tempe, AZ 85287-0202. **EMAIL** scolina@asu.edu

COLKER, MARVIN L.
PERSONAL Born 03/19/1927, Pittsburgh, PA, m, 1959, 1 child **DISCIPLINE** LATIN **EDUCATION** Univ Pitts, BA summa cum laude, 48; Harvard Univ, PhD 51. **CAREER** Univ Virginia, inst, asst prof, assoc prof, prof, ch dept classics, prof emeritus, 53 to 98-. **HONORS AND AWARDS** Sheldon Fel Harvard; Litt D hon Trinity Col; ACLS Fel; Guggenheim Fel; Fulbright Fel; BSA Fel; Phi Beta Kappa. **MEMBERSHIPS** MAA; AMARC; North American Assoc. of Medieval Latin; CAMW&S. **RESEARCH** Medieval latin; latin palaeography; cataloguing of medieval manuscripts. **SELECTED PUBLICATIONS** Auth, Latin poems from Paris Codex B N lat 8433, Medievalia et Humanistica, 58; De nobilitate animi, Mediaeval Studies, 61; Richard of Saint Victor and the anonymous of Bridlington, Traditio, 62; Analecta Dublinensia, Mediaeval Acad Am, 75; A Hagiographic polemic, Mediaeval Studies, 77; Galteri De Castellione Alexandreis, Antenore, 78; Trinity College Dublin Library: Descriptive Catalogue of the Medieval and Renaissance Latin Manuscripts, 2 vols, 91; auth, "A Previously Unpublished History of the Trojans," Journal of Medieval Latin, 98. **CONTACT ADDRESS** Dept of Classics, Univ of Virginia, Charlottesville, VA 22903. **EMAIL** mlcolker@cstone.net

COLL-TELLECHA, REYES
PERSONAL Born 11/17/1960, Spain, s **DISCIPLINE** HISPANIC STUDIES **EDUCATION** Univ Mass, PhD. **CAREER** Vis Prof, Wellesley Col; vis prof Wash Univ; assoc prof, Univ of Mass. **MEMBERSHIPS** Amnesty Intl. **RESEARCH** Literature and Society. **SELECTED PUBLICATIONS** Ed, La Vida de Lazarillo de Tormes, Akal (Madrid, Spain), 97. **CONTACT ADDRESS** Dept Hisp Studies, Univ of Massachusetts, Boston, 100 Morrissey Blvd, Dorchester, MA 02125-3300.

COLLINS, DEREK B.
PERSONAL Born 08/24/1965, Washington, DC, m, 1990, 2 children **DISCIPLINE** COMPARATIVE LIT; CLASSICS; FOLKLORE & MYTHOLOGY **EDUCATION** Univ CA, Los Angeles, MA, 91; Harvard Univ, PhD, 97. **CAREER** Asst Prof Classics, Univ Texas at Austin, 97-. **HONORS AND AWARDS** Nat Academy of Sciences, Ford Found, Doctoral Dissertation fel, 9/96--6/97. **MEMBERSHIPS** Am Philos Asn; Classical Asn of the Middle West and South; Am Folklore Soc. **RESEARCH** Greek lit; comparative lit (German); witchcraft. **SELECTED PUBLICATIONS** Trans, Greek selections in the Appendix to Claude Calame, The Craft of Poetic Speech in Ancient Greece, Cornell Univ Press, 95; auth, The Myth and Ritual of Ezili Freda in Hurston's Their Eyes Were Watching God, Western Folklore 55, 96; trans with J. Orion, Claude Calame, Young Women's Choruses in Ancient Greece: Their Morphology, Religious Role, and Social Functions, Lanham, MD, Rowman & Littlefield Pubs, 97; auth, Fatum, in the Dictionaire International des Termes Litteraitres, gen ed, Jean-Marie Grassin, A. Francke-Berne, Saur-Vg Pub, Berne, Munich, Paris, New York, 97; On the Aesthetics of the Deceiving Self in Nietzsche, Pindar, and Theognis, Nietzsche-Studien 26, 97; Review of Jacob Rabinowitz, The Rotting Goddess: The Origin of the Witch in Classical Antiquity, Scholia 7 (ns), 16, 98; Immortal Armor: The Concept of Alke in Archaic Greek Poetry, Lanham, MD, Rowman & Littlefield Pubs, 98; Hesiod and the Divine Voice of the Muses, Arethusa, forthcoming, 99. **CONTACT ADDRESS** Dept of Classical Studies, Univ of Michigan, Ann Arbor, 2160 Angell Hall, 435 S State St, Ann Arbor, MI 48109-1003. **EMAIL** dbcollin@umich.edu

COLOMBAT, ANDRE P.
DISCIPLINE FRENCH **EDUCATION** Universite Lyon II, Fr, MA ; Washington Univ, PhD. **CAREER** Assoc prof. **RESEARCH** Bilingual writers, Beckett, Green, Bianciotti, Semprun, Huidobro, del Castillo, Wiesel, Feyderman, Agosin, Chavez; contemporary philosophy and criticism, Deleuze, French film and the Holocaust; Modern France and francophone literature. **SELECTED PUBLICATIONS** Auth, The Holocaust In French Film, 93; Deleuze et la litterature, 90. **CONTACT ADDRESS** Dept of Foreign Languages, Loyola Col, 4501 N Charles St, Baltimore, MD 21210. **EMAIL** apc@loyola.edu

COMFORT, KATHLEEN
DISCIPLINE FRENCH **EDUCATION** Ill State Univ, BA, 82; MA, 83; Univ Kans, PhD, 97. **CAREER** Instr, Univ Mo, 97-. **HONORS AND AWARDS** Graduate Honors Fel, Univ Kans, 94; Awd for Outstanding Teaching, Univ Kans, 90. **MEMBERSHIPS** Am Asn of Teachers of French, Mod Lang Asn, Pi Delta Phi. **RESEARCH** 19th century French novel, Naturalism. **SELECTED PUBLICATIONS** Auth, "Andre Cide's L'Immoralists: Portrait of a Male Hysteric," Romance Notes, (forthcoming); auth, "Blood Memory: Hereditary Metaphors in Emile Zola's Le Docteur Pascal," Romance Quarterly, (98): 195-202; auth, "Images of Flora as Emblems of Health in Balzac's Le Lys dans la Vallee," Dalhousie French Studies, (98): 31-38. **CONTACT ADDRESS** Dept Romance Lang, Univ of Missouri, Columbia, 143 Arts & Sci Bldg, Columbia, MO 65211-7080. **EMAIL** comfortk@missouri.edu

COMPAGNON, ANTOINE M.
PERSONAL Born 07/20/1950, Brussels, Belgium, s **DISCIPLINE** FRENCH, COMPARATIVE LITERATURE **EDUCA-**

TION Ancien eleve de l'Ecole polytechnique, 73; Ingenieur des Ponts et Chaussees, 75; Univ Paris 7, Licence de Lettres modernes, 72; Maitrise, 73; Doctorat de troisieme cycle, 77. **CAREER** Attache de recherche, Ctr Nat de la Recherche Sci, 75-78; charge de cours, Univ Paris, 75-80; Maitre de conferences, Ecole des Hautes Etudes en Sci Soc, 77-79; prof, Bennington Col Prog, 78-82; Maitre de conferences, Ecole polytechnique, 78-80; prof, Inst francais du Royaume-Uni, 80-81; Maitre asst, Univ de Rouen, 81-84; Maitre de confr, Ecole polytechnique, 81-85; Maitre de confr, Univ de Rouen, 84-85; prof, Columbia Univ, 85-91; vis prof, Univ of Pa, 86; Maitre de confr, Ecole polytechnique, 88; prof, Univ du Mans, 89-90; vis prof, Univ of Pa, 90; Blanche W. Knopf prof of French and Comparative Literature, Columbia Univ, 91-; chemn of dept of french and romance philology, Columbia Univ, 92-94; prof, Univ de Paris IV, 94-. **HONORS AND AWARDS** Pensionnaire de la Foundation Thiers, 76-78; fel, John Simon Guggenheim Memorial Found, 88; listed in The International Who's Who, 89-; listed in Who's Who in America, 92-; vis fel, All Souls Col, 94; Chevalier des Palmes academiques, 95; fel, Am Acad of Arts and Sci, 97; listed in Who's Who in France, 98-. **SELECTED PUBLICATIONS** Auth, Les Cinq Paradoxes de la modernite, Editions du Seuil (Paris, France) 90 & 97; auth, Chat en poche: Montaigne et l'allegorie, Editions du Seuil (Paris, France), 93; co-ed, "L'Esprit de l'Europe," Flammarion, 93; ed, Charles Baudelaire, Les Flurs du mail, L'Ecole des lettres-Editions du Seuil (Paris, France), 93; auth, Connaissez-vouse Brunetiere? Enquete sur un antidryfusard et ses amis, Editions du Seuil (Paris, France), 97; ed, Les Classiques Decoiffes: Special Issue of Critique (98); auth, Le Demon de la theorie. Litterature et sens commun, Editions du Seuil (Paris, France), 98. **CONTACT ADDRESS** Dept French, Columbia Univ, 513 Philosophy Hall, New York, NY 10027. **EMAIL** amc6@columbia.edu

COMPITELLO, MALCOLM ALAN
PERSONAL Born 02/09/1946, Brooklyn, NY, m, 1977, 1 child **DISCIPLINE** SPANISH LANGUAGE AND LITERATURE **EDUCATION** St John's Univ, BA, 68, MA, 70; Ind Univ, PhD(Span), 77. **CAREER** Asst prof, 77-81, Assoc Prof Span, Mich State Univ, 81-, Ed, The Am Hisp, 75- & An Annual Bibliog Post-Civil-War Span Fiction, 77-; vis prof, Span Sch, Middlebury Col, 80. **MEMBERSHIPS** Am Asn Teachers Span; MLA. **RESEARCH** Contemporary Spanish literature; literary sociology; contemporary Spanish cultural history. **SELECTED PUBLICATIONS** Auth, Reflections on the Act of Narrating, Benet, Vargasllosa and Dacunha,Euclides, Insula-Revista de Letras y Ciencias Humanas, Vol 0048, 93. **CONTACT ADDRESS** Dept Romance Lang, Michigan State Univ, East Lansing, MI 48824. **EMAIL** compitel@u.arizona.edu

CONACHER, DESMOND J.
PERSONAL Born 12/27/1918, Kingston, ON, Canada **DISCIPLINE** CLASSICS **EDUCATION** Queen's Univ, BA, 41, MA (Classics), 42; Univ Chicago, PhD (Greek Lang & Lit), 50; LLD(hon), Dalhousie Univ, 92; DLitt(hon), Univ Victoria, 93; LLD(hon), Queen's Univ, 95; LLD(hon), Univ Sask, 97. **CAREER** Lectr, Dalhousie Univ, 46-47; asst prof to assoc prof, Univ Sask, 47-58; assoc prof to prof, 58-84, dept head, 66-72, prof emer, Trinity Col, Univ Toronto, 84-, mem, sch grad stud, 84-90. **HONORS AND AWARDS** Fel, Royal Soc Can, 76. **MEMBERSHIPS** Class Asn Can; Am Philol Asn. **RESEARCH** Greek tragedy; Euripides; Aeschylus. **SELECTED PUBLICATIONS** Auth, Euripedean Drama, 67; auth, Aeschylus' 'Prometheus Bound': A Literary Study, 80; auth, Aeschylus' 'Oresteia': A Literary Commentary, 87; auth, Euripides' 'Alcestis': with Introduction, Translation and Commentary, 88; contribur, Sources of Dramatic Theory, vol 1, 91; contribur, Aeschylus: The Earlier Plays and Related Studies, 96. **CONTACT ADDRESS** Trinity Col, Univ of Toronto, 6 Hoskin Ave, 336 Larkin Bldg, Toronto, ON, Canada M5S 1H8. **EMAIL** djconacher@idirect.com

CONANT, JONATHAN BRENDAN
PERSONAL Born 12/16/1941, Hartford, CT, m, 1964, 1 child **DISCIPLINE** GERMANIC PHILOLOGY, PEDAGOGY **EDUCATION** Yale Univ, AB, 64, MPhil, 68, PhD(Ger), 69. **CAREER** Asst prof Ger, Brown Univ, 69-75, vis assoc prof, Univ Minn, Minneapolis, 75-77, Assoc Prof Foreign Lang & Lit, Univ Minn, Duluth, 77-, Assoc ed, Unterrichtspraxis, 77-. **MEMBERSHIPS** Am Asn Teachers Ger. **RESEARCH** Old Icelandic poetry; runology and foreign language pedagogy. **SELECTED PUBLICATIONS CONTACT ADDRESS** Dept of Foreign Lang & Lit, Univ of Minnesota, Duluth, 10 University Dr, Duluth, MN 55812-2496.

CONE, ANNABELLE
PERSONAL Born 12/14/1950, Washington, DC, d, 2 children **DISCIPLINE** FRENCH, ITALIAN **EDUCATION** Williams Col, BA, 82; Brown Univ, PhD, 93. **CAREER** Teaching Asst, Brown Univ, 89-90; Sen Lectr, Dartmouth Col, 87-. **MEMBERSHIPS** MLA. **RESEARCH** Women and the city. **SELECTED PUBLICATIONS** Auth, "Misplaced Desire: Women and the City in Colette and Rohmer," Film/Lit Quart (96); auth, "A Man's Home is his Castle But the House Tells Her Story: The Domes politics of Marguerite Duras," Poetics of Space Conf (00). **CONTACT ADDRESS** Dept Lang, Dartmouth Col, 6087 Dartmouth Hall, Hanover, NH 03755-3511. **EMAIL** annabelle.cone@dartmouth.edu

CONGER, SYNDY MCMILLEN
PERSONAL Born 10/14/1942, Waterloo, IA, m, 1967 **DISCIPLINE** ENGLISH AND COMPARATIVE LITERATURE **EDUCATION** Univ Iowa, BA, 65; MA, 69; PhD, 76. **CAREER** Asst prof, 72-80, Assoc Prof, 80-84, Prof, English, 84-, ch, English & Journ Dept, Western Ill Univ, 98- . **HONORS AND AWARDS** Phi Beta Kappa, 64; Phi Kappa Phi, 82; Fulbright Fels (Germany), 73-74, 83-84; DAAD Fel, 82; NEH Summer Sem, 77, 81, 93; Newberry Library Fel, 89; ACLS travel grant, 89; Clifford Prize, Am Soc for 18th Century Studies, 86. **MEMBERSHIPS** MLA; Am Soc 18th Century Studies; N Am Soc for Study of Romanticism; NCTE **RESEARCH** Pros fiction; Gothic literature; 18th century Anglo-German literary relations; women's lit, 1680-1840. **SELECTED PUBLICATIONS** Auth, Matthew G. Lewis, Charles Robert Maturin, and the Germans, Arno Pr (New York, NY), 80; auth, "A German Ancestor for Mary Shelley's Monster: Kahlert, Schiller, and the Buried Treasure of Northanger Abbey," Philol Q 59; auth, "Hans Robert Jauss's 'Rezeptionsaesthetik' and England's Reception of Eighteenth Century German Literature," Eighteenth Century: Theory and Interpretation 22; auth, "Fellow Travellers: Eighteenth-Century Englishwomen and German Literature," Studies in Eighteenth Century Culture 14; auth, "The Sorrows of Young Charlotte: Werther's English Sisters 1785-1805," Goethe Yearbook 3; auth, "Another Secret of the Rue Morgue: Poe's Transformation of the 'Geisterseher' Motif," Studies in Short Fiction 24; auth, "Reading 'Lovers' Vows': Jane Austen's Reflections on English Sense andGerman Sensibility," Studies in Philol 85; auth, Mary Wollstonecraft and the Language of Sensibility, Fairleigh Dickinson Univ Pr, 94; auth, Prophecy and Sensibility: Mary Wollstonecraft in Frankenstein, 1650-1850: Ideas, Aesthetics, and Inquiries in the Early Modern Era,"AMS Pr, 97; auth, "Multivocality in Mary Shelley's Unfinished Biography of her Father," Europ Roman Rev 9. **CONTACT ADDRESS** Dept of English, Western Illinois Univ, 1 University Cir, Macomb, IL 61455-1390. **EMAIL** syndy_conger@ccmail.wiu.edu

CONLEY, KATHARINE
PERSONAL Born 08/10/1956, Washington, DC, m, 1997 **DISCIPLINE** LITERATURE, FRENCH **EDUCATION** Harvard Univ, BA, 79; Univ Colo, MA, 88; Univ Pa, MA, 90; PhD, 92. **CAREER** Asst prof to assoc prof, Dartmouth Col, 92-. **HONORS AND AWARDS** Whiting Found Travel Grant, 96; Jr Fac Fel, Dartmouth Col, 96; Burke Res Grant, Dartmouth Col, 92; Mellon Fel, 91-92. **MEMBERSHIPS** MLA; AATF; ACQS; WIF. **RESEARCH** Surrealism; Quebec fiction; writing by women. **SELECTED PUBLICATIONS** Auth, Automatic Women, Nebr, 96; auth, Le Femme S'Entite: La Part du Feminin dans le Surrealisme, Pleine Marge, 98; auth, Robert Desnos pour l'am 2000, Gallimard, 00; auth, "Anamorphic Love: The Surrealist Poetry of Desire," in Desire Unbound, eds. Mundy, Ady (Tate Gallery, 01). **CONTACT ADDRESS** 334 Turnpike Rd, Norwich, VT 05055-9559. **EMAIL** katharine.conley@dartmouth.edu

CONLEY, TOM C.
PERSONAL Born 12/07/1943, New Haven, CT, m, 1967, 2 children **DISCIPLINE** FRENCH STUDIES **EDUCATION** Lawrence Univ, BA, 65; Columbia Univ, MA, 66; Univ Wis, PhD, 71. **CAREER** Asst prof to prof, Univ Minn, 71-95; vis prof, Univ Mich, 78; vis assoc prof, Univ Calif Berkeley, 78-79; vis prof, CUNY, Grad Center, 85-87; vis prof, Miami Univ Ohio, 89-93; vis prof, Univ Calif Los Angeles, 95; prof, Bryn Mawr Col, 01. **HONORS AND AWARDS** Fulbright Fel, 68; Ford Diss Fel, 71; ACLS Fel, 76; MEH Fel, 75, 89; Inst for Res in Humanities Fel, 90; Hermon Dunlap Smith Fel, 91; Cornell Soc fof the Humanities Fel, 98. **MEMBERSHIPS** MLA, Renaissance Soc of Am, Asn for the Study of Dada, Surrealism, Soc for Cinema Studies, Soc for the Hist of Discoveries. **RESEARCH** Early modern French literature and culture, film and visual studies, contemporary criticism and writing. **SELECTED PUBLICATIONS** Auth, Film Hieroglyphics: Ruptures of Classical Cinema, Univ Minn Pr, 91; auth, The Graphic Unconscious in Early Modern French Writing, Cambridge Univ Pr, 92; transl, ed, The Fold: Leibniz and the Baroque, by Gilles Deleuze, Univ Minn Pr, 93; coed, Identity Papers: Contested Nationhood in 20th Century France, Univ Minn Pr, 96; transl and ed, The Capture of Speech and Cultural in the Plural by Michel de Certeau, Univ Minn Pr, 97; auth, The Self-Made Map: Cartographic Writing in Early Modern France, 97; coed, The World and its Rival: Essays in Honor of Per Kykrog, Rodopi Editions, 99; auth, L'inconscient graphique: essai sur la lettre a la Renaissance, 00. **CONTACT ADDRESS** Dept Romance Lang, Harvard Univ, Boylston Hall, Cambridge, MA 02138. **EMAIL** tconley@fas.harvard.edu

CONNER, MAURICE WAYNE
PERSONAL Born 08/20/1938, Houston, TX, m, 1966 **DISCIPLINE** GERMANIC LANGUAGE & LITERATURE **EDUCATION** Univ Tex-Arlington, BA, 64; Univ Nebr-Lincoln, MA, 66, PhD(Ger), 73. **CAREER** Instr English as second lang, Stuttgarter Fremdsprachenschule, 63-64; instr Ger, Univ Wis-Green Bay, 66-68; instr, 71-73, asst prof, 73-76, assoc prof, 76-81, asst dean, Col Arts & Sci, 79-80, vchair, Dept Foreign Lang, 81-82, prof Ger, Univ Nebr, Omaha, 81-, lab dir, Univ Wis-Green Bay, 66-68; co-ed, Schatzkammer der deutschen Sprachlehre, 75-77; consult, Central States Conf Teaching Foreign Lang, 81-82. **HONORS AND AWARDS** Fellow, Center for Great Plains Study, 95; Certificate of Merit, Am Asn of Teachers of Ger, 88; Excellence in Teaching Awd, Univ of Nebr at Omaha, 84; Outstanding Ger Teacher in Nebr, 82; Who's Who in Am Education; Who's Who among America's Teachers. **MEMBERSHIPS** MLA; Am Asn Teachers Ger; Soc for Ger-Am Studies; Am Asn of Univ Profs; Ger-Texan Heritage Soc. **RESEARCH** Austrian literature; German-Americana; foreign language pedagogy. **SELECTED PUBLICATIONS** Coauth, A German Dialect Spoken in South Dakota: Swiss-Volhynian, Ger-Am Studies, 74; Language Camp Guidelines, Die Unterrichtspraxis, 74; auth, New Curricular Connections, In: The Language Connection: From the Classroom to the World, 77; From Switzerland to South Dakota: A Two Century Journey, Schatzkammer, 79; Schnitzler's Sterben and Durrenmatt's Der Meteor: Two Responses to the Prospect of Death, Ger Notes, 80; ed, New Frontiers in Foreign Language Education, 80 & A Global Approach to Foreign Language Education, 81, Nat Textbk Co; auth, Teaching Global Perspectives, Mod Lang J, 81; Thinking Styles in Foreign Language Learning, Improving College and Univ Teaching, 83; German-American Reminiscences of Early Life in Austin County, Texas, Yearbook of Ger-Am Studies, 93; Anti-German Ku Klux Klan Activity in a Texas Community, Schlatzkammer, 97. **CONTACT ADDRESS** Dept Foreign Lang, Univ of Nebraska, Omaha, 6001 Dodge St, Omaha, NE 68182-0002. **EMAIL** mconner@unomaha.edu

CONNER, PATRICK WAYNE
PERSONAL Born 07/31/1946, Marion Station, MD, m, 1968, 1 child **DISCIPLINE** MEDIEVAL LITERATURE, ENGLISH AND GERMANIC PHILOLOGY **EDUCATION** Univ Md, BA, 68, MA, 70, PhD(English), 75. **CAREER** Instr English, Univ Md, 70-74, instr & adv, 74-76; lectr ling, Goucher Col, 75-76; Asst Prof English, WVA Univ, 76-. **MEMBERSHIPS** MLA; AAUP; Early English Text Soc; Southeastern Medieval Asn. **RESEARCH** Old English literature; oral-formulaic studies; diachronic linguistics. **SELECTED PUBLICATIONS** Auth, Schematization of oral-formulaic processes in Old English poetry, Lang & Style, 72; The Liturgy and the Old English Descent into Hell, JEGP, 80; Bloom, the Masons and the Benstock connection, James Joyce Quart, 80. **CONTACT ADDRESS** Dept of English, West Virginia Univ, Morgantown, P O Box 6296, Morgantown, WV 26506-6296.

CONNOLLY, JOY P. T.
PERSONAL Born 04/07/1970, Lowell, MA, s **DISCIPLINE** CLASSICS **EDUCATION** Princeton Univ, AB, 91; Univ Pa, MA, 95; PhD, 97. **CAREER** Asst prof, Univ Wash, 97-00; asst prof, Stanford Univ, 00-. **HONORS AND AWARDS** Simpson Center for the Humanities Fel, Univ Wash, 98; Fel, Stanford Univ, 99-00. **MEMBERSHIPS** Am Philol Asn; Class Asn of the Atlantic States. **RESEARCH** Greek and Roman rhetoric; Feminist theory; The ancient novel; Pastoral and elegy; Ancient education; Greek and Roman cultural relations. **SELECTED PUBLICATIONS** Auth, "Mastering corruption: constructions of identity in Roman oratory," in Women and Slaves in Greco-Roman Culture, 98; auth, "Asymptotes of pleasure: thoughts on the nature of Roman erotic elegy," Arethusa, (00): 71-98. **CONTACT ADDRESS** Dept Class, Stanford Univ, Main Quad, Bldg 20, Stanford, CA 94305-2080. **EMAIL** jptc@stanford.edu

CONNOLLY, JULIAN WELCH
PERSONAL Born 10/19/1949, Newburyport, MA, m, 1991 **DISCIPLINE** LANGUAGES & LITERATURE **EDUCATION** Harvard Col, AB, 72; Harvard Univ, AM, 74, PhD(Slavic lang & lit), 77. **CAREER** Asst Prof Slavic Lang & Lit, Univ Va, 77- **HONORS AND AWARDS** All-University Outstanding Teacher Awd, 99. **MEMBERSHIPS** Am Asn Advan Slavic Studies; Am Asn Teachers Slavic & E Europ Lang; MLA. **RESEARCH** Symbolism; 1912-Century Russian prose; Nabokov. **SELECTED PUBLICATIONS** Auth, The role of duality in Sologub's Tvorimaja Legenda, Die Welt der Slaven, 74-75; A modernist's palette: Color in the prose fiction of Eugenij Zamjatin, Russ Lang J, 79; Bunin's Petlistye Ushi: The Deformation of a Byronic Rebel, Can-Am Slavic Studies, 80; Desire and renunciation: Buddhist elements in the prose of Ivan Bunin, Can Slavonic Papers, 81; The function of literary allusion in Nabokov's Despair, Slavic and East Europ J, 82; Ivan Bunin, G K Hall & Co, 82; Nabovov's Earl, Early Fiction: Patterns of Self and Other, Cambridge: Cambridge Univ Press, 92; Nabovov's "Invitation to a Beheading": A Critical Companion, Evanston: Northwestern Univ Press, 97; auth, Nabokov and His Fiction: New Perspectives (Cambridge), Cambridge Univ Press, 99. **CONTACT ADDRESS** Dept Slavic Lang & Lit, Univ of Virginia, 109 Cabell Hall, PO Box 400783, Charlottesville, VA 22904-4738. **EMAIL** jwc4w@virginia.edu

CONNOR, CAROLYN
PERSONAL Born 11/03/1943, Binghamton, NY, m, 1968, 2 children **DISCIPLINE** CLASSICS **EDUCATION** NY York Univ, PhD. **CAREER** Prof, Univ NC, Chapel Hill. **HONORS AND AWARDS** Hettleman Prize for Teaching and Scholarship, UNC-CH, 98. **MEMBERSHIPS** Medieval Acad of Am, Int Comt on Byzantine Studies Conf, Hagiography Soc, Col Art Assoc **RESEARCH** Byzantine art and civilization. **SELECTED PUBLICATIONS** Auth, Americans and the Unconscious,

Oxford Univ, 86; auth, Religion and the Life Cycle, Fortress Press, 88; auth, Art and Miracles in Medieval Byzantium: The Crypt at Hosios Loukas and Its Frescoes, Princeton UP, 91; auth, New Perspectives on Byzantine Ivories, Gesta, Vol 30, 91; Hosios Loukas as a Victory Church, Greek, Roman and Byzantine Stud, Vol 33, 92; auth, Alternative Medicine and American Religious Life, Oxford Univ Press, 92; coauth, The Life and Miracles of Saint Luke of Steiris, A Translation and Commentary, Hellenic Col Orthodox Press, 94; auth, Naming the Antichrist, Oxford Univ Press, 95; auth, The Color of Ivory: Polychromy on Byzantive Ivories, Princeton Univ Press, 98; auth, Stairways to Heaven, Westview Press, 00. **CONTACT ADDRESS** Dept of Classics, Univ of No Carolina, Chapel Hill, CB#3145, Chapel Hill, NC 27599-3145. **EMAIL** clconnor@email.unc.edu

CONNOR, PETER T.
PERSONAL Born 04/12/1960, Ireland, s **DISCIPLINE** FRENCH **EDUCATION** Trinity Col Dublin, BA, 82; Univ Calif at Irvine, MA, 85; Univ Calif at Berkeley, PhD, 91. **CAREER** Asst/Assoc Prof, Columbia Univ Barnard Col, 91-. **HONORS AND AWARDS** Contemplative Practice Fel, Am Coun of Learned Soc, 98. **RESEARCH** 19th and 20th century French Literature, Literary Theory, Contemporary French Philosophy. **SELECTED PUBLICATIONS** Co-transl, Duras by Duras, by Marguerite Duras (San Francisco: City Light Books, 87); transl, The Tears of Eros, by Georges Bataille (San Francisco: City Light Books, 89); transl, The Inoperative Community, by Jean-Luc Nancy (Univ of Minn Press: Theory and Hist of Lit Ser, 91); auth, Georges Bataille and the Mysticism of Sin, The Johns Hopkins Univ Press (Baltimore), 00. **CONTACT ADDRESS** Dept French, Barnard Col, 3009 Broadway, New York, NY 10027-6501. **EMAIL** ptc4@columbia.edu

CONNOR, W. ROBERT
PERSONAL Born 08/30/1934, Worcester, MA, m, 1968, 2 children **DISCIPLINE** CLASSICS **EDUCATION** Hamilton Col, BA, 56; Princeton Univ, PhD, 61. **CAREER** Instr, Univ Mich, 60-63; asst prof to prof emeritus, Princeton Univ, 64-89; pres and dir, Nat Humanities Center, 89-. **HONORS AND AWARDS** Fulbright Fel, Univ Col Oxford, 56-57; Woodrow Wilson Fel; ACLS Fel; LHD Knox Col; LHD Hamilton Col; Behrman Award; Phi Beta Kappa. **MEMBERSHIPS** Am Philol Asn; Am Acad of Arts and Sci; Am Philos Soc. **RESEARCH** Athenian cultural history, classical period; Greek religion; Historiography. **SELECTED PUBLICATIONS** Auth, Thucydides, Princeton Univ Press, 84; auth, New Politicians of Fifth Century Athens, Princeton Press, 72. **CONTACT ADDRESS** Nat Humanities Center, 3017 Frank Perry Rd, Hillsborough, NC 27278. **EMAIL** connor@ga.unc.edu

CONRAD, CHARLES R.
DISCIPLINE ORGANIZATIONAL COMMUNICATION, RHETORICAL THEORY **EDUCATION** Univ Kansas, PhD. **CAREER** Prof, Texas A&M Univ. **HONORS AND AWARDS** Southern Commun Journal's Outstanding Article Awd; Distinguished Tchg Awd, Asn Former Stud at Texas A&M Univ. **SELECTED PUBLICATIONS** Auth, Strategic Organizational Communication; ed, The Ethical Nexus; assoc ed, Quart J Speech. **CONTACT ADDRESS** Dept of Speech Communication, Texas A&M Univ, Col Station, College Station, TX 77843-4234.

CONRAD, JOSEPH LAWRENCE
PERSONAL Born 06/26/1933, Kansas City, MO, m, 1955, 3 children **DISCIPLINE** RUSSIAN LANGUAGE AND LITERATURE **EDUCATION** Univ Kans, BA, 55; Univ Tex, PhD, 61. **CAREER** From instr to asst prof, Ger & Russ, Fla State Univ, 59-62; asst prof, Univ Tex, 62-66; chmn dept Slavic lang, 66-75, Prof Russ Lang & Lit, Univ Kans, 66-, Int Res & Exchanges Bd scholar, Moscow Univ, spring 74; Fulbright res scholar, Zagreb, Yugoslavia, 81. **MEMBERSHIPS** Am Asn Advan Slavic Studies; Am Asn Teachers Slavic & E Europ Lang; Am Asn S Slavic Studies; Am Asn Southeast Europ Studies. **RESEARCH** Slavic Languages and Literatures, Slavic Folklore, Slavic and East Europe Folklore Association. **SELECTED PUBLICATIONS** Auth, Practical Sorcery--Incantations, Charms-Russian, Slavic and E Europ Jour, Vol 0037, 93; Folk Remedies in the Angara Region--Russian, Slavic and E Europ Jour, Vol 0037, 93. **CONTACT ADDRESS** Dept of Slavic Lang, Univ of Kansas, Lawrence, 1445 Jay Hawk Blvd, Rm 2134, Lawrence, KS 66045-7590. **EMAIL** jlconrad@ku.edu

CONROY, PETER VINCENT
PERSONAL Born 04/09/1944, New York, NY, m, 1967 **DISCIPLINE** FRENCH **EDUCATION** Queens Col, BA, 65, MA, 67; Univ of Wis, PhD, 70. **CAREER** ASST PROF, 70-74, ASSOC PROF, 74-86, PROF, 86-, UNIV OF ILL AT CHICAGO. **MEMBERSHIPS** MLA; ASECS: AATF. **RESEARCH** 18th Century novel; Montesquieu; J.J. Rousseau. **SELECTED PUBLICATIONS** Auth, Intimate, Intrusive, and Trimphant: Readers in the 'Liaisons dangereuses', Purdue Univ Monographs in Romance Langs, 87; auth, Montesquieu Revisited, Twayne World Authors Series, 92; transl, "New History in France: The Triumph of the Annales, Univ of Ill Pr, 94; auth, Jean-Jacques Rousseau, Twayne World Authors Series, 98. **CONTACT ADDRESS** Dept of Spanish & French, M/C 315, Univ of Illinois, Chicago, 601 S Morgan, Chicago, IL 60607-7117.

CONSENSTEIN, PETER
DISCIPLINE FRENCH STUDIES **EDUCATION** SUNY at Plattsburgh, BA, 81; Univ Laval, MA, 86; Columbia Univ, PhD, 93. **CAREER** Preceptor, Columbia Univ, 87-92; Coord, Columbia Univ, 92-93; Assoc Prof, Bor Manhattan Community Col, 93-. **HONORS AND AWARDS** Presidents Fel, Columbia Univ, 90, 91-92; New York Jr Fac Awd, CUNY, 94, 96; NISOD Excellence Awd, Nat Inst for Staff and Orgn Develop, 97; Who's Who Among America's Teachers, 01; Who's Who in the World, 18th ed, 01. **RESEARCH** French poetry after World War II, 20th-century French literature, the group Oulipo, literary criticism and theory, Francophone literature. **SELECTED PUBLICATIONS** Auth, "The Asian Influences in the Poetry of Jacque Roubaud and Raymond Queneau," W Va Univ Philol Papers 40 (94): 56-63; auth, "Memory and 'Oulipian' Constraints," Postmodern Culture 6:1 e-J, Oxford Univ Pr (95); auth, "The Rhythm of Irony," Cincinnati Romance Rev XV (96): 8-19; auth, "Dominique Fourcade-Confluences," Sites 3:1 (99): 203-216. **CONTACT ADDRESS** Dept Lang, Borough of Manhattan Comm Col, CUNY, 205 W 88th St, #12C, New York, NY 10024-2350. **EMAIL** pconsenstein@bmcc.cuny.edu

CONTRERAS, HELES
PERSONAL Born 08/01/1933, Victoria, Chile, m, 1955, 5 children **DISCIPLINE** SPANISH LINGUISTICS AND SYNTACTIC THEORY **EDUCATION** Concepcion Univ, Profesor de Estado, 57; Ind Univ, MA, 59, PhD(ling), 61. **CAREER** Prof ling, Concepcion Univ, 61-64; vis asst prof ling & Romance lang, 64-65, asst prof, 65-67, assoc prof, 67-79, Prof Ling & Romance Lang, Univ Wash, 79-. **RESEARCH** Spanish grammar. **SELECTED PUBLICATIONS** Auth, On Null Operator Structures, Natural Lang and Ling Theory, Vol 0011, 93; On the Position of Subjects, Syntax and Semantics, Vol 0025, 91. **CONTACT ADDRESS** Dept of Ling, Univ of Washington, Seattle, WA 98105.

CONWELL, DAVID
PERSONAL Born 01/13/1959, Philadelphia, PA, m, 1992, 2 children **DISCIPLINE** CLASSICAL STUDIES **EDUCATION** Trinity Col, BA, 82; Univ Pa, PhD, 92. **CAREER** Instr, Baylor School, 95-. **HONORS AND AWARDS** NEH Teacher Exchange Fel, 97. **MEMBERSHIPS** Archaeol Inst of Am; Am Philol Asn; Classical Asn of the Midwest and South. **RESEARCH** Archaeology of Cyprus, Greece, and Italy; Ancient fortifications; Art history. **SELECTED PUBLICATIONS** Auth, "The White Poros Wall on the Athenian Pnyx: Character and Context," in The Pnyx in the Hist of Athens, 96; "Rediscovering the Athenian Long Walls," in Am School of Class Studies Newsletter, 95; "Topography and Toponyms between Athens and Piraeus," in J of Ancient Topography, 93. **CONTACT ADDRESS** Baylor School, P O Box 1337, Signal Mountain, TN 37377. **EMAIL** david_conwell@baylor.chattanooga.net

COOEY, PAULA M.
PERSONAL Born Hays, KS, m, 1 child **DISCIPLINE** RELIGION, THEOLOGY AND SOCIAL THEORY **EDUCATION** Univ Ga, BA, philos, 68; Harvard Divinity Sch, MTS, 74; Harvard Univ, grad sch of arts & sci, PhD, 81. **CAREER** Visiting instr, Conn Col, 9/79-9/80; instr part-time, relig, Univ Mass, Harbor Campus, 9/80-1/81; asst prof, relig, Trinity Univ, 9/81-7/87; assoc prof, relig, Trinity Univ, 8/87-8/93; prof, relig, Trinity Univ, 8/93-99; Margaret W. Harmon Prof of Christian Theol and Culture, Macalester College, 9/99- . **HONORS AND AWARDS** Co-dir, Southwest Regional Amer Acad of Relig workshop on teaching for jr facul, 94-96; Sears-Roebuck Found award for excellence in teaching & campus leadership, 91; Trinity Univ nom for CASE award, 88. **MEMBERSHIPS** Amer Acad of Relig; Soc for Buddhist-Christian Studies; Soc for the Sci Study of Relig; Amer Asn of Univ Prof. **RESEARCH** Death and dying from a feminist perspective. **SELECTED PUBLICATIONS** Auth, Family, Freedom, and Faith: Building Community Today, Westminster John Knox Press, ix-131, 96; auth, Religious Imagination and the Body: A Feminist Analysis, Oxford Univ Press, vii-184, 94; auth, After Patriarchy: Feminist Reconstructions of The World Religions, Orbis Press, ix-169, 91; article, Bad Women: The Limitations of Theory and Theology, Horizons in Feminist Theology, Fortress, 97; article, Kenosis, Popular Religiosity, Religious Pluralism, Dict of Feminist Theol, John Knox Westminster Press, 96; article, Re-Membering the Body: A Theological Resource for Resisting Domestic Violence, Theol & Sexuality, 3, 27-47, 95; article, Mapping the Body through Religious Symbolism: The Life and Work of Frida Kahlo as Case Study, Imagining Faith: Essays in Honor of Richard R. Niebuhr, Scholars Press, 105-125, 95; article, Backlash, Jour of Feminist Studies, 10, 1, 109-111, 94. **CONTACT ADDRESS** Dept. of Religious Studies, Macalester Col, 1600 Grand Ave., Saint Paul, MN 55105. **EMAIL** cooey@macalester.edu

COOK, ELIZABETH HECKENDORN
DISCIPLINE EIGHTEENTH-CENTURY BRITISH AND FRENCH LITERATURE **EDUCATION** Stanford Univ, PhD, 90. **CAREER** Assoc Prof, Eng, Univ Calif, Santa Barbara. **RESEARCH** Intersection of natural history; Landscape aesthetics; Property law in the period 1789-1832. **SELECTED PUBLICATIONS** Auth, "The Limping Woman and the Public Sphere," Body and Text in the Eighteenth Century, Stanford Univ Press, 94; Epistolary Bodies: Gender and Genre in the Eighteenth-Century Republic of Letters, Stanford Univ Press, 96. **CONTACT ADDRESS** Dept of Eng, Univ of California, Santa Barbara, Santa Barbara, CA 93106-7150. **EMAIL** ecook@humanitas.ucsb.edu

COOK, ERWIN
PERSONAL Born 04/27/1957, Edinburgh, Scotland, 1 child **DISCIPLINE** CLASSICS **EDUCATION** Univ Calif, Berkeley, MA, 85, PhD, 90. **CAREER** Asst prof, Univ Texas, Austin, 90-93, 94-96; vis assoc prof, 93-94, assoc prof, Johns Hopkins, 97-, UT-Austin. **MEMBERSHIPS** Am Philol Asn; Classical Asn of the Midwest and South. **RESEARCH** Epic poetry, Greek religion, mythology, archaic Greek history. **SELECTED PUBLICATIONS** Auth, A Note on the Text of Sextus Empiricus, Adv. Math, Hermes, 91; auth, Ferrymen of Elysium and the Homeric Phaeacians, J of Indo-European Stud, 92; auth, Some Remarks on Odyssey 3.2 16-38, Class Philol, 94; auth, The Odyssey in Athens: Myths of Cultural Origins, Cornell, 95; auth, rev, Homer: His Art and His World, by Latacz, Bryn Mawr Class Rev, 96; auth, Heroism, Suffering and Change, Proceedings of a Conference Sponsored by the Smithsonian Institution and the Society for the Preservation of the Greek Heritage, 98; auth, Active and Passive Heroics in the Odyssey, Classical World 93:2 (99): 149-67; rev, The Returns of Odysseus: Colonization and Ethnicity, by I. Malkin, (Berkeley, 98), Bryn Mawr Class Rev 00. **CONTACT ADDRESS** Dept of Classics, Univ of Texas, Austin, 123 WAG, Austin, TX 78212. **EMAIL** efcook@mail.utexas.edu

COOK, HARUKO M.
PERSONAL Born 01/02/1948, Tokyo, Japan **DISCIPLINE** LINGUISTICS **EDUCATION** Sophia Univ, Japan, BA, 70; BA, 72; Cal State Univ, MA, 78; Univ S Cal, PhD, 88. **CAREER** Lectr, Cal State Univ, 80-81, 83-84; lectr, San Diego state Univ, 82-83; asst lectr, Univ S Cal, 85-88; asst prof, Univ Hawaii, 88-94; assoc prof, 94-. **MEMBERSHIPS** IPA; ATJ; AAS; AAAL; AAA. **RESEARCH** Sociolinguistics; discourse analysis; language socialization and pragmatics. **SELECTED PUBLICATIONS** Auth, "The use of addressee phonetics in Japanese elementary school classroom," in Japanese/Korean Linguistics, eds. Noriko Akatsuka, Shoichi Iwasaki, Susan Strauss (Stanford, CA: Cen Study of Lang Info, 96), 67-81; auth, "Japanese language socialization: Indexing the modes of self," Discourse Processes 22 (96): 71-197; auth, "The Japanese verbal suffixes as indicators of distance and proximity," in Construal of Space in Language and Thought, eds. Martin Putz, Rene' Dirven (Berlin & New York: Mouton de Uruyter, 96), 3-27; auth, "The role of the Japanese masu form in caregiver-child conversation," J Pragmatics 28 (97): 695-718; auth, "Situational meaning of the Japanese social deixis: The mixed use of the masu and plain form," J Ling Anthro 8 (98): 87-110; auth, "Students' use of the impersonal style in a Japanese elementary school classroom," Crossroads of Lang, Interaction, Cult (98): 43-58; auth, "Language socialization in Japanese elementary schools: Attentive listening and reaction turns," J Pragmatics 31 (99): 1443-1465. **CONTACT ADDRESS** Dept east Asian Lang and Lit, Univ of Hawaii, Manoa, 1890 East West Rd, Honolulu, HI 96822-2318. **EMAIL** hkcook@hawaii.edu

COOK, KENNETH WILLIAM
PERSONAL Born 01/30/1947, Long Beach, CA **DISCIPLINE** LINGUISTICS **EDUCATION** Los Angeles Harbor Col, AA, 66; Calif State Univ, BA, 68; MA, 77; Univ Calif, PhD, 88. **CAREER** Inter-American School, Guatemala, 68-69; Banning High School, 71-75; Univ of Calif, San Diego, 83-88; prof, Haw Pacific Univ. **HONORS AND AWARDS** Univ of Calif Regents Fel, 82-83; Diss Fel, Univ of Calif, 87-88; Fel, Japan Soc for the Promotion of Sci, 99. **MEMBERSHIPS** Ling Soc of Am; Int Cognitive Ling Assoc; Haw Teachers of English to Speakers of Other Lang; Haw Lang Soc. **RESEARCH** Cognitive linguistics, Polynesian linguistics, the phonology and syntax of Italian, Japanese, Samoan, Spanish and Hawaiian. **SELECTED PUBLICATIONS** Auth, "A Cognitive Account of Samoan Case Marking and Cliticization", Studi Italiani di Linguistica Teorica ed Applicata 22 (93): 509-530; auth, "A Cognitive Account of Samoan Lavea and Galo Verbs", Conceptualizations and Mental Processing in Language, eds Richard a. Geiger, and Brygida Rudzka-Ostyn, Mouton de Gruyter, (93): 567-592; auth, "The Empathy Hierarchy and Samoan Clitic Pronouns", Cognitive Ling 5 (94): 57-75; rev, Samoan Reference Grammar by Ulrike Mosel and Evan Hovdhaugen, Oceanic Ling 33 (94): 567-581; auth, "The Cia Suffix as a Passive Marker in Samoan", Oceanic Linguists 35 (96): 57-76; auth, "The Temporal Use of Hawaiian Directional Particles", The Construal of Space in Language and Thought, eds Rene Dirven and Martin Putz, Mouton de Gruyter, (96): 455-66; auth, "Subject Pronoun Fronting in Samoan and Hawaiian", Rongorongo Studies: A Forum for Polynesian Philology 7 (97): 4-18; auth, "The Samoan Transitive Suffix as an Inverse Marker", Lesical and Syntactical Constructions and the Construction of Meaning, eds Marjolin, Verspoor, Kee Dong Lee and Eve Sweetser, John Benjamins Pub, (Amsterdam, Philadelphia, 97): 347-361; auth, "Samoan as an Active Zone Language", Issues in Cognitive

Linguistics, ed Leon de Stadler and Christoper Eyrich, Mouton de Gruyter, (Berlin, 99): 391-405; auth, Hawaiian he, 'o, and I: Copular Verbs, Prepositions, or Determiners?", Oceanic Linguistics 38, (99): 43-65. **CONTACT ADDRESS** English Found Prog, Hawaii Pacific Univ, 1188 Fort St Mall, Honolulu, HI 96813.

COOK, ROBERT FRANCIS
PERSONAL Born 10/24/1944, Atlanta, GA **DISCIPLINE** MEDIEVAL FRENCH LANGUAGE & LITERATURE **EDUCATION** King Col, AB, 65; Vanderbilt Univ, MA, 68, PhD(-French), 70; Univ Pittsburgh, MS, 75. **CAREER** Asst prof French, Univ Pittsburgh, 69-75; assoc Prof French, 75-91, Full Prof, Univ VA, 91-. **MEMBERSHIPS** MLA; Am Asn Teachers Fr; Mediaeval Acad Am; Int Arthurian Soc; Soc Rencesvals. **RESEARCH** The chansons de geste; textual criticism. **SELECTED PUBLICATIONS** Auth, Les manuscrits de Baudouin de Sebourc, Romania, 70; ed, Le batard de Bouillon, chanson de geste, Droz-Minard, 72; coauth, Le deuxieme Cycle de la Croisade, Droz, 72; auth, Foreign language study and intellectual power, ADFL Bull, 5/77; coauth, The Legendary Sources of Flaubert's Saint Julien l'Hospitalier, Univ Toronto, 77; coauth, Chanson d'Antioche, Chanson de geste, 80; Aucassin et Nicolete, a Critical Bibliography, 82; The Sense of the Song of Roland, 87. **CONTACT ADDRESS** Dept of French, Univ of Virginia, 302 Cabell Hall, Charlottesville, VA 22903. **EMAIL** rfc@virginia.edu

COOKE, MIRIAM
DISCIPLINE ASIAN LITERATURE, MIDDLE EASTERN LITERATURE **EDUCATION** Edinburgh Univ, MA, 71; St Anthony's Col, PhD, 80. **CAREER** Lectr, Islamic and Arabian Develop Studies, 8-81; asst prof, Center for Int Studies, 81-87; assoc prof to prof, Duke Univ, 87-. **HONORS AND AWARDS** Grant, Oxford, 79; Grant, Duke Univ Res Counc, 82; Josiah Trent Found, 85; AAUP Fel, 86; SSRC Scholar, 86; Duke Univ Res Coun, 86, 87; Guggenheim, 90; Dartmouth Col Grant, 90; NCar Humanities Grant, 94; Fulbright Scholar, 95-96; Who's Who in the World, 99; Provost's Fund Awd, 99; Trent Found Awd, 00; Outstanding Scholars of the 21st Century, 00. **MEMBERSHIPS** MLA, MESA. **RESEARCH** War/Gender Studies, Postcolonial Theory, Prison Narratives, Islam and Feminism. **SELECTED PUBLICATIONS** Auth, The Anatomy of an Egyptian Intellectual. Yahya Haqqi, Three Continents Pr, (Washington, DC), 84; ed and transl, Good Morning and Other Stories by Yahya Haqqi, Three Continents Pr, (Washington, DC), 94; auth, War's Other Voices. Women Writers on the Lebanese Civil War, Cambridge Univ Pr, (London/NY), 88; coed, Opening The Gates: A Century of Arab Feminist Writing, Virago/Ind Univ Pr, (London), 90; coed Gendering War Talk, Princeton Univ Pr, 93; coed, Blood into Ink: 20th Century South Asian and Middle Eastern Women Write War, Westview Pr, 94; auth, Women and the War Story, Univ of Calif Pr, 97; auth, Women Clair Islam. Creating Islamic Feminism Through Literature, Routledge, 00, auth, Hayati, My Life. A Novel, Syracuse Univ Pr, 00. **CONTACT ADDRESS** Asian & African Lang & Lit, Duke Univ, 2101 Campus Dr, Durham, NC 27708. **EMAIL** mcw@duke.edu

COOLEY, ROBERT E.
PERSONAL Born Kalamazoo, MI, m, 1952, 2 children **DISCIPLINE** HEBREW STUDIES; NEAR EASTERN ARCHAEOLOGY **EDUCATION** Wheaton Col, BA; Wheaton Col Grad Sch, MA; NYork Univ, PhD. **CAREER** Asst to the pres, Dropsie Univ; acad dean, Evangel Col; prof, Southwest Mo State Univ; dir, Ctr Archaeol Res, Southwest Mo State Univ; pres, 81-97; chancellor, Gordon-Conwell Theol Sem, 97-00; Exec. Dir., CTI Found, 00-. **HONORS AND AWARDS** Ch bd dir(s), World Relief Corp; pres, Assn Theol Sch(s), US, Can; bd dir(s), InTrust mag; pres, In Trust, Inc. **MEMBERSHIPS** SBL **SELECTED PUBLICATIONS** Sr ed, Christianity Today. **CONTACT ADDRESS** Gordon-Conwell Theol Sem, 130 Essex St, South Hamilton, MA 01982. **EMAIL** recgets@aol.com

COOLIDGE, JOHN STANHOPE
PERSONAL Born 07/26/1926, Laramie, WY, m, 1964, 2 children **DISCIPLINE** ENGLISH AND COMPARATIVE LITERATURE **EDUCATION** Harvard Univ, BA, 49, MA, 51, PhD(English), 57. **CAREER** Instr English, Swarthmore Col, 56-60; asst prof, 60-67, assoc prof, 67-80, Prof English, Univ Calif, Berkeley, 80-, Huntington Libr grant-in-aid, 64-65. **MEMBERSHIPS** MLA; Renaissance Soc Am; NCTE. **RESEARCH** Puritanism and the Bible; influence of classical on later literature. **SELECTED PUBLICATIONS** Auth, Fielding and conservation of character, 5/60 & Marvell and Horace, 11/65, Mod Philol; Great things and small: The Virgilian progression, Comp Lit, winter 65. **CONTACT ADDRESS** Dept of English, Univ of California, Berkeley, Berkeley, CA 94720.

COONS, DIX SCOTT
PERSONAL Born 07/11/1930, Mesa, AZ, m, 1956, 5 children **DISCIPLINE** SPANISH; LATIN AMERICAN LITERATURE **EDUCATION** Brigham Young Univ, BA, 55, MA, 57; Univ Tex, PhD, 64. **CAREER** Asst Span, Univ Tex, 56-57; asst, St Stephen's Episcopal Sch, 57-63; from instr to asst prof, Brown Univ, 63-66; asst prof, 66-68, Assoc Prof Span, RI Col, 68-; coord, Latin Am Studies prog, RI Col. **MEMBERSHIPS** Am Asn Teachers Span & Port. **RESEARCH** Latin-American novel and short story; modernismo; Mexican novel. **CONTACT ADDRESS** Latin American Studies, Rhode Island Col, 600 Mt Pleasant, Providence, RI 02908-1924.

COOPER, CRAIG
DISCIPLINE GREEK; ROMAN **EDUCATION** Univ Alberta, BA, 83; Univ Brit Columbia, MA, 85, PhD, 92. **CAREER** Asst prof **RESEARCH** Greek historiography; Athenian law; Athenian orators and rhetoric. **SELECTED PUBLICATIONS** Auth, Hyperides and the Trial of Phryne, Phoenix 49, 95. **CONTACT ADDRESS** Dept of Classics, Univ of Winnipeg, 515 Portage Ave, Winnipeg, MB, Canada R3B 2E9. **EMAIL** craig.cooper@uwinnipeg.ca

COOPER, DANIELLE CHAVY
PERSONAL Born 12/11/1921, Paris, France, m, 1947, 1 child **DISCIPLINE** FRENCH STUDIES **EDUCATION** Univ Paris, BA, 39, MA, 41, PhD(Am lit), 42; Univ Southern Calif, PhD, 63. **CAREER** Teacher English & Span, Sec Schs, France, 42-44; asst French, Whalley Range High Sch & Univ Manchester, 45-46; Marcelle Parde teaching fel, Bryn Mawr Col, 46-47; lang coordr, Isabelle Buckley Schs, Los Angeles, Calif, 55-56; instr French & Ger, Immaculate Heart Col, 57-60, asst prof French, 60-63; lectr, Univ Colo, 63-65; from assoc prof to prof, Keuka Col, 65-70, chmn dept mod lang, 65-70; chmn div lang & civilizations, 71-73, chmn dept lang & humanities, 75-77, Prof French, Monterey Inst Int Studies, Instr French, Fr Found Calif, Los Angeles, 56-58; bd reviewer, Bks Abroad/World Lit Today, 58-; instr, Univ Southern Calif, 58; mem, Alliance Francaise. **HONORS AND AWARDS** Chevalier, Ordre des Palmes Academiques, 72. **MEMBERSHIPS** Am Asn Teachers Fr; MLA; African Studies Asn; Am Name Soc; Philol Asn Pac Coast. **RESEARCH** French phonetics; African and Caribbean literature of French expression; translation theory and practice. **SELECTED PUBLICATIONS CONTACT ADDRESS** Monterey Inst of Intl Studies, PO Box 1978, Monterey, CA 93940.

COOPER, HENRY RONALD, JR.
DISCIPLINE SLAVIC LANGUAGES AND LITERATURES **EDUCATION** City Col of New York, BA (summa cum laude, Russian Lit), 67; Columbia Univ, MA (Russian Lit), 69; Russian Inst, Columbia Univ, Cetificate, 69; Columbia Univ, PhD (Slavic Lit), 74. **CAREER** US Dept of State, escort-interpreter, Serbian and Croatian, 84-; asst tour guide, Lipson Travel, Inc, USSR and East Europe, 68; counter-intelligence special agent, US Army, 69-71; preceptor in Slavic, 73, res asst, 73-74; asst prof, Northwestern Univ, 74-81; asst prof, 81-84, assoc prof, 84-91, prof, IN Univ, 91-, prof and chair, Slavic Dept, 91-, acting dean, Int Prog, 91-92; dir, summer workshop in Soviet & East European Langs, IN Univ, 86, 87; dir, Russian and East European Inst, 86-91. **HONORS AND AWARDS** Phi Beta Kappa; Pi Delta Phi; Grad Honors in Slavic, CCNY, 66-67; Prize for Papers in Problems of Slovene Culture, 76-77; Order of the Yugoslav Flag with Gold Star, 89; Zahvala (Acknowledgement), Govt of the Republic of Slovenia, 92; John W Ryan Awd for Int Service, IN Univ, 94; corresponding member, Slovene Academy of Sciences and Arts, 95. **MEMBERSHIPS** Asn of Literary Scholars and Critics; Am Asn for the Advancement of Slavic Studies; Am Asn of Teachers of Slavic and East European Langs; Soc for Slovene Studies; North Am Serbian Studies Asn; Am Asn for Southeast European Studies; The Fellowship of SS Alban and Sergius; Bulgarian Studies Asn; Early Slavic Lit Asn. **RESEARCH** Slavic lits (especially Old Russian, South Slavic), Slavic Bible translations. **SELECTED PUBLICATIONS** Auth, Marin Drzic and France Preseren, in Vasa D Mihailovich, ed, South Slavic Writers before World War II (Dictionary of Literary Biography, vol 147, Bruccoli, Clark, and Layman, 95; Translating the Freising Manuscripts to Reflect Assumptions about Their Literary and Historical Context, in Janos Kos, et al, Zbornik Britinski spomeniki, ZRC/SAZU, Institut za slovensko literaturo in literarne vede, 96; Intro, Death and the Dervish, English trans by Bogdan Radic and Stephen Dickey, Northwestern Univ Press, 96; The Translation of the Bible Into Slavic Languages: Biblical Citations in the Vitas of Cyril and Methodius, Slavica Tergestina, Trieste, Italy, 5, 97; Kajetan Kovic in Vasa D Mihailovich, ed, South Slavic Writers after World War II (Dictionary of Literary Biography, vol 181), Bruccoli, Clark, Layman, 97; The Origins of the Church Slavonic Version: An Alternative Hypothesis, Proceedings, Int Symposium on the Interpretation of the Bible, Slovene Academy of Sciences and Arts, Ljubljana, Slovenia, 86; The Tense Situation of Slavic: Past, Present, and Future, ADFL Bul, 98; four translations, 28 other publications. **CONTACT ADDRESS** Dept of Slavic Languages and Literatures, Indiana Univ, Bloomington, Ballantine Hall 502, Bloomington, IN 47405-6616. **EMAIL** Cooper@Indiana.edu

COPJEC, JOAN
DISCIPLINE ENGLISH, COMPARATIVE LITERATURE, MEDIA STUDY **EDUCATION** Univ Wis, MA; Univ College Of London, Dipl.; New York Univ, PhD. **CAREER** Prof/Dir Ctr Study Psychoanalysis and Cult. **HONORS AND AWARDS** Fellow, Inst for Arch and Urban Studies; Fellow, Society for the Humanities, Cornell; Fellow, Center for Cultural Analysis of Contemporary Culture, Rutgers. **RESEARCH** Comp lit; cinema; lit criticism. **SELECTED PUBLICATIONS** Auth, Read My Desire: Lacan Against the Historicists, MIT, 94; ed, Jacques Lacan: Television, Norton, 90; Shades of Noir, Verso, 93; Radical Evil, Verso, 93; Supposing the Subject, Verso, 94; Giving Ground, Verso, 99. **CONTACT ADDRESS** Dept Comp Lit, SUNY, Buffalo, 639 Clemens Hall, Buffalo, NY 14260. **EMAIL** joancopjec@hotmail.com

COPPOLA, CARLO
PERSONAL Born 10/01/1938, Wooster, OH, d, 2 children **DISCIPLINE** COMPARATIVE LITERATURE, LINGUISTICS **EDUCATION** John Carroll Univ, BS, 60; Univ Chicago, MA, 61, PhD(comp lit), 75. **CAREER** Lectr Hindi & Urdu ling, 68-70, asst prof, 70-75, assoc prof, 75-82, Prof Hindi & Urdu Ling, Oakland Univ, 82-, Chmn Area Studies Prog, 76-00, SAsian bibliogr, Publ MLA, 71-76; ed, J SAsian Lit, 63-00; asst ed, J Asian Studies, 78-81. **HONORS AND AWARDS** Rockerfeller Fel, 83. **MEMBERSHIPS** Asn Asian Studies, SAsia Lit Asn. **RESEARCH** Modern Hindi; Urdu literature, Indian writing in English, Marxist aesthetics, psychoanalytic lit crit. **SELECTED PUBLICATIONS** Auth, Marxist Influences and South Asian Lit, 88; auth, Husband, Lover, Holy Man, an Intercultural Comedy, World Lit Today, Vol 0067, 93; Footsteps, World Lit Today, Vol 0070, 96; The State Witness, World Lit Today, Vol 0069, 95; Sensuous Horizons--The Stories and Plays, World Lit Today, Vol 0071, 97; The Novel in Javanese--Aspects of Its Social and Literary Character, World Lit Today, Vol 0067, 93; Contemporary Urdu Short-Stories--An Anthology, World Lit Today, Vol 0066, 92. **CONTACT ADDRESS** Dept of Mod Lang & Lit, Oakland Univ, Rochester, MI 48063. **EMAIL** coppola@oakland.edu

CORBEILL, ANTHONY
DISCIPLINE CLASSICAL LANGUAGES AND LITERATURE **EDUCATION** Univ MI, AB, 83; Univ CA, Berkeley, MA, 85, PhD, 90. **CAREER** Assoc prof, Univ KS. **HONORS AND AWARDS** APA fel, Thesaurus Linguae Latinae, Ger, 90-91; Rome Prize fel, Am Acad Rome, 94-95; adv coun, aar; contrib, tocs-in. **MEMBERSHIPS** Mem, Am Philol Assn; CAMWS; Am Class League; Soc of Fellows Am Acad Rome; outsanding acad book, Controlling Laughter. Polit Humor in the Late Roman Republic, Princeton, 97. **RESEARCH** Latin lit and Roman cult hist. **SELECTED PUBLICATIONS** Auth, Controlling Laughter. Political Humor in the Late Roman Republic, Princeton, 96; Deviant Diners in Roman Political Invective, Roman Sexualities, Princeton, 98. **CONTACT ADDRESS** Dept of Class, Univ of Kansas, Lawrence, Admin Building, Lawrence, KS 66045. **EMAIL** corbeill@ku.edu

CORBETT, NOEL L.
PERSONAL Born 11/23/1938, Bowmanville, ON, Canada, m, 1963 **DISCIPLINE** FRENCH LANGUAGE AND LINGUISTICS **EDUCATION** Univ Toronto, BA, 60, MA, 63, PhD(-French), 67. **CAREER** Teaching asst French, Victoria Col, Univ Toronto, 62-66, lectr, 66-67; asst prof, 67-72, prog coordr fac educ, 77-81, Assoc Prof French, York Univ, 72-, Fac Fel, York Univ, 79-80. **HONORS AND AWARDS** Can Coun Res, Fel, 69-70, Can Secy of State Grant, 72. **MEMBERSHIPS** MLA; Ling Soc Am; Soc Ling Romane; Can Asn Univ Teachers; Can Ling Asn. **RESEARCH** Diachronic study of French and Romance languages; medieval French language and literature; synchronic structure of French and Canadian French. **SELECTED PUBLICATIONS** Transl, The Knight of the Two Swords: A Thirteenth-Century Arthurian Romance, Univ Pr of Fla, 96. **CONTACT ADDRESS** Dept of French Studies, York Univ, 4700 Keele St, Downsview, ON, Canada M3J 1P3. **EMAIL** ncorbett@yorku.ca

CORDOVA, SARAH DAVIES
PERSONAL Born 01/23/1960, France, d **DISCIPLINE** FRENCH **EDUCATION** Cal State Univ, BA, 85; Univ Calif at Los Angeles, MA, 86; PhD, 93. **CAREER** Teach asst, Univ Calif, Los Angeles, 85-91; lectr, Loyola Marymount Univ, 92; instr, MoorPk Col, 87-95; instr, Univ Calif, Los Angeles, 92-95; lectr, Univ S Cal, 93-95; asst prof, Marq, 95-. **HONORS AND AWARDS** Fulbright-hays Fel; Hortense Fishbaugh Mem Schlp; Chan Diss Fel; CSW Gnt; Univ Geo Gnt; Bourse Marandon, SPFFA; Camargo Found Fel; Cult Ser Gnt; CLAT Gnt. **MEMBERSHIPS** AATF; HAS; IFTR; Phi Delta Phi; Pi Delta Phi; MLA; SCMLA; RAD; Women in French; UWM. **RESEARCH** 19th century literature and culture; cultural studies; women and gender issues; colonial and post-colonial Maghrebi and Caribbean Francophone literatures. **SELECTED PUBLICATIONS** Co-ed, "Medievalism: Testing Ground for Historicism(s)?," Paroles Gelees 9 (91): 1-32; rev, "Narrative: an International Conference (Albany)," Dance Res J 25 (93): 61-62; auth, " 'La Danse des djinns': notice necrologique d'une danseuse," Bulletin Soc Theophile Gautier 18 (96): 347-357; auth, "Germinie Lacerteux: The Dance of the Cliniciens es lettres," Excavatio 9 (97): 20-31; auth, "Recits de la danse et Graphies dansees au dix-neuvieme siecle," Litterature 112 (98): 26-36; auth, "Writing Dance; Textualizing Narrative Poetics in Maupassant's "Menuet" and "Le Masque," Romance Lang Ann 9 (98): 40-45; auth, Paris Dances: Textual Choreographies in the Nineteenth-Century French Novel, Intl Schl Pub (Bethesda), 99; auth, "Stepping out of attitude - [La Fanfarlo and autobiog-

raphy]," (Banff; Canada: Banff Cen Press, forthcoming); auth, "The Socio-Politics of Orientalist Representations: Delacroix, Djebar, and the Femmes d'Alger," Nineteenth Cent French Stud (forthcoming). **CONTACT ADDRESS** Dept Foreign Language, Marquette Univ, PO Box 1881, Milwaukee, WI 53201-1881. **EMAIL** cordovas@marquette.edu

CORGAN, MARGARET M.
PERSONAL Born 08/24/1936, Wilkes-Barre, PA **DISCIPLINE** FRENCH LANGUAGE & LITERATURE **EDUCATION** Marymount Col, NYork, BA, 58; Univ Rennes, dipl French Lang & Lit, 59; Fordham Univ, MA, 62, PhD(French), 67. **CAREER** Instr French, Col Misericordia, 59-61; asst, Fordham Univ, 61-63; instr, St John's Univ, NY, 64-65; from asst prof to assoc prof, 65-74, prof French, King's Col, PA, 74-, chmn Dept Foreign Lang & Lit, 77-. **HONORS AND AWARDS** Fulbright Scholar, Univ of Paris, 63-64; French Government Grantee, Chambre de Commerce et d'Industrie, Paris, Summer, 82; Herve Le Blanc Distinguished Service Prof, King's Coll, 92-97; National French Contest Admin of the Year, 92. **MEMBERSHIPS** Am Asn Teachers Fr; Am Coun Teaching For Lang. **RESEARCH** Twentieth century French literature; bibliography of twentieth century French authors; translation. **CONTACT ADDRESS** Dept of Foreign Lang & Lit, King's Col, 133 N River St, Wilkes-Barre, PA 18711-0801. **EMAIL** mmcorgan@kings.edu

CORMIER, RAYMOND
PERSONAL Born 11/23/1938, Bridgeport, CT, m, 1960, 2 children **DISCIPLINE** FRENCH **EDUCATION** Univ Bridgeport, AB, 60; Stanford Univ, AM, 62; Harvard Univ, PhD, 67. **CAREER** Teaching Asst, Stanford Univ, 60-62; Instructor, Harvard Univ, 63-67; Instructor, Tufts Univ, 65-67; Asst Prof, Univ Va, 67-72; Assoc Prof to Prof and Chair, Temple Univ, 72-79; Prof, Wilson Col, 84-95; Instructor, Cent Piedmont Cmty Col, 94-96; Vis Prof, Longwood Col, 96-. **HONORS AND AWARDS** Distinguished Service Awd, Mod Lang Asn, 82; Fulbright Sen Res Fel, France, 83-84; NEH, Brussels, 86; Certificate for Excellence in Education, Valley Forge, 87; Fulbright Res Fel, Barcelona, 92-93; Innovation grant, Central Piedmont Community Col, 95-96. **MEMBERSHIPS** Intl Courtly Lit Soc; Capitol Film Soc; MLA; Comparative Studies in Med Lit; Oakhurst Homeowners Asn; Alliance Francaise de Charlotte; Am Asn of Teachers of French; Anglo-Norman Texts Soc; Irish Texts Soc. **RESEARCH** Medieal Comparative Literature: French, Latin and Celtic, with special focus on the Trasmission of Antiquity; Translation and gocnitive theories; Mythology; Women's studies, and the figure of the hero. **CONTACT ADDRESS** Dept Eng & Lang, Longwood Col, 201 High St, Farmville, VA 23909-1800. **EMAIL** rcormier@longwood.lwc.edu

CORNGOLD, STANLEY ALAN
PERSONAL Born 06/11/1934, Brooklyn, NY, m, 1995, 1 child **DISCIPLINE** GERMAN AND COMPARATIVE LITERATURE **EDUCATION** Columbia Univ, AB, 57; Cornell Univ, MA, 63, PhD(comp lit), 69. **CAREER** Instr English, Univ Md, Europ div, 59-62; teaching asst, Cornell Univ, 63-64, teaching asst French, 64-65; from lectr to asst prof Ger, 66-72, assoc prof, 72-79, assoc prof Ger & comp lit, 79-81, Prof Ger & Comp Lit, Princeton Univ, 81- . **HONORS AND AWARDS** Nat Endowment for Humanities fel, 73-74; Guggenheim fel, 77-78; Acad of Lit Stud, 83-88; listed, Who's Who in America; Fulbright Res Fel, 86-87; pres, Kafka Soc of Am, 87-88; Princeton Univ grant-in-aid, 90-97; consult for German Lit, Guggenheim Found, 92-99; publ comt, MLA, 93-95; invited mem, Heidelberg Club Int, 95- ; fac assoc, Int School of Theory in the Hum at Santiago de Compostela, 96- ; bd of dir, Literature da Quieli, 98. **MEMBERSHIPS** MLA; PEN Club; Am Comparative Lit Asn. **RESEARCH** European Romanticism; modern German literature; modern poetics. **SELECTED PUBLICATIONS** Ed & transl, Ausgewaehlte Prosa by Max Frisch, Harcourt Brace, 68; ed & transl, Franz Kafka, The Metamorphosis, Bantam, 72, Norton, 96; co-ed, Thomas Mann, 1875-1975, Princeton Univ Library, 75; co-ed, Aspekte der Goethezeit, Vandenhoeck & Ruprecht, 77; auth, The Commentators' Despair: The Interpretation of Kafka's Metamorphosis, Assoc Faculty Press, 73; auth, The Fate of the Self: German Writers and French Theory, Columbia, 86, 2nd ed., 94; auth, Franz Kafka: The Necessity of Form, Cornell, 88; coauth, Borrowed Lives, SUNY Albany, 91; transl, Walter Benjamin, Goethe's Elective Affinities, Harvard, 96; auth, Complex Pleasure: Forms of Feeling in German Literature, Stanford, 98. **CONTACT ADDRESS** Dept of Germanic Languages & Literatures, Princeton Univ, Princeton, NJ 08544-5264. **EMAIL** corngold@princeton.edu

CORRE, ALAN DAVID
PERSONAL Born 05/02/1931, London, England, m, 1957, 4 children **DISCIPLINE** SEMITIC STUDIES, LINGUISTICS **EDUCATION** Univ London, BA, 51; Univ Manchester, MA, 53; Univ Pa, PhD(ling), 62. **CAREER** Minister, Congregation Mikveh Israel, Pa, 55-63; from asst prof to assoc prof, 63-68, Prpf Hebrew Studies, Univ Wis-Milwaukee, 68-, Chmn Dept, 80-, Nat Endowment for Humanities younger scholar fel, Univ Col, Univ London, 67-68. **HONORS AND AWARDS** Res in Humanities Prize, Wis Acad Sci, Arts & Lett, 66; Standard Oil of Ind Awd for teaching excellence, 73. **MEMBERSHIPS** Ling Soc Am; Am Orient Soc. **RESEARCH** Semitic linguistics; Sefardic studies; Judeo-Arabic studies. **SELECTED PUBLICATIONS** Auth, A Lexicon of the Hebrew and Aramaic Elements in Modern Judezmo, Jour Amer Oriental Soc, Vol 0115, 95. **CONTACT ADDRESS** Dept of Foreign Languages & Linguistics, Univ of Wisconsin, Milwaukee, Milwaukee, WI 53201. **EMAIL** corre@uwm.edu

CORREDOR, EVA LIVIA
PERSONAL Born 03/07/1936, Budapest, Hungary, d, 1 child **DISCIPLINE** LINGUISTICS, FRENCH, GERMAN **EDUCATION** Univ Sorbonne, Dip, 59; Columbia Univ, MA, 68; PhD, 75. **CAREER** Instr, Barnard Col, 68-73; instr, Columbia Univ, 68-73; asst prof, Rutgers Univ Douglas Col, 73-78; vis asst prof, Reed Col, 78-79; vis asst prof, Univ Wash, 78-80; asst prof, Mills Col, 80-83; prof, US Naval Acad, 83-00. **HONORS AND AWARDS** Merit Civ Awd, USNA; Excellence Res Awd, USNA; Vis Prof, Brit Roy Nav Col and Harvard Univ. **MEMBERSHIPS** MLA; JAPL; AATF; AATG. **RESEARCH** Literary theory; philosophy; Gyorgy Lukacs and contemporary French theory and philosophy; exile literature; autobiography. **SELECTED PUBLICATIONS** Auth, Gyorgy Lukacs and the Literary Text as a Pretext, Peter Lang; auth, Lukacs After Communism: Interviews with Contemporary Intellectuals. **CONTACT ADDRESS** 4 Horizon Rd, Apt 627, Fort Lee, NJ 07024-6743. **EMAIL** elc49@columbia.edu

CORRIGAN, KEVIN
PERSONAL Born 08/04/1948, United Kingdom, m, 1976, 4 children **DISCIPLINE** PHILOSOPHY; CLASSICS **EDUCATION** Lancaster, BA, 75; MA, 77, PhD, 80, Dalhousie **CAREER** Asst Prof, Col of Notre Dame, Saskatchewan, 82-86; Asst Prof, Assoc Prof, Full Prof, 86-, Dean, 91-, St. Thomas More Col, Univ of Saskatchewan. **RESEARCH** Philosophy; Classics; Ancient/Medieval Plato; Aristotle; Plotinus **SELECTED PUBLICATIONS** Auth, Plotinus Theory of Matter-Evil and the Question of Substance:Plato, Aristotle, and Alexander of Aphrodisias, 96. **CONTACT ADDRESS** 1437 College Dr., Saskatoon, SK, Canada S7N 0W6. **EMAIL** k.corrigan@usask.ca

CORTES, JULIO
PERSONAL Born 01/23/1924, Bilbao, Spain, m, 1967, 1 child **DISCIPLINE** LINGUISTICS **EDUCATION** Univ Complutense Madrid, MA, 52; PhD, 65. **CAREER** Dir & prof, Centro Cultural Hispanico, 56-60 & 62-67; lectr, Univ of Damascus, 65-67; prof, Univ of NC at Chapel Hill, 80-00-. **HONORS AND AWARDS** Orden del Merito, Spain; Tanner Awd. **MEMBERSHIPS** AOS, AEO, AATA, MESA, MLA, UEAI. **RESEARCH** Qur'anic Arabic, modern Arabic lexicography. **SELECTED PUBLICATIONS** Auth, Diccionario de Arabe Culto Moderno, Madrid, 96; auth, El Coran, Barcelona, 99. **CONTACT ADDRESS** Dept Romance Lang, Univ of No Carolina, Chapel Hill, 440 W Franklin St, Chapel Hill, NC 27599-2319.

CORTIJO, ANTONIO
PERSONAL Born 08/03/1967, Madrid, Spain, m, 1995 **DISCIPLINE** SPANISH LITERATURE **EDUCATION** Univ Ottawa, MA, 93; Universidad Cenpluteuse, Madric, BA; Universidad de Alcala de Henares, PhD, 93; Univ Calif Berkeley, PhD, 97. **SELECTED PUBLICATIONS** Auth, "Ejemplo de declamatio en el Examen de maridos de Juan Ruiz de Alarcon", Bulletin Hispanique 95 (93): 541-56; auth, "Noticia sobre un nuevo manuscrito de Las firmezas de Isabela", Rivista de Filologia Espanola 75, (95): 131-138; auth, "La leyenda del caballero de Olmedo a la luz de un Mx inedito de la Fernan Nunez Collection", Criticon 68 (96): 101-11; coauth, Universal Enciclopedia Multimedia, Historia de la Literatura Espanola (letras A-D), Historia de la Literatura Catalana, Micronet, (Madrid), 96; auth, "Commerical Rivalry Between Valencia and Barcelona in the Fourteenth-Century", La Coronica 26.1 (97): 45-52; auth, "Los primeros conatos de literatura en espanol en Centroamerica: Las cartas familiares de Alonso y Gomez Diax de la Reguera", Ventana abierta 2.6 (99): 75-79; auth, La ficcion sentimental espanola de los sigmox XV y XVI, Tamesis (London), 99; auth, "Teoria de la historia y teoria politica en el siglo XVI. De Historia institutione de Sebastian Fox Morcillo", Alcala de Henares Univ Pr, 00; auth, Los Suppositi de Juan Perez Petreyo: teatro escolar e influjo italiano, Pamplona Univ Pr, 00. **CONTACT ADDRESS** Dept Span and Port, Univ of California, Santa Barbara, 552 University Rd, Santa Barbara, CA 93106-0002. **EMAIL** costijo@humanitas.ucsb.edu

CORUM, ROBERT T., JR.
PERSONAL Born 09/19/1947, Great Lakes, IL, m, 1966, 2 children **DISCIPLINE** FRENCH LITERATURE **EDUCATION** Old Dominion Univ, BA, 69; Univ Va, MA, 71; PhD, 75; Middlebury Col, Ecole francaise d'ete, 69. **CAREER** Instr, Univ Va, 71-75; instr, Sweet Briar Col, 75; asst prof, Univ of Southern Calif, 75-77; asst prof to prof, dept head, Kans State Univ, 77-. **HONORS AND AWARDS** Univ Outstanding Teacher Awd, 83; Am Philos Soc Grant, 84, 87; NEH Grant, 84, 87, 90; Stamey Teaching Awd, 89, 93; ACLS Grant, 90; Pres Awd for Distinction in Undergraduate Teaching, 00. **MEMBERSHIPS** MLA, ADFL. **RESEARCH** 17th Century French Literature **SELECTED PUBLICATIONS** Auth, "Other Worlds and Other Seas: Art and Vision in Saint-Amant's Nature Poetry," Fr Forum, 79; ed, Cesar de Nostredame, les Perles, ou les Larmes de la Saincte Magdeleine, Exeter Univ Pr, 86; auth, Reading Boileau: An Integrative Study of the Early Satires, Purdue Univ Pr, 98. **CONTACT ADDRESS** Dept Mod Lang, Kansas State Univ, Manhattan, KS 66506. **EMAIL** corum@ksu.edu

CORY, MARK E.
PERSONAL Born 07/01/1942, Carmel, CA, m, 1984, 3 children **DISCIPLINE** GERMAN LITERATURE **EDUCATION** Dartmouth Col, BA, 63; Ind Univ, MA, 68; PhD, 71. **CAREER** From asst prof to assoc prof, Univ of Nebr, 71-82; prof, Univ of Ark, 82-. **HONORS AND AWARDS** Fulbright Travel Grants; Awd for Distinguished Teaching, Univ of Nebr, 77; Master Teacher Awd, Fulbright Col at Univ of Ark, 99. **MEMBERSHIPS** Ger Studies Asn. **RESEARCH** Twentieth-Century German Literature, Holocaust Studies. **SELECTED PUBLICATIONS** Co-ed, Politics in German Literature, Camden, 98. **CONTACT ADDRESS** Dept For Lang, Univ of Arkansas, Fayetteville, 425 Kimpel, Fayetteville, AR 72701-1201. **EMAIL** mcory@comp.uark.edu

COSTA, GUSTAVO
PERSONAL Born 03/21/1930, Rome, Italy, m, 1963, 1 child **DISCIPLINE** ITALIAN, HISTORY **EDUCATION** Univ Rome, DPhilos, 54. **CAREER** Asst hist of mod & contemporary philos, Univ Rome, 57-60; lectr Ital, Univ Lyon, 60-61; from instr to assoc prof, 61-72, chmn dept, 73-76, 88-91, Prof Ital, Univ Calif, Berkeley, 72-91, prof emer, 91-; vis prof, Naples, 84; vis prof, Inst of Philos, Univ of Rome, 92; ed staff, Cuadernos sobre Vico, New Vico Studies, Forum Italicum & Nouvelles de la Republique des lettres. **HONORS AND AWARDS** Ist Ital Studi Storici, Naples fel, 54-57; French & Belg govt grants, 56; Am Philos Soc grant, 67; Nat Endowment for Humanities fel, 70-71; Guggenheim Mem Found fel, 76-77. **MEMBERSHIPS** AATI; Renaissance Soc Am; Am Soc Aesthet. **RESEARCH** Literary criticism; history; philosophy. **SELECTED PUBLICATIONS** Auth, La leggenda dei secoli d'oro nella letteratura italiana, Laterza, 72; auth, Le antichita germaniche nella cultura italiana da Machiavelli a Vico, Bibliopolis, 77; auth,Il sublime e la magia da Dante a Tosso, Edizioni Scientifiche Italiane, 94; auth, Vico e l'Europa: Contro la "boria delle nazioni", Guerini e Associati, 96. **CONTACT ADDRESS** Dept of Ital, Univ of California, Berkeley, Berkeley, CA 94720.

COSTELLO, JOHN ROBERT
PERSONAL Born 09/12/1942, New York, NY, m, 1967 **DISCIPLINE** LINGUISTICS **EDUCATION** Wagner Col, BA, 64; NYork Univ, MA, 66, PhD(Ger ling), 68. **CAREER** Instr Ger, Univ Col, 67-68, asst prof, 68-72, Assoc Prof Ling, Washington Sq Col, NY Univ, 73-, Consult, Universe Bks & Lexik Houser Publ. **MEMBERSHIPS** Ling Soc Am; Int Ling Asn (pres, 81-82); Soc Ger-Am Studies. **RESEARCH** Historical linguistics; linguistic reconstruction; language acquisition. **SELECTED PUBLICATIONS CONTACT ADDRESS** Dept of Ling, New York Univ, 719 Broadway, New York, NY 10003-6806.

COTNAM, JACQUES
PERSONAL Born 07/20/1941, m, 1964, 1 child **DISCIPLINE** FRENCH-CANADIAN LITERATURE **EDUCATION** Laval Univ, BA & BPh, 62, Lic es Lett, 64, Dipl Etudes Super, 66, D es L, 78. **CAREER** From lectr to asst prof, 64-72, Assoc Prof French Lit, York Univ, 72-, Lectr, MLA, 69 & Col de France, Paris, 70; lectr at var foreign univs, 73-; vis prof, Univ de Guenoble III, 80-82. **MEMBERSHIPS** Amis Andre Gide; Can Asn Comp Lit; Can Asn Univ Teachers; Asn Can Univ Teachers Fr. **RESEARCH** Influence of nationalism on literature; Andre Gide and English and American literatures; cosmopolitism and the French symbolist movement. **SELECTED PUBLICATIONS** Auth, Bilbiographie Chronologique De L'Uvre D'AndrE Gide (1889-1973), by Jacques, Cotnam; auth, Le thaeaatre quaebaecois: instrument de contestation sociale et politique, by Jacques Cotnam; auth, Contemporary Quebec: an analytical bibliography, by Jacques Cotnam; auth, Poetes Du Quebec, by Jacques Cotnam, 82; auth, coed, La didactique al'oeuvre: Perspectives theoriques et patiques, by Jacques Cotnam, Janet M. Paterson, 95. **CONTACT ADDRESS** Dept of Fr Stud, York Univ, N727 Ross Building, 4700 Keele St, North York, ON, Canada M3J 1P3. **EMAIL** jcotnam@yorku.ca

COTTRELL, ROBERT DUANE
PERSONAL Born 02/20/1930, Farmersburg, IA, m, 1965, 2 children **DISCIPLINE** FRENCH LITERATURE **EDUCATION** Columbia Univ, BS, 57; Yale Univ, PhD(Romance lang), 61. **CAREER** From instr to asst prof Romance lang, Northwestern Univ, 60-65; asst prof, Amherst Col, 65-68; assoc prof, 68-71, chmn dept, 74-78, Prof Romance Lang, Ohio State Univ, 71-, Vis prof, Univ Pittsburgh, 72. **MEMBERSHIPS** MLA; Am Asn Teachers Fr; Mod Humanities Res Asn; Soc Amis Montaigne. **RESEARCH** French Renaissance literature. **SELECTED PUBLICATIONS CONTACT ADDRESS** Dept of Romance Lang, Ohio State Univ, Columbus, 1841 Millikin Rd, Columbus, OH 43210-1229.

COUGHLIN, EDWARD V.
PERSONAL Born 03/02/1932, Norwood, MA, m, 1989, 2 children **DISCIPLINE** SPANISH LANGUAGE & LITERATURE **EDUCATION** Col Holy Cross, BA, 54; Boston Col, MA, 55; Univ Mich, PhD, 65. **CAREER** Asst prof, 64-74, assoc prof, 74-81, Prof Span Lit, Univ Cincinnati, 81-; Prof Emeritus. **MEMBERSHIPS** Am Asn Teachers Span & Port; Am Soc 18th Century Studies; Ctr Estud del Siglo XVIII. **RESEARCH** Eighteenth and 19th century Spanish literature. **SELECTED PUBLICATIONS** Coauth, Bibliografia selecta y critica de Octavio Paz, Univ San Luis Potosi, 73; ed, Habides de Ignacio Lopez de Ayala, Ed Hisp, 74; co-ed, Homenaje a Octavio Paz, Univ San Luis Potosi, 76; auth, Adelardo Lopez de Ayala, Twayne, 77; ed, Tres obras ineditas de Ramon de la Cruz, Puvill, 79; coauth, Cambios: La cultura hisp nica, Heinle & Heinle, 83; transl, Poems of Roberto Sosa, Span Publ, 84; ed, Ten Unedited Plays of Ramon de la Cruz, Hispanofila, 87; Nicasio Alvarez de Cienfuegos, Twayne, 88. **CONTACT ADDRESS** Dept of Romance Lang, Univ of Cincinnati, PO Box 210377, Cincinnati, OH 45221-0377. **EMAIL** coughlev@email.uc.edu

COULET DU GARD, RENE
PERSONAL Born 12/29/1919, Saint-Denis-du Sig, Algeria, m, 1940, 5 children **DISCIPLINE** FRENCH LITERATURE **EDUCATION** Univ PA, MS, 63; Univ Besancon, PhD(lit), 66. **CAREER** Prin, Ecole d'Apprentissage, Morocco, 46-52; teacher, high sch, NY, 53-57 & Kimberton Sch, Pa, 57-62; teacher French, Ursinus Col, 62-63; asst prof French & Span, West Chester State Col, 63-66; from asst prof to assoc prof, 66-80, Prof French, Univ Del, 80-, Ed, Thursday Page, Maroc Press, Morocco, 47-52; foreign corresp, Echos Monde Roman Inedit, Morocco, 52-55. **HONORS AND AWARDS** Adventure Novel Prize, Soc Arts et Let Algeria, 52; Poetry Awd, Acad Jeux Floraux Tunisia, 53; Chevalier, Soc Philanthropique at Culturelle France, 66, Commandeur, 68; Chevalier, Palmes Academiques, 67, Officier, 77; Medaille d'argent, Concours Lit: Acad Int Lutece, Paris, 73; Medaille d'OR Concours Litteraire, Acad Int Lutece, Paris, 74; Prix d'Hist Maritime, Soc Arts et Lettres Acad Bordeaux, France, 80; Prix de la Langue Francaise, Acad Francaise, 80. **MEMBERSHIPS** Am Asn Tchrs Fr; Soc des Gens Lett et auteurs France. **RESEARCH** Eighteenth and 19th century French lit; origin of French geog names in the US. **SELECTED PUBLICATIONS** Auth, L'Arithmosophie de Gerard de Nerval, Ed Deux Mondes, 72; Reine (novel), Ed La Revue Mod, Paris, 73; The Handbook of French Place Names in the USA, Ed Des Deux Mondes, 74 & 77; La France Contemporaine de 1900 a 1976, 76 & L-Oiseau de feu (poetry), 76, Slavuta, Can; Le fruit defendu (poetry), Ed Chantecler, France, 76; Pleure pas P'tit Bonhomme (novel), Ed Du Vent, France, 77; The Handbook of AmCounties, Parishes and Independent Cities, Ed Deux Mondes, 81; Dictionary of Spanish Place Names in the USA, 5v; auth, L'Epopee Algerienne, Ed des Deux Mondes, 97; auth, Eglantine, Ed des Deux Mondes; auth, Vie et Mort des Indiens d'Amerique du Nord, Ed France-Empire; auth, La Rage, Ed des Deux Mondes. **CONTACT ADDRESS** PO Box 251, Elkton, MD 21921.

COUNTRYMAN, L. WM
PERSONAL Born 10/21/1941, Oklahoma City, OK, 1 child **DISCIPLINE** CLASSICS, NEW TESTAMENT **EDUCATION** Univ of Chicago, BA, 62, MA, 74, PhD, 77; General Theol Sem, STB, 65 **CAREER** Lect, 74-76, Univ of Chicago; Asst Prof, 76-79, SW Mission St Univ; Asst Prof, 79-83 TX Christ Univ; Prof, 83-pres, Church Div Sch of the Pac **HONORS AND AWARDS** Phi Beta Kappa **MEMBERSHIPS** Soc of Bibl Lit; Assoc of Anglican Bibl Schols; Soc for Study of Christian Spirituality **RESEARCH** Spirituality; Sexual Orientation **SELECTED PUBLICATIONS** Auth, The Rich Christian in the Church of the Early Empire, Edwin Mellen Press, 80; Auth, The Mystical Way in the Fourth Gospel, Crossing Over into God, Fortress Press, 87; Living on the Border of the Holy: The Priesthood of Humanity and the Priesthoods of the Church, Morehouse Publ, 99; Forgiven and Forgiving, Morehouse Publ, 98 **CONTACT ADDRESS** Church Divinity Sch of the Pacific, 2451 Ridge, Berkeley, CA 94709. **EMAIL** bcountryman@cdsp.edu

COURTEAU, JOANNA
DISCIPLINE SPANISH, PORTUGUESE **EDUCATION** Univ Minn, Minneapolis, BA, 60; Univ Wis-Madison, MA, 62, PhD, 70. **CAREER** Instr Span, Sullins Col, 63-65; asst prof, Univ Ark, Fayetteville, 67-71; asst prof Span & Port, 71-76, assoc prof, Foreign lang & lit, 76-80, Prof Span & Port, Iowa State Univ, 76-; Vis prof, Warsaw Univ, Poland, 79; Assoc ed, Hispania, 93-99. **HONORS AND AWARDS** NDEA fel, 60-65; Ford fel, 66-67; ICA grant, 79; Garlbenkian Found grant 88; Wilton Park award, 97. **MEMBERSHIPS** AAUP (comt, 91-93, exec counc 94-97, govt relation comt, 95-97); AATSP (exec comt, 92-95); AIL (exec comt, 84-90); APSA (pres, 96-98, exec comt, 98-01, founding mem, 93-96). **RESEARCH** Modernist Brazilian novel; modernist peninsular poetry; XIX Spanish poetry; feminist literature. **SELECTED PUBLICATIONS** More than fifty articles & book chpt; co-ed vol on Hispanic Women's writing in the XIX Century and an encycl on Hispanic poetry. **CONTACT ADDRESS** Foreign Lang & Lit Dept, Iowa State Univ of Science and Tech, Ames, IA 50011-0002. **EMAIL** courteau@iastate.edu

COURTNEY, EDWARD
PERSONAL Born 03/22/1932, Belfast, Ireland, m, 1962, 2 children **DISCIPLINE** CLASSICS **EDUCATION** Trinity College Dublin, BA, 54; Christ Church Oxford, MA, 57. **CAREER** Lectr, Christ Church Oxford 55-59; Lectr 59-70, reader 70-77; Prof 77-82, Univ London King's College; Prof, 82-93, Stanford Univ; Gildersleeve Prof, classics, 93-, Univ Virginia. **MEMBERSHIPS** APA; CAMWS; CAV. **RESEARCH** Latin language and literature; Textual criticism and transmission of texts. **SELECTED PUBLICATIONS** Auth, Commentary on the Satires of Juvenal, 80; The Poems of Petronius, 91; The Fragmentary Latin Poets, 93; Musa Lapidaria, 95, Archaic Latin Prose, 99; texts edited; Valerius Flaccus, Argonatica, 70; coauth, Ovid, Fasti, 78, 4th edition, 97; auth, Juvenal, Satires, 84; Statins, Silvae, 90. **CONTACT ADDRESS** 1500 West Pines Dr, Charlottesville, VA 22901. **EMAIL** EC4S@virginia.edu

COWART, WAYNE
DISCIPLINE LINGUISTICS **EDUCATION** City Univ NYork, PhD, 83. **CAREER** Assoc prof, 89-. **RESEARCH** Psychology and biology of language; philosophy of mind. **SELECTED PUBLICATIONS** Auth, Experimental Syntax: Applying objective methods to sentence judgments, Sage, 97; pubs in Lang, Perceptual and Motor Skills, Memory and Cognition, Cognition, The Jour of Psycholinguistic Research, and The Jour of Verbal Lrng and Verbal Behav. **CONTACT ADDRESS** Dept of Linguistics, Univ of So Maine, 37 Col Ave, Gorham, MN 04038-1083.

COWEN, ROY C.
PERSONAL Born 08/02/1930, Kansas City, MO, w, 1956 **DISCIPLINE** GERMAN LITERATURE **EDUCATION** Yal Univ, BA, 52; Univ Gottingen-Ger, PhD, 61. **CAREER** Instr, 60-64, asst prof, 64-67, assoc prof, 67-70. Prof, 70- , chr Ger dept, 79-85, Univ Mich. **HONORS AND AWARDS** Wms Teaching Awd Hum, 68; Sr Fel NEH, 72-73; Bundesverdientskreuz 1. Klasse, 75. **MEMBERSHIPS** Am Asn Teachers Ger; Brabbe-Gesellschaft; Grillparzar Soc; G. Hauptmann-Gesellschaft; Forum Vormarz Forschung; Immermann-Gesellschaft. **RESEARCH** German literature, 18th Century to present. **SELECTED PUBLICATIONS** Auth, Hauptmann-Kommentar zum dramatischen Werk, (80); auth, Hauptmann-Kommentar zum nichtdramatischen Werk, (81); auth, Der Naturalismus, (81); auth, Der Poetische Realismus, (85); auth, Das deutsche Drama im 18. Jahrhundert (88); auth, Christian Deitrich Grabbe-Dramatiker ungeloster Widerspruche (98). **CONTACT ADDRESS** Dept Ger Lang, Univ of Michigan, Ann Arbor, 812 E Washington St, 3110 MLB, Ann Arbor, MI 48109-1275. **EMAIL** rcowen@umich.edu

COX, JERRY LYNN
PERSONAL Born 04/14/1945, Wichita, KS, m, 1973, 2 children **DISCIPLINE** GERMAN, APPLIED LINGUISTICS **EDUCATION** Wichita State Univ, BA, 68; Univ Colo Boulder, MA, 72; Ind Univ Bloomington, MS, 75, PhD(Ger ling), 77. **CAREER** Instr, 76-77, Asst Prof Ger and English as a Second Lang, Furman Univ, 77- Dir Lang Lab, 76-, Fulbright fel ling, Univ Hamburg, 72-73. **MEMBERSHIPS** Am Asn Teachers Ger; Ling Soc Am; Teachers English to Speakers of Other Lang; Am Asn Appl Ling; Am Coun Foreign Lang Teachers. **RESEARCH** Foreign language methodology; applied linguistics-language acquisition; comparative Germanic linguistics. **SELECTED PUBLICATIONS CONTACT ADDRESS** Dept of Mod Foreign Lang, Furman Univ, 3300 Poinsett Hwy, Greenville, SC 29613-0002.

COX, ROGER LINDSAY
PERSONAL Born 03/23/1931, Manson, IA, m, 1951, 4 children **DISCIPLINE** ENGLISH & COMPARATIVE LITERATURE **EDUCATION** Morningside Col, BA, 51; Univ Calif, Los Angeles, MA, 52; Columbia Univ, PhD, 61. **CAREER** Instr English, Bates Col, 58-61; from asst prof to assoc prof, DePauw Univ, 61-71; assoc prof, 71-75, Prof English, Univ Del, 75-, vis prof, Jean-Moulin Univ, Lyon, Fr, 93; **HONORS AND AWARDS** Great Lakes Cols Asn award, 67-68; Am Coun Learned Soc fel, 67-68; Andrew Mellon fel, Univ Pittsburgh, 69-70. **RESEARCH** Tragedy; Comedy; Shakespeare; the novel. **SELECTED PUBLICATIONS** Auth, Hamlet's Hamartia: Aristotle or St Paul?, Yale Rev, 66; Tragedy and the gospel narratives, Yale Rev, 68; Between Earth and Heaven: Shakespeare, Dostoevsky and the Meaning of Christian Tragedy, Holt, 69; The invented self: An essay on comedy, Soundings, summer 74; The structure of comedy, Thought, 3/75; Dostoevsky and the Ridiculous, Dostoevsky Studies, 80; Time and timelessness in Dostoevsky's fiction, Forum Int, fall 80; Stavrogin and Prince Hal, Canadian Slavonic Papers, 84; Kirillov, Stavrogin, and Suicide, Dostoevsky and the Human Condition after a Century, Greenwood Press, 86; Shakespeare's Comic Changes: The Time-Lapse Metaphor as Plot Device, Univ Georgia Press, 91. **CONTACT ADDRESS** 404 Vassar Dr, Newark, DE 19711. **EMAIL** ROGERLC@EROLS.COM

COZEA, ANGELA
DISCIPLINE FRENCH LITERATURE **EDUCATION** Univ Calgary, BA; Univ Montreal, MA; PhD. **RESEARCH** Modern presentations of the concepts of perspective and style in the literary, visual, clinical discourses; figures of encounter between the ethical and the aesthetic in German and French philosophy; limits of experience-conceptualising history, practising rememoration after Shoah. **SELECTED PUBLICATIONS** Auth, La fidelite aux choses: pour une perspective benjaminienne, 96. **CONTACT ADDRESS** Dept of French, Univ of Western Ontario, London, ON, Canada N6A 5B8. **EMAIL** acozea@julian.uwo.ca

CRACOLICI, STEFANO
PERSONAL Born 05/16/1965, Padova, Italy **DISCIPLINE** FRENCH, ITALIAN **EDUCATION** Albert-Ludwig Univ Freiburg, MD, 94; Univ delgi Studi di Trento, Laurea, 95; Univ of Toronto, MA, 96; PhD, 00. **CAREER** Asst prof, Dartmouth Col, 00-. **MEMBERSHIPS** AAIS, MLA, SILBA, Renaissance Soc of Am. **RESEARCH** Renaissance Studies, Literature and Medicine, Visual Studies (Leon Battista Alberti), Italian and French Petrarchism. **CONTACT ADDRESS** Dept Fr and Ital, Dartmouth Col, Hinman Box 6087, Hanover, NH 03755. **EMAIL** stefano.cracolici@dartmouth.edu

CRAIG, CHARLOTTE MARIE
PERSONAL Born 01/14/1929, Ostrava, Czechoslovakia, m, 1954 **DISCIPLINE** GERMAN LANGUAGE AND LITERATURE **EDUCATION** Univ Puget Sound, BA & teaching cert, 57; Univ Ariz, MA, 60; Rutgers Univ, PhD(Ger), 64. **CAREER** Teacher English & hist, Alaska Pub Schs, 57-59; asst prof Ger, Univ Kans, 64-68; lectr, George Washington Univ, 68-69; prof & chairperson Ger & comp lit, Schiller Col, Heidelberg, Ger, 69-73; Prof Ger, Kutztown State Col, 74-, Watkins fac fel Ger lit, Univ Kans, 65. **MEMBERSHIPS** MLA; Asn Teachers Ger; Am Soc 18th Century Studies; Northeastern Am Soc 18th Century Studies. **RESEARCH** Eighteenth century German literature; 18th century comparative literature. **SELECTED PUBLICATIONS** Auth, Christoph Martin Wieland as the Originator of the Modern Travesty in German Literature, Chapel Hill: UNC Press, 70; ed, contrib. auth, Lichtenberg. Essays Commemorating the 250th Anniversary of his Birth, New York: Peter Lang, 92; ed, "A Rigid Issue: Litchenberg versus Lavater," Anthropology and the German Enlightenment: Perspectives on Humanity; Bucknell Review. Ed. Katherine M. Faull, Lewisburg: Bucknell UP, 95; ed, "August Wilhelm Schlegel 1767-1845," Encyclopedia of German Literature, Vol 2, Chicago, London: Fitzroy Dearborn, 00. **CONTACT ADDRESS** Kutztown Univ of Pennsylvania, Kutztown, PA 19530. **EMAIL** craigrbcm@aol.com

CRAIG, CHRISTOPHER P.
DISCIPLINE CLASSICAL STUDIES **EDUCATION** Oberlin Col, AB, 74; Univ NC, PhD, 79. **CAREER** Instr, Stockley Inst, 83-84; Tchg fel, Univ NC, 78-79; instr, Univ Ca, 79-80; asst prof, 80-86, assoc prof, Univ Tenn, 86-. **HONORS AND AWARDS** Dir, Vergilian Soc Am, 85-93. **MEMBERSHIPS** Am Philol Asn; Archaeol Inst Am; Class Asn Middle W and S; Am Class League; Vergilian Soc Am; Tennessee Lang Tchr Asn; Tennessee Class Asn; Int Soc Hist Rhet; Am Soc Hist Rhet; Speech Commun Asn. **RESEARCH** Classical rhetoric and oratory; Cicero. **SELECTED PUBLICATIONS** Auth, "Cicero's Strategy of Embarrassment in the Speech for Plancius," Am Jour Philol, 90; auth, Form as Argument in Cicero's Speeches, Scholars, 93; auth, "Three Simple Questions for Teaching Cicero's First Catilinarian Oration," Class Jour, 93; auth, "Teaching Cicero's Speech for Caelius: What Enquiring Minds Want to Know," Class Jour, 95. **CONTACT ADDRESS** Dept of Classics, Univ of Tennessee, Knoxville, Knoxville, TN 37996-0413. **EMAIL** ccraig@utk.edu

CRAIG, HERBERT EUGENE
PERSONAL Born 12/13/1946, Chardon, OH, m, 1995 **DISCIPLINE** LITERATURE, SPANISH **EDUCATION** Ohio State Univ, BA, 69; Univ Wis Madison, MA, 72; PhD, 83; Univ Ill, MA, 85. **CAREER** Asst prof, Bethany Col, 79-89; asst prof to assoc prof, Univ Nebr Kearney, 89-. **HONORS AND AWARDS** Phi Beta Kappa; Fulbright/Hays Fel, 76-77; NEH, 85; Res Grant, Univ Nebr, 97; Sab, Bethany Col, 85-86; Univ Nebr, 97-98. **MEMBERSHIPS** AATSP; MLA. **RESEARCH** Literary relation between Marcel Proust and Spanish America; Hispanic film; translation studies. **SELECTED PUBLICATIONS** Auth, "Proust y Mujica Lainez: La Memoria Asociativa," Cuadernos Hisp (84); auth, "Ideas de Ortega y Gasset Sobre la Novella Proustiana," Bulletin Hisp 88 (86); auth, "La Memoria Proustiana en Rayuela," Nueva Rev de Filol Hisp 37 (89); auth, "Proustian Time in Elamor en los Tiempos del Colera," Confluen 5 (90); auth, "Proustian in Spanish: The Old and New translations of Du Cote de Chez Swann," Platt Val Rev 23 (95); auth, "Proust en Espana y en Hispano-Americana: La Recepcion 1920-1929," Bulletin Hisp 101 (99). **CONTACT ADDRESS** 2111 9th Ave, Kearney, NE 68845-5016. **EMAIL** craigh@unk.edu

CRAIG, VIRGINIA ROBERTSON
PERSONAL Born 10/16/1935, Ft Worth, TX, m, 1954, 1 child **DISCIPLINE** SPANISH LANGUAGE; LITERATURE **EDUCATION** Bethel Col, Tenn, BA, 56; Univ Mo-Columbia, PhD, 68. **CAREER** Chairperson dept mod foreign lang, 76-80; asst prof Span, Ind Univ, Ft Wayne, 69-; Ind Univ grant-in-aid, 70-71; dir, Ind Univ Overseas Study Prog, Madrid, 77-78. **HON-**

ORS AND AWARDS Distinguished Tchg Awd, Ind Univ, 75. **MEMBERSHIPS** MLA; Am Asn Tchrs Span & Port; Comediantes. **RESEARCH** Seventeenth century Spanish drama; Spanish civilization and culture. **SELECTED PUBLICATIONS** Contribur, Manual of Hispanic Bibliography, Univ Wash, 70; Annotated Analytical Bibliography of Tirso de Molina Studies, 1627-1977, Univ Mo, 79. **CONTACT ADDRESS** Dept of Mod Foreign Langs, Indiana Univ-Purdue Univ, Fort Wayne, 2101 Coliseum Blvd E, Fort Wayne, IN 46805-1445. **EMAIL** craig@IPFW.edu

CRAMER, OWEN C.
PERSONAL Born 12/01/1941, Tampa, FL, m, 1962, 4 children **DISCIPLINE** CLASSICS **EDUCATION** Oberlin Col, AB, 62; Univ Tex, PhD, 73. **CAREER** Instr to prof, Colo Col, 65-; vis prof, Univ Chicago, 87-88. **HONORS AND AWARDS** Woodrow Wilson Fel, 62. **MEMBERSHIPS** Am Philol Asn; Class Asn of the Middle W and S; Am Comparative Lit Asn; Mod Greek Studies Asn. **RESEARCH** Home; Greek historiography. **SELECTED PUBLICATIONS** Auth, "Speech and Silence in the Iliad," Class j, (76): 300-304; auth, "Ulysses the Good? What is the Formula at Od," Transactions of the Am Philol Asn, (74): 77-80. **CONTACT ADDRESS** Dept Class, Colo Col, 14 E Cache la Poudre St, Colorado Springs, CO 80903. **EMAIL** ocramer@coloradocollege.edu

CRANNELL, KENNETH C.
PERSONAL Born 04/05/1934, Lynn, MS, m, 1960, 2 children **DISCIPLINE** ORAL INTERPRETATION **EDUCATION** Emerson Col, BA, 55, MA, 57; Northwestern Univ, PhD, 70. **CAREER** From instr to assoc prof, 57-69, Prof Speech & Comm Studies & Chmn Div Oral Interpretation, Emerson Col, 69-, Asst, Northwestern Univ, 61-62, instr interpretation, 64-65; speech consult, St John's Sem, 67-68; vis instr homiletics, Pope John XXIII Sem, 70-78; consult, Harvard Divinity Sch, 73; Consul, Crannell Consulting. **MEMBERSHIPS** Speech Commun Asn; Eastern States Commun Asn; New Eng Speech Asn; Eastern Commun Asn. **RESEARCH** Prosody; oral performance; modern poetry. **SELECTED PUBLICATIONS** Coauth, Oral interpretation: graduate programs, Speech Teacher, 72; contribr, Oral interpretation bibliography, NC Speech J, 73; auth, A prosodic analysis of The Hill Wife, Rodophi, Studies Interpretation, Vol II; auth, Voice and Articulation, 4th ed, Wadsworth. **CONTACT ADDRESS** Div of Oral Interpretation, Emerson Col, 100 Beacon St, Boston, MA 02116-1596. **EMAIL** kcrhapsode@aol.com

CRANSTON, EDWIN AUGUSTUS
PERSONAL Born 10/18/1932, Pittsfield, MA, m, 1960 **DISCIPLINE** JAPANESE LITERATURE **EDUCATION** Univ Ariz, BA, 54; Stanford Univ, MA, 63, PhD(Japanese lit), 66. **CAREER** Instr Japanese, 65-66, from asst prof to assoc prof, 66-72, prof Japanese Lit, Harvard Univ, 72-, Fulbright-Hays res grant, 69-70. **HONORS AND AWARDS** MA, Harvard Univ, 72. **MEMBERSHIPS** Am Asn Asian Studies; Asn Teachers Japanese. **RESEARCH** Heian literature; Man'yoshu; poetry of Izumi Shikibu. **SELECTED PUBLICATIONS** Auth, The Izumi Shikibu Diary: A Romance of the Heian Court, Harvard Univ, 69; The poetry of Izumi Shikibu, Monumenta Nipponica, 70; Water-plant imagery in the Man'yoshu, Harvard J Asiatic Studies, 71; Murasaki's Art of fiction, Japan Quart, 4-6/71; coauth, Nihon Koten Bungei: The Courtly Tradition in Japanese Art and Literature, Kodansha Int, Tokyo, 73; auth, Young Akiko: The Literary Debut of Yosano Akiko (1878-1942), Lit East & West, 74; The Dark Path: Images of Longing in Japanese Love Poetry, Harvard J Asiatic Studies, 75; contribr, Toward a Reconsideration of Makurakotoba: An Analysis of Preposited Figurative Elements in a Choka by Hitomaro, In: Man'yoshu Kenkyu, Hanawa Shobo, Vol V, 76; A Waka Anthology, Vol I: The Gem-Glistening Cup, Stanford Univ, 93. **CONTACT ADDRESS** Dept of E Asian Lang & Civilizations, Harvard Univ, 2 Divinity Ave., Cambridge, MA 02138-2020.

CRANSTON, MECHTHILD
PERSONAL Born 10/12/1938, Berlin, GER, m, 1962, 0 child **DISCIPLINE** FRENCH **EDUCATION** Univ Calif-Berkeley, BA, 58; PhD, 66. **CAREER** Instr, Univ Calif-Berkeley, 95-96; asst prof, Univ San Fran, 66-68; asst prof, CSU-Hayward, 68-89; vis prof, Philipps Univ, Marburg, 70; assoc prof, Univ N Car, 71-77; instr to prof, Clemson Univ, 80- . **HONORS AND AWARDS** Provost Awd Sch Ach, 95, Clemson Univ; Bd Trustees Awd Fac Exc, 97 & 99, Clemson Univ; Bradbury Awd Outstanding Contribur Hon Col, 99, Clemson Univ; Phi Beta Kappa; Palma Accad, Fr Min Educ. **MEMBERSHIPS** Mod Lang Asn; S Atlantic Mod Lang Asn; Am Asn Teachers Fr; Am Lit Schol Asn; Women's Fr; S Comp Lit Asn. **RESEARCH** Modern poetry, in particular, Apollinaire, Saint-John Perse, and Rene Char, The writings of Marguerite Duras. **SELECTED PUBLICATIONS** Auth, In Language and in Love: The Unspeakable. Essays for Marguerite Duras, Scripta Hum, 92; auth, Beyond the Book. Marguerite Duras: Infans, Scripta Hum, 96; auth, "Rehearsals in Bas Relief: Le Marin de Gibraltar of Marguerite Duras," Stud in Twentieth Cent Lit, vol 17:2 (93): 287-307; auth, "From Blick to Augenblick: Rilke's Panther on the Move," Neophilologus 78 (94): 283-288; auth, "Dancing at Mecca: Circling The Square of Marguerite Duras." Dalhousie French Stud 34 (96): 103-118; auth, "Words, Images, Crossings: La mer ecrite of Marguerite Duras," Puni Jahaj Pe Aawe, Hardvar, (90). **CONTACT ADDRESS** Dept Mod Lang, Clemson Univ, 113 Houston St, Clemson, SC 29631-1311. **EMAIL** cransto@clemson.edu

CRAWFORD, RONALD LEE
PERSONAL Born 03/28/1939, Warren, OH, m, 1973, 2 children **DISCIPLINE** GERMAN LITERATURE **EDUCATION** Heidelberg Col, BS, 61; Kent State Univ, MA, 67; Rutgers Univ, PhD(Ger), 74. **CAREER** Temp instr, Hiram Col, 61-63; from instr to asst prof, 66-77, Assoc Prof Ger, Kent State Univ, 77-, Nat Endowment for Humanities, summer, 80. **MEMBERSHIPS** Am Asn Teachers Ger. **RESEARCH** Classical German literature; Schiller. **SELECTED PUBLICATIONS** Auth, The Complete Correspondence of Clara and Robert Schumann, trans by H. Fritsch and R. Crawford, Vol I 94; Vol II 96. **CONTACT ADDRESS** 1615 Bobwhite Trail, Stow, OH 44224.

CRAWFORD, SIDNIE WHITE
PERSONAL Born 01/08/1960, Greenwich, CT, m, 1994 **DISCIPLINE** NEAR EASTERN LANGUAGES AND CIVILIZATIONS **EDUCATION** Trinity Col, BA, 81; Harvard Divinity Sch, MTS, 84; Harvard Univ, PhD, 88. **CAREER** Instr, Harvard Div Sch, 87-88; asst prof, St Olaf Col, 88-89; asst prof, 89-96, ch of fac, 95-96, assoc prof, Relisios Studies, Albright Col, 96 -; assoc prof & ch, Classics, Unic Neb-Lincoln, 96- . **HONORS AND AWARDS** Abraham Joshua Heschel Prize, 81; Cert of Distinct in Tchg, Harvard Univ, 87; Jacob Albright Awd, Fac Mem of the Yr, 91; United Methdist Church Awd, Albright Col, 95. **MEMBERSHIPS** Am Acad Rel; Am Schs of Oriental Res; Int Org for the Study of Qumran; Soc of Bib Lit. **RESEARCH** Second Temple Judaism, Dead Sea Scrolls, Hebrew Bible Textual Criticism. **SELECTED PUBLICATIONS** Co-auth, 4Qdeuteronomy a, c, d, f, g, I, n, o, p, Discoveries in the Judaean Desert XIV, Oxford Univ, 95; coauth, 4Qreworked Pentateuch: 4Q364-367, Discoveries in the Judaean Desert XIII, Oxford Univ, 94; auth, A Response to Elizabeth Owen's "4Qdeut": A Pre-Samaritan Manuscript, Dead Sea Discoveries 5, 98; Has Esther been Found at Quamran?, 4Qproto-Esther and the Esther Corpus, Revue ke Qumran 17, 96; Amram, Testament of, "Angelic Liturgy" and eighteen other entries in Dictionary of Biblical Judaism, NY, Macmillan, 95. **CONTACT ADDRESS** Dept of Classics, Univ of Nebraska, Lincoln, 236 Andrews Hall, Lincoln, NE 68588-0337. **EMAIL** scrawfor@unl.edu

CREEL, BRYANT L.
PERSONAL Born 04/24/1944, Berkeley, CA, M, 1989, 1 child **DISCIPLINE** SPANISH LITERATURE **EDUCATION** Stanford Univ, BA, 95; Univ Ca, PhD, 78. **CAREER** Prof, Univ Tenn. **HONORS AND AWARDS** NEH Summer Grant, 80; Gubbenhian Foundation Fellowship, 77-78, 85. **MEMBERSHIPS** MLA; ATTSP; Assoc Internacional de Hisperistas, Asociacion Intl Siglo de Oro. **RESEARCH** 16th and 17th Century Spanish, Portugese, Poetry and Prose, Cervanllo. **SELECTED PUBLICATIONS** Auth, pubs on sixteenth and seventeenth century Peninsular prose and poetry, and contemporary Portuguese. **CONTACT ADDRESS** Dept of Mod For Langs & Lits, Univ of Tennessee, Knoxville, 701 McClung Tower & Plaza, Knoxville, TN 37996. **EMAIL** bcreel@utk.edu

CRIBIORE, RAFFAELA
PERSONAL Born 03/27/1948, Varese, Italy, m, 1970, 2 children **DISCIPLINE** CLASSICS **EDUCATION** Universita Cattolica Milan, BA, 72; M Philos, 90; Columbia Univ, PhD, 93. **CAREER** Lectr, High School A Mosso Italy, 72-76; Scuola D'Italia NY, 79-85; tchg asst, Columbia Univ, 86-89; preceptor, 90; instr, 96, 97; res assoc, Columbia Univ, 96-; assoc curator of Papyri Rare Book and Manuscripts Library, 94-. **HONORS AND AWARDS** President's Fel, 86-89; Polychronis Fel, 89-90, Bd Dir of the Am Soc of Papyrologists, 95-98; Vis Comm to the Grad Fac of Political and Soc Sci, New School for Soc Res, 94-96. **RESEARCH** Greek and Latin Education; Greek Literature; Papyrology. **SELECTED PUBLICATIONS** Writing, Teachers, and Students in Graeco-Roman Egypt, 96. **CONTACT ADDRESS** 17 Sutton Pl, New York, NY 10022. **EMAIL** rc141@columbia.edu

CRICHFIELD, GRANT
PERSONAL Born 02/28/1941, Orange, NJ, s, 2 children **DISCIPLINE** FRENCH LANGUAGE, LITERATURE **EDUCATION** Univ Mass Amherst, BA, 62; Univ Wis Madison, MA, 66; PhD, 72. **CAREER** Lectr as Fulbright Teaching Fel, Universite de Dijon Fr, 63-64; Teaching Asst, Univ of Wis Madison, 64-67; Proj Asst, Univ of Wis Madison, 67-68; From Instr to Assoc Prof, Univ of Wis Madison, 72-; Dir, Vt Overseas Study Prog, Nice, Fr, 70-71; co-dir, Vt Overseas Study Prog, Burlington, 69-70, 71-73; 87-88. **HONORS AND AWARDS** Fulbright Teaching Fel, Universite de Dijon, Fr, 63-64; Outstanding Teacher Asst Awd, Univ of Wis-Madison, 67; Int Travel Grants, Univ of Wis-Madison, 69; Res Fel, Univ of Vt, 91, 74; Institutional Grant, Univ of Vt, 74; Instructional Incentive Grant, Univ of Vt, 83; Int Travel Grants, Univ of Vt, 92; Int Travel Grants, Am Coun of Learned Soc, 94; Grant for Participation in Int Conf on Slavery in the Francophone World, Univ of Ga, 97; Sabbatical Leaves, 77, 90, 97. **MEMBERSHIPS** Fulbright Asn, MLA, Am Asn of Teachers of Fr, La Societe des Etudes romantiques et dix-neuviemistes, Nineteenth Century Fr Scholars Asn, Int Asn fo Word and Image Studies, Vt For Lang Asn, Alliance Fr of Vt-Cercle Quebecois. **RESEARCH** 19th century French literature, especially narratives of travel to the "orient", relationships between text and image, the representation of history, Charles Nodier, Alphonse de Lamartine, Theophile Gautier. **SELECTED PUBLICATIONS** Auth, Three Novels of Madam de Duras: "Ourika," "Edouard," "Olivier," Mouton (The Hague), 75; auth, "Nodier's Numbers: Multiplicity, Accelaeration, Unity in La Fee aux Miettes," Nineteenth Century Fr Studies 17-1/2 (Fall/Winter 88-89); auth, "La Constantinople de Gauiter: Un Miroir en Orient," Etudes francaise 26-1 (Printemps 90), special issue: "La Tentation de l'Orient;" auth, "Fantasmagoria and Optics in Theophile Gautier's 'Arria Marcella'," in Shape of the Fantastic, ed. Olena H. Saciuk (NY: Greenwood Press, 90); auth, "Gautier's Orient: Mask, Mirage and 'decor d'opera' in Constantinople'," Romance Notes 32-3 (Spring 92); auth, "Charles Nodier," in Dictionary of Literary Biography 119: Nineteenth Century French Fiction Writers: Romanticism and Realism, 1800-1860," ed. Catharine Savage Brosman (Detroit: Gale Res, 92); auth,"Decamps, Orientalist Intertext, and Counter-Discourse in Gautier's Constantinople," Nineteenth Century Fr Studies 21-3/4 (Spring-Summer 93); auth, "Geography, Wonder, and Politics in Lamartine's 'Voyage en Orient'," in Romantic Geographies, ed. Colin Smethurst (Glasgow: Univ of Glasgow Fr and Ger Publication, 96); auth, "Terrors Between Old Friends: Nodier's 'Souvenirs et portraits' and Dumas Pere's 'Les Blancs et les Bleus'," Lit and Hist third series 7-1 (Spring 98). **CONTACT ADDRESS** Dept Romance Lang, Univ of Vermont, Waterman Bldg, Burlington, VT 05405-0160.

CRISPIN, JOHN
PERSONAL Born 05/03/1936, Tienen, Belgium, m, 1966, 1 child **DISCIPLINE** SPANISH LANGUAGE AND CONTEMPORARY LITERATURE **EDUCATION** Univ St Thomas, Tex, BA, 60; Univ Wis-Madison, MA, 62, PhD(Span & French), 67. **CAREER** Prof Exp: From instr to asst prof, 65-71, Assoc Prof Span, Vanderbilt Univ, 71-, Chmn Span-Portt, 79-. **MEMBERSHIPS** MLA; Am Asn Teachers Span & Port. **RESEARCH** Contemporary poetry and novel; intellectual history; comparative literature. **SELECTED PUBLICATIONS CONTACT ADDRESS** Dept of Span & Port, Vanderbilt Univ, Box 1518-B, Nashville, TN 37203.

CRIST, LARRY S.
PERSONAL Born 01/16/1934, Harrisburg, PA, m, 1961, 3 children **DISCIPLINE** FRENCH **EDUCATION** Western Md Col, BA, 55; Princeton Univ, MA, 59, PhD(French), 63. **CAREER** Lectr French, Queens Col, NY, 61-63; from asst prof to assoc prof, 63-75, Prof French, Vanderbilt Univ, 75-, Chmn Dept French & Ital, 80- **MEMBERSHIPS** Am Asn Teachers Fr; Mediaeval Acad Am; MLA; AAUP; Soc Rencesvals. **RESEARCH** Medieval French cycle of the Crusade; semiotics of medieval French literature. **SELECTED PUBLICATIONS CONTACT ADDRESS** 6609 Rolling Fork Dr., Nashville, TN 37205.

CRO, STELIO
PERSONAL Born 04/07/1936, Rome, Italy, m, 1973 **DISCIPLINE** ITALIAN, SPANISH **EDUCATION** Univ Buenos Aires, Lic en Let, 63, Univ Venice, DLing e Lett Straniere(-Span), 66. **CAREER** Assoc prof Ital, Univ Buenos Aires, 67-69; asst prof Ital & Span, Fla State Univ, 69-72; from asst prof to assoc prof, 72-78, Head Dept, McMaster Univ, 76-00, Prof Ital, 78-. **MEMBERSHIPS** MLA, Am Asn Teachers Span & Port, Am Asn Teachers Ital. **RESEARCH** Italian 19th century literature, Spanish 19th and 20th century literature, Cervantes. **SELECTED PUBLICATIONS** Auth, Realidad Y Utopia En El Descubrimiento Y Conquista De LA America Hispana 1492-1682; auth, The Noble Savage: Allegory of Feedom, 90. **CONTACT ADDRESS** Dept of Modern Lang, McMaster Univ, Togo Salmon Hall 611, Hamilton, ON, Canada L8S 4M2. **EMAIL** crostel@mcmaster.ca

CROFT, LEE B.
PERSONAL Born 09/19/1946, Cut Bank, MT, m, 1981, 4 children **DISCIPLINE** RUSSIAN **EDUCATION** Ariz State Univ, BS, 68; Univ Ariz, MA, 70; Cornell Univ, PhD, 73. **CAREER** From asst prof to assoc prof to prof, 73-, Ariz State Univ. **HONORS AND AWARDS** Dean's Distinguised Tchg Awd, 78, ASU CLAS; Distinguised Fac Achievement Awd, 85, Bulington Northern Found; Joe Malik Jr Ariz Slavic Stud Awd, 93; Alpha Mu Gamma Honorary Stud Mentorship Awd, 95; dept coordr, 75-, dir of critical lang inst, 91-98, ariz state univ. **MEMBERSHIPS** AATSEEL; AAASS; RMMLA; ACTR. **RESEARCH** Linguistic iconicity; poetry translation; mnemonotactics. **SELECTED PUBLICATIONS** Auth, art, Triplicity and Textual Iconicity: Russian Literature Through a Triangular Prism, 95. **CONTACT ADDRESS** Arizona State Univ, DLL-0202, Tempe, AZ 85287-0201. **EMAIL** lee.croft@asu.edu

CRONE, ANNA LISA
PERSONAL Born 06/09/1946, Brooklyn, NY, 1 child **DISCIPLINE** RUSSIAN LITERATURE, LITERARY THEORY **EDUCATION** Educ: Goucher Col, BA, 67; Harvard Univ, MA, 69, PhD, 75. **CAREER** Instr, Goucher Col & Johns Hopkins Univ, 71-74; Prof Russ, Univ Chicago, 77-, Senator, 91-94,

Founder, Slavic Forum; Fel, Radcliffe Inst Independent Study, 76-77; mem ed bd, Russ Lang J. **HONORS AND AWARDS** Quantrell Awd for Excellence in Teaching, 85; Honorary Docorate, Goucher Col, 88; Honorary Sr Res Fel, Inst Slavonic and Eastern Europ Studies, Univ London, 98-99. **MEMBERSHIPS** Am Asn Teachers Slavic & Eastern Europ Lang; MLA; Phi Beta Kappa. **RESEARCH** Late nineteenth and early twentieth-century Russian; literature and religious thought; Russian poetry and poetics. **SELECTED PUBLICATIONS** Auth, The disintegration of the mystical body: The church in Balzac and Rozanov, Die Welt der Slawen, 78; Unnamuno and Dostoevskij: Some thoughts on atheistic humanitarianism, Hispanofila, 78; Blok as Don Juan in Axmatora's Poems bez geoja & Gnosticism in Bely's Fotile Letaer, 82, Russ Lang J; Axmatora's Imitation of Annenskij, Wiener Slawistiches Jahrbueh, 81; Difference in Saussure and Derrida, Neophilologus, 78; Rozanov and the End of Literature, JAL Verlag, 78; Pasternak's Pushkinien Variations, Die Weit der Slawen, 79; The Presence of Mandelstham in the Dedication to Poema bez geroja, Russ Lit, 82; co-ed, New Studies in Russian Language & Literature, Slavic Press, 86; author of numerous articles on Russian literature of Silver Age and other topics; auth, The Daring of Derzhavin, IN Press, 00 **CONTACT ADDRESS** Dept of Slavic Lang, Univ of Chicago, 1130 E 59th St, Chicago, IL 60637-1539. **EMAIL** acrone@midway.uchicago.edu

CROSBY, DONALD H.

PERSONAL Born 04/03/1927, New York, NY, m, 1973, 4 children **DISCIPLINE** GERMANIC STUDIES **EDUCATION** NYork Univ, AB, 51; Princeton Univ, AM, 53, PhD, 55. **CAREER** Instr Ger, Princeton Univ, 54-55; asst prof, Union Col, NY, 55-56; from instr to asst prof, Ind Univ, Bloomington, 58-63; vis assoc prof Ger lang, Queens Col, NY, 64-65; from assoc prof to prof, Univ Kans, 65-70; Prof Ger Lang, Univ Conn, 70-, Consult, US Dept Defense, 56-61; Am Coun Learned Soc studies fel, 63-64; vis prof, Dartmouth Col, 70; Fulbright fel, Univ Munich, 78. **MEMBERSHIPS** Am Asn Teachers Ger; Heinrich von Kleist Ges. **RESEARCH** Literature of the Goethezeit; Heinrich von Kleist; musical-literary relations. **SELECTED PUBLICATIONS** Auth, Kleist on Stage, 1804-1987, Jour Eng and Ger Philol, Vol 0094, 95. **CONTACT ADDRESS** Dept of Ger Lang, Univ of Connecticut, Storrs, Storrs, CT 06268.

CROSSGROVE, WILLIAM C.

PERSONAL Born 06/06/1965, Archbold, OH, m, 1965, 2 children **DISCIPLINE** GERMAN **EDUCATION** Ohio Univ, AB, 59; Univ of Texas at Austin, PhD, 62. **CAREER** From Instr to Assoc Prof, Brown Univ, 62-64; Asst Prof of German, Brown Univ, 64-69; Research Assoc in Linguistics, Univof Kiel, 65-66; Visiting Prof of German, Columbia Univ, 70; Prof of German 78-92; Prof of German and Comparative Literature, Brown Univ, 92-; Assoc Dean of the Faculty, Brown Univ, 99-. **HONORS AND AWARDS** Phi Beta Kappa, Ohio Univ, 59, NDEA Title IV Graduate Fellowship, 59-62, Research Fellowship, Alexander von Humboldt-Stiftung (Germay) 70-71, renewed in 80 and 98. **MEMBERSHIPS** Medieval Academy of America, American Assoc of Teachers of German, Gesellschaft fur Wissenchaftsgeschichte, American Assoc of Higher Educ. **RESEARCH** Medieval German scientific and technical literature, especially herbals. **SELECTED PUBLICATIONS** Auth, Deprivation, Basil Blackwell (Cambridge, MA and Oxford), 90; auth, Graded German Reader: Erste Stufe, with Hannelore Crossgrove, D.C. Heath and Company (Lexington, MA), 92; auth, Die deutsche Sachliteratur des Mittelalters, Germanistische Lehrbuchsammlung 63, berne et al: Peter Lang Verlag, 94; auth, "Das landwirtschaftliche Handbuch von Petrus de Crescentiis in der deutschen Fassung des Bruder Franciscus," Sudhoffs Archiv 78 (94): 97-106; auth, "Medicine in the Twelve Books on Rural Practices of Petrus de Cresentiis, "In: Margaret Schleissner (ed.), Manuscript Sources of Medieval Medicine: A Book of Essays Garland Medieval Casebooks, (New York: Garland, 95), 81-103; auth, "Medical parody and medical practice in medieval German, "Wurzburger medizinhistoriche Mitteilungen, 14 (96): 269-277; auth, "The Vernacularization of Science, Medicine, and Technology in Late Medieval Europe: Broadening our Perspective," Early Science and Medicine 4 (00). **CONTACT ADDRESS** Dept German, Brown Univ, Box 1857, Providence, RI 02912-1857. **EMAIL** william_crossgrove@brown.edu

CROWDER, DIANE GRIFFIN

PERSONAL Born Denison, TX **DISCIPLINE** FRENCH, WOMEN'S STUDIES **EDUCATION** TX Christian Univ, BSEd, 70; Univ Wis, MA, 72; PhD, 77. **CAREER** Asst Prof to Full Prof, Cornell Col, 77-. **HONORS AND AWARDS** Richard & Norma Small Chair for Distinguished Senior Fac, Cornell Col, 00; McConnell Grant, 99; Mellon Grant, 98; Awd for Outstanding Achievement in the Advancement of Women in Higher Education, IA, 97. **MEMBERSHIPS** Mod Lang Asn, Nat Women's Studies Asn. **RESEARCH** Feminist theory, Queer theory, Contemprary French novel. **SELECTED PUBLICATIONS** Auth, "Lesbians and the (Re/De)Construction of the Female Body", in Queer Looks (NY: Haworth); auth, "Amazons", The Gay and Lesbian Literary Heritage (95); transl Colette Guillaumin, "The Constructed Body", Reading the Social Body, (Univ of IA Press, l993); auth, "Separatism and Feminist Utopian Fiction", Sexual Practice/Textual Theory: Lesbian Cultural Criticism (93): 237-250. **CONTACT ADDRESS** Dept Modern & Classical Lang, Cornell Col, 600 1st St W, Mount Vernon, IA 52314. **EMAIL** dcrowder@cornell-iowa.edu

CROWE, P. S.

PERSONAL Born 05/16/1953, Fraserburgh, Scotland, s **DISCIPLINE** ARMENIAN LANGUAGE AND LITERATURE **EDUCATION** Univ Aberdeen, MA; Univ Oxford, BA, 78; Hebrew Univ Jerusalem, PhD, 78. **CAREER** From asst prof to assoc prof, Columbia Univ, 84-96; vis assoc prof, Univ Calif at Los Angeles, 96-. **HONORS AND AWARDS** Fel of Alexander von Humboldt-Stiftung; Byzantine Fel, Dumbarton Oaks; Awd, Netherlands Inst for Advanced Study in the Humanities and Soc Sci; IREX Fel. **MEMBERSHIPS** Asn des Etudes Armeniennes, Middle E Studies Asn, Soc for Armenian Studies, Soc for the Study of Caucasia, Asn for the Study of Nationalities. **RESEARCH** Armenian Nationalism, Lyric Tradition and Drama. **SELECTED PUBLICATIONS** Auth, Commentary on the Divine Liturgy by Xosrov Anjewacci, St Vartan's Press (New York), 91; auth, The Armenian Version of Daniel, Scholars Press (Atlanta, GA), 92; auth, Mkhitar Sasneci's Theological Discourses, Peeters, 93; auth, The Armenian Manuscripts in the Cambridge University Library, Peeters, 94. **CONTACT ADDRESS** Dept Near Eastern Lang & Cultures, Univ of California, Los Angeles, 295 Kinsey Hall, PO Box 151105, Los Angeles, CA 90095-1511.

CROWHURST, MEGAN J.

DISCIPLINE LINGUISTICS **EDUCATION** Univ BC, BA, 85; Univ Ariz, MA, 89, PhD, 91. **CAREER** Assoc, 91-93, lectr, 92-93, Univ Tex, Austin; asst prof, Yale Univ, 93-94; ASST PROF, LINGUISTICS, UNIV NC, CHAPEL HILL, 94-. **CONTACT ADDRESS** Dept of Linguistics, Univ of No Carolina, Chapel Hill, CB 3155, Chapel Hill, NC 27599-3155.

CROWNER, DAVID L.

DISCIPLINE GERMAN LANGUAGE **EDUCATION** Pacific Lutheran Univ, BA, 61; Rutgers Univ, PhD, 67. **CAREER** Instr, Hartwick Col, 64-67; Asst Prof to Prof of German, 67-, Gettysburg Col. **CONTACT ADDRESS** Gettysburg Col, Box 398, Gettysburg, PA 17325. **EMAIL** crowner@gettysburg.edu

CSAKI, LUCIANA CUPPO

PERSONAL Born 05/30/1941, Trieste, Italy **DISCIPLINE** CLASSICAL LANGUAGES **EDUCATION** Univ of Heidelberg, BA, Univ of Kansas, MA, 70; Fordham Univ, MA, 85, PhD, 95. **CAREER** Instr, 77-83, Penn Valley Comm Coll; Frances Schwartz Fel, 86-87, Amer Numismatic Society; teach fel, 83-87, Fordham Univ; Lectr, 86-88, Mount St Mary's Coll; inst & dept head Classics, 89-92, Manhattanville Coll, Purchase; teacher of Latin, 91-98, CUNY Graduate School; adj Prof, 95-, SUNY Westchester & Albany. **MEMBERSHIPS** APA **RESEARCH** Late antiquity early medieval history, medieval & classical latin, palaeography manuscript studies. **SELECTED PUBLICATIONS** Auth, The Year 680 as caput saeculi in Cas 641 in Roma magistras Melanges offerts au Pere L E Boyle a l'occasion de son 75e anniversaire, Beatus Cassiodorus, Vivarium Scyllacense, 97; Contra Voluntatem fundatorum, il monasterium Vivariense di Cassiodoro dopo il 575, in Acta of the XIII International Cogress for Christian Archaeology, Rome/Split, 96; La catacomba di S Domittilla come centro di culto e pellegrinaggio nel sesto secolo ed alto Medioevo, in: Akten des XII, Internationalen Kongresses fur Christliche Archaologie, Munster, 95; The Copper Coinage of Theodahad, a Reappraisal, in: Proceedings of the XIth International Numismatic Congress, ed, T Hackens, Louvain-la-Neuve, 93. **CONTACT ADDRESS** 24 Pecoho Rd, Lake Peekskill, NY 10537. **EMAIL** vivario@geocities.com

CUENCA, JOSE RAMON ARALUCE

DISCIPLINE SPANISH LITERATURE **EDUCATION** Fla State Univ, PhD. **CAREER** Assoc prof, Univ Southern Calif. **SELECTED PUBLICATIONS** Auth, El libro de los estados: Don Juan Manuel y la sociedad de su tiempo and Sintaxis de la paremia en el Arcipreste de Talavera. **CONTACT ADDRESS** Dept of Spanish and Portuguese, Univ of So California, University Park Campus, Los Angeles, CA 90089. **EMAIL** araluce@usc.edu

CUEVA, EDMUND

PERSONAL Born 10/26/1964, Esmeraldas, Ecuador, m, 1987 **DISCIPLINE** CLASSICS **EDUCATION** Univ S Fla, BA, 87; Univ Fla, MA, 89; Loyola Univ, MA 93; PhD, 95. **CAREER** Lecturer, Northwestern Univ, 91-92; Teaching Fel to Lecturer, Univ Chicago, 92-94; Vis Asst Prof, Xavier Univ, 94-96; Lecturer, Univ Cincinnati, Lecturer, 95-96; Asst Prof to Dept Chair, 96-. **HONORS AND AWARDS** Wheeler Grant, Xavier Univ , 99, 98; Publication Grant, Univ S Fla, 99; Nomination NEH Summer Fel, Xavier Univ, 97. **MEMBERSHIPS** Am Classical League, Am Philol Asn, Classical Asn of the Middle West and South, Eta Sigma Phi, Intl Plutarch Soc, Soc of Biblical Literature, Women's Classical Caucus. **SELECTED PUBLICATIONS** Co-ed, Humor in the Ancient World, Special issue of Classical Bulletin, forthcoming; co-auth, Longus: Text, Commentary and vocabulary, forthcoming; co-ed, Veritatis Amicitaeque Causa: Essays in Honor of Anna Lydia Motto and John R Clark, Bolchazy-Carducci Pub, 99; auth, "Art and Myth in Cupid and Psyche," in Veritatis Amicitiaeque Causa: Essays in Honor of Anna Lydia Motto and John R Clark, , Bolchazy-Carducci Pub, forthcoming; auth, "The state of Research on the ancient Novel," Classical Bulletin, (99)l; 47-59; auth, "The analogue of the Hero of Heliodorus' Aethiopica," Sylecta Classica, (98): 103-113; auth, Plutarch's Ariadne I Chariton's Chaereas and Callirhoe," American Journal of Philology, (96): 473-484; auth, "Anth. Pal. 14.34 and Achilles Tatius 2.14," Greek, Roman, and Byzantine Studies, (94): 281-288; auth, "Divine Indigestion: Ghosts, Cannibalism and the Ancient Novel," Classical Bulletin, forthcoming; auth, "Tacitean Necrologies," Journal of Ancient Civilizations, forthcoming. **CONTACT ADDRESS** Dept Classics, Xavier Univ, Ohio, 3800 Victory Pkwy, Cincinnati, OH 45207-1035.

CULBERTSON, DIANA

PERSONAL Born 09/18/1930, Atlanta, GA **DISCIPLINE** COMPARATIVE LITERATURE, RELIGION **EDUCATION** Siena Heights Col, BA, 52: John Carroll Univ, MA, 58; Univ NC, Chapel Hill, PhD(comp lit), 71; Aquinas Inst Theol, Iowa, MA, 80. **CAREER** Lectr world lit, St John Col Cleveland, 63-65; instr English, Univ NC, Chapel Hill, 70-71; asst prof, 71-76, Assoc Prof Comp Lit, Kent State Univ, 76-, Danforth Found fel, 76. **MEMBERSHIPS** MLA; Am Acad Relig; Am Comp Lit Asn; Cath Theol Soc Am. **RESEARCH** Comparative literature; religion; theology. **SELECTED PUBLICATIONS** Auth, Aint-Nobody-Clean, the Liturgy of Violence in Glory--Self-Sacrificing Racial Violence in Zwick, Edward Film, Rel and Lit, Vol 0025, 93; Inscribing the Other, So Hum Rev, Vol 0028, 94; The Jews Body, So Hum Rev, Vol 0028, 94. **CONTACT ADDRESS** Dept of English, Kent State Univ, PO Box 5190, Kent, OH 44242-0001.

CULL, JOHN T.

DISCIPLINE SPANISH **EDUCATION** Parkland Jr Col, Champaign and Univ Ill at Urbana-Champaign, BA, 75; Univ Ill at Urbana-Champaign, MA, 78, PhD, 84. **CAREER** Assoc prof. **RESEARCH** European emblem literature; Grupo de investigacion sobre literatura Emblematica Espanola; a compendium of Illustrated Spanish emblems; Spanish golden age comedia; Spanish golden age prose; medieval Spanish medicine; Spanish sentimental fiction. **SELECTED PUBLICATIONS** Auth, Hablan poco y dicen mucho: The Function of Discovery Scenes in the Drama of Tirso de Molina, Mod Lange Rev 91 3, 96; Purging Humor(s): Medical and Scatalogical Imagery in Tirso de Molina, Bull of the Comediantes 47 2, 95; Emblems in the Secular Drama of Calderon: A Review Article, Romance Quart 41 2, 94. **CONTACT ADDRESS** Dept of Modern Languages and Literatures, Col of the Holy Cross, 1 College St, PO Box 113A, Worcester, MA 01610-2395. **EMAIL** jcull@holycross.edu

CUMMINS, FRED

PERSONAL m, 1 child **DISCIPLINE** LINGUISTICS **EDUCATION** Trinity Col Dublin, BA, 91; Ind Univ, MA, 96, PhD, 97. **CAREER** Postdoctoral res, 97-; tchg, 97-98; led working sessions Rhythm Study Group, Ind Univ, 96; res asst to Dr Robert Port, 92-95; assoc instr, 95; crse instr; assoc instr, 96; invited sem, Dept Colloquium, Northwestern Univ, 97. **HONORS AND AWARDS** Cognitive Sci Dissertation awd, Ind Univ, 98; Mellon postdoctoral fel, Northwestern Univ, 97; Res Incentive Dissertation yr fel awd, Ind Univ, 96; Cognitive Scie Summer res awd, Ind Univ, 96 Best Student Paper in Speech Communication, Acoust Soc Am, St Louis, Mo, 95; Cognitive Sci Summer res awd; Ind Univ, 95; Connectionist Models Summer Sch Fel, Univ Colo, 93; Cognitive Sci Summer Res Awd, Ind Univ, 93; Cognitive Sci Fel, Ind Univ, 91. **MEMBERSHIPS** Acoust Soc Am; Cognitive Sci Soc; Cognitive Sci Soc Ireland; Irish Res Sci Asn. **RESEARCH** Speech; prosdy; timing; motor control; temporal pattern processing; phonetics; cognitive sci. **SELECTED PUBLICATIONS** Rhythmic constraints on English stress timing, Proceedings of the Fourth International Conference on Spoken Language Processing, Alfred duPont Inst, Wilmington, Delaware, 96; Rhythmic Commonalities Between Hand Gestures and Speech, Proceedings of the 18th Annual Conf of the Cognitive Sci Soc, Lawrence Erlbaum Assoc, 96; A Dynamic Approach to Rhythm in Language: Toward a Temporal Phonology, Proceedings of the Chicago Ling Soc, Dept Ling, Univ Chicago, 96; Self-Entrainment in Animal Behavior and Human Speech, Online Proceedings of the 1996 Midwest Artificial Intelligence and Cognitive Sci Conf, 96; Coauth, Rhythmic Coordination in English Speech: An Experimental Study, PhD thesis, Ind Univ, Also Technical Report 198, Ind Univ Cognitive Sci Prog, 97; coauth, "Language identification from prosody without explicit features To appear in Proc. EUROSPEECH, 99; auth, "Some lengthening factors in English speech combine additively at most rates, Journal of the Acoustical Society of America, 105: 476-480; auth, "Synergetic organization in speech rhythm, In Tschacher, W. and Dauwalder, J. -P., Editors, Dynamics, Synergetics, Autonomous Agents, 99: 256-267, World Scientific; coauth, "Speech and rhythmic behavior," In Savelsburgh, G.J.P., van der Maas, H., and van Geert, P. C. L., editors, The Non-linear Analysis of Developmental Processes, Elsevier, Amsterdam. **CONTACT ADDRESS** Dept of Linguistics, Northwestern Univ, 1801 Hinman, Evanston, IL 60208. **EMAIL** fred.cummins@ucd.ie

CUMMINS, W. JOSEPH
DISCIPLINE PHILOSOPHY; CLASSICS **EDUCATION** Xavier Univ, AB, 70; Emory Univ, MA, 71, PhD, 75; Univ Cincinnati, MA, 76, PhD, 89. **CAREER** Asst prof, Old Dominion Univ, 76-80; from asst prof to assoc prof, 84-, Grinnell Col. **RESEARCH** Greek and Roman philosophy; intellectual history **CONTACT ADDRESS** Dept of Philosophy, Grinnell Col, Grinnell, IA 50112. **EMAIL** cummins@grinnell.edu

CUNLIFFE, WILLIAM GORDON
PERSONAL Born 03/25/1929, Southport, England, m, 1957, 2 children **DISCIPLINE** GERMAN **EDUCATION** Univ London, BA, 53; Univ Hamburg, PhD(Ger), 63. **CAREER** Lektor transl & interpretation, Univ Saarlandes, 55-60; lectr Ger, Univ Bradford, 60-62; asst prof, 62-68, Assoc Prof Ger, Univ Wis-Madison, 68- **MEMBERSHIPS** MLA **RESEARCH** Medieval and modern German literature; modern English and American literature. **SELECTED PUBLICATIONS CONTACT ADDRESS** Dept of Ger, Univ of Wisconsin, Madison, Madison, WI 53706.

CUNNINGHAM, WILLIAM
PERSONAL Born 07/15/1939, Cleveland, OH, m, 1963, 2 children **DISCIPLINE** GERMAN **EDUCATION** Oberlin Col, AB, 61; Univ Ill, MA, 64; Univ Tex, PhD, 69. **CAREER** Asst prof, Univ Southern Calif, 68-73; assoc & full prof, Univ of Louisville, 73-. **HONORS AND AWARDS** Dankstipendium, Berlin, 64-65; NDEA Fel, Univ Tex, 65-68. **RESEARCH** German Baroque, J C Gunther, German literature of the Nineteenth-Century, Theodor Storm's fiction, German literature in English translation, Arthur Schnitzler's dramas. **SELECTED PUBLICATIONS** Auth, "Baroque Poetry & American Students," Unterrichtspraxis (73); auth, G C Gunther's 'Trostaria'," Monatshefte (76); auth, "Zur Wassersymbolik in 'Aquis submersus'," Schriften der Theodor-Storm-Gesellschaft (79); auth, "Zur Wassersymbolik in T Storm's 'Schimmelreiter'," Germanic Notes and Rev (81); auth, German Literature in English," Germanic Notes (99). **CONTACT ADDRESS** Dept Lang, Univ of Louisville, 2301 S 3rd St, Louisville, KY 40292-0001.

CURLEY, MICHAEL JOSEPH
PERSONAL Born 12/23/1942, Hempstead, NY, 2 children **DISCIPLINE** MEDIEVAL LITERATURE, LATIN **EDUCATION** Fairfield Univ, BA, 64; Harvard Univ, MA, 65; Univ Chicago, PhD, 72. **CAREER** Prof Eng, dir Honors Prog, Univ Puget Sound, 71-; NEH fel classics, Univ Tex, Austin, 77-78; Am Coun Learned Soc fel Celtic, Harvard Univ, 79-80; Graves fel Celtic, Univ Wales, Aberystwyth, 82-83. **MEMBERSHIPS** Medieval Acad Am; Medieval Assn of Pac. **RESEARCH** Latin literature; palaeography; Celtic. **SELECTED PUBLICATIONS** Auth & trans, Physiologus, Univ of Texas Press, 79; auth & trans, Marie de France, Purgatory of Saint Patrick, Binghamton: Center for Medieval and Renaissance Texts, 93; auth, Geoffrey of Monmouth, New York: Macmillan, 94. **CONTACT ADDRESS** Honor's Program, Univ of Puget Sound, 1500 N Warner St, Tacoma, WA 98416-0005. **EMAIL** curley@ups.edu

CURRAN, LEO C.
DISCIPLINE CLASSICS **EDUCATION** Oxford Univ, MA, 58; Yale Univ, BA; PhD, 61. **CAREER** Fac, 67-; to assoc prof emer, present, SUNY Buffalo. **HONORS AND AWARDS** Chancellor's Awd Excel Tchg, 80; found assoc ed, arethusa. **RESEARCH** Software for computer analysis of Latin lit and for Latin instruction; poetry of the late Republic and early Empire. **SELECTED PUBLICATIONS** Auth, Identification of Latin Poets by Sound, Syllecta Classica 2, 90; Identification of Latin Poets by Sound II, Syllecta Classica 3, 91. **CONTACT ADDRESS** Dept Classics, SUNY, Buffalo, 707 Clemens Hall, Buffalo, NY 14260. **EMAIL** lccurran@acsu.buffalo.edu

CURRAN, MARK JOSEPH
PERSONAL Born 08/30/1941, Abilene, KS, m, 1969 **DISCIPLINE** SPANISH, PORTUGUESE **EDUCATION** Rockhurst Col, BSBA, 63; St Louis Univ, PhD(Span & Latin Am studies), 68. **CAREER** Asst prof, 68-73, Assoc Prof Span & Port, Ariz State Univ, 73- **MEMBERSHIPS** Am Asn Teachers Span & Port; Pac Coast Coun Latin Am Studies; Am Folklore Soc. **RESEARCH** Folklore and popular culture of Brazil; Latin American civilization; northeastern literature of Brazil. **SELECTED PUBLICATIONS** Auth, Brazil Literatura-De-Cordel String-Literature--Poetic Chronicle and Popular History, Stud Latin Amer Pop Cult, Vol 0015, 96. **CONTACT ADDRESS** Dept of Foreign Lang, Arizona State Univ, Tempe, AZ 85281.

CURRY, CORRADA
DISCIPLINE ITALIAN LITERATURE AND CULTURE **EDUCATION** La State Univ, PhD, 85. **CAREER** Asst prof, La State Univ. **SELECTED PUBLICATIONS** Auth, Immagini letterarie e arti figurative, in Can J of Ital Stud, 93; Ritorno in Sicilia (poems), in Voices in Ital Am, 96; Description and Meaning in Three Novels by Gustave Flaubert, 96. **CONTACT ADDRESS** Dept of French and Ital, Louisiana State Univ and A&M Col, 129A Prescott, Baton Rouge, LA 70803. **EMAIL** corrada@compuserve.com

CURSCHMANN, MICHAEL J.
PERSONAL Born 01/11/1936, Cologne, Germany, m, 1961, 1 child **DISCIPLINE** GERMAN **EDUCATION** Universitat Munchen 56; PhD, 62. **CAREER** Asst Prof, Universitat Munchen, 62-63; Prof, Princeton Univ, 63-. **HONORS AND AWARDS** Fel, Medieval Acad of Am, 00; Guggenheim Fel, 70-71. **MEMBERSHIPS** Bavarian Acad of Sci, Inst for Germanic Studies, School for Adv Studies. **RESEARCH** Medieval German literature 1100-1600; Medieval orality; Literature and music; Literature and the visual arts. **SELECTED PUBLICATIONS** Auth, Vom Wandel im bildlichen Umgang mit literarischen Gegenstanden. Rodenegg, Wildenstein und das flaarsche Haus in Stein am Rhein, Freiburg, 97; auth, "Ein Zyklus profaner Wandmalerei auf Burg Wildenstein an der donau: Sietrich und Sigenot," Kunstchronik, (95): 41-46; auth, "Constantine-Heraclius: German Texts and picture cycles," in Piero della Francesca and his Legacy, Washington, 95; auth, "Hofische Laienkultur zwischen Mundlichkeit und Schriftlichkeit. Das Zeugnis Lamberts von Ardres," in Auffuhrung und Schrift in Mittelalter und fruher Neuzeit, Stuttgart, 96; auth, "Wolfgang Stammler und die folgen: wort und Bild als interdisziplinaeres Forschungsthema in internationalem Rahmen," in Das Mittelalter un ie Germanisten. Zur neueren Methodengeschichte der Germanischen Philologie, Schweiz, 98; auth, "Wort - Schrift - Bild: Zum Verhaeltnis von volkssprachigem Schrifttum und bildender Kunst vonm 12. Bis zum 16. Jahrhundert," in Mittelalter und fruehe Neuzeit. Uegergaenge, Umbrueche und neuansaetxze, 99. **CONTACT ADDRESS** Dept Germanic Lang & Lit, Princeton Univ, 230 E Pyne Hall, Princeton, NJ 08544-0001. **EMAIL** micur@princeton.edu

CURTIS, ALEXANDER ROSS
PERSONAL Born 08/06/1931, Tredegar, Wales, m, 1964 **DISCIPLINE** FRENCH **EDUCATION** Univ Wales, BA, 53, MA, 57, Univ Paris, DUniv(French), 66. **CAREER** From instr to asst prof, 57-70, acad secy, 66-70, assoc chmn dept, 70-71, Assoc Prof French, Univ Toronto, 70-. **MEMBERSHIPS** Asn Can Univ Teachers Fr, Can Asn Appl Ling. **RESEARCH** Seventeenth century French theatre, comparative stylistics. **CONTACT ADDRESS** Dept of French, Univ of Toronto, 50 St Joseph St, 2nd Fl., Toronto, ON, Canada M5S 1J4.

CURTIS, JAMES MALCOLM
PERSONAL Born 04/16/1940, Florence, AL, m, 1962, 1 child **DISCIPLINE** RUSSIAN LITERATURE **EDUCATION** Vanderbilt Univ, BA, 62; Columbia Univ, MA, 64; PhD(Russ), 68. **CAREER** Actg asst prof Russ, Univ Calif, Berkeley, 66-68; asst prof, 68-72, assoc prof, 72-78, Prof Russ, Univ MO-Columbia 79-, Am Coun Learned Soc fel, 76-77. **MEMBERSHIPS** Am Asn Teachers Slavic & E Europ Lang; Am Asn Advan Slavic Studies. **RESEARCH** Tolstoy; Dostoevsky; critical theory. **SELECTED PUBLICATIONS** Auth, Culture as Polyphony: An Essay on the Nature of Paradigms; auth, Solzhenitsyn's Traditional Imagination. **CONTACT ADDRESS** Dept of Ger & Russian Studies, Univ of Missouri, Columbia, Columbia, MO 65211. **EMAIL** CurtisJM@missouri.edu

CYPESS, SANDRA M.
PERSONAL Born 01/05/1943, Brooklyn, NY, m, 1964, 2 children **DISCIPLINE** SPANISH **EDUCATION** Brooklyn Col, BA, 63; Cornell Univ, MA, 65; Univ of IL, PhD, 68. **CAREER** Instr to vis asst prof, Duke Univ 67-70; asst prof, Point Park Col, 70-74; vis prof, Univ of Ky, 73; vis asst prof, Carnegie-Mellon Univ, 75-76; asst prof to prof SUNY, 84-93; prof, Univ of Md, 94-. **HONORS AND AWARDS** Fel, Univ of IL, 66; Fel, SUNY, 77; Fel, Cornell Univ, 88; Grants, SUNY, 79-80, 85, 86, 88; NEH Fel, Mexico, 89; Fe., Univ of Md, 96, 00. **MEMBERSHIPS** Lat Am Studies Assoc; Feministas Unidas. **RESEARCH** Latin American and Caribbean Literature, Women's Studies, Cross-Cultural Studies, Comparative Drama, Translation Practice, Latin American Area Studies. **SELECTED PUBLICATIONS** Coauth, Modern Women Writers: A Bibliography of Criticism and Interpretation: Part I, South America, Scarecrow Pr, (NJ), 89; auth, La Malinche in Mexican Literature: From History to Myth, Univ Tex Pr, 91; coed, Essays in Honor of Frank Dauster, Juan de la Cuesta Pr, 95; auth, "Re-Vision de la figura de la Malinche en la dramaturgia mexicana contemporanea", La Malinche, sus padres y sus hijos, ed Margo Glantz, UNAM Pr, (95): 179-96; auth, "Dramatic Strategies Made Clear: The Feminist Politics in 'Puesta en claro' by Griselda Gambaro", Studies in Twenthieth Century Lit 20.1 (96): 125-145; auth, "Tennessee Williams en Argentina" in De Eugene O'Neill Al 'Happening", ed Osvaldo Pellettieri and George Woodyard, Editorial Gaerna, (Buenos Aires, 96), 47-60; auth, "Myth and Metatheatre: Malinche and Medea in Magana's (Re) Vision of the Conquest" in The Bucknell Review, Perspectives on Contemporary Spanish American Theatre, Ed Frank Dauster, Bucknell Univ Pr, (96): 37-52; auth, "Twentieth Century Spanish American Drama", in Cambridge History of Latin American Literature, Vol 2, eds Enrique Pupo-Walker and Roberto Gonzalez Echevarria, Cambridge Univ Pr, (96): 497-525; auth, "La Malinche, historia y leyenda de la unica mujer importante durante la conquista de Mexico" in Las desobedientes: Historias de mujeres latinoamericanas, eds Betty Osorio and Mercedes Jaramillo, Panamericana, (Santafe de Bogota, 97), 3-24; auth, "Del corpus dramatico al corpus politico: el dialgo entre Elena Garro y la historia de Mexico" , in Homenaje a Elena Garro, eds Robert Anderson and Mara Garcia, Univ of Tlaxcala Pr, (99): 85-97. **CONTACT ADDRESS** Dept Span & Port, Univ of Maryland, Col Park, 2215 Jimenez Hall, College Park, MD 20742-4835. **EMAIL** smcypess@wam.umd.edu

CZERWINSKI, EDWARD J.
PERSONAL Born 06/06/1929, Erie, PA **DISCIPLINE** SLAVIC DRAMA AND THEATRE, COMPARATIVE LITERATURE **EDUCATION** Grove City Col, BA, 51; Pa State Univ, MA, 55; Univ Wis, MA, 64, PhD(Russ, Polish), 65. **CAREER** Instr English, Ga Tech, 57-59; asst prof English & drama, McNeese State Col, 59-60: assoc prof Russ & Polish lit, Univ Pittsburgh, 65-66; assoc prof Slavics & chmn dept, State Univ NY, Buffalo & Millard Fillmore Eve Div, 66-67; assoc prof Russ & Polish, Univ Kans, 67-70; Prof Russ & Comp Lit, State Univ NY Stony Brook, 70-, Chmn Comt Acad Exchange With Poland, 73-, Special ed & mem ed bd, Comp Drama; ed, Slavic & EEurop Theatre J. **HONORS AND AWARDS** Distinguished Teaching Awd, NY State Asn Foreign Lang Teachers, 75. **MEMBERSHIPS** MLA; Am Asn Teachers Slavic & EEurop Lang; Int Fedn Mod Lang & Lit; AAUP; Am Asn Advan Slavic Studies. **SELECTED PUBLICATIONS CONTACT ADDRESS** Dept of Ger & Slavic Lang, SUNY, Stony Brook, Stony Brook, NY 11790.

D

D'ANDREA, ANTONIO
PERSONAL Born 11/22/1916, Messina, Italy **DISCIPLINE** ITALIAN **EDUCATION** Univ Pisa, Dottorato in Filosofia, 39. **CAREER** Assoc prof to prof, 56-86, ch Ital, 64-76, PROF EMER ITALIAN, McGILL UNIV, 86-; dir, Ital Cultur Inst Montreal, 62-64. **HONORS AND AWARDS** Stella della Solidarieta italiana; Grande Ufficiale, Ordine al Merito della Repubblica (Ital); Queen's Silver Jubilee Medal; Royal Soc Can. **MEMBERSHIPS** Can Mediter Int; Can Soc Ital Stud; Asn Profs Ital Que; Can Soc Renaissance Stud. **SELECTED PUBLICATIONS** Auth, Il nome della storia, 82; auth, Strutture inquiete, 93; co-ed, Discours contre Machiavel, 74; co-ed, Yearbook of Italian Studies, 71-75. **CONTACT ADDRESS** Dept of Ital, McGill Univ, 1001 Sherbrooke St W, Montreal, QC, Canada H3A 1G5.

D'ARMS, JOHN H.
PERSONAL Born 11/27/1934, Poughkeepsie, NY, m, 1961, 2 children **DISCIPLINE** CLASSICAL PHILOLOGY **EDUCATION** Princeton Univ, AB, 56; New College, Oxford, BA (Literae Humaniores), 59; Harvard Univ, PhD (Classical Philol), 65. **CAREER** Chmn, dept classical studies, Univ MI, 72-75, 76-77, 80-85; dir, Am Academy in Rome and A W Mellon Prof, School of Classical Studies, 77-80; dean, Horace H Rackham School of Graduate Studies, Univ MI, 85-95, prof history, 86-97, Vice Provost for Academic Affairs, 90-95, G F Else Prof Humanities, Univ MI, 95-97; adjunct prof Classics and History, Columbia Univ, 97-; pres, AM Coun of Learned Societies, 97-. **HONORS AND AWARDS** Phi Beta Kappa, Princeton Univ, 56; Princeton Univ, Keasbey Scholar, 56; Honorary Woodrow Wilson fel, 56; Fulbright fel, Univ Rome, 61-62; Am Coun Learned Societies fel, 71-72; fel, John Simon Guggenheim Memorial Found, 75-76; vis member, School of Historical Studies, Inst for Advanced Study, Princeton, 75-76; corresponding member, German Archaeological Inst, Rome, 80-; Distinguished Faculty Achievement Awd, Univ MI, 82; fel, Am Academy of Arts and Sciences, 92-; Centennial Medal, Am Academy in Rome, 95; Presidential Medal for Outstanding Service, Univ MI, 95; member, Am Philos Soc, 98; Docteur Honoris Causa (honorary), Univ Montreal, 98. **MEMBERSHIPS** Archaeolog Inst of Am; Am Hist Asn; Soc for the Promotion of Roman Studies (England); Am Philol Asn. **RESEARCH** Roman social, cultural, and economic history; Roman historiography; Latin epigraphy; Roman art, architecture, and archaeology; Latin prose and poetry. **SELECTED PUBLICATIONS** Auth, Romans on the Bay of Naples: A Social and Cultural Study of the Villas and their Owners from 150 BC to AD 400, Harvard Univ Press, 70; co-ed with E C Kopff, Roman Seaborne Commerce: Studies in Archaeology and History (Memoirs of the Am Academy in Rome), 80; auth, Commerce and Social Standing in Ancient Rome, Harvard Univ Press, 81; Control, Companionship, and Clientela: some Social Functions of the Roman Communal Meal, Echos du Monde Classique, N S 3, 84; The Roman Convivium and the Idea of Equality, in O Murray, ed, Sympotica: A Symposium on the Symposium, Claredon Press, Oxford, 90; Slaves at Roman Convivia, in W J Slater, ed, Dining in a Classical Context, Univ MI Press, 91; Heavy Drinking and Drunkenness in the Roman World: Questions for Historians, in O Murray, ed, In Vino Veritas, British School at Rome, 95; Funding Trends in the Academic Humanities, 1970-1995: Reflections on the Stability of the System, in A Kernan, ed, What's Happened to the Humanities, Princeton Univ Press, 97; auth, "Performing Culture: Roman Spectacle and the Banquets of the Powerful," in The Art of Ancient Spectacle, ed. B. Bergman and C. Kondoleon (Yale Univ Press, 99). **CONTACT ADDRESS** American Council of Learned Societies, 228 E 45th St, New York, NY 10017-3398.

DA CUNHA-GIABBAI, GLORIA E.
PERSONAL Born, Uruguay **DISCIPLINE** LATIN AMERICAN LITERATURE, SPANISH **EDUCATION** Instituto Magisterial, Uruguay, BA; Ga State Univ, MA; Univ Ga, PhD. **CAREER** Assoc prof, Morehouse Col, 93-. **HONORS AND AWARDS** Centro de Estudios Iberoamericanos "Mario Benedetti"; Instituto Literario y Cultural Hispanico, Phi Kappa Phi. **MEMBERSHIPS** LASA, AATSP, MLA, AHF, SCOLAS, CLA, ACTFL. **RESEARCH** Latin American Essay, Literature and History, Narrative of Latin American Women Writers. **SELECTED PUBLICATIONS** Auth, El exilio: realidad y ficcion, 92; auth, Humanidad: la utopia del hispanoamericano, 92; auth, Mujer e historia. La narrativa de Ana teresa Torres, 94; coed, Cuentistas hispanoamericanas, 96; auth, La cuentistica de Renee Ferrer: continuidad y cambio de nuestra expresion, 97; auth, El pensamiento de Marietta de Veintemilla, 98; coed, Narradoras ecuatorianas de hoy, 00; auth, Marion Benedetti y la nacion posible, 01. **CONTACT ADDRESS** 5652 Buttonwood Ct, Stone Mountain, GA 30087-1611. **EMAIL** gdacunha@morehouse.edu

DAEMMRICH, HORST S.
PERSONAL Born 01/05/1930, PA, m **DISCIPLINE** GERMAN **EDUCATION** Wayne State Univ, BA, 58; MA, 59; Univ Chicago, PhD, 64. **CAREER** Instr, Univ Chicago, 61-62; instr, asst, assoc to full prof, Wayne State Univ, 62-80; prof to prof emeritus, 81-. **HONORS AND AWARDS** WSU Bd of Governors Fac Recognition Awd, 75; WSU Distinguished Grad Awd 79; Ira H Abrams memorial Awd, Univ Penn, 90. **MEMBERSHIPS** ACLA, AATG, CCLA, ETA Hoffmann Gesellschaft, Lenz Soc. **RESEARCH** Themes and Motifs in literature. **SELECTED PUBLICATIONS** Auth, Spirals and Circles: A Key to Thematic Patterns in Classicism and Realism, New York, 94; auth, Themen und Motive in der Literatur, Ein Handbuch, Tubingen: Francke, 95. **CONTACT ADDRESS** Dept German, Univ of Pennsylvania, 745 Williams Hall, Philadelphia, PA 19104-6305. **EMAIL** hdaemmri@sas.upenn.edu

DAINARD, JAMES A.
PERSONAL Born 05/26/1930, Golden, BC, Canada **DISCIPLINE** FRENCH **EDUCATION** Univ BC, BA, 51, MA, 61, BLS, 62; Univ Alta, PhD, 67. **CAREER** Instr to asst prof, Romance lang, Univ Alta, 63-68; asst prof to prof, 68-95, Prof Emer French, Univ Toronto, 95-. **SELECTED PUBLICATIONS** Ed, Editing Correspondence, 79; contrib ed, Correspondance generale d'Helvetius, vols 1-4, 81-; gen ed, La Correspondance de Madame de Graffigny, vols 1-5, 85-. **CONTACT ADDRESS** Univ Col, Univ of Toronto, Toronto, ON, Canada M5S 3H7. **EMAIL** adainard@chass.utoronto.ca

DALZELL, ALEXANDER
PERSONAL Born 05/08/1925, Belfast, Northern Ireland **DISCIPLINE** CLASSICS **EDUCATION** Trinity Col (Dublin), BA, 50, MA, 53, BLitt, 56. **CAREER** Lectr, Kings Col, Univ London, 51-53; lectr, Univ Sheffield, 53-54; lectr to prof, 54-88, dean arts, 68-73, vice provost, 72-79, acting provost, 73, 79, PROF EMER, TRINITY COL, UNIV TORONTO, 88-. **MEMBERSHIPS** Class Asn Can (pres 80-82); Am Philol Asn (mem publ comt), 81-84. **SELECTED PUBLICATIONS** Auth, The Criticism of Didactic Poetry, 96; contribur, Correspondence of Erasmus, vols 10 & 11, 92, 93; assoc ed/ed, Phoenix, 60-71; ed bd, Collected Works of Erasmus. **CONTACT ADDRESS** 344 Saunders St, Fredericton, NB, Canada E3B 1N8. **EMAIL** adalzell@nbnet.nb.ca

DAMIANI, BRUNO MARIO
PERSONAL Born 04/15/1942, Pola, Italy **DISCIPLINE** SPANISH, ITALIAN **EDUCATION** Ohio State Univ, BA, 63, MA, 64; Johns Hopkins Univ, PHD(romance lang & lit), 67. **CAREER** Asst prof, 67-69, Assoc Prof Romance Lang & Lit, Cath Univ Am, 69-, Consult Title VII & prog qual consult, Task Group C, Dept Health, Educ & Welfare, 72; prog off, Nat Endowment for Humanities, 76. **MEMBERSHIPS** Asoc Int Hispanistas; MLA; Am Asn Teachers Span & Port. **RESEARCH** Medieval, Renaissance and Baroque periods; Spanish Renaissance literature; Spanish and Italian medieval literature. **SELECTED PUBLICATIONS CONTACT ADDRESS** Dept of Mod Long, Catholic Univ of America, Washington, DC 20017.

DAMROSCH, DAVID N.
PERSONAL Born 04/13/1953, Bar Harbor, ME, m, 1974, 3 children **DISCIPLINE** COMPARITIVE LITERATURE **EDUCATION** Yale Univ, BA, 75, PhD(comp lit), 80. **CAREER** Speechwriter & ed, Off Special Asst to the Pres for Health, White House, Washington, DC, 79; asst prof, 80-; prof comp lit, Columbia Univ, 87-. **MEMBERSHIPS** MLA; Pres, Am Comp Lit Asn, 01-02. **RESEARCH** The novel; epic and romance; scripture. **SELECTED PUBLICATIONS** Auth, The Narrative Covenant, 87; We Scholars, 95; ed, The Longman Anthology of British Literature, 98; auth, Meeting of the Mind, 00. **CONTACT ADDRESS** Dept of English & Comp Lit, Columbia Univ, 2960 Broadway, New York, NY 10027-6900. **EMAIL** dnd2@columbia.edu

DANA, MARIE IMMACULEE
PERSONAL Born 10/28/1931, Albany, NY **DISCIPLINE** FRENCH LANGUAGE & LITERATURE **EDUCATION** Rosemont Col, BA, 53; McGill Univ, MA, 62; Fulbright, 63-64; Univ Pa, PhD(French), 68. **CAREER** Teacher, St Agnes Sch, 53-54; teacher French, Latin & hist, Our Lady of Mercy Acad, 55-60 & St Peter High Sch, 60-63; instr, 54-63, asst prof, 67-73, assoc prof French, Carlow Col, 73-, chemn dept lang 67-, chemn, dept educ, 75-, prof, 92-, vice pres acad affairs, 92-, travel grant, Bibliotheque Nationale, Paris, 66; consult, Duquesne-Carlow Pupil-Personnel Serv Prog; Acad Am Coun Educ Admin fel, 74; consult, Pa Dept Educ, 77-; Adv bd mem, Project 81, 78-. **MEMBERSHIPS** MLA; Am Coun Teaching For Lang. **RESEARCH** Twentieth century French literature. **SELECTED PUBLICATIONS** Auth, Lope de Vega in the work of Moliere, Hispanofila. **CONTACT ADDRESS** Carlow Col, 3333 Fifth Ave, Pittsburgh, PA 15213-3165. **EMAIL** midanarsm@carlow.edu

DANESI, MARCEL
PERSONAL Born 10/01/1946, Lucca, Italy **DISCIPLINE** ITALIAN STUD **EDUCATION** Univ Toronto, BA, 69, MA, 71, PhD, 74; Royal Conserv, ARCT, 83. **CAREER** Vis prof, Rutgers Univ, 72-74; PROF ITALIAN STUD, VICTORIA COL, UNIV TORONTO, 74-, dir, prog semiotics & commun theory; vis prof, Catholic Univ Milan, 91; permanent vis prof, Univ Lugano, 95-. **SELECTED PUBLICATIONS** Auth, Vico, Metaphor and the Origin of Language, 93; auth, Cool: The Signs and Meanings of Adolescence, 94; auth, Messages and Meanings: Introduction to Semiotics, 94; auth, Giambattista Vico and the Cognitive Science Enterprise, 95; auth, Increase Your Puzzle IQ, 97; coauth, Applied Psycholinguistics, 85; coed, Ital Asn Applied Ling, 90-. **CONTACT ADDRESS** Victoria Col, Univ of Toronto, NF 217, Toronto, ON, Canada M5S 1K7. **EMAIL** marcel.danesi@utoronto.ca

DANIEL, LEE A.
PERSONAL Born 11/17/1945, Dublin, TX, m, 1969, 3 children **DISCIPLINE** SPANISH AMERICAN LITERATURE **EDUCATION** Tarleton State Univ, BA, 68; Univ N Tex, MA, 72; Tex Tech Univ, PhD, 79. **CAREER** Lectr, Univ Ark, 79-80; asst prof, SW Okla State Univ, 80-85; prof, chair, Tex Christian Univ, 85-. **HONORS AND AWARDS** Phi Beta Delta, Finalist, Chancellor's Award for Distinguished Res; Nat Dir of Latin Americanists, 85; Mortar Board Preferred Prof, 88, 92, 94. **MEMBERSHIPS** MLA, SW Coun of Latin Am Studies. **RESEARCH** The imaginary town in Latin American Literature, The Works of Rosa Maria Britton, The theatre of Sor Juana Ines de la Cruz. **SELECTED PUBLICATIONS** Auth, "Sor Juana's pentad of Carlosian Loas," Sor Juana Ines de la Cruz: Selected Studies, (89); auth, "El 'Dixie Gongorism' de joaquin Bestard y 'La obsesion de German Ortiga,'" Confluencia, (92); auth, "Sor Juana's Baroque Martyr-Auto, El martir del Sacramento, San Hermenegildo," Latin Am Theatre Rev, (94); auth, The Los of Sor Juana Ines de la Cruz, York Pr, 94; ed, Cuentos de Beyhuale, York Pr, 94; auth, "Angustia y evasion en la narrativa de Rima de Vallbona," Revista de Filogia y Linguistica de la Universidad de Costa Rica, (95); auth, 'Influencia faulkneriana o experiencia mundovista': Las cronicas de Beyhuale y Maravillas," Confluencia (97); auth, "Mythical Worlds of Latin American Writers," Confluencia, (99); auth, "Entrevista a Rosa Mariqa Crespo de Britton," Mester, (00); auth, "El pueblo ficticio en la literatura mexicana: Una cartografia," Confluencia (01). **CONTACT ADDRESS** Span and Latin Am Studies, Texas Christian Univ, TCU Box 297220, Fort Worth, TX 76129. **EMAIL** 1.daniel@tcu.edu

DANKER, FREDERICK W.
PERSONAL Born 07/12/1920, Frankenmuth, MI, m, 1948, 2 children **DISCIPLINE** NEW TESTAMENT THEOLOGY, LINGUISTICS **EDUCATION** Concordia Sem, BA, 42, BD, 50; Univ Chicago, PhD, 63. **CAREER** From asst prof to prof New Testament exec theol, 54-74; Prof New Testament Exec Theol, Christ Sem-Seminex, 74-. **MEMBERSHIPS** Am Philol Asn; Soc Bibl Lit; Am Soc Papyrologists; Societas Novi Testamenti Studiorum; Cath Bibl Asn. **RESEARCH** Greek tragedy; Greek and Latin Epigraphy; Greek Lexicography. **SELECTED PUBLICATIONS CONTACT ADDRESS** 6928 Plateau Ave, Saint Louis, MO 63139.

DARHOWER, MARTIN L.
PERSONAL Born 05/29/1969, Harrisburg, PA **DISCIPLINE** LINGUISTICS, ENGLISH **EDUCATION** Millersville Univ, BS, 92; MA, 94; Univ Pitts, PhD, 00. **CAREER** Adj instr, Harrisburg CC, 93-96; adj instr, Millersville Univ, 95-97; adj instr, Gettysburg Col, 94-97; teaching asst, Univ Pitts, 07-00; asst prof, Univ PR, 00-. **MEMBERSHIPS** AATSP; CALLICO; TESOL. **RESEARCH** Computer mediated communication; computer assisted language learning; second/foreign language pedagogy. **SELECTED PUBLICATIONS** Auth, "Some Interactional Features of Synchronous Computer Mediated Communication in the Intermediate L2 Class: A Sociocultural Case Study," CALICO J (01). **CONTACT ADDRESS** English Dept, Univ of Puerto Rico, Humacao Univ Col, Humacao, PR 00791. **EMAIL** markdarhower@aol.com

DARST, DAVID HIGH
PERSONAL Born 06/08/1943, Greensboro, NC, m, 1969, 2 children **DISCIPLINE** GOLDEN AGE SPANISH LITERATURE **EDUCATION** Univ of the South, AB, 65; Univ NC, Chapel Hill, MA, 67; Univ Ky, PhD, 70. **CAREER** Asst prof, 70-76, assoc prof span, 76-81, asst dir humanities, 78-81, full prof Spanish & assoc dir humanities, Fla State Univ, 81-, Nat Endowment for Humantities grants, 74, 78 & 81-82. **RESEARCH** Renaissance and baroque; humanities. **SELECTED PUBLICATIONS** Auth, The comic art of Tirso de Molina, Estudios de Hispanofila, The two worlds of La Ninfa del Cielo, Hisp Res & The thematic design of El Condemado por Desconfiado, Kentucky Romance Quart, 74; Tirso de Molina's The Trickster of Seville: A Critical Commentary, Simon & Schuster, 76; Lope de Vega y Cervantes o la modernidad literaria, Arbor, Madrid, 77; Juan Buscan, Twayne, 78; Andrenio's perception of reality and the structure of El Criticon, Hispania, 77; Witchcraft in Spain: The testimony of Martin de Castanega's Treatise on Superstition and Witchcraft, Proc Am Philos Soc, 79. **CONTACT ADDRESS** Dept of Mod Lang, Florida State Univ, 600 W College Ave, Tallahassee, FL 32306-1096. **EMAIL** ddarst@mailer.fsu.edu

DASSONVILLE, MICHEL
PERSONAL Born 12/27/1927, Lille, France, m, 1949, 3 children **DISCIPLINE** FRENCH LITERATURE **EDUCATION** Univ Lille, BA, 46, Lic es Let, 48; Univ Sacre-Coeur, MA, 51; Laval Univ, DLet, 53. **CAREER** Asst prof French lit, Laval Univ, 53-58; charge de cours, Cath Inst Paris, 58-60; from vis asst prof to assoc prof, 60-63, Prof French Lit, Univ Tex, Austin, 63-, Res grants, French Govt, 53 & 58 & Can Arts Coun, 57; Casgrain Prize, 58, Minnie Stevens Piper prof, 65; cult secy, Alliance Francaise, Paris, 58-60; pres, Alliance Francaise, Austin, Tex, 63-67. **HONORS AND AWARDS** Chevalier des Palmes Academiques, French Govt, 76. **MEMBERSHIPS** S Cent Mod Lang Asn. **RESEARCH** Sixteenth century French literature. **SELECTED PUBLICATIONS CONTACT ADDRESS** Univ of Texas, Austin, Sutton Hall 215, Austin, TX 78712.

DAUGHERTY, GREGORY NEIL
DISCIPLINE CLASSICS **EDUCATION** Univ Richmond, BA, 70; Vanderbilt Univ, MA,75; PhD, 77. **CAREER** Instr, 76-78, asst prof, 78-84, assoc prof, 84-94, prof Class, Randolph-Macon Col, 94-; vis asst prof, Univ Richmond, 77, 91, 93; vis asst prof, Va Commonwealth Univ, 82, 85; vis assoc prof, Col William and Mary, 87. **HONORS AND AWARDS** Woodrow Wilson fel, Univ Richmond, 70; Fulbright scholar, Univ Pavia, Italy, 70-71; Thomas Branch Awd for Excellence in Tchg, Randolph-Macon Col, 78, 82; Fulbright grant, Italy, 79; NEH Summer Inst on Women in Antiquity, 83, Phi Beta Kappa, 70. **MEMBERSHIPS** Secy, Richmond Soc of the Archaeol Inst of Am, 82-95; mem, Va Dept of Educ, Lat Textbk Selection Comt, 84; consult, Va Dept of Educ, Standards of Lrng for Lat, 86-87.; Mem at Large, Exec Bd of the Class Asn of Va, 87-89; ed, Prospects Newsletter of the Nat Comt on Lat and Greek, 90-96; dir, Class Essay Contest, Class Asn of Va, 90-95; exec secy, Nat Comt on Lat and Greek, 91-93; mem, Joint Comt on Class in Am Educ, Am Philol Asn, 91-94; ch, Comt on Local Arrangements, Class Asn of the Midwest and S; mem, Final Rev Bd NEH Fel Prog for For Lang Tchr K-12, 94; ch, Membership Comt, Class Asn of the Midwest and S, 94-96; pres, For Lang Asn of Va, 95-96; secy-treas, Class Asn of the Midwest and S, 96-. **SELECTED PUBLICATIONS** Auth, Rev of John E. Stambaugh, The Ancient Roman City: The Johns Hopkins Univ Press 88, Class World 84.3, 91; Rev of Walter Ellis, Alcibiades. Classical Lives, Routledge, 89, Class World 84, 91; The Cohortes Vigilum and the Great Fire of 64 AD, Class J 87.3, 92; coauth, Preparation and Training for Teachers of Latin, Class J 86, 91. **CONTACT ADDRESS** Dept of Class, Randolph-Macon Col, Ashland, VA 23005-5505. **EMAIL** gdaugher@rmc.edu

DAUSTER, FRANK NICHOLAS
PERSONAL Born 02/05/1925, Irvington, NJ, m, 1949, 2 children **DISCIPLINE** SPANISH **EDUCATION** Rutgers Univ, AB, 49, MA, 50; Yale Univ, PhD(Span), 53. **CAREER** From instr to asst prof Romance lang, Wesleyan Univ, 50-55; from asst prof to assoc prof, 55-61, Prof Romance Lang, 61-97, Prof Eneritus, Rutgers Univ, New Brunswick, 92. **MEMBERSHIPS** MLA; Am Asn Teachers Span & Port; Inst Int Lit Iberoam. **RESEARCH** Contemporary Latin America, particularly the theater and poetry. **SELECTED PUBLICATIONS** Auth, Breve Historia de la Poesia Mexicana, 56, Ensayos sobre Poesia Mcxicana, 63 & Breve Historia del Teatre Hispanoamericano, Siglox XIX-XX, 66, 2nd ed, 73, Studium; coed, Literatura de Hispanoamericana, Harcourt, 70; auth, Xavier Villaurrutia, Twayne, 71; co-ed, En un acto, Van Nostrand, 74; Ensayos sobre Teatro Hispanoamericana, Sepsetentas, 75; coed, 9 dramaturgos hispanamericanos, Ginol, 79, 2d ed, 98. **CONTACT ADDRESS** 159 Lakeside Dr N, Piscataway, NJ 08854.

DAVIAU, DONALD G.
PERSONAL Born 09/30/1927, Medway, MA, m, 1950 **DISCIPLINE** GERMAN **EDUCATION** Clark Univ, BA, 50; Univ Calif, MA, 52, PhD, 55. **CAREER** From instr to assoc prof Ger, 55-75, chmn dept Ger & Russ, 69-75, prof German,

Univ Calif, Riverside, 75-, ed, Mod Austrian Lit, 71-. **HONORS AND AWARDS** Ehrenkreuz fur Wissenschaft und Kunst, Austrian Govt, 77. **MEMBERSHIPS** MLA; Am Asn Teachers Ger; Int Arthur Schnitzler Res Asn (pres, 78-); Hugo von Hofmannsthal Gesellschaft; Am Coun for Study Austrian Lit (pres, 80-). **RESEARCH** Modern Austrian and German literature. **SELECTED PUBLICATIONS** Co-ed, The Correspondence of Arthur Schnitzler and Raoul Auernheimer, Univ NC, 72; coauth, The Correspondence of Hugo von Hofmannsthal and Raoul Auernheimer, Mod Austrian Lit, 74; coauth, The Ariadne auf Naxos of Hugo von Hoftmannsthal and Richard Strauss, Univ NC, 76; Hermann Bahr and decadence, Mod Austrian Lit, 77; auth, The Letters of Arthur Schnitzler to Hermann Bahr, Univ NC, 78; Das junge und das jungste Wien, In: Osterreichiche Gegenwart, Francke Verlag, 80; Hermann Bahr and the secessionist art movement in Vienna, In: The Turn of the Century, Bouvier Verlag, 81; Das Exilerlebnis, 82; coed, The Correspondence of Stefan Zweig with Raoul Auernheimer and Richard Beer-Hofmann, 83; Der Mann von Ubermorgen, 84; ed, Stefan Zweig/Paul Zech. Briefe 1910-1942, 84 & 87; Hermann Bahr, 85; coed, Exil: Wirkung und Wertung, 85; ed, Major Figures of Comtemporary Austrian Literature, 87; ed, Major Figures of Modern Austrian Literature, 88; coed, Austrian Fiction Writers 1875-1913, 89; coed, Austrian Fiction Writers after 1914, 89; ed, Major Figures of Turn-of-the-Century Austrian Literature, 91; ed, Austrian Writers and the Anschluss, 91; ed, Osterreichische Tagebuchschriftsteller, 94; ed, Major Figures of the Austrian Inteerwar Years 1918-1938, 95; ed, Jura Soyfer and His Time, 95; coed, Geschichte der osterreichischen Literatur, 97; ed, Major Figures of Nineteenth-Century Austrian Literature, 98. **CONTACT ADDRESS** Dept of Literature & Language, Univ of California, Riverside, 900 University Ave, Riverside, CA 92521-0001. **EMAIL** donald.daviau@ucr.edu

DAVIDHEISER, JAMES CHARLES

PERSONAL Born Reading, PA, 1 child **DISCIPLINE** GERMAN LITERATURE, COMPARATIVE LITERATURE **EDUCATION** La Salle Col, BA, 63; Univ Pittsburgh, MA & PhD(Ger lang & lit), 72. **CAREER** Instr English, Univ Mainz, 67-68; instr Ger, Univ Pittsburgh, 68-69; asst prof Ger lang & lit, Univ Del, 69-76, fac res grant, 73; Assoc Prof Ger & Chmn Dept, Univ of the South, 76-, Fulbright grant, 77; Exxon Found grant, 81. **MEMBERSHIPS** Am Asn Teachers Ger; Lessing Soc; Southern Comp Lit Asn. **RESEARCH** Modern German literature; comparative literature; 18th century literature. **SELECTED PUBLICATIONS** Auth, Grammar Groups in the Student-Centered Classroom, For Lang Annals, Vol 0029, 96; Intermediate Conversation and Composition Courses--What Makes Them Successful, For Lang Annals, Vol 0028, 95. **CONTACT ADDRESS** Dept of Ger, Univ of the South, Sewanee, TN 37375.

DAVIDSON, HUGH MACCULLOUGH

PERSONAL Born 01/21/1918, Lanett, AL, m, 1951, 1 child **DISCIPLINE** FRENCH **EDUCATION** Univ Chicago, AB, 38, PhD, 46. **CAREER** From instr to asst prof French, Univ Chicago, 46-53, asst dean col, 49-52, chmn col French staff, 51-53; asst prof Romance lang, Dartmouth Col, 53-56, prof, 56-62, chmn dept, 57-59; prof French, Ohio State Univ, 62-76; mem fac, 76-79, Prof French, Univ VA, 79-, Carnegie fel, Univ Chicago, 48-49; Fulbright res scholar, France, 59-60; Nat Found Arts & Humanities sr fel, 67-68; mem ed comt, PMLA, 68-73. **HONORS AND AWARDS** MA, Dartmouth Col, 56. **MEMBERSHIPS** Am Asn Teachers Fr; MLA; Int Asn Fr Studies. **RESEARCH** Seventeenth and 18th century French literature; methods of literary study and criticism; literature and philosophy. **SELECTED PUBLICATIONS** Auth, Playing with Truth--Language and the Human Condition in Pascal Pensees, Fr Forum, Vol 0020, 95. **CONTACT ADDRESS** Dept of French, Univ of Virginia, Charlottesville, VA 22903.

DAVIES, LAURENCE J.

PERSONAL Born 02/24/1943, Llanwrtyd, Wales, d **DISCIPLINE** COMPARATIVE LITERATURE **EDUCATION** Univ Oxford, BA, 63; MA, 68; Univ Sussex, D Phil, 72. **CAREER** Sr teach fel, Monash Univ, Aust, 64-68; vis asst prof, Dickinson Col, 75-77; vis asst prof, Dartmouth Col, 69-71; 77-; assoc prof, Dartmouth Coll. **HONORS AND AWARDS** Res fel, NEH; fel NEA; Woodrow Wilson fel. **MEMBERSHIPS** ICLA; MLA; Soc Utopian Stud; Joseph Conrad Soc US and UK. **RESEARCH** Modernist fiction; speculative fiction; Anglo Celtic lit and politics. **SELECTED PUBLICATIONS** Coauth, Cunninghame Graham: A Critical Biography, Cambridge Univ Press (79); coauth, The Collected Letters of Joseph Conrad, Cambridge Univ Press (83), vol 1-5, vol 6-8 in progress; auth, "At Play in the Fields of our Ford: Utopian Dystopianism," in Zanyatin, Huxley and Atwood; auth, "Seductions of the Word: Conrad's Kurtz, Soyinka's Professor."; auth, "The Evils of a Long Peace: Longing for the Great War."; auth, "Conrad Woman Readers." **CONTACT ADDRESS** Comp Lit Prog, Dartmouth Col, 6051 Dartmouth Hall, Hanover, NH 03755. **EMAIL** laurence.davies@dartmouth.edu

DAVIES, MORGAN

DISCIPLINE MEDIEVAL ENGLISH, WELSH, IRISH LANGUAGE, LITERATURE AND CULTURE **EDUCATION** Stanford, BA; Univ CA, MA, Cphil, PhD. **CAREER** Asst prof, Colgate Univ. **HONORS AND AWARDS** NEH Fel, Col Tchr-(s), 95. **RESEARCH** Old Eng lit, old and middle Irish lit, middle Welsh lit. **SELECTED PUBLICATIONS** Auth, Dafydd Ap Gwilym and the Friars: The Poetics of Antimendicancy, Studia Celtica; Aed I'r Coed I Dorri Cof: Dafydd Ap Gwilym and the Metaphorics of Carpentry, Cambrian Medieval Celtic Studies. **CONTACT ADDRESS** Dept of Eng, Colgate Univ, 13 Oak Drive, Hamilton, NY 13346.

DAVILLA-LOPEZ, GRACE

PERSONAL Born 04/10/1959, Arroyo, Puerto Rico, m, 1981, 2 children **DISCIPLINE** SPANISH **EDUCATION** Univ Puerto Rico, BA, 80; Univ Calif Berkeley, MA, 82; Univ Calif Irvine, PhD, 89. **CAREER** Visiting Asst Prof, Scripps Col, 90-91; Assoc Adj Prof, Pomona Col, 91-. **HONORS AND AWARDS** UCI Teaching Asst Teaching Awd, 86. **MEMBERSHIPS** Latin Am Studies Asn. **RESEARCH** Latin American Theater; Latin American Women's Narrative. **SELECTED PUBLICATIONS** Auth, "La construccion visual de la identidad nacronal, Society etnica en al teatro yotras artes visuales," Gestos 13 (98): 25. **CONTACT ADDRESS** Dept Romance Lang, Pomona Col, 333 N Col Way, Claremont, CA 91711-4429. **EMAIL** gdavilalopez@pomona.edu

DAVIS, DALE W.

DISCIPLINE COMPARATIVE LITERATURE AND VICTORIAN LITERATURE **EDUCATION** Univ OK, PhD, 68. **CAREER** Assoc prof Eng, mem, grad fac, instr, Hum Stud, mem, Univ Honors Coun, dir, Bachelor of Gen Stud degree prog, TX Tech Univ. **RESEARCH** Interdisciplinary educ. **SELECTED PUBLICATIONS** Publ articles on Victorian lit, pedag, lit theory, and criticism, and co-auth a standard two-volume textbook on interdisciplinary hum--The Humanities in Western Culture (8th Edition). **CONTACT ADDRESS** Texas Tech Univ, Lubbock, TX 79409-5015. **EMAIL** ditdd@ttacs.ttu.edu

DAVIS, GAROLD N.

PERSONAL Born 10/14/1932, Downey, ID, m, 1954, 5 children **DISCIPLINE** GERMAN AND COMPARATIVE LITERATURE **EDUCATION** Brigham Young Univ, BA, 58, MA, 59; Johns Hopkins Univ, PhD(Ger lit), 62. **CAREER** Instr Ger, Univ Pa, 62-63; asst prof, Southern Ore Col, 63-66; asst prof Ger & comp lit, Univ Colo, 66-68; Prof Ger, Brigham Young Univ, 68-, Assoc Dean, Col Humanities, 80-. **MEMBERSHIPS** MLA **RESEARCH** Anglo-German literary relations; Romanticism; Austrian Heimat literature. **SELECTED PUBLICATIONS** **CONTACT ADDRESS** Dept of Ger Lang, Brigham Young Univ, 4094 Jkhb, Provo, UT 84602-0002.

DAVIS, GREGSON

PERSONAL Born 10/20/1940, St. John's, Antigua, m, 1980, 4 children **DISCIPLINE** CLASSICS AND COMPARATIVE LITERATURE **EDUCATION** Harvard Univ, AB, 60; Univ Cal Berkeley, PhD, 68. **CAREER** Asst prof, Stanford Univ, 69-75; assoc prof, 75-85; prof, 85-89; prof, Cornell Univ, 89-94; prof, Duke Univ, 94- . **HONORS AND AWARDS** Latin Orator, Harvard Commencement, 60; Arthur D. Cory Travelling Fel, Harvard Univ, 61-63. **MEMBERSHIPS** Am Phil Asoc; MLA; Vergilian Soc; Caribbean Studies Asoc. **RESEARCH** Latin and Greek literature; Caribbean literature; rhetoric and poetics. **SELECTED PUBLICATIONS** Auth, Polyhymnia: The Rhetoric of Horatian Lyric Discourse, 91; auth, Desire and the Hunt in Ovid's Metamorphoses, The Burnett Lectures: A Quarter Century, 93; auth, Between Cultures: Toward a Redefinition of Liberal Education, African Studies and the Undergraduate Curriculum, 94; guest ed of spec issue, The Poetics of Derek Walcott: Intertextual Perspectives, South Atlantic Quart, 97; auth, Aime Cesaire, 97. **CONTACT ADDRESS** Dept. of Classical Studies, Duke Univ, 234A Allen Bldg., Durham, NC 27708-0103.

DAVIS, JACK L.

PERSONAL Born 08/13/1950, Wooster, OH **DISCIPLINE** CLASSICS **EDUCATION** Univ Akron, BA, 72; Univ Cincinnati, PhD, 77. **CAREER** Vis Fel, Fitzwilliam Col; Carl W. Blegen Chaired Prof, Univ Cincinnati, 93-; Asst prof, Univ Ill, 77-83; Assoc prof, 84-91; Prof, 91-93. **HONORS AND AWARDS** Silver Circle award, 82; AMOCO award, 82; Univ Scholar award, 85-87; Joanne Stolaroff Cotsen Prize; james rignall wheeler fel, eugene vanderpool fel. **MEMBERSHIPS** Archaeol Inst Am; Am Sch Classical Studies Athens; Institute for Aegean Prehistory; Archaeometry Comt; Nat Endowment Hum; Nat Hum Ctr. **SELECTED PUBLICATIONS** Co-ed, Papers in Cycladic Prehistory, UCLA, 79; auth, Period V, Meinz, 86; coauth, Landscape Archaeology as Long-Term History: Northern Keos in the Cycladic Islands, UCLA, 91; auth, Sandy Pylos: An Archaeological History from Nestor to Navarino, Univ of Tex Press, 98. **CONTACT ADDRESS** Dept of Classics, Univ of Cincinnati, PO Box 210226, Cincinnati, OH 45210-0226. **EMAIL** jack.davis@uc.edu

DAVIS, KENNETH G.

PERSONAL Born 09/16/1957, Louisville, KY **DISCIPLINE** PASTORAL THEOLOGY, CROSS-CULTURAL COMMUNICATION **EDUCATION** St. Louis Univ, BA, cum laude, 80; Washington Theol Union, MA, 85; Pacific Sch of Theol, DMin, 91. **CAREER** Deaconate in Honduras, 85-86; found dir, Hispanic ministry, 86-88; assoc pastor, St. Paul the Apostle Church, San Pablo, CA, 88-91; staff, intl office RENEW, 91-94; found dir, DMin, Oblate Sch Theol, 94-97; asst prof, Mundelein Sem, 97- . **MEMBERSHIPS** ACHTUS; Amer Acad Rel; Asn DMin Educ; CORHIM; Inst de Litugia Hispana; Nat Org Catechesis for Hispanics; Nalt Catholic Coun Hispanic Ministry. **RESEARCH** Religious faith of US Hispanics. **SELECTED PUBLICATIONS** Auth, Child Abuse in the Hispanic Community: A Christian Perspective, Apuntes, 12(3), Fall, 92, 127-136; Auth, Cuando El Tomar Ya No Es Gozar, LA, Franciscan Comm Press, 93; What's New in Hispanic Ministry, Overheard, Fall 93; auth, Primero Dios, Susquehanna UP, 94; Following the Yellow Brick Road: Rahner Reasons Through Petitionary Prayer, Living Light, 30(4), Summer, 94, 25-30; The Hispanic Shift: Continuity Rather than Conversion, in An Enduring Flame: Studies on Latino Popular Religiosity, NY, Bildner Ctr W Hemispheric Studs, 94, 205-210; The Hispanic Shift: Continuity Rather Than Conversion, Jour Hispanic/Latino Theol, 1(3), May 94, 68-79; Preaching in Spanish as a Second Language, in Perspectivas, Kansas City, Sheed and Ward, 95; Presiding in Spanish as a Second Language, AIM, Wint 95, 22-24; Encuentros, in New Catholic Encycl, vol 19, Wash DC, Catholic UP, 95; Afterward, in Discovering Latino Religion, NY, The Bildner Ctr W Hemispheric Studs, 95; Selected Pastoral Resources, in Perspectivas, Kansas City, Sheed and Ward, 95; Las Bodas de Plata de Una Lluvia de Oro, Revista Latinoamericana de Teologia, 12(37), April, 96, 79-91; coauth, The Attraction and Retention of Hispanics to Doctor of Ministry Programs, Theol Ed, 33(1), Autumn, 96, 75-82; Presiding in Spanish as a Second Language, in Misa, Mesa y Musa, Schiller Park, IL, J.S. Paluch Co, 97; Misa, Mesa y Musa, Schiller Park, IL, J. S. Paluch, 97; From Anecdote to Analysis: A Case for Applied Research in the Ministry, Pastoral Phychol, 46(2), 97, 99-106; La Catequesis ante la Experiencia Rligiosa, Catequetica, 1, 97, 3-8; Introduction, Listening: Jour of Rel and Cult 32(3), Fall, 97, 147-151; Challenges to the Pastoral Care of Central Americans in the United States, Apuntes 17(2), Summer 97, 45-56; A New Catholic Reformation? Chicago Studs, 36(3), Dec 97, 216-223; Petitionary Prayer: What the Masters Have to Say, Spiritual Life, Summer 97, 91-99; A Survey of Contemporary US Hispanic Catholic Theology, Theol Dig, 44(3), fall 97, 203-212; co-ed, Listening: Journal of Religion and Culture, vol 32, no 3, Fall, 97; co-ed, Chicago Studies, vol 36, no 3, Dec, 97; co-ed, Theol Today, vol 54, no 4, Jan, 98; Visions and Dreams, Theol Today, 54(4), Jan 98, 451-452. **CONTACT ADDRESS** Dept of Theology, Saint Meinrad Sch of Theol, 1 Hill Dr, Saint Meinrad, IN 47577. **EMAIL** kdavis@saintmeinrad.edu

DAVIS, STUART

PERSONAL Born 01/23/1957, San Francisco, CA **DISCIPLINE** LINGUISTICS **EDUCATION** Univ Calif, Los Angeles, BA, 79; Univ Arizona, MA, 81; PhD, 85. **CAREER** Asst Prof, 89-95, assoc prof, 95-, Ind Univ, Bloomington. **MEMBERSHIPS** Linguistic Soc of Am (LSA); Middle East Studies Asn (MESA). **RESEARCH** Linguistics; Diabetes. **SELECTED PUBLICATIONS** Auth, "On the Representation of Initial Geminates, Phonology, 16:93-104, 99; auth, "Emphasis Spread in Arabic and Grounded Phonology," Linguistic Inquiry 26, 465-498, 95. **CONTACT ADDRESS** Dept Linguistics, Indiana Univ, Bloomington, 1021 East 3rd St., Bloomington, IN 47405-7005. **EMAIL** davis@indiana.edu

DAVIS, WILLIAM

PERSONAL Born 06/08/1958, Ashland, Ore, m, 1988, 2 children **DISCIPLINE** COMPARATIVE LITERATURE; GERMAN **EDUCATION** Brigham Young Univ, BA, 81; Stanford Univ, MA, 82; Stanford Univ, PhD, 89. **CAREER** Asst prof Ger, Brigham Young Univ, 89-93; asst prof to assoc prof human, Colorado Col, 93- . **HONORS AND AWARDS** Fulbright. **MEMBERSHIPS** Mod Lang Asn; N Am Soc for Studenty of Romantics; Am Comp Lit Asn; Goethe Soc N Am. **RESEARCH** Romanticism, Philosophy and literature, Goethe, Novalis, British Romanticism. **SELECTED PUBLICATIONS** Auth, Frauenzimmerliche Handarbeiten: Reflections on Goethe's Poem 'Magisches Netz.'" Jahrbuch fur Int Germanistik 22, Heft 2:58-79, (91); auth, "Alittle Night Music: An Intertextual Reading of Goethe's 'Nachtgesang.' "Goethe Yearbook 6, 87-113, (92); auth, "Subjectivity and Exteriority in Goethe's 'Dauer im Wechsel.'" The German Quart 66.4, 452-467, (93); auth, " 'Menschwerdung der Menschen': Poetry and Truth in Hardenberg's Hymnen an die Nacht and the Jnal of 1797." Athendum: Jahrbuch fur Romantik 4: 239-259, (94); auth, "The Intensification of the Body in Goethe's Die Leiden des jungen Werther." The Ger Rev 69.3: 106-117, (94); " ' What More do You Want?': Iterability and Meaning in Lyric Texts." "Repetition, Readers, Irony." Der unzirtierbare Text, Bern: Lang Verlag: 69-74, 99-104, (97). **CONTACT ADDRESS** Dept English, Colo Col, 14 E Cache La Poudre St, Colorado Springs, CO 80903-3243. **EMAIL** wdavis@coloradocollege.edu

DAVISON, ALAN R.

DISCIPLINE SPANISH LITERATURE **EDUCATION** Univ Utah, BA, 81, PhD, 91; Univ Ca, MA, 85. **CAREER** Assoc prof. **SELECTED PUBLICATIONS** Auth, The Adventures of

Captain Harvey, Odyssey Shield, 97; El corno emplumado/The Plumed Horn: A Voice of the Sixties Textos Toledanos, 94. **CONTACT ADDRESS** Westminster Col of Salt Lake City, 1840 S 1300 E, Salt Lake City, UT 84105. **EMAIL** a-daviso@wcslc.edu

DAVISON, JEAN MARGARET
PERSONAL Born 04/19/1922, Glens Falls, NY **DISCIPLINE** CLASSICAL LANGUAGES, ANCIENT HISTORY **EDUCATION** Univ Vt, AB, 44; Yale Univ, AM, 50, PhD(class archaeol), 57; Univ Ital Stranieri, Perugia, dipl, 60. **CAREER** Cryptanalyst, US Dept War, 44-45; foreign serv clerk, US Dept State, Athens, 45-46 & Vienna, 47-49; instr ancient hist, Latin, Greek & Greek art, 55-59, from asst prof to prof, 59-72, Roberts Prof Class Lang & Lit, Univ VT, 72-, Am Philos Asn res grant, 67-68; mem managing comt, Am Sch Class Studies, Athens, 65, mem exec comt, 73, vis prof, 74-75. **MEMBERSHIPS** Archaeol Inst Am; Vergilian Soc Am; Class Asn New England; Am Sch Orient Res; Asn Field Archaeol. **RESEARCH** Greek Archaeology; Homeric studies; pre-Roman Italy. **SELECTED PUBLICATIONS** Auth, Vitruvius on Acoustical Vases in Greek and Roman Theaters, Amer Jour Archaeol, Vol 0100, 96. **CONTACT ADDRESS** Dept of Classics, Univ of Vermont, Burlington, VT 05401.

DAVISON, ROSENA
PERSONAL Born, United Kingdom **DISCIPLINE** FRENCH **EDUCATION** McGill Univ, BA, 71, MA, 74, PhD, 81. **CAREER** Asst prof, 92-90, assoc prof French, Simon Fraser Univ, 90-, dept ch, 91-94. **MEMBERSHIPS** MLA; Asn interdisciplinaire de recherche sur l'epistolaire; Can Soc Eighteenth Century Stud; Am Soc Eighteenth Century Stud; Asn des profs de francais aux univ et col can. **RESEARCH** France in the eighteenth century including literature, especially women writers, pedagogy and correspondence, salons, le journal intime. **SELECTED PUBLICATIONS** Auth, Diderot et Galiani: etude d'une amitie philosophique, 85; auth, Diderot, Galiani, et Vico: un itineraire philosophique (Diderot Studies, 88); co-ed, Man and Nature, vol 8, 90; auth, Mme d'Epinay's Contribution to Girls' Education, in Women Intellectuals of the French Eighteenth Century, 94; auth, "Conversations d'Emilie," in Studies on Voltaire and the Eighteenth Century, Vol. 342, (96). **CONTACT ADDRESS** Dept of French, Simon Fraser Univ, 8888 Univ Dr, Burnaby, BC, Canada V5A 1S6. **EMAIL** rosena_davison@sfu.ca

DAVISSON, MARY H. T.
PERSONAL Born 12/05/1952, Baltimore, MD, m, 1980, 3 children **DISCIPLINE** CLASSICS **EDUCATION** Brown Univ, AB, 74, MA, 74; Univ CA, Berkeley, PhD (Classics), 79. **CAREER** Asst prof, Univ VA, 81-83; adjunct asst prof, Loyola Col in Maryland, 84-. **HONORS AND AWARDS** Phi Beta Kappa; Sather Res assistantship, 75-76. **MEMBERSHIPS** Am Philol Asn; Classical Asn of the Middle West and South; Classical Asn of the Atlantic States; Am Classical League; Maryland Junior Classical League. **RESEARCH** Ovid; Virgil; pedagogy. **SELECTED PUBLICATIONS** Auth, Sed sum quam medico notior ipse mihi: Ovid's Use of Some Conventions in the Exile Epistles, Clasical Antiquity 2, 83; Magna Tibi Imposita Est Nostris Persona Libellis: Playwright and Actor in Ovid's Epistulae ex Ponto 3-1, Classical J 79, 84; Parents and Children in Ovid's Poems from Exile, Classical World 78, 84; Tristia 5-13 and Ovid's Use of Epistolary Form and Content, Classical J 80, 85; Quid moror exemplis?: Mythological Exempla in Ovid, Phoenix 47, 93; The Treatment of Festering Sores in Virgil, Classical World 86, 93; Mythological Exempla in Ovid's Remedia Amoris, Phoenix 50, 96; The Observers of Daedalus in Ovid, Classical World 90, 97. **CONTACT ADDRESS** Classics Dept, Loyola Col, 4501 N Charles St, Baltimore, MD 21210. **EMAIL** mdavisson@loyola.edu

DAVYDOV, SERGEI
DISCIPLINE RUSSIAN **EDUCATION** Charles Univ, AB; Ludwig Maximillian Univ, MA; Yale Univ, PhD. **CAREER** Prof; Middlebury Col, 88-. **RESEARCH** Literature; Alexander Pushkin; Vladimir Nabokov. **SELECTED PUBLICATIONS** Auth, Tekstymatreshki' Vladimira Nabokova, Slavistische Beitraege, Band 152, Munich: Otto Sagner, 82; The Passions of Young 'Sirin', NY Times Bk Rev, 90; Weighing Nabokov's The Gift on Pushkin's Scales, in Cult Mythologies of Russ Modernism: From the Golden Age to the Silver Age, Berkeley: Univ Calif Press, Calif Slavic Stud, 91; Pushkin i christianstvo, in Transactions of the Asn Russ Amer Scholars in USA, vol25, NY: 92-93 & Pushkin's Easter Triptych: 'Otcy pustynniki i zheny neporochny,'Podrazhanie italianskomu,' and 'Mirskaja vlast', in Pushkin Today, Indi UP, 93. **CONTACT ADDRESS** Dept of Russian, Middlebury Col, Middlebury, VT 05753. **EMAIL** Davydov@Middlebury.edu

DAWSON, ROBERT LEWIS
PERSONAL Born 07/26/1943, Buenos Aires, Argentina **DISCIPLINE** FRENCH LITERATURE, PORTUGUESE **EDUCATION** Trinity Col, BA, 65; Yale Univ, MPhil, 68, PhD(French), 72. **CAREER** Actg asst prof French & Ital, Univ Santa Clara, Calif, 70-72; asst prof, Rol lins Col, Fla, 73-75; asst prof, 75-78, Assoc Prof French, Univ Texas, Austin, 79-, Fel, La Fondation Camargo, Cassis, France, 72-73. **MEMBERSHIPS** Am Soc 18th Century Studies; Soc d-etude dix-huitieme siecle. **RESEARCH** Eighteenth-century French literature. **SELECTED PUBLICATIONS** Auth, Baculard d'Arnaud: life & prose fiction, Studies on Voltaire & 18th Century, 76; ed, International Directory of 18th Century Research and Scholars, Int Soc 18th Century Studies, 79; Additions to the Bibliographies of 17th and 18th Century French Prose Fiction, Voltaire Found, 88; auth, The French booktrade and the Pemission Sample of 1777, Studies in Voltaire, 92. **CONTACT ADDRESS** Dept of French & Ital, Univ of Texas, Austin, Austin, TX 78712-1026.

DAY, JAMES T.
PERSONAL Born 02/28/1948, St Louis, MO, m, 1990, 2 children **DISCIPLINE** FRENCH **EDUCATION** Princeton Univ, AB, 70; Univ Pa, PhD, 78. **CAREER** Lectr, Wash Univ, 78-79; asst prof, Univ Ga, 79-85; asst to assoc prof, Univ SCar, 85-. **HONORS AND AWARDS** Grant, Fr Govt, 87; SCar Honors Col Outstanding Humanites Prof, 91. **MEMBERSHIPS** MLA, Am Assoc of Teachers of Fr, Assoc des Amis d'Andre Gide. **RESEARCH** 19th and 20th century French literature, foreign language instruction. **SELECTED PUBLICATIONS** Auth, "The Hero as Reader in Stendhal," Fr Rev, 81; auth, "Student Motivation, Academic Validity, and the Summer Language Program Abroad," Mod Lang Jour, 87; auth, Stendhal's Paper Mirror, Peter Lang, 87; auth, "Stendhal," Dict of Lit Biog: Fr Authors 1800-1850, ed Catharine Savage Brosman, (Detroit: Gale Res, 92); coauth, "Foreign Language Curricular Needs of Students Preparing for an Internship Abroad," Mod Lang Jour, (93); coauth, Video Verite, Houghton Mifflin, 94; auth, "Gide, Stendhal et la sensibilite musicale," Bull des Amis d'Andre Gide, (96); auth, "A Story of Reading and Writing, or the Poetics of Self-Reference," Approaches to Teaching Stendhal's The Red and the Black, ed Stirling Haig and Dean de la Motte, (NY: MLA, 99); auth, "Theater, Texts, and Ambiguity in Gide's L'Immoraliste," Fr Rev, (02). **CONTACT ADDRESS** Dept Fr and Class, Univ of So Carolina, Columbia, Columbia, SC 29208. **EMAIL** james.t.day@sc.edu

DE ARMAS, FREDERICK A.
PERSONAL Born 02/09/1945, Havana, Cuba, s **DISCIPLINE** SPANISH **EDUCATION** Stetson Univ, BA, 65; Univ NC, PhD, 69. **CAREER** Asst Prof to Assoc Prof, La State Univ, 68-78; Vis Assoc Prof, Univ Mo, 77; Prof, La State Univ, 78-88; Vis Prof, Univ Mo, 86; Prof to Distinguished Prof, PaState Univ, 88-98; vis Prof, Duke Univ, 94; Prof, PaState Univ, 98-00; Prof, Univ Chicago, 00-. **HONORS AND AWARDS** Audrey Lumsden-Kouvel Fel, Newberry Library, 95; Nat Endowment for the Humanities, Penn State, 94; Nat Endowment for the Humanities summer stipend, Penn State, 89; Nat Endowment for the Humanities Fel, Newberry Library, 85; Nat Endowment for the Humanities summer stipend, 79. **MEMBERSHIPS** Am Asn of Teachers of spanish and Portuguese, Asn Internacional de Hispanistas, Mod Lang Asn, Renaissance Soc of Am. **RESEARCH** Spanish literature of the Golden Age, Relations between Italian Renaissance art, classical mythology and spanish literature. **SELECTED PUBLICATIONS** Auth, Cervantes, Raphael and the Classics, Cambridge Univ Press, 98; auth, The Return of Astraea: An Astral-Imperial Myth in Calderon, Univ Press of Kentucky, 86; auth, The Invisible Mistress. Aspects of Feminism and Fantasy in the Spanish Golden Age. Biblioteca Siglo de Oro, Charlottesville, 76; auth, Paul Scarron, Twayne's World Authors Series, No. 194, New York, 72; auth, The Four Interpolated Stories in the Roman Comique: Their sources and Unifying function, Univ of North Carolina, 71; ed, A Star-Crossed Golden Age: Myth and the Spanish comedia, Lewisburg, 98; ed, Heavenly Bodies: The Realms of 'La estrella de Sevilla', Lewisburg, 96; ed, The Prince in the Tower: Perceptions of 'La vida es suefio', Lewisburg, 93; ed, Critical Perspectives on Calderon de la Barca, Lincoln, 81; ed, Luis de Belmonte Bermudez, El sastre del Campillo. Coleccion Siglio de Oro, Chapel Hill, 75. **CONTACT ADDRESS** Dept Spanish & Ital, Pennsylvania State Univ, Univ Park, 352 Burrowes Bldg, University Park, PA 16802-6203.

DE CRUZ-SAENZ, MICHELE S.
PERSONAL Born 01/05/1949, Mt Vernon, NY, d, 2 children **DISCIPLINE** FRENCH, SPANISH **EDUCATION** Conn Col, AB, 71; Univ Pa, MA, 74; PhD, 76. **CAREER** Lectr, Univ of Pa, 74-76; lectr, Swarthmore Col, 74-76, lectr, Haverford Col, 75-76; asst prof, Beaver Col, 76-78; asst prof, George Washington Univ, 78-82; chair, For Lang Wallingford-Swarthmore School Dist, 82-. **HONORS AND AWARDS** APS Grants, 73, 76, 82; Ludwig Vogelstein Grant, 85; IMPACT Awd, 90; NEH, 90; Businessweek Awd, 91; Sp Govt Grant, 95. **MEMBERSHIPS** MLA, NEMLA, AATSP, ACTFL. **RESEARCH** Medieval French and Spanish Language and Literature, Spanish/Hispanic Romances, romance Philology. **SELECTED PUBLICATIONS** Auth, The Life of St Mary of Egypt, Purvill, (Barcelona), 76; auth, El Romancero tradicional de Costa Rica, Juan de la Cuesta, 86; auth, Resource Guide for Medieval Ballads of Hispania, Villanova, PA, 90; auth, Ms K-III-4, Hispanic Medieval Seminary, 92; auth, Traditional Ballads of Aragaon, Bushnell Univ Pr, 95. **CONTACT ADDRESS** 739 Windsor Pl, Wallingford, PA 19086-6730. **EMAIL** mcruzsaenz@aol.com

DE LEY, HERBERT C.
PERSONAL Born 11/24/1936, Altadena, CA, m, 1990, 1 child **DISCIPLINE** FRENCH **EDUCATION** Yale Univ, PhD, 63. **CAREER** Vis assoc prof French, Univ Cal-Riverside, 67-68, Univ Chicago, 69, UCLA, 76-77; prof of French, Univ Ill-Urbana, 77-; Chevalier, Palmas Academies, 93. **MEMBERSHIPS** MLA; NASSCFL. **RESEARCH** La Fontaine; Brantome; Saint Simon. **SELECTED PUBLICATIONS** Auth Marcel Proust et le duc de Saint-Simon, Univ Ill Press, 66; Saint-Simon Memorialist, Univ Ill Press, 75; The Movement of Thought, Univ Ill Press, 85; Le jeu classique, Jeu et theorie des jeux au Grand Siecle, Tubingen, 88; Fixing up Reality, La Fontaine and Levi-Strauss, Tubingen, 96. **CONTACT ADDRESS** Dept of French, Univ of Illinois, Urbana-Champaign, Urbana, IL 61801. **EMAIL** h_deley@staff.uiuc.edu

DE LOOZE, LAURENCE
DISCIPLINE FRENCH LITERATURE **EDUCATION** Univ Oregon, BA; Univ Toronto, MA; PhD. **RESEARCH** Medieval and Renaissance culture/literature; theories of autobiography and textuality, film; role of the poet; gender issues; metaphor and analogy. **SELECTED PUBLICATIONS** Auth, The Pseudo-Autobiography of the Fourteenth Century, 97; pub(s) on autobiography and subjectivity, film, Gustav Mahler, medieval literature and medievalism, Racine, and Wallace Stevens. **CONTACT ADDRESS** Dept of Modern Languages, Univ of Western Ontario, London, ON, Canada N6A 5B8. **EMAIL** ldelooze@julian.uwo.ca

DE RAFOLS, WIFREDO
DISCIPLINE SPANISH LITERATURE, CULTURE, AND LITERARY THEORY **EDUCATION** Johns Hopkins Univ, MA; Univ Calif, Davis, PhD. **CAREER** Assoc prof Span, dir, grad stud, Univ Nev, Reno. **RESEARCH** Hermeneutics; artificial reading. **SELECTED PUBLICATIONS** Published widely within his area of specialization -- 19th- and 20th-century Spanish literature; his publications examine works by Zorrilla, Perez Galdos, Valle-Inclan, and Jimenez. **CONTACT ADDRESS** Univ of Nevada, Reno, Reno, NV 89557. **EMAIL** fdrafols@unr.edu

DE TEJADA, CRISTINA SAENZ
DISCIPLINE SPANISH, LATIN AMERICAN LITERATURE **EDUCATION** Univ Central de Barcelona, Lic en Hist, 84; Pa State Univ, MA, 90; PhD, 94. **CAREER** Prof, Colegio La Salle Bonanoba, 85-88; TA, Pa State Univ, 88-92; vis asst prof, Bucknell Univ, 92-93; asst prof, Goucher Col, 94-. **HONORS AND AWARDS** Grant, Goucher Col; Who's Who Among Am Teachers, 00. **MEMBERSHIPS** AATSP, BRASA, MLA, ACTFL, LASA, Amnesty Int, Phi Sigma Iota. **RESEARCH** Brazilian Historical Narratives, Brazilian Women Writers, Cuban Writers of the Exile. **SELECTED PUBLICATIONS** Cotransl, of "Aprendizaje o el libro de los placeres," by Clarice Lispector, Siruela, (Madrid, 90); auth, "The Eternal Non-Difference: Clarice Lispector's Concept of Androgyny," Luso-Brazilian Rev 31.1, (94): 39-56; auth, "Autobiografia, identidad y ficcion en Mulher no Espelho," Travessia 29/30, (94-95): 225-248; auth, "Raza y Genero en la narrativa femenina afrobrasilena," Revista de Critica Literaria Latinoamericana XXIII.46, (97): 269-285; auth, "Ecologist and Ecofeminist Awareness in Agua Viva: A Brazilian Woman Rereading Nature," Brasil/Brazil 18.10, (97): 39-58; auth, "Yo tambien soy brasilena: Historia y sociedad en la obra de Carolina Maria de Jesus," Confluencia, Revista Hispanica de cultura y literatura, Univ of N Colo, 13.2, (98); auth, La (re)construccion de la identidad femenina en la narrativa autobiografica latinoamericana, Peter Lang, (NY, Berlin), 98; auth, "S Sumico da Santa: A Post-modern Reconstruction of Racial Dynamics in Contemporary Bahian Society," Jorge Amado: New Critical Essays, ed Keith Brower, Earl Fitz and Enrique Martinez-Vidal, (01): 203-220. **CONTACT ADDRESS** 1021 Dulaney Valley Rd, Goucher C, Baltimore, MD 21204-2753.

DEAGON, ANN FLEMING
PERSONAL Born 01/19/1930, Birmingham, AL, w, 1951, 2 children **DISCIPLINE** CLASSICS, CREATIVE WRITING **EDUCATION** Birmingham-Southern Col, BA, 50; Univ NC, MA, 51, PhD(Latin), 54. **CAREER** Asst prof classics, Furman Univ, 54-56; from asst prof to assoc prof, 56-75, prof Classics, Guilford Col, 75-92; Nat Endowment for Arts literary fel, 82. **MEMBERSHIPS** Am Philol Asn; Class Asn Midwest & S; Poetry Soc Am; Archaeological Inst Am. **SELECTED PUBLICATIONS** Auth, Poetics South, Blair, 74; Carbon 14, Univ Mass, 74; Indian Summer, Unicorn Press, 75; Women and Children First, Iron Mountain, 76; There is No Balm in Birmingham, Godine, 78; The Flood Story, Winthrop Col, 81; Habitats, Green River Press, 82; auth, The Diver's Tomb, St martins, 84; auth, The Polo Poems, Nebraska, 90. **CONTACT ADDRESS** 802 Woodbrook Dr, Greensboro, NC 27410. **EMAIL** anndeagon@worldnet.att.net

DEAN, DENNIS RICHARD
PERSONAL Born 05/29/1938, Belvidere, IL, m, 1968 **DISCIPLINE** ENGLISH, HISTORY OF SCIENCE **EDUCATION** Stanford Univ, AB, 60, AM, 62; Univ Wis-Madison, PhD(English), 68. **CAREER** Instr English, Kenosha Ctr, Univ Wis, 67-68; asst prof, 68-73, assoc prof English, 73-82, Prof English &

Humanities, Univ Wis-Parkside, 82-, Fulbright award, Korea, 77; NSF grant, New Zealand, 82. **MEMBERSHIPS** AAUP; Hist Sci Soc; Keats-Shelley Asn. **RESEARCH** Literature and science; British romantics; history of science, especially geology. **SELECTED PUBLICATIONS** Auth, The San-Francisco Earthquake of 1906, Annals of Sci, Vol 0050, 93. **CONTACT ADDRESS** Humanities Div, Univ of Wisconsin, Parkside, Kenosha, WI 53140.

DEARMAS, FREDERICK A.
PERSONAL Born 02/09/1945, Havana, Cuba, s **DISCIPLINE** COMPARATIVE LITERATURE, SPANISH **EDUCATION** Stetson Univ, BA, 65; Univ NCar Chapel Hill, PhD, 69. **CAREER** Asst prof to assoc prof to prof, La State Univ, 68-88; prof to distinguished prof to Edwin Erle Sparks prof, Penn State Univ, 89-00; prof to Andrew W. Mellon prof, Univ Chicago, 00-. **HONORS AND AWARDS** NEH Fel, 95; Dir NEH Summer Inst, 94. **MEMBERSHIPS** MLA; RSA; AIH. **RESEARCH** Early modern Spanish literature; comparative approaches; mythology; Italian art. **SELECTED PUBLICATIONS** Auth, Paul Scarron, Twayne (NYork), 72; auth, The Invisible Mistress: Aspects of Feminism and Fantasy in the Golden Age (Charlottesville), 76; auth, The Return of Astraca: An Astral-Imperial Myth in Calderon, Univ Ky Pr, 86; ed, The Prince in the Tower: Perspectives on 'La Vida es Sueno,' Bucknell UP, 93; ed, Heavenly Bodies: The Realms of 'La Estrella de Seville,' Bucknell UP, 96; auth, Cervantes, Raphael and the Classics, Cambridge Univ Pr, 98; ed, A Star-Crossed Golden Age: Myth and the Spanish Comedia, Bucknell UP, 98. **CONTACT ADDRESS** Romance Lang Dept, Univ of Chicago, 1050 E 59th St, Chicago, IL 60637-1559. **EMAIL** fdcarmas@uchicago.edu

DEBICKI, ANDREW PETER
PERSONAL Born 06/28/1934, Warsaw, Poland, m, 2 children **DISCIPLINE** SPANISH **EDUCATION** Yale Univ, BA, 55, PhD, 60. **CAREER** Instr Span, Trinity Col, Conn, 57-60; asst prof, Grinnell Col, 60-62, from assoc prof to prof Span, 62-68; prof, 68-76, Distinguished Prof Span, 76-, Vice-Chancellor, Res & Grad Studies, 94-96, Dean, Graduate School, 93-, Dean, Graduate School & Int Progs, Univ KS, 96-00; Fulbright grant, 66; fels, Am Coun Learned Soc, 66-67, Guggenheim, 71-72, 80 & Nat Humanities Ctr, 80, 92-93; NEH, 92-93; Bellagio, 93. **HONORS AND AWARDS** Prize, Hispania, 71; Teaching Awd, Univ KS, 72; Balfour Jeffrey Res Awd, Univ KS, 83. **MEMBERSHIPS** MLA; Am Asn Teachers Span & Port. **RESEARCH** Spanish and Latin American contemporary poetry; poetics and literary theory. **SELECTED PUBLICATIONS** Auth, La poesia de Jose Gorostiza, Andrea, Mex, 62; Estudios sobre poesia espanola: La generacion de 1924-1925, Gredos, Madrid, 68 & 81; Damaso Alonso, Twayne, 70 & Catedra, Madrid, 74; La poesia de Jorge Guillen, 73 & Poetas hispanoamericanos contemporaneos, 76, Gredos, Madrid; ed, Pedro Salinas, Taurus, Madrid, 76; Antologia de la poesia mexicana moderna, Tamesis, London, 77; Poetry of Discovery: The Spanish Generation of 1956-71, Kentucky, 82; Angel Gonzalez, Jucar, 89; Spanish Poetry of the Twentieth Century, KY, 94, Gredos, 97. **CONTACT ADDRESS** Spanish and Port, Univ of Kansas, Lawrence, Lawrence, KS 66045-0001. **EMAIL** adebicki@ukans.edu

DEBOO, EDWARD L.
PERSONAL Born 05/07/1967, Chicago, IL **DISCIPLINE** CLASSICS **EDUCATION** Knox Col, BA, 91; Brown Univ, MA; PhD, 01. **CAREER** Instr, Univ RI, 94-95, 01-. **HONORS AND AWARDS** Fel, Brown Univ Grad Res, 96-97; Fel, Javits Found, 91-95; Fel, Ford Found, 90; Phi Beta Kappa, 91. **MEMBERSHIPS** Am Philol Asn. **RESEARCH** Classical rhetoric and literary theory; Greco-Roman philosophic literature; Greek and Latin poetry; Roman comedy; Early Christianity. **SELECTED PUBLICATIONS** Auth, "Phrynichus Fragment 27K-A: A pun," Class Quart, 98. **CONTACT ADDRESS** Dept Classics, Univ of Rhode Island, 83 John St, Providence, RI 02903-1803. **EMAIL** Edward_DeBoo@Brown.edu

DEBRECZENY, PAUL
PERSONAL Born 02/16/1932, Budapest, Hungary, m, 1959, 2 children **DISCIPLINE** RUSSIAN LITERATURE **EDUCATION** Eotvos Univ, Hungary, BA, 53, BA, 55; Univ London, PhD(Russ), 60. **CAREER** Res asst Russ lit, Inst Lit Hist, Hungarian Acad Sci, 55-56; trans ed, Pergamon Press, Oxford, England, 59-60; asst prof Russ & chm dept, Tulane Univ, 60-66, assoc prof, 66-67; assoc prof, 67-74, chm dept, 74-79, prof Russ, 74-83, alumni distinguished prof Russ and Comp Lit, 83-99 , Univ NC, Chapel Hill; Emer, 99-. **HONORS AND AWARDS** Int Res & Exchanges Bd res fel, 73 & 82; Nat Endowment for Humanities fel, 78 & 79. **MEMBERSHIPS** Am Asn Teachers Slavic & EEurop Lang (vpres, 78-79); Am Asn Advan Slavic Studies; MLA; Southern Conf Slavic Studies (pres, 77). **RESEARCH** Nineteenth century Russian literature; comparative literature; sociology of literature. **SELECTED PUBLICATIONS** Auth, Niklolay Gogol and His Contemporary Critics, Am Philos Soc, 66; co-ed, Literature and National Identity: 19th Century Russian Critical Essays, Univ Nebr, 70; ed, 2 special issues devoted to Pushkin, Can-Am Slavic Studies, summer 76 & spring 77; co-ed, Chekhov's Art of Writing: A Collection of Critical Essays, Slavica Publ, 77; trans & ed, Alexander Pushkin: Complete Prose Fiction, 83 & auth, The Other Pushkin: A Study of Alexander Pushkin's Prose Fiction, 83, Stanford Univ Press; auth, Temptations of the Past, historical novel, Hermitage Publ, 82; co-ed, Russian Narrative and Visual Arts: Varieties of Seeing, 94; auth, Social Functions of Literature: Alexander Pushkin and Russian Culture, 97. **CONTACT ADDRESS** Dept of Slavic Lang, Univ of No Carolina, Chapel Hill, Chapel Hill, NC 27599-3165. **EMAIL** pdebrecz@email.unc.edu

DECK, ALLAN F.
PERSONAL Born 04/19/1945, Los Angeles, CA, s **DISCIPLINE** THEOLOGY; LATIN AMERICAN STUDIES **EDUCATION** St Louis Univ, BA, 69, PhD, 74; Jesuit Sch of Theol at Berkeley, MDiv, 76; Gregorian Univ, STD, 88. **CAREER** Admin, Our Lady of Guadalupe Church, 76-79; Dir, Hispanic Ministry, Diocese of Orange, 79-85; Asst Prof of Theology, Jesuit Sch of Theol, 87-92; Assoc Prof of Theol, Loyola Marymt Univ, 92-96; Exec Dir, Loyola Inst for Spirituality, 97-. **HONORS AND AWARDS** Catholic Press Asn 1st Place Awd Pro Book Category, 89. **MEMBERSHIPS** Acad of Catholic Hispanic Theol of the US, (co-founder & 1st pres); Nat Catholic Counc for Hisp Ministry, (co-founder & 1st pres). **RESEARCH** Hispanic religious expressions & spirituality, faith and culture. **SELECTED PUBLICATIONS** Auth, Francisco Javier Alegre: A Study in Mexican Literary Criticism, Historical Inst of the Soc of Jesus, 76; auth, The Second Wave, Paulist Press, 89; auth, Perspectivas: Hispanic Ministry, Sheed & Ward, 95; Hispanic Catholic Culture in the US, Univ Notre Dame Press, 94. **CONTACT ADDRESS** 480 S Batavia St, Orange, CA 92868. **EMAIL** deck8@juno.com

DECOSTA-WILLIS, MIRIAM
PERSONAL Born 11/01/1934, Florence, AL, w, 1972 **DISCIPLINE** SPANISH **EDUCATION** Wellesley Coll, BA 1956; Johns Hopkins Univ, MA 1960, PhD 1967. **CAREER** Owen Coll, instructor 1960-66; Memphis State Univ, assoc prof of Spanish 1966-70; Howard Univ, assoc prof of Spanish 1970-74, prof & chmn of dept 1974-76; LeMoyne-Owen Coll, prof, Romance Languages, prof of Spanish & dir of DuBois program, 79-88. **HONORS AND AWARDS** Phi Beta Kappa 1956; Johns Hopkins Fellowship 1965. **MEMBERSHIPS** Mem, Coll Language Assn; bd of dirs, MSU Center for Rsch on Women; chair TN Humanities Council; bd Federation of State Humanities Councils; editorial bd Sage & Afro-Hispanic Review; life mem NAACP; chmn, Exec bd/mem, TN Humanities Council, 1981-87; chmn & founding mem, Memphis Black Writers' Workshop, 1980-. **SELECTED PUBLICATIONS** Ed, Blacks in Hispanic Literature Kennikat Pr 1977; articles in CLAJ, Journal of Negro History, Black World Negro History Bulletin, Revista Interamericana, Caribbean Quart; Sage Afro-Hispanic Review; Outstanding Faculty Mem of the Year, LeMoyne-Owen Coll, 1982; Homespun Images: An Anthology of Black Memphis Writers & Artists, 1988; editor, The Memphis Diary of Ida B Wells, Beacon Press, 1994. **CONTACT ADDRESS** Visiting Commonwealth Prof of Spanish, George Mason Univ, Fairfax, Dept of Foreign Languages & Literature, Fairfax, VA 22030.

DEE, JAMES H.
PERSONAL Born 12/30/1943, Albany, NY, m, 1969, 1 child **DISCIPLINE** PHILOLOGY **EDUCATION** Univ Rochester, AB, 66; Univ Tex at Austin, PhD, 72. **CAREER** Asst prof to prof emer, Univ Ill at Chicago, 72-. **HONORS AND AWARDS** NEH Fel in Residence, 77-78; NEH Fel for Col Teachers, 89-90. **MEMBERSHIPS** Am Philol Asn; Class Asn of the Mid Wand S. **RESEARCH** Homeric diction and lexicography; Latin literature. **SELECTED PUBLICATIONS** Auth, Epithetic Phrases for the Homeric Gods, Garland Pub, 94; auth, Lexicon of Latin Derivatives in Italian, Spanish, French, and English, 2 Vols, Olms-Weidmann, 97; auth, Epitheta Hominum apud Homerum, Olms-Weidmann, 00; auth, Vocabula Homerica: Four Sets of Word-Frequency Lists for the Iliad and the Odyssey, Olms-Weidmann, 01. **CONTACT ADDRESS** 7004 Juneberry Cove, Austin, TX 78750. **EMAIL** jhdee1243@aol.com

DEFOREST, MARY MARGOLIES
PERSONAL Born 09/11/1946, Washington, DC, s **DISCIPLINE** CLASSICS **EDUCATION** Holyoke Col, BA, 67; Univ Chicago, MA, 70; Univ Colo Boulder, PhD, 81. **CAREER** Teaching asst, Univ Colo Boulder, 76-81; asst prof, Creighton Col, 81-81; asst prof, Hamilton Col, 82-89; vis asst prof, Univ Iowa, 89-90; lectr, Wayne State Univ, 90-91; vis asst prof, Creighton Univ, 91; lectr, Wayne State Univ, 92; vis asst prof, Univ Colo Boulder, 92-96; vis asst prof, Metropolitan State Col, 96-97; instr, Univ Colo Denver, 00-. **HONORS AND AWARDS** Feminist Essay Prize, Rocky Mountain, MLA, 93; Summer Res Grant, Hamilton Col, 88; Cornelia Coulter Award, Holyoke Col, 67. **MEMBERSHIPS** RMMLA; ACLA. **RESEARCH** Classical literature and the classical tradition. **SELECTED PUBLICATIONS** Auth, "Mary Poppins and the Great Mother," Class and Mod Lit, (91): 139-154; auth, "Eighteenth-Century Women and the Languages of Power," Class and Mod Lit, (92): 191-207; ed, Women's Power, Man's Game: Essays in Honor of Joy King, Wauconda, 93; auth, "Clytemnestra's Breast and the Evil Eye," in Women's Power, Man's Game: Essays in Honor of Joy King, Wauconda, 93; auth, "Female Choruses in Greek Tragedy," Didaskalia, 98. **CONTACT ADDRESS** Dept Class, Univ of Colorado, Denver, 1220 Marion St, Denver, CO 80218. **EMAIL** crypto@ecentral.com

DEFRANCIS, JOHN
PERSONAL Born 08/31/1911, Bridgeport, CT, m, 1938, 1 child **DISCIPLINE** CHINESE **EDUCATION** Yale Univ, BA, 33; Columbia Univ, MA, 41, PhD(Chinese), 48. **CAREER** Asst prof Chinese, Seton Hall Univ, 62-66; prof, 66-76, Emer Prof Chinese, Univ Hawaii, Manoa, 76-, Assoc ed, J Am Orient Soc, 50-55. **HONORS AND AWARDS** Am Philos Soc grant, 51-52; Soc Sci Res Conn & Am Coun Learned Soc grants Chinese math, 59-63; US Off Educ grants, 62-67. **MEMBERSHIPS** Chinese Lang Teachers Asn; MLA; Am Orient Soc. **CONTACT ADDRESS** Dept of E Asian Lang and Lit, Univ of Hawaii, Manoa, 1890 E-W Rd, Moore Hall 382, Honolulu, HI 96822. **EMAIL** johnd@hawaii.edu

DEGRAFF, AMY
DISCIPLINE FRENCH CIVILIZATION, FRENCH CONVERSATION, FRENCH LITERATURE **EDUCATION** Sorbonne, Univ Paris, Diplome d'Etudes Superieures; Univ Va, PhD. **CAREER** Assoc prof Fr, ch, dept Romance Lang, Randolph-Macon Col. **RESEARCH** Psychological criticism in film and literature; the 17th century French fairy tale **SELECTED PUBLICATIONS** Auth, The Tower and the Well: A Psychological Interpretation of the Fairy Tales of Mme d'Aulnoy; From Glass Slipper to Glass Ceiling, or 'Cinderella', the Endurance of a Fairy Tale, Merveilles et Contes. **CONTACT ADDRESS** Dept of Romance Lang, Randolph-Macon Col, Ashland, VA 23005-5505. **EMAIL** adegraff@rmc.edu

DEHON, CLAIRE L.
PERSONAL Born 12/17/1941, Uccle, Belgium, m **DISCIPLINE** FRENCH **EDUCATION** Inst Hist I'Art, Brussels, MA, 64; Univ KS, MA, 69, PhD, 73. **CAREER** From Asst Prof to Assoc Prof, 72-89, Prof French, KS State Univ, 89. **HONORS AND AWARDS** Nat Endowment for Hum fel, 81-82; Phi Beta Kappa. **MEMBERSHIPS** Am Asn Tchr(s) Fr; African Lit Asn; ALSC; KFLA; MAAAS. **RESEARCH** Novels in French in Black Africa. **SELECTED PUBLICATIONS** Auth, Le theatre d'Emile Verhaeren: quelques interpretations, Le Flambeau, 75; Allegory in E Verhaeren plays, Philol Quart, 7/78; La Dame du photographe: sa structure, son sens, Rev Pacifique, fall 78; Corinne: une artiste heroine de roman, 19th Cent Fr Studies, 80; Colette and Art Nouveau, Colette, the Woman, the Writer, 81; De Nouvelles Valeurs dous le roman camerounais, Presence Francophone 26, 85; Les Influences de la Litterature Traditionnelle sur le roman camerounais, Neohelicon, 16.2, 89; Le roman camerounais d'expression Francaise, SUMMA, 89; Le Roman en Afrique noire francophone, French Rev 68.6, 95; Women in Black African Novels in French, NWSA 8.1, 96; auth, Le Realisme Africain: Le Roman Francophonen Afrique Sub-Sakarienne, Harmattan, 01. **CONTACT ADDRESS** Dept of Mod Lang, Kansas State Univ, 104 Eisenhower Hall, Manhattan, KS 66506-2800. **EMAIL** dehoncl@ksu.edu

DEHORATIUS, EDMUND F.
PERSONAL Born Philadelphia, PA **DISCIPLINE** CLASSICAL LANGUAGES **EDUCATION** Duke Univ, BA, 95. **CAREER** Tchr, Bancroft Sch, 95- , dept chemn, 89- . **HONORS AND AWARDS** MA For Lang Asn, David Taggart Clancy Prize, Chester Middlesworth Awd, Duke Univ. **MEMBERSHIPS** APA, Class Asn New England; Medieval Acad Am; Renaissance Soc Am. **RESEARCH** Classical tradition; paleography; Latin literature; pedagogy. **CONTACT ADDRESS** 102 Central St., Concord, MA 01742-2911. **EMAIL** edehorat@bancroft.pvt.k12.ma.us

DEINERT, HERBERT
PERSONAL Born 12/13/1930, Germany, m, 1957, 2 children **DISCIPLINE** GERMAN LITERATURE **EDUCATION** Yale Univ, PhD(Ger lit), 60. **CAREER** Asst prof Ger lit, Univ Ga, 59-61 & Duke Univ, 61-65; chmn dept, 68-74, Prof Ger Lit, Cornell Univ, 74-, Consult, Nat Endowment for Humanities, 74-78. **MEMBERSHIPS** MLA; Am Asn Teachers Ger; German Studies Assoc; Goethe Soc of North America. **RESEARCH** Baroque; 19th century realism; the 20th century; Intellectual History. **SELECTED PUBLICATIONS** Auth, Colonialism and the Postcolonial Condition, Pmla-Pub(s) Mod Lang Assn Am, Vol 0110, 95; Crazy Ideas--Heilbrun Method in Madness--Comment, Opera News, Vol 0058, 94; Boehme--An Intellectual Biography of the 17th-Century Philosopher And Mystic, Jour Eng and Ger Philol, Vol 0093, 94; Dithyrambists of the Fall--Gnosticism in Modern Aesthetics and Philosophy--German, Jour Eng and Ger Philol, Vol 0095, 96; auth, "Pelikan Faust the Theologian," JEGP vol 97, 198; auth, "The Protestant Revolution," Dimensions, Verlag Van Acken, 93. **CONTACT ADDRESS** Dept of Ger Lit, Cornell Univ, Ithaca, NY 14853. **EMAIL** hd11@cornell.edu

DEKEYSER, R. M.
DISCIPLINE LINGUISITICS **EDUCATION** Stanford Univ, PhD, (Education), 86. **CAREER** Vis asst prof, 88-91, asst prof, 91-97, assoc prof, Linguistics Dept, Univ Pittsburgh, 97-. **HONORS AND AWARDS** ACTFL Emma Birkmaier Awd for

doctoral dissertation res on foreign lang ed, 87; Mellon Fel, Inst for Advance Studies Prog, administered by the Nat Foreign Lang Center, 97. **MEMBERSHIPS** AAAL; TESOL. **RESEARCH** Second lang acquisition; cognitive psychology. **SELECTED PUBLICATIONS** Auth, The Effect of Error Correction on Grammar Knowledge and Oral Proficiency, The Modern Language J, 77, 93; How Implicit Can Adult Second Language Learning Be?, AILA Rev, 11, 94; Learning Second Language Grammar Rules: An Experiment with a Miniature Linguistic System, Studies in Second Language Acquisition, 17, 95; The Differential Role of Comprehension and Production Practice, Language Learning, 46, 96; Beyond Explicit Rule Learning: Automatizing Second Language Morphosyntax, Studies in Second Language Acquisition, 19, 97; Beyond Focus on Form: Cognitive Perspectives on Learning and Practicing Second Language Grammar, in C Doughty & J Williams, eds, Focus on Form in Classroom Language Acquisition, Cambridge Univ Press, 98; auth, The robustness of critical period effects in second language acquision, Studies in Second Language Acquisition 22 (00): 499-533; coauth, Explaining the natural order of L2 morpheme acquision in English: A meta-analysis of multiple determinants, Language Learning 5 (01): 1-50. **CONTACT ADDRESS** Dept of Linguistics, Univ of Pittsburgh, Pittsburgh, PA 15260. **EMAIL** rdk1@pitt.edu

DEKYDTSPOTTER, LAURENT

DISCIPLINE FRENCH LITERATURE **EDUCATION** Cornell Univ, PhD, 95. **CAREER** Asst prof, Ind Univ. **HONORS AND AWARDS** Nat Sci Found funding. **SELECTED PUBLICATIONS** Auth, The Syntax and Semantics of the French Ne Que Construction, 93; Nested Variable and Locality, 92; The Syntax of Predicate Clefts, 91. **CONTACT ADDRESS** Dept of French and Ital, Indiana Univ, Bloomington, 1020 E Kirkwood Ave, Ballantine Hall 642, Bloomington, IN 47405. **EMAIL** ldekydts@indiana.edu

DEL CARO, ADRIAN

PERSONAL Born 12/29/1952, Eveleth, MN, m, 1985, 1 child **DISCIPLINE** GERMAN, GERMAN LITERATURE, COMPARATIVE LITERATURE **EDUCATION** Univ Minn, MA, 77, PhD, 79. **CAREER** Lect, Univ Calif, Riverside, 79-80; from asst prof to assoc prof to prof, 80-92, La State Univ; prof, chamn, Univ Colo, Boulder, 92-. **HONORS AND AWARDS** Graduate School Dissertation Fel, 87-79; phd with distinction, 79. **MEMBERSHIPS** Am Asn Tchrs German; Modern Lang Asn; N Am Heine Soc; N Am Nietzsche Soc; German Stud Asn; Am Asn Univ Profs. **RESEARCH** Late 18th, 19th, 20th, century literature and thought; literature and philosophy; poetry. **SELECTED PUBLICATIONS** Auth, Nietzsche contra Nietzsche: Creativity and the Anti-Romantic, 89; auth, Holderlin: The Poetics of Being, 91; auth, Hugo von Hofmannsthal: Poets and the Language of Life, 93; auth, The Early Poetry of Paul Celan: In the beginning was the word, 97; auth, art, Nietzsche, Sacher-Masoch, and the Whip, 98; co-ed, Geman Studies in the Post-Holocaust Age, 00. **CONTACT ADDRESS** 886 W Chestnut Cir, Louisville, CO 80027. **EMAIL** adrian.delcaro@colorado.edu

DEL PLIEGO, JOSE B.

PERSONAL Born 07/16/1970, Madrid, Spain **DISCIPLINE** SPANISH **EDUCATION** Univ Autonoma de Madrid, BA, 94; ABD, 96; Univ Complutense de Madric, Applied Linguistics, 95. **CAREER** Instr, Tutorlingua Lang Sch, 95-97; instr, La Corrala, 96-97; instr, Tulane Univ, 97-98; instr, CARE-USA, 01. **HONORS AND AWARDS** Univ Autonoma de Madrid Fel, 94-96. **MEMBERSHIPS** MLA. **RESEARCH** 20th century Spanish literature, Literary relationships between Spain and Latin America, Avant-garde theory. **SELECTED PUBLICATIONS** Coauth, "Presupuesto editorial," La escena alternativa. Actas de los Encuentros de Editories Independientes; auth, "Juan Larrea. Continuidad y cambio en los escritos de la Guerra Civil," Sesenta anos despues, La cultura del exilio Vasco, (00); ed, Juan Larrea: Orbe, El Signo del Gorrion 21, (00); auth, "Juan Larrea: su razon de ser en el contexto actual de la literatura espanola," hablar/Falar de poesia 4, (01); auth, "Juan Larrea: cubismo y discurso poetico del Nuevo Mundo, Sesenta anos despues, La cultura del exilio republicando espanol de 1939, (01). **CONTACT ADDRESS** 1078 Lanier Blvd, Atlanta, GA 30306-3569. **EMAIL** jdelpl@hotmail.com

DEL VALLE, JOSE

DISCIPLINE SPANISH AND PORTUGUESE **EDUCATION** SUNY at Buffalo, MA, 90; Georgetown Univ, PhD, 94. **CAREER** Asst prof, Miami Univ **RESEARCH** Spanish historical linguistics; history of Hispanic linguistics; minority languages. **SELECTED PUBLICATIONS** Auth, El trueque s/x en espanol antiguo: Aproximaciones teoricas, Tubingen, Germany: Max Niemeyer, 96; Modern linguistics in Menendez Pidal, In Multiple Perspectives on the Historical Dimension of Language, Munster, Germany: Nodus, 96; La historificacion de la linguestica historica: Los oregenes de Ramon Menendez Pidal, Historiographia Ling 24, 97. **CONTACT ADDRESS** Dept of Spanish and Portugise, Miami Univ, Oxford, OH 45056. **EMAIL** delvalj@miavx1.muohio.edu

DELGADO, LUISA ELENA

DISCIPLINE SPANISH LITERATURE **EDUCATION** Univ Calif Santa Barbara, PhD, 89. **CAREER** Assoc prof, Univ Ill Urbana Champaign. **RESEARCH** Modern and contemporary Spanish literature; Spanish culture and film; literary theory. **SELECTED PUBLICATIONS** Auth, El interes del relato: Estrategias narrativas en la serie de Torquemada, Anales Galdosianos, 90; El derecho de revision: La de Bringas y el discurso de la alienacion femenina, Romance Lang Annual, 92; Palabras contra palabras: el lenguaje de la historia en Tirano Banderas, Anthropos, 92; Mas estragos que las revoluciones: detallando lo feminino en La de Bringas, Rev Hispanica Moderna, 95; Cambiando de genero: lenguaje e identidad en dos textos galdosianos, Insula, 95; Pliegos de (des)cargo: las paradojas discursivas de La incognita, 96. **CONTACT ADDRESS** Spanish, Italian, and Portuguese Dept, Univ of Illinois, Urbana-Champaign, 52 E Gregory Dr, Champaign, IL 61820. **EMAIL** ldelgado@uiuc.edu

DELISLE, JEAN

PERSONAL Born 04/13/1947, Hull, PQ, Canada **DISCIPLINE** TRANSLATION STUDIES, HISTORY **EDUCATION** Laval Univ, BA, 68; Univ Montreal, LTrad, 71, MTrad, 75; Sorbonne Nouvelle (Paris), DTrad, 78. **CAREER** Prof, School Transl & Interpretation, Univ Ottawa, 74-. **HONORS AND AWARDS** Can Coun schol, 76. **MEMBERSHIPS** Soc traducteurs Que, 72-92; Union ecrivains que, 87-94; Can Asn Transl Stud, 87- (pres 91-93); pres, Comt Hist Transl, 90-. **SELECTED PUBLICATIONS** Auth, L'Analyse du discours comme methode de traduction, 80; auth, Les Obsedes textuels, 83; auth, Au coeur du trialogue canadien/Bridging the Language Solitudes, 84; auth, La Traduction au Canada/Translation in Canada 1534-1984, 87; auth, The Language Alchemists, 90; auth, La Traduction raisonee, 93; coauth, Bibliographic Guide for Translators, Writers and Terminologists, 79; coauth, International Directory of Historians of Translation, 3rd ed 96; ed, L'enseignement de l'interpretation et de la traduction: de la theorie a la pedagogie, 81; ed, Les Traducteurs dans l'histoire, 95; ed, Translators Through History, 95. **CONTACT ADDRESS** School of Transl & Interpretation, Univ of Ottawa, 70 Laurier Ave E, Room 401, PO Box 450, Station A, Ottawa, ON, Canada K1N 6N5. **EMAIL** jdelisle@uottawa.ca

DELLANEVA, JOANN

PERSONAL Born 02/28/1955, Philadelphia, PA, m, 1983, 1 child **DISCIPLINE** FRENCH, ITALIAN, COMPARATIVE LITERATURE **EDUCATION** Bryn Mawr Col, AB, 76; Univ Pa, MA, 78; Princeton Univ, MA, 80; PhD, 82. **CAREER** From Asst Prof to Assoc Prof, Univ Notre Dame, 82-. **HONORS AND AWARDS** NEH Fel for Col Teachers, 87, 92. **MEMBERSHIPS** Renaissance Soc of Am, Sixteenth-Century Studies Conf, Am Asn of Teachers of Fr, Am Asn of Ital Studies. **RESEARCH** French Renaissance poetry, Franco-Italian literary relations in the Renaissance, petrarchism, Renaissance imitation theory, women writers of the Renaissance, Maurice Sceve, Pleiade poets. **SELECTED PUBLICATIONS** Auth, Song and Counter-Song: Sceve's Delie and Petrarch's Rime, Fr Forum (Lexington), 83; auth, "Reflecting Lesser Lights: The Imitation of Minor Authors in the Renaissance," Renaissance Quart, 42 (89): 449-479; auth, "Image and (Un)Likeness: Mirroring Other Texts in Sceve's 'Delie'," A Sceve Celebration: Delie 1544-1994 (Saratoga, CA: Anma Libri, 94), 43-54; auth, "Petrarch at the Portal: Opening Signals," in Rivista de Letterature Moderne e Comparate, 50 (97): 259-272; auth, "Teaching De Bellay A Lesson: Ronsard's Rewriting of Ariosto's Sonnets," Fr Forum, 24 (99): 285-301. **CONTACT ADDRESS** Dept Lang, Univ of Notre Dame, 343 O'Shaugnessy Hall, Notre Dame, IN 46556-5639. **EMAIL** dellaneva.1@nd.edu

DELLEPIANE, ANGELA B.

PERSONAL Born 05/13/1926, Rio Cuarto, Argentina, m, 1962 **DISCIPLINE** SPANISH AMERICAN LITERATURE **EDUCATION** Univ Buenos Aires, MA, 48, PhD, 52. **CAREER** Prof Latin, Teacher's Col, Buenos Aires, 48-57; asst prof Span lit, Fordham Univ, 61-63; from asst prof to assoc prof philol, phonetics & Span lit, 63-72, Prof Span Am Lit, City Col New York, 73-; Prof emer, Prof Span Am Lit, Grad Ctr, City Univ New York, 69-. **HONORS AND AWARDS** Consult & panelist, Fel Div, Nat Endowment for Humanities, 77-79; vis prof, Univ Ky, 78. **MEMBERSHIPS** Int Inst Ibero-Am Lit; Asn Int de Hispanistas; Am Asn Teachers Span & Port; Latin Am Studies Asn. **RESEARCH** Spanish American narrative; Gauchesca literature; structural stylistics. **SELECTED PUBLICATIONS** Auth, A Tribute to Earle, Peter,G., Hisp Rev, Vol 0061, 93. **CONTACT ADDRESS** Span Doctoral Frog Grad Ctr, Graduate Sch and Univ Ctr, CUNY, 33 W 42nd St, New York, NY 10016-4309.

DELLINGER, MARY ANN

PERSONAL Born 01/22/1949, Lancaster, PA, m, 1994, 1 child **DISCIPLINE** LINGUISTICS, SPANISH **EDUCATION** Univ NM, BA, 71; Univ Ariz, MA, 93; Ariz State Univ, MA, 01. **CAREER** Instr, Univ Phoenix, 94-01; asst prof, Vir Mil Inst, 01-. **MEMBERSHIPS** AATSP; AHH; ALSC; MLA. **RESEARCH** Twentieth-century Spanish; female essayists of Spain; Spanish Civil War; 1939 exile; Franco era; pedagogy; writing as a process and the incorporation of authentic literature in lower division Spanish courses. **SELECTED PUBLICATIONS** Auth, Sendas literarias: Manual de asesoramiento, Heinle and Heinle, 97; auth, Sendas literarias: Cuaderno de lenguaje y practica, Heinle and Heinle, 98; contrb auth, En espanol! Teacher's Manual, McDougal Little, 98; auth, Sendas literarias: Manual de Asesoramiento, 2nd ed, Prentice Hall; co-auth, Sendas literarias: Cuaderno delenguaje y practica, Prentice Hall, 01; co-auth, Sendas literarias I, 2nd ed, Prentice Hall, 01; co-auth, Sendas literarias II, 2nd ed, Prentice Hall, 01; co-auth, Vistas: Introduccion a la lengua Espanola, Vista Higher Learn (01). **CONTACT ADDRESS** 8340 N Thornydale, Ste 110-264, Tucson, AZ 85741. **EMAIL** mj12@ix.netcom.com

DELPECHE, BERNARD

PERSONAL Born 01/04/1954, Haiti, d, 1 child **DISCIPLINE** LITERATURE, LANGUAGE, FRENCH **EDUCATION** Univ Man, BA, 88; Univ Brit Colum, MA, 92; Univ Toronto, PhD, 96. **CAREER** Asst prof, Univ Toronto, 96-98; asst prof, Univ Guelph, 98-00; asst prof, Acadia Univ, 00-. **HONORS AND AWARDS** Louise Bennett Awd, 94. **MEMBERSHIPS** MLA; Cief. **RESEARCH** Francophone literature; 20th-century French literature; post colonial literature. **CONTACT ADDRESS** English Dept, Acadia Univ, PO Box 6853, Wolfville, NS, Canada B0P 1E1. **EMAIL** bernard.delpeche@acadia.ca

DEMBOWSKI, PETER FLORIAN

PERSONAL Born 12/23/1925, Warsaw, Poland, m, 1954, 3 children **DISCIPLINE** ROMANCE PHILOLOGY **EDUCATION** Univ BC, BA, 52; Univ Paris, DUniv, 54; Univ Calif, Berkeley, PhD, 60. **CAREER** Instr French & Russ, Univ BC, 54-56; from asst prof to assoc prof French, Univ Toronto, 60-66; assoc prof French & ling, 66-69, dean students, Div Humanities, 68-70, Prof French, Univ Chicago, 69-, Chmn Dept Romance Lang & Lit, 76-83; Distinguished service prof, 89-95, emeritus, 95-; Guggenheim fel, 70-71; resident master, Smell & Hitchcock Halls, Univ Chicago, 73-79; vis mem, Sch Hist Studies, Inst Advanced Study, Princeton, 79-80. **HONORS AND AWARDS** Chevalier, Acad Palms, France, 81; Fel, Am Acad of Arts and Science, 90; the Norman Macdlean fac award, Univ Chicago. **MEMBERSHIPS** Soc Ling Romane; Mediaeval Acad Am. **RESEARCH** Linguistics; medieval French literature; Old French hagiography. **SELECTED PUBLICATIONS** Auth, La Chronique de Robert de Clari, Univ Toronto, 63; auth, Ami et Amile, Chanson de Geste: Classiques Francais du Moyen Age, Champion Paris, 68; auth, Jourdain de Blaye: Chanson de Geste, Univ Chicago & London, 69; auth, La Vie de Sainte Marie l'Egyptienne: Version en Ancien et Moyen Francais, Droz (Geneva-Paris), 77; auth, Jean Froissart and his Meliador, French Forum (Lexington), 77; auth, La Paradis d'Amour et l'Orloge Amoureus, Droz (Geneva), 86; auth, "Erec et Enide, edition et traduction en francais moderne," in Chretien de Troyes (OEuvres completes, Gallimard, Paris, 94); L'Estrif de Fortune et Vertu, Droz (Geneva), 99. **CONTACT ADDRESS** Dept of Romance Lang, Univ of Chicago, Chicago, IL 60637.

DEMERS, RICHARD ARTHUR

PERSONAL Born 09/10/1941, Portland, OR, 2 children **DISCIPLINE** LINGUISTICS **EDUCATION** Ore State Univ, BA, 63; Univ Wash, MA, 65, PhD(Ger), 68. **CAREER** Asst prof ling, Univ Mass, Amherst, 68-73, assoc prof, 74-75; assoc prof, 75-80, Prof Ling, Univ Ariz, 80-, Fel, Mass Inst Technol, 71-72; reader squibs & arts, Ling Inquiry & mem bd ed, Ling Anal, 74-. **MEMBERSHIPS** Ling Soc Am. **RESEARCH** Lummi (structure, syntax, grammar) 1972 to present; Old Icelandic phonology 1973 to present; native American languages of Arizona 1975 to present. **SELECTED PUBLICATIONS** Auth, Predicates and Pronominal Arguments in Straits Salish, Lang, Vol 0070, 94. **CONTACT ADDRESS** Dept of Ling Math, Univ of Arizona, P O Box 210028, Tucson, AZ 85721-0028.

DENDLE, BRIAN JOHN

PERSONAL Born 03/30/1936, Oxford, England, m, 1962, 2 children **DISCIPLINE** SPANISH **EDUCATION** Oxford Univ, BA, 58, MA, 62; Princeton Univ, MA, 64, PhD(Romance lang), 66. **CAREER** Instr French, Kenyon Col, 61-63; instr Span, Princeton Univ, 66; asst prof, Univ Mich, 66-69; assoc prof, Univ Ala, 69-71; assoc prof, 71-78, Prof Span, Univ KY, 78- **MEMBERSHIPS** MLA; Int Inst Spain. **RESEARCH** Galdos; Spanish Romanticism; Spanish novel on the 19th century. **SELECTED PUBLICATIONS** Auth, On the Origin of the Phrase La Virgen-De-Los-Ultimos-Amores--Espronceda Debt to Chateaubriand, Bulletin Hisp, Vol 0097, 95; Solar Imagery in 3 Novels of Espina,Concha, Anales de la Literatura Espanola Contemporanea, Vol 0022, 97; The Suplemento-Literario of La-Verdad 1923-1926--Spanish, Hisp Rev, Vol 0061, 93; Galdos and the Visit of President Loubet, 1905, Bulletin Hisp, Vol 0095, 93; Las Ruinas de mi Convento, A Romantic Novel by Patxot, Fernando 1851, Critica Hisp, Vol 0018, 96; History and Fiction in Galdos Narratives, Rev Estudios Hispanicos, Vol 0028, 94; Marianela, the Discovery of a New World and the Limitations of Science, Insula-Rev de Letras y Ciencias Humanas, Vol 0048, 93. **CONTACT ADDRESS** Dept of Span & Ital, Univ of Kentucky, 500 S Limestone St, Lexington, KY 40506-0003. **EMAIL** dendle@ukcc.uky.edu

DENHAM, SCOTT
DISCIPLINE GERMAN LANGUAGE & LITERATURE **EDUCATION** Univ of Chicago, BA, 84; Harvard Univ, AM, 89, PhD, 90. **CAREER** Tutor, teaching fel, instr, Harvard Univ, 85-90; assoc prof, Davidson Col, 90-; Chair, Dept. of German & Russian, Davidson College, 99-02 **HONORS AND AWARDS** B.Blume Prize for acad excellence, 84-86; Danforth Ctr for Teaching and Learning Cert of Distinction in Teaching, 85-89; William R. Kenan Fund Grant, Harvard Univ, 89; Davidson Col fac summer res grant, 91; Nat Endowment for the Hums Summer Stipend, 92; Salzburg Sem Fel, 93; Southern Reg. Educ Bd., Small Grants Prog, 94; Am Coun on Germany Fel, 95; DAAD grants, 95, 96; Davidson Col fac res grants, 96, 97, 98; Davidson Col Mellon Found Grant, 98; DAAD Summer Study Visit Scholar, 98; Modern Language Assoc, Member, Executive Committee on Nineteenth and Early Twentieth-Century Literature, (sec'y, 97; chair, 98), 96-01. **MEMBERSHIPS** MLA; German Studies Asn; Soc of Architectural Hists; Kafka Soc of Am; Arnold-Zweig Gesellschaft; Am Coun on Germany; Am Asn of Teachers of German; Am Historical Assoc **RESEARCH** Gropius, the Bauhaus, and Modernism; Cultural studies; Friedrieh Torberg; Ernst Junger's political journalism **SELECTED PUBLICATIONS** Auth, Walter Gropius Papers, 2., In-house publication of the Houghton Library, Harvard University, 90, Housed in the reading rooms at Houghton and at the Bauhaus-Archiv, Berlin; auth, Visions of War: The Ideology and Imagery of War Fictions in German Literature Before and After the Great War, Germanic Studies in America Series, New York, Berne: Peter Lang, 92; auth, "The American Council on Germany Seventeenth German-American Young Leaders Conference, 95," American Council on Germany Council on Germany Occasional Paper, New York: American Council on Germany, 96; auth, "Morderische Mentalitat? Die doppelte Goldhagen-Rezeption in den USA," With Christopher R. Jackson, Evangelische Kommentare (5/97): 272--74; ed, "How to Read a Novel" (with Irene Kacandes), and "How to View a Building" (with Wallis Miller) in A User's Guide to German Cultural Studies, eds Scott Denham, Irene Kacandes, and Jonathan Petropoulos, Ann Arbor: University of Michigan Press, 97, 456-57, 474-76; ed., A User's Guide to German Cultural Studies, Edited by Scott Denham, Irene Kacandes, and Johnathan Petropoulos, Ann Arbor: University of Michigan Press, 97; auth, "Schindler's List in Germany and Austria: A Reception Study," In Memory, Memorialization, and Denial, ed. Peter Hayes, Evanston: Northwestern UP, 99, 193-210; Transl and intro, Internal and External Emigration: A Dialogue, by Friedrich Torberg, Transl. And intro. By Scott Denham, The New England Review 20.4, Fall 99: 36-56; transl, "The Weimer Myth: From City of the Arts to Global Village," by Gert Theile, Transl by Scott Denham, In Unwrapping Goethe's Weimar: Essays in Cultural Studies and Local Knowledge, eds. Burkhard Henke, Susanne Kord, and Simon Richter, Rochester: Camden House, 00, 310-328; ed, History and Literature: Essays in Honor of Karl S. Guthke, edited by William C. Donahue and Scott Denham, Tubingen: Stauffenburg Verlag, forthcoming Oct., 00. **CONTACT ADDRESS** Dept of German & Russian, Davidson Col, Davidson, NC 28036-1719. **EMAIL** scdenham@davidson.edu

DENNIS, HARRY JOE
PERSONAL Born 01/16/1940, Cisco, TX, m, 1962, 1 child **DISCIPLINE** SPANISH AND PORTUGUESE LANGUAGES AND LITERATURES **EDUCATION** Univ Ariz, BA, 62, MA, 65; PhD(Span & Port), 70. **CAREER** Instr Span, Tex, Instr Spanisa University Arizona 1962-1965; instr English for foreign studies, English Lang Inst, Univ Ariz, summers 64-69; vis prof Span, Univ Nev, Las Vegas, 69-70; Adm Span & Port, Calif State Univ, Sacramento, 70-, Assoc mem bd, Luso Am Educ Found, San Francisco, 72-; dir, Calif State Univ, Guanajuato, Mex, 75-77 & Spain, 81; Dir Spain Program, 89. **MEMBERSHIPS** Am Asn Teachers Span & Port; Foreign Lang Assoc Greater Sacramento. **RESEARCH** Contemporary Latin American prose fiction; Brazilian literature of the 20th century. **SELECTED PUBLICATIONS** Auth, Explicacion de Textos Literarios, Vol 0023, 94; Florilegio de Literatura Hispanoamericana, 00. **CONTACT ADDRESS** Dept of Span & Port, California State Univ, Sacramento, 6000 J St, Sacramento, CA 95819-2694. **EMAIL** dannis@csus.edu

DENOMME, ROBERT T.
PERSONAL Born 05/17/1930, Fitchburg, MA **DISCIPLINE** FRENCH **EDUCATION** Assumption Col, AB, 52; Boston Univ, MA, 53; Univ Paris, dipl, 59; Columbia Univ, PhD, 62. **CAREER** Instr French & Span, St Joseph's Col, Pa, 56-60; from instr to asst prof French, Univ Va, 60-64; asst prof, Univ Chicago, 64-66; assoc prof, 66-70, Prof French Lit, Univ VA, 70-, Chmn Dept French, 77-, Reader French lang & lit, Educ Testing Serv, 71-77; mem adv bd, Nineteenth-Century French studies, 72-; Am Philos Soc grant, 75; vis prof Fr, Univ Orleans, France, 78. **MEMBERSHIPS** MLA; Am Asn Teachers Fr; SAtlantic Mod Lang Asn. **RESEARCH** Romanticism; realism and symbolism; 19th century French literature. **SELECTED PUBLICATIONS** Auth, Madame Bovary, Fr Rev, Vol 0067, 94; A Critical Bibliography of French Literature, Vol 5, the 19th-Century, Fr Forum, Vol 0020, 95; Contemplation and Dream--Hugo,Victor, Poet of Intimateness-French, Fr Rev, Vol 0068, 94; Complete Poetic Works, Vol 3, Odes--French, Nineteenth-Century Fr Stud, Vol 0024, 95; Oeuvres-Poetiques-Completes, Vol 4, Les Exiles, Amethystes--French, Nineteenth-Century Fr Stud, Vol 0023, 95. **CONTACT ADDRESS** Dept of French, Univ of Virginia, 302 Cabell Hall, Charlottesville, VA 22903.

DER-HOUSSIKIAN, HAIG
PERSONAL Born 08/16/1938, Cairo, Egypt, m, 1961 **DISCIPLINE** LINGUISTICS **EDUCATION** Am Univ Beirut, BA, 61, MA, 62; Univ Tex Austin, PhD, 69. **CAREER** Instr English, Brit Lebanese Training Col, Beirut, 60-62; asst prof Swahili & ling, 67-70, assoc prof foreign lang & ling, 70-77, acting dir ling, Univ, 71-72, dir, Ctr African Studies, 73-79, Prof Foreign Lang & Ling, Univ Fla, 77-, Chair, Dept African & Asian Lang & Lit, 82-91; Res assoc, Univ, Dar es Salaam, 66. **HONORS AND AWARDS** Fulbright-Hays res award, EAfrica, 66-67; sr Fulbright lectr, Univ Luanda, Angola, 72-73, Univ Benin, Togo, 79-80 & 81 & Univ Ouagadougou, Upper Volta, 81; Acad specialist grant, vis prof, Univ Marien Ngouabi, Barazzaville, Congo 5-8/88; invited vis prof, Dept of African Langs & Lits, Univ Zimbabwe, Harare, Zimbabwe, 89. **MEMBERSHIPS** Ling Soc Am; African Lang Teachers Asn; Ling Asn of Can and the U.S. **RESEARCH** Bantu linguistics, Swahili, morphology, discourse, creolization, multilingualism, sociology of language. **SELECTED PUBLICATIONS** Auth, The semantic content of class in Bantu and its syntactic significance, Linguistics, 70; Educated urban Swahili, J Lang Asn EAfrica, 71; The evidence for a Niger-Congo hypothesis, Cahiers d'Etudes Africaines, 72; A Bibliography of African Linguistics, Ling Res, Inc, 72; co-ed, Language and Linguistic Problems in Africa, Hornbeam, 77; Tem Grammar Handbook, Tem: Communication and Culture, Tem: Special Skills, Peace Corps Lang Handbk Series, 80; auth, Togo's Choice, The Linguistic Connection, Univ Press of Am, 83; auth, Case Assignment in Armenian, Proceedings of the Fifth International Conference on Armenian Linguistics, Caravan Press, 96; auth, Reduplication in Colloquial Western Armenian, LACUS, 98; auth, The State of a Nation: Kiswahili: A Window on Kenya, ERIC-CAL, 98. **CONTACT ADDRESS** Ctr for African Studies, Univ of Florida, Univ Station, PO Box 14105, Gainesville, FL 32604. **EMAIL** haig@aall.ufl.edu

DERBYSHIRE, WILLIAM W.
PERSONAL Born 12/30/1936, Philadelphia, PA, 3 children **DISCIPLINE** RUSSIAN AND SLAVIC LINGUISTICS **EDUCATION** Univ Pa, BA, 58, MA, 59, PhD (Slavic ling), 64. **CAREER** Asst instr Russ lang, Univ Pa, 59-61; asst prof Russ lang and lit, Lycoming Col, 61-63; from asst prof to assoc prof, State Univ NY Binghamton, 64-59, chmn dept, 67-69; assoc prof Russ and Slavic ling, 69-76, chmn, Dept Slavic Lang and Lit, 69-80, Prof Slavic Ling, Rutgers Univ, 76-, Fulbright res fel, Inst Ling, Univ Zagreb, 72-73; mem exec coun, Soc for Slovene Studes, 77-. **MEMBERSHIPS** Am Asn Teachers Slavic and East Europ Lang; MLA; AAUP; Am Asn Advan Slavic Studies; Soc for Slovene Studies. **RESEARCH** Russian lexicology and lexicography; homonymy in Slavic languages; Slovene language. **SELECTED PUBLICATIONS CONTACT ADDRESS** Dept of Slavic Lang and Lit, Rutgers, The State Univ of New Jersey, New Brunswick, New Brunswick, NJ 08903.

DERSOFI, NANCY
PERSONAL Born Boston, MA **DISCIPLINE** ITALIAN, COMPARATIVE LITERATURE **EDUCATION** Radcliffe Col, AB, 57; Harvard Univ, AM, 59, PhD(comp lit), 66. **CAREER** Asst prof Ital, Conn Col, 66-68 & Queens Col, 68-71; asst prof, 72-80, assoc Prof Ital, Bryn Mawr Col, 80-, Sibley fel Greek, 65-66; I Tatti fel Ital, Harvard Univ, 76-77; prof Comp Lit, 89-. **MEMBERSHIPS** MLA; Renaissance Soc Am; Am Assoc of Teachers of Italian; Am Assoc of Italian Studies. **RESEARCH** Renaissance theater; early modern actresses. **SELECTED PUBLICATIONS** Auth, Arcadia and the Stage: An Introduction to the Dramatic Art of Angelo Beolco, Called Ruzante, Jose Porrua Turanzas, 78; Ruzente L'Auconitana The Woman from Ancena, trans with intro ed notes, Univ of Calif Press, Berkeley, 94. **CONTACT ADDRESS** Bryn Mawr Col, 101 N Merion Ave, Bryn Mawr, PA 19010-2899. **EMAIL** ndersofi@brynmawr.edu

DESMIDT, BEN
PERSONAL Born 08/04/1973, Madison, WI **DISCIPLINE** CLASSICS **EDUCATION** Univ Chicago, BA, 95; Columbia Univ, MA; MPhil, 01 **CAREER** Teaching Asst to Preceptor, Columbia Univ, 96-. **HONORS AND AWARDS** Pres Fel, Columbia Univ, 95-00. **MEMBERSHIPS** Am Philol Asn. **RESEARCH** Roman moral philosophy and philosophical rhetoric. **CONTACT ADDRESS** Dept Class, Columbia Univ, 617 Hamilton Hall, New York, NY 10011. **EMAIL** dbd5@columbia.edu

DESROCHES, RICHARD HENRY
PERSONAL Born 10/17/1927, Worcester, MA, d, 2 children **DISCIPLINE** FRENCH **EDUCATION** Clark Univ, AB, 47; Yale Univ, PhD, 62. **CAREER** Master French, Span & Latin, Tabor Acad, Marion, Mass, 49-51; asst, Yale Univ, 53-57; from instr to asst prof Romance lang, 57-69, asst fir, NDEA French Inst, Tours, France, 62-68, instr, 63-65, 67-68, acting chmn dept Romance lang, Univ, 73-74, Assoc Prof Romance Lang, Univ Ore, 69-98, Master Span, Hamden Hall Country Day Sch, Conn, 56-57. **MEMBERSHIPS** Am Asn Tchr(s) Fr; Philol Asn Pac Coast. **RESEARCH** Eighteenth century French novel. **SELECTED PUBLICATIONS** Coauth, Guide for French, Curric Publ, Portland Pub Sch, Ore, 62; auth, An eighteenth century philosopher's literary protest against slavery, Proc Pac Northwest Conf Foreign Lang, 4/64; Pre-romantic melancholy and the philosophical mind, Pac Coast Philol, 4/68; Reality behind the myth in Giraudoux's La Guerre de Troie n'aura pas lieu, Rev Langues Vivantes, 6/68. **CONTACT ADDRESS** Dept of Romance Lang, Univ of Oregon, Eugene, OR 97403-1205. **EMAIL** rdesroch@oregon.uoregon.edu

DESROSIERS-SCHOLT, NICOLE
PERSONAL Born 06/06/1941, m, 2 children **DISCIPLINE** FRENCH **EDUCATION** Mt Holyoke, MA, 68; Univ de Clermont-Ferrand, MA, 70; Univ Mass, PhD, 80. **CAREER** Lectr, Williams Col, 75-; tchr, Lenox Memorial High Sch; coordr, high sch stud exchange prog. **HONORS AND AWARDS** Founding mem, For Acad Alliance in Berkshire County, 88-. **RESEARCH** Translation; composition; teaching of culture; computers use in teaching foreign languages; High school student exchange program. **SELECTED PUBLICATIONS** Auth, En Direct: A French Activity Workbook and Teacher's Manual; transl, J. Gaudemet's Marriage in the Western World. **CONTACT ADDRESS** Center for Foreign Languages, Literatures and Cult, Williams Col, Williamstown, MA 01267. **EMAIL** drosiers@massed.net

DETIENNE, MARCEL
PERSONAL Born 10/22/1935, Liege, Europe, s **DISCIPLINE** FRENCH CLASSICS **EDUCATION** Doctor Research, Paris, 60; Doctor Philosophy and Anthropology, Liege, 65. **CAREER** Dir D'Etudes, Ecole des Hautes Etudes, Paris, 68-92; prof, Basil L Gildersleeve Ch, Dept Classics, John Hopkins Univ, 92-. **SELECTED PUBLICATIONS** Auth, Dionysos a cie Louvert, Machette Littetatures (Paris), 98; auth, Appollon le Couteau a la Main, Gallmard (Paris), 98; auth, The Masters of Truth in Archaic Greece, Zone Books, MIT, 99; auth, Comparer L'Incomparable, Le Seuil (Paris), 00; coauth, The Everyday Life of the Greek Gods, Stanford Univ Press, 00. **CONTACT ADDRESS** Dept Classics, Johns Hopkins Univ, Baltimore, 3400 North Charles St, Baltimore, MD 21218-2608.

DETMER, HELLENA R.
PERSONAL Born 12/09/1950, Huntington, IN, m, 1989, 5 children **DISCIPLINE** CLASSICS **EDUCATION** IN Univ, BA, 72; Univ MI, PhD, 76. **CAREER** Act ch, 82-89;co-supvr, Elem Latin prog, 89; ch, 93-. **HONORS AND AWARDS** Mellon fel, Duke Univ, 78-79; May Brodbeck Awd, 83; Faculty Scholar 85-87; pres-elect, CAMWS, 95-96; vp, camws, 88-91; ch, camws col awards comm for transl, 90-92; ch, tchg award comm camws, 94-96; exec comm, camws, 94-98; pres, camws, 96-97. **SELECTED PUBLICATIONS** Auth, Horace: A Study in Structure, Hildesheim, 83; A Workbook to Ayers' English Words From Latin And Greek Elements, Tucson 86; Love by the Numbers: Form and Meaning in the Poetry of Catullus, NY, 97; co-ed, Syllecta Classica 1, 89; Syllecta Classica 2, 90; Syllecta Classica 3, 92; Syllecta Classica 4, 93; Syllecta Classica 5, 94; Syllecta Classica 6, 96; The First and Last of Catullus, Syllecta Classica 5, 94; rev(s), Murgatroyd's Tibullus Elegies II, Class Outlook 74, 96; Catullus: Advanced Placement Edition, Class Outlook 75, 97; Thomspon's Catullus Rel Stud Rev, 97. **CONTACT ADDRESS** Dept of Class, Univ of Iowa, 202 Schaeffer Hall, Iowa City, IA 52242. **EMAIL** helena-dettmer@uiowa.edu

DETWILER, LOUISE A.
PERSONAL Born 02/01/1965, Norristown, PA, m, 2000 **DISCIPLINE** SPANISH LANGUAGE, HISPANIC LITERATURE, CULTURE **EDUCATION** Dick Col, BA, 87; Miami Univ OH, MA, 91; Ind Univ, PhD, 99. **CAREER** Vis instr, Miami Univ, 91-94; assoc instr, Ind Univ, 95-99; asst prof, Butler Univ, 99-. **HONORS AND AWARDS** GAANN Fel, 94-99; M/MLA Wom Cau Dis Pap Awd, 00; Teach Excel Recog Awd, 98; Leon P. Irvin Essay Prize for Excel Schl Comp, 92; Phi Beta Kappa, 87. **MEMBERSHIPS** MLA; MLAWC; MWMLA; MWMLAWC; Fem Unidas. **RESEARCH** Spanish American testimonio; gender and genre; feminist and literary theory; literature and politics. **SELECTED PUBLICATIONS** Auth, "The Ins and Outs of Cervantes's 'El celoso extremeno' and 'El viejo celoso': A Study of Narrative Sequence," Confluencia (93); auth, "The Question of Cultural Difference and Gender Oppression in Estela Portillo's The Day of the Swallows," Biling Rev (96); auth, "Deconstructing the Role of Love in Two of Pablo Neruda's Veinte poemas de amor y una cancion desesperada," Hispanofila (98); auth, "The Blindfolded (Eye)witness of Alicia Partnoy's The Little School" J Midwest MLA (01). **CONTACT ADDRESS** Dept. Mod Lang, Butler Univ, 4600 Sunset Ave, Indianapolis, IN 46208. **EMAIL** ldetwile@butler.edu

DEWEESE, PAMELA
DISCIPLINE SPANISH LANGUAGE AND LITERATURE **EDUCATION** Univ NC Greensboro, BA; Univ NC Chapel Hill, MA; PhD. **CAREER** Prof, Sweet Briar Col. **RESEARCH** Mod Span lit; comp lit. **SELECTED PUBLICATIONS** Auth, articles and papers on the works of contemp Span novelist, Luis Goytisolo; auth, Approximations to Luis Goytisolo Antagonia, Peter Lang Pr, 00. **CONTACT ADDRESS** Sweet Briar Col, Sweet Briar, VA 24595. **EMAIL** deweese@sbe.edu

DI MAIO, IRENE S.
PERSONAL Born New York, NY, 1 child **DISCIPLINE** GERMAN STUDIES **EDUCATION** Vassar Col, BA; Univ Chicago, MA, La State Univ, PhD, 76. **CAREER** From instr to assoc prof, La State Univ, 65-. **HONORS AND AWARDS** DAAD; SCMLA Travel Grant; NEH Summer Sem; IREX; Southern Region Educ Travel Board; Fulbright Summer Sem. **MEMBERSHIPS** AATG, MLA, SCMLA, INCS, Women in German, Forum Vormurz Forschung. **RESEARCH** German-Jewish Relations, Cultural Diversity, Eighteenth- through Twentieth-Century German Literature--especially Realism, Raabe, Lewald, Auerbach, Gerstucker. **SELECTED PUBLICATIONS** Auth, The Multiple Perspective: Wilhelm Raabe's Third-Person Narratives of the Braunschweig Period, John Benjamins, 81; auth, "The Frauenfrage and the Reception of Wilhelm Raabe's Female Characters," in Wilhelm Raabe: Studien zu seinem Leben und Werk, eds. Leo Lensing and Hans-Werner Peter (Braunschweig: pp-Verlag, 81), 406-413; auth, "Nochmals zu den Akten: Sphinx, Indianerprinzessin, Nilschlange," Jarbuch der Raabe-Gesellschaft (87): 228-242; auth, "Heimat, Ortlichkeiten, and Mother-Tongue: The Cases of Jean Amery and Elias Canetti," in The Concept of "Heimat" in Contemporary German Literature, ed. H. W. Seliger (Munich: Iudicium Verlag, 87), 211-224; auth, "Berthold Auerbach's Dichter und Kaufmann: Enlightenment Thought and Jewish Identity," Lessing Yearbook (88): 265-283; auth, "Fanny Lewald," in Dictionary of Literary Biography. Nineteenth-Century German Writers, 1841-1900, eds. James Hardin and Siegfried Mews (MI: Gale Research, Inc., 93), 202-213; auth, "Borders of Culture: The Native American in Friedrich Gerstacker's North American Narratives," Yearbook of German-American Studies Vol 28 (93): 53-75; auth, "Fanny Lewald and Bismarck: Forty-Eighter Turned Monarchist?," Forum Vormarz Forschung, Jahrbuch (98): 233-250. **CONTACT ADDRESS** Dept For Lang & Lit, La State Univ, Baton Rouge, LA 70803-5306. **EMAIL** idmaio@lsu.edu

DI NAPOLI, THOMAS JOHN
PERSONAL Born 10/02/1944, Providence, RI, m, 1986, 1 child **DISCIPLINE** MODERN GERMAN LITERATURE, GERMAN LANGUAGE **EDUCATION** Univ Tex, Austin, PhD, 71. **CAREER** Assoc prof Ger, undergrad adv, La State Univ. **RESEARCH** East German studies; German children's literature. **SELECTED PUBLICATIONS** Auth, Thirty Years of Children's Literature in the German Democratic Republic, in Ger Stud Rev, No 2, 84; The Children's Literature of Peter Hacks, Peter Lang Publ, 87. **CONTACT ADDRESS** Dept of For Lang and Lit, Louisiana State Univ and A&M Col, 220A Prescott Hall, Baton Rouge, LA 70803. **EMAIL** dinapoli@lsu.edu

DIAZ, LIDIA
PERSONAL Born 02/09/1948, Buenos Aires, Argentina, m, 1968, 2 children **DISCIPLINE** SPANISH **EDUCATION** Licenciada In Educ Sci. Univ Cordoba, Argentina, 81; Univ Pittsburgh, MA, 91; PhD, 94. **CAREER** Asst prof, Univ of Cordoba, 84-85; asst prof, San Martin Training Inst for Teachers, 85-86; prof, Adult Educ Prog, Argentina, 86-87; instr, Berlitz Sch of Lang, 88; instr Duquesne Univ, 90; TA, Univ of Pittsburgh, 88-92; asst prof, Pa State Univ, 93-96; instr to asst prof, Univ of Tex, 96-. **HONORS AND AWARDS** Res Fel, Univ of Pittsburgh, 89; Andrew Mellon Fel, 92-93; Grant, Tex Counc for the Humanities, 99. **MEMBERSHIPS** Sigma Delta Pi; ACTFL; Am Assoc of Univ Women; Amnesty Int; Instituto de Lit Iberoamericana; Int Reading Assoc; SpanSig. **SELECTED PUBLICATIONS** Auth, "Sobre La Edad de oro, de Jose Marti", La Habana (Cuba, 91): 24-30; auth, "Oliverio Girondo y sus espantapajaros para ser leidos en cualquier medio de transporte", Hispanic Culture Rev, 1.3 (92): 40-52; auth, "aproximaciones a una lectura de Raucho, de ricardo Guiraldes", Tropos, (94): 8-13; transl, Giving Thanks, a Native American Good Morning Message by Chief Jake Swamp, Lee and Low Books (NY), 96; transl, Scary Stories to Tell in the Dark, ed Alvin Schwarts, Harper Collins (NY) 96; transl, The Birthday Swap, by Loretta Lopez, Lee & Low, (NY), 97; auth, "La otredad reivindicada en un texto zapoteca para ninos", Revista de Literatura Mexicana Contemporanea, (forthcoming). **CONTACT ADDRESS** Dept Mod Lang, Texas Southmost Col, 83 Fort Brown St, Brownsville, TX 78520-4956. **EMAIL** ldiaz@utb1.utb.edu

DIAZ, LOMBERTO
PERSONAL Born 04/16/1914, Pinar del Rio, Cuba, m, 1940, 2 children **DISCIPLINE** SPANISH AND SPANISH AMERICAN LITERATURE **EDUCATION** Univ Havana, Dr, 38, Dr and Master, 44; Ind State Univ, Terre Haute, BA, 65, MA, 66; Fla State Univ, PhD (philos), 69. **CAREER** Prof polit sci, Interam Ctr Econ and Soc Studies, Dominican Repub, 63; instr Span, Ind State Univ, Terre Haute, 65-66; assoc prof, Northeastern Mo State Col, 66-67; instr, Fla State Univ, 67-69; assoc prof, 69-73, dir summer prog, 71, 72 and 74, prof, 73-80, Emer Prof Span, Ind State Univ, Evansville, 80-, Vis prof, Inst Filologia Hispanica, Saltillo, Mex, 71, Univ San Luis Potosi, 72. **MEMBERSHIPS** Am Asn Teachers Span and Port; Circulo Cult Panam; MLA; AAUP. **RESEARCH** Latin American studies. **SELECTED PUBLICATIONS** Auth, To Gullon,Ricardo in From His Students, Critica Hispanica, Vol 18, 1996. **CONTACT ADDRESS** Dept of Foreign Lang, Indiana State Univ, Terre Haute, IN 47712.

DIAZ, LUIS FELIPE
PERSONAL Born 03/19/1950, Puerto Rico **DISCIPLINE** LINGUISTICS **EDUCATION** Univ PR, BA, 74; Univ Ill Chicago, MA, 77; Univ Minn, PhD, 83. **CAREER** Asst prof, InterAm Univ PR, 84-87; prof, Univ Puerto Rico, 87-01. **HONORS AND AWARDS** Ford Found Fel, 78-82. **RESEARCH** 19th and 20th-century Spanish literature; 20th-century Latin American novel; Caribbean literature. **SELECTED PUBLICATIONS** Auth, Irony and Ideology in 'La Regenta' by Leopoldo Alas, Peter Lang, 97; auth, Semiotica, Psicoanalisis y Postmodernidad, 99; auth, Globalizaciou, Naciou, Postmodernidad, Estudios Culturales Puerto Riqueues, LALASA, 01. **CONTACT ADDRESS** Hisp Studies Dept, Univ of Puerto Rico, San Juan, PO Box 364984, San Juan, PR 00936-4984. **EMAIL** lfd7@coqui.net

DIAZ, ROBERTO IGNACIO
DISCIPLINE SPANISH AMERICAN LITERATURE **EDUCATION** Harvard Univ, PhD. **CAREER** Asst prof, Univ Southern Calif. **RESEARCH** Literary-historical study of Spanish American writing in English and French. **SELECTED PUBLICATIONS** Publ on, 19th and 20th century Spanish American literature. **CONTACT ADDRESS** Dept of Spanish and Portuguese, Univ of So California, University Park Campus, Los Angeles, CA 90089. **EMAIL** rdiaz@bcf.usc.edu

DIAZ-JIMENO, FELIPE
PERSONAL Born 08/09/1937, Madrid, Spain, m, 2 children **DISCIPLINE** SPANISH GOLDEN AGE LITERATURE, CONTEMPORARY LITERATURE **EDUCATION** Univ Kans, BA, 68; Univ Tex at Austin, MA, 73; PhD, 78. **CAREER** Vis lectr, Univ Ill, 76-77; translator and assoc ed, Span Archives of Tex Translations; vis prof, Pa State Univ, 79-80; Prof of Span, West Ga Col, 80-83; Prof of Span, Univ Col at Denver, 83-88; vis prof of Span Medieval Lit, Univ of Calif at Irvine, 98-; Prof of Span, Calif State Univ, 88-. **HONORS AND AWARDS** Fulbright Grant, 74; Span Ministry of Foreign Affairs Grant, 75; Span Univ Found Grant, 75-78; Prof of the Year, Cal State Univ at Los Angeles, 91. **MEMBERSHIPS** AATSP, MLA, PAMLA. **RESEARCH** Spanish Medieval, Renaissance, and Golden Age literature, Contemporary Spanish and Spanish American narrative, satire and social criticism in literature, interaction and contacts between history and literature, early California history and Southwest Spanish Culture. **SELECTED PUBLICATIONS** Auth, Fate and Fortune in Sixteenth Century Spain, FUE (Madrid, Spain), 87; auth, "Savonarola in Salamouco, The Reprobatio of 1546," Studies in Honor of Enrique Ruiz-Fornells (91); auth, "Theme and Structure in Pero Mexia's Silva," Discurso Literario (90). **CONTACT ADDRESS** Dept Foreign Lang, California State Univ, Los Angeles, 5151 State Univ Dr, Los Angeles, CA 90032-8112. **EMAIL** fdiaz@calstatela.edu

DICK, ERNST S.
PERSONAL Born 04/07/1929, Grabenhof, Germany, m, 1961, 2 children **DISCIPLINE** GERMAN **EDUCATION** Univ of Sheffield, 55; Johns Hopkins Univ, 56-57; Univ of Munster, PhD, 61. **CAREER** Vis Scholar, Johns Hopkins Univ, 56-57; Instr, Univ of Montana, 57-58, 61-62; Asst/Assoc Prof, Univ of Va, 62-67; Prof, Univ of Wis Milwaukee, 67-68; Prof, Univ of Kans, 68-. **HONORS AND AWARDS** Grant-in-Aid, ACLS, 64; Hall Center Res Fel, Univ of Kans, 89; Festschrift (in hohem prise), 89; Grad Teaching Awd, Kans Univ Center for Teaching Excellence, 99. **MEMBERSHIPS** Medieval Acad of Am, Internationale Vereinigung fur germanische Sprach- und Literatuewissenschaft, Int Courtly Lit Soc, Int Arthurian Soc, Am Asn of Teachers of Ger, Wolfram von Eschenbach-Gesellschaft, Soc for Ger Renaissance and Baroque Lit, Soc for Medieval Ger Studies. **RESEARCH** Germanic word studies, Medieval epic and romance, Epic theory, German Novelle, Durrenmatt. **SELECTED PUBLICATIONS** Auth, Ae. Dryht und seine Sippe: Eine worthundliche, kultur- und religionsgeschichtliche Betrachtung zur altgermanischen Glaubensvorstellung vom wachstumlichen Heil, 65; co-ed, Rilke: The Alchemy of Alienation, 80; co-ed, Festschrift fur Karl Schneider zum 70. Geburstag am 18. April 1982, 82; auth, "Epos-Romance-Roman: Zu den Anfangen einer historischen Poetik der mittelalterlichen Epik nach 1750," in Kunstgriffe: Auskunfte zur Reichweite von Literaturtheorie und Literaturkritik. Festschrift fur Herbert Mainusch, ed. Ulrich Horstmann and Wolfgang Zach (Frankfurt a M: Lang, 89), 34-50; auth, "The Grimms' 'Hilderbrandslied'," in The Grimm Brothers and the Germanic Past, ed. Elmer H. Antonsen, Amsterdam Studies in the Theory and Hist of Ling Sci 3-43 (Amsterdam: Benjamins, 90), 71-87; auth, "Tristan the Hunter: Toward a Metanarrative Reading of Gottfried's Stag Ritual," in Fide et amore: A Festschrift for Hugo Bekker on his Sixty-Fifth Birthday, ed. William C. McDonald and Winder McConnel, Goppinger Arbeiten zur Germanistil 526 (Goppingen: Kummerle, 90), 41-69; auth, "Durrenmatts Dramaturgie des Einfalls: Der Besuch der alten Dame und Der Meteor," in Europaische Komodie, ed. Herbert Mainusch (Darmstadt: Wissenschaftliche Buchgesellschaft, 90), 389-435; auth, "Minne im Widerspruch: Modellrevision und Fiktionalisierung in Wolframs 'Titurel'," in Der Buchstab todt-der Geist macht lebendig, Festschrift zum 60. Geburtstag von Hans-Gert Roloff von Freunden, Schulern und Kollegen, ed. James Hardin and Jorg Jungmayr (Bern: Lang, 92) 1: 399-420; auth, "Bast and Bastard: Ein Versuch zu einer ungeklarten Wortgruppe," in Comparative-Historical Linguistics: Indo-European and Finno-Ugric. Papers in honor of Oswald Szemerenyi III, ed. Bela Brpgyanyi and Reiner Lipp, Current Issued in Ling Theory 97 (Amsterdam: Benjamins, 93), 307-340; auth, "The Hundred Stag and the Renewal of Minne: bast in Gottfried's Tristan," Tristania 17 (96): 1-25. **CONTACT ADDRESS** Dept Ger Lang and Lit, Univ of Kansas, Lawrence, 1 Univ of Kans, Lawrence, KS 66045-0001. **EMAIL** esdick@ukans.edu

DICKERSON, GREGORY WEIMER
PERSONAL Born 03/08/1937, Hanover, NH, m, 1967, 2 children **DISCIPLINE** CLASSICAL LANGUAGES & LITERATURE **EDUCATION** Harvard Univ, AB, 59; Princeton Univ, MA, 65, PhD, 72. **CAREER** Teaching fel classics, Phillips Acad, Andover, Mass, 59-60; secy, Am Sch Class Studies, Athens, 63-64; instr, Gilman Sch, Baltimore, 64-66; instr classics, 67-70, asst prof Greek, 70-76, assoc prof Greek, Bryn Mawr Col, 76-. **MEMBERSHIPS** Am Phil Asn. **RESEARCH** Greek drama. **SELECTED PUBLICATIONS** Auth, Aristophanes' Ranae 862: A note on the anatomy of Euripidean Tragedy, Harvard Studies Class Philol, 74; coauth, Sophocles' Women of Trachis, Oxford Univ, 78. **CONTACT ADDRESS** Dept of Greek, Bryn Mawr Col, 101 N Merion Ave, Bryn Mawr, PA 19010-2899. **EMAIL** gdickers@brynmawr.edu

DICKIE, MATTHEW WALLACE
PERSONAL Born 11/20/1941, Edinburgh, Scotland **DISCIPLINE** CLASSICAL PHILOLOGY **EDUCATION** Univ Edinburgh, MA, 64; Univ Toronto, PhD (Greek), 72. **CAREER** Instr classics, Swarthmore Col, 67-68; asst prof, 72-78, Assoc Prof Classics, Univ Ill, Chicago Circle, 78-, Chmn Dept, 80-. **RESEARCH** Early Greek poetry; Greek ethics; Greek history. **SELECTED PUBLICATIONS CONTACT ADDRESS** Dept of Classics, Univ of Illinois, Chicago, Chicago Circle, Box 4348, Chicago, IL 60680.

DICKISON, SHEILA KATHRYN
PERSONAL Born 11/14/1942, Walkerton, ON, Canada **DISCIPLINE** CLASSICS, ANCIENT HISTORY **EDUCATION** Univ Toronto, BA, 64; Bryn Mawr Col, MA, 66, PhD (Latin and Greek), 72. **CAREER** From instr to asst prof Greek, Latin and ancient hist, Wellesley Col, 69-76; actg chmn classics, 77-78, Assoc Prof Classics, Univ Fla, 76-. **MEMBERSHIPS** Archaeol Inst Am; Am Class League. **RESEARCH** Roman historiography; ancient social history **SELECTED PUBLICATIONS** Auth, The Reasonable Approach to Beginning Greek and Latin, Class J, Vol 87, 92. **CONTACT ADDRESS** ASB-3C, Univ of Florida, 3c Arts and Sciences, Gainesville, FL 32611-9500.

DICKSTEIN, MORRIS
PERSONAL Born 02/23/1940, New York, NY, m, 1965, 2 children **DISCIPLINE** ENGLISH & COMPARATIVE LITERATURE **EDUCATION** Columbia Univ, AB, 61; Yale Univ, MA, 63, PhD, 67. **CAREER** From instr to asst prof Eng & comp lit, Columbia Univ, 66-71; from Assoc Prof to Prof, 71-94, Distinguished Prof Eng, Queens Col, NY, 94-; vis prof Am studies, Univ Paris, 80-81; dir, Ctr for the Hum, CUNY Grad Sch, 93-. **HONORS AND AWARDS** Soc Relig Higher Educ fel, 69-70; Chamberlain fel, Columbia Univ, 69-70; Guggenheim fel, 73-74; Am Coun Learned Socs fel, 77; Rockefeller Found Hum fel, 81-82; NEH Fel, 86-87; Mellon Fel, Nat Hum Ctr, 9-90. **MEMBERSHIPS** MLA; PEN Club; Nat Book Critics Circle (bd mem 83-89); Nat Soc Film Critics. **RESEARCH** Eng and Europ romanticism; mod lit and criticism; film and lit; Am cult hist. **SELECTED PUBLICATIONS** Auth, Allen Ginsberg and the 60's, Commentary, 1/70; Keats and His Poetry: A Study in Development, Univ Chicago, 71; The Black aesthetic in white America, Partisan Rev, winter 71-72; Coleridge, Wordsworth, and the conversation poems, Centennial Rev, fall 72; Fiction hot and kool: Dilemmas of the experimental writer, Tri Quart, 75; Seeds of the sixties: The growth of Freudian radicalism, Partisan Rev, 76; Gates of Eden: American Culture in the Sixties, Basic Bks, 77; co-ed, Great Film Directors: A Critical Anthology, Oxford Univ, 78; auth, Double Agent: The Critic and Society, Oxford Univ, 92; ed, The Revival of Pragmatism: New Essays on Social Thought, Law, and Culture, Duke Univ, 98; coauth, Cambridge History of American Literature, Vol 8, Cambridge Univ, 99. **CONTACT ADDRESS** Center for the Hum, Queens Col, CUNY, 65-30 Kissena Blvd, Flushing, NY 11367. **EMAIL** mdickste@gc.cuny.edu

DIETZ, DONALD T.
PERSONAL Born 09/09/1939, Chicago, IL, m, 1963, 6 children **DISCIPLINE** SPANISH **EDUCATION** Univ Notre Dame, BA, 61; Univ Ariz, PhD (Span), 68. **CAREER** Instr Span, Univ Dayton, 65-66; from asst prof to assoc prof and admin asst to chmn dept, Ball State Univ, 66-72; prof Span and chmn dept mod lang, Univ Louisville, 72-76; Prof Span and Chairperson Dept, Tex Tech Univ, 76-. **MEMBERSHIPS** Am Asn Teachers Span and Port; MLA. **RESEARCH** The Autos Sacramentales; Spanish Renaissance. **SELECTED PUBLICATIONS** Auth, Baroque Art and Sacramental Drama, Calderon No Hay Instante Sin Milagro, Bull Comediantes, Vol 46, 94. **CONTACT ADDRESS** Dept of Class and Mod Lang and Lit, Texas Tech Univ, Lubbock, TX 79409.

DIJKSTRA, BRAM
PERSONAL Born 07/05/1938, Tandjung Pandan, Indonesia, m, 1964 **DISCIPLINE** AMERICAN & COMPARATIVE LITERATURE **EDUCATION** Ohio State Univ, BA, 61, MA, 62; Univ Calif, Berkeley, PhD, 67. **CAREER** From actg instr to asst prof, 66-73, assoc prof, 73-85, prof Am & comp lit, Univ Calif, San Diego, 85-. **RESEARCH** Visual arts and literature; sociology of literature; literature and ideology. **SELECTED PUBLICATIONS** Auth, Faces in Skin, Oyez, 65; The Hieroglyphics of a New Speech; Cubism, Stieglitz and the early Poetry of William Carlos Williams, Princeton, 69; contribr, Encounters: Essays in Literature and the Visual Arts, Studio Vista, London, 71; Un Reve Americain: Norman Mailer et l'esthetique de la domination, Temps Mod, Paris 4/72; The androgyne in nineteenth-century art and literature, Comp Lit, winter 74; Painting and ideology: Picasso and Guernica, Praxis, 76; ed, William Carlos Williams on Art and Artists, New Directions, 78; Nicht-repressive rhythmische Strukturen in einigen Formen afro-amerikanischer und westindischer Musik, Die Zeichen, Fischer Verlag, Frankfurt, 81; auth Idols of Perversity: Fantasies of Feminine Evil in Fin-de-siecle Culture. Oxford Univ, 86; Defoe and Economics: The Fortunes of ROXANA in the History of Interpretation, MacMillan, 87; The High Cost of Parasols: Images of Women in Impressionist Art, California Light, Chronicle Books, 90; America and Georgia O'Keefe, Georgia O'Keefe, The New York Years, A A Knopf, 91; Early Modernism in Southern California: Provincialism or Eccentricity Modernist Art 1900-1950, Univ Calif, 96; Evil Sisters: The Threat of Female Sexuality and the Cult of Manhood, A A Knopf, 96; Georgia O'Keefe and the Eros of Place, Princeton Univ, 98. **CONTACT ADDRESS** Dept Lit, Univ of California, San Diego, 9500 Gilman Dr., La Jolla, CA 92093-5003.

DIK, HELMA
DISCIPLINE CLASSICS **EDUCATION** Univ Amsterdam, PhD, 95. **CAREER** Asst prof, Univ Chicago. **HONORS AND AWARDS** Junior Fel; Fel Lexikon des fruhgriechischen Epos; Graduate fel. **SELECTED PUBLICATIONS** Auth, 'Senex: een case-study uit de oudheid', Pentecostalia, 92; auth, 'Gekloofde zinnen langs de lijn', ICG, 94; auth, 'Vrij maar niet willekeurig: Pragmatische aspecten van constituentvolgorde in twee fragmenten uit Herodotus', Lampas, 94; auth, 'Ancient Greek warfare--a case study in constituent ordering, Mouton de Gruyter, 94; auth, Word Order in Ancient Greek. A Pragmatic Account of Word Order Variation in Herodotus, Gieben, 95. **CONTACT ADDRESS** Univ of Chicago, 5801 S Ellis, Chicago, IL 60637.

DILLER, GEORGE THEODORE
PERSONAL Born 01/01/1940, Hanover, NH, m, 1961, 3 children **DISCIPLINE** MEDIEVAL FRENCH **EDUCATION** Princeton Univ, AB, 61; Middlebury Col, MA, 63; Stanford Univ, PhD (French), 68. **CAREER** Instr French, Brandeis Univ, 66-68; asst prof, 68-73, Assoc Prof French, Univ Fla, 73-. **MEMBERSHIPS** Soc Anciens Textes Francais; SAtlantic Mod Lang Asn; Repertoire Int Medievistes. **RESEARCH** Medieval French historians, especially Froissart; Romans antiques. **SELECTED PUBLICATIONS** Auth, Froissart, Historiography, The University Curriculum and Isabeau of Bavaria, Romance Quart, Vol 41, 94. **CONTACT ADDRESS** Dept of RLL, Univ of Florida, PO Box 117405, Gainesville, FL 32611-7405.

DILTS, MERVIN R.
PERSONAL Born 02/26/1938, Flemington, NJ **DISCIPLINE** CLASSICS **EDUCATION** Gettysburg Col, BA, 60; Ind Univ, MA, 61, PhD (classics), 64. **CAREER** Asst prof classics, Knox Col, 64-65 and Univ Ill, Urbana, 65-69; assoc prof, 69-79, Prof Classics, NY Univ, 79-, Am Philol Soc grant, 71; Am Coun Learned Soc grant-in-aid, 77. **MEMBERSHIPS** Am Philol Asn; Class Asn Atlantic States; Soc Textual Scholarship. **RESEARCH** Greek textual criticism; Greek codicology. **SELECTED PUBLICATIONS** Auth, Hiatus in the Orations of Aeschines, Am J Philol, Vol 115, 94. **CONTACT ADDRESS** Dept of Classics, New York Univ, 25 Waverly Pl, New York, NY 10003-6701.

DIMAIO, MICHAEL
PERSONAL Born 06/05/1949, Providence, RI, d, 1980, 2 children **DISCIPLINE** CLASSICS **EDUCATION** Johns Hopkins Univ, BA, 70; Univ Mo, MA, 73, PhD, 77; Univ of RI, M.L.S., 80. **CAREER** Grad Teaching Asst, Univ of Mo-Columbia, 73; Instr, Dundee, Ill, 74-76; Substitute Teacher, Geneva Sch District, 77-78; Instr, St. Johns Country Day Sch, 78-79; Grad Asst, Univ of RI, 80; Instr, Nash Library, Gannon Univ, 80-83; Asst prof, Salve Regina Col, 83-87; Asst prof, Salve Regina Col, 87-88; Asst prof, Salve Regina Col, 88-90; Assoc prof, Salve Regina Univ, 90-97; Prof, Salve Regina Univ, 97-. **HONORS AND AWARDS** Dept & general honors, Johns Hopkins Univ; NDEA Title IV grant, MU; chemn, De Imperatonibus Romains, 96-97. **MEMBERSHIPS** APA; Asn of Ancient Hist. **RESEARCH** Roman history; Byzantine literature. **SELECTED PUBLICATIONS** Auth, "Zonaras, Julian, and Philostorgios on the Death of Constantine I," GOTR 26 (81): 118-124; auth, "Infaustis Ductoribus Praeviis: The Antiochene Connection, Part II," Byzantion 51 (81): 501-511; auth, The Early Church and State, Fortress Press, 82; auth, "History and Myth in Zonaras Epitome Historiarum," Byzantine Studies/Etudes byzantines, 10 (83): 230-255; auth, "Smoke in the Wind: Zonaras Use of Philostorgius in his Account of the Late Neo-Flavian Emperors, Byzantion 58 (88): 230-255; auth, "Ambiguitas Constantiniana: The Caeleste Signum Dei of Constantine the Great," Byzantia, 58 (88): 334-360; auth, "The Emperor Julian's Edicts of Religious Toleration," Ancient World, 20 (89): 99-110; auth, "The Proelium Cibalense et Proelium Campi Ardiensis: The First Civil War of Constantine I and Licinius I," Ancient World 21, (90): 67-91; auth, "Per Vim, Per Caedem, Per Bellum: A Study of Murder and Ecclesiastical Politics in the Year 337 A.D.," Byzantion 72 (92): 158-211; auth, "Imago Veritatis aut Verba in Speculo: Athanasius, the Meletians, and Linguistic Frontiers in Fourth Century Egypt," in Shifting Frontiers in Late Antiquity, ed. Ralph W. Mathisen and Hagith S. Sivan, (Aldershot, 96), 271-278. **CONTACT ADDRESS** 226 Davis St., Fall River, MA 02720. **EMAIL** mdimaio@atsids.net

DIMARIA, SALVATORE
DISCIPLINE ITALIAN LITERATURE **EDUCATION** Univ Wisc, PhD, 78. **CAREER** Assoc prof, Ital, Univ Tenn. **RESEARCH** Dramatic theater in the Italian Renaissance. **CONTACT ADDRESS** Dept of Mod For Langs & Lits, Univ of Tennessee, Knoxville, 701 McClung Tower & Plaza, Knoxville, TN 37996. **EMAIL** sdimaria@utk.edu

DIMIC, MILAN VELIMIR
PERSONAL Born 03/15/1933, Belgrade, Yugoslavia, m, 1959, 2 children **DISCIPLINE** COMPARATIVE AND GERMAN LITERATURE **EDUCATION** Univ Belgrade, MA, 56; Univ Vienna, dipl, 56. **CAREER** Instr Ger, Serbian Acad Sci and Inst Exp Phonetics, 56-57; asst prof comp lit, Univ Belgrade, 57-62; from asst prof to assoc prof, 66-72, chmn dept comp lit, 69-75 and 81, prof German and Comp Lit, Univ Alta, 72-, Chmn Comp Lit Prog, 67-, Res asst, Inst Theory of Lit and Aesthet, Belgrade, 60-62; mem, Can Coun Acad Panel, 74-78, chmn 76-78; ed, Can Rev Comp Lit, Univ Alta Press and Univ Toronto Press, 74-; prof emer; dir, Res Institute for Comp Lit. **MEMBERSHIPS** MLA; Asn Can Univ Teachers Ger; Can Asn Slavists; Am Comp Lit Asn; Can Comp Lit Asn. **RESEARCH** Romanticism; Expressionism; Popular Literature; Literary Theory; Methods of Literary Scholarship; Value Judgements; Literary Translation. **SELECTED PUBLICATIONS** Auth, Greene, E. J. H.--In-Memoriam, Can Rev Comp Lit-Rev Can Litt Comp, Vol 22, 95; Why Study Canonization, Can Rev Compa Lit Rev Can Litt Com, Vol 20, 93; 20 Years of The Canadian Review of Comparative Literature, Can Rev Compa Lit Rev Can Litt Com Vol 20, 93; Canons and Canonization, from Theory to Practice, Can Rev Compa Lit Rev Can Litt Com, Vol 20, 93; The New Editorship and the Future of the Canadian Review Of Comparative Literature Revue Canadienne De Litterature Comparee, Can Rev Compa Lit Rev Can Litt Com, Vol 23, 96; Re VisionS of Canadian Literature--Introduction, Can Rev Compa Lit Rev Can Litt Com, Vol 20, 93. **CONTACT ADDRESS** Dept of Comp Lit, Univ of Alberta, Edmonton, AB, Canada T6G 2E6. **EMAIL** mdimic@gpu.srv.ualberta.ca

DIMLER, GEORGE RICHARD
PERSONAL Born 10/21/1931, Baltimore, MD **DISCIPLINE** GERMAN LANGUAGE & LITERATURE **EDUCATION** Fordham Univ, AB, 56, MA, 60; Woodstock Col, STB, 62, STL, 64; Middlebury Col, MA, 66; Univ Calif, Los Angeles, PhD(Germanic lang), 70. **CAREER** Instr Ger, Marquette Univ, 62-; Asst prof, Loyola Col, Md, 70-71; assoc prof, 72-81, Prof Lang, Fordham Univ, 82-; NDEA fel, 67-70; Nat Endowment for Humanities grant, 74; Am Coun of Learned Socs fel, 75; Ger Acad Exchange Serv fel, 76-77 & 78-79; Herzog August bibliothek, Wolfenbuttek Stipendium, 79. **MEMBERSHIPS** Am Asn Teachers Ger; MLA; Mid Atlantic Lang Asn; Goethe Soc Am (treas, 72); Renaissance Soc Am **RESEARCH** German baroque literature, Jesuit drama; Jesuit emblematics. **SELECTED PUBLICATIONS** Auth, Friedrich Spee's Trutznachtigall, Herbert Lang, Bern, 73; The genesis and development of Spee's love imagery in the Trutznachtigall, Germanic Rev, 73; Don Quixote and Simplicius Simplicissimus: Study in alienation, Thought, 74; Gottfried Von Strassburg's Tristan, Amsterdamer Beitrage, 75; The egg as emblem: Genesis and structure of a Jesuit emblem book, Studies in Iconography, 76; A bibliographical survey of Jesuit emblem books in Early Jesuit colleges, Archivum Hist Soc Jesu, 76; Friedrich Spees Trutznachtigall, Univ Press Am, 81; Imago Primi Saeculi: The secular tradition and the Jesuit emblem book, Thought, 81; Jesuit Series, Corpus Librorum Emblematum, vol 1, McGill-Queens Press, 97; auth, Research Professor of Jesuit Emblem Studies, 99; Vol 2, University of Toronto Press, 00. **CONTACT ADDRESS** Fordham Univ, 501 E Fordham Rd, Bronx, NY 10458-5191. **EMAIL** dimler@fordham.edu

DINNEEN, DAVID A.
PERSONAL Born 06/24/1931, New York, NY, m, 1956, 3 children **DISCIPLINE** LINGUISTICS, AND ROMANCE PHILOLOGY **EDUCATION** Harvard Univ, PhD. **CAREER** Prof; dept ch, Coord, French Basic Conversation Program, Univ KS. **MEMBERSHIPS** LSA; MLA; AATF; ALTFL. **RESEARCH** For lang pedag. **SELECTED PUBLICATIONS** Co-auth, a first-yr textbk in French, Chapeau! **CONTACT ADDRESS** Dept of French and Italian, Univ of Kansas, Lawrence, Lawrence, KS 66045. **EMAIL** dad@ukans.edu

DIONNE, RENE
PERSONAL Born 01/29/1929, Saint-Philippe-de-Neri, PQ, Canada **DISCIPLINE** FRENCH **EDUCATION** Univ Laval, BA, 50; Univ Montreal, MA, 55, LL, 60; L'Immaculee-Conception Montreal, LPh, 58; Univ Sherbrooke, DL, 74. **CAREER** Prof, Col Saint-Ignace, 54-56, 58-59; prof, Col Sainte-Marie, 65-69; prof, Univ Montreal, 67-69; prof, Univ Sherbrooke, 69-70; Prof Lettres Francaises, Univ Ottawa, 70-, dir dept, 75-78; prof invite, Univ Kiel, 88; prof associe, Univ Moncton, 89-95. **HONORS AND AWARDS** Prix de l'Ambassade suisse, 60; Prix litteraire de La Press, 79; Prix litteraire Champlain, 80; LittD(hon), York Univ, 95. **RESEARCH** French-Canadian literature. **SELECTED PUBLICATIONS** Auth, "Anthologie de la poesie franco-ontarienne," des origines a nos jours, Sudbury, Prise de parlole, (91), 223; auth, "La Litterature regionale aux confins de l histoire et de la geographie," Sudbury, la societe historique du Nouvel Onterio, (93), 89; co auth, "Anthologie de la litterature quebecoise, sous la direction de Gilles Marcotte, tome II: La Patrie litteraire, 1760-1895," et tome IV (en collaboration avec Gabrielle Poulin) : Lage de l interrogation, 1937-1952, Montreal. La Presse, (revisee), (94), 463, 516; co auth, "Bibliographie de la critique de la litterature quebecoise et canadienne-francaise dans les revues canadiennes," en colaboration avec Pierre Cantin, 4 vol, (94), 328; auth, "1910, Une premiere prise de parole colloective en Ontarieo francais," dans Chiers Charlevoix. 1, Etudes franco-ontariennes, sudbury, societe Charlevoix et Prise de parole, (95), 15-124; auth, Lettres des nouvelles missions du Canada, 1972-1852, dans Cahiers Charlevoix, 2, etudes franco-ontariennes, Sudbury, societe Charlevoix et Prise de parole, (97), 389-486; auth, Anthologie de la litterature franco-ontarienne des origines a nos jours, tome 1,: les origines francaises (1610-1760): les origines franco-ontariennes (1760-1865), sudbury, Prise de parole, (97) 592; Histoire de la litterature franco-ontarienne des origines a nos jours, tome 1: les origines francaises (1610-1760): les origines franco-tome 1: les origines francaises (1610-1760): les origines franco-ontariennes(1760-1865), sudbury, Prise de parole, (97), 363; auth, Trois Litteratures francophones au Canada, 1972-1992," dans Cahiers charlevoix, 3, etudes franco-ontariennes, Sudbury, Societe charlevoix et Prise de parole, (98), 199-232. **CONTACT ADDRESS** Dept of Lettres Francaises, Univ of Ottawa, Pavillon Simard, Local 200, C.P. 450, Succ. A, Ottawa, ON, Canada K1N 6N5.

DIOP, SAMBA
PERSONAL Born 06/13/1957, Dakar, Senegal, 1 child **DISCIPLINE** FRENCH LANGUAGE & LITERATURE **EDUCATION** Univ Mas Amherst, BA, 89; Univ Calif Berkeley, MA, 90; PhD, 93. **CAREER** Vis asst prof, Univ Calif, Los Angeles, 93-94; asst prof, SUNY, Buffalo, 94-97; asst prof, Harvard Univ, 97-. **HONORS AND AWARDS** Phi Beta Kappa. **MEMBERSHIPS** ASA; CIEF. **RESEARCH** African Epic Literature, Oral Traditions, Francophone Film and Cinema, Francophone Literature, Post Colonial Studies. **SELECTED PUBLICATIONS** Auth, The Oral History and Literature of the Wolof of Senegal, Mellen Pr, 95; auth, Dis coups nationaliste et identite ethnique a travers le roman Selegalais, Nouvelles du Sud, (Paris), 99; auth, the Epic of El Hadj Uman Tall, Univ of Wisc, (Madison), 00. **CONTACT ADDRESS** Dept Romance Lang, Harvard Univ, 507 Boylston Hall, Cambridge, MA 02138.

DISTERHEFT, DOROTHY
PERSONAL Born Los Angeles, CA, d, 1 child **DISCIPLINE** LINGUISTICS **EDUCATION** Univ Calif at Los Angeles, BA, 68; PhD, 77. **CAREER** From asst prof to assoc prof, Univ of SC, 79-. **HONORS AND AWARDS** Fulbright Res Awd, Ireland Univ Col, 85-86. **MEMBERSHIPS** LSA. **RESEARCH** Historical Linguistics (especially syntax), Old and Middle Irish Syntax, Theory of Language Change. **SELECTED PUBLICATIONS** Auth, The Syntactic Development of the Infinitive in Indo-European, Slavica Press (Columbus, OH), 80; auth, "The role of adaptive rules in language change," Diachronica 7 (90): 181-198; auth, "Parameter resetting," Hist Ling 1991, John Benjamins, 93; auth, "Syntactic innovation in Early Irish," Dan do oide. Essays in memory of Conn R. O Cleirigh 1927-1995, Institiuid Teangeolaichta Eireann (Dublin, Ireland), 97; co-ed, Studies in Honor of Jaan Puhvel, Part I: Ancient Languages and Philology, Inst for the Study of Man (Washington, DC), 97. **CONTACT ADDRESS** Dept English, Univ of So Carolina, Columbia, Columbia, SC 29225. **EMAIL** disterh@vm.sc.edu

DIX, JENNIFER A.
PERSONAL m, 2001 **DISCIPLINE** COMPARATIVE LITERATURE **EDUCATION** Ind Univ, BA, 98; Univ Maryland, MA, 01. **CAREER** Teach asst, Univ Maryland, 00-01. **HONORS AND AWARDS** Grad Sch Univ MD, 98-99. **MEMBERSHIPS** MLA. **RESEARCH** Contemporary literature; culture and film of the Americas. **CONTACT ADDRESS** Comp Lit Prog, Univ of Maryland, Col Park, 2107 Susquehanna Hall, College Park, MD 20742. **EMAIL** jdix@wam.umd.edu

DJEBAR, ASSIA
DISCIPLINE FRENCH STUDIES **EDUCATION** Univ Paris-Sorbonne, DES, 59. **CAREER** LSU Found Distinguished Prof,

La State Univ, Dir, Ctr for Fr and Francophone Stud. **HONORS AND AWARDS** Doctor Honoris Causa, Univ of Vienna, 95; elected mem of the Belgian Royal Acad of French Lang and Lit, 99; Medal of Francophony, Academie Francaise de Paris, 99; Prize from the Review: Etudes Francaises, Montreal for Ces voix qui m'assiegent, 99; Int Prize of Palmi (Italy) for all creative work, 98; Marguerite Yourcenar Prize for Literature, Boston, for Oran Langue Morte, 97; Fonlon-Nichols Prize, African Lit Asn, USA, for all creative work, 97; Int Literary Neustadt Prize, World Lit Today, Oklahoma, for all creative work, 96; Maurice Maeterlinck Int Prize, Societe des gens de Lettres, Brussels, for all creative work, 95. **SELECTED PUBLICATIONS** Auth, Chronique d'un ete Algerien Paris: Plume, 93; auth, Vaste est la prison Paris, Albin Michel, 94; auth, Le blanc de l'Algerie Paris: Albin Michel, 96; auth, Oran, langue morte Paris: Actes Sud, 97; auth, Les nuits de Strasbourg Paris: Actes Sud, 97; auth, Ces voix qui m'assiegent: En marge de ma francophonie Paris: Albin Michel and Montreal: Les presses de l'universite de Montreal, 99. **CONTACT ADDRESS** Dept of Fr Grad Stud, Louisiana State Univ and A&M Col, Baton Rouge, LA 70803.

DOBSEVAGE, ALVIN P.
PERSONAL Born 11/29/1922, New York, NY, m, 1976, 4 children **DISCIPLINE** PHILOSOPHY, FRENCH, LATIN **EDUCATION** City Col New York, BA, 42; Harvard Univ, MA, 48; Columbia Univ, MPhilos, 52; Cent Conn State Univ, MA, 82. **CAREER** Instr philos, Brooklyn Col, 51-53; vconsul info off, US Info Serv, Salisbury, Rhodesia, 55-58; teacher Latin, Wilton High Sch, Conn, 58-65; asst prof, 65-82, Assoc Prof French, Latin and Ling, Western Conn State Col, 82-, Chmn Dept Mod Lang, 81-, Adj asst prof Latin, Saturday Sch Lang, NY Univ, 60-68; adj asst prof philos, Danbury State Col, 60-; lectr, Univ Conn, Stamford Br, 63-64; ed, Hermes Americanus, 90-95; Nat Endowment for Humanities grant, Am Acad Rome, 82. **HONORS AND AWARDS** Letter of Commendation from Off Personnel, Dept of Army for Work as Mem Haines Bd Study Group, 40, regarding civil affairs, Psychol Oper, 67. **MEMBERSHIPS** Am Philos Asn; Am Philol Asn; Mediaeval Acad Am; Class Asn New England; MLA. **RESEARCH** Gaston Bachelard's theory of imagination; aesthetics and metaphysics; teaching French and Latin. **SELECTED PUBLICATIONS** Auth, The Metamorphoses of Apuleius--On Making an Ass of Oneself, Class W, Vol 89, 96. **CONTACT ADDRESS** 45 Dodgingtown Rd, Bethel, CT 06801.

DOCKERY, CHARLES D.
DISCIPLINE FRENCH LANGUAGE **EDUCATION** Earlham Col, BA, 61; IA Univ, PhD, 74. **CAREER** Prof, Davidson Col, 74. **HONORS AND AWARDS** 2 Mellon grants; res dir montpellier study abroad prog, davidson col. **RESEARCH** Cult and lit of Quebec; the Francophone short story; tchg vocab and grammar through traditional and contemp songs; transl theory; multimedia courseware develop. **SELECTED PUBLICATIONS** Coauth, software program devel at Middlebury to teach French phonetics. **CONTACT ADDRESS** Davidson Col, 102 N Main St, PO Box 1719, Davidson, NC 28036.

DOCTER, MARY K.
DISCIPLINE HISPANIC LANGUAGES AND LITERATURES **EDUCATION** Univ Calif, LA, PhD, 91. **CAREER** Assistant Professor of Spanish, Westmont College, 92-present Assistant Professor, Department of Hispanic Studies, Scripps College, Claremont, 88-92 Bilingual Instructor, Colegio Eton, Mexico City, Mexico, 81-82 **HONORS AND AWARDS** UCLA Distinguished Teaching Awd, 1986-87 **RESEARCH** 20th cent Latin Am lit; romance ling. **SELECTED PUBLICATIONS** Auth, La Piedra y la masa: Un analisis comparativo de dos textos de Vallejo, Hispania 72:1, 89. **CONTACT ADDRESS** Dept of Eng, Westmont Col, 955 La Paz Rd, Santa Barbara, CA 93108-1099.

DOENGES, NORMAN ARTHUR
PERSONAL Born 08/23/1926, Ft Wayne, IN, m, 1952, 3 children **DISCIPLINE** ANCIENT HISTORY, CLASSICS **EDUCATION** Yale Univ, BA, 47; Oxford Univ, BA, 49; Princeton Univ, MA, 51, PhD (classics), 54; American School Classical Studies, 51-52. **CAREER** Instr classics, Princeton Univ, 49-50 and 52-53; from instr to assoc prof, 55-65, chmn dept classics, 59-63, 67-71 and 78-79, chmn div humanities, 63-67, assoc dean fac, 64-66, prof-in-chg, Intercol Ctr Class Studies, Rome, Italy, 66-67, Prof Classics, Dartmouth Col, 65-, Mem managing comt, Am Sch Class Studies; mem adv coun, Am Acad in Rome; Field Dir Excavation of the Roman colony of Pollentia, Mallorca, Spain, 84-97. **HONORS AND AWARDS** Woodrow Wilson Fellow, 50-51; Fulbright Fellow, 51-52. **MEMBERSHIPS** Soc Prom Hellenic Studies; Am Philol Asn; Class Asn Can; Class Asn New Eng(secy-treas, 63-68); Asn of Ancient Historians. **RESEARCH** Greek and Roman history; Greek pseudonymic letters. **SELECTED PUBLICATIONS** Auth, The Letters of Themistokles, New York: Arno Press, 81; auth, A. Arribas y N. Doenges, Piezas Singulares de una Estancia del Area Commercial del Foro de Pollentia, Travalhos de Antropologia e Etnologia 35, 95, 397-412; auth, Ostracism and the Boulai of Kleisthenes, Hist Zeitschrift Alte Geschichte, Vol 45, 96; The Campaign and Battle of Marathon, Historia 47 (1998)1-17. **CONTACT ADDRESS** Dept of Classics, Dartmouth Col, Hanover, NH 03755. **EMAIL** doenges@dartmouth.edu

DOERKSEN, VICTOR GERARD
PERSONAL Born 01/09/1934, Winnipeg, MB, Canada, m, 1960, 2 children **DISCIPLINE** GERMAN LITERATURE AND CRITICISM **EDUCATION** Univ Man, BA, 58, MA, 60, Univ Zurich, DPhil(Ger), 64. **CAREER** Asst prof Ger, Univ NB, 60-61; lectr, 61-62 and 64-65, from asst prof to assoc prof, 66-74, Prof Ger, Univ Col, Univ Man, 74-, Head Dept, 68-, Can Coun Res Grant, 67-. **MEMBERSHIPS** Asn Can Univ Teachers Ger, Int Germanistenverband. **RESEARCH** Nineteenth Century German literature, literary criticism. **CONTACT ADDRESS** Dept of Ger and Slavic Stud, Univ of Manitoba, 327 Fletcher Argue, Winnipeg, MB, Canada R3T 2N2.

DOHERTY, LILLIAN E.
DISCIPLINE GREEK AND LATIN LITERATURE **EDUCATION** St Mary's Col, BA; Univ Chicago, MA, PhD. **CAREER** Instr, George Mason Univ; Howard Univ; asst prof, 87; assoc prof, Univ of Md, 93-. **HONORS AND AWARDS** Affil, women's stud prog; comp lit prog. **RESEARCH** Homeric epic, classical mythology, and women in classical antiquity. **SELECTED PUBLICATIONS** Auth, Tyro in Odyssey 11: Closed and Open Readings, Helios, 92; Gender and Internal Audiences in the Odyssey, Amer Jour of Philol, 92; Siren Songs: Gender, Audiences, and Narrators in the Odyssey, Univ Mich Press, 95; Sirens, Muses and Female Narrators in the Odyssey, The Distaff Side: Representing the Female in Homer's Odyssey, Oxford UP, 95 y **CONTACT ADDRESS** Dept of Class, Univ of Maryland, Col Park, 2407 Marie Mount Hall, College Park, MD 20742-1335. **EMAIL** LL21@umail.umd.edu

DOLEZEL, LUBOMIR
PERSONAL Born 10/03/1922, Lesnice, Czechoslovakia **DISCIPLINE** SLAVIC & COMPARATIVE LITERATURE **EDUCATION** Charles Univ Prague, grad, 49; Czeck Acad Sci, PhD, 58. **CAREER** High sch tchr, Czeck, 49-54; res fel, Czeck Acad Sci, 58-68; assoc prof, Charles Univ Prague, 61-68; vis prof, Univ Mich, 65-68; vis prof, 68-71, prof, 71-88, ch dept, 80-83, prof emer Slavic & Comparative Lit, Univ Toronto, 88-; vis prof, Univ Amsterdam, 76; vis prof, Univ Munich, 77. **HONORS AND AWARDS** Can Coun leave fel, 77-78; Connaught sr fel, 83-84; Mem Medal Resistance; fel, Royal Soc Can. **MEMBERSHIPS** Toronto Semiotic Cir; Can Comp Lit Asn; Asn Czeck Writers. **SELECTED PUBLICATIONS** Auth, Narativni zpusoby v ceske literature, Prague, Cesky spisovatel, 93; auth, "The Themata of Eco's Semiotics of Literature," in Rocco Capozzi, ed., Reading Eco: An Anthology, (Bloomington: Indiana Univ Press, 97): 111-20; auth, "Fictional Worlds: Density, Gaps, and Inference," Style vol. 25, (95): 201-14; auth, "De la diversite des poetiques," in Pierre Laurette and Hans-George Ruprecht, eds., Poetiques et imaginaires: Francopolyphonie litteraire des Ameriques, (Paris: L'Harmattan,95): 135-47; auth, "Roman Jakobson as a Student of Communication," in Elen Semek-Pankratov, ed., Studies of Poetics: Commemorative Vol, Krystna omorska (1928-1986), (Columbus, OH: Slavic Publishers, 95): 27-38; auth, "Structuralism of the Prague School," in Raman Selden, ed., Cambridge Hist of Literary Criticism, vol. 8, (Cambridge: Cambridge Univ Press, 95): 33-57; auth, "Prazska skols v exilu," Svetova literarnevedna bohemistika, Prague: Ustav pro ceskou literaturu AV CR, sv. 2, (96): 506-11; auth, "In Search of Implicit Meaning: From Rhetoric to Cognitive Text Theory," Canadian Journal for Rhetorical Studies/La Revue Canadienne d'etudes rhetoriques, vol. 6, (96): 63-72; auth, "Mundos de Ficcion: densidad, vacios e inferencias," in J.M. Pozuelo Yvancos and F. Vicente Gomez, eds., Mundos de Ficcion, (Universidad de Murcia: Servicio de Publicationes, 96): 13-26; auth, "Polyfunctional or Monofunctional Language?" in H. Hendrix, et al., eds., The Search for a New Alphabet: Literary Studies in a Changing World, (In Honor of Douwe Fokkema), (Amsterdam: Benjamins, 96): 73-77; auth, "The Themata of Eco's Semiotics of Literature," in Rocco Capozzi, ed., Reading Eco: An Anthology, (Bloomington: Indiana Univ Press, 97): 111-20. **CONTACT ADDRESS** Univ of Toronto, Robarts Libr, 14th Fl, Toronto, ON, Canada M5S 1A1.

DOLEZVELOVA-VELINGEROVA, MILENA
PERSONAL Born Prague, Czechoslovakia **DISCIPLINE** CHINESE LANGUAGE & LITERATURE **EDUCATION** Charles Univ, Prague, MA, 55; Oriental Inst, Prague, PhD, 65. **CAREER** Res assoc, Oriental Inst, Czeck Acad Sci, 54-68; res assoc, Inst Lit, Chinese Acad Sci, Beijing, 58-59; res assoc, Ctr Chinese Studs, Univ Mich, 67-68; assoc prof, 69-75, Prof, Univ Toronto 75-. **HONORS AND AWARDS** Sr. Res Vis Fel, Corpus Christi Col, Cambridge Univ, 84-85; Res Scholar, The Rockfeller Found Stud & Conf Ctr, Bellagio, Italy, 85; vis scholar, Harvard Univ, 90-91. **MEMBERSHIPS** Asn Asian Studs; Toronto Semiotic Circle; Can Asn Comparative Lit. **SELECTED PUBLICATIONS** Coauth/transl, The Ballad of the Hidden Dragon, 71; coauth, The Chinese Novel at the Turn of the Century, 80; coauth/ed, A Selective Guide to Chinese Literature 1900-1949, 88; coauth/ed, Poetics East and West, 89. **CONTACT ADDRESS** Dept of East Asian Studies, Univ of Toronto, Toronto, ON, Canada M5S 1S3.

DOLLENMAYER, DAVID BRISTOL
PERSONAL Born 04/05/1945, TN, m **DISCIPLINE** LINGUISTICS, LITERATURE **EDUCATION** Princeton Univ, BA, 67; PhD, 77. **CAREER** Instr, Middlebury Col, 75-76; instr, Smith Col, 76-78; asst prof, MIT, 78-88; prof, Worcester Poly Inst, 88-. **HONORS AND AWARDS** Fulbright-Hays Fel, 67-68; Woodrow Wilson Fel, 71-72. **MEMBERSHIPS** MLA; AATG. **RESEARCH** 20th-century German literature. **SELECTED PUBLICATIONS** Auth, The Berlin Novels of Alfred Dobun, 88; auth, Neve Horizonte, 99, 5th ed. **CONTACT ADDRESS** Dept Humanities and Arts, Worcester Polytech Inst, 100 Institute Rd, Worcester, MA 01609-2247. **EMAIL** dbd@wpi.edu

DOMINGO-FORASTE, DOUGLAS
PERSONAL Born 05/04/1954, Los Angeles, CA, m, 1999, 2 children **DISCIPLINE** COMPARATIVE LITERATURE, CLASSIC STUDIES **EDUCATION** Univ Calif Davis, AB, 76; Univ Calif Santa Barb, MA, 81; PhD, 88. **CAREER** Res, Univ Calif Irvine, assoc prof, ICCS, Rome, 99-00; 86-90; lectr, asst prof, assoc prof, prof, Calif State Long Beach, 88-. **HONORS AND AWARDS** CSULB Col Lib Arts, Most Val Prof, 96, 98. **MEMBERSHIPS** ANS; AIA; APA; CCA; BSC. **RESEARCH** Greek numismatics; Greek law; Menander. **SELECTED PUBLICATIONS** Trans, "Life of Sts. David, Symeon, and George of Lesbos," in Byzantine Defenders of Images, ed. A. M. Talbot (DC: Dumbarton Oaks, 98): 143-241; ed, Claudius Aelianus Epistulae et Fragmenta, Bibliotheca Teubneriana (Leipzig: Teubner, 94)); ed, Lysias On the Murder of Eratosthenes (Amherst, Mass: CANE, 94); auth, "Walcott's Other: Philoctete and Philoctetes," Genre 16 (95): 84-93; auth, "The Dual Number," Athen NL (95): 18-20; auth, "The Fourth Century Mint of Anaktorion" in La Monetazione corinzia in Occidente: Atti del IX Convegno del Centro Internazionale di Studi Numismatici, eds. A. Stazio, M. Taliercio Mensitieri, R. Vitale (Rome, 93): 43-59; auth, "Piety in Menander, " Laetaberis 7 (89): 1-8; auth, "The Fourth Century Mint at Anaktorion, " Am J Arch 88 (84): 242-243. **CONTACT ADDRESS** Dept of Comp Lit and Classics, California State Univ, Long Beach, 1250 Bellflower Rd, Long Beach, CA 90840-2404. **EMAIL** dforaste@csulb.edu

DOMINGUEZ, SYLVIA
DISCIPLINE SPANISH **EDUCATION** Our Lady of the Lake Col, Med; Univ Ariz, MA; PhD, 71. **CAREER** Visiting Prof, Univ Ariz, 78-85; Prof, Univ Tex Pan Am, 60-. **HONORS AND AWARDS** Nat Honor Scholarship, Alpha Chi; Sigma Delta Pi; Kappa Delta Phi; Kappa Gamma Phi; Sigma Tau Delta; Alpha Psi Omega; Intl Book of Honor, 82; Honor Student, Nat Univ of Mex; Who's Who in the South and Southwest, 82-83; Cervantes Awd, Am Asn of Teachers of Spanish and Port; NEH Grant. **MEMBERSHIPS** Am Asn of Teachers of Spanish and Port, SW Coun of Latin Am Studies; Tex Asn of Col Teachers. **RESEARCH** Spanish Language and Literature; Golden Age Spanish Literature (Peninsular); Spanish American Literature--Poetry, Novel, and Drama; Original and Creative Activity (Drama) and Hispanic Studies. **SELECTED PUBLICATIONS** Auth, "Curanderismo: A Dramatic Portrayal," Dept of State Pub, 76; auth, La comadre Maria, Am Universal Art Forms Co, 73; auth, La comadre Maria. Instruction-Production System, Am Universal Art Forms Co, 76; auth, "The Chekhov Theatre," "The Christmas Twins - Zonia and Antonia," and "Lest We Forget," Journal of sigma Tau Delta, 56. **CONTACT ADDRESS** Dept Mod Lang, Univ of Texas, Pan American, 1201 W Univ Dr, Edinburg, TX 78539-2909.

DONADEY, ANNE
DISCIPLINE FRENCH, WOMEN'S STUDIES **EDUCATION** Universite de Nice, France, BA, 84; MA, 85; Northwestern Univ, PhD, 93. **CAREER** Lectr, Univ Tex Austin, 85-87; TA, Northwestern Univ, 88-93; asst to assoc prof, Univ Iowa, 93-01; assoc prof, San Diego State Univ, 01-. **HONORS AND AWARDS** Diss Recognition Awd, Northwestern Univ, 91; Awd, Iowa Cult Affairs Coun, 95-96; Awd, Obermann Ctr for Adv Studies Humanities Symposium Awd, 95-96; Who's Who in the Midwest, 96, 98-99. **MEMBERSHIPS** African Lit Assoc, AAUW, AATF, AAUP, Midwest Mod Lang Assoc, MLA, Women in Fr. **RESEARCH** Postcolonial literature (especially North African and Caribbean women writers), postcolonial theory, feminist theory and criticism, colonialism, race and gender in France and the US. **SELECTED PUBLICATIONS** Auth, "Assia Djebar's Poetics of Subversion," L'Esprit createur 33.2 (93): 107-17; auth, "'Une certaine idee de la France': The Algeria Syndrome and Struggles over 'French' Identity," Identity Papers: Contested Nationhood in Twentieth-Century France, ed Steven Unger and Tom Conley, Univ of Minn Pr, (Minneapolis, 96): 215-32; auth, "Rekindling the Vividness of the Past Assia Djebar's Films and Fiction," World Lit Today 70.4 (96): 885-92; coed, Empire and Occupation and the Francophone World, Studies in Twentieth-Century Literature 23.1 (99); auth, "Cultural Multilingual Strategies of Postcolonial Literature: Assia Djebar's Algerian Palimpsest," World Lit Today 74.1 (00): 27-36; auth, "'Y' a bon Banania': Ethics and Cultural Criticism in the Colonial Context," Fr Cult Studies 11. 1.31, (00): 9-29; auth, "Portrait of a Maghrebian Feminist as a Young Girl: Fatima Mernissi's 'Dreams of Trespass,'" Edebiyat: Jour of Middle Eastern Lit 11.1 (00): 85-103; auth, "Anamnesis and National Reconciliation: Re-Membering October 17, 1961," Immigrant Narratives in Contemporary France, ed Susan

Ireland and Patrice J Proulx, Greenwood Pr, (01): 47-56; auth, Recasting Postcolonialism: Women Writing between Worlds, Heinemann, 01. **CONTACT ADDRESS** European Studies, San Diego State Univ, 5500 Campanile Dr, San Diego, CA 92182.

DONAHUE, JOHN F.
DISCIPLINE CLASSICAL STUDIES **EDUCATION** Col Holy Cross, AB, 80; Univ NC at Chapel Hill, MA, 90, PhD, 96. **CAREER** Adj instr; Col William and Mary, 97; adj asst prof, Williamsburg, Va; tchg asst, Med Word Formation and Entymology, 94 & Latin, 91-93, Univ NC at Chapel Hill; Fay Sch, 86-88; UNC res ast, L'Annee Philiologique, 89-91, 94; Latin tutor, 91-93; fact checker, Amer Nat Biog, Oxford UP, 95-. **HONORS AND AWARDS** UNC Grad Sch Dissertation fel, 95; UNC Grad Sch Dept Class Travel Awd(s), 94 & Kappa Delta Pi Honor Soc, Colombia Univ, 84. **MEMBERSHIPS** Amer Philol Asn; Asn Int d'Epigraphie Grecque et Latine; Class Asn Mid W and S. **RESEARCH** Roman social history; Ancient dining; Latin inscriptions. **SELECTED PUBLICATIONS** Auth, Feasts and Females: Sex Roles, Public Recognition and Community Banquets in the Western Roman Empire, Class Asn Mid W and S, Nashville, 96; Public Banqueting in the Roman Empire: Issues for Consideration, Class Asn Mid W and S, Southern Section, Chapel Hill, 94 & Distributions of Bread During the Later Roman Empire: Some Chronological Problems, Class Asn Mid W and S, Atlanta, 94. **CONTACT ADDRESS** Dept of Classical Studies, Col of William and Mary, Morton Hall, PO Box 8795, Williamsburg, VA 23187-8795. **EMAIL** jfdona@facstaff.wm.edu

DONAHUE, THOMAS JOHN
PERSONAL Born 01/09/1943, Philadelphia, PA, 2 children **DISCIPLINE** FRENCH LITERATURE, THEATRE **EDUCATION** Univ Pa, AM, 67 PhD, 73. **CAREER** Asst prof, 65-80, Assoc Prof, 80-91, prof, 91-, St Joseph's Univ. **HONORS AND AWARDS** Scholarship of the Alliance Francaise de Philadelphie, 64-65; fel Camargo Found, 78; Awd for Tchg, Awd for Scholarship, St Joseph's Univ. **MEMBERSHIPS** Am Asn of Tchrs of French; Alliance Francaise de Philadelphie. **RESEARCH** Auth, 20th-Century French theater; French theater history; theater semiotics. **SELECTED PUBLICATIONS** The Theater of Fernando Arrabal, New York Univ Press, 80; auth, Structures of Meaning: A Semiotic Approach to the Play Text, Fairleigh Dickinson. **CONTACT ADDRESS** Dept of French, Saint Joseph's Univ, 5600 City Ave, Philadelphia, PA 19131-1376. **EMAIL** tdonahue@sju.edu

DONLAN, WALTER
PERSONAL Born 07/30/1934, Boston, MA **DISCIPLINE** CLASSICS **EDUCATION** Harvard Col, BA, 56; Northwestern Univ, PhD, 68. **CAREER** Asst prof to prof, classics, Penn St Univ, 67-86; prof classics, Univ of Calif, Irvine, 86- . **HONORS AND AWARDS** Pres, Class Asn of the Atlantic states, 79-80. **MEMBERSHIPS** Am Philol Asn; Archaeol Inst of Am; Asn of Ancient Hist; Calif Class Asn. **RESEARCH** Early Greek literature, Greek social history. **SELECTED PUBLICATIONS** Auth, Duelling with Gifts in the Illiad: As the Audience Saw It, in Colby Q, 93; coauth, The Village Community of Ancient Greece: Neolithic, Bronze and Dark Ages, in Studi Micenei ed Egeo-Anatolici, 93; auth, Chief and Followers in Pre-State Greece, in From Political Economy to Anthropology: Situating Economic Life in Past Societies, Black Rose, 94; auth, The Homeric Economy, in A New Companion to Homeric Studies, Brill, 97; auth, The Relations of Power in the Pre-State and Early State Politics, in The Development of the Polis in Archaic Greece, Routledge, 97; auth, Political Reciprocity in Dark Age Greece: Odysseus and his Hetairoi, in Reciprocity in Ancient Greece, Oxford,, 97; coauth, Ancient Greece: A Political, Social, and Cultural History, Oxford, 99; auth, The Aristocratic Ideal and Selected Papers, Bulchazy-Carducci, 99. **CONTACT ADDRESS** Dept of Classics, Univ of California, Irvine, 120 Humanities Office Bldg 2, Irvine, CA 92697. **EMAIL** wdonlan@uci.edu

DOOLITTLE, JAMES
PERSONAL Born 10/08/1917, Morristown, NJ, m, 1944, 6 children **DISCIPLINE** FRENCH LANGUAGE & LITERATURE, FRENCH HISTORY **EDUCATION** Princeton Univ, AB, 39, MA, 42, PhD, 48. **CAREER** Teacher French and English, Thacher Sch, Calif, 39-40; instr French, Princeton Univ, 46-49; from asst prof to prof, Ohio State Univ, 49-61; prof Romance lang and head dept, Univ Cincinnati, 61-65; Prof French Lit, Univ Rochester, 65-, Ohio State Univ fel, 59-60; Guggenheim fel, 62-63 and 65; Am Coun Learned Soc grant, 69-70. **RESEARCH** History of ideas in France, 1600-1900; French literature of the 17th, 18th and 19th centuries; 17th century French memoirs. **SELECTED PUBLICATIONS** Auth, The Hungry Spirit, Selected Plays and Prose of Gowan, Elsie, Park, Theatre Rsrc Can Recherches Theatrales Can, Vol 13, 1992 The Nowlan, Alden Papers--An Inventory of the Archive at the University Of Calgary Libraries, Theatre Rsrc Int, Vol 19, 94. **CONTACT ADDRESS** Dept of Foreign Lang, Lit and Ling, Univ of Rochester, Rochester, NY 14627.

DORENLOT, FRANCOISE
PERSONAL Born 03/28/1934, Paris, France **DISCIPLINE** FRENCH LANGUAGE AND LITERATURE **EDUCATION** Univ Aix-Marseille, Lic en Droit, 55; Univ Paris, Lic es Let, 57; Univ Cincinnati, MA, 58; Univ Calif, Los Angeles, PhD (French), 66. **CAREER** Lectr French, McGill Univ, 61-65; lectr, 65-66, from instr to asst prof, 66-72, Assoc Prof French, City Col New York, 72-. **SELECTED PUBLICATIONS** Auth, THE MISSING CENTER OR NIHILISM AND LITERATURE - PAPERS WRITTEN IN HONOR OF TISON-BRAUN,MICHELINE/, ESPRIT CREATEUR, Vol 34, 1994 **CONTACT ADDRESS** Dept of Romance Lang City, City Col, CUNY, New York, NY 10031.

DORIAN, NANCY CURRIER
PERSONAL Born 11/05/1936, New Brunswick, NJ **DISCIPLINE** LINGUISTICS, GERMANIC AND CELTIC LANGUAGES **EDUCATION** Conn Col, BA, 58; Univ Mich, MA, 61, PhD (ling), 65. **CAREER** Lectr, 65-66, from asst prof to assoc prof, 66-78, prof ling, Ger and anthrop, 78-79, William R Kenan, Jr, Prof Ling, Bryn Mawr Col, 80-. **MEMBERSHIPS** Ling Soc Am; Int Ling Asn; Celtic Studies Asn; Scottish Oral Hist Group. **RESEARCH** Linguistic change; language death; Scottish Gaelic and Pennsylvania Dutch. **SELECTED PUBLICATIONS** Auth, A Response to Ladefoged Other View of Endangered Languages, Lang, Vol 69, 93; An Introduction to the Ecology of Written Language, Lang, Vol 71, 95; Multilingualism, Lang, Vol 72, 96; Language Selection and Switching in Strasbourg, Lang, Vol 69, 93; Language Conflict and Language Planning, Language in Society, Vol 25, 96; Sustaining Local Literacies, Lang Soc, Vol 24, 95; 1st Language Attrition, Lang, Vol 68, 92; Language of the Islenos--Vestigial Spanish in Louisiana, Romance Philol, Vol 47, 94; Foundations of Bilingual Education and Bilingualism, Lings, Vol 32, 94; Sociolinguistics--A Sociological Critique, Lang, Vol 70, 94; Varieties of Variation in a Very Small Place--Social Homogeneity, Prestige Norms, and Linguistic Variation, Lang, Vol 70, 94; Endangered Languages, Lang, Vol 70, 94; Purism Vs Compromise in Language Revitalization and Language Revival, Lang Soc, Vol 23, 94. **CONTACT ADDRESS** Dept English, Bryn Mawr Col, 101 N Merion Ave, Bryn Mawr, PA 19010-2899.

DORON, PINCHAS
PERSONAL Born 07/05/1933, Poland, m, 1969, 5 children **DISCIPLINE** HEBREW LANGUAGE, BIBLE **EDUCATION** Hebrew Univ, Jerusalem, BA, 62, MA, 64; NYork Univ, PhD (Hebrew studies), 75. **CAREER** Instr Hebrew and Talmud, Jewish Theol Sem, 64-65; lectr Hebrew, Hunter Col, 65-66; Asst Prof Hebrew, Queens Col, 66-, Instr, The Ulpan Ctr, 69-70. **MEMBERSHIPS** Asn Jewish Studies; Nat Asn Professors Hebrew. **RESEARCH** Biblical research; Hebrew language and literature; medieval Hebrew literature. **SELECTED PUBLICATIONS CONTACT ADDRESS** 730 E 7th St, Brooklyn, NY 11218.

DORSEY, JAMES
DISCIPLINE ASIAN AND MIDDLE EASTERN LANGUAGES AND LITERATURES **EDUCATION** Colgate Univ, BA, 83; IN Univ, MA, 92; Univ WA, PhD, 97. **CAREER** Asst prof, Dartmouth Col; lecturer and teaching asst, 90-96; dir, 97; Darthmouth Japan Foreign Study prog, 98-99. **HONORS AND AWARDS** Soc Sci Res Coun/Japan Soc for the Promotion for Sci res grant, 00-01. **RESEARCH** Mod Japanese lit, criticism, and intellectual hist; class Japanese drama and lit theory. **SELECTED PUBLICATIONS** Transl, Japanese fiction; transl "The Unsinkable Molly Brown, " by Kageyama Tamio. In New Japanese Voices: The Best Contemporary Fiction, Atlantic Monthly Pr, 91; auth, "Escaping the Impasse in the Discourse on National Identity: Hagiwara Sakutaro, Sakaguchi Ango, and Nishitani Keiji," In New Historicism and Japanese Library Studies: Proceedings of the Midwest Association for Japanese Literary Studies, 98. **CONTACT ADDRESS** Dept of Asian an Middle Eastern Lang and Lit, Dartmouth Col, 6191 Bartlett Hall, Hanover, NH 03755. **EMAIL** james.dorsey@dartmouth.edu

DORSINVILLE, MAX
PERSONAL Born 01/30/1943, Port-au-Prince, Haiti, m, 1964, 1 child **DISCIPLINE** ENGLISH, COMPARATIVE LITERATURE **EDUCATION** Univ Sherbrooke, BA, 66, MA, 68; City Univ New York, PhD (comp lit), 72. **CAREER** Lectr, 70-72, asst prof, 72-75; dir, Ctr for French-Can Studies, 75-80, Assoc Prof English, McGill Univ, 75-, Can Coun fel, 77-78. **HONORS AND AWARDS** Canada Coun leave fel, Humanities Research Council and Multiculturalism Directoraate publication grants, McGill Graduaate Fac interntional travel and res grants. **MEMBERSHIPS** Can Comp Lit Asn (treas, 75-77); Asn Can Univ Teachers English. **RESEARCH** 20th century lit (Canadian, Am, Caribbean), Modernism, fiction, Derek Waalcott's poetry. **SELECTED PUBLICATIONS** Auth, Caliban without Prospero: Essay on Quebec and Black Literature, 74; auth, Le Pays natal: Essais sur les litteratures du Tiers-Monde et du Quebec, 83; auth, Solidarites: Tiers-Monde et litterature comparee, 88; auth, "Remembering Rogeer Dorsinvill," Res in African Literatures 25, (94), 171-175; auth, James Wait, novel, 95; auth, Ronald Sutherland, in The Oxford Companion to Canadian Literature, 2nd ed, 97; auth, Erzulie Loves Shango, novel, 98; auth, "The Heat of Home: Metaphors of Incorporation in Derek Walcott's Poetry," Anglistica 3:1, 99; auth, The Rule of Francois ("Papa Doc") Duvalier Realism and Magic Realism in Haiti, 00. **CONTACT ADDRESS** Dept of English, McGill Univ, 853 Sherbrooke W, Montreal, QC, Canada H3A 2T6. **EMAIL** mdorsi@po-box.mcgill.ca

DOSWALD, HERMAN K.
PERSONAL Born 03/24/1932, Oakland, CA, m, 1956, 2 children **DISCIPLINE** GERMAN **EDUCATION** Univ Calif, Berkeley, AB, 55; Univ Wash, MA, 59, PhD, 65. **CAREER** Instr Ger, Oberlin Col, 59-60, Univ Wash, 60-61, Seattle Univ, 61-62; actg asst prof, Univ Kans, 64-65, asst prof, 65-67; from asst prof to assoc prof, Fresno State Col, 67-72; prof Ger and chmn dept Ger and Slavic lang and lit, Kent State Univ, 72-79; Prof Ger and Head Dept Foreign Lang and Lit, Va Polytech Inst and State Univ, 79-. **MEMBERSHIPS** Int Vereinigung fur Germanische Sprach-und Literaturwissenschaft. **RESEARCH** Hugo von Hofmannsthal; modern German literature; East German literature. **SELECTED PUBLICATIONS CONTACT ADDRESS** Dept of Foreign Lang and Lit, Virginia Polytech Inst and State Univ, Blacksburg, VA 24061.

DOUBLES, MALCOLM CARROLL
PERSONAL Born 08/14/1932, Richmond, VA, m, 1956, 3 children **DISCIPLINE** RELIGION, PHILOLOGY **EDUCATION** Davidson Col, BA, 53; Union Theol Sem, Va, BD, 57; Univ St Andrews, PhD, 62. **CAREER** Pastor, Lebanon & Castlewood Presby Churches, VA, 60-65; asst prof Old Testament, St Andrews Presby Col, 65-69, mem Christianity & cult team, 65-74, chmn freshman Christianity & cult team, 67-71, assoc prof relig, 69-76, dean students, 74-76; prof Relig & Dean Col, 76-97, Distinguished Prof Intl Studies, Coker Col, 97-; Fulbright fel, Pakistan, 84, P R China, 88; NEH younger humanist fel, 71-72; managing ed, St Andrews Rev, 72-76; managing ed, Prog for Comput & Publ Targumic Lit, 74-. **MEMBERSHIPS** Soc Bibl Lit; Int Orgn for Study Old Testament; Asn Targumic Studies 2E **RESEARCH** Aramaic language and literature, with particular reference to Targumic studies; linguistics, with particular reference to Hebrew and Greek; New Testament background, with particular reference to Jewish history. **SELECTED PUBLICATIONS** Auth, Toward the publication of the Palestinian Targum(s), Vetus Testamentum, Vol XV, No 1; Indications of antiquity in the Fragment Targum, in In Memoriam Paul Kahle, Topelmann, 68; contribr, The History of the Jews in the Time of Christ, T&T Clark & Sons, 73. **CONTACT ADDRESS** Coker Col, 300 E College Ave, Hartsville, SC 29550-3797. **EMAIL** mdoubles@aol.com

DOUBROVSKY, SERGE
PERSONAL Born 05/22/1928, Paris, France, m, 1955, 2 children **DISCIPLINE** FRENCH **EDUCATION** Sorbonne, Lic philos, 49, Lic English, 51, Dd'Etat(Fr lit), 64; Nat Ministry Educ, France, Agrege, 54. **CAREER** Instr French, Harvard Univ, 55-57; asst prof, Brandeis Univ, 57-61; from assoc prof to prof, Smith Col, 61-66; Prof French, NY Univ, 66-, Guggenheim fels, 65-66, 68-69. **MEMBERSHIPS** MLA. **RESEARCH** Seventeenth century literature; contemporary cirticism and fiction. **SELECTED PUBLICATIONS** Auth, Excerpts From Le Livre Brise, Genre Forms of Discourse and Culture, Vol 26, 93; The Fact is That Writing is a Profoundly Immoral Act--An Interview with Doubrovsky, Serge, Genre Forms Discourse Cult, Vol 26, 93; Autobiography Truth Psychoanalysis Reprinted from Autobiographies, Pg 68-79, 88; Genre Forms Discourse Cult, Vol 26, 93. **CONTACT ADDRESS** Dept of French, New York Univ, 19 University Pl, New York, NY 10003-4556.

DOUDOROFF, MICHAEL JOHN
PERSONAL Born 04/26/1939, Carmel, CA, m, 1963, 1 child **DISCIPLINE** SPANISH LANGUAGE & LITERATURE **EDUCATION** Stanford Univ, AB, 61, MA, 65, PhD(Span), 69. **CAREER** From acting asst prof to asst prof, 65-76, assoc prof, 76-88, Prpf Span, Univ KS, 88-. **MEMBERSHIPS** MLA; Am Asn Teachers Span & Port; Latin Am Studies Asn; AAUP; MMLA; IILI. **RESEARCH** Hispanic folklore; Spanish American literature; Venezuelan poetry. **SELECTED PUBLICATIONS** Auth, Tensions and triangles in Al Filo del Agua, Hispania, 74; El auto de los reyes magos en tradicion reciente, Rev Dialectologia y Tradiciones Populares, 74; Coordinate design in a Chilean Nueva Novels, Latin Am Lit Rev, 75; Lectura de La boba y el Buda, In: Aproximaciones a G Alvarez Gardeazabal, Bogota, Plaza Y Janes, 77; N S Momaday y la novela indigenista en ingles, Texto Critico, 79; Moros y Cristianos in Zacatecas, Lawrence, Amadeo Concha, 81; Lesbia y liron, SFQ, 78; Ruben Dario y las primas de Euterpe, in RD Azul y Prosas profanas, ed, Debicki & Doudoroff, Madrid, Alhambra, 85; Jose Emilio Pacheco: an Overview of the Poetry, Hispania, 89, rev and trans in Verani, La hoguera y el viento, MEX, UNAM/Era, 93; Prologo, Juan Liscano, Nuevo mundo Orinoco, Caracas, Monte Avila, 93; ed, Romulo Gallegos, Canaima, Pittsburgh UP, 96; translations of works by Juan Liscano, Santa Lopez, Jose Balza, Rafael Castillo Zapata. **CONTACT ADDRESS** Dept of Span & Port, Univ of Kansas, Lawrence, 3062 Wescoe, Lawrence, KS 66045-2166. **EMAIL** mdoudoroff@ukans.edu

DOUGHERTY, RAY CORDELL
PERSONAL Born 09/18/1940, Brooklyn, NY, m, 1982, 3 children **DISCIPLINE** LINGUISTICS, PHILOSOPHY OF LANGUAGE **EDUCATION** Dartmouth Col, BA, 62, MS, 64; Mass Inst Technol, PhD, 68. **CAREER** Res assoc ling, Mass Inst Technol, 68-69; asst prof, 69-72, Assoc Pr of Ling, NY Univ, 72-; Fulbright prof ling, Univ Salzburg, Austria, 76-77. **MEMBERSHIPS** Ling Soc Am; Philos Sci Asn. **RESEARCH** Grammar; Computational Linguistics; history of science. **SELECTED PUBLICATIONS** Auth, A grammar of coordination: I,II, Language, 12/70; coauth, Appositive NP constructions, 1/72 & auth, A survey of linguistic methods, 11/73, Found Lang. **CONTACT ADDRESS** Dept of Ling, New York Univ, 719 Broadway, New York, NY 10003-6806. **EMAIL** doughert@acfz.nyu.edu

DOUGLASS, R. THOMAS
PERSONAL Born 06/24/1932, Morristown, NY, m, 1981 **DISCIPLINE** SPANISH, LINGUISTICS **EDUCATION** George Washington Univ, BA, 54; Univ Pa, PhD (Romance ling), 64. **CAREER** Teacher high sch, NY, 58-62; from asst prof to assoc prof Span and ling, Millersville State Col, 63-67; assoc prof French, Span and ling and head dept foreign lang, Simpson Col, 67-70; Assoc Prof Span, Univ Iowa, 70-, Vis lectr ling, St Joseph's Col, Pa, 64-66; textbk consult, Xerox Col Publ, 72-73; Co-Ed, Iowa Foreign Lang Bull, 72-; lang arts consult, Scott, Foresman and Co, 73; Textbk Consult, Holt-Rinehart, Random House and Prentice-Hall, 76-. **MEMBERSHIPS** Am Asn Teachers Span and Port; Am Coun Teaching Foreign Lang. **RESEARCH** Spanish spelling; historical Spanish grammar; teaching methods in foreign languages. **SELECTED PUBLICATIONS** **CONTACT ADDRESS** Univ of Iowa, 218 Schaeffer Hall, Iowa City, IA 52242.

DOUTHWAITE, JULIA V.
PERSONAL Born 03/10/1958, Seattle, WA, m, 2 children **DISCIPLINE** FRENCH LITERATURE **EDUCATION** Univ Wash, BA, 81, MA, 84; Princeton Univ, MA, 86, PhD, 90. **CAREER** Assoc prof. **HONORS AND AWARDS** NEH Fel, 95-96; Summer NEH Fel, 93. **MEMBERSHIPS** MLA; ASECS. **RESEARCH** Prose fiction; voyage literature; enlightenment philosophy and history; feminist criticism; comparative studies; french revolution. **SELECTED PUBLICATIONS** Auth, Exotic Women: Literary Heroines and Cultural Strategies in Ancien Regime France, 92; Between Monster and Model, Eighteenth C Life, 97. **CONTACT ADDRESS** Romance Languages and Literatures Dept, Univ of Notre Dame, Notre Dame, IN 46556.

DOW, JAMES RAYMOND
PERSONAL Born 01/02/1936, D'Lo, MS **DISCIPLINE** GERMAN FOLKLORE **EDUCATION** MS Col, BA, 57; Univ IA, MA, 61, PhD(Ger), 66. **CAREER** Instr Ger, Univ IA, 64-66; asst prof, Univ WY, 66-70; asst prof, 71-74, assoc prof, 74-80, prof Ger, IA State Univ, 80-. **RESEARCH** Hermann Hesse's Marchen; Romantic Kunstmarchen; American-German folkloristic studies. **SELECTED PUBLICATIONS** Co-ed, Internationale Volkskundliche Bibliographie, 82; German Volkskunde; Nazification of an Academic Discipline; Volkische Wissenschaft. **CONTACT ADDRESS** Dept of Foreign Lang and Lit, Iowa State Univ of Science and Tech, Ames, IA 50011-0002. **EMAIL** jrdow@iastate.edu

DOWLING, JOHN CLARKSON
PERSONAL Born 11/14/1920, Strawn, TX, m, 1949 **DISCIPLINE** SPANISH **EDUCATION** Univ Colo, BA, 41; Univ Wis, MA, 43, PhD (Span), 50. **CAREER** Markham traveling fel from Univ Wis, Spain, 50-51; instr Span and Port, Univ Wis, 51-53; prof foreign lang and head dept, Tex Tech Col, 53-63; prof Span and Port and chmn dept, Ind Univ, Bloomington, 63-72; prof span and head dept Romance lang, 72-79, Alumni Found Distinguished Prof Romance Lang, Univ GA, 80-91, Dean Grad Sch, 79-89, Guggenheim Fel, 59-60; Am Philos Soc grants, 71, 74 and 81; dir, Nat Endowment for Humanities Sem Col Teachers, 77; vis prof, Univ Iowa, 93; interim dean, Schmidt Col of Arts and Humanities, Florida Atlantic Univ, 95. **HONORS AND AWARDS** Awd, Acad Alfonso X el Sabio, Spain, 55. **MEMBERSHIPS** MLA; Am Asn Teachers Span and Port; Asoc Int Hispanistas; Am Soc 18th Century Studies; Hispanic Soc Am. **RESEARCH** Spanish Golden Age prose; 18th and 19th century Spanish literature; modern Spanish drama. **SELECTED PUBLICATIONS** Auth, Moratin, Saavedra Fajardo, Jose Melchor Gomis. **CONTACT ADDRESS** Dept of Romance Lang, Univ of Georgia, 145 Hancock Lane, Athens, GA 30605-4747. **EMAIL** constance.dowling@worldnet.att.net

DOWNING, PAMELA A.
PERSONAL Born 12/25/1948, Rockford, IL, m, 1990, 2 children **DISCIPLINE** LINGUISTICS **EDUCATION** Univ of Iowa, BA, 70; Univ Calif Berkeley, MA, 75; PhD, 84. **CAREER** Visiting lectr, Univ Calif Santa Barbara, 85-86; visiting asst prof, UCLA, 84-85, 86-87; visiting lectr, San Diego State Univ, 83-84; visiting prof, Seijo Univ, Tokyo, Japan, summer, 96; assoc prof, Univ Wisc Milwaukee, 87-. **MEMBERSHIPS** Ling Soc of Amer; Intl Pragmatics Asn. **RESEARCH** Functional syntax and semantics; Discourse analysis; Sociolinguistics; Lexical Semantics. **SELECTED PUBLICATIONS** Auth, Proper names as a referential option in English conversation, Studies in Anaphora, Amsterdam, John Benjamins, 95-143, 96; auth, Numeral Classifier Systems: the case of Japanese, Amsterdam, John Benjamins, 96; auth, Word order in discourse: by way of introduction, Word Order in Discourse, Amsterdam, John Benjamins, 1-27, 95; co-ed, Word Order in Discourse, Amsterdam, John Benjamins, 95; auth, Pragmatic and semantic constraints on numeral quantifier float in Japanese, Jour of Ling, 29, 1, 65-93, 93; co-ed, The Linguistics of Literacy, Amsterdam, John Benjamins, 92; auth, The use of wa as a cohesion marker in Japanese oral narratives, Perspectives on Topicalization: the case of Japanese wa, Amsterdam, John Benjamins, 3-56, 87; auth, The anaphoric use of numeral classifiers in Japanese, Noun Classification and Categorization, Amsterdam, John Benjamins, 345-75, 86; auth, The relation between word formation and meaning, Quaderni di Semantica, 5, 67-75, 84; auth, Factors influencing lexical choice in narrative, The Pear Stories: cognitive, cultural and lexical aspects of narrative production, Norwood, NJ, Ablex, 89-126, 80; auth, On the creation and use of English compound nouns, Lang, 53, 810-842, 77. **CONTACT ADDRESS** English Dept, Univ of Wisconsin, Milwaukee, PO Box 413, Milwaukee, WI 53201. **EMAIL** downing@uwm.edu

DOYLE, RUTH LESTHA
PERSONAL Born 12/13/1944, Doylestown, PA **DISCIPLINE** FRENCH LANGUAGE AND LITERATURE **EDUCATION** Univ NC, Chapel Hill, AB, 66, MA, 68, PhD (Romance lang and lit), 76. **CAREER** Asst prof French, Elon Col, 67-71; asst prof French and head dept, Univ Charleston, 72-75; Asst Prof French and Ital, Cent MO State Univ, 76-. **MEMBERSHIPS** Am Asn Teachers French; MLA. **RESEARCH** French romanticism; computer aided instruction in modern languages; Italian language. **SELECTED PUBLICATIONS** **CONTACT ADDRESS** Dept of Mod Lang Cent Mo, Central Missouri State Univ, Warrensburg, MO 64093-8888.

DRAKE, DANA BLACKMAR
PERSONAL Born 12/18/1926, Macon, GA **DISCIPLINE** SPANISH **EDUCATION** Davidson Col, AB, 48; Univ Va, LLB, 51; NYork Univ, LLM, 52; Middlebury Col, MA, 66; Univ NC, Chapel Hill, PhD (Span), 67. **CAREER** Jr Partner, Young and Hollis, Columbus, Ga, 52-55; attorney, Joint Comt Taxation, 55-59; asst mgr real estate, Trust Dept, Citizens Southern Nat Bank, 59-62; instr Span, Univ NC, Chapel Hill, 62-67; asst prof, 67-71, assoc prof, 71-82, Prof Span, VA Polytech Inst and State Univ, 82-. **MEMBERSHIPS** Am Asn Teachers Span and Port; MLA; Cervantes Soc Am. **RESEARCH** Cervantes. **SELECTED PUBLICATIONS** Auth, Rossetti Goblin Market, Explicator, Vol 51, 92; Ibsen A Doll House, Explicator, Vol 53, 94. **CONTACT ADDRESS** 210 University Club, Blacksburg, VA 24060.

DRAKE, HAROLD A.
PERSONAL Born 07/24/1942, Cincinnati, IL, m, 1969, 1 child **DISCIPLINE** HISTORY, CLASSICS **EDUCATION** Univ S Calif, AM, 63; Univ Wis, MA, 66; MA, 69; PhD, 70. **CAREER** Teach asst, Univ Wis, 62-65; lectr, asst prof, assoc prof, prof, UCSB, 70-. **HONORS AND AWARDS** NEH Fel, Inst Adv Stud, 73-74; Sr Fel, Annenburg Res Inst, 91-92; Asn Stud Out Teach Awd, 73-74; Plous Memo Awd, Out Asst Prof, 76; Mortar Bd Prof of Yr, 86-87; Alumni Dist Teach Awd, 95-96. **MEMBERSHIPS** Phi Beta Kappa; APA; AIA; SPRS; AAH; NAPS; BSA; ASCH; SBL. **RESEARCH** Late Roman empire; early Christianity; late antiquity; ancient histiography. **SELECTED PUBLICATIONS** Auth, In Praise of Constantine, Univ Calif Press, 76; co-auth, Eudoxia and the Holy Sepulchre, Cisalpino Golliardica (Milan), 81; auth, "Eusebius on the True Cross," Eccle Hist (85); auth, "Lambs Into Lions," Past and Pres (96); auth, Constantine and the Bishops, John Hopkins Press, 00. **CONTACT ADDRESS** Hist Dept, Univ of California, Santa Barbara, Santa Barbara, CA 93106-9410. **EMAIL** drake@humanities.ucsb.edu

DREES, HAJO
PERSONAL Born 12/08/1962, Frankfurt, Germany, m, 1992, 1 child **DISCIPLINE** GERMAN CULTURE **EDUCATION** Univ Nebr at Lincoln, DS, 88; MA, 90; PhD, 94. **CAREER** Instr, Univ NC, 87-92; coord, Univ NC, 92-93; prog dir, Creighton Prep, 96-98; asst prof, Grand Valley State Univ, 96-98; prof dir, Samford Univ, 98-. **MEMBERSHIPS** AATY, AATFL, MLA. **RESEARCH** Christa Wolf, Contemporary German Authors, Pedagogy. **SELECTED PUBLICATIONS** Auth, "Mirror, Mirror on the Wall, Who is the Selfest of Them All? The Myth of Fact and Fiction in Autobiography," J of the Midlands Confr on Lit & Lang Volume 7 (96): 50-54; coauth, "Prismatischen Balintgruppen. Ein methodischer Ansatz fur Beratung, Therapien, Supervisionen und Unterricht," Integrative Therapie 1.2 (97): 60-84; auth, "Stranger in a Strange Land. A Quest for Identity in the German Literature of the 1990," J of the Midlands Confr on Lit & Lang Volume 8 (99): 32-36; auth, "Voicing the Void: From Vergangenheitsbewaltigung to the Wunderkinder. Exploring Germany's Fiction of the Nineties," in European Voices: Trends and Themes in Contemporary Fiction (forthcoming); auth, "Never Mind Freud! Who Nees Psychoanalysis, When You Can Write Poetry? Rainer Maria Rilke's Torture, Therapy, and Salvation," in Rainer Maria Rilke (forthcoming). **CONTACT ADDRESS** World Lang & Cultures, Samford Univ, 800 Lakeshore Dr, Birmingham, AL 35229-0001.

DREW, SHIRLEY K.
PERSONAL Born 11/28/1956, m, 1998 **DISCIPLINE** INTERPERSONAL & PUBLIC COMMUNICATION **EDUCATION** Bowling Green State Univ, BA, MA, PhD. **CAREER** Assoc prof. **MEMBERSHIPS** Nat Commun Assoc; Central States Commun Assoc; Phi Kappa Phi. **RESEARCH** Relationship disengagement; Interpersonal, Group & Organizational Communication; Ethnography & Communication. **SELECTED PUBLICATIONS** Publ, health communication, personal narratives; auth, Group communication; Orgn Personal Narratives. **CONTACT ADDRESS** Dept of Commun, Pittsburg State Univ, 1701 S Broadway St, Pittsburg, KS 66762.

DRINKA, BRIDGET
DISCIPLINE INDO-EUROPEAN HISTORICAL LINGUISTICS **EDUCATION** Univ IL at Champaign-Urbana, BA; Georgetown Univ, MS; Univ TX at Austin, PhD. **CAREER** Asst prof; taught at, L'Istituto Am in Florence, Italy; Am Univ; Univ TX at Austin & Univ MO at Kansas City; adv, Sigma Tau Delta. **HONORS AND AWARDS** Fac Develop Leave awd; Fac Res Awd, UTSA, 93; special Facu Res Grant, 94; Fulbright-Hays Gp Proj Grant; Personal Enrichment Grant, UTSA. **RESEARCH** Hist of Eng; principles of linguistics; hist and sociolinguistics; linguistic methods of analyzing lit. **SELECTED PUBLICATIONS** Auth, The sigmatic aorist in Indo-European, J of Indo-Europ Stud, 95; publ in, Indogermanische Forschungen, Word, J of Indo-Europ Stud. **CONTACT ADDRESS** Col of Fine Arts and Hum, Univ of Texas, San Antonio, 6900 N Loop 1604 W, San Antonio, TX 78249. **EMAIL** bdrinka@lonestar.utsa.edu

DRIVER, EDDY BEVERLEY
PERSONAL m **DISCIPLINE** GERMAN **EDUCATION** Col Wooster, BA, 58-62; Ind Univ, MA, 62-64; Freie Univ, Berlin, 64-66; Ind Univ, PhD, 66-69. **CAREER** Instr, Middlebury Col, 69-70; dir, Middlebury Col Grad Sch, 71-72; asst prof, Middlebury Col, 70-73; ch, dept ger and russ, 74-76; asst prof, Dickinson Col, 73-77; dir, Ctr Pa Consitorium, 78-83; instr, Dickinson, Franklin and Marshall, Gettysburg, Wilson col(s), 77-83; assoc prof, 83-94; ch, ger dept, 94-97; prof, 94-97. **MEMBERSHIPS** Mem, Soc Advan Scand Study; Am Scand Found; Am Assn Tchr(s) Ger. **SELECTED PUBLICATIONS** Auth, Brecht in Dialogue with Karin Michaelis, James K. Lyon and Hans-Peter Breuer, Univ Del Press, London: AUP, 95; Herta Muller: Art Transcends Boundaries, Provincetown Arts, 13, 97-98; rev(s), Herta Muller, The Land of Green Plums, Metropolitan Bk(s), 96; Herlinde Nitsch Ayers, Rollenkonflikte im Werk von Hebbel, Ibsen und Strindberg, 97. **CONTACT ADDRESS** Dept of Ger, Dickinson Col, PO Box 1773, Carlisle, PA 17013-2896.

DRULINER, MARCIA M.
PERSONAL Born 12/18/1946, Auburn, NE, s **DISCIPLINE** LINGUISTICS, EDUCATION **EDUCATION** Nebr Wesleyan, BA, 69; Univ Nebr, MSE, 74; Marquette Univ, Doctor Philos, 92. **CAREER** Lect, Univ Nebr, Lincoln, 91-93; assoc prof, Concordia Col, Bronxville, NY, 93-95; asst prof, Northwestern Col, Orange City, Iowa, 98-. **HONORS AND AWARDS** PiLambda Theta; Who's Who Among America's Teachers; Who's Who in America; Universidad de Madrid, summer study prog in Spain; Instituto Antonio Machado, summer study prog in Spain; Universidad de Guadalajara, summer study prog in Mexico; CEUCA, summer study prog in Bogota, Columbia. **MEMBERSHIPS** Nat Asn Multicultural Ed, Delta Kappa Gamma, Philos of Ed Soc, AmAsn Teachers of Spanish & Portuguese, Lutheran Ed Asn. **RESEARCH** Paulo Freire and education for critical consciousness. **CONTACT ADDRESS** Dept Teacher Ed, Northwestern Col, Iowa, 101 7th St S W, Orange City, IA 51041. **EMAIL** druliner@nwciowa.edu

DRUMMOND, RICHARD HENRY
PERSONAL Born 12/14/1916, San Francisco, CA, m, 1943, 3 children **DISCIPLINE** CLASSICS **EDUCATION** UCLA, BA, 38, MA, 39; Univ Wisc, PhD, 41; Luth Theol Sem, BD, 44. **CAREER** Pastor, The Japanese Church of Christ, San Fran, 47-49; fraternal worker in Japan, 49-62; prof Christian Stud & Class Lang, 58-62, vis prof, 68-69, 76-78, & 86-87, Meiji Gakuin Univ, Tokyo; prof Ecumenical Mission & Hist of Relig, 62-85, Florence Livergood Warren Prof Comp Relig, 84-87, Prof Ecumenical Mission & Hist of Relig Emer, 87- , Univ Dubuque Theol Sem; vis prof, Atlantic Univ, 87-89 & Old Dominion Univ, 89. **HONORS AND AWARDS** Phi Beta Kappa, 38; Outstanding Educ Am, 72 & 74; Univ fel, Univ Dubuque, 91. **SELECTED PUBLICATIONS** Auth, Missiological Lessons-From Events New and Old, Missiology, 94; A New History of Japanese Theology, Mission Studies, 94; A Broader Vision, Stud in Interreligious Dialogue, 96; A Boarder Vision: Perspectives on the Buddha and the Christ, ARE Press, 95. **CONTACT ADDRESS** Univ of Dubuque, 2000 University Ave, Dubuque, IA 52001.

DRUXES, HELGA
DISCIPLINE GERMAN **EDUCATION** Brown Univ, MA, 85, Ph, 87. **CAREER** Assoc prof, Williams Col, 87-. **RESEARCH** Contemporary Germany after 1945; 19th-century Realist Novel; Contemporary German Women Writers; Critical Theory; French Feminist Theory; Women's Studies; Comparative Literature French, American, British; Identity Psychology; Cultural Studies. **SELECTED PUBLICATIONS** Auth, Queerbeet: An Intermediate German Reader, Peter Lang, 88; The Feminization of Dr Faustus: Female Identity Quests from Stendhal to Morgner, Pa State Univ Press, 93; Remembering as Revision: Fictionalizing Nazism in Postwar Germany, MLN 94; Resisting Bodies: The Negotiation of Female Agency in Twentieth-Century Women's Fiction, Wayne State Univ Press, 96. **CONTACT ADDRESS** Center for Foreign Languages, Literatures and Cult, Williams Col, 995 Main St., Williamstown, MA 01267. **EMAIL** Helga.Druxes@williams.edu

DRYER, MATTHEW S.
PERSONAL Born 04/27/1950, Toronto, ON, Canada, m, 1979 **DISCIPLINE** LINGUISTICS **EDUCATION** Univ Toronto, BA, 72, MSc, 73; Univ Mich, AM, 75, PhD (ling), 79. **CAREER** Vis asst prof ling, Univ Windsor, 78-79; sessional instr, Univ Calgary, 79; Vis Asst Prof Ling, Univ Alta, 80-. **RESEARCH** Typology and universals; syntactic theory. **SELECTED PUBLICATIONS** Auth, Languages of the World--Classical Ethiopic, Language, Vol 71, 95; A Grammar of Tauya, Can J Ling Revue Canadienne De Linguistique, Vol 39, 94; A Grammar of Lezgian, Can J Ling Revue Canadienne De Linguistique, Vol 41, 96; A Grammar of Supyire, Can J Lin Revue Canadienne De Linguistique, Vol 41, 96; Barasano Syntax--Jones, W, Jones ,P, Word J Int Ling Assn, Vol 45, 94; On The 6 Way Word Order Typology, Studs Lang, Vol 21, 97; Languages of The World--Gunin-Kwini, Lang, Vol 71, 95; Languages of the World - Mbalanhu - Fourie,Dj/, Language, Vol 71, 95; Languages Of The World--Cantonese, Lang, Vol 71, 95; Focus, Pragmatic Presupposition, and Activated Propositions, J Pragmatics, Vol 26, 96. **CONTACT ADDRESS** Dept of Ling, Univ of Alberta, Edmonton, AB, Canada T6G 2E7.

DUBE, PIERRE
PERSONAL Born 08/23/1943, Toronto, ON, Canada, m, 2 children **DISCIPLINE** FRENCH LITERATURE **EDUCATION** Univ Toronto, BA; MA; Ohio State Univ, PhD. **CAREER** Prof. **HONORS AND AWARDS** SSHRC, 3-year grant for A Critical Bibliography of Alexandre Dumas pere; SSHRC, 3-year grant for A Critical Bibliography of Francois Rene de Chateaubriand: and Update. **RESEARCH** Early Romantic writers. **SELECTED PUBLICATIONS** Coauth, A concordance of Flaubert's Trois Contes, New York: Garland, 79; coauth, A Concordance of Flaubert's La Tentaation de Saint Antoine, Garland, 79; coauth, A Concordance of Flaubert's Bouvard et Pecuchet, New York: Garland, 79; coauth, A Concordance of Pascals Lettres Provinciales, New York: Garland Publishing, 80; auth, Bibliographie de la Critique sur Francois-Rene de Chateaubriand, 1801-1986, Paris: A-G Nizet, (88): 485; auth, Chateaubriand's Les Aventures du dernier Abencerage: Past and Present, Frankfurt: Verlang Peter Lang, (89): 119; coauth, Patrimoines: La Francophonie en Amerique du nord, Toronto: HBJ Holt, (92): 265; auth, Bibliographie de la critique sur Porsper Merimee, Geneve: Librairie Droz, (97): 398; auth, Bibliographie de la critique sur Madame de Stael, Geneve: librarie Droz, (98): 427. **CONTACT ADDRESS** Dept of French Studies, Univ of Waterloo, Waterloo, ON, Canada N2L 3G1. **EMAIL** phdube@watarts.uwaterloo.ca

DUBOIS, BETTY LOU
PERSONAL Born 12/13/1927, Oklahoma City, OK **DISCIPLINE** APPLIED LINGUISTICS **EDUCATION** Univ Okla, BA, 49, MA, 54; Univ NMex, PhD (ling and lang pedag), 72. **CAREER** Asst prof, 73-76, assoc prof, 76-80, Prof Speech, NMex State Univ, 80-, Consult, Southwest Multicult Ethnic Study Ctr, Univ Tex, El Paso, 73-; head ed comt, Papers in Southwest English, Trinity Univ, 76-. **MEMBERSHIPS** Ling Asn of Can and US; Int Asn Appl Ling; Int Asn Study Child Lang; Ling Asn of Southwest; Teachers English to Speakers Other Lang. **RESEARCH** Elementary school language arts; nonstandard southwest English; sex-linked communicative behavior. **SELECTED PUBLICATIONS CONTACT ADDRESS** New Mexico State Univ, Box 3W, University Park, NM 88003.

DUBRUCK, EDELGARD E.
PERSONAL Born 11/01/1925, Breslau, Germany, m, 1957, 1 child **DISCIPLINE** FRENCH LITERATURE **EDUCATION** Univ Mich, MA, 55, PhD (Romance lang and lit), 62. **CAREER** Vis lectr French, Oakland Univ, 62-65; from asst prof to assoc prof, 65-75, Prof French, Marygrove Col, 75-, Chmn Dept Foreign Lang, 73-, US Govt scholar, Mich State Univ, 51-52; vis lectr, Kalamazoo Col, 61. **HONORS AND AWARDS** Awd of MI Academy of Sciences, Arts, and Letters in 78; President of the Academy 81-93; Grant of $3,000 from NEH in 1984, to search and acquire 23 MSS of the Passion Isabeau 1398. **MEMBERSHIPS** MLA. **RESEARCH** Humor and humorous intent in French literature of the Middle Ages; late-medieval theater; all countries; violence in text and image. **SELECTED PUBLICATIONS** Auth, The Theme of Death in French Poetry of the Middle Ages and the Renaissance (TheHague: Mouton, 64); auth, Pierre Riviere: La Nef des folz du monde 1498, 2 vols, Critical Edition, (Ann Arbor: UMI, 77); auth, Fifteenth-Century Studies, vols 1-25, founder and editor, 78; auth, Medieval and Renaissance Monograph Series, vols 1-6, ed (Ann Arbor: McNaughton and Gunn, 81-84); auth, New Images of Medieval Women: Essays Toward a Cultural Anthropology, ed., Lewiston, Mellen, 89; auth, La Passion Isabeau. Une Edition du manuscrit fr. 966 de la Bibliotheque Nationale de Paris, avec une introduction et des notes, New York: Peter Lang, 90; auth, Aspects of Fifteenth-Century Society in the German Carnival Comedies: Speculum hominis, Lewiston: Mellen, 93; auth, The Current State of Research in Fifteenth-Century Literature: Germania-Romania, ed. With W.C. McDonald, vol 2, (1985-95) Lewiston: Mellen, 96; auth, Death and Dying in the Middle Ages., eds, Edelgard E. DuBruck and Barbara I. Gusick, New York: Peter Lang, 99. **CONTACT ADDRESS** Dept of Foreign Lang, Marygrove Col, Modern Languages, Detroit, MI 48221. **EMAIL** dubruck@cs.com

DUCKERT, AUDREY ROSALIND
PERSONAL Born 03/28/1927, Cottage Grove, WI **DISCIPLINE** ENGLISH PHILOLOGY & LINGUISTICS **EDUCATION** Univ Wis, BS, 48, MA, 49; Radcliffe Col, PhD, 59. **CAREER** Res asst, WI Eng Lang Surv, Univ WI, 48-52; ed asst, G&C Merriam Co, Mass, 53-56; from instr to assoc prof, 59-72, Prof Eng, Univ MA, Amherst, 72-, Assoc ed & columnist, Names, Am Name Soc, 61-65; mem adv bd, Ling Atlas US & Can, 64- & Dict Am Regional English, 65-; vis res assoc, Univ Wis-Madison, 66-67; consult, Oxford Eng Dict, Suppl II, 68-; Am Coun Learned Soc sr fel, 73-74; vis prof Eng, Emory Univ, 78; adj ed, Dict Am Regional Eng, 81. **MEMBERSHIPS** Am Dialect Soc (pres, 74); Am Name Soc (pres, 71); Mediaeval Acad Am; Mod Hum Res Asn, Gt Brit; Ling Soc Am. **RESEARCH** Lexicography; medieval lang and lit; dialectology. **SELECTED PUBLICATIONS** Coauth, A Method for Collecting Dialect, Am Dialect Soc, 53; auth, The linguistic atlas of New England revisited, Publ Am Dialect Soc, 4/63; co-ed, Handbook of the Linguistic Geography of New England, AMS, 72; Lexicography in English, NY Acad Sci Annal, 73; auth, Tbe second time around: Methods in dialect revisiting, Am Speech, 74; The winds of change, In: James B McMillan: (festschrift), Essays in Linguistics by His Friends and Colleagues, Univ AL, 77;adj ed, Dictionary of American Regional Ehglish, 80. **CONTACT ADDRESS** Dept of Eng, Univ of Massachusetts, Amherst, Amherst, MA 01003-0002.

DUDLEY, EDWARD J.
PERSONAL Born 07/18/1926, St. Paul, MN, m, 1959, 2 children **DISCIPLINE** SPANISH, ENGLISH **EDUCATION** Univ MN, Minneapolis, BA, 49, MA, 51, PhD, 63. **CAREER** Tchr, Am Sch, Managua, Nicaragua, 54-55; instr Span, St John's Univ, MN, 56-60; asst prof, UCLA, 63-70; chmn & prof Hisp lang & lit & dir comp lit prog, Univ Pittsburgh, 70-74; chmn dept Span, Ital & Port, 74-77, chmn dept French & Dept Ger & Slavic, 76-77, Prof Span & Comp Lit, State Univ NY Buffalo, 74-, Chmn Dept Mod Lang & Lit, 77-, Consult, Nat Bd Consult, Nat Endowment for Hum, 76. **MEMBERSHIPS** MLA; Mediaeval Acad Am; Asn Int Hispanistas; Cervantes Soc Am; Conrad Soc Am. **RESEARCH** Cervantes; early prose fiction; comp lit. **SELECTED PUBLICATIONS** Auth, Three patterns of imagery in Conrad's Heart of Darkness, Rev des Langues Vivantes, 65; coauth, El cuento, Holt, 66; auth, Court and country: The fusion of two images of love in Juan Rodriguez's El siervo libre de amor, PMLA, 67; Don Quixote as magus: The rhetoric of interpolation, Bull Hisp Studies, 72; co-ed, The Wild Man Within: An Image in Western Thought from the Renaissance to Romanticism, Univ Pittsburgh, 72; co-ed, 2nd ed, El cuento, Holt, 84; co-ed, American Attitudes toward Foreign Languages and Foreign Cultures, Bouvier, Bonn, 83; auth, The Endless Text: Don Quijote and The Hermeneutics of Romance, SUNY Press, 97; various other articles and essays on Cervantes. **CONTACT ADDRESS** Dept of Mod Lang & Lit, SUNY, Buffalo, PO Box 604620, Buffalo, NY 14260-4620. **EMAIL** edudley@acsu.buffalo.edu

DUFFEY, JOHN PATRICK
PERSONAL Born 11/19/1963, Grand Prairie, TX, m, 1988, 2 children **DISCIPLINE** HISPANIC LITERATURE **EDUCATION** Washington Univ in St. Louis, AB, 85; Univ Tx at Arlington, BA, 90; Univ Tx at Austin, MA, 92; PhD, 94. **CAREER** Asst prof to assoc prof, Austin Col, 94-. **HONORS AND AWARDS** NEH Summer Inst Stipend Awd, 00. **MEMBERSHIPS** MLA, Ist Int de Lit Iberoamericana, Latin Am Studies Asn, Am Asn of Teachers of Spain and Portugal. **RESEARCH** Mexican narrative, the influence of film on Hispanic narrative, Hispanic film, Mexican-American fiction and film. **SELECTED PUBLICATIONS** Auth; "Cinematic Techniques in Spanish Vanguard Prose, 1927-1932: Slow Motion and Zoom," West Va Univ Philol Papers 39 (94): 132-137; auth, "Documentaries of the Mexican Revolution: The Influence of Film on Martin Luis Guzman's El aguila y la serpiente," La Chispa 95: Selected Proceedings (95): 143-152; auth, "Montage in Hispanic Vanguard Prose, 1926-1934: Neurasthenia, Back Projection, and Chase Scenes," Hispanofila 118.4 (96): 29-38; auth, "Virgenes, madres y prostitutas: la figura femenina en El llano en llamas," Generos 4.10 (96): 16-22; auth, De la pantalla al texto: La influencia del cine en la narrativa mexicana del siglo XX, Univ Nac Autonoma de Mex, 96; co-ed, Que pais es este?: Los Estados Unidos y los gringos vistos por autores mexicanos de los siglos XIX y XX, Consejo Nac para la Cult y las Artes, 96; auth, "A War of Words: Orality and Literacy in Azuela's Los de abajo," Romance Notes 38.2 (98): 173-178; auth, "Pancho Villa at the movies: Cinematic Techniques in the Works of Guzman and Munoz," Latin American Literature and Mass Media (NY: Garland, 00). **CONTACT ADDRESS** Dept Foreign Lang, Austin Col, 900 North Grand Ave, Sherman, TX 75090-4440. **EMAIL** pduffey@austinc.edu

DUGGAN, ANNE E.
PERSONAL Born 04/16/1967, Milwaukee, WI, m, 1991 **DISCIPLINE** FRENCH LANGUAGE AND LITERATURE **EDUCATION** Univ Minn, BA, 89; MA, 92; PhD, 98. **CAREER** Lectr, Univ Minn, 98-99; asst prof, Wayne State Univ, 99-; asst ed, Oxford Compan to Fairy Tales, 00; assoc ed, Marvels and Tales, 00-. **HONORS AND AWARDS** WSA Univ Res Grnt Prog, 00-01; WSU Hum Cen Fac Fel, 99-00; WSU Min Women Sum Grnt, 00; Univ Minn Doct Dis, Spec Grnt, 95; Newberry Lib Res Grnt, 94. **MEMBERSHIPS** MLA; MMLA; Women in French. **RESEARCH** Fairy Tales; early modern American authors; 17th-century literature and culture; French theater. **SELECTED PUBLICATIONS** Auth, "Review of The Classic Fairy Tales," ed. Maria Tatar, Marvels and Tales: J Fairy Tale Stud 15 (99); auth, "Gossip and/as History: Madeleine de Scudery's Gazette de Tendre," Work Pap Roman Lits and Philo 1 (96); auth, "Lovers, Salon and State: La Carte de Tendre and the Mapping of Socio-Political Relations," Dalhousie Fr Stud 36 (96); auth, "The Ticquet Affair as Recounted in Madame Dunoyer's Lettres Historiques et Galantes: the Defiant Galante Femme," Pap French 17th-Cen Lit 46 (97); auth, "Feminine Genealogy, Matriarchy, and Utopia in the Fairy Tale of Marie-Catherine d'Aulnoy," Neophil 82 (98); contrb, "Alcott, Louisa May," "Babbitt, Natalie," "Bain, R. Nisbet," "Belasco, David," "Bignon, Jean Paul," "Bruna, Dick," "Chorpenning, Charlotte," "Curtin, Jeremiah," "Delessert, Etienne," "Gueulette, T.-Simon," "Haviland, Virginia," "Hughes, Richard," in The Oxford Companion to Fairy Tales: The Western Fairy Tale Tradition from Medieval to Modern, ed. Jack Zipes (Oxford: OUP, 00); auth, "Nature and Culture in the Fairy Tale of Marie-Catherine d'Aulnoy" Marv and Tales: J of Fairy Tale Stud 15 (01). **CONTACT ADDRESS** Dept Romance Lang and Lit, Wayne State Univ, 487 Manoogian, Detroit, MI 48202. **EMAIL** ag7230@wayne.edu

DUGGAN, HOYT NOLAN
PERSONAL Born 04/05/1938, Atlanta, TX, m, 1962, 2 children **DISCIPLINE** MEDIEVAL LANGUAGES & LITERATURE **EDUCATION** Centenary Col La, BA, 60; Pembroke Col, BA, 63; Oxford Univ, MA, 68; Princeton Univ, PhD(English), 69. **CAREER** From assist to prof english, Univ VA, 68-; NEH fel, 73-74. **HONORS AND AWARDS** Fel, 93-94, assoc Fel, Inst for Advanced Technology in the Humanities, 94; NEH Fel, 73-74; Sesquicentennial Fel, 73-74; NEH Summer Fel, 70; Charles G. Osgood Fel, 68-69; Rhodes Scholar, 60-63. **MEMBERSHIPS** Chemn, Mediaeval Acad Am, 94-; MLA; Early English Text Soc; Soc Study Medieval Lang & Lit; Dir, Soc for Early English and Norse Electronic Texts, 93-; Envoi; Labyrinth; CLH-L. **RESEARCH** Critical edition of the Middle English Wars of Alexander; Ovidian commentaries in the Middle Ages; Middle English alliterative poetry. **SELECTED PUBLICATIONS** Co-ed, Piers Plowman: Corpus Christi College, Oxford MS 201, Univ Mich Press and SEENET, 00; auth, Creating an Electronic Archive of Piers Plowman, Pub of the Inst for Advanced Tech in the Humanities, Res Reports, Second Series, 94; The Role and Distribution of -ly Adverbs in Middle English Alliterative Verse, Loyal Letters: Studies on Mediaeval Alliterative Poetry and Prose, 94; Libertine scribes and maidenly editors: Meditations on textual criticism and metrics, English Historical Metrics, 96; Meter, Stanza, Vocabulary, Dialect, A Companion to the Gawain-Poet, 97; Some Unrevolutionary Aspects of Computer Editing, The Literary Text in the Digital Age, 96. **CONTACT ADDRESS** Dept of English, Univ of Virginia, Bryan Hall, Charlottesville, VA 22903. **EMAIL** hnd@virginia.edu

DUGGAN, JOSEPH J.
PERSONAL Born 09/08/1938, Philadelphia, PA, m, 1981, 3 children **DISCIPLINE** COMPARATIVE LITERATURE, MEDIEVAL ROMANCE LITERATURES **EDUCATION** Fordham Univ, BA, 60; Ohio State Univ, PhD,64. **CAREER** Asst prof, 64-78; prof, 78-, Univ California, Berk. **HONORS AND AWARDS** Woodrow Wilson Fel, 60; Woodrow Wilson Diss Fel 64; NEH, 68,94; Guggenheim Fel. **MEMBERSHIPS** SIRER; MAA. **RESEARCH** Comparative epic and lyric in the romances; French and Occitan romance; texual criticism; romance philology. **SELECTED PUBLICATIONS** Auth, The 'Cantar de mio Cid': Poetic Creation in its Economic and Social Contexts, Cam Stud Medi Lit, Cam Univ Press (89); auth, The Romances of Chretien de Troyes: A Study, Yale Univ Press (New Haven), in press. **CONTACT ADDRESS** Dept Comparative Literature, Univ of California, Berkeley, Berkeley, CA 94720-2510. **EMAIL** roland@socrates.berkeley.edu

DUKAS, VYTAS
PERSONAL Born 02/14/1923, Lithuania, m, 1957, 2 children **DISCIPLINE** SLAVIC LANGUAGES **EDUCATION** Univ Mich, BA, 54, MA, 55 and 56, PhD (comp lit), 65. **CAREER** Asst prof Russ and Ger, 59-66, assoc prof Russ, 66-69, chmn dept Russ and Ger, 68-71, Prof Russ, San Diego State Univ, 69-. **MEMBERSHIPS** Am Asn Teachers Ger; Am Asn Teachers Slavic and East Europ Lang. **RESEARCH** Russian literature; Soviet poetry; Russian and German comparative literature. **SELECTED PUBLICATIONS CONTACT ADDRESS** Dept of Ger and Russ, San Diego State Univ, San Diego, CA 92182.

DULAI, SURJIT SINGH
PERSONAL Born 11/06/1930, Danubyu, Burma, m, 1965, 2 children **DISCIPLINE** COMPARATIVE LITERATURE, SOUTH ASIAN STUDIES **EDUCATION** Panjab Univ, BA, 50, MA, 54; Mich State Univ, PhD, 65. **CAREER** Lectr English, Urdu, Panjab Univ, 54-59; headmaster, G N High Sch, Partab, Pura, 59-60; asst English & comp lit, Mich State Univ, 62-67, fel, 64-65; asst prof English, Long Island Univ, 65-66; asst prof humanities, 66-70, assoc prof humanities & Asian studies, 70-74, prof English, 74-, Mich State Univ; co-ed, J SAsian Lit, 69-. **HONORS AND AWARDS** Fulbright-Hays fel, Off Health, Educ, Welfare, 70-71; Rockefeller Found award, 76; Mich State Univ Excellence in Diversity Award, 95. **MEMBERSHIPS** Asn Asian Studies; Can Asn SAsian Studies; MLA; Popular Cult Asn; Asn Gen & Lib Studies. **RESEARCH** Interdisciplinary humanities; Indian & comparative literature; Anglo-Indian literature. **SELECTED PUBLICATIONS** Co-ed, Punjab in Perspective, 91; coauth, Contemporary Poets, St James Press, 95; co-ed, World Literature and Thought, 4 v, 00. **CONTACT ADDRESS** Dept of English, Michigan State Univ, 201 Morrill Hall, East Lansing, MI 48824-1036. **EMAIL** dulai@pilot.msu.edu

DUMAS, BETHANY K.
PERSONAL Born 04/01/1937, Corpus Christi, TX, s **DISCIPLINE** LINGUISTIC **EDUCATION** Lamar Univ, BA, 55-59; Univ Ark, MA, PhD, 59-71. **CAREER** Instr, Aug 64-May 66, MO State Univ; asst prof, Aug 66- June 73, Southern Univ (Baton Rouge); asst prof, visiting assoc prof, Aug 73-74, Summer 75, English Trinity Univ; adjunct prof, 93, Univ TN, Knoxville, Spring 93; professional lectr, fall 97, Georgetown Univ; assoc prof, Aug 74- , Univ TN, Knoxville. **HONORS AND AWARDS** Univ TN Intl Travel Grant, 96; Univ TN English Dept Hodges Travel/Research Grants 93, 97, 98. **MEMBERSHIPS** South Atlantic Amer Dialect Soc (vice president, 80, president, 81), 73-present; Linguistic Soc of Amer, 74-present; Amer Dialect Soc (Executive Committee, 81-84; Assn for Computational Linguistics, 85-88; Amer Bar Assn, 84, 90, 98- ; Law and Soc Assn, 90-94, 96- ; Intl Assn of Forensic Linguists (Membership Secetary, 93-94), 93- . **SELECTED PUBLICATIONS** Auth, Warning Labels on the Locite RC/609 Containers and the Material Safety Data Sheets on Loctite RC/609, Language in Action: New Studies of Language in Society, Hampton, 97; auth,English in the American Midwest, review of Heartland English: Variation and Transition in the American Midwest, 97; auth, Linguistic Ambiguity in Non-Statutory Language: Problems in The Search Warrant in the Matter of 7505 Derris Drive, Forensic Linguistics: The Intl Journal of Language and the Law, 98; auth,Southern Mountain English: The Language of The Ozarks and Southern Appalachia, a chapter in Living English, Praeger, July 99. **CONTACT ADDRESS** Dept of English, Univ of Tennessee, Knoxville, 301 McClung Tower, Knoxville, TN 37996-0430. **EMAIL** dumasb@utk.edu

DUNAWAY, JOHN MARSON
PERSONAL Born 06/24/1945, Washington, GA, m, 1966, 2 children **DISCIPLINE** FRENCH LANGUAGE AND LITERATURE **EDUCATION** Emory Univ, BA, 67; Duke Univ, MA, 71, PhD (French), 72. **CAREER** Asst prof, 72-77, chmn, Dept Mod Foreign Lang, 76-79, 83-86, 95-98, Assoc Prof French, Mercer Univ, 77-85, Prof, 85-. **HONORS AND AWARDS** Don Quixote Awd, Valdosta State Col, 76; Spencer B. King Distinguished Prof, 93. **MEMBERSHIPS** Am Asn Teachers Fr; SAtlantic Mod Lang Asn; Am Weil Soc; Am Maritain Assoc. **RESEARCH** Twentieth century French literature, philosophy, and religious thought. **SELECTED PUBLICATIONS** Auth, Exiles & Fugitives: The Letters of Jacques Maritain, Caroline Gordon & Allen Tate, LSUP, 92; auth, The Double Vocation: Christian Presence in 20th Century Fr. Fiction, Summa, 96; co-ed, The Beauty That Saves: Essays on Aesthetics and Language in Simone Weil, Merer Up, 96. **CONTACT ADDRESS** Dept of Foreign Lang & Lit, Mercer Univ, Macon, 1400 Coleman Ave, Macon, GA 31207-0003.

DUNCAN, BRUCE
PERSONAL Born 02/17/1942, Bryn Mawr, PA, m, 1964, 2 children **DISCIPLINE** GERMAN LITERATURE, GERMAN LINGUISTICS **EDUCATION** Williams Col, BA, 64; Cornell Univ, MA, 66, PhD, 69. **CAREER** Asst prof, 69-75, assoc prof, 75-81, Prof Ger, Dartmouth Col, 81-, assoc dean of fac hum, 89-93, Vis prof Ger, Univ Cincinnati. **HONORS AND AWARDS** Woodrow Wilson Fel, 64; DAAD Fel, 66-67; Am Coun Learned Socs Grant-in-Aid Fel, 76; DAAD Res Travel Fel, 93. **MEMBERSHIPS** Am Asn Tchr(s) Ger; Intern Arnim Soc. **RESEARCH** Eighteenth century Ger lit; Ger Romanticism; second lang acquisition. **SELECTED PUBLICATIONS** Auth, Hand, heart, and language in Minna von Barnhelm, 72 & The Marchese's story in Wilhelm Meisters Lehrjahre, 72, Seminar; A Cool Medium as social corrective: J M R Lenz's Concept of Comedy, Colloquia Ger, 75; Some correspondences between Arnim's Majoratsherren and Fichte's Concept of the Ich, Monatshefte, 76; The Comic Structure of Lenz's Soldaten, Mod Lang Notes (Ger issue), 76; Ich Pflanzel Gerstenberg's Ugolino and the mid-life crisis, Ger Rev, 78; The implied reader in Lessing's Theory of Comedy, Lessing Yearbk, 78; Fate and Coincidence in Arnim's Seltsames Begegnen und Wiedersehen, 79, Seminar; Die Versohnung in der Sommerfrische. Eine ungedruckte Erzahlung Achim von Arnims, Aurora, 80; Emilia Galotti lag auf dem Tisch aufgeschlagen: Werther as (Mis-)Reader, Goethe Yearbook 82; An Worte labt sich trefflich glauben. Die Sprache der Luise Millerin, In: Friedrich Schiller: Kunst Humanitat und Politik in der spaten Aufklarung, Max Niemeyer Verlag, 82; Werther's Reflections on the Tenth of May, In: Exile and Enlightenment: Studies in Honor of Guy Stern on His 65th Birthday, Wayne State Univ Press, 87; Werke von und uber Achim von Arnim seit Volker Hoffmanns Die Arnim-Forschung 1945-1972, In: Neue Tendenzen der Arnim-Forschung, Edition, Biographie, Interpretation, mit unbekannten Dokumenten, Lang, 90; Some Common Themes in Sturm und Drang Reception, In: Momentum Dramaticum: Aufsatze zu Ehren von Eckehard Catholy aus Analass seines 75; Geburtstages, Univ Waterloo Press, 90, Ontario; Co-auth (with Otmar Foelsche) Doch ein Begriff mub bei dem Worte sein: Teaching Literature with an Electronically Annotated Text, Die Unterrichtspraxis, 95; auth, Remembering Schiller: The Centenary of 1859, Seminar, 99; Achim von Arnim's Novellas of 1812, Mellen, 97; Lovers, Parricides and Highwaymen: Aspects of Sturm und Drang Drama, Camden, 99. **CONTACT ADDRESS** Dept of Ger, Dartmouth Col, 6084 Dartmouth Hall, Hanover, NH 03755-3511. **EMAIL** Bruce.Duncan@dartmouth.edu

DUNCAN, JANICE MARIE
PERSONAL Born 05/05/1945, Rolla, MO **DISCIPLINE** FRENCH **EDUCATION** Univ Mo, BS, 67; MA, 69; Univ Nebr, PhD, 91. **CAREER** Teaching asst, Univ Mo, 67-69; asst prof, SW Baptist Univ, 69-84; teaching asst to lectr, Univ Nebr, 84-92; asst prof, NE State Univ, 94-00; assoc prof, Ouachita Baptist Univ, 00-. **HONORS AND AWARDS** Phi Sigma Iota; Delta Kappa Gamma; George Rogers Scholar; Finalist, Teaching Asst Award, Univ of Nebr; Fel, Alternate Maude Hammond Fling; Mayme C.Hamilton Scholar; Nominee, Arts and Sci Outstanding Teaching Asst Award. **MEMBERSHIPS** MLA; AATF; SCMLA; APLTA. **RESEARCH** 19th Century French Literature; 20th Century French Literature. **SELECTED PUBLICATIONS** Co-auth, "The VCR Revolution. Feature Films for Language and Culture Proficiency," in Proficiency, Policy and Professionalism in Foreign Language Education, (87), 92-105. **CONTACT ADDRESS** Dept Lang, Ouachita Baptist Univ, 2617 Golden St, Arkadelphia, AR 71923-6517. **EMAIL** duncanj@obu.edu

DUNHAM, VERA S.
PERSONAL Born 12/13/1912, Moscow, Russia, m, 1942, 1 child **DISCIPLINE** SLAVIC LANGUAGES AND LITERATURE **EDUCATION** Univ Erlangen, PhD (slavic philol), 35; Univ Brussels, lic-lettres, 38. **CAREER** Prof, Wayne State Univ, 61-75; Prof, Queens Col, City Univ New York, 75-, Res analyst, Off Strategic Serv, Washington, DC, 44-45; assoc ed, Common Cause, Univ Chicago, 46-47; res consult, Inst Int Social Res, Princeton Univ, 59-60; vis prof, Slavic Dept, Univ Mich, 65 and Columbia Univ, 67. **MEMBERSHIPS** Am Asn Avan Slavic Studies; Am Asn Teachers Slavic and Eastern Europ, Lang. **RESEARCH** A Literary study of the worker and the Soviet system--the 1960's and 1970's. **SELECTED PUBLICATIONS** Auth, Literary Politics in the Soviet Ukraine, 1917-1934, Russ Hist Histoire Russe, Vol 21, 94. **CONTACT ADDRESS** 15 Stephens Path, Port Jefferson, NY 11777.

DUNN, PETER NORMAN
PERSONAL Born 03/23/1926, London, England, m, 1953, 6 children **DISCIPLINE** SPANISH **EDUCATION** Univ London, BA, 47, MA, 49, DLitt, 73. **CAREER** Asst lectr Span, Aberdeen Univ, 49-50, lectr, 50-66; prof Span lit, Univ Rochester, 66-77; Prof Romance Lang, Wesleyan Univ, 77-97, Examr Span, Scottish Univs Entrance Bit, 51-60; Joint Matriculation Bd, Northern Univ, England, 60-66; vis prof Span, Western Reserve Univ, 64-65. **MEMBERSHIPS** MLA; Asn Hispanists Gt Brit; Cervantes Soc Am; Internation Asn Hispanists. **RESEARCH** Spanish literature; medieval, Renaissance and 17th century. **SELECTED PUBLICATIONS** The Picaresque--A Symposium on the Rogues Tale, Hisp Rev, Vol 63, 95; Framing the Story, Framing the Reader, Modern Lan Rev, Vol 91, 96; The Concept of Genre and Picaresque Literature, Bull Hisp Stud, Vol 72, 95 Shaping Experience, Narrative Strategies In Cervantes, Mln Modern Lang Notes, Vol 109, 94. **CONTACT ADDRESS** Dept of Romance Lang, Wesleyan Univ, Middletown, CT 06457.

DUNN, SUSAN
PERSONAL Born 07/19/1945, New York, NY **DISCIPLINE** FRENCH LITERATURE **EDUCATION** Smith Col, BA, 66; Harvard Univ, PhD, 73. **CAREER** Teaching fel Romance lang, Harvard Univ, 67-70, instr French, 70-73; Prof French, Williams Col, 73-; Instr French, Wellesley Col, 71-73; NEH fel in residence, Princeton Univ, 75-76; fel, Camargo Found, 81; NEH, 90 & 97. **MEMBERSHIPS** ASECS. **RESEARCH** French and American Revolutions. **SELECTED PUBLICATIONS** Auth, Nerval et le roman historique, Minard, Paris, 81; The Deaths of Louis XVI, Princeton Univ Press, 94; co-auth, The Lion, the Fox, and the President, Harvard Mag, 95; ed, Diversity and Citizenship, Rowman and Littlefield, 96; Sister Revolutions, French Lightning, American Light, Farrar, Strauss, Giroux, 99; Revolutionary Men of Letters and the Pursuit of Radical Change, William & Mary Quart, 53; co-auth, Revolutionary Myths in France and America, Partisan Rev, 58. **CONTACT ADDRESS** Dept of Romance Lang, Williams Col, Stetson Hall, Williamstown, MA 01267-2600. **EMAIL** sdunn@williams.edu

DUPUY, BEATRICE
DISCIPLINE FRENCH, LINGUISTICS **EDUCATION** Univ Southern Calif, PhD, 94. **CAREER** Asst prof, La State Univ. **SELECTED PUBLICATIONS** Auth, "Lecture-cadeau, lecture-plaisir: Des Etudiants en FLE et les benefices derives de la lecture libre," The French Review 71.2 (97): 182-191; coauth, "From Lower to Upper-Division Foreign Language Classes: Obstacles to Reaching the Promised Land," ITL: Review of Applied Linguistics 119-120 (98): 1-7; auth, "Cercles de lecture: Une autre approache de la lecture dans la classe intermediaire de francais langue etrangere," The Canadian Modern Language Review 54.4 (98): 579-585; coauth, "Cross Linguistic Evidence for the Early Acquisition of Discourse Markers as Register Variables," Journal of Pragmatics 31.10 (99): 1339-1351; auth, "Narrow Listening: An Alternative Way to Develop Listening Comprehension in the Foreign Language Classroom," System 27.3 (99): 351-361; auth, "Content-Based Instruction: Can it Help Ease the Transition from Beginning to Advanced Foreign Language Classes?," Foreign Language Annals 33.2 (00): 205-223. **CONTACT ADDRESS** Dept of Fr Grad Stud, Louisiana State Univ and A&M Col, Baton Rouge, LA 70803. **EMAIL** bdupuy@lsu.edu

DUQUETTE, JEAN-PIERRE
PERSONAL Born 06/27/1939, Valleyfield, PQ, Canada **DISCIPLINE** FRENCH LITERATURE **EDUCATION** Univ Montreal, LL, 63; Doctorat de 3e cycle Lettres modernes, Paris X, 1969. **CAREER** Asst, 69-85, French Prof, McGill Univ, 85-, Dept Chmn, 85-96. **SELECTED PUBLICATIONS** Ed, Centenaire de Jean Cocteau, 90; ed, Montreal 1642-1992; auth, Seurat, la science et l'art, Ecrits du Canada francais, 92; rev, L'espace du regard, 94; auth, Lectures de la vingtaine, Ecrits du Canada francais, 94; auth, Saint-Denys Garneau peintre et dessinateur, Litteratures, 94; auth, Journak de Prague, Les Ecrits, 96; coauth, Jean Ethier-Blais: dictionnaire de lui-meme, 98; ed, Boccace: decameron 1414, G. Di Stefano, 98. **CONTACT ADDRESS** Dept of French, McGill Univ, 3460 McTavish St, Montreal, QC, Canada H3A 1X9. **EMAIL** jpduquet@leacock.lan.mcgill.ca

DURAN, JAIME
PERSONAL Born 03/04/1967, Oviedo, Spain, m, 2000 **DISCIPLINE** LINGUISTICS, LITERATURE, SPANISH LANGUAGE **EDUCATION** Univ Oviedo, Lic Filo Ing, 94; Villanova Univ, MA, 97; Temple Univ PhD, 00. **CAREER** Teach asst, Villanova Univ, 95-97; teach asst, Temple Univ, 98-00; vis asst prof, Villanova Univ, 00-. **HONORS AND AWARDS** Dis Teach Awd, Temple Univ; Villa Univ Fel, 95-97; Temple Univ Fel, 98-00; Sec Span Hon Soc, Sigma Delta Phi. **MEMBERSHIPS** MLA. **RESEARCH** Peninsular literature, modern and contemporary. **SELECTED PUBLICATIONS** Auth, Miguel Espinosa y Camilo Jose Cela, dos clasicos (00). **CONTACT ADDRESS** Dept. of Classical and Mod Lang and Lit, Villanova Univ, 800 Lancaster Ave, Villanova, PA 19085. **EMAIL** jaime.duran@villanova.edu

DURAND, ALAIN-PHILIPPE
PERSONAL Born 04/25/1968, Marseille, France **DISCIPLINE** FRENCH **EDUCATION** Emporia State Univ, BA, 92; Univ Kans, MA, 94; MA, 95; Univ NCar Chapel Hill, PhD, 99. **CAREER** TA, Univ Kans, 92-95; teaching fel, Univ NCar Chapel Hill, 95-98; vis instr, NCar Central Univ, 98-99; asst prof, Univ RI, 99-, vis asst prof, Ecole Superieure de Commerce Marseille-Provence, 00-. **HONORS AND AWARDS** Pi Delta Phi, 89; Sigma Delta Pi, 89; Galloo-Neuenschwander Fel, 93; Fel, Univ Kans, 95; Florence T McCullouch Fel, 98; URI Found, 99,00. **MEMBERSHIPS** AATF, MLA, Int Comp Lit Asn. **RESEARCH** Contemporary French Novel, French Cinema, Cultural Studies and Criticism, Contemporary Latin American Literature, French Travel Accounts in Latin America, Balzac, Bret Easton Ellis. **SELECTED PUBLICATIONS** Auth, "Grassou et Frenhofer: Chef d'oeuvre connu ou inconnu?" Romance Quart, (97); auth, "Le troisieme texte," Romance Lang Annual, (98); auth, "Discotheques. Sur Phinx d'Anne Garreta," L'Atelier du Roman, (99); auth, "Le Cote de Belleville: Negociation de l'espace migratoire chez Calixthe Beyala," Etudes Francophones, (99); auth, "Quartre mariages et deux enterrements: helena de Machado de Assis," Romance Notes, (00); auth, "Le Francais est la langue des champions," AATF Nat Bulletin, (00); auth, "Lucien Chardon - de Rubempre: Champi-

on du Monde en titre(s)," Romance Quart, (01); auth, "Les envahisseurs. Sur La television de Jean-Philippe Toussaint," L'Atelier du Roman, (01); auth, "Understanding and Overcoming the Telephone Interview," ADFL Bulletin (forthcoming); auth, "La Mondovision," Fr Rev, (forthcoming). **CONTACT ADDRESS** Dept Mod and Class Lang and Lit, Univ of Rhode Island, Kingston, RI 02881-0812. **EMAIL** adurand@uri.edu

DURAND, FRANK
PERSONAL Born 05/12/1932, Brooklyn, NY, m, 1955, 2 children **DISCIPLINE** SPANISH LITERATURE AND LANGUAGE **EDUCATION** NYork Univ, BA, 53; Northwestern Univ, MA, 54, Univ Mich, PhD, 62; Brown Univ, MA, 65. **CAREER** Teaching asst Span, Northwestern Univ, 53-54; teaching fel, Univ Mich, 56-60; asst prof, 60-65, assoc prof Span lit, 65-72, Prof Hisp Studies and Chmn Dept Hisp and Ital Studies, Brown Univ, 72-, Howard Found Fel, 68-69. **MEMBERSHIPS** MLA; Am Asn Teachers Span and Port. **RESEARCH** Nineteenth and 20th century Spanish literature; literary criticism; Latin American novel. **SELECTED PUBLICATIONS CONTACT ADDRESS** Dept of Hisp and Ital Studies, Brown Univ, Providence, RI 02912.

DURER, CHRISTOPHER
PERSONAL Born 09/15/1928, Warsaw, Poland, m, 1967, 1 child **DISCIPLINE** ENGLISH, COMPARATIVE LITERATURE **EDUCATION** Chicago Teachers Col, BEd, 61; Univ Calif, Berkeley, MA, 63, PhD (comp lit), 69. **CAREER** Instr humanities, Univ Mo, Rolla, 63-64; instr comp lit, San Francisco State Col, 65-67, Univ Calif, Berkeley, 68-69; asst prof English, 69-73, Assoc Prof English and Mod Lang, Univ Wyo, 73-. **MEMBERSHIPS** MLA; Am Comp Lit Asn; Int Comp Lit Asn; Am Soc 18th Century Studies. **RESEARCH** Comparative theory and history; English 18th century literature; 20th century drama. **SELECTED PUBLICATIONS** Auth, Musical Metamorphoses--Forms and History of Arrangement, Musik und Kirche, Vol 63, 93; The International Glen Gould Festival in Groningen , Musica, Vol 47, 93; Report on the 17th Edition of the Tage Alter Musik Held in Herne, December 1992, Musica, Vol 47, 93; Kagel Die Erschopfung Der Welt, Musica, Vol 48, 94; Freyer Distanzen, Musica, Vol 48, 94; 100 Years of Opera in Essen 1893-1993, Musica, Vol 47, 93; Fortner in Seinem Garten Liebt Don Perlimplin Belisa, Musica, Vol 48, 94; Geister Der ModerneReport on a Recent Concert Series in Recklinghausen March 7-14, 1993, Musica, Vol 47, 93; Hummel Gorbatschow, Musica, Vol 48, 94; Freyer Flugel Schlage, Musica, Vol 48, 94. **CONTACT ADDRESS** Dept of English, Univ of Wyoming, Laramie, WY 82070.

DURHAM, CAROLYN ANN
PERSONAL Born 02/13/1947, Plainview, NE **DISCIPLINE** FRENCH LANGUAGE AND LITERATURE **EDUCATION** Wellesley Col, BA, 69; Univ Chicago, MA, 72, PhD, 76. **CAREER** Lectr French, Univ Chicago, 76; asst prof, 76-80, Assoc Prof French, Col Wooster, 81; Inez K. Gaylord Prof of French, 86; **HONORS AND AWARDS** Nat Endowment for Hum seminar, The Problematics of L'Ecriture Feminine, summer 79; Fulbright Grant, 74-75; Camargo Foundation, 88; NEH Summer Seminar: "Images of the Nation in Interwar France, 94 **MEMBERSHIPS** MLA; Nat Women's Studies Asn. **RESEARCH** Twentieth-century novel; feminist lit criticism; film. **SELECTED PUBLICATIONS** Auth, The contradictory become coherent: La Religieuse and Paul et Virginic, Eighteenth Century: Theory & Interpretation, spring 82; L'Art Romanesque de Raymond Roussel, French Literature Publications, Inc, 82; Noman, Everywomen: Claudine Hermann's Les Voleuses de Langue, Buckncll Rev: Lit, Arts & Ideology 82; The Contexture of Feminism: Marie Cardinal and Multicultural Literacy, univ IL press, 91; auth, At the Crossroads of Gender and Culture: Where Feminism and Sexism in The mod lang jrnl, 95; auth, "Foreword" to Marie Cardinal, In Other Words, Indiana UP, 95; auth, Double Takes: Culture and Gender in French Films and Their American Remakes, UP of New England, 98; auth, "Codes of Contagion: Cyril Collard's Les Nuits Fauves," French Forum 99; auth, "Euzhan Palcy's Feminist Filmmaking," Women in French Studies, 99; auth, Missing Masculinity: Re-Reading Dorothy Arzner's Christopher Strong, Quarterly Review of Film and Video, 01 **CONTACT ADDRESS** Dept of French, The Col of Wooster, 1189 Beall Ave, Wooster, OH 44691-2363. **EMAIL** cdurham@acs.wooster.edu

DURHAM, KEN R.
PERSONAL Born 03/21/1948, m, 1973, 2 children **DISCIPLINE** RELIGION AND COMMUNICATION **EDUCATION** David Lipscomb Col, BA, 70; La State Univ, MA, 72, PhD, 74; post doc grad work Austin Presbyterian theol sem, Abilene Christian Univ. **CAREER** Instr, Inst Christian Studies, 77-78; vis fac, 88; lectr, Okla Christian Univ, 91; David Lipscomb Univ, 89; adjunct fac, Harding Univ Grad Sch Rel, 89; contrib ed, 21st Century Christian, 93-; vis fac, 97-. **SELECTED PUBLICATIONS** Auth, Speaking From the Heart: Richer Relationships Through Communication, Sweet Publ, 86; Jesus, Our Mentor and Model, Baker Bk House, 87; co-auth, Becoming Persons of Integrity, Baker Bk House, 88; Anchors For the Asking, Baker Bk House, 89. **CONTACT ADDRESS** Dept of Relig, Pepperdine Univ, 24255 Pacific Coast Hwy, Malibu, CA 90263. **EMAIL** kdurham@pepperdine.edu

DURHAM, SCOT
DISCIPLINE FRENCH **EDUCATION** Yale Univ, PhD. **CAREER** Asst prof, Northwestern Univ; lect, Univ de Paris IV, Sorbonne; Univ Ca, Riverside; Univ Pa; SUNY, Binghamton; Stanford Univ; Miami Univ; Le College Int de Philos. **RESEARCH** 20th century literature; Foucault & Deleuze. **SELECTED PUBLICATIONS** Auth, "Genet's Shadow Theatre: Memory and Utopian Phantasy in Un captif amoureux," in L'Esprit Createur, 95; auth, Phantom Communities: The Simulacrum and the Limits of Postmodernism, Stanford Univ Press, 98; auth, "From Margarite to Klossowski: The Simulacrum Between Painting and Narrative," 99; auth, Deleuze, Godard, and Djebar. **CONTACT ADDRESS** Dept of French, Northwestern Univ, 1859 Sheridan Rd, Evanston, IL 60208. **EMAIL** spd594@northwestern.edu

DURMELAT, SYLVIE
DISCIPLINE FRENCH AND FRANCOPHONE 20TH CENTURY LITERATURES **EDUCATION** Univ Mich, PhD, 95. **CAREER** Asst prof, La State Univ. **SELECTED PUBLICATIONS** Auth, Faux et d? de langue dans les romans d'Azouz Begag, in Francophone Plurielle, 95; L'apprentissage de l'ecriture dans Geogette! de Farida Belghoul, L'ecriture d?centr?e dans le roman contemporain en France, 96. **CONTACT ADDRESS** Dept of Fr Grad Stud, Louisiana State Univ and A&M Col, Baton Rouge, LA 70803. **EMAIL** durmelas@georgetown.edu

DURR, VOLKER
DISCIPLINE GERMAN **EDUCATION** Princeton Univ, PhD. **CAREER** Assoc prof, Northwestern Univ. **RESEARCH** A monograph on Rilke. **SELECTED PUBLICATIONS** Auth, essays and articles on, poetry; fiction; relation of history to literature; interaction of literature and philosophy; Lessing; Goethe; Bettina von Arnim; Nietzsche: Literature and Values; Coping with the Past; a monograph on Flaubert's Sallamb. **CONTACT ADDRESS** Dept of German, Northwestern Univ, 1801 Hinman, Evanston, IL 60208. **EMAIL** v-durr@nwu.edu

DUSSIAS, PAOLA E.
DISCIPLINE SPANISH LITERATURE **EDUCATION** Univ Ariz, PhD. **CAREER** Asst prof, Univ Ill Urbana Champaign. **RESEARCH** Constraints on Spanish/English codeswitching; sentence processing in bilinguals. **SELECTED PUBLICATIONS** Auth, Sentence Matching and the Functional Head Constraint in Spanish/English Codeswitching, Spanish Applied Ling, 97. **CONTACT ADDRESS** Spanish, Italian, and Portuguese Dept, Univ of Illinois, Urbana-Champaign, 52 E Gregory Dr, Champaign, IL 61820. **EMAIL** dussias@staff.uiuc.edu

DUST, PATRICK
DISCIPLINE TWENTIETH-CENTURY SPANISH LITERATURE **EDUCATION** Univ Chicago, PhD. **CAREER** Literature, Carleton Univ. **MEMBERSHIPS** Auth, Ortega y Gasset and the Question of Modernity. **CONTACT ADDRESS** Carleton Col, 100 S College St., Northfield, MN 55057-4016.

DUVAL, JOHN
PERSONAL Born 19/10/1940, Philadelphia, PA, m, 1967, 2 children **DISCIPLINE** TRANSLATION THEORY AND PRACTICE **EDUCATION** Franklin & Marshall, AB, 62; Univ Pa, MA, 65; Univ Ark, PhD, 77; Univ Ark, MFA, 79. **CAREER** Assist Prof English, French, and Spanish, Albany Junior College, 78-82; Prof, Univ Ark, 82-; Dir, Prog on Literary Translation, Univ Ark, 89. **HONORS AND AWARDS** Outstanding Acad Bk, 82; Harold Morton Landon Translation Awd (Acad of Poets), 92; Nat Endowment Arts, 99; dir, prog literary translation. **MEMBERSHIPS** Exec Coun, Am Lit Transl Assoc, 96-98, present mem; Soc Trilasa **RESEARCH** Translations of Old French poetry and Romanesco poetry. **SELECTED PUBLICATIONS** Auth, Cuckolds, Clerics, and Countrymen: Medieval French Fabliaux, 82; Transl, Long Blues in A Minor, 88; Tales of Trilussa by Carlo Salustri, 90; The Discovery of America by Cesare Pascarella, 91; Auth, Fabliaux, Fair and Foul, 92; Auth, Where the Bee Sucks:Translation Failure #34, Delos Vol 17, 96; Auth, The Man with Twelve Wives and the Translator with More than One Manuscript, Modern Poetry in Transl Vol 8, 96; Auth, Proverbs, Translation Rev Vol 50, 96; Auth, A Good Year, Exchanges Vol 8, 97; Auth, From Language to Language, Culture to Culture, Phi Beta Delta Rev, 98. **CONTACT ADDRESS** Dept of English, Univ of Arkansas, Fayetteville, Fayetteville, AR 72701.

DVORAK, PAUL FRANCIS
PERSONAL Born 05/26/1946, Queens, NY, m, 1969, 2 children **DISCIPLINE** GERMAN LANGUAGE & LITERATURE **EDUCATION** La Salle Col, BA, 68; Univ Md, MA, 70, PhD(Ger), 73. **CAREER** Instr, Univ Md, 70-74; asst prof Ger, Va Commonwealth Univ, 74-, res grant, Va Commonwealth Univ, 78-79, 82-83, 93-94; Fulbright grant, Summer, 81. **HONORS AND AWARDS** Faculty Research Grant, Virginia Commonwealth University, 93-94; Faculty Development Grant, College of H&S, VCU, 95. **MEMBERSHIPS** Am Asn Teachers Ger; Am Coun Teaching of Foreign Lang; Am Coun Study Austrian Lit; Am Transl Assn. **RESEARCH** Post-War German literature; Austrian literature; foreign language pedagogy. **SELECTED PUBLICATIONS** Auth, Adapting personalized questions to second-year foreign language courses, Die Unterrichtspraxis, 75; transit, Ezekiel, humanizing the slave laws in Israel, hope in the OT, letter to the Romans, In: Interpreter's Dictionary of the Bible, Suppl, Abingdon, 76; auth, Communication, small groups and the interview in the foreign language classroom, For Lang Annals, 78; Notation for nouns continued, Die Unterrichtspraxis, 81; Joachim Unseld, Franz Kafka, A Writer's Life, (Translation from the German of Franz Kafka, Ein Schrifstellerleben), Riverside: Ariadne Press, 94; Robert Schneider, Dirt, (Translation from the German of Franz Kafka. Ein Schrifstellerleben), Riverside: Ariadne Press, 96. **CONTACT ADDRESS** Dept of Foreign Lang, Virginia Commonwealth Univ, Box 2021, Richmond, VA 23284. **EMAIL** pdvorak@atlas.vcu.edu

DWORKIN Y MENDEZ, KENYA C.
DISCIPLINE SPANISH **EDUCATION** Univ Hawaii, PhD. **CAREER** Languages, Carnegie Mellon Univ. **SELECTED PUBLICATIONS** Coauth, Manifestaciones del habla afrocubana: La literatura como fuente dialectal, Jour Iberian & Latin Am Studies, 90; Rigoberta Menchu: 'Los indegenas no nos quedamos como bichos aislados, inmunes, desde hace 500 anos. No, nosotros hemos sido protagonistas de la Historia', Nuevo Texto Cretico 93; Rigoberta Menchu: Con quien nos identicamos?, Jour Iberian & Latin Am Studies 3, 92. **CONTACT ADDRESS** Carnegie Mellon Univ, 5000 Forbes Ave, Pittsburgh, PA 15213.

DYCK, ANDREW R.
PERSONAL Born 05/24/1947, Chicago, IL, m, 1978 **DISCIPLINE** CLASSICS **EDUCATION** Univ of Wis, BA; Univ of Chicago, PhD. **CAREER** Lect, Univ of Alberta, 75-76; Vis Asst Prof, UCLA, 76-77; Asst Prof, Univ MN, 78-79; Asst Prof, Prof, UCLA, 79-. **HONORS AND AWARDS** Fel, Alexander VonHumboldt-Stiftung, 81-82; Fel, Nat Endowment for Humanities, 91-92; Mem, Ints for Adv Stud, 91-92; Vis Fel, All Souls Col Oxford, 98; Vis Fel and Life Member, Clare Hall, Cambridge, 99. **MEMBERSHIPS** APA; Calif Class Asn; US Nat Com on Byzantine Studies **RESEARCH** Cicero's Philosophical Essays **SELECTED PUBLICATIONS** Epimerismi Homerici, Berlin-NY, 83-95; The Essays on Euripides and George of Pisidia and on Heliodorus and Achilles Tatius, ed Michael Psellus, Vienna, 86; A Commentary on Cicero, De Officiis, AA, 96; Schliemann on the Excavation of Troy: Three Unpublished Letters, Greek, Roman and Byzantine Stud, 90; Cicero the Dramaturge, Qvi Miscvit Vtile Dvlci: Festschrift Essays for Paul Lachlan MacKendrick, 98; Narrative Obfuscation, Philosophical Topoi, and Tragic Patterning in Cicero's Pro Milone, Harvard Stud in Class Philo, 98. **CONTACT ADDRESS** 405 Hilgard Ave, Los Angeles, CA 90095-1417.

DYCK, MARTIN
PERSONAL Born 01/16/1927, Gruenfeld, Ukraine, 4 children **DISCIPLINE** GERMAN LITERATURE, LITERATURE AND MATHEMATICS **EDUCATION** Univ Man, BA, 53, MA, 54; Univ Cincinnati, PhD, 56. **CAREER** Asst prof Ger and Russ, Mass Inst Technol, 56-58; from asst prof to prof Ger, Univ Mich, 58-65; Prpf Ger and Humanities, Mass Inst Technol, 65-, Guggenheim and Am Coun Learned Soc fels, 61-62; Am Philos Soc award, 69; assoc ed, Hist Mathematica, 72-76. **MEMBERSHIPS** MLA; Hist Sci Soc; Int Soc Ger Lang and Lit; AAUP; Lessing Soc Am. **RESEARCH** German literature of the 18th and 20th centuries, especially Goethe, Novalis, Schiller and Kafka; theory of poetry, major fiction, and comedy; foundations of literature and mathematics. **SELECTED PUBLICATIONS** Auth, The Age of Goethe Today--Critical Reexamination and Literary Reflection, Ger Stud Rev, Vol 15, 92; Performing Schiller--The Critics Speak, 1946-1985, Ger Stud Rev, Vol 15, 92. **CONTACT ADDRESS** Massachusetts Inst of Tech, 77 Massachusetts Ave, Cambridge, MA 02139.

DYE, ROBERT ELLIS
PERSONAL Born 03/21/1936, m, 1959, 3 children **DISCIPLINE** GERMAN LANGUAGE AND LITERATURE **EDUCATION** Univ Utah, BA, 60; Rutgers Univ, MA, 63, PhD (Ger), 66. **CAREER** Teaching asst Ger, Univ Utah, 59-60; teaching asst, Rutgers Col, Rutgers Univ, 61-62, instr, 63-64; instr, Douglass Col, 64-66; asst prof, 66-71, Assoc Prof, 71-79, Prof Ger, MaCalester Col, 79-, Chmn Dept Ger and Russ, 77 **MEMBERSHIPS** MLA; Goethe-Gesellschaft. **RESEARCH** Goethe; literature and religion. **SELECTED PUBLICATIONS** Auth, Women, Water, and the Males Deliquescence, In Goeth, Ger Notes Rev, Vol 24, 93. **CONTACT ADDRESS** Dept of Ger Lang and Lit, Macalester Col, 1600 Grand Ave, Saint Paul, MN 55105.

DYSON, STEVEN L.
DISCIPLINE CLASSICS **EDUCATION** Brown Univ, BA; Yale Univ, PhD, 63. **CAREER** Mellon prof, Intercollegiate Ctr Class Studies; Charles Eliot Norton Lectureship, Archaeolog Inst Am, 93-94; chr class dept, SUNY Buffalo, present. **HONORS AND AWARDS** Fellow, Am Coun Learned Soc; fellow, NEH; pres, archaeolog inst am. **RESEARCH** Romanization of Sardinia; urban develop and soc hist of ancient Rome; the hist of Class archaeol. **SELECTED PUBLICATIONS** Auth, The Roman Villas of Buccino, 83; The Creation of the Roman Fron-

tier, 85; Community and Society in Roman Italy, 92. **CONTACT ADDRESS** Dept Classics, SUNY, Buffalo, 712 Clemens Hall, Buffalo, NY 14260.

E

EARLE, PETER G.
PERSONAL Born 05/31/1923, Yonkers, NY, m, 1949, 3 children **DISCIPLINE** SPANISH AND LATIN AMERICAN LITERATURE **EDUCATION** Mexico City Col, BA, 49, MA, 51; Univ Kans, PhD, 59. **CAREER** Instr Span, Princeton Univ, 56-59; asst prof, Wesleyan Univ, 59-63; assoc prof, 63-69, Prof Span to Prof Emer, Univ Pa, 69-, Assoc ed, Hisp Rev, 64-73, ed, 73-; adv ed, Latin Am Lit Rev, 72-. **MEMBERSHIPS** Am Asn Teachers Span and Port; MLA; Mod Humanities Res Asn; Inst Int Lit Iberoamericana. **RESEARCH** Modern Spanish literature; modern Latin American literature. **SELECTED PUBLICATIONS** Auth, Mexican Narrative from Los De Abajo to Noticias Del Imperio, Hisp Rev, Vol 63, 95; Rereading the Spanish American Essay--Translations of 19th and 20th Century Womens Essays, Hisp Rev, Vol 65, 97; The Elusive Self--Archetypal Approaches to the Novels of Unamuno, Miguel,De, Hisp Rev, Vol 62, 94. **CONTACT ADDRESS** Dept of Romance Lang, Univ of Pennsylvania, 3451 Walnut, Philadelphia, PA 19104.

EASTMAN, CAROL M.
PERSONAL Born 09/27/1941, Boston, MA **DISCIPLINE** LINGUISTICS, ANTHROPOLOGY **EDUCATION** Univ Mass, BA, 63; Univ Wis, PhD (ling), 67 **CAREER** Asst prof anthrop and ling, 67-73, assoc prof, 73-79, Prof Anthrop, Univ Wash, 79-, Vis prof, Univ Nairobi, 79-80; Adj Prof Ling and Women Studies, Univ Wash, 79-. **MEMBERSHIPS** Ling Soc Am; fel African Studies Asn; Am Anthrop Asn; Current Anthrop. **RESEARCH** Bantu linguistics and literature; Northwest Indian languages; language and culture. **SELECTED PUBLICATIONS CONTACT ADDRESS** Dept of Anthrop, Univ of Washington, Seattle, WA 98195.

EBERT, ROBERT P.
PERSONAL Born 08/05/1944, Mt Vernon, NY, m, 2 children **DISCIPLINE** LINGUISTICS **EDUCATION** Union Col, BA, 66; Univ Wisconsin, MA, 68; PhD, 72. **CAREER** Asst prof, Univ Chicago, 72-79; vis asst prof, Univ Calif, Berkeley, 77-78; assoc prof, Princeton Univ, 79-87; prof, 87-. **HONORS AND AWARDS** Fulbright Fel, Nurnberg, 66-67; Phi Beta Kappa. **SELECTED PUBLICATIONS** Auth, Historische Syntax des Deutschen II: 1300-1750, Peter Lang (Bern, Ger), 86; coauth, Fruhneuhochdeutsche Grammatik, Niemejer (Tubingen, Ger), 93; auth, Verbstellungswandel bei lugendlichen, Frauen und Mannern im 16, Jahrhundert, Niemeyer (Tubingen, Ger), 98; auth, Historische Syntax des Deutschen 11: 1300-1750, Weidler (Berlin), 99; auth, "Presuppositions and Contrastive Analysis. Polar Adjectives in English and German," in Paners from the International Symposium on Applied Contrastive Linguistics, ed. Gerhard Nickel (Bielefeld: Cornelsen-Velhagen, 72), 107-127; auth, "A Functional Explanation of the Development of Extended Prenominal Participial Constructions in German and Why It Fails," in Papers from the Parasession on Functionalism (Chicago: Chicago Linguistic Society, 75), 150-155; auth, "Subject Raising, the Clause Squish and German Scheinen Constructions,¤ in Papers from the Eleventh Regional Meeting (Chicago: Chicago Linguistic Society, 75), 177-187. **CONTACT ADDRESS** Dept Ger Lang/Lit, Princeton Univ, 230 East Pyne Hall, Princeton, NJ 08544-0001.

EBLE, CONNIE C.
PERSONAL Born 11/20/1942, New Orleans, LA **DISCIPLINE** LINGUISTICS, ENGLISH **EDUCATION** St Mary's Dominican Col, BA, 64; Univ NCar, MA, 67; PhD, 70. **CAREER** Instr, Univ Ky, 68-71; prof, Univ NCar, 71-. **HONORS AND AWARDS** ACLS Fel, 75; CNDCT Fel, Brazil, 94; IBM Fel, 67; NDEA Fel, 64-67. **MEMBERSHIPS** ADS; SAMLA; LACUS; SCL; LSA; MLA; DSNA; AAUP. **RESEARCH** American slang; college slang; English's of Louisiana; history of American English. **SELECTED PUBLICATIONS** Auth, College Slang 101, Spectacle Lane Pr, 89; auth, "Prolegomenon to the Study of Cajun English," Secol Rev 17 (93): 164-177; ed, American Speech, Duke Univ Pr, 95-; auth, Slang and Sociability: In Group Language Among College Students, Univ NCar Pr, 96. **CONTACT ADDRESS** Ling Dept, Univ of No Carolina, Chapel Hill, PO Box CB3520, Chapel Hill, NC 27599-3520. **EMAIL** cceble@email.unc.edu

ECKHARD, ROLZ
PERSONAL Born Kaufbeuren, Germany **DISCIPLINE** GERMAN LANGUAGE, LITERATURE **EDUCATION** Ut State Univ, BA, 94; Univ NCar Chapel Hill, MA, 96; PhD, 00. **CAREER** Asst prof, Idaho State Univ, 00-. **HONORS AND AWARDS** James Kent Brown Fel, 96-00; Tanner Teaching Award, 97; Mem ADTS, 00-. **MEMBERSHIPS** AATG; MLA; RMMLA; IATLC. **RESEARCH** Childhood in 18th-century Germany; gender issues; Heinrich von Kleist; language pedagogy. **SELECTED PUBLICATIONS** Auth, "Genderless Childhood: Narrative Literature and the Case Study in Eighteenth-Century Germany," SUNY Pr (forthcoming). **CONTACT ADDRESS** Dept For Lang, Idaho State Univ, MSC 8372, Pocatello, ID 83209. **EMAIL** rolzeckh@isu.edu

ECKHARDT, CAROLINE DAVIS
PERSONAL Born 02/27/1942, New York, NY, m, 1964, 4 children **DISCIPLINE** ENGLISH AND COMPARATIVE LITERATURE **EDUCATION** Drew Univ, BA, 63; Ind Univ, Bloomington, MA, 65; Univ Mich, Ann Arbor, PhD (comp lit), 71. **CAREER** Asst prof, 71-76, Assoc Prof English and Comp Lit, PA State Univ, 76-, Dir Comp Lit Prog, 77-, Co-ed, JGE (jour), 74-; fel palaeography, Univ Pa Medieval Inst, 76. **MEMBERSHIPS** MLA; Mediaeval Acad Am; Int Arthurian Soc; Am Comp Lit Asn; Conf Ed Learned Jours. **RESEARCH** Medieval romance; medieval lyric; Chaucer. **SELECTED PUBLICATIONS** Auth, The Meaning of Ermonie in Sir Tristrem, Stud Philol, Vol 93, 96; The Historia Regum Britannie of Geoffrey of Monmouth, Vol 4--Dissemination and Reception in the Later Middle Ages, Speculum J Medieval Stud, Vol 69, 94; Comparative Poetics--An Intercultural Essay on Theories of Literature, World Lit Today, Vol 67, 93; The Meaning of Ermonie in Sir Tristrem, Stud in Philol, Vol 93, 96; The Historia Regum Britannie of Geoffrey of Monmouth, Vol 4--Dissemination and Reception in The Later Middle Ages, Speculum J Medieval Stud, Vol 69, 94. **CONTACT ADDRESS** Dept of English, Pennsylvania State Univ, Univ Park, 434n Burrowes Bldg, University Park, PA 16802-6204.

EDGEWORTH, ROBERT J.
PERSONAL Born 01/02/1947, Chicago, IL, m, 2000, 2 children **DISCIPLINE** CLASSICS **EDUCATION** Loyola Univ, AB, 67; Univ Mich, MA, 68; PhD, 74. **CAREER** Lecturing Fel, Australian Nat Univ, 74-80; Lecturer, San Diego State Univ, 81; Asst Prof to Prof, La State Univ, 81-. **MEMBERSHIPS** Am Philol Asn, Classical Asn of the Middle West and South, La Classical Asn, Vergilian Soc. **RESEARCH** The Epic; Ancient color terminology. **SELECTED PUBLICATIONS** Auth, the colors of the Aeneid, Peter Lang, 92. **CONTACT ADDRESS** Dept For Lang, La State Univ, Baton Rouge, LA 70803-0104.

EDMUNDS, LOWELL
PERSONAL Born 10/11/1938, Franklin, NH, m, 1966, 2 children **DISCIPLINE** CLASSICS **EDUCATION** Harvard, PhD, 70. **CAREER** Teaching asst, Classics, Berkeley, 63-64; teaching fel, Classics, Harvard, 67-69; teaching fel, Harvard summer school, 68, 69; instr Classics, Wheaton Col, 69-70; tutor, St John's Col, Santa Fe, NM, summers 70, 71; asst prof Classics, Harvard, 70-75; asst prof Classics, Harvard Univ Extension, 72-73; assoc prof Classics, Harvard, 75-78; assoc prof Classics, Harvard Univ Exrension, 76-80; assoc prof Classics, Boston Col, 78-83; ed, Comparative Civilizations Bul, 79-82; chmn, Dept Classical Studies, Boston Col, 83; prof Classics and chmn, Johns Hopkins Univ, 83-88; member, fac ed bd, Johns Hopkins Univ Press, 83-86; member ed bd, Am J of Philol, 83-87; member, subcommittee on the Thesaurus Linguae Graecae of the Res Comm of the Am Philol Asn, 86-; chmn, Ed Adv Comm, Perseus: A New Curriculum on Ancient Greek Civilization, Harvard based, 86-92; first vice pres, Baltimore Soc of the Archaeological Inst of Am, 87-88; member, ed bd, Lexis (Univ Venice), 87-; co-dir, Coppin-Hopkins Prog in the Baltimore City Schools, 87-89; prof Classics, Rutgers Univ, 88-, dir, graduate prog in Classics, 88-90, chair, 90-96, acting dir, graduate prog in Classics, 94-96; professore a contratto, Universita degli Studi di Venezia, April 90; prof a contratto, Universita degli Studi di Trento, Nov 93; vis prof, Princeton Univ, spring 95; asst ed, Classical World, 97-00. **HONORS AND AWARDS** Pushcart Prize for "Choosing Your Names," 93-94. **MEMBERSHIPS** Am Philol Asn; Int Soc for Folk Narrative Res. **RESEARCH** Greek lit; Greek mythology; Roman lit. **SELECTED PUBLICATIONS** Auth, Choosing Your Names, Raritan 11 3, winter 92, under pseudonym, Kothar wa-Khasis, reprinted in The 1993-1994 Pushcart Prize XVIII: Best of the Small Presses; Intertextuality Today, Lexis 13, 95; Theatrical Space and Historical Place in Sophocles' Oedipus at Colonus, Rowman and Littlefield, 96; Poet, Public, and Performance: Essays in Ancient Greek Literature and Literary History, ed with Robert Wallace, The Johns Hopkins Univ Press, 97; Myth in Homer, in New Companion to Homer, ed by Barry Powell and Ian Morris, Brill, April 97; The Silver Bullet: The Martini in American Civilization, Contributions in Am Studies 52, Greenwood Press, 81, 2nd ed, titled Martini Straight Up: The Classic American Cocktail, Johns Hopkins Univ Press, 98. **CONTACT ADDRESS** 440 Grant Ave, Highland Park, NJ 08904. **EMAIL** edmunds@rci.rutgers.edu

EDWARDS, DON R.
PERSONAL Born 05/26/1955, Lafayette, IN **DISCIPLINE** CLASSICS **EDUCATION** St. John's Col, BA, 78; Johns Hopkins, MS, 96; Brown Univ, PhD, 84. **CAREER** Author **RESEARCH** Philosophy **CONTACT ADDRESS** 218 East Del Ray Ave, Alexandria, VA 22301.

EEKMAN, THOMAS
PERSONAL Born 05/20/1923, Middelharnis, Netherlands, m, 1946, 4 children **DISCIPLINE** SLAVIC LITERATURES **EDUCATION** Univ Amsterdam, MA, 46, PhD (Slavic lang), 51. **CAREER** Docent S Slavic lang and lit, Univ Amsterdam, 55-66; vis prof, 60-61, res grants, 66-78, Prof Slavic Lang, Univ Calif, Los Angeles, 66-, Vis prof Russ lit, Univ Hamburg, 72-73 and Aarhus Univ, 73; Am Coun Learned Soc res grants, 72-73, 73-74 and 78-; Univ Calif Humanities Inst res grant, 73; co-ed, Calif Slavic Studies, 73-. **HONORS AND AWARDS** Order of Yugoslav Flag, Yugoslav Govt, 65; Martinus Nijhoff Awd, Netherlands, 81. **MEMBERSHIPS** Philol Asn Pac Coast; Am Asn S Europ Studies; W Slavic Asn; Asn Int des Lang et Litt Slaves. **RESEARCH** Nineteenth and 20th century Russian literature; comparative Slavic literature; poetics. **SELECTED PUBLICATIONS CONTACT ADDRESS** Dept of Slavic Lang, Univ of California, Los Angeles, 405 Hilgard Ave, Los Angeles, CA 90024.

EGAN, RORY BERNARD
PERSONAL Born 02/06/1942, Sutton West, ON, Canada, m, 1970 **DISCIPLINE** CLASSICS **EDUCATION** Assumption Univ, Windsor, BA, 63; Univ Western Ont, MA, 65; Univ Southern Calif, PhD (classics), 71. **CAREER** Asst prof classics, Univ Southern Calif, 70-77; Assoc Prof Classics and Dept Head, Univ Man, 77-. **MEMBERSHIPS** Am Class League; Am Inst Archaeol; Am Philol Asn; Class Asn Can; Philol Asn Pac Coast. **RESEARCH** Classical mythology; Greek literature; Greek language. **SELECTED PUBLICATIONS** Auth, Stesichorus and Helen, Dallan and Columba, Class World, Vol 87, 93; Corydon Winning Words in Eclogue 7, Phoenix J Class Assn Can, Vol 50, 96. **CONTACT ADDRESS** Dept of Classics, Univ of Manitoba, Winnipeg, MB, Canada R3T 2N2. **EMAIL** regan@ms.umanitoba.ca

EGEA, ESTEBAN R.
DISCIPLINE SPANISH AND FRENCH LITERATURE **EDUCATION** Harvard Univ, PhD, 74. **CAREER** Assoc prof. **RESEARCH** Linguistics; English as a second language. **SELECTED PUBLICATIONS** Auth, Los adverbios terminados en mente en el espanol contemporaneo, Inst Caro y Cuervo, 80; Using a Computer-generated Concordance to Analyze and Document Stylistic Devices in Robert Pinget's Fable, Comput Humanities, 77. **CONTACT ADDRESS** Dept of Literature, Univ of Texas, Dallas, Richardson, TX 75083-0688. **EMAIL** egea@utdallas.edu

EGERT, EUGENE
PERSONAL Born 12/29/1935, Rudnik, Poland, m, 1961, 2 children **DISCIPLINE** GERMANIC LANGUAGES **EDUCATION** Univ BC, 58, MA, 61; Univ Tex, PhD (Ger), 77. **CAREER** Instr Ger, Univ Wash, 64-67; from asst prof to assoc prof, 67-77, Prof Ger, Univ Alta, 77-, **MEMBERSHIPS** Am Asn Teachers Ger; Asn Can Univ Teachers Ger; Mediaeval Acad Am. **RESEARCH** Early Middle High German literature; Middle High German lyric; Middle High German courtly epic. **SELECTED PUBLICATIONS** Auth, The Presentation and Function of Artistic Elements in Gottfried Von Strassburg Tristan, Seminar J Ger Stud, Vol 30, 94. **CONTACT ADDRESS** Dept of Mod Langs, Univ of Alberta, Edmonton, AB, Canada T6G 2M7.

EGGINTON, WILLIAM
PERSONAL Born 03/24/1969, Syracuse, NY, m, 1999 **DISCIPLINE** ENGLISH, COMPOSITION, LITERATURE, SPANISH **EDUCATION** Dartmouth Univ, AB, 91; Univ Minn, MA, 94; Stanford Univ, AM, 96; PhD, 99. **CAREER** Asst prof, SUNY Buffalo, 99-. **HONORS AND AWARDS** Stanford Hum Cent Fel, 96-97; Bradley Rubidge Mem Dis Prize, Stan Univ. **MEMBERSHIPS** MLA; SLS; IAPL. **RESEARCH** European literary history; continental philosophy; psychoanalysis. **SELECTED PUBLICATIONS** Auth, "Gracidn and the Emergence of the Modern Subject," Hisp Issue (97); auth, "On Relativism, Rights and Differends, or, Ethics and the American Holocaust," Qui Parle (95); auth, "A Wrinkle in Historical Time," Substance (96); auth, "An Epistemology of the Stage: Subjectivity and Theatricality in Early Modern Spain," New Lit Hist (96); auth, "From the End of History to the Death of Man," Annalecta Husserlina (96); auth, "On Dante, Hyper spheres, and the Curvature of the Medieval Cosmos," J Hist Ideas (99); auth, "Psychoanalysis and the Comedia: Skepticism and the Paternal Function in La vida es sueno," Bullit Comediantes (00); auth, Borges: The Passion of an Endless Quote, SUNY P, forthcoming; auth, How the World Became a Stage, SUNY, forthcoming; auth, The Pragmatic Turn in Philosophy, SUNY P, forthcoming. **CONTACT ADDRESS** Eng Dept., SUNY, Buffalo, 910 Clemens, Buffalo, NY 14260-4620. **EMAIL** egginton@ascu.buffalo.edu

EHRE, MILTON
PERSONAL Born 04/15/1933, New York, NY, m, 1963, 2 children **DISCIPLINE** RUSSIAN LITERATURE **EDUCATION** City Col New York, BA, 55; Columbia Univ, MA, 66, PhD, 70. **CAREER** Asst prof, 67-72, assoc prof, 72-81, prof Russ & humanities, Univ Chicago, 81-. **HONORS AND AWARDS** Am Coun Learned Soc grant, 70-71; Guggenheim fel, 75-76. **MEMBERSHIPS** Am Assn Advan Slavic Studies; Am Assn Teachers Slavic & East Europ Lang. **RESEARCH** Russian literature of the 19th & 20th century; Russian prose fiction; Russian drama. **SELECTED PUBLICATIONS** Auth,

Oblomov and His Creator: The Life and Art of Ivan Goncharov, Princeton: Princeton Univ Press, 73; co-ed, The Theater of Nikolay Gogol: Plays and Selected Writings, Chicago: Univ of Chicago Press, 80; transl, Chekhov for the Stage, Northwestern Univ Press, 92; auth, Fedor Sologub's The Petty Demon: Erotica, Time and Decadence, The Silver Age, London: MacMillan, 92; auth, Meaning in Oblomov, Ivan A. Goncarov: Leben, Werk und Wirkung, Cologne: Bohlau, 95; auth, Ivan Goncharov's A Usual Story and the Precipice, Alexander Ostrovsky's Forest, Alexander Pushkis's Boris Godunov, Guide to Russian Literature, London: Fitzzroy, 97, auth, Issac Babel, Boston: Twayne, 86, CD-ROM version, New York, Macmillan, 97; **CONTACT ADDRESS** Dept of Slavic, Univ of Chicago, 1130 E 59th St, Chicago, IL 60637-1539. **EMAIL** m-ehre@uchicago.edu

EHRET, CHRISTOPHER

PERSONAL Born 07/27/1941, San Francisco, CA **DISCIPLINE** AFRICAN HISTORY, HISTORICAL LINGUISTICS **EDUCATION** Univ Redlands, BA, 63; Northwestern Univ, Evanston, MA and cert African studies, 66, PhD (African hist), 68. **CAREER** Asst prof, 68-72, assoc prof, 72-78, Prof African Hist, Univ Calif, Los Angeles, 78-, Ford Found grant African relig hist, 71-74; Fulbright grant, 82. **MEMBERSHIPS** Kenya Hist Soc; Hist Soc Tanzania; African Studies Association life member. **RESEARCH** Development and use of linguistic evidence in historical reconstruction; eastern and southern African history; African historical linquistics. **SELECTED PUBLICATIONS** Auth, "Southern Nilotic History," 71; auth, "Ethiopians and East Africans," 74; auth, "The Archaeological and Linguistic Reconstruction of African History," 82; auth, "Reconstructing Proto-Afroasiatic, 95; auth, An African Classical Age," 98 **CONTACT ADDRESS** Dept of Hist, Univ of California, Los Angeles, Los Angeles, CA 90024. **EMAIL** ehret@history.ucla.edu

EHRLICH, CARL S.

PERSONAL Born 05/15/1956, New Haven, CT, m, 1982, 2 children **DISCIPLINE** HEBREW **EDUCATION** Univ Mass at Amherst, BA, 76; Harvard Univ, AM, 84; PhD, 91. **CAREER** Sen Lectr, Hochschule fur Judische Studien, Heidelberg, 91-95; Vis Lectr, Humboldt Univ Berlin, 93; Vis Prof, Kirchliche Hochschule, Wuppertal Germany, 96; Asst Prof to Assoc Prof, York Univ, 96-; Vis Prof, Hochschule fur Judische Studien Heidelberg, 00-01. **HONORS AND AWARDS** Fel, Mem Found for Jewish Culture, 79-80; Fel, Dorot Found, 81; Fel, Nat Found for Jewish Culture, 85-86. **MEMBERSHIPS** Am Sch of Oriental Res; Asn for Jewish Studies; Can Soc of Biblical Studies; Deutscher Palastina-Verein; Europ Asn for Jewish Studies; Soc of Biblical Lit. **RESEARCH** Hebrew Biblical and Ancient Near Eastern Studies. **SELECTED PUBLICATIONS** Auth, Coalition Politics in Eighth Century B.C.E. Palestine: The Philistines and the Syro-Ephraimite War, Zeitschrift des Deutschen Palastina-Vereins 107, 91; auth, "Sklavenauslieferung in der Bibel und im alten Orient," Trumah 4, 94; auth, "'Anti-Judaismus' in der hebraischen Bibel. Der Fall: Exechiel," Vetus Testamentum 46, 96; auth, The Philistines in Transition: A History from ca. 1000-730 BCE, Leiden-New York-Koln: E.J. Brill, 96; auth, "How the Mighty Are Fallen: The Philistines in Their Tenth Century Context," in The Age of Solomon: Scholarship at the Turn of the Millennium, (Leiden: E.J. Brill, 97)m 179-201; auth, "Judaism", in The Illustrated Guide to World Religions, (Duncan Baird Pub, 98(, 14-51; auth, "Du sollst dir kein Gottesbildnis machen. Das zweite Wort vom Sinai im Rahmen der judischen Auslegung des Dekalogs," in Im Anfang war das Wort: Interdisziplinare theologische Perspektiven, (Foedus Werlag, 98), 40-55; auth, ""Ezekiel: The Prophet, His Times, His Message," European Judaism 32, 99; auth, "Joshua, Judaism and Genocide," in Jewish Studies at the Turn of the 20th Century, (Leiden-Boston-Koln: Brill, 99), 117-126; auth, "Moses, Torah, and Judaism," in The Rivers of Paradise, (Eerdmans, 01), 11-119. **CONTACT ADDRESS** Div of Humanities, York Univ, Toronto, ON, Canada M3J 1P3. **EMAIL** ehrlich@yorku.ca

EICHENLAUB, CONSTANCE

PERSONAL Born 01/08/1954, Chicago, IL, m, 1985, 1 child **DISCIPLINE** ENGLISH, COMPARATIVE LITERATURE **EDUCATION** Duquesne Univ, BA, 84; MS, 85; Univ Wash, MA, 87; PhD, 98. **CAREER** Adj fac, Antioch Univ, 95, 98-99; lectr, Univ Wash, 98-00; adj fac, Trinity Luth Col, 00-01; fac, Cornish Col, 99-. **HONORS AND AWARDS** David C Fowler Trav Awds; Cornish Col Fac Dev Fund; Beinecke Fel, 01-02. **MEMBERSHIPS** CAAS; APA; ISSEI; MLA; ACLA. **RESEARCH** The life and work of Marguerite Young, American author (1908-1995). **SELECTED PUBLICATIONS** Auth, "Overview essay of the life and work of Marguerite Young," Rev Contemp Fict (00): 121-148; auth, "Aristotelian katharsis as Ethical Conversion in Plotinian Aesthetics," in Dionysius XVII (99): 57-82; auth, "Anamnesis and the Unconscious: Ancient Concepts of Memory in Plato, Aristotle and Plotinus," Pro Fifth ISSEI Conf (98); auth, "Rediscovery of Anima - American Culture in Search of Soul," Euro Legacy: Toward New Paradigms 2 (97): 668-674; auth, "Transformative Aisthesis," in Western Esoteric Traditions, SUNY Press, forthcoming. **CONTACT ADDRESS** Eng Dept, Univ of Washington, 321 W Garfield, Seattle, WA 98119. **EMAIL** connieei@u.washington.edu

EICHMANN, RAYMOND

DISCIPLINE MEDIEVAL FRENCH FABLIAUX AND DRAMA **EDUCATION** Univ Ark, BA, 65; Univ Ark, MA, 67, Univ Ky, PhD, 73. **CAREER** From asst prof to prof & dept ch, For Langs, Univ Ark, 69- . **HONORS AND AWARDS** Chair, dept; Chair, European Studies prog. **CONTACT ADDRESS** Dept of For Langs, Univ of Arkansas, Fayetteville, Fayetteville, AR 72701. **EMAIL** reichman@comp.uark.edu

EICHNER, HANS

PERSONAL Born 10/30/1921, Vienna, Austria **DISCIPLINE** GERMAN LANGUAGE AND LITERATURE **EDUCATION** Univ London, BA, 44, BA(Hons), 46, PhD, 49; Queen's Univ, LLD, 74. **CAREER** Asst lectr, Bedford Col (London), 48-50; asst prof to prof, Queen's Univ, 50-67; prof, 67-88, ch grad dept Ger, 67-72, ch Ger, 75-84, Prof Emer German, Univ Toronto, 88-; hon prof hum, Univ Calgary, 78; adj prof, Queen's Univ, 90-. **HONORS AND AWARDS** Fel, Royal Soc Can, 67. **MEMBERSHIPS** Can Asn Univ Tchrs Ger. **SELECTED PUBLICATIONS** Auth, Thomas Mann, 53, 2nd rev ed 61; auth, Reading German for Scientists, 59; auth, Four German Authors: Mann-Rilke-Kafka-Brecht, 64; auth, Friedrich Schlegel, 70; auth, Deutsche Literatur im klassisch-romantischen Zeitalter 1795-1805, 1 Teil, 90; ed, Friedrich Schlegel: Literary Notebooks 1797-1801, 57, 2nd (Ger) ed, 80; ed, Kritische Friedrich Schlegel-Ausgabe, vols 2-6, vol 16, 58-81; ed, 'Romantic' and its Cognates: The European History of a Word, 72; ed, Der Artushof und andere Erzahlungen (Eichendorff), 91; ed, Ausgewahlte Schriften, 94; gen ed, Canadian Studies in German Language and Literature. **CONTACT ADDRESS** Box 41, Rockwood, ON, Canada N0B 2K0.

EINBECK, KANDACE

PERSONAL Born 03/13/1952, New York, NY, s **DISCIPLINE** GERMAN **EDUCATION** Swarthmore Col, BA, 74; Univ New Hamp, MA, 79; Univ Conn, PhD, 95. **CAREER** Teach, Mt Desert HS, 74-81; inst, Lang Coord, 81-86; teach asst, Univ Conn, 84-88; instr, Goethe Inst, 86-; instr, Univ Rhode Island, 88-94; resid dir, Univ Salzburg, 94-96; vis asst prof, Univ Conn, 98-99; asst prof, Univ Colorado, 98-. **HONORS AND AWARDS** Predoc Fel Univ Conn. **MEMBERSHIPS** AATG; CCFLA; GACC; Hagiography Soc. **RESEARCH** Languages for specific purposes; content-based instruction; learning style of foreign language learning; learning cross-cultural awareness; medieval and renaissance; German saints legends. **SELECTED PUBLICATIONS** Coauth, "The Changing Goals of Language Instruction," in Languages for a Multi-cultural World in Transition, ed. Heidi Byrnes (NTC, 93); auth, "Crossing Cultures and a Millennium With Kas Tai,' Global Bus Lang (00). **CONTACT ADDRESS** Univ Colorado Boulder, Univ of Colorado, Boulder, Campus Box 276, Boulder, CO 80309-0276. **EMAIL** kandace.einbeck@colorado.edu

EISENBICHLER, KONRAD

PERSONAL Born 03/18/1949, Lussinpiccolo, Istria, s **DISCIPLINE** ITALIAN **EDUCATION** McMaster Univ, BA, 73; BA, 74; Univ Toronto, PhD, 81. **CAREER** Curator to Dir, Center for Reformation and Renaissance Studies, 79-; Asst Prof to Prof, Univ Toronto, 85-. **HONORS AND AWARDS** Gold Medal, Trieste, 95; Howard Marraro Prize, Catholic Hist Asn of Am, 99. **MEMBERSHIPS** Am Asn of Italian Studies; Can Soc for Italian Studies; Can Soc for Renaissance Studies; Renaissance Soc of Am. **RESEARCH** Medieval and Renaissance Italy; Florence; Theatre; Confraternities; Giuliano-Dalmata history and culture. **SELECTED PUBLICATIONS** Co-trans, Giovanni Della Casa, Galateo, Toronto, 90; auth, Confraternities, Medieval Inst Press, 91; co-trans, Agnolo Firenzuola, On the Beauty of Women, Univ Penn Press, 92; co-ed, Desire and Discipline. Sex and Sexuality in the Premodern West, Univ Toronto Press, 96; auth, An Italian Region in Canada. The Case of Friuli-Venezia Giulia, Toronto, 98; auth, The Boys of the Archangel Raphael. A Youth Confraternity in Florence, 1411-1785, Univ Toronto Press, 98; auth, Crossing the Boundaries. Christian Piety and the Arts in Italian Medieval and Renaissance; co-ed, Carnival and the Carnivalsque, The Fool, The Reformer, The Wildman, and Others in Early Modern Teatre, Amsterdam, 99. **CONTACT ADDRESS** Univ of Toronto, Victoria Col, 71 Queen's Pk Cres E, Toronto, ON, Canada M5S 1K7. **EMAIL** konrad.eisenbichler@utoronto.ca

ELAM, HELEN REGUEIRO

PERSONAL Born 09/18/1943, Montevideo, Uruguay **DISCIPLINE** COMPARATIVE LITERATURE **EDUCATION** Brandeis Univ, BA, 64; Brown Univ, PhD (comp lit), 69. **CAREER** Asst prof English and comp lit, Columbia Univ, 69-75; asst prof English, Yale Univ, 75-77; Assoc Prof English, State Univ NY Albany, 77-, Chamberlain fel, Columbia Univ, 74; Soc for Humanities jr fel, Cornell Univ, 73-74. **MEMBERSHIPS** MLA; Am Comp Lit Asn. **RESEARCH** Nineteenth and 20th century English, American, French, German and Greek poetry; literary criticism and literary theory; 19th and 20th century novel. **SELECTED PUBLICATIONS** Auth, Introduction--Romantic Poets and Their Critics, The Case of Hartman, Geoffrey, H, Stud Romanticism, Vol 35, 96. **CONTACT ADDRESS** Dept of English, SUNY, Albany, 1400 Washington Ave, Albany, NY 12222-1000.

ELARDO, RONALD JOSEPH

PERSONAL Born 08/25/1948, Buffalo, NY, m, 1972, 3 children **DISCIPLINE** GERMAN LANGUAGE & LITERATURE **EDUCATION** State Univ NYork Buffalo, BA, 70; Purdue Univ, MA, 72; Univ Mich, PhD(Ger lang & lit), 79. **CAREER** Teaching asst Ger, Purdue Univ, 70-72; lectr, Univ Mich, 79-80 & Oakland Univ, 80-81; Asst Prof Ger & English, Adrian Col, 81-. **MEMBERSHIPS** MLA; Am Asn Teachers Ger **RESEARCH** The writings of Friedrich Wilhelm Joseph von Schelling; German romantic fairy tales; Alchemy and the medieval German epics. **SELECTED PUBLICATIONS** Auth, Lanzelet, alchemy and individuation, Symp, summer 80; E T A Hoffmann's Klein Zaches, the Trickster, Sem, 9/80; E T A Hoffman's Nussknacker und Mausekonig: The mouse-queen in the tragedy of the hero, Ger Rev, winter 80; The maw as infernal medium in Ritter Gluck and Die Bergwerke zu Falun, New Ger Studies, spring 81. **CONTACT ADDRESS** Dept of Foreign Lang, Adrian Col, 110 S Madison St, Adrian, MI 49221-2575. **EMAIL** r.elardo@adrian.adrian.edu

ELBAZ, ANDRE ELIE

PERSONAL Born 03/19/1937, Fez, Morocco, 2 children **DISCIPLINE** FRENCH AND COMPARATIVE LITERATURE **EDUCATION** Univ Bordeaux, Lic es Lett, 62; Sorbonne, DUniv(lit), 69. **CAREER** Teacher French, Universal Israelite Alliance, Meknes, Morocco, 56-61; prof English, UNESCO Emergency Prog, Niamey, Niger, 61-63; lectr French, Western Wash State Col, 63-65; assoc prof, 65-80, adj res prof french, Carleton Univ, 80-, Mem bd dirs, Can Serv Overseas Students and Trainees, 66-68; Can Coun and Humanities Res Coun Can grants, 69-78; fac consult, Acad Coun World Inst Sephardic Studies, 73-; guest lectr Sephardic Studies, Yeshiva Univ, 73-; researcher folk lit, Can Ctr Folk Cult Studies, Nat Museum Man, Ottawa, 76-78; Can Coun leave fel, 78-69. **HONORS AND AWARDS** Numerous Res Awds from Can Coun and Carleton Univ. **MEMBERSHIPS** Int Comp Lit Asn; Can Asn Folklore Studies; World Union Jewish Studies; Acad Coun World Inst Sephardic Studies; Int Res Prog Zola and Naturalism. **RESEARCH** French literataure and the Dreyfus affair; French and North American Jewish literature; Sephardic popular literature. **CONTACT ADDRESS** Dept of French, Carleton Univ, 1125 Colonel By Dr, 1602 Dunton Tower, Ottawa, ON, Canada K1S 5B6.

ELDER, ARLENE ADAMS

PERSONAL Born 05/11/1940, Los Angeles, CA, 1 child **DISCIPLINE** AFRICAN, ETHNIC AMERICAN, & AUSTRALIAN-ABORIGINAL LITERATURE **EDUCATION** Immaculate Heart Col, AB, 61; Univ Denver, MA, 62; Univ Chicago, PhD(English), 70. **CAREER** Instr English, Emmanuel Col, 62-65; lectr, 70-71, asst prof, 71-76, assoc prof, 76-90, prof English & comp lit, Univ Cincinnati, 91-; vis Fulbright lectr lit, Univ Nairobi, Kenya, 76-77. **MEMBERSHIPS** MLA, member exec coun, division of African lit, 95-2000; MELUS Soc Study Multi-Ethnic Lit US; AAUP; member, exec coun, African Lit Asn, 94-2000; member of the Delegate Assembly 00-02; African Studies Cert Prog. **RESEARCH** African lit; ethnic Americans; Australian-Aboriginal lit.; orature int literature. **SELECTED PUBLICATIONS** Auth, The Hindered Hand: Cultural Implications of Early African-American Fiction, Greenwood, 79; and many essays on African, African-Am, and women's literature. **CONTACT ADDRESS** Dept of English, Univ of Cincinnati, PO Box 210069, Cincinnati, OH 45221-0069. **EMAIL** elder2@fuse.net

ELDRED, KATHERINE O.

DISCIPLINE CLASSICS **EDUCATION** Brown Univ, BA, 89; Princeton Univ, MA, 93, PhD, 97. **CAREER** Prof, Northwestern Univ; Mellon postdoctoral fel, 97-99. **RESEARCH** Latin poetry; Roman violence; Roman cultural studies. **SELECTED PUBLICATIONS** Auth, Off With Her Head! Reading Lucan's Medusa, Bristol Univ Dept Class and Ancient Hist, 98; Telemachus Strings the Bow, in Aspects of the Hero: A Colloquium on Violence, Gender, and Self-Definition in Homer, Northwestern Univ, 98; Face/Off: Lucan's Medusa and the Gaze of Tyranny, Northwestern Univ, 98; Lucan's Medusa: Resisting Civil War, Am Philol Asn,97; All for One: the Sacrifice of Vulteius, Am Philol Asn, 96. **CONTACT ADDRESS** Dept of Classics, Northwestern Univ, 1801 Hinman, Kresge 17, Evanston, IL 60208. **EMAIL** koeldred@nwu.edu

ELDREDGE, LAURENCE MILTON

PERSONAL Born 05/21/1931, Melrose, MA, m, 1979, 2 children **DISCIPLINE** MIDDLE ENGLISH AND MEDIEVAL LATIN LITERATURE **EDUCATION** Colgate Univ, AB, 53; Columbia Univ, MA, 59, PhD (English), 63. **CAREER** From instr to asst prof lit, Antioch Col, 62-69; assoc prof, 69-72, Prof English, Univ Ottawa, 72-. **MEMBERSHIPS** Medieval Acad Am; Asn Can Univ Teachers English; Early English Text Soc; New Wyclif Soc; New Chaucer Soc. **RESEARCH** Fourteenth century poetry; 14th century philosophy, 14th and 15th century culture. **SELECTED PUBLICATIONS** Auth, Sciences and the Self in Medieval Poetry--Alan-Of Lille Anticlaudianus and Gower, John Confessio Amantis, Mod Lang Rev, Vol 92, 97; 9 Medieval Latin Plays, Medium Aevum, Vol 64, 95; Sciences and the Self in Medieval Poetry--Alan of Lille Anticlaudianus and Gower, John Confessio Amantis, Mod Lang Rev, Vol 92,

97; The Textual Tradition of Benvenutus Grassus De Arte Probatissima Oculorum, Studi Medievali, Vol 34, 93; The Rise and Decline of the Scholastic Quaestio Disputata with Emphasis on its Use in the Teaching of Medicine and Science, Medium Aevum, Vol 63, 94; A History of Anglo Latin Literature 1066-1422, Medium Aevum, Vol 63, 94; The Latin and German Etymachia, Medium Aevum, Vol 66, 97. **CONTACT ADDRESS** Dept of English, Univ of Ottawa, Ottawa, ON, Canada K1N 6N5.

ELLIOTT, THOMAS G.
PERSONAL Born 09/12/1938, Toronto, ON, Canada, m, 1983, 1 child **DISCIPLINE** CLASSICS **EDUCATION** Harvard, PhD, 71 **CAREER** Inst Class Lang, 64-67, Trinity Col; asst assoc Prof, 67-98, Univ of Toronto. **RESEARCH** Constantine, Athanasius. **SELECTED PUBLICATIONS** Auth, Ammianus Marcellinus and Fourth-Century History, Toronto, 83; auth, "Constantine's Conversion: Do we really need it?" Phoenix 41, (87): 420-438; auth, "The Language of Constantine's Propaganda" TAPA 120, (90): 359-363; auth, "Eusebian frauds in the Vita Constantini," Phoenix 45, (91): 162-171; auth, "Constantine's Preparation for the Council of Nicaea", Journal of Religious Hist 17, (92): 127-37; auth, "Constantine's Explanation of His Career," Byzantion 62, (92): 212-234. **CONTACT ADDRESS** Dept of Classics, Erindale Col, 97 St. George St, Toronto, ON, Canada M5S 2E8. **EMAIL** telliott@credit.erin.utoronto.ca

ELLIS, BRADFORD
PERSONAL Born 01/20/1968, Bellefonte, PA, m, 1994 **DISCIPLINE** SPANISH **EDUCATION** Bates Col, BA, 90; Univ Wis, MA, 92; PhD, 00. **CAREER** Teaching asst, Univ Wis, 90-96; asst prof, Aquinas Col, 97-. **HONORS AND AWARDS** Outstanding Fac of the Month Awd, Aquinas Col, 98; Mich Campus Compact Faculty/Staff Community Service-Learning Awd, 99. **MEMBERSHIPS** MLA, Am Asn of Univ Professors, Cervantes Soc of Am. **RESEARCH** Spanish Golden Age Literature (especially prose), Spanish Novella Corta Tradition. **CONTACT ADDRESS** Dept Modern & Classical Lang, Aquinas Col, Michigan, 1607 Robinson Rd SE, Grand Rapids, MI 49506-1741. **EMAIL** ellisbra@aquinas.edu

ELLIS, KEITH A. A.
PERSONAL Born 04/05/1935, Jamaica **DISCIPLINE** HISPANIC LITERATURE **EDUCATION** Univ Toronto, BA, 58; Univ Wash, MA, 61, PhD, 62. **CAREER** Prof Spanish & Portugese, Univ Toronto, 62-. **HONORS AND AWARDS** Fel, Royal Soc Can; Can Hispanists' Prize Best Bk. **MEMBERSHIPS** MLA; Can Asn Hispanists; Can Asn Latin Am Stud; Jamaican Can Asn; Can-Cuban Friendship Asn. **RESEARCH** Modern Spanish Am poetry and prose. **SELECTED PUBLICATIONS** Auth, El arte narrativo de Francisco Ayala, 64; auth, Critical Approaches to Ruben Dareo, 74; auth, Tres ensayos sobre Nicolas Guillen, 80; auth, Cuba's Nicolas Guillen: Poetry and Ideology, 84; auth, Nicolas Guillen: poesia y ideologea, 87; auth, Nicolas Guillen (1902-1989): A Life of Poetic Service, 91; coauth, Mirrors of War, 85; coauth, La poesia de Emilio Ballagas, 90; ed, La cabeza del cordero de Francisco Ayala, 70; co-ed, El ensayo y la cretica literaria en Iberoamerica, 70; co-ed, Encyclopedia of Spanish American Literature, 90. **CONTACT ADDRESS** Dept of Spanish & Portuguese, Univ of Toronto, Toronto, ON, Canada M5S 1A1. **EMAIL** keith.ellis@utoronto.ca

ELLIS, MARION LEROY
PERSONAL Born 03/27/1928, Georgetown, SC **DISCIPLINE** FRENCH **EDUCATION** Univ SC, AB, 38, MA, 50; Univ Aix-Marseille, Dr Univ, 55. **CAREER** Asst prof English, Va Polytech Inst, 57-60; prof French and chmn dept lang, Erskine Col, 60-61; assoc prof French and Span, Va Polytech Inst, 61-64; assoc prof French, Lewis and Clark Col, 65-68 and N Tex State Univ, 68-69; prof foreign lang and head dept, 69-79, Prof English Second Lang and Foreign Lang, Lamar Univ, 79-, Acad leader, Exp in Int Living, 64-65. **HONORS AND AWARDS** Chevalier, Palmes Academiques, 67, Officier, 77. **MEMBERSHIPS** Am Asn Teachers Fr. **RESEARCH** Acadian culture in Southeast Texas; contemporary French theater; history of the Russian colony in the department of Alpes-Maritimes, France. **SELECTED PUBLICATIONS CONTACT ADDRESS** Dept Foreign Lang, Lamar Univ, Beaumont, Beaumont, TX 77710.

ELLIS, ROBERT
PERSONAL Born 07/08/1955, Fort Worth, TX, m, 1989, 2 children **DISCIPLINE** OLD TESTAMENT AND BIBLICAL HEBREW **EDUCATION** Hardin Simmons Univ, BS, 77; Southwest Baptist Theol Sem, MDiv, 81; PhD, 88. **CAREER** Instr, Hardin-Simmons Univ, 84-86; assoc prof, Southwest Baptist Theol Sem, 86-96; prof, Hardin-Simmons Univ, 96-. **HONORS AND AWARDS** Distinguished Alumnus of Logsdon School of Theol. **MEMBERSHIPS** Nat Asn of baptist Porf of Rel; Soc of Bibl Lit. **RESEARCH** Old Testament Prophets and Wisdom Literature; Biblical Hebrew. **SELECTED PUBLICATIONS** Auth, Divine Gift and Human Response: An Old Testament Model for Stewardship, Southwestern J of Theol, 95; Are There Any Cows of Bashan on Seminary Hill?, Southwestern J of Theol, 95; articles in New Int Dictionary of Old Testament Theol and Exegesis, 97; The Theological Boundaries of Inclusion and Exclusion in the Book of Joshua, Rev and Expositor, 98. **CONTACT ADDRESS** Box 16235, Abilene, TX 79698-6235. **EMAIL** rellis@hsutx.edu

ELLRICH, ROBERT JOHN
PERSONAL Born 01/15/1931, Bridgeport, CT **DISCIPLINE** FRENCH LITERATURE **EDUCATION** Harvard Univ, BA, 52, MA, 53, PhD, 60. **CAREER** From instr to asst prof Romance lang, Princeton Univ, 59-64, coordr French sect, NDEA Inst, 63; asst prof, 64-69, dir, arts and sci honors prog, 77-80, Assoc Prof French and Comp Lit, Univ Wash, 69-, Princeton Univ Coun Humanities res fel, 63-64. **MEMBERSHIPS** MLA; Int Asn Fr Studies; Am Soc 18th Century Studies. **RESEARCH** French literature of the 17th and 18th centuries; development of the novel; Dante. **SELECTED PUBLICATIONS CONTACT ADDRESS** Dept of Romance Lang GN-60, Univ of Washington, Seattle, WA 98195.

ELLSWORTH, JAMES DENNIS
PERSONAL Born 10/25/1939, Los Angeles, CA **DISCIPLINE** CLASSICS **EDUCATION** Univ Calif, Berkeley, BA, 62, PhD(classics), 71. **CAREER** From instr to asst prof classics, Univ Conn, 67-73; asst prof, Southern Ill Univ, Carbondale, 73-74; asst prof, 74-79, assoc prof, 79-86, prof classics, Univ Hawaii, 86-. **HONORS AND AWARDS** Dean's Awd for Excellence in Teaching, Univ Hawaii **MEMBERSHIPS** Am Philol Asn. **RESEARCH** Greek mythology; Greek pedagogy; Classical Philology. **SELECTED PUBLICATIONS** Auth, Ovid's Iliad (Met 12.1-13.622), Prudentia, 80; Ovid's Odyssey (Met 13.623-14.608), Mnemosyne, 88; Ovid's Aeneid Reconsidered (Met 13.623-14.608), Vergilius, 86; Reading Ancient Greek: A Reasonable Approach (2nd ed), McGraw-Hill, 97; Reading Ancient Greek: The Second Year (2nd ed), McGraw-Hill, 98. **CONTACT ADDRESS** Dept Europ Lang & Lit, Univ of Hawaii, Manoa, 1890 E West Rd, Honolulu, HI 96822-2318. **EMAIL** ellswort@hawaii.edu

ELSON, MARK JEFFREY
DISCIPLINE SLAVIC AND GENERAL LINGUISTICS **EDUCATION** Univ Mich, Ann Arbor, BA, 68; Harvard Univ, MA, 72, PhD (ling), 73. **CAREER** Asst prof Russ, Amherst Cot, 73-74; asst prof, 75-81, Assoc Prof Slavic Lang and Lit, Univ Va, Charlottesville, 81-. **MEMBERSHIPS** Ling Soc Am; Am Asn Teachers Slavic and E Europ Lang; Southeastern Conf Ling; MLA. **SELECTED PUBLICATIONS CONTACT ADDRESS** Univ of Virginia, 1 Cabell Hall, Charlottesville, VA 22903-3125.

ELSTUN, ESTHER NIES
PERSONAL Born 02/22/1935, Berkshire Heights, PA, w, 1 child **DISCIPLINE** GERMANIC LANGUAGES & LITERATURES **EDUCATION** Colo Col, BA, 60; Rice Univ, MA, 64, PhD(Ger), 69. **CAREER** Instr Ger, Colo Col, 60-61; from asst prof to assoc prof Ger, 68-76, chm dept foreign lang, 71-76, prof Ger, George Mason Univ, 76- ; consult, State Coun for Higher Ed in Va, 71-72, 77, 96-97, 99; Va Dept of Educ, 79, US Dept of Educ, 80-81; pres, Va Coun for Study Abroad, 81-82, Va Hum Conf, 89-90; dir, George Mason Univ/Univ Wuerzburg exchange prog, 90-; Fulbright Commission, Regional Selection Comm 98, 99. **HONORS AND AWARDS** Phi Beta Kappa; Delta Phi Alpha. **MEMBERSHIPS** MLA; Am Asn Teachers Ger; AAUP. **RESEARCH** Twentieth-century German literature; the Young Vienna Circle; post-war and contemporary novel in German. **SELECTED PUBLICATIONS** Auth, Richard Beer-Hofmann: His Life and Work, Pa State, 83; ed, Human Rights: A Cross-Disciplinary Symposium, Va Tech Center for Programs in the Humanities, 90. **CONTACT ADDRESS** Dept of Modern & Classical Languages, George Mason Univ, Fairfax, 4400 University Dr, Fairfax, VA 22030-4444. **EMAIL** eelstun@gmu.edu

EMBLETON, SHEILA
PERSONAL Born Ottawa, ON, Canada **DISCIPLINE** LANGUAGE, LITERATURE, LINGUISTICS **EDUCATION** Univ Toronto, BS, 75, MS, 76, PhD, 81. **CAREER** Lectr, 80-81, asst prof, Grad Prog Interdisciplinary Studs, 83-84, asst prof, 82-84, Assoc Prof Langs, Lit & Ling, York Univ 84-, assoc dean, Fac Arts, 94-97. **HONORS AND AWARDS** Queen Elizabeth II Scholar, 79-80; Gov Gen Gold Medal, 75; Dr. Harold C. Parsons Scholar, 72-73; Archibald Young Scholar, 73-74. **MEMBERSHIPS** Can Soc Stud Names; Finno-Ugic Stud Asn; Int Soc Hist Ling Asn; Ling Soc Am; Int Coun Onomastic Sci; Can Friends Finland. **RESEARCH** Historical linguistics and language change, sociolinguistics, dialectology, onomastics, finnish literature, and women and language. **SELECTED PUBLICATIONS** Auth, Statistics in Historical Linguistics, 86; ed, the Fourteenth LACUS Forum, 88; co-ed, Indo-Europian and the Indo-Eurpeans, 92/93; ed, Twenty-Fourth LACUS Forum, 98; co-ed, The Emergence of the Modern language Sciences: Studies on the Transition form Historical-Comparative to Structural Linguistics, 99 **CONTACT ADDRESS** Dept of English, York Univ, 208 Stong College, 4700 Keele St, Toronto, ON, Canada M3J 1P3. **EMAIL** embleton@yorku.ca

EMENEAU, MURRAY BARNSON
PERSONAL Born 02/28/1904, Lunenburg, Canada, m, 1940 **DISCIPLINE** SANSKRIT, LINGUISTICS **EDUCATION** Dalhousie Univ, BA, 23; Oxford Univ, BA, 26, MA, 35; Yale Univ, PhD, 31. **CAREER** Instr classics, Yale Univ, 26-31, researcher, 31-40; from asst prof to prof Sanskrit, gen ling and fac res lectr, 40-71, Emer Prof Sanskrit and Gen Ling, Univ Calif, Berkeley, 71-, Guggenheim fel, 49 and 56; LittD, Univ of Hyderabad (India), 87. **HONORS AND AWARDS** LHD, Univ Chicago, 68; LLD, Dalhousie Univ, 70. **MEMBERSHIPS** Am Orient Soc (pres, 53-54); Ling Soc Am (vpres, 48, pres, 49); hon fel Royal Asiatic Soc; Int An Tamil Res (vpres, 66-); hon mem Ling Soc India. **SELECTED PUBLICATIONS** Auth, Dravidian Linguistics--An Introduction, J Am Orient Soc, Vol 113, 93; Tamil Expressives with Initial Voiced Stops, Bulletin of the School of Oriental and African Studies University of London, Vol 56, 93; The Palatalizing Rule in Tamil Malayalam and Telugu, J Am Orient Soc, Vol 115, 95. **CONTACT ADDRESS** Dept of Ling, Univ of California, Berkeley, Berkeley, CA 94720.

EMERY, TED
DISCIPLINE ITALIAN EIGHTEENTH CENTURY **EDUCATION** Trinity Col, BA; Brown Univ, MA, PhD. **CAREER** Asst prof-. **HONORS AND AWARDS** Commentator on Giacomo Casanova, Arts and Entertainment Network's biog prog. **RESEARCH** Singing and acting, scenery, costumes and dance. **SELECTED PUBLICATIONS** Auth, monograph on the opera libretti of Carlo Goldoni, Peter Lang, 91; ed, co-transl, Five Tales for the Theatre by Carlo Gozzi, Univ Chicago Press, 89. **CONTACT ADDRESS** Dept of Fr and Ital, Dickinson Col, PO Box 1773, Carlisle, PA 17013-2896.

EMMA, RONALD DAVID
PERSONAL Born 07/21/1920, London, England, m, 1948, 1 child **DISCIPLINE** ENGLISH, PHILOLOGY **EDUCATION** City Col New York, BBA, 41; Duke Univ, MA, 51, PhD, 60. **CAREER** Instr English, Col William & Mary, 54-60; asst prof, Cent Mich Univ, 60-61; from asst prof to assoc prof, Southern Conn State Col, 61-66; prof English, Windham Col, 66-78, chmn dept English, 66-70, chmn div humanitites, 66-74; Asst Prof Acct, Albertus Magnus Col, 81-, Asst, Duke Univ, 52-53; Col William & Mary res grants-in-aid, 58 & 59; vis lectr English, Univ Mass, 76-77; consult ed, English Literary Renaissance. **MEMBERSHIPS** MLA; Milton Soc Am; Yeats Soc; Int Asn Philos & Lit; Am Acct Asn. **RESEARCH** Grammar and style in Milton; Milton and 17th century poetry; contemporary Irish poetry. **SELECTED PUBLICATIONS** Auth, Milton's Grammar, Mouton The Hague, 63; co-ed, Language and Style in Milton, Ungar, 67 & Seventeenth-Century English Poetry, Lippincott, 69; The exordium and Paradise Lost, S Atlantic Quart, autumn 72; Milton's grammar, In: Milton Encyclopedia, Vol II; Poetry (a variety), in var Jours, US & Abroad. **CONTACT ADDRESS** 61 Elizabeth St, West Haven, CT 06516.

EMPLAINCOURT, EDMOND ARTHUR
PERSONAL Born 08/02/1943, Roux, Belgium, m, 1975, 2 children **DISCIPLINE** ROMANCE PHILOLOGY **EDUCATION** Col William & Mary, BA, 69; Univ Ala, MA, 72, PhD(French), 75. **CAREER** From Asst Prof to Assoc Prof, 75-92, Prof French, Miss State Univ, 92-, Head, Dept For Lang, 97-. **HONORS AND AWARDS** Outstanding Honors Fac, 95. **MEMBERSHIPS** Soc Rencesvals. **RESEARCH** Epic, especially Old French; textual criticism. **SELECTED PUBLICATIONS** Auth, CR. of Jean-Marie d'Heur Sur la date, la composition et la destination de La Chanson de la croisade albigeoise, M langes offerts Charles Rostaing, Olifant 4, 78; Lettres in dites de Marie-Angelique Arnauld des religieuses, Yearbook of the Am Philos Soc, 80; La Geste du Chevalier au Cygne, vol 9 of The Old French Crusade Cycle, Univ Ala Press, 89; Sur la destination de La Chanson du Chevalier au Cygne, Olifant 17, 92; CR. of Douglas A. Kibbee, for to Speke French Trewely: The French Language in England, 1000-1600, Modern Lang Note 77, 93; author and coauthor of numerous other articles. **CONTACT ADDRESS** Dept of Foreign Lang, Mississippi State Univ, P O Box Fl, Mississippi State, MS 39762-5720. **EMAIL** eaempl@ra.msstate.edu

ENGEL, BARBARA
PERSONAL Born 06/28/1943, New York, NY **DISCIPLINE** RUSSIAN **EDUCATION** CCNY, BA, 65; Harvard Univ, MA, 67; Columbia Univ, PhD, 74. **CAREER** Part-time instr, Drew Univ, 72-73; adjunct lectr, CCNY, 73-74; instr, Columbia Univ, summer, 74; asst prof, Sarah Lawrence Col, 74-76; asst prof, Univ Colo, 76-82; assoc prof, Univ Colo, 82-92; prof, Univ Colo, 92-; dir, Central and Eastern Europ Studies Prog, Univ Colo, 93-95; chair, dept of hist, Univ Colo, 95-98. **HONORS AND AWARDS** Phi Beta Kappa, 65; Harvard Univ scholar, 65-66, 66-67; NY State regents fel, 65-66; NDEA Columbia Univ facul fel, 65-66, 66-67; Chancellor's writing award, Univ Colo, spring, 84; AWSS Heldt Article award, 91; Elizabeth Gee award for excellence, 93; Boulder facul assembly award, 93; Mortar Bd Sr Hon Soc, 94; AWSS Heldt prize, 96. **MEMBERSHIPS** AHA; AAASS; CCWH. **RESEARCH** Russian family, women; Soviet family, women. **SELECTED PUBLICATIONS** Auth, Women in Imperial, Soviet and Post-Soviet Russia, Am Hist Asn (Washington D.C.), 99; co-ed, A Revolution

Of Their Own: Russian Women Remember their Lives in the Twentieth Century, Westview Press, 98; auth, Between the Fields and the City: Women, Work and Family in Russia, 1861-1914, Cambridge Univ Press, 94; article, Not by Bread Alone: Subsistence Riots in Russia during World War I, Jour of Mod Hist, 69, n 4, 696-721, dec, 97; article, Les Femmes dans la Russie des Revolutions, Encycl politique et hist des femmes: Europe, Amer du Nord, Presses Univ de Fr, 433-471, 97; article, Women, Men and the Languages of Peasant Resistance, 1870-1914, Cultures in Flux: Lower Class Values, Practices and Resistance in Late Imperial Russia, Princeton Univ Press, 34-53, 94; article, Russian Peasant Views of City Life, 1861-1914, Slavic Rev, 52, no 3, 445-459, fall, 93; article, Socially Deviant Women and the Russian Peasant Community, 1861-1914, Gender Restructuring in Russian Studies, Tampere, Finland, 53-64, 93. **CONTACT ADDRESS** Dept. of Hist, CB 234, Univ of Colorado, Boulder, Boulder, CO 80309. **EMAIL** engelb@spot.colorado.edu

ENGEL, DAVID M.
PERSONAL Born 12/11/1964, Charleston, WV, m, 1998 **DISCIPLINE** CLASSICS **EDUCATION** Univ Calif Berkeley, PhD **CAREER** Pa St Univ **MEMBERSHIPS** Amer Philolog Assoc; Amer Philos Assoc, Amer Inst of Archaeol. **RESEARCH** Ancient Greek' ancient philos; mind; lang; ethics. **CONTACT ADDRESS** Pennsylvania State Univ, Univ Park, 108 Weaver Bldg, University Park, PA 16802. **EMAIL** dme8@psu.edu

ENGELBERG, EDWARD
PERSONAL Born 01/21/1929, Germany, m, 1950, 3 children **DISCIPLINE** COMPARATIVE LITERATURE AND ENGLISH **EDUCATION** Brooklyn Col, BA, 51; Univ Ore, MA, 52; Univ Wis, PhD, 57; Fulbright Research Scholar, St. Catharine's College, Cambridge, 55-57. **CAREER** From instr to assoc prof English, Univ Mich, 57-65; assoc prof, 65-67, chmn, Comp Lit Prog, 65-72, chmn, Dept Romance and Comp Lit, 71-75, chmn, Joint Prog Lit Studies, 71-75, Prof Comp Lit, Brandeis Univ, 67-, Nat Endowment for Humanities sr fel, 75; fac rep, Bd Trustees, Brandeis Univ, 76-78, mem, Acad Planning Comt, 75-78; mem, exec comt, Eastern Comp Lit Conf. **HONORS AND AWARDS** Phi Beta Kappa, Brooklyn College; Honorary Alumnus Awd, Brooklyn College, 94. **MEMBERSHIPS** MLA; Am Comp Lit Asn; AAUP. **RESEARCH** Romanticism and literary history; modern poetry; English-German relations. **SELECTED PUBLICATIONS** Auth, "The Vast Design: Pattern in W. B. Yeats's Aesthetic," 64; (Second Edition, revised and enlarged, 88; auth, "The Unknown Distance: From Consciousness to Conscience, Goethe to Camus," 72; auth, "The Symbolist Poem: The Development of the English Tradition," 67; auth, "Elegiac Fictions: The Motif of the Unlived Life," 89. **CONTACT ADDRESS** Dept of Romance and Lit Comp, Brandeis Univ, Waltham, MA 02154. **EMAIL** engelberg@brandeis.edu

ENGELHARDT, KLAUS HEINRICH
PERSONAL Born 11/17/1936, Wurzburg, Germany, m, 1967, 2 children **DISCIPLINE** FRENCH LITERATURE **EDUCATION** Univ Munich, Staatsexamen, 62, PhD(Romance lang), 68. **CAREER** Teaching asst Ger, Lycee Descartes, Tours, France, 60-61; asst prof French, Univ Munich, 65-69; asst prof French & Ger, 69-74, acting chmn dept foreign lang, 70-71, assoc prof, 74-82, prof French & Ger, Lewis & Clark Col, 82-; chmn, dept foreign lang,Lewis & Clark Col, 99-. . **MEMBERSHIPS** MLA; AAUP; Am Asn Teachers Fr. **RESEARCH** French novel; French theatre; Occitan culture. **SELECTED PUBLICATIONS** Auth, Contributions on French literature, In: Kindler Literatur Lexikon, Munich, 64-73; Le Langage des yeux dans la Chartreuse de Parme de Stendhal, Stendhal Club, Grenoble, 7/72; Une Source Roumaine du Tueur Sans Gages d'Eugene Ionesco, Neueren Sprachen, Ger, 1/72; coauth, Daten der Franzosischen Literatur, dtv, Munchen, 79. **CONTACT ADDRESS** Dept of Foreign Lang, Lewis and Clark Col, 0615 SW Palatine Hill Rd, Portland, OR 97219-7879. **EMAIL** klaus@lclark.edu

ENGELS, DONALD W.
PERSONAL Born 05/15/1946, Rockville Centre, NY, s **DISCIPLINE** HISTORY, CLASSICS **EDUCATION** Univ of Fla, Ba, 69; Univ of Tex, MA, 72; Univ of Pa, PhD, 76. **CAREER** Instr for Greek & Roman Hist, Univ of Pa, 77; vis asst prof in Hist & Classics, Brandeis Univ, 77-78; asst prof of Hist & Greek & Latin, Wellesley Col, 78-85; from asst prof to prof, Univ Ark, 83-; vis asst prof o fhist & classics, Univ of Chicago, 83; vis asst prof, Boston Col, 85-86. **HONORS AND AWARDS** Tchg fel for Greek and Roman Hist, Univ of Pa, 75-76; Ford Found Archaeol Traineeship, 70; res & tchg fels, Univ of Pa, 73-76; Am Philos Soc Grant, 79; travel grant, Wellesley Col, 79; NEH summer stipend, Brown Univ, 81; res fel, Wolfson Col, Cambridge Univ, 00-01. **MEMBERSHIPS** Am Philol Asn; Asn of Ancient Historians; Friends of Ancient Hist; Soc for Ancient Medicine; Historical Soc. **RESEARCH** Greek and Roman history. **SELECTED PUBLICATIONS** Auth, Alexander the Greant the Logistics of the Macedonian Army, Univ Calif Pr, 78; auth, Roman Corinth: An Alternative Model for the Classical City, Univ of Chicago Press, 90; Classical Cats: The Rise and Fall of the Sacred Cat, Routledge, 99; Ptolemy I, World Book Encycl, 81; The Use of Historical Demography in Ancient History, Classical Quart, 84; The Length of Eratosthenes' Stade, Am J of Philol, 85; The Classical City Reconsidered, The Eye Expanded, Berkeley, 98. **CONTACT ADDRESS** Dept of Hist, Univ of Arkansas, Fayetteville, Fayetteville, AR 72701. **EMAIL** dengles@comp.uark.edu

ENNS, PETER
PERSONAL Born 01/02/1961, Passaic, NJ, m, 1984, 3 children **DISCIPLINE** NEAR EASTERN LANGUAGE AND CIVILIZATIONS **EDUCATION** Messiah Col, BA, 82; Harvard, MA, 93; Harvard, PhD, 94 **CAREER** Assoc prof Old Testament, Westminister Theolog Seminary, 94- **MEMBERSHIPS** Soc Bibl Lit; Inst Bibl Res; Evangelical Theolog Soc **RESEARCH** Early Jewish Biblical Interpretation; Old Testament Theology; New Testament's use of the Old Testament; Wisdom Literature **SELECTED PUBLICATIONS** Exodus, Zondevan, forthcoming; ed, The New Testament's Use of the Old in Its Historical-Hermeneutical Milieu, Zondervan, forthcoming; auth, Exodus Retold: Ancient Exegesis of the Departure from Egypt in Wis 10:15-21 and 19:1-9, Scholars Press, 97 **CONTACT ADDRESS** Westminster Theol Sem, Pennsylvania, PO Box 27009, Philadelphia, PA 19118.

EPPLE, JUAN ARMANDO
PERSONAL Born 04/26/1946, Osorno, Chile, m, 1967, 1 child **DISCIPLINE** SPANISH AMERICAN LITERATURE **EDUCATION** Austral Univ Chile, BA, 71; Harvard Univ, MA, 77, PhD (romance lang), 80. **CAREER** Asst prof lit theory, Austral Univ Chile, 72-74; instr Span, Ohio State Univ, 79-80; Asst Prof Romance Lang, Univ Ore, 80-. **MEMBERSHIPS** MLA; Inst Internac Lit Iberoamericana; Midwest Mod Lang Asn; Pac Coast Coun Latin Am Studies. **RESEARCH** Chicano literature; Latin American literary historiography. **SELECTED PUBLICATIONS** **CONTACT ADDRESS** Dept Romance Lang, Univ of Oregon, Eugene, OR 94703.

EPSTEIN, EDMUND LLOYD
PERSONAL Born 10/15/1931, New York, NY, m, 1965, 3 children **DISCIPLINE** ENGLISH, LINGUISTICS **EDUCATION** Queens Col, NYork, BA, 51; Yale Univ, MA, 53; Columbia Univ, PhD(English), 67. **CAREER** Ed dict, various publ, 53-55; instr English, Univ Buffalo, 55-57; ed trade-and-text-bks, G P Putnam's Sons, 57-63 & Farrar, Straus & Giroux, 63-65; from assoc prof to prof English, Southern Ill Univ, Carbondale, 65-74; prof English, Queens Col City Univ New York 74-; The Graduate Center CUNY; Ed-in-chief, James Joyce Rev, 57-61; consult, James Joyce Quart, 63-; ed-in-chief, Lang & Style, 68-; vis scholar, Univ Col, Univ London, 71-72; prof English,Grad Ctr., City Univ New York, 81-; exchange prof , Univ Paris, 82, 95. **HONORS AND AWARDS** Excellence in Teaching Awd, Standard Oil Found, Ind, 71, nominated Distinguished Prof of English, 97; nominated for Awd for Excellence in Teaching, 97. **MEMBERSHIPS** MLA; Ling Soc Am; Mediaeval Acad Am. **RESEARCH** Modern British literature; linguistics, the analysis of style, structural semantics, the analysis of meaning. **SELECTED PUBLICATIONS** Coauth, Linguistics and English prosody, Studies Ling, 58; Interpretation of Finnegans Wake, James Joyce Quart, summer 66; auth, The Ordeal of Stephen Dedalus: Conflict of the Generations in James Joyce's A Portrait of the Art as a Young Man, Southern Ill Univ, 71; Language and Style, Methuen, London, 78; auth Women's Language and Style: Studies in Contemporary Language #1, Queens Col, 78; auth A Starchamber Quiry: a Joyce Centennial Publication, 1882-1982, Methuen, London, 82; auth Joyce Centenary Essays, Southern Ill Univ, 1983; auth Mythic Worlds, Modern Worlds: the Writings of Joseph Campbell on James Joyce, Harper-Collins, 93; auth The Language of African Literature, Africa World Press, 98. **CONTACT ADDRESS** Dept of English, Queens Col, CUNY, 6530 Kissena Blvd, Flushing, NY 11367-1597. **EMAIL** bloom1866@aol.com

EPSTEIN, RICHARD
DISCIPLINE LINGUISTICS **EDUCATION** UCSD, San Diego, PhD. **CAREER** Asst prof, Rutgers, State Univ NJ, Camden Col of Arts and Sci. **RESEARCH** Semantics; pragmatics; Kumeyaay, a native American language. **SELECTED PUBLICATIONS** Auth, Some Uses of the Demonstrative Clitic pu in Jamul Diegueo, Hokan-Penutian Lang Workshop, 91; The Development of the Definite Article in French, Perspectives on Grammaticalization, John Benjamins, 94; L'article dQ-fini en anciens frantais: l'expression de la subjectivitQ, Langue Fr, 95; Le temps dans la linguistique cognitive, ModQles ling 95; Viewpoint and the Definite Article in Conceptual Structure, Discourse and Language, Cambridge, 96. **CONTACT ADDRESS** Rutgers, The State Univ of New Jersey, Camden, Camden Col of Arts and Sci, Camden, NJ 08102-1405. **EMAIL** repstein@camden.rutgers.edu

ERICKSON, DANIEL NATHAN
PERSONAL Born 07/30/1958, Sioux Falls, SD, s **DISCIPLINE** LATIN, GREEK **EDUCATION** Concordia Col, Moorhead Minn, BA, 81; Tex Tech Univ, MA, 85; Syracuse Univ, DA, 90. **CAREER** Instr, Newport High School, 82-86; instr, The Louisiana School LA,86-93; asst prof, Univ NDak, 98-. **HONORS AND AWARDS** Grad magna cum laude, Concordia Coll, 81; Who's Who Among America's Teachers, 94. **MEMBERSHIPS** Am Philol Asn; Am Council on the Teaching of Foreign Lang; Am Classical League. **RESEARCH** Teaching of Latin and Greek; Roman History. **SELECTED PUBLICATIONS** Auth, Eutropius' Compendium of Roman History: Introduction, translation, and notes. **CONTACT ADDRESS** Dept of Modern and Classical Lang, Univ of No Dakota, P O Box 8198, Grand Forks, ND 58202. **EMAIL** danieric@badlands.nodak.edu

ERICKSON, GERALD M.
PERSONAL Born 09/23/1927, Amery, WI, m, 1951, 3 children **DISCIPLINE** CLASSICAL LANGUAGES **EDUCATION** Univ Minn, BS, 54, MA, 56, PhD (classics), 68. **CAREER** Teacher, Edina-Morningside Pub Schs, 56-65 and 66-67; vis lectr Latin, 65-66, asst prof Latin and Greek, 67-70, Assoc Prof Classics, Univ Minn, Minneapolis, 70-, Consult classics, Am Coun Teaching Foreign Lang Annual Bibliog Foreign Lang Teaching, 69-; reader, Col Entrance Exam Bd, Advan Placement, 75-76, chief reader designate, 77, chief reader, 78. **MEMBERSHIPS** Am Class League; Class Asn Mid W and S; Am Philol Asn. **RESEARCH** Language teaching, methods and materials; madness and deviant behavior in Greece and Rome; computer based instruction for teaching vocabulary development, technical terminology and ancient Greek. **SELECTED PUBLICATIONS** Auth, Reading Classical Latin--The 2nd Year, Mod Lan J, Vol 77, 93. **CONTACT ADDRESS** Dept of Classics, Univ of Minnesota, Twin Cities, 330 Folwell Hall, Minneapolis, MN 55455. **EMAIL** gerald.m.erickson-1@tc.umn.edu

ERICKSON, JOHN
PERSONAL Born 01/09/1934, Aitkin, MN, m, 1959, 2 children **DISCIPLINE** COMTEMPORARY FRENCH AND COMPARATIVE LITERATURE **EDUCATION** Univ Minn, BA, 58, MA, 61, PhD (French), 63; Harvard Univ, MA, 59. **CAREER** From instr to asst prof French and comp lit, Univ Iowa, 63-65; assoc prof French lit, Univ Kans, 65-70; vis prof French and Am lit, Mohammed V Univ, Morocco, 70-72; prof French lit, Univ Kans, 72-80; Prof and Chmn French, La State Univ, 80-, Founder and cd, L'Esprit Createur, 61-; Fulbright lectr to Morocco, 70-72; vis prof Univ Damascus, 76; Adv bd, Oeuvres et critiques and French lit pubs Fulbright, 61, 70-72 and 81; Mellon fel, spring, 79; Nat Endowment for Humanities, summer, 79. **MEMBERSHIPS** MLA; Am Asn Teachers Fr; Asn Univ Teachers Gr Brit; Soc Fr Studies, Gt Brit; Soc Fr Prof Am. **RESEARCH** Contemporary literature; modern novel; modern criticism. **SELECTED PUBLICATIONS** Auth, Veiled Women and Veiled Narrative in Benjelloun, Tahar The Sandchild, Boundary 2 Int J Lit Cult, Vol 20, 93. **CONTACT ADDRESS** Dept of Fr, Univ of Kentucky, 500 S Limestone St, Lexington, KY 40506-0003.

ERLICH, VICTOR
PERSONAL Born 11/22/1914, Petrograd, Russia, m, 1940, 2 children **DISCIPLINE** SLAVIC LANGUAGES AND LITERATURES **EDUCATION** Free Polish Univ, MA, 37; Columbia Univ, PhD, 51. **CAREER** Asst lit ed, New Life, Warsaw, 37-39; rcs writer, Yiddish Encycl, 42-43; from asst prof to prof Slavic Lang and lit, Univ Wash, 48-62; Bensinger Prof Russ Lit, Yale Univ, 62-, Rockefeller fel, 49; Ford fel, 53-54; Fulbright lectr, 57-58; Guggenheim fel, 57-58, 64 and 76-77; Nat Endowment Humanities sr fel, 68-69. **HONORS AND AWARDS** MA, Yale Univ, 63. **MEMBERSHIPS** MLA; Am Asn Advan Slavic Studies (vpres, 73-77). **RESEARCH** Methodology of literary scholarship; modern Russian poetry; Soviet criticism **SELECTED PUBLICATIONS** Auth, Art and Reality, A Note on Babel, Issak Metaliterary Narratives, Can Slavonic Papers Revue Canadienne Slavistes, Vol 36, 94; Exploring Gogol, Slavic Rev, Vol 54, 95. **CONTACT ADDRESS** Dept of Slavic Lang and Lit, Yale Univ, New Haven, CT 06520.

ERMOLAEV, HERMAN
PERSONAL Born 11/14/1924, Tomsk, Russia, m, 1975, 3 children **DISCIPLINE** SOVIET AND RUSSIAN LITERATURE **EDUCATION** Stanford Univ, BA, 51; Univ Calif, Berkeley, MA, 54, PhD (Slavic lang and lit), 59. **CAREER** Instr Russ, Army Lang Sch, 55; from instr to assoc prof, Russ and Soviet lit, 59-70, McCosh fel, 67-68, Prof Russ and Soviet Lit, Princeton Univ, 70-. **HONORS AND AWARDS** McCosh Fel, Princeton Univ, 67-68 **MEMBERSHIPS** Am Asn Advan Slavic Studies; Am Asn Teachers Slavic and E Europ Lang (pres, 71-73); Asn Russ Am Scholars USA. **RESEARCH** Sholokhov; Soviet censorship; Solzhenitsyn. **SELECTED PUBLICATIONS** Auth, Soviet Literary Theories, 1917-1934: The Genesis of Socialist Realism; auth, Mikhail Sholokhov and His Art, Censorship in Soviet Literature, 1917-1991; coauth, Sholokhov's Tikhii Don, A Commentary; auth, Untimely Thoughts: Essays on Revolution, Culture and the Bolshevuks, 1917-1918. **CONTACT ADDRESS** Dept of Slavic Lang and Lit, Princeton Univ, Princeton, NJ 08544. **EMAIL** ermolaev@princeton.edu

ERTL, WOLFGANG
PERSONAL Born 05/27/1946, Sangerhausen, Germany, m, 1969 **DISCIPLINE** GERMANIC LANGUAGES AND LITERATURE **EDUCATION** Univ Marburg, Ger, BA, 69; Univ NH, MA, 70; Univ Pa, PhD (Ger lang and lit), 75. **CAREER** Lectr, Univ of Pa, 74-76; asst prof, Swarthmore Col, Pa, 76-77;

asst prof, Univ of Iowa, 77-82, assoc prof, 82-88, chair of the dept of Ger, 88-96, Acting chair of the Dept of Ger, 99; resident dir, Academic Yr in Freiburg, Ger, 00-01; Prof Ger, Univ of Iowa, 88-. **HONORS AND AWARDS** Univ of Iowa Old Gold Summer Fel, 79, 81, 82; Univ of Iowa; Semester Development Leave, 84, 91; May Brodbeck Humanities Fel, 87; Special Collegiate Res Assignment, 96. **MEMBERSHIPS** Mod Lang Asn of Am; Am Asn of Teachers of Ger; Ger Studies Asn; Northeast Mod Lang Asn; South Atlantic Mod Lang Asn. **RESEARCH** 20th century German literature and culture; GDR and postunification literature; German lyric poetry; 19th century German literature; interdisciplinary studies in literature and ecology. **SELECTED PUBLICATIONS** Auth, Stephan Hermlin und die Tradition, Bern, Frankfurt am Main, Las Vegas: Peter Lang, 77; auth, Natur und Landschaft in der Lyrik der DDR: Walter Werner, Wulf Kirsten und Uwe Grebmann, Stuttgart: Akademischer Verlag Hans-Dieter Heinz, 82; coauth, Zur Lyrik Volker Brauns: Konigstein/Ts: Verlagsgruppe Athenaum, 84; co-ed, DDR-Lyrik im Kontext, Amsterdamer Beitrage zur Germanistik, 26, Amsterdam: Rodopi, 88; co-ed, glossen eine internationale zweisprachige publikation zu literatur, film und kunst in den deutschsprachigen landern nach 1945, 97; auth, "Dichtung und Wahrheit: Zum Fall Stephan Hermlin," glossen, eine internationale zweisprachige publikation zu literatur, film und kunst in den deutschsprachigen landern nach 1945, (97); auth, "Refugium und Ortsbestimmung: Zu Wulf Kirstens neuer Lyrik," Colloquia Germanica 30, (97): 323-333; auth, "brandflecke im teppich der natur': Zur okologischen Problematik in Wulf Kirstens lyrischem Werk," Literatur und Okologie, hrsg. V. Axel Goodbody, Amersterdam: Rodopi (98): 123-138; co-ed, Bestandsaufnahme-Zur deutschen Literatur nach der Vereinigung: Beitrage zum 1. Carlisler Symposium zur modernen deutschsprachigen Literatur, glossen: Sonderausgabe 10, 00; auth, "Von der Komik der deutsch-deutschen Vereiningung zum Ernst der Vergangenheitsaufarbeitung: Thomas Rosenlochers Prosa seit der Wende," Bestandsaufnahme-Zur deutschen Literatur nach der Vereinigung: Beitrage zum 1, Carlisler Symposium zur modernen deutschsprachigen Literatur, hrsg. V. Christine Cosentino, Wolfgang Ertl und Wolfgang Muller, glossen: Sonderausgabe 10 (00); **CONTACT ADDRESS** Dept of Ger, Univ of Iowa, 526 Phillips Hall, Iowa City, IA 52242-1409. **EMAIL** wolfgang-ertl@uiowa.edu

ESCOBAR, ANNA MARIA
DISCIPLINE SPANISH LITERATURE **EDUCATION** State Univ NYork, MA; PhD, 86. **CAREER** Assoc prof, Univ Ill Urbana Champaign. **RESEARCH** Spanish variation; language contact theory; Andean sociolinguistics. **SELECTED PUBLICATIONS** Auth, Los bilingues y el castellano en el Peru, Inst de Estudios Peruanos, 90; Evidential uses in the Spanish of Quechua speakers in Peru, SW J Ling, 94; From time to modality in Spanish in Contact with Quechua, Hisp Ling, 97; Contrastive and innovative uses of the present perfect and the preterite in Spanish in contact with Quechua, Hispania, 97; co-auth, Practical Review of Spanish Grammar, Univ Ill, 98. **CONTACT ADDRESS** Spanish, Italian, and Portuguese Dept, Univ of Illinois, Urbana-Champaign, 52 E Gregory Dr, Champaign, IL 61820. **EMAIL** aescobar@uiuc.edu

ESSIF, LES
DISCIPLINE FRENCH LITERATURE **EDUCATION** Brown Univ, PhD, 91. **CAREER** Assoc prof, French, Univ Tenn. **RESEARCH** Dramatic and performance theories concerning contemporary French theatre; foreign language performance pedagogy; twentieth century critical theory. **SELECTED PUBLICATIONS** Auth, Empty Figure on an Empty Stage: The Theatre of Samuel Beckett and His Generation, Indiana UP, 01. **CONTACT ADDRESS** Dept of Mod For Langs & Lits, Univ of Tennessee, Knoxville, 701 McClung Tower & Plaza, Knoxville, TN 37996. **EMAIL** essif@utk.edu

ETZKORN, GIRARD J.
PERSONAL Born 09/18/1927, Kirkwood, MO **DISCIPLINE** PHILOSOPHY, FRENCH **EDUCATION** Quincy Col, BA, 53; St Joseph Sem, Ill, STB, 57; Cath Univ Louvain, PhD (philos), 61. **CAREER** From instr to assoc prof philosophy, Quincy Col, 61-71; assoc prof, Southern Ill Univ, CArbondale, 71-72; RES PROF CRITICAL ED OF WILLIAM OCKHAM, FRANCISCAN INST, 73-, Am Philos Soc grant, 65-66. **MEMBERSHIPS** Int Soc Study Medieval Philos; Am Philos Asn; AAUP. **RESEARCH** Critical editions of medieval manuscripts; French and German phenomenology and existentialism; translating of French philosopher Michel Henry. **SELECTED PUBLICATIONS** Auth, William De La Mare, Scriptum in Secundum Librum Sententiarum, Speculum J Medieval Stud, Vol 72, 97; Bonaventure Sermons de Diversis, Speculum J Medieval Stud, Vol 70, 95. **CONTACT ADDRESS** Franciscan Inst, Saint Bonaventure, NY 14778.

EVANS, ARTHUR BRUCE
PERSONAL Born 10/24/1948, Salem, MA **DISCIPLINE** FRENCH **EDUCATION** Tufts Univ, BA, 70; Goddard Col, MA, 72; Middlebury Col, MA, 79; Columbia Univ, MPhil, 82, PhD, 85. **CAREER** Teaching asst, Tufts Univ, 69-70; High Sch Teacher, Montpelier High Sch, Vermont, 70-78; adjunct instr, Community Col of Vermont, 74-75; preceptor, Columbia Univ, 81-83; asst prof, DePauw Univ, 85-90, assoc prof, 91-99, chair, dept of Romance Langs, 94-98, chair, Dept of Modern Langs, 98-99, full prof, 99-. **HONORS AND AWARDS** Ed and pub, Science Fiction Studies; referee/consult/book reviewer, Nineteenth-Century French Studies, Para doxa, PMLA, Utopian Studies, Heinle and Heinle Pubs, Nat Endowment for the Humanities, Duke Univ Press, Wesleyan Univ Press. **MEMBERSHIPS** Modern Lang Asn, Societe Jules Verne, Am Asn of Teachers of French, Coun of Eds of Learned Js, Amnesty Int. **SELECTED PUBLICATIONS** Auth, Jean Cocteau and his Films of Orphic Identity, Assoc Univ Presses (77); contrib ed, En Route! Review Grammar, Harcourt Brace, Jovanovich (85); auth, Jules Verne Rediscovered: Didacticism and the Scientific Novel, Greenwood Press (88); co-ed, On Philip K. Dick, SF-TH, Inc (92); auth, "Jules Verne," TCLC 52: Twentieth-Century Literary Criticism, Gale (94): 336, 351-361; coauth, "Jules Verne et la persistence retinjenne," Cahier du Musee Jules Verne #13 (96): 11-17; auth, "North American College Courses in Science Fiction, Utopian Literature, and Fantasy," Science-Fiction Studies Vol 23, #70 (96): 437-524; auth, "Vehicular Utopias of Jules Verne," Transformations of Utopia: Changing Views of the Perfect Society, eds George Slusser, et al, NY: AMS Press (99): 99-108; auth, "Scholarly SF Journals as 'Authorities'," Science Fiction and Contests for Authority, Univ of Ga Press (forthcoming 2000); auth, "Jules Verne and the French Literary Canon," Jules Verne: Narratives of Modernity, Liverpool Univ Press (forthcoming, 2000). **CONTACT ADDRESS** L-08 E College, DePauw Univ, Greencastle, IN 46135. **EMAIL** aevans@depauw.edu

EVANS, DALE WILT
PERSONAL Born 09/27/1939, Philadelphia, PA **DISCIPLINE** PHILOSOPHY, CLASSICS **EDUCATION** Pa State Univ, BA, 65, MA, 66, PhD (Philos), 73. **CAREER** Instr philos, Univ Wyo, 69-72; programmer, Sperry Univac, 74-75; ASST PROF PHILOS, PA STATE UNIV, 75-, Fulbright fel, 70-71. **MEMBERSHIPS** Am Philos Soc. **RESEARCH** Contemporary philosophy; contemporary man. **SELECTED PUBLICATIONS** Auth, Prisoners of objective thinking, 81 & The heterogeneous symmetry of nature, 82, Contemp Philos. **CONTACT ADDRESS** Dept of Philos, Pennsylvania State Univ, DuBois, Du Bois, PA 15801.

EVANS, HARRY B.
PERSONAL Born 03/27/1942, Scranton, PA, s **DISCIPLINE** LATIN POETRY, ROMAN TOPOGRAPHY **EDUCATION** NC Univ, PhD. **CAREER** Prof, Fordham Univ. **SELECTED PUBLICATIONS** Auth, Publica Carmina: Ovid's Books from Exile, 83; Water Distribution in Ancient Rome: The Evidence of Frontinus, 94; ed, Shaped of City Life n Rome and Pomoeii, 98. **CONTACT ADDRESS** Dept of Class Lang and Lit, Fordham Univ, 441 E Fordham Rd, New York, NY 10458. **EMAIL** hevans@fordham.edu

EVANS, JAMES A. S.
PERSONAL Born 03/24/1931, Galt, ON, Canada **DISCIPLINE** CLASSICS **EDUCATION** Univ Toronto, BA, 52; Yale Univ, MA, 53, PhD, 57. **CAREER** Prof, Univ Western Ont, 55-60; vis lectr, Victoria Col, 60-61; vis asst prof, Univ Texas Austin, 61-62; fac mem hist, McMaster Univ, 62-72; prof, 72-96, dept head, 86-93, PROF EMER CLASSICS, UNIV BC, 96-; Gertrude Smith prof, Am Sch Class Stud (Athens), 91; non-resident fac mem, Cecil Green Col, 93-94; vis prof, Univ Wash, 97; Whitehead prof, Am Sch Class Stud (Athens), 98-99. **HONORS AND AWARDS** Fel, Royal Soc Can, 92. **MEMBERSHIPS** Mng comt, Am Sch Class Stud (Athens); Class Asn Can (pres 82-84); Asn Ancient Hist (secy treas 79-82). **SELECTED PUBLICATIONS** Auth, Social and Economic History of an Egyptian Temple in Greco-Roman Egypt, 61; auth, Procopius, 72; auth, Herodotus, 82; auth, Herodotus, Explorer of the Past: Three Essays, 91; auth, The Age of Justinian: The Circumstances of Imperial Power, 96; ed, Waterloo Rev, 57-60; ed, Vergilius, 63-73; ed Polis and Imperium: Studies in Honour of Edward Togo Salmon, 74; co-ed, Studies in Medieval and Renaissance History, 77-96;. **CONTACT ADDRESS** Classics Dept, Univ of British Columbia, Buch C625, Vancouver, BC, Canada V6T 1Z1. **EMAIL** jaevans@interchange.ubc.ca

EVANS, MARTHA NOEL
PERSONAL Born 02/21/1939, Philadelphia, PA, m, 1964, 2 children **DISCIPLINE** FRENCH LITERATURE **EDUCATION** Wellesley Col, BA, 60; Yale Univ, PhD (Fr lang and Lit), 67. **CAREER** Instr French, Peace Corps, 62 and 63; from instr to asst prof, 65-69, asst prof, 74-76, Assoc Prof French, Mary Baldwin Col, 76-. **MEMBERSHIPS** AAUP; Am Asn Teachers Fr; SAtlantic Mod Lang Asn. **RESEARCH** Preromantic French literature; nineteenth-century French novel; psychoanalysis, Lacan. **SELECTED PUBLICATIONS CONTACT ADDRESS** Dept of French, Mary Baldwin Col, Staunton, VA 24401.

EVANS-GRUBBS, JUDITH
PERSONAL Born 11/30/1956, Atlanta, GA, m, 1979, 1 child **DISCIPLINE** CLASSICS **EDUCATION** Emory Univ, BA, 78; Amer School of Classical Studies, 78-79; Stanford Univ, PhD, 87. **CAREER** Prof, 00-; Assoc prof Classical Studies, Sweet Briar Col, 93-98; asst prof Classical Studies, Sweet Briar Col, 87-93; Tchg Fel, Stanford Univ, 83-84, 85-87; lctr, Intercollegiate Center for Classical Studies, 84-85. **HONORS AND AWARDS** Nat Endowment for Humanities Fel for Col Tchrs, 97-98; NEH Summer Sem for Col Tchrs, Amer Acad Rome, 95; Jessie Ball Dupont Fel, Nat Humanities Center, 93-94; Nat Endowment Humanities Summer Stipend, 88; Mednick Grant, Va Found Independent Cols, 88. **MEMBERSHIPS** Am Philoi Asn; Am Soc Greek & Latin Epigraphy; Am Soc Papyrologists; Asn Ancient Historians; Classical Asn Middle West & South; Classical Asn Va; N Amer Patristics Soc; Women's Classical Caucus. **RESEARCH** Marriage and Family in Ancient Roman Society; Roman Imperial Law; Slavery in Ancient Rome; Women and Gender in Antiquity. **SELECTED PUBLICATIONS** Auth, 'Pagan' and 'Christian' Marriage: the State of the Question, Jour Early Christian Studies, 94; auth, Law and Family in Late Antiquity: the Emperor Constantine's Marriage Legislation, Oxford Univ Pr, 95; auth, articles on "Marriage," "Divorce," and "Concubinage" in Guide to Late Antiquity, ed. G. Bowersock, P. Brown, and O. Grabar; auth, "The Slave who Avenged her Master's Death," Ancient History Bulletin (00). **CONTACT ADDRESS** Dept of Classical Studies, Sweet Briar Col, Sweet Briar, VA 24595. **EMAIL** evansgrubbs@sbc.edu

EWALD, OWEN M.
PERSONAL Born 11/18/1969, Washington, DC, m, 1995, 2 children **DISCIPLINE** CLASSICS **EDUCATION** Yale Univ, BA, 92; Univ Wash, PhD, 99. **CAREER** Instr, Univ Wash, 92-01; Asst Prof, Seattle Pac Univ, 01-. **HONORS AND AWARDS** Simpson Humanities Fel, 98-99. **MEMBERSHIPS** Am Philol Asn; Class Asn of the Pac NW. **RESEARCH** Roman Historiography; Greco-Roman Mythology; Ancient comedy; Ancient Jobs. **SELECTED PUBLICATIONS** Auth, "Virgilian End Rhymes: Geo 1.393-423," Harvard Studies in Class Philol, (90): 311-313. **CONTACT ADDRESS** Dept Class, Seattle Pacific Univ, 3307 3rd Ave W, Seattle, WA 98119. **EMAIL** ewald@spu.edu

EXNER, RICHARD
PERSONAL Born 05/13/1929, Niedersachsewerfen, Germany, m, 1955, 2 children **DISCIPLINE** GERMAN AND COMPARATIVE LITERATURE **EDUCATION** Univ Southern Calif, AB, 51, PhD (Ger), 57. **CAREER** Instr Ger, Univ Rochester, 55-56; from instr to asst prof, Princeton Univ, 56-60; assoc prof, Oberlin Col, 60-65; Prof Ger, Univ Calif, Santa Barbara, 65-, Fulbright sr res award and Guggenheim fel, 67-68; vis prof humanities, Mass Inst Technol, 69-70; Mem Comt Advan Placement In Ger, Col Entrance Exam Bd, 72-, chief reader Ger lit, 76-77; vis prof Ger lit, Stanford Univ, 73-74; mem, Bavarian Acad Fine Arts, 79; vis prof, Univ de Nice, 80. **MEMBERSHIPS** Am Coun Studies Austrian Lit (vpres, 72-); MLA; Inst Compt Lit Asn; Thomas Mann Ges; Am Literary Translr Asn. **RESEARCH** Lyric poetry; German and comparative literature of the 19th and 20th centuries. **SELECTED PUBLICATIONS CONTACT ADDRESS** Dept of Ger and Slavic Lang, Univ of California, Santa Barbara, Santa Barbara, CA 93106.

EYKMAN, CHRISTOPH WOLFGANG
PERSONAL Born 12/06/1937, Frankfurt, Germany, 2 children **DISCIPLINE** GERMAN LITERATURE **EDUCATION** Univ Bonn, PhD, 64. **CAREER** Asst prof Ger, Antioch Col, 64-68; from asst prof to prof Ger, Boston Col, 68-. **MEMBERSHIPS** MLA. **RESEARCH** Comp lit; 20th century Ger lit; theory of lit. **SELECTED PUBLICATIONS** Auth, Die Funktion des Hasslichen in der Lyrik G Heyms, G Trakls und G Benns, Bouvier, Bonn, 65; Der Verlust der Geschichte in der Deutschen Literatur des 20 Jahrhunderts, Neophilologus, 70; Geschichtspessimismus in der Deutschen Literatur des 20, Jahrhunderts, Francke, Berne, 70; Zur Sozialphilosophie des deutschen Expressionismus, Z Deut Philol, 72; Denk-und Stilformen des Deutschen Expressionismus, Francke, Berne, 73; Phanomenologie der Interpretation, Francke, Berne, Munich, 77; Schreiben als Erfahrung, Bouvier, Bonn, 85; Der Intellektuelle in der Westeuropaischen und Amerikanischen Romanliteratur ab 1945, hitzeroth, Marburg, 92; Asthetische Erfahrung in der Lebenswelt des Westeuropaischen und Amerikanischen Romans, Francke, Tubingen and Basel, 97; auth, Die geringen Dinge, Shaker, Aachen, 99; numerous articles on German and Austrian Exile Literature. **CONTACT ADDRESS** Dept of Ger Studies, Boston Col, Chestnut Hill, 140 Commonwealth Ave, Chestnut Hill, MA 02167-3800. **EMAIL** cykman@bc.edu

F

FABER, SEBASTION
PERSONAL Born Amsterdam, Netherlands **DISCIPLINE** HISPANIC LITERATURE **EDUCATION** Univ Amsterdam, Doctorandus, 95; Univ Calif Davis, PhD, 99. **CAREER** Asst prof, Oberlin Col, 99-. **HONORS AND AWARDS** George Watt Mem Prize, 00; SSRC/ACLS, 99; Span Ministry For Affairs Fel, 99; Prog Cult Coop, Spanish Ministry Cult. **MEMBERSHIPS** MLA; MMLA; LASA; IILI; AEMIC. **RESEARCH** Literature of Spanish Civil war Exile; representations of the Spanish Civil War; constructions of Pan-Hispanic identity since Latin-American independence; theory of ideology; contemporary Spanish fiction; journalism and fiction in Latin-American literature. **SELECTED PUBLICA-**

TIONS Auth, "La Metonimia en una Cronica de Monsivais: Hacia un Peridismo Democratico," Lit Mex 10 (99): 249-280; auth, "Can the Female Muse Speak? Chacel and Poniatowaska Read Against the Grain," Rocky Mtn Rev Lang Lit 53 (99): 47-66; auth, "'El Norte Nos Devora:' La Construccion de un Espacio Hispanico en el Exilio Anglosajon de Luis Cernuda," Hisp 83 (01): 733-744. **CONTACT ADDRESS** Hisp Studies Dept, Oberlin Col, Oberlin, OH 44074. **EMAIL** sebastiaan.faber@oberlin.edu

FABIAN, HANS JOACHIM
PERSONAL Born 08/01/1926, Elbing, Germany, m, 1951, 2 children **DISCIPLINE** GERMAN **EDUCATION** Syracuse Univ, BA, 50, MA, 52, MSLS, 54; Ohio State Univ, PhD (Ger lit), 63. **CAREER** Dir libr, Wilmington Col, 54-61; asst Ger, Ohio State Univ, 61-62, asst prof libr admin, 63-64; instr Ger, Ohio Univ, 62-63; dir jr year abroad, 68-69, Asst Prof Ger, Univ Mich, Ann Arbor, 64-, Rackham fel, 67. **MEMBERSHIPS** Am Asn Teachers Ger; MLA. **RESEARCH** German expressionism; Georg Kaiser. **SELECTED PUBLICATIONS CONTACT ADDRESS** Dept of Ger, Univ of Michigan, Ann Arbor, Ann Arbor, MI 48104.

FAGER, JEFF
PERSONAL Born 11/04/1952, Redkey, IN, m, 1975 **DISCIPLINE** HEBREW BIBLE **EDUCATION** Univ Evansville, BA, 75; So Methodist Univ, MTh, 79; Vanderbilt Univ, PhD, 87. **CAREER** Prof relig and philos, Kentucky Wesleyan Col, 86- . **MEMBERSHIPS** Soc of Bibl Lit; Am Acad of Relig. **RESEARCH** Ethics of the Hebrew Bible. **SELECTED PUBLICATIONS** Auth, Land Tenure in the Biblical Jubilee: A Moral World View, Hebrew Annual Rev, 88; auth, Back to the Past: Two Instances of Mentoring in the Hebrew Bible, Int J of Mentoring, 88; auth, Land Tenure and the Biblical Jubilee: Discovering a Moral World View through the Sociology of Knowledge, Sheffield Academic, 93; auth, Chaos and the Deborah Tradition, Q Rev, 93; auth, Miriam and Deborah: Legends of women in Power in an Ancient Patriarchal Society, Bible Tod, 94; auth, rev of Janzen, Old Testament Ethics: A Paradigmatic Approach, Princeton Sem Bull, 95; auth, book note on Habel, The Land is Mine: Six Biblican Land Ideologies, Theol Today, 96. **CONTACT ADDRESS** Kentucky Wesleyan Col, PO Box 1039, Owensboro, KY 42302-1039. **EMAIL** jeffreyf@kwc.edu

FAGLES, ROBERT
PERSONAL Born 09/11/1933, Philadelphia, PA, m, 1956, 2 children **DISCIPLINE** COMPARATIVE LITERATURE, ENGLISH **EDUCATION** Amherst Col, AB, 55; Yale Univ, MA, 56, PhD (English), 59. **CAREER** LTjg, United States Navy, 6th Fleet, 58-61; Instr English, Yale Univ, 59-60; from instr to asst prof, 60-65, assoc prof English and comp lit, 65-70, dir prog comp lit, 66-75, PROF COMPLIT, PRINCETON UNIV, 70-, chair of department, 75-94, Arthur W. Marks 19 prof of comp lit, vis prof, The Hebrew Univ, 74-75; vis prof, Comparative Lit, Yale Univ, 90; NY State Summer Writers Inst, Sem on Translation. **HONORS AND AWARDS** Calif Commonwealth Club Gold Medal for Non-fiction, 80; British Comparative Lit Asn, First Prize, Translation Competition, 91, British Comparative Lit Asn, Second Prize, Translations on a Jewish theme, 91; Coun for Advancement and Support of Education, Gold Medal for Looking for Kafka, 91; Landon Translation Award, The Acad of Am Poets, 91; Nat Bk Critics Circle award for nonfiction, Finalist, 95; PEN/Ralph Manheim Medal for Translation, 97; Truman Capote Prize for Literary Criticism, 97; Behrman Award, Princeton; Commander, Order of the Phoenix, Hellenic Republic. **MEMBERSHIPS** Am Acad of Arts and Letters; Am Acad of Arts and Sciences, Am Philosophical Soc. **RESEARCH** The epic tradition; Greek tragedy; Greek, Latin and English lyric poetry. **SELECTED PUBLICATIONS** Auth, Translations, Aeschylus Oresteia, Sophocles Three Theban Plays, Homer Iliad and Odyssey; auth, The Lies of Art: Max Beerbohm's Parody and Caricature, New York: Alfred A Knopf, 72, London: Victor Gollancz, 73; co-transl, The Dark Room and other Poems, by Enrique Lihn, New York: New Directions, 78, 2nd ed, 00; auth, Translating Neruda: The Way to Macchu Picchu, Stanford Univ Press, 80, paperback edition, 86; auth, Paul Celan: Poet, Survivor, Jew, Yale Univ Press, 95, paperback edition, 97, Nota Bene edition, 01, Verlag C.H. Beck, Munich, 97, pocketbook, 01; auth, Heights of Macchu Picchu/ Alturas de Macchu Picchu, Nevada, with photographs by Edward Ranney, Limited Editions Club, 98; coed, Jewish American Literature: A Norton Anthology, W.W. Norton, 00; ed and translator, Selected Poems and Prose of Paul Celan, W.W. Norton, 00; auth, Deathfugue/Todesfuge (Celan), Limited Editions Club, 01. **CONTACT ADDRESS** Dept of Comp Lit, Princeton Univ, Princeton, NJ 08540. **EMAIL** fagles@princeton.edu

FAGUNDO, ANA MARIA
PERSONAL Born 03/13/1938, Santa Cruz de Tenerife, Spain **DISCIPLINE** COMPARATIVE LITERATURE, SPANISH AND ENGLISH LITERATURE **EDUCATION** Univ Redlands, BA, 62; Univ Wash, MA, 64, PhD (comp lit), 67. **CAREER** Asst prof Span lit, 67-76, Assoc Prof Contemp Span Lit, Univ Calif, Riverside, 76-, Ed-in-Chief, Alaluz. **HONORS AND AWARDS** Carabela de Oro poetry prize. **MEMBERSHIPS** Am Asn Teachers Span and Port; Sociedad Colegial de Escritores. **RESEARCH** Contemporary Spanish poetry; contemporary American poetry. **SELECTED PUBLICATIONS** Auth, Cantico or a Tribute to Mother, Insula Revista De Letras Y Ciencias Humanas, Vol 48, 93. **CONTACT ADDRESS** Dept of Span, Univ of California, Riverside, Riverside, CA 92502. **EMAIL** ana.fagundo@ucr.edu

FAINGOLD, EDUARDO D.
PERSONAL Born 09/06/1958, La Plata, Argentina, m, 1 child **DISCIPLINE** LANGUAGE, LINGUISTICS **EDUCATION** Hebrew Univ Jerusalem, BA, 84; MA, 87; Tel-Aviv Univ, PhD, 92. **CAREER** Lectr, Tel-Aviv Univ, 88-89; lectr, SUNY, Stony Brook, 92-95; prof, Univ of Tulsa, 95-. **HONORS AND AWARDS** Fel, Hebrew Univ, 86; fel, DAAD, 89; Fozis Prize, Tel-Aviv Univ, 89; Rothschild Prize nominee, Tel-Aviv Univ, 91; Grant, Ger Sci Found, 96; Teaching Awd, Univ of Tulsa, 97; Who's who in the South and Southwest, 99-00; Fel, Kellogg Found Grant, Austria, 99; Grant, NEH, 99; Who's Who in the World, 00. **MEMBERSHIPS** Ling Soc of Am; MLA; Int Ling Assoc; Am Assoc of Teachers of Span and Port, Int Clinical Phonetics and Ling Assoc; Ling Assoc of the SW; Salzburg Sem Alumni Assoc; DAAD Alumni Assoc. **RESEARCH** Spanish and Portugese linguistics, English linguistics, applied linguistics, Judeo-Spanish, language variation and change, child language, creole linguistics, second language acquisition and learning, bilingualism. **SELECTED PUBLICATIONS** Auth, The case for fusion: (Jewish) Ladino in the Balkans and the Eastern Turkish Empire, Res Center for Multilingualism (Hamburg, Germany), 89; ed, Southwest Journal of Linguistics, Vol 13, 94; auth, "The genesis of the article system in creolization and historical change", Papiere zur Linguistik 50 (94): 51-63; auth, "Variation in the application of natural processes: Language-dependent constraints in the phonological acquisition of bilingual children", J of Psycholinguistic Res 25, (96): 515-526; auth, Child Language, Creolization, and Historical Change. Spanish in Contact with Portuguese, Gunter Narr Verlag (Tubingen, Ger), 96; auth, Codice de Composicion. Guia para Escribir Trabajos, ERIC Center for Applied Ling, (Arlington, VA), 98; auth, "Naturalness, functionalism, and principles of linguistics change", Papiere zur Linguistik 58 (98): 223-226; auth, "the acquisition, learning, change, and history of Spanish Mood in Mexico and the U.S. (with reference to South America and Spain", Papiere zur Linguistik 58 _98): 137-156; auth, "Lexical strategies in early trilingual acquisition", Travaux du LILLA, ed Henri Zingle, Univ de Nice, (France, 99); auth, "The re-emergence of Spanish and Hebrew in a multilingual adolescent", Int J of Bilingual Educ and Bilingualism 2 (99): 283-295. **CONTACT ADDRESS** Dept For Lang, Univ of Tulsa, 600 S College Ave, Tulsa, OK 74104-3126. **EMAIL** eduardo-faingold@utulsa.edu

FAIRLEY, IRENE R.
PERSONAL Born 01/02/1940, Brooklyn, NY, 2 children **DISCIPLINE** LINGUISTICS, ENGLISH **EDUCATION** Queens Col, NYork, AB, 60; Harvard Univ, MA, 61, PhD (ling), 71. **CAREER** From instr to asst prof English, C W Post Col, Long Island Univ, 68-73; from asst prof English and ling to prof, Northeastern Univ, 73-. **HONORS AND AWARDS** Am Coun Learned Soc grant-in-aid, 77-78; Guggenheim fel, 79-80. **MEMBERSHIPS** Ling Soc Am; MLA; Semiotic Soc Am; Millay Colony for Arts. **RESEARCH** Linguistic approaches to literature, stylistics, poetics. **SELECTED PUBLICATIONS** Auth, Millay, Edna, Stvincent Gendered Language and Form, Sonnets from an Ungrafted Tree, Style, Vol 29, 95. **CONTACT ADDRESS** 34 Winn St, Belmont, MA 02478. **EMAIL** irfairley@nev.edu

FAJARDO, SALVADOR J.
PERSONAL Born 01/06/1940, Zaragoza, Spain, m, 1970, 4 children **DISCIPLINE** SPANISH, LITERATURE **EDUCATION** Col Stemisles, BA, 58; Univ Montreal, MA, 62; Univ Chicago, PhD, 68. **CAREER** Asst prof, N Ill Univ, 65-66; asst prof, Univ Fla, 66-67; asst prof, Univ SCar, 67-68; asst prof, Univ West Ont, 70-71; asst prof, Neth Hawthorn Col, 72-75; asst prof, New Eng Col, 75-78; assoc prof to prof to dept chmn, Wesleyan Univ, 78-90; prof to dept chmn, SUNY Binghamton, 90-. **HONORS AND AWARDS** Woodrow Wilson Fel, 63; Univ Chicago Humanities Fel, 64; NEH, 92, 94, 95, 98, 00. **MEMBERSHIPS** MLA; AATSD; SSSAS; Cervantes Soc. **RESEARCH** Contemporary Spanish poetry; Cervantes. **SELECTED PUBLICATIONS** Auth, Claude Simon; auth, Luis Cernude; auth, Multiple Species; auth, The Poetry of Rafael Alseih; auth, The Word and the Mirror; ed, Essays on the Poetry of Luis Cernude; co-ed, At Home and Beyond: New essays on Spanish Poets of the Twenties; co-ed, After the War: essays on Recent Spanish Poetry; co-ed, Don Quixote. **CONTACT ADDRESS** Span Studies Dept, SUNY, Binghamton, PO Box 6000, Binghamton, NY 13902-6000. **EMAIL** farardo@binghamton.edu

FALK, JULIA SABLESKI
PERSONAL Born 09/21/1941, Englewood, NJ, m, 1967, 1 child **DISCIPLINE** LINGUISTICS **EDUCATION** Georgetown Univ, BS, 63; Univ WA, MA, 64, PhD, 68. **CAREER** From instr to assoc prof, 66-78, Prof Ling, MI State Univ, 78-, Assoc Dean Col Arts & Lett, 79-86, Sr researcher educ, Inst Res on Teaching, 76-77; vis prof, Univ Hong Kong, 95. **HONORS AND AWARDS** Woodrow Wilson fel, 63; Nat Defense Educ Act Title IV fel, 63-66; Nat Sci Found fel, 65; MI State Univ Paul Varg Alumni Awd, 93. **MEMBERSHIPS** Ling Soc Am; North Am Assoc Hist Lang Sciences. **RESEARCH** Hist of linguistics. **SELECTED PUBLICATIONS** Auth, Equational clauses in Bengali, Language, 65; A Generative Phonology of a Spanish Dialect, 65 & Nominalizations in Spanish, 68, Univ Wash; auth, Linguistics and Language, Wiley, 1st ed, 73, 2nd ed, 78; Language and linguistics: Bases for a curriculum, In: Language in Education, Ctr Appl Ling, 78; Lang acquisition and the teaching and learning of writing, Col English, 79; coauth, Speaking Black English and reading, J Negro Educ, 82; Otto Jespersen, Leonard Bloomfield, and American Structural Linguistics, Language, 92; To Be Human: A History of the Study of Language, In: Language: Readings in Language and Culture, St Martins Press, 5th ed, 94, 6th ed, 95; co-auth, The Saleski Family and the Founding of the LSA Linguistics Institutes, Historiographia Linguistica, 94; The Women Foundation Members of the Linguistic Society of America, Language 94; Portraits of Women Linguistics: Louise Pound, Edith Claflin, Adelaide Hahn, In: History of Linguistics 1993: Papers from the Sixth International Conference on the History of the Language Sciences, John Benjamins Publ, 95; Roman Jakobson and the History of Saussurean Concepts in North American Linguistics, Historiographia Linguistica, 95; Words without Grammar: Linguists and the International Auxiliary Language Movement in the United States, Lang & Commun, 95; co-auth, Further Notes on Reinhold E Saleski, Historiographia Linguistica, 96; Territoriality, Relationships, and Reputation: The Case of Gladys A Reichard, Southwest Jour Ling, 97; The American Shift from Historical to Non-Historical Linguistics, Language and Commun, 98; auth, Women. Language and Linqustics: Three American Stories from the First Half of the Twentieth Century, Routledge, 99. **CONTACT ADDRESS** 8939 Caminito Verano, La Jolla, CA 92037. **EMAIL** jsfalk@san.rr.com

FALKNER, THOMAS M.
PERSONAL Born 11/09/1947, Buffalo, NY, m, 1972, 3 children **DISCIPLINE** GREEK AND LATIN LITERATURE **EDUCATION** LeMoyne Univ, AB, 69; SUNY, MA, 71, PhD, 75. **CAREER** Vis scholar Cambridge Univ, 96-97; prof; dean of fac, Col Wooster, 99-. **HONORS AND AWARDS** Six different grants, NEH; fel in residence; dit, wooster-in-greece prog, 84. **SELECTED PUBLICATIONS** Co-ed, Old Age in Greek and Latin Literature; co-ed, Contextualizing Classics; auth, Euripides' Orestes, The Poetics of Old Age in Greek Epic, Lyric, and Tragedy; articles on Greek and Latin poetry, articles on Sophoclean tragedy. **CONTACT ADDRESS** Dept of Classics, The Col of Wooster, Wooster, OH 44691. **EMAIL** tfalkner@wooster.edu

FALLON, JEAN
DISCIPLINE 16TH CENTURY FRENCH LITERATURE, 19TH CENTURY POETRY **EDUCATION** Univ VA, PhD. **CAREER** Instr, Hollins Col, 90. **RESEARCH** French lyric poets of the 16th century. **SELECTED PUBLICATIONS** Auth, Voice and Vision in Ronsard's Les Sonnets pour Helene. **CONTACT ADDRESS** PO Box 9576, Roanoke, VA 24020.

FALLON, ROBERT THOMAS
PERSONAL Born 06/06/1927, New York, NY, d, 2 children **DISCIPLINE** ENGLISH AND COMPARATIVE LITERATURE **EDUCATION** US Mil Acad, BS, 49; Canisius Col, MA, 60; Columbia Univ, PhD, 65. **CAREER** Asst prof English, US Mil Acad, 61-64; chmn dept mil sci, 69-70, asst to the pres, 70-71, assoc prof, 70-79, prof English, 79-95, prof Emer, 95-, Lasalle Col. **HONORS AND AWARDS** James Holly Hanford Awd, 94, NEH fel, 90-91; Outstanding Acad Book, Choice, 96. **MEMBERSHIPS** Milton Soc Am (treas, 77-86, vpres, 87, & pres, 88); MLA; John Donne Soc; ALSC. **RESEARCH** John Milton--military and political imagery; English history -- The Interregnum; contrib ed, The Variorum Edition of the Poetry of John Donne. **SELECTED PUBLICATIONS** Auth, John Milton and the honorable artillery company, Milton Quart, 5/75; Filling the gaps: New perspectives on Mr Secretary Milton, Milton Studies XII, 78; Miltonic documents in the public records office, London, Studies Bibliog, 78; Milton's defenseless doors: The limits of irony, Milton Quart, 12/79; Milton in the anarchy, 1659-1660: A question of consistency, Studies English Lit, winter 81; Milton's Epics and the Spanish War: Toward a Poetics of Experience, In: Milton Studies XV, Univ Pittsburgh Press, 82; Captain or Colonel: The Soldier in Miltons Life and Art, Univ Missouri Press, 84; Milton in Government, Penn State Univ Press, 93; Divided Empire: Miltons Political Imagery, Penn State Univ Press, 95; Shakespeare: A Theater goer's Guide, Ivan R. Dee, Pub, 00. **CONTACT ADDRESS** River Rd, Lumberville, PA 18933. **EMAIL** fallon@lasalle.edu

FANGER, DONALD LEE
PERSONAL Born 12/06/1929, Cleveland, OH, m, 1955, 3 children **DISCIPLINE** RUSSIAN & COMPARATIVE LITERATURE **EDUCATION** Univ CA, Berkeley, BA, 51, MA, 54; Harvard Univ, PhD, 62. **CAREER** Instr Russ lang & lit, Brown Univ, 60-62; from asst prof to assoc prof Russ lang & lit & dir Slavic Div, Stanford Univ, 66-68; chmn slavic dept, 73-82, Prof Slavic & Comp Lit, Harvard Univ, 68-98, Harry Levin Research Prof of Lit, 98-, Mem nat adv comt, Inter-Univ

Comt Travel Grants, 67-68; Am Coun Learned Soc res grant, 68-69; mem prog comt, Int Res & Exchanges Bd, 69-73; Guggenheim fel, 75-76; fel, Am Acad Arts & Sci, 80-; res fel, Rockefeller Found Ctr Advan Study, Bellagio, summer 81. **HONORS AND AWARDS** Christian Gauss Award, Phi Beta Kappa, 80. **MEMBERSHIPS** MLA; Am Asn Tchr(s) Slavic & East Europ Lang; Am Comp Lit Asn, Am Acad of Arts & Sci. **RESEARCH** Develop of the Russian novel. **SELECTED PUBLICATIONS** Auth, Dostoevsky today, Survey, 4/61; Romanticism and comparative literature, Comp Lit, spring 62; ed, Brown Univ Slavic Reprint Series, 61-66; auth, Dostoevsky and Romantic Realism, Harvard Univ, 65, Univ Chicago, 67, Northwestern 98; The Peasant in 19th Century Russia, Stanford Univ, 68; The Creation of Nikolai Gogol, Harvard Univ, 79. **CONTACT ADDRESS** Dept of Slavic Lang & Lit, Harvard Univ, Barker Center, Cambridge, MA 02138-3800. **EMAIL** fanger@fas.harvard.edu

FANT, J. CLAYTON
DISCIPLINE CLASSICAL STUDIES **EDUCATION** Williams Coll, BA, 69; Univ of Mich, PhD, 76. **CAREER** Asst Prof, 76-79, Wellesley Coll; Instr, 79-81, St Stephen's School Rome; vis Asst Prof, 81-83, Univ of Mich; Asst Prof, Assoc Prof, 84-, Univ of Akron. **HONORS AND AWARDS** Amer Acad Rome Fel. **MEMBERSHIPS** AIA, APA, ASMOSIA, Vergilian Society. **RESEARCH** Roman Archaeology **SELECTED PUBLICATIONS** Auth, Cavum Antrum Phrygiae, The Organization and Operations of the Roman Imperial Marble Quarries at Docimium, BAR Intl Series, 89; Ancient Marble Quarrying and Trade, BAR Intl Series, 88; Ideology Gift and Trade, A Distribution Model for the Roman Imperial Marbles, in: The Inscribed Economy, Production and Distribution in the Roman Empire in the Light of Instrumentum Domesticum, ed W V Harris & S Panciera, JRA, 93; The Imperial Marble Yard at Portus, in: Ancient Stones, Quarrying Trade and Provenance. Interdisciplinary Studies on Stones and Stone Technology in Europe and Near East from the Prehistoric to the Early Christian Period, ed, M Waelkens, N Herz & L Moens, 92. **CONTACT ADDRESS** Dept of Classics, Univ of Akron, 326 Olin, Akron, OH 44325-1910. **EMAIL** cfant@uakron.edu

FANTHAM, ELAINE
PERSONAL Born 05/25/1933, Liverpool, England, w, 1958, 2 children **DISCIPLINE** CLASSICS **EDUCATION** Oxford Univ, MA, B.Litt, 57; Liverpool Univ, PhD, 62. **CAREER** Vis prof, 66-68, Indiana Univ; from asst to full Prof of Classics, 68-86, Univ Toronto; Giger Prof of Latin, Princeton Univ, 86-99. **HONORS AND AWARDS** Former vpres, Res Div, APA; trustee, Am Acad in Rome. **MEMBERSHIPS** Am Philol Asn; Class Asn of Canada; Int Soc for the Hist of Rhetoric. **RESEARCH** Latin epic; rhetoric; Roman social history; women's history. **SELECTED PUBLICATIONS** Auth, A Commentary on Lucan De Bello Civili Book 2, Cambridge, 92; co-auth, Women in the Classical World: Image and Text, Oxford, 94; auth, Roman Literary Culture: from Cicero to Apuleius, Johns Hopkins, 96; transl, The Hidden Author by Gian Biagio Conte, Berkeley, 96; ed. and commentator , Ovid: Fasti Book IV, Cambridge, 96; auth, Envy and Fear the Begetters of Hate: Statius Thebaid and the Genesis of Hatred, in, Gill, ed, The Passions in Latin Literature and Thought, Cambridge, 97; auth, Occasions and Contexts of Roman Public Oratory, in Dominik, ed, Roman Eloquence, London, 97; auth, Propertius' Old New Rome, in Habinek, ed, The Roman Cultural Revolution, Cambridge, 97; auth, Allecto's First Victim, in, Vergil's Aeneid in Its Political Context, Duckworth, 98; auth, "Fighting Words; Turnus at bay in the Latin council," Am Journal of Philology, 99. **CONTACT ADDRESS** 28 1/2 Wiggins St, Princeton, NJ 08540. **EMAIL** fantham@ariel.princeton.edu

FARAONE, CHRISTOPHER
DISCIPLINE CLASSICS **EDUCATION** Stanford Univ, PhD, 88. **CAREER** Asst prof, Va Polytech Inst & State Univ, 88-91; Asst prof, Univ Chicago, 91-93; Assoc prof, Univ Chicago, 93-. **HONORS AND AWARDS** John Simon Guggenheim Memorial Foundation Fel; Nat Endowment Hum; Jr Fel; ACLS Grant; NEH Summer Stipend; State Coun Higher Educ Va (SCHEV) Grant; Phi Beta Kappa Sch; Whiting Dissertation Fel; Stanford Grad Fel. **MEMBERSHIPS** Am Philol Asn; Clas Asn Midwest & South; Int Plutarch Soc; Soc Ancient Med; Soc Biblical Lit; Women's Clas Caucus. **SELECTED PUBLICATIONS** Auth, Talismans and Trojan Horses: Guardian Statues in Ancient Greek Myth and Ritual, Oxford Univ Press, 92, 96; auth, Ancient Greek Love Magic, Harvard Univ Press, 98; Co-ed, Magika Hiera: Ancient Greek Magic and Religion, Oxford Univ Press, 91; co-ed, Masks of Dionysus, Cornell Univ Press, 93. **CONTACT ADDRESS** Univ of Chicago, 5801 S Ellis, Chicago, IL 60637.

FARBER, GERALD HOWARD
PERSONAL Born 03/21/1935, El Paso, TX, m, 1967, 4 children **DISCIPLINE** COMPARATIVE LITERATURE, ENGLISH & AMERICAN LITERATURE **EDUCATION** Univ CA, Los Angeles, BA, 58; CA State Univ, Los Angeles, MA, 62; Occidental Col, PhD, 70. **CAREER** Lectr English, 62-65, asst prof, CA State Univ, Los Angeles, 66-68; from lectr to asst prof, 68-74, assoc prof, 74-81, Prof Comp Lit, San Diego State Univ, 81-; Maitre assistant associe, 74 & maitre de conferences associe, 77, Univ Paris VII. **HONORS AND AWARDS** Outstanding Fac Awd, SDSU, 93. **RESEARCH** Aesthetics; the teaching of literature; comedy; eighteenth-century European lit; Marcel Proust. **SELECTED PUBLICATIONS** Auth, The Student as Nigger, 70 & The University of Tomorrowland, 72, Simon & Schuster; A Field Guide to the Aesthetic Experience, Foreworks Press, 82; The Third Circle: On Education and Distance Learning, Sociological Perspectives, vol 41, no 4, 98; auth, Scott Moncrieff's Way: Proust in Translation, Proust Said That, no 6, March 97; Aesthetic Resonance: Beyond the Sign in Literature, Reader: Essays in Reader-Oriented Theory, Criticism, and Pedagogy, no 32, fall, 94; Golden Grove Unweaving (and not a moment too soon), Fiction International, no 27, 94; Learning How To Teach: A Progress Report, College English, vol 52, no 2, Feb 90. **CONTACT ADDRESS** Dept of English and Comp Lit, San Diego State Univ, San Diego, CA 92182-8140. **EMAIL** jfarber@mail.sdsu.edu

FARBER, JAY JOEL
PERSONAL Born 11/06/1932, Philadelphia, PA, m, 1952, 2 children **DISCIPLINE** CLASSICAL LANGUAGES AND LITERATURES **EDUCATION** Univ Chicago, BA, 52, MA, 54; Yale Univ, PhD (Greek and ancient hist), 59. **CAREER** Instr classics, Univ Chicago, 57-60; asst prof, Rutgers Univ, 60-63; assoc prof, 63-70, chmn dept, 63-79, Prof Classics, Franklin and Marshall Col, 70-95, Rutgers Univ Res Coun grants, 61 and 62; vis res assoc, Ctr Int Studies, Princeton Univ, 62-63; examnr, comt advan placement classics, Col Entrance Exam Bd, 71-74; Shirley Watkins Seinman Prof of Classics Emer, 95-. **MEMBERSHIPS** Am Philol Asn; Am. Soc Papyrologists; Class Asn Atlantic States. **RESEARCH** Greek myth; Greek tragedy; Greek political theory. **SELECTED PUBLICATIONS** Auth, "Family Financial Disputes in the Patermouth's Archive," Bul Am Soc Papyrologists, Vol 27, 90. **CONTACT ADDRESS** Dept of Classics, Franklin and Marshall Col, 1415 Hillcrest Rd, Lancaster, PA 17603. **EMAIL** farberjoel@aol.com

FARINA, LUCIANO FERNANDO
PERSONAL Born 01/03/1943, Milan, Italy, m, 1982, 2 children **DISCIPLINE** ITALIAN, COMPUTATIONAL LINGUISTICS, APPLIED LINGUISTICS, TRANSLATOR **EDUCATION** Catholic Univ, BST, 70; Ohio State Univ, MA, 72, PhD (Romance Ling), 77. **CAREER** Teach asst, 70-76, instr, 76-77, Asst Prof Ital, Ohio State Univ, 77- and Dir Ital Lang Prog, 76-92, Res Dir Computer Appln Ital, Instruct and Res Computer Ctr, Ohio State Univ, 75-, Dir Individualized Lang Instr, 77-80; res guest, Vocabolario Dialetti Svizzera Italiana, Lugano, Switz, summer 76 and consult, 79; consult, Archivio Storico Ticinese, Bellinzona, Switzerland, 80, Assessorato Cult, Regione Lombardia, Milano, Italy, 80 and Pyramid Serv Corp, Columbus, Ohio, 80-92; vis prof, Univ of Catania, Italy, 80-. **MEMBERSHIPS** Asn Comput Ling; Asn Ling and Lit Comput; Soc Ling Ital; MLA; Am Asn Applied Ling; AATI; AAIS; ACH. **RESEARCH** Lexicography; dialectology; pedagogy; semantics; developed LDMS for Latin; Old French; Medieval & Modern Italian. **SELECTED PUBLICATIONS** Auth, Bravo,Italian Grammar for Foreigners--Course In Italian Language And Civilization, Mod Lang J, Vol 77, 93. **CONTACT ADDRESS** Dept French & Italian, Ohio State Univ, Columbus, 1841 Millikin Rd, Columbus, OH 43210-1229. **EMAIL** farina.1@osu.edu

FARKAS, DONKA F.
DISCIPLINE LINGUISTICS **EDUCATION** Univ Bucharest, Romania, BA; Univ Chicago, PhD, 81. **CAREER** Prof, Lang, Univ Calif, Santa Cruz. **RESEARCH** Semantics of complementation, quantifier scope and modality. **SELECTED PUBLICATIONS** Auth, Intensional Descriptions and the Romance Subjunctive Mood, Garland Publ, 85; On Obligatory Control, Ling and Philos, 88; Two Cases of Underspecification in Morphology, Ling Inquiry, 90; On the Semantics of Subjunctive Complements, Romance Lang and Mod Ling Theory, John Benjamins Publ, 92. **CONTACT ADDRESS** Dept of Ling, Univ of California, Santa Cruz, Stevenson Col, 1156 High St, Santa Cruz, CA 95064. **EMAIL** farkas@cats.ucsc.edu

FARNHAM, ANTHONY EDWARD
PERSONAL Born 07/02/1930, Oakland, CA, m, 1957, 2 children **DISCIPLINE** ENGLISH, PHILOLOGY **EDUCATION** Univ Calif, Berkeley, AB, 51; Harvard Univ, MA, 57, PhD(English), 64. **CAREER** From instr to assoc prof, 61-72, Prof English, Mt Holyoke Col 72-, Vis asst prof, Amherst Col, 64-65; lectr, Smith Col, 65-66; vis asst prof, Univ Calif, Berkeley, 66-67; Prof, Emeritus, 99-. **MEMBERSHIPS** Mediaeval Acad Am; MLA; Am Cath Hist Asn; Asn Literary Scholars & Critics; Dante Soc Am; New Chaucer Soc; Phi Beta Kappa **RESEARCH** Old and Middle English language and literature; history of the English language. **SELECTED PUBLICATIONS** Ed, A Sourcebook in the History of English, Holt, Rinehart & Winston, 69; auth, Statement and Search in the Confessio Amantis, Mediaevalia, 93. **CONTACT ADDRESS** Dept of English, Mount Holyoke Col, 50 College St, South Hadley, MA 01075-1461. **EMAIL** afarnham@mtholyoke.edu

FARRONATO, CRISTINA
PERSONAL Born 06/06/1967, Bassano Del Grappa, Italy, m, 1999 **DISCIPLINE** ITALIAN LANGUAGE, ITALIAN LITERATURE **EDUCATION** Univ Venice, Laurea, 92; Univ Calif San Diego, MA, 98; PhD, 00. **CAREER** Asst prof, Colgate Univ, 00-. **HONORS AND AWARDS** Teaching Excellence Awd, 98-99; Distinguished Fel, 98; Friends Intl Cen Fel, 98; Grad Scholar, Univ Venice, 93-94. **MEMBERSHIPS** MLA; AAIS; SSA. **RESEARCH** Italian studies; film and film theory; semiotics. **SELECTED PUBLICATIONS** Auth, "Holbein's Christ and the Horror of the Broken Narrative," in Interdisciplinary Journal for German Linguistics and Semitic Analysis (Berkeley: Intl Area Studies, 98); auth, "Survey of Italian Long Fiction," in Critical Survey of Long Fiction, ed. Carl Rollyson (Salem Pr, 99); auth, "The Theory of Abduction and the Name of the Rose," in SSA Proceedings (Peter Lang, 99). **CONTACT ADDRESS** 71 Hamilton St, Hamilton, NY 13346-1319. **EMAIL** cfarronato@mail.colgate.edu

FARROW, J. G.
PERSONAL Born 09/19/1948, England **DISCIPLINE** CLASSICS **EDUCATION** Oxford, Master of Letters, 79 **CAREER** Head class, relig stud, Haberdashers' Monmouth, Wales, 80-86; ADJ PROF CLASS, WAYNE STATE UNIV, 88-; PROF HUM, MACOMB COMMUNITY COL, 89-. **CONTACT ADDRESS** Dept of Classics, Wayne State Univ, Manoogian Hall 430, Detroit, MI 48101. **EMAIL** farrowj@exchange.macomb.cc.mi.us

FARTHING, JOHN L.
DISCIPLINE RELIGION AND CLASSICAL LANGUAGES **EDUCATION** Univ Tulsa, BA, 69; Duke Univ, MDiv, 74, PhD, 78. **CAREER** Prof Relig and Clas Lang, 78, ch, dept Relig, Hendrix Col. **RESEARCH** Medieval, Reformation, and Renaissance theology. **SELECTED PUBLICATIONS** Auth, Thomas Aquinas and Gabriel Biel; transl, Jean-Claude Margolin, auth, Humanism in Europe at the Time of the Renaissance. **CONTACT ADDRESS** Hendrix Col, Conway, AR 72032.

FAULHABER, CHARLES BAILEY
PERSONAL Born 09/18/1941, East Cleveland, OH, m, 1971 **DISCIPLINE** MEDIEVAL SPANISH LITERATURE **EDUCATION** Yale Univ, BA, 63, MPhil & PhD, 69; Univ Wis-Madison, MA, 66. **CAREER** Actg instr Span, Yale Univ, 68-69; from Asst Prof to Assoc Prof, 69-80, Prof Span, Univ CA, Berkeley, 80-, Chmn, Dept Span & Port, 89-94, James D. Hart Dir, The Bancroft Libr, 95-; ed, Romance Philol, 82-95, ed-in-chief, 86-87; assoc ed, Hispania, 95-98. **HONORS AND AWARDS** Prin investr, Hispanic Soc Am, Nat Endowment for Hum, 76 & 78-80; Guggenheim fel, 82-83; mem, Hisp Soc Am, 83; Fulbright fel, 67-68; Ministerio de Asuntos Exteriores de Espana, beca de investigacion, 89, 95; NEH grants, 89-91, 91-93, 94-95, 99-00; Quincentenary Postdoctoral Fel, Spain, 91. **MEMBERSHIPS** MLA; Assoc Int Hispanistas; Medieval Acad Am; Am Acad Res Hist Medieval Spain; Am Asn Tchr(s) Span & Port; AAUP; Asn Hisp Lit Medieval; Asn Computers and the Hum; Medieval Asn Pacific. **RESEARCH** Medieval rhetoric; computers and hum. **SELECTED PUBLICATIONS** Auth, Latin Rhetorical Theology in Thirteenth and Fourteenth Century, Univ of Calif Press, 72; auth, Libros y bibliotecas en la Espana medieval. Una bibliografia de fuentes impresas, Research Bibliographies and Checklists, Grant & Cutler, 87; Medieval Manuscripts in the Library of the Hispanic Society of America. Documents and Letters, The Hisp Soc Am, 93; Necrology: Ruth House Webber (1918-1997), La Coronica 25.2, 97; Sobre la cultura ibrica medieval: Las lenguas vern¤a culas y la traduccion, Actas del VI Congreso Internacional de la Asociacion Hispanica de Literatura Medieval, Univ Alcal¤, 97; author numerous other articles and publ; coed, Philosophy, The Bancroft Library, 99. **CONTACT ADDRESS** The Bancroft Library, Univ of California, Berkeley, Berkeley, CA 94720-6000. **EMAIL** cfaulhab@library.berkeley.edu

FEAL, CARLOS
PERSONAL Born 03/06/1935, La Coruna, Spain **DISCIPLINE** SPANISH **EDUCATION** Univ Madrid, PhD(Romance lang), 63. **CAREER** Lectr Span, Univ Lyon, 60-61 & Univ Nantes, 63-66; asst prof, Univ Mich, Ann Arbor, 66-69; assoc prof, 69-75, prof Span, State Univ NY Buffalo, 75-, fac res fels, Univ Mich, 69 & State Univ NY, 70, 74 & 79. **MEMBERSHIPS** MLA; Am Asn Teachers Span & Port. **RESEARCH** Modern Spanish literature; Golden Age Drama. **SELECTED PUBLICATIONS** Auth, La poesia de Pedro Salinas, Gredos, Madrid, 65; Eros y Lorca, Edhasa, Barcelona, 73; Unamuno: El Otro y Don Juan, Planeta, Madrid, 76; auth, Ennombre de Don Juan Estructura de un mito literario, John Benjamins, Amsterdam, 84; Lorca: Tragedia y mito, Dovehouse, Ottawa, 89; ed, Miguel de Unamuno, El resentimiento tragico de la vida, Notas sobre la revolucion y guerra civil espanolas, Alianza, Matrit, 91; coauth, Painting on the Page: Interartistic Approaches to Modern Hispanic Texts, SUNY Press, Albany, 95; auth, Poesia y narrativa de Petro Salinas, Gredos, Madrid, 00. **CONTACT ADDRESS** Dept of Mod Lang & Lit, SUNY, Buffalo, PO Box 604620, Buffalo, NY 14260-4620. **EMAIL** feal@acsu.buffalo.edu

FEAL, GISELE C.
PERSONAL Born 07/05/1939, Froges, France, 2 children **DISCIPLINE** SPANISH, FRENCH **EDUCATION** Univ Grenoble, France, Lic es Lett, 62; Sorbonne, Agreg l'Univ, 65; Unich Mich, PhD(French), 72. **CAREER** Prof Span, Nantes, France, 65-66; asst prof French, Eastern Mich Univ, 67-68; lectr French, Univ Mich, 68-69; Prof French & Span, State Univ Col Buffalo, 73-, Dir, NY State Span Hon Soc; fel, Res Found, State Univ NY. **MEMBERSHIPS** MLA; Am Asn Teachers Fr; Am Asn Teachers Span. **RESEARCH** Psychoanalytically oriented criticism of Spanish and French literature. **SELECTED PUBLICATIONS** Auth, La Mythologie matriarcale chez Claudel, Montherlant, Crommelynck, Ionesco et Genet, Peter Lang, New York, 93; Le Theatre onirique d'Eugene Ionesco, Un itineraire psychologique editions Imago, Paris, 00. **CONTACT ADDRESS** Dept of Foreign Lang, SUNY, Col at Buffalo, 1300 Elmwood Ave, Buffalo, NY 14222-1095. **EMAIL** Fealgc@buffalo.state.ede

FEAL, ROSEMARY GEISDORFER
PERSONAL Born, NY **DISCIPLINE** SPANISH **EDUCATION** Instituto Belga Guatemalteco, Bachillerato en Letras, 72; Univ Paul Valery, Diplome d'Etudes Francaises, 76; Allegheny Col, BA (magna cum laude), 77; State Univ of NYork at Buffalo, PhD (with distinction), 84. **CAREER** Lectr, Canisius Col, 82-86; asst prof of Spanish, Univ of Rochester, 87-90, assoc Prof of Spanish, 90-96, prof of Spanish, 96-98; Prof of Spanish, State Univ of NY, 99-. **HONORS AND AWARDS** Grad School Fel, 80, Excellence in Tchg Awd, Univ at Buffalo, 80; Mellon postdoctoral Fel, 86-87, Bridging Fel with Art Hist, 89, Outstanding Woman Awd, Univ of Rochester, 98; grant for publication, Ministerio de Cultura, 94; resident fel, Humanities Inst, Univ at Stony Brook, 97. **MEMBERSHIPS** MLA; Feministas Unidas, Asociacion de Literatura Hispanica Femenina, Latin Am Studies Asn, Afro-Latin Am Res Asn. **RESEARCH** Latin American Lit with specialization in: Afro-Hispanic Lit; contemporary novel; women's writing; autobiographical studies; feminist theory; queer theory. **SELECTED PUBLICATIONS** Auth, Novel Lives: The Fictional Autobiographies of Guillermo Cabrera Infante and Mario Vargas Llosa, Univ of NC Studies in the Romance Languages and Lits, 86; The Double Bind: Feminism and Afro-Hispanism, Afro-Hispanic Rev, 91; Feminist Interventions in the Race for Theory: Neither Black Nor White, Afro-Hispanic Rev, 91; Latin American Feminist Criticism and the Realm of the Real, Letras Femeninas, 94; coauth, Painting on the Page: Interartistic Approaches to Modern Hispanic Texts, State Univ of NY Press, 95. **CONTACT ADDRESS** Dept of Modern Lang and Lit, SUNY, Buffalo, 910 Clemens Hall, Buffalo, NY 14260. **EMAIL** efeal@acsu.buffalo.edu

FEARS, J. RUFUS
PERSONAL Born 03/07/1945, Atlanta, GA, m, 1966, 2 children **DISCIPLINE** CLASSICS; HISTORY **EDUCATION** Emory Univ, BA, 66; Harvard Univ, MA, 67, PhD, 71. **CAREER** Asst Prof Classical Lang, Tulane Univ, 71-72; from Asst Prof to Prof Hist, Ind Univ, 72-86; Prof Classics and Dept Chair, Boston Univ, 86-90; Prof Classics, 90-92, G.T. and Libby Blankenship Prof Classics, Univ Okla, 92-, Dean Col Arts & Sci, 90-92. **HONORS AND AWARDS** Woodrow Wilson Fel, 66-67; Danforth Fel, 66-71; Harvard Prize Fel, 66-71; Sheldon Traveling Fel, 69-71; Fel of the Am Acad in Rome, 69-71; Howard Found Fel, 77-78; Guggenheim Fel, 76-77; Alexander von Humboldt Fel, 77-78, 80-81; Distinguished Fac Res Lectr, Ind Univ, 80; NEH Fel, 86; Woodrow Wilson Ctr Fel, 86; ACLS Fel, 86; Nat Humanities Ctr Fel, 86; Wash Univ Ctr Hist Freedom Fel, 89-90; Judah P. Benjamin Nat Merit Awd, 96; 15 awards for outstanding teaching, 76-00; Univ of Okla Prof of Year, 96, 99. **MEMBERSHIPS** Phi Beta Kappa; Golden Key Nat Honor Soc; Am Philol Asn; Archaeol Inst Am; Classical Asn Middle West and South; Vergilian Soc; Soc for Classical Tradition. **RESEARCH** Ancient history; history of freedom. **SELECTED PUBLICATIONS** Auth, Atlantis and the Myth of the Minoan Thalassocracy, Atlantis: Fact of Fiction, 78; Princeps A Diis Electus, 77; The Cult of Jupiter and Roman Imperial Ideology, 81; The Theology of Victory at Rome, 81; The Cult of Virtues and Roman Imperial Ideology, 81; Roman Liberty, 80; Gottesgnadentum, Reallexikon fur Antike und Christentum XI, 81; Herrscherkult, Reallexikon fur Antike und Christentum XIV, 88; Selected Writings of Lord Acton (3 vols), 85-88; Michael Rostovtzeff, Classical Scholarship: A Biographical Encyclopedia, 90; Antiquity: The Model of Rome, An Uncertain Legacy: Essays in Pursuit of Liberty, 97; Natural Law: The Legacy of Greece and Rome, Common Truths, 00; The Lessons of Rome for Our Own Day, Preparing America's Foreign Policy for the 21st Century, 99. **CONTACT ADDRESS** Dept of Classics, Univ of Oklahoma, Norman, OK 73019. **EMAIL** jrfears@ou.edu

FEDERMAN, RAYMOND
PERSONAL Born 05/15/1928, Paris, France, m, 1960, 1 child **DISCIPLINE** ENGLISH, COMPARATIVE LITERATURE **EDUCATION** Columbia Univ, BS, 57; Univ Calif, MA, 59, PhD, 63. **CAREER** Tchg asst French, Univ CA, Los Angeles, 57-59; lectr, Univ CA, Santa Barbara, 59-62, asst prof, 62-64; from Assoc Prof to Prof French, 64-68, Prof English & Comp Lit, 73-90, Distinguished Prof Eng and Comp Lit, State Univ NY-Buffalo, 90-, Melodia E. Jones Ch of Lit, 94-; mem bd consult, Coord Coun Lit Mags, 73-76. **HONORS AND AWARDS** Guggenheim fel, 66-67; Frances Steloff Fiction Prize, 71; Panache Exp Fiction Prize, 72; Fulbright Fel, Israel, 82-83; NEH Fel/Fiction, 86; Am Bk Awd, 86; DAAD Fel, Berlin, 89-90. **MEMBERSHIPS** PEN Am; MLA; Am Comp Lit Asn; Am Asn Tchr(s) Fr. **RESEARCH** Twentieth century French lit; contemp fiction; creative writing. **SELECTED PUBLICATIONS** Auth, Double or nothing (novel), 71 & ed, Surfiction (essays on modern fiction), 75, Swallow; auth, Amer Eldorado (novel), Ed Stock, 74; Take it or leave it (novel), Fiction Collective, 76; Me too (poems), Westcoast Rev, 76; co-ed, Cahier de L'herne: Samuel Beckett, Eds L'Herne Paris-France, 77; auth, Imagination as plagiarism, New Lit Hist, 77; The voice in the closet (fiction), Tri-Quart, 77; The Two Fold Vilration (novel), Ind Univ Press, 82; Smiles on Washington Square, 85; To Whom it May Concern, 90; CRITIFICTION, 94; La Fourrure de oya Tante Rachel, 96. **CONTACT ADDRESS** Dept of Eng, SUNY, Buffalo, PO Box 604610, Buffalo, NY 14260-4610. **EMAIL** moinous@aol.com

FEIN, DAVID
PERSONAL Born 05/15/1949, Cambridge, MA, m, 1971, 3 children **DISCIPLINE** FRENCH **EDUCATION** Brown Univ, BA, 71; Cornell Univ, PhD, 76. **CAREER** Asst prof, Univ NC, Greensboro, 77-81, assoc prof, 81-90; prof, 90-; head, dept of romance lang, 96-00. **HONORS AND AWARDS** Phi Beta Kappa; NC AATF; Teacher of the Year, 95. **MEMBERSHIPS** Am Asn of Teachers French; Southeastern Medieval Asn; MLA. **RESEARCH** Medieval French lyric poetry; 15th-century French literature. **SELECTED PUBLICATIONS** Auth, "Time and Timelessness in Villon's Testament," Neophilogus (87); auth, Francois Villon and His Reader, Wayne State Univ Press, 89; auth, "Joined Hearts and Severed Tongues," Philological Quarterly (92); auth, "Villon on the Road to Emmaus," Fifteenth-Century Studies (92); auth, "Authorial Reliability in the Twelfth-Century French Narrative," Philological Quarterly (92); auth, "Audience Collusion in Twelfth-Century French Narrative," Neophilologus (92); auth, "Problematic Aspects of Narrative Authority in Twelfth-Century French literature," French Review (93); auth, "Acts of Nature and Preternatural Acts in Le Journal d' un bourgeois de Paris," Fifteenth-Century Studies (93); auth, Francois Villon Revisited, Twayne Publishers, 97; auth, Architextes, Harcourt Brace, 97; auth, "Representations of the Female Body in the Cent Nouvelles Nouvelles," Romance Notes (99); auth, "Guyot Marchant's Danse Macabre: The Relationship Between Image and Text," Mirator (00). **CONTACT ADDRESS** Dept of Romance Lang, Univ of No Carolina, Greensboro, 1000 Spring Garden St., Greensboro, NC 27412-0001. **EMAIL** dafein@uncg.edu

FEINBERG, LAWRENCE E.
PERSONAL Born 11/13/1941, New York, NY, m, 1994 **DISCIPLINE** SLAVIC LINGUISTICS **EDUCATION** Middlbury Col, BA, 62; Harvard Univ, MA, 64; PhD, 69. **CAREER** Asst prof, Univ of Colo, 67-70; asst prof to assoc prof, Univ of NC Chapel Hill, 70-. **HONORS AND AWARDS** IREX Summer Exchange, USSR, 81. **MEMBERSHIPS** Ling Soc of Am; Am Assoc for the Advan of Slavic Studies. **RESEARCH** Comparative Slavic linguistics, history and structure of Russian, Russian poetics, 19th/20th century Russian Poetry. **SELECTED PUBLICATIONS** Auth, "Measure and Complementarity in Akhmatova", Russ Lit 5 (77): 303-14; auth, "The Morphology of Russian Imperfective Derivation", Slavic and E Europ J 24.2 (80): 145-54; coauth, "Development and Stasis in Blok's 'O doblestjax, o podvigax, o slave'", Int J of Slavic Ling and Poetics 23 (81): 133-46; auth, "Theme and Desinence in Common Slavic Declension" Studia Slavica Hungarica 27 (81): 270-80; auth, "Of Two Minds: Linear vs. Non-Linear in Blok" in Aleksandr Blok Centenary Conference, ed Walter N. Vicery and B. Sagatov, Columbus (82): 141-58; auth, "Stem Structure, Hierarchy and Russian Verbal Accent", in New Studies in Russ Lang and Lit Presented to Bayara Aroutunova, ed C.V. Chvany and A.L. Crone, Columbus (87): 104-16; auth, "Markedness and the typology of Russian Verb Stems", in Towards a Calculus of Meaning: Studies in Markedness, Distinctive Features and Deixis, Amsterdam-Philadelphia, (96): 140-58; auth, "An Automorphic Model of Paradigm Structure. Toward a New Model of Russian Case Morphology", J of Slavic Ling 5.1, (97): 51-79; auth, "The Automorphism of Slavic Declension in Synchronic and Diachronic Perspective", in Am Contributions to the Twelfth Int Congress of Slavists, ed R.A. Maguire and A. Timberlake, Bloomington (98): 326-43; auth, "Slavistics in the U.S. : 1945-1995", Slavistics in Non-Slavic Countries (forthcoming). **CONTACT ADDRESS** Dept Slavic Lang and Lit, Univ of No Carolina, Chapel Hill, 440 W Franklin St, Chapel Hill, NC 27599-2319. **EMAIL** lfeinber@email.unc.edu

FELDER, MIRA B.
PERSONAL Born 05/05/1938, Poland, m, 1959, 3 children **DISCIPLINE** LINGUISTICS, ENGLISH **EDUCATION** Brooklyn Col, BA; Temple Univ, MA. **CAREER** Asst prof, Touro Col, New York, NY, 78-, E. S. L. Divisional Officer, 78-, assoc dean, 91-. **SELECTED PUBLICATIONS** Coauth, Light and Lively, 2nd ed, Addison Wesley Longman (97); coauth, Laugh and Learn, 2nd ed, Addison Wesley Longman (97). **CONTACT ADDRESS** Dept Lang & Lit, Touro Col, New York, 27 W 23rd St #33, New York, NY 10010-4202.

FELDMAN, LOUIS H.
PERSONAL Born 10/29/1926, Hartford, CT, m, 1966, 3 children **DISCIPLINE** CLASSICAL STUDIES **EDUCATION** Trinity Col, BA, 46; Trinity Col, MA, 47; Harvard Univ, PhD, 51. **CAREER** Instr, Harvard Sem Found, 51-52; Instr, Trinity Col, 52-53; Instr, Hobart and William Smith Cols, 53-55; Instr, Yeshiva and Stern Cols, 55-56; Asst Prof, Yeshiva Col, 55-61; Assoc Prof, Yeshiva Col, 61-66; Prof, Yeshiva Univ, 66-. **HONORS AND AWARDS** Guggenheim Found Fel; Senior Fel, Am Coun of Learned Soc; Awd for Excellence, Am Philol Asn, 81; Judaica Ref Book Awd, Asn of Jewish Libr, 85; Fel, Annenberg Acad for Jewish Res, 93; Fel, Inst for Advancaed Study, Princeton, 94. **MEMBERSHIPS** Am Acad for Jewish Res, Assoc for Jewish Studies, Am Philol Asn, Soc of Bibl Lit. **RESEARCH** Hellenistic Judaism, especially Josephus. **SELECTED PUBLICATIONS** Auth, Scholarship on Philo and Josephus (1937-1962), Yeshiva Univ Pr (New York, NY), 63; auth, Josephus and Modern Scholarship (1937-1980), de Gruyter (Berlin, Germany), 84; ed, Josephan Studies (Japanese), 4 vols, Yamamoto Shoten (Tokyo, Japan), 85-86; auth, Josephus: A Supplementary Bibliography, Garland (New York, NY), 86; ed, Josephus, Judaism and Christianity, Wayne st Univ Pr (Detroit, MI), 87; ed, Josephus, The Bible and History, Wayne St Univ Pr (Detroit, MI), 89; auth, Jew and Gentile in the Ancient World: Attitudes and Interactions from Alexander to Justinian, Princeton Univ Pr, 93; auth, Studies in Hellenistic Judaism, Brill (Leiden), 96; coauth, Jewish Life and Thought Among Greeks and Romans: Primary Readings, Fortress Pr (Minneapolis, MN), 96; ed, Josephus' Contra Apionem: Studies in its Character and Context with a Latin Concordance to the Portion Missin in Greek, Brill (Leiden), 96; auth, Studies in Josephus' Rewritten Bible (Leiden: Brill) 96; auth Josephus's Interpretation of the Bible, (Berkeley: Univ Ca Pr) 98; auth, Flavius Josephus, Judean Antiquities 1-4: Translation and Commentary, (Leiden: Brill) 00. **CONTACT ADDRESS** Dept Humanities, Yeshiva Univ, 500 W 185th St, New York, NY 10033-3201. **EMAIL** lfeldman@ymail.yu.edu

FELDSTEIN, RONALD FRED
PERSONAL Born 08/15/1947, Newark, NJ, m, 1975, 2 children **DISCIPLINE** SLAVIC LINGUISTICS, RUSSIAN **EDUCATION** Princeton Univ, MA, 69, PhD (Slavic lang), 73. **CAREER** Instr Russian and ling, State Univ NY, Binghamton, 69-73, asst prof, 73-76, dir, Critical Lang Prog, 74-76; asst prof, 76-80, Assoc Prof Slavic Ling, Ind Univ, 80-, Co-dir Slavic workshop, Ind Univ, Bloomington, 78-81. **MEMBERSHIPS** Am Asn Teachers of Slavic and East Europ Lang. **RESEARCH** Slavic accentology; Slavic historical phonology; contemporary Slavic phonology. **SELECTED PUBLICATIONS CONTACT ADDRESS** 603 Plymouth Rd, Bloomington, IN 47401.

FELLBAUM, CHRISTIANE
DISCIPLINE FRENCH, GERMAN **EDUCATION** Northeastern Univ, BA; Princeton Univ, PhD. **CAREER** Res staff, Princeton Univ, 87-; vis scholar, LADL, Univ Paris, 86-88; assoc prof, 80-. **MEMBERSHIPS** Mem, ed bd ling jour(s). **SELECTED PUBLICATIONS** Auth, articles, Intl Jour Lexicography, Revue Quebecoise de Linguistique, Revue Linguistique de Vincennes, The Psychol Rev. **CONTACT ADDRESS** Dept of Art and Sci, Westfield State Col, 577 Western Ave., Westfield, MA 01085.

FELSTINER, JOHN
PERSONAL Born 07/05/1936, Mt. Vernon, NY, m, 1966, 2 children **DISCIPLINE** LITERARY TRANSLATION, MODERN POETRY; JEWISH LITERATURE **EDUCATION** Harvard Col, AB, 58--Magna Cum Laude and Class Odist, PhD, 65. **RESEARCH** Poetry; Art; Music from The Holocaust; Poetry and the Environment. **SELECTED PUBLICATIONS** Auth, Celan, Paul--Holograms of Darkness, Compar Lit, Vol 45, 93; Translation as Reversion--Celan, Paul Jerusalem Poems, Judaism, Vol 43, 94. **CONTACT ADDRESS** Dept of English, Stanford Univ, 660 Salvatierra St, Stanford, CA 94305-2087. **EMAIL** felstiner@stanford.edu

FENVES, PETER
DISCIPLINE GERMAN **EDUCATION** Johns Hopkins Univ, PhD. **CAREER** Prof German, Northwestern Univ; Dir of Graduate Stud. **SELECTED PUBLICATIONS** Auth, A Peculiar Fate: Metaphysics and World-History in Kant; Chatter: Language and History in Kierkegaard; ed, Raising the Tone of Philosophy: Late Essays by Kant, Transformative Critique by Derrida; essays and articles on, Marx; Kant; George Eliot; Nietzsche; Adorno; Benjamin; Jan-Luc Nancy; Kierkegaard; Kleist; H"lderlin; auth, "From an Awkward Perspective: Essays on Literature, Philosophy, and Legal Theory from Leibniz to Irigaray. **CONTACT ADDRESS** Dept of German, Northwestern Univ, 1801 Hinman, Evanston, IL 60208. **EMAIL** p-fenves@nwu.edu

FERGUSON, MARGARET WILLIAMS
PERSONAL Born 12/28/1948, Columbus, OH **DISCIPLINE** ENGLISH LITERATURE, COMPARATIVE LITERATURE **EDUCATION** Cornell Univ, BA, 69; Yale Univ, MPhil, 72, PhD (comp lit), 74. **CAREER** ASST PROF ENGLISH, YALE UNIV, 74-, Morse fel, Yale Univ, 77-78. **MEMBERSHIPS** MLA; Shakespeare Asn Am. **RESEARCH** Renaissance litera-

ture; literary theory. **SELECTED PUBLICATIONS** Auth, Dangerous Familiars--Representations of Domestic Crime in England, 1550-1700, Mod Philol, Vol 94, 96. **CONTACT ADDRESS** Dept English, Univ of California, Davis, 1 Shields Ave, Davis, CA 95616-5271.

FERGUSON, WILLIAM ROTCH
PERSONAL Born 02/14/1943, Fall River, MA, m, 1983 **DISCIPLINE** SPANISH **EDUCATION** Harvard Univ, BA, 65, MA, 70, PhD, 75. **CAREER** Clark Univ, Worcester, Assoc Prof Spanish, 83, Asst Prof, 79-83, Vis Prof, 77-79; Adjunct Prof Eng, 89, Univ PA, Philadelphia, Vis Lectr Spanish Renaissance Lit, 86-87; Assoc Ed, 86-87, Hispanic Review; Asst Prof Spanish, 75-77, Inst Spanish, 71-75, Boston Univ. **HONORS AND AWARDS** Don Membership, Phi Beta Kappa; Clark Chapter, Sigma Delta Pi, (Spanish Natl Hon Soc), 87. **MEMBERSHIPS** AAUP; MLA; NEMLA; Intl Inst in Spain; Assoc Intl del Siglo de Oro. **RESEARCH** Spanish Lit, espec Golden Age and 20th Century; Latin Am Lit; Creative Writing in Eng. **SELECTED PUBLICATIONS** Auth, La versificacion imitativa en Fernando de Herrera, London: Tamesis, 81; Freedom and Other Fictions, New York, Knopf, 84; A De lo suave a lo aspero: Notas sobre las estetica de Herrera, Revista de Estudios Hispanicos, Universidad de Puerto Ricom, Rio Piedras, 81; I Was Not Always A Magician, Mississippi Review, Hattiesburg, MS, 80; Space Invaders, Fiction NY vol 6 no 3, 81; Aubade, Canto, Andover, MA, vol 3, no 2, 80; On The Beach, Harvard Advocate, civ, 1, 70; Poem For Mirko In Which He Appears Near the End, Sumac, 69. **CONTACT ADDRESS** Clark Univ, Estabrook 302, Worcester, MA 01610. **EMAIL** wferguson@clarku.edu

FERNANDEZ-OLMOS, MARGARITE
PERSONAL Born 02/24/1949, New York, NY, m, 1973 **DISCIPLINE** SPANISH LANGUAGE, LINGUISTICS **EDUCATION** Montclair State Col, BA, 70; NY Univ in Spain, MA, 72; NY Univ, PhD, 79. **CAREER** Lectr, NYork Univ, 72-76; adj lectr, Hostos Community Col, 73-76; adj lectr, Fordham Univ, 75-76; instr to prof, Brooklyn Col, 76-. **HONORS AND AWARDS** Ford Found Fel, 70-75; Penfield Fel, NY Univ 77; Ford Fel, Princeton, 85-86; PSC-CUNY Res Awd, 86, 88, 90, 92-94; Wolf Inst Fac Fel, Brooklyn Col, 93-94; Res Grant, Recovering the US Hispanic Literary Heritage Project, 96. **RESEARCH** Spanish language and linguistics, Latin American and Caribbean Literatures and Cultures; U.S. Latino Studies, Afro-Caribbean Culture, Latin American Women's Writing. **SELECTED PUBLICATIONS** Coed, Contemporary Women Authors of Latin America: Introductory Essays and New Translations, (NY: Brooklyn Col Pr, 83); auth, Sobre la literatura puertorriquena de aqui y de alla: aproximachiones feministas, (Santo Domingo: Editora Alfa y Omega, 89); coed, El Placer de la palabra: literatura erotica femenina de America Latina (antologia critica)", (Mexico: Editorial Planeta Mexicana, 91); coed, Pleasure in the Word: Erotic Writings by Latin American Women, (NY: White Pine Pr, 93), coed, cotransl, of "Remaking a Lost Harmony: Short Stories from the Hispanic Caribbean", (NY: White Pine Pr, 95); coed, The Latino Reader: An American Literary Tradition from 1542 to the Present, (NY: Houghton Mifflin, 97); coed, Sacred Possessions: Vodou, Santeria, Obeah and the Caribbean, (NJ: Rutgers Univ Pr, 97); auth, Rudolfo A. Anaya: A Critical Companion, Greenwood Pr, (Westport), 99; coauth, Healing Cultures: Art and Religion as Curative Practices in the Caribbean and its Diaspora, St. Martins Pr, 00; coauth, U.S. Latino Literature: A Critical Guide for Students and Teachers, Greenwood Pr, 00. **CONTACT ADDRESS** Dept Modern Lang, Brooklyn Col, CUNY, 2901 Bedford Ave, Brooklyn, NY 11210-2813. **EMAIL** mfolmos@aol.com

FERNANDEZCIFUENTES, L.
PERSONAL Born 07/31/1945, Leon, Spain, m, 1995, 2 children **DISCIPLINE** HISPANIC LITERATURES **EDUCATION** Madrid Univ, MA, 70; Princeton Univ, PhD, 76. **CAREER** Asst prof, 76-83, assoc prof, 83-88, Princeton Univ; prof, Harvard Univ, 88-. **RESEARCH** Hispanic literatures. **SELECTED PUBLICATIONS** Ed, Los majos de Cadiz, Cadiz, 98; ed, Don Juan Tenorio, Barcelona, 93; auth, Garcia Lorca en el teatro: la norma y la diferencia, Zaragoza, 83; auth, Teoria y mercado de la novela en Espana, Madrid, 83. **CONTACT ADDRESS** Harvard Univ, 516 Boylston Hall, Cambridge, MA 02138. **EMAIL** cifuent@fas.harvard.edu

FERRAN, OFELIA
DISCIPLINE SPANISH AND PORTUGUESE LITERATURE **EDUCATION** Syracuse Univ, BA, 88; Cornell Univ, PhD, 97. **RESEARCH** Contemporary Spanish peninsular literature; contemporary Spanish women writers; exile literature; narrative constructions and representations of memory; autobiography. **SELECTED PUBLICATIONS** Auth, 'Cuatro anos en Pares', de Victoria Kent: la 'doble voz' en la escritura femenina del exilio, 98; La escritura y la historia: Entrevista con Paloma Deaz-Mas, 9 de diciembre, 1995, 97; 'Una palabra, ya sabes: un cadaver': la poetica del trauma en Paul Celan, 95; Ekfrasis y Exilio: dos versiones de 'un amor interrumpido', 94. **CONTACT ADDRESS** Spanish and Portuguese Dept, Univ of Minnesota, Twin Cities, 34 Folwell Hall, 9 Pleasant St SE, Minneapolis, MN 55455. **EMAIL** ferra007@tc.umn.edu

FERRANTE, JOAN M.
PERSONAL Born 11/11/1936, Jersey City, NJ **DISCIPLINE** COMPARATIVE MEDIEVAL LITERATURE **EDUCATION** Barnard Col, Columbia Univ, BA, 58; Columbia Univ, MA, 59, PhD(comp medieval lit), 63. **CAREER** From asst prof to assoc prof, 66-74, dir, Casa Italiana, 78-80, PROF ENGLISH & COMP LIT, COLUMBIA UNIV, 74-, Am Coun Learned Soc fel, 69-70; Adv Bd, Speculum, Medieval Acad Am, 75-78; Consult Ed, Records of Civilization, Columbia Univ Press, 75-; Nat Endowment for Humanities fel, 80-81. **MEMBERSHIPS** Mediaeval Acad Am; Renaissance Soc Am; Dante Soc Am (vpres, 79-82); Int Arthurian Soc. **RESEARCH** Medieval romance and allegory; Dante; Provencal poetry. **SELECTED PUBLICATIONS** Coauth, introd to & transl, The Lais of Marie de France, Dutton, 78; auth, Narrative patterns in the Decameron, Romance Philol, 78; Florence and Rome, the Two Cities of Man, In: Divine Comedy, Acta, Binghampton Conf Early Renaissance, 78; Ab joi mou lo vers e'l comens, The Interpretation of the Medieval Lyric, Macmillan, 79; Artist Figures in the Tristan Stories, Tristania, 79; Some thoughts on the application of modern critical methods to medieval literature, Yrbk Comp & Gen Lit, 28; The education of women in the middle ages in theory, fact and fantasy, In: Beyond Their Sex, Learned Women of the European Past, NY Univ, 80; Cortes' Amor in Medieval Texts, Speculum, 80. **CONTACT ADDRESS** Dept of English & Comp Lit, 2960 Broadway, New York, NY 10027-6900.

FERREIRA, DEBORA R. S.
PERSONAL Born 07/29/1964, Recife, PE, Brazil, m, 1987, 2 children **DISCIPLINE** CLASSICS **EDUCATION** Univ Fed de Pern, BA, 89; Univ Ga, MA, 94; PhD, 99. **CAREER** Res asst, Univ Fed de Pern, 88-92; teaching asst to instr, Univ Ga, 92-. **HONORS AND AWARDS** Grad Sch Asstshp, 99; Outstanding Teaching Awd, 94; Merit Awd, 94-95; Hon Soc Phi Kappa Phi; Hon Soc Phi Lambda Beta; Res Asstshp, 88-91. **MEMBERSHIPS** AATSP; BSA; MLA; SAMLA; ALFH. **RESEARCH** Latin American novel; post-colonial studies, negotiating power; feminist theory, gender relations; literary and cultural relations in the Lusephone world; production of teaching media. **SELECTED PUBLICATIONS** Auth, "O Imaginario Nacionalistico na Obra Clarice Lispector," Romance Lang Ann (98): 472-73; auth, "Carolina Maria de Jesus and Clarice Lispector: Constructing Brazil and Brasileiras," Torre de Papel. **CONTACT ADDRESS** Dept Romance Lang, Univ of Georgia, Gilbert Hall, Athens, GA 30602-1815. **EMAIL** ferreira@arches.uga.edu

FERRIOL, ANTONIA
PERSONAL Born 10/04/1969, Spain, s **DISCIPLINE** LITERATURE, LANGUAGE, SPANISH **EDUCATION** Univ de la Islas, Lic, 92; Pa State Univ, PhD, 98. **CAREER** Grad teaching asst, Pa State Univ, 93-98; vis asst prof, Middlebury Col, 98-99; asst prof, Denison Univ, 99-01. **HONORS AND AWARDS** Distinguished Fel, Pa State Univ, 96-97. **MEMBERSHIPS** MLA; ALFH; ISLHHS. **RESEARCH** Contemporary Spanish novel and humor; women novels; teaching methodologies and culture. **CONTACT ADDRESS** Dept Modern Lang, Denison Univ, Granville, OH 43023. **EMAIL** ferriol@denison.edu

FETZER, GLENN W.
PERSONAL Born 09/20/1955, Woodbury, NJ, m, 1985 **DISCIPLINE** FRENCH **EDUCATION** CUNY Grad Sch, PhD, 88. **CAREER** Asst de langue anglaise, Lycee Jacques Decours, Paris, 85-86; inst, King's Col, 84-85, 86-87; asst prof, assoc prof, French Calvin Col, 87- . **MEMBERSHIPS** Am Assoc Tchrs Fr; Int Assoc Philos and Lit. **RESEARCH** Contemporary French poetry. **SELECTED PUBLICATIONS** Auth, Immutability and Change in the Poetics of Emmanuel Hocquard, in Romance Lang Annual, 93; auth, Dream Imagery and the Dialectics of Consciousness in Andre du Boucher's 'et la nuit,' in LitteRealite, 94; auth, Memory, Absence, and the Consciousness of Self in the Novels of Mehdi Charef, in CLA J, 95; auth, Avenement de la parole: Illusion et Realite Chez Anne Teyssieras et Celine Zins, in Thirty Voices in the Feminine, Rodopi, 96; auth, Andre du Bouchet: Imaging the Real, Seeing the Unseeable, in, Nottingham, in Fr Stud, 96; auth, Finding One's Way: Poetry and the Mind's Eye in the Work of Celine Zins, in Romance Notes, 98; auth, Le Shakespeare d'Emmanuel Hocquard, in ALFA, 97/98; auth, French Poetry of Our Time: Crisis and Response, in Literature and the Renewal of the Public Sphere, Macmillan, 00; auth, Palimpsests of the Real in Recent French Poetry, Rodopi, 01. **CONTACT ADDRESS** Dept of French, Calvin Col, 3201 Burton St SE, Grand Rapids, MI 49546. **EMAIL** fetzer@calvin.edu

FETZER, JOHN FRANCIS
PERSONAL m, 2 children **DISCIPLINE** GERMAN **EDUCATION** NYork Univ, AB, 53; Columbia Univ, MA, 57; Univ Calif, Berkeley, PhD(Ger), 65. **CAREER** Instr Ger, Northwestern Univ, 62-65; from asst prof to assoc prof, 65-76, PROF GER LANG & LIT, EMERITUS, UNIV CA, DAVIS, 76-93; Chmn, Dept Ger & Russ, 81-84, 96-97, Am Philos Soc & Humanities Inst fels, 69-70; vis prof: Dartmouth, 76, Univ Exeter, 89-90; retired, 93. **HONORS AND AWARDS** Fulbright, 54, 80, 89; Am Phil Soc & Humanities Inst fels, 69-70; Guggenheim 80-81. **MEMBERSHIPS** MLA; Am Asn Teachers Ger; Ger Studies Asn. **RESEARCH** German Romanticism; relationships between music and literature; modern German lit. **SELECTED PUBLICATIONS** Auth, Ritter Gluck's Ungluck: The crisis of creativity in the Age of Epigone, 71, Ger Quart; Schatten ohne Frau: Marginalia on a Werther motif, Ger Rev, 71; The scales of injustice: Comments on Heinrich Boll's Die Waage der Baleks, Ger Quart, 72; Recent trends in Clemens Brentano research (1968-1970), Lit Wiss Jahrbuch, 72; Romantic Orpheus: Profiles of Clemens Brentano, Univ Calif, 74; Paul Elbogen, In: Deutsche Exilliteratur I, Francke, 76; coauth, Bibliographie der Buchrezensionen fur deutsche Literatur, Univ Microfilms, 77; Clemens Brentano, Twayne, 81; On the Threshold of German Romanticism, in Englishand German Romanticism, winter 85; Ludwig Tieck, in European Writers: The Romantic Century, Scribner's, 85; From the Blue Flower to the True Blue, Anna Seghers' Variations on a Romantic Theme from her Exile Years in Mexico, in Literarische Wege zwischen den Kontinenten, Niemeyer, 85; Jakob: Guardian of the Musical Threshold, in Franz Grillparzer: Der Arme Spielmann, Wayne State, 88; Annette Kolb, in Deutschsprachige Exilliteratur seit 1933, Francke, 89; Romantic Irony, in European Romanticism: Literary Cross-Currents, Modes, and Models, Wayne State, 89; Music, Love, Death, and Doctor Faustus, Camden, 90; Mediation as Medication for the Romantic Malady?, in Romantik--eine lebendige Krnakheit, Rodopi, 91; Music on the Threshold of German Romanticism, in The Romantic Tradition, Univ Press, 92; Visconti's Cinematic version of Death in Venice, in Approaches to Teaching Mann's Death in Venice and Other Short Stories, MLA, 92; Die musikalische Muse und Annette Kolb, in Ich habe etwas zu sagen: Annette Kolb 1870-1967, Diederichs, 93; Mignon's Minions: ambroise Thomas' opera Mignon, in Goethe's Mignon und ihre Schwestern, Lang, 93; Das Drama der Romantik/Die romantische Lyrik, in Romantik-Handbuch, Jahrbuch des Freien Deutschen Hochstifts, 95; Changing Perspectives of Thomas Mann's Doctor Faustus: Criticism 1947-1992, Camden, 96; auth, Threshold Metaphors in Goethe's 'Werther' in Sweden. Germanistische Erkundungen einer Metapher, Konigshausen & Neumann 99; auth, Anna Katharina Emmerick als literarishces und geistiges Phanomen einer Schwellenzeit, in Anna Katharina Emmerick, Passio-Compassio-Mystik, 00. **CONTACT ADDRESS** Dept of Ger & Russ, Univ of California, Davis, Davis, CA 95616-8606. **EMAIL** jffetzer@ucdavis.edu

FICHTNER, EDWARD G.
PERSONAL Born 00/00/1931 **DISCIPLINE** GERMANIC PHILOLOGY, GERMAN LINGUISTICS **EDUCATION** Univ Ill, AB, 57; Ind Univ, MA, 60; Univ Pa, PhD (Ger), 66. **CAREER** Instr Ger, St Joseph's Col, Pa, 62-63 and Columbia Univ, 63-67; from asst prof to assoc prof, 67-77, Prof Ger, 78-95, emeritus, 95, adjunct prof, Dept of Foreign Langs, Sch of Continuing and Professional Studies, New York Univ, 97-, Mem Doctoral Fac Ger Lang, Grad Ctr, Queens Col, City Univ New York, 73-, Managing ed, Word, 80-83. **MEMBERSHIPS** MLA; Ling Soc Am; Int Ling Asn. **RESEARCH** Structure of modern German; medieval German literature; medieval Scandinavian language and literature. **SELECTED PUBLICATIONS** Auth, English and German Syntax, Munich, 79; auth, Cleft Sentences in English, A Comprehensive View, Word J Int Ling Assoc, Vol 44, 93. **CONTACT ADDRESS** Dept of Germantic and Slavic Langs, Queens Col, CUNY, P O Box 022301, Brooklyn, NY 11202-2301. **EMAIL** edgefine@compuserve.com

FIDO, FRANCO
PERSONAL Born 07/15/1931, Venice, Italy, m, 1958, 2 children **DISCIPLINE** ITALIAN AND COMPARATIVE LITERATURE **EDUCATION** Univ Pisa, DLett(Ital lit), 53; Ital govt, Lib Doc, 69; Brown Univ, MA, 71. **CAREER** French govt fel, Sorbonne, 53-54; lectr Ital, Faculte des Lett, Dijon, 54-58; instr, Univ Calif, Berkeley, 58-61; lectr, Faculte des Lett, Grenoble, 61-63; from asst prof to prof Ital, Univ Calif, Los Angeles, 63-69, chmn dept, 66-69; prof, Brown Univ, 69-78; R Pierotti prof Ital lit, Stanford Univ, 78-79; Univ Prof, Brown Univ, 79-. **MEMBERSHIPS** MLA; Am Asn Teachers Ital; Dante Soc Am; Am Soc 18th Century Studies. **RESEARCH** Italian literature and theatre from the 18th to the 20th century; Boccaccio; Italian Renaissance, especially Machiavelli. **SELECTED PUBLICATIONS** Auth, Goldoni, Carlo and Voltaire, Revue D Histoire Du Theatre, Vol 45, 93; The Philosophes, America and the Indians, Rivista Di Letterature Moderne E Comparate, Vol 48, 95; Aspects of Baretti, Giuseppe, Marcantonio English Works--Didactics and So Called Nonsense, Invective and Theater, Rivista Di Letterature Moderne E Comparate, Vol 46, 93. **CONTACT ADDRESS** Dept of Hisp and Ital Studies, Brown Univ, Providence, RI 02512.

FIEDLER, THEODORE
PERSONAL Born 10/01/1942, Altenburg, MO, m, 1963, 1 child **DISCIPLINE** GERMAN, LANGUAGE AND LITERATURE **EDUCATION** Washington Univ, AB, 64, MA(Ger) and MA(comp lit), 66; Univ Tubingen, PhD (Ger), 69. **CAREER** Asst prof, Univ Calif, Irvine, 68-75; assoc prof, Univ Tex, San Antonio, 76-77; Assoc Prof Ger, Univ KY, 77-, Fulbright fel, 66-68; Am Philos Soc grant-in-aid, 73. **MEMBERSHIPS** MLA; Int Brecht Soc; Semiotic Soc Am. **RESEARCH** Twentieth century German literature and literary theory; poetics; film.

SELECTED PUBLICATIONS Auth, Continuity and New Beginning Colloquia Germanica Past and Present, Colloquia Germanica, Vol 26, 93. **CONTACT ADDRESS** Dept of Ger, Univ of Kentucky, 500 S Limestone St, Lexington, KY 40506-0003.

FIELD, NORMA
DISCIPLINE PREMODERN JAPANESE POETRY AND PROSE **EDUCATION** IN Univ, MA, 74; Princeton Univ, PhD, 83. **CAREER** Lit, Univ Mich. **SELECTED PUBLICATIONS** Auth, And Then, La State Univ press & Tokyo Univ Press, 78, The Splendor of Longing in the Tale of Genji, Princeton Univ Press, 78; In the Realm of a Dying Emperor, Pantheon, 93. **CONTACT ADDRESS** Univ of Chicago, 5801 S Ellis Ave, Chicago, IL 60637-5418. **EMAIL** n-field@uchicago.edu

FIELD, THOMAS TILDEN
PERSONAL Born 09/09/1949, Hardwick, VT, m, 1977, 2 children **DISCIPLINE** ROMANCE LINGUISTICS **EDUCATION** Wheaton Col, BA, 71; Cornell Univ, MA, 75, PhD (ling), 78. **CAREER** Instr French, State Univ NY Col Oswego, 78-79; prof Ling and French, Univ of MD, Baltimore County, 79-; dir, UMBC Cntr for the Humanities, 99-. **HONORS AND AWARDS** Gilbert Chinard Prize in Pedagogy, 82; Carnegie Case MD, Prof of Year, 96; UMBC pres tching prof, 92-95. **MEMBERSHIPS** Ling Soc Am; MLA; Am Asn Teachers French; Asn Int d'Etudes Occitanes. **RESEARCH** Occitan and French linguistics; textual analysis; literacy. **SELECTED PUBLICATIONS** Co-auth, A Linguistic and Semiotic Approach to Textual Analysis, The French Review, 82; co-auth, Revising/Reviving Textual Analysis in the Modern Language Curriculum, ADFL Bulletin, 83; co-auth, Introducing 'The World of Language': A Linguistic Basis for Language Study, The Modern Language Journal, 84; auth, Language Attitudes and Language Death in the French Pyrenees, The SECOL Review, 85; auth, La recherche de l'orlite en gascon pyreneen a l'aube de l'epoque moderne, Actes du XVIIe Congres International de Linguistique et de Philogie Romanes (Tubingen), Max Niemeyer, 1988; co-auth, Semiotic and Sociolinguistic Paths to Understanding Culture, Toward a New Integration of Language and Culture (Middlebury, VT), Northeast Conference on the Teaching of Foreign Languages, 88; auth, L'auxiliaire en gascon pyreneen, Langues en Bearn (Toulouse, France), Presses Universitaires du Mirail, 89; auth, Ideologies et contacts linguistiques dans le sud de la Gascogne, Contacts de langues, de civilisations et intertextualite (Montpellier), Centre d'Etudes Occitanes de l'Universite de Montpellier, 92; auth, Comportements linguistiques dans les Pyrenees a la find du Moyen Age: effets de l'ecrit, Actas do XIX Congreso Internacional de Linguistica e Filoloxia Romanicas (A Coruna), Fundacion Pedro Barrie de la Maza, 92; co-auth, Ouvertures: cours intermediaire de francais (Fort Worth), Holt Rinehard and Winston, 93, 2nd ed, 97. **CONTACT ADDRESS** Center for the Humanities, Univ of Maryland, Baltimore County, Baltimore, MD 21250. **EMAIL** tfield@umbc.edu

FIFER, ELIZABETH
PERSONAL Born 08/05/1944, Pittsburgh, PA, m, 1970, 1 child **DISCIPLINE** COMPARATIVE LITERATURE, ENGLISH **EDUCATION** Univ MI, Ann Arbor, BA, 65, MA, 66, PhD, 69. **CAREER** Lectr hum, Res Col, Univ MI, 69-72; asst prof, 73-80, Assoc Prof Eng, Lehigh Univ, 80-, prof eng, Lehigh Univ. **HONORS AND AWARDS** Stabler Awd for Excellence in Teaching, 99. **MEMBERSHIPS** MLA; Asn Theater Res. **RESEARCH** Gertrude Stein; Contemp lit; Contemp drama; Contemp fiction (U S & World). **SELECTED PUBLICATIONS** Auth, The Confessions of Italo Sveno, Contemp Lit, 73: Sex-stereo Typing in Geography & Plays, Univ Mich Papers Women's Studies, 75; Tragedy into Melodrama, Lex et Scientia, 77; The Interior Theater of Gertrude Stein, Signs, 78; Rescued Readings: Reconstruction of Gertrude Stein's Difficult Texts, Wayne State Univ, 92; auth, 'Black is Black' The Other in Jewish Thought and Hist, 95. **CONTACT ADDRESS** Dept of Eng, Lehigh Univ, 35 Sayre Dr, Bethlehem, PA 18015-3076. **EMAIL** EF00@lehigh.edu

FIGUEIRA, DOROTHY
DISCIPLINE COMPARATIVE LITERATURE **EDUCATION** Univ Chicago, PhD, 85. **CAREER** Asst prof, Univ IL Urbana Champaign. **RESEARCH** Europ rel with the cult of India; Indo-Europ mythology; lit and relig; transl theory; comp drama and epic. **SELECTED PUBLICATIONS** Auth, Translating the Orient; Exoticism: A Doctrine of Decadence; publ(s) on the reception and construct of Indian class texts and cult in Europ thought of the 18th, 19th and 20th centuries. **CONTACT ADDRESS** Comp Lit Dept, Univ of Illinois, Urbana-Champaign, E Gregory Drive, PO Box 52, Champaign, IL 61820. **EMAIL** figueira@arches.uga.edu

FIGUEREDO, DANILO H.
DISCIPLINE LATIN AMERICAN LITERATURE, LIBRARY SCIENCE, COMPARATIVE LITERATURE **EDUCATION** Montclair State Univ, BA, 76; Rutgers Univ, MLS, 78; New York Univ, MA, 88. **CAREER** Asst prof lit, Montclair State Univ, dir, bilingual prog, Lat Am bibliog, asst ch map div, Newark Pub Libr; LIBR DIR, BLOOMFIELD COL, 90-; exec dir NJ Libr Assoc. **CONTACT ADDRESS** Library, Bloomfield Col, Bloomfield, NJ 07003. **EMAIL** Danilo_Figueredo@Bloomfield.edu

FIGURITO, JOSEPH
PERSONAL Born 11/24/1922, Gaeta, Italy, m, 1956 **DISCIPLINE** FRENCH **EDUCATION** Boston Col, AB, 47; Middlebury Col, MA, 49, DML, 53; Univ Rome, cert, 52. **CAREER** Instr French, 47-48, instr Romance lang, 48-54, asst prof, 55-68, actg chmn dept, 71, Assoc Prof Mod Lang, Boston Col, 68-88, prof emeritus, 88-; Asst prof, exten, Harvard Univ, 57-68 & assoc prof, 68-81. **HONORS AND AWARDS** Silver Medal of Cult, Italy, 62; Knight, Order of Merit, Italy, 68; French Honor Society, Pi Delta Phi, Honorary mem, 97. **MEMBERSHIPS** Asn of Alumni & Friends of Ital Sch of Middlebury Col (pres 60-62); MLA; Am Asn Tchr(s) Ital (pres New Engl chap 62-64); Dante Soc Am (council mem 64-66); Mediaeval Acad Am; Honorary mem Harvard Univ Exten Alumni Asn, 81. **RESEARCH** Dante, Boccaccio, Petrarch and Leopardi; Lit and opera; 17th century French lit. **SELECTED PUBLICATIONS** Auth, A Student Guide to the Divina Commedia, Eaton, 59; L'Ultimo Baluardo dei Borboni nel Risorgimento, Italica, 9/61; contribr, A Concordance to Dante's Divine Comedy, Harvard Univ, 65; auth, Dante, Divine Comedy, Bk Notes, Barnes & Noble, 69; Leopardi Ribelle, In: Leopardi e l'Ottocento, Acts of II International Congress of Studies on Leopardi, Olschki, Florence, 70; Leopardi e Macchiavelli, In: Leopardi e la Letteratura Italiana dal Duecento al Trecento, Acts of IV Int Cong of Studies on Leopardi, Olschki, Florence, 78; Leopardi e Frontone, In: Leopardi e il Mondo Antico, Acts of the V Int Cong of Studies on Leopardi, Olschki, Florence, 82; Opinioni Politico-Religiose di Leopardi, In: Il Pensiero Storico e Politico di Giamcomo Leopardi, Acts of VI Int Cong of Studies on Leopardi, Olschki, Florence, 89; La Vita e le Opere di Don Salvatore Buonomo, In: Gaeta e Dintorni, Collana, Nova et Vetera, No 3, Gaeta, 91. **CONTACT ADDRESS** Dept of Romance Lang & Lit, Boston Col, Chestnut Hill, Chestnut Hill, MA 02467-3804.

FILER, MALVA ESTHER
PERSONAL Born 02/25/1933, Argentina, m, 1964, 2 children **DISCIPLINE** SPANISH AMERICAN LITERATURE **EDUCATION** Univ Buenos Aires, BA, 58; Columbia Univ, PhD(philos), 66. **CAREER** Lectr Span, 63-66, instr, 66-68, asst prof, 69-72, Assoc Prof Span, Brooklyn Col, 73- **MEMBERSHIPS** MLA; Inst Int Lit Iberoam; Assoc Int de Hispanistas **RESEARCH** Contemporary Spanish American literature. **SELECTED PUBLICATIONS** Coauth, Voces de Hispanoamerica: Antologia literia, 88, 96; auth, Salvador Elizondo and Servero Sarduy: Two Borgesian Writers, Borges and his Successors, Univ of MO, 90; auth, Los perros del paraiso y la nueva novela historica, En este aire y Iuz de America: Homenaje a Alfredo A. Roggiano, Inst Unt de Lit Iberoam, 90; auth, La vision de America en la obra de Abel Posse, La novel argentina de los aflos 80; Vervuert Verlag, 91; auth, Cesar Aira y su aprcrifa historia de los caciques cura, VII Congreso Nacional de Literatura Argentina, Univ Nacional de Tueuman, 93; auth, Los nuevos narradores de la Conquista, Reflejos, Vol 1, No 2, 93; auth, Maluco: re-escritura de los relatos de la expedicion de Mafallanes, Actas Irvine, 92; auth, La historia apocrifa en las novelas de los postmodernistas rioplatenses, Alba de America, 12:22-23, 94; auth, Hispanoamerica en la obra de Jose Maria Merino, Actas XXIX Congreso del Instituto Internacionnal del Literatura Iberoamericana, Univ Barcelona, 94. **CONTACT ADDRESS** Dept of Mod Lang, Brooklyn Col, CUNY, 2900 Bedford Ave, Brooklyn, NY 11210. **EMAIL** mfiler@brooklyn.cuny.edu

FILIPS-JUSWIGG, KATHERINA P.
PERSONAL Born Poltava, USSR, d, 1 child **DISCIPLINE** RUSSIAN LITERATURE; EUROPEAN LITERATURE **EDUCATION** Pedag Inst, Vinnitsa, USSR, BA, 41; Univ Montreal, MA, 55, PhD, 61. **CAREER** Asst prof Russ & Ukrainian lang & lit, Univ Alta, 61-62; assoc prof Russ lang, lit & cult, Ore State Univ, 62-67; assoc prof, 67-71; chmn dept Slavic lang, 68-74; prof Russ lang, lit & cult, Univ Wis-Milwaukee, 71, consult Russ lit, Slavic & EEurop Jour, 78. **HONORS AND AWARDS** Nat Joe Malik Serv Awd, Am Asn Tchrs Slavic & European lang, 87. **MEMBERSHIPS** MLA; Am Asn Tchrs Slavic & Europ Lang; Am Asn Advan Slavic Studies; Asn Russ-Am Scholars US; Int Dostoevsky Soc; Int PEN Club; Am Mikhail Bulgakov Society. **RESEARCH** Russ & European novel. **SELECTED PUBLICATIONS** Auth, Russian words in the German post-war memoirs, Slavic & EEurop Jour, 64; Names of poets in the poetry of Georgij Ivanov, Names, 67; Innokentij Volodin in Solzhenitsyn's First Circle.., Trans Asn Russ-Am Scholars, 74; New chapters for Solzenicyn's V Kruge Pervom .., Russ Lang Jour, 75; ed, Boris Singermann (Moskau), Brechts' Zur Aesthetik der Montage, Dreigroschenoper, Brecht-Jahrbuch 1976, 76; auth, Nemtsy o Russkikh (Russians in German Memoirs), Slavica (Volga Bks), 76; Russkaja religioznaia zizn' . . . , 76 & Anglo-American books on L N Tolstoy: A critical bibliography for the 70's, 78, Trans Asn Russ-Am Scholars; Paradigmy metafory krehcheniia v Mastere I Margarite Bulgakova, Trans Asn Russ-Am Scholars, 85; Novyj Zhurnal 164, Kontinent, 87; Ivan Elagin in Memoriam, Novyj Zhurnal 165, 87; Bulgakovs Master I Margarita: Metaphor and Method, ed Munir Sendich, Studies in Slavic Literatures and Culture, 88; rev., ed V. Sechkarev, Otkliki. Sbornik statej pamjati N.N. Uljanova, 88; Igrajushchij chelovek Ju. Ivaska, Novyi Shurnal 171, 88; ed Katharina Wilson, three articles (Aleksadra Tolstaya, Rina Levinson, Eugenia Dimer), Encyclopedia of Continental Women Writers, 91; Mikhail Bulgakov's Master and Margarita and Oscar Wilde's Salome: Motif Pattern and Allusions, Trans Asn Russ-Am Scholars, 91; (A Biographical Note and Complete Bibliography of Prof. Z.O.Yurieff), Trans Asn Russ-Am Scholars, 92-93; ed M. Ledkovskaia, A. Tolstaya, Dictionary of Russian Women Writers, 94; Dolgopolov - Professor, Scholar, Literary Critic, Novyj Zhurnal, 95; ed E. Etkind, Am Doctoral Diss on Derzhavin, Symposium Dedicated to Gavriil Derzhavin, 95; Pamiati I.V. Chinnova, Trans Asn Russ-Am Scholars, 96-97; auth, Ukazatel; (four indexes) for M. Chudakova's Zhizneopisanie Mikhaila Bulgakova, Russkij Aktsent, 97. **CONTACT ADDRESS** Dept of Foreign Languages and Linguistics, Univ of Wisconsin, Milwaukee, PO Box 413, Milwaukee, WI 53201-0413. **EMAIL** kfj@uwm.edu

FINCH, PATRICIA S.
PERSONAL Born Mexico City, Mexico, 1 child **DISCIPLINE** SPANISH LANGUAGE AND LITERATURE **EDUCATION** Bowling Green State Univ, BA, MA; Catholic Univ Am, PhD. **CAREER** Fac, 91-; assoc prof Span. **RESEARCH** Don Quijote in Western Art and Thought; preparing Spanish-language edition of La Celestina. **SELECTED PUBLICATIONS** Auth, published articles on La Celestina, Don Quijote, magic and witchcraft in medieval and Golden Age Spain. **CONTACT ADDRESS** Centre Col, 600 W Walnut St, Danville, KY 40422. **EMAIL** finch@centre.edu

FINCO, ALDO
PERSONAL Born 01/05/1921, Asiago, Italy, m, 1958, 2 children **DISCIPLINE** ITALIAN, FRENCH **EDUCATION** Collegio Colombo, BA, 49; Boston Univ, BA, 55; Middlebury Col, MA, 63, DML, 67. **CAREER** Teacher French & Latin, Millis High Schs, Mass, 55-60; lectr Ital, Univ NH, 60-64; asst prof Ital, Univ Iowa, 65-68; assoc prof, 68-76, Prof Romance Lang, Tex Tech Univ, 76-; Teacher, French, Berwick Acad, Maine, 60-64. **MEMBERSHIPS** Am Asn Teachers Ital; Cent States Mod Lang Asn; Inst Ital Cult. **RESEARCH** Italian trecento and ottocento. **SELECTED PUBLICATIONS** Auth, Grafica Toscana, Firenze, Italy; Appunti, Tex Tech Univ, 72; Una Donna Fogazzariana: Iole Moschini, Studies by mem SCent Mod Lang Asn, 73; L'umorismo di Antonio Fogazzaro, Romance Notes, 73; Dante and the Laurel Crown, Studies by the Members of SCMLA, winter 76; The Italian-Americans: Their Contribution in the Field of Literature, in Proceedings of the Comparative Literature Symposiu, Tex Tech Univ, 78; Dino Buzzati's Un caso clinico and Boris Vian's Les Batisseurs d'empire, Francia, 82; Buzzati's poetic solitude, Studies by the Members of SCMLA, 83; Buzzati fumettista e Pittore, Romance Notes, 89; Buzzati e la musica, Rivista di Studi Italiani, 93; Primo Levi: Lo spettro di Auschwitz, Rivista di Studi Italiani, 94; Mario Rigoni Stern: la voce della montagna, Asiago, ieri, oggi, domani; auth, Primo Levi sopravvivere per raccontare, Rivista di Studi Italiani, 97; auth, Debenedetti: The Sixteen of October, 97; auth, Rivista di Studi Italiani, Woolf: The memory of the Offense, 97; auth, Rivista di Studi Italiani, auth, Dino Buzzati's Il Deserto dei Tartari e il Corriere della Sera, Analogie, 99. **CONTACT ADDRESS** Dept of Class & Romance Lang, Texas Tech Univ, Lubbock, TX 79409-0001. **EMAIL** aldo.finco@ttu.edu

FINDLEY, CARTER VAUGHN
PERSONAL Born 05/12/1941, Atlanta, GA, m, 1968, 2 children **DISCIPLINE** HISTORY; MIDDLE EASTERN STUDIES **EDUCATION** Yale Col, BA, 63; Harvard Univ, PhD, 69. **CAREER** Asst prof, 72-79, assoc prof hist, Ohio State Univ, 79-86, prof hist, 86-; Soc Sci Res Coun fel, 76-77, 79, 86-87, Inst Adv Study, 81-82; Fulbright-Hays Sr Res Fel, 94 & 98; vis prof, Ecole des Hautes en Sci Soc, Paris, 94; vis lect Dept Hist, Bilkent Univ, Ankara, 97. **HONORS AND AWARDS** OH Acad Publ Awd and M Fuat Koprulu Book Prize Turkish Stud Assoc. **MEMBERSHIPS** Fel MidE Inst; fel MidE Studies Asn NAm; AHA; Am Oriental Soc; Comite Int pour les Etudes Pre-Ottomanes et Ottomanes; Oh Acad Hist; Turkish Stud Assoc (pres 90-92), Economic Soc Hist Found Turkey; World Hist Assoc vpres, 98-00, pres elect, 00-02. **RESEARCH** Ottoman history; Turkish studies; world history. **SELECTED PUBLICATIONS** Auth, Bureaucratic Reform in the Ottoman Empire: The Sublime Porte, 1789-1922, Princeton Univ, 80; Ottoman Civil Officialdom: A Social History, Princeton Univ, 89; Economic Bases of Revolution and Repression in the Late Ottoman Empire, Comparative Studies in Society and History, 86; La soumise, la subversive: Fatma Aliye, romanciere et feministe, Turcica, 95; Ebu Bekir Ratib's Vienna Embassy Narrative: Discovering Austria or Propagandizing for Reform in Istanbul, Wiener Zeitschrift fur die Kunde des Morgenlandes, 95; An Ottoman Occidentalist in Europe, Ahmed Midhat Meets Madame Gulnar, 1889, Am Hist Rev, 98; coauth Twentieth-Century World, Houghton Mifflin, 98. **CONTACT ADDRESS** Dept Hist, Ohio State Univ, Columbus, 230 W 17th Ave, Columbus, OH 43210-1361. **EMAIL** findley.1@osu.edu

FINE, ELLEN SYDNEY
PERSONAL Born 09/30/1939, New York, NY, d **DISCIPLINE** FRENCH LITERATURE AND LANGUAGE **EDUCATION** Smith Col, BA, 61; Univ Calif, Berkeley, MA, 64; NYork Univ, PhD (French), 79. **CAREER** Researcher dept doc, French Embassy Press and Info Serv, 63-64; asst prof, 64-80, Assoc Prof French, Kingsborough Community Col, 80-, Vis

lectr, Jack P Eisner Inst Holocaust Studies of the City Univ New York, 81-82. **MEMBERSHIPS** MLA; Northeastern Mod Lang Asn; Am Asn Teachers Fr. **RESEARCH** Holocaust studies; Elie Wiesel. **SELECTED PUBLICATIONS CONTACT ADDRESS** 130 E 18th St, New York, NY 10003.

FINEGAN, EDWARD J.
PERSONAL Born 06/25/1940, New York City, NY **DISCIPLINE** LINGUISTICS LAW **EDUCATION** Iona Col, BS; Ohio Univ, MA; Ohio Univ, PhD. **CAREER** Prof; post-doc, Univ Southern Calif; Ohio State Univ, Ling Inst & Harvard Law Sch. **HONORS AND AWARDS** Liberal Arts fel, Harvard Law Sch. **MEMBERSHIPS** Past dir, Amer Lang Inst/Nat Iranian Radio and Tv, past chair, linguistics dept, USC. **RESEARCH** Legal writing, register variation. **SELECTED PUBLICATIONS** Auth, Language: Its Structure and Use; coauth, Looking at Languages; coed, Sociolinguistic Perspectives on Register. **CONTACT ADDRESS** School of Law, Univ of So California, Los Angeles, CA 90089. **EMAIL** finegan@usc.edu

FINELLO, DOMINICK LOUIS
PERSONAL Born 03/17/1944 **DISCIPLINE** SPANISH RENAISSANCE & BAROQUE LITERATURE **EDUCATION** Brooklyn Col, BA, 65; Univ IL, Urbana-Champaign, MA, 67, PhD(Span), 72. **CAREER** Asst prof, 71-75, assoc prof, 75-87, prof span, Rider Univ, 88-. **MEMBERSHIPS** Inst Asn Hispanists; Cervantes Soc Am; Am Asn Teachers Span & Port; MLA. **RESEARCH** Cervantes; 16th century Spanish literature; southern European Renaissance. **SELECTED PUBLICATIONS** Auth, Temas y formas de la literature espanola, Revista Filol Espanola, 75; Cervantes y lo pastoril a nueva luz, Anales Cervantinos, 77; co-ed with R Rodriguez, La cornada by Alfonso Sastre, with notes and intro, Ed Abra, 78; auth, The Galatea: Theory and practice of the pastoral novel, In: Cervantes, his World and his Art, Fordham Univ, 78; Una olvidada defensa de la poesia del s 16, Anuario de Letras, 78; En la Sierra Morena--Actas del 6th Cong Int de Hisp, Toronto, 77; Don Quijote's Profession and Mark Van Doren's Profession, Actac del I Cong Int Sobre Cervantes, Madrid, 81; An Analytical and Biographical Guide to Criticism on Don Quijote (1790-1893), with Dana Drake, Newark, DE: Juan de la Cuesta-Hispanic Monographs, 87; Pastoral Themes and Forms in Cervantes's Fiction, Lewisburg, PA: Bucknell Univ Press, 94; Cervantes: Essays on Social and Literary Polemics, London: Boydell & Brewer, Tamesis, 98. **CONTACT ADDRESS** Dept Foreign Lang, Rider Univ, 2083 Lawrenceville, Lawrenceville, NJ 08648-3099. **EMAIL** finello@rider.edu

FINK, BEATRICE
PERSONAL Born 09/13/1933, Vienna, Austria, w, 3 children **DISCIPLINE** FRENCH LITERATURE, HISTORY OF IDEAS **EDUCATION** Bryn Mawr Col, BA, 53; Yale Univ, MA, 56; Univ Pittsburgh, PhD (French), 66. **CAREER** From instr to asst prof French, 64-72; assoc prof, 72-91, prof french, U MD Col Par, 91-99, emer, 99. **HONORS AND AWARDS** Sec General, Int Soc 18th Cont Studies, 79-87. **MEMBERSHIPS** Am Soc 18th Century Studies; Soc Fr Etude XVIIIe Siecle; Asn Benjamin Constant; East-Central Am Soc 18th Century Studies (past pres.); Soc Diderot; Soc Etudes Staeliennes. **RESEARCH** Benjamin Constant; aulinary history/discourse in Enlightenment. **SELECTED PUBLICATIONS** Auth, Les Liaisons savoureuses, 95; coed, Etre materialisle a l'age des Lumieres, 99. **CONTACT ADDRESS** 629 Constitution Ave, NE, No. 305, Washington, DC 20002. **EMAIL** bf5@umail.umd.edu

FINK, HILARY L.
PERSONAL Born 05/11/1966, 1 child **DISCIPLINE** LINGUISTICS, SLAVIC, LANGUAGE **EDUCATION** Smith Col, BA, 87; Columbia Univ, PhD, 96. **CAREER** Asst prof, Yale Univ, 96-. **HONORS AND AWARDS** Pepsico Jr Fel, 91-92; Whiting Found Fel, 94-95; IREX, Ind Adv Res Fel, Moscow, 95; Morse Fel, 00-01; Sarai Ribicoff Awd for Encour of Teach, Yale Col, Univ, 00; Sarai Ribicoff Asst Prof of Slavic Lang Lit, 00-03. **MEMBERSHIPS** MLA; AAASS; AATSEEL; IAPL. **RESEARCH** 19th and 20th-century Russian literature; Russian intellectual history, religious thought; comparative literature; Western philosophy in Russian literature. **SELECTED PUBLICATIONS** Auth, "Bergson and Russian Modernism, 1900-1930," (Evanston: Northwestern UP, 99); auth "From the Aesthetic to the Ethical: A Kierkegaardian Reading of Blok's 'Neznakomka,'" Slav East Euro J 44 (00): 79-91; auth, "The Kharmsian Absurd and the Bergsonian Comic: Against Kant and Causality," Russ Rev 57 (98): 526-38; auth, "Andrei Bely and the Music of Bergsonian Duration," Slav East Euro J 41 (97): 287-302. **CONTACT ADDRESS** Slavic Dept., Yale Univ, New Haven, CT 06520. **EMAIL** hilary.fink@yale.edu

FINK, KARL J.
PERSONAL Born 11/12/1942, Delmont, SD, m, 1964, 3 children **DISCIPLINE** GERMAN LANGUAGE & LITERATURE **EDUCATION** Wartburg Col, BA, 64; Univ Ariz, MA, 66; Univ Ill, PhD(Ger), 74. **CAREER** Asst prof Ger, Univ Ill, 74-77, Southern Ill Univ, 77-78 & Univ Ky, 78-82; assoc prof Ger & chmn dept, St Olaf Col, 82-87, 95-97; dir, Ill-Austria Exchange Prog, Univ Ill, 74-77; Minnesota German Festival, coordinator, 98. **HONORS AND AWARDS** Grawemeyer Awd, Univ Louisville, 79. **MEMBERSHIPS** MLA; Am Asn Teachers Ger; Am Soc Eighteenth Century Studies; Goethe Soc NAm; Int Herder Soceity; History of Science Society. **RESEARCH** Goethe studies; 18th century science; foreign language methodology. **SELECTED PUBLICATIONS** Auth, Learning to read German: A search for relevant models, Studies in Lang Learning, 77; The ecospace concept for the bicultural classroom abroad, Int Educ, 79; contribr, The meta-language of Goethe's history of color theory, In: The Quest for the New Science, Southern Ill Univ Press, 79; auth, Atomism: A counterpoint tradition in Goethe's writings, Eighteenth Century Studies, 80; contribr, Herder's theory of origins: From poly to palingenesis, In: Herder: Innovator through the Ages, Bouvier Press, 81; auth, Herder's stages of life as forms in geometric progression, Eighteenth Century Life, 81; Goethe's West-Ostlicher Divan: Orientalism restructured, Int J Mid East Studies, 82; Dualisten, Trinitarier, Solitarier: Formen der Autoritat in Goethes Geschichte der Farbenlehre, Goethe-Jahrbuch, 82; Goethe as Critic of Literature, American University Press, 84; co-ed Goethe's History of Science, Cambridge, 91; The Eighteenth Century German Book Review, Winter, 95; Goethe Shides in North American, Eighteenth-Century Life, 96; The Politics of Heners' Pluralism, The European Legacy, 96; auth, "Immagini virtuali nella scienza di Goethe," Milan, 98; auth, "Goethes Morphologie der Bewegung," Frankfurt, 99. **CONTACT ADDRESS** St. Olaf Col, 1520 St Olaf Ave, Northfield, MN 55057-1099. **EMAIL** kjfink@stolaf.edu

FINLEY, THOMAS JOHN
PERSONAL Born 10/29/1945, Jacksonville, FL, m, 1995, 2 children **DISCIPLINE** OLD TESTAMENT, ANCIENT SEMITIC LANGUAGES **EDUCATION** Biola Col, BA, 67, MDiv, 71; Univ Calif, Los Angeles, MA, 74, PhD, 79. **CAREER** Prof Old Testament & Semitics, Talbot Sch Theol, Biola Univ, 77-. **MEMBERSHIPS** Soc Bibl Lit; Evangel Theol Soc. **RESEARCH** Old Testament biblical Hebrew, Aramaic & Akkadian languages; Studies on Joel, Amos and Obadiah. **SELECTED PUBLICATIONS** Auth, Joel, Amos, Obadiah, Wycliffe Exegetical Commentary, Moody, 90; Auth, Joel, Obadiah, and Micah, Everymen Bible Commentary; Moody, 95; auth, A Bilingual Concordance to the Targum of the Prophets: Ezekiel, Brill, 99. **CONTACT ADDRESS** Talbot Theol Sem, Biola Univ, 13800 Biola Ave, La Mirada, CA 90639-0002. **EMAIL** tom.finley@truth.biola.edu

FINN, MARGARET R.
PERSONAL Born 08/03/1916, Jersey City, NJ **DISCIPLINE** CLASSICS **EDUCATION** Col St Elizabeth, AB, 37; Fordham Univ, MA, 42, PhD, 50. **CAREER** Instr Latin, Col St Elizabeth, 37-38; teacher, St Michael's High Sch, Jersey City, NJ, 38-43; teacher Latin and math, pub high schs, Jersey City, 43-50; asst to prin, Ferris High Sch, 50-62, from vprin to prin, 62-72; coordr non-pub secular educ prog, 72-73, actg dir, 72-80, Dir Adult Educ, Jersey City Bd Educ, 80-, Instr Latin, Seton Hall Univ, 51-54; adj asst prof, Fordham Univ, 55-69. **HONORS AND AWARDS** Women of Achievement, Jersey J, 69. **MEMBERSHIPS** Am Class League; Am Philol Asn. **RESEARCH** History of Latin paleography; medieval Latin literature. **SELECTED PUBLICATIONS CONTACT ADDRESS** 144 Erie St, Jersey City, NJ 07302.

FIORE, ROBERT L.
PERSONAL Born 08/02/1935, New York, NY, m, 1986, 2 children **DISCIPLINE** SPANISH **EDUCATION** Iona Col, BA, 61; Middlebury Col, MA, 62; Univ NC, Chapel Hill, PhD(Romance lang), 67. **CAREER** Instr Span, Univ NC, Greensboro, 62-67; asst to assoc prof, 67-75, Prof, Mich State Univ, 76-, Assistant Dean, Col of Arts & Letters, 80-86. **HONORS AND AWARDS** Honors in Italian, Iona Col, 61; Cultura Hispanica Scholarship, 62; Paul Varg Col of Arts & Letters Alumni Teacher's Awd, 94. **MEMBERSHIPS** Am Asn Teachers Span & Port; Comediantes; MLA. **RESEARCH** Spanish. **SELECTED PUBLICATIONS** Auth, Towards a Bibliography on Jorge Luis Borges (1923-69), In: The Calderon de la Barca Studies 1951 69, Univ Toronto, 71; El gran teatro del mundo: An ethical Interpretation, Hisp Rev, 72; Drama and Ethos: Natural-Law Ethics in Spanish Golden Age Theater, Univ KY, 75; Desire and Disillusionment in Lazarillo de Tormes, Studies Lang & Lit, 76; The Interaction of Motives and Mores in La Verdad Sospechosa, Hispanofila, 77; Lazarillo de Tormes: Estructura narrative de una novela picaresca, In: Actas del 1 Congr Int Sobre la Picaresca, 78; Lazarillo de Tormes and Midnight Cowboy: The Picaresque Model and Myth, In: Studies in Honor of Everett W Hesse, 81; Lazarillo de Tormes, Twayne, 84; co-ed, Studies in Honor of William C. McCrary, Univ of NE Press, 86; La Jezebel de Tirso: Reina astuta, muer que manda en casa, Critica Hispanica 8, 86; Alarcon's El dueno de las estrallas: Hero and Pharmakos, Hispanic Rev, 61, 93; Fuenteovejuna: Philosophical Views on the State and Revolution, Hispanic Essays in Honor of Frank P. Casa, 97; Lazarillo de Tormes: The Sceptic Histor and the Poetics of Silence, Critica Hispanica, 19, 97; ed, Critica Hispanica, 19, 97. **CONTACT ADDRESS** Dept of Romance Lang, Michigan State Univ, 161 Old Horticulture, East Lansing, MI 48824-1112. **EMAIL** fiore@pilot.msu.edu

FIRCHOW, EVELYN SCHERABON
PERSONAL Born Vienna, Austria, m, 1969, 2 children **DISCIPLINE** GERMANIC LANGUAGES & LITERATURES **EDUCATION** Univ Tex, Austin, BA, 56; Univ Man, MA, 57; Harvard Univ, PhD, 63. **CAREER** Teacher math, Balmoral Hall Sch, Winnipeg, Man, 53-55; teaching fel, German, Harvard Univ, 57-58, 61-62; lectr, Univ Md Br Munich, 61; from instr to asst prof Ger, Univ Wis-Madison, 62-65; assoc prof Ger philol, 65-69, acting chair, Ger Philol prog, Univ Minn, 77 & 84, Prof Ger & Ger Philol, Univ Minn, Minneapolis, 69-; NDEA-Fulbright-Hays fac fel, Univ Iceland, 67-68; vis prof Ger philol, Univ Fla, 73; Inst Advan Studies res fel, Univ Edinburgh, 73; Alexander von Humboldt-Stiftung res fel, 60-61, 77, 81, 85, 90, 93; vis scholar res grant, Austria, 77; Fulbright res prof, Univ Iceland, 80-94; NEH fel, independent study & res, 80-81; vis prof, Univ FL, 72; vis res prof, Nat Cheng Kung Univ, Tainan, Taiwan, 82-83; vis prof, Jilin Univ, Chang Chun, China, 87; vis prof, Univ Graz, Austria, 89 & 91; vis prof, Univ Vienna, Austria, 95; vis prof, Univ Bonn, Germany, 96; vis prof, Universidad Nacional de Costa Rica, Heredia, 00. **HONORS AND AWARDS** Corresponding mem, Center for Multilingualism, Brussels, Belgium, 86; Am Inst Indian Studies, fel, India, 88; Bush fel, Univ Minn, 89-90; Thor Thors fel, Univ Iceland, 94; Fac fel, Univ Minn, summer 95 & 96; McKnight fel, Univ Minn, summer, 95 & 96; De consolatione philologiaei: A Festschrift in Honor of Evelyn Scherabon Firchow, 00. **MEMBERSHIPS** AAUP; ICLA; ACLA; ALLC; Alexander von Humboldt Asn of Am; Fulbright Alumni Asn; Oswald von Wolkenstein Gesellschaft; Mediavisten-Verband Deutschlands; Asn Literary Scholars & Critics. **RESEARCH** Germanic philology; medieval studies; linguistics. **SELECTED PUBLICATIONS** Co-ed, Taylor Starck-Festschrift, 64, Studies by Einar Haugen, 72 & Studies for Einar Haugen, 72, Mouton, The Hague; The Latin Text with a New English Translation, introduction, notes and illustrations, Univ Miami, 72 and Biblioteca Germanica 3/85; co-ed, Was Deutsche Lesen: Modern German Short Stories, McGraw, 73; Deutung und Bedeutung, Mouton, The Hague, 73; ed & transl, Modern Icelandic Short Stories, 74 & East German Short Stories, 79, Twayne; co-ed (with K Grimstad), The Old Icelandic Elucidarius, Reykjavik, 87; The Old Norse Elucidarius: Original Text and English Translation,Camden House, 92; Notker der Deutsche von St Gallen: De interpretatione, Boethius Bearbeitung von Aristoteles Schrift peri hermeneias, Konkordanzen, Wortlisten und Abruck des Textes nach dem Codex Sangallensis 818, de Gruyter, 95; Notker der Deutsche von St Gallen: Categoriae, Boethius Bearbeitung von Aristoteles Schrift kategoriai, Konkordanzen, Wortlisten und Abdruck der Texte nach den Codices Sangallensis 818 und 825, Walter de Gruyter, 96; reprint, Einhard: Vita Caroli magni, Das Leben Karls des Grossen, 3rd rev ed, Philipp Reclam, 97; Alois Brandstetter: The Abbey, Ariadne Press, 98; Notker der Deutsche von St Gallen: Martianus Capellas De nuptiis Philologiae et Mercurii, Textabdruck, Konkordanzen und Wortlisten nach dem Codex Sangallensis 872, forthcoming, 98; Notker di Rentsl von St. Gallen (950-1022): Ausfuhrlire Bibliographie, 00. **CONTACT ADDRESS** Dept of Ger, Scand & Dutch, Univ of Minnesota, Twin Cities, 9 Pleasant St SE, Minneapolis, MN 55455-0194. **EMAIL** Firch001@tc.umn.edu

FIRCHOW, PETER EDGERLY
PERSONAL Born 12/16/1937, Needham, MA, 1 child **DISCIPLINE** ENGLISH & COMPARATIVE LITERATURE **EDUCATION** Harvard Univ, BA, 59, MA, 61; Univ Wis, PhD, 65. **CAREER** Asst prof English, Univ Mich, 65-67; from asst prof to assoc prof, 67-73, chmn comp lit prog, 72-78, Prof English & Comp Lit, Univ Minn, Minneapolis, 73-; Fel, Inst Advan Studies in Humanities, Univ Edinburgh, Scotland, 77; Distinguished vis prof, Chong King Univ, Taiwan, 82-83; vis prof, Jipin Univ, PRC, 87; vis prof, Univ Munidu, 88-89; vis prof, Univ Graz, 90; Fulbright vis prof, Univ Bonn, 95-96. **HONORS AND AWARDS** Fulbright Vis Prof, Natl Univ of Costa Rica, 00. **MEMBERSHIPS** Midwest Mod Lang Asn; Am Comp Lit Asn; Asn of Literary Scholars & Critics; Aldous Huxley Literary Soc. **RESEARCH** Modern literature, English, European and American. **SELECTED PUBLICATIONS** Auth, Aldous Huxley: Satirist and Novelist, Univ Minn Press, 72; auth, "Margaret Drabble's The Millstone: Rosamund's Complaint," in Old Lines, New Forces, Fairleigh Dickinson Univ, 76; ed & co-transl, East German Short Stories: An Introductory Anthology, Twayne, 79; auth, Hilda Doolittle, in American Writers, Supplement I, Scribner's, 79; auth, "Germany and Germanic Mythology," in E M Forster's Howards End, Comp Lit, winter 81; auth, Lewis Mumford, in American Writers, Supplement II, Scribner's, 81; auth, The End of Utopia: A Study of Brave New World, Buckwell Univ Press, 84; auth, The Death of the German Cousin, Buckwell Univ Press, 86; co-ed & transl, Alois Brandstetter, The Abbey, Ariadne Press, 98; auth, Envisioning Africa: Racism and Imperialism in Conrad's 'Heart of Darkness', Univ of Ky Pr, 00. **CONTACT ADDRESS** Dept of English, Univ of Minnesota, Twin Cities, 207 Church St SE, Minneapolis, MN 55455-0156. **EMAIL** firch002@tc.umn.edu

FIRESTONE, RUTH H.
PERSONAL Born 08/19/1936, Baltimore, MD, m, 1970, 2 children **DISCIPLINE** GERMAN **EDUCATION** Univ PA, BA, 59; Univ Colo, MA, 65, PhD, 72. **CAREER** Asst prof German, Otterbein Col, 69-70; from asst to assoc prof German, 73-86, dept chair, Germanic and Slavic Stud, Univ Mo, Columbia; Prof German, Chair, Dept Mod Langs, Fort Hays State Univ, 86-. **HONORS AND AWARDS** Shumway Prize German, Univ Pa, 59; Baur-van Sweringen Awd German, Univ Colo,

66;2d prize, Univ Chicago, dept Germanic Lang Lit Folklore Prize Comp, 72; Fulbright for Col Teachers of German Civ, 77; Purple Chalk for teaching, Univ Mo, 84; NEH Summer Seminar, "Beowulf and the Reception of Germanic Antiquity," Harvard Univ, 93; delta phi alpha, phi sigma iota, phi kappa phi. **MEMBERSHIPS** Mod Lang Asn; Am Asn of Teachers of German; Medieval Acad. **RESEARCH** Medieval German Literature; heroic narrative; Arthurian narrative. **SELECTED PUBLICATIONS** Auth, Queen Helche the Good: Model for Noblewomen," Women as Protagonists and Poets in the German Middle Ages: Feminist Approaches to the Study of Middle High German Literature, 91; auth, "Boethian Influence on Gottfried's Tristan: A preliminary Assessment,"in Tristan-Tristant: Melanges en l'honneur de Danielle Buschinger, 96. **CONTACT ADDRESS** Dept Modern Languages, Fort Hays State Univ, 600 Park St, Hays, KS 67601-4099. **EMAIL** rfiresto@fhsu.edu

FISCHLER, ALEXANDER
PERSONAL Born 12/28/1931, Reichenberg, Czechoslovakia, m, 1958, 2 children **DISCIPLINE** COMPARATIVE LITERATURE **EDUCATION** Univ Wash, BA, 54, PhD (compt lit), 61. **CAREER** Teaching asst and assoc, Univ Wash, 52-56, assoc 57-59; teaching asst, Ind Univ, 56-57; from instr to asst prof English, Whitman Col, 59-62; asst prof foreign lang, Univ Ore, 62-64; asst prof, 64-66, Assoc Prof French and Comp Lit, State Univ NY Binghamton, 66-. **MEMBERSHIPS** Am Comp Lit Asn; MLA, Am Asn Teachers Fr. **RESEARCH** English-French literature, 19th and 20th centuries. **SELECTED PUBLICATIONS CONTACT ADDRESS** Dept of Romance Lang and Lit, SUNY, Binghamton, Binghamton, NY 13901.

FISHER, JOHN C.
PERSONAL Born 11/27/1927, Mendon, NY, m, 1956, 2 children **DISCIPLINE** LINGUISTICS, LITERATURE **EDUCATION** Champlain Col, BA, 53; Univ Mich, AM, 54, EdD(English lang and lit), 62. **CAREER** From instr to assoc prof, 57-62, dir summer instr, 62-68, chmn dept, 72-74, Prof English, State Univ NY Col, Oswego, 63-, Vis lectr, English Lang Inst, Univ Mich, 57-61; instr, State Univ NY, Ford Found Indonesia Proj, 62-63; Fulbright lectr, Univ Rome, 63-64; dir, NEA Inst English, 65; coordr, BA Ling Prog, State Univ NY Col, Oswego, 66-73; exec secy, NY State English Coun, 68-70, fel, 70; vis prof, ling, Univ Hawaii, Hilo, 70; vis prof, English, Inter-Am Univ PR, 70. **MEMBERSHIPS** MLA; NCTE. **RESEARCH** Nineteenth century British literature; linguistics, especially in literary criticism; English as a foreign language. **SELECTED PUBLICATIONS** Auth, Reinventing a Livelihood--How United States Labor Laws, Labor Management Cooperation Initiatives, and Privatization Influence Public Sector Labor Markets, Harvard J Legislation, Vol 34, 97. **CONTACT ADDRESS** Perry Hill RD 3, Oswego, NY 13126.

FISHMAN, JOSHUA AARON
PERSONAL Born 07/18/1926, Philadelphia, PA, m, 1951, 3 children **DISCIPLINE** SOCIOLINGUISTICS **EDUCATION** Univ Pa, BA and MS, 48; Columbia Univ, PhD (social psychol), 53. **CAREER** Res assoc social psychol, Jewish Educ Comt New York, 50-54; res assoc and res dir, Col Entrance Exam Bd, 55-58; assoc prof psychol and Human rels, Univ Pa, 58-60; prof psychol and sociol, 60-66, Distinguished Univ Res Prof Soc Sci, Yeshiva Univ, Soc Sci Res Coun fel, 54-55; fels, Ctr Advan Study Behav Sci, 63-64, Inst for Advan Study, NJ, 75-76 and Nat Inst Educ, 76-77; consult, Ministry Finance, Repub Ireland, 65-; sur sr specialist, East-West Ctr, Univ Hawaii, 68-69; ed, Int J Sociol Lang, 74-. **HONORS AND AWARDS** PedD, Yeshiva Univ, 68. **MEMBERSHIPS** Am Psychol Asn; Am Sociol Asn; Am Anthrop Asn; Ling Soc Am; Yivo Inst Jewish Res. **RESEARCH** Sociology of language; bilingual education; applied linguistics. **SELECTED PUBLICATIONS CONTACT ADDRESS** Soc Sci Div, Yeshiva Univ, 500 W 185th St, New York, NY 10033.

FISHWICK, DUNCAN
PERSONAL Born 05/12/1929, Adlington, England **DISCIPLINE** CLASSICS **EDUCATION** Manchester Univ, BA, 50; Oxford Univ, BA, 53, MA, 56. **CAREER** Lectr, McGill Univ, 56-57; asst prof, Univ Toronto, 57-64; assoc prof, St Francis Xavier Univ, 74-71; assoc prof to prof classics, 71-86, univ prof, 86-94, ch classics, 87-92, Univ Prof Emer, Univ Alberta, 94-. **HONORS AND AWARDS** Univ Alta Res Prize, 85; McCalla Res Prof, 85-86. **SELECTED PUBLICATIONS** Auth, Studies in Roman Imperial History, 76; auth, The Imperial Cult in the Latin West, vol I, 87, vol II, 91/92; coauth, The Foundations of the West, 64. **CONTACT ADDRESS** Dept of Hist and Classics, Univ of Alberta, Edmonton, AB, Canada T6G 2F6.

FITCH, BRIAN T.
PERSONAL Born 11/19/1935, London, England **DISCIPLINE** FRENCH **EDUCATION** Kings Col, Univ Durham, BA, 58; Univ Strasbourg, Dr de l'U, 62. **CAREER** Asst lectr, Manchester Univ, 62-65; vis assoc prof, 65-66, head Fr, 71-75, assoc ch grad stud Fr, 77-81, Univ prof, 89-, Gerald Larkin prof French, Trinity Cof, Univ Toronto, 96-; vis sr res fel, Merton Col, Oxford, 70; vis prof, Bar-Ilan Univ, Israel, 83; vis prof, Montpellier Univ, 93. **HONORS AND AWARDS** Can Coun leave fel, 70-71, 76-77, 82-83; Connaught sr fel, 88-89. **MEMBERSHIPS** MLA; Can Asn Univ Tchrs; Can Comp Lit Asn. **SELECTED PUBLICATIONS** Auth, Dimensions et structures chez Bernanos: essai de methode critique, Paris, Minard, "Situations", (69): 247; auth, Un texte, ses lecteurs, leurs lectures: etude methodologique de "L'Etranger" de Camus, Paris, Lrousse, Collection "L", (72): 176; auth, Essai de bibliographie des etudes en langue francaise consacrees a Allbert Camus (1937-71), 2eme Edition, Paris, Montreal, "Calepins de Bibliographie," (72): 480; auth, Dimensions, structures et textualite dans la triologie romanesque de Samuel Becket, Paris, Minard, "Situations", (77): 205; auth, The Naricssistic Text: A Reading of Camus Fiction, Toronto, Univ of Toronto Press, (82): 152; auth, Monde a l'envers/Texte reversible: la fiction de Bataille, Paris, Minard, (82): 188; auth, Beckett and Babel: An Investigation into the Status of the Bilingual Work, Toronto, Univ of Toronto Press, (88): 242; auth, Reflections in the Mind's Eye: Reference and its Problematization in Twentieth-Century Fiction, Toronto, Univ of Toronto Press, Theory/Culture Series, (91): 234; auth, Lire les recits de Blanchot, "Collection Monographique Rodopi en litterature francaise contemporine," (92): 92; auth, A Matter of Guilt: Camus' "The Fall", Boston, G.K. Hall, "Twayne Masterwork Studies," (95): 138. **CONTACT ADDRESS** Dept of French, Univ of Toronto, 50 St. Joseph St., Toronto, ON, Canada M5S 1J4. **EMAIL** bfitch@chass.utoronto.ca

FITZ, BREWSTER
DISCIPLINE COMPARATIVE LITERATURE **EDUCATION** Yale, PhD, 73. **CAREER** Engl, Okla St Univ. **RESEARCH** Non-Western World Literature, Multi-cultural Literatures, Native American Literature and Critical Theory. **SELECTED PUBLICATIONS** Auth, Rapture in Liminality: Leslie Marmon Silko's 'Yellow Woman', Univ Tex, El Paso, 96; Some Theoretical Reflexions in Leslie Marmon Silko's Gloss on 'Coyote and Lark', 96; Dialogistic Witchery in 'Tony's Story', 97; Undermining Narrative Stereotypes in Simon Ortiz's 'The Killing of a State Cop', 97. **CONTACT ADDRESS** Oklahoma State Univ, Stillwater, 101 Whitehurst Hall, Stillwater, OK 74078.

FITZ, EARL EUGENE
PERSONAL Born 03/07/1946, Marshalltown, IA, m, 1973, 1 child **DISCIPLINE** LUSO-BRAZILIAN STUDIES **EDUCATION** Univ Iowa, BA, 68, MA, 70; City Univ New York, MA, 73, PhD (comp lit), 77. **CAREER** Vis lectr Span and Port, Univ Mich, Ann Arbor, 76-77; asst prof, Dickinson Col, 77-78; Asst Prof Luso-Brazilian Studies and Span Am Lit, PA State Univ, 78-. **MEMBERSHIPS** MLA; Am Asn Teachers Span and Port; Am Translr Asn; Midwest Mod Lang Asn. **RESEARCH** Spanish Am Lit and culture; comparative literature. **SELECTED PUBLICATIONS CONTACT ADDRESS** Dept of Span Ital and Port, Pennsylvania State Univ, Univ Park, 352 Burrowes Bldg, University Park, PA 16802-6203.

FIZER, JOHN
PERSONAL Born 06/13/1925, Ukraine, m, 1957, 4 children **DISCIPLINE** SLAVIC AND COMPARATIVE LITERATURE **EDUCATION** Columbia Univ, MA, 52, PhD, 60. **CAREER** Analyst & interviewer, Harvard Univ, 51; asst prof Russ, Univ Notre Dame, 54-60; Prof Slavic & Comp Lit, Rutgers Univ, New Brunswick, 60-; Academician of the Natl Acad of Sciences of Ukraine, Hon prof of the Natl Univ of Kiev-Mohyla Acad, Kiev Unkraine. **MEMBERSHIPS** AATSEEL **RESEARCH** Lit aesthetics and theory; aesthetics; psychol. **SELECTED PUBLICATIONS** Auth, Philosophy in the Soviet Union: A Survey of the Mid-Sixties, De Reydel, Dordrecht, 67; Conceptual affinities and differences between A A Potebnja's theory of internal form and Roman Ingarden's stratum of aspects, In: American Contributions to the Seventh International Congress of Slavists, Mouton, The Hague, 73; The concept of strata in Roman Ingarden's theory of literary structure, In: The Personality of the Critic, Pa State Univ, 73; Some correlations in the aesthetics of A A Potebnja and Benedetto Croce, In: Sumbolae in Honorarem Georgii Y Shevelov, Logos, Munich, 73; Ingarden's prhases, Bergson's durree reele and William James' stream: metaphoric variants or mutually exclusive concepts on the theme of time, In: Analecta Husserliana, Dortrecht, 76; Psychologism and Psychoaesthetico: A Historical and Critical View of Their Relations, John Benjamin's BV, Amsterdam, 81; Psychologism and Psychoaesthetics: A Historical View of Their Relations, Amsterdam: John Benjamin B.V. 81; Psychologizm i psychoestetyka, Warsaw: PWN, 91; Alexander A. Potebja's Psycholinguistic Theory of Literature: A Metacritical Inquiry, Harvard Univ Press, 86. **CONTACT ADDRESS** Dept of Slavic Lang & Lit, Rutgers, The State Univ of New Jersey, New Brunswick, PO Box 5062, New Brunswick, NJ 08903-5062. **EMAIL** fizer@rci.rutgersledu

FLECK, JERE
PERSONAL Born 03/02/1935, New York, NY, m, 1966 **DISCIPLINE** GERMANIC LINGUISTICS **EDUCATION** Univ Munich, Dr Phi l(Ger philol), 66. **CAREER** Asst prof Ger lang, Univ Cincinnati, 66-67 and Vanderbilt Univ, 67-70; asst prof, 70-73, Assoc Prof Ger Lang, Univ MD, College Park, 73-. **MEMBERSHIPS** Pedagog Sem Ger Philol; MLA; Am Asn Teachers Ger; SAtlantic Mod Lang Asn; Mongolia Soc. **RESEARCH** Pre-Christian Germanic religion and cultural history; Germanic, Indo-European and general historic linguistics; language pedagogics and methodology. **SELECTED PUBLICATIONS** Auth, Knowing Engineers--Response, Soc Stud Sci, Vol 24, 94. **CONTACT ADDRESS** Dept of Ger and Slavic Lang, Univ of Maryland, Col Park, College Park, MD 20742-0001. **EMAIL** jfl7@umail.umd.edu

FLEISCHER, GEORGETTE
PERSONAL Born 07/31/1957, New York, NY **DISCIPLINE** ENGLISH, COMPARATIVE LITERATURE **EDUCATION** Univ Mich, BA, 79; Columbia Univ, MFA, 94; MA, 95; MPhil, 98; PhD, 01. **CAREER** Teaching fel, Brooklyn Col, CUNY, 91-92; TA, preceptor, Columbia Univ, 95-01; assoc prof, Barnard Col, 00-01. **HONORS AND AWARDS** Fel, Univ of Mich, 75-79; Louise B. Goodman Awd, 92; Fel, Columbia Univ, 92-93, 95-01; Edward F. Albee Found Fel, 94; Miron Christo-Levaunu Awd, 95. **MEMBERSHIPS** MLA, ACLA, Virginia Woolf Soc, Samuel Beckett Soc. **RESEARCH** Genre Departures: Women Writers and the Crisis of Representing National Socialism and World War II. **SELECTED PUBLICATIONS** Auth, "Light on Nightwood," Nation, (95); auth, "Hitler Was Their Boy," Nation, (96); auth, "Under the Sign of Wittgenstein: Postmodernist Poetics Explained," Contemp Lit, (97); auth, "Djuna Barnes and T.S. Eliot: The Politics and Poetics of Nightwood," Studies in the Novel, (98) auth, "Ingeborg Bachmann's Malina (1971): Wittgensteinian Poetics Out of the Austrian National Socialist Past," how2, (90); rev, "Her Own Lambs and Falcons" of Selected Letters of Rebecca West, Nation, (00); auth, "(Judith) Butler: Is It All Greek?" Nation, (00). **CONTACT ADDRESS** Barnard Col, 19 Cleveland Pl, #4A, New York, NY 10012. **EMAIL** gf24@columbia.edu

FLEISHMAN, LAZAR
PERSONAL Born 05/15/1944, Dvrutch, Ukraine, d, 2 children **DISCIPLINE** RUSSIAN LITERATURE **EDUCATION** Latvia State Univ, Riga, MA equivalent, 66; passed PhD exams in Riga and Tartu, 67-68. **CAREER** Sr lectr, Hebrew Univ, Jerusalem, 77-81; asst prof, 81-85, prof, Stanford Univ, 85-, chairman, 91-94; vis prof, Univ Calif, Berkeley, 78-79, 80-81, 99; vis prof, Univ Tex, Austin, 81-82; vis prof, Harvard and Yale, 94; vis prof, Russian State Univ for the Humanities, 98. **HONORS AND AWARDS** The Pew Found grant, 86; The Guggenheim Found Fel, 87; Humboldt-Stiftung-Forschungspreis, 94-95; German-Am Cooperative Res grant, 92-93; IREX grant, 2000. **MEMBERSHIPS** Am Asn of Literary Scholars and Critics. **RESEARCH** History and poetics of Russian literature; Boris Pasternak; culture of Russian emigration; Soviet literature and literary politics. **SELECTED PUBLICATIONS** Coauth with H. B. Harder and Sergej Dorzweiler, Boris Pasternak's Lehriahre: Neopublikovannye filosofskie konspekty I zametki Borisa Pasternaka (unpublished Philosophical Notes, Abstracts, and Synopses), Stanford Slavic Studies, vol 11, part 1-2, Stanford (96); coauth with Iu. Abyzov and B. Ravdin, Russkaia pechat' v Rige: Iz istorii gazety "Segodnia" 1930-kh godov (Russian Press in Riga: A History of the Newspaper "Segodnia" in the 1930s), Vols I-V, Stanford Slavic Studies, vol 13-17, Stanford (97); ed, Studies in Modern Russian and Polish Culture and Bibliography, Essays in Honor of Wojciech Zalewski, Stanford Slavic Studies, vol 20, Stanford (99); ed, Poetry and Revolution: Boris Pasternak's "My Sister Life," Stanford Slavic Studies, vol 21, Stanford (99). **CONTACT ADDRESS** Slavic Lang & Lit, Stanford Univ, Bldg 40-42 L, Stanford, CA 94305. **EMAIL** hf.lsf@forsythe.stanford.edu

FLEMING, RAYMOND RICHARD
PERSONAL Born 02/27/1945, Cleveland, OH, m, 1969 **DISCIPLINE** ITALIAN **EDUCATION** Univ of Notre Dame, IN, BA, 1967; Univ of Florence, Italy, 1967-68; Harvard Univ, Cambridge MA, 1968-69, PhD, 1976. **CAREER** Univ of Notre Dame, Notre Dame IN, instructor, 69-72; Univ of CA, San Diego CA, asst prof, 73-80; Miami Univ, Oxford OH, assoc prof of Italian and asst dean of graduate school, 80-, assoc dean of graduate school, 85-87; PA State Univ, Univ Park PA, prof of com lit and Italian, currently. **HONORS AND AWARDS** Ford Foundation Fellowships, 1966, 1972; Fulbright Grant to Florence Italy, 1967; Woodrow Wilson Fellowship to Harvard Univ, 1968; Ingram-Merrill Poetry Awd, 1971; Alexander Von Humboldt Fellowship to Germany, 1978; American Philosophical Society Research Grant, 1982; author of Diplomatic Relations (book), 1982; author of Keats, Leopardi, and Holderlin (book), 1987; Natl Endowment for the Humanities, grant, 1989, endowed professorship, 1991. **MEMBERSHIPS** Dante Society of Amer, Amer Council of Learned Societies. **SELECTED PUBLICATIONS** Author of Ice and Honey (book), 1979. **CONTACT ADDRESS** Professor of Comparative Literature and Italian, Pennsylvania State Univ, Univ Park, 433 N Burrowes Building, University Park, PA 16802.

FLETCHER, ROBERT E.
PERSONAL Born 12/12/1938, Detroit, MI, m **DISCIPLINE** LAW, FILM **EDUCATION** Fisk Univ, attended 1956-59; Wayne State Univ, BA 1961; Natl Educ TV Film Training Sch, attended 1970; Comm Film Workshop Council TV News Cinematography Prog 1971; Natl Acad of TV Arts & Sci/Third World Cinema Prod Inc 1976-77; New York University School of Law, JD, 1990. **CAREER** No Student Movement Harlem,

field organizer 63-64; SNCC Jackson MS, Selma AL Atlanta GA, photographer field coord editorial & air dir 64-68; freelance photographer journalist & film maker 68-; Brooklyn Coll, adj prof dept of film studies 75-76; "Vote for Your Life", prod/dir 77; "Weatherization, What's It all About?"; Video & TV Prod, summer 77; WPIX-TV, bi-weekly talk show; "A Nation in View", co-producer; Cravath, Swaine & Moore, attorney, 91-. **HONORS AND AWARDS** Cinematographer dir "A Luta Continva" 1971; documentary film on liberation struggle in Mozambique "O Povo Organizado" 1975; panelist "Voices of the Civil Rights Movement" Smithsonian Inst 1980. **MEMBERSHIPS** Mem Intl Photographers of the Motion Picture Indus; chmn bd dir Rod Rodgers Dance Co 1973-; photographs pub in Ebony, Essence, Black Enterprises, Tuesday, Life, Redbook, NY Mag; author of publ in MS. **CONTACT ADDRESS** Cravath, Swaine & Moore, 825 Eighth Ave, New York, NY 10019-7415.

FLEURANT, KEN
PERSONAL m, 2 children **DISCIPLINE** FRENCH LITERATURE **EDUCATION** Holy Cross Col, BA; Princeton Univ, MA, PhD. **CAREER** Adv French prog. **RESEARCH** French and Francophone cultural studies; cultural and political history of Quebec; European Renaissance and Enlightenment studies; all aspects of French literature. **SELECTED PUBLICATIONS** Auth, pubs on contemporary literature. **CONTACT ADDRESS** Dept of French, Univ of Wisconsin, Green Bay, 2420 Nicolet Dr, Green Bay, WI 54311-7001. **EMAIL** fleurank@uwgb.edu

FLIER, MICHAEL S.
PERSONAL Born 04/20/1941, Los Angeles, CA, s **DISCIPLINE** SLAVIC LANGUAGES & LITERATURES **EDUCATION** Univ of Calif at Berkeley, BA, 62, MA, 64, PhD, 68. **CAREER** Vis acting asst prof of Slavic Languages and Lit, Univ of Calif at Berkeley, 68; asst prof of Slavic Languages, 68-73, assoc prof of Slavic Languages, 73-79, prof of Slavic Languages and Lit, Univ of Calif at Los Angeles, 79-91; vis prof of Slavic Languages, Columbia Univ, 88; Vis prof of Slavic Languages and Lit, 89, Oleksandr Potebnja Prof of Ukrainian Philology, Harvard Univ, 91-. **HONORS AND AWARDS** Travel grant, Inter-University Comt on Travel Grants, Moscow State Univ, 66-67; travel grant, Int Res and Exchanges Board, Moscow State Univ & Charles Univ, 71; summer fel for jr fac, UCLA, 77; travel grant, Int Res and Exchanges Board, Russian Language Inst of the Acad of Sci of the U.S.S.R., 78; summer col inst fel, Col of Letters and Sci, UCLA, 84; study grant, Kennan Inst for Advanced Russian Studies, 85; President's Fel in the Humanities, Univ of Calif, 90; John Simon Guggenheim Memorial Found Fel, 90-91; IREX Grant, 96. **MEMBERSHIPS** Am Asn for Teachers of Slavic and East European Languages; Am Asn for the Advancement of Slavic Studies; Linguistic Soc of Am. **RESEARCH** Slavic Linguistics, Semiotics of Medieval East Slavic Culture. **SELECTED PUBLICATIONS** Auth, Aspects of Nominal Determination, Mouton & Co, 74; co-ed, Medieval Russian Culture II, Univ of Calif Press, 94; For SK: In Celebration of the Life and Career of Simon Karlinsky, Berkeley Slavic Specialties, 94; The Language and Verse of Russia. In Honor of Dean S. Worth on his Sixty-fifth Birthday, Vostochnaya Literatura Pub, 95; ed, Ukrainian Philology and Linguistics, 94. **CONTACT ADDRESS** Dept of Slavic Languages and Literatures, Harvard Univ, Barker Center, 12 Quincy St., Cambridge, MA 02138. **EMAIL** flier@fas.harvard.edu

FLORES, YOLANDA
PERSONAL Born 03/02/1962, Bakersfield, CA, s **DISCIPLINE** SPANISH **EDUCATION** Univ Calif, BA, 87; Univ Chicago, MA, 89; Cornell Univ, MA, 92; Cornell Univ, PhD, 95. **CAREER** Lectr, Cornell Univ, 94-95; Asst Prof, Chapman Univ, 95-99; Asst Prof, Univ Vt, 99-. **HONORS AND AWARDS** Grad Fel, Cornell Univ, 91-94; Spring Res Travel Grant, Cornell Univ, 94; Summer Fac Res Grant, Chapman Univ, 97; Phi Beta Delta; Who's Who in the W, 97-98; Fac Grand-in-Aid, Chapman Univ, 98; Who's Who in Am, 99-00. **MEMBERSHIPS** MLA, LASA, Am Soc for Theatre Res, S Calif Chicano/Latino Educr, Feministas Unidas. **RESEARCH** Comparative literature of the Americas, Contemporary Spanish American, Brazilian and United States Latino literatures, cultural studies, cultural politics, race studies and critical pedogogy, women's writing, feminist criticism, feminist dramatic criticism. **SELECTED PUBLICATIONS** Auth, "Subverting Scripts: Identity and Performance in Play by U S Latinas," Latinas on Stage, (95); auth, "On Borders, Multiple Migrations, Cultural Diversity and the Politics of Identity," The Global Citizen (96); auth, "Performing Difference: Intra-Ethnic Theatricalities," Feministas Unidas, vol 17.2 (97); auth, The Drama of Gender: Feminist Theater by Women of the Americas, Peter Land Publ (New York, NY), 00; rev, "Julia Alvarez Yo!," Letras Femeninas, forthcoming. **CONTACT ADDRESS** Dept Lang, Univ of Vermont, Waterman Bldg, Burlington, VT 05405-0001.

FLORI, MONICA ROY
PERSONAL Born 09/17/1944, Montevideo, Uruguay, m, 1968 **DISCIPLINE** LATIN AMERICAN & SPANISH LITERATURE **EDUCATION** Inst Uruguayo de Estudios Prepatorios, 63; Univ Repub Uruguay, Lic Philos, 70; Univ Hawaii, MA, 71; Univ Ore, PhD(Romance lang & lit), 79. **CAREER** Instr Span & Fr, Portland Community Col, 71-74; lectr Span & Fr, 77-79, Prof Lang & Lit, Lewis & Clark Col, 79-. **MEMBERSHIPS** Southwestern States Latin Am Studies Asn; MLA, Instituto Literio y Cultural Hispanico. **RESEARCH** Contemporary Latin American fiction; Latin American women writers; fiction of the River Plate area. **SELECTED PUBLICATIONS** Auth, Simbolismo existencial en la narrative de Juan Carlos Onetti, Vol I, 80 & Las ventanas en Paseo de Jose Donoso, Vol II, 81, Selecta; Las imagenes sensoriales en El pozo y El astillero de Juan Carlos Onetti, Explicacion de Textos Literarios, Vol X, 81-82; The Hispanic community as resource for a practical Spanish program, Foreign Lang Ann, spring 82; Streams of Silver: Six Contemporary Women Writers from Argentina, Lewisburg, Bucknell University Press, 95, 97; De almibares, perfumes y sedas: La recuperacion historica-biografica en Perfumes de Cartago de Teresa Porzekanski, in Alba de America, 99; auth, " Familia hauon de fin de siglo " Una lectura de Lamuerte como efecto secundario de Ana Maria Shva; auth, " In Rhonda Buchanan, ed Elrio de los sueuos" Aproxiamuanes critcas a la obra de Ana Maria Shava, Washington, DC Colecceou Interamer, 00. **CONTACT ADDRESS** Foreign Lang Dept, Lewis and Clark Col, 0615 SW Palatine Hill Rd, Portland, OR 97219-7879. **EMAIL** flori@lclark.edu

FLORY, MARLEEN BOUDREAU
PERSONAL Born 01/02/1944, CT, m, 1970 **DISCIPLINE** CLASSICS **EDUCATION** Mount Holyoke Col, BA, 65; Yale Univ, PhD, 75. **CAREER** Inst, Asst Acad Dean, 70-73, Asst Prof, 70-77, Classics, Mount Holyoke Coll, Classics; Res Fel, 74-75, Sr Assoc Member, 82-83 and 91-92, Amer School of Classical Stud, Athens; Asst Prof, Assoc Prof to Prof, Classic, 78-, Gustavus Alodolophus Coll, Asst Prof, 77-78, Salem Coll, Classics; Andrew W. Mellon Fellow, 85-86, Amer Acad in Rome. **HONORS AND AWARDS** Phi Beta Kappa; Fellow of the Amer Acad. **MEMBERSHIPS** Chair, Classical Association of the Midwest and South; Member of Ed Bd; Consult Evaluator; Executive Bd. **RESEARCH** Roman Society History. **SELECTED PUBLICATIONS** Auth, Octavian's Felicitas, Rheinisches Museum fur Philology, 107, pp 89-112, 94; Deification of Roman Women, Ancient History Bulletin, 95; The Meaning of the Name Augusta in the Julio-Claudian Period, Amer J of Ancient Hist, 97; The Integration of Women in the Roman Triumph, forthcoming in Historia, 98; Review, The Late Roman Army, by P Southern & KR Dixon, in: Religious Studies Review, 98, Atia and Julia and late Republic Political propaganda, CAMWS, 98. **CONTACT ADDRESS** Dept of Classics, Gustavus Adolphus Col, 800 W College Ave, Saint Peter, MN 56082-1498. **EMAIL** mflory@gustavus.edu

FLORY, STEWART GILMAN
PERSONAL Born 10/28/1941, New York, NY, m, 1970 **DISCIPLINE** CLASSICAL LANGUAGES & LITERATURES **EDUCATION** Yale Univ, BA, 64, MA, 67, MPhil, 68, PhD(classics), 69. **CAREER** Asst prof classics, Amherst Col, 69-77; Chmn Dept Classics, Gustavus Adolphus Col, 79-, Am Sch Class Studies fel, Athens, 74-75 & sr assoc, 82-83; Nat Endowment for Humanities fel, Rome, summer, 80 & foreign col teachers, 82-83. **MEMBERSHIPS** Am Philol Asn; Archaeol Inst Am. **RESEARCH** Herodotus; Homer; Plato. **SELECTED PUBLICATIONS** Auth, The Personality of Herodotus, Arion, 69; Laughter, tears and wisdom in Herodotus, Am J Philol, 78; Medea's right hand, Tapa, 78; Who read Herodotus' histories, Am J Philol, Vol 101. **CONTACT ADDRESS** 800 W College Ave, Saint Peter, MN 56082-1498. **EMAIL** sflory@gac.edu

FLOWERS, RONALD BRUCE
PERSONAL Born 01/11/1935, Tulsa, OK, m, 1959, 3 children **DISCIPLINE** RELIGION, AMERICAN CHURCH HISTORY **EDUCATION** Tex Christian Univ, BA, 57; Vanderbilt Univ, BD, 60, STM, 61; Univ Iowa, PhD(relig, Am church hist), 67. **CAREER** Asst prof, 66-72, assoc prof relig, Tex Christian Univ, 72-83, prof 84-. **HONORS AND AWARDS** Danforth assoc, 71-; Weatherly Prof of Religion, 98. **MEMBERSHIPS** Disciples of Christ Hist Soc; Am Acad of Relig. **RESEARCH** The history of religion in America; church and state relationships in America. **SELECTED PUBLICATIONS** Auth, An Introduction to Church-State Relationships, Encounter, summer 71; Piety in Public Places, Christianity & Crisis, 11/71; A Selected Bibliography on Religion and Public Education, J Church & State, autumn 72; The Supreme Court's Three Tests of the Establishment Clause, Religion in Life, spring 76; coauth, Toward Benevolent Neutrality: Church, State, and the Supreme Court, Baylor Univ, 77, rev ed, 82, 5th rev ed, 94; Freedom of Religion Versus Civil Authority in Matters of Health, Ann Am Acad Pol Soc Sci, 11/79; The Supreme Court's Interpretation of the Free Exercise Clause, Relig Life, fall 80; The 1960's: A Decisive Decade in American Church-State Relationships, Encounter, summer 82;auth, Religion in Strange Times: The 1960's and 1970's, 84; co-auth, The Naturalization of Rosika Schwimmer, Journal of Church and State, spring 90; auth, In Praise of Conscience: Marie Averil Bland, Angelican and Episcopal History, March 93; Government Accomodation of Religious-Based Conscientious Objection, Seton Hall Law Rev, 93; That Godless Court?: Supreme Court Decisions on Church-State relationships, 94. **CONTACT ADDRESS** Dept of Relig, Texas Christian Univ, Box 298100, Fort Worth, TX 76129-0002. **EMAIL** r.flowers@tcu.edu

FLOYD, EDWIN DOUGLAS
PERSONAL Born 05/19/1938, Prescott, AZ, m, 1967, 4 children **DISCIPLINE** CLASSICS **EDUCATION** Yale Univ, BA, 58; Princeton Univ, MA, 60, PhD (classics), 65. **CAREER** Instr ancient lang, Col William and Mary, 62-66; asst prof, 66-72, Assoc Prof Classics, Univ Pittsburgh, 72-. **MEMBERSHIPS** Am Philol Asn; Archaeol Inst Am; Ling Soc Am; Am Oriental Soc. **RESEARCH** Greek poetry; Greek historical linguistics; Sanskrit poetry. **SELECTED PUBLICATIONS** Auth, Homeric Epios Friendly and Vedic Api Friend, Glotta Zeitschrift Griechische Lateinische Sprache, Vol 71, 93; Bacchylides 18.31 and Indo European Poetics, J Indo Europ Stud, Vol 20, 92; Homer Iliad, Book 1, Line 191, Explicator, Vol 53, 95. **CONTACT ADDRESS** Dept of Classics, Univ of Pittsburgh, 1518 Cathedral of Learning, Pittsburgh, PA 15260-0001. **EMAIL** edfloyd@pitt.edu

FOELL, KRISTIE A.
PERSONAL Born 10/22/1962, Monterey, CA, m, 1984 **DISCIPLINE** GERMAN **EDUCATION** Yale Univ, BA, 84; Univ Calif Berkeley, MA, 92. **CAREER** Vis asst prof, Gustavus Adolphus Col, 91-92; vis asst prof, Vassar Col, 92-95; asst prof, Bowling Green State Univ, 95-. **HONORS AND AWARDS** Fulbright Grant, 89-90, 95. **MEMBERSHIPS** MLA, GSA, AATG. **RESEARCH** Elias Canetti (Viennese and exile contexts), German unificiation, interdisciplinary studies of film, music. **SELECTED PUBLICATIONS** Auth, Blind Reflections: Gender in Elias Canetti's 'Die Blendung', Ariadne Pr, (Riverside), 94; auth, "July 15, 1927: The Vienna Palace of Justice is burned in a mass uprising of Viennese workers, a central experience in the life and work of Elias Canetti," Yale Companion to Jewish Writing and Thought in German Culture, 1096-1996, ed Zipes and Gilman, (97): 464-470; dir, A Year in Salzburg, video, BGSU-AYA Prog, 00; coed, Textual Responses to German Unification, Walter de Gruyter, 01; auth, "Elias Canetti and the intellectual debates of his time," A Companion to Elias Canetti, Camden House, (02). **CONTACT ADDRESS** Dept GREAL, Bowling Green State Univ, Bowling Green, OH 43403. **EMAIL** kfoell@bgnet.bgsu.edu

FOGEL, HERBERT
PERSONAL Born 04/24/1931, New York, NY **DISCIPLINE** FRENCH **EDUCATION** NYork Univ, BA, 52, MA, 55, PhD (Romance lang), 63. **CAREER** Instr French, NY Univ, 56-59; instr, Queens Col, NY, 60-61; from instr to asst prof, 61-67, Assoc Prof French, Long Island Univ, 67, Fulbright fel, Sorbonne, 59-60. **MEMBERSHIPS** MLA; Am Asn Teachers Fr. **SELECTED PUBLICATIONS** Auth, The Complete Discography of Mitropoulos, Dimitri, Association for Recorded Sound Collections J, Vol 23, 92; Rosbaud, Hans--A Biobibliography, Assoc Rec Sound Collect J, Vol 24, 93; The Devils Music Master--Furtwangler, Wilhelm, Assoc Rec Sound Collec J, Vol 24, 93. **CONTACT ADDRESS** Dept of Mod Lang, Long Island Univ, Brooklyn, Brooklyn, NY 11201.

FOGEL, JERISE
PERSONAL Born 11/30/1964 **DISCIPLINE** CLASSICS **EDUCATION** Smith Col, AB, 85; Columbia Univ, MA, 87, MPhil, 90, PhD, 94. **CAREER** Vis asst prof, Smith Col, 90; asst prof, Univ Il Urbana-Champaign, 94-97; asst prof, Gettysburg Col, Pa, 97-98; asst prof, Mich St Univ, 98- . **HONORS AND AWARDS** Mellon Fel, 86-91 **MEMBERSHIPS** Amer Philol Assoc; Archaeol Inst of Amer; AAUW; AAUP; Int Soc for Hist of Rhetoric; Lesbian/Gay/Bisexual Classical Caucus. **RESEARCH** Greek & Roman rhetoric; oratory; political theory. **SELECTED PUBLICATIONS** Auth, Order for Payment to a Banker, Business Letter, Columbia Papyri, 97; Clientela System, Papian-Poppacan Law(Lex Papia-Poppaea, Pax romana, Roman Republic, of The Historical Encyclopedia of world Slavery, 97; Formalized speech in twentieth-century Madagascar and the Late Republic, in Retorica, Politica e Ideologia: Desde la Antiguedad hasta nuestros dias, Salamanca, Spain, 98; Cicero, On Friendship, translation, Copley Publ Co, forthcoming. **CONTACT ADDRESS** Dept of Romance & Classical Lang, Michigan State Univ, East Lansing, MI 48824. **EMAIL** fogell@ux1.cso.uiuc.edu

FOLEY, JOHN MILES
PERSONAL Born 01/22/1947, Northampton, MA, m, 1983, 4 children **DISCIPLINE** COMPARATIVE LITERATURE **EDUCATION** Univ Mass, PhD, 74. **CAREER** Prof, researcher. **HONORS AND AWARDS** NEH; ACLS; Guggenheim Fel; IREX; Fulbright; Mellon; founded, ctr stud in oral tradition. **MEMBERSHIPS** Russ Acad Sci; Folklore Fellows. **RESEARCH** Oral tradition; ancient Greek; medieval English; South Slavic. **SELECTED PUBLICATIONS** Auth, The Theory of Oral Composition (Indiana); auth, Traditional Oral Epic (California); auth, Immanent Art (Indiana); auth, Homer's Traditional Art, Penn State; ed, Teaching Oral Traditions, Modern Language Assoc; ed, Oral Tradition, 86-. **CONTACT ADDRESS** Center for Studies in Oral Tradition, Univ of Missouri, Columbia, 316 Hillcrest Hall, Columbia, MO 65211. **EMAIL** foleyj@missouri.edu

FONTANELLA, LEE
PERSONAL Born 07/23/1941, Stafford Springs, CT, m, 1974, 1 child **DISCIPLINE** HISPANIC STUDIES, COMPARA-

TIVE LITERATURE. **EDUCATION** Williams Col, BA, 63; New York Univ, MA, 66; Princeton Univ, MA, 68, PhD (Romance lang and lit), 71. **CAREER** Instr Span, Williams Col, 63-64; asst prof, 70-76, Assoc Prof Span, Univ Tex, Austin, 76-, Coun Int Exchange Scholars fel, 77-78. **MEMBERSHIPS** SCent Mod Lang Asn; SCent Soc 18th Century Studies; Am Asn Teachers Span and Port; MLA; Am Soc 18th Century Studies. **RESEARCH** Spanish romantic literature and essay; comparative literature; 19th century popular science and photohistory. **SELECTED PUBLICATIONS CONTACT ADDRESS** Dept of Span and Port, Univ of Texas, Austin, Batts Hall, Austin, TX 78712.

FONTES, MANUEL D.
PERSONAL Born 07/02/1945, Azores, Portugal, m, 1974, 3 children **DISCIPLINE** CLASSICS, LANGUAGE **EDUCATION** Modesto Jr Col, AB, 64; Stanislaus State Col, BA, 69; Univ Calif Berkeley, MA, 72; Univ Calif Las Angeles, PhD, 75. **CAREER** Lectr, Stanford Univ, 72, 73; asst prof to assoc prof to prof, Kent State Univ, 75-. **HONORS AND AWARDS** NEH Fel, 78, 80-81; Guggenheim Fel 84-85; Distinguished Scholar Award, 97. **MEMBERSHIPS** AATSP; CSA; AIL; MLA; SRBHP; SCSM. **RESEARCH** Medieval and renaissance Spanish and Portuguese literature; relations between folklore and literature; the role of conversos in Spanish literature; crypto-Judaism in Portugal and Spain. **SELECTED PUBLICATIONS** Ed, Romanceiro Portuguese do Canada, Acta Univ, 79; ed, Romanceiro Portuguese dos Estados Unidos, 1: Nova Inglaterra; 2: California, Acta Univ, 80; ed, Romanceiro da Ilha de Sao Jorge, Acta Univ, 83; auth, "The Ballad of 'Floresvento' and Its Epic Antecedents," Ky Romance Quart 32 (85): 309-319; co-ed, Romanceiro da Provincia de Trds-os-Montes, Acta Univ, 87; auth, "Four Portuguese Crypto-Jewish Prayers and Their Inquisitorial Counterparts," Mediterranean Lang Rev 6-7 (90): 67-104; auth, "The Holy Trinity in 'La Lozana Andaluza," Hisp Rev 62 (90): 249-266; auth, "Celestina as an Antithesis of the Virgin Mary," J Hisp Philol 14 (90): 7-41; auth, Portuguese and Brazil Bibliographic Index, Hisp Sem Medieval Studies, 97; auth, Folklore and Literature: Studies in the Portuguese, Brazilian, Sephardic, and Hispanic Oral Traditions, SUNY Pr, 00. **CONTACT ADDRESS** Dept Class, Kent State Univ, Kent, OH 44242. **EMAIL** mfontes@neo.rr.com

FORCADAS, ALBERTO M.
PERSONAL Born 11/25/1935, Barcelona, Spain, m, 1966 **DISCIPLINE** SPANISH LANGUAGE & LITERATURE **EDUCATION** Univ Ga, BBA, 62; Univ Mo-Columbia, MA, 64, PhD (Span), 66. **CAREER** Asst prof, 66-70, Assoc Prof, 70-79, Prof Span and Catalan, Univ Alta, 80-, Univ Alta Res Grant-in-aid, 67-68; Can Coun Res Grant Catalan-English Dict, 68-69. **MEMBERSHIPS** MLA; Am Asn Teachers Span and Port, Can Asn Hispanists, Can Asn Latin Am Studies, Assoc Int Llenqua and Lit Catalanes. **RESEARCH** Golden Age Literature (especially theatre), Catalan Language and Literature, Ruben Dario and Modernism. **CONTACT ADDRESS** Dept of Modern Lang & Cultural Stud, Univ of Alberta, 200 Arts Bldg, Edmonton, AB, Canada T6G 2E6.

FORCE, PIERRE
PERSONAL Born 04/04/1958, Toulon, France, m, 1997, 2 children **DISCIPLINE** FRENCH LITERATURE **EDUCATION** Sorbonne, BA, 79; MA, 80; PhD, 87; Hab, 94. **CAREER** Lectr, Yale, 84-86; lectr, J Hopkins, 86-87; asst prof, assoc prof, prof, Nell Singer prof, Col Univ, 87-. **HONORS AND AWARDS** Ecole normale superieure, Paris, 78-81, 83-84; Col Univ Cou for Res Human, 88, 89; Chevalier dans l'Ordre des palmes academiques, 99. **MEMBERSHIPS** Cen Intl Blaise Pascal, Soc des Amis de Port-Royal, NA Soc for Seventeenth Cen Fr Lit, Col Univ Sem on Eighteenth Cen Euro Cul, MLA. **RESEARCH** Seventeenth and eighteenth-cen European intellectual history, French classicism and its reception, history of hermeneutics. **SELECTED PUBLICATIONS** Auth, Le Probleme hermeneutique chez Pascal, Vrin (Paris), 89; auth, Moliere ou le Prix des choses: Morale, economie et comedie, Nathan (Paris), 94; auth, De la morale A l'economie politique: Dialogue Franco-American sur les moralistes franqais, PUP (Pau: France), 96; auth, Pensees, Pascal, Resume analytique: Commentaire critique, Nathan (Paris), 97. **CONTACT ADDRESS** Dept French, Columbia Univ, New York, NY 10027. **EMAIL** pf3@columbia.edu

FORD, ALVIN EARLE
PERSONAL Born 11/07/1937, Edmonton, AB, Canada **DISCIPLINE** FRENCH LITERATURE **EDUCATION** Univ BC, BA, 59, MA, 62; Univ Pa, PhD, 71. **CAREER** Instr French, Univ Sask, Regina, 62-65; lectr, 68-71, asst prof, 71-76, assoc prof, 76-81, prof French, 81-, Calif State Univ, Northridge. **MEMBERSHIPS** Am Assn Teachers Fr; Am Soc 18th Century Studies Res. **RESEARCH** Medieval apocrypha; enlightenment. **SELECTED PUBLICATIONS** Auth, L'evangile de Nicodeme: Les Versions Courtes en Ancien Francais et en Prose, Droz, Geneva, 73; auth, La vengeance de Nostre-Seigneur: The old French prose versions, Vol I: The version of Japheth, Pontifical Inst Mediaeval Studies, 82; co-ed, Paradigms in Medieval Thought: Applications in Medieval Disciplines, Mellon, Lewiston, 90; auth, La Vengeance de Nostre-Seigneur, vol 2, Pontifical Institute of Medieval Studies, 93. **CONTACT ADDRESS** Dept of Mod & Classical Langs & Lits, California State Univ, Northridge, 18111 Nordhoff St, Northridge, CA 91330-8247. **EMAIL** alvin.ford@csun.edu

FORD, ANDREW
PERSONAL Born New York, NY, m, 2 children **DISCIPLINE** CLASSICS **EDUCATION** Cornell Univ, BA, 74; Yale Univ, PhD, 81. **CAREER** Instr, Smith Col, 80-85; fel, Cornell Univ, 85-87; asst/assoc prof, Princeton Univ, 87-; Prof. **HONORS AND AWARDS** NEH fel. **MEMBERSHIPS** Am Philol Asn. **RESEARCH** Classics. **SELECTED PUBLICATIONS** Auth, Aomen: the poetry of the past. **CONTACT ADDRESS** 75 Dryads Green, Northampton, MA 01060. **EMAIL** aford@princeton.edu

FORD, JAMES
DISCIPLINE LANGUAGE AWARENESS **EDUCATION** Henderson State Univ, BSE, 62; Univ Central Ark, MSE, 67, Univ Ark, MA, 68; Ohio State Univ, PhD, 74. **CAREER** English and Lit, Univ Ark. **HONORS AND AWARDS** Acting Chair, Dept; Chair, dept, 77-86. **SELECTED PUBLICATIONS** Areas: language attitudes, and foreign language acquisition/learning. **CONTACT ADDRESS** Univ of Arkansas, Fayetteville, Fayetteville, AR 72701.

FORD, JAMES FRANCIS
PERSONAL Born 02/15/1937, Russell County, AL, m, 1972, 4 children **DISCIPLINE** SPANISH, SOCIOLINGUISTICS **EDUCATION** Henderson State Univ, BSE, 62; Univ Cent Ark, MSE, 67; Univ Ark, MA, 68; Ohio State Univ, PhD (for lang educ), 74. **CAREER** Instr Spanish methods, Ark State Univ, 68-69 and Univ Ark, 69-70; asst prof Spanish methods, Okla State Univ, 72-74; asst prof, 74-77, Assoc Prof Spanish and Chmn Dept for Lang, 77-, Bd of dir, Cent State Conf Teaching For Lang, 76-80. **MEMBERSHIPS** MLA; Am Coun Teaching For Lang; Am Asn Teachers Span and Port; Teachers English Speakers Other Lang. **RESEARCH** Language acquisition; sociolinguistics; teacher training. **SELECTED PUBLICATIONS** Auth, Intermediate Spanish, Mod Lan J, Vol 79, 95; Facetas--Conversation and Writing, Mod Lan J, Vol 78, 94; Personajes, Mod Lan J, Vol 77, 93; Claro--Impressions and Ideas, Mod Lan J, Vol 79, 95; Intermediate Spanish--Civilization and Culture, 5th Edition, Mod Lan J, Vol 79, 95; Intermediate Spanis Conversation Review, 5th Edition, Mod Lan J, Vol 79, 95; Claro--Tapescript, Mod Lan J, Vol 79 95; Intermediate Spanish Lit Art, 5th Eition Spanish, Mod Lan J, Vol 79, 95; Facetas--Reader, Mod Lan J, Vol 78, 94; Intermediate Spanish--Laboratory Manual and Creative Exercises, Mod Lan J, Vol 79, 95. **CONTACT ADDRESS** Dept For Lang, Univ of Arkansas, Fayetteville, Fayetteville, AR 72701-1202.

FOREST, JEAN
PERSONAL Born 03/03/1942, Montreal, PQ, Canada **DISCIPLINE** FRENCH LITERATURE **EDUCATION** Laurentian Univ, BA, 63; Laval Univ, MA, 66, PhD (French lit), 71. **CAREER** Assoc Prof French Lit, Univ Sherbrooke, 70-. **RESEARCH** French 19th century prose and poetry; modern criticism. **SELECTED PUBLICATIONS** Auth, "Des femmes de Balzac," Montreal, P.U.M., (84), 232; auth, "L'affaie Maiget," Monteral, P.U.M., (94),1190; auth, "Les archives Maiget," Montreal, P.U.M., (94,) 286; auth, "Anatomie du quebecois," Montrreal, Triptyque, (96), 340. **CONTACT ADDRESS** 2990 Rue Savard, Sherbrooke, QC, Canada JIK 1S4.

FORMAN, MICHAEL LAWRENCE
PERSONAL Born 06/30/1940, Kansas City, MO, m, 1963, 4 children **DISCIPLINE** LIMGUISTICS, ANTHROPOLOGY **EDUCATION** John Carroll Univ, AB, 61; Cornell Univ, PhD, 72. **CAREER** Asst researcher, Pac & Asian Ling Inst, 68-69, acting asst prof, 69-72, asst prof, 72-73, chmn Southeast Asian studies, 77-80, Assoc Prof Ling, Univ Hawaii, Manoa, 73-, Second Language Acquisition faculty; assoc ed, Oceanic Ling; coed, The Carrier Pidgeon, 93-96; contribr, Biography: An Interdisciplinary Quart. **HONORS AND AWARDS** Nat Endowment for Humanities study fel, 74-75; Soc Sci Res Inst, 80-82, 93-95; Excellence in Teaching Awd, Univ Hawaii Board of Regents, 84, Univ Hawaii Col Lang, Ling, & Lit, 84; Robert W. Clapton Awd for Distinguished Community Service, 86. **MEMBERSHIPS** Am Anthrop Asn; Ling Soc Am; Ling Soc Philippines. **RESEARCH** Child language acquisition; pidginization and creolization; Philippine descriptive linguistics. **SELECTED PUBLICATIONS** Auth Kapampangan Grammar Notes, 71 & Kapampangan Dictionary, 71, Univ Hawaii; coauth, Riddles: Expressive models of interrogation, Ethnology, Vol X , Nov 4 & In: Directions in Sociolinguistic Holt, 72; ed, World Englishes 2000, Univ Hawaii Press, 97. **CONTACT ADDRESS** Dept of Ling, Univ of Hawaii, Manoa, 1890 E West Rd, Honolulu, HI 96822-2318. **EMAIL** forman@hawaii.edu

FORNARA, CHARLES WILLIAM
PERSONAL Born 11/19/1935, New York, NY **DISCIPLINE** CLASSICS **EDUCATION** Columbia Col, AB 56; Univ Chicago, AM, 58; Univ Calif, Los Angeles, PhD, 61. **CAREER** Instr classics, Ohio State Univ, 61-63; from asst prof to prof, 63-77, Prof Class and Hist, Brown Univ, 77-. **MEMBERSHIPS** Am Philol Asn; Am Hist Asn; Am Asn Ancient Hists; Soc Promotion of Hellenic Studies. **RESEARCH** Greek history; epigraphy and historiography; late antiquity. **SELECTED PUBLICATIONS** Auth, Diodorus Siculus and the 1st Century, Classic Philol, Vol 87, 92; Studies in Ammianus Marcellinus .2. Ammianus Knowledge and Use of Greek and Latin Literature, Hist Zeitschrift Alte Geschichte, Vol 41, 92; Studies in Ammianus Marcellinus .2. Ammianus Knowledge and Use of Greek And Latin Literature, Historia Zeitschrift Alte Geschichte, Vol 41, 92. **CONTACT ADDRESS** Dept of Classics, Brown Univ, 1 Prospect St, Providence, RI 02912-9127.

FORSTER, MERLIN HENRY
PERSONAL Born 02/24/1928, Delta, UT, m, 1952, 5 children **DISCIPLINE** SPANISH AND PORTUGUESE **EDUCATION** Brigham Young Univ, BA, 56; Univ Ill, MA, 57, PhD, 60. **CAREER** Instr Romance lang, Univ Tex, 60-61, asst prof, 61-62; from asst prof to assoc prof, Univ Ill, Urbana-Champaign, 62-69, prof, 69-78, dir, Ctr Latin Am Studies, 72-78; Prof Span and Port and Chmn Dept, Univ Tex, Austin, 79-, Soc Sci Res Coun res grant, 65-66; Fulbright-Hays res fel, Arg, Uruguay, Chile, Brazil and Peru, 71; res assoc, Ctr Advan Study, Univ Ill, 76. **MEMBERSHIPS** Am Asn Teachers Span and Port; Latin Am Studies Asn; Inst Int Lit Iberoam (pres, 79-81). **RESEARCH** Spanish American poetry and drama; Mexican literature; Brazilian and Portuguese literature. **SELECTED PUBLICATIONS** Auth, The Concept of Ars Poetica in the Poetry of Rojas, Gonzalo, Chasqui Revista Lit Latinoamericana, Vol 22, 93. **CONTACT ADDRESS** Dept of Span and Port, Univ of Texas, Austin, Austin, TX 78712.

FORSYTH, PHYLLIS
PERSONAL Born Boston, MA, m, 1969 **DISCIPLINE** CLASSICAL STUDIES, HISTORY, FINE ART **EDUCATION** Mount Holyoke Col, BA, 66; Univ Toronto, MA, 67, PhD, 72. **CAREER** Tchr Fel, Univ Toronto, 67-69; prof, Univ Waterloo, 69-, founding ch, dept class studs, 79-88, acting ch 94-. **HONORS AND AWARDS** Distinguished Tchr Awd. **MEMBERSHIPS** Ont Class Asn; Can Fedn Hum; Archeol Inst Am; Can Mediter Inst. **RESEARCH** The Aegean Bronze Age; Thera in the Bronze Age; Minoan Civilization; Cycladic Civilization; Volcanic Eruptions in Antiquity; Natural Caatastrophes in the Ancient World; The Myth of Atlantis; Catullus. **SELECTED PUBLICATIONS** Auth, Atlantis: The Making of Myth, 80; ed, Labyrinth: A Classical Magazine for Secondary Schs, 73-84, 88-94; auth, Thera in the Bronze Age, Peter Lang Publ, 97. **CONTACT ADDRESS** Dept of Classical Studies, Univ of Waterloo, 200 University Ave W, Waterloo, ON, Canada N2L 3G1. **EMAIL** forsyth@watarts.uwaterloo.ca

FORTENBAUGH, WILLIAM WALL
PERSONAL Born 07/10/1936, Philadelphia, PA, m, 1959, 3 children **DISCIPLINE** CLASSICS **EDUCATION** Princeton Univ, BA, 58; Oxford Univ, BA, 61; Univ PA, PhD(classics), 64. **CAREER** From instr to asst prof, 64-68, assoc prof, 68-80, prof I, classics, 79-91, prof II, Rutgers Univ, 91-; Ctr Hellenic Studies jr fel, 67-68; Am Coun Learned Soc study fel & hon res fel, Univ Col, London, 72-73; Alexander von Humboldt-Stiftung res fel, Univ Heidelberg, 76-77; vis prof, Univ WA, spring 87; res fel, Netherlands Inst for advanced study, 90-91; Alexander von Humboldt-Stiftung, res fel, Univ Saarbrucken, 92; Study fel, Bogliasco Found, 99. **HONORS AND AWARDS** Phi Beta Kappa, 58; NEH, summer stipend, 67, project grants, 80-83, 84-85, 88. **MEMBERSHIPS** Am Philol Asn; Soc for Ancient Greek Philos (pres, 76-77, prog comm, 82-98). **RESEARCH** Ancient philosophy. **SELECTED PUBLICATIONS** Auth, Nicomachean Ethics 1096 b26-29, Phronesis, 66; Recent Scholarship on Aristotle's Psychology, Class World, 67; Aristotle on Emotion, Duckworth, London, NY: Barnes & Noble, 74; Quellen zur Ethik Theophrasts, Amsterdam: B R Gruener Verlag, 84; Theophrastus of Eresus: Sources for His Life, Writings, Thought & Influence, 2 vols, ed and trans with P Hughby, R Sharples, & D Gutas, Leiden: E J Brill, 92, reprinted with corrections, 93. **CONTACT ADDRESS** Dept Classics, Rutgers, The State Univ of New Jersey, New Brunswick, PO Box 270, New Brunswick, NJ 08903-0270. **EMAIL** fortenb@rci.rutgers.edu

FOSTER, DAVID W.
PERSONAL Born 09/11/1940, Seattle, WA, m, 1966, 1 child **DISCIPLINE** SPANISH, WOMEN'S STUDIES **EDUCATION** Univ of Wash, BA, 61; MA, 63; PhD, 64. **CAREER** Teaching Asst to instr, Univ of Wash, 61-64; vis instr, Fresno State Col, 62; vis asst prof, Vanderbilt Univ, 64; asst prof, Univ of Mo, 64-66; fulbright prof, Inst del Profesorado Superior en Lenguas Vivas, Universidad Nacional de La Plata, 67; asst prof to prof, Ariz State Univ, 70-; fulbright prof, Univ de Buenos Aires, 73; Inter-American Development Bank Prof of Ling, Univ Catolica de Chile, 75; fulbright prof, univ Federal do parana, 85; fulbright prof, Univ Catolica del Uruguay, 88; vis prof, Univ of Calif at Los Angeles, 89; vis prof, Univ of Ariz, 89. **HONORS AND AWARDS** Outstanding Graduate Mentor, Graduate Col, 89; res of the year, Alumni Asn, 94. **RESEARCH** Urban culture in Latin America, with emphasis on issues of gender construction and sexual identity, Jewish culture. **SELECTED PUBLICATIONS** Auth, Violence in Argentine Literature: Cultural Responses to Tyranny, Univ of Mo Press, 95; auth, Sexual Textualities: Essays on Queer/ing Latin

American Writing, Univ of Tex (Austin, TX), 97; auth, Espacio escenico y lenguaje, Galerna (Buenos Aires, Mexico), 98; auth, A Funny Dirty Little War/No habra mas penas ni olvido, Flicks Books (Trowbrdige, Eng), 98; coauth, Culture and Customs of Argentina, Greenwood Press (Westport, CT), 98; coauth, The Writer's Reference Guide to Spanish, Univ of Tex Press (Austin, TX), 99; auth, Gender and Society in contemporary Brazilian Cinema, Univ of Tex Press (Austin, TX), 99. **CONTACT ADDRESS** Dept Lang and Lit, Arizona State Univ, PO Box 870202, Tempe, AZ 85287-0202. **EMAIL** david.foster@asu.edu

FOUCHEREAUX, JEAN
DISCIPLINE FRENCH LITERATURE **EDUCATION** Univ Iowa, MA, PhD. **CAREER** Assoc prof. **SELECTED PUBLICATIONS** Auth, pubs on francophone studies in North America and implementation of new teaching strategies through technology. **CONTACT ADDRESS** 37 Col Ave, Gorham, MN 04038-1083. **EMAIL** jeanf@usm.maine.edu

FOURNIER, HANNAH
DISCIPLINE FRENCH LITERATURE **EDUCATION** Univ Toronto, BA; Univ Western Ontario, MA; PhD. **RESEARCH** Sixteenth century renaissance; reformation literature; history of French women writers. **SELECTED PUBLICATIONS** Auth, pub(s) on Marie de Gournay and Marguerite de Navarre; co-ed, Les Jumeaux martirs 1650. **CONTACT ADDRESS** Dept of French, Univ of Waterloo, 200 University Ave W, Waterloo, ON, Canada N2L 3G1. **EMAIL** hsfourer@watarts.uwaterloo.ca

FOURNY, DIANE
DISCIPLINE SEVENTEENTH- AND EIGHTEENTH-CENTURY FRENCH LITERATURE **EDUCATION** Stanford Univ, PhD. **CAREER** Assoc prof, Univ KS. **HONORS AND AWARDS** H Bernerd Fink distinguished Tchg award. **RESEARCH** Psychoanalytic and anthrop approaches to lit. **SELECTED PUBLICATIONS** Auth, articles on Corneille, Diderot, and Rousseau. **CONTACT ADDRESS** Dept of French and Italian, Univ of Kansas, Lawrence, Admin Building, Lawrence, KS 66045.

FOWKES, ROBERT ALLEN
PERSONAL Born 04/07/1913, Harrison, NY **DISCIPLINE** LINGUISTICS **EDUCATION** NYork Univ, AB, 34, AM, 35; Columbia Univ, PhD, 47. **CAREER** Asst Ger, NY Univ, 35-36; asst, Columbia Univ, 37-38, from instr to prof, 38-73, chmn dept Ger lang, 57-68; prof and chmn dept Ger lang, 73-78, Emer Prof Ling and Ger, NY Univ, 78-, Lectr Celtic lang, Univ Pa, 67. **MEMBERSHIPS** Ling Soc Am; MLA; Int Ling Asn. **RESEARCH** Germanic Indo-European and comparative linguistics; Welsh and other Celtic languages; Welsh etymological dictionary. **SELECTED PUBLICATIONS** Auth, Spirit Pond Runestones--A Study in Linguistics, Verbatim, Vol 22, 96; Eyebrows and Lowbrows, Verbatim, Vol 19, 93; The International Linguistic Association, A Subjective History, Word J Int Ling Assoc, Vol 45, 94. **CONTACT ADDRESS** 632 Van Cortland Park Ave, Yonkers, NY 10705.

FOWLER, CAROLYN A.
DISCIPLINE FRENCH LITERATURE **EDUCATION** Univ Pa, PhD. **CAREER** Prof. **RESEARCH** Haitian culture and literature; Cameroonian literature; French heritage of Madagascar; African American literature; literature and culture as reflected in literary and general interest periodicals. **SELECTED PUBLICATIONS** Auth, pubs on Haitian authors, and African American aesthetics. **CONTACT ADDRESS** For Lang and Lit, Colorado State Univ, 1Colorado State Univ, Fort Collins, CO 80523-0001. **EMAIL** cfowler@vines.colostate.edu

FOX, DIAN
PERSONAL Born 04/10/1951, Seattle, WA **DISCIPLINE** SPANISH LITERATURE **EDUCATION** Univ Ore, BA, 75; Duke Univ, MA, 77, PhD (Romance lang), 79. **CAREER** Lectr Span, Duke Univ, 79-80; Asst Prof Span and Humanities, Columbia Univ, 80-, Am Coun Learned Soc fel, 83; res assoc, Univ Calif, Berkeley, 83. **MEMBERSHIPS** MLA; Am Asn Teachers Span and Port. **RESEARCH** Spanish Golden Age theater, especially political aspects of Calderon; narrative theory of Cervantes; medieval Spanish literature. **SELECTED PUBLICATIONS** Auth, The Prince in the Tower, Perceptions of La Vida Es Sueno, Mln Mod Lan Notes, Vol 110, 95; Parallel Lives--Spanish and English National Drama 1580-1680, Comp Lit Stud, Vol 30, 93; The Prince in the Tower, Perceptions of La Vida Es Sueno, Mln Mod Lan Notes, Vol 110, 95; An Ideological Reading of Calderon, El Medico de Su Honra, Bull Comediantes, Vol 45, 93; Fatal Union, A Pluralistic Approach to the Spanish Wife Murder Comedias, Bull Hisp Stud, Vol 70, 93. **CONTACT ADDRESS** Dept Roman Langs, Brandeis Univ, 415 S St, Waltham, MA 02453-2700.

FOX, EDWARD INMAN
PERSONAL Born 08/22/1933, Nashville, TN **DISCIPLINE** SPANISH STUDIES **EDUCATION** Vanderbilt Univ, BA, 54, MA, 58; Princeton Univ, MA, 59, PhD, 60. **CAREER** Asst prof Span, Vanderbilt Univ, 60-64, assoc prof, 64-66; assoc prof Romance lang Univ Mass, 66-67; Prof Hispanic studies and chmn dept, Vassar Col, 67-71, John Guy Vassar prof mod lang, 71-74, dean fac, 71-72, dir long range educ planning, 72-73; pres, Knox Col, Ill, 74-82; Prof Span and Port, Northwestern Univ, 82-, Vis prof, Escuela Verano, Mex, 58-60 and 62; Am Philos Soc grants, 63 and 68; Fulbright res grant, Spain, 65-66; mem exec and nominating comt, Spanish IV, MLA, 65-68, secy, Spanish V, 67, chmn, 68; delivered lect, Spain and Brit Isles, 66,74 and 77, US, 67-68 and 77-82; vis prof Romance lang, Wesleyan Univ, 71; Miguel de Unamuno prof, Univ Salamanca, 73; chmn, Great Lakes District Rhodes Scholarship Comt, 79-81; mem exec comt, Spanish V, MLA, 80-84; Nat Endowment Humanities fel, 82-83. **MEMBERSHIPS** Asoc Int Hispanistas; MLA. **RESEARCH** Nineteenth and twentieth century Spanish literature and intellectual history. **SELECTED PUBLICATIONS CONTACT ADDRESS** Northwestern Univ, Evanston, IL 60201.

FOX, LINDA CHODOSH
PERSONAL Born 05/20/1943, Charlottesville, VA, m, 1967, 2 children **DISCIPLINE** SPANISH, WOMEN'S STUDIES **EDUCATION** Douglass Col, BA, 65; Ind Univ, Bloomington, MA 67; Univ Wis-Madison, PhD(Span), 74. **CAREER** Lectr, 71-74, asst prof Span, Ind Univ-Purdue Univ, Fort Wayne, 74-95; assoc prof Span, 96-; dir of Women's Studies, 82-88; 95, newsletter ed, Feministas Unidas: A coalition of feminist scholars in Span, Span-Am, Luso-Brazilian, Afro-Port & Chicano-Riqueno Studies; 81-96. **HONORS AND AWARDS** Phi Beta Kappa, 65; Sigma Delta Pi Honorary, 65; Outstanding Teacher Awd Indiana U-Purdue U, Fort Wayne, 96; Best Teachers in America; 98; Zonta Summit Awd, 00. **MEMBERSHIPS** MLA; Am Asn Teachers Span & Port; Assoc Lit Hisp Femenina; Ferninistas Unidas. **RESEARCH** Power in the family and beyond: Dona Perfecta and Bernarda Alba as manipulators of their destinies; characterization of women in Hispanic literature. **SELECTED PUBLICATIONS** Auth, Vision of Cain and Abel in Spain's generation of 1898, CLA J, 6/78; Las lagrimas y la tristeza en el Lazarillo de Tormes, Revista Estudios Hisp, 10/79; Making Bonds, Breaking Bonds: The Mother-Daughter Relationship in Chicana Poetry 1975-1985, in En homenaje a Victoria Urbano, ed, Adelaida Lopez de Martinez, Madrid: Editorial Fundamentos, 93; From Chants to Borders to Communion: Pat Mora's Journey to Nepantla, Bilingual Review, Revista Bilingue, Sept-Dec, 96; auth, "Four imaginarios femeninos in Pat Mora's 'Cuarteto Mexicano,'" in The Americas Review, valedictorian issue, 99. **CONTACT ADDRESS** Dept of Mod Foreign Lang, Indiana Univ-Purdue Univ, Fort Wayne, 2101 Coliseum Blvd E, Fort Wayne, IN 46805-1499. **EMAIL** fox@ipfw.edu

FRADIN, JOSEPH I.
DISCIPLINE COMPARATIVE LITERATURE **EDUCATION** Columbia Univ, BA; PhD. **CAREER** Fac, Columbia Univ; fac, Cornell Univer; prof, SUNY Buffalo, present. **RESEARCH** Novels of Dickens; writing and violence; art and the ethical. **SELECTED PUBLICATIONS** Auth, articles in a number of jour(s) including PMLA, 19th century fiction; TX studies in lang(s) and lit, and Conradiana. **CONTACT ADDRESS** Dept Comp Lit, SUNY, Buffalo, 639 Clemens Hall, Buffalo, NY 14260.

FRAIOLI, DEBORAH
PERSONAL Born Ithaca, NY, m, 2 children **DISCIPLINE** FRENCH **EDUCATION** Cornell Univ, BA, 65; Syracuse Univ, MA, 72; PhD, 81. **CAREER** Instr, Syracuse Univ, 72-73; teaching asst, Harvard Univ, 81; prof, Simmons Col, 83-. **HONORS AND AWARDS** Woodrow Wil Dissertation Fel, 81; Am Coun of Learned Soc Fel, 82-83. **MEMBERSHIPS** Medieval Acad of Am, Am Asn of Teachers of French. **RESEARCH** Joan of Arc (Literature, History, Theology); Abelard and Heloise. **SELECTED PUBLICATIONS** Auth, Joan of Arc: The Early Debate, Boydell & Brewer, 00; auth, "Pierre Bayle's Reflections on a Much Talked About Woman: The 'Heloise' Article in the Dictionaire historiue et critique," in Listening to Heloise: Essays on the Abbess of Abelard's Paraclete, St Martins Press, 00; auth, "Why Joan of Arc Never Became an Amazon," in Fresh Verdicts on Joan of Arc, Garland, 96; auth, "L'Origine des sources ecrites et leur fonction pour Le Titie de Jehanne d'Arc de Christine de Pizan," Bulletin de L'Association des amis du Centre Jeane d'Arc, (93): 5-17; auth, "The Importance of Satire in St. Jerome's Adversus jovinianum as an Argument against the Authenticity of the Historia Calamitatum," Falschungen im Mettelalter, (88): 167-200. **CONTACT ADDRESS** Dept of Mod Lang, Simmons Col, 300 Fenway, Boston, MA 02115-5820. **EMAIL** fraioli@simmons.edu

FRAJZYNGIER, ZYGMUNT
PERSONAL Born 04/03/1938, Radom, Poland, m, 1971, 2 children **DISCIPLINE** LINGUISTICS, AFRICAN LANGUAGES AND LINGUISTICS **EDUCATION** Univ Warsaw, MA, 63, PhD (philol), 68; Univ Ghana, MA, 65. **CAREER** Doktorant African lang, Univ Warsaw, 65-68, adjunct, 68-69; asst prof, 70-76, assoc prof, 76-82, Prof Ling, Univ Colo, 82-, Sr lectr, Bayero Col, Ahmadu Bello Univ, Kano, Nigeria, 74-75. **MEMBERSHIPS** Ling Soc Am. **RESEARCH** Semantics; syntax. **SELECTED PUBLICATIONS CONTACT ADDRESS** Dept Ling, Univ of Colorado, Boulder, Box 295, Box 295, Boulder, CO 80309-0295.

FRAKES, JEROLD C.
PERSONAL Born 11/02/1953, Peoria, IL **DISCIPLINE** COMPARATIVE LITERATURE, GERMAN, LATIN **EDUCATION** Univ of MN, PhD, 82 **CAREER** Asst Prof, 82-87, USC; Guest Prof, 87-, Medieval Latin Univ Heidelberg; Prof, USC, 88-. **HONORS AND AWARDS** Austro-Am Soc, Commission Travel Awd, 78; Fulbright, 79; Deutscher Adademischer Austauschdienst, commission Tavel award, 79; Germanistic Soc of Am/Fulbright, 80-81; Alexander von Humboldt Found Fel, 93, 98; Skirball Visting Fel, 01-02; Nat Endowment for the Humanities Fel, 01-02. **MEMBERSHIPS** Am Assoc of Prof of Yiddish Lit, Assoc for Jewish Studies, Medieval Acad of Am, Medieval Assoc of the Pacific, Modern Language assoc, World Congress of Jewish Studies. **RESEARCH** Medieval Europena literature, German, Latin, Yiddish, Norse **SELECTED PUBLICATIONS** Auth, The Fate of Fortune in the Early Middle Ages: The Boethian Tradition, Leiden: E.J. Brill, 87; auth, The Politics of Interpretation: Alterity and Ideology in Old Yiddish studies, Albany: Suny Press, 88; transl, Walter Berschin, Greek Letters and the Latin Middle Ages: From Jerome to Nicholas of Cusa, Washington: Catholic Univ Press, 88; ed, Max Weinreich, Geschichte der jiddischen Sprachforschung, Atlanta: Scholars Press, 93; auth, Brides and Doom: Gender, Property and Power in Medieval German Women's Epic, Philadelphia: Univ of Pennsylvania Press, 94 **CONTACT ADDRESS** Dept of German, Univ of So California, MC 0351, Los Angeles, CA 90089. **EMAIL** frakes@usc.edu

FRANCESCHETTI, ANTONIO
PERSONAL Born 10/13/1939, Padova, Italy, m, 1965, 3 children **DISCIPLINE** ITALIAN **EDUCATION** Univ Padova, Dr Lett, 63; Columbia Univ, PhD (Ital), 68. **CAREER** Lectr Ital, Univ Reading, 64, lectr, Barnard Col, Columbia Univ, 64-66, from instr to asst prof, 66-69, asst prof, 69-71, assoc prof, 71-80, Prof Ital, Scarborough Col, Univ Toronto, 80-, Can deleg, Asn Int Studi Ling and Lett Ital, 76-, rep Ital, Humanities Res Coun Can, 77-. **MEMBERSHIPS** MLA; Am Asn Teachers Ital, Asn Int Studi Ling and Lett Ital, Soc Dante Alighieri. **RESEARCH** Chivalric literature in the Middle Ages and the Renaissance, 18th century poetics and poetry. **SELECTED PUBLICATIONS** Auth, "On the Saracen in Early Italian Chivalric Literature" in Comparative Literatue East and West: Traditions and Trends, Selected Conference Papers, ed, Cornelia N. Moore and Raymond A. Moody, (Honolulu: Col Lang Haw, 86), 203-11. **CONTACT ADDRESS** Div of Humanities Scarborough Col, Univ of Toronto, 100 St Joseph St, Carr Hall, Room 204, West Hill, ON, Canada M5S 1J4. **EMAIL** francesc@chass.utoronto.ca

FRANCESE, JOSEPH
PERSONAL Born 09/05/1955, Westerly, RI, m, 1979, 2 children **DISCIPLINE** ITALIAN LITERATURE, AMERICAN LITERATURE **EDUCATION** Univ RI, BA, 77; Univ Rome, LL, 81; Univ Ct, PhD, 90. **CAREER** From Asst Prof to Prof, Mich St Univ, 90-. **HONORS AND AWARDS** NEH Summer Fel, Mich St Univ, 94; Global Competence Grant, Mich St Univ, 95; Int Activities Res Grant, Midwest Univs Consortium, 95, 97. **MEMBERSHIPS** MLA, ACLA, AATI, AAIS, IGS. **RESEARCH** 16th and 20th Century Italian literature, contemporary American literature. **SELECTED PUBLICATIONS** Auth, Il realismo impopolare de Pier Paolo Pasolini, Bastogi Editrice Ital (Foggia), 91; auth, Narrating Postmodern Time and Space, St Univ NY Pr (Albany, NY), 97; auth, Cultura e politica negli anni Cinquanta. Salinari Pasolini Calvino, Lithos Editrice (Rome, Italy), 00; ed, "The Critic and His Craft: Essays in Memory of Glauco Cambon, Bordighera Pr (00). **CONTACT ADDRESS** Dept Lang, Michigan State Univ, East Lansing, MI 48824-1112.

FRANCIS, WINTHROP NELSON
PERSONAL Born 10/23/1910, Philadelphia, PA, m, 1939, 3 children **DISCIPLINE** LINGUISTICS **EDUCATION** Harvard Univ, AB, 31; Univ Pa, AM, 35, PhD, 37. **CAREER** From instr to prof English, Franklin and Marshall Col, 37-62; prof, 62-76, chmn dept ling, 68-75, Emer Prof Ling and English, Brown Univ, 76-, Fulbright res scholar, Univ Leeds, 56-57; Nat Endowment for Humanities sr fel, 72-73; vis sr lectr, Univ Trondheim, Norway, 76-77. **MEMBERSHIPS** MLA; NCTE; Ling Soc Am; Am Dialect Soc; Int Ling Asn. **RESEARCH** English language; dialectology; mechanolinguistics. **SELECTED PUBLICATIONS** Auth, The Oxford Companion to the English Language, Language in Society, Vol 22, 93; The Science of Words, Language, Vol 73, 97; Automating the Lexicon--Research and Practice in a Multilingual Environment, Lan, Vol 73, 97; English in Britain and Overseas--Origins and Developments, Lan Soc, Vol 25, 96; Historical Linguistics 1993, Lan, Vol 73, 97; New Directions in English Language Corpora--Methodology, Results, Software Developments, Lan, Vol 70, 94. **CONTACT ADDRESS** Brown Univ, 355 Blackstone Blvd, Apt 337, Providence, RI 02906.

FRANCO, CHARLES
PERSONAL Born 12/09/1941, Italy, m, 1978, 2 children **DISCIPLINE** ITALIAN LITERATURE **EDUCATION** Rutgers Univ, PhD, 77. **CAREER** Assoc prof, chemn dept, SUNY Stony Brook. **MEMBERSHIPS** AATI. **RESEARCH** Medieval Italian literature. **SELECTED PUBLICATIONS** Auth,

Dante: Summa Medievalis. **CONTACT ADDRESS** Dept of European Languages, SUNY, Stony Brook, Stony Brook, NY 11794-3359. **EMAIL** cfranco@notes.cc.sunysb.edu

FRANK, ELFRIEDA
PERSONAL Born 02/06/1916, Vienna, Austria **DISCIPLINE** LATIN **EDUCATION** Univ Milan, LittD, 38; Bryn Mawr Col, MA, 41; Univ Va, PhD (classics), 51. **CAREER** Asst prof classics, Cornell Col, 53-56; from asst prof to assoc prof, Tex Tech Univ, 56-61; from asst prof to assoc prof, 61-70, Prof Classics, Univ New Orleans, 70-. **MEMBERSHIPS** Am Philol Asn; Class Asn Mid W and S. **RESEARCH** Latin philology; Latin epic poetry; Ovid. **SELECTED PUBLICATIONS CONTACT ADDRESS** Dept of Foreign Lang, Univ of New Orleans, New Orleans, LA 70122.

FRANK, FRANCINE
PERSONAL Born 04/18/1931, New York, NY, d **DISCIPLINE** LINGUISTICS SPANISH **EDUCATION** NYork Univ, BA, 52; Cornell Univ, MA, 53; Univ IL, Urbana, PhD, 55. **CAREER** Instr Span, Univ IL, Urbana, 55-57; asst lang training supvr, Inter-govt Comt Europ Migration, 59-66; asst prof, 66-80, asst dean, Col Arts & Sci, 73-74, coordr, curric & interdisciplinary studies, div Humanities, 75-77, assoc prof Span & Ling, State Univ NY Albany, 80-87, dir Ling, 73-85, Consult Span proficiency exam, NY State Educ Dept, 70-80; Fulbright sr lectr appl ling, Rome, Italy, 71-72; lectr, English Lang, US Embassy, Yugoslavia, 71-72; mem, Regents External Degree Bachelors Comt, NY State, 73-84; Fulbright sr lectr ling & English as a second lang, Buenos Aires, Argentina, 80; vis prof, Sofia Univ, Bulgaria, 94; assoc Dean Col of Humanities & Fine Arts, 85-86, Dean Col of Hum & Fine Arts, 86-93, prof Linguistics and Women's Studies, 87-97, dir Ling & Cognitive Science, 94-97, dir Center for the Arts and Humanities, 94-97, Prof Emerita, SUNY, 97. **HONORS AND AWARDS** Research fel, Univ Awds Prog, SUNY Research Found, summer 82; Presidential Awd for Excellence in Academic Service, SUNYA, 86; Making Waves Awd for Community Service and Commitment to Feminist Goals, Albany Area Chapter, Nat Org for Women (NOW), 89; Book Language, Gender, and Professional Writing selected by Choice as an Outstanding Academic Book for 89-90; Bread and Roses Awd for extraordinary contributions on behalf of gender equity, from the Council of Women's Groups at the Univ at Albany, 92; Evan R. Collins Awd in recognition of distinguished service and devotion to the Univ at Albany by members of the faculty, 93; co-dir, Ford Found three-year Grant for Internationalizing Women's Studies, 95-98; Named Professor Emerita, Univ at Albany, SUNY, 97. **MEMBERSHIPS** Int Ling Asn; Ling Soc Am; MLA; Fulbright Alumni Asn; Linguistic Assoc of CAN and the US (LACUS); Nat Women's Studies Asn; Societas Linguistica Europaea. **RESEARCH** Spanish linguistics, especially syntax; pidgin and creole languages; sociolinguistics, especially language and gender. **SELECTED PUBLICATIONS** Auth, Taxemic redundancy in Spanish, In: Structural Studies on Spanish Themes; Acta Salmanticensia, Filos y Letras, Salamanca, Vol XII, No 3; The training of an English teacher, Lingua & Nuova Didattica, 9/72; Language and education in the Leeward Netherlands Antilles, Caribbean Studies, 1/74; Women's language in America: Myth and reality, In: Women's Language and Style, Studies in Contemporary Language, No 1, Akron, 78; co-ed, Colloquium on Spanish and Luso-Brazilian Linguistics, Georgetown Univ Press, 79; coauth, Language and the Sexes, SUNY Press, 84;auth, Language Planning and Sexual Equality: Guidelines for Non-Sexist Usage, in Sprachwandel und feministische Sprachpolitik: Internationale Perspektiven, Westdeutscher Verlag, 85; El genero gramatical y los cambios sociales, Espanol actual 43, 85; El Sexo como Factor Sociolinguistico: Algunas Consideraciores Teoricas y Metodologicas, Actas del V Congrso Internacional de la Asociacion de Linguistica y Filologia de la America Latina (ALFAL), Caracas, 86; coauth, Language, Gender, and Professional Writing: Theoretical Approaches and Guidelines for Nonsexist Usage, The Modern Language Asn, 89; Planificacion linguistica y cambio social, Seminario de Estudios sobre la Mujer (proceedings of the joint 86 Seminar in Women's Studies, SUNY/Univ Costa Rica), San Jose, Costa Rica, Ministry of Culture, 89; A Dean's Perspective on Women in Academe, The Cornell Lectures: Women in the Linguistics Profession, Comm on the Status of Women in Linguistics, Linguistic Soc of Am, 90; Japanese trans of Language and the Sexes, Kansai Univ Press, 95. **CONTACT ADDRESS** 489 State St., Albany, NY 12203. **EMAIL** fwf@cnsvax.albany.edu

FRANK, RICHARD MACDONOUGH
PERSONAL Born 12/04/1927, Louisville, KY, m, 1950, 4 children **DISCIPLINE** SEMITIC STUDIES, ARABIC **EDUCATION** Cath Univ Am, AB, 53, PhD, 55. **CAREER** From instr to assoc prof Semitic and Egyptian lang, 55-73, Prof Semitic and Egyptian Lang and Lit, Cath Univ Am, 73-. **HONORS AND AWARDS** Pres of Am Oriental Soc, 95-96; honorary mem of Societe Asiatique, 00. **MEMBERSHIPS** Am Orient Soc; Cath Bibl Asn Am. **RESEARCH** Islamic philosophy and theology. **SELECTED PUBLICATIONS** Auth, The Physical Theory of Kalam--Atoms, Space and Void in Basrian Mutazili Cosmology, J Am Orient Soc, Vol 116, 96; Dona Lambra and Family Conflict in the Legend of the Siete Infantes De Lara Found in the Chronicles and Old Romances, Confluencia Revista Hisp Cult Y Lit, Vol 5, 90; Theology and Society in the 2nd Century and the 3rd Century of the Hijra--A History of Religious Thought in Early Islam, J Am Orient Soc, Vol 114, 94; Dona Lambra and Family Conflict in the Legend of the Siete Infantes de Lara Found in the Chronicles and Old Romances, Confluencia Revista Hisp Cult Y Lit, Vol 5, 90. **CONTACT ADDRESS** Dept of Semitic Lang, Catholic Univ of America, Washington, DC 20017.

FRANK, YAKIRA H.
PERSONAL Born 11/15/1923, New York, NY, m, 1945, 2 children **DISCIPLINE** LINGUISTICS **EDUCATION** Honter Col, AB, 43; Univ Pa, MA, 45; Univ Mich, PhD, 49. **CAREER** From instr to assoc prof, 62-74, PROF ENGLISH and DIR STAMFORD CAMPUS, UNIV CONN, 74-, Am Coun Learned Soc fel, 49; lectr, Hunter Col, 51-55 and 58 and Univ Conn, Stanmford, 61-62; mem bd, Conn Humanities Coun, 77-. **MEMBERSHIPS** Ling Soc Am; NCTE; MLA; Teachers English as Second Lang. **RESEARCH** Stylistics; dialect geography; bilingualism. **SELECTED PUBLICATIONS** Auth, Oxford Yiddish, Vol 3--Studies in Yiddish Language, Literature and Folklore, J Jewish Stud, Vol 47, 96. **CONTACT ADDRESS** Univ of Connecticut, Stamford, Stamford, CT 06903.

FRANKE, WILLIAM
DISCIPLINE COMPARATIVE LITERATURE **EDUCATION** Williams Col, BA, 78; Oxford Univ, MA, 80, Univ Calif, Berkeley, MA, 88; Stanford Univ, PhD, 91. **CAREER** Adj fac, 84-86, Columbia Col; assoc prof, 91-, Vanderbilt Univ. **RESEARCH** Dante, Phil of lit, Poetry & Poetics, theory **CONTACT ADDRESS** Program in Comparative Literature, Vanderbilt Univ, Box 1709 - Station B, Nashville, TN 37235.

FRANKEL, MARGHERITA
PERSONAL Born Sao Paulo, Brazil, m, 1963 **DISCIPLINE** ITALIAN AND FRENCH LITERATURE **EDUCATION** Brooklyn Col, BA, 68; NYork Univ, PhD (French), 73. **CAREER** Asst prof, 73-76, Assoc Prof Ital, NY Univ, 76-. **HONORS AND AWARDS** Gustav O Arlt Awd in Humanities, Nat Coun Grad Schs, 75. **MEMBERSHIPS** Dante Soc Am; MLA; Renaissance Soc Am; Mediaeval Acad Am; Am Comp Lit Asn. **RESEARCH** Dante; Renaissance literature; Vico. **SELECTED PUBLICATIONS** Auth, Public and Private Concerns, Index Censorship, Vol 24, 95; Mikve and Philosophy of Halakha, Tradition J Orthodox Jewish Thought, Vol 31, 97. **CONTACT ADDRESS** Dept of French and Ital, New York Univ, 19 University Pl, New York, NY 10003.

FRANKLIN, JAMES L.
PERSONAL Born 07/19/1947, Dayton, OH, s **DISCIPLINE** CLASSICS **EDUCATION** Denison Univ, BA, 69; Queen's Univ, MA, 70; Duke Univ, PhD, 75. **CAREER** Asst Prof, Columbia Univ, 75-76; Asst Prof, Wellesley Col, 76-77; Vis Asst Prof, Univ Mich, 77-80; From Asst Prof to Prof, Ind Univ, 81-. **HONORS AND AWARDS** Phi Beta Kappa, 69; Fel, Am Acad of Rome, 73-75; ACLS Grand-in-Aid, 76; NEH Category B Fel, 80-81; Amoco Found Distinguished Teaching Awd, 87. **MEMBERSHIPS** APA, Am Soc of Greek and Latin Epigraphy, Archaeol Inst of Am, Asn Int d'Epigraphie Grecque et Latine, Class Asn of the Middle East and S. **RESEARCH** Pompeian studies, Roman archaeology, Latin literature. **SELECTED PUBLICATIONS** Auth, Games and a Lupanar: Prosopography of a Neighborhood in Ancient Pompeii," Class J 81 (86): 319-328; auth, "Pantomimists at Pompeii: Actius Anicetus and his Troupe," Am J of Philol 108 (87): 95-107; auth, "Literacy and the Parietal Inscriptions of Ancient Pompeii," J of Roman Archaeol (91): 77-98; auth, "Cn. Alleius Nigidius Maius and the Amphitheatre: Munera and a Distinguished Career at Ancient Pompeii," Historia 46 (97): 434-447; auth, Pompeis Difficile Est: Studies in the Political Life of Imperial Pompeii, Ann Arbor, 99; auth, "Aulus Vettius Caprasius Felix of Ancient Pompeii," Qui Miscuit Utile cum Dulci, (98), 165-175. **CONTACT ADDRESS** Dept Classical Studies, Indiana Univ, Bloomington, 1020 E Kirkwood Ave, Bloomington, IN 47405-7103. **EMAIL** franklin@indiana.edu

FRANKLIN, URSULA
PERSONAL Born 06/03/1929, Widdersberg, Germany, m, 1949 **DISCIPLINE** FRENCH LANGUAGE AND LITERATURE **EDUCATION** Mich State Univ, BA, 64, MA, 66, PhD (French), 71. **CAREER** Instr French, Mich State Univ, 70-71; asst prof, 71-74, assoc prof, 74-80, Prof French, Grand Valley State Col, 80-, Am Coun Learned Soc fel, 78-69. **MEMBERSHIPS** MLA; Am Asn Teachers Fr; Am Coun Teaching Foreign Lang; AAUP. **RESEARCH** Stephane Mallarme; French symbolism; prose peom in French literature. **CONTACT ADDRESS** Dept of French, Grand Valley State Univ, Allendale, MI 49401. **EMAIL** frankliu@river.it.gvsu.edu

FRANKS, J. RICHARD
DISCIPLINE CCC-AUDIOLOGY **EDUCATION** Brigham Young Univ, BA, 52, MA, 59; Mich State Univ, PhD, 64. **CAREER** Prof, Washington State Univ. **SELECTED PUBLICATIONS** Auth, A Training Program for Native Americans in Communication Disorders, Amer Speech-Lang-Hearing Asn, 88 & Testing Auditory Selective Attention, Wash Speech and Hearing Asn, 88. **CONTACT ADDRESS** Dept of Speech and Hearing Sciences, Washington State Univ, 201 Daggy Hall, Pullman, WA 99164-2420. **EMAIL** franks@wsu.edu

FRANKS, STEVEN
PERSONAL Born 05/18/1955, London, England, m, 1985, 3 children **DISCIPLINE** LINGUSITICS **EDUCATION** Princeton, AB, 77; UCLA, MA, 79; Cornell, PhD, 85. **CAREER** Lang analyst, US Dept of Defense, 84-87; asst prof, 87-94, assoc prof, IN Univ, 94-, chmn, Linguistics Dept, 98-. **HONORS AND AWARDS** Fulbright, 77-78; NSF Graf fel; Prize for an Outstanding Work of Linguisitics Scholarship, AATSEEL, Dec 96; short-term guest professorship, Univ CT, 96-97. **MEMBERSHIPS** Ling Soc of Am; Am Asn of Teachers of Slavic and East European Lang. **RESEARCH** Syntactic theory and analysis; Slavic linguistics; Clitics. **SELECTED PUBLICATIONS** Auth, On parallelism in across-the-board dependencies, Linguistic Inquiry, 24.3, 93; auth, Parametric Properties of Numeral Phrases in Slavic, Natural Lang an dLing Theory, 12.4, (94): 570-649; auth, Parameters of Slavic Morphosyntax, Oxford Univ Press, 95; coauth, Asymmetries in the scope of Russian negation, Journal of Slavic Linguistics, 3.2, (95): 239-287; coauth, Knowledge of binding in normal and SLI children, Journal of Child Lang, 23.2, (96): 431-464; coauth, Formal Appraoches to Slavic Linguistics: the Connecticut Meeting, Mich Slavic Materials, 98; auth, Parameters of Slavic Morphosyntax Revisited; A Minimalist Retrospective, in Formal Approaches to Slavic Linguistics: The Connecticut Meeting, ed. by Z. Boskovic, (98): 134-165; coauth, The Syntax of Adverbial Participles in Russian Revisited, Slavic nad East European Journal 42.3, (98): 117-149; auth, A Copy and Delete Analysis of Second Position Clitics, Zeitschrift fur Slawistik, 44.2, (99): 155-166. **CONTACT ADDRESS** Dept of Linguistics, Indiana Univ, Bloomington, Memorial Hall, Bloomington, IN 47401. **EMAIL** FRANKS@Indiana.Edu

FRANTZ, BARBARA
PERSONAL Born, Germany, m, 2 children **DISCIPLINE** GERMAN, FEMINIST STUDIES **EDUCATION** Univ Calif Santa Barbara, BA, 89; MA, 91; PhD, 95. **CAREER** Lectr, Calif Poly San Luis Obispo, 95-. **HONORS AND AWARDS** Teaching Asst of the Year Awd, UCSB, 94; General Affiliates Dissertation Fel, 94; Grad Student Fee Fel, 94, 95; Hayman Fel Awd, 95. **MEMBERSHIPS** AATG, Calif For Lang Teachers Asn, MLA, Women in Ger, Prof Women's Asn. **RESEARCH** Issues related to women, age, gender, Social issues related to women. **SELECTED PUBLICATIONS** Auth, "Jewish Working Women in Weimar Fiction: being a Flapper was not for Everyone," in Weimas Culfare: Issues of Modernity and the Metropolis, ed. C. Gannon and S. Melto, 94; contrib, Feminist Encyclopedia of German Literature, Greenwood Publ Press, 97; auth, Gertrud Kolmar's Prose, Peter Lang Publ (NY), 97. **CONTACT ADDRESS** Dept Mod Lang, California Polytech State Univ, San Luis Obispo, 1 Grand Ave, San Luis Obispo, CA 93407-9000. **EMAIL** bfrantz@calpoly.edu

FRANZ, THOMAS RUDY
PERSONAL Born 04/07/1942, South Milwaukee, WI, 4 children **DISCIPLINE** SPANISH LITERATURE **EDUCATION** Carroll Col, BA, 64; Univ Kans, MA, 67, PhD(Span), 70. **CAREER** Instr Span & English, Plymouth Wis Pub Schs, 65-66; asst prof, 70-75, assoc prof, 75-80, Prof Mod Lang, Ohio Univ, 80-, Ohio Univ Res Inst res grant, 74. **MEMBERSHIPS** MLA; Midwest Mod Lang Asn; Am Asn Teachers Span & Port **RESEARCH** Miguel de Unamuno; 19th and 20th century Spanish novel; comparative literature. **SELECTED PUBLICATIONS** Auth, The figure of the civil guard in the novels of Camilo Jose Cela, Occas Papers Lang, Lit & Ling, 12/71; Ancient rites and the structure of Unamuno's Amor y Pedagogia, Romance Notes, 12/71; Humor in Unamuno's Paz en la Guerra, Horizontes, 4/72; Cela's La familia del heroe, the nouveau roman, and the creative act, Mod Lang Notes, 3/73; Menendez y Pelayo as Antolin S Paparrigopulos of Unamuno's Niebla, Papers Lang & Lit, spring 73; El sentido de humor y adquisicion de autoconciencia en Niebla, Cuadernos Catedra Miguel de Unamuno, 73; The philosophical bases of Fulgencio Entrambosmares in Amor y Pedagogia, Hispania, 9/77; Remaking Reality in Galdos, Strathmore Press, 82. **CONTACT ADDRESS** Dept of Mod Lang, Ohio Univ, Athens, OH 45701-2979. **EMAIL** franz@oak.cats.ohiou.edu

FRASER, HOWARD MICHAEL
PERSONAL Born 11/11/1943, New York, NY, m, 1967, 1 child **DISCIPLINE** SPANISH AM LIT **EDUCATION** Columbia Univ, BA, 64; Univ NMex, MA, 66, PhD (Span), 70; Harvard Univ, AM, 67. **CAREER** Res asst Span, Hisp Inst US, 63-64; grad asst, Univ NMex, 64-66, instr English, col educ, 67; teaching asst Port, 69-70, instr Span, 70; lab asst Englsih, Southwestern Coop Educ Lab, 68; asst prof Span, Univ Wis-Madison, 70-74; asst prof, 74-77, Assoc Prof Mod Lang, Col William and Mary, 77-, Reader Span, Columbia Col, 63-64; instr Span, Peace Corps Training Ctr, NMex, 65-66 and Ithaca, NY, 66. **MEMBERSHIPS** MLA; Am Asn Teachers Span and Port; AAUP; Midwest Mod Lang Asn; Inst Int Lit Iberoam. **RESEARCH** Modernist fiction in Spanish America; Spanish American theatre. **SELECTED PUBLICATIONS** Auth, Apocalyptic Vision and Modernisms Dismantling of Scientific Discourse--Lugones Yzur, Hispania J Devoted Teaching of Span Portug, Vol 79, 96; Apocalyptic Vision and Modernisms Dismantling of Scientific Discourse--Lugones Yzur, Hispania J Devoted Teaching Port, Vol 79, 96; Using Spanish Synonyms, Mod Lan J, Vol 79, 95. **CONTACT ADDRESS** Dept of Mod

Langs, Col of William and Mary, PO Box 8795, Williamsburg, VA 23185-8795.

FRASER, THEODORE
DISCIPLINE FRENCH, COMPARATIVE LITERATURE **EDUCATION** Fordham Univ, AB, 56; Brown Univ, MA, 63, PhD, 67. **CAREER** Prof. **RESEARCH** Modern religious themes/structures in fiction and film; 20th-Century French literature and civilization; French Intellectuals from WWII to the present; 19th-century French Literature. **SELECTED PUBLICATIONS** Auth, The Modern Catholic Novel in Europe, NY: Twayne/Macmillan, 94; The French Essay, NY: Twayne, 86 & The Moralist Tradition in France, Wash/NY: Assoc Fac Press, 82; Le Duchat, 1st ed of Rabelais, Geneva: Droz, 71. **CONTACT ADDRESS** Dept of Modern Languages and Literatures, Col of the Holy Cross, 1 College St, PO Box 145A, Worcester, MA 01610-2395. **EMAIL** tfraser@holycross.edu

FRAUTSCHI, RICHARD LANE
PERSONAL Born 11/14/1926, Rockford, IL, m, 1973, 4 children **DISCIPLINE** FRENCH **EDUCATION** Univ Wis, AB, 49; Harvard Univ, MA, 53, PhD, 58. **CAREER** Instr French, Smith Col, 54-58; from asst prof to prof, Univ NC, Chapel Hill, 58-70; Prof French & Head Dept, 70-89, prof, 89-90, Prof Emeritus, 96-, PA State Univ; Am Coun Learned Soc grant, 68; vis prof French, St Augustine's Col, NC, 60-70; mem advan placement comt French, Col Entrance Exam Bd, 70-76, consult, 76-88. **HONORS AND AWARDS** Nat Sci Found-Pa State Univ grant, 71; Am Philos Soc Grant, 72; Int Res & Exchanges Bd grant, Soviet Union, 75; Int Res & Exchange Bd grant, Poland & Czech Rep, 80-81; Camargo Found grant, 81; res fel, Macquarie Univ, Australia, 82; NEH grants, 91-95 **MEMBERSHIPS** MLA; Am Asn Teachers Fr; Soc Fr Etude XVIIIe Siecle; Am Soc 18th Century Studies; Asn Computing Machinery. **RESEARCH** 16th and 18th century literary and cultural prose, lexicography and quantitative textual modeling, SLA theory and practice, business French, International eudcation, and curriculum dev. **SELECTED PUBLICATIONS** Coauth, Pour et Contre, Manuel de Conversations Graduees, Dodd, 72 & 2nd ed, Harper, 78; auth, The authorship of certain unsigned articles in the Encyclopedie, Computer Studies Humanities & V erbal Behav, 70; Styles de roman et styles de censure dan la 2de moitie du 18e siecle, Studies on Voltaire, 72; A project for computer-assisted analysis of French prose fiction, 1751-1800, In: The Computer and Literary Studies, Edinburgh Univ, 73; coauth, Bibliographie due Genre Romanesque Francais, 1751-1800, Mansell, 77; A Model for Chi-Square Analysis of Regression Vocabularyy in H de Crenne's Les Angoysses douloureuses, Comput & Humanities, 79; Le comportement verbal du narrateur dans Gil Bias: Quelques observations quantitatives, Studies Voltaire, 81; Le jeu des axes de narration dans Les Liaisons dangereuses: Etude de focalisation enonciative, Marche Romane, 82; co-auth, Bibliographie du genre romanesque, 1700-1800, Oxford: Voltaire Fdn, forthcoming. **CONTACT ADDRESS** Dept of French, Pennsylvania State Univ, Univ Park, 5325 Burrowes Bldg, University Park, PA 16802. **EMAIL** rlf11@psu.edu

FRAZER, TIMOTHY C.
PERSONAL Born 07/11/1941, Sterling, IL, m, 1970, 4 children **DISCIPLINE** ENGLISH LANGUAGE, LINGUISTICS **EDUCATION** Univ Chicago, MA, 61, PhD, 73; Western IL Univ, BS, 67. **CAREER** Asst prof to prof, Western IL Univ, 72-. **HONORS AND AWARDS** NEH Summer Fel, 83, 87. **MEMBERSHIPS** Ling Soc of Am; Am Dialect Soc; Am Names Soc. **RESEARCH** American Dialects, Spanish in the USA. **SELECTED PUBLICATIONS** Auth, "South Midland Pronunciation in the North Central States", Dialect and Language Variation, ed Harold B Allen and Michael D Linn, Acad Pr, (London, 86): 142-150; auth, "Microdialectology" Am Speech 61.3 (86): 307-17; auth, "Attitudes Toward Regional Pronunciation", J of English Ling 20, (87): 89-100; auth, Midland Illinois Dialect Patterns, Univ of Ala Pr, (Tuscaloosa), 87; auth, "More on the Semantics of A-Prefixing", Am Speech 65.1 (90): 89-93; auth, "The Language of Yankee Cultural Imperialism", Heartland English, (93): 59-66; auth, "Problems in Midwest English, Heartland English, (93): 1-19; ed, Heartland English, Univ of Ala Pr, 93; auth, "Perception and Gender in Virginia Speech: the Case of /aw/", Am Speech 69.2 (94); 145-154; auth, "The Dialects of the Middle West", Focus on the USA, ed Edgar Schneider, John Benjamins, (Amsterdam, 96): 81-102. **CONTACT ADDRESS** Dept English and Jour, Western Illinois Univ, 1 University Circle, Macomb, IL 61455-1367. **EMAIL** mftcf@wiu.edu

FRAZIER, EARLENE
PERSONAL Born Atlanta, GA, m, 1971, 1 child **DISCIPLINE** SPANISH LANGUAGE & LITERATURE **EDUCATION** InterAm Univ, MA, 71; PhD, 75. **CAREER** Prof, chair Dept Mod For Lang, Morris Brown Col, 72- ; prof & vis prof, Spelman Col, Clark Atlanta Univ, 78-00; vis prof, Atlanta Metrop Col, 76- , Ga State Univ. **HONORS AND AWARDS** Nat Wom of Achievement Awd, 99; Outstanding Community Serv Awd, 99; MVA Community Serv Awd; Int Wom of Distinction Pres Awd. **MEMBERSHIPS** AATSP, Acad Alliance, ADFL. **RESEARCH** Language development during childhood, Second Language Acquisition. **SELECTED PUBLICATIONS** Auth, Foreign Language as an Influence on Student Achievement in the Grade, Afr Am J of Children & Youth Lit; auth, Language Learning During Childhood, Afr Am J of Children & Youth Lit, 00. **CONTACT ADDRESS** Dept Commun, Morris Brown Col, PO Box 310804, Atlanta, GA 30331.

FRAZIER, LYN
DISCIPLINE LINGUISTICS **EDUCATION** Univ Wis, BA, 74; Univ Conn, PhD, 78. **CAREER** Prof. **HONORS AND AWARDS** Netherlands Institute for Advanced Study Fellowship, 89-90; NSF Advisory Board 90-92; Distinguished Rescon Awd, Univ of Mssachusetts, 94; Max Planck Institute Advisory Board, 94-98; Outstanding Teacher Awd, Univ of Massachusetts, 00. **RESEARCH** Syntax; relation between theories of grammar and theories of the mental representation and processing of language. **SELECTED PUBLICATIONS** Auth, Syntactic Complexity, Cambridge, 85; Syntactic Processing: Evidence from Dutch, Natural Lang Ling Theory, 87; Focus in relative clause construal, MIT, 96; co-auth, Filler-Driven Parsing: A Study of Gap-Filling in Dutch, J Memory Lang, 89; Argument Structure and Associate Preferences, Cognition, 95; Constraint satisfaction as a theory of sentence processing, J Psycholinguistic Res, 95. **CONTACT ADDRESS** Linguistics Dept, Univ of Massachusetts, Amherst, S College 225, Amherst, MA 01003.

FREDRICKSMEYER, ERNST A.
PERSONAL Born 01/14/1930, Bismarck, ND, m, 1957, 3 children **DISCIPLINE** CLASSICS **EDUCATION** Lakeland Col, BA, 52; Univ Wis, MA, 53, PhD, 58. **CAREER** Instr, Cornell Col, 58-59; instr, Dartmouth Col, 59-60; instr, Bryn Mawr Col, 60-61; asst prof, Univ Wash, 61-66; assoc prof, Univ Colo, 66-71; vis prof, Univ Ore, 71; vis prof, Univ Wis, 78-79; prof, Univ Colo, 71-98. **HONORS AND AWARDS** Tchg Excellence Awd, Univ Colo, 87. **MEMBERSHIPS** Am Philos Asn; Class Asn Middle W & S; Am Archeol Inst; Nat Asn Scholars. **RESEARCH** Golden Age Latin poetry; fourth century Greek history. **CONTACT ADDRESS** Dept of Classics, CB 348, Boulder, CO 80309-0248.

FREED, BARBARA
DISCIPLINE FRENCH AND SECOND LANGUAGE ACQUISITION **EDUCATION** Univ Pa, PhD. **CAREER** Languages, Carnegie Mellon Univ. **SELECTED PUBLICATIONS** Auth, The Linguistic Consequences of Study Abroad Experiences. In preparation for the "Studies in Bilingualism Series.". John Benjamins Publ Co; Foreign Language Acquisition Research and The Classroom, Lexington, MA: D. C. Heath & Co, 91; The Foreign Language Requirement in Teaching Languages at College: Curriculum and Content, NTC Publ Gp, 92; Language Learning in a Study Abroad Context: The Effects of Interactive and Non-Interactive Out-of Class Contact on Grammatical Achievement and Oral Proficiency, 90. **CONTACT ADDRESS** Carnegie Mellon Univ, 5000 Forbes Ave, Pittsburgh, PA 15213.

FREEDMAN, DAVID NOEL
PERSONAL Born 05/12/1922, New York, NY, m, 1944, 4 children **DISCIPLINE** SEMITIC LANGUAGES AND LITERATURE **EDUCATION** Univ Calif, Los Angeles, AB, 39; Princeton theol Sem, ThB, 44; Johns Hopkins Univ, PhD, 48; DLitt, Univ of the Pac, 73; DSc, Davis and Elkins Col, 74. **CAREER** Instr, Johns Hopkins Univ, 47-48; asst prof Hebrew and Old Testament lit, Western Theol Sem, 48-51, prof, 51-60; prof, Pittsburgh Theol Sem, 60-61, James Anderson Kelso prof, 61-64; prof, Grad Theol Union Berkeley, 64-71; prof, San Francisco Theol Sem, 64-70, Gray prof, 70-71, actg dean fact 66-67, dean, 67-71; prof to prof emer, Univ of Mich, 71-; Assoc ed, J Bibl Lit, Soc Bibl Lit, 52-54, ed, 55-59; guest prof, McCormick Theol Sem, 59; dir, Ashdod Excavation Proj, 62-64; co-ed, Anchor Bible Ser, Doubleday, 64-71, ed, 71-; William Copley Winslow lectr archaeol and Bible, 66; Danforth vis prof, Int Christian Univ, Tokyo, 67; Am Coun Learned Soc grant-in-aid, 68; dir, Am Sch Orient Res, Jerusalem, 69-70 and 76-77; vis prof, Hebrew Univ, Jerusalem, 76-77, Macquarie Univ, Sydney, Australia, 80, Univ Queensland, Brisbane, Australia and Texas Christion Univ, 81, Brigham Univ, Utah, 81-82. **HONORS AND AWARDS** Guggenheim fel, 58-59; lectr, Uppsala Univ, 59 and Int Cong old Testament Scholars, Bonn, Ger, 62; Am Asn Theol Sem fel, 63-64. **MEMBERSHIPS** Soc Bibl Lit; Am Orient Soc; Am Schs Orient Res (vpres, 70-); Cath Bibl Asn Am; Bibl Colloquium (secy-treas 65-). **CONTACT ADDRESS** Near Eastern Studies Dept, Univ of Michigan, Ann Arbor, Ann Arbor, MI 48104.

FREEDMAN, MORRIS
PERSONAL Born 10/06/1920, New York, NY, d, 2 children **DISCIPLINE** ENGLISH & COMPARATIVE LITERATURE **EDUCATION** City Col New York, BA, 41; Columbia Univ, MA, 50, PhD, 53. **CAREER** Lectr & instr English, City Col New York, 46-54; assoc ed, Commentary, 54-55; from asst prof to prof English, Univ NMex, 55-66; head dept, 67-72, prof English & Comp Lit, Univ Md, College Park, 66- **MEMBERSHIPS** MLA; NCTE; Milton Soc Am. **RESEARCH** Later seventeenth century; Milton; creative writing and contemporary drama, American studies. **SELECTED PUBLICATIONS** Auth, Dryden's Miniature Epic, J English & Ger Philol, 58; Milton and Dryden on Rhyme, Huntington Libr Quart, 61; ed, Essays in the Modern Drama, Heath, 64; auth, The Compact English Handbook, McKay, 65; Success and the American Dramatist, Am Theatre, 67; The Moral Impulse, Southern Ill Univ, 67; co-ed, Controversy in Literature, Scribner's, 68; auth, American Drama in Social Context, Southern Ill Univ, 71. **CONTACT ADDRESS** Dept of English, Univ of Maryland, Col Park, College Park, MD 20742. **EMAIL** mf18@umail.umd.edu

FREEMAN, BRYANT C.
PERSONAL Born 06/26/1931, Richmond, VA, m, 1986, 1 child **DISCIPLINE** SEVENTEENTH-CENTURY FRENCH LITERATURE **EDUCATION** Yale Univ, PhD. **CAREER** Prof and Dir, Inst of Haitian Studies of Univ of Kansas, Prof of French. **HONORS AND AWARDS** Lifetime achievement award from U.S. Embassy, Haiti. **MEMBERSHIPS** Life mem MLA and Am Assoc of Teachers of French. **RESEARCH** Haitain language, history, and culture. **SELECTED PUBLICATIONS** Auth, Concordance du Theatre et des Poesies de Jean Racine; auth, Haitai-English Dictionary; auth, Ann Bay Lodyans; auth, Haitian Folktales in Haitian. **CONTACT ADDRESS** Dept of French an Italian, Univ of Kansas, Lawrence, Lawrence, KS 66045.

FREEMAN, DAVID
DISCIPLINE LINGUISTICS **EDUCATION** Dartmouth Col, BA; Stanford Univ, MA; Univ AZ, MA, PhD. **CAREER** Prof; dir, Lang Devel and TESOL. Programs, **MEMBERSHIPS** Mem, Nat Conf Res Lang and Lit; Ctr Expansion of Lang and Thinking; Mod Lang Assn; Intl Reading Assn; CA Reading Assn; Tchr(s) Eng to Speakers of Other Lang; CA TESOL; Nat Coun Tchr(s) Eng; Nat Assn Bilingual Edu; CA Assn Bilingual Edu. **SELECTED PUBLICATIONS** Co-auth, Whole Language for Second Language Learners, N.H.: Heinemann, 92; Between Worlds: Access to Second Language Acquisition, Heinemann, 94; Teaching Reading and Writing in the Spanish/English Bilingual Classroom, Heinemann, 97. **CONTACT ADDRESS** Div Lang, Lit and Cult, Fresno Pacific Col, 1717 S Chestnut, Fresno, CA 93702.

FREEMAN, THOMAS PARRY
PERSONAL Born 05/22/1944, Chicago, IL, m, 5 children **DISCIPLINE** GERMAN LITERATURE **EDUCATION** Haverford Col, AB, 65; Stanford Univ, MA, 66, PhD(Ger & humanities), 70. **CAREER** Teaching asst Ger, Stanford Univ, 67-68; instr Ger & humanities, Columbia Univ, 68-71; asst prof Ger, State Univ NY, Brockport, 71-75, assoc prof, 75-81; Assoc Prof Ger, Beloit Col, 81-, Mem fac literature, New Sch Social Res, spring 71; Ger Acad Exchange Serv fel, 72; **HONORS AND AWARDS** State Univ NY Res Found grants-in-aid, 72-73 & 74-75; Mellon fel, Ger, Univ Pittsburgh, 76-77; Alexander von Humboldt fel, 79-80, 96; Cullister Fnd Grants; Hewlett-Mellon Grants, NEH Summer fels; Sr Fulbright Res fels; **MEMBERSHIPS** Midwest MLA; Fulbright Alum Asn; Alexander von Humboldt Asn Am.Am Asn Prof Yiddish; MLA. **RESEARCH** Modern German literature; German exile literature; Holocaust studies. **SELECTED PUBLICATIONS** Auth, El uso del sueno en la poesia de Benn y Mallarme, Folia Humanistica, 9/69; The lotus and the tigress--symbols of mediation in Hans Henny Jahnn's Perrudja, Genre, summer 74; co-ed, Hans Henny Jahnn--Gesammelte Werke 7 Banden, Hoffmann und Campe, 74; auth, Zu Hans Henny Jahnns Leben, und Werk, Freie Akademie der Kunste in Hamburg, 80; Hans Henny Jahnn, 80 & Hans Erick Nossack, 80, Columbia Dict of Modern European Literature, Columbia Univ Press; Mythische Strukturen in Hans Henny Jahnns Perrudja, text und Kritik, 1/80; Hans Henny Jahnns Schweizerr Aufenthalt, Akten des VI Internationalen Germanistenkongresses, Peter Lanf, 80; auth, The Cowboy and the Astronaut - The American Image in German Periodical Advertisements, Jou of Popular Culture, 72; auth, Heinrich Hoffman's Der Struwelpeter, Violence in German Children's Literature, Jour of Popular Cult, 77; auth, Zu Pastor Ephraim Magnus, Programsheft Staatstheater Kassel, 79/80; auth, Umstrittener Dichter Hans Henny Jahn, Kultur fur alle, Hamburger Kulturbegorde, 84; auth, Haupttendenzen der Jahn-Forschung Ein Oberblick, Archaische Moderne der Dichter, Architekt und Orgelbauer Hans Henny Jahn, Metzher & Poeschel, 96; auth, Deutschland als multikulturelle Gesellschaft Stimmen der Minderheiten in der neuren literatir, Fremdverstehen in Sprache, literature und medien, Peter Lang, 97; auth, Jewish Identity and the Holocaust in Robert Schindel's Geburtig, Modern Austrian Literatur, 97; auth, Kurt Tucholsky, Yale Companion to Jewish Writing and Thought in German Culture, 1096-1996, Yale Univ, 97. **CONTACT ADDRESS** Dept of Mod Lang, Beloit Col, 700 College St, Beloit, WI 53511-5595. **EMAIL** freemant@beloit.edu

FREIERT, WILLIAM K.
PERSONAL Born 04/26/1941, Baltimore, MD, m, 1970, 1 child **DISCIPLINE** CLASSICS **EDUCATION** St. Louis Univ, AB, 65, MA 66; Univ Minn, PhD, 72. **CAREER** Prof, Gustavus Adolphus Col, 72-; exchange prof, Kansai Gaidai Univ, 92. **HONORS AND AWARDS** Fulbright lectr. **MEMBERSHIPS** Am Philol Asn; Am Class League; Class Asn of Middle West and South; Int Soc for the Class Tradition. **RESEARCH** Classical studies. **SELECTED PUBLICATIONS**

Auth, Paul T. Granlund: Spirit of Bronze, Shape of Freedom, 91; "Classical Myth in Post-War American Fiction" in The Class Tradition and the Am, 99; "Platonism in Saul Bellow's 'More Die of Heartbreak'" in J of Inquiry and Res, 93; "Bellow's 'Golden Ass': Greco-Roman Antecedents in 'More Die of Heartbreak'" in Saul Bellow J, 92. **CONTACT ADDRESS** 721 N Washington, Saint Peter, MN 56082-1847. **EMAIL** wfreiert@gac.edu

FREIS, CATHERINE RUGGIERO
PERSONAL Born 10/18/1940, New York, NY, m, 1964, 2 children **DISCIPLINE** CLASSICAL STUDIES **EDUCATION** Brooklyn Col, CUNY, BA, 63; UC Berkeley, MA, 66; PhD, 80 **CAREER** From asst prof to prof & ch dept of classical studies, Millsaps Col, 75- . **HONORS AND AWARDS** Am Philol Soc Awd for Excel in the Tching of Classics; Millsaps Col Teaching Awd; Mississippi Humanities Coun Teach Awd. **MEMBERSHIPS** Am Philol Soc; Classical Assoc of Midwest & South **RESEARCH** Tragedy & East & South Asian Dance Drama **SELECTED PUBLICATIONS** Auth, "Intensive Latin and Greek Courses as adjuncts to the Humanities Core Curriculum", in Intensive and Innovative Methods of Teaching Latin and Greek, 81; auth, "The Ancient City", Arts Alliance, 87; rev, "The Roman Cookery of Apicius", Classical World, 89; ed, Introduction to Liberal Studies Reader, Copley Press, 95, 97; auth, "Kathakali and Greek Drama," Didaskalia, Ancient Theatre Today, 98; coauth, Ancient Greek Alive, Univ NCar Pr, 99. **CONTACT ADDRESS** Classical Studies Dept, Millsaps Col, Box 150223, Jackson, MS 39210. **EMAIL** freiscr@millsaps.edu

FREIS, RICHARD
PERSONAL Born 11/22/1939, New York, NY, m, 2 children **DISCIPLINE** GREEK AND LATIN LANGUAGES AND LITERATURES **EDUCATION** Univ Calif, PhD. **CAREER** Dept Classics, Millsaps Col **HONORS AND AWARDS** Amer Philol Asn awd & Millsaps Col Distinguished prof awd. **RESEARCH** Greek philosophy; religious studies and comparative literature. **SELECTED PUBLICATIONS** Publ on, class and mod lit & publ poet. **CONTACT ADDRESS** Dept of Classics, Millsaps Col, 1701 N State St, Jackson, MS 39210. **EMAIL** freissr@millsaps.edu

FREIXAS, ERIK CAMAYD
DISCIPLINE SPANISH LITERATURE **EDUCATION** Tufts Univ, BA, 80; Harvard Univ, MA, PhD. **CAREER** Lang instr, Tufts Univ, 80; tchg fel, Harvard Univ, 84-86; asst prof, Marquette Univ, 94-97; asst prof, Fla Int Univ, 97-. **MEMBERSHIPS** MLA; Latin Am Studies Asn; Am Studies Asn. **SELECTED PUBLICATIONS** Auth, Heteroglosia y parodia historiográfica en Cien alos de soledad, 96; Reflections on Magical Realism: A Return to Legitimacy, The Legitimacy of Return, 96; 'Alturas de Macchu Picchu': Forma y sentido en su retorica elegiaca, 95; Teoria y sentido del realismo m gico, 95; coauth, Encyclopedia of Contemporary Latin American and Caribbean Cultures, Routledge, 97; Benet's Readers' Encyclopedia, 96. **CONTACT ADDRESS** Dept of Modern Languages, Florida State Univ, 11200 SW 8th St, Miami, FL 33174. **EMAIL** camayde@fiu.edu

FRENCH, HAROLD WENDELL
PERSONAL Born 01/14/1930, Wichita, KS, m, 3 children **DISCIPLINE** ASIAN RELIGIOUS TRADITIONS, PSYCHOLOGY OF RELIGION **EDUCATION** York Col, Nebr, BA, 52; United Sem Dayton, MDiv; Boston Univ, STM; McMaster Univ, PhD (relig hist India), 72. **CAREER** Asst prof Asian relig tradition, St Andrews Col, NC; Assoc Prof Asian Relig Tradition, Univ SC, 72-; prof & chair of dept, 89-95; distinguished prof emer, 95. **HONORS AND AWARDS** Amoco Teacher of Year, Univ SC, 77. **MEMBERSHIPS** Am Acad Relig; Asn Asian Studies; World Coun Relig. **RESEARCH** The Ramakrishna movement and the West; modern Indian religious movements; death perspectives. **SELECTED PUBLICATIONS** coauth, Religious Ferment in Modern India, N.Y.: St. Martin's Press, 81; auth, A Study of Religious Foundation & Response to It Adversary Identity, Edwin Mellen Press, 90; auth, Maurice, F. D. and Unitarianism, Victorian Stud, Vol 37, 94; auth, Zen & The Art of Anything, Summerhouse Press (Columbia, SC), 99; auth, "L.P. Jacks" in Dictionary of Literary Biography (Detroit: Gale Research Co), 94; auth, "Poe Victorian Broad Church, Selected of Twentieth Century Religions Pluralism and Implicit Religion," (Implicit Religion, 98). **CONTACT ADDRESS** Dept of Relig Studies, Univ of So Carolina, Columbia, Columbia, SC 29208. **EMAIL** french@sc.edu

FRENCH, PAULETTE
PERSONAL Born 06/16/1941, Laconia, NH **DISCIPLINE** COMPARATIVE LITERATURE, FRENCH **EDUCATION** Colby Col, BA, 63; Univ Paris at the Sorbonne, cert prof francais, 64; Univ Md, College Park, MA, 67; Univ Colo, Boulder, PhD (comp lit), 71. **CAREER** Instr French and Span, Bowie State Col, 65-66; assoc French, Univ Colo, Boulder, 67-69; asst prof Romance lang, Univ Maine, Orono, 69-72, asst to vpres, 72-73; asst vchancellor acad affairs, Univ Calif, Irvine, 73-76; Assoc Prof French and Lit and Chmn Lang and Classics, Univ Maine, 76-, Conf interpreter, US State Dept, Washington, DC, 64-66; instr English as foreign lang, Econ Opportunity COmn, San Jose, Calif, 66-67; Am Coun Educ fel, 73-74. **HONORS AND AWARDS** Prix Litteraire Hachette et Larousse laureate, 63-64. **MEMBERSHIPS** Medieval Acad Am; Am Asn Teacher Fr; MLA; AAUP; Nat Asn Women Deans and Counr. **RESEARCH** Moliere; Medieval lyric poetry; academic administration. **SELECTED PUBLICATIONS** Auth, Moving Pictures, Still Words, Poetry Rev, Vol 83, 93; Malle, Louis--In Memoriam, Sight Sound, Vol 6, 96; No End in Sight , Index Censorship, Vol 24, 95; Fieldwork, 95 6, J Egyptian Archaeol, Vol 82, 96. **CONTACT ADDRESS** Dept of Lang and Classics, Univ of Maine, Orono, ME 04473.

FRESCO, ALAIN D.
DISCIPLINE FRENCH LITERATURE **EDUCATION** Univ Delaware, BA, 69; Univ Ind, PhD, 81. **CAREER** Asst prof, Univ Ill Urbana Champaign. **SELECTED PUBLICATIONS** Auth, 'Les Vies Africaines': A Series of Popular Literature Today, 82. **CONTACT ADDRESS** French Dept, Univ of Illinois, Urbana-Champaign, 52 E Gregory Dr, Champaign, IL 61820. **EMAIL** a-fresco@staff.uiuc.edu

FRESCO, KAREN
DISCIPLINE FRENCH LITERATURE **EDUCATION** Carleton Col, BA, 69; Univ Ind, PhD, 83. **CAREER** Assoc prof, Univ Ill Urbana Champaign. **HONORS AND AWARDS** Fac Res Grants, 83, 84; Res Initiation Grant, Univ of Houston, 86; Res Board Grant, Univ of Ill, 88; Humanities Released Time Res Board, Univ of Ill, 91; Melon Corley Petit Professorship, Univ of Ill, 93-94. **MEMBERSHIPS** International Arthurian Soc; International Courtly Lit Soc; Medieval Academy of Am; Medieval Asn of the Midwest; Modern Lang Asn; Member of editorial board for Illinois Medieval Monographs. **SELECTED PUBLICATIONS** Auth, The Troubadour Lyric: A Psychocritical Reading (rev), Manchester Univ, 90; ed, Le Bel Inconnu, Garland; Les Posies de Gillebert de Berneville, Droz, 88. **CONTACT ADDRESS** French Dept, Univ of Illinois, Urbana-Champaign, 2040 flb, mc 158, 707 s mathews, Urbana, IL 61801. **EMAIL** k-fresco@staff.uiuc.edu

FREY, HERSCHEL J.
PERSONAL Born 12/27/1935, Waco, TX, m, 1964 **DISCIPLINE** SPANISH LINGUISTICS, APPLIED LINGUISTICS **EDUCATION** Tex Christian Univ, BA, 57; Univ Wis, MA, 58; Univ NC, PhD (Romance lang), 63. **CAREER** Instr Spanish, Univ NC, 62-63; asst prof Spanish ling, Univ Wash, 63-66; asst prof, Univ Calif, Los Angeles, 66-69; Assoc Prof Spanish Ling, Univ Pittsburgh, 70-, Chmn Spanish I, Mod Lang Asn Am, 68; Fulbright lectr ling, Buenos Aires, Arg, 69-70. **MEMBERSHIPS** MLA; Am Asn Teachers Span and Port; Am Coun Teaching Foreign Lang. **RESEARCH** Linguistics, especially Spanish; Spanish applied linguistics. **SELECTED PUBLICATIONS** Auth, Observations on the Border of Text, Mln Mod Lan Notes, Vol 109, 94. **CONTACT ADDRESS** Dept of Hisp Studies, Univ of Pittsburgh, 1309 Cathedral/Learn, Pittsburgh, PA 15260-0001.

FREY, JOHN ANDREW
PERSONAL Born 08/29/1929, Cincinnati, OH **DISCIPLINE** FRENCH **EDUCATION** Univ Cincinnati, BA, 51, MA, 52; Cath Univ Am, PhD (Romance lang), 57. **CAREER** Assoc prof French, 60-70, chmn dept, 66-69, Prof Romance Lang and Lit, George Washington Univ, 70-. **RESEARCH** Nineteenth century French literature; stylistics. **SELECTED PUBLICATIONS** Auth, Rimbaud 1891-91, Fr Rev, Vol 70, 96; Les Illuminations--A Different Reader, Fr Rev, Vol 70, 96; Mallarme--The Poetics of theater and Writing, Fr Rev, Vol 70, 96; Performance in the Texts of Mallarme, Fr Rev, Vol 68, 94; Desire for the Virgin--The Herodiade According to Mallarme, Fr Rev, Vol 68, 95. **CONTACT ADDRESS** Dept of Romance Lang and Lit, The George Washington Univ, Washington, DC 20006.

FRICKEY, PIERRETTE M.
DISCIPLINE FRENCH LITERATURE **EDUCATION** Augusta Col, BA; Univ SC, MA, PhD. **RESEARCH** Twentieth century French literature; literature of the Caribbean. **SELECTED PUBLICATIONS** Auth, pubs on Caribbean theater, French poet Aragon, and Jean Rhys. **CONTACT ADDRESS** Dept Foreign Languages and Literature, State Univ of West Georgia, Carrollton, GA 30118.

FRIEDBERG, MAURICE
PERSONAL Born 12/03/1929, Rzeszow, Poland, m, 1956, 2 children **DISCIPLINE** SLAVIC LANGUAGES & LITERATURE **EDUCATION** Brooklyn Col, BSc, 51; Russian Inst, cert & Columbia Univ, AM, 53, PhD (Slavic Lang & Lit), 58. **CAREER** Lectr Russ, Hunter Col, 55-58, from instr to asst prof, 58-62, assoc prof & in charge Russ Div, 62-65; prof Slavic Lang & Lit, Ind Univ, Bloomington, 66-75, dir Russ & E Europ Inst, 67-71; prof Russ Lit & head Dept Slavic Lang & Lit, Univ Ill, Urbana, 75-; Center for Adv Study, prof, 95-; assoc, Russ Res Ctr, Harvard Univ, 53; lectr, Brooklyn Col, 54, 62, & Middlebury Col, 60, 61; vis asst prof Russ Lit, Columbia Univ, 61-62; travel grant, St Antony's Col, Oxford Univ, 62; inst study USSR, Munich, Ger, 63, 68; Fulbright vis prof, Hebrew Univ, Israel, 65-66; mem fel comt, Nat Endowment for Humanities, 70: mem bd dirs, Int Res & Exchanges Bd, 70-73; Guggenheim fel, 71 & 81-82; juror, Nat Bk Award, 73. **MEMBERSHIPS** MLA; Am Asn Advan Slavic Studies; Am Asn Teachers Slavic & East Europ Lang; corresp mem Polish Inst Arts & Sci, US. **RESEARCH** Soviet and 19th century Russian literature; Polish literature. **SELECTED PUBLICATIONS** Auth, Russian Classics in Soviet Jackets, Columbia Univ, 62: The Party and the Poet in the USSR, NY Univ, 63; ed, A Bilingual Collection of Russian Short Stories, Vols I & II, 64 & 65, Random House; auth, The Jew in Post-Stalin Soviet Literature, B'nai B'rith, 70: A Imagem do Judeu na Literatura Sovietica Pos-Stalinista, Ed Grijalbo, Sao Paulo, 71; co-ed & contribr, Encyclopedia Judaica (16 vols), Macmillan, 71-72: ed, Leon Trotsky, The Young Lenin, Doubleday, 72; A Decade of Euphoria: Western Literature in Post-Stalin Russia 1954-64, Ind Univ, 77; Literary Translation in Russia, Penn State Univ, 97. **CONTACT ADDRESS** Dept of Slavic Lang & Lit, Univ of Illinois, Urbana-Champaign, 707 S Mathews Ave, Urbana, IL 61801-3625. **EMAIL** friedbrg@uiuc.edu

FRIEDEN, KEN
PERSONAL Born 12/04/1955, New Rochelle, NY, m, 1996, 2 children **DISCIPLINE** COMPARATIVE LITERATURE **EDUCATION** Yale Col, BA, 77; Univ Chicago, MA, 78; Yale Univ, MPhil, 83; PhD, 84. **CAREER** Teaching Asst to Lecturer, Yale Univ, 82-85; Assoc Prof to Asst Prof, Emory Univ, 85-93; Visiting Assoc Prof, Hochschule fur Judische Studien, 92; visiting Prof, Tel Aviv Univ, 97; visiting Prof, Univ Calif, 99; Visiting Prof, Univ Haifa, 00; Prof, Syracuse Univ, 93-. **HONORS AND AWARDS** Fel, Alexander von Humboldt Foundation, 95; Luce Fel, Emory Fac Sem, 91; Summer Awd, Emory Univ Res Committee, 90; visiting Scholarship, Oxford Ctr for Postgraduate Studies, 89; ACLS Grant, Israel, 88-89; Grant, Memorial Foundation for Jewish Culture, 88-80; Fel, Hebrew Univ, 88-89; NEH Grant, 87-88; Development Awd, Emory Univ Summer Fac Awd, 87; Lady Davis Trust Res Fel, 85-86; Grant, Memorial Foundation for Jewish Culture, 85-86; Fel, YIVO Inst, 85-86; Grant, Winston Foundation , 85; Fel, Yale Univ, 81-84; Thomas Enders Fund Fel, Yale Univ, 82-83; Hillel Foundation Stipend, 82; Grant, Goethe Inst, 78; Fel, Univ Chicago, 77-79. **MEMBERSHIPS** Am Asn of Comparative Literature, Mod Lang Asn, Asn for Jewish Studies, Am Asn of Prof of Yiddish, Nat Asn of Prof of Hebrew. **RESEARCH** Translation; Hasidic and Neo-Hasidic Stories. **SELECTED PUBLICATIONS** Ed, Judaic Literature: Identity, displacement, and Destruction, Vol 52, 99; auth, "The Displacement of Jewish Identity in Stefan Zweig's 'Buchmendel'," Symposium, 99; auth, "Oral Torah: sholem aleichem as a Performer of his Monologues," Yiddisher kemfer, 98; ed, Sholem aleichem, Nineteen to the dozen: Monologues and Bits and Bobs of Other Things, Syracuse Univ Press, 98; auth, "A Century in the Life of Sholem Aleichem's Tevye," The B.G. Rudolph Lectures in Judaic Studies, Syracuse Univ Press, 97; ed, S.Y. Abramovitsch, Tales of Mendele the Book Peddler: fishke the Lame and Benjamin the Third, Schocken, 96; auth, classic Yiddish Fiction: Abramovitsh, Sholem aleichem, and Peretz, SUNY Press, 95; auth, "New(s) Poems: Y.L. Teller's Lider fun der tsayt(ung)," AJS Review: The Journal of the Association for Jewish Studies, (90): 269-289; auth, Freud's Dream of Interpretation, SUNY Press, 90; auth, Genius and Monologue, Cornell Univ Press, 85. **CONTACT ADDRESS** Dept Judaic Studies, Syracuse Univ, 441 Hall of Lang, Syracuse, NY 13244-1170. **EMAIL** kfrieden@syr.edu

FRIEDMAN, DONALD F.
DISCIPLINE COMPARATIVE LITERATURE **EDUCATION** New York Univ, PhD, 85. **CAREER** Winthrop Univ, 88-; prof, 95-. **HONORS AND AWARDS** Belgium Am Found Awd; ECLT Gnt. **MEMBERSHIPS** ICL; ACL; MLA; CIEF. **RESEARCH** Belgian studies; literary translation; literature interrelations; turn of the century; dream and modern literature. **SELECTED PUBLICATIONS** Ed, transl of, An Anthology of Belgian Symbolist Poets (NY: Garland, 90); transl of, The Drowned Land, by Paul Willems (NY: Peter Lang, 92); transl of, Dreams and Destinies, by Marguerite Yourenar (NY: St Martins, 00). **CONTACT ADDRESS** Dept Modern, Classical Languages, Winthrop Univ, 701 West Oakland Ave, Rock Hill, SC 29733-0001. **EMAIL** friedmand@winthrop.edu

FRIEDMAN, EDWARD HERBERT
PERSONAL Born 01/19/1948, Richmond, VA, m, 1974 **DISCIPLINE** SPANISH LITERATURE **EDUCATION** Univ Va, BA, 70; Johns Hopkins Univ, MA, 71, PhD (Romance lang), 74. **CAREER** Asst prof, Kalamazoo Col, 74-77, asst prof, 77-80, Assoc Prof Span, Ariz State Univ, 80-89; Prof, Ind Univ, 89-. **MEMBERSHIPS** MLA, Rocky Mountain Mod Lang Asn: Rocky Mountain Medieval and Renaissance Asn Am Asn Teachers Span and Port. **SELECTED PUBLICATIONS** Auth, The Unifying Concept: Approaches to the Structure of Cervantes' Comedias, 81; auth, The Anitheroine's Voice: Narrative Discourse and Transformations of the Picaresque, 87; coed, Aproximaciones el estudio de la literatura hispanica, 3rd ed, 83. **CONTACT ADDRESS** Dept of Comp Lit, Indiana Univ, Bloomington, 1020 E Kirkwood Ave, Bloomington, IN 47405-7103. **EMAIL** edfriedm@indiana.edu

FRIEDMAN, EVA MARY
PERSONAL Born 10/21/1926, Berlin, Germany, m **DISCIPLINE** GERMAN **EDUCATION** Hunter Col, BA, 49; Johns Hopkins Univ, MA, 51, PhD(German), 54. **CAREER** Instr mod lang, Cedar Crest Col, 52-53; from instr to assoc prof, 53-73, dir Ger prog, 73-74, PROF GER, ADELPHI UNIV, 73-. **HONORS AND AWARDS** Senner Prize, 49. **MEMBERSHIPS** MLA; Am Asn Teachers Ger. **RESEARCH** Nineteenth century German literature; foreign languages in the elementary school; Theodor Storm; business German program development. **SELECTED PUBLICATIONS** Auth, Rainer Maria Rilkes Aufzeichmumgen des Malte Laurids Brigge oder das Problem der menschlichen Existenz; T The child in German literature: From marionette through symbol to reality, winter 69 & The generation gap 100 years ago: The father-son conflict in Theodor Storm's novellen, winter 74, Univ Dayton Rev; Existence and alienation in Rainer Maria Rilke's Notebooks of Malte Laurids Brigge, Univ Dayton Rev, 81; Amerikaspiegelung in Theodor Storm's Novelle, Botjer Basch, In: Schriften Der Theodor Storm Gesellschaft, 83; Lessing's Nathan der Weise and Ronetti Roman's Manesse: A Comparison in Lessing and the Enlightenment, ed Alexej Ugrinsky, Greenwood Press, 86. **CONTACT ADDRESS** Dept of Lang & Int Studies, Adelphi Univ, 1 South Ave, Garden City, NY 11530-4299. **EMAIL** Friedman@ADLIBV.adelphi.edu

FRIEDMAN, MELVIN JACK
PERSONAL Born 03/07/1928, Brooklyn, NY, m, 1958, 2 children **DISCIPLINE** ENGLISH, COMPARATIVE LITERATURE **EDUCATION** Bard Col, AB, 49; Columbia Univ, AM, 52; Yale Univ, PhD (comp lit), 54. **CAREER** Assoc ed, French Studies, Yale Univ, 51-53; assoc prof comp lit, Univ Md, 62-66; PROF COMP LIT, UNIV WIS-MILWAUKEE, 66-, Vis sr fel, Univ EAnglia, 72; mem fel comt, Nat Endowment for Humanities, 73-74; Fulbright sr lectr, Univ Antwerp, 76. **MEMBERSHIPS** MLA; PEN. **RESEARCH** Twentieth century novel; 20th century literary criticism. **SELECTED PUBLICATIONS** Auth, 3 Views Of Modernism, Mississippi Quart, Vol 46, 93; Wandering and Home, Beckett Metaphysical Narrative, Contemporary Lit, Vol 36, 95; The Beckett Studies Reader, Contemporary Literature, Vol 36, 95; Beckett Dying Words, Contemporary Lit, Vol 36, 95; Nobodys Home, Speech, Self, and Place in American Fiction from Hawthorne to Delillo, Novel Forum Fiction, Vol 28, 95; Cabell, James, Branch and Richmond In Virginia, Am Lit, Vol 66, 94; Innovation in Beckett, Samuel Fiction, Contemporary Lit, Vol 36, 95; Accidents of Influence, Writing as a Woman and a Jew in America, Int Fiction Rev, Vol 20, 93. **CONTACT ADDRESS** Dept of Comp Lit, Univ of Wisconsin, Milwaukee, Milwaukee, WI 53201.

FRIEDMAN, RICHARD ELLIOTT
DISCIPLINE BIBLE, NEAR EASTERN LANGUAGES AND CIVILIZATIONS **EDUCATION** Harvard Univ, ThD, 78. **CAREER** Prof Hebrew and Comp Lit, Katzin Prof of Jewish Civilization, Univ Calif, San Diego, 76-. **HONORS AND AWARDS** Fel, Am Coun of Learned Soc, 82; Outstanding Fac Awd, Revelle Col, Univ Calif, San Diego, 92; Pres Res Fel in the Humanities, Univ Calif, 97; Sr Fel, Am Schools of Orient Res, 97; Res Awds, Univ Calif, 78, 79, 84, 88, 97. **RESEARCH** Literary and historical research in Bible. **SELECTED PUBLICATIONS** Auth, The Exile and Biblical Narrative, 81; ed, The Creation of Sacred Literature, 81; ed, The Poet and the Historian, 83; ed, The Future of Biblical Studies: The Hebrew Scriptures, 87; auth, Who Wrote the Bible?, 87; The Disappearance of God, 95; auth, The Hidden Face of God, 97; auth, The Hidden Book in the Bible, 98; auth, Commentary on the Torah, 00. **CONTACT ADDRESS** Dept of Lit, Univ of California, San Diego, 9500 Gilman Dr, La Jolla, CA 92093-0410. **EMAIL** refriedm@ucsd.edu

FRIEDMAN, VICTOR A.
PERSONAL Born 10/18/1949, Chicago, IL **DISCIPLINE** LINGUISTICS, EAST EUROPEAN LITERATURE **EDUCATION** Reed Col, BA, 70; Univ Chicago, MA, 71; PhD, 75. **CAREER** From Asst Prof to Prof, Univ NC, 75-93; Prof, Univ Chicago, 93-; Sen Polit and Policy Analyst, UN, 94; Vis Prof, Cornell Univ, 97; Vis Prof, Central European univ, 99. **HONORS AND AWARDS** Woodrow Wilson Fel, Univ Chicago, 70; Phi Beta Kappa, Reed Col, 70; Category A Fel, Nat Endowment Humanities, 80-81; Skopje Gold Plaque Awd, Cyril and Methodius Univ, 91; ACLS Grant for E European Studies, 99; **MEMBERSHIPS** ACLS, Macedonian Acad of Arts & Sci, APS, Int Res & Exchanges Board, AASES, ASASS, Bulgarian Studies Assoc, Gypsy Lore Soc, Soc for Albanian Studies, AATSEEL, AATT, EEAG, LSA, SSC, SECOL. **RESEARCH** Linguistics, East European literature. **SELECTED PUBLICATIONS** Auth, "Surprise! Surprise! Arumanian Has Had an Admirative!" Ind Slavic Studies, vol 7 (94): 79-89; auth, "Romani Standardization and Status in the Republic of Macedonia," Romani in Contact: The Hist, Structure and Soc of a Lang, Benjamins (95): 203-217; auth, "The Differentiation of Macedonian and Bulgarian in a Balkan Context," Balkan Forum, vol 3, no 3 (95): 291-305; auth, "Persistence and Change in Ottoman Patterns of Codeswitching in the Republic of Macedonia: Nostalgia, Duress and Language Shift in Contemporary Southeastern Europe," Summer Sch: Code-Switching and Lang Contact, Fryske Akad (95): 58-67; auth, "Introduction: A Handbook of Vlax Romani, by Ian Hancock (Columbus: Slavica, 95), 13-15; auth, "The Turkish Lexical Element in the Languages of the Republic of Macedonia from the Ottoman Period to Independence," Zeitschrift fur Balkanologie, vol 32, no 2 (96): 133-150; auth, "Linguistic Form and Content in the Romani-Language Press," The Typology and Dialectology of Romani, Benjamins (97): 181-196; auth, "The Grammatical Expression of Presumption and Related Concepts in Balkan Slavic and Balkan Romance," Am Contributions to the 12th Int Cong of Slavists, Bloomington (98): 390-405; auth, "Linguistic Emblems and Emblematic Languages: On Language as Flag in the Balkans," Oh St UP (99). **CONTACT ADDRESS** Dept Lang, Univ of Chicago, 1130 E 59th St, Chicago, IL 60637--1539. **EMAIL** vfriedm@midway.uchicago.edu

FRIEDRICH, PAUL
PERSONAL Born 10/22/1927, Cambridge, MA, m, 1996, 6 children **DISCIPLINE** LINGUISTICS, ANTHROPOLOGY, POETRY **EDUCATION** Harvard Univ, BA, 50, MA, 51; Yale Univ, PhD, 57. **CAREER** Res assoc, Russ Res Ctr, 49-50; asst prof anthrop, Harvard Univ, 57-58; asst prof jr ling, Deccan Col, India, 58-59; asst prof anthrop, Univ Pa, 59-62; assoc prof, 62-67, prof anthrop & ling, Univ Chicago, 67-; prof anthrop, ling & soc thought, 92. **MEMBERSHIPS** Ling See Am; Amer Anthro Assoc; Amer Acad Arts & Sci . **RESEARCH** Homeric Greek; Russian, Comp. Poetics. **SELECTED PUBLICATIONS** Auth, Russia and Eurasia, Encyclopedic 1 World, Cultures, 94; auth, Music in Russian Poetry, Lang, 98. **CONTACT ADDRESS** Dept of Anthrop, Univ of Chicago, 1126 E 59th St, Chicago, IL 60637-1539.

FRIEDRICHSMEYER, ERHARD MARTIN
PERSONAL Born 08/09/1933, Rugby, ND, 3 children **DISCIPLINE** GERMAN **EDUCATION** Lakeland Col, BA, 58; Univ Wis, MA, 59; Univ MN, PhD, 64. **CAREER** Instr Ger, Concordia Col, Moorhead, MN, 59-60; instr, Univ MN, 61-63; asst prof, Univ WI-Milwaukee, 63-66; from asst prof to assoc prof, 66-70, Prof Ger, McMicken Col, Univ Cincinnati, 70. **HONORS AND AWARDS** UC Distinguished Tchg Awd. **RESEARCH** Nineteenth and Twentieth century Ger lit. **SELECTED PUBLICATIONS** Auth, Schnitzler's Der Grune Kakadu, Z Deutsche Philol, 69; The Dogmatism of Pain-Grass' Local Anaesthetic, Dimension, 71; The Bertram Episode in Hesse's Glass Bead Game, Ger Rev, 74; Hagiography and Humor in Hesse's Glass Bead Game, In: Hermann Hesse Heute, Bouvier, Bonn, 80; Die satirische Kurzprosa Heinrich Bolls, Univ NC Press, 81; The Swan Song of a Male Chauvinist, In: Of The Fisherman and His Wife: Gunter Grass, The Flounder in Critical Perspective, AMS Press, 82; Adrian Leverbuhn: Thomas Mann's Lachender Faust; Colloquia Germanica, 1/2, 84; Gunter Grass's The Rat: Making Room for Doomsday, South Atlantic Rev, 89; Hermat, Utopie und Sprachsuche in Boll's Frauen von Flusslandscharft, In: Geschichte und Melancholia, 95. **CONTACT ADDRESS** Dept of Ger Lang & Lit, Univ of Cincinnati, P O Box 210372, Cincinnati, OH 45221-0372.

FRIER, BRUCE W.
PERSONAL Born 08/31/1943, Chicago, IL, s **DISCIPLINE** HISTORY OF LAW, CLASSICAL STUDIES **EDUCATION** Trinity Col, BA, 64; Fel, Am Acad in Rome, 68; Princeton Univ, PhD, 70. **CAREER** Asst prof to prof, Univ Mich, 69-. **HONORS AND AWARDS** Fel, Am Coun of Learned Soc; Fel, NEH, 76-77; Goodwin Awd, Am Philol Asn, 83; Guggenheim Fel, 84-85; Fel, Clare Hall, 84-85; Fel, NEH, 92-93; Fel, Am Acad of Arts and Sci, 93-; LS and A Excellence in Res Awd, 96. **MEMBERSHIPS** Am Philol Asn; Am Soc for Legal Hist. **RESEARCH** Roman law and legal history; Roman social, economic, and demographic history; Hellenistic and Roman historiography, especially Polybius, Sallust, and Livy; Legal theory and the sociology of law; Classical and modern rhetoric. **SELECTED PUBLICATIONS** Co-auth, The Demography of Roman Egypt, Cambridge Univ Press, 94; co-auth, The Census Register P.Oxy 984: The Reverse of Pindar's Paeans, Univ Brussels, 97; auth, Libri Annales Pontificum Maximorum: The Origins of the Annalistic Tradition, rev ed, Univ Mich Press, 99; co-auth, A Casebook on Roman Family Law, Scholars Press, (forthcoming); auth, Roman Law and the Social Sciences, Verlag, (forthcoming). **CONTACT ADDRESS** Sch of Law, Univ of Michigan, Ann Arbor, Univ Mich, Ann Arbor, MI 48109-1215. **EMAIL** bwfrier@umich.edu

FRISCHER, BERNARD D.
PERSONAL Born 05/23/1949, Cleveland, OH, m, 1979 **DISCIPLINE** CLASSICAL STUDIES **EDUCATION** Wesleyan Univ, BA, 71; Univ Heidelberg, PhD, 75. **CAREER** Asst Prof to Full Prof and Dir, 76-. **HONORS AND AWARDS** Fel, Woodrow Wilson, 71; Mich Soc of Fel, 71-74; Fel, Am Acad in Rome, 74-76, 96; Fel, Am Coun of Learned Soc, 81-82, 96-97; Fel, Ctr for Adv Study in the Visual Arts, 97; Phi Beta Kappa, 70. **MEMBERSHIPS** Archaeol Inst of Am; Am Philol Asn; Renaissance Soc of Am. **RESEARCH** Virtual reality applied to cultural heritage; Roman archaeology and topography; Roman literature; Stylometrics; The reception of Antiquity. **SELECTED PUBLICATIONS** Auth, Shifting Paradigms. New Approaches to Horace's Ars Poetica, Am Philol Ans, 91; auth, "Rezeptionsgeschichte and Interpretation: The Quarrel of Antonio Riccoboni and Niccolo Cologno about the Structure of Horace's Ars Poetica," Zeitgenosse Horaz, 96; co-auth, "'Sentence' Length and Word-Type at 'Sentence' Beginning and End: Reliable Authorship Discriminators for Latin Prose? New Studies on the Authorship of the Historia Augusta," Res in Humanities Computing 96; co-auth, "Word-Order and Transference Between Latin and Greek: the Relative Position of the Accusative Director Object and the Governing Verb in Cassius Dio and Other Greek and Roman Prose Authors," Harvard Studies in Class Philol, 99; co-auth, "Virtual Reality and Ancient Rome: The UCLA Cultural VR Lab's Santa Maria Maggiore Project," Brit Archaeol Reports Intl Series, 00; co-auth, "Notes on the New Excavations at Horace's Villa near Licenza (Roma), Italy," in Memoirs of the American Academy in Rome, 01; co-auth, "From CVR to CVRO: The Past, Present, and Future of Cultural Virtual Reality," in British Archaeol Reports, 01; co-auth, Allan Ramsay and the Search for Horace's Villa, London, 01. **CONTACT ADDRESS** Dept Classics, Univ of California, Los Angeles, 405 Hilgard Ave, Los Angeles, CA 90095-1417. **EMAIL** frischer@ucla.edu

FRITZ, ANNICK
DISCIPLINE FRENCH LANGUAGE, LITERATURE, AND CULTURE **EDUCATION** Univ Besancon, France, BA, 71, MA, 72, PhD, 91. **CAREER** Prof, Univ of Besancon, 73-78; lectr, Macalester Col, St. Paul, MN. **MEMBERSHIPS** Women in French, MMLA, MLA, Alliance Francaise, AATF. **RESEARCH** French cinema, contemporary French novel. **SELECTED PUBLICATIONS** Auth, Francois Pouge: De l'eaiture a l'oevre, New York: Peter Lang (97). **CONTACT ADDRESS** Dept French, Macalester Col, 1600 Grand Ave, Saint Paul, MN 55105-1801. **EMAIL** fritz@macalester.edu

FROEHLICH, CHARLES DONALD
PERSONAL Born 05/07/1927, Goose Creek, TX **DISCIPLINE** THEOLOGY, CLASSICS **EDUCATION** Concordia Sem, BA, 52, BD, 55, STM, 58; Univ Tex, Austin, MA, 52. **CAREER** Instr hist, Greek & Latin, St John's Col, Kans, 50-52; instr, New Testament & Greek, Concordia Sem, 55-57; instr, theol & Latin, Lutheran High Schs, St Louis, 57-62; assoc prof, 62-80, Prof Theol & Class Lang, Concordia Teachers Col, Ill, 80- **MEMBERSHIPS** Class Asn Midwest & S. **RESEARCH** New Testament; medieval Christianity; patristics. **SELECTED PUBLICATIONS** Auth, Logophiles of the world, unite!, Lutheran Educ, 11-12/73. **CONTACT ADDRESS** Dept of Theol, Concordia Univ, Illinois, 7400 Augusta St, River Forest, IL 60305-1402.

FROMENT-MEURICE, MARC
PERSONAL Born 10/30/1953, Tokyo, Japan, m, 3 children **DISCIPLINE** FRENCH LITERATURE, PHILOSOPHY **EDUCATION** Univ Paris, Doctorat de 3 Cycle (PhD), 79; Univ Nice-Sophia Antipolis, Doctorat D'Etat, 92. **CAREER** Vis prof, Univ of Washington, 89-91; vis prof, Univ de Montreal, 92; vis prof, Univ Calif, Irvine, 93; vis prof, La State Univ, 95-96; full prof, Vanderbilt Univ, 96-. **HONORS AND AWARDS** Fel, Centre National Du Livre, Paris, France, 93-94. **MEMBERSHIPS** MLA, Colleoe International de Philosophie. **RESEARCH** Continental philosophy (Heideguer)- Deconstruction theory; XIXth and XXth century French literature (emphasis on poetry). **SELECTED PUBLICATIONS** Auth, Les Intermittences de la raison, Penser Cage, Entendre Heidegger, Paris: Klincksieck (82); auth, La Disparue, Paris: Gallimard (87); auth, Solitudes, De Rimbaud a Heidegger, Paris: Galilee (89); auth, La Chose Meme, Solitudes II, Paris: Galilee (92); auth, Tombeau de Trakl, Paris: Berlin (92); auth, Solitudes, From Rimbaud to Heidegger, transl by D. Brick & P .Walsh, Albany, NY: SUNY Press (95); auth, That Is To Say. Heidegger's Poetics, transl by Jan Plug, Stanford, CA: Stanford Univ Press (98); auth, Lignes de Fuite, with graphics by Roberto Altmann, La Souterraine: La Main Courante (98); auth, "Personne a/a ce nom," in L'animal autobiographique. Autour du travail de Jacques Derrida, ed Marie-Louise Mallet, Paris: Galilee (99); auth, "In No Way," Po&sie, 90, Paris: Berlin (99); auth, "Aphasia or the Last Word," in Philosophy and Tragedy, ed Miguel de Beistegui and Simon Sparks, London: Routledge (2000). **CONTACT ADDRESS** Dept French & Italian, Vanderbilt Univ, 2201 W End Ave, Nashville, TN 37235-0001. **EMAIL** Mfment@ctrvax.vanderbilt.edu

FROMKIN, VICTORIA A.
PERSONAL Born 05/16/1923, Passaic, NJ, m, 1948, 1 child **DISCIPLINE** LINGUISTICS, EXPERIMENTAL PHONETICS **EDUCATION** Univ Calif, Berkeley, AB, 44, MA, 63, PhD (ling), 65. **CAREER** Asst prof English, Calif State Univ, 65; asst prof speech, 66-67, asst prof ling, 67-69, actg dir phonetics lab, 68-69, chmn dept, 72-76, Prof Ling, Univ Calif, Los Angeles, 69-, Dean Grad Div, 79-, Nat Insts Health grant, 63-; asst prof lang sem, Calif State Col Los Angeles, spring 65; Off Naval Res contract, 66-; mem ling panel, Nat Sci Found, 76-78: ling deleg, Nat Acad Sci, China, 74; vis prof, Univ Stockholm, 77. **MEMBERSHIPS** Fel Acoust Soc Am; Ling Soc Am; Int Phonetic Asn; Asn Machine Transl and Computational Ling; Am Assoc Applied Ling. **RESEARCH** Electromyographics studies of speech **SELECTED PUBLICATIONS** Auth, Linguistic Representational and Processing Analyses of Agrammatism--Introduction, Brain and Language, Vol 50, 95p; The Mind of a Savant Language Learning and Modularity, Lingua, Vol 99, 96; Some Thoughts about the Brain Mind Language Inter-

face, Lingua, Vol 100, 97; Comprehension and Acceptability Judgments in Agrammatism--Disruptions in the Syntax of Referential Dependency, Brain Lan, Vol 45, 93; Jakobson, Roman--A Linguists View of Aphasia, Brain Lan, Vol 47, 94. **CONTACT ADDRESS** Dept of Ling, Univ of California, Los Angeles, Los Angeles, CA 90024.

FRYDMAN, ANNE
PERSONAL Born 05/27/1947, New York, NY, m, 1982 **DISCIPLINE** RUSSIAN AND COMPARATIVE LITERATURE **EDUCATION** Sarah Lawrence Col, BA, 68; Columbia Univ, MA, 69, PhD (Russ lit), 78. **CAREER** Kenan fel humanities, Soc Fels in Humanities, Columbia Univ, 77-79; vis asst prof, State Univ NY, Purchase, 79-82; Vis Asst Prof Russ Lit, State Univ NY, Purchase, 79-, Preceptor Slavic lang, Columbia Univ, 73-76, vis lectr, 79; vis lectr Slavic lang and lit, Princeton Univ, 80; consult, Theatre Dept, State Univ NY, Purchase, 80; vis asst prof Slav lang, Princeton, 80-81. **MEMBERSHIPS** Int Chekhov Soc (exec secy, 80-82); Am Asn Advan Slavic Studies. **RESEARCH** Anton Chekhov's short stories, form and vision; the prose of Isaac Babel. **SELECTED PUBLICATIONS** Auth, Pirozhkova Memoir of Babel--Introduction, Can Slavonic Papers Rev Can Slavistes, Vol 36, 94. **CONTACT ADDRESS** 425 Riverside Dr Apt 7J, New York, NY 10025.

FRYER, T. BRUCE
PERSONAL Born 01/21/1941, Philadelphia, PA, m, 1964, 2 children **DISCIPLINE** SPANISH **EDUCATION** Muhlenberg Col, BA, 62; Middlebury Col, MA, 66; Univ Tex, Austin, PhD (foreign lang educ), 70. **CAREER** Teacher Span, Spring-Ford Area Schs, 62-67, head dept foreign lang, 64-67; teaching assoc Span educ, Univ Tex, Austin, 67-70; asst prof, 70-74, Assoc Prof Span, Univ SC, 74-90; prof 90-, Coordr, Div Span and Port, 75-, Mem Bd Dirs, Southern Conf Lang Teaching, 76-. **MEMBERSHIPS** Am Asn Teachers Span and Port; MLA; Am Coun Teaching Foreign Lang; Am Translators Assoc. **RESEARCH** Foreign language teaching methodology; spanish for international business. **SELECTED PUBLICATIONS** Auth, Beyond Borders--Profiles in International Education, Mod Lan J, Vol 80, 96; Foreign Language Curricular Needs of Students Preparing for an Internship Abroad, Mod Lan J, Vol 77, 93; Understanding Global Cultures--Metaphorical Journeys Through 17 Countries, Mod Lan J, Vol 81, 97; auth, Spanish & Portuguese for Business and the Professions, National Textbook Co, 97; auth, Exitocomericial: practicas Administrative y contextos comerciales, 3rd ed., Harcourt, 01. **CONTACT ADDRESS** Dept of Spanish, Italian, & Portuguese, Univ of So Carolina, Columbia, Columbia, SC 29208. **EMAIL** bfryer@sc.edu

FUCHS, ESTHER
PERSONAL Born 02/26/1953, Tel Aviv, Israel **DISCIPLINE** HEBREW LITERATURE **EDUCATION** Brandeis Univ, PhD, 80. **CAREER** Univ Texas, asst prof, 80-85; Univ Arizona Tucson, assoc prof, 85-00; prof, 00-. **MEMBERSHIPS** AJS, SBL, NAPH. **RESEARCH** Women in Biblical literature; women in modern Hebrew literature; S.Y. Agnon. **SELECTED PUBLICATIONS** Auth, Encounters with Israeli Authors, Marblehead: Micah, 83; auth, Cunning Innoncence: The Ironic Art of S.Y. Agon, Tel Aviv Univ, 85; auth, Israeli Mythogynies: Women in Contemporary Hebrew Fiction, Albany: SUNY Press, 87; auth, Sexual Politics in the Biblical Narrative: Reading the Hebrew Bible as a Women, Sheffield Academic Press, 00. **CONTACT ADDRESS** Dept of Judaic Studies, Univ of Arizona, Franklin Bldg 305, Tucson, AZ 85721. **EMAIL** fuchs@u.arizona.edu

FUEGI, JOHN B.
PERSONAL Born 05/09/1936, London, England, 2 children **DISCIPLINE** COMPARATIVE LITERATURE **EDUCATION** Pomona Col, BA, 61; Univ Southern Calif, PhD(comp lit), 67. **CAREER** Lectr Am lit, Free Univ Berlin, 66-67; from asst prof to prof comp lit, Univ Wis, Milwaukee, 67-76; Prof Ger, Slavic & Comp Lit & Dir Comp Lit, Univ MD, 76-86. **HONORS AND AWARDS** Vis fel, Wesleyan Ctr for Humanities, 69; Am Coun Learned Soc sr res fel in East Europ Studies, 73-74; Univ Wis, Milwaukee sr res fel in 20th century studies, 73-74; co-ed, Brecht Jahrbuch, 73-89; Rockefeller Found award, 82-83; Kurt Weill Found fel, 84, 85; Guggenheim fel, 84-85; PBS award for Beckett Directs Beckett, 88-89; Maryland Hum Coun award, 97-98, 99-00. **MEMBERSHIPS** MLA; Am Comp Lit Asn; Int Comp Lit Asn. **RESEARCH** Relationship of German, Russian and English literatures; the drama, especially Shakespeare and Brecht; E. Hauptmann; R. Berlau; M. Steffin; Virginia Woolf; Hildegard von Bingen; Ada Byron-Lovelace; the relationship of literature and film. **SELECTED PUBLICATIONS** Auth, producer & dir, The Wall (film), Flare Productions, 61; auth, The Essential Brecht, Univ Calif, Studies Comp Lit, 72; ed, Brecht Today: Yearbook of International Brecht Society, 71-79 & 82-89; auth, Explorations in no man's land: Shakespeare's poetry as theatrical film, Shakespeare Quart, 72; The Form and the Pressure: Shakespeare's Haunting of Bertolt Brecht, Mod Drama, 72; Moliere and Brecht: The Authorship of Brecht's Don Juan, Comp Lit Studies, 74; auth, Bertolt Brecht: Chaos According to Plan, Cambridge, 87; producer, dir & auth, Red Ruth, Nordisk Film, 90 and The War Within: A Portrait of Virginia Woolf; auth, Brecht and Company, Grove, 94; auth, Brecht et Cie, Fayard, 95; auth, Brecht und Co, Eva Hamburg, 97; auth, "In the Symphony of the World" A Portrait of Hildegard of Bingen," 98. **CONTACT ADDRESS** 2701 Curry Dr, Adelphi, MD 20783. **EMAIL** jfuegi@wam.umb.edu

FUKUYAMA, FRANCIS
PERSONAL Born 10/27/1952, Chicago, IL, m, 1986, 3 children **DISCIPLINE** CLASSICS **EDUCATION** Cornell Univ, BA, 74. **CAREER** Social sci, Rand Corp, 80-81, 83-89, 90-95; State Dept policy planning, 81-82, 89; George Mason Univ Inst of Public Policy, 95- . **HONORS AND AWARDS** Hon doctorate, Conn Col; Permio Capri; Los Angeles Times Critics Awd. **MEMBERSHIPS** Am Polit Sci Asn. **RESEARCH** Democracy, economic culture; social capital. **SELECTED PUBLICATIONS** Co-ed, The Soviet Union and the Third World: The Last Three Decades, Cornell, 87; auth, The End of History and the Last Man, Free Press, 92; auth, Trust: The Social Virtues and the Creation of Prosperity, Free Press, 95; auth, The Primacy of Culture, J of Democracy, 95; auth, Confucianism and Democracy, J of Democracy, 95; auth, Immigration, in Alexander, ed, The New Promise of American Life, Hudson Inst, 95; auth, Virtue and Prosperity, Natl Interest, 95; auth, On the Possibility of Writing a Universal History, in Melzer, ed, History and the Idea of Progress, Cornell, 95; auth, Social Capital and the Global Economy, For Aff, 95; auth, Trust Still Counts in a Virtual World, Forbes ASAP, 96; auth, The Illusion of Exceptionalism, J of Democracy, 97; auth, Is It All In the Genes? Commentary, 97; auth, Asian Values and the Asian Crisis, Commentary, 98; auth, Women and the Evolution of World Politics, For Aff, 98; auth, The great Disruption, Free Press, 99. **CONTACT ADDRESS** Esther Newberg International Creative Mgt, 40 West 57th St, New York, NY 10019. **EMAIL** ffukuyam@gmu.edu

FULCO, WILLIAM J.
PERSONAL Born 02/24/1936, Los Angeles, CA, s **DISCIPLINE** NEAR EASTERN LANGUAGES & LITERATURE **EDUCATION** Univ Santa Clara, AB, 59; Univ Santa Clara, MA, PhL, 60; STM, STL, 67; Yale Univ, PhD, 70. **CAREER** Ntl Endowment for Humanities Prof Ancient Mediterranean Studies, Loyola Marymount Univ, 98-; Organizer & Host Loyola Marymount Univ Intl Conf in Near Eastern Archaeology, 96-98; correspondent, Annotazioni Numismatiche, 91-; assoc ed, Cath Bibl Quart; Corp Representative of Univ S Calif to Amer Schools of Oriental Res; co-dir, Univ S Calif & Jordanian Dept of Antiquities joint archaeological excavation, Jordan, 90; adjunct prof Archaeology, Univ S Calif, 89-98; participant, Dept of Antiquities, Jordan, Amman Citadel Project; lctr, Univ Judaism, 84-90; lctr Theolog Dept, Loyola Marymount Univ, 84-97. **HONORS AND AWARDS** Mortar Board (Pi Sigma Alpha), Univ S Calif, Faculty of the Month, 95; Megiddo Expedition Israel, 94-. **MEMBERSHIPS** Cath Bibl Assoc Archaeology Committee, 96-; Amer Numismatic Assoc; Amer Numismatic Soc; Amer Oriental Soc; Amer Schools of Oriental Res; Cath Bibl Assoc Amer; Ntl Assoc Afroasiatic Linguistics; Numismatic Soc India; Soc Bibl Lit. **RESEARCH** Linguistics; Archaeologty **SELECTED PUBLICATIONS** Coauth, Tyre: The Shrine of Apollo, Coins & Stamped Handles, 96; Searching for Revelations at Megiddo, in Loyola Marymount Univ VISTAS, 96; coauth, Coins from the Excavations at Tell Nimrin, in Amer Jour of Numismatics, 95-96. **CONTACT ADDRESS** Department of Classics, Loyola Marymount Univ, 7900 Loyola Blvd., PO Box 45041, Los Angeles, CA 90045-0041. **EMAIL** wfulco@lmu.edu

FULLER, CLARENCE
PERSONAL Born 01/17/1927, Foxboro, MA **DISCIPLINE** FRENCH, PHONETICS **EDUCATION** Brown Univ, AB, 50; Middlebury Col, MA, 51. **CAREER** Lectr French, Sch Gen Studies, Columbia Univ, 55-56, instr, Columbia Col, 59-61; asst prof, 61-65, Assoc Prof French and Span, Bloomfield Col, 65-. **RESEARCH** Phonetics; French. **SELECTED PUBLICATIONS CONTACT ADDRESS** Dept of Lang, Bloomfield Col, Bloomfield, NJ 07003.

FULLER, M. A.
DISCIPLINE CHINESE LITERATURE **EDUCATION** Yale, BA, 74, PhD, 82. **CAREER** Asst prof, Harvard, 84-90; asst prof, 92-93, assoc prof, Univ CA, Irvine, 93-. **RESEARCH** Classical Chinese poetry; literary theory. **SELECTED PUBLICATIONS** Auth, Road to East Slope: the Development of Su Shi's Poetic Voice, Stanford, 90; auth, An Introduction to Literary Chinese, Harvard, 99. **CONTACT ADDRESS** Univ of California, Irvine, Irvine, CA 92717. **EMAIL** mafuller@uci.edu

FULLERTON, GERALD LEE
PERSONAL Born 08/03/1941, San Francisco, CA **DISCIPLINE** GERMANIC LINGUISTICS **EDUCATION** Stanford Univ, AB, 63, MA, 65; Univ Mich, Ann Arbor, PhD(Ger), 71. **CAREER** Instr Ger, Meramec Community Col, 64-66; instr, Drake Univ, 66-68; asst prof, State Univ NY Buffalo, 71-75; asst prof, Univ Tex San Antonio, 76-77; Asst Prof Ger, Univ Minn, Twin Cities, 77- **MEMBERSHIPS** Ling Soc Am. **RESEARCH** Comparative Germanic grammar; syntax of modern Ger. **SELECTED PUBLICATIONS** Auth, The source of the Gothic fourth weak conjugation, Language, 71; The development of obstruents in four Germanic endings, 74 & Grimm's law and WGmc 2sg verb endings -s, 75, Linguistics; Historical Germanic Verb Morphology, Walter de Grunter, Berlin, 77; On teaching the subjective use of modal auxiliaries, Die Unterrichtspraxis, 77; Subjective modals, assessment adverbs and source phrases, In: Studies in Descriptive German Grammar, Julius Groos, Heidelberg, 82; auth, The Gothic Genitive Plural: An Analysis of Morphological Structure, Michigan Germanic Stud, 83; auth, The Germanic Weak Nonpresent Formations, Beitrage zur Geschichte der Deutschen Sprache und Literatur, 89; auth, Reduplication and the Prosody of Ancient Germanic, Beitrage zur Geschichte der Deutschen Sprache und Literatur, 91; auth, PIE Syllabification and Germanic Nominal Inflection, in, On Germanic Linguistics, de Gruyter, 92. **CONTACT ADDRESS** Dept Germ, Scandinavian & Dutch, Univ of Minnesota, Twin Cities, 9 Pleasant St. SE, 205 Folwell Hall, Minneapolis, MN 55455. **EMAIL** fulle001@tc.umn.edu

FUQUA, CHARLES
PERSONAL Born 10/05/1935, Paris, France, m, 1961, 3 children **DISCIPLINE** CLASSICS **EDUCATION** Princeton Univ, BA, 57; Cornell Univ, MA, 62, PhD(classics), 64. **CAREER** From instr to asst prof classics, Dartmouth Col, 64-66; chmn dept, 66-78, assoc prof, 66-72, Garfield Prof Ancient Lang, Williams Col, 72-, Mem adv coun, Am Acad Rome, 66- & exec comt, 71-74. **HONORS AND AWARDS** Phi Beta Kappa, 57; Phi Kappa Phi, 64. **MEMBERSHIPS** Am Philol Asn; Class Asn New Eng; Classical Asn Mass; Vergilian Soc. **RESEARCH** Greek epic & drama; Latin lyric poetry. **SELECTED PUBLICATIONS** Auth, Possible implications of the ostracism of Hyperbolus, Trans Am Philol Asn, 65; Horace, Carmina 1.23-25, 1/68 & Aeschylus: Agamemnon 1446-47, 7/72, Class Philol; Studies in the use of myth in Sophocles' Philoctetes and the Orestes of Euripides, 76, The World of myth in Euripides Orestes, 78 & Heroism, Heracles, and the Trachiniae, 80, Traditio; Tyrtaeus and the cult of heroes, Greek, Roman & Byzantine Studies, 81; Hector, Sychaeus, and Deiphobus: Three mutilated figures in Aeneid, Class Philol, 1-6/82; auth, Proper Bevavior in the Odyssey, Ill Classical Stud, 46-58/91; auth, Moral Clusters in the Odyssey, Scholia, 56-68/93. **CONTACT ADDRESS** Dept of Classics, Williams Col, 880 Main St, Stetson Hall B25, Williamstown, MA 01267-2600. **EMAIL** cfuqua@williams.edu

FURNESS, EDNA LUE
PERSONAL Born 01/26/1906, Knox Co, NE **DISCIPLINE** ENGLISH & SPANISH **EDUCATION** Univ CO, AB & BE, 28, MA, 39, EdD, 51. **CAREER** Teacher, High Schs, CO, 28-33 & WY, 33-39; instr Span, Pueblo Col, 42-45; instr English & mod lang, Casper Col, WY, 45-47; from asst prof to prof English & foreign lang educ, Univ WY, 47-61; prof English & Span, 61-72, Emer Prof Lang & Lit, WY State Univ 72-; Instr, Univ CO, 50-51; fac res grant, Univ WY, 57; Coe fel Am studies, Coe Found, 59; Delta Kappa Gamma res grant, 60-61; US Off Educ res grant, 66-67, humanities res grant, 71-72. **HONORS AND AWARDS** Haiku Awd, Washington Poets Asn, 80. **MEMBERSHIPS** NEA; Int Platform Asn; Nat Coun Teachers English. **RESEARCH** Comparative literature; translation; children's literature. **SELECTED PUBLICATIONS** Coauth, New Dimensions in the Teaching of English, Pruett, 67; auth, Trends in Literature on Teaching the Language Arts, contribr, Teaching of Listening, Scarecrow, 71, Linguistics in the Elementary School Classroom, Macmillan, 71 & Language Arts in the Elementary School, Lippincott, 72; auth, Mediterranean magic, 74 & Spelling is Serious Stuff, 78, Delta Kappa Gamma Bull; contribr, Educational Assessment of Learning Problems, 78; Assessment and Correction of Language Arts Difficulties, 80; Spelling for the Millions, 66; Guide to Better English Spelling, 91. **CONTACT ADDRESS** 725 S Alton Way Windsor Gardens-6B, Denver, CO 80231.

FURST, LILLIAN R.
PERSONAL Born 06/30/1931, Vienna, Austria, s **DISCIPLINE** COMPARATIVE LITERATURE, GERMAN **EDUCATION** Univ Manchester, England, BA, 52; Cambridge Univ, England, PhD, 57. **CAREER** Vis, Dartmouth, 71-72; vis, Case Western Reserve, 78-79; vis, Stanford Univ, 81-82; vis, Harvard Univ, 83-84; Prof, Univ NC, 86-. **HONORS AND AWARDS** Fel, ACLS, 74-75; Guggenheim Fel, 82-83; Stanford Human, 82-83; Nat Human, 88-89; NEH, 93-94. **MEMBERSHIPS** MLA; CLA. **RESEARCH** 19th C literature and medicine. **SELECTED PUBLICATIONS** Auth, Romanticism in Perspective (69), 2nd ed (76); auth, Contours of European Romanticism (77); auth, Fictions of Romantic Irony (84); auth, Home is Somewhere Else (92); auth, All is True: The Claims and Strategies of Realist Fiction (95); auth, Between Doctors and Patients (98); auth, Just Talk: Narratives of Psychotherapy (99). **CONTACT ADDRESS** Dept Comp Literature, Univ of No Carolina, Chapel Hill, 342 Dey Hall, Chapel Hill, NC 27599-3150.

G

GABBARD, KRIN
PERSONAL Born 01/29/1948, Charleston, IL, m, 1973 **DISCIPLINE** COMPARATIVE LITERATURE **EDUCATION** Univ Chicago, BA, 70; IN Univ, PhD, 79. **CAREER** Asst prof, Classics and Modern Lang, Univ SD, 77-79; asst prof, English,

Stephens Col, 79-81; asst prof, 81-87, assoc prof, 87-97, prof, Comparative Lit, SUNY Stony Brook, 98-. **MEMBERSHIPS** Soc for Cinema Studies; ACLA; MLA; Sonneck Soc. **RESEARCH** Jazz; film hist and theory; psychoanalysis. **SELECTED PUBLICATIONS** Auth, The Circulation of Sado-Masochistic Desire in the Lolita Texts, J of Film and Video, 94, repeated in Psyart: A Hyperlink J for Psychological Study of the Arts (http://www.clas.ufl.edu/ipsa/journal/articles/gabbar01.htm); ed, Representing Jazz, Duke Univ Press, 95; ed, Jazz Among the Discourses, Duke Univ Press, 95; auth, Psychoanalysis and Film Study in the 1990s, The Am Psychoanalyst 29 4, 96; Jammin' at the Margins: Jazz and the American Cinema, Univ Chicago Press, 96; Louis Armstrong and His Audiences, Jazz: A Century of Change, ed Lewis Porter, Schirmer, 97; The Ethnic Oedipus: The Jazz Singer and Its Remakes, Play It Again, Sam: Retakes on Remakes, ed Andrew Horton and Stuart Y McDougal, Univ CA Press, 98; Borrowing Black Masculinity: The Role of Johnny Hartman in The Bridges of Madison County, in Soundtrack Available: Essays on Film and Popular Music, ed Arthur Knight and Pamela Robertson, Duke Univ Press, 99; Kansas City Dreamin': Robert Altman's Jazz History Lesson, to appear in Music and Cinema, ed James Buhler, Caryl Flinn, and David Neumeyer, Wesleyan Univ Press, 99; Psychiatry and the Cinema, with Glen O Gabbard, MD, 1st ed, 86, rev and expanded, AM Psychiatric Press, 99; Stanley Kubrick and the Art Cinema, to appear in an anthology on A Clockwork Orange, Cambridge Univ Press. **CONTACT ADDRESS** Dept of Comparative Lit, SUNY, Stony Brook, Stony Brook, NY 11794. **EMAIL** kgabbard@notes.cc.sunysb.edu

GABRIELE, JOHN P.
DISCIPLINE SPANISH LITERATURE **EDUCATION** Univ Conn, BA, 75, MA, 77; Univ NC, PhD, 81; Univ de Salamanca, Spain. **CAREER** Prof. **RESEARCH** Nineteenth and Twentieth-Century Spanish Theatre **SELECTED PUBLICATIONS** Auth, Suma valleinclaniana, Barcelona: Anthuopos, 92; auth, De lo particula a lo universal: el teatro espanol del siglo XX y su contexto. Frankfurt am Main: Vervuert Verlag, 94; auth, "Gender in the Mirror: A feminist Perspective on the Esperpento de la hija del capitan," revista Hispanica Moderna 48.2, (95), 307-314; auth, Panoramica del teatro espanol actual, Madrid: editorial Fundamentos, 96; auth, El teatro breve de Lidia Falcon, editorial fundamentos, 97; auth, "Towards a Radical Feminist Stage Rhetoric in the Short Plays of Lidia Falcon," Symposium 51.1, (97), 3-19; auth, Nuevas perspectivas sobre el 98, Madrid: Iberoamericana, 99; auth, "Manuel Martinez Mediero: deslindes de un teatro de urgencia social, Madrid: Fundamentos, 00; auth, "House and Body: Confinement in Lorca's Woman-Conscious Trilogy, " Hispanic research Journal 1.3, (00), 275-285 **CONTACT ADDRESS** Dept of Span, The Col of Wooster, Wooster, OH 44691. **EMAIL** jgabriele@acs.wooster.edu

GAEFFKE, PETER
PERSONAL Born 12/06/1927, Breslau, m, 1958, 2 children **DISCIPLINE** INDOLOGY, COMPARATIVE LITERATURE **EDUCATION** Univ Mainz, WGer, MA, 51, PhD(Indoeurop ling), 52. **CAREER** Prof Hindi, Univ Utrecht, Netherlands, 64-75; Prof Indian Lit, Univ PA, 75-. **HONORS AND AWARDS** MA, Univ Pa, 75. **MEMBERSHIPS** Ger Orient Soc; Dutch Orient Soc; Am Orient Soc; Am Asn Comp Lit. **RESEARCH** Medieval and modern literatures in Hindi, Urdu and Bengal. **SELECTED PUBLICATIONS CONTACT ADDRESS** S Asia Regional Studies Dept, Univ of Pennsylvania, Philadelphia, PA 19174.

GAGARIN, MICHAEL
PERSONAL Born 01/04/1942, New York City, NY, m, 1974, 2 children **DISCIPLINE** CLASSICS **EDUCATION** Stanford Univ, BA, 63; Harvard Univ, MA, 65; Yale Univ, PhD(classics), 68. **CAREER** From instr to asst prof classics, Yale Univ, 68-73; asst prof, 73-80, Assoc Prof Classics, Univ Tex, Austin, 80-86; prof classics, 86-; Jr fel, Ctr Hellenic Studies, Washington DC, 72-73; vis asst prof classics, Univ Calif, Berkeley, 76-77; Am Coun Learned Soc fel, 80-81. **HONORS AND AWARDS** NEH fellow 85-86 and 97-98. **MEMBERSHIPS** Am Philol Asn; Am Inst Archaeol; Soc Ancient Greek Philos. **RESEARCH** Greek literature; Greek law; Greek philosophy. **SELECTED PUBLICATIONS** Auth, Aeschylean Drama, Univ of CA Press, 76; auth, Drakon and Early Athenian Homicide Law, Yale Univ Press, 81; auth, Early Greek Law, Univ of CA Press, 86, paperback ed, 89; auth, The Murder of Herodes: A Study of Antiphon 5, Frankfurt, 89; ed, Symposion 1990. Akten der Gesellschaft fur griechische and hellenistische Rechtsgeschichte, vol. 8, Cologne, 92; co-auth, Early Greek Political Thought from Homer to the Sophists, Cambridge, 95; ed & comment, Antiphon, the speeches, Cambridge Greek and Latin Classics, Cambridge, 97; co-trans, Antiphon and Andocides, vol. 1 of Classical Greek Oratory, Austin, 98. **CONTACT ADDRESS** Classics Dept, Univ of Texas, Austin, Austin, TX 78712. **EMAIL** gagarin@mail.uTexas.edu

GAGLIARDI, FRANK M.
DISCIPLINE CLASSICAL LANGUAGES **EDUCATION** Carleton Col, BA, 72; Univ Mich, PhD, 76. **CAREER** Prof & dir, Oakley Ctr for the Humanities & Soc Sci. **RESEARCH** Greek Tragedy; archaic Greek literature and culture, especially Homer and lyric poetry; critical theory, especially gender studies and anthropological approaches to Greek culture; Roman comedy. **SELECTED PUBLICATIONS** Publ on, Horace Odes 1.5; Sophocles' Philoctetes. **CONTACT ADDRESS** Classics Dept, Williams Col, Stetson Hall, Williamstown, MA 01267. **EMAIL** mhoppin@williams.edu

GAICHAS, LAWRENCE EDWARD
PERSONAL Born 03/30/1942, Chicago, IL, m, 1967, 2 children **DISCIPLINE** CLASSICS **EDUCATION** Xavier Univ, Ohio, HAB, 64; Ohio State Univ, MA, 68, PhD(classics), 72. **CAREER** Teaching asst classics, Ohio State Univ, 66-68; instr classics and English, Kalamazoo Col, 70-72; instr Columbus Pub Schs, 72-73; asst prof, 73-77, Assoc Prof Classics, 77-83, prof classics, 83-, Duquesne Univ, Chmn Dept, 78- Concurrent Pos: Circulation mgr, Class World, 78-. **MEMBERSHIPS** Am Philol Asn. **RESEARCH** Graeco-Roman historiography; Graeco-Roman epic; etymology. **SELECTED PUBLICATIONS** Auth, Latin Skills 1 and Latin Skills 2 for the IBM-PC and the PS/2, Version 1.0, Class World, Vol 0089, 1996. **CONTACT ADDRESS** Dept of Classics, Duquesne Univ, Pittsburgh, PA 15259. **EMAIL** gaichas@duq.edu

GAINES, JAMES FREDERICK
PERSONAL Born 05/31/1949, Somerville, MA, m, 1975 **DISCIPLINE** FRENCH LITERATURE **EDUCATION** Mich State Univ, BA, 71; Univ Pa, MA, 75, PhD(Fr), 77. **CAREER** Asst prof, 77-80, Assoc Prof French, Southeastern LA Univ, 80-, Coordr, Univ Hon Prog, Southeastern La Univ, 80-. **MEMBERSHIPS** NAm Soc 17th Century Fr Lit; MLA; Am Asn Teachers Fr. **RESEARCH** Moliere; history and sociology of literature, especially comic theatre; ideologies of French seventeenth century literature. **SELECTED PUBLICATIONS** Auth, Moliere 'Tartuffe,' Theatre J, Vol 0044, 92; Moliere 'George Dandin,' Theatre J, Vol 0044, 92; Valincour, G S--the Limits of Honnetete, Fr Rev, Vol 0066, 93; Costume and Fashion in the Plays of Moliere, Jean, Baptiste, Poquelin--A 17th-Century Perspective, Fr Rev, Vol 0067, 94; Tragedy at the Time of Henri-II and Charles-IX, Bibliotheque D Humanisme Et Renaissance, Vol 0057, 95; Moliere and Marx--Prospects For A New Century, Esprit Createur, Vol 0036, 96; The Awakening of Feelings and the Paradox of Conscience in L'ecole-Des-Femmes' in Play By Moliere, Fr Rev, Vol 0070, 97. **CONTACT ADDRESS** Southeastern Louisiana Univ, 500 Western Ave, PO Box 724, Hammond, LA 70402-0001.

GAIR, JAMES WELLS
PERSONAL Born 12/27/1927, Buffalo, NY, w, 1950, 2 children **DISCIPLINE** LINGUISTICS **EDUCATION** Univ Buffalo, BA, 49, MA, 56; Cornell Univ, PhD(ling), 63. **CAREER** Instr English, Univ Buffalo, 49-51; instr gen educ, State Univ NY Utica, 51-54; instr commun & lit, Univ Buffalo, 54-57, lectr gen stud & asst to dean, Col Arts & Sci, 57-58; res asst NDEA Sinhalese proj, 61-62, from asst prof to assoc prof, 62-74, dir NDEA SAsia Ctr, 67-69, Prof Ling, Cornell Univ, 74-, Instr, Can Ling Inst, Univ Alta, 62-66. **HONORS AND AWARDS** Fulbright-Hays res grant, Ceylon, 64-65 & 69-70, lectr award, Sri Lanka, 76-77; D Litt, Kelaniya Univ, 93. **MEMBERSHIPS** Ling Soc Am; Asn Asian Studies; Ling Soc India; Royal Asiatic Soc, Ceylon. **RESEARCH** South Asian languages and linguistics; English linguistics. **SELECTED PUBLICATIONS** Auth, The alphabet, Collier's Encyclopedia, 66; coauth, Colloquial Sinhalese, Cornell Univ SAsia Prog, 68; auth, Colloquial Sinhalese Clause Structures, Mouton, 70; Sinhalese digiossia, Anthrop Ling, Vol X, No 8; coauth, Literary Sinhala, Cornell Univ SAsia Prog, 74; coauth, Spoken Sri Lanka (Jaffna) Tamil, Sri Lanka Univ, 78; auth, Papers in South Asian Linguistics: Sinhala and Other South Asian Languages, Oxford Univ Press, 98; coauth, A New Course in Reading Pali, Motilal Banarsidass, Delhi, 98; co-ed and co-auth; Lexical Anaphors and Pronouns in Selected South Asian Languages, Maston de Gruyler, 00. **CONTACT ADDRESS** Dept of Modern Lang & Ling, Cornell Univ, 203 Morrill Hall, Ithaca, NY 14853-4701. **EMAIL** jwg2@cornell.edu

GAISSER, JULIA HAIG
PERSONAL Born 01/12/1941, Cripple Creek, CO, m, 1964, 1 child **DISCIPLINE** CLASSICAL PHILOLOGY **EDUCATION** Brown Univ, AB, 62; Harvard Univ, AM, 66; Edinburgh Univ, PhD, 66. **CAREER** Asst prof classics, Newton Col, 66-69, Swarthmore Col, 70-72 & Brooklyn Col, 73-75; Assoc Prof, 75-84, Prof Latin, Bryn Mawr Col, 84-. **HONORS AND AWARDS** NEH Sr Fel, 85-86, 93-94, 99; ACLS Fel, 89-90; MBE, 90; Res, Bellagio Study & Conf Ctr, Bellagio, Italy, 94; Vis Schol, Phi Beta Kappa, 96-97; Martin Classical Lecturer, Oberlin College, 00. **MEMBERSHIPS** Class Asn Atlantic States; Pres of Am Philol Asn, 00; Renaissance Soc. **RESEARCH** Greek epic; Latin poetry; classical tradition. **SELECTED PUBLICATIONS** Auth, A structural analysis of the digressions in the Iliad and the Odyssey, Harvard Studies Class Philol, 68; Adaptation of traditional material in the Glaucus-Diomedes episode, Trans Am Philol Soc, 69; Structure and tone in Tibullus 1 6, Am J Philol, 71; Tibullus 1 7: A tribute to Messalla, Class Philol, 71; Noun-epithet combinations in the Homeric hymn to Demeter, Trans Am Philol Soc, 74; coauth, Partons in antiquity, Am J Physics, 77; auth, Mythological Exempla in Propertius 1 2 and, Am J Philol, 77; Tibullus 2 3 and Vergil's Tenth Eclogue, Trans Am Philol, 77; Catullus and his Renaissance Readers, Oxford, 93; auth, Pierio Valeriano On The Ill Fortune of Learned Men: A Renaissance Humanist and his World, Mich, 99. **CONTACT ADDRESS** Dept of Latin, Bryn Mawr Col, 101 N Merion Ave, Bryn Mawr, PA 19010-2899. **EMAIL** jgaisser@brynmawr.edu

GALAND, RENE
PERSONAL Born 01/27/1923, France, m, 1959, 2 children **DISCIPLINE** FRENCH **EDUCATION** Univ Rennes, Lic es Let, 44; Yale Univ, PhD(French), 52. **CAREER** Instr French, Yale Univ, 49-51; from asst prof to assoc prof, 51-63; chmn dept, 68-72, Prof French, Wellesley Col, 63-, Asst ed, Fr Rev, 67-74; reviewer Breton Lit, World Lit Today, 78-93. **HONORS AND AWARDS** Chevalier, Palmes Academiques, French Govt, 71; Xavier de Langlais Prize for Breton Literature, 79. **MEMBERSHIPS** Am Asn Teachers Fr; Soc Fr Prof Am. **RESEARCH** Nineteenth and twentieth century French literature; Breton language and literature. **SELECTED PUBLICATIONS** Auth, L'Ame celtique de Renan, 59; auth, Baudelaire: poetiques et poesie, 69; auth, Saint-John Perse, 72; contr, The Binding of Proteus: Perspectives on Myth and Literature, 80; contr, A Critical Biography of French Literature. The Twentieth Century, 80; contr, Bretagne et pays celtiques, 82; auth, Canevas: etudes sur la poesie francaise de Baudelaire a L'OULIPO, 86; auth, Strategie de la lecture, 90; contr, The New Princeton Encyclopedia of Poetry and Poetics, 93; contr, Bretagne et pays d'Europe, 99. **CONTACT ADDRESS** Dept of French, Wellesley Col, Wellesley, MA 02481.

GALINSKY, KARL
PERSONAL Born 02/07/1942, Strassburg, m, 1986, 2 children **DISCIPLINE** CLASSICS **EDUCATION** Bowdoin, AB, 63; Princeton, PhD, 66. **CAREER** Instr, Princeton, 65-66; asst prof, 66-68; assoc prof, 68-72; dept chair, 74-90; Univ Tex Austin, Prof, 72-; Cailloux Centennial prof, 84-; Distinguished Teaching Prof., 99-. **HONORS AND AWARDS** Fellowhips at NEH, ACLS, Guggenheim, Humboldt; Tchg Excellence at Univ Tex, Am Philol Asn. **MEMBERSHIPS** Am Philos Asn; Archaeol Inst of Am; Mommsen Gesellschaft. **RESEARCH** Roman Civilization, Augustan Age. **SELECTED PUBLICATIONS** Auth, Aeneas, Sicily, and Rome, 69; The Herakles Theme, 72; Perspectives of Roman Poetry, 74; Ovid's Metamorphoses, 75; Classical and Modern Interactions, 92; The Interpretation of Roman Poetry, 92; Augustan Culture, 96. **CONTACT ADDRESS** Dept of Classics, Univ of Texas, Austin, Austin, TX 78712-1181. **EMAIL** galinsky@utxvms.cc.utexas.edu

GALLAGHER, EDWARD J.
PERSONAL Born 10/09/1943, Philadelphia, PA, m, 1977 **DISCIPLINE** FRENCH LITERATURE **EDUCATION** La Salle Univ, AB, 65; Brown Univ, AM, 67, PhD, 72. **CAREER** Asst prof, Wash Univ, 72-74; asst prof, Rosemont Col, 74-75; vis asst prof, Wash Univ, St Louis, 75-77; from asst prof to assoc prof to prof, 77-, Wheaton Col. **MEMBERSHIPS** AAUP, Hagiographic Soc. **RESEARCH** Medieval french literature; the French Novel. **SELECTED PUBLICATIONS** Auth, art, Bedier and the Tristan Legend: The Case of the Bride Quest Episodes, 96; auth, art, Last Writes: Extreme Unction and Flaubert's Madame Bovary, 97; auth, art, Undiscovered Countries: The Role of Some Minor Characters in Flaubert's Madame Bovary, 97; auth, art, Narrative Uncertainty in Flaubert's Madame Bovary, 98; auth, art, The Eucharist in Flaubert's Madame Bovary and Mauriac's Therese Desqueyroux, 98; auth, "Monsieur Bourisien: Flaubert's Cure de Campagne," 00; auth, "Displacements of the Maternal in Flaubert's Madame Bovary," 00. **CONTACT ADDRESS** Dept of French, Wheaton Col, Massachusetts, Norton, MA 02766. **EMAIL** egallagh@wheatonma.edu

GALLANT, CHRISTEL
PERSONAL Born Troisdorf, Germany **DISCIPLINE** TRANSLATION **EDUCATION** Univ Neuchatel (Switz) LL, 69, DL, 78. **CAREER** Instr, 64, prof adj, 69, prof agregee, 78, Prof Titulaire, Dir Dep De Traduction Et Des Langues, Univ Moncton, 85-, dir du dep, 93-96. **HONORS AND AWARDS** SSHRCC grant. **SELECTED PUBLICATIONS** Auth, L'Acadie, le berceau de la traduction officielle au Canada, in Cultures de Canada francais, 2, 85; auth, L'influence des religions catholique et protestante sur la traduction des textes sacres a l'intention des Micmacs dans les provinces Maritimes: du livre de prieres de l'abbe Maillaird (1717-1762) a la traduction des Evangiles par Silar Tertius Rand (1810-1899), in TTR-Etudes sur le texte et ses transformations, 3(2), 90; auth, Paul Mascarene, in Circuit, automne, 95. **CONTACT ADDRESS** Dep de traduction et des langues, Univ of Moncton, Moncton, NB, Canada E1A 3E9. **EMAIL** gallanc@umoncton.ca

GALLATI, ERNST
PERSONAL Born 10/12/1934, Switzerland **DISCIPLINE** GERMAN AND COMPARATIVE LITERATURE **EDUCATION** Engelberg Col, Switz, BA, 54; Univ Zurich, MA, 58; McGill Univ, PhD(ger lit), 66. **CAREER** Tenure Ger, French and hist, Schinznach High Sch, Switz, 59-62; teaching asst Ger, MCGill Univ, 62-64; asst prof, San Diego State Univ, 64-67; lectr, Col Geneva, Switz, 67-70; asst prof 70-75, Assoc Prof

German, McGill Univ, 75-, Can Coun res fel, 73-74; vis prof, Univ Montreal, 72-73. **MEMBERSHIPS** Swiss Teachers Soc, Swiss Asn Univ Prof Ger; MLA; Can Asn Univ Teachers Ger. **RESEARCH** German and French literature 1815-1850; German poetry 18th to 20th century. **SELECTED PUBLICATIONS** Auth, Haller, Albrecht, Von Fame as a Poet--A History of Reception, Colloquia Germanica, Vol 0025, 92. **CONTACT ADDRESS** Dept of Ger, McGill Univ, PO Box 6070, Montreal, QC, Canada H3A 2T6.

GALLI, BARBARA E.
PERSONAL Born 12/01/1949, Montreal, PQ, Canada, d **DISCIPLINE** GERMANIC LANGUAGES; LITERATURE **EDUCATION** Carleton Univ Ottawa, BA 73; Univ Toronto, MA 76; McGill Univ, PhD 90. **CAREER** Univ Alabama, Aaron Aronov Ch, 97; assoc and lect, McGill Univ. **MEMBERSHIPS** AAR; AJS; ALA; MLA. **RESEARCH** Franz Rosenzweig; Jewish theology and literature. **SELECTED PUBLICATIONS** Auth, Franz Rosenzweig and Jehuda Halevi: Translating Translation Translators, McGill-Queen's Univ Press, 95; God Man and the World: Lectures and Essays, trans and ed, Syracuse Univ Press, 98; Franz Rosenzweig and the New Thinking, trans and ed, Afterward by Alan Udoff, SUP, 98; Orientation in the Modern World: Franz Rosenzweig's Writings in a Cultural Vein, trans and ed, SUP, forthcoming, March 99. **CONTACT ADDRESS** Fac of Religious Studies, McGill Univ, 3520 Univer, Montreal, Canada PQH3A2A7. **EMAIL** bgalli2@po-box.mcgill.ca

GALLUCCI, JOHN
DISCIPLINE RENAISSANCE AND CLASSICAL FRENCH LITERATURE **EDUCATION** BS License es lettres, BS, Strasbourg, 79; Maitrise Avignon, 83; Yale Univ, MA, 82, PhD, 88. **CAREER** Instr, Yale Univ; Actg ch, Comm Acad Advising, 97; ch, Working Comm on FLAC, 92-96; assoc prof-. **HONORS AND AWARDS** Picker fel; fel, Am Coun Learned Soc; co-organizer, weekend colloquium on for lang tchg, 93. **SELECTED PUBLICATIONS** Auth, Entre copie et autographe: le texte des Pensees de Pascal, Travaux de Litterature; Pascal, Henry Adams and American Modernity, De la morale a l'economie politique; Politique et ecriture: la 'disposition' pascalienne comme principe de liberte, Justice et force: politiques au temps de Pascal; Poetic Pascal, or the Pensees as an Infinite Text, Dalhousie Fr Studies; Pascal and Kenneth Burke: An Argument for a 'Logological' Reading of the Pensees, Fr Seventeenth-Century Lit; Faith and Language: Allegories of Interpretation in Pascal, Fr Forum; Pascal poeta-theologus, Fr Seventeenth-Century Lit; rev(s), The Fr Rev, Papers on Fr Seventeenth-Century Lit; transl, Yale Fr Studies. **CONTACT ADDRESS** Dept of Romance Lang, Colgate Univ, 13 Oak Drive, Hamilton, NY 13346. **EMAIL** jgallucci@mail.colgate.edu

GALOPPE, RAUL A.
PERSONAL Born 04/12/1957, Santa Fe, Argentina **DISCIPLINE** SPANISH LITERATURE **EDUCATION** Inst Superior de Profesorado A Brown, BA, 80; BA, 84; Univ Mo Columbia, MA, 95; PhD, 99. **CAREER** Instr, Inst Superior de Profesorado A Brown, 85-93; TA to vis instr, Univ Mo Columbia, 93-99; asst prof, Ind Univ - Purdue Univ, 99-. **HONORS AND AWARDS** Fulbright Grant, 90-91; Outstanding TA, Univ Mo Columbia, 95; Grant, Ind Univ - Purdue Univ, 00, 01. **MEMBERSHIPS** MLA, Am Transl Assoc, Sigma Delta Phi. **RESEARCH** The dialogue between gender and genre in literature and the construction of subjectivity. **SELECTED PUBLICATIONS** Coed, Tirso de Molina: His Originality Then and Now, Ottawa Hispanic Studies - Dovehouse Ed, 96; coed, La comedia espanola y el teatro europea del siglo SVII, Tamesis (England), 99; auth, "El Juego de los significantes: tirso de Molina y la critica al gobierno de los privados," Romance Lang Annual X, (99); auth, Genero y confusion en el teatro de Tirso de Molina, Editorial Pliegos (Spain), 01. **CONTACT ADDRESS** Indiana Univ-Purdue Univ, Fort Wayne, 2101 E Coliseum Blvd, Fort Wayne, IN 46805. **EMAIL** galopper@ipfw.edu

GALTON, HERBERT
PERSONAL Born 10/01/1917, Vienna, Austria, m, 2 children **DISCIPLINE** SLAVIC LANGUAGES **EDUCATION** Univ London, PhD(Slavic ling), 51. **CAREER** Sr monitor, Brit Broadcasting Corp Monitoring Serv, Reading, Eng, 56-62; translr-ed, US Dept State Foreign Broadcast Info Serv, US Embassy, Vienna, 56-62; from asst prof to assoc prof, 62-69, Prof Slavic Lang, Univ Kans, 69-, Inter-univ comt travel grants exchange scholar, Bulgaria, 65, Czech, 67-68 and Yugoslavia, 70-71. **MEMBERSHIPS** Am Asn Advan Slavic Studies; Am Asn Teachers Slavic & EEurop Lang. **RESEARCH** Comparative Slavic syntax and phonology-synchronic and diachronic; functional morphology; philosophy. **SELECTED PUBLICATIONS** Auth, On the Possibility of Reciprocal Influence between Altaic and Proto-Slavic, Wiener Slavistisches Jahrbuch, Vol 0038, 92; Did Proto-Bulgarian Influence Old-Bulgarian, Zeitschrift Fur Slawistik, Vol 0039, 94; Neither Universals nor Preferences--The Genesis fo Slavic, Folia Linguistica Historica, Vol 0017, 96. **CONTACT ADDRESS** Dept of Slavic Lang, Univ of Kansas, Lawrence, Lawrence, KS 66044.

GALVAN, DELIA V.
PERSONAL Born Mexico City, Mexico **DISCIPLINE** LITERATURE AND CIVILIZATION OF SPANISH AMERICA **EDUCATION** Univ Cincinnati, BA, MA, PhD. **CAREER** Instr, Bucknell Univ; John Carroll Univ; assoc prof, 91-. **SELECTED PUBLICATIONS** Publ, Spanish American Women Writers of Fiction. **CONTACT ADDRESS** Dept of For Lang, Cleveland State Univ, 83 E 24th St, Cleveland, OH 44115.

GAMAL, ADEL SULAIMAN
PERSONAL Born 03/14/1937, Cairo, Egypt, m, 1963, 2 children **DISCIPLINE** CLASSICAL ARABIC LITERATURE, ARABIC LANGUAGE **EDUCATION** Cairo Univ, BA, 59, MA, 64, PhD, 70. **CAREER** Instr Arabic lang & lit, Am Univ in Cairo, 62-70; asst prof, Univ Calif, Berkeley, 71-73 & Am Univ in Cairo, 73-75; assoc prof, Univ Ariz, 75-76 & Am Univ in Cairo, 76-78; assoc prof Arabic lang & lit, 78-80, prof, 80-, Univ Ariz. **HONORS AND AWARDS** First prize, Arabic Lang Acad, 94. **MEMBERSHIPS** MidE Studies Asn Nam; Am Asn Teachers Arabic. **RESEARCH** Classical Arabic literature; Arabic language; classical Arabic manuscripts. **SELECTED PUBLICATIONS** Transl, Who's Afraid of Virginia Woolf, In: Majallat al-Masrah, J Theater Art, 3/65; auth, Arabic poetry and the phenomenon of multiple usage of certain verses, 5/66 & The fortitude (Hamasa) books in classical Arabic literature, 3/68, Al-Majalla; The collected Poetry of Al-Ahwas Al-Ansary, Ministry Cult, Cairo, 70; The dissemination of Arabic language in Egypt after the Arab conquest, Majallat ath-Thaqafa, 3/74; Diwan Hatim al-Ta-i, Cairo, Egypt, 75; The basis of selections in the Hamasa Collection, J Arabic Lit, Scotland, 11/76; The conception of nobility in Early Arabic literature, Journal of American Asn Arabic Teachers; auth, al-Muntakhab, 2 vol, 94; auth, Al-Hamasa al-Basriyya, Edinting and Critical Study, vols. 1-4, 99-00. **CONTACT ADDRESS** Dept of Oriental Studies, Univ of Arizona, Franklin Rm 403A, Tucson, AZ 85721-0001. **EMAIL** gamal@u.arizona.edu

GAMLIN, GORDON S.
PERSONAL Born 10/26/1964, Frankfort, Germany, s **DISCIPLINE** LINGUISTICS **EDUCATION** McGill Univ, MA, 92; Univ Brit Colum, BA, 88, MEd, 99; Univ Constance, PhD, 95. **CAREER** Teaching asst , McGill Univ, 90-92; ESL instr, ELI, Univ Brit Colum, 96, 97, 99-; On-line Tutor, 97-99; Interface-Ed, 96-99; session lectr, 96-99; lectr, Col Asia Pac Studies, Japan, 00-. **HONORS AND AWARDS** Teaching Fel For Lang, Bard Col. **MEMBERSHIPS** MLA; AUTG; ASNLE; TEAL. **RESEARCH** Media English. **SELECTED PUBLICATIONS** Auth, "Michael Ondaatje's In the Skin of a Lion and the Oral Narrative," Can Lit 135 (92): 68-77; auth, Synergetische Sinnkonstitution und das Bild des Macbeth in Friedrich von Schillers Einrichtung der Gleichnamigen Trag? die von William Shakespeare am Weimarer Hoftheater am 13 Mai 1800 Unter der Leitung von Johann Wolfgang von Goethe, Constance (Hartung-Gore Verlag), 95; auth, "Besprechung: Martin Kuester, Framing Truths: Parodic Structures in Contemporary English Canadian Historical Novels," J Can Studies 30 (96); auth, "Die Nachschlagewerke von Duden, Langenscheidt und Meyer auf CD-Rom," Forum Deutsch 8 (96); ed, Reading German: A Multimedia Reading Course on German for Professional and Technical Purposes, by Jorge Roche (Ctr Continuing Studies, Univ Brit Colum, 97); auth, A Study Guide to Reading German: A Multimedia Reading Course on German for Professional and Technical Purposes, Distance Edu Tech, Univ Brit Colum Pr, 98; auth, "Language Acquisition and the Role of Graphic Representation in the Study of Oral Lit," Polyglossia 1 (99): 37-44; transl, Austrian Lit in the Liberal Era, by Karl Wagner (Univ Vienna/McMaster Univ, 1999); transl, CAD Interface Software Code, by Tim Evans (Transoft Solutions, Richmond, Brit Colum, 1999). **CONTACT ADDRESS** 317 55th St, Delta, BC, Canada V4M 3L4. **EMAIL** gordongamlin@hotmail.com

GANIM, JOHN MICHAEL
PERSONAL Born 02/18/1945, Weehawken, NJ **DISCIPLINE** ENGLISH, LINGUISTICS **EDUCATION** Rutgers Univ, BA, 67; IN Univ, MA, 69, PhD, 74. **CAREER** From asst prof to assoc prof, 74-88, prof eng, Univ CA, Riverside, 88, ch Eng Dept, 96. **HONORS AND AWARDS** Jr Fac Awd, Ctr Medieval and Renaissance Studies, 77. **MEMBERSHIPS** MLA; Medieval Acad Am; Medieval Asn Pacific. **RESEARCH** Middle Eng lit; Chaucer; Old Eng lit. **SELECTED PUBLICATIONS** Auth, Disorientation, style and consciousness in Sir Gawain and the Green Knight, PMLA, 76; Tone and Time in Chaucer's Troilus, ELH, 76; Style and Consciousness in Middle English Narrative, Princeton Univ Press; Bakhtin, Chaucer, Carnival, Lent, Studies in the Age of Chaucer, 87; Chaucer, Boccaccio and the Problme of Popularity, In: Assays, Pittsburgh Univ Press, 87; Carnival Voices in the clerk's Envoy, Chaucer Rev, 87; Chaucer and the Noise of the People; Exemplaria, spring 90; Chaucerian Theatricality, Princeton Univ Press, 90; Forms of Talk in the Canterbury Tales, Poetica, 91; The Literary Uses of New History, In: The Idea of Medieval Literature: New Essays on Chaucer and Medieval Culture in Honor of Donald R Howard (James M Dean and Christian K Zacher, ed); Univ Del Press, 92; Chaucerian Ritual and Patriarchal Romance, Chaucer Yearbook, 92; Literary Anthropology at the Turn of the Centuries: E K Chambers' The Mediaeval Stage, Envoi, 93; The Devil's Writing Lesson, In: Oral Poetics in Middle English Poetry (Mark Amodio, ed), Garland, 94; Medieval Literature as Monster: The Grotesque Before and After Bakhtin, Exemplaria, 95; Recent Studies on Literature, Architecture, and Urbanism, MLQ, 9/95; The Myth of Medieval Romance, In: Medievalism and the Modernist Temper (R Howard Bloch and Stephen G Nichols, ed), Johns Hopkins Univ Press, 96; Double-Entry in the Shipman's Tale: Chaucer and Bookkeeping Before Pacioli, Chaucer Rev, 96; auth, "Urbanism, Experience and Rhetoric in Some Early Descriptions of London," in The Performance of Middle English Culture, ed James Paxon et al (D.S. Brewer, 98); auth, "Chaucer, Boccaccio, Confession and Subjectivity," in The Decameron and the Canterbury Tales, ed Brenda Schildgen and Leonard Koff (Farleigh Dickinson Press, 99); auth, "Native Studies: Orientalism and the Middle Ages," in The Postcolonial Middle Ages, ed Jeffrey Jerome Cohen (Garland, 00). **CONTACT ADDRESS** Dept of Eng, Univ of California, Riverside, 900 University Ave, Riverside, CA 92521-0001. **EMAIL** john.ganim@ucr.edu

GANS, ERIC L.
PERSONAL Born 08/21/1941, Bronx, NY, m, 1999, 2 children **DISCIPLINE** FRENCH **EDUCATION** Columbia Col, BA, 60; Johns Hopkins Univ, MA, PhD, 66. **CAREER** Instr to Asst Prof, SUNY at Fredonia, 65-67; Asst Prof, Ind Univ, 67-69; Asst Prof to Prof, UCLA, 69-. **HONORS AND AWARDS** Prix de la langue francaise, Acad Francaise, 77; Chevalier des Palmes Acad, 82. **RESEARCH** Generative anthropology; French literature (19th century); Critical theory; film. **SELECTED PUBLICATIONS** Auth, Science and Faith: The Anthropology of Revelation, Rowman & Littlefield, 90; auth, Originary Thinking: Elements of Generative Anthropology, Stanford Univ Press, 93; auth, Signs of Paradox: Irony, Resentment, and Other Mimetic Structures, Stanford Univ Press, 97. **CONTACT ADDRESS** Dept French, Univ of California, Los Angeles, Box 951550, Los Angeles, CA 90095-1550. **EMAIL** gans@humnet.ucla.edu

GANTT, BARBARA N.
PERSONAL Born 07/22/1947, FL, s **DISCIPLINE** SPANISH **EDUCATION** Fla State Univ, BA, 69; MA, 72; PhD, 77. **CAREER** From asst prof to assoc prof, Northern Ariz Univ, 77-. **HONORS AND AWARDS** NEA Transl Inst, 93. **MEMBERSHIPS** Am Transl Asn, Am Lit Transl Asn, Ariz Lang Asn. **RESEARCH** Early Twentieth-century Latin American Women Writers. **SELECTED PUBLICATIONS** Co-ed & co-transl, "Poems," by Rosalia de Castro, SUNY Pr (Albany, NY), 91. **CONTACT ADDRESS** Dept Modern Lang, No Arizona Univ, Box 6004, Flagstaff, AZ 86011-0001. **EMAIL** barbara.gantt@nau.edu

GAO, Q.
PERSONAL Born 03/28/1955, Lanzhou, China, m, 2 children **DISCIPLINE** CHINESE GRAMMAR **EDUCATION** Ohio State Univ. PhD, 00. **CAREER** Ohio State Univ, tchr assoc; Wright State Univ, adj fac instr. **MEMBERSHIPS** LSA **RESEARCH** Syntactic Structure; Sentence Structure; Argument Structure; Chinese Grammar. **SELECTED PUBLICATIONS** Auth, Chinese NP Structure, Linguistics, 94; auth, Resultative Verb Compounds and BA Construction in Chinese, Journal of Chinese Linguistics, 96. **CONTACT ADDRESS** Dept of Linguistics, Ohio State Univ, Columbus, 5702 Davidson Road, Columbus, OH 43026. **EMAIL** gao.4@osu.edu

GARAUD, CHRISTIAN
DISCIPLINE FRENCH LITERATURE **EDUCATION** Univ Poitiers, PhD. **CAREER** Prof, Univ MA Amherst. **RESEARCH** 17th century lit; French cult studies autobiography; play and lit. **SELECTED PUBLICATIONS** Auth, pubs on Segalen, Paulhan, Aury, and Ernaux. **CONTACT ADDRESS** Dept of French and Italian Studies, Univ of Massachusetts, Amherst, Mass Ave, Amherst, MA 01003. **EMAIL** cgaraud@frital.umass.edu

GARCIA, JOSE LUIS SUAREZ
DISCIPLINE SPANISH LITERATURE **EDUCATION** Univ Ill Urbana-Champaign, PhD. **CAREER** Assoc prof. **SELECTED PUBLICATIONS** Auth, pubs on Spanish Golden Age, medieval bibliography, poetic and dramatic theory, and contemporary theater. **CONTACT ADDRESS** Foreign Languages and Literature Dept, Colorado State Univ, Fort Collins, CO 80523. **EMAIL** jsuarez-garcia@vines.colostate.edu

GARCIA-CASTELLON, MANUEL
PERSONAL Born 06/10/1945, Spain, s **DISCIPLINE** COLONIAL SPANISH LITERATURE **EDUCATION** Univ Valencia, BA; W Va Univ, MA, Univ Ga, PhD. **CAREER** Assoc prof, Univ New Orleans, 95. **HONORS AND AWARDS** Dolores Artau Schol. **MEMBERSHIPS** MLA; AATSP **RESEARCH** Spanish essays, Filipino Spanish literature. **SELECTED PUBLICATIONS** Auth, Guaman Poma, Pionero de la Teologia de Liberacion, Madrid, (92); auth, El Siglo XX, persistencias y rupturas, Madrid, (95); auth, Terra, pontus, astra, Murcia, (95). **CONTACT ADDRESS** Dept For Lang, Univ of New Orleans, 2000 Lakeshore Dr, New Orleans, LA 70148-0001. **EMAIL** mgarciac@uno.edu

GARCIA-OSUNA, ALFONSO
PERSONAL Born 05/23/1953, Havana, Cuba, m, 1976, 2 children **DISCIPLINE** SPANISH LITERATURE **EDUCATION** Queen's Col, BA, 76, MA, 78; Citu Univ NY, PhD, 89. **CAREER** Assoc prof, Kingsborough Community Col, Univ of NY. **MEMBERSHIPS** MLA, AATSP. **RESEARCH** Medieval and Renaissance Spanish literature. **SELECTED PUBLICATIONS** Auth, Incidents of Travel on the Road to Santiago, NY: McGraw-Hill (98); plus several articles in learned journals. **CONTACT ADDRESS** Dept Foreign Lang, Kingsborough Comm Col, CUNY, 2001 Oriental Blvd, Brooklyn, NY 11235-2333. **EMAIL** agarcia-osuna@kbcc.cuny.edu

GARCIA-SANCHEA, JOSE
PERSONAL Born 12/14/1964, Salamanca, Spain, m, 1990, 4 children **DISCIPLINE** SPANISH **EDUCATION** Univ Salamanca, Spain, 90; Ariz State Univ, PhD, 96. **CAREER** Adj prof, Jainet A Coll; asst prof, ESU. **MEMBERSHIPS** MLA; AATSP. **RESEARCH** Spanish literature; Spanish American modernism. **SELECTED PUBLICATIONS** Coauth, "Un motivo etnoliterano andino: la deslealtad," Escritos (92): 85-101; auth, " 'Edgar Allan Poe': foto-sintesis de una maquina reproductora en Los raros de Ruben Dano," Cuadernopara la investliteratura hisp 20 (95): 189-95; auth, "El nacionalismo de Jose' Maria Vargas Vila en Ibis," Revista estud colombianos 16 (96): 6-11; auth, "Jose' Maria Vargas Vila," in Gay & Lesbian Encyclopedia of Spanish Literature, ed. David William Foster (Westport: Greenwood Press, 99); auth, "Jose' Maria," iLa novela corta de Jose' Maria Vargas Vila, Univ Press South (New Orleans), 99; auth, "Jose' Maria Vargas Vila," in Feminist Encyclopedia of Latin American Literature, ed. Eva Paulino Bueno, Ivonne Gordon Vailakis (Greenwood Pub Group), forthcoming. **CONTACT ADDRESS** Dept Modern Languages, Eastern Washington Univ, 526 5th St, Cheney, WA 99004-1619. **EMAIL** jgarcia@mail.ewu.edu

GARFINKEL, ALAN
PERSONAL Born 09/06/1941, Chicago, IL, m, 1965, 2 children **DISCIPLINE** SPANISH EDUCATION **EDUCATION** Univ Ill, Urbana, BA, 63, MA, 64; Ohio State Univ, PhD(educ), 68. **CAREER** Teacher Span, Waukegan Twp High Sch, Ill, 64-66; asst prof foreign lang educ, Okla State Univ, 69-72; asst prof, 72-74, Assoc Prof Foreign Lang Educ, Purdue Univ, West Lafayette, 72-, Asst Dir, Div Sponsored Prog, 81-85, Ed Notes and News, Mod Lang J, 74--90; prof of Span and edu, Purdue Univ, 93-. **HONORS AND AWARDS** Fulbright, US Dept of State Academic Specialist. **MEMBERSHIPS** Am Coun Teaching Foreign Lang; MLA; Nat Soc Studies Educ; Am Asn Teachers Span & Port; Rotary Int. **RESEARCH** Language teaching methodology and curriculum; language teacher education; continuing education. **SELECTED PUBLICATIONS** Coauth, Explorando en la Cast de los Monstruos, Teacher's Discovery (Auburn Hills, MI), 97; auth, Capitan Cataplum y Sargento Sapo . . ., Carlex (Rochester, MI), 00; articles and revs in Hispania, Foreign Lang Annals, and Modern Lang Jrnl. **CONTACT ADDRESS** FLL/SC, Purdue Univ, West Lafayette, West Lafayette, IN 47907-1359. **EMAIL** alangarf@purdue.edu

GARIANO, CARMELO
PERSONAL Born 03/04/1922, Nicosia, m, 1953, 2 children **DISCIPLINE** SPANISH, LINGUISTICS **EDUCATION** Univ Catania, Italy, DLet, 46; Univ Buenos Aires, Arg, Prof en Let, 51, Lic en Let, 53; De Paul Univ, MA, 56; Univ Chicago, PhD(-Spanish), 64. **CAREER** Lectr Latin Am lit, Univ Buenos Aires, 51-52, aesthet and stylistics, 52-53; instr Span, Univ Detroit, 57-60; asst prof, Roosevelt Univ, 60-62; asst prof, 62-68, Prof Romance Lang, Calif State Univ, Northridge, 68, Assoc prof classics, Nat Univ Litoral, Arg, 51-53; mem, Nat Fed Mod Lang Teachers Asn, 59-. **MEMBERSHIPS** MLA; Am Asn Teachers Span & Port. **RESEARCH** Diachronic linguistics; Spanish medieval literature; medieval and Renaissance studies. **SELECTED PUBLICATIONS** **CONTACT ADDRESS** Dept of Foreign Lang, California State Univ, Northridge, 18111 Nordhoff St, Northridge, CA 91324.

GARLINGER, PATRICK P.
PERSONAL Born 04/08/1972, Fontana, CA **DISCIPLINE** SPANISH, LITERATURE **EDUCATION** Wash Univ, BA, 94; Emory Univ, PhD, 00. **CAREER** Asst prof, Univ Iowa, 00-. **MEMBERSHIPS** MLA. **RESEARCH** Twentieth-century Spanish literature; gay and lesbian studies; queer theory; feminist theory. **SELECTED PUBLICATIONS** Auth, "'Homoness' and the Fear of Femininity," Diacritics 29 (99): 57-71; auth, "Lost Lesbian Love Letters? Epistolary Erasure and Queer Readers in Martin Gaite's El Cuarto de Atras," Bulletin of Hisp Studies 76 (99): 513-33; auth, "Dragging Spain into the Post-Franco Era: Transvestism and National Identity in Eduardo Mendicutti's Una Mala Noche la Tiene Cualquiera," Rev Can de Estud Hisp 24 (00): 363-82. **CONTACT ADDRESS** Dept Mod Lang, Univ Iowa, 111 Phillips Hall, Iowa City, IA 52242. **EMAIL** patrick-garlinger@uiowa.edu

GARNER, RICHARD
PERSONAL Born 03/06/1953, Tahlequah, OK, s **DISCIPLINE** CLASSICAL LANGUAGE, CLASSICAL LITERATURE **EDUCATION** Princeton Univ, BA, 75; Harvard Univ, MA 76; Univ Chicago, MA, 80; PhD, 83. **CAREER** Asst prof to assoc prof, Yale Univ, 83-93; Olin prof, Yale Univ. 93-94; Dean, Honors Col, Adelphi, 94-. **HONORS AND AWARDS** Banchko Prize, Princeton, 75; Phi Beta Kappa; Fel, Harvard Univ, 80-83; Galler Prize, Univ of Chicago, 83; Sidonie Miskimin Clauss Prize, Yale Col, 86; Sarai Ribicoff Awd, Yale, 86; Heyman Prize, Yale, 86; Devane/Phi Beta Kappa Medal, Yale, 92; Fel, Olin Fac, 93-94; Loeb Lect, Harvard, 94. **SELECTED PUBLICATIONS** Auth, Law and Society in Classical Athens, St. Martin's, Croom Helm, 87; auth; "Death and Victory in Euripides 'Alcestis'", Classical Antiquity 7, (88): 58-71; auth, From Homer to Tragedy: The Art of Allusion in Greek Poetry, Routledge, 90; auth, "Mules, Mysteries, and Song in Pindar's Sixth Olympian", Classical Antiquity 11 (92): 45-67; auth, "Countless Deeds of Valor: Bacchylides 11", Classical Quarterly 42 (92): 523-25; auth, "Achilles in Locri: P.Oxy 3876, frr. 37-77", Zeitschrift fur Papyrologie und Epigraphik 96 (93): 153-65; auth, "Stesichorus' Althaia: P.Oxy. 3876", Zeitschrift fur Papyrologie und Epigraphik 100 (94): 25-37. **CONTACT ADDRESS** Dept Lang & Lit, Adelphi Univ, 1 South Ave, Garden City, NY 11530-4213. **EMAIL** garner@adelphi.edu

GARNETT, MARY ANNE
DISCIPLINE 19TH CENTURY FRENCH LITERATURE **EDUCATION** Wisc State Univ, BA, 70; Univ Wisc, MA, 71, PhD, 80. **CAREER** English and Lit, Univ Ark **SELECTED PUBLICATIONS** Ed, Women in French Newsletter. **CONTACT ADDRESS** Univ of Arkansas, Little Rock, 2801 S University Ave., Little Rock, AR 72204-1099. **EMAIL** magarnett@ualr.edu

GARR, W. RANDALL
PERSONAL Born 12/21/1954, Norwalk, CT **DISCIPLINE** SEMITIC LANGUAGES **EDUCATION** Vassar Col, AB, 77; Yale Univ, MA, 79, MPhil, 80, PhD(Near East lit), 82. **CAREER** Lectr Norhtwest Semitic Lang, Univ PA, 82-. **MEMBERSHIPS** Am Orient Soc; Soc Bibl Lit; Am Schs Orient Res; Ling Soc Am; Asn Jewish Studies. **RESEARCH** History of the Hebrew language; comparative semitics; history of Syria-Palestine. **SELECTED PUBLICATIONS** Auth, The Grammar and Interpretation of Exodus-Vi,3 and An Analysis of the Literary Construction of the Divine Names El-Shaddai and Yahweh Within the Context of the Priestly (P) Document, J Biblical Lit, Vol 0111, 92. **CONTACT ADDRESS** Dept of Religious Studies, Univ of California, Santa Barbara, Santa Barbara, CA 93106-3130. **EMAIL** wrgarr@humanita.ucsb.edu

GARRETSON, DEBORAH
DISCIPLINE RUSSIAN LANGUAGE **EDUCATION** NYork Univ, PhD. **CAREER** Assoc prof, Dartmouth Col. **HONORS AND AWARDS** Interp, INF and the START I and START II treaties, as well as at the US-USSR summit meetings, 85-. **RESEARCH** Second lang acquisition **SELECTED PUBLICATIONS** Auth, numerous articles on var aspects of 2nd lang acquisition ranging from the psycholinguistics of reading in a second lang to cult frameworks for Second Language Methodology. **CONTACT ADDRESS** Russ Dept, Dartmouth Col, 44 N College St, Hanover, NH 03755-1801. **EMAIL** deborah.garretson@dartmouth.edu

GARRISON, DANIEL H.
PERSONAL Born 12/24/1937, Hamilton, NY, m, 1992, 1 child **DISCIPLINE** CLASSICS **EDUCATION** Harvard Univ, BA, 59; Univ NC Chapel Hill, MA, 63; Univ Cal Berk, PhD, 68. **CAREER** Northwestern Univ, prof, 66-. **MEMBERSHIPS** APA; Classical Assoc Middle W & S; Soc Ancient Medicine; AAHM. **RESEARCH** Lyric poetry; Medical history. **SELECTED PUBLICATIONS** Coauth, "Vesalius on the Variability of the Human Skull: Book I Chapter V of De humani corporis fabrica," Clinical Anatomy 13, (00): 311-320; auth, Sexual Culture in Ancient Greece, Univ Oklahoma Press, 00; auth, Horace Epodes and Odes, A New Annotated Latin edition, Univ OK Press, 91, rev, Class Wld 92, Greece and Rome, 92, Classical Outlook, 93; coauth, "Andreas Vesalius on the Teeth: An Annotated translation from De humani corporis fabrica," Clinical Anatomy, 95; coauth, "Andreas Vesalius on the Larynx and Hyoid Bone", Medical History, 93; auth, The Locus Inamoenus: Another Part of the Forest, Arion II, 92; **CONTACT ADDRESS** Dept of Classics, Northwestern Univ, 1859 Sheridan Rd, Evanston, IL 60208. **EMAIL** d-garrison@northwestern.edu

GARRISON, DAVID LEE
PERSONAL Born 05/10/1945, Bremerton, WA, m **DISCIPLINE** SPANISH, PORTUGUESE **EDUCATION** Wesleyan Univ, BA, 68; Catholic Univ, MA, 72; Ind Univ, MA, 78; Johns Hopkins Univ, PhD, 75. **CAREER** Vis Asst Prof, Ind Univ, 75-76; Vis Asst Prof, Washington Col, 77; Vis Asst Prof, Univ Kans, 78-79; Asst Prof, Prof and Dept Chair, Wright State Univ, 79-. **HONORS AND AWARDS** Presidential Awd, Wright State Univ, 98; Culture Works Grant, Montgomery County Arts Coun, 96; Alumni Awd, Wright State Univ, 94; Presidential Awd, Wright State Univ, 88; Fourth Prize, Nat Poetry Contest of the Am Poetry Asn, 85; Third Prize, Nat Poetry Contest, Cowan Col, 83. **MEMBERSHIPS** Am Asn of Teachers of Spanish and Portuguese, Soc for Renaissance and Baroque Hispanic Poetry. **RESEARCH** Spanish poetry of 16th, 17th and 20th Centuries; Translation; Language pedagogy. **SELECTED PUBLICATIONS** Ed and trans, Pedro Salinas, Certain Chance, Bucknell Univ Press, forthcoming; co-ed, Food Poems, Bottom Dog Press, 98; auth, Inside the Sound of Rain, Vincent Brothers Pub, 97; auth, Gongora and the 'Pyramus and Thisbe" Myth from Ovid to Shakespeare, Juan de la Cuest, 94; ed and trans, Poems of Jose Bergamin (1895-1983): Echoes of a Distant Sea, Edwin Mellen Press, 91; ed, Luis de Gongora y Argote, La Fabula de Piramo y Tisbe, Jose Esteban, 87; co-auth, Instructor's Manual, habla espanol? Essentials, 3rd ed, Holt, Rinehart, and Winston, 85; auth, Blue Oboe, Wyndham Hall Press, 84; trans, A Bird of Paper: Poems of Vincent Alexandria, Ohio Univ Press, 82. **CONTACT ADDRESS** Dept Mod Lang, Wright State Univ, Dayton, 3640 Colonel Glenn Hwy, Dayton, OH 45435-0001. **EMAIL** david.garrison@wright.edu

GARROTT, CARL L.
PERSONAL Born 12/04/1948, Indianapolis, IN, s **DISCIPLINE** LINGUISTICS **EDUCATION** Kentucky State Univ, BA, 70; Tennessee State Univ, MA, 74; Western KY Univ, Ed.S, 77; Univ KY, Ed.D, 85; add grad, Univ Guadalajara, Mexico. **CAREER** Instr, Univ KY, 81-85; div hd, Chowan Col, 85-96; assoc prof, Hampton Univ, 96-98; assoc prof, VA State Univ, 98-. **HONORS AND AWARDS** Nat Woodrow Wilson Fel, 70; Excell Coll Teach, Chowan Coll, 97; Fac Res Grants; Ford Found Grant; Starr Found Grant; VA Found Human Pub Policy Grant; Who's Who Am Edu; Who's Who S SE; Woodrow Wilson Schol; UK Doctoral Fel. **MEMBERSHIPS** Am Asn Teachers of French; Am Asn Teachers of Span Port; AAAL; CLA. **RESEARCH** Applied linguistics; Afro-French cultural hist; Afro-Span lit; Haiti; Caribbean studies; Creoles; Business Span. **SELECTED PUBLICATIONS** Auth, Cultural descriptors of Hispanics by African American university students of Spanish, Cen Applied Ling (Washington, DC), 97; auth, Erroneous feature migration: Subject-verb agreement in French using linear differences, Cen Applied Ling (Washington, DC), 98; auth, Resistance strategies in the university Spanish classroom, Cen Applied Ling (Washington, DC), 99; ed, An Afro-Hispanic Forum, VSU Dept Lang Lit and the VA Found Humanities, forthcoming. **CONTACT ADDRESS** Dept Lang Lit, Virginia State Univ, 1 Hayden Dr, Petersburg, VA 23806-1000.

GARTON, CHARLES
PERSONAL Born 08/13/1926, Yorkshire, England, m, 1960, 2 children **DISCIPLINE** CLASSICS **EDUCATION** Cambridge Univ, BA, 49, MA, 53. **CAREER** Asst lectr classics, Univ Hull, 51-53; lectr, Univ Newcastle upon Tyne, 53-65; assoc prof, 65-72, actg chmn dept, 73-74, Prof Classics to Prof Emer, SUNY, Buffalo, 72-; Ed, Arethusa, 68-71, assoc ed, 74-. **MEMBERSHIPS** Class Asn England & Wales. **RESEARCH** Classical and comparative literature; theatre; educational history. **CONTACT ADDRESS** Dept of Classics, SUNY, Buffalo, 338 MFAC, Buffalo, NY 14261.

GASCHE, RODOLPHE
DISCIPLINE COMPARATIVE LITERATURE **EDUCATION** Freie Universitat, MA; PhD **CAREER** Fac, Freie Universitat; fac, Johns Hopkins Univ; fac, SUNY Buffalo. **HONORS AND AWARDS** ACLS Fel, 81-82. **RESEARCH** 19th- and 20th-century French lit; critical theory and its rel to continental philos since early romanticism. **SELECTED PUBLICATIONS** Auth, Die hybride Wissenschaft, Metzler, 73; System und Metaphorik in der Philosophie von Georges Bataille, Lang, 78; The Tain of the Mirror: Derrida and the Philosophy of Reflection, Harvard, 86; Interventions of Difference: On Jacques Derrida, Harvard, 94; auth, The Wildcard of Reading: On Paul de Mau, Harvard, 98; auth, Of Minimal Things, Studies on the Notion of Relation, Stanford, 99; trans, works by Derrida and Lacan into German. **CONTACT ADDRESS** Dept Comp Lit, SUNY, Buffalo, 639 Clemens Hall, Buffalo, NY 14260. **EMAIL** gasche@acsu.buffalo.edu

GASIENICA-BYRCYN, ANNA ZOFIA
PERSONAL Born 04/25/1962, Zakopane, Poland, s **DISCIPLINE** CLASSICS, LITERATURE, LANGUAGE, SLAVIC, POLISH **EDUCATION** Univ Ill Chicago, MA, 89; PhD, 00. **CAREER** Teaching asst to vis lectr, Univ Ill, 84-90, 92-99, 00-. **HONORS AND AWARDS** Tracy Awd, Univ Ill, 93; ACLS Teaching Grant, 96, 97. **MEMBERSHIPS** PIASA; AATSEEL; MLA. **RESEARCH** Polish women's poetry, 20th-century; Marta Fox; Halina Powiatowska. **SELECTED PUBLICATIONS** Auth, "I'll Dance for You in Words," Lit 47 (01): 5-22; trans, intro, "Halina Powiatowska's Verbal Paintings," (Sarmat Rev, 1996): 363-370. **CONTACT ADDRESS** Dept Classics, Univ of Illinois, Chicago, 601 S Morgan St, MC 306, Chicago, IL 60607-7100. **EMAIL** anna-gb@uic.edu

GASPERETTI, DAVID
DISCIPLINE RUSSIAN LITERATURE **EDUCATION** Lawrence Univ, BA, 76; Univ Calif, Los Angeles, MA, 78, PhD, 85. **CAREER** Vis asst prof, Univ Tulsa, 83-85; asst prof, Univ Tulsa, 85- 89; asst prof, 89-96, ASSOC PROF RUSSIAN, UNIV NOTRE DAME, 96-. **CONTACT ADDRESS** Dept of German & Russian Lang, Lit, Univ of Notre Dame, Notre Dame, IN 46556.

GASTA, CHAD M.
PERSONAL Born 04/04/1971, MI **DISCIPLINE** SPANISH **EDUCATION** Mich State Univ, BA, 89; BA, 93; MA, 96; PhD, 00. **CAREER** TA to vis asst prof, Mich State Univ, 94-00; lectr, Univ Ariz, 00-01; asst prof, Iowa State Univ, 01- **HONORS AND AWARDS** Fel, Mich State Univ, 99. **MEMBERSHIPS** MLA, Bull of the Comediantes, Assoc of Teachers of Span and Port, Cervantes Soc of Am. **RESEARCH** Spanish Golden Age Literature and Culture, technology and teaching, Critical Theory, Spanish for the professions. **SELECTED PUBLICATIONS** Auth, "A Text for His Viewing Public: El Buscon as an Open and Enduring Source of Criticism," TROPOS, (99); auth, "El proceso ciclico de la violencia y su culminacion catartica en La familia de Pascual Duarte," Dactylus, (99); auth, "Political Texts and Contexts of the Golden Age: A Cultural Study of Spanish and Spanish-American Theater and Opera," Diss Abstract Int, (00); auth, Counter-Reformation Spirituality in Francisco de Zurbaran's The Vision of Saint Anthony of Padua, MSU Pr, 01. **CONTACT ADDRESS** Iowa State Univ, 300 Pearson Hall, Ames, IA 50011. **EMAIL** gasta@msu.edu

GATTO, KATHERINE M.
PERSONAL Born 11/27/1945, Braunau, Austria, m, 1968, 4 children **DISCIPLINE** SPANISH **EDUCATION** John Carroll Univ, AB, 67; Case Western Univ, MA, 71; PhD, 75. **CAREER** Vis Asst Prof to Prof and Dept Chair, John Carroll Univ, 75-. **HONORS AND AWARDS** NDEA Fel, Case Western Univ, 67-70; Fulbright Hays Res Scholar, Madrid, 72-73; NEH grant, 87, 90; George E Gravel Fac Fel, 81-82, 95-96; Summer Res Fel, 94, 00. **MEMBERSHIPS** MLA, Hungarian Lit Discussion Group, Am Asn of the Teachers of Spanish and Portuguese, Am Hungarian Educators Asn, Fulbright Asn, Am Asn for the Advancement of Slavic Studies, Am Asn of Teachers of Slavic and East European Lang. **RESEARCH** Medieval Spanish Literature and History; Feminist Theory; Film Studies; Hungarian and Hungarian-American Studies, Latino Cultures, War and Memory. **SELECTED PUBLICATIONS** Auth, Of Kings and Poets: Canionero Poetry of the Trastamara Courts, New York, 92; co-ed, The Lapidary of King Alfonso X, the Learned, Univ Press of the South, 97; ed, Treasury of Hungarian Love Poems, Quotations and Proverbs in Hungarian and English, Hippocrene Books, 96. **CONTACT ADDRESS** Dept Mod & Classical Lang, John Carroll Univ, 700 N Park Blvd, Cleveland, OH 44118-4520. **EMAIL** gatto@jcu.edu

GAUGGEL, KARL H.
PERSONAL s **DISCIPLINE** SPANISH **EDUCATION** San Francisco State Univ, BA, 66; Univ Colo, MA, 72, 78; PhD, 86 **CAREER** Vis asst prof, Univ Mont, 85-87; instr, Univ Colo, 87; asst prof, Concordia Col, 88-90; asst prof, Mesa Col, 90-96; vis asst prof, S Colo Univ, 97-98; instr, N Colo Univ, 98-99. **MEMBERSHIPS** Colo Educ Asn; Ling Circle of Man and N Dak; Midlands Conf on Lang and Lit; Minn Coun on the Teaching of For Lang; MLA; Cervantes Soc of Am. **RESEARCH** Modernist poetry; Peninsular mediaeval literature; Spanish American colonial poetry; Spanish mediaeval Latin. **SELECTED PUBLICATIONS** Auth, El cisne modernista, Peter Lang, 87; trans, "Pablo Antonio cuadra. Seven Trees Against the Sunset," in Another Chicago Magazine, (89): 31-49; trans, "Jean Paul Mestas. Among Silent Violins." Minn, Intl Writers and Artists Asn, 90. **CONTACT ADDRESS** Dept Mod Lang & Class, Ball State Univ, Dept Mod Lang, Muncie, IN 47306.

GAVRONSKY, SERGE
PERSONAL Born 08/16/1932, Paris, France, m, 1960, 1 child **DISCIPLINE** FRENCH **EDUCATION** Columbia Univ, BA, 54, MA, 55, PhD, 65. **CAREER** From lectr to assoc prof, 60-75, prof French & chmn dept, 75-, Barnard Col, Columbia Univ; Sterling Currier grant, Columbia Univ & NEH pilot grant, 78; John Simon Guggenheim Found fel, Camargo Found fel, French Govt grant & Mellon Fac grant, 79; NEH implementation grant, 82; vis, 83, Natl Human Ctr; judge, 90, Acad Amer Poets's Harold Morton Landon Prize in Transl; NY St Coun on Arts, transl grant, 91; judge, Jeanne Scaglione Prize in transl, MLA, 98. **HONORS AND AWARDS** Chevalier, 81, Officier, 91, Chevalier, 98, dans l'Ordre des Palmes Academiques, French Govt; Whitney Olin Professor of French, 94. **MEMBERSHIPS** Pen Club. **SELECTED PUBLICATIONS** Auth, Louis Zukofsky, l'Homme/poete, transl De A 1 A 7 Ulysse fin de Siecle, 94; auth, Toward a New Poetics: Contemporary Writing in France, Univ Calif Press, 94; auth, Joyce Mansour Cris/Screams, trans Post-Apollo Press, 95; auth, Parlons de lui, poems, pierre Annette, 95; auth, Reduction du Tryptique, poemes, Philippe Millereau, 96; auth, Six Contemporary French Women Poets, S Ill Univ Press, 97; auth, Mallarme Spectal ou Zukofsky au travail, La Main Courante, 98. **CONTACT ADDRESS** Dept of French, Barnard Col, 3009 Broadway, New York, NY 10027-6598. **EMAIL** sgavronsky@barnard.columbia.edu

GAY-CROSIER, RAYMOND
PERSONAL Born 08/30/1937, Basel, Switzerland, m, 1963, 1 child **DISCIPLINE** FRENCH LITERATURE **EDUCATION** Univ Berne, PhD(Romance), 65. **CAREER** Asst Ger lit, Stanislas, Lycee Louis-le-Grand, Paris, 60-61; prof French & philos, Lycee de Berthoud, Switz, 62-66; asst prof French, Trent Univ, 66-67; assoc prof, 67-73, grad coordr, 70-80, fac develop grant, 73-74, Prof French, Univ Fla, 73-, Chmn, 80-93; Chair, Ed Bd, Humanities Monograph Series, Presses of the Univ Fla, 77-92; Gen Ed, Ars interpretandi series, Peter Lang, 86-; Asst Ed, The Fr Rev, 86-; Ed-in-chief of the Camus series, Revue des Lettres Modernes, 87-; For Books Ed, S Atl Rev, 90-93. **HONORS AND AWARDS** Am Coun Learned Soc grant, 82; Chevalier, 87, Officier, 93, Palmes Acad¤miques Pres, SAMLA, 93-94. **MEMBERSHIPS** MLA; Am Asn Teachers Fr. **RESEARCH** Twentieth-century French literature, criticism and history of ideas. **SELECTED PUBLICATIONS** Auth, Les envers d'un echec, Etude sur le theatre d'Albert Camus, Paris, Minard, 67; contribr & ed, Albert Camus, 70, Sherbrooke, Celef, 70; Religious Elements in the Secular Lyrics of the Troubadours, NC Univ Press, 71; ed, Albert Camus series, Revue des Lettres Modernes, Vol 7, 74, Vol 9, 78, Vol 11, 82, Vol 12, 85, Vol 13, 89, Vol 14, 91, Vol 15, 94, Vol 16, 95, Vol 17, 96 vol. 18, 99; Albert Camus, Darmstadt, Wissenschaftliche Buchgesellschaft, 76; contribr & ed, Albert Camus 1980, Univ Fla, 80; International Camus Criticism, Critical Bibliography of French Literature, Syracuse Univ, 80; ed and contribr, Albert Camus: oeuvre fermee, oeuvre ouvert?, Gallimard, 84; La navette entre l'exil et le royaume: le voyage comme apprentissage du desenchantement chez Albert Camus, Lendemains XXI:81, 96; Points de rencontre et points de choc. Desir transformateur et violence geneatrice: Claude Simon et l'acte de lecture, In: Point de recontre: le roman, Oslo, Res Coun of Norway, Kult Skriftserie, no 37, vol II, 96; Lyrisme et ironie: le cas du Premier Homme, Camus et le lyrisme, SEDES, 97; auth, des enjeux de la pensee de uidi, Perspectives, Revue de l'Universite-hebraique de Jerusalem 5, 98; auth, Les wasques de l'impossible: le theatre de Camus anjourd hui, Europe, 846, 99; author of numerous other journal articles and book chapters since 1980. **CONTACT ADDRESS** Dept of Romance Lang & Lit, Univ of Florida, P O Box 117405, Gainesville, FL 32611-7405. **EMAIL** gaycros@rll.ufl.edu

GAYLIN, ANN E. E.
PERSONAL Born 04/01/1962, Chicago, IL **DISCIPLINE** COMPARATIVE LITERATURE **EDUCATION** Brandeis Univ, BA, 84; Princeton Univ, MA, 90; PhD, 95. **CAREER** Lectr to asst prof to assoc prof, Yale Univ, 94-. **HONORS AND AWARDS** Fac Leave, Yale Univ, 01-02; Jr Fac Fel, Whitney Humanities Ctr, 99-00; Vis Fel, Univ London, 98-99; Morse Jr Fac Fel, 98-99; Griswold Fac Res Grant, 97-98; Paul Moore Fund Grant, 96-97; Whiting Fel, 91-92; Princeton Univ Fel, 87-91; Penn L'Aquila Scholar, Italy, 87; Dorothy Brewer Cohen Award, 84; Valedictorian, Brandeis Univ, 84; Phi Beta Kappa. **MEMBERSHIPS** MLA; SSN; ACLA. **RESEARCH** Nineteenth and early twentieth-century British and French literature; the European novel; the Gothic tradition in fiction; narrative literature and the visual arts; nineteenth-century female detectives. **SELECTED PUBLICATIONS** Auth, "The Mad Woman Outside the Attic: Eavesdropping and Narrative Agency in the Woman in White," Tex Studies Lit/Lang (01); auth, Eavesdropping: Privacy and Transgression in the Nineteenth-Century Novel, Cambridge Univ Pr (forthcoming). **CONTACT ADDRESS** Dept Comp Lit, Yale Univ, PO Box 208299, New Haven, CT 06520. **EMAIL** ann.gaylin@yale.edu

GAYLORD, INEZ K.
DISCIPLINE FRENCH LANGUAGE AND LITERATURE **EDUCATION** Wellesley Col, BA; Univ Chicago, MA, PhD. **CAREER** Prof. **RESEARCH** Twentieth-century novel. **SELECTED PUBLICATIONS** Auth, numerous articles on fiction and film. **CONTACT ADDRESS** Dept of French, The Col of Wooster, Wooster, OH 44691.

GEARHART, SUZZANE
DISCIPLINE FRENCH LANGUAGE **EDUCATION** Johns Hopkins Univ, PhD. **CAREER** Prof, Fr, Univ Calif, Irvine. **SELECTED PUBLICATIONS** Auth, The Open Boundary of History and Fiction; The Interrupted Dialectic: Philosophy, Psychoanalysis, and Their Tragic Other; pub(s), articles on Fr lit, hist, philos, and psychoanalysis. **CONTACT ADDRESS** Dept of Fr and Ital, Univ of California, Irvine, Irvine, CA 92697.

GEARY, JOHN STEVEN
PERSONAL Born 08/18/1948, Oakland, CA, m, 1978 **DISCIPLINE** MEDIEVAL LITERATURE, ROMANCE PHILOLOGY **EDUCATION** Univ Calif, Berkeley, AB, 70, MA, 72, PhD(Romance philol), 79. **CAREER** Asst Prof Spanish Lit, Univ Colo, Boulder, 79-. **MEMBERSHIPS** MLA; Am Asn Teachers of Spanish & Portuguese. **RESEARCH** Medieval Spanish epic poetry; Medieval Catalan poetry; comparative Romance linguistics. **SELECTED PUBLICATIONS CONTACT ADDRESS** Dept of Spanish Lit, Univ of Colorado, Boulder, Box 278, Boulder, CO 80309-0278.

GELBER, LYNNE LEVICK
PERSONAL Born 02/06/1939, Philadelphia, PA, m, 1959, 2 children **DISCIPLINE** FRENCH & COMPARATIVE LITERATURE **EDUCATION** Bryn Mawr Col, AB, 60, MA, 62; Univ Colo, Boulder, PhD, 71. **CAREER** From instr to asst prof, 68-77, assoc prof, 77-81, prof French, Skidmore Col, 81-, coordr, Skidmore Jr Yr Abroad, 80-86, 89-90; chairperson, Dept Foreign Lang & Lit, 79-86, 89-90; Chair French Section 98-; adj prof, Union Grad Sch, 72-75. **HONORS AND AWARDS** Nat Endowment for Humanities teaching fel, Princeton Univ, 75-76; NYork Univ Scholar in residence and research fellow, 86-87. **MEMBERSHIPS** Paul Claudel Soc; MLA; AM Asn Teachers Fr; AAUP; Am Asn Univ Women. **RESEARCH** Modern French literature; French poetry; women in French literature, Food in Literature. **SELECTED PUBLICATIONS** Auth, The art criticism of Paul Claudel, Claudel Newslett, 2/72; Camille Claudel's art and influence, Claudel Studies, fall 72; Women in France since the revolution, Empire State Col, spring 73; Claudel on Rodin: Sweet vengeance and bitter memory, Claudel Studies, spring 76; ed, Dialogues with the Unseen and the Unknown: Essays in Honor of Andre Malraux, 78; In/Stability: The Shape and Space of Claudel's Art Criticism, UMI Res Press, 80; auth, "Creation and Annihiliation: Uses of Food in Contemporary French Narrative," in Cooking by the book, ed. Schofield, Bowling Green: Popular Press, 89, 159-69. **CONTACT ADDRESS** Dept For Language & Literature, Skidmore Col, 815 N Broadway, Saratoga Springs, NY 12866-1698. **EMAIL** lgelber@skidmore.edu

GELERNT, JULES
PERSONAL Born 07/13/1928, Berlin, Germany, m, 1958, 2 children **DISCIPLINE** ENGLISH & COMPARATIVE LITERATURE **EDUCATION** City Col New York, BA, 49; Columbia Univ, MA, 50, PhD(comp lit), 63. **CAREER** Instr English, Hofstra Univ, 56-63; from asst prof to assoc prof, 63-71, PROF ENGLISH & CHMN DEPT, BROOKLYN COL, 75-78; Professor Emerites, 96; Mem, Comt Comp & World Lit, NCTE, 67-. **MEMBERSHIPS** Dante Soc Am; Renaissance Soc Am. **RESEARCH** Renaissance and comparative literature. **SELECTED PUBLICATIONS** Auth, Review Notes on Dante's Divine Comedy, Monarch, 63; World of Many Loves: The Heptameron of Marguerite de Navarre, Univ NC, 66. **CONTACT ADDRESS** Dept English, Brooklyn Col, CUNY, 2901 Bedford Ave, Brooklyn, NY 11210-2813. **EMAIL** jrgelernt@worldnet.att.net

GELLRICH, MICHELLE
DISCIPLINE GREEK LITERATURE AND PHILOSOPHY, LITERARY THEORY, DRAMA **EDUCATION** Univ Calif, Berkeley, PhD, 82. **CAREER** Assoc prof, La State Univ. **HONORS AND AWARDS** Lily Found tchg grant, 84; ACLS fel, 86; LSU summer fac res stipend, 92; Alpha Lambda Delta, 96; Phi Beta Kappa. **RESEARCH** Greek literature and philosophy; classical rhetoric. **SELECTED PUBLICATIONS** Auth, Tragedy and Theory: The Problem of Conflict Since Aristotle, 88; auth, "Aristotle's Poetics and the Problem of Tragic Conflict," Ramus (94); auth, "Aristotle's Rhetoric: Theory, Truth, and Metarhetoric," Cabinet of the Muses (90); auth, "Socratic Magic: Enchantment, Irony, and Persuasion in Some Dialogues of Plato," Classical World (94); auth, "On Interpreting Greek Tragedy: History, Theory, and the New Philology," Tragedy, History, Theory (forthcoming). **CONTACT ADDRESS** Dept of Eng, Louisiana State Univ and A&M Col, 223E Allen Hall, Baton Rouge, LA 70803. **EMAIL** mgellri@lsu.edu

GEMUNDEN, GERD
DISCIPLINE GERMAN AND COMPARATIVE LITERATURE **EDUCATION** Univ OR, PhD, 88. **CAREER** Assoc prof, Dartmouth Col. **RESEARCH** Contemp Ger lit and film, lit theory, and travel lit. **SELECTED PUBLICATIONS** Auth, Die hermaneutische Wende: Disziplin und sprachlosigkeit nach 1800, 90; coed, Wim Wenders, einstellungen, 93; coed, The Cinema of Wim Wenders: Image, Narrative, and the Postmodern Condition, 97; auht, Framed Visions: Popular Culture, Americanization, and the Contemporary German and Austrian Imagination, 98. **CONTACT ADDRESS** Dept of German Studies, Dartmouth Col, 6084 Dartmouth Hall, Hanover, NH 03755-3511. **EMAIL** gerd.gemunden@dartmouth.edu

GENDZIER, STEPHEN J.
PERSONAL Born 07/14/1930, New York, NY, m, 1958, 4 children **DISCIPLINE** FRENCH LITERATURE **EDUCATION** Oberling Col, BA, 52; Columbia Univ, MA, 53, PhD, 59. **CAREER** Instr, 56-60, Columbia Univ; asst prof, 60-62, Mass Inst Technol; asst prof, 62-66, assoc prof, 66-, co-chmn, romance & comp lit, 97-, Brandeis Univ. **MEMBERSHIPS** Am Assn Tchrs Fr; MLA; Soc Fr Etude XVIIIe Siecle. **RESEARCH** The French enlightenment; the English and French novel of the eighteenth century. **SELECTED PUBLICATIONS** Auth, L'Interpretation de la figure humaine chez Diderot et chez Balzac, L'Annee Balzacienne, 62; art, Balzac's Changing Attitudes Toward Diderot, Fr Studies, 4/65; auth, Denis Diderot: The Encyclopedia, Harper, 69; auth, Diderot and the Jews, Diderot Studis, 73. **CONTACT ADDRESS** 36 Hayes Ave, Lexington, MA 02173. **EMAIL** gendzier@binah.cc.brandeis.edu

GENNO, CHARLES N.
PERSONAL Born 11/19/1934, Toronto, ON, Canada **DISCIPLINE** GERMAN **EDUCATION** Univ Toronto, BA, 57, MA, 59, PhD, 61. **CAREER** Alexander von Humboldt res fel (Ger), 60-61; asst to assoc prof, 63-87, prof to prof emer, Univ Toronto, 87-, dept ch, 89-94; vis prof, Univ BC, 67; guest prof, Univ Trier (Germany), 73. **SELECTED PUBLICATIONS** Auth,

Structured Language Practice and Grammatical Review, 2nd ed, 90; auth, German for Advanced Intermediates, 3rd ed, 92; ed, The First World War in German Narrative Prose, 80. **CONTACT ADDRESS** German Dept, Univ of Toronto, 50 St Joseph St, Toronto, ON, Canada M5S 1J4.

GENOVESE, EDGAR NICHOLAS

PERSONAL Born 09/18/1942, Baltimore, MD, m, 1969, 2 children **DISCIPLINE** CLASSICS **EDUCATION** Xavier Univ, Ohio, AB, 64; Ohio State Univ, PhD(classics), 70. **CAREER** From asst prof to assoc prof, 70-76, Prof Classics, San Diego State Univ, 76-, Chmn Dept Class & Humanities, 77-. **HONORS AND AWARDS** Phi Beta Kappa; Phi Kappa Phi. **MEMBERSHIPS** Amer Philol Assoc; Amer Assoc Univ Profs. **RESEARCH** Greek and Latin poetry; mythology. **SELECTED PUBLICATIONS** Auth, Propertius' tardus Amor, Class J, 1/73; Cicero and Sallust: Catiline's ruina, Class World, 74; Symbolism in the Passer poems, Maia, 74; Deaths in the Aeneid, Pac Coast Philol, 75; Case of the poor preposition, Class Outlook, 76; Serpent Leitmotif in the Metamorphoses, Latomus, 83; The Burnett Lectures: A Quarter Century, 93; Mythology: Texts and Contexts, 98. **CONTACT ADDRESS** Dept Class & Humanities, San Diego State Univ, 5500 Campanile Dr, San Diego, CA 92182-8143. **EMAIL** genovese@mail.sdsu.edu

GENTRY, FRANCIS G.

PERSONAL Born 06/08/1942, Boston, MA, m, 1972 **DISCIPLINE** GERMAN **EDUCATION** Boston Col, BS, Ger and Eng, 63; Indiana Univ, MA, Ger, 66, PhD, Ger, 73. **CAREER** Instr, SUNY-Albany, 69-74; asst prof, SUNY-Albany, 74-75; asst prof, Univ Wis Madison, 75-80; assoc prof, Univ Wis Madison, 80-84; guest prof, Lehrstuhl Schupp, Univ Freiburg, 84; prof, Univ Wis Madison, 84-91; prof, Penn State Univ, 91-. **HONORS AND AWARDS** Alpha & Omega, Boston Col Sch of Educ Honor Soc, 62; Alpha Sigma Nu, Nat Jesuit Honor Soc, 62; Delta Phi Alpha, Nat Ger Honor Soc, 64, pres, Beta Chap, 68; Campion Distinguished Alumnus Awd, Boston Col, 77; Seal of the Univ Freiburg, 85; fel, Vilas assoc, Univ Wis Madison, 86-88; Alexander von Humboldt-Stiftung fel, 78, 79, summer 82; Inst for Res in the Humanities, 77; Indiana Univ-Kiel Univ Exchange fel, 64. **MEMBERSHIPS** Alexander-von-Humboldt Assoc of Amer; Amer Assoc of Tchrs of Ger; Fulbright Assoc; Ger Studies Assoc; Gesellschaft fur interkulturelle Germnaistik; Intl Arthurian Soc; Intl Courtly Lit Soc; Intl Vereinigung fur Ger Sprachund Lit; Mediavisten-Verband; Medieval Acad of Amer; Mod Lang Asn; Oswald-von-Wolkenstein-Gesellschaft; Wolfram-von-Eschenbach-Gesellschaft. **RESEARCH** Medieval literature and culture. **SELECTED PUBLICATIONS** Co-ed, with James K. Walter, Heroic Epic, The Ger Libr, vol 1, NY, 95; Bibliographie zur fruhmittelhochdeutschen, Dichtung, Berlin, 92; ed, German Medievalism, Studies in Medievalism 3/4, Cambridge, 91; ed, Gottfried von Strasburg, The Ger Libr, vol 3, NY, 88; articles, Owe armiu phaffheite: Heinrich von Melk's Views on Clerical Life, Medieval Purity and Piety: Essays on Medieval Clerical Celibacy and Religious Reform, NY, Garland, 337-52, 98; Kaiserchronik, Dict of Lit Bio: Ger Writers and Works of the Early Middle Ages, 800-1170, vol 148, NY/London, Gale Res, 202-207,95; Notker von Zwiefalten, Dict of Lit Bio: Ger Writers and Works of the Early Middle Ages 800-1170, vol 148, NY/London, Gale Res, 106-109, 95; Der Arme Hartmann, Dict of Lit Bio: Ger Writers and Works of the Early Middle Ages, 800-1170, vol 148, NY/London, Gale Res, 10-13, 95; Silent that Others Might Speak: Notes on the Ackermann aus Bohmen, Ger Quart, 67, 484-492, 94. **CONTACT ADDRESS** Pennsylvania State Univ, Univ Park, 305 Burrowes Bldg., University Park, PA 16802. **EMAIL** fgg1@psu.edu

GEORGE, EDWARD

PERSONAL Born 12/10/1937, Buffalo, NY, m, 1968, 3 children **DISCIPLINE** CLASSICS **EDUCATION** Niagara Univ, BA, 59; Canisius Col, MEd, 62; Univ Wis, PhD, 66. **CAREER** Univ of Tex, 66-71; Tex Tex Univ, 71-, prof, 77-. **HONORS AND AWARDS** Acad Achievement Awd, Tex Tech Univ, 00. **MEMBERSHIPS** Am Philological Assoc; Classical Assoc of Middle West and S; AAUP; Renaissance Soc of Am; Int Assoc of Neo-Latin Studies. **RESEARCH** Greek and Latin Rhetoric, Renaissance Rhetoric, Jan Luis Vives, Greco-Roman Cultural Background to Hispanic New World Culture. **SELECTED PUBLICATIONS** Ed, Juan Luis Vives, Somnium et Vigilia in Somnium Scipionis, Attic Pr, 89; ed, Juan Luis Vives, Declamationes Sullanae: Part One, EJ Brill (Leiden, Netherlands), 89; auth, "Rhetoric in Vives", Opera Omnia Ioannis Lodovici Vivis, ed Antonio Mestre, Edicions Alfons el Magnanim, (Valencia, 92): 113-77; auth, "Justice and Discourse: New Light on Juan Luis Vives (1493-1540)", Recapturing the Renaissance: New Perspectives on Humanism, Dialogue and Texts, ed Diane S Wood and Paul Allen Miller, New Paradigm Pr, (96): 33-62; auth, "Persuading a Feminine Audience? Gratuitious Invective Apostrophe in Juan Luis Vives' On the Education of a Christian Woman", Scholia: Natal Studies in Classical Antiquity (96): 94-111; auth, "Latin and Spanish: Roman Culture and Hispanic America", Latin in the 21st Century, ed Richard A LaFleur, Scott Foresman-Addison Wesley (Reading, MA, 97): 227-236. **CONTACT ADDRESS** Dept Mod Lang and Lit, Texas Tech Univ, Lubbock, TX 79409-2071. **EMAIL** ed.george@ttu.edu

GEORGE, EMERY EDWARD

PERSONAL Born 05/08/1933, Budapest, Hungary **DISCIPLINE** GERMANIC LANGUAGES, EAST EUROPEAN STUDIES **EDUCATION** Univ Mich, BA, 55, MA, 59, PhD(-Ger), 64. **CAREER** Instr Ger, Univ Mich, 62-64; from instr to asst prof, Univ Ill, Urbana, 64-66; from asst prof to assoc prof, 66-75, off res admin res grant, 67-68, Prof Ger Lang and Lit, Univ Mich Ann Arbor, 75-, Assoc ed Russ lit, Triquarterly, 73-; found ed, Mich Ger Studies, 75-76; Fel, Int Acad Poets, England, 76-; Int Res and Exchanges Bd fel, 81. **HONORS AND AWARDS** Hopwood Awd in Poetry, 60. **MEMBERSHIPS** MLA; AM Soc Aesthet; Holderlin Ges; Poetry Soc Am; Int Poetry Soc. **RESEARCH** German literature of the Age of Goethe; English literature; Russian and Hungarian literataure. **SELECTED PUBLICATIONS CONTACT ADDRESS** Dept of Ger, Univ of Michigan, Ann Arbor, Ann Arbor, MI 48109.

GEORGE, HERMON, JR.

PERSONAL Born 11/22/1945, Tampa, FL, d **DISCIPLINE** SPANISH **EDUCATION** Wilkes College, Wilkes-Barre, PA, BA, 1967; Middlebury College, Middlebury, VT, MA, 1968; University of California, Irvine, CA, PhD, 1979. **CAREER** Wartburg College, Waverly, IA, instructor of Spanish, 68-70; Fisk University, Nashville, TN, instructor of Spanish, 70-71; Spelman College, Atlanta, GA, instructor of Spanish, 71-73; California State University, Fresno, CA, assistant professor of ethnic studies, 78-81; SUNY College, New Paltz, NY, assistant professor, Black Studies, 81-85; University of Northern Colorado, Greeley, CO, associate professor and coordinator, 85-91; professor, 91-. **MEMBERSHIPS** Member-at-large, executive board, National Council for Black Studies, 1980-87; reviewer, Social Science Journal, 1980-81, 1985-; reviewer, Science & Society, 1987-; regional editor, Western Journal of Black Studies, 1991-96; member, National Conference of Black Political Scientists, 1988-89. **SELECTED PUBLICATIONS** The Black Scholar, advising & contributing editor, 1994; Western Social Science Assn, exec council, 1993-96; The Social Science Journal, assoc editor, 1994-95; Contemporary Authors, V 126, 1989;American Race Relations Theory, Lanham MD, Univ Press of America, 1984; "Black Power in Office: The Limits of Electoral Reform", reprinted in Talmadge Anderson Ed, Black Studies: Theory, Method, and Critical Perspectives 1990; Fellowship, NEH, Summer Institute on African-American Culture, 1987; Faculty Excellence Award, Univ of Northern Colorado, 1987; "Clarence Thomas: 'Loyal Foot Soldier' for Reaganism"; Court of Appeal: The Black Community Speaks Out on the Racial and Sexual Politics of Thomas vs Hill, 1992. **CONTACT ADDRESS** Dept of Africana Studies, Univ of No Colorado, Greeley, CO 80639. **EMAIL** hhgeorg@bentley.unco.edu

GEORGES, ROBERT A.

PERSONAL Born 05/01/1933, Sewickley, PA, m, 1956, 1 child **DISCIPLINE** FOLKLORE, LINGUISTICS **EDUCATION** Ind State Col, BS, 54; Univ Pa, MA, 61; Ind Univ, PhD, 64. **CAREER** Teacher English, Bound Brook High Sch, NJ, 54-56; Southern Regional High Sch, Manahawkin, 58-60; from instr to asst prof English, Univ Kans, 63-66; from asst prof to assoc prof English and folklore, 66-76, vchmn, Folklore and Mythology Group, 67-68, chmn 68-76, PROF ENGLISH and FOLKLORE, UNIV CALIF, LOS ANGELES, 76-, Guggenheim fel, 69-70. **MEMBERSHIPS** MLA; Ling Soc Am; Am Folklore Soc. **RESEARCH** Narrating process; narrative analysis; conceptual foundations of folklore and mythology studies. **SELECTED PUBLICATIONS CONTACT ADDRESS** Folklore and Mythology Studies Univ of Calif Los, Los Angeles, CA 90024.

GERATO, ERASMO GABRIELE

PERSONAL Born 03/24/1943, Formia, Italy, m, 1989, 1 child **DISCIPLINE** ITALIAN & FRENCH LANGUAGE & LITERATURE **EDUCATION** City Univ New York, BS, 66; Univ Wis, MA, 68, PhD(Ital-French), 74. **CAREER** Teaching asst Ital, Univ Calif, Los Angeles, 66-67; teaching asst Ital, Univ Wis, 67-70; from asst prof to prof Ital, French, Fla State Univ, 70-. **HONORS AND AWARDS** Ward Medal, City Univ New York, 66; Fullbright Scholarship, 71; Cofrs Univ Scholar, 74-75; Pi Delta Phi-National French Honor Society; The Dante Society Univ S. Florida (life membership); Director of International Linkage Institutes 80-99 (State of Florida); French Academic Palms, 93 (Chevalier); Promotion, French Academic Palms, 98 (Officer). **MEMBERSHIPS** Am Assoc of Teachers of Fr; Am Assoc of Teachers of Ital; Am Soc of Fr Acad Palms. **RESEARCH** Italian and French language, literature and linguistics. **SELECTED PUBLICATIONS** Auth, A Critical Study of the Life and Works of Alessandro Poerio, Casa Editrice C Maccari, 75; Thematic fragments in Alessandro Poerio's poetry, La Parola del Popolo, 5/75; La Chartreuse de Parme: A study of its origins A discussion of several possible sources, La Stagione, 1/76; Reality of illusion and illusion of reality in Leopardi's Zibaldone, SAtlantic Bull, 5/76; Un capolavoro della lett italiana del 600: La Reina de Scotia--Studio critico della sua lingua e stile, Neuphilolische Mitteilungen, 6/76; Vittorio Alfieri, the artist and his creation: An exposition of Alfieri's personal nature as reflected in his protagonists, Rocky Mt Rev, 81; Guido Gustavo Gozzano: A Literary Interpretation, Madrid: Jose Porrua Turanzas, 83; Salvatore Quasimodo Nobel Laureates in Literature. Ed. R. Pribic, New York, Garlando, 90, 341-344. **CONTACT ADDRESS** Dept of Mod Lang, Florida State Univ, 371 DIF, Tallahassee, FL 32306-1540. **EMAIL** egerato@mailer.fsu.edu

GERBER, BARBARA LESLIE

PERSONAL Born 10/29/1941, New York, NY, m, 1986, 4 children **DISCIPLINE** COMPARATIVE LITERATURE, FRENCH **EDUCATION** Brooklyn Col, BA, 62; Univ Wis-Madison, MA, 65; PhD, 68. **CAREER** Asst prof French, St Lawrence Univ, 68-73; asst prof, 73-77, assoc prof, 77-81, prof comp lit, 82-, Brooklyn Col; Dir, St Lawrence Jr Year in France, 71-72; dir, Spec Baccalaureates Degree Prog Adults, 79-86; dir Master of Arts in Liberal Studies, 82-97; dir, Comparative Lit Prog, Brooklyn Col, CUNY. **HONORS AND AWARDS** Fulbright Fel; Ford Fund grants. **MEMBERSHIPS** AAUP; MLA; Am Comp Lit Asn. **RESEARCH** Twentieth century French novel and theatre. **SELECTED PUBLICATIONS** Contrib, Twentieth Century French Fiction, Rutgers Univ, 75; coauth, Dictionary of Modern French Idioms, Garland, 77; transl, Color of Time, Zone Press, 80; auth, arts on: John Ciardi, Adele Simpson, and Isaac Bashevis Singer, in Encyl of Am Lives, 99, 00. **CONTACT ADDRESS** 2901 Bedford Ave, Brooklyn, NY 11210. **EMAIL** bgerber@brooklyn.cuny.edu

GERBER, DOUGLAS E.

PERSONAL Born 09/14/1933, North Bay, ON, Canada, m, 1986, 1 child **DISCIPLINE** CLASSICS **EDUCATION** Univ Western Ontario, BA, 55, MA, 56; Univ Toronto, PhD, 59. **CAREER** Lectr, Univ Toronto, 58-59; lectr, 59-60, asst prof, 60-64, assoc prof, 64-69, prof, 69- , dept ch, 69-97, Univ Western Ontario; prof emer. **HONORS AND AWARDS** William Sherwood Fox Ch of Classics, 77- ; Pres, Class Asn Canada, 88-90; ed, Transactions Amer Philol Asn, 74-82. **MEMBERSHIPS** Amer Philol Asn; Class Asn, Great Brit; Class Asn Canada; Class Asn Middle West and South. **RESEARCH** Greek Lyric Poetry. **SELECTED PUBLICATIONS** Ed and transl, Greek Iambic Poetry, LOEB, 99; ed and transl, Greek Elegiac Poetry, LOEB, 99; auth, "Pindar, Nemean Six: A Commentary," Harvard Studies in Classical Philology 99, (99): 33-91. **CONTACT ADDRESS** Dept of Classics, Univ of Western Ontario, London, ON, Canada N6A 3K7. **EMAIL** degerber@julian.uwo.ca

GERDES, NEIL W.

PERSONAL Born 10/19/1943, Moline, IL **DISCIPLINE** LIBRARIAN; SPIRITUALITY **EDUCATION** Univ Ill, AB, 65; Harvard Univ, BD, 68; Columbia Univ, MA, 71; Univ Chicago, MA, 75; Univ St Mary of the Lake, DMin, 94. **CAREER** Instr, Tuskegee Institute, 69-71; libr asst, Augustana Col, 72-73; libr prof, Meadville Theol Sch, 73-; libr, program dir, Chicago Cluster Theol Sch, 77-80; dir, Hammond Libr, 80-; libr prof, Chicago Theol Sem, 80-. **HONORS AND AWARDS** Ordained to ministry Unitarian Universalist Assn, 1975. **MEMBERSHIPS** ALA; Am Theol Libr Asn; Chicago Area Theol Libr Asn; Unitarian Universalist Mins Asn; Assn Liberal Religious Scholars; Phi Beta Kappa. **RESEARCH** Spirituality, liberal religious history. **CONTACT ADDRESS** Meadville/Lombard Theol Sch, 5701 S Woodlawn Ave, Chicago, IL 60637-1602. **EMAIL** ngerdes@meadville.edu

GERICKE, PHILIP OTTO

PERSONAL Born 12/24/1936, Ukiah, CA, 4 children **DISCIPLINE** SPANISH LANGUAGE & LITERATURE **EDUCATION** Univ Calif, Riverside, BA, 58; Univ Calif, Berkeley, MA, 60, PhD, 65. **CAREER** Assoc Span, Univ Calif, Riverside, 62-63, lectr, 63-64; asst prof foreign lang, San Fernando Valley State Col, 64-66, asst prof, 66-71, assoc prof, 71-78, assoc dean, grad div, 75-81, Prof Span, Univ Calif, Riverside, 78-94, Prof Emer, 94-. **MEMBERSHIPS** MLA; Am Asn Teachers Span & Port; PAMLA; Asn Intl de Hispanists. **RESEARCH** Spanish literature of the Middle Ages and early Renaissance. **SELECTED PUBLICATIONS** Coauth, El Vencimjento del mundo, tratado ascetico del siglo XV: edicion, Hispanofila, 64; auth, El Invencionario de Alfonso de Toledo, Rev Arch, Bibliot & Mus, 1-12/67; The narrative structure of the Laberinto de fortuna, Romance Philol, 5/68; ed & transl, Manuel C Rojo's Historical Notes on Lower California, Dawson's 72; The turtledove in four sixteenth-century versions of Fontefrida, El Romancero, Hoy, 79; On the structure of the Libro de Buen Amor: A question of method, Ky Romance Quart, 2/81; Apostillas a Sacome de la prision y romances relacionados actas del congreso Romancero-Caucimero, UCLA, 84; Porrua Turanzsi, 87; ed, Alfonso de Toledo's Invencionario, Hispanic Sem of Medieval Studies, 92. **CONTACT ADDRESS** Dept of Hispanic Studies, Univ of California, Riverside, 900 University Ave, Riverside, CA 92521-0001. **EMAIL** gericke@aol.com

GERIG, WESLEY LEE

PERSONAL Born 09/17/1930, Ft Wayne, IN, m, 1952, 4 children **DISCIPLINE** RELIGION, HEBREW, THEOLOGY **EDUCATION** Ft Wayne Bible Col, AB, 51; Fuller Theol Sem, M div, 54, ThM, 56; Univ Iowa, PhD(relig), 65. **CAREER** From instr to assoc prof Bible & theol, 57-69, acad dean, 71-73, Prof Bible & Theol, Ft Wayne Bible Col, 69-91, Chmn Dept Bibl Studies, 62-91; Taylor Univ, 92-;Instr Bibl lang & dir admis, prof Bibl & theol; Winona Lake Sch Theol, 64-. **MEMBER-**

SHIPS Evangel Theol Soc; Am Acad Relig. **RESEARCH** The Hebrew-Gentile relations in the Old Testament; the social ethics of the Apostolic Fathers; Koine Greek. **CONTACT ADDRESS** Div Bibl Studies, Taylor Univ, Fort Wayne, 1025 W Rudisill Blvd, Fort Wayne, IN 46807-2197. **EMAIL** wsgerig@ tayloru.edu

GERLACH, U. HENRY
PERSONAL Born 06/29/1938, Berlin, Germany, m, 1965, 4 children **DISCIPLINE** GERMAN LITERATURE **EDUCATION** Univ Utah, BA, 64; Cornell Univ, MA, 66, PhD (Ger Lit), 68. **CAREER** Asst prof, Univ Ill, Urbana, 68-74; Alexander von Humboldt-Stiftung Dozentenstipendiat, 74-75; assoc prof, Univ Ill, Urbana, 74-87; prof, Univ Ill, Urbana, 87-; Hd, Dept Germanic Lang and Lit, Univ Ill, Urbana, 00-. **HONORS AND AWARDS** Knight's Cross for Science and Art (Austria). **MEMBERSHIPS** MLA; AATG, Hebbel-Ges, Storm-Ges, E. T.A. Hoffmann-Ges. **RESEARCH** Nineteenth and Twentieth Century German Lit. **SELECTED PUBLICATIONS** Hebbel-Bibliography 1910-1970, 73, hebbel-briefe, 75, Briefe von und an hebbel, 78, C. F. Meyer-Bibliographie, 94, Hebbel Briefwechsel vol 1, 99, Contributions to the following periodicals, Hebbel-Jahrbuch, Maske u Kothurn, Wirkendes Wort, Zeitschr F Dt Philologie, and others. **CONTACT ADDRESS** Dept Germanic Lang & Lit, Univ of Illinois, Urbana-Champaign, 707 S Mathews Ave, Urbana, IL 61801-3625. **EMAIL** ugerlach@ uiuc.edu

GERLI, E. MICHAEL
PERSONAL Born 03/11/1945, San Jose, Costa Rica, m, 1966, 2 children **DISCIPLINE** SPANISH, HISPANIC STUDIES **EDUCATION** Univ Calif, BA, 68; Middlebury Col, MA, 69; Univ Calif at Los Angeles, PhD, 72. **CAREER** From asst prof to prof, Georgetown Univ, 72-00; vis prof, Univ Calif at Los Angeles, 80; vis prof, Univ Md, 86-87 & 90; vis prof, Johns Hopkins Univ, 91-92; vis prof, Univ Pa, 93; vis prof, Univ Va, 94; Commonwealth of Va Prof of Hispanic Studies, Univ Va, 00-. **HONORS AND AWARDS** Competitive Grants in Aid for Res, Georgetown Univ, 77, 84, 86, 88, & 89; res & travel grants, Am Philos Soc, 78; res & travel grants, ACLS, 81 & 89; res & travel grants, Comite Conjunto Hispano-Norteamericano, 83; NEH Sr Summer Stipend, 86 & 93; Comt for Cultural Coop Between U.S. Universities and Spain, 87, 90, 92, &95; NEH Sr Res Fel, 94. **MEMBERSHIPS** MLA, Asn Int de Hispanistas, Asn de Lit Hispanica Medieval, Am Asn of Res Historian on Medieval Spain, Int Courtly Lit Soc, Medieval Acad of Am. **RESEARCH** Medieval and Early Modern Iberian Literature and Culture. **SELECTED PUBLICATIONS** Auth, Alfonso Martinez de Toledo, 76; co-ed, Studies in Honor of Gerald E. Wade, 78; ed, Arcipreste de Talavera, 76, 81, & 87; ed, Triste deleytacion: An Anonymous Fifteenth-Century Castilian Romance, 82; ed, Milagros de Nuestra Senora, 85, 87, & 90; ed, La poesia cancioneril: Historia y texto, 90; co-ed, Hispanic Medieval Studies in Honor of Samuel G. Armistead, 92; auth, Refiguring Authority: Reading, Writing, and Rewriting in Cervantes, Univ Press of Kent, 95; co-ed, Studies on the Spanish Sentimental Romance, Tamesis, 97; co-ed, Poetry at Court in Trastamaran Spain: from the Cancionero de Baena To the Cancionero general, Ctr for medieval and Renaissance Studies, Univ Ariz Press, 98. **CONTACT ADDRESS** Dept Span, Ital, & Port, Univ of Virginia, 115 Wilson Hall, Charlottesville, VA 22903.

GERMAIN, CLAUDE
PERSONAL Born 06/27/1941, St. Tite, PQ, Canada **DISCIPLINE** LINGUISTICS **EDUCATION** Univ Montreal, LL, 65, CAPES, 67, MA, 68; Univ Aix-Marseille (France), PhD(Ling), 70; Univ Ottawa, PhD(Philos), 89. **CAREER** Tchr, Royal Mil Col, St-Jean, 65-67; prof ling, Univ Ottawa, 70-79; prof educ, Univ Montreal, 79-87; CH LINGUISTICS, UNIV QUEBEC MONTREAL, 87-. **HONORS AND AWARDS** Can Mod Lang Rev Best Article Awd, 85; Ghyslaine Coutu-Vaillancourt Awd, 85. **SELECTED PUBLICATIONS** Auth, Le Point sur l'approche communicative, 91, 2nd ed 93; auth, Evolution de l'enseignement des langues: 5000 ans d'histoire, 93; coauth, L'evaluation de la communication ecrite au primaire, 2 vols, 85; ed, Le point sur la grammaire en didactique des langues, 95; ed, Les eleves sourds: Style cognitif et education bilinguel/ biculturelle, 95. **CONTACT ADDRESS** Lnguistics Dept, Univ of Quebec, Montreal, CP 8888, Succ Centre-ville, Montreal, QC, Canada H3C 3P8. **EMAIL** germain.claude@uqam.ca

GERRARD, CHARLOTTE
DISCIPLINE FRENCH LITERATURE **EDUCATION** Univ Pittsburgh, PhD, 66. **CAREER** Assoc prof. **RESEARCH** Philosophy of Camus and Sartre. **SELECTED PUBLICATIONS** Auth, Montherlant and Suicide, 77; pubs on Camus, Vian, Montherlant, Maulnier, Sartre, Ionesco, Ribemont-Dessaignes and antitheism in drama. **CONTACT ADDRESS** Dept of French and Italian, Indiana Univ, Bloomington, 1020 E Kirkwood Ave, Ballantine Hall 642, Bloomington, IN 47405.

GESELL, GERALDINE C.
DISCIPLINE CLASSICAL STUDIES **EDUCATION** Vassar Col, BA, 53; Univ Okla, MA, 55; Univ NC, PhD, 72. **CAREER** Asst prof, 72-79, assoc prof, 79-85, prof, Univ Tenn, 85-. **MEMBERSHIPS** Advis Counc Am Acad Rome; Archaeol Inst Am; Class Asn Mid W and S; Tenn Class Asn. **SELECTED PUBLICATIONS** Auth, Town, Palace, and House Cult in Minoan Crete, 85. **CONTACT ADDRESS** Dept of Classics, Univ of Tennessee, Knoxville, Knoxville, TN 37996-0413. **EMAIL** ggesell@utk.edu

GESNER, B. EDWARD
PERSONAL Born 09/22/1942, Middleton, NS, Canada, m, 1971, 3 children **DISCIPLINE** DIALECTOLOGY, APPLIED LINGUISTICS **EDUCATION** Univ King's Col, BA Hons, 63; Dalhousie Univ, MA, 67; Univ Toulouse II, Dr 3 cycle ling, 77. **CAREER** Teacher French, Queen Elizabeth High Sch, 65-66; lectr, 67-69, asst prof, 69-80, Assoc Prof French, Dalhousie Univ, 80-, Res assoc, Int Ctr Res Biling, Laval Univ, 80-81. **MEMBERSHIPS** Am Asn Teachers Fr. **RESEARCH** Acadian morphology and syntax; pedagogy of French as second language. **SELECTED PUBLICATIONS** Auth, Ecrivons--Strategies for Writing in French as a 2nd-Language, Can Mod Lang Rev-Revue Canadienne Des Langues Vivantes, Vol 0049, 93; Invitation--Contexts, Culture and Communication, 4th ed, Can Mod Lang Rev-Revue Canadienne Des Langues Vivantes, Vol 0051, 95. **CONTACT ADDRESS** French Dept, Dalhousie Univ, Halifax, NS, Canada B3H 3J5.

GESS, RANDALL S.
PERSONAL Born 07/26/1963, Fort Worth, TX **DISCIPLINE** LINGUISTICS **EDUCATION** Univ Tex, BA, 87; MA, 89; Univ Wash, PhD, 96. **CAREER** Vis asst prof to asst prof, Univ Ut, 95-. **HONORS AND AWARDS** Univ Ut Fel, 00. **MEMBERSHIPS** LSA; MLA; AATF. **RESEARCH** Phonological change; phonological theory; historical French. **SELECTED PUBLICATIONS** Auth, "Alignment and Sonority in the Syllable Structure of Late Latin and Gallo-Romance," Theoret Anal Romance Lang (98); auth, "Old French NoCoda Effects From Constraint Interaction," Probus (98); auth, "Compensatory Lengthening and Structure Preservation Revisited," Phonology (98); auth, "Positional Faithfulness vs. Cue Preservation: The Case of Nasal Sequence Resolution in Gallo-Romance," Formal Perspective Romance Lang (99); auth, "Rethinking the Dating of Old French Syllable-final Consonant Loss," Diachronica (99); auth, "Distinctive Vowel Length in Old French: Evidence and Implications," Hist Ling (01). **CONTACT ADDRESS** Dept Ling, Univ of Utah, 255 S Central Campus Dr, Rm 2328, Salt Lake City, UT 84103. **EMAIL** randall.gess@m.cc.utah. edu

GIBALDI, JOSEPH
PERSONAL Born 08/20/1942, Brooklyn, NY, m, 1962, 2 children **DISCIPLINE** ENGLISH, COMPARATIVE LITERATURE **EDUCATION** City Col New York, BA, 65; MA, 67; NYork Univ, PhD(comp lit), 73. **CAREER** Instr English, Brooklyn Col, 71-73; asst prof comp lit, Univ Ga, 73-76; ASSOC DIR, BK PUBL AND RES PROG, MOD LANG ASN AM, 76-, Southeastern Inst Medieval and Renaissance Studies fel, 76; adj prof English, Fairleigh Dickinson Univ, 77-. **MEMBERSHIPS** MLA; Am Comp Lit Asn; Renaissance Soc; New Chaucer Soc. **RESEARCH** Medieval and Renaissance literature; interdisciplinary studies; professional subjects. **SELECTED PUBLICATIONS** Auth, Anatomy of the Novella; auth, Approaches to Teaching Chaucer's 'Cantebury Tales'; auth, Teaching Literature & Other Arts; auth, MLA Handbook for Writers of Research Papers. **CONTACT ADDRESS** New Sch for Social Research, 66 W 12th St, New York, NY 10011.

GIBBS, VIRGINIA
DISCIPLINE SPANISH **EDUCATION** Univ Wis, BA; NYork Univ, MA; Univ Minn, PhD. **CAREER** Assoc prof. **HONORS AND AWARDS** Co-founder & member bd dir, Northeast Iowa People for Animal Welfare, PAW. **SELECTED PUBLICATIONS** Auth, Las Sonatas du Valle-Indan, Madrid. **CONTACT ADDRESS** Dept of Modern Languages, Luther Col, 700 College Dr, Decorah, IA 52101. **EMAIL** gibbsvir@luther.edu

GIBSON, TODD
DISCIPLINE TIBETAN STUDIES **EDUCATION** Ind Univ, PhD, 91 **CAREER** Inst, Antioch Univ, 91-; inst, Teikyon Univ, 94-96; inst, Denver Univ, 97. **MEMBERSHIPS** Am Acad of Relig **RESEARCH** Inner Asian and Tibetan History; Culture; Relig **SELECTED PUBLICATIONS** Auth, Two Figures in the Early Great Perfection," in Tibet Jrnl, 99; "Notes on the History of the Shamanic in Tibet and Inner Asia," Numen 44, 97 **CONTACT ADDRESS** 31646 Broadmoor, Evergreen, CO 80439.

GIEBER, ROBERT L.
PERSONAL Born 01/22/1944, Clifton, KS **DISCIPLINE** FRENCH LANGUAGE AND LITERATURE **EDUCATION** Kans State Teachers Col, BEd, 65; Univ Iowa, MA, 66; Univ Nebr, PhD, 71. **CAREER** Instr French, Ft Hays State Col, 66-69; Prof French, Simpson Col, 71-, Chmn Dept, 74-, Nat Endowment Humanities res grant, 75. **MEMBERSHIPS** Am Asn Teachers French; Mediaeval Acad Am. **RESEARCH** Medieval hagiography; medieval & Renaissance civilization. **SELECTED PUBLICATIONS** Ed, A critical edition of La Vie Saint-Jehan-Baptiste, an old French poem of the early 14th century, Z Romanische Philol, 78; An English-French Glossary of Educational Terminology, Univ Press Am, 81; Poetic elements of rhythm in the ballades, Rondeaux and Virelais of Guillaume de Machaut, Romantic Rev, 82. **CONTACT ADDRESS** Dept of Foreign Lang, Simpson Col, Iowa, 701 N C St, Indianola, IA 50125-1297. **EMAIL** gieber@simpson.edu

GIES, DAVID THATCHER
PERSONAL Born 08/18/1945, Pittsburgh, PA, m, 1994 **DISCIPLINE** SPANISH LITERATURE **EDUCATION** PA State Univ, BA, 67; Univ Pittsburgh, MA, 70, PhD(Span), 72. **CAREER** Assoc prof, St Bonaventure Univ, 70-79; vis lect, Univ Birmingham, England, 78; assoc prof Span, 79-91, Commonwealth Prof Span, Univ VA, 92-, chair, dept span, 83-90, 92-95; ed, Dieciocho: Hispanic Enlightenment. **HONORS AND AWARDS** John Simon Guggenheim fel, 83-84; NEH Sr fels. **MEMBERSHIPS** MLA; Am Asn Teachers Span & Port; Assoc Int de Hispanistas. **RESEARCH** Spanish Enlightenment and Romanticism. **SELECTED PUBLICATIONS** Auth, Agustin Duran: A Biography and Literary Appreciation, Tamesis, London, 75; Nicolas Fernandez de Moratin, Twayne, 79; Theatre and Politics in Nineteenth-Century Spain, Cambridge, 88; The Theatre in Nineteenth-Century Spain, Cambridge, 94; ed, Grimaldi, La pata de cabra, Rome, Bulzoni, 86; ed, Romanticismo, Madrid, Taurus, 89; ed, Historia y critica de la literatura espanola, siglo XVIII, Barcelona, Critica, 92; ed, Zorrilla Don Juan Tenorio, Madrid, Casalia, 94; ed, Moratin La petimetra, Madrid, Castalia, 95; ed, Cambridge Companion to Modern Spanish Culture, Cambridge, 99; seventy-five scholarly articles and 100+ book reviews. **CONTACT ADDRESS** Dept Span, Univ of Virginia, 115 Wilson Hall, Charlottesville, VA 22903-3125. **EMAIL** dtg@virginia.edu

GIGNAC, FRANCIS THOMAS
PERSONAL Born 02/24/1933, Detroit, MI **DISCIPLINE** PHILOLOGY, THEOLOGY **EDUCATION** Loyola Univ, Ill, AB, 55, MA, 57, MA, 68; Oxford Univ, DPhil(Greek), 64. **CAREER** Instr Greek, Loyola Univ, Ill, 65-67; from asst prof to assoc prof Theol, Fordham Univ, 68-74; assoc prof Bibl Studies & chmn dept, Cath Univ Am, 74-, NSF travel grant, 67. **MEMBERSHIPS** Cath Bibl Asn; Am Philol Asn; Am Soc Papyrologists. **RESEARCH** The language of the non-literary Greek papyri; the language of the Greek New Testament; textual criticism. **SELECTED PUBLICATIONS** Auth, The language of the non-literary Greek papyri, Am Studies Papyrology, 70; The text of Acts in Chrysostom's homilies, Traditio, 70; The pronunciation of Greek stops in the papyri, Trans & Proc Am Philol Asn, 70; An Introductory New Testament Greek Course, Loyola Univ, 73; A Grammar of the Greek Papyri of the Roman and Byzantine Periods (2 vols), Cisalpino-La Goliardica, Milan, 76 & 81. **CONTACT ADDRESS** Dept of Biblical Studies, Catholic Univ of America, 620 Michigan Ave NE, Washington, DC 20064-0002. **EMAIL** gignac@cua.edu

GILES, MARY E.
PERSONAL Born 09/18/1934, Missoula, MT, m, 1953, 2 children **DISCIPLINE** SPANISH LITERATURE **EDUCATION** Univ Idaho, BA, 55; State Univ Wash, MA, 57; Univ Calif, Berkeley, PhD, 61. **CAREER** Teaching asst, State Univ Wash, 55-57 and Univ Calif, Berkeley, 58-61; from instr to asst prof foreign lang, Calif State Col Hayward, 61-64; from asst prof to assoc prof Span, 64-71, Prof Humanities, Univ Sacranento, 71-, Part-time instr, Univ Idaho, 56-57; ed, Studia Mystica, 78-**MEMBERSHIPS** Philol Asn Pac Coast; Am Asn Teachers Span & Port; MLA; Asn Advan Humanities. **RESEARCH** Nineteenth century and contemporary Spanish novel. **SELECTED PUBLICATIONS CONTACT ADDRESS** Dept of Humanities, California State Univ, Sacramento, Sacramento, CA 95818.

GILLIS, DANIEL J.
PERSONAL Born 09/25/1935, New Bedford, MA, s **DISCIPLINE** CLASSICS **EDUCATION** Harvard, AB, 57; Cornell Univ, MA, 59, PhD(classics), 63. **CAREER** Instr classics, Brown Univ, 59-60; asst prof, Univ Tex, 64-65 & Swathmore Col, 65-66; from ast prof to assoc prof, 66-76, Prof Classics, Haverford Col, 76-, Ger govt fel, Univ Munich, 63-64; Ford Found humanities res grant, 73. **MEMBERSHIPS** Am Philol Asn. **RESEARCH** Latin poetry; Roman history; Greek politics. **SELECTED PUBLICATIONS** Auth, Furtwangler Recalled, DeGraff, 66; Furtwangler and America, Manyland Bks, 70; Vita, Westworks, 79; Collaboration with the Persians, Steiner, 79; Measure of a Man, Iona Fdn, 82; Eros and Death in the Aeneid, Bretschneider, 82. **CONTACT ADDRESS** Dept of Classics, Haverford Col, 370 Lancaster Ave, Haverford, PA 19041-1392.

GILLON, ADAM
PERSONAL Born 07/17/1921, Kovel, Poland, m, 1946, 2 children **DISCIPLINE** ENGLISH AND COMPARATIVE LITERATURE **EDUCATION** Hebrew Univ, Jerusalem, MA, 48; Columbia Univ, PhD, 54. **CAREER** Lectr English, Sch Higher Studies, Jerusalem, 44-45; lectr English lang and lit, Hascalla Col, prin and teacher English, Montefiore Tech High Sch, Tel-Aviv, 49-50; instr English, Univ Kans, 56-57; assoc prof, Acadia Univ, 58-59, prof and head dept, 59-61; prof English and World Lit, 61-80, EMER PROF ENGLISH, STATE UNIV NY, NEW PALTZ, 80-; PROF ENGLISH LIT, UNIV HAIFA, IS-

RAEL, 81-, Can Res Coun grant-in-aid, 61; Polish ser ed, Twayne's World Auth Ser, 64-, Hebrew ser, 65-; State Univ NY Res Found res grants-in-aid, 65, 66, 68, 70 and 72-73; Alfred Jurzykowski Found award, 67; US Govt res grant, Israel, 68-69; Joseph Fels Found res grant, Israel, 68-69; ed, Joseph Conrad Today. **MEMBERSHIPS** Joseph Conrad Soc Am (pres, 75-82); MLA; Am Comp Lit Asn; NCTE; Int Comp Lit Asn. **RESEARCH** English, American, Polish, Russian and Hebrew literatures; creative writing of fiction, poetry and drama comparative and world literature. **SELECTED PUBLICATIONS** Auth, The 'Affair in Marseilles,' Another Polish Novel about Conrad, Conradiana, Vol 0025, 93. **CONTACT ADDRESS** Dept of English and World Lit, SUNY, New Paltz, New Paltz, NY 12561.

GILMAN, DONALD
PERSONAL Born 02/24/1945, Newport News, VA **DISCIPLINE** FRENCH, COMPARATIVE LITERATURE **EDUCATION** Univ NC, Chapel Hill, AB, 67, PhD(French, comp lit), 76; Univ Harvard, AM, 70. **CAREER** Instr French, Christopher Newport Col, Col William & Mary, 67-70; asst prof, 74-79, assoc prof French & Humanities 79-87; prof 87-; vis prof, Univ de Nancy II, 97-98; Pres, Medieval Asn Midwest, 96-97; res assoc and fel, Northrop Frye Centre and Centre for Reformation and Renaissance Studies, Univ Toronto, 99. **HONORS AND AWARDS** Grants, Government of PQ and Canadian Embassy, 91-92; Travel Grants, CNRS (France), 91, Learned Societies of Canada, 91, Univ Toronto, 88, Univ Cent. MI, 83 & 81, Univ BC, 81; National Endowment for the Humanities, 89 & 80; Newberry Library, Chicago, 83-84. **MEMBERSHIPS** Renaissance Soc Am; Medieval Asn Midwest, pres, 96-97; Midwest Mod Lang Asn; 16th-century Studies. **RESEARCH** 16th-century French lit; Renaissance lit in France and Italy; history of literary criticism, from Plato to French structuralism. **SELECTED PUBLICATIONS** Ed., Everyman and Company: Essays on the Theme and Structure of European Moral Play, 89; co-ed, Louis Le Caron, Dialogues, 86; auth, Petrarch's Sophonisba: Seduction, Sacrifice, and Patriarchal Politics in Sex and Gender in Medieval Renaissance Lit: The Latin Tradition, 97; auth, Theories of Dialogue, in The Dialogue in Early Modern France, 1547-1630: Art and Argumentation, 93; auth, Ronsard's concept of the Poete Humain, Bibliotheque d'Humanisme et Renaissance; 83, plus numerous other articles. **CONTACT ADDRESS** Dept of Modern Languages and Classics, Ball State Univ, 2000 W University, Muncie, IN 47306-0465. **EMAIL** dgilman@bsw.edu

GILMORE, ROGER H.
DISCIPLINE SPANISH **EDUCATION** Univ Nebr, PhD. **CAREER** Assoc prof emer, Spanish, Univ Neb. **RESEARCH** Second lang acquisition; second lang pedagogy & teaching methodologies; linguistics; hist of Span lang. **CONTACT ADDRESS** Foreign Languages and Literature Dept, Colorado State Univ, Fort Collins, CO 80523. **EMAIL** rgilmore@vines.colostate.edu

GILROY, JAMES PAUL
PERSONAL Born 08/30/1947, Worcester, MA **DISCIPLINE** FRENCH LITERATURE **EDUCATION** Col Holy Cross, BA, 68; Princeton Univ, MA, 70, PhD, 72. **CAREER** Asst prof, 72-79, assoc prof, 79-90, Prof French, Univ Denver, 90-. **HONORS AND AWARDS** Knight Acad Palms, France, 92; Univ Scholar/Teacher of the Year, Univ Denver, 92; Top Honors Prof Award, 95, 96, 97 & 98; Managing Editor, The French Review, 98-01. **MEMBERSHIPS** Rocky Mountain Mod Lang Asn; Soc Prof Fr Am; Am Asn Teachers Fr; Les Amis Lang Francaise; Philol Asn Pac Coast; Fr Women authors of the Revolution and Empire; Victor Hugo and musical drama. **RESEARCH** Romanticism and Pre-Romanticism; French fiction of 18th and 19th centuries; French Enlightenment; non-metropolitan French literature. **SELECTED PUBLICATIONS** Auth, The Theme of Etre and Paraitre in the Works of Agrippa d'Aubigne, Bull Rocky Mountain Mod Lang Asn, 73; Theatricality in the Universe of Balzac's Le Pere Goriot, Degre 2nd, 77; Prevostian themes in the Suite de Manon Lescaut, in Enlightenment Essays, 77; Peace and the Pursuit of Happiness in the French Utopian Novel, in Studies on Voltaire and the Eighteenth Century, Voltaire Found, 79; The Romantic Manon and Des Grieux, Naaman, Sherbrooke, 80; The theme of the woman in Balzac's La Cousine Bette, Rocky Mountain Rev, 80; Structures epiques et liturgiques dans Maria Chapdelaine, Bull Societe des Professeurs Francais en Amerique, 81; ed, Francophone literatures of the New World, Vol II, in Occasional Papers, 82; Prevost's Le Doyen de Killerine: The Career of an Imperfect Mentor, Studies on Voltaire, 84; The Pursuit of the Real in Rina Lasnier's Presence de l'absence, in Traditionalism, Nationalism, and Feminism: Women Writers of Quebec, Greenwood Press, 85; Rabelais, the Good Doctor: Health and Sanity in the Quart Livre, European Studies J, 85; Prevost Theophe: A Liberated Heroine in Search of Herself, French Rev, 87; Food, Cooking and Eating in Proust's A la recherche du temps perdu, Twentieth Century Lit, 87; Variations of the Theme of Mentor in the Later Abbe Prevost, Studies on Voltaire, 89; Prevost's Mentors: The Master-Pupil Relationship in the Major Novels of the Abbe Prevost, Studia Humanitatis, 90; Erik Satie and Le Piege de Meduse, Ars Musica Denver, 89; Educators of Kings and Commoners in the Abbe Prevost's Semi-Fictional Works, Nottingham French Studies, 90; Self-Educated Women in the Novels of Abbe Prevost, Studies on Voltaire, 92; Teaching a Literature Course on the French Revolution, French Rev, 93. **CONTACT ADDRESS** Dept of Langs & Lits, Univ of Denver, 2040 S Race St, Denver, CO 80210-4308. **EMAIL** jgilroy@du.edu

GIMENEZ, ANTONIO
DISCIPLINE SPANISH **EDUCATION** Ohio State Univ, MA; PhD, 73. **CAREER** Prof, Williams Col, 74-; dir in residence, Hamilton Col Acad Yr in Spain, 77-78, 82-83, 91-92; ch, Romance Lang dept, Williams Col, 84-88, 95-97. **HONORS AND AWARDS** NEH fel, Univ Pittsburgh, 75; NEH fel, Cornell Univ, 81. **RESEARCH** Contemporary Spanish narrative; 19th-century travel literature on and about Spain; 20th-century history and civilization of Spain. **SELECTED PUBLICATIONS** Co-ed, From Dante to Garcea Marquez: Studies in Romance Literatures and Linguistics, Williams Col, 87; Los espanoles y la guerra, an ed with introduction, transl and notes of Richard Ford's, An Historical Enquiry into the Unchangeable Character of a War in Spain, Madrid: Editorial Tayo, 90; George Borrow and the Spanish Press, Proceedings of the George Borrow in Wales Conf, Toronto, 90; Cosas de los ingleses! La Espana vivida y sonada en la Correspondencia entre George Borrow and Richard Ford, Madrid: Editorial Complutense, 97. **CONTACT ADDRESS** Center for Foreign Languages, Literatures and Cult, Williams Col, Williamstown, MA 01267. **EMAIL** Antonio.Gimenez@williams.edu

GINSBERG, ELLEN SUTOR
PERSONAL Born 04/18/1935, South Bend, IN, m, 1962 **DISCIPLINE** FRENCH LANGUAGE & LITERATURE **EDUCATION** Northwest Univ, BA, 55, MA, 56; Univ Chicago, PhD, 63; Univ Vienna, cert Ger, 63. **CAREER** Lectr Eng, Ecole Norm Super de Jeunes Filles, France, 61-62, asst prof, Bryn Mawr, 63-69; asst prof, 65-69; vis asst prof, Univ MD, 71-72; asst prof, 72-80, Chmn Dept of Mod Lang, 86-94; Assoc Prof French, Cath Univ AM, 81-00. **MEMBERSHIPS** MLA; SAtlantic Mod Lang Asn; Northeast Mod Lang Asn; Renaissance Soc Am; Southeast Renaissance Conf; Am Asn of Professors of French. **RESEARCH** French lit of the Renaissance; comp lit of the Renaissance; drama; poetry. **SELECTED PUBLICATIONS** Ed, Le Cesar de Jacques Grevin: Edition Critique, Droz, Geneva, 71; auth, The Legacy of Muret's Julius Caesar, Acta Conventus Nen-Latini Lovaniensis, Wilhelm Fink, Munich, 73; coauth, Fictional material and philosophic method, Mod Lang Studies, fall, 73; auth, Genre theory in the French Renaissance, French Lit Ser Vol IV, 77; Joachim du Bellay's Latin poem Patriae Desiderium and his vernacular poetry, In: Acta Conventus Neo-Latini Turonensis, Vrin, Paris, 80; The Amores of Joachim Du Bellay: A Neo-Latin Cycle of Love Poems, Acta Conventus Neo-Latini Bono, Nensis, MRT,, Binghamton, 85; Peregrinations of the Kiss: Thematic Relationships between Neo-Latin and French Poetry in the Sixteenth Century, Acta Conventus Neo-Latini Sanctandreani, MRTS, Binghamton, 86; Marc-Antoine de Muret: A Re-Evaluation, Acta Conventus Neo-Latini Guelpherbytani, MRTS, Binghamton, 88; Translation, Imitation, Transofrmation: Du Bellay as Self Translator, Acta Conventus neoo-Latini Hafnienis, MRTS, Binghamton, 94; ed, Tragedie Nouvelle Appelee Pompee: La Tragedie a l'epoque d'Henri III, Olschki & Presses Universitaires de France, Florence & Paris, 00; ed, Du Bellay's Six Latin Poems in Praise of Ronsard, Acta Conventus neo-Latini Abulensis, Arizona Center for Medieval and Renaissance Studies, Tempe, AR, 00. **CONTACT ADDRESS** Dept of Mod Lang, Catholic Univ of America, 7129 Maple Ave, Takoma Park, MD 20912. **EMAIL** ginsberg@cua.edu

GINSBURG, MICHAL P.
DISCIPLINE FRENCH **EDUCATION** Yale Univ, PhD. **CAREER** Prof and ch, Northwestern Univ; co-dir, Interdisciplinary Group on Fr Culture Soc; co-organizor, Narrative Int Conf; past fel, Wissenschaftskolleg, Berlin; former dir, Program in Comparative Lit and Theory; ed bd, Comp Lit Studies. **HONORS AND AWARDS** Lect, Am Comp Lit Asn conf; Int Soc for the Study European Ideas ,Utrecht; Dickens conf, Dijon. **RESEARCH** 19th-century novel in France and England; contemporary theory. **SELECTED PUBLICATIONS** Auth, Flaubert Writing: A Study of Narrative Strategies, Stanford Univ Press, 86; Economics of Change: Form and Trans- formation in the Nineteenth-Century Novel, Stanford Univ Press, 96; Framing Narrative, Poetics Today, 97; La Tentation du biographique, Gustave Flaubert: Intersections. **CONTACT ADDRESS** Dept of French, Northwestern Univ, 1859 Sheridan Rd, Evanston, IL 60208. **EMAIL** m-ginsburg@northwestern.edu

GIRALDEZ, SUSAN C.
PERSONAL m, 1986, 2 children **DISCIPLINE** HISPANIC LANGUAGE, LITERATURE **EDUCATION** Univ Pac, BA; Middlebury Col, MA; Univ Calif Santa Barb, PhD. **CAREER** Lectr, Univ Calif Berkeley, 91-93; assoc prof, Univ Pac, 93-. **MEMBERSHIPS** MLA; ACTFL. **RESEARCH** Chivalric novel; 15th-17th-century Spanish literature. **SELECTED PUBLICATIONS** Auth, Las Sergas de Esplandian y la Espana de Los Reyes, Peter Lang, 01. **CONTACT ADDRESS** Hisp Lang Dept, Univ of the Pacific, Stockton, 3601 Pacific Ave, Stockton, CA 95211. **EMAIL** sgiralde@uop.edu

GIRO, JORGE A.
PERSONAL Born 10/21/1933, Havana, Cuba, m, 1961, 2 children **DISCIPLINE** SPANISH **EDUCATION** Jose Marti Univ, LLB/PhD, 57; Ind State Univ, BA, 63, MS, 64. **CAREER** Full prof to chemn, Towson Univ, 66-. **CONTACT ADDRESS** Dept of Mod Langs, Towson State Univ, Towson, MD 21252. **EMAIL** jgiro@towson.edu

GITTLEMAN, SOL
PERSONAL Born 06/05/1934, Hoboken, NJ, m, 1956, 3 children **DISCIPLINE** GERMAN, COMPARATIVE LITERATURE **EDUCATION** Drew Univ, MA, 55; Columbia Univ, AB, 56; Univ Mich, 61. **CAREER** From instr to asst prof Ger, Univ Mich, 59-64; from asst prof to assoc prof & chemn dept, 64-72, Prof Ger, Tufts Univ, 72-, Sr Vpres & Provost, Tufts Univ; Consult & reviewer, Choice, 63-. **HONORS AND AWARDS** Harbison Awd for Gifted Teaching, Danforth Found, 71; hon degrees, Dr. Humane Letters, Hebrew Col, 95, Stonehill Col, 96. **MEMBERSHIPS** Am Asn Teachers Ger; MLA. **RESEARCH** Anglo-German literary relations in 19th century; German expressionism; works of Frank Wedekind. **SELECTED PUBLICATIONS** Auth, John Hay as a critic, Victorian Newsletter, autumn 63; Image of America in Wedekind, Ger Quart, 3/66; Wedekind and Brecht: A literary relationship, Mod Drama, 2/68; Frank Wedekind, Twayne, 68; Sholom Aleichem: A Non-Critical Introduction to His Works, Mouton, 74; Thomas Mann and the Jews: A final word, Dayton Univ Rev, spring 76; Sternheim and Wedekind, Ger Quart, 1/76; Shtetl to Suberbia: The Family In Jewish Literary Imagination, Beacon, 78. **CONTACT ADDRESS** Office of the Provost, Tufts Univ, Medford, Medford, MA 02155. **EMAIL** sol.gittleman@tufts.edu

GLADE, HENRY
PERSONAL Born 10/08/1920, Germany, m, 1958 **DISCIPLINE** GERMAN, RUSSIAN **EDUCATION** Elizabethtown Col, AB, 42; Univ Pa, MA, 48, PhD(Ger), 58. **CAREER** Prof mod lang, Hershey Jr Col, 50-53; instr Ger, Bates Col, 53-54; asst prof French and Ger, 54-55, assoc prof Ger, 55-62, Prof Ger and Russ, Manchester Col, 62-, Chmn Dept Mod Lang, 67-, Sr Fulbright fel and Int Res and Exchanges Bd grant, sr exchange scholar, Gorky Inst World Lit, 70-71; Am Philos Soc grant res Moscow, 72; vis prof, Slavisches Inst der Univ zu Koln, 79-80. **MEMBERSHIPS** MLA; Am Asn Teachers Slavic & Europ Lang; Am Asn Teachers Ger. **RESEARCH** Modern German drama; Soviet-German literary relations. **SELECTED PUBLICATIONS** Auth, Der Engel Schwieg, World Lit Today, Vol 0068, 94; Gegen Die Laufrichtung, World Lit Today, Vol 0069, 1995; The Russian-German Literary Exchange in the Postcommunist Era, 1992-1995, Germano-Slavica, Vol 0009, 96; Hope is Like a Wild Animal--Correspondence 1945-1953, World Lit Today, Vol 0070, 96. **CONTACT ADDRESS** Manchester Col, Box 36, North Manchester, IN 46962.

GLADNEY, FRANK Y.
PERSONAL Born 01/20/1936, Mt. Vernon, NY, m, 1958, 3 children **DISCIPLINE** SLAVIC LANGUAGES **EDUCATION** Harvard Univ, AB, 57, AM, 59, PhD(Slavic Lang & Lit), 66. **CAREER** Assoc Prof Slavic Lang, Univ Ill, Urbana-Champaign, 63-, Ed Slavic & E Europ J, 7O-75. **MEMBERSHIPS** Am Asn Teachers Slavic & E Europ Lang; Am Asn Advan Slavic Studies; Ling Soc Am. **RESEARCH** Russian, Polish and Czech grammar. **SELECTED PUBLICATIONS** Auth, Item and process in Russian verbal inflection, In: American Contributions to the VIII International Congress of Slavists, 78; auth, Handbook of Polish, 83. **CONTACT ADDRESS** Dept of Slavic Lang & Lit, Univ of Illinois, Urbana-Champaign, 707 S Mathews Ave, Urbana, IL 61801-3625. **EMAIL** gladney@uiuc.edu

GLATZ, LAWRENCE F.
PERSONAL Born 05/03/1961, Pittsburgh, PA **DISCIPLINE** GERMAN LANGUAGES AND LITERATURES **EDUCATION** Univ Pa, BA, 84; Penn State Univ, MA, 88, PhD, 95. **CAREER** Asst prof of German, Metropolitan State Col of Denver, 96-. **HONORS AND AWARDS** BA with honors, Univ Pa, 84; DAAD/German Academic Exchange Service Scholarship, 91-92. **MEMBERSHIPS** AATG, MLA, IALLT, ACTFL, AAUP. **RESEARCH** Postwar German literature, German culture, language pedagogy, computers in education. **SELECTED PUBLICATIONS** Auth, Heinrich Boll als Moralist, Peter Lang, New York (99). **CONTACT ADDRESS** Dept Modern Langs, Metropolitan State Col of Denver, PO Box 173362, Denver, CO 80217-3362. **EMAIL** glatz@mscd.edu

GLEASON, MAUDE
DISCIPLINE CLASSICS **EDUCATION** BA, 75; Oxford Univ, MA, 77; Univ CA Berkeley, PhD, 90. **CAREER** Lctr, Stanford Univ. **RESEARCH** Relig and soc in Late Antiquity and the High Empire; rhetoric; gender. **SELECTED PUBLICATIONS** Auth, Festive Satire: Julian's Misopogon and the New Year at Antioch, JRS, 86; The Semiotics of Gender: Physiognomy and Self-Fashioning in Before Sexuality, 90; Making Men: Sophists and Self-Presentation in the Roman Empire, 95. **CONTACT ADDRESS** Stanford Univ, Bldg 20, Main Quad, Stanford, CA 94305.

GLEASON, MICHAEL
PERSONAL Born 11/02/1958, Camden, NJ, m, 1991, 2 children **DISCIPLINE** COMPARATIVE LITERATURE **EDUCATION** Brown Univ, PhD. **CAREER** Dept Classics, Millsaps Col **SELECTED PUBLICATIONS** Publ on, medieval Latin. **CONTACT ADDRESS** Dept of Classics, Millsaps Col, 1701 N State St, PO Box 150174, Jackson, MS 39210. **EMAIL** gleasm@okra.millsaps.edu

GLEAVES, ROBERT MILNOR
PERSONAL Born 03/18/1938, Nashville, TN, m, 1964, 2 children **DISCIPLINE** SPANISH LANGUAGE, SPANISH AMERICAN LITERATURE **EDUCATION** David Lipscomb Col, BA, 60; Vanderbilt Univ, MA, 63, PhD(Span), 68. **CAREER** From instr to asst prof Span, Univ SFla, 65-69; asst prof, 69-72, Assoc Prof Span, Univ NC, Charlotte, 72-. **MEMBERSHIPS** Am Asn Teachers Span & Port; Int Inst Iberoam Lit; SAtlantic Mod Lang Asn. **RESEARCH** Contemporary Spanish-American prose fiction; Spanish-American poetry. **SELECTED PUBLICATIONS** Auth, The Reaffirmation of Analogy, an Introduction to Carreraandrade, Jorge Metaphoric System, Confluencia-Rev Hispanica de Cult y Lit, Vol 0010, 94. **CONTACT ADDRESS** Dept of Foreign Lang, Univ of No Carolina, Charlotte, 9201 University City, Charlotte, NC 28223-0002.

GLENN, JERRY
PERSONAL Born 09/05/1938, Little Rock, AR **DISCIPLINE** GERMAN **EDUCATION** Yale Univ, BA, 60; Univ Tex, MA, 62, PhD(Ger), 64. **CAREER** Asst prof Ger, Univ Wis-Milwaukee, 64-67; from asst prof to assoc prof, 67-72, dir hon prog, 77-79, Prof Ger, Univ Cincinnati, 72-, Head Dept, 80-. **MEMBERSHIPS** MLA; Am Asn Teachers Ger; Am Lessing Soc (secy-treas, 68-74); Am Lit Transl Asn; Mid-E Hons Asn (pres, 79-80). **RESEARCH** German lyric, literature and classics. **SELECTED PUBLICATIONS CONTACT ADDRESS** Dept of Ger, Univ of Cincinnati, P O Box 210372, Cincinnati, OH 45221-0372.

GLENN, JUSTIN MATTHEWS
PERSONAL Born 04/10/1945, Little Rock, AR, d, 1971, 2 children **DISCIPLINE** GREEK & LATIN LITERATURE **EDUCATION** Stanford Univ, BA, 67; Princeton Univ, MA, 69, PhD(classics), 70. **CAREER** Asst prof Classics, Univ Ga, 70-72; asst prof, 72-76, from assoc prof to prof Classics, Fla State Univ, 76-82; vice pres Classical Assoc of Fla, 85-87. **HONORS AND AWARDS** Teacher of the Year, Classical Assoc of Fla, 92. **MEMBERSHIPS** Class Asn Mid W & S. **RESEARCH** Classical mythology; psychoanalytic criticism; Greek and Latin poetry. **SELECTED PUBLICATIONS** Auth, Mezentius and Polyphemus, Am J Philol, 71; The Polyphemus folktale, Trans Am Philol Asn, 71; Psychoanalytic writings on Greek and Latin authors, Class World, 72; Virgil's Polyphemus, Greece & Rome, 72; Psychoananlytic writings on classical mythology and religion, Classical World, 76-77. **CONTACT ADDRESS** Dept of Classics, Florida State Univ, 205 Dodd Hall, Tallahassee, FL 32306-1510. **EMAIL** jglenn@mailer.fsu.edu

GLENN, KATHLEEN MARY
PERSONAL Born 06/12/1936, Exeter, CA **DISCIPLINE** SPANISH LITERATURE **EDUCATION** Stanford Univ, BA, 57, MA, 61, PhD(Span), 70; Univ Madrid, dipl Hisp studies, 59. **CAREER** Instr, Univ Victoria, 64-66; instr, Col San Mateo, 67-69; asst prof, Univ Santa Clara, 69-73 and Kans State Univ, 73-74; Assoc Prof Span, Wake Forest Uvin, 74-, Assoc Ed, Anales De La Literature Espanola Contemporaries, 76-. **MEMBERSHIPS** MLA; Am Asn Teachers Span & Port; S Cent Mod Lang Asn; SAtlantic Mod Lang Asn; Asn Lit Femenina Hisp. **RESEARCH** Twentieth century Spanish novel; 20th century Spanish theater. **SELECTED PUBLICATIONS CONTACT ADDRESS** Dept of Romance Lang, Wake Forest Univ, Winston-Salem, NC 27109.

GLINERT, LEWIS
DISCIPLINE ASIAN AND MIDDLE EASTERN LANGUAGES AND LITERATURES **EDUCATION** Oxford Univ, BA; Univ London, PhD. **CAREER** Fac Schl Oriental and African Studies, Univ London; vis assoc prof Hebrew, Univ Chicago; asst prof Linguistics, Haifa and Bar-Ilan Univ; prof, Dartmouth Col. **HONORS AND AWARDS** Int Adv Bd, Israel Ctr Lang Policy. **MEMBERSHIPS** Int Advisory Bd to Israel Ctr for Lang Policy. **RESEARCH** Cult and linguistics of Israeli and Jewish soc in lang policy and in tech and safety discourse. **SELECTED PUBLICATIONS** Auth, The Grammar of Modern Hebrew; The Joys of Hebrew; Hebrew in Ashkenaz: A Language in Exile; Mamme Dear: A Turn-of-the-Century Collection of Model Yiddish Letters; Product Safety Information and Language Policy in an Advanced Third World Economy; We Never Changed our Language: Attitudes of Hasidic Educators to Yiddish Language Acquisition; BBC documentaries: Tongue of Tongues: The Rebirth of Hebrew and Golem: The Making of a Modern Myth. **CONTACT ADDRESS** Dartmouth Col, 6161 Bartlett Hall, Hanover, NH 03755. **EMAIL** lewis.glinert@dartmouth.edu

GLON, DANIEL
PERSONAL Born 04/07/1950, Rennes, France, m, 1983, 4 children **DISCIPLINE** INTERPRETATION, TRANSLATION, LINGUISTICS **EDUCATION** Univ Saarbrucken, BA; ESIT, Interpreter's Diploma; Translator's Diploma; Univ Provence, PhD. **CAREER** Confr interpreter, Govt of Canada, 75 & 76; confr interpreter, European Comn, 77-79; chief interpreter and terminologist, Aerospatiale, 79-83; prof, 83-00; founder & dir, Armell Int, Inc., 92-00; sr transl, Atlanta Olympic Games, 96; transl mgr, Salt Lake City Games, 00-02. **MEMBERSHIPS** Int Confr Interpreter Asn; Asn Int Des Ling Olympiques Et Sportifs. **RESEARCH** Computer Aided Translation, Sports Lingo and Terminology. **SELECTED PUBLICATIONS** Auth, Language International 2.4. **CONTACT ADDRESS** Transl, Monterey Inst of Intl Studies, 425 Van Buren St, Monterey, CA 93940-2623. **EMAIL** danglon@pacwan.fr

GLOWACKI, KEVIN T.
DISCIPLINE CLASSICAL STUDIES **EDUCATION** Loyola Univ, AB, 83, MA, 85; Bryn Mawr Col, MA, 87, PhD, 91. **CAREER** Asst prof, Indiana Univ-Bloom. **RESEARCH** Greek art and archaeology; Greek sculpture; topography & monuments of Athens; Aegean Bronze & Iron Ages; mythological representation in art. **SELECTED PUBLICATIONS** Auth, A New Fragment of the Erechtheion Frieze, Hesperia, 95; The Acropolis of Athens before 566 B.C, Univ Pa, 97. **CONTACT ADDRESS** Dept of Classical Studies, Indiana Univ, Bloomington, 547 Ballatine Hall, 1020 E Kirkwood Ave, Bloomington, IN 47405. **EMAIL** kglowack@indiana.edu

GLOWKA, ARTHUR WAYNE
PERSONAL Born 03/18/1952, Weimar, TX, m, 1992, 2 children **DISCIPLINE** MEDIEVAL LITERATURE, ENGLISH LINGUISTICS **EDUCATION** Univ Tex, BA, 73, MA, 75; Univ Del, PhD, 80. **CAREER** From asst prof to prof, Ga Col, 80-. **HONORS AND AWARDS** Fulbright-Hays, 89; Excellence in Res/Publ Award, Ga Col Found, 92; Post-Tenure Rev Fac Dev Award, Univ System of Ga, 99. **MEMBERSHIPS** S Atlantic Mod Lang Asn; New Chaucer Soc; Am Dialect Soc; Dictionary Soc of N Am. **RESEARCH** Prosody; history of the English language; neology; medieval literature. **SELECTED PUBLICATIONS** Auth, Yachtjacking, Boatnapping, or Getting Seajacked by Ship-jackers, Am Speech 62, 87; A Simplified Model of Language Variation and Change: A History of the Bot People, Glowka and Lance; A Guide to Chaucer's Meter, Univ Press of Am, 91; co-ed, Language Variation in North American English: Research and Teaching, MLA, 93; auth, The Poetics of Layamon's Brut, In: Text and Tradition in Layamon's Brut, Arthurian Studies 33, 94; Lawman and the Sabellian Heresy, Int J for the Semiotics of Law 8.24, 95; Layamon's Heathens and the Medieval Grapevine, In: Literacy and Orality in Early Middle English Literature, ScriptOralia 83, 96; coauth, Among the New Words, Am Speech 72, Fall and Winter 97. **CONTACT ADDRESS** Dept of English & Speech, Georgia Col, Milledgeville, GA 31061-0490. **EMAIL** wglowka@mail.gcsu.edu

GOBERT, DAVID LAWRENCE
PERSONAL Born 10/18/1932, Decatur, IL, m, 1956, 5 children **DISCIPLINE** FRENCH LANGUAGE AND LITERATURE **EDUCATION** Millikin Univ, BA, 54; State Univ Iowa, MA, 56, PhD(Fr), 60; Chambre de Commerce et de'Industire de Paris, Diplome Superieur Francais des Affaires, 89. **CAREER** Asst prof French and Span, Coe Col, 58-61, assoc prof French, 62-65, actg chmn dept foreign lang, 64-65; assoc prof, 65-70, asst dean, col lib arts and sci, 68-70, assoc dean humanities, 71-74, Prof French, Southern Ill Univ, 71-, Admin intern, Am Coun Educ, Syracuse Univ, 69-70; French reader, Educ Testing Serv, 77-78. **HONORS AND AWARDS** Minisabbatical grant: "stage" in commercial French, 80; Minisabbatical grant: Purdue Univ, 82; Teaching Inprovement grant in commercial French, 86; Title VI, USED Grant, 88; Outstanding Teacher Awd, COLA, 88; SIU Sphinx Club, 91; CIBER Grant, Seminar, Bus Lang Texts, 91; CIBER Grant, ESC Grenoble, 92; CIBER Grant, Seminar, Internships Abroad, 92; CIBER Grant, Internships Abroad, 93; Illinois Lt. Governor's Awd, Outstanding Serv in prof, 94. **MEMBERSHIPS** Modern Lang Asn (MLA), 75-76; Am Asn of Teachers of French, 87-; Illinois Foreign Lang Teachers Asn, 87-; Club Francais d'Amerique, 84; Amis D'Edith Piaf, 88-92; Assoc, Int Correspondence Network, 92. **RESEARCH** Textbooks, French language, culture, business; 19th and 20th century French novel and short story; Voltaire and 18th century French literature; Classical popular French music, 20th century; Translations: English to French; French to English. **SELECTED PUBLICATIONS** Auth, Oudot and Gobert, Conversational French, National Textbook Company, 88; auth, Oudot and Godert, La France: Culture, Economie, Commerce - An Introduction to Business French, Houghton-Mifflin, 83; rev, "Valeurs modales du futur et du conditionnel et leurs emplois en francais contemporain," with V. Maisier, French Rev, Vol 68, No 6, (95): 1003-1014; auth, "The Essential Character in Queneau's Zazie dans le Metro, "Symposium, Vol 40, No 2, (86): 91-106; auth, "Merimee Revisited," Symposium, Vol 26, No 2, (72): 128-46; rev, "Des Reflects du beylisme dans la sturcture episodique du Rouge," French Rev, Vol 43, No 4, (70): 426-33; auth, "Identity in Diversity: Montherlant;s Celles qu'on prend dans ses bras' and 'La Ville don't le prince est un enfant," Symposium, Vol 22, No 1, (67): 22-28; auth, "Tense Variation in Complex Hypothetical Utterances in Contemporary French Speech," Iowa Philological Quarterly, Vol 45, No 2, (66): 464-68; auth, "Aspective Agreement between Verbs and Conjunctions in French, Language Learning, Vol 15, No 3 and 4, (65): 111-14; auth, "Comic in Micromegas as Expressive of Theme," Studies on Voltaire and the 18th Century, Vol 37, (65): 53-60. **CONTACT ADDRESS** Dept of Foreign Lang, So Illinois Univ, Carbondale, Faner Hall, Carbondale, IL 62901. **EMAIL** dfll1@siu.edu

GODFREY, AARON W.
PERSONAL Born 01/10/1929, New York, NY, m, 1981, 7 children **DISCIPLINE** CLASSICS **EDUCATION** Fordham Univ, BA, 58; Hunter Col, MA, 60. **CAREER** Asst Latin-Am rels, Grace Nat Bank, 52-60; instr lang, Newton Col Sacred Heart, 60-61, asst prof hist and class lang, 61-65; dir spec proj, 65-74, Dir Upware Bound Proj, State Univ NY Stony Brook, 66-, Lectr Classics, 67-, Consult, State Educ Dept NY, 67-73; Secy-Treas, Nat Coord Coun Educ Opportunity, 70-, ed, Review; consult, Esea Title I, New York Schs, 70-72. **MEMBERSHIPS** AHA; Medieval Acad Am; Liturgical Arts Soc; Class Asn Atlantic States; Asn Equality & Excellence Educ (secy, 77-). **RESEARCH** Ancient and medieval history; compensatory education; classical and medieval Latin. **SELECTED PUBLICATIONS** Auth, Catalogus-Translationum-Et-Commentariorum, Vol 7, Medieval and Renaissance Latin Translations and Commentaries, Class World, Vol 0087, 94; Theodoric in Italy, Class World, Vol 0088, 95; Suetonius 'De Grammaticis Et Rhetoribus,' Class World, Vol 0090, 97. **CONTACT ADDRESS** SUNY, Stony Brook, Stony Brook, NY 11794-3359.

GODFREY, GARY M.
PERSONAL Born 08/29/1942, Ogden, UT, m, 1967, 4 children **DISCIPLINE** FRENCH **EDUCATION** Weber State Univ, BA, 67; Univ Wash, MA, 69; PhD, 74. **CAREER** Grad asst, Univ Wash, 68-72; asst prof, Southwest Mo State Univ, 72-75; assoc prof, St Mary-of-the-Woods Col, 76-85; prof, Weber State Univ, 85-. **HONORS AND AWARDS** NEH, Princeton Univ; NEH, Univ Pittsburgh; Best Paper, Ut Acad, 93; Fulbright Teacher Exchange Awd. **MEMBERSHIPS** MLA, Am Asn of Teachers of French. **RESEARCH** French Literature, Nineteenth-Century French Literature. **SELECTED PUBLICATIONS** Auth, "Balzac's La Peau de chagrin: A Dantesque Reading," Enclycia (93); auth, "Animal Symbolism and the Language of Transformation in Heptameron 70," Encyclia (in press). **CONTACT ADDRESS** Dept For Lang, Weber State Univ, 1403 University Cr, Ogden, UT 84408-1403. **EMAIL** ggodfrey@weber.edu

GODIN, JEAN CLEO
PERSONAL Born 08/13/1936, Petit-Rocher, NB, Canada, m, 1963, 4 children **DISCIPLINE** FRENCH AND QUEBEC LITERATURE **EDUCATION** Boston Col, BA, 61; Univ Montreal, Lic es Lett, 64; Aix-Marseille, D Univ, 66. **CAREER** Chmn dept French studies, 74-77, Prof Lit, Univ Montreal, 66-, Mem jury Coun Arts, Gov Gen Prize, 71-73. **MEMBERSHIPS** Asn Can Univ Teachers Fr; MLA; Can Lit Asn; Asn Can Theatre Hist. **RESEARCH** French novel of the 19th and 20th centuries; theatre Quebecois. **SELECTED PUBLICATIONS** Auth, Julien Daoust: Dramaturge 1866-1943, Theater Hist in Can vol 4 no 2, fall (83): 113; auth, Alain Grandbois et le theatre, Theater Hist in Can vol 7 no 2, fall (86): 149; auth, Dramaturgies quebecoises des annes quatre-vingt, Lemeac, (Montreal, QC), 99. **CONTACT ADDRESS** Dept of French Studies, Univ of Montreal, CP 6128, Succ Centre-ville CP 6128, SUCC. Centre-ville, Montreal, QC, Canada H3C 3J7. **EMAIL** jeancleo@sympatico.ca

GODSALL-MYERS, JEAN
PERSONAL Born 05/26/1951, Bryn Mawr, PA, m, 1973, 2 children **DISCIPLINE** GERMAN LITERATURE **EDUCATION** Smith Col, BA, 73; Univ Mich, MA, 76; Bryn Mawr Col, PhD, 81. **CAREER** From Asst Prof to Prof, Widener Univ, 82-. **HONORS AND AWARDS** Fulbright Fel, 83; CIEE Fel, 91; A&S Fac Awd for Teaching Excellence, 96; Phi Kappa Phi, 99. **MEMBERSHIPS** AATG, GSA, IAS, ICLS, MLA. **RESEARCH** Discourse analysis in medieval and modern German literature. **SELECTED PUBLICATIONS** Rev, "Anna Seghers im Exil," by Alexander Stephan, Colloquia Germanica 27 (94): 298-299; rev "Women Writers and Fascism," by Marie-Luise Gattens, Col Lit 25.2 (98): 208-209; auth, "Anna Seghers' Craft and Kraft," Pa For Lang Conf 1991-1992 (Pittsburgh, PA: Duquesne Univ Pr, 95), 109-115; auth, "Enite's Loss of Voice When She Speaks from the Heart," Speculum Medii Aevi 2-3 (96): 57-67; auth, "The Seventh Cross and 'Das siebte Kreuz': More Betrayal or Loyalty to Higher Ideals?" Annual of For Films and Lit IV (98): 61-73. **CONTACT ADDRESS** Dept Humanities, Widener Univ, Pennsylvania, 1 University Pl, Chester, PA 19013. **EMAIL** jean.e.godsall-myers@widener.edu

GOETSCHEL, WILLI
PERSONAL Born 03/13/1958, Zurich, Switzerland, m, 1998, 1 child **DISCIPLINE** GERMAN **EDUCATION** Univ Zurich, MPhil, 82; Harvard Univ, PhD, 89. **CAREER** Instructor, Harvard Univ, 88-89; Visiting Asst Prof, Bard Col, 89-91; Asst

Prof to Assoc Prof, Columbia Univ, 91-00; Prof, Stanford Univ, 00-. **HONORS AND AWARDS** Alexander von Humboldt Fel, 96-97; Andrew W. Mellon Fel, Stanford Univ, 00-01. **MEMBERSHIPS** MLA; Lessing Soc. **RESEARCH** German Intellectual History; German-Jewish Culture. **SELECTED PUBLICATIONS** Auth, Kant als schriftsteller, Wien, 90; Ed, Perspektiven der dialogik. Zurcher Kolloquium zu Ehren von Hermann Levin Goldschmidt, Vienna, 94; auth, Constituting Critique: Kant's Writing as Critical Praxis, Duke Univ Press, 94; co-ed, Gershom Scholem. Special Issue, 97; co-ed, Heinrich Heine's Jewish Con/Texts. Special Issue, 99; ed, Moses Mendelssohn, jerusalem oder uber religiose Macht und Jedentum, Hamburg, forthcoming; auth, Spinoza's Modernity: Mendelssoh, Lessing, heine, forthcoming. **CONTACT ADDRESS** Dept German Studies, Stanford Univ, Pigott Hall, Bldg 260, Stanford, CA 94305-2030.

GOETZ, THOMAS HENRY
PERSONAL Born 02/09/1936, Philadelphia, PA, m, 1970, 1 child **DISCIPLINE** FRENCH LITERATURE **EDUCATION** La Salle Col, BA, 61; Syracuse Univ, MA, 63, PhD, 67. **CAREER** Asst prof French, Ill Wesleyan Univ, 66-67; from asst prof to prof, 67-91, Distinguished Service prof French, State Univ NY Col Fredonia, 91-, chmn, Dept Foreign Lang & Lit, 79-89; ed, Nineteenth-Century Fr Studies, 72-; consult, La Bd Regents, 82. **HONORS AND AWARDS** Chevalier, Ordre des Palmes Academiques, 81; NEH fel, 77, 79, 84, 87, 88; Chevalier, 81, Officier, 89, Ordre des Palmes Academiques; NY State UUP Excellence Awd. **MEMBERSHIPS** MLA; Am Asn Teachers Fr; Soc Etudes Romantiques; Asn de l'Ordre des Palmes Academiques; Am Soc de l'Ordre des Palmes Academiques. **RESEARCH** Nineteenth-century French literature; Hippolyte Taine. **SELECTED PUBLICATIONS** Auth, Taine and the Fine Arts, Ed Playor, 73; Poetry and Civilization: An Essay on the Humanities and the Human Condition, in Studies in the Humanities, Indiana Univ, Pa, 6/73; A Partially Unpublished Taine Letter, Romance Notes, 73; Poe and Taine: A Neglected French Critic, Poe Studies, 73; transl, The Defeat of the Armouchiquois Savages, Nat Museum of Man Mercury Ser, Can, 75; Paul Bourget's Le Disciple and the Text-Reader Relationship, Fr Rev, 78; auth, Edmond Louis Antoine and Jules Alfred Huot de Goncourt, in European Writers, The Romantic Century, Charles Scriber's, 85; The Uses of Translation: French Literature in 19th Century America, Laurels, 86; ed, articles on 19th-century French authors for the World Book Encycl, 89-90; auth, section on Goncourt brothers, in A Critical Bibliography of French Literature, Syracuse Univ Press, 94. **CONTACT ADDRESS** SUNY, Col at Fredonia, 1 Suny at Fredonia, Fredonia, NY 14063-1143. **EMAIL** goetz@ait.fredonia.edu

GOETZ-STANKIEWICZ, MARKETA
PERSONAL Born 02/15/1927, Liberec, Czechoslovakia **DISCIPLINE** GERMANIC STUDIES **EDUCATION** Univ Toronto, BA, 54, MA, 55, PhD, 57. **CAREER** Instr to prof, 57-92, dept head, 80-85, Prof Emer Germanic Stud, Univ British Columbia, 92-. **HONORS AND AWARDS** UBC Cert Merit Excellence Tchg, 72, 92; Ordo Libri Bohemici, 88; Boeschenstein Medal, Can Asn Univ Tchrs Ger, 92; Hlavka Medal, Czech Acad Sci, 92. **MEMBERSHIPS** Ed bd, Seminar, 65-70; ed comt, Can Rev Comp Lit, 75-. **SELECTED PUBLICATIONS** Auth, The Silenced Theatre: Czech Playwrights Without A Stage, 79; ed, The Filter of Translation, 80; ed, Drama contemporary: Czechoslovakia, 85; ed, The Vanek Plays: Four Authors, One Character, 87; ed, Good-Bye, Samizdat: Twenty years of Czechoslovak Underground Writing, 92; co-ed, "Critical Essays on Vaclav Havel (with introduction)," New York: G.K. Halll, 99. **CONTACT ADDRESS** Dept of Germanic Stud, Univ of British Columbia, Vancouver, BC, Canada V6T 1Z1. **EMAIL** marketa@interchange.ubc.ca

GOFF, BARBARA E.
PERSONAL Born 01/23/1958, London, England, m, 1989, 1 child **DISCIPLINE** CLASSICS **EDUCATION** Berkeley, PhD, 85. **CAREER** Jr Res fel, Kings Col Cambridge, 86-90; Asst prof, 91-98, Assoc Prpf, Univ Texas-Austin, 98- . **MEMBERSHIPS** APA **RESEARCH** Greek tradegy; women in antiquity. **SELECTED PUBLICATIONS** Auth, Euripedes Ion, 88; The Tent, PCPS, 88; The shields of the Phoenissae, GRBS, 88; The Noose of Words: readings of desire, violence and language in Euripide's Hippolytos, Cambridge Univ Press, 90; The sign of the fall: the scars of Orestes and Odysseus, CA, 91; rev Synnove des Bouvrie, Women in Greek Tragedy, AJP, 92; rev, Ruth Padel, In and Out of the Mide, CPhil, 94; auth, Aithra at Eleusis, Helios, 95; The Women of Thebes, CJ, 95; The Figure of Antiquity in the Memoirs of Mme Roland: the classical, the revolutionary, and the feminine, CML, 96. **CONTACT ADDRESS** Classics Dept, Univ of Texas, Austin, Waggener Hall 123, Austin, TX 78712-1181.

GOHEEN, JUTTA
PERSONAL Born 06/29/1935, Zwickau, Germany, m, 1965 **DISCIPLINE** GERMAN **EDUCATION** Padagogische Hochsch Potsdam, Staatsexamen, 56, PhD(Ger), 57; Univ Bonn, Staatsexamen(English), 61. **CAREER** Asst Ger, Padagogische Hochsch Potsdam, 56-58; lectr, McMaster Univ, 63-64, asst prof, 64-65; asst prof, 65-68, assoc prof, 68-81, Prof Ger, Carleton Univ, 81-. **RESEARCH** Medieval literature: linguistic stylistics; language as means of manipulation. **SELECTED PUBLICATIONS** Auth, Mensch und Moral im Mittelalter: Geschichte und Fiktion in Hugo von Trimbergs "Der Renner", by Jutta Goheen; auth, Mittelalterliche Liebeslyrik von Neidhart von Reuental bis zu Oswald von Wolkenstein: eine Stilkritik, by Jutta Goheen. **CONTACT ADDRESS** Dept of Ger, Carleton Univ, 1125 Colonel By Dr, Ottawa, ON, Canada K1S 5B6. **EMAIL** jutta_goheen@carleton.ca

GOIC, CEDOMIL
PERSONAL Born 03/03/1928, Antofagasta, Chile, m, 1956, 5 children **DISCIPLINE** SPANISH AMERICAN AND CHILEAN LITERATURE **EDUCATION** Univ Chile, Santiago, Profesorde Estado, 53, Dr en Filos(Romance philol), 65. **CAREER** Prof, Dept Span, Univ Chile, 55-76; Prof Span Am Lit, Dept Romance Lang, Univ Mich, 76-, Vis prof Span Am lit, Dept Romance Lang, Univ Tex, Austin, 65-67 and Dept Span and Port, Univ Wis, 67-68; res evaluator humanities, Nat Comn Sci Invest, 71 and Cath Univ Chile, 75. **MEMBERSHIPS** Int Inst Iberoam Lit; MLA; Asoc Int Hispanistas. **RESEARCH** Spanish American novel; Spanish American poetry; Spanish American colonial literature. **SELECTED PUBLICATIONS** Auth, Huidobro, Vicente, an Analysis of the Poems El 'Espejo de Agua' and 'Ano Nuevo,' Rev Iberoamericana, Vol 0060, 94. **CONTACT ADDRESS** Dept of Romance Lang, Univ of Michigan, Ann Arbor, 812 E Washington St, Ann Arbor, MI 48109-1275.

GOINS, SCOTT
PERSONAL Born 05/02/1961, Cleveland, TN, s **DISCIPLINE** CLASSICS **EDUCATION** Univ Tenn, BA, 83; Fla State Univ, MA, 85, PhD, 88. **CAREER** Vis asst Prof, Classics, Univ of South, 88-89; asst prof, 89-95, assoc prof & asst dept head dept of languages, 95-, Mcneese State Univ, 89-; ed, McNeese Rev. **MEMBERSHIPS** Amer Philol Asn; Class Asn Midwst & S; La Class Asn; Class Asn Can. **RESEARCH** Virgil; Boethius; Fable; Greek drama. **SELECTED PUBLICATIONS** Auth, Penelope and Melantho: A Question of Jealousy in Odyssey 19?, Class Bull, 87;Horace, sermo 1.5.61, Latomus, 87; The Influence of Old Comedy on the Vita Aesopi, Class World, 89; Euripides Fr 863 Nauck, Rheinisches Museum fur Philologie, 89; The Heroism of Odysseus in Euripides, Cyclops Eos, 91; Birds and Erotic Fantasies in Catullus and Goethe, Goethe Yearbook, 92; Two Aspects of Virgils Use of Labor in the Aeneid, Class Jour, 93; Pain and Authority in the Aeneid and Henry V, Class and Modern Lit, 95; The Date of Aeschylus Perseus Tetralogy, Rheinisches Museum fur Philol, 97; The Poetics in the Mythology Syllabus: Nothing to do with Dionysus, Class Bull, 97. **CONTACT ADDRESS** Dept of Languages, McNeese State Univ, Box 93465, Lake Charles, LA 70609-2655. **EMAIL** sgoins@mcneese.edu

GOLB, NORMAN
PERSONAL Born 01/15/1928, Chicago, IL, m, 1949, 3 children **DISCIPLINE** JEWISH HISTORY, HEBREW AND JUDEO-ARABIC STUDIES **EDUCATION** Roosevelt Col, BA, 48; Johns Hopkins Univ, PhD, 54. **CAREER** Warburg res fel Judaeo-Arabic studies, Hebrew Univ, Jerusalem, 55-57; vis lectr Semitic lang, Univ Wis, 57-58; from instr to asst prof Mediaeval Jewish studies, Hebrew Union Col, 58-63; from asst prof to prof Hebrew and Judeo-Arabic Studies, Univ Chicago, 63-88, Rosenberger Prof Jewish Hist and Civilization, 88-. **HONORS AND AWARDS** Adler res fel, Dropsie Col, 54-55; Am Philos Soc grants-in-aid, 59, 63 & 67; Am Coun Learned Soc grants-in-aid, 63 & 65; Guggenheim Mem Found fels, 64-65 & 66-67; vis fel, Clare Hall, Cambridge Univ, 70; Nat Endowment for Humanities grant, 70-72; Grand Medal of Honor of the City of Rouen, 85; Docteur Honoris Causa (Histoire), Univ of Rouen, 87; Medal of Haute Normandie, 87. **MEMBERSHIPS** Fel Am Acad Jewish Res; life mem, Clare Hall, Cambridge Univ, 80-; Soc de l'Histoire de France, 87-; Founder and vice-pres, Soc for Judeo-Arabic Studies, 84-. **RESEARCH** Jewish History, Hebrew and Judeo-Arabic Studies; Voting mem, Orient Inst, 61-. **SELECTED PUBLICATIONS** Auth, A Judaeo-Arabic Court Document of Syracuse, AD 1020, J Near Eastern Studies, 73; The Problem of Origin and Identification of the Dead Sea Scrolls, Proc Am Philos Soc, 80; Nature et destination du monument hebraique decouvert a Rouen, Proc Am Acad Jewish Res, 81; coauth (with Omeljan Pritsak), Khazarian Hebrew Documents of the Tenth Century, Cornell Univ Press, 82, trans to Russ, 97; auth, Les Juifs de Rouen au Moyen Age, Presses Univ de Rouen, 85; Who Wrote the Dead Sea Scrolls?, Scribner, 95, translated in Ger, Dutch, Port, Fr, Japanese; The Jews of Medieval Normandy, Cambridge Univ Press, 98; ed, Judeo-Arabic Studies, Harwood Acad Press, 97. **CONTACT ADDRESS** Univ of Chicago, Oriental Inst, 1155 E 58th St, Chicago, IL 60637-1540. **EMAIL** n-golb@uchicago.edu

GOLD, BARBARA K.
PERSONAL Born 03/23/1945, Brooklyn, NY, m, 1986, 1 child **DISCIPLINE** CLASSICS **EDUCATION** Univ Michigan, BA, 66; Univ N Carolina, Chapel Hill, MA, 68, PhD, 75. **CAREER** Lectr, actg asst prof, Univ Calif, Irvine, 71-75; asst prof, Univ Richmond, 76-77; asst prof, Univ Va, 77-78; asst prof classics and comp lit, Univ Texas, 78-86; assoc prof classics, women's stud, Santa Clara Univ, 86-89; assoc prof to prof, 89- , Leonard C Ferguson Prof of Class, 94-97, Prof of Classics and Assoc Dean; 97- , Hamilton Col. **HONORS AND AWARDS** NDEA Fel, 67-68; Mellon Fel, 79; Univ Res Inst sum fel, 79, 81; Univ Res Inst res grant, 79-83, 80, 84; Thomas Terry Awd, 88-89; NEH summer stipend, 92. **MEMBERSHIPS** Am Class League; Am Philol Asn; Archaeol Inst Am; Calif Class Asn; Class Asn of the Atlantic States; Class Asn of the Empire State; Class Asn of the Middle West and South; Philol Asn of the Pacific Coast. **RESEARCH** Greek and Roman literature; Roman elegy, lyric and satire; Pindar; Greek tragedy; Plato; comparative literature; women in antiquity. **SELECTED PUBLICATIONS** Ed, Literary and Artistic Patronage in Ancient Rome, Univ Texas, 82; auth, Literary Patronage in Greece and Rome, Univ North Carolina, 87; co-ed, Sex and Gender in Medieval and Renaissance Texts: The Latin Tradition, SUNY, 97; co-ed, Vile Bodies: Roman Satire and Corporeal Discourse, special issue Arethusa, 98. **CONTACT ADDRESS** Dept of Classics, Hamilton Col, New York, Clinton, NY 13323. **EMAIL** bgold@hamilton.edu

GOLDBERG, RITA MARIA
PERSONAL Born 10/01/1933, New York, NY **DISCIPLINE** SPANISH **EDUCATION** Queens Col, NYork, BA, 54; Middlebury Col, MA, 55; Brown Univ, PhD, 68. **CAREER** Lectr Span, Queens Col, NY, 56-57; from asst prof to prof, 57-71, Harriet Lewis prof mod lang, 71-75, chmn dept, 72-75, Charles A Dana Prof Mod Lang & Lit, St Lawrence Univ, 75-; Danforth Found grants, 60-61 & 63-64; Assoc Newman Alumni, NY fel, 63; chmn Regional Conf Am Prog in Spain, 71-72, 75-76 & 79-81. **HONORS AND AWARDS** Phi Betta Kappa; Sigma Delta Pi. **MEMBERSHIPS** MLA; Am Asn Teachers Span & Port; AAUP; ACT FL; NYSFLT. **RESEARCH** Romance; 17th century poetry and music; modern novel and theatre. **SELECTED PUBLICATIONS** Auth, Una nueva version manuscrita del romance de Lope De pechos sobre uan torre, Hisp Rev, 67; Un modo de subsistencia del romancero nuevo: romances de Gongora y Lope de Vega en bailes del Siglo de Oro, Bull Hisp, 70; Don Fernando Cortes, III Marques de Valle: su boda con dona Mencia de la Cerda y el inventario de bienes de 1602, 70 & Mas datos sobre Don Pedro Cortes, IV Marques del Valle de Oaxaca, 71, Bull Nat Arch Gen, Mex; La Familia de Calderon y la Calle de la Nao o Henao, ABC, Madrid, 9/74; The Impossible Dream of Integration, in Fornells and Cynthia: Ruiz-Fornells; The United States and the Spanish World, SGEL, Madrid, 79. **CONTACT ADDRESS** Dept of Mod Lang & Lit, St. Lawrence Univ, Canton, NY 13617-1499. **EMAIL** rgol@music.stlawu.edu

GOLDBERG, SANDER M.
DISCIPLINE CLASSICS **EDUCATION** Univ Rochester, 66-70, BA, 70; Univ Tex, 70-71; Ind Univ, MA, 74, PhD, 77; Univ Col London, 76-77. **CAREER** Vis asst prof, Ind Univ, 77-78; vis lectr, Univ Calif-Berkeley, 80-81; asst prof, Univ Colo, 81-85; asst prof, 85-87; assoc prof, 87-91; Prof, UCLA, 91-. **HONORS AND AWARDS** Phi Beta Kappa, 70; Woodrow Wilson fel, 70; NDEA Title IV fel, Univ Tex, 70-71; Ind Univ grad sch fel, 72-73, 76-77; Wheeler fel, Amer Sch Class Stud, Athens, 76; Fulbright-Hays scholar, 76-77; A.W. Mellon post-doc fel, Stanford Univ, 78-80; NEH fel, 84-85; President's res fel, Univ Calif, 89-90; ed, transactions of the amer philol assn, 91-95; ed bd, the class jour, 82-83; helios, 84-90; bryn mawr class rev, 96-; comparative drama, 96-; referee: amer jour philol; class antiquity; class jour; class philol; comparative drama; phoenix; transactions **SELECTED PUBLICATIONS** Auth, The Making of Menander's Comedy, Univ Calif Press, 80; Understanding Terence, Princeton Univ Press, 86; Epic in Republican Rome, Oxford Univ Press, 95; "Improvisation, Plot, and Plautus' Curculio," Plautus und die Tradition des Stegreifspiels, Tubingen, 95. **CONTACT ADDRESS** Dept of Classics, Univ of California, Los Angeles, PO Box 951436, Los Angeles, CA 90095-1436.

GOLDEN, BRUCE
PERSONAL Born 06/18/1933, Rochester, NY, m, 1969 **DISCIPLINE** ENGLISH AND COMPARATIVE LITERATURE **EDUCATION** Northwestern Univ, BS, 55; Columbia Univ, AM, 58, PhD(English & comp lit), 66. **CAREER** Mem acad fac humanities, Juilliard Sch Music, 62-65; from instr to assoc prof English, 65-77, PROF ENGLISH, CALIF STATE COL, SAN BERNARDINO, 77-, Nat Endowment Humanities younger humanist fel, 71-72. **MEMBERSHIPS** MLA; Renaissance Soc Am; Malon Soc. **RESEARCH** Renaissance dramatic literature; literature and the other arts; popular culture. **SELECTED PUBLICATIONS** Coauth, The Good Soldier: A tragedy of self-deception, Mod Fiction Studies, 63; auth, Calderon's tragedies of honor: Topos, emblem, and action in the popular theatre of the Siglo de oro, Renaissance Drama, 70; The Beach Boys: Southern California Pastoral, Newcastle/Borgo, 76. **CONTACT ADDRESS** Dept of English, California State Univ, San Bernardino, 5500 University Pky, San Bernardino, CA 92407-7500.

GOLDEN, LEON
PERSONAL Born 12/25/1930, Teasley City, NJ **DISCIPLINE** CLASSICS **EDUCATION** Univ Chicago, BA, 50, MA, 53, PhD, 58. **CAREER** Instr to asst prof, Col of William & Mary, 58-65; assoc prof to prof, Fl St Univ, 65- . **HONORS AND AWARDS** Phi Beta Kappa **MEMBERSHIPS** Amer

Philol Assoc; Classical Assoc of Midwest & South; Amer Comparative Lit Assoc. **RESEARCH** Greek tragedy; Homer; classical literary criticism. **SELECTED PUBLICATIONS** Auth bibliogr, In Praise of Prometheus: Humanism and Rationalism in Aeschylean Thought, Chapel Hill, 66; The Clarification Theory of Catharsis, Hermes, 76; Comic Pleasure, Hermes, 87; Aristotle on Tragic and Comic Mimesis; 92; coauth bibliogr, Horace for Students of Literature: the Ars Poetica and its Tradition, 95. **CONTACT ADDRESS** Dept of Classics, Florida State Univ, Tallahassee, FL 32306. **EMAIL** lgolden@mallen.fsu.edu

GOLDEN, MARK
PERSONAL Born 06/08/1948, Winnipeg, MB, Canada, m, 1985, 2 children **DISCIPLINE** CLASSICS **EDUCATION** Univ Col, Toronto, BA, 70; Univ Toronto, PhD, 81. **CAREER** Lectr, asst prof, Univ British Columbia, 80-82; asst prof, prof, Univ Winnipeg, 82- . **HONORS AND AWARDS** Fel, Nat Hum Ctr. **MEMBERSHIPS** Class Asn of Can; APA; Asn of Ancient Hist; Soc for Socialist Stud. **RESEARCH** History of childhood; ancient family history; Greek sport. **SELECTED PUBLICATIONS** Co-ed, Inventing Ancient Culture: Historicism, Periodization and the Ancient World, Routledge, 97; auth, Sport and Society in Ancient Greece, Cambridge, 98. **CONTACT ADDRESS** Dept of Classics, Univ of Winnipeg, Winnipeg, MB, Canada R3B 2E9. **EMAIL** m.golden@uwinnipeg.ca

GOLDIN, FREDERICK
PERSONAL Born 11/03/1930, Brooklyn, NY, m, 3 children **DISCIPLINE** MEDIEVAL AND COMPARATIVE LITERATURE **EDUCATION** City Col New York, BA, 52; Columbia Univ, MA, 54, PhD, 64. **CAREER** Instr, Brooklyn Col, 60-61; from instr to asst prof, Rutgers Univ, 61-67; from asst prof to assoc prof, 67-76, Prof English and Comp Lit, City Col New York, 77-, Prof to distinguished prof emer, Ger, French, English and Comp Lit, Grad Sch, City Univ NY, 77-. **HONORS AND AWARDS** Fulbright sr res fel, Vienna, 68-69; Am Coun Learned Soc grant, 68-69; Fulbright sr res scholar, Vienna, 75-76; Am Coun Learned Soc travel grant, 78 and fel, 80-81; City Univ NY Res Found grant, 81. **MEMBERSHIPS** Soc Rencesvals; MLA; Mediaeval Acad Am; Int Arthurian Soc; Int Courtly Lit Soc. **RESEARCH** Medieval courtly literature; medieval and Renaissance epic; medieval and Renaissance drama **SELECTED PUBLICATIONS** Auth, The Age-de-Parage--Essay on Poetics in 13th-Century Occitania, Romance Philol, Vol 0047, 94. **CONTACT ADDRESS** Dept of Comp Lit Grad Sch, City Univ, NY 33 W 42nd St, New York, NY 10016-4309.

GOLDSTEIN, DARRA
PERSONAL Born 04/28/1951, Lakewood, NJ, m, 1980, 1 child **DISCIPLINE** RUSSIAN **EDUCATION** Vassar Col, AB, 73; Stanford Univ, PhD, 83. **CAREER** Prof, Williams Col, 83-; ed, gastronomica, 00-. **HONORS AND AWARDS** Res grants, Int Res & Exchanges Bd, Amer Coun of Learned Soc(s), Kennan Inst, Mellon Found; Julia Child Awd, 93; Sophie Coe Subsidiary Prize, 97; NEH fel. **MEMBERSHIPS** AAASS, IACP. **RESEARCH** Russian poetry; modernism; Russian Avant-Garde Art; Russian cultural studies; culinary history. **SELECTED PUBLICATIONS** Auth, A Taste of Russia, HarperCollins, 83, 93; Art for the Masses, Williams College Museum of Art, 85; Russian Houses, Stewart, Tabori & Chang, 91; The Georgian Feast: The Vibrant Culture and Savory Food of the Republic of Georgia, Harper Collins, 93, Univ of CA, 99; auth, Nikolai Zabolotsky: Play for Mortal Stakes, Cambridge UP, 93; coauth, Graphic Design in the Mechanical Age, Yale Univ Press, 98. **CONTACT ADDRESS** Center for Foreign Languages, Literatures and Cult, Williams Col, Williamstown, MA 01267. **EMAIL** Darra.Goldstein@williams.edu

GOLLRAD, GARETH E.
PERSONAL Born 12/10/1965, Chicago, IL **DISCIPLINE** FRENCH **EDUCATION** Reed Col, BA, 87; Univ Chicago, MA, 90; Univ Paris, DEA, 93; Univ Chicago, PhD, 99. **CAREER** Lectr to instr, Univ Chicago, 94-01. **HONORS AND AWARDS** Whiting Dissertation Fel, 95-96. **MEMBERSHIPS** MLA. **RESEARCH** The modern French novel; eighteenth and nineteenth century French fiction and historiography; enlightenment political philosophy; visual theory. **SELECTED PUBLICATIONS** Auth, "The Decline of Painting as a Rhetorical Figure of Written History in the Works of Gaston de Levis and Madame de Stael," Chicago Art J, 99. **CONTACT ADDRESS** Dept Lang and Lit, Univ of Chicago, 4850 S Lake Park Ave, Apt 2409, Chicago, IL 60615-2045. **EMAIL** gegollra@midway.uchicago.edu

GOLSTON, CHRIS
PERSONAL Born 02/03/1961, Fort Hood, TX, m, 1990, 2 children **DISCIPLINE** LINGUISTICS **EDUCATION** Univ Calif - Los Angeles, PhD, 91. **CAREER** Teacher, San Francisco Chinese Parents Comt Sch, 83-84; Teacher, Maybeck High Sch, 84-86; Vis External Lectr, Univ Ariz, 91-92; Vis Asst Prof, Stanford Univ, 92-93; Vis Asst Prof, UCLA, 94; Asst Prof Linguistics, Calif State Univ Fresno, 96-. **MEMBERSHIPS** Ling Soc Am. **RESEARCH** Phonology; Morphology; meter. **SELECTED PUBLICATIONS** Co-auth, The Hopi Coyote Story as Narrative: The Problem of Evaluation, J Pragmatics, 87; Zero morphology and constraint interaction: subtraction and epenthesis in German dialects, Yearbook of Morphology, 95; The phonology of Classical Arabic meter, Linguistics, Stockholm Univ, 97; Idre germansk vers kvantifierande, Meter Medel, Stockholm Univ, 98; The structure of the German root, Phonology and Morphology of the Germanic Languages, Niemeyer, 98; auth, Syntax outranks phonology: evidence from Ancient Greek, Phonology, 95; Prosodic constraints on roots and words, In: Studia Grammatica: Interfaces in Phonology, Akademie Verlag, 96; Direct Optimality Theory: representation as pure markedness, Lang, 96. **CONTACT ADDRESS** Lingusitics Dept, California State Univ, Fresno, PO Box 92, Fresno, CA 93740-0001. **EMAIL** chrisg@csufresno.edu

GOMEZ, GILBERTO
PERSONAL Born 05/29/1957, Columbia, d, 1 child **DISCIPLINE** SPANISH AMERICAN LITERATURE **EDUCATION** Licenciatura en Edrcacion/Universidad del Quindio, Columbia; Washington Univ, St Louis, Mo, PhD. **CAREER** Assoc prof, Spanish, Wabash Col, 96-. **HONORS AND AWARDS** Fulbright scholar. **MEMBERSHIPS** MLA, Inst Int de Literatura Iberoamericana, Latin Am Studies Asn, Asn de Columbidinistos. **RESEARCH** Latin American narrative of the 19th and 20th centuries. **SELECTED PUBLICATIONS** Auth, Entre Maria y La Voragine: literatura columbiona Ginisecular 1886-1903, Bogota, Fondo Cultural Capetero (89). **CONTACT ADDRESS** Dept Modern Langs, Wabash Col, PO Box 352, Crawfordsville, IN 47933-0352. **EMAIL** gomezg@wabash.edu

GOMEZ-MORIANA, ANTONIO
PERSONAL Born 09/13/1936, Malaga, Spain **DISCIPLINE** SPANISH **EDUCATION** Univ Pontificia de Salamanca, Lic, 58, PhD, 62; Ludwig-Maximilians Univ (Munich, Ger), MA, 64, PhD, 65. **CAREER** Tchr, Sanlucar de Barrameda (Spain), 58-59; lectr, Spanisches Kulturinstitut (Munich, Ger), 62-65; Ruhr-Univ (Bochum, Ger), 65-71; prof, 71-74, ch Span, Univ Ottawa, 73-74, ; dir, dept d'etudes anciennes et mod, 74-78, prof, 74-96, prog de litt comp, 87-89, dir-fond, dep de litt comp, Univ Montreal, 89-90; ch Span & Latin Am stud, 92-94, PROF INTERDISCIPLINARY STUD, SIMON FRASER UNIV, 97-. **MEMBERSHIPS** Royal Soc Can; Acad Hum & Soc Sci; Inst Int Sociocritique; Asn Can Hispanistas; Can Semiotic Asn. **SELECTED PUBLICATIONS** Auth, uber den Sinn von 'Congo-ja' bei Unamuno, 65; auth, Derecha de resistencia y tiranicido, Estudio de una tematica en las 'comedias' de Lope de Vega, 68; auth, Die sprach- und literarhistorische Entwicklung des Spanischen, 73; auth, La subversion du discours rituel, 85; auth, Discourse Analysis as Sociocriticism, 93; coauth, Lecture ideologieue du Lazarillo de Tormes, 84. **CONTACT ADDRESS** Dept of Humanities, Simon Fraser Univ, Burnaby, BC, Canada V5A 1S6. **EMAIL** antonio_gomez-moriana@sfu.ca

GONTARSKI, S. E.
PERSONAL Born 02/27/1942, Brooklyn, NY, m, 1968, 1 child **DISCIPLINE** ENGLISH, IRISH, LITERATURE **EDUCATION** Long Island Univ, BA, 66; MA, 68; Ohio State Univ, PhD, 74. **CAREER** Asst prof to assoc prof, 74-84; vis assoc prof, Univ Calif Riverside, 82-83; assoc prof, Ga Inst Tech, 84-86; distinguished vis prof, Calif State Univ Long Beach, 87-88; prof, Fla State Univ, 88; distinguished vis prof, Univ Dublin, 94; Fulbright prof, Univ Col, 98-99; Sarah Herndon prof, distinguished res prof, Fla State Univ, 99-. **HONORS AND AWARDS** Distinguished Res Prof Awd, 00; TIP Awd, 99; Profess Excellence Awd, 99; Fla State Univ Awd, 91-92, 96-97; Rockefeller Found Grant, 01; Sr Fulbright Fel, 98-99; William Evans Vis Fel, Univ Otago, 94; NEH Fel, 93, 94. **MEMBERSHIPS** PEN; NBCC; MLA; Samuel Beckett Soc. **RESEARCH** 20th-century Irish studies, in British, US and European modernism, and in critical theory. **SELECTED PUBLICATIONS** Auth, Beckett's Happy Days: A Manuscript Study, Ohio State Univ Lib Pub, 77; co-ed, Samuel Beckett, Humanistic Perspectives, Ohio State UP, 83; auth, The Intent of Undoing in Samuel Beckett's Dramatic Texts, Ind UP, 85; ed, On Beckett: Essays and Criticism, Grove Pr, 86; auth, The Beckett Studies Reader, UP Fla, 93; ed, The Theatrical Notebooks of Samuel Beckett, Faber and Faber, 93 and Grove Pr, 93; ed, notes, Samuel Beckett. The Complete Short Prose, 1928-1989, Grove Pr, 96; ed and notes, The Theatrical Notebook of Samuel Beckett: The Shorter Plays, Vol. IV, Faber and Faber, 99 and Grove Pr, 99; auth, Modernism, Censorship, and the Politics of Puhlishing: The Grow Pr Legacy, Univ NCar, 00; ed, The Grove Pr Reader, 1951-2001, Grove Pr, 01. **CONTACT ADDRESS** English Dept, Florida State Univ, Tallahassee, FL 32306-1580. **EMAIL** sgontarski@english.fsu.edu

GONTRUM, PETER B.
PERSONAL Born 02/13/1932, m, 1956, 3 children **DISCIPLINE** GERMAN & COMPARITIVE LITERATURE **EDUCATION** Haverford Col, BA, 54; Princeton Univ, MA, 56; Univ Munich, PhD, 58. **CAREER** Instr Ger, Univ Chicago, 58-61; from asst prof to assoc prof, 61-72, prof Ger, Univ Ore, 72-, head Dept Ger Lang & Lit, 78-84; prof Emeritus, 98; Am Philos Soc grant, 60, 65-66; Am Coun Learned Soc grant & Alexander von Humboldt fel, 65-66; Alexander von Humboldt fel, 71 & 79; mem Nat Fulbright Selection Comn, 71-73; Fulbright lectr, Univ Mannheim, 74. **MEMBERSHIPS** Am Asn Teachers Ger; MLA; Philol Asn Pac Coast; Am Comp Lit Asn; Int Comp Lit Asn. **RESEARCH** Rilke; modern German literature; Hesse, Brecht, Durrenmatt and Frisch. **SELECTED PUBLICATIONS** Auth, Natur und Dingsymbolik als Ausdruck de Inneren Welt Hermann Hesses, Univ Munich, 58; The legend of Rip van Winkle in Max Frisch's Stiller, Studies Swiss Lit, 71; Max Firsch and the theatre of Bertolt Brecht, German Life and Letters, 1/80. **CONTACT ADDRESS** Dept of German Language & Lit, Univ of Oregon, Eugene, OR 97403-1205.

GONZALEZ, ALFONSO
PERSONAL Born 01/07/1938, Mexico City, Mexico, m, 1963, 3 children **DISCIPLINE** MEXICAN LITERATURE, SPANISH LANGUAGE **EDUCATION** Univ Kans, BA, 67, MA, 68, PhD(Span), 71. **CAREER** Asst prof Span, Ohio Univ, 71-75; prof Span, 82-83, Calif State Univ Los Angeles, 78-, Ohio Univ res inst grants Mex Cult, 72-73 & 73-74; vis prof Lat Am Lit, Univ Southern Calif, 75-76. **HONORS AND AWARDS** MPPP Awd for Spring 87-Summer 88, CSULA; Lottery Funds Awd, Spring 94, 87, CSULA; PPSI Awd, CSULA. **MEMBERSHIPS** Am Asn Teachers Span & Port; MLA; Philol Asn Pac Coast; Pac Coast Coun Latin Am Studies. **RESEARCH** Latin American literature; Latin American studies. **SELECTED PUBLICATIONS** Auth, El novumundismo en la prosa de ficcion de Altamirano, Palabra & Hombre, 10-12/72; Onomasticas and creativity in Dona Barbara and Pedro Paramo, Names, 3/73; Narrative techniques in twentieth-century Spanish American novomundismo, Grad Studies Latin Am, Fall 73; Elementos del Quijote en la caracterizacion de La Voragine, Romance Notes, 74; Elementos hispanicos y clasicos en la caracterizacion de La Voragine, Cuadernos Am, 5-6/75; introd to chap on Julieta Campos, In: Mujeres en la Literature, Fleischer Ed, Mex, 78; Indice de la Cultura en Mexico (1962-1971), Univ Microfilms Int, 78; Entrando en la posmodernidad, Mexico: UNAM, 98. **CONTACT ADDRESS** 5151 Rancho Castilla, Los Angeles, CA 90032-4202. **EMAIL** alfonso.Gonzalez@worldnet.atl.net

GONZALEZ, BERNARDO ANTONIO
PERSONAL Born 06/20/1950, San Pedro, CA, m, 1976, 2 children **DISCIPLINE** MODERN SPANISH LITERATURE **EDUCATION** Univ Calif, Berkeley, AB, 72, MA, 74, PhD(Romance lang and lit), 79. **CAREER** Prof Span, Wesleyan Univ, 79-. **MEMBERSHIPS** MLA; Am Asn Teachers of Span and Portuguese; Northeastern MLA. **RESEARCH** Modern Spanish Theater. **SELECTED PUBLICATIONS** Auth, Cuando Acabe la Guerra, Anales de la Lit Espanola Contemporanea, Vol 0018, 93; Theater in Spain, Between Tradition and Avant-Garde, Rev de Estudios Hispanicos, Vol 0027, 93; Ultima Batalla En El Pardo, Estreno-Cuadernos del Teatro Espanol Contemporaneo, Vol 0020, 94; Popular National Theater--On the Theory and Practice of Rodriguezmendez, Jose, Maria, Estreno-Cuadernos del Teatro Espanol Contemporaneo, Vol 0020, 94; The Theory of Theater Criticism During the 2nd-Republic, the Case of Chabas, Juan, Anales de la Lit Espanola Contemporanea, Vol 0020, 95; Yo Fui Actor Cuando Franco, Manana, Aqui, A la Misma Hora, Estreno-Cuadernos del Teatro Espanol Contemporaneo, Vol 0021, 95; Puigserver, Fabia, Man of Theater, Estreno-Cuadernos del Teatro Espanol Contemporaneo, Vol 0021, 95; Olmo, Lauro El 'Perchero' (1953)--Playwrighting in the Social, Economic and Political Contexts of the Times, Estreno-Cuadernos del Teatro Espanol Contemporaneo, Vol 0022, 96; Spanish Alternative Theater Today, Estreno-Cuadernos del Teatro Espanol Contemporaneo, Vol 0022, 96; Reflections on Theatrical Politics, Estreno-Cuadernos del Teatro Espanol Contemporaneo, Vol 0023, 97. **CONTACT ADDRESS** Dept of Romance Lang, Wesleyan Univ, Middletown, CT 06457.

GONZALEZ, ELOY
DISCIPLINE MEDIEVAL AND GOLDEN AGE SPANISH LITERATURE **EDUCATION** Ohio State Univ, PhD, 74. **CAREER** Assoc prof, Wash State Univ 81-. **RESEARCH** Medieval and golden age Spanish literature. **SELECTED PUBLICATIONS** Auth, Metafora y simetria en el prologo del Abencerraje, Explicacion de textos literarios 5, 76; Carnival on the Stage: Cefalo y Pocris, a comedia burlesca, Bull Comediantes 30, 78; La muerte, entierro y honras de Chrespina Marauzmana, gata de Juan Chrespo, de Bernardino de Albornoz Edition of the poem, with a prologue and notes, Revista de lit 51, 89, publ Consejo Superior de Investigaciones Cientificas, Madrid, Spain; Las batallas en el Amadis de Gaula, Selecta, J Pacific Northwest Coun on For Lang 10, 89 & Tipologia literaria de los personajes en el Amadis de Gaula, Nueva Revista de Filologia Hisp 39, 91; coauth, Montalvo's Recantation, Revisited, Bull Hisp Stud 55, 78. **CONTACT ADDRESS** Dept of Foreign Languages and Literatures, Washington State Univ, 1 SE Stadium Way, Pullman, WA 99164. **EMAIL** eloygonz@wsunix.wsu.edu

GONZALEZ-CRUZ, LUIS F.
PERSONAL Born 12/11/1943, Cardenas, Cuba, s **DISCIPLINE** HISPANIC LANGUAGES **EDUCATION** Inst Jose Smith Comas, BS, 60; Univ Pittsburgh, MA, 68; PhD, 70. **CAREER** Instr to prof, Pa State Univ, 69-94. **HONORS AND AWARDS** Excellence in Teaching Award, Pa State Univ, 89; Finalist, Golden Letters Award, Univ Miami, 87; Res Award, Am Coun of Learned Soc, 84; Honorary Distinction, Mairena Poetry Contest, Puerto Rico, 81; Director's Award, Pa State Univ, 73. **MEMBERSHIPS** MLA; AATSP; LAS. **RESEARCH** Latin American and Peninsular Literature; Spanish

poetry; Pre-Columbian Cultures and Civilizations; Modern Theater; Cuban Theater; Cuban Letters in general; Pablo Neruda; Cesar Vallejo; Federico Garcia Lorca; Virgilio Pinera; Eugenio d'Ors. **SELECTED PUBLICATIONS** Auth, Cuban Theater in the United States. A Critical Anthology, Bilingual Press, 92; auth, Three Masterpieces of Cuban Drama, Green Integer, 00; auth, Olorun's Rainbow. Anatomy of a Cuban Dreamer, 01. **CONTACT ADDRESS** 6445 Indian Creek Dr, Bldg B Penthouse Unit 501, Miami Beach, FL 33141-5834.

GONZALEZ-DEL-VALLE, LUIS T.
PERSONAL Born 11/19/1946, Cuba, m, 1969, 2 children **DISCIPLINE** SPANISH **EDUCATION** Univ NC, BA, 68; Univ Mass Amherst, MA, 72; PhD, 72. **CAREER** Asst prof to assoc prof, Kans State Univ, 72-77; assoc prof to prof, Univ Nebr, 77-86; prof and dept chair, Univ Colo Boulder, 86-; vis prof, Univ Valladolid, 92, 94; vis prof, Univ Complutense, 97; vis prof, Univ Salamanca, 98. **HONORS AND AWARDS** Silver Medal, Xunta de Galicia, 00; Diploma de Honor, Asociacion Castellano Manchega de Escritores, 96; Woodrow Wilson Dissertation Fel, 71-72. **MEMBERSHIPS** Asn Intl de Hispanistas; Conf of Ed of Learned Journals; MLA; Midwest MLA; Rocky Mountain MLA; Am Asn of Teachers of Spanish and Portuguese; Cervantes Soc of Am; Twentieth Century Spanish Asn of Am. **RESEARCH** 19th and 20th Centuries Spanish and Spanish American Drama and Narrative Fiction; Modernity; Narratology; Literary Theory. **SELECTED PUBLICATIONS** Auth, La ficcion breve de Valle-Inclan (Hermeneutica y estrategia narrativas), Barcelona, 90; auth, El canon. Reflexiones sobre la recepcion literaria-teatral (Perez de Ayala ante Benavente), Madrid, 93; auth, Ecos de Cuba. Revista del Avisador Comercial de la Habana, Xunta de Galicai, 97; co-auth, La generacion de 1898 ante Espana. Antoloia de literatura moderna de temas nacionales y universales, 2nd ed, Boulder, 97. **CONTACT ADDRESS** Dept Spanish and Portuguese, Univ of Colorado, Boulder, Campus PO Box 278, Boulder, CO 80309-0278.

GOODE, WILLIAM OSBORNE
PERSONAL Born 06/22/1939, Chase City, VA, m, 1972, 3 children **DISCIPLINE** FRENCH LITERATURE **EDUCATION** Washington and Lee Univ, BA, 60; Duke Univ, MA, 63, PhD(French), 68. **CAREER** Asst prof French, Univ Md, 67-68 and Univ Pa, 68-73; asst prof, 74-78, Assoc Prof French, Univ NC, Greensboro, 78-, Advert Mgr, The Fr Rev, 80-. **MEMBERSHIPS** MLA; Am Asn Teachers Fr; S Atlantic Mod Lang Asn; AAUP. **RESEARCH** Seventeenth century French literature; classical theater; tragedy. **SELECTED PUBLICATIONS** **CONTACT ADDRESS** Dept of Romance Lang, Univ of No Carolina, Greensboro, 1000 Spring Garden, Greensboro, NC 27412-0001.

GOODMAN, DAVID G.
PERSONAL Born Racine, WI, m, 1968, 2 children **DISCIPLINE** ASIAN LANGUAGES **EDUCATION** Yale Univ, BA, 69; Cornell Univ, MA, 80; PhD, 82. **CAREER** Ed-Publisher, Concerned Theatre Japan, 69-73; writer, 74-78; vis asst prof, Univ of Kansas, 81-82; asst prof to prof, Univ of IL, 82-. **HONORS AND AWARDS** Transl Center Awd, Columbia Univ, 90; Fel, Univ of IL; Grants from NEH, Japan Found, Pola Found, 93-98; Silver Medal, 78th Annual NY Directors Club Competition, 99. **RESEARCH** Modern Japanese drama; modern Japanese literature and poetry, modern Japanese intellectual history, Japanese stylistics and original writing in Japanese, cultural dimensions of international security. **SELECTED PUBLICATIONS** Auth, Hashiru, Iwanami shoten, 89; auth, "Long, Long Autumn Nights: Selected Poems of Oguma Hideo, 1901-1940", Mich Monographs Series in Japanese Studies, 3, 89; coauth, "Jews in the Japanese Mind: the History and Uses of a Cultural Stereotype", The Free Press, 95; auth, "Concerned Theatre Japan: the Graphic Art of Japanese Theatre, 1960-1980", CD-ROM, Krannert Art Museum, 98; auth, Angura: Posters of the Japanese Avant-Garde, Princeton Archit Pr, 99. **CONTACT ADDRESS** Dept E Asian Lang and Cult, Univ of Illinois, Urbana-Champaign, 707 s. Mathews Ave, Rm 2090A, Urbana, IL 61801. **EMAIL** dgoodman@uiuc.edu

GOODSON, ALFRED CLEMENT
PERSONAL Born 11/30/1946, Houston, TX, m, 1984, 1 child **DISCIPLINE** COMPARATIVE LITERATURE, ENGLISH **EDUCATION** Rice Univ, BA, 68; State Univ NYork Buffalo, PhD(comp lit), 73. **CAREER** Asst prof, 72-77, ASSOC PROF ENGLISH, MICH STATE UNIV, 77-, Alexander von Humboldt Stiftung res grant, Deutsches Seminar, Tubingen, 79; prof english, 88; dir, 91-. **RESEARCH** Romantic Lang Theory and Poetics; Critical History and Theory; Literature and Medicine. **SELECTED PUBLICATIONS** Auth, Verbal Imagination: Coleridge and the Language of Modern Criticism, Coxford, 88; auth, Frankenstein in the Age of Prozac: Artistic Creativity, Depression, Modern Medicine, Lit and Med, Vol 0015, 96; auth, Coleridge's Writing, on Language, Vol 3, MacMillan, 98. **CONTACT ADDRESS** 403 Kensington Rd, East Lansing, MI 48823. **EMAIL** goodson@pilot.msu.edu

GOPNIK, MYRNA
PERSONAL Born 06/21/1935, Philadelphia, PA, m, 1954, 6 children **DISCIPLINE** LINGUISTICS, SEMIOTICS **EDUCATION** Univ Pa, BA, 62, MA, 64, PhD(ling), 68. **CAREER** Instr hist and philos sci, Phila Col Arts, 67-68; invited lectr info sci, Drexel Inst Technol, 68; res, assoc auto transl, Univ Montreal, 68-69; Assoc Prof Ling, Mcgill Univ, 69-. **MEMBERSHIPS** Ling Soc Am; Can Ling Asn; Ling Asn Can & US; Can Asn Hist & Philos Sci; MLA. **RESEARCH** Linguistic metatheory; textlinguistics; semiotics. **SELECTED PUBLICATIONS** Auth, Impairments of Tense in a Familial Language Disorder, J Neurolinguistics, Vol 0008, 94; Compensatory Strategies in Genetic Dysphasia--Declarative Memory, J Neurolinguistics, Vol 0010, 97; Neuroanatomical Correlates of Familial Language Impairment--A Preliminary-Report, J Neurolinguistics, Vol 0010, 97; Genetic Dysphasia--Introduction, J Neurolinguistics, Vol 0010, 97; What Underlies Inflectional Error Patterns in Genetic Dysphasia, J Neurolinguistics, Vol 0010, 97. **CONTACT ADDRESS** Dept of Ling, McGill Univ, 1001 Sherbrooke, Montreal, QC, Canada H3A 1G5.

GORBATOV, INNA
PERSONAL Born 03/04/1955, Moscow, Russia, d, 1 child **DISCIPLINE** LINGUISTICS **EDUCATION** Queens Col, BA, 77; City Univ Grad Sch, NY, MA; 79; CUNY Grad Sch, PhD, 89. **CAREER** Adj, assoc, asst, prof, City Univ NYork; State Univ NYork; NYork Univ; LIU; Manhattan Col; Touro Col; Yeshiva Univ; Marymont Col; 78-. **HONORS AND AWARDS** USSR Govt Scholar, Odessa State Univ, 73-74; Univ Scholar, CUNY, 77-79; Fr Govt Scholar, Sorbonne, Univ Paris, 79-80. **MEMBERSHIPS** MLA; AATSEEL; CLA. **SELECTED PUBLICATIONS** Auth, Fornation du Concept do Setimentalisme dans la Literature Russe, Peter Lang Pub; auth, "La Nouvelle Heloise de J -J Rousseau and La Pauvre Liza de N.M. Kararamzine," The Univ of Dayton Rev. **CONTACT ADDRESS** Dept Modern Lang, Borough of Manhattan Comm Col, CUNY, 199 Chambers St, New York, NY 10007-1044.

GORDON, ALEXANDER LOBBAN
PERSONAL Born 04/12/1935, Grantown-on-Spey, Scotland **DISCIPLINE** FRENCH **EDUCATION** Aberdeen Univ, MA, 58; Sorbonne, DUniv (French), 65. **CAREER** Asst English, Univ Rennes, 58-59; from lectr to asst prof French, 61-70, Assoc Prof French, Univ Man, 70-. **MEMBERSHIPS** MLA; Int Soc Hist Rhetoric. **RESEARCH** French poetry of the 16th century; modern French poetry. **CONTACT ADDRESS** Dept of French and Span & Ital, Univ of Manitoba, 430 Fletcher Argue Bldg, Winnipeg, MB, Canada R3T 2N2. **EMAIL** gordonal@cc.umanitoba.ca

GORDON, LOIS G.
PERSONAL Born 11/13/1938, Englewood, NJ, m, 1961, 1 child **DISCIPLINE** ENGLISH & COMPARATIVE LITERATURE **EDUCATION** Univ MI, BA, 60; Univ Wis, MA, 62, PhD, 66. **CAREER** Lectr Eng, City Col NY, 64-66; asst prof, Univ MO, KS City, 66-68; from asst prof to assoc prof, 68-75, prof eng & comp lit, Fairleigh Dickinson Univ, 75-, vis prof, Rutgers Univ, 94, Asst ed, Lit & Psychol, 68-71. **HONORS AND AWARDS** Teaching Fel, 62-64; Univ of Wis: Tuition Scholarship; Dissertation Completion Fel, 66; Univ of Mo Res Grant, 67-68; Fairleigh Dickinson Univ Res Grant, 85-86, 89-90, 96-97; **MEMBERSHIPS** MLA; Pinter Soc; Beckett Soc; PEN; Acad of Am Poets; Int Bach Soc; Int League for Human Rights; Authors Guild; U.S. Nat Landmarks Commission. **RESEARCH** Twentieth century Eng and comp lit; postmoderism. **SELECTED PUBLICATIONS** Auth, Stratagems to Uncover Nakedness: The Dramas of Harold Pinter, Univ MO Press, 69; Donald Barthelme, G K Hall, 81; Robert Coover--The Universal Fictionmaking Process, Southern Ill Univ Press, 83; co-auth, American Chronicle: Six Decades in American Life, 1920-1979, Atheneum/Random House, 87; co-auth, American Chronicle: Seven Decades in American Life, 1920-1989, Random House, 80; Harold Pinter: A Caseboo, Garland Publ, 90; co-auth, The Columbia Chronicles of American Life, 1910-1992, Columbia Univ Press, 95; The World of Samuel Beckett, 1906-1946, Yale Univ Press, 96, reprint, 98; American Chronicle: Decade by Decade through the Twentieth Century, Yale Univ Press, 99. **CONTACT ADDRESS** Dept of Eng, Fairleigh Dickinson Univ, Teaneck-Hackensack, 1000 River Rd, Teaneck, NJ 07666-1996. **EMAIL** loisgord@aol.com

GORDON, LYNN
DISCIPLINE LINGUISTICS AND TESOL **EDUCATION** Univ Calif, Los Angeles, PhD. **CAREER** Assoc prof, Washington State Univ. **SELECTED PUBLICATIONS** Auth, Maricopa Morphology and Syntax, 86. **CONTACT ADDRESS** Dept of English, Washington State Univ, 1 SE Stadium Way, PO Box 645020, Pullman, WA 99164-5020. **EMAIL** gordonl@wsunix.wsu.edu

GORMAN, JOHN
PERSONAL Born 08/28/1938, Hoboken, NJ **DISCIPLINE** GERMAN **EDUCATION** Manhattan Col, BA, 60; Johns Hopkins Univ, MA, 61, PhD, 67. **CAREER** Asst prof foreign lang, Lamar State Col, 65-66 and Univ Miami, 67-74; Writer, 74-; prof, Univ Houston Clear Lake. **RESEARCH** German-Spanish literary relations; comparative literature. **SELECTED PUBLICATIONS** Auth, Lost in the City, Am Bk Rev, 93. **CONTACT ADDRESS** Univ of Houston, Clear Lake, 2700 Bay Area Blvd., Box 143, Houston, TX 77058. **EMAIL** gorman@clu.uh.edu

GORUP, RADMILA J.
PERSONAL Born Yugoslavia, m, 1963, 2 children **DISCIPLINE** SLAVIC LANGUAGES **EDUCATION** Univ Belgrade, BA; St John's University, MA; Columbia Univ, PhD & MA. **CAREER** Prof. **HONORS AND AWARDS** Fulbright Fellowship; ACLS Grant. **MEMBERSHIPS** MLA; LSA; AAASS; AATSEEL; NASSS **RESEARCH** Theoretical linguistics; sociolinguistics; South Slavic cultures; Serbian literature. **SELECTED PUBLICATIONS** Auth, Semantic Organization of the Serbocroatian Verb, 87; Women in Andric's Writing, 95; History as Human Construct: Radoslav Petkovic's Sudbina i Komentari, Serbian Studies, 96; ed, The Prince of Fire: An Anthology of Serbian Contemporary Short Stories, Pittsburgh U. of Pittsburgh Press, 98; ed., Milorad Pavic, The Review of Contemporary Fiction, summer 98, guest editor; ed., In a Foreign Harbor: Essays in Honor of Vasa D. Mihailovich, Slavica, 00. **CONTACT ADDRESS** Dept of Slavic Languages, Columbia Col, New York, 2960 Broadway, New York, NY 10027-6902. **EMAIL** rjg26@columbia.edu

GOSS, NOBLE T.
PERSONAL Born 08/11/1944, Heppner, OR, m, 1973, 4 children **DISCIPLINE** SPANISH, SPANISH LITERATURE **EDUCATION** Pepperdine Col, BA, 66; Portland State Univ, MA, 73; Univ Ore, MA, 79, PhD, 87. **CAREER** Res asst, Univ Ore, 84-96; instr, Lane Commun Col, 84-96; Asst Prof, Harding Univ, 96-. **HONORS AND AWARDS** Dissertation, The Theme of Chastity in Ariosto and Spenser, 87. **MEMBERSHIPS** AATSP; AFLTA. **RESEARCH** Golden age, Spain, drama & poetry; Renaissance Epic; FL teaching methodology. **CONTACT ADDRESS** Dept of Foreign Languages, Harding Univ, Box 12263, Searcy, AR 72143. **EMAIL** ngoss@harding.edu

GRAF, ERIC
DISCIPLINE SPANISH LANGUAGE AND LITERATURE **EDUCATION** Univ VA, PhD, 96. **CAREER** Span, Smith Col **SELECTED PUBLICATIONS** Auth, Forcing the Poetic Voice: Garcilaso de la Vega's Sonnet XXIX as a Deconstruction of the Renaissance Idea of Harmony, MLN 109 2, 94; auth, "Forcing the Poetic Voice: Garcilaso de la Vega's Sonnet XXIX as a Demonstration of the Renaissance Idea of Harmony," Modern Lang Notes 109.2, (94): 163-85; auth, May I Have This Dance? Unveiling Vicente Aleixandre's El vals, Romanic Rev 85 2, (94): 313-26; auth, "Escritor/Excretor: Cervantes's 'Humanism' on Philip II's Tomb," Cervantes 19 1, (99): 66-95; auth, "When an Arab Laughs in Toledo: Cervantes's Interpellation of Early Modern Spanish Orientalism," Diacritics 29.2, (99): 68-85; auth, "Heullas de la violencia mimetica y su resolucion falico-politica en el Poema de mio Cid: Girard y Lacan," La coronica 28.2, (00): 101-27; auth, "Appellative, Cultural and Geographical Liminality in the Poema de mio Cid," (forthcoming); auth, "Axolotl de Julio Cortazar: Dialectica entre las mitologias azteca y dantesca," (forthcoming); auth, "From Scipio to Nero to the Self: The Exemplary Politics of Stoicism in Garcilaso de la Vega's Elegies," (forthcoming). **CONTACT ADDRESS** Dept of Span and Portuguese, Smith Col, Northampton, MA 01063. **EMAIL** egraf@sophia.smith.edu

GRAGG, GENE BALFORD
PERSONAL Born 08/24/1938, Amsterdam, NY, m, 1969, 2 children **DISCIPLINE** LINGUISTICS, SUMEROLOGY **EDUCATION** Loyola Univ, Chicago, BA, 60; West Baden Col, Lic Phil, 62; Univ Chicago, PhD, 66. **CAREER** Res assoc Sumerian, Univ Amsterdam, 67-69; from Asst Prof to Assoc Prof, 69-82, Prof, Univ Chicago, 82-, Chmn 79-85; Dir, Oriental Inst, 97-. **MEMBERSHIPS** Ling Soc Am; Am Orient Soc. **RESEARCH** Historical linguistics; Sumerian; Cushitic. **SELECTED PUBLICATIONS** Auth, The Sumerian Dimensional Infixes, Butzon, 73; Oromo, of Wallagga, In: Non-Semitic Languages of Ethiopia, 75; Dictionary of Oromo, 82; Achaemenid Royal Inscriptions (elec), 97. **CONTACT ADDRESS** Oriental Inst, Univ of Chicago, 1155 E 58th St, Chicago, IL 60637-1540. **EMAIL** g-gragg@uchicago.edu

GRAGNOLATI, MANUELE
PERSONAL Born 01/11/1968, Pavia, Italy, s **DISCIPLINE** ITALIAN LITERATURE **EDUCATION** Univ Pavia, Laurea in lettere Classiche, 92; Paris IV Sorbonne, DEA, 94; Columbia Univ, PhD, 99. **CAREER** Asst prof, Dartmouth Col, 99-. **HONORS AND AWARDS** Collegio Ghislieri Mem, Univ of Pavia, 87-92; Collegio Ghislieri Fel, 88; Europ Community Erasmus Fel, 91; President's Fel, Columbia Univ, 94-99; Whiting Fel, Columbia Univ, 99; Presidential Awd for Outstanding Teaching, Columbia Univ, 99. **MEMBERSHIPS** Am Assoc of Ital Studies, Medieval Acad of Am, Dante Soc of Am. **RESEARCH** Human identity and significance of the body in Dante and medieval popular culture (especially uguccione Da Lodi, giacomino Da Verona, and Bonvesin Da La riva), Medieval Eschatology, the Italian Lyric Tradition. **SELECTED PUBLICATIONS** Auth, "Giovanni Pascoli: Varianti conviviali (1895-1905)," Fevue des Etudes Italiennes, XLI.1-4 (95): 133-156; auth, "Love, Lust and Avarice: Leodilla between Dante and Ovid," Fortune and Romance: Boiardo in America, eds Jo Ann Cavallo and Charles Ross, (Temple, AZ: Medieval and Renaissance Texts and Studies, 98): 151-174; auth, "Marinetti e la lingua francese alle soglie del Futurismo: l'eclettismo

ambiguo de 'La ville charnelle, '" Revue des Etudes Italiennes XLV.1-2 (99): 115-132; auth, "From Decay to Splendor: Body and Pain in Bonvesin da la Riva's 'Book of the Three Scriptures,'" Last Things: Death and Apocalypse in the Middle Ages, eds Caroline Bynum and Paul Freedman (Philadelphia: Univ of Pa Pr, 99): 83-97; auth, "From Plurality to (Near) Unicity of Forms: Embryology in Purgatorio 25," Dante 2000, Proceedings of the NY Int Conf, eds Wayne Storey and Teodolinda Barolini (NY: Fordham Univ Pr, forthcoming); auth, Dante Alighieri, 'Rime', a cura di Teodlinda Barolini; note di Manuele Gragnolati, Rizzoli, (Milano), forthcoming; auth, "Bonvesin da la riva," Italian Literature of the Thirteenth Century, ed Zygmunt Baranski and Theodore Cachey, Bruccoli Clark Layman (NY, forthcoming). **CONTACT ADDRESS** Dept Fr & Ital, Dartmouth Col, Hb 6087, Hanover, NH 03755. **EMAIL** manuele.gragnoloti@dartmouth.edu

GRAHAM, A. JOHN
PERSONAL Born 03/09/1930, Lowestoft, England, m, 1963, 2 children **DISCIPLINE** CLASSICS **EDUCATION** Cambridge Univ, BA, 52, MA, 56, PhD, 57. **CAREER** Asst Lectr, Univ London, 55-57; Asst Lectr to Sr Lectr, Univ Manchester, 57-77; Prof Classical Studies, 77-95, Prof Emeritus, Univ Pa, 95-. **HONORS AND AWARDS** Cromer Greek Prize, British Acad, 56; Hare Prize, Univ Cambridge, 60; NEH Fel, 81-82. **MEMBERSHIPS** Soc Hellenic Studies; British Sch at Athens; Cambridge Philol Soc. **RESEARCH** Greek history; Greek colonization; Greek prose authors; ancient beekeeping. **SELECTED PUBLICATIONS** Auth, Colony and Mother City in Ancient Greece, 2nd ed, 83; Thucydides 7.13.2 and the Crews of Athenian Triremes, Transactions Am Philol Asn 122, 92; A Dedication from the Chersonese at Olympia, Nomodeiktes. Greek Studies in of Martin Ostwald, 93; The Odyssey, History and Women, The Distaff Side, 95; Themistocles' Speech before Salamis: the Interpretation of Herodotus 8.83.1, Classical Quart 46, 96; auth, "Thasos: the Topography of the Ancient City," Annual of the British School at Athens 95 (00); auth, Collected Papers on Greek Colonization, 01. **CONTACT ADDRESS** Classical Studies Dept, Univ of Pennsylvania, Logan Hall, Philadelphia, PA 19104-6304.

GRAMBERG, ANNE-KATRIN
PERSONAL Born 12/10/1957, Norderney, Germany, s **DISCIPLINE** GERMAN **EDUCATION** Georg August univ Gottingen, Germany, MA; Mich State Univ, PhD, 91. **CAREER** Instr, Central Mich Univ, 89; lectr, Univ of Mich, 90-93; asst prof to assoc prof, Auburn Univ, 93-. **SELECTED PUBLICATIONS** Coauth, "Discourse Strategies: Innovative Methods for the Subjective and Its Implicit Message," Die Unterrichtspraxis 26.2 (93): 185-193; auth, "Gender and Foreign Cultures in Business Language Classes," Dimension 96, (96): 69-78; auth, "Intensifiers and Politeness Markers in German and American Persuasive Communication," Schatzkammer der duetschen Sprachlehre, Dichtung und Geschichte XXII.2 (96): 29-42; coauth, "The Implications of Lexical Variation for the Reassessment of Erik Pontoppidan's 19th Century Creole Proverbs," SECON Rev XXI.2 (97): 126-140; auth, "Persuasive Strategies in Cultural Context: Discourse Analysis of German and North American Car Advertisements," Deutsche Sprache: Zeitschrift fur Theorie, Praxis 26, (98): 174-189; coauth, Business German: The Next Step, The Birth of a New Discipline", Die Unterrichtspraxis 33.2 (00): 148-171; coauth, German for Business and Economics 2nd Ed., Vols. I, II, Mich State Univ Pr, (East Lansing), 00; coauth, German for Business and Economics, 2nd Ed., Vols I, II, Teachers Resource Handbook, Mich State Univ Pr, (East Lansing: 00). **CONTACT ADDRESS** Auburn Univ, Auburn, AL 36849-0002. **EMAIL** gramban@mail.auburn.edu

GRANROSE, KATHLEEN
PERSONAL Born 08/12/1965, Ann Arbor, MI, m, 1999, 2 children **DISCIPLINE** SPANISH **EDUCATION** Oberlin Col, BA, 86; Univ Ga, MA, 96; Univ Va, PhD, 00. **CAREER** Asst prof, Univ of Nebr Omaha, 00-. **HONORS AND AWARDS** Fel, Dana Found, Oberlin Col, 85; Paul Patrick Rogers Prize, Oberlin Col, 86; Res Grant, Univ of Ga, 95-96; DuPont Fel, Univ of Va, 99-00; Dean, Fac Fel, Univ of Va, 99-00. **MEMBERSHIPS** MLA. **RESEARCH** Hispanic poetry, especially Federico Garcia Lorca and contemporary women poets of Spain. **SELECTED PUBLICATIONS** Auth, "Entrevista con Mempo Giardinelli", Hispamerica (forthcoming), auth, "Dialogue between Cinema and Novel: the case of Casablanca and El invierno en Lisboa", Espana Contemporanea (forthcoming). **CONTACT ADDRESS** Dept Foreign Lang, Univ of Nebraska, Omaha, 6001 Dodge St, Omaha, NE 68182.

GRANT, JOHN NEILSON
PERSONAL Born 05/03/1940, Edinburgh, Scotland, m, 1962, 3 children **DISCIPLINE** CLASSICS **EDUCATION** Univ Edinburgh, MA, 62; Cambridge Univ, BA, 64; Univ of St Andrews, PhD(Latin), 70. **CAREER** Lectr classics, Univ Man, 65-67; asst prof, 67-72, assoc prof, 72-80, prof Classics, Univ Toronto, 80-, Chmn, 82-, Can Coun fel, 77-78. **MEMBERSHIPS** Class Asn Can; Am Philol Asn. **RESEARCH** Roman comedy; transmission of texts; republican Latin literature. **SELECTED PUBLICATIONS** Auth, Studies in the Textual Tradition of Terence, Toronto, 86; auth, 2 Syntactic Errors in Transcription, Seneca, 'Thyestes 33' and Lucan, 'BC 2.279,' Class Quart, Vol 0044, 94; Taide in 'Inferno 18' and Terence 'Eunuchus 937,' Quaderni D Italianistica, Vol 0015, 94. **CONTACT ADDRESS** Dept Class, Univ of Toronto, 97 St. George St, Toronto, ON, Canada M5S 2E8. **EMAIL** grant@chass.utoronto.ca

GRANT, RICHARD BABSON
PERSONAL Born 01/18/1925, Boston, MA, m, 2 children **DISCIPLINE** FRENCH **EDUCATION** Harvard Univ, PhD(Romance lang), 52. **CAREER** From instr to prof Romance lang, Duke Univ, 52-71; prof French, Univ Tex, Austin, 71-; prof. Emeritus 96- . **RESEARCH** French naturalism; French romanticism. **SELECTED PUBLICATIONS** Auth, The Perilous Quest: Image, Myth, & Prophecy in the narratives of Victor Hugo (Duke Univ Pr, 1968), 93; Hugo, Victor Le 'Rhin' and the Search for Identity, 19th-Century Fr Stud, Vol 0023, 95. **CONTACT ADDRESS** Dept of French and Ital, Univ of Texas, Austin, Austin, TX 78712.

GRAY, EUGENE FRANCIS
PERSONAL Born 04/22/1936, Flint, MI, m, 1964, 2 children **DISCIPLINE** FRENCH LITERATURE **EDUCATION** Univ Mich, Ann Arbor, BSE, 60, MA, 62, PhD, 68. **CAREER** Instr lang & phys sci, Detroit Inst Technol, 62-67; asst prof, 67-71, acting chmn dept, 71-72, assoc prof, 71-81, prof French, Mich State Univ, 81-, dir, lang learning ctr, 91; dir, Lang Learning Center, 91-01. **MEMBERSHIPS** Am Asn Teachers Fr; CALICO. **RESEARCH** Nineteenth century French novel; French literary style; history of science. **SELECTED PUBLICATIONS** Auth, Gustave Flaubert, in A Critical Bibliography of Nineteenth-Century French Literature, 94; ed Madame Bovary: A Collection of Essays, 95; auth, "Hypermedia Approaches to Baudelaire's Poetry," in Approaches to Teaching Baudelaire's Flowers of Evil," 00. **CONTACT ADDRESS** Dept of Romance Lang, Michigan State Univ, 161 Old Horticulture, East Lansing, MI 48824-1112. **EMAIL** graye@pilot.msu.edu

GRAY, FLOYD FRANCIS
PERSONAL Born 08/12/1926, Meadville, PA, m, 1998 **DISCIPLINE** FRENCH **EDUCATION** Syracuse Univ, BA, 50; Inst Phonetique, Univ Paris, 51, Ecole Prof Francais a l'Etranger, cert, 51; Univ Wis, MA, 52, PhD, 56. **CAREER** Asst English, Lycee Henri-Martin, Saint-Quentin, 50-51; instr French, Univ Wis, 55-56; from instr to assoc prof, 56-65, univ fel, 58, prof French, Univ Mich, Ann Arbor, 65-; vis prof 16th century French lit, Univ Calif, Santa Barbara, 70-71; managing ed, Mich Romance Studies; Visting Prof, Univ of Liverpool, 92; Visting Prof, Mich State Univ, 95. **HONORS AND AWARDS** Palmes Academiques, French Govt, 75; Phi Beta Kappa, 50; Officer Palmes academiques 91; Julia Lockwood Awd, 95. **MEMBERSHIPS** Am Asn Teachers Fr; Soc ALmis Montaigne; MLA. **RESEARCH** French 16th and 17th century literature, especially Montaigne; Du Bellay; Rabelais; Renaissance Soc of Am. **SELECTED PUBLICATIONS** Auth, Le Style de Montaigne, Nizet, Paris, 58; Albert Thibaudet's Montaigne, Gallimard, Paris, 63; ed & transl, Gargantua and Pantagruel, 66 & auth, Anthologie de la Poesie francaise du XVIe siecle, 67, Appleton; Rabelais et l'ecriture, Nizet, Paris, 74; La Poetique de Du Bellay, 78 &; ed, Textes et Intertextes, Etudes sur le XVIe siecle pour Alfred Glauser, 79, Nizet, Paris; Poetiques: Theorie et critique litteraires, Mich Romance Studies, Vol 1, 80; auth, La Balance de Montaigne, Nizet, Paris, 82; La Bruyere amateur de caracteres, Nizet, 86; Montaigne bilingue, Champion, Paris, 91; Rabelais et le comique du discontinu, Champion, 94; ed, Rabelais, Gargantua, Champion, 95; auth, Rabelais, Pantagruel, Champion, 97; auth, Gender, Rhetoric, and Print Culture in French Renaissance Wrinting, Cambridge Univ Press, 00. **CONTACT ADDRESS** Univ of Michigan, Ann Arbor, Ann Arbor, MI 48109. **EMAIL** FGray@umich.edu

GRAY, MARGARET
DISCIPLINE FRENCH LITERATURE **EDUCATION** Yale Univ, PhD, 86. **CAREER** Assoc prof. **RESEARCH** Narrative dynamics and their relation to historical, cultural and theoretical frameworks. **SELECTED PUBLICATIONS** Auth, Postmodern Proust, 92; articles on Proust, George Sand, Beckett, and Toussaint. **CONTACT ADDRESS** Dept of French and Italian, Indiana Univ, Bloomington, 1020 E Kirkwood Ave, Ballantine Hall 642, Bloomington, IN 47405. **EMAIL** megray@indiana.edu

GRAY, RICHARD T.
DISCIPLINE GERMAN **EDUCATION** Univ NC, Greensboro, BA, 74; Univ Cincinnati, MA, 76; Univ Va, PhD, 81. **CAREER** Asst prof, Univ Va, 81-82; vis asst prof, Reed Col, 82-84; asst prof, 84-88, assoc, 88-91, Mills Col; assoc prof, 91-93, PROF GER, UNIV WASH. **CONTACT ADDRESS** Dept of Germanics, Univ of Washington, Box 35310, Seattle, WA 98195-3130. **EMAIL** woyzeck@u.washington.edu

GREELEY, JUNE-ANN T.
PERSONAL Born 03/21/1955, Brookline, MA, m, 1983, 1 child **DISCIPLINE** CLASSICS **EDUCATION** Conn Col, BA, 76; Univ Conn, MA, 82; Rutgers Univ, BA, 88; Fordham Univ, MA, 89; PhD, 00. **CAREER** Instr, Fordham Univ, 87-89; Instr, Univ Conn, 97; Instr, Fairfield Col Prep, 97-; Instr, Sacred Heart Univ, 95-. **MEMBERSHIPS** Am Philol Asn; Medieval Acad of Am; Dante Soc; Intl Center for Medieval Art; N Am Medieval Latin Asn; Vergilian Soc; Hagiography Soc; Class Asn of N Eng. **RESEARCH** Poetry of late antiquity; Early Christian poets; Medieval Latin literature; Medieval religion (mysticism); Sacred art/architecture; Classical tradition in (early) medieval literature; Gender studies (esp women in religious traditions); Sufism and medieval Islam. **CONTACT ADDRESS** 4 Merritt Lane, Westport, CT 06880. **EMAIL** june-ann@vocanda.com

GREEN, ANNE
DISCIPLINE GERMAN LANGUAGE AND CULTURE **EDUCATION** Univ Ill, PhD. **CAREER** Languages, Carnegie Mellon Univ. **MEMBERSHIPS** Study Abroad Scholarships Comt; Lang Learning Resource Lab Advisory Comt; Western Pa Am Asn Tchrs German. **SELECTED PUBLICATIONS** Coauth, The Most Noble Diet: Food Selection and Ethics, New York: Diet Ethics, 94; Adapting Games for the Foreign Language Classroom, 94; Mod Lang Undergrad Handbook, 95; Games for the German Classroom, 95. **CONTACT ADDRESS** Carnegie Mellon Univ, 5000 Forbes Ave, Pittsburgh, PA 15213.

GREEN, GEORGE
PERSONAL Born 01/26/1937, Urbana, IL, m, 1977, 4 children **DISCIPLINE** HISPANIC LITERATURE, LINGUISTICS, TRANSLATION, FOLKLORE **EDUCATION** Columbia Univ, BA, 68; MA, 71; MPhil, 74; PhD, 76. **CAREER** Prof, Univ Tex at Brownsville, 76-. **HONORS AND AWARDS** NDF, 71. **MEMBERSHIPS** Ed Bd, Novosantanderino; Ed Bd, Mesquite Rev. **RESEARCH** Latin American poetry and novel, esp, Mexico and Central America; 19th and 20th Centuries. **SELECTED PUBLICATIONS** Auth, El Lenguaje Poetico De Ruben Dario, Univ America (Managua, Nicaragua), 99. **CONTACT ADDRESS** Dept Arts, Sci, Univ of Texas, Brownsville, 1614 Ridgely Rd, Brownsville, TX 78520-4964.

GREEN, GEORGIA MARKS
PERSONAL Born 04/16/1944, Atlanta, GA **DISCIPLINE** LINGUISTICS **EDUCATION** Univ Chicago, BA, 66, MA, 69, PhD(ling), 71. **CAREER** Asst prof, 71-73, Assoc Prof Ling, Univ Ill, Urbana, 73-, Fels, Ctr Advan Study, Univ Ill, 70-71 and 78-79. **MEMBERSHIPS** MLA; Ling Soc Am. **RESEARCH** Syntax; semantics; pragmatics. **SELECTED PUBLICATIONS** **CONTACT ADDRESS** Dept of Ling, Univ of Illinois, Urbana-Champaign, 707 S Mathews Ave, Urbana, IL 61801-3625.

GREEN, LISA
DISCIPLINE LINGUISTICS **EDUCATION** Grambling State Univ, BS, 85; Univ Ky, MA, 87; Univ Mass, PhD, 93. **CAREER** Asst prof, Univ of Mass, Amherst; asst prof, Univ of Tex. **RESEARCH** Syntactic theory; African-American English syntax and semantics. **SELECTED PUBLICATIONS** Auth, Verb Phrase patterns in Black English and Creole (rev), J Pidgin Creole Lang, 94; A Unified Account of Auxiliaries in African American English, CLS, 94. **CONTACT ADDRESS** Dept of Ling, Univ of Texas, Austin, Austin, TX 78712. **EMAIL** lgreen@mail.utexas.edu

GREEN, PAUL J.
PERSONAL Born 07/27/1936, Seattle, WA, s **DISCIPLINE** COMPARATIVE LITERATURE **EDUCATION** Seattle Pac Col, BA, 57; Univ Wash, MA, 58; Univ Calif Berkeley, MLS, 68; Wash State Univ, PhD, 81. **CAREER** Teaching asst, Univ Wash, 63-66; instr, Cen Wash Univ, 66-67; res asst, Univ Calif Berkeley, 67-68; asst ser lib, Univ Ore, 68-69; teaching asst, Wash State Univ, 74-76; independent critic scholar, Spokane, Seattle, Pullman, 81-. **HONORS AND AWARDS** Phi Sigma Iota, China, 97; Int Biog Asn Life Fel; ABIRA Dep Gov; Order Int Ambassadors. **MEMBERSHIPS** IPA; MLA; ACLA; ICLA; NASSR; Kafka Soc; AAUP; People to People Intl; Univ Wash Alumni; NGS; Sierra Club; AAP. **RESEARCH** The novel; comparative literature of the 19th and 20yh centuries; psychoanalysis and literature; European studies; evaluation bibliography; Franz Kafka; Foreign language pedagogy. **SELECTED PUBLICATIONS** Ed, Student Writing, 66-67; auth, The Life of Jack Gray: An Education in Living and in Love. **CONTACT ADDRESS** 630 NE Maiden Ln, Unit 10, Pullman, WA 99163.

GREEN, PETER
PERSONAL Born 12/22/1924, London, England, m, 1975, 3 children **DISCIPLINE** CLASSICS **EDUCATION** Cambridge Univ, BA, 50; MA, 54; PhD, 54. **CAREER** Vis Prof, Univ Tex, 71-72; Vis Prof, Univ Calif, 76; Prof, Tulane Univ, 86; Prof, Univ Tex, 72-97; Vis Prof, Univ Iowa, 97-98; Adjunct Prof, Univ Iowa, 98-. **HONORS AND AWARDS** Heinemann Awd for Lit, 57; Grad Teaching Awd, Univ Tex, 84; NEH Sen Feel, 83-84. **MEMBERSHIPS** APA, CAMWS, Hellenic Assoc. (UK), ATA. **RESEARCH** Greek history, classical and Hellenistic, Latin satire and elegy, modern Greek and Anglo-American poetry. **SELECTED PUBLICATIONS** Auth, Alexander of Maredon, 356-323 B C: A Historical Biography, Rev Ed (London, UK), 74; auth, Alexander to Actium: The Historical Evolution of the Hellenistic Age, Rev Ed (Berkeley, CA), 93; auth, The Greco-Persian Wars (Berkeley, CA), 96; auth,

Classical Beanings: Interpretive Ancient History and Culture (New York, NY), 98; auth, Juvenile: The Sixteen Satires, 3rd Rev Ed (New York, NY), 98. **CONTACT ADDRESS** Dept Class, Univ Iowa, 1268 Chamberlain Dr, Iowa City, IA 52240. **EMAIL** peter-green-1@uiowa.edu

GREEN, VIRGINIA M.
DISCIPLINE FRENCH **EDUCATION** B.A., University of Puget Sound; Ph.D., Duke University. **CAREER** Asst prof; dir Assessment. **SELECTED PUBLICATIONS** Publ, sev articles on French Renaissance lit. **EMAIL** vmgreen@enid.com

GREENBERG, MARC L.
PERSONAL Born 11/09/1961, Los Angeles, CA, m, 1988, 2 children **DISCIPLINE** LANGUAGE; LITERATURE **EDUCATION** Univ Calif Los Angeles, BA, 83, PhD, 90; Univ Chicago, MA, 84. **CAREER** Asst prof to assoc prof, Univ Ks, 90-; chair, Slavic dept, 00-. **HONORS AND AWARDS** Zahvala, Republic of Slovenia, 92; neh res fel, 93; fulbright-hays fel, 88-89. **MEMBERSHIPS** Soc of Slovene Stud, Amer Assoc of Teachers of Slavic & E Eur Lang; SE Eur Stud Assoc; Amer Assoc for the Adv of Slavic Stud. **RESEARCH** Hist Slavic & Indo-Eur ling; dialectology. **SELECTED PUBLICATIONS** Auth, Archaisms and Innovations in the Dialect of Sredisce; In Slavic Stud, 95; The vowel system of the Sredisce dialect based on the descriptions of Karel Ozvald, Rodopi, 96; The Sociolinguistics of Slovene, ed. Mouton de Gruyter, 97; auth, Sound Repetition and Metaphorical Structure in the Igor' Tale, Slavic, 98; Is Slavic ceta an Indo-European Archaism? In J of Slavic Ling & Poetics, 00; auth, A Historical Phonology of the Slovene Language, C Winter Universitatsverlag (Heidelberg), 00. **CONTACT ADDRESS** Dept Slavic Lang & Lit, Univ of Kansas, Lawrence, 2134 Wescoe Hall, Lawrence, KS 66045-2174. **EMAIL** m-greenberg@ukans.edu

GREENBERG, NATHAN ABRAHAM
PERSONAL Born 08/23/1928, Boston, MA, m, 1952, 3 children **DISCIPLINE** CLASSICAL PHILOLOGY **EDUCATION** Hebrew Teachers Col, Boston, BJEd, 48; Harvard Univ, AB, 50, AM, 52, PhD, 55. **CAREER** From instr to assoc prof, 56-69, assoc dean humanities, 67-68, chmn dept, 70-76, Prof Classics, Oberlin Col, 69-, Fulbright scholar, Italy, 55-56; Rockefeller Found study grant, 62-63; Am Coun Learned Soc study grant, 68; Fulbright sr res fel, Belgium, 69-70; vis fel, Wolfson Col, Oxford Univ, 76-77; Am Coun Learned Soc res fel, 76-77. **MEMBERSHIPS** AAUP; Am Philol Asn; Archaeol Inst Am; Vergilian Soc. **RESEARCH** Ancient poetics; political philosophy; computer use in literary study. **SELECTED PUBLICATIONS** Auth, The Attitude of Agamemnon: Homer, 'Iliad', Book-1, Class World, Vol 0086, 93. **CONTACT ADDRESS** Dept of Classics, Oberlin Col, King Bldg, Oberlin, OH 44074. **EMAIL** nate71@usa.net

GREENBERG, WENDY
PERSONAL Born 12/31/1951, Philadelphia, PA **DISCIPLINE** FRENCH, COMPARATIVE LITERATURE **EDUCATION** Columbia Univ, BA, 73, MA, 74, PhD(Fr), 79. **CAREER** Preceptor, Columbia Univ, 74-77; Asst Prof French, PA State Univ, Fogelsville, 79-, Nat Endowment for Humanities fel, Harvard Univ, 81. **MEMBERSHIPS** MLA; Am Asn Teachers Fr; Alliance Francaise. **RESEARCH** Theory of metaphor; Victor Hugo; 19th century French romanticism. **SELECTED PUBLICATIONS** Auth, Hugo and Whitman: Poets of totality, Whitman Rev, 3/78; coauth & transl, The object-event, Yale French Studies, No 59; auth, Is there a text in this class?, Teaching Lang Through Lit, spring 82. **CONTACT ADDRESS** Pennsylvania State Univ, Univ Park, University Park, PA 16802.

GREENE, ROBERT WILLIAM
PERSONAL Born 01/03/1933, Boston, MA, m, 1959, 2 children **DISCIPLINE** FRENCH **EDUCATION** Boston Col, AB, 54; Middlebury Col, MA, 58; Univ Pa, PhD(Romance lang), 63. **CAREER** From instr French to asst prof, Univ Calif, Berkeley, 63-69; assoc prof, Univ Iowa, 69-74; vis prof, 74-75, Prof Emer French, State Univ NY, Albany 97-, Am Coun Learned Soc grant-in-aid, 73; Am Philos Soc grant, 75; Nat Endowment for Humanities res fel, 80-81. **MEMBERSHIPS** MLA; Am Asn Teachers Fr; Asn Lit Scholars & Critics. **RESEARCH** Modern French poetry, fiction, art criticism. **SELECTED PUBLICATIONS** Auth, The Poetic Theory of Pierre Reverdy , U of Cal Press, 67; auth, Six French Poets of Our Time, Princeton UP, 79; ed, Dalhousie French Studies, 21 91, Art Criticism by French Poets Since World War II; auth, Lost Beyond Telling--Representations of Death and Absence in Modern French Poetry, Fr Forum, Vol 0017, 92; auth, Just Words: Moralism and Metalanguage in Twentiety-Century French Fiction, Penn State UP, 93; The Presence of the Image--Bonnefoy, Yves Critique of 9 Painters and Sculptors, Fr Forum, Vol 0021, 96; When Apollinaire, Malraux and Bonnefoy Write about Art, Esprit Createur, Vol 0036, 96. **CONTACT ADDRESS** Dept of French, SUNY, Albany, 25 Birchwood Pl, Delmar, NY 12054.

GREENFIELD, SUMNER M.
PERSONAL Born 12/13/1921, Boston, MA, m, 1946, 2 children **DISCIPLINE** SPANISH **EDUCATION** Boston Col, AB, 44; Boston Univ, AM, 47; Harvard Univ, AM, 51, PhD(Romance lang), 57. **CAREER** From instr to assoc prof, 51-67, Prof Span, Univ Mass, Amherst, 67-. **MEMBERSHIPS** MLA; Am Asn Teachers Span & Port; New England Coun Latin Am Studies. **RESEARCH** Twentieth century Spanish literature; the modernist movement. **SELECTED PUBLICATIONS CONTACT ADDRESS** Dept of Span and Port, Univ of Massachusetts, Amherst, Amherst, MA 01003.

GREGG, ROBERT C.
DISCIPLINE CLASSICS **EDUCATION** BA, 60; MDiv, 63; Univ PA, PhD, 74. **CAREER** Prof relig studies/class. **RESEARCH** Early Christianity , institutions, thought, ritual, Jews, Pagans, and Christians in Late Antiquity, asceticism in the late Roman and Early Christian periods, Comparative exegesis in Judaism, Christianity, and Islam. **SELECTED PUBLICATIONS** Auth, Jews, Pagans, and Christians in the Ancient Golan Heights, 96; coauth, Early Arianism, 81; ed, Arianism: Historical and Theological Assessments, 85. **CONTACT ADDRESS** Stanford Univ, Bldg 70, Main Quad, Stanford, CA 94305. **EMAIL** rgregg@stanford.edu

GREGORY, ELMER RICHARD
PERSONAL Born 09/25/1938, Baytown, TX, m, 1981, 1 child **DISCIPLINE** ENGLISH, COMPARATIVE LITERATURE **EDUCATION** Univ Tex, Austin, BA, 60; Rice Univ, MA, 61; Univ Ore, PhD(comp lit), 65. **CAREER** Asst prof English, Univ Ga, 65-67; from asst prof to assoc prof, 67-77, PROF ENGLISH, UNIV TOLEDO, 77-. **MEMBERSHIPS** Conf Christianity and Lit; Milton Soc Am; MLA. **RESEARCH** John Milton; 17th century British literature; detective stories. **SELECTED PUBLICATIONS** Auth, Milton and Tradition, Milton Stud, Vol 0029, 92; Moore, Marianne 'Poetry,' Explicator, Vol 0052, 93; Milton Protestant Sonnet Lady--Revisions in the Donna-Angelicata Tradition, Comp Lit Stud, Vol 0033, 96. **CONTACT ADDRESS** Dept of English, Univ of Toledo, Toledo, OH 43606.

GREGORY, JUSTINA
PERSONAL Born 09/24/1946, Brattleboro, VT, m, 2 children **DISCIPLINE** CLASSICS **EDUCATION** Smith Col, AB, 67; Harvard Univ, MA, 72; PhD, 74. **CAREER** Asst prof, Yale Univ, 74-75; asst prof to prof, Smith Col, 75-. **HONORS AND AWARDS** ACLS Fel; Fulbright Fel; Woodrow Wilson Fel. **MEMBERSHIPS** Am Philol Assoc, Women's Class Caucus, New England Class Assoc, Phi Beta Kappa. **RESEARCH** Greek tragedy, fifth-century intellectual history. **SELECTED PUBLICATIONS** Transl, Aesop's Fables, 75; auth, "Some Aspects of Seeing in the Bacchae," Greece and Rome 32.1 (85): 22-31; auth, Euripides and the Instruction of the Athenians, 91; auth, "The Encounter at the Crossroads in Sophocles' Oedipus Tyrannus," Jour of Hellenic Studies 115, (95): 141-6; auth, "Intertextuality and Genealogy in Hecuta," Am Jour of Philol 116, (95): 389-97; auth, Euripides' Hecuba: Introduction, Text and Commentary, 99; auth, "Comic Elements in Euripides," Ill Class Studies 24-25, (99-00). **CONTACT ADDRESS** Smith Col, Northampton, MA 01063-0001. **EMAIL** jgregory@smith.edu

GRENOBLE, LENORE A.
DISCIPLINE RUSSIAN LANGUAGE AND LITERATURE **EDUCATION** Univ CA Berkeley, PhD, 86. **CAREER** Assoc prof and chr, Prog Ling and Cog Sci and Dept of Russian. **RESEARCH** Semantics and discourse analysis; Slavic and Tungusic lang(s); deixis; verbal categories; lang endangerment. **SELECTED PUBLICATIONS** Coauth, The Role of Deictics in Discourse Coherence: French voici/voila and Russian vot/von, Jour Pragmatics, 96; Endangered Languages: Current Issues and Future Prospects, Int Jour Soc Lang, 96; ed, Essays in the Art and Theory of Translation, Edwin Mellen, 97; co-ed, Essays in the Art and Theory of Translation, Lewiston, NY: Edwin Mellen Press, 97; co-ed, Endangered Languages: Current Issues and Future Prospects, Cambridge: Cambridge Univ Press, 98; auth, Deixis and Information Packaging in Russian Discourse, Pragmatics and Beyond, Cambridge UP, 98; coauth, Languages of the World Materials/141, Munich: Lincom, 99; coauth, "Revisiting Tungusic Classification from the Bottom Up: A Comparison of Evenki and Oroqen," Language 75/2, (99): 286-321. **CONTACT ADDRESS** Dartmouth Col, 44 N Col St, Hanover, NH 03755-1801. **EMAIL** lenore.grenoble@dartmouth.edu

GREPPIN, JOHN AIRD COUTTS
PERSONAL Born 04/02/1937, Rochester, NY, m, 2 children **DISCIPLINE** LINGUISTICS **EDUCATION** Univ Rochester, AB, 61; Univ Wash, MA, 66; Univ Calif, Los Angeles, PhD, 72. **CAREER** Asst prof, Univ Fla, 71-72; asst prof, Cleveland State Univ, 75-80; assoc prof, 80-83; full prof, 83-; vis prof, Marburg Univ, Germany, 93. **HONORS AND AWARDS** Russell Mumford Tuttle Awd for Proficiency in Greek, Univ Rochester, 61; Silver medal, Melchiatarist Congregation, Venice, Italy; recipient of numerous IREX grants, NEH fellowships, and other grants; acls fel, 65; neh fel, 66, 67, 69, 78; irex grant, 74-75, 79, 80, 81, 84, 85, 87, 92, 94; agbu alex manoogian grant, 79-00. **MEMBERSHIPS** Am Philol Asn; Am Oriental Soc; Soc Armenian Studies; Assoc Int des Etudes Armeniennes. **RESEARCH** Classical and Middle Armenian Philology; Classics; Indo-European linguistics. **SELECTED PUBLICATIONS** Auth, A Medieval Arabic-Armenian Pharmaceutical Dictionary, Vienna, Mechitaristen-Buch-druckerei, Studien zur armenischen Geschichte XVI, 97; co-ed, Studies in Honor of Jaan Puhvel, Part I: Ancient Languages and Philology, J Indo-Europ Studies Monograph No 20, Inst for the Study of Man, 97; Studies in Honor of Jaan Puhvel, Part II: Mythology and Religion, J Indo-Europ Studies Monograph No 21, Inst for the Study of Man, 97; auth, The Diffusion of Greek Medicine into the Middle East and the Caucasus, Caravan Books, 00; author and editor of numerous other books and articles. **CONTACT ADDRESS** Program in Ling, Cleveland State Univ, 1983 E 24th St, Cleveland, OH 44115-2440. **EMAIL** j.greppin@csuohio.edu

GRIBBLE, CHARLES EDWARD
PERSONAL Born 11/10/1936, Lansing, MI, m, 1 child **DISCIPLINE** SLAVIC LANGUAGES **EDUCATION** Univ MI, BA, 57; Harvard Univ, AM, 58, PhD, 67. **CAREER** From lectr to asst prof Russ, Brandeis Univ, 61-68; asst prof Slavic, Ind Univ, Bloomington, 68-75, asst chmn dept Slavic lang & lit & dir Slavic Workshop, 68-70; assoc prof, 75-89, Prof Slavic Lang, OH State Univ, 89-, chmn dept, 90-96; Pres, Slavica Publ, 68-97; Slavic area fel, 72; partic sr scholar exchange to USSR, Int Res & Exchanges Bd, 72. **HONORS AND AWARDS** Phi Beta Kappa; Phi Kappa Phi; Phi Eta Sigma; Boynton Sch, 56-57 **MEMBERSHIPS** Ling Soc Am; Am Asn Tchr Slavic & East Europ Lang; Am Asn Advan Slavic Studies; Am Asn Southeast Europ Studies; Ling Soc Europe; MLA. **RESEARCH** Hist and struct of Russ; comp Slavic linguistics; South Slavic lang(s). **SELECTED PUBLICATIONS** Ed, Studies Presented to Professor Roman Jakobson by His Students, 68, auth, Russian Root List with a Sketch of Russian Word Formation, 73, Medieval Slavic Texts, vol I, 73 & A Short Dictionary of 18th Century Russian, 76, Slavica. **CONTACT ADDRESS** Dept of Slavic Lang, Ohio State Univ, Columbus, 1841 Millikin Rd, Columbus, OH 43210-1229. **EMAIL** gribble3@osu.edu

GRIES, FRAUKE
PERSONAL Born 09/06/1922, Berlin, Germany, m, 1945 **DISCIPLINE** GERMAN LANGUAGE, GERMAN LITERATURE **EDUCATION** San Francisco State Col, BA, 62; Stanford Univ, MA, 64; PhD, 67. **CAREER** Asst prof to assoc prof to prof to emer, Calif State Univ Hayward, 66-. **HONORS AND AWARDS** NDEA Fel, 62-65; FRG Foreign Off, Fel, 71; PhilolSoc Grant, 74; ACLS, Grant, 73-74; Intl Hochschulferienkurs fur Germanistik, Halle Univ, 85. **MEMBERSHIPS** KLA; AATG; IVG; Simone de Beauvoir Soc. **RESEARCH** German romanticism; modern German literature; contemporary and modern drama. **SELECTED PUBLICATIONS** Auth, "A Model for In-Service Education," Am Foreign Lang Teaching (70); auth, "Fine Unbeachtet Gebliebene Rezension von Ludwig Tieck: Belisar Trauerspiel in Funf Akten von Ed v Schenk," Zeitschrift fur Deut Philol (71); auth, "Two Critical Essays by Ludwig Tieck: on Literature and its Sociological Aspects," Monatshefte (74); auth, "Edition of Two Previously Unpublished Essays by Ludwig Tieck," Am PhilolSoc (75); auth, "Anna Seghers and Simone de Beavoir," Simone de Beavoir Soc (87). **CONTACT ADDRESS** 135 Amber Dr, San Francisco, CA 94131-1625. **EMAIL** kafragries@msn.com

GRIFFEN, TOBY DAVID
PERSONAL Born 05/12/1946, Washington, DC **DISCIPLINE** LINGUISTICS, GERMAN **EDUCATION** The Citadel, BA, 68; Univ Va, MA, 69; Univ Fla, PhD(ling). **CAREER** Asst prof Ger, Wichita State Univ, 75-77; Asst Prof Ger, Southern Ill Univ, Edwardsville, 77-82, Assoc prof, 82-86; Prof, 86-. **HONORS AND AWARDS** Res scholar awards, Southern Ill Univ, 78, 81, 84, Outstanding scholar award, 92. **MEMBERSHIPS** Ling Asn Can and US; Celtic Studies Asn N Am. **RESEARCH** Linguistics; celtic studies. **SELECTED PUBLICATIONS** Auth, An Applied Linguistic Approach to German Word-Order, Wichita State Univ, Studies, No. 106, 76; auth, Aspects of Dynamic Phonology, Current Issues in Linguistic Theory No. 37, (Amsterdam): John Benjamins, 85; auth, Germano-European: Breaking the Sound Law, Carbondale: Southern Ill Univ Press, 88; auth, The Linguistics of Welsh Literature, editor, special issue of Lang Sciences, vol 15, Number 2, 93; auth, Names from the Dawn of British Legend: Taliesin, Aneirin, Myrddin/Merlin, Arthur, Felinfach, Lampeter (Wales): Llanerch Publications, 94; auth, Celebrating the Celtic Saints: As Candles on a Stand, Templegate (Springfield, IL) 98; auth, The Last Battle of the Gododdin: The Hidden Poem in Armes Prydein, Felinfach, Lampeter Llanerch Publications (Wales), in press 01. **CONTACT ADDRESS** Dept Foreign Lang & Lit, So Illinois Univ, Edwardsville, Edwardsville, IL 62026-1432. **EMAIL** tgriffe@siue.edu

GRIFFIN, DAVID ALEXANDER
PERSONAL Born 01/25/1919, Buffalo, NY, m, 1942, 5 children **DISCIPLINE** LINGUISTICS, SPANISH **EDUCATION** Univ Chicago, AB, 47, AM, 49, PhD(Span), 56. **CAREER** Instr Romance lang, Oberlin Col, 52-56; vis asst prof Span, Newcomb Col, Tulane Univ, 56-57; asst prof mod lang, Univ Okla, 57-59; sci linguist and asst head dept Southwestern Europ and Latin Am lang, Foreign Serv Inst, US Dept State, 59-61; assoc prof Romance lang, 61-74, acting chmn dept, 71-72, Prof

Romance Lang, Ohio State Univ, 74-, Chmn Dept, 72-. **MEMBERSHIPS** Ling Soc Am; Int Ling Asn; Ling Soc Europe. **RESEARCH** General linguistics; Romance linguistics; Spanish dialectology. **SELECTED PUBLICATIONS** Auth, On the Origin of Spanish Eres, Hisp Rev, Vol 0062, 94. **CONTACT ADDRESS** Dept of Romance Lang, Ohio State Univ, Columbus, 190 N Oval Dr, Columbus, OH 43210.

GRIGGS, JOHN W.

PERSONAL Born 10/05/1948, Three Rivers, MI, d **DISCIPLINE** SPANISH LITERATURE, SPANISH HISTORY **EDUCATION** Ariz State Univ, BA, 70, MA, 71, PhD, 83. **CAREER** Chemn, 71-, Glendale Comm Col. **MEMBERSHIPS** AATSP **RESEARCH** Spanish civil war; modern Spanish poetry, drama, novel. **CONTACT ADDRESS** Glendale Comm Col, Arizona, 6000 W Olive Ave, Glendale, AZ 85302. **EMAIL** jgriggs@gcmail.maricopa.edu

GRIGORUT, CONSTANTIN

PERSONAL Born 04/03/1955, Romania, m, 1988, 2 children **DISCIPLINE** FRENCH **EDUCATION** Stefan cel Mare Univ, BA, 82; McMaster Univ, MA, 97. **CAREER** Professeur Agrege, Lycee Mihail Sadoveanu, Romania, 82-96; instr, McMaster Univ, 96-97; instr, Univ Brit Columb, 97-99. **HONORS AND AWARDS** Arthur W Patrick Awd, 96; SSHRC Fel, 99-01. **MEMBERSHIPS** MLA, CIEF. **RESEARCH** 20th Century French Novel, 20th Century French Drama, 20th Century French History of Ideas, Myths and Literary Symbols in French Liteature, Theory of Intertexuality, French Literature after 1945, Postmodern French Canadian Literature. **SELECTED PUBLICATIONS** Auth, "Un mythe voyageur et son ancrage intertextuel," Etudes francophones, (00). **CONTACT ADDRESS** Univ of British Columbia, 297-1873 East Mall, Vancouver, BC, Canada V6T 1N3. **EMAIL** grigorut@interchange.ubc.ca

GRIMM, REINHOLD

PERSONAL Born 05/21/1931, Nuremberg, Germany, m, 1954, 1 child **DISCIPLINE** GERMAN, COMPARATIVE LITERATURE **EDUCATION** Univ Erlangen-Nurnberg, 51-52; Univ Colo, 52-53; Univ Erlangen-Nurnberg, DPhil, 56. **CAREER** Asst prof, Univ Erlangen-Nurnberg, 57-61; asst prof, Univ Frankfurt, 61-67; A. Hohlfeld Prof, Univ Wis; prof, Univ Calif at Riverside, 90-. **HONORS AND AWARDS** A. Hohlfeld Prof of German, Univ Wis, 67-80; Guggenheim Fel, 69 & 70; Vilas Res Prof of Comparative Lit and German, Univ Wis, 80-90; Presidential Chair, Univ Calif, 90-92; Distinguished Prof of German and Comparative Lit, Univ Calif, 97-. **MEMBERSHIPS** Int P.E.N. Club, Am Asn of Teachers of German. **RESEARCH** German and Comparative Literature of the Nineteenth- and Twentieth-centuries, Blacks in German Art and Literature, the Picaresque Novel, Translation. **SELECTED PUBLICATIONS** Auth, Love, Lust, and Rebellion: New Approaches to George Buchner, 85; auth, Echo and Disguise: Studies in German and Comparative Literature, 89; auth, Versuche zur europaischen Literatur, 94. **CONTACT ADDRESS** Dept Comparative Lit & For Lang, Univ of California, Riverside, 900 University Ave, Riverside, CA 92521-0001.

GRIMSTAD, KAAREN

DISCIPLINE OLD ICELANDIC LANGUAGE AND LITERATURE **EDUCATION** Harvard Univ, PhD. **CAREER** Assoc prof, Univ Minn, Twin Cities. **RESEARCH** Children's literature. **SELECTED PUBLICATIONS** Auth, Text Editing as Dialogue, Ger Stud in Honor of Anatoly Liberman, Nowele 31/32, Odense UP, 97; coauth, Munu vit ekki at thve aettask: A Closer Look at Dialogues in Hrafnkels saga, Arkiv for nordisk filologi 111, 96. **CONTACT ADDRESS** Dept of Ger, Scand & Dutch, Univ of Minnesota, Twin Cities, 231 Folwel, Minneapolis, MN 55455. **EMAIL** grims001@tc.umn.edu

GRIMSTAD, KIRSTEN J.

PERSONAL Born 11/17/1944, Milwaukee, WI **DISCIPLINE** COMPARATIVE LITERATURE **EDUCATION** Barnard Col, BA, 68; Columbia Univ, MA, 71; Union Inst, PhD, 97. **CAREER** Preceptor, Columbia Univ, 69-73; exec ed, Chrysalis, 76-81; acquisitions ed, JP Tarcher, 80-81; assoc prof, Norwich Univ, 88-. **HONORS AND AWARDS** Ger Prize, Barnard Univ, 67; Fel, Columbia Univ, 70-72; Fel, Norwich Univ, 95; Fel, Am Asn of Univ Women, 95; Charles A Dana Awd, Norwich Univ, 99. **MEMBERSHIPS** MLA, Ger Studies Assoc, Thomas Mann Gesellschaft, Modernist Studies Assoc. **RESEARCH** European modernism, Gnosticism and literature, Psychoanalysis and literature. **SELECTED PUBLICATIONS** Ed, Women's Work and Women's Studies, Barnard Col, 71-72; coauth, The New Woman's Survival Catalogue, Coward, McCann, 73; coauth, the New Woman's Survival Sourcebook, Knopf, 75; ed, Conservation of Tapestries and Embroideries, Getty Conserv Inst, 89; auth, The Modern Revival of Gnosticism in Thomas Mann's Doktor Faustus, Camden House, 01. **CONTACT ADDRESS** 14709 Bestor Blvd, Pacific Palisades, CA 90272. **EMAIL** grimstad@mindspring.com

GRISE, YOLANDE

PERSONAL Born 08/05/1944, Montreal, PQ, Canada **DISCIPLINE** FRENCH LITERATURE **EDUCATION** Univ Montreal, BA, 64, BPed, 65; Univ Laval, LL, 71; Univ Sorbonne, ML, 72, DL 3e cycle, 77. **CAREER** Prof hist, Univ Laval, 78-79; prof adj, 80, prof agregee, 83, Prof Litterature, Lettres Francaises, Univ Ottawa, 80-, prof titulaire, 90. **HONORS AND AWARDS** Boursiere, Govt Que, 71-72, 72-75; Conseil des arts du Can, 72-75. **MEMBERSHIPS** Soc des etudes latines (Paris); l'Union des ecrivains quebecois; l'Assoc des etudes canadiennes; l'Assoc des litt can et quebecoise. **SELECTED PUBLICATIONS** Auth,"Melanges de litterature candienne-francaise et quebecoise offerts a Refean Robioux," textes reunis par Yolande Grise et Robert Major, (Ottawa, P.U.O. 92), 430; auth, "Aspects de la mort dans les debuts de la poesie au Canada francais," dans Melanges de litterature canadienne-francaise et quebecoise offerts a Refena Robidoux, texts reunis par yolande Grise et Robert Major, (Ottawa, P.U.O. 92), 56-76; auth, "Pistes de reflecion sur l'avenir de la recherche en litterature quebecoise," dans Pour un bilan prospectif de la recherche en litterature quebecois, sous la direction de Louise Milot et Francois Demont, Quebec, Nuit blan-che Editeur, (93), 115-130; auth, "emile Nelligan, " cinquante ans apres sa mort, sous la direction de Yolnade Grise, Rejean robidoux et Paul wyczynski, Montreal, Fides, (93), 352; auth, "Etats generaux de la recherche sure la francophonie a l exterieur du Quebec," textes reunis par Yolande Grise, Ottawa, P.U.O. (95), 284; co auth,"Les Textes poetiques du Canada francais, 1606-1867," Edition integrale, par Yolande Grise et Jeanne dArc Lortie, s.c.o. (en collaboration avec Pierre Savard et Paul Wyczynski), Montreal, fides, (vol 9: 1861-1862), (96), 797; auth, "La Presence de Thgomas Moore, auteur de A canadian Boat Song," dans la poesie canadienne-francais, au XIX siecle, J of Canadian Studies/La Revue d etudes canadiennes, vol 32, (97), 48-71; auth, "Les Textes poetiques du Canada fracais, 1606-1867" Edition integrale, (vol 10: 1863-1864), Montreal, fides, (97), 843; auth, "La Poesie quedbecoise avant Nelligan," anthologie, Montreal, Fides, (98), 369. **CONTACT ADDRESS** Dep des lettres francaises, Univ of Ottawa, Ottawa, ON, Canada K1N 6N5.

GRITTNER, FRANK MERTON

PERSONAL Born 02/12/1927, Ashland, WI, m, 1949, 5 children **DISCIPLINE** GERMAN, SPANISH **EDUCATION** Northland Col, BA, 50; Univ Wis, MA, 52, PhD(foreign lang educ), 72. **CAREER** Teacher Ger, Fond du Lac Pub Schs, Wis, 52-56; teacher Ger and Span, Madison Pub Schs, 56-60; State Supvr Foreign Lang, WIS Dept Pub Instr, 60-, Comt mem, MLA studies of effectiveness of NDEA Title XI Foreign Lang Summer Inst Prog, 67; ed, Cent States Conf Teaching Foreign Lang publ, 68-74; educ auditor, Milwaukee Biling Prog, and State Off Educ ESEA Title VII grant, 69-72. **MEMBERSHIPS** Am Coun Teaching Foreign Lang (pres, 75); Am Asn Teachers Ger (pres, 84); Cent States Conf Teaching Foreign Lang; Asn Dept Foreign Lang (secy, 65-68); Nat Coun State Supvr Foreign Lang (pres, 64-65). **RESEARCH** History of foreign language acquisition. **SELECTED PUBLICATIONS** Auth, Books: Teaching Foreign Languages, Harper & Row, 69 revised & expanded 77; auth, Individualized Foreign Language Instruction, w. Fred LaLeike, 73, Chap. 2, Pluralism in FL Ed., National Textbook Britannica Review of FL ed., 71; ed or auth of over 50 books, articles, or chapters published nationally or internationally, including in MLJ, FL Annals, French Review, Unterrichts-Praxis, Editor of FL Annals, 92-00; ed., In a Class by Itself--Focus on Instruction, For Lang Ann, Vol 0026, 93; ed., Curriculum Renewal in School Foreign-Language Learning, Mod Lang J, Vol 0077, 93; ed., In a Class by Itself--Focus on Instruction, For Lang Ann, Vol 0027, 94; ed.,In a Class by Itself--Focus on Instruction, For Lang Ann, Vol 0028, 95; ed., Toward a Definition of Learning-Disabled (LD) as Applied to the Foreign-Language Student, For Lang Ann, Vol 0028, 95; ed.,Strategies and Techniques in Foreign-Language Teaching--Introduction, For Lang Ann, Vol 0029, 96; ed.,In a Class by Itself--Focus on Instruction, For Lang Ann, Vol 0029, 96; ed. ,Introduction to this Special Edition on Culture, For Lang Ann, Vol 0029, 96; ed.,Focus on Illustration, For Lang Ann, Vol 0030, 97. **CONTACT ADDRESS** 6230 Onwentsia Trl., Oregon, WI 53575. **EMAIL** fgrittner@mailbag.com

GROCH, JOHN R.

DISCIPLINE COMPUTER-MEDIATED COMMUNICATION **EDUCATION** PhD **CAREER** Coordr, Commun Stud in Continuing Educ. **RESEARCH** Film; mass cult; postmodernism. **SELECTED PUBLICATIONS** Written on, popularity of The Wizard of Oz & comic authorship in the films of the Marx Brothers. **CONTACT ADDRESS** Commun Dept, Chatham Col, Woodland Rd., Pittsburgh, PA 15232.

GROOS, ARTHUR

PERSONAL Born 02/05/1943, Fullerton, CA, m, 1979, 2 children **DISCIPLINE** GERMAN STUDIES **EDUCATION** Princeton Univ, BA, 64; Cornell Univ, MA, 66, PhD, 70. **CAREER** Asst prof, UCLA, 69-73; asst prof, Cornell Univ, 73-76, assoc prof, 76-82, prof, 82-, Dir, Medieval Studies, 74-79, 81-86, chair, dept of German, 86-91, 96-99. **HONORS AND AWARDS** Fulbright Sr Res Fel to Germany, 79-80; Guggenheim Fel; ASCAP Deems Taylor Prize, 93; Fel, Cornell Soc for the Humanities, 99; Alexander von Humboldt Res Prize, 99; founding co-ed, Cambridge Opera J, 89-; founding mem and Bd of Dirs, Centro Studi Giacomo Puccini (Lucca), 96-; founding ed, Studi pucciniani, 98-. **MEMBERSHIPS** Am Musicological Soc, Modern Lang Asn, Medieval Acad, Wolfram-von-Eschenbach Gesellschaft. **RESEARCH** Opera (German, Italian); postcolonial studies; medieval German literature; history of science. **SELECTED PUBLICATIONS** Auth, "Matthijs Jolles," Dichtkunst und Lebenskunst: Studien zum Problem der Sprache bei Friedrich Schiller, ed, Arthur Groos, Bonn: Bouvier (80); coauth, "Puccini: La boheme," Cambridge Opera Handbooks, Cambridge: Cambridge Univ Press (86); auth, "Magister Regis: Studies in Honor of Robert Earl Kaske, ed Arthur Groos, NY: Fordham Univ Press (86); coauth, Medieval Christian Imagery: A Guide to Interpretation, Toronto: Univ of Toronto Press (86); co-ed, Reading Opera, Princeton, NJ: Princeton Univ Press (88); auth, Romancing the Grail: Genre, Science, and Quest in Wolfram von Eschenbach's Parzival, Ithaca: Cornell Univ Press (95); co-ed, Studi pucciniani I, Lucca: Centro Studi Giacomo Puccini (98). **CONTACT ADDRESS** Dept German Studies, Cornell Univ, 183 Goldwin Smith Hall, Ithaca, NY 14853. **EMAIL** abg3@cornell.edu

GROSS, DAVID STUART

PERSONAL Born 02/22/1942, Mineola, NY, m, 1971, 1 child **DISCIPLINE** ENGLISH, COMPARATIVE LITERATURE **EDUCATION** Wesleyan Univ, BA, 65; Univ Iowa, MA, 69, PhD(comp lit), 73. **CAREER** Asst prof English, Winona State Col, 71-73; asst prof to prof, Univ of Okla, 73-. **MEMBERSHIPS** MLA; Soc Amis Flaubert. **RESEARCH** The novel; literature and society; Marxist theory. **CONTACT ADDRESS** Dept of English, Univ of Oklahoma, 760 Van Vleet Oval, Room 113, Norman, OK 73069. **EMAIL** david-gross@ou.edu

GROSS, IRENA GRUDZINSKA

PERSONAL Born 12/15/1946, Poland, d, 2 children **DISCIPLINE** FRENCH **EDUCATION** Columbia Univ, MA, 76; MPhil, 78; PhD, 82. **CAREER** Vis lectr, Yale Univ, 83-84; asst prof to assoc prof, Emory Univ, 84-95; vis assoc prof to vis scholar, NY Univ, 96-. **HONORS AND AWARDS** Knight's Cross, Poland, 96; Mellon Fel, Harvard Univ, 86; Pres Fel, Columbia Univ, 74-78. **MEMBERSHIPS** MLA; AAASS. **RESEARCH** 18-20th century European history and culture, especially national identity. **SELECTED PUBLICATIONS** Auth, The Scar of Revolution: Custine, Tocqueville and the Romantic Imagination, Univ Calif Press, 91; ed, Constitutionalism in East Central Europe, Am Coun of Learned Soc, 94; ed, Constitutionalism and Politics, Am Coun of Learned Soc, 94; ed, Adam Michnik, Letters from Freedom, Univ Calif Press, 98; ed, Alexis de Tocqueville, Selected Letters, Znak Pub, 99; auth, Joseph Brodsky and the Fellowship of Poets, forthcoming; auth, Mickiewicz and the Nationality Question, forthcoming. **CONTACT ADDRESS** Dept Lang, New York Univ, 3 Washington Sq Village, Apt 3B, New York, NY 10012. **EMAIL** iggl@ny.edu

GROSS, SABINE

PERSONAL Born 09/11/1957, Frankfurt, Germany **DISCIPLINE** GERMAN LITERATURE **EDUCATION** Univ Calif - Santa Barbara, PhD, 91. **CAREER** Asst Prof, 92-97, Assoc Prof, Univ Wis - Madison, 97-. **HONORS AND AWARDS** Lilly Foundation Fellowship, 94-95; Chancellor's Distinguished Teaching Awd, 99; Vilas Research Fellowship, 99-01. **MEMBERSHIPS** MLA; AATG; Women in Ger; IVG; IAPL; Int Soc Study of Time; International Brecht Society; International Herder Society. **RESEARCH** 20th-century German literature; literary theory; reader response & narratology; theater; film; study of time. **SELECTED PUBLICATIONS** Auth, Lese-Zeichen: Kognition, Medium und Materialitat im LeseprozeÑ, Wissenschaftliche Buchgesellschaft, 94; Narrative Time and the Reader, Semiotics Around the World: Synthesis in Diversity. IASS Congress Proceedings, Mouton de Gruyter, 97; The World Turned Image: Reading Pattern Poems, Poetics Today, Spring 97; Cognitive Readings or the Disappearance of Literature in the Mind, Poetics Today, Summer 97; ed, Monatshefte, Winter 97; author of numerous other articles and book chapters. **CONTACT ADDRESS** Univ of Wisconsin, Madison, 1220 Linden Dr, Madison, WI 53706.

GROSSFELD, BERNARD

PERSONAL Born 06/13/1933, Vienna, Austria, m, 1964, 3 children **DISCIPLINE** HEBREW LANGUAGE AND LITERATURE **EDUCATION** Univ Calif, Los Angeles, BA, 59, Berkeley, MA, 62; Johns Hopkins Univ, PhD(Near Eastern studies), 68. **CAREER** Chaplain, US Air Force, 62-64; grad student Near Eastern studies, Johns Hopkins Univ, 64-68; asst prof, 69-73, chmn dept, 70-73, assoc prof, 73-80, Prof Hebrew and Aramaic, Univ Wis-Milwaukee, 80-, Chmn Dept, 76-. **MEMBERSHIPS** Soc Biblical Lit; Am Orient Soc; Asn Jewish Studies; Asn Targumic Studies; Nat Asn Prof Hebrew. **RESEARCH** Targum, Aramaic Bible translation; Bible language and literature; Rabbinic language and literature. **SELECTED PUBLICATIONS** Auth, Bible versions--Aramaic: The Targumim: 841-851, Encyclopaedia Judaica, 72; A Bibliography of Targum Literature Bibliographica Judaica, KTAV Publ House, 72; Targum Onkelos and Rabbinic interpretation to Genesis 2: 1-2, J Jewish Studies, 73; A critical note on Judges 4: 21, Z Alttestamentliche Wiss, 73; Targum Neofiti 1 to Deuteronomy 31: 7, the problem re-analyzed, Australian Biblical Rev, 76; coauth, Targum Onkelos on Genesis 49; Translation and Analytical Commentary, Scholars Press, 76; auth, Targum Literature Vol II: Bibliographica Judaica, KTAV Publ House,

77. **CONTACT ADDRESS** Dept of Hebrew Studies, Univ of Wisconsin, Milwaukee, Curtin Hall 904, Milwaukee, WI 53201.

GROSSI, VERONICA
DISCIPLINE SPANISH **EDUCATION** Univ Tex, Austin, MA, 90, PhD, 96. **CAREER** Lectr, Univ Tex, Austin, 96-99; asst prof, Univ NC, Greensboro, 97. **CONTACT ADDRESS** Dept of Romance Langs, Univ of No Carolina, Greensboro, 321 McIver Bldg, PO Box 26170, Greensboro, NC 27402-6170. **EMAIL** vgrossi@uncg.edu

GROSSMAN, JEFFREY
PERSONAL Born 01/19/1961, Mt Vernon, NY, m **DISCIPLINE** GERMAN **EDUCATION** Tufts Univ, BA, 82; MA, 86; Univ Tex, PhD, 92. **CAREER** Engl instr & transl, Univ Jena, 83-85; tchg asst, Tufts Univ, 85-86; asst instr, Univ Tex, 86-88, 90-91; resrchr, Hebrew Univ, 94-95; instr, Univ Freiburg, 95; asst prof, German, Univ Va, 96-. **HONORS AND AWARDS** Sesquicentennial Res Fel, Univ Va, 99-00; Univ Tchg Fel, Tchg Res Ctr, Univ Va, 99-00; Fac Dev Res Grant, Univ Va, 97; Fel, Ctrfor Judaic Studies, Univ of Pennsylvania, 95-96; Fulbright Postdoctoral Research Grant, Israel Junior Researcher Awd, 92-94; DAAD-Dissertation Research in Federal Republic of Germany. **MEMBERSHIPS** Modern Language Association; Amer Assoc of Teachers of German; German Studies Assoc; YIVO Institute of Jewish Research; Assoc of Jewish Studies. **RESEARCH** German Literature 19th-20th C; German-Jewish Culture, Yiddish Lit. **SELECTED PUBLICATIONS** Auth, "Far vos ignorirn di literatur-kritiker A.N. Shtentslen?" Oksforder Yidish: A Yearbook of Yiddish Studies 1, 90: 91-105; auth, "The Reception of Walter Benjamin in the Anglo-American Literary Institution," The German Quarterly 65.3-4, 92: 414-428; auth, "Herder and the Language of Diaspora Jewry," Monatshefte 86.1, 94: 59-79; auth, "Wilhelm von Humboldt's Linguistic Ideology: The Problem of Pluralism and the Absolute Difference of National Character-Or, where do the Jews fit in?" German Studies Review 20.1, 97: 23-47; rev, "The Berlin Jewsih Community, Jewish Studies Series," New York and London: Oxford UP, 94, Jewish Quarterly Review 87.3-4, 97: 396-401. **CONTACT ADDRESS** Dept German, Univ of Virginia, 108 Cocke Hall, Charlottesville, VA 22903-3248. **EMAIL** jg2t@virginia.edu

GROSSMAN, JOAN DELANEY
PERSONAL Born 12/12/1928, Dubuque, IA **DISCIPLINE** SLAVIC LANGUAGES **EDUCATION** Clarke Col, AB, 52; Columbia Univ, MA, 62; Harvard Univ, PhD(Slavic lang & lit), 67. **CAREER** Asst prof Russ, Mundelein Col, 67-68; asst prof, 68-80, Assoc Prof Slavic Lang and Lit, Univ Calif, Berkeley, 80-, Consult, US-USSR summer lang teachers enchange, Int Res and Exchanges Bd, 69-72; Am Coun Learned Soc fel, 71-72; Guggenheim fel, 78-79. **MEMBERSHIPS** Am Asn Advan Slavic Studies; Western Slavic Asn; Mod Lang Asn. **RESEARCH** Russian literary and cultural trends at the end of the 19th and the early 20th century; Russian novel. **SELECTED PUBLICATIONS** Auth, Turgenev's Sportsman: Experiment in unity, Slavic & E Europ J, 64; Edgar Allan Poe in Russia: A Study in Legend and Literary Influence, Jal, Wurzburg, 73; Genius and madness: Return of the Romantic concept of the poet in late nineteenth-century Russia, In: American Contributions to the Seventh International Congress of Slavists, Vol II, Mouton, The Hague, 74; Tolstoy's Portrait of Anna: Keystone in the arch, Criticism, winter 76; Feminine images in Old Russian literature and art, California Slavic Studies XI, Univ Calif, 78; Dostoevsky and Stendhal's Theory of Happiness, American Contributions to the Eighth International Congress of Slavists, Vol II, Columbus: Slavica, 78. **CONTACT ADDRESS** Dept of Slavic Lang, Univ of California, Berkeley, 366 Le Conte Hall, Berkeley, CA 94720-7301.

GROSSMAN, KATHRYN MARIE
PERSONAL Born 12/06/1945, New York, NY **DISCIPLINE** FRENCH LITERATURE, UTOPIAN STUDIES **EDUCATION** Bryn Mawr Col, AB, 67; Yale Univ, MPhil, 70, PhD(Romance lang), 73. **CAREER** Asst prof, 73-80, Assoc Prof French Lang and Lit, PA State Univ, 81-, Actg Asst Dean, Col Lib Arts, 82-. **MEMBERSHIPS** MLA; Am Asn Teachers Fr; Am Coun Teaching Foreign Lang; Soc Utopian Studies; Am Asn Advan Humanities. **RESEARCH** Victor Hugo (prose fiction); romanticism; utopias. **SELECTED PUBLICATIONS** Auth, Gautier's Dream of Stone: The plastic aesthetics of Emaux et camees, Les Bonnes Feuilles, spring 75; Jean Valjean and France: Outlaws in search of integrity, Stanford Fr Rev, winter 78; Playing surrealist games: Parataxis and creativity, Fr Rev, 4/79; Monsieur Teste as modern parable, Dalhousie Fr Studies, 10/79; Hugo's romantic sublime: Beyond chaos and convention in Les Miserables, Philol Quart, fall 82. **CONTACT ADDRESS** Pennsylvania State Univ, Univ Park, University Park, PA 16802.

GROSSVOGEL, DAVID I.
PERSONAL Born 06/19/1925, San Francisco, CA, m, 1974, 2 children **DISCIPLINE** FRENCH, ROMANCE STUDIES **EDUCATION** Univ Calif, BA, 49; Univ Grenoble, cert, 50; Columbia Univ, MA, 51, PhD(French), 54. **CAREER** Instr French lang & lit, Columbia Univ, 53-56; vis lectr, Harvard Univ, 56-57, asst prof Romance lit, 57-60; assoc prof Romance Studies, 60-64, prof, 64-70, Goldwin Smith Prof Comp Lit & Romance Studies, Cornell Univ, 70-; Fulbright fel, Paris, 59-60; Guggenheim fel, 63-64; found & ed, Diacritics, 71-. **MEMBERSHIPS** MLA **RESEARCH** Criticism; cinema; modern European literature. **SELECTED PUBLICATIONS** Auth, Self-Conscious Stage, Columbia Univ; Anouilh's Antigone, Integral Ed, 58; Four Playwrights and a Postscript, Cornell Univ, 62; Sagan's Bonjour Tristesse, Integral Ed, 64; Limits of the Novel, Cornell Univ, 68; co-ed, Divided We Stand: Reflections on the Crisis at Cornell, Doubleday, 70; Mystery and Its Fictions: From Oedipus to Agatha Christie, Johns Hopkins Univ, 79; Dear Ann Landers, Contemporary Books, 87; auth, VISHNU in Hollywood: The Changing Image of the American Male, Scarecrow Press, 00; co-auth, Changing Channels: America in T V Guide, Univ Ill Press, 92. **CONTACT ADDRESS** Dept of Romance Studies, Cornell Univ, 288 Coldwin Smith Hall, Ithaca, NY 14853-4701. **EMAIL** dig3@cornell.edu

GROSZ, ELIZABETH
DISCIPLINE COMPARATIVE LITERATURE **CAREER** Teacher, Univ of Sydney 78-91; Associate prof philos Monash Univ 92-95; Director, Inst for Cultural & Critical Theory 92-95; Personal Chair, 95; Julian Park Prof Comp Lit. 99-. **SELECTED PUBLICATIONS** Auth, Crossing Boundaries: Feminisms and the Critique of Knowledges, 88; Jacques Lacan: A Feminist Introduction, 90; Sexual Subversions: Three French Feminists, 89; Sexy Bodies: The Strange Carnalities of Feminism, 95; Space, Time and Perversion: Essays on the Politics of Bodies, 95; Volatile Bodies: Toward a Corporeal Feminism, 94. **CONTACT ADDRESS** Dept Comp Literature, SUNY, Buffalo, 638 Clemens Hall, Buffalo, NY 14260. **EMAIL** egrosz@acsu.buffalo.edu

GROTANS, ANNA A.
PERSONAL Born 03/23/1962, Minneapolis, MN **DISCIPLINE** GERMAN STUDIES, PALEOGRAPHY **EDUCATION** Univ Minn, BA, 84, PhD, 92; Univ Toronto, MA, 85. **CAREER** Asst prof, Brigham Young Univ, 92-93; asst prof, Ohio State Univ, 93-99; assoc prof, 99-. **HONORS AND AWARDS** DAAD, 88-89; Tchg Fulbright, 89-90; NEH Summer Stipen, 97; Fulbright Jr Res, 97-98. **MEMBERSHIPS** Medieval Acad; AATG; MLA; AABS. **RESEARCH** Medieval German studies; Paleography. **SELECTED PUBLICATIONS** Coauth, art, Pride and Prejudice: Notker Labeo and his Editors, 94; coauth, art, The Altdeutsche Textbibliothek Notker Labeo Edition, 95; coauth, The St. Gall Tractate: A Classroom Guide to Rhetorical Syntax, 95; auth, art, Notker's De rhetorica in Early Modern Bavaria, 96; auth, art, Sih tir selbo lector: Lexical and Graphic Cues for Reading in Tenth-Century St. Gall, 97; auth, "Utraque lingua: Deutschunterricht in Notkers St. Gallen," 99; auth, "Simplifying Latin in Notker's Classroom: Tradition and Innovation, 99; auth, Consolatio Philologiae, Festschrift for Evelyn S. Firchow, Anna Grotans, Heinrich Bech and Anton Schwob, eds., Goppingen: Kummerle, 00; auth, "The Scrives and Notker Labeo," 00. **CONTACT ADDRESS** Dept of German, Ohio State Univ, Columbus, 314 Cunz Hall, Columbus, OH 43210-1229. **EMAIL** grotans.1@osu.edu

GROTON, ANNE H.
PERSONAL Born 04/08/1954, Oak Park, IL **DISCIPLINE** CLASSICAL STUDIES **EDUCATION** Wellesley Coll, AB, 76; Univ of Michigan, MA. 77, PhD 82. **CAREER** Asst Prof, Assoc Prof to Prof, 81-, St Olaf Coll. **HONORS AND AWARDS** Awd for Excellence in the Tchg of Class, Amer Philos Assoc. **MEMBERSHIPS** Amer Philos Assoc; Class Assoc Middle West and South; Class Assoc of Minnesota; Amer Soc Papyrologists; Vergilian Soc. **RESEARCH** Ancient Greek and Roman Drama, especially comedy. **SELECTED PUBLICATIONS** Auth, From Alpha to Omega: A Beginning Course in Classical Greek, Focus Publishing, 95. **CONTACT ADDRESS** Dept Classics, St. Olaf Col, 1520 St Olaf Ave, Northfield, MN 55057-1098. **EMAIL** groton@stolaf.edu

GRUBER-MILLER, JOHN C.
DISCIPLINE CLASSICS **EDUCATION** Ohio State Univ, MA, 79; Xavier Univ, PhD, 87. **CAREER** Vis Instr, Ohio Wesleyan Univ, 86-87; Asst Prof to Prof, Cornell Col, 87-. **HONORS AND AWARDS** Fulbright Fel, 89; Fel, NEH, 94, 96. **MEMBERSHIPS** Am Philol Asn; Am Class League; Class Asn of the Mid W and S; Comput Assisted Lang Inst Consortium; AMICI; Women's Class Caucus; Am Coun of Teachers of For Lang; Archaeol Inst of Am. **SELECTED PUBLICATIONS** Site Ed, Riley Collection of Roman Portrait Sculpture, http://vroma.org/~riley/; site ed, Let's Review Greek!, http://cornellcollege.edu/classical_studies/reviewgreek/; co-auth, "How Do You Say MOO in Latin? Assessing Student Learning and Motivation in Beginning Latin," CALICO J, 01; auth, When Dead Tongues Speak: Teaching Beginning Latin and Greek, Oxford Univ Press, 01. **CONTACT ADDRESS** Dept Class and Mod Lang, Cornell Col, 515 Third St NW, Mount Vernon, IA 52314. **EMAIL** jgruber-miller@cornellcollege.edu

GRUBISIC, VINKO
PERSONAL Born 04/05/1943, Posuski Gradac, Herzegovina **DISCIPLINE** SLAVIC LITERATURE **EDUCATION** Aix En Provence Univ, PhD, 74. **SELECTED PUBLICATIONS** Auth, O Hrvatskom Jeziku, Ziral, 75; Grafija hrvatske lapidarne cirilice, 78; Bibliography of the Croatian Language, Norval, 87; Elementary Croatian I, Zagreb, 94; Druzenje s tijelom, Napredak, 95; Elementary Croatian II, Zagreb, 96; coauth, Illustrated Dictionary for Children, Zagreb, 89. **CONTACT ADDRESS** Dept of German and Slavic Literature, Univ of Waterloo, 200 University Ave W, Waterloo, ON, Canada N2L 3G1. **EMAIL** vggrubis@watstar.uwaterloo.ca

GRUETTNER, MARK
PERSONAL Born Dallas, TX, 2 children **DISCIPLINE** GERMAN **EDUCATION** Tex A&M Univ, BS, 84; BA, 84; Tex Tech Univ, MA, 87; Wash Univ, PhD, 93. **CAREER** Asst to assoc prof, Centenary Col, 93-. **HONORS AND AWARDS** Delta Phi Alpha; Theodor W Alexander Scholar, 86-87; Fel, Hamburg Univ, 89-90; German Acad Exchange Serv Grant, 94; Centenary Col Res Grant, Ger, 95, 96, 00. **MEMBERSHIPS** Am Assoc of Teachers of Ger; Assoc for the Study of Lit and Environ; Ger Studies Assoc; MLA; Am Coun on the Teaching of For Lang; Am Comp Lit Assoc. **SELECTED PUBLICATIONS** Auth, "Die Rezeption historischer Dichterfiguren in der deutschsprachigen Literatur der siegziger Jahre", wirkendes Wort 42.1 (92): 76-93; auth, "Eichendorffs Sehnsucht und Die Heimat. An meinen Bruder: Die Konstruktion der Illusion", Mountain Interstate For Lang Conf Rev 5, (95): 38-50; auth, "Zwischen Waldromantik und Kahlschlag: Tote Walder bei Gunter Grass, Richard Manning, William Dietrich und Robert Bateman", Natur, Raume, Landschaftern: 2, Internationales Kingstoner Symp, (Munchen, Ger, 96): 221-233; auth, Intertextualitat und Zeitkritik in gunter Grass' Kopfgeburten und Die Rattin, Stauffenburg Verlag, (Tubingen, Ger), 97; auth, "Gunter Grass", Modern Germany: An Encycl of History, People, and Culture, 1871-1990, Garland (NY/London, 98): 415-416; auth, "zur Okologie von Schopfung und Verwanglung: Die Achte Elegie von Rainer Maria Rilke", Unreading Rilke: Unorthodox Approaches to a Cultural Myth, Peter Lang, (forthcoming). **CONTACT ADDRESS** Dept For Lang, Centenary Col, PO Box 41188, Shreveport, LA 71134-1188. **EMAIL** mgruettn@centenary.edu

GRUNFELD, MIHAI
DISCIPLINE LATIN AMERICAN LITERATURE **EDUCATION** Univ Toronto, Can, BA; Univ Mich, Arbor, MA; Univ Calif, PhD. **CAREER** Act in, Latin Amer stud prog & Int stud prog **RESEARCH** Modern Latin American poetry, especially the Avant-Garde; representation of indigenous culture in Latin America. **CONTACT ADDRESS** Dept of Hispanic Studies, Vassar Col, Mail Drop 451, Poughkeepsie, NY 12604-0451. **EMAIL** grunfeld@vassar.edu

GRUZINSKA, ALEKSANDRA
PERSONAL Born Poznan, Poland **DISCIPLINE** FRENCH LANGUAGE, 19TH CENTURY FRENCH LITERATURE **EDUCATION** State Univ of NYork, Buffalo, BA, 64; MA, 66; Pa State Univ, PhD, 73. **CAREER** Instr, Rosary Hill Col, 66-68; instr, Sweet Briar Col, 71-73; asst prof, Ariz State Univ, 73-. **HONORS AND AWARDS** Phi Beta Kappa, 64; Graduate Fel, 64; Fulbright res fel in Paris, France, 68-69; ASU Women's Studies Summer Res Grant, 00. **MEMBERSHIPS** MLA; Friends of George Sand; Women in French; Rocky Mt Modern Lang Asn; Ariz Lang Asn; Societe Octave Mirbeau; ARA; Polish Inst of Arts and Sci of Am. **RESEARCH** The works of George Sand, Madame de Stael, Octave Mirbeau, EM Cioran, 19th Century Short Story, the poetry of Wislawa Szymborska. **SELECTED PUBLICATIONS** Auth, "Octave Mirbeau", Dict of Literary Biography. Nineteenth-Century French Fiction Writers: Naturalism and Beyond, 1860-1900, Bruccoli Clark Layman (92): 215-231; transl, "Diverse Thoughts on Man", by Antoine Pecquet, Peter Lang, (NY), 99; ed, auth, "Essays on E M Cioran. Rasinara 1911 - Paris 1995, ARA Pub, (Costa Mesa, CA), 99. **CONTACT ADDRESS** Dept of Languages and Literatures, Arizona State Univ, MC 0202, Tempe, AZ 85287. **EMAIL** gruzinska@asu.edu

GUERRERO, VLADIMIR
DISCIPLINE SPANISH **EDUCATION** Univ Calif Davis, PhD, 99. **CAREER** Vis prof, Univ Oslo, 00; vis prof, Univ Calif Davis, 99-. **MEMBERSHIPS** MLA; Cervantes Soc; Asn Hispanica de Lit Medieval; Soc Intl Rencesvals; Soc for Renaissance and Baroque Hispanic Poetry. **RESEARCH** Orality in medieval literature; Oral-aural retention; Transition to writing. **SELECTED PUBLICATIONS** Auth, "Gender, Class, Theology and the First Don Juan," Romansk Forum, (00): 43-50; auth, "Tradition and Renewal of a Spanish Ballad," Caliope; auth, "Literatura, oraltura y el 'Canter de Fernan Gonzalez'," Revista de Poetica Medieval, 01; auth, "Diegesis y realidad en 'Niebla'," Revue Romane, (forthcoming). **CONTACT ADDRESS** Dept Spanish and Class, Univ of California, Davis, Dept Spanish, Davis, CA 95616. **EMAIL** vguerrero@ucdavis.edu

GUI, MING C.
PERSONAL Born 07/01/1946, Kunming, Yannan, China, m, 1983, 2 children **DISCIPLINE** CHINESE LANGUAGE **EDUCATION** Quangzhou Inst For Lang, BA, 69; Univ Tex, MA, 85; PhD, 90. **CAREER** Lectr, Quangzhou Inst For Lang, 81-83; Asst Prof, Univ Tex, 84-90; Ed & Trans, PCH Co Calif, 91-

93; Asst Prof, Univ Okla, 94-. **HONORS AND AWARDS** Fel, Univ Tex; Cecil W Woods Teaching Excellence Awd, Univ Okla; Summer Res Fel, Univ Okla; LPresidential Int Travel Fel, Univ Okla. **MEMBERSHIPS** Ling Asn of Am & Can, Chinese Teacher Asn of Am. **RESEARCH** Chinese dialectology, Chinese teaching pedagogy. **SELECTED PUBLICATIONS** Auth, The Impact of Reduplication Structure on Tones and Semantics of words in Kunming Chinese, Yuyan Yanjiu (Wuhan, China), 99; auth, Kunming Chinese, Lincoln Europa Acad Publ (Muenchen, Germany), 00. **CONTACT ADDRESS** Dept Mod Lang, Univ of Oklahoma, 780 Van Vleet Oval, Room 206, Norman, OK 73019-2032. **EMAIL** mgui@ou.edu

GUIEU, JEAN-MAX
PERSONAL Born 10/24/1943, Marseille, France **DISCIPLINE** FRENCH LITERATURE **EDUCATION** Univ Aix en Provence, Lic es Lett, 67, Maitrise de lett, 68; Univ Md, PhD(French), 75. **CAREER** Instr ling and phonetics, Univ Aix en Provence, 67-68; instr French, Univ Md, 68-73; prof, Lycee Francais Int Wash, 73-76; ASST Prof French, Sch Foreign Serv, Georgetownn Univ, 76-, Collabr res comt, Complete Corresp of Emile Zola, 75-. **MEMBERSHIPS** Am Asn Teachers Fr. **RESEARCH** Emile Zola's lyric dramas; literature and politics. **SELECTED PUBLICATIONS** Auth, 'Mireio' and 'Mireille'--Mistral Poem and Gounod Opera, Opera Quart, Vol 0010, 93; Bruneau, Alfred and Zola, Emile--Naturalism on the Lyric Stage, Opera Quart, Vol 0010, 94. **CONTACT ADDRESS** Dept of French Sch Foreign Serv, Georgetown Univ, Washington, DC 20067.

GUINAN, MICHAEL DAMON
PERSONAL Born 02/16/1939, Cincinnati, OH **DISCIPLINE** SEMITICS, SYRIAC PATRISTICS **EDUCATION** San Luis Rey Col, BA, 61; Old Mission Theol Sem, STB, 65; Cath Univ Am, STL, 67, MA, 70, PhD(Semitics), 72. **CAREER** Prof Bibl Theol & Semitic Lang, Franciscan Sch Theol, Grad Theol Union, 72-. **MEMBERSHIPS** Cath Theol Soc Am; Cath Bibl Asn; Soc Bibl Lit; Soc for Study of Christian Spirituality. **RESEARCH** Old Testament; Syriac patristic theology. **SELECTED PUBLICATIONS** Auth, The Making of Many Images: Scripture Film and Religious Education, Multimedia Int, 73; Convenant in the Old Testament, Franciscan Herald, 75; Where are the dead?, Purgatory and immedicate retribution in James of Sarug, Proc Syriac Symp of 1972; Jacob of Sarug, In: New Cath Encycl, Vol XVI; The Creation Story of Genesis: Does It Really Establish Evolution?; Angels: Their Meaning for Today; The Messiah and the Millenium; Christian Spirituality: Many Styles, One Spirit-Catholic Update, 94, 95, 97, 98. **CONTACT ADDRESS** Franciscan Sch of Theol, 1712 Euclid Ave, Berkeley, CA 94709-1294. **EMAIL** mdguinan@aol.com

GUITART, JORGE
PERSONAL Born 09/15/1937, Havana, Cuba, m, 1969, 2 children **DISCIPLINE** LINGUISTICS **EDUCATION** George Wash Univ, BA, 67; Georgetown Univ, MS, 70, PhD, 73. **CAREER** Asst prof of Spanish Linguistics, SUNY, Buffalo, 73-77, assoc prof, 77-82, prof, 82-. **MEMBERSHIPS** LSA, AATSP. **RESEARCH** Phonology, semantics, pedagogical grammar. **SELECTED PUBLICATIONS** Auth, "The NP-based, class/member analysis of mood choices in Spanish relative clauses," Papers in Second Language Teaching and Linguistics in Honor of Tracy D. Terrell, ed by Peggy Hashemipour, Margaret von Naerssen, and Ricardo Maldonado, NY: McGraw Hill (95): 385-398; auth, "Spanish in Contact with Itself and the Phonoligical Characterization of Conservative and Radical Styles," Spanish in Contact, ed by John Jensen and Ana Roca, Somerville, MA: Casadilla Press (96): 151-157; auth, Film Blanc, Buffalo, NY: Meow Press (96); co-ed with William Fischer, David Gerber, and Maxine Seller, Identity, Community, and Pluralism in American Life, NY: Oxford Univ Press (97); auth, Nociones de psicolinguistica: adquisicion de la primera lengua, Lima, Peru: Dept de Linguistica y Lit de la Univ Nacional Federico Villarreal (97); auth, "Variability, Multilectalism, and the Organization of Phonology in Caribbean Spanish," Issues in the Phonology and Morphology of the Major Iberian Languages, ed by Alfonso Morales-Front and Fernando Martinez-Gil, Washington, DC: Georgetown Univ Press (97): 515-536; auth, "Actives, Passives, Impersonals and the Semantic Roles of Spanish Noun Phrases," Linguistic Studies in Honor of Bohdan Saciuk, ed by Robert M. Hammond and Marguerite G. MacDonald, West Lafayette, In: Learning Systems, Inc (97): 45-52; auth, El caso gramatical en el espanol en la teoria de los roles semanticos, Lima, Peru: Editorial Runasimi (98). **CONTACT ADDRESS** Dept Modern Lang, SUNY, Buffalo, 910 Clemens Hall, Buffalo, NY 14260-0001. **EMAIL** guitart@acsu.buffalo.edu

GULSOY, J.
PERSONAL Born 08/15/1925, Ordu, Turkey, m, 1959, 2 children **DISCIPLINE** SPANISH LANGUAGE & LITERATURE **EDUCATION** Univ BC, BA, 53; Univ Toronto, MA, 55; Univ Chicago, PhD, 61. **CAREER** From instr to assoc prof, 58-70; Can Coun grant, 67-68. Prof Span, Univ Toronto, 70-00; Prof emer, Univ Toronto, 00-. **MEMBERSHIPS** Am Asn Teachers Span & Port; Soc Ling Romance; Medieval Acad Am. **RESEARCH** Lexicographical compilations; Catalan and Spanish linguistics; Hispanic dialectology; Old Span; Catalan; Romance Philology. **SELECTED PUBLICATIONS** Coauth, Diccionari etimologic i complementari de la llengua catalana, Barcelona: Curial-La Caixa, 95; auth, Estudis de gramatica historica. **CONTACT ADDRESS** Dept of Span and Port, Univ of Toronto, 73 Queen's Park Crescent, Toronto, ON, Canada M5S 1K7. **EMAIL** jgulsoy@chass.utoronto.ca

GUMPEL, LISELOTTE
PERSONAL Born Berlin, Germany **DISCIPLINE** GERMAN, GERMAN LITERATURE **EDUCATION** San Francisco State Col, BA, 64; Stanford Univ, MA, 66, PhD, 71. **CAREER** From Asst Prof to Full Prof; Prof Ger Lang & Lit, 68-98, Prof Emeritus, Univ Minn, Morris, 98-. **HONORS AND AWARDS** NEH Fel, 72; Helen Cam res fel, 77-78. **MEMBERSHIPS** MLA (life member); AAUP; Am Asn Teachers Ger; GIG; IVG; Women in Ger. **RESEARCH** German literature; semantics; esthetics. **SELECTED PUBLICATIONS** Auth, The essence of reality as a construct of language, Found Lang, 3/74; The structure of idioms: A phenomenological approach, Semiotica, J Int Asn Semiotic Studies, 12-1/74; Metaphor as nominalized meaning: A phenomenological analysis of the lyrical genre, Jarhbuch Int Germanistik, 76; Concrete Poetry from East and West Germany: The Language of Exemplarism and Experimentalism, Yale Univ, 76; Metaphor Reexamined: A Non-Aristotelian Perspective, (Bloomington: Ind Univ, 85); Meaning and Metaphor: The World in Verbal Translation, Schmidt-Verlag. **CONTACT ADDRESS** 111 Marquette Ave S, No 1008, Minneapolis, MN 55401-2028.

GUMPERZ, JOHN J.
DISCIPLINE LINGUISTICS, ANTHROPOLOGY **EDUCATION** Univ Cincinnati, BA, 47; Univ Mich, PhD(Ger ling), 54. **CAREER** Instr ling, Cornell Univ, 52-54; from instr to assoc prof S Asian lang and ling, 56-67, Prof Anthrop, Univ Calif, Berkeley, 67-, Ford Found fel ling, India, 54-56; mem comt socioling, Soc Sci Res Coun, 66-73; Trainers of Teachers of Teachers comt, Berkeley sch bd, 69-71. **MEMBERSHIPS** Ling Soc Am; Am Anthrop Asn; Ling Soc India; AAAS. **RESEARCH** Sociolinguistics; linguistics and cognitive anthropology; applied linguistics. **SELECTED PUBLICATIONS** Auth, Treacherous Words--Gender and Power in Academic Assessment, Folia Linguistica, Vol 0030, 96. **CONTACT ADDRESS** Dept of Anthrop, Univ of California, Berkeley, 232 Kroeber Hall, Berkeley, CA 94720.

GUNDEL, JEANNETTE K.
PERSONAL Born 07/16/1942, Krakou, Poland, m, 1964, 1 child **DISCIPLINE** LINGUISTICS **EDUCATION** Pa State Univ, BA, 63; MA, 66; Univ Texas, PhD, 74. **CAREER** Vis asst prof, Univ Hawaii, 78-80; asst prof, 80-87, assoc prof, 87-92, prof, linguis, 92-, Univ Minn. **MEMBERSHIPS** Linguistic Soc Amer **RESEARCH** Semantics; pragmatics; syntax; lang processing; lang & cognition. **SELECTED PUBLICATIONS** Coauth, Cognitive Status and Form of Referring Expressions in Discourse, Language 69.2, 93; art, Shared Knowledge, Encycl of Lang & Ling, Pergamon Press, 93; art, Focus and Natural Language Processing vol 3 Discourse, Working Papers of the Inst for Logic & Ling, IBM Deutschland Info-syst GMbH Heidleberg, 94; art, Understanding Reference: Where Communication and Cognition Meet, Form & Function in Lang, Odense Univ press, 95; co-ed, Reference and Referent Accessibility, John Benjamins & Co, 96; coauth, Prosodic Tune and Information Structure, Proceed 1995 Ann Conf of the Can Ling Soc, Toronto Working Papers in Ling, 95; art, Relevance Theory Meets the Givenness Heirarchy: an Account Of Inferrables, Reference and Referent Accessibility, John Benjamins & Co, 96; art, Pragmatic Function And Linguistic Form, J Korean Ling 21.1, 97; coauth, Relevance, Referring Expressions and the Givenness Hierarchy, Proceed Workshop On Relevance Theory, Univ Herfordshire, 97; art, Shared Knowledge, Concise Encycl of The Phil of Lang, Oxford Elsevier Science Ltd, 97; coauth, What Brings A Higher-Order Entity Into Focus of Attention?, Proceed Workshop on Anaphora 35th Ann Mtg Assoc Of Computational Ling, 97; art, Centering Theory And The Givenness Hierarchy: A Proposed Synthesis, Centering Theory In Discourse, Oxford Univ Press, 98. **CONTACT ADDRESS** Dept of Linguistics, Univ of Minnesota, Twin Cities, 192 Klaeber Ct, 320 16th Ave SE, Minneapolis, MN 55455. **EMAIL** gunde00@umn.edu

GUNTERMANN, GAIL
PERSONAL Born 10/09/1938, Miles City, MT, s **DISCIPLINE** SPANISH **EDUCATION** Univ Mont, BA, 60, Univ NMex, MA, 69; Ohio State Univ, PhD(foreign lang educ), 77. **CAREER** Teacher Span, Whitefish Schs, Mont, 60-62 and Albany Union High Sch, Ore, 62-65; lang coordr and instr Span, Brockport State Col, New York, 69-71; lang coordr, Avance, SA, El Salvador, 74-76; methods instr and supvr student teachers Span and French, Fredonia State Col, New York, 77; Asst Prof Span and Methods, Ariz State Univ, 77-; prof, Ariz State univ, 00-. **HONORS AND AWARDS** Southwest Conference on Language Teaching, Outstanding Post-Secondary Educator, 85; American Council on the Teaching of Foreign Languages and New York State Assoc of Foreign Language Teachers, Anthony Papalia award, 95; Arizona Language Assoc Service award, 98; American Assoc of Teachers of Spanish and Portuguese, Robert G Mead award, 99. **MEMBERSHIPS** Arizona Language Assoc **RESEARCH** Curriculum design; languages for specific purposes; national standards and classroom language learning. **SELECTED PUBLICATIONS** coauth, " The Case for Foreign Languages: Both the Student and the Nation Benefit." Today's Education 71, 1, (82), 46-49; auth, " Los errores y la communicacion: Un sumario," Lenguas Modernas Nos 9-10 (82-83), 57-68, Departmento de Linguistica, Universidad de Chile; coauth, " Espanol para profesiones internacionales: un programa 'funcional' intensivo," The Journal of Language for International Business 1. (84), 37-46; coauth, " Languages for International Professions: A Pilot Project," ADFL Bulletin 16, (84), 31-34; auth, " Designing Basic Programs for Special Needs Plus General Proficiency," Foreign Language Annals 17, 6, (84). 585-591; auth, " Designing Programs for Foreign Languages," Theory into Practice 26, 4 (87), 276-281; auth, " An Analysis of Interlanguage Development Over Time: Part I, por and para," Hispania 75,5, (92), 177-187; auth, " An Analysis of Interlanguage Development Ofer Time; Part II, se and estar," Hispania 75, 5, (92), 1294-1303; auth, " Prospects for Significan Teacher Education Reform," ADFL Bulletin 28, 3,(97); auth, " Issues of Performance and Assessment Related to the Entry Level Teacher," Proceedings of Naitonal Pedagogical Summit, American Association of Teachers of Spanish and Portuguese, 97. **CONTACT ADDRESS** Dept of Languages and Literatures, Arizona State Univ, MC 0202, Tempe, AZ 85287. **EMAIL** gailg@asu.edu

GUNTSCHE, MARINA
PERSONAL Born 04/24/1962, Ann Arbor, MI **DISCIPLINE** SPANISH **EDUCATION** Univ Nacional de Buyo, Lic, 87; Univ Mich, MA, 89; PhD, 93. **CAREER** Assoc prof, Ball State Univ, 94-. **MEMBERSHIPS** AATSP. **RESEARCH** Twentieth Century Argentine novels; Peronism and the Argentine novel Literature from the province of Mendoza. **SELECTED PUBLICATIONS** Auth, "La epifania sismica en la novela de Mendoza, Argentina," in Pedra y Canto, (Argentina, 95), 127-136; auth, "El cronotopo de la carcel laberintica en Una sombra ya pronto seras de Osvaldo Soriano," Hispanic Prison Lit, (95): 302-315; auth, "El triunfo secreto de la novela argentina contemporanes," Cincinnati Romance Rev, (96): 127-133; auth, Entre la locura y la cordura: Cinco novelas argentinas del siglo, EDIUNC, 97; auth, "Latin American Novel: Argentina," in Encyclopedia of the Novel, (Fitzroy Dearborn Pub, 98), 707-714; auth, "La poesia edenica de Alfredo Bufano," Hispania, (00): 198-209; auth, "Oro y barro en la Argentina del XX: La novela de Peron, de Tomas Eloy Martinez," Cincinnati Romance Rev, (00): 94-101. **CONTACT ADDRESS** Dept Mod Lang and Class, Ball State Univ, Ball State Univ, Muncie, IN 47306. **EMAIL** 00m0guntsche@bus.edu

GURA, TIMOTHY
PERSONAL Born 09/03/1947, Peoria, IL, s **DISCIPLINE** INTERPRETATION **EDUCATION** Northwestern Univ, BS, 69, PhD, 74; Univ Mich, AM, 71. **CAREER** Prof Speech Commun and Dept Chair, Brooklyn Col, City Univ New York, 84-. **HONORS AND AWARDS** Tow Awd. **MEMBERSHIPS** NCA. **RESEARCH** Performance of literature; shakespeare; teaching. **SELECTED PUBLICATIONS** Coauth, Oral Interpretation, 10th ed, 2000. **CONTACT ADDRESS** 275 W. 12th St., New York, NY 10014. **EMAIL** tgura@brooklyn.cuny.edu

GURVAL, ROBERT ALAN
PERSONAL Born 08/02/1958, Kingston, PA **DISCIPLINE** CLASSICS **EDUCATION** Brown Univ, BA, 80; Univ Calif Santa Barbara, MA, 82; Univ Calif Berkeley, PhD, 88. **CAREER** Lectr, 88-89; asst prof, Univ Ore, 89-90; asst prof, 90-96; ASSOC PROF, UCLA, 96-, chair, 00-. **HONORS AND AWARDS** Fel, Am Acad at Rome, 96-97; UCLA Honors Prog, Distinguished Teacher Awd, 00. **MEMBERSHIPS** APA; Am Numis Soc. **RESEARCH** Roman history; Latin literature; Roman coinage. **SELECTED PUBLICATIONS** Auth, Actium and Augustus, Mich, 96. **CONTACT ADDRESS** Dept of Classics, Univ of California, Los Angeles, Dodd 100, Los Angeles, CA 90095-1417. **EMAIL** gurval@humnet.ucla.edu

GUSTAFSON, RICHARD FOLKE
PERSONAL Born 06/17/1934, Hartford, CT **DISCIPLINE** RUSSIAN LANGUAGE AND LITERATURE **EDUCATION** Yale Univ, AB, 56; Columbia Univ, PhD, 63. **CAREER** Instr Russ, Brown Univ, 60-62; from lectr to asst prof, Yale Univ, 62-65; assoc prof, 65-72, Prof Russ, Barnard Col, Columbia Univ, 72-, Chmn Dept, 65-. **MEMBERSHIPS** MLA; Am Asn Advan Slavic Studies; Am Asn Teachers Slavic & East Europ Lang. **RESEARCH** Russian poetry; 19th-century fiction; Tolstoy; and Russian religion and philosophy. **SELECTED PUBLICATIONS** Auth, The Upas Tree: Pushkin and Erasmus Darwin, PMLA, 1/60; auth, Tjutcev's Imagery and What It Tells Us, 6/60 & The Suffering Usurper: Gogol's Diary of a Madman, 3/65, Slavic & East Europ J; The Imagination of Spring: The Poetry of Afanasy Fet, Yale Univ, 66; auth, Leo Tolstoy, Resident and Stranger: A Study in Fiction and Theology, Princeton Univ, 86. **CONTACT ADDRESS** Dept of Russ Barnard Col, Columbia Univ, 3009 Broadway, New York, NY 10027-6598. **EMAIL** rgustafson@barnard.columbia.edu

GUTHKE, KARL SIEGFRIED
PERSONAL Born 02/17/1933, Lingen, Germany, m, 1965, 1 child **DISCIPLINE** GERMAN LITERATURE **EDUCATION** Univ Tex, MA, 53; Univ Gottingen, PhD, 56; MA, Harvard Univ, 68. **CAREER** From instr to prof Ger lit, Univ Calif, Berkeley, 56-65; prof Ger, Univ Toronto, 65-68; Prof Ger, Harvard Univ, 68-, Am Philos Soc grant-in-aid, 61-62; vis prof, Univ Colo, 63 and Univ Mass, 67; Guggenheim fel, 65; Am Coun Learned Soc fel, 72-73. **HONORS AND AWARDS** Walter C Cabot Prize, Harvard Univ, 77. **RESEARCH** Anglo-German literary relations; 18th century German literature; Cultural history. **SELECTED PUBLICATIONS** Auth, der Stand der Lessing-Forschung, 65; auth, Das Geheimnis um B. Traven entdeckt--und ratselvoller denn je, 84; auth, B. Traven: Biographie eines Ratsels, 87. Engl.: B. Traven: The Life Behind the Legends, 91; auth, Letzte Worte: Variationen uber ein Thema der Kulturgeschichte des Westerns, 1990, Engl.: Las Words: Variations on a Theme in Cultural History, 1992, Jap.: Ojosai no meiserifu, 95; auth, Trails in No-Man's-Land: Essays in Literary and Cultural History, 93; auth, Die Entdeckung des Ich: Studien zur Literatur, 93; auth, Schillers Dramen: Idealismus und Skepsis, 94; auth, Ist der Tod eine Frau? Geschlecht und Tod in Kunst und Literatur, 97, 2. Aufl. 98; Engl.: The Gender of Death: A Cultural History in Art and Literature, 99; auth, auth, Der Blick in die Fremde: Das Ich u. das and ere I.d. Lit., 00; auth, Ist der Tod eine Frau? Geschlecht und Tod in Kunst und Literatur, 97, 2. Aufl, 98; **CONTACT ADDRESS** Dept of Ger, Harvard Univ, Barker Center, Cambridge, MA 02138-3800.

GUTHRIE, ELIZABETH M.
DISCIPLINE FRENCH LANGUGE **EDUCATION** Univ Ill, PhD. **CAREER** Dir, Fr Lang Prog, Lectr, Univ Calif, Irvine. **SELECTED PUBLICATIONS** Auth, "Classroom Discourse and Linguistic Intake"; "Intake, Communication, and Second-Language Teaching." **CONTACT ADDRESS** Dept of Fr and Ital, Univ of California, Irvine, Irvine, CA 92697.

GUTHRIE, J. RICHARD, JR.
PERSONAL Born 11/11/1939, Newport News, VA, s **DISCIPLINE** LINGUISTICS, FRENCH, GERMAN, LANGUAGE, LITERATURE **EDUCATION** Col Will Mary, AB, 62; Middlebury Col, MA, 66; Univ NCar Chapel Hill, PhD, 78. **CAREER** Instr, Chris Newport Col, 67-75; asst prof to assoc prof, Col Will Mary, 78-90; prof, Chris Newport Col, 91-. **HONORS AND AWARDS** AATG, Germ Cult, Cert Merit, 00; Phi Mu Alpha Hon Mem; Nat Beta Soc Memo; LLS Cert Apprec. **MEMBERSHIPS** AATG; AATF; MLA. **RESEARCH** French and German existentialism; the 'new' Germany since the fall of the wall. **CONTACT ADDRESS** Modern Lang Dept, Chris Newport Univ, 1 University Pl, Newport News, VA 23606-2949. **EMAIL** rguthrie@cnu.edu

GUTIERREZ, JESUS
PERSONAL Born 10/31/1928, Santander, Spain **DISCIPLINE** SPANISH LANGUAGE AND LITERATURE **EDUCATION** Univ Comillas, PhBach, 49; Inst Cath, Paris, Dipl, 59; Fordham Univ, MA, 63; Hunter Col, MA, 70; City Univ New York, PhD(Span and Span Am), 73. **CAREER** Asst prof Span lang and lit, Col Guizar Valencia, 52-57; instr sociol and Span, Marymount Manhattan Col, 65-68; lectr Span, Queens Col, NY, 70-73, asst prof, 73-74; asst prof, Hofstra Univ, 74-76; vis prof, Wellesley Col, 76-77; assoc prof, Douglass Col, Rutgers Univ, 77-78 and York Col, City Univ New York, 78-81; Assoc Prof Span Golden Age, Wayne State Univ, 81-, Examr NY Reg Interviewing Comt Teacher Exchange Prof, Europe and Latin Am, 66-68; consult, Bilingual Educ Prog Girl Scouts Am, 73-75. **MEMBERSHIPS** MLA; Asoc Int Hispanistas; Am Asn Teachers Span & Port; Soc Menendez Pelayo. **RESEARCH** Spanish literature and thought of the Renaissance and Golden Age; the 18th century. **SELECTED PUBLICATIONS** Auth, Denina, Carlo and His Defense of Spain: Introduction, Dieciocho-Hisp Enlightenment, Vol 0015, 92. **CONTACT ADDRESS** Dept of Span Lang and Lit, Wayne State Univ, Detroit, MI 48202.

GUTIERREZ, JOHN R.
PERSONAL Born 03/02/1952, Santa Fe, NM, m, 1999, 2 children **DISCIPLINE** LINGUISTICS **EDUCATION** NMex State Univ, BA, 74; MA, 77; Univ NMex, PhD, 83. **CAREER** Asst prof, Ind Univ Bloomington, 80-84; asst prof, Univ of Va, 84-88; assoc prof, Pa State Univ, 88-98; assoc prof, Univ of Ariz, 99-00, prof, Univ of Miss, 00-. **HONORS AND AWARDS** Sigma Delta Pi, 72; Gulbenkian Found Scholar, 81; Who's Who in the Midwest, 84; Distinguished Serv Awd, Foreign Lang Asn of Va, 88; Phi Sigma Iota, 92; Who's Who Among Hispanic Am, 92; George W. Atherton Awd, Pa State Univ, 95; Outstanding Leadership and Serv, Univ or Ariz, 00. **MEMBERSHIPS** MLA; Am Assoc of Teachers of Span and Port; Am Assoc of Univ Supvrs and Coordrs of Foreign Lang Prog; Am Counc on the Teaching of Foreign Lang. **SELECTED PUBLICATIONS** Coauth, Ya veras: Primer nivel, Heinle and Heinle (Boston), 97; coauth, Ya veras: Segundo nivel, Heinle and Heinle, (Boston), 97; coauth, Ya veras: Tercer nivel, Heinle and Heinle (boston), 97; coauth, Tu diras: Introduccion a la lengua y cultura hispanicas, Heinle ane Heinle (Boston), 99. **CONTACT ADDRESS** Dept Mod Lang, Univ of Mississippi, 213 Cr 102, Oxford, MS 38677.

GUTIERREZ, MANUEL HIERRO
PERSONAL Born 09/08/1957, Grajal de Campos, Spain, m, 2000 **DISCIPLINE** LITERATURE, HISTORY, LANGUAGE, SPANISH **EDUCATION** Univ del Pais Vasco, Lic, 83; Wash Univ, PhD, 99. **CAREER** Teaching asst, Wash Univ, 91-95; lectr to asst prof, Univ Wis Madison, 00-. **HONORS AND AWARDS** Eva Sichel Essay Prize, Wash Univ, 93; Mellon Dissertation Fel, 93-94; Mellon Fel, 90-91 **MEMBERSHIPS** TCSAA; MLA; FAPE. **SELECTED PUBLICATIONS** Auth, Verano del 36. Aspectos de la Vida Cotidiana en Bilbao. Una Vision Desde la Prensa, Pergola, 93; auth, Antonio Pinto: La Logica del Caos, Reverso, 96; auth, "Por los Territorios del Anti-Edipo: La Genealogia Indeseada de Juan Goytisolo en Coto Vedado," Mono Rev (93); auth, La Memoria Sitiada de Juan Goytisolo en El Sitio de los Sitios, 96; auth, El Pensamiento Oral: El Caso Lewinsky, Antipods, 98; auth, La Comunicacion Callada de la Literatura: Excurso Tedrico Sobre el Diario Intimo, Eusko Ikaskuntza, 99. **CONTACT ADDRESS** Dept Span Port, Univ of Wisconsin, Madison, Curtin Hall, PO Box 413, Milwaukee, WI 53201. **EMAIL** mhierro@uwm.edu

GUTIERREZ-VEGA, ZENAIDA
PERSONAL Born 06/23/1924, Union del Reyes, Cuba **DISCIPLINE** SPANISH, SPANISH AMERICAN LITERATURE **EDUCATION** Inst Sec Educ, Matanzas, Cuba, BA, 45; Univ Havana, PhD(Span lit), 50; Univ Madrid, PhD(Romance philol), 66. **CAREER** Prof Span & lit, Inst Sec Educ Velado, Havana, 52-62; prof, Univ Las Villas, Cuba, 59-62; asst prof Span & Span Am lit, Univ Mo, St Louis, 67-68; asst prof, State Univ NY Col Oswego, 68-72; Prof Span, Hunter Col, 72-; Mem, Ministry Educ, Cuba, 56-57; mem, Inst Hisp Cult, Madrid, 62-66. **HONORS AND AWARDS** Lit Prize, Inst Hisp Cult, Madrid, 66; Summa cum Laude, 66; fel, Inst de Cultura Hispanica, 62-67; PSC-CUNY grants, 84, 85, 87. **MEMBERSHIPS** MLA; Am Asn Teachers Span & Port. **RESEARCH** Hispanic American literature; poets, essayists, novelists of the twentieth century of Spain and Latin America. **SELECTED PUBLICATIONS** Auth, Jose Maria Chacon y Calvo, Hispanista Cubano, Ediciones Cultura Hispanica, 69; auth, Epistolario Alfonso Reyes-Jose Ma. Chacon, Fundacion Universitaria Espanola, 76; auth, Estudio Bibliografico de Jose Ma. Chacon, Fundacion Universitaria Espanola, 82; auth, Fernando Ortiz en sus Cartas a Jose Ma. Chacon, Fundacion Universitaria Espanola, 82; auth, Corresponsales Espanoles de Jose Ma. Chacon, Fundacion Universitaria Espanola, 86; auth, Carmen Conde: de Viva Voz, Senda Nueva de Ediciones, 92. **CONTACT ADDRESS** 220 E 63rd St, Apt 4L, New York, NY 10021.

GUTWIRTH, MADELYN
PERSONAL Born 01/04/1926, Brooklyn, NY, m, 1948, 3 children **DISCIPLINE** FRENCH LITERATURE, WOMEN'S STUDIES **EDUCATION** Brooklyn Col, BA, 47; Bryn Mawr Col, MA, 49; PhD(French), 58. **CAREER** Instr French, Haverford Col, 50-51; assoc prof, 66-69, Prof French, West Chester State Col, 69-, FAC Coordr, Arts and Sci, 79-, Vis lectr French, Univ Pa, 67-68; Am Count Learned Soc fel, 71-72. **MEMBERSHIPS** MLA; Northeast Mod Lang Asn (pres, 73-74); Am Soc 18th Century Studies; Soc d'Etudes Staeliennes; AAUP. **RESEARCH** Madame de Stael; Romanticism; the 18th century. **SELECTED PUBLICATIONS** Auth, Madame de Stael's debt to Phedre: Corinne, Studies Romanticism, spring 64; Madame de Stael, Rousseau and the woman question, PMLA, 1/71; co-ed, Sources et Reflets de l'Histoire de France, Oxford Univ, 71; auth, Corinne et l'esthetique du camee, Acta Collogue de Clermont sur le preromantisme, 72; Madame de Stael, Novelist, Univ Ill, 78; Laclos and le sexe: The rack of ambivalence, Studies Voltaire & 18th Century, 80; Femme, Revolution et mode epistolaire, Cahiers Staeliens, 81. **CONTACT ADDRESS** Dept of Foreign Lang, West Chester Univ of Pennsylvania, West Chester, PA 19380.

GUTZWILLER, KATHRYN
PERSONAL Born 09/25/1948, Hinton, WV, m, 1971, 1 child **DISCIPLINE** CLASSICS **EDUCATION** Marshall Univ, BA, 70; Bryn Mawr Col, MA, 71; Univ of Wis Madison, PhD, 77. **CAREER** Asst to assoc prof, Case Western Reserve, 86-89; asst prof to prof, Univ of Cincinnati, 78-85, 89-. **HONORS AND AWARDS** Gildersleeve Prize, Am Jour of Philol, 92; McMicken Dean's Awd, 99; Charles J. Goodwin Awd of Merit, Am Philog Assoc, 01. **MEMBERSHIPS** Am Philol Assoc, Classical Assoc of Middle West and South, Ohio Classical Conf. **RESEARCH** Greek and Latin Poetry, Women in Antiquity and Gender Studies, Literary Theory. **SELECTED PUBLICATIONS** Auth, Studies in the Hellenistics Epyllion, 81; auth, "The Lorer and the Lena: Propertius 4.5," Ramus, (85); auth, "Women and Other Strangers: Feminist Perspectives in Classical Literature," (En)gendering Knowledge, (91); auth, Theocritus' Pastoral Analogirds: the Formation of a Genre, Madison, 91; auth, "Callimachus' Lock of Berenice," Am Jour of Philol, (92); auth, "The Evidence for Theocritean Poetry Books," Hellenistica Groningana 2, (96); auth, "The Poetics of Editing in Melenger's Garland," Transactions of Am Philol Assoc, (97); auth, Poetic Garlands: Hellenistic Epigrams in Context, Berkeley, 98; auth, "The Tragic Mask of Comedy: Metatheatricality in Menender," Classical Antiquity, (00). **CONTACT ADDRESS** Dept Classics, Univ of Cincinnati, Cincinnati, OH 45221-0226. **EMAIL** kathryn.gutzwiller@uc.edu

GUYNN, NOAH
PERSONAL Born 11/02/1968, Berkeley, CA, s **DISCIPLINE** FRENCH **EDUCATION** Yale Univ, MA, 93; MPhil, 95; PhD, 98. **CAREER** Asst prof, Univ of Iowa, 97-98; asst prof, Univ of Calif at Davis, 98-. **HONORS AND AWARDS** Pauline Jones Prize, Bryn Mawr, 90; Fulbright Fel, 90-91; Richard J. Franke Fel, Yale, 91-95; res grant, Whiting Fel, Yal, 96-97; John F. Eiders Res Grant, Yale, 97; Jr Fac Res Fel, Univ of Calif at Davis, 98; undergraduate instructional improvement grant, Univ of Calif at Davis, 99; fac res grant, Univ of Calif at Davis, 99-00. **MEMBERSHIPS** Medieval Acad of Am. **RESEARCH** Medieval literature and old French, classical and medieval Latin literature, gender studies, queer theory, feminism, and critical theory, music and literature. **SELECTED PUBLICATIONS** Transl, "Travels in Eucharistia: Formosa and Ireland from George Psalmanaazaar to Jonathan Swift," by Frank Lestringant, Corps Mystique, Corps Sacre, Yale French Studies vol 86 (94); transl, "The Question of the Other," by Luce Irigaray, Another Look, Another Woman, Yale French Studies vol 87 (95); transl, "The Role of Female Homosexuality in Casanova's Memoirs," by Chantal Thomas, Libertinage and Modernity, Yale French Studies vol 94 (98); co-ed, Rereading Allegory: Essays in Honor of Daniel Poirion, Yale French Studies vol 95 (99); auth, "Eternal Flame: State-Building, Deviant Architecture, and the monumentality of Sexual Deviance in the Eneas," GLQ (00); auth, "Historicizing Shame, Shaming History: Origination and Negativity in the Eneas," L'esprit createur (00). **CONTACT ADDRESS** Dept French & Italian, Univ of California, Davis, 1 Shields Ave, Davis, CA 95616-5270. **EMAIL** ndguynn@ucdavis.edu

GUZMAN-MERCED, ROSA MARIA
PERSONAL Born 12/06/1954, Puerto Rico, m, 1974, 1 child **DISCIPLINE** BUSINESS COMMUNICATION, SPANISH **EDUCATION** Univ Puerto Rico, BA, 76; PhD, 96; Univ Paris, MA, 81. **CAREER** Head, CPN, 85-96; asst to assoc prof, Univ Puerto Rico, 96-. **HONORS AND AWARDS** Who's Who Among America's Teachers, 94, 96; Fel, AAUW, 95; Premio Luis Llorens Torres, 96. **MEMBERSHIPS** MLA, AAUW, AATSP, LASA. **RESEARCH** Autobiography, cultural studies, communication. **SELECTED PUBLICATIONS** Coauth, Historia y geografia de Puerto Rico, Serie Norma Estudios Sociales, (Colombia), 99; auth, Las narraciones autobiograficas puertoriquenas, Publicaciones Puertorrequenas, (San Juan), 00. **CONTACT ADDRESS** calle 7 F-21, Riberas del Rio, Bayamon, PR 00959. **EMAIL** miromi@coqui.net

H

HAASE, DONALD P.
PERSONAL Born 03/20/1950, Cincinnati, OH, m, 1972, 3 children **DISCIPLINE** COMPARATIVE LITERATURE, GERMAN STUDIES **EDUCATION** Univ Cincinnati, BA, 72; MA, 73; Univ NC Chapel Hill, PhD, 79. **CAREER** Vis asst prof, Miami Univ, 78-81; asst prof to assoc prof, Wayne State Univ, 81-; Chair, 89-. **HONORS AND AWARDS** President's Awd for Excellence in Teaching; NEH Summer Stipend; Ger Acad Exchange Serv Fel. **MEMBERSHIPS** MLA; Am Assoc of Teachers of Ger; Bruder Grimm-Gesellschaft. **RESEARCH** Folktale, Fairytale, European Romanticism, Reception Studies, Children's Literature, Exile and Holocaust. **SELECTED PUBLICATIONS** Ed, the Reception of Grimm's Fairy Tales, 93; ed, Marvels and Tales: Journal of Fairy-Tale Studies 97-. **CONTACT ADDRESS** Dept Ger and Slavic Lang, Wayne State Univ, 443 Manoogian, Detroit, MI 48202. **EMAIL** d.haase@wayne.edu

HABERL, FRANZ P.
PERSONAL Born 03/08/1935, Nurnberg, Germany, d **DISCIPLINE** GERMAN LANGUAGE AND LITERATURE **EDUCATION** Ursinus Col, BA, 59; Cornell Univ, MA, 61, PhD(-Ger & comp lit), 64. **CAREER** Instr Ger, Ohio Univ, 62-63; from instr to asst prof, C W Post Col, Long Island Univ, 63-65; asst prof, Univ Md, 65-66; asst prof, Brooklyn Col, 66-69; assoc prof and chmn dept, Mt Allison Univ, 69-73; Prof Ger, Dawson Col, 73-. **MEMBERSHIPS** MLA; Can Asn Univ Teachers Ger. **RESEARCH** German literature especially the Age of Goethe; modern drama and modern novel. **SELECTED PUBLICATIONS** Auth, Midas Oder die Schwarze Leinwand, World Lit Today, Vol 0066, 92; Dreck, World Lit Today, Vol 0067, 93; Der Traum des Konditors, World Lit Today, Vol 0067, 93; Dramas, Vol 3, World Lit Today, Vol 0069, 95; Das Kliff, World Lit Today, Vol 0070, 96; Inselgeschichten, World Lit Today, Vol 0070, 96. **CONTACT ADDRESS** Dept of Mod Lang, Dawson Col, 535 Viger Ave, Montreal, QC, Canada H2L 2P3.

HABERLAND, PAUL MALLORY
PERSONAL Born 09/24/1935, Milwaukee, WI, m, 1962, 2 children **DISCIPLINE** GERMAN LITERATURE & LANGUAGE **EDUCATION** Haverford Col, BA, 57; Johns Hopkins Univ, MA, 60, PhD(Ger), 69. **CAREER** Actg asst prof Ger, Univ Calif, Riverside, 64-66; from instr to asst prof, Lawrence Univ, 66-72; lectr English, Univ Gottingen, Ger, 72-73; from assoc prof Ger to prof Ger, Western Carolina Univ, 74-99;

head Dept Mod Lang, Western Carolina Univ, 81-90. **HONORS AND AWARDS** Fulbright scholar, US, Austria, Germany; Am Philos Soc res grant; Austrian Govt res grant. **MEMBERSHIPS** MLA; Am Asn Teachers Ger; SAtlantic Mod Lang Asn. **RESEARCH** Eighteenth century German literary criticism; 19th century German literature; 20th century Austrian literature. **SELECTED PUBLICATIONS** Auth, The Development of Comic Theory in Germany during the Eighteenth Century, Goppinger Arbeiten Ger Alfred Kummerle, 71; The reception of German literature in Baltimore's literary magazines 1800-1875, Ger-Am Studies, 74; Number symbolism: The father-daughter relationship in E T A Hoffmann's Rat Krespel, 75 & A Fabian's view of Goethe--an unpublished letter from Sidney Webb to Beatrice Potter, 76, Lang Quart; Duality, the artist, and Wolfgang Bauer, Mod Austrian Lit, 78; The role of art in the writings of Barbara Frischmuth, Mod Austrian Lit, 81; auth, Literary Censorship in Austria since 1945, Germanic Rev, 65, No. 2, 90; auth, Amerika als das Andere - Das Amerikabild in den Schriften von Wolfgang Bauer und Gerhard Roth, Akten des VIII. Int Germisten-Kongresses, Band 9, 91.

HABERLY, DAVID T.
PERSONAL Born 12/11/1942, Tucson, AZ, m, 1963, 2 children **DISCIPLINE** SPANISH **EDUCATION** Harvard Univ, AB, 63, AM, 64, PhD(Romance lang), 66. **CAREER** From instr to asst prof romance lang, Harvard Univ, 66-73; chmn, Dept Span, Ital and Port, 73-78, Assoc Prof Port, Univ VA, 73-. **MEMBERSHIPS** MLA; Am Asn Teachers Span & Port. **RESEARCH** Brazilian and Portuguese literature; Spanish American and North American literature. **SELECTED PUBLICATIONS CONTACT ADDRESS** Dept of Span Ital and Port, Univ of Virginia, 1 Cabell Hall, Charlottesville, VA 22903-3125.

HADLEY, MICHAEL LLEWELLYN
PERSONAL Born 04/06/1936, Campbell River, BC, Canada, m, 1959, 4 children **DISCIPLINE** GERMAN LANGUAGE AND LITERATURE **EDUCATION** Univ BC, BA, 59; Univ Man, MA, 64; Queen's Univ, Ont, PhD(Ger), 71. **CAREER** Foreign Serv officer, Can Govt, 59-62; lectr Ger, St John's Col, Univ Man, 62-64; asst prof, Univ Winnipeg, 65-70; asst prof, 70-73, chmn dept, 74-80, Assoc Prof Ger Lang and Lit, Univ Victroia, 74-, Chmn, External Rels Comt, Humanities Res Coun Can, 78-. **MEMBERSHIPS** Can Asn Univ Teachers Ger (vpres, 76-78, pres, 78-80); Am Asn 18th Century Studies; Can Asn 18th Century Studies; Am Lessing Soc; Maritime Defense Asn Can. **RESEARCH** Eighteenth-century literature; Deutsche Schauerromantik; U-Boat warfare in Canadian waters. **SELECTED PUBLICATIONS** Auth, Understanding Remarque, Erich, Maria, Seminar-J Ger Stud, Vol 0029, 93; Understanding Bernhard, Thomas, Seminar-J Ger Stud, Vol 0029, 93; Understanding Canetti, Elias, Seminar-J Ger Stud, Vol 0029, 93; The Longest Battle--The Royal-Canadian-Navy in the Atlantic, 1939-1945, Am Neptune, Vol 0054, 94; The Kaisers Pirates--German Surface Raiders in World-War-I, Mariners Mirror, Vol 0081, 95; The Defeat of the U-Boats--The Battle of the Atlantic, Am Neptune, Vol 0055, 95; Graf-Spees Raiders--Challenge to the Royal-Navy, 1914-1915, Mariners Mirror, Vol 0082, 96. **CONTACT ADDRESS** Dept of Ger Lang and Lit, Univ of Victoria, Victoria, BC, Canada V8W 2Y2. **EMAIL** mlhadley@uvvm.uvic.ca

HAENICKE, DIETHER H.
PERSONAL Born 05/19/1935, Hagen, Germany, m, 1962, 2 children **DISCIPLINE** GERMAN LITERATURE **EDUCATION** Univ Munich, Ger, PhD, 62. **CAREER** Prof, dean, provost, Wayne State Univ, 63-78; prof, dean, provost, Ohio State Univ, 78-85; pres, Western Mich Univ, 85-98; dist prof, pres, emer, 98-. **HONORS AND AWARDS** Fulbright Scholar, 63, 64; DHL, 86, 98; Phi Beta Kappa. **MEMBERSHIPS** AAUP; MLA; AATC. **RESEARCH** German literature of 19th and 20th Centuries. **SELECTED PUBLICATIONS** Coauth, The Challenge of German Literature, 71; ed, L Tieck-Werke, 3 vols, 69; auth, Das Versepos Des 20, Jahrhunderts, 62. **CONTACT ADDRESS** Dept Lang, Ling, Western Michigan Univ, 3019 Waldo Library, Kalamazoo, MI 490008-3804.

HAFTER, MONROE Z.
PERSONAL Born 06/28/1926, New York, NY, m, 1957, 2 children **DISCIPLINE** SPANISH LITERATURE **EDUCATION** Harvard Univ, PhD, 56. **CAREER** Teaching fel Span, Harvard Univ, 51-56; from instr to asst prof Romanic lang, Williams Col, 56-60; from asst prof to assoc prof, 60-67, Prof Span, Univ Mich, Ann Arbor, 67-, Am Philos Soc grant, 58; Williams Col Class of 1900 Fund grant, 58; grant, Rackham Sch Grad Studies, Univ Mich, Ann Arbor, 62; Fulbright and Guggenheim Found res grants, 67-68. **MEMBERSHIPS** MLA; Am Soc 18th Century Studies. **RESEARCH** Transition in Spanish literature from Golden Age to nineteenth century; moralist literature, satire and novel. **SELECTED PUBLICATIONS CONTACT ADDRESS** Dept of Romance Lang, Univ of Michigan, Ann Arbor, Ann Arbor, MI 48109.

HAGENS, JAN LUBER
DISCIPLINE GERMAN LITERATURE **EDUCATION** Univ Va, MA, 83; Univ Tubingen, staatsexamen, 88; Princeton Univ, MA, 90, PhD, 93. **CAREER** Asst prof, Carleton Col, 93-95; asst prof, Eckerd Col, 95- 97; ASST PROF GER, UNIV NOTRE DAME, 97-. **CONTACT ADDRESS** Dept of German & Russian, Univ of Notre Dame, 318 O'Shaughnessy Hall, Notre Dame, IN 46556. **EMAIL** jan.l.hagens.2@nd.edu

HAGIWARA, TAKAO
DISCIPLINE JAPANESE AND COMPARATIVE LITERATURE **EDUCATION** Sophia Univ, BA, 71;Univ British Columbia, MA, 79, PhD, 86. **CAREER** English, Case Western Reserve Univ. **SELECTED PUBLICATIONS** Auth, The Idea of Innocence in Kenji Miyazawa,Tokyo: Meijishoin, 88; Coed, The Mother in Japanese Literature,Tokyo: Shinyosha, 97. **CONTACT ADDRESS** Case Western Reserve Univ, 10900 Euclid Ave, Cleveland, OH 44106. **EMAIL** txh13@po.cwru.edu

HAHM, DAVID EDGAR
PERSONAL Born 09/30/1938, Milwaukee, WI, m, 1964, 4 children **DISCIPLINE** CLASSICAL LANGUAGES, ANCIENT PHILOSOPHY, INTELLECTUAL HISTORY **EDUCATION** Northwestern Col, BA, 60; Univ Wis-Madison, MA, 62, PhD(classics), 66. **CAREER** Asst prof class lang, Univ Mo-Columbia, 66-69; from asst to assoc prof class, 69-78, Prof Classics, Ohio State Univ, 78-, Fel, Ctr Hellenic Studies, Wash, DC, 68-69. **MEMBERSHIPS** Am Philol Asn; Am Philos Asn; Hist Sci Soc; Class Asn Midwest & South. **RESEARCH** Ancient philosophy and science, Greek literature. **SELECTED PUBLICATIONS** Auth, The origins of Stoic cosmology, Columbus, 77; auth, "A neglected Stoic argument for human responsibility," Illinois Classical Studies 17, (92): 23-48; auth, "Galen and Chrysippus on the soul: argument and refutation in the 'De placitis, bks. 2-3," Bulletin of the Hist of Medicine 73, (99): 302-3; auth, "Plato, Carneades and Cicero's Philus, (Cicero, Rep. 3.8-31)," Classical Quarterly ns. 49, (99): 167-83. **CONTACT ADDRESS** Dept of Greek & Latin, Ohio State Univ, Columbus, 230 N Oval Mall, Columbus, OH 43210-1335. **EMAIL** hahm.1@osu.edu

HAHN, FRANCIS V. HICKSON
DISCIPLINE CLASSICS **EDUCATION** Univ NC, Chapel Hill, PhD, 86. **CAREER** Assoc Prof, Univ Calif, Santa Barbara. **RESEARCH** Religion of the Roman Republic. **SELECTED PUBLICATIONS** Auth, Roman Prayer Language: Livy and the Aeneid of Vergil, Teubner, 93; "Patruus: Paragon or Pervert? The Case of a Literary Split Personality," Syllecta Classica 4, 93; "Augustus Triumphator: Manipulation of the Triumphal Theme in the Political Program of Augustus," Latomus, 91; "Roman Religion," The Dictionary of Religion, Harper-Collins and Amer Acad of Rel, 95. **CONTACT ADDRESS** Dept of Classics, Univ of California, Santa Barbara, Santa Barbara, CA 93106-7150. **EMAIL** fhahn@humanitas.ucsb.edu

HAHN, HANNELORE
DISCIPLINE SPANISH **EDUCATION** San Jose State Univ, BA, MA; Columbia Univ, PhD. **CAREER** Assoc prof, Col St. Elizabeth. **RESEARCH** Kafka's influence on Latin Am writers; Cuban writers in exile; Orlando Saa Thomas Mann's influence on Latin Am writers; transl tech. **SELECTED PUBLICATIONS** Auth, Las novelas de J Leyra, 97; Los Balseros de la libertad de J Leyva, WPU, 97; Tierrade Extranos de J A Albertini, Pensamiento, 97; Reacion to U Hegi's book:Tearing the Silence, CSE, 97; Las novelas de J Leyva, Youngstown State Univ, 97; El desafio existential en la obra de Josefina Leyva, Circulo de Cultura, WPU, 97; El Tiempo Inagotado de Irene Marquina de J Leyva, Simposio en la Univ de Bariloche, Argentina, 97; Las novelas de J Leyva, Circulo de Escritores y Poetas de Nueva York, 97; rev, El Tiempo Inagotado de Irene Marquina de J Leyva, Pensamiento, Fla, 97; Los balseros de la libertad de Josefina Leyva, Pensamiento, Fla, 1997 & El veranito de , Circulo de Cult, 97; article on, Los Balseros de la Libertad de J Leyva, Pensamiento Lit Mag, 97; Los Balseros de la libertad de Josefina Leyva, Pensamiento, 97. **CONTACT ADDRESS** Dept of For Lang, Col of Saint Elizabeth, 2 Convent Rd., Morristown, NJ 07960. **EMAIL** hahn@liza.st-elizabeth.edu

HAHN, OSCAR
PERSONAL Born 07/05/1938, Iquique, Chile, m, 1971, 1 child **DISCIPLINE** SPANISH AMERICAN POETRY, LITERARY THEORY **EDUCATION** Univ Chile, Profesor Span, 63; Univ Iowa, MA, 72; Univ Md, PhD(Span), 77. **CAREER** Prof Hisp lit, Univ Chile Arica, 65-73; instr, Univ Md, 74-77; asst prof Span Am poetry, 77-79, Assoc Prof Span Am Lit, Univ Iowa, 79-, Hon fel writing, Int Writing Prog, Univ Iowa, 72; contrib ed Span Am poetry, Handbook of Latin American Studies, Libr Cong, 77-. **MEMBERSHIPS** MLA; Inst Lit Iberoam. **RESEARCH** Spanish American literature; literary theory. **SELECTED PUBLICATIONS** Auth, 20th-Century Chilean Literature, Rev Iberoamericana, Vol 0060, 94; Huidobro, Vicente, from the Mechanic Kingdom to the Apocalypse, Rev Iberoamericana, Vol 0060, 94. **CONTACT ADDRESS** Dept of Span, Univ of Iowa, Iowa City, IA 52240.

HAIDT, REBECCA
PERSONAL Born 10/26/1961, New York, NY, 1 child **DISCIPLINE** SPANISH **EDUCATION** Washington Univ, AB, 83, AM, 89, PhD, 92. **CAREER** Asst Prof of Spanish, 92-98, Assoc Prof of Spanish, Ohio State Univ, 98-. **HONORS AND AWARDS** Fulbright fel for independent res, 84-85; DAAD Direktstipendium, 87-88; Katherine Singer Kovacs Prize; Modern Language Assn, 99. **MEMBERSHIPS** ASECS; MLA; Iber-American Soc for Eighteenth-Century studies; Society of Dance Hist Scholars; Society of Spanish & Portuguese Hist scholars. **RESEARCH** Eighteenth-Century Spain; enlightenment; gender; cultural studies; urban hist; consumer cultues. **SELECTED PUBLICATIONS** Auth, Fray Gerundio and Luxury: The Rococo Aesthetics of Feminized Form, Dieciocho, 94; How Should Medicine Know the Body?: Feijoo's El medico de si mismo, Dieciocho, 96; Los besos de amor and La maja desnuda: The Fascination of the Senses in the Ilustracion, Revista de Estudios Hispanicos, 95; auth, Embodying Enlightenment: Knowing the Body in Eighteenth-Century Spanish Lit and Culture, St. Martin's Press, 98; auth, "Luxury, Consumption and Desire: Theorizing the Petimetra" Arizona Journal of Hispanic Cultural Studies, 99; auth, "Fashion, Effeminacy, and Homoerotic Desire: The Question of the Petimetres" Letras Peninsulares, 99; **CONTACT ADDRESS** Dept of Spanish & Portuguese, Ohio State Univ, Columbus, Columbus, OH 43210. **EMAIL** haidt.1@osu.edu

HAIDU, PETER
PERSONAL Born 03/07/1931, Paris, France, 2 children **DISCIPLINE** FRENCH **EDUCATION** Univ Chicago, BA, 52; Columbia Univ, MA, 59, PhD(French), 66. **CAREER** From instr to asst prof French, Columbia Univ, 61-68; from asst prof to assoc prof, Yale Univ, 68-72; assoc prof, Univ Va, 72-74; Prof French and Sch Humanities, Univ Ill, 74-, Morse fel, Yale Univ, 70-71; Nat Endowment for Humanities fel, 77-78; Camargo Found fel, 77-78. **RESEARCH** Semiotics; French and medieval literature; theory of literature. **SELECTED PUBLICATIONS** Auth, The Art of Medieval French Romance, Mod Lang Quart, Vol 0054, 93. **CONTACT ADDRESS** Dept of Fr, Univ of California, Los Angeles, PO Box 951550, Los Angeles, CA 90095-1550.

HAIG, I. R. STIRLING
PERSONAL Born 05/20/1936, Washington, DC, m, 1960, 2 children **DISCIPLINE** FRENCH **EDUCATION** Univ NC, BA, 58; Yale Univ, PhD, 64. **CAREER** Instr, Yale Univ, 62-64; from instr to asst prof, Princeton Univ, 64-67; from asst prof to prof, Univ of NC, 67-. **HONORS AND AWARDS** Phi Beta Kappa; Fulbright Scholar; Ordre des Palmes Acadmiques. **MEMBERSHIPS** MLA, AAFT. **RESEARCH** Stendhal, Flaubert, Nineteenth-Century novel. **SELECTED PUBLICATIONS** Auth, Flaubert and the Gift of Speech, Cambridge Univ Press, 86; auth, The Madame Bovary Blues, La State Univ Press, 87; auth, Approaches to Teaching Stendahal's 'The Red and the Black,' MLA, 99; auth, Resonant Themes, Univ of NC Press, 99. **CONTACT ADDRESS** Dept Romance Lang, Univ of No Carolina, Chapel Hill, Chapel Hill, NC 27599-3170. **EMAIL** shaig@email.unc.edu

HAILE, GETATCHEW
PERSONAL Born 04/19/1931, Shenkora, Shoa, Ehtiopia, m, 1964, 6 children **DISCIPLINE** LINGUISTICS, RELIGION **EDUCATION** Am Univ Cairo, BA, 57; Coptic Theol Col, Cairo, BD, 57; Univ Tubingen, PhD(semitic philol), 62. **CAREER** Lectr, Amharic, Ge'ez and Arabic, HSI Univ, Ethiopia, 62-64, asst prof Amharic, Ge'ez and Arabic and chmn dept Ethiopian lang, 64-69; exchange scholar ling, Univ Calif, Los Angeles, 69-70; vis prof African studies, Okla State Univ, 70-71; assoc prof Amharic, Ge'ez and Arabic, HSI Univ, Ethiopia, 71-75; Cataloguer of Oriental Manuscripts and Regents Prof of Medieval History, Hill Monastic Manuscript Libr, St John's Univ, Minn, 76-, Contrib ed, Northeast African Studies, Mich State Univ. **HONORS AND AWARDS** MacArthur Foundation Awd. **MEMBERSHIPS** Corresponding Fellow of the British Academy. **RESEARCH** Ge'ez literature; Amharic grammar. **SELECTED PUBLICATIONS** Auth, A Catalogue of Ethiopian Manuscripts Micorfilmed for the Ethiopian Manuscript Microfilm Library, addis Ababa and for The Hill Monastic Manuscript Library, Collegeville, 83; auth, The Faith of the Unctionists in the Ethiopian Church, 90; auth, The Epistle of Humanity, 91; auth, The Mariology of Emperor Zar'a Yaeqob of Ethiopia, 92; auth, From Emperor Selassie, Haile to Polotsky, H. J.--An Ethiopian and Semitic Miscellany, J Royal Asiatic Soc, Vol 0006, 96. **CONTACT ADDRESS** Hill Monastic Ms Libr, St. John's Univ, Collegeville, MN 56321. **EMAIL** ghaile@csbsju.edu

HAILE, HARRY G.
PERSONAL Born 07/31/1931, TX, m, 1952, 3 children **DISCIPLINE** GERMAN LITERATURE **EDUCATION** Univ Ark, BA, 52, MA, 54; Univ Ill, PhD, 57. **CAREER** Instr Ger, Univ Pa, 56-57; from asst prof to assoc prof, Univ Houston, 57-63; assoc prof, 63-65, chmn dept, 64-67, head dept, 67-73, assoc mem, Ctr Advan Studies, 69-70, Prof Ger, Univ ill, Urbana, 65-, Am Coun Learned Soc grant, 60; Deut Forschungsgemeinschaft grant, 62-63; vis prof Ger, Univ Mich, 78. **MEMBERSHIPS** MLA; Am Asn Teachers Ger; Goethe Soc; Wiener Goethe Verein. **RESEARCH** Humanities education and higher education in the United States; pre-industrial German literature; Martin Luther biography. **SELECTED PUBLICATIONS** Auth,

Luther An Experiment in Biography, Das Fastbuch n.d. Wolfenbuttler MS Artist in Chrysalis, Invitation to Goethe's Faust, Hist of Dr. Johannfastus. **CONTACT ADDRESS** 706 Hessel Blvd., Champaign, IL 61820-6341. **EMAIL** harryhaile@aol.com

HAJIBASHI, ZJALEH

PERSONAL Born 12/15/1962, Denton, TX, s **DISCIPLINE** LANGUAGE, LITERATURE, PERSIAN **EDUCATION** Rice Univ, BA, 83; Univ Tex Austin, MA, 88; PhD, 98. **CAREER** Lectr, Univ Vir, 00-. **MEMBERSHIPS** MESA; SIS; MLA. **RESEARCH** Modern Persian literature; cultural studies; translation theory; feminist theory; women's studies. **SELECTED PUBLICATIONS** Auth, "Feminism or Ventriloquism: Western Representations of Middle Eastern Women," Mid E Report 21 (91): 43-45; auth, "Heaven's Fruit," and "Morning Exercise," in A World Between, eds. P. Karim, M. Meldi (NY: George Braziller, 98). **CONTACT ADDRESS** 2527 Hydraulic Rd, Apt 44, Charlottesville, VA 22901-2367. **EMAIL** zhzf@virginia.edu

HAKUTANI, YOSHINOBU

PERSONAL Born 03/27/1935, Osaka, Japan, m, 1967, 2 children **DISCIPLINE** AMERICAN LITERATURE, LINGUISTICS **EDUCATION** Hiroshima Univ, Japan, BA, 57; Univ Minn, Minneapolis, MA, 59; Pa State Univ, PhD(English), 65. **CAREER** Instr English, SDak State Univ, 59-61; asst prof, Calif State Univ, Northridge, 65-68; asst prof, 68-71, assoc prof, 71-80, Prof English, Kent State Univ, 80-, Res fel, Kent State Univ, 71-72. **HONORS AND AWARDS** Choice Awd, 88; Acad of Am Poets, 99, Nat Poetry Month. **MEMBERSHIPS** MLA; ALA; Dreiser Soc. **RESEARCH** Modern American Literature, African American Literature, Cross-Cultural Studies. **SELECTED PUBLICATIONS** Auth, Young Dreiser: A Critical Study, Assoc Uiv Presses, 80; ed, Selected Magazine Articles of Theodore Dreiser: Life and Art in the American 1890s, Assoc Univ Presses, 85-87; ed, Selected English Writings of Yone Noguchi: An East-West Literary Assimilation, Assoc Univ Presses, 90-92; co-ed, The City in African-American Literature, Assoc Univ Presses, 95; ed, Postmodernity and Cross Culturalism, Fairleigh Dickinson UP, 01; ed, Modernity in East-West literary Criticism, Fairleigh Dickinson UP, 01; ed, Art, Music, and Literature, 1897-1902, by Theodore Dreiser, U of IL P, 01; ed, Theodore Dreiser and American Culture, U of Delaware P, 00. **CONTACT ADDRESS** Dept of English, Kent State Univ, PO Box 5190, Kent, OH 44242-0001. **EMAIL** yhakutan@kent.edu

HALE, MARK

DISCIPLINE LINGUISTICS **EDUCATION** Univ Mich, BA, 76; Ind Univ, MA, 80; Harvard Univ, PhD, 87. **CAREER** Assoc prof, Concordia Univ, 94-; visiting prof, Cornell Univ, 97; vis prof, Harvard Summer Sch, 95, 96; visiting prof, Univ Wien, 95; assoc prof, Harvard Univ, 90-94; vis prof, Univ Wien, 91; asst prof, Harvard Univ, 87-90; tchg fel, Harvard Univ, 82-86; tchg asst, Ind Univ, 79-80. **HONORS AND AWARDS** FRDP Res grant, 94-97; Whiting fel, Harvard Univ, 86-87; Fulbright Stud grant, Univ Regensburg, Ger, 85-1986; grad stud fel, Ind Univ, 78-79; class distinction and univ hon(s), Univ Mich, 76; Harry Helfman Fund Alumni scholar, Univ Mich, 75. **SELECTED PUBLICATIONS** Auth, "Preliminaries to the study of the relationship between syntax and sandhi in Rigvedic Sanskrit," Munchner Studien zur Sprachwissenschaft 51, (90), 77-96; auth, "Tmesis in Old Iranian," Indo-Iranian J, 34, (91); auth, Harvard Working Papers in Linguistics, vol 2, Dept of Ling, Harvard Univ, 93; coauth, On the Initial Ranking of OT Faithfulness Constraints in Universal Grammar, Concordia Univ, 95; auth, "Deriving Wackernagel's Law: prosodic and syntactic factors determing clitic placement in the language of the Rigveda," in the Approaching Second: Second position clitics and related phenomena, A. Zwicky and A. Halpern ed(s), Stanford Univ, 96; auth, "Commentary on Epstein, Flynn and Martohardjono, Second language acqustion: theoretical and experimental issues in contemporary research," Behavioural and Brain Sci, 96; auth, auth, Some Cases of So-called Metrical Lengthening in the Rigveda, in the Felicitation Vol for George Cardona, Madhav Deshpande and Peter Hook ed(s), 96; coauth, The Phonology-Syntax Interface in Rotuman, in the Proceedings of the Third Meeting of the Austronesian Formal Ling Assic, UCLA, 97; auth, Regular Syntactic Change, in th premier vol of the J Interdisciplinary syntax, Basil Blackwell, 97; auth, Noun-incorporation in Micronesian: A Historical Account, in Canadian J of Ling, D. Massam and B. Miller ed(s), 97. **CONTACT ADDRESS** Dept of Classics, Mod Lang and Ling, Concordia Univ, Montreal, 7141 Sherlbrooke St., W, Montreal, QC, Canada H4G 1M6. **EMAIL** hale1@alcor.concordia.ca

HALE, THOMAS ALBERT

PERSONAL Born 01/05/1942, Boston, MA, m, 1968, 1 child **DISCIPLINE** AFRICAN AND FRENCH LITERATURE **EDUCATION** Tufts Univ, BA, 64, MA, 68; Univ Rochester, PhD(French), 74. **CAREER** Agr co-op asst, Peace Corps, Union Nigerienne de Credit et de Cooperation, 64-66; admin asst, NDEA French Inst, Tufts Univ, 67; Assoc Prof French and Comp Lit, Pa State Univ, 73-, Co-ed, Cahiers Cesairiens, 74- and African Lit Asn Newsletter, 74-78; Fulbright sr lectr, Univ de Niamey, Niger, 80-81. **MEMBERSHIPS** MLA; African Lit Asn (secy-treas, 74-79, press, 81-82); Am Asn Teachers French; African Studies Asn; Am Comp Lit Asn. **RESEARCH** Caribbean literature; French literature outside France. **SELECTED PUBLICATIONS** Auth, Sur Une tempete d'Aime Cesaire, Etudes Lit, 4/73; Aime Cesaire: A bio-bibliography, Africana J, spring 74; From Afro-America to Afro-France: The literary triangle trade, French Rev, 5/76; Structural dynamics in a Third World classic: Aime Cesaire's Cahier d'un retour au pays natal, Yale French Studies, No 53, 76; co-ed, The Teaching of African Literature, Univ Tex Press, 77; auth, Les Ecrits d'Aime Cesaire: Bibliographie commentee, Univ Montreal Press, 78; co-ed, Artist and Audience: African Literature as a Shared Experience, Three Continents Press, 79; auth, From written literature to the oral tradition and back: Camara Laye, Babou Conde, and Le Maitre de la Parole: Kouma Lafolo Kouma, French Rev, 5/82. **CONTACT ADDRESS** French Dept, Pennsylvania State Univ, Univ Park, 434 N Burrowes Bldg, University Park, PA 16802-6204.

HALEY, MICHAEL

PERSONAL Born 12/30/1947, Birmingham, AL **DISCIPLINE** LINGUISTICS **EDUCATION** Fla State Univ, PhD. **CAREER** Univ Alaska. **HONORS AND AWARDS** Phi Beta Kappa, 69; Moss Chair of Excellence, Univ of Memphis, 98. **SELECTED PUBLICATIONS** Coauth, Noam Chomsky, Twayne, 94; The Semeiosis of Poetic Metaphor, Indiana Univ Press, 89; Managing ed, Peirce Seminar Papers: Essays in Semiotic Analysis, 93, 94, 97, 99. **CONTACT ADDRESS** Univ of Alaska, Anchorage, 3211 Providence Dr., Anchorage, AK 99508. **EMAIL** afmch@uaa.alaska.edu

HALFORD, PETER W.

PERSONAL Born Essex County, m, 3 children **DISCIPLINE** FRENCH LANGUAGE; LITERATURE **EDUCATION** Univ Windsor, BA, MA; l'Universite des Sciences Humaines in Strasbourg, Fr, PhD. **CAREER** Couns, Univ of Windsor; adj assoc prof, Univ of Windsor. **HONORS AND AWARDS** Excellence in univ tchg, Ont Coun Univ Fac Assoc, 83. **RESEARCH** 300 year history of the French language of our area. **SELECTED PUBLICATIONS** Auth, Le Francais des Canadiens a la veille de la Conquete. **CONTACT ADDRESS** Dept of French Language and Literature, Univ of Windsor, 401 Sunset Ave, Windsor, ON, Canada N9B 3P4. **EMAIL** dadotoo@uwindsor.ca

HALL, JOHN

PERSONAL Born 01/02/1969, Gadsden, AL, m, 1997, 1 child **DISCIPLINE** SPANISH, LINGUISTICS **EDUCATION** Univ W Fla, BA, 92; Fla State Univ, MA, 94; Fla State Univ, PhD, 97. **CAREER** Teacher, Acad Teocali, 90-91; Asst Teacher, Fla State Univ, 92-95; Vis Instr, Purdue Univ, 95-96; Asst Prof, Ball State Univ, 96-98; Asst Prof, Univ Montevallo, 98-. **HONORS AND AWARDS** Int Travel Grant, Ball State Univ, 97-98; Ford Found Fel, 99; Ford Found Grant, 99. **MEMBERSHIPS** SCOLAS **RESEARCH** Central American cultures and literature, Spanish linguistics. **SELECTED PUBLICATIONS** Auth, "Tres Motivos en la poesia de Juan Ramon Molina," Visiones y Revisiones de la Lit Cent Am, Coleccion Centro Int de Lit Cent Am, vol 3 (00): 71-79. **CONTACT ADDRESS** Dept Lang & Ling, Univ of Montevallo, PO Box 6000, Montevallo, AL 35115-6000. **EMAIL** johngretah@cs.com

HALL, JONATHAN M.

DISCIPLINE CLASSICS **EDUCATION** Univ Oxford, BA, 88, MA, 91; Univ Cambridge, PhD, 93. **CAREER** Tchg fel, Marlboro Col, 88-89; Undergrad Supvr, Univ Cambridge, 89-96; Lectr, British Sch at Athens Summer Sch, 92-93; Res Fel, Downing Col, 93-96; Aff lectr, Univ Cambridge, 95-96; Asst prof, Univ Chicago, 96-. **HONORS AND AWARDS** Open Exhibition, Hertford Col, Univ of Oxford, 84; College Scholarship, Hertford Col, 87; Univ Prize for Fieldwork in Ancient Hist and Archaeology, Univ of Oxford, 87; British Academy Major State Studentship, Univ of Cambridge, 89-93; L.H. Jeffery Studentship in Archaic Greek Archaeology and Epigraphy, 91-92; Junior Fel, Center for Hellenic Studies, 98-99; Charles J. Goodwin Awd, 99. **RESEARCH** The social and cultural hist of archaic Greece, Greek history, hsitoriography, and archaeology. **SELECTED PUBLICATIONS** Auth, Ethnic identity in Greek antiquity, Cambridge, 97. **CONTACT ADDRESS** Dept of Classical Lang & Literature, Univ of Chicago, 1010 E 50th St, Chicago, IL 60637. **EMAIL** jhall@midway.uchicago.edu

HALLE, MORRIS

PERSONAL Born 07/23/1923, Liepaja, Latvia, m, 1955, 3 children **DISCIPLINE** SLAVIC LANGUAGES **EDUCATION** Univ Chicago, MA, 48; Harvard Univ, PhD(Slavic lang & lit), 55. **CAREER** Teaching fel Russ & Ger, Univ Chicago, 47-48; teaching fel Russ, Harvard Univ, 49-51; from asst prof to prof, 51-76 Ferrari P Ward prof, 76-81, Inst Prof Mod Lang & Ling, Mass Inst Technol, 81-96, Prof Emeritus, 96-. **HONORS AND AWARDS** Guggenheim fel, 60-61; fel, Ctr Advan Studies Behav, 60-61; J.R. Killian Jr Fac Achievement Awd lectr, 78-79; Sci prize of Union de Assurances de Paris, 91; DSC (hon), Brandeis, 89; DHL (hon), Univ Chicago, 92. **MEMBERSHIPS** Fel Am Acad Arts & Sci; Ling Soc Am (vpres, 73, pres, 74); Nat Acad of Sci. **RESEARCH** Phonetics; general linguistics; Slavic languages and linguistics. **SELECTED PUBLICATIONS** Auth, The Sound Pattern of Russian, Mouton, The Hague, 59; coauth, Preliminaries to Speech Analysis, MIT Press, 63; The Sound Pattern of English, MIT Press, 92; auth, The accentuation of Russian words, Language, 49/73; coauth, An Essay on Stress, MIT Press, 87; auth, On Stress and Accent, Indo-Euro Lang, 73/97. **CONTACT ADDRESS** Massachusetts Inst of Tech, E39-218, Cambridge, MA 02139-4307. **EMAIL** halle@mit.edu

HALLECK, GENE B.

DISCIPLINE TESL, PSYCHOLINGUISTICS **EDUCATION** Penn State Univ, PhD, 90. **CAREER** Assoc Prof, eng Dept, OK State Univ. **MEMBERSHIPS** TESOL; AAAL; ILTA; ACTFL. **RESEARCH** Oral Proficiency **SELECTED PUBLICATIONS** Auth, Interrater reliability of the OPI: Using academic trainee raters, Foreign Lang Annals, 96; Assessing oral proficiency: A comparison of holist and objective measures, Modern Lang J, 95; coauth, Testing language and teaching skills of international teaching assistants: The limits of contemporary strategies, TESOL Qtly, 95; coauth, Solving the plagiary puzzle: Role plays for intl students, TESOL J, 95; coauth, Probing above the ceiling in oral interviews: What's up there?, in: Current developments and alternatives in language assessment, eds, S Hunta, V Kohonen, L Kurki-Suonio, S Luoma, Jyvaskyla, U of Jyvaskyla, 97; coauth, The OPI as speech event: Native and non-native speaker's questions, in: Language proficiency interviews, eds, Richard Young, Agnes He, Benjamins, 98; coauth, Let them eat cake! Or how to avoid losing your head in cross-cultural conversations, in: Lang Prof Interviews, eds, Richard Young, Agnes He, Benjamins, 98; rev, Traveling through idioms: An exercise guide to the world of Amer idioms, Kadden, Modern Lang J, 98. **CONTACT ADDRESS** TESL Program, Oklahoma State Univ, Stillwater, 205 Marrill Hall, Stillwater, OK 74078.

HALLEN, CYNTHIA L.

PERSONAL Born 06/01/1955, Greenbay, WI **DISCIPLINE** LINGUISTICS & PHILOLOGY **EDUCATION** Univ Arizona, PhD, 91. **CAREER** Assoc prof, 7 yrs, Brigham Young Univ **MEMBERSHIPS** Emily Dickinson International Soc; Found for Ancient Res and Mormon Stud, Univ Fac for Life. **RESEARCH** Dickinson, Lexicography, Philology, Translation Poetry, Aymara. **SELECTED PUBLICATIONS** Transl, "Translation and the Emily Dickinson Lexicon," with Laura M. Harvey, Emily Dickinson Journal 2:2, (93): 130-146; auth, "Student Lexicographers: Pioneers for the Emily Dickinson Lexicon," Dicitonaries 15, (94): 100-115; auth, Brave Columbus, Brave Columbia: Emily Dickinson's Search for Land," Emily Dickinson Journal 5:2, (96): 169-75; auth, "Cognitive Circuits: The Circumference of Dickinson's Lexicon," The Emily Dickinson Journal: Special Issue on Translating Dickinson, 6:2, (97): 76-83; auth, "Glossary, "Linguistics at Work: A Reader of Applications, ed. Dallin D. Oaks, Dallas, Texas: Harcourt, (98): 727-745; auth, "Student Lexicographers: Pioneers for the Emily Dickinson Lexicon," Linguistics at Work: A Reader of Applications, ed. Dallin D. Oaks, Dallas, Tex: Harcourt, (98): 536-552. **CONTACT ADDRESS** Linguistics Dept, Brigham Young Univ, 2140 JKHB, Provo, UT 84602-6278. **EMAIL** cynthia_hallen@byu.edu

HALLER, HERMANN W.

PERSONAL Born 06/02/1945, Aarau, Switzerland **DISCIPLINE** ITALIAN LINGUISTICS, ROMANCE PHILOLOGY **EDUCATION** Univ Bern, SWI, PhD, 71. **CAREER** Sci asst Romance philol, Univ Bern, 70-72; instr, 73-74, asst prof, 74-80, assoc prof Romance Lang, 80-83, Prof Romance Lang, Queens Col and Grad Ctr, City Univ New York, 84-; vis prof, NY Univ, 80, Brown Univ, 80-81, Johns Hopkins Univ, 93-01, Middleburg Col, 94, Univ of Trett, ITA, 96. **HONORS AND AWARDS** International Dino Compana Prize, 91; Fellow, NEH, 94-95; Scaglione Publication Awd MLA, 98. **MEMBERSHIPS** MLA; Am Asn Teachers Ital; Int Ling Asn; Ling Soc Am; Soc Ling Italiana. **RESEARCH** Early Italian texts; history of Italian language; Italian stylistics; Italian dialectology; dialect literature. **SELECTED PUBLICATIONS** Auth, Der Deiktische Gebrauch des Demonstrativums im Altitalienischen, Lang, Bern, 73; ed & auth, Il Panfilo veneziano, Edizione critica, Olschki, Firenze, 82; The Hidden Italy. A Bilingual Edition of Italian Dialect Poetry, Detroit, Wayne State Univ Press, 86; Una lingua perduta e ritrovata: l'italiano degli italo-americani, Firenze, La Nuova Italia, 93; Italian, Joshua A. Fishman and Ofelia Garcia, eds, in The Multilingual Apple. Languages in New York City, Berlin-New York: Mouton De Gruyter, 97; The Dialects Abroad, Martin Maiden and Mair Parry, eds, in The Dialects of Italy, London-New York: Routledge, 97; The Other Italy. The Literary Cenon in Dialect, Univ of Toronto, (Toronto), 99. **CONTACT ADDRESS** European Languages and Literature, Queens Col, CUNY, 6530 Kissena Blvd, Flushing, NY 11367-1597. **EMAIL** haller@forbiu.qc.edu

HALLETT, JUDITH PELLER

PERSONAL Born 04/04/1944, Chicago, IL, m, 1966, 2 children **DISCIPLINE** CLASSICAL PHILOLOGY **EDUCATION** Wellesley Univ, BA, 66; Harvard Univ, MA, 67, PhD, 71. **CAREER** Lectr and Vis Asst Prof, Clark Univ, 72-74; Asst

Prof, Boston Univ, 74-82; Asst Prof Mellon Found, Brandeis Univ, 82-83; Assoc Prof, 83-93, Prof, Univ Md, 93-, Dept Chair, 96-. **HONORS AND AWARDS** Blegen Vis Schol, Vassar Col, 80; NEH Fel Col Teachers, 86-87; Distinguished Scholar-Teacher, Univ Md, 92-93. **MEMBERSHIPS** Am Philol Asn; Classical Asn Atlantic States, 99-00; Phi Beta Kappa; Am Asn Univ Prof; Women's Classical Caucus, 72; Am Philological Asn, Dir, 96-99. **RESEARCH** Latin lang and lit; Roman culture; women, sexuality, and the family in classical antiquity; the classical tradition. **SELECTED PUBLICATIONS** Auth, Fathers and Daughters in Roman Society: Women and the Elite Family, Princeton Univ Press, 84; Feminist Theory, Historical Periods, Literary Canons and the Study of Greco-Roman Antiquity, Feminist Theory and the Classics, 93; Martial's Sulpicia and Propertius, Women in Classical Antiquity: Essays in Honor of Joy K. King, Oak Park, 93; ed and contribr, Six [North American] Women Classicists, special issue of Classical World, Nov/Dec 96-Jan/Feb 97; co-ed and contribr, The Personal Voice in Classical Scholarship, Routledge, 96; Roman Sexualities, Princeton, 97; co-ed and contribr, Rome and Her Monuments: Essays on the City and Literature of Rome in honor of Katherine A. Geffcken, Bolchazy-Carducci, 00; author of numerous articles and other publications. **CONTACT ADDRESS** Classics Dept, Univ of Maryland, Col Park, 2407 Marie Mount Hall, College Park, MD 20742. **EMAIL** jh10@umail.umd.edu

HALLIBURTON, C. LLOYD
PERSONAL Born 07/31/1934, Shreveport, LA, m, 1993, 6 children **DISCIPLINE** SPANISH **EDUCATION** Century Col, AB, 55; La State Univ, MA, 61; PhD, 70; Univ de Valladolid, C en FyL, 65. **CAREER** Instr, Univ of Notre Dame, 62-63; asst prof, Centenary Col, 63-66; asst to assoc prof, Va Milit Inst, 66-80; prof, Ga Milit Col, 80-81; asst prof to prof, La Tech Univ, 81-. **HONORS AND AWARDS** Phi Kappa Phi; Omicron Delta Kappa; Phi Sigma Iota; Alpha Chi; Sigma Delta Pi; Pi Mu Sigma; Sigma Tau Delta; NDEA Fel, 59-62; Fulbright Fel, 65; NEH Fel, 71-72; LittD, London Inst for Appl Res, 93; La Tech Univ Grants. **SELECTED PUBLICATIONS** Auth, Colombia en la poesia, Ediciones Dos Mundos, (Madrid), 67; Auth, "The Novios", New Orleans Rev 2.1 (70): 15-18; auth, Hendaye, Colonial Pr, (Bessemer, AL), 90; auth, Saddle Soldiers: The Civil War Correspondence of General William Stokes of the 4th South Carolina Cavlary, Sandlapper Pub, (Orangeburg, SC), 93; auth, "Hemingway's Use of Maquinna in For Whom the Bell Tolls: A Reconsideration", NDak Quarterly 62.2 (94-95): 183-192; auth, "Benning Revisited: 25 June 1994", Centenary Today 2.1 (95): 7; auth, "Corrington, Bukowski, and the Loujon Prress", La Lit 13.1 (96): 103-109; auth, The Cemaco Seed, Northwest Pub (Salt Lake City), 97. **CONTACT ADDRESS** Dept For Lang, Louisiana Tech Univ, 305 Wisteria St, Ruston, LA 71270-4235.

HALLOCK, ANN HAYES
PERSONAL Born 05/13/1941, Los Angeles, CA **DISCIPLINE** ITALIAN LITERATURE **EDUCATION** Stanford Univ, BA, 63; Middlebury Col, MA, 66; Harvard Univ, PhD(Romance lang & lit), 74. **CAREER** Asst prof Ital lang & lit, Univ Calif, Rkiverside, 71-72; asst prof, 72-80, Assoc Prof Ital Lang & Lit, Tulane Univ, 80-, Consult, Nat Bilingual/Bicultural Resource Ctr Southern US, 75-77 & Nat Endowment for Humanities, 76-. **HONORS AND AWARDS** Cultural Achievement Awd, Greater New Orleans Ital Cult Soc, 77; Cavaliere Ufficiale nell'Ordine di Merito, Repub of Italy, 77. **MEMBERSHIPS** Dante Soc; MLA; Am Asn Teachers Ital; SCent Mod Lang Asn; SAtlantic Mod Lang Asn. **RESEARCH** Dante and Italian literature from 13th to 14th centuries; poetry of Michelangelo. **SELECTED PUBLICATIONS** Auth, Dante's Selva Oscura and other obscure Selvas, Forum Italicum, 3/72; The pre-eminent role of Babilonia in Petrarch's Theme of the Two Cities, Italica, 77; Ugo Foscolo and the critics of Michelangelo's Rime, SAtlantic Bull, 11/77; Ensuring an Italian Renaissance, Asn Dept Foreign Lang Bull, 3/78; Michelangelo the Poet, Page-Ficklin, 78; Explication of Michelangelo's obscure pastoral poem, Rom Notes, spring 79; The origin of Michelangelo's poetic expression, Ital Quart, summer 80; Fantasticheria: Verga's declaration of transition, Ital Cult, 3/82. **CONTACT ADDRESS** Dept of French & Ital, Tulane Univ, 6823 St. Charles Ave, New Orleans, LA 70118-5698.

HALLSTEIN, CHRISTIAN W.
DISCIPLINE GERMAN **EDUCATION** Pa State Univ, PhD. **CAREER** Languages, Carnegie Mellon Univ. **SELECTED PUBLICATIONS** Auth, Four Short Stories by Arnold Krieger, Studio Schaffen und Forschen, 93; Interactive Grammar Practice in a Communicative Context, Mod Lang Dept. Duquesne Univ; A New Look at Interactive Computer-Aided Language Learning, Jour Computing Small Cols, 90; Information Access and Interactive Learning: Two Modes of Computer-Aided Language Instruction, Coauth, Prospectives In Foreign Language Teaching, Youngstown State Univ, 89. **CONTACT ADDRESS** Carnegie Mellon Univ, 5000 Forbes Ave, Pittsburgh, PA 15213.

HALPERN, CYNTHIA L.
PERSONAL Born 05/11/1952, Rochester, NY, m, 1973, 3 children **DISCIPLINE** SPANISH **EDUCATION** Bryn Maur Col, PhD, 91. **CAREER** Assoc prof, Cabrini Col, 94-. **HONORS AND AWARDS** Tchr Year; Linback Awd for Dist Tchg, Cabrini Col, 98. **MEMBERSHIPS** AATSP; PASE; MLA **RESEARCH** Golden age theater. **SELECTED PUBLICATIONS** Auth, The Political Theater of Early Seventeenth Century Spain, with Special Reference to Juan Ruiz de Alarcon. **CONTACT ADDRESS** Cabrini Col, 610 King of Prussia Rd, Radnor, PA 19087. **EMAIL** cynthia.halpern@cabrini.edu

HALPORN, JAMES W.
PERSONAL Born 01/14/1929, New York, NY, m, 1960, 2 children **DISCIPLINE** CLASSICAL STUDIES **EDUCATION** Columbia Univ, AB, 49; MA, 50; Cornell Univ, PhD, 53. **CAREER** Instr, Columbia Col, 54-58; Vis Lectr, Carleton Univ, 58-59; Vis Asst Prof, Univ Mo, 59-60; Prof to Prof Emeritus, Ind Univ, 60-; Vis Prof, Univ Calif Berkeley, 71-72; Prof, Ind Univ, 75-90; Assoc in the Class, Harvard Univ, 93-. **HONORS AND AWARDS** Fulbright Scholar, Univ Vienna, 53-54; Fel, Am Coun of Learned Soc, IBM, 65-66. **MEMBERSHIPS** Am Philol Asn; Class Asn of N Eng; Hagiography Soc. **RESEARCH** Late Latin literature; Latin palaeography; Early Saints' Lives. **SELECTED PUBLICATIONS** Auth, "Roman Comedy and Greek Models," in Theatre and Society in the Ancient World, *Univ Mich Press, 93), 191-213; co-auth, The Meters of Greek and Latin Poetry 2nd ed, Methuen and Bobbs Merrill, 94; auth, "Women and Classical Archaeology at the Turn of the Century: Abby Leach of Vassar College," in Assembling the Past: Studies in the Professionalization of Archaeology, (Univ N Mex Press, 00), 121-132; auth, "After the Schools: Grammar and Rhetoric in Cassiodorus," in Latin Grammar and Rhetoric: Classical Theory and Medieval Practice, (Continuum Press, forthcoming); auth, "Cassiodorus on the Soul and Institutiones, translation and commentary," in Translated Texts for Historians, (Liverpool Univ Press, forthcoming.) **CONTACT ADDRESS** 320B Harvard St, Cambridge, MA 02139-2002. **EMAIL** halporn@fas.harvard.edu

HALSEY, MARTHA T.
PERSONAL Born Richmond, VA **DISCIPLINE** SPANISH **EDUCATION** Goucher Col, AB, 54; State Univ Iowa, MA, 56; Ohio State Univ, PhD(Span), 64. **CAREER** Instr Span & French, Iowa State Univ, 56-59; asst instr Span, Ohio State Univ, 59-64; asst prof, 64-70, assoc prof, 70-79, Prof to Prof Emer Span, PA State Univ, University Park, 79-, Ed assoc, Mod Int Drama, Ky Romance Quart & Estreno. **MEMBERSHIPS** Am Asn Teachers Span & Port; MLA; Northeast Mod Lang Am; S Atlantic Mod Lang Asn. **RESEARCH** Nineteenth and twentieth century Spanish literature. **CONTACT ADDRESS** Dept of Span, Pennsylvania State Univ, Univ Park, 352N Burrowes Bldg, University Park, PA 16802. **EMAIL** mth1@psu.edu

HALTON, THOMAS
PERSONAL Born 02/06/1925, Cavan, Ireland **DISCIPLINE** GREEK, LATIN **EDUCATION** Maynooth Col, Ireland, BA, 46, STB, 49; Univ Col, Dublin, MA, 58; Cath Univ Am, PhD, 63. **CAREER** Assoc prof, 60-75, Prof Greek & Latin, Cath Univ AM, 75- **MEMBERSHIPS** Early Christian Greek **SELECTED PUBLICATIONS CONTACT ADDRESS** Dept of Greek & Latin Cath, Catholic Univ of America, 620 Michigan Ave N E, Washington, DC 20064-0002.

HAMALIAN, LEO
PERSONAL Born 01/13/1920, New York, NY, m, 1943, 3 children **DISCIPLINE** ENGLISH, COMPARATIVE LITERATURE **EDUCATION** Cornell Univ, BS, 42; Columbia Univ, MA, 47, PhD(English), 54. **CAREER** Instr English, New York Univ, 47-54; from instr to assoc prof, 54-67, PROF ENGLISH LIT, CITY COL NEW YORK, 67-, DIR, GRAD CREATIVE WRITING, 72-, Smith-Mundt grant, Syria, 62-64; Am Studies Sem fel, Columbia Univ, 68-; dean, Calif Inst of Arts, 70-72; mem, bd dir, Tuum Est Drug Rehabil Ctr, Venice, 71-; Fulbright lectr, Univ Tehran, 74-75 & Univ Hamburg, 80; ed, Ararat. **MEMBERSHIPS** MLA; NCTE; Am Studies Asn; English Union; PEN Club. **RESEARCH** T S Eliot; D H Lawrence; comparative continental literature. **SELECTED PUBLICATIONS** Auth, The secret career of Samuel Roth, J Popular Cult, summer 68; ed, In the Modern Idion, 73 & An Invitation to Semantics, 73, Crowell; auth, Hemingway as hunger artist, Lit Rev, winter 73; Amid bounty, longing, New York Times, 12/76; The figures in the window: Design in T S Eliot's The Family Reunion, Col Lit, 77-78; Sole: Stories of Women Alone, Dell Bks, 78; New Writing from the Middle East, New Am Libr, 78; Burn After Reading, 79 & As Others See Us: The Armenian Image in Literature, 80, Ararat Press; ed, In Search of Eden, New Am Libr, 80; ed & auth, Ladies on the Loose: Women Travellers of the 18th and 19th Centuries, Dodd, 81; auth, D H Lawrence in Italy, Tapinger, 82. **CONTACT ADDRESS** Dept of English, City Col, CUNY, New York, NY 10031.

HAMILTON, JAMES FRANCIS
PERSONAL Born 12/09/1939, Cleveland, OH, m, 1963, 2 children **DISCIPLINE** FRENCH LITERATURE & LANGUAGE **EDUCATION** Kent State Univ, BSEd, 62; Ohio State Univ, MA, 65, PhD(Romance lang), 70. **CAREER** Teacher French, Lincoln High Sch, Cleveland, Ohio, 62-63; instr & asst supvr, Ohio State Univ, 63-69; asst prof, Denison Univ, 69-70; asst prof, 70-76, assoc prof, 76-81, Prof French, Univ Cincinnati, 81-, Taft fac grant, 72. **MEMBERSHIPS** Am Asn Teachers Fr; MLA; Soc Fr Etude VIIIe Siecle; Am Soc Eighteenth Century Studies. **RESEARCH** Rousseau and romanticism; Montesquieu to Zola. **SELECTED PUBLICATIONS** Auth, The novelist an historian: A contrast between Balzac's Les Chouans and Hugo's Quatrevingt-treize, Fr Rev, 6/76; From art to nature in George Sand's La Mare au Diable, Fr Lit Ser: Fr Lit & Arts, 78; Rousseau's Theory of Literature: The Poetics of Art and Nature, Fr Lit Publ Co, 79; The anti-Rousseauism of Madame Bovary, Romance Notes, fall 80; Zola's Nana and Jeanne d'arc: Contrary myths and the creative process, USF Lang Quart, fall-winter, 80; Two psychodramatic scenes in Stendhal's Armance, Ky Romance Quart, 81; Pagan ritual and human sacrifice in Merimee's Mateo Falcone, Fr Rev, 10/81; The impossible return to nature in Maupassant's Bel-Ami, Nineteenth-Century Fr Studies, springsummer, 82. **CONTACT ADDRESS** Dept of Romance Lang, Univ of Cincinnati, P O Box 210377, Cincinnati, OH 45221-0377.

HAMILTON, JOHN DANIEL BURGOYNE
PERSONAL Born 10/19/1939, Los Angeles, CA **DISCIPLINE** CLASSICAL LANGUAGES, GREEK MYTHOLOGY & RELIGION **EDUCATION** St Louis Univ, AB, 63; AM, 64; Weston Col, Cambridge, MS, MDiv, 69; Univ MN, PhD, 73. **CAREER** Instr classics, Univ Santa Clara, 65-66; asst prof, 72-76, assoc prof Classics, 77-, Grad Studies Adv, Classics, Col of the Holy Cross, 89-. **MEMBERSHIPS** Am Philol Asn; Class Asn New England; Class Asn Midwest & South; Soc Promotion Hellenic Studies; Class Asn Gt Brit. **RESEARCH** Greek epic and drama; mythology; Roman satire. **SELECTED PUBLICATIONS** Auth, Justin's Apology 66: A review of scholarship, 72 & The church and the language of mystery, 77, Ephemerides Theol Lovanienses; transl (with B Nagy), L Gernet, The Anthropology of Ancient Greece, Johns Hopkins, 81; Antigone: Kinship, Justice and the Womb, in Myth and the Pelis, Cornell, 91; At Sea with Myth: A Bibliography for Charting a Course, NE Clas J, Dec 89; contrib, articles in The World Book Encyclopedia, 93. **CONTACT ADDRESS** Dept of Calssics, Col of the Holy Cross, 1 College St, Worcester, MA 01610-2395. **EMAIL** jhamilto@holycross.edu

HAMILTON, RICHARD
PERSONAL Born 12/19/1943, Bryn Mawr, PA, m, 1965, 2 children **DISCIPLINE** GREEK LITERATURE **EDUCATION** Harvard Col, AB, 65; Univ Mich, PhD(class), 71. **CAREER** From Asst Prof to Assoc Prof, 71-88, Prof Greek, Bryn Mawr Col, 88-. **HONORS AND AWARDS** NEH Sr Fel, 94. **MEMBERSHIPS** Am Philol Asn. **RESEARCH** Greek literature; Greek religion. **SELECTED PUBLICATIONS** Auth, Epinikion: General Form in the Odes of Pindar, Mouton, The Hague, 74; The Architecture of Hesiod's Theogany and Works and Days, Hopkins, 89; Choes and Anthesteria, Mich, 92; Treasure Map, Mich (forthcoming 98). **CONTACT ADDRESS** Dept of Greek, Bryn Mawr Col, 101 N Merion Ave, Bryn Mawr, PA 19010-2899. **EMAIL** rhamilto@brynmawr.edu

HAMLIN, FRANK RODWAY
PERSONAL Born 04/10/1935, Wolverhampton, England, m, 1968, 2 children **DISCIPLINE** ROMANCE LINGUISTICS **EDUCATION** Univ Birmingham, BA, 57, PhD(French), 59 Cambridge Univ, MA, 61. **CAREER** Lectr mediaeval French, Queen's Univ, Belfast, 60-61; res fel French, Gonville & Caius Col, Cambridge, 61-63; asst prof, 63-68, assoc prof, 68-78, Prof French, Univ BC, 78-, Can Coun fel, 68-69, 76-77 & 82-83. **MEMBERSHIPS** Soc Ling Romane; Soc Fr Onomastique; English Place-Name Soc; Can Soc Study Names; Am Name Soc. **RESEARCH** Toponymy, especially of Southern France; Old Provencal language and literature. **SELECTED PUBLICATIONS** Auth, The Adventure of Languages in the West--Their Origins, Their History, Their Geography, J Int Ling Asn, Vol 0047, 96; A History of Indo-European Verb Morphology, J Int Ling Asn, Vol 0046, 95. **CONTACT ADDRESS** Dept of French, Univ of British Columbia, Vancouver, BC, Canada V6T 1W5.

HAMMERMEISTER, KAI
PERSONAL Born 07/15/1967, Gottingen, Germany **DISCIPLINE** GERMAN STUDIES **EDUCATION** Univ Va, MA, 92, PhD, 95. **CAREER** Instr, Univ Va, 95-96; asst prof, Ohio State Univ, 98-. **MEMBERSHIPS** MLA **RESEARCH** German intellectual history; literary theory; aesthetics; hermeneutics. **SELECTED PUBLICATIONS** Auth, art, Inventing History: Toward a Gay Holocaust Literature, 96; auth, art, Pragmatismus als Anti-Asthetik, 96; auth, art, Literature between Social Change and the Valuation of Tradition, 99; auth, Hans-Georg Gadamer, 99. **CONTACT ADDRESS** Dept of Germanic Languages and Literatures, Ohio State Univ, Columbus, 1841 Millikin Rd, 314 Cunz Hall, Columbus, OH 43210. **EMAIL** hammermeister.2@osu.edu

HAMMOND, MASON
PERSONAL Born 02/14/1903, Boston, MA, m, 1935, 3 children **DISCIPLINE** ROMAN HISTORY, LATIN LITERATURE **EDUCATION** Harvard Univ, AB, 25; Oxford Univ, BA, 27, BLitt, 30. **CAREER** From instr to Pope prof, 28-73, Emer Pope Prof, Latin Lang & Lit, Harvard Univ, 73-, From

instr to prof, Radcliffe Col, 28-42; prof in charge class studies, Am Acad Rome, 37-39 & 55-57, vis prof, 51-52 & 63; actg dir, Villa I Tatti, Harvard Ctr Renaissance Studies, Florence, Italy, 72 & 73; vis prof classics, Univ Wis-Madison, 74; emer trustee, Am Acad Rome & St Mark's Sch; trustee, Isabella Stewart Gardner Mus, Boston. **HONORS AND AWARDS** LHD, St Bonaventure Univ, 78. **MEMBERSHIPS** Am Philol Asn; Archaeol Inst Am; Am Acad Arts & Sci; hon mem Ger Archaeol Inst. **RESEARCH** Roman history; Latin literature. **SELECTED PUBLICATIONS** Auth, The Augustan Principate, 33 & Russell, 68, co-ed, Plautus, Menaechmi, 33 & rev ed, 68, auth, City-State and World State, etc, 51 & Biblo & Tannen, 66, Harvard; The Antonine Monarch, Am Acad Rome, 57; coauth, From Aeneas to Augustus, 62 & 2nd ed, 67, ed, Plautus, Miles, 63 & rev ed, 69, coauth, The City in the Ancient World, 72 & auth, Latin: A Historical and Linguistic Handbook, 76, Harvard. **CONTACT ADDRESS** Harvard Univ, Widener Libr H, Cambridge, MA 02138.

HAMMOND, MICHAEL
PERSONAL Born 03/30/1957, Los Angeles, CA, m, 1999, 1 child **DISCIPLINE** LINGUISTICS **EDUCATION** Univ Calif at Los Angeles, BA, 79; MA, 81; PhD, 84. **CAREER** Asst prof, Univ Min, 83-84; asst prof, Univ Wis, 84-88; asst prof, Univ Ariz, 88-92; assoc prof, 92-99; prof, 99-. **HONORS AND AWARDS** Phi Beta Kappa; Univ Calif, Los Angeles, Reg Awd; Japan Found Schlp; Grad Sch Res Gnt; Fr Sci Miss Gnt; NIH Fogarty Sr Intl Fel; Res Prof, SBSRI; NLEIT Gnt, 98, 99; NSF Con Pro; Sun Micro Sys Acad Gnt. **MEMBERSHIPS** LSA. **RESEARCH** Phonology; Morphology; Poetry; English; Psycholinguistics; computational linguistics. **SELECTED PUBLICATIONS** Auth, "Lexical stresses in Macedonian and Polish," Phonology 6 (89): 19-38; auth, "The 'Name Game' and Onset Simplification," Phonology 7 (90): 159-162; coauth, "Waves, Spectra, and Pendula: Acoustics by Computer," Inn Ling Edu 5 (91): 10-20; auth, "Poetic meter and the arboreal grid," Lang 67 (91): 240-259; auth, "Morphemic circumscription," YB Moroph (91): 195-210; auth, "On the absence of category-changing prefixes in English 24 (93): 562-567; auth, "Heavy trochees in Choctaw," Phonology 10 (94): 325-336; coauth, "Onglides in American English," Phonology 12 (95): 159-182; auth, "Vowel quantity and syllabification in English," Language 73 (97): 1-17; auth, English Phonology, Oxford Univ Press (Oxford), 99. **CONTACT ADDRESS** Dept Linguistics, Univ of Arizona, PO Box 210028, Tucson, AZ 85721-0028. **EMAIL** hammond@u.arizona.edu

HAMP, ERIC PRATT
PERSONAL Born 11/16/1920, London, England, m, 1951 **DISCIPLINE** LINGUISTICS **EDUCATION** Amherst Col, BA, 42; Harvard Univ, MA, 48, PhD(ling), 54. **CAREER** Chief lend-lease, Govt Union SAfrica, 42-46; from instr to assoc prof, 50-62, chmn, Dept Ling, 66-69, Prof Indo-Europ Ling, Univ Chicago, 62-, Prof Behav Sci, 71-, Prof Slavic Lang, 80-, Dir, Ctr Balkan & Slavic Studies, 65-, Vis lectr, Univ Mich, 53, Univ Wash, 62, Europe, 65-67 & 73-78 & US cult exchange lectr, Univ Bucharest, USSR, 75 & 76; Fulbright res scholar, Greece, 55-56 & Fulbright-Hays fel, Copenhagen Univ, 66-67; mem staff, Gaelic Dialect Surv, Edinburgh, 56-58; secy comt lang prog, Am Coun Learned Soc, 59-63, chmn, 63-69; Am Coon Learned Soc-Soc Sci Res Coun grant Albanian res, Greece & Yugoslavia, 60-61; mem, Nat Sci Found Sem Comput Ling, Rand Corp, 63; mem, Comt Automatic Lang Processing, Nat Acad Sci-Nat Res Coun, 64- & Comt Ling Info, Ctr Appl Ling, 64-68; vis prof, Ind Univ, 64, Univ Belgrade, 64 & 67, Univ Ill, 68 & Univ Salzburg, 79 & 82; mem, Comt Hist & Theory Ling, Ind Univ Press, 65-73, Adv Comt East Europ Coun Int Exchange Scholars, 66-78, Comt Lang & Lit, Ctr Neo-Hellenic Studies, 67-78, US Nat Comn, UNESCO, 72-78 & Phillips Fund Comt, Am Philos Soc, 77-; chmn, Comt Ill Place-Name Surv, 66-; consult, US Off Educ, 66-72, Harper & Row, 71-, Nat Endowment for Humanities, 76-82, Nat Sci Found Subcomt Linguistics, 77-79 & Am Printing House for Blind, 77-; adv, Encycl Britannica, 69-; assoc ed, Int J Am Ling, 69-; vis scholar, Inst Arts & Humanistic Studies, Pa State Univ, 69; Guggenheim fel, 73-74. **HONORS AND AWARDS** Ling Soc Am Collitz prof, Univ Tex, 60; Vernam Hull lectr Celtic studies, Harvard Univ, 71; Innaugural lectr, Ctr Celtic Studies, Aberystwyth, 79; lhd, amherst col, 72. **MEMBERSHIPS** Fel Am Acad Arts & Sci; Am Philos Soc; Ling Soc Am (vpres, 63 & 70, pres, 71); MLA; fel Am Anthrop Asn. **RESEARCH** General linguistics; Indo-European language and culture; Celtic, Balkan and Amerindian languages. **SELECTED PUBLICATIONS** Auth, A Glossary of American Technical Linguistic Usage 1925-1950, Spectrum, Ultrecht, 57, 63 & 3rd rev ed, 66; coauth, Readings in Linguistics II, Univ Chicago, 66; auth, Albanian, In: Vol IX, Current Trends in Linguistics, 72; Problems of Multilingualism in Small Linguistic Communities, Georgetown Round Table, 78; A Glance from Here On, The Languages of Native America, 79; Indo-European *gwen-Ha, Kuhns Zeitschrift, 79; Imbolc, Oimelc, Studia Celtica, 80; IE *( )kuondog, Indogermanische Forschungen, 80. **CONTACT ADDRESS** Dept of Ling, Univ of Chicago, Chicago, IL 60637.

HAN, MIEKO
DISCIPLINE EAST ASIAN LANGUAGES **EDUCATION** Univ Tex, PhD, 61. **CAREER** Prof, Univ Southern Calif. **RESEARCH** Japanese language; linguistics and phonetic study of Asian languages. **SELECTED PUBLICATIONS** Auth, Living in Japan: Intermediate Conversational Japanese; Acoustic Manifestations of Mora Timing in Japanese. **CONTACT ADDRESS** East Asian Studies Center, Univ of So California, University Park Campus, Los Angeles, CA 90089.

HANAN, PATRICK DEWES
PERSONAL Born 01/04/1927, New Zealand, m, 1951, 1 child **DISCIPLINE** CHINESE LITERATURE **EDUCATION** Univ NZ, BA, 48, MA, 49; Univ London, BA, 53, PhD, 60. **CAREER** Lectr Chinese, Sch Orient & African Studies, Univ London, 54-63; from assoc prof to prof, Stanford Univ, 63-68; prof Chinese lit, Harvard Univ, 68-89, Victor S. Thomas Prof of Chinese Lit, Harvard Univ, 89-98, Victor S Thomas Res Prof of Chinese Lit, Harvard Univ, 98-. **HONORS AND AWARDS** Guggenheim fel, 77; fel, Am Acad of Arts & Sci, 77-; Levenson Awd of Asn Asian Stud, 90; Concurrent Prof of Nanjimg Univ, 95-; Officer of New Zealand Order of Merit, 99-. **MEMBERSHIPS** Asn Asian Studies; **RESEARCH** Chinese literature. **SELECTED PUBLICATIONS** Auth, The Chinese Short Story, 73; auth, The Chinese Vernacular Story, 81; auth, The Invention of Li Yu, 88; transl, The Carnal Prayer Mat, 90; auth, A Tower for the Summer Heat, 92; transl, The Sea of Regret, 95; transl, The Money Demon, 99. **CONTACT ADDRESS** Dept of East Asian Lang, Harvard Univ, 2 Divinity Ave, Cambridge, MA 02138-2020. **EMAIL** hanan@fas.harvard.edu

HANKAMER, JORGE
PERSONAL Born 09/12/1940, Alvin, TX **DISCIPLINE** LINGUISTICS **EDUCATION** Rice Univ, BA, 62, MA, 66; Yale Univ, PhD(Ling), 71. **CAREER** Fel Ling, Mass Inst Technol, 71-73; asst prof, Tufts Univ, 72-73; asst prof, Harvard Univ, 73-78, assoc prof Ling, 78-80; from assoc prof to prof Ling, Univ Calif, Santa Cruz, 80-83; ed, Ling Inquiry, Squibs & Discussions, 75-77 & Dissertations in Ling ser, Garland Publ Co, 75-95; vis asst prof Ling, Bogazici Univ, Istanbul, 76-77; assoc ed, Language, 81-; assoc vice chancellor, Planning and Programs, UCSC, 90-95; dean of Humanities, 95-. **MEMBERSHIPS** Ling Soc Am; New Eng Ling Soc. **RESEARCH** Syntax and semantics of natural language; Turkish syntax. **SELECTED PUBLICATIONS** Auth, Unacceptable ambiguity, 73 & coauth, Deep and surface anaphora, 76, Ling Inquiry; auth, On the interpretation of anaphoric expressions, Georgetown Univ Round Table, 76; Multiple analysis, In: Mechanisms of Syntactic Change, 77; coauth, Ambiguity, Encycl Einandi, 78. **CONTACT ADDRESS** Cowell Commons, Univ of California, Santa Cruz, 1156 High St, Santa Cruz, CA 95064-0001. **EMAIL** hank@atscats.ucsc.edu

HANLIN, TODD
PERSONAL Born 11/09/1941, Buchanan, MI, m, 1969, 2 children **DISCIPLINE** CONTEMPORARY DRAMA AND PROSE OF THE GERMAN-SPEAKING COUNTRIES **EDUCATION** Wabash Col, BA, 64, Univ Kans, MA, 67; Bryn Mawr Col, PhD, 75. **CAREER** English and Lit, Univ Ark. **HONORS AND AWARDS** Outstanding Tchr Awd; Fulbright grant. **SELECTED PUBLICATIONS** Area: Franz Kafka. **CONTACT ADDRESS** Univ of Arkansas, Fayetteville, Fayetteville, AR 72701.

HANNA, BLAKE THOMPSON
PERSONAL Born 08/02/1927, Boston, MA, m, 1950, 3 children **DISCIPLINE** FRENCH, LANGUAGE EDUCATION **EDUCATION** Bowdoin Col, BA, 48; Univ Montreal, MA, 53, PhD(French), 64. **CAREER** Instr English, Col Stanislas, Montreal, 53-57; from asst prof to assoc prof, 57-69, Prof Ling, Univ Montreal, 69-, Can Coun res grant, 66. **MEMBERSHIPS** MLA; Soc Transl & Interpreters Can (vpres, 67-68); Soc Fr Etude XVIIIe Siecle; Am Soc 18th Century Studies; Can Soc 18th Century Studies. **RESEARCH** Translating and interpreting; 18th century French literature; teaching English as a second language. **SELECTED PUBLICATIONS** Auth, How to Write a Precis, Meta, Vol 0038, 93; Comparative Stylistics of French and English, A Methodology for Translation, Meta, Vol 0041, 96. **CONTACT ADDRESS** Sch of Transl, Univ of Montreal, PO Box 6128 Br, Montreal, QC, Canada H3C 3J7.

HANREZ, MARC
PERSONAL Born 08/15/1934, Brussels, Belgium, 3 children **DISCIPLINE** FRENCH LANGUAGE & LITERATURE **EDUCATION** Free Univ Brussels, Lic en Philos et Lett & Agrege, 58; Univ Paris, VII, Dr 3e Cycle, 73. **CAREER** Asst prof Romance lang, Univ Mass, Amherst, 67-70; assoc prof, 70-76, Prof French, Univ Wis-Madison, 76-, Guggenheim fel, 72-73. **RESEARCH** Contemporary French literature, especially Abellio, Celine, Drieu la Rochelle, Malraux, Proust; the war fiction, ideology and fine arts. **SELECTED PUBLICATIONS** Auth, Celine, Gallimard, Paris, 61, 69; ed, Les Ecrivains et la Guerre d'Espagne, Dossiers H, Paris, 75; auth, Sous les signes d'Abellio, L'Age d'Homme, Lausanne, 76; ed, Drieu la Rochelle, Cahiers de l'Herne, Paris, 82; auth, La Grande Chose Americaine, Cadex Editions, 92. **CONTACT ADDRESS** Dept of French & Ital, Univ of Wisconsin, Madison, 1220 Linden Drive, Madison, WI 53706-1557.

HANSEN, ELENA S.
PERSONAL Born 12/14/1959, Kharkov, Ukraine, m, 1997, 1 child **DISCIPLINE** RUSSIAN, FRENCH **EDUCATION** Kharkov State Univ, MA, 83; Belgorod State Pedagogical Inst, MA, 87; Moscow Regional Pedagogical Inst, 90. **CAREER** Prof, Russian Branch of Serendipity, 93-97; Adj Prof, St Ambrose Univ, 98-. **MEMBERSHIPS** Mod Lang Asn of Am, Am Asn of Teachers of Slavic and East European Lang. **RESEARCH** Russian language and literature, Russian culture, Russian civilization. **SELECTED PUBLICATIONS** Auth, Getting Your Russian sounds Right!, McGraw-Hill, 99; auth, Aspects of the Russian Verb, McGraw-Hill, 99; auth, "Leo Tolstoy: an Outside Look (American Literary Criticism from 1980's), Yoprosy literaty. **CONTACT ADDRESS** Dept For Lang, St. Ambrose Univ, 518 W Locust St, Davenport, IA 52803-2829. **EMAIL** rossika@juno.com

HANSEN, HELYNNE
PERSONAL Born 10/19/1951, Salt Lake City, UT, m, 1979, 2 children **DISCIPLINE** FRENCH, ENGLISH **EDUCATION** Univ Ut, BA; MA; PhD. **CAREER** Asst prof, Western State Col, 88-97; vis asst prof, Brigham Young Univ, 91-92. **MEMBERSHIPS** MLA, George Sand Asn, Rocky Mountain MLA, Women in French, Am Asn of Teachers of French. **RESEARCH** Nineteenth- and Twentieth-century Women Writers in French, Feminist Theory, French and Francophone Cinema and Film Theory, Napoleonic Era, Romanticism. **SELECTED PUBLICATIONS** Auth, Hortense Allart: The Woman and the Novelist. **CONTACT ADDRESS** Dept Commun Arts, Western State Col of Colorado, 600 N Adams St, Gunnison, CO 81231-7000. **EMAIL** hhansen@western.edu

HANSEN, WELLS S.
PERSONAL Born 12/08/1964, Southport Island, ME, s **DISCIPLINE** CLASSICAL LANGUAGE AND LITERATURE **EDUCATION** Boston Col, BA, 87; Univ Chicago, MA,88. **CAREER** Tchr, Mount Alvernia Acad, 87; lectr, Univ Chicago, 98-92; tchr, Princeton Day Sch, 93; tchr, Milton Acad, 93-. **HONORS AND AWARDS** Weiner Classics Medal, 87; Shorey Fel and Bobrinsky Fel, 90, 92; Klingenstein Sum Fel, 94; Fulbright Grant, 98; McKinlay Fel, 98. **MEMBERSHIPS** Am Philol Asn; Class Asn Mass; Pearl River Gibonian Soc. **RESEARCH** Latin literature, pedagogy of classical languages in secondary schools. **SELECTED PUBLICATIONS** "Catullus 75 and the Poetics of Separation," New Engl Classic J, 98. **CONTACT ADDRESS** Ware Hall, Suite 516, Milton, MA 02186. **EMAIL** wells_hansen@milton.edu

HANSEN, WILLIAM F.
PERSONAL Born 06/22/1941, Fresno, CA, m, 1994, 1 child **DISCIPLINE** CLASSICAL STUDIES, FOLKLORE **EDUCATION** Univ Calif, Berkeley, BA, 65, PhD, 70. **CAREER** From asst prof to prof, Class Stud & Folklore, Inst, Indiana Univ Bloomington, 70-; assoc dean fac, Indiana Univ Bloomington, 86-92; chmn, Class Stud, Indiana Univ Bloomington, 97-; co-dir, Program in Mythology Stud, 98-. **HONORS AND AWARDS** Phi Beta Kappa, 65; NEH Younger Hum Fel, 72-73; Am Coun Learned Soc fel, 77-78, 92. **MEMBERSHIPS** Am Philol Asn; Class Asn of the Middle West and South; Am Folklore Soc; Calif Folklore Soc; Hoosier Folklore Soc; Int Soc for Folk-Narrative Res; Int Soc for Contemp Legend Res. **RESEARCH** Mythology; folklore; early Greek epic; early fiction. **SELECTED PUBLICATIONS** Auth, The Theft of the Thunderweapon: A Greek Myth in Its International Context, Classica et Mediaevalia, 95; auth, Abraham and the Grateful Dead Man, in Bendix, ed, Folklore Interpreted: Essays in Honor of Alan Dundes, Garland, 95; auth, The Protagonist on the Pyre: Herodotean Legend and Modern Folktale, Fabula, 96; auth, Phlegon of Tralles' Book of Marvels, Univ Exeter, 96; auth, Homer and the Folktale, in Morris, ed, A New Companion to Homer, Brill, 97; auth, Idealization as a Process in Ancient Greek Story-Formation, Symbolae Osloenses, 97; auth, Mythology and Folktale Typology: Chronicle of a Failed Scholarly Revolution, J of Folklore Res, 97; ed, Anthology of Ancient Greek Popular Literature, Indiana, 98. **CONTACT ADDRESS** Classical Studies Dept, Indiana Univ, Bloomington, 1020 E Kirkwood Ave, Bloomington, IN 47405-7103. **EMAIL** hansen@indiana.edu

HANSON, KLAUS D.
DISCIPLINE GERMAN **EDUCATION** Univ IL, PhD, 72. **CAREER** Prof; Univ WY, 73-; taught in, Ger & Japan; supvr, UW's stud exchange-Univ Oldenburg; dept head, 84-89; dir, lang lab. **RESEARCH** Contemp Ger theater and cult; pedag; Renaissance and Baroque lit. **SELECTED PUBLICATIONS** Publ, bk, articles, on Ger theater and Baroque poetry. **CONTACT ADDRESS** Dept of Mod and Class Lang(s), Univ of Wyoming, PO Box 3964, Laramie, WY 82071-3964. **EMAIL** HANSON@UWYO.EDU

HARDIN, JAMES NEAL
PERSONAL Born 02/17/1939, Nashville, TN **DISCIPLINE** GERMAN & COMPARATIVE LITERATURE **EDUCATION** Washington & Lee Univ, AB, 60; Univ NC, Chapel Hill, MA, 64, PhD(Ger & comp lit), 67. **CAREER** Asst Ger, Univ NC, 62-67; from asst prof to assoc prof, 69-73, Ger Acad Exchange Serv grant, 73, Prof Ger, Univ SC, 73-, Fulbright fel, 60-

61; Alexander von Humboldt fel, 74-75. **MEMBERSHIPS** MLA; SAtlantic Mod Lang Asn; Am Asn Tchrs Ger; Am Soc Ger Lit 16th & 17th Centuries. **RESEARCH** Sixteenth and 17th century Ger lit; Ger Baroque novel; descriptive bibl. **SELECTED PUBLICATIONS** Auth, Theme of salvation in the novels of Hermann Broch, PMLA, 70; George B Shaw's Saint Joan, Diesterweg, 74; Hermann Broch's theories of mass psychology, Ger Quart, 74; Johann Beers Parodie Printz Adimantus, Jahrbuch int Ger, 75; Descriptive bibliography and the works of Johann Beer, Wolfenbutteler Barocknachrichten, 77; ed, Der verliebte Oesterreicher von Johann Beer, Lang, Bern, 78; auth, Eine Beschreibende Bibliographie der Werke Johann Beers, Francke Verlag, 78; Johann Beer, Twayne Series, 79; co-ed, Figures of German Literature in Dictionary of Literacy, 93-97, ed, Camden House in Print, Boydell and Brewer, 98-. **CONTACT ADDRESS** Dept of Ger and Slavic, Univ of So Carolina, Columbia, Columbia, SC 29208. **EMAIL** camdenhouse@compuserve.com

HARDING, GEORGE E.
PERSONAL Born 08/11/1950, Birmingham, AL, m, 1974, 2 children **DISCIPLINE** GERMANIC LANGUAGES & LITERATURE **EDUCATION** Birmingham-Southern Col, BA, 72; Miss State Univ, MA, 74; Univ Tenn, Knoxville, PhD, 85. **CAREER** Teacher, Knoxville City Schs, 81-86; Instr, for lang, Univ Kentucky Community Col, 86-87; from asst to Assoc Prof, German, Francis Marion Univ, 87-. **HONORS AND AWARDS** Gerti Wunderlich Awd, 80; Delta Phi Alpha, 71; Phi Delta Phi, 74; Phi Kappa Phi, 79. **MEMBERSHIPS** S Atlantic Mod Lang Asn; Philogical Asn Carolinas. **RESEARCH** Medieval literature **SELECTED PUBLICATIONS** Ed, The Gast of Gy, 95; ed, Golf: The Thinking Game, 95; auth, rev of The Pilgrimage Motif in the Works of the Medieval German Author Hartmann von Aue, Arturiana, 97 **CONTACT ADDRESS** Francis Marion Univ, CEMC 113, Florence, SC 29501. **EMAIL** gharding@fmarion.edu

HARGRAVES, JOHN A.
PERSONAL Born 12/02/1944, m **DISCIPLINE** GERMAN **EDUCATION** Dartmouth Col, AB, 66; Yale Univ, MA, 90; MPhil, 91; PhD, 93. **CAREER** Instructor, Yale Univ, 88-94; Asst Prof, Conn Col, 94-. **MEMBERSHIPS** ALTA; Goethe Soc. **RESEARCH** Music and Literature; Translation. **SELECTED PUBLICATIONS** Trans, Elias Canetti- Nachtrageous Hampstead, Notes from Hampstead, 98. **CONTACT ADDRESS** Dept German, Connecticut Col, 270 Mohegan Ave, New London, CT 06320-4125. **EMAIL** jhargraves@aol.com

HARLOW, L. L.
PERSONAL Born 06/10/1949, Batesville, IN, m, 1973, 1 child **DISCIPLINE** FRENCH **EDUCATION** Ball St Univ, BA, 71; Purdue Univ, MAT, 78, PhD, 82. **CAREER** Tchr, 71-72, Port Huron Schl Corp; Tchr, 74-76, Tippecanoe Schl Corp; Tchng Asst, 76-82, Purdue Univ; Asst Prof, 82-85, Atlantic Christian Col; Asst Prof, 85-91, Assoc Prof, 91-, Assoc Dean, 97-, Ohio St Univ. **HONORS AND AWARDS** Fondation Franco-Americaine, Voyage d'etudes, 94; MLA/NEH Awd, Middlebury Col, 91; Univ Res Grant, 90; Intl Trvl Grant, College of Humanities, 87, 92, 96; Grant-in-Aid, 86; David Ross Fel, 81, 79; Phi Delta Kappa Ed Hon; Phi Kappa Phi Honor Soc; Pi Delta Phi French Hon; Harvard Inst of Higher Educ Mgt Dev Prog, Harvard Univ, 99. **MEMBERSHIPS** Amer Coun on the Tchng of Foreign Lang; Amer Assoc of Tchrs of French; Amer Assoc of Univ Supv Coor and Dir of Foreign Lan Prog; Ohio Foreign Lang Tchrs Assoc. **RESEARCH** Foreign Language Pedagogy; TA Training; Sociopragmatics. **SELECTED PUBLICATIONS** CoAuth, Bravo Culture et Litterature, Heinle & Heinle, 93; CoAuth, Bravo Communication et Grammaire, Heinle & Heinle, 93 & 94; Bravo Communication, Grammaire, Culture et Litterature, Heinle & Heinle, 98; CoAuth, Collaborative Partnerships for Articulation: Asking the Right Questions, For Lang Ann, 96; CoAuth, Politeness Strategies in French and English: Implications for Second Language Acquisition, Speech Acts Across Cultures, 95; Priorities for Intermediate-Level Language Instruction, Mod Lang Jour, 94; The Effects of the Yellow Highlighter - Second Language Learner Strategies and Their Effectiveness A Research Update, Canadian Mod lang Rev, 88. **CONTACT ADDRESS** Ohio State Univ, Columbus, College of Humanities, 230 N Oval, Columbus, OH 43210. **EMAIL** harlow.1@osu.edu

HARMON, DANIEL P.
PERSONAL Born 05/03/1938, Chicago, IL **DISCIPLINE** CLASSICS **EDUCATION** Northwestern Univ, MA, 65, PhD, 68. **CAREER** Asst prof, 67-75, assoc prof, 75-89, prof, 84- , chemn, Dept of Classics, 76-91, co-dir, 92-00 , Univ Washington Rome Ctr. **MEMBERSHIPS** APA; Archaeol Inst of Am; AAUP; Societe des Etudes Latines. **RESEARCH** Greek and Roman religion; Roman archaeology; classical linguistics. **SELECTED PUBLICATIONS** Auth, The Poet's Initiation and the Sacerdotal Imagery of Propertius 3.1-5, Stud in Latin Lit and Roman Hist, Coll Latomus, 79; auth, Religion in the Latin Elegists, in Haase, ed, Augstieg und Niedergang der Romischen Welt: Geschichte und Kultur Roms im Spiegel der Neuren Forschung, Walter de Gruyter, 85; auth, The Religious Significance of Games in the Roman Age, in Raschke, ed, The Archaeology of the Olympics, Univ Wisconsin, 87; auth, contribur, World Book Encyclopedia, 93; auth, Feriae, Der Neue Pauly, v.4, J.B. Metzger Verlag. **CONTACT ADDRESS** Dept of Classics, Univ of Washington, PO Box 353110, Seattle, WA 98195. **EMAIL** dph@u.washington.edu

HARMS, ROBERT THOMAS
PERSONAL Born 04/12/1932, Peoria, IL, m, 1956, 4 children **DISCIPLINE** LINGUISTICS **EDUCATION** Univ Chicago, AB, 52, AM, 56, PhD, 60. **CAREER** From instr to asst prof Russ & ling, 58-65, assoc prof ling & Slavic lang, 65-67, actg chmn, 72-73, chmn dept, 73-77, prof ling, Univ Tex, Austin, 67-, Grant, Inter-Univ Comt Travel Grants, Leningrad State Univ, USSR, 62-63, res grant, Hungarian Acad Sci, Budapest & Univ Szeged, 67-68; Fulbright res scholar, Univ Helsinki, 68; res grant, USSR Acad of Sci, Tallinn & Syktyvkar, 78. **MEMBERSHIPS** Ling Soc Am. **RESEARCH** Phonology; historical linguistics; Uralic linguistics. **SELECTED PUBLICATIONS** Auth, Estonian Grammar, 62 & Finnish Structural Sketch, 64, Uralic & Altaic Ser, Ind Univ; The Measurement of Phonological Economy, Language, 66; Introduction to Phonological Theory, Prentice-Hall, 68; coauth, How do Languages Get Crazy Rules, In: Linguistic Change and Generative Theory, Ind Univ, 72; auth, Uralic languages, In: Encycl Britannica, 74. **CONTACT ADDRESS** Dept of Ling, Univ of Texas, Austin, Austin, TX 78712-1026. **EMAIL** harms@mail.utexas.edu

HARPER, A. DIANNE
PERSONAL Born 10/24/1947, VA, s **DISCIPLINE** LINGUISTICS **EDUCATION** NC State Univ, BA, 69; Brown Univ, MAT, 71, PSU, PhD, 79. **CAREER** Assoc prof, Fisk Univ, 82-88; asst prof, E Mich Univ, 88-91; assoc prof, Middle Tenn State Univ, 91-. **HONORS AND AWARDS** Rockefeller Fel, 69; Brown Univ Grant, 70; Fulbright Fel, Fulbright-Hays Found, 71; Fel, Univ of Kiel, Germany, 72; Outstanding Woman of the Year, Montgomery Board of Adv, 83-84; UNCF Summer Humanities Fac Inst Grant, Morehouse Col, 85; Fac Travel Grants, Mich Univ, 90; Fac Appreciation Awd, E Mich Univ, 91; Outstanding Lib Arts Adv, Middle Tenn State Univ, 97. **MEMBERSHIPS** Am Asn of Teachers of German, Am Council on the Teaching of For Langs. **RESEARCH** Foreign language teaching in the public school system, minority recruitment for foreign languages, use of audiovisual aids for foreign language teaching. **SELECTED PUBLICATIONS** Auth, "Foreign Language Days at EMU for Minority High School Students," Treffpunkt Deutsch 1 (91); auth, "The Hidden Agenda: Minority Concerns in Academe," Mosaics (91). **CONTACT ADDRESS** Dept For Lang, Middle Tennessee State Univ, 1301 E Main St, Murfreesboro, TN 37132-0001.

HARPER, SANDRA NADINE
PERSONAL Born 06/28/1938, Fostoria, OH, m, 1959 **DISCIPLINE** SPANISH **EDUCATION** Ohio State Univ, BS, 59, MA, 65, PhD(Span theater), 68. **CAREER** Teacher pub schs, Ohio, 59-62; instr, 68-69, asst prof, 69-79, from assoc prof to prof, Spanish, Ohio Wesleyan Univ, 79-, Chairperson, Romance Lang Dept, 81-83, chair, Mod For Langs Dept, 83-84, 86-94 Mellon grant, Ohio Wesleyan Univ, 72-73, 76 & 80. **MEMBERSHIPS** MLA; Am Asn Teachers Span & Port; AAUP. **RESEARCH** Contemporary Spanish theater, especially Alfonso Sastre; developing real communication in the foreign language classroom; the works of Rosario Castellanos. **SELECTED PUBLICATIONS** Auth, Puntos de vista: narrativa espanola moderna, 93. **CONTACT ADDRESS** Dept of Mod For Langs, Ohio Wesleyan Univ, 61 S Sandusky St, Delaware, OH 43015-2398. **EMAIL** snharper@cc.owu.edu

HARRIES, ELIZABETH WANNING
PERSONAL Born 05/22/1938, East Orange, NJ, d, 3 children **DISCIPLINE** ENGLISH, COMPARATIVE LITERATURE **EDUCATION** Vassar Col, AB, 59; Yale Univ, MAT, 60; PhD, 73. **CAREER** Lectr, Yale Univ, 73-74; asst prof to prof, Smith Col, 74-. **HONORS AND AWARDS** Danforth Fel for Women, 67-73; Walker Cowen Mem Prize, Univ of Va, 93. **MEMBERSHIPS** MLA, ASECS, ACLA. **RESEARCH** European fairy tales, 18th century literature. **SELECTED PUBLICATIONS** Auth, The Unfinished Moment: Essays on the Fragment in the Later Eighteenth Century, Charlottesville: Univ Press of Va (94); auth, "Simulating Oralities: French Fairy Tales of the 1690's," Col Lit 23 (June 96): 100-115; auth, "Fairy Tales about Fairy Tales: Notes on Canon Formation," in Out of the Woods: The Origins of the Literary Fairy Tale in Italy and France, ed Nancy Canepa, Detroit: Wayne State Univ Press (97): 152-175; auth, " 'Out in Left Field': Charlotte Smith's Prefaces, Bourdieu's Categories, and the Public Sphere," Modern Lang Quart, 58 (97): 457-473; auth, "The Mirror Broken: Fairy Tales in Women's Autobiographies," Marvels and Tales (April 2000); auth, " 'Excited Ideas': Description, the Monstrous, and the Sublime," Recueil d'essais sur l'estetique et l practique de l'ecriture fragmentaire, ed Rosa Maria Losito (forthcoming); auth, Twice Upon a Time: Re-Reading the History of the Fairy Tale (tentative title), Princeton Univ Press (forthcoming 2001). **CONTACT ADDRESS** Dept English, Smith Col, 98 Green St, Northhampton, MA 01063-1000. **EMAIL** eharries@sophia.smith.edu

HARRINGTON, KAREN A.
DISCIPLINE FRENCH LITERATURE **EDUCATION** Ca State Univ, BA, 73, MA, 78; Univ Ca, PhD, 86. **CAREER** Tchg asst, 80-83; tchg fel, Univ Ca, 83-84; instr, Valley Jr Col, 82-86; asst prof, 86-94; assoc prof, 94-. **HONORS AND AWARDS** Outstanding Tchg Awd. **MEMBERSHIPS** MLA; Tennessee For Lang Tchr Asn; Am Coun Tchg For Lang. **SELECTED PUBLICATIONS** Fragmentation and Irony in Les Fleurs du Mal, 92; Tirman, Alvin, and Karen Harrington; French Dominance at the Forefront of Modern Mathematics, 92; Harrington, Karen, and Josette Penso, 96. **CONTACT ADDRESS** Dept of Foreign Language, East Tennessee State Univ, PO Box 70717, Johnson City, TN 37614-0717. **EMAIL** harringk@etsu.edu

HARRIS, ALICE C.
PERSONAL Born 11/23/1947, Columbus, GA, m, 1976, 2 children **DISCIPLINE** LINGUISTICS **EDUCATION** Randolph-Macon Woman's Col, AB, 69; Univ Essex, MA, 72; Harvard Univ PhD, 76. **CAREER** Assoc Prof to Prof and Dept Chair, Vanderbilt Univ, 85-. **HONORS AND AWARDS** Phi Beta Kappa, 87; Leonard Bloomfield Book Awd, Linguistic Soc of am, 98; Earl Sutherland Prize for Achievement, Vanderbilt Univ, 98; Vis Erskine Fel, Univ Canterbury, 99; NEH Fel, 90-91. **MEMBERSHIPS** Intl Soc for Hist Linguistics, Linguistic Soc of Am, Soc for the study of Caucasia, Soc Caucasologica Europaea. **RESEARCH** Historical syntax and morphology, Universals (morphology and syntax), Languages of the Caucasus. **SELECTED PUBLICATIONS** Auth, "Georgian: A Language with Active Case Marking," Lingua, (90: 347-365; auth, "The Particle -a in Udi, the Non-Slavic Languages of the USSR: Linguistic Studies, Chicago Linguistic Soc, 92; auth, "Ergative-to=Accusative Shift in agreement: Tabassaran," in Linguistic Studies in the Non-Slavic Languages of the Commonwealth of Independent States and the Baltic Republics, Chicago Linguistic Soc, 94; auth, "On the History of Relative Clauses in Georgian," Non-Slavic Languages of the USSR: Papers from the Fourth Conference, Slavica Pub, 94; auth, "Focus in UDI," NSL.8: Linguistic Studies in the Non-Slavic Languages of the Commonwealth of Independent States and the Baltic Republics, Chicago Linguistic Soc, 96; auth, "Where in the Word is the Udi Clitic?," Language, in press. **CONTACT ADDRESS** Dept German, Vanderbilt Univ, 2201 West End Ave, Nashville, TN 37235-0001. **EMAIL** alice.c.harris@vanderbilt.edu

HARRIS, FREDERICK J.
PERSONAL Born 07/29/1943, New York, NY **DISCIPLINE** FRENCH **EDUCATION** Fordham Col, BA, 65; Columbia Univ, MA, 66, PhD, 69. **CAREER** Instr, Barnard Col, Columbia Univ, 68-70; asst prof to prof, Fordham Univ, 70-, Chair of the Humanities Div at Lincoln Center, 79-85, Chair of the bi-campus Dept of Modern Langs and Lits, 95-99. **HONORS AND AWARDS** Phi Beta Kappa, 64; graduated summa cum laude, Fordham Univ, BA, 65; Bourse Romain Rolland Fel, 67-68; mem, Conseil d'Administration, Societe des Professeurs Francais et Francophones d'Amerique, 95-98; advisory comt, Kreig und Literatur/War and Literature, published by the Erich Maria Remarque Archiv at the Univ of Osnabruck, Germany, 90-. **MEMBERSHIPS** Modern Lang Asn, Am Asn of Teachers of French, the Int Comparative Lit Asn, Am Comparative Lit Asn, Asn des Amis d'Andre Gide, Societe des Professeurs Francais et Francophones d'Amerique, the Pen American Center. **RESEARCH** Twentieth century French literature; 19th century French literature; 20th century comparative literature. **SELECTED PUBLICATIONS** Auth, Andre Gide and Romain Rolland: Two Men Divided, New Brunswick, NJ: Rutgers Univ Press (73); auth, Encounters with Darkness: French and German Writers on World War II, New York: Oxford Univ Press (83); auth, "Realite et imagination dans la tragedie allemande de Louis-Ferdinand Celine," in Francographies, numero speciale I (95): 33-44; auth, "The Debacle to the Debarquement: World War II France on the Stage," in Wolfgang Gortschacher and Holger Klein, eds, Modern War on Stage and Screen/Der Moderne Krieg auf der Buhne, Lewiston, NY, Queenston, Ontario, Lampeter, Wales: Edwin Mellon Press, Ltd (97): 317-332; auth, "Remarque's Der Funke Leben. The Concentration Camp as Text," in Enrich Maria Remarque: Leben, Werk und weltweite Witrkung, Thomas Schneider, ed, Osnabruck, Germany: Universitatsverlag Rasch (98): 227-288; auth, "L'Occupation au theatre: trois apercus," in Francographies, numero speciale I (98): 1-10; auth, "Pilote de guerre de Saint-Exupery" le role de la technologie," in Francographies, numero speciale 2, Nouvelle Serie, tome II, (99): 271-279. **CONTACT ADDRESS** Dept Modern Langs, Fordham Univ, 441 E Fordham Rd, Bronx, NY 10458-5149.

HARRIS, JANE GARY
PERSONAL Born New York, NY, 2 children **DISCIPLINE** SLAVIC LANGUAGE & LITERATURE **EDUCATION** Stanford Univ, BA, 59; Columbia Univ, MA & PhD, 69. **CAREER** Instr, Univ Pittsburgh, 67-69; asst prof, Indiana Univ, Bloomington, 73-74; assoc prof & chairperson dept Slavic lang & lit, full prof Russian lang, lit, & cult, Univ Pittsburgh, 75-, corresp ed, Canadian-American Slavic Studies, 73-; dir summer sem, Nat Endowment for Humanities, 81 & 83; acad dean, Semester at Sea, 84 **HONORS AND AWARDS** Nat Bk Awd, 80. **MEMBERSHIPS** AAAS; MLA; Am Asn Teachers Slavic & East Europ Lang, Pres 95-97; Am Soc Eighteenth Century Studies;

Asn Dept Foreign Lang; CIEE. **SELECTED PUBLICATIONS** Auth, History of a feminine image: Towards an analysis of Boris Pasternak's esthetic vision, Russian Lit Triquart, 74; transl, Osip Mandelstam's poetry, The Silver Age of Russian Culture, Ardis, 75; Osip Mandelstam's prose fiction, Russian Lit Triquart, 75; Osip Mandelstam's critical essays, Modern Russian Poets on Poetry, Ardis, 76; auth, An inquiry into the use of autobiography as a stylistic determinant of the modernist aspect of Osip Mandelstam's literary prose, American Contributions to the VIIIth International Congress of Slavists, Slavica Publ, 78; Osip Mandelstam: The Complete Critical Prose and Letters, Ardis, 79 & 97, 3rd ed; G R Derzhavin: The Poetic Imagination in Evolution (in prep); Osip Mandelstam, G K Hall, 88; ed, American Contributions to the Xth International Congress of Slavists, Slavica Publ, 88; Autobiographical Statements: Essays on the Autobiographical Mode in Twentieth-Century Russian Literature, Princeton Univ, 90; Lydia Ginzburg: In Memorium, Essays, C-ASS, 94. **CONTACT ADDRESS** Dept of Slavic Languages & Literaature, Univ of Pittsburgh, 1417 C/L, Pittsburgh, PA 15260. **EMAIL** jgh@pitt.edu

HARRISON, ANN TUKEY
PERSONAL Born 04/19/1938, Geneva, NY **DISCIPLINE** FRENCH LANGUAGE, LINGUISTICS **EDUCATION** Mich State Univ, BA, 57; Univ Mich, MA, 58, PhD(Romance ling), 62. **CAREER** Teaching asst French, Univ Mich, 57-61; instr, Univ Wis, 61-63, asst prof French & ling, 63-65; from asst prof to assoc prof Romance lang, 65-73, Prof French, Mich State Univ, 73- **HONORS AND AWARDS** Ruth Dean Annual Lectr, Mt Holyoke Col, 76. **MEMBERSHIPS** MLA; AAUP; Medieval Acad; Am Asn Teachers French. **RESEARCH** French medieval language and literature; French linguistics. **SELECTED PUBLICATIONS** Auth, 'Ballades Et Rondeaux', French Rev, Vol 0067, 94; The 'Romance of the Rose' and its Medieval Readers--Interpretation, Reception, Manuscript Transmission, French Rev, Vol 0068, 95. **CONTACT ADDRESS** 277 Maplewood Dr, Lansing, MI 48823.

HARRISON, JAMES W.
PERSONAL Born 05/31/1945, Lebanon, PA, m, 1966, 5 children **DISCIPLINE** GERMAN **EDUCATION** Univ of North Carolina at Chapel Hill, PhD, 76. **CAREER** Prof of German and humanities, Southern Utah Univ, 76-98. **HONORS AND AWARDS** Distinguished Faculty Dir; Thunderbird Prof of the Year; Outstanding Educator of the Year; mem of Speakers Bureau for Utah Endowment for the Humanities; Fulbright Fel; Distinguished Faculty Lecture Awd; Distinguished Educator Awd. **MEMBERSHIPS** Arizona Ctr for Medieveal and Renaissance Studies. **RESEARCH** German High Middle Ages. **SELECTED PUBLICATIONS** Auth, "Hartmann's 'Der Arme Heinrich': A Precartesian View of Medicine", in Selecta 13, 92; auth, "Schopenhauer, Wagner, and the 'Ring'", Selecta 14, 93; auth, A Concise History of the West, Stipes, 93; coauth, Hartmann von aue. 'Der Arme Heinrich', Stipes, 93. **CONTACT ADDRESS** Department of Language and Literature, So Utah Univ, 351 W. Center St., Cedar City, UT 84702. **EMAIL** harrison@suu.edu

HART, GAIL K.
DISCIPLINE GERMAN LANGUAGE **EDUCATION** SUNY, BA, 72; Univ Rochester, MA, 77; Univ Va, MA, 79, PhD, 83. **CAREER** Instr, Yale Univ, 84-87; Reed Col, 87-90; Assoc Dean, Hum for Undergrad Stud, Prof, German, Univ Calif, Irvine, 90-. **SELECTED PUBLICATIONS** Auth, Readers and their Fictions in the Novels and Novellas of Gottfried Keller, Univ NC Stud Germ Lang and Lit, 89; Tragedy in Paradise: Family and Gender Politics in German Bourgeois Tragedy 1750-1850, Camden House, 96; Verleiblichungen: Literatur- und kulturgeschichtliche Studien uber Strategien, Formen und Funktionen der Verleiblichung in Texten von der Fruhzeit bis zum Cyberspace, St. Ingbert: Rohrig Universitatsverlag, 96. **CONTACT ADDRESS** Dept of Ger, Univ of California, Irvine, Irvine, CA 92697. **EMAIL** gkhart@uci.edu

HART, PATRICIA
PERSONAL Born 03/03/1954, Provo, UT **DISCIPLINE** SPANISH LITERATURE **EDUCATION** Univ NC, Chapel Hill, PhD. **CAREER** Prof Span, Purdue Univ. **RESEARCH** 20th century Hispanic fiction; Detective fiction; Catalan. **SELECTED PUBLICATIONS** Auth, Little Sins, Tower Books, 80; auth, The Spanish Sleuth, Fairleigh Dickinson Univ Press, 87; auth, Narrative Magic in the Fiction of Isabel Allende, Fairleigh Dickinson Univ Press, 89; auth, More Heaven and Less Mud: The Precedence of Catalan Unity Over Feminism in Francesc Betriu's Filmic Vision of MercS Rodoreda's La Plaoa del Diamant, The Garden Across the Border: MercS Rodoreda's Fiction, Susquehanna Univ Press, 94; auth, Magic Feminism in The Stories of Eva Luna, by Isabel Allende, in Feminism/Postmodernism/Multiculturalism, Assoc Univ Press, 94; auth, The Deconstruction of the Soldadera in Laura Esquivel's Como agua para chocolate, Cincinnati Romance Rev, Vol XIV, 95; auth, Visual Strategies in Gabriel Retes' Film, El bulto, Portland State Univ Press, 95; auth, Can a Good Feminist Sit Through Kika? Rape, Recovery, and Submission Fantasies in the Films of Pedro Almodovar, Anuario de Cine y Lit en Espanol, Vol III, 97; co-ed, Romance Lang Annual, Vol VI, 94; Vol VII, 95; Vol VIII, 96; transl, Julia, by Isabel-Clara Simo (UP of the South, 99); transl, Women, by Carme Riera, (00). **CONTACT ADDRESS** Dept of For Lang and Lit, Purdue Univ, West Lafayette, 1080 Schleman Hall, West Lafayette, IN 47907-1080. **EMAIL** hartp@omni.cc.purdue.edu

HART, PIERRE
PERSONAL Born 05/06/1935, Baraboo, WI, m, 1958, 2 children **DISCIPLINE** RUSSIAN LITERATURE **EDUCATION** Antioch Col, BA, 57; Univ Wis-Madison, MS, 60, MA, 66, PhD(Russ lit), 68. **CAREER** Asst prof Russ, State Univ NY Buffalo, 67-72, assoc prof, 72-79; Prof Russ, LA State Univ, 80-, Am Coun Educ fel, 78-79. **MEMBERSHIPS** Am Asn Teachers Slavic & E Europ Lang. **RESEARCH** Russian 18th century poetry; symbolist prose; fictional representations of childhood. **SELECTED PUBLICATIONS** Auth, Metaphor, Metonymy and Myth in the 'Petty Demon', Slavic East Europ J, Vol 0041, 97; Metaphor, Metonymy and Myth in the 'Petty Demon', Slavic East Europ J, Vol 0041, 97; Narrative Oscillation in Gogol 'Nevsky Prospect', Studies Short Fiction, Vol 0031, 94. **CONTACT ADDRESS** For Lang, La State Univ, Baton Rouge, Baton Rouge, LA 70803-0001.

HART, THOMAS ROY
PERSONAL Born 01/10/1925, Raleigh, NC, m, 1945, 2 children **DISCIPLINE** SPANISH **EDUCATION** Yale Univ, BA, 48, PhD, 52. **CAREER** Visiting prof, Oxford Univ, 86; Univ of Chicago, 97-98; Instr Span, Amherst Col, 52-53; instr Romance lang, Harvard Univ, 53-55; asst prof, Johns Hopkins Univ, 55-60; assoc prof, Emory Univ, 60-64; Prof Romance Lang, Univ Ore, 64-95, Fulbright res grants, Univ Montpellier, 50-51 & Univ Madrid, 66-67; ed, Comp Lit, 72-95. **HONORS AND AWARDS** NEH fell, 85-86; Camargo found fell, 90, 94. **RESEARCH** Spanish literature of the Middle Ages and Golden Age; Portuguese and Catalan literature. **SELECTED PUBLICATIONS** Auth, Cervantes and Ariosto: Renewing Fiction, Princeton UP, 89; auth, Cervantes' Exemplary Fictions, Univ Press of Kent, 94. **CONTACT ADDRESS** Dept of Romance Lang, Univ of Oregon, Eugene, OR 97403. **EMAIL** trhart@oregon.uoregon.edu

HARTH, ERICA
PERSONAL Born New York, NY, m, 1984 **DISCIPLINE** FRENCH LITERATURE **EDUCATION** Barnard Col, BA, 59; Columbia Univ, MA, 62, PhD, 68. **CAREER** Instr French, NY Univ, 64-66; from instr to asst prof, Columbia Univ, 67-71; lect, Tel-Aviv Univ, Israel, 71-72; asst prof, 72-75, assoc prof, 75-85, prof French & Comp Lit, 85-92, Prof Humanities & Women's Studies, Brandeis Univ, 92-; Fel, NEH, 70, 89-90, Am Coun Learned Socs, 78, ACLS, 89-90 & Bunting Inst, 89-90. **MEMBERSHIPS** MLA. **RESEARCH** Seventeenth century French literature; sociology of literature. **SELECTED PUBLICATIONS** Auth, Cyrano de Bergerac and the Polemics of modernity, Columbia Univ, 70; The tragic moment in Athalie, Mod Lang Quart, 12/72; Exorcising the beast: Attempts at rationality in French classicism, MLA Publ, 1/73; Classical innateness, Yale Fr Studies, 6/73; The creative alienation of the writer: Sartre, Camus and Simone de Beauvoir, Mosiac, spring 75; Classical disproportion: La Bruyere's Caracteres, L'Esprit Createur, spring-summer 75; Sur des vers de Virgile (III, 5): Antinomy and totality in Montaigne, Fr Forum, 1/77; Ideology and Culture in Seventeenth-Century France, Cornell Univ Press, 83; Cartesian Women: Versions and Subversions of Rational Discourse in the Old Regime, 92. **CONTACT ADDRESS** Dept of Romance & Comp Lit, Brandeis Univ, ROCL - MS024, Waltham, MA 02215-2700. **EMAIL** harth@binah.cc.brandeis.edu

HARTIGAN, KARELISA V.
PERSONAL Born 03/05/1943, Stillwater, OK, m, 1992, 5 children **DISCIPLINE** CLASSICS **EDUCATION** Col of Wooster, BA, 65; Univ Chicago, AM, 66, PhD, 70. **CAREER** Asst prof, St Olaf Col, 69-73; asst prof, 73-76, assoc prof, 76-90, Prof, Univ FL, 90-. **HONORS AND AWARDS** Various undergraduate awards, including Phi Beta Kappa; Woodrow Wilson fel, 65; Ford Found MA fel, 66; Univ Chicago fel, 66-68; Woodrow Wilson Dissertation fel, 68-69; numerous teaching awards, Univ FL; Amer Philos Assoc Nat Teaching Awd; Distinguished Alumni Prof, Univ FL; Classical Assoc of Middle West and South Ovatio Awd. **MEMBERSHIPS** Classical Assoc of Middle West and South, pres 92-93; Amer Philol Assoc; Modern Greek Studies Assoc. **RESEARCH** Greek drama; mythology; ancient cities; comparative lit. **SELECTED PUBLICATIONS** Auth, The Poets and the Cities, Anton Hain, 79; Ambiguity and Self Deception, Apollo & Artemis Plays of Euripides, Peter Lang, 91; Greek Drama on the American Stage, Greenwood, 95; Myths Behind Our Words, Forbes, 98; over 2 dozen articles on Greek drama, comparative lit, and myth in film; also slide sets with commentary: 4, with Pictures of Record. **CONTACT ADDRESS** Dept of Classics Dauer 3-C, Univ of Florida, Box 117435, Gainesville, FL 32611. **EMAIL** kvhrtgn@classics.ufl.edu

HARTMAN, C.
PERSONAL Born 11/26/1946, Phoenixville, PA, m, 1978, 1 child **DISCIPLINE** CHINESE LITERATURE **EDUCATION** Indian Univ, BA, 67; Indiana Univ, MA, 70; Indiana Univ, PhD, 75 **CAREER** Asst prof, Ntl Taiwan Univ, 77-79; asst prof, Univ Wis, 79-80; asst prof, St Univ NY Albany, 80-85; assoc prof, St Univ NY Albany, 85-93; prof, St Univ NY Albany, 93- **HONORS AND AWARDS** Assoc Asian Studies, Joseph Levenson Prize; National Endowment for the Humanities, Fellowship for College Teachers, 88-89; first place, best book in the humanities, State Univ of New York at Albany, 86 **MEMBERSHIPS** Assoc Asian Studies **RESEARCH** Literary Inquisitions during the Sung dynasty; Iconology and Meaning in the Chinese Literary Visual Arts; Traditional Chinese Literature, especially poetry. **SELECTED PUBLICATIONS** Auth, "LiuTsung-yuan", Twayne, (73); Han Yu and the T'ang Search for Unity, Princeton Univ Pr, 86; The Indiana Companion to Traditional Chinese Literature, Ind Univ Pr, 86; auth, ThePurloined Plum and the Heart of Iron: A Contribution to the History of Flowering Plum Imagery in the Sung and Yuan Dynasties," Journal of Sung-Yuan Studies, (95); auth, "Stomping Songs: Word and Image," Chinese Literature: Essays, Articles, Reviews, (95); "The Making of a Villian: Ch'in Kuei and Tao-hsueh," Harvard Jrnl Asiatic Studies, 98 **CONTACT ADDRESS** Dept E Asian Studies, SUNY, Albany, Humanities 210, Albany, NY 12222. **EMAIL** Hartman@albany.edu

HARTMAN, JAMES WALTER
PERSONAL Born 01/28/1939, Newark, OH **DISCIPLINE** ENGLISH LANGUAGE, LINGUISTICS **EDUCATION** OH Univ, BA, 61; Univ MI, MA, 62, PhD, 66. **CAREER** Instr Eng, Eastern IL Univ, 63-64; asst prof Eng & ling, OH Univ, 66-67; asst prof Eng lang, Univ WI-Madison, 67-70; Assoc Prof, 70-85, Prof Eng & Ling, Univ KS, 85-, Asst dir, Dict Am Regional Eng, 67-70; Assoc Ed, 70-; Assoc Ed, Am Speech, 72-97; Ed Publ, Am Dialect Soc, 76-85. **MEMBERSHIPS** Am Dialect Soc; NCTE. **RESEARCH** Dialectology; sociolinguistics; lexicography; Am Eng pronunciation. **SELECTED PUBLICATIONS** Auth, Phonological Variation in the United States, In: Dictionary of American Regional English, Vol I, 85; Some Possible Changes in the Pronunciation of Young Americans (maybe), Am Speech 59.3, 84; ed, Cambridge International Dictionary of English, Cambridge Univ Press, 96; co-ed, English Pronouns Dictionary, 15th, Cambridge Univ Press, 97; auth, Dictionary Pronunciations: Mine or Yours or Theirs, Am Speech Vol 75, No. 3, (00): 250-253. **CONTACT ADDRESS** Dept of Eng Wescoe Hall, Univ of Kansas, Lawrence, Lawrence, KS 66045-0001. **EMAIL** jwhartma@eagle.cc.ukans.edu

HARTMAN, STEVEN LEE
PERSONAL Born 05/04/1946, Lexington, VA, m, 1987 **DISCIPLINE** SPANISH LINGUISTICS **EDUCATION** Univ Wis, BA, 66, MA, 68, PhD(Span), 71. **CAREER** Asst Prof Span, Southern Ill Univ Carbondale, 71-, Vis prof, Univ Veracruzana, Mexico, 73. **MEMBERSHIPS** Am Asn Teachers Span & Port; MLA; Ling Soc Am; Asn Comput Ling. **RESEARCH** Historical linguistics; generative phonology; computational linguistics. **SELECTED PUBLICATIONS** Auth, "On the histor of Spanish macho," Hispanic Linguistics, Vol 1, 84; auth, "Historia interna del espanol moderno," Lexikon der Romanistischen Linguistik, Vol 6; auth, "Writing Rules for a Computer Model of Sound Change," So. Illinois Working Papers in Linguistics & Language Teaching, Vol 2. **CONTACT ADDRESS** Dept of Foreign Lang & Lit, So Illinois Univ, Carbondale, Carbondale, IL 62901-4521. **EMAIL** lhartman@siu.edu

HARVEY, CAROL
PERSONAL Born 04/18/1941, Heckmondwike, United Kingdom, m, 1964, 2 children **DISCIPLINE** FRENCH **EDUCATION** Univ Edinburgh, MA, 63, PhD, 69; Univ Caen, LL, 64. **CAREER** Lectr, Univ Caen, 63-64; ed asst lexicography, WM Collins, Glasgow, 66-69; asst prof, 70-76, assoc prof, 76-84, Prof French, Univ Winnipeg, 84-; vis fel, Corpus Christi Col, Cambridge, 89; vis prof, Univ Perpignan (France), 91-92. **HONORS AND AWARDS** Chevalier, Ordre des Palmes Acad, France. **MEMBERSHIPS** Int Courtly Lit Soc; Can Soc Medievalists; Medieval Acad Am; MLA. **SELECTED PUBLICATIONS** Auth, Intertextuality in the Anglo-Norman Lyric, in J Rocky Mt Medieval Renaissance Asn, 89; auth, Gabrielle Roy: institutrice: reportage et texte narratif, in Cahiers franco-canadiens de l'Ouest, 91; auth, Le cycle manitobain de Gabrielle Roy, 93; auth, Georges Bugnet et Gabrielle Roy: paysages litteraires de l'ouest canadien, in LitteRealite, 94; auth, La litterature au feminin, 95. **CONTACT ADDRESS** French Dept, Univ of Winnipeg, 515 Portage Ave, Winnipeg, MB, Canada R3B 2E9. **EMAIL** caroll.harvey@uwinnipeg.ca

HARVEY, MARIA-LUISA ALVAREZ
PERSONAL Born Torreon, Mexico, 1 child **DISCIPLINE** TWENTIETH CENTURY SPANISH LITERATURE **EDUCATION** TX Western Col, BA, 65; Univ TX, El Paso, MA, 66; Univ AZ, PhD, 69; Jackson State Col, M Sci in Ed, 72; postdoctoral work, Harvard Univ, summers 72 and 73. **CAREER** Teaching assoc Span, Univ Ariz, 69; asst prof & head dept mod lang, Col Artesia, 69-70; assoc prof, 70-74, prof Span, 74-80, Prof Mod Foreign & Dir, Hons Prog, Dean of W. B. Dubois Honors Col and Prof of MFL, Jackson State Univ, 81-. **HONORS AND AWARDS** Phi Beta Kappa; Danforth Assoc, Teacher of the Year, 78; Outstanding Educator Awd, 90 (during the Salute to Prominent Women in MS). **MEMBERSHIPS** Nat Collegiate Hons Coun; Southern Regional Honors Council. **RESEARCH** Twentieth century Spanish poetry; bilingual edu-

cation; human development. **SELECTED PUBLICATIONS** Auth, Cielo y tierra en la poesia lirica de Manuel Altolaguirre, Univ & Col Press Miss, 72; Where is the critical period of development for the disadvantaged, fall-winter, 73 & Is teaching selection the answer, fall, 74, IL Schs J; Teach Spanish to Black students? Make it relevant! Make it Black!, J Negro Educ, summer 74; A good teacher and an eclectic approach: The hopeful answer to successful reading instruction, fall 74 & Teach them reading while you teach them Spanish .. or French .. or any other subject, summer 75, Reading Horizons; One egg has the subject, another has the predicate: A Spanish (or English) teaching game, Elem English, 4/75; Lorca's Yerma: Frigid .. or mismatched?, Col Lang Asn J, 6/80; Minorities and Women and Honors Education, in P. G. Friedman, R. C. Jenkins-Friedman, eds, Fostering Academic Excellence Through Honors Programs, New Directions for Teaching and Learning, No 25, San Francisco, Jossey-Bass, March 86; I Like to Examine Insects: An Honors Program Comes of Age, The College Bd Rev, summer 87; An Honors Program Approach to the Making of Professionals, The Gifted Child Today, May/June 90. **CONTACT ADDRESS** W. B. DuBois Honors Col, Jackson State Univ, 1400 Lynch St, Jackson, MS 39217-0001.

HARVEY, ROBERT
DISCIPLINE COMPARATIVE LITERATURE **EDUCATION** Univ Ca, BA, 72; Univ Paris, DUEL, 72; DEA, 84; San Francisco State Univ, MA, 75; Univ Calif, PhD, 88. **CAREER** Asst prof, 88-94; assoc prof, French, 94- , assoc prof, comp lit SUNY-Stony Brook, 97- ; vis prof, Univ de Poitiers, 99; Prof HDR, Univ Paris, 01. **HONORS AND AWARDS** President's and Chancellor's Awds for Excellence in Teaching, 96; ACLS Grant for Travel, 96; Provost's Merit Awd, 96; NYS/UUP PDQWL Continuing Faculty Development Awd, 95; NYS/UUP PDQWL Term Faculty Development Awd, 93; Provost's Merit Awd for Teaching, 90; SUNY Research Development Travel Grant, 90; SUNY Research Development Summer Stipend, 89; NYS/UUP PDQWL New Faculty Development Awd, 89; SUNY Research Development Travel Grant, 89; Exchange Fel, 84-85; French Government Scholarship, 84-85; Regents' Travelling Fel, 83-84; Regents' Fel, 83-84. **MEMBERSHIPS** Am Asn Tchr French; Asn des Amis de Pontigny-Cerisy; Can Soc Hermeneutics Postmodern Thought; Int Asn Philos Lit; MRAP; MLA; Sartre Soc; Soc Cinema Studies; Amities Internationales Andre Malraux; Ancien Eleve de l'Ecole Normale Superieure; Asn Antoine Berman; Conseil Int d'Etudes Francophones; Duras Soc of the United Kingdom; Groupe d'Etudes Sartriennes; Societe d'Etudes de la Litterature de xxeme siecle **SELECTED PUBLICATIONS** Auth, Search for a Father: Sartre, Paternity and the Question of Ethics, Univ Mich, 91; ed, Toward the Postmodern, Humanities, 93; co-auth, Marguerite Duras: A Bio-Bibliography, Greenwood, 97; co-auth, "Introduction: Marguerite Duras: Writing as Life," Marguerite Duras: A Bio-Bibliography, Greenwood, (97); co-auth, "Adrift in the Realm of the Senses," Situating Sartre in Twentieth-Century Thought and Culture, St. Martin's Press, (97); co-auth, "Purloined Letters: Intertextuality and Intersexuality in Tahar Ben Jelloun's The Sand Child," Articulations of Difference: Gender Studies and Writing in French, Stanford, (97); co-auth, "Genet's Open Enemies: Sartre and Derrida," Yale French Studies, (97); co-auth, "Lyotard in Passing," October, (98); ed, "Afterwords: Essays in Memory of Jean-Francois Lyotard," (99); ed, "Jean-Francois Lyotard: Time and Judgement," Yale French Studies, (01). **CONTACT ADDRESS** Dept of Comp Studies, SUNY, Stony Brook, PO Box 863, Stony Brook, NY 11790-0863. **EMAIL** rharvey@sunysb.edu

HARVEY, WILLIAM D.
PERSONAL Born 12/24/1958, Peterborough, ON, Canada, m, 1998, 2 children **DISCIPLINE** LINGUISTICS **EDUCATION** Trent Univ, BA, 80; BA, 81; Univ Toronto, MA, 94; PhD, 99. **CAREER** Instr, Dorset Col, 99-. **RESEARCH** Linguistics. **SELECTED PUBLICATIONS** Auth, "Linguistic Relativity in French, English, and German Philosophy," Philos Today, (96): 273-288. **CONTACT ADDRESS** Dept Ling, Dorset Col, 222 N Templeton, Vancouver, BC, Canada V5L 3E4. **EMAIL** wharvey76@hotmail.com

HASHIMOTO, I. Y.
DISCIPLINE LANGUAGE AND WRITING **EDUCATION** Stanford Univ, BA, 67; Univ Wis, MA, 69; Univ Mich, PhD, 78. **CAREER** Instr, Univ Mich; Idaho State Univ; prof, 83-. **HONORS AND AWARDS** Dir, Whitman Col Wrtg Ctr; exec comm, Conf Col Compos and Commun. **RESEARCH** Academic writing, modern non-fiction prose. **SELECTED PUBLICATIONS** Auth, Thirteen Weeks: A Guide to Tchg Col Writing. **CONTACT ADDRESS** Dept of Eng, Whitman Col, 345 Boyer Ave, Walla Walla, WA 99362-2038. **EMAIL** hashimiy@whitman.edu

HASLAM, GERALD WILLIAM
PERSONAL Born 03/18/1937, Bakersfield, CA, m, 1961, 5 children **DISCIPLINE** AMERICAN LITERATURE, LINGUISTICS **EDUCATION** San Francisco State Col, AB, 63, MA, 65; Union Grad Sch, PhD, 80. **CAREER** Teaching asst English, Wash State Univ, 65-66; instr, San Francisco State Col, 66-67; from asst prof to assoc prof, 67-71, prof Eng, Sonoma State Univ, 71-, Gen Semantics Found res grant, 66; invitational scholar, Polish Acad Sci, Warsaw, 66; mem nat acad adv bd, Multi-Cult Inst, 67-; dir, Okie Studies Proj & Arch, Sonoma State Col, 76-; ed, Lit Hist Am West, Nat Endowment for Humanities, 79- **HONORS AND AWARDS** Honoable Mention (finalist) PEN USA West Nonfiction Award. **MEMBERSHIPS** Col Lang Asn; Western Am Lit Asn; Multi-Ethnic Lit of US. **RESEARCH** The West in Am lit; non-white Am writers; Am dialects. **SELECTED PUBLICATIONS** Auth, Hawk Flights: Visions of the West, Seven Buffaloes Press, 83; auth, Snapshots: Glimpses of the Other Californi, Devil Mountain Books, 85; auth, The Man Who Cultivated Fire and Other Stories, Capra Press, 87; auth, That Constant Coyote: California Stories, Univ of Nevada Press, 90; auth, The Great Central Valley: California's Heartland, Univ of Calif Press, 93; auth, The Other California: The Great Central Valley in Life and Letters, Univ of Nevada, 94; auth, Condor Dreams and Other Fictions, Univ of Nevada Press, 94; auth, The Great Tejon Club Jubilee, Devil Mountain Books, 95; auth, Workin' Man Blues: Country Music in California, Univ of Calif Press, 99; auth, Coming of Age in Califonia, Devil Mountain Books, 00. **CONTACT ADDRESS** Dept of English, Sonoma State Univ, Rohnert Park, CA 94928.

HASSELBACH, INGRID TIESLER
PERSONAL Born Rabishau, Germany, m, 1972 **DISCIPLINE** GERMAN LITERATURE **EDUCATION** Goethe Univ, GER, Staatsexamen; Tulane Univ, PhD, 78. **CAREER** Asst prof German, FL State Univ, 65-73; Lectr German, Loyola Univ, 75-; Lectr German, Tulane Univ, 78-. **MEMBERSHIPS** Mod Foreign Lang Asn. **RESEARCH** Modern German literature (Gunter Grass); women in German literature of the 19th century; medieval German literature. **SELECTED PUBLICATIONS** Auth, Gunter Grass Katz u Maus Interpretation, Oldenbourg Verlag Munchen, 2nd ed, 71. **CONTACT ADDRESS** 6363 St Charles Ave, New Orleans, LA 70118-6195.

HASSELBACH, KARL HEINZ
PERSONAL Born Giessen, Germany **DISCIPLINE** GERMAN LANGUAGES & LITERATURE **EDUCATION** Univ Marburg, DPhil(Ger), 71. **CAREER** Actg asst prof, Fla State Univ, 65-72; from asst prof to prof, Tulane Univ, 72-. **MEMBERSHIPS** AAUP **RESEARCH** Nineteenth and twentieth century German literature; German dialectology. **SELECTED PUBLICATIONS** Auth, German Dialectology, Elwert (Marburg, Germany), 71; auth, "T. Mann, 'Doktor Faustus,'" Oldenbourg (Munchen, Germany), 77; auth, "G. Buchner, 'Lenz,'" Oldenbourg (Munchen, Germany), 86; auth, "B. Brecht, 'Kalendergeschichten,'" Oldenbourg (Munchen, Germany), 90; auth, "Georg Buchner," Reclam (Stuttgart, Germany), 97. **CONTACT ADDRESS** Dept Ger & Slavic Lang, Tulane Univ, 6823 St Charles Ave, New Orleans, LA 70118-5698. **EMAIL** hasselk@mailhost.tcs.tulane.edu

HATASA, KAZUMI
DISCIPLINE JAPANESE LANGUAGE **EDUCATION** Waseda Univ, BA, 80; Univ Ill, Urbana-Champaign, MA, 85; Univ Ill, Urbana-Champaign, PhD, 89. **CAREER** Asst, ESL lang lab, Univ Ill, Urbana-Champaign, 82-83; instr, Middlebury Col, 83, 84, 86, 88, tchg asst, Univ Ill, Urbana-Champaign, 83-85; res asst, Univ Ill, 85-88; prof, Middlebury Col, 86; asst prof Japanese, 88-94, dir, For Lang Media Ctr, 93-, assoc prof Japanese, 94-, dir, Ctr for Technol-Enhanced Lang Lrng and Instr, Purdue Univ, 97-. **HONORS AND AWARDS** Global Initiative grant, Purdue Univ, 94; fel, Japan Found, 96; mem, bd of dir of asn of tchr of japanese. **MEMBERSHIPS** Mem, Asn for Asian Stud; Asn of Tchr of Japanese; Can Asn of Tchr of Japanese; Nihongo Kyoiku Gakkai; Comput Assisted Lang Lrng and Instr Consortium; Int Asn of Lang Lab. **RESEARCH** Technology enhanced language learning and instruction; Japanese language. **SELECTED PUBLICATIONS** Auth, Nihongo kyoshi no tameno computer literacy, Gekkan Nihongo , ALC Press, 96; Computer Literacy for Japanese Language Professionals-What do we need to know about applications of the computer?, in Progress in Japanese Linguistics and Pedagogy: A Collection in Honor of Professor Akira Miura, ed by Hubbard, Sakamoto & Davis, ALC Press, 97; coauth, Making Electronic Communication Possible in Japanese on the Internet, in Tele-collaboration in foreign languages: proceedings of the Hawaii Symposium 95,Univ Hawaii Second Lang Tchg and Curric Ctr, 96; co-ed, Bridging Gaps Proceedings of the Sixth Annual Lake Erie Teachers of Japanese Conference, LETJC, 94. **CONTACT ADDRESS** Dept of For Lang and Lit, Purdue Univ, West Lafayette, 1080 Schleman Hall, West Lafayette, IN 47907-1080. **EMAIL** khatasa@purdue.edu

HATCH, MARY G.
PERSONAL Born 02/17/1913, Omaha, NE, m, 1940, 4 children **DISCIPLINE** GERMANIC LANGUAGES **EDUCATION** Vassar Col, AB, 35; Univ Mich, MA, 37; Syracuse Univ, PhD, 52. **CAREER** Teach, Montclair HS, 38-40; teach, Dana Hall Sch, 40-42; prof, Columbia Univ, 60-. **HONORS AND AWARDS** Vassar Fel; Syr Univ Schl. **MEMBERSHIPS** Phi Beta Kappa; AATG; SAMLA. **RESEARCH** Life and works of Goethe; medieval German epic. **SELECTED PUBLICATIONS** Auth, Under the Elms: Yesterday and Today, Syracuse Univ, 49; auth, "Werther and Student Protest," Mod Lang Asn (74). **CONTACT ADDRESS** Dept Foreign Language, Columbia Col, So Carolina, 1301 Columbia College Dr, Columbia, SC 29203-5949.

HATHAWAY, ROBERT L.
DISCIPLINE SPANISH LITERATURE OF THE XVI AND XVII CENTURIES **EDUCATION** Williams Col, BA, 53; Georgetown Univ, MS, 57; Brown Univ, MA, 63, PhD, 69. **CAREER** Prof, Colgate Univ, emer. **HONORS AND AWARDS** NEW fel in residence, Harvard Univ, 76-77. **SELECTED PUBLICATIONS** Auth, Not Necessarily Cervantes: Readings of the Quixote, Juan de la Cuesta-Hispanic Monogr, 95; ed, The "Villancicos" from The "Cancionero" of Pedro Manuel Jimenez de Urrea, and Ximenez de Urrea, Penitencia de amor, Exeter Univ Press 76, 90; articles and rev(s), Anales Cervantinos, Boletin de la Biblioteca Menendez Pelayo, Bulletin of the Comediantes, Celestinesca, Cervantes, Hisp Rev, Jour of Hisp Philol, Nueva Revista de Filologea Hispanica. **CONTACT ADDRESS** Dept of Romance Lang, Colgate Univ, 13 Oak Drive, Hamilton, NY 13346.

HATTON, ROBERT WAYLAND
PERSONAL Born 02/05/1934, Columbus, OH, m, 1954, 3 children **DISCIPLINE** SPANISH **EDUCATION** Capital Univ, AB, 57; Middlebury Col, AM, 59. **CAREER** Teacher pub schs, Ohio, 58-60; Binat Cult Ctr Grantee, US Info Agency, Colombia, 60-62; instr Span, Ohio Wesleyan Univ, 62-63; from asst prof to assoc prof, 63-70, prof mod lang, Capital Univ, 70-, escort interpreter, US Dept State, 66-70. **MEMBERSHIPS** Am Asn Teachers Span & Port; Taurine Bibliophiles Am; Am Coun Teaching Foreign Lang; Midwest Asn Lang Studies. **RESEARCH** Editing of student texts. **SELECTED PUBLICATIONS** Co-ed, La gloria de Don Ramiro, Heath, 66; ed, Hombre hispanico, C E Merrill, 70; Los clarines del miedo, Xerox, 71; coauth, The Bullfight: A Teaching and Study Guide, Advan Press Am, 74; ed, Just a Little Bit of the Civil War as seen by W J Smith, Co M, 2nd OVC, Ohio Hist, Parts I & II, summer-autumn 75; coauth, A Day at the Bullfight: A Viable Alternative to the Language Fair, Foreign Lang Ann, 2/77; auth, The Sideline Show, NAWDAC J, fall 78; Louis Bromfield Revisited, Ohioana Quart, summer 80. **CONTACT ADDRESS** Dept of Mod Lang, Capital Univ, 2199 E Main St, Columbus, OH 43209-2394.

HAVILAND, BEVERLY
DISCIPLINE COMPARATIVE LITERATURE **EDUCATION** Sarah Lawrence Col, BA, 74; Princeton Univ, MA, 75, PhD, 82. **CAREER** Adj asst prof, Occidental Col, 89; asst prof, 84-92; assoc prof, Vassar Col, 92-96; assoc prof, 96-00; SUNY Stony Brook; vis assoc prof, sr lectr, Brown Univ. **HONORS AND AWARDS** Univ Learning Communities Teaching Fel NYS/UUP PDQWL Continuing Fac Dev Grant, 99; The Margaret Church Memorial Prize, 98; Nat Endowment for the Humanities Focus Grant for New Am Studies at Stony Brook, 97; Stony Brook Acad of Teacher-Scholars Grant, 97-98; Fac Ctr Fel, Vassar Col for Dilemmas of Person and Property, 90; The John N McGinnis Awd, 89; Nat Endowment for the Humanities Fel, 87-88; Am Coun of Learned Soc, Grant-in-Aid, 85; Princeton Univ Fel, 75-81. **MEMBERSHIPS** MLA; The Henry James Soc; Nat Book Critics Circle; Am Comp Lit Asn; Soc for Cinema Studies; Midwest MLA. **SELECTED PUBLICATIONS** Auth, Henry James's Last Romance: Making Sense of the Past and the American Scene, Cambridge, 97; Passing from Paranoia to Plagiarism: The Abject Authorship of Nella Larsen, Modern Fiction Studies, 97; The Return of the Alien: Henry James on the Lower East Side 1904, Henry James Rev, 95; 'Psychic Mulattos': The Ambiguity of Race, Common Knowledge, 94; Waste Makes Taste: Thorstein Veblen, Henry James, and the Sense of the Past, Int Jour Polit, Culture, Soc, 94; co-auth, Opening the Gap on Depression: From Monotony to Meaning, Psychoanalysis and Contemporary Thought 24:2 (01). **CONTACT ADDRESS** Dept of Comp Lit, Brown Univ, Box E, Providence, RI 02912. **EMAIL** Beverly_Haviland@brown.edu

HAWKINS, JOHN A.
PERSONAL Born 08/10/1947, Liverpool, England, m, 1979, 2 children **DISCIPLINE** SYNTAX, SEMANTICS, HISTORICAL LINGUISTICS AND PSYCHOLINGUISTICS **EDUCATION** Cambridge Univ, PhD. **CAREER** Prof, Univ Southern Calif. **MEMBERSHIPS** LSA, LAGB, ALT. **RESEARCH** Syntax & semantics; historical linguistics; psycholinguistics. **SELECTED PUBLICATIONS** Auth, Definiteness &Indefiniteness, 78; Word Order Universals, 83; Comparative Typology of English and German, 86; ed, Explaining Language Universals, 88; ed, with Murray Gell-Mann, The Evolution of Human Languages, 92; A Performance Theory of Order and Constituency, 94. **CONTACT ADDRESS** Dept of Linguistics, Univ of So California, University Park Campus, Los Angeles, CA 90089. **EMAIL** hawkins@mizar.usc.edu

HAWTHORNE, GERALD F.
PERSONAL Born 08/16/1925, Los Angeles, CA, m, 1955, 3 children **DISCIPLINE** CLASSICAL GREEK, NEW TESTAMENT **EDUCATION** Wheaton Col, Ill, BA, 51, MA, 54; Univ Chicago, PhD, 69. **CAREER** From instr to assoc prof, 53-73, Prof Class Greek & New Testament Exegesis, Wheaton Col, Ill, 73- **MEMBERSHIPS** Am Acad Relig; Soc Bibl Lit; Evangel Theol Soc; Studiorum Novi Testamenti Soc; Inst Bibl Res (treas, 73-). **RESEARCH** Early Christian literature and church history; New Testament studies. **SELECTED PUBLICA-**

TIONS Auth, Chained in Christ--The Experience and Rhetoric of Paul Imprisonments, J Biblical Lit, Vol 0116, 97. **CONTACT ADDRESS** Dept of Bibl and Theol Studies, Archaeol and World Relig, Wheaton Col, Illinois, Wheaton, IL 60187. **EMAIL** gerald.f.hawthorne@wheaton.edu

HAYDAR, ADNAN
DISCIPLINE MODERN AND CLASSICAL ARABIC LITERATURE **EDUCATION** Am Univ Beirut, BA, 63, MA, 68; Univ Calif, PhD, 77. **CAREER** English and Lit, Univ Ark. **HONORS AND AWARDS** Dir, King Fahd Middle East Studies Prog; Ed, Syracuse Univ Press. **SELECTED PUBLICATIONS** Area: modern Arabic literature. **CONTACT ADDRESS** Univ of Arkansas, Fayetteville, Fayetteville, AR 72701.

HAYDEN, GEORGE A.
DISCIPLINE EAST ASIAN LANGUAGES **EDUCATION** Stanford Univ, PhD, 72. **CAREER** Assoc prof, Univ Southern Calif. **RESEARCH** Classical Chinese language; pre-modern Chinese literature. **SELECTED PUBLICATIONS** Auth, Crime and Punishment in Medieval Chinese Drama: Three Judge Pao Plays. **CONTACT ADDRESS** East Asian Languages and Cultures Dept., Univ of So California, University Park, Taper Hall of Humanities 226 A, Los Angeles, CA 90089-0357.

HAYMANN, MARY
PERSONAL Born, CT **DISCIPLINE** FRENCH **EDUCATION** Simmons Col, BA, 66; Rutgers Univ, MA, 84; PhD, 90. **CAREER** Translator, 72-80; teaching asst, Turgers Univ, 81-82; instr, Caldwell Col, 79-86; instr, Rutgers Univ, 90-91; asst to assoc prof, Caldwell Col, 91--. **HONORS AND AWARDS** Jeanne Marandon Grant, 91-92; Am Fel, Am Asn of Univ women, 89-90; Dissertation Res Gran, Rutgers Univ, 88-89. **MEMBERSHIPS** Mod Lang Asn, Am Asn of Univ Women, Societe des Amis de Colette. **RESEARCH** Colette, Autobiography, Interdisciplinary studies. **SELECTED PUBLICATIONS** Co-auth, Alice Parizeau: l'epopee romanesque, Editions Pierre Tisseyre: Montreal, 00; auth, "La Naissance de l'ecriture chez Alice Poznanska Parizeau," in Femme de tous les combats, Montreal, 96; auth, "Identite, langue et liberte: la venue a l'ecriture d'Alice Parizeau," in francographies, 94; auth, "Le quatuor quebecois d'Alice Parizeau," in Francographies, 93; auth, Les Vrilles de la vigne - l'exil fertile," Cahiers colette, 92; auth, "Colette: En Marge d'une page blanche," Bulletin de la Societe des Professeurs Francais et Francophone en Amerique, 90-91; auth, "La Spirale et sa dynamique: La Naissance de l'imaginaire colettien dans les Vrilles de la vigne de Colette, Paris, 90; auth, "Paralleles entre le lisible et le visible: Nathalie Sarraute et Claude Simon," in Bulletin de la Societe des Professeurs Francais et francophone en Amerique, 89-90. **CONTACT ADDRESS** Dept For Lang, Caldwell Col, 9 Ryerson Ave, Caldwell, NJ 07006-6109. **EMAIL** mhaymann@caldwell.edu

HAYNE, DAVID MACKNESS
PERSONAL Born 08/12/1921, Toronto, ON, Canada, m, 1955 **DISCIPLINE** FRENCH **EDUCATION** Univ Toronto, BA, 42; Univ Ottawa, MA, 44, PhD, 45. **CAREER** From lectr to assoc prof, 45-61, registr univ col, 56-61, Prof French to Prof Emer, Univ Toronto, 61-, Mem, Nat Res Coun Can, 42-43; Dir Mil Intel, Dept Nat Defence, 43-45; gen ed, Dictionary Can Biog, 65-69; assoc ed, Univ Toronto Quart, 65-76. **MEMBERSHIPS** Fel Royal Soc Can; Asn Can Univ Teachers Fr; Bibliog Soc Can; Can Ling Asn; Can Comp Lit Asn. **RESEARCH** French-Canadian literature; 17th century French literature. **CONTACT ADDRESS** Dept of French, Univ of Toronto, 50 St Joseph St, 2nd Floor, Toronto, ON, Canada M5S 1J4. **EMAIL** david.hayne@utoronto.ca

HAYNES, HOLLY
PERSONAL Born 11/02/1965, TX **DISCIPLINE** CLASSICS **EDUCATION** Univ Washington, PhD 96. **CAREER** NY Univ, asst prof 95 to 98-. **MEMBERSHIPS** APA **RESEARCH** Critical Theory; Historiography **CONTACT ADDRESS** Dept of Classics, New York Univ, 25 Waverly Pl, 7th Fl, New York, NY 10003. **EMAIL** hh13@is5.nyu.edu

HECHT, LEO
PERSONAL Born 03/16/1927, Vienna, Austria, m, 1954, 1 child **DISCIPLINE** RUSSIAN LANGUAGE & LITERATURE **EDUCATION** Columbia Univ, BS, 60; MA, 61; PhD, 73; Doctorate in the Humanities, Shenandoah Univ, 95. **CAREER** Instr polit sci, US Govt Sch, Dept Defense, 56-60; instr Ger, Univ Md, 69-70; assoc prof Russ & chmn dept foreign lang & lit, 72-80, Fulbright fel to Moscow Univ, 76, 82, 86, 90; ed, Newsnotes on Soviet & E Europ Drama & Theatre; prof and chmn Russian Studies, George Mason Univ, 80-. **MEMBERSHIPS** Am Asn Teachers Slavic & E Europe Lang; MLA. **RESEARCH** Russian cultural history; contemporary Soviet affairs. **SELECTED PUBLICATIONS** Auth, Tolstoy the Rebel, Revisionist Press, 76; auth, The USSR Today, Scholastics, 76; 2nd revised ed, 83; 3rd revised ed 87; auth, The Soviet Union Through Its Laws, Praeger, 83; auth, "Vladimir Vysotskii--Hamlet With a Guitar," Slavic East Europ J, Vol 0037, 93. **CONTACT ADDRESS** Dept of Foreign Lang & Lit, George Mason Univ, Fairfax, 4400 University Dr, Fairfax, VA 22030-4444.

HEGSTROM, VALERIE
PERSONAL Born Boise, ID **DISCIPLINE** SPANISH, COMPARITIVE LITERATURE **EDUCATION** Brigham Young Univ, BA, 82; MA, 86; Kansas Univ, MA, 88; PhD, 92. **CAREER** Instr, 90-92, asst prof, 92-94, UNM; asst prof, 94-98; assoc prof, 98-, Brigham Young Univ., **HONORS AND AWARDS** Res and Trav Gnts, BYU Coll Hum, BYU Wom Res Inst, BYU Kennedy Cen, Cult Coop Prog, UNM Res Alloc Comm. **MEMBERSHIPS** MLA; AATSP; ACLA; ICLA; AHCT; Comediantes. **RESEARCH** Early modern literature, esp theater; early modern woman writers. **SELECTED PUBLICATIONS** Co-ed, Engendering the Early Modern Stage: Woman Playwrights in the Spanish Empire, (New Orleans, Univ Press South, 99); ed and notes, La traicion en la amistad/ Friendship Betrayed, by Maria de Zayas, (Lewisburg, Bucknell Univ Press, 99). **CONTACT ADDRESS** Dept Spanish Portuguese, Brigham Young Univ, PO Box 26119, Provo, UT 84602-6119. **EMAIL** valerie_hegstrom@byu.edu

HEIDEN, BRUCE A.
PERSONAL Born 09/04/1951, Brooklyn, NY, d, 2 children **DISCIPLINE** CLASSICAL PHILOLOGY **EDUCATION** Columbia, BA, 72; Cornell, PhD, 84. **CAREER** Asst prof, 84-80, assoc prof, 90-, Ohio State Univ, 84-. **MEMBERSHIPS** Amer Philol Asn; Brit Class Asn; Class Asn of Midwst & S **RESEARCH** Homer; Greek drama; Cognitive science. **SELECTED PUBLICATIONS** Rev, Journal of Hellenic Studies, 93; auth, Sic te servato: An Interpretation of Propertius 1.21, Class Philol, 95; The Three Movements of the Iliad, Greek, Roman, and Byzantine Studies, 96; The Ordeals of Homeric Song, Arethusa, 97; The Simile of the Fugitive Homicide: Analogy, Foiling and Allusion, Am Jour Philol, 98; The Placement of Book-Divisions in the Iliad, Jour Hellenic Studies, 98. **CONTACT ADDRESS** Dept of Greek & Latin, Ohio State Univ, Columbus, Columbus, OH 43210. **EMAIL** heiden.1@osu.edu

HEIDENREICH, ROSMARIN
DISCIPLINE GERMAN AND ENGLISH LITERATURE **EDUCATION** Moorehead State Univ, BA, 64; Univ Man, MA, 66; Univ Toronto, PhD, 83. **CAREER** Prof, Schiller Univ, Ger, 68-69; prof, Univ Tubingen, Ger, 69; prof, Univ Freiburg, Ger, 69-74; Prof English & Translation, St. Boniface Col, Univ Manitoba, 93-. **HONORS AND AWARDS** Can Coun Doctoral Fel, 76-79. **MEMBERSHIPS** Can Asn Comp Lit; Can Asn Transl Studs. **SELECTED PUBLICATIONS** Auth, The Postwar Novel in Canada: Narrative Patterns and Reader Response, 89; auth, Recent Trends in Franco-Manitoban Fiction and Poetry, in Prairie Fire, 11, 90; auth, Causer l'amour dans le Far-West du Canada, in Poetiques de la Francophonie, 96. **CONTACT ADDRESS** Dept of English, St. Boniface Col, Winnipeg, MB, Canada R2H 0H7. **EMAIL** rheidenr@ustboniface.mb.ca

HEIDSIECK, ARNOLD
PERSONAL Born 02/20/1937, Germany, s **DISCIPLINE** GERMAN **EDUCATION** Free Univ Berlin, PhD, 66. **CAREER** Instr, NY Univ, 66-72; Prof, Stanford Univ, 73-74; Prof, Univ S Calif, 75-. **HONORS AND AWARDS** NEH Summer Fel, 86; DAAD Fel, 89; Fac Res Fund Fel, Univ S Calif, 89. **MEMBERSHIPS** MLA, AATG **RESEARCH** 20th-Century literature, 18th-Century intellectual history, literary semantics. **SELECTED PUBLICATIONS** Auth, Das Groteske & das Absurde im modernen Drama, 69; auth, The Intellectual Contexts of Kafka's Fiction: Philosophy, Law, Religion, 94. **CONTACT ADDRESS** Dept German, Univ of So California, 3501 Trousdale Pkwy, Los Angeles, CA 90089-0091. **EMAIL** heidsiec@usc.edu

HEIMONET, JEAN-MICHEL
PERSONAL Born 05/15/1948, Niort, France, m, 1983, 1 child **DISCIPLINE** FRENCH **EDUCATION** Univ Paris, Doctorat d'Etat, 83. **CAREER** Vis Prof, Univ Washington, 83-85; Asst Prof, Univ NC, 8-88; Assoc Prof to Prof, Catholic Univ, 88-. **RESEARCH** Critical theory; relationships; Literature/Politics/ Society. **SELECTED PUBLICATIONS** Auth, Le Mal a l'oeuvre, Georges Bataille et l'ecriture du sacrifice, Chemin de Ronde, 86; auth, De la revolte a l'exercice: essai sur l'hedonisme contemporain, Summa Pub, 90; auth, Negativite et communication, J-M Place, 90; auth, Politiques du symbole: l'humanisme critique dans la tradition romantique et moderne, Kime, 93; auth, Tocqueville et le devenir de la democratie: la perversion de l'ideal, Paris, 99; auth, Pourquoi Bataille? Trajets intellectuels et politiques d'une negativite au chomage, Paris, 00; auth, Le Mysticisme seculier, Editions Le Seuil, in press. **CONTACT ADDRESS** Dept Mod Lang, Catholic Univ of America, 620 Mich Ave NE, Washington, DC 20064-0001. **EMAIL** heimonet@netkonnect.net

HEINEMANN, EDWARD ARTHUR
PERSONAL Born 09/16/1941, New York, NY, m, 1964, 2 children **DISCIPLINE** FRENCH **EDUCATION** Hamilton Col, AB, 63; Princeton Univ, MA, 66, PhD(French), 70. **CAREER** From lectr to asst prof, 66-74, Assoc Prof French, Univ Toronto, 74- **MEMBERSHIPS** MLA; Soc Rencesvals; Medieval Acad Am. **RESEARCH** Chanson de geste; history of the French language. **SELECTED PUBLICATIONS** Auth, L'art metrique de la chanson de geste, Essai sur la musicalite du recit, Publications Romanes et Francaises, 205, Geneva: Droz, 93; auth, "Mapping Echoes in the Charroi de Nimes with the Aid of the Computer" in Significations: Essais en l'honneur d'Henry Schogt/Essays in honour of Henry/Schogt, Parth Bhatt, ed. (Toronto: Canadian Scholars' Press, 1997): 77-86; auth, "Patterns of Narrative and Poetic Organization in the Kernel William Cycle", Reading Around the Epic: A Festschrift in Honour of Professor Wolfgang van Emden, eds., Marianne Ailes, Philip E. Bennett and Karen Pratt, King's College London Medieval Studies, XIV, King's College London Centre for Late Antique & Medieval Studies, (98): 249-267; auth, "Laisse and Echo in the Opening Scence of the Prise d'Orange as Found in the Three Verse Versions (Toward a History of the Metric Art of the Chanson de geste)" in Echoes of the Epic: Studies in Honor of Gerard J. Grault (98). **CONTACT ADDRESS** Dept of French, Univ of Toronto, 50 St Joseph St, 2nd Fl, Toronto, ON, Canada M5S 1J4. **EMAIL** heineman@atschass.utoronto.ca

HEINEN, HUBERT
PERSONAL Born 03/05/1937, Houston, TX, m, 1959, 3 children **DISCIPLINE** GERMAN LANGUAGE & LITERATURE **EDUCATION** Univ Tex, BA, 58, PhD(Ger), 64. **CAREER** Instr, Univ of Penn, 63-64; asst prof, Univ of Pitts, 64-68; assoc prof, Univ of Pitts, 68-69; vis prof, Die deutsche Sommerschule von New Mexico; assoc prof, The Univ of Tex at Austin, 69-90; prof, The Univ of Tex at Austin, 90-; prof, The Univ of Texas at Austin, 90- **HONORS AND AWARDS** Univ Fel, The Univ of Texas, 61-62; Fel, Southeastern Medieval Instit, Durham, NC, 76; Two-Week Summer Seminar by Goethe Instit in Berlin, 84; Fac Res Assignment, The Univ of Texas at Austin, 85. **MEMBERSHIPS** MLA; Am Asn Teachers Ger; Scent Mod Lang Asn; Medieval Acad Am. **RESEARCH** Middle and Early New High German language and literature; German-American cultural history. **SELECTED PUBLICATIONS** Auth, Die ryhthmisch-metrische Gestaltung des Knittelverses bei Hans Folz, Marburger Beitrage zur Germanistik 12, Marbug: Elwert, 66; coauth, Paths to German Poetry: An Introductory Anthology, with Lore B. Foltin, New York: Dodd, Mead, Harper & Row, 69; coauth, Basic Spoken German Grammar, with J. Alan Pfeffer et al, Englewood Cliffs, NJ: Prentice Hall, 74; coauth, Basic Spoken German Grammar: Workbook and Guide to Tapes, with J. Alan Pfeffer, Englewood Cliffs, NJ: Prentice Hall, 75; coed, Bertolt Brecht: Political Theory and Literary Practice, with Betty Nance Weber, Athens, Georgia: U of George P, 80; coed, Thomas Brunner, Isaac, with Wolfgang F. Michael, Bern: Peter Lang, 83; coed, Genres in Medieval German Literature, Goppinger Arbeiten zur Germmanistik 439, with Ingeborg Henderson, Goppingen: Kummerle, 86; auth, Mutabilitat im Minnesang: mehrfach uberlieferte Lieder des 12. Und fruhen 13. Jahrhunderts, Goppinger Arbeiten zur Germanistik 515. Goppingen: Kummerle, 89. **CONTACT ADDRESS** Dept of Ger Lang, Univ of Texas, Austin, Austin, TX 78712-1026. **EMAIL** hubert.heinen@mail.utexas.edu

HEINRICH, AMY VLADECK
PERSONAL Born 06/05/1945, New York, NY, m, 1965, 2 children **DISCIPLINE** JAPANESE & COMPARATIVE LITERATURE **EDUCATION** Columbia Univ, BA, 67, MA, 76, PhD(Japanese lit), 80. **CAREER** Lectr East Asian Studies, Columbia Univ, 80-, Res assoc, East Asian Inst, Columbia Univ, 80-81; consult, Nat Humanities Fac, 80-81. **MEMBERSHIPS** Asn Asian Studies; Am Comp Lit Asn. **RESEARCH** Modern Japanese poetry; women's literature: Japanese & English; comparative literature: Japanese, Chinese, English. **SELECTED PUBLICATIONS** Auth, My mother is dying: Saito Mokichi's Shinitamau haha, Monumenta Nipponica, winter 78; Ame furihajimu: 5 poems, 2/79, Furusato: 6 poems, 8/79, & Hyakuendama no tsuki: 15 poems, 80, Uchufu; ed, Contemporary Japan: A Teaching Workbook, East Asian Inst, Columbia Univ, 81; auth, Tanka no kozo o megutte, Uchufu, 10-12/81; Blown in flurries: The role of Waka in Ukifune, In: Ukifune: Love in The Tale of Genji, 82 & Fragements of Rainbows: The Life and Poetry of Saito Mokichi (in press), Columbia Univ Press. **CONTACT ADDRESS** Columbia Univ, 250 W Broadway, New York, NY 10013.

HELBLING, ROBERT E.
PERSONAL Born 05/06/1923, Lucerne, Switzerland, m, 1956 **DISCIPLINE** GERMAN & FRENCH LITERATURE **EDUCATION** Univ Utah, MA, 49; Stanford Univ, PhD, 59. **CAREER** Instr Ger & French, Univ Utah, 50-53; asst, Stanford Univ, 53-55; from instr to assoc prof, 55-66, traveling scholar, 61 & 63, honrs dir, 64-66, chmn dept lang, 65-77, Prof Ger & French, Univ Utah, 66- **MEMBERSHIPS** MLA; Asn Depts Foreign Lang (pres, 74). **RESEARCH** Modern German and French literature, especially existentialist literature; Heinrich von Kleist. **SELECTED PUBLICATIONS CONTACT ADDRESS** Dept of Lang, Univ of Utah, Orson Spencer Hall, Salt Lake City, UT 84112-8916.

HELD, DIRK
PERSONAL Born 03/24/1939, New York, NY, m, 1962, 2 children **DISCIPLINE** CLASSICS **EDUCATION** Brown **CAREER** Instr Classics and Inst for Lib Arts, Emory Univ, 68-71; asst prof to prof of Classics, Conn Col, 71-; NEH fel for Interrelations Sci and Hum, 74-75. **HONORS AND AWARDS** Univ fel philos, Univ Penn, 66-67; NEH fel for Interrelations Sci and Hum, 74-75. **MEMBERSHIPS** Am Philol Asn; Soc

Ancient Greek Philos; Int Soc Classical Tradition. **RESEARCH** Greek philosophy; Classical tradition 18th-19th Century. **SELECTED PUBLICATIONS** Auth Why Individuals didn't exist in classical Antiquity, N Eng Classical Newsl & Jour, 91; Megalopsychia in Nicomachean Ethics IV, Ancient Philos, 93; Bernard Williams Shame and Necessity, Int Jour Philos Stud, 95; Shaping Eurocentrism: The Uses of Greek Antiquity, Greeks and Barbarians: Essays on the Interactions between Greeks and Non-Greeks in Antiquity and the Consequences of Eurocentrism, CDL Press, 97; Plato and Aristotle on Memory, Knowledge and the Self, Memory, History and Critique, European Identity at the Millenium, Proceedings of the Fifth Conference of the International Society for the Study of European Ideas, Utrecht, 98. **CONTACT ADDRESS** Classics Dept, Connecticut Col, 270 Mohegan Ave, New London, CT 06320. **EMAIL** dthel@conncoll.edu

HELFANT, IAN M.
DISCIPLINE RUSSIAN **EDUCATION** Harvard Univ, BS, 86, MA, 92, PhD, 96. **CAREER** Vis asst prof, Williams Col,97-98. **HONORS AND AWARDS** Mellon fel, 89-91, 94-95; USIA/ACTR Res Scholar in Petersburg, 94; FLAS fel, 90-91, 92-93; Harvard Frederick Sheldon Traveling fel in Eastern Europe, 86-87. **RESEARCH** 19th-century Russian literature; cultural and gender studies; Autobiographical genres; reader response and risk theory. **SELECTED PUBLICATIONS** Auth, Sculpting a Persona: The Path from Pushkin's Caucasian journal to Puteshestvie v Arzrum, Russ Rev, 97. **CONTACT ADDRESS** Center for Foreign Languages, Literatures and Cult, Williams Col, Williamstown, MA 01267. **EMAIL** Ian.M.Helfant@williams.edu

HELGERSON, RICHARD
PERSONAL Born Pasadena, CA, m, 1967, 1 child **DISCIPLINE** ENGLISH & COMP LIT **EDUCATION** Johns Hopkins Univ, PhD, 70. **CAREER** Prof, Eng, Univ Calif, Santa Barbara, Dept Chair 89-93. **HONORS AND AWARDS** Woodrow Wilson Fellowship, 63-63; NEH Fellowship, 79-80; 98-99; Huntington Library Fellowship, 84-85; Guggenheim Fellowship, 86; Folger Library Fellowship, 93-94; James Russell Lowell Prize, 94; British Council Prize in the Humanities 94; UCSB Faculty Research Lecturer 98; VC President's Fellowship 98-99. **MEMBERSHIPS** Modern Language Association; Renaissance Society of America, International Spenser Society; Shakespeare Association of America; North American Conference on British Studies. **RESEARCH** Early mod Europ drama and paint; Renaissance lit and cult. **SELECTED PUBLICATIONS** Auth, The Elizabethan Prodigals, Univ Calif Press, 77; Self-Crowned Laureates: Spenser, Jonson, Milton, and the Literary System, Univ Calif Press, 83; Tasso on Spenser: The Politics of Chivalric Romance, Yrbk Eng Stud, 88; "Writing Against Writing: Humanism and the Form of Coke's Institutes," Mod Lang Quart, 92; "Camoes, Hakluyt, and the Voyages of Two Nations," Cult and Colonial, 92; Forms of Nationhood, Univ Chicago Press, 92; Doing Literary History on a Large Scale, Eng Stud and Hist, 94; auth Adulterous Alliances: Home, State, and History in Early Modern European Drama and Painting, Univ Chicago Press, 00. **CONTACT ADDRESS** Dept of Eng, Univ of California, Santa Barbara, Santa Barbara, CA 93106-7150. **EMAIL** rhelgers@humanitas.ucsb.edu

HELGUERO, GRACE
PERSONAL Born 06/05/1957, New York, NY, s **DISCIPLINE** SPANISH **EDUCATION** St John's Univ, BA, 79; NYU, BA, 82; Univ Salamanca, PhD. **CAREER** Instr and curriculum develop, Fla Lang Center, 96-99; asst prof, Broward Cmty Col, 99-00; asst prof, Lynn Univ, 00-. **HONORS AND AWARDS** Who's Who in the South and SW, 96-97; Who's Who in Educ, 95-96; Who's Who of am Women, 96; Broward Prop Appraisers Serv Award, 00. **MEMBERSHIPS** ACTFL; AATSP; TESOL; AATI; BEC; MLA; Inst Cervantes. **RESEARCH** Miguel de Unamuno - works (novels and theater); Pedagogy - ESL/Foreign language; 20th Century History, Politicis and Literature in Spain; Curriculum Development in ESL, ESP, Foreign Languages - Spanish, Italian. **SELECTED PUBLICATIONS** Auth, Explorando La Gramatica Castellana: apuntes y Ejercicios. **CONTACT ADDRESS** Dept Lang, Lynn Univ, 6350 Longboat Ln W, Boca Raton, FL 33433-8082. **EMAIL** ghelguero@lynn.edu

HELLENBRAND, HAROLD
DISCIPLINE EARLY AMERICAN LITERATURE, WORLD LITERATURES **EDUCATION** Stanford Univ, PhD. **CAREER** Prof, Dean, Col Liberal Arts, Univ Minn, Duluth. **SELECTED PUBLICATIONS** Auth, The Unfinished Revolution: Education and Politics in the Thought of Thomas Jefferson, Univ Del Press, 89. **CONTACT ADDRESS** Dept of Eng, California Polytech State Univ, San Luis Obispo, San Luis Obispo, CA 93433. **EMAIL** hhellenb@calpoly.edu

HELLER, JANET
PERSONAL Born 07/08/1949, Milwaukee, WI, m, 1982 **DISCIPLINE** ENGLISH, LITERATURE, LINGUISTICS, CREATIVE WRITING, WOMEN'S STUDIES **EDUCATION** Oberlin Col, 67-70; Univ Wis at Madison, BA, 71; MA, 73; Univ Chicago, PhD, 87. **CAREER** Ed, Primavera, 73-92; coord of the Writing Prog, Univ of Chicago, 76-81; instr, Northern Ill Univ, 82-88; asst prof, Nazareth Col, 89-90; asst prof, Grand Valley State Univ, 90-97; asst prof, Albion Col, 98; asst prof, Western Mich Univ, 99-. **HONORS AND AWARDS** Winner, Friends of Poetry Contest, Kalamazoo, 89; listed in Directory of Am Poets & Fiction Writers, 79-. **MEMBERSHIPS** MLA, Mich Col English Asn, Soc for the Study of Midwestern Lit. **RESEARCH** Nineteenth-Century British Literature, Contemporary American Poetry, Prose Non-fiction, the Drama, Linguistics Applied to Literature, Women's Studies (Women Writers, Literature & Social Sciences, American Literature Since 1800). **SELECTED PUBLICATIONS** Auth, Coleridge, Lamb, Hazlitt, and the Reader of Drama, 90; articles have appeared in Poetics, Concerning Poetry, Lan and Style, Theatre J, Shakespeare Bulletin, The Eighteenth Century, PBSA, Libr Quart, Twentieth Century Lit, and others; poetry has appeared in Anima, Cottonwood, Organic Gardening, Ky Poetry Rev, Earth's Daughters, Lilith, Modern Maturity, and others. **CONTACT ADDRESS** Dept English, Western Michigan Univ, 1201 Oliver St, Kalamazoo, MI 49008-3804. **EMAIL** janet.heller@wmich.edu

HELLERSTEIN, NINA
PERSONAL Born 03/29/1946, New York, NY, m, 1970, 2 children **DISCIPLINE** FRENCH **EDUCATION** Univ Chicago, MA, 69; PhD, 74. **CAREER** Adj Asst Prof, Baruch Col, 74-75; vis Asst Prof, Vassar Col, 75-76; Instr, Rosary Col, 76-78; Instr, Roosevelt Univ, 76-78; Asst Prof to Prof, Univ Ga, 78-. **HONORS AND AWARDS** Phi Beta Kappa, 68; Ford Foundation Fel, 68-72; Grants, Univ Ga, 82, 85, 91. **MEMBERSHIPS** AATF, SAMLA, MMLA, NEMLA, MLA, Paul Claudel Soc, Soc Paul Claudel, women in French, Simone de Beauvoir Soc, Conseil Intl des Etudes Francophones. **RESEARCH** Modern French poetry; Paul Claudel; Francophone literature; French and francophone women writers; French cinema; Asia in French literature; Art; Music and Literature. **SELECTED PUBLICATIONS** Auth, "Narrative Innovation and the construction of Self in Marguerite Andoux's Marie-Claire," French Review, (95): 246-254; auth, "L'Ecriture des Conversations dans le Loir-et-Cher de Paul Claudel," in Ecritures Claudeliennes: Actes du Colloque de Besancon, 97; auth, "Food and the Female Existentialist Body in L'Invitee," French Forum, (97): 203-215.; auth, "Phenomenology and Ekphrasis in Claudel's Connaissance de l'Est," Nottingham French Studies, (97): 34-44; auth, "Violence, Mythe et Destin dans l'Univers Antillais de Gisele Pineau," LitteRealite , (98): 47-58; auth, "Phenomenological Structures in Duras's Cinema: the Universe of Nathalie Granger," Dalhousie French Studies, (98): 135-146; auth, "The Aesthetics of the Oriental Gardenin Claudel's Connaissance de l'Est," Claudel Studies, (99): 43-54. **CONTACT ADDRESS** Dept Romance Lang, Univ of Georgia, Athens, GA 30602-1815. **EMAIL** hellerst@arches.uga.edu

HELM, JAMES JOEL
PERSONAL Born 12/17/1937, Chicago, IL, m, 1960, 2 children **DISCIPLINE** CLASSICAL STUDIES **EDUCATION** Elmhurst Col, BA, 59; Union Theol Sem, MDiv, 63; Univ Mich, Ann Arbor, MA, 65, PhD(class studies), 68. **CAREER** Instr class studies, Univ Mich, Ann Arbor, 66-68; asst prof, 68-74, chmn dept, 76-82, 90-96, Assoc Prof Classics, Oberlin Col, 74-82, Prof 82-, Vis assoc prof classics, Scripps Col, 78-79; assoc dean, Oberlin Col, 86-89, Actg Dean, 91-92, 96-. **MEMBERSHIPS** Am Philol Asn; Archaeol Inst Am; Class Asn Mid West & South. **RESEARCH** Greek paleography; computer applications in classical studies; poetry of Catullus. **SELECTED PUBLICATIONS** Auth, Koros--From Satisfaction to Greed, Classical World, Vol 0087, 93. **CONTACT ADDRESS** Dept of Classics, Oberlin Col, 135 W Lorain St, Oberlin, OH 44074-1076. **EMAIL** james.helm@oberlin.edu

HELMETAG, CHARLES HUGH
PERSONAL Born 04/07/1935, Camden, NJ, m, 1959, 2 children **DISCIPLINE** GERMAN **EDUCATION** Univ Pa, BA, 57; Univ Ky, MA, 59; Princeton Univ, PhD(Ger), 68. **CAREER** Instr, Ger Purdue Univ, 60-62; asst prof, 64-75, assoc prof, 75-80, Prof Ger, Villanova Univ, 80-, Chmn Dept Mod Lang, 73-, **MEMBERSHIPS** Am Asn Teachers Ger; MLA; AAUP; Northeast Mod Lang Asn. **RESEARCH** Nineteenth and 20th century German literature; German film. **SELECTED PUBLICATIONS** Auth, Recapturing the 1950s in Schlondorff,Volker Film Adaptation of 'Homo Faber', Germanic Notes Rev, Vol 0027, 96. **CONTACT ADDRESS** Dept of Mod Lang & Lit, Villanova Univ, 845 E Lancaster Ave, Villanova, PA 19085.

HELZLE, MARTIN
PERSONAL Born 08/17/1961, Stuttgart, Germany, m, 1987, 3 children **DISCIPLINE** CLASSICS **EDUCATION** Univ of Leeds, BA, 83; Univ of Cambridge, PhD, 88. **CAREER** Univ of Bristol, 80-87; Univ Wales, 87-88; Cleveland State Univ, 89, part time; John Carroll Univ, 89, part time; asst prof, 89-95; assoc prof, 96-, Case Western Reserve Univ. **HONORS AND AWARDS** Jopson research fel; RIG from State of Ohio; Humboldt Fel. **MEMBERSHIPS** APA; CAMWS; OCC; Mommsengesellschaft. **RESEARCH** Latin Poetry **SELECTED PUBLICATIONS** Auth, P Ouidii Nasonis Epistualarum ex Ponto liber IV: A commentary on Poems 1-7 and 16, 89; auth, Die Charakterisierung Scipios in Silius Italicus' Classica et Mediaevalia, 95; auth, Der Stil ist der Mensch, Redner und Reden im romischen Epos, 96. **CONTACT ADDRESS** Dept of Classics, Case Western Reserve Univ, 10900 Euclid Ave, Cleveland, OH 44106-7111. **EMAIL** mxh13@po.cwru.edu

HEMAND, JOST
PERSONAL Born 04/11/1930, Kassel, Germany, m, 1956 **DISCIPLINE** GERMAN LITERATURE, HISTORY, PHILOSOPHY **EDUCATION** Univ Marburg, Ger, PhD, 55. **CAREER** From Asst Prof to Vilas Res Prof, Univ Wis, 58-. **HONORS AND AWARDS** ACLS Fel, 63; Vilas Res Prof, 67; Mem of Saxon Acad, 85. **RESEARCH** German Culture 1750 to the Present, German-Jewish History, Comparative Arts, Fascism and Exile. **SELECTED PUBLICATIONS** Auth, Judentum und deutsche Kultur, 96; auth, A Hitler Youth to Poland, 97; auth, Deutsche Diditer bunde, 98; auth, Formen des Eses tu der Kunst, 00. **CONTACT ADDRESS** Dept German, Univ of Wisconsin, Madison, 1230 Linden Dr, Van Hise Hall, Madison, WI 53706-1525.

HENDERSON, CHARLES, JR.
PERSONAL Born 08/22/1923, Lynchburg, VA, m, 1944, 5 children **DISCIPLINE** CLASSICS **EDUCATION** Davidson Col, AB, 42; UNC Chapel, MA, 46; PhD, 50. **CAREER** Instr, NYU, 50-55; asst prof, assoc prof, dean, UNC Chapel, 55-62; prof, asst pres, emeritus, Smith Col, 64-. **HONORS AND AWARDS** Fulbright, 53; Phi Beta Kappa, 42. **MEMBERSHIPS** APA; CANE; MAA. **RESEARCH** Ancient rhetoric; Latin literature. **SELECTED PUBLICATIONS** Co-auth, Latin for Americans, Macmillan, 68; McGraw Hill, 90; ed, Classical, Mediaeval and Renaissance Studies in honor of B. L. Ullman, Edizioni di Storia a Letteratura, 63; asst ed, Humanities in the South, 58-61; auth, "Cato's Pine Cone," TAPhA 86 (55): 256-67; auth, "The Career of the Younger Marcus Aemilius Scaurus," CJ 53 (58): 194-206; auth, "Quorum Parva Fui," TAPhA 130 (00). **CONTACT ADDRESS** 2 Dabney Lane, York Harbor, ME 03911. **EMAIL** chmn@cybertours.com

HENDERSON, JEFFREY
PERSONAL Born 06/21/1946, Montclair, NJ, m, 1996 **DISCIPLINE** CLASSICS **EDUCATION** Kenyon Col, BA, 68; Harvard Univ, MA, 70, PhD, 72. **CAREER** Asst prof, 72-78, Yale Univ; assoc prof, 78-82, Univ Mich; prof, 82-91, USC; prof, chmn, 91-, Boston Univ. **HONORS AND AWARDS** LHD, Kenyon Col, 94; Guggenheim fel, 97-98. **MEMBERSHIPS** APA; Asn of Literary Scholars & Critics. **RESEARCH** Greek lit, esp. drama; textual criticism. **SELECTED PUBLICATIONS** Auth, The Maculate Muse: Obscene Language in Attic Comedy, Yale Univ Press, 75, Oxford Univ Press, 90; auth, Aristophanes: Essays in Interpretation, contr ed, Yale Classical Studies XXVI, Cambridge Univ Press, 80; ed with intro and commentary, Aristophanes Lysistrara, Clarendon Press, 87, 90; ed and transl, Aristophanes, Loeb Class Lib, Harvard Univ Press, 98. **CONTACT ADDRESS** Dept of Classical Studies, Boston Univ, 745 Commonwealth Ave, Boston, MA 02215. **EMAIL** jhenders@bu.edu

HENRY, ERIC PUTNAM
PERSONAL Born 03/15/1943, Greensboro, NC, m, 1976, 3 children **DISCIPLINE** CHINESE LITERATURE & HISTORY **EDUCATION** Amherst Col, BA, 72; Yale Univ, Mph, 76, PhD, 79. **CAREER** Vis asst prof Chinese lang & lit, Dartmouth Col, 80-82; Lectr Chinese Lang, Univ NC, 82- . **MEMBERSHIPS** Asn Asian Studies; Warring States Project. **RESEARCH** Chinese drama and fiction; Chinese legendary history; Chinese social history; Vietnamese lang, lit, and hist. **SELECTED PUBLICATIONS** Auth, Chinese Amusement: The Lively Plays of Li Yu, Shoe String Press, 80; auth, "The Motif of Recognition in Early China,: Harvard Journal of Asiatic Stud, 47:1, 87; auth, "Chu-ko Liang in the Eyes of His Contemporaries," Harvard Journal of Asiatic Stud 52.2, 92; auth, "Junzi Yue Varsus Zhongni Yeu in Zuo Zhuan," Harvard Journal of Asiatic Stud 59.1, 99; auth, "The Social Significance of Nudity in Early China," Fashion Theory 3.4, 99. **CONTACT ADDRESS** Asian Studies Curric, Univ of No Carolina, Chapel Hill, Campus Box 3267, Chapel Hill, NC 27514. **EMAIL** henryhme@bellsouth.net

HENRY, FREEMAN GEORGE
PERSONAL Born 09/08/1942, Pontiac, MI, m, 1999, 1 child **DISCIPLINE** FRENCH COMPARATIVE LITERATURE, COMPARATIVE LITERATURE **EDUCATION** Ashland Col, BA, 64; Wash State Univ, MA, 66; Univ Colo, PhD(French), 73. **CAREER** Asst prof, English, Lycee Janson de Sailly, Paris, 67-68; from instr to asst prof French, Univ Ga, 70-77; asst prof, 77-80, assoc prof, French, Univ SC, 80-87, Grad Dir, 82-; Assoc ed, Fr Lit Ser, 79- **HONORS AND AWARDS** Sarah H Moss Fel, 72-73; NEH Inst Fel, 93; USC Class Fel, 00. **MEMBERSHIPS** MLA; Am Asn Teachers Fr; SAtlantic Mod Lang Asn. **RESEARCH** Nineteenth century French literature; French poetry and theatre. **SELECTED PUBLICATIONS** Auth, "Les Fleurs du Mal and the Onomastics of Religion", Lit Onomastics Studies, 83; auth, Les Fleurs expliques, Rodopi, 83; auth, Le Message4 humaniste des Fleus du Mal, Nized, 84; auth, Le Debut du Me chapitre de Mademoiselle de Maupin, Bul Soc t. Galtier, 85; auth, Historical Synthesis in 'Les Fleurs du Mal,' Cin Rom Rev, 85; transl, the Caretakers, Viking-

Penguin, 88; authauth, A Case of Questionalble Motives: T Gautier and 'La Gaze he des Femms,' Bul Soc T. Gautier, 94; auth, Twenty Years of French Criticism, Summer 94; auth, T. Gauteier: enluminures et dans macabre, Bul Soc T. Gautier, 96; auth, Gautier/Baudelaire: homo ludens versus homo duplex, 19th Cent Fr Studies, 96. **CONTACT ADDRESS** Dept French & Classics, Univ of So Carolina, Columbia, Columbia, SC 29208. **EMAIL** henryf@sc.edu

HENS, GREGOR
PERSONAL Born 11/25/1965, Cologne, Germany **DISCIPLINE** GERMAN **EDUCATION** Univ MO-Columbia, MA, 91; Univ Calif, Berkeley, PhD, 95. **CAREER** Asst prof, Ohio State Univ, 95-. **MEMBERSHIPS** MLA; LSA; Soc Germanic Philol. **RESEARCH** Germanic linguistics (syntax, semantics, pragmatics); contemporary German/Austrian literature. **SELECTED PUBLICATIONS** Auth, art, The Definition of a Grammatical Category: Gothic Absolute Constructions, 95; auth, art, (jm) einen Brief schreiben: Zur Valenz in der Konstruktionsgrammatik, 96; auth, art, Constructional Semantics in Germany: The Dative of Inaction, 97; auth, art, What Drives Herbeck? Schizophrenia, Immediacy, and the Poetic Process, 99, auth, Thomas Bernhards Triligie der Kunste: Der Untergeher, Holzfallen, Alte Meister, 99. **CONTACT ADDRESS** 314 Cunz Hall, Columbus, OH 43210-1229. **EMAIL** gregor@hens.net

HENSEY, FREDERICK GERALD
PERSONAL Born 10/30/1931, Albany, NY, m, 1956, 2 children **DISCIPLINE** LINGUISTICS **EDUCATION** Univ Am, MEX, BA, 56; Univ TX, Austin, PhD, 67. **CAREER** Teaching asst English, Univ Nacional Autonoma, MEX, 60-62; vis prof ling, Pontificia Cath Univ, Brazil, 65; Prof Span & Port, Univ Tx, Austin, 66-; Vis prof ling, Vanderbilt Univ, Nashville, 68, Tulane Univ, New Orleans, 69, Univ los Andes, Bogota, 77, Universidad Autonoma de Guadalajara, MEX, 93, 96; Fulbright Comn sr lectr, Colombia, 77; Univ Mobile, Latin Am Campus, San Marcos, Nicaragua, 98; Vis Prof, National Yunlin Univ of Sci and Tech, Taiwan, 00. **MEMBERSHIPS** Am Asn Teachers Span & Port; Ling Soc Am; Asoc Latinoam Ling Filol; Universala Esperanto-Asocio; North Am Catalan Soc; Am Translators Asn; Nat Asn of Judiciary Translators and Interpreters; Am Soc of Interpreters; Asn de Linguistica y Filologia de la America Latina. **RESEARCH** Sociological linguistics; general Romance linguistics; translation; Professional interpreter education. **SELECTED PUBLICATIONS** Coauth, Modern Portuguese: A Project of the Modern Language Association (and Accompanying Teacher's Guide), Random House & Knopf, 70; auth, Portuguese inflectional morphology, Lang Quart, 71; The Sociolinguistics of the Brazilian Uruguayan Border, Mouton, 72; Portuguese Vowel Alternations in Casagrande and Saciuk: Generative Studies in Romance Linguistics, Newbury House, 72; Grammatical variation in Southwestern United States Spanish, Linguistics, The Hague, 73; Toward a grammatical analysis of Southwestern Spanish, In: Studies in Southwestern Bilingualism, Newbury House, 76; coauth, Three Essays on Linguistic Diversity in the Spanish-Speaking World, Mouton, 76; co-ed, Contemporary Studies in Romance Linguistics, Georgetown Univ, 77. **CONTACT ADDRESS** Dept of Span & Port, Univ of Texas, Austin, Austin, TX 78712-1026. **EMAIL** f.hensey@mail.utexas.edu

HENTON, CAROLINE G.
DISCIPLINE PHONETICS **EDUCATION** Univ E Anglia, England, BA, 76; Royal Soc Arts, MA, 78; Univ Oxford, MPhil, 82; Univ Ozford, PhD, 85. **CAREER** Dir, Lang Dev, Voice Proc Corp, 95-96; Dir, DECtalk Ling Dev, Digital Equip Corp, 96-96; consult, Claris Corp, Digital Equip Corp, 97-98; VPRES, STRATEGIC TECH, FONIX CORP, 98-. **HONORS AND AWARDS** National Science Foundaation Travel, 87-90, Apple Scholar Incentive Awards, 91-93 **RESEARCH** Product development in speech technology **CONTACT ADDRESS** 160 Commonwealth Ave, #406, Boston, MA 02116. **EMAIL** henton@ling.ucsc.edu

HERIQUE, EMMANUEL
DISCIPLINE FRENCH LITERATURE; LINGUISTICS **EDUCATION** Univ Nancy II, PhD. **CAREER** Fac, Univ of Victoria. **RESEARCH** Irregularities in language; phonetics and phonology; linguistic readings of literary texts. **SELECTED PUBLICATIONS** Auth, A Case Study of the Emergence and Evolution of an Interjection in the French Language, Proc of the Fourteenth Intl Cong of Ling, Akademie-Verlag, 87; auth, "Les mots de l'oubli: les interjections," Actualite scientifique: La memoie des mots, Montreal, Proceedings of the Veme Journees Scientifiques, (97), 627-35; auth, "L'evaluation des professeus de langue a l'univesite de Victoria," Les langues modernes, Paris: Association des Professeus de Langues Vivantes, (98), 66-75. **CONTACT ADDRESS** Dept of French, Univ of Victoria, PO Box 3045 STN CSC, Victoria, BC, Canada V8W 3P4. **EMAIL** herique@uvic.ca

HERMANN, E. C.
PERSONAL Born 10/13/1930, Argentina, m, 1956, 3 children **DISCIPLINE** SPANISH LITERATURE **EDUCATION** Univ BsAs Argentina, MS 57; Occidental Col, MA honors 77, life tchg cred 78. **CAREER** Sweet Briar Col, vis asst prof 89-96, vis assoc prof, 98-; Randolph-Macon Woman's Col, act assoc prof 96-97; Lynchburg Col asst prof, assoc prof, 88 to 98-; Col of William and Mary, asst prof 87-88; High Point Acad, prof 84-87; Flintridge Sacred Heart Acad, lang Dept ch 78-83; Occidental Col, inst 76-78; Northwestern Univ, lectr 68-72. **HONORS AND AWARDS** Jessie Ball duPont Sem Participant; James A Huston Excel Sch Awd Nom; LCVA Fac Gnts. **MEMBERSHIPS** AATSP; NEMLA; MACLAS; AHI; LASA; MIFLIC. **RESEARCH** Literary works produced by contemporary Argentine Women writers. **SELECTED PUBLICATIONS** Auth, Contemporary Argentinean Women Writers, co-ed, Univ Press Florida, 98; Viajes en la palabra y en la imagen, ed, Buenos Aries, Ediciones de Arte Gaglianone, 96; Escritoras Argentinas Contemporaneas, co-ed, U of Texas, Stud in Contemporary Spanish-Amer, NY, Peter Lang, 93; La utopia de escribir, Alina Diaconu Los devorados, Alba de Amer, 96; Exilios internos: El viage en cinco escritoras argentinas, coauth, Hispanic Jour, 94; Francisca Lopez, Mito y discurso ed la novela femenina de posguerra en Espana, ed, Hispanic Jour, forthcoming; Anibal Gonzalez, ed, Jour and the Development of Spanish Amer Narrative, Revista Iberoaamerica, 96; Doris Meyer, Interpreting the Spanish American Essay, Chasqui, 95; Teresa Mendez-Faith, Breve diccionario de la literature paraguaya, Hispanic Jour, 95. **CONTACT ADDRESS** Dept of Spanish, Lynchburg Col, 3172 Woodcreek Dr, Charlottesville, VA 22911. **EMAIL** herman@sbc.edu

HERMINGHOUSE, PATRICIA A.
PERSONAL Born 03/13/1940, IL, m, 1964, 2 children **DISCIPLINE** GERMAN STUDIES, LANGUAGE **EDUCATION** Knox Col, BA, 62; Wash Univ, MA, PhD, 63-68. **CAREER** Asst prof, Univ Mo, 66-67; asst prof, Wash Univ, 67-83; prof, Univ Rochester, 83-. **HONORS AND AWARDS** Karl F./Bertha A. Fuchs Prof; NEH Fel, 91; Fulbright Fel, 62-63; IREX Fel, 76. **MEMBERSHIPS** GSA; MLA; WIG; AATG. **RESEARCH** Women in literary history; German political emigres in the US; history of German feminism; literature; history and politics in east-west German relations. **SELECTED PUBLICATIONS** Co-ed, Literatur und Literatur Theorie in der DDR, Suhrkamp, 76; co-ed, Literatur der DDR in den Siebziger Jahren, Suhrkamp, 83; ed, Frauen im Mittelpunkt: Contemporary German Women, Suhrkamp, 87; co-ed, Women in German Yearbook, vol 11-17, Univ Neb Pr, 95-01; co-ed, Gender and Germaness: Cultural Construction of Nation, Berghahn, 97; co-ed, ed, Ingeborg Bachman and Christa Wolf, Continuum, 98; auth, Teaching German in Twentieth Century America, Univ Wis Pr, 99; co-ed, German Feminist Writings, Continuum, 01; auth, The German American Encounter: Conflict and Cooperation Between Two Cultures, Berghahn, 01. **CONTACT ADDRESS** Dept Mod Lang Cult, Univ of Rochester, PO Box 270082, Rochester, NY 14627-0082. **EMAIL** pahe@troi.cc.rochester.edu

HERNADI, PAUL
PERSONAL Born 11/09/1936, Budapest, Hungary, m, 1964, 2 children **DISCIPLINE** COMPARATIVE LITERATURE **EDUCATION** Univ Vienna, PhD, Hist of Theater, 63; Yale Univ, PhD, Compar Lit, 67. **CAREER** Prof, Eng, Univ Calif, Santa Barbara. **RESEARCH** Lit theory; Hist of crit; Europ drama. **SELECTED PUBLICATIONS** Auth, Beyond Genre: New Directions, Literature Classification, Cornell Univ Press, 72; Interpreting Events: Tragicomedies of History on the Modern Stage, Cornell Univ Press, 85; Cultural Transactions: Nature, Self, Society, Cornell Univ Press, 95; ed, What is Literature? and What is Criticism?, Ind Univ, 78, 81; The Horizon of Literature, Univ Nebr Press, 82; The Rhetoric of Interpretation and the Interpretation of Rhetoric, Duke Univ Press, 89. **CONTACT ADDRESS** Dept of Eng, Univ of California, Santa Barbara, Santa Barbara, CA 93106-7150. **EMAIL** hernadip@humanitas.ucsb.edu

HERNANDEZ, CONSUELO
PERSONAL Born, Columbia, m, 1999 **DISCIPLINE** SPANISH **EDUCATION** Univ Antioquia, BA, 78; Simon Bolivar Univ, MA, 84; NY Univ, PhD, 91. **CAREER** Adj Instr to Adj Asst Prof, NYork Univ, 90-95; Asst Prof to Chair, Manhattanville Col, 91-95; Asst Prof to Assoc Prof, Am Univ, 95-. **HONORS AND AWARDS** Included in 15 Colombian Poets in United States, Immigrant Poetry, 98; New Fac Awd, Am Univ, 95; Dr. Carol S. Russett Awd, Am Coun of Educ, 94; Celia Siegel Awd for Excellence in Teaching, NY Univ, 90, 89; finalist in literary contest, Univ Miami, 88, **MEMBERSHIPS** Mod Lang Asn, Instituto Internacional de Literatura Iberoamericana, Am Bibliographical Res Inst, Instituto Literario y cultural Hispanico, Prometeo: Revista Latino Americana de Poesfia, Latin Am Indian Literatures Asn, LASA, Asn of colombianistas, Asn of Venezolanistas, MACLAS. **SELECTED PUBLICATIONS** Auth, Sos de violin, Poemario para musicos y pintores, 97; auth, Alvaro Mutis: una estetica del deterioro, Monte avila Editores, 96; auth, Voces de la sledad, Onda Uraniana, 82; auth, "Las historias prohibidas: Una aritmetica del dolor vivisimo,"î in Los otros roques. La Poetica multiple de Roque Dalton, Univ Press of the South, 99; auth, "Tulio Mora, archivista de america," in Neoindigenismo in the andean Countries, Catholic Univ, 97; auth, "Cronica, historiografia e imaginacion en las novelas de Manuel Scorze," in Beyond Indigenous voices, Penn state Univ, 96; auth, "La arquitectura poetica de eugenio Montejo," Venezuela. Literatura de fin de siglo, INTI Revista de Literatura Hispanica, Brown Univ, 93; auth, "Three Women, Three poetics, Writing in Spanish in USA," Cuadernos de ALDEEU, (99): 59-69; auth, "Reconstruyendo a Centroamerica a traves de la poesfa," Inti Revista de literatura Hispanica, (98): 45-56. **CONTACT ADDRESS** Dept For Lang, American Univ, 4400 Mass Ave NW, Washington, DC 20016. **EMAIL** chdez@american.edu

HERNANDEZ, JUAN
DISCIPLINE LATIN AMERICAN LITERATURE **EDUCATION** Tex Christ Univ, PhD, 81. **CAREER** Assoc prof. **RESEARCH** Translation studies; 20th century Latin American and U.S. American literature; poetry writing. **SELECTED PUBLICATIONS** Auth, Poetas de los Angeles, Univ de Guanajuato, 92; Poetry from Chile: 26 New Voices, Ca State Univ, 93; 21 Voces de Humo y Rafaga: Poesea de Jalisco, Ca State Univ, 94; Poesea contemporanea de los Angeles, Univ de Guadalajara, 94; Vida sin fin, confusiones de Pocho y otros poemas/Endless Life, Pocho Confusions and other poems, Guadalajara, 94. **CONTACT ADDRESS** Dept of Literature, Univ of Texas, Dallas, Richardson, TX 75083-0688. **EMAIL** juan@utdallas.edu

HERRERA, ENRIQUE
PERSONAL Born 02/22/1965, Peru, m **DISCIPLINE** SPANISH, ECONOMICS **EDUCATION** Pontificia Univ Catolica del Peru, BS; Fla State Univ, MA; PhD. **CAREER** Instr, Luther Col, 92-93; asst prof, Valparaiso Univ, 98-00. **RESEARCH** Golden Age Narrative and Theater, Contemporary Hispanic Narrative. **CONTACT ADDRESS** Dept For Lang, Valparaiso Univ, 651 College Ave, Valparaiso, IN 46383-6461. **EMAIL** enrique.herrera@valpo.edu

HERRERO, JAVIER
PERSONAL Born 08/12/1926, Murcia, Spain, m, 1962, 3 children **DISCIPLINE** SPANISH, COMPARATIVE LITERATURE **EDUCATION** Univ Madrid, LLB, 49, BA, 51, PhD(philos), 56. **CAREER** Asst philos, Univ Madrid, 54-55; asst Span, Univ Edinburgh, 56-60, lectr, 60-66; assoc prof, Duke Univ, 66-67, prof, 67-68; prof, Univ Pittsburgh, 68-74, Mellon prof, 74-79; William R Kenan Jr Prof Span, Univ Va, 79-, Univ Edinburgh res grant, 62; Sir Ernest Cassel res grant, 65; Guggenheim fel, 68; Am Philos Soc grant, 73; Nat Endowment for Humanities grant, 73. **MEMBERSHIPS** MLA; SAtlantic Mod Lang Asn; Asoc Int Hispanistas. **RESEARCH** Spanish and comparative literature, 17th to 20th centuries; literary criticism. **SELECTED PUBLICATIONS** Auth, The Jewish Dragon, Apocalypse, Intolerance and Magic, Critica Hisp, Vol 0015, 93. **CONTACT ADDRESS** Dept of Span, Univ of Virginia, 1 Cabell Hall, Charlottesville, VA 22903-3125.

HERRON, ROBERT DEUPREE
PERSONAL Born 06/29/1935, Roanoke, VA, m, 1964, 3 children **DISCIPLINE** SPANISH, PORTUGUESE **EDUCATION** Univ Richmond, BA, 57; Univ Wis, MA, 59, MA, 63, PhD Span, 68. **CAREER** Instr Span & Port, Miami Univ, 63-68; asst prof Port, Univ NMex, 68-73, actg dir, Lang & Area Ctr Latin Am, 69-70; assoc prof Span & Port, 73-76, chmn dept, 73-82, prof Mod Lang, St Louis Univ, 76-, dir, Andean Studies & Res Ctr, Univ NMex in Quito, Ecuador, 71-72; prof emeritus Mod Lang, St Louis Univ. **MEMBERSHIPS** MLA; Am Asn Teachers Span & Port; Midwest Mod Lang Asn. **RESEARCH** Brazilian and Portugues prose fiction of 19th and 20th centuries; Spanish American literature; Chicano literature. **SELECTED PUBLICATIONS** Auth, Lima Barreto's Isias Caminha as a psychological novel, Luso-Brazilian Rev, Winter 71; Personajes y paises en Adalberto Ortiz, Suplemento Domincal, El Comercio, Quito, Ecuador, 4/72; O tema da amizade em O amanuense Belmiro, de Cyro dos Anjos, Suplemento lit, Minas Gerais, Belo Horizonte, Brazil, 9/72; Three Fables; Translations from A Dor da Bruxa e outras Fabulas by Robert Reis, Vol VI, Webster Rev, Spring 81. **CONTACT ADDRESS** Dept of Mod & Class Lang, Saint Louis Univ, 221 N Grand Blvd, Saint Louis, MO 63103-2097.

HERTLING, GUNTER H.
PERSONAL Born 06/14/1930, Pasadena, CA, m, 1953, 2 children **DISCIPLINE** GERMAN **EDUCATION** Univ Calif, Berkeley, BA, MA, PhD(Ger), 61. **CAREER** Assoc Ger, Univ Calif, Berkeley, 60-61; from instr to assoc prof, 61-74, Grad Sch res Fund grant, 65, sen, fac senate, 72-74, Prof Germanic, Univ Wash, 74-; prof emer, 99-. **HONORS AND AWARDS** Osterreichische Gesil Lit, Vienna, 80. **MEMBERSHIPS** MLA; Am Asn Teachers Ger; Philol Asn Pac Coast; Stifter-Gesellschaft. **RESEARCH** 18th and 19th century German literature, literary theories, aesthetics and culture; pacific realism. **SELECTED PUBLICATIONS** Books and essays on C.F. Meyer, T. Fontaine, T. Storme, A. Stilter, F. Keller, Goeth, Lessing, etc. **CONTACT ADDRESS** Dept of Germanics, Univ of Washington, PO Box 353130, Seattle, WA 98195-3130. **EMAIL** hertgh@u.washington.edu

HERTZ, DAVID M.
PERSONAL Born 05/30/1954, Bay Shore, NY, m **DISCIPLINE** COMPARATIVE LITERATURE **EDUCATION** NYU, PhD, 83; IU, MA, 79; BS, 77; IU, BA (MIT), 76. **CA-**

REER Chair, Comparative Literature, Indiana Univ, 99-; Prof of Comparative Literature, Indiana Univ, 94. **HONORS AND AWARDS** Mellon Postdoctural Fel, NYU. **MEMBERSHIPS** ACLA, Pen Club, Ameri Society for Aesthetics. **RESEARCH** Modern Poetry; Music History; Architectural History. **CONTACT ADDRESS** Dept Comparative Literature, Indiana Univ, Bloomington, 1020 East Kirkwood Ave, Bloomington, IN 47405-7103. **EMAIL** hertzd@indiana.edu

HERZ, JULIUS MICHAEL
PERSONAL Born 02/04/1926, Vienna, Austria **DISCIPLINE** GERMAN **EDUCATION** Univ Vienna, PhD(Ger); Vanderbilt Univ, MA, 58. **CAREER** Teacher, Austria, 49-50; instr English, Austro-Am Inst Educ, 52, Western civilization, Ithaca Col, 55-56 & Ger & French, Univ Maine, 56-57; asst prof, 57-75, Assoc Prof Ger, Temple Univ, 75- **MEMBERSHIPS** MLA; AAUP; Int Arthur Schnitzler Res Asn. **RESEARCH** German and Austrian literature; bibliography; German-American studies. **SELECTED PUBLICATIONS** Auth, Ein Lese-Und-Bilderbuch-Von-Menschen--Unpublished Letters of Thomas Mann, Alfred Knopf, and Loweporter, 1929-1934, Seminar, Vol 0030, 94; Lenau--His Life, Work and Influence, Modern Austrian Lit, Vol 0027, 94. **CONTACT ADDRESS** Dept of Ger & Slavic Lang, Temple Univ, Philadelphia, PA 19122.

HERZFELD, ANITA
PERSONAL Born 01/22/1932, Buenes Aires, Argentina, s **DISCIPLINE** CREOLISTICS, SOCIOLINGUISTICS **EDUCATION** Teacher's Col, Argentina, BS, 53; Technical Col, Wales, GCE, 55; Instituto Superior del Profesorado, Argentina, BA, 65; Univ of Kans, MA, 65; MPhil, 74; PhD, 78. **CAREER** Assoc prof, Univ of Kans, 84-. **HONORS AND AWARDS** Fel, Univ of Concepcion, 58; Fulbright Fel, 61, 74, 79, 94; Sigma Delta Pi; Danforth Grad Fel, 73; Ford Found Grant, 73; Outstanding Int Woman Awd, 75; Tinker Grant, 82-83; Women's Hall of Fame Awd, 82; USAID Grant, 86; Anita Herzfeld Awd, CIPRA, AIT, 88; Phi Beta Delta; OIP Awd, 99; Teaching Awd, Center for Teaching Excellence, 00. **MEMBERSHIPS** AAUP; Ling Soc of Am; Soc for Caribbean Ling; Lat Am Studies Assoc; Fulbright Assoc; Soc for Pidgin and Creole Ling; ALFAL; SSILA. **SELECTED PUBLICATIONS** Auth, "Language and Identity: Limonese Creole and the Black Minority of Costa Rica", Exploration in Ethnic Studies 18.1, (95): 77-95; rev, of "Language and the Social Construction of Identity in Creole Situations", ed Marcyliena Morgan, Explorations on Sights and Sounds 15, (95): 54-55; auth, "La estrategia del vacilar en el criollo limonense", Antropologia e identidades en Centroamerica", Univ of Costa Rica, (96): 201-210; coauth, "Limonese Creole Proverbs and Sayings", Revista de Filologia y Linguistica XXII.1 , Univ of Costa Rica, (96): 155-193; auth, "No Powerless Women These: Gender in Limonese Creole", Proceedings of the Mid America Linguistics Conf, (Lawrence, KS), 96; auth, "Language and Identity in Central America: A History of Oppression, Struggle and Achievement", Latin America: An Interdisciplinary Approach, eds Julio Lopez-Arias and Gladys M. Varona-Lacey, Peter Lang, (NY), 98; auth, "Cohesion in Limonese Creole", Soc for Caribbean Linguistics, Univ of the W Indies, (99): 163-177; auth, "Integracion o Pluralismo: la educacion intercultural bilingue de los Mayahablantes", Actas del XI Congreso Internacional de la Asociacion de Linguistics y Filogia de la America Latina, Univ de las Palmas de Gran Canaria (00): 1745-1753. **CONTACT ADDRESS** Latin Am Studies, Univ of Kansas, Lawrence, 107 Lippincott Hall, Lawrence, KS 66045-2168. **EMAIL** herzfeld@ukans.edu

HESS, WILLIAM HUIE
PERSONAL Born 12/24/1933, Arkadelphia, AR, m, 1954, 2 children **DISCIPLINE** CLASSICS **EDUCATION** Univ TX, BA, 55, MA, 59; Princeton Univ, MA, 62, PhD, 63. **CAREER** Spec instr class, 59-60, from instr to asst prof classics, Univ TX, 62-68; assoc prof, 68-78, Prof Lang & Chmn Dept, Univ UT, 78-83, Prof Emer, 98. **MEMBERSHIPS** Camus **RESEARCH** Greek comedy; ancient relig; hist of ideas. **CONTACT ADDRESS** 1860 Laurelwood Cir, Salt Lake City, UT 84121-1220.

HESTER, RALPH M.
PERSONAL Born 12/22/1931, Fort Worth, TX, m, 1966, 2 children **DISCIPLINE** FRENCH **EDUCATION** Univ Calif, Los Angeles, BA, 54, MA, 56, PhD(Romance lang), 63. **CAREER** Asst French, Univ Calif, Los Angeles, 54-56, assoc, 56-57, asst 58-59, assoc, 59-60, lectr, 61-63; from asst prof to assoc prof, 63-78, Prof French, Stanford Univ, 78-, Chmn, Dept Fr & Ital, 79- **MEMBERSHIPS** MLA; Am Asn Teachers Ft; Renaissance Soc Am. **RESEARCH** French Renaissance literature; methodology in teaching of French. **SELECTED PUBLICATIONS** **CONTACT ADDRESS** Dept Ft & Ital, Stanford Univ, Stanford, CA 94305-1926.

HEWITT, ANDREW
DISCIPLINE COMPARATIVE LITERATURE **EDUCATION** Sidney Sussex Col, BA; MA; Cornell Univ, PhD. **CAREER** Assoc prof, SUNY Buffalo. **RESEARCH** Critical theory and the dialogue between French and Ger intellectual; cult traditions in the 20th century; the relationship of mass cult to the historical avant-garde; aesthetic constructions of gender and sexuality; mod dance. **SELECTED PUBLICATIONS** Auth, Fascist Modernism; Political Inversions. **CONTACT ADDRESS** Dept Comp Lit, SUNY, Buffalo, 639 Clemens Hall, Buffalo, NY 14260. **EMAIL** ahewitt@acsu.buffalo.edu

HEWSON, JOHN
PERSONAL Born 12/19/1930, Tugby, England, m, 1954, 3 children **DISCIPLINE** LINGUISTICS **EDUCATION** Univ Col, London, BA, 52; Inst Educ, London, PGCE, 53; Univ Laval, MA(Fre), 58, MA(ling), 60, DUn, 64. **CAREER** Asst to assoc prof Fr, 60-68, prof ling, 68-, HENRIETTA HARVEY PROF LINGUISTICS, MEMORIAL UNIV NFLD, 97-. **HONORS AND AWARDS** Fel, Royal Soc Can. **MEMBERSHIPS** Can Ling Asn; Ling Soc Am; Ling Asn Great Brit; Philol Soc; Soc Linguistique Romane. **SELECTED PUBLICATIONS** Auth, Oral French Pattern Practice, 63; auth, La Pratique du francais, 65; auth, Article and Noun in English, 72; auth, The Beothuk Vocabularies, 78; auth, A Computer-Generated Dictionary of Proto-Algonquian, 93; auth, The Cognitive System of the French Verb, 97; coauth, Fundamentals for a Science of Language, 84; coauth, The Micmac Grammar of Father Pacifique, 90; coauth, Tense and Aspect in Indo-European Languages, 97. **CONTACT ADDRESS** Dept of Linguistics, Mem Univ of Newfoundland, Saint John's, NF, Canada A1B 3X9. **EMAIL** jhewson@morgan.ucs.mun.ca

HIGGINBOTHAM, VIRGINIA
PERSONAL Born 11/06/1935, Dallas, TX **DISCIPLINE** SPANISH LITERATURE **EDUCATION** Southern Methodist Univ, BA, 57, MA, 62; Tulane Univ, PhD, 66. **CAREER** Teaching asst Span, Southern Methodist Univ, 60-62 & Tulane Univ, 62-66; asst prof, 66-73, Assoc Prof Span & Port, Univ Tex, Austin, 73-. **MEMBERSHIPS** Am Asn Teachers Span & Port; MLA. **RESEARCH** Contemporary Spanish literature. **SELECTED PUBLICATIONS** Auth, The Comic Spirit of Federico Garcia Lorca, Univ Tex, 74; Luis Bunuel, Twayne, 79; Spanish Film Under Franco, Univ Tex, 88; Spirit of the Beehive, Flicks Books, 98. **CONTACT ADDRESS** Dept of Span & Port, Univ of Texas, Austin, Austin, TX 78712-1026. **EMAIL** vhigginbotham@mail.utexas.edu

HIGGINS, LYNN ANTHONY
PERSONAL Born 07/21/1947, Ann Arbor, MI, m, 1968, 1 child **DISCIPLINE** FRENCH LANGUAGE & LITERATURE **EDUCATION** Oberlin Col, BA, 69; Univ MN, Minneapolis, MA, 73, PhD, 76. **CAREER** Vis lectr French, Hamline Univ, fall 73; Grad tchg asst and assoc, Univ MN, Minneapolis, 70-76; Vis lectr Comp Lit, Univ of Pittsburgh, fall 83; from Asst Prof French to Prof, 76-91, Ch, French & Ital Dept, 93-99, Dartmouth Col, Nat Endowment for Hum fel, 79 & Camargo fel, 81; Vis scholar and lectr, Vt and NH Coun for Hum Lit Series, 80. **HONORS AND AWARDS** Choice Outstanding Acad Bk Awd, 96; MLA Jeanne and Aldo Scaglione Prize, Best Bk in French and Francophone Studies, 97; Who's Who of Am Women. **MEMBERSHIPS** MLA; Nat Women's Studies Asn; Asn for French Cult Studies; New Novel Asn. **RESEARCH** 20th-Century French fiction & film. **SELECTED PUBLICATIONS** Auth, Nouvelle nouvelle autobiography: Monique Wittig's Le Corps Lesbien, Sub-Stance, 77; coauth, Conversation w Christiane Rochefort, Esprit Createur, 79; Godard and Rochefort: Two or three things about prostitution, Fr Rev, 75; auth, Typographical eros: Reading Ricardou in the third demension, Yale Fr Studies, 79; Literature a la lettre: Ricardou and the poetics of Anagram, Romanic Rev, 82; Barthes' imaginary voyages, Studies in Twentieth Century Lit, 82; Parables of theory: Jean Ricardou's metafiction, Summa Publ, 84; Ed, contr, History and Literature, Studies in Twentieth Century Lit, fall 85; Coed, contr, Screen/Memory: Rape and its alibis in Last Year at Marienbad, In: Rape and Representation, Columbia Univ Press, 91; If looks could kill: Louis Malle's portraits of collaboration, In: Fascism, Aesthetics, and Culture (Richard J Golsan, ed), Univ Press New England, 92; Sexual fantasies and war memories: Claude Simon's Narratology, In: Gendering War Talk (Miriam Cooke & Angela Woollacott, ed), Princeton Univ Press, 93; Gender and war narrative in La Route des Flandres, In: Claude Simon (Celia Britton, ed), Longman, 93; Pagnol and the paradoxes of Frenchness, In: Identity Papers: Scenes of Contested Nationhood in Twentieth-Century France (Tom Conley & Steven Ungar, ed), Univ Minn Press, 96; New Novel, New Wave, New Politics: Fiction and the Representation of History in Post War France, Univ Nebr Press, 96; Le Langage, l'etrangete et les formes de l'histoire dans La Route Des Flandres de Claude Simon, In: Lectures de La Route des Flandres (Francine Dugast-Portes & Michele Touret, ed), Presses Univ de Rennes; The Barbie affair and the trial of memory, In: Fascism's Return: Scandal, Revision and Ideology since 1980 (Richard J Golsan, ed), Univ Nebr Press, 98. **CONTACT ADDRESS** Dept of French & Italian, Dartmouth Col, 6087 Dartmouth Hall, Hanover, NH 03755-3511. **EMAIL** lynn.higgins@dartmouth.edu

HIGGINS, ROGER F.
DISCIPLINE LINGUISTICS **EDUCATION** Cambridge Univ, BA, 63; Yale Univ, MPhil, 69; Univ Mass, PhD, 73. **CAREER** Asst prof. **RESEARCH** Historical syntax of English. **SELECTED PUBLICATIONS** Auth, The Pseudo-cleft Construction in English, Garland, 79; On J. Emonds's Analysis of Extraposition, Seminar, 73. **CONTACT ADDRESS** Linguistics Dept, Univ of Massachusetts, Amherst, S College 124, Amherst, MA 01003.

HIGGINS, WILLIAM E.
PERSONAL Born 01/18/1945, Newark, NJ, s **DISCIPLINE** CLASSICS **EDUCATION** Georgetown Univ, BA, 66; Harvard Univ, PhD, 71; New York Univ, MBA, 81. **CAREER** Asst prof, Brandeis Univ, 71-79. **HONORS AND AWARDS** Phi Beta Kappa, Jr Fel, Ctr for Hellenic Stud, Washington, DC, 77-78. **MEMBERSHIPS** Am Philol Asn. **RESEARCH** Greek literature; ancient history. **SELECTED PUBLICATIONS** Auth, Aspects of Alexander's Imperial Administration, Athenaeum, 80; Deciphering Time in the Herakles of Euripides, Quaderni Urbinati, 84; rev of Osborne, Demos, AHR, 86; rev of Hirsch, The Friendship of the Barbarians, AHR, 87; rev of Garner, Law and Society in Classical Athens, AHR, 89. **CONTACT ADDRESS** 489 Summit Ave, Maplewood, NJ 07040. **EMAIL** wehigg@bellatlantic.net

HILGAR, MARIE-FRANCE
PERSONAL Born 06/19/1933, St. Palais, France, m, 1954, 4 children **DISCIPLINE** FRENCH LITERATURE **EDUCATION** Indiana Univ Pa, BA, 63; San Francisco State Col, MA, 66; Univ Calif, Davis, PhD(French), 71. **CAREER** Prof French, Peace Corps, 66; lectr, San Francisco State Col, 67; Prof French, Univ Nev, Las Vegas, 71-, Nat chmn, N Am Soc for 17th Century Fr Lit, 77; ed, Tape Hiss, Nev Foreign Lang Newslett, 77-; conf chmn, Pacific Northwest Conf Foreign Lang, 79. **MEMBERSHIPS** MLA; Int Asn Fr Studies; Asn Caracterologie; Am Soc 17th Century; Soc Fr Etude XVIIe Siecle. **RESEARCH** French theater of the 17th century; women authors; Madame Deshoulieres. **SELECTED PUBLICATIONS** Auth, La Mode des Stances dans le Theatre Tragique Francias 1610-1687, Nizet, 73; Un nerveux par excellence: Theophile de Viau, Caracterologie, 73; La mort d'Agis, Proc Pacific Northwest Conf Foreign Lang, 74; La folie dans le theatre du XVIIe siecle en France, Romance Notes, winter 75; La condition d'une heroine feminine: Medee, Papers in 17th Century Fr Lit, 77-78; Grandeur et decadence d'Hercule, Australian J Fr Studies, 78. **CONTACT ADDRESS** Dept of Foreign Lang, Univ of Nevada, Las Vegas, P O Box 455047, Las Vegas, NV 89154-5047.

HILL, STEVEN PHILLIPS
PERSONAL Born 04/25/1936, Estherville, IA, s **DISCIPLINE** SLAVIC LANGUAGES & LITERATURES **EDUCATION** Stanford Univ, BA, 57; Univ Mich, Ann Arbor, MA, 58, PhD, 65. **CAREER** From instr to asst prof, 61-69, Assoc Prof Russ, Univ Ill, Urbana, 69-. **MEMBERSHIPS** Am Asn Teachers Slavic & EEurop Lang; Soc Cinema Studies; Early Slavic Studies Asn; Am Asn for Advance Slavic Studies. **RESEARCH** Russian film history; East European film history; Russian 20th century drama. **SELECTED PUBLICATIONS** Auth, Kuleshov--prophet without honor?, Film Cult, spring 67; The Soviet film today, Film Quart, summer 67; coauth, Russian drama after Chekhov: A guide to English translations, 1900-1969, Theatre Doc, fall 69; A quantitative view of Soviet cinema, Cinema J, spring 72; Ilia Frez and Russian children's films, Film Cult, 74; The N-Factor and Russian Prepositions, Mouton, The Hague, 77; auth, Strange case of the vanishing epigraphs, in Eisenstein's Battleship Potemkin, Avon, 78; Career survey of Capra, Lubitsch, Sternberg, and Wyler, in Master Space--Film Images, Greenwood, 92. **CONTACT ADDRESS** Dept of Slavic, Univ of Illinois, Urbana-Champaign, Slavic, 3092 FLB, 707 S Mathews St., Urbana, IL 61801-3625. **EMAIL** s-hill4@uiuc.edu

HILL, SUSANNE
PERSONAL Born 08/18/1964, Germany, m, 1995, 1 child **DISCIPLINE** GERMAN **EDUCATION** Univ Mannheim, BA, 90; Univ Fla, MA, 93; PhD, 96. **CAREER** Visiting Asst Prof, Ohio Univ, 97-. **HONORS AND AWARDS** Gibson Fel, 95. **MEMBERSHIPS** MLA, AATG, SAMLA, WIG. **RESEARCH** East German. **CONTACT ADDRESS** Dept Mod Lang, Ohio Univ, 1 Ohio Univ, Athens, OH 45701-2942.

HILLEN, GERD
PERSONAL Born 10/18/1935, Ehren, Germany, m, 1965, 1 child **DISCIPLINE** GERMAN LITERATURE **EDUCATION** Stanford Univ, PhD(Ger), 68. **CAREER** Asst prof, 65-71, assoc prof & chmn dept, 71-77, Prof Ger, Univ Calif, Berkeley, 77- **MEMBERSHIPS** Lessing Soc; Philol Asn Pac Coast; MLA; Int Arbeitskreis fur Barockliterature. **RESEARCH** Seventeenth and 18th century German literature. **SELECTED PUBLICATIONS** Auth, Andreas Gryphius' Cardenio und Celinde, Mouton, The Hague, 71; coed, G E Lessing Werke II, Hanser, Munich, 71; auth, Reisemotive in den Romanen von Max Frisch, Wirkendes Wort, 19: 126-133; Ideologic und Humanitat in Lessings Dramen, 1; 150-161 & Die Halsstarrigkeit der Tugend: Bemerkungen zu Lessings Trauerspielen, II: 83-97, Leasing Jahrbuch; Lessings theologische Schriften im Zusammenhang seines Werks, In: Lessing in Heutiger Sicht, Bremen und Wolfenbuttel, 76; Lessing Chronik, Hanser, Muchen, 79; Allegorie im kontext, form und funktion der allegorie in Lit texten des 17, Jhds, 592-604, Formen und Funktionen der Allegorie, Metzler, Stuttgart, 79. **CONTACT ADDRESS** Dept of Ger, Univ of California, Berkeley, 5315 Dwinelle Hall, Berkeley, CA 94720-3244.

HILLERS, DELBERT ROY
PERSONAL Born 11/07/1932, Chester, SD, m, 1958, 2 children **DISCIPLINE** OLD TESTAMENT, SEMITIC LANGUAGES **CAREER** Instr Hebrew, Concordia Sr Col, 58-60; from asst prof to assoc prof Hebrew & Old Testament, 63-70, Prof Semitic Lang, Johns Hopkins Univ, 70-, Ann prof, Am Sch Orient Res, Jerusalem, 68-69; Am Philos Soc grant, 68-69. **MEMBERSHIPS** Soc Bibl Lit; Am Orient Soc. **RESEARCH** Northwest Semitic languages; Old Testament. **SELECTED PUBLICATIONS** Auth, Treaty-Curses and the Old Testament Prophets, Pontif Bibl Inst, Rome, 64; An alphabetic cuneiform tablet from Taanach, Bull Am Schs Orient Res, 64; Delocutive verbs in Biblical Hebrew, J Bibl Lit, 68; Covenant: The History of a Biblical Idea, Johns Hopkins Univ, 69; Lamentations, Anchor Bible, Doubleday, 72. **CONTACT ADDRESS** Dept of Near Eastern Studies, Johns Hopkins Univ, Baltimore, 3400 N Charles St, Baltimore, MD 21218.

HIMELBLAU, JACK J.
PERSONAL Born 02/06/1935, Chicago, IL, d, 2 children **DISCIPLINE** SPANISH **EDUCATION** Univ Chicago, AB, 58; MA, 59; Univ Mich, PhD, 65. **CAREER** Asst prof, Univ Mich, 65-69; assoc prof, Columbia Univ, 69-72; assoc prof, Mills Col, 72-76; prof, Univ Tex at San Antonio, 76-. **HONORS AND AWARDS** NEH grant, 77; Who's Who in the South and Southwest, 95; Men of Achievement, Cambridge, England: Int Biographical Centre, 96; Dictionary of Int Biography, Cambridge, England: Int Biographical Centre, 96; elected Miembro Correspondiente Extranjero, Academia Venezolana de la Lengua, Correspondiente de la Real Espanola, March 20, 95. **MEMBERSHIPS** AATSP. **RESEARCH** Spanish-American contemporary novel; literature of the Conquest of the Americas; nineteenth-century Spanish novel; nineteenth-century Spanish-American novel; twentieth-century Spanish-American theatre. **SELECTED PUBLICATIONS** Auth, "Miguel Angel Asturias' Dawn of Creativity (1920-30): The Minstrel of Merriment," (excerpts), Contemporary Literary Criticism, Vol 8, Detroit: Gale Res Co (78): 25-27; auth, Alejandro O. Deustua: Philosophy in Defense of Man, Gainesville: Univ Presses of Fla (79); auth, Quiche Worlds in Creation: The Popol Vuh as a Narrative Work of Art, Culver City, Calif: Labyrinthos (89); auth, "The Popul Vuh of the Quiche Maya of Guatemala: Text, Copyist, and Time Frame of Transcription," Hispania 72 (Mar 89): 97-122; auth, "Chronologic Deployment of Fictional Events in M. A. Asturias El Senor Presidente," Hispanic J 12 (fall 91): 181-209; auth, "Indigenous Cultures: Views by Spanish-American Social Thinkers of the Nineteenth and Twentieth Centuries," Quincentennial: A Critical Exploration (1492-1992), eds., Amalia Mondriguez and Melissa Walschak, San Antonio: Incarnate Word, The Col (Oct 12, 92): 62-90; ed, The Indian in Spanish America: Centuries of Removal, Survival, and Integration, A Critical Anthology, Vol 1 and 2, Lancaster, Calif: Labyrinthos (94, 95). **CONTACT ADDRESS** Dept Foreign Lang, Univ of Texas, San Antonio, 6900 N Loop 1604 W, San Antonio, TX 78249-1130. **EMAIL** jhimelbl@utsa.edu

HINDERER, WALTER
PERSONAL Born 09/03/1934, Ulm, Germany, m, 1966 **DISCIPLINE** GERMAN LITERATURE, PHILOSOPHY **EDUCATION** Abitur, Kepler Gymnasium, Ulm, 54; Univ Tuebingen, German & Eng Lit, European History & Phil, 54-55; Univ Munich, 55-60, PhD, 60. **CAREER** Dir, Acad Div, 61-66, R. Piper & Co (publ), Munich, 61-66; asst prof, German, 66-69, Penn St Univ; assoc prof, German, 69-71, Univ CO; vis prof, 70-71, Stanford Univ; prof, German, 71-78, Univ MD; prof, German, 78-, Princeton Univ. **HONORS AND AWARDS** Fel, Inst for Res in Humanities, Univ WI, 76-77; DAAD Res Grant, 84; Fel, Inst for Advanced Study Berlin, 85-86; Fel, Franz Rosenzweig Res Center, 95, Hebrew Univ; Order of Merit of the Fed Rep of Germany, 95; Alexander von Humboldt Awd, 98. **MEMBERSHIPS** Intl Vereinigung fuer Germanische Sprac und Lit; Modern Language Asn; AATG; Schiller-Gesellschaft; Buechner-Gesellschaft; Heine-Gesellschaft; Gesellschaft fuer Interkulturelle Germanistik. **RESEARCH** German & European lit of the 18th, 19th, and 20th centuries; concepts and ideas of German drama; political poetry; politics and lit; German soc and cult history; rhetoric and oratory; lit theory; poetics and aesthetics; history of criticism. **SELECTED PUBLICATIONS** Auth, Arbeit an der Gegenwart. Zur deutschen Literatur nach 1945, Wuerzburg: Verlag Koenigshausen und Neumann, 94; ed, Brechts Dramen, Intrepretationen, Verlag Philipp Reclam jun, 95; ed, Kleists Dramen Literaturstudium, Interpretationen, Verlag Philipp Reclam jun, 97; ed, Codierungen von Liebe in der Kunstperiode, Verlag Koenigshausen & Neumann, 97; auth, Von der Idee des Menschen, Ueber Friedrich Schiller, Verlag Konigshausen & Neumann, 98; ed, Kleists Erzahlungen, Literaturstudium, Interpretationen, Reclam Verlag, 98; auth, Die Rhetorik der Parabel. Zu ihrem asthetischen Funktionszuusammenhang und Funktionswechsel bei Friedrich Schiller, Fabel und Parabel Kulturgeschichtliche Prozesse im 18, Jahrhundert. 94; auth, Die Depotenzierung der Vernunft: Kompensationsmuster im praeromantischen und romantischen Diskurs, Romantiches Erzahlen, Verlag Koenigshausen & Neumann, 95; auth, Den Dichtern geht es wie dem Araukaner, Anmerkungen zu Gunter Kunerts Poetik, Kunert Werkstatt, Materialien und Studien zu Gunter Kunerts literarischem Werk, Aisthesis Verlag, 95; auth, Das Roecheln der Mona Lisa. Aspeckt von Ernst Jandyls Lyrik im Kontext der sechziger Jahre, Text & Kriktik. Zeitschrift fur Literatur, 96; auth, Die Entmuendigung der Muendigkeit. Zum Paradigmawechsel eines anthropologischen Konzepts im philosophischen und literarischen Diskurs der Kinstperiode, Lit und Erfahrungswandel 1789-1930, Intl Corvey-Symposiums 9 & 12, 93; auth, Im babylonischen Turm, oder: Steine aus dem Glashaus, Amerikas Kampf um den Kanon und um kulturelle Einheit, Neue Rundschau. Der postkoloniale Blick. Eine neue Weltliteratur?, Jahrgang 96; auth, Das Reich der Schatten In Interpretationen. Gedichte von Friedrich Schiller, Stuttgart Philipp Reclam Verlag, 96; auth, Torquato Tasso, Goethe-Handbuch Vol II, JB Metzler Verlag, 96; auth, Literatur als Anweisung zum Fremdverstehen, Deutsch und fur Asien, IDV-Regionaltagung Asien - Beijing, 94, Intl Cul Pub, 96; ed, Zur Liebesauffassung der Kunstperiode, Codierungen von Liebe in der Kunstperiode, Verlag Konigshausen & Neumann, 97; auth, Liebessemantik als Provokation, Codierunger von Liebe in der Kunstperiode, Verlag Koenigshausen & Neumann, 97; auth, Prinz Friedrich von Homburg. Zweideutige Vorfaelle, Kleists Dramen, Literaturstudium, Interpretationen, Verlag Philipp Reclam jun, 97; auth, Literarisch-Aesthetische Auftakte zur Romantischen Musik, Jahrbuch der deutschen Schillergesellschaft, 1997, Alfred Kroener Verlag, 97; auth, Das Kollektivindividuum Nation im deutschen Kiontext. Zu seinem Bedeutungswandel im vor-und nachrevolutionaren Diskurs, Volk-Nation-Europa. Zur Romantisierung und Entromantisierung politischer Begriffe, Verlag Koenigshausen & Neumann, 98; auth, Die heilige Caecilie oder die Gewalt der Musik, Kleists Erzaehlungen. Literaturstudium, Interpretationen, Reclam Verlag, 98; auth, Erzaehlte Bilder und eingebildete Texte, Bild und Schrittinder Tomantik, Verlag Koenigshausen & Neumann, 99; auth, Diskursueber Judustrialisierung und Natur im deutschen Roman des A9 Jahrhunderts, Erich Schmidt Verlag, 99. **CONTACT ADDRESS** Dept of Germanic Lang and Lit, Princeton Univ, 230 E Pyne, Princeton, NJ 08544-5264. **EMAIL** Hinderer@Princeton.edu

HINDS, LEONARD
DISCIPLINE FRENCH LITERATURE **EDUCATION** Emory Univ, PhD, 95. **CAREER** Asst prof. **RESEARCH** French narrative prose; philosophical prose; literary theory. **SELECTED PUBLICATIONS** Auth, pubs on Montaigne, Charles Sorel, and Madeleine de Scudery. **CONTACT ADDRESS** Dept of French and Italian, Indiana Univ, Bloomington, 1020 E Kirkwood Ave, Ballantine Hall 642, Bloomington, IN 47405. **EMAIL** lhinds@indiana.edu

HINER, SUSAN
PERSONAL Born 06/06/1964, Richmond, VA, m, 1999 **DISCIPLINE** FRENCH **EDUCATION** Univ Va, BA, 86; Columbia Univ, MA, 88; M Phil, 92; PhD, 96. **CAREER** Vis Asst Prof, Skidmore Col, 95-98; Vis Asst Prof, Vassar Col, 98-. **HONORS AND AWARDS** Phi Beta Kappa, 86; Mellon Fel in Humanities; President's Fel, Columbia Univ. **RESEARCH** 19th Century French Literature and Culture. **SELECTED PUBLICATIONS** Rev, of "Struggling Under the Destructive Glance: Androgyny in the Novels of the Guy de Maupassant" by Rachel M. Hartig, Nineteenth-Century French Studies (Fall-Winter 92-93): 224-226; rev, of "Narrative Strategies in the Aftermath of the French Revolution," by Doris Kadish, Romantic Rev (May 93): 340-342; rev, of "Where Flaubert Lies: Chronology, Mythology, and History," by Claire Addison, Romantic Rev (Nov 97); auth, "In Cool Blood: Mourning Landscapes in 'Therese raquin'," Excavatio (Spring 98); auth, "Paris Pastoral: Cultivating Anarchy in Zola's Fin de Siecle," in Confrontations: Politics and Aesthetics in Nineteenth-Century France (Rodopi, forthcoming). **CONTACT ADDRESS** Dept French, Vassar Col, 124 Raymond Ave, Poughkeepsie, NY 12604-0001. **EMAIL** suhiner@vassar.edu

HINES, THOMAS MOORE
PERSONAL Born 06/28/1936, Columbia, SC, m, 1970 **DISCIPLINE** FRENCH **EDUCATION** Univ Ga, BA, 58; Johns Hopkins Univ, MA, 60; Emory Univ, PhD, 73. **CAREER** Instr, Va Military Inst, 61-64; instr, Univ SC, 64-65; teaching asst, Emory Univ, 71-73; asst prof, Univ Ala Birmingham, 73-80; assoc prof to prof, Samford Univ, 82-. **HONORS AND AWARDS** Teaching Fel, Emory Univ, 71-73; Pi Delta Phi; Phi Kappa Phi; Study Grant, Univ Ala Birmingham; Study Grant, Samford Univ. **MEMBERSHIPS** S Atlantic MLA; Am Asn of Teachers of French; MLA; Ala Asn of Teachers of For Lang. **RESEARCH** Twentieth-century French literature and culture; Business French; Translation. **SELECTED PUBLICATIONS** Auth, " Le Reve et l'action: Une etude de 'L'Homme a Cheval' de Drieu la Rochelle, 78; trans, "The Man on Horseback," by Drieu la Rochelle, 78; auth, "Myth, Misogyny, and Fascism in the Works of Drieu la Rochelle," Purdue Univ. **CONTACT ADDRESS** Dept Lang, Samford Univ, 1801 Mission Rd, Birmingham, AL 35216-2241. **EMAIL** TMHines@Samford.edu

HINTZ, ERNST RALF
PERSONAL Born 12/16/1948, m, 1998, 2 children **DISCIPLINE** GERMAN **EDUCATION** Fordham Univ, BA, 72; Ruprecht-Karl Universitat, Heidelberg, MA, 76; Univ Wisc, PhD, 86. **CAREER** Teaching Asst, Univ Wisc, 80-86; Vis Asst Prof, Chatham Col, 86-87; Vis Lecturer, Univ Otago, 88; Instructional Designer, Macquarie Univ, 89-91; Lecturer, Univ S Australia, 91-93; Lecturer, PaState Univ, 94-96; Asst Prof to Assoc Prof, Fort Hays State Univ, 96-. **HONORS AND AWARDS** Vilas Traveling Grant, Univ Wisc, 83; Kans Humanities Coun Grant, 97, 98, 99. **MEMBERSHIPS** German Studies Asn, Medieval Acad of Am, Mod Lang Asn, Kans For Lang Teachers Asn. **RESEARCH** Rhetorical theory and practice in medieval narrative; Early women writers in German and Latin; 13th Century authors (Konrad von Wurzburg); reception of the Middle ages (Scheffel's Ekkehard); concepts of learning and teaching in German literature. **SELECTED PUBLICATIONS** Auth, "Der Wilde Mann: ein Mythos vom Andersartigen," in Mittelalter Mythen: damonen, Monster, Ungeheuer, St Gallen, 99; auth, leaning and persuasion in the German Middle Ages, Garland Pub, 97; auth, "Frau Ava," in Dictionary of Literary Biography, Vol 148: German Writers and Works of the Early Middle ages: 800-1170, Charleston 95. **CONTACT ADDRESS** Dept Mod Lang, Fort Hays State Univ, 600 Park St, Hays, KS 67601-4099. **EMAIL** ehintz@fhsu.edu

HINTZ, SUZANNE S.
DISCIPLINE SPANISH, LITERATURE **EDUCATION** Purdue Univ, BA, 67; Univ of Va, Med, 78; George Mason Univ, MA, 91; Cath Univ of Am, PhD, 93 **CAREER** Prof, 93-98, Germanna Cmnty Col; Div Chair, 98-, Northrn VA Cmnty Col **HONORS AND AWARDS** Embassy of Spain awd, 91; DeFerrari Sch, 90-93; Lee-Hatzfeld Sch, 90-92 **MEMBERSHIPS** MLA, SAMLA, LASA, MACLAS, AATSP **RESEARCH** Puerto Rican and Catalan lit. **SELECTED PUBLICATIONS** Auth, "Rosario Ferre, A Search for Identity," Literal books, 95; Essays in Honor of Josep M. Sola-Sole: Linguistic and Literary Relations of Catalan and Castilian, Peter Lang, 96; transl, "The War of the Christs and Amelia's Case, Peterlang, 92. **CONTACT ADDRESS** No Virginia Comm Col, Woodbridge, VA 22191. **EMAIL** shintz@nv.cc.va.us

HINZE, KLAUS-PETER WILHELM
PERSONAL Born 09/06/1936, Berlin, Germany, m, 1967, 2 children **DISCIPLINE** GERMAN & COMPARATIVE LITERATURE **EDUCATION** Frere Univ Berlin, Staatsexamen, 65; Wash Univ, MA & PhD, 69. **CAREER** Asst prof Ger, Case Western Reserve Univ, 67-71; assoc prof, 71-78, Prof Ger & Comp Lit, Cleveland State Univ, 78-, Asst Dean Arts & Sci, 80-, Lit agent, Kreisselmeier Publ, Munich, 76-; scholar, Austrian govt, 76, W Ger Govt, 77, Akad Wiss, 78 & Stiller Soc, 79. **HONORS AND AWARDS** Scholar, Austrian govt, 76. **MEMBERSHIPS** MLA; Am Asn Teachers Ger; Int Arthur Schnitzler Res Asn; Goethe Soc; Wiener Goethe-Soc. **RESEARCH** Goethe; German 20th century literature. **SELECTED PUBLICATIONS** Auth, Goethes Spiegelungstechnik im Bereich seiner Erzahlungen, Orbis Litterarum, 70; Goethes Dialogerzahlung Die Guten Weiber, Neophilologus, 71; Neue Aspekte zum Kafka-Bild, Mod Austrian Lit, 71; Kom Strukt Goethes Erzahl, Boehlau, Cologne, 75; Ernst Weiss Bibliographie, Engel, Hamburg, 77; ed, Der Andere Augenzeuge: Ich der Augenzeuge, Heyme, Munich, 79; auth, Die Gruppe 1925, Dvjs, Der Zweite Augenzeuge, GRM, 81. **CONTACT ADDRESS** Dept of Mod Lang, Cleveland State Univ, 1983 E 24th St, Cleveland, OH 44115-2440.

HIRSCH, MARIANNE
PERSONAL Born 09/23/1949, Timisoara, Romania, 3 children **DISCIPLINE** COMPARATIVE LITERATURE, FRENCH **EDUCATION** Brown Univ, BA, & MA, 70, PhD, 75. **CAREER** Vis instr French, Dartmouth Col, 74-75, asst prof, 75-77; Mellon asst prof humanities, Vanderbilt Univ, 77-78; asst prof French & Comp Lit, 78-82, assoc prof French & Cmp Lit, 82-89, prof, 89-; parents distinguished res prof, Dartmouth Col, 95-99. **HONORS AND AWARDS** Magna Cum Laude, 70; Phi Beta Kappa, 70; Fulbright Fellowship (declined), 70; DAAD Fellowship (declined), 70; NDEA Title IV Fellowship, 71-72; AAUW Dissertation Fellowship, 73-74; Dartmouth Col Jr Faculty Fellowship, 79; Faculty Development Grant, Wellesley Center for Research on Women, 80; Stanford Humanities Center Fellowship (declined), 84-85; Dartmouth Col Sr Faculty Grant, 85; Mary Ingraham Bunting Institute Fellowship, 84-85; Mellon Course Development Award, 86; Mellon Humanities Institute on Gender and War, Dartmouth Col,. 90; Nat Humanities Center Fel, 92-93; Rockefeller Foundation Bellagio Residence Fel, 95; Mellon Humanities Institute, Cultural Memory and the Present, Dartmouth Col, 96; Distinguished Graduate School Alumna Award, Brown Univ, 96; Fac, School of Criticism and Theory, 98; Nat Humanities Center Distinguished Lectr, 98-01; Brown Univ Alumni Magazine, featured as one of the 100 alumni who had the greatest influence on the twentieth century, 00. **MEMBERSHIPS** MLA; Am Comp Lit Asn. **RESEARCH** Contemporary fiction; hist and theory of narrative; women's studies; holocaust studies, photography. **SELECTED PUBLICATIONS** Auth, The Novel of Formation as Genre: Between Great Expectations and Lost Illusions, Genre, 79; Michel Buton: The Decentralized Vision, Contemp Lit, summer 81; Mothers and Daughters: A Review Essay, Signs, fall 81; A Mother's Discourse: Incorporation and Repetition in La Princesse de Cleves, Yale Fr Studies, Vol 62, 81; auth, The Mother/Daughter Plot: Narrative, Psychoanalysis, Feminism (Choice Outstanding academic book of the year), IN Univ Press, 89; auth, "Past Lives: Postmemories in Exile," Poetics Today 17, 4, 96; Family Frames: Photography, Narrative and Postmemory, Harvard Univ Press, 97; auth, "Projected Memory: Holocaust Photographs in Personal and Public Fanta-

sy," in Acts of Memory, ed. Mieke Bal, Jonathan Crewe, Leo Spitzer, (Hanover: Univ Press of New England, 99); auth, "Surviving Images: Holocaust Photographs and the Work of Postmemory," in Yale Journal of Criticism, 01; and in Visual Culture and the Holocaust, ed. Barbie Zelizer, (New Brunswick: Rutgers Univ Press, 01); auth of several articles and ed of five volumes. **CONTACT ADDRESS** Dept French & Italian, Dartmouth Col, 6087 Dartmouth Hall, Hanover, NH 03755-3511. **EMAIL** marianne.hirsch@dartmouth.edu

HIRSCHBACH, FRANK DONALD
PERSONAL Born 05/13/1921, Berlin, Germany, s **DISCIPLINE** GERMAN LITERATURE **EDUCATION** Southern Conn State Col, BA, 46; Yale Univ, MA, 49, PhD, 52. **CAREER** Instr Ger, Yale Univ, 52-57; asst prof, Clark Univ, 57-58; from asst prof to assoc prof, 58-66, Prof Ger, Univ Minn, Minneapolis, 66-, Dir Honors Div, Col Lib Arts, 71-, Chmn Dept, 82-, Morse fel, 54-55; Ger Acad Exchange Serv grant, 74-75; Int Res & Exchanges Bd res fel, 79. **MEMBERSHIPS** MLA; Am Asn Teachers Ger. **RESEARCH** Modern German literature; literature of German Democratic Republic. **SELECTED PUBLICATIONS** Auth, Nazi Germany and the American Germanists--A Study of Periodicals, 1930-1946, Germanic Notes Rev, Vol 0028, 97; Anna Seghers in Exile--Essays, Texts, Documents, Germanic Notes Rev, Vol 0026, 95. **CONTACT ADDRESS** Univ of Minnesota, Twin Cities, 9 Pleasant St. SE, 205 Folwell Hall, Minneapolis, MN 55455. **EMAIL** hirsc006@tc.umn.edu

HIRTLE, WALTER HEAL
PERSONAL Born 08/23/1927, Lunenburg, NS, Canada, m, 1959, 4 children **DISCIPLINE** LINGUISTICS **EDUCATION** Univ BC, BA, 48; Dalhousie Univ, MA, 50; Laval Univ, MA, 59, PhD(ling), 63. **CAREER** From asst prof to assoc prof, 59-69, Prof English Ling, Laval Univ 69- **MEMBERSHIPS** Can Ling Asn; Can Asn Appl Ling; Ling Asn Can-US. **RESEARCH** English grammar; psychomechanics of language; Guillaumean lingusitics. **SELECTED PUBLICATIONS** Auth, Syntax-Autonomous or Meaning Motivated, Can J Ling, Vol 0039, 94; The Simple Form Again--An Analysis of Direction-Giving and Related Uses, J Pragmatics, Vol 0024, 95. **CONTACT ADDRESS** Dept of Lang & Ling, Univ of Laval, Quebec, QC, Canada G1K 7P4.

HISLOPE, KRISTI A.
PERSONAL Born 11/14/1969, Somerset, KY **DISCIPLINE** SPANISH, ESL **EDUCATION** Morehead State Univ, BS, 92; Univ Ky, MA, 94; Purdue Univ, PhD, 01. **CAREER** TA, Univ Ky, 92-95; Instr, Lexington Community Col, 95; TA, Purdue Univ, 95-01; ESL instr, Purdue Village Eng as a Second Lang School, 98-01; asst prof, N Ga Col and State Univ, 01-. **HONORS AND AWARDS** Purdue Res Grant, 97, 99-01. **MEMBERSHIPS** Am Assoc of Applied Ling, Am Assoc of Teachers of Span and Port, MLA, Am Coun on the Teaching of Foreign Lang. **RESEARCH** Teaching Spanish to Spanish-Speakers, Writing Processes, Written Focus-on-Form methods for grammar acquisition, second language acquisition, Spanish linguistics, ESL. **SELECTED PUBLICATIONS** Coauth, "(Re)experiencing hegemony: The linguistic imperialism of Robert Phillipson," Int Jour of Applied Ling 8.2 (98); coauth, "Hegemonic Discourse Revisited," Int Jour of Applied Ling 9.1, (99); coauth, "A Study of syllable final /r/ neutralization in Puerto Rican Spanish," Romance Lang Annuals 10, (99); auth, "Issues in Teaching Writing in Spanish to Hispanic Bilinguals at the University Level," Multiplicities: Mediating Cultural Productions, (Purdue Univ, 00). **CONTACT ADDRESS** FLL Dept, 134 Stanley Coulter Bldg, West Lafayette, IN 47906. **EMAIL** hislopek@omni.cc.purdue.edu

HIZ, HENRY
PERSONAL Born 10/08/1917, Leningrad, Russia, m, 1943 **DISCIPLINE** LINGUISTICS, PHILOSOPHY **EDUCATION** Free Univ Brussels, lic en philos, 46; Harvard Univ, PhD(-philos), 48. **CAREER** Asst philos, Underground Univ Warsaw, 40-44; adj math, Univ Warsaw, 49-50; asst prof, Univ Utah, 52-54 & Pa State Univ, 55-60, assoc prof, 60-64, Prof Ling, Univ Pa, 64-, Vis lectr, Univ Pa, 51, 53, 54 & 58-59; investr, NSF Tranformation & Discourse Analysis Proj, 58-; vis prof philos, NY Univ, 69- 71 & Jagiellonian Univ, 77; vis fel philos, Clare Hall, Cambridge, Eng, 76-77; Guggenheim fel ling, 76-77. **MEMBERSHIPS** Ling Soc Am; Semiotic Sco Am (pres, 75-76); Am Philos Asn. **RESEARCH** Formal grammars; mathematical logic; philosophy of art; ethics. **SELECTED PUBLICATIONS** Auth, Zellig Harris, 23-October-1909 May-22-1992, In-Memoriam, Proceedings Am Philos Soc, Vol 0138, 94; auth, Autobiography, in First Person Singular III, ed E.F.K. Koerner, 98. **CONTACT ADDRESS** Dept of Ling, Univ of Pennsylvania, Philadelphia, PA 19174. **EMAIL** hiz@babel.ling.upenn.edu

HODDIE, JAMES HENRY
PERSONAL Born 01/16/1936, Attleboro, MA, m, 1965, 2 children **DISCIPLINE** SPANISH LANGUAGE & LITERATURE **EDUCATION** Boston Univ, AB, 58; Univ Wis, MA, 59; Brown Univ, PhD, 65. **CAREER** From instr to asst prof Span, Univ Pittsburgh, 62-65; asst prof, Yale Univ, 65-67; from Asst Prof to Assoc Prof, 67-92, Prof Spanish, Col Lib Arts, Boston Univ, 92-. **HONORS AND AWARDS** Schol on Augustus Howe Buck Educ Fund, Boston Univ, 54-58; Kemper K. Knapp Fel, Univ Wisc, 58-59; Univ Fel, Brown Univ, 60-62; Phi Beta Kappa, Mass Epsilon, 57; Phi Sigma Iota, Omega Chapter, 58; Phi Beta Delta, Boston Univ, 90. **MEMBERSHIPS** Asn Int de Hispanistas. **RESEARCH** Spanish biography in the 20th century, especially Maranon and Gomez de la Serna; Spanish novel. **SELECTED PUBLICATIONS** Auth, Vivencias Hispanicas: Cuentos del Siglo XX, Harcourt Brace Jovanovich, Inc, 88; Jose Echegaray, El gran Galeoto, Introduction, edition and notes, Letras Hispanicas, Ediciones Catedra, 89; La unidad y universalidad en la ficcion modernists de Gabriel Miro, Origenes, 92; Auth, El contraste en la obra de Ramon Gomez de la Serna, Madrid, Editorial Pliegos, 99; author of numerous articles and papers. **CONTACT ADDRESS** Dept of Lang, Boston Univ, 718 Commonwealth Ave, Boston, MA 02215-2423. **EMAIL** jhhoddie@bu.edu

HODGES, CAROLYN RICHARDSON
PERSONAL Born 11/25/1947, Roebling, NJ, m, 1972 **DISCIPLINE** GERMAN **EDUCATION** Beaver College, BA, 1969; University of Chicago, MA, 1971, PhD, 1974. **CAREER** Central YMCA Community College, instructor of German, 70-72; Kennedy-King Jr College, assistant professor of humanities, 75-82; Univ of Tennessee, Knoxville, assistant professor of German, 82-88, associate professor of German, 88-. **HONORS AND AWARDS** Chancellor's Citation for Extraordinary Service, Univ of Tennessee, 1987; Merrill Research Awd, College of Education, Univ of Tennessee-Knoxville, 1990, 1992; Outstanding Advising, College of Liberal Arts, 1991; Dissertation Year Awd, Ford Foundation, 1973-74; Trustee Fellowship, Univ of Chicago, 1969-73; Faculty Travel Awd, Univ of Tennessee, 1983. **MEMBERSHIPS** Secretary/treasurer, Southern Comparative Literature Assn, 1990-; vice-president, Tennessee American Assn of Teachers of German, 1987-89; board member, Tennessee Foreign Language Teacher Assn, 1989-92; editorial reviewer, Soundings an Interdisciplinary Journal, 1985-91; member, Tennessee Collaborative Council on Foreign Language, 1986-. **CONTACT ADDRESS** Univ of Tennessee, Knoxville, 701 McClung Tower, Knoxville, TN 37996-0470.

HOEFERT, SIGFRID
PERSONAL Born 08/14/1925, Poland, m, 1954, 3 children **DISCIPLINE** GERMAN **EDUCATION** Univ Toronto, BA, 58, MA, 60, PhD(Ger), 63. **CAREER** Lectr, 61-63, from asst prof to assoc prof, 63-69, Prof Ger, Univ Waterloo, 69-, Soc Sci & Humanities Res Coun Can awards & fac res grants. **MEMBERSHIPS** Am Asn Teachers Ger; Can Asn Univ Teachers Ger; Can Comp Lit Asn Int Ver Ger Sprach-u Literaturwiss; MLA. **RESEARCH** Naturalism; literature of the German Democratic Republic. **SELECTED PUBLICATIONS** Auth, Das Drama des Naturalismus; auth, Gerhart Hauptmann; auth, Gerhart Hauptmann und der Film: mit unvereoffentlichten Filmentweurfen des Dichters; auth, Internationale Bibliographie zum Werk Gerhart Hauptmanns; auth, Russische Literatur in Deutschland: Texte z. Rezeption von d. achtziger Jahren bis z. Jahrhundertwende. **CONTACT ADDRESS** Dept of Ger & Slavic Langs & Lits, Univ of Waterloo, 200 Univ Ave W, Waterloo, ON, Canada N2L 3G1.

HOENG, PETER
PERSONAL Born 03/05/1960, s **DISCIPLINE** GERMAN LITERARY HISTORY & CULTURE **EDUCATION** Univ Siegen, MA, 88; Univ Wis, PhD, 94. **CAREER** From asst prof to assoc prof, Univ Tenn, 94-. **HONORS AND AWARDS** Fac Res Awd, Univ Tenn, 95, 96, & 99; Promising Young Scholar Awd, Univ Tenn, 99. **MEMBERSHIPS** Asn of Teachers in Ger, Soc for Eighteenth-Century Studies, Ger Studies Asn. **RESEARCH** German Literature and Culture since the Eighteenth-Century, Beethoven's Intellectual Life, Ger Jewish Culture, Censorship, Authors: Schiller, Goethe, Tabori, Bernhard. **SELECTED PUBLICATIONS** Ed, Embodied Projections on History: George Tabori's Theater Work, 98; auth, Die Sterne, Die Zensur. Das Vaterland: Geschichte Und Theater Im Spaten 18. Jahr Hun Dert, 00. **CONTACT ADDRESS** Ger & Slavic Lang, Univ of Tennessee, Knoxville, 1345 Circle Park, Knoxville, TN 37996-0001. **EMAIL** hoeyng@utk.edu

HOENIGSWALD, HENRY M.
PERSONAL Born 04/17/1915, Breslau, Germany **DISCIPLINE** LINGUISTICS **EDUCATION** Univ Florence, D Litt, 36. **CAREER** Mem staff, Inst Studi Etruschi, 36-38; lectr ling, Yale Univ, 39-42, res asst, 45-46; lectr phonetics & ling, Hartford Sem Found, 42-43, instr, 45-46; in charge army specialized training in Hindustani, Univ Pa, 43-44; mem staff, foreign serv inst, US Dept State, 46-47; assoc prof classic lang, Univ Tex, 47-48; assoc prof, 48-59, chmn dept, 63-70, Prof Ling, Univ PA, 59-, Am Coun Learned Soc fel, 42-43, 44-45; lectr, Hunter Col, 42-43 & 46; Guggenheim fel, 50-51; vis assoc prof, Georgetown Univ, 52-53 & 54; assoc ed, J Am Orient Soc, 52-54, ed, 54-58; sr linguist, Deccan Col, India, 55; Newberry Libr fel, 56; chmn Am comt, SAsian Lang, 56; vis assoc prof, Princeton Univ, 59-60; vis prof, Yale Univ, 61-62; Nat Sci Found sr fel, Ctr Advan Study Behav Sci, 62-63; mem comt lang prog, Am Coun Learned Soc, 63-70; mem univ sem, Columbia Univ, 64-; mem corp vis comt, Mass Inst Technol, 68-74; Fulbright lectr, Oxford Univ, 76-77; fel, St John's Col, Oxford, 76-77; chmn, overseers comt to vis Dept of Ling, Harvard Univ, 78- **HONORS AND AWARDS** LHD, Swarthmore Col, 81; LHD, Univ Pennsylvania. **MEMBERSHIPS** Ling Soc Am (pres, 58); Am Orient Soc (pres, 66-67); Am Philos Soc; Am Acad Arts & Sci; Philol Soc; Nat Academy of Sciences; British Academy. **RESEARCH** History of linguistics; Indo-European comparative linguistics; theory of change and reconstruction. **SELECTED PUBLICATIONS** Auth, Language change and linguistic reconstruction, 60; auth, Studies in Formal Historical Linguistics, 73; numerous articles. **CONTACT ADDRESS** Univ of Pennsylvania, 618 Williams Hall, Philadelphia, PA 19104. **EMAIL** henryh@babel.ling.upenn.edu

HOFFER, PETER T.
PERSONAL Born 05/27/1942, Providence, RI, s **DISCIPLINE** GERMAN STUDIES **EDUCATION** Columbia Univ, BA, 64; Tufts Univ, MA, 65; Univ Pa, PhD, 75. **CAREER** Instr, asst prof, Lincoln Univ, 71082; asst prof to assoc, prof, Univ Sci, 82. **HONORS AND AWARDS** Psych Cen, Fel Assoc. **MEMBERSHIPS** MLA; AATG; GSA; Fulbright Asn. **RESEARCH** History of psychoanalysis; applied psychoanalysis; history of science; intellectual history; modern German literature; translation. **SELECTED PUBLICATIONS** Auth, Monograph: Klaus Mann, GK Hall, 78; transl, Sigmund Freud: A Phylogenic Fantasy: Overview of the Transference Neuroses (Harvard Univ Pr, 1987); transl, The Correspondence of Sigmund Freud and Sandor Ferench (Harvard Univ Pr, 1993, 1996, 2000). **CONTACT ADDRESS** 151 Bishop Ave, Apt L14, Secane, PA 19018. **EMAIL** p.hoffer@usip.edu

HOFFMANN, GEORGE
DISCIPLINE FRENCH **EDUCATION** UCSB, MA, 84; Univ Aix-Marseille, DEA, 86; Univ Va, PhD, 90. **CAREER** Assoc Prof, Boston Univ. **HONORS AND AWARDS** C.A.I.E.P. article of the year Awd in Fr Studies, 96; Seaghorie Awd, best book in Fr Studies, 99. **MEMBERSHIPS** MLA. **RESEARCH** Renaissance Literature. **SELECTED PUBLICATIONS** Auth, Mointagne's Career, Claredon (Oxford), 98. **CONTACT ADDRESS** Dept For Lang, Boston Univ, 718 Commonwealth Ave, Boston, MA 02215-2423. **EMAIL** hoffmann@bu.edu

HOFFMANN, KLAUS D.
DISCIPLINE GERMAN LITERATURE **EDUCATION** Univ Iowa, PhD. **CAREER** Assoc prof. **RESEARCH** Study of the heritage of Germans from Russia. **CONTACT ADDRESS** Foreign Languages and Literature Dept, Colorado State Univ, Fort Collins, CO 80523. **EMAIL** khoffmann@vines.colostate.edu

HOFFMEISTER, GERHART
PERSONAL Born 12/17/1936, Giessen, Germany, d, 1966, 1 child **DISCIPLINE** GERMAN & COMPARATIVE LITERATURE **EDUCATION** Univ Md, College Park, PhD(Ger), 70. **CAREER** Referendar English & Ger, Cologne Sch Syst, 64-66; instr Ger, Univ Md, 66-70; asst prof, Univ Wis-Milwaukee, 70-74; assoc prof, Wayne State Univ, 74-75; assoc prof, 75-79, Prof Ger, Univ Calif, Santa Barbara, 79-, Am Philos Soc grant, 75. **MEMBERSHIPS** MLA; Am Asn Teachers Ger; Philol Asn Pac Coast. **RESEARCH** German baroque; German-Hispanic relations; European romanticism. **SELECTED PUBLICATIONS** Auth, The Influence of Italian Humanism on the German Literature Before 1600, German Quarterly, Vol 0067, 94; Early Romanticism--Epoch, Work, Influence, German Quarterly, Vol 0067, 94; Italian-European Cultural Ties During the Baroque Period, German Quarterly, Vol 0065, 92. **CONTACT ADDRESS** Dept of Ger & Slavic Lang, Univ of California, Santa Barbara, 552 University Rd, Santa Barbara, CA 93106-0001. **EMAIL** hoffmeis@humanities.ncsb.edu

HOFFMEISTER, WERNER
DISCIPLINE GERMAN AND COMPARATIVE LITERATURE **EDUCATION** Brown Univ, PhD, 62. **CAREER** Emeritus Prof Ger and Comp Lit. **RESEARCH** Ger and comparative lit of the 19th and 20th centuries, particularly prose fiction. **SELECTED PUBLICATIONS** Auth, publ(s) about Fontane, Kleist, Grass, Thomas Mann, Musil, and Ger-Am lit rel(s). **CONTACT ADDRESS** Dept of German Studies, Dartmouth Col, 6084 Dartmouth Hall, Hanover, NH 03755.

HOGELAND, L. M.
PERSONAL Born 08/16/1959, Glendale, CA, s **DISCIPLINE** MODERN THOUGHT AND LITERATURE **EDUCATION** Stanford Univ, AB, 81; PhD, 92. **CAREER** Assoc Prof English & Women's Studies, Univ Cincinnati. **RESEARCH** American women writers; Feminist criticism and theory. **SELECTED PUBLICATIONS** Auth, Fear of Feminism, MS, 94; Feminism and Its Fictions: The Consciousness-Raising Novel and the Women's Liberation Movement; Univ Penn Press, 98. **CONTACT ADDRESS** Univ of Cincinnati, PO Box 0069, Cincinnati, OH 45221-0069. **EMAIL** lisa.hogeland@uc.edu

HOHENDAHL, PETER U.
PERSONAL Born 03/17/1936, Hamburg, Germany, m, 2 children **DISCIPLINE** GERMAN STUDIES **EDUCATION** Univ Hamburg, PhD, 64. **CAREER** Asst prof Ger, PA State Univ, 65-68; assoc prof, WA Univ, 68-69, prof, 70-77, chmn dept, 72-

77; Prof Ger & Comp Lit, Cornell Univ, 77-, Chmn Dept, 81-86; Jacob Gould Shurman Prof Ger & Comp Lit, 85-; Merton vis prof, Free Univ Berlin, 76; Distinguished vis prof, OH state Univ, 87. **HONORS AND AWARDS** Choice Outstanding Acad Bk Awd, 96. **MEMBERSHIPS** MLA; Am Asn Tchr(s) Ger; Ger studies Asn; Heinnoh Heine soc; AHA. **RESEARCH** Theory of lit; 18th and 19th century Europ lit; mod Ger lit. **SELECTED PUBLICATIONS** Auth, Literaturkritik und Offentlichkeit, Piper, 74; auth, Der europaische Roman der Empfindsamikeit, Athenaion, 77; The Institution of Criticism, Cornell Univ Press, 82; Building a National Literature, The Case of Germany, 1830-1870, 89; Reappraisals: Shifting Alignments in Postwar Critical Theory, 91; Geschichte Opposition Subersion: Studien zur Literatur des 19 Jahrhunderts, 93; Prismatic Thought: Theodore W. Adorno, 95. **CONTACT ADDRESS** Dept of Ger Studies, Cornell Univ, 193 Goldwin Smith Hall, Ithaca, NY 14853-3201. **EMAIL** puh1@cornell.edu

HOJI, HAJIME

DISCIPLINE LINGUISTICS AND EAST ASIAN LANGUAGES AND CULTURES **EDUCATION** Univ Wash, PhD, 85. **CAREER** Assoc prof, Univ Southern Calif. **RESEARCH** East Asian linguistics. **SELECTED PUBLICATIONS** Auth, Anaphora and Japanese Syntax; Japanese/Korean linguistics. **CONTACT ADDRESS** East Asian Studies Center, Univ of So California, University Park Campus, Los Angeles, CA 90089.

HOLLAND, NORMAN

DISCIPLINE HISPANO-AMERICAN LITERATURES **EDUCATION** Johns Hopkins Univ, PhD. **CAREER** Assoc prof, Hampshire Col. **SELECTED PUBLICATIONS** Writes on Latin Am and Latino lit and cult. **CONTACT ADDRESS** Hampshire Col, Amherst, MA 01002.

HOLLANDER, ROBERT

PERSONAL Born 07/31/1933, Manhattan, NY, m, 1964, 2 children **DISCIPLINE** ITALIAN, COMPARATIVE LITERATURE **EDUCATION** Princeton AB, 55; Columbia PhD, 62. **CAREER** Col Sch, NYC, teacher, latin eng, 55-57; Colum Col, instr eng, 58-62; Princeton, lectur euro lit, dept RLL, 62; Princeton, prof euro lit, depots RLL and CL, 75-98; Butler Col, Master, 91-95, chmn comp lit, 94-98; Fellowships, Guggenheim, Fulbright, NEH 2, Rockefeller Found, Bellagio; Founding Memb of Intl Dante Seminar, pres, 92-2000; Mem, Bd trust, Collegiate Sch NYC, 90-96, 98-2001; Vs prof, Univ Florence, 88; Nat Humanities Cen, Mem, Bd trust, 81-, Chmn Comm on Schol Affairs, 87-88, Vice Chmn and VP of the center, 87-88, Chmn Bd, 88-91; Emer Stat, 91-. **HONORS AND AWARDS** The Howard T Behrman Awd, Princ, 86; Gold Medal of the Cty Florence, behalf of Dante, 88; John Witherspoon Awd in Humanities, NJ Comm, 88; Bronze Medal of the Cty of Tours, 93; Hon Cit of Certaldo, behalf of Boccaccio, 97. **MEMBERSHIPS** Dante Soc Am; Soc Dante Italiana; Am Boccaccio Asn. **RESEARCH** Dante; Boccaccio; late Medieval Europe **SELECTED PUBLICATIONS** Allegory in Dante's Commedia, Prin, 69; Boccaccio's Two Venuses, Colum, 77; Studies in Dante, Longo, 80; Il Virgilio dantesco, Olschki, 83; Boccaccio's Last Fiction, Il Corbaccio, Penn, 88; Dante's Letter to Cangrande, Mich, 93; Boccaccio's Dante and the Shaping Force of Satire, Mich, 97; auth, Dante Alighieri Editalia, 00. **CONTACT ADDRESS** Princeton Univ, Dept Romance Languages, Princeton, NJ 0854. **EMAIL** bobh@princeton.edu

HOLLIDAY, VIVIAN LOYREA

PERSONAL Born 02/25/1935, Manning, SC **DISCIPLINE** CLASSICS, ANCIENT HISTORY **EDUCATION** Winthrop Col, AB, 57; Univ Mo, MA, 59; Univ NC, PhD(classics), 61. **CAREER** Instr classics, 61-63, from asst prof to assoc prof, 63-69, Aylesworth Prof Classics, Col Wooster, 69-, Dean Fac, 77-85, mem managing comt, Am Sch Class Studies, Athens, 67. **MEMBERSHIPS** Am Philol Asn; Am Inst Archaeol. **RESEARCH** Republican Rome; comparative literature; modern Greek literature. **SELECTED PUBLICATIONS** Auth, Pompey in Cicero's Letters and Lucan's Civil War, Mouton, The Hauge, 69; Kazantzakis, Odyssey, Neo-Hellenika, Vol III, 78; Job Satisfaction for the Faculty, Academic Job Satisfaction: Varieties and Values, 80; Classical and Modern Narratives of Leadership, (pub 1999). **CONTACT ADDRESS** Dept of Classics, The Col of Wooster, 1189 Beall Ave, Wooster, OH 44691-2363. **EMAIL** IN%vholliday@acs.wooster.edu

HOLLINGSWORTH, ANTHONY L.

PERSONAL Born 09/10/1967, Rockford, IL, m, 1995, 1 child **DISCIPLINE** CLASSICS, GERMAN LANGUAGE AND LITERATURE **EDUCATION** Univ Dallas, BA, 89; Brown Univ, AM, 93; PhD, 98. **CAREER** Asst prof, Roger Williams Univ, 97-; dept chair, 98-. **HONORS AND AWARDS** Fulbright Fel; DAAD Diss Fel; Den's Grad Fel; Rotary Schl; Cardinal Spellman Awd; Phi Beta Kappa. **MEMBERSHIPS** APA; CANE; RICA; ACL; ATFL. **RESEARCH** Latin and Greek literature; German language and literature; comedy and tragedy (ancient and modern); computing applications. **SELECTED PUBLICATIONS** Auth, "Let The Play Begin: The Origin of the Greek Theater," Class Calliope 8 (97); auth, "Octavian's Triple Triumph," Class Calliope 8 (97); auth, "Recitation and Senecan Tragedy: Where is The Similarity?," Class World (97); auth, "Love Leads to War: The Origins of The Trojan War," Class Calliope 9 (98); auth, "Defeat and Victory: Hannibal's March," Class Calliope (98); auth, "Hadrian: Emperor By Adoption," Classical Calliope (99); auth, "A Loud No to The Demand For Food & Water," Classical Calliope (99); auth, "Charlemagne, According to Einhard," Class Calliope (99); auth, "If You Build It, They Will Enroll: The Formation of a Language Department," NECJ (forthcoming). **CONTACT ADDRESS** Dept Humanities, Roger Williams Univ, 1 Old Ferry Rd, Bristol, RI 02809-2923. **EMAIL** alh@alpha.rwu.edu

HOLLIS, SUSAN T.

PERSONAL Born 03/17/1939, Boston, MA, d, 2 children **DISCIPLINE** RELIGION; ANCIENT NEAR EASTERN LANGUAGES & CIVILIZATIONS **EDUCATION** Harvard, PhD, 82 **CAREER** Prof, Union Inst Los Angeles, 91-93; dean & prof, Sierra Nevada Col, 93-95; center dir & assoc dean, Central NY Center, State Univ of NY, Empire State Col, 96-; Assoc Prof, Genesee Valley Century, State University of New York, Empire State Col, 99- **HONORS AND AWARDS** Teaching Excellence, Harvard Col; Who's Who in the West, East, America, World, Women **MEMBERSHIPS** Amer Res Egypt; Amer Acad Relig; Soc Bibl Lit; Int Assoc Egyptologist; Amer Folklore Soc **RESEARCH** Ancient Egypt; Ancient Israel; Egyptian Relations; Folklore; Ancient Women's Studies **SELECTED PUBLICATIONS** auth, The Ancient Egyptian "Tale of Two Brothers": The Oldest Fairy Tale in One World, u. and OK Press, 90; co-ed & contributor, Feminist Theory and the Study of Folklore, Univ Ill, 93; ed, Ancient Egyptian Hymns, Prayers, and Songs. An Anthology of Ancient Egyptian Lyric Poetry, Scholar's Press, 95; contri, Civilizations of the Ancient Near East, "Tales of Magic and Wonder" (Scribner 95); auth, "Otiose Deities and the Ancient Egyptian Pantheon," Jrnl Amer Res Center in Egypt, 98; contri, "Two Brothers"; contri, "Oval Tradition"; contri, The Oxford Encyclopedia and Ancient Egypt, Oxford, 01 **CONTACT ADDRESS** SUNY, Empire State Col, 1475 Winton Rd. N, Rochester, NY 14609. **EMAIL** susan_hollis@esc.edu

HOLMBERG, I. E.

DISCIPLINE GREEK LITERATURE **EDUCATION** Univ Vermont, BA, 80; Yale Univ, PhD, 90. **CAREER** Asst prof, Univ of Victoria, 91. **RESEARCH** Early Greek hexameter poetry; construction of gender and representations of women in ancient Greek literature. **SELECTED PUBLICATIONS** Auth, "Euripides Helen: Most Noble and Most Chaste," AJP 116, (95): 19-42; auth, "The Odyssey and Female Subjectivity," Helios 22.2, (95): 1-21; auth, "The Sign of Metis," Arethusa 30.1, (97): 1-33. **CONTACT ADDRESS** Dept of Greek and Roman Studies, Univ of Victoria, PO Box 1700 STN CSC, Victoria, BC, Canada V8W 2Y2. **EMAIL** ingrid@uvic.ca

HOLMLUND, CHRISTINE

DISCIPLINE FRENCH LITERATURE **EDUCATION** Univ Wis, PhD, 84. **CAREER** Assoc prof, Cinema Studies & French, Univ Tenn. **RESEARCH** Film studies; women's studies; critical theory. **SELECTED PUBLICATIONS** Auth, pubs on mainstream and experimental films from Canada, France, the U.S., Austria, Sweden, Costa Rica, and Ecuador, and French feminist theory. **CONTACT ADDRESS** Dept of Mod For Langs & Lits, Univ of Tennessee, Knoxville, 701 McClung Tower & Plaza, Knoxville, TN 37996. **EMAIL** cholmlun@utk.edu

HOLOKA, JAMES P.

PERSONAL Born 01/19/1947, Rochester, NY, m, 1968, 3 children **DISCIPLINE** CLASSICS AND ANCIENT HISTORY **EDUCATION** Univ Rochester, BA, 69; SUNY-Binghamton, MA, 72; Univ Mich, PhD, 74. **CAREER** Teaching asst/fel, 69-72; lectr, Eastern Mich Univ, 74-76; from asst prof to prof, Eastern Mich Univ, 76-. **HONORS AND AWARDS** Rackham Prize Fel, Univ Mich, 73-74; NEH Summer Stipend, 76; Distinguish Fac Award for Excellence in Teaching and Commitment to Students, 80; Scholarly Recognition Award, 91. **MEMBERSHIPS** Am Philol Asn; Class Asn of the Mid West and South; Cen Intl d'Etudes Homeriques. **RESEARCH** Greek and Roman epic, lyric, and satire; Ancient history; Women in antiquity; Comparative literature and literary theory. **SELECTED PUBLICATIONS** Auth, "Homeric Originality: A Survey," 78; "Homer Studies 1971-1977," 79; "Looking Darkely: Reflections on Status and Decorum in Homer," 83; "Homer Studies 1978-1983 Pt. 1," 90; "Homer Studies 1978-1983 Pt. 2," 90; "Homer, Oral Poetry Theory and Comparative Literature: Major Trends and Controversies in Twentieth-Century Criticism," 91; World History, 91; "Nonverbal Communication in the Classics: Research Opportunities," 92; Lives and Times: A World History Reader, 95; trans, Homer: His Art and His World, 96; Co-auth, A Survey of Western Civilization, 97; auth, Marathon and the Myth of the Same-Day March 97, 00. **CONTACT ADDRESS** Foreign Language Dept, Eastern Michigan Univ, 7685 Paint Creek Dr, Ypsilanti, MI 48197. **EMAIL** fla_holoka@online.emich.edu

HOLSCHUH, ALBRECHT

PERSONAL Born 02/28/1937, Voklingen, Germany, m, 1968, 5 children **DISCIPLINE** GERMANIC STUDIES **EDUCATION** Princeton Univ, AM, 61, PhD(Ger), 64. **CAREER** Instr Ger, Princeton Univ, 62-64; asst prof, 64-68, Assoc Prof Ger, Ind Univ Bloomington, 68-, Chmn Dept, 78-, Am Coun Learned Soc fel, 81. **MEMBERSHIPS** MLA; Am Asn Teachers Ger; Midwest Mod Lang Asn; Am Coun Teaching Foreign Lang; AAUP. **RESEARCH** Twentieth century German literature. **SELECTED PUBLICATIONS** Forum--Relevance, Philology and Baackmann Essay on Bachmann 'Undine Geht', German Quarterly, Vol 0068, 95. **CONTACT ADDRESS** Dept of Ger Studies, Indiana Univ, Bloomington, 1020 E Kirkwood Ave, Ballantine Hall 644, Bloomington, IN 47405. **EMAIL** holschuh@indiana.edu

HOLUB, ROBERT C.

PERSONAL Born 08/22/1949, Neptune, NJ, m, 1998, 1 child **DISCIPLINE** GERMAN LITERATURE, LITERARY THEORY **EDUCATION** Univ Pa, BA, 71; Univ Wis, Madison, MA, 73, MA, 76, PhD, 79. **CAREER** Teaching asst, Univ Wis, Madison, 72-78; asst prof of German, Univ Calif, Berkeley, 79-. **HONORS AND AWARDS** Emmy Kleist Fel, Univ of Wis, Madison, 77; WARF Dissertation Fel, Univ Wis, Madison, 78-79; Alexander von Humboldt Fel, 83-85; Humanities Res Fel, Univ Calif, Berkeley, 89; DAAD Study Visit Grant, 95; NEH Summer Stipend, 95. **MEMBERSHIPS** MLA; Am Asn Teachers of German; Heinrich Heine Soc. **RESEARCH** German intellectual, cultural, and literary history of the 19th & 20th century. **SELECTED PUBLICATIONS** Auth, Heinrich Heine's Reception of German Grecophilia: The Function and Application of the Hellenic Tradition in the First Half of the Nineteenth Century, Carl Winter (Heidelberg), 81; auth, Reflections of Realism: Paradox, Norm, and Ideology in Nineteenth-Century German Prose, Wayne State Univ Press (Detroit, MI), 91; auth, J¤rgen Habermas: Critic in the Public Sphere, Routledge (London), 91; auth, Crossing Borders: Reception Theory, Poststructuralism, Deconstruction, Univ of Wis Press (Madison, WI), 92; coed, Impure Reason: Dialectic of Enlightenment in Germany, Wayne State Univ Press (Detroit, MI), 93; auth, Friedrich Nietzsche, Twayne Publishers (New York, NY), 95; coed, Responsibility and Commitment: Ethische Posulate der Kulturvermittlung: Festschrift f¤r Jost Hermand, Lang (Frankfurt), 96; coed, Heine's Contested Identities: Politics, Religion, and Nationalism in Nineteenth-Century Germany, Lang (New York, NY), 99. **CONTACT ADDRESS** Dept German, Univ of California, Berkeley, 5315 Dwinelle Hall, Berkeley, CA 94720-3243. **EMAIL** RCHolub@socrates.berkeley.edu

HONG, RAN-E

PERSONAL Born 05/20/1960, Seoul, South Korea, 1 child **DISCIPLINE** LITERATURE, FRENCH **EDUCATION** Ewha Woman's Univ, BA, 81; MA, 83; Univ Paris, Doct de 3e Cycle, 87; Brown Univ, PhD, 00. **CAREER** Lectr, Ewha Woman's Univ, 87-94; lectr, Hongik Univ, 92-93; lectr, Hankook Univ, 93-95; lectr, Konkuk Univ, 94-96; asst prof, Rivier Col, 00-01. **MEMBERSHIPS** MLA; NASSCFL; ASEF; CIBP; Soc du XVIIe Siecle; Soc des Amis de Port-Royal. **RESEARCH** 17th-century French literature and culture. **SELECTED PUBLICATIONS** Auth, "Le Paradoxe Dans les Premieres Liasses de L'Apologie," Cahiers de Asn Intl des Etudes (88); auth, "La Force et Ses Aspects Selon Pascal," Equinox (88); auth, "L'ideal de L'honnete Homme Selon Pascal et la Figure de L'homme de Qualite Selon Confucius Pascalienne," Pascal (90); auth, "La Recriture de Deux Contes de La Fontaine et Sq Signification," Fr 17th-Century Lit (00); auth, L'impossible Social Selon Moliere, Gunter Narr (forthcoming). **CONTACT ADDRESS** Dept Mod Lang, Grand Valley State Univ, 1 Campus Dr, Allendale, MI 49401-9403.

HONG, WEI

PERSONAL Born 11/05/1962, China, m, 1986, 2 children **DISCIPLINE** LINGUISTICS **EDUCATION** Tongj Univ, China, BA, 83; MA, 86; Pur Univ, PhD, 94. **CAREER** Assoc prof, Pur Univ, 97-. **MEMBERSHIPS** IACL; ACTFL. **RESEARCH** Sociolinguistics; pragmatics; business Chinese. **SELECTED PUBLICATIONS** Auth, Practical Business Chinese, China Books (San Francisco), 98; auth, Chinese and German Requests: A Cross-cultural Study, Lincom (Munich, Ger), 98. **CONTACT ADDRESS** Dept Foreign Language, Purdue Univ, West Lafayette, West Lafayette, IN 47907. **EMAIL** hongwei@purdue.edu

HONIG, EDWIN

PERSONAL Born 09/03/1919, New York, NY, d, 2 children **DISCIPLINE** SPANISH **EDUCATION** Univ Wis, BA, 41, MA, 47. **CAREER** Instr English, Purdue Univ, 42, Ill Inst Technol, 46 & Univ NMex, 47-48; instr Harvard Univ, 49-52, Briggs-Copeland asst prof, 52-57; assoc prof, Brown Univ57-60, chmn dept, 67-68, prof, 60-82, EMER PROF ENGLISH & COMP LIT, BROWN UNIV, 82-, Guggenheim fel, 48 and 62; Bollingen Found grant, 63; vis prof, Univ Calif, Davis, 64-65; Nat Inst Arts & Lett grant, 66; Nat Transl Ctr Grant, 66; RI Comn on Arts, 67, sr poet, Poetry in Schs Prog, 67-72, mem spec comt, Arts-in-Educ, 70-72; Arts Award Comt, 72-73; Amy Lowell traveling scholar, 68-69; Nat Endowment for Humanities, co-transl fel, 77- & sr fel grant for independent studies, 75. **HONORS AND AWARDS** Guggenheim fel, 48, 62; Bollingen Foung Grant, 63; NEA Creative Writing Awd, Nat Endowment of Arts, 77, Music Awd, 80; ma, brown univ, 58. **MEMBERSHIPS** Dante Soc Am; PEN Club Am; Am Lit Transl Asn. **RESEARCH** Renaissance; theory of translation; theory of persona in literature and other disciplines. **SELECTED PUBLICATIONS** Auth, Mich Quarterly Rev, Vol 0036, 97. **CONTACT ADDRESS** Dept of English, Brown Univ, Providence, RI 02912.

HOOD, EDWARD
PERSONAL Born 04/10/1954, Burlington, NC, m **DISCIPLINE** LATIN AMERICAN LITERATURE **EDUCATION** West Ill Univ, BA, 77; BA, 79; MA, 79; San Diego State Univ, MA, 84; Univ Calif, PhD, 90. **CAREER** Asst prof, Coastal Carolina Col, 89-91; asst prof to assoc prof, Northern Ariz Univ, 91-. **HONORS AND AWARDS** Fulbright Fel, Research and teaching in Honduras, 97. **MEMBERSHIPS** S East Coun for Latin Am Studies, ILCH, CILCA. **RESEARCH** Central American literature, Gabriel Garcia Marquez. **SELECTED PUBLICATIONS** Auth, La ficcion de Gabriel Garcia Marquez: repeticion e intertextualidad, Peter Lang: New York, 93; trans, The Bugler/El corneta; Bilingual Edition (81) by Roberto Castillo, Univ Press of America: Lantham, 00; trans, "Face of the Earth, Heart of the Sky (seflores bajo los arboles (94)" by Mario Roberto Morales, Bilingual Review Press, 99; trans, Little Red Riding Hood in the Red Light District (Caperucita en la zona roja (77) by Manlio Argueta, Curbstone Press, 98; trans, The Lost Chronicles of Terra Firma (La nifa blanca y los pajaros sin pies (92) by Rosario Aguilar, White Pine Press, 97; trans, El corneta (81) by Roberto Castillo, Kendall Hung Publ, 96; auth, "La novela en Nicaragua: una bibliografia tentativa," Revista interamericana de bibliografia (98): 143-152; auth, "Tragedia de la paz, Milagro de la Paz: Del testimonio al intimismo en las novelas de Manlio Argueta," Antipodas, (98): 119-127; auth, "La larga vida feliz de Margarito Duarte, Milagro en Roma y La santa de Gabriel Garcia Marquez: del periodico al cine al cuento," Quaderni Ibero-Americani, (96): 97-104; auth, "Busqueda de identidad historico-literaria en La nina blanca y los pajaros sin pies de Rosario Aguilar," in Visiones y revisiones de la literatura centroamericana, Ciudad de Guatemala: Oscar de Leon Palacios, (00): 189-199; auth, "El proceso revolucionario en Nicaragua visto por tres narradoras: Rosario Aguilar, Gioconda Belli y Monica Zalaquett," Proceedings of the Pacific Coast Council on Latin American Studies, (94): 99-109. **CONTACT ADDRESS** Dept Mod Lang, No Arizona Univ, PO Box Nau, Flagstaff, AZ 86011-0001. **EMAIL** edward.hood@nau.edu

HOOLEY, DANIEL M.
PERSONAL Born 08/08/1950, Stillwater, MN, m, 1 child **DISCIPLINE** LATIN AND GREEK LITERATURE **EDUCATION** Minn Univ, MA, PhD, Class, PhD, Engl. **CAREER** Assoc prof, Univ MO, 92-; taught at Allegheny Col, Carleton Col & Princeton Univ; ed, Classical and Modern Lit. **HONORS AND AWARDS** ACLS fel. **MEMBERSHIPS** Am Philol Asn; Classical Asn of the Midwest and South; the Classical Asn. **RESEARCH** Satire; later Latin; Classical tradition; translation studies. **SELECTED PUBLICATIONS** Auth, The Classics in Paraphrase: Ezra Pound and Modern Translators of Latin Poetry & The Knotted Thong: Structures of Imitation in Persius; and a number of articles and reviews. **CONTACT ADDRESS** Dept of Classics, Univ of Missouri, Columbia, 420 GCB, Columbia, MO 65211. **EMAIL** hooleyd@missouri.edu

HOOVER, DAVID LOWELL
PERSONAL Born 02/10/1949, Goshen, IN, m, 1974, 1 child **DISCIPLINE** MEDIEVAL LITERATURE, LINGUISTICS **EDUCATION** Manchester Col, BA, 71; Ind Univ, MA, 74, PhD(English lang), 80. **CAREER** Instr English, Ind Cent Univ, 80-81; ASST PROF ENGLISH, NY UNIV, 81- **MEMBERSHIPS** MLA. **RESEARCH** Medieval language and literature; metrics; stylistics. **SELECTED PUBLICATIONS** Auth, Theory, Fact, and Grammar, 2 Approaches to Old-English Meter, Modern Philol, Vol 0092, 94. **CONTACT ADDRESS** English Dept, New York Univ, 19 University Pl, New York, NY 10003-4556.

HOOVER, POLLY
PERSONAL Born 08/28/1956, Yokosuka, Japan, m, 1986 **DISCIPLINE** CLASSICS **EDUCATION** Beloit Col, BA, 78; Univ Chicago, MA, 84; Univ Wisc, MA, 90; PhD, 95. **CAREER** Teaching Asst, Univ Chicago, 81-83; Teaching Asst to Instructor, Univ Wisc, 89-95; Visiting Instructor, Ohio State Univ, 95-97; part-time Instructor, Columbia Col, 97-98; Instructor, Wilbur Wright Col, 97-. **HONORS AND AWARDS** NEH Summer Sem Fel, 99; Pressey Honors Course Enrichment Fund, 96; Travel-Study Awd, CAMWS, 93; Distinguished Teaching Awd, 91-92; Univ Fel, 88-89. **MEMBERSHIPS** Am Philol Asn, Classical Asn of the Midwest and South. **RESEARCH** Literary Theory and Art; Technology in the Classroom. **SELECTED PUBLICATIONS** Auth, "Contextual Learning and the Latin Language Textbooks," Classical World, forthcoming; auth, The boundaries of Transgression, forthcoming. **CONTACT ADDRESS** Dept Humanities, Wilbur Wright Col N, 4300 N Narragansett Ave, Chicago, IL 60634-1591. **EMAIL** phoover@ccc.edu

HOPKINS, LEROY TAFT, JR.
PERSONAL Born 08/19/1942, Lancaster, PA **DISCIPLINE** RUSSIAN, GERMAN **EDUCATION** Millersville St Coll, BA 1966; Harvard U, PhD 1974. **CAREER** Millersville State Coll, asst prof of German, 79-; Prof of German, 92-; Chair Foreign Languages dept, 98-; Urban League of Lancaster Co Inc, acting exec dir, 79, asso dir, 76-79; Hedwig-Heyle-Schule (W Germany), instr English 74-76; NE Univ, instructor German, 71-72. **HONORS AND AWARDS** Received Travelling Fellowship Harvard Univ 1969-70; Study/Visit Grant for Research, German Academic Exchange Service, 1989; Member of Honor Society, Phi Kappa Phi, 1991. **MEMBERSHIPS** Adv Com on Black History PA Hist & Mus Commn 1979-; com person City of Lancasters Overall Econ Devel Prog; Bd Mem Lancastger Co Library/Lancaster Neighborhood Hlth Ctr 1977-; chmn PA Delegation to White House Conf on Libraries 1978-79; Past Pres, Lancaster Co. Historical Society, member of board 83-99, 00; 1st vice pres, Lancaster Historical Society, 1989-; mem, Pennsylvania Humanities Council, 1988-. **CONTACT ADDRESS** Dept of For Lang, Millersville Univ of Pennsylvania, Millersville, PA 17551. **EMAIL** leroy.hopkins@millersv.edu

HOPPER, EDWARD W.
PERSONAL Born 09/12/1939, Macon, MO, m, 1984, 1 child **DISCIPLINE** SPANISH **EDUCATION** North TX State, BA, 61; Univ Mo, MA, 64; PhD, 70. **CAREER** Instr, Univ Mo, 65-67; instr to assoc prof, Univ NC, 67-. **HONORS AND AWARDS** Bank of Am Awd for Teaching Excellence, Charlotte, 85-86. **MEMBERSHIPS** SAMLA. **RESEARCH** Spanish Golden Age, Don Quixote, Golden Age drama, Spanish and Spanish American Civilization, culture. **CONTACT ADDRESS** Dept For Lang, Univ of No Carolina, Charlotte, 9201 University City Blvd, Charlotte, NC 28223-0001. **EMAIL** ewhopper@email.uncc.edu

HOPPER, PAUL
DISCIPLINE ENGLISH AND LINGUISTICS **EDUCATION** Univ Tex, PhD. **CAREER** Lit, Carnegie Mellon Univ. **HONORS AND AWARDS** Ed, Jour Lang Scis; 's Language, Collitz Prof LSA's Linguistics Inst, Fulbright Fel; Guggenheim Fel. **MEMBERSHIPS** MLAl; Ling Soc Am. **SELECTED PUBLICATIONS** Coauth, Grammaticalization, Cambridge, 93. **CONTACT ADDRESS** Carnegie Mellon Univ, 5000 Forbes Ave, Pittsburgh, PA 15213.

HORAN, ELIZABETH R.
PERSONAL Born 07/06/1956, Boston, MA, m, 1980, 1 child **DISCIPLINE** LITERATURE IN ENGLISH & SPANISH **EDUCATION** Barnard Col, BA 78; Univ Calif-Santa Cruz, MA, 84, PhD, 88. **CAREER** Lectr, Wheelock Col, 87-88; vis asst prof, Tufts Univ, 88-89; from asst prof to assoc prof, Ariz State Univ, 89-; vis assoc prof, Grand Valley State, 00-01. **HONORS AND AWARDS** Fulbright Schol, 85-87, 95-96; Gabriela Mistral Awd, Org Am States, 90. **MEMBERSHIPS** MLA; ACLA; Letras Feministas; Emily Dickinson Int Soc. **RESEARCH** US & Latin American women writers; translations; biography. **SELECTED PUBLICATIONS** Co-transl, Happiness, White Pine Press, 93; auth, Gabriela Mistral, an Artist and Her People, Org Am States, 94; To Market: The Dickinson Copyright Wars, Emily Dickinson J, 96; Santa Maestra Muerta: Body and Nation in Portraits of Gabriela Mistral, Taller de Letras, 97; Reading the Book of Memory, Always from Somewhere Else: A Memoir of My Jewish Father, The Feminist Press at CUNY, 98; auth, The Subversive Voice of Carmen Lyra, Univ Pr Florida, 00; author of numerous other articles and publications. **CONTACT ADDRESS** English Dept, Arizona State Univ, Tempe, AZ 85287-0302. **EMAIL** elizabeth.horan@asu.edu

HORN, PIERRE LAURENCE
PERSONAL Born 11/13/1942, Paris, France, m, 1968 **DISCIPLINE** FRENCH, COMPARATIVE LITERATURE **EDUCATION** Brooklyn Col, City Univ New York, BA, 64; Columbia Univ, MA, 65, PhD, 74. **CAREER** Instr French, Columbia Univ, 68-69; asst prof, Clark Univ, 69-75; asst prof, 75-78, assoc prof French, 78-84, Prof, Wright State Univ, 84-; Contract escort & interpreter, US Dept State, 64-68; mem, bd dirs, Am Soc Interpreters, 72-77. **HONORS AND AWARDS** Chevalier de l'Ordre des Palmes academiques, French Govt, 78; Col of Liberal Arts, Wright State Univ, Merit Awd for Outstanding Teaching, 82; WSU Bd of Trustees Awd for Faculty Excellence, 88; WSU Presidential Awd for Outstanding Faculty Member, 89; Braye Golding Distinguished Prof of Research, 92-95. **MEMBERSHIPS** MLA; Am Asn Teachers Fr; Am Soc Interpreters; Popular Cult Asn. **RESEARCH** Nineteenth-century French literature; 20th century French literature; comparative novel. **SELECTED PUBLICATIONS** Auth, On a Whitman quotation in Les Caves du Vatican, Fr-Am Rev, winter 76; Un correspondent oublie de Victor Hugo: George J Harney, Revue Hist Lit France, 3-4/77; Isabelle: a detective novel by Andre Gide, Romance Notes, fall 77; Reflections on Mme de Renal's first name, Nineteenth-Century Fr Studies, fall-winter 77; L'episode des banquiers dans Cesar Birotteau et Jerome Paturot, L'Annee Balzacienne, 78; Marguerite Yourcenar's Le Labyrinthe du Monde: A Modern Autobiography In: The Writer and the Past, ed, Donald L. Jennermann, IN State Univ Press, 81; Victor Hugo's Theatrical Royalties during his Exile Years, Theatre Res Int, spring 82; co-ed, The Image of the Prostitute in Modern Literature, NY: Frederic Ungar Pubs, 84; auth, Marguerite Yourcenar, Boston: Twayne Pubs, 85; Louis XIV, NY: Chelsea House, 86; Lafayette, NY: Chelsea House, 89; ed, Handbook of French Popular Culture, Westport, CT: Greenwood Press, 91; auth, Modern Jewish Writers of France, Lewisburg, NY: Edwin Mellon Press, 97; Dictionary of French Cinema, Westport, CT: Greenwood Press, forthcoming; and numerous articles appearing in the following publications: The World Encyclopedia of Cartoons, Phenix, French-Am Rev, Modern Lang J, English Lang Notes, Cyclopedia of Literary Characters II, Contemp Graphic Artists, Cyclopedia of World Authors II, Great Lives from History: Twentieth Century, Identities and Issues in Literature (and several other publications). **CONTACT ADDRESS** Wright State Univ, Dayton, 3640 Colonel Glenn, Dayton, OH 45435-0001. **EMAIL** phorn@wright.edu

HORNING, ALICE S.
DISCIPLINE ENGLISH, LINGUISTICS **EDUCATION** Mich State Univ, 77, PhD, Boston Univ, BA, 71. **CAREER** Prof of Rhetoric and Linguistics, 94-, Oakland Univ; Assoc Prof, 88-94, Oakland Univ; Asst Prof, Oakland Univ, 82-88; Asst Prof, English, Wayne State Univ, 78-82. **HONORS AND AWARDS** Advising Excellence Awd, Oakland Univ, 85. **MEMBERSHIPS** NCTE; CCCC; Amer Assoc for Applied Linguistics, Michigan Linguistic Society, Assoc for Psychological Type. **RESEARCH** Language and Literacy acquisition, psycholinguistics; reading and writing processes. **SELECTED PUBLICATIONS** Auth, "The Psycholinguistics of Readable Writing," Ablex Publishing, 93; auth, "Understanding Literacy," co-edited with Ron Sudol, Hampton Press, 97; auth, "The Literacy Connection," co-edited with Ron Sudol, Hampton Press, 99. **CONTACT ADDRESS** Department Rhetoric, Oakland Univ, Rochester, MI 48309. **EMAIL** horning@oakland.edu

HORNSBY, ROGER ALLEN
PERSONAL Born 08/08/1926, Nye, WI, m, 1960 **DISCIPLINE** CLASSICS **EDUCATION** Western Reserve Univ, BA, 49; Princeton Univ, MA, 51, PhD(classics), 52. **CAREER** Instr Latin & Greek, 54-58, from asst prof to assoc prof classics, 58-67, chmn dept, 66-81, Prof Classics, Univ Iowa, 67-, Coun Learned Soc fel, 70-71; consult, Nat Endowment for Humanities, 71-72; ed, Text Book Series APA, 75-81, Am Acad Rome resident, 83. **HONORS AND AWARDS** Ovatio, Classic Asn Midwest & South, 80. **MEMBERSHIPS** Am Philol Asn; Classic Asn Midwest & South (pres, 68-69); Archaeol Inst Am; Am Numis Soc; Mediaeval Acad Am. **RESEARCH** Latin poetry; stoicism; Greek poetry. **SELECTED PUBLICATIONS** Auth, The Vergilian Simile as Means of Judgement, 60: 337-344, Classics J; The Armor of the Slain, Philol Quart, 4/66; The Works of Luther; Reading Latin Poetry, Okla Univ, 67; The Pastor in the Poetry of Vergil, Classics J, 1/68; Patterns of Action in the Aeneid, Univ Iowa, 70. **CONTACT ADDRESS** Dept Classics, Univ of Iowa, Iowa City, IA 52242.

HORSLEY, RITTA JO
PERSONAL 2 children **DISCIPLINE** GERMAN LANGUAGE & LITERATURE **EDUCATION** Radcliffe Col, AB, 62; Harvard Univ, MA, 64, PhD(Ger lang & lit), 70. **CAREER** Asst prof Ger, 69-76, assoc dean spec prog & interdisciplinary studies, Col Arts & Sci, 76-77, assoc prof Ger, Univ Mass, Boston, 76-. **HONORS AND AWARDS** Fulbright Senior Professor; DAAD Study. **MEMBERSHIPS** Am Asn Teachers Ger; MLA; Women in Ger. **RESEARCH** Age of Goethe; 20th century German fiction; women in literature; European Witch Persecutions; Lesbian Studies. **SELECTED PUBLICATIONS** Articles concerning Irmgard Keun, Iugeborg Bachmaun, and European Witch Persecutions. **CONTACT ADDRESS** Dept of Mod Lang, Univ of Massachusetts, Boston, 100 Morrissey Blvd, Boston, MA 02125-3393. **EMAIL** horsley@umbsky.cc.umb.edu

HORWATH, PETER
PERSONAL Born 06/27/1929, Petrovgrad, Yugoslavia, 3 children **DISCIPLINE** GERMAN **EDUCATION** Ind Univ, Bloomington, BA, 52, MA, 53; Univ Mich, PhD, 59. **CAREER** Ind Univ, 52-53; Holy Cross Col, 55-59; Univ Ariz, 60-63; E Wash State Univ, 67; Prescott Col, 68-73; Prof, 67-, assoc prof, 73, chair, 84-92, coord German, 92, grad dir, Arizona State Univ. **HONORS AND AWARDS** Golden Cross of Honor (Austria); Cross of Honor for the Scis and the Arts (Austria); Internationales Forschungszentrum Kulturwissenschaft (Vienna), 96. **MEMBERSHIPS** World Fedn of Humanists (Budapest); Int Asn of Intercultural Studies; Fedn Internationale des Langues et Litteratures Modernes; Mod Lang Asn of Am; Societe Europeenne de Culture (Venice). **SELECTED PUBLICATIONS** Publications & Video Recording in German, Austrian, Serb Literature & Cultural History; Folklore; Curricular Matters. **CONTACT ADDRESS** Dept of Languages and Literatures, Arizona State Univ, MC 0202, Tempe, AZ 85287. **EMAIL** peter.horwath@asu.edu

HORWEGE, RONALD EUGENE
PERSONAL Born 03/05/1944, St. Francis, KS, m, 1970, 2 children **DISCIPLINE** GERMANIC LINGUISTICS **EDUCATION** Univ Kans, BA, 66; Ind Univ, Bloomington, MA, 68, PhD, 71. **CAREER** Asst prof, 71-79, Assoc Prof Ger, Sweet Briar Col, 79-; Chmn, Dept Mod Lang, 81-, Guest lectr, Cent Va Community Col, 72-; Fulbright Sem on Ger Cult fel, 76; Sweet Briar Col res grant, 77-78, 81 & 82; Danish teacher, Gen

Electric Plant, Lynchbung, 78-79; consult, NEH grant, 79. **MEMBERSHIPS** Am Asn Teachers Ger; Am Coun for Study Austrian Lit. **RESEARCH** Early New High German; German literature and German nationalism; Old Icelandic. **SELECTED PUBLICATIONS** Auth, Marquard von Lindau: De nabuchodonosor, Jahrbuch fur internationale Germanistik, 76, 79. **CONTACT ADDRESS** Dept of Mod Lang, Sweet Briar Col, Box 35, Sweet Briar, VA 24595-1056. **EMAIL** horwege@sbc.edu

HOTTELL, RUTH A.
PERSONAL Born Corydon, IN, m, 2000 **DISCIPLINE** FRENCH **EDUCATION** Western Ky Univ, BA, 74; Univ Louisville, MA, 81; Univ Ill, PhD, 87. **CAREER** Assoc prof French; prof of French. **HONORS AND AWARDS** Outstanding Univ Woman, 97. **SELECTED PUBLICATIONS** Auth, A Poetics of Pain: Evelyne Accad's Critical and Fictional World, World Lit Today, 97; Chanter son pays-La Rue Cases-Negres d'Euzhan Palcy, Martinique, 97; The Diabolic Dialogic: Les Diaboliques by Henri-Georges Clouzot, Lit Film Quarterly, 96; The Delusory Denouement and other Narrative Strategies in Maupassant's Fantastic Tales, Romanic Rev, 94; The Time of Ecofeminism, Humanities, 94; co-auth, The Pedantic Eye/I: Feminist Theory and Pedagogy, State Univ NY, 97; auth, Including Ourselves: The Role of Female Spectators in Le Bonheur and L'Une chante, l'autre pas by Agnes Varda, Cinema Journal, 99; auth, Flying through Southern France: Sans toit ni loi by Agnes Varda, Women's Studies, 99. **CONTACT ADDRESS** Foreign Languages Dept, Univ of Toledo, Univ Hall 5210, Mail stop 930, Toledo, OH 43606. **EMAIL** ruth.hottell@utoledo.edu

HOUNG, CAROLINE C.
DISCIPLINE LINGUISTICS, CHINESE LANGUAGE **EDUCATION** Chengchi Univ, Taiwan, BA, 75; Occidental Col, MA; Univ TX, Austin, PhD, 87. **CAREER** Instr, Univ TX, Austin; instr, Univ Houston; instr, Soochow Univ, Taiwan; instr, Nat Ocean Univ, Taiwan; instr, Fort Bend Independent Sch Dist; Prof, Rice Univ. **SELECTED PUBLICATIONS** Auth, Popular Chinese Expressions in American English; Communicating in Chinese Workbook. **CONTACT ADDRESS** Rice Univ, PO Box 1892, Houston, TX 77251-1892. **EMAIL** houng@ruf.rice.edu

HOUSTON, GEORGE W.
PERSONAL Born 11/15/1941, New York, NY, m, 1962, 2 children **DISCIPLINE** CLASSICS **EDUCATION** Haverford Col, BA, 63; Univ NC, PhD, 71. **CAREER** Instr to Prof and Dept Chair, Univ NC, 71-. **HONORS AND AWARDS** Fulbright Grant, Italy, 67-68; Rome Prize Fel, Am Acad, Rome, 67-69; Am Philos Soc Res Grant, 82; Bowman and Gordon Gray Assoc Prof, 86-89; Lurcy Fel, Inst for the Arts and Humanities, 89. **MEMBERSHIPS** Am Philol Asn; Archaeol Inst of Am; Am Soc of Greek and Latin Epigraphy; Vergilian Soc. **RESEARCH** Roman history and historiography; Latin Epigraphy; Roman social history and the history of technology. **SELECTED PUBLICATIONS** Auth, "A Revisionary Note on Ammianus Marcellinus 14.6.18: When Did the Public Libraries of Ancient Rome Close?" Library Quarterly, (88): 258-264; auth, "Ports in Perspective: Some Comparative Materials on Roman Merchant Ships and Ports," Am Journal of Archaeol, (88): 553-564; auth, "The State of the Art: Current Work in the Technology of Ancient Rome," Classical Journal (89): 63-80; auth, "What Uses Might Roman Farmers Have Made of the Loans They Received in the Alimenta Program?" Rivista Storica dell'Antichita, (93): 97-105; auth, "The Slave and Freedman Personnel in Roman Public Libraries," Preatti del CI Congresso Internazionale di Epigrafia Greca e Latina, (97): 819-827. **CONTACT ADDRESS** Dept Classics, Univ of No Carolina, Chapel Hill, CB 3145, Chapel Hill, NC 27599. **EMAIL** gwhousto@email.unc.edu

HOUSTON, MONA T.
DISCIPLINE FRENCH LITERATURE **EDUCATION** Yale Univ, PhD, 64. **CAREER** Assoc prof emer, Indiana Univ. **RESEARCH** History of the theater and performance. **SELECTED PUBLICATIONS** Coed, Mauriac's Genitrix, 66; auth, French Symbolist Poetry: An Anthology, 80; coauth, Harper's Grammar of French. **CONTACT ADDRESS** Dept of French and Italian, Indiana Univ, Bloomington, 1020 E Kirkwood Ave, Ballantine Hall 642, Bloomington, IN 47405-7103.

HOWARD, JOAN E.
PERSONAL Born 08/25/1951, Augusta, ME, 1 child **DISCIPLINE** TRANSLATION **EDUCATION** Univ New Hamp, BA, 73; Univ RI, MA, 76; Univ Conn, PhD, 87. **CAREER** Dir, 91-, Word Works; Instr, Asst Prof, 81-89, Univ New Hamp. **HONORS AND AWARDS** Ludwig Vogelstein Foun Fel; Florence Gould Foun Gnt; NH Dept Cult Affs; UNH Cen Hum; AAUW Diss Fel; CRIC Gnt; Phi Kappa Phi; Pi Sigma, Alpha. **MEMBERSHIPS** MLA; WSP; WBC. **RESEARCH** Marguerite Yourcenar **SELECTED PUBLICATIONS** Trans, Carson McCullers: A young Girl's Heart, by Josyane Savigneau, Boston, Houghton Mifflin, in press; coed, Les Visages de la mort dans l' oeuve de Marguerite Yourcenar, Tours FR, SIEY, 93; trans, Marguerite Yourcenar: Inventing a Life, by Josyane Savigneau, Chicago, U of Chicago Press, 93; auth, From Violence to Vision: Sacrifice in the Works of Marguerite Yourcenar, Carbondale, S IL U Press, 92. **CONTACT ADDRESS** Word Works, 78 Congress St, Portsmouth, NH 03801-4018. **EMAIL** wrdwks@nh.ultranet.com

HOWARD, LLOYD H.
PERSONAL Born 12/08/1951, Los Angeles, CA **DISCIPLINE** ITALIAN AND MEDIEVAL STUD **EDUCATION** Univ BC, BA, 73; Johns Hopkins Univ, MA, 75, PhD, 76. **CAREER** Instr to asst prof, 76-90, prof, State Univ NY Oswego, 90-; ch, dept Hispanic & Ital stud, 89-94, Dir, Medieval Stud Prog, Univ Victoria, 96-99; . **HONORS AND AWARDS** Gilman fel, SSHRCC grants. **MEMBERSHIPS** Can Soc Ital Stud (adv bd). **RESEARCH** Guido Cavalcanti, Dante's Divine Comedy. **SELECTED PUBLICATIONS** Ed bd, Quaderni d'italianistica; ed bd, Can J Ital Stud. **CONTACT ADDRESS** Medieval Stud Prog, Univ of Victoria, PO Box 3045, Victoria, BC, Canada V8W 3P4. **EMAIL** lhoward@uvic.ca

HOWES, GEOFFREY C.
PERSONAL Born 11/06/1955, Detroit, MI, m, 1979, 1 child **DISCIPLINE** GERMAN **EDUCATION** Mich State Univ, BA, 77; AM, 78; Mich State Univ, PhD, 85. **CAREER** Instr, Univ of Minn, 85-86; asst to assoc prof, Bowling Green State Univ, 86-. **HONORS AND AWARDS** Fulbright Grad, 82-83. **MEMBERSHIPS** MLA, Am Assoc of Teachers of Ger, Ger Studies Assoc, Int Arthur Schnitzler Res Assoc, Int Assoc for Philos and Lit. **RESEARCH** Austrian Literature and Culture, Contemporary Austrian Literature, Robert Musil, Joseph Roth, Peter Rosei, Madness and Literature. **SELECTED PUBLICATIONS** Auth, "Emerson's Image in Turn-of-the-Century Austria: The Cases of Kassner, Friedell, and Musil," Mod Austrian Lit, (89); auth, "Joseph Roth's Kapuzinergruft as a Document of 1938," Austrian Writers and the Anschluss, ed D. Daviau, Ariadne, (CA: Riverside, 91); auth, "Ein Genre ohne Eigenschaften: Musil, Montaigne, Sterne und die essayistische Tradition," Robert Musil: Essayismus und Ironie, ed G. Brokoph-Mauch, Francke, (Tubingen, 92); auth, "Flying Blind: A Neglected Early Essay by Bachmann," Thunder Rumbling at My Heels: Tracing Ingeborg Bachman, ed G. Brokoph-Mauch, Ariadne, (CA: Riverside, 98); auth, "Therapeutic Murder in Elfriede Cruzda and Lilian Faschinger," Mod Austrian Lit, (99); auth, "Rosei's I's: The (De-) Composition of the Self in Peter Rosei's Fiction," The Fiction of the I: Contemporary Austrian Writers and Autobiography, ed N. Meyerhofer, Ariadne, (CA: Riverside, 99); auth, "Antipsychiatrie bei Thomas Bernhard?" Thomas Bernhard: Die Zurichtung des Menschen, ed A. Honold and M. Joch, Konigshausen & Neumann, (Wurzburg, 99); auth, "A Proletarian Bildungsroman? Michael Scharang's 'Charly Traktor,'" Toward the Millenium: Interpreting the Austrian Novel 1971-1996, ed G. Chapple, Stauffenberg (Tubingen, 00); auth, "The Idea of Austria in Djuna Barnes Nightwood," Austria in Literature, ed D. Davaiu, Ariadne, (CA: Riverside, 00); auth, "Die Poetik der Poetik Peter Roseis," Basic Rosei, ed W. Vogl, Sonderzahl (Vienna, 00). **CONTACT ADDRESS** Dept Ger, Russ and E Asian Lang, Bowling Green State Univ, 438 N Prospect St, Bowling Green, OH 43402. **EMAIL** ghowes@bgnet.bgsu.edu

HOYT, GILES REID
PERSONAL Born 07/28/1943, Binghamton, NY, m, 1965, 1 child **DISCIPLINE** GERMAN LITERATURE **EDUCATION** Harpur Col, BA, 65; State Univ NYork, Binghamton, MA, 68; Univ Ill, PhD(Ger), 73. **CAREER** Instr English, Jamestown Community Col, 71-73; lectr Ger, Univ Wis-Milwaukee, 74-75; asst prof, 76-81, Assoc, 81-93, Prof Ger, Assoc Dean, Ind Univ-Purdue Univ, Indianapolis, 93-; NEH grant-in-residence Ger, Univ Cincinnati, 75-76. **MEMBERSHIPS** Am Asn Teachers Ger; MLA; Int Arbeitskreis Barockliteratur; Midwest Mod Lang Asn, Asn Intl Educators; Soc Ger-Am Stud. **RESEARCH** Seventeenth cent Ger lit; Ger novel; immigration hist. **SELECTED PUBLICATIONS** Auth, Johann Hellwig--A Descriptive Bibliography, German Quarterly, Vol 0069, 96; Sebastian Brant, the 'Ship Of Fools' in Critical Perspective, 1800-1901, German Studies Rev, Vol 0020, 97; Wolfgang Hildesheimer and His Critics, Seminar, Vol 0032, 96; Physics, Classics, and the Bible--Elements of the Secular and the Sacred in Heinrich Barthold Brockes 'Irdisches Vergnugen In Gott', 1721, German Quarterly, Vol 0066, 93; Previously Unknown Poetry of Sigmund-Von-Birken, German Quarterly, Vol 0067, 94. **CONTACT ADDRESS** Off Intl Affairs, Indiana Univ-Purdue Univ, Indianapolis, 620 Union Dr, Indianapolis, IN 46202. **EMAIL** hoyt@iupui.edu

HSIEH, HSIN-I
PERSONAL Born, Taiwan **DISCIPLINE** LINGUISTICS, CHINESE **EDUCATION** Taiwan Univ, BA, 63, MA, 6; Univ Calif, Berkeley, PhD(ling), 71. **CAREER** Asst prof Chinese, Univ Detroit, 70-71; asst res linguist, Univ Calif, Berkeley, 72; asst prof, 72-76, from assoc prof to prof Chinese, Univ Hawaii 76-83. **MEMBERSHIPS** Ling Soc Am; Assoc Asian Stud. **RESEARCH** Application of logic and mathematics to linguistics; Chinese linguistics; philosophy of language. **SELECTED PUBLICATIONS** Auth, The psychological reality of Taiwanese tone Sandhi rules, In: Papers from the Sixth Regional Meeting of Chicago Ling Soc, 70; coauth, The time variable in phonological change, J Ling, 7 1:1-13, 71; auth, Lexical diffusion: Evidence from child language acquisition, Glossa, 6 1:89-104, 72 & In: The Lexicon in Phonological Change, Mouton, 77; A new method of dialect subgrouping, J Chinese Ling, 1 1:64-92, 73 & In: The Lexicon in Phonological Change, Mouton, 77; Time as a cause of phonological irregularities, Lingua, 33 3: 253-264, 74; contribr, How generative is phonology?, In: The Transformational-Generative Paradigm and Modern Linguistic Theory, John Benjamins, Amsterdam, 75; auth, On the unreality of some phonological rules, Lingua, 38 1:1-19, 76; Set theory as a meta-language for natural languages, Papers in Ling, 13 3: 529-542, 80. **CONTACT ADDRESS** Dept East Asian Lang, Univ of Hawaii, Manoa, 1890 E West Rd, Honolulu, HI 96822-2318. **EMAIL** hhsieh@hawaii

HSIEH, YVONNE Y.
DISCIPLINE 20TH-CENTURY FRENCH LITERATURE **EDUCATION** Univ Stanford, PhD. **RESEARCH** East-West literary relations; exoticism in French Literature. **SELECTED PUBLICATIONS** Auth, Segalen's Literary Encounter with China: Chinese Moulds, Western Thoughts, U of Toronto P, 88; From Occupation to Revolution: China Through the Eyes of Loti, Claudel, Segalen and Malraux (1895-1933), Summa Publ, Inc Birmingham, 96; auth, "Andrre Dhotel: sage taoiste?" Ande Dhotel," Angerrs: Presses de l'univerrsite d'Angerrs, 98; auth, "Le probleme de l'alterite dans Les Immemoriaux de Victor Segalen," Revue Francophone XIII:I, (98), 43-54. **CONTACT ADDRESS** Dept of French, Univ of Victoria, PO Box 3045 STN CSC, Victoria, BC, Canada V8W 3P4. **EMAIL** yhsieh@uvic.ca

HSU, KYLIE
PERSONAL Born 07/03/1957, Taiwan **DISCIPLINE** APPLIED LINGUISTICS, CHINESE STUDIES **EDUCATION** Univ Mich, BA, 80; Cal State Univ, Northridge, MA, 94; Univ Calif at Los Angeles, PhD, 96. **CAREER** Instr, Univ Mich, 76-80; res, admin asst, Am GNC Corp, 80-86; exec vpres, 86-93; instr, Univ Calif, Los Angeles, 94-95; dir, pres asst, Pacific States Univ, 96-97; asst prof, Cal State Univ, LA, 97-; assoc cen dir, 99-. **HONORS AND AWARDS** Who's Who in World, Am, Am Women; 2000 Outstand Scholars; 1000 World Leaders of Influence; Inn Inst Awd; Pres Fel Res Grant; St Cal Fel; ALT Scholar; Bausch & Lomb Hon Sci Awd; Dept Edu Scholar; James B Angell Scholar; Martin Luther King Scholar; Nat Deans List; Olive M Roosenraad Mem Scholar; Regents Alumni; Vieta Vogt Woodlock Scholar; WK Kellogg Found Scholar. **MEMBERSHIPS** AAAL; ACTFL; AAS; ROCLING; ALT; CIBER; CLIC; CLTA; IACL; IBA; IPA; LASSO; LSA; MLA; ROCMELLA; TESOL. **RESEARCH** Contextual analysis of written and spoken discourse; language and cultural socialization; heritage language pedagogy; intercultural communication. **SELECTED PUBLICATIONS** Auth, A Discourse Analysis of Temporal Markers in Written and Spoken Mandarin Chinese: The Interaction of Semantics, Syntax, and Pragmatics, Edwin Mellen Press (Lewiston, NY), 98; auth, "Business Chinese through the world wide web," Global Bus Lang 4 (99): 122-135; rev of, Heinle & Heinle's Complete Guide to TOEFL Test: Practice Tests by Bruce Rogers, CATESOL NL 30 (98): 20-22; auth, "Joint attention in a father-child-mother triad: A Chinese-American case study," Issues in Applied Ling 7 (96): 77-90; rev of "Culture and Language Learning in Higher Education," Issues in Applied Ling 6 (95): 112-116; rev of, "Second-Language Classroom Interaction; Questions and Answers in ESL Classes," Issues in Applied Ling 6 (95): 155-157; auth, "How do Immigrant Chinese parents in the U.S. help their children to acquire literacy," in Literacy Instruction in English for Bilingual Students (Northridge: Cal St Univ, 94): 112-127. **CONTACT ADDRESS** Dept Modern Languages, Lit, California State Univ, Los Angeles, 5151 State University Dr, Los Angeles, CA 90032-8112.

HUALDE, JOSE IGNACIO
DISCIPLINE SPANISH LITERATURE **EDUCATION** Univ Southern Calif, MA, 85; PhD, 88. **CAREER** Assoc prof, Univ Ill Urbana Champaign. **RESEARCH** Cognitive approach to phonology; Integrating synchrony and diachrony; Acoustic investigation of Spanish spriantization; Basque accented systems. **SELECTED PUBLICATIONS** Auth, Catalan, Descriptive Grammars Series, London & New York: Routledge, 92, pp. I-xxx, 451; coauth, A Phonological Study of the Basque Dialect of Getxo, Donostia-San Sebastian: Diputacion Foral de Gipuzkoa, (Supplement 29 of Anuario del Seminario de Filologia Vasca 'Julio de Urquijo'), 92, J. I. Hualde & Xabier Bilbao, pp. 117; coed, Generative Studies in Basque Linguistics, Benjamins: Amsterdam & Philadelphia, 93, J. I. Hualde & Jon Ortiz de Urbina, pp.I-vi, 333; coauth, The Basque Dialect of Lekeitio, Bilbao & Donostia-San Sebastian: Univ. of the Basque Country Press & Diputacion Foral de Gipuzkoa, 94, J. I. Hualde, G. Elordieta & A. Elordieta, pp. 1-xx, 314; coed, Towards a History of the Basque Language, Amsterdam & Philadelphia: Benjamins, 95, J. I. Hualde, J. A. Lakarra & R. L. Trask, pp. 365; auth, "Accentuation and empty vowels in Ondarroa Basque: Against the concept of phonological derivation," Lingua 99, 96, 197-206; auth, "Spanish /l/ and related sounds: an exercise in phenemic analysis," Studies in the Linguistic Sciences 27.2, 97, 61-79; auth, Euskararen azentuerak [The accentual systems of the Basque language], Servicio Editorial de la Universidad del Pais Vasco/Euskal Herriko Unibertsitatea [Univ. of the Basque Country Press], 97, pp. 248; auth, "A gap filled: Postpostinitial

accent in Azkoitia Basque," Linguistics 36, 98, 99-117. **CONTACT ADDRESS** Spanish, Italian, and Portuguese Dept, Univ of Illinois, Urbana-Champaign, 52 E Gregory Dr, Champaign, IL 61820. **EMAIL** jhualde@staff.uiuc.edu

HUANG, ALEXANDER C. Y.

PERSONAL Born 03/30/1973, Taipei, Taiwan, s **DISCIPLINE** GERMAN **EDUCATION** Nat Tsinghua Univ, BA, 97; Oxford Univ, Cert, 96; Univ Trier, PNdS, 96. **CAREER** Teacher, Taiwan Sr High Sch, 96-97; teaching asst, Nat Tsing-Hua Univ, 96-97; interpreter, Management of New Art, Co, 98-99; tutor, Palo Alto, 00; teaching asst to instr and tutor, Stanford Univ, 00-. **HONORS AND AWARDS** Res Creativity Award, Nat Sci Coun, 97; Grant, Found for the Adv of Outstanding Scholar, 96; Fel, Nat Sci Coun Res, 96; Award, Chinese Asn of Confucian and Mencius Studies, 92. **MEMBERSHIPS** CLTA; English and Am Lit Asn of the Rep of China; Comp Lit Asn of the Rep of China; ACTFL; AATG; ACLA; SCLA; Folio Soc; Die Deutsche Shakespeare-Gesellschaft; ANZSA; ISA; MLA. **RESEARCH** Intercultural performance/theatre; Shakespeare in Germany and China; Cultural hermeneutics; Adaptations of Shakespeare. **SELECTED PUBLICATIONS** Auth, "Can You Sort Out What It's All About? Bona Fide Tykes versus New Comers," Peagasus (94): 2-4; auth, "The Chinese Shakespeare: Implications of Cultural Hermeneutics," in Intl Conf on Hermeneutic Traditions in Chinese Culture, Rutgers, 96; auth, "Tatsachen und 'Taschensachen' uber deutsche Stadte und Gegenden," J of For Lang Dept, (96): 51-56; auth, "Unser Shakespeare - das Rezeption Shakespeares in der deutsche Literature," J of For Lang Dept, 97; auth, "Shakespeare in Germany and Modern China: Toward a Cultural Hermeneutics," in 1997 Nat Conf on English/American Lit and Ling, Taipei, 97; co-auth, Sailing to Ellis Island, Taipei, 97; auth, Peregrinatio: Poetry Landscape of a Mind, 2nd ed, Taipei, 97; auth, "Caution! Artists at Work! The Hermeneutic Relevance of Intentionality and Literary Criticism," in The 2000 Interdisciplinary Symposium: The Portraits of Artist, Stanford Univ, 00; auth, "Conjunction and Disjunction: The German Shakespeare and its Chinese Counterpart," in Dislocating Shakespeare: The 6th Biennial Conf of the Australia and New Zealand Shakespeare Asn, Auckland, 00; auth, "A Form Unknown? The vicissitudes of the Tragic in Classical Chinese and Renaissance English Drama," in Interpretation and Perversion, Stanford Univ, 01. **CONTACT ADDRESS** Dept Lang and Lit, Stanford Univ, 74 Barnes Ct, Stanford, CA 94305-7197. **EMAIL** acyhuang@leland.stanford.edu

HUANG, J.

PERSONAL Born 06/04/1948, Taiwan, m, 1977, 2 children **DISCIPLINE** LINGUISTICS **EDUCATION** PhD, 82, MIT. **CAREER** Prof, 83-85, Natl Tsing-Hua Univ; Prof, 85-90, Cornell Univ; Prof, 90-, Univ California-Irvine. **HONORS AND AWARDS** Guggenheim Fel, 89; Fel, Ctr for Advanced Study in the Behavioral Sciences, 97-98. **MEMBERSHIPS** Linguistics Soc of Amer. **RESEARCH** Linguistic theory; syntax **CONTACT ADDRESS** Dept of Linguistics, Univ of California, Irvine, 3151 SSPA, Irvine, CA 92697-5100. **EMAIL** jhuang@uci.edu

HUBER, THOMAS

PERSONAL Born 03/23/1937, Berlin, Germany, m, 1988, 2 children **DISCIPLINE** GERMAN LANGUAGE AND LITERATURE **EDUCATION** Univ VT, MA, 62; Princeton Univ, MA, 64, PhD, 65. **CAREER** Instr Ger, Univ Vt, 61-62 & Princeton Univ, 64-65; lectr philol, Univ Bergen, Norway, 65-66; from asst prof to assoc prof Ger, 66-77, dir studies, Sch Ger, 66-67, 69-70 & 72-73, 87-88, 91-92, 96-97; Prof Ger, Middlebury Col, 77-, Dean, Sch Ger & Chmn Dept, 73-91, Consult int educ, Inst Int Educ, 67-68; bd men, Coun Int Educ Exchange, 76-81. **HONORS AND AWARDS** Ger-Am Friendship Awd, 85. **MEMBERSHIPS** MLA; AATC. **RESEARCH** Period of enlightenment in Germany; contemp Ger novel; popular Europ fiction. **SELECTED PUBLICATIONS** Auth, Studien zur Theorie des Ubersetzens, Hain: Meisenheim, 67; US Programs in Germany: Problems and Perspectives, IIE, New York; coauth, Modern German, Harcourt Brace Jovanovich, 71, 2nd ed, 78; auth, Studium in den USA, 74 & Studium in den USA--a case study, 74, aspekte, Frankfurt; coauth, Thomas Mann's Tonio Kroger, Harcourt Brace Jovanovich, 78. **CONTACT ADDRESS** Dept Ger, Middlebury Col, Middlebury, VT 05753-6001. **EMAIL** thomas_huber@flannet.middlebury.edu

HUBERT, JUDD D.

PERSONAL Born 01/17/1917, Toledo, OH, m, 1950, 1 child **DISCIPLINE** SEVENTEENTH CENTURY FREND LITERATURE, SYMBOLIST POETRY, THEATER ARTISTS' BOOKS **EDUCATION** Bac. Es L., Lille, France, 36; B.A. Middlebury, 41; M.A., Columbia Univ, 42; PhD, 51. **CAREER** Air Corps, 42-46; U.S. Merchant Marine Acad, Kings Point, NYork, 46-47; instr, Rutgers Univ, 47-50; teaching assoc, Columbia Univ, 50-52; asst prof, Harvard Univ, 53-57; assoc prof, UCLA, 57-62; prof, 62-65; prof, Univ of Ill, Urbana, 65-67; prof, Univ of Calif, Irvine, 67-87; prof emer, 87-. **HONORS AND AWARDS** Fulbright Res fel, France, 56-57; Guggenheim fel, 62-63; Camargo Found fel, 88; **SELECTED PUBLICATIONS** Auth, L'Esthetique des Fleurs du Mal: Essai sur l'ambiguite poetique, Cailler (Geneva), 53; auth, Essai d'exegese racinienne: les secrets temoins, Nizet (Paris), 56; auth, Moliere and the Comedy of the Intellect, Univ of Calif Press, 62; auth, Metatheater: The Example of Shakespeare, Nebr Univ Press, 91; auth, Corneille's Performative Metaphors, Rockwood Press (Charlottesville), 97; coauth, The Cutting Edge of Reading: Artists' Books, Granary Books (NYork), 99. **CONTACT ADDRESS** Dept of Fr and Ital, Univ of California, Irvine, Irvine, CA 92697. **EMAIL** jhubert@uci.edu

HUBERT, MARIE LOUISE

PERSONAL Born 06/25/1914, New York, NY **DISCIPLINE** FRENCH **EDUCATION** St Joseph's Col NYork, AB, 36; Columbia Univ, AM, 39; Yale Univ, PhD(French), 50. **CAREER** Pres, 56-71, prof French, Albertus Magnus Col, 42-, dir Inst Res, 72-, pres, Conn Coun Higher Educ, 65-67. **HONORS AND AWARDS** LLD, Albertus Magnus Col, 72. **MEMBERSHIPS** Am Asn Teachers Fr; Asn for Inst Res. **SELECTED PUBLICATIONS** Auth, Pascal's Unfinished Apology, Yale Univ & Presses Univs de France, 52; coauth, Pascal, In: The Seventeenth Century, Vol 4, A Critical Bibliography of French Literature, Syracuse Univ, 62; contribr, New Structures of Campus Power, Jossey-Bass, 78. **CONTACT ADDRESS** Dir Inst Res, Albertus Magnus Col, 700 Prospect St, New Haven, CT 06511-1189.

HUBERT, RENEE RIESE

DISCIPLINE FRENCH AND COMPARATIVE LITERATURE **EDUCATION** Columbia Univ, PhD. **CAREER** Prpf Emer, Fr and Compar Lit, Univ Calif, Irvine. **SELECTED PUBLICATIONS** Auth, Surrealism and the Book; Magnifying Mirrors: Women, Surrealism, and Partnership. **CONTACT ADDRESS** Dept of Fr and Ital, Univ of California, Irvine, Irvine, CA 92697.

HUBERT, RENEE RIESE

PERSONAL Born 07/02/1916, Wiesbaden, 1, Germany, m, 1950 **DISCIPLINE** FRENCH, COMPARATIVE LITERATURE, ARTISTS' BOOKS **EDUCATION** B. ed L., Lyon, 36; Licence es L., Sorbonne, 39; Columbia Univ, MA, 46, PhD, 51. **CAREER** Teacher, secondary school, England, 39-44; Instr French & German, Wilson Col, 45-47; instr French, Columbia Univ, 48-49; mem fac, Sarah Lawrence Col, 49-53; instr, Harvard Univ, 53-55; asst prof, Suffolk Univ, 55-56; asst prof French & German, San Fernando Valley State Col, assoc prof French & chmn dept foreign lang, 62-65; assoc prof French, Univ Ill, Urbana, 65-66, prof, 66-67; Prof French & Comp Lit, Univ Calif, Irvine, 67-87, prof emerita, 87-. **HONORS AND AWARDS** Guggenheim fel, 64-65; Sr fel Nat Endowment for Humanities, 79; Bellagio fel, 89; Camargo fel, 85, 88; Panunzio Prize, Univ of Calif Distinguished Emeriti Awd in Humanities & Social Sciences, 98. **MEMBERSHIPS** MLA; Am Asn Teachers Fr; Int Fed Mod Lang & Lit; Int Asn Studies Fr. **RESEARCH** Modern Poetry; relation of literature and art; surrealism. **SELECTED PUBLICATIONS** Auth, Le Verceau d'Eve, Ed de Minuit (Paris), 56; cotrans, Aragon, The Adventures of Telemachus, Univ of Nebraska Press, 88; auth, Surrealism and the Book, Univ of Calif press, 88; auth, Magnifying Mirrors: Women, Surrealism, and Partnership, Univ of Nebraska Press, 94; cotrans, Exact Change, (Cambridge), 97; coauth, The Cutting Edge of Reading: Artists' Books, Granary Books (NYork), 99. **CONTACT ADDRESS** Dept of French and Comp Lit, Univ of California, Irvine, Irvine, CA 92664. **EMAIL** rhubert@uci.edu

HUFFINES, MARION LOIS

PERSONAL Born 10/01/1945, Chester, PA **DISCIPLINE** GERMAN, SOCIOLINGUISTICS **EDUCATION** Maryville Col, TN, BA, 67; Ind Univ, Bloominton, MA, 69, PhD, 71. **CAREER** Prof Ger & Ling, Bucknell Univ, 71-, assoc vice pres, acade affairs; Nat Endowment for Humanities fel, 80. **MEMBERSHIPS** AAHE **RESEARCH** Sociolinguistics; Am dialects; PA Ger. **SELECTED PUBLICATIONS** Auth, Sixteenth century printers and standardization of new high German, J English & Ger Philol, 74; OE aglaeca: Magic and moral decline of monsters and men, Semasia, 74; The original manuscript of Ulrich Schmidt: Chivalry and Peasantry of the Late Middle Ages, Gordon, 77; English in contact with Pennsylvania German, Ger Quart, 53: 352-366; Pennsylvania German: Maintenance and shift, Int 3 Soc Lang, 25: 43-57; over 40 articles on the Language and Culture of the Pennsylvania Germans. **CONTACT ADDRESS** Academic Affairs, Bucknell Univ, Lewisburg, PA 17837-2029.

HUFFMAN, CARL A.

PERSONAL Born 12/27/1951, Denver, CO, m, 1986, 3 children **DISCIPLINE** CLASSICS **EDUCATION** Univ Colo, BA, 74, MA, 76; Univ Tex, PhD, 81. **CAREER** From asst prof to assoc prof to prof, DePauw Univ, 81-. **HONORS AND AWARDS** John Simon Guggenheim Found Fel, 95-96; Howard Found Res Fel, 89-90; NEH Fel Independent Study & Res, 83-84; Bye Fel, Robinson Col, Cambridge Univ, 83-84. **MEMBERSHIPS** Am Philological Asn; Soc Ancient Greek Philos. **RESEARCH** Ancient philosophy. **SELECTED PUBLICATIONS** Auth, Philolaus of Croton: Pythagorean and Presocratic, 93; auth, The Pythagorean Tradition, Cambridge Companion to Early Greek Philos, 99; auth, Die Pythagoreer, Philosophen der Antike I, 96; auth, Pythagorisme, Le Savior Grec, 96; auth, Philolaus' Cosmogony, Ionian Philos, 89; auth, The Role of Number in Philolaus' Philosophy, Phronesis, 88; auth, The Authenticity of Archytas Fragment 1, Class Quart, 85. **CONTACT ADDRESS** Dept of Classics, DePauw Univ, 400 S Locust, Greencastle, IN 46135. **EMAIL** cahuff@depauw.edu

HUFFMAN, CLAIRE

DISCIPLINE ITALIAN, FRENCH, RUSSIAN **EDUCATION** Harvard Univ, PhD, 72. **CAREER** Visiting Mellon Fel, Harvard Univ, 78; asst prof to full prof, CUNY Brooklyn Col, 78-. **HONORS AND AWARDS** World's Who's Who of Women in Educ; dictionary of Am Scholars; Directory of Distinguished Am; Intl Who's Who, Woodrow Wilson Fel, Fulbright Fel, Harvard Univ Fel, Nat Endowment of the Humanities, Andrew Mellon Fel, Am Coun of Learned Soc Fel. **MEMBERSHIPS** Asn of Literary Scholars & Critics, Acad of Sci and Humanities, Fondazione Schlesinger, Lugano. **RESEARCH** Modern comparative literatures and languates (Italy, England, France, Russia), Theater and cultural history, Issues of translation. **SELECTED PUBLICATIONS** Auth, Eugenio Montale and The Occasions of Poetry, Princeton Univ Press, 83; auth, "Montale for the English Speaking: The Case of 'In limine,'" Forum Italicum, (89): 121-146; auth, "Eugenio Montale and Giacomo Leopardi," Italian Quarterly, (80): 63-82; auth, "The Earliest Influences of 'Tasso' in Elizabethan England," rivista di letterature moderne e comparate, (79): 45-61; auth, "Vitaliano Brancati," columbia Dictionary of Modern European Literature, 80. **CONTACT ADDRESS** Dept Modern Lang, Brooklyn Col, CUNY, 2901 Bedford Ave, Brooklyn, NY 11210-2813.

HUGHES, WILLIAM NOLIN

PERSONAL Born 05/21/1918, Raymond, WA, m, 1953, 3 children **DISCIPLINE** GERMAN **EDUCATION** Univ Wash, BA, 41; Northwestern Univ, MA, 52, PhD(Ger lit), 55. **CAREER** Personnel supvr, Boeing Aircraft Co, Seattle, Wash, 41-46; asst to labor adv, Allied Comn for Austria, 46-49; asst, Econ Coop Admin Mission to Austria, 49-50; instr, Univ Mich, 55-60; asst prof, Columbia Univ, 60-63; assoc prof, 63-66, chmn dept 65-75, asst dean, Col Arts & Sci, 75-80, Prof Ger, Mich State Univ, 66-. Ed, Ger Lit Sect, MLA Intern Biblioq, 81-. **MEMBERSHIPS** MLA; Am Asn Teachers Ger; Thomas Mann Gesellschaft. **RESEARCH** Modern literature; German literature of the 17th century. **SELECTED PUBLICATIONS** **CONTACT ADDRESS** 513 Ardson Rd, East Lansing, MI 48823.

HULL, ALEXANDER

PERSONAL Born 07/17/1928, Portland, OR, m, 1952 **DISCIPLINE** FRENCH **EDUCATION** Univ Wash, BA, 45, MA, 47, PhD(Romance ling), 55. **CAREER** From instr to asst Prof French, Univ Mass, 54-60; vis asst prof, Univ Mich, 60; assoc prof, St John's Col, Man, 60-62; asst prof, 62-66, Assoc Prof Romance Lang, Duke Univ, 66-93; Fulbright grant, France, 49-50; Emer, 93-. **MEMBERSHIPS** MLA; Am Asn Teachers Fr; Ling Soc Am. **RESEARCH** North American French dialects; history of the French language; applied linguistics. **SELECTED PUBLICATIONS** Auth, Linguistic and Ethnographic Atlas of Reunion Island, J Pidgin Creole Lang, Vol 0009, 94; Teaching of Mother-Tongues--Current Issues in Different Parts of the World, French Rev, Vol 0067, 93; The Creoles, French Rev, Vol 0069, 96; Tense and Aspect in Seychelles Creole--Values and Interferences, French Rev, Vol 0068, 95; French in the Francophone World, French Rev, Vol 0069, 96. **CONTACT ADDRESS** Dept of Romance Lang, Duke Univ, Durham, NC 27706.

HULVEY, S. YUMIKO

PERSONAL Born 08/23/1949, Tokyo, Japan, m, 1973, 1 child **DISCIPLINE** JAPANESE **EDUCATION** Univ N Fla, BA, 74; Fla State Univ, MA, 79; Univ Calif Berkeley, PhD, 89. **CAREER** Asst Prof, Miami Univ, 88-90; Asst/Assoc Prof, Univ of Fla, 90-. **MEMBERSHIPS** Asn for Asian Studies, Southeast Conf of Asn for Asian Studies, Asn of Teachers of Japanese, Asn of Fla Teachers of Japanese, Asn of Japanese Lit Studies, Southwestern Japan Sem. **RESEARCH** Japanese literature, Women's Studies, Art History, Translation, Myth. **SELECTED PUBLICATIONS** Auth, "Nocturnal Muse: Ben no Naishi Nikki," Monumenta Nipponica 44.4 (Winter 89): 391-413; trans, "The Old Woman Who Eats Flowers," ("Hana Kui Uba"), by Enchi Fumiko, Manoa: A Pac J of Int Writing (Honolulu: Univ of Haw Press) 6.2 (94): 162-168; auth, "Izumi Shikubu," "Enchi Fumiko," "Ben no Naishi," "Abutsu-ni," in Japanese Women Writers: A Bio-Critical Sourcebook, ed. Cheiko Mulhern (Westport: Greenwood Press, 94), 153-160, 40-60, 19-26, 3-8; auth, "The Intertextual Fabric of Narratives by Enchi Fumiko (1905-1986)," in Japan in Traditional and Postmodern Perspectives, ed. Steven Heine and Charles W. Fu (SUNY Press, 95), 169-224; transl, "Wicked Gate," ("Kuguri"), by Enchi Fumiko, Manoa: New Writing from America, the Pacific, and Asia (Honolulu: Univ of Haw Press) (Winter 97): 160-167; transl, "Transformation," ("Kesho"), by Enchi Fumiko, Manoa: New Writing from America, the Pacific, and Asia (Honolulu: Univ of Haw Press) 10.1 (Summer 98): 100-110; auth, "Enchi Fumiko's Portal to Desire," Jap Studies Rev 2 (98): 37-55; auth, "Man-Eaters: Women Writers and the Appropriation of the Yamauba Motif," PMAJLS (Proceedings of Midwest Asn of Japanese Lit Studies) 5 (98): 240-249; auth, "Ben no Naishi," in Dictionary of Literary Biography, ed. Steven D. Carter (Columbia, SC: Bruccoli, Clark, Layman Publ, 99) vol 203, 10-14. **CONTACT ADDRESS** Dept African/Asian Lit and Lang, Univ of Florida, 470 Grinter Hall, Gainesville, FL 32611.

HUME, ELIZABETH

PERSONAL Born 10/29/1956, London, ON, Canada, s, 1 child **DISCIPLINE** LINGUISTICS **EDUCATION** Universite Laval, BA, 81; McMaster Univ, MA, 86; Cornell Univ, MA,89; PhD, 92. **CAREER** Fac, Ohio State Univ, 93; asst prof to assoc prof, Ohio State Univ. 92-. **HONORS AND AWARDS** Phi Kappa Phi; Sage Fel, Cornel Univ, 88-89; Res Scholarship, Res Coun of Can, 89-90, 91-93; Mary Bates Stecker Fel, Cornell Univ, 90-91; Res Fel, Univ of Utrecht, The Netherlands; Virginia Hull Res Awd, Ohio State Univ, 99; Nat Sci Found Res Grant, 99-02. **MEMBERSHIPS** Ling Soc of Am. **RESEARCH** Understanding the sound structure of human languages, particularly underdocumented languages, metathesis of speech sounds, the interplay of speech perception and phonology, phonological variation. **SELECTED PUBLICATIONS** Auth, Front Vowels, Coronal Consonants and their Interaction in Nonlinear Phonology, Garland (NY), 94; coauth, "The Internal Organization of Speech Sounds", in Handbook of Phonological Theory, ed, J. Goldsmith, (Oxford: Blackwell, 95), 245-306; auth, "Coronal Consonant, Front Vowel Parallels in Maltese", Nat Lang and Ling Theory 14.1 (96): 165-203; coauth, "Reconsidering (consonantal)", Phonology 13.3 (96): 345-376; coauth, "Nonmoraic Geminates in Leti", Phonology 14.3 (97): 371-402; coauth, "Metathesis in Phonological Theory: The Case of Leti, Lingua 104, (98): 147-186; auth, "The Role of Perceptibility on Consonant/Consonant Metathesis", Proceedings of W Coast Conf on formal Ling 17, ((*): 293-307; coauth, The Role of Speech Perception in Phonology, Academic Pr (NY), 00. **CONTACT ADDRESS** Dept Ling, Ohio State Univ, Columbus, 1712 Neil Ave, Columbus, OH 43210-1219. **EMAIL** ehume@ling.ohio-state.edu

HUMPHRIES, JOHN J.

PERSONAL Born 08/24/1955, Tuscaloosa, AL, m, 1998 **DISCIPLINE** FRENCH & COMPARATIVE LITERATURE **EDUCATION** Duke Univ, hist & romance lang, AB, 77; Yale Univ, fr & comp lit, MA, 78, M Phil, 80, PhD, 81. **CAREER** Chemn, dept of fr & ital, 97-, assoc chemn, dept of fr, 93-95, dir of grad studies in fr, 85-90, mem, steering comt for prog in comp lit, 94-, prof, fr, eng, and comp lit, 82-, La State Univ. **HONORS AND AWARDS** Nat Endow for the Humanities fel, 95-96; LSU Found Distinguished Facul award, 93; principal scholar, LEH Summer Seminar for high sch teachers, 88; co-dir, proj on Intertextuality and Civilization in the Americas, merit scholar, Duke Univ, 73-77; Acad of Amer Poets prize, 77; Distinction in Romance Lit, Duke Univ, 77; Phi Beta Kappa, Duke Univ; Univ fel, Yale Univ; Phi Kappa Phi, 85; nom, SC Rev and The Mass Rev; General Electric awards for Younger Writers, 86; Distinguished Short Stories Published award, 87; Thomas York Mem award for short fiction, 88; nom, Southwest Rev, CCLM/General Electric awards for younger writers, 89; Manship Summer res grant; Artist's fel in creative writing, La Div of the Arts, 92; Summer res stipend, LSU Coun on Res, 84, 87; Amer Coun of Learned Soc grant-in-aid, 86; Nat Endow for the Humanities travel to collections grant, 86; Lyndhurst Found regrant, 86. **MEMBERSHIPS** MLA. **RESEARCH** Nineteenth and twentieth century French lit; Asian studies; Am lit; Literary theory and comparative lit. **SELECTED PUBLICATIONS** Auth, The Meaning Behind Miyoshi's Lament: A Response to Masao Miyoshi's Reply to Japan in Theory, New Lit Hist, 97; auth, The Idea of Japan, New Lit Hist, 97; auth, The Karmic Text: A Buddhist Reading of Jacques Derrida and Paul de Man Rading Walter Benjamin's The Task of the Translator, Univ of Toronto Quart, 97; co-ed, Poetics of the Americas: New Perspectives on Intertextuality and Civilization, LSU Press, 97; auth, The Discourse of Southerness, or How We Can Know There Will Be Such a Thing as the South and Southern Literary Culture in the Twenty-First Century, The Future of Southern Letters, Oxford Univ Press, 96; co-ed, The Future of Southern Letters, Oxford Univ Press, 96; auth, A Bestiary (poems), Blue Pond Press, 95; auth, The Perry and Harris Treaties and the Invention of Modern Japan, Tamkang Rev, 95; auth, Images of the Floating World: The Idea of Japan, Antioch Rev, 95; auth, Proust and the Bonsai Tree, a Comparative Discussion of Eastern and Western Theories of Art, Southwest Rev, 94. **CONTACT ADDRESS** Dept. of French and Italian/Dept. of English/ Prog, Louisiana State Univ and A&M Col, 205 Prescott Hall, Baton Rouge, LA 70803-5309. **EMAIL** jhumphries125@msn.com

HUNT, IRMGARD

DISCIPLINE GERMAN LITERATURE **EDUCATION** Univ of Alaska, MA, 75; Univ of Wash, PhD, 82. **CAREER** Asst prof to prof, Colo State Univ, 89-. **HONORS AND AWARDS** NEH grant, 79; dissertation grant, 82; career enhancement grant, 90; res and travel grants annually; Elizabeth Frazer de Bussy Prose Prize, 97. **MEMBERSHIPS** AATG, GSA, Heinrich Boll-Stiftung, Eise Lasker-Schuler Gesellsdraft, Soc for Utopian Studies, Soc for the Interdisciplinary Study of Soc Imagery. **RESEARCH** Art and literature, ecology in literature, utopian thought, 20th century German literature, contemporary authors, migrant literature, Gunter Grass, Christa Wolf, Lugeborg Bachmann, and Urs Taeggi. **SELECTED PUBLICATIONS** Auth, Mutter und Muttermythos in Gunter Grass' Roman Der Butt (Frankfurt), 83; auth, Krieg und Frieden in der Deutschen Literatur: Vom Barock bis heule (Frankfurt), 86; auth, Urs Taeggi: Werkbiographie (New York), 93; co-ed, Twentieth Century German Poetry (New York), 00. **CONTACT ADDRESS** Dept Foreign Lang and Lit, Colorado State Univ, Fort Collins, CO 80523-0001. **EMAIL** ihunt@vines.colostate.edu

HUNT, JOHN M., JR.

PERSONAL Born 09/21/1943, Bryn Mawr, PA, s **DISCIPLINE** CLASSICS **EDUCATION** Lafayette Col, AB, 65; Cornell Univ, Post-grad fel, 65-66; Bryn Mawr Col, MA, 68, PhD, 70 **CAREER** Inst, Lafayette Col, 70; Asst Prof, 70-76, Villanova Univ; Visit Assoc Prof, 78-80, Univ of CA, Santa Barbara; Assoc Prof, 84-90, Prof, 91-, Villanova Univ **HONORS AND AWARDS** Who's Who in Am Educ **MEMBERSHIPS** Soc of Mayflower Descendants in PA; Sons of the Revolution; PA Soc **RESEARCH** Latin lit; textual criticism **CONTACT ADDRESS** Dept of Mod Lang, Villanova Univ, Villanova, PA 19085. **EMAIL** john.hunt@villanova.edu

HUNT, PATRICK

DISCIPLINE CLASSICS **EDUCATION** BA, 77; Dallas Theol Sem, MA, 82; Univ London, PhD, 91. **CAREER** Lctr, Stanford Univ. **RESEARCH** Archaeol and papyrology. **SELECTED PUBLICATIONS** Auth, Holy Moountian, Sacred Stone, Precolumbian Art Res Inst, 94; Maya and Olmec Stone Contests: Basalt and Limestone Weathering Contrasts, Precolumbian Art Res Inst, 94; Sensory Images in the Song of Solomon, 95. **CONTACT ADDRESS** Stanford Univ, Bldg 20, Main Quad, Stanford, CA 94305.

HUPPAUF, BERND

PERSONAL Born 10/19/1942, Waldenburg, Poland, m, 3 children **DISCIPLINE** GERMAN, LITERATURE **EDUCATION** Univ of Tubingen, Ger, PhD, 70. **CAREER** Prof, 74-93, Univ of NSW; Prof, 94-, NYU. **RESEARCH** Literature and philosophical anthropology; literature and culture of the Weimar Republic; the construction of space in literature and photography; representations of war and violence. **SELECTED PUBLICATIONS** Auth, Methodendiskussion, 95; War, Violence and the Modern Condition, 97; Unzeitgemasses uber den Krieg: Ernst Junger, Von Boll bis Buchheim, 97; auth, Signale aus der Bleecker Street, Deutsche Texte aus New York, 99; auth, "Uber ein unzeitgemabes Vergessen," 99; auth, "Walter Benjamins imaginare Landschaft," 99; auth, "Das Weltbild der modernen Physik in Robert Musils Der Mann ohne Eigenschaften," 99. **CONTACT ADDRESS** Fac of Arts & Sci, New York Univ, New York, NY 10003. **EMAIL** bernd.huppauf@nyu.edu

HURST, MARY JANE

DISCIPLINE LINGUISTICS, ENGLISH LANGUAGE AND LITERATURE **EDUCATION** Miami Univ, BA, 74; Univ of Md, MA, 80; PhD, 86. **CAREER** From asst prof to prof, Tex Tech Univ, 86-; assoc dean of col of arts and sci, Tex Tech Univ, 00-. **HONORS AND AWARDS** Coun of the Col of Arts and Sci Awd for Outstanding Undergraduate Teaching, Tex Tech Univ, 88; President's Excellence in Teaching Awd, 95. **MEMBERSHIPS** Ling Asn of the Southwest, S Central MLA, Ling Soc of Am, MLA, Southeast Confr on Ling. **RESEARCH** Language in Literature, Linguistic and Other Interdisciplinary Approaches to Literature. **SELECTED PUBLICATIONS** Tech ed, HTLV-1 and the Nervous System, Alan R. Liss, 89; auth, The Voice of the Child in American Literature, Univ Press of Ky, 90; auth, "Tolstoy's Description of Tourette Syndrome in Anna Karenina, J of Child Neurology 9.4 (94): 53-57; auth, "Reintroducing Aubrey Menen," World Lit Written in English 34.1 (94): 129-141; auth, "The Road to the White House: A Comparison of language in Candidate Clinton's Acceptance Speech and Language in President Clinton's Inaugural Address, SECOL Rev 19.1 (95): 80-103; auth, "Language, Gender, and Community in American Fiction at the End of the Century," Southwest J of Ling 17.1 (98): 1-13; auth, "Language and Style in Anne Tyler's The Accidental Tourist," Lang and Style (forthcoming). **CONTACT ADDRESS** Dept English, Texas Tech Univ, Lubbox, TX 79409-0999. **EMAIL** ditmg@ttacs.ttu.edu

HUTCHEON, LINDA

PERSONAL Born Toronto, ON, Canada **DISCIPLINE** ENGLISH, COMPARATIVE LITERATURE **EDUCATION** Cornell Univ , MA, 71; Univ Toronto, BA, 69, PhD, 75. **CAREER** Asst prof, 76-82, assoc prof, 82-85, prof, McMaster Univ, 85-88; Prof English, Univ Toronto, 88-. **HONORS AND AWARDS** Woodrow Wilson Fel, 69-79; Killam Postdoc fel, 78-79; John P. Robarts Ch Can Studs, 88-89; Guggenheim Fel, 92-93. **MEMBERSHIPS** MLA; Int Comp Lit Asn; Can Comp Lit Asn; Toronto Semiotic Circle; Ctr Italian Can Studs; Asn Can Col Univs Tchrs Eng. **RESEARCH** Interdisciplinary methodologies; comparative literary history. **SELECTED PUBLICATIONS** Auth, Narcissistic Narrative: The Metafictional Paradox, 80; auth, Formalism and the Freudian Aesthetic, 84; auth, A Theory of Parody, 85; auth, A Poetics of Postmodernism , 88; auth, The Canadian Postmodern: A Study of Contemporary English-Canadian Fiction, 88; auth, The Politics of Postmodernism, 89; auth, Irony's Edge: The Theory and Politics of Irony, 95; coauth, Opera: Desire, Disease, Death, 96; auth, Bodily charm: Living Opera, 00. **CONTACT ADDRESS** Dept of English, Univ of Toronto, Toronto, ON, Canada M5S 1A1.

HUTTON, LEWIS J.

PERSONAL Born 07/26/1921, New York, NY, m, 1948, 4 children **DISCIPLINE** SPANISH **EDUCATION** Columbia Univ, AB, 42, MA, 46; Princeton Theol Sem, BD, 44; Princeton Univ, MA, 48, PhD(Romance lang, Span), 50; Union Theol Sem, STM, 50. **CAREER** Instr Span, Princeton Univ, 45-48; instr, NY Univ, 48-49; minister, First Presby Church, Gowanda, NY, 51-55; sr minister, Capitol Hill Presby Church, Wash, DC, 55-62; sr minister, First Presby Church, Kirksville, Mo, 62-64; from asst prof to assoc prof Span, Drake Univ, 64-66; assoc prof, 66-72, Prof Span, Univ RI, 72-, Assoc Span, George Washington Univ, 57-62. **MEMBERSHIPS** MLA; Am Asn Teachers Span & Port; Am Soc Church Hist; Soc Bibl Lit. **RESEARCH** Sixteenth and seventeenth century Spanish literature; contemporary intellectual thought; sixteenth century ecclesiastical history. **SELECTED PUBLICATIONS** **CONTACT ADDRESS** Dept of Span, Univ of Rhode Island, Kingston, RI 02881.

HUTTON, WILLIAM E.

PERSONAL Born 07/26/1961, Bellefonte, PA, m, 1991 **DISCIPLINE** CLASSICS **EDUCATION** Penn State Univ, BA, 82; Univ Tex Austin, MA, 85; PhD, 95. **CAREER** Vis asst prof, Univ Wis Madison, 91-92; instr, Univ Calgary, 92-96; vis asst prof, Truman State Univ, 96-97; vis asst prof, Coll of William and Mary, 97-. **HONORS AND AWARDS** Phi Beta Kappa; Phi Alpha Theta; Phi Kappa Phi; James R Wheeler Fel; Jacob Hirsch Fel; Eugene Vaderpool Fel, Am School of Classical Studies in Athens. **MEMBERSHIPS** Am Philol Asn; Archaeol Inst of Am; Classical Asn of the Middle W and S; Classical Asn of Va. **RESEARCH** Greek Prose; Greek History; Greek Historiography; Greek topography. **SELECTED PUBLICATIONS** Auth, The Meaning of ge-te-o in Linear B, Minos, 90-91. **CONTACT ADDRESS** Dept of Classical Studies, Col of William and Mary, Box 8795, Williamsburg, VA 23185-8795. **EMAIL** wehutt@wm.edu

HUYSSEN, ANDREAS

PERSONAL Born 05/15/1942, Dusseldorf, Germany, m, 1975, 2 children **DISCIPLINE** GERMAN **EDUCATION** Univ Munich, PhD, 69. **CAREER** Prof, Univ of Wis Milwaukee, 71-86; Villard Prof, Columbia Univ, 86-. **HONORS AND AWARDS** Phi Beta Kappa. **RESEARCH** 18th - 20th Century Germany literature and culture, European modernization, aesthetic and central theory, postmodernism. **SELECTED PUBLICATIONS** Auth, Twilight Memories: Marking Time in a Culture of Amnesia, Routledge, (NY/London), 95; auth, "Monumental Seduction", New Ger Critique 69, (Fall 96): 101-200; auth, Memorias do Modernismo, Editora UFRJ, (Rio de Janeiro), 97; auth, "Von Mauschwitz in die Catskills und zuruck: Art Spiegelmans Holocaust-Comic Maus", Bilder des Holocaust, eds Manuel Koeppen and Klaus R. Scherpe, Koln Weimar Wien (Bohlau), (97): 171-190; auth, "Fear of Mice: The Transformations of times Square", Harvard Des Mag, (98): 26-28; auth, "The Disturbance of Vision in Vienna Modernism", Modernism/Modernity 5.3 (98): 33-48; auth, "Sculpture, Materiality, and Memory in an Age of Amnesia", Displacements, Art Gallery of Ontario, (Toronto), 98; auth, "La Cultura de la Memoria: Medios, Politca y Amnesia", Revists de Critica Cultural 18, (99): 8-15; auth, "Andreas Huyssen: El boom de la memoria y el olvido", Graciela Speranza, Razones intensas, Libros Perfil (Buenos Aires, 99): 93-108; auth, "After the War: Berlin as Palimpsest" Harvard Des Mag, (00): 70-75. **CONTACT ADDRESS** Dept Ger, Columbia Univ, 2960 Broadway, New York, NY 10027-6944. **EMAIL** ah26@columbia.edu

HYATTE, REGINALD L.

PERSONAL Born 05/09/1943, La Porte, IN, m, 1982 **DISCIPLINE** FRENCH, COMPARATIVE LITERATURE **EDUCATION** Ind Univ, BA, 65; Ind Univ, MA, 66; Univ Pa, PhD, 71. **CAREER** From Asst Prof to Assoc Prof, Ripon Col, 79-87; Prof, Univ Tulsa, 95-. **HONORS AND AWARDS** Fulbright-Hays Grant, 81; NEH Summer Stipend, 84; Camargo Found Fel, 91. **MEMBERSHIPS** Int Arthurian Soc, Fifteenth-Century Soc. **RESEARCH** Medieval and Renaissance French, Italian, and Latin literature and philosophy. **SELECTED PUBLICATIONS** Auth, "Reconfiguring Ancient 'Amicitia perfecta' in the 'Decameron' 10, 8," Ital Quart, 32 (95): 125-126; auth, "Muhammad's Prophethood in Two Old French Narratives: Divergent Traditions and Converging Ends," Allegorica 18 (97): 3-19; auth, "Praise and Subversion of Romance Ethos in the Prose 'Lancelot'," Neophilologus 82 (98): 11-18; auth, "Complimentary Humanistic Models of Marriage and Male 'Amicitia' in Fifteenth-Century Literature," in Friendship in Medieval Europe (Stroud, UK: Sutton, 99), 251-261; auth, "Dream-Engendering Dreams in the Old French 'Lancelot'," Mediaevalia, 22.2 (99): 343-358; auth, "Reading Affective Companionship in the Prose 'Lancelot'," Neophilologus 83 (99): 19-32. **CONTACT ADDRESS** Dept Lang, Univ of Tulsa, 600 S College Ave, Tulsa, OK 74104-3 74104-3126. **EMAIL** reginald-hyatte@utulsa.edu

HYE, ALLEN EDWARD
PERSONAL Born 12/01/1944, New Brunswick, NJ, m, 1967, 2 children **DISCIPLINE** GERMAN & SCANDINAVIAN LITERATURE **EDUCATION** Franklin & Marshall Col, BA, 66; Middlebury Col, MA, 67; Univ CT, PhD(Ger), 72. **CAREER** Instr Ger, Franklin & Marshall Col, 72-73; asst prof, Lehigh Univ, 73-78; assoc prof Ger, Wright State Univ, 78-96, prof Ger, Wright State Univ, 96-. **MEMBERSHIPS** Am Asn Teachers Ger; Soc Advan Scand Studies; German Studies Asn. **RESEARCH** Modern German drama; modern Danish drama; science and literature. **SELECTED PUBLICATIONS** Ed, Modernes Deutschland im Brennpunkt, W W Norton, 78; Shoeless Joe and the American Dream, The Markham Rev, 15, 86; An American Apocalypse: Religious Parody in The Iowa Baseball Confederacy, Aethlon 6.2, 89; The Baseball Messiah: Christy Mathewson and the Celebrant, Aethlon 7.1, 90; Fantasy + Involvement = Thought: Kjeld Abell's Conception of Theater, Scandinavian Studies 63, 90; Se alting i spejle: The Mirror and Other Key Symbols in the Plays of Kjeld Abell, Univ of Dayton Rev, 23,2, 95; The Moral Dilemma of the Scientist in Modern Drama, Edwin Mellen Press, 96; Kaj Munk, Dictionary of Literary Biography: Twentieth-Century Danish Writers, Vol 214, 99. **CONTACT ADDRESS** Dept of Mod Lang, Wright State Univ, Dayton, 3640 Colonel Glenn, Dayton, OH 45435-0001. **EMAIL** allenhye@wright.edu

HYERS, M. CONRAD
PERSONAL Born 07/31/1933, Philadelphia, PA, m, 1955, 3 children **DISCIPLINE** COMPARATIVE MYTHOLOGY & HISTORY OF RELIGIONS **EDUCATION** Carson-Newman Col, BA, 54; Eastern Theol Sem, BD, 58; Princeton Theol Sem, ThM, 59, PhD(phenomenol relig), 65. **CAREER** From instr to assoc prof hist relig, Beloit Col, 65-77; assoc prof, 77-81, Prof Hist Relig, Gustavus Adolphus Col, 81-97, Prof Emer, 97-. **HONORS AND AWARDS** Humanities develop grant, 69; Assoc Col Midwest non-Western studies fel, East-West Ctr, 70; Nat Found Humanities fel, 70-71; Fund Studies Great Relig fel, 71; Nat Found Humanities res fel, 75-76. **MEMBERSHIPS** Am Acad Relig **RESEARCH** A phenomenological study of the mythological motifs of Paradise Lost, fall and degeneration; a phenomenological study of the nature and function of comedy and humor in relation to the sacred; interfaith relations. **SELECTED PUBLICATIONS** Auth, Holy Laughter: Essays on Religion in the Comic Perspective, Seabury, 69; The Dialectic of the Sacred and the Comic, Cross Currents, winter 69; The Ancient Ch'an Master as Clown Figure and Comic Midwife, Philos East & West, winter, 69-70; The Comic Perspective in Zen Literature and Art, Eastern Buddhist, 72; Zen and the Comic Spirit, Rider, London, 73; The Chickadees: A Contemporary Zen Fable, Westminster, 74; The Comic Vision and the Christian Faith, Pilgrim, 81; The Meaning of Creation: Genesis and Modern Science, John Knox, 84; And God Created Laughter, The Bible as Divine Comedy, John Knox, 86; Once-Born, Twice-Born Zen, The Soto and Rinzai Schools of Japan, Hollowbrook, 89; The Laughing Buddha, Hollowbrook, 90; The Spirituality of Comedy, Comic Heroism in a Tragic World, Transaction Publ, 96. **CONTACT ADDRESS** 2162 Harbor View Drive, Dunedin, FL 34698.

HYNER, BERNADETTE H.
PERSONAL Born 10/03/1957, Germany, m, 1980, 2 children **DISCIPLINE** GERMAN **EDUCATION** Univ Ariz, BA, 94; MA, 96; Vanderbilt Univ, PhD, 01. **CAREER** Grad asst instr, Univ of Ariz, 94-96; grad asst instr, Vanderbilt Univ, 96-01; asst prof, Wash State Univ, 01-. **HONORS AND AWARDS** Grant, Vanderbilt Univ; Exchange Prog, Vanderbilt-Freie Universitat Berlin. **MEMBERSHIPS** MLA, AATG, Delta Phi Alpha Ger Honor Soc, Women in Ger, ACTFL, Psi Chi. **RESEARCH** German Travel Literature, Romanticism, Sensibility, Women's Studies, Feminist Theory, Gender and Language, Foreign Language Acquisition. **SELECTED PUBLICATIONS** Auth, "Eine Fietze erzahlt," Das Fenster 3.4 (95): 2; auth, "Wenn Eine eine Reise tut. Reisende Fraven in 18 und 19 Jahrhunclert," Schriften zur Hochschul-Sozialpolitik ISB, (Berlin: Studenten werk, 99): 128-131. **CONTACT ADDRESS** 304 1/2 4th, Albion, WA 99102. **EMAIL** hynerbh@wsu.edu

I

IANNUCCI, AMILCARE ALFREDO
PERSONAL Born 03/13/1946, Casalvieri, Italy, m, 1970 **DISCIPLINE** ITALIAN LITERATURE **EDUCATION** Univ Toronto, BA, 70; Harvard Univ, AM, 72, PhD(Ital lit), 77. **CAREER** From instr to asst prof, 73-78, Assoc Prof Ital, Univ Toronto, 78-. **MEMBERSHIPS** Mediaeval Acad Am; Dante Soc Am; Can Soc Ital Studies; Can Soc Renaissance Studies; Humanities Asn Can. **RESEARCH** Dante; Medieval and Renaissance Italian literature. **SELECTED PUBLICATIONS** Auth, The 'Gospel of Nicodemus' in Medieval Italian Literature, Quaderni D Italianistica, Vol 0014, 93. **CONTACT ADDRESS** Italian Studies, Univ of Toronto, 21 Sussex Ave, Toronto, ON, Canada M5S 1A1. **EMAIL** iannucci@chass.utoronto.ca

IBSEN, KRISTINE L.
DISCIPLINE SPANISH LITERATURE **EDUCATION** Calif State Univ, BA, 83; Univ Calif Los Angeles, MA, 84, PhD, 91. **CAREER** Assoc prof. **RESEARCH** Spanish American literature. **SELECTED PUBLICATIONS** Auth, pubs on Sor JuanA Ines de la Cruz, Julio Cortazar and Pablo Neruda. **CONTACT ADDRESS** Romance Languages and Literatures Dept, Univ of Notre Dame, Notre Dame, IN 46556.

IFRI, PASCAL A.
PERSONAL Born Flers, France, m, 1988, 1 child **DISCIPLINE** LINGUISTICS, FRENCH, LITERATURE, LANGUAGE **EDUCATION** Caen Univ, Lic d'Anglais, 76; WVa Univ, MA, 78; Brown Univ, PhD, 82. **CAREER** Asst prof to assoc prof, Wash Univ, 82-. **MEMBERSHIPS** MLA; AATF. **RESEARCH** 20th-century French novel. **SELECTED PUBLICATIONS** Auth, Proust et Son Narrataire, Droz, 83; auth, Celine et Proust: Correspondances Proustiennes dans L'oeuvre de L F Celine, Summa Pub, 96; auth, Les Deux Etendards, De Lucien Rebatet: Dossier D'un Chef D'oeuvre Maudit, L'age D'homme, 02. **CONTACT ADDRESS** Language Dept, Washington Univ, PO Box 1077, Saint Louis, MO 63130. **EMAIL** paifri@artsa.wustl.edu

IGEL, REGINA
PERSONAL Born 04/26/1942, Sao Paulo, Brazil **DISCIPLINE** PORTUGUESE **EDUCATION** Univ Sao Paulo, BA, 64; Univ Iowa, MA, 70; Univ N Mex, PhD(Port), 73. **CAREER** Instr Port, Univ Iowa, 68-70 & Univ N Mex, 70-73; asst prof, 73-77, Assoc Prof Port, Univ MD, 78-. **MEMBERSHIPS** MLA; Am Asn Teachers Span & Port (secy, 76); Mid-Atlantic Asn Port High Sch (vpres, 75). **RESEARCH** Brazilian literature of the 19th and 20th centuries. **SELECTED PUBLICATIONS** Auth, The Sugarcane Plantation in the Poetry of Cabraldemeloneto, Joao, World Lit Today, Vol 0066, 92. **CONTACT ADDRESS** Dept of Span & Port, Univ of Maryland, Col Park, 2215 Jimenez Hall, College Park, MD 20742. **EMAIL** ri1@umail.umd.edu

IGGERS, WILMA ABELES
PERSONAL Born 03/23/1921, Mirkov, Czechoslovakia, m, 1948, 3 children **DISCIPLINE** MODERN GERMAN & CZECH LITERATURES **EDUCATION** McMaster Univ, BA, 42; Univ Chicago, AM, 43, PhD, 52. **CAREER** Instr French & Ger, Univ NB, 46; asst prof mod lang, Philander Smith Col, 50-55; asst prof Ger, Dillard Univ & Tulane Univ, 57-63; asst prof, Loyola Univ, Ill, 63-65; from asst prof to assoc prof Ger, 65-75, actg chmn mod lang, 76-77, Prof Ger, Canisius Col, 75-. **HONORS AND AWARDS** DAAD Awd, Ger Acad Exchange Serv, 78. **MEMBERSHIPS** MLA; AAUP; Mod Humanities Res Asn; Czech Soc Arts & Sci in US; Soc Hist Czech Jews. **RESEARCH** Cultural History of the Jews in Boehmia and Moravia; recent Czech literature; Karl Kraus. **SELECTED PUBLICATIONS** Auth, Carl Kraus, A Viennese Critic of the Twentieth Century, Nijhoff, 67; The Bohemian Jewish writers: Their attitudes toward their roots, Vol III, In: Czechoslovakia Past and Present, Czech Soc Arts & Sci; Leopold Kompert, romancier of the Bohemian ghetto, Mod Austrian Lit, 73; Vojtech Rakous, A Forgotten Czech Story Teller, In: Czechoslovakia, Past and Present, Vol II, The Hague, Mauton, 66; Karl Kraus Then and Now, In: Kankrete Reflexion Festschrift in Honor of Prof Herman Wein, The Hague, Nijhoff, 75; Karl Kraus and his critics, Mod Austrian Lit, Vol 8, No 1/2; From Socialist to Realism to New Individualism: Some Trends in Recent East German Literature, In: East Central Europe, III:69-83. **CONTACT ADDRESS** Dept of Mod Lang, Canisius Col, 2001 Main St, Buffalo, NY 14208.

ILIE, PAUL
PERSONAL Born 10/11/1932, Brooklyn, NY, m, 1969 **DISCIPLINE** SPANISH AND COMPARATIVE LITERATURE **EDUCATION** Brown Univ, PhD, 59; Brooklyn Col, BA, 54. **CAREER** Prof, Univ Southern Calif., 82-96; Univ of Mich, 59-82. **HONORS AND AWARDS** Guggenheim, NEH, ACLS fellowships; distinguished alumnus Brown Univ. **MEMBERSHIPS** MLA, ASECS, NAS, AIH. **RESEARCH** Hispano-French relations; Spanish lit 18-20 centuries. **SELECTED PUBLICATIONS** Auth, the Age of Minerva trilogy, 2 vol; publ on, Voltaire; Goya; Span Romantic poets; Unamuno; Cela; Surrealism, the Literature of Exile & Post-Spanish Civil war; fiction. **CONTACT ADDRESS** Col Letters, Arts & Sciences, Univ of So California, University Park Campus, Los Angeles, CA 90089. **EMAIL** pilie@usc.edu

ILIESCU, NICOLAE
PERSONAL Born 05/21/1919, Romania, m, 1953, 2 children **DISCIPLINE** ITALIAN **EDUCATION** Univ Padua, Dr in Lett, 47; Harvard Univ, PhD, 58. **CAREER** From instr to asst prof Italian, 58-63, assoc prof, 63-68, Prof Romance Lang & Lit, Harvard Univ, 68-, UNESCO grant, Fiesole, Italy, 50-51; Guggenheim fel, Rome, 61-62. **HONORS AND AWARDS** Presidency of Ital Govt, 63; Ital foreiga Ministre, Medaglia della Cultura, 63. **MEMBERSHIPS** MLA; Renaissance Soc Am; Mediaeval Acad Am; Dante Soc Am; Am Asn Teachers Ital. **RESEARCH** Nineteenth century Italian literature; medieval Italian literature and Dante; Renaissance Italian literature, especially Petrarch. **SELECTED PUBLICATIONS** Auth, Da Manzoni a Nievo (considerazioni sul romanzo ital), 59 & Il Canzoniere petrarchesco e Sant Agostine, 62, Soc Acad Romena, Rome. **CONTACT ADDRESS** Harvard Univ, Cambridge, MA 02138.

ILLIANO, ANTONIO
PERSONAL Born 04/21/1934, Monte di Procida, Italy, m, 1962, 1 child **DISCIPLINE** ITALIAN **EDUCATION** Univ Naples, DottL, 58; Univ Calif, Berkeley, PhD(Romance lang & lit), 66. **CAREER** Asst Ital, Univ Ill, 59-60 & Univ Calif, Berkeley, 60-63; assoc, Univ Calif, Santa Barbara, 63-66; asst prof Romance lang, Univ Tex, Austin, 66-68, res & acad excellence prog fel, 66; vis asst prof Romance Lang, Univ Ore, 68-69; asst prof, 69-71, assoc prof, 71-82, Prof Romance Lang, Univ NC, Chapel Hill, 82-, Pogue leave, Univ NC, Chapel Hill, 77; mem fac, Ital Sch, Middlebury Col, summer 81, Univ Ga Cortona Prog, summer, 82. **MEMBERSHIPS** MLA; Am Asn Teachers Ital; Dante Soc Am. **RESEARCH** Medieval and modern literature. **SELECTED PUBLICATIONS** Auth, Per una definizione della vena cosmogonica di Calvino, Italica, fall 72; Italian without a master, Mark Twain J, 74; Metapsichica e letteratura in Pirandello, 82; auth, Per l'esegesi del Corbaccio, 91; auth, Morfologia della narrazione manzoniana, 93; auth, Sulle sponde del Prepurgaturio, 97; auth, From Boccaccio to Pirandello, 97; auth, From Vita Nuova to Palomar, 99. **CONTACT ADDRESS** Dept of Romance Lang, Univ of No Carolina, Chapel Hill, 238 Dey Hall Campus Box 3170, Chapel Hill, NC 27599. **EMAIL** ailliano@email.unc.edu

IMAMURA, SHIGEO
PERSONAL Born 08/14/1922, San Jose, CA, m, 1963 **DISCIPLINE** LINGUISTICS, ENGLISH AS A SECOND LANGUAGE **EDUCATION** Matsuyama Univ Commerce, Dipl, 43; Univ Mich, Ann Arbor, BA, 53, MA, 64. **CAREER** Teacher supvr English as second lang, Ehime State Bd Educ, Japan, 49-55; asst prof, Ehime Univ, Japan, 55-61, assoc dir English teaching inst, 56-61; asst prof English as second lang, Mich State Univ, 61-62; asst prof, Ehime Univ, 62-63; asst prof, 63-64, dir English lang ctr, 64-73, Assoc Prof English as a Second Lang, Mich State Univ, 66-, Dir Spec Progs, English Lang Ctr, 78-, Dir, Konan-Ill Ctr, Kobe, Japan, 77-78. **MEMBERSHIPS** Nat Asn Foreign Student Affairs; Asn Teachers English as Second Lang; Teachers English to Speakers Other Lang. **RESEARCH** Pronunciation and grammar in teaching English as a second language; teaching Japanese as a second language, especially grammar; inter-cultural understanding. **SELECTED PUBLICATIONS** Coauth, Readings from Samuel Clemens, 69 & Readings on American Society, 69, Blaisdell; auth, Basic knowledge for Studies in the United States, Kenkyusha, Tokyo, 72; Teaching of English in the Middle East and Indonesia, 72 & Cultural interference in language learning, 73, English Lang Educ Coun Bull, Tokyo; International Understanding and the Teaching of English, Lang Educ Coun Tokyo, 74. **CONTACT ADDRESS** English Lang Ctr, Michigan State Univ, East Lansing, MI 48824.

IMBERT, PATRICK L.
PERSONAL Born 02/04/1948, Paris, France **DISCIPLINE** FRENCH LITERATURE **EDUCATION** Institut catholique de Paris, Licence, 69; Univ Ottawa, MA, 70, PhD, 74. **CAREER** Asst prof, McMaster Univ, 74-75; from asst prof to prof, Univ of Ottawa, 75-. **MEMBERSHIPS** Societe de Philosophie de l'Outaouais; Int Asn Semiotic; Can Semiotic Asn; Can Comp Lit Asn; Asn Can Que Lit. **SELECTED PUBLICATIONS** Auth, Roman quebecois contemporain et cliches, 83; auth, L'Objectivite de la Presse, 89; auth, Les discours du Nouveau Monde au Canada francais et en Amerique latinel/Los discursos del Nuevo Mundo en el Canada francofono y en America latina, 95. **CONTACT ADDRESS** Dept of French, Univ of Ottawa, 309 Simard Hall, PO Box 450, Station A, Ottawa, ON, Canada K1N 6N5. **EMAIL** pimbert@uottawa.ca

IMHOFF, BRIAN
DISCIPLINE SPANISH **EDUCATION** Pa State Univ, BA, 84; Univ Ill, Urbana-Champaign, MA, 88, PhD, 96. **CAREER** Asst prof, Texas A & M Univ, 97-. **HONORS AND AWARDS** Texas A & M Univ, Prog to Enhance Schol and Creative Activities, Off of the VP for Res, 98; Texas A & M Univ, Undergrad Res Opportunities Prog, Dept Mod and Classical Lang, 97; FLAS Title VI Summer Fel for For Lang Study, Brazilian Portuguese, 88; Univ Ill List of Excellent Teachers, 85, 88; Univ Scholars Prog of Penn State Univ, 82-84; Phi Sigma Iota, Beta Chap, 83. **MEMBERSHIPS** MLA, 91-; Amer Asn Tchrs Span and Portuguese, 95-; Ling Asn Southwest, 96-; Medieval Acad Amer, 97-; Southeast Conf on Ling, 98-; South Atlantic Mod Lang Asn, 98-. **SELECTED PUBLICATIONS** Auth, On the Chronology and Recession of the Old Spanish -ie Imperfect, La coronica 26 2, 98; Bibliography of Spanish Linguistics, Comp Romance Ling Newsl 41 2, 92 & Bibliography of Spanish Linguistics, Comp Romance Ling Newsl 40 2, 91; coauth, Bibliography of Spanish Linguistics, Comp Romance Ling Newsl 39 2, 90; auth, Dialect Contact and Historical Linguistic Variation: The Old Spanish - I E Imperfect; Socio - Historic Network Ties and Medieval Navarro - Aragonese. **CONTACT ADDRESS** Dept of Modern and Classical Languages, Texas A&M Univ, Col Station, College Station, TX 77843-4238. **EMAIL** b-imhoff@tamu.edu

IMMERWAHR, HENRY R.
PERSONAL Born 02/28/1916, Breslau, Germany, m, 1944, 1 child **DISCIPLINE** GREEK, CLASSICS **EDUCATION** Univ Florence, Dottore in Letters, 38; Yale Univ, PhD, 43. **CAREER** Instr to Asst Prof, Yale Univ, 47-57; Asst Prof to Emeritus, Univ NC, 57-. **HONORS AND AWARDS** John S. Guggenheim Fel, 46-47; Morse Fel, Yale Univ, 55-56; Kenan Leave, Univ NC, 70-71. **MEMBERSHIPS** ASCSA; Center for Hellenic Studies; Am Philol Assoc; Archaeol Inst of Am; AAUP. **RESEARCH** Greek historiography and Greek epigraphy (especially inscriptions on Attic pottery). **SELECTED PUBLICATIONS** Auth, "The Signatures of Pamphaios," Am J of Archaeol (84): 341-352; auth, "Herodotus," "Thucydides," and "Common Elements of Fifth-Century Historiography," in The Cambridge History of Classical Literature, (85), 426-458; auth, Attic Script: A Survey, Oxford Univ Press, 90; auth, A Corpus of Attic Vase Inscriptions, Parts i-vi, 98-01. **CONTACT ADDRESS** Dept Class, Univ of No Carolina, Chapel Hill, 750 Weaver Dairy Rd, Chapel Hill, NC 27514-1441. **EMAIL** HRI@email.unc.edu

IMPEY, OLGA TUDORICA
PERSONAL Born 09/25/1937, Constanta, Romania, m, 1967, 2 children **DISCIPLINE** SPANISH MEDIEVAL & RENAISSANCE LITERATURE **EDUCATION** Univ Bucharest, BA, 61; Univ Ky, PhD(Span), 72. **CAREER** Asst prof Span & romance ling, Univ Bucharest, 61-67; teaching asst, Univ Ky, 68-72; instr, Princeton Univ, 72-74; asst prof, 75-80, Assoc Prof Span, Ind Univ, 80-, Lectr Span & Romance ling, Princeton Univ, 74-75. **MEMBERSHIPS** MLA; Midwest Mod Lang Asn; Asociacion Internacional de los Hispanistas; Soc Romanian Studies. **RESEARCH** Spanish and European medieval prose and poetry; Spanish Renaissance poetry; rhetoric and stylistics (theory and practice). **SELECTED PUBLICATIONS** Coauth, Quelques remarques sur la flexion nominale romane, Societe Roumaine de Linguistique Romane, Bucharest, 70; auth, Alfonso de Cartagena, traductor de Seneca y precursor del humanismo espanol, Prohemio, Madrid, Vol 3, 72; Apuntes sobre el estilo romancistico del Duque de Rivas, In: Acta, Cong Romance Ling & Philol, Acta, Quebec, 76; Los topoi y los comentarios literarios en el Libro de buen amor, Nueva revista de filolgia hispanica, Vol 25, 76; La estructura unitaria de Razon feyta d'amor, J Hisp Philol, Vol 4, No 1; Ovid, Alfonso X and Juan Rodriguez del Padron: Two Castilian Translations of the Heroides and the Beginnings of Spanish Sentimental Prose, Bull Hisp Studies, Vol 57, 80; The Literary Emancipation of Juan Rodriguez del Padron: From the Fictional Cartas to the Siervo libre de amor, Speculum, Vol 55, No 2; Un dechado de la prosa literaria alfonsi: el relato cronistico de los amores de Dido, Romance Philol, Vol 34, 80. **CONTACT ADDRESS** Dept of Spanish & Portuguese, Indiana Univ, Bloomington, Ballantine Hall Rm 855, Bloomington, IN 47405. **EMAIL** impey@indiana.edu

INGBER, ALIX
PERSONAL Born 02/07/1945, New York, NY, m, 1975, 1 child **DISCIPLINE** SPANISH **EDUCATION** Brooklyn College CUNY, BA; Univ IL, MA; CUNY, PhD. **CAREER** Prof, Sweet Briar Col. **HONORS AND AWARDS** Phi Beta Kappa. **MEMBERSHIPS** MLA; AATSP. **RESEARCH** Golden Age Span lit and transl; computer assisted instruction in Span. **SELECTED PUBLICATIONS** Auth, El bien mas alto, A Reconsideration of Lope de Vega's Honor Plays, Univ Presses FL; articles on Span and Latin Am lit; original programs for computer-assisted instruction in Span. **CONTACT ADDRESS** Sweet Briar Col, Sweet Briar, VA 24595. **EMAIL** ingber@sbc.edu

INGEMANN, FRANCES
PERSONAL Born 10/25/1927, Trenton, NJ **DISCIPLINE** LINGUISTICS **EDUCATION** Montclair State Univ, BA, 49; Columbia Univ, MA, 50; Ind Univ, PhD, 56. **CAREER** Instr English, Univ PR, 50-52; instr, Columbia Univ, 50, 51, 56; linguist, Haskins Labs, 56-57; asst prof English, 57-61, assoc prof English & ling, 61-66, Univ Edinburgh, 59-60, prof ling, Univ Kans, 66-00. **MEMBERSHIPS** Ling Soc Am; Acoust Soc Am; Am Assn Phonetic Sci. **RESEARCH** Acoustic phonetics; New Guinea languages; Liberian languages. **SELECTED PUBLICATIONS** Coauth, Studies in Cheremis, the Supernatural; Eastern Cheremis Manual, Ind Univ, 61. **CONTACT ADDRESS** Dept of Ling, Univ of Kansas, Lawrence, Lawrence, KS 66045-2140. **EMAIL** fing@ukans.edu

INGHAM, NORMAN WILLIAM
PERSONAL Born 12/31/1934, Holyoke, MA **DISCIPLINE** SLAVIC LANGUAGES & LITERATURES **EDUCATION** Middlebury Col, AB, 57; Univ Mich, MA, 59; Harvard Univ, PhD(Slavic), 63. **CAREER** Asst prof Slavic lang & lit, Ind Univ, 64-65; asst prof, Harvard Univ, 65-71; from assoc prof Slavic lang & lit to prof, Univ Chicago, 71-; chemn, comt on Slavic & East Europ Studies, 82-91; dir, Center for East Europ and Russ/Eurasian Studies, 91-96; **HONORS AND AWARDS** Inter-Univ Comt Travel Grants study & res grant, Charles Univ, Prague, 63-64; vis fel, Dumbarton Oaks Ctr Byzantine Studies, 72-73. **MEMBERSHIPS** Am Asn Teachers Slavic & East Europ Lang; Am Asn Advan Slavic Studies; Early Slavic Studies Asn. **RESEARCH** Medieval Russian and Slavic literature. **SELECTED PUBLICATIONS** Auth, The Limits of Secular Biography in Med-Slavic Literature, Particularly Old Russian, In: American Contributions to the Sixth International Congress of Slavists, Mounton, The Hague, 68; The Sovereign as Martyr, East and West, Slavic & East Europ J, 73; E T A Hoffman's Reception in Russia, Jal, 74; co-ed, Mnemozina: Studia Litteraria Russica in Honorem Vsevolod Setchkarev, Wilhelm Fink, 74; auth, Irony in Povest' o Gore: Zlocastii, Slavic & East Europ J, 80; The Martyred Prince and the Question of Slavic Cultural Continuity in the Early Middle Ages, Calif Slavic Studies, 82; ed, The Church and Religious Culture in Old Russ, Canadian-Am Slavic Studies, 91; Early East-Slavic Lit as Sociocultural Fact, California Slavic Studies, 19, 94. **CONTACT ADDRESS** Dept of Slavic Lang & Lit, Univ of Chicago, 1130 E 59th St, Chicago, IL 60637. **EMAIL** ningham@midway.uchicago.edu

INGRAM, MARK
PERSONAL Born 04/19/1957, Tocoma, WA, m **DISCIPLINE** FRENCH **EDUCATION** Western Washington, BA, 79; Univ Washington, MA, 86; New York Univ, PhD, 96. **CAREER** French Instr, Bellevue Community Col, 86-88; Vis Instr, Cent Conn State Univ, 95-96; Vis Asst Prof, Univ of Conn, 95-96; Asst Prof of French, Goucher Col, 96-. **HONORS AND AWARDS** Dean's Dissertation Fel, New York Univ, Andrew W. Mellon Foundatin Fellowship in Modern Europena Studies, National Science Foundation Dissertation Improvement Fel, Chateaubriand Dissertation Fel, French Government, Bourse Marandon, Societe des Professerus Francais et Francophones d' Amerique, Pre-Dissertation Fel, Council for European Studies, Columbia Univ. **MEMBERSHIPS** Am Anthropological Assoc, Am Assoc of Teachers of French, Anthropology of Francophone Cultures Network, Council on European Studies, Modern Languages Assoc, Society for the Anthropology of Europe. **RESEARCH** Cultural policy, national culture, French Studies. **SELECTED PUBLICATIONS** Auth, "Le Francais - En Route!", Delta Video Productions (Bainbridge Island, WA), 87; auth, "La culture passe-frontieres: les performances europeennes d'un groupe theatral francais" in Quaderni. La revue de la communication, 27 (95): 23-47; auth, "Review of Vintages and Traditions: An Ethnohistory of Southwest French Wine Cooperatives, by Robert Ulin, for Anthropological Quarterly, (97): 204-205; auth, "A Nationalist Turn in French Cultural Policy," The French Review, 71 (98): 797-808; auth, "Voices Unveiled: Memories d' immigres, L heritage maghrebin," 99, auth, "Envisioning Anthropology: David MacDougall and the next culture," A Review Essay in Para.Doxa. Studies in World Literary Genres, 00, auth, "Interdisciplinary Perspectives in the French Civilization Class," French Review, 01. **CONTACT ADDRESS** Dept Modern Languages, Goucher Col, 1021 Dulaney Valley Rd, Towson, MD 21204-2753.

INGWERSEN, NIELS
PERSONAL Born 05/18/1935, Horsens, Denmark, m, 1961 **DISCIPLINE** SCANDINAVIAN LITERATURE **EDUCATION** Copenhagen Univ, Cand Mag, 63. **CAREER** Adj Danish lit & lang, Hellerup Seminarium, Denmark, 64-65; from asst prof to assoc prof, 65-73, Prof Scand Lit, Univ Wis-Madison, 73-, Res assoc, Odense Univ, Denmark, 71-72; assoc ed, Scand Studies, 71-; vis prof, Aarhus Univ, Denmark, 78-79. **MEMBERSHIPS** Soc Advan Scand Studies (pres, 69-71); Dansklaerer-foreningen. **RESEARCH** Danish novel; Danish prose of 1890's; theory of the novel. **SELECTED PUBLICATIONS** Auth, Sandemoses Ryg, World Lit Today, Vol 0067, 93; Ubekraeftede Forlydender, World Lit Today, Vol 0067, 93; Mellem ar og Dag, World Lit Today, Vol 0068, 94; Krigen, World Lit Today, Vol 0068, 94; The Rags--Studies on Common Danish-Norwegian Literature After 1814, Scand Stud, Vol 0067, 95; The Need for Narrative--The Folktale as Response to History, Scand Stud, Vol 0067, 95; Literary-Criticism, a Selection, Scanddinica, Vol 0034, 95; Peddling My Wares, J Engl and Germanic Philol, Vol 0096, 97. **CONTACT ADDRESS** Dept of Scand Studies, Univ of Wisconsin, Madison, 1306 Van Hise Hall, Madison, WI 53706. **EMAIL** ningwers@students.wisc.edu

INMAN, BEVERLY J.
PERSONAL Born 06/17/1944, Cedar Rapids, IA, s **DISCIPLINE** GERMAN, HISTORY **EDUCATION** Coe Col, BA, 66; Univ Iowa, MA, 69; PhD, 84; EdS, 88. **CAREER** Teaching asst, Univ Wash, 66-67; teaching asst, Univ Iowa, 71-73, 74-75, & 83-84; teacher, Geschwister-Scholl-Schule, 73-74; instr, Quincy Univ, 75-76; assoc ed, Univ Iowa, 78-83; instr, Kirkwood Community Col, 82-83; asst prof, Winona State Univ, 84-85; instr, Iowa State Univ, 86; instr, Univ Memphis, 89-93; instr, Talladega Col, 93-95; instr, Kirkwood Community Col, 96-. **HONORS AND AWARDS** Grant, NDEA Ger Lang Inst of Northwestern Univ, 65; Fulbright Ger Studies Sem, 76; Fel, DAAD Sem, Cornell Univ, 91; Berlin Sem, Loyola of Md & European Acad for Urban Affairs, 94; Teagle Found, 94. **MEMBERSHIPS** MLA, AATG, Fulbright Alumni, GSA. **RESEARCH** Interdisciplinary German Studies: Late Nineteenth- and Early Twentieth-Century German Regional and Heimat Literature, Folklore, Cultural Studies, Nineteenth- and Twentieth-Century German History, Reformation, Higher Education: liberal arts, humanities, international and general education. **SELECTED PUBLICATIONS** Auth, "The Influence of the Kulturkampf on Austro-Bavarian Heimatliterature," SCHATZKAMMER 7.2 (86). **CONTACT ADDRESS** Kirkwood Comm Col, PO Box 2068, Cedar Rapids, IA 52406-2068. **EMAIL** bjinman@juno.com

INSLER, STANLEY
PERSONAL Born 06/23/1937, New York, NY **DISCIPLINE** INDO-IRANIAN LINGUISTICS **EDUCATION** Columbia Col, AB, 57; Yale Univ, PhD, 63. **CAREER** From instr to asst prof, 63-70, assoc prof, 70-80, prof Sanskrit & chemn dept, grad sch, Yale Univ, 80-, Morse fel, 67-68. **MEMBERSHIPS** Am Orient Soc; Ling Soc Am; fel Royal Asiatic Soc; Deut Morganlaandische Ges. **RESEARCH** History of Sanskrit language; comparative Indo-Iranian linguistics; Zoroastrianism. **SELECTED PUBLICATIONS** Auth, The Indra Hymns of the Rg-Veda, J Amer Oriental Soc, Vol 0113, 93; The Question Sentences in the Rg-Veda, J Amer Oriental Soc, Vol 0113, 93; Asura in Early Vedic Religion, J Amer Oriental Soc, Vol 0113, 93. **CONTACT ADDRESS** Dept East Asian Languages, Yale Univ, PO Box 208236, New Haven, CT 06520-8236.

IPPOLITO, CHRISTOPHE
PERSONAL Born Paris, France **DISCIPLINE** FRENCH **EDUCATION** Univ Paris, DEA, 86; MA, 92; Columbia Univ, PhD, 98. **CAREER** Instr, French Cult Ctr, 87-88; Lectr, Acad de Versailles, 88-90; Instr, Alliance Francaise de Paris, 91, 93; Asst Ed, French Music Off NY, 93; Instr, Alliance Francaise de NY, 93-94; Interim Admin to Teaching Asst, Columbia Univ, 93-98; Vis Asst Prof, Hamilton Col, 98-99; Vis Asst Prof, Amherst Col, 99-01. **HONORS AND AWARDS** Peter H. Kauffman Mem Fel, Columbia Univ, 97-98; Pres Fel, Columbia Univ, 93-98; Res Fel, French Ministry of For Affairs and Egyptian Govt, 86-88. **MEMBERSHIPS** MLA; Women in French; Nineteenth-Century French Studies; Paul Claudel Soc; Asn des Amis d'Andre Gide. **RESEARCH** 19th and 20th Century French and Francophone Literature and Culture; French Language and applied Linguistics; French Civilization after 1789; Flaubert; Middle Eastern Francophone Literature; Literary Theory; Cultural Studies; Comparative Literature. **SELECTED PUBLICATIONS** Auth, "Le Syndrome Borel chez Baudelaire: comment peut-on etre lycanthrope au second degre?" in L'oeuvre d'identite. Essais sur le romantisme de Nodier a Baudelaire, eds Didier Maleuvre & Catherine Nesci, (Montreal: Paragraphes, 96); auth, "La Verite toute nue sort du puits: communication et sexualite dans la Fortune des Rougon," Excavatio, 97; auth, "Systeme du bonnet flaubertien," in Fashion and Fashionability in Modern French & Francophone Culture, 97; auth, "Flaubert's Literary Shop in Times of 'Industrial' Art," LitteRealite, 97; co-auth, "Histoires d'engendrements et engendrement d'Histoire," in Lectures de Histoire, Paris, 00; auth, "Flaubert's Pearl Necklace: Weaving a Garland of Images in the Reader's Memory," Symposium, 00; auth, "Paris, 1890: la decadence au miroir alexandrin," Romance Studies, 00; auth, "Subtexts in Flaubert: The Underlying Currents of Meaning," Recherches semiotiques, forthcoming; auth, "Flaubert's Chateaubriand: Plagiarism or Palimpsest?" Romance Notes, forthcoming; auth, "Narrative Memory in Flaubert's Works," in Currents in Comparative Romance Languages and Literatures, Peter Lang, forthcoming. **CONTACT ADDRESS** Dept French, Amherst Col, Box 2255, Amherst, MA 01002-5000. **EMAIL** cippolito4@yahoo.com

IRIZARRY, ESTELLE
PERSONAL Born 11/13/1937, Paterson, NJ, m, 1963, 3 children **DISCIPLINE** LINGUISTICS **EDUCATION** Montclair State Univ, BA; 59; Rutgers Univ, MA, 63; George Washington Univ, PhD, 70. **CAREER** Prof, Georgetown Univ, 70-; ed, J of Am Assoc Teach Span Port, 93-01. **HONORS AND AWARDS** Mem, AASP, Mem, RSA; Civ Ord Alphonse the Sage, Spain; Inst of PR, Prize, 96; Alumni Cit, Montclair State Univ, 96; Outstand Contrib Awd, NJ, 93. **MEMBERSHIPS** AATSP; IPR, NY. **RESEARCH** Hispanic literature; computer analysis of literature; literature and art. **SELECTED PUBLICATIONS** Auth, La inventiva surrealista de F. F. Granell, 76; auth, Francisco Ayala, 77; auth, La broma literaria en nuestros dias, 79; auth, Enrique A. Laguerre, 82; auth, Writer-Painters of Contemporary Spain, 84; auth, "La ilamarada," clasico puertorriqueflo, 85; auth, Infortunios de Alonso Ramirez, 90; auth, Estudios sobre Rafael Dieste, 92; auth, Inforinatica y literatura, 97; auth, Altruisino y literatura: Oddn Betanzos Palacios, 99. **CONTACT ADDRESS** Dept Spanish and Portuguese, Georgetown Univ, PO Box 571039, Washington, DC 20057-1039. **EMAIL** irizarre@gusun.georgetown.edu

IRVINE, MARGOT ELISABETH
PERSONAL Born 05/28/1969, New Haven, CT, m, 1992, 2 children **DISCIPLINE** WOMAN'S STUDIES, FRENCH **EDUCATION** Univ Toronto, BA, 92; MA, 93; PhD, 00. **CAREER** Asst prof, Univ Toronto, 00-. **HONORS AND AWARDS** SSHRC Awd, 97-99; Ont Grad Study Fel 94-96; Univ Toronto Fel, 99-00; Senior Doct Teaching Assocshp. **MEMBERSHIPS** MLA; Women in Fr; 19th-centruy Fr Studies; SERN; CWSA. **RESEARCH** Nineteenth century French women's writing. **CONTACT ADDRESS** Humanities Soc Sci Dept, Univ of Toronto, 130 St George St, Roberts Library 14th Fl, Toronto, ON, Canada M5S 3H1. **EMAIL** mirvine@chass.utoronto.ca

IRWIN, AMANDA LEE
PERSONAL Born Kansas City, MO **DISCIPLINE** SPANISH, LANGUAGE, LITERATURE **EDUCATION** Univ de Ciencias Humanas, Lic; Univ Chicago, MA; PhD. **CAREER** Asst prof, Rhodes Col. **MEMBERSHIPS** MLA; MMLA; ACTFL; LASA. **RESEARCH** Latin American literature; US Hispanic literature; novel of dictatorship. **CONTACT ADDRESS** 5060 Sea Isle Rd, Memphis, TN 38117-6336. **EMAIL** irwin@rhodes.edu

IRWIN, ELEANOR
PERSONAL Born Toronto, ON, Canada **DISCIPLINE** CLASSICS **EDUCATION** Univ Toronto, BA, 59, MA, 60, PhD, 67. **CAREER** Asst prof, 68-73, Assoc Prof, Scarborough Col, Univ Toronto, 73-, assoc ch, 80-82, 94-, vice prin & assoc dean, 89-93. **HONORS AND AWARDS** D.R. Campbell Awd Outstanding Contrib Scarborough Col, 84. **MEMBERSHIPS** Class Asn Can; Can Soc Patristic Studs; Int Soc Class Tradition. **RESEARCH** Flowering plants in the Classical Greek world; connections between medicinal plants and mythological figures; women and goddesses in the ancient world; reasons for the virginity of the Greek goddesses Hestia, Athena and Artemis. **SELECTED PUBLICATIONS** Auth, Colour Terms in Greek Poetry, 74; auth, Evadne, Iamos and Violets in Pindar's Sixth Olympian in Hermes, 96. **CONTACT ADDRESS** Dept of Humanities, Univ of Toronto, 1265 Military Trail, Scarborough, ON, Canada M1C 1A4. **EMAIL** irwin@scar.utoronto.ca

ISAAC, EPHRAIM
PERSONAL Born 05/29/1936, Nedjio, Ethiopia, m **DISCIPLINE** HISTORY, PHILOLOGY **EDUCATION** Concordia Coll, BA 1958; Harvard Univ Div School, BD 1963; Harvard Univ, PhD 1969. **CAREER** Harvard Univ, instr, 68-69, lecturer, 69-71, assoc prof, 71-77; Hebrew Univ, visiting prof, 77-79; Inst for Advanced Study Princeton, fellow, 79-80; Princeton Theol Sem/Hunter Coll, visiting prof, 80-81; Bard Coll, visiting prof, 81-83; Lehigh Univ, visiting prof of religion Princeton Univ, visiting prof, 83-85; Institute of Semitic Studies, dir, 85. **HONORS AND AWARDS** Second Prize Ethiopian HS Matric Awd 1954; Ethiopian Natl Prize for literacy (Humanity) 1967; Outstanding Educators of Amer 1972; Fellow Endowment for the Humanities 1979; NEH Rsch Grant 1976-77; Harvard Univ Faculty Fund Rsch Grants; Concordia Coll Scholarships 1956-58; Univ Coll of Addis Ababa Fellowship 1954-56. **MEMBERSHIPS** Dir general Natl Literacy Campaign of Ethiopia 1966-72; bd mem Amer Assn for Ethiopian Jews 1973-; pres Ethiopian Student Assn in North Amer 1959-62; vice chmn Ethiopian Famine Relief Comm 1984-; bd mem African Studies Heritage Assoc 1969-73; chmn Comm for Ethiopian Literacy 1963-68; treas Harvard Graduate Student Assoc 1962-65; chorale dir Harvard Graduate Chorale 1962-64. **SELECTED PUBLICATIONS** Ethiopic Book of Enoch, Doubleday, 1983; A History of Religions in Africa, Oxford. **CONTACT ADDRESS** Inst of Semitic Studies, 9 Grover Ave, Princeton, NJ 08540-3601.

ISBELL, JOHN
PERSONAL Born 06/25/1963, Seattle, s **DISCIPLINE** FRENCH **EDUCATION** Cambridge Univ, BA, 85; PhD, 91. **CAREER** Lecturer in French, Univ of Durham, 92-93; Asst Prof in French, Indiana Univ, 93-. **HONORS AND AWARDS** Indiana Univ TERA teaching award, 97. **MEMBERSHIPS** Executive committees, Societe des Etudes stac liennes Associazione di studi sismordiani. **RESEARCH** International Romanticism; French Revolution and Napoleonic Europe; Women's Studies. **SELECTED PUBLICATIONS** Auth, "The Birth of European Romanticism: Truth and Propaganda in Stael's De l'Auemagne Cambridge: Cambridge UP, 94; auth, "The People's Voice: a Romantic Civilization, 1779-1848, Bloomington: Lilly Library, 96. **CONTACT ADDRESS** Dept French & Italian, Indiana Univ, Bloomington, 1020 E Kirkwood Ave, Ballantine Hall 642, Bloomington, IN 47405-7103. **EMAIL** jisbell@indiana.edu

ISHAM, WILLIAM P.
PERSONAL Born 05/30/1955 **DISCIPLINE** LINGUISTICS **EDUCATION** Univ of Kans, BA, 79; Gallaudet Univ, MA, 82; Northeastern Univ, PhD, 91. **CAREER** Staff interpreter, 83-85, acting coord, 85, Gallaudet Interpreting Service, Gllaudet Univ; freelance Amer sign lang/English interpreter, 85-86; teaching asst, Dept of Psychology, 86-90, isntr, 91-92, Northeastern Univ; ASST PROF, DEPT OF LINGUISTICS, UNIV OF NMex, 93-. **HONORS AND AWARDS** Grant-In-Aid, Univ of NMex, 98; Int Travel Grant, Am Coun of Learned Soc, 94; Post-Doctoral fel, Fyssen Found, Univ of Paris, 91-92 & 92-93; Biomedical Sci Support Comt, Northeastern Univ, 87-90. **MEMBERSHIPS** Community Task Force on Interpreting in Legal Settings, Community Outreach Prog for the Deaf; Nmex Am Sign Lang Teachers Asn; Interpreting: Int J of Res and Practice in Interpreting; Seminar on Interpreting Res, Aarhus Business School; Registry of Interpreters for the Deaf, Inc; Nat Asn of the Deaf; Conf of Interpreter Trainers. **RESEARCH** Translation studies; American sign language and the deaf community; language and cognition; inferential statistics. **SELECTED PUBLICATIONS** Auth, Interpreting Property Concepts, At the Turn of the Century: The AVLIC 98 Conf Papers, AVLIC Inc, in press; auth, Phonological Interference in Interpreters of Spoken-Languages: An Issue of Storage or Process?, Language Processing and Interpreting: Interdisciplinary Perspectives, in press; auth, On the Relevance of Signed Languages to Research in Interpretation, Target, 95; auth, Memory for Sentence Form after Simultaneous Interpretation: Evidence Both for and against Deverbalization, Bridging the Gap: Empirical Research in Simultaneous Interpretation, 94; auth, Signed Language Interpreting, Routledge Encyc of Translation Studies, 98; auth, Memory for Form after Simultaneous Interpretation: Comparisons of Language, Modality, and Process, Proceedings of the Thirteenth Nat Conv of the Registry of Interpreters for the Deaf, RID Pub, 95; Pride and Pluralism, TBC News, 93; coauth, A Common Conceptual Code in Bilinguals: Evidence from Simultaneous Interpretation, Sign Language Studies, 94; coauth, Blackness, Deafness, IQ and g, Intelligence, 93; coauth, Simultaneous Interpretation and the Recall of Source-language Sentences, Language and Cognitive Processes, 93. **CONTACT ADDRESS** Dept of Linguistics, Univ of New Mexico, Albuquerque, Humanities 526, Albuquerque, NM 87131-1196. **EMAIL** ISHAM@unm.edu

ISHIKAWA, MINAKO
DISCIPLINE JAPANESE **EDUCATION** Georgetown Univ, PhD, 93. **CAREER** Asst prof. **RESEARCH** Sociolinguistics; discourse analysis; language acquisition. **SELECTED PUBLICATIONS** Auth, Iconicity in Discourse: The Case of Repetition, Text, 91. **CONTACT ADDRESS** Center for Foreign Languages, Literatures and Cult, Williams Col, Williamstown, MA 01267. **EMAIL** Minako.Ishikawa@williams.edu

ISHIMATSU, GINETTE
PERSONAL Born 05/30/1958, San Jose, CA **DISCIPLINE** SOUTH ASIAN STUDIES **EDUCATION** Univ Calif, Berkeley, BA, 79, MA, 85, PhD, 94. **CAREER** Vis asst prof, relig stud, Whittier Col, 93-94; fac dir, South India Term Abroad, Madurai, India, 97; asst prof, Asian relig, Univ Denver, 94- . **MEMBERSHIPS** AAR; JAAR. **RESEARCH** South Indian Hindu temples and temple rituals; Saiva Siddhanta; Siva. **SELECTED PUBLICATIONS** Auth, Book Notes, Relig Stud Rev, 93-94; auth, rev, Home of Dancing Sivan: The Traditions of the Hindu Temple in Citamparam by Paul Younger, Critical Rev of Books in Relig, 96; auth, The Making of Tamil Saiva Siddhanta, Contrib to Indian Sociol, 99. **CONTACT ADDRESS** Dept of Religious Studies, Univ of Denver, 2000 Ashbury Ave, Storm Hall, Ste 166, Denver, CO 80208. **EMAIL** gishimat@du.edu

ITO, JUNKO
DISCIPLINE THEORETICAL PHONOLOGY **EDUCATION** ICU, Tokyo, BA, MA; Univ Mass-Amherst, PhD, 86. **CAREER** Prpf, Ling, Univ Calif, Santa Cruz. **RESEARCH** Structure of the phonological lexicon; Prosodic morphology and phonology. **SELECTED PUBLICATIONS** Auth, A Prosodic Theory of Epenthesis, Natural Lang and Ling Theory, 89; Melodic Dissimilation in Ainu, Ling Inquiry, 84; Licensed segments and safe paths, Can Jour of Ling, 93. **CONTACT ADDRESS** Dept of Ling, Univ of California, Santa Cruz, 1156 High St, Santa Cruz, CA 95064.

IUDIN-NELSON, LAURIE
DISCIPLINE RUSSIAN **EDUCATION** St. Olaf Col, BA; Univ Minn, MA; Univ Wis-Madison, PhD. **CAREER** Asst prof; dir, Luther Col Balalaika Ensemble; resident dir, Univ Wis-Moscow State Univ Exch Prog; vis Dana fel, Dartmouth Col, 93;employed in, Concordia Lang Vlg, 84-; dean, Russ Vlg, 89-. **RESEARCH** Utilizing music in L2 pedagogy, integration of this methodology into the Russian language. **SELECTED PUBLICATIONS** Auth, An Anthology of Russian Song, Concordia Lang Villages. **CONTACT ADDRESS** Dept of Modern Languages, Luther Col, 700 College Dr, Decorah, IA 52101. **EMAIL** iudinnel@luther.edu

IVANOV, VYACHESLAV V.
DISCIPLINE BALTIC, INDO-EUROPEAN LINGUISTICS **EDUCATION** Moscow State Univ, Eng Philology, 51, Hittite, Indo-Euroepan Grammar, PhD, 54; Univ Vilnius, Doct, Baltic, Indo-European Ling, 80. **CAREER** PROF, SLAVIC LANGS, LITS, UNIV CALIF, LOS ANGELES, 91-; prof, Stanford Univ, 90-91; RES FEL, INST SALVIC & BALKAN STUD, RUSSIAN ACAD SCIS, MOSCOW, 89-; DIR, INST WORLD CULTURE and PROF, PHILOS, MOSCOW STATE UNIV, 92-; dir, All-Union Libr For Lit, Moscow, 89-93; chair, dept structural typology, Inst Salvic, Balkan Studies, Acad Scis USSR, 63-69; prof, Archival & Hist Inst, Moscow, 88-89; chair, Res Grp Computer Trans, Inst Computer Tech & Exact Mechanics, Acad Scis USSR, 59-61; asst prof, Lab Comput Trans, State Pedagogical Inst For Langs, Moscoq, 59-61. **CONTACT ADDRESS** Dept of Slavic Langs, Lit, Univ of California, Los Angeles, 115 Kinsey Hall, Box 951502, Los Angeles, CA 90095-1502. **EMAIL** ivanov@ucla.edu

IVERSON, STANLEY
PERSONAL Born 05/07/1940, Gays Mills, WI, m, 1972, 2 children **DISCIPLINE** CLASSICS **EDUCATION** Luther Col, BA, 62; Vanderbilt Univ, MAT, 63; MA, 69; PhD, 75. **CAREER** Teacher, Phoenix Union High Sch, 63-65; Prof, Concordia Col, 65-66, 69-. **MEMBERSHIPS** Am Philol Assoc, Am Classical League, Classical Assoc of Minn. **RESEARCH** Teaching of Latin. **SELECTED PUBLICATIONS** Co-ed, Fabulae Graecae: Longman's. **CONTACT ADDRESS** Dept Classics, Concordia Col, Minnesota, 3627 Rivershore Dr, Moorhead, MN 56560-5556. **EMAIL** iverson@gloria.cord.edu

IVLIYEVA, IRINA
PERSONAL Born 10/30/1966, Moscow, Russia, m, 1994, 1 child **DISCIPLINE** LINGUISTICS, RUSSIAN, FRENCH **EDUCATION** Moscow State Univ, MA, 89; Russ Acad Sci, PhD, 97. **CAREER** Prof, Moscow Energy Inst, 89-96; Prof, Univ Mo, 97-. **HONORS AND AWARDS** Outstanding Teaching Awds, Univ Mo, 97-00. **MEMBERSHIPS** AATSEEL, AAASS. **RESEARCH** Linguistics, morphology and word formation (Russian and comparative). **SELECTED PUBLICATIONS** Auth, "Word Formation Possibilities of the Verbs of Sound in the Modern Russian Language," Russ Lang: System, Rhetoric, Poetics (91); auth, "Analysis Criteria of Semantic Modification Parameters of the Verbs of Sound in the Modern Russian Language," Russ Lang Inst (96); auth, "Classification of the Modifiers of the Verbs of Sound in the Modern Russian Language," Russ Lang Inst (96); auth, "Semantic Modification Possibilities of the Verbs of Sound in the Russian Language," Russ Lang Inst (97). **CONTACT ADDRESS** Dept Ling, Univ of Missouri, Rolla, 1870 Miner Circle, Rolla, MO 65409-0001. **EMAIL** ivliyeva@umr.edu

IWAMOTO, YOSHIO
PERSONAL Born 11/25/1931, New Westminster, BC, Canada **DISCIPLINE** MODERN JAPANESE LITERATURE **EDUCATION** Univ Mich, BA, 58, MA, 59, PhD(Japanese lit), 64. **CAREER** Asst prof Japanese lang & lit, Univ Mich, 64-68; asst prof, Univ Ill, 68-69; Assoc Prof Japanese & Comp Lit, Ind Univ, Bloomington, 69-, Vis assoc prof Japanese lit, Univ Hawaii, 71. **MEMBERSHIPS** Asn Asian Studies; Am Orient Soc; MLA; Asn Teachers Japanese. **RESEARCH** Modern Japanese novel; politics and literature in modern Japan; Japanese-Western literary relations. **SELECTED PUBLICATIONS** Auth, Sanso to Tenko (War and conversion), Hihyo (criticism), winter 66; The changing hero image in Japanese fiction of the thirties, J Newslett Asn Teachers Japanese, 8/66; Suehiro Tetcho: a Meiji political novelist, Monumenta Nipponica, 9/68; Oe Kenzaburo's existentialist novel: A Personal Matter, Papers CIC Far Eastern Lang Inst, Vol IV, 71; Aspects of the proletarian literary movement in Japan, In: Japan in Crisis: Essays on Taisho Democracy, Princeton Univ, 74; coauth, Yukio Mishima; dialectics of mind and body, Contemp Lit, winter 75; The last sad sigh: Time and Kawabata's The Master of Go, Lit E & W, Vol XVIII, 78. **CONTACT ADDRESS** Dept of EAsian Lang & Lit, Indiana Univ, Bloomington, Goodbody Hall, Bloomington, IN 47401.

J

JACKENDOFF, RAY SAUL
PERSONAL Born 01/23/1945, Chicago, IL, 2 children **DISCIPLINE** LINGUISTICS **EDUCATION** Swarthmore Col, BA, 65; MA Inst Technol, PhD(ling), 69. **CAREER** Lectr ling, Univ CA, Los Angeles, 69-70; asst prof, 71-73, assoc prof, 73-78, prof ling, Brandeis Univ, 78-; Special ling, Rand Corp, 69-70; Guggenheim fel, 93-94; fel, Center for Advanced Studies in Behavioral Science, 83-84; Fellow, Wissenschattskolleg zu Berlin, 99-00. **HONORS AND AWARDS** Gustave Art Humanities Award, 75; Fel, Am Assoc for The Advancement of Science, 99; Fel, Am Acad of Arts and Sciences, 00. **MEMBERSHIPS** Ling Soc Am; Soc for Philos and Psychol (pres, 90-91). **RESEARCH** Semantics; syntactic theory; musical cognition; consciousness. **SELECTED PUBLICATIONS** Auth, Semantic Interpretation in Generative Grammar, 72, X-Bar Syntax, 75, coauth (with Fred Lerdahl), A Generative Theory of Tonal Music, 82 & Semantics and Cognition, Mass Inst Technoll Press, 83; Consciousness and the Computational Mind, 87; Semantic Structures, 90; Languages of the Mind, 92; Architecture of the Language Faculty, 97; Patterns in the Mind, Basic Books, 94. **CONTACT ADDRESS** Volen Center, Brandeis Univ, 415 South St, Waltham, MA 02254.

JACKMAN, JARRELL C.
PERSONAL Born 12/05/1943, Kenosha, WI, m, 1998, 1 child **DISCIPLINE** GERMAN AND AMERICAN STUDIES **EDUCATION** UCLA, BA, 66; Cal State Univ, MA, 69; Univ Cal, SB, PhD, 77. **CAREER** Exec Dir, 81-, Santa Barbara Trust for Hist Preservations. **HONORS AND AWARDS** Fulbright Fel; U of Cal Fel; DAAD; Spanish Min Cult Res Gnt. **MEMBERSHIPS** CMSA; SBDO; SBHA; SCIF; SMRC; CHS. **RESEARCH** German History and Literature; Spanish Colonial History. **SELECTED PUBLICATIONS** Coed, Santa Barbara Presido Area 1840-present, Univ California, Santa Barbara CA, 93; Presidos of the Big Bend Area, by James E Ivey, in: Public Historian, 92; Felipe de Goicoechea: Santa Barbara Presidio Commandante, in: The Spanish Beginnings in CA, UCSB, 90, pub, Anson Luman Press, Santa Barb, 93. **CONTACT ADDRESS** Santa Barbara Trust for Historic Preservation, 123 E. Canon Perdido, PO Box 388, Santa Barbara, CA 93102. **EMAIL** sbthp@rain.org

JACKSON, ELIZABETH R.
PERSONAL Born 05/13/1926, Boston, MA, m, 1970, 2 children **DISCIPLINE** FRENCH LITERATURE **EDUCATION** Reed Col, BA, 47; Univ Toulouse, cert philos, 51; Wellesley Col, MA, 59; Univ Paris, DUniv(French lit), 63. **CAREER** Statist asst, Nat Bur Econ Res, 47-48; teacher, Putney Sch, 48-49; tutor French, Goddard Col, 53-55; vis lectr, Knox Col, 63-65; assoc, humanities & French, Univ Calif, San Diego, 65-66; chmn, Dept French & Ital, 75-80, Prof French, San Diego State Univ, 69-, Fr Govt grant & Fulbright travel grant, 60-62; Am Philos Soc grant-in-aid, 63; grant, Centre national de la recherche scientifique, 65. **MEMBERSHIPS** MLA; Am Asn Teachers Fr; Asn Studies Dada & Surrealism. **RESEARCH** Modern French poetry; Chenier; modern French novel. **SELECTED PUBLICATIONS CONTACT ADDRESS** Dept of French & Ital, San Diego State Univ, San Diego, CA 92182.

JACKSON, K. DAVID
PERSONAL Born 07/21/1944, Henderson, TX, m, 1980, 3 children **DISCIPLINE** PORTUGUESE LANGUAGE & LITERATURE **EDUCATION** Univ Ill, BA, 66; Univ Wisc, MA, 67; PhD, 73. **CAREER** Assoc prof, prof, Univ Tex, Austin, 80-93; prof, Yale Univ, 93-. **MEMBERSHIPS** IAL. **RESEARCH** Brazilian and Portuguese literatures. **SELECTED PUBLICATIONS** Auth, A Hidden Presence: 500 Years of Portuguese Culture in India and Sri Lanka/A Presenca Oculta: 500 Anos de Cultura Portuguesa na India e no Sri Lanka, Macau Foundation/Territorial Comm of Macau for the Commemoration of the Portuguese Discoveries (Macau), 95; auth, Cantha Sen Vargonya: Thadicoes Orais em Verso Crioulo Indo-Portugue, Macau Foundation/Territorial Commission of Macau for the Commemoration of the Portuguese Discoveries (Macau), 96; auth, Builders of the Oceans. Notebooks of the Portuguese Pavillion, Assino & Alvim; Portuguese Pavillion, EXPO '98, 97; (in Portuguese) Os Construtores dos Ocean os (Lisboa), 98; auth, A Van guarda Literaria no Bras il: Bibliografia e Antologia Critica. Bibliografia e Antologia Critica das Vanguardas Literarias, vol 1, Vervuert/Interamericana (Frankfurt and Madrid), 98; co-ed, Experimental, Visual, Concrete: Avant-Garde Poetry Since 1960, Rodopi (Amsterdam and Atlanta), 96; auth, "The Indo-Portuguese Folklore Text: The Cantigas." Rev Culture 26, Portuguese ed, "0 Texto Folclorico e Os Crioulos Asia ticos: 0 Cancioneiro IndoPortugues," (96): 62-76; auth, "Macacos e Ratos. a transformacao do conto oral no crioulo indoportugues." In Os Sentidos e 0 Sen tido: Literatura e Cultura Portuguesas em Debate, eds. Ana Hatherly, Silvina Rodrigues Lopes (Homenageando Jacinto Prado Coelho, Lisboa: Edicoes Cosmos, 97), 185-198; auth, "A Fatalidade Linguistica da Ilba de Ceilao: Tavares de Mello em Colombo, 1905-1908." Intraducao: In Folclores Ceilonenses, Comissao Nacional pelas Comemoracoes dos Descobrimentos (Lisboa), Portugueses, 98; auth, "Utopia and Identity in the Voyages: Camoes between India and Portugal." In Arquivos do Centro Cultural Calouste Gulbenkian, Homenagem a Maria de Lourdes Belchior (Lisboa-Paris: Centro Cultural Calouste Gulbenkian, 98),185-94; auth, "Invencao e Razao na Poesia de Almada," in Almada Negreiros: A Descoberta como Necessidade, coord, Celina Silva, Actas do Coloquio Intemacional, Porto, 12, 13, (96). **CONTACT ADDRESS** Dept Spanish, Portuguese, Yale Univ, PO Box 208204, New Haven, CT 06520-8204.

JACKSON, KENT PHILLIPS
PERSONAL Born 08/09/1949, Salt Lake City, UT, m, 1975, 5 children **DISCIPLINE** ANCIENT NEAR EASTERN LANGUAGES **EDUCATION** Brigham Young Univ, BA, 74; Univ Mich, MA, 76, PhD(Near Eastern studies), 80. **CAREER** Prof Ancient Scripture, Brigham Young Univ, 80- **MEMBERSHIPS** Soc Bibl Lit; Am Schs Orient Res. **RESEARCH** Canaanite inscriptions; West Semitic personal names; Biblical history. **SELECTED PUBLICATIONS** Auth, Revolutionaries in the First-Century + Zealots, Rebellion, and the 1st Jewish Revolt Against the Roman-Empire, Brigham Young Univ Stud, Vol 0036, 97. **CONTACT ADDRESS** Dept of Ancient Scriptures, Brigham Young Univ, Joseph Smith Bldg 375 JSB, Provo, UT 84602. **EMAIL** kent-jackson@byu.edu

JACKSON, ROBERT LOUIS
PERSONAL Born 11/10/1923, New York, NY, m, 1951, 2 children **DISCIPLINE** SLAVIC LANGUAGES AND LITERATURES **EDUCATION** Cornell Univ, BA, 44; Columbia Univ, MA, 49; Univ Calif, PhD(Slavic Lang & Lit), 56. **CAREER** Instr, 54-59 ; asst prof Russ Lang & Lit, 59-62, assoc prof, 62-67, prof Russ Lit, Yale Univ, 67-, chmn, B E Bensinger Prof Slavic Languages and Literatures, 91; auth, B.E. Bensinger Prof Emeritus Slavic Languages and Literatures, 00. **HONORS AND AWARDS** Fel, Am Coun of Learned Soc, 50-51; Phi Beta Kappa, 53; Morse Fel, Yale Univ, 61; Guggenheim Fel, 67; Honorary M.A., Yale Univ, 67; Nat Endow for the Humanities Fel, 74; Honorary Doctor's Degree, Moscow State Univ; 94; Am Assoc of Teachers of Slavic and East European Languages, 94; Prize for Outstanding Work in the field of Slavic Languages and Literature for Dialogues with Dostoevsky: The Overwhelming Questions, Stanford Univ Press, (93) 94. **MEMBERSHIPS** Int Dosteovsky Soc (vpres, 71-); NAm Dostoevsky Soc (pres, 70-); Vyacheslav I. Ivanov Convivium, Pres, 81-; North Am Chekhov Soc, Pres, 88; Yale Conf in Slavic Lit and Culture, Dir, 80-. **RESEARCH** Interaction of aesthetic and philosophical thought in the 19th century Russian literature; chance and fate in 19th century literature; tragedy and the Brothers Karamazov; Chekhov; Goethe and Russian Lit. **SELECTED PUBLICATIONS** Auth, Dostoevsky's Underground Man in Russian Literature," 58; auth, "The Art of Dostoevsky," 58; auth, Dostoevsky's Quest for Form: A Study of His Philosophy of Art, Yale Univ, 66; The Testament of F M Dostoevsky, Russ Lit, 73; Miltonic Imagery and Design in Pushkin's Mozart and Salieri: The Russian Satan, Am Contributions to Seventh Int Congr Slavists, 73; auth, introd & ed, Crime and Punishment, a collection of critical essays, In: Twentieth Century Interpretations, Prentice-Hall, 74; Dialogues with Dostoevsky, The Overshelming Questions, Stanford Univ Press, 93; articles on Pushkin, Gogol, Turgenev, Tolstoy, Chekhov, V.I. Ivanov, Solzhenitsyn and others. **CONTACT ADDRESS** Slavic Languages & Literature, Yale Univ, P O Box 208236, New Haven, CT 06520-8236. **EMAIL** robert.l.jackson@yale.edu

JACKSON, WILLIAM EDWARD
PERSONAL Born 12/01/1936, Creedmoor, NC, m, 1961, 3 children **DISCIPLINE** GERMAN LANGUAGE & LITERATURE **EDUCATION** NC Col, BA, 58; NYork Univ, MA, 61; Univ Pa, PhD(Ger), 72. **CAREER** Lectr Ger, City Col New York, 61-64; acting instr, 70-71, asst prof, 71-75, assoc prof Ger, Yale Univ, 75-80; prog officer, Gen Res Prog, Nat Endowment for Humanities, 80-81; assoc prof Ger & assoc Dir, Carter G Woodson Inst, Univ VA, 81-. **MEMBERSHIPS** Am Asn Teachers Ger; MLA. **RESEARCH** Medieval German lang; medieval German lit; medieval Austrian culture. **SELECTED PUBLICATIONS** Auth, Reinmar Studies--A Commentary on the So-Called Spurious Poems of Reinmar Der Alte, J Engl and Germanic Philol, Vol 0092, 93; The Crusade Motif in the Poetry of Reinmar Der Alte, Germanisch-Romanische Monatsschrift, Vol 0043, 93; Reinmar Studies--A Commentary on the So-Called Spurious Poems of Reinmar Der Alte, J Engl and Germanic Philol, Vol 0092, 93; auth, "Das Kreuzzugsmotiv in Reinmars Lyrik, Germanisch-romanische Monatsschrift, 93; auth, "Poet, Woman, and Crusade, Mediaevalia, 99. **CONTACT ADDRESS** Dept of Ger Lang, Univ of Virginia, 108 Cocke, Charlottesville, VA 22903. **EMAIL** wej@virginia.edu

JACOBS, CAROL F.
DISCIPLINE COMPARATIVE LITERATURE **EDUCATION** Cornell Univ, MA; Johns Hopkins Univ, PhD. **CAREER** Prof, NYork Univ. **RESEARCH** Lit theory as it appears in Eng, French, and Ger lits in the 18th, 19th, and 20th centuries; critical theory of the same periods. **SELECTED PUBLICATIONS** Auth, The Dissimulating Harmony on Nietzsche, Rilke, Artaud, and Benjamin, Johns Hopkins UP, 78; Uncontainable Romanticism: Shelley, Bronte, Kleist, Johns Hopkins, 89; Telling Time on Lessing, Ford Madox Ford, Wordsworth, Rilke, de Man, Benjamin, and Levi-Strauss, Johns Hopkins, 93; auth, In the Language of Walter Benjamin, Johns Hopkins Univ Pr, 99. **CONTACT ADDRESS** Dept Ger, New York Univ, New York, NY 10003.

JACOBS, RODERICK ARNOLD
PERSONAL Born 05/29/1934, London, England, m, 1962, 2 children **DISCIPLINE** DIACHRONIC LINGUISTICS, STYLISTICS, DISCOURSE **EDUCATION** Univ London, BA, 56; Harvard Univ, EdM, 62; Univ Ca, San Diego, MA, 70, PhD, 72. **CAREER** Teacher English & French, Pub Schs, London, England, New Brunswick, Can & Newton, Mass, 56-64; curric supvr English & reading, Tuxedo Pub Schs, NY, 64-66; assoc prof lit, State Univ NY Col Oneonta, 66-68; res fel ling, Univ Calif, San Diego, 68-72; teacher & researcher Amerindian lang & cult, Pala Indian Band Calif, 72-73; prof ling & English lang, Univ Hawaii, Manoa, 73-, consult, Peace Corps Training Div, 70-71; consult bilingual educ, Trust Territory Micronesia, 78-; dir bilingual studies, Dept English Second Lang, 77-79, ch dept English Second Lang, 94-, Univ Haw, Manoa, 77-99; Dean, College of Lang, Ling, & Lit, Univ Haw, Monoa, 99-. **MEMBERSHIPS** Ling Soc Am; NCTE; TESOL. **RESEARCH** Syntactic change; discourse analysis; stylistics; cognitive linguistics. **SELECTED PUBLICATIONS** Co-ed, Vanity Fair, 64 & Wuthering Heights, 65, Harper; coauth, English Transformational Grammar, Ginn-Blaisdell, 68; auth, On Transformational Grammar, NCTE, 69; coauth, Transformations, Style, and Meaning, 71 & auth, Studies in Language, 73, Xerox; Syntactic Change, Univ Calif, 75; English Syntax, Oxford, 95. **CONTACT ADDRESS** Col of Languages, Linguistics & Literature,, Univ of Hawaii, Manoa, Bilger 101, Honolulu, HI 96822-2318. **EMAIL** rjacobs@hawaii.edu

JACOBSON, RODOLFO
PERSONAL m, 1944, 4 children **DISCIPLINE** LINGUISTICS, BILINGUAL EDUCATION **EDUCATION** Univ Panama, AB, 52; Univ Mich, MA, 64, PhD(ling), 66. **CAREER** Teacher, Escuela Prof, Panama, 52-62; instr English as foreign lang, English Lang Inst, Univ Mich, 65, lectr, 65-66; assoc prof English, State Univ NY Col Cortland, 66-69, prof English & dir English socioling prog, 69-74; Prof Ling, Univ Tex, San Antonio, 74-, Consult, Ministry Educ, Panama, 60-62; lectr, Am Univ Beirut & Am Univ Cairo, 73; consult, United Independent Sch Dist, Laredo, Tex, 75-79; dir, Title VIII Training fel, demonstration proj, 77-; interpreter & examr, Adm US Courts, Washington, DC, 80-81. **MEMBERSHIPS** Teachers English to Speakers Other Lang; Nat Asn Bilingual Educ; Int Sociol Asn; Ling Asn Southwest; Am Educ Res Asn. **RESEARCH** Sociolinguistics; Spanish language varieties and use; methods in bilingual instruction. **SELECTED PUBLICATIONS** Auth, Incorporating sociolinguistic norms into an EFL program, TESOL Quart, 76; La reinvindicacion de parole, Estudios Filol, 76; The social implications of intrasentential codeswitching, in: Chicano Scholarship (the New Scholar), 77; Anticipatory embedding and imaginary content, in: Swallow VI Proc, 78; Semantic compounding in the speech of Mexican American bilinguals, in: Bilingualism & Bilingual Educ, 79; Beyond ESL: The teaching of content other than language arts in bilingual education, Southwest Educ Development Lab, Austin, Tex, 79; Can bilingual teaching techniques reflect bilingual community behavior?, in: Bilingual Educ and Public Policy, Ypsilanti, Mich, 79; Can and should the Laredo experiment be duplicated elsewhere?, in: NABE Proc, 81. **CONTACT ADDRESS** 14222 Golden Woods, San Antonio, TX 78285.

JACOBY, SALLY
PERSONAL Born Paterson, NJ **DISCIPLINE** LINGUISTICS; COMMUNICATION; APPLIED **EDUCATION** Northwestern Univ, BS, 69; Tel Aviv Univ, BA, 78; Univ Birmingham, UK, MA, 86; UCLA, PhD, 98. **CAREER** Instr, Tel Aviv Univ, 77-88; adj asst prof, Soka Univ, 95-96; asst prof, Dept of Commun, Univ New Hampshire, 96- . **MEMBERSHIPS** AAAL; AAUP; AILA; CIOS; ICA; NCA. **RESEARCH** Language and social interaction; conversation analysis; situated interpersonal communication; ethnographic and discourse analytic approaches to communicative competence; language and discourse socialization; multi-modal communication; ethnography of communication; expert-novice interaction; Hebrew conversation. **SELECTED PUBLICATIONS** Co-auth, Interpretive journeys: H ow Physicists Talk and Travel Through Graphic Space, in Configurations, 94; ed, sp issue, and co-auth, Co-Construction, Res on Lang and Soc Interaction, 95; co-auth, A Genre-based Developmental Writing course for Undergraduate ESL Science Majors, in Academic Writing in a Second Language: Essays on Research and Pedagogy, Ablex, 95; auth, When I Come Down I'm in the Domain State: Grammar and Graphic Representation in the Interpretive Activity of Physicists, in Ochs, co-ed, Interaction and Grammar, Cambridge, 96; co-auth, Down to the Wire: The Cultural Clock of Physicists and the Discourse of Consensus, Lang and Soc, 97; co-auth, Saying What Wasn't Said: Negative Observation as a Linguistic Resource for the Interactional Construction of performance feedback, in The Language of Turn and Sequence, Oxford, 00. **CONTACT ADDRESS** Dept of Communication, Univ of New Hampshire, Durham, 20 College Rd, Durham, NH 03824-3586. **EMAIL** swj@hopper.unh.edu

JAEGER, C. STEPHEN
PERSONAL Born 09/01/1940, Hanford, CA, m, 2 children **DISCIPLINE** GERMAN LITERATURE **EDUCATION** Univ Calif, Berkeley, BA, 63; MA, 65; PhD, 70. **CAREER** Asst prof, Univ of Chicago 68-70; asst prof, Northwestern Univ, 71-76; assoc prof to prof, Bryn Mawr Col, 76-85; prof, Univ of Wash, 85-. **HONORS AND AWARDS** Fulbright Fel, 79-80, 91-92; Guggenheim Fel, 85-86; Jacques Barzun Prize, Am Philos Soc, 95; Alex von Humboldt Found 96-97; Inst for Advan Study, Princeton, 99-00. **RESEARCH** Medieval German and Latin Literature of the Middle Ages, Medieval Cultural and Intellectual History. **SELECTED PUBLICATIONS** Auth, the Origins of Courtliness, 85; auth, The Envy of Angels: Cathedral Schools, 97; Ennobling Love, 99. **CONTACT ADDRESS** Dept Germanics, Univ of Washington, PO Box 353130, Seattle, WA 98195-3130. **EMAIL** jaeger@u.washington.edu

JAEN-PORTILLO, ISABEL
PERSONAL Born Madrid, Spain **DISCIPLINE** HISPANIC LITERATURE **EDUCATION** Univ of Madrid, BA, 93; PhD, 96; Univ of Salamanca, Nat Cert of Pedagogical Aptitude, 94; Purdue Univ, MA, 98; PhD, 00. **CAREER** Instr, AR Castelao Sch, Spain, 89-93; TA, St Michael's Grammar Sch, UK, 93-94; TA, Coptall Grammar Sch, UK, 93-94; Instr, Cult Dept of the City of Mostoles, Spain, 94-; instr, Estudio Int Sampere, Spain, 95-96; instr, TA, Purdue Univ, 98-01; lectr, Yale Univ, 01-. **HONORS AND AWARDS** First Nat Prize of Narrative Dia de Europa, Spain, 85; Award, Purdue Univ, 01. **MEMBERSHIPS** MLA. **RESEARCH** Golden Age and 20th Century Literature, Poetry, Literary Theory and Cognition, Neuroscience, Cervantes, Bakhtin, Drama, Music, Film World History. **SELECTED PUBLICATIONS** Auth, "The Hidden Pleasure of Cleaning a Toilet," Purdue Exponent, (Purdue Univ, 96); auth, "Poemas," Babel: Revista literaria internacional (Madrid: Acaal, 97); auth, "El laboratorio critico. Categorias y contextualizaciones (Especimen y muestras: Francisco de Aldana)," Romance Lang Annual XI, (99): 503-506; auth, "Fagundes Varela and the Romantic Syndrome: A Neurcognitive Approach to 'Arquetipo,'" Romance Notes, (Univ of NCar Chapel Hill, forthcoming); auth, "States of Consciousness: Dreams, Literature and the Neurochemistry of the Brain," Dept For Lang and Lit, (forthcoming). **CONTACT ADDRESS** Purdue Univ, West Lafayette, Stanley Coulter Hall, West Lafayette, IN 47907. **EMAIL** ljaen@omni.cc.purdue.edu

JAGASICH, PAUL A.
PERSONAL Born 03/30/1934, Budapest, Hungary, m, 1960, 2 children **DISCIPLINE** GERMAN, LINGUISTICS **EDUCATION** Pedagogini Foiskola, MA, 55; UNC Chapel Hill, MA, 70; UNC Chicago, MA, 71; PhD, 73; Middlebury Col, MA, 83. **CAREER** St. Bernard's School, 66-68; instr, UNC Chapel Hill, 68-73; prof, Hampden Sydney Col 73-. **HONORS AND AWARDS** Trustees Awd, Hampden Sydney Col, 86; Mettauer Res Awd, 86, 88, Hampden Sydney Col. **MEMBERSHIPS** AATG; AATSEEL; ATA; ALTA; AATG of Va. **RESEARCH** Translations from Czech and German into English, comp. Linguistics. **SELECTED PUBLICATIONS** Auth, The Casting of Bells, Spirit that Moves Us Pr, 84; auth, Mozart in Prague, Spirit That Moves Us Pr, 86; 8 Days, Spirit that Moves Us Pr, 86; trans, Halley's Comet, 86; trans, Dressed in Light, 90, auth, Two Faces of the English Channel, 91. **CONTACT ADDRESS** Dept Mod Lang, Hampden-Sydney Col, PO Box 81, Hampden-Sydney, VA 23943. **EMAIL** paulj@tiger.hsc.edu

JAHN, GARY ROBERT
PERSONAL Born 09/29/1943, Minneapolis, MN, m **DISCIPLINE** RUSSIAN LITERATURE **EDUCATION** Univ Minn, BA, 65; Univ Wis, MA, 68; PhD, 72. **CAREER** Asst prof, St Olaf Coll, 71-72; asst prof, SUNY Buffalo, 72-77; asst prof, Univ MN, 77-82; assoc prof, 82-98; prof, 98-. **HONORS AND AWARDS** Student Asn Awd for Excellence in Teaching (SUNY/Buffalo), 77; IREX Exchange of Lang Teachers with USSR (Moscow State Univ), 78; Slav East Euro J, ed, 89-94; McKnight Summer Fel, 97; Innovation in Technology Enhanced Learn Awd, Univ Minn, 98; Selected as Univ of Minn Fac Ambassador **MEMBERSHIPS** AATSEEL; AAASS; ALSC. **RESEARCH** Russian literature of the 19th century, esp works of Leo Tolstoy; electronic scholarly editions of major literary works; computer-assisted language learning, (for Russian language). **SELECTED PUBLICATIONS** Auth, Sentences, Exceller Software, (Ithaca NY), 89; auth, "Donna Tussing Orwin, Tolstoy's Art and Thought," in the Roundtable Discussion, Tolstoy Studies J 6 (93): 161-67; auth, "Brother or Other: Tolstoy's Equivocal Surrender to the Concept of Brotherhood," in Lev Tolstoy and the Concept of Brotherhood, Legas (96): 71-87; auth, "On the Syle of a Story for the People," Tolstoy Studies J (98): 42-49; **CONTACT ADDRESS** Dept Slavic and Central Asian Langs and Literatures, Univ of Minnesota, Twin Cities, 210 Nolte Center, Minneapolis, MN 55455. **EMAIL** gjahn@umn.edu

JAINI, PADMANABH S.
PERSONAL Born 10/23/1923, Mangalore, India **DISCIPLINE** LINGUISTICS, SOUTH & SOUTHEAST ASIAN RELIGIONS **EDUCATION** HPT Col, India, BA, 47; BJ Inst Res, Ahmedabad, MA, 49; Vidyodaya Pirivena, Ceylon, Tripitakacarya, 51; Univ London, PhD (Sanskrit Lit) 59. **CAREER** Lectr Sanskrit & Pali, Benaras Hindu Univ, 52-56; Pali & Buddhist Sanskrit, Univ London, 56-64, reader, 65-67; vis lectr Buddhism, Univ Mich, Ann Arbor, 64-65, prof Indic Lang, 67-72; prof Buddhism, Univ Calif, Berkeley, 72-94; prof Emeritus, grad school, 94. **RESEARCH** Pali and Buddhist Sanskrit language and literature; Abhidharma studies; comparative study of Indian religions; Jaina studies. **SELECTED PUBLICATIONS** Auth, "Silonmam be Varsh, Gujarat Vidyasabha, Ahmedabad," 52; auth, "Abhidharmadipa with Vibhasaprabha-vrtti," K.P. Jayaswal Research Institute, Patna, 59; reprinted 77; auth, "Milinda-tika, Pali Text Society," London, 61; auth, "Laghutattvasphota by Amrtacandra," Sanskrit text with English translation, L. D. Institute of Indology Series, No. 62, Ahmedabad, 78; auth, "Saratama: A Panjika on the Astasahasrika-Prajnaparamita by Ratnakarasanti," K. P. Jayaswal Research Institute, Patna, 79; auth, "The Jaina Path of Purification," University of California Press, Berkeley, 79, Reprinted by Motilal Banarsidass, Delhi, 97; auth, "Pannasa-Jataka or Zimme Pannasa (in Burmese Recension), vol I Jatakas 1-25, Pali Text Society, London, 81; auth, "Jaina Sampradaya men Moksa, Avatara our Punarjanma," B. J. Institue of Learning and Research, Ahmedabad, 82 (in Hindi); auth, "Pannasa-Jataka or Zimme Pannasa (in Burmese ecension), vol. II (Jatakas 30-50), Pali Text Society, London, 83; auth, "Apocryphal Birth-Stories (translation of the Pannasa-Jataka), vol. I (with I.B. Horner), Pali Text Society, London, 85. **CONTACT ADDRESS** Dept of South and Southeast Asian Lang & Lit, Univ of California, Berkeley, 7303 Dwinelle Hall, Berkeley, CA 94720-0001.

JAMES, DOROTHY
DISCIPLINE GERMAN **EDUCATION** Univ London, UK, PhD. **CAREER** Prof, Hunter Col, 78-; ch, Ger Dept, 13 yrs; fac, Grad Sch, CUNY; trained tester, oral proficiency on the ACTFL model, 83 & trainer, testing, 85; past dir, NEH funded Hunter Col proj to institute a proficiency-based curric in an urban univ; proj dir, NEH funded Proj, CUNY: A Model Curric in Ger, 94-97. **HONORS AND AWARDS** NYSAFLT awd, 89; Northeast Conf awd, 93; ADFL awd, 94. **MEMBERSHIPS** Pres, Asn Departments For Languages, 90; interim dir, For Languages at the MLA & ed, ADFL Bull, 90-91; ch, MLA Adv Comt For Languages and Literatures, 95-96. **SELECTED PUBLICATIONS** Auth, Raimund and Vienna, Cambridge UP, 70 & Georg Bnchner's Dantons Tod, Mod Humanities Res Asn, 82; ed, Patterns of Change, German Drama and the European Tradition, Peter Lang, 90. **CONTACT ADDRESS** Dept of German, Hunter Col, CUNY, 695 Park Ave, New York, NY 10021.

JAMESON, MICHAEL H.
PERSONAL Born 10/15/1924, United Kingdom, m, 1946, 4 children **DISCIPLINE** CLASSICS **EDUCATION** BA, 42; Univ Chicago, PhD, 49. **CAREER** Edward Clark Crossett Prof Emeritus Hum Studies and prof emeritus class. **RESEARCH** Greek hist; relig; epigraphy; archaeol. **SELECTED PUBLICATIONS** Auth, Sophocles, The Women of Trachis in Complete Greek Tragedies, 57; A Decree of Themistokles from Troizen, Hesperia, 60; Agriculture and Slavery in Classical Athens, CJ, 77-8; Sacrifice Before Battle in Hoplites, 91; coauth, A Greek Countryside: The Southern Argolid from Prehistory to Present Day, 92. **CONTACT ADDRESS** Stanford Univ, Bldg 20, Main Quad, Stanford, CA 94305. **EMAIL** michael.jameson@stanford.edu

JAMME, ALBERT W. F.
PERSONAL Born 06/27/1916, Senzeille, Belgium **DISCIPLINE** ENGLISH, FRENCH **EDUCATION** Cath Univ Louvain, DTheol, 47, DOr, 52; Pontif Bibl Comm, Rome, Lic, 48. **CAREER** Res Prof Semitics, Cath Univ Am, 55-, Epigraphical adv, Govt Saudi Arabia, 68-69. **MEMBERSHIPS** Cath Bibl Asn Am; Am Orient Soc. **RESEARCH** Pre-Islamic Arabian sci. **SELECTED PUBLICATIONS** Auth, Pieces Epigraphiques de Heid bin Aqil, la Necropole de Timna, (Hagr Kohlan), Biblio Mus, Louvain, 52; La Kynastie de Sarahbiil Yakuf et la documentation epigraphique sud-arabe, Ned Hist Archaeol Inst, Istanbul, 61; Sabaean inscriptions from Mahram Bilquis (Marib), Johns Hopkins Univ, 62; Miscellanees d'ancient arabe, I-XX, Washington, 71-98; Carnegie Museum 1974-1975 Yemen Expedition, Carnegie Natural Hist Spec Publ No 2, Pittsburgh, 76. **CONTACT ADDRESS** Dept of Semitics, Catholic Univ of America, 620 Michigan Ave N E, Washington, DC 20064-0002.

JANC, JOHN J.
PERSONAL Born 07/24/1945, Blue Island, IL, s **DISCIPLINE** FRENCH LANGUAGE, LITERATURE **EDUCATION** Univ Wis Eau Clair, BA; Univ Mich, MA, 68; Universite de la Sorbonne Nouvelle, Doctorat de troisieme cycle, 77; Univ Wis Madison, MA, 74; PhD, 81. **CAREER** Teacher, Durand Unified High School, 67; instr, St. Benedict col, 68-69; instr, Univ of Wis Stout, 69-72; lectr, Centre Audio-Visuel de l'Universite de Pointiers, 72-74; TA, Univ of Wis Madison, 74-76, 77-79; prof, Minn State Univ, 79-. **HONORS AND AWARDS** Woodrow Wilson Fel, 67-68; Fulbright Fel, France, 76-77; Outstanding Fac Member, Minn State Univ, 82-83; Chevalier dans l'Order des palmes Academiques, 86; Merit Awd, Minn State Univ, 85; Emma Birkmaier Awd, 94; Founders Awd, 99. **MEMBERSHIPS** Alpha Mu Gamma; Kappa Delta Pi; Phi Kappa Phi; Pi Delta Phi; Sigma Tau Delta; AATF; ACTFL; MAATF; MCTLC; Central States Conf; Soc des Etudes Romantiques et Dix-Neuviemistes. **RESEARCH** Nineteenth-century French theatre, the theatre of Victor Hugo. **SELECTED PUBLICATIONS** Auth, Victor Hugo, Les deux Trouvailles de Gallus, Univ Pr of Am, (NY), 83; auth, Victor Hugo, Torquemada, Univ Pr of Am (NY), 89; auth, Faisons des progres. Manuel de conversation, Univ Pr of Am (NY), 97; auth, "Le Francais tel qu-on le parle en cours, revu, mis a Jet augmente", Minn Lang Rev 26.2 (97-98): 18-19; auth, "Victor Hugo", in French Dramatists from 1789 to 1914. Dictionary of Literary Biography 192, Bruccoli clark Layman, (98): 175-194; auth, "Proverbes, dictons et expressions imagees pour les cours de francias", Minn Lang Rev 27.4 (99): 3-12; auth, Victor Hugo, Hernandi (forthcoming). **CONTACT ADDRESS** Dept Modern Languages, Mankata State Univ, PO Box 8400, Mankato, MN 56002-8400. **EMAIL** john.janc@mankato.msus.edu

JANKOFSKY, KLAUS P.
DISCIPLINE MEDIEVAL AND COMPARATIVE LITERATURE, HISTORICAL LINGUISTICS, SHAKESPEARE **EDUCATION** Univ Saarlandes, Ger, Dr phil. **CAREER** Prof, hd, dept Eng, Univ Minn, Duluth. **RESEARCH** Death and dying in literature and historical documents. **SELECTED PUBLICATIONS** Auth, John Ciardi's Medievalism." Medievalism in North America, ed, Kathleen Verduin, Bury St. Edmunds, D S Brewer, Cambridge, 94; ed, The South English Legendary: A Critical Assessment, Francke, 92. **CONTACT ADDRESS** Dept of Eng, Univ of Minnesota, Duluth, Duluth, MN 55812-2496.

JARA, RENE
DISCIPLINE SPANISH AND PORTUGUESE LITERATURE **EDUCATION** Univ Cath Valparaiso, BA, 61; Ariz State Univ, PhD, 79. **RESEARCH** Seventeenth century Spanish American narratives and poetry; colonial writing in Spanish America; colonial heritage in the New Latin American novel. **SELECTED PUBLICATIONS** Auth, Los pliegues del silencio, 96; Amerindian Images and the Legacy of Columbus, Univ Minn, 92; co-auth, Perfil historiografico de una literatura colonial, 92. **CONTACT ADDRESS** Spanish and Portuguese Dept, Univ of Minnesota, Twin Cities, 34 Folwell Hall, 9 Pleasant St SE, Minneapolis, MN 55455.

JARVIS, DONALD KARL
PERSONAL Born 04/06/1939, Ithaca, NY, m, 1965, 6 children **DISCIPLINE** RUSSIAN LANGUAGE & CULTURE **EDUCATION** Brigham Young Univ, BA, 64; Ohio State Univ, PhD, 70. **CAREER** Teacher foreign lang, Beaver Pub Schs, 65-66; teacher Russ, Salt Lake City Pub Schs, 66-67; assoc prof, 70-80, chmn dept Asian & Slavic lang, 76-79, prof Russ, Brigham Young Univ, 80-; assoc dir Gen Educ, 81-84; Ed, Newslett, Am Assn Teachers Slavic & E Europ Lang, 71-73; dir, Gen Ed, 84-86; dir, Faculty Center, 92-94; **HONORS AND AWARDS** NDEA title IV fel, Ohio State Unv, 67-70; Maeser General Bdocation Prof, 91-94;Joe Malik Awd for Outstanding Service to AATSEEL, 99. **MEMBERSHIPS** Am Assn Teachers Slavic & E Europ Lang; Am Coun Teaching Russ. **RESEARCH** Language teaching; Russian linguistics; Russian culture. **SELECTED PUBLICATIONS** Auth, Teaching foreign etiquette in the foreign language class: Student involvement techniques, Foreign Lang Ann, 5/75; coauth, Russian Language Study in 1975: A Status Report, MLA, 76; art, The Langugage Connection: From the Classroom to the World, Nat Textbk, 77; ed, Techniques for increasing Slavic program enrollments: A collection of success stories, Am Assn Teachers Slavic & E Europ Lang, 78; auth, Krazvitiiu kommunikativinoi sposobnosti uchashchixsia (obsor amerikanskix eksperimentov i metodov) Russkii iazyk za rubezhom, 1/78; coauth, Viewpoints: A Listening and Conversation Course in Russian, Brigham Young Univ Press, 79; art, A study of the effect of parallel translations on second language reading and syntax acquisition, Mod Lang J, 82; co-ed, Russian Language Teaching, Slavica, 82. **CONTACT ADDRESS** Dept of Germanic & Slavic Lang, Brigham Young Univ, Provo, UT 84602. **EMAIL** don_jarvis@byu.edu

JEANNET, ANGELA MARIA
PERSONAL Born 08/08/1931, Pergine, Italy, 5 children **DISCIPLINE** FRENCH **EDUCATION** Univ Florence, DLet, 54. **CAREER** Teaching asst, Lycee Fenelon, Lille, France, 52-54; instr Ital & French, Univ Colo, 56-62; asst prof Romance lang, Pa State Univ, 62-67; asst prof French, 67-71, Assoc Prof Ital & French, Franklin & Marshall Col, 71-, Danforth assoc. **MEMBERSHIPS** AAUP; MLA; Am Asn Teachers Ital; Asn Ital Studies. **RESEARCH** Contemporary literature; women's studies. **SELECTED PUBLICATIONS** Auth, Nell officina carducciana, Italica, IXIII: 3; The poet as magician, Symposium, spring 68; From Florence, Italy: on Zabriskie Point, Ital Quart, fall 70; co-ed, New World Journeys, Greenwood, 77; Italo Calirno's Invisible City, Perpectives Contemp Lit, 5/77; If America did not exist ..: Italian writings on America from 1925-1970, Ital Am, fall-winter/80. **CONTACT ADDRESS** Dept of French & Ital, Franklin and Marshall Col, Lancaster, PA 17604.

JELINSKI, JACK BERNARD
PERSONAL Born 10/01/1943, Wisconsin Rapids, WI, m, 1968, 2 children **DISCIPLINE** SPANISH LITERATURE **EDUCATION** Univ Wis-Madison, BA, 67, PhD(Span), 74; Ind Univ, Bloomington, MA, 69. **CAREER** Teaching assoc Span, Ind Univ, Bloomington, 68-69; lectr, Univ Wis-Madison, 71-72; asst prof, 73-77, Assoc Prof Span & Head Dept Mod Lang, Mont State Univ, 77-, Prog consult lang & ethnic studies, Nat Endowment Humanities, 78-79, reviewer/panelist, Div Res Prog. **HONORS AND AWARDS** Montana Asn of Teachers Awd as the Outstanding Spanish Teacher in the State. **MEMBERSHIPS** Am Asn Teachers Span & Port; MLA; AAUP. **RESEARCH** Twentieth-century novel; literary criticism. **SELECTED PUBLICATIONS** Auth, Unamuno: Descubridor de Don Quijote y Sancho Panza, 4/75 & Unamuno: Su ensayo como poesia, 4/76, Proc Pac Northwest Conf Foreign Lang; La vida de Don Quijote y Sancho: Nueva interpretacion y analisis, Revista Estudios Hispanicos, 1/76; contribr, Ignacio Aldecoa: A Forgotten Master: A Critical Re-examination of Gran Sol, Univ Wyo, 77; auth, A new look at teaching the Spanish subjunctive, Hispania, 5/77; auth, El fulgor y la songre: Novela del tiempo in Aproximacion critica a Fgnacio Aldecon, Espasa-Calpe, Sapnia, 84. **CONTACT ADDRESS** Dept of Mod Lang, Montana State Univ, Bozeman, 329 Reid Hall Rm 329, Bozeman, MT 59717. **EMAIL** umljj@montana.edu

JENKINS, FRED W.
PERSONAL Born 04/13/1957, Cincinnati, OH, s **DISCIPLINE** CLASSICAL PHILOLOGY **EDUCATION** Univ Cincinnati, BA, 79; Univ Ill Urbana-Champaign, AM, 81, PhD, 85, MS, libr & info sci, 86. **CAREER** Catalog spec and asst prof, 87-96, coord & head collection mgt and assoc prof, 96-, Univ Dayton Libr. **HONORS AND AWARDS** Phi Beta Kapp, 78; Acad Libr Asn of Oh Res grant, 93, 97; Choice Outstanding Acad Book, 96; Oh Libr Found Res award, 97. **MEMBERSHIPS** Amer Soc of Papyrologists; Amer Libr Asn. **RESEARCH** Later Latin literature; Papyrology; History & bibliography of classical studies. **SELECTED PUBLICATIONS** Co-auth, Reorganizing Collection Development and Acquisitions in a Medium-sized Academic Library, Libr Acquisitions: Practice and Theory, 22.3, 287-293, fall, 98; auth, Classical Studies, Mag for Libr, 9th ed, 356-362, 97; co-auth, Internet Resources for Classical Studies, Col & Res Libr News, 58.4, 255-259, apr, 97; auth, A Ptolemaic Account, Bull of the Amer Soc of Papyrologists, 33, 21-23, 96; auth, Classical Studies: A Guide to the Reference Literature, Libr Unlimited, 96; auth, A Coptic Account from the Michigan Collection, Archiv fur Papyrusforschung, 41.2, 191-193, 95; auth, A Fourth-Century Receipt from the Michigan Collection, Bull of the Amer Soc of Papyrologists, 31.3-4, 137-139, 94; "A Lease of Land from the Tebtunis Grapheion Archive", in Papyri in honorem Johannis

Bingen octogenarii. **CONTACT ADDRESS** Univ of Dayton, 105F Roesch Library, Dayton, OH 45469-1360. **EMAIL** fredjenkins@udayton.edu

JENKINS, FREDERIC MAGILL
PERSONAL Born 01/28/1930, Oakland, CA, m, 1956, 1 child **DISCIPLINE** CONTEMPORARY FRENCH, LINGUISTICS **EDUCATION** Swarthmore Col, BA, 52; Univ Calif, Berkeley, MA, 57, PhD(ling), 63. **CAREER** Asst prof French, San Diego State Col, 61-64; asst prof, 64-67; Assoc Prof French & Ling, Univ IL, 67-00; Exec Dir Am Asn Teachers Fr, 79-97. **HONORS AND AWARDS** Palmes academiques, Chevalier 86, Officier 97. **MEMBERSHIPS** Am Asn Teachers Fr; Am Translators Assoc. **RESEARCH** Contemporary French linguistics; normative French grammar; translation theory. **CONTACT ADDRESS** Dept of French, Univ of Illinois, Urbana-Champaign, 2090 Foreign Language Bldg 707 S Mathews, Urbana, IL 61801. **EMAIL** fmajatf@uiuc.edu

JENNERMANN, DONALD L.
DISCIPLINE COMPARATIVE LITERATURE **EDUCATION** Univ Wis, BA, 63, MA, 64; Ind Univ, PhD, 74. **CAREER** Instr, 64-69, asst prof, 79-74, assoc prof, 74-84, prof, 84-,dir honors, 78-, chair hum, 86-, Ind State Univ. **HONORS AND AWARDS** Lilly Fac Open Fel 84-85. **MEMBERSHIPS** Nat Col Hon Coun. **RESEARCH** History of literary criticism. **SELECTED PUBLICATIONS** Ed, The Writer and the Past, (80); auth, Born of a Cretan Spring, (81); ed, The Poem of the Mind, (99); auth, Bearing North, (95); auth, The Insistent Second, (99). **CONTACT ADDRESS** Dept Hum-Root Hall, Indiana State Univ, 210 N 7th St, Terre Haute, IN 47809-0001. **EMAIL** hujenn@root.indstate.edu

JENNINGS, LEE B.
PERSONAL Born 05/03/1927, Willard, OH, m, 1974 **DISCIPLINE** GERMAN **EDUCATION** Ohio State Univ, BA, 49; Univ Ill, Urbana, MA, 51, PhD(Ger), 55. **CAREER** Instr Ger, Univ Colo, 56; instr Harvard Univ, 56-57; from instr to asst prof, Univ Calif Los Angeles, 57-62; assoc prof, Univ Tex, 62-68; Prof Ger, Univ Ill, Chicago Circle, 68-, Alexander von Humboldt Found res fel, Munich & Marbach, Ger, 65-67; Ger Acad Exchange Serv res fel, fall 73; Nat Endowment for Humanities grant, 82. **MEMBERSHIPS** MLA Am Asn Teachers Ger. **RESEARCH** German 19th century literature; psychology and literature; the absurd and the grotesque in literature. **SELECTED PUBLICATIONS** Auth, Bending the Frame in the German Cyclical Narrative--Arnim, Achim, Von Der 'Wintergarten' and Hoffmann,E.T.A. Die 'Serapionsbruder', Seminar-J Ger Stud, Vol 0029, 93; Keller, Gottfried 'Sieben Legenden'--A Description of His Narrative Writing, Colloquia Germanica, Vol 0027, 94; Keller, Gottfried 'Sieben Legenden'--A Description of His Narrative Writing, Colloquia Germanica, Vol 0027, 94; Life, A Death--Grillparzer Der 'Traum Ein Leben', Modern Austrian Lit, Vol 0028, 95; Uhland,Ludwig and the Critics, Seminar-J Ger Stud, Vol 0032, 96; Eichendorff Scholarly Reception--a Survey, Colloquia Germanica, Vol 0029, 96; Eichendorff Scholarly Reception--a Survey, Colloquia Germanica, Vol 0029, 96. **CONTACT ADDRESS** Dept of Ger, Univ of Illinois, Chicago, Chicago Circle, Box 4348, Chicago, IL 60680. **EMAIL** lbj@uic.edu

JENSEN, BIRGIT A.
PERSONAL Born 12/23/1960, Duisburg, West Germany, m, 1994, 1 child **DISCIPLINE** GERMAN LITERATURE **EDUCATION** Univ Fla, BA, 86; Ohio State Univ, MA, 88; PhD, 93. **CAREER** Vis Asst Prof, Oberlin Col, 93; Vis Asst Prof, Middlebury Col, 94; Asst Prof, John Carroll Univ, 94-00; Asst Prof, East Carolina Univ, 00-. **HONORS AND AWARDS** distinguished Grad Assoc Teaching Awd, 93; Phi Beta Kappa 86; Fulbright Dissertation Fel, 90-92. **MEMBERSHIPS** AATG, ACTFL, GSA, MLA. **RESEARCH** Nineteenth-Century German Literature; Social History of family and childhood in German literature; autobiography of the working class in late 19th Century German Literature. **SELECTED PUBLICATIONS** Auth, auf der morschen Gartenschaukel: Kindheit als Problem bei Theodor Fontane, Amsterdam, 98; auth, "die entfachung der kindlichen Vitalitat in Theodor Fontane Grete Minde," German life and Letters, (97):339-353. **CONTACT ADDRESS** Dept For Lang, East Carolina Univ, 110 Bramblewood Dr, Greenville, NC 27858.

JENSEN, FREDE
PERSONAL Born 02/17/1926, Auning, Denmark, m **DISCIPLINE** ROMANCE PHILOLOGY **EDUCATION** Univ Copenhagen, MA, 53; Univ Salamanca, dipl, 55; Univ Calif, Los Angeles, PhD, 61. **CAREER** Asst prof French, Univ Alta, Calgary, 61-64, Univ Calif, Los Angeles, 64-67; assoc prof, 67-73, Prof French, Univ Colo, Boulder, 73-, Mem ed bd, Semasia, 73- **MEMBERSHIPS** MLA; Rocky Mountain Mod Lang Asn; Centre Guillaume IX, Assoc Int d'Etudes Occitanes (pres, 81-). **RESEARCH** Old Provencal (Occitan) historical grammar; troubadour poetry; the medieval poetry of Portugal, Italy, and Sicily. **SELECTED PUBLICATIONS** Auth, From Vulgar Latin to Old Provencal, Univ of NC, 72; auth, The Old Provencal Noun and Adjective Declension, Odense Univ Press, 76; auth, The Earliest Portuguese Lyrics, Odense Press, 78; auth, The Poetry of the Sicilian School, Garland (NYork), 86; auth, Old French and Comparative Gallo-Romance Syntax, Niemeyer (Tubingen), 90; auth, Medieval Galician, Garland (NYork), 92; auth, Syntaxe del'ancien occitan, Niemeyer (Tubingen), 94; auth, Tuscan Poetry of the Duecento, Garland (NYork), 94; auth, Troubadour Lyrics, Lang (NYork), 98; auth, A Comparative Study of Romance, Land (NYork), 99. **CONTACT ADDRESS** Dept of Fr, Univ of Colorado, Boulder, Box 238, Boulder, CO 80309-0238. **EMAIL** frenital@spot.colorado.edu

JENSEN, JOHN BARRY
PERSONAL Born 12/30/1943, Provo, UT, m, 1969, 4 children **DISCIPLINE** PORTUGUESE, LINGUISTICS **EDUCATION** Brigham Young Univ, BA, 65; Harvard Univ, AM, 68, PhD(Port & ling), 71. **CAREER** Vol educr, Peace Corps, Brazil, 65-67; asst prof Port, Univ Va, 70-78; Assoc Prof Mod Lang, Fla Int Univ, 78-, Chairperson, 80-, Nat Endowment for Humanities younger humanist fel, 74-75; vis lectr Span & Port, State Univ NY Albany, 77-78; Fulbright lectr, Columbia, 81. **MEMBERSHIPS** Am Asn Teachers Span & Port; Ling Soc Am; Am Coun Teaching Foreign Lang; Southeast Coun Ling; Asn Brasileira Ling. **RESEARCH** Portuguese and Brazilian sociolinguistics; Spanish linguistics; applied linguistics. **SELECTED PUBLICATIONS** Auth, Writing Portuguese Electronically--Spontaneous Spelling Reform, Hispania-J Devoted to the tchg Span and Port, Vol 0078, 95; Writing Portuguese Electronically--Spontaneous Spelling Reform, Hispania-J Devoted to the tchg Span and Port, Vol 0078, 95. **CONTACT ADDRESS** Dept of Mod Lang, Florida Intl Univ, 1 F I U South Campus, Miami, FL 33199-0001.

JENSEN, JOHN T.
PERSONAL Born 06/23/1944, Philadelphia, PA, m, 1972 **DISCIPLINE** PHONOLOGY, ENGLISH LINGUISTICS **EDUCATION** Univ Pa, BA, 66; McGill Univ, PhD, 72. **CAREER** Mem fac, Univ Colo, Boulder, 73-76; Mem Fac, Univ Ottawa, 76-, NIH fel, Mass Inst Technol, 72-73; ed, Cahiers Linguistiques d'Ottawa, 76-82. **MEMBERSHIPS** Ling Soc Am; Can Ling Asn. **RESEARCH** Syntax; morphology. **SELECTED PUBLICATIONS** Auth, Case and Thematic Role in Latin: Evidence from Passive Constructions, 83; auth, English Phonology (Amsterdam Studies in the Theory and History of Linguistic Science, Series IV: Current Issues in Linguistic Theory, vol 99), 93. **CONTACT ADDRESS** Dept of Linguistics, Univ of Ottawa, Arts Bldg, 70 Laurier, Ottawa, ON, Canada K1N 6N5. **EMAIL** jjensen@aix1.uottawa.ca

JENSEN, THEODORE WAYNE
PERSONAL Born 08/31/1944, Sacramento, CA, m, 1967, 3 children **DISCIPLINE** HISPANIC LANGUAGES & LITERATURE **EDUCATION** Univ Mont, BA, 66, MA, 70; State Univ NYork Buffalo, PhD(Hisp Lang & Lit) 76. **CAREER** Instr, State Univ NY Buffalo, 70-74; lectr, Canisius Col, 72-73; prof Span, Montana State Univ-Billings, 74-, Nat Endowment for Humanities fel, Duke Univ, Summer, 76; Am Coun Learned Soc res grant, 78; Board of Dir, pacific Northwest Coun for Languages, Assoc of Language Teachers. **HONORS AND AWARDS** Men of Achievement; Outstanding Young Men of America; National Directory of Latin Americanists; Billings Latino Club's Chris Rosas Award; Who's Who Among America's Teachers; International Directory of Distinguished Leadership. **MEMBERSHIPS** Inst Int Lit Iberoamericana; Am Asn Teachers Span & Port, MALT, PNCFL, VFW. **RESEARCH** Spanish American modernismo; contemporary short fiction of Latin America; Spanish Theatre of the Golden Age. **SELECTED PUBLICATIONS** El pitagorismo en Las fuerzas extranas de Lugones, In: Fantasia y Realismo Magico en Iberoamerica, Mich State Univ, 75; Modernista Pythagorean literature: The symbolist inspiration, In: Waiting For Pegasus: Studies of the Presence of Symbolism and Decadence in Hispanic Letters, West Ill Univ, 79; The Phoenix and folly in Lope's La noche de San Juan, Forum for Mod Lang Studies, 80; Christian-Pythagorean dualism in Nervo's El donador de almas, Ky Romance Quart, 81; Ruben Dario's final profession of Pythagorean Faith, Latin Am Lit Rev, 82; auth, The Hispanization of America, MALT Bulletin, 85; auth, The Case for Foreign Language Study, MALT Bulletin, 85; El jardin encantado y las vislumbres del oro: La disimulada fantasia apolinea en los primeros cuentos de Dario, Anales de literatura hispanoamericana, 92. **CONTACT ADDRESS** Dept of Foreign Lang & Lit, Montana State Univ, Billings, 1500 N 30th St, Billings, MT 59101-0298. **EMAIL** fl_jensen@vixen.emcmt.edu; fuzzybear3@imt.net

JEREZ-FARRAN, CARLOS
PERSONAL Born 02/14/1950 **DISCIPLINE** SPANISH LITERATURE **EDUCATION** Univ Sheffield, England, BA, 80; Univ Mass, Amherst, MA, 82; PhD, 87. **CAREER** Assoc prof, Dept of Romance Langs and Lits, Univ Notre Dame. **HONORS AND AWARDS** Univ Nominee, NEH Summer Stipend Competition, 91; NEH Fel for Col Teachers, 91-92; Inst for Scholarship in Liberal Arts, Univ Notre Dame, summer 92 and 93; Prog for cultural cooperation between Spain's Ministry of Culture and US Univs, summer 94; mem, Senat Ciutada Barcelona 2001, Ciutat Europea de la Cultura. **MEMBERSHIPS** N Am Catalan Soc, Am Asn for Teachers of Spanish and Portuguese, Asociacion de Licenciados de Espana en los Estados Unidos, Asociacion Int de Hispanistas, Asociacion Int de Valleinclanistas, Fundacion Federico Garcia Lorca. **RESEARCH** Modern Spanish literature, gay and lesbian studies. **SELECTED PUBLICATIONS** Auth, El expresionismo en Valle-Inclan: Una reinterpretacion de su vision esperpentica, Sada-A Coruna (Spain): Edicios do Castro (89); auth, "Homosexual Literary Themes Prompt Reflection," The Observer (April 14, 94); auth, "Gay Literature Course Offers a 'Brave New World''," The Observer (April 15, 94), reproduced both of the latter, in Lesbian and Gay Studies Newsletter, Vol 22, 5 (summer 95): 4-6; auth, "Sadomasoquismo homoerotico como vehiculo de homofobia internalizada en el Cuadro II de El publico de Garcia Lorca," Modern Philol, 93 (May 96): 468-497; auth, "Garcia Lorca y El Paseo de Buster Keaton: Alegoria del amor homosexual sublimado," Romanic Rev, 85, 3 (97): 629-655; auth, La homosexualidad sublimada: Texto y subtexto en al teatro de Garcia Lorca (in prep). **CONTACT ADDRESS** Dept Romance Langs, Univ of Notre Dame, 343 O Shaugnessy Hall, Notre Dame, IN 46556-5639. **EMAIL** Jerez.1@nd.edu

JEWERS, CAROLINE
PERSONAL Born 02/20/1961, Ramford, EX, England **DISCIPLINE** COMPARATIVE MEDIEVAL LITERATURE **EDUCATION** Univ OR, PhD. **CAREER** Assoc prof, Univ KS. **RESEARCH** Medieval Studies. **SELECTED PUBLICATIONS** Articles on women troubadours, medieval romance, and the poet Eustache Deschamps. **CONTACT ADDRESS** Dept of French and Italian, Univ of Kansas, Lawrence, 2044 Wescoe Hall, Lawrence, KS 66045. **EMAIL** cjewers@falcon.cc.ukans.edu

JIMENEZ, CARLOS
PERSONAL Born 08/16/1963, Jerez de la Frontera, Spain **DISCIPLINE** SPANISH **EDUCATION** Villanova Univ, MA, 90; Univ Pa, PhD, 97. **CAREER** Asst prof, Cabrini Col, 98-. **HONORS AND AWARDS** Fel, Univ of Pa, 94-95; Mellon Grant, 95-96. **MEMBERSHIPS** MLA, AATPS. **RESEARCH** Contemporary Spanish Peninsular poetry. **SELECTED PUBLICATIONS** Auth, Fernando Ortiz. Collection Adelfos de Poesia, Quasyeditorial, (Sevila), 90; auth, Aventuia Ed Abelardo Linares, Collection Galle del Aire XXXIV, Renaicimiento (Sevila), 92; auth, "Poems in Cuaderno de Literatura n 24," Aula de Literatura Jose Cadalso, ed Juan macias, Ayuntamiento de San Rogue, (San Rogue, 94). **CONTACT ADDRESS** 1524 County Line Rd, Bryn Mawr, PA 19010-1048.

JIMENEZ, FRANCISCO
PERSONAL Born 06/29/1943, Jalisco, Mexico, m, 1968, 3 children **DISCIPLINE** LATIN AMERICAN LITERATURE **EDUCATION** Santa Clara Univ, BA, 66; Columbia Univ, MA, 69, PhD(Latin Am lit), 72. **CAREER** Precepter Span & Port, Columbia Univ, 69-70, assoc, fall 70, instr 71-72, asst prof, spring 73; from Asst Prof to Prof, 73-86, Sanfilippo Prof Mod Lang & Lit, Santa Clara Univ, 86-, Chmn Dept, 97-, Dir Arts & Humanities, 81-89, VPres Acad Affairs, 90-94; Mem, Western Asn Schs & Cols Accrediting Comn, 89-95; Mem, Bd Far West Labs for Educ Res and Develop, 88-91; consult & mem, WNET-TV Nat Adv Comt proj, 75-77; vchmn, Calif State Comn Teacher Prep & Lic, 76-77, chmn, 77-79; West Coast ed, Bilingual Rev. **HONORS AND AWARDS** Ariz Quart Ann Awd, Univ Ariz, 73; Pres Special Recognition Awd for Fac, 78; Mem, Bd Trustees, Santa Clara Univ, 81-87; Mem, Bd Trustees, Archbishop Mitty High Sch, 95-98; James Barnes Farmer Distinguished Guest Prof, Miami Univ, 96-97; John and Patricia Beatty Awd, Calif Libr Asn, for: The Circuit; Americas Awd, for: The Circuit, 97; Boston Globe Horn Book Awd for Fiction for The Circuiit, 98; Jane Addams Honor Book Awd for The Circuit, 98. **MEMBERSHIPS** MLA; Am Asn Teachers Span & Port; Hispanic Inst US; Pac Coast Coun Latin Am Studies; Nat Chicano Counc Higher Educ. **RESEARCH** Mexican literature; Chicano literature; Latin American literature. **SELECTED PUBLICATIONS** Contribr, Encycl of World Literature in the 20th Century, Vol IV, Ungar, 75; coauth, Viva la Lengua?, 75 & Spanish Here and Now, 78, Harcourt; ed, Identification and Analysis of Chicano Literature, 78 & co-ed, Hispanics in the United States: An Anthology of Creative Literature, 80, Bilingual Press; Mosaico de la vida: Prosa chicana, cubana y puertorriquena, Harcourt, 81; co-ed, Hispanics in the United States: An Anthology of Creative Literature, Vol II, Bilingual Press, 82; contribr, Dict of Mexican American History, Greenwood Press, 82; auth, Poverty and Social Justice, Bilingual Press, 87; The Circuit: Stories from the Life of a Migrant Child, Univ NMex Press, 97; La Mariposa, Houghton Mifflin, 98; auth, Cajas de Carton, Houghton Mifflin, 00; auth, The Christmas Gift, Houghton Mifflin, 00. **CONTACT ADDRESS** Dept of Mod Lang, Santa Clara Univ, 500 El Camino Real, Santa Clara, CA 95053-0001. **EMAIL** fjimenez@scu.edu

JIMENEZ, QIU Y.
DISCIPLINE SPANISH **EDUCATION** Beijing Univ, BA, 85; MA, 88; Univ Cincinnati, MA, 92; UCLA, PhD, 97. **CAREER** Asst prof, Beijing Univ, 88-89; TA, Univ Cincinnati, 90-92; Teaching Fel, UCLA, 92-97; assoc prof, Bakersfield Col, 97-. **HONORS AND AWARDS** Del Amo Grad Fel, 95-96; UCA Fel, 97. **MEMBERSHIPS** MLA, Calif Teachers Asn. **RESEARCH** Teaching the Spanish language, Researching on the Contemporary Latin American literature, particularly Jorge Luis Borges. **SELECTED PUBLICATIONS** Transl, of The

Pied Pier of Hamlin, AIMS Int Books, (Cincinnati, OH, 92); auth, "El proposito enmascarado: Pineda y Bascunan y El cautiverio feliz," Mester XXIII.2 (94); 101-111; auth, Chinese Sources in the Writings of Jorge Luis Borges, Univ Mi Pr, (Ann Arbor, MI), 97. **CONTACT ADDRESS** Bakersfield Col, 1801 Panorama Dr, Bakersfield, CA 93305. **EMAIL** yqiu@bc.cc.ca.us

JOBIM, JOSE LUIS
PERSONAL Born 05/23/1953, Rio de Janeiro, m **DISCIPLINE** COMPARATIVE LITERATURE **EDUCATION** Univ Rio de Janeiro, PhD, 86. **CAREER** Prof, Univ Santa Ursula, 78-85; prof, Univ Fed Fluminense, 86-01; prof, Univ Rio de Janeiro, 94-01. **MEMBERSHIPS** MLA; AATSP; ABLC; ANPPGL; BSA. **SELECTED PUBLICATIONS** Auth, Palavras da Critica, 92; auth, A Poetica do Fundamento, 96; auth, Introducao ao Romantismo, 99; auth, Literatura e Indentidades, 99; auth, Introducao Aos Termos Literarios, 00; auth, "Gonsalves Dias," Port Lit Cult Studies (00); auth, "Quinhentos Anos Depois: Entre o Nacioalismo e a Globalizacio," Rev Bibli Mar Andrade 58 (00). **CONTACT ADDRESS** 1765 Ednamary Way, Apt D, Mountain View, CA 94040-2361. **EMAIL** jobim@verj.br

JOCHNOWITZ, GEORGE
PERSONAL Born 08/01/1937, Brooklyn, NY, m, 1962, 2 children **DISCIPLINE** FRENCH **EDUCATION** Columbia Univ, AB, 58, MA, 60, PhD(ling), 67. **CAREER** Instr French & Ital, Temple Univ, 61-63; instr French, NY Univ, 63-65; lectr Romance lang, Queens Col, NY, 65-68; asst prof ling, 68-72, Assoc Prof Ling, Col Staten Island, City Univ New York, 72-, Nat Sci Found grant, 68-69; vis lectr Yiddish, Yale Univ, 72-73. **MEMBERSHIPS** Ling Soc Am; MLA; Soc Ling Romane; Am Dialect Soc. **RESEARCH** French dialects; Judeo-Italian dialects. **SELECTED PUBLICATIONS** Auth, Bilingualism and dialect mixture among Lubavitcher Hasidic children, Am Speech, 10/68; Forme meridionali nei dialetti degli ebrei dell'Italia centrale, Rassegna Mensile di Israel, 9/72; Dialect Boundaries and the Question of Franco-Provencal, Mouton, The Hague, 73; Parole di origine romanza ed ebraica in giudeo-italiano, XIV Cong Int Ling & Filologia Romanza, 77. **CONTACT ADDRESS** Col of Staten Island, CUNY, Staten Island, NY 10301.

JOFEN, JEAN
PERSONAL Born 11/13/1922, Vienna, Austria, m, 1944, 4 children **DISCIPLINE** GERMAN LITERATURE **EDUCATION** Brooklyn Col, BA, 43; Brown Univ, Ma, 45; Columbia Univ, PhD, 53; Yeshiva Univ, MS, 60, cert psychol, 62. **CAREER** Assoc prof Ger, Stern Col for Women, Yeshiva Univ, 53-60; chmn dept, 60-78, Prof Ger & Slavic Lang, Baruch Col, 60-, Chmn Dept Mod Lang, 77- . **HONORS AND AWARDS** Littaure res fel, 63-64; univ scholar spec fund, 65-66; univ res fel, 68; Am Asn Univ Women fel, 68-69; Ford Found grant, 70; Population Coun grant, 71-72; Nat Endowment for Humanities fel, 74; organized first int cong the marlowe soc of am, sheffield, england, 83. **MEMBERSHIPS** MLA; Am Psychol Asn; Col Yiddish Asn; Marlowe Soc Am (pres, 75-); Am Asn Yiddish Prof (vpres). **RESEARCH** Yiddish linguistics and general philology; literature and psychology. **SELECTED PUBLICATIONS** Auth, Yiddish for Beginners, 55 & A Linguistics Atlas of Eastern European Yiddish, 60, Edwards Bros; A Freudian interpretation of Freud's Moses, Brit Ivrit Olamit, 74; The Yiddish idiom and proverb as mirror of Jewish cultural values Mosaic; Traces of the book of Esther in the works of Shakespeare, Studies Cult Life of Jews in England, Vol V, 75; Yiddish Literature for Beginners 75, coauth, Hebrew for Beginners, 76 & Chinese for Beginners, 77, Edwards Bros; Das letzte Geheimnis, Francke Verlag, Bern, 72; auth, The Jewish Mystic in Kafke; ed, Elizabethan COncordance Series, A concordance to the works of Christopher Marlow, The Shakespeare Apocrypha, 87; auht, The First American Attempt to Produce a Yiddish Language Atlas, in Language and Communication, Vol 18, 88; auth, Kafka and the Rebbe of Gur, in MJS Annual VII, 90. **CONTACT ADDRESS** Dept of Mod Lang and Comp Lit, Baruch Col, CUNY, 17 Lexington Ave, New York, NY 10010.

JOHN, DAVID GETHIN
PERSONAL Born 03/24/1947, Wales, m, 1972, 3 children **DISCIPLINE** GERMAN LITERATURE & LANGUAGE **EDUCATION** Univ Toronto, BA, 67, MA, 70, PhD(Ger), 75. **CAREER** Asst Prof Ger, Univ Waterloo, 74-. **MEMBERSHIPS** Can Asn Univ Teachers Ger; Can Soc 18th Century Studies; Am Soc 18th Century Studies; Lessing Soc; Deutsche Ges fur die Erforschung des 18 Jahreshundert. **RESEARCH** German theatre, especially 18th century; German language pedagogy. **SELECTED PUBLICATIONS** Auth, Johann Christian Kruger, Werke, Kritische Gesamtausgabe, 86; auth, The German "Nachspiel" in the Eighteenth Century, 91; coed, Momentum dramaticum, (1993; ed with Linda Dietrick); auth, Margarete von Parma in Goeth's Egmont: Text and Performance, Christophy Lorey and John L. Plews, eds, Queering the Canon, Defying Sights in German Literature and Culture, Columbia, SC: Camden House, 98; auth, Images of Goethe through Schiller's Egmont, Montreal, Kingston: McGill-Queen's UP, 98. **CONTACT ADDRESS** Dept of Ger, Univ of Waterloo, 200 University Ave W, Waterloo, ON, Canada N2L 3G1. **EMAIL** djohn@watarts.uwaterloo.ca

JOHN, JAMES J.
PERSONAL Born 07/25/1928, Long Prairie, MN, w, 1952, 6 children **DISCIPLINE** LATIN, MEDIEVAL HISTORY **EDUCATION** Univ Notre Dame, BA, 48, MA, 50, MMS, 51, DMS-(mediaeval studies), 59. **CAREER** Asst paleography, Inst Advan Studies, 51-61, res assoc, 62-64; Prof Paleography & Medieval Hist, Cornell Univ, 65-, Vis lectr, Princeton Univ, 59, Bryn Mawr Col & Fordham Univ, 61-62; consult, Free Libr Philadelphia, 60-65; fel, Inst Res Humanities, Univ Wis, 64-65; Am Philos Soc grant, 69-70; Am Coun Learned Soc grant, 69-70, fel, 72-73; mem, Inst Advan Studies, 69-70 & 72-73; Nat Endowment for Humanities grant, 72-73; vis prof, State Univ NY Binghamton, 74. **HONORS AND AWARDS** Member, Comite Intl de Paleographie Latine, 79. **MEMBERSHIPS** Am Cath Hist Asn; Mediaeval Acad Am **RESEARCH** Medieval intellectual history; Latin paleography. **SELECTED PUBLICATIONS** The Ex-Libris in 'Codices Latini Antiquiores' Scriptorium, Vol 50, 96; auth, "Latin Paleography," in Medieval Studies: An Introduction, ed James M. Powell, 2nd rev ed, (Syracuse: Syracuse Univ Press, 92) 3-81; coauth, "Addenda to Codices Latini Antiquiores (II)," Mediaeval Studies, Vol 54 (92): 286-307; auth, "The Named (and Namable) Scribes in Codices Latini Antiquiores," in Scribi e colofoni: Le sottoscrizioni di copiste dalle origini all'avvento della stampa, ed Emma Condello and Giuseppe DeGregorio (Spoleto, 95) 107-121. **CONTACT ADDRESS** Dept of Hist, Cornell Univ, McGraw Hall Rm 450, Ithaca, NY 14853-0001. **EMAIL** jjj2@cornell

JOHN-STEINER, VERA P.
PERSONAL Born 06/13/1930, Budapest, Hungary, w, 2 children **DISCIPLINE** LINGUISTICS **EDUCATION** Columbia Univ, BA, 50; Univ Chicago, Social and Developmental Psychology, PhD, 56. **CAREER** Lecturer to Asst Prof, Univ Rochester, 59-63; Assoc Prof, Yeshiva Univ, 63-72; Assoc Prof, Univ N Mex, 80-86; Vis Prof, Univ Haw, 88; Prof, Univ N Mex, 74-. **HONORS AND AWARDS** Fel, Am Psychol Asn, 93; Fac Scholar, Univ N Mex, 92; William James Awd, Am Psychol Asn, 90; UNM Presidential Professorship Awd, 85-90; Sigma XI; Regents' Prof. **MEMBERSHIPS** Am Psychol Asn, Am Educ Res Asn, Am Anthropol Asn. **RESEARCH** Psycholinguistics (cognitive processes in bilingual education, language acquisition, relationship of language to thought), Creativity and collaboration, Gender issues, Development of cultural-historical theory. **SELECTED PUBLICATIONS** Auth, Creative collaboration, Oxford Univ Press, in press; auth, Notebooks of the mind, 2nd ed, Oxford Univ Press, 97; co-auth, Sociocultural approaches to language and literacy; An interactionist perspective, Cambridge Univ Press, 94; co-auth, "Creativity and collaboration in knowlege construction," in Vygotskian perspectives on literacy research: Constructing meaning through collaborative inquiry, Cambridge Univ Press; auth, "Sociocultural and feminist theory: Mutuality and relevance," in Activity theory and social practice: Cultural historical approaches, Aarhus Univ Press, 99; co-auth, "The challenge of studying collaboration," American Educational Research Journal, (98): 773-784; co-auth, "A functional systems approach to concept development," Mind, culture and activity, (98): 127-134; co-auth, "Introduction to special issue on concept formation," Mind, culture and activity, (98): 81-88; co-auth, "Sociocultural approaches to learning and development: A Vygotskian framework," Educational Psychologist, (96): 191-206; auth, "Women's collaborative Interactions," in Social Interaction, social context and language: Essays in honor of Susan Ervin-Tripp, Lawrence Erlbaum Assoc, 96. **CONTACT ADDRESS** Dept Ling, Univ of New Mexico, Albuquerque, 1 Univ Campus, Albuquerque, NM 87131-0001. **EMAIL** vygotsky@unm.edu

JOHNSON, ANITA L.
DISCIPLINE CONTEMPORARY SPANISH THEATER, POST CIVIL WAR SPANISH NOVEL **EDUCATION** BA, Carlow Col, 74; Middlebury Col, MA, 76; Univ Wis-Madison, PhD, 88. **CAREER** Act dir, Vassar Wesleyan Colgate prog, Spain, 88-89, 95; ed, Esterno, 96-; assoc prof. **HONORS AND AWARDS** Grant,program for coop, Span Ministry Cult and Am Univ(s), 90; travel grant, Am Coun Learned Soc, 90. **SELECTED PUBLICATIONS** Publ, articles on Garcia Lorca, Domingos Miras, Alfonso Sastre, Concha Romero, the contemporary Span stage, Anales de La Lit Espanola Contemporanea, Gestos, Estreno, Critica Hisp, Confluencias. **CONTACT ADDRESS** Dept of Romance Lang, Colgate Univ, 13 Oak Drive, Hamilton, NY 13346. **EMAIL** ajohnson@center.colgate.edu

JOHNSON, CARROLL B.
PERSONAL Born 01/09/1938, Los Angeles, CA **DISCIPLINE** SPANISH LITERATURE **EDUCATION** Univ Calif, Los Angeles, BA, 60, MA, 61; Harvard Univ, PhD(Romance lang), 66. **CAREER** Acting asst prof, 64-66, from asst prof to assoc prof, 66-75, vchmn dept, 72-75, chmn dept Span & Port, 75-81, 91-96, Prof Span, Univ Calif, Los Angeles, 75-. **MEMBERSHIPS** MLA; Renaissance Soc Am; Cervantes Soc Am, (pres 98-00); Asn Int Hisp. **RESEARCH** Seventeenth century Spanish prose fiction; 16th century Spanish drama; literature and psychoanalysis. **SELECTED PUBLICATIONS** Auth, Matias de los Reger and the Craft of Fiction, 73; auth, Inside Guzman de Alfarache, 78; auth, Madness and Last, A Psychoanalytical Approach to Don Quixote, 83; auth, Don Quixote: The Quest for Modern Fiction, 90; auth, Molho, Maurice + Obituary, Hispania-J Devoted to the tchg Span and Port, Vol 0079, 96; Economies and Lineages in La 'Gitanilla' + The Contrast Between Gypsies and Aristocrats in the Cervantine Text, Mester, Vol 0025, 96; From One Subject to the Next--Social Criticism and Psychoanalysis, Mester, Vol 0026, 97; auth, Cervantes and the Material World, 00. **CONTACT ADDRESS** Dept of Span & Port, Univ of California, Los Angeles, Los Angeles, CA 90095-1532. **EMAIL** johnson@humnet.ucla.edu

JOHNSON, DONALD BARTON
PERSONAL Born 06/15/1933, Indianapolis, IN, m, 1975 **DISCIPLINE** RUSSIAN LITERATURE **EDUCATION** Ind Univ, BA, 54; Univ Calif, Berkeley, MA, 58; Univ Calif, Los Angeles, PhD(Slavic ling), 66. **CAREER** Asst prof Russ & Slavic ling, Ohio State Univ, 65-66; asst prof, 66-72, assoc prof, 72-80, Prof Russ & Slavic Ling, Univ Calif, Santa Barbara, 80-, Consult, Rand Corp, 67-69; Inter-Univ Comt Travel Grants grant, Bulgaria & Russia, 68-69; prof & actg chmn dept Russ, Monash Univ, Australia, 75-76. **MEMBERSHIPS** Am Asn Teachers Slavic & E Europ Lang; Am Asn Advan Slavic Studies; Philol Asn Pac Coast; MLA. **RESEARCH** Literary structuralism; Nabokov; Russian modernism. **SELECTED PUBLICATIONS** Auth, Toward a typology of the Slavic verb: The verbs of body position, In: American Contributions to the Sixth International Congress of Slavists, Mouton, 68; Transformations and Their Use in the Resolution of Syntactic Homomorphy, Mouton, 69; coauth, Russian Derivational Dictionary, Elsevier, 70; Synesthesia, polychromatism and Nabokov, Russ Lit Triquart, 72; translr & ed, Analysis of the Poetic Text, Ardis, 76; A Structural Analysis of Sasha Sokolou's School for Fools: A Paradigmatic Novel, In: Fiction and Drama in Eastern and Southeastern Europe, Columbus, 80; The Scrabble Game in Ada or Taking Nabakov Clitorally, J Mod Lit, 4/82. **CONTACT ADDRESS** Dept of Ger & Russ, Univ of California, Santa Barbara, Santa Barbara, CA 93106.

JOHNSON, EMILY
DISCIPLINE RUSSIAN **EDUCATION** UCLA, BA, 87; Columbia Univ, MA, 90, MPhil, 93. **CAREER** Vis asst prof, Williams Col, 98-99. **HONORS AND AWARDS** ACTR res fel, 96-97; Meier's fel, 97-98. **RESEARCH** Russian language and culture; 19th and 20th century Russian literature; travel literature; contemporary Russian films. **SELECTED PUBLICATIONS** Auth, NP Antsiferov and the Origin of the Literary Excursion, AATSEEL Conf, 97; Morbid Dread: Vampires in Bolshevik Propaganda from the 1920s, Northeast Reg Conf, 95. **CONTACT ADDRESS** Center for Foreign Languages, Literatures and Cult, Williams Col, Williamstown, MA 01267. **EMAIL** Emily.Johnson@williams.edu

JOHNSON, JULIE GREER
PERSONAL Born 09/06/1945, Hartford, CT, s **DISCIPLINE** SPANISH AMERICAN LITERATURE **EDUCATION** Memphis State Univ, BA, 67; Ind Univ, MA, 70, PhD(Span lit), 75. **CAREER** From instr to asst prof Span, Univ NC, Asheville, 74-77; from asst prof to full prof Span, Univ Ga, 77-. **HONORS AND AWARDS** John Carter Brown Fel, 84; Columbian Quincentennial Fel, 88; Outstanding Honors Prof, 88, 97; NEH Senior Fel, 99-00. **MEMBERSHIPS** MLA; Am Asn Teachers Span & Port; Latin Am Studies Asn; S Atlantic MLA; Southeastern Council for Latin Am Studies; Luso-Hispanic Humor Soc. **RESEARCH** Colonial Spanish American literature; Women, Satire, Printing, Theater **SELECTED PUBLICATIONS** Auth, Women in Colonial Spanish America: Literary Images, Greenwood Press, 83; auth, The Book in the Americas: The Role of Books and Printing in the Development of Culture and Society in Latin America, John Carter Brown Library, 88; auth, Satire in Colonial Spanish America: Turning the New World Upside Down, Texax, 93. **CONTACT ADDRESS** Dept Romance Lang, Univ of Georgia, Gilbert Hall, Athens, GA 30602. **EMAIL** jjohnson@arches.uga.edu

JOHNSON, KYLE B.
DISCIPLINE LINGUISTICS **EDUCATION** Univ Calif Irvine, BA, 81; Univ Mass, PhD, 85. **CAREER** Assoc prof. **RESEARCH** Syntactic theory; comparative Germanic data. **SELECTED PUBLICATIONS** Auth, When Verb Phrases Go Missing, 97; In Search of the Middle Field, 96; Object Positions, Nat Lang Ling Theory, 94; co-auth, On the Acquisition of Word Order in Nominals, 96; Lowering and Mid-Size Clauses, 97. **CONTACT ADDRESS** Linguistics Dept, Univ of Massachusetts, Amherst, S College 122, Amherst, MA 01003. **EMAIL** kbj@linguist.umass.edu

JOHNSON, LEONARD WILKIE
PERSONAL Born 09/01/1931, Oakland, CA **DISCIPLINE** FRENCH LITERATURE **EDUCATION** Dartmouth Col, AB, 53; Harvard Univ, AM, 55, PhD(Romance lang & lit), 62. **CAREER** Acting instr French, 61-62, from instr to asst prof, 62-71, Assoc Prof French, Univ Calif, Berkeley, 71-, Asst dir, studies ctr, Univ Calif in Bordeaux, France, 63-65. **MEMBERSHIPS** MLA; Am Asn Teachers Fr; Renaissance Soc Am. **RESEARCH** Neo-Platonism in French literature, especially 16th and 17th centuries; emblem literature. **SELECTED PUBLICATIONS** Auth, Princes or Princes + France--15th-Century Politics and Poetry, Fr Rev, Vol 0068, 95. **CONTACT ADDRESS** Dept of French, Univ of California, Berkeley, 4125 Dwinelle Hall, Berkeley, CA 94720-2581.

JOHNSON, MAYUMI YUKI
PERSONAL Born Tokyo, Japan, s **DISCIPLINE** JAPANESE **EDUCATION** Seijo Univ, BA, 79; Tokyo Univ, MA, 80; Univ Minn, MA, 89; PhD, 94. **CAREER** Teaching Asst to Instructor, Univ Minn, 86-94; Instructor, Intl Christian Univ, 90-91, 94; Asst Prof, Univ Mich, 95-. **HONORS AND AWARDS** Grant, Japan Foundation, 97; Grant, Intl Inst Univ MI, 97; Grant, Univ MI, 97. **MEMBERSHIPS** AAS; ATJ **SELECTED PUBLICATIONS** Co-auth, Japanese for College Students Vol 1, 2 and 3, Kodan-sha, 96; auth, "Proficiency Guidelines and Language Curriculum: Making ACTFL Proficiency Guidelines Effective in Furthering Japanese Language Proficiency," Journal of Applied Language Learning, (97): 229-251; auth, "Modality Riron no Meikaku-ka o Motomete (Seeking a better understanding of the theory of modality)," Nihongo-gaku to Nihongo Kyooiku, (Kurosio Press, 98), 145-160; auth, "Mada-bun ni okeru Agentivity no Yakuwari (The Role of Agentivity in Mada Sentences)," Nihongo-gaku to Nihongo Kyooiku, (Kuosio Press, 00); auth, "Conditionals and Modality: A Reexamination of the Function of B a and Volitional Expressions," in Japanese-Language Education around the Globe, (Tokyo, 00), 165-189; auth, Modality and the Japanese Language, Univ MI Press, forthcoming. **CONTACT ADDRESS** Dept Asian Lang, Univ of Michigan, Ann Arbor, 105 S State St, Ann Arbor, MI 48109-1285. **EMAIL** yukijohn@umich.edu

JOHNSON, VIDA
PERSONAL Born 03/05/1947, Belgrade, Yugoslavia, m, 1969, 2 children **DISCIPLINE** RUSSIAN **EDUCATION** Harvard Univ, BA, 68; MA, 71; PhD, 77. **CAREER** Assoc prof to prof, Tufts, Univ, 77-; Chair, 77-. **HONORS AND AWARDS** Marion and Jasper Whiting Found Awd, 89, 91; NEH Awd, 90; Am Philos Soc Fel, 91; Tufts Univ Fac Res Awds, 84, 86, 88, 93, 89, 95. **SELECTED PUBLICATIONS** Auth, "Laughter Beyond the Mirror: Humor and Satire in the Films of Andrei Tarkovsky?", Inside Soviet Satire: Laughter with a Lash, ed Andrew Horton, Cambridge Univ Pr, (93): 98-113; coauth, "Tarkovsky", Five Filmmakers: Tarkovsky, Forman, Polanski, Szabo, Makaveyev, ed Daniel J. Goulding, Ind Univ Pr, (94): 1-49; coauth, The Films of Andrei Tarkovsky: A Visual Fugue, Ind Univ Pr, 94; auth, "Russian After the Thaw", Oxford History of World Cinema, ed Geoffrey Nowell-Smith, Oxford Univ Pr, (96): 640-651; auth, "The Search for a New Russia in an Era of Few Films", Russ Rev, (97): 287-91; auth, "Georgy Haindrava's A Century of Dreams", Kinotavr 2, (Sochi, Russia), June 97; auth, "A New Russian Hero?", Kinotavr 4 (Sochi, Russia), June 98. **CONTACT ADDRESS** Dept Ger and Slavic Lang, Tufts Univ, Medford, Olin Bldg, Medford, MA 02155. **EMAIL** vjohnson@tufts.edu

JOHNSON, W. RALPH
PERSONAL Born Trinidad, CO, 2 children **DISCIPLINE** CLASSICS **EDUCATION** Univ Calif, BA, 61, MA, 63, PhD, 66. **CAREER** Asst to Assoc Prof, UC Berkeley, 66-74; Assoc Prof to Prof, Cornell, 74-81; Prof, Univ Chicago, 81-98; Emeritus. **HONORS AND AWARDS** Distinguished Tchg Awd; Christian Gauss Awd; Martin Lectures; Townsend Lectures. **SELECTED PUBLICATIONS** Auth, Luxuriance and Economy: Cicero and the Alien Style, Ucal Press,71; auth, Darkness Visible: A Study of Vergil's Aeneid, Univ Calif Press,76; auth, The Idea of Lyric, Univ Calif Press, 82; auth, Momentary Monsters: Lucan and his Heroes, Cornell, 87; auth, Horace and the Dialectic of Freedom, Cornell Univ Press, 93; auth, Lucretius and the Modern World, Duckworth, 00. **CONTACT ADDRESS** Univ of Chicago, 1010 E 59th St, Chicago, IL 60637. **EMAIL** 1johnson@uchicago.edu

JOHNSON, WARREN
PERSONAL Born 04/16/1958, Geneva, IL **DISCIPLINE** COMPARATIVE LITERATURE **EDUCATION** Univ Iowa, BA, 78; Univ Mich, AM, 84; PhD, 89. **CAREER** Asst prof, Moorhead State Univ, 90-91; asst prof, Univ of Ala, 91-95; asst prof, Ark state Univ, 98-. **MEMBERSHIPS** Soc des Etudes Romantiques, Am Asn of Teachers of French, Am Asn of Teachers of Span and Port, Midwest MLA, S Central MLA, MLA. **RESEARCH** Nineteenth-Century French Novel, Contemporary French Novel, the Comic. **SELECTED PUBLICATIONS** Auth, "Paralyzed with Terror: Desire and Eterminism in Zola," French Forum 19 (94): 295-307; auth, "Machines and Malaise: Technology and the comic in Villiers and Allais," Nineteenth-Century French Studies 24 (95-96): 192-202; auth, "Edison's Comic Dualism," in Jerring Dreamers: Villiers de l'Isle-Adam's L'Eve future at Our Fin de Siecle, ed. John Anzalone (Amsterdam: Rodopi, 96), 167-175; auth, "That Sudden Shrinking Feeling: Exchange in La peau de chagrin," French Rev 70 (97): 543-553; auth, "The Veiled Laugh: Women, the Body, and the Comic in Nineteenth-Century France," in Performing Gender and Comedy: Theories, Texts and Contexts, ed. Shannon Hengen (Amsterdam: Gordon and Breach, 98), 47-58; auth, "The Dialogic Self: Language and Identity in Annie Ernaux," Studies in Twentieth-Century Lit 23 (99): 297-314. **CONTACT ADDRESS** Dept Lang, Arkansas State Univ, PO Box 2400, State University, AR 74267-2400. **EMAIL** wjohnson@toltec.astate.edu

JOHNSTON, OTTO WILLIAM
PERSONAL Born 02/26/1942, Staten Island, NY, m, 1966, 1 child **DISCIPLINE** GERMANIC LANGUAGES & LITERATURES, PHILOLOGY **EDUCATION** Wagner Col, BA, 63; Columbia Univ, MA, 66; Princeton Univ, PhD, 69. **CAREER** Instr English & Ger, Berlitz Sch Lang, 61-62; Instr Ger, Columbia Univ, 63-64; Prof Ger, Univ Fla, 69-, Chmn Dept Ger & Slavic Lang & Lit, 79-. **HONORS AND AWARDS** Standard Oil Good Teaching Citation, 71-72; ODK Outstanding Professor, 72-73; Teacher of the Year, Col of Arts and Sciences, 73-74; Alexander von Humboldt fel, 74 & 82; Exxon Impact grant, 78; Goethe Institute Study Grant, 78; Fulbright Res Awd to Innsbruck, Austria, 87; TIP Awd, 94. **MEMBERSHIPS** MLA; Am Asn Teachers Ger; Am Coun Teachers Foreign Lang; S Atlantic Mod Lang Asn. **RESEARCH** Nineteenth century German literature; literary sociology; philology. **SELECTED PUBLICATIONS** Auth, Nestroy and the Critics, Colloquia Germanica, Vol 0029, 96; Narration as Natural Relationship--Die 'Wahlverwandschaften'--The Problem of the Portrayability of Nature and Society Since Goethe Plan for a So-Called Novel about the Universe, Ger Quart, Vol 0069, 96; Nestroy and the Critics, Colloquia Germanica, Vol 0029, 96. **CONTACT ADDRESS** Dept Ger & Slavic Lang & Lit, Univ of Florida, P O Box 117430, Gainesville, FL 32611-7430. **EMAIL** ot1942@nersp.nerdc.ufl.edu

JOHNSTON, PATRICIA A.
PERSONAL Born 07/30/1937, Chicago, IL, m, 1959 **DISCIPLINE** CLASSICS **EDUCATION** UCLA, AB, 67; Univ Calif Berkeley, MA, 72; PhD, 75. **CAREER** TA, Univ of Calif Los Angeles, 67-69; Univ Calif Berkeley, 70-75; asst prof to prof, Brandeis Univ, 75-. **HONORS AND AWARDS** Phi Beta Kappa; Sloan Fel. **MEMBERSHIPS** APA, Women's Class Caucus of APA, Vergilian Soc, Class Asn, CANE, CAMWS, Phi Beta Kappa. **RESEARCH** Greek and Latin Literature, specializing in Vergil and his precedessors, Religion, specializing in the Mystery Cults, Classical mythology, ancient Italy. **SELECTED PUBLICATIONS** Auth, "Eurydice and Proserpina in the Georgics," TAPA 107, (77): 161-172; auth, Vergil's Agricultural Golden Age: A Study of the Georgics, Leiden, 80; auth, "Poenulus I, 2 and Roman Women," TAPA 110 (80): 143-159; auth, "The Storm in Aeneid VII," Vergilius 27, (81): 23-30; auth, "Dido, Berenice, and Arsinoe," AJPh 108 (87): 649-654; auth, Traditio: An Introduction to the Latin Language and its Influence, Macmillan, 88; auth, "Love and Laserpicium in Catallus 7," CPh 88 (93): 329; auth, "Under the Volcano: Volcanic Myth and Metaphor in Vergil's Aeneid," Vergilius 42 (96): 55-65; auth, "Cybele and Her Companions on the Northern Littoral of the Black Sea," Cybele, Attis and Related Cults: Essays in Memory of MJ Vermaseren (Leiden, 96): 101-116; transl Vergil's Aeneid, Focus Publ, (forthcoming). **CONTACT ADDRESS** Dept Classics, Brandeis Univ, MS 016, Waltham, MA 02454-9110. **EMAIL** johnston@brandeis.edu

JOHNSTON, SARAH ILES
PERSONAL Born 10/25/1957, Bowling Green, OH, m, 2001, 2 children **DISCIPLINE** GREEK, LATIN **EDUCATION** Univ Kans, BS, 79; BA, 80; Cornell Univ, MA, 83; PhD, 87. **CAREER** Lectr, Princeton Univ, 87-88; asst prof to prof, Ohio State Univ, 88-. **HONORS AND AWARDS** Mellon Fel, Inst for Adv Study; Fel, ACLS; Fel, Fondation Hardt; Den Fel, Inst for the Adv Study of Relig. **MEMBERSHIPS** Am Philol Asn; Am Acad of Relig; Soc for Biblical Lit; Women's Class Caucus. **RESEARCH** Ancient Mediterranean religions and myths, especially Greek. **SELECTED PUBLICATIONS** Auth, Hekate Soteira, Scholars Press, 90; co-ed, Medea: Essays on Medea in Myth, Literature, Philosophy and Art, Princeton Univ Press, 97; auth, Restless Dead: Encounters Between the Living and the Dead in Ancient Greece, Univ Calif Press, 99. **CONTACT ADDRESS** Dept Relig Studies, Ohio State Univ, Columbus, 414 University Hall, 230 N Oval Mall, Columbus, OH 43210-1319. **EMAIL** sjohnston@postbox.acs.ohio-state.edu

JONAS, KLAUS WERNER
PERSONAL Born 06/22/1920, Stettin, Germany, m, 1945 **DISCIPLINE** GERMAN LANGUAGE & LITERATURE **EDUCATION** Rutgers Univ, MLS, 55; Univ Munster, PhD, 55. **CAREER** Instr Ger, Douglass Col, Rutgers Univ, 50-55; librn Ger lit, Yale Univ Libr, 55-57; from asst prof to assoc prof, 57-65, chmn dept, 59-61, Prof Ger, Univ Pittsburgh, 65-, MLA res grants, 56 & 60; Caroline Newton grant, Yale Univ, 57; Am Coun Learned Soc res grant, 58; cur Thomas Mann Arch, Deut Akad Wiss Berlin, 60-; Bollingen Found res grants, 61 & 63; Charles E Merrill Found fac fel, 63; Ford Found fels, 66 & 67; Guggenheim Mem Found fel, 73-74. **MEMBERSHIPS** MLA; Rilke Soc; Am Asn Teachers Ger; Bibliog Soc Am; Int Ver Ger Sprach-u Literaturwiss. **RESEARCH** Modern German literature and culture; bibliography; Anglo-German literary relations. **SELECTED PUBLICATIONS** Auth, Fifty Years of Thomas Mann Studies, Univ Minn, 55; The World of Somerset Maugham, Peter Owen, London, 59; Der Kronprinz Wilhelm, H Scheffler, Frankfurt & Univ Pittsburgh, 62; Thomas Mann Studies, Univ Pa, Vol II, 67; ed, Deutsche Weltliteratur von Goethe bis Ingeborg Bachmann, Max Niemeyer, Tubingen, 72; Die Thomas Mann--Literatur, Erich Schmidt, Berlin, Vols I & II, 72 & 78. **CONTACT ADDRESS** Dept of Ger Lang & Lit, Univ of Pittsburgh, 1409 Cathedral of Learning, Pittsburgh, PA 15260.

JONASSAINT, JEAN
DISCIPLINE FRENCH **EDUCATION** Universite du Quebec a Montreal, BA, 77, MA, 81, PhD, 90 **CAREER** Sr lectr, Universite du Quebec a Montreal, 79-96; asst prof to Andrew W. mellow asst prof, Duke Univ, 96- . **HONORS AND AWARDS** Andrew W. Mellow Asst prof; Etudes ethniques canadiennes, ministere du Patrimoine canadien, res grant; Fonds FCAC, PhD grant; Canada Arts Coun/Explorations res grant. **MEMBERSHIPS** Amer Comparative Lit Assoc; Consiel int d' etudes francophones; Modern Lang Assoc of Amer; S Atlantic Modern Lang Assoc of Amer. **RESEARCH** Francophone lit; theory & hist of lit; comparative lit; postnational lit & lit prod in immigration, creative writing & publ. **SELECTED PUBLICATIONS** Auth, Migration et etudes litteraires, J of Canadian Stud, 96; Des recits haitiens au Quebec, Neue Romania, 97; Le Nomade enracine, in Rene Depestre, Le Metier a metisser, Paris, Stock, 98; Haitian Literary Production in the United States, 1948-1986, in American Literatures and Languages, Harvard Engl Stud, (forthcoming); Les Romans de tradition haitienne: des recits tragiques, (forthcoming). **CONTACT ADDRESS** Dept of Romance Stud, Duke Univ, Box 90257, Durham, NC 27708. **EMAIL** jonj1996@duke.edu

JONES, BRUCE WILLIAM
PERSONAL Born 08/28/1935, Palo Alto, CA, d, 3 children **DISCIPLINE** HEBREW BIBLE **EDUCATION** Amherst Col, BA, 56; Grad Theol Union, PhD(Old Testament), 72; Azusa Pac Univ, MA, 80. **CAREER** Prog secy, Student Christian Movement India, 60-62; minister, United Church of Christ, Petersburg, Ill, 62-64; lectr Old Testament, Pac Sch Relig, 68-69; asst prof relig studies, Holy Names Col, 70-73; asst prof, 73-75, ASSOC PROF RELIG STUDIES, CALIF STATE COL, BAKERSFIELD, 76-, Lectr Bible, Mills Col, 69-73; therapist, Bakersfield Family Therapy Group, 81-. **MEMBERSHIPS** Soc Bibl Lit; Am Acad Relig; Am Asn Marriage & Family Therapy. **RESEARCH** Apocalyptic literature; the Book of Esther; computer assisted instruction in Bible and religion. **SELECTED PUBLICATIONS** Auth, The prayer in Daniel 9, Vetus Testamentum, 18: 488; More about the apocalypse as apocalyptic, J Bibl Lit, 87: 325; Religious studies as a test case for computer assisted instruction in the humanities, Proc 4th Conf Comput in Undergrad Curricula, Claremont Col, 73; Computer assisted instruction in religious studies, Bull Coun Study Relig, 74; Two misconceptions about the Book of Esther, Cath Bibl Quart, 39: 171; The so-called appendix to the Book of Esther, Semitics, 6: 36; Antiochus Epiphanes and the persecution of the Jews, in: Scripture in Context: Essays on the Comparative Method, Pickwick Press, 80; Using the computer to teach methods and interpretative skills in the humanities: Implementing a project, Resourses Educ, 82. **CONTACT ADDRESS** Dept of Philosophy & Religious Studies, California State Univ, Bakersfield, 9001 Stockdale Hwy, Bakersfield, CA 93311.

JONES, CALVIN N.
PERSONAL Born 06/28/1947, Danville, KY, m, 1977, 3 children **DISCIPLINE** GERMAN **EDUCATION** Davidson Col, AB, 69; Univ NCar, PhD, 76. **CAREER** Asst prof to prof, Univ of S Ala, 77-. **HONORS AND AWARDS** Fulbright, 74-75; DAAD, 79, 81; Ala Comm on Higher Educ, 88; Goethe Inst, 89; Dean's Lectr, USA Col of Arts and Sci, 96. **MEMBERSHIPS** MLA, AATG, SAMLA. **RESEARCH** 19th and 20th-centry German Literature, Else Lasker Schuler. **SELECTED PUBLICATIONS** Auth, "Learning to See, to Experience, to Write: Peter Handke's Die Lehre der Sainte-Victoire as Narrative," Ger Rev 59, (84); auth, "Past Idyll or future Utopia: Heimat in German Lyric Poetry of the 1030s and 1940s," Ger Studies Rev 8, (95); auth, "The Dialectics of Despair and Hope: The Modernist Volksstuck of Jura Soyfer," Maske und Kothurn: Int Beitrage zur Theaterwissenschaft 32.1/2, (86); auth, "The Teacher as Failure - The Text as Teacher: Hermann Broch's Die vier Reden des Studienrats Zacharias," W Va Univ Philol Papers 36, (90); auth, "Ferdinand Raimund and Odon von Horvath: the Volksstuck as Negation and Utopia," Ger Quart 64, (91); auth, "Sarah Kirsch: Naturschutzgebiet," Die Mauersegler, Annaherungen an die deutsche Lyriik, ed Ernst-Ullrich Pinkert, Aalborg Univ, 17, (92); auth, Negation and Utopia: The German Volksstuck from Raimund to Kroetz, Peter Lang, (NY), 93; auth, "Representing the People: Darstellung and Vertretung in Else Lasker-Schuler's Drama Die Wupper," Ger Rev 69, (94); auth, The Literary Reputation of Else Lasker-Schuler: Criticism 1901-1993, Camden House, (Columbia, SC), 94; auth, "The Play's the Thing: Subject, Author, and History as Drama in Ichundich," Else Lasker-Schuler. Ansichten und Perspecktiven/Views and Reviews, ed Ernst Schurer and Sonja Hedgepeth, Francke Verlag, (Tubingen, 99). **CONTACT ADDRESS** Dept For Lang & Lit, Univ of So Alabama, Mobile, AL 36688. **EMAIL** cnjones@jaguar1.usouthal.edu

JONES, CHRISTOPHER M.
DISCIPLINE FRENCH **EDUCATION** Univ Mass, PhD. **CAREER** Languages, Carnegie Mellon Univ. **HONORS AND AWARDS** Dir, Lang Learning Resource Ctr. **SELECTED PUBLICATIONS** Auth, Portes Ouvertes: an interactive multimedia approach to first-year French; Coauth, Fort Worth: Holt Rinehart and Winston, 97. Language-related Technology: Notes from Carnegie Mellon, Pa Lang Forum, 96; The Oral Language Archive: A Digital Audio Database for Foreign Language Study, CALL Journal, 96; The passe-blanc: Boris Vian

and the New French Literary Establishment, Cincinnati Romance Rev,94. **CONTACT ADDRESS** Carnegie Mellon Univ, 5000 Forbes Ave, Pittsburgh, PA 15213.

JONES, CHRISTOPHER P.
PERSONAL Born 08/21/1940, Chislehurst, England **DISCIPLINE** CLASSICS, ANCIENT HISTORY **EDUCATION** Oxon (Oxford), BA, 61, MA, 67; Harvard, PhD, 65. **CAREER** Lect, 65-66, Univ Toronto; asst prof, 66-68, assoc prof, 68-75, prof, 65-92, prof of class & hist, 92-97, George Martin Lane Prof of Classics & Hist, 97-, Harvard Univ. **HONORS AND AWARDS** Fel, Royal Soc of Canada; Corresp mem, Ger Archaeol Inst, 92; fel, Am Numismatic Soc, 93; The Am Philos Soc, 96; fel, Am Acad of Arts & Sci, 98. **MEMBERSHIPS** APA; Bd of Sr Fellows, Byzantine Stud, Dumbarton Oaks Res Lib & Collection, Harvard Univ; Class Asn of Canada; Inst for Advanced Stud, Princeton, Sch of Hist Stud; Soc for the Promotion of Hellenic Stud; Soc for Promotion of Roman Stud. **RESEARCH** Greek lit of the Roman period; Hellenistic and Roman hist; Greek epigraphy. **SELECTED PUBLICATIONS** Auth, Philostratus: Life of Apollonius of Tyana, Penguin Books, 71; auth, Plutarch and Rome, Oxford Univ Press, 71, 72; auth, The Roman World of Dio Chrysostom, Harvard Univ Press, 78; auth, Culture and Society in Lucian, Harvard Univ Press, 86; coed, Louis Robert, Le Martyre de Pionios, pretre de Smyrne, mis au point et complete par G. W. Bowersock et C. P. Jones, Dumbarton Oaks Res Lib & Collection, Wash, 94; auth, Kinship Diplomacy in the Ancient World, Harvard Univ Press, forthcoming 99. **CONTACT ADDRESS** Dept of Classics, Harvard Univ, 226 Boylston Hall, Cambridge, MA 02138. **EMAIL** cjones@fas.harvard.edu

JONES, LARRY BERT
PERSONAL Born 11/11/1953, Kansas City, MO, m, 1977, 1 child **DISCIPLINE** LINGUISTICS **EDUCATION** Brown Univ, AB, 76; Univ Tex, Arlington, MA, 78, PhD(ling), 80. **CAREER** Transl & Consult, Summer Inst Ling, Indonesia BR, 77-, Vis consult, Summer Inst Ling, Mex Br, 77; vis consult & lectr, Summer Inst Ling, Philippine Br, 81-82; vis lectr, Nat Ctr Indonesian Lang, Jakarta Indonesia, 82. **MEMBERSHIPS** Ling Asn Can & US. **RESEARCH** Prag and the context of speech as it relates to linguistic and translation theory; Papuan languages; discourse analysis. **SELECTED PUBLICATIONS** Coauth, Levels of significant information in discourse, Mid-Am Linquistics Conf Okla, Univ Okla, 79; A discourse particle in Cajonos Zapotec & Multiple levels of information in discourse, in: Discourse Studies in Mesoamerican Languages, Summer Inst Lings, summer 79; auth, Pragmatic information in the fourth Gospel, Summer Inst Ling, Dallas, 79; Pragmatic influences on English written discourse, in: The Sixth Lacus Forum 1979, Hornbeam Press, 80; Pragmatic Aspect of English Text Sucture, Summer Inst Ling, 82; coauth, Verb morphology and discourse structure in Mesoamerican languages, in: Paper in Text Ling, Buske Press, 82. **CONTACT ADDRESS** 1009 J St, La Porte, IN 46350.

JONES, MARGARET E. W.
PERSONAL Born 02/04/1938, New York, NY, m, 1964, 2 children **DISCIPLINE** SPANISH **EDUCATION** SUNY Albany, BA, 59; Univ Wis, MA, 61; PhD, 63. **CAREER** Asst prof span, Salem Col, 63-64; from asst prof to assoc prof, NC Col Durham, 64-67; from asst prof to assoc prof, 67-75, assoc dean grad sch, 77-79, prof span, Univ Ky, 75-. **HONORS AND AWARDS** Am Counc on Educ fel in Acad Admin, 79-80; Eugene M. Kayden Transl Awd for transl of The Same Sea As Every Summer, 89; Nat Endowment for the Arts transl fel, 00. **MEMBERSHIPS** Am Asn Univ Women; Women's Caucus Mod Lang; MLA; Am Asn Teachers Span & Port. **RESEARCH** Modern and contemporary Spanish literature; Spanish women's literature. **SELECTED PUBLICATIONS** Books and publications on contemporary Spanish literature and Spanish women's literature. **CONTACT ADDRESS** Dept of Span, Univ of Kentucky, 1115 Patterson Office Tower, Lexington, KY 400506-0027. **EMAIL** jonesmw@pop.uky.edu

JONES, MICHELE
PERSONAL Born 06/18/1944, France, m, 1967, 2 children **DISCIPLINE** FRENCH **EDUCATION** Univ Nantes, MA, 66; CUNY, PhD, 72. **CAREER** Adj Asst Prof to Assoc Prof, St John's Univ, 89-. **HONORS AND AWARDS** BCLE Scholarship, NY French Embassy, 95. **MEMBERSHIPS** Am Asn for Teachers of French. **RESEARCH** Translation Studies; Francophone Literature. **SELECTED PUBLICATIONS** Auth, Le Theatre national en France de 1800a 1830, Klincksieck, 75; auth, The Beginning Translator's Workbook, or the ABC of French to English Translation, Univ Press of Am, 97; auth, "Teaching French-English Translation to Beginning Translators: A Linguistic Approach, Am Translators Asn chronicle, (99): 50-54. **CONTACT ADDRESS** Dept Mod Lang, St. John's Univ, 8150 Utopia Pkwy, Jamaica, NY 11439-0001.

JONES, NICHOLAS FRANCIS
PERSONAL Born 08/22/1946, Los Angeles, CA, m, 1971, 4 children **DISCIPLINE** ANCIENT HISTORY, CLASSICAL PHILOLOGY **EDUCATION** Univ Southern Calif, BA, 68; Univ Calif, Berkeley, MA, 72, PhD(classics), 75. **CAREER** Instr, 75-76, asst prof 76-81, assoc, 82-97, Prof Classics, Univ Pittsburgh, 97-. **HONORS AND AWARDS** Fulbright Fel, 72-73; Am Coun of Learned Societies Fel, 79; Nat Endowment for the Humanities Fel, 84-85; Inst for Advanced Study, Princeton, visitor, 84-85. **MEMBERSHIPS** Am Philol Asn; Archaeol Inst Am; Asn Ancient Historians. **RESEARCH** Greek and Roman hist; classical philol. **SELECTED PUBLICATIONS** Auth, Public Organization in Ancient Greece, Am Philos Soc, 87; auth, Ancient Greece: State and Society, Prentice Hall, 97; auth, The Associations of Classical Athens. The Response to Democracy, Oxford Univ Press, 99. **CONTACT ADDRESS** Dept of Classics, Univ of Pittsburgh, 1518 Cathedral, Pittsburgh, PA 15260-0001. **EMAIL** nfjones@pitt.edu

JONES, RANDALL LEE
PERSONAL Born 02/21/1939, Cedar City, UT, m, 1962, 5 children **DISCIPLINE** LINGUISTICS, GERMANIC LANGUAGES **EDUCATION** Brigham Young Univ, BA, 63, MA, 65; Princeton Univ, MA, 66, PhD, 70. **CAREER** Asst prof ling, Cornell Univ, 68-72; ling consult, Cent Intel Agency Lang Sch, 72-74; asst prof ling, Cornell Univ, 74-78; assoc prof, 78-82, prof Ger, 82-, dean, Coll of Hum, Brigham Young Univ, 91-97; **MEMBERSHIPS** Ling Soc Am; MLA; Assn Comput Ling; Am Assn Teachers Ger; Am Coun Teaching Foreign Lang. **RESEARCH** German syntax; language testing. **SELECTED PUBLICATIONS** Art, TICCIT and CLIPS: The Early Years, 84-97, Thirty Yars of Computer Assisted Language Instruction, Festschrift for John R. Russell, CALICO Monograph Series 3, Durham, NC: CALICO, 95. **CONTACT ADDRESS** Dept of Germanic & Slavic Languages, Brigham Young Univ, 4094 jkhb, Provo, UT 84602. **EMAIL** randall_jones@byu.edu

JONES, TOBIN H.
PERSONAL Born 04/13/1939, Minneapolis, MN, m, 1962 **DISCIPLINE** FRENCH LITERATURE **EDUCATION** Univ Minn, Minneapolis, BA, 62, MA, 65, PhD(French), 69. **CAREER** Assoc prof. **RESEARCH** Development of the French novel; contemporary poetry; literary theory and criticism; French cultural studies. **SELECTED PUBLICATIONS** Auth, pubs on French novels and the aesthetics of narrative fiction of the eighteenth, nineteenth, and twentieth centuries. **CONTACT ADDRESS** Foreign Languages and Literature Dept, Colorado State Univ, Fort Collins, CO 80523. **EMAIL** thjones@vines.colostate.edu

JONES, WARD
DISCIPLINE CLASSICAL STUDIES **EDUCATION** Univ Richmond, BA, 52; Univ NC at Chapel Hill, MA, 57, PhD, 59. **CAREER** Instr, Ohio State Univ, 59-61; assoc prof, 61-67; prof, 67- & Chancellor prof, 68-, Col William and Mary; vis assoc prof, Tufts Univ in Naples, Italy, 65-66 & Univ NC, 66. **HONORS AND AWARDS** Ovatio awd, Class Asn Mid W and S, New Orleans, 88; Listed in Whols Who in Am, 85-; VP, 65-66 & pres, 66-67, Class Asn Va; sec-treas, 66-68 & pres, 80-82, Class Asn Mid W and S, Southern Sect; exec comt, Class Asn Mid W and S, 79-82; mng ed, Class J, 70-80; nominating comt, Class Asn Mid W and S; dir, 70-, VP, 78-80 & pres, 80-, Mediter Soc Am; VP, 86-88 & Marshal, 90-92, Alpha Chap of Phi Beta Kappa & pres, Alpha Delta Gamma, Hon Medieval and Renaissance Fraternity, 94-95; fel Inst Advanced Study in Arts and Humanities, Univ Minn, 67 - $300,00; fel Southeastern Inst Medieval and Renaissance Stud, Duke Univ & Univ NC, 66 - $600,00; 67 -600,00; 68 - $600.00 & 69-70 - $14,000,00; fac res assignments, William and Mary, 78 & 92-93. **RESEARCH** Vergil; Legend of the Sack of Troy; early history of the College of William and Mary. **SELECTED PUBLICATIONS** Auth, A New Latin Quitrent Poem of the College of William & Mary, Va Mag Hist and Biog, vol 96, 88; The So-Called Silvestris Commentary on the Aeneid and Two Other Interpretations, Speculum, 89 & A Latin Munusculum among the Papers of Francis Nicholson, Bodleian Libr Record, 93; coauth, The Commentary on the First Six Books of the Aeneid of Vergil Commonly Attributed to Bernardus Silvestris, Univ Nebr Press, 77 & An Aeneid Commentary of Mixed Type: the Glosses in MSS Harley 4946 and Ambrosianus Glll inf, The Pontifical Inst Mediaeval Stud, Toronto, 96; co-ed, Solomon Henning's Chronicle of Courland and Livonia, Baltic Stud Ctr, Madison, 92; rev, Schreiber and Maresca, Commentary on the First Six Books of Vergilis Aeneid by Bernardus Silvestris, in Vergilius, 80. **CONTACT ADDRESS** Dept of Classical Studies, Col of William and Mary, Morton Hall, Williamsburg, VA 23187-8795. **EMAIL** jwjone@facstaff.wm.edu

JORDAN, BORIMIR
PERSONAL Born 11/05/1933, Sofia, Bulgaria, m, 1961, 3 children **DISCIPLINE** CLASSICS **EDUCATION** Univ Calif, Berkeley, PhD, 68. **CAREER** Asst prof, Univ So Calif, 67-68; asst prof, assoc prof, prof, Univ Calif, Santa Barbara, 68- . **MEMBERSHIPS** APA. **RESEARCH** Ancient Greek history; Greek historical writers; Greek religion. **SELECTED PUBLICATIONS** Auth, The Athenian Navy, Berkeley, 75; Servants of the gods, Gottingen, 79. **CONTACT ADDRESS** Dept of Classics, Univ of California, Santa Barbara, Santa Barbara, CA 93106-3120. **EMAIL** bjordan@humanitas.ucsb.edu

JORDAN, GREGORY D.
PERSONAL Born 12/19/1951, Jackson, MS, m, 1973, 3 children **DISCIPLINE** HEBRAIC, COGNATE STUDIES **EDUCATION** Belhaven Col, BA, 73; Trinity Evangel Div Sch, MA, 76, MDiv, 77; Hebrew Union Col-Jewish Inst of Relig, PhD, 86. **CAREER** Chr, 84-89, Bible & Relig Dept, King Col; mem, Bd of dir, 85-87, Inst of Holy Land Stud; Chr of the Hum div, 87-89, v pres, acad affairs/dean Fac, 90-97, actng dean, Admis, 96-97, provost & actng pres, 96-97, pres, 97-, King Col. **HONORS AND AWARDS** Paul Harris Awd, Bristol Rotary Club; Erna and Julius Krouch Scholar, Hebrew Union Col; Joseph and Helen Regenstein Fel, Hebrew Union Col; S H Scheur Fel, Hebrew Union Col; Isle Hitchman Fel, Hebrew Union Col; Tchng Awd, King Col. **MEMBERSHIPS** Soc of Bibl Lit; Am Soc of Oriental Res; Inst for Bibl Res; Rotary Club of Bristol; Bristol Chamber of Commerce, Pres-Elect; United Way of Bristol. **RESEARCH** Near Eastern history. **CONTACT ADDRESS** President, King Col, 1350 King College Rd, Bristol, TN 37620-2699. **EMAIL** gdjordan@king.edu

JORDAN, SABINE D.
PERSONAL Born 06/14/1933, Berlin, Germany, m, 1961, 1 child **DISCIPLINE** GERMAN **EDUCATION** N Sch for Soc Res, BA, 57; MA, 61; Columbia Univ, MA, 63; PhD, 77. **CAREER** Instr, Columbia Univ, 61-65; instr, Univ N Colo, 71-74; prof, Deep Springs Col, 88; instr, Univ Wyo, 88-91; cultural consult, private practice, 93-. **HONORS AND AWARDS** Humanities Award, Ind State Governor, 82; Res Fel, DAAD, 66-67; Res Fel, Germanistic Soc of Am, 65-66; NY State Scholar Incentive Awards, 62-65; Louis S. Weiss Award, N Sch for Soc Res, 57. **MEMBERSHIPS** MLA; AATG; Deutsche Schillergesellschaft; Nat Coalition of Indep Scholars. **RESEARCH** 18th Century German literature; German-Americana; Music Theory. **SELECTED PUBLICATIONS** Auth, Das grosse Schauspiel. Ludwig Ferdinand Hubers ausgewahlte Schriften zur Franzosischen Revolution, Stuttgart, 94. **CONTACT ADDRESS** 733 Oxford Ln, Fort Collins, CO 80525-2211.

JORGENSEN, BETH E.
PERSONAL Born 10/11/1953, Staten Island, NY, m, 1975, 2 children **DISCIPLINE** SPANISH **EDUCATION** Oberlin Col, BA, 75; Univ Wisc - Madison, MA, 78, PhD, 86. **CAREER** Lectr, 82-83, Univ Wisc - Madison; asst prof, 86-93, assoc prof, 93-, chmn, dept of Modern Lang & Cult, 94-98, assoc prof, 98-, Univ Rochester. **CONTACT ADDRESS** Dept. of Modern Languages & Cultures, Univ of Rochester, PO Box 270082, Rochester, NY 14627. **EMAIL** bjgn@mail.rochester.edu

JORGENSEN, PETER A.
PERSONAL Born 07/31/1941, Jersey City, NJ **DISCIPLINE** LINGUISTICS **EDUCATION** Princeton Univ, AB, 63; Harvard Univ, MA, 71, PhD, 72. **CAREER** Asst Prof, Univ of Calif at Riverside, 71-76; Prof, Univ of Ga, 76-. **HONORS AND AWARDS** Fulbright; M.G. Michael Awd; Creative Res Medal; Outstanding Honors Prof; Honoratus Medal; Sr Teaching Fel. **MEMBERSHIPS** Med Acad of Am, Phi Beta Delta. **RESEARCH** Bear's Son folktale, editing Old Icelandic manuscripts; saga forgeries; linguistic classification of loanwords; medieval German pilgrimage of Arnold von Harff. **SELECTED PUBLICATIONS** Auth, The Story of Jonatas in Iceland, Reykjavick, 97; auth, Valla-Ljots saga, Saarbrucken, 91; auth, "Tristrams saga ok Isondar," in Norse Romance I; auth, "The Gift of the Useless Weapon in Beowulf and the Icelandic Sagas," in ANF, 79; coauth, "Die handschriftlichen Verhaltnisse der spatmittelalterlichen Pilgerfahrt des Arnold von Harff," in ZDPh, 91; auth, The Neglected Genre of Rimur-Derived Prose and Post-Reformation Jonatas Saga," in Gripla, 90; auth, Hafgeirs saga Flateyings: An Eighteenth-Century Forgery," in JEGP, 77; auth, "Four Literary Styles in Three Centuries: The Old Icelandic Theophilus Legend," in Samtidarsogur (Akureyri, 94). **CONTACT ADDRESS** Dept of Ger and Slavic Lang, Univ of Georgia, Athens, GA 30602-0002. **EMAIL** jorgy@arches.uga.edu

JOSEPH, BRIAN DANIEL
PERSONAL Born 11/22/1951, New York, NY, m, 1975, 1 child **DISCIPLINE** LINGUISTICS, INDO-EUROPEAN STUDIES **EDUCATION** Yale Univ, AB, 73; Harvard Univ, AM, 76, PhD(ling), 78. **CAREER** Lectr, Univ Alta, 78-79; Asst Prof Ling, Ohio State Univ, 79. Izaak Walton Killam fel, Univ Alta, 78-79. **MEMBERSHIPS** Ling Soc Am; Can Ling Asn; Mod Greek Studies Asn; Am Asn Teachers Slavic & East Europ Lang; Am Asn Southeast Europ Studies. **RESEARCH** Indo-European linguistics; relational grammar and the syntax of Modern Greek; Balkan linguistics. **SELECTED PUBLICATIONS** Auth, Envy--a functional analysis, Ling Inquiry, 76; Morphology and Universals in Syntactic Change: Evidence from Medieval and Modern Greek, Ind Univ Ling Club, 78; Linguistic universals and syntactic change, Lang, 80; Locatives and obviation in Cree, Int J Am Ling, 80; Recovery of information in relative clauses: Evidence from Greek and Hebrew, J Ling, 80; A new convergence concerning the Balkan loss of the infinitive, Indogermanische Forschungen, 80; On the synchrony and diachrony of Modern Greek na, Byzantine & Mod Greek Studies, 81; The Synchrony and Diachrony of the Balkan Infinitive, Cambridge Univ Press (in press). **CONTACT ADDRESS** Dept Ling, Ohio State Univ, Columbus, 1712 Neil Ave 222 Oxley Hall, Columbus, OH 43210-1298. **EMAIL** Joseph.1@osu.edu

JOSEPHS, ALLEN
PERSONAL Born 11/20/1942, Charlotte, NC, 3 children **DISCIPLINE** MODERN SPANISH LITERATURE, MODERN LITERATURES **EDUCATION** Univ NC, Chapel Hill, BA, 65; NYork Univ, MA, 66; Rutgers Univ, PhD(Span), 73. **CAREER** Asst prof, 69-76, assoc prof, 76-79, Prof Span, Univ W Fla, 79-, Consult, Westinghouse Elec Corp, Spain, 74-75; Nat Endowment for Arts fel, 79-80. **MEMBERSHIPS** MLA; SAtlantic Mod Lang Asn; Am Asn Teachers Span & Port. **RESEARCH** The work of Federico Garcia Lorca; Spanish culture and civilization; Hemingway and other writers on Spain. **SELECTED PUBLICATIONS** Co-ed, F G Lorca's La Casa de Bernarda Alba, Catedra, 76; F G Lorca Poema del Cante Jondo/ Romancero Gitano, Catedra, 77; auth, At the heart of Madrid, Atlantic Monthly, 7/79; Homage to Andalucia, Va Quart Rev, summmer 79; The Andaluian Picasso, New Boston Rev, 11-12/ 80; F G Lorca Antologia poetica, Plaza y Janes, 81; auth, Terra Nostra: Whose land?, Secolas Annals, 3/82; Hemingway's poor Spanish: Chauvinism and the loss of credibility in For Whom the Bell Tolls, In: Hemingway: A Revaluation, Whitson, 82. **CONTACT ADDRESS** Dept Foreign Lang, Univ of West Florida, 11000 Univ Pkwy, Pensacola, FL 32514.

JOSEPHS, HERBERT
PERSONAL Born 11/11/1932, New York, NY, m, 1958, 1 child **DISCIPLINE** FRENCH **EDUCATION** Brooklyn Col, BA, 53; Fordham Univ, MA, 57; Princeton Univ, MA, 59, PhD, 63. **CAREER** Asst instr, Princeton Univ, 57-59; Instr French, Amherst Col, 60-62; from instr to assoc prof, 62-72, PROF FRENCH LIT, 72- , Mich State Univ, 72-, Nat Endowment for Humanities, summer grant, 75 & 81; Am Coun Learned Soc grant-in-aid, 76; Mich State Univ Found Res Grant, 81, 84, 86; Mich Coun Hum Bicentennial Celebration Fr Revolution; prof emer, 00. **HONORS AND AWARDS** Paul Varg Award Tchg & Scholar: Col Arts & Lett, Mich State Univ, 90; Mich Prof Yr-CASE Award, 93; Apollo Award, 95; Honors Col Award for Teaching, 99. **RESEARCH** Lit of the French Enlightenment; Denis Diderot; French novel of the Enlightenment; Opera and Lit. **SELECTED PUBLICATIONS** Auth, Manon Lescaut: A rhetoric of intellectual evasion, Romanic Rev, 10/68; Le Neveu de Rameau: Diderot's Dialogue of Language and Gesture, Ohio State Univ, 69; Metaphor and discovery in Diderot's Lettre sur les Sourds et Muets, Ky Romance Quart, Vol XX, No 2; La Religieuse: The dark cave of the Libertine soul, Mod Lang Notes, 76; The Marquis de Sade and women: Exorcising the awe of the sacred, Studies in Burke & His Time, 77; Diderot's Eloge de Richardson: A Paradox on Praising, In: Essays on the Age of Enlightment in Honor of Ira 0 Wade, Droz, 77; At the frontiers of the real: Forms and shadows of Diderot's narrative art, Forum, XVI, 78; Le paysan parvenu: Satire and the fiction of innocence, Fr Forum, Vol V, 80; ed Diderot, Digression and Disperion: A Bicentennial Tribute, Fr Forum Publ, 84; Diderot and teh Dramatization of Philosophical Thought, Skill and Education: Reflection and Experience, Springer-Verlag, 92; Une Guerre a l'Opera, De la Litterature Francaise, Bordas, 93; rev Crisis beneath the Tears: Identitiy and Ideology: Diderot, Sade and the Serious Genre, EMF: Stud in Early Fr, Signs of the Early Modern, 96; Manon, Marguerite, Violetta: On Angelism in Literature and Opera Ars Lyrica, 97. **CONTACT ADDRESS** Dept of Romance & Class Lang, Michigan State Univ, 161 Old Horticulture Rm 258, East Lansing, MI 48824-1112. **EMAIL** josephsh@pilot.msu.edu

JOUBERT, ANDRE
PERSONAL Born 07/01/1924, Lyon, France **DISCIPLINE** FRENCH **EDUCATION** Sorbonne, Lic, 46, dipl, 47, cert, 56. **CAREER** Lectr, French-German Inst, Ludwigsburg, 56-57, Tech Univ, Hannover, 58; lects, 58-59, from asst profto assoc prof, 59-72, Prof French, Univ Man, 72-. **RESEARCH** Contemporary French novel; literary criticism in France; philosophy of time. **SELECTED PUBLICATIONS** Auth, Colette et Cheri, Ed Nizet, Paris, 72. **CONTACT ADDRESS** Dept of French, Spanish, & Italian, Univ of Manitoba, Rm 431 Fletcher Argue Bldg, Winnipeg, MB, Canada R3T 2N2.

JOYCE, DOUGLAS A.
PERSONAL Born 07/20/1922, Carbonear, NF, Canada, m, 1960 **DISCIPLINE** GERMANIC LANGUAGES **EDUCATION** McGill Univ, BA, 43; Harvard Univ, AM, 44, PhD, 52. **CAREER** Lectr, Ger, 50-54, from asst prof to assoc prof, 54-67, Prof Ger & Head Dept, Trinity Col, Univ Toronto, 67-, Founding mem & asst ed, Seminar: J Ger Studies, 64-; Can Coun grant, 73-74. **MEMBERSHIPS** MLA; Asn Can Univ Teachers Ger (secy, 60-62); Hofmannsthal Soc. **RESEARCH** Literary criticism of the post-romantic period in Germany; German drama of the nineteenth century; Hugo von Hofmannsthal. **SELECTED PUBLICATIONS** Auth, Hugo Von Hofmannsthal's Der Schwierige: A Fifty-Year Theater History. **CONTACT ADDRESS** Dept of Ger Trinity Col, Univ of Toronto, 58 Colin Ave., Toronto, ON, Canada M5P 2B9.

JOYCE, JANE W.
DISCIPLINE CLASSICS **EDUCATION** Bryn Mawr Col, BA; Univ Tex Austin, MA and PhD. **CAREER** Fac, 78-; prof. **HONORS AND AWARDS** Disting Prof Hum, Centre Col. **RESEARCH** Latin language and literature, ancient epic and lyric poetry, Greco-Roman drama, classical mythology and creative writing. **SELECTED PUBLICATIONS** Auth, Beyond the Blue Mountains; The Quilt Poems, Mill Springs Press, 84/ 86, Gnomon, 91; transl, Lucan's Pharsalia, Cornell Univ Press, 93. **CONTACT ADDRESS** Centre Col, 600 W Walnut St, Danville, KY 40422. **EMAIL** joycej@centre.edu

JRADE, CATHY L.
PERSONAL Born 03/12/1949, New York, NY, m, 1973, 1 child **DISCIPLINE** SPANISH AMERICAN LITERATURE **EDUCATION** Queens Col, CUNY, BA, 69; Brown Univ, AM, 71; PhD, 74. **CAREER** Asst prof, Vir Polytech Inst, 75-76; asst prof, assoc prof, Indiana Univ, 76-87; assoc prof, prof, Vanderbilt Univ, 87-; chmn dept span and port, Vanderbilt Univ, 98-. **HONORS AND AWARDS** Spence Wilson Fel; Fel and Co-Dir of the Fellows Prog of the Robt Penn Warren Cen for Human, 94-95, 00-01; Univ Res Coun Grnt, 97; Res Coun Fac Fel 89, 93; Kenan-Venture Fund Grnt, 88; Grnt-in-Aid of Res, Indiana Univ, 87; West Euro Fac Res Grnt, IN U, 86; Woodrow Wilson Fac Dev Grnt, 84-85; IN U Fac Fel, 79; Woodrow Wilson Dis Fel, 72, 73; Choice Mag, Outst Acad Title, 99; Exec Com of the MLA Div "Latin Am Literature from Independence to 1900, 82 and 97- 00; Hispania Awd, 79-80, 81; Phi Beta Kappa; Sigma Delta Pi; Summa Cum Laude, 69. **MEMBERSHIPS** MLA, AATSP, Inst of Intl de Lit Iberoamericana. **RESEARCH** Spanish American literature of the 19th and 20th centuries; modernisms; **SELECTED PUBLICATIONS** Auth, "Annotated Bibliography on Modernist Poetry," in The Cambridge History of Latin American Literature (Cambridge Univ Press, 96); auth, "Modernism on Both Sides of the Atlantic," Anales de la literatura espanola contemporanea 23 (98): 181-196; auth, "Modernist Poetry," in The Cambridge History of Latin American Literature (Cambridge Univ Press, 96); auth, Ruben Dario y la busqueda romantica de la unidad, Fondo de Cultura Economica (86); auth, Modernismo, Modernity, and the Development of Spanish American Literature Writings (Univ Tex Press, 98); auth, Modernismo, Modernity, and the Development of Spanish American Literature, netlibrary.com (00). **CONTACT ADDRESS** Dept. Spanish and Port, Vanderbilt Univ, PO Box 35-1616, Stn. B, Nashville, TN 37235. **EMAIL** cathy.1.jrade@vanderbilt.edu

JUAREZ, ENCARNACION
PERSONAL Born 08/14/1951, Granada, Spain, m, 2 children **DISCIPLINE** SPANISH LITERATURE **EDUCATION** Univ Barcelona, Spain Licenciatura, 77; Univ Calif Berkeley, MA, 81; PhD, 87. **CAREER** TA to lectr, Univ Calif Berkeley, 79-88, asst prof, St Mary's Col, 88-95; vis asst prof to asst prof, Univ of Notre Dame, 95-. **HONORS AND AWARDS** Grant, Univ Calif Berkeley, 84; Sigma Delta Pi, 84; Charles E Keny Grad Scholarship, Univ of Calif Berkeley, 84-85; Outstanding Grad Student Instr Awd, Univ of Calif Berkeley, 85-86; Grant, St Mary's Col, 89; NEH Grant, 93, 99; Fel, Medieval Inst, Univ of Notre Dame, 00. **MEMBERSHIPS** Am Assoc of Teachers of Span and Port, Asociacion de Literatura Femenina Hispanica, Assoc for Hispanic Classical Theater, Assoc Int de Hispanistas, Assoc Int Siglo de Oro, Medieval Inst, Lang Assoc of Am, Soc for Renaissance and Baroque Poetry, Renaissance Soc of Am. **RESEARCH** Golden Age literature, with a focus on 17th century prose, 16th and 17th century culture and intellectual European history, Cultural, Gender, and Disability Studies, Spanish Medieval literature, Colonial Spanish-American Literature. **SELECTED PUBLICATIONS** Auth, Italia en la vida y obra de quevedo, Peter Lang, (NY), 90; auth, "Quevedo, lince de la crisis europea de principios del XVII," Hispanic Jour 14.1 (93): 133-142; auth, "La hora de todos:ambiguedad calculada o cambio de actitud de Quevedo?' Revista Canadiense de Estudios Hispanicos 19, (95): 505-21; auth, "Senora Catalina, donde es el camino? La autobiografia como busqueda y afirmacion de identidad en 'Vida I sucesos de la Monja Alferez,'" LA CHISPA '95: Selected proceedings, (95): 185-195; auth, "Alonso de Contreras: politica del vestido y construccion del sujeto autobiografico en el barroco," Bull of Hispanic Studies 74, (97): 179-195; auth, "La mujer militar en la america colonial: elcaso de la Monja Alferez," Ind Jour of Hispanic Lit 10.11 (97): 147-164; auth, "Autobiografias de mujeres en la Edad Media y el Siglo de Oro y el canon literario," Monographic Rev/Revista Monografica 13, (97): 154-168; auth, "el manuscrito del Lince de Italia de Francisco de Quevedo en la Biblioteca Bancroft," La Perinola 3, (99): 375-382; auth, "auth, "The Autobiography of the Aching Body in Teresa de Cartagena's 'Arboleda de los enfermos,'" Enabling the Humanities, ed Brenda Jo Brueggemann, Sharon L Snyder and Rosemarie Garland (NY: MLA, forthcoming); auth, "El discurso sartorial y el conflicto amoroso social en 'El caballero de Olmedo,'" Bull of the Comediantes 54.1, (forthcoming). **CONTACT ADDRESS** 3427 Creekview Dr, South Bend, IN 46635-2000. **EMAIL** juarez.6@nd.edu

JUFFS, ALAN
PERSONAL Born 09/28/1959, London, England **DISCIPLINE** LINGUISTICS **EDUCATION** Univ London, UK, BA (Combined honors in French and German), 82; Univ Durham, UK, MA, (Applied Linguistics), 85; McGill Univ, Montreal, PhD (Linguistics), 94. **CAREER** Lect, Hunan Agricultural Col, Hunan, P R of China, 82-84; asst prof, Int Univ of Japan, Grad School of Int Relations, 85-89; asst prof, 93-98, assoc prof, Dept of Linguistics, Univ of Pittsburgh, 98-. **MEMBERSHIPS** Am Asn of Applied Ling; Ling Soc of Am. **RESEARCH** Second lang acquistition; lang processing; semantics; syntax; lang pedagogy. **SELECTED PUBLICATIONS** Auth, An Introduction to Communicative Methodology in English Teaching, Hunan Provincial Service Foreign Languages Asn, 84; Learnability and the Lexicon: Theories and Second Language Acquisition Research (Language Acquisition and Language Disorders, vol 12), John Benjamins, 96; Garden Paths and Error Data in Second Language Sentence Processing, with Michael Harrington, Language Learning, 46, 96; Parameters in the Lexicon, Language Variation, and Language Development, in A Stringfellow, D Cahana-Amitay, E Hughes, & A Zukowski, eds, Proceedings of the 20th Annual Boston Univ Conference on Language Development, vol 1, Cascadilla Press, 96; Semantics-Syntax Correspondences in Second Language Aquisition, Second Language Res, 12, 96; Constraints on Wh-Movement in Two Different Contexts of Non-Native Language Acquisition: Competence and Processing, with Lydia White, in S Flynn, G Martohardjono, & W O'Neill, eds, The Generative Study of Second Language Acquisition, Lawrence Erlbaum Assocs, 97; Individual Processing Performance in Second Language Acquisition Research, Second Lang Res, 14, 98; The Acquisition of Semantics-Syntax Correspondences and Verb Frequencies in ESL Materials, Language Teaching Res, 2, 98; Main Verb vs Reduced Relative Clause Ambiguity Resolution in Second Language Sentence Processing, Lang Learning, 48, 98; numerous other articles. **CONTACT ADDRESS** Dept of Linguistics, Univ of Pittsburgh, 2816 CL, Pittsburgh, PA 15260. **EMAIL** juffs@pitt.edu

JULIEN, HELENE
DISCIPLINE 20TH CENTURY FRENCH LITERATURE **EDUCATION** Ecole Normale Superieure, DEA., Maitrise Universite de Paris IV-Sorbonne; Princeton Univ, MA, PhD. **CAREER** Asst prof, Colgate Univ. **HONORS AND AWARDS** Intl travel and res grant, AR State Univ, 94; McMahon grant, Princeton Univ, 91; grant, Fulton-McMahon Fund, 89; Armstrong fel, Princeton Univ, 88-92; French government scholar, Ecole Normale Superieure, 84-89; nominated, prof yr award, ar state univ, 96. **RESEARCH** 20th Century French Literature; First Person Narratives Women Studies; European Intellectual History. **SELECTED PUBLICATIONS** Le Roman de Karin et Paul: Le Journal de Cathering Pozzi et les Cahiers de Paul Valery, L'Harmattan, (Paris); "Catherine Pazzi: parcours de l'initiation, parcours poetique," Romanic Review; "Voyage, xeferentialite et la question des origines dans L'immoraliste et la modification," French Literature Series; "Christiane Rochefort: una vie de femme, revue et corrigee," Dalhousie French Studies; auth, L'Orphee meurtrier des Cahiers: regard sur la poetique de Valery, Bulletin des Etudes Valeryennes; Catherine Pozzi, Feminist Companion to Fr Lit; Les Cahiers de Valery 1920-1928: problemes de genre et de statut, Rocky Mountain Rev; 1920: une annee de reflexion poetique dans les Cahiers, Paul Valery: Vers anciens et poietique des Cahiers. **CONTACT ADDRESS** Dept of Romance Lang, Colgate Univ, 13 Oak Drive, Hamilton, NY 13346. **EMAIL** hmjulien@yahoo.com

JUN, SUN-AH
PERSONAL Born 11/06/1959, South Korea, m, 1986, 1 child **DISCIPLINE** LINGUISTICS **EDUCATION** Oh State Univ, PhD, 93. **CAREER** Assoc prof, dept of ling, Univ Calif Los Angeles, 93-. **MEMBERSHIPS** Ling Soc of Amer; Acoust Soc of Amer. **RESEARCH** Phonetics and Phonology. **SELECTED PUBLICATIONS** Auth, The Accentual Phrase in the Korean Prosodic Hierarchy, Phonology, 98; co-auth, Rate Effects on French Intonation: Phonetic Realization and Prosodic Organization, Jour of Phonetics, 98; auth, The Phonetics and Phonology of Korean Prosody: intonational phonology and prosodic structure, Garland, 96; co-auth, A Prosodic analysis of three types of wh-phrases in Korean, Lang and Speech, 96; auth, Asymmetrical prosodic effects on the laryngeal gesture in Korean, Phonology and phonetic evidence: Papers in Laboratory Phonology, Cambridge, 95; co-auth, Distribution of Devoiced High Vowels in Korean, Proceedings of the Intl Conf on Spoken Lang Processing, 94. **CONTACT ADDRESS** Dept. of Linguistics, Univ of California, Los Angeles, 3125 Campbell Hall, 405 Hilgard, Ave, Los Angeles, CA 90095-1543. **EMAIL** jun@humnet.ucla.edu

JUNOD, SAMUEL A.
PERSONAL Born 06/07/1967, Geneva, Switz, s **DISCIPLINE** LINGUISTICS, LITERATURE **EDUCATION** Univ Geneva, 94, 96; John Hopkins Univ, PhD, 00. **CAREER** Asst prof, Univ Colo Boulder, 99-. **HONORS AND AWARDS** Jr Fac Dev Awd, 00. **MEMBERSHIPS** MLA; ACLA; SCSC. **RESEARCH** French renaissance; Rubelais; D'Aubigne; French Swiss literature. **SELECTED PUBLICATIONS** Auth, "Lectures du Physet¤re ou le Physet¤re se D¤gonfle," Etude Rabelaisiennes (98); auth, "Resingenies et Surgissement: Deux Modalites de la Parole Dam les Tragiques d'Agrippa d'Aubign¤," Etude de Lettres (99). **CONTACT ADDRESS** Fr and Ital Dept, Univ of Colorado, Boulder, Boulder, CO 80309-0001. **EMAIL** junod@spot.colorado.edu

JUNTUNE, THOMAS WILLIAM
PERSONAL Born 05/27/1940, Astoria, OR, m, 1968, 2 children **DISCIPLINE** GERMANIC LINGUISTICS **EDUCATION** Stanford Univ, AB, 63, MA, 64; Princeton Univ, MA, 66, PhD(ling), 68. **CAREER** Asst prof, 67-71, assoc prof, 71-

80, Prof Ger, Mich State Univ, 80-, Res grant, Alexander von Humboldt Found, Ger, 74-75; 89-90; resident dir jr yr, Freiburg, Ger, 82-83. **MEMBERSHIPS** MLA; Ling Soc Am; Am Asn Teachers Ger; Sem Germanic Philol; Soc Advan Scand Studies. **RESEARCH** Germanic syntax; Germanic phonology; old Icelandic; Germanic-Finnousric Language content. **SELECTED PUBLICATIONS** Auth, The informational value of Germanic loanwords into Finnish, Amsterdamer Beitrage zur alteren Germanistik, 73; Reflexivization and reflexive verbs in old Icelandic, Nordic Lang & Mod Ling, Vol 3, 78; Using parallel Bible translations in teaching the history of the German language, Yrbk Sem Germanic Philol, 80; Subject and Reflexure in Old Icelandic in Recent Developments in Germaic Linguistics, CILT, 93, 92; Languages and Peoples in Contrast; Early Germanic & Early Finnu in The Germanic Mosaic: Cultural and Linguistic Diversity in Society, 94. **CONTACT ADDRESS** Dept of Ling & Lang, Michigan State Univ, A615 Wells Hall, East Lansing, MI 48824-1020. **EMAIL** juntune@pilot.msu.edu

JURADO, JOSE
PERSONAL Born 12/22/1925, Madrid, Spain, m, 1961, 1 child **DISCIPLINE** SPANISH LITERATURE **EDUCATION** Univ Madrid, Bachiller, 49, lic, 56, Dr(philos & lett), 63. **CAREER** Asst Latin philol, Univ Madrid, 58-59; prof Span philol & lit, Univ Caldas, Colombia, 60-62; vis asst prof, Univ Chicago, 62-63; asst prof, Univ Va, 63-64; from asst prof to assoc prof, 64-73, Prof Span Lit, Carleton Univ, 73-, Can Coun grant, 67. **MEMBERSHIPS** Am Asn Teachers Span & Port. **RESEARCH** Eighteenth century and Old Spanish literature. **SELECTED PUBLICATIONS** Auth, On the Lesson Yelos/ Yergos From the 'Libro De Buen Amor', Boll De La Real Acad Espanola, Vol 0074, 94; A Critical-Study of the Word Feste in Ruiz, Juan 'Libro De Buen Amor', Revista De Filologia Espanola, Vol 0075, 95; John of the Cross--'Cantico Espiritual, Poesias, Codice Inedito De Marchena Del Cb-Mch--, Revista De Filologia Espanola, Vol 0077, 97. **CONTACT ADDRESS** Dept of Span, Carleton Univ, 1125 Colonel By Dr, Ottawa, ON, Canada K1S 5B6.

JURKEVICH, GAYANA
PERSONAL Born Montreal, PQ, Canada **DISCIPLINE** SPANISH; COMPARATIVE LITERATURE **EDUCATION** Mount Holyoke Col, AB, 74; Univ Minn, MA, 77; NYork Univ, MPhil, 85; NYork Univ, PhD, 87. **CAREER** Teaching assoc, Univ Minn, 75-77; personnel mgt, US Dept of State, 77-81; actress, adm coord, GALA, Teatro Hispano, Inc, 77-81; instr, The Key Sch, 86-87; instr, Anne Arundel Comm Col, 86-87; adjunct asst prof, Baruch Col/CUNY, 87-88; sub asst prof, Baruch Col/ CUNY, 88-89; asst prof, Baruch Col/CUNY, 89-92; assoc prof, Baruch Col/CUNY, 93-98; prof, 99-. **HONORS AND AWARDS** Fel, Mount Holyoke Col; fel, Univ Minn; fel, NYU; Prog for Cultural Cooperation btw. US Universities and the Spanish Ministry of Culture, 95-96, 98. **MEMBERSHIPS** Phi Kappa Phi; MLA; AATSP. **SELECTED PUBLICATIONS** Auth, The Elusive Self: Archetypal Approaches to the Novels of Miguel de Unamuno, Univ Mo, 91; auth, Defining Castile in Literature and Art: Institucionismo, The Generation of 1898, and the Origins of Modern Spanish Landscape,Revista Hispanica Moderna, 47, 94; auth, A Poetics of Time and Space: Ekphrasis and the Modern Vision in Azorin and Velazquez, MLN, 110.2, 95; auth, Azorin's Magic Circle: The Subversion of Time and Space in Dona Ines, Bull of Hisp Studies, LXXIII, 96; auth Azorin's Painted Lady: Maria Fontan and the Economics of Ekphrasis in La Chispa '97. Selected Proceedings of the Eighteenth Louisiana Conference of Hisp Lang and Lit, Tulane UP, 97; auth, In Pursuit of the Natural Sign: Azorin and the Poetics of Ekphrasis, Bucknell, 00. **CONTACT ADDRESS** Dept of Modern Languages, Baruch Col, CUNY, 17 Lexington Ave, Box G-1224, New York, NY 10010. **EMAIL** gayana_jurkevich@bcnwh.cuny.edu

K

KABAKOFF, JACOB
PERSONAL Born 03/20/1918, New York, NY, m, 1944, 3 children **DISCIPLINE** HEBREW LANGUAGE & LITERATURE **EDUCATION** Yeshiva Univ, BA, 38; Jewish Theol Sem, MHL, 44, DHL, 58. **CAREER** Asst rabbi, Har Zion Temple, Philadelphia, 44-46; rabbi, B'nai Israel of Olney, 44-48; educ dir, Flatbush Jewish Ctr, 48-50; mem ed staff, Encycl Hebraica, Jerusalem, 50-52; prof Hebrew & dean, Cleveland Col Jewish Studies, 52-68; assoc prof Hebrew, 68-72, Prof Hebrew, Lehman Col, 72-, Am Philos Soc grant, 67; Mem Found Jewish Cult grant, 67-68; ed, Jewish Bk Annual, Jewish Bk Coun, 77-; Asn Prof of Hebrew (pres, 74-76). **HONORS AND AWARDS** DD, Jewish Theol Sem, 72. **MEMBERSHIPS** Am Acad Jewish Res; Am Jewish Hist Soc; World Union Jewish Studies; Nat Orgn Hebrew Cult (vpres, 77-). **RESEARCH** Current Israeli literature; American Hebrew literatary and cultural history. **SELECTED PUBLICATIONS** Auth, Some East European Letters on Emigration--Rethinking the American Jewish Experience, Amer Jewish Arch, Vol 0045, 93. **CONTACT ADDRESS** Div Hebraic & Judaic Studies, Lehman Col, CUNY, Bronx, NY 10468.

KACANDES, IRENE
DISCIPLINE GERMAN LANGUAGE **EDUCATION** Harvard Univ, PhD, 91. **CAREER** Fac, Univ Tex; Asst prof, Dartmouth Col. **RESEARCH** Goethe, Kleist, Grass, and Christa Wolf; narrative theory; 20th-century cult studies. **SELECTED PUBLICATIONS** Auth, publ(s) about orality and literacy, feminist linguistics, and the Holocaust. **CONTACT ADDRESS** Dartmouth Col, 3529 N Main St, #207, Hanover, NH 03755.

KACHRU, BRAJ BEHARI
PERSONAL Born 05/15/1932, Srinagar, India, m, 1965, 1 child **DISCIPLINE** NON-NATIVE ENGLISHES, SOCIOLINGUISTICS **EDUCATION** Jammu & Kashmir Univ, BA, 52; Allahabad Univ, MA, 55; Edinburgh Univ, dipl, 59, PhD(ling), 61. **CAREER** Lectr ling, Lucknow Univ, 62-63; res assoc, 63-64, from asst prof to assoc prof, 64-70, head dept, 69-79, Prof Ling, Univ Ill, Urbana, 70-, Coordr, Div Applied Ling, 74-, Mem SAsia lang comt, Comt Instnl Coop, 65-; consult, Dict English Lang, Random House, 66; Am Inst Indian Studies fac fel, 67-68; chmn comt varieties English, Asn Commonwealth Lit & Lang Studies, 68; assoc Ctr Advan Studies, Univ Ill, 71-72; ed, Papers on SAsian Ling, 73; consult, Ford Found, 74 & 75; mem lang comt, SAsia Regional Coun, 77-; dir, Ling Inst Ling Soc Am, 78; chmn, Int Conf SAsian Lang & Ling, 80- **MEMBERSHIPS** Philol Soc, Eng; Ling Soc Am, Ling Soc India; Ling Asn Can & US. **RESEARCH** South Asian English and linguistics; Kashmiri language and literature; varieties of English. **SELECTED PUBLICATIONS** Auth, English in South Asia, Current Trends in Ling, 69; co-ed, Current Trends in Stylistics, Ling Res, 72; Issues in Linguistics: Papers in Honor of Henry and Renee Kahane, Univ Ill, 73; ed, Dimensions of bilingualism, Unit Foreign Lang Study & Res, Univ Ill, 76; co-ed, Aspects of sociolinguistics in South Asia, Int J Sociol Lang, 78; Kashmiri Literature, 81; The Indianization of English: The English Language in India, 82; ed, The Other Tongue: English Across Cultures, 82. **CONTACT ADDRESS** Dept of Ling, Univ of Illinois, Urbana-Champaign, 707 S Mathews Ave, Urbana, IL 61801-3625. **EMAIL** b-kachru@staff.uiuc.edu

KACHRU, YAMUNA
PERSONAL Born 03/05/1933, Purulia, India, m, 1965, 2 children **DISCIPLINE** LINGUISTICS **EDUCATION** Bihar Univ, BA, 53; Patna Univ, MA, 55; Univ London, PhD, 65. **CAREER** Lectr Hindi, Ranchi Women's Col, India, 56-58; lectr, Sch Orient & African Studies, Univ London, 59-65; asst res prof ling, 65-66, asst prof ling & Eng, 67-68, assoc prof ling, Eng & Hindi, 68-71, Prof Ling & Eng as Second Lang, Univ IL, Urbana, 71-94, Prof Ling, 94-98; Act Dir, Div Eng as an Int lang, Univ IL, 84-85, 85-89; Rockefeller fel, Deccan Col, 58-59; Am Inst Indian Studies fac fels, 67-68, 71-72 & 85-86; assoc, Ctr Advan Study, Univ IL, 75. **HONORS AND AWARDS** Two Gold Medals, Panta Univ, 55; Distinction in Ling, Deccan Col, 58-59; Assoc, Center for Advan Study, Univ IL, 75; Grants from Res Bd, Univ IL, Am Coun Learned Soc & Smithsonian Found; mem, ed bd, World Englishes Blackwell, Oxford) and Eng in Asia, Nat Inst Educ, Singapore. **MEMBERSHIPS** Ling Soc Am; IAWE; Lling Soc India. **RESEARCH** Generative grammars of South Asian languages; pragmatics; contrastive rhetoric; Second Lang acquisition; world Eng. **SELECTED PUBLICATIONS** Auth, An Intro to Hindi Syntax, Univ Ill, 66; ed, Studies in Linguistics Sciences, Special Issues on Hindi Linguistics, 71; Topics in a Transformational Grammar of Hindi (in Hindi), Agra, Central Inst of Hindi, 74; On the semantics of the causative construction in Hindi-Urdu, In: The Grammar of Causative Constructions, Syntax and Semantics set VI, Acad Press, 76; On relative clause formation in Hindi-Urdu, Ling, 78; Aspects of Hindi Grammar, Manohar Publ, India, 80; ed, Dimensions of South Asian Linguistics, fall 81; Cross-cultural texts, discourse strategies and discourse interpretation, In: Discourse Across Cultures: Strategies in World Englishes, Prentice-Hall, 87; Ergativity, Subjecthood and Topicality in Hindu-Urdu, In: Studies on Ergativity (spec vol Lingua), North-Holland Elsevier, The Netherlands, 87; Hindi-Urdu, In: World's Major Languages, Croom-Helm, 87; ed, Special Issue on Pedagogical Grammars of English: Approaches and Resources, winter 87; Writers in Hindi and English, In: Contrastive Rhetoric: Theory and Case Studies, Written Commun Annual, vol 3, Sage Publ, 88; Cognitivie and cultural styles in second language acquisition, Annual Rev Applied Ling, 88; co-ed, Pragmatics and Language Learning, monogr 1-V, 90-94; Social meaning and creativity in Indian English speech acts, In: Language, Communication and Social Meaning, Georgetown Univ Monogr Series on Lang and Ling, 92; Self, identity and creativity: Women writers in India, In: Self as Person in Asian Theory and Practice, SUNY Press, Albany, 94; Lexcial components of cultural contact: Speech act verbs in Hindi-English dictionaries, In: Cultures, Ideologies, and the Dctionary: Studies in Honor of Ladislav Zgusta, Max Niemeyer Verlag, 95; co-ed, Language, Gender, and Power, 95; Culture and argumentative writing in world Englishes, In; World Englishes 2000, Univ Hawaii Press, 97. **CONTACT ADDRESS** Dept of Ling, Univ of Illinois, Urbana-Champaign, 707 S Mathews Ave, Urbana, IL 61801-3625. **EMAIL** ykachur@staff.uiuc.edu

KAGA, MARIKO
DISCIPLINE JAPANESE LANGUAGE **EDUCATION** Kobe Kaisei Women's Col, BA; Univ Ill, MA, PhD.Columbia Univ, PhD. **CAREER** Japanese, Carleton Col **SELECTED PUBLICATIONS** Auth, Exercise in Japanese Counters. **CONTACT ADDRESS** Carleton Col, 100 S College St., Northfield, MN 55057-4016.

KAILING, JOEL
PERSONAL Born Atlanta, GA, m, 4 children **DISCIPLINE** SPEECH, INTERCULTURAL COMMUNICATION **EDUCATION** Univ Ky, PhD. **CAREER** Assoc prof, Lee Univ, 94-. **MEMBERSHIPS** Lee Comm Club; Lee Univ Vindagua, Missions Alive. **SELECTED PUBLICATIONS** Inside, Outside, Upside Down, Int Rev Missions, 88; A New Solution to the African Christian Problem; Missiology, 94. **CONTACT ADDRESS** Lee Col, Tennessee, 1120 N. Ocoee St, Cleveland, TN 37320-3450. **EMAIL** jkailing@leeuniversity.edu

KAIMOWITZ, JEFFREY H.
PERSONAL Born 11/03/1942, New York, NY, m, 1987, 1 child **DISCIPLINE** CLASSICS **EDUCATION** Johns Hopkins, AB, 64; Univ of Cincinnati, PhD, 70; Columbia Univ, MS, 76 **CAREER** Asst Prof, 69-73, Miami Univ, OH; Libr Trainee, 73-77, NY Pub Lib; Curator, 77-, Watkinson Lib, Trinity Col, Hartford **HONORS AND AWARDS** Phi Beta Kappa, 64; Woodrow Wilson Fel, 64-65; Fulbright Fel, 66-67 **MEMBERSHIPS** Am Lib Asc; Grolier Club **RESEARCH** Translating Latin poetry; Printing hist **CONTACT ADDRESS** Watkinson Lib, Trinity Col, Connecticut, Hartford, CT 06106. **EMAIL** jeffrey.kaimowitz@trincoll.edu

KALBOUSS, GEORGE
PERSONAL Born 06/21/1939, New York, NY, m, 1962, 2 children **DISCIPLINE** RUSSIAN LANGUAGE & LITERATURE, DRAMA **EDUCATION** Columbia Univ, AB, 60, AM, 61; NYork Univ, PhD(Slavic lang), 68. **CAREER** Vis instr Russ, Dartmouth Col, 66; instr, Purdue Univ, 66-67; asst prof, Dartmouth Col, 67-73, asst dean, 68-73; assoc prof Slavic Lang & Lit, Ohio State Univ, 73-. **HONORS AND AWARDS** Distinguished Teaching Awd, Ohio State Univ, 77. **MEMBERSHIPS** Am Asn Teachers Slavic & E Europ Lang; Am Asn Advan Slavic Studies. **RESEARCH** Works of Fiodor Sologub; poetry and prose of Russian symbolism; computer-assisted instruction. **SELECTED PUBLICATIONS** Auth, From Mystery to Fantasy: An Attempt to Categorize the Plays of the Russian Symbolists, Canadian American Slavic Studies, Winter 1974; On 'Armenian Riddles' and Their Offspring 'Radio Erevan', Slavic and East European J, Fall 1977; Andrei Bely and the Modernist Movement in Russian Drama, In: "Andrey Bely: A Critical Review" (ed. Gerald Janacek), Univ of Kentucky Press, 78; The Many Faces Behind the Masks of Zoloto v Iazuri, In: "Andrey Bely Centenary Papers" (ed. Boris Christa), Hakkert, 80; The Plays of the Russian Symbolists, E. Lansing, Russian Language J, 82; Sologub and Myth, Slavic and East European J, Winter 83; Echoes of Nietzsche in the works of Fedor Sologub, "Nietzsche in Russia" (ed. Bernice Rosenthal), Princeton Univ Press, 86; Rhyming Patterns in Griboedov's "Gore ot Uma", Slavic and East European J, Spring 95; Russian Culture, Simon and Schuster, 98. **CONTACT ADDRESS** Dept of Slavic Lang & Lit, Ohio State Univ, Columbus, 1841 Millikin Rd, Columbus, OH 43210-1229. **EMAIL** kalbouss.1@osu.edu

KALLAUR, CONSTANTINE H.
PERSONAL Born 02/03/1934, Horedno, Poland, m, 1963, 3 children **DISCIPLINE** RUSSIAN LITERATURE **EDUCATION** Columbia Univ, BS, 58; Hofstra Univ, MA, 66; New York Univ, PhD, 81. **CAREER** Regional Study Fel, Princeton Univ, 66-67; dept chair, Nassau Cmty Col, 80-99, (retired in 99 prof emeritus). **HONORS AND AWARDS** Fac Distinguished Achievement Awd, 92. **MEMBERSHIPS** AAJSEEL, MLA. **RESEARCH** 19th Century Russian literature. **SELECTED PUBLICATIONS** Auth, "The Writing History of Tolstoy's 'The Devil' with particular emphasis on the ending," The Nassau Review, 71; auth, "Imagery in V.M. Garshin's "The Scarlet flower'," The Nassau Review, 72. **CONTACT ADDRESS** Dept For Lang, Nassau Comm Col, 1 Educ Dr, Garden City, NY 11530-6719.

KAMENISH, PAULA K.
DISCIPLINE WORLD LITERATURE, EUROPEAN LITERATURE, DRAMA, NOVELLA, AND NOVEL **EDUCATION** Ctr Col Ky, BA; Univ NC, Chapel Hill, MA, PhD. **CAREER** Assoc prof, Univ NC, Wilmington. **RESEARCH** German and French theatre of the 20th century; Dada movement. **SELECTED PUBLICATIONS** Published articles on Shakespeare, French Canadian author Roch Carrier, and various modern dramatists. **CONTACT ADDRESS** Univ of No Carolina, Wilmington, Morton Hall, Wilmington, NC 28403-3297. **EMAIL** kamenishp@uncwil.edu

KAMLA, THOMAS A.
DISCIPLINE MEDIEVAL GERMAN LITERATURE, GERMAN LITERATURE, GERMAN LANGUAGE **EDUCATION** St John's Univ, BA, 61; Univ Wis, MA, 69; PhD, 73. **CAREER** Asst prof, Carnegie Mellon Univ, 72-76; vis asst

prof, Univ Nebr, 76-78; prof, Univ Scranton, 78-. **MEMBERSHIPS** Am Asn of Teachers of Ger; Ger Studies Asn. **RESEARCH** 19th-20th century Ger lit; psychoanalytic criticism; turn of the century; expressionism; exile lit. **SELECTED PUBLICATIONS** Auth, Confrontation with Exile: Studies in the German Novel, 75; auth, "The Officer-Figure Aestheticized: Some Biographical Speculations on Hofmannsthal's 'Reitergeschichte,'" Perspectives on Contemp Lit 14 (88): 64-72; auth, "The Aestheticism-Decadence Dialectic in Hofmannsthal's 'Reitergeschichte,'" Orbis Litterarum 44 (89): 327-40; auth, "Bruno Frank," in Twentieth-Century German Dramatists 1889-1918, ed. Wolfgang D. Elfe and James Hardin (MI: Gale Res Inc., 92), 49-59; auth, "Thomas Mann's 'Gefallen': Etats d'ame and the Bahrian New Psychology," Ger Quart 66 (93): 510-523. **CONTACT ADDRESS** Dept of For Lang and Lit, Univ of Scranton, Scranton, PA 18510. **EMAIL** Kamlatl@uofs.edu

KAMUF, PEGGY
DISCIPLINE FRENCH AND COMPARATIVE LITERATURE **EDUCATION** Cornell Univ, PhD. **CAREER** Prof, Univ Southern Calf; Visiting Professor at the Centre d'Etudes Feminines, Universite de Paris VIII and from 1991-96; Directeur de Programme at the College International de Philosophie in Paris. **RESEARCH** Translation theory; philosophy and literature; 18th-century aesthetics; post-structuralist literary and feminist theory. **SELECTED PUBLICATIONS** Auth, Fictions of Feminine Desire: Disclosures of Heloise, 82; Signature Pieces: On The Institution of Authorship, 88; ed, A Derrida Reader: Between the Blinds, 91. **CONTACT ADDRESS** Col Letters, Arts & Sciences, Univ of So California, University Park Campus, Los Angeles, CA 90089. **EMAIL** kamuf@.usc.edu

KANDE, SYLVIE
PERSONAL Born 10/13/1957, Paris, France, d, 2 children **DISCIPLINE** FRENCH **EDUCATION** Sorbonne Univ, Licence, 78; Maitrise, 79; DEA, 84; Doctorat, 92. **CAREER** Res Asst to Lecturer, Stanford Univ, 89-91; Lecturer, Col of Notre-Dame, 91-92; Asst Prof, San Jose State Univ, 91-94; Asst Prof, New York Univ, 94-. **HONORS AND AWARDS** Finalist, RATP-Paris Poetry in Motion Contest, 99; NYU Golden Dozen Teaching Awd, 98; NYU Goddard Fel, 98; NEH Institute of African Literature, 93. **MEMBERSHIPS** Pen Am Center, African Studies Asn, African Lit Asn, Asn Pour l'Etude des Litteratures Africaines, Modern Lang Asn, Asn des anciens eleves de Louis-le-Grand, NYU ABFAS-Black Fac Administrators & Staff Asn. **RESEARCH** African and Caribbean History and Literature. **SELECTED PUBLICATIONS** Auth, Black, White and Tan Fantasy: Fictions of metissage in Francophone Literature, in press; co-ed, The Haitian Revolution Revisited, in press; auth, Metissage et hybridite. L'etat de la question au debut du 2eme millenaire, in press; auth, "Mosaique," Services culturels francais, 00; auth, "I Love Harlem," Revue Noire, forthcoming; auth, Terres, urbanisme et architecture creoles en Sierra Leone XVIIIe-XIXe siecles, Paris, 98; auth, Discours sur le metissage, identites metisses. En quete d'Ariel, Paris, 99; auth, Lagon, lagunes. Collection Continents Noirs, Paris, 00. **CONTACT ADDRESS** Dept French, New York Univ, 19 Univ Place, New York, NY 10003-4556. **EMAIL** skk1@is.nyu.edu

KANE, LESLIE
DISCIPLINE COMPARATIVE LITERATURE **EDUCATION** Brooklyn Col, BA; Fairleigh Dickinson Univ, MA; NYork Univ, PhD. **CAREER** Pres, David Mamet Soc; ed, David Mamet Newsletter; former VP, Harold Pinter Soc. **RESEARCH** Stage and screenplays of David Mamet and the drama of Harold Pinter. **SELECTED PUBLICATIONS** Publ, lit jour(s); The Language of Silence: On the Unspoken and the Unspeakable in Modern Drama; David Mamet: A Casebook; Israel Horovitz: Critical Essays. **CONTACT ADDRESS** Dept of Engl, Westfield State Col, 577 Western Ave., Westfield, MA 01085.

KANELLOS, NICOLAS
PERSONAL 1 child **DISCIPLINE** LANGUAGE, LITERATURE, PUBLISHING **EDUCATION** Univ Autonoma Mex, Mex Lit & Cult, 64-65; Farleigh Dickinson Univ, BA, Span, 66; Univ Tex, MA, Roman Lang, 68; Univ Lisboa Portugal, Portuguese Lit & Cult, 69070; Univ Tex, PhD, Span & Portuguese, 74. **CAREER** PROF, UNIV HOUSTON, 80-. **SELECTED PUBLICATIONS** America's Hispanic People: Their Images Through History, 97; edr, Biographical Dictionary of Hispanic Literature in the United States, Greenwood Press, 89; Mexican-American Theater Legacy and Reality, Lat Am Rev Press, 87; Hispanic-American Almanac: A Reference Work on Hispanics in the United States, Gale Res, 93, Hispanic Firsts, Gale Res, 97; auth, Hispanic Periodicals in the United States: A Brief History and Comprehensive Bibliography, 00. **CONTACT ADDRESS** Dept Hisp & Class Lang, Univ of Houston, Houston, TX 77204-3128.

KANES, MARTIN
PERSONAL Born 09/21/1927, Philadelphia, PA, m, 1953, 2 children **DISCIPLINE** FRENCH **EDUCATION** Univ Paris, Dr(comp lit), 53; Univ Pa, PhD, 59. **CAREER** Instr Romance lang, Univ Pa, 53-59; asst prof French, Univ Calif, Davis, 59-66; assoc prof French lit, Univ Calif, Santa Cruz, 66-71, Prof French & Comp Lit, 71-79; SUNY, Albany, 79-96. **HONORS AND AWARDS** Officer daus l'Ordre des Palmes Academiques; Fels, Guggenheim & Fulbright, 65-66. **MEMBERSHIPS** MLA. **RESEARCH** French and comparative literature of the 19th century; Zola; Balzac. **SELECTED PUBLICATIONS** Auth, Zola's LaBete humaine: A Study in Literary Creation, California Univ Pr, Berkeley, 62; auth, Balzac's Comedy of Words, Princeton Univ Pr, 75; auth, Critical Essays on Balzac, G.K. Hall, (Boston), 90; auth, Pere Goriot Anatomy of a Troubled World, Twayne, (New York) 93. **CONTACT ADDRESS** SUNY, Albany, Albany, NY 12222.

KANEVSKAYA, MARINA
PERSONAL Born 04/18/1956, Moscow, Russia, 1 child **DISCIPLINE** RUSSIAN LITERATURE **EDUCATION** Moscow State Univ, MA, 79; Indiana Univ, PhD, 97. **CAREER** Asst instr, 89, 90, 93, 94, 96, 97, 98, Summer Workshop Slavic E Europ Lang Ind Univ; res asst, 89, asst instr, 90, 93-95, Dept Slavic Lang & Lit, Ind Univ; tchr, 91, 92, Summer Lang School, Beloit Col; lectr, Dept Slavic Lang, Univ Texas Austin, 90-92; lectr, Depauw Univ, 97; lectr, Georgetown Univ, 97-98; lectr, George Wash Univ, 98; Asst Prof, Univ Montana, 98- . **HONORS AND AWARDS** Grad Stud Res Awd, Ind Univ, 94; Mellon grant, 93, 94, 96; Am Assoc of Univ Women Educ Found, Car Devel Grant, 95-96; IREX predissertation res grant (Moscow) 96; Salaroglio Mod For Lang Scholar, 96. **MEMBERSHIPS** Am Asn Advan Russian Studies; Am Asn Tchrs Russian & E Europ Langs. **RESEARCH** 19th & 20th Century Russian literature. **SELECTED PUBLICATIONS** Auth, Nikolai Pavlovich Antsiferov-Teacher of Human Science, E/W Educ, 93; Petty Demon by Fedor Sologub as a Travesty, Selected Stories by Fedor Sologub, Zapizdat Publ, 94; A Corrupted Quotation as a Key to a New Meaning: Chekhov on Gogol, Gogolevskii sbornik, Obrazovanie, 94; Moscow as a Host of Pushkin's Celebrations of 1880, Grad Essays on Slavic Lang & Lit, Univ Ctr Russian & E Europ Stud, 95; A Diary of a Writer from Tioplyi Stan: The Beautifulness of Life by Evgenii Popov, NW Univ Press, 98; Pushkin as a 'Universal' Poet: Varnhagen von Ense and Dostoevsky, Proceedings of the 1966 Cent Slavic Conf, Univ Missouri-Columbia, 98; Icon in the Structure of Dostoevsky's Notes from the House of the Dead, Znamia, 98; The Semiotic Validity of the Mirror Image in Vladimir Nabokov's Despair, Proceedings of Vladimir Nabokov's Centennial Festival, Cornell Univ Press, 99. **CONTACT ADDRESS** Dept For Lang, Univ of Montana, Missoula, MT 59812. **EMAIL** MKANEV@selway.umt.edu

KAPLAN, EDWARD HAROLD
PERSONAL Born 01/09/1936, New York, NY, m, 1957, 2 children **DISCIPLINE** CHINESE HISTORY & LANGUAGE **EDUCATION** Georgetown Univ, BS, 60; Univ Iowa, MA, 63, PhD, 70. **CAREER** Instr hist, Univ Del, 64-68; from lectr to asst prof, 68-74, assoc prof hist, Western Wash Univ 74-; Ed, Studies on East Asia, WWC CEAS, 94-. **MEMBERSHIPS** Asn Asian Studies; Am Orient Soc; AHA. **RESEARCH** Sung history; Chinese economic history. **SELECTED PUBLICATIONS** Transl & ed, Maxims for the Well Governed Household, Occasional Papers No 1, Prog EAsian Studies, 71 & An Economic History of China, by Chou Chin-sheng, Occasional Papers No 7, 74, Western Wash Univ; A Monetary History of China, East Asian Res Aids and Translations, no 5, Western Wash Univ Ctr East Asian Studies, 94; . **CONTACT ADDRESS** Dept of Hist, Western Washington Univ, M/S 9056, Bellingham, WA 98225-9056. **EMAIL** kaplan@cc.wwu.edu

KAPLAN, EDWARD KIVIE
PERSONAL Born 03/04/1942, Boston, MA, m, 1986, 3 children **DISCIPLINE** FRENCH & COMPARATIVE LITERATURE **EDUCATION** Brown Univ, BA, 64; Columbia Univ, MA, 66, PhD, 70. **CAREER** Instr French, Barnard Col, Columbia Univ, 67- 71; asst prof, Amherst Col, 71-78; asst prof, prof French & comparative literature, Brandeis Univ, 78-; res assoc Tauber Inst Study Europ Jewry; NEH fel, 85-86. **HONORS AND AWARDS** Lewis Galantiere Prize, 90. **MEMBERSHIPS** MLA; Am Asn Teachers Fr; Soc Etud Romantiques; Soc Values Higher Educ; Assoc Jewish Stud. **RESEARCH** 19th century French literature; Michelet; Baudelaire; Bonnefoy; Heschel. **SELECTED PUBLICATIONS** Auth, Gaston Bachelard's Philosophy of Imagination, Philos & Phenomenol Res, 9/72; Language and reality in A J Heschel's Philosophy of Religion, J Am Acad Relig, 3/73; Les Deux sexes de l'esprit: Michelet phenomenologue de l'imagination .., Europe, 12/73; Michelet's Poetic Vision: A Romantic Philosophy of Nature, Man, and Woman, Univ Mass, 77; Mysticism and despair in Abraham J Heschel's religious thought, J Relig, 1/77; Michelet's revolutionary symbolism: From Hermencutics in politics, 4/77 & The courage of Baudelaire and Rimbuad: The anxiety of faith, 12/78, Fr Rev; ed Baudelaire and the Vicissitudes of Venus: Ethical Irony in Fleurs du Mal, The Shaping of Text: Style, Imagery, and Structure in French Literature, Bucknell Univ, 93; Sacred versus Symbolic Religion: Abraham Joshua Heschel and Martin Buber, Mod Judaism, 94; auth Holiness in Words: Abraham Joshua Heschel's Poetics of Piety, SUNY, 96; Abraham Heschel, Yale Companion to Jewish Writing and Thought in Germany, 1096-1996, Yale Univ, 97; The Voices of Marceline Desbordes-Valmore: Deference, Self-Assertion, Accountability, Fr Forum, 97; La Spiritualite de Michelet: Une nouvelle religion republicaine, Litterature et Nation Michelet et la question sociale, Univ Fr Rabelais, 97; auth Abraham Joshua Heschel, Prophetic Witness, Yale Univ, 98; Recovering the Origins, ADFL Bull, 98; Ecstasy and Insight: Baudelaire's Fruitful Tensions, Romance Quart, 98; L'Internet de Michelet: Evolution, Immortalite, Fragilite du Moi, Europe, 98. **CONTACT ADDRESS** Dept Romance & Comp Lit, Brandeis Univ, MS-024, Waltham, MA 02254-2700. **EMAIL** edwkaplan@brandeis.edu

KAPLAN, ELIZABETH ANN
DISCIPLINE COMPARATIVE LITERATURE **EDUCATION** Univ Birmingham, BA, 58; Rutgers Univ, PhD, 70. **CAREER** Prof, 87-. **RESEARCH** 19th and 20 century American Literature; feminist theory; women in film; cultural studies. **SELECTED PUBLICATIONS** Auth, Fritz Lang: A Guide to References and Resources, Hall, 81; Women and Film: Both Sides of the Camera, 90; co-auth, Talking About the Cinema, 74; co-ed, Late Imperial Culture, 95. **CONTACT ADDRESS** English Dept, SUNY, Stony Brook, Stony Brook, NY 11794. **EMAIL** eakaplan@notes.cc.sunysb.edu

KAPLAN, GREGORY
DISCIPLINE SPANISH LITERATURE **EDUCATION** Univ Pa, PhD, 94. **CAREER** Asst prof, Span, Univ Tenn. **RESEARCH** Literature of the Spanish conversos. **CONTACT ADDRESS** Dept of Mod For Langs & Lits, Univ of Tennessee, Knoxville, 701 McClung Tower & Plaza, Knoxville, TN 37996. **EMAIL** gkaplan@utk.edu

KAPLAN, JAMES MAURICE
PERSONAL Born 03/16/1943, Worcester, MA **DISCIPLINE** FRENCH LITERATURE **EDUCATION** Univ Mass, Amherst, BA, 64; Univ Calif, Berkeley, PhD(French), 71. **CAREER** Teaching asst French, Univ Calif, Berkeley, 65-66, 67-69; asst English, Lycee Bellevue, Toulouse, France, 66-67; escortinterpreter French & Swed, US Dept State, 72-76; asst prof, 76-80, Prof French, Moorhead State Univ, 80-, Fulbright fel, 66-67; Swed Govt fel, 69-70; Nat Endowment for Humanities grants, 78 & 81; resident dir, St Cloud State Univ prog in France, 81. **HONORS AND AWARDS** Knight of the Swedish Royal Order of the Polar Star. **MEMBERSHIPS** MLA. **RESEARCH** French 18th century poetry; French 18th century opera; Jungian literary analysis. **SELECTED PUBLICATIONS** Auth, Une Demarmontelisation de Marmontel: LaNeuvaine de Marmontel et Polymnie, 83; cythere, 75. **CONTACT ADDRESS** Dept of Foreign Lang, Moorhead State Univ, 1104 7th Ave, Moorhead, MN 56563. **EMAIL** kaplan@mha1.moorhead.msus.edu

KAPLAN, JANE PAYNE
PERSONAL Born 10/03/1937, Richmond, VA, d, 1964, 2 children **DISCIPLINE** FRENCH LANGUAGE & LITERATURE, LINGUISTICS **EDUCATION** Univ NC, Chapel Hill, BA, 59; La State Univ, Baton Rouge, PhD(Romance philol), 70. **CAREER** Lectr French, Yale Univ, 64-65; instr, Southern Conn State Col, 65-67; asst prof, Quinnipiac Col, 69-70; asst prof French & ling, 71-74, from assoc Prof to Prof French, Ithaca Col, 74-83. **HONORS AND AWARDS** Danforth Associate; Fulbright, 63-64; Dana Teaching Fel for excellence in teaching, 84-85; Oracle Society, faculty inductee, 89; Sears-Roebuck Teaching Excellence & Campus Leadership Awd, 90; Chevalier dans l'Ordre des Palmes Academique, awarded by French govt. **MEMBERSHIPS** AATF; MLA. **RESEARCH** Eighteenth century literature; seventeenth century theater. **SELECTED PUBLICATIONS** Auth, Complexity of character and the overlapping of a single personality in Cocteau's Les Enfants Terribles, Australian J Fr Studies, XII: 89-104; A visual and temporal decoding of the pragmatic structure of Jaques le fataliste, Semiotica, 36: 1-25; Diderot, In: Encyclopedic Dictionary of Semiotics, 87; Food as a Structural Catalyst in Lesage's Gil Blas, Food & Foodways, vol 2, 88; The Role of the Active Listener, The French Review, Feb, 88. **CONTACT ADDRESS** Dept of Modern Lang, Ithaca Col, 953 Danby Rd, Ithaca, NY 14850-7002. **EMAIL** kaplan@ithaca.edu

KAPLAN, ROBERT B.
PERSONAL Born 09/20/1920, New York, NY, m, 1951, 3 children **DISCIPLINE** APPLIED LINGUISTICS; WRITTEN DISCOURSE ANALYSIS; LANGUAGE POLICY & PLANNING **EDUCATION** Willamette Univ, BA, 52; Univ of Southern Calif, MA, 57; PhD, 63. **CAREER** Lectr, Univ of Ore, 57-60; from instr to prof emer, 60-, dir, Am Lang Inst, 60-73, 86-92, assoc dean continuing educ, 73-76, Univ of Southern Calif. **HONORS AND AWARDS** Hon life mem, TESOL; Rita H. Small Found Grant; Hon life mem, NAFSA; Dist Fac Service Awd, Acad Senate, Univ of Southern Calif, 95; Philip C. Holland Lectureship, Wash State Univ, 97; Dist Scholar and Service Awd, Am Asn for Applied Ling, 98. **MEMBERSHIPS** Am Anthrop Asn; Am Asn for the Advan of Sci; Am Asn for Appl Ling; Am Asn of Univ Prof; Asn Int de Ling Applique; Asn of Teachers of Engl as a Second Lang; Nat Asn for For Student Affairs. **RESEARCH** Analysis of written discourse (contrastive rhetoric), language policy and planning. **SELECTED PUBLICATIONS** Coauth, Writing across languages: Analysis of L2 text, Addison Wesley, 86; coauth, Introduction to Applied Linguistics, Addison Wesley, 92; auth, "The teaching of Writing in the Pacific Basin," J of Asian Pacific Commun 6 (95); coauth, Theory and practice of Writing: An Applied linguistic

perspective, Longman, 96; coauth, Language Planning From Practice to Theory, Multilingual Matters, 97; coauth, Language planning Malawi, Mozambique, and The Philippines, Multilingual Matters, 97; coauth, Language planning in Nepal, Sweden and Taiwan, Multilingual Matters, 00; auth, Language planning Botswana, Hungary, Ivory Coast and Vanuatu, Multilingual Matters, in press. **CONTACT ADDRESS** PO Box 577, Port Angeles, WA 98362. **EMAIL** rkaplan@olypen.com

KARCH, DIETER
PERSONAL Born 11/29/1927, Ludwigshafen/Rhine, Germany, m, 1959 **DISCIPLINE** GERMANIC LINGUISTICS, GENERAL LINGUISTICS **EDUCATION** Univ of Washington, MA, 64, PhD(Ger Philol), 67. **CAREER** From instr to assoc prof Ger, 66-76, Prof Mod Lang, Univ Nebr, 76-, Woodsfac fel, Univ Marburg, 71-72; sr fac res, IDS Mannheim, 77. **MEMBERSHIPS** MLA; Am Asn Teachers Ger. **RESEARCH** Dialectology; Standard German; Colloquial German. **SELECTED PUBLICATIONS** Auth, Gimmeldingen Krs Neustadt an der Weinstrasse/Mutterstadt Krs Ludwigshafen am Rhein Phonai 13, 73, Mannheim-Umgangssprache Phonai 16, 75 & Zur Morphologie vorderpfalzischer Dialekte Phonai Beiheft 3, 75, Niemeyer, Tubingen; Siedlungspfalzisch im Kreis Waterloo, Ontario Kanada Phonai 18, 77 & Braunschweig-Veltenhof Pfalzische Sprachinsel in Ostfalischen Phonai 20, 78, Niemeyer, Tubingen; Neuburg am Rhein Eine alemannische Sprachinsel in der sudlichen Vorderpfalz, Univ Nebr, 78; Jockgrim Krs Germersheim/Niederhorbach Krs Landau-Bad Berrgzabern Niemeyer Tubingen Phonai 22, 80; Phonemidistribution Dargestellt an rheinhessischen Ortsmundarten DDG 107 I/II Elwert, Marburg. **CONTACT ADDRESS** Dept of Mod Lang & Lit, Univ of Nebraska, Lincoln, PO Box 880315, Lincoln, NE 68588-0315. **EMAIL** dkarch@unlinfo.unl.edu

KARLINSKY, SIMON
PERSONAL Born 09/22/1924, Harbin, Manchuria **DISCIPLINE** SLAVIC LANGUAGES & LITERATURES **EDUCATION** Univ Calif, Berkeley, BA, 60, PhD(Slavic), 64; Harvard Univ, MA, 61. **CAREER** Acting asst prof, 63-64, from asst prof to assoc prof, 64-67, chmn dept, 67-69, Prof Slavic Lang & Lit, Univ Calif, Berkeley, 67-, Vis assoc prof, Harvard Univ, 66; Guggenheim Mem Found fel, 69-70 & 77-78. **HONORS AND AWARDS** Woodrow Wilson Fellow, 60-61; Guggenheim Fellowship, 69-70; Guggenheim Fellowship, 78; Humanities Research Fellowship, 78. **MEMBERSHIPS** MLA; Am Asn Advan Slavic Studies; Am Asn Teachers Slavic & East Europ Lang; Philol Asn Pac Coast. **RESEARCH** Modern Russian literature; comparative literature. **SELECTED PUBLICATIONS** Auth, Marina Cvetaeva: Her Life and Art, Univ of CA Press, 66; auth, Letters of Anton Chekhov, Harper and Row, 73; auth, Anton Chekhov's Life nad Thought, Univ of CA Press, 75; auth, The Nabokov-Wilson Letters, 1940-1971, Harper and Row, 79; auth, Russian Drama from Its Beginnings to the Age of Pushkin, Univ of CA Press, 85; Marina Tsvetaeva: The Woman, Her World and Her Poetry, Cambridge Univ Press, 86. **CONTACT ADDRESS** Dept of Slavic Lang & Lit, Univ of California, Berkeley, 5416 Dwinelle Hall, Berkeley, CA 94720.

KARSEN, SONJA PETRA
PERSONAL Born 04/11/1919, Berlin, Germany **DISCIPLINE** SPANISH **EDUCATION** Carleton Col, BA, 39; Bryn Mawr Col, MA, 41; Columbia Univ, PhD, 50. **CAREER** Instr Span, Lake Erie Col, 43-45; instr mod lang, Univ PR, 45-46; instr Span, Syracuse Univ, 47-50; instr, Brooklyn Col, 50-51; personal asst to dept dir-gen, 51-52, UNESCO, Paris; Latin Am desk, prog div tech assistance dept, 52-54, mem tech assistance mission, Costa Rica, 54; asst prof mod lang, Sweet Briar Col, 55-57; assoc prof Span, 57-61, chmn dept Romance lang; 57-65, fac res lectr 63, chmn dept mod lang, 65-79, prof Span, 61-87, prof emerita, 87-, Skidmore Col; contribr ed, Bks Abroad, 65-67; Fulbright lectr, Free Univ Berlin, 68; mem, Fulbright North-East Regional Screening Comt, 70-71, chmn 71 & 74. **HONORS AND AWARDS** Chevalier, Palmes Academiques, 63; Foreign Language Leadership Awd, New York State Asn Foreign Lang Teachers, 73; Nat Distinguished Leadership Awd, NY State Asn Lang Teachers, 79; elected to Phi Sigma Iota, 79; Spanish Heritage Awd, 81; Alumni Achievement Awd, Carleton Col, 82; NY State Asn For Lang Tchrs Capitol District For Lang, Distinguished Service Awd, 87; elected hon mem, Sigma Delta Pi; International Woman of the year, 91-92, Int Biog Ctr, Cambridge Eng. **MEMBERSHIPS** MLA; Am Asn Teachers Span & Port; Nat Asn Self-Instr Lang Prog (treas, 73-77, vpres, 81-82); Am Asn Univ Women; Asn Int Hispanistas. **RESEARCH** Spanish American literature; Latin American literature and culture; translation. **SELECTED PUBLICATIONS** Auth, Guillermo Valencia, Colombian Poet 1873-1943, New York: Hispanic Institute in the United States, 51; auth, Educational Development in Costa Rica with UNESCO's Technical Assistance, 1951-1954, San Jose: Ministerio de Educacion Publica, 54; auth, Jaime Torres Bodet: A Poet in a Changing World, Saratoga Springs, NYork: Skidmore Col, 63; auth, Selected Poems of Jaime Torres Bodet, Bloominton: Indiana Univ Press, 64; auth, Versos y Prosas de Jaime Torres Bodet, Madrid: Ediciones Iberoamericanas, 66; auth, Jaime Torres Bodet, Twayne, 71; auth, Essays on Iberoamerican Literature and History, Peter Lang, 88; ed, Papers on Foreign Languages, Literature and Culture, 1982-87, New York State Association of Foreign Language Teachers, 88; transl, Leopoldo Zea, The Role of the Americas in History, Rowman and Littlefield, 92; auth, Bericht uber den Vater: Fritz Karsen (1885-1951), Overall Verlag, 93; **CONTACT ADDRESS** 1755 York Ave, Apt 37A, New York, NY 10128-6875.

KARTTUNEN, FRANCES
PERSONAL Born 04/16/1942, Boston, MA, m, 1983, 2 children **DISCIPLINE** LINGUISTICS **EDUCATION** Radcliffe Col/Harvard Univ, AB, 64; Ind Univ, MA, 68, PhD, 70. **CAREER** Sr Univ Res Scientist, Univ Tex, 78-. **RESEARCH** Language contact and language change; the social dimensions of language and culture contact; language learning in children and adults; descriptive linguistics; non-Indo-European languages, especially Mesoamerican and Finno-Ugric languages. **SELECTED PUBLICATIONS** Auth, Between Worlds: Interpreters, Guides, and Survivors, Rutgers Univ Press, 94; coauth, Language Death, Language Genesis, and World History, J World Hist 95; auth, Rethinking Malinche, Indian Women of Early Mexico, Univ Okla Press, 97; Raising the Alarm for Endangered Languages, Univ Helsinki Quart, 97; What I Might Have Been: Ella Simon (1902-1981), Arvot, analyysi, tulkinta [studies in honor of Professor Seikko Eskola], Finnish Hist Soc, 97; Indigenous Writing as a Vehicle of Postconquest Continuity and Change in Mesoamerica, Native Traditions in the Postonquest World, Dumbarton Oaks, 98. **CONTACT ADDRESS** Univ of Texas, Austin, Linguistics Res Ctr, Austin, TX 78712. **EMAIL** fkarttunen@mail.utexas.edu

KASKE, CAROL VONCKX
PERSONAL Born 02/05/1933, Elgin, IL, w, 1958, 1 child **DISCIPLINE** ENGLISH & COMPARATIVE LITERATURE **EDUCATION** Wash Univ, AB, 54; Smith Col, MA, 55; Johns Hopkins Univ, PhD(English), 64. **CAREER** Instr English, Duke Univ, 59-60, Women's Col, Univ NC, 61 & Univ Ill, Urbana, 61-64; from lectr to sr lectr, 64-73, asst prof English, Cornell Univ, 73-; from assoc prof to prof English, Cornell, 85-92. **HONORS AND AWARDS** Am Philos Soc grant-in-aid, 75, 86; Am Coun Learned Soc travel grant, 79, 86. **MEMBERSHIPS** MLA; Renaissance Soc Am; Spenser Soc; Int Assn Neo-Latin Studies; AAUP; Medieval Academy of Am; Int Asn of Univ Profs of English. **RESEARCH** Renaissance literature; theology; Edmund Spenser. **SELECTED PUBLICATIONS** Auth, The dragon's spark and sting and the structure of Red Cross's dragon fight, Studies Philol, 69; Mount Sinai and Dante's Mount Purgatory, Dante Studies, 71; contribr, Spenser's Pluralistic Universe, In: Contemporary Thought on Spenser, Univ Southern Ill, 75; Getting around the Parson's Tale, In: Chaucer at Albany, Burt Franklin, 75; auth, The Bacchus who wouldn't wash, Renaissance Quart, 76; Spenser's Amoretti and Epithalamion of 1595, English Lit Renaissance, 78; Religious Reverence doth Buriall Teene, Rev English Studies, 79; Auth, with John R Clark: Marsilio Ficino, Three Books on Life, a Critical Edition and Translation with Introduction and Notes, Binghamton, NY: Medieval and Renaissance Texts and Studies, 89; contribr, "How Spenser Really Used Stephen Hawes in the Legend of Holiness," in Unfolded Tales, ed. George Logan and Gordon Teskey (Ithaca: Cornell Univ Pr, 89), 119-136; auth, "The Audiences of the Faerie Queene: Iconoclasm and Related Issues in Books I, V, and VI," Lit and Hist 3 (94); auth, Spenser and biblical Poetics, Cornell Univ Pr (Ithaca, NYork), 99. **CONTACT ADDRESS** Dept of English, Cornell Univ, 250 Goldwin Smith Hall, Ithaca, NY 14853-0001. **EMAIL** cvk2@cornell.edu

KASTAN, DAVID SCOTT
PERSONAL Born 01/04/1946, New York, NY, m, 1983, 1 child **DISCIPLINE** ENGLISH AND COMPARATIVE LITERATURE **EDUCATION** Princeton Univ, AB, 67; Univ Chicago, MA, 68 PhD, 74. **CAREER** Instr, Dartmouth Col, 73; prof, Columbia Univ, 87. **HONORS AND AWARDS** Gen ed, Arden Shakespeare; distinguished vis prof, Univ of Copenhagen, 98; distinguished vis prof, American Univ Cairo, 94. **SELECTED PUBLICATIONS** Auth, essays on Shakespeare and Renaissance lit, Daedalus, ELH, Renaissance Drama, Shakespeare Quarty, Shakespeare Stud, Stud in Philol; auth, Shakespeare and the Shapes of Time, 82; co-ed, Staging the Renaissance: Essays on Elizabethan and Jacobean Drama, 91; ed, Critical Essays on Shakespeare's Hamlet, 95; New History of Early English Drama, 97; A Companion to Shakespeare, 99; Shakespeare After Theory, 99. **CONTACT ADDRESS** Dept of Eng, Columbia Col, New York, 2960 Broadway, New York, NY 10027-6902. **EMAIL** dsk1@columbia.edu

KASTER, ROBERT A.
PERSONAL Born 02/06/1948, New York, NY, m, 1969, 2 children **DISCIPLINE** LATIN LANGUGE AND LITERATURE. **EDUCATION** Dartmouth Coll, AB, 69; Harvard Univ, MA, 71; PhD, 75. **CAREER** Harvard Univ: Tchg Fel, 72-73; Instr, Colby Col, 73-74; asst prof, 75-82, assoc prof, 82-89, prof, 89-97 Univ Chicago; prof, Princeton Univ; 97- **HONORS AND AWARDS** Nat Endowment Hum Fel, 80-81; John Simon Guggenheim Memorial Found Fel, 91-92; Charles J. Goodwin Awd of Merit, 91; Kennedy Found Prof of Latin, 97-; pres, am philol asn, 96; avalon found distinguished service prof, 96-97. **MEMBERSHIPS** Am Philol Asn; Asn Ancient Historians; Women's Class Caucus. **RESEARCH** Latin literature; Roman culture. **SELECTED PUBLICATIONS** Auth, Guardians of Language: The Grammarian and Society in Late Antiquity, TheTransformation of the Classical Heritage, /vik 11, Berkeley-Univ Calif Press, 88; Studies on the Text of Suetonius De Grammaticis et Rhetoribus, The American Philological Association: American Classical Studies, Scholars Press, 92; Suetonius: De Grammaticis et Rhetoribus, Clarendon Press, 95. **CONTACT ADDRESS** Dept of Classics, Princeton Univ, 104 East Pyne, Princeton, NJ 08544. **EMAIL** kaster@princeton.edu

KATARZYNA, OLGA B.
DISCIPLINE SPANISH **EDUCATION** Univ Warsaw, MA, 90; Univ Chicago, PhD, 98. **CAREER** Vis asst prof, Williams Col, 98-99. **HONORS AND AWARDS** Univ Warsaw Merit fel, 87-90; Nat Jour Students' Awd, 85. **RESEARCH** Contemporary Spanish Literature and Culture; Romanticism in Europe and Latin America; 19th and 20th Century Hispanic Literature; Medieval Spanish Literature and History; Spanish Language and Culture. **SELECTED PUBLICATIONS** Auth, Indifference and Catastrophe: Spanish Short Story on the Threshold of the 21st Century, XXII Congreso de Letras Hispanicas, 96. **CONTACT ADDRESS** Center for Foreign Languages, Literatures and Cult, Williams Col, Williamstown, MA 01267. **EMAIL** Katarzyna.O.Beilin@williams.edu

KATH, RUTH R.
PERSONAL Born 04/17/1948, New Britain, CN, s, 2 children **DISCIPLINE** GERMAN **EDUCATION** Syracuse Univ, BA; Univ Conn, MA; Univ Iowa, PhD, MA Lores College Theology. **CAREER** Prof, Luther Col, 79-; listed in, World's Who's Who of Women, Who's Who Among Amer Women, Who's Who in the Midwest; 1969 and 1970, instr, Lindau Sailing Sch, Ger, 69 & 70; Fulbright sr awd, 85; Coordinator for Prayer Services, International Ecumenical Seminar, Strasbourg, France, 00. **HONORS AND AWARDS** Oral Proficiency Testing Workshop--German scholar, Iowa Dept Edu, 86; 1988-1991, charter member, Iowa Governor's Commn on For Lang & Int Edu; pres, Iowa Chap, 83-85; proj, monuments to jewish tradition in berlin, e ger, 90; co-founded, distinguished ecumenical lect ser, 93. **MEMBERSHIPS** Delta Phi Alpha, Nat Ger Honorary Soc, 70-; Amer Asn Tchr(s) Ger, 75-; Iowa For Lang Asn, 74-. **RESEARCH** Ecumenical Dialogues, esp. Roman Catholic-Lutheran Joint Declaration on the Doctrine of Justification. **SELECTED PUBLICATIONS** Auth, The Correspondence of Gerhard Marcks and Marguerite Mildenhain, 1970-1981:A Mingling of Souls, Iowa State Univ Press & Luther Col Press, 91; Children in the Poetry of Bertolt Brecht:Images of Young People and Examples for Youthful Audiences, Bern Switzerland, Peter Lang Verlag, 82. **CONTACT ADDRESS** Dept of Modern Languages, Luther Col, 700 College Dr, Decorah, IA 52101. **EMAIL** kathruth@luther.edu

KATRITZKY, LINDE
PERSONAL Born 07/28/1928, Ansbach, Germany, m, 1952, 4 children **DISCIPLINE** GERMAN **EDUCATION** Univ of Munich, Staatsexamen in Hist, German and English, 47-52; Univ FL, MA, 82-84, PhD, 84-88. **CAREER** Graduat Teaching Asst, 82-84, Lectr, 84-88, Adjunct Assoc Prof, 88-94, Adjunct Prof, 95-present, Univ FL. **MEMBERSHIPS** Honor Soc of Phi Kappa Phi; Lichtenberg-Gesellschaft; Howe Soc of the Univ FL; President's Council, Univ FL (distinguished member); Soc for German-Amer Studies; MLA (Modern Language Assn); Amer Soc for Eighteen-Century Studies; Amer Assn of Teachers of German Studies; E.T.A. Hoffmann Gesellschaft; Mid Western Section ASECS; South Eastern Section of ASECS. **RESEARCH** German and English eighteeth-century culture; literature and science; Samuel Johnson, The Letters of Junius; Georg Christoph Lichtenberg; Nachtwachen. Von Bonaventura. **SELECTED PUBLICATIONS** Lichtenbergs Gedankensystem: Denkanleitung fur Jedermann, The Enlightenment, German Interdisciplinary Studies, 95; Johnson and The Letters of Junius: New Perspectives on an Old Enigma, Ars Interpretandi/The Art, 96; A Guide to Bonaventura's Nightwatches, auth, Ars Interpretandi/the Art, Peter Lang, 99. **CONTACT ADDRESS** Dept Germanic & Slavic Studies, Univ of Florida, Gainesville, FL 32601.

KATZ, MARILYN A.
DISCIPLINE CLASSICAL LANGUAGES **EDUCATION** Columbia Univ, BA, 66, Yale Univ, MA, 68, PhD, 75. **CAREER** Trinity Col, Hartford, CT, 66; Lectr Trinity Col, Hartford, CT, 67, 68; Vis Instr, Wesleyan Univ, Middletown, CT, 70-71; Tchng Intern, Brooklyn Col, CUNY, 72-73, P/T Instr; 73-75, F/T Instr; 75, Instr, Sarah Lawrence Col, 75, 76; Vis Instr, Columbia Col, Columbia Univ, 75-77; Asst Prof; 76, 77, Asst Prof, Vis Lectr, Yale Col, Guest Fel, Morse Col, 80, Wesleyan Univ, Asst Prof, 78-83; Assoc Prof, 83-90; Prof 90-. **HONORS AND AWARDS** Yale Univ fel, 68; Mary Cady Tew Profize, 68; Samuel K. Bushnell Fel, 69-70; Elizabeth & A. Varvick Stout Fel, 71-72; Biddle Travel Sch, 73; Mem, Sch Hist, Studies, Inst Adv Study, 77-78; ACLS Fel Recent Ph.D.'s, 78; Nat Endowment Hum, 79, 80, 89, 90-91; Fac fel, Ctr Hum, 82; Elected mem, Am Philol Asn, 84-87, 87-90; Nat Endowment Hum, 87; Chair, Am Philol Asn, 89-90; Guggenheim Found, 93. **MEMBERSHIPS** Am Philological Asn, 67; Women's Classical Caucus, 72; Columbia Univ Seminar on

Women and Society, 74; Am Asn Univ Prof, 79; Mod Lang Asn, 79, Columbia Univ Sem Clas Civilization, 83; Gardiner Seminar, 86; Soc Biblical Lit, 86; Yale Univ Judaic Studies Fac Seminar, 86. **SELECTED PUBLICATIONS** Sexuality and the Body in Ancient Greece, Metis. Revue d'anthropologie du monde grec ancient 4.1, 89, 155 - 79; Profoblems Sacrifice in Ancient Cultures, In The Bible in the Light Cuneiform Literature. Scripture in Context III, Edwin Mellen Profess, 90; Patriarchy and Inheritance in Greek and Biblical Antiquity: The Epiclerate and the Levirate. Profoceedings the Xth World Congress Jewish Studies, Magnes Profess, 90; Penelope's Renown: Meaning and Indeterminacy in Homer's Odyssey. Profinceton, New Jersey: Profinceton Univ Profess, 91; Review Suzanne Dixon, The Roman Mother, New England Clas Newsl & Jour 17, 90; Review Robert Garland, The Greek Way Life, The Classical Outlook 69, 91-92; Bouphonia and Goring Ox: Homicide, Animal Sacrifice, and Judicial Profocess, invited contribution to refereed volume, Nomodeiktes: Greek Studies in Honor Martin Ostwald, Univ Mich Profess, 92; Did the Greeks Believe in Their Myths? An Essay on the Constitutive Imagination History and Theory 31, 92; Ox Slaughter and Goring Oxen: Homicide, Animal Sacrifice, and Judicial Profocess, Yale Jour Law & Hum, 92; Politics and Pomegranates, in Essays on the Homeric Hymn to Demeter, Profinceton Univ Profess, 93; Ideology and 'the Status Women' in Ancient Greece, History and Theory Beiheft 31: History and Feminist Theory, 92; Homecoming and Hospitality: Recognition and the Construction Identity in the Odyssey,' in Epic and Epoch, Texas Tech Univ Pess, 94; The Character Tragedy: Women and the Greek Imagination, Arethusa 27.1, 94; Ideology and 'the Status Women' in Ancient Greece, in Feminists Revision History, Rutgers Univ Profess, 93; Ideology and 'the Status Women' in Ancient Greece, in Women in Antiquity: New Assessments, Routledge, 95. **CONTACT ADDRESS** Wesleyan Univ, Middletown, CT 06459. **EMAIL** mkatz@wesleyan.edu

KATZ, MICHAEL RAY
PERSONAL Born 12/09/1944, New York, NY **DISCIPLINE** RUSSIAN LANGUAGE AND LITERATURE **EDUCATION** Williams Col, BA, 66; Oxford Univ, BA, MA and DPhil(Russ), 72. **CAREER** Asst prof, 72-78, chmn prog comp lit, 77-78, Assoc Prof Russ, Williams Col, 78-, Chmn Dept Ger and Russ, 80-, Vis scholar, Univ Calif, Berkeley, 75-76. **MEMBERSHIPS** Am Asn Advan Slavic Studies; Am Asn Teachers Slavic and E Europ Lang. **RESEARCH** Russian romantic poetry; dreams in Russian fiction; Russian intellectual history. **SELECTED PUBLICATIONS** Auth, The Literary Ballad in Early Nineteenth Century Russian Literature, Oxford Univ, 76. **CONTACT ADDRESS** Dept of Russ, Univ of Texas, Arlington, Arlington, TX 76019.

KATZ, PHYLLIS
PERSONAL Born 05/23/1936, New Haven, CT, 4 children **DISCIPLINE** CLASSICS **EDUCATION** Wellesley Col, BA, 58; Univ Calif, Los Angeles, MA, 63; Columbia Univ, phD, 69. **CAREER** Lectr, Mount St Mary's Col, 62-63; Lectr, Barnard Col, 65- 66; asst prof, 69, instr, 68-69, Univ Ill; instr, CUNY, City College NY, 71-72; vis asst prof, Col New Rochelle, 74; lectr, 76, vis asst prof, 74-75; SUNY, Purchase; teach, 77-83, Miss Porter's Sch; lectr, fac mem, Class Asn New Eng, Summer Inst, summers 87-97; vis lectr, Univ Mass, 93; vis lectr, Wesleyan Univ, Grad Lib Stud Prog, 92; vis scholar, vis lectr, sen lectr, DARTMOUTH COL, 90-. **HONORS AND AWARDS** Barlow-Beach Awd, Classical Assoc of New England, 97; National Endowment for the Humanities; Reader's Digest Teacher Scholar, 90-91; National Endowment for the Humanities Faculty Adviser, Younger Scholar Awd, Summer 89; National Endowment for the Humanities Council for Basic Education Fellowship for Independent Study in the Humanities Summer 88; Miss Porter's School, Craven Summer Sabbatical, Columbia University, Summer 87; Columbia University, Woodbridge Honorary Fellowship, 65. **MEMBERSHIPS** Am Philogical Assoc, 86-; Am Classical League, 85-; Vergilian Society, 85-, Trustee, 97-00; Classical Assoc of New England, 83-, Pres, 89, Exec.Sec., 98-03; Women's Classical Caucus, 66-; Am Institute of Archaeology, 65-. **RESEARCH** Women in Antiquity: coming of age rituals of young girls, portrayals of girls and women in Greek poetry and on Attic and Corinthian pottery, literary and artistic depictions of gender and the body; women's voices in ancient and modern poetry. **SELECTED PUBLICATIONS** Auth, Hill-Stead 46.1.95: A Lost Work of the Painter of Athens, 931, BABESCH, No. 72, 97-1-20; auth, Io in the Prometheus Bound: A Coming of Age Paradigm for the Athenian Community, in Rites of Passage in Ancient Greece: Literature, Religion, Society, The Bucknell Review, 99, (Vol. XLIII, Number 1), 129-147; Selections from Ovid: Amores, Metamorphoses, with Charbra A. Jestin, 2nd Edition, Summber 00, Bolchazy-Carducci Press. **CONTACT ADDRESS** Dept of Classics, Dartmouth Col, HB 6086, Reed Hall, PO Box 1048, Hanover, NH 03755. **EMAIL** phyllis.b.katz@dartmouth.edu

KAUFFMAN, JANET
DISCIPLINE VISUAL AND MIXED TEXTS **EDUCATION** PhD. **CAREER** E Mich Univ **SELECTED PUBLICATIONS** Auth, Award The Weather Book, Tex Tech Univ Press, 81; World a Woman Could Walk, Knopf, 83; Collaborators, Knopf, 86; Where the World Is, Montparnasse Press, 88; Obscene Gestures for Women, Knopf, 89; The Body in Four Parts, Graywolf, 94; Characters on the Loose, Graywolf, 97. **CONTACT ADDRESS** Eastern Michigan Univ, Ypsilanti, MI 48197.

KAUFFMANN, RUTH A.
PERSONAL Born 02/12/1957, IL, m, 1982, 2 children **DISCIPLINE** LITERATURE, LANGUAGE, SPANISH **EDUCATION** Goshen Col, BA, 79; Univ Ill Chicago, MEd, 83; MA, 90; Univ Chicago, PhD, 94. **CAREER** Asst prof, Rockford Col, 93-96; assoc prof, William Jewell Col, 97-. **HONORS AND AWARDS** Teaching of Year Awd, 99; Distinguished Christ Edu Prof, Pkwy Bap, 01. **MEMBERSHIPS** FLA; MLA; AATSP. **RESEARCH** San Juan de la Cruz; service learning for tolerance; Chicano literature; San Juana Ine's de la Cruz. **CONTACT ADDRESS** Dept Lang, William Jewell Col, 500 College Hill, Liberty, MO 64068-1843. **EMAIL** kauffmannr@william.jewell.edu

KAUFMAN, STEPHEN ALLAN
PERSONAL Born 09/11/1945, Minneapolis, MN, m, 1972, 2 children **DISCIPLINE** ANCIENT NEAR EASTERN LANGUAGES, OLD TESTAMENT **EDUCATION** Univ Minn, BA, 62; Yale Univ, PhD(Near Eastern lang and lit), 70. **CAREER** Asst prof North-West semitics, Univ Chicago, 71-76; assoc prof, 76-81, Prof Bible and Cognate Lit, Hebrew Union Col, 81-, Vis sr lectr, Haifa Univ, Israel, 74-76; Ed, Soc Bibl Lit, Aramaic Series, 79- **MEMBERSHIPS** Am Oriental Soc; Soc Bibl Lit. **RESEARCH** Aramaic studies; humanities micro computing. **SELECTED PUBLICATIONS** The Causative Stem in Ugartic and the Causative Form in Semitic--A Morphologic-Semantic Analysis of the S-Stem and Disputed Non-Sibilant Causative Stems in Ugartic, J Am Oriental Soc, Vol 113, 93; Old Aramaic Grammar of Texts from 7th-8th Century BC, J Am Oriental Soc, Vol 115, 95; A Scholars; Dictionary of Jewish Palestinian Aramaic--An Article Rev of Sokoloff, Michael Dictionary, J Am Oriental Soc, Vol 114, 94; The Dead Sea Scrolls on Microfiche--A Comprehensive Facsimile Edition of the Texts from the Judean Desert, Vol 3, Inventory List of Photographs, J Am Oriental Soc, Vol 116, 96; The Function of the Niphal in Biblical Hebrew in Relationship to Other Passive-Reflexive Verbal-Systems and to the Pual and Hophal in Particular--Siebesma,Pa, Cath Bibl Quart, Vol 56, 94; Living Waters--Scandinavian orientalistic Studies Presented to Lokkegaard,Frede on His 75th Birthday, January 27th, 1990, J Am Oriental Soc, Vol 113, 93; The Dead-Sea-Scrolls on Microfiche--A Comprehensive Facsimile Edition of the Texts from the Judean Desert, Vol 2, Companion Volume, J Am Oriental Soc, Vol 116, 96; The Dead-Sea-Scrolls Catalog--Documents, Photographs, and Museum Inventory Numbers, J Am Oriental Soc, Vol 116, 96. **CONTACT ADDRESS** Dept Bible and Cognate Lit, Hebrew Union Col-Jewish Inst of Religion, Ohio, Cincinnati, OH 45220.

KAUFMAN, TERRENCE SCOTT
PERSONAL Born 06/12/1937, Portland, OR, d, 1 child **DISCIPLINE** ANTHROPOLOGY; LINGUISTICS **EDUCATION** Univ Chicago, AB, 59; Univ Calif, Berkeley, PhD(ling), 63. **CAREER** Asst prof ling, Ohio State Univ, 63-64; asst prof, Univ Calif, Berkeley, 64-70; Assoc Prof Anthrop, Univ Pitts, 71-80, Tech dir ling, Francisco Marroquin ling proj, Antigua, Guatemala, 71-79; prof, Anthrop, Univ Pitts, 80- . **MEMBERSHIPS** Ling Soc Am. **RESEARCH** Mayan synchronic and diachronic linguistics; comparative and historical linguistic method and theory; Romani linguistics. **SELECTED PUBLICATIONS** Auth, Teco: A new Mayan language, Int J Am Ling, 69; Tzeltal Phonology and Morphology, Univ Calif, 69; El proto Tzeltal-Tzotzil, Nat Univ Mex, 72; Areal linguistics and Middle America, In: Current Trends in Linguistics, Mouton, The Hague, 73; auth, A Decipherment of epi-Olmec Hieroglyphic Writing, Science, 93. **CONTACT ADDRESS** Dept of Anthrop, Univ of Pittsburgh, 3H01 WWPH, Pittsburgh, PA 15260. **EMAIL** topkat@pitt.edu

KAULBACH, ERNEST NORMAN
PERSONAL Born 01/03/1935, Bridgeport, CT, m, 1970, 2 children **DISCIPLINE** MEDIEVAL STUDIES AND PHILOSOPHY **EDUCATION** St Mary's Univ, AB, 57, STL, 61; Fairfield Univ, MA, 61; Cornell Univ, PhD(medieval studies), 70. **CAREER** Instr English, St Joseph's Col, 61-62; instr English and theol, St Mary's Col, 63-66; vis assoc prof English, classics and philos, 70-73, Assoc Prof English and Classics, Univ Tex, Austin, 73- **MEMBERSHIPS** Mediaeval Acad Am; Dante Soc Am. **RESEARCH** Medieval philosophy, literature and theology. **SELECTED PUBLICATIONS** Auth, Inferno XIX, 45: The Zanca of temporal power, Dante Studies, 68; Piers Plowman B IX, 18, 52: Further refinements of Inwit, In: Festschrift for A A Hill, 73. **CONTACT ADDRESS** Dept of English, Univ of Texas, Austin, 0 Univ of Texas, Austin, TX 78712-1026.

KAYE, ALAN STEWART
PERSONAL Born 03/02/1944, Los Angeles, CA, d, 2 children **DISCIPLINE** LINGUISTICS, NEAR EASTERN STUDIES **EDUCATION** Univ Calif, Los Angeles, BA, 65; Univ Calif, Berkeley, MA, 68, PhD(ling), 71. **CAREER** Asst prof, Univ Colo, 69-71; asst prof, 71-74, assoc prof and chmn ling, 74-78, Prof and Dir, Lab Phonetic Res, Calif State Univ, Fullerton, 78-, Nat Endowment Humanities grant, 73-74; Am Philos Soc grant, 73-74 and 75-76; Fulbright res grant, 78-79; instr, Pepperdine Univ, 74-76; Consult, Rockwell Int, 76-; Instr, Univ Calif, Irvine, 77- **MEMBERSHIPS** Am Orient Soc; Ling Soc Am; Am Assoc of Teachers of Arabic. **RESEARCH** Arabic dialectology; Semitic linguistics; field linguistics (Africa, S Asia). **SELECTED PUBLICATIONS** Auth, Modern standard Arabic and the colloquials, Lingua, 71; Arabic/ziim/: A synchronic and diachronic study, Ling, 72; Towards a generative phonology of Arabic, Int J Mid East Studies, 74; More on diglossia in Arabic, Int J Mid-East Studies, 75 Nigerian Arabic and diachronic linguistics, In: From Meaning to Sound, Univ Nebr, 75; Chadian and sudanese Arabic, Mouton, 76; The Hebrew grammarians and the history of linguistics, In: Festschrift for Robert A Hall Jr, 77; More on Moolah, Am Speech, 81; Spinoza as linguist, Hebrew Ann Rev, 81; A Dict of Nigerian Arabic, Undena, 82. **CONTACT ADDRESS** Ling Prog, California State Univ, Fullerton, 800 N State College Blvd, Fullerton, CA 92834. **EMAIL** akays@exchange.fullerton.edu

KAZAZIS, KOSTAS
PERSONAL Born 07/15/1934, Athens, Greece, m, 1958, 2 children **DISCIPLINE** BALKAN LINGUISTICS **EDUCATION** Univ Lausanne, Lic es Sci Polit, 57; Univ Kans, MA, 59; Ind Univ, PhD(ling), 65. **CAREER** Instr ling, Univ Ill, Urbana, 64-65; from asst prof to assoc prof, 65-77, Prof Ling, Univ Chicago, 77-, NDEA grant, 67-68. **MEMBERSHIPS** Ling Soc Am; Mod Greek Studies Asn; Soc Romanian Studies; Soc Albanian LStudies; Am Asn Southeast Europ Studies. **RESEARCH** Languages in contact; bilingualism; sociolinguistics. **SELECTED PUBLICATIONS** coauth, Reference Grammar of Literary Dhimotiki, Mouton, The Hague, 64; auth, On a Generative Grammar of the Balkan Languages, Found Lang, 67; Sunday Greek, Papers 4th Regional Meeting Chicago Ling Soc, 68; The status of turkisms in the present day Balkan languages, Aspects of Balkans, 72; On some aspects of linguistic hellenocentrism, Proc 11th Int Cong Ling, 75; coauth, Reduplication of indefinite direct objects in Albanian and modern Greek, Lang, 76; Learnedisms in Costas Taktsis's Third Wedding, Byzantine & Mod Greek Studies, 79; On Modern Greek poi-, Who?, In: Papers from the Parasession on Pronouns and Anaphora, Chicago Ling Soc, 80. **CONTACT ADDRESS** Dept of Ling, Univ of Chicago, 1010 E 59th St, Chicago, IL 60637-1512.

KE, C. R.
PERSONAL Born 09/23/1954, China, m, 1982, 1 child **DISCIPLINE** LINGUISTICS **EDUCATION** Indiana Univ Bloom, PhD 92. **CAREER** Univ Iowa, asst prof, Chinese lang co-or, 93-. **MEMBERSHIPS** AAAL; ACTFL; CLTA **RESEARCH** Second language acquisition; Chinese language and pedagogy; Experimental psycholinguistics; language assessment; curriculum and teacher development. **SELECTED PUBLICATIONS** Auth, Effects of strategies on the learning of Chinese characters among foreign language students, Jour of the Chin Lang Teach Assoc, 98; Effects of language background on the learning of Chinese characters among foreign language students, Foreign Lang Annals, 98; An Inquiry into the Reading Strategies of Intermediate and Advanced Learners of Chinese as a Foreign Language, coauth, Jour of the CLTA, 97; An empirical study on the relationship between Chinese character recognition and production, Modern Lang Jour, 96; A Gating Experiment with Chinese, Lang Teach and Ling Stud, 95; Aspects of Accuracy in a Proficiency-Oriented Program, ADFL Bulletin, 95. **CONTACT ADDRESS** Dept of Asian Languages and Literature, The Univ of Iowa, 659 Phillips Hall, Iowa City, IA 52242. **EMAIL** chuanren-ke@uiowa.edu

KEANEY, JOHN J.
DISCIPLINE CLASSICS **EDUCATION** Boston Coll, AB, 53; Harvard Univ, PhD, 59. **CAREER** Prof, Princeton Univ. **RESEARCH** Greek paleography and lexicography; Greek political theory. **SELECTED PUBLICATIONS** Auth, The Composition of Aristotle's Athenaion Politeia; ed, Harpocration: Lexeis of the Ten Orators; Contributing ed, Theophrastus of Eresus: Sources for his Life, Writings, Thought, and Influence. **CONTACT ADDRESS** Princeton Univ, 103 E Pyme, Princeton, NJ 08544.

KECK, CHRISTIANE ELISABETH
PERSONAL Born 07/19/1940, Jena, Germany, m, 1990 **DISCIPLINE** GERMANIC LANGUAGES & LITERATURE **EDUCATION** Col New Rochelle, AB, 61; Columbia Univ, MA, 62; Univ Tex, Austin, PhD(Ger), 66. **CAREER** Prof Ger and Head, Dept For Lang and Lit, Purdue Univ, West Lafayette, 92-; Assoc Dir, Ctr for Int Bus Educ and Res, 92-. **HONORS AND AWARDS** Amoco Awd for Outstanding Univ Teaching, 84; Federal Cross of Merit, Ger, 89; Goethe Medaille, 92; Ind Ger Teacher of the Year, 98. **MEMBERSHIPS** MLA; Am Asn Teachers Ger; Am Comp Lit Asn; ADFL; ACTFL. **RESEARCH** Italian Renaissance as an influence on German literature; 19th century German drama and novelle; the European historical novel; business German; women in literature. **SELECTED PUBLICATIONS** Auth, Renaissance and Romanticism: Tieck's Conception of Cultural Decline as Portrayed in his Vittoria Accorombona, In: Ser, German Studies in America, Vol 20, 76; Handbook on Business German; ed, Global Business Languages. **CONTACT ADDRESS** Dept of Foreign Lang & Lit, Purdue Univ, West Lafayette, West Lafayette, IN 47907-4359. **EMAIL** ckeck@purdue.edu

KEEL, WILLIAM D.
DISCIPLINE GERMAN DIALECTOLOGY, GERMANIC PHILOLOGY **EDUCATION** IN Univ, PhD, 77. **CAREER** Instr, Inst fur deutsche sprache, Mannheim; prof; ch, 90-. **HONORS AND AWARDS** Ger-Am collab res grants, Am Coun Learned Soc(s); Ger Acad Exchange Serv, (DAAD); ed, yrbk of ger-am stud, 86; exec comm, soc ger-am stud; exec comm ks assn of tchr(s) ger, 94-97. **MEMBERSHIPS** Mem, Speakers' Bureau Kans Hum Coun. **RESEARCH** Volga Ger settlements and dialects in KS. **SELECTED PUBLICATIONS** Co-ed, German Emigration from Bukovina to the Americas, Univ Munch, 96; auth, articles treating Hannoverian Low German, German-Bohemian and Mennonite Low German dialects in KS and Mo as well as the settlement history of Pa Germans in KS. **CONTACT ADDRESS** Dept of Ger Lang and Lit, Univ of Kansas, Lawrence, Admin Building, Lawrence, KS 66045. **EMAIL** wkeel@falcon.cc.ukans.edu

KEELE, ALAN F.
PERSONAL Born 11/17/1942, Provo, UT, m, 1966, 6 children **DISCIPLINE** GERMAN LANGUAGE AND LITERATURES **EDUCATION** Brigham Young Univ, BA, 67; Princeton Univ, PhD, 71. **CAREER** Prof Ger, assoc dean honors & gen educ, dept chr, 92-98, Brigham Young Univ, 71- . **HONORS AND AWARDS** NOEA fel, Princeton Univ, 68-71. **MEMBERSHIPS** Mod Lang Asn; Rocky Mtn Mod Lang Asn. **RESEARCH** Gunter Grass, Postwar German literature, Rainer Marie Ritke, Resistance to Nazis. **SELECTED PUBLICATIONS** Auth, The Apocalyptic Vision: A Thematic Approach to D. W. German Lit, Studia humanitatis, (83); auth, Understanding Gunter Frass, Univ S. Carolina Press, (89); auth, When Truth was Treason: Teens Against Hitler, Univ Ill Press, (96). **CONTACT ADDRESS** Dept Ger & Slavic Lang, Brigham Young Univ, 4082 JKHB, Provo, UT 84602. **EMAIL** Alan_keele@byu.edu

KEENAN, J. G.
PERSONAL Born 01/19/1944, New York, NY, m, 2000 **DISCIPLINE** CLASSICS **EDUCATION** Col of the Holy Cross, AB 65; Yale Univ, MA 66, PhD 68. **CAREER** Univ Cal Berk, asst prof 68-73; Loyola Univ, assoc to full prof 74 to 98-. **HONORS AND AWARDS** NEH **MEMBERSHIPS** ASP; AIP; APA; ARCE; CAMWS **RESEARCH** Papyrology, ancient, social, economic and legal history; Byzantine and medieval Egypt. **SELECTED PUBLICATIONS** Auth, Egypt A.D. 425-600, Cambridge Ancient History, forthcoming; Review of Stanley Burstein, Ancient African Kingdoms, and Derek A. Welsby, The Kingdom of Kush, for The Classical Bull, forthcoming; Review of David Tandy, Warriors into Traders: The power of the Market in Early Greece, for Classical Bull, forthcoming; More From the Archive of the Descendents of Eulogius, with Todd Hickey, Analecta Papyrologica, 98; Gilgamesh: An Appreciation, in: Danny P. Jackson, trans, The Epic of Gilgamesh, rev ed, Bolchazy Carducci Pub, Wauconda Il, 97; George Sphrantzes: A Brief Review, The Ancient World, 96; The Aphrodito Murder Mystery: A Return to the Scene of the Crimes, BASP, 95; The Will of Gaius Longinus Castor, BASP, 94. **CONTACT ADDRESS** Dept of Classic Studies, Loyola Univ, Chicago, 6525 N Sheridan Rd, Chicago, IL 60626. **EMAIL** jkeenan@orion.it.luc.edu

KEENER, FREDERICK M.
PERSONAL Born 12/28/1937, New York, NY, m, 1961, 2 children **DISCIPLINE** ENGLISH, COMPARATIVE LITERATURE **EDUCATION** St John's Univ, NYork, AB, 59; Columbia Univ, MA, 60, PhD(English), 65. **CAREER** From instr to asst prof English, St John's Univ, NY, 61-66; from asst prof to assoc prof, Columbia Univ, 66-72, dean summer session, 72-74; from assoc prof to prof, 74-78; Prof English, Hofstra Univ, 78-, Lectr, Hunter Col, 66; Nat Endowment for Humanities res fel, 76-77; vis prof, Columbia Univ, 81. **MEMBERSHIPS** MLA; Conf Brit Studies; Am Soc 18th Century Studies. **RESEARCH** Eighteenth century British literature; 18th century comparative literature. **SELECTED PUBLICATIONS** Critical Essays on Pope, Alexander, Scriblerian and the Kit-Cats, Vol 27, 95. **CONTACT ADDRESS** Dept of English, Hofstra Univ, 1000 Fulton Ave, Hempstead, NY 11550-1091.

KEFFER, CHARLES K., JR.
DISCIPLINE FRENCH LANGUAGE AND LITERATURE **EDUCATION** Univ NC Wilmington, BA; Univ NC Chapel Hill, MA and PhD. **CAREER** Fac, 79-; prof. **HONORS AND AWARDS** Rookie of Yr Awd, Centre Col; David Hughes Mem Awd Excel Tchg, Centre Col, 88; dir res study-abroad prog, centre col;fulbright exch tchr, ger. **RESEARCH** French language and literature. **SELECTED PUBLICATIONS** Auth, scholarly articles on Michel de Montaigne. **CONTACT ADDRESS** Centre Col, 600 W Walnut St, Danville, KY 40422. **EMAIL** keffer@centre.edu

KELLER, GARY D.
PERSONAL Born 01/01/1943, San Diego, CA, m, 1967, 1 child **DISCIPLINE** SPANISH-ENGLISH BILINGUALISM, CHICANO LITERATURE **EDUCATION** Univ of the Ams, BA, 63; Columbia Univ, MA, 67, PhD(Span), 71; New Sch Social Res, MA, 72. **CAREER** Instr Span, Pace Col, 67-69; instr, Columbia Col, Columbia Univ, 69-70; asst prof, City Col New York, 70-74; assoc prof, Dept Foreign Lang and Humanities, York Col, City Univ New York, 74-78, chmn dept, 74-76; prof, William Paterson Col NJ, 78-79; Dean, Grad Sch, Eastern Mich Univ, 79-, Vis asst prof, NY Univ, 73 and 77; adj prof, Teachers Col, Columbia Univ, 77-79. **MEMBERSHIPS** MLA; Ling Soc Am; Int Ling Asn. **RESEARCH** Spanish-English bilingualism; higher education administration. **SELECTED PUBLICATIONS** Tijuana--Stories On The Border, Revista De Estudios Hispanicos, Vol 30, 96. **CONTACT ADDRESS** Grad Dean Eastern, Eastern Michigan Univ, Ypsilanti, MI 48197.

KELLER, HOWARD HUGHES
PERSONAL Born 09/05/1941, Brooklyn, NY, m, 1969 **DISCIPLINE** THEORETICAL LINGUISTICS, RUSSIAN LITERATURE **EDUCATION** Fordham Univ, AB, 63; Georgetown Univ, PhD(Russ), 67. **CAREER** Asst prof ling, Southern Ill Univ, Carbondale, 66-67; Fulbright lectr, Univ Sofia, 67-68; assoc prof, 70-80, Prof Russ, Murray State Univ, 80-, Bk Rev Ed, Slavic and East Europ J, 78-; Nat Endowment for Humanities fel, 78; Presidential res fel, Murray State Univ, 79; ED, Slavic and East Europ J, 80-; Nat Endowment for Humanities fel, 81. **MEMBERSHIPS** Am Asn Teachers Slavic and East Europ Lang; Ling Soc Am; Am Asn Advan Slavic Studies; Am Asn Teachers Ger; Ling Soc Am. **RESEARCH** Slavic and Germanic word formation; language teaching methodology; language and the brain. **CONTACT ADDRESS** Dept of Foreign Lang, Murray State Univ, Murray, KY 42071. **EMAIL** keller@indiana.edu

KELLER, JOHN ESTEN
PERSONAL Born 09/27/1917, Lexington, KY **DISCIPLINE** SPANISH **EDUCATION** Univ Ky, AB, 40, AM, 42; Univ NC, PhD, 46. **CAREER** Insts, Univ NC, 43-46; asst prof, Univ Ky, 46-47; from asst prof to assoc prof, Univ Tenn, 47-50; from asst prof to prof Romance lang, Univ NC, Chapel Hill, 50-67, exec secy curric in folklore, 63-67; assoc dean, Col Arts and Sci, 67-72, Prof Span and Chmn Dept Span and Ital, Univ KY, 67-. **HONORS AND AWARDS** Distinguished Prof Award, UK, 75; UK Sang Award Outstanding Contribr to Grad Educ, 73; Dr. of Humane Letters, Plymouth State Col, 82; Dr. Honoris Causa, Univ of Granada, 86. **MEMBERSHIPS** MLA; Mediaeval Acad Am; Am Asn Teachers Span and Port; SAtlantic Mod Lang Asn (pres, 67-68); corresp mem Hisp Soc Am. **RESEARCH** Roman philology; Old Spanish literature; iconography of brief medieval Spanish narrative. **SELECTED PUBLICATIONS** Auth, Motif-index of Mediaeval Spanish Exempla, Univ Tenn; ed, El libro de los gatos, 58, El libro de los Exemplos por a b c, 61 Calila et Digna, Barlaam e Josafat, 67 and 79; Consejo Super Inves Cient, Madrid, 67; auth, Alfonso X, el sabio, 67 & Gon alo de Berceo, Twayne, 72; The Book of Count Lucanor and Patronio, Univ Ky, 77; auth, Iconography in Medieval Spanish Literatuta, with Richard Kinkade, 84; auth, Daily Life Depicted in the Cantigas de Santa, with Annette Cash, 98; auth, Libro de los exenplos por a.b.c., Ars Libris 00. **CONTACT ADDRESS** Dept of Span and Ital, Univ of Kentucky, Lexington, KY 40506.

KELLEY, ALITA
PERSONAL Born 11/19/1932, Bradford, England, m, 1970, 2 children **DISCIPLINE** SPANISH **EDUCATION** Univ Ariz, BA, 81; MA, 86; PhD, 92. **CAREER** Asst prof to assoc prof, Pa State Univ, 92-; vis prof, Univ of Sheffield, England, 97. **HONORS AND AWARDS** Grant, Tinker Found, 86-87; NEH, 93; Grant Pa State Univ Res Dev; Grant, Fund for Excellence in Learning and Teaching. **MEMBERSHIPS** Am Lit Transl Assoc; Am Transl Assoc; Am Assoc of Teachers of Spanish and Portuguese; Int Soc for Humor Studies; Latin Am Studies Assoc; Int Soc for Luso-Hispanic Humor Studies; Latin Am Indian Lit Assoc; MLA. **RESEARCH** Translation - Spanish to English, Latin American Literature, specifically of Peru, Humor Studies in Latin American Literature. **SELECTED PUBLICATIONS** Transl, The Identity of Hispanoamerica: An Interpretation of Colonial Literature by Jose Promis, 91; transl, Goodbye, Ayacucho and Moscow's Gold by Julio Ortego, 94; auth, Target Practice, 94; transl, Path Through the Canefields by Jose Watanabe, 97. **CONTACT ADDRESS** Dept Foreign Lang, Pennsylvania State Univ, Delaware County, 25 Yearsley Mill Rd, Media, PA 19063-5522. **EMAIL** kak7@psu.edu

KELLEY, E. MORGAN
PERSONAL Born 09/14/1943, Hartford, CT, m, 1993, 3 children **DISCIPLINE** LINGUISTICS **EDUCATION** Washington & Lee Univ, BA, 65; Mich State Univ, MA, 67, PhD, 68. **CAREER** Asst prof, Col of William & Mary, 68-2000. **HONORS AND AWARDS** Woodrow Wilson Fel, 65; NDEA Title IV Fel, 65-68; Fulbright Scholar, year abroad, 65, summer abroad, 79. **MEMBERSHIPS** AAUP, AATG, ASLIP, MES, SEAPM. **SELECTED PUBLICATIONS** Auth, "Tanith: Patron Saint of Carthaginian Sailors," Epigraphic Soc Occasional Pubs, 18:52-55 (89); auth, "North American Indian Tribal Names," Epigraphic Soc Occasional Pubs, 19:83-91 (90); auth, "Abraxas etait-il (aussi) le dieu guerrier dse Mayas?' Mediterranea, 40:2-13 (90); auth, "Mithras und Perseus: Ein Beitrag zu dem Werke Prof. Dres. Heinsohns," Vorzeit-Fruhzeit-Gegenwart, 2-3:53 (90); auth, "Die Entzifferung der Stammesnamen: Deutsch und die Franken," Vorzeit-Fruhzeit-Gegenwart, 5:53-64 (91); auth, "Colibri Gaucher: Dieu Guerrier des Azteques," Mediterranea, 43:2-9 (91); auth, The Metaphorical Basis of Language: A Study in Cross-Cultural Linguistics, Edwin Mellon Press (92). **CONTACT ADDRESS** Dept Modern Lang, Col of William and Mary, PO Box 8795, Williamsburg, VA 23187-8795.

KELLEY, MICHAEL ROBERT
PERSONAL Born 08/20/1940, Washington, DC, m, 1994, 1 child **DISCIPLINE** ENGLISH LITERATURE, LINGUISTICS **EDUCATION** Cath Univ Am, BA, 62, MFA, 65, PhD(English), 70. **CAREER** Asst prof, 70-75, assoc prof, 75-80, prof English, George Mason Univ, 80-, Contrib ed, Mod Humanities Res Asn Bibliog, 75-. **MEMBERSHIPS** MLA; Mediaeval Acad Am. **RESEARCH** Medieval English drama; Chaucer; literary aesthetics. **SELECTED PUBLICATIONS** Auth, Fifteenth Century Flamboyant Style and the Castle of Perseverance, Comp Drama, spring 72; English for Foreign Speakers--a Television Solution, AV instr, 11/72; Flamboyant Drama, Southern Ill Univ, 7; auth, "Antithesis as the Principle of Design in Chaucer's Parlement of Foules," Chaucer Rev 14 (79), 61-73. **CONTACT ADDRESS** George Mason Univ, Fairfax, Mail Stop 1D2, Fairfax, VA 22030-4444. **EMAIL** mkelley@gmu.edu

KELLEY, PAUL B.
PERSONAL Born 04/23/1967, Columbia, SC **DISCIPLINE** FRENCH **EDUCATION** Univ SCar, BA, 89; MA, 93; Univ de Haute-Alsace, Maitrise, 92; Columbia Univ, PhD, 99. **CAREER** Adj prof, Drew Univ, 99-; vis asst prof, Wake Forest Univ, 01-. **HONORS AND AWARDS** James Buttenwieser Res Fel; Phi Beta Kappa, 89; President's Fel, 93-99. **MEMBERSHIPS** MLA, Samuel Becket Soc, N Am Satire Soc. **RESEARCH** 20th Century Prose Fiction, Philosophical Approaches to Literature, Life Writing, Cinema and Literature. **SELECTED PUBLICATIONS** auth, "Nausea and Space in La Nausee and Voyage au bout de la nuit," LittleRealite 9.1, (97); auth, "Memory, Narration and the Gendering of the Confessional Text: Samuel Beckett's Enough," Dalhousie Fr Studies 45, (00); auth, "Marcel Proust's Remembrance of Things Past: The Long-lost Galley Proofs," Dict of Lit Biography: Yearbook 2000, (01); auth, "Gilles Deleuze, L'Epuise in Quad et autre pieces pour la television (forthcoming). **CONTACT ADDRESS** Drew Univ, 36 Madison Ave, Madison, NJ 07940-1493. **EMAIL** pbkelley@hotmail.com

KELLING, HANS-WILHELM L.
PERSONAL Born 08/15/1932, Schwerin, Germany, m, 1958, 4 children **DISCIPLINE** GERMAN LANGUAGE & LITERATURE **EDUCATION** Brigham Young Univ, BA, 58; Stanford Univ, MA, 60, Ph, 67. **CAREER** Teaching asst Ger, Brigham Young Univ, 57-58; asst, Stanford Univ, 58-61; from asst prof to assoc prof, 62-72, chmn, Dept Germanic Lang, 77-82, Prof Ger, Brigham Young Univ, 72-, Chmn Dept Germanic & Slavic Lang, 82- **MEMBERSHIPS** MLA; Rocky Mountain Mod Lang Asn; Am Asn Teachers Ger. **RESEARCH** German literature of the classical period; cultural history. **SELECTED PUBLICATIONS** Coauth, Deutsche Aufsatzhilfe, Brigham Young Univ, 67 & 68; auth, Bettina von Arnim--a study in Goethe idolatry, Bull Rocky Mountain Mod Lang Asn, 6/69; The idolatry of poetic genius, Yearbk English Goethe Soc, 70; The Idolatry of Poetic Genius in German Goethe Criticism Herbert Lang, Berne, 70; coauth, Deutschwie Man's Sagt und Schreibt, 72 & auth, Deutsche Kulturgeschichte, 73; Holt; Goethe the Dichterprophet, Ger Life & Lett, 73; auth, Deutsche Kueturgeschichte, 96, 99, McGraw-Hill. **CONTACT ADDRESS** Brigham Young Univ, 2007A JKHB, Provo, UT 84602-0002. **EMAIL** hans-wilhelm_kelling@byu.edu

KELLMAN, STEVEN G.
DISCIPLINE COMPARATIVE LITERATURE **EDUCATION** State Univ NYork, Binghamton, BA, 67; Univ of Calif Berkeley, MA, 69; PhD, 72. **CAREER** Asst prof, Bemidji State Univ, 72-73; lectr, Tel-Aviv Univ, 73-75; vis lectr, Univ of Calif Irvine, 75-76; vis assoc prof, Univ of Calif Berkeley, 82; asst prof to prof, Univ of Tex San Antonio, 76-. **HONORS AND AWARDS** Fulbright Lectr, 80; UTSA Awd, 85-86; HL Mencken Writing Awd, 86; Partners of the Am Lectr, 88, 95; Fulbright Hays Travel Grant, China, 95; NEH Summer Sem, 96; John E Sawyer Fel, Harvard, 97. **MEMBERSHIPS** MLA; Nat Book Critics Circle; PEN Am Center, PEN USA West. **RESEARCH** Narrative, Film, 20th Century, Translingualism, Biography of Henry Roth. **SELECTED PUBLICATIONS** Auth, The Self-Begetting Novel, Columbia Univ Pr, (NY), 80; auth, Loving Reading: Erotics of the Text, Archon, (Hamden, CT), 85; auth, The Modern American Novel, Salem Pr, (Englewood Cliffs, NJ), 91; auth, The Plague: Fiction and Resistance, Twayne, (Boston), 93; auth, "Sayles Goes Spanish", Hopscotch I.1 (99): 24-35; auth, "Colliding Selves: Ariel Dorfman Spans the Gap Between North and South", Hopscotch I.2 (99): 112-17; auth, "Requiem for Henry Roth", USA Today Mag 128 2658 (00): 75-6; Auth, The Translingual Imagination, Lincoln Univ Nebraska Press, 00; Auth, Fulbright Distinguished Lecturer, Univ of Sofia, 00; Ed, "Torpid Smoke: Vladimir Nabokov's Short Stories," Amsterdam, Rodopi, 00. **CONTACT ADDRESS** Dept For Lang, Univ of Texas, San Antonio, 6900 N Loop 1604 W W, San Antonio, TX 78249-0644. **EMAIL** kellman@lonestar.utsa.edu

KELLY, DAVID H.
PERSONAL Born 09/23/1929, Philadelphia, PA, m, 1997, 3 children **DISCIPLINE** CLASSICAL LINGUISTICS **EDUCATION** Cath Univ Am, BA, 52; Univ PA, MA, 54, PhD, 58. **CAREER** From asst prof to assoc prof class & ling, La Salle Univ, 61-70, chmn dept for lang, 67-69, dean arts & sci, 69-70; Prof Class, Montclair State Col, 70; asst, Montclair St Univ, 70-00. **HONORS AND AWARDS** MSU Distinguished Tchr, 98. **MEMBERSHIPS** Am Philol Asn; Class Asn Atlantic States (pres, 77-78). **RESEARCH** Lang tchg methodology; class hum; syntax of Greek and Latin. **SELECTED PUBLICATIONS** Auth, Distinctive feature analysis in Latin phonology, Am J Philol, 67; Transformations in the Latin nominal phrase, Class Philol, 68; Tense in the Latin independent operative, Glotta, 72; Latin the tool subject, Class Outlook, 73; Revolution in classical studies, Class J, 73; Egyptians and Ethiopians: Color, race, and racism, Class Outlook, 91; Case: Grammar and terminology, Class World, 93. **CONTACT ADDRESS** Dept of Class, Montclair State Univ, 1 Normal Ave, Montclair, NJ 07043-1699. **EMAIL** kellyd@mail.montclair.edu

KELLY, DOROTHY J.
PERSONAL Born 08/27/1952 **DISCIPLINE** FRENCH LITERATURE **EDUCATION** Smith Col, BA, 74; Yale Univ, MA, 75; PhD, 80. **CAREER** Instr, Yale Univ, 77-78; Lectr to Prof and Chair, Boston Univ, 80-. **HONORS AND AWARDS** Sen Fel, Boston Univ, 91-92; Grant, Boston Univ, 83-84; Grant, Whiting Found, 82-83; Fel, Yale Univ; Phi Beta Kappa, 74; Phi Sigma Iota, 87. **MEMBERSHIPS** MLA. **RESEARCH** French literature of the 19th and 20th centuries; Literary theory; Psychoanalysis and literature; Gender and literature. **SELECTED PUBLICATIONS** Auth, Telling glances, Rutgers Univ Press, 92; auth, "Experimenting on Women," in Spectacles of Realism, 95; auth, "Teaching Madame Bovary through the Lens of Post-structuralism" in Approaches to Teaching Madame Bovary, 95; auth, "Singes, meres, et langage dans les textes de Flaubert," in A la Recherce du XIXe siecle, 98; auth, "Between Bodies and Texts," in Approaches to Teaching Balzac's Old Goriot, 00. **CONTACT ADDRESS** Dept French, Boston Univ, 718 Commonwealth Ave, Boston, MA 02215.

KELLY, LOUIS G.
DISCIPLINE LINGUISTICS **EDUCATION** Univ Laval, PhD. **CAREER** Prof, Univ Ottawa. **RESEARCH** Translation theory; history of linguistics; sociolinguistics. **SELECTED PUBLICATIONS** Auth, Twenty-five Centuries of Language Teaching, Newbury House, 69; Quaestiones Alberti de modis significandi: A Critical Edition, Benjamins, 77; The True Interpreter: A History of Translation Theory in the West, Blackwells, 79; Prorsus Taliter. The Latin Text of Kipling's Just So Stories, Centaur Bk(s), 85; A Critical Edition of Basil Valentine, His Triumphant Chariot of Antimony. London, Garland Publishing, 90. **CONTACT ADDRESS** Dept of Linguistics, Univ of Ottawa, 70 Laurier Ave, PO Box 450, Ottawa, ON, Canada K1N 6N5.

KELLY, VAN
DISCIPLINE FRENCH LITERATURE **EDUCATION** Univ NC, Chapel Hill, PhD. **CAREER** Assoc prof, Univ KS. **RESEARCH** French moralists and mod poetry. **SELECTED PUBLICATIONS** Auth, Pascalian Fictions: Antagonism and Absent Agency in the Wager and Other Pensees, Summa, 92; co-ed, Epic and Epoch: Essays on the History and Interpretation of a Genre, Tex Tech UP, 84. **CONTACT ADDRESS** Dept of French and Italian, Univ of Kansas, Lawrence, Admin Building, Lawrence, KS 66045.

KELZ, ROCHELLE KANTER
PERSONAL Born Chicago, IL, m, 2 children **DISCIPLINE** SPANISH **EDUCATION** Northwestern Univ, BS, 66; MA, 67, PhC., 69; PhD, 71. **CAREER** Prof, North Park Univ, 69-90; prof, Roosevelt Univ, 90-94; dean, Mott Community Col, 94-98; assoc, prof, Ind Univ Kokomo, 98-. **HONORS AND AWARDS** Grant, Northwestern Univ, 69-70; Pi Sigma Alpha, Pi Lambda Theta, Alpha Lambda Delta; Pan Hellenic Awd, 66; Outstanding Univ Prof of Span in US, 87; Outstanding Univ Prof of Span in Ill, 87; Athena Awd, 97; 2000 Notable Am Women. **MEMBERSHIPS** AAHE, Am Assoc of Teachers of Span and Port, AAUE, CASE, Am Coun on the Teaching of For Lang, Nat Assoc for Bilingual Educ. **RESEARCH** Language for Career Purposes: Spanish for Health Professionals, Spanish for Business, Spanish for Social Services. **SELECTED PUBLICATIONS** Auth, Conversational Spanish for Medical Personnel: Essential Expressions, Questions and Directions for Medical Personnel to Facilitate Conversation with Spanish-Speaking Patients and Coworkers, John Wiley & Sons, 77; auth, Conversational Spanish for Medical Personnel: Essential Expressions, Questions and Directions for Medical Personnel to Facilitate Conversation with Spanish-Speaking Patients and Coworkers, Delmar Publ, 82; coauth, Delmar's English/Spanish Pocket Dictionary for Health Professionals, Delmar Publ, 96; coauth, Conversational Spanish for Health Professionals, Delmar Publ, 99. **CONTACT ADDRESS** 5605 Four Mile Dr, Kokomo, IN 46901-3829. **EMAIL** skelz@iuk.edu

KEMMER, SUZANNE E.
PERSONAL Born 11/07/1959, Chicago, IL, m, 1987 **DISCIPLINE** LINGUISTICS **EDUCATION** Rice Univ, BA. **CAREER** Res Fel Stanford Univ, 81-87; asst prof, Univ Cal at San Diego, 88-93; asst prof, Rice Univ, 93-94; assoc prof, 94-; Sr res fel, MPI Evolutionary Anthrop, 00; prof, LSA, Summer Inst, 01. **HONORS AND AWARDS** Phi Beta Kappa. **MEMBERSHIPS** LSA; CLA; BD Consult Eds, Cognitive Ling; co-ed, Typological Stud Lang Series. **RESEARCH** Language and cognition; language change; language universals; English Lexicon; Lexical Semantics. **SELECTED PUBLICATIONS** Auth, The Middle Voice, Typol Studies Lang Series, Benjamins (Amsterdam and Philadelphia), 93; co-ed, On Language: Selected Writings of Joseph H Greenberg, Stanford UP (Stanford), 90; co-ed, Usage Based Models of Language, CSLI Pub (Stanford), 00. **CONTACT ADDRESS** Dept Linguistics, Rice Univ, 6100 Main St, Houston, TX 77005-1827. **EMAIL** kemmer@rice.edu

KEMP, HENRIETTA J.
DISCIPLINE GERMAN, HISTORY, LIBRARY SCIENCE **EDUCATION** Univ Iowa, BA, 66; Univ Pittsburgh, MLS, 71. **CAREER** LIBR, 81-, SUPERV, FINE ARTS COLLECT, 89-, LUTHER COL. **CONTACT ADDRESS** Library, Luther Col, 700 College Dr, Decorah, IA 52101. **EMAIL** kempjane@luther.edu

KENKEL, KONRAD
DISCIPLINE GERMAN LANGUAGE **EDUCATION** IN Univ, PhD, 75. **CAREER** Dir, Middlebury Ger Summer Schl; Assoc prof, Darmouth Col. **HONORS AND AWARDS** Bundesverdienstkreuz, Fed Repub Ger, 96. **RESEARCH** Ger lit and art from the turn of the century through the Weimar Repub. **SELECTED PUBLICATIONS** Auth, comp studies about the treatment of myth; publ(s) about Gryphius, Hofmannsthal, Gustav Mahler, and var postwar Ger auth(s). **CONTACT ADDRESS** Dartmouth Col, 3529 N Main St, #207, Hanover, NH 03755.

KENNEDY, CHRIS
DISCIPLINE LINGUISTICS **EDUCATION** Univ Calif Santa Cruz, PhD. **CAREER** Prof, Northwestern Univ. **RESEARCH** Syntax; semantics; syntax-semantics interface; adjectives and comparatives; anaphora and ellipsis; natural language processing. **SELECTED PUBLICATIONS** Auth, Cross-polar anomaly and the ontology of degrees, 98; Antecedent contained deletion and the syntax of quantification, Ling Inquiry, 97; Verb phrase deletion and 'Nonparasitic' Gaps, Ling Inquiry, 97; coauth, Attributive comparatives and bound ellipsis, Ling Res Center Report LRC-97-03, Univ Calif, Santa Cruz, 97; An indexical account of certain ambiguities, Proceedings of ESCOL '95, Ithaca, Cornell LingClub, 96; Comparatives, indices, and scope, Proceedings of FLSM VI. Bloomington: Ind Univ Ling Club, 95; Morphological alignment and head projection: Towards a nonderivational account of stress in Dakota, Phonology at Santa Cruz 3, Ling Res Center, Univ Calif, Santa Cruz, 95; Argument contained ellipsis, Ling Res Center, Report LRC-94-03, Univ Calif, Santa Cruz, 94. **CONTACT ADDRESS** Dept of Linguistics, Northwestern Univ, 2016 Sheridan Rd #10, Evanston, IL 60208-3118. **EMAIL** kennedy@northwestern.edu

KENNEDY, GEORGE A.
PERSONAL Born 11/26/1928, Hartford, CT, m, 1955, 1 child **DISCIPLINE** CLASSICS **EDUCATION** Princeton Univ, AB, 50; Harvard Univ, AM, 52, PhD, 54. **CAREER** Kennedy Traveling Fel, 54-55, instr and tutor of Classics, Hist, & Lit, 55-58, visiting asst prof, Harvard Univ, 59; asst prof of Greek, 58-59, asst prof of Classics, 59-63, assoc prof of Classics, 63-65, chemn, Haverford Col; prof of Classics & chemn, Dept of Classics, Univ of Pittsburgh, 65-66; prof of Classics, 66-72, dir, Am Office of L'Annee Philologique, 68-74, Paddison Prof of Classics, 72-95, chemn, Dept of Classics, 66-76, chemn, Dept of Linguistics, 75-76, chemn, Curriculum of Comparative Lit, 89-93, chemn of Univ fac, 85-88, Univ of NC at Chapel Hill; auth, Classical Rhetoric & Its Christian and Secular Tradition, Univ of NC Press, 99. **HONORS AND AWARDS** Fulbright fel, 64-65; Guggenheim fel, 64-65; Charles J. Goodwin Awd, Am Philological Asn; Distinguished Scholar Awd, Nat Commun Asn; Thomas Jefferson Awd, UNC-CH; Phi Beta Kappa, 50; member, National Humanities Council, 80-87, vice chemn, Board of Governors, Univ of NC Press, 73-88. **MEMBERSHIPS** Am Acad of Arts & Sci; Am Philosophical Soc; Am Philological Asn, 79-80; Int Soc for the Hist of Rhetoric, 79-80; National Humanities Council, 80-87, vice chemn, 83-85; chemn, Board of Governors, Univ of NC Press, 73-88 **SELECTED PUBLICATIONS** Auth, The Art of Persusion in Greece, Princeton Univ Press, 63; auth, Quintilian, Twayne Pubs, 69; auth, The Art of Rhetoric in the Roman World, Princeton Univ Press, 72; auth, Greek Rhetoric Under Christian Emperors, Princeton Univ Press, 83; auth, New Testament Interpretation through Rhetorical Criticism, Univ of NC Press, 84; auth, Aristotle, On Rhetoric: A Theory of Civic Discourse, Newly Translated with Introduction, Notes, and Appendices, Oxford Univ Press, 91; auth, A New History of Classical Rhetoric, Princeton Univ Press, 94; auth, Comparative Rhetoric: An Historical and Cross-Cultural Introduction, Oxford Univ Press, 98. **CONTACT ADDRESS** PO Box 271880, Fort Collins, CO 80527-1880.

KENNEDY, WILLIAM JOHN
PERSONAL Born 04/26/1942, Brooklyn, NY, m, 1967, 2 children **DISCIPLINE** RENAISSANCE & COMPARATIVE LITERATURE **EDUCATION** Manhattan Col, BA, 63; Yale Univ, PhD(comp lit), 69. **CAREER** Instr Eng, Fairleigh Dickinson Univ, 67-70; asst prof comp lit, 70-76, assoc prof, 76-82, Prof comp lit, Cornell Univ, 82-, Vis assoc prof comp lit, NY Univ, 82. **HONORS AND AWARDS** MLA Howard R. Marraro Prize, 83; Guggenheim fel 87-88; Villa Serbelloni, 98. **MEMBERSHIPS** MLA; Am Comp Lit Asn; Renaissance Soc Am. **RESEARCH** Lit theory; rhetorical criticism; lyric poetry. **SELECTED PUBLICATIONS** Auth, Rhetorical Norms in Renaissance Literature, Yale Univ Press, 78; Jacopo Sannazaro and the Uses of Pastoral, Univ New England Press, 83; Authorizing Petrarch, Cornell Univ Press, 94. **CONTACT ADDRESS** Comp Lit Dept, Cornell Univ, Ithaca, NY 14850. **EMAIL** WJK3@cornell.edu

KENNEDY-DAY, KIKI
PERSONAL Born Chicago, IL, m, 1988 **DISCIPLINE** NEAR EASTERN LANGUAGES AND LITERATURE-ARABIC (ISLAMIC PHILOSOPHY) **EDUCATION** NYork Univ, PhD, 96. **CAREER** St John's Univ Jamaica; Adj Asst Prof, Hofstra Univ NY, 98-. **MEMBERSHIPS** APA. **RESEARCH** Islamic Philosophy; Ibn Sina. **SELECTED PUBLICATIONS** Auth, articles about Al-Kindi, Aristotelianism in Islamic Philos, Routledge Encycl of Islamic Philos, 98. **CONTACT ADDRESS** Fort Washington Ave, 4A, New York, NY 10033.

KENSHUR, OSCAR S.
PERSONAL Born 11/27/1942, m, 1994, 2 children **DISCIPLINE** COMPARATIVE LITERATURE **EDUCATION** N Western Univ, BA, 64; MA, 68; Univ Iowa, PhD, 77. **CAREER** Asst prof to assoc prof to adj assoc prof to dir to prof to adj prof to dept chmn, Ind Univ, 78-. **HONORS AND AWARDS** Res Fel, Univ Iowa, 72-76; Lilly Endowment Fel, 79-80; Ind Univ Summer Fel, 83-00; NEH Fel, 89-90, 97-98; Teaching Excellence Award, Ind Univ, 98, 99. **MEMBERSHIPS** ASECS; ACLA; MLA. **RESEARCH** Interrelations between literature and philosophy, particularly in the context of early-modern religio-political culture; contemporary theoretical debates concerning ideology and the status of evidence in the sciences and humanities. **SELECTED PUBLICATIONS** Auth, "The Rhetoric of Incommensurability," J Aesthetics and Art Criticism (84); auth, Open Form and the Shape of Ideas: Literary Structures as Representations of Philosophical Concepts in the Seventeenth and Eighteenth Centuries, Bucknell Univ Pr, 86; auth, "Scriptural Deism and the Politics of Dryden's Religio Laici," ELH (87); auth, "Demystifying the Demystifiers: Metaphysical Snares of Ideological Criticism," Critical Inquiry (88); auth, "Pierre Bayle and the Structures of Doubt," Eighteenth Century Stud (88); auth, Dilemma's of Enlightenment: Studies in the Rhetoric and Logic of Idealism, Univ Calif Pr, 93; auth, "Virtue and Defilement: Moral Rationalism and Sexual Prohibitions in the Lettres Persanes," SVEC (forthcoming). **CONTACT ADDRESS** Dept Comp Lit, Indiana Univ, Bloomington, Bloomington, IN 47405. **EMAIL** okenshur@indiana.edu

KERN, RICHARD G.
DISCIPLINE FRENCH **EDUCATION** Univ Calif, BA, 79; MA, 83; PhD, 88. **CAREER** Asst Prof, Univ Tex, 88-92; Assoc Prof, Univ Calif, 92-. **HONORS AND AWARDS** Spencer Found Grant; McEnerney Endowment Grant. **MEMBERSHIPS** Am Asn of Applied Ling, AATF, MLA. **RESEARCH** Foreign language acquisition, psycholinguistics, literacy, technology and literacy. **SELECTED PUBLICATIONS** Auth, Literacy and Language Teaching, Oxford UP, 00; auth, Network-Based Language Teaching: Concepts and Practice, Cambridge UP, 00. **CONTACT ADDRESS** Dept Lang, Univ of California, Berkeley, 4125 Dwinelle Hall, Berkeley, CA 84720-2580. **EMAIL** kernrg@socrates.berkeley.edu

KERR, LUCILLE
DISCIPLINE LATIN AMERICAN LITERARY STUDIES **EDUCATION** Barnard Col, BA; Yale Univ, M.Phil; PhD. **CAREER** Prof, Univ Southern Calif; ch, Northwestern Univ; prof, Northwestern Univ. **HONORS AND AWARDS** Am Philos Soc Res Grant, 78-79; Social Science Res Council/Am Counc of Learned Societies Joint Comt on Latin Am Studies Advanced Res Grant, 89; Albert S. Raubenheimer Distinguished Fac Award, Univ S CA, 96; NEH Fel for Univ Teachers,, 97-98. **MEMBERSHIPS** Am Asn of Teachers of Spanish and Portuguese; Am Comparative Lit Asn; Latin Am Studies Asn; Latin Am Jewish Studies Asn; Modern Lang Asn. **RESEARCH** Modern fiction and the critical theory of narrative; texts from the Spanish American tradition; modern Latin Am lit and literary hist; narrative fiction; literary theory. **SELECTED PUBLICATIONS** Auth, Suspended Fictions: Reading Novels by Manuel Puig & Reclaiming the Author: Figures & Fictions from Spanish America. **CONTACT ADDRESS** Dept of Hispanic Studies, Northwestern Univ, 1859 Sheridan Rd, Evanston, IL 60208-2202. **EMAIL** lckerr@northwestern.edu

KERSHNER, R. BRANDON
PERSONAL Born 11/17/1944, Cumberland, MD, d, 3 children **DISCIPLINE** ENGLISH AND COMPARATIVE LITERATURE **EDUCATION** Johns Hopkins Univ, BA, 66; MA, 66;

Stanford Univ, MA, 68; PhD, 72. **CAREER** Grad tchg asst, Stanford Univ, 68-69; asst prof, 71-76; vis prof, Univ Utrecht, 78; vis prof, Univ Col Dublin, 84; vis prof, Univ Utrecht, 94; ch, SAMLA, 90; assoc prof, 76-90; prof, 90-. **HONORS AND AWARDS** Danforth fel, 66-72; Woodrow Wilson fel, 66; Amer Conf on Irish Stud award, 90; res grant, 93; Alumni Prof of English, 99. **MEMBERSHIPS** MLA; Intl James Joyce Found; Amer Conf Irish Stud. **RESEARCH** James Joyce. **SELECTED PUBLICATIONS** Auth, Dylan Thomas: The Poet and His Critics Chicago: Amer Lib Assn, 77; Joyce, Bakhtin and Popular Literature: Chronicles of Disorder, Univ NC Press, 89; ed, James Joyce, A Portrait of the Artist as a Young Man, St. Martin's Press, 92; The Twentieth-Century Novel: An Introduction, St Martin's Press, 97; ed, Joyce and Popular Culture, 96. **CONTACT ADDRESS** Dept of Eng, Univ of Florida, 226 Tigert Hall, Gainesville, FL 32611. **EMAIL** kershner@ufl.edu

KESLER, LINC
DISCIPLINE LINGUISTICS **EDUCATION** Yale Univ, BA, 71; Univ Toronto, MA, 72, PhD, 81. **CAREER** Engl, Oregon St Univ. **RESEARCH** Semiotics; renaissance & 17th century Brit, native Am & Asian lit. **SELECTED PUBLICATIONS** Auth, The Idealization of Women in the Renaissance: Morphology and Change in Three Poetic Texts, Mosaic, 90; Fate and Narrative Sturcture in Lermontov's A Hero of Our Time, Texas Studies in Language & Literature, 90; Ben Jonson Johns Hopkins Guide to Literary Theory and Criticism, 93. **CONTACT ADDRESS** Oregon State Univ, Corvallis, OR 97331-4501. **EMAIL** lkesler@orst.edu

KEUMSIL, KIM YOON
DISCIPLINE LINGUISTICS **EDUCATION** Univ Paris III-Sorbonne, PhD, 84. **CAREER** Prof & dir, Bilingual-ESL Grad prog. **RESEARCH** Machine-mediated discourse and ethnolinguistic identity. **SELECTED PUBLICATIONS** Publ in the areas of, sociolinguistics, psycholinguistics, second language acquisition, and pragmatics. **CONTACT ADDRESS** Dept of Language and Cultures, William Paterson Col of New Jersey, 300 Pompton Rd., Wayne, NJ 07470.

KEVRA, SUSAN
PERSONAL Born 03/26/1963, New Brunswick, NJ, m, 1991 **DISCIPLINE** FRENCH **EDUCATION** Oberlin Col, BA, 85; Univ of Mich, MA, 88; Univ of Mass at Amherst, PhD, 98. **CAREER** Vis prof, Marlboro Col. **HONORS AND AWARDS** Women in French Graduate Student Essay Prize, 94; Phi Kappa Phi Honor Soc, 92; Micheline Dufau Prize for Excellence in Tchg French, 92. **MEMBERSHIPS** MLA; Am Coun for Quebec Studies; Women in French; Conseil Int d'etudes francophones. **RESEARCH** Quebec Lit; women's studies. **SELECTED PUBLICATIONS** Auth, Indigestible Stew and Holy Piss: The politics of Food in Rodolphe Girard's marie Calumet, Quebec Studies, Vol 27, 99; Of Pigs and Princesses: Corporeal Currency in the Meat Market: Themes of Consumption in Les Trois petits cochons, Women in French Studies Vol 2, 94. **CONTACT ADDRESS** Marlboro Col, Marlboro, VT 05346. **EMAIL** skevra@marlboro.edu

KIBBEE, DOUGLAS
DISCIPLINE FRENCH LITERATURE **EDUCATION** Colgate Univ, BA, 71; Univ Ind, MA, 75; PhD, 79 **CAREER** Prof, Univ Ill Urbana Champaign. **RESEARCH** History of French language; lexicography; politics of language; history of linguistics. **SELECTED PUBLICATIONS** Auth, "Language Variation and Linguistic Description in the 16th-Century France," Historiographia Linguistics 18, (90): 49-65; auth, For to Speke French Trewely The French Language in England, 1000-1600: Its Status, Description and Instruction, Amsterdam: John Benjamins, (91): 268; ed, New Analysis of Romance Languages: Proceedings of the Eighteenth Linguistic Symposium on Romance Languages, Amsterdam: John Benjamins, 91; auth, "Renaissance notions of medieval language and the development of historical linguistics," Journal of Medieval and Renaissance Studies, 22, (92): 41-54; auth, "16th-Century Bilingual Dictionaries (French-English): Organization and Access, Then and Now," Toronto: Centre for Computing in the Humanities, 92; auth, "World French Takes on World English: Competing Visions of National and International Languages," World englishes 12, (93): 209-221; auth, "Emigrant Languages and Acculturation: The Case of Anglo-French," Rasmus Rask Quarterly 2, (95): 1-20; auth, "Assertion/attenuation, subjectivite/objectivite en anglais et en francais: seem/ sembler Relations discursives et traduction, Lille: Presses universitaires, (95): 73-87; auth, "The New Historiography, the History of French and Le Bon Usage in Nicot's Dictionary (1606)", Tubingen: Niemeyer, (95): 103-118; auth, Language Legislation and Linguistic Rights, Amsterdam/Philadelphia: John Benjamins, 98. **CONTACT ADDRESS** French Dept, Univ of Illinois, Urbana-Champaign, 52 E Gregory Dr, Champaign, IL 61820. **EMAIL** dkibbee@staff.uiuc.edu

KIBLER, LOUIS WAYNE
PERSONAL Born 07/23/1939, Clifton Forge, VA, m, 1960, 3 children **DISCIPLINE** ITALIAN, FRENCH **EDUCATION** Ind Univ, BA, 61, PhD(French), 65. **CAREER** Asst prof Ital & French, Ind Univ, Bloomington, 65-72; assoc prof mod lang, Sweet Brair Col, 72-74; assoc prof Ital, Wayne State Univ, 74- **MEMBERSHIPS** Am Asn Teachers Ital; AAIS; AAUP. **RESEARCH** Twentieth century Italian and French prose and theater; medieval Italian theater. **SELECTED PUBLICATIONS** Coauth, Giorno per Giorno, Macmillian, 71; auth, Imagery as expression; Moravia's Indifferenti, Italica, fall 72; Reality and Realism of Moravia, Ital Quart, summer 73; Imagery in Georges Bataille's Le Bleuduciel, Fr Rev, spring 74; Patterns of time, In: Pavese's La luna e ifalo, Forum Italicum, fall 78; Moravia and Guttuso: A la recherche de la realite perdue, Italica, summer 79; ed, Ezio d'Errico's Theater of the Absurd: Three Plays, Fairleigh Dickinson Univ Press, 91; auth, Myth and Meaning in D'Annunzio's La figlia di Iorio, Annali d'Italianistica, 87; Moravia as Journalist, Homage to Moravia, Forum Italicum, 93. **CONTACT ADDRESS** Dept of Romance, Wayne State Univ, 487 Manoogian Hall, Detroit, MI 48202-3919. **EMAIL** l.kibler@wayne.edu

KIEFFER, BRUCE
DISCIPLINE GERMAN **EDUCATION** Columbia Univ, BA, 73; Princeton Univ, PhD, 79. **CAREER** Prof, Williams Col, 78-; dir, Ctr For Lang, Lit & Cult, 86-90. **HONORS AND AWARDS** NEH res fel, 82-83. **RESEARCH** German literature and thought 1750-1900; American and German comparative political history. **SELECTED PUBLICATIONS** Auth, The Storm and Stress of Language: Linguistic Catastrophe in the Early Works of Goethe, Lenz, Klinger and Schiller, 86. **CONTACT ADDRESS** Center for Foreign Languages, Literatures and Cult, Williams Col, Williamstown, MA 01267. **EMAIL** Bruce.Kieffer@williams.edu

KILLIAM, MARIE-THERESE
PERSONAL Born Frejus, France, 2 children **DISCIPLINE** FRENCH LANGUAGE AND LITERATURE **EDUCATION** Univ of Nice, BA; Columbia Univ, MA; PhD. **CAREER** Prof, Sweet Briar Col. **HONORS AND AWARDS** Fulbright Fel, 77. **RESEARCH** 20th century lit and mod literary criticism. **SELECTED PUBLICATIONS** Auth, The Art Criticism of Paul Claudel; coauth, L'Analyse du texte; articles on modern French writers and on French cinema. **CONTACT ADDRESS** Sweet Briar Col, Sweet Briar, VA 24595. **EMAIL** killiam@sbc.edu

KILPATRICK, ROSS S.
PERSONAL Born 10/03/1934, Toronto, ON, Canada, m, 1960, 3 children **DISCIPLINE** CLASSICS **EDUCATION** Univ Toronto, BA, 57, MA 64; Yale Univ, MA, 65, PhD, 67. **CAREER** Tchr, East York Collegiate, 57-64; instr, 67-68, asst prof, classics, 68-70, Yale Univ; assoc prof, 70-85, actg head dept, 84, asst to VP, 85, head dept, 85-95, prof, Queen's Univ, 85- . **HONORS AND AWARDS** OVATIO, Classical Assoc of the Middle West and South, 96. **MEMBERSHIPS** Am Philol Asn; Class Asn Can; Class Asn Middle West and South; Int Soc for Class Tradition; Ontario Class Asn; Soc of Fel of Am Acad in Rome; Vergilian Soc Am. **RESEARCH** Latin and Greek literature; classical tradition in Renaissance art and in English and Canadian literature. **SELECTED PUBLICATIONS** Ed, Smethurst, Classics at Queens: A Short History, Queen's Univ, 93; auth, In Praise of Nurses: T.R. Glover, Queen's Q, 94; auth, The Sea Took Pity, Studies, 95; auth, The Stuff of Doors and Dreams, Vergilius, 95; auth, Old Friends and Good Temper: T.R. Glover and Horace, Arethusa, 95; auth, Fortuna Regum: An Anonymous Landscape in the Bader Collection at Queen's, Int J for Class Trad, 97; auth, Yoshio Markino: A London Portfolio, Queen's Q, 97; auth, Yoshio Markino in the West London Hospital, J of Med Biog, 97; auth, A Missed Literary Source for Sir Charles G.D. Roberts' Out of Pompeii, Can Poetry, 97; auth, Giorgione's Tempest and the Flight of Hagar, Artibus et Historiae, 97; auth, Amicus Medicus: Medicine and Epicurean Therapy in Lucretius, Mem of the Am Acad in Rome, 97; ed, Sir Charles G D Roberts' Orion, and Other Poems, Canadian Poetry, forthcoming 98; auth, Education, Culture, and the Classics in Haliburton's Nova Scotia, Stud in Honor of Margaret Thomson, in Cahiers des Etudes Class, forth 98; auth, Nam Unguentum Dabo: Catullus 13 and Servius' Unguent of Phaon, Class Q, 98; auth, Horace, Vergil,and the Jews of Rome, Dionysius, forthcoming 98; auth, T R Glover at Queen's, Class Views, forthcoming 98; auth, Winnie-the-Pooh and the Canadian Connection, Queen's Q, forthcoming 98. **CONTACT ADDRESS** Dept of Classics, Queen's Univ at Kingston, 502 Watson Hall, Kingston, ON, Canada K7L 3N6. **EMAIL** kilpatri@post.queensu.ca

KIM, NAM-KIL
DISCIPLINE LINGUISTICS **EDUCATION** Univ of Wash, PhD, 74. **CAREER** Prof, Univ of Southern Calif; dir, Univ of Southern Calif Korean Studies Inst. **MEMBERSHIPS** Ling Soc of Am, Int Circle of Korean Ling, Int Asn of Korean Lang Educ. **RESEARCH** Linguistics, East Asian Linguistics, Korean Language Teaching. **SELECTED PUBLICATIONS** Auth, "On Experiential Sentences," Studies in Ling 22.1 (98): 161-204; auth, Modern Korean: An Intermediate Reader, Univ of Haw Press, 00. **CONTACT ADDRESS** Dept Asian Lang & Lit, Univ of So California, 3501 Trousdale Pkwy, Los Angeles, CA 90089-0091. **EMAIL** nkum@usc.edu

KIM-RENAUD, YOUNG-KEY
DISCIPLINE LANGUAGE, LINGUISTICS, & CULTURE **EDUCATION** Ewha Woman's Univ, BA, 63; Univ Calif at Berkeley, MA, 65; Inst des Professeurs de Francais a l'Etranger at Univ de Paris, Diploma in French, 66; Univ Haw, PhD, 74. **CAREER** Asst prog dir for Ling, U.S. Nat Sci Found, 78-79; vis lectr, Dept of E Asian Lang and Civilizations at Harvard Univ, 86-87; from asst professorial lectr to prof, The George Wash Univ, 83-. **HONORS AND AWARDS** Phi Kappa Phi, 75-; Fulbright Awds, 85, 94, & 97-98; Phi Beta Delta, 93; Achievement Awd, Int Asn of Korean Language Educ, 99. **MEMBERSHIPS** Ling Soc of Am, Int Circle of Korean Ling, Ling Soc of Korea, Korean Lang Asn, Korean Lang Soc, Int Asn for Korean Lang Educ, Asn for Asian Studies, The Asia Soc, The Korea Club, The Phonological Soc of Korea, The Fulbright Asn. **RESEARCH** Theoretical and Applied Linguistics (Phonology, Historical Linguistics, Sociolinguistics, Second Language Acquisition, Syntax, Language Pedagogy), Literary Translation: Intercultural Communication. **SELECTED PUBLICATIONS** Ed, King Sejong the Great: The Light of Fifteenth Century Korea, Int Circle of Korean Ling (Washington, DC), 92 & 97; ed, Theoretical Issues in Korean Linguistics, Ctr for the Study of Lang and Info at Stanford Univ, 94; ed, The Korean Alphabet: Its History and Structure, Univ of Haw Press (Honolulu, HI), 97; co-ed, "Creation and Re-Creation: Modern Korean Fiction and Its Translation," Sigur Center Asia papers 8 (00). **CONTACT ADDRESS** Dept Asian Lang & Lit, The George Washington Univ, 801 22nd St, NW, Washington, DC 20052. **EMAIL** kimrenau@gwu.edu

KING, ADELE C.
PERSONAL Born 07/26/1932, Omaha, NE, m, 1955, 1 child **DISCIPLINE** FRENCH **EDUCATION** Univ Iowa, BA, 54; Univ Leeds, MA, 60; Univ Paris, DU, 70. **CAREER** Lectr, Univ of Ibadan, 65; lectr, asst prof, and Head of French, Univ of Lagos, 67-70; from assoc prof to prof, Ahmadu Bello Univ, 73-76; vis assoc prof, Univ of Mo, 76-77; from assoc prof to prof, Ball State Univ, 86-. **HONORS AND AWARDS** AAVW Postdoctoral Fel, 77-78; Outstanding Fac Res Awd, Ball State Univ, 98. **MEMBERSHIPS** MLA, Women in French. **RESEARCH** Twentieth-Century Novel, Women's Writing, Francophone Literature of West Africa and the Caribbean, Camus, Contemporary Black Writing in France. **SELECTED PUBLICATIONS** Auth, Camus, Grove Press and Barnes & Noble, 66, Capricorn Books, 71; auth, Proust, Oliver & Boyd, 68; auth, Paul Nizan: ecrivain, Didier, 76; auth, The Writings of Camara Laye, Heinemann, 80; auth, French women Novelists: Defining a Female Style, Macmillan and St Martin's Press, 89; ed, Camus's L'Etranger: Fifty Years On, Macmillan and St Martin's Press, 92. **CONTACT ADDRESS** Dept For Lang, Ball State Univ, 2000 W Univ Ave, Muncie, IN 47306-1022.

KING, BEN L.
PERSONAL Born 01/31/1967, Bloomington, IN, s **DISCIPLINE** CLASSICS **EDUCATION** Princeton Univ, PhD, 97. **CAREER** Vis asst prof, Univ VA, 96-97; lectr, Univ Cal Riverside, 97-. **MEMBERSHIPS** Amer Philol Asn **RESEARCH** Greek intellectual history; Homer; Greek and Roman historigraphy. **SELECTED PUBLICATIONS** Auth, The Rhetoric of the Victim: Odysseus at the Swineherds Hut, Classical Antiquity, 99. **CONTACT ADDRESS** 600 Central Ave., #30, Riverside, CA 92507. **EMAIL** BENKING@veracl.ucr.edu

KING, CHARLOTTE P.
PERSONAL Born 09/04/1944, Mexia, TX, d, 1 child **DISCIPLINE** FRENCH, SPANISH **EDUCATION** Univ Tex, Austin, BA, 66; MA, 70; Middlebury Col, DML, 85. **CAREER** Dept ch, assoc prof, Gannon Univ, 97-. **HONORS AND AWARDS** Dean's List; Fac Res Grant; ISFL Grant. **MEMBERSHIPS** MLA; AATF; NE MLA; S MLA. **RESEARCH** Business French; 19th and 20th Century French Literature. **SELECTED PUBLICATIONS** Auth, "A Linguistic and a Cultural Competence - Can They Live Happily Together?" For Lang Annals (90); auth, Los Ojos Verdes: Un Analisis Semiotico del Uso del Titulo en La Casa Verde, de Mario Vargas Llosa, Univ Complutense de Madrid; auth, "Exito and C'est Tres Facile: A Study in the Use of Computers in Foreign Language Learning, J Lang Intl Business, AGSB (96); auth, "From Twenty Questions to the Internet: Activities of the Business Language Classroom," Global Bus Lang 996); auth, "Simone de Beauvoir Julia Kristeva: A Multiplication of the Loaves? Simone de Beauvoir J 14 (98). **CONTACT ADDRESS** Dept Foreign Language, Gannon Univ, 109 University Sq, Erie, PA 16541-0002. **EMAIL** king001@gannon.edu

KING, KATHERINE CALLEN
PERSONAL Born 10/27/1942, OR, s, 2 children **DISCIPLINE** COMPARATIVE LITERATURE **EDUCATION** Vassar Col, Poughkeepsie, AB, 67; Columbia Univ NYork, MA, 69; Princeton, PhD, 78. **CAREER** John Jay Col, NY, lectr, 70-72; UCLA, comp lit, asst prof, 78-85, UCLA ASSOC PROF COMP LIT AND CLASSICS, 85-; UCLA, comp lit, ch, 96-99;UCLA, PROF COMP LIT,99- **HONORS AND AWARDS** UCLA distg teach awd; Annual facul recog awd; Mortarbd facul of the quarter. **MEMBERSHIPS** ACLA; ICLA. **RESEARCH** Classical tradition; epic; gender stud; Cultural Stud. **SELECTED PUBLICATIONS** Achilles: Paradigms of the War Hero from Homer to the Middle Ages, Univ Cal Press, 87; paperbk ed, Univ Cal Press, 94; Homer, ed, classical heritage series, Garland Press, 94; Hybrid Genre? Leslie Marmon

Silko's Epic Almanac?, auth, Forthcoming in: The Postcolonial Cond of Hybridity, ed Najib Mokhtari, Univ Ibn Tofail Faculte des Lettres et des Sciences Humaines, Kenitra Morocco, 98; many numerous articles. **CONTACT ADDRESS** Dept of Comparative Lit, Univ of California, Los Angeles, 212 Royce Hall, Los Angeles, CA 90095-1536. **EMAIL** king@humnet.ucla.edu

KING, PETER
PERSONAL Born New York, NY **DISCIPLINE** CLASSICS, ANCIENT HISTORY **EDUCATION** Fordham Univ, MA; Univ NC, JD; PhD. **MEMBERSHIPS** Am Philol Asn. **RESEARCH** Roman Law, History and Society; Latin Language. **CONTACT ADDRESS** Dept Class, Temple Univ, 213 E 84th St, New York, NY 10028. **EMAIL** pking002@astro.temple.edu

KING, SAMUEL C.
PERSONAL Born 06/18/1944, Jena, LA, m, 1968, 1 child **DISCIPLINE** SPANISH **EDUCATION** La State Univ, BA, 66; MA, 66; PhD, 71. **CAREER** From asst prof to prof, Clemson Univ, 71-; chemn of dept of lang, Clemson Univ, 95-. **HONORS AND AWARDS** NEH Endowment Fund, 94. **MEMBERSHIPS** MLA, Asn of Departments of For Lang. **RESEARCH** History of Spanish Photography, Pictorialism, Photographic Printing Processes. **SELECTED PUBLICATIONS** Auth, The Photographic Impressionists of Spain: A History of the Aesthetics and Technique of Pictorial Photography, The Edwin Mellen Press (New York), 89; auth, "El Libro del Carbon: Introduccion y Guia de Trabajo para la Impresion en Carbon Monochromo," Cuadernos de Fotografia Alternativa, 98; auth, Schmidt de las Heras: Fotografias 1944-1960, Xunta de Galica, 99; co-ed, La Goma Bicromatada: Procedimiento Basico, Novelda, 99. **CONTACT ADDRESS** Dept Modern Lang, Clemson Univ, Clemson, SC 29634-0001. **EMAIL** sanking@hubcap.clemson.edu

KINGERY, SANDRA L.
PERSONAL Born 11/22/1964, IL, d **DISCIPLINE** SPANISH **EDUCATION** Lawrence Univ, BA, 86; Univ Wis Madison, MA, 89; PhD, 95. **CAREER** TA, Univ Wis Madison, 88-94; asst prof, Lycoming Col, 94-96, 98-; asst prof, Wake Forest Univ, 96-97. **HONORS AND AWARDS** Junior Fac Teaching Awd, Lycoming Col, 99. **MEMBERSHIPS** MLA, AATSP, ACTFL, AAUP, Feministas Unidas, Asociacion de literatura femenina hispanica. **RESEARCH** Contemporary Spanish female writers. **SELECTED PUBLICATIONS** Auth, "Monster Mothers: Ana Maria Moix's 'Julia,'" Women and Creativity, Greenwood Pr, forthcoming; auth, Memories of Love: Ana Maria Moix and Esther Tusquets Remember, Mester, forthcoming; transl, Julia by Ana Maria Moix, Univ Nebr Pr, forthcoming. **CONTACT ADDRESS** Dept Span, Lycoming Col, Box 2, Williamsport, PA 17701. **EMAIL** kingery@lycoming.edu

KINGSTON, JOHN
DISCIPLINE LINGUISTICS **EDUCATION** Univ Chicago, BA, 76, MA, 77; Univ Calif Berkeley, PhD, 85. **CAREER** Assoc prof. **RESEARCH** Relationship of phonetic theory; methods to phonology. **SELECTED PUBLICATIONS** Auth, Articulatory Binding, Cambridge, 90; Integrating Articulations in the Perception of Vowel Height, Phonetica, 91; co-auth, The Inadequacy of Underspecification, NE Ling Soc, 89; Resonance Versus Source Characteristics in Perceiving Spectral Continuity between Vowels and Consonants, Univ Wis; Phonetic Knowledge, Language, 94. **CONTACT ADDRESS** Linguistics Dept, Univ of Massachusetts, Amherst, S College 321, Amherst, MA 01003. **EMAIL** jkingston@linguist.umass.edu

KINGSTONE, BASIL D.
DISCIPLINE TRANSLATION ENGLISH-FRENCH; FRENCH-ENGLISH **EDUCATION** Oxford, BA, MA, DPhil; Ottawa, MA. **CAREER** Prof & ch French prog; ed, Can Jour Neth Stud & Newsl the Can Asn for the Advancement of Neth Stud and the Can Asn for Transl Stud. **RESEARCH** Netherlandic Dutch and Flemish studies; Andre Gide. **SELECTED PUBLICATIONS** Transl, Quebec short stories into English & Mijn vriend Andre Gide into French. **CONTACT ADDRESS** Dept of French Language and Literature, Univ of Windsor, 401 Sunset Ave, Windsor, ON, Canada N9B 3P4. **EMAIL** bkingst@uwindsor.ca

KINKADE, RICHARD PAISLEY
PERSONAL Born 01/07/1939, Los Angeles, CA, m, 1962, 5 children **DISCIPLINE** SPANISH **EDUCATION** Yale Univ, BA, 60, PhD(Span), 65. **CAREER** Instr Span, Yale Univ, 60-62, 63-65; from asst prof to assoc prof Romance Lang, Univ Ariz, 65-71; prof Romance Lang & chmn dept, Emory Univ, 71-74; prof Romance Lang & head dept Romance & Class Lang, Univ Conn, 77-82; prof Span & dean, fac of Humanities, Univ Ariz, 82-87, bus mgr, La Coronica, 72-76; consult, Div Educ, Nat Endowment for Humanities, 76-77, res grant, 78-79; reviewer Jacob K Javits Fel Prog, US Dept of Ed, 97. **MEMBERSHIPS** MLA; Mediaeval Acad Am; SAtlantic Mod Lang Asn; Asn Int Hispanistas; Am Asn Teachers Span & Port. **RESEARCH** Medieval Spanish language and literature. **SELECTED PUBLICATIONS** Ed, "Los Lucidarios espanoles" critical edition, Madrid: Ed. Gredos, 68; auth, The historical date of the coplas and the death of Jorge Manrique, Speculum, 3, 70; A new Latin source for Berceo's Milagros: MS 110 of Madrid's Biblioteca Nacional, Romance Philol, 11, 71; Sancho IV: puente literario entre Alfonso el Sabio y Juan Manual, PMLA, 10, 72; coauth (with John E Keller), Iconography and Narrative Art in Medieval Spanish Fiction, Univ Press Ky, 84; auth, of Alfonso X, Cantiga 235, and the Events of 1269-1278, Speculum 67, (92), 284-323; ed., of "Juan Manuel, Ordenamjentos dados a la villa de Penafiel, 10 de abril de 1345: A Reconstruction of the Manuscript Text with an Introduction and Annotated English Translation, Spanish Series, 112, Madison, Wisconsin: Hispanic Seminary of Medieval Studies, 96; auth, of "A Thirteenth-Century Precursor of the Libro de buen amor: The Art d'amors, La coronica 24.2, (96), 123-139; auth, of "Myth and Reality in the Miracle of Cantiga 29" La coronica 28.1, (99), 35-69. **CONTACT ADDRESS** Dept of Spanish and Portuguese, Univ of Arizona, Tucson, AZ 85721-0067. **EMAIL** rpk@u.arizona.edu

KIPA, ALBERT ALEXANDER
PERSONAL Born 09/10/1939, Kiev, Ukraine, m, 1966, 2 children **DISCIPLINE** GERMAN & SLAVIC LITERATURE **EDUCATION** City Col NYork, BA, 62; Univ Pa, AM, 64, PhD(Ger), 72. **CAREER** Vis lectr English, Univ Freiburg, 64-65; from instr to prof Ger & Russ, 66-96, J & F Seeger Prof of Comp Lit, Muhlenberg Col, 96-, head, Dept For Lang and Lit, 89-93, 97-; Mem Nat Adv Coun, Ethnic Heritage Studies, US Dept Educ, 80-82. **HONORS AND AWARDS** NEH study grant, 78; Lindback Found Awd for Distinquished Teaching, 80; sr Fulbright fel, Germany, 81; Cert of Merit, Am Asn Teachers Ger & Goethe Inst, 87; Citation for Outstanding Service in For Lang Educ, PA Dept Educ, 91; IREX grant, to Ukraine, 95. **MEMBERSHIPS** AAUP; Am Asn Teachers Ger; Am Asn Teachers Slavic & EEurop Lang; PA State Mod Lang Asn (pres, 90-92). **RESEARCH** Germano-Slavic literary relations; translation theory and practise. **SELECTED PUBLICATIONS** Auth, Gerhart Hauptmann in Russia: First notices, Mod Lang Notes, 10/73; Gerhart Hauptmann in Russia: 1880-1917, Helmut Buske, 74; K D Bal'mont and Gerhart Hauptmann, In: Views and Reviews of Modern German Literature, Delp, 74; Ivan Franko's view of Gerhart Hauptmann, In: Probleme der Komparatistik und Interpretation, 77 & co-ed, Probleme der Komparatistik und Interpretation, 77, Bouvier; Aufnahme--Weitergabe: Literarische Impulse um Lessing und Goethe, Helmut Buske, 82; auth, The Poet as Translator: Paulo Hrabous'kyj and Goethe's Faust, In: Aufnahrue-Weiter-gabe.., 82; Lesja Ukrainka and Gerhart Hauptmann: Anatomy of an Admiration, In: Hauptmann Research. New Directions, Peter Lang, 86; Das Hauptmannbild Lesja Ukrainkas und seine Rolle in ihrem Schaffen, In: Lesia Ukrainka und die europaische Literatur, B"hlau Verlag, 94; coauth, Goethe's Weimar and the Slavic Realm: The Ukrainian Dimension, In: A Reassessment of Weimar Classicism, Edwin Mellon Press, 96. **CONTACT ADDRESS** Dept of Foreign Lang, Muhlenberg Col, 2400 W Chew St, Allentown, PA 18104-5586. **EMAIL** kipa@muhlenberg.edu

KIRBY, CAROL
PERSONAL Born 10/12/1946, Akron, OH, m, 1969 **DISCIPLINE** LINGUISTICS **EDUCATION** Univ Akron, BA, 67; Univ Wisc-Madison, MA, 69; Univ Ky, PhD, 77. **CAREER** From instr to asst prof, Purdue Univ, 75-83; instr, Slippery Rock Univ, 83-85; vis assoc prof, Mich State Univ, 92-93; from asst prof to prof, Buffalo State Univ, 85-. **HONORS AND AWARDS** Valedictorian, Univ of Akron, 67; Sigma Delta Pi, 72. **MEMBERSHIPS** Int Asn of Hispanists, Int Asn of the Golden Age, Soc for Textual Scholar, Soc for Emblem Studies. **RESEARCH** Spanish golden age drama, textual criticism and editing. **SELECTED PUBLICATIONS** Auth, Critical Edition, El rey don Pedro en Madrid (Kassel: Edition Reichenberger, 98). **CONTACT ADDRESS** Dept For Lang, Buffalo State Col, 1300 Elmwood Ave, Buffalo, NY 14222-1004.

KIRBY, JOHN T.
PERSONAL Born 05/09/1955, New Haven, CT, 2 children **DISCIPLINE** CLASSICS & COMPARATIVE LITERATURE **EDUCATION** Choate Sch, diploma, 73; Univ NC Chapel Hill, AB, 77; Univ NC Chapel Hill, MA, 81; Univ NC Chapel Hill, PhD, 85. **CAREER** Asst prof, class lang and lit, Smith Col, 85-87; founding chair, prog in class studies, Purdue Univ, 88-94; chair, prog in comparative lit, Purdue Univ, 94-. **HONORS AND AWARDS** Phi Eta Sigma, 74; Phi Beta Kappa, 76; Morehead Scholar, Univ NC, 73-77; Univ Res Asst, Univ NC, 80-81; Classics Teaching fel, Univ NC, 83-84; Software develop grant, ACIS Found of IBM, 85; Robert E. Frane Memorial Scholar, 85; Morris House fel, Smith Col, 86; Facul Teaching Awd nominee, Smith Col, 86; Libr Scholars grant prog award, Purdue Univ, 87; Facul teaching award nominee, Smith Col, 87, 88; XL Summer facul grant, Purdue Res Found, 88; Univ Outstanding Undergraduate Teaching Awd nominee, Purdue Univ, 88; XL summer facul grant, Purdue Res Found, 90; XL Intl Travel grant, Purdue Res Found, 91; res leave, dept foreign lang and lit, Purdue Univ, spring, 91; NEH fel, Univ Iowa, fall, 91; fel, Ctr for Humanistic Studies, Purdue Univ, spring, 93; Scholar-in-residence, Choate Rosemary Hall, fall, 93; Sch of Liberal Arts Outstanding Teaching award, Purdue Univ, 93; Amer Philol Asn award for Excellence in the Teaching of the Classics, 96; Twentieth Century award for achievement, Intl Bio Ctr, 97; man of the year, am biog inst, 96; international man of the year, int biog ctr, 96-97; listed in int dir of distinguished leadership, 7th ed, 97; listed in int who's who of intellectuals, 12th ed, 97. **MEMBERSHIPS** Mod Lang Asn; Amer Comparative Lit Asn; Amer Philol Asn; Calif Class Asn; Class Asn of the Middle West and South; Amer Soc for the Hist of Rhetoric. **RESEARCH** Classical Greek and Latin literature; Classical rhetoric and poetics; Literary theory. **SELECTED PUBLICATIONS** Auth, The Rhetoric of Cicero's Pro Cluentio, 90; ed, The Comparative Reader: A Handlist of Basic Reading in Comparative Literature, 98; jour articles, Amer Jour of Philol, 118, 517-554, 97; Philos and Rhetoric, 30, 190-202, 97; Voices in Italian Amer, 7, 207-211, 96; Ill Class Studies, 20, 77-81, 95; Voices in Italian Amer, 6, 71-76, 95; book chap, Ciceronian Rhetoric: Theory and Practice, 13-31, Roman Eloquence: Rhetoric in Society and Literature, 97; Classical Greek Origins of Western Aesthetic Theory, 29-45, 96; The Great Triangle in Early Greek Rhetoric and Poetics, 3-15, 94; The Neo-Latin Verse of Joseph Tusiani, 180-204, Joseph Tusiani: Poet, Translator, Humanist, 94; auth, Secret of the Muses Retold: Classical Influences on Itlaian Authors of the Twentieth Century, Chicago: University of Chicago Press, in press; ed, Landmark Essays on Ciceronian Rhetoric, Davis CA: Hermagoras Press/Erlbaum, in press. **CONTACT ADDRESS** Dept of For Lang and Lit, Purdue Univ, West Lafayette, 1080 Schleman Hall, West Lafayette, IN 47907-1354. **EMAIL** corax@purdue.edu

KIRBY, STEVEN D.
PERSONAL Born 02/21/1945, Waukegan, IL, m, 1969 **DISCIPLINE** SPANISH **EDUCATION** Univ Virginia, BA, 67, MA, 68; Univ Kent, PhD, 76. **CAREER** Asst prof Span, Purdue Univ, 76-81; asst to assoc prof, 84-91; prof, E Mich Univ, 91- . **HONORS AND AWARDS** Phi Beta Kappa, 67. **MEMBERSHIPS** Asn Int de Hisp. **RESEARCH** Juan Ruiz and his Libro De Buen Amor, Medieval Spanish narrative poetry, Old Spanish language and linguistics. **SELECTED PUBLICATIONS** Auth, "La Funcion Estetica de la Rima Consecutive en el Libro de Buen Amor," Revista de Filol Espanola, Madrid, pp 101-121, (99). **CONTACT ADDRESS** Dept For Lang, Eastern Michigan Univ, 219 Alexander Hall, Ypsilanti, MI 48197-2255. **EMAIL** Steven.Kirby@emich.edu

KIRKHAM, VICTORIA E.
PERSONAL Born 05/07/1942, Jersey City, NJ, s **DISCIPLINE** ITALIAN **EDUCATION** Wellesley Col, BA, 64; Univ Ill, MA, 67; Johns Hopkins Univ, MA, 69; PhD, 72. **CAREER** Asst Prof, SUNY, 70-72; Asst Prof to Full Prof, Univ Pa, 72-. **HONORS AND AWARDS** Fulbright, Italy, 64-65; Fel, Harvard Univ,777-78; NEH Fel. 96; Newberry Fel, 00-01. **MEMBERSHIPS** Am Asn of Italian Studies, Am Asn of Teachers of Italian, Dante Soc of Am, Italian Art Soc, Mod Lang Ans. **RESEARCH** Italian literature and culture of Middle Ages and Renaissance; Women's Studies; film. **SELECTED PUBLICATIONS** Auth, Diana's Hunt. La Caccia di Diana. Boccaccio's First Fiction, Univ. Penn Press, 91; auth, The Sign of Reason in Boccaccio's Fiction, Leo S Olschki Pub, 93; auth, Fabulous Vernacular: Boccaccio's Filocolo and the Art of Medieval Fiction, Univ Mich Press, forthcoming; ed, Boccaccio 1990. The Poet and his Renaissance Reception, 90; auth, "Early Portraits of Boccaccio. A Doorway to the Decameron," in Approaches to Teaching Boccaccio's Decameron, forthcoming; auth, "Dante's Ravenna and Antonioni's Red Desert," in Dante at the Movies, Univ of Toronto Press; forthcoming; auth, "Cosimo and Eleonora in Shepherdland: A Lost Eclogue by Laura Battiferra degli Ammannati," in The Cultural Politics of duke Cosimo I de Medici, forthcoming. **CONTACT ADDRESS** Dept Romance Lang, Univ of Pennsylvania, 34th and Spruce St, Philadelphia, PA 19104.

KIRKPATRICK, PETER S.
PERSONAL Born 09/13/1964, WV, m, 1990 **DISCIPLINE** FRENCH **EDUCATION** Univ Richmond, BA, 86; Univ Va, MA, 88; PhD, 92. **CAREER** Asst prof to assoc prof, Va Commonwealth Univ, 92-; foreign correspondent, L'Humanite, 88-. **HONORS AND AWARDS** Phi Betta Kappa; Fulbright; Palmes Academiques Nomination. **MEMBERSHIPS** MLA, AATF, AFCS, Societe Jaures. **RESEARCH** French cinema, French media, French regional culture, French political discourse. **SELECTED PUBLICATIONS** Auth, "La capitalisme horizon indepassable?" La Pensee; auth,"Semiotics and Gestures in French Political Discourse," Semiotics, 93; auth, "L'avenir du marxisme aux Etats-Unis," La Pensee; auth, "La contexte et ses effets sur la gestualite dans le discours politique," in Semiotics Around the World; auth, "La gestuelle dans le discours politique francais," Echos. **CONTACT ADDRESS** Dept For Lang, Virginia Commonwealth Univ, Box 842021, Richmond, VA 23284. **EMAIL** pkirkpat@atla.vcu.edu

KIRKPATRICK, SUSAN
PERSONAL Born 01/16/1942, Newcastle, WY, 1 child **DISCIPLINE** SPANISH LITERATURE, FEMINIST CRITICISM **EDUCATION** Univ Wyo, BA, 63; Cambridge Univ, MA, 65; Harvard Univ, PhD(comp lit), 72. **CAREER** Instr Span, Brandeis Univ, 70-71; asst prof Span Lit, 71-78, from assoc to prof Span Lit, Univ Calif, San Diego, 78-88. **HONORS AND AWARDS** Guggenheim Fellowship, 86-87. **MEMBERSHIPS**

MLA; Int Asn Hispanists; Exec Council 93-96. **RESEARCH** Spanish nineteenth century literature; romanticism. **SELECTED PUBLICATIONS** Auth, From Octavia Santino to El yermo de las almas, Rev Hispanica Mod, Vol 37, 72-73; Tirano Banderas y la estructura de la historian Nueva Rev Filologia Hispanica, Vol 24, 76; Spanish romaniticism and the liberal project: The crisis of Larra, Studies Romanticism, Vol 16, 77; Larra: El laberinto inextricable de un romantics liberal, Gredos, Madrid, 77; The Ideology of Costumbrismo, Ideologies & Lit, Vol 2, No 7; auth, Las Romanticas: Women and Subjectivity in Spain, Univ Calif Pr (Berkeley), 89; auth, Antologia poetica de escritoras del siglo XIX, Castalia (Madrid), 92; On the threshold of the realist novel: Fernan Caballero, Publ Mod Lang Asn; Fantasy, Seduction and the Woman Reader: Rosalia de Castro's Novels, in The Politics/Poetics of Gender, ed. Lou Charnon-Deutsch and Jo Labanyi, New York, Oxford Univ Press, 95; auth, "Constituting the Subject: Race, Gender and Nation in the Early Nineteenth Century," in Culture and the State in Spain, ed. Tom Lewis and Francisco Sanchez (NYork: Garland Pr, 99). **CONTACT ADDRESS** Lit Dept, Univ of California, San Diego, 9500 Gilman Dr, La Jolla, CA 92093-5003. **EMAIL** skirkpatrick@ucsd.edu

KIRKWOOD, GORDON MACDONALD
PERSONAL Born 05/07/1916, Toronto, ON, Canada, m, 1940, 2 children **DISCIPLINE** CLASSICAL PHILOLOGY **EDUCATION** Univ Toronto, AB, 38; Cornell Univ, AM, 39; Johns Hopkins Univ, PhD(Greek), 42. **CAREER** Latin master, Lower Can Col, 45-46; from instr to prof, 46-73, chmn dept, 63-72, Frederic J Whiton Prof Classics, Cornell Univ 73-, Ford fel, 53-54; Guggenheim fel, 56-57; Am Coun Learned Soc fel, 62-63; co-ed, Cornell Studies in Class Philol; Nat Endowment for Hum fel, 77. **MEMBERSHIPS** Am Philol Asn; Class Asn Atlantic States; AAUP. **RESEARCH** Greek lit. **SELECTED PUBLICATIONS** Auth, A Study of Sophoclean Drama, Cornell Univ, 58; A Short Guide to Classical Mythology, Holt, 60; Early Greek Monody, 74 & ed, Poetry and Poetics, Studies in Honor of James Hutton, 75, Cornell Univ; Selections from Pindar, Am Philol Asn, 82. **CONTACT ADDRESS** Dept of Classics, Cornell Univ, Ithaca, NY 14850. **EMAIL** GMK4@Cornell.edu

KISACKY, JULIE
DISCIPLINE ITALIAN **EDUCATION** Wells Col, BA, 87; Rutgers Univ, MA, 90; PhD, 95. **CAREER** Vis instr, Ohio Univ, 91-94; lectr, Baylor Univ, 95-. **HONORS AND AWARDS** Grant, Baylor Univ Res Coun Grant, 98. **MEMBERSHIPS** MLA, SCMLA, AATI, AAIS, RSA, Am Boccaccio Asn, Phi Beta Kappa, Phi Sigma Iota. **RESEARCH** Ariosto, Boiardo, Boccaccio, Italian Renaissance. **SELECTED PUBLICATIONS** Auth, Magic in Boiardo and Ariosto, Peter Lang, 00. **CONTACT ADDRESS** Dept Modern Lang, Baylor Univ, Waco, PO Box 97391, Waco, TX 76798-7391. **EMAIL** julia_kisacky@baylor.edu

KITCHELL, KENNETH F.
PERSONAL Born 10/24/1947, Brockton, MA, m, 1970, 1 child **DISCIPLINE** CLASSICAL STUDIES **EDUCATION** Coll of Holy Cross, BA, 69; Loyola Univ Chicago, MA, 73; PhD, 76. **CAREER** Loyola Univ, 74; Quigley Preparatory Sem S Chicago, 74-76; Cath High School Baton Rouge, 80-81; Am School of Class Studies Athens Greece, 89; co-dir, Program in Greece Vergilian Soc of Am, 90; instr, 76-78; asst prof, 83-94, assoc prof, 94-97, prof, LA State Univ, 97-; vis prof to full prof, Univ Mass, 98-. **HONORS AND AWARDS** Amoco Found award for Outstanding Undergraduate Techg, 80; Am Philol Asn Awd for excellence in Tchg of Classics, 83; LSU Student Govt Asn Fac Awd, 91; Robert L Amborski Distinguished Honors Prof Awd, 93; Ovatio, Clasical Asn of the Middle W and S, 94; Summer Scholar Centre for Hellenic Studies Wash DC, 97; LSU Alumni Asn Distinguished Fac Awd, 97; Who's Who in the South and Southwest; Who's Who of Emerging Leaders in America; Men of Achievement; Dictionary of International Biography; Who's Who in American Education; Full Prof, Classics, Univ of Mass, 99-. **MEMBERSHIPS** Am Philol Asn; Archaeol Inst Am; Am Class League; Asn of Ancient Hist; Class Asn of the Middle west and S; Class Asn of New England, Joint Asn of Class Tchrs; Mass Foreign Lang Asn; Class Asn of Mass; Class Asn of the Pacific Northwest Am Council on the Tchg of Foreign Lang. **RESEARCH** Latin and Greek Pedagogy; Crete. **SELECTED PUBLICATIONS** Entering the Stadium, Approaches to Ancient Greek Athletics, Class Bull, 98;coauth, A Trilogy on the Herpetology of Linnaeus's Systema Naturae X, Smithsonian Herpetological Service, 94; Albertus Magnus De Animalibus: A Medieval Summa Zoologica, 99. **CONTACT ADDRESS** The Dept of Classics, Univ of Massachusetts, Amherst, 520 Herter Hall, Amherst, MA 01003. **EMAIL** kkitchel@classics.umass.edu

KLAUSENBURGER, JURGEN
PERSONAL Born 07/22/1942, Reghin, Romania, m, 1967, 3 children **DISCIPLINE** ROMANCE LINGUISTICS **EDUCATION** Univ Mich, Ann Arbor, BA, 64, MA, 66, PhD(Romance ling), 69. **CAREER** Asst prof, 69-75, assoc prof, 75-81, Prof French and Romance Ling, Univ Wash, 81-95, prof Linguistics, 95-. **HONORS AND AWARDS** Fel, Camargo Found, Cassis, France, 82, 85. **MEMBERSHIPS** Ling Soc Am. **RESEARCH** Historical Romance linguistics; French phonology; phonological theory; grammaticalization. **SELECTED PUBLICATIONS** Auth, French Prosodics and Phonotactics: An Historical Typology, 70 & Historische Franzosische Phonologie aus Generativer Sicht, 74, Max Niemeyer, Tubingen, Ger; Rule inversion, opacity, conspiracies: French liaison and elision, Lingua 34, 74; Latin vocalic quantity to qualit: A pseudo-problem?, In: Diachronic Studies in Romance Linguistics, Mouton, The Hague, 75; (De)-morphologization in Latin, Lingua 40, 76; French linking phenomena: A natural generative analysis, Lang, 78; Morphologization: Studies in Latin and Romance Morphophonology, Max Niemeyer, Tubingen Ger, 79; Romance Phonological Studies in the 70's, In: Proceedings of the Tenth Anniversary Symposium on Romance Linguistics, Univ Wash, 81; auth, French Liaison and Linguistic Theory, Steiner, Stuttgart, Ger, 84; auth, Grammaticalization: Studies in Latin and Romance Morphosyntax, Benjamins, Amsterdam, the Netherlands, 00. **CONTACT ADDRESS** Dept of Linguistics, Univ of Washington, Seattle, WA 98195. **EMAIL** jklaus@u.washington.edu

KLEE, CAROL A.
PERSONAL Born 09/06/1953, Royal Oak, MI, m, 1987, 1 child **DISCIPLINE** HISPANIC LINGUISTICS EDUCATION **EDUCATION** Col of Wooster, BA, 75; Univ of Tex Austin, MA, 80; PhD, 84. **CAREER** Lectr, Univ of IL Urbana, 83=85; asst prof to assoc prof, chair, Univ of Minn, 85-. **HONORS AND AWARDS** Nat Presby Scholar, 71-75; Tinker Field Res Grant, 85; Grant, Univ of Minn, 86, 88, 89, 94-96, 99, 00; Diploma in Recognition of Outstanding Serv, Univ of Minn, 92; Emma Birkmaier Awd, 97. **MEMBERSHIPS** Am Assoc of Appl Ling; Am Assoc of Teachers of Span and Port; AAUP; Am Assoc of Univ Supervisors, Coordinators and Directors of Lang Prog; MLA; AM Coun on the Teaching of For Lang; Minn Coun on the Teaching of Lang and Cult. **RESEARCH** Spanish Sociolinguistics, Quechua-Spanish language contact, the acquisition of Spanish as a second language, foreign language teaching and learning. **SELECTED PUBLICATIONS** Auth, "Spanish language contact in the Andes", Word 41 (90): 35-46; coauth, "Reconsidering the FL requirement: From seat-time to proficiency in the Minnesota experience", Problems Confronting Foreign Language Programs in the 1990's, ed Sally Sieloff Magnan, Heinle & Heinle (91): 55-69; ed, Sociolinguistics of the Spanish-speaking world: Spain, Latin America and the United States, Bilingual Rev Pr, (Tucson, AZ), 91; ed, Faces in a crowd: the individual learner in multisection courses, AAUSC Series on Issues in Lang Prog Direction, Heinle & Heinle, 94; coauth, "The expression of past reference in Spanish narratives of Spanish/Quechua bilingual speakers", Spanish in contact with other languages, ed Carmen Silva-Corvalan, Georgetown Univ Pr, (95): 52-70; auth, "The Spanish and Peruvian Andes: The influence of Quechua on Spanish Language structure", Spanish in contact: Studies in bilingualism, eds John B Jensen and Ana Roca, Cascadilla Pr, (96): 73-91; coauth, "The undergraduate foreign language immersion program in Spanish at the University of Minnesota", Content-Based Instruction in the Foreign Language Classroom, ed Steven Stryker and Betty L Leaver, Georgetown Univ Pr, (97): 140-173; auth, "Communication as an Organizing Principle in the National Standards: Sociolinguistic Aspects of Spanish Language Teaching", Hispania 81, (98): 321-333; auth, "Foreign Language Instruction: Past, Present, and Future", Handbook of Undergraduate Second Language Education: ESL, Bilingual, and Foreign Language Instruction for a Multilingual World, ed Judith Rosenthal, Lawrence Erlbaum, 00; coed, The interaction of social and cognitive factors in second language acquisition, Proceedings of the 1999 Second Lang Res Forum, Cascadilla Pr, (Somerville, MA), (forthcoming). **CONTACT ADDRESS** Dept Span, Univ of Minnesota, Twin Cities, 9 Pleasant St SE, Minneapolis, MN 55455-0194. **EMAIL** klee@umn.edu

KLEE, ILDORA
PERSONAL Born 03/25/1930, New York, NY, d, 3 children **DISCIPLINE** SPANISH **EDUCATION** Middlebury Col, BA; Fairfield Univ, MA; Yale Univ, PhD. **CAREER** Instructor, Sacred Heart Univ, 92, 93-94, 98-99; Instructor, Univ Bridgeport, 66-71; Instructor, Yale Univ, 79-80; Adj Prof, Fairfield Univ, 98-. **HONORS AND AWARDS** Phi Beta Kappa. **MEMBERSHIPS** Am Trans Asn, Phi Beta Kappa. **CONTACT ADDRESS** Dept Mod Lang, Fairfield Univ, 1073 N Benson Rd, Fairfield, CT 06430-5171.

KLEIN, ANNE
DISCIPLINE RELIGIOUS STUDIES, TIBETAN BUDDHISM, CLASSICAL TIBETAN LANGUAGE **EDUCATION** Univ VA, PhD, 81. **CAREER** Prof, ch, dept Relig Stud, Rice Univ. **HONORS AND AWARDS** Fulbright dissertation res fel, India and Nepal, 80; NEH summer grant, 94; NEH transl grant, 94; adv bd, Women & Religion Prog, Harvard Divinity Sch; Ford Found Fel, 99-01. **MEMBERSHIPS** AAR; Int Asn of Tibetan Scholars. **RESEARCH** Bon & Buddhis Dzogchen philos/epistemology in early Tibetan tradition; issues of gender & embodiment. **SELECTED PUBLICATIONS** Auth, Knowing, Naming, and Negation: A Sourcebook on Tibetan Sautrantika; Knowledge and Liberation; Path to the Middle: Oral Madhyamika Philosophy in Tibet: The Spoken Scholarship of Kensur Yeshey Tupden; Meeting the Great Bliss Queen: Buddhists, Feminists, and the Art of the Self, Beacon Press, 94. **CONTACT ADDRESS** Rice Univ, PO Box 1892, Houston, TX 77251-1892. **EMAIL** klein-A@rice.edu

KLEIN, DENNIS ALLAN
PERSONAL Born 10/19/1943, New York, NY, 1 child **DISCIPLINE** SPANISH **EDUCATION** Univ Kans, BSEd, 65, MA, 67; Univ Mass, PhD, 73. **CAREER** Asst prof, Southwest Mo State Univ, 73-75; vis instr, Univ Mo-Rolla, 75-76; asst prof, 76-78, assoc prof, 78-83, prof, 83-, Span, Univ S Dak, Bibliog, MLA; Nat Endowment for Humanities summer fel, 79, 84, 93, 94, 95; Exxon Foreign Lang Workshop, 81. **HONORS AND AWARDS** Fulbright Fel, 97; NEH grants, 99; Writer-in-Residene; Fundacion Valparaiso, Majacar, Spain, 01. **MEMBERSHIPS** Sigma Delta Pi, Pi Delta Phi, Phi Kappa Phi. **RESEARCH** Spanish drama; bibliography; comparative drama. **SELECTED PUBLICATIONS** Auth, Asi que pasen cinco anos: A Search for Sexual Identity, J Span Studies: 20th Century, 75; The Old Women in the Theatre of Garcia Lorca, 75 & Christological Imagery in Lorca's Yerma, 78, Garcia Lorca Rev; coauth, Garcia Lorca: A Selectively Annotated Bibliography of Criticism, Vol I, 79 & Vol II (in press), Garland; auth, Peter Shaffer, Twayne, 79, Rev Ed. 93; "Literary Onomastics in Peter Shaffer's Shrivings and Equus," Lit Onomastic Studies, 80; Peter and Anthony Shaffer: A Reference Guide, G K Hall, 82; auth, "Amadeus: The Third Part of Peter Shaffer's Dramatic Trilogy," Modern Language Studies, 83; auth, Blood Wedding, Yerma, and the House of Bernarda Alba: Federico Garcia Lorca's Tragic Trilogy, Twayne, 91; auth, "The Influence of Aeschylus's Oresteia on Israel Horowitz's Alfred Trilogy," in Israel Horovitz: A Collection of Critical Essays, Greenwood, 94; auth, "Sex, War, and Jewish Law in Four Plays about King David and His Family," Modern Jewish Studies 11, (99): 101-34; auth, Spanish Writers on Gay and Lesbian Themes: A Bio-Critical Sourcebook; auth, Contemporary Jewish-American Dramatists and Poets: A Bio-Critical Sourcebook. **CONTACT ADDRESS** Dept of Modern Lang, Univ of So Dakota, Vermillion, 414 E Clark St, Vermillion, SD 57069-2390. **EMAIL** dklein@sunflowr.usd.edu

KLEIN, ILONA
PERSONAL Born 03/16/1956, Geneva, Switzerland **DISCIPLINE** ITALIAN **EDUCATION** Laurea Univ, Rome, 81; Univ Wis Madison, MA, 82; PhD, 86. **CAREER** Asst prof, Loyola Univ, 86-94; assoc prof, Brigham Young Univ, 94-. **MEMBERSHIPS** AAIS; AATI; MLA; ACR. **RESEARCH** Italian and German romanticism; Italian Shoah (Holocaust); Primo Levi. **SELECTED PUBLICATIONS** Transl, Dana Perocco (Ca' Foscari, Venezia), "Avvicinarsi alle "Terre Nuove" nella realta e nella fantasia: Italian del '500 che scrivono sull'America," WPSWL (Erdman Press: Greensburg, PA), forthcoming; rev, Primo Levi, Italica 75 (98): 131-132; rev, Novella Bellucci, eds. Walter Binni, Lezioni Leopardiane, Italica 74 (97): 102-103; rev, Understanding Primo Levi, Rocky Mountain Rev 50 (96), 86-87; auth, "Walters W2O: Chapters to Be Observed by the Singers of the Cappella Giulia (1574)," forthcoming; auth, "Goethe's Die Leiden des jungen Werthers: An Epistolary Novel, or A Stage Drama in Disguise?," European Romantic Rev 7 (97): 134-158; auth, "Let's Surf-the-Net! World-Wide Web (WWW) Sites in Italy, or: How/Why Include a Web-Browser Component in Culture and Civilization Classes," Mid-Atlantic J Foreign Lang Pedagogy, 5 (96): 1-20; auth, "Primo Levi and Bruno Piazza: Auschwitz in Italian Literature," Remembrance, Repentance, Reconciliation, Studies in the Shoah, XXI, ed. Douglas Tobler (Lanham, MD: Univ Press of America, 98): 127-135; auth, "Science, Science Fiction and Memory in Primo Levi," pending; auth, "La science, la science-fiction et la memoire clans l'oeuvre de Primo Levi," Shoah, Memoire et Ecnture: Primo Levi et le dialogue des savoirs (Paris: L'Harmattan, 97), 87-96; auth, "Primo Levi," Dictionary of Literary Biography (DLB): Italian Novelists Since World War II, ed. Augustus Pallotta (Detroit-Washington DC-London: Bruccoli Clark Layman, 97), 162-170; auth, "Leopardi e la critica contemporanea: nuove prospettive," Italica 72 (95), 400-406. **CONTACT ADDRESS** Dept Italian, Brigham Young Univ, 4002 Jkhb, Provo, UT 84602.

KLEIN, JARED S.
PERSONAL Born 08/05/1946, Cleveland, OH, m, 1974, 2 children **DISCIPLINE** LINGUISTICS **EDUCATION** Case Western Reserve Univ, BA, 68; Yale Univ, MPhil, 71; MA, 72; PhD, 74. **CAREER** Temp asst prof to prof, Univ of Ga, 72-. **HONORS AND AWARDS** Mellon Fel, 78-79; Lady Davis Vis Prof, Hebrew Univ of Jerusalem, 85; NEH Stipend, 77, 91. **MEMBERSHIPS** Ling Soc of Am; Am Oriental Soc; Am Philog Assoc; Philog Soc; Soc de Ling de Paris; Indogermanische Fesellschaft; Soc Ling Europaea. **RESEARCH** Indo-European Linguistics, especially Indo-Iranian, Germanic, Classical Armenian, Gothic and Iranian. **SELECTED PUBLICATIONS** Auth, The Particle u in the Rigveda, Vandenhoeck and Ruprecht, (Gottengen), 78; auth, Toward a Discourse Grammar of the Rigveda, Vol 1: Coordinate Conjunction, Parts 1 and 2, Carl Winter (Heidelberg), 85; auth, On Verbal Accentuation in the Rigveda, Am Oriental Soc (New Haven), 92; auth, On Personal Deixis in Classical Armenian, J.H. Roll (Dettelbach), 95. **CONTACT ADDRESS** Dept Classics, Univ of Georgia, Athens, GA 30602-6203. **EMAIL** jklein@arches.uga.edu

KLEINHENZ, CHRISTOPHER
PERSONAL Born 12/29/1941, Indianapolis, IN, m, 1964, 2 children **DISCIPLINE** ITALIAN LITERATURE, PHILOLOGY **EDUCATION** Ind Univ, Bloomington, AB, 64, MA, 66,

PhD(Ital), 69. **CAREER** From instr to asst prof Ital, Univ Wis-Madison, 68-70; vis asst prof Ital, Ind Univ, Bloomington & resident dir foreign studies prog, Bologna, Italy, 70-71; asst prof, 71-75, assoc prof, 75-80, prof Ital & chmn Medievl Studies, Univ Wis-Madison, 80-; pres, Am Asn of Teachers of Italian, 99-01 (vice-pres)93-98; counr, Dante Soc of Am, 85-91; pres, Am Boccaccio Asn, 93-98; ch, Comm on Centers and Regional Asns (CARA) of the Medieval Acad of Am, 93-98; pres, Medieval Asn of the Midwest, 84-85; Exec comm, Medieval and Renaissance Italian Literature, MLA, 86-90; member, Delegate Assembly, Modern Language Asn, 91-93. **HONORS AND AWARDS** Fulbright Fellowship to Italy, 64-65; Fellow, Institute for Research in the Humanities. 74-75; dir, Development Grant, NEH, 76-79; co-dir, research Tools Grant, NEH, 80-84; Vilas Assoc, Univ of Wisconsin, 85-87; Newberry Library/NEH Fellowship, 88-89; Carol Mason Kirk, Prof of Italian, 00-03. **MEMBERSHIPS** MLA; Medieval Acad Am; Dante Soc Am; Int Arthurian Soc; Am Asn Teachers Ital. **RESEARCH** Medieval Italian literature; Romance philology; textual criticism. **SELECTED PUBLICATIONS** Ed, Medieval Manuscripts and Textual Criticism, 76; co-ed, Medieval Studies in North America, 82; auth, The Early Italian Sonnet, 86; co-ed, Saint Augustine, the Bishop: A Book of Essays, 94; numerous articles and chapters in: Dante Studies, Italica, Forum Italicum, Filologia e critica, Alighieri, Traditio, Romance Philology, Aevum, Studi e problemi di critica testuale, Lectura Dantis, Thought, Journal of Medieval and Renaissance Studies, Quaderni d'italianistica, Annali d'Italianistica, Romance Quart, and others; ed, Dante Studies, 89-; book review ed, Italica, 84-93; mem, ed board, Medieval Acad Reprints for Teaching, 78-93, ch, 81-93; Bibliographer, Studi e problemi di critica testuale, 70-; Dante Soc of Am, 84-; and Am Boccacio Asn, 83-; and BIGL-LI, 94- ; auth, "Fearfulhope: Approaching the New Millennium," 99; contr, "Dante, The Fiore and Detto d'Amne," 00. **CONTACT ADDRESS** Dept of Fr & Ital, Univ of Wisconsin, Madison, 1220 Linden Drive, Madison, WI 53706-1557. **EMAIL** ckleinhe@atsfacstaff.wisc.edu

KLIBBE, LAWRENCE H.
PERSONAL Born 10/07/1923, Utica, NY, m, 1952, 2 children **DISCIPLINE** SPANISH **EDUCATION** Syracuse Univ, AB, 49, MA, 51, PhD, 54. **CAREER** From instr to assoc prof mod lang, Le Moyne Col, 53-59; assoc prof, St Johns Univ, NY, 59-65, dept rep, Brooklyn Ctr, 60-65; Assoc Prof Span, NY Univ, 65-. **MEMBERSHIPS** Am Asn Teachers Span and Port. **RESEARCH** Spanish 19th and 20th century literature; United State-Spanish literary relations. **SELECTED PUBLICATIONS CONTACT ADDRESS** Dept of Span, New York Univ, 19 University Pl, New York, NY 10003.

KLIMA, EDWARD STEPHENS
PERSONAL Born 06/21/1931, Cleveland, OH, m, 1968 **DISCIPLINE** LINGUISTICS, THEORY OF LANGUAGE **EDUCATION** Dartmouth Col, BA, 53; Harvard Univ, MA, 55, PhD (ling), 65. **CAREER** From instr to assoc prof ling, Mass Inst Technol, 57-67; Prof Ling, Univ Calif, San Diego, 67-; Consult, Bolt, Beranek and Newman, 65-66 and lang acquisition proj, Harvard Univ, 65-67; Nat Sci Found fel, 66-67; Partic, Edinburgh Conf Psycholing, 66 and Ciba Found Conf, London, Eng, 68. **MEMBERSHIPS** Ling Soc Am; Int Ling Asn. **RESEARCH** Linguistics; psycholinguistics; historical linguistics. **SELECTED PUBLICATIONS** Auth, Right-Hemisphere Damage Aphasia in American Sign Language, Brain Lang, Vol 0060, 97. **CONTACT ADDRESS** Dept of Ling, Univ of California, San Diego, San Diego, PO Box 109, La Jolla, CA 92093.

KLINE, THOMAS JEFFERSON
PERSONAL Born 07/16/1942, Washington, DC, m, 1984, 3 children **DISCIPLINE** FRENCH LITERATURE **EDUCATION** Oberlin Col, BA, 64; Columbia Univ, MA, 66, PhD(French), 69. **CAREER** Instr French, Columbia Univ, 68-69, asst prof, 70; asst prof, 70-72, assoc provost, Fac Arts & Lett, 76-79, mem prof comp lit, 78-79, assoc prof, State Univ NY, Buffalo, 72-79; Prof French & Chmn Mod Lang & Lit, Boston Univ, 79-, Adj prof, Univ Grenoble, 72-73. **MEMBERSHIPS** Malraux Soc; Northeast Mod Lang Asn; AATF. **RESEARCH** Modern French novel; contemporary European drama and film. **SELECTED PUBLICATIONS** Auth, Andre Malraux and the Metamorphosis of Death, Columbia Univ, 73; Bertolucci's Dream Loom: A Psychoanalytic Study of Cinema, Univ Mass Press, 87; ed, The Film and the Book, L'Esprit Createur, summer 90; auth, Screening the Text: Intertextuality in New Wave French Cinema, Johns Hopkins, 92; I film di Bernardo Bertolucci, Gremese, Rome, 93; coed, Bernardo Bertolucci Interviews, Univ MS Press, 99; author of numerous articles on French and European Cinema, French Novel and Theater. **CONTACT ADDRESS** Dept Mod For Lang & Lit, Boston Univ, 718 Commonwealth Ave, Boston, MA 02215-2423. **EMAIL** jkline@bu.edu

KLOCK, SHELDON, JR
PERSONAL Born 07/04/1938, Evanston, IL, m, 1962, 2 children **DISCIPLINE** SPANISH AND PORTUGUESE LANGUAGE AND LITERATURE **EDUCATION** Pan American Col (now Univ Tex at Pan Am), BA, 60; Tulane, MA, PhD, 96. **CAREER** Teaching asst (Spanish), Tulane Univ, 62-63; asst prof, Tex Tech Univ, 63-. **HONORS AND AWARDS** Woodrow Wilson Fel; Mortar Board, Tex Tech Univ; Nominated for Teaching Excellence, Tex Tech Univ. **MEMBERSHIPS** AATSP, SCOLAS. **RESEARCH** Brazilian and Portuguese literature. **SELECTED PUBLICATIONS** Auth, Themes in the Novels of Aluisto Azevedo, York Press, Toronto, Ont, Can (99). **CONTACT ADDRESS** Dept Modern & Classical Lang, Texas Tech Univ, 1 Tex Tech Univ, Lubbock, TX 79409-0999'. **EMAIL** sheldon.klock@ttu.edu

KLOPP, CHARLES
PERSONAL Born 04/14/1937, Palatine, IL, m, 3 children **DISCIPLINE** ITALIAN LITERATURE **EDUCATION** Princeton Univ, AB, 59; Harvard Univ, MA, 65, PhD(Ital lit), 70. **CAREER** Instr English, Robert Col, Istanbul, 59-64; teaching fel humanities, Harvard Univ, 65-67; lectr Ital, Stanford Univ, 68-69; asst prof Ital, Princeton Univ, 69-76; asst prof, 76-80, Assoc Peod Ital, Ohio State Univ, 80-99, Prof, 99-. **MEMBERSHIPS** Am Asn Teachers Ital; Midwest Mod Lang Asn; MLA; Am Asn Univ Prof Ital; Am Asn for Italian Studies. **RESEARCH** Modern Italian literature. **SELECTED PUBLICATIONS** Gabnele D'Annuuzio, Boston, 88; Sentences: The Memoirs and Letters of Italian Political Prisoners for Benvenuto Cellini to Aldo Moyo, Toronto, 99. **CONTACT ADDRESS** Dept of French and Italian, Ohio State Univ, Columbus, 1841 Millikin Rd, Columbus, OH 43210-1229. **EMAIL** klopp.2@osu.edu

KNAPP, BETTINA
PERSONAL Born 05/09/1926, New York, NY, m, 1949, 2 children **DISCIPLINE** FRENCH LITERATURE; COMPARATIVE LITERATURE **EDUCATION** Barnard Col, BA; Columbia Univ, MA, PhD; Sorbonne, Paris: Certificat. **CAREER** Lectr French lit, Columbia Univ, 52-60; prof, Hunter Col, 60-73, full prof; Prof Romance Lang, Hunter Col and Grad Ctr City, Univ NY, 61. **HONORS AND AWARDS** Guggenheim Fel; Grant from the Am Philosophical Soc; Fac Res Award (three times); Shuster Grant; Officer of the Palmes Academiques; Medal from the Alliance Francaise; President of the North-East Modern Lang Asn, 81-2; Mem of Nat Humanities Fac; Mem of P.E.N.; Thomas Hunter Prof: The President's Award for Excellence in Scholarship/Creative Activity, 93; Awarded honorary membership in Rome's Accademia Tiberina, 93; Awarded Chevalier dans l'Ordre des Lettres from the French Government, 00. **RESEARCH** French theatre, poetry, novel; comparative mythology and literature. **SELECTED PUBLICATIONS** Auth, Louis Jouvet, Man of the Theatre, New York: Columbia Univ Press, 57; auth, Louise Labe, Paris: Lettres Modernes, 54; coauth, That Was Yvette, A Biography of Yvette Guilbert, New York: Holt, Rinehart, Winston, 64; auth, Cymbalum Mundi, New York: Twayne Pub, 65; auth, Aristide Bruant, A Biography, Paris: Nouvelles Editions Debresse, 68; auth, Jean Genet, A Critical Study, New York: Twayne Pub, 68; auth, Antonin Artaud, Man of Vision, New York: David Lewis, 69; auth, Jean Cocteau, A Critical Study, New York: Twayne Pub, 72; auth, Celine, Man of Hate, University: University of Alabama Press, 74. **CONTACT ADDRESS** 334 W 86 St., New York, NY 10024-3106.

KNAPP, RICHARD GILBERT
PERSONAL Born 11/24/1940, Litchfield, CT **DISCIPLINE** FRENCH LITERATURE & LANGUAGE **EDUCATION** Wesleyan Univ, BA, 62; Columbia Univ, MA, 64, PhD(Fr), 69. **CAREER** From inst to asst prof French, Lafayette Col, 67-71; asst prof, 71-74, assoc prof, Prof French, Mars Hill Col, 74-. **MEMBERSHIPS** AAUP; MLA; Am Coun Teaching Foreign Lang; Am Soc 18th Century Studies; Am Asn Teachers Fr **RESEARCH** Voltaire; Diderot; history of ideas. **SELECTED PUBLICATIONS** Auth, The fortunes of Poe's Essay on Man in 18th century France, Vol 82, In: Studies on Voltaire and the Eighteenth Century, Inst et Musee Voltaire, Geneva, 71. **CONTACT ADDRESS** Dept of Mod Foreign Lang, Mars Hill Col, Mars Hill, NC 28754. **EMAIL** rknapp@mhc.edu

KNAPP, ROBERT C.
PERSONAL Born 02/12/1946, m, 1974, 2 children **DISCIPLINE** ANCIENT HISTORY, CLASSICS **EDUCATION** Cent MI Univ, BA, 68; Univ PA, PhD, 73. **CAREER** Vis asst prof classics, Colby Col, 73; asst prof of hist, Univ of Utah, 73-74; asst prof, 74-80, Assoc Prof Classics, Numismatics, Univ CA, Berkeley, 80-87; Prof 87. **HONORS AND AWARDS** Am Council of Learned Societies Fellowship, 82-83. **MEMBERSHIPS** Asn Ancient Historians; Am Philol Asn; Archaeological Institute of Am Fellow; Royal Numismatic Society. **RESEARCH** Roman Spain; Roman Cult Studies. **SELECTED PUBLICATIONS** Auth, Aspects of the Roman Experience in Iberia, 206-100 BC, Anejos IX Hisp Antiqua, 77; The date and purpose of the Iberian denarii, Numis Chronicle, 77; The origins of provincial prosopography in the West, Ancient Soc, 78; Cato in Spain, 195-194 BC, In: Studies in Latin Literature and Roman History II, C Deroux, Brussells, 80; La epigrafia y la historia de la Cordoba romana, Annario, de Filologia, 80; Festus 262L and Praefecturae in Italy, Athenaeum, 80; L Axius Naso and Pro legato, Phoenix, 81; Roman Cordoba, Univ Calif press, 83; Latin Inscriptions from Central Spain, Univ Calif, 92; Mapping Ancient Iberia: Progress and Perspectives, intro, ed (and contribution, Ptolemy Mapping Baetica, pp 29-36) Classical Bulletin, special issue, 96; auth, Finis Rei Publicae, Eyewitneses to the End of the Roman Republic, with P. Baughn, Focus Publishing, 99; ed, Barrington Atlas of the Greek and roman World, ed. By R.J. A Talbert, Princeton, 00. **CONTACT ADDRESS** Dept Class, Univ of California, Berkeley, 7233 Dwinelle Hall, Berkeley, CA 94720-2520. **EMAIL** RCKNAPP@SOCRATES.Berkeley.edu

KNAUER, GEORG NICOLAUS
PERSONAL Born 02/26/1926, Hamburg, Germany, m, 1951, 1 child **DISCIPLINE** CLASSICAL STUDIES **EDUCATION** Hamburg Univ, PhD, 52. **CAREER** Asst Prof to Prof, Freie Univ Berlin, 54-66; Vis Prof, Yale Univ, 65; Prof, Univ Pa, 75-88; Guest Prof, Columbia Univ, 76-. **HONORS AND AWARDS** Guggenheim Fel, 79-80; NEH Fel, 84-85. **MEMBERSHIPS** APA; Renaissance Soc of Am. **RESEARCH** Latin translations of Homer (1360-1620). **SELECTED PUBLICATIONS** Auth, Psalmenzitate in Augustins Konfessionen, 55; auth, Die Aeneis und Homer, 64. **CONTACT ADDRESS** Dept Class Studies, Univ of Pennsylvania, 3300 Darby Rd, Haverford, PA 19041-1070. **EMAIL** gknauer@sas.upenn.edu

KNELLER, JOHN WILLIAM
PERSONAL Born 10/15/1916, Oldham, England, m, 1943, 1 child **DISCIPLINE** FRENCH LITERATURE **EDUCATION** Clark Univ, BA, 38; Yale Univ, MA, 48, PhD, 50. **CAREER** From instr to prof French, Oberlin Col, 50-69, chm dept Romance lang, 58-65, provost, 65-69; prof mod lang & pres, 69-79 emer pres, Brooklyn Col, 79-; prof to prof emer Humanities & Arts, Hunter Col & Grad Ctr, City Univ New York, 79-, **HONORS AND AWARDS** Managing ed, Fr Rev, 62-65, ed, 65-68; trustee, Clark Univ, 68-74 & Brooklyn Inst Arts & Sci, 71-79; Chevalier, Ordre Palmes Academiques, 72, officer, 82; chm, subcomt enrollment goals & projections, NY State Educ Comn Adv Coun on Higher Educ & mem adv coun; littd, clark univ, 70. **MEMBERSHIPS** MLA; Am Asn Teachers Fr. **RESEARCH** J J Rousseau; 19th century French literature; music and literature. **SELECTED PUBLICATIONS** Coauth, The Poet and His Moira, El Disdichado, PMLA, 60; Introduction a la Poesie Francaise, Ginn, 62; Initiation au Francais, Macmillan, 63; auth, The Changing College, Oberling Alumni Mag, 66; Translation and Transformation: New Roles for Research, Proc MLA Conf, 72; Newer Clothes for Emperors, Centerpoint, fall 74; The Terrifying Pips of Reality, Fr Rev, 3/78. **CONTACT ADDRESS** PhD Prog Fr Grad Ctr City, New York Univ, 33 W 42nd St, New York, NY 10016-4309.

KNIGHT, ALAN EDGAR
PERSONAL Born 09/07/1931, Plant City, FL, d, 2 children **DISCIPLINE** FRENCH AND COMPARATIVE LITERATURE **EDUCATION** Fla State Univ, BA, 58; Fordham Univ, MA, 60; Yale Univ, PhD, 65. **CAREER** Acting instr French lang and lit, Yale Univ, 63-64; asst prof French lit, 64-70, assoc prof, French and comp lit, PA State Univ, University Park, 70-84; prof, French, Penn State Univ, 84-97; prof emeritus, French, 97-. **HONORS AND AWARDS** NEH grants, 85-88, 93-95. **MEMBERSHIPS** Mediaeval Acad Am; Soc Int lEtude Theatre; Medieval, Medieval, and Renaissance Drama Soc; Soc for Textual Scholarship. **RESEARCH** Medieval drama; literature and society; textual criticism; paleography. **SELECTED PUBLICATIONS** Auth, "The Medieval Theater of the Absurd," PMLA 86 (71): 183-189; auth, "Drama and Society in Late Medieval Flanders and Picardy," The Chaucer Review 14 (80): 379-389; auth, Aspects of Genre in Late Medieval French Drama, Manchester Univ Press (Manchester), 83; auth, "The Condemnation of Pleasure in Late Medieval French Morality Plays," The French Review 57 (83): 1-9; auth, "Editing the Unique Manuscript: The Case of the Lille Plays," Text: Transactions of the Society for Textual Scholarship 5 (91): 145-155; auth, "The Bishop of Fools and His Feasts in Lille," in Festive Drama, ed. Meg Twycross (Cambridge, D.S. Brewer, 96), 157-166; ed, The Stage as Mirror: CivicTheatre in Late Medieval Europe, D.S. Brewer (Cambridge), 97; auth, "Processional Theatre and the Rituals of Social Unity in Lille," in Drama and Community: People and Plays in Medieval Europe, ed. Alan Hindley (Turnhout, Brepols, 99), 99-109; auth, "The Roman 'Saint Plays' of Lille," Medieval English Theatre 19 (99): 15-25; auth, Les Mysteres de la Procession de Lille, Vol 1, Librairie Droz (Geneva), 01. **CONTACT ADDRESS** Dept of French, Pennsylvania State Univ, Univ Park, 325 Burrowes Bldg, University Park, PA 16802. **EMAIL** aek@psu.edu

KNIGHT, DEIRDRE SABINA
PERSONAL Born 11/16/1966, London, England, s **DISCIPLINE** LANGUAGE, LITERATURE **EDUCATION** Univ Wisconsin-Madison, BA, 88; MA, 94; PhD, 98; Univ Calif, MA, 92. **CAREER** Graduate Student instr, Univ of Calif, 90-91 and 92-93; Teaching Asst, Univ Wis, Madison, 94-95; Research Assoc, National Central Library, 95-96; Lecturer in East Asian Studies and Political Science, Univ of Wis, Madison, 97-98; Research Assoc, Harvard Univ, 99-00; Asst Prof, Smith Col, 98-. **HONORS AND AWARDS** Jean Picker Fel, Smith College, 00; Committee on Fac Compensation & Development (CFCD) Funding for Research; Student Asst, Smith College, 99; Univ Dissertation Fel, UW-Madison, 96; J. William Fulbright Scholarship for study and research, 95-96; Foreign Language and Area Studies (FLAS) Scholarship, 94; Dobroe Slovo, National Slavic Honors Society, 94; Univ WARF Fel, UW-Madison, 93-94; Four-year Univ Predoctoral Humanities Fel,

UC-Berkeley, 89-92; Harvard Univ Graduate Fel, 89; Rotary Foundation Graduate Scholarship fr International Understanding, 88-89; Helen C. White Scholarship, UW-Madison, 88; Florence Waste Pulver Scholarship, UW-Madison, 88; Ralph B. Adams Scholarship, UW-Madison, 87; Phi Beta Kappa, UW-Madison, 87; Phi Kappa Phi National Honor Society, UW-Madison, 87; Crucible the UW Chancellor's Active Women's Honorary Organization, 86-87; Swarthmore College Scholarship, 84-85; International Exchange Scholarship, UW Foundation, 86; Recipient of an All-American Collegiate Awd, 87; College of Letters and Science Dean's List, UW-Madison, 85-88; **MEMBERSHIPS** American Comparative Literature Association, Association of Asian Studies, Chinese Language Teachers Assoc, Modern Language Assoc. **RESEARCH** Modern and Traditional Chinese Literature, Ethics: East and West, Comparative Literary and Cultural Studies, Women's Studies. **SELECTED PUBLICATIONS** Auth, Translation of Liu Heng's story "Dogshit Food," Columbia Anthology of Modern Chinese Literature, ed. Joseph S. M. Lau and Howard Goldblatt (New York: Columbia Univ Press, 95) 416-428; auth, "Agency Beyond Subjectivity: The Unredeemed Project of May Ficitin," Journal of Modern Literature in Chinese (98): 1-36; auth, "decadence, Revolution and Self-Determination in Su Tong's Fiction," Modern Chinese Literature 10 (98): 91-111; rev, Thinking from the Han: Self, Truth, and Transcendence in Chinese and Western Culture, by David L. Hall and Roger T. Ames (SUNY Press, 98), China Review International (99), 449-52; rev, Chinese Modernism in the Era of Reforms, by Zhang Xudong (Duke, UP,, 97), Journal of Asian Studies, (99), 180-82; rev, Misogyny, Cultural Nihilism and Oppositional Politics, by Lu Tonglin (Stanford UP, 95), Journal of Modern Literature in Chinese (99), 175-78; auth, "Literature of the Wounded, " The Columbia Companion to Modern East Asian Literature, ed. Joshua Mostow, Columbia Univ Press, (forthcoming), (00). **CONTACT ADDRESS** Dept East Asian Lang & Lit, Smith Col, 98 Green St, Northampton, MA 01063-1000. **EMAIL** dsknight@sophia.smith.edu

KNOPP, SHERRON ELIZABETH

PERSONAL Born 04/11/1947, Fort Worth, TX **DISCIPLINE** MEDIEVAL & COMPARATIVE LITERATURE **EDUCATION** Loyola Univ, Chicago, AB, 71; Univ Calif, Los Angeles, MA, 72, PhD(English), 75. **CAREER** Asst prof, 75-80, assoc prof, 80-86, prof English, Williams Col, 86-. **MEMBERSHIPS** Mediaeval Acad Am; MLA; New Chaucer Soc. **RESEARCH** Chaucer; medieval romance; medieval dream poetry. **SELECTED PUBLICATIONS** Auth, Chaucer and Jean de Meun as Self-Conscious Narrators, Comitatus, 73; Catullus 64 and the Conflict Between Amores and Virtutes, Class Philol, 76; Artistic design in the stanzaic Morte Arthur, English Literary Hist, No 45; The Narrator and His Audience in Chaucer's Troilus and Criseyde, Studies in Philol, 78; A Zeer Zernes Ful Zerne: Teaching Sir Gawain and the Green Knight in the Survey for Majors, Approaches to Teaching Sir Gawain and the Green Knight, MLA, 86; Augustinian Poetic Theory and the Chaucerian Imagination, The Idea of Medieval Literature, Univ of Del Press, 91. **CONTACT ADDRESS** Dept of English, Williams Col, 880 Main St, Williamstown, MA 01267-2600. **EMAIL** Sherron.E.Knopp@williams.edu

KNORR, ORTWIN

PERSONAL Born 02/12/1966, Bremen, Germany, m, 1994, 1 child **DISCIPLINE** CLASSICS **EDUCATION** Univ Gottingen, PhD, 99. **CAREER** Wissen asst, Univ Gott, 92-93; lectr, Univ Calif Berkeley, 95; instr, Univ Gott, 96-99; lectr, John Hopkins Univ, 00; vis asst prof, Georgetown Univ, 00-01; asst prof, Willamette Univ, 01-. **HONORS AND AWARDS** Univ Gott and Univ Calif Berkeley, Fel, 93-94; Georgetown Univ Sum Grnt, 01. **MEMBERSHIPS** AAP. **RESEARCH** Latin poetry; Roman satire; Roman comedy; Greek and Roman material, culture, customs, beliefs. **SELECTED PUBLICATIONS** Auth, "The Character of Bacchis in Terence's Heautontimorumenos," Am J Philo (95); auth, "Zur Oberlieferungsgeschichte des Liber de Haeresibus des Johannes von Damascus," Byzant Zeitsch (98); auth, "Die Paralleluberlieferung zum Panarion des Epiphanius," Wiener Stud (99). **CONTACT ADDRESS** Dept of Classics, Willamette Univ, 900 State St, Salem, OR 20720. **EMAIL** oknorr@willamette.edu

KNOWLTON, EDGAR C., JR.

PERSONAL Born 08/14/1921, Delaware, OH, s **DISCIPLINE** SPANISH, LINGUISTICS **EDUCATION** Harvard, AB, 41, AM, 42; Stanford, PhD, 59. **CAREER** Instr to PROF EMERITUS, EUROPEAN LANG, UNIV HAWAII, MANOA, 48. **HONORS AND AWARDS** Translation Prize, Lisbon, Portugal, 73; Phi Beta Kappa, 91, Hawaii. **MEMBERSHIPS** MLA; AATSP; Maui Portuguese Cultural Club; Puerto Rican Heritage Soc of Hawaii. **SELECTED PUBLICATIONS** Coauth, An Indian Baroness in Hawaii, Honolulu Soc, Boston: Twayne, 72; auth, The Conquest of Malacea, Univ of Melaye Press, 72; auth, Esteban Echeverria, Bryn Dorrance; Mawr, 86. **CONTACT ADDRESS** Dept European Langs, Univ of Hawaii, Honolulu Comm Col, 1026 Kalo PL, Apt 403, Honolulu, HI 96826.

KNOX, BERNARD MACGREGOR WALKER

PERSONAL Born 11/24/1914, Bradford, England, m, 1 child **DISCIPLINE** CLASSICAL PHILOLOGY **EDUCATION** Cambridge Univ, BA, 36; Yale Univ, PhD, 48, LHD, 83. **CAREER** Instr Classics, Yale Univ, 47-48; asst prof & fel, Branford Col,48-54, from assoc prof to prof, 54-60; Dir, Ctr Hellenic Studies, Washington DC 61-85, Guggenheim fel, 56-57; Sather lectr, Univ Calif, Berkeley, 63; chmn, Soc Preserv Greek Heritage, 77-; Martin lectr, Oberlin Col, 81; West lectr, Stanford Univ, 84; Nellie Wallace lectr, Oxford Univ, 75; Spielvogel-Diamonstein award Pen, 90; Frankel priize, NEH, 90; NEH Jefferson lectr, 92. **HONORS AND AWARDS** Awd for Lit, Nat Inst Arts & Lett, 67; George Jean Nathan Awd for Dramatic Criticism, Mfrs Hanover Trust, 78; ma, harvard univ, 61; littd, princeton univ, 64; dhl, george washington univ, 77; georgetown univ, lhd, 88; lhd (hon) univ mich, 85. **MEMBERSHIPS** Am Philol Soc; Am Archaeol Inst; AAAS; Am Philol Asn (pres 80). **RESEARCH** Greek tragedy; Latin and Greek literature. **SELECTED PUBLICATIONS** Auth, Oedipus at Thcbes, Yale Univ, S7; The Heroic Temper, Univ Calif, 64, reissued 98; Word and action: Essays on the ancient theater, Johns Hopkins Press, 79; asst ed & contribr, Cambridge History of Classical Literature, Vol I (1985); coauth (with Robert Foyles), The Theban plays of Sophocles, Viking Press (1982); coauth with Robert Foyles, Homer, The Iliad 90; The Odyssey, 96; Essays Ancient and Modern, 89; The Oldest Dead White European Males, 93; Backing into the Future, 94 **CONTACT ADDRESS** 13013 Scarlet Oak Dr, Darnestown, MD 20878-3551.

KNOX, EDWARD CHAPMAN

PERSONAL Born 10/05/1939, Meriden, CT, m, 1965 **DISCIPLINE** FRENCH **EDUCATION** Wesleyan Univ, BA, 61; Yale Univ, PhD(French), 66. **CAREER** Asst prof Romance lang, Case Western Reserve Univ, 66-69; asst prof French, 69-74, dean French sch, 73, assoc prof, 74-79, Prof French, Middlebury Col, 80-; Dean French Sch, 76-. **MEMBERSHIPS** MLA; Am Asn Teachers Fr; Am Coun Teaching Foreign Lang. **RESEARCH** Literary style. **SELECTED PUBLICATIONS** Auth, Culture Studies in the Teaching of French in Reply, Fr Rev, Vol 0069, 95. **CONTACT ADDRESS** Dept of French, Middlebury Col, Middlebury, VT 05753-6001.

KNUST, HERBERT

DISCIPLINE COMPARATIVE LITERATURE **EDUCATION** PA State Univ, PhD, 61. **CAREER** Prof, Univ IL Urbana Champaign . **RESEARCH** 19th-and 20th-century Ger lit; drama; literary thematics; Am-Ger rel(s); lit and the other arts. **SELECTED PUBLICATIONS** Auth, Wagner, the King and The Waste Land; Theatrical Drawings and Watercolors (rev); Leben des Galilei (rev); ed, Montage, Satire and Cultism: Germany between the Wars; George Grosz: Briefe 1913-59; pubs on T.S. Eliot, Camus, Brecht, Frisch, Grosz, Hofmannsthal, Kastner, Piscator, Tucholsky, satire, the Everyman theme, the Faust theme, and sci in lit. **CONTACT ADDRESS** Comp Lit Dept, Univ of Illinois, Urbana-Champaign, E Gregory Drive, PO Box 52, Champaign, IL 61820. **EMAIL** h-knust@staff.uiuc.edu

KNUTSON, HAROLD CHRISTIAN

PERSONAL Born 12/18/1928, Minneapolis, MN, m, 1967 **DISCIPLINE** FRENCH **EDUCATION** Univ Minn, AB, 49, MA, 52; Univ Calif, Berkeley, PhD(Romance lit), 62. **CAREER** Teaching asst, Univ Minn, 51-52 and Univ Calif, Berkeley, 55-59; from instr to assoc prof, 60-75, asst dean, fac arts, 69-72 and assoc dean, 77-82, Prof French, Univ BC, 75-; Can Coun Leave fel, 72-73; Social Sci and Humanities Res Coun Can leave fel, 79-80. **MEMBERSHIPS** Asn Can Univ Teachers Fr; MLA; NAm Soc 17th Century Fr Lit; Can Comparative Lit Asn. **RESEARCH** French drama of the 17th century; comedy; criticism. **SELECTED PUBLICATIONS** Auth, An Enemy of the People and Ibsen, Henrik in Ibsen Reluctant Comedy, Comparative Drama, Vol 0027, 93; Forms of Address in Ibsen Ghosts, Scandinavica, Vol 0033, 94; Moliere, Don Juan, Essays in Theatre-Etudes Theatrales, Vol 0014, 96. **CONTACT ADDRESS** Dept of French, Univ of British Columbia, Vancouver, BC, Canada V6T 1W5.

KOC, RICHARD

DISCIPLINE GERMAN LITERATURE **EDUCATION** SD State Univ, BA; Stanford Univ, MA, PhD. **CAREER** Prof. **HONORS AND AWARDS** Fulbright, 72-3. **MEMBERSHIPS** AATG. **RESEARCH** German drama; history of German cabaret; German film, literature and music; Thomas Mann, psychological approaches to literature. **SELECTED PUBLICATIONS** Auth, pubs on Goethe, Schiller and Thomas Mann. **CONTACT ADDRESS** German Dept, Colorado Col, 14 E Cache La Poudre St, Colorado Springs, CO 80903. **EMAIL** rkoc@coloradocollege.edu

KOCH, EREC R.

PERSONAL Born 04/05/1958, Philadelphia, PA, m, 1987, 2 children **DISCIPLINE** FRENCH LITERATURE **EDUCATION** Harvard Univ, AB, 81; Yale Univ, MA, 83; MPhil, 85; PhD, 88. **CAREER** Asst to assoc prof, assoc dean, Tulane Univ, 88-. **HONORS AND AWARDS** NEH Fel, 92-93; Comm on Res Summer Fel, Tulane Univ, 89, 96; Georges Lurcy Trust, 99; Florence Gould Found, 99; LAS Centre for Scholars, 99; Newcomb Found, 00; Mellon Found 01-03. **MEMBERSHIPS** MLA, SCMLA, N Am Soc for 17th Century Fr Lit. **RESEARCH** Pascal and Jansenism, history and theory of rhetoric, French Classical theater, the moralists, power and the representation of power, philosophy and the history of ideas, literary/critical theory. **SELECTED PUBLICATIONS** Auth, "Tragic Disclosures of Racine's 'Iphigenie,'" Romanic Rev, (90); auth, "Rhetorical Aesthetics and Rhetorical Theory in Pascal," Papers on Fr 17th Century Lit, (93); auth, "Pascal/de Man: Rhetoric, Reading, and Raison des effets," De la Morale a la politique, (Pau: PU De Pau, 96); auth, "Pascal and Rhetoric: Figural and Persuasive Language in the Scientific Treatises, the Provinciales, and the Pensees, EMF Monograph Series, (Charlottesville), 97; auth, "The Truth of Painting: Eloquence and Color in the Logique de Port-Royal and Rogers de Piles's Conversations sur la connoissance de la peinture," Papers on Fr 17th Century Lit, (98); auth, "Deferred Acts: Bajazet, Untimeliness, and Tragic Orthodoxy," 17th Century Fr Studies, (99); ed, Classical Unities: Place, Time, Action. Actes du 32e congres annuel de la North American Soc for 17th Century Lit, (Tubingen: Gunter Narr Verlag), 01. **CONTACT ADDRESS** Tulane Univ, Office of the Assoc Dean, Robert C Cudd Hall, New Orleans, LA 70118-5698. **EMAIL** erkoch@tulane.edu

KOCH, ERNST

PERSONAL Born 10/20/1906, Berlin, Germany, m, 1946, 2 children **DISCIPLINE** GERMANIC LANGUAGES AND LITERATURES **EDUCATION** Pa State Univ, AB, 28, AM, 31; NYork Univ, PhD(Ger), 34. **CAREER** Teacher, Jr High Sch, NJ, 28-29; instr Ger, Pa State Univ, 29-31; from instr to asst prof, NY Univ, 33-46; from asst prof to prof, 46-73, chmn dept, 52-56, assoc dean students, 67-68, asst dean acad adjustments, 68-73, Emer Prof Ger, Brooklyn Col, 73-; Consult, Ger, col text dept, Am Bk Col, 47-52. **MEMBERSHIPS** MLA **RESEARCH** Eighteenth century German literature, especially Schiller and Lessing; Scandinavian literature, especially Ibsen; problems of administration in higher education. **SELECTED PUBLICATIONS CONTACT ADDRESS** 780 E 32nd St, Brooklyn, NY 11210.

KOCH, KENNETH

PERSONAL Born 02/27/1925, Cincinnati, OH, m, 1957, 1 child **DISCIPLINE** ENGLISH, COMPARATIVE LITERATURE **EDUCATION** Harvard Univ, AB, 48; Columbia Univ, MA, 53, PhD, 59. **CAREER** Asst, Univ Calif, Berkeley, 51; from instr to assoc prof, 59-71, Prof English and Comp Lit, Columbia Univ, 71-; Guggenheim fel, 61; Fulbright grant, 78, 82. **HONORS AND AWARDS** Harbison Awd, Danforth Found, 70. **RESEARCH** Twentieth century American poetry; modern European literature. **SELECTED PUBLICATIONS** Auth, The Villino, Raritan-a Quart Rev, Vol 0012, 93; One Train May Hide Another, NY Rev Books, 93; One Train May Hide Another, Parabola-Myth Tradition and the Search for Meaning, Vol 0019, 94; Introduction to the Green Lake is Awake, Selected Poems, Am Poetry Rev, Vol 0023, 94; A Heroine of the Greek Resistance, Am Poetry Rev, Vol 0023, 94; A New Guide, Am Poetry Rev, Vol 0023, 94; Your Genius Made Me Shiver, Am Poetry Rev, Vol 0025, 96; An Interview With Koch, enneth, Am Poetry Rev, Vol 0025, 96; The True Life, Am Poetry Rev, Vol 0025, 96; How in Her Pirogue She Glides, Am Poetry Rev, Vol 0025, 96; What Makes This Statue Noble Seeming, Am Poetry Rev, Vol 0025, 96; Au Coconut School, Am Poetry Rev, Vol 0025, 96; Allegheny Menaces, Am Poetry Rev, Vol 0025, 96; Might I Be the First, Am Poetry Rev, Vol 0025, 96; In Ancient Times, Am Poetry Rev, Vol 0025, 96; Vous Etes Plus Beaux Que Vous Ne Pensiez, Poetry, Vol 0168, 96; Diving Along, Am Poetry Rev, Vol 0025, 96; Lets Pour, Am Poetry Rev, Vol 0025, 96; They Say Prince Hamlets Found a Southern Island, Am Poetry Rev, Vol 0025, 96; Mediterranean Suns, Am Poetry Rev, Vol 0025, 96; Africa Paese Notturno, Am Poetry Rev, Vol 0025, 96; Let Us Praise The Elephant, Am Poetry Rev, Vol 0025, 96. **CONTACT ADDRESS** Dept of English, Columbia Univ, New York, NY 10027.

KOCH, PHILIP

PERSONAL Born 12/31/1927, New York, NY, m, 1952, 2 children **DISCIPLINE** FRENCH **EDUCATION** Harvard Univ, AB, 49, AM, 51, PhD(French and Ital), 55. **CAREER** Instr French lang, Phillips Exeter Acad, 49; instr French lang, Northwestern Univ, 55-56; from instr to asst prof French, Bryn Mawr Col, 56-61; from asst prof to assoc prof, 61-66, chmn dept French and Ital, 66-72, Prof French, Univ Pittsburgh, 66-; Reader advan placement French, Educ Testing Serv, 60-65; consult French, Regents Doc Eval Proj, NY State, 75-76 and Masters Rev Proj, City Univ New York, 82. **MEMBERSHIPS** Am Asn Teachers Fr; NAnt Soc 17th Century Fr Lit; Am Soc 18th Century Studies; Societe Francaise dEtude du XVIIIe Siecle. **RESEARCH** French literature of the 17th and 18th centuries; modern Italian literature; influence of the Commedia dellarte on French comedy. **SELECTED PUBLICATIONS** Auth, On Marivaux's expression, Se donner la comedie Romanic Rev, 2/65; Reflections on Racine's Oreste, Ky Romance Quart, Vol XV, No 4; ed, F Galiani's Dialogues entre M Marquis de Roquemaure et M le Chevalier Zanobi, Vittorio Klostermann, 68; auth, Innocent Hippolyte, Fr Rev, 4/70; Les veritables dialogues de Galiani, Problemi Attuali de Scienza e di Cultura, 75; Regnard and Collin d'Harleville, Studies 18th Century Cult, Vol VIII; Les Dernieres Annees de Mezzetin, XVIIIe

Siecle, 79; L'Histoire de l'Ancien Theatre-Italien, Studies Voltaire & 18th Century, Vol CXCIX. **CONTACT ADDRESS** Dept of Fr and Ital, Univ of Pittsburgh, Pittsburgh, PA 15260.

KOCHER, SUZANNE A.
PERSONAL Born Boston, MA **DISCIPLINE** FRENCH **EDUCATION** Reed Col, BA, 90; Univ Wisc Madison, MA, 91; Univ Ore, PhD, 99. **CAREER** Teaching asst, Univ Wisc Madison, 90-91; discussion section leader, Portland State Univ, 93-94; teaching fel, Univ Ore, 94-99; asst prof, Univ La Lafayette, 00-. **HONORS AND AWARDS** Outstanding Teacher Award, Univ La Lafayette, 00; Jane Grant Dissertation Fel, 97-98; Scholar, Medieval Acad, 97; Stickels Scholar, 96; Res Award, Univ Ore, 95. **MEMBERSHIPS** MLA; Phi Beta Delta Honor Soc; Soc for Medieval Feminist Scholar; Feministas Unidas; The Medieval Acad; Nat Women's Studies Asn; Intl Arthurian Soc. **RESEARCH** Medieval French literature; Marguerite Porete studies; Medieval religion and mysticism; Arthurian literature; The Roman de Silence; Marguerite of Navarre studies; Allegory and personification; Women's studies' Gender studies; Medieval history; Manuscript studies. **SELECTED PUBLICATIONS** Auth, "Undermining Oppositionality: The Romance of Silence's Nature/Nurture Debate Complicated by the Rhymes of Apieler (To Name) and Celer (To Conceal)," Romance Lang Ann, (95): 95-99; auth, "Marguerite de Navarre's Portrait of marguerite Porete: A Renaissance Queen Constructs a Medieval Woman Mystic," Medieval Feminist Newsletter, (98): 17-23; auth, Gender and Power in marguerite Porete's Mirouer des Simples Ames, Univ Ore, 99; auth, "Tricky Lessons: Didactic Elements and Narrative Structure in the Roman de Silence," Arthuriana, (forthcoming). **CONTACT ADDRESS** Mod Lang Dept, Univ of Louisiana, Lafayette, PO Box 43331, Lafayette, LA 70504-3331. **EMAIL** skocher@louisiana.edu

KODA, KEIKO
DISCIPLINE JAPANESE AND SECOND LANGUAGE ACQUISITION **EDUCATION** Univ Ill, PhD. **CAREER** Languages, Carnegie Mellon Univ. **SELECTED PUBLICATIONS** Auth, Second language reading research: Problems and possibilities. Applied Psycholinguistics, 94; Development of L2 word recognition, 94; Cognitive consequences of L1 and L2 orthographies, 95; L2 Word Recognition Research: A Critical Rev, Mod Lang Jour , 96, Cross-linguistic transfer of orthographic knowledge, 97; Cambridge Univ Press. **CONTACT ADDRESS** Carnegie Mellon Univ, 5000 Forbes Ave, Pittsburgh, PA 15213.

KOEKKOEK, BYRON J.
PERSONAL Born 05/19/1924, MI, m, 1955, 2 children **DISCIPLINE** GERMANIC AND GERMAN LINGUISTICS **EDUCATION** Olivet Col, BA, 49; Univ Mich, MA, 50; Univ Vienna, PhD, 53. **CAREER** From instr to assoc prof, 53-65, chmn dept Germanic and Slavic, 71-76, Prof to prof emer Ger, State Univ NY, Buffalo, 65-; Corresp Overseas Mem; Inst Fur Deutsche Sprache, Mannheim, Ger, 69-. **MEMBERSHIPS** MLA; Ling Soc Am; Ling Asn Can and US; Am Asn Teachers Ger. **RESEARCH** Germanic and German linguistics. **SELECTED PUBLICATIONS** Auth, The Dictionary of German in German, Engl Ger Philol, Vol 0092, 93; Principles of German Orthography in German, Vol 0070, 94; Learning and Teaching Grammar in Unit I in German, Mod Lang J, Vol 0078, 94; Language as Organism in Metaphors, A Key to Grimm, Jacob, Concept of Language in German, J Engl Ger Philol, Vol 0094, 95. **CONTACT ADDRESS** Dept of Mod Lang and Lit, SUNY, Buffalo, 1027 Clemens Hall, North Campus, Buffalo, NY 14260.

KOELB, CLAYTON L.
PERSONAL Born 11/12/1942, New York, NY, m, 1999, 2 children **DISCIPLINE** GERMAN, COMPARATIVE LITERATURE **EDUCATION** Harvard Univ, BA, 64; MA, 66; PhD, 70. **CAREER** Asst to assoc prof, Univ of Chicago, 69-91; Chair, 78-82; Guy B. Johnson Prof, Univ of NC, 91-; Chair, 97-. **HONORS AND AWARDS** David McCord Prize; Woodrow Wilson Fel; Danforth Found Fel; Ger Soc of Am Fel; Susan Anthony Potter Prize; Guggenheim Fel. **MEMBERSHIPS** MLA; Kafka Soc of N Am. **RESEARCH** Literary criticism and theory, Franz Kafka, Thomas Mann. **SELECTED PUBLICATIONS** Auth, Thomas Mann's Death in Venice: A New Translation, Backgrounds and Contexts, Criticism, W.W. Norton (NY, London), 94; auth, "Castration Envy: Nietzsche and the Figure of Woman", Nietzsche and the Feminine, ed Peter J. Burgard, Univ Pr of Va, (94): 71-81; auth, "Rede als Erlebnis: Die Tagebucher Kafkas", Osterreichische Tagebuchschriftsteller, ed Donald Daviau, Edition Atelier, (94): 171-190; auth, "The Metamorphosis of the Classics: John Barth, Philip Roth, and the European Tradition", Traditions, Voices and Dreams: The American Novel Since the 1960s, ed Melvin J. Friedman and Ben Siegel, Univ of Del Pr, (95): 108-128; auth, "Wrestling with Proteus: Irony in Kierkegaard's Either/Or", Narrative Ironies, ed Raymond A. Prier and Gerald Gillespie, Rodopi (Amsterdam, Atlanta), 97: 21-31; auth, Legendary Figures: Ancient History in Modern Novels, Univ of Nebr Pr, (Lincoln, London), 98; auth, "Thomas Mann", Encarta Encycl CD-ROM, Microsoft Corp, 98. **CONTACT ADDRESS** Dept Ger, Univ of No Carolina, Chapel Hill, 414 Dey Hall, Campus Box 3160, Chapel Hill, NC 27599. **EMAIL** ckoelb@email.unc.edu

KOENEN, LUDWIG
PERSONAL Born 04/05/1931, Cologne, Germany, m, 1955, 4 children **DISCIPLINE** CLASSICAL PHILOLOGY, PAPYROLOGY **EDUCATION** Univ Cologne, Dr(class philol), 57, Drhabil(class philol), 69. **CAREER** From asst prof to assoc prof and from cur to chief cur class philol and papyrology, Univ Cologne, 56-75; Prof Papyrology, Univ Mich, Ann Arbor, 75-; Res study papyri Cairo, Univ Cologne, 62-65; field dir papyri, Photog Arch Egyptian Mus, Cairo Int Asn Papyrologists, 69, 71, 73 and 76; corresp mem, Ger Archaeol Inst, 75. **MEMBERSHIPS** Am Philol Asn; Am Soc Papyrologists (vpres, 78-80, pres, 81-); Int Asn Papyrologists. **RESEARCH** Classical philology; papyrology; patristics. **SELECTED PUBLICATIONS** Auth, Phoenix From the Ashes in the Burnt Archive from Petra, Mich Quart Rev, Vol 0035, 96. **CONTACT ADDRESS** 1312 Culver, Ann Arbor, MI 48103.

KOENIG, JEAN-PAUL FRANCOIS XAVIER
PERSONAL Born 03/12/1933, Tananarive, Madagascar, m, 1961, 3 children **DISCIPLINE** FRENCH, AFRICAN LITERATURE **EDUCATION** Univ NC, Chapel Hill, MA, 67; Universite de Toulouse, France, Doctorat (compt lit), 73. **CAREER** From Instr to Asst Prof, 67-91, Assoc Prof French, Univ NC, Greensboro, 91-. **HONORS AND AWARDS** Elected mem of the Malagasy Acad, 90. **MEMBERSHIPS** SAtlantic Mod Lang Asn. **RESEARCH** Malagasy literature. **SELECTED PUBLICATIONS** Auth, L'influence de la Litterature Francaise dans l'oeuvre de Jacques Rabemananjara, 12/77 & L'histoire Malgache dans l'oeuvre de Jacques Rabemananjara, 5/78, Univ Sherbrooke. **CONTACT ADDRESS** Dept of Romance Lang, Univ of No Carolina, Greensboro, 1000 Spring Garden, Greensboro, NC 27412-0001. **EMAIL** koenigj@fagan.uncg.edu

KOEPKE, WULF
PERSONAL Born 09/24/1928, Luebeck, Germany, m, 1953, 4 children **DISCIPLINE** GERMAN LANGUAGE AND LITERATURE **EDUCATION** Univ Freiburg, PhD(Ger lit), 55. **CAREER** Lectr Ger, Univ Malaya, 55-59; head div, Goethe-Inst, Munich, 59-65; assoc prof Ger, Univ Ill, Chicago, 65-68; assoc prof, Rice Univ, 68-71; assoc prof, 71-73, Prof Ger, Tex Am Univ, 73-. **MEMBERSHIPS** MLA; Jean-Paul-Ges; Lessing Soc; Am Soc 18th Century Studies; Western Asn Ger Studies. **RESEARCH** Eighteenth century and 20th century German literature; the structure of the German language; German culture and civilization. **CONTACT ADDRESS** Dept of Mod Lang, Texas A&M Univ, Col Station, Station, TX 77843.

KOERNER, E. F. K.
PERSONAL Born 02/05/1939, Mlewiec, Poland **DISCIPLINE** LINGUISTICS **EDUCATION** Univ Gottingen, 62-63; Freie Univ Berlin, 63-64, BPhil, 65; Univ Edinburgh, 64-65; Justus Liebig Univ Giessen, 66-68, MA, 68; Simon Fraser Univ, PhD, 71; DScPhil(hon), Univ Sofia, Bulgaria, 94. **CAREER** Assoc prof, 76-88, prof general linguistics, Univ Ottowa, 88-; chief ed, Historiographia Linguistica, 73-; chief ed, Diachronica, 84-. **HONORS AND AWARDS** Can Coun scholar, 68; Diploma & Bronze Medal, Lille, Fr, 81; Medal Acad Merit, Nicholas Copernicus Univ, Poland, 95; fel, Royal Soc Can, 97; fel, Royal Soc Arts, London, 98; fel in residence, Netherlands Inst for Advanced Study, Wassenaar, 01-02; Konrad Adenauer Res Award of the Alexander von Humboldt Found, Bonn-Bad Godesberg, Germany, 00. **SELECTED PUBLICATIONS** Auth, Contribution au debat post-saussurien sur le signe linguistique: Introduction generale et bibliographie annotee, Mouton (The Hague, Paris), 72; auth, Ferdinand de Saussure: Origin and Development of His Linguistic Thought in Western Studies of Language. A Contribution to the History and Theory of Linguistics, Friedrich Vieweg & Sohn (Braunschweig), xl, 73; auth, The Importance of Techmer's 'Internationale Zeitschrift fur Allgemeine Sprachwissenschaft' in the Development of General Linguistics, John Benjamins (Amsterdam), vii, 73; auth, Western Histories of Linguistics, 1822-1976: An Annotated, Chronological Bibliography, John Benjamins (Amsterdam), ix, 78; auth, Toward a Historiography of Linguistics: Selected Essays," John Benjamins (Amsterdam), xx, 78; auth, Noam Chomsky: A Personal Bibliography, 1951-1986, John Benjamins (Amsterdam, Philadelphia), xi, 86; auth, Saussurean Studies/Etudes saussuriennes, Avant-propos de Rudolf Engler (Geneve, Editions Slatkine, 88), xxi; auth, Practicing Linguistic Historiography: Selected Essays, John Benjamins (Amsterdam, Philadelphia), xii, 89; auth, Professing Linguistic Historiography, John Benjamins (Amsterdam, Philadelphia), viii, 95; auth, Linguistic Historiography: Projects & Prospects, John Benjamins (Amsterdam, Philadelphia), x, 99. **CONTACT ADDRESS** Dept of Ling, Univ of Ottawa, Arts Building, 70 Laurier, Ottawa, ON, Canada K1N 6N5. **EMAIL** koerner@uottawa.ca

KOESTER, RUDOLF ALFRED
PERSONAL Born 03/16/1936, m, 1973 **DISCIPLINE** GERMANIC LANGUAGES & LITERATURES **EDUCATION** Univ Calif, Los Angeles, BA, 58, MA, 59; Harvard Univ, PhD, 64. **CAREER** Acting instr Ger, Univ CA, Los Angeles, 62-64, asst prof, 64-69; assoc prof, 69-76, Prof Ger, Univ NV, Las Vegas, 76-. **HONORS AND AWARDS** UNLV Found Outstanding Grad Fac Awd, 93. **MEMBERSHIPS** Rocky Mountain Mod Lang Asn; Int Ver Ger Sprach-u Literaturwiss; Am Asn Tchr(s) Ger. **RESEARCH** Nineteenth and 20th century Ger lit. **SELECTED PUBLICATIONS** Auth of numerous studies on Kleist, Fontane, Thomas Mann, Hesse, Georg Kaiser, Hofmannsthal, Hauptmann and others in Monatshefte, Ger Rev, Ger Life & Lett, Rev des Langues Vivantes, Orbis Litterarum, Ger Quart & Librarium; Hermann Hesse, Metzler, Stuttgart, 75; Die Hesse-Rezeption in den USA, In: Hermann Hesses weltweite Wirkung-Internationale Rezeptionsgeschichte, Suhrkamp, Frankfurt/Main, 77; Joseph Roth, Colloquium Verlag, Berlin, 82; Hermann Broch, Colloquium Verlag, Berlin, 87; Jakob Wassermann, Morgenbuch Verlag, Berlin, 96. **CONTACT ADDRESS** Dept of For Lang, Univ of Nevada, Las Vegas, PO Box 455047, Las Vegas, NV 89154-5047.

KOGAN, VIVIAN
PERSONAL Born Cairo, Egypt, m, 1969, 2 children **DISCIPLINE** FRENCH **EDUCATION** Grinnell Col, AB, 62; Brown Univ, AM, 66, PhD(French), 72. **CAREER** Instr, 69-71, Asst Prof French, Dartmouth Col, 71-. **MEMBERSHIPS** MLA. **RESEARCH** The contemporary French novel; 19th century fiction. **SELECTED PUBLICATIONS** Auth, Signs and signals in La Chartreuse de Parme, 19th Century Fr Studies, 11/73; Le jeu de la regle et du hasard, Fr Rev, 12/75; L'emploi du temps, l'emploi des temps, Teaching Lang Through Lit, 4/76; Raymond Queneau: A critical bibliography, In: A Critical Bibliography of French Literature; The Flowers of Fiction: Time and Space in Raymond Queueau's Les Flurs Bliues, French Forum, 82; Le Jules d'Athenais, Roman, 88; Michelet et les di erences, Lectures de la di erence sexuelle, de Femmes, 90. **CONTACT ADDRESS** Dept of French, Dartmouth Col, 315 Dartmouth Hall, Hinman Box 6087, Hanover, NH 03755-3511. **EMAIL** vivian.kogan@dartmouth.edu

KOHL, STEPHEN WILLIAM
PERSONAL Born 04/23/1944, Grand Island, NE, m, 1989, 1 child **DISCIPLINE** JAPANESE LANGUAGE & LITERATURE **EDUCATION** Univ Wash, BA, 67, PhD(Japanese), 74. **CAREER** Instr, 72-74, asst prof, 74-79, assoc prof Japanese Lang & Lit, Univ Ore, 79-, dir, Ore Japan Study Ctr, Waseda Univ, 74-75, 88-89; chmn, Asian Studies Prog, Univ Ore, 78-80, dept chmn, East Asian Lang, 81-87. **MEMBERSHIPS** Asn Asian Studies; Asn Teachers Japanese; Am Orient Soc; Japan Soc; Philol Asn Pac Coast. **RESEARCH** Contemporary Japanese literature; Japanese-Americans in the Northwest; translation. **SELECTED PUBLICATIONS** Coauth, The White Birch School of Japanese Literature, Asian Studies Prog, Univ Ore, 75; auth, Shiga Naoya and the literature of experience, Monumenta Nipponica, Vol 32, No 2; coauth, The Three Crabs, Japan Quart, Vol XXV, No 3; auth, I for the Mysterious, Dread Japan: The quest of Ronald McDonald, The East, 78; An Early Account of Japanese life in the Pacific Northwest, Pac Northwest Quart, 79; The Cliff's Edge, 80 & Withered Fields, 82, Midwest Publ Int; Strangers in a Strange Land: Japanese Castaways and the Opening of Japan, Pac Northwest Quart, 82; auth, The Saint of Mt. Koya and the Song of the Troubadour, Takakuwa Bujutsu, 90; Wind and Stone, Stonebridge Press, 92. **CONTACT ADDRESS** Dept of East Asian Lang, Univ of Oregon, Eugene, OR 97403-1205. **EMAIL** kohl@oregon.uoregon.edu

KOIKE, DALE A.
DISCIPLINE ROMANCE LINGUISTICS **EDUCATION** Univ New Mexico, PhD 81. **CAREER** Univ Tex, assoc prof 85-; N Carolina State Univ, asst prof 82-85; Univ Cal SB, lectr 80-82. **MEMBERSHIPS** AATSR; ACTFL. **RESEARCH** Spanish and Portuguese pragmatics; Discourse analysis; Second language acquisition. **SELECTED PUBLICATIONS** Auth, Language and Social Relationship in Brazilian Portuguese: The Pragmatics of Politeness, Austin TX, Univ of TX Press, 92; auth, Romance Linguistics: The Portuguese Context, coed, Westport CT, Bergin and Garvey, 92; auth, Christina Makara Biron and Dale A Koike, Puntos de vista: Converscacion, Boston, Heinle & Heinle, 94; auth, Vamos ao Brasil: Exploratory Portuguese Language and Culture for Middle School Students, coauth, Newburyport MA, Focus Pub, forthcoming; Transfer of Pragmatic Competence and Suggestions in Spanish Foreign Language Learning, Susan Gass, Joyce Neu, eds, Speech Acts Across Cultures, Berlin, Mouton de Gruyter, 95; auth, Perspectives on Second Language Acquisition from Spanish, co-ed, Austin TX, Cen for Lang Edu Studies, 98; auth, Function of the Adverbial ya in Spanish Narrative Discourse, Jour of Pragmatics, 96; Negation in Spanish and English Suggestions and Requests: Mitigating Effects?, Jour of Pragmatics, 94. **CONTACT ADDRESS** Dept of Spanish and Portuguese, Univ of Texas, Austin, Austin, TX 78712. **EMAIL** d.koike@mail.utexas.edu

KOLB, JOCELYNE
PERSONAL Born 02/21/1951, Urbana, IL, m, 1981, 1 child **DISCIPLINE** GERMAN **EDUCATION** Smith Col, BA, 72; Yale Univ, PhD, 79. **CAREER** Vis instr, Amherst Col, 76-78; asst prof, Dartmouth Col, 79-87; assoc prof to prof, Smith Col, 88-. **HONORS AND AWARDS** Yale Univ Fel, 72-76; Alexander von Humboldt Fel, 87-88; Book Awd, Am Conf of Romanticism, 95. **MEMBERSHIPS** AATG; ASECS; N Am Goethe Soc; N Am Heine Soc; ETA Hoffmann Gesellschaft; Am Conf on Romanticism. **RESEARCH** European Romanticism,

questions of taste, genre, decorum, Heine. **SELECTED PUBLICATIONS** Auth, "E.T.A. Hoffmann's Kreisleriana: A la recherche d'une forme perdue?", Monatshefte 69, (77): 34-44; auth, "The Sublime, The Ridiculous, and The Apple Tarts in Heine's Ideen. Das Buch Le Grand", Ger Quarterly 56, (81): 392-404; auth, "Heine and Music: Let It Sound No More", Heine-Jahrbuch (84): 90-113; auth, "Presenting The Unpresentable. Goethe's Translation of Le Neveu de Rameau", Goethe Yearbook 3, (86): 149-163; auth, "Thomas Mann's Translation of Wagner into Buddenbrooks", Ger Rev 61, (86): 146-153; auth, "Die Puppenspiele meines Humors: Heine and Romantic Irony", Studies in Romanticism 26, (Fall 87): 399-419; auth, "Heine as Freud's Double in Der Witz und seine Beziehung zum Unbewubten", Heine-Jahrbuch, (92): 137-162; auth, "Die Lorelei oder die Legende um Heine", Hein-Gedichte: Interpretationen, ed Bernd Kortlander, Reclam, 95; auth, The Ambiguity of Taste. Freedom and Food in European Romanticism, Univ of Mich Pr, (Ann Arbor), 95; ed, "Philip Kolb and Proust", Afterward to Marcel Proust. Selected Letters, Vol 4, HarperCollins, (London), 00. **CONTACT ADDRESS** Dept Ger Studies, Smith Col, Seelye 414, Northampton, MA 01063-1000. **EMAIL** jkolb@smith.edu.

KOLONOSKY, WALTER F.
PERSONAL Born 01/16/1938, Danville, PA, m, 1963, 2 children **DISCIPLINE** RUSSIAN LANGUAGE AND LITERATURE **EDUCATION** Lycoming Col, BA, 63; Univ Pa, MA, 65; Univ Kans, PhD(Russian), 72. **CAREER** Instr Russ and French, Kans State Col, 65-67; asst prof Russ lang and lit, Pa State Univ, 70-73; Assoc Prof Russ Lang and Lit, Kans State Univ, 73-; Assoc Ed, Studies in 20th Centruy Lit, 76-; Dir, Off Study Abroad, Kans State Univ, 77-; exchange prof, Int Res and Exchanges Bd, summer 78; Fulbright adv, Kans State Univ, 78-. **MEMBERSHIPS** AM Asn Teachers Slavic and East Europ Lang; Nat Asn For Student Affairs. **RESEARCH** Twentieth century Russian literature; comparative literature; Russian folklore. **SELECTED PUBLICATIONS CONTACT ADDRESS** 514 Wickham Rd, Manhattan, KS 66502.

KOM, AMBROISE
PERSONAL Born, Cameroon, m, 3 children **DISCIPLINE** FRANCOPHONE STUDIES **EDUCATION** Universite de la Sorbonne Nouvelle, Paris III, Doctorat d'Etat es lettres, 81. **CAREER** Eleanor Howard O'Leary prof; dir, Presence Francophone, International Journal of lang and lit. **RESEARCH** Literary production and its institutions; Colonial education and creativity; Francophonie; Imperialism and African cultures. **SELECTED PUBLICATIONS** Auth, Education et democratie en Afrique, le temps des illusions, Paris: l'Harmattan, 96; Le Cas Chester Himes, Paris: Nouvelles du Sud, 94; George Lamming et le destin des Caraibes, Montreal: Didier, 86; Le Harlem de Chester Himes, Sherbrooke: Naaman, 78; et al, Dictionnaire des oeuvres litteraires de langue francaise en Afrique au Sud du sahara, vol 2, 79-89, San Francisco, Bethesda, London: Int Scholars Publ, 96; Dictionnaire des oeuvres litteraires de langue francaise en Afrique au Sud du Sahara, Vol 1, des Origines a 78, San Francisco, Bethesda, London: Int Scholars Publ, 96; Mongo Beti, 40 ans d'ecriture, 60 ans de dissidence, Presence Francophone 42, 93 & Litteratures africaines, Paris: Silex, 87; auth, La Malediction francophone, Cle/Lit Verlag, Yaounde/Hamburg, 00. **CONTACT ADDRESS** Dept of Modern Languages and Literatures, Col of the Holy Cross, 1 College St, PO Box 89A, Worcester, MA 01610-2395. **EMAIL** akom@holycross.edu

KOMAR, KATHLEEN LENORE
PERSONAL Born 10/11/1949, Joliet, IL, m, 1988 **DISCIPLINE** COMPARATIVE LITERATURE; MODERN GERMAN; ENGLISH LITERATURE **EDUCATION** Univ Chicago, BA, 71; Princeton Univ, MA, 75; PhD, 77. **CAREER** From asst prof to full prof, Univ Calif, Los Angeles, 77-; chair, Prog in Comp Lit, Univ Calif, Los Angeles, 86-89; dir, Humanities Cluster Prog, Univ Calif, Los Angeles, 91-92; assoc dean, Grad Div, Univ Calif, Los Angeles, 92-. **HONORS AND AWARDS** Goethe Prize, Univ Chicago, 70; DAAD Fel, 71-72; Kent Fel, 74-77; Career Dev Grant for Jr Fac, Univ Calif, Los Angeles, 79, 81; Am Coun of Learned Soc Travel Grant, 86; Dist Teaching Awd for Fac, Univ Calif, Los Angeles, 88-89. **MEMBERSHIPS** MLA; Am Comp Lit Asn; Philol Asn Pac Coast; Western Asn Ger Studies. **RESEARCH** Fragmented, multilinear narratives in the early 20th century: German and American; the poetry of Rainer Maria Rilke and Wallace Stevens; the works of Hermann Broch; contemporary women writers. **SELECTED PUBLICATIONS** Auth, Pattern and Chaos: Multilinear Novels by Dos Passos, Faulkner, D¤blin, and Koeppen, Camden House Publ (Columbia, SC), 83; auth, Transcending Angels: Rainer Maria Rilke's "Duino Elegies", Univ Nebr Press (Lincoln, NE), 87; auth, "Christa Wolf," in Magell's Survey of World Literature, Supplement, ed. Frank N. Magill (NY: Marshall Cavendish Corp, 95), 2835-2843; auth, "Visions and Re-Visions: Contemporary Women Writers Re-present Helen & Clytemnestra," in Visions in History: Visions of the Other, ed. Margaret R. Higonnet and Sumie Jones (Tokyo: Univ Toyko Press, 95), 593-600; auth, "Rilke: Metaphysics in a New Age," in Rilke-Rezeptionen: Rilke Reconsidered, ed. Sigrid Bauschinger and Susan Cocalis (T¤bingen/Basel: Francke Verlag, 95), 155-169; auth, "Seventh Duino Elegy," in Reference Guide to World Literature, ed. Laura Berger (MI: St James Press, 95), 1012-1013; auth, "Christa Wolf's 'Cassandra,'" in Masterplots II: Women's Literature, ed. Frank N. Magill (CA: Salem Press, 95), 318-323; auth, "Kassandra as a Rebel Against War: The Theme of Heroism in Christa Wolf's Re-Vision of the Trojan War," in Themes and Structures: Studies in German Literature from Goethe to the Present, ed. Alexander Stephan (SC: Camden House, 97), 234-253; coed, Lyrical Symbols and Narrative Transformations, Camden House Publ (Columbia, SC), 98. **CONTACT ADDRESS** Dept of Comp Lit, Univ of California, Los Angeles, Los Angeles, CA 90095-1536. **EMAIL** komar@ucla.edu

KONSTAN, DAVID
PERSONAL Born 11/01/1940, New York, NY, m, 1994, 2 children **DISCIPLINE** CLASSICS **EDUCATION** Columbia Col, BA, 61; Columbia Univ, MA, 63, PhD, 67. **CAREER** Lectr classics, Hunter Col, 64-65, Brooklyn Col, 65-67; dir Hum prog, 72-74, chr, 75-77, 78-80, asst prof, 67-72, assoc prof, 72-77, Jane A. Seney prof Greek, 77-87, Wesleyan Univ; Dir Grad Stud, 88-89, CHR, 89-90, 92-94, 98-2001, Prof Classics & Comp Lit, 87- , John Rowe Workman Distinguished Prof Classics & Humanistic Trad, Brown Univ; vis prof, Am Univ Cairo, 81-83; vis schol Univ Texas-Austin, 86-90; vis prof, UCLA, 87; Fulbright lectr, 88; vis prof, Univ Sydney, 90-91; vis prof, Univ Natal, 93, Univ La Plata, 97. **HONORS AND AWARDS** President, American Philol. Assn., 99; Guggenheim, ACLS, NEH Fellowships. **MEMBERSHIPS** Am Philol Asn. **RESEARCH** Ancient literature; culture. **SELECTED PUBLICATIONS** Auth, Sexual Summetry: Love in the Anceint Novel and Related Genres, Princeton Univ Press, 94; Greek Comedy and Ideology, Oxford Univ, 95; Friendship in the Classical World, Cambridge Univ Press, 97; Philodemus on Frank Criticism: Introduction, Translation and Notes, Soc Bibl Lit Texts & Transl, 98; The greek Commentaries on Aristotle's Nicomachean Ethics 8 and 9, Cornell Univ Press. **CONTACT ADDRESS** Dept Classics, Brown Univ, Providence, RI 02912. **EMAIL** dkonstan@brown.edu

KOONTZ, CHRISTIAN
PERSONAL Born 06/22/1930, Juniata, PA, s **DISCIPLINE** ENGLISH LITERATURE, LINGUISTICS **EDUCATION** Mercyhurst Col, BA; Cath Univ Amer, MA, PhD. **CAREER** Prof, 80-. **RESEARCH** Writing to learn, heal, and create. **SELECTED PUBLICATIONS** Auth, Cultivating Multiple Intelligences through the Living Journal. **CONTACT ADDRESS** Dept of Eng, Univ of Detroit Mercy, 4001 W McNichols Rd, PO BOX 19900, Detroit, MI 48219-0900. **EMAIL** ckoontzrsm@juno.com

KOOP, MARIE-CHRISTINE W.
PERSONAL Born St Raphael, France, d, 1 child **DISCIPLINE** FRENCH **EDUCATION** Teachers Col Aix-en-Provence, Cert, 76; SUNY, MA, 79; Mich State Univ, PhD, 87. **CAREER** Teacher, CES Ranguin Cannes France, 76-77; Instructor, Allegheny Col, 83-84; Visiting Asst Prof, La Tech Univ, 84-85; Instructor, Middlebury Col, 86; Asst Prof, Univ Tex, 87-90; Asst Prof to Assoc Prof, Univ N Tex, 90-. **HONORS AND AWARDS** Nelson Brooks Awd, Am Coun on the Teaching of For Lang, 99; Intl Ed Awd, Univ N TX, 97; Professing Women Awd, Univ N TX, 96; Developing Scholar Awd, Univ N TX, 96; Nat Awd for Excellence, Am Asn of Teachers of French, 95; Chevalier in the Order of the Palmes Academiques, France, 94; Who's Who of Am Teachers, 94. **MEMBERSHIPS** AATF; MLA; ACTFL; AFCS; ASMCF; AECSE; WIF; ANEF. **RESEARCH** The French Education System; Status of Women in France; The Teaching of Culture. **SELECTED PUBLICATIONS** Auth, "Taking Teachers to France: Organizing a Summer Immersion Program Supported by Grants," Foreign Lang Annals, (95): 424-436; auth, "La reforme du baccalaureat en France," The French Review, (96): 566-582; auth, "Ecole libre et loi Falloux," Contemporary French Civilization, (96): 59-75; co-auth, "France," in Acquiring Cross-Cultural Competence: Four Stages for Students of French, (Nat Textbook Co, 96), 19-25; auth, Bien Sur! Culture et Communications, Upper Saddle River, Prentice Hall, 96; auth, "Importance des echanges d'etudiants accompagnes de stages professionnels pour revitaliser l'etude du francais aux Etats-Unis," Dialogues et Cultures, (98): 88-92; auth, "La violence dans les etablissements scolaires en France," Contemporary French Civilization, (00): 54-74; auth, "Democratisation de l'enseignement en France: illusion ou realite?," in France at the Dawn of the Twenty-First Century: Trends and Transformations, (Summa Pub, 00), 97-114; ed, France at the Dawn of the Twenty-First Century: Trends and Transformations, Summa Pub, 00. **CONTACT ADDRESS** Dept For Lang, Univ of No Texas, PO Box 311127, Denton, TX 76203-1127. **EMAIL** koop@unt.edu

KOOREMAN, THOMAS EDWARD
PERSONAL Born 02/07/1936, St. Louis, MO, m, 1967, 2 children **DISCIPLINE** SPANISH, SPANISH AMERICAN LITERATURE **EDUCATION** Northeast Mo State Univ, BS, 59; Univ Mo, Columbia, MAT, 66, PhD(Span), 70. **CAREER** Asst prof, 70-74, assoc prof, 74-82, Prof Span, Butler Univ, 82-99, prof emer, 99-. **HONORS AND AWARDS** Foreign Lang Teacher of the Year, Indiana, 96; CIBER Workshop, U Ill, 98. **MEMBERSHIPS** Am Asn Teachers Span and Port; AAUP; Am Literary Translators Asn; Asn of Colombianists. **RESEARCH** Spanish American literature; Literary Translation; Spanish for Business. **SELECTED PUBLICATIONS** Auth, Manuel Zapata Olivella, A Saint Is Born in China, U Texas, 91; auth, "Poetic Vision and the Creation of Character in Elcoronel no tiene quien le escrio," Romance Notes 23 (93); ed, Breves Cuentos Hispanos, Prentice Hall, 00. **CONTACT ADDRESS** Dept of Mod Foreign Lang, Butler Univ, 4600 Sunset Ave, Indianapolis, IN 46208-3443. **EMAIL** tkoorema@butler.edu

KOPFF, EDWARD CHRISTIAN
PERSONAL Born 11/22/1946, Brooklyn, NY, M, 1986, 2 children **DISCIPLINE** GREEK, LATIN **EDUCATION** Haverford Col, BA, 68; Univ NC, Chapel Hill, PhD(classics), 74. **CAREER** Asst dir classics, Intercol Ctr Class Studies, Rome, Italy 72-73; asst prof, 73-76, Assoc Prof Classics, Univ Colo, Boulder, 76, Bk Rev ed, Class J, 77-; Nat Endowment for the Humanities fel, Am Acad Rome, 78-79; Assoc Dir, Honors Prog, 90-. **HONORS AND AWARDS** National Endowment for the Humanities fellow, American Academy in Rome, 78-90; CU-Student Alumni (SOAR) Teaching Recognition Awd, 83, 97. **MEMBERSHIPS** Am Philol Asn; Class Asn Midwest and South. **RESEARCH** Transmission of ancient literature; Greek palaeography; ancient drama. **SELECTED PUBLICATIONS** Critical Edition of Euripides, Bacchae Tuebner, 82; The Devil Knows Latin: Why America Needs the Classical Tradition, ISI Books, 99. **CONTACT ADDRESS** Honors Prog., Univ of Colorado, Boulder, Campus Box 184, Norlin M 400, Boulder, CO 80309-0184. **EMAIL** kopff@spot.colorado.edu

KOPP, RICHARD L.
PERSONAL Born 06/23/1934, New York, NY, m, 1958, 2 children **DISCIPLINE** FRENCH LANGUAGE, FRENCH LITERATURE **EDUCATION** Queens Col, BA, 55; State Univ Iowa, MA, 57; NYork Univ, PhD(French), 67. **CAREER** From instr to asst prof French, Col of the Holy Cross, 59-69; asst prof, 69-74, chmn dept, 73, assoc prof, 74-78, prof Mod Lang, Fairleigh Dickinson Univ, 78, Ford Found grant, 69; fac res grant, Fairleigh Dickinson Univ, 72-73. **HONORS AND AWARDS** Founders Day Awd, NY Univ, 68. **MEMBERSHIPS** MLA; Soc Amis Marcel Proust; Asn Study Higher Educ; Am Asn Higher Educ. **RESEARCH** Proust; Gide; Svevo. **SELECTED PUBLICATIONS** Auth, Proust's Elstir and the meaning of social success, Laurel Rev, Fall 70; Marcel Proust as a Social Critic, Fairleigh Dickinson Univ, 71; The presentation of the artist in Proust and Svevo, Univ SFla Lang Quart, Winter 76; contribr, Critical Bibliography of French Literature, 79; The Moralist Tradition in France, Asn Fac Press, 82. **CONTACT ADDRESS** Dept of Mod Lang, Fairleigh Dickinson Univ, Florham-Madison, 285 Madison Ave, Madison, NJ 07940-1099.

KOPPISCH, MICHAEL SEIBERT
PERSONAL Born 07/12/1942, Baltimore, MD, m, 1973 **DISCIPLINE** FRENCH **EDUCATION** Johns Hopkins Univ, BA, 64, MA, 67, PhD(French), 70. **CAREER** Instr French, Northwestern Univ, 67-70; asst prof, 70-76, assoc prof, 76-81, Prof French, Mich State Univ, 81-. **HONORS AND AWARDS** Palmes Academiques, 95. **MEMBERSHIPS** MLA; Am Asn Teachers Fr; North Am Soc 17th Century Fr Lit. **RESEARCH** Seventeenth century French literature; European novel; Literature of the Holocaust. **SELECTED PUBLICATIONS** The Dissoulition of Character: Changing Perspectives in La Bruyere's Caracteres, Fr Forum Publ, Inc, 81; coed, Approaches to Teaching Moliere: Tartuffe and Other Plays, with James Gaines, MLA, 95. **CONTACT ADDRESS** Dept of Romance Lang, Michigan State Univ, East Lansing, MI 48823. **EMAIL** koppisch@msn.edu

KORNBLATT, JUDITH DEUTSCH
PERSONAL Born 10/26/1955, Chicago, IL, m, 1985, 2 children **DISCIPLINE** PHILOSOPHY, RUSSIAN, LITERATURE; LANGUAGE **EDUCATION** Williams Col, BA, 77; Columbia Univ, MA, 80; MPhil, 82; PhD, 85. **CAREER** Instr, Dalhousie Univ, 81; precept, Columbia Univ, 82-85; vis lectr, Williams Col, 84; adj vis asst prof, Columbia Univ, 86; vis asst prof, Ind Univ, 86-87; vis scholar, Hebrew Univ, 98; vis asst prof to asst prof to assoc prof to prof to chmn to assoc dean, Univ Wis Madison, 87-. **HONORS AND AWARDS** H. I. Romnes Fel, 97; IREX Grant, 97; NEH, 93, 91-92; ACLS/SSRC Fel, 92-94; Postdoc Fel, 85-86. **MEMBERSHIPS** AAASS; AATSEEL; MLA; ACTR; AAR; AAUW; Phi Beta Kappa. **RESEARCH** Russian religious philosophy; Jews in Russia; 19th and 20th-century Russian literature. **SELECTED PUBLICATIONS** Auth, The Cossack Hero in Russian Literature: A Study in Cultural Mythology, Univ Wis Pr (Madison): 92; co-ed, Russian Religious Thought, Univ Wis Pr (Madison), 96; auth, "Gogol and the Muses of Mirgorod," Slavic Rev 50 (91): 309-316; auth, "Solov'ev's Androgynous Sophia and the Jewish Kabbalah," Slavic Rev 50 (91): 486-496; auth, "The Transfiguration of Plato in the Erotic Philosophy of Vladimir Solov'ev," Relig/Lit 24 (92): 35-50; auth, "Vladimir Solov'ev on Spiritual Nationhood, Russia, and the Jews," Russian Rev 56 (97): 157-77; auth, "On Laughter and Vladimir Solov'ev's 'Three Encounters,'" Slavic Rev 57 (98): 563-84; auth, "Why a Ladies' Tailor: Ladies' Tailor and the End of Soviet Jewry," Jewish Soc Studies 5 (99): 180-195; co-auth, "Vladimir Solov'ev: Confronting Dostoevsky on the Jewish and Christian

Questions," J Am Acad Relig 68 (00): 69-98; auth, "When Fiction Meets Philosophy: Solov'ev's Three Conversations and Tolstoy's Resurrection," SEED 45 (01); auth, Doubly Chosen: The Question of Jews in the Post-Stalinist Russian Orthodox Church, (forthcoming). **CONTACT ADDRESS** Dept Slavic Lang, Univ of Wisconsin, Madison, 1220 Linden Dr, Madison, WI 53706-1525. **EMAIL** jkornbla@falstaff.wisc.edu

KOROPECKYJ, ROMAN
PERSONAL Born 04/03/1954, New York, NY, m, 1980 **DISCIPLINE** SLAVIC LANGUAGES AND LITERATURE **EDUCATION** Columbia Univ, BA, 76; Harvard Univ, PhD, 90. **CAREER** Instr, Univ of Ottawa, 84-86; Preceptor, Harvard Univ, 90-92; Managing Ed, Harvard Libr of Early Ukrainian Lit, 88-93; Adj Instr, Columbia Univ, 89-90; Univ Calif, Los Angeles, 92-. **MEMBERSHIPS** AAASS, AATSEEL, MLA. **RESEARCH** Polish Literature, Ukrainian Literature, Slavic Romanticism. **SELECTED PUBLICATIONS** Co-ed, Lev Krevza's 'Defense of Church Unity' and Zaxarija Kpystenes'kyj's 'Palinodia', Harvard Ukrainian Res Inst (Cambridge), 95; auth, "'The Weakly-Colored Dahlia': The Ruthenian Langauge Questions in Jan Zachariasiewicz's 'Swiety Jur'," Die Welt der Slaven 60 (95): 1-21; auth, "Konstrukcje homoseksualizmu w 'Dzienniku' Jana Lechonia (Proba innej lektury)," ("The construction of homosexuality in Jan Lechon's 'Diary': An attempt at a different reading"), Teksty Drugie 4 (96): 154-168; auth, "Narrative and Social Drama in Adam Mickiewicz's 'Pan Tadeusz'," Slavonic and E Europ Rev 76 (98): 467-483; auth, "Between Deybel and the Deep Blue Sea: Edmond Mainard's Biography of Adam Mickiewicz," in Mickiewicz 1798-1998: bicentenaire de la naissance, special issue of Actes de la Societe Historique et Litteraire Polonaise 4 (98): 101-119; auth, The Poetics of Revitalization: Adam Mickiewicz between 'Forefathers' Eve, pt.3' and 'Pan Tadeusz', Boulder: E Europ Monographs, 00. **CONTACT ADDRESS** Dept Slavic Lang, Univ of California, Los Angeles, PO Box 951584, Los Angeles, CA 90095-1584. **EMAIL** koropeck@humnet.ucla.edu

KOSTA, BARBARA
DISCIPLINE GERMAN LITERATURE **EDUCATION** Univ Calif, Berkeley, 89. **CAREER** Assoc Prof, Univ Ariz, 95-. **HONORS AND AWARDS** German Acad Exchange, 96; Fulbright Res Fel, 96-97. **MEMBERSHIPS** Women in German; Women's Caucus of the Modern Lang; Modern Lang Asn; German Stud Asn; Assoc Am Tchrs German. **RESEARCH** German cinema; autobiography; weemae republic and contemporary German literature. **SELECTED PUBLICATIONS** Coauth, Auf deutsch: Arbeitsbuch, 90; coauth, Auf deutsch: Instructor's Manual and Testing Program, 90; coauth, Auf deutsch; First Year German Textbook, 90; auth, art, Employed Bodies: The Female Servant in Works by Marieluise Fleiser, 92; auth, Recasting Autobiography: Women's Counterfictions in Contemporary German Literature, 94. **CONTACT ADDRESS** Dept of German Studies, Univ of Arizona, Tucson, AZ 85721. **EMAIL** bkosta@u.arizona.edu

KOVACH, THOMAS A.
PERSONAL Born 10/22/1949, Providence, RI, m, 1999, 3 children **DISCIPLINE** COMPARATIVE LITERATURE **EDUCATION** Columbia Univ, BA, 71; Princeton Univ, PhD, 78. **CAREER** Asst prof, assoc prof, Univ Utah, 78-85; dept chemn, assoc prof, Univ Ala, 90-94; dept head, assoc prof, Univ Ariz, 94-. **HONORS AND AWARDS** Fulbright-hays Grad Fel, 74-75; Fulbright-Hays Grant, 83; Phi Beta Kappa; grad col fel, princeton univ, 71-74; deutscher verein prize, columbia univ, 71. **MEMBERSHIPS** MLA; German Stud Asn; Am Asn Tchrs German. **RESEARCH** Rilke; Hofmannsthal; German-Jewish writers; German and Comparative Lit from the mid-eighteenth through the early twentieth centuries. **SELECTED PUBLICATIONS** Auth, Hofmannsthal and Symbolism: Art and Life in the Work of a Modern Poet, Am Univ Stud III/18, Berne/Frankfurt/New York: Peter Lang Verlag, 85; auth, " Essay on Jaroslav Hasek in Contemporary Authors 129, Detroit/New York/London: Gale Publishing, 90; auth, "Traditionalist Modernism or Modernist Trarditionalism: The Case of Hugo von Hofmannsthal," Philogical Papers 39, 93; ed, "Rilke's Die Insel der Sirenen and the Music of Silence," Lyric Symbols and Narrative Transformations: Essays in Honor of Ralph Freedman, co-ed. Kathleen L. Komar and Ross Shideler, (Columbia, SC: Camden House, 98). **CONTACT ADDRESS** Dept of German Studies, Univ of Arizona, Tucson, AZ 85721-0067. **EMAIL** tkovach@u.arizona.edu

KOVACS, P. DAVID
PERSONAL Born 11/12/1945, Kenosha, WI, m, 1969, 2 children **DISCIPLINE** CLASSICS **EDUCATION** Col Wooster, BA, 67; Harvard Univ, AM, 69; PhD, 76. **CAREER** Asst prof, Univ Va, 76-82, assoc prof, 82-90, prof, 90-. **HONORS AND AWARDS** NEH, 90-92, 96-97. **MEMBERSHIPS** AMA; CAMWS; CA. **RESEARCH** Greek tragedy; Ovid. **SELECTED PUBLICATIONS** Auth, The Andromache of Euripides: An Interpretation, Scholars Press (Chico, CA), 80; auth, The Heroic Muse: Studies in the Hippolytus and Hecuba of Euripides, Johns Hopkins Univ Press (Baltimore), 87; auth, Euripidea, E J Brill (Leiden), 94; Auth, Euripides. The Loeb Classical Library Euripides, Greek text and English translation, Harvard Univ Press (94) vol 1; auth, Euripides. The Loeb Classical Library Euripides, Greek text and English translation, Harvard Univ Press (95) vol vol2; auth, Euripides. The Loeb Classical Library Euripides, Greek text and English translation, Harvard Univ Press (98) vol 3; auth, Euripides. The Loeb Classical Library Euripides, Greek text and English translation, Harvard Univ Press (99) vol 4; Auth, "Euripides, Troa des 95-97: Is Sacking Cities Really Foolish?" Classical Quart 33 (1983), 334-338; auth, "On Medea's Great Monologue (Eur. Medea 1021-1080)," CQ 36 (86): 343-352; auth, "Ovid, Metamorphoses 1.2," CQ 37 (1987):458-465; auth, "Zeus in Euripides Medea," AJP 114 (93): 45-70; auth, "The Theology of Euripides' Trojan Trilogy," Colby Quarterly 33.2 (97): 162-76. **CONTACT ADDRESS** Dept Classics, Univ of Virginia, 401 New Cabell Hall, Charlottesville, VA 22903-3125.

KOZMA, JANICE M.
PERSONAL Born 12/20/1945, Wyandotte, MI, m, 1981 **DISCIPLINE** ITALIAN LANGUAGE & LITERATURE **EDUCATION** Univ Florence, dipl/cert Ital, 65; Univ MI, Ann Arbor, BA, 68, MA, 70, PhD, 73. **CAREER** Vis asst prof Ital, Univ KY, Lexington, 73-74; adj prof, FL Int Univ, 74-75; asst prof, 77-80, Assoc Prof Ital, Univ KS, 80-, Tchg fels, Univ MI, 68-73. **HONORS AND AWARDS** Cavaliere dello Stato: Knight of the Order of Merit of the Italian Republic. **MEMBERSHIPS** MLA; Am Asn Tchr(s) Ital; Am Asn Univ Profs Ital; Midwest Mod Lang Asn. **RESEARCH** Italy's post-war neo-realistic novels; narrative techniques. **SELECTED PUBLICATIONS** Auth, Carosello: A Cultural Reader, Holt, Rinehart & Winston, 78, 2nd ed, 82; Vasco Pratolini, In: Columbia Dictionary of Modern European Literature, Columbia Univ Press, 2nd ed, 80; Pratolini's Il Quartiere: The metaphor, Ky Romance Quart, XXIX: 37-45; Metaphor in Pratolini's novels: Il Quartiere and Cronache Di Poveri Amanti, Romance Notes, XX: 1-6; Scholl, Bianco, V, 60--Glod, A Quattr' Occhi, Italica, 57: 215; Functions of Metaphor in Pratolini's Cronache Di Pover Amanti: Maciste and the Signora, Ital Cult, 81; Omen and Image: Presage and Sacrifice in Moravia's La Ciociara, Italica, 84; The Racconti romani and the Nuovi racconti romani: Moravia's Romani de Roma, Papers in Romance, 85; The Architecture of Imagery in Alberto Moravia's Fiction, Univ NC Press, 93; Say it with Flowers: Imagistic Represenations of Women in Alberto Moravia's Prose, Italica, 93; Francesca Duranti, In: Dictionary of Literary Biography, 95; Bio-Fictive Conversations and the Uncentered Woman in Francesca Duranti's Novels, The Italianist, 96; Pratolini, Vasco, Il Quartiere, Harcourt Brace, 96; Grow Up! Grazia Deledda's Adult-Adolescent Males of Arrested Maturation, Annali d'italianistica, 97. **CONTACT ADDRESS** Dept of French & Ital, Univ of Kansas, Lawrence, Lawrence, KS 66045-0001. **EMAIL** jkozma@ukans.edu

KRA, PAULINE
PERSONAL Born 07/30/1934, Lodz, Poland, m, 1955, 2 children **DISCIPLINE** FRENCH LITERATURE **EDUCATION** Barnard Col, BA, 55, Columbia Univ, MA, 63, PhD, 68; Queens Col CUNY, MA , 90. **CAREER** Lectr French, Queens Col, 64-65; vis lectr, Rutgers Univ, 3/68; asst prof, 68-74, assoc prof, 74-82, Prof French, Yeshiva Univ, 82. **HONORS AND AWARDS** Phi Beta Kappa, 55. **MEMBERSHIPS** Am Soc for 18th Century Studies; Northeast Am Soc for 18th Century Studies; Am Asn Tchr(s) French; MLA. **RESEARCH** Montesquieu; computer appl to lit anal; conceptual struct. **SELECTED PUBLICATIONS** Auth, The invisible chain of the Lettres persanes, Studies on Voltaire and the 18th Century, 63; Religion in Montesquieu's Lettres persanes, Institut et Musee Voltaire, 70; Note on the derivation of names in Voltaire's Zadig, Romance Notes, 75; The Role of the Harem, In: Imitations of Montesquieu's Lettres persanes, Studies on Voltaire and the Eighteenth Century, 79; L'Enchaninement des chapitres de l'Espirt des lois, Studi Francesi, 82; Jean de La Bruyere, In: European Writers (George Stade, ed), NY, 84; Montesquieu and Women, In: French Women and the Age of Enlightenment (Samia I Spencer, ed), Bloomington, 84; The Politics of National Character, In: Studies on Voltaire and the 18th Century, 89; Multiplicity of voices in the Lettres persanes, Revue belge de philologie et d'histoire, 92; Montesquieu's Lettres persanes and George Lyttelton's Letters from a Persian in England, Transactions of the Eighth Int Cong on the Enlightenement, Studies on Voltaire and the 18th Century, 92; In Search of National Character, ARTFL Proj Newsletter, 94-95; les Chaines argumentatives dans l'Espirit des lois, La fortune de Montesquieu: Montesquieu Ecrivain, Bordeaux, 95; The Name Rica and the Veil in Montesquieu's Lettres persanes, Studi Francesi, 98. **CONTACT ADDRESS** Dept of French, Yeshiva Univ, 245 Lexington Ave, New York, NY 10016-4699. **EMAIL** kra@ymail.yu.edu

KRAABEL, ALF THOMAS
PERSONAL Born 11/04/1934, Portland, OR, m, 1956, 3 children **DISCIPLINE** RELIGIOUS STUDIES, CLASSICS **EDUCATION** Luther Col, BA, 56; Univ Iowa, MA, 58; Luther Theol Sem, BD, 61; Harvard Univ, ThD, 68. **CAREER** Asst prof classics and relig studies, 67-70, assoc prof classics and chmn rclig studies, 70-76, Prof Classics and Relig Studies, Univ Minn, Minneapolis, 76-; Chmn Dept and Dir Grad Study, 80-; Assoc dir, Joint expedition to Khirbet Shema, Israel, 69-73; Sabbatical fel, Am Coun Learned Soc, 77-78. **MEMBERSHIPS** Soc Bibl Lit; Am Acad Relig; Am Soc Study Relig; Soc Values Higher Educ. **RESEARCH** Greco-Roman religions; archaeology. **SELECTED PUBLICATIONS** Auth, Jewish Communities in Asia-Minor, Cath Bibl Quart, Vol 0055, 93; Ancient Jewish Epitaphs in An Introductory Survey of a Millennium of Jewish Funerary Epigraphy Cath Bibl Quart, Vol 0055, 93; From Synagogue to Church in Public Services and offices in the Earliest Christian Communities Interpretation-A, J Bible Theol, Vol 0048, 94; Mission and Conversion in Proselytizing in the Religious History of the Roman Empire, J Early Christian Studies, Vol 0004, 96; Early Christian Epitaphs from Anatolia, Cath Bibl Quart, Vol 0058, 96. **CONTACT ADDRESS** Dept of Classics, Univ of Minnesota, Twin Cities, 310A Folwell Hall, Minneapolis, MN 55455.

KRABBE, JUDITH
DISCIPLINE GREEK, LATIN & SANSKRIT LANGUAGES & LITERATURES **EDUCATION** Cath Univ, PhD. **CAREER** Dept Classics, Millsaps Col **SELECTED PUBLICATIONS** Auth, The Metamorphoses of Apuleius; coauth, An Introduction to Sanskrit. **CONTACT ADDRESS** Dept of Classical Studies, Millsaps Col, 1701 N State St, Jackson, MS 39210. **EMAIL** krabbjk@orka.millsaps.edu

KRABBENHOFT, KENNETH
PERSONAL Born 12/21/1946, Detroit, MI, m, 1979, 1 child **DISCIPLINE** SPANISH, PORTUGUESE **EDUCATION** Yale Univ, BA, 68; NY Univ, MA, 79; PhD, 82. **CAREER** From asst prof to assoc prof, NYork Univ, 82-; dir, NYork Univ Master of Arts & Liberal Studies, 91-93; dir, NYork Univ--Spain, 94-97. **MEMBERSHIPS** Phi Beta Kappa, Alpha Connecticut Chapter. **RESEARCH** Spanish Literature, Luso--Brazilian Literature, Mysticism, Science Fiction, Translation. **SELECTED PUBLICATIONS** Auth, El precio de la cortesía, Univ de Salamanca, 94 & 95; transl, "Odes to Opposites," by Pablo Neruda, Bulfinch Press, 95, 97, & 99; auth, "Gongora's Stoic Pilgrim," Bullet of Hispanic Studies 73.1 (96): 1-12; auth, "Don Quixote and Lolita," Atlantis 18.10 (97): 213-227; transl, "The Poems of St John of the Cross," Harcourt Brace and Co., 99; auth, Neoestoicismo y genero popular, Univ de Salamance Pr, forthcoming; auth, "The uses of madness in Cervantes and Philip K. Dick," Science-Fiction Studies, forthcoming. **CONTACT ADDRESS** Dept Span & Port, New York Univ, 19 University Place, New York, NY 1003-4556.

KRAMER, KARL D.
PERSONAL Born 01/19/1934, Seattle, WA, m, 1955, 1 child **DISCIPLINE** RUSSIAN LANGUAGES AND LITERATURE **EDUCATION** Univ Wash, AB, 55, MA, 57, PhD(comp lit), 64. **CAREER** From instr to asst prof Russ, Northwestern Univ, 61-65; asst prof Slavic lang and lit, Univ Mich, Ann Arbor, 65-70; Assoc Prof Slavic Lang and Lit, Univ Wash, 70-. **MEMBERSHIPS** MLA; Am Asn Advan Slavic Studies; Am Asn Teachers Slavic and EEurop Lang. **RESEARCH** Nineteenth century Russian literature; Soviet literature. **SELECTED PUBLICATIONS** **CONTACT ADDRESS** Dept of Slavic Lang and Lit, Univ of Washington, Seattle, WA 98105.

KRAMER-HELLINX, NECHAMA
PERSONAL Born 09/26/1940, Jerusalem, Israel, m, 1985, 2 children **DISCIPLINE** SPANISH **EDUCATION** CUNY Queens Col, BA, 73; CUNY Graduate Center, MA, 78; PhD, 88. **CAREER** Adj lectr, CUNY Queens Col, 73-78; adj asst prof, CUNY York Col, 89-. **HONORS AND AWARDS** NY SABE, Bilingual Teacher of the Year, 88. **MEMBERSHIPS** MLA, AATSP. **RESEARCH** Siglo de Oro, Spain, Literature by Spanish Conversos, The Image of the Spanish Inquisition in Literature, Sephardic Studies. **SELECTED PUBLICATIONS** Auth, "antonio Enriques gomez y la Inquisicion: Vida y Literatura," Peamin 46.7, (91): 196-221; auth, Antonio Enriques Gomez: Literatura y Sociedad en El siglo pitagorico y Vida de don Gregorio Guadana, Peter Lang, 93; auth, "Aspectos picarescos en El siglo pitagorico y Vida de (1600-1663)," Actes del Simposi Internacional Sobre Cultura Sefardita, ed Josep Ribera, (Univ Barcelona, Spain, 93); auth,"Dedicatoria in Memoriam de Guerra Da Cal da Versao Hebraica do 'romance al Divin Martir Juda Creyente' de Antonio Enriquez Gomez (1600)," Congresso Int de Lingua, Cultra e Literaturas Lusofonas, (94): 261-280; auth, "El Aspecto de la Inquisicion en la obra de Antonio Enriquez gomez (1600-1663)," the Culture of Spanish Jewry: Proceeding of the First Int Congress, ed Aviva Doron, (Levinsky Col of Educ Publ House, Israel, 94); auth, "La Prudente Abigail y A los que obliga el honor: Honor, prudencia, amor, celos y muerte. Dos comedias de Antonio Enriquez gomez (1600-1663),' Los judaizantes en Europa y la literatura castellana del Siglo de Oro, ed Fernando Diaz Esteban, (Madrid, Spain: Editorial Letrumero, 94); auth, "La Literatura como espejo de la Historia: Los historicos malsines inquisitoriales, en la literatura de A Enriquez Gomez," Melanges de la Casa de Velazquiex, (94): 139-150; auth, "La figura del malsin en El Siglo pitagorico y Vida de don Gregorio Guadana de Antonio Enriquez Gomez (1600-1663)," Hispano-Jewish Civilization after 1492, eds Michel Abitol, Assis Yom-Tov and Galit, Hasn-Rokem, (97); auth, "Honor y desafio en La Soberbia de Nimrod," and "Resonancias biblicas en el Sanson Nazareno," Cuenca: Antonio Enriquez gomez, eds Carlos de la Rica y Antonio Lazaro Cebrian, (99). **CONTACT ADDRESS** York Col, CUNY, Guy Brewer Blvd, Jamaica, NY 11451: **EMAIL** nechamakr@worldnet.att.net

KRATZ, BERND
PERSONAL Born 01/25/1935, Saarbruecken, Germany **DISCIPLINE** GERMANIC LINGUISTICS, MEDIEVAL GERMAN LITERATURE **EDUCATION** Univ Marburg, Staatsexamen, 62, PhD, 63. **CAREER** Wiss asst Ger, Univ Marburg, 63-66; assoc prof, 67-74, Prof Ger, Univ Ky, 74-; Ed, Colloquia Germanica, Franke, Bern, 76-. **MEMBERSHIPS** MLA **RESEARCH** Germanic linguistics; Medieval German literature. **SELECTED PUBLICATIONS** Auth, "Die altdeutschen Sprueche 'Pro Nessia' und ein franzoesischer Hippiatrie-Traktat des 15," Amsterdamer Beitraege zur aelteren Germanistik 34 (91): 23-31; auth, "Der Computer als Zugang zum altislaendishcen Kalender," Am J of Ger Ling and Lit 4 (92): 19-42; auth, "'Vnbyllich het sye eb gedan': Die Inschrift des 'Gothaer Liebespaar'-Gemaeldes," Zeitschrift fuer Kunstgeschichte 63 (00): 120-132. **CONTACT ADDRESS** Dept of Ger, Univ of Kentucky, 1065 Patterson Office Tower, Lexington, KY 40506-0003. **EMAIL** bkratz@pop.uky.edu

KRATZ, HENRY
PERSONAL Born 03/23/1922, Albany, NY, m, 1997 **DISCIPLINE** GERMANIC LANGUAGES **EDUCATION** NYork State Col Teachers, BA, 42; Oh State Univ, MA, 46, PhD, 49. **CAREER** Asst Ger, Ohio State Univ, 45-48, instr, 48-49; instr, Univ Mich, 49-53; instr, Univ Mass, 53-55; asst ed, G and C Merriam Co, 55-60; from asst prof to assoc prof Ger, Univ Ore, 60-65; Prof Ger, Univ Tenn, Knoxville, 65-92; Head Dept Ger and Slavic Lang, 72-87; prof emer, 92-. **RESEARCH** Middle High and Old High German; Old Norse. **SELECTED PUBLICATIONS** Auth, Fr[illegible]hes Mittelalter, Bern, 70; auth, Wolfram von Eschenbach's Parzival: An Attempt at a Total Evaluation, Bern, 73; ed, Adelbert von Chamisso, Voyage around the World with the Romanzov Exploring Expedition in the Years 1815-1818 in the Brig Rurik, 86. **CONTACT ADDRESS** Dept of Mod and For Lang, Univ of Tennessee, Knoxville, Knoxville, TN 37996-0470.

KRATZER, ANGLELIKA
DISCIPLINE LINGUISTICS **EDUCATION** Univ Konstanz, BA, 73, PhD, 79. **CAREER** Prof. **RESEARCH** Formal semantics; syntax-semantics interface. **SELECTED PUBLICATIONS** Auth, Stage Level and Individual Level Predicates, Univ Chicago, 95; Severing the External Argument from its Verb, Kluwer, 96; Scope or Pseudoscope? Are there Wide Scope Indefinites?, Kluwer, 98. **CONTACT ADDRESS** Linguistics Dept, Univ of Massachusetts, Amherst, Amherst, MA 01003. **EMAIL** kratzer@linguist.umass.edu

KRAUEL, RICARDO
PERSONAL Born Granada, Spain, m, 2 children **DISCIPLINE** LANGUAGE, LITERATURE, SPANISH **EDUCATION** Univ Malaga, Kaw, 90; BA, 90; Univ Ottawa, MA, 93; Brown Univ, PhD, 98. **CAREER** Asst prof, Princeton Univ, 98-. **HONORS AND AWARDS** Res Hum Fel, 250th Ann Fund Fel, Princeton Univ; Mary Ann Lippitt Pres Awd, Manning Fel, Kossoff Prize, Kenyon Fel, Brown Univ. **MEMBERSHIPS** MLA; IAH; IAGS. **RESEARCH** Modern Spanish literature; gender studies; literary theory; cinema and literature. **SELECTED PUBLICATIONS** Auth, "Funambulismo Sobre la Frontera de un Genero," Anal Lit Espan Cont 23 (98); auth, "La Sinrazon de la Eazon: Revision de la Cordura en 'Fortunata y Jacinta,'" Anal Galdos 31-32 (96); auth, "Incesto y Escritura en El Sur, de Adelaida Garcia Morales," in Elerotismo en la Narrativa Espanola e Hispano-Americana Actual, ed. Elvita Huelbes (Fundacion L. Goytisolo, 00); auth, Voces Desde el Silenco: Heterologias Generico Sexuales en la Narrativa Espanola Moderna, 1875-1975, Libertarias (Madrid), 01. **CONTACT ADDRESS** Romance Lang Dept, Princeton Univ, 201 E Pyne, Princeton, NJ 08544-0001. **EMAIL** rkrauel@princeton.edu

KRAUS, MATTHEW A.
PERSONAL Born 08/21/1963, Cincinnati, OH, m, 1991, 3 children **DISCIPLINE** CLASSICS **EDUCATION** Harvard-Radcliffe, BA, 85; Hebrew Union Col, Jewish Inst of the Religion, Rabbinic ordination, 91; Univ MI, PhD, 96. **CAREER** Asst Prof Classics and Jewish Studies, Williams Col, 96-. **MEMBERSHIPS** AJS; AAR-SBL; APA. **RESEARCH** Jerome; Judaism and the Greco-Roman world; late Antique Latin lit. **CONTACT ADDRESS** Dept of Classics, Williams Col, Stetson Hall, Williamstown, MA 01267. **EMAIL** mkraus@williams.edu

KRAUSE, MAUREEN THERESE
PERSONAL Born Evanston, IL **DISCIPLINE** GERMAN **EDUCATION** Northwestern Univ, BA, 69; Ohio State Univ, MA, 70, PhD(Ger), 80. **CAREER** Instr Ger, Ohio State Univ, 80-81; Asst Prof Ger, Rose-Hulman Inst Technol; 81-. **MEMBERSHIPS** MLA; Am Asn Teachers Ger; E T A Hoffmann Ges; Am Coun Teaching Foreign Lang. **RESEARCH** German romanticism, novel theory, pedagogy. **SELECTED PUBLICATIONS** Auth, Paragraphs on Translation, Mod Lang J, Vol 0078, 94; Durrenmatt, Friedrich, German Quart, Vol 0068, 95. **CONTACT ADDRESS** Div of Humanities, Rose-Hulman Inst of Tech, Terre Haute, IN 47803.

KRAUSS, MICHAEL
PERSONAL Born 08/15/1934, Cleveland, OH, m, 1962, 4 children **DISCIPLINE** LINGUISTICS **EDUCATION** Harvard Univ PhD 59. **CAREER** Univ Alaska Fairbanks, prof 60-, dir of Native Lang Cen, 72-. **HONORS AND AWARDS** NSF; NEH **MEMBERSHIPS** LSA; SSILA **RESEARCH** Alaskan Eyak Languages, Eskim-Aleut, endangered languages, Celtic Scandinavian. **SELECTED PUBLICATIONS** Auth, Alaska Native Languages: Past, Present and Future, 80; In Honor of Eyak, 82; The World's languages in Crisis, 92. **CONTACT ADDRESS** Alaska Native Language Center, Univ of Alaska, Fairbanks, Fairbanks, AK 99775. **EMAIL** ffmek@uaf.edu

KRAWCZENIUK, JOSEPH V.
PERSONAL Born 10/07/1924, Tarnopol, Ukraine, m, 1957, 4 children **DISCIPLINE** GERMAN, RUSSIAN **EDUCATION** Univ Munich, PhD(Ger), 51; Columbia Univ, MSLS, 60. **CAREER** Cataloguer, Butler Libr, Columbia Univ, 60-62; from asst prof to assoc prof mod lang, 62-72, Prof Ger, King's Col, PA, 72-. **MEMBERSHIPS** MLA; Shevchenko Sci Soc. **RESEARCH** Comparative literature; bibliography; problems of ecumenism. **SELECTED PUBLICATIONS** Auth, The giant from St George's Hill: Metropolitan Andrew Sheptytzky, Redeemer's Voice, Can, 63; The cult of Sts Cyril and Methodius in Ukraine, Lohos, Can, 64; Ucrainica in foreign languages, Asn Ukrainian Writers Almanach, 65; Ivan Franko and his foreign friends, 68 & Gerhart Hauptmann's works in Ukrainian: A bibliographic review, 78, Shevchenko Sci Soc Proc; transl, Taras Schevchenko's works, America, 79; auth, Reverend John Volansky, First Ukrainian Priest in the US, Lohos, Can, 81; Henrik Ibsen and Ukrainian literature, Ukrainian Nat Asn Almanach, 81; Rev John Wolansky in Brazil, Almanac of the Ukr Natl Assn, 94; First Ukrainian Diplomatic Mission in American, Almanac of the Ukr Fratl Assn, 94. **CONTACT ADDRESS** King's Col, 133 N River St, Box 24, Wilkes-Barre, PA 18711-0801. **EMAIL** jvkrawcz@kings.edu

KREISS, PAUL THEODORE
PERSONAL Born 05/11/1926, Riedisheim, France, m, 1952, 10 children **DISCIPLINE** FRENCH, GERMAN **EDUCATION** Concordia Teachers Col, Ill, BSEd, 52; Boston Univ, MEd, 57; Northwestern Univ, PhD(French), 68. **CAREER** Teacher-prin elem sch, Mass, 52-56; teacher elem sch, Mo, 56-60; from instr to asst prof French & Ger, 60-73, assoc prof French, Concordia Teachers Col, Ill, 73-, ed Foreign Lang Sect, Instruct Mat Guide for Lutheran Elem Schs, 68-; mem, Lutheran Curric Resource Comt, 68-. **MEMBERSHIPS** Am Asn Teachers Fr; Am Coun Teaching Foreign Lang. **RESEARCH** French literature of the 17th and 18th centuries; teaching foreign language in the elementary schools. **SELECTED PUBLICATIONS** Auth, Foreign languages in elementary schools, Lutheran Educ, 6/61; Fleshpots or Angels Food, Motif, Fall 62. **CONTACT ADDRESS** Dept of Foreign Lang, Concordia Univ, Illinois, 7400 Augusta St, River Forest, IL 60305-1499. **EMAIL** crfkreisspt@crfdngrad.edu

KRETZSCHMAR, WILLIAM A., JR.
PERSONAL Born 09/13/1953, Ann Arbor, MI, m, 1976, 2 children **DISCIPLINE** ENGLISH, LINGUISTICS **EDUCATION** Univ Mich, AB, 75; Yale Univ, MA, 76; Univ Chicago, PhD, 80. **CAREER** Asst prof, Univ of Wis Whitewater, 82-86; asst to prof, Univ of Ga, 86-. **MEMBERSHIPS** MLA; LSA; ADS; Assoc Computers and the Humanities; AAAL; AAAS; Medieval Acad of AM; IAUPE. **RESEARCH** American English, Language Variation/Sociolinguistics, Humanities, Computing, Medieval Literature. **SELECTED PUBLICATIONS** Coed, Dialects in culture: Essays in General Dialectology by Raven I. McDavid, Jr., Univ of Ala Pr, 79; auth, "Isoglosses and Predictive Modeling", Am Speech 67 (92): 227-49; coed, Handbook of the Linguistic Atlas of the Middle and South Atlantic States, Univ of Chicago Pr, 93; coauth, "Spatial Analysis of Linguistic Data with GIS Functions", Int Jof Geog Info Systems 7, (93): 541-60; auth, "Quantitative Area Analysis of Dialect Features", Lag Variation and Change 8, (96): 13-39; coauth, Introduction to Quantitative Analysis of Linguistic Survey Data, Sage (Thousand Oaks, CA), 96; auth, "Foundations of American English", in Focus on the USA, ed Edgar Schneider (Philadelphia: John Benjamins, 96), 25-50; auth, "Dimensions of Variation in American English Vocabulary" English Worldwide 17, (96): 189-211; auth, "American English for the 21st Century", in Englishes Around the World, Vol 1, ed Edgar Schneider (Amsterdam: John Benjamins, 97), 307-23; coed, Concise Dictionary of Pronunciation, Oxford Univ Pr, (forthcoming). **CONTACT ADDRESS** Dept English, Univ of Georgia, Athens, GA 30602-0002. **EMAIL** billk@atlas.uga.edu

KREUTER, KATHERINE
PERSONAL Born Rockford, IL **DISCIPLINE** FRENCH **EDUCATION** Sorbonne, Magistere, 73; Univ Calif, Los Angeles, PhD, 79. **CAREER** French Dept, Scripps Col, Claremont, Calif, 80-85; ESL Dept, Col of the Desert, Palm Desert, Calif, 95-2000. **HONORS AND AWARDS** Teaching fel, Univ Calif, Los Angeles, 75-79. **MEMBERSHIPS** MLA. **RESEARCH** 20th century French literature (Samuel Beckett). **SELECTED PUBLICATIONS** Auth, Fool Me Once (94); auth, Cloud Nine Affair (97). **CONTACT ADDRESS** Communs Div, Col of the Desert, 43500 Monterey Ave, Palm Desert, CA 92260-9305. **EMAIL** Romietkk@cs.com

KREVANS, NITA
DISCIPLINE CLASSICS **EDUCATION** Yale Col, BA, 75; Cambridge Univ, BA, 77; Princeton Univ, PhD, 84. **CAREER** Assoc prof, Univ Minn, Twin Cities. **RESEARCH** Hellenistic and Latin lyric. **SELECTED PUBLICATIONS** Auth, Print and the Tudor Poets, in Reconsidering the Renaissance, ed. M.A. Di Cesare, Medieval and Renaissance Texts and Studies, 93, Binghamton, 92; Ilia's Dream: Ennius, Virgil, and the Mythology of Seduction, HSCP 95, 93; Fighting against Antimachus: the 'Lyde' and the 'Aetia' Reconsidered, in Hellenistica Groningana. 1. Callimachus, eds, M A Harder, R F Regtuit, and G C Wakker, Groningen, 93; Medea as Foundation-heroine, in Medea, eds, Clauss and Johnston, Princeton UP, 97. **CONTACT ADDRESS** Dept of Class and Near Eastern Studies, Univ of Minnesota, Twin Cities, 9 Pleasant St. SE, 330 Folwell Hall, Minneapolis, MN 55455. **EMAIL** nkrevans@tc.umn.edu

KROEGER, CATHERINE CLARK
DISCIPLINE CLASSICAL STUDIES **EDUCATION** Bryn Mawr Col, AB, 47; Univ Minn, MA, 82; PhD, 87. **CAREER** Prot Chaplain, Hamilton Col, 87-88; Adj Prof, Hamilton Col, 92-. **MEMBERSHIPS** Am Acad of Relig; Soc of Bibl Lit; Am Inst of Archaeol; Am Philol Asn; Evangel Theol Soc **RESEARCH** Women in the biblical world; Africans of the Bible and early Church; Biblical response to violence against women. **SELECTED PUBLICATIONS** Auth, I Suffer Not a Woman: Re-examining I Timoth 2: 9-15 in Light of Ancient Evidence, Baker Books, 92; ed, Women, Abuse and the Bible: How the Scriptures Can Be Used to Hurt or to Heal, Baker Books, 95; ed, A Study Bible for Women: The New Testament, Baker Books, 98; co-auth, No Place for Abuse, Downers Grove IVP, 01; ed, InterVarsityPress Women's Bible Commentary, forthcoming. **CONTACT ADDRESS** 1073 Stony Brook Rd, Brewster, MA 02631. **EMAIL** ckroeger@world.std.com

KROGSTAD, ALLISON D.
PERSONAL Born 09/25/1970, m, 2000 **DISCIPLINE** SPANISH **EDUCATION** North Central Col, BA, 92; Univ Minn, MA, 96; PhD, 99. **CAREER** Instr, Bethel Col, 97-98; asst prof, Central Col, 99-. **HONORS AND AWARDS** Grant, Univ of Minn, 99. **MEMBERSHIPS** MLA, Am Assoc of Teachers of Span and Port, Iowa World Lang Assoc. **RESEARCH** Colonial Latin American Literatur and Culture, Service Learning, Early 20th Century Hispanic Literature. **CONTACT ADDRESS** Central Col, Iowa, Pella, IA 50219. **EMAIL** krogstada@central.edu

KRONEGGER, MARIA ELISABETH
PERSONAL Born 09/23/1932, Graz, Austria **DISCIPLINE** FRENCH **EDUCATION** Sorbonne, dipl, 54; Univ Kans, ME, 57; Fla State Univ, PhD, 60; Univ Graz, MA, 60. **CAREER** Asst prof French, Ger, English lit, Rosenberg Col, Switz, 61-62; asst prof French lit and humanities, Hollins Col, 62-64; Prof French and Comp Lit to Prof Emer, Mich State Univ, 64-; Chmn and adv, Nat Screening Comt for Grants Grad Study Abroad, Inst Int Educ, Fulbright Hays and other progs, 71-77. **HONORS AND AWARDS** Certificate Distinguished Serv, Int Int Educ, 77. **MEMBERSHIPS** MLA; Int Comp Lit Asn; Soc Fr Prof Am; AAUP; Chinese Comp Lit Asn. **RESEARCH** Baroque literature and the other arts; impressionist literature and the other arts; phenomenology and structuralism. **SELECTED PUBLICATIONS** Auth, James Joyce and Associated Image Makers; auth, Literary Impressionism; auth, Allegory Old and New in Literature, the Fine Arts, Music and Theatre, and its Continuity in Culture, 94; coed, Life, The Human Quest for an Ideal, 96; ed, Esthetique Baroque et Imagination Creatrice, 97; auth, Life Differentiation and Harmony: Vegetal, Animal, Human, Analecta Husseliana LVII, 98; auth, The Orchestration of the Arts, 00. **CONTACT ADDRESS** Dept of Romance Lang, Michigan State Univ, 313 Old Horticulture, East Lansing, MI 48823. **EMAIL** kronegge@msu.edu

KRONIK, JOHN W.
PERSONAL Born 05/05/1931, Vienna, Austria, m, 1955, 2 children **DISCIPLINE** LINGUISTICS **EDUCATION** Queens Col, BA, 52; Univ Wis Madison, MA, 53; PhD, 60. **CAREER** Asst prof Hamilton Col, 58-63; assoc prof, Univ Ill, Urbana, 63-66; assoc prof, Cornell Univ, 66-71; prof, Cornell Univ, 71-. **HONORS AND AWARDS** Fulbright Fel; Guggenheim Fel; APS Grant; ACLS Grant; Rockefeller Res Residency; NEH Stipend; NEH Summer Sem for Coll Teachers; Doctor of Humane Letters, Chicago, IL; Editor of PMLA, Anales Galdosianos; Pres Intl Galdos Assoc; Visit Prof Univ Cal Berk, Univ CO, BYU, Middlebury Coll. **MEMBERSHIPS** MLA; Intl Asn Hispanists; Intl Galdos Assoc; Am Asn Teachers Spanish; **RESEARCH** 19th- and 20th-century Spanish literature; Latin Am drama; literary theory. **SELECTED PUBLICATIONS** Auth, "La Farsa" y el teatro espanol de preguerra, Castalia (Madrid), 71; coed, Textos y contextos de Galdos, Castalia (Madrid), 94; coauth, Creacion de una realidad ficticia: las novelas de Torquemada, Castalia (Madrid), 97; coed, Intertextual Pursuits: Literary Meditations in Modern Spanish Narrative, Bucknell Univ Press (Lewisburg, PA), 98; auth, :Invasions from Outer Spaces: Narration and the Dramatic Art in Spanish America", Latin Am Thea Rev 26.2 (93): 25-47; auth, "La Abeja of Barcelona and German Literature in Spain", The Lion and the Eagle: Interdisciplinary Essays on German-Spanish Relations over the Centu-

ries, (NY: Berg Hahn, 00), 235-254. **CONTACT ADDRESS** Dept Romance Studies, Cornell Univ, 283 Goldwin Smith Hall, Ithaca, NY 14853. **EMAIL** jwk4@cornell.edu

KROTKOFF, GEORG
PERSONAL Born 05/21/1925, Vienna, Austria, m, 1952 **DISCIPLINE** ARABIC PHILOLOGY **EDUCATION** Univ Vienna, PhD, 50 **CAREER** Lectr Ger, Ain Shams Univ, Cairo, 51-55; from lectr to asst prof, Univ Baghdad, 55-59; asst prof Arabic, Orient Sem, 60-66, assoc prof arabic, 66-89, prof, 89-90, prof emeritus, 90-, Johns Hopkins Univ. **MEMBERSHIPS** Am Orient Soc; MidE Studies Asn NAm. **RESEARCH** Arabic philology and linguistics; dialects of Arabic and modern Aramaic. **SELECTED PUBLICATIONS** Auth, Taschenbuch der russischen Grammatik, Globus Verlag (Wien), 50; auth, Lehrbuch der deutschen Sprache mit arabischer Anleitung, Cairo, 54; auth, Langenscheidts Taschenworterbuch der arabischen und deutschen Sprache, Langenscheidt (Berlin), 76; auth, A Neo-Aramaic Dialect of Kurdistan, American Oriental Series Vol 64, American Oriental Soc (New Haven), 82; auth, Langenscheidts Taschenworterbuch der arabischen und deutschen Sprache, Langenscheidt (Berlin), 93. **CONTACT ADDRESS** Dept of Near Eastern Studies, Johns Hopkins Univ, Baltimore, 3400 N Charles St, Baltimore, MD 21218.

KRUEGER, ROBERTA L.
PERSONAL Born Cincinnati, OH, m, 3 children **DISCIPLINE** FRENCH LANGUAGE, LITERATURE **EDUCATION** Wesleyan Univ, BA, 73; Univ Calif, PhD, 80. **CAREER** Prof, Chair of Dept Romance Lang, Hamilton Col NY, -. **HONORS AND AWARDS** Leonard C. Ferguson Prof of French; NEH Fel for Col Teachers. **RESEARCH** Medieval French Literature, Medieval Studies, Women's Writing. **SELECTED PUBLICATIONS** Auth, "Women Readers and the Ideology of Gender in Old French Verse Romance, " Cambridge Companion to Medieval Romance. **CONTACT ADDRESS** Dept Romance Lang, Hamilton Col, New York, 198 College Hill Rd, Clinton, NY 13323-1218. **EMAIL** rkrueger@hamilton.edu

KRUGER, CAROLE A.
PERSONAL m, 2 children **DISCIPLINE** FRENCH LANGUAGE AND LITERATURE **EDUCATION** Univ NC Greensboro, BA, 79; MA, 83; Duke Univ, PhD, 91. **CAREER** Assoc prof, Davidson Col, 87-; res dir Jr Yr Abroad prog, 93-94. **HONORS AND AWARDS** Dir self-directional progs, Davidson Col; ed, Women in French. **RESEARCH** 19th century French novel and theater; soc and polit discourse in mid-century France; lit and cult of Quebec; female autobiography, humor, and Colette. **SELECTED PUBLICATIONS** Auth, publ articles on var aspects of Colette's works, on Benonte Groult and the contemp novel in France, and an interview of Elisabeth Badinter. **CONTACT ADDRESS** Davidson Col, 102 N Main St, PO Box 1719, Davidson, NC 28036.

KRZYZANOWSKI, JERZY ROMAN
PERSONAL Born 12/10/1922, Lublin, Poland, m, 1948, 3 children **DISCIPLINE** SLAVIC LANGUAGES **EDUCATION** Univ Warsaw, Phil Mag, 59; Univ Mich, PhD(comp lit), 65. **CAREER** Vis lectr Polish, Univ Calif, 59-60; lectr, Univ Mich, 60-63; asst prof Slavic, Univ Colo, 63-64; assoc prof, Univ Kans, 64-67; assoc prof, 67-70, Prof Slavic, Ohio State Univ, 70-91; prof emeritus, 91-. **HONORS AND AWARDS** Phi Beta Kappa, 63; Delta Tau Kappa, 76; Union of Polish Writers Abroad Awd, 97; Boleslaw Prus Honorary Awd, 98. **MEMBERSHIPS** Asn Advan Polish Studies (pres, 77-79); Polish Inst Arts and Sci Am; The Kosciuszko Found. **RESEARCH** Polish literature; Comparative literature. **SELECTED PUBLICATIONS** Auth, Ernest Hemingway, Wiedza Powszechna (Warsaw), 63; auth, Wladyslaw Stanislaw Reymont, Twayne (NYork), 72; auth, General Leopold Okulicki, Odnowa (London), 80; ed, Janta czlowiek I pisararz, PKF (London), 82; auth, Diana, Bicentennial (NYork), 86; auth, Legenda Somosietty, Czytelnik (Warsaw), 87; auth, Katyn w literaturze, Nobertinum (Lublin), 95; auth, U Szarugi, Norbertinum (Lublin), 95; auth, "Polish Novel" in Encyclopedia of the Novel, Fitzroy (Dearborn, Chicago), 98; auth, Afrodyte, Norbertinum (Lublin), 99. **CONTACT ADDRESS** Dept of Slavic Lang and Lit, Ohio State Univ, Columbus, Columbus, OH 43210. **EMAIL** kryzynowoki.1@osu.edu

KUBIAK, DAVID PAYNE
PERSONAL Born 08/13/1950, Milwaukee, WI, s **DISCIPLINE** PHILOLOGY **EDUCATION** Loyola Univ, BA, 72; Harvard Univ, AM, 74; PhD, 79. **CAREER** Prof Classics, Wabash Col, 97-; assoc prof Classics, Wabash Col, 85-97; asst prof Classics, Wabash Col, 79-85; instr Latin, Buckingham, Browne and Nichols School, 78-79; asst Senior Tutor, Kirkland House, Harvard Col, 77-79; Tchg Fel Classics, Harvard Univ, 73-79. **HONORS AND AWARDS** NEH Summer Seminar Member, Amer Acad in Rome, 91; McLain-McTurnan-Arnold Res Scholar, Wabash Col, 89; Bowdoin Prize in Latin Composition, Harvard Univ, 77; Competitive Grant, Harvard Classics Dept, 76. **MEMBERSHIPS** Amer Philoi Assoc; Classics Assoc of Middle West & South; Ind Classical Conf; Vergilian Soc. **RESEARCH** Late Republican and Augustan Roman Poetry; Early Christian Poetry **SELECTED PUBLICATIONS** Lucan IX, in Bryn Mawr Classical Commentary Series, 85; Epic and Comedy in Prudentius' Humn to St. Eulalia (Peristephanon 3), Philogus, 99; auth, Ciceros, Vergil, and the Rejection of Friendship in Marcel Proust's A la recherche du temps perdu," Classical & Mod Lit, 97. **CONTACT ADDRESS** Dept of Classics, Wabash Col, Crawfordsville, IN 47933. **EMAIL** kubiakd@wabash.edu

KUCERA, HENRY
PERSONAL Born 02/15/1925, Czechoslovakia, m, 1951, 2 children **DISCIPLINE** SLAVIC LANGUAGES & LINGUISTICS **EDUCATION** Charles Univ, Prague, MA, Harvard Univ, PhD(Slavic lang), 52; Brown Univ, MA, 58. **CAREER** Asst prof for lang, Univ FL, 52-55; asst prof mod lang, 55-58, assoc prof, 58-63, Prof Slavic Lang, Ling & Cognitive Sci, 63-, prof cognitive sci, 81-90, Fred M Seed prof ling and cognitive scis, 82- , Brown Univ; Ford fel, 60-61; Guggenheim Found fel, 60-61; Howard Found fel, 60-61, mem admin bd, 78-; Int Bus Machines Corp res assoc, Mass Inst Technol, 60-63; mem, Am Comt Slavists, 65-68; vis prof, Univ MI, 67; consult, ling panel, Am Heritage Dictionary, 67-69; Nat Endowment for Hum sr fel, 68-69; vis prof, Univ CA, Berkeley, 69; Am Coun Learned Soc fel, 69-70; res assoc, Harvard Univ, 77-79. **HONORS AND AWARDS** Phi Beta Kappa; DSc, hon, Bucknell Univ, 84; PhD, hon, Masaryk Univ, Brno, Czech, 90. **MEMBERSHIPS** Ling Soc Am; MLA; Asn for Comput Ling; Am Asn Tchrs Slavic & East Europ Lang; Cognitive Sci Soc; Czech Soc Arts and Sci in Am; Prague Ling Circle. **RESEARCH** General and Slavic linguistics; computers in linguistic research; language and cognition. **SELECTED PUBLICATIONS** Auth, The Phonology of Czech, Mouton, The Hague, 61; coauth, Computational Analysis of Present-Day AmEnglish, Brown Univ, 67; A Comparative Quantitative Phonology of Russian, Czech, and German, Am Elsevier, 68; ed, American Contributions to the 6th International Congress of Slavists, Mouton, The Hague, 68; auth, Computers in Linguistics and in Literary Studies, Brown Univ, 69; coauth, Time in Language, Univ Mich, 75; Frequency Analysis of English Usage, Houghton Mifflin Co, 82. **CONTACT ADDRESS** Dept of Slavic Lang, Brown Univ, PO Box E, Providence, RI 02901-1674. **EMAIL** Henry_Kucera@brown.edu

KUDSZUS, WINFRIED G.
PERSONAL Born 09/10/1941, Dillingen, Germany, m, 1995, 3 children **DISCIPLINE** GERMAN LITERATURE **EDUCATION** Univ Calif, Berkeley, MA, 66, PhD(Ger), 68. **CAREER** From actg asst prof to asst prof Ger, Stanford Univ, 67-68; asst prof, Univ Calif, Berkeley, 68-70; res fel humanities, Soc Humanities, Cornell Univ, 69-70; assoc prof Ger, Univ Calif, Berkeley, 70-74; vis prof, Univ Tubingen, Ger, 71-72; Prof Ger, Univ Calif, Berkeley, 74-; Vis res prof lit theory and psychiat, Univ Mainz, Ger, 75-76; spec appt lit theory and psychoanal, Univ Frankfurt, Ger, 76. **HONORS AND AWARDS** Guggenheim Fel, 84. **MEMBERSHIPS** MLA. **RESEARCH** German literature 18th-20th centuries; translation theory; literature and psychology. **SELECTED PUBLICATIONS** Auth, Sprachverlust und Sinnwandel, 69; coed, Austriaca: Beitrage zur osterreichischen Literatur, 75; ed, Literatur und Schizophrenie, 77; auth, "Reflections on the Double Bind of Literature and Psychopathology", 78; coed, Contemporary Germany: Politics and Culture, 84; auth, "Kafka's Cage and Circus", 87; auth "Between the Tongues", 89; auth, Poetic Process, 95; auth, " The Possibility of Extremes", 99. **CONTACT ADDRESS** Dept of Ger, Univ of California, Berkeley, 5319 Dwinelle Hall, Berkeley, CA 94720-3244. **EMAIL** kudszus@uclink4.berkeley.edu

KUENZLI, RUDOLF ERNST
PERSONAL Born 07/28/1942, Switzerland, m, 1968, 2 children **DISCIPLINE** ENGLISH LITERATURE, COMPARATIVE LITERATURE **EDUCATION** Univ Wis-Madison, MA-(English), 68, MA(Ger), 69, PhD(comp lit), 71. **CAREER** Asst prof 70-76, assoc prof, 76-82, Prof English and Comp Lit, Univ Iowa, 82-; Res fel English and comp lit, Univ Iowa, 76; fel, Sch Criticism and Theory, Univ Calif, 78; Dir, Dada Arch Res Ctr, 78-; Inst Res Humanities fel, 79-80; chmn program comp lit, Univ Paul Valery, 80-83; vis prof, Montpellier, France, 81-82. **MEMBERSHIPS** MLA; Midwestern Mod Lang Asn; Comp Lit Asn; Asn Study Lit and Philos; Asn Study Dada and Surrealism. **RESEARCH** Avant-garde; Nietzsche; philosophies of language. **SELECTED PUBLICATIONS** Auth, Identities and Introduction, J Midwest Mod Lang Asn, Vol 0028, 95. **CONTACT ADDRESS** Dept of Lit, Univ of Iowa, 308 English Phil Bld, Iowa City, IA 52242-1492.

KUEPPER, KARL JOSEF
PERSONAL Born 08/08/1935, Cologne, Germany, m, 1963, 2 children **DISCIPLINE** GERMAN LINGUISTICS **EDUCATION** Univ Cologne, MA, 62, MEd, 64; Univ Muenster, DPhil, 70. **CAREER** From asst prof to assoc prof, Univ NB, 65-78, prof, 78-79, actg assoc dean arts, 75-76 and 77-78; Dean of Fac, Bishops Univ, 80-. **MEMBERSHIPS** Can Asn Univ Teachers Ger; Can Ling Asn; Can Asn Advan Netherlandic Studies; Can Asn Applied Ling. **RESEARCH** Historical German linguistics; contrastive and applied linguistics. **SELECTED PUBLICATIONS** Auth, Pretext and Subtext in Reflections on Form and Function of German Late Medieval Texts Containing Reports of Urban Events, Zeitschrift Deutsche Philol, Vol 0116, 97. **CONTACT ADDRESS** Dean's Office, Bishop's Univ, Lennoxville, QC, Canada J1M 1Z7.

KUHN, ROSE MARIE
PERSONAL m **DISCIPLINE** FRENCH LANGUAGE **EDUCATION** Facultes Universitaires Saint-Louis, BA, 71; Universite Catholique de Louvain, MA, 74; Cath Univ, MA, 77; PhD, 88. **CAREER** Vis Lectr, Oberlin Col, 79-80; Lectr, Cath Univ, 80-82; Vis Lectr, Hope Col, 82-83; Asst Prof, Rhodes Col, 83-87; Asst Prof, Christian Bros Univ, 87-88; Prof, Calif State Univ, 88-. **HONORS AND AWARDS** Instructional Technol Initiative Awd, Calif State Univ; Travel & Res Fel, Fr Govt; **MEMBERSHIPS** Calif Lang Teachers Asn, Calif Fac Asn, Central Valley For Lang Asn, Conseil Int d'Etudes Francophones, MLA, Women in Fr. **RESEARCH** Contemporary French & Francophone literature and culture, women in Twentieth-Century literature, comparative literature, distance learning technology and teaching methodology. **SELECTED PUBLICATIONS** Auth, "L'imaginaire dans l'oeuvre romanesque de Jean Echenoz," Studies in Mod and Class Lang & Lit, 5 (96): 27-32; auth, "La roue d'eau," de J M G Le Clezio ou le mirage de desert: Reve nostalgique du paradis perdu d'un peuple? (Toronto: Editions du GREF), forthcoming; co-ed, La representation du desert dans le litterature froncophones, Editions du GREF (Toronto, CAN), forthcoming. **CONTACT ADDRESS** Dept Lang, California State Univ, Fresno, 2320 E San Ramon Ave, Fresno, CA 93740-8030. **EMAIL** rose_marie_kuhn@csufresno.edu

KUHN-OSIUS, ECKHARD
PERSONAL Born 02/01/1948, Kassel, Germany, m, 2000, 2 children **DISCIPLINE** GERMAN **EDUCATION** Univ Colo at Boulder, PhD. **CAREER** Assoc prof; ch, AATG Testing Comn; dir, Hunter summer prog, Ger. **RESEARCH** 18th-century enlightenment literature; Goethe, and the 20th century up to the present. **SELECTED PUBLICATIONS** Main auth, 3-vol series of introductory textbk(s), used and/or tested at various col in CUNY; publ on, lit and pedagogical topics. **CONTACT ADDRESS** Dept of German, Hunter Col, CUNY, 695 Park Ave, New York, NY 10021. **EMAIL** ekuhnos@hunter.cuny.edu

KUIZENGA, DONNA
PERSONAL Born 01/30/1947, Princeton, NJ **DISCIPLINE** FRENCH LANGUAGE AND LITERATURE **EDUCATION** Adelphi Univ, AB, 68; City Univ New York, PhD, 74. **CAREER** Instr French, Adelphi Univ, 69-71; asst prof, 74-79, Assoc Prof French, Univ MO-Collumbia 79-; Vis assoc prof Fr, Univ Wis-Madison, 79-80; assoc dean, Col of Arts and Sciences, Univ of Vermont. **MEMBERSHIPS** MLA; Am Asn Teachers French; NAm Soc Study Seventeenth Century French Lit; Asn Int Etudes Fr; AAUP. **RESEARCH** Seventeenth-century French literature; womens studies. **SELECTED PUBLICATIONS** Auth, Et In Arcadia Ego in Essais on the Pastoral Novel, Fr Rev, Vol 0066, 93; Le Prince Deguise, La Mort De Cesar, Fr Rev, Vol 0068, 95; Gherardi, Evariste Italian Theater, Vol 1, Fr Rev, Vol 0069, 96; Bolduc, Benoit Andromede Delivree, Intermede Anonyme 1623, Fr Rev, Vol 0069, 96. **CONTACT ADDRESS** Univ of Vermont, Col of Arts and Sciences, Columbia, MO 65211. **EMAIL** dkuizeng@zoo.uvm.edu

KUMAYAMA, AKIHISA
PERSONAL Born 03/26/1942, m, 1975, 3 children **DISCIPLINE** JAPANESE LANGUAGE **EDUCATION** Kansai Univ, BA, 65; Univ Ariz, MA, 73; MA, 73; Am Grad Sch Int Mgt, Master Int Mgt, 89. **CAREER** Assoc prof, Thunderbird, the Am Grad Sch of Int Mgt, 73-. **HONORS AND AWARDS** Grant, Am Grad Sch of Int Mgt, 85; grant, Am Grad Sch of Int Mgt, 86; grants, CIBER Projects, U.S. Dept of Educ, 94-00. **MEMBERSHIPS** Eastern Mich Univ Confr, Ariz TESOL, Teachers of Ariz Japanese Lang Asn. **RESEARCH** Cross-cultural Aspects of Doing Business with the Japanese, Job Search with Japanese Companies, American Subsidiaries in Japan, English Grammar (especially countable and uncountable nouns). **SELECTED PUBLICATIONS** Auth, Eigo Kanshi Yoho Jiten (Dictionary of Usage of the English Articles- a, an, and the), Taishukan Pub Co., (Tokyo, Japan), 85; contribur, "An Examination of the Role of business Socialization in Japan--with Some Comparisons to Taiwan and Singapore," Proceedings of the Acad of Int Business Southeast Asia Regional Confr Vol 1, 86; auth, "Japanese/American Cross-Cultural Business Negotiations," Pacific Northwest Coun on For Lang Newsletter (88); auth, "Gift giving in Japan," The Int Exec (90); auth, Suisei Bunka to Yusei Bunka--Nichibeibunka Kiban no Hikaku (Water Culture and Oil Culture--Fundamental Comparison of Japanese and American Cultures), Taishukan pub Co., (Tokyo, Japan), 91; auth, "Japanese/American Cross Cultural Business Negotiations," Intercultural Commun Studies Vol 1.1 (91); rev, of "Advanced Japanese Social and Economic Issues in Japan and the U.S.," The J of Lang for Int Business 5.2 (94); coauth, "What are Japanese Employers looking for?" Global Business Lang (99). **CONTACT ADDRESS** Dept Modern Lang, Thunderbird, The Am Grad Sch of Intl Management, 15249 n 59th Ave, Glendale, AZ 85306-6000.

KUMPF, MICHAEL
DISCIPLINE CLASSICAL LANGUAGE **EDUCATION** Luthe Col, BA, 68; MA, 72, PhD, 74, Ohio State Univ. **CAREER** Prof, Classics, 75-98, Chr, Foreign Lang and Lit, 81-84 and 98-, Valparaiso Univ; **CONTACT ADDRESS** Dept of Foreign Languages and Literature, Valparaiso Univ, Valparaiso, IN 46383. **EMAIL** michael.kumpf@valpo.edu

KUNO, SUSUMU
PERSONAL Born 08/11/1933, Tokyo, Japan, m, 1967, 2 children **DISCIPLINE** LINGUISTICS **EDUCATION** Univ Tokyo, AB, 56, AM, 58; Harvard Univ, PhD, 64. **CAREER** From instr to assoc prof, 64-69, Prof Ling, 69-, Chmn Dept, 72-77, 78-91, Harvard Univ. **HONORS AND AWARDS** Guggenheim fel, 77-78; Hon Doc, Univ Paris VII, 97. **MEMBERSHIPS** Asn Comput Mach; Asn Comput Ling (pres, 67); Ling Soc Am. **RESEARCH** Generative grammar; functional syntax; Japanese and English syntax; computational linguistics; discourse analysis. **SELECTED PUBLICATIONS** Auth, Computer Analysis of Natural Languages, Proc Symp Applied Math, 67; auth, "Locatives in Existential Sentences," Linguistic Inquiry, 72; auth, "Functional Sentence Perspective," Linguistic Inquiry, 72; auth, The Structure of the Japanese Language, MIT, 73; coauth, Functional Syntax and GB Theory, U Chicago, 93; coauth, "Remarks on Negative Islands," Linguistic Inquiry, (97); coauth, "Quantifier Scope in English, Chinese, and Japanese," Language, (99). **CONTACT ADDRESS** Dept of Ling, Harvard Univ, 315 Boylston Hall, Cambridge, MA 02138-3800. **EMAIL** kuno@fas.harvard.edu

KUNTZ, MARION L.
PERSONAL Born 09/06/1934, Atlanta, GA, w, 2 children **DISCIPLINE** FRENCH, ITALIAN **EDUCATION** Agnes Scott Col, BA; Emory Univ, MA; PhD, 69. **CAREER** Asst Prof to Prof, Ga State Univ, 66-. **HONORS AND AWARDS** Distinguished Alumni, Agnes Scott Col, 95; Distinguished Prof, GA State Univ, 94. **MEMBERSHIPS** Renaissance Soc of Am; Am Philol Asn. Sixteenth Century Studies. **RESEARCH** Classics; 16th Century Itellectual History (French & Italian). **SELECTED PUBLICATIONS** Auth, Colloquium of the Seven About Secrets of the Sublime, Princeton Univ Press, 75; auth, Guillaume Postef. Prophet of the Restitution of All Things, 81; auth, Jacob's Ladder and the Tree of Life. Concepts of Hierarchy and the Great Chain of Being, 84; auth, Postello Venesia est suo monto, Firenze, 88; auth, Venice Myth and Utopian Thought, Ashgate Pub, 99; auth, The Anointment of Dionisio, Penn State Press, 01. **CONTACT ADDRESS** Dept For Lang, Georgia State Univ, 33 Gilmer St, SE, Atlanta, GA 30303-3044. **EMAIL** marion@gsu.edu

KUPPER, NELLY J.
PERSONAL Born 03/13/1964, Moscow, Russia, m, 1994, 1 child **DISCIPLINE** LINGUISTICS, FRENCH, RUSSIAN, LITERATURE **EDUCATION** Va Commonwealth Univ, BFA, 87; Univ Tenn Knoxville, MA, 96; PhD, 98. **CAREER** Teacher, Louisa Cty Sch, 88-89; teacher, Hanover Cty Sch, 91-93; teaching assoc to instr, Univ Tenn Knoxville, 93-00; asst prof, N Mich Univ, 00-. **MEMBERSHIPS** MLA; AATF; SAMLA. **RESEARCH** 19th and 20th-century French literature; 19th-century Russian literature; critical theory; women's studies; issues of identity such as in Francophone literature. **SELECTED PUBLICATIONS** Auth, "The Sacrificial Woman in Archetypal Triads of Provost, Vigny and Alain-Fournier," Romance Notes 38 (98): 207-14; auth, "Review of Malraux Romancier," Revue Andre Malraux Rev 27 (98): 118-119; auth, "A Woman's Choice: Duty and Desire in La Princesse de Cleves," Symposium (01). **CONTACT ADDRESS** Dept Mod Lang/Lit, No Michigan Univ, 1401 Presque Isle Ave, Marquette, MI 49855. **EMAIL** nkupper@nmu.edu

KURMAN, GEORGE
PERSONAL Born 06/10/1942, Tallinn, Estonia, m, 1965, 4 children **DISCIPLINE** COMPARATIVE AND ESTONIAN LITERATURE **EDUCATION** Cornell Univ, BA, 62; Columbia Univ, MA, 66; Ind Univ, PhD(comp lit), 69. **CAREER** Transl Estonian epic poetry, UNESCO, 69-70; from asst prof to assoc prof, 70-80, Prof English and Comp Lit, Western Ill Univ, 80-; Int Res and Exchanges Bd fel, Estonian lit, 72-73. **MEMBERSHIPS** Asn Advan Baltic Studies; corresp mem Inst Estonian Lang and Lit. **SELECTED PUBLICATIONS** Auth, The Development of Written Estonian, Uralic & Altaic Ser, Ind Univ, 68; Negative comparison in literary epic narrative, Comp Lit, 69; Literatures in contact: Finland and Estonia, Estonian Learned Soc Am, 72; Ecphrasis in epic poetry, Comp Lit, 73; Entropy and the death of tragedy: Notes for a theory of drama, Comp Drama, 75; Literary censorship in general and in Soviet Estonia, J Baltic Studies, 77; A methodology of thematics: The literature of the palgue, Comp Lit Studies, 82; Kaleripreg, Symposia Press, 82. **CONTACT ADDRESS** Dept of English, Western Illinois Univ, Macomb, IL 61455.

KURTH, WILLIAM CHARLES
PERSONAL Born 10/23/1932, Waterloo, IA, d, 3 children **DISCIPLINE** LATIN, GREEK **EDUCATION** Univ Northern Iowa, AB, 53; Univ Tex, MA, 59, Univ NC, PhD, 65. **CAREER** Tchr, 55-56, high Sch, Wis; instr Latin, 57-59, Baylor Univ; from instr to asst prof classics, 62-67, Univ Ill; assoc prof, 67-73, chmn dept, 67-76, prof classics, 73-98, prof emer, 98-, Luther Col, Iowa; consult programmed Latin, 67, Macalester Col; NEH fel, Univ Tex, 77-78. **MEMBERSHIPS** Am Philol Assn; Class Assn Mid W & S. **RESEARCH** Aulus Gellius; the minor Latin rhetoricians. **CONTACT ADDRESS** Dept of Classics, Luther Col, 700 College Dr, Decorah, IA 52101-1045. **EMAIL** kurthwmc@luther.edu

KURTZ, HORST
DISCIPLINE GERMAN LANGUAGE, LITERATURE, CULTURE **EDUCATION** Ohio State Univ, MA, 86; PhD, 92. **CAREER** Grad asst, Oh State Univ, 84-89; instr, Col Wooster, 89-93; asst prof, Ga S Univ, 93-. **HONORS AND AWARDS** AATG Prof of Year, 98. **MEMBERSHIPS** AATG; ACTFL; FLAG; SCOLT. **RESEARCH** Oswald Wiener, Wiener Gruppe; 20th century; post WWII; Austrian literature; Landeskunde. **SELECTED PUBLICATIONS** Coauth, "Commercial Language, Business Economics and the Liberal Arts Curriculum: Implementation at the College of Wooster," in Languages and Cultures for Business and the Professions, eds. Geoffrey M Voght, Ray Schaub (Ypsilanti: World College/Eastern Mich Univ, 92). **CONTACT ADDRESS** Dept Foreign Language, Georgia So Univ, PO Box 8081, Statesboro, GA 30460-1000. **EMAIL** hkurz@gasou.edu

KUSCH, MANFRED
PERSONAL Born 10/11/1941, Germany **DISCIPLINE** FRENCH LITERATURE, COMPARATIVE LITERATURE **EDUCATION** Univ Gottingen, Ger, MA, 66; Univ Calif, Berkeley, PhD(comp lit), 73. **CAREER** Asst prof, 71-80, Assoc Prof French, Univ Calif, Davis, 80-. **MEMBERSHIPS** MLA; Am Soc 18th Century Studies; Philol Asn Pac Coast. **RESEARCH** French novel of the 18th century; theory of the novel; comparative literature. **SELECTED PUBLICATIONS** Auth, Manon Lescaut, or voyage du chevalier des Grieux dans la basse Romancie, Studies Voltaire & 18th Century, 75; Narrative technique and cognitive modes in La Princesse de Cleves, Symposium, 76; Landscape and literary form: Structural parallels in La Nouvelle Heloise, L'Esprit Createur, 77; The river and the garden: Basic spatial models in Candide and La Nouvelle Heloise, Eighteenth Century Studies, 78. **CONTACT ADDRESS** Dept of French and Ital, Univ of California, Davis, Davis, CA 95616.

KUSHNER, EVA
PERSONAL Born 06/18/1929, Prague, Czechoslovakia **DISCIPLINE** COMPARATIVE LITERATURE **EDUCATION** McGill Univ, BA, 48, MA, 50, PhD, 56. **CAREER** Lectr philos, Sir George Williams Univ, 52-53; lectr Fr, McGill Univ, 52-55; lectr, Univ Col, London, 58-59; lectr to prof Fr & comp lit, Carleton Univ, 61-76; prof Fr & comp lit, McGill Univ, 76-87; prof, 87-94, PROF EMER, UNIV TORONTO, 94-, SR FELLOW, COMPARATIVE LITERATURE, 97-. **SELECTED PUBLICATIONS** Auth, Patrice de la Tour du Pin, 61; auth, Le mythe d'Orphee dans la litterature francaise contemporaine, 61; auth, Chants de Boheme, 63; auth, Saint-Denys Garneau, 67; auth, Francois Mauriac, 72; ed, Renewals in the Theory of Literary History, 84; ed, La problematique du sujet chez Montaigne, 95; ed, Constraints to Freedom of Scholarship and Science, 96; co-ed, Proceedings of the VIIth Congress of the Int Comp Lit Asn. **CONTACT ADDRESS** Victoria Univ, Univ of Toronto, 73 Queen's Park Cr, Pratt 322, Toronto, ON, Canada M5S 1K7. **EMAIL** eva.kushner@utoronto.ca

KUSMER, ROBERT L.
PERSONAL Born Cleveland, OH **DISCIPLINE** GERMAN LANGUAGE **EDUCATION** Cleveland State Univ, BA, 72; Northwestern Univ, PhD, 83; Kent State Univ, MLS, 88. **CAREER** Cataloger, 90-92; head Tech Serv, 92-96, Mentor Public Libr; cataloger, Univ Notre Dame, 97-. **HONORS AND AWARDS** Beta Phi Mu, 89; Sidney L. Jackson Memorial Awd, Kent State Univ, 89; DAAD, 79-80. **MEMBERSHIPS** ALA, ACRL; ALCTS **RESEARCH** Librarianship; German literature in English; philosophy; theology; general humanities. **CONTACT ADDRESS** Theodore M. Hesburg Library, Univ of Notre Dame, Cataloging Dept, Notre Dame, IN 46556. **EMAIL** kusmer.1@nd.edu

KUSSI, PETER
DISCIPLINE SLAVIC LANGUAGES **EDUCATION** Queens Col, BS; Univ Wis, MS; Columbia Univ, PhD. **CAREER** Prof. **RESEARCH** Czech literature; comparative literature; theory of translation. **SELECTED PUBLICATIONS** Ed, Toward the Radical Center; ed, A Karel Capek Reader; Writing on the Wall, An Anthology of Czech Literature. **CONTACT ADDRESS** Dept of Slavic Languages, Columbia Col, New York, 2960 Broadway, New York, NY 10027-6902. **EMAIL** pk10@columbia.edu

KUSTANOVICH, KONSTANTIN
PERSONAL Born 08/22/1945, Soviet Union, 1 child **DISCIPLINE** RUSSIAN LITERATURE AND CULTURE **EDUCATION** Columbia Univ, PhD, 86. **CAREER** Asst prof, Lafayette Col, 86-87; asst prof, Vanderbilt Univ, 87-94; assoc prof, 94-; dean, Russian Sch Norwich Univ, 92-97. **HONORS AND AWARDS** Fulbright Awd, Russian Federation, 01-02. **MEMBERSHIPS** AATSEEL, AAAASS. **RESEARCH** Russian literature; Russian culture; theory of literature and culture. **SELECTED PUBLICATIONS** Auth, The Two Worlds in Jurij Zivago's Poem Zimnjaja noc, Russian Lit, 92; auth, The Naturalistic Tendency in Contemporary Soviet Fiction: Thematics, Poetics, Functions, New Directions in Soviet Literature, 92; auth, The Artist and the Tyrant: Vasily Aksenov's Works in the Brezhnev Era, 92; auth, Erotic Glasnost: Sexuality in Recent Russian Literature, World Lit Today, 93; Venichka Erofeev's Grief and Solitude: Existentialist Motifs in the Poema, Venedikt Erofeev's Moscow-Petushki: Critical Perspectives, 97. **CONTACT ADDRESS** Vanderbilt Univ, Box 1567-B, Nashville, TN 37235. **EMAIL** konstantin.kustanovich@vanderbilt.edu

KUSTUS, GEORGE L.
DISCIPLINE CLASSICS **CAREER** Fac, Harvard Univ, 53; prof emer, SUNY Buffalo, present. **RESEARCH** Ancient rhetoric; Class and Medieval lit, drama, educational hist. **SELECTED PUBLICATIONS** Auth, Studies in Byzantine Rhetoric, Thessalonica, 73; publ on rhetoric. **CONTACT ADDRESS** Dept Classics, SUNY, Buffalo, 712 Clemens Hall, Buffalo, NY 14260.

KUXDORF, MANFRED
PERSONAL Born 07/04/1933, Cologne, Germany, m, 1963, 2 children **DISCIPLINE** GERMAN LITERATURE **EDUCATION** Univ Waterloo, BA, 63, MA, 65; Univ Alta, PhD(Ger), 69. **CAREER** Assoc chmn dept Ger lang, 74-75, from assoc prof to prof Ger, Univ Waterloo, 74-; Humanities Res Coun Can publ grant, 71; Can Coun res grants, 71, 72 and leave fel, 75-76; vis prof, Univ Mannheim, 72-73; Ger Acad Exchange Serv stipend, 72-73; Assoc Ed, German-Slavica, 73-. **MEMBERSHIPS** Can Asn Univ Teachers Ger; Int Arthur Schnitzler Res Asn; MLA; Int Vereinigung fur Germanistische Sprach - u Literaturwissenschaft. **RESEARCH** Modern German literature, especially expressionism. **SELECTED PUBLICATIONS** Auth, Love in Expressionism in A Study of Poetry Published in the Js Die Aktion and Der Sturm from 1910-1914, J Ger Studies, Vol 0029, 93; auth, Der Schriftsteller Salomo Friedlaender/Mynona: Kommentator einer Epoche: eine Monographie. **CONTACT ADDRESS** Dept Ger and Slavic Lang and Lit, Univ of Waterloo, Waterloo, ON, Canada N2L 3G1. **EMAIL** mkuxdorf@watarts.uwaterloo.ca

KUZNIAR, A. A.
PERSONAL Born 10/31/1956, Hamilton, ON, Canada, s **DISCIPLINE** GERMAN LITERATURE **EDUCATION** Princeton Univ, PhD, 83. **CAREER** Prof, Univ NC, 83- . **HONORS AND AWARDS** Humboldt Fel, 97-98. **SELECTED PUBLICATIONS** Auth, Deyaled Endings: Nomencalture in Novais and Hoelderlin, 83; ed, Outing Goethe and His Age, 96; auth, The Queer German Cinema, 00. **CONTACT ADDRESS** German Dept., Univ of No Carolina, Chapel Hill, CB #3160, Chapel Hill, NC 27599-3160. **EMAIL** akuzniar@email.unc.edu

KUZNIEWSKI, ANTHONY JOSEPH
PERSONAL Born 01/28/1945, Carthage, MO **DISCIPLINE** AMERICAN HISTORY, CHURCH HISTORY **EDUCATION** Marquette Univ, AB, 66; Harvard Univ, AM, 67, PhD(hist), 73; Loyola Univ Chicago, MDiv, 80. **CAREER** Teaching fel hist, Harvard Univ, 68-72; asst prof, Col Holy Cross, 74-76 and Loyola Univ Chicago, 80-81; Asst Prof Hist, Col Holy Cross, 81-; Res tutor hist, Kirkland, House Harvard Col, 70-72; Vis lectr, Loyola Univ Chicago, 76-77. **HONORS AND AWARDS** Oscar Halecki Awd, Polish Am Hist Asn and Am Hist Asn, 81. **MEMBERSHIPS** Polish Am Hist Asn (pres, 82-83); Am Cath Hist Asn; Orgn Am Historians. **RESEARCH** Polish immigrants in the United States; the religious life of Polish Americans; the interaction of various Catholic immigrant groups in the United States. **SELECTED PUBLICATIONS** Auth, Boot straps or book learning?: Reflections on the education of Polish Americans, Polish Am Studies, 75; Polish Catholics in America, In: Catholics in America, Nat Conf Cath Bishops, 76; Milwaukee's Poles, 1866-1918: The rise and fall of a model community, Milwaukee Hist, 1/78; The Catholic Church in the life of the Polish Americans, In: Poles in America: Bicentennial Essays, Worzalla Publ Co, 78; Faith and Fatherland: The Polish Church War in Wisconsin, 1896-1918, Univ Notre Dame Press, 80. **CONTACT ADDRESS** Dept of Hist, Col of the Holy Cross, Worcester, MA 01610.

KYES, ROBERT L.
PERSONAL Born 07/08/1933, Allegan, MI, m, 1985, 3 children **DISCIPLINE** GERMAN **EDUCATION** Univ Mich, BA, 58; PhD, 64; Brown Univ, MA, 59. **CAREER** Instr to asst prof, Univ of Mich, 62-68; vis assoc prof, Univ of Colo, 68-69; assoc prof to prof, chair, Univ of Mich, 69-95. **HONORS AND AWARDS** Woodrow Wilson Fel, 58-59; Fulbright Fel, 59-60; Distinguished Serv Awd, Univ Mich, 66; Awd for Excellence in Undergrad Advising, Univ of Mich, 99; Recipient, Studies in Honor of Robert L Kyes, Am Jour of Ger Ling and Lit, 00. **MEMBERSHIPS** MLA, Ling Soc of Am, Soc for Ger Ling, Am Assoc of Teachers of Ger. **RESEARCH** Comparative Germanic linguistics, history and structure of German, medieval Germanic dialects, language attitudes, historiography of grammar in the German speaking countries, oral narratives from early 20th century, Austrian cultural history. **SELECTED PUBLICATIONS** Auth, The Old Low Franconian Psalms and Glosses, Univ of Mich Pr, (Ann Arbor), 69; coauth, Germanic and Its Dialects: A Grammar of Proto-Germanic, vol 3, Benjamins (Amsterdam), 77; auth, Dictionary of the Old Low and Central Franconian Psalms and Glosses, Niemeyer (Tubingen), 83; auth, "Phonological Changes: Evidence," Research Guide on Language Change, ed Edgar Polome (NY, Berlin: Mouton de Gruyter, 91) 303-306; auth, "Neutralization of Final Obstruents in German," Semper idem et novus: Festschrift for Frank

Banta, ed F Gentry, (Goppingen: Kummerle, 88), 59-73; auth "German Vowel Lengthening: Causes and Conditions", am Jour of Ger Ling and Lit 1 (89): 153-176; coed, On German Linguistics: Issues and Methods, Mouton de Gruyter (NY, Berlin), 92; auth, "Assimilation in Germanic", On German Linguistics: Issues and Methods, eds I Rauch, G Carr and R Kyes, (NY, Berlin: Mouton de Gruyter, 92); auth, "Grammar and Grammars in 17th Century Germany: The Case of Christian Gueintz," Insights in German Linguistics, ed I Rauch and G Carr, NY, Berlin: Mouton de Gruyter, 95); auth, "Language Attitudes in Sixteenth and Seventeenth Century Germany," Interdigitations: Essays for Irmengard Rauch, ed G Carr, W Harbert and L Zhang, (NY: Peter Lang, 99), 285-293. **CONTACT ADDRESS** Dept German Lang and Lit, Univ of Michigan, Ann Arbor, 3110 Mod Langs Bldg, Ann Arbor, MI 48109-1275. **EMAIL** rlkyes@umich.edu

KYM, ANNETTE
DISCIPLINE GERMAN **EDUCATION** Univ Cincinnati, PhD. **CAREER** Assoc prof, chair, Hunter Col; Grad Sch & Univ Ctr, CUNY; Hunter Col, 85-; coordr, basic lang sequence; supvr, adj fac & mentor, grad stud doing tchg practica at Hunter Col; past tchr, distance learning crse over interactive tv, Hunter and Brooklyn Col; expert tester for, Prnfung Wirtschaftsdeutsch Int. **HONORS AND AWARDS** Distinguished Tchr Awd, NY State Asn of For Lang Teachers. **MEMBERSHIPS** AATG; ACTFL; NEMLA; NYSFLT. **RESEARCH** GDR literature; Swiss literature; FL Pedagogy. **SELECTED PUBLICATIONS** Auth, bk on Hesse's Role As A Critic & on pedagogical topics. **CONTACT ADDRESS** Dept of Ger, Hunter Col, CUNY, 695 Park Ave, New York, NY 10021. **EMAIL** akym@shiva.hunter.cuny.edu

L

L'ALLIER, LOUIS
PERSONAL Born 02/27/1961, PQ, Canada **DISCIPLINE** CLASSICAL STUDIES **EDUCATION** Univ Ottawa, MA, 89; Laval Univ, PhD, 96. **CAREER** Lectr, Laval Univ, 96-. **MEMBERSHIPS** Am Philol Asn; Class Asn of Can; Soc des Etudes Anciennes du Quebec. **RESEARCH** Ancient Greek literature. **SELECTED PUBLICATIONS** Auth, "Le Heros Xenophontique et les Femmes," 98; "Le Domaine de Scillonte; Xenophon et l'Exemple Perse," 98; "Xenophon's Park at Scillua: Some Ancient and Modern Views on Nature," 97. **CONTACT ADDRESS** 24 Benedict St, Hull, QC, Canada J8Y 5G1. **EMAIL** l.lallier@sympatico.ca

LABORDE, ALICE M.
DISCIPLINE FRENCH LITERATURE **EDUCATION** UCLA, PhD. **CAREER** Prof Emer, Fr, Univ Calif, Irvine. **SELECTED PUBLICATIONS** Auth, Diderot et Madame de Puisieux; Le Mariage du Marquis de Sade. **CONTACT ADDRESS** Dept of Fr and Ital, Univ of California, Irvine, Irvine, CA 92697.

LABRADOR, JOSE J.
PERSONAL Born 04/08/1941, Castejon, Spain, m, 1966, 1 child **DISCIPLINE** SPANISH LANGUAGE & LITERATURE **EDUCATION** Univ Madrid, BA, 61; Case Western Reserve Univ, MA, 68, PhD, 71. **CAREER** From instr to assoc prof, 69-88, prof, 88-; Span, Cleveland State Univ, 88-; vis prof, Middlebury Col, Summer 76. **HONORS AND AWARDS** CSU Distinguished Fac Awd for Res and Schol, 97. **MEMBERSHIPS** Mediaeval Soc Am; Midwest Mod Lang Asn. **RESEARCH** Spanish medieval literature and history; European literature and history; Medieval philosophy. **SELECTED PUBLICATIONS** Co-ed, Cancionera de poeseas varias. Manuscrito 3902 de la Bibblioteca Nacional de Madrid, in Coleccion Cancioneros Castellanos, vol 2, Cleveland State Univ, 89; Estudios en homenaje a Enrique Ruiz-Fornells, ALDEEU, 90; Poeseas del Maestro Leon y de Fray Melchor de la Serna y otros, in Codice numero 961 de la Biblioteca Real de Madrid, Cleveland State Univ, 91; coauth, Tabla de los principios de la poeseas espanola, in Siglos XVI-XVII, Cleveland State Univ, 93; co-ed, Cancionera de poeseas varias, in Manuscrito No. 1587 de la Biblioteca Real de Madrid, Visor Libros, Madrid, 94; Cancionero sevillano de Nueva York, Univ Sevilla, 96; coauth, Manuscrito Fuentelsol (Madrid, Palacio II-973). Con poemas de Fray Luis de Leon, Fray Melchor de la Serna, Hurtado de Mendoza, Linan, Gongora, Lope y otros, in Seguido ahora de un apendice con las poeseas del fraile benito Fray Melchor de la Serna, Cleveland State Univ, 97; co-ed, Romancero de Palacio, Univ Penn, Visor Libros, Madrid, 98; author of numerous journal articles and book contributions. **CONTACT ADDRESS** Dept of Modern Lang, Cleveland State Univ, 1983 E 24th St, Cleveland, OH 44115-2440. **EMAIL** J.labrador@popmail.csuohio.edu

LABRIE, GILLES R.
PERSONAL Born 09/10/1939, Springfield, MA **DISCIPLINE** FRENCH LANGUAGE AND LITERATURE **EDUCATION** Univ Montreal, BA, 60; Univ Mass, MA, 66, PhD, 71; Central Mich Univ, MS, 88. **CAREER** Teacher, Easthampton, Mass, Public Schs, 62-64; teacher, Northampton (Mass) Sch for Girls, 65-66; asst prof, Central Mich Univ, 70-77, assoc prof, 77-93, prof, 93-, acting chair, 93, 94-95, chair, Dept of French Langs, Lit and Culture, 95-99. **HONORS AND AWARDS** Central Mich Univ Excellence in Teaching Awd, 89. **MEMBERSHIPS** Modern Lang Asn, Am Asn of Teachers of French, Mich Acad of Sci, Arts and Letters, Computer Animated Learning and Instruction Asn. **RESEARCH** Computer animated language learning, Quebec culture and literature, twentieth century French literature. **SELECTED PUBLICATIONS** Transl, "L'Espagnol Chicano," by David Lawton, Etudes de Lingistique Appliquee 15 (juillet-sept 74): 69-75; coauth with L. P. S. Singh, "Parsing, Error Diagnostics and Instruction in a French Tutor," Calico J 9, 1 (autumn 91): 9-25; rev of The Tragic Middle: Racine, Aristotle, Euripides by Richard Goodwin, Classical and Modern Lit, 12, 4 (summer 92): 389-391; auth, "Models of Computer-Assisted Language Instruction," Mich Academician, 25, 2 (winter 93): 109-122; auth, "A French Vocabulary Tutor for the Web," Calico J, 17, 3 (spring 2000): 1-25; auth, "Student Web Pages in Advanced French," French Rev (forthcoming March 2001). **CONTACT ADDRESS** Dept Foreign Lang, Central Michigan Univ, 100 W Preston Rd, Mount Pleasant, MI 48859-0001. **EMAIL** gilles.labrie@cmich.edu

LACAVA, J.
PERSONAL Born 03/10/1961, Versailles, France, m, 1988, 1 child **DISCIPLINE** FRENCH **EDUCATION** Paris VII Univ, BA; MA; PhD, 94. **CAREER** Co-director & teacher, French Cultural Center of Malabo, 86-87; private french tutor, President of Equatorial Guinea, 86-87; sr french transl, Rotary Int Headquarters, 89-; prof, North Park Col, 94. **HONORS AND AWARDS** Grant, French Ministry of Culture, 86. **MEMBERSHIPS** Am Asn of Teachers of French, MLA, Chicago Area Transl Asn. **SELECTED PUBLICATIONS** Auth, "Julio Finn: Du blues au reggae, de la musique a la litterature," Soul Bag 115 (89); auth, "Sterling Plumpp: A Blues Poet," Living Blues Magazine 21.1 (90); auth, "The Theatricality of the Blues, Black Music Res J 12.1 (92); auth, "Blues Poetics," The Original Chicago Blues Annual 4 (92). **CONTACT ADDRESS** Dept Humanities, No Park Univ, 3225 W Foster Ave, Chicago, IL 60625-4823. **EMAIL** lacavaj@lacava.net

LACKEY, ROBERT SAM
DISCIPLINE LANGUAGE ARTS AND DISTANCE LEARNING **EDUCATION** Univ Tulsa, PhD, 70. **CAREER** Southwest Tex State Univ **MEMBERSHIPS** Channel One, Chapbook, Okla Eng Jour. **SELECTED PUBLICATIONS** Area: poetry. **CONTACT ADDRESS** Southwestern Oklahoma State Univ, Weatherford, 100 Campus Dr, Weatherford, OK 73096. **EMAIL** lackeys@swosu.edu

LACURE, JON W.
PERSONAL Born Portland, OR, m, 2 children **DISCIPLINE** JAPANESE LITERATURE **EDUCATION** Univ Ore, BA, 71; Ohio State Univ, MA, 77; Ind Univ, PhD, 91. **CAREER** Assoc prof, Univ Tenn at Knoxville, 91-. **MEMBERSHIPS** Asn for Asian Studies, Asn of Teachers of Japanese, Haiku Soc of Am, Southern Comparative Lit Asn, Midwest Asn for Japanese Literary Studies, MLA, S Atlantic MLA, Am Lit Translators Asn. **RESEARCH** Classical and modern Japanese poetry, literature of the Heian period, translation studies. **SELECTED PUBLICATIONS** Auth, "The Tales of Ise: Critical Evaluation and Bibliography," in Masterplots: Twentieth Anniversary Revised Second Edition (CA: Salem Press, 96), 6399-6402; auth, "The Tales of Ise," in Great Literature of the Eastern World, ed. Ian P. McGreal (NY: Harper-Collins,96), 273-276; auth, "Found Along the Side of the road: Basho and the Japanese Poetic Tradition," Modern Haiku 29.1 (98): 57-61; auth, The rhetorical Devices of the Kokinshu: A structural Analysis of Japanese Waka Poetry. Japanese Studies Volume 4, The Edwin Mellen Press (Lewiston, NY), 97. **CONTACT ADDRESS** Dept Modern For Lang & Lit, Univ of Tennessee, Knoxville, 701 McClung Tower, Knoxville, TN 37996-0460. **EMAIL** lacure@utkux.utcc.utk.edu

LACY, NORRIS J.
PERSONAL Born 03/08/1940, Hopkinsville, KY **DISCIPLINE** FRENCH **EDUCATION** Murray St Univ, AB, 62; Ind Univ, MA, 63, PhD, 67. **CAREER** Lectr, 65-66, Ind Univ; asst prof, 66-70, assoc prof, 70-75, prof, 76-88, Univ Kansas; vis assoc prof, 75-76, UCLA; prof, 88-98, Wash Univ, St Louis; Edwin Erle Sparks Prof, 98-, Penna St Univ. **HONORS AND AWARDS** Honory Pres of the Int Arthurian Soc, 87-; Decorated by Fr Govt: Chevalier in the Ordre des palmes academiques, 88. **MEMBERSHIPS** Medieval Acad of Am, Int Arthurian Soc, Mod Lang Asn, Soc Rencesvals. **RESEARCH** Arthurian lit, medieval romance, fabliaux **SELECTED PUBLICATIONS** Ed, 26 Chansons d'amour de la Renaissance (Paris) Klincksieck, Lawrence: Univ Press of Kansas, 75; auth, The Craft of Chretien de Troyes: An Essay on Narrative Art, Leiden: Brill, 80; ed, L'Istoyre de Jehan Coquault: A Literary Forgery, French Literature Publications (York, SC), 83; coauth, The Arthurian Handbook, Garland (New York), 88, 97; ed, The Romance of Tristan, by Beroul, Garland Publishing, (New York), 89; coed, Continuations: Essays on Medieval French Literature and Language in Honor of John L. Grigsby, Summa, (Birmingham, AL), 89; ed, The Vows of the Heron Les Voeux du heron: A Middle French Vowing Poem, Critical edition, Garland (New York), 92; coed, Conjunctures: Medieval Studies in Honor of Douglas Kelly, Rodopi (Amsterdam), 94; coed, Perceval/Parzival, Arthurian Characters and Themes, Garland (New York), 01. **CONTACT ADDRESS** Dept of French, Pennsylvania State Univ, Univ Park, University Park, PA 16802. **EMAIL** njl2@psu.edu

LADEFOGED, PETER
PERSONAL Born 09/17/1925, Sutton, England, m, 1953, 3 children **DISCIPLINE** LINGUISTICS, ENGLISH **EDUCATION** Univ Edinburgh, MA, 51, PhD, 59. **CAREER** Lectr phonetics, Univ Edinburgh, 53-61; W African Lang Surv fel, 61-62; from asst prof to assoc prof English, 62-65, Prof Ling, Univ Calif, Los Angeles, 65-, Team leader, Uganda Lang Surv, 68. **MEMBERSHIPS** Acoust Soc Am; Int Phonetic Asn; Int Asn Voice Identification; Am Speech and Hearing Asn; Ling Soc Am (pres). **RESEARCH** Experimental phonetics; African languages; phonology. **SELECTED PUBLICATIONS** Auth, Another View of Endangered Languages, Lang, Vol 0068, 92; Clicks and Their Accompaniments, J Phonetics, Vol 0022, 94; The Status of Phonetic Rarities, Lang, Vol 0072, 96; Phonetic Structures of Banawa, an Endangered Language, Phonetica, Vol 0054, 97; Abercrombie, David and the Changing Field of Phonetics, J Phonetics, Vol 0025, 97. **CONTACT ADDRESS** Dept of Ling, Univ of California, Los Angeles, Los Angeles, CA 90024.

LADUSAW, WILLIAM A.
DISCIPLINE LINGUISTICS **EDUCATION** Univ Ky, BA; Univ Tex, Austin, PhD, 79. **CAREER** Prof, Dept Ch, Univ Calif, Santa Cruz. **RESEARCH** Syntax and semantics of negation, negative concord, and negative polarity items. **SELECTED PUBLICATIONS** Auth, Polarity Sensitivity as Inherent Scope Relations, Garland Publ, 80; "Logical Form and Conditions on Grammaticality," Ling and Philos, 82; "A Proposed Distinction between Levels and Strata," Ling in the Morning Calm, The Linguistic Society of Korea, 87; co-auth, Towards a Non-grammatical Account of Thematic Roles, Thematic Relations, Acad Press, 88. **CONTACT ADDRESS** Dept of Ling, Univ of California, Santa Cruz, 1156 High St, Santa Cruz, CA 95064.

LAFAYETTE, ROBERT
DISCIPLINE LANGUAGE LEARNING AND TEACHING, APPLIED LINGUISTICS **EDUCATION** Ohio State Univ, PhD, 71. **CAREER** Prof, La State Univ. **SELECTED PUBLICATIONS** Auth, The Culture Revolution in Foreign Language Teaching, 75; Conna?tre la France, 83; L'enseignement du fran-(ais aux Etats-Unis, 88; La Francophonie: R?flexions sur la culture et la civilization, 93. **CONTACT ADDRESS** Dept of Fr Grad Stud, Louisiana State Univ and A&M Col, Baton Rouge, LA 70803.

LAFLEUR, RICHARD ALLEN
PERSONAL Born 09/22/1945, Newburyport, MA, m, 1967, 3 children **DISCIPLINE** CLASSICAL STUDIES **EDUCATION** Univ Va, BA, 68, MA, 70; Duke Univ, PhD, 73. **CAREER** Asst prof, 72-77, Assoc Prof Classics, Univ GA, 77-, Head Dept, 80-, Ed, Class Outlook, 79-; chmn, comt Prom Latin, 79-81, exec comt, 79-83, S sect secy-treas, 78-; Class Asn Midwest & South. **HONORS AND AWARDS** Am Philol Asn Awd, Excellence in Teaching Classics, 84; Classical Asn Midwest & South, Ovatio, 85; Am Classical League, pres, 84-86, hon pres for life, 86-; Univ GA, Bronze Medallion, Public Service, 88; For Lang Asn Ga, Teacher of the Year, 88; Ga Governors Awd, Humanities, 89. **MEMBERSHIPS** Am Class League; Am Philol Asn; Archaeol Inst Am; Class Asn Mid W & S; Vergilian Soc. **RESEARCH** Juvenal; Roman satire; Latin pedagogy. **SELECTED PUBLICATIONS** Auth, The Teaching of latin in American Schools, Scholars Press, 87; Latin Poetry for the Beginning Student, Longman, 87; Wheelock's Latin, Harper Collins, 95; Love and Transformation: An Ovid Reader, Scott Foresman-Addison Wesley 98; Latin for the 21st Century: From Concept to Classroom, Scott Foresman-Addison Wesley, 98. **CONTACT ADDRESS** Dept Classics, Univ of Georgia, Athens, GA 30602-0001. **EMAIL** rlafleur@parallel.park.uga.edu

LAFONTANT, JULIEN J.
PERSONAL Born Port-au-Prince, Haiti, m **DISCIPLINE** FRENCH, BLACK STUDIES **EDUCATION** SUNY Binghamton, MA (distinction) 1974, PhD 1976. **CAREER** Exec Mansion Morovia Liberia, translator 1961-63; Ivory Coast Embassy Monrovia Liberia, translator 1963-66; Cuttington Coll Suakoko Liberia, asst prof 1966-72; SUNY Binghamton, teaching asst 1972-76; Univ of NE Lincoln, asst prof 1976-77; Acting Chair Black Studies UNO, asst prof 1977-78; Univ of NE, assoc prof 1978-82, full prof French Chair Black Studies UNO 1983-85; full prof French and Black Studies 1986-98; full prof french, 98-. **HONORS AND AWARDS** Great Teacher Awd Univ of NE Omaha 1982. **MEMBERSHIPS** Fr Review; Nineteenth Century Fr Studies. **SELECTED PUBLICATIONS** book on Montesquieu; book entitled Understanding A Culture; several articles dealing with the Black exper in general and the French encounter with Blacks. **CONTACT ADDRESS** Dept of Foreign Languages, Univ of Nebraska, Omaha, Omaha, NE 68182-0001. **EMAIL** julien_lafontant@unomaha.edu

LAGO, MARY MCCLELLAND
PERSONAL Born 11/04/1919, Pittsburgh, PA, m, 1944, 2 children **DISCIPLINE** MODERN ENGLISH AND BENGALI LITERATURE **EDUCATION** Bucknell Univ, BA, 40; Univ Mo-Columbia, MA, 65, PhD(English), 69. **CAREER** Instr, 64-70, lectr, 70-75, res grants, 71-74, assoc prof, 75-78, Prpf English, Univ MO-Columbia, 78-, Am Philos Soc res grants, 67, 68 and 70; Am Coun Learned Soc/Ford Found Joint SAsia Prog grant, 72-73; Nat Endowment for Humanities grant, 80-83. **HONORS AND AWARDS** DLitt, Bucknell Univ, 81. **MEMBERSHIPS** MLA; Midwest Mod Lang Asn; Asn Asian Studies; Soc of Authors, London; Virginia Woolf Soc. **RESEARCH** Modern Indian literature; late 19th and early 20th century English literature and art history. **SELECTED PUBLICATIONS** Auth, A 'River Called Titash', World Lit Today, Vol 0069, 95. **CONTACT ADDRESS** Dept of English, Univ of Missouri, Columbia, Columbia, MO 65201.

LAHTI, KATHERINE
PERSONAL Born 11/20/1958, Portland, OR, m, 1994 **DISCIPLINE** RUSSIAN **EDUCATION** Wesleyan Univ, BA, 81; Yale Univ, MA, 83; Yale Univ, PhD, 91. **CAREER** Asst Prof, Trinity Col, 91; Assoc Prof, Trinity Col, 98-. **HONORS AND AWARDS** Res Grant, IREX Advanced Res for Senior Scholars, 94. **MEMBERSHIPS** AAASS, SHERA, AATSEEL, Linguistic Soc of Am. **RESEARCH** Russian literature and theater. **SELECTED PUBLICATIONS** Auth, "On Loving Statues and Pandora," Kamennye Baby; Auth, "Futuristic Aesthetics: The Female Body in 'Vladeinir Mayakorsky: A Tradgedy,'" Russian Review 58: 432-455; auth, "Vladimir Mayakorsky: A Dithyramb," SEEJ 40: 257-77. **CONTACT ADDRESS** Dept Mod Lang, Trinity Col, Connecticut, 300 Summit St, Hartford, CT 06106. **EMAIL** katherine.lahti@trincoll.edu

LAIRET, DOLORES PERSON
PERSONAL Born 12/27/1935, Cleveland, OH, w **DISCIPLINE** FRENCH **EDUCATION** Wheaton Coll, AB 1957; Middlebury Coll, AM 1958; Univ of Paris; Case Western Reserve U, PhD 1972. **CAREER** Cleveland State Univ, assoc prof 1972-77, instructor 1971-72, lecturer 1969-71; City of Cleveland, sr personnel asst 1969-71; Western Reserve Univ, teaching fellow lecturer 1965-67; John Marshall HS, French teacher 1963-65; Fox Lane Sch Bedford NY, Educator 1960-62; Southern Univ Baton Rouge, instructor 1959. **HONORS AND AWARDS** Recipient of various Fellowships. **MEMBERSHIPS** Mem Am Assn of Tchrs of French 1971-; Am Assn of Univ Prof 1971; Am Council on Tching of Foreign Lang 1972-; NE Modern Lang Assn 1974-; African Lit Assn; Music Critics Assn; OH Mod Lang Tchrs Assn; past sec & pres Cleveland Chap Tots & Teens Inc 1963-73; mem of bd Glenville Health Assn 1974-; mem Champs Inc 1964-; Am Spec Lctr for US Dept of State in Niger Mali Upper Volta Senegal & Togo. **SELECTED PUBLICATIONS** The Francophone African Novel Perspectives for Critical Eval; Presence Africaine; various articles on Jazz Cleveland Press Showtime. **CONTACT ADDRESS** E 24 St & Euclid Ave, Cleveland, OH 44115.

LAKER, JOSEPH ALPHONSE
PERSONAL Born 03/17/1941, Indianapolis, IN, m, 1987 **DISCIPLINE** HISTORY, JAPANESE STUDIES **EDUCATION** Marian Col, BA, 63; IN Univ, MA, 67, PhD, 75. **CAREER** Instr hist, St Olaf Col, 67-70; asst prof, 74-80, assoc prof, 80-94, Prof Hist, Wheeling Col, 94-; NEH Summer Seminar, Brown Univ, 79; Fulbright/Hays Summer Seminar, Korea, 87; co-dir, NEH Summer Inst for High Sch Tchr(s), summer 95. **MEMBERSHIPS** Asn Asian Studies; Econ Hist Asn; Bus Hist Asn. **RESEARCH** The develop of the Japan beer industry; mod Japan economic and soc hist; Japan Colonialism. **SELECTED PUBLICATIONS** Encyclopedia of World War II, Cord Publ, 78; Oligopoly at home and expansion abroad: The develop of the Japan beer industry, 1907-1937, Proc Second Int Symp Asian Studies, 80; coauth, Tchr Outreach in Japanese Studies, Educ About Asia, fall 96. **CONTACT ADDRESS** Wheeling Jesuit Col, 316 Washington Ave, Wheeling, WV 26003-6243. **EMAIL** lakerj@wju.edu

LALLY, TIM DOUGLAS PATRICK
PERSONAL Born 11/11/1942, Los Angeles, CA, m, 1973, 1 child **DISCIPLINE** OLD & MIDDLE ENGLISH LANGUAGE & LITERATURE **EDUCATION** Harvard Col, AB, 68; State Univ NYork, Stony Brook, MA, 72, PhD(English), 80. **CAREER** Instr, Bowling Green State Univ, 76-80; Asst Prof, 80-84, Assoc Prof English, Univ South Ala, 84-98, retired, 98-; Ed, J Advan Compos, 80-86. **MEMBERSHIPS** MLA; Medieval Acad Am; NCTE; Conf on Col Compos & Commun; Early English Text Soc. **RESEARCH** Medieval English poetry and drama; teaching of advanced composition. **SELECTED PUBLICATIONS** Auth, The nature of innovation in writing instruction, English Lang Arts Bull, 78; Thought and feeling in the Old English Wanderer, In Geardagum III, 79; The Gothic aesthetic of the Middle English St Erkenwald, Ball State Univ Forum, 79; The intellectual content of freshman English, English Lang Arts Bull, 80; Synchronic vs diachronic popular culture studies and the Old English elegy, In: 5000 Years of Popular Cult Before Printing, Bowling Green Univ Press, 80. **CONTACT ADDRESS** Dept English, Univ of So Alabama, Mobile, AL 36688-0002. **EMAIL** tlally@jaguar1.usouthal.edu

LALONDE, GERALD VINCENT
PERSONAL Born 05/18/1938, Bellingham, WA, m, 1969, 2 children **DISCIPLINE** CLASSICS, ANCIENT HISTORY **EDUCATION** Univ Wash, BA, 62, MA, 64, PhD(classics), 71. **CAREER** Instr classics, Univ Wash, 68-69; from instr to asst prof, 69-74, assoc prof, 74-79, Prof Class, Grinnell Col, 80. **MEMBERSHIPS** Archaeol Inst Am; Am Philol Asn; Brit Class Asn. **RESEARCH** Greek epigraphy, history and archaeology. **SELECTED PUBLICATIONS** Auth, A fifth century Hieron southwest of the Athenian Agora, 68 & A Boiotien decree in Athens, 77, Hisperia. **CONTACT ADDRESS** Dept of Classics, Grinnell Col, P O Box 805, Grinnell, IA 50112-0805.

LAMB, MARGARETE
PERSONAL Born 09/06/1954, Austria, m, 1980, 3 children **DISCIPLINE** GERMAN **EDUCATION** Univ Ill, MA, 81; Rice Univ, MA, 91; PhD, 92. **CAREER** Instr, Goethe Inst, 88-92; teaching asst, 88-92; assoc prof, Lafayette, 92-. **HONORS AND AWARDS** Thomas Roy and Lura Forrest Jones Lecture Awd, 99; Andrew W Mellon Grant, 96-99. **MEMBERSHIPS** MLA, NEMLA, AATG, Central PA of AATG. **RESEARCH** Contemporary Austrian Literature and Film; Austrian Theater; 19th and 20th Century German Literature; GDR/Wende Literature and Film; Feminist Theory. **SELECTED PUBLICATIONS** Auth, "Auf dem 'Holzweg des modernen Daseins," Modern Austrian Literature, (99): 133-147; auth, "Threats to Establishment: A Portrait of Valie Export," Austria Kultur, (98): 12-13; auth, "Heimat is a Political Space: A Dimension of Peter Turrini's and elfriede Jelinek's Criticism of the Heimat-Myth," in I Am Too Many People, Peter Turrini: Playwright, Poet, Essayist., Ariadne Press, (98): 97-109; auth, "Nobel Prize Recipients," The Feminist Encyclopedia of German Literature, Greenwood Press, 97, 368-369; ed, Out from the Shadows. A Collection of Articles on Austrian Literature and Film by Women since 1945, Riverside: Ariadne, 97; auth, "Vergangenheitsbewaltigung," The Feminist Encyclopedia of German Literature, Westport, (97): 54-542; auth, "L'avant-garde feministe autrichienne. Innovations esthetique: Valie Export et elfriede Jelinek," Continuites et Ruptures Dans la Litterature Autrichienne, (96): 231-245; auth, "Avantgard-Filmj=kunst und ihre Presse-Rezeption: Valie Exports feministische Asthetisierung," Modern Austrian Literature, (96): 93-107; auth, "Die Kunst ist geschlechtsfrie. Zur 'Sein/Schein'-Asthetik als seelischgeistige Haltung," Literaturkritik und erzahlerische Praxis, (95): 147-152; auth, "Ein Gesprach mit Julian Schutting," Literaturkritik und erzahlerische Praxis, (95):153-160. **CONTACT ADDRESS** Dept For Lang, Lafayette Col, Easton, PA 18042. **EMAIL** lambafm@lafayette.edu

LAMOUREUX, NORMAND J.
PERSONAL m, 4 children **DISCIPLINE** FRENCH **EDUCATION** Boston Col, MA, 60, BA, 57; Ind Univ, PhD, 67. **CAREER** Prof & ch dept lang & lit, Col of Holy Cross. **RESEARCH** French language and pedagogy. **SELECTED PUBLICATIONS** Auth, Tout Ensemble, Fort Worth: Holt, Rinehart and Winston, 96; Ensemble: Grammaire, 5th ed, Fort Worth: Holt, Rinehart and Winston, 94; Ensemble: Litterature, 6th ed, Fort Worth: Holt, Rinehart and Winston, 99; Ensemble: Culture et Societe, 6th ed, Fort Worth: Holt, Rinehart and Winston, 99 & Ensemble: Histoire, Fort Worth: Holt, Rinehart and Winston, 92. **CONTACT ADDRESS** Dept of Modern Languages and Literatures, Col of the Holy Cross, 1 College St, PO Box 182A, Worcester, MA 01610-2395. **EMAIL** nlamoure@holycross.edu

LANCE, DONALD M.
PERSONAL Born 07/10/1931, Gainesville, TX, s **DISCIPLINE** ENGLISH LINGISTICS **EDUCATION** Texas A&M Col, BA, 52; Univ Tx-Austin, MA, 62; PhD, 68. **CAREER** High sch teacher, English & Spanish, 57-64; grad instr, Univ Tx-Austin, 64-67; asst prof, Texas A&M Univ, 67-69; asst prof, Univ Mo - Columbia, 69-72; assoc prof, 72-78; prof, 78-94; prof emeritus, 94- . **HONORS AND AWARDS** Strathmore's Who's Who, 98. **MEMBERSHIPS** Ling Soc of Am; Am Dial Soc; Am Name Soc; Dict Soc N Am; MLA; Mo Folklore Soc; Coun of Geog Names Authorities. **RESEARCH** Phonology; syntax; pedagogical linguistics, discourse, toponymy. **SELECTED PUBLICATIONS** auth, Pronunciation in The Century Dictionary, Dictionaries, 96; auth, Regional Vocabulary in Missouri, Language Variety in the South, 97; auth, Discourse, Information, and Syntax, Papers from the 1997 Mid-America Linguistics Conference, 97; auth with Martha D. Patton, Sequential Chains of Connections: A Linguistic Analyis of Written Expository Discourse, Papers from the 1997 Mid-America Linguistics Conference; auth, Regional Variation in Subjective Dialect Divisions in the United States, A Handbook of Perceptual Dialectology. **CONTACT ADDRESS** 2208-F Bushnell Dr., Columbia, MO 65201. **EMAIL** LanceDM@missouri.edu

LANDY, FRANCIS
PERSONAL Born 07/10/1947, London, England, m, 1995, 1 child **DISCIPLINE** ENGLISH, COMPARATIVE LITERATURE **EDUCATION** Cambridge Univ, BA, 69; Sussex Univ, PhD, 83; **CAREER** From Asst Prof to Prof, Univ Alta, 84-. **MEMBERSHIPS** Soc of Bible lit, Am Acad of Relig, Can Soc of the Old Testament/Hebrew Bible. **RESEARCH** Literary Study of the Old Testament and Hebrew bible. **SELECTED PUBLICATIONS** Auth, "In the Wilderness of Speech: Problems of Metaphor in Hosea," Bibl Interpretation, 3 (95): 35-59; auth, Sex and Sadism in Hosea," in Jewish Explorations of Sexuality (London: Duckworth, Providence: Berghahn, 95), 17-26; auth, "Hosea" in Readings (Sheffield: Sheffield Acad Pr, 95); auth, "Do We Want Our Children to Read This Book?" The Bible and the Ethics of Reading (97): 155-175; auth, "Strategies of Concentration and Diffusion in Isaiah 6," Bibl Interpretation, 6 (99): 58-86; auth, "Flood and Fludd," in Bibl Studies/Cult Studies: The Third Sheffield Colloquium (Sheffield: Sheffield Acad Pr, 98), 117-159; auth, "Seraphim and Poetic Process," in The Labour of Reading: Essays in Hon of Robert C. Culley at the Time of This Retirement (Atlanta, GA: ScholarsPress, 99); auth, "Isaiah," in An Anthrop of Bibl Autobiographies (Sheffield: Sheffield Acad Pr, forthcoming). **CONTACT ADDRESS** Dept Comparative Lit, Univ of Alberta, Old Arts Bldg, Edmonton, AB, Canada T6G 2E1. **EMAIL** francis.landy@ualberta.ca

LANG, MABEL LOUISE
PERSONAL Born 11/12/1917, Utica, NY **DISCIPLINE** CLASSICAL PHILOLOGY **EDUCATION** Cornell Univ, AB, 39, Bryn Mawr Col, AM, 40, PhD, 43. **CAREER** From instr to assoc prof class philol, 43-59, actg dean, 58-59 & 60-61, Prof Greek to Prof Emeritus, Bryn Mawr Col, 59-, Fulbright res grant, Greece, 59-60; chmn comt admis & fels, Am Sch Class Studies, Athens, 67-72, chmn managing comt, 75-80; Blegen Distinguished Vis Res prof, Vassar Col, 76-77; Martin lectr, Oberlin Col, 82. **HONORS AND AWARDS** LittD, Holy Cross Col, 75, Colgate Univ, 78. **MEMBERSHIPS** Archaeol Inst Am; Am Philol Asn; Am Philos Soc. **RESEARCH** Greek history, literature and epigraphy. **SELECTED PUBLICATIONS** Auth, Pylos tablets, 1957-1962, Am J Archaeol, 58-63; The Athenian Citizen, 60 & Weights and Measures of the Athenian Agora, 64, Am Sch Class Studies, Athens; The palace of Nestor, Vol II, in The Frescoes, Princeton Univ, 68; The Athenian Agora, XXI, Graffiti and Dipinti, 76 & Socrates in the Agora, 78, Am Sch Class Studies, Athens; auth, Herodotean Narrative and Discourse, Harvard Univ Press, 84; auth, The Athenian Agora, Ostraca, 90. **CONTACT ADDRESS** Dept of Greek, Bryn Mawr Col, Bryn Mawr, PA 19010. **EMAIL** mlang@brynmawr.edu

LANGACKER, RONALD WAYNE
PERSONAL Born 12/27/1942, Fond du Lac, WI, m, 1966 **DISCIPLINE** LINGUISTICS **EDUCATION** Univ Ill, AB, 63, AM, 64, PhD(ling), 66. **CAREER** From asst prof to assoc prof, 66-76, Prof Ling, Univ Calif, San Diego, 76-, Assoc ed, Language 71-77; Nat Endowment for Humanities sr fel, 73-74; Guggenheim fel, 78-79. **MEMBERSHIPS** Ling Soc Am; AAUP. **RESEARCH** Linguistic theory; Uto-Aztecan languages. **SELECTED PUBLICATIONS** Auth, Raising and Transparency, Lang, Vol 0071, 95; Constituency, Dependency, and Conceptual Grouping + Cognitive Grammar, Cognitive Ling, Vol 0008, 97. **CONTACT ADDRESS** Dept of Ling, Univ of California, San Diego, San Diego, 9500 Gilman Dr, La Jolla, CA 92093.

LANGE, HORST
DISCIPLINE GERMAN LANGUAGE, LITERATURE, AND CULTURE **EDUCATION** Univ Tubingen, MA; Univ Va, PhD. **CAREER** Asst prof Ger, Univ Nev, Reno. **RESEARCH** 18th- and early 19th-century German literature. **SELECTED PUBLICATIONS** Published a book on Kant and articles on Frege and Goethe. **CONTACT ADDRESS** Univ of Nevada, Reno, Reno, NV 89557. **EMAIL** lange@unr.edu

LANGENDOEN, TERENCE
PERSONAL Born 06/07/1939, Paterson, NJ, m, 1984, 1 child **DISCIPLINE** LINGUISTICS **EDUCATION** Mass Inst Technol, SB, 61; PhD, 64. **CAREER** Asst Prof to Assoc Prof, Ohio State Univ, 64-69; Prof, CUNY, 69-88; Prof, Univ Ariz, 88-. **HONORS AND AWARDS** Sen Fulbright-Hays Lectureship, Univ Utrecht, 77; Fel, NY Acad of Sci, 77; Summer Fac Fel, Ohio State Univ, 66; Nat Merit Scholarship, Johnson Motor Lines Co, 57-61. **MEMBERSHIPS** Am Asn for the Advancement of Sci, Linguistic Soc of Am, Mod Lang Asn, NY Acad of Sci. **RESEARCH** Eng syntax; linguistic theory; psycholinguistics. **SELECTED PUBLICATIONS** Auth, Optimality theory: An overview, Blackwell Pub, 97; auth, The vastness of natural language, Blackwell Pub, 84; auth, "The logic of reflexivity and reciprocity," in Anaphora: A guidebook, Blackwell Pub, in press; auth "Limitations on embedding in coordinate structures," Journal of Psycholinguistic Research, (98): 235-259; auth, "Bloomfield," in The MIT encyclopedia of the cognitive sciences, MIT Press, 90-91; auth, "Linguistic theory," in a companion to cognitive science, Blackwell Pub, 98; auth, "foreword," in Optimality theory: an overview, Blackwell Pub, 97; auth, "Sobre las llamadas clausulas relativas en yaqui," in Tercer Encuentro de Linguistica en el Noroeste, Editorial Unison, 96; auth, "A rationale for the Text Encoding Initiative recommendations for feature-structure markup," Computers and the Humanities, (95): 191-210. **CONTACT ADDRESS** Dept of Ling, Univ of Arizona, PO Box 210028, Tucson, AZ 85721-0028. **EMAIL** langendt@arizona.edu

LANGLEY, STEPHEN G.
PERSONAL Born 12/25/1938, Gardner, MA **DISCIPLINE** THEATRE, SPEECH **EDUCATION** Emerson Col, BA, 60, MA, 61; Univ Ill, Urbana, PhD, 65. **CAREER** Lectr speech, 63-65, from instr to assoc prof, 65-76, bus mgr, Theatre Div, 66, gem mgr, Ctr Performing Arts, 68-75, prof theatre, Brooklyn Col, 76-, dir div Performing Arts Mgt, 75-, grad dept chp, Theatre Dept, 78-. **MEMBERSHIPS** Dramatists Guild; Am Theatre Asn. **RESEARCH** Puritanism and the American drama; performing arts administration. **SELECTED PUBLICATIONS** Auth, Theatre management in America: Principle and practice, and producers on producing, Drama Bk Specialists, 73, rev ed, 80. **CONTACT ADDRESS** Performing Arts Ctr, Brooklyn Col, CUNY, 2901 Bedford Ave, Brooklyn, NY 11210-2813.

LANGLOIS, WALTER G.
DISCIPLINE FRENCH **EDUCATION** Yale Univ, PhD, 55. **CAREER** Prof to prof emer, Univ Wyo, 74-. **RESEARCH** 20th century French lit and espec Andre Malraux. **CONTACT ADDRESS** Dept of Mod and Class Lang, Univ of Wyoming, Hoyt Hall 228, Laramie, WY 82071.

LANGSTON, DWIGHT E.
PERSONAL Born 07/17/1944, Greenville, SC, m, 1990, 3 children **DISCIPLINE** GERMAN **EDUCATION** Furman Univ, BA, 86; Tulane Univ, PhD, 73. **CAREER** Instr, Lingua-Schule Germany; Instr, Wesleyan Coll; Asst prof to assoc prof, Univ Central Ark, 86- . **HONORS AND AWARDS** Fulbright Sch. **MEMBERSHIPS** Am Asn Tchrs German. **RESEARCH** For. Lang Pedagogy. **SELECTED PUBLICATIONS** Auth, Langston, D.E., Letter Cueing in Oral Translation Exercises, Die Unterrichtspraxis, 75, No. 2, 102-103; -------------, English-Language Cartoons in the Intermediate German Class, Schatzkammer, XIV, No. 1, Spring, 88, 176-178; -------------, Is the Infinitive Really So Basic? Die Unterrichtspraxis, 88, No. 2, 208-211; ---------------, Acts, Turns and Routines: Strategies for Foreign Language Teaching Suggested by Disclosure Analysis, SELECTA, A Journal of the NCFL, 18, 97, 13-22. **CONTACT ADDRESS** Univ of Central Arkansas, 201 Donaghey Ave, Conway, AR 72035-0001. **EMAIL** dwightl@mail.uca.edu

LANHAM, CAROL D.
PERSONAL Born 01/18/1936, m, 1957 **DISCIPLINE** MEDIEVAL LATIN **EDUCATION** Conn Col, AB, 57; UCLA, MA, 68; PhD, 73. **CAREER** Vis Asst Prof, Brown Univ, 73-74; Ed to Res Assoc, UCLA Ctr for Medieval and Renaissance Studies, 75-; Ed Consult, Rhetorica, Inc, 88-. **HONORS AND AWARDS** Phi Beta Kappa. **MEMBERSHIPS** am Philol Asn; Medieval Acad of Am; Medieval Asn of the Pac; Medieval Latin Asn of N Am. **RESEARCH** Latin epistolography; Early medieval education; Rhetoric. **SELECTED PUBLICATIONS** Auth, "Freshman Composition in the Early Middle Ages: Epistolography and Rhetoric before the 'ars dictaminis'," Viator, 92; auth, "Writing Instruction from Late Antiquity to the Twelfth Century," in A Short History of Writing Instruction from Ancient Greece to Modern America, (Lawrence Erlbaum Assoc, 91), 79-121. **CONTACT ADDRESS** Ctr for Medieval & Renaissance Studies, Univ of California, Los Angeles, 927 Bluegrass Lane, Los Angeles, CA 90049. **EMAIL** lancd@aol.com

LANOUX, ANDREA
DISCIPLINE RUSSIAN LITERATURE **EDUCATION** Brown Univ, BA, 89; Univ Calif at Los Angeles, MA, 93; PhD, 99. **CAREER** Asst prof, Connecticut Col, 99-. **HONORS AND AWARDS** Woodrow Wilson Jr Schol, 99; Metchie J E Budka Awd, 97; ACLS Diss Fel, 97; SSRC Diss Fel, 98; IREX Diss Res Fel, 96, 97. **MEMBERSHIPS** MLA; AAASS; AATSEEL; Kosciusko Found; AWSS. **RESEARCH** 19th C Russian and Polish literature. **SELECTED PUBLICATIONS** Transl, Dictionary of Russian Women Writers, thirteen articles, ed. M Ledkovsky, C Rosenthal, M Zirin (Westport, CT, Greenwood Press, 94); rev, "Rewriting Capitalism: Literature and the Market in Late Tsarist Russia and the Kingdom of Poland," by Beth Holmgren, in SELl (00); rev, " Women and the Spirit of Otherness (Kobiety i duch innosci)," by Maria Janion, in Women East- West (98); rev, "Women of a Foreign Land (Cudzoziemki)," by Grazyna Borkowska, in Women East-West (98); transl, "The End and the Beginning," by Wistawa Szymborska, Suitcase (97); transl, "Anew," by Anna Swirszczynska, Suitcase (98); auth, "Nadezhda Sokhanskaia," in Russian Women Writers, ed. Christine Tomel (NY: Garland Publishing, 99); auth, "The Making of National Poets: Figures of Nation and Empire in the Early Critical Reception Of Mickiewicz and Pushkin, 1823-1829," in Polish Literature in the European Context, ed. Ntricia Brodsky (London: Harwood Acad Pub, 00). **CONTACT ADDRESS** Dept Russian, Connecticut Col, 270 Mohegan Ave, New London, CT 06320-4125. **EMAIL** alano@conncoll.edu

LANSING, RICHARD H.
PERSONAL Born 05/14/1943, Rochester, NY, m, 1972, 1 child **DISCIPLINE** ITALIAN & COMPARATIVE LITERATURE **EDUCATION** Columbia Col, NYork, AB, 65; Univ Calif, Berkeley, MA, 67, PhD(comp lit), 72. **CAREER** Teaching asst Ital, Univ Calif, Berkeley, 67-69, assoc, 69-70, actg instr comp lit, 70-71; from asst prof to prof and chemn Dept Comp Lit, Brandeis Univ, 72-. **HONORS AND AWARDS** Mabelle McLeod Lewis mem fund grant, 72. **MEMBERSHIPS** MLA; Dante Soc Am; Mediaeval Acad Am; Am Asn Univ Prof Ital; Am Asn Teachers Ital. **RESEARCH** Dante; comparative medieval literature; epic and romance. **SELECTED PUBLICATIONS** Auth, Two similes: The shipwrecked swimmer and Elijah's ascent, Romance Philol, 74; Submerged meanings in Dante's similes, Dante Studies, 76; Stylistic and structural duality in Manzoni's I Promessi Sposi, Italica, 75; From Image to Idea: A Study of the Simile in Dante's Commedia, Longo, Ravenna, 77; The structure of meaning in Lampedusa's Il Gattopardo, PMLA, 5/78; Dante's unfolding vision, approaches to teaching Dante's divine comedy, MLA, 82; trans, Il Convivio (The Banquet), Garland Libr of Medieval Lit, series B, no. 65, 90; auth, "Ariosto's 'Orlando furioso' and the Logic of Paradox," Italiana VI (94): 82-90; auth, "Narrative Design in Dante's Earthly Paradise," Dante Studies 113 (95): 101-113; ed, The Dante Encyclopedia, Garland Publishing (NYork and London), 00. **CONTACT ADDRESS** Dept of Romance & Comp Lit, Brandeis Univ, 415 South St, MS 024, Waltham, MA 02454-9110 02454-9110. **EMAIL** lansing@brandeis.edu

LANZINGER, KLAUS
PERSONAL Born 02/16/1928, Woergl, Austria, m, 1954, 2 children **DISCIPLINE** LANGUAGE, LITERATURE, GERMAN, RUSSIAN **EDUCATION** Bowdoin Col, BA, 51; Univ Innsbruck, PhD, 52. **CAREER** Res asst, Univ Innsbruck, 57-67; assoc prof to prof to emer to chmn, Univ Notre Dame, 67-. **HONORS AND AWARDS** Foreign Studies Grant, Bowdoin Col, 50-51; Fulbright Res Grant, 61; Thomas Wolfe Soc Zelda Gitlin Lit Prize, 93. **MEMBERSHIPS** MLA, TWS; EAAS; DGA. **RESEARCH** 19th-century and early 20th-century American literature; early 20th-century German literature; American-European literary relations. **SELECTED PUBLICATIONS** Auth, Epik im Amerikanischen Roman, 65; auth, Jason's Voyage: The Search for the Old World in American Literature, 89. **CONTACT ADDRESS** German Russian Dept, Univ of Notre Dame, 318 O'Shaugnessy Hall, Notre Dame, IN 46556-5639.

LAPAIRE, PIERRE J.
PERSONAL Born 01/07/1954, Boulogne, France, m, 1997, 2 children **DISCIPLINE** FRENCH LANGUAGE **EDUCATION** Univ Perpionan, Fr, BA, 76, MA, 77; Univ No Carolina, Chapel Hill, MA, 80, PhD, 84. **CAREER** Asst prof, High Point Col, 83-85; asst prof, 85-90, assoc prof, 90-94, prof, 94-, Chair 95-99, Univ No Carolina, Wilmington. **MEMBERSHIPS** MLA; SEMLA; AATF. **RESEARCH** Stylistics; Camus; twentieth century French drama; Supervielle Djian; Montherlant. **SELECTED PUBLICATIONS** Auth, Montherland La Reine Marie Revisited Lang quarterly, 86; auth, Aspects de l'Antitheatre Chez Montherant Pr rev 89; auth, Aspects de la dualite du discours Montherlantien, Dalhousie Fr Stud, 93; auth, Elements de la binarite stylistique chez Camus: Un Style polarise, Fr Rev, 93; auth, Montherlant et la parole: Etude d'un language dramatique, Summa, 93; auth, Racine, Corneillè, Flaubert, Balzac, Camus, in, Reference Guide to World Literature, St James, 95; auth, L'esthetique binaire de Baudelaire: A Une Passante et la beaute fugitive, Romance Notes, 95; auth, Heliotropies, Caracteres, 95; auth, Aspects de L'antitheatre chez Montherlant, Fr. Rev., 89; auth, Montherlant -- La Reine Morte Revisited, Language Quarterly, 86. **CONTACT ADDRESS** Dept of Foreign Languages and Literatures, Univ of No Carolina, Wilmington, 601 S College Rd, Wilmington, NC 28403-3297. **EMAIL** lapairep@uncwil.edu

LAPIERRE, ANDRE
DISCIPLINE FRENCH AND FRENCH CANADIAN LINGUISTICS **EDUCATION** Univ Ottawa, BA, 64, MA, 68; Univ Strasbourg, PhD(ling), 72. **CAREER** Lectr French, 66-69, asst prof ling, 72-82, Assoc Prof Ling, Univ Ottawa, 82-Book rev ed, Onomastica, 81-. **MEMBERSHIPS** Can Soc Study Names (pres, 82-); Am Name Soc; Can Ling Asn. **RESEARCH** North American French place-names; French and French Canadian lexicology and dialectology. **SELECTED PUBLICATIONS** Auth, Quelques aspects quantitatifs de la conjugaison en francais contemporain, Le francais moderne, 74; Situation du francais ontarien, Protee, 79; L'orthographe de la langue maternelle: le cas des Franco-Ontariens, Can Mod Lang J, 79; Le Manuel de l'abbe Thomas Maguire et la langue quebecoise au XIXe siecle, Rev hist Am francaise, 81; Toponymie francaise en Ontario, Etudes vivantes, Montreal, 81; ed, L'Ontario francais du sud-ouest: temoignages oraux, Univ Ottawa Press, 82. **CONTACT ADDRESS** Dept of Ling, Univ of Ottawa, 70 Laurier, Arts Building, Ottawa, ON, Canada K1N 6N5. **EMAIL** lapierre@ottawa.ca

LAPPRAND, MARC
DISCIPLINE TWENTIETH CENTURY FRENCH LITERATURE **EDUCATION** Univ Toronto, PhD. **RESEARCH** Boris Vian; Raymond Queneau and Oulipo; literary theory. **SELECTED PUBLICATIONS** Auth, Boris Vian la vie contre: biographie critique, Ottawa, Presses de l'Universite d'Ottawa, Paris, Nizet, 93; Trois Fous du langage: Vian, Queneau, Prevert, Nancy, Presses universitaires de Nancy, 93; Poetique de l'Oulipo, Amsterdam, Rodopi, 98. **CONTACT ADDRESS** Dept of French, Univ of Victoria, PO Box 3045 STN CSC, Victoria, BC, Canada V8W 3P4. **EMAIL** lapprand@uvic.ca

LARDINOIS, ANDRE P. M. H.
PERSONAL Born 06/14/1961, Watford, England **DISCIPLINE** CLASSICS **EDUCATION** Free Univ, Neth, BA, 84; MA, 88; Princeton Univ, MA, 91; PhD, 95. **CAREER** Asst prof, Univ Minn, Twin Cities. **RESEARCH** Archaic Greek poetry; greek tragedy; greek and roman mythology. **SELECTED PUBLICATIONS** Auth, Lesbian Sappho and Sappho of Lesbos, in J N Bremmer, ed, From Sappho to de Sade: Moments in the History of Sexuality, London-NY, 89; Greek Myths for Athenian Rituals: Religion and Politics in Aeschylus' Eumenidesand Sophocles' Oedipus Coloneus, GRBS 33/4, 92; Subject and Circumstance in Sappho's Poetry, TAPA 124, 94; Who Sang Sappho's Songs?, in E Greene, ed, Reading Sappho: Contemporary Approaches, Berkeley, 96; Modern Paroemiology and the Use of Gnomai in Homer's Iliad, CP 92, 97; coauth, Tragic Ambiguity: Anthropology, Philosophy and Sophocles' Antigone, Leiden, 87; coedit, Making Silence Speak: Women's Voices in Greek Literature and Society, Princeton Univ Press, 01. **CONTACT ADDRESS** Dept of Class and Near Eastern Studies, Univ of Minnesota, Twin Cities, 9 Pleasant St. SE, 330 Folwell Hall, Minneapolis, MN 55455-0125. **EMAIL** lardi001@tc.umn.edu

LAROCHE, ROLAND ARTHUR
PERSONAL Born 03/04/1943, Berlin, NH, m, 1965, 3 children **DISCIPLINE** CLASSICS **EDUCATION** Boston Col, BA, 65; Tufts Univ, MA, 66, PhD(classics), 72. **CAREER** Teacher French, Latin and Greek, Pingree Sch, S Hamilton, Mass, 66-70; asst prof classics, State Univ NY, Potsdam, 70-77; teacher Latin and French, Cheshire Acad, Conn, 77-81; Teacher Latin and Greek and Chmn, Foreign Lang Dept, Albany Acad, 81-. **MEMBERSHIPS** Am Class League; Class Asn Atlantic States. **RESEARCH** Greek and Roman numerical practices; Livy; early Roman historiography. **SELECTED PUBLICATIONS** Auth, Popular Symbolic-Mystical Numbers in Antiquity, Latomus, Vol 0054, 95; Number Symbolism, Latomus, Vol 0055, 96. **CONTACT ADDRESS** Albany Acad, Albany, NY 12210.

LARRAGA, MARIBEL
PERSONAL Born 12/12/1969, Veracruz, Mexico, m, 1 child **DISCIPLINE** SPANISH, PORTUGUESE **EDUCATION** Our Lady of the Lake Univ, BA, 92; Univ N Mex, MA, 95; PhD, 99. **CAREER** Asst prof, Our Lady of the Lake Univ, 97-. **MEMBERSHIPS** Am Asn of Teachers of Spanish and Portuguese. **RESEARCH** Spanish Colonial Latin America. **SELECTED PUBLICATIONS** Auth, "Indios, blancos y mulatos: 'Si todos somos Hermanos Y, todos bamos aun Fin ya no ay criollo O, Gachupin, todos sean Americanos," Colonial Latin American Historical Review, (96): 47-73; auth, "Paletitas de guayaba: un novela postmoderna de descubrimiento," Cuicuilco: Revista de la Escuela Nacional de Antropologia e Historia (95): 97-110. **CONTACT ADDRESS** Dept Humanities, Our Lady of Lake Univ, 411 Southwest 24th St, San Antonio, TX 78207-4617. **EMAIL** larrm@lake.ollusa.edu

LARSEN, KEVIN
DISCIPLINE SPANISH **EDUCATION** Harvard Univ, PhD, 83. **CAREER** Assoc prof; Univ WY, 89-. **RESEARCH** 19th-century Peninsular Spanish lit. **SELECTED PUBLICATIONS** Auth, bk on, Gabriel Miro, 92. **CONTACT ADDRESS** Dept of Mod and Class Lang(s), Univ of Wyoming, PO Box 3964, Laramie, WY 82071-3964. **EMAIL** KLARSEN@UWYO.EDU

LARSON, ANN R.
DISCIPLINE MODERN, CLASSICAL LANGUAGES **EDUCATION** Hope Col, BA, 70; Columbia Univ, MA, 71; PhD, 75. **CAREER** Instr, Colgate Univ, 74-75; asst prof, 75-79; asst prof, Univ Tulsa, 79-84; assoc prof, Hope Col, 84-93; prof, 93-. **HONORS AND AWARDS** Josephine A. Roberts Awd, 99; NEH Fel, 97. **MEMBERSHIPS** MLA; AATF; SFESS. **RESEARCH** French renaissance and 17th century women writers; epistolarity; literary theory' translation; poetic theory. **SELECTED PUBLICATIONS** Co-ed, Renaissance Women Writers: French Texts/American Contexts (Detroit: Wayne State Univ Press, 94), 235; auth, co-ed, Women Writers in Pre-Revolutionary France: From Marie de France to Elisabeth Viggee-Le Brun (NY, and London: Garland Publishing, 00), 592. **CONTACT ADDRESS** Dept Modern Classical Languages, Hope Col, 137 East 12th St, Holland, MI 49423-3607.

LASARTE, PEDRO
PERSONAL Born Lima, Peru, m, 1998, 1 child **DISCIPLINE** SPANISH LANGUAGE **EDUCATION** Univ Tex, BA, 71; MA, 73; Univ Mich, PhD, 83. **CAREER** Vis Instr, Vassar Col, 80-81; Vis Assoc Prof, Univ of Mich, 84; From Instr to Asst Prof, Univ of Rochester, 81-87; From Asst Prof to Assoc Prof, Boston Univ, 87-. **HONORS AND AWARDS** Humanities Fel, Boston Univ; John Carter Brown Fel; Horale H. Rackham Predoctoral Fel. **MEMBERSHIPS** MLA, Inst Iberommericano. **RESEARCH** Spanish-American literature and culture, Textual criticism. **SELECTED PUBLICATIONS** Auth, "Mateo Rosas de Oquendo: la satira y el carnaval," Hisp Rev 53 (85): 415-436; auth, "Don Catrin, Don Quijote y la picaresca," Revista de estudios hispanicos 23 (89): 101-112; auth, "Mateo Rosas de Oquendo y la escritura autobiografica," MLN 105 (90): 373-

384; auth, "'No oyes ladrar los perros' de Juan Rulfo: peregrinaje hacia el origen," Int Revista de lit hispanica 29 (90): 101-118; auth, "Satira hecha por Mateo Rosas de Oquendo a las cosas que pasan en la Piru, ano de 1589," in Estudio y edicion critica (Masidon: Hisp Sem of Medieval Studies, Univ of Wis, 90); auth, "Jose Maria Roe Barcena y la narracion fantastica," Chasqui, Revista de Lit Latinoamericana 20 (91): 10-16; auth, "Sin rumbo en la texto de Schopenhauer," Int Revista de Lit Hispanica 39 (94): 81-96; auth, "Francisco de Terrazas, Pedro de Ledesma y Jose de Arrazola: algunos poemas novohispanos ineditos," Nueva revista de filologia hispanica 45 (97): 45-66; auth, "La Vieja y el Periquillo: una aproximacion a la Lima de Juan del Valle y Caviedes," Caliope, J of the Soc for Renaissance and Baroque Hisp Poetry 4 (98): 125-139; auth, "Hacia un estudio del cancionero peotico 'Ms. Codex 193' de la Universidad de Pensilvania," in Edicion y anotacio de textos coloniales hispanoamericanos, ed. I Arellano, and J.A. Rodriguez Garrido (Pamplona-Madrid: Universidad de Navarra-Iberoamericana, 99), 233-244. **CONTACT ADDRESS** Dept For Lang, Boston Univ, 718 Commonwealth Ave, Boston, MA 02215-2423. **EMAIL** lasarte@bu.edu

LASERSOHN, PETER
PERSONAL Born 06/09/1959, Cleveland, OH, m, 1999 **DISCIPLINE** LINGUISTICS **EDUCATION** Earlham Col, BA, 81; Ohio State Univ, MA, 85; PhD, 88. **CAREER** Lecturer, Univ of TX, 88-89; postdoctoral fel, Univ Calif, 89-91; asst prof, Univ Rochester, 91-96; asst prof, Univ Ill, 96-. **HONORS AND AWARDS** Arthur Charles Fel, Earlham Col, 81; Univ Fel, Ohio State Univ, 82; Pres Fel, Ohio State Univ, 87. **MEMBERSHIPS** Ling Soc of Am, European Asn for logic, lang and information. **RESEARCH** Formal semantics. **SELECTED PUBLICATIONS** Auth, "On the Readings of Plural Noun Phrases," Linguistic Inquiry, (89): 130-134; auth, "Group Action and Spatio-Temporal Proimity," Linguistics and Philosophy, (90): 179-206; auth, A Semantics for Groups and Events, Garland Pub, 90; auth, Plurality, conjunction and Events, Kluwer Academic Press, 95; auth, "Pragmatic Halos," Language 75, (99): 522-552. **CONTACT ADDRESS** Dept Linguistics, Univ of Illinois, Urbana-Champaign, 707 S Mathews Ave, Urbana, IL 61801-3625.

LASNIK, HOWARD
PERSONAL Born 07/03/1945, Washington, DC, m, 1973, 1 child **DISCIPLINE** LINGUISTICS **EDUCATION** Carnegie Inst of Tech, BS, 67; Harvard Univ, MA, 69; Mass Inst of Tech, PhD, 72. **CAREER** Prof, Univ Conn, 81-00; assoc prof, Univ Conn, 76-81; asst prof, Univ Conn, 72-76. **HONORS AND AWARDS** Phi Kappa Phi; Di Delta Epsilon; Woodrow Wilson Fel; Harvard Grad Prize Fel; NIH Trainee; NSF Grad Fel; Univ Conn Res Grant, 75, 86, 87, 88, 89, 99; Sloan Found Vis Scientist, Univ Calif Irvine, 78-79; Postdoctorate Fel, Mass Inst of Tech, 84-85; Ntl Sci Found Res Grant, 95-96; Univ Conn Alumni Assoc Fac Res Awd, 88; AAUP Teaching Excellence Awd, 98; Chanellor's Res Excellence Awd, 99; Fel Center for Advanced Study in the Behavioral Sciences, 00; Board of Trustees Distinguished Prof, 00. **MEMBERSHIPS** Generative Linguists of the Old World; N Eastern Linguistic Soc; Linguistic Soc Amer; Languages & Linguistics Ed Brd; Rivista di Linguistics Advisory Brd; Lincom Studies in Theoretical Linguistics Advisory Brd. **RESEARCH** Syntactic Theory; Logical Form; Learnability **SELECTED PUBLICATIONS** Auth, A Course in GB Syntax, with J. Uriagereka, MIT Press, 88; auth, Essays on Araphora, Kluwer, 89; auth, Essays on restrictiveness and Learnability, Kluwer, 90; auth, Move, with M. Saito, MIT Press, 92; auth, A Course in Minimalist Syntax, with J. Uriagereka, Blackwell, forthcoming; auth, Minimalist Investigations in Linguistic Theory, Routledge, forthcoming; auth, Minimalist Analysis, Blackwell, 99. **CONTACT ADDRESS** Dept Linguistics, U-145, Univ of Connecticut, Storrs, 341 Mansfield Rd, Storrs, CT 06269-1145. **EMAIL** lasnik@sp.uconn.edu

LATEINER, DONALD
PERSONAL Born 06/01/1944, New Rochelle, NY, m, 1976, 2 children **DISCIPLINE** CLASSICAL STUDIES, ANCIENT HISTORY **EDUCATION** Univ Chicago, BA, 65; Cornell Univ, MA, 67; Stanford Univ, MA, 70, PhD(classics), 72. **CAREER** Lectr hist, San Francisco State Col, 68-69; acting asst prof classics, Stanford Univ, 71-72; asst prof class studies, Univ PA, 72-79; asst prof, 79-82, Assoc Prof Humanities-Classics, 82-85, prof, 85-92, JOHN WRIGHT PROF GREEK & HUMANITIES, OH WESLEYAN UNIV, 93-. **HONORS AND AWARDS** Am School of Classical Studies @ Athens, Seymour fel, 69-70; Center for Hellenic Studies, Washington, D.C., vis Sr Scholar, 99. **MEMBERSHIPS** Am Philol Asn; Am Asn Ancient Historians; Archaeol Inst Am; Friends Ancient Hist. **RESEARCH** Greek epic; nonverbal behaviors in ancient lit; Greek historiography; Latin elegy; Greek oratory. **SELECTED PUBLICATIONS** Auth, The Speech of Teutiaplus, Greek, Roman & Byzantine Studies, 75; Tissaphernes and the Phoenician fleet, Trans Am Philol Asn, 76; Obscenity in Catullus, Ramus, 77; No Laughing Matter: A Literary Tactic in Herodotus, Trans Am Philol Asn, 77; An Analysis of Lysias' Defense Speeches, Rivista Storica dell' Antichita, 81; The Historical Method of Herodotus, Toronto, 89; The Failure of the Ionian Revolt, Historia, 82; Mimetic Syntax: Metaphor from World Order, Am J of Philol, 90; Sardonic Smile, Nonverbal Behavior in Homeric Epic, Ann Arbor, 95; auth, "Abduction Marriage in Heliodorus' Aethiopica," GRBS (97). **CONTACT ADDRESS** Dept of Humanities-Classics, Ohio Wesleyan Univ, 61 S Sandusky St, Delaware, OH 43015-2398. **EMAIL** dglatein@cc.owu.edu

LATHROP, THOMAS A.
PERSONAL Born 04/18/1941, Los Angeles, CA, m, 1969, 1 child **DISCIPLINE** SPANISH **EDUCATION** Univ Calif, Los Angeles, AB, 64, MA, 65, PhD, 70. **CAREER** Instr, Univ Wyo, 66-68; asst prof, Mt St Mary's Col, 69-71; asst prof, Transylvania Univ, 73-76; asst prof, Lafayette Col, 76-80; asst to assoc prof, Univ Del, 80-. **HONORS AND AWARDS** Alliance for Progress grant, 68; Del Amo Found Grant, 72; Gulbenkian Found Grant, 73; Ed, Juan la Cuesta--Hispanic Monographs, 78-. **MEMBERSHIPS** MLA, Cervantes Soc of Am, Asn de Cervantistas, Soc Cervantina. **SELECTED PUBLICATIONS** Auth, The Evolution of Spanish--An Introductory Historical Grammar, 3rd ed, Newark, Del: Juan de la Cuesta (96); auth, "Mais sobre a origem portuguese da Cronica General de Espanha de 1344," in Ecos de ume viagem: En honra de Eduardo Mayone Dias, ed, Francisco Costa Fagundes, Providence: Gavea-Brown Pubs (99): 17-25; auth, "Había realmente siete Infantes de Lara," Hispanica Polonarum, 2 (99):17-25; ed and annotator, Don Quijote de la Mancha, Newark, Del: Juan de la Cuesta--Hispanic Monographs (99); auth, Don Quijote Dirionary, Newark: Del: Juan de la Cuesta--Hispanic Monographs (99); auth, "Contradictions in the Quijote Explained," in Jewish Culture and the Hispanic World, ed Mishael M. Caspi and Samuel Armistead, Newark, Del: Juan de la Cuesta (2000): 242-46; coauth with Frede Jensen, La Vie de Saint Eustace, Newark, Del: LinguaText, Ltd (2000). **CONTACT ADDRESS** Dept Foreign Lang, Univ of Delaware, 18 Amstel Ave Rm 325, Newark, DE 19716-2599. **EMAIL** lathrop@udel.edu

LATIMER, DAN RAYMOND
PERSONAL Born 07/15/1944, San Angelo, TX, m, 1970, 1 child **DISCIPLINE** COMPARATIVE LITERATURE, ENGLISH STUDIES **EDUCATION** Univ Tex, Austin, BA, 66; Univ Mich, Ann Arbor, MA, 67, PhD(comp lit), 72. **CAREER** Asst prof, 72-78, assoc prof Eng, Auburn Univ, 78-; Res and Writing, 82-, Asst Ed, Southern Humanities Rev. **MEMBERSHIPS** MLA; Am Comp Lit Asn; Southern Comp Lit Asn. **RESEARCH** Symbolism; modern criticism; Goethe. **SELECTED PUBLICATIONS** Auth, Contemporary Critical Theory, 89; auth, "Oedipus in the South Seas: The Case of Herman Melvilles Typee," Essays in Lit, 94; auth, "Piracopuios Missing Finger: Schiler, Batarille, and the Fate of English Studies," The Comparatist, 98. **CONTACT ADDRESS** Dept of English, Auburn Univ, University, AL 36849.

LATOUSEK, ROB
PERSONAL Born 07/10/1956, Evanston, IL **DISCIPLINE** CLASSICS **EDUCATION** Holy Cross Col, BA, 78; Loyola Univ, Chicago, MA, 85. **CAREER** Univ Wisconsin, Madison, proj asst, 86-88, Centaur Systems Ltd, Pres, 84-. **HONORS AND AWARDS** HCC, Bean Scholarship, 74-78, Loyola Univ., Condon Fel, 82-84 **MEMBERSHIPS** APA, ACL, CAMS **RESEARCH** Classical computing **SELECTED PUBLICATIONS** Auth, Software Directory for the Classics, ACL, 93-95, Random Access, Classical Outlook, ACL, 89-, Survey of latin Instructional Software for the Microcomputer, ACL, 85-91, software pub, Tutrix, 88; Latin Vocab Drill, 87; Latin Flash Drill, 85; Centaur Sys Ltd. **CONTACT ADDRESS** Centaur Systems Ltd, 407 North Brearly St, Madison, WI 53703-1603. **EMAIL** Latousek@centaursystems.com

LATTA, ALAN DENNIS
PERSONAL Born 06/28/1940, Wichita, KS, m, 1962, 1 child **DISCIPLINE** GERMAN LANGUAGE AND LITERATURE **EDUCATION** Univ Kans, AB, 62; Yale Univ, MA, 65, PhD(Ger), 69. **CAREER** From lectr to asst prof, 67-76, Assoc Prof Ger, Trinity Col, Univ Toronto, 76-. **MEMBERSHIPS** MLA; Can Asn Univ Teachers Ger. **RESEARCH** Thomas Mann; German literature since 1945; novel. **SELECTED PUBLICATIONS** Auth, The Mystery of Life: A Theme in Der Zauberberg, Monatshefte, 74. **CONTACT ADDRESS** Dept of Ger, Univ of Toronto, 50 St Joseph St, Toronto, ON, Canada M5S 1J4. **EMAIL** german@chass.utoronto.ca

LATTA, SUSAN M.
DISCIPLINE ENGLISH LITERATURE AND LINGUISTICS **EDUCATION** Ind State Univ, BA, MA; Purdue Univ, PhD. **CAREER** Dir, wrtg prog; asst prof, 96-. **RESEARCH** Participatory action research and computer assisted instruction. **SELECTED PUBLICATIONS** Pub(s), essays on mass media in the classroom, student self-assessment, and critical research methodologies. **CONTACT ADDRESS** Dept of Eng, Univ of Detroit Mercy, 4001 W McNichols Rd, PO BOX 19900, Detroit, MI 48219-0900. **EMAIL** LATTAS7@udmercy.edu

LATTIMORE, STEVEN
PERSONAL Born 05/25/1938, Bryn Mawr, PA **DISCIPLINE** CLASSICS, CLASSICAL ARCHEOLOGY **EDUCATION** Dartmouth Col, AB, 60; Princeton Univ, MA, 64, PhD(class archaeol), 68. **CAREER** Instr class archaeol, Dartmouth Col, 64; instr Greek, Haverford Col, 65-66; asst prof classics and class archaeol, Intercol Ctr Class Studies, Rome, 66-67; asst prof, 67-74, Assoc Prof Classics, Univ Calif, Los Angeles, 74-, Guggenheim Found fel, 75-76. **MEMBERSHIPS** Archaeol Inst Am; Am Philol Asn. **RESEARCH** Classical sculpture; Greek literature; mythology. **SELECTED PUBLICATIONS** Auth, The bronze apoxyomenos from Ephesos, Am J Archaeol, 72; Battus in Theocritus' fourth Idyll, Greek, Roman & Byzantine Studies, 73; A Greek pediment on a Roman temple, Am J Archaeol, 74; The Marine Thiasos in Greek Sculpture, Archaeol Inst Am, 76. **CONTACT ADDRESS** Dept of Classics, Univ of California, Los Angeles, Los Angeles, CA 90024.

LAUER, JANICE M.
PERSONAL Born Detroit, MI **DISCIPLINE** RHETORIC, LINGUISTICS **EDUCATION** Marygrove Col, BA, 54; St Louis Univ, MA, 61; Univ Mich, EdD(English rhetoric), 67. **CAREER** Prof English, Marygrove Col, 62-; Dir Writing Prof English, Univ Detroit, 72-, Bd dirs, Rhetoric Soc Am, 78-78; dir writing, Cranbrook Writers Conf, 76-. **MEMBERSHIPS** Rhetoric Soc Am; Conf Col Compos and Commun; NCTE. **RESEARCH** Heuristics; creative process; rhetoric. **SELECTED PUBLICATIONS CONTACT ADDRESS** Dept of English, Univ of Detroit Mercy, Detroit, MI 48221.

LAURENTI, JOSEPH L.
PERSONAL Born 12/10/1931, Hesperange, Luxembourg **DISCIPLINE** SPANISH, ITALIAN **EDUCATION** Univ Ill, AB, 58, MA, 59; Univ Mo, PhD(Span), 62. **CAREER** Instr Span, Univ Mo, 59-62; asst prof Span, Ital and Ger, 62-66, Prof Span and Ital, Ill State Univ, 66-, US corresp, Quad Ibero-Am; consult, PMLA. **MEMBERSHIPS** Am Asn Teachers Span and Port. **RESEARCH** Modern Italian literature; Spanish Golden Age. **SELECTED PUBLICATIONS CONTACT ADDRESS** Dept of Span, Illinois State Univ, Normal, IL 61761.

LAVALVA, ROSEMARIE
DISCIPLINE ITALIAN LANGUAGE AND LITERATURE **EDUCATION** Rutgers Univ, PhD. **CAREER** Prof/Dir grad studies. **RESEARCH** Romantic and late Romantic lit; the transition to "modernism": Pascoli, D'Annunzio, Pirandello, and Svevo; philosophical, anthropological, and psychoanalytical views of early 20th century thinkers in rel to the lit text. **SELECTED PUBLICATIONS** Auth, I Sacrifici Humani, 91. **CONTACT ADDRESS** SUNY, Binghamton, PO Box 6000, Binghamton, NY 13902-6000. **EMAIL** rlavalva@binghamton.edu

LAVERY, GERARD B.
PERSONAL Born 02/03/1933, Brooklyn, NY **DISCIPLINE** CLASSICAL LANGUAGES **EDUCATION** Fordham Univ, AB, 55, MA, 56, PhD(classics), 65. **CAREER** Asst prof, 61-72, Assoc Prof Class Lang, Col of the Holy Cross, 72-, Batchelor Ford fac fel, 69. **MEMBERSHIPS** Am Philol Asn; AAUP. **RESEARCH** Plutarch; Roman history and politics; Lucretius. **SELECTED PUBLICATIONS** Auth, Plutarch 'Lucullus' and the Living Bond of Biog, Class J, Vol 0089, 94; Never Seen in Public--Seneca and the Limits of Cosmopolitanism, Latomus, Vol 0056, 97. **CONTACT ADDRESS** Col of the Holy Cross, Box 89 A, Worcester, MA 01610.

LAWALL, GILBERT WESTCOTT
PERSONAL Born 09/22/1936, Detroit, MI, m, 1957, 2 children **DISCIPLINE** CLASSICS **EDUCATION** Oberlin Col, AB, 57; Yale Univ, PhD, 61. **CAREER** Instr classics, Yale Univ, 61-63 & 64-65, jr fel, Ctr Hellenic Studies, 63-64; asst prof classics, Amherst Col, 65-67; from asst prof to assoc prof, 67-72, Prof Classics, Univ MA, Amherst, 72-. **HONORS AND AWARDS** Barlow-Beach Awd Distinguished Serv, Class Asn New England, 79; Oustanding contrib For Lang Educ, Class Asn Empire State, 79. **MEMBERSHIPS** Am Philol Asn; Class Asn New Eng (vpres, 72-73, secy-treas, 80-87); Vergilian Soc; Archaeol Inst Am; Am Class League (pres, 76-80). **RESEARCH** Hellenistic Greek poetry; Senecan tragedy; Catullus; Horace; Latin pedagogy. **SELECTED PUBLICATIONS** Auth, Theocritus' Coan Pastorals: A Poetry Book, Ctr Hellenic Studies, 67; The Phaedra of Seneca: Latin Text and Study Materials, Bolchazy-Carducci Publ, 81; Petronius: Selections from the Satyricon: Introduction, Notes, and Vocabulary by Gilbert Lawall, Bolchazy-Carducci Pubs, 3rd rev ed, 95; Plautus' Menaechmi: ed with Introduction and Running Vocabularies by Gilbert Lawall and Betty Nye Quinn, Bolchazy-Carducci Pubs, Chicago, 81; Euripides Hippolytus: A Companion and Translation by Gilbert and Sarah Lawall, Bristol Classical Press, 86; ed and coauth, Cicero's Somnium Scipionis: The Dream of Scipio, Sally Davis and Gilbert Lawall, Prentice Hall, 88; The Aulularia of Plautus: The Pot of Gold, Gilbert Lawall and Betty Nye Quinn, Prentice Hall, 88; ed, The Romans Speak for Themselves: Books I and II, Prentice Hall, 89, rev ed, 95; coauth, Maurice Balme and Gilbert Lawall, Athenaze: An Introduction to Ancient Greek, Book I, NY: Oxford Univ Press, 90, Book II, NY: Oxford Univ Press, 91; coauth rev, Fabulae Graecae: A Revised Edition of Richie's Fabulae Faciles, ed by Gilbert Lawall, Stanley Iverson, and Allen Wooley, Prentice Hall, 91; coauth rev and ed with David Perry, Fabulae Romanae: Stories of Famous Romans, Prentice Hall, 93; chief rev ed, Ecce Romani: A Latin Reading Program, 3rd ed, Prentice Hall, 00; auth, Love and Betrayal: A Catullus Reader by Bruce Arnold, Andrew Aronson, and Gilbert Lawall, Prentice Hall, 00. **CONTACT AD-**

DRESS Dept of Classics, Univ of Massachusetts, Amherst, Amherst, MA 01003-3905. **EMAIL** glawall@classics.umass.edu

LAWALL, SARAH NESBIT
PERSONAL Born Wellesley, MA, m, 1957, 2 children **DISCIPLINE** COMPARATIVE LITERATURE, FRENCH **EDUCATION** Oberlin Col, AB, Phi Beta Kappa, 56; Yale Univ, PhD(comp lit), 61. **CAREER** From asst prof to assoc prof French, 66-74, actg chmn dept comp lit, 69, chmn dept, 74-78, prof Comp Lit, Univ Mass, Amherst, 74-, adj prof French, 78-, ed, modern period, Norton World Masterpieces, 77-, gen ed, Norton World Masterpieces, 98-. **HONORS AND AWARDS** Director, NEH Institute ("The Theory and Teaching of World Literature"): six-week summer session, 87; grant 9/1/86-6/30/88. **MEMBERSHIPS** Am Comp Lit Asn; Int Comp Lit Assoc, MLA; AAUP; Am Asn Teachers Fr; Int Soc Comp Study Civilizations. **RESEARCH** Theory and practice of world literature; the surrealist tradition; phenomenological literary theory. **SELECTED PUBLICATIONS** Auth, Critics of Consciousness: The Existential Structures of Literature, Harvard Univ, 68; Ponge and the Poetry of Self-Knowledge, Contemp Lit, 70; Poetry from Dada to Tel Quel, Wayne State Univ, 74; coauth, Decouverte de l'essai, Harcourt, 74; auth, A style of silence: Two Readings of Yves Bonnefoy's Poetry, Contemp Lit, 75; The Poem as Utopia, Fr Forum, 76; Poetry Taking Place, World Lit Today, 79; The Time and Space of Translation, Pac Quart, 80; Euripides' Hippolytus, Introduction, Translation and Commentary by Gilbert and Sarah Lawall, Bristol Classical Press, 86; Rene Wellek and Modern Literary Criticism, Comparative Lit, 40, 1, winter 88; Richard Moulton: Literature and Cultural Studies in 1911, Yearbook of Comparative and Gen Lit, 39, 90-91; Bonnefoy's Pierre ecrite: Progressive Ambiguity as The Many in the One, in The Ladder of High Designs: Structure and Interpretation of the French Lyric Sequence, ed by Doranne Fenoalta and David Lee Rubin, Univ Va Press, 91; Naguib Mahfouz and the Nobel Prize: A World of Expectations, in Naguib Mahfouz, ed by Michael Beard and Adnan Haydar, Syracuse Univ Press, 93; World Literature in Context, in Global Perspectives on Teaching Literature, ed by Sandra Lott, NCTE, 93; Preface and "Reading World Literature" in Reading World Literature: Theory, History, Practice: edited and with an introduction by Sarah Lawall, Austin:Univ Tx P, 94; Richard Moulton and World Literature from the English Point of View, in No Small World, New Quests, New Canons, New Directions in Theory and Pedagogy of World Literature, ed Michael Carroll, National Council of Teachers of English, 96; Introduction and Rene Wellek and Perspectivism in Rene Wellek, ed Sarah Lawall, Yearbook of Comp and Gen Lit, 44, 96; ed, Norton World Masterpieces:The Western Tradition, 7th ed, 2 vols, WW Norton (New York), 98. **CONTACT ADDRESS** Dept of Comp Lit, Univ of Massachusetts, Amherst, Amherst, MA 01003-1114. **EMAIL** lawall@complit.umass.edu

LAWLER, JAMES RONALD
PERSONAL Born 08/15/1929, Melbourne, Australia, m, 1954, 2 children **DISCIPLINE** FRENCH LITERATURE **EDUCATION** Univ Melbourne, BA, 50, MA, 52; Univ Paris, DUniv, 54. **CAREER** Lectr French, Univ Queensland, 55-56; sr lectr, Univ Melbourne, 57-62; prof and head dept, Univ Western Australia, 63-71; prof and chmn dept, Univ Calif, Los Angeles, 71-74; McCulloch prof, Dalhousie Univ, 74-79; Edward Carson Waller Distinguished Ser Prof Emer; Prof French, Univ Chicago, 79-, Brit Coun interchange scholar, 67; Australian Acad Humanities fel, 70-; Guggenheim Found fel, 74; ed, Dalhousie French Studies, 79; vis fel, Australian Nat Univ, 81. **HONORS AND AWARDS** Officier, Palmes Academiques, 70; NEH Sr Fel, 85. **MEMBERSHIPS** MLA; Am Asn Teachers Fr; Int Asn Fr Studies, 74-; pres, 99-. **RESEARCH** Modern French poetry; poetics; 20th century novel. **SELECTED PUBLICATIONS** Auth, Form and Meaning in Valery's Le Civetiere Marin, 59; auth, An Anthology of French Poetry, 61; auth, Lecture de Valery, 63; auth, The Language of French Symbolism, 69; auth, Poure Valery: Poems, 71; auth, The poet et Analyst, 74; auth, Paul Valery, An Anthology, 76; auth, Rene Char: The Myth and the Poem, 78; Edgar Poe et Les Poetes frrancais, 89; auth, Paul Valery, 91; Rimbaud's Theaatre of the Self, 92; auth, Poetry and Moral Dialectic: Baudelaire's Les Fleun du mal, 97. **CONTACT ADDRESS** Univ of Chicago, Chicago, IL 60637.

LAWRENCE, SAMUEL G.
DISCIPLINE INTERPERSONAL AND INTERCULTURAL COMMUNICATION **EDUCATION** PhD. **CAREER** Univ Albany - SUNY **SELECTED PUBLICATIONS** Auth, Normalizing stigmatized practices: Achieving co-membership by 'doing being ordinary, Res Lang & Soc Interaction, 96. **CONTACT ADDRESS** SUNY, Albany, 1400 Washington Ave, Albany, NY 12222.

LAWSON, RICHARD H.
PERSONAL Born 01/11/1919, San Francisco, CA, m, 1950 **DISCIPLINE** GERMAN **EDUCATION** Univ Ore, BA, 41; MA, 48; UCLA, PhD, 56. **CAREER** Instr, Wash State Univ, 53-57; asst prof to prof and dept chair, San Diego State Univ, 57-76; prof to prof emeritus, Univ NC, 76-. **HONORS AND AWARDS** Outstanding Prof Award, Calif State Univ, 72 **MEMBERSHIPS** MLA; S Atlantic MLA; Pac Ancient and Mod Lang Asn; Kafka Soc of Am; Soc for Germanic Philol. **RESEARCH** Old High German; Middle High German; Modern Austrian Literature; Comparative Literature. **SELECTED PUBLICATIONS** Auth, Understanding Elias Canetti; Univ SC Press, 91; auth, Brother Hermann's Life of the Countess Yolanda, Camden House, 95; ed, New Anthology of Contemporary Austrian Folk Plays, Ariadne, 96; co-ed, An Anthology of German Literature Waveland, 98; auth, Arthurian Romances, Tales, and Lyric Poetry: the complete Works of Hartmann von Aue, Pa State Univ Press, 01. **CONTACT ADDRESS** Dept Germanic Lang, Univ of No Carolina, Chapel Hill, 8816 Jackie Dr, San Diego, CA 92119-1418.

LAZAR, MOSHE
DISCIPLINE DRAMA AND COMPARATIVE LITERATURE **EDUCATION** Sorbonne, Paris, PhD. **CAREER** Prof, Univ Southern Calif; diplomado de Filologia Hispanica, Salamanca, Spain; res assoc, Ctr for Medieval and Renaissance Stud, UCLA. **RESEARCH** Spanish and Judeo-Spanish biblical and para-biblical texts. **SELECTED PUBLICATIONS** Auth, Provencal literature: Amour Courtois et Fin'Amors; Bernard de Ventadour; Lo Jutgamen General. **CONTACT ADDRESS** Col Letters, Arts & Sciences, Univ of So California, University Park Campus, Los Angeles, CA 90089. **EMAIL** lazar@.usc.edu

LAZARUS, JOYCE B.
PERSONAL Born 09/26/1946, New York, NY, m, 1978, 2 children **DISCIPLINE** FRENCH LANGUAGE & LITERATURE **EDUCATION** Queens Col, CUNY, BA, 67; Harvard Univ, MA, 68; PhD, 74. **CAREER** Prof, Framingham State Col, 72-. **HONORS AND AWARDS** Phi Beta Kappa; Pi Delta Phi. **MEMBERSHIPS** AATF; Mass Teachers Assoc. **RESEARCH** 20th Century French and Francophone literature. **SELECTED PUBLICATIONS** Auth, "Elie Wiesel's La Nuit and l'Oublie: In Pursuit of Silence", Essays in Fr Lit 28, (91); auth, Parole Aux Jeunes, Heinle & Heinle, 92; auth, "Expanding Time: The Art of Elie Wiesel in the Gates of the Forest", Mod Lang Studies, Fall 94; auth, "Gifts", Mind in Motion 37, 95; auth, "Still Waters", Inside, Summer 96; auth, "Yahrzeit", "Jerusalem: 30 July, 1997", Midstream 98; auth, Strangers and Sojourners: Jewish Identity in Contemporary Francophone Fiction, Peter Lang Pub, 99. **CONTACT ADDRESS** Dept Mod Lang, Framingham State Col, 100 State St, Framingham, MA 01702-2460. **EMAIL** joycelazarus@hotmail.com

LE HIR, MARIE-PIERRE
DISCIPLINE FRENCH AND COMPARATIVE LITERATURE **EDUCATION** Freie Universitat, MA, 79; Univ Iowa, PhD, 86. **CAREER** Mod langs, Case Western Reserve Univ; Fr Ital, Univ of Ariz. **HONORS AND AWARDS** Dir, French Studies Prog. **RESEARCH** Linguistics **SELECTED PUBLICATIONS** Auth, book Le Romantisme aux Encheres: Ducange, Pixere court, Hugo Benjamins, 92; Bridging National Fields: XIXth-Century Scholarship in French and American Perspectives. Nineteenth-Century French Studies 24, 95-96, Defining French Cultural Studies, Jour Midwest Mod Lang Asn, 96; The Societe des Gens de Lettres and French Socialism: Association as Resistance to the Industrialization and Censorship of the Press. Nineteenth-Century French Studies 24, 96; Imagining the discipline: beyond Frenchness and Francophilia, Contemporary French Civilization 21, 97; French Cultural Studies in the United States: a Case Study in French Cultural Studies, Jour Contemporary French Studies, 97. **CONTACT ADDRESS** Dept of Mod Langs, Univ of Arizona, PO Box 210067, Rm 549, Tucson, AZ 85721-0067. **EMAIL** mlehir@u.arizona.edu

LE MOINE, ROGER
PERSONAL Born 11/06/1933, La Malbaie, PQ, Canada **DISCIPLINE** LETTRES FRANCAISES **EDUCATION** Univ Ottawa, BA, 57; Univ Laval, MA, 72, DES, 64, DL, 70. **CAREER** Prof Titulaire, Lettres Francaises, Univ Ottawa. **HONORS AND AWARDS** Prix Champlain, 68; mem, Soc royale Can, 93. **MEMBERSHIPS** Soc des Dix. **SELECTED PUBLICATIONS** Auth, Un Quebecois bien tranquille, Quebec, La Liberte, (85): 187; auth, La Fran-Maconneri sous lel regime francais, Etat de la question, les Cahiers des Dix, vol. 444, (89): 115-134; auth, Charles Guerin et engagement politique de Chauveau, les Cahiers des Dix, vol. 45, (90): 141-167; auth, Deux loges montelaises du Grand Orient de France, Ottawa, P. U.O, (91): 189; auth, L'Epopee abandonnee de Felix-Antoine Savard, dans Melanges de litterature canadienne-francaise et quebecoise offerts a Rejean Robidoux, Ottawa, P.U.O, (92): 134-151; auth, "Le Quartrieme fauteuil, (Edouard-Zotique massicotte et Raymond Douville)," Cahiers des Dix, vo. 51, (96): 77-109; auth, "L'Aereique des ecrivains francais de la Renaissance, Actes du colloque Impressions de la Renaissance, Bibliotheque nationale du Canada, dans Impresions de la Renaissance, Histoire, Lettres, Arts, Sciences, Ottawa Lycee Claudel, (97): 21-31. **CONTACT ADDRESS** Dep lettres francaises, Univ of Ottawa, CP 450, Succ A, Ottawa, ON, Canada K1N 6N5.

LEA, HENRY A.
PERSONAL Born 05/08/1920, Berlin, Germany, m **DISCIPLINE** GERMAN LANGUAGE & LITERATURE **EDUCATION** Univ Pa, BSEd, 42; MA, 51; PhD, 62. **CAREER** Univ Mass Amherst, instr to prof emeritus, 52-. **MEMBERSHIPS** MLA, AATG, Soc for Exile Studies, Int Gustav Mahler Soc. **RESEARCH** Franz Werfel, Gustav Mahler, expressionism, Wolfgang Hildesheimer, exile literature. **SELECTED PUBLICATIONS** Auth, "Prodigal Sons in Werfel's Fiction," Ger Rev 40, (65): 41-54; auth, "The Failure of Political Activism in Werfel's Plays," Symposium 22 (68): 319-334; auth, "Expressionist Literature and Music," Expressionism as an International Literary Phenomenon, ed Ulrich Weisstein, (Paris: Didier, Budapest: Akademiai Kiado, 73): 141-160; auth, Gustav Mahler: Man on the Margin, Bouvier (Bonn), 85; auth, "Mahler's Extraterritoriality," Mass Rev 31.3 (90): 341-354; auth, Wolfgang Hildesheimers Weg als Jude und Deutscher, Verlag Hans-Dieter Heinz, (Stuttgart), 97. **CONTACT ADDRESS** 103 Fairway Vlg, Leeds, MA 01053-9720.

LEACH, ELEANOR W.
DISCIPLINE CLASSICAL STUDIES **EDUCATION** Bryn Mawr Col, BA, 59; Yale Univ, PhD, 63. **CAREER** Prof, Ind Univ, Bloomington. **RESEARCH** Latin texts. **SELECTED PUBLICATIONS** Auth, Absence and Desire in Cicero's De Amicitia, CW, 93; Oecus on Ibycus: Investigating the Vocabulary of the Roman House, Oxbow, 97; auth, "Personal and Communal Time in the Reading of Horace's 'Odes,' Books 1-3," Arethusa (98). **CONTACT ADDRESS** Dept of Classical Studies, Indiana Univ, Bloomington, 1020 E Kirkwood Ave, 547 Ballantine Hall, Bloomington, IN 47405. **EMAIL** leach@indiana.edu

LEAHY, DAVID G.
DISCIPLINE CLASSICS **EDUCATION** St. Peter's Col, BA, 59; Fordham Univ, MA, 64. **CAREER** Lectr, Iona Col, 63-64; Assoc Prof, NY Univ, 64-72; Assoc Prof, C.W. Post Col LIU, 72-76; Mgt Consult, 76-89; Adj Assoc Prof, Brooklyn Col CUNY, 85-92; Vis Assoc Prof & Dir Undergrad Relig Studies, NY Univ, 91-98; Distinguished Vis Prof Philos, Loyola Col Md, 98-; Vis Assoc Prof, SUNY - Stony Brook, 95. **HONORS AND AWARDS** Scholarship to St. Peter's Col; Nat Oratorical Contest Col & Univ Scholarships; Scholarship to Fordham Univ; NYU Lindback Found Awd for Distinguished Teaching; **MEMBERSHIPS** Am Philos Asn; Soc Advancement Am Philos; Am Acad Relig. **SELECTED PUBLICATIONS** Auth, To Create The Absolute Edge, J Am Acad Relig, 89; The New Beginning: Beyond the Post-Modern Nothingness, J Am Acad Relig, 94; Novitas Mundi: Perception of the History of Being, SUNY Press, repr, 94; Foundation: Matter The Body Itself, SUNY Press, 96; The Golden Bowl Structure, Geodesic Math Links, Geodesic Designs, Inc, 96-98 (http://www.geod.com/main/geomath.htm) **CONTACT ADDRESS** 104 Yorkleigh Rd., Towson, MD 21204. **EMAIL** dgl@dgleahy.com

LEAL, LUIS
PERSONAL Born 09/17/1907, Linares, Mexico, m, 1936, 2 children **DISCIPLINE** SPANISH **EDUCATION** Northwestern Univ, BA, 40; Univ Chicago, AM, 41, PhD, 50. **CAREER** Instr Span, Univ Chicago, 42-43, 46-48, asst prof, 48-52; assoc prof mod lang, Univ Miss, 52-56; assoc prof, Emory Univ, 56-59; assoc prof, 59-62, prof, 62-76, Emer Prof Span, Univ Ill, Urbana, 76-, Vis prof, Univ Ariz, 55-56, Univ Calif, Santa Barbara, 76-77 and Univ Calif, Los Angeles, 77-78; Actg Dir, Ctr for Chicano Studies, Univ Calif, Santa Barbara, 80-. **MEMBERSHIPS** Am Asn Teachers Span and Port; MLA. **RESEARCH** Spanish American literature, especially the short story; Mexican literature; Chicano literature. **SELECTED PUBLICATIONS** Auth, Historia del Cuento Hispanoamericano, Studium, 66; Panorama de la Literatura Mexicana Actual, Pan Am Union, 68; Mariano Azuela, Twayne, 71; Breve Historia de la Literatura Hispanoamericana, Knopf, 71; ed, Cuentistas Hispanoamericanos del Siglo XX, Random, 72; Mariano Azuela: Paginas Escogidas, 73 & Cuentos de la Revolucion, 77, Nat Univ Mex, 77; coauth, A decade of Chicano literature, 1970-1979, La Causa, 82. **CONTACT ADDRESS** Univ of California, Santa Barbara, Santa Barbara, CA 93106.

LEBANO, EDOARDO A.
DISCIPLINE ITALIAN LITERATURE **EDUCATION** Cath Univ Am, PhD, 66. **CAREER** Prof. **RESEARCH** Renaissance epic; nineteenth century narrative; advanced language and Italian American studies. **SELECTED PUBLICATIONS** Auth, pubs on teaching of Italian in United States. **CONTACT ADDRESS** Dept of French and Italian, Indiana Univ, Bloomington, 1020 E Kirkwood Ave, Ballantine Hall 642, Bloomington, IN 47405. **EMAIL** lebano@indiana.edu

LEBLANC, W. JAMES
PERSONAL Born 11/01/1928, Abbeville, LA, m, 1961, 3 children **DISCIPLINE** LINGUISTICS **EDUCATION** Univ Southwestern La, BA, 52; State Univ IA, MA, 54. **CAREER** From instr to assoc prof Span, Loras Col, 54-67, chmn dept mod for lang, 64-67; jr instr Span, Univ VA, 68-70; asst prof, Madison Col VA, 70-71; instr, Univ VA, 71-72; asst prof French & Eng, 72-75, Assoc Prof Eng, For Lang and Speech, Paul D Camp Community Col, 75. **MEMBERSHIPS** Am Asn Tchr(s) Span & Port; Am Asn Tchrs Fr. **RESEARCH** Hist of the Span lang; Golden Age, Span Am and contemp Span drama. **CONTACT ADDRESS** Bus/Soc Sci and Humanities, Paul D. Camp Comm Col, PO Box 737, Franklin, VA 23851-0737. **EMAIL** jleblanc@pc.cc.va.us

LEBOFSKY, DENNIS STANLEY
PERSONAL Born 10/28/1940, Philadelphia, PA, m, 1965, 5 children **DISCIPLINE** LINGUISTICS; ENGLISH **EDUCATION** Temple Univ, BA, 61; Princeton Univ, MA, 65, PhD(l-ing), 70. **CAREER** From Instr to Asst Prof, 65-84, Assoc Prof English, Temple Univ, 84-. **RESEARCH** Philadelphia English. **CONTACT ADDRESS** Dept of English, Temple Univ, 1114 W Berks St, Philadelphia, PA 19122-6029. **EMAIL** dlebofsk@nimbus.temple.edu

LEDERER, HERBERT
PERSONAL Born 06/09/1921, Vienna, Austria, m, 1948, 2 children **DISCIPLINE** GERMAN **EDUCATION** Brooklyn Col, BA, 48; Univ Chicago, MA, 49, PhD(Ger), 53. **CAREER** Instr Ger, Univ Chicago, 49-52; asst prof, Wabash Col, 52-53 assoc prof and chmn dept, 53-57; assoc prof, Ohio Univ, 57-61 and Queens Col NY, 61-69; head, Dept Ger and Slavic Lang, 69-79, Prof Ger, Univ Conn, 69-, Mem staff, Ger Summer Sch, Middlebury Col, 53-69; chief reader Ger Advan Placement, Educ Testing Serv, 64-67; chmn Ger comt, Col Entrance Exam Bd, 67-; Leo Baeck Soc Am Coun Learned Soc res grant, 68-69; vpres, Nat Fed Mod Lang Teachers Asn, 71, pres, 72; pres, Am Coun Study Austrian Lit, 72-80, Asn Depts Foreign Lang, 78. **HONORS AND AWARDS** Austrian Cross of Honor for Arts and Letters, First Class, 76. **MEMBERSHIPS** Am Asn Teachers Ger; MLA; Int Arthur Schnitzler Res Asn; AAUP; Am Coun Studies Austrian Lit. **RESEARCH** Modern German literature, especially Schnitzler and the young Vienna school; contemporary theater; linguistics and teaching methodology. **SELECTED PUBLICATIONS** Auth, Nestroy, Johann 1801-1862--World Vision and Dramatic Writings, Colloquia Germanica, Vol 0025, 92; Schnitzler, Arthur and Beerhofmann, Richard--Correspondence, 1891-1931, J Engl and Ger Philol, Vol 0094, 95. **CONTACT ADDRESS** Dept of Ger and Slavic Lang, Univ of Connecticut, Storrs, Storrs, CT 06268.

LEDFORD-MILLER, LINDA
DISCIPLINE LITERATURE OF THE AMERICAS (EXCLUDING CANADA) **EDUCATION** Univ CA, Irvine, BA, 78; Univ TX at Austin, MA, 83, PhD, 88; PA State Univ, MA, 86. **CAREER** Dept For Lang & Lit, Univ Scranton **HONORS AND AWARDS** Fulbright lectureship,San Carlos Univ, Guatemala City, 90; Fulbright-Hayes fel, Brazil, 79-80. **MEMBERSHIPS** Am Asn of Tchrs Span and Port; Latin Am Stud Asn; Brazilian Stud Asn; Northeast Asn Luso-Brazilianists; AAUP; Soc for Am Travel Writing. **RESEARCH** Travel Narratives, esp. Guatemala; biblical influences in Robert Coover and Dalton Trevisan **SELECTED PUBLICATIONS** Auth, Shoes for Little Peter: Narrative Technique in Trevisan's Not at All Exemplary Novella, Pedrinho, Brasil/Brazil, 4, 90; transl, Benedito Nunes, Narrativo .. muitas vozes, translated as, Narration in Many Voices, Rev Contemp Lit XV.3, 95; auth, Voice to the Visited: Indigenous Presence in the Guatemala Travel Writings of the Abbot Brasseur de Bourboug and Alfred Valois, Monografica: Hispanic Travel Lit, XII, 96; If the River Was Whiskey by T. Coraghessan Boyle, 1500 word ref essay for Masterplots II, Short Story, Suppl, Pasadena, Salem Press, 96; "Ephraim George Squier," essay, Dict of Lit Biog, Am Travel Writers 1865-1915, (Gale Research, 98), 274-282; "Harriet Doerr," essay, Critical Survey of Long Fiction: Second Rev Ed, (Pasadena, CA: Salem Press, 00), 898-902; "Stones for Ibarra: essay, Masterplosts II: Am Fiction, Rev, (Pasadena, CA: Salem Press, 00), 2397-2400; "Barren Lives," essay, Masterplots II: Am fiction, rev, (Pasadena, CA:Salem Press, 00), 175-178; "Las vieajeras a Guatemala: algunas impresiones de viaje," actas del IV Congreso Internacional de Camineria Hispanica, vol II, Madrid, (Spain: AACHE Ed, 00) 895-900; "Juan Rulfo," essay, Critical Survey of Short Fiction, Second Rev ed, (Pasadena, CA: salem Press, 01), 2064-2068. **CONTACT ADDRESS** Dept of For Lang(s) and Lit(s), Univ of Scranton, Scranton, PA 18510. **EMAIL** LedfordLl@uofs.edu

LEE, CECILIA CASTRO
DISCIPLINE SPANISH LITERATURE **EDUCATION** Emory Univ, PhD. **SELECTED PUBLICATIONS** Auth, pubs on Spanish and Latin-American writers; ed, The Literature of Democratic Spain: 1975-1992; co-ed, On Men and Monsters. **CONTACT ADDRESS** Dept Foreign Languages and Literature, State Univ of West Georgia, Carrollton, GA 30118.

LEE, CHARLES NICHOLAS
PERSONAL Born 07/27/1933, Washington, DC, m, 1956, 4 children **DISCIPLINE** RUSSIAN LITERATURE **EDUCATION** Univ Md, BA, 55, MA, 58; Harvard Univ, PhD Russ, 64. **CAREER** Instr French, Ger & Russ, Univ Md, 56-60; asst prof Ger & Russ, Bucknell Univ, 63-65; from asst prof to assoc prof, 65-74, chmn, Dept Slavic Lang & Lit, 67-69, prof Russ, Univ Colo, Boulder, 74-, chmn, Dept Slavic Lang & Lit, 80-, NDEA summer fel, 65; Am Coun Learned Soc humanities fel, 75-76; prof, emer, Russ, 98. **MEMBERSHIPS** Am Asn Advan Slavic Studies; Am Asn Teachers Slavic & E Europ Lang. **RESEARCH** Russian prose of the 20th century emigration; Tolstoy in Russian & Western literature; A I Solzhenitsyn. **SELECTED PUBLICATIONS** Auth, The philosophical tales of M A Aldanov, Slavic & East Europ J, 71; Mark Aleksandrovic Aldanov: Zizn'i tvorcestvo, Russkaja lit v emigracii, 72; Dreams and daydreams in the early fiction of L N Tolstoy, Am Contrib Seventh Int Congr Slavists, 73; The short stories of M A Aldanov, In: Mnemozina; studia litteraríca in honorem Vsevolod Setchkarev, 74; Man and the land in the fiction of Solzhenitsyn, Rocky Mountain Soc Sci J, 74; Mark Aldanov, In: Mod Encycl Russ & Soviet Lit, 77; Ecological ethics in the fiction of L N Tolstoj, Am Contrib Eighth Int Congr Slavists, 78; Mark Aldanov: Russian, Jewry and the World, Midstream, 81; Darwin, Degeneracy, & Regeneration in Cexov's Fiction, in Russian Language J, 97; M A Aldanov, in Reference Guide to Russian Literature, 98. **CONTACT ADDRESS** Dept of Germanic & Slavic Lang & Lit., Univ of Colorado, Boulder, Box 276, Boulder, CO 80309-0276. **EMAIL** leecn@prodigy.net

LEE, HUGH MING
PERSONAL Born 02/10/1945, Honolulu, HI **DISCIPLINE** CLASSICS **EDUCATION** St Mary's Col, Calif, BA, 66; Stanford Univ, MA, 71, PhD(classics), 72. **CAREER** Instr classics, Ind Univ, Bloomington, 71-72, asst prof, 72-78; asst prof, Miami Univ, Ohio, 78-79; Asst Prof Classics, Univ MD, College Park, 79-, Nat Endowment for Humanities fel, 79-80. **HONORS AND AWARDS** Year-long res fel from the Fulbright Found (Rome); NEH; Am Coun of Learned Societies (Cologne). **MEMBERSHIPS** Am Philol Asn; Archaeol Inst Am; Vergilian Soc; Classical Asn Atlantic States. **RESEARCH** Greek and Roman athletics. **SELECTED PUBLICATIONS** Auth, "Running and the Stadium," Archaeology, (96): 35; auth, "Yet Another Scoring System for the Ancient Pentathlon," Nikephoros 8, (96): 41-55; auth, "The Later Greek Boxing Glove and the Roman Caestus: A Centennial Reevaluation of Juthner's Uber antike Turngerathe, Nikephoros 10, (forthcoming). **CONTACT ADDRESS** Dept of Classics, Univ of Maryland, Col Park, Marie Mount Hall, Rm 2407, College Park, MD 20742-7532. **EMAIL** hlee@deans.umd.edu

LEE, JOSEPH PATRICK
PERSONAL Born 11/30/1942, Leitchfield, KY, m, 1972 **DISCIPLINE** FRENCH LANGUAGE & LITERATURE **EDUCATION** Brescia Col, BA, 63; Fordham Univ, PhD, 71. **CAREER** Asst prof French, Brescia Col, 67-71 & Univ Ga, 71-78; acad dean & assoc prof French, Belmont Abbey Col, 78-81; Provost & Sr VPres Acad Affairs & Prof French, Barry Univ, 81-; Am Philos Soc res grant, 74. **HONORS AND AWARDS** Woodrow Wilson Fellow, 63-64; Danforth Fellow, 63-67; Fulbright Fellow, 66-67. **MEMBERSHIPS** MLA; Am Asn Teachers Fr; Am Soc 18tb Century Studies; Soc Fr Etude XVIIIe Siecle; S Atlantic Mod Lang Asn. **RESEARCH** Eighteenth century French literature; Voltaire; Anglo-French literary relations. **SELECTED PUBLICATIONS** Contrib, The Complete Works of Voltaire, Voltaire Found, 68; Dictionnaire des journalistes de langue francaise (1600-1789), Univ Grenoble, 76; auth, Voltaire and Cesar de Missy, Studies Voltaire & 18th Century, 76; Le Sermon philosophique: A Voltairean creation, Studies Lang & Lit, Eastern Ky Univ, 76; Voltaire and Massillon: Affinities of the heart, Fr Rev, 77; The Textual History of Voltaire's Sermon des cinquante, Studies on Voltaire & 18th Century, 92; contrib, Dictionaire de Voltaire, 94; Voltaire et ses combats, 97; La Philosophie clandestine a l'age classique, 97; auth, The Genesis and Publication of Voltaire's Sermon du rabbin Akib, Studies in Voltaire & 18th Century, 97. **CONTACT ADDRESS** Sr VPres for Acad Affairs, Barry Univ, 11300 NE 2nd Ave, Miami, FL 33161-6695. **EMAIL** jplee@mail.barry.edu

LEE, M. OWEN
PERSONAL Born 05/28/1930, Detroit, MI **DISCIPLINE** CLASSICS **EDUCATION** Univ Toronto, BA, 53, MA, 57; St Michael's Col, Univ Toronto, STB, 57; Univ BC, PhD, 60. **CAREER** From lectr to asst prof classics, St Michael's Col, Univ Toronto, 60-68; from assoc prof to prof, Univ St Thomas, Tex, 68-72; assoc prof, Loyola Univ Chicago, 72-75; assoc prof, 75-79, Prof Classics, Univ Toronto, 79-. **MEMBERSHIPS** Am Philol Asn. **RESEARCH** Myth of Orpheus; Roman poets; Wagner. **SELECTED PUBLICATIONS** Auth, Correspondence + Amara, Lucine, Opera Quart, Vol 0009, 92; Die 'Aeneis' as the Subject of Opera--Dramaturgical Changes From the Early Baroque to Berlioz, Phoenix-J Class Assoc of Can, Vol 0046, 92; Correspondence + Burroughs, Bruce, Opera Quart, Vol 0009, 93; Wagner 'Schwarzschwanenreich' + Johanning, Raffeiner, Quandt, Bach--Marco Polo 8 223777 8, Opera Quart, Vol 0012, 96; Correspondence + Farkas Rev of Lee 'First Intermissions'--Comment, Opera Quart, Vol 0012, 96; Wagner die 'Meistersinger Von Nurnberg' + Wiener, Thomas, Watson, Keilberth-Eurodisc 69008 2 Rg, Opera Quart, Vol 0012, 96; Wagner 'Tristan Und Isolde' + Jerusalem, Meier, Barenboim--Teldec 94568 2, Opera Quart, Vol 0013, 96; Wagner die 'Meistersinger Von Nurnberg' + Schoffler, Seider, Seefried, Bohm Preiser 90234, Opera Quart, Vol 0012, 96. **CONTACT ADDRESS** St. Michael's Col, 81 St Mary St, Toronto, ON, Canada M5S 1A1.

LEE, SONIA M.
PERSONAL Born 01/25/1938, Paris, France, m, 1958, 3 children **DISCIPLINE** FRENCH LITERATURE **EDUCATION** Univ Wis, BS, 64, MA, 66; Univ Mass, PhD(French lit), 74. **CAREER** Instr French, Univ Mass, 67-72; instr French, Univ PR, 72-73; asst prof to prof, Trinity College, 73-; coordr of African Concentration and African Minor, Trinity Col, 92-. **HONORS AND AWARDS** Summer Melon Grant to work on Women Writers of Francophone Can, 78; Summer Melon Grant to work on a new course on African Lit, 84; Summer Women's Studies Grant, Ford Foundation, to prepare a new course in French and Women's studies: French Women Writers and Women Writers in French, 87; NEH Summer Fellowship to study Modern Critical Theory in French Narrative with Prof Rigolot, Princeton Univ, 88. **MEMBERSHIPS** Am Asn Teachers Fr; Soc Study Multi-Ethnic Lit US; Secy of the Francophone African Lit Sect, NEMLA Conv, 75, 81; Elected Pres of the Francophone African Lit Sect, NEMLA Conv, 76; Chercheur Assoc- Centre d'Etudes Afro-Americaines and Tiers Monde Anglophone, 87; Advisor to the Institut National de Recherche Pedagogque for the French Ministry of Educ, 87; Elected Pres of Francophone Lit Sect, Mid-hudson MLA Conf, 88; Coop Prof in Hall High School: Project on the French Revolution, 88-89; co-chair of two panels: Les Nouvelles critures Africaines, ALA meeting, NY, 90; Conseil International d'Etudes Francophones CIEF-elected member of lte Council. **RESEARCH** Women writers of French speaking world. **SELECTED PUBLICATIONS** Auth, The Awakening of the Self in the Heroines of Sembene Ousmane, Critique, 12/75; The Image of the Woman in the African Folk-tale from the Sub-Saharan Francophone Area, Yale Fr Studies, 76; Franco-American Literature of New England: Two Significant Writers, Multi-Ethnic Lit US, 78; A selective bibliography of three prominent African authors, In: Critical Bibliography of French Literature of the 20th Century, Syracuse Univ, 79; A Critical Essay on Camara Laye, Twayne; Camara Laye, Chantre Malink, in: Hommage Camara Laye, Arts et Lettres, Magazine culturel du Soleil, 82; Camara Laye, Twayne's Series, G.K. Hall Publ, 83; Le Theme du bonheur chez les romancieres de l'Afrique occidentale, Presence Francophone, Univ Sherbrooke, no 29, 87; Changes in the Mother Image in West African fiction, Neohelicon, June 88; Entretiens avec Aminata Sow Fall, ALA Bull, Fall 88; Conversations with Miriam Tlali, ALA Bull, Summer 91; auth, Les Romancieres du continent noir, Hatier, 94; Daughters of Hagar: Daughters of Muhammad, The Marabout and the Muse (ed. Kenneth Harrow), Heinemann, 96; African Women Writers, and The Francophone Novels in West Africa, Encyclopedia of Sub-Saharan Africa (ed. John Middleton), Charles Scribner's Sons, Summer 97; auth, From Colonialism to Immigration: The French School in Francophone African fiction-in RACE and Racism in Theory and Practice edited by Berel Lang, Rowmans Littlefield Publishers, 99. **CONTACT ADDRESS** Trinity Col, Connecticut, 300 Summit St, Box 1355, Hartford, CT 06106-3186. **EMAIL** sonia.lee@trincoll.edu

LEEB, CAROLYN
PERSONAL m, 6 children **DISCIPLINE** HEBREW SCRIPTURES **EDUCATION** Mass Inst Tech, BS; San Francisco Theol Sem, MDiv, 93; Lutheran Sch Theol, ThM, 96; PhD, 98. **CAREER** Adj asst prof, McCormick Theol Sem, Lutheran Sch Theol, 98-99; vis asst prof, Valparaiso Univ, 99-. **MEMBERSHIPS** SBL. **RESEARCH** Social world of ancient Israel. **SELECTED PUBLICATIONS** Auth, Away From the Father's House: The Social Location of the Na'ar and Na'arah in Ancient Israel, Sheffield Acad (Sheffield), 00. **CONTACT ADDRESS** Dept Theology, Valparaiso Univ, 651 College Ave, Valparaiso, IN 46383-6461.

LEEBER, VICTOR F.
PERSONAL Born 02/18/1922, Elkins, WV **DISCIPLINE** SPANISH LANGUAGE & LITERATURE **EDUCATION** Boston Col, AB, 46, MA, 47; Weston Col, STL, 54; Univ Madrid, PhD(Span), 57. **CAREER** From instr to assoc prof, 47-66, Prof Mod Lang, Fairfield Univ, 66-, Chmn Dept, 57- **MEMBERSHIPS** MLA; Am Asn Cols Teacher Educ; Am Asn Teachers Span & Port. **RESEARCH** Golden Age Spanish literature; neoclassical Mexican literature; Romance philology. **SELECTED PUBLICATIONS** Auth, Perfiles Literarios, Holt, 63; El P Abad y su obra Poetica, Porrua, Spain, 65. **CONTACT ADDRESS** Dept of Mod Lang, Fairfield Univ, 1073 N Benson Rd, Fairfield, CT 06430-5195.

LEER, NORMAN ROBERT
PERSONAL Born 02/25/1937, Chicago, IL **DISCIPLINE** ENGLISH, COMPARATIVE LITERATURE **EDUCATION** Grinnell Col, AB, 58; Ind Univ, MA, 60, PhD(English), 64. **CAREER** Instr English, State Univ NY Stony Brook, 63-65; asst prof, Beloit Col, 65-67; assoc prof Roosevelt Univ, 67-72, assoc prof, 72-78, prof English, 78-, mem bd, Urban Life Ctr, 72-; coordr, Educ Network, Asn Humanistic Psychol, 72-74 & Midwest Regional Newslett, 78-; Fulbright lectr English, Odense Univ, Denmark, 74-75; lectr, Center for Older Adults, Fourth Presbyterian Church of Chicago, 96-. **HONORS AND AWARDS** Phi Beta Kappa, Grinnell College, 58; Poetry Prize, All Nations Poetry Contest, Triton Col, 76, 77, 78, 79 & 81; Burlington Northern Awd, Roosevelt Univ (for teaching and scholarship), 86; Illinois Significant Poet's Awd, 90; Samuel Ortrowski Awd, Roosevelt Univ (for best creative work), 98. **RESEARCH** Modern literature in the light of existential philosophy and humanistic psychology; writing poetry; application of some of the techniques of humanistic psychology to college teaching. **SELECTED PUBLICATIONS** Auth, Escape and Confrontation in the Stories of Philip Roth, Christian Scholar, summer 66; The Limited Hero in the Novels of Ford Madox Ford, Mich State Univ, 67; The Double Theme in Malamud's

Assistant: Dostoevsky with Irony, Mosaic, spring 71; Innovation and power struggles: An Experiential Deadlock, J Humanistic Psychol, winter 73; To Doris Lessing: Inside the Apocalypse, Oyez Rev, spring 75; Riding Commas to the Moon: Teaching Maleness and Imagination, New Directions in Teaching, winter 78; Slightly Crumpled Survival Flower (poems), Spoon River Poetry Press, 85; I Dream My Father in a Stone (poems), Mellen Poetry Press, 91; Second Lining (poems), Mellen Poetry Press, 97; Over 100 individual poems in Spoon River Quart, Willow Review, Rhino, Oyez Review, The Wolf Head Quart, Poetry Digest, and American Poets and Poetry. **CONTACT ADDRESS** Dept of English, Roosevelt Univ, 430 S Michigan Ave, Chicago, IL 60605-1394.

LEFFEL, KATHERINE
DISCIPLINE ENGLISH LINGUISTICS AND SYNTACTIC THEORY **EDUCATION** Univ FL, PhD, 88. **CAREER** Dept Eng, Univ Ala **HONORS AND AWARDS** Dir, eng dept ling prog. **SELECTED PUBLICATIONS** Auth, Views on Phrase Structure, Kluwer Academic Press. **CONTACT ADDRESS** Univ of Alabama, Birmingham, 1400 University Blvd, Birmingham, AL 35294-1150.

LEFKOWITZ, MARY ROSENTHAL
PERSONAL Born 04/30/1935, New York, NY, m, 1982, 2 children **DISCIPLINE** CLASSICS **EDUCATION** Wellesley Col, BA, 57; Radcliffe Col, MA, 59, PhD, 61. **CAREER** Instr Greek, 59-63, from asst prof to assoc prof Greek & Latin, 63-75, chemn dept, 70-72, 75-78, 81-87, 91-94, & 96-, prof Greek & Latin, Wellesley Col, 75-; Andrew W Mellon prof humanities, 79-; fel, Radcliffe Inst, 66-67, 72-73, Am Coun Learned Soc fel, 72-73; mem managing comt, Am Sch Class Studies, Athens, 71-; vis prof, Univ Calif, Berkeley, 78; vis fel, St Hilda's Col, Oxford, 79-80; dir Nat Endowment Summer Seminar, 84-85; Nat Endowment for Humanities fel, 79-80, 91. **HONORS AND AWARDS** Honorary Fel, St. Hilda's Col, 94-; LHD, Trinity College, 96; Honorary Ph.D., Univ of Patras, 99; L.H.D., Grinnell Col, 00. **MEMBERSHIPS** Am Philol Asn; Archaeol Inst Am. **RESEARCH** Greek poetry; classical mythology; ancient biography. **SELECTED PUBLICATIONS** Auth, The Victory Ode, Noyes, 76; Heroines and Hysterics, St Martin's, 81; The Lives of the Greek Poets, 81; co-ed, Women's Life in Greece and Rome, Johns Hopkins, 82, 2nd ed, 92; auth, Women in Greek Myth, John's Hopkins, 86; First-Person Fictions, Oxford, 91; Not Out of Africa, Basic Books, 96; co-ed Black Athena Revisited, North Carolina, 96. **CONTACT ADDRESS** Dept of Classical Studies, Wellesley Col, 106 Central St, Wellesley, MA 02481-8252. **EMAIL** mlefkowitz@wellesley.edu

LEHISTE, ILSE
PERSONAL Born 01/31/1922, Tallinn, Estonia **DISCIPLINE** LINGUISTICS **EDUCATION** Univ Hamburg, PhD, 48; Univ Mich, PhD(ling), 59. **CAREER** Mem fac, Univ Hamburg, 48-49; assoc prof Ger philol, Kans Wesleyan Univ, 50-51; assoc prof mod lang, Detroit Inst Technol, 51-56; res assoc acoustic phonetics, Commun Sci Lab, Univ Mich, 57-63; assoc prof ling and Slavic lang and lit, 63-65, chmn, dept of ling, 65-71, Prof Ling, Ohio State Univ, 65-, Nat Sci Found res grants, 61-63 and 63-65; guest prof, Univ Cologne, 65; Guggenheim fel, 69 and 75-76; guest prof ling, Univ Vienna, Austria, 74; Ctr Advan Study Behav Sci fel, 75-76; guest prof, Univ Tokyo, 80. **HONORS AND AWARDS** Distinguished Res Awd, Ohio State Univ, 80. DU, Univ Essex, Eng, 77, Univ Lund, Sweden, 82; Univ Tartu, Estonia, 89; Am Acad of Arts and Scis, 90; Ohio State Univ, 99; Foreign Mem, Finnish Acad of Scis, 98; du, univ essex, eng, 77, univ lund, sweden, 82. **MEMBERSHIPS** Fel Acoust Soc Am; Ling Soc Am; Ling Soc Europe; Int Soc Phonetic Sci. **RESEARCH** Acoustic phonetics; perception of spoken language; historical phonology. **SELECTED PUBLICATIONS** Auth, Perception of Prominence by Estonian and English Listeners, Lang and Speech, Vol 0035, 92; Bilingualism, Lang, Vol 0068, 92; Lost Prosodic Oppositions--a Study of Contrastive Duration in Estonian Funeral Laments, Lang and Speech, Vol 0037, 94; Introduction to Phonetics, J Phonetics, Vol 0022, 94. **CONTACT ADDRESS** Dept of Ling, Ohio State Univ, Columbus, 222 Oxley Hall, 1712 Neil, Columbus, OH 43210. **EMAIL** ilsele@ling.ohio-state.edu

LEHMANN, WINFRED PHILIPP
PERSONAL Born 06/23/1916, Surprise, NE, m, 1940, 2 children **DISCIPLINE** LINGUISTICS AND GERMANIC PHILOLOGY **EDUCATION** Northwestern Col, AB, 36; Univ Wis, AM, 38, PhD(Ger philol), 41. **CAREER** From instr to asst prof, Wash Univ, 46-49; from assoc prof to prof Ger, 49-63, Ashbel Smith Prof Ling and Ger Lang, Univ Tex, Austin, 63-83, Fulbright fel, Norway, 50-51; dir Georgetown Univ English Lang Prog, Ankara, Turkey, 55-56; Guggenheim fel, 72-73; mem bd dirs, Am Coun Learned Soc, 72- and Inst Deut Sprache, 73-; chmn, Ling Deleg to Peoples Repub China, 74; Louann and Larry Templ Centennial Prof in the Humanities, 83-86; Emeritus, 86. **HONORS AND AWARDS** Brothers Grimm Prize, Philipps-Univ, Marburg, Ger, 75; Nehru Mem Lectr, 81. **MEMBERSHIPS** Ling Soc Am (pres, 73); MLA (pres 87), Indogermanische Gesellschaft; foreign mem, Royal Acad Sci, Denmark. **RESEARCH** Indo-European linguistics; general linguistics. **SELECTED PUBLICATIONS** Auth, proto-Info-European, Phonology Austin, 52; auth, The Development of Germanic Verse Form, Austin, reprint New York, 71, 56; auth, Historical Linguistics: an Introduction, Third ed 92, New York, 62; auth, Descriptive Lingusitics. An Introduction, New York, 72; auth, Proto-Indo-European Syntax, reprint 80, Austin, 74; auth, An Introduction to Old Irish, with Ruth P.M. Lehmann, New York, 75; auth, A Gothic Etymological Dictionary, Leiden, 86; auth, Theoretical Bases of Indo-European Linguistics, London, 93; auth, Residues of Indo-European Active Structure and their Implications for the Relationships among the Dialects, Innsbruck, 95; auth, Biblical Hebrew, with Esther Raizen and Helen-Jo Jakusz Hewitt, San Antonio, 99. **CONTACT ADDRESS** 3800 Eck Lane, Austin, TX 78734. **EMAIL** lehmaun@mail.utexas.edu

LEHNERT, HERBERT HERMANN
PERSONAL Born 01/19/1925, Luebeck, Germany, m, 1952, 2 children **DISCIPLINE** GERMAN **EDUCATION** Christian Albrechts Universitat, PhD, 52. **CAREER** Instr, Secondary Schools in Schleswig Holstein, Germany, 51-57; Lectr in German, Univ of Western Ontario, 57-58; instr, NY Univ, summer 58; lectr in German, 58-59, asst prof to prof of German, Rice Univ, 59-68; prof of German, Univ of Kans, 68-69; vis prof of German, Harvard Univ, 70; Prof of German, 69-94, Prof Emeriturs Recalled, Res Prof of German, Univ of Calif at Irvine, 95-. **HONORS AND AWARDS** Thomas Mann Medaille of the Deutsche Thomas Mann Gesellschaft, 98; NEH Fel, 73 & 77; NEH seminar for col teachers, 81; Guggenheim Fel, 78. **MEMBERSHIPS** MLA; AATG. **RESEARCH** German lit, especially in the 20th-Century. **SELECTED PUBLICATIONS** Auth, Thomas Mann: Fiktion, Mythos, Religion, Kohlhammer, 65 & 68; Struktur und Sprachagie, Kohlhammer, 66 & 72; Geschichte der deutschen Literatur rom Ingendstil Zum Expressionismus, Reclam, 78 & 96; coauth, Nihilismus der Menschenfreundlichkeit: Thomas Manns Wandlung und sein Essay Goethe und Tolstoi, Klostermann, 91; co-ed, Thomas Mann's Doctor Faustus: A Novel at the Margin of Modernism, Camden House, 91. **CONTACT ADDRESS** Dept of German, Univ of California, Irvine, Irvine, CA 92697-3150. **EMAIL** hlehnert@uci.edu

LEHOUCK, EMILE
PERSONAL Born 06/25/1935, Brussels, Belgium, m, 1962, 1 child **DISCIPLINE** FRENCH LITERATURE **EDUCATION** Free Univ Brussels, Lic en philol romane and Agrege, 57, PhD, 65. **CAREER** Aspirant, Belgian Nat Found Sci Res, 61-66; asst prof, Univ Congo, 66-67; asst prof, 67-72, assoc prof, 72-79, Prof French, Univ Col, Univ Toronto, 80-. **RESEARCH** Charles Fourier and the French literature; the romantic theatre. **CONTACT ADDRESS** Dept of French, Univ of Toronto, 50 St Joseph St, 2nd Floor, Toronto, ON, Canada M5S 1J4. **EMAIL** elouc@interlog.com

LEIGHTON, LAUREN GRAY
PERSONAL Born 06/21/1934, Virginia, MN, m, 1991, 2 children **DISCIPLINE** RUSSIAN LITERATURE, ROMANTICISM **CAREER** Instr Russian, Mercer Univ, 62-63; instr, Grinnell Col, 63-64; asst prof Slavic, Univ Va, 67-72; assoc prof, Northern Ill Univ, 72-78; Prof Slavic, Univ Ill, Chicago, 78-97, US-USSR Acad Exchange, IREX-USSR Ministry Higher Educ, 70 and IREX-USSR Acad Sci, 77, 89-90; ed, Slavic and East Europ J, 76-80. **MEMBERSHIPS** Asn Advan Slavic Studies; Am Asn Univf, Am Asn Teachers Slavic and East Europ Lang. **RESEARCH** Russian romanticism; Pushkin; translation theory. **SELECTED PUBLICATIONS** Auth, Literary Translation in Russia and America, 19: The Esoteric tradition in Russian Romantic Literature, 1994; A bibliography of Alexander Pushkin in English, 1999. **CONTACT ADDRESS** Dept of Slavic Lang and Lit, Univ of Illinois, Chicago, 601 S Morgan, Chicago, IL 60607. **EMAIL** laurengl@ptwi.net

LEINIEKS, VALDIS
PERSONAL Born 04/15/1932, Liepaja, Latvia **DISCIPLINE** CLASSICS **EDUCATION** Cornell Univ, BA, 55, MA, 56; Princeton Univ, PhD, 62. **CAREER** From instr to asst prof classics, Cornell Col, 59-64; assoc prof, Ohio State Univ, 64-66; assoc prof, 66-71, Prof Classics, Univ Nebr, Lincoln, 71-, Chm Dept, 67-95, Chm Comp Lit Prog, 70-86. **MEMBERSHIPS** Am Philol Asn; Am Classical League; Classical Asn of the Middle West and South. **RESEARCH** Greek and Latin literature and linguistics; linguistic theory. **SELECTED PUBLICATIONS** Auth Morphosyntax of the Homeric Greek Verb, Mouton, 64; The Structure of Latin: An Introductory Text Based on Caesar and Cicero, MSS Educ Publ, 75; Index Nepotianus, Univ Nebr, 76; The plays of Sophokles, Grîner, 82; The City of Dionysos, Teubner, 96. **CONTACT ADDRESS** Dept of Classics, Univ of Nebraska, Lincoln, 234 Andrews, Lincoln, NE 68588-0337. **EMAIL** vleinieks2@unl.edu

LEITAO, DAVID
PERSONAL Born 06/18/1964, CT, m, 1988 **DISCIPLINE** CLASSICS **EDUCATION** Dartmouth, AB, 86; Univ Mich, MA, 90, PhD, 93. **CAREER** Vis asst prof, 93-95, Ohio St Univ; asst prof, 95-, San Francisco St Univ. **RESEARCH** Gender and sexuality; anthropology of ancient world; computers in classics. **SELECTED PUBLICATIONS** Art, Classical Antiquity; art, Mnemosyne; art, Bucknell Review; art, Neue Parly; auth, Materialie Discussion. **CONTACT ADDRESS** 1600 Holloway Ave, San Francisco, CA 94132. **EMAIL** dleitao@sfsu.edu

LEKI, ILONA
PERSONAL Born 12/24/1947, Dieburg, Germany **DISCIPLINE** FRENCH LITERATURE, ENGLISH AS A SECOND LANGUAGE **EDUCATION** Univ Ill, AB, 68, AM, 70, PhD(French), 75. **CAREER** Instr English, Knox County Adult Educ, 74-76; instr, 76-80, Asst Prof English, Univ Tenn, 80-, Translr French, US Govt Joint Publ Res, 74-; sr ed fac publ, Univ Tenn, 75-77; asst prof French, Knoxville Col, 75-77. **MEMBERSHIPS** MLA;SAtlantic Mod Lang Asn; Am Asn Teachers Fr; Southern Comp Lit Asn; Alliance Francaise (treas, 77-78). **RESEARCH** French New Novel, particularly novels of Alain Robbe-Grillet; prose works of Henri Michaux; second language acquisition. **SELECTED PUBLICATIONS** Auth, Assessing 2nd-Language Writing in Academic Contexts, Coll Composition and Commun, Vol 0044, 93; Students Perceptions of Eap Writing Instruction and Writing Needs Across the Disciplines, Tesol Quart, Vol 0028, 94; Coping Strategies of Esl Students in Writing Tasks Across the Curriculum, Tesol Quart, Vol 0029, 95; Completely Different Worlds--Eap and the Writing Experiences of Esl Students in University Courses, Tesol Quart, Vol 0031, 97. **CONTACT ADDRESS** Univ of Tennessee, Knoxvill, 502 Longview Rd Apt E, Knoxville, TN 37996.

LENZ, JOHN RICHARD
PERSONAL Born 07/03/1957, New York, NY, m, 1994, 1 child **DISCIPLINE** CLASSICAL STUDIES **EDUCATION** Columbia Univ, PhD, 93. **CAREER** 90-91, Union College; 91-94, Chmn 94-, Drew Univ. **HONORS AND AWARDS** Fulbright Travel Grant, Greece, 88-89. **MEMBERSHIPS** Bertrand Russell Society, Pres; NJ Classical Assoc, VP. **RESEARCH** Bertrand Russell, ancient Greece. **CONTACT ADDRESS** Dept of Classics, Drew Univ, Madison, NJ 07940. **EMAIL** jlenz@drew.edu

LEON, PIERRE R. A.
PERSONAL Born 03/12/1926, Ligre, France **DISCIPLINE** PHONETICS **EDUCATION** Sorbonne, LL, 52, DL, 72; Univ Besancon, DUn, 60. **CAREER** Asst prof, Sorbonne, 50-58; asst prof, Ohio State, 58-60, 63-64; dir, ctr appl ling, Univ Besancon, 60-63; prof, founder & dir, Exp Phonetics Lab, Univ Toronto, 65-91, Prof Emer French, Univ Toronto. **HONORS AND AWARDS** Prix de l'acad francaise, 66; Commandeur palmes acad, 94. **MEMBERSHIPS** Soc Ling Paris; Ling Soc Can; Int Soc Phonetic Sci; Soc des auteurs de l'Ontario. **SELECTED PUBLICATIONS** Auth, Prononciation du francais standard, 66, 72, 77, 86; auth, Le dialogue, 85; auth, Chants de la Toundra, 85; auth, Le conte, 87; auth, Structure du francais moderne, 89; auth, Phonetisme et prononciations du francais, 90; auth, Precis de phonostylistique, 93. **CONTACT ADDRESS** Dept of French, Univ of Toronto, 50 St Joseph St, 2nd Floor, Toronto, ON, Canada M5S 1J4. **EMAIL** pleon@chass.utoronto.ca

LERNER, ISAIAS
PERSONAL Born 03/13/1932, Buenos Aires, Argentina, m, 1967, 1 child **DISCIPLINE** SPANISH LITERATURE **EDUCATION** Univ Buenos Aires, professor, 59; Univ Ill, Urbana-Champaign, PhD(Span), 69. **CAREER** Instr Latin and Span, Univ Buenos Aires, 60-66; asst prof Span lit, Univ Ill, Urbanna-Champaign, 69-71; assoc prof, 71-79, Prof Span Lit and Chmn Dept, Herbert H Lehman Col, CUNY, 79-, Prof Letters, 80-, Guggenheim fel Span lit, 77-78; fel, Herbert H Lehman Col, 77-78. **HONORS AND AWARDS** Premio Extraordinario Augusto Malaret, Real Acad Espanola, 73. **MEMBERSHIPS** MLA; Am Asn Teachers Span and Port. **RESEARCH** Spanish literature of the XVI and XVII century; history of the Spanish language; XVIII century Spanish lexicography. **SELECTED PUBLICATIONS** Auth, Rhetorics and Narration in Mexia, Pero, 'Historia Imperial', Bull Hisp Stud, Vol 0070, 93. **CONTACT ADDRESS** Lehman Col, CUNY, New York, NY 10021.

LESMAN, ANN ST CLAIR
DISCIPLINE SPANISH **EDUCATION** Rollins Col, BA; Duke Univ, Med; Univ MD, MA, PhD. **CAREER** Prof & prog coordr; pres, For Lang Asn of VA, 89-91; Fulbright-Hayes sponsored gp proj, Mexico, 96. **HONORS AND AWARDS** Outstanding fac mem & received the campus Alumni Fedn Fac of the Yr Awd, 96; Awd for Excellence in For Lang Educ, For Lang Asn of VA, 80. **SELECTED PUBLICATIONS** Publ on, tchg of conversational skills. **CONTACT ADDRESS** Dept of Span, Shenandoah Univ, 1460 University Dr., Winchester, VA 22601.

LESSL, THOMAS M.
PERSONAL Born 10/11/1954, Milwaukee, WI, m, 1976, 2 children **DISCIPLINE** SPEECH COMMUN **EDUCATION** Univ Tex, Austin. **CAREER** Assoc Prof, Speech Commun, Univ GA, 85-. **MEMBERSHIPS** Nat Commun Asn **RESEARCH** Rhetoric of Science **SELECTED PUBLICATIONS** "Toward a Definition of Religious Communication: Scientific and Religious Uses of Evolution, Jour Commun & Relig, 93; "Naturalizing Science: Two Episodes in The Evolution of a Rhetoric of Scientism," West Jour of Commun, 96; "The Social Implications of Genre: A Burkean Interpretation Aristotle," Speaker & Gavel, 97; "Conceptualizing Rhetoric Through Analogy. The speech Commun Tchr, 97; "Heresy, Or-

thodoxy, and the Politics of Science," Quart Jour of Speech, 98. **CONTACT ADDRESS** Dept Speech Commun, Univ of Georgia, Athens, GA 30602. **EMAIL** tlessl@arches.uga.edu

LETTS, JANET TAYLOR
PERSONAL Born 09/19/1930, Ho-Ho-Kus, NJ **DISCIPLINE** FRENCH LITERATURE **EDUCATION** Swarthmore Col, BA, 52; Univ Strasbourg, dipl, 55; Yale Univ, PhD, 62. **CAREER** Instr French, Wellesley Col, 59-60; from instr to assoc prof, 67-76, Prof French, Wheaton Col Mass, 76-, Chmn Dept, 66-, Mem adv comt, Jr Year in France, Sweet Briar Col. **MEMBERSHIPS** MLA; Int Asn Fr Studies; Soc Fr Hist Studies. **RESEARCH** Seventeenth century French literature. **SELECTED PUBLICATIONS** Auth, Le Cardinal de Retz, Historien et Moraliste du Possible, Nizet, Paris, 66. **CONTACT ADDRESS** Dept of French, Wheaton Col, Massachusetts, Norton, MA 02766.

LETZRING, MONICA
PERSONAL Born 02/01/1935, Grafton, ND **DISCIPLINE** ENGLISH AND COMPARATIVE LITERATURE **EDUCATION** Col St Scholastica, BA, 57; Univ Md, MA, 60, PhD, 63. **CAREER** Instr English lit, Col Notre Dame, Md, 63; instr English, Ctr Ling, Bergamo, Italy, 63-65; asst prof, 65-75, Assoc Prof English, Temple Univ, 75-. **MEMBERSHIPS** MLA; Am Soc 18th Century Studies. **RESEARCH** Eighteenth century English literature. **SELECTED PUBLICATIONS** Auth, Influence of Camoens in English literature, Rev Camoneana, 64, 65, 71; Strangford's poems from the Portuguese of Camoens, Comp Lit, fall 71; The Adamastor episode and 18th century theory of the sublime in England, Actas da I Reuniao Int de Camonistas, 73; Mickle, Boswell, Liberty and the Prospects of Liberty and Slavery, Mod Lang Rev, 74; Sarah Prince Gill and the John Adams-Catharine Macaulay correspondence, Proc Mass Hist Soc, 76. **CONTACT ADDRESS** Dept of English, Temple Univ, 1114 W Berks St, Philadelphia, PA 19122-6029.

LEUNG, KAI-CHEONG
PERSONAL Born 06/19/1936, Hong Kong, m, 1968, 2 children **DISCIPLINE** CHINESE LANGUAGE AND CULTURE **EDUCATION** Hong Kong Univ, BA and MA, 63; Leeds Univ, Dipl, 66; Int Phonetic Asn, Cert, 66; Univ Calif, Berkeley, PhD(Orient lang), 74. **CAREER** Lectr English and educ, Grantham Col Educ, 64-69; lectr, English and extra-mural studies, Chinese Univ Hong Kong, 67-69; asst prof Chinese, 73-79, Assoc Prof Chinese, San Jose State Univ, 79-, Consult, Asian-Am Bilingual Ctr, Berkeley, 80-81. **MEMBERSHIPS** Int Phonetic Asn; Asn Asian Studies; Philol Asn PACIFIC Coast; Chinese Lang Teachers Asn. **RESEARCH** Chinese drama; East-West literary relations; pedagogy. **SELECTED PUBLICATIONS** Auth, Turbulence, World Lit Today, Vol 0067, 93; 'Masks and Crocodile'--a Contemporary Chinese Poet and his Poetry, World Lit Today, Vol 0067, 93; The Transparent Eye--Reflections on Translation, Chinese Literature and Comparative Poetics, World Lit Today, Vol 0068, 94; The Short Stories of Chen Ruoxi Translated From the Original Chinese--a Writer at the Crossroads, World Lit Today, Vol 0068, 94; The 'Remote Country of Women', World Lit Today, Vol 0069, 95; The 'Butchers Wife' and Other Stories, World Lit Today, Vol 0070, 96. **CONTACT ADDRESS** Dept of Foreign Lang, San Jose State Univ, San Jose, CA 95192.

LEUSHUIS, REINIER
PERSONAL Born 09/16/1969, Tiel, Netherlands **DISCIPLINE** FRENCH, ITALIAN RENAISSANCE **EDUCATION** Utrecht Univ, MA, 93; MA, 93; Princeton Univ, PhD, 00. **CAREER** Grad asst to grad lect, Princeton Univ, 95-00; asst prof, Fla State Univ, 00. **HONORS AND AWARDS** Charlotte Elisabeth Procter Fel, 98-99. **MEMBERSHIPS** MLA, Renaissance Soc of Am; SAMLA. **RESEARCH** 16th Century French and Italian literature, focusing mostly on narrative genres and the representation of humanist ideals in literature. **SELECTED PUBLICATIONS** Auth, Le Mariage et l'amitie courtoise dans le dialogue et le recit bref a la Renaissance, Leo S Olschki Editore, Florence, It, forthcoming. **CONTACT ADDRESS** Dept Mod Lang & Ling, Florida State Univ, 262 Diffenbaugh, Tallahassee, FL 32308-1540. **EMAIL** rleushui@mailer.fsu.edu

LEVI, JOSEPH ABRAHAM
DISCIPLINE LINGUISTICS, LITERATURE, PORTUGUESE **EDUCATION** Univ Wis Madison, MA, 88; MA, 89; PhD, 93. **CAREER** Vis asst prof, Cen de Estudos Tec Intl, 85-86; vis instr, Univ Ga, 93-94; vis instr to adj asst prof to adj prof, Univ Iowa, 94-. **HONORS AND AWARDS** Tri Delta Recognition, Acad Teaching Excellence, Univ Iowa, 95; Alpha Delta Pi Teaching App, 93; Outstanding Teacher, 91-92; Grad Teaching Awd, 86-91; Outstanding Teacher, Univ Wis Madison, 87, 88, 90; Alpha Chi Omega Hon, Univ Wis, 87. **MEMBERSHIPS** AATSP; APSA; ASHAHS; ASSS; AATI; MLA. **RESEARCH** Romance philology; dialectology and linguistics; concentration: Portuguese, Hispanic, and Italian; Portuguese language, Portuguese and Brazilian history; culture, and literature; lusophone history, literatures, and cultures of Africa, Asia, and Oceania; history of the Portuguese Overseas Expansion; medieval history, literature, culture, and civilization of Portugal, Spain, and Italy; Sephardic Iberia; Italian Jewry/the Sephardic diaspora in the Americas (16 and 18th centuries); history of Africa; Islamic studies; English as a second language. **SELECTED PUBLICATIONS** Ed, Text and Concordance of the Biblioteca Apostolica Vaticana, MS 8174 Libro di Sapere di Astronomia, Alfonso X, El Sabio. (14th-Century Italian Translation by Guerruccio Federighi), Hisp Sem Medieval Studies (93); auth, Hernando del Pulgar: Los Claros Varones de Espana (c1483). A Semi -Paleographic Ed, Peter Lang, 96; auth, Alfonso X, El Sabio, Estonia de Alexandre el Grand, General Estonia (Quanta Parte). Manuscript U, Vatican Urb, Latin 539, Edwin Mellen Pub, 96; auth, O Dicionario Portugues-Chines de Padre Matteo Ricci, (1552-1610): Uma abordagem historico-linguistica, UP South, 98; auth, "Um Uso Mais Criativo no Laboratorio de Linguas: Como Usar a Console Multimedia a Nossa Vantagem no Ensino da Lingua Portuguesa," Vida Hisp 18 (98): 19-24; auth, "La Ienti de Sion: Linguistic and Cultural Legacy of an Early 13th-Century Judeo-Italian Kinah," Italica 1 75 (98): 1-21; co-trans, Francisco Varo's Grammar of the Mandarin Language (1703), (John Benjamin, 2000); auth, "A Diaspora Sefardita nas Americas Durante os Seculos XVII-XVIIL," Cad da Catedra de Estud 1 (01): 1-45; auth, "The People of the Book Jews, Muslims, and Christians in Medieval Iberia: Minorities and Hegemony at the Service of Science," Mediaev (01); auth, "AI-Andalus e a sua heranqa islamica," Nos Revista de Lusofonia (01). **CONTACT ADDRESS** Dept Modern Lang, Rhode Island Col, 600 Mt Pleasant St, CL 141, Providence, RI 02908. **EMAIL** jalevi@juno.com

LEVI, JUDITH N.
DISCIPLINE LINGUISTICS **EDUCATION** Univ Chicago, PhD. **CAREER** Prof, Northwestern Univ; language consultant to attorneys. **RESEARCH** Language and the Law; semantics; word formation. **SELECTED PUBLICATIONS** Evaluating Jury Comprehension of Illinois Capital Sentencing Instructions, Am Speech, 93; coauth, Plain Meaning and Hard Cases, Yale Law J, 94; Language as Evidence: The Linguist as Expert Witness in North American Courts, Forensic Linguistics: The Int J Speech, Lang and the Law, 94; Language and Law: A Bibliographic Guide to Social Science Research in the USA, Chicago: Am Bar Asn, 94; auth, What is Meaning in a Legal Text, A First Dialogue for Law and Linguistics,. Wash Univ Law Quart, 95; coauth, Bringing Linguistics into Judicial Decisionmaking: Semantic Analysis Submitted to the US Supreme Court, Forensic Ling: The Int J Speech, Lang, and the Law, 95; coauth, Regulatory Variables and Statutory Interpretation, Wash Univ Law Quart, 95; coauth, Improving Decisions on Death by Revising and Testing Jury Instructions, Judicature, 96. **CONTACT ADDRESS** Dept of Linguistics, Northwestern Univ, 2016 Sheridan Rd, Evanston, IL 60208-4090. **EMAIL** j-levi@northwestern.edu

LEVIN, BETH
DISCIPLINE LINGUISTICS **EDUCATION** MIT, PhD. **CAREER** Prof, Northwestern Univ. **RESEARCH** Lexical semantics; syntax; morphology; language typology. **SELECTED PUBLICATIONS** Auth, Approaches to Lexical Semantic Representation, Automating the Lexicon I: Research and Practice in a Multilingual Environment, Oxford UP, 95; Coauth, Morphology and Lexical Semantics, Handbook of Morphology, Blackwell, Oxford, 98; Making Sense of Corpus Data: A Case Study of Verbs of Sound, Int J Corpus Ling, 97; Lexical Semantics and Syntactic Structure, The Handbook of Contemp Semantic Theory, Blackwell, Oxford, 96; Two Types of Derived Accomplishments, Proceedings of the First LFG Conf, 96; Building on a Corpus: A Linguistic and Lexicographical Look at Some Near-synonyms, Int J Lexicography, 95; Unaccusativity: At the Syntax-Lexical Semantics Interface, Linguistic Inquiry Monograph 26, MIT Press, Cambridge, Mass, 95; The Elasticity of Verb Meaning, Proceedings of the 10 Annual Conf Israel Asn for Theoret Ling and Workshop on the Syntax-Semantics Interface, 95. **CONTACT ADDRESS** Dept of Linguistics, Northwestern Univ, 2016 Sheridan Rd, Evanston, IL 60208.

LEVIN, DAVID J.
DISCIPLINE PERFORMANCE STUDIES, GERMANIC STUDIES, CINEMA STUDIES **EDUCATION** Brown Univ, BA, 82; Univ Cal, Berk, MA, 86; PhD, 92. **CAREER** Asst prof, Columbia Univ, 92-98; vis asst prof, Univ Chicago, 97; assoc prof, 98-. **HONORS AND AWARDS** SSRC Postdoc Fel, Berlin; Coun Res Hum, Colum Univ. **MEMBERSHIPS** MLA; AATC; AMS; SCS. **RESEARCH** Opera; theater; cinema; interdisciplinary performance studies. **SELECTED PUBLICATIONS** Co-ed, Opera Through Other Eyes, Stanford Univ Press (Stanford, CA), 94; auth Richard Wagner, Fritz Lang, and the Nibelungen: The Dramaturgy of Disavowal, Princeton Univ Press, 98; auth, "Taking Liberties with Liberties Taken: On the Aesthetic Politics of Helke Sander's Liberators take Liberties," MIT Press 72 (95): 65-77; auth, "Staging a Reading/Reading a Staging: Die Meistersinger von Nurnberg in Performance," Cambridge Opera J 9 (97), 47-71; auth, "Are We Sisters Yet? The Rhetoric of Reconciliation in Percy Adlon's Bagdad Cafe," in Triangulated Visions: Gender, Race, and New German Cinema, ed. I Majer-O'Sickey (SUNY Press, 98); auth, "War of the White Roses: Resistance, Reification, and Community," in The Nasty Girl, The White Rose, and Five Last Days, Germanic Rev 73 (98): 86-100. **CONTACT ADDRESS** Dept Germanic Lang, Literature, Univ of Chicago, 1050 East 59th St, Chicago, IL 60637-1559. **EMAIL** dlevin@midway.uchicago.edu

LEVIN, JULES FRED
PERSONAL Born 01/25/1940, Chicago, IL, m, 1967, 1 child **DISCIPLINE** LINGUISTICS **EDUCATION** Univ Calif, Los Angeles, BA, 61, MA, 64; PhD(Balto-Slavic ling), 71. **CAREER** Vis lectr Russ, Univ Calif, Santa Barbara, 68-69; acting asst prof Russ and ling, 69-71, asst prof, 71-77, Assoc Prof Russ and Ling, Univ Calif, Riverside, 77-. **MEMBERSHIPS** Ling Soc Am; Am Asn Teachers Slavic and EEurop Lang; Asn Advan Baltic Studies. **RESEARCH** Linguistics: historical and dialectology; Balto-Slavic linguistics: historical, dialectology, phonology. **SELECTED PUBLICATIONS** Auth, Semiotics of Inspired Illustration in a Molokan Sacred Text, Amer J Semiotics, Vol 0009, 92. **CONTACT ADDRESS** Dept of Lit and Lang, Univ of California, Riverside, 900 University Ave, Riverside, CA 92521-0001.

LEVIN, MAURICE IRWIN
PERSONAL Born 02/13/1931, Boston, MA, m, 1953, 2 children **DISCIPLINE** SLAVIC LINGUISTICS **EDUCATION** Boston Univ, BA, 53; Harvard Univ, MA, 58, PhD(Slavic), 64. **CAREER** Instr mod lang, Mass Inst Technol, 61-63; asst prof Russ, Bowdoin Col, 63-65; asst prof Slavic, Ind Univ, Bloomington, 65-68; assoc prof, 68-72, Prof Slavic, Univ Mass, Amherst, 72-97; Emer, 97. **MEMBERSHIPS** Am Asn Teachers Slavic and EEurop Lang; Am Coun Teachers Russ. **RESEARCH** Russian language; structure of Russian; pedagogy of Russian. **SELECTED PUBLICATIONS** The Stress Patterns of the Russian Verb, Russ lang J, 71; Variant Forms in Russian Conjugation, Slavic and EEurop J, 72; Some Uses of the Accusative Case in Time Expressions, 73 and Stress Notation in the Russian adjective, 75, Russian Lang J, 75; Irregularities in Imperfective Derivation, Slavic and EEurop J, 77; Russian Declension and Conjugation: a Structural Description with Exercises, Slavica Publ, 78; Stress Notation in Russian Declension, Folia Slavica, 78; On Predicting the Genitive Case of Pluralia Tantum Nouns, Russ Lang J, 80. **CONTACT ADDRESS** 5 Evergreen LA, Amherst, MA 01002-2804. **EMAIL** mlevin@slavic.umass.edu

LEVIN, SAUL
PERSONAL Born 07/13/1921, Chicago, IL, m, 1951, 6 children **DISCIPLINE** CLASSICS **EDUCATION** Univ Chicago, AB, 42; PhD, 49. **CAREER** Instr, Univ Chicago, 49-51; from asst prof to assoc prof, Wash Univ, 51-61; prof, SUNY Binghamton, 61-; Dist Prof of Ancient Lang, 90-00; prof emer, 00-. **HONORS AND AWARDS** Fac Fel, Ford Found, 53-54; grants & fels, Res Found and Joint Awds Coun, SUNY, 61, 63, 65, 66, 68, 69, 75. **MEMBERSHIPS** Am Philol Asn; Soc Bibl Lit; Ling Asn Can and US; Class Asn of the Atlantic States; Class Asn of the Empire State; Int Orgn for Septuagint and Cognate Studies; Asn for the Study of Lang in Prehistory; Soc for Ancient Greek Philos; Golden Key Nat Honor Soc. **RESEARCH** Comparison of Semitic and Indo-European languages; Classical Greek, especially the Homeric dialect; Hebrew scriptures. **SELECTED PUBLICATIONS** Auth, Guide to the Bible, Part I: Genesis to Malachi (The Pentateuch, the Former Prophets or Historical Books, the Latter Prophets), SUNY-Binghamton, 87; auth, Guide to the Bible, Part II: The Hagiographia (or "Writings"), selected Apocrypha, the New Testament, SUNY-Binghamton, 87; auth, Guide to the Bible: The Hebrew Scriptures (or Old Testament), selected Apocrypha, the New Testament, 2nd ed, SUNY-Binghamton, 89; cotransl, Rerum senilium libri, by Petrarch (Baltimore: Johns Hopkins Univ Press, 92); auth, Semitic and Indo-European: The principal etymologies, with observations on Afro-Asiatic, John Benjamins (Amsterdam), 95; auth, "Greek as the Superstrate Written Language of Jews and Other Semitic Populations," Israel Oriental Studies 15 (95): 265-279; auth, "Rejoinder to Lamberti," Anthropos 94 (99): 646-647; auth, "'Achilles' Grudge' and 'Groveling before the Lord': Some Impediments to an Accurate Translation," LACUS Forum 25 (98): 421-431; auth, "The Forerunners of Scientific Phonology: Diacritical Marks and Other Reforms in Orthography," in Functional Approaches to Language, Culture and Cognition, ed. David G. Lockwood et al (Amsterdam: John Benjamins, 00), 569-592; auth, "How Polyglots Enlarge the Lexicon of Their Primary Language," LACUS Forum 26 (99). **CONTACT ADDRESS** Dept of Class and Near Eastern Studies, SUNY, Binghamton, Binghamton, NY 13902-6000. **EMAIL** slevin@binghamton.edu

LEVIN, THOMAS Y.
PERSONAL Born 09/14/1957, Cincinnati, OH, s **DISCIPLINE** GERMAN **EDUCATION** Yale Col, BA, 79; Yale Univ, MA hist of art, 81; MA philosophy, 83; PhD, 89. **CAREER** Asst Prof, Princeton Univ, German Dept, 90-97; Assoc Prof 97-; Acting Chmn, Fall 98. **HONORS AND AWARDS** Fel, J. Paul Getty Ctr for Hist of Art and Humanities, 90-91; Fel, Inst for Advanced Studey/Collegium Budapest, Hungary, 94; Research Scholar, Int Forschungszentrum Kulturwissenschaften, 95; Pro Helvetia Found, Geneva, Switz, 97. **MEMBERSHIPS** MLA, AATG, IAPL, Society for Cinema Studies. **RESEARCH** Media and Cultural Theory; Frankfurt Sch; Aesthetics and Politics **SELECTED PUBLICATIONS** coed, Siegried Kracauer. Neue Interpretationen, Tubingen: Stauffenburg Verlag 90; auth, Musical Quarterly, Elements of a Radio Theory: Adorno and the Princeton Radio Research Project, Summer 94; auth, Technophonia: Essays in Sound 2, After the Beep: A Short History of Voice Mail, Contemporary Sound

Arts, Darlinghurst, Australia, 95; auth, Meaning in the Visual Arts: Views from the Outside. A Centennial Commemoration of Erwin Panofsky (1892-1968), Iconology at the Movies: Panofsky's Film Theory, Inst for Adv Study, Princeton, 95; ed, Siegfried Kracauer, The Mass Ornament. Weimar Essays, Harvard Univ Press, 95; auth, Situacionistas: arte, politica, urbanismo/Situationist: art, politics, urbanism, Geopolitics of Hibernation: The Drift of Situationist Urbanism, Museu d'art contemporani, Barcelona, 96; **CONTACT ADDRESS** German Dept, Princeton Univ, 230 E Pyne, Princeton, NJ 08544. **EMAIL** tylevin@princeton.edu

LEVINE, DANIEL BLANK
PERSONAL Born 09/22/1953, Cincinnati, OH **DISCIPLINE** CLASSICAL LANGUAGE AND LITERATURE **EDUCATION** Univ Minn, BA, 75; Univ Cincinnati, PhD(classics), 80. **CAREER** Asst Prof Classics, Univ Ark, 80-, Ed, Ark Class Newslett, 80-. **MEMBERSHIPS** Class Asn Mid West and South; Am Philol Asn. **RESEARCH** Epic poetry; archaic Greek history. **SELECTED PUBLICATIONS** Auth, "Counterfeit Man," (in Greek and Hebrew Literature) in Classical Texts and their Traditions: Studies in Honor ofo C.R. Trahman, (Scholars Press: Chico, Calif, 84): 125-137; auth, "Symposium and Polis," in Theognis of Megara: Poetry and the Polis, eds. T.J. Figueira and G. Nagy, (Johnss Hopkins: Baltimore, 85): 176-196; auth, "Pittacus of Mytilene," in Great Lives from History: Ancient and Medieval Series, ed. F.N. Magil, (Salem Press: Pasadena, 88): 1644-1649; auth, "Phidias," in Great Lives from History: Ancient and Medieval Series, ed. F.N. Magill, (Salem Press: Pasadena, 88): 1592-1597; auth, "Eupalinus of Megara," in Great Lives from History: Ancient and Medieval Series, ed. F.N. Magill, (Salem Press: Pasaden, 88): 704-708; auth, "Acorns and Primitive Life in Greek and Latin Literature," Classical and Modern Literature 9, (89): 87-95; auth, "Uses of Classical Mythology in Rita Mae Brown's Soutehrn Discomfort," Classical and Modern Literature 10, (89): 63-70; auth, "John Clinton Futrall," "Henry Harrison Strauss," biographical essays Some illustious Educators of Old Main, Univ of Ark, 91; auth, "Hubris in Josephus Jewish Antiquities 1-4," Hebrew Union Col Annual, 64, (93): 51-87; auth, "Classica Americana Troglodytica: V.T. Hamlin' Alley Oop April 1939-Febrary 1940, The Epics Meet the Comics," Classical and Modern Literature: A Quarterly 14.4, (94): 365-386. **CONTACT ADDRESS** Dept of Foreign Lang, KIMP 425, Univ of Arkansas, Fayetteville, 904 Park Ave, Fayetteville, AR 72701. **EMAIL** dlevine@comp.uark.edu

LEVINE, MOLLY MYEROWITZ
PERSONAL Born 12/18/1942, Hartford, CT, m, 2 children **DISCIPLINE** CLASSICS **EDUCATION** Radcliffe Col, BA, 64; Yale Univ, MPhil , 71; Bar-Ilan Univ, PhD, 80. **CAREER** Instr to asst prof, Bar-Ilan Univ, 66-83; lectr to prof, Howard Univ, 84-. **HONORS AND AWARDS** Women's Class Caucus Award, Howard Univ, 90-91, 96-97, 99-00; Blegen Res Fel, Vassar Col, 90-91; Andrew W. Mellon Fac Enrichment Stipend, Howard Univ, 86; NEH summer seminar, Am Acad Rome, 86. **MEMBERSHIPS** Am Philol Asn; Class Asn of the MidAtlantic States; Wash Class Soc. **RESEARCH** Augustan poetry; Myth and religion; Gender; Cultural studies; Greece and the Near East; Translation theory. **SELECTED PUBLICATIONS** Auth, "Multiculturalism and the Classics," Arethusa, (92): 215-220; auth, "The Domestication of Desire: Ovid's Parva Tabella and the Theater of Love," in Pornography and Representation in Greece and Rome, (Oxford, 92(, 131-157; rev, of "The Use and Abuse of Black Athena," in The Am Hist Rev, (92): 440-460; auth, "The Gendered Grammar of Ancient Mediterranean Hair," in Off With Her Head: The Denial of Women's Identity in Myth, Religion, and Culture, (Univ Calif Press, 95), 76-130; auth, "Bernal and the Athenians in the Multicultural World of the Ancient Mediterranean," in Classical Studies in Honor of David Sohlberg, (Bar-Ilan Univ Press, 96), 1-56; auth, "Women Who Wait: Akiva's Rahel and Odysseus' Penelope," in Papers from the Howard Gilman Intl Conf, (Tel-Aviv Univ Press, 98), 303-335; rev, of "The Marginalization of Martin Bernal," Class Philol, (98): 345-363. **CONTACT ADDRESS** Dept Class, Howard Univ, 6106 Dunleer Ct, Bethesda, MD 20817. **EMAIL** myerowitz@aol.com

LEVITINE, EDA MEZER
PERSONAL Born 02/16/1927, Russia, m, 1944, 3 children **DISCIPLINE** FRENCH LITERATURE **EDUCATION** Boston Univ, AB, 50, MA, 52. **CAREER** From instr to asst prof French, Lesley Col, 57-64; asst prof, 64-69, Assoc Prof French, Trinity Col, 69-, Chmn Dept, 70-. **MEMBERSHIPS** Am Asn Teachers Fr. **RESEARCH** French 19th century literature; Baudelaire, Flaubert; relationship between French literature and French art. **SELECTED PUBLICATIONS** Auth, Baudelaire: Fashion and modernity, In: Hommage a Baudelaire, Univ Md, 68; transl, Flaconet, Reflexions sur la peinture, In: George Levitine, The Sculpture of Falconet, NY Graphic, 72; transl, Twentieth century masterpieces from the Musee de Grenoble, Univ Md, 11/73; transl, Couffignal, Apollinaire, Ala Univ, 75. **CONTACT ADDRESS** Dept of French, Trinity Col, Washington, DC, 125 Michigan Ave N E, Washington, DC 20017-1090.

LEVITSKY, ALEXANDER
PERSONAL Born 07/22/1947, Prague, Czech Republic, m, 1976, 3 children **DISCIPLINE** SLAVIC LANGUAGES **EDUCATION** Univ Minn, BA, 70; Univ Mich, MA, 72; PhD, 77. **CAREER** Teaching Asst, Univ Mich, 74-75; Lecturer, Middlebury Col, 75; Instructor to Full Prof and Dept Chair, Brown Univ, 75-; Visiting Prof, Middlebury Col, 82. **HONORS AND AWARDS** Woodrow Wilson Fel, 70-71; NDFL Title VI Fel, 70-72; H.H. Rackam Prize Fel, Univ Mich, 72-73; Fulbright-Hays Fel, 73-74; Teaching Fel, Univ Mich, 74-75; Fel of the Russian Res Ctr, Harvard Univ, 80-82; Henry Wriston Fel, Brown Univ, 81; Who's Who of Emerging Leaders in Am, 87; IREX Short Term Res Grant, 92. **SELECTED PUBLICATIONS** Co-ed, Czech Language News #14, 00; co-ed, Modern Czech Studies, Brown Slavic contributions Vol XIII, Brown Univ, 00; co-ed, Czech Language News #13, 99; ed, G.R. Derzhavin: Select Poetry. A Bilingual Reader, Brown Univ, 00; co-ed, Czech Language News #12, 99; co-ed, Modern Czech Studies, Brown Univ, 99; co-ed, Czech Language News #11, 98; auth, Collected Works by G.R. Derzhavin, Terra, 00; ed, A.P. Sumarokov, Psalter 1773, Schoningh, forthcoming; ed, A Laurel Wreath for Derzhavin (Venok Derzhavinu), Discovery House, 96; auth, Zamorozki Pamiati, Khudozhestvennaja Literatura, 93; auth, Adrian, Svenska Barncancerfonden, 91; auth, Russian Sacred Verse from Simeon of Polotsk to the Epoch of Derzhavin, V.K. Trediakovskij, 89; ed, V.K. Trediakovskij. Psalter 1753, First Ed, Schoningh, 89; ed, anthology of Czech Poetry, Univ of Mich Press, 73. **CONTACT ADDRESS** Dept Slavic Lang & Lit, Brown Univ, 20 Manning Walk, Providence, RI 02912-9100. **EMAIL** Alexander_Levitsky@brown.edu

LEVITT, JESSE
PERSONAL Born 06/15/1919, New York, NY, m, 1958, 2 children **DISCIPLINE** FRENCH **EDUCATION** City Col New York, BA, 38; Columbia Univ, MA, 40, PhD(Romance philol), 63. **CAREER** Trans & later info specialist, Foreign Broadcast Information Service, 41-54; teacher high schs, Md, 55-56; teacher, Jr High Sch, NY, 56: teacher high sch, NY, 57-59; from instr to asst prof French & Span, Wash State Univ, 60-65; assoc prof French & Romance lang, 65-70, chm dept foreign lang, 75-81, prof For Lang, Univ Bridgeport, 70-89, Ed, Geolinguistics, Am Soc Geoling, 73- **HONORS AND AWARDS** Phi Beta Kappa; magna cum laude, 38; Who's Who In America, 01. **MEMBERSHIPS** Am Soc Geoling; MLA; Am Name Soc; Int Soc of Dialectology and Geolinguistrics **RESEARCH** French linguistics, 17th to 20th centuries; French literature of the 20th century; Spanish linguistics. **SELECTED PUBLICATIONS** Auth, The Grammaire des Grammaires of Girault-Duvivier: A Study of Nineteenth-Century French, Mouton, The Hague, 68; The Concept of Euphony in Traditional French Grammar, In: Studies in Honor of Mario A Pei, Univ NC, 72; The Agreement of the Past Participle in Modern French, Linguistics, 10/73; The Influence of English on Spanish, English Around World, 11/75 & 11/77; Names in Beckett's Theater: Irony and Mystification, 77 & Irony and Allusiveness in Gide's Onomastics, 76, Lit Onomastics; The Influence of Orthography on Phonology: A Comparative Study (English, French, Spanish, Italian, German), Linguistics, 78; From Literature to the Lexicon: Names of Authors, Books and Literary Characters as Vocabulary in the Romance Languages, Papers in Onomastics, Univ Mo-Rolla, 11/81; ed and contrib, Geolinguistic Perspectives, Proceedings of the 1985 Conf of the Am Soc of Geolinguistics, Univ Press of Am; co-ed and contribur, Justice, Interdisciplinary and Global Perspectives, Univ Press of Am, 88; ed, " Constructed Languages and Language Construction," American Society of Geolinguistics, Cummings and Hathatway1, containing, " French and English Influence On Spanish Construction," 96; ed and contrib, Language in Contemporary Society, Proceedings of the 1992 Conference of the American Society of Geolinguistics; ed and contrib, Language and Communication in the New Century, Cummings & Hathaway, 99; auth, " The Franks: Their Onomastic and Semantic Legacy," Geolinguistics, 00; auth, " Ny Twenty-Five Years as Editor of 'Geolinguistics,'" Geolinguistics, 00 **CONTACT ADDRESS** Univ of Bridgeport, 485 Brooklawn Ave, Fairfield, CT 06432.

LEVY, DIANE WOLFE
PERSONAL Born 06/06/1944, Washington, DC, m, 1966, 1 child **DISCIPLINE** FRENCH LITERATURE, COMPARATIVE LITERATURE **EDUCATION** Barnard Col, BA, 66; Columbia Univ, MA, 69, PhD(French and Romance philol), 73. **CAREER** Asst prof French, Columbia Univ, 73-74; Asst Prof French, State Univ NY, Albany, 74-80. **MEMBERSHIPS** MLA; Nat Asn Teachers Fr; Northeast Mod Lang Asn. **RESEARCH** Urban literature; narrative structure. **SELECTED PUBLICATIONS** Auth, History as art: Ironic parody in Anatole France's Les Sept Femmes de la Barbe-Bleue, Nineteenth-Century Fr Studies, spring 76; coauth, How to Use French Verbs, Barron's Educ Ser, 77; auth, Cityscapes: Towards a definition of urban literature, Mod Fiction Studies, spring 78; Ironic Techniques in the Short Stories of Anatole France, NC Ser Romance Lang and Lit (in press). **CONTACT ADDRESS** 9317 Ocala St, Silver Spring, MD 20901.

LEVY, GAYLE A.
PERSONAL Born 01/18/1965, San Francisco, CA **DISCIPLINE** FRENCH LITERATURE **EDUCATION** Univ Calif Berkeley, AB, 87; Johns Hopkins Univ, MA, 90; Duke Univ, PhD, 95. **CAREER** Asst prof, Univ of Mo, 96-. **HONORS AND AWARDS** Univ of Mo Grant, 98, 99; NEH Inst, 99; Phi Beta Kappa. **MEMBERSHIPS** MLA, MMLA. **RESEARCH** French Cultural Studies, 19th and 20th century French fiction and poetry, feminist theory, interdisciplinary studies. **SELECTED PUBLICATIONS** Auth, "Teaching French Cultural Studies," Contemp Fr Civilization, (98); auth, Refiguring the Muse, Peter Lang, 99; auth, "La Genie Scientifique et le hasard poetique," Regles du genre et inventions du genie, (99). **CONTACT ADDRESS** Univ of Missouri, Kansas City, 5100 Rockhill Rd, 211 Scofield Hall, Kansas City, MO 64110. **EMAIL** levyg@umkc.edu

LEVY, KAREN D.
DISCIPLINE FRENCH LITERATURE **EDUCATION** Univ Ky, PhD, 71. **CAREER** Prof, French, Univ Tenn. **RESEARCH** Twentieth century French fiction, poetry, and literary criticism. **SELECTED PUBLICATIONS** Co-ed, Revue Andre Malraux Review, Univ Tenn, 96- . **CONTACT ADDRESS** Dept of Mod For Langs & Lits, Univ of Tennessee, Knoxville, 701 McClung Tower & Plaza, Knoxville, TN 37996. **EMAIL** klevy@utk.edu

LEVY, KURT LEOPOLD
PERSONAL Born 07/10/1917, Berlin, Germany, m, 1947, 5 children **DISCIPLINE** SPANISH **EDUCATION** Univ Toronto, BA, 45, MA, 46, PhD(Span), 54. **CAREER** Instr Span lang and lit, 45-50, lectr Span and Span Am lit, 50-55, from asst prof to assoc prof, 55-65, dir Latin Am studies and assoc chmn dept Hisp studies, 65-70, Prof Hisp Studies, Univ Toronto, 65-, Chmn Dept Span and Port, 78-, Govt Columbia lectr, SAm, 55; Can Coun sr res fel, Columbia and Latin Am Univs, 65; external examr Span, Univ West Indies, 69-71; Rockefeller vis prof lit, Univ Valle, Columbia, 71-73; Treas, Int Fedn Insts Teaching Span, 72-. **MEMBERSHIPS** Can Asn Latin Am Studies (pres, 69-71); MLA; Am Asn Teachers Span and Port; Inst Int Lit Iberoam (pres, 67-69); Am Coun Teaching Foreign Lang. **RESEARCH** Spanish American prose fiction, specifically Colombian. **SELECTED PUBLICATIONS** Auth, Tomas Carrasquilla (Twayne's World Author Series, 546); auth, Efe Gaomez; auth, Mi deuda con Antioquia. **CONTACT ADDRESS** Dept of Span & Port, Univ of Toronto, 73 Queen's Park Crescent, Toronto, ON, Canada M5S 1K7.

LEWES, ULLE ERIKA
PERSONAL Born 03/22/1942, Tallinn, Estonia, w, 1989 **DISCIPLINE** MEDIEVAL & COMPARATIVE LITERATURE **EDUCATION** Cornell Univ, AB, 64; Harvard Univ, MA, 65, PhD, 72. **CAREER** Instr, Temple Univ, 71-72, asst prof, 72-78; Assoc Prof, 78-82, Prof English, Ohio Wesleyan Univ, 82-, Dir Writing Ctr, Ohio Wesleyan Univ; writing consult, Muskingum Col, Denison Col, Col DuPage & Rice Univ; Dir, Project Writing across the Curriculum, Mellon Found Grant, 79-82; Lead Prof, NEH Summer Inst on Renaissance Drama, Secondary School Teachers-Ohio Wesleyan, 86; dir, various Ohio Wesleyan grants, 84, 85, 86, 94. **HONORS AND AWARDS** Phi Beta Kappa, 63; S.A. Potter Awd, Harvard Univ, 72; Medieval Acad Younger Schol grant, Int 12th Century Renaissance Conf, Medieval Acad, 77; Benjamin T. Spencer Lectureship, 94-96. **MEMBERSHIPS** MLA; Medieval Acad Am; Asn Teachers Advanc Compos; Conf Col Comp and Commun; Coun Writing Prog Admin; Estonian Learned Soc; Nat Coun Teachers English; Tristan Soc. **RESEARCH** The Tristan legend; Women's Studies; Shakespeare Studies; the theory and practice of teaching composition. **SELECTED PUBLICATIONS** Auth, Is America Losing Her Folklore Heritage?, Town and Country, 78; The Life in the Forest: Influence of the Saint Giles Legend on the Courtly Tristan Story, Univ Tenn, Chattanooga, 79; A Rejoinder to C.S. Jaeger on the Tristan Story, Tristania, 81; The Uses of Peer Editing in Advanced Writing Courses, J Advanced Comp, 85; The Originality of the Farewell Scene in Gottfield's Tristan, Tristania, 89; Writing as Learning: A Workbook for Teachers of Jefferson County Schools, 90. **CONTACT ADDRESS** Dept of English, Ohio Wesleyan Univ, 61 S Sandusky St, Delaware, OH 43015-2398. **EMAIL** uelewes@cc.owu.edu

LEWIS, BART L.
PERSONAL Born 06/29/1946, Dallas, TX, s **DISCIPLINE** LATIN AMERICAN LITERATURE **EDUCATION** Southern Methodist Univ, BA; Univ NM, MA, PhD. **CAREER** J William Fulbright prof, Lyon Col. **MEMBERSHIPS** Southwest Coun of Latin Am Studies; Modern Lang Asn; Am Asn of Teachers of Spanish & Portuguese. **SELECTED PUBLICATIONS** Auth, Mexican Modernism in A Hist Mex Lit. **CONTACT ADDRESS** Dept of Mod Lang, Lyon Col, 300 Highland Rd, PO Box 2317, Batesville, AR 72503. **EMAIL** blewis@lyon.edu

LEWIS, DAVID WILFRID PAUL
PERSONAL Born 01/24/1932, Clacton-on-Sea, England, m, 1959, 4 children **DISCIPLINE** FRENCH **EDUCATION** Oxford Univ, BA, Hons, 53, MA, 68; Col Europe, dipl int relat, 57; Univ Paris, Dr, 73. **CAREER** Dean students, Col Europe, 57-58; Coun of Europe, Strasbourg, info off, 58-62, adminr educ prog, 62-65; secy, Europ Comt Conserv Nature and Natural Resources, 65-68; assoc prof mod lang, Lakehead Univ, 68-77, chmn dept, 68-70; Prof Mod Lang and Chmn Dept Mod

Foreign Lang, Lehigh Univ, 77-, Vis prof, Univ Ottawa, 71, Univ Prince Edward Island, 74 and Univ Ottawa, 77; campus dir admin, Champlain Regional Col, St Lambert, Quebec, 75-76; transl consult, secy state, Govt Can, 76-77. **HONORS AND AWARDS** French Govt Awd of Merit for Contrib to Europ Coop in Educ, 63; ODK Nat Honor Soc, 80. **MEMBERSHIPS** Int Arthurian Soc; Asn Int Etud Fr; Am Asn Teachers Fr; Asn Int Docteurs Univ Paris. **RESEARCH** Modern languages, especially 19th century French poetry and French for business and international affairs; international relations, especially European integration. **SELECTED PUBLICATIONS** Coauth, Higher Civil Servants, Col Europe, 58; Youth and Development Aid, Coun of Europe, 66; auth, Albert Glatigny et la Tradition Boheme, Can Asn Univ Teachers Fr, 72; Dans le Sillon des Voyageurs: Experiment in French (educational) television, Can Rev Mod Lang, 74. **CONTACT ADDRESS** Dept of Mod Foreign Lang, Lehigh Univ, Bethlehem, PA 18015.

LEWIS, GERTRUD JARON
PERSONAL Born 10/27/1931, Frankfurt-Main, Germany, m, 1960, 3 children **DISCIPLINE** MEDIEVAL GERMAN LITERATURE **EDUCATION** Univ Alta, MA, 67, PhD(Ger), 71. **CAREER** Instr Ger and French, Univ Redlands, 59-62; asst prof Ger, 72-78, Assoc Prof Ger, Laurentian Univ, 78-, Can Coun publ grant, 73; Laurentian Univ publ grant, 74; Soc Sci and Humanities Res Coun Can fel, 80; Soc Sci and Humanities grant, 82. **MEMBERSHIPS** MLA; Can Asn Univ Teachers Ger; Can Comp Lit Asn; Mediaeval Acad Am; Int Arthurian Soc. **RESEARCH** Middle high German epic; German women mystics of the Middle Ages. **SELECTED PUBLICATIONS** Auth, The Heart as the Center of Mystical Experience--Mysticism in Cistercian Convents in 13th-Century Helfta, Speculum-J Medieval Stud, Vol 0068, 93; In Search of Woman in the Middle Ages, Seminar-J Ger Stud, Vol 0029, 93; Tears and Saints, Arachne, Vol 0003, 96. **CONTACT ADDRESS** Dept of Mod Lang, Laurentian Univ, 935 Ramsey Lake Rd, Sudbury, ON, Canada P3E 2C6.

LEWIS, MARTHA HOFFMAN
PERSONAL Born 11/08/1922, Newton, MA, m, 1954, 2 children **DISCIPLINE** CLASSICS **EDUCATION** Univ Calif, Berkeley, AB, 43; Bryn Mawr Col, MA, 49, PhD, 51. **CAREER** Teacher Latin and English, Red Bluff High Sch, Calif, 44-45, Piedmont High Sch, 45-48; asst prof classics and educ, Univ Ill, 53-56; asst prof Latin, 63-66; assoc prof Latin and English, Rockhurst Col, 66-82. **HONORS AND AWARDS** Fulbright scholar and fel, Am Acad Rome, 51-53. **MEMBERSHIPS** Am Philol Asn; Am Asn Ancient Historians. **RESEARCH** Roman history, especially late republic and early empire; modern poetry. **SELECTED PUBLICATIONS** Auth, The Official Priests of Rome Under the Julio-Claudrasus, Am Acad in Rome, Papers and Monographs 16, 55. **CONTACT ADDRESS** 716 W 109th Terr, Kansas City, MO 64114.

LEWIS, MARVIN A.
PERSONAL Born 10/09/1942, VA, m, 2 children **DISCIPLINE** SPANISH **EDUCATION** Morgan State Univ, BA, 68; Purdue Univ, MA, 68-69; Univ Calif Berkeley, MA, 70; Univ Wash, PhD, 74. **CAREER** Asst prof, Univ Minn, 75-76; from asst to assoc prof to dir, Univ Ill, 76-89; dir, 86-89, prof 89-, Univ Mo. **HONORS AND AWARDS** NEH, 89; NEH Travel Grant, 90; Fulbright Grant, 89, 99; ACLS Grant 88, 91; martin luther king grant, woodrow wilson found; charles e. kany scholar, 69-70; ndea fel, 71-74. **MEMBERSHIPS** MLA; Afro-Latin/Am Res Asn. **RESEARCH** Afro Hispanic and Latin American Literature. **SELECTED PUBLICATIONS** Auth, From Lima to Leticia: The Peruvian Novels of Mario Vargas Llosa, 83; auth, Afro-Hispanic Poetry, 1940-1980: From Slavery to Negritud in South American Verse, 83; auth, Treading the Ebony Path: Ideology and Violence in Contemporary Afro-Colombian Prose Fiction, 87; auth, Ethnicity and Identity in Contemporary Afro-Venezuelan Literature: A Culturalist Approach, 92; auth, Afro-Argentine Discourse: Another Dimension of the Black Diaspora, 96. **CONTACT ADDRESS** Dept of Romance Languages, Univ of Missouri, Columbia, 143 Arts and Science Bldg, Columbia, MO 65211. **EMAIL** lewism@missouri.edu

LEWIS, PHILIP EUGENE
PERSONAL Born 09/08/1942, Kingsport, TN, m, 1966, 2 children **DISCIPLINE** FRENCH LITERATURE **EDUCATION** Davidson Col, BA, 64; Yale Univ, PhD(French), 69. **CAREER** Asst prof, 68-74, chm dept, 73-76, assoc prof, 74-79, ed, Diacritics, 76-81, chm dept, 78-80, Prof Romance Studies, 79- , dean Arts & Sciences, 95- , Cornell Univ. **RESEARCH** Seventeenth century French literature; Semiotics. **SELECTED PUBLICATIONS** Auth, La Rochefoucauld: The Art of Abstraction, Cornell Univ, 76; auth, Seeing Through the Mother Goose Tales, Stanford, 96. **CONTACT ADDRESS** College of Arts and Sciences, Cornell Univ, 147 Goldwin Smith, Ithaca, NY 14853-3201. **EMAIL** as_dean@cornell.edu

LEWIS, WARD B.
PERSONAL Born 05/08/1938, m, 3 children **DISCIPLINE** GERMAN **EDUCATION** Amherst Col, BA, 60; Univ Minn, MA, 65; Univ Pa, PhD, 68. **CAREER** Teaching fel, Univ of Pa, 66-67; asst prof, Univ of Iowa, 68-71; from asst prof to assoc prof, Univ of Ga, 71-. **HONORS AND AWARDS** Germanistic Soc of Am Fel, 66; Disstertation Fel, Univ of Pa, 67-68; res fel, Alexander von Humboldt Found, 79-80. **MEMBERSHIPS** Lambda Alpha Psi, Delta Phi Alpha, MLA, Northeast MLA, S Atlantic MLA, Eugene O'Neill Soc, Soc for Exile Studies, Int Brecht Soc, Ger Studies Asn. **SELECTED PUBLICATIONS** Auth, "Arnolt Bronnen," Twentieth-Century German Dramatists 1919-1992, Dictionary of Literary Biography 124, The Gale Group (Farmington Hills, MI), 92; auth, "Bibliography of Kurt Pinthus," International Biographical Dictionary of Central European Emigres, Saur, 93; auth, "Patrick Suskind," Encyclopedia of Popular Fiction," Beacham (Osprey, FL), 96; auth, "Dennis Lynds (Michael Collins, American Hardboiled Detective and Mystery Writers," Dictionary of Literary Biography, forthcoming; auth, "Egon Erwin Kisch" and "Frank Wedekind's Fruhlings Erwachen," Encyclopedia of German Literature, forthcoming. **CONTACT ADDRESS** Dept Ger & Slavic Lang, Univ of Georgia, Athens, GA 30602-0002.

LI, AUDREY
DISCIPLINE EAST ASIAN LANGUAGES AND CULTURES **EDUCATION** Univ Southern Calif, PhD, 85. **CAREER** Asso prof, Univ Southern Calif. **RESEARCH** Linguistics; English, Mandarin and Taiwanese language; language policies in Taiwan. **SELECTED PUBLICATIONS** Auth, New Horizons in Chinese Linguistics; Syntax of Scope; Order and Constituency in Mandarin Chinese. **CONTACT ADDRESS** East Asian Studies Center, Univ of So California, University Park Campus, Los Angeles, CA 90089.

LI, CHARLES N.
PERSONAL Born 02/06/1940, Shanghai, China, m, 1983, 2 children **DISCIPLINE** LINGUISTICS **EDUCATION** Bowdoin Col, BA, 63; Stanford Univ, PhD, 66; Univ Calif, Berkeley, PhD, 71. **CAREER** From Vis Asst Prof to Prof, Univ Calif, 71-. **HONORS AND AWARDS** Phi Beta Kappa, 63; Nat Danforth Fel, 63-69; NSF Summer Res Fel, 63; Fac Res Fel, Univ Calif, 73; Postdoctoral Study Fel, ACLS, 74-75; Fel, NAIS, 97-98. **MEMBERSHIPS** ACLS. **RESEARCH** Origin of language, language change, Chinese languages, Mongolic languages. **SELECTED PUBLICATIONS** Coauth, "An Explanation of Word Order Change: SVO---SOV," Found of Lang, 12 (74): 201-214; co-ed, "Subject and Topic: A New Typology of Language," in Subject and Topic (Acad Pr, 76), 457-490; auth, Mandarin Chinese: A Functional Reference Grammar, Univ Calif Pr (Berkeley, CA), 81; co-ed, "Beyond Borrowing and Interference: Contact-Induced Morphosyntactic Change in Chinese," in Morphosyntactic Changes in Chinese (John Benjamin Publ, forthcoming); auth, The Evolutionary Origin of Language, Harper-Collins Publ, forthcoming. **CONTACT ADDRESS** Dept Ling, Univ of California, Santa Barbara, 552 University Rd, Santa Barbara, CA 93106-0002.

LIBERMAN, ANATOLY
PERSONAL Born 03/10/1937, Leningrad, Russia, m, 1969, 1 child **DISCIPLINE** PHILOLOGY **EDUCATION** Hertzen Pedagogical Inst, BA, 59; Leningrad Univ, PhD, 65; Acad Sci, USSR, PhD, 71. **CAREER** Teach, Leningrad, 59-62; instr, Leningrad Polytech Inst, 62-65; res asst, Leningrad Inst Ling, 65-75; prof, Univ Minn, 75-. **HONORS AND AWARDS** Guggenheim Fel; Fulbright Fel; NEH, 80, 91, 95; Bush Fel; Festschrift. **MEMBERSHIPS** SASS; DSNA; NAS; ALSC; SPLS. **RESEARCH** General and historical linguistics; history of linguistics; medieval literature and folklore; Russian literature. **SELECTED PUBLICATIONS** Transl of, On the Heights of Creation: The Lyrics of Fedor Tyutchev JAI Press (Greenwich and London), 93; transl of, Word Heath, Wortheide, Ortheioti, Il Calamo (Rome), 94; transl of, Vrachevanie dukha (Healing of the Spirit), Effect (NY), 96; co-transl and ed, Theory and History of Folklore, Univ Minn Press, Manchester Univ Press (Minneapolis and Manchester), 84; co-transl and ed, Studies in Germanic Philology, Helmut Buske (Hamburg), 86; co-transl and ed, Writings on Literature, Univ Minn Press (Minneapolis), 90; co-transl and ed, The Legacy of Genghis Khan and Other Essays on Russia's Identity, Mich Slavic Prod (Ann Arbor), 91; co-ed, Aspects of Change, Univ Minnesota, 85; co-ed, Science and Pseudoscience, Univ Minneapolis, 87. **CONTACT ADDRESS** Dept German, Scand, Dutch, Univ of Minnesota, Twin Cities, 9 Pleasant St SW, 205 Folwell Hall, Minneapolis, MN 55455-0124. **EMAIL** liber002@tc.umn.edu

LICHTBLAU, MYRON IVOR
PERSONAL Born 10/10/1925, New York, NY, m, 1956, 3 children **DISCIPLINE** LATIN AMERICAN LITERATURE **EDUCATION** City Col NY, BA, 47; Univ Nac Mex, MA, 48; Columbia Univ, PhD, 57. **CAREER** Instr, Ind Univ, 57-59; lang coord, Peace Corps, Syr Univ, 66; vis prof, Colgate Univ, 70; vis prof, SUNY Binghamton, 75; asst prof to assoc prof to prof to chmn, Syracuse Univ, 59-98. **HONORS AND AWARDS** Hon Dip, Univ de Nuevo Leon, 64; NEH, 93. **MEMBERSHIPS** MLA; AATSP; IILI. **RESEARCH** Latin American prose and fiction; Argentine novel; Latin American theater. **SELECTED PUBLICATIONS** Auth, The Argentine Novel in the Nineteenth-Century (NYork), 59; ed, Las dos Vidas del Pepre Napoleon (NYork), 63; auth, Elarte Estilistico de Eduardo Mallea (Buenos Aires), 67; auth, Manuel Galvez (NYork), 72; auth, A Practical Reference Guide to Reading Spanish (NYork), 77; ed, Manuel Pacho (Bogot'), 80; transl, History of an Argentine Passion (Pittsburgh, 1983); auth, "Rayvela," Creatividad Artistica (89); ed, La Maestra Normal (Miami) 91; auth, The Argentine Novel: An Annotated Bibliography, Lanham, 97. **CONTACT ADDRESS** 111 Saybrook Ln, Syracuse, NY 13214-2119. **EMAIL** mlichtbl@syr.edu

LIDA, DENAH LEVY
PERSONAL Born 09/09/1923, New York, NY, m, 1955 **DISCIPLINE** SPANISH **EDUCATION** Hunter Col, BA, 43; Columbia Univ, MA, 44; Nat Univ Mex, Dr Let(Span), 52. **CAREER** From instr to asst prof Span, Smith Col, 45-53; asst prof mod lang, Sweet Briar Col, 54-55; from instr to assoc prof Span, 55-67, chmn dept Romance & comp lit, 64-66 & 74-77, Prof Span, Brandeis Univ, 67-, Assoc scholar, Radcliffe Inst Independent Study, 61-62, chmn, Joint Prog Lit Studies, 78-81, chmn, Hum Coun, 81-82; Prof Emerita, 86. **MEMBERSHIPS** MLA; Renaissance Soc Am; Asoc Int Hispanistas; Asoc Int Galdositas. **RESEARCH** Comp lit, the Don Juan theme; Sephardic Spanish; 19th century Spanish lit. **SELECTED PUBLICATIONS** Ed, Pronunciation of Smyrnian Judeo-Spanish 52 & On Almudena and his speech, Nueva Rev Filol Hispanica, 61; El amigo manso, Oxford Univ, 63; Sobre el Krausismo de Galdos, Anales Galdosianos, 68; El crimen de la calle de Fuencarral, Homenaje a Casalduero, 72; Galdos entre cronica y novela, 73 & Galdos y sus santas modernas, 75, Anales Galdosianos; The Catalogues of Don Giovanni and Don Juan Tenorio, Hispano-Italic Studies, 79; auth, "Galdo's y el teatro: teoria y practica" in Homanaje a A.M. Barrenechea, NY, 83; auth, "Secularizacion De instituciones y ralores espritiuales eu Misericordia" in Studies in Honor of Sumner M. Greenfield, Nebraska, 85; auth, " Ma's reframes judeo-espanoles de Esmirna" in Homenaje a Celina Sabor de Cortazar, Filologia, Bs.As., 87; auth, "Grality and Characterization in Galdo's," Nueva Revista De Filologia Hispanica, 92; auth, "Don Juan en Italia en el siglo XVIII", NRFH, 92; auth, "The Language of the Sephardin in Anglo-America" in Sephardin in the Americas, Studies in Culture and History, Univ of Alabama, 93; auth, "Galdo's freute al romanticismo in Filologia, Temas Galdosicanos, Bo.As., 95. **CONTACT ADDRESS** Dept of Romance & Comp Lit, 19 Chauncy St, 3A, Cambridge, MA 02138.

LIDOV, JOEL
PERSONAL Born 03/13/1945, Chicago, IL, m, 2 children **DISCIPLINE** GREEK & LATIN LANGUAGE & LIT **EDUCATION** Columbia Coll, BA, 66; Columbia Univ, MA, 67, PhD, 72. **CAREER** Visiting/acting, asst prof, Univ of CA Berkely, 70-73; Visiting asst prof, 73-75, Stanford Univ; asst to assoc prof, Queens College & graduate sch, City Univ of NY, 75-. **HONORS AND AWARDS** Phi Beta Kappa, 65; Earle Prize in classics, 66; Woodbridge distinguished fel, 70; Gildersleev prize (John Hopkins Univ Press), 93. **MEMBERSHIPS** Amer Philogical Assn **RESEARCH** Classical Greek Lit (especially Archaic, classical poetry) **SELECTED PUBLICATIONS** Auth, Alternating Rhythm in Archaic Greek Poetry, Trans, American Philological Assoc, 89; What am I? What am I not?: Three Recent Pindars, Classical Journal, 93; The Second Stanza of Sappho 31, Another Look, American Journal of Philology, 93; Pindar's Hym to Cybele, Meter, Form and Syncretism, Greek, Roman and Byzantine Studies, 96. **CONTACT ADDRESS** Dept of Classical Middle-Eastern & Asian Langs, Queens Col, CUNY, 6530 Kissena Blvd, Flushing, NY 11367. **EMAIL** joel_lidov@qc.edu

LIEBERMAN, STEPHEN JACOB
PERSONAL Born 03/21/1943, Minneapolis, MN **DISCIPLINE** ASSYRIOLOGY, LINGUISTICS **EDUCATION** Univ Minn, BA, 63; Harvard Univ, PhD(Near Eastern lang), 72. **CAREER** From asst prof to assoc prof Near Eastern studies, New York Univ, 71-75; res specialist, Sumerian Dict, Univ Mus, Univ Pa, 76-79; Assoc Prof Assyriol and Semitic Ling, Dropsie Univ, 82-, Fel Mesopotamian civilization, Baghdad Ctr Comt, Am Schs Orient Res, 70-71; Nat Endowment for Humanities fel, 75-76; Guggenheim fel, 79-80; Inaugural fel, Found for Mesopotamian Studies, 80- **MEMBERSHIPS** Am Orient Soc; AHA; Archaeol Inst Am; Ling Soc Am; NAm Conf Afro-Asiatic Ling. **RESEARCH** Sumerian and Akkadian languages and cultures; Semitic linguistics; Mesopotamian history. **SELECTED PUBLICATIONS** Auth, Bar Ilan Studies in Assyriology Dedicated to Artzi, Pinhas, J Amer Oriental Soc, Vol 0112, 92. **CONTACT ADDRESS** Dept Assyriol and Semitic Ling, Dropsie Univ, Philadelphia, PA 19132.

LIESBSCHER, GRIT
PERSONAL Born 02/08/1968, Leipzig, Germany, m, 2000, 1 child **DISCIPLINE** APPLIED LINGUISTICS **EDUCATION** Univ Leipzig, Ger, MA, 92; Univ Tex Austin, PhD, 99. **CAREER** Asst prof, Univ Waterloo, 99-. **HONORS AND AWARDS** DAAD Fel, 93-94; Univ Tex Prof Dev Awd, 95, 96, 96, 97; Univ Tex Austin Fel, 97-98; Univ Waterloo/SSHRC, 00-01; Univ Waterloo Grant, 00-02. **MEMBERSHIPS** MLA, Am Assoc of Applied Ling, Am Assoc of Teachers of Ger, Can Assoc of Teachers of Ger, Int Pragmatics Assoc. **RESEARCH** Codeswitching, Conversation Analysis, Language and Identity, Second Language Acquisition, Computer-Assisted Language Learning. **SELECTED PUBLICATIONS** Coauth, Aktuelle Videos fur Wirtschaftsdeutsch, AATG, 95; auth, "Unified Ger-

many (?): Processes of Identifying, Redefining and Negotiating in Interactions between East and West Germans," Salsa IV, ed A Chy, AM Guerra, C Tetreault, (97); coed, Salsa VI, Proceedings of the Sixth Annual Symposium about Languages and Society Austin, Tex Ling Forum Austin, 99; auth, "Arriving at identities: positioning of speakers in German TV talkshows," Relocating Germanness - Discursive Disunity in Unified Germany(Basingstoke: Macmillan/St Martin, 00); auth, "Perspectives in Conflict: An Analysis of German-German Conversations," Beyond Misunderstanding - The Linguistic Reconstruction of Intercultural Communication, ed Kristin Buhrig and Jan D ten Thije, (Amsterdam: John Benjamins, 01). **CONTACT ADDRESS** Dept Ger and Slavic Studies, Univ Waterloo, 200 University Ave W, Waterloo, ON, Canada N2L 3G1. **EMAIL** gliebsche@uwaterloo.ca

LIHANI, JOHN

PERSONAL Born 03/24/1927, Slovakia, m, 1950, 3 children **DISCIPLINE** SPANISH LANGUAGE AND LITERATURE **EDUCATION** Case Western Reserve Univ, BS, 48; Ohio State Univ, MA, 50; Univ Tex, PhD(Romance lang), 54. **CAREER** Asst Span, Tulane Univ, 50-51; instr, Univ Tex, 53-54; from instr to asst prof, Yale Univ, 54-62; assoc prof Romance lang, Univ Pittsburgh, 62-69; Prof Span Ling and Lit, Univ KY, 69-92; prof emer, 92-. **HONORS AND AWARDS** Morse fel, 60-61; Fulbright prof, Inst Caro y Cuervo, Colombia, 65-66; ed, La Coronica, 72-73; assoc ed, Bull Comediantes, 73-; Int Res and Exchanges Bd res award, 74; Am Philos Soc res awd, 77; Am Coun Learned Soc grant, 80; Phi Beta Kappa. **MEMBERSHIPS** MLA; Am Asn Teachers Span and Port; SAtlantic Mod Lang Asn; AAUP. **RESEARCH** Romance linguistics; Spanish medieval and classical literature; general linguistics; ESL. **SELECTED PUBLICATIONS** Auth, La pronunciacion del ingles de los EEUU, Univ Javeriana, 66; Lucas Fernandez, Farsas y eglogas, Las Americas, 69; Observations on the Spanish of South America, Ky Romance Quart, summer 69; New biographical ideas on B de Torres Naharro, Hispania, 12/71; El lenguaje de Lucas Fernandez, Inst Caro y Cuervo, Bogota, 73; Lucas Fernandez, 73 & Bartolome de Torres Naharro, 79, Twayne; La tecnica de recapitulacion autentica en el teatro del siglo XVI, Actas del Primer Congreso sobre Lope de Vega, 81; ed, Poema de Fernan Gonzalez, Collegues Pr, 92; auth, Transitional English (for speakers of Slovak, 96; for speakers of Span, 98). **CONTACT ADDRESS** Dept Span and Ital, Univ of Kentucky, Lexington, KY 40506. **EMAIL** lihani.prof@prodigy.net

LILLO-MARTIN, DIANE C.

DISCIPLINE LINGUISTICS **EDUCATION** Univ Calif, San Diego, PhD. **CAREER** Assoc prof and prof, Univ Conn; dept ch. **RESEARCH** Language acquisition, structure of American Sign Language. **SELECTED PUBLICATIONS** Auth, Universal Grammar and American Sign Language: Setting the Null Argument Parameters, Dordrecht: Kluwer Acad Press, 91; Two Kinds of Null Arguments in American Sign Language, Natural Lang and Ling Theory 4, 86; coauth, Language and Cognition: The View from Sign Language and Deafness, Oxford, UK: Oxford UP, 97; Wh-Movement and the Position of SPEC CP: Evidence from American Sign Language, Lang 73, 97. **CONTACT ADDRESS** Dept of Linguistics, Univ of Connecticut, Storrs, Monteith Bldg, Unit 1145, 1266 Storrs Rd, Storrs, CT 06269-1085. **EMAIL** lillo.martin@uconn.edu

LILLYMAN, WILLIAM J.

PERSONAL Born 04/17/1937, Sydney, Australia, m, 1962 **DISCIPLINE** GERMAN COMPARATIVE LITERATURE **EDUCATION** Sydney Univ, BA, 59; Stanford Univ, PhD(Ger), 64. **CAREER** Asst prof Ger lit, Stanford Univ, 64-67; from asst prof to assoc prof, Univ Calif, Santa Cruz, 67-72; assoc prof and chmn dept, 72-73, Prof Ger and Dean Humanities, 73-82, Vice Chancellor, Univ Calif, Irvine, 82-, Humanities res fel, Univ Calif, Irvine, 73; dir, Goethe Res Prog, 81-**MEMBERSHIPS** MLA; Am Asn Teachers Ger. **RESEARCH** Nineteenth century German and comparative literature. **SELECTED PUBLICATIONS CONTACT ADDRESS** Office of Vice Chancellor, Univ of California, Irvine, Irvine, CA 92717.

LIMA, ROBERT F.

PERSONAL Born 11/07/1935, Havana, Cuba, m, 1964, 4 children **DISCIPLINE** SPANISH LANGUAGE, COMPARATIVE LITERATURE **EDUCATION** Villanova Univ, BA, 57; MA, 61; New York Univ, PhD, 68. **CAREER** Lectr, Hunter Col, 62-65; vis prof, poet in res, Univ Nacional Mayor de Marcos, 76-77; vis prof, Pontifica Univ, 76-77; vis prof, Univ Yaounde, 86; asst prof to prof, PaState Univ, 65-; ch, 70-75; prof Span Comp Lit, 73-. **HONORS AND AWARDS** Alpha Psi Omega; NYU Founders Day Awd; Cintas Found Fel; MID Awd; Sr Fulbright Fel; Phi Sigma Iota; Phi Kappa Phi; Who's Who in World, Am, Hisp Am, East, of Authors, Am Edu. **MEMBERSHIPS** AATSP; Fulbright Asn; Intl PEN; PSA; Poets and Writers; ALA; AIA; IAFA; RAE; Foro Manuel Fraga; ANLE. **SELECTED PUBLICATIONS** Transl of, Savage Acts, Four Plays, by Ramon del Valle-Inclan, Estreno Contemporary Span Plays (University Park), 93; auth, Dark Prisms: Occultism in Hispanic Drama, Univ Press KY (Lexington), 95; co-ed, Homenafe a /Tribute to Martha T Halsey, Estreno (University Park), 95; auth, "Valle-Inclan, Spanish Precursor of the Absurdist Mode," in Contemporary Theatre Rev, ed. Maria A. Delgado (London), 97; auth, "The Mystery Women of Elche," in Essays in Honor of Gilbert Paolini, ed. Mercedes Vidal Tibbits (Potomac, MD: Studia Hispanistica, 97); auth, "Yule: The Ancient Roots of Christmas," in First Light Poems, Stories and Essays of the Winter Holiday Season, ed. Susan Richardson (Cheyenne, WY: Calypso Pub, 97); auth, "Gift Bearers of the Epiphany," in First Light: Poems, Stories and Essays of the Winter Holiday Season, ed. Susan Richardson (Cheyenne, WY: Calypso Pub, 97); auth, "The Orishas: African Gods in Cuban Literature," in The Growth of African Literature, eds. Edris Makward, Thelma Ravell-Pinto, Aliko Songolo (Trenton--Asmara: Africa World Press, 98); auth, "The Arcane Paganism of Celestina: Plutonic Magic Versus Satanic Witchcraft," in Tragicomedia de Calixto y Melibea. In Neophilologus (The Netherlands, 98). **CONTACT ADDRESS** Dept Spanish, Italian, Portuguese, Pennsylvania State Univ, Univ Park, 352 Burrowes Bldg, University Park, PA 16802-6203. **EMAIL** rxl2@psu.edu

LIMBRICK, ELAINE

DISCIPLINE SIXTEENTH; SEVENTEENTH CENTURY FRENCH LITERATURE **EDUCATION** Univ Poitiers, PhD. **CAREER** Prof, Univ of Victoria. **RESEARCH** Montaigne's literary influence; relationship between literature and the arts. **SELECTED PUBLICATIONS** Auth, Franciscus Sanches, That nothing is known, Cambridge UP, 88; The use of the vernacular in the popularization of philosophy: Descartes' case, History of European Ideas, Pergamon Press, 91; Montaigne: metamorphose d'un philosophe en theologien, Conclusion, Bibliographie, Montaigne Penseur et Philosophe, Champion, 90; L'oeil du poete: vision et perspective dans la poesie francaise de la Renaissance, Etudes litteraires, 87. **CONTACT ADDRESS** Dept of French, Univ of Victoria, PO Box 3045 STN CSC, Victoria, BC, Canada V8W 3P4. **EMAIL** French@uvvm.uvic.ca

LINDENBURGER, HERBERT S.

PERSONAL Born 04/04/1929, Los Angeles, CA, m, 1961, 2 children **DISCIPLINE** ENGLISH, COMPARATIVE LITERATURE **EDUCATION** Antioch Col, BA, 51; Univ Washington, PhD, 55. **CAREER** Instr to prof, Univ of Calif, Riverside, 54-66; prof, Washington Univ, 66-69; Avalon Prof of Humanities, Stanford Univ, 69-. **HONORS AND AWARDS** Guggenheim Fel, 68-69; Nat Endowment for Humanities Fel, 75-76, 82-83; Stanford Humanities Ctr Fel, 82-83; Pres, MLA, 97. **MEMBERSHIPS** MLA, Am Comp Lit Asn. **RESEARCH** Romanticism, modernism, relation of literature to other arts, opera. **SELECTED PUBLICATIONS** Auth, On Wordsworth's Prelude, Princeton Univ Press (63); auth, Historical Drama, Univ Chicago Press (75); auth, Saul's Fall, Johns Hopkins Univ Press (79); auth, Opera: The Extravagant Art, Cornell Univ Press (84); auth, The History in Literature, Columbia Univ Press (90); auth, Opera in History: From Monteverdi to Cage, Stanford Univ Press (98); auth, Literature and the Other Arts, Cambridge History of Criticism (2000). **CONTACT ADDRESS** Dept English Bldg 460, Stanford Univ, Stanford, CA 94305-2087. **EMAIL** Lindenberger@stanford.edu

LINDERSKI, JERZY

DISCIPLINE CLASSICS **EDUCATION** Univ Cracow, MA, 55, PhD, 60. **CAREER** Prof, Univ NC, Chapel Hill; vis mem, Inst for Advan Stud, Princeton Univ, 77-78. **HONORS AND AWARDS** Ford Found fel, 62-63; Deut Forschungsgemeinschaft fel, Univ Cologne, 70-71; Guggenheim fel, 77-78; NEH fel, 85-86. **RESEARCH** Cicero; Roman law. **SELECTED PUBLICATIONS** Auth, Broughton, Thomas Robert Shannon, in W.W. Briggs, Jr, ed, Biog Dictionary of N Am Classicists, Westport, Ct., 94; Zum Wandel d/l: medulla / melila, Glotta 71 93, 94; Thomas Robert Shannon Broughton, Gnomon 67, 95; A Missing Ponticus, Am J of Ancient Hist 12, 87, 95; Games in Patavium, Ktema 17, 92, 96; Q. Scipio Imperator, in Jerzy Linderski, ed, Imperium Sine Fine: T.R.S. Broughton and the Roman Republic, Hist Einzelschriften 105, 96; Cato Maior in Aetolia, in Robert W. Wallace and Edward M. Harris, eds, Transitions to Empire. Essays in Greco-Roman History 360 -146 B.C. in Honor of Ernst Badian, Norman, OK, 96; Agnes Kirsopp Michels and the Religio, Class J 92.4, 97; Fatalis: A Missing Meretrix, Rheinisches Mus 140, 97; ed, Imperium Sine Fine: T.R.S. Broughton and the Roman Republic, Hist Einzelschriften 105, Steiner Verlag, 96; coauth, T. Robert S. Broughton, In Memoriam, Am Philol ASn Newsl 17.2, 94. **CONTACT ADDRESS** Univ of No Carolina, Chapel Hill, Chapel Hill, NC 27599.

LINDHEIM, SARA H.

DISCIPLINE CLASSICS **EDUCATION** Brown Univ, PhD, 95. **CAREER** Asst Prof. **MEMBERSHIPS** Am Philol Asn; Women's Classical Caucus. **RESEARCH** Latin poetry, Sappho, critical and feminist theory. **SELECTED PUBLICATIONS** Auth, "Hercules Cross-Dressed, Hercules Undressed: Unmasking the Construction of the Propertian Amator in Elegy 4.9," in Am Jour of Philology 119.1 (98), 43-66; auth, I Am Dressed, Therefore I Am?: Vertumnus in Propertius 4.2 and in Metamorphoses 14.662-771, Ramus 27.1 (98), 27-38; auth, Omnia Vincit Amor: Or, Why Oenone Should Have Known It Would Never Work Out (Eclogue 10 and Heroides 5), Material e discussioni per l'analisi dei testi classici 44 (00), 83-101. **CONTACT ADDRESS** Dept of Classics, Univ of California, Santa Barbara, Santa Barbara, CA 93106-7150. **EMAIL** lindheim@humanitas.ucsb.edu

LINDSTROM, NAOMI

PERSONAL Born 11/21/1950, Chicago, IL, s **DISCIPLINE** SPANISH & PORTUGUESE **EDUCATION** Univ Chicago, AB, 71; Ariz State Univ, MA, 72; PhD, 74. **CAREER** From Asst Prof to Prof, Univ Tex, 75-. **HONORS AND AWARDS** Andrew W Mellon Found Grant, 90, 94. **MEMBERSHIPS** Latin Am Jewish Studies Asn, Ist Int de Lit Iberoamericana, Latin Am Studies Asn, MLA. **RESEARCH** Spanish-American narrative, Brazilian narrative, 20th-Century Jewish thought. **SELECTED PUBLICATIONS** Auth, Jewish Issues in Argentine Literature: From Gerchunoff to Szichman, Univ Mo Pr (Columbia, MO), 89; auth, "Women's Voice in Latin American Literature," Three Continents Pr (Washington, DC), 89; auth, Jorge Luis Borges: A Study of the Short Fiction, Twayne Publ (Boston, MA), 90; auth, Twentieth-Century Spanish American Fiction, Univ Tex Pr (Austin, TX), 94; auth, The Social Conscience of Latin American Writing, Univ Tex Pr (Austin, TX), 98;. **CONTACT ADDRESS** Dept Spanish & Portugese, Univ of Texas, Austin, 0 University of Texas, Austin, TX 78712-1155. **EMAIL** lindstrom@mail.utexas.edu

LINN, MICHAEL D.

PERSONAL Born 03/07/1936, Aberdeen, SD, m, 1962, 1 child **DISCIPLINE** LINGUISTICS, AMERICAN ENGLISH **EDUCATION** Univ Mont, BA, 60, MA, 62; Univ Minn, MA, 70, PhD(commun), 74. **CAREER** Instr English, Lamara State Col of Tech, 63-65; res asst ling, Univ Minn, 68-71 and Cent Midwest Regional Educ Lab, 71-72; from instr to asst prof English, Va Commonwealth Univ, 72-77; asst prof, 77-80, Assoc Prof English and Anthrop, Univ Minn, Duluth, 80-, Consult, Cent Midwest Regional Educ Lab, 72-73, Richmond Pub Sch, 74-75 and Va State Dept of Educ, 74-75; tape collector, US Dialect Tape Depository, 75-78; reader and consult, Choice, 75-; lectr, Arrowhead Speaker Serv, 78-81; manuscript reader, Halcyon, 78-; res fel, Mass Inst of Technol, 78; manuscript referee, J Teacher Educ, 79-81. **MEMBERSHIPS** NCTE; Am Dialect Soc; MLA; Ling Soc Am; Asn Appl Ling. **RESEARCH** American dialects; language variation; the teaching of writing. **SELECTED PUBLICATIONS** Auth, Papers From the Special Session in Honor of Professor Sibata, Takesi--Introduction, Amer Speech, Vol 0071, 96. **CONTACT ADDRESS** English Dept, Univ of Minnesota, Duluth, 10 University Dr, Duluth, MN 55812-2496.

LINTZ, BERNADETTE C.

DISCIPLINE 19TH-CENTURY FRENCH LITERATURE, FRENCH THEATER **EDUCATION** DUEL, License es Lettres Modernes, Maitrise d'Anglais Univ de Strasbourg; Rice Univ, MA, 82, PhD, 84. **CAREER** Act ch, 95; dir, Dijon Study Group, 86, 89, 94; instr, Univ IN, Univ Houston, Rice Univ; assoc prof-; Dijon Study Group, 00. **HONORS AND AWARDS** Sr Picker research fel, Colgate Univ, 90; travel grant, Am Coun Learned Societies, 85. **MEMBERSHIPS** NCFS, MLA, AATF. **RESEARCH** Victor Hugo, Romantic Drama, Emile Zola, naturalism, intertextuality. **SELECTED PUBLICATIONS** Auth, Victor Hugo: Oeuvres et critique, 81-83; co-auth, Minard, 92; co-ed, The French Novel from Lafayette to Desvignes, New Paradigm Press, 95; Nana: le savoir de l'alcove, The Fr Novel from Lafayette to Desvignes, New Paradigm Press, 95; contrib, Critical Bibliography of Fr Lit: The XIX Century (Syracuse UP, 91; articles, Analecta Husserliana, The Fr Rev, Nineteenth-Century Fr Studies, Symposium, Travaux de Litterature; rev(s), L'Esprit Createur, Nineteenth-Century Fr Studies; Excavatio; co-auth, Victor Hugo: Oeuvres et critique, 81-83, Minard, 92; The XIX Century, Syracuse UP, 91. **CONTACT ADDRESS** Dept of Romance Lang, Colgate Univ, 13 Oak Drive, Hamilton, NY 13346. **EMAIL** blintz@mail.colgate.edu

LIONNET, FRANCOISE

PERSONAL Born 07/28/1948, Mauritius, m, 1972, 2 children **DISCIPLINE** FRENCH **EDUCATION** Univ d'Aix-en-Provence, BA, 69; Univ Mich, MA, 71; PhD, 86. **CAREER** Asst prof to assoc prof and dir and prof, Northwestern Univ, 87-98; prof and chair, UCLA, 98-. **HONORS AND AWARDS** MLA Women's Florence Howe Awd, 87; Fel, Cornell Univ, 87-88; Travel grant, Am Philos Soc, 88; Travel grant, Am Coun of Learned Soc, 89; Sen Rockefeller Fel, Univ Minn, 91-92; Fel, Univ Calif, 92; Res Fel, Northwestern Univ, 92-93; Grant, NEH, 95; Fac Recognition Awd, Northwestern Univ, 96; Grant, Soc Sci Res Coun, 96; UNFPA grant, 97. **MEMBERSHIPS** MLA; ACLA; AATF; Soc for the Study of Narrative; Auto/Biography Studies. **RESEARCH** French and Francophone Studies; Comparative Literature; African Studies; African American Studies; Gender and Women's Studies. **SELECTED PUBLICATIONS** Auth, Autobiographical Voices: Race, Gender, Self-Portraiture, paperback ed, Cornell Univ Press, 91; co-ed, "Post/Colonial Conditions: Exiles, Migrations, and Nomadisms," Yale French Studies, 93; co-ed, "Postcolonial, Indigenous, and Emergent Feminisms," Signs: J of Women in Culture and Soc, 95; auth, Postcolonial Representations: Women, Literature, Identity, Cornell Univ Press, 95; auth, "The Francophone

Novel," in Cambridge Companion to the Modern French Novel, (Cambridge Univ Press, 97), 194-213; auth, "Reframing Baudelaire: Literary History, Biography, Postcolonial Theory, and Vernacular Languages," Diacritics, (98): 63-85; auth, "Questions de methode: Itineraires ourles de l'autoportrait et de la critique," in Postcolonialisme et autobiographie, (Rodopi, 99), 5-22; auth, "Transnationalism, Postcolonialism, or Transcolonialism? Reflections on Los Angeles, Geography, and the Uses of Theory," Emergences: J for the Study of Media and Composite Cultures, (00): 25-35; ed, Cities, Modernity, and Cultural Memory in France and the Francophone World, 01; auth, "The Mirror and the Tomb: Africa, Museums, and Representation," African Arts, 01. **CONTACT ADDRESS** Dept French, Univ of California, Los Angeles, 212 RH, Box 951536, Los Angeles, CA 90095-1536.

LIPOVETSKY, MARK

PERSONAL Born 06/02/1964, Sverdlovsk, Russia, M, 1986, 1 child **DISCIPLINE** RUSSIAN LITERATURE AND CULTURE **EDUCATION** Ural State Univ, Russia, BA/MA, 86; PhD, 89, Dr Sci, 96. **CAREER** Lect, Ural Theatre Col, 89-91; assoc prof, Ural State Pedagogical Univ, 91-94; vis assoc prof, Univ Pittsburgh, 94-95; vis asst prof, Ill Wesleyan Univ, 96-99; asst prof, Univ Colo Boulder, 99-. **HONORS AND AWARDS** Prize for Best Critical Article in Znamia, 93; Fulbright Fel, 94; Kennan Inst for Advan Russ Studies Grant, 95; Winner, Best Textbook for Russ Univ in Lit Studies, Open Soc Inst, Soros Grant, 98; Woodrow Wilson Fel, 98; SSRC Res Grant, 00-01. **MEMBERSHIPS** Am Asn for the Advan of Slavic Studies, Acad of Contemp Russ Lit. **RESEARCH** Russian literature and culture of the 20th Century, Russian Postmodernism, Poststructuralism. **SELECTED PUBLICATIONS** Auth, Poetics of the Literary Fairy Tale, Ural State Univ Pr, (Ekateriburg), 91; auth, Russian Postmodernist Fiction: Dialogue with Chaos, ME Sharpe Inc, (Armonk, NY), 99; coauth, Modern Russian Literature, 3 vols, Editorial URSS, (Moscow), 01. **CONTACT ADDRESS** Dept Ger, Slavic Lang and Lit, Univ of Colorado, Boulder, UCB 276, Boulder, CO 80309. **EMAIL** leiderma@colorado.edu

LIPSCHUTZ, ILSE HEMPEL

PERSONAL Born 08/19/1923, Bonnigheim, Germany, m, 1952, 4 children **DISCIPLINE** FRENCH **EDUCATION** Inst Prof Francais a l'Etranger, dipl, 43, Sorbonne, Lic es Let, 43, dipl Etudes Super, 44; Univ Madrid, dipl Estud Hisp, 45; Harvard Univ, MA, 49, PhD, 58. **CAREER** Teaching fel French and Span, Harvard Univ and Radcliffe Col, 47-51; instr, 51-58, asst prof, 58-63, assoc prof, 63-72, prof French, 72-81, Andrew W Mellon Prof Humanities, Vassar Col, 81-, Chmn Dept, 75-, Am Asn Univ Women fel, 50-51; Anne Radcliffe fel, 50-51; Vassar Col fac fel, 60-61 and 66-67; US-Spain Treatise of Friendship res fel, 79-80 and 81. **MEMBERSHIPS** MLA; AAUP; Am Asn Univ Women; Int Soc Fr Studies; Soc Etudes Romantiques; Soc Theophile Gautier. **SELECTED PUBLICATIONS** Auth, El despojo de obras de arte durante la Guerra de Independencia, 61 & El pintor y las poetas, Goya y los romanticos franceses, summer 68, Arte Espanol; Spanish Painting and the French Romantics, Harvard Univ, 72, Span ed, Taurus (Madrid), 88; Victor Hugo, Louis Boulanger, Francisco de Goya: Amities, affinites, influences, Nineteenth-Century Fr Studies, fall-winter 75-76; Theophile Gautier, su Espana legendaria y los Caprichos de Goya, Revista de Occidente, 12/76; Theophile Gautier et son Espagne retrouvee dans l'oeuvre grave de Goya, Bull Soc Theophile Gautier, 80; Imagenes y palabras, los franceses ante la pintura espanola, in La Imagen Romantica de Espana, Madrid, 81; auth, Gautier, Theophile, Life and Work, 19th-Century Fr Stud, Vol 0026, 97. **CONTACT ADDRESS** 11 Park Ave, Poughkeepsie, NY 12603.

LISKER, LEIGH

PERSONAL Born 12/07/1918, Philadelphia, PA, m, 1947, 3 children **DISCIPLINE** LINGUISTICS **EDUCATION** Univ Pa, BA, 41, MA, 46, PhD(ling), 49. **CAREER** Asst instr Ger, 47-48; from instr to assoc prof ling and Dravidian ling, 48-64, chmn dept, 76-80, PROF LING, UNIV PA, 64-, Am Coun Learned Soc fel, 47-48; Fulbright grant, India, 51-52, 59-60; Res Consult, Hasking Labs, NY, 53-; vis lectr, Deccan Col Post-Grad and Res Inst Poona, India, 59-60. **MEMBERSHIPS** Acoust Soc Am. **RESEARCH** Structural and Dravidian linguistics; acoustic and physiological phonetics. **SELECTED PUBLICATIONS** Auth Introduction to Spoken Telugu, Am Coun Learned Soc, 63. **CONTACT ADDRESS** Dept of Ling, Univ of Pennsylvania, Philadelphia, PA 19104.

LITTLE, GRETA D.

PERSONAL Born 12/03/1943, Asheville, NC **DISCIPLINE** ENGLISH, LINGUISTICS **EDUCATION** Carleton Col, BA, 65; Univ NC, MA, 69, PhD(ling), 74. **CAREER** Peace Corps teacher English, Haile Selassie 1st Sch, Ethiopia, 65-67; teaching asst Swahili, Univ NC and Duke Univ, 72; inst ling, Univ NC, 72-73; Fulbright lectr English, Cyril and Methodius Univ, Skopje, 73-74; dir English for Foreign Students, 77-79, Asst Prof English and Ling, Univ SC, 74-, Assoc Ed, Southeastern Conf Ling Rev, 77-. **MEMBERSHIPS** Ling Soc Am; Ling Asn Can and US; Southeastern Conf Ling; Southern Asn Africanists; Teachers English to Speakers Other Lang. **RESEARCH** Syntactic change; African languages. **SELECTED PUBLICATIONS** **CONTACT ADDRESS** English Dept, Univ of So Carolina, Columbia, Columbia, SC 29208.

LITTMAN, ROBERT J.

PERSONAL Born 08/23/1943, Newark, NJ, m, 1966, 3 children **DISCIPLINE** ANCIENT HISTORY, CLASSICS **EDUCATION** Columbia Univ, BA, 64, PhD(class philol), 70; Oxford Univ, BLitt, 68. **CAREER** Instr hist, Rutgers Univ, 67-68; instr classics, Brandeis Univ, 68-70; asst prof, 70-75, assoc prof, 75-79, Prof Classics, Univ Hawaii, Manoa, 79-, Herodotus fel and vis mem, Inst Advan Study, Princeton, 77. **MEMBERSHIPS** Am Philol Asn; Am Hist Asn; Soc Prom Hellenic Studies, Friends Ancient Hist. **RESEARCH** Greek history; historiography; Greek literature. **SELECTED PUBLICATIONS** Auth, Epidemiology of the Plague of Athens, Transactions of the American Philol Asn, Vol 0122, 92; Athens, Persia and the Book of Ezra, Transactions of the Amer Philol Asn, Vol 0125, 95; Kinship and Politics in Athens, 90; Jewish History in 100 Nutshells, 96. **CONTACT ADDRESS** Dept of Europ Lang and Lit, Univ of Hawaii, Manoa, 1890 E. West Rd., Honolulu, HI 96822-2362. **EMAIL** littman@hawaii.edu

LIU, CATHERINE

DISCIPLINE EARLY MODERN FRENCH NOVEL; LITERARY THEORY; PSYCHOANALYSIS; COMPARATIVE LITERATURE **EDUCATION** CUNY, PhD. **CAREER** Instr, Univ Minn, Twin Cities. **HONORS AND AWARDS** McKnight Land-grant prof. **MEMBERSHIPS** MLA; AAUW. **RESEARCH** The fiction of Lafayette; historiography; psychoanalytic theory; modernism and modernity. **SELECTED PUBLICATIONS** Published in the fields of psychoanalytic theory and art criticism. **CONTACT ADDRESS** Dept of Cult Studies and Comp Lit, Univ of Minnesota, Twin Cities, 9 Pleasant St. SE, 350 Folwell Hall, Minneapolis, MN 55455. **EMAIL** liuxx@tc.umn.edu

LIU, JUN

PERSONAL Born 12/15/1959, Changshu, China, 1 child **DISCIPLINE** LINGUISTICS **EDUCATION** Suzhou Univ, BA, 81; E China Normal Univ, MEd, 89; Ohio State Univ, PhD, 96. **CAREER** Acad Prof to Vis Asst Prof, Ohio State Univ, 96-98; Asst Prof, Univ Ariz, 98-. **HONORS AND AWARDS** Newbury House Excellence of Teaching Awd, TESOL, 99; Prof Develop Awd, TESOL, 99; Grad Res Forum Awd, Ohio State Univ, 95; Univ Excellence of Teaching Awd, 89. **MEMBERSHIPS** TESOL; AAAL; AERA; CCCC; AZTESOL. **RESEARCH** Second Language Acquisition and Teaching; Research Methodology; Second Language Reading and Writing; Non-native English Speakers Empowerment; Teaching Methodology and Teacher Education. **SELECTED PUBLICATIONS** Co-auth, "Theoretical and Methodological Considerations of Social Identity," TESOL Quart, 97; auth, "non-native English Speaking Professionals," TESOL Quart, 99; auth, "The Power of Readers' Theater," ELT J, 00; auth, "Methodological Options for Classroom Research," J of Intensive English Studies, 00; auth, "Factors affecting Asian Students' Classroom Participation in US universities," J of Asian Pac Comm, 00; auth, "Writing from Chinese to English: My Cultural Transformation," Reflections on Multiliterate Lives, 01; auth, Asian Students' Classroom Communication Patterns in U.S. Universities, Greenwood Pub group, 01; co-auth, Peer Response in L2 Writing, Univ Mich Press; co-ed, Michigan Series on Teaching Multilingual Writers, Univ Mich Press, 01. **CONTACT ADDRESS** Dept Ling, Univ of Arizona, ML 488, PO Box 210067, Tucson, AZ 85721. **EMAIL** junliu@arizona.edu

LIVORNI, ERNESTO

PERSONAL Born 03/27/1959, Pescara, Itlay, m, 1991, 3 children **DISCIPLINE** ITALIAN LITERATURE **EDUCATION** Univ Urbino, Italy, Laurea, 82; Univ Conn, PhD, 90. **CAREER** Lectr to assoc prof, Yale Univ, 88-00; asst prof, Univ of Wis, 00-. **HONORS AND AWARDS** Mellon Fel, 92-93. **MEMBERSHIPS** Am Assoc for Ital Studies, Am Assoc for teachers of Ital, MLA. **RESEARCH** Modern and contemporary Italian literature, comparative literature, poetry, cinema and literature, literary criticism. **SELECTED PUBLICATIONS** Auth, Avanguardia e tradizione: Ezra Pound e Giuseppe Ungaretti, Casa Editrice Le Lettere, Florence, 98. **CONTACT ADDRESS** Dept Fr and Ital, Univ of Wisconsin, Madison, 618 Van Hise Hall, Madison, WI 53706. **EMAIL** elivorni@facstaff.wisc.edu

LLOYD, CARYL

DISCIPLINE FRENCH LITERATURE **EDUCATION** Univ Iowa, PhD. **SELECTED PUBLICATIONS** Auth, pubs on eighteenth and nineteenth century literature, French women writers, and Leona Queyrouze. **CONTACT ADDRESS** Dept Foreign Languages and Literature, State Univ of West Georgia, Carrollton, GA 30118.

LLOYD, PAUL M.

PERSONAL Born 09/15/1929, Rochester, NY, m, 1952, 2 children **DISCIPLINE** ROMANCE PHILOLOGY **EDUCATION** Oberlin Col, AB, 52; Brown Univ, AM, 54; Univ Calif, Berkeley, PhD, 60. **CAREER** Teaching asst Span, Brown Univ, 52-54 & Univ Calif, 54-58; instr, Dartmouth Col, 58-60 & Ling Sci Romance Lang, Sch Lang, Foreign Serv inst, 60-61; from asst prof to assoc prof, 61-70, prof Romance Lang, Univ PA, 70-, assoc ed, Hisp Rev, 65-; Fulbright lectr English, Univ Deusto, Spain, 66-67. **HONORS AND AWARDS** John Frederick Lewis Awd from American Philosophical Society, 88. **MEMBERSHIPS** Ling Soc Am; Am Asn Teachers Span & Port; Soc Ling Romane; Ling Asn Can & US; Sci Fiction Res Asn. **RESEARCH** Romance philology; general and Spanish linguistics. **SELECTED PUBLICATIONS** Auth, Verb-complement Compounds in Spanish, Max Niemeyer, Tubingen, 68; L'action du substrat et la structure linguistique, In: Actele celui de-al XII-les Congres International de Linguistica si Filologie Romanica, 1968, 71; Contribucion al estudio del tema de Don Juan en las comedias de Tirso de Molina, In: Homenaje al Prof William L Fichter, 71; coauth, A Graded Spanish Review Grammar with Composition, Prentice-Hall, 73; auth, La metafonia vocalica y el sistema verbal romanico, In: Proceedings of the 14th International Congress of Romance Linguistics and Philology, Amsterdam, Benjamins, 77; On the definition of Vulgar Latin, Neuphilogische Mitteilungen, 79; From Latin to Spanish, American Philosophical Society, 87, Spanish translation: Del Latin al espanol, 93. **CONTACT ADDRESS** Dept of Romance Lang, Univ of Pennsylvania, Philadelphia, PA 19104-6305. **EMAIL** plloyd@sas.upenn.edu

LLOYD, ROSEMARY

PERSONAL Born 09/19/1949, Adelaide, South Australia, m, 1971 **DISCIPLINE** FRENCH LITERATURE **EDUCATION** Univ Adelaide, BA, 72, MA, 75; Univ Cambridge, MA, 78, PhD, 78. **CAREER** Fel, New Hall, Cambridge, UK, 78-90; Univ lectr (prof), Cambridge, UK, 79-90; prof, Indiana Univ, 90-99, Rudy Prof of French, 99-. **HONORS AND AWARDS** NEH, 98. **MEMBERSHIPS** MLA, Nineteenth-century French Studies. **RESEARCH** 19th century French novel and poetry, 20th century novel and poetry, literature and the visual arts. **SELECTED PUBLICATIONS** Transl, The Master Pipers, by George Sand, Oxford: Oxford Univ Press (94); auth, Closer & Closer Apart: Jealousy in Literature, Ithaca, NY: Cornell Univ Press (95); transl, Revolutions in Writing: Nineteenth-Century French Prose, Bloomington: Indiana Univ Press (96); co-ed, "Roses de noel," (Vol 6) and "Le Sang de la coupe" (vol 2), plus other volumes of Theodore de Banville, Euvres completes, Geneva: Slatkine (95-); auth, Mallarme: The Poet and His Circle, Ithaca, NY: Cornell Univ Press (99); auth, Women Seeking Expression: France 1789-1914, Monash Romance Studies (forthcoming); auth, Women Seeking Expression: France 1789-1914: Translations, Monash Romance Studies (forthcoming); **CONTACT ADDRESS** Dept French and English, Indiana Univ, Bloomington, 1020 E Kirkwood Ave, Ballantine Hall 642, Bloomington, IN 47405-7103. **EMAIL** rolloyd@indiana.edu

LO, CHIN-TANG

PERSONAL Born 07/27/1929, Lungsi, China, m, 1959, 2 children **DISCIPLINE** CHINESE **EDUCATION** Nat Taiwan Univ, BA, 52, MA, 56, LittD, 61. **CAREER** Assoc prof, New Asian Col, Chinese Univ Hong Kong, 60-61; lectr, Univ Hong Kong, 61-66; assoc prof, 66-70, Prof Chinese, Univ Hawaii, Manoa, 71-; Vis prof, Univ Hamburg, 72-73, Nat Taiwan Univ, 79-80; Chair Prof of Tung-Hai Univ, 86-87. **SELECTED PUBLICATIONS** Auth, An introduction to the literary value of Confucian classics, 67; The development of Chinese fiction, 68; translr, Early Chinese Literature, B Watson, 69; Clues leading to the discovery of Hsi Yu Chi Ping-hua, 69; Popular stories of Wei and Chin period, 71; Goethe and the novels of Ming Dynasty, 73; Chinese point of view to drama, 73; On Classical Chinese drama, 77; Chinese Study and Sinology, 79; The Development of Chinese Drama, 80. **CONTACT ADDRESS** Dept of East Asian Lang & Lit, Univ of Hawaii, Manoa, 1890 E West Rd, Honolulu, HI 96822-2318.

LOBNER, CORINA DEL GRECO

PERSONAL Born 02/22/1927, Italy, m, 1945, 1 child **DISCIPLINE** COMPARATIVE LITERATURE **EDUCATION** Dominican Col, BA, 66; Univ Wis, MA, 68; Univ Tulsa, PhD, 81. **CAREER** Lectr, Univ Wis Racine, Loyola Univ, 64-68; asst prof, Dominican Col, 68-74; assoc prof to emer, Univ Tulsa, 81-97. **HONORS AND AWARDS** Adv Ed, James Joyce Quart and Studies; Pres Invitational Papers of James Joyce Intl Symposium, 82-97; Speaker at Joyce Symposium Univ Trieste, Italy, 97; Women Studies Awd, 92; Who's Who Am; Phi Kappa Phi Scholshp, 68; Lamba Iota Tau, Domin Col, 66; Grad Fel, Irish Studies, Univ Tulsa, 77-81. **MEMBERSHIPS** Phi Kappa Phi; Gabinetto Viesseux, Florence, Italy. **RESEARCH** James Joyce; modernism; Dante; Italian and Sicilian literature; Italian Cirierraa. **SELECTED PUBLICATIONS** Auth, James Joyce's Italian Connection: The Poetics of the Word, Iowa UP, 89; auth, "A Lexicon for Both Sexes: Natalia Ginzburg and the Family Saga," in Contemporary Women Writers in Italy (Mass UP, 90); co-ed, "Dante and Modernism," Lectura Dantis 12 (93); ed, "The Italian Joyce," James Joyce Quart (99). **CONTACT ADDRESS** 7405 E 20th Pl, Tulsa, OK 74112-7709.

LOCKE, JOHN

PERSONAL Born New York, NY, s **DISCIPLINE** COMPARATIVE LITERATURE **EDUCATION** Univ Iowa, PhD. **CAREER** English and Lit, Univ Ark. **HONORS AND AWARDS** Dir, Comp Lit. **RESEARCH** Wisdom Lit. **SELECTED PUBLICATIONS** Transl, Nine Plays by Rainer Maria Rilke, Ungar, 79. **CONTACT ADDRESS** Univ of Arkansas, Fayetteville, Kimpel Hall 333, Fayetteville, AR 72701.

LOCKHART, PHILIP N.
PERSONAL Born 05/03/1928, Smicksburg, PA, m, 1959, 2 children **DISCIPLINE** CLASSICAL STUDIES **EDUCATION** Univ Pa, BA, 50; Univ NC, MA, 51; Yale Univ, PhD(classical lang), 59. **CAREER** Teacher, Ezel Mission Sch, Ky, 51-52; instr class lang, Univ Mo, 54-56; instr class studies, Univ Pa, 57-61, asst prof, 61-63; assoc prof class lang and chmn dept, 63-68, prof, 68-71, Asbury J Clarke Prof Latin and Chmn Dept, Dickinson Col, 71- , prof emer, 90-; Vis prof, Ohio State Univ, 69-70. **HONORS AND AWARDS** Ganoe Awd Teaching, Dickinson Col, 69, 73, 81; 2000 Outstanding Scholars, Who's Who, 00. **MEMBERSHIPS** Am Philol Asn; Archaeol Inst Am; Am Class League; Vergilian Soc Am. **RESEARCH** Latin poetry; fourth century AD; Homeric background. **SELECTED PUBLICATIONS** Auth, Moser, Mary, E. 1950-1996--in Memoriam, Class World, Vol 0089, 96. **CONTACT ADDRESS** Dept of Class Lang, Dickinson Col, Carlisle, PA 17013. **EMAIL** lockhart@dickinson.edu

LOEWEN, LYNN
DISCIPLINE SPANISH LANGUAGE **EDUCATION** Univ Wis, BA, MA, PhD. **CAREER** Languages, Carthage Col. **SELECTED PUBLICATIONS** Area: teaching English as a second language. **CONTACT ADDRESS** Carthage Col, 2001 Alford Dr., Kenosha, WI 53140. **EMAIL** loewen@carthage.edu

LOFSTEDT, BENGT
PERSONAL Born 11/14/1931, Lund, Sweden, m, 1961, 4 children **DISCIPLINE** LATIN **EDUCATION** Univ Uppsala, MA, 54, Phil lic, 57, PhD(Latin), 61. **CAREER** Asst prof Latin, Univ Uppsala, 62-67; assoc prof, 67-68, Prof Medieval Latin, Univ Calif, Los Angeles, 68- Alexander von Humbolt-Stiftung fel, 61-62; Univ Calif fel, Humanities Inst, 68 and 72; Am Coun Learned Soc grant, 72. **MEMBERSHIPS** Am Philol Asn; Soc Etudes Latines; Indoger Ges. **RESEARCH** History of the Latin language, with emphasis on the later periods; medieval Latin grammarians; patristics. **SELECTED PUBLICATIONS** Auth, Studien Uber die Sprache der langobardischen gesetze, 61; auth, Der hibeadolateinische Grammatiker Malsachanus, 65; auth, Zenonis Veronensis Tractatus, 71; auth, Ars Laureshamensis, 77; auth, Sedulius Scottus: In donati artem minorem, in Priscianum, in Eutychem, 77; auth, Ars Ambrosiana, 82; coauth, Maturin cordier: De Corrupti Sermonis Emendatione, 89; auth, Sedulius Scottus: Kommentar zum Evangelium nach Matthaus, 11,2, bis Schluss, 91; coauth, Anonymus ad Cuimnanum, 92. **CONTACT ADDRESS** Dept of Classics, Univ of California, Los Angeles, 405 Hilgard Ave, Los Angeles, CA 90024.

LOGAN, PAUL ELLIS
PERSONAL Born 10/05/1945, Washington, DC **DISCIPLINE** GERMAN LANGUAGE & LITERATURE **EDUCATION** Howard Univ, BA, 66; Univ Md, MA, 70, PhD(Ger), 74. **CAREER** Instr German, Univ Md, 69-73; assoc prof, Morgan State Univ, 73-77; chm dept Ger/Russian, Howard Univ, 77-, assoc dean humanities, Col of Arts and Sci, 91-. **HONORS AND AWARDS** Faculty res grant, Morgan State Univ, 76; Fulbright scholar, 76 & 82; German Acad Exchange Serv fel, 79 & 81; Distinguished Alumni Awd from Nat Asn for Equal Opportunity in Educ. **MEMBERSHIPS** Col Lang Asn; Mod Lang Asn; Frobenius-Gesellschaft; Am Asn Teachers Ger; Afrika-Gesellschaft. **RESEARCH** German Africa travelogs of the 16th and 17th century; American Slavery as a theme in German literature of the 18th and 19th century. **SELECTED PUBLICATIONS** Auth, Gottfried Finckelthaus Rediscovered, CLA J, 75; Leo Frobenius and Negritude, Negro Hist Bull, 78; Leo Frobenius: The Demonic Child, CLA J, 78: transl, The Sign and the Sense(Le signe et le sens-Der Sinn und das Mittel), CLA J, 78; Leo Frobenius, Negritude and the Escape of Caliban, In: Festschrift for Leon-Gontran Damas, 79; The Image of the Black in J LE Kolb's Erzahlungen von den Sitten und Schicksalen der Negersklaven, Monatshefte, 81; J E Kolb's Der Neger Makandal, Negro Hist Bull, 81; A Howard Reader: An Intellectual and Cultural Quilt of the African-American Experience, Houghton Mifflin, 97. **CONTACT ADDRESS** Office of the Dean, Col of Arts and Sci, Howard Univ, 2400 6th St N W, Washington, DC 20059-0002.

LOMBA, ARTHUR J.
DISCIPLINE FRENCH **EDUCATION** Eastern Nazarene Col, BA; Am Univ, MA; Boston Univ, PhD. **CAREER** Eng Dept, Eastern Nazarene Col **RESEARCH** Cult and hist of the Cape Verde Islands; Cape Verde immigrants; Cape Verdean Crioulo (CVC) lang. **SELECTED PUBLICATIONS** Auth, Basic CVC Pedagogical Grammar. **CONTACT ADDRESS** Eastern Nazarene Col, 23 East Elm Ave, Quincy, MA 02170-2999.

LOMBARDO, STANLEY
DISCIPLINE GREEK AND LATIN LITERATURE **EDUCATION** Loyola Univ, BA; Tulane Univ, MA; Univ TX, PhD, 76. **CAREER** Dept ch; prof, Univ KS. **HONORS AND AWARDS** Kemper tchg fel; Nat Transl Ctr award. **RESEARCH** Transl of Homer's Odyssey; transl Sappho. **SELECTED PUBLICATIONS** Transl, Greek poetry, including Homer's Iliad, Hackett, 97, 00; Parmenides and Empedocles, The Fragments in Verse Co-transl, Callimachus' Hymns, Epigrams & Select Fragments, Johns Hopkins, 88; Tao Te Ching, Hackett, 93; Hesiod's Works & Daysand Theogony, Hackett, 93; Horace's Odes in Latin Lyric and Elegiac Poetry, Garland, 95; Transl, Greek poetry, including Homer's Iliad, Hackett, 97, 00. **CONTACT ADDRESS** Dept of Class, Univ of Kansas, Lawrence, Admin Building, Lawrence, KS 66045. **EMAIL** lombardo@ukans.edu

LONG, ANTHONY A.
PERSONAL Born 08/17/1937, Manchester, United Kingdom, m, 2 children **DISCIPLINE** CLASSICS **EDUCATION** Univ Col London, BA, 60; Univ London, PhD, 64. **CAREER** Prof, Univ Liverpool, 73-83; Prof, Univ Calif, 83-. **HONORS AND AWARDS** Guggenheim Fel, 86; NEH Fel, 91; Fel, Am Acad of Arts & Sci, 89-; Corresponding Fel of Brit Acad, 92-. **RESEARCH** Ancient Greek and Roman philosophy, Greek literature. **SELECTED PUBLICATIONS** Auth, Language and Thought in Sophacles, 68; auth, Problems in Stoicism, 71; auth, Hellenistic Philosophy, 74, 2nd Ed, 86; , The Hellenistic Philosphies, 87; auth, The Question of Eclecticism, 88; coauth auth, Stoic Studies, 96; ed, The Cambridge Companion to Early Greek Philosophy, 99. **CONTACT ADDRESS** Dept Classics, Univ of California, Berkeley, 5303 Dwinelle Hall, Berkeley, CA 94720-2520. **EMAIL** aalong@uclink4.berkeley.edu

LONG, MARY
PERSONAL Born 06/12/1964, Denver, CO, m, 1990, 1 child **DISCIPLINE** SPANISH **EDUCATION** Colo State Univ, BA, 86; Princeton Univ, MA, 91; PhD, 95. **CAREER** Sen instr and co-dir, Univ Colo Boulder, 98-. **HONORS AND AWARDS** IMPART Awd, Univ Colo Boulder, 00; FDIB Fel, Univ Colo Denver, 00; Mellon Fel, 88-90, 93; Phi Beta Kappa, 84; Phi Kappa Phi Grad Fel, 88. **MEMBERSHIPS** MLA; Latin Am Studies Asn; Am Asn of Teachers of Spanish and Portuguese; Am Asn of Teachers of Spanish and Portuguese. **RESEARCH** Mexican literature and culture; Effects of globalization on concepts of traditional cultural identity; Pedagogical topics related to teaching Spanish for professional uses and ethics for international business. **SELECTED PUBLICATIONS** Auth, "Novo y la fragmentacion del yo," Biblioteca de Mexico, (94): 36-40; auth, "Salvadors Novo's continente Vacio," Latin Am Lit Rev, 96; auth, "Nota introductoria," Salvador Novo: viajes y Ensayos II: Cronicas y periodismo, 99. **CONTACT ADDRESS** Dept Span and Port, Univ of Colorado, Boulder, McKenna Lang Bldg, Campus Box 278, Boulder, CO 80309-0278. **EMAIL** mary.long@colorado.edu

LONG, SHERI SPAINE
PERSONAL Born 12/02/1958, Waterloo, IA, m, 1980, 2 children **DISCIPLINE** SPANISH **EDUCATION** Univ Iowa, BA, 80; MA, 83; UCLA, 90. **CAREER** Instr to asst prof, Samford Univ, 89-92; lectr to assoc prof, Univ Ala, 92-; **HONORS AND AWARDS** Outstanding For Lang Teacher Award, S Conf on Lang Teaching; Finalist, Birmingham Nat Alumni Soc Award, Univ Ala, 99; Outstanding For Lang Teacher Award, Ala Asn of For Lang Teachers, 00. **MEMBERSHIPS** Del Amo Endowment Dissertation Fel; UAB Fac Res Grant. **RESEARCH** Contemporary Spanish Novel: Madrid as a Literary Construct; Foreign Language Pedagogy: Content-Based Foreign Language Instruction; Foreign Language Policy and the Profession. **SELECTED PUBLICATIONS** Auth, En train d'ecrire: A Process Approach to French Composition with Lisa Gerrard, McGraw-Hill, 93; auth, Redaccion y revision: Estrategias para la composicion en espanol with Lisa Gerrard, McGraw-Hill, 93; auth, "Pedagogy and the Emerging Spanish Canon," Dimension, 97; auth, "Montero's Metafictional Children's Tale: El nido de los suenos," Romance Lang Annual, (97): 666-669; auth, Hacia la literatura with Susan Villar, John Wiley and Sons, 98; auth, "A Case for Common Ground: K-12 Foreign Language Teacher Recruitment in Higher Education," For Lang Annals, (00): 433-437; auth, "A Case for Common Ground: K-12 Standards and Higher Education," Assoc Dept of For Lang Bulletin, (00): 72-74. **CONTACT ADDRESS** Dept For Lang and Lit, Univ of Alabama, Birmingham, 1530 3rd Ave S, HB 407 F, Birmingham, AL 35294-1260. **EMAIL** espanol@uab.edu

LONG, TIMOTHY
PERSONAL Born 01/31/1943, Cincinnati, OH, s **DISCIPLINE** CLASSICS **EDUCATION** Xavier Univ, BA, 65; Princeton Univ, MA, 67; PhD, 71. **CAREER** Lectr to prof, Ind Univ, 69-; Chair, 93-97. **HONORS AND AWARDS** Alexander von Humboldt Fel, Ger, 77-78; Fulbright Lectr, Ger, 87-88. **MEMBERSHIPS** Am Philol Assoc; Class Assoc of the Middle West and South; Am Class League. **RESEARCH** Ancient comedy, comic theory. **SELECTED PUBLICATIONS** Auth, Barbarians in Greek Comedy, Univ of Southern Il Pr, 87; auth, Repetition and Variation in the Short Stories of Herodotous, Atheneaeum, (Frankfurt), 87. **CONTACT ADDRESS** Dept Class Studies, Indiana Univ, Bloomington, 1020 E Kirkwood Ave, Bloomington, IN 47405-7103. **EMAIL** longt@indiana.edu

LONIGAN, PAUL R.
PERSONAL Born 05/27/1935, New York, NY, m, 1965, 4 children **DISCIPLINE** CLASSICS **EDUCATION** Queens Col, BA, 60; Johns Hopkins Univ, PhD, 67. **CAREER** Instructor, Russell Sage Col, 63-65; Assoc Prof, SUNY, 65-67; Prof, Queens Col, 67-. **HONORS AND AWARDS** Nat Defense Fel; Phi Beta Kappa; Nat German Honor Soc; Men of Achievement; Presidential Cert, Queens Col; Plaque of Distinction, Queens Col; Intl Order of Merit, 99. **MEMBERSHIPS** Phi Beta Kappa; Circulo de Cultura Panamerican; Cumann na Scribheann nGaedhilge; Irish Am cultural Inst; Delta Phi Alpha; Asn of Literary Scholars and critics; Archaeol Inst of Am; Biblical Archaeol Soc; Intl Order of Merit. **RESEARCH** Medieval literature; Renaissance literature; Classics; Mythology; Philology; Celtic Studies; Indo-European Studies. **SELECTED PUBLICATIONS** Auth, The Druids: Priests of the Ancients Celts, Greenwood Pub Groups, 96; ed, Maria Victoria Carreno Montas, Santo Domingo, 99; auth, "Napoleon Bonaparte: sus estrategias de expansion en America y el Caribe," forthcoming. **CONTACT ADDRESS** Dept Romance Lang, Queens Col, CUNY, 6530 Kissena Blvd, Flushing, NY 11367-1575. **EMAIL** garwaf@juno.com

LOONEY, DENNIS
PERSONAL Born 08/18/1955, Springfield, TN, m, 1983, 2 children **DISCIPLINE** ITALIAN, CLASSICS **EDUCATION** Boston Univ, BA, 78; MA, 80; UNC Chapel Hill, PhD, 87. **CAREER** Asst prof to acad dean, Univ Pittsburgh, 86-. **HONORS AND AWARDS** Pres Distinguished Teaching Awd, Univ Pittsburgh, 92. **MEMBERSHIPS** MLA, Am Assoc Ital Studies, Renaissance Soc of Am. **RESEARCH** Dante, The reception of Dante and The Divine Comedy, Renaissance Humanism, The reception of Classical Culture in Medieval and Renaissance Italy, Renaissance Italian Literature. **SELECTED PUBLICATIONS** Auth, Comprosming the Classics: Romance Epic Narrative in the Italian Renaissance, Wayne State Univ Pr, (Detroit), 96. **CONTACT ADDRESS** Dept Fr & Ital, Univ of Pittsburgh, 1328 Cthdrl of Lrng, Pittsburgh, PA 15260. **EMAIL** looney@pitt.edu

LOPEZ, IGNACIO JAVIER
PERSONAL Born 02/25/1956, Galdakao, Spain, m, 1979, 3 children **DISCIPLINE** SPANISH LANGUAGE & LITERATURE **EDUCATION** Instituto Simancas, Madrid, Spain, Bachilerato, 73; Universidad Autonoma, Madrid, Spain, Licenciado, 79; Univ of Wi Madison, PhD, 84. **CAREER** Asst prof to assoc prof, Univ Va, 84-90; assoc prof to prof to dept chair, 90- . **HONORS AND AWARDS** Book rev ed, Hispanic Review, 90-97; gen ed, Hispanic Review, 97- ; Ed Bd, Siglo XIX, Univ Valladolid, Spain, Dialogos, Univ Amsterdam, Netherlands; colaborador universitario, univ autonoma, madrid, spain, 76; knapp fel, univ wi, 83-84. **MEMBERSHIPS** MLA; NEMLA; Asociacion Internacional de Hispanistas. **RESEARCH** Modern period; Spanish lit; hist of ideas; aesthetics; lit theory. **SELECTED PUBLICATIONS** Auth, Caballero de novela, Barcelona, 86; Realismo y ficcion, Barcelona, 89; Galdos y el arte de la prosa, Barcelona, 93; ed, La madre Naturaleza, Madrid, 92; Jardin cerrado, Malaga, 95; Dibujo de la muerte, Madrid, 98; Homenaje a Russell P. Sebold, Alicante, 99. **CONTACT ADDRESS** Dept of Romance Languages, Univ of Pennsylvania, Philadelphia, PA 19104. **EMAIL** ilopez@sas.upenn.edu

LOPEZ, OSCAR R.
PERSONAL Born Medellen, Columbia, m, 1994 **DISCIPLINE** LITERATURE, SPANISH **EDUCATION** BEd, Ude A Medellin, Colombia, 78; BPh, 86; Wash Univ, MA, 90; Univ Cincinnati, PhD, 98. **CAREER** prof, Univ de Antioquia, Colombia, 86-90, 92-94; dir, Univ Medellin, 92-94; asst prof, St Louis Univ. **HONORS AND AWARDS** Book Publication Awd, Medellin, 96; Fel, Wash Univ, 90; Res Fel, Univ of Cincinnati, 96; Taft Mem Res, Univ of Cincinnati, 97; Mellon Res, St Louis Univ, 00. **MEMBERSHIPS** MLA; INTI; Revista of Lit. **RESEARCH** Contemporary Latin American Literature. **SELECTED PUBLICATIONS** Auth, "El carnero: o de la tecnica narrativa", Con-textos, Revista de semiotica literaria 16, (95): 19-31; auth, "Acerca del cuento: o de las mudanzas de la narracion", Dominical, (Dec 95): 9-13; auth, La critica latinoaericana: o del dialogo cultural con los otros, Martin Vieco Ltda, (Medellin), 96; auth, "Una carta a Martin Romana: La realidad ficcionalizada, La ficcion Real (izada)", Cincinnati Romance Review 15, (96): 166-173; auth, "Algunas contradicciones en las ideas ilustradas de Jose Cadalso", Con-Textos: Revista de semiotica literaria 19, (April 97): 25-40; auth, "Las sagas literarias: de los griegos a Armando Romero", Domincal (Nov 97): 9-12; auth, "Un bel morir: novela clave en el ciclo del Gaviero", Hojas Univ 44 (Nov 97): 86-93; auth, "El vampiro de la colonia Roma: o del travestismo posmoderno", Revists de Lit Mexicana Contemporanea 10 (99). **CONTACT ADDRESS** Dept Mod and Class Lang, Saint Louis Univ, 221 N Grand Blvd, Saint Louis, MO 63103-2006. **EMAIL** arieslop@yahoo.com

LOPEZ-CALVO, IGNACIO
PERSONAL Born 08/05/1968, Segora, Spain, m, 1998 **DISCIPLINE** SPANISH **EDUCATION** Univ Complutense, BA; Univ Ga, MA, 94; PhD, 97. **CAREER** Teaching asst, Univ Ga, 91-97; asst prof, Calif State Univ at Los Angeles, 97-. **HONORS AND AWARDS** Listed in Who's Who; Sigma Delta Pi. **MEMBERSHIPS** MLA, AATSP, ILCH. **RESEARCH** Twentieth-Century Latin American Literature, Literary Theory. **SELECTED PUBLICATIONS** Auth, "Rapports entre la pensee

de la liberation et les portraits de femmes dans le roman antillais," Francographies 7 (98): 57-68; auth, "El fluir de conciencia en Cesar Vallejo," Confluencia 14.1 (98): 82-86; auth, "Entrevista a Marcos Aguinis," Alba de Am 17.32 (99): 395-404; auth, "La piedra como refugio de la Historia en la poesia de Ruben Vela," Alba de Am 17.32 (99): 85-90; auth, "La pasividad como terapia y mecanismo de transformacion social en Realidad nacional desde la cama de Luisa Valenzuela," Alba de Am 17.32 (99): 291-298; auth, "El compromiso social involuntario en la obra de Enrique Anderson Imbert," Alba de Am 18.33-4 (99): 51-60; auth, The Chilean Novel in Exile, Garland Publ, forthcoming. **CONTACT ADDRESS** Dept For Lang, California State Univ, Los Angeles, 5151 State University Dr, Los Angeles, CA 90032-4226. **EMAIL** lopezcalvo@cs.com

LOPEZ-MORILLAS, CONSUELO
PERSONAL Born 07/07/1944, Iowa City, IA, m, 1971, 2 children **DISCIPLINE** ROMANCE AND HISPANIC LINGUISTICS; HISPANO-ARABIC LITERATURE **EDUCATION** Bryn Mawr Col, BA, 65; Univ Calif, Berkeley, PhD, 74. **CAREER** Asst prof, Ohio State Univ, 74-77; from Asst Prof to Assoc Prof, 77-94, Prof Spanish and Near Eastern Lang, Ind Univ, 94-; Vis asst prof Arabic, Ohio State Univ, 79. **MEMBERSHIPS** MLA; Asociacion Int de Hispanistas. **RESEARCH** Hispano-Arabic language and literature; Romance linguistics; Hispanic linguistics (historical). **SELECTED PUBLICATIONS** Auth, Aljamiado akosegir and its old provencal counterparts, Romance Philol, 75; Los bereberes Zanata en la historia y la leyenda, Al-Andalus, 77; Trilingual Marginal notes in a Morisco manuscript from Toledo, J of the Am Oriental Soc, 82; La oracion como dialogo en un comentario morisco sobre la Fatiha, Nueva Revista de Filologia Hisp, 82; The Quran in 16th Century Spain: Six Morisco Versions of Sura 79, Tamesis Books, London, 82; Was the Muwashsah Really Accompanied by the Organ?, La Coronica, 85; Hispano-Semitic Calques and the Context of Translation, Bulletin of Hispanic Studies, 90; Language and Identity in Late Spanish Islam, Hispanic Rev, 95; Textos aljamiados sobre la vida de Mahoma: El profeta de los moriscos, CSIC, Madrid, 94. **CONTACT ADDRESS** Dept of Span and Port, Indiana Univ, Bloomington, 1020 E Kirkwood Ave, Bloomington, IN 47405. **EMAIL** lopez@indiana.edu

LORE, ANTHONY GEORGE
PERSONAL Born 02/21/1922, Cleveland, OH, m, 1 child **DISCIPLINE** SPANISH **EDUCATION** La State Univ, BA, 48, MA, 49; Univ NC, PhD(Romance lang), 65. **CAREER** Assoc Prof Span and Methodol and Dir Lang Lab, Univ NC, Chapel Hill, 60-. **MEMBERSHIPS** Am Asn Teachers Span and Port; MLA; Nat Asn Lang Lab Dir, NEA; Nat Soc Prog Instr. **CONTACT ADDRESS** Univ of No Carolina, Chapel Hill, 105 Dey Hall, Chapel Hill, NC 27514.

LORENZI, PAOLA G.
DISCIPLINE ITALIAN LITERATURE **EDUCATION** Col Edu Univ Florence, PhD, 81;post grad studies, Art Ctr Col Design Pasadena, Calif. **CAREER** Asst prof, CA State Univ; vis asst prof, Texas A&M Univ; instr, Univ Houston, Col Arch; vis lectr, 89-. **RESEARCH** Hist of Italian Cinema **SELECTED PUBLICATIONS** Auth, Commercial Terminology for the Oil & Gas Industry, Agip Petroleum Company, Inc, 87; transl, The Rose of Yesterday, Alessandro Carrera, Rev Contemp Fiction, 92; The Prodigal Son, Alessandro Carrera, SW Lit Arts Coun, 88. **CONTACT ADDRESS** Dept of Commun, Pepperdine Univ, 24255 Pacific Coast Hwy, Malibu, CA 90263. **EMAIL** plorenzi@pepperdine.edu

LOREY, CHRISTOPH R.
DISCIPLINE GERMAN STUDIES **EDUCATION** Asst prof, assoc prof, Univ NBruns, 94-. **CAREER** Editor, The International Fiction Rev, 95-; Mem Ed Advisory Committee, J Can Lesbian Gay Study Asn, 98-00; Mem Ed Bd, Torquere, 00-. **RESEARCH** German culture and civilization; Queer theory; Gay and Lesbian literature; German enlightenment and classicism. **SELECTED PUBLICATIONS** Auth, Lessings Familienbild im Wechselbereich von Gesellschaft and Individuum, Bouvier (Bonn), 92; auth, "'Alles Ist so Schon, Dab es Fast zu Schon Ist': Die Sozialkritischen Motive in Adalbert Stifters Roman Der Nachsommer," Ger Quart 66 (94): 477-89; auth, "Glaube und Zweifel, Luge and Wahrheit, Genialitat and Einfalt: Georg Buchners Dantons Tod und Bertolt Brechts Leben des Galilei," Deuts Vierteljahr Lit Geistes 68 (94): 251-77; co-ed, "Die Schuld-Verhaltnisse in Hartmanns Iwein," in Analogon Rationis: Festschrift fur Gerwin Marahrens Zum 65, Geburtstag (Edmonton: Pub by the Eds, 94): 19-47; co-ed, Analogon Rationis: Festschrift fur Gerwin Marahrens zum 65, Geburtstag 95; auth, Die Ehe im Klassischen Werk Goethes, Rodopi Pr, 95; auth, "Zur Innen- und Aubenperspektive in Stephan Hermlin's Erzahlung Die Kommandeuse," J Ger Studies 33 (97): 134-48; co-ed, Queering the Canon: Defying Sights in German Literature and Culture, Camden House, 98; auth, "Warum es sinnvoll and notwendig ist, die Lesbenliteratur zu kanonisieren. Ein Beitrag zur Neuorientierung der deutschen Literaturgeschichtsschreibung," in Erinnern and Wiederentdecken: Tabuisierung and Enttabuisierung der mannlichen and weiblichen Homosexualitdt in Wissenschaft and Kritik, eds. Dirck Linck, Wolfgang Popp, Annette Runte (Berlin: Verlag rosa Winkel, 99): 149-168; co-auth, A New Guide to Reading German, Captus Pr, 00. **CONTACT ADDRESS** Dept Culture Lang Studies, Univ of New Brunswick, Fredericton, Carleton Hall Rm 334, PO Box 4400, Fredericton, NB, Canada E3B 5A3. **EMAIL** lorey@unb.ca

LOSADA, LUIS ANTONIO
PERSONAL Born 01/07/1939, New York, NY, m, 1966 **DISCIPLINE** CLASSICS, ANCIENT HISTORY **EDUCATION** Hunter Col, AB, 60; Columbia Univ, MA, 62, PhD(Greek and Latin), 70. **CAREER** From lectr to asst prof classics, 68-74, Assoc Prof Classics, Lehman Col, 74-, Chmn Dept Class and Orient Lang, 73-, Assoc mem, Univ Sem Class Civilization, Columbia Univ, 72-. **MEMBERSHIPS** Am Philol Asn; Petronian Soc; Am Inst Archaeol. **RESEARCH** Greek history and numismatics; the teaching of classical languages. **SELECTED PUBLICATIONS** Auth, The Aetolian indemnity of 189 and the Agrinion hoard, Phoenix, 65; coauth, The time of the shield signal at Marathon, Am J Archaeol, 70; auth, Fifth columns in the Peloponnesian War: How they worked and the defense against them, Klio, 72; The Fifth Column in the Peloponnesian War, E J Brill, 72. **CONTACT ADDRESS** Lehman Col, CUNY, Bronx, NY 10468.

LOSEFF, LEV V.
PERSONAL Born 06/15/1937, Lemingzad, m, 1959, 2 children **DISCIPLINE** RUSSIAN LITERATURE **EDUCATION** Univ MI, PhD. **CAREER** Prof, Dartmouth Col. **HONORS AND AWARDS** Phi Beta Kappa; Honarary Member, 00; Guggenheim Fellowship, 00; The Liberty Awd for the Outstanding contributions Russian American Culture, 99; Palmyra of the North Awd for the best book of poetry, 97. **RESEARCH** 19th and 20th century Russ prose and poetry. **SELECTED PUBLICATIONS** Auth, On the Beneficence of Censorship: Aesopian Language in Modern Russian Literature, Poetika Brodskogo, six collections of poetry in Rus; co-ed, Joseph Brodsky: The Art of a Poem; Brodsky's Poetics and Aesthetics; A Sense of Place: Tsarskoe Selo and Its Poets. **CONTACT ADDRESS** Dartmouth Col, 44 N College St, #208, Hanover, NH 03755-1801. **EMAIL** lev.loseff@dartmouth.edu

LOSSE, DEBORAH N.
PERSONAL Born 05/06/1944, Boston, MA, m, 1966, 2 children **DISCIPLINE** FRENCH LANGUAGE **EDUCATION** Conn Col, BA, 66; Univ NC Chapel Hill, MA, 70; PhD, 73. **CAREER** From Asst Prof to Prof, Ariz State Univ, 73-; Assoc Dean Grad Col, Ariz State Univ, 95-. **HONORS AND AWARDS** Dean's Quality Teaching Awd, 82; Barlington Northern Fac Achievement Awd in Excellence in Teaching, 89. **MEMBERSHIPS** Renaissance Soc of Am, MLA, Africa Lit Asn, Societe Francaise d'Etude du seiziene siecle, Societe des Amis de Montaigne. **RESEARCH** Renaissance Nouvelle, Montaigne, Rabelais, Marguerite de Navarre, Jacques Yvere. **SELECTED PUBLICATIONS** Auth, Rhetoric at Play. Rabelais and Satirical Eulogy, Peter Lang (Berne), 80; auth, "From Auctor to Auteur: Authorization and Appropriation in the Renaissance," Medievalia et Humanistica New Ser 16 (88): 153-163; auth, "Nue verite ou invention poetique? History and Fiction in the Prologue of the Renaissance Nouvelle," Symposium (Summer 89): 107-117; auth, "Sampling the Book. Beginning Metaphors and their Poetic Function," Neophilologus 74 (90): 192-201; auth, "Conter et Raconter: Montaigne and the Tradition of the Conte," Neophilologus 76 (92): 24-41; auth, Sampling the Book. Renaissance Prologues and the French Conteurs, Bucknell Univ Press (Lewisburg), 94; auth, "'Se Peindre de la Plume': History, Biography, and Self-Portraiture in Monataigne's Rewriting of History," MLN 110-5 (95): 1054-1066; auth, "Triple contexture: La Boetie, Montaigne, Marie de Gournay et l'amitie. Pretexte, texte et edition de 1595 des Essais," Bull de la Societe des Amis de Montaigne VII Serie 1-2-3 (Janvier-Juin 96): 145-151; coauth, "Preparing Doctoral Students and Faculty Roles: The Arizona State University Model," The J of Grad Asst Develop 5-3 (97-98): 119-125; auth, "Rewriting Culture: Montaigne Recounts New World Ethnography," Neophilologus (99): 1-11. **CONTACT ADDRESS** Dept Lang and Lit, Arizona State Univ, Tempe, AZ 85287-0202. **EMAIL** dlosse@asu.edu

LOTT, ROBERT EUGENE
PERSONAL Born 11/30/1926, Miami, FL, m, 1954 **DISCIPLINE** SPANISH, ROMANCE STYLISTICS **EDUCATION** Athens Col, AB, 51; Univ Ala, MA, 52; Cath Univ Am, PhD, 58. **CAREER** Teaching asst, Univ Ala, 51-52; instr, Cath Univ Am, 52-56, teaching asst, 56-58; from asst prof to assoc prof Span, Univ Ga, 58-66; assoc prof mod Span, 66-68, assoc mem ctr advan studies, 72, Prof Mod Span Lit to Prof Emer, Univ Ill, Urbana, 68- **MEMBERSHIPS** MLA; Am Asn Teachers Span and Port; Midwest Mod Lang Asn. **RESEARCH** Modern and Contemporary Spanish literature; Romance stylistics; the modern novel. **CONTACT ADDRESS** Dept Spanish, Italian, and Portugese, Univ of Illinois, Urbana-Champaign, 707 S Mathews Ave, 4080 FLB MC-176, Urbana, IL 61801.

LOUDEN, BRUCE
PERSONAL Born 11/08/1954 **DISCIPLINE** CLASSICS, COMPARATIVE LITERATURE **EDUCATION** Univ Calif at Santa Cruz, BA, 77; San Francisco State Univ, MA, 83; Univ of Calif at Berkeley, PhD, 90. **CAREER** Vis asst prof, Univ Wis Madison, 90-91; from asst prof to assoc prof, Univ Tex at El Paso, 91-. **HONORS AND AWARDS** Summer Scholar, The Ctr for Helenic Studies, 96 & 00. **RESEARCH** Epic Poetry, Mythology, the Bible. **SELECTED PUBLICATIONS** Auth, The Odyssey: Structure, Narration and Meaning, Johns Hopkins Univ Pr, 99. **CONTACT ADDRESS** Dept Lang & Ling, Univ of Texas, El Paso, 500 W Univ Ave, El Paso, TX 79968-8900. **EMAIL** blouden@miners.utep.edu

LOUNSBURY, RICHARD CECIL
PERSONAL Born 01/03/1949, Yorkton, SK, Canada **DISCIPLINE** CLASSICAL LANGUAGES, CLASSICAL TRADITION, AMERICAN INTELLECTUAL HISTORY **EDUCATION** Univ Calgary, BA, 70; Univ Tex, Austin, MA, 72, PhD(classics), 79. **CAREER** Lectr classics, Univ Witwatersrand, 79-81; asst prof, Univ Victoria, 81-82; Prof Classics & Comp Lit, Brigham Young Univ, 82- **RESEARCH** Roman literature of the early Empire; classical rhetoric; intellectual history of the American South. **SELECTED PUBLICATIONS** Auth, The death of Domitius in the Pharsalia, Trans Am Philol Asn, 75; History and motive in book seven of Lucan's Pharsalia, Hermes, 76; Restoring the generous past: Recent books of rhetoric and criticism, Mich Quart Rev, 79; contribr, Intellectual Life in Antebellum Charleston, Tennessee, 86; auth, The Arts of Suetonius: An Introduction, peter Lang, 87; ed, Louisa S. McCord: Political and Social Essays, Univ Press of Virginia, 95; ed, Louisa S. McCord: Poems, Drama, Biography, Letters, Univ Press of Virginia, 96; ed, Louisa S. McCord: Selected Writings, Univ Press of Virginia, 97. **CONTACT ADDRESS** Dept of Humanities Classics & Comp Lit, Brigham Young Univ, 3010 Jhkb, Provo, UT 84602-0002. **EMAIL** richard_lounsbury@byu.edu

LOVELADY, EDGAR JOHN
PERSONAL Born 11/12/1937, Grand Rapids, MI, m, 1958, 2 children **DISCIPLINE** ENGLISH, GREEK **EDUCATION** Toronto Bible Col, dipl bible, 58; Grace Col, BA, 60; Grace Theol Sem, MDiv, 63; St Francis Col, MA, 66; Purdue Univ, PhD(English), 74; Grace Theol Sem, ThM, 76. **CAREER** Teacher English, W Noble Sch Corp, 63-66; Prof English & Greek, Grace Col, 66-. **HONORS AND AWARDS** Alva J McClain Awd, Grace Col, 75; Distinguished Alumnus, 75; Delta Epsilon Chi; Phi Kappa Phi; Int Who's Who in Educ. **MEMBERSHIPS** MLA; Ind Coun of Teachers of English. **RESEARCH** Old English grammar; Greek grammar. **SELECTED PUBLICATIONS** Auth, The Logos concept in John 1:1, Grace J, spring 63; The rise of Silas Lapham as problem novel, Ind English J, 73-74. **CONTACT ADDRESS** Grace Col, 200 Seminary Dr., Box 397, Winona Lake, IN 46590-1294. **EMAIL** lovelaej@grace.edu

LOWENSTAM, STEVEN
PERSONAL Born 12/14/1945, Springfield, IL **DISCIPLINE** CLASSICAL LANGUAGES **EDUCATION** Univ Chicago, BA, 67; Harvard Univ, MA, 69, PhD(classics), 75. **CAREER** Asst prof, 75-81, Assoc Prof Classics, Univ Ore, 81-; Asn Prof, 81-93; Prof, 93-. **MEMBERSHIPS** Am Philol Asn; Archaeol Inst Am; Philol Asn PACIFIC Coast. **RESEARCH** Archaic epic; literary criticism; glyptics. **SELECTED PUBLICATIONS** Auth, The Death of Patroklos: A Study in Typology, 81; auth, The Uses of Vase Depictions in Homeric Studies, Transactions of the Amer Philol Asn, Vol 0122, 92; The Arming of Achilleus on Early Greek Vases, Class Antiquity, Vol 0012, 93; Is Literary Criticism an Illegitimate Discipline--a Fallacious Argument in Plato 'Ion', Ramus Critical Studies in Greek and Roman Literature, Vol 0022, 93; auth, The Scepter and the Spear, 93; The Pictures on Junos Temple in the 'Aeneid', Class World, Vol 0087, 93; Vatican 35617 and Iliad 16, Amer J Archaeol, Vol 0098, 94; auth, "Talking Vases," Transactions of Amer Philol Asn, 97; auth, "Seneca's Epistle 65" Memoirs of American Academy in Rome, 98; auth, "The Shroud of Laertes and Penelope's Guile" Classical Journal, 00; auth, The Extramural Sanctuary of Demeter and Persephone, Libya; auth, "The Sources of the Odyssey Landscapes," Echos du Monde. **CONTACT ADDRESS** Dept of Classics, Univ of Oregon, Eugene, OR 97403-1205. **EMAIL** slowenst@oregon.uoregon.edu

LOWRIE, JOYCE OLIVER
PERSONAL Born 12/16/1936, Curitiba, Brazil, m, 1959, 1 child **DISCIPLINE** FRENCH **EDUCATION** Baylor Univ, BA, 57; Yale Univ, PhD, 66. **CAREER** Asst prof, 66-71, assoc prof, 71-77, Prof French, Wesleyan Univ, 77-. **MEMBERSHIPS** Am Asn Teachers Fr. **SELECTED PUBLICATIONS** Auth, Motifs of kingdom and exile in Atala, Fr Rev, 4/70; The structural significance of sensual imagery in Paul et Virginie, Romance Notes, spring 71; The structural and ideological significance of Vigny's man of destiny in Stello, PMLA, spring 71; The Violent Mystique: Thematics of Retribution and Expiation in Balzac, Barbey d'Aurevilly, Bloy and Huysmans, Droz, Geneva, 74; The function of repetition in Pinget's Lettre Morte, Fr Rev, 4/76; The question of Mimesis in Gautier's Contes Fantastiques, Nineteenth-Century Fr Studies, fall-winter 79-80; The Rota Fortunae, In: Pieyre de Mandiargues's La Motocyclette, 2/80 & Entretien avec Andre Pieyre de Mandiargues, 12/81, Fr Rev. **CONTACT ADDRESS** Dept of Romance Lang, Wesleyan Univ, Middletown, CT 06459. **EMAIL** jlowrie@wesleyan.edu

LOWRIE, MICHELE
PERSONAL Born 04/24/1962, New Haven, CT, m, 1988, 1 child **DISCIPLINE** CLASSICS **EDUCATION** Yale Univ BA 84; Harvard Univ PhD 90; Institute for Advance Study. **CAREER** New York Univ, asst prof 90-96, assoc prof, 97-. **HONORS AND AWARDS** Presidential Fell NYU; Burkhardt Fellowship, ACLS; Inst for Advanced Study. **MEMBERSHIPS** CS **RESEARCH** Latin lit; Augustan poetry. **SELECTED PUBLICATIONS** Auth, Horace's Narrative Odes, Oxford, Clarendon Press, 97, rev by Bryn Mawr Classical Rev 98; Spleen and the Monumentum: Memory in Horace and Baudelaire, Comp Lit, 97; A Parade of Lyric Predecessors, Horace Odes, Phoenix, 95; Lyric's Elegos and the Aristotelian Mean: Horace Odes, Class World, 94; Myrrha's Second Taboo, Ovid Metamorphoses, Class Philology, 93; Classical Review, Classical Philology, 99; Journal of Roman Studies, 99. **CONTACT ADDRESS** Dept of Classics, New York Univ, 25 Waverly Pl, New York, NY 10003. **EMAIL** michele.lowrie@nyu.edu

LOWRY, EDDIE R., JR.
PERSONAL Born 11/18/1945, Fredericksburg, VA, m, 1978, 2 children **DISCIPLINE** GREEK, LATIN **EDUCATION** Hampden Sydney Col, BA, 68; Harvard Univ, MDiv, 71; PhD, 80. **CAREER** Lectr to asst prof, Yale Univ, 78-82; asst prof, Univ of Dayton, 82-88; assoc prof to prof, Ripon Col, 88-; Marie Zarwell Chair, 88-. **HONORS AND AWARDS** Phi Beta Kappa; Eta Sigma Phi; Rockefeller Fel, 68-69; Woodrow Wilson Fel, 68; World Coun of Churches Scholar, 71-72; Mellon Fel, 82-83; Univ of Dayton Grants, 83, 84; Latin Teacher of the Year Awd, 95; Nicholas Campus Communicator Awd, 97; Ovatio Awd, 00. **MEMBERSHIPS** Wis Assoc of For Lang Teachers; Am Philogical Assoc; Am Class League; Class Assoc of the Middle W and S. **RESEARCH** Classical epic, Greek and Roman mythology and religioun, foreign language teaching. **SELECTED PUBLICATIONS** Auth, Thersites: A Study in Comic Shame, Garland Pub, (NY), 91; auth, "Glaucus, the Leaves, and the Heroic Boast of Iliad 6.146-211", The Ages of Homer, eds Jane B Carter and Sarah P Morris, Univ of Tex Pr, (Austin, 95): 193-203. **CONTACT ADDRESS** Dept Romance and Class Lang, Ripon Col, PO Box 248, Ripon, WI 54971-0248. **EMAIL** lowrye@ripon.edu

LOZANO-RENIEBLAS, ISABEL
PERSONAL Born 12/25/1958, Moureal de Ariza, Spain, s **DISCIPLINE** LINGUISTICS, LITERATURE, SPANISH, MEDIEVAL **EDUCATION** Univ de Zauapoza, Lic, 89; CUNY, PhD, 95. **CAREER** Teaching asst, CUNY Hunter Col, 90-95; teaching asst, CUNY Lehman Col, 90-95; asst prof, Dartmouth Col, 96-. **MEMBERSHIPS** AIH; MLA; AISO; AILM; Cervantes. **RESEARCH** Medieval literature; Cervantes. **SELECTED PUBLICATIONS** Auth, Cervantes y el Mundos del 'Persile', 98; co-ed, Silva Studia Philologica in Honorem Isaias Lerner, Castalia, 01. **CONTACT ADDRESS** Span Port Dept, Dartmouth Col, Hanover, NH 03755.

LOZOVAYA, ELIZAVETA V.
PERSONAL Born 06/17/1972, Samara, Russia, m, 1999 **DISCIPLINE** RUSSIAN **EDUCATION** Samara State Univ, MA. **CAREER** Chief Ed, Newspaper, Russia, 95-98; fac mem, Moscow Acad of Humanities, 97-98; instr, Center of Prof Educ, Russia, 94-98; prof, Samara Acad of Humanities, 97-98; prof, Samara State Univ, 94-98; tutor, Univ of New Orleans, 99-; instr, Tulane Univ, 00-. **HONORS AND AWARDS** Cert of Achievement, Adv Eng Course for Sr Teachers, 97; Cert of Achievement, Methodology of Eng Teaching Course for Sr Eng Teachers, 98. **RESEARCH** Foreign Language Teaching, Cognition, Professional Education (training of a future specialist). **SELECTED PUBLICATIONS** Auth, "Cognitive Activity as Means of Development of a Future Professional," Samara State Univ, (96); auth, "Means of Activization of Cognition through Teaching Foreign Languages," Samara State Univ, (98); auth, "Innovative Approach to Modelling of Professional Education," Samara State Univ, (00). **CONTACT ADDRESS** Dept Ger and Slavic Studies, Tulane Univ, 305 Newcomb Hall, New Orleans, LA 70118. **EMAIL** elozova@tulane.edu

LUBENSKY, SOPHIA
PERSONAL Born 01/21/1935, Kharkov, Russia **DISCIPLINE** RUSSIAN, LINGUISTICS **EDUCATION** Kharkov Univ, MA, 63; Leningrad Univ, MA, 57, PhD, 72. **CAREER** From asst prof 77 to prof 96-, Univ Albany, State Univ NY. **HONORS AND AWARDS** Geraldine R. Dodge Foundation, 89; Dept of Defense, 84-93; US Dept of Education, 90-94; IREX, 94-95; SUNY Faculty Research Awd, 00. **MEMBERSHIPS** Euralex; Dictionary Society of North Am; American Asn of Teachers of Slavic and East European Lang (AATSEEL). **RESEARCH** Bilingual Lexicography, semantics, translation, methodology. **SELECTED PUBLICATIONS** Russian-English Dictionary of Idioms, Random House, 95 and publ in Russia: Russko-angliiskii frazeologicheskii slovar, Iazyki russkoi kul'tury, 97; Approaches to a Russian-English Dictionary of Idioms, In Dictionaries, 91; Aspectual Properties of Verba Percipiendi, In The Scope of Slavic Aspect, UCLA Slavic Ser 12, Slavica, 85; coauth, Nachalo: When in Russia.. a Basal Russian Textbook with a Video Component, McGraw-Hill, 96. **CONTACT ADDRESS** Dept of Languages, Literatures, and Cultures, SUNY, Albany, 1400 Washington Ave, Humanities 254, Albany, NY 12222. **EMAIL** lubensky@cnsvax.albany.edu

LUCIANI, FREDERICK
DISCIPLINE LATIN AMERICAN LITERATURE OF THE COLONIAL PERIOD, NINETEENTH AND TWENTIETH **EDUCATION** Rutgers Univ, BA, 72-76; Yale Univ, MA, 76-77, PhD, 77-82. **CAREER** Dir, Vassar-Wesleyan-Colgate prog, Spain, 94; dept ch, 91-92, 94, 96-; ch, assoc prof-. **HONORS AND AWARDS** NEH fel, 95; res fel, Am Coun of Learned Soc, 84; summer res fel, Cornell Univ, 87; Picker res fel, 88; res assoc, ctr latin am studies, univ ca, berkley, 91; ed bd, latin am lit rev, 90-96; colonial latin-am rev, 1995-. **MEMBERSHIPS** Mem, Mod Lang Assn Comm Prof Employment, 96-97. **SELECTED PUBLICATIONS** Auth, The Man in the Car/in the Trees/behind the Fence: From Cortazar's 'Blow-Up' to Stone's JFK, anthology of critical essays on Julio Cortazar, Cambridge UP, 97; Spanish American Theatre of the Colonial Period and Spanish American Theatre of the Eighteenth Century, The Cambridge History of Latin American Literature, vol 1, Cambridge UP, 96; articles, Colonial Latin Am rev, Discurso Literario, Latin American Lit Rev, Bulletin of Hisp Studies, Romance Quart, Revista Iberoamericana, Hisp Jour, Texto Cretico; rev(s), NY Times Bk Rev; Hispanofila; Colonial Latin Am Rev; Revista Iberoamericana, Boleten de la Biblioteca Menendez Pelayo. **CONTACT ADDRESS** Dept of Romance Lang, Colgate Univ, 13 Oak Drive, Hamilton, NY 13346. **EMAIL** fluciani@center.colgate.edu

LUKACHER, NED
PERSONAL Born 09/03/1950, York, PA, m, 1978 **DISCIPLINE** ENGLISH LITERATURE, COMPARATIVE LITERATURE **EDUCATION** Dickinson Col, BA, 72; Univ Ariz, MA, 74; Duke Univ, PhD(English), 78. **CAREER** Asst Prof English, Univ Ill, Chicago, 80-. **SELECTED PUBLICATIONS** Auth, K(Ch)ronosology, Sub-stance, Vol 25, 80; Notre-Homme-des-Fleurs: Wolf Solent's Metaphoric Legends, Powys Rev, Vol 6, 80; Schreber's juridical opera: A reading of the Denkwsrdigkeiten Eines Nervenkranken, Structuralist Rev, Vol 2, 81; Freud's Phantom, In: Psychoanalysing Psychoanalysis: Freud and the Hidden Fault of the Father, Johns Hopkins Univ Press, 82. **CONTACT ADDRESS** Univ of Illinois, Chicago, Chicago, IL 60680.

LUMPKINS, DAVID W.
PERSONAL Born 11/16/1944, Lafollette, TN, m, 1964 **DISCIPLINE** SLAVIC LANGUAGES **EDUCATION** Univ Tn, BA, 66; Vanderbilt Univ, PhD, 74. **CAREER** Prof, Univ South, 68- **MEMBERSHIPS** AME; Assoc of Teachers of Slavic & East-Eur Lang **RESEARCH** Nineteenth cent Russian lit **CONTACT ADDRESS** 735 University Ave, Sewanee, TN 37383-1000. **EMAIL** dlumpkin@sewanee.edu

LUND, JEROME A.
PERSONAL Born 09/12/1948, Willmar, MN, m, 1988, 3 children **DISCIPLINE** ANCIENT SEMITIC LANGUAGES **EDUCATION** Hebrew Univ, PhD, 89; LA Baptist Theol Sem, MDiv, 73. **CAREER** Senior res scholar, 90-, Hebrew Union College. **HONORS AND AWARDS** James Montgomery fel. **MEMBERSHIPS** AOS; SBL; IBR. **RESEARCH** Aramaic and Hebrew Languages; Ancient Bible Versions. **SELECTED PUBLICATIONS** The Old Testament in Syriac according to the Peshitta Version, Concordance to the Pentateuch, prepared by PG Borbone, J Cook, KD Jenner, DM Walter in collaboration with JA Lund and MP Weitzman, Leiden Brill, 97; Sepher Bereshit Jerusalem: Caspari Center, 94, a study book on the book of Genesis; The Third and Forth Oracles of Balaam in the Peshitta and Targums, in: Targum Studies 2: Targum and Peshitta, ed, Paul V Flesher, Atlanta, Scholars Press, 98; The Noun mattar Prison: A possible Ghost Word in the Lexicon of Middle Western Aramaic, Orientalia, 97; auth, "Morphological Variation in the Imperfect of hewa in Onqelos and Jonathan," Sefarad 58, 98: 260-70; auth, "Articles on Noah; Shem; Ham; Japheth; Moab; Korah, Dathan, Abiram (The Rebellion of); in the New International Dictionary of Old Testament Theology and Exegesis, ed. Willem A. VanGemeren, Grand Rapids: Zondervan, 97; auth, "Grecisms in the Peshitta Psalms, in The Peshitta as a Translatin, ed. P.B. Dirksen and A. Van der Kooij, Leiden: E.J. Brill, 95: 85-102; auth, "On Yerushalmi Baba Mesia 6.1, 10D," Jewish Quarterly Review 84, 93-94: 253-259; auth, "The Language of Jesus," Mishkan 17-18, (1992/2-1993/1) 139-55; auth, "The Syntax of the Numeral 'One' as a Noun Modifier in Jewish Palestinian Aramaic of the Amoraic Period, Part 1. Journal of the American Oriental Society 106, 86, 413-23; auth, "On the Interpretation of the Palestinian Targumic Reading wqht in Genesis 32:25," Journal of Biblical Literature 105, 86: 99-103; auth, "The Interchange of (d l (l in Targum Neofiti 1. Bulletin of the School of Oriental and African Studies, 42, 79: 541. **CONTACT ADDRESS** 3101 Clifton Ave, Cincinnati, OH 45220. **EMAIL** jlund@cn.huc.edu

LUNDELL, TORBORG LOVISA
PERSONAL Born Stockholm, Sweden, 1 child **DISCIPLINE** COMPARATIVE LITERATURE, FOLKTALE **EDUCATION** Univ Calif, Berkeley, PhD(comp Lit), 73. **CAREER** Assoc 69-70, Act ass prof 70-72; lectr, 72-73, asst prof, 73-77, Assoc Prof Swed, Univ Calif, Santa Barbara, 77-83, prof 84-. **MEMBERSHIPS** Soc Advan Scand Studies; Philol Asn Pacific Coast; C G Jung Found Anal Psychol. **SELECTED PUBLICATIONS** Auth, Gender Related Biases in the Type and Motif Indexes as a Aaron and Thompson in Fairy Tales and Society, ed. R. Boehipeimen, 86; auth, Lars Ahlin, Fairytale Mathers, 90; auth, Canada in Sweden, Scand Studies, 99. **CONTACT ADDRESS** Dept of Ger and Slavic Lang, Univ of California, Santa Barbara, 552 University Rd, Santa Barbara, CA 93106-0001.

LUNT, HORACE GRAY
PERSONAL Born 09/12/1918, Colorado Springs, CO **DISCIPLINE** SLAVIC LINGUISTICS **EDUCATION** Harvard Univ, AB, 41; Univ Calif, AM, 42; Columbia Univ, PhD, 50. **CAREER** Teaching asst Slavic langs, Univ Calif, 46; lectr Serbocroatian, Columbia Univ, 48-49; from asst prof to assoc prof, 49-59; Prof Slavic Lang and Lit, Harvard Univ, 59-, Guggenheim fel, 60-61. **MEMBERSHIPS** Ling Soc Am; Am Asn Advan Slavic Studies; MLA; Am Asn Teachers Slavic and East Europ Lang. **RESEARCH** Church Slavonic; comparative Slavic linguistics. **SELECTED PUBLICATIONS** Auth, Grammar of the Macedonian Literary Language, Skopje, 52; Fundamentals of Russian, Norton, 2nd ed, 68; Old Church Slavonic Grammer, Mouton, The Hague, 6th ed, 74; Progressive Palatalization of Common Slavic, Skopje, 81. **CONTACT ADDRESS** Dept of Slavic Lang, Harvard Univ, Cambridge, MA 02138.

LUSHNIG, CECILIA EATON
PERSONAL Born New York, NY, m, 1970 **DISCIPLINE** CLASSICS **EDUCATION** City Col NYork, BA, 62; Univ Cincinnati, MA, 63; PhD, 72. **CAREER** Instr, Ohio Univ, 66-70; asst prof, Univ Wash, 73-74; prof, Univ Idaho, 75-. **HONORS AND AWARDS** APA Teach Awd; Phi Kappa Phi; Cen Hellenic Studies Scholar. **MEMBERSHIPS** CAPN; WCC; AFT. **RESEARCH** Greek Tragedy; language teaching. **SELECTED PUBLICATIONS** Auth, An Introduction to Ancient Greek: A Literary Approach, Charles Scribner's Sons, 76; auth, Latin and Literacy: An Essay on How and Why to Revive Latin in the Schools, Am Class League, 78; coauth, ETYMA: An Introduction to Vocabulary Building from Latin and Greek, UP Am, 82; auth, Vocabula: A Course in Latin Vocabulary Building, Class Asn New Eng Pub, 87; auth, Time Holds the Mirror: A Study of Knowledge in Euripides Hippolytus, EJ Brill, 88; auth, Tragic Aporia: A Study of Euripides' Iphigenia at Aulis, Ramus Monographs, 89; auth, Etymidion, rev ed, UPA, 94; auth, The Gorgon's Severed Head: A Study of Euripides' Alcestis, Electra, and Phoenissae, EJ Brill, 95. **CONTACT ADDRESS** Dept Foreign Lang, Univ of Idaho, 375 S Line St, Moscow, ID 83844-0001. **EMAIL** luschnig@uidaho.edu

LUTCAVAGE, CHARLES
DISCIPLINE GERMAN **EDUCATION** La Salle Col; Lessing Kolleg in Marburg; Univ Vienna; Harvard Univ, PhD. **CAREER** Sr preceptor & coordr Ger Lang Instr. **HONORS AND AWARDS** Created interactive comput and video prog for Ger and Austrian Landeskunde. **MEMBERSHIPS** AATG; ACTFL; Goethe Society; IVN; AAUSC; AANS. **RESEARCH** Language pedagogy; technology in language teaching; Austrian and Dutch history and literature. **SELECTED PUBLICATIONS** Publ on, methodology. **CONTACT ADDRESS** Dept of Germanic Languages and Literatures, Harvard Univ, Barker Center 348, Cambridge, MA 02138. **EMAIL** lutcavag@fas.harvard.edu

LUTES, LEASA
DISCIPLINE SPANISH **EDUCATION** Wheaton Col, BA, 78; Middlebury Col, MA, 79; MA, 87; DML, 95. **CAREER** Teacher, Evanston Twp High Sch, 81-83; from asst prof, Wheaton Col, 83-93; from assoc prof to prof & chair of for lang, Gordon Col, 93-. **MEMBERSHIPS** AATSP, AATG, ACTFL, MLA, ACLA, NACFLA, AAUP. **RESEARCH** Latin American Female Bildungsroman, Technology in Foreign Language Instruction. **SELECTED PUBLICATIONS** Auth, Allende, Buitrago, Luiselli: Aproximaciones teoricas al concepto del Bildungsroman femenino, Peter Lang, forthcoming. **CONTACT ADDRESS** Dept For Lang & Ling, Gordon Col, Massachusetts, 255 Grapevine Rd, Wenham, MA 01984-1813. **EMAIL** lutes@gordon.edu

LUTHY, MELVIN JOSEPH
PERSONAL Born 11/15/1936, Logan, UT, m, 1965, 4 children **DISCIPLINE** LINGUISTICS, FINNISH, ENGLISH LANGUAGE **EDUCATION** UT State Univ, BS, 62; IN Univ, PhD, 67. **CAREER** Asst prof Eng & ling, Univ WI-Oshkosh, 69-71; assoc prof, 71-80, prof Eng & Ling, Brigham Young Univ, 80; assoc dean of Humanities, Brigham Young Univ, 96-. **MEMBERSHIPS** Tchr(s) of Eng Speakers Other Lang; Phi Kappa Phi; Soc for Advancement Scandinavian Studies. **RESEARCH** Mod grammars; lang pedag; Finnish lang and lit. **SELECTED PUBLICATIONS** Auth, Phonological and Lexical Aspects of Colloquial Finnish, Ind Univ, 73-, coauth, TICCIT Composition and Grammar Course, 74 & auth, Finnish Noun/Adjective/Verb Wheels, 76, Brigham Young Univ; Why transformational grammar fails in the classroom, Col Compos & Commun, 77; The case of Prufrock's grammar, Col English, 78; A comparative generative junction approach to Finnish morphosyntax, J Uralic & Altaic Studies, 82; Study in English Grammars, Brigham Young Univ Homestudy, 90; auth, "Early Finnish Number Parallelism and Classical Hebrew Analogs," in Scandinavian Studies, 95; auth, "A Place for Phonetics in High Technology,"

in Linguistics at Work, 98. **CONTACT ADDRESS** Dept of Linguistics, Brigham Young Univ, 2129 Jkhb, Provo, UT 84602-0002. **EMAIL** melvin_luthy@byu.edu

LUTKUS, ALAN
PERSONAL Born 09/28/1940, East Chicago, IN, m, 1966 **DISCIPLINE** ENGLISH, LINGUISTICS **EDUCATION** Harvard Univ, BA, 62; Ind Univ, MA, 66, PhD, 75. **CAREER** Ndea Lectr Ling, Trinity Col, Conn, 68; Instr Eng & ling, Northern IL Univ, 69-71; Assoc Prof Eng & Ling, State Univ NY Col Geneseo, 73-; Chief Ling Consul, Amer Inst Tech, vocab series Wordscape, 90; media consult, NEH Amer radio Project, 96-97. **RESEARCH** Stylistics; film. **SELECTED PUBLICATIONS** Coauth, Arts and Skills of English: Daybook, Grades 3-6, Holt, 72-73; auth, Troublespeaking the approach to public doublespeaking: Purism and our concept of language, Col English, 76; coauth, Spelling Matters, 77 & The World of Spelling, Grades 1-8, 78, Heath; coauth, Spelling Worlds, Grades 2-6, Ditto Master Series, Heath, 79; Composition Theory Meets Practice and They Pretty Well Get Along Twice, Journal of Teaching Writing, 3, 84; Literacy Reconsidered For Better and Worse, Review essay, Journal of Teaching Writing, 2, 83. Buster Keaton, p265-272, Sir John Falstaff, p176-184, Touchstone, p466-470, in Fools and jesters in Literature, Art, and History: A Bio-Biographical Sourcebook, Greenwood Press, 98; **CONTACT ADDRESS** Dept of Eng, SUNY, Col at Geneseo, 1 College Cir, Geneseo, NY 14454-1401. **EMAIL** lutkus@genesco.edu

LUTZELER, PAUL M.
PERSONAL Born 11/04/1943, Doveren, m, 1972, 2 children **DISCIPLINE** GERMAN LITERATURE **EDUCATION** Ind Univ, MA, 70; PhD, 72. **CAREER** Prof, 81. **HONORS AND AWARDS** Guggenheim; Humboldt Awd; Outstanding Teacher Awd, AATG; Ger Cross of Merit; Austrian Cross of Honor in Arts and Sciences; Rosa May Distinguished Univ Prof in the Humanities, 93. **MEMBERSHIPS** MLA; AATG; GSA; Acad in Mainz; Acad in Dusseldorf. **RESEARCH** German and European romanticism, European identity, Literature and History, Exile Literature, Hermann Broch. **SELECTED PUBLICATIONS** Auth, A Biography (also in German, Spanish, and Japanese) 85); auth, History and Literature: The Modern German Novel, 87; auth, Hermann Broch, Ethics and Politics, 92; auth, Authors and Europe from Romanticism to the Present, 92; auth, Multiculturism and European Identity (also in Italian), 98; auth, Cleo or Calliope: Literature and History, 98; auth, Human Enthropy: Studies in the Works of Hermann Broch, 00. **CONTACT ADDRESS** Ger Lang, Washington Univ, 1 Brookings Dr, Campus Box 1104, Saint Louis, MO 63130-4862. **EMAIL** europe@artsci.wustl.edu

LUZBETAK, LOUIS JOSEPH
PERSONAL Born 09/19/1918, Joliet, IL **DISCIPLINE** LINGUISTIC ANALYSIS, CULTURAL ANTHROPOLOGY **EDUCATION** Divine Word Sem, BA, 42; Pontif Gregorian Univ, STL, 46, JCB, 47; Univ Fribourg, PhD(anthrop), 51. **CAREER** Prof anthrop, ling and missiology, Divine Word Sem, Ill, 51-52, 56-58; lectr and summer asst prof appl anthrop, Cath Univ Am, 60-65; exec dir, Ctr Appl Res in Apostolate, Washington, DC, 65-73; pres, Divine Word Col, Iowa, 73-78; Ed, Anthropos, Int Rev Ethnology and Ling, 79-, Dir, Anthropos Inst, St Augustin bei Sieberg, WGer, 51-; Ford Found fel, 52-54; cult anthrop and ling field work, New Guinea, 52-56; lectr appl anthrop, Ctr Intercult Formation, Cuernavaca, Mex, 60-65; Ctr for Intercult Commun, Cath Univ PR, 60-65; rector, Divine Word Col, DC, 68-73; Walsh-Price fel, Ctr Mission Studies, Maryknoll, NY, 78-79. **HONORS AND AWARDS** Pierre Charles Awd, Fordham Univ, 64. **MEMBERSHIPS** Fel Am Anthrop Asn; Cath Anthrop Asn (vpres, 61-62, pres, 62-69); Ling Soc Am; Soc Appl Anthrop; Am Soc Missiology (pres, 75-76). **SELECTED PUBLICATIONS** Auth, The Church and Cultures: New Perspectives in Missiological Anthropology, Orbis, 95. **CONTACT ADDRESS** 1985 Waukegan Rd, PO Box 6067, Techny, IL 60082-6067.

LYMAN-HAGER, MARY ANN
DISCIPLINE ITALIAN, FRENCH **EDUCATION** Univ Ariz, MA, 75; Univ Idaho, MEd, 81; PhD, 86. **CAREER** Asst prof, 87-90, Univ Mass, Amherst; asst, assoc, prof, Pa State Univ, 90-97; PROF, SAN DIEGO STATE UNIV, 97-. **CONTACT ADDRESS** Dept French, Italian, San Diego State Univ, San Diego, CA 92182. **EMAIL** mlymanha@mail.sdsu.edu

LYON, JAMES K.
PERSONAL Born 02/17/1934, Rotterdam, Netherlands, m, 1959, 8 children **DISCIPLINE** GERMAN LANGUAGE, LITERATURE **EDUCATION** Univ Utah, BA, 58; MA, 59; Harvard Univ, PhD, 63. **CAREER** Instr, Harvard Univ, 62-63; US Army, 63-66; asst prof, Harvard Univ, 67-71; assoc prof, Univ Fla, 71-74; prof, Univ Calif San Diego, 74-94; vis prof, Univ Augsburg, 93; prof, Brig Young Univ, 94-. **HONORS AND AWARDS** Guggenheim Fel, 74; NEH Fel, 70-71; APS Fel, 79; Ford Found Fel, 87-90, 92-95; Excellence Teaching, Revelle Col, 80; Scheuber-Yeinz Endow Prof, 94-. **MEMBERSHIPS** MLA; AATG; IBS. **RESEARCH** 20th-century German poetry and drama; Holocaust studies; works of Bertolt, Brecht, Paul Celan; Celan and Martin Heideggor. **SELECTED PUBLICATIONS** Auth, Bertolt Brecht in America; auth, Bertolt Brecht and Rudyard Kipling; auth, Bertolt Brecht's American Cicerone; auth, Brecht Unbound; auth, Konkondanz zur Lyrik Gottfried Benns; auth, "Paul Celan and Martin Buber: Poetry as Dialogue," PMLA 86 (71): 110-119; auth, "Paul Celan's Language of Stone," Colloq Germ (74): 298-318; auth, "Die Patho-Physiologies des Ichs inder Lyrik Paul Celans," Zeit Deutsche Philol106 (87): 591-609; auth, "Der Holocaust und Nicht Referentielle Sprache in der Lyrik Paul Celan," Celan J 5 (93): 247-270. **CONTACT ADDRESS** 4335 Mile High Dr, Provo, UT 84604-6308. **EMAIL** james_lyon@byu.edu

LYONS, DECLAN P.
PERSONAL Born 12/03/1961, Galway, Ireland **DISCIPLINE** ANCIENT CLASSICS, FRENCH **EDUCATION** Nat Univ Ireland, BA; Univ Dublin, MLitt, 90; SUNY-Buffalo, PhD, 98. **CAREER** Tchg asst, SUNY-Buffalo, 88-92; res scholar, Univ de Geneve-Suisse, 92-93; asst prof Classics, Franciscan Univ, 94- . **HONORS AND AWARDS** Coun Euro res fel, Switz, 92-93; Ital Cult inst res awd, 98. **MEMBERSHIPS** APA; CAAS. **RESEARCH** Hellenistic Philosophy; Neronian Rome; SENECA; Hellenistic Poetry; Psychology and Classics. **CONTACT ADDRESS** Dept of Mod & Classical Lang, Franciscan Univ of Steubenville, 1235 Univ Blvd, Steubenville, OH 43952. **EMAIL** lyons@fran.u.edu

LYONS, JOHN D.
PERSONAL Born 10/14/1946, Springfield, MA **DISCIPLINE** FRENCH **EDUCATION** Brown Univ, AB, 67; Yale Univ, MA, 68; PhD, 72. **CAREER** Asst prof to prof, Dartmouth Col, 72-87; prof, Univ of Va, 87-92; Commonwealth Prof of French, Univ of Va, 92-. **HONORS AND AWARDS** Phi Beta Kappa, 67; Woodrow Wilson Fel, 67; Robert Fish Awd for Excellence in Teaching, Dartmouth Col, 78; ACLS Study Fel, 79-80; NEH Res Fel, 85-86, 92-93; Outstanding Teacher Awd, Univ of Va, 96. **RESEARCH** Seventeenth-century French literature. **SELECTED PUBLICATIONS** Auth, "L'Economie des marques dans La Princesse de Cleves," Neuphilologische Mitteilungen LXXXI (80): 326-336; auth, "The Cartesian Reader and the Methodic Subject," Espirit Createur XXI (81): 37-47; auth, Exeplum: The Rhetoric of Example in Early Modern France and Italy, Princeton Univ Press, 89; auth, "Tacit History," Montaigne Studies VI (94): 37-47; auth, The Tragedy of Origins. Pierre Corneille and Historical Perspective, Stanford Univ Press, 96; auth, Kingdom of Disorder. The Theory of Tragedy in Seventeenth-Century France, Purdue Studies in Romance Lit, Purdue Univ Press (W Lafayette, LA), 99. **CONTACT ADDRESS** Dept French, Univ of Virginia, PO Box 400770, Charlottesville, VA 22904-4770.

LYOVIN, ANATOLE VLADIMIROVICH
PERSONAL Born 11/13/1938, Leskovats, Yugoslavia, m, 1963, 2 children **DISCIPLINE** CHINESE LINGUISTICS, PHONOLOGY **EDUCATION** Princeton Univ, AB, 64; Univ Calif, Berkeley, PhD(Ling), 72. **CAREER** Asst prof, 68-73, assoc prof Ling, Univ Hawaii, Manoa, 73-, co-prin investr, Northwest Lang Relationships Proj, Pac & Asian Ling inst, 72-73. **MEMBERSHIPS** Ling Soc Am. **RESEARCH** Phonological change; historical phonology of Chinese; Classical Tibetan. **SELECTED PUBLICATIONS** Auth, Notes on the addition of final stops in Maru, 6/68; A Chinese dialect dictionary on computer: Progress report, Proj Ling Anal Reports, 6/68; co-ed, CLIBOC: Chinese Linguistics Bibliography on Computer, Cambridge Univ, 70; auth, Sound change, homophony and lexical diffusion, Proj Ling Analy Reports, 11/71; Intro to the Languages of the world, Oxford, Univ, 97. **CONTACT ADDRESS** Dept of Ling, Univ of Hawaii, Manoa, 1890 E West Rd, Honolulu, HI 96822-2318. **EMAIL** lyovin@hawaii.edu

LYS, FRANZISKA
PERSONAL Born 05/06/1955, Berne, Switzerland, m, 1981 **DISCIPLINE** GERMAN **EDUCATION** Northwestern Univ, PhD. **CAREER** Col lectr; Asst Chair, German; dir, Undergraduat Studies; ch, Coun Lang Instr. **HONORS AND AWARDS** ACTFL/FOP Houghton Mifflin Awd for Excellence in Foreign Language Instruction using Technology, 99; AATG/Goethe Institute Awd, Certificate of Merit, 98; Charles Deering McCormick Univ distinguished lectr, 97-98; Lieutenant Governor's Awd, Ill Coun Tchr(s) For Lang, 96; outstanding tchg Col Arts Sci(s), Northwestern Univ, 87-88; Fac Honor Roll Dept of German, Northwestern Univ, 84-87; developer, cd-rom multimedia software drehort: neubrandenburg interaktiv and azubi interaktiv. **MEMBERSHIPS** ACTFL, AAUSC, CALICO (Board Member), AATG. **RESEARCH** Intermatik, an interactive German grammar on the internet and a new multi-media application for language teaching. **SELECTED PUBLICATIONS** Producer and auth educ documentaries, Drehort: Neubrandenburg; AZUBI; Drehort: Bern; Gesichter einer Stadt, Berne; Faces of a City. **CONTACT ADDRESS** Dept of German, Northwestern Univ, Kresge 113, 1859 Sheridan, Evanston, IL 60208-2203. **EMAIL** flys@northwestern.edu

M

MA, JOHN T.
DISCIPLINE GREEK **EDUCATION** Oxford Univ, BA, 91; D Phil, 97. **CAREER** Asst prof Classics, Princeton Univ **RESEARCH** Greek history, especially Hellenistic, Greek epigraphy, the classical and post-classical polis. **SELECTED PUBLICATIONS** Articles on: Greek epigraphy and history. **CONTACT ADDRESS** Dept of Classics, Princeton Univ, 105 E Pyne, Princeton, NJ 08544. **EMAIL** johnma@princeton.edu

MAAZAOUI, ABBES
PERSONAL Born 03/01/1953, Tunisia, m, 1 child **DISCIPLINE** FRENCH **EDUCATION** Maitrise, Univ of Tunis, Tunisia, 78; Doctorat de 3e cycle, Univ Provence, France, 82. **CAREER** Asst prof, 82-87, assoc prof, Univ Tunis, Sousse, Tunisia, 87-89, co-dir, French Dept, 88, co-dir, Study Abroad Prog, CREDIF in Paris, France, spring 88; vis asst prof, Bowdoin Col, Brunswick, ME, 90-91; vis asst prof, Colby Col, Waterville, ME, 91-92; asst prof, Ramapo Col, Mahwah, NJ, 92-93, dir, Lang Lab, 92-93; Assoc Prof French, Lincoln UNIV, PA, 93-, academic dir, Int Inst for Public Policy Summer Lang Inst, 97-98 (co-founder), acting chair, Dept of Langs and Linguistics, 96-97, supervisor, Foreign Lang Teaching Assts, fall 95-spring 98, coord, Lang Placement Exam, 95-, dir, Lang Lab, 93-94. **HONORS AND AWARDS** Lincoln fac develoment grant, fall 98; Inst for Int Public Policy, 5 year grant, for a Summer Lang Inst at Lincoln Univ, summer 97; Who's Who Among America's Teachers, 96; Who's Who in the East, 95; numerous grants and scholarships from France and Tunisia. **MEMBERSHIPS** Northeast Modern lang Asn; Conseil Int d'Etudes Francophones; Am Asn of Teachers of French; Modern Lang Asn. **RESEARCH** French and Francophone lit and cultures; literary theories; Marcel Proust. **SELECTED PUBLICATIONS** Auth, Ethnicity, Race, and Gender: A Colonial Perspective in French Film, The Humanities Newsletter, Vol 1, no 3, summer 95; Steven Ungar, Scandal and Aftereffect: Blanchot and France since 1930, Univ MN Press, 95, forthcoming in Romance Quart; Representation et alterite dans les romans de Robbe-Grillet, the French Rev, Vol 68, no 3, 95; L'Enfant de sable et La Nuit sacree ou le corps tragique, the French Rev, Vol 69, no 1, 95; A World of Films: The International Film Series, The Humanities Newsletter, Vol 2, no 1, fall 96; A World of Films: The International Film Series (Part II), The Humanities Newsletter, vol 2, no 2, spring 97; The 1997-98 International Film Series, The Humanities Newsletter, Vol 3, no 1, fall 97; Les traces du terroir dans Talismano de Meddeb et Le Conclave des plseureuses de Mellah, in Tunisie Plurielle, Vol 1, ed Hedi Bouraoui, L'Or du temps, 97; Literary Theories and Minority Literature, the Humanities Newsletter, Vol 3, no 2, spring 98; L'Erotisme et le sacre: Ben Jelloun, Djebar, Mellah, Romance Notes, 38, no 2, winter 98; Poetique des marges et marges de la poetique, in Transgressing Boundaries: the Poetics of Marginality, spring 98. **CONTACT ADDRESS** Dept of Langs and Linguistics, Lincoln Univ, Pennsylvania, Lincoln University, PA 19352. **EMAIL** maazaoui@lu.lincoln.edu

MAC ADAM, ALFRED J.
PERSONAL Born 11/02/1941, Newark, NJ, m, 1967, 2 children **DISCIPLINE** SPANISH **EDUCATION** Rutgers Col, BA, 63; Princeton Univ, MA, 65, PhD, 69. **CAREER** Barnard Col, Columbia Univ, 83-. **MEMBERSHIPS** MLA, ALSC. **RESEARCH** Latin American culture. **SELECTED PUBLICATIONS** Auth, Textual Confrontations. **CONTACT ADDRESS** Dept Spanish, Barnard Col, 3009 Broadway, New York, NY 10027-6501. **EMAIL** AJM19@Columbia.edu

MACARY, JEAN LOUIS
PERSONAL Born 01/26/1931, Paris, France, m, 1959, 3 children **DISCIPLINE** FRENCH LITERATURE **EDUCATION** Sorbonne, Lic Lett & dipl etudes super, 54, Agregation Lett, 62; Doctorat d'etat es Lettres, Pantheon-Sorbonne, 74. **CAREER** Asst French lit, Sorbonne, 65-68; lectr, Princeton Univ, 69-70, asst prof, 70-76; assoc prof, 76-80, Prof French Lit & Chmn Dept Fordham Univ, 80-. **MEMBERSHIPS** Am Soc 18th Century Studies; Int Soc Studies 18th Century; MLA. **RESEARCH** Seventeenth & 18th century French literature; history of ideas. **SELECTED PUBLICATIONS** Ed, Voltaire, Faceties, Presses Univ, France, 73; auth, Mas que et lumieres au XVIIIe: A-F2 des landes, citoyen et philosophe 1680-1757, Nijhoff, The Hague, 75; ed, Essays on the Age of Enlightenment, In Honor of Ira O Wade, Droz, Geneva, 77. **CONTACT ADDRESS** Dept of Mod Lang, Fordham Univ, 501 E Fordham Rd, Bronx, NY 10458-5191. **EMAIL** voldid@aol.com

MACAULEY, BETH
DISCIPLINE CCC-SPEECH-LANGUAGE PATHOLOGY **EDUCATION** Univ Fla, BA, 87, MA, 89, PhD, 98. **CAREER** Assoc prof, Wash State Univ, 95-; grad tchg asst, Dept Commun Processes and Disorders, Univ Fla, 94-95 & grad res asst, 91-95; speech lang pathologist, Tacachale, 90-95, Res-Care cluster and group homes, 90-95. **SELECTED PUBLICATIONS** Coauth, Limb Apraxia Results From a Fractionation of Movement Representations I: Deficits in Spatial Planning, In Press - Brain, 94; Joint Coordination Deficits in Limb Apraxia.

In Press - Brain, 94; Ecological Implications of Limb Apraxia: Evidence From Mealtime Behavior, In Press - J the Int Neuropsychological Soc, 94; Lateralized Hand Use in Gestural Communication, In Press - Brain & Cognition, 94 & Left Hemisphere Movement Control, Soc for Neuroscience Abstracts, vol 20, 94. **CONTACT ADDRESS** Dept of Speech and Hearing Sciences, Washington State Univ, 201 Daggy Hall, Pullman, WA 99164-2420. **EMAIL** macauleyb@wsu.edu

MACCHIARULO, LOUIS
PERSONAL Born 01/04/1958, Queens, NY, m, 1983, 2 children **DISCIPLINE** CLASSICS **EDUCATION** Fordham Univ, PhD, 86. **CAREER** Instr Latin, Greek & Italian, Regis High School. **HONORS AND AWARDS** Assistantship, Fordham Univ, 79-81; Fordham Univ Fel, 81-83. **MEMBERSHIPS** APA; Virgilian Soc **RESEARCH** Homer; Virgil, Dante, Roman History **SELECTED PUBLICATIONS** The Life and Times of Fortunato, PhD Thesis. **CONTACT ADDRESS** 55 E 84th St, New York, NY 10028.

MACCOULL, LESLIE
PERSONAL Born 08/07/1945, New London, CT, s **DISCIPLINE** CLASSICS; SEMITICS (COPTIC) **EDUCATION** Vassar Col, AB, 65, summa cum laude; Yale Univ, MA, 66; Catholic Univ of Amer, PhD with distinction, 73. **CAREER** Curator, 74-78, Inst of Christian Oriental Research, Catholic Univ; dir of studies, 78-84, Soc for Coptic Archaeology Cairo; senior research scholar (North Am), 84- , adjunct, 97, AZ Ctr for Medieval and Renaissance Studies, AZ State Univ. **HONORS AND AWARDS** Phi Beta Kappa 64; Dumbarton Oaks jr fel 69-71; summer fel, 83; fel, 90-91; fel, Ameri Research Ctr in Egypt, 78-79; NEH Fel, 93-94. **MEMBERSHIPS** Amer Soc of Papyrologists; Intl Assn for Coptic Studies; US Natl Committee for Byzantine Studies, Mensa. **RESEARCH** Coptic papyrology; Byzantine papyrology; social and cultural hist of lat antiquity. **SELECTED PUBLICATIONS** Auth, Dated and datable Coptic documentary hands before A.D. 700, Le Museon, 97; auth, The Triadon: an English translation, Greek Orthodox Theological Review, 97; auth, Chant in Coptic pilgrimage, in Pilgrimage and Holy Space in Late Antique Egypt, 98; auth, BM 1075: A Sixth-Century Tax Register from the Hermopolite, in press; coauth, Catalogue of the Illustrated Manuscripts in the Coptic Museum, in press; auth, The Historical Background of John Philoponus' De Opificio Mundi in the Culture of Byzantine-Coptic Egypt, Zeitshrift fur Autkes Christeutum, in press. **CONTACT ADDRESS** 914 E Lemon St, #137, Tempe, AZ 85281. **EMAIL** haflele@imap4.asu.edu

MACDONALD, MARYELLEN
DISCIPLINE PSYCHOLOGY, LINGUISTICS, AND THE NEUROSCIENCE PROGRAM **EDUCATION** Univ Calif, Los Angeles, PhD, 86. **CAREER** Assoc prof, Univ Southern Calif. **RESEARCH** Human language comprehension; Speech production & its relationship to comprehension; role of working memory in language processing; decline of language processing abilities in patients with Alzheimer's Disease. **SELECTED PUBLICATIONS** Coauth, The lexical nature of syntactic ambiguity resolution, Psycholog Rev, 101, 94; ed, Lexical representations & sentence processing, Hove, Sussex, UK: Psychology Press, Publ simultaneously as Issues 2-3 jour Lang and Cognitive Processes, 97. **CONTACT ADDRESS** Dept of Linguistics, Univ of So California, University Park Campus, Los Angeles, CA 90089-2520. **EMAIL** mcm@gizmo.usc.edu

MACE, CARROLL E.
PERSONAL Born 12/05/1926, Neosho, MO **DISCIPLINE** SPANISH **EDUCATION** Drury Col, BA, 49; Tulane Univ, MA, 52, PhD(Span), 66. **CAREER** Asst prof, Univ SC, 60-63; instr Span, Tulane Univ, 63-65; asst prof, 65-67, assoc prof, 67-70, prof Span, Xavier Univ LA, 71-, chmn Dept Mod Lang, 72-; chmn Dept Mod Lang of Xavier 1970-90; retired, 98. **MEMBERSHIPS** Am Asn Teachers Span & Port; SCent Mod Lang Asn. **RESEARCH** Cervantes and the generation of 1898; folk literature of Guatemala. **SELECTED PUBLICATIONS** Auth, The Patzca dance of Rabinal, El Palacio, fall 61; translr, The day of the dead of 1836: Figaro in the cemetery by Larra, Shenandoah, Winter 65; auth, New information about dance-dramas of Rabinal and the Rabinal-Achi, Xavier Univ Studies, 2/67; Two Spanish-Quiche Dance-Dramas of Rabinal, Tulane Studies Romance Lang & Lit, 70; Charles Etienne Brasseur de Bourbourg, Handbk Mid Am Indians, 73; Los Negritos: A Maya Christmas comedy, Xavier Rev, 1/81; Algunos apuntes sobre los bailes de Guatemala y de Rabinal, Mesoamerica, 2/81; Bailes y Teatro Prehispanicos en Guatemala, in vol one, gen ed, Dr Jorge Lujan Munoz, 98. **CONTACT ADDRESS** Dept of Mod Lang, Xavier Univ, Louisiana, 7325 Palmetto St, New Orleans, LA 70125-1098.

MACE, SARAH
DISCIPLINE CLASSICS **EDUCATION** Colby Col, BA, 82, Univ Penn, MA, 85; Yale Univ, PhD, 92. **CAREER** Lectr, Univ Penn, 92-93; vis asst prof, Columbia Univ, 93-94; vis asst prof, Dartmouth Col, 94-95; vis asst prof, 95-97, asst prof, 97- , Union Col. **HONORS AND AWARDS** Charles C Sherman fel, 86-87; Yale Univ fel, 87-89; 85-86; Whiting Diss Fel, 90-91. **RESEARCH** Homer, Hesiod and the epic tradition; Presocratica; Archaic Greek lyric; Epinician; Aeschylus; Lucretius. **SELECTED PUBLICATIONS** Auth, Utopian and Erotic Fusion in a New Elegy of Simonides, APE, 96; rev of Lesbian Desire in the Lyrics of Sappho by Snyder, AJP, forthcoming. **CONTACT ADDRESS** Dept of Classics, Union Col, New York, Schenectady, NY 12308. **EMAIL** maces@idol.union.edu

MACEWEN, SALLY
PERSONAL Born Abington, PA **DISCIPLINE** CLASSICAL LANGUAGES AND LITERATURES **EDUCATION** Mt Holyoke Col, BA, 70; Univ Pa, PhD, 81. **CAREER** Vis Lectr, Univ Ut, 79-82; Asst Prof to Assoc Prof, Agnes Scott Col, 82-. **HONORS AND AWARDS** Human Relations Awd, Agnes Scott Col; Liberty Bell Awd, Decatur-DeKalb Bar Asn; DuPont Fac Develop Grant; Grant, NEH. **MEMBERSHIPS** Am Philol Asn; Class Asn of the Middle W and S; Ga Class Asn; Am Class League; Women's Class Caucus; Asn for Moral Educ. **RESEARCH** Greek Drama; Greek history; Diversity studies; Latin poetry; Gender studies. **SELECTED PUBLICATIONS** Auth, "Classical Drama and the American Western," Classical Bulletin, 97; auth, "Observations by a Classicist on Teaching Diversity on a Predominantly White Campus," Classical World, 02. **CONTACT ADDRESS** Dept Lang, Agnes Scott Col, 141 E College Ave, Decatur, GA 30030. **EMAIL** smacewen@agnesscott.edu

MACHONIS, PETER A.
DISCIPLINE FRENCH LINGUISTICS **EDUCATION** Pa State Univ, PhD, 82. **CAREER** Assoc prof. **HONORS AND AWARDS** Excellence Teaching Awd; Am Asn of Teachers of Fr (AATF); Am Dialect Soc (ADS); Southeastern Conf on Lings (SECOL). **RESEARCH** Evolution of the French Language; Lexicon-grammar. **SELECTED PUBLICATIONS** Auth, "Old French Diphthongization and Syncope in the New Paradigm," Papers in Romance 3 (85): 147-165; auth, "Transformations of Verb Phrase Idioms: Passivization, Particle Movement, Dative Shift, Am Speech 60.4, (85): 291-308; auth, "The Lexicon-Grammar of English: Support and Operator Verbs, Proceedings of the XIVth International Congress of Linguists, (87): 992-995; auth, "Support Verbs: An Analysis of BE + PREP + Xidioms, The Secol Review 2, (88): 95-125; auth, The Support Verb make, In: Ferenc Kiefer, ed. International Conference on Computational Lexicography: Conference Proceedings, Budapest: Hungarian Academy of Sciences (91): 141-153; auth, "Neutral Verbs in English: A Preliminary Classification, Lingvisticae Investigationes XXI:2 (97): 293-320; auth, Histoire de la langue: du latin a l'ancien francais, Landham, MD: Univ Press of America, 90. **CONTACT ADDRESS** Dept of Modern Languages, Miami, FL 33174. **EMAIL** machonis@fiu.edu

MACIAS, MANUEL JATO
PERSONAL Born 03/25/1929, Portland, OR **DISCIPLINE** SPANISH **EDUCATION** Univ Portland, AB, 51, AM, 52; Univ Madrid, DrPhil & Let, 56; Northwestern Univ, PhD, 63; Univ Coimbra, dipl, 70; Univ Portland, MA, 77. **CAREER** Instr mod lang, Marquette Univ, 55-57, asst prof Span, 57-58; from Asst Prof to Prof, 58-95, Prof Emeritus Span, Univ Portland, 95-, admin dir prog in Spain, Univ Navarre, 70-72, Chmn Dept For Lang, 72, Lectr, Portland State Col, 59; Fulbright exchange prof, Gt Brit, 59-60; vis assoc prof Span, Lewis & Clark Col, 68-69; lectr Span, Portland State Univ, 76-78. **MEMBERSHIPS** Am Asn Tchr(s) Span & Port; Philol Asn Pac Coast; AAUP; Pac Northwest Foreign Lang Conf (pres, 68-69); Am Coun For Lang Tchg. **RESEARCH** Nineteenth and twentieth century Span drama; mod Galician lit. **SELECTED PUBLICATIONS** Auth, La ensenanza del espanol en los EEUU de American, Ed Cult Hisp, 61. **CONTACT ADDRESS** Dept of Eng & Mod Lang, Univ of Portland, 5000 N Willamette, Portland, OR 97203-5798. **EMAIL** manuel@hevanet.com

MACK, SARA
PERSONAL Born 05/01/1939, New Haven, CT, w, 2 children **DISCIPLINE** CLASSICS **EDUCATION** AM, 64, PhD, 74, Harvard Univ. **CAREER** Asst/Assoc/Full Prof, 76-, UNC-Chapel Hill. **HONORS AND AWARDS** Bowman and Gordon Gray Professorship, 94-97; Fellowship, Natl Humanities Ctr. **MEMBERSHIPS** Amer Philological Assoc; Assoc of Literary Scholars and Critics; Classics Assoc of the Midwest and South; NC Classical Assoc; Virgilian Soc. **RESEARCH** Latin Poetry; Greek and Latin epic; Euripides. **SELECTED PUBLICATIONS** Auth, Ovid (Hermes Books), 88; reviews, Allen Mandelbaum, The Metamorphoses of Ovid: A New Verse Translation, 94; Carole Newlands, Playing with Time, Ovid and the Fasti, 97; auth, "Pattern of Time in Vergil's Aeneid, Oklahoma 99; auth, "Ruit Oceano Nox," cq 80; auth, "The Single Supplie" Ramus 81; auth, "Teaching Ovid's Orpheus to Beginners" CJ 96; auth, "Acis and Galatea," Arion 99; rev, "Wiltshire, Public & Private in Vergil's Aenerd," 90; auth, "Cairs, Virgil's Augustan Epic," 92; auth, "Farreu, Virgil's Georgies & The Traditaes or Aenerd Epic, Mynas, Virgil Geargics, 94. **CONTACT ADDRESS** Univ of No Carolina, Chapel Hill, 212 Murphey Hall, CB #3145, Chapel Hill, NC 27599-3145. **EMAIL** smack@email.unc.edu

MACKENZIE, LOUIS A.
DISCIPLINE FRENCH LITERATURE **EDUCATION** Univ Notre Dame, BA, 69; Middlebury Col, MA, 72; Cornell Univ, PhD, 77. **CAREER** Assoc prof. **RESEARCH** 17th century literature. **SELECTED PUBLICATIONS** Auth, Strategies of Fragmentation in Pascal's Lettres provinciales. **CONTACT ADDRESS** Romance Languages and Literatures Dept, Univ of Notre Dame, Notre Dame, IN 46556.

MACKEY, LOUIS HENRY
PERSONAL Born 09/24/1926, Sidney, OH, d, 4 children **DISCIPLINE** PHILOSOPHY, COMPARATIVE LITERATURE **EDUCATION** Capital Univ, BA, 48; Yale Univ, MA, 53, PhD(philos), 54. **CAREER** From instr to asst prof philos, Yale Univ, 53-59; from assoc prof to prof, Rice Univ, 59-67; vis prof, 67-68, prof Philos, Univ Tex, Austin, 68-, Morse fel, Yale Univ, 57-58; vis prof, Haverford Col, 71-72; Nat Endowment for Humanities res fel, 76-77; vis prof, Univ of Tulsa, 83. **HONORS AND AWARDS** Harry Ransom Awd for Undergraduate Teaching, 87; President's Assoc Teaching Excellence Awd, 91; Awd for Outstanding Grad Teaching, 94. **MEMBERSHIPS** Amer Comparative Lit Assoc, Inter Assoc for Philo and Lit. **RESEARCH** Literary theory; medieval philosophy; Kierkegaard. **SELECTED PUBLICATIONS** Auth, Kierkegaard: A Kind of Poet, Univ Pa, 71; auth, Points of View: Readings of Kierkegaard, Florida State, 86; auth, "Fact, Fiction, and Representation: Four Novels by Gilbert Sorrentino, Camden House, 97; auth, "Peregrinations of the Word: Essays on Medieval Philosophy," Michigan, 97; Theory and Practic in the Rhetoric of I A Richards, Rheoric Soc Quarterly, 97. **CONTACT ADDRESS** Univ of Texas, Austin, Austin, TX 78712-1180.

MACKEY, WILLIAM FRANCIS
PERSONAL Born 01/26/1918, Winnipeg, MB, Canada, m, 1949, 2 children **DISCIPLINE** LINGUISTICS, BILINGUALISM **EDUCATION** Univ Man, BA, 40; Laval Univ, MA, 42; Harvard Univ, MA, 47; Univ Geneva, DLitt, 65. **CAREER** Sr lectr ling method, Univ London, 48-50; assoc prof English philol, 50-54, prof English philol and ling, 54-61, dir lang lab, 57-69, dir div lang didactics, 61-69, prof lang didactics, 61-71, exec dir, Int Ctr Res Bilingualism, 67-70, Res Prof, Lalval Univ, 71-, Consult, Comt Educ of Poles, English, 48; Commonwealth Off Educ, Australia, 49; Intergovt Comt Europ Migration, Geneva, 55-56; Dept Citizenship and Immigration, Can, 57-69; mem Humanities Res Coun Can, 60-70; US Dept Health, Educ and Welfare, 66-70; Royal Comn Bilingualism and Biculturalism, 66, consult, 66-68; mem acad senate, Can Coun, 67; mem Lang Attitudes Res Comt, Irish Govt, 71-; ed, Studies Bilingual Educ, 71-; fed comnr, Bilingual Districts Adv Bd, Can Govt, 72-; comnr, Kommission fur sprachpolitische Integrationsfragan europaischen Gerneinschaft, 75-; chmn, lang policy, Can Coun Develop Comt on Individual, Lang and Soc, 75-77, comnr, Fed Govt Comn Lang Training in Pub Serv Can, 75-77. **HONORS AND AWARDS** 1974 Jubilee Medal, Inst Ling, London, England, 75. **MEMBERSHIPS** Ling Soc Am; Can Ling Asn; Ling Soc Paris; Int Phonetic Asn; fel Royal Soc Can. **RESEARCH** Bilingualism; geolinguistics; lexicometrics. **SELECTED PUBLICATIONS** Auth, Literary Diglossia, Biculturalism and Cosmopolitanism in Literature, Visible Lang, Vol 0027, 93; The English Infinitive, Can J Ling-Revue Canadienne De Linguistique, Vol 0040, 95. **CONTACT ADDRESS** Int Ctr Language Management Re, Univ of Laval, Quebec, QC, Canada G1K 7P4.

MACKIE, HILARY S.
DISCIPLINE CLASSICS **EDUCATION** BA, 87; Princeton Univ, PhD, 93. **CAREER** Vis prof, Stanford Univ. **RESEARCH** Archaic Greek poetry; lit theory; Augustan poetry. **SELECTED PUBLICATIONS** Auth, Talking Trojan: Difference and Conversational Style in the Iliad, 96. **CONTACT ADDRESS** Dept of Span and Class, Rice Univ, 6100 Main St., Houston, TX 77005-1892.

MACKSEY, RICHARD ALAN
PERSONAL Born 07/25/1931, Glen Ridge, NJ, m, 1956, 1 child **DISCIPLINE** COMPARATIVE LITERATURE, ENGLISH **EDUCATION** Johns Hopkins Univ, MA, 53, PhD, 57. **CAREER** Jr instr English, Johns Hopkins Univ, 53-55; from instr to asst prof, Loyola Col, 56-58; asst prof writing sem, 58-63, assoc prof humanistic studies, 64-73, Carnegie lectr sem hist ideas, 62-64, chmn sect lang, lit and cult, 66-72, actg dir humanities ctr, 68-69, Prof Humanistic Studies and Chmn Humanities Ctr, Johns Hopkins Univ, 73-, Chmn comt internal evidence, Bibliog Conf, 62; lectr, Baltimore Mus Art, 64-65; dir, Bollingen Poetry Festival, Turnbull lect, Theatre Hopkins, Center Stage, Tantamount Films, Carroll House and Levering Hall; moderator, Dialogue of the Arts, CBS; ed comp lit, Mod Lang Notes and Structure. **MEMBERSHIPS** MLA; Am Soc Aesthet; Renaissance Soc Am; Mediaeval Acad Am; Col English Asn. **RESEARCH** European and English novel; poetics, rhetoric, and theory of literature; interrelation of arts, comparative methodology and intellectual history. **SELECTED PUBLICATIONS** Auth, Poems from the Hungarian Revolution, Cornell Univ, 66; Forerunners of Darwin, 2nd ed, 68, The Languages of Criticism and the Sciences of Man, 69 & Interpretation: Theory and Practice, Johns Hopkins, 69; coauth, Negative metaphor and Proust's rhetoric of absence, Mod Lang Notes, 70; co-ed,

The Structuralist Controversy, 72 & auth, Velocities of Change, Johns Hopkins; Gloria Victis, Nemzetor, Munich, 66. **CONTACT ADDRESS** Ctr for Humanities, Johns Hopkins Univ, Baltimore, 3400 N Charles St, Baltimore, MD 21218-2680.

MACLEISH, ANDREW
PERSONAL Born 08/30/1923, Philadelphia, PA, m, 1950, 3 children **DISCIPLINE** LINGUISTICS, PHILOLOGY **EDUCATION** Roosevelt Univ, AB, 50; Univ Chicago, MA, 51; Univ Wis, PhD(English philol), 61. **CAREER** Instr English, Valparaiso Univ, 51-53 and Rockford Col, 56-58; from asst prof to assoc prof, Northern Ill Univ, 58-67; assoc prof English, Univ Minn, Minneapolis, 67-68, assoc prof English and ling, 68-71, Prof to Prof Emer English and Ling, 71-80. Dir, US Off Educ English Proj, Curric Ctr Ling, 64-67; Peace Corps res grant, 65-67; consult, Hilo Lang Develop Proj, Hawaii, 65-68. **MEMBERSHIPS** Nat Coun Teachers English; Ling Soc Am; Midwest Mod Lang Asn. **RESEARCH** English in Southeast Asia; descriptive historical English linguistics; materials for teaching standard English in Hawaii. **CONTACT ADDRESS** 4141 Aldrich Ave S, Minneapolis, MN 55409. **EMAIL** macle001@umn.edu

MACPHAIL, ERIC
DISCIPLINE FRENCH LITERATURE **EDUCATION** Princeton Univ; PhD, 88. **CAREER** Assoc prof. **SELECTED PUBLICATIONS** Auth, The Voyage to Rome in French Renaissance Literature; pubs on Rabelais, Du Bellay, Montaigne, Cervantes, Cyrano, Prophecy, Astrology, and Antiquarianism. **CONTACT ADDRESS** Dept of French and Italian, Indiana Univ, Bloomington, 1020 E Kirkwood Ave, Ballantine Hall 642, Bloomington, IN 47405. **EMAIL** macphai@indiana.edu

MACRIS, PETER JOHN
PERSONAL Born 10/06/1931, Buffalo, NY, m, 1963, 3 children **DISCIPLINE** GERMAN LANGUAGE AND LITERATURE **EDUCATION** State Univ NYork, Buffalo, BS, 56; Middlebury Col, MA, 63; NYork Univ, PhD(Ger lang and lit), 68. **CAREER** From asst prof to assoc prof, 64-70, Prof Ger Lang and Lit, State Univ NY, Col Oneonta, 70-. **MEMBERSHIPS** AAUP; Am Asn Teachers Ger; Int Brecht Soc. **RESEARCH** Modern drama; Bertolt Brecht; literary texts used in music. **SELECTED PUBLICATIONS** Stephen Zwieg as dramatist, State Univ NY (in prep). **CONTACT ADDRESS** Dept of Foreign Lang, SUNY, Col at Oneonta, P O Box 4015, Oneonta, NY 13820-4015.

MACRO, ANTHONY DAVID
PERSONAL Born 07/10/1938, London, England, m, 1967, 2 children **DISCIPLINE** CLASSICAL PHILOLOGY, ANCIENT HISTORY **EDUCATION** Oxford Univ, BA, 61, MA, 64; Johns Hopkins Univ, PhD, 69. **CAREER** Teaching assoc classics, Ind Univ, Bloomington, 61-62; instr, Univ Md, College Park, 65-67; jr instr, Johns Hopkins Univ, 67-69; asst prof classics, 69-75, assoc prof, 75-85, prof, 85-, Hobart Prof Class Lang, 92-, Trinity Col. **HONORS AND AWARDS** Leverhulme Commonwealth fel, Univ Wales, 75-76. **MEMBERSHIPS** Am Philol Asn; Soc Prom Hellenic Studies; Soc Prom Roman Studies. **RESEARCH** Greek epigraphy; Roman imperial history; comparative linguistics. **SELECTED PUBLICATIONS** Auth, Sophocles, Trachiniai, 112-21, American Journal of Philology, 73; Imperial provisions for Pergamum: OGIS 484, Greek, Roman & Byzantine Studies, 76; "A Confirmed Asiarch," American Journal of Philology, 79; The Cities of Asia Minor under the Roman imperium, Aufstieg und Niedergang der romischen Welt, Vol 2, No 7, Berlin, 80; Applied classics: Using Latin and Greek in the modern world, Class Outlook, 81; auth, "Asiarch Reconfirmed," American Journal of Philology, 85; auth, Prolegemena to the Study of Galatian-Celtic Name Formations, Celtic Connections, ACTA, 94. **CONTACT ADDRESS** Dept of Classics, Trinity Col, Connecticut, 300 Summit St, Hartford, CT 06106-3186. **EMAIL** ad.macro@mail.trincoll.edu

MADDOX, DONALD
DISCIPLINE FRENCH; ITALIAN LITERATURE **EDUCATION** Duke Univ, PhD. **CAREER** Prof, Univ MA Amherst. **HONORS AND AWARDS** Pres, Int Courtly Lit Soc. **RESEARCH** Medieval lit; Old French; Medieval and Early Modern Studies. **SELECTED PUBLICATIONS** Auth, Voix et textualites du recit eschatalogique; The Arthurian Romances of Chretien de Troyes: Once and Future Fictions; auth, Fictions of Identity in Medieval France; co-ed, The Medieval French Alexander; co-ed, Froissart Across the Genres; co-ed; Melusine of Lusignan; co-ed, Literary Aspects of Courtly Culture. **CONTACT ADDRESS** Dept of French and Italian Studies, Univ of Massachusetts, Amherst, Mass Ave, Amherst, MA 01003. **EMAIL** maddox@frital.umass.edu

MADDUX, STEPHEN
DISCIPLINE FRENCH **EDUCATION** Univ Dallas, BA, 71; Univ Chicago, MA, 73; PhD, 79; addn stud, Univ Paris, 71-72; Univ Toronto, 75-76; Wilhelms Univ, 77-78. **CAREER** Assoc prof; hd, Fr prog. **RESEARCH** Montaigne, Pascal. **SELECTED PUBLICATIONS** Auth, The Fiction of the Livre in Robert de Boron's Merlin, Jour Rocky Mountain Medieval and Renaissance Assn, 85; Satan With and Without a Human Face in the Novels of Georges Bernanos, Claudel Studies, 86; Cocteau's Tristan and Iseut: A Case of Overmuch Respect, Tristan and Isolde: A Casebook New York: Garland, 95. **CONTACT ADDRESS** Dept of Mod Lang and Lit, Univ of Dallas, 1845 E Northgate Dr, Irving, TX 75062. **EMAIL** maddux@acad.udallas.edu

MADISON, CHARLES L.
DISCIPLINE CCC-SPEECH-LANGUAGE PATHOLOGY **EDUCATION** State Univ NYork, BS, 66; Ohio Univ, MA, 67, PhD, 70. **CAREER** Prof, Wash State Univ, 70-. **HONORS AND AWARDS** Cert Clinical Competence in Speech Pathology, 71-; Wash Speech Lang Hearing Asn, 96. **MEMBERSHIPS** Amer Speech-Language-Hearing Asn; Int Asn for the Study of Child Lang; Int Soc Applied Psycholing; Wash Speech and Hearing Asn. **RESEARCH** Voice disorders, research methods, advanced speech and hearing sciences, and current literature. **SELECTED PUBLICATIONS** Auth, Attitudes Toward Mild Misarticulation Disordered Peers, Lang Speech and Hearing Services in Schools 23, 92; coauth, A Survey of Program Selection and Expectations of Current and Prospective Graduate Students, National Stud Speech-Lang-Hearing Asn J 20, 93. **CONTACT ADDRESS** Dept of Speech and Hearing Sciences, Washington State Univ, 201 Daggy Hall, Pullman, WA 99164-2420. **EMAIL** madisonc@wsu.edu

MADLAND, HELGA STIPA
PERSONAL Born Klodnitz, Upper Silesai **DISCIPLINE** GERMAN LITERATURE AND LANGUAGE **EDUCATION** Idaho State Univ, BA, 74; Univ Wash, MA, 79, PhD(German and Span), 81. **CAREER** Asst Prof German, Univ Okla, 81-. **MEMBERSHIPS** MLA; SCent Mod Lang Asn; Lessing Soc; Am Asn Teachers German. **RESEARCH** Eighteenth century German literature; dramatic theory. **SELECTED PUBLICATIONS** Auth, Aristotelian Drama in Eighteenth-Century Germany and its Modernity, J.M.R. Lenz, 82; auth, Reason and Emotion: The Life and Works of Marianne Ehrmann, 98. **CONTACT ADDRESS** Dept Mod Lang, Lit, and Ling, Univ of Oklahoma, 780 Van Vleet Oval, Room 206, Norman, OK 73019-2032. **EMAIL** hmadland@ou.edu

MAGLIOLA, ROBERT
PERSONAL Born, NJ, 3 children **DISCIPLINE** COMPARATIVE LITERATURE, HERMENEUTICS CONCENTRATION **EDUCATION** Princeton Univ, PhD, 70. **CAREER** Asst prof of comparative lit, Purdue Univ, W Lafayette, IN, 70-73, assoc prof, 74-80, full prof, 81-84; Distinguished chair prof, National Taiwan Univ, Taipei, Taiwan, 90-93; distinguished prof of Philosophy and Religions, ABAC Univ, Bangkok, Thailand, 94-. **HONORS AND AWARDS** Resident NHC grantee, 79; NSC/Taiwan grants, 97. **MEMBERSHIPS** SPEP; IAPL; MLA; AAR; Centre Cultural International Cerisy-la-Salle, France. **RESEARCH** Hermeneutics (European and Asian); Buddism and Cathoicism in dialogue; Jacques Derrida. **SELECTED PUBLICATIONS** Auth, Phenomenology and Literature, Purdue Univ Press, 77; Derrida on the Mend, Purdue Univ Press, 84; On Deconstructing Life-Worlds: Buddhism, Christianity, Culture, Atlanta: Scholars Press, Am Academy of Relig, 97. **CONTACT ADDRESS** 100 Barbados Dr, Toms River, NJ 08757-4024. **EMAIL** jmagliola@lycos.com

MAGNARELLI, SHARON
PERSONAL Born 10/03/1946, Seneca Falls, NY, m, 1969 **DISCIPLINE** SPANISH **EDUCATION** State Univ NY Oswego, BA, 68; Cornell Univ, PhD, 75. **CAREER** Prof, Albertus Magnus Col, 76-94; prof, Quinnipiac Univ, 94-. **HONORS AND AWARDS** Fulbright Fel, 84; Awd, NE Mod Lang Soc Women's Caucus. **MEMBERSHIPS** MLA; AATS; Inst Int de Lit Iberoamericana; Feministas Unidas; Assoc de Lit Femenina. **RESEARCH** Contemporary Spanish-American narrative and theatre. **SELECTED PUBLICATIONS** Auth, The Lost Rib: Female Characters in the Spanish-American Novel, Bucknell Univ Pr, (Lewisburg, PA), 85; auth, Reflections/Refractions: Reading Luisa Valenzuela, Peter Lang (NY), 88; auth, Understanding Jose Donoso, Univ SC Pr, (Columbia, SC), 93. **CONTACT ADDRESS** Dept Lang & Fine Arts, Quinnipiac Col, 275 Mt Carmel Ave, Hamden, CT 06518-1961. **EMAIL** sharon.magnarelli@quinnipiac.edu

MAHARG, JAMES
PERSONAL Born 05/12/1940, Glasgow, Scotland, m, 1967, 2 children **DISCIPLINE** SPANISH AMERICAN AND BRAZILIAN LITERATURES **EDUCATION** Univ Glasgow, MA, 67; Univ Ill, Urbana, PhD(Span-Am lit), 70. **CAREER** Asst prof, Univ Mich, Ann Arbor, 70-76; Assoc Prof Span and Port, Univ Ill, Chicago Circle, 76-, Nat Endowment for Humanities res grant, 73; reader Span, Col Entrance Bd, 77. **RESEARCH** Reputation of Jose Ortega y Gasset in Latin America; modern Brazilian and Spanish American literatures; realism and naturalism in Brazil. **SELECTED PUBLICATIONS** Auth, Reflexiones en torno a la ideologia de Ezequiel Martinez Estrada, Cuadernos Hispanoam, 11/72; Meditaciones americanas sobre Ortega y Gasset, Rev Occidente, Madrid, 1/73; The paradises of Walter Beneke, Latin Am Theatre Rev, spring 75; From romanticism to modernism: The peomaspiadas of Oswald de Andrade as parodies, Luso-Brazilian Rev, winter 76; Fructiferous exile: Martinez Estrada and the encounter with Marti, Estudos Ibero-Am, 12/76; A Call to Authenticity: The Essays of Ezequiel Martinez Estrada, Romance Monogr, Miss, 77. **CONTACT ADDRESS** Dept Span Ital and Port, Univ of Illinois, Chicago, Chicago Circle, Chicago, IL 60680.

MAHLENDORF, URSULA R.
PERSONAL Born 10/24/1929, Strehlen **DISCIPLINE** GERMAN LITERATURE **EDUCATION** Brown Univ, PhD, 58. **CAREER** Asst Ger, Brown Univ, 54-57; from instr to assoc prof, 57-77, Prof Ger, Univ Calif, Santa Barbara, 77-, Chmn Dept Ger and Slavic Lang, 80-, Assoc dir, Educ Abroad Prog, 68-71. **MEMBERSHIPS** MLA; Int Asn of Social Psychol; Am Asn of Social Psychiat; Asn Applied Psychoanal. **RESEARCH** Nineteenth and 20th century literature; psychology. **SELECTED PUBLICATIONS** Auth, Niedere Gangarten, World Lit Today, Vol 0066, 92; Unstete Leute, World Lit Today, Vol 0067, 93; Between the Past and the Future-Women Writers of the Gdr From an American Point-of View, Ger Quart, Vol 0069, 96. **CONTACT ADDRESS** Dept of German and Slavic Lang, Univ of California, Santa Barbara, 399 Loma Media, Santa Barbara, CA 93106. **EMAIL** mahlendo@humanitas.ucsb.edu

MAHONEY, CHRISTINA HUNT
PERSONAL Born 01/10/1949, m, 1973, 1 child **DISCIPLINE** IRISH LITERATURE **EDUCATION** Marquette Univ, BA, 70; Univ Col Dublin, Nat Univ Ireland, MA, 71; PhD, 88. **CAREER** Assoc dir, Center for Irish Studies, The Cath Univ of Am, Washington, DC, 84-. **MEMBERSHIPS** MLA, CAIS, ACIS, IASIL, 19th Century Ireland Soc. **RESEARCH** 19th and 20th century Irish literature. **SELECTED PUBLICATIONS** Auth, "Politicization of Women in the Writings of Julia O'Faolain: No Country for Young Men and The Irish Signorina," Troubled Histories, Troubled Fictions, 4, The Literature of Politics, The Politics of Literature, Amsterdam: Rodopi (95): 151-58; auth, "Poetry in Modern Ireland-Where Post-Colonial and Postmodern Part Ways," The Comparist (spring 96); auth, "Women's Education, Edward Dowden and the University Curriculum in English Literature-- An Unlikely Progression," Gender and Nineteenth Century Ireland, Dublin: Irish Acad Press (96); auth, Contemporary Irish Literature: Transforming Tradition, NY: St Martin's Press (98). **CONTACT ADDRESS** Center for Irish Studies, Catholic Univ of America, 620 Mich Ave NE, Washington, DC 20064-0001. **EMAIL** mahoney@cua.edu

MAHONEY, JOHN FRANCIS
PERSONAL Born 05/19/1929, Detroit, MI, m, 1980, 4 children **DISCIPLINE** ENGLISH, CLASSICS **EDUCATION** Univ Detroit, BA, 50, MA, 52; Univ NC, PhD, 56. **CAREER** Instr English, Univ NC, 53-56; instr Latin, Duke Univ, 54-56; asst prof Mid English, Duquesne Univ, 56-59, assoc prof English & chm grad studies, 59-61; assoc prof English & comp lit, Univ Detroit, 61-63, chm grad comt, 61-64, prof, chem dept and English, 64-69, dean col arts & sci, 69-73; dean, Walden Univ, 73-74; vpres acad affairs, William Paterson Col NJ, 74-78; Dean, Walden Univ, 79-, Southern Fels Fund fel, 56; mem bd, Am Grad & Prof Comn, 66-; pres, Vri, Inc, 79-90; admin dir, Beli-Laddi farm, 80- ; ed & publ Imperial Beach & South County Times, 85-98; columnist, Imperial Beach Eagle & Times, 98- ; Project Develop Officer, B.E.L.I., Inc., 96- . **MEMBERSHIPS** MLA; Mediaeval Acad Am; Dante Soc Am; Soc Exceptional Children. **RESEARCH** Mixed media; mediaeval languages; Dante. **SELECTED PUBLICATIONS** Ed, The Structure of Purgatorio, Dante Soc Bull, 62; Chaucerian Tragedy and the Christian Tradition, Ann Mediaevale, 62; American Authors and Critics (12 vols), Holt, 62-; coauth, Studies in Honor of U T Holmes, Jr, Univ NC, Chapel Hill, 66; The Insistent Present, Houghton, 70; co-ed, New Poets, New Music, Winthrop, 71; coauth, Early Help (film), Medianovations, 73; The House of Tenure (play), Medianovations, 80. **CONTACT ADDRESS** PO Box 5429, Playa del Rey, CA 92293. **EMAIL** mahwis@gte.net

MAIER, CAROL SMITH
PERSONAL Born 06/10/1943, Pittsburgh, PA, m, 1962, 2 children **DISCIPLINE** HISPANIC LITERATURE **EDUCATION** Douglass Col, BA, 68; Rutgers Univ, MA, 72, PhD(Span), 75. **CAREER** Asst prof, 76-80, Assoc Prof Span, Bradley Univ, 80-. **MEMBERSHIPS** MLA; Am Asn Teachers Span and Port; Am Lit Translr Asn; Women's Caucus Mod Lang; Asoc Int de Hispanistas. **RESEARCH** Ramon del Valle-Inclan; literary translation; women's studies. **SELECTED PUBLICATIONS** Auth, La aportacion cerrvantina a Yo soy aquel que ayer no mas decia, Mester, 5/66; Symbolist Aesthetics in Spanish: the concept of language in Valle-Inclan's La lampara maravillosa, Waiting for Pegasus, Studies of the Presence of Symbolism and Decadence in Hispanic Letters, Essays in Lit, 79; The poetry of Ana Castillo: a dialogue between poet and critic, Letras Femeninas, spring 80; Notas sobre melancolia y creacion en dos narradores valleinclanescos: El Marques de Brandomin y el poeta de La lampara marvillosa, Revista de Estudios Hispanicos, 1/81; Notas hacia una definicion del concepto de la historia en La lampara maravillosa, Explicacion de Textos Literarios, Vol IX, No 2; Xose Conde Corbal e a estetica do grabado: Una reforma do ollo por medio da deformacion da lina, Grial, Vol 70, 80; Transl, Imagination and (Un) academic Activity, Transl Rev, winter 80; Por tierras de Portugal y de Espana e Galicia:

Unha rectificacion da perspectiva caztiza, planteada por Valle-Inclan, Grial, Vol 75, 82. **CONTACT ADDRESS** Dept of English and Foreign Lang, Bradley Univ, Peoria, IL 61625.

MAIER, LINDA
PERSONAL Born 11/01/1957, Jefferson City, MO **DISCIPLINE** SPANISH AMERICAN LITERATURE **EDUCATION** WA Univ, AB, 80; Univ VA, MA, 82; PhD, 87. **CAREER** Univ Ala in Huntsville. **MEMBERSHIPS** Am Asn of Teachers of Span and Port; Int Asn of Hispanists; MLA; South American MLA. **SELECTED PUBLICATIONS** Auth, Borges and the European Avant-garde, Lang, 96. **CONTACT ADDRESS** Univ of Alabama, Huntsville, Huntsville, AL 35899. **EMAIL** maierl@email.uah.edu

MAIERHOFER, WALTER
PERSONAL Born Burghausen, Germany **DISCIPLINE** GERMAN LITERATURE **EDUCATION** Univ Regensburg, Germany, MA, 85, PhD, 88. **CAREER** Lectr, Univ Calif Santa Barbara, 89-90; asst prof to assoc prof, Univ Iowa, 90- . **HONORS AND AWARDS** Alexander von Humboldt fel, 98. **MEMBERSHIPS** MLA; ASECS; N Amer Goethe Soc; Heine Soc. **RESEARCH** German literature, mainly of eighteenth & nineteenth century; narrative prose; interrelations of lit & art; German cultural hist. **SELECTED PUBLICATIONS** Auth, Wilhelm Meisters Wanderjahre' und der Roman des Nebeneinander, 90; auth, Angelika Kauffman, dargestellt von Waltraud Maierhofer, 97; auth, Wahrheit und Dichtung, Historiographie und Fiktion im Erzahlwerk Ricarda Huchs, Euphorion, 94; auth, Krieg und Frieden in Gemalden und Briefen Angelika Kauffmanns, Jahrbuch des Vorarlberger Landesmuseumsvereins, 97; auth, Vetter Grune Goetherezeption in Julian Schuttings Zuhorerbehelligungen und Leserbelastigungen, Zeitschrift fur Deutsche Philologie, 97; co-ed, Angelika Kauffmann. Briefe einer Malerin, Excerpta Classica 17, 99; auth, "Goethe on Emma Hamilton's 'Attitudes': Can Classicist Art Be Fun?" Goeth Yrbk 9, 99; co-ed, Resonanzen, Festschrift for Hans Joachim Kreutzer, Koeningshausen & neumann (Wuerzburg), 00. **CONTACT ADDRESS** German Dept, Univ of Iowa, Iowa City, IA 52242-1323. **EMAIL** waltraud-maierhofer@uiowa.edu

MAIR, VICTOR H.
PERSONAL Born 03/25/1943, Canton, OH, m, 1969, 1 child **DISCIPLINE** CHINESE **EDUCATION** Dartmouth Col, BA, 65; Univ London, BA, 72; Harvard Univ, MA, 73; PhD, 76; Univ London, MPhil, 84; Univ Pa, MA, 85. **CAREER** Lecturer, Tunghai Univ Taiwan, 70-72; Lecturer to Asst Prof, Harvard Univ, 73-79; Asst Prof to Prof, Univ Pa, 79-. **HONORS AND AWARDS** Marshall Scholar; Grant, Am Coun of Learned Soc; NEH Grant; Grant, Sloan foundation; Fel, Inst for Adv Study; Fel, Nat Humanities Center. **MEMBERSHIPS** Tang Stud Soc; Asn for Asian Studies; Chinese Lang Soc of Hong Kong. **RESEARCH** Chinese lexicography; The Chinese script; Silk Road; Interaction of China with ancient India and Iran; Chinese popular literature and vernacular language. **SELECTED PUBLICATIONS** Co-auth, "The Sanskrit Origins of Recent Style Prosody," Harvard Journal of Asiatic Studies, (91): 375-470; auth, "Script and Word in Medieval Vernacular Sinitic," Journal of the American Oriental Society, (92): 269-278; trans, Wandering on the Way: Early Taoist Tales and Parables of Chuang Tzu, Bantam, 94; auth, "The Bronze Age and Iron Age Peoples of Eastern Central Asia: Progress Report," Early China News, (95): 5-11; auth, "Language and Script: Biology, Archaeology, and (Pre)history," International Review of Chinese Linguistics, (96): 31-41, 47-50; co-ed, ABC Chinese-English Dictionary, Univ Hawaii Press; auth, "Canine conundrums: Eurasian Dog ancestor Myths in Historical and Ethnic Perspective," Sino-Platonic Papers, (98): 74; ed, The Bronze Age and Early Iron Age Peoples of Eastern Central Asia, Univ PA, 98. **CONTACT ADDRESS** Dept Asian Studies, Univ of Pennsylvania, 255 S 36th St., Philadelphia, PA 19104-3805. **EMAIL** vmair@sas.upenn.edu

MAJOR, JEAN-LOUIS
PERSONAL Born 07/16/1937, Cornwall, ON, Canada **DISCIPLINE** FRENCH LITERATURE **EDUCATION** Univ Ottawa, BA, BPh, 59, BA(Hon), LPh, 60, MA, 61, PhD, 65; Ecole Pratique des Hautes Etudes, Paris, 68-69. **CAREER** Prof, Col Bruyere d'Ottawa, 60-61; dept phil, Univ d'Ottawa, 61-65; prof adjoint, 65-67, prof agrege, 67-71, prof Titulaire dept de lettres Francaises, Univ d'ottawa, 71-, doyen associe a la recherche, faculte des arts, 91-97; vis prof, Univ Toronto, 70-71. **MEMBERSHIPS** Soc Royale Can. **SELECTED PUBLICATIONS** Auth, Ringuet, Trente arpents, Montreal, P.U.M., (91): 521; auth, Louis Dantin, Emile Nelligan et son Oeuvre, Monteal, Les Presses de l'Universite de Montreal, (97): 300; auth, Diereville, Relation du voyage du Port Royal de l'Acadie suivie de Poesies diverses, Montreal, Les Presses de l'Universite de Montreal, (97): 600; auth, Gabriel Sagard, Le Grand Voyage du pays des Hurons, suivi du Dictionnaire de la langue huronne, Montreal, Les Presses de l'Universite de Monteal, (98): 528; auth, Gilbert La rocque, Les Masques, Montreal, Les Presses de l'Universite de Montreal, (98): 302. **CONTACT ADDRESS** Dept de Lettres Francaises, Univ of Ottawa, Simard Hall, 60 Universite, Ottawa, ON, Canada K1N 6N5. **EMAIL** corpus@uottawa.ca

MAJOR, WILFRED E.
DISCIPLINE CLASSICS **EDUCATION** Southern IL Univ Carbondale, BA, 89; IN Univ, MA, 91; IN Univ, PhD, 96. **CAREER** Assoc instr, IN Univ, 90-94; instr, Hobart and William Smith Col, 94-96; instr, Loyola Univ New Orleans, 95-97; adj instr, Tulane Univ, 96-97; asst prof, St Anselm Col, 97-00; vis asst prof, Loyola Univ, 00-. **HONORS AND AWARDS** Phi Kappa Phi, Southern Ill Univ, 88; Indiana Univ Grad Sch Fel, 89; Dr. Lola Case Bk Awd, 93; Grad Student Travel Awd, 95; Help Our Peers Execl (HOPE) Awd for Teaching Excellence, 97 **MEMBERSHIPS** Am Philological Asn; Classical Asn of New England; Classical Asn of the Middle West and South; Lousiana Classical Asn. **SELECTED PUBLICATIONS** Auth, Gorgias' Undeclared Theory of Arrangement Revisited, Southern Comm Jour, 97; Gorgias' "Undeclared" Theory of Arrangement: A Postscript to Smeltzer, Southern Comm Jour, 96; ed, Euripides: Andromache in Aris and Phillips 1994, Didaskalia, 95; auth, "Menander in Macedonian World," Greek Roman and Byzantine Studies 38 (97): 41-73; auth, "Social Class System and the Economy," The Roman Republic and Empire 264 BCE-476CE, World Eras Series, (Columbia, SC: Manly, 01); auth, "Antiphon, Crates, Cratinus," "Demetrius Phalereus," "Diocles of Carystus," "Eupolis," "Gelon of Syracuse," "Menander," and "Theron of Acragas," in Encyclopedia of the Ancient World, (Salem Press, forthcoming). **CONTACT ADDRESS** Dept of Classical Studies, Loyola Univ, New Orleans, 6363 St Charles Ave, Box 113, New Orleans, LA 70118. **EMAIL** wemajor@loyno.edu

MAKKAI, ADAM
PERSONAL Born 12/16/1935, Budapest, Hungary, m, 1966, 2 children **DISCIPLINE** LINGUISTICS **EDUCATION** Harvard Univ, BA, 58; Yale Univ, MA, 62, PhD(gen ling), 65. **CAREER** Asst prof English, Calif State Univ, Long Beach, 66-67; from asst prof to assoc prof ling, 67-74, Prof Ling, Univ Ill Chicago Circle, 74-, Exec Dir and Dir Publ, Ling Asn Can and US, 74-, Paderewski Found grant ling, Univ Malaya, Kuala Lumpur, 63-64; Am Coun Learned Soc, Yale Univ, 64-65; NSF grant comput ling, Rand Corp, Santa Monica, Calif, 65-66; asst prof Russ, Occidental Col, 66-67; managing ed jour, Word, Int Ling Asn, 73-74; exec dir and dir publ and ed jour, Forum Ling, Ling Asn Can and US. **MEMBERSHIPS** Ling Soc Am; MLA; Int Ling Asn; Ling Asn Can and US. **RESEARCH** Idomaticity and English semantics; English lexicography, poetry and translation; stratificational grammar. **SELECTED PUBLICATIONS** Auth, In Search of a Revolution--Discussion, Lang and Commun, Vol 0015, 95; Idiomatic Adaptive vs Literal Traditional Translation + Macleod, Ian Translation of Madach, Imre the 'Tragedy of Man', Hungarian Quart, Vol 0037, 96. **CONTACT ADDRESS** Dept of Ling, Univ of Illinois, Chicago, Chicago, IL 60637.

MAKWARD, CHRISTIANE PERRIN
PERSONAL Born 01/06/1941, Hyeres, France, m, 1960, 2 children **DISCIPLINE** FRENCH LITERATURE, WOMEN'S STUDIES **EDUCATION** Sorbonne, Lic es Lett, 63, DLit, 74; Univ Dakar, DES, 65. **CAREER** From asst lectr to lectr French lang & lit, Univ Ibadan, Nigeria, 62-67; lectr French lit, Univ Wis, 68-69 & 74-75; lectr, Univ Que-Rimouski, 76-77; asst prof, 77-80, assoc prof French, prof French, 96-, Pa State Univ, 80-96, Ed, Breff, Pa State Univ, 76-. **MEMBERSHIPS** MLA; Am Asn Teachers Fr; Women's Caucus Mod Lang; Asn Int Femmes Ecrivians; Asn Amis Cerisy-la-Salle. **RESEARCH** Contemporary French literature; psychoanalysis; stylistics. **SELECTED PUBLICATIONS** Auth, Mallarme and Ricardou: Echoes, 73, Claude Simon: Earth, Eros and Death, 74 & Interview with Helene Cixous, 76, Sub-Stance; La critique feministe: Elements d'une problematique, Revue Sci Humanies, Lille, 12/77; auth, Aspects of bisexuality in Claude Simon's works, In: Blinded Orion, Bucknell Univ; Structures du silence/du delire: Marguerite Duras/Helene Cixous, Poetique, Paris; Nouveau regard sur la critique feministe, Revue de l'Univ d'Ottawa, Vol 50, No 1; Colette and signs, In: Colette, The Woman, The Writer, Pa State Univ Press, 81. **CONTACT ADDRESS** Dept of French, Pennsylvania State Univ, Univ Park, 316 Burrowes Bldg, University Park, PA 16802-6203. **EMAIL** cjm9@psu.edu

MALAMUD, MARTHA A.
PERSONAL Born Boston, MA, m, 2 children **DISCIPLINE** CLASSICS **EDUCATION** Bryn Mawr, BA, 78; Cornell, PhD, 85. **CAREER** Asst, assoc prof, Univ of Southern Cal, 84-92; assoc prof, classics dept, Univ of Buffalo (SUNY), 92-. **HONORS AND AWARDS** Mellon fel; Rome prize: NEH sr fel, Amer Acad in Rome, 88-89; ACLS grant. **MEMBERSHIPS** Amer Philol Asn. **RESEARCH** Late antique lit; Latin epic; Allusion and the development of the Roman Imperial period **SELECTED PUBLICATIONS** Ed, Arethusa;m auth, A Poetics of Transformation: Prudentius and Classical Mythology **CONTACT ADDRESS** Classics Dept., SUNY, Buffalo, Clemens Hall, Buffalo, NY 14260. **EMAIL** malamud@acsu.buffalo.edu

MALANDRA, WILLIAM
DISCIPLINE CLASSICAL AND NEAR EASTERN STUDIES **EDUCATION** Haverford Col, BA, 64; Brown Univ, BA, 66; Univ Pa, PhD, 71. **CAREER** Assoc prof, Univ Minn, Twin Cities. **RESEARCH** Indo-Iranian philological studies. **SELECTED PUBLICATIONS** Auth, Avestan zanu-drajah: an Obscene Gesture, Indo-Iranian J 22, 80; An Introduction to Old Iranian Religion, Univ Minn Press, 83; Rasnu and the Office of Divine Judge: Comparative Reconstructions and the Varuna Problem, Festschrift for Ludo Rocher, Madras: Adyar Libr, 87. **CONTACT ADDRESS** Univ of Minnesota, Twin Cities, 9 Pleasant St. SE, 330 Folwell Hall, Minneapolis, MN 55455.

MALBY, MARIA BOZICEVIC
PERSONAL Born 05/16/1937, Zagreb, Yugoslavia, d, 1 child **DISCIPLINE** RUSSIAN AND SERBO-CROATIAN LANGUAGES AND LITERATURES **EDUCATION** Fla State Univ, BA, 62; Harvard Univ, AM, 63, PhD(Slavic lang and lit), 70. **CAREER** Asst prof, Frostburg State Col, 66-70; assoc prof, 70-80, Prof Ger and Russ, East Carolina Univ, 80-. **MEMBERSHIPS** AAUP; MLA; SAtlantic Mod Lang Asn; Am Asn Teachers Slavic and East Europ Lang; Am Asn Slavic Scholars. **RESEARCH** Comparative Russian and Serbo-Croatian literature; German. **SELECTED PUBLICATIONS** Transl mod Yugoslav lit in anthologies & jour, Fairleigh Dickinson Univ Lit Rev, 68 & Nin, Zagreb, 72; auth, Yugoslav literature, Twayne, 73. **CONTACT ADDRESS** Dept of Foreign Lang and Lit, East Carolina Univ, Greenville, NC 27834.

MALDONADO-DEOLIVEIRA, DEBORA
PERSONAL Born 09/13/1966, San Juan, Puerto Rico, m **DISCIPLINE** LINGUISTICS, LITERATURE, SPANISH **EDUCATION** Univ Puerto Rico, BA, 89; Univ Rochester, MA, 93; PhD, 00. **CAREER** Asst prof, Wayne State Univ, 97-99; asst prof, Meredith Col, 00-; instr, Durham Tech Community Col, 00-. **HONORS AND AWARDS** Univ Rochester Fel, 90-96; Ford Found PreDoct. **MEMBERSHIPS** MLA; Feminists Unidas; SHC. **RESEARCH** Caribbean and Latin American literature and culture; literary theory; feminism; popular culture; US Latino literature (esp Puerto Rican); visual arts; film studies; post-colonial theory. **CONTACT ADDRESS** Dept Foreign Lang and Lit, Meredith Col, 3800 Hillsborough St, Raleigh, NC 27607. **EMAIL** deoliveirad@meredith.edu

MALL, LAURENCE
DISCIPLINE FRENCH LITERATURE **EDUCATION** Faculte des Lettres d'Avignon, France, BA, 80; Univ Pa, PhD, 90. **CAREER** Prof, Univ Ill Urbana Champaign. **RESEARCH** Rousseau, 18th Century Novel, techniques, history, 18th Century novelists, Prevost, Marivaux, Grafligny, Charriere, 18th Century history of ideas, narraiology stylistics. **SELECTED PUBLICATIONS** Auth, "Les Aberrations de l'errance: le voyage dans La Nouvelle Heloise," Australian Journal of French Studies XXXI, 2, (64): 175-187; auth, "Langues etrangeres et etrangete du langage dans Les Leures d'une Peruvienne de Madame de Grafigny," Studies on Voltaire and the Eighteenth Century 323, (94): 323-343; auth, "Moins seule et factice': la part autobiographique dans Une Femme d'Annie Ernaux," The French Review 69, 1, (95): 45-54; auth, "Rhetorique et pouvoir dans De la cour des Caracteres de la Bruyere," Romanic Review, 87.1, (96): 35-58; auth, "Traduction et original dans les Leures d'une Peruvienne de Graffigny," Romance Quarterly 44, 1, (97): 13-23; auth, "Perdues dans les details: les Leures de Mistriss Henley de Charriere et l'ecriture de la desintegration," Orbis Liuerarum, 52, (97): 178-193; auth, "Les luxes de l'autoportrait par hypothese: la digression 'Si j'etais riche' dans l'Emile" Poetique, 112, (97): 387-407; auth, "La Theartralisation generalisee dans Emile et la Leure a d'Alembert de Rousseau," Pensee libre 6, (97): 43-51; auth, Origines et retraites dans La Nouvelle, Peter Lang, 97; L'ethnotexte de la banlieue: Journal du dehors d'Annie Ernaux, 98. **CONTACT ADDRESS** French Dept, Univ of Illinois, Urbana-Champaign, 2038 flb, mc 158, 707 s mathews, Urbana, IL 61801. **EMAIL** l-mall@staff.uiuc.edu

MALL, RITA SPARROW
PERSONAL Born New York, NY **DISCIPLINE** FRENCH LITERATURE **EDUCATION** Brooklyn Col, BA, 57; NYork Univ, MA, 60; Univ Ill, Urbana, PhD(French), 69. **CAREER** Instr French, Univ Mass, Amherst, 60-62; asst prof, 68-76, Assoc Prof French, 76-00; Asst Dean Arts and Sci, La Salle Col, 76-86, Asst French, NY Univ, 58-59 and Univ Ill, Urbana, 64-65 and 67-68. **HONORS AND AWARDS** Phi Beta Kappa; Undergrad Fulbright; NEH Fellowship. **MEMBERSHIPS** Am Asn Teachers Fr. **RESEARCH** Nineteenth and twentieth century French novel. **SELECTED PUBLICATIONS** Auth, Tragic Muse--Rachel of the Comedie Francaise, 19th-Century Fr Stud, Vol 0024, 95. **CONTACT ADDRESS** Dept of Foreign Lang, La Salle Univ, 1900 W Olney Ave, Philadelphia, PA 19141-1199.

MALONE, JOSEPH LAWRENCE
PERSONAL Born 07/02/1937, New York, NY, m, 1964, 2 children **DISCIPLINE** LINGUISTICS **EDUCATION** Univ Calif, Berkeley, BA, 63, PhD(ling), 67. **CAREER** From instr to assoc prof, 67-75, Prof Ling, Barnard Col, Columbia Univ, 75-, Chmn Dept, 67-, Contrib consult ling, Grolier Publ Co, NJ, 77-. **MEMBERSHIPS** Ling Soc Am; Am Orient Soc; North Am Conference on Afrnasiatic Lings. **RESEARCH** Linguistic theory; Semitic linguistics; translation. **SELECTED PUBLICATIONS** Auth, The Science and Linguistics in the Art of Translation, SUNY, Albany, 88; Tiberian Hebrew Phonology,

Eisenbrauns, Winona Lake, 93; Carmina Gaiana, Linear Arts Books, NY, 97; auth, Above The Salty Bay, Linear Arts Books, 01. **CONTACT ADDRESS** Dept of Ling Barnard Col, Columbia Univ, 3009 Broadway, New York, NY 10027-6598. **EMAIL** jmalone@barnard.columbia.edu

MALONEY, ELLIOTT CHARLES
PERSONAL Born 04/17/1946, Pittsburgh, PA **DISCIPLINE** NEW TESTAMENT STUDIES, BIBLICAL LANGUAGES **EDUCATION** St Vincent Col, AB, 68; Pontifical Atheneum of St Anselm, Rome, STL, 72; Fordham Univ, PhD(New Testament), 79. **CAREER** Instr, 76-81, Assoc Prof New Testament Studies & Bibl Lang, 81-92; Professor New Testament Studies & Bibl Lang, 92-, St Vincent Sem, 76. **MEMBERSHIPS** Soc Bibl Lit; Cath Bibl Asn. **RESEARCH** Greek language of the New Testament; Gospel of Mark; Epistles of Paul. **SELECTED PUBLICATIONS** Auth, Semitic interference in Marcan Syntax, Soc Bibl Lit Dissertation Series, 81; transl, Epistles of James, 1-2 Peter, Jude, In: New American Bible, rev New Testament, 86. **CONTACT ADDRESS** Saint Vincent Col, 300 Fraser Purchase, Latrobe, PA 15650-2690. **EMAIL** emaloney@stvincent.edu

MALPEZZI PRICE, PAOLA
DISCIPLINE ITALIAN AND FRENCH LITERATURE **EDUCATION** Univ Oregon, PhD. **CAREER** Assoc prof. **RESEARCH** Italian language and culture; French language, literature, and culture. **SELECTED PUBLICATIONS** Auth, pubs on French and Italian women writers. **CONTACT ADDRESS** Foreign Languages and Literature Dept, Colorado State Univ, Fort Collins, CO 80523. **EMAIL** pmalpezziprice@vines.colostate.edu

MALSBARY, GERALD HENRY
PERSONAL Born 11/06/1952, Oakland, CA, m, 1979, 5 children **DISCIPLINE** CLASSICS **EDUCATION** Univ Calif, Berkeley, BA, 74, MA, 76; Univ Toronto, PhD, 88. **CAREER** Asst prof, St. Michael's Col, 87-89; res, Thesaurus Linguae Latinae, Munich, 89-91; prof, St. Charles Borromeo Sem, 91- . **HONORS AND AWARDS** Am Philol Asn, TLL fel, 89. **MEMBERSHIPS** APA; NAMLA. **RESEARCH** Trivium; ethics; metaphysics; education history; Vatican II doctrines; Chinese and Indian philosophy. **SELECTED PUBLICATIONS** Three articles on Early Christian Latin; four books translated from German and Italian. **CONTACT ADDRESS** 260 Ballymore Rd, Springfield, PA 19064. **EMAIL** drmalsbary@juno.com

MAMOOJEE, ABDOOL-HACK
DISCIPLINE CLASSICS **EDUCATION** Merton Col, Oxford, BA, 65, MA, 68; Univ Ottawa, PhD, 78. **CAREER** Instr, Royal Col, Port-Louis, Mauritius; Univ Quebec, Univ Ottawa; prof, 69-. **HONORS AND AWARDS** Ch, dept lang; deputy-dean, Fac Arts; corresponding mem, Can Fed for the Hum; act mem, Class Assn Can. **MEMBERSHIPS** Classical Asn of Canada. **RESEARCH** Works of Cicero and the history of the Late Roman Republic. **SELECTED PUBLICATIONS** Auth, "Le proconsulat de Q. Ciceron en Asie," Echos du monde classique, vol. 38, (94): 23-50; auth, "Cicero, in togo candida fr. 8", Classical Views, vol. 39.3, (95): 401-412; rev, of A. Vasaly, representations: Images of the world in Ciceronian oratory, Classical Views, vol. 49.33, (95): 428-432; auth, Le proconsulat de Q. Ciceron en Asie, Echos du monde classique, 94; Cicero, In toga candida fr 8, Class Views, 95; rev, of J. W. Crawford, Cicero: the fragmentary speeches, Phoenix vol. 49.2, (95): 168-170, vol. 50.2, (96): 167; auth, "Cicero, ad Atticum 11.8.2: a note on Furnius", Classical Views, vol. 41.2, (97): 317-324; auth, "Cicero's choice of a deputy in Cilicia: the Quintus option," Ancient History Bulletin, vol. 12.1-1, (98): 19-28; auth, "Cicero: agrestis versus rusticus," Melanges Margaret Thomson, Cahier des etudes anciennes, vol. 34, (98): 95-102; auth, "Gratiarum actio iv Kal. Iun. Habita A.D. MIM", Classical Views, vol. 43.1, (99): 163-164. **CONTACT ADDRESS** Dept of Lang, Lakehead Univ, 955 Oliver Rd, Thunder Bay, ON, Canada P7B 5E1. **EMAIL** aketonen@sky.lakeheadu.ca

MAMOON, TRINA
PERSONAL Born, Bangladesh, m **DISCIPLINE** RUSSIAN **EDUCATION** Peoples' Friendship Univ Moscow, MA, 84; Univ Ill, MA, 97; PhD, 98 **CAREER** Adj Prof, Rose-Hulman Inst of Technol, 89-90; Lecturer, Ind State Univ, 90-91; Asst Prof, Univ Alaska, 98-. **HONORS AND AWARDS** IREX Bulgarian summer Seminar, 94. **MEMBERSHIPS** AATSEEL, AFLA. **RESEARCH** 19th and 20th Century Russian Literature; Medieval Russian Literature; Women Studies. **SELECTED PUBLICATIONS** Auth, "Olga Berggol'tts" in Anthology of Russian Women Writers, Garland Pub, 99. **CONTACT ADDRESS** Dept For Lang, Univ of Alaska, Fairbanks, PO Box 756440, Fairbanks, AK 99775-6440.

MANGAN, JACQUELINE J. SAMPERI
PERSONAL Born 01/09/1960, Florentin, France, m, 1988, 4 children **DISCIPLINE** ITALIAN **EDUCATION** Concordia Univ, BA, 86; McGill Univ, MA, 91; PhD, 00. **CAREER** Teacher, PICAI, 80-93; teacher, Boi-De-Boulogne Col, 93-97; TA, McGill Univ, 87-98; Director, Univ de Montreal, 99-00; prof, Vanier Col, 90-01; prof, Concordia Univ, 93-01. **HONORS AND AWARDS** Ger Lit Prize, 86; Best Teacher, PICAI, 87; Anne Dudley Noad Mem Awd, 87; Ital LitStudy Achievement Prize, 93; AATI Grant, 96. **MEMBERSHIPS** Am Assoc of Ital Studies, Am Assoc of Teachers of Ital, Can Soc for Ital Studies, MLA, Am Coun on the Teaching of For Lang. **RESEARCH** Contemporary Italian Literature and de-centralized literatures in the global world. **SELECTED PUBLICATIONS** Auth, "Error Analysis of Italian Childrens' Compositions in a Multilingual Context (Montreal)," L2 and Beyond. Teaching and Learning Modern Languages, ed V Adamantova, L Sbrocchi, R Williamson, (NY: Legas, 93); auth, "La morte onnipresente: visioni tetre in tre romanzi di donne svizzere," Minstry of For Affairs, Italy, (01). **CONTACT ADDRESS** Dept Class, Mod Lang and Ling, Concordia Univ, Montreal, 1455 de Maisonneuve Blvd W, PO Box H 663, Montreal, QC, Canada H3G 1M8. **EMAIL** jacqueline_samperi@yahoo.ca

MANIQUIS, ROBERT MANUEL
PERSONAL Born 09/04/1940, Newark, NY, m, 1961, 2 children **DISCIPLINE** ENGLISH LITERATURE, COMPARATIVE LITERATURE **EDUCATION** Rutgers Univ, BA, 62; Columbia Univ, MA, 63, PhD(English), 67. **CAREER** Asst prof English, 66-77, dir freshman English, 75-76, Assoc Prof English, Univ Calif, Los Angeles, 77-, Am Coun Learned Soc fel, 72-73. **MEMBERSHIPS** MLA; Philol Asn PACIFIC Coast. **RESEARCH** Nineteenth century Romanticism, English, French, and German; 19th century novel, English, French, and German. **SELECTED PUBLICATIONS** Auth, Comparison, intensity, and time in Tintern Abbey, Criticism, fall 69; The puzzling Mimosa: Sensitivity and plant symbols in Romanticism, Studies Romanticism, spring 69; Lonely empires: Personal and public visions of Thomas De Quincey, In: Literary Monographs, Univ Wis, 76. **CONTACT ADDRESS** Dept of English, Univ of California, Los Angeles, Los Angeles, CA 90024.

MANLEY, JOAN
PERSONAL Born, England **DISCIPLINE** LINGUISTICS **EDUCATION** Univ Col, London, BA; Univ Tex at Austin, PhD. **CAREER** Past ch, ACTFL/Texas Proj; past pres, Tex For Lang Asn; undergrade stud adv; dept adv, over 20 yrs; actg dir, university's Acad Adv Ctr, 90-93; main tchr, Methods of For Lang Instruction. **MEMBERSHIPS** Bd, Southwest Conf Lang Tchg; bd, Amer Coun on the Teaching of For Languages. **RESEARCH** Renaissance theatre; preparation and certification of foreign language teachers; French language programs for beginners. **SELECTED PUBLICATIONS** Lead auth, 1st beginning Fr Prog, Qu'est-ce qu'on dit, Heinle and Heinle, 94; sec, Horizons, Heinle and Heinle, 98; **CONTACT ADDRESS** Dept of Languages and Linguistics, Univ of Texas, El Paso, 500 W University Ave, El Paso, TX 79968. **EMAIL** jmanley@utep.edu

MANN, JOAN DEBBIE
PERSONAL Born 09/19/1955, Lakeland, FL, m, 1981, 1 child **DISCIPLINE** FRENCH **EDUCATION** Berry Col, BA, 76; Univ Fla, MA, 78, PhD, 87. **CAREER** From asst prof to assoc prof, Southern Ill Univ, 88-. **HONORS AND AWARDS** Phi Beta Kappa. **MEMBERSHIPS** MLA; AATF. **RESEARCH** 20th century French prose; francophone novel; short story genre. **SELECTED PUBLICATIONS** Auth, art, Andree Chedid, 95; auth, art, Andree Chedid Nouvelliste, 96. **CONTACT ADDRESS** Dept of Foreign Languages, So Illinois Univ, Edwardsville, Box 1432, Edwardsville, IL 62026-1432. **EMAIL** jmann@siue.edu

MANN, MARIA A.
PERSONAL Born Perugia, Italy, 2 children **DISCIPLINE** ITALIAN, FRENCH **EDUCATION** Univ of Perugia Italy, lauria in lingue, 75; Univ for foreigners, Perugia Italy, certificate, 78; CUNY Graduate Center, PhD, 87. **CAREER** Lectr, Queens Col, 81-85; adj asst prof, Hofstra Univ, 85-89; instr to assoc prof, chair, Nassau Community Col, 89-. **HONORS AND AWARDS** Queens Col Fel, 81-83. **MEMBERSHIPS** MLA, Am Asn Teachers of Ital, Am Soc for 18th Century Studies, Asn of Italian Am Educ. **RESEARCH** 18th-century French and Italian women writers, women's advancement and education in the 18th century, writers of the illuminismo lombardo. **SELECTED PUBLICATIONS** Auth, La mere dans la litterature francaise 1678-1831, Lang, 89; auth, "Twentieth-Century thoughts in eighteenth-century Milan," Rivista di Studi Italiani, (97). **CONTACT ADDRESS** Dept For Lang, Nassau Comm Col, Garden City, NY 11530. **EMAIL** mannm@sunynassau.edu

MANNETTER, TERRANCE
PERSONAL Born 08/26/1959, Waukesha, WI, m, 1988, 2 children **DISCIPLINE** SPANISH LITERATURE, LINGUISTICS, PEDAGOGY **EDUCATION** Univ Wis, BA; MA; PhD. **CAREER** Lectr, Univ Wis, Madison; lectr, Univ Wis, Oshkosh; asst prof, Univ Wis, River Falls. **HONORS AND AWARDS** Fac Res Gnt; Stud Fac Res Gnt. **MEMBERSHIPS** MLA; MMLA; WAA; WAFLT. **RESEARCH** Development of Spanish language; old Spanish lexicography; Spanish Pedagogy. **SELECTED PUBLICATIONS** Ed, Cronica de once (veinte) reyes, Escorial MS (Madison: Hispanic Seminary of Medieval Studies, Ltd., 89); ed, Leyes del estilo, Escorial MS (Madison: Hispanic Seminary of Medieval Studies, Ltd., 90); ed, Leyes del estilo, MS.5764, Biblioteca Nacional (Madison: Hispanic Seminary of Medieval Studies, Ltd., 89); ed, Texts and Concordances of Leyes del estilo Escorial MSS, and the 1497 and 1500 Salamanca Incurables, (Madison: Hispanic Seminary of Medieval Studies, Ltd., 93). **CONTACT ADDRESS** Dept Modern Lang, Univ of Wisconsin, River Falls, 410 South 3rd St, River Falls, WI 54022-5013. **EMAIL** terrence.mannetter@uwrf.edu

MANNING, ALAN
PERSONAL Born 11/12/1945, London, England, m, 1971, 2 children **DISCIPLINE** MEDIEVAL LITERATURE AND LANGUAGE **EDUCATION** Univ Wales, BA Hons, 69; Univ Wis-Milwaukee, MA, 72; Pa State Univ, PhD(French), 76. **CAREER** Asst prof transl, Laurentian Univ, 76-80; Asst Prof Transl, Univ Laval, 80-, Can Coun res grant, Res Coun Can, 78. **RESEARCH** French Medieval treatises on heraldry; Medieval French literature and language. **SELECTED PUBLICATIONS** Auth, Articulation of the Text in English and French, Meta, Vol 0037, 92. **CONTACT ADDRESS** Dept of Transl, Univ of Laval, Quebec, QC, Canada G1K 7P4. **EMAIL** alan.manning@lli.ulaval.ca

MANNING, JOSEPH G.
DISCIPLINE CLASSICS **EDUCATION** BA, 81; Univ Chicago, PhD, 92. **CAREER** Asst prof, Stanford Univ. **RESEARCH** Papyrology; Hellenistic, Near Eastern, and Egyptian hist. **SELECTED PUBLICATIONS** Auth, Land and Social Status in Hellenistic Egypt in Grund und Boden in Altagypten, Tubingen, 95; Demotic Egyptian Instruments of Conveyance as Evidence of Ownerswhip of Real Property in Chicago-Kent Law Review, 96; The Hauswaldt Papyri: A Third Century Family Archive from Edfu, Upper Egypt , Demotische Studien, 96. **CONTACT ADDRESS** Stanford Univ, Bldg 20, Main Quad, Stanford, CA 94305. **EMAIL** jmanning@stanford.edu

MANOPOLOUS, MONIQUE M.
PERSONAL Born 01/05/1957, Marseille, France, m, 1995, 1 child **DISCIPLINE** FRENCH, ITALIAN **EDUCATION** Univ de Provence, Licence es-Lettres, 78; Ariz State Univ, MA, 89; Univ Iowa, PhD, 94. **CAREER** Vis asst prof, Univ Utah, 94-95; prof, Supdeco, 95-97; vis asst prof, Univ of Memphis, 97-. **HONORS AND AWARDS** Ariz State Univ Fel, 88; ASUU Student's Choice Award for Teaching, 95. **MEMBERSHIPS** MLA, AATF, Congres Int des Etudes Francophones. **RESEARCH** Post Francophonie, Post colonialite, 20th Century French Literature, Renaissance French Literature. **SELECTED PUBLICATIONS** Auth, "L'ecriture decentree: La langue de l'autre dans le roman contemporain, L'Harmattn, (96); auth, "Decentrage et pluri-identities dans Les ANI du Tassili d'Akli Tadjer, Le Maghreb litteraires, (99); auth, Une difficle fin de moi d'Ahmed Zitouni: les sans-papiers, greve de la faim et identite, 00; auth, Voix narratrices et (de) canonisation de la litterature chez Ahmed Zitouni, LitteRealite, 00; auth, Maghrebian Mosaic: A Literature in Transition, Lynne Rienner, 00. **CONTACT ADDRESS** Univ of Memphis, 375 Dunn Hall, Memphis, TN 38152. **EMAIL** monimanop@netscape.com

MANSOUR, GEORGE PHILLIP
PERSONAL Born 09/04/1939, Huntington, WV, m, 1961, 2 children **DISCIPLINE** SPANISH LITERATURE **EDUCATION** Marshall Univ, AB, 61; MI State Univ, MA, 62, PhD, 65. **CAREER** From instr to asst prof, 64-68, assoc prof, 68-77, assoc chairperson romance & class lang, 72-82, Prof Span, MI State Univ, 77. **MEMBERSHIPS** Am Asn Tchrs Span & Port; MLA. **RESEARCH** Nineteenth century Span lit; Don Juan theme; Span Romanticism. **SELECTED PUBLICATIONS** Auth, El convidado de piedra: A zarzuela by Rafael de Castillo, Hispania, 12/65; Time in the prose of J Echegaray, Ky Foreign Lang Quart, 68; Algunos Don Juanes olvidados del siglo XIX, Rev Estudios Hisp, 11/69; Concerning Rivas unexplained localization of Don Alvaro, Romance Notes, winter 78; Parallelism in Don Juan Tenorio, Hispania, 5/78; The poetization of experience, Hisp J, 81. **CONTACT ADDRESS** Dept of Romance Lang, Michigan State Univ, 248 Old Horticulture, East Lansing, MI 48824-1112. **EMAIL** mansour@msu.edu

MANTEIGA, ROBERT CHARLES
PERSONAL Born 06/08/1947, Brooklyn, NY, m, 1970, 1 child **DISCIPLINE** SPANISH LETTERS & COMPARATIVE LITERATURE **EDUCATION** Univ Va, BA, 69, PhD(Span), 77; NYork Univ, MA, 71. **CAREER** Instr Span, Univ Va, 72-73; instr, Univ RI, 73-75; lectr, Rutgers Univ, 75-76; asst prof, 76-80, Assoc Prof Span, Univ RI, 81-86, prof, 87-. **MEMBERSHIPS** MLA; Am Asn Teachers Span & Port; AAUP. **RESEARCH** Medieval lyric poetry; 20th century peninsular literature. **SELECTED PUBLICATIONS** Auth, The Poetry of Rafael Alberti: A Visual Approach, Tamesis, 79; coed, Critical Approaches to the Writings of Juan Benet, Univ Press of New England, 84; coed, Feminine Concerns in Contemporary Spanish Fiction by Women, Scripta Humanistica, 88; auth, "From Empathy to Detachment: The Author-Narrator Relationship in Several Spanish Novels by Women," Monographic Rev 8 (93): 19-35; auth, "El lector-viajero de Juan Benet," Insula (93): 23-24; auth, "Hacia un teatro popular," Letras Peninsulares (99). **CONTACT ADDRESS** Dept of Mod Lang, Univ of Rhode Island, 60 Upper Col Rd, 161 Independence Hall, Kingston, RI 02881. **EMAIL** roberto@uri.edu

MANTERO, MANUEL
PERSONAL Born 07/29/1930, Seville, Spain, m, 1963, 5 children **DISCIPLINE** SPANISH **EDUCATION** Univ Seville, Licenciado, 53; Univ Salemanca, Doctorate, 57. **CAREER** Prof, Univ Seville; Prof, Univ Madrid; Prof, Western Mich Univ; Res Prof, Univ Ga, 73-. **HONORS AND AWARDS** Nat Prize of Literature, Spain; Prize "Andalucia de la Critica", The Royal Acad of the Lang, Spain; The Albert Christ Janer Awd. **MEMBERSHIPS** Am Asn of Teachers of Spanish and Portuguese, S Atlantic Mod Lang Asn, Consejo Superior de Invetigaciones Cientificas, Order de Don Quijote. **RESEARCH** Spanish and Spanish-American Literature: poetry, novel, essay. **CONTACT ADDRESS** Dept Romance Lang, Univ of Georgia, 245 Forest Heights Dr, Athens, GA 30606. **EMAIL** mantero@arches.uga.edu

MANUEL, SHARON Y.
DISCIPLINE PRODUCTION, ACOUSTICS, AND PERCEPTION OF SPEECH **EDUCATION** IA State Univ, BS; ID State Univ, MS; Yale Univ, Mphil, PhD. **CAREER** Speech, Emerson Col. **SELECTED PUBLICATIONS** Areas: variations among lang, speaking styles, and normal and disordered speech. **CONTACT ADDRESS** Emerson Col, 100 Beacon Street, Boston, MA 02116-1596.

MAPA, MARINA VARGAS
PERSONAL Born 09/04/1925, Iloilo, Philippines **DISCIPLINE** SPANISH LANGUAGES & LITERATURE **EDUCATION** San Francisco Col Women, BA, 52, MA, 55; Stanford Univ, PhD(Span), 60. **CAREER** Instr Span & Latin, San Francisco Col Women, 56-61, from asst prof to assoc prof Span, 61-69, chmn dept, 63-69, lang lab dir, 65-69, registr, 66-68; Assoc Prof Span & Lang Lab Dir, Univ San Diego, 69- **MEMBERSHIPS** Nat Asn Lang Lab Dirs; Am Asn Teachers Span & Port; AAUP; Am Coun Teaching Foreign Lang. **RESEARCH** Methods of teaching Spanish. **CONTACT ADDRESS** Dept of Foreign Lang, Univ of San Diego, 5998 Alcala Park, San Diego, CA 92110-2492. **EMAIL** mmapa@acusd.edu

MAPLES, ROBERT JOHN BARRIE
PERSONAL Born 05/01/1934, Rochester, NY, m, 1961, 1 child **DISCIPLINE** FRENCH **EDUCATION** Univ Rochester, AB, 56; Yale Univ, PhD(French), 65. **CAREER** Instr French, Univ Rochester, 62-65; asst prof, Univ Mich, Ann Arbor, 65-69; Assoc Prof French, Lycoming Col, 69-99. **MEMBERSHIPS** Am Asn Teachers Fr. **RESEARCH** French Romantic literature. **SELECTED PUBLICATIONS** Auth, Individuation in Nodier's La fee aux miettes, Studies Romanticism, fall 68. **CONTACT ADDRESS** Dept of Foreign Lang & Lit, Lycoming Col, 700 College Pl, Williamsport, PA 17701-5192. **EMAIL** maples@lycoming.edu

MARAHRENS, GERWIN
PERSONAL Born 12/12/1929, Breslau, Germany, m, 1962, 1 child **DISCIPLINE** GERMAN LANGUAGES AND LITERATURE **EDUCATION** Univ Freiburg, PhD, 58. **CAREER** Asst lectr Ger lang and lit, Univ Edinburgh, 58-61; from asst prof to assoc prof, 62-72, actg chmn dept, 70, Prof Ger Lang, Univ Alata, 72-, Chmn Dept, 71-. **MEMBERSHIPS** Can Asn Univ Teachers Ger; Am Asn Teachers Ger; MLA; Am Soc 18th Century Studies. **RESEARCH** Eighteenth to 20th century literature; Goethe. **SELECTED PUBLICATIONS** Auth, Redefining Goethe Aphorisms, Goethe Jahrbuch, Vol 0110, 93; Goethe Other 'Faust'--the Drama, Part II, Seminar-J Ger Stud, Vol 0031, 95. **CONTACT ADDRESS** Dept of Ger Lang, Univ of Alberta, 183 Quesnell Crescent, Edmonton, AB, Canada T6G 2E1.

MARANTZ, ENID GOLDSTINE
PERSONAL Born 12/25/1923, Winnipeg, MB, Canada, m, 1961 **DISCIPLINE** FRENCH **EDUCATION** Univ Man, BA, 46; Univ Paris, DUniv, 49. **CAREER** Lectr, 51-52, 53-58, asst prof, 58-68, dep registr, 66-67, registr, Univ Col, 68-71, Assoc Prof French, Univ Man, 68-, Vpres, Alliance Francaise de Winnipeg, 64-70; mem, Second Lang Curric Coun, Prov Man, 69-73; pres, Alliance Francaise, Man, 70-73; adv, Fed Alliances Francaises du Can, 71-; mem bd teacher educ and certification, Prov Man, 77-78; mem senate, Univ Man, 76-81, senate exec, 79-81. **MEMBERSHIPS** Asn Can Univ Teachers Fr; Can Comp Lit Asn; Soc des Amis de Marcel; Praust et des Amis de Combray; MLA. **RESEARCH** Comparative literature; Marcel Proust; 20th century novel and drama. **SELECTED PUBLICATIONS** Auth, The Infinite, the Uncompleted and the Ending in the Proustian Text--the Case of Mlle De Stermaria, Etudes Francaises, Vol 0030, 94. **CONTACT ADDRESS** Dept of French, Spanish, and Italian, Univ of Manitoba, 467 Univ Col, Winnipeg, MB, Canada R3T 2N2.

MARCH, WALLACE EUGENE
PERSONAL Born 07/08/1935, Dallas, TX, m, 1957, 2 children **DISCIPLINE** THEOLOGY; ANCIENT LANGUAGES **EDUCATION** Austin Col, BA, 57; Austin Presby Theol Sem, BD, 60; Union Theol Sem, NYork, PhD(Old Testament), 66. **CAREER** From instr to assoc prof, Austin Presby Theol Sem, 64-73, prof, 73-82; Arnold B Rhodes Prof Old Testament, Louisville Presby Theol Sem, 82-, Dean, 92-99. **HONORS AND AWARDS** Rockefeller Schol, 64; Advanced Rel Study Fel, 66, 74; Asn Theol Schs Theol Scholar res grant, 80. **MEMBERSHIPS** Soc Bibl Lit; Am Acad of Rel. **RESEARCH** Prophetic literature, particularly the sixth and eighth centuries; form criticism and literary criticism; Biblical theology. **SELECTED PUBLICATIONS** Contribr, Laken: its functions and meanings, In: Rhetorical Criticism, Pickwick, 74; Prophecy, In: Old Testament Form Criticism, Trinity Univ, 74; auth, Basic Bible Study, German Press, 78; Ed, Texts and Testaments: Critical Essays on the Bible and Early Church Fathers, Trinity Univ, 80; auth, Biblical Theology, authority and the Presbyterians, J Presby Hist, 81; Israel and the Politics of Land, John Knox Press, 94; Haggai, The New Interpreter's Bible, Abingdon Press, 96. **CONTACT ADDRESS** Louisville Presbyterian Theol Sem, 1044 Alta Vista Rd, Louisville, KY 40205-1758. **EMAIL** emarch@lpts.edu

MARCHAND, JAMES WOODROW
PERSONAL Born 11/11/1926, Birmingham, AL, m, 3 children **DISCIPLINE** GERMANIC LANGUAGES **EDUCATION** George Peabody Col, BA, 50; Vanderbilt Univ, MA, 51; Univ Mich, PhD(Ger lang), 55. **CAREER** Asst prof mod lang, Cumberland Univ, 50-51; asst prof, Howard Col, 51-52; instr Ger, Wayne Univ, 53-54; instr, Univ Mich, 54-55; asst prof, Wash Univ, 55-58; assoc prof, Univ Calif, 58-60; prof, Vanderbilt Univ, 60-67; prof, Cornell Univ, 67-69; prof, univ, 69-71, Prof Ger, Ctr Advan Study, Univ Ill, Urbana, 71-, Vis lectr, Harvard Univ, 57; Guggenheim fel, 58; researcher, Nat Endowment for Humanities, 76-77. **MEMBERSHIPS** MLA; Ling Soc Am; Soc Advan Scand Studies. **RESEARCH** Mediaeval literature; Ger linguistics; general linguistics. **CONTACT ADDRESS** Ctr for Advan Study, Univ of Illinois, Urbana-Champaign, Urbana, IL 61801. **EMAIL** marchand@uiuc.edu

MARCHI, DUDLEY M.
PERSONAL Born 04/14/1955, Myers, FL, m, 1984, 2 children **DISCIPLINE** FRENCH, COMPARATIVE LITERATURE **EDUCATION** Univ Mass Amherst, BA, 81; Univ NCar, MA, 84; Columbia Univ, PhD, 91. **CAREER** Assoc prof, NCar State, 89-. **HONORS AND AWARDS** Outstanding Teacher of the Year, NCar State, 95. **MEMBERSHIPS** MLA, AATF, Am Comp Lit Assoc, Am Coun on the Teaching of For Lang, S Comp Lit Assoc, For Lang Assoc of NCar. **RESEARCH** International Relations, Masterpieces of Literature, History of Western Culture, French Civilization, Cultural Literacy, Second Language Acquisition. **SELECTED PUBLICATIONS** Auth, "Vocabularies of Innovation and Repetition in Montaigne, Nietzsche, and de Man," Montaigne Studies, (92); auth, "Montaigne and the New World: The Cannibalism," Mod Lang Studies, (93); auth, Montaigne Among the Moderns, Berghahn Books, 94; auth, "Montaigne among the Postmoderns: Chaillou," Fr Rev, (95); auth, "Participatory Aesthetics: Reading Mallarme and Joyce," Comparatist, (95); auth, "Virginia Woolf Essaying the French Renaissance," Comparative Lit Studies, (97); auth, "Baudelaire"s America: Contrary Affinities," Yearbook of Gen and Comp Lit, (99); auth, "Montaigne: A Practical Philosophy for the Twenty-first Century," Montaigne Studies, (00). **CONTACT ADDRESS** No Carolina State Univ, Box 8016, Raleigh, NC 27695. **EMAIL** dmm@unity.ncsu.edu

MARCHIONE, MARGHERITA FRANCES
PERSONAL Born 02/19/1922, Little Ferry, NJ **DISCIPLINE** ITALIAN, AMERICAN HISTORY **EDUCATION** Georgian Court Col, AB, 43; Columbia Univ, AM, 49, PhD(Ital), 60. **CAREER** Teacher parochial & private high schs, 43-54; instr lang, Villa Walsh Col, 54-67; assoc prof, 67-77, chmn dept lang, 67-68, Prof Ital, Fairleigh Dickinson Univ, Florham-Madison Campus, 77-, Res grants, Fairleigh Dickinson Univ, 68-69, 71-82; NDEA grant Ital inst undergrad, US Off Educ, 68; consult & rep, Gallery Mod Art, 68, 69; dir Ital Inst, Univ Salerno, 72, Tivoli, 73, Rome, 74; mem exec coun, Am Ital Hist Asn, 77-79; mem adv bd, NJ Cath Hist Rec Comn, 77-; NJ Hist Comn, 78-; Nat Hist Publ & Records Comn, 78, 79, 80 & 81; Nat Endowment for Humanities grant, 80-83. **HONORS AND AWARDS** Am-Ital Achievement Award in Educ, 71; UNICO Nat Rizzuto Award, 77; Star of Solidarity of Ital Repub, Pres Italy, 77. **MEMBERSHIPS** Am Asn Teachers Ital; MLA; Am Coun Teaching Foreign Lang; Am Inst Ital Studies (pres, 77-80); Am Ital Hist Asn. **RESEARCH** Contemporary Italian Culture and lit; Dante; the papers of Philip Mazzei. **SELECTED PUBLICATIONS** Auth, A Pitcorial History of St. Lucy Filippini Chapel, Edizioni del Palazzo, Prato, (92): 130; auth, Legacy and Misison: Religious Teachers Filippini, Villa Walsh, Morristown, NJ, (92): 50; auth, Philip Mazzei: World Citizen (Jefferson's "Zealous Whig"), Univ Press of Am, Lanham, MD, (94): 158; auth, Yours is a Presicous Witness (Memoirs of Jews and Catholics in Wartime Italy), Paulist Press, Mahwah, NJ, (96): 300; auth, Yours Is a Precious Witness: Memoirs of Jews and Catholics in Wartime Italy, 97; auth, Pio XII e gli ebrei, Editoriale Pantheon, Rome, (99): 288; auth, Pope Pius XII: Architect for Peace, 00; auth, Pope Pius XII: Architect for Peace, Paulist Pres, Mahwah, NJ, (00): 350; auth, Pio XII: Architetto di pace, Editoriale Pantheon, Rome, (00): 413; auth, Carteggio Giovanni Abbo-Giuseppe Prezzolini, Edizioni di Storia e Letteratura, Rome, (00): 233. **CONTACT ADDRESS** Col of Arts & Sci Fairleigh, Fairleigh Dickinson Univ, Florham-Madison, Madison, NJ 07940.

MARCONE, ROSE MARIE
PERSONAL Born 11/05/1938, White Plains, NY **DISCIPLINE** SPANISH **EDUCATION** Mary Washington Col, BA, 60; Johns Hopkins Univ, PhD(Span), 64. **CAREER** Asst prof, 64-67, assoc prof, 67-74, Prof Span and Ital, Univ Richmond, 74-, Chmn Dept Mod Foreign Lang, 72-. **MEMBERSHIPS** MLA; AAUP; Am Asn Teachers Span and Port. **RESEARCH** Contemporary Spanish literature; Golden Age drama. **SELECTED PUBLICATIONS** Auth, The Role of Augusto-Perez + Unamuno--a Study of 'Niebla', Confluencia-Revista Hisp De Cultura Y Lit, Vol 0005, 89; an Approach to Unamuno 'Cuentos', Neophilologus, Vol 0078, 94. **CONTACT ADDRESS** Dept of Mod Foreign Lang, Univ of Richmond, 28 Westhampton Way, Richmond, VA 23173-0002.

MARCUS, DAVID
PERSONAL Born 06/24/1941, Dublin, Ireland, m, 3 children **DISCIPLINE** BIBLE AND ANCIENT SEMITIC LANGUAGES **EDUCATION** Trinity Col Dublin, BA; Cambridge Univ, MA; Columbia Univ, PhD. **CAREER** Fac, Columbia Univ; prof, chr, Bible and Ancient Semitic Languages, Jewish Theol Sem Am. **MEMBERSHIPS** Soc of Biblical Lit; Columbia Univ Hebrew Bible Seminar. **RESEARCH** The Bible and the Ancient Near East; presently working with an international team of scholars revising the critical edition of the Hebrew Bible. **SELECTED PUBLICATIONS** Auth, From Balaam to Jonah: Anti-prophetic Satire in the Hebrew Bible, Brown Judaic Studies series; numerous scholarly articles; two language manuals, Akkadian, the ancient language of Mesopotamia, Tthe Aramaic of the Babylonian Talmud. **CONTACT ADDRESS** Jewish Theol Sem of America, 3080 Broadway, New York, NY 10027. **EMAIL** damarcus@jtsa.edu

MARCUS, MARVIN H.
PERSONAL Born 10/16/1944, Baltimore, MD, m, 1976, 3 children **DISCIPLINE** JAPANESE LANGUAGE AND LITERATURE **EDUCATION** Cornell Univ, BA, 66; Johns Hopkins Univ, MLA, 69; Univ Mich, MA, 81; Univ Mich, PhD, 86. **CAREER** Assoc prof, dir, Int Affairs Prog, Washington Univ, 85-; dir, East Asian Studies Prog, Washington Univ, 95-98. **HONORS AND AWARDS** Fulbright-Hayes Diss Fel; Japan Found Fel; NEH Fac Res Fel. **MEMBERSHIPS** Assoc for Asian Studies; Assoc of Japanese Lit Studies; Midwest Japan Sem; Midwest Coun on Asian Affairs. **RESEARCH** Modern Japanese Literature; autobiography and literary reminiscence; literary journalism. **SELECTED PUBLICATIONS** Auth, Paragons of the Ordinary: the Biographical Literature of Mori Ogai, (Haw Univ Pr), 93; auth, The Writer Speaks: Late Meiji Reflections on Literature and Life, (in thomas Hate, et al, eds, The Distant Isle, (Univ of Mich Pr), 96. **CONTACT ADDRESS** Asian Studies, Washington Univ, 1 Brookings Dr, Campus B 1111, Saint Louis, MO 63130-4862. **EMAIL** mhmarcus@artsci.wustl.edu

MARCUS, SHARON
DISCIPLINE ENGLISH AND COMPARATIVE LITERATURE **EDUCATION** Brown Univ, BA, 86; Johns Hopkins Univ, PhD, 95. **CAREER** Assoc prof, eng dept, Univ Calif Berkeley. **RESEARCH** 19th century British and French novel; Feminist theory; Lesbian and gay studies; Urban and architectural history. **SELECTED PUBLICATIONS** Auth, Apartment Stories: City and Home in Nineteeth Century, Paris and London. **CONTACT ADDRESS** Dept. of English, Univ of California, Berkeley, Berkeley, CA 94720-1030. **EMAIL** smarcus@socrates.berkeley.edu

MARECAUX, MARIE-LAURE
PERSONAL Born 12/23/1956, Suresnes, France, w **DISCIPLINE** FRENCH **EDUCATION** Inst d'Etudes Politiques de Paris/Sciences - PO, 78; Sorbonne Univ, Certificat de Maitrise, 80; Univ Minn, PhD, 98. **CAREER** Int auditor, Dannon Group, 81-83; audit supervisor, Price Waterhosue CPA, 83-87; instr, Colo State Univ, 87-90; instr, Univ Minn, 90-98; lectr, Univ N Colo, 00-. **HONORS AND AWARDS** Deutscher Akademischer Austausch Dienst Fel, 78-79; Norman Johnston Dewitt Fel, 94-95; PT3 Colo Grant, 01. **MEMBERSHIPS** MLA, MWMLA, Thompson Valley Rotay Club, Club Price Waterhouse Paris. **RESEARCH** Interdisciplinary studies, Literature and medicine, Chaos Theory, Women's Studies, Technology and Teacher Education. **SELECTED PUBLICATIONS** Auth, "Pour une critique excoloniale excentice," Preface to L'Ectriture Casterale et le discourse juridique, Frieda Ekotta, (Yaounde and Paris, 99). **CONTACT ADDRESS** PO Box 5203, Greeley, CO 80634. **EMAIL** mmareca@unc.edu

MARGOLIN, URI
PERSONAL Born 12/22/1942, Tel Aviv, Israel, m, 1968, 1 child **DISCIPLINE** COMPARATIVE LITERATURE, POETICS **EDUCATION** Hebrew Univ, Jerusalem, BA, 64; Cornell Univ, MA, 70, PhD(comp lit), 72. **CAREER** Teaching Asst, Cornell Univ, 69-70; Asst Prof, Univ of Alberta, 72; Assoc Prof, 76; Prof, 83. **HONORS AND AWARDS** Univ of Alberta Res Grant, 72; Univ of Alberta Res Grant, 75; CRF travel grant, 89, 90, 92, 94, 95, 97. **MEMBERSHIPS** Int Comp Lit Asn; Can Comp Lit Asn. **RESEARCH** Poetics; theory of genres; literary methodology. **SELECTED PUBLICATIONS** Auth, "Narrative 'You' Revisited" Language and Style, 23, 4, (90):

425-446, published Dec 95; auth, "Characters and their Versions" in Fiction Updated, eds, Calin-Andrei Mihailescu and Wand Hamarneh, Univ of Toronto Press, (96): 113-132; auth, "Telling Our Story: On 'We' Literary Narratives" Language and Literature, 5, 2 (96): 115-33; auth, "Formal, Sematic and Pragmatic Aspects of Metatetuality: Comparatism Revisited," eds, de Zepetnek and Dimic, Comparative Literature Today: Theroies and Practice, Paris: Honore Champion, 99; auth, "Collective Perspective, Individual Perspective and the Speaker in between: On 'We' Literary Narratives," eds, Chatman & van Peer, Narrative Perspective Cognition and Emotion, SUNY Press, 99; auth, "Character, Types of" & "Person in Narrative" in Encyclopedia of the Novel, Fitzroy Dearborn Publishers, Chicago, 88. **CONTACT ADDRESS** Dept of Comp Lit, Relig, & Film/Media Studs, Univ of Alberta, 347 Arts, Edmonton, AB, Canada T6G 2E6. **EMAIL** uri.margolin@ualberta.ca

MARGOLIS, NADIA
PERSONAL Born 04/27/1949, Neuilly-sur-Seine, France **DISCIPLINE** MEDIEVAL LITERATURE, FRENCH POETRY **EDUCATION** Univ NH, AB, 71; Stanford Univ, PhD (French), 77. **CAREER** Ed asst, Speculum, Mediaeval Acad Am, 77-78; Asst Prof French, Amherst Col, 78-, Attache res humanisme francais, Ctr Nat Res Sci, 73-; Nat Endowment for Humanities independent res fel, 81-82. **MEMBERSHIPS** MLA; Mediaeval Acad Am; Soc Rencesvals; Int Courtly Lit Soc. **RESEARCH** Fifteenth century France; French poetic theory; comparative Medieval literature. **SELECTED PUBLICATIONS** Auth, The prison motif in Christine de Pizan, Charles d'Orleans, and Francois Villon, 15th Century Studies, 78. **CONTACT ADDRESS** Dept of Romance Lang, Amherst Col, Amherst, MA 01002.

MARIANI, BETHANIA S. C.
PERSONAL Born 02/07/1959, Rio de Janeiro, Brazil **DISCIPLINE** LINGUISTICS, SEMANTICS **EDUCATION** Universidade Estadual de Campinas, PhD. **CAREER** Pontifica Universidade Catouca do Rio de Janeiro; Universida de Federal Fluminense. **MEMBERSHIPS** AASTP, MLA, ABRALIN, SBPC, ANPOLL, ALED. **RESEARCH** Discourse Analysis, History of Linguistic Ideas, Policies of Language. **SELECTED PUBLICATIONS** Auth, "O PCB E A Imprensa (1922/1989), o imaginaino sobre os comunisheas nos jornais coriecas," Rio de Janeiro/Campirnas, (98); auth, "L'institucionalisation de la langue, de la memoire et de la citoyennete au Bresil durant le XVIII," Langages 130, ed S Auroux, E Orlandi, (Paris: Larousse, 98); auth, "Sobre um percurso de analise do discurso journalistico: A revolucao de 30', IM: Indursky, ed, M.C. Ferreire, (Porto Alegro: Editorie Sagra Luzzah, 99); auth, "el estade y la iglesia en la question de la lengue hablade en Brasil," Language y illustacion in Americe, (Buenos Aires: Eudeba, 00); ed, E. Arnoux, C. Luis, Leng **CONTACT ADDRESS** 1765 Ednamary Way, Mountain View, CA 94040-2361. **EMAIL** bemariani@aol.com

MARICHAL, JUAN
PERSONAL Born 02/02/1922, Teneriffe, Spain, m, 1947, 2 children **DISCIPLINE** SPANISH **EDUCATION** Univ Algiers, bachelier, 41; Princeton Univ, MA, 48, PhD(Romance lang), 49. **CAREER** Instr Span, Princeton Univ, 46-48 and Johns Hopkins Univ, 48-49; asst prof Romance lang, Harvard Univ, 49-53; assoc prof Span, Bryn Mawr Col, 53-58; assoc prof Romance lang, 58-61, prof, 61-80, Smith Prof Romance Lang and Lit, Harvard Univ, 80-, Guggenheim fel, 59 and 71-72; syndicator, Univ Press, Harvard Univ, 65-69; mem educ adv bd, Guggenheim Found, 67-. **HONORS AND AWARDS** Hon chair, San Marcos Univ, Lima, 65. **MEMBERSHIPS** Corresp mem Hisp Soc Am; MLA; Am Asn Teachers Span and Port. **RESEARCH** Spanish history, 1898-1936; Latin American intellectual history, 1810-1960. **SELECTED PUBLICATIONS** Auth, an Interview With Marichal, Juan, Insula Revista De Letras Y Ciencias Humanas, Vol 0051, 96. **CONTACT ADDRESS** Widener Libr, Harvard Univ, Cambridge, MA 02138.

MARINCOLA, JOHN
PERSONAL Born 12/14/1954, Philadelphia, PA, s **DISCIPLINE** CLASSICS **EDUCATION** Swarthmore Col, BA, 79; Brown Univ, PhD, 85. **CAREER** Instr to asst prof, Col of the Holy Cross, 84-86; vis asst prof to assoc prof, Union Col, 86-97; exec dir, Am Philol Asn, 97-98; assoc prof, NY Univ, 00-. **HONORS AND AWARDS** Fel, Center for Hellenic Studies, 99-00. **MEMBERSHIPS** Am Philol Asn, Asn of Ancient Hist, Cambridge Philol Soc, Class Asn, Class Asn of the Atlantic States, Class Asn of the Middle W and S. **RESEARCH** Greek and Roman historiography, Ancient Rhetoric, Greek History. **SELECTED PUBLICATIONS** Transl, Herodotus: The Histories, Penguin Books, 96; auth, "Odysseus and the Historians," Histos 1, (97); auth, Authority and Tradition in Ancient Historiography, Cambridge, 97; auth, "Genre, Convention and Innovation in Greco-Roman Historiography,", The Limits of Historiography: Genre and Narrative in Ancient Historical Texts, ed C Kraus, (Leiden, 99): 281-324; auth, Greek Historians, Greece and Rome New Surveys in the Classics, Oxford, 01. **CONTACT ADDRESS** Dept Classics, New York Univ, New York, NY 10003. **EMAIL** john.marincola@nyu.edu

MARINONI, R. MAX
DISCIPLINE FRENCH LANGUAGE **EDUCATION** Univ Grenoble, BA, 61; Univ WA, MA, 65, Doctorate, 75. **CAREER** Instr, Seattle Univ. **MEMBERSHIPS** Northwest Asn Lang Lab; MLA; WAFLT; Puget Sound Alliance For FL. **SELECTED PUBLICATIONS** Transl, Paul Bleton, auth, Paraliterature and Serialization, Para-Doxa; Marc Richir, auth, Merleau Ponty and the Question of Phenomenological Architectonics in Patrick Burke and Jan Van Der Veke, eds, Merleau Ponty in Contemporary Perspective, Klower, 93. **CONTACT ADDRESS** Seattle Univ, Seattle, WA 98122-4460. **EMAIL** marinoni@seattleu.edu

MARKEY, CONSTANCE D.
PERSONAL Born Waukesha, WI, m, 1973, 3 children **DISCIPLINE** ITALIAN LITERATURE **EDUCATION** Rosary Col, BA, 65; Univ Chicago, MA, 70; Univ Ill Urbana, PhD, 80. **CAREER** Adj prof, Loyola Univ, 79-85; instr to prof, DePaul Univ, 84-. **HONORS AND AWARDS** Loyola Univ Grant, 80-81, 82-83; DePaul Univ Grant, 92. **MEMBERSHIPS** MLA, AAIS, AATI. **RESEARCH** Postmodeern literature and film. **SELECTED PUBLICATIONS** Auth, Federico Fellini: A Guide to References and Resources, CK Hart, 78; auth, Italo Calvino: A Journey toward Postmodernism, Univ of Fla Pr, 99. **CONTACT ADDRESS** 1814 N Howe St, Chicago, IL 60614-5126.

MARKS, ELAINE
PERSONAL Born 11/13/1930, New York, NY, d **DISCIPLINE** FRENCH STUDIES **EDUCATION** Bryn Mawr Col, AB(magna cum laude with Honors in French), 52; Univ PA, MA, 53; New York Univ, PhD, 58. **CAREER** Graduate asst, NY Univ, 54-56, instr, 57-60, asst prof, 60-62; assoc prof, Univ WI-Milwaukee, 63-65; prof, Univ MA-Amherst, 65-66; prof, Univ WI-Madison, 66-68; vis prof, Univ MA-Amherst, 71, prof, 71-73; lect, Univ WI-Madison, 77, prof to Germaine Bree prof, Dept of French and Italian and Women's Studies Prog, Univ WI-Madison, 80-. **HONORS AND AWARDS** Fulbright fel to Paris, 56-57; NY Univ Alumnae Pin for Scholarship, 58; Johnson fel, Inst for Res in the Humanities of the Univ WI, 62-63; grants from the Ford Found, the Johnson Found, the Stackner Family, 79-84; YWCA Women of Distinction Awd, 82; grad school res support (summer), 86, 88; WARF/Univ Houses professorship, 88; Vilas Assoc awarded and declined, 88; Univ WI Fac Development grant, 90; elected second vice pres, MLA, 91; John Simon Guggenheim Memorial Fund fel, 92; Chancellor's Awd for Excellence in Teaching, 93; pres, MLA, 93; NYU, Distinguished Alumni Awd, 94; Officier dans l'Ordre des Palmes Academiques, 94; Hilldale Awd in the Humanities, 95-96. **MEMBERSHIPS** MLA; MMLA; AATF; Nat Women's Studies Asn; Societe des Amis de Colette; Simone de Beauvoir Soc; Women in French. **RESEARCH** 19th and 20th Century French Lit; women writers. **SELECTED PUBLICATIONS** Auth, Marrano as Metaphor: the Jewish Presence in French Writing, Columbia Univ Press, 96. **CONTACT ADDRESS** Dept of French and Italian, Univ of Wisconsin, Madison, 1220 Linden Dr, 618 Van Hise Hall, Madison, WI 53706. **EMAIL** emarks@faestaff.wisc.edu

MARMURA, MICHAEL ELIAS
PERSONAL Born 11/11/1929, Jerusalem, Palestine, m, 1962, 3 children **DISCIPLINE** ISLAMIC PHILOSOPHY, ARABIC **EDUCATION** Univ Wis, BA, 53; Univ Mich, MA, 55, PhD(Near Eastern studies), 59. **CAREER** Lectr Islamic philos and theol, 59-62, from asst prof to assoc prof, 62-69, assoc chmn dept Mid E and Islamic studies, 69-78, Prof Islamic Philos and Theol, Univ Toronto, 69, Chmn Dept Mid E and Islamic Studies, 78-. **MEMBERSHIPS** Am Orient Soc; Can Philos Asn. **RESEARCH** Islamic theology. **SELECTED PUBLICATIONS** Auth, Islamic Theology and Philosophy; ed, Islamic Theology and Philosophy: Studies in Honor of George F. Hourani, ed, Michael E. Marmura, Hardcover, 84; cotransl, The Incoherence of the Philosophers (Islamic Translation Series), Al-Ghazali, Michael E. Marmura, Hardcover, 98; coauth, The Incoheence of the Philosophers (Islamic Translation Series), 00. **CONTACT ADDRESS** Dept of Near & Mid E Civilizations, Univ of Toronto, 4 Bancroft Ave, Toronto, ON, Canada M5S 1C1.

MARQUESS, HARLAN EARL
PERSONAL Born 01/23/1931, Sheridan, WY, m, 1958, 3 children **DISCIPLINE** SLAVIC LINGUISTICS, RUSSIAN LANGUAGE **EDUCATION** Univ Calif, Berkeley, AB, 58, MA, 60, PhD, 66. **CAREER** From instr to prof, 64-98, prof emer Slavic Lang, Univ Wis, Madison, 98-. **MEMBERSHIPS** Ling Soc Am; Int Ling Asn; Am Asn Teachers Slavic & E Europ Lang; Am Asn Advan Slavic Studies. **RESEARCH** Structure of Russian; nonstandard Russian speech; morphology of Czech. **SELECTED PUBLICATIONS** Coauth, Soviet Prison Camp Speech, Univ Wis, 72. **CONTACT ADDRESS** Dept of Slavic Lang, Univ of Wisconsin, Madison, 1220 Linden Drive, Madison, WI 53706-1557. **EMAIL** hemarque@facstaff.wisc.edu

MARQUEZ, ANTONIO
DISCIPLINE AMERICAN AND COMPARATIVE LITERATURE **EDUCATION** Univ Nmex, PhD, 77. **CAREER** Instr, Univ NMex, 77-. **HONORS AND AWARDS** Fulbright scholar/lectr. **SELECTED PUBLICATIONS** Auth, Richard Rodriguez's Hunger of Memory and New Perspectives on Ethnic Autobiography, Tchg Am Ethnic Lit, UNM, 95. **CONTACT ADDRESS** Univ of New Mexico, Albuquerque, Albuquerque, NM 87131. **EMAIL** amarquez@unm.edu

MARQUEZ-VILLANUEVA, FRANCISCO
PERSONAL Born 03/21/1931, Seville, Spain, m, 1960, 3 children **DISCIPLINE** SPANISH LANGUAGE AND LITERATURE **EDUCATION** Univ Seville, Spain, PhD(lit), 58. **CAREER** Prof adj Span lit, Univ Seville, Spain, 55-59; instr Romance lang, Harvard Univ, 59-62; asst prof, Univ BC, 62-65 and Harvard Univ, 65-67; prof, Rutgers Univ, 67-68 and Grad Ctr, City Univ New York, 68-78; Prof Span, Harvard Univ, 78-. **MEMBERSHIPS** MLA; Int Asn Hispanists; Soc Span and Port Hist Studies. **RESEARCH** Mediaeval and Golden Age Spanish literature; intellectual and religious history; comparative literature. **SELECTED PUBLICATIONS** Auth, A Modest Tribute to Widener Library, Harvard Libr Bull, Vol 0006, 95. **CONTACT ADDRESS** Dept of Romance Lang, Harvard Univ, Boylston Hall, Cambridge, MA 02138-3800.

MARRONE, NILA GUTIERREZ
PERSONAL Born La Paz, Bolivia **DISCIPLINE** SPANISH LINGUISTICS, SPANISH AMERICAN LITERATURE **EDUCATION** Columbia Univ, BA, 70, NYork Univ, MA, 72, PhD(Span and ling), 75. **CAREER** Lectr Span, New York Univ, 72-73; assoc, Columbia Univ, 73-74; Asst Prof Span, Univ Conn, 75-. **MEMBERSHIPS** Am Asn Teachers Span and Port; MLA. **RESEARCH** Descriptive Spanish linguistics; applied and sociolinguistics. **SELECTED PUBLICATIONS** Auth, Remembering Mead, Robert, G., Hispania-J Devoted tchg Span Port, Vol 0079, 96. **CONTACT ADDRESS** Dept of Span, Univ of Connecticut, Storrs, Storrs, CT 06268. **EMAIL** nila.marrone@uconn.edu

MARSHALL, DAVID
PERSONAL Born 01/06/1938, Perry, OK, m, 1966, 2 children **DISCIPLINE** LINGUISTICS **EDUCATION** Tex Christian Univ, BA, 60; Union Theol Sem, MDiv, 64; NY Univ, PhD, 75. **CAREER** Editor-in-Chief, Pilgrim Press, 69-72; from asst prof to assoc prof, Barton Col, 72-80; NEH vis scholar, Stanford Univ, 79 & 84; from assoc prof to prof, Univ NDak, 80-; vis prof, Univ Ariz, 88; NEH vis scholar Univ Wis Madison, 90. **HONORS AND AWARDS** Fulbright, Nanjing Univ; Fulbright, Eotvos Lorand Univ; Fulbright, St Cyril and St Methodius Univ, 00-01. **MEMBERSHIPS** Nat Coun of Teachers of English, Am Asn of Univ Professors, Nat Educ Asn and NDak Higher Educ Asn, NDak Public Employees Asn, MLA, Ling Soc of Am, Southeastern Confr on Ling, Ling Circle of Manitoba and NDak. **RESEARCH** How language laws impact and shape nationalistic and ethnic identity and how they can be used to create national coherence and avoid ethnic conflict. **SELECTED PUBLICATIONS** Ed, Language Planning: Focusschrift in honor of Joshua A. Fishman. Volume III: Language Planning, John Benjamins, 91; auth, "Language Maintenance and Revival," in Review of Applied Linguistics XIV: Language Planning, ed. William Grabe (Cambridge Univ Press, 94), 20-33; auth, "The Politics of Language in America: Attempts to Prevent an Emerging Renationalization in the United States," in What Became of the Great Society? Comparative Perspectives on the U.S.A. in the 1960s and 1990s, ed. W. Herget (Wessenschaftlicher Verlag, 96), 67-80; coauth, "Ethnicity and Language in the United States and Canada," in Handbook of Language and Ethnic Identity, ed. Joshua A. Fishman (Oxford Univ Press, 99), 244-264. **CONTACT ADDRESS** Dept English, Univ of No Dakota, PO Box 2709, Grand Forks, ND 58202-2709. **EMAIL** dmarshal@badlands.nodak.edu

MARSHALL, GROVER EDWIN
PERSONAL Born 03/28/1930, Portland, ME, m, 1966, 1 child **DISCIPLINE** FRENCH; ITALIAN **EDUCATION** Bowdoin Col, BA, 51; Princeton Univ, MA, 54, PhD(French), 71. **CAREER** Instr French & Ital, Princeton Univ, 54-58; instr, Williams Col, 58-60, asst prof Romanic lang, 60-64, lectr, 64-65; Asst Prof, 65-90, Assoc Prof French & Ital, Univ NH, 90-00, Chmn Dept, 73-80, 81-83, 88-91. **HONORS AND AWARDS** Phi Beta Kappa, 50. **MEMBERSHIPS** Am Asn Teachers Fr; NE Mod Lang Asn. **RESEARCH** Francophone Caribbean **CONTACT ADDRESS** Dept of Languages, Literatures, and Cultures, Univ of New Hampshire, Durham, 15 Library Way, Durham, NH 03824-3596. **EMAIL** groverm@cisunix.unh.edu

MARSHALL, PETER K.
PERSONAL Born 07/02/1934, Cardiff, Wales, m, 1984, 2 children **DISCIPLINE** CLASSICAL LANGUAGES, MEDIEVAL LITERATURE **EDUCATION** Univ SWales, BA, 54; Oxford Univ BA, 56, MA, 60. **CAREER** Instr classics, 59-61, asst prof, 62-68, assoc prof, 68-73, Prof Classics, Amherst Col, 73-, Asst lectr Latin & Greek, Univ Liverpool, England, 61-62. **HONORS AND AWARDS** ACLS fel, 76-77; Guggenheim fel, 80-81; ma, amherst col, 73. **MEMBERSHIPS** Class Asn Gt Brit; Am Philol Asn; Medieval Acad Am. **RESEARCH** The textual transmission of classical Latin authors; the Commentarii of Servius; the De Proprietatibus Rerum of Bartholomaeus Anglicus. **SELECTED PUBLICATIONS** Auth, Utopia, Sir Thomas More, Washington Sq Press, 65; ed, A Gellii Noctes

Atticae, 2 vols, Oxford Univ Press, 68; auth, The Manuscript Tradition of Cornelius Nepos, Univ London, 77; ed, Cornelii Nepotis Vitae cum Fragmentis, Teubner, Leipzig, 77; Isidore, Etymologies Book II, Les Belles Lett, Paris, 82; coauth, Texts and Transmission, Clarendon Press, 83; auth, Servati Lupi Epistulae, Teubner, 84; Hyginus Fabulae, Teubner, 93; Servius and Commentary on Virgil, CEMERS, 97. **CONTACT ADDRESS** Dept of Classics, Amherst Col, Amherst, MA 01002-5000. **EMAIL** pkmarshall@amherst.edu

MARSILIO, MARIA S.
PERSONAL Born 05/21/1963, Glenside, PA, m, 2001 **DISCIPLINE** CLASSICAL STUDIES **EDUCATION** Col New Rochelle, BA, 85; Univ Pa, MA, 89; PhD, 93. **CAREER** Lectr, Univ of Pa, 93-95; vis asst prof to assist prof, Saint Joseph's Univ, 95-. **HONORS AND AWARDS** Grant, St Joseph's Univ, 98; Awd for Res, St Joseph's Univ, 00. **MEMBERSHIPS** Am Philog Assoc, Classical Assoc of the Atlantic States, Am Classical League, Pa Classical Assoc, Philadelphia Classical Soc. **RESEARCH** Greek Epic and Lyric Poetry, Greek and Roman Drama, Gender and Sexuality in Antiquity. **SELECTED PUBLICATIONS** Auth, "Hesiod's Winter Maiden," Helios 24.2, (97): 101-111; auth, "The Poetics of Hesiod's Winter," Annali della Scuola Normale Superiore di Pisa, IV.II.2, (97): 411-425; auth, "Two Ships in the Menaechmi," Classical World 92.2, (98): 131-139; auth, Farming and Poetry in Hesiod's Works and Days, Univ Pr of Am (Lanham), 00. **CONTACT ADDRESS** Sch of Arts and Sciences, Saint Joseph's Univ, 5600 City Ave, Philadelphia, PA 19131. **EMAIL** marsilio@sju.edu

MARTEINSON, PETER
DISCIPLINE FRENCH LITERATURE **EDUCATION** International Baccalaureate, 87; Univ Toronto, BA, 93; MA, 94; PhD, 97. **CAREER** Ed, 95-; Ancien Pensionnaire de l'Ecole Normale Superieure, 97; doctor of Philos, Toronto, 97; lectr, Victoria Univ, 97-98; asst prof, Univ of Waterloo, 98-. **HONORS AND AWARDS** Ed, Applied Semiotics. **SELECTED PUBLICATIONS** Rev, Wynton Marsalis: enorme succes au festival de jazz duMaurier, rev for L'Express de Toronto, 91; rev, Ivry Gitlis a Massey Hall, classical music review in monthly Franco-Ontarian paper Le courrier, 91; auth, "Picasso et la modalisation de l'espace scriptural et pictural moderne," David Mendelson, Applied Semiotics, No. 8, 99; auth, "John Donne and the Anthropomorphic Map Tradition," Noam Flinker, Applied Semiotics, No. 8, 99; coauth, "Till Versus Until: A Sign-Oriented Approach," Applied Semiotics, No. 8, 99; coauth, "La semiotique de la metastabilite chez Claude Gandelman," Applied Semiotics, No.8, 99; coauth, "Semiotic Aspects of the Transformation of Legal Systems," Applied Semiotics, No. 6/7, 99; coauth, "The Interconnectedness Principle and the semiotic Analysis of Discourse," Applied Semiotics, No. 6/7, 99; coauth, "The Sign Science and the Life Science," Applied Semiotics, No. 6/7, 99; coauth, "A Discursive Analysis of TV Soap Opera: Eastenders," Applied Semiotics, No. 6/7, 99. **CONTACT ADDRESS** Dept of French, Univ of Waterloo, 200 Univ Ave W, Waterloo, ON, Canada N2L 3G1. **EMAIL** marteinson@watarts.uwaterloo.ca

MARTIN, CAROLE
PERSONAL Born 05/15/1960, France, m, 1 child **DISCIPLINE** FRENCH LITERATURE **EDUCATION** Sorbonne Nouvelle, Licence es Lettres, 83; Sorbonne Nouvelle, Maitrije es Lettres, 85; NY Univ, PhD, 91. **CAREER** Vis Asst Prof, Colby Col, 90-91; Asst Prof, Tufts Univ, 91-99; Asst Prof, Southwest Tex State Univ, 99-. **HONORS AND AWARDS** Fel, NY Univ, 89-90; Mellon Res Fel, 95. **MEMBERSHIPS** MLA, SATOR, NAASR, ASECS, Soc for Utopian Studies, Robert Challe Soc, Soc des Amiscle. **RESEARCH** Space or time in Early Modern Europe as represented in literary works, Rousseau on education. **SELECTED PUBLICATIONS** Auth, "Imposture utopique et froces colonial: Denis Veiras - Robert Challe," Early Mod Fr Crtiques (00). **CONTACT ADDRESS** Dept Lang, Southwest Texas State Univ, 601 University Dr, San Marcos, TX 78666-4685. **EMAIL** cmartin@modlang.swt.edu

MARTIN, CHARLES EDWARD
PERSONAL Born 09/03/1930, Mantee, MS, m, 1953, 3 children **DISCIPLINE** SPANISH **EDUCATION** Miss Col, BA, 51; US Army Lang Sch, dipl, 52; Tulane Univ, MA, 58, PhD(Span), 65. **CAREER** Asst prof mod lang, 57-62, assoc prof, 62-67, head, Dept Foreign Lang, 66-69, Prof Span, Miss Col, 67-, Vpres Acad Affairs, 69-, Chmn, Southern Baptist Col Deans, 80 & Nat Deans' Conf, 81. **MEMBERSHIPS** Am Asn Teachers Span & Port. **RESEARCH** The generation of 1898 in Spain. **CONTACT ADDRESS** Dept of Foreign Lang, Mississippi Col, Clinton, Clinton, MS 39056.

MARTIN, DANIEL
PERSONAL Born 12/07/1932, Madrid, Spain, m, 1960, 1 child **DISCIPLINE** FRENCH RENAISSANCE LITERATURE **EDUCATION** Univ IL, Chicago Circle, BA, 69; Yale Univ, MPhil, 72, PhD, 73. **CAREER** Asst prof, 73-80, assoc prof, 80-84, Prof French, Univ MA, Amherst, 85-. **MEMBERSHIPS** Soc Amis Montaigne Paris; MLA; Renaissance Soc Am. **RESEARCH** Montaigne; structural criticism; the philos of chance and mnemonics. **SELECTED PUBLICATIONS** Ed, Michel de Montaigne, Essais 1580 avec une introduction et des notes sur les variantes, Libr Slatkine, Geneva, 76; auth, Montaigne et la Fortune: Essai sur le hasard et le language, Paris: Honore Champion, 77; ed, The Order of Montaigne's Essays, Amherst, MA: Herstia Press, 89; auth, L'Architecture des Essais de Montaigne: memoire artificielle et mythologie, Paris: Nizet, 92; ed, Montaigne and the Gods: The Mythological Key to the Essays, Amherst, MA: Hestia Press, 93; auth, Le Triptyque des Essais de Montaigne et l'heraldique des dieux greco-remains, Paris & Tours, Nizet, 96; Montaigne et son cheval ou les sept couleurs du discours De la servitude volontaire, Paris & Tours, Nizet, 98. **CONTACT ADDRESS** Dept of French & Ital, Univ of Massachusetts, Amherst, Amherst, MA 01003-0002. **EMAIL** dmartin@frital.umass.edu

MARTIN, DELLITA LILLIAN
PERSONAL Born 10/27/1946, New Orleans, LA, m, 2 children **DISCIPLINE** SPANISH LITERATURE, COMPARATIVE LITERATURE **EDUCATION** La State Univ, BA, 68; Ohio State Univ, MA, 71, PhD(Romance lang & lit), 75. **CAREER** Instr Span & French, St Matthias Cath Sch, 76; asst prof, 76-82, Assoc Prof Span & Am Lit, Univ Ala, Birmingham, 82-, Univ Col fac res grant, Univ Ala, Birmingham, 78-79; secy, Comt Humanities Ala, 78-81. **MEMBERSHIPS** African Lit Asn; AAUP; Asn of Caribbean Studies; Col Lang Asn; MLA. **RESEARCH** Contemporary Latin American prose fiction and poetry; the Francophone writers of West Africa and the Caribbean; Afro-American and Afro-Hispanic literatures. **SELECTED PUBLICATIONS** Auth, Labe, Louise 'Elegies'--The Burden of Love and the Burden of Being a Writer, Etudes Lit, vol 0027, 94. **CONTACT ADDRESS** Dept of Foreign Lang Univ of Ala, Univ of Alabama, Birmingham, Birmingham, AL 35294.

MARTIN, JANET MARION
PERSONAL Born 10/24/1938, Bogalusa, LA **DISCIPLINE** CLASSICS **EDUCATION** Radcliffe Col, AB, 61; Univ MI, MA, 63; Harvard Univ, PhD, 68. **CAREER** From instr to asst prof classics, Harvard Univ, 68-72; asst prof, 73-76, Assoc Prof Classics, Princeton Univ, 76-, Fel Post-classical & humanistic studies, Am Acad Rome, 71-73. **MEMBERSHIPS** Am Philol Asn; Mediaeval Acad Am. **RESEARCH** Medieval Latin lit: ancient and medieval rhetoric and poetics; the class tradition. **SELECTED PUBLICATIONS** Ed, Peter the Venerable: Selected Letters, Pontifical Inst Mediaeval Studies, 74; auth, John of Salisbury's manuscripts of Frontinus and of Gellius, J Warburg & Courtauld Insts, 77; Uses of tradition: Gellius, Petronius, and John of Salisbury, Viator, 79; contribr, chap, In: The Renaissance of the Twelfth Century, Harvard Univ, 82. **CONTACT ADDRESS** Dept of Class, Princeton Univ, 104 E Pyne, Princeton, NJ 08544-1098. **EMAIL** jmmartin@princeton.edu

MARTIN, LAURA
DISCIPLINE LANGUAGES OF MESOAMERICA **EDUCATION** Degrees of BA (Spanish), MA, and PhD, (Linguistics) from the Univ of FL. **CAREER** Prof CSU fac in both Anthrop and Mod Lang since 71. **RESEARCH** Mayan lang **SELECTED PUBLICATIONS** Publ, Spanish Dialectology, Language, Culture, Second-lang Acquisition. **CONTACT ADDRESS** Dept of For Lang, Cleveland State Univ, 83 E 24th St, Cleveland, OH 44115.

MARTIN, PHILIPPE JEAN
PERSONAL Born 01/04/1944, Brussels, Belgium **DISCIPLINE** LINGUISTICS, ACOUSTICS **EDUCATION** Free Univ Brussels, Ingenieur civil, 67, Dr(sci), 73; Univ Nancy, Dr 3rd cycle, 72. **CAREER** Res engr acoustics, 68-70, lectr phonetics, 70-72, asst prof, 72-75, assoc prof, 75-77, Prof Phonetics, Univ Toronto, 81-, Res assoc, Royal Mus Cent Africa, Brussels, 71-; sr researcher, Inst Phonetics, Univ Bruxelles, 74-77; lectr phonetics, Univ Provence, 78-81. **RESEARCH** Syntax; intonation. **SELECTED PUBLICATIONS** Coauth, Prolegomenes a l'Etude des Structures Intonatives, Didier, Paris, 70; Classification Formelle Automatique et Industries Lithiques, Mus Tervuren, 72; auth, Analyse phonologique de la phrase Francaise, Linguistics, 75; Questions de phonosyntaxe et de phonosemantique en Francais, Linquisticae Investigationes, 78; coauth, Toronto English, Didier; auth, Vets une theorie syntaxique de l'intonation, In: Intonation: de l'acoustique a la semantique, Klincksieck, Paus, 81; Pitch Analysis by Spectral Combination Method, Proc ICASSP, 82. **CONTACT ADDRESS** Exp Phonetics Lab, Univ of Toronto, 39 Queen's Park Crescent E, Toronto, ON, Canada M5S 1A1.

MARTIN, RICHARD PETER
PERSONAL Born 05/19/1954, Dorchester, MA, d, 2 children **DISCIPLINE** GREEK AND LATIN: LANGUAGE COURSES **EDUCATION** Harvard, AB, 76, AM, 78; PhD, 81. **CAREER** The Boston Globe, gen assignment reporter, 74-78; Harvard, tchg fellow, 78-81; asst prof, 81-88, assoc prof, 89-94 Princeton Univ; Vis assoc prof, Univ Calif, 91; Prof, Princeton Univ, 94-99; Prof, Stanford Univ, 00. **HONORS AND AWARDS** Harvard, Bowdoin Prize, 79; Howard Behrman tchg fel, 96-00; Grants, Stanley Seeger fel res Cyclades,94; Stanley Seeger fel res, Ionian islands, 95; Onassis Found grant, fieldwork in oral tradition Crete, 96; Princeton 250th anniversary Awd for Innovative Tchg, 97. **RESEARCH** Latin poetry; Hesiod; Greek hymns; Pindar. **SELECTED PUBLICATIONS** Auth, The Language of Heroes: Speech and Performance in the Iliad. Cornell Univ Press, 89; Bulfinch's Mythology, Harper Collins, 91; Similes in Performance; The Scythian Accent: Anacharsis and the Cynics, Univ Calif Press 97. **CONTACT ADDRESS** Stanford Univ, Stanford, CA 94305-1926. **EMAIL** rpmartin@stanford.edu

MARTIN, SAMUEL ELMO
PERSONAL Born 01/29/1924, Pittsburg, KS **DISCIPLINE** LINGUISTICS **EDUCATION** Univ Calif, AB, 47, AM, 49; Yale Univ, PhD, 50. **CAREER** From instr to asst prof Japanese & Korean, 50-58, assoc prof Far Eastern ling, 58-62, chmn dept East & South Asian lang, 63-65, chmn dept ling, 66-80, Prpf Far Eastern Ling, Yale Univ, 62-, Vis prof, Georgetown Univ, 55, Univ Mich, 56, Univ Alta, 59 & Univ Wash, 62-63; secy, Comt Uralic & Altaic Studies, Am Coun Learned Soc, 58-64; vis prof ling & dir Pac & Asian ling inst, Univ Hawaii, 65-66. **MEMBERSHIPS** Ling Soc Am; Am Orient Soc; Asn Asian Studies. **RESEARCH** Phonemics, morphophonemics and historical phonology of Japanese, Korean and Chinese. **SELECTED PUBLICATIONS** Auth, On ohe Finite Forms of Old Japanese Verbs, J E Asian Ling, vol 0005, 96; How Did Korean Get--For Middle-Chinese Words Ending in + Articulation and Ling Change, J E Asian Ling, vol 0006, 97. **CONTACT ADDRESS** Dept of Linguistics, Yale Univ, New Haven, CT 06520. **EMAIL** semartin@pantheon.yale.edu

MARTIN, SUSAN D.
PERSONAL Born 11/30/1951, Berkeley, CA, m, 1989 **DISCIPLINE** CLASSICS **EDUCATION** Univ Calif, BA, 73; BA, 76; Univ Mich, PhD, 81. **CAREER** Asst prof to assoc prof to dept head to assoc dean to prof, Univ Tenn, 81-. **HONORS AND AWARDS** Chancellor's Citation; Public Serv Award, Univ Tenn; NEH Fel, 91; Harvard Law Sch Fel, 88-89; Am Acad Rome Fel, 80-81; Horace Rackham Fel, 79-80. **MEMBERSHIPS** APA; CAMWS; ASLH; ACVAAR; AIA; CSAAR; TFLTA; TCA; SFAAR. **RESEARCH** Roman law; Roman social and economic history; women in antiquity. **SELECTED PUBLICATIONS** Auth, "A Reconsideration of Probatio Operis," APA 103 (86); auth, The Roman Jurists and the Organization of Private Building in the Late Republic and Early Empire, Collection Latomas (Brussels), 89; auth, "Servum Meum Mulionem Donduxisti: Mules, Muleteers and Transport in Classical Roman Law," MLA 120 (90); auth, "Imeritia: The Responsibility of Skilled Workers in Classical Roman Law," Am J Philol 122 (01); auth, "Roman Law and the Study of Land Transportation," in Speculum Iuris: Roman Law as a Reflection on Economic and Social Life in Antiquity, eds. J. J. Aubert, B. Sirks (01); auth, Roman Land Transportation, Univ Mich Pr (forthcoming). **CONTACT ADDRESS** Class Dept, Univ of Tennessee, Knoxville, 1101 McClung Tower, Knoxville, TN 37996-0413. **EMAIL** sdmartin@utk.edu

MARTIN, VINCENT
PERSONAL Born 02/05/1963, CA **DISCIPLINE** SPANISH LITERATURE **EDUCATION** Univ Calif Berkeley, AB, 85; NY Univ, MA, 87; PhD, 97. **CAREER** Asst prof, Univ of N Fla, 97-98; asst prof, Utah State Univ, 98-00; asst prof, Univ of Del, 00-. **MEMBERSHIPS** MLA, Cervantes Soc of Am, Asociacion de Hispanismo Filosofico. **RESEARCH** Calderon, The art and thought of Counter-Reformation Spain, The classical tradition in Spain. **SELECTED PUBLICATIONS** Auth, "Corpus Christi Simplicioribus: alegorias y representacion de autoridad en Valencia," Revists de Dialectologia y Tradiciones Populares 47, (92); auth, "El Calderon de regalado y el ano 2000," Revists Hispanica Moderna 51, (98); auth, Calderon (1600-1681), Ediciones del Orto, Madrid, 00; auth, "Cervantes's Critique of Verisimiltitude as Intertext for the New Comedy," Bull of the Comediantes 52.2, (00); auth, El concepto de representacion en los autos sacramentales de Calderon, Reichenberg, (Kassel), 00; auth, "Mirabile Visu: The Wonderful World of Calderon," Romantic Rev, forthcoming. **CONTACT ADDRESS** Univ of Delaware, 326 Smith Hall, Newark, DE 19716-2550. **EMAIL** vmartin@udel.edu

MARTIN-OGUNSOLA, DELLITA LILLIAN
PERSONAL Born 10/27/1946, New Orleans, LA, m, 1979 **DISCIPLINE** SPANISH, FRENCH **EDUCATION** Louisiana State Univ, New Orleans, BA, 1968; Ohio State Univ, MA, 1971, PhD, 1975. **CAREER** St Mathias High School, instructor of Spanish/French, 75-76; Univ of Alabama-Birmingham, asst prof of Spanish, 76-82, assoc prof of Spanish, 82-99; prof of Spanish, 99-; chair of dept of foreign langs, 93-. **HONORS AND AWARDS** Presidential Awd for Excellence in Teaching, 1997; Outstanding Faculty-UAB Honors Program, 1998; Faculty Rep to the Bd of Trustees, Univ of Alabama System, 1994-95; Phi Beta Delta, Beta Nu Chapter, Charter Member Honor Soc for International Scholars, 1992; Alpha Lambda Delta, UAB Honorary Faculty Member, 1992; UAB-Univ College, Ingalls Finalist for Teaching Excellence, 1979-80, 1983, 1989; Sigma Delta Pi, Omicron Mu Chapter, UAB Faculty/Assoc Member, 1985. **MEMBERSHIPS** Afro-Hispanic Association, consulting and contributing editor, 1990-; Alabama Association of Teachers of Spanish, 1977-; Association of Caribbean

Studies, liaison sec, 1979, 1982-84; College Language Association, 1977-; Hispanic Conf of Greater Birmingham, 1984-; Modern Language Association, 1976, sec 1977-78, chair Afro-Am ex com, 1979; South Atlantic Modern Lang Assn, 1979-; Alabama Humanities Foundation, sec exec sub-committee 1978-80, chair nominations sub-committee, 1979. **SELECTED PUBLICATIONS** Selected Poems of Langston Hughes and Nicolas Guillen, Doctoral Dissertation, Ohio State Univ, 1975; "West African & Hispanic Elements in NG's La cancion del bongo," South Atlantic Bulletin, 45:1, p 47-63, 1980; "Langston Hughes & the Musico-Poetry of the African Diaspora," in Langston Hughes Review, 5:1, p 1-17, 1986; "Translation as a Poetic Experience/Experiment: Short Fiction of Quince Duncan," Afro-Hispanic Review, 10:3, p 42-50, 1991; Las mejores historias de Quince Duncan/The Best Short Stories of Quince Duncan editorial, San Jose, Costa Rica, 1995; Female Characters in the Fiction of Quince Duncan, 1999. **CONTACT ADDRESS** Univ of Alabama, Birmingham, 900 S 13th St, Arts & Humanities Bldg Rm 407-B, Birmingham, AL 35294-1260.

MARTIN-RODRIGUEZ, MANUEL M.

PERSONAL Born 09/26/1962, Sevilla, Spain **DISCIPLINE** HISPANIC LANGUAGE & LITERATURE **EDUCATION** Universidad de Sevilla, Spain, Licenciature en Filologia Hispanica, 85; Univ Houston, MA, 87; Univ Calif Santa Barbara, PhD, 90. **CAREER** Lectr, 90, Univ Calif Santa Barbara; asst prof, 90-96, Yale Univ; assoc prof, 96-98, Wayne St Univ; assoc prof, dir, 98-, Univ Wi Milwaukee. **HONORS AND AWARDS** Grad Scholar, 88-89; Special Regents Fel, 87-90; Samuel Wofsy Mem Prize for Outstanding PhD Stud, 90; Grad Dissertation Fel, 90; A Whitney Griswold Fac Awd, 92; Morse Fel, 92-93, Hilles Publ Fund, 94; Summer Res Grant, 97; Humanities Center Fel, 97; Small Res Grant, 97. **SELECTED PUBLICATIONS** Auth, Rolando Hinojosa y su 'cronicon' chicana: Una novela del lector, Universidad de Sevilla, 93; auth, La voz urgente: Antologia de literature chicana en espanol, Fundamentos, 95; auth, Life in Search of Readers: Reading Chicano/ a Literature, Univ NM Press, 99; auth, La nueva novela de la tierra: conflicto cultural y fronterizo en la narrativa chicana de Texas, La Torre, 99. **CONTACT ADDRESS** Robert Hernandez Center, Univ of Wisconsin, Milwaukee, PO Box 413, Milwaukee, WI 53201. **EMAIL** mmartin@uwm.edu

MARTINES, LAURO

PERSONAL Born 11/22/1927, Chicago, IL, m, 1957, 1 child **DISCIPLINE** RENAISSANCE HISTORY, ITALIAN LITERATURE **EDUCATION** Drake Univ, AB, 50; Harvard Univ, PhD(hist), 60. **CAREER** From instr to asst prof hist, Reed Col, 58-62; Prof Hist, Univ Calif, Los Angeles, 66-, Am Philos Soc grants, 60, 61, 66; Am Counc Learned Soc fel, 62-63; Harvard Ctr Ital Renaissance Studies fel, Villa I Tatti, Florence, Italy, 62-65; John Simon Guggenheim Mem Found fel, 64-65; Ford Found grant, 68-69; Nat Endowment for Humanities sr fel, 71, fel, 78-79; Rockefeller Fel, Villa Serbeloni, 90. **HONORS AND AWARDS** Harvard, Bayard-Cutting fel, 55-56; Sheldon Travelling fel, 57-58. **MEMBERSHIPS** AHA; Renaissance Soc Am; fel Mediaeval Acad Am. **RESEARCH** Seventeenth century Europe; the Italian Renaissance; the social analysis of English Renaissance verse. **SELECTED PUBLICATIONS** Auth, The Social World of the Florentine Humanists: 1390-1460, 63 & Lawyers and Statecraft in Renaissance Florence, 68, Princeton Univ; ed, Violence and Civil Disorder in Italian Cities, 1200-1500, Univ Calif, 72; coauth, Not in God's Image: A History of Women from the Greeks to the Nineteenth Century, Harper, 73; auth, Power and Imagination: City-States in Renaissance Italy, Knopf, 79; auth, Society and History in English Renaissance Verse, 85; auth, An Italian Renaissance Sextet, 94; auth, Strong Words: Writing and Social Strain in the Italian Renaissance, 01. **CONTACT ADDRESS** 8 Gloucester Crescent, London, England NW1 7DS. **EMAIL** lauromartines@talk21.com

MARTINEZ, ELIZABETH COONROD

PERSONAL Born 06/03/1954, Austin, TX **DISCIPLINE** LATIN AMERICAN LITERATURE & CULTURE **EDUCATION** Portland State Univ, 83 BA; NYork Univ, MA, 91; Univ NM in Albuquerque, PhD, 95. **CAREER** Journalist; prof, Mod Langs & Lits, Sonoma St Univ. **HONORS AND AWARDS** Poynter Institute Summer Fel for Journalism Teachers, 95; SSU Summer Res Fel, 98, 99; NEH Summer Institute on "The Maya World", 00. **MEMBERSHIPS** MLA, AATSP, NACCS, Letras Femeninas, MALCS. **RESEARCH** 20th century and colonial Latin Am narrative, indigenous studies, cultural and gender studies. **SELECTED PUBLICATIONS** Auth, Henry Cisneros: Mexican-American Leader, 93; Sor Juana Ines de la Cruz: A Trail-blazing Thinker, 93; Edward James Olmos: Mexican-American Actor, 94; Coming to America: The Mexican-American Experience, 95; auth, "Before the Boom: Latin Am Revolutionary Novels of the 1920s," Lanham, MD: Univ Press of Am, 01. **CONTACT ADDRESS** Dept of Modern Lang & Lit, Sonoma State Univ, 1801 E. Cotati Ave., Rohnert Park, CA 94928-3609. **EMAIL** elizabeth.martinez@sonoma.edu

MARTINEZ, ESTHER M.

DISCIPLINE SPANISH MEDIEVAL LITERATURE **EDUCATION** Univ Mich, PhD, 89. **CAREER** Assoc prof. **RESEARCH** Cuaderna via narrative poetry of the 13th century. **SELECTED PUBLICATIONS** Publ on, cohesion theory and 13th-century cuaderna via, several aspects of the Libro de Alexandre and the circular structure of the Libro de buen amor; Traditional material in the Poema de Yucuf, Perez de Guzm n's translation of Seneca's Epistulae, rhetoric in the Novelas ejemplares, and holymorphism in the poetry of Sor Juana Ines de la Cruz. **CONTACT ADDRESS** Dept of Language and Cultures, William Paterson Col of New Jersey, 300 Pompton Rd., Wayne, NJ 07470.

MARTINEZ, H. SALVADOR

PERSONAL Born 03/31/1936, Leon, Spain **DISCIPLINE** MEDIEVAL SPANISH LITERATURE, PHILOSOPHY OF HISTORY **EDUCATION** Univ Rome, Dr Laurea, 60; Gregoriana Univ, Rome, Laurea, 68; Univ Toronto, PhD, 72. **CAREER** Prof Span lit & philos, Angelo State Univ, 72-76; Prof Medieval Span Lit, NY Univ, 76-. **MEMBERSHIPS** Soc Rencesvals; Asoc Int Hispanistas; Mediaeval Acad Am; MLA; Am Acad Res Historians Medieval Spain. **CONTACT ADDRESS** Dept of Span & Port, New York Univ, 19 University Pl, New York, NY 10003-4556. **EMAIL** hsm1@is.nyu.edu

MARTINEZ, JACQUELINE M.

DISCIPLINE SEMIOTICS, PHENOMENOLOGY, FEMINIST THEORY, INTERCULTURAL COMMUNICATION **EDUCATION** Southern Ill Univ, PhD, 92. **CAREER** Asst prof, Purdue Univ. **SELECTED PUBLICATIONS** Auth, Radical Ambiguities and the Chicana Lesbian; Body Topographies on Contested Lands, in Spoils of War: Women of Color, Cultures, Revolutions, 97; coauth, Signifying Harassment: Communication, Ambiguity, and Power, Human Stud, 95. **CONTACT ADDRESS** Dept of Commun, Purdue Univ, West Lafayette, 1080 Schleman Hall, West Lafayette, IN 47907-1080. **EMAIL** martinez@purdue.edu

MARTINEZ, RONALD L.

DISCIPLINE COMPARATIVE MEDIEVAL AND RENAISSANCE (ITALIAN, ENGLISH, SPANISH AND FRENCH) **EDUCATION** Univ Calif, Santa Cruz, PhD. **CAREER** Instr, Univ Minn, Twin Cities. **RESEARCH** Dante studies. **SELECTED PUBLICATIONS** Auth, Time and the Crystal. **CONTACT ADDRESS** Univ of Minnesota, Twin Cities, 9 Pleasant St. SE, 260 Folwell Hall, Minneapolis, MN 55455.

MARTINEZ-BONATI, FELIX

PERSONAL Born 03/07/1929, Santiago, Chile, m, 1957, 2 children **DISCIPLINE** SPANISH & COMPARATIVE LITERATURE **EDUCATION** Univ Goettingen, DrPhil, 57; Univ Chile MPhil, 58. **CAREER** Prof Span, Univ Chile, 57-62; pres, Univ Austral Valdivia, 62-68; Alexander von Humboldt fel, 69-70; prof Span & comp lit, Univ Iowa, 71-77; prof Span, Univ IL, Chicago, 77-78; Prof Span, Columbia Univ, 78-; Vis prof philos, Univ Goettingen, 64-66; Vis prof Span, Princeton Univ, 83. **HONORS AND AWARDS** Dr honoris causa Univ Austral Chile, 74. **RESEARCH** Theory of literature; intellectual history. **SELECTED PUBLICATIONS** Auth, La concepcion del lenguaje en la filosofia de Husserl, & Las ideas esteticas de Schiller, Univ Chile, 60; La estructura de la obra literaria, Seix-Barral, Barcelona, 60, 72, 85; Fictive Discourse and the Structures of Literature, Cornell Univ Press, 82; Don Quixote and the Poetics of the Novel, Cornell Univ Press, 92; La ficcion narrativa, Univ Murcia, 92; El Quijote y la poetica de la novela, Madrid, 95. **CONTACT ADDRESS** Dept of Span, Columbia Univ, 2960 Broadway, Box 4348, New York, NY 10027-6900.

MARTINEZ-LOPEZ, ENRIQUE

PERSONAL Born 08/18/1928, Granada, Spain, m, 1954, 3 children **DISCIPLINE** IBERIAN, LITERATURE **EDUCATION** Univ Granada, BA; Univ Madrid, MA; PhD, 64. **CAREER** Instr, Univ da Paraiba, 54-56; instr, Univ do Recife, 56-59; asst prof, Univ Houston, 59-63; asst prof to assoc prof to dept chmn to prof to emer, Univ Calif Santa Barbara, 63-; vis lectr, Univ Wis Madison, 66, 67. **HONORS AND AWARDS** Inst Miguel de Cervantes Fel, Madrid, 52-54; Cruz de Caballero, Orden del lento Civil, 55; Pres Inst Brasil de Cult Hisp, Recife, 57-59; Hon Mem, Inst de Cult Hisp, Madrid, 57; APS Grant, 71; Univ Calif Santa Barbara Fac Fel, 65; Humanities Inst Fel, 66-67, 74; Acad Senate, Community on Res, 63-77, 80, 88-90, 95. **MEMBERSHIPS** MLA; AATSP; IILI; AISO; ASSS. **RESEARCH** Sixteenth to Eighteenth Centuries literature in Spain, Portugal and Ibero-Americana; New Christians: racial purity and cultural conflicts; Slavery and the Inquisition; Contemporary Spanish and Ibero-American poetry and drama; Spanish, Mexican and Brazilian balladry; Medieval Spanish literature. **SELECTED PUBLICATIONS** Auth, "Sor Juana Ines de la Cruz en Portugal: Un Desconocido Homenaje y versos Ineditos," Rev de Lit 33 (68): 53-84; auth, "Sobre 'Aquella Bestialidad' de Garcilaso," PMLA 87 (72): 12-25; auth, "La Variacion en el Corrido Mexicano," in The Hispanic Ballad Today: Poetics, ed, Diego Catalan et al (Madrid: Gredos, 79): 65-120, 373-77; auth, "El rival de Garcilaso," Bolet de la Real Acad Espah 61 (81): 191-281; auth, Camoniana Californiana, Bandanna Books, Santa Barbara, 85; auth, Federico Garcia Lorca: Granada, Paraiso Cerrado, y Otras Paginas Granadinas, Biblioteca de Escritores y Temas Granadinos, 71 (89); co-ed, "La Leyenda del Judio Errante en la Literatura de Cordel Espanola," Bull Hisp 92 (90): 789-825; auth, "Mezclar Berzas con Capachos: Armonia y Guerra de Castas en el Extremes del Retablo de lass Mara villas, de Cervantes," Bull de la Real Acad Espan 72 (92): 67-171; auth, "Erotismo y Ejemplaridad en El Viejo Celoso de Cervantes," in Erotismo err las Letras Hispanics, eds, L. Lopez-Baralt, F. Marquez (Villanueva, Pub de la Nuem Rev de Filo Hisp, 95): 335-85; auth, Tablero de Ajedrez: Imagenes del Negro Heroico en la Comedic Espanola y eri la Literatura e Iconografia Sacra del Brasil Esclavista, Cen Cultural C. Gulbenkian, 98. **CONTACT ADDRESS** 503 Miramonte Dr, Santa Barbara, CA 93209-1400.

MARTINEZ-SAN MIGUEL, YOLANDA M.

PERSONAL Born 05/10/1966, Santurce, Puerto Rico, m, 1988 **DISCIPLINE** LATIN AMERICAN AND CARIBBEAN LITERATURE **EDUCATION** Univ Puerto Rico, BA, 89; Univ Calif, MA, 91; PhD, 96. **CAREER** Instr, Univ of Calif, 94-96; asst prof, Univ of Puerto Rico, 96-97; asst prof, Princeton Univ, 97-00; asst prof, Rutgers Univ, 00-. **HONORS AND AWARDS** Am Awd of Excellence, 88-89; Fel, Univ of Calif, 92-94; Ford Found Fel, 90-92, 94-95, 95-96; Proyecto Atlantea, 97; Princeton Univ Grant, 97, 98, 99; Ford Found Fel, 99, 00, Who's Who in Am, 01. **MEMBERSHIPS** MLA, Latin Am Studies Assoc, Brazilian Studies Assoc, Puerto Rican Studies Assoc, Caribbean Studies Assoc, Am Assoc of teachers of Span and Port, Instituto Internacional de Literatura Iberoamericana, Asociacion de Literatura Femenina Hispanica. **RESEARCH** Latin American Literature, Colonial, Hispanic Caribbean, and Latino Literature, Literary Theory, Colonial and Postcolonial Theory, Migration Studies. **SELECTED PUBLICATIONS** Auth, "Saberes americanos: la constitucion de una subjetividad colonial en los villancicos de Sor Juana," Rivista Iberoamericana, (98); auth, "Hacia unos estudios culturales latinoamericanos: algunas notas sobre el impacto en la ensenanza," Revista de Ciencias Sociales, (98); auth, "Cartografias pancaribenas: representaciones culturales de los enclaves caribenos en Puerto Rico y Estados Unidos," Rivista de Estudios Hispanicos; auth, "Saberes americanos: constitucion de una subjetividad intelectual femenina en la poesia lirica de Sor Juana," Revista de Critica Literaria Latinoamericana; auth, Saberes americanos: subalternidad y epistemologia en los escritos de Sor Juana, Instituto Int de Literatura Iberoamericana, 99; auth, "Bitextualidad y bilingueismo: reflexiones sobre el lenguaje en la escritura latina contemporanea," Centro: Jour of the Center for Puerto Rican Studies, (00); auth, "Poder y narracion: representacion y mediacion de un deseo americano en la Segunda carta de relacion," Agencias criollas: hacia una redefinicion del adjetivo colonial en la litertura y la historia hispanoamericanas, (00); auth, "De lo invisible a los innombrable: los trajes vadios en Frida Kahlo y las reapropiaciones fantasticas de la historia en Carmen Bullosa," Nomada, (00); auth, "Narrativas bilingues/bitextuales: escenas de lo intraducilbe en la escritura Latina contemporanea," Postdata, (00); auth, "A Caribbean Confederation?: Cultural Representations of Cuban and Dominican Migrations to Puerto Rico," Jour of Caribbean Lit, (00). **CONTACT ADDRESS** Dept Span, Rutgers, The State Univ of New Jersey, New Brunswick, 3306 Birchwood Crt, New Brunswick, NJ 08902. **EMAIL** yolamsm@rci.rutgers.edu

MARTINSON, STEVEN D.

PERSONAL Born 08/10/1949, Puyallup, WA, m, 1975, 3 children **DISCIPLINE** GERMANIC STUDIES **EDUCATION** Univ of WA, PhD, 77, MA, 73; Seattle Pac Univ, BA, 71; Univ of Heidelberg, 69-70 **CAREER** Prof, 91-, Spec Asst, 96-98, Assoc Prof, 88-91, Univ of AZ; Asst Prof, 80-88, Univ of CA; Asst Prof, 77-80, Northwestern Univ **HONORS AND AWARDS** Alexander von Humboldt fel, 99; Choice awd, 97 **MEMBERSHIPS** The Lessing Soc; The German Studies Asn **RESEARCH** Modern Ger Lit **SELECTED PUBLICATIONS** Auth, Vergleichung Shakespears und Andreas Gryphius, 84; auth, Between Luther and Munzer: The Pesant Revolt in German Drama and Thought, 88; auth, Harmonious Tensions: The Writings of Friedrich Schiller, Associated Univ Presses, 96. **CONTACT ADDRESS** Dept of German Stud, Univ of Arizona, Tucson, AZ 85721. **EMAIL** martinso@u.arizona.edu

MARULLO, THOMAS GAITON

DISCIPLINE SLAVIC LANGUAGES **EDUCATION** Col The Holy Cross, BA, 70; Cornell Univ, MA, 71, PhD, 75; Ind Univ, S Bend, MBA, 89. **CAREER** Instr, Ithaca Col, 73-75; asst prof, 75-81, ASSOC PROF, 81-, UNIV NOTRE DAME. **CONTACT ADDRESS** Dept of German, Russian Langs & Lit, Univ of Notre Dame, Notre Dame, IN 46556. **EMAIL** Thomas.G.Marullo.1@nd.edu

MARUN, GIOCONDA

PERSONAL Born 11/21/1942, San Juan, Argentina **DISCIPLINE** LATIN AMERICAN LITERATURE **EDUCATION** Univ Nac San Juan, BA, 64; St John's Univ, MA, 74; Univ Nac Buenos Aires, PhD, 79. **CAREER** Prof, Fordham Univ, 83-. **HONORS AND AWARDS** Fondo Nacional de Las Artes Fel, 70; NEH Fel, 82; Fordham Univ Fel, 88, 91, 97, 01. Acls Fel, 90; Org of Am States Fel, 92. **MEMBERSHIPS** MLA, Am Asn of teachers of Span and Port, Inst Int de Lit Iberoamericana, Centre d'Etude des Litteratures et des Civilisations du Rio de la Plata. **RESEARCH** Argentine Literature, Latin American Literature. **SELECTED PUBLICATIONS** Auth, Origenes del costumbrismo etico-social. Addison y Steele: antecedentes del articulo costumbrista espanol y argentino, Ediciones Universal (Miami, FL), 83; auth, "Relectura de Sin rumbo: floracion de la novela moderna," Revista Iberoamerican, (86); auth, "Revista literaria una ignorada publicacion del modernismo argentino," Revista iberoamericana, (89); auth, El modernismo argentino incognito en la Ondina del Plata y Revista Literaria (1875-1880), Inst Caro y cuervo (Botota), 93; ed, Olimpio Pitango de Monalia, Solar (Buenos Aires), 94; auth, "Edicion pnincipe de la novela Olimpio Pitango de Monalia de Eduardo L Holmberg," Revista Iberoamericana, (96), auth, "Darwin y la literatura Argentina," La Torre: Revista de la Universidad de Puerto Rico, (98); ed, La figura del intelectual en la produccion cultural rioplatense de fines del siglo XIX a fines del XX, Rio de la Plata (Paris), 00. **CONTACT ADDRESS** Fordham Univ, 441 E Fordham Rd, Bronx, NY 10458. **EMAIL** marun@fordham.edu

MARX, LEONIE

DISCIPLINE GERMAN LITERATURE **EDUCATION** Univ IL, PhD. **CAREER** Instr, Univ Ger, Denmark; Univ WI; prof-. **RESEARCH** Ger and Danish lit and Ger-Scandinavian lit rel. **SELECTED PUBLICATIONS** Auth, pioneering analysis of the contemp Danish author Benny Andersen, Eng ed, 83; Danish ed, 8; comprehensive study of the Ger short story since the late nineteenth century, Metzler, 2nd, augmented ed, 97; pub(s), bk chapters, Der deutsche Frauenroman im 19. Jahrhundert, Handbuch des Romans; Thomas Mann und die Literaturen Skandinaviens, Thomas-Mann-Handbuch; Die deutsche Kurzgeschichte, Formen der Literatur. **CONTACT ADDRESS** Dept of Ger Lang and Lit, Univ of Kansas, Lawrence, 2080 Wescoe Hall, Lawrence, KS 66045-2127. **EMAIL** marx@eagle.cc.ukans.edu

MASANAT, LYDIA

PERSONAL Born 03/29/1961, Badalona, Spain, m, 1992, 2 children **DISCIPLINE** SPANISH LITERATURE **EDUCATION** Univ S Calif, PhD. **CAREER** Asst prof, Mercer Univ, 97-; vis instr, Citadel Col, 97-99. **RESEARCH** Women's Literature, Contemporary Spain Narrative. **SELECTED PUBLICATIONS** Auth, "La autobiografia fememine espanola contemporanee", Ed Fundamentos, 98. **CONTACT ADDRESS** Dept Foreign Lang, Mercer Univ, Macon, 1400 Coleman Ave, Macon, GA 31207-0001. **EMAIL** masanat_l@mercer.edu

MASON, H. J.

PERSONAL Born 07/29/1943, Norwich, United Kingdom, m, 1970, 3 children **DISCIPLINE** CLASSICS **EDUCATION** McGill Univ, BA, 64; AM, 65, PhD, 68, Harvard Univ. **CAREER** Teaching Fel, Harvard Univ, 65-66, 67-68; Asst Prof, 68-72, Assoc Prof, 72-, Undergrad coordinator, 95-, Univ Toronto. **RESEARCH** Ancient novel; classical linguistics; topography. **SELECTED PUBLICATIONS** Auth, "The distinction of Lucius," Phoenix 37, (83): 135-43; auth, "The literature of Classical Lesbos and the Fiction of Stratis Myrivilis," C&ML 9, (89): 347-57; auth, Salmonella typhi and the Throne of Spain, Canadian Bulletin of Medical History, 90; Ancient Novels and Opera libretti, The Ancient Novel: Classical Paradigms and Modern Perspectives, 90; auth, "Mytilene and Methymna," EMC 37, (93): 225-50; auth, "Greek and Latin Versions of the Ass-Story," ANRW 34.2, (94): 1665-1770; auth, "Romance in a limestone landscape, CP 90, (95): 263-66; auth, "The End of Antissa," AJP 116, (95): 399-410 **CONTACT ADDRESS** Dept of Classics, Univ of Toronto, 97 St. George St, Toronto, ON, Canada M5S 2E8. **EMAIL** hmason@chass.utoronto.ca

MASTERS, GEORGE MALLARY

PERSONAL Born 06/19/1936, Savannah, GA **DISCIPLINE** FRENCH **EDUCATION** Columbia Univ, BS, 60; Johns Hopkins Univ, MA, 62, PhD, 64. **CAREER** Asst prof French, Univ Mo, 64-66; asst prof Romance lang, State Univ NY, Binghamton, 66-69, assoc prof, 69-70; assoc prof, 70-78, Prof Romance Langs & Lits, Univ NC, Chapel Hill, 78-, Univ Mo Res Coun Grants-in-aid, 64-66; State Univ NY Res Found grant-in-aid, 67-69, grant-in-aid & fel, 69-70; Am Coun Learned Soc fel, 76-77. **MEMBERSHIPS** SAtlantic Mod Lang Asn; Am Asn Teachers Fr; Renaissance Soc Am. **RESEARCH** Renaissance French Literature; Rabelais; Montaigne; Marguerite de Navarre; Montpellier; Pellicier (Guillaume); La Peruse; 16th-century French theater; 17th-century French theater. **SELECTED PUBLICATIONS** Auth, Heroic Virtue, Comic Infidelity--Reassessing Marguerite de Navarre 'Heptameron', Philos and Lit, vol 0019, 95. **CONTACT ADDRESS** Dept of Romance Langs, Univ of No Carolina, Chapel Hill, 230 Dey Hall, PO Box 907, Chapel Hill, NC 27244-0907. **EMAIL** gmasters@triad.rr.com

MASTRONARDE, DONALD JOHN

PERSONAL Born 11/13/1948, Hartford, CT, m, 1971, 2 children **DISCIPLINE** CLASSICAL PHILOLOGY **EDUCATION** Amherst Col, BA, 69; Oxford Univ, BA, 71; Univ Toronto, PhD(classical studies), 74. **CAREER** From Asst Prof to Assoc Prof, 73-84, Prof Classics, Univ Calif, Berkeley, 84-, Dept Chair, 93-00. **HONORS AND AWARDS** Am Coun Learned Soc, fel, 78-79, 96-97; Guggenheim Fel, 84-85; Charles J. Goodwin Awd of Merit, Am Philol Asn, 97. **MEMBERSHIPS** Am Philol Asn. **RESEARCH** Greek tragedy; Greek and Latin poetry. **SELECTED PUBLICATIONS** Auth, Theocritus' Idyll 13: love and the hero, Trans Am Philol Asn, 99, 68; Seneca's Oedipus: the drama in the word, Trans Am Philol Asn 101, 70; Iconography and imagery in Euripides' Ion, Calif Studies in Class Antiquity 8, 75; Are Euripides' Phoinissai 1104-1140 interpolated?, Phoenix, Vol 32; Contact and Discontinuity: Some conventions of speech and action on the Greek tragic stage, Univ Calif Publ Class Studies, Vol 21, 79; P Strasbourg WG 307 re-examined (Eur Phoin 1499-1581, 1710-1736), Zeitschrift fuer Papyrologie und Epigraphik 38, 1; coauth, The Textual Tradition of Euripides' Phoinissai, Univ Calif Publ Class Studies, Vol 27, 82; auth, Euripides, Phoenissae, Teubner edition, 88; Introduction to Attic Greek, Univ Calif Press, 93; Euripides, Phoenissae, Cambridge Classical Texts and Commentaries, 29, 94. **CONTACT ADDRESS** Dept of Class, Univ of California, Berkeley, 7303 Dwinelle Hall, Berkeley, CA 94720-2520. **EMAIL** pinax@socrates.berkeley.edu

MATEJIC, MATEJA

PERSONAL Born 02/19/1924, Smederevo, Yugoslavia, m, 1949, 5 children **DISCIPLINE** SLAVIC LANGUAGES AND LITERATURES **EDUCATION** Theol Acad, Eboli, Italy, degree theol, 46; Wayne State Univ, BA, 63; Univ Mich, PhD(Slavic lang & lit), 67. **CAREER** Asst prof Slavic lang & lit, Case Western Reserve Univ, 67-68; Prof Slavic Lang & Lit, Ohio State Univ, 68-, Priest, Monroe, Mich, 56-67 & Columbus, Ohio, 67-; Ed, Path of Orthodoxy; 68-; Dir, Hilandar Microfilming Proj, 70-. **MEMBERSHIPS** Am Asn Teachers Slavic & E Europ Lang; Am Asn Advan Slavic Studies. **RESEARCH** Medieval Slavic manuscripts; medieval Russian and Serbian literature; theology.Medieval Slavic manuscripts; medieval Russian and Serbian literature; theology. **SELECTED PUBLICATIONS** Coauth, Phrase Book: Serbian-English, YMCA, WGer, 49; auth, Njegoseva Luca Mikrokozma ..., Avala, Windsor, Ont, 64; Pesme (poems), privately publ, 64; coauth, Na stazama izbeglickim ..., Thought, Melbourne, 68; auth, The Eastern Orthodox Church, Mid East in Transition, 70; On contemporary Yugoslav novel, Can Slavic Studies, 71; Hilandar Slavic Codices, Ohio State Univ, 76; Biography of St Sava, 76. **CONTACT ADDRESS** Dept Slavic Lang and Lit, Ohio State Univ, Columbus, Columbus, OH 43210.

MATHEWS, GARY

PERSONAL Born 09/15/1953, Owensboro, KY, s **DISCIPLINE** COMPARATIVE LITERATURE **EDUCATION** Univ Calif Berkeley, PhD, 92. **CAREER** Tchg asst, Dept Comp Lit & Dept Rhetoric, 83-85, instr, Dept Comp Lit & Dept Classics, 85-92, Univ Calif Berkeley; lectr, Dept Classics, 93, vis instr, Dept World & Comp Lit & Dept Classics, 93-95, lectr, Dept World & Comp Lit & Dept Hum & Dept Classics & NEXA Interdisciplinary Prog, 95-97, San Francisco State Univ; Hum tchr, Div gen studies, N Carolina Sschool or Arts, 97- . **HONORS AND AWARDS** Charles Eliot Norton Fellowship, Harvard, 76-77; McKay Latin Verse Translation Prize, Univ of CA, Berkeley, 87. **MEMBERSHIPS** Mod Lang Asn; Am Comp Lit Asn; Am Philol Asn; N Carolina Class Asn; Am Class League; Womens Class Caucus; S Comp Lit Asn; Lesbian, Gay, Bisexual Classical Caucus. **RESEARCH** Euripides; Latin elegy; Mythology; Japanese Noh drama. **SELECTED PUBLICATIONS** Auth, Finding What One Wants: Desire and Interpretation in Euripides' Iphigeneia at Aulis, Laetaberis, 94; Walter Benjamins Origin of German Tragic Drama and the Baroque World View of Euripedes and Thucydides, Mag, 95; auth, There For Me: Interpersonal Connection and separation in the Noh Drama Hagoromo and the Ballet Our Town, Symp, 96; auth, An Atypical Exemplar: Zeami's Noh Drama Yamamba, Symp, 97; Aristophanes High Lyrics Reconsidered, Maia, 97. **CONTACT ADDRESS** Gen Studies, No Carolina Sch of the Arts, 1533 S Main St., Winston-Salem, NC 27127. **EMAIL** garym@ncarts.edu

MATHEWS, THOMAS J.

DISCIPLINE SPANISH **EDUCATION** Weber State Col, BA, 81; Middlebury Col, MA, 84; Univ Del, PhD, 92 **CAREER** Assoc prof, Weber State Univ, 96-; asst prof, Brigham Young Univ, 91-96. **MEMBERSHIPS** Amer Asn Teachers Span and Portuguese; Amer Coun for the Tchg For Lang; Golden Spike Empire Lang Alliance; Rocky Mt Mod Lang Asn; Southwest Conf on Lang Tchg; Utah For Lang Asn. **SELECTED PUBLICATIONS** Auth, The Acquisition of Sexist Language by Native and Non-Native Speakers of Spanish, Hisp, 98; A case for Increasing Negative Effect in Foreign Language Classes, Lang Learning J 13, 96; Avoiding Sexist Language in Composition: Complementary Solutions in Spanish and English, Mid-Atlan J For Lang Pedagogy, 95; rev, Aprendizaje: Tecnicas de composicion, In Hisp 81, 98. **CONTACT ADDRESS** Dept of Foreign Language and Literature, Weber State Univ, 1403 University Cir, Ogden, UT 84408-1403. **EMAIL** tmathews@weber.edu

MATHIAS, GERALD BARTON

PERSONAL Born 07/09/1935, Berkeley, CA, m, 1959, 2 children **DISCIPLINE** JAPANESE LANGUAGE & LITERATURE, LINGUISTICS **EDUCATION** Univ Calif, Berkeley, AB, 61, MA, 65, PhD(Orient Lang), 68. **CAREER** From lectr to asst prof East Asian Lang & Lit, Ind Univ, 67-75; assoc prof Japanese, Univ Hawaii, Manoa, 75-. **MEMBERSHIPS** Asn Asian Studies; Asn Teachers Japanese; Ling Soc Am; Asn Computational Ling. **RESEARCH** Prehistory of Japanese language; semantic structure of language; mechanical parsing. **SELECTED PUBLICATIONS** Auth, Toward the semantics of -te-i- attachment, J Newslett Asn Teachers Japanese, 69; On the modification of certain reconstructions of proto-Korean-Japanese, 73 & Some problems with word meaning, 73, Papers Japanese Ling; Seven tales of Yamato, In: K'uei Hsing, Ind Univ, 74; Subject and topic in Korean, Japanese, and English, Korean Ling, 78. **CONTACT ADDRESS** Dept of East Asian Lang, Univ of Hawaii, Manoa, 1890 E West Rd, Honolulu, HI 96822-2318. **EMAIL** mathias@hawaii.edu

MATHIOT, MADELEINE

PERSONAL Born 06/11/1927, Saulxures-sur-Moselotte, France, m, 1960, 1 child **DISCIPLINE** LINGUISTICS, ANTHROPOLOGY **EDUCATION** Georgetown Univ, BS, 54, MS, 55; Cath Univ Am, PhD(anthrop), 66. **CAREER** Asst prof anthrop, Univ Calif, Los Angeles, 67-69; assoc prof ling, 69-74, Prof Ling & Anthrop, State Univ NY Buffalo, 74-, Dir, Ctr Studies Cult Transmission, 74- **MEMBERSHIPS** Am Anthrop Asn; Ling Soc Am; Semiotic Soc Am. **RESEARCH** Lexicology; ethnosemantics; face-to-face interaction. **SELECTED PUBLICATIONS** Auth, An Approach to the Cognitive Study of Language, 68 & A Papago Dictionary of Usage, vol 1, 73, vol 2, 78, Ind Univ; ed, Approaches to the Analysis of Face-to-Face Interaction, Semiotica, 78; Ethnolinguistics: Boas, Sapir, Whorf Revisited, Mouton, 79; A meaning based theory of face to face interaction, Int J Soc Ling (in prep). **CONTACT ADDRESS** Dept Ling, SUNY, Buffalo, Buffalo, NY 14260. **EMAIL** mathiotm@acsu.buffalo.edu

MATHISEN, RALPH WHITNEY

PERSONAL Born 02/17/1947, Ashland, WI, m, 1979 **DISCIPLINE** ANCIENT HISTORY, CLASSICS **EDUCATION** Univ Wis, BS, 69, MA, 73, PhD(hist), 79; Rensselaer Polytech Inst, MS, 72. **CAREER** Vis asst prof Roman hist, Univ Ill, Chicago Circle, 79-80; ASST PROF ANCIENT & BYZANTINE HIST, UNIV SC, 80-. **MEMBERSHIPS** Asn Ancient Historians; Am Philol Asn; Am Hist Asn; Soc Ancient Numis. **RESEARCH** Late Roman society and religion; late Roman prosopography; Greek and Roman numismatics. **SELECTED PUBLICATIONS** Auth, Hilarius, Germanus and Lupus: The aristocratic background of the Chelidonius affair, Phoenix, 79; Resistance and reconciliation: Majorian and the Gallic aristocracy, Francia, 79; Sidonius on the reign of Avitus: A study in political prudence, 79 & Epistolography, literary circles and family ties in late Roman Gaul, 81, Trans Am Philol Asn; Antigonus Gonatas and the silver coinages of Macedonia circa 280-270 BC, Am Numis Soc Mus Notes, 81; Avitus, Italy and the East in AD 455-456, Byzantion, 81; The last year of Saint Germanus of Auxerre, Analecta Bollandiana, 81; Petronius, Hilarius and Valerianus: Prosopographical notes on the conversion of the Roman aristocracy, Hist, 81. **CONTACT ADDRESS** Dept of Hist, Univ of So Carolina, Columbia, Columbia, SC 29208.

MATIJEVICH, ELKE

PERSONAL Born Klingenberg, Germany **DISCIPLINE** GERMAN **EDUCATION** Univ Tex, BA, 78; MA, 80; PhD, 88. **CAREER** Prof, Collin County Col, 89-. **HONORS AND AWARDS** Fulbright Summer Study Grant, 98. **MEMBERSHIPS** Mod Lang Asn, German Studies Asn, Am Teachers of German. **RESEARCH** Literature and Culture of 20th Century Germany. **SELECTED PUBLICATIONS** Auth, "The Zeitroman of the Late Weimar Republic", 95. **CONTACT ADDRESS** Dept Humanities, Collin County Comm Col, 2800 E Spring Creek Pkwy, Plano, TX 75074-3300. **EMAIL** ematijevich@ccccd.edu

MATISOFF, JAMES ALAN

PERSONAL Born 07/14/1937, Boston, MA, m, 1962, 2 children **DISCIPLINE** LINGUISTICS, SOUTHEAST ASIAN STUDIES **EDUCATION** Harvard Univ, AB, 58, AM, 59; Univ Calif, Berkeley, PhD(ling), 67. **CAREER** From instr to asst prof, Columbia Univ, 66-70; assoc prof, 70-80, Prof Ling, Univ Calif, Berkeley, 80-, Am Coun Leanred Soc grant for res in Asia, 70; vis scholar, Summer Inst Ling Soc Am, Ann Arbor, Mich, 73. **MEMBERSHIPS** Ling Soc Am; Northern Thai Soc. **RESEARCH** Psycho-semantics. **SELECTED PUBLICATIONS** Auth, Verb concatentation in Lahu, Acta Ling, 69; Glottal dissimulation and the Lahu high-rising tone, J Am Orient Soc, 70; The Loloish Tonal Split Revisited, Ctr S & Southeast Asian Studies, Univ Calif, 72; The Grammar of Lahu, Univ Calif, 73; Psycho-ostensive expressions in Yiddish, Ha-sifrut, Jerusalem, 73. **CONTACT ADDRESS** Dept of Ling, Univ of California, Berkeley, 2337 Dwinelle Hall, Berkeley, CA 94720-2651.

MATLON, RONALD

DISCIPLINE LEGAL COMMUNICATION **EDUCATION** Purdue Univ PhD, 66. **CAREER** Instr, chp, dept Mass Commun and Commun Stud, Towson Univ. **SELECTED PUBLICATIONS** Auth, Communication in the Legal Process; Communication Strategies in the Practice of Lawyering; Opening Statements/Closing Arguments; Index to Journals in Communication Studies. **CONTACT ADDRESS** Towson State Univ, Towson, MD 21252-0001. **EMAIL** rmatlon@towson.edu

MATSUDA, PAUL KEI
PERSONAL Born 09/11/1970 **DISCIPLINE** COMPOSITION STUDIES, APPLIED LINGUISTICS **EDUCATION** Univ Wis, BA, 93; Miami Univ, MA, 95; Purdue Univ, PhD, 00. **CAREER** Asst prof, Miami Univ, 00-01; asst prof, Univ of NHamp, 01-. **MEMBERSHIPS** MLA, NCTE, Conf on Col Comp and Commun, Teachers of Eng to Speakers of Other Lang, Am Assoc for Appl Ling, Coun of Writing Program Admin, Soc for the Hist of Ling and Lang Studies, N New Eng TESOL, Japan Assoc for Lang Teaching, Ohio Teachers of Eng to Speakers of Other Lang. **RESEARCH** Second language writing, contrastive rhetoric, written discourse analysis. **SELECTED PUBLICATIONS** Auth, "Contrastive Rhetoric in Context: A Dynamic Model of L2 Writing," Jour of Second Lang Writing, (97); auth, "Situating ESL Writing in a Cross-Disciplinary Context," Writing Commun, (98); auth, "Composition Studies and ESL Writing: A Disciplinary Division of Labor," Col Comp and Commun, (99); coauth, "Cross-cultural Composition: Mediated Integration of US and International Students," Composition Studies, (99); coauth, "Beyond the L2 Metaphor: Towards a Mutually Transformative Model of ESL/WAC Collaboration," Acad Writing, (00); coauth, "On the Future of Second Language Writing: A Colloquium," Jour of Second Lang Writing, (00); auth, "Re-examing Audiolingualism: On the Genesis of Reading and Writing in L2 Studies," Linking Literacies: Perspectives on Second Language Reading/Writing Connects, ed Diane Belcher and Alan Hirvele, Univ of Mich Pr, (Ann Arbor, 01); coed, Landmark Essays on ESL Writing, Lawrence Erlbaum Assoc, 01; coed, On Second Language Writing, Lawrence Erlbaum Assoc, 01. **CONTACT ADDRESS** Dept English, Univ of New Hampshire, Durham, 95 Main St, Hamilton Smith Hall, Durham, NH 03824-3574. **EMAIL** matsuda@jslw.org

MATTEO, SANTE
PERSONAL Born 07/08/1948, Petrella, Italy, m, 1978, 1 child **DISCIPLINE** ITALIAN **EDUCATION** Kenyon Col, BA, 71; Miami Univ, MA, 76; Johns Hopkins Univ, MA, 77; PhD, 83. **CAREER** Instructor, Miami Univ, 76-79; Instructor to Assoc Prof, Brigham Young Univ, 80-90; Asst Prof to Prof, Miami Univ, 90-. **HONORS AND AWARDS** NEH Summer Sem, Univ Chicago, 83. **MEMBERSHIPS** Am Asn for Italian studies, Am Asn of Teachers of Italian, Mod Lang Asn, Dante Soc of Am, Boccaccio Soc of Am, Am Ital Hist Asn. **RESEARCH** Italian Romanticism; Italian cinema; Other periods of Italian literature. **SELECTED PUBLICATIONS** Auth, Textual Exile: The reader in Sterne and foscolo, Lang Pub, 85; ed, The Reasonable Romantic: Essays on Alessandro Manzoni, Lang Pub, 86; ed, Italian Echoes in the rocky Mountains: Papers from the 1988 conference on the american Association of Italian Studies, Brigham Young Univ, 90; co-ed, Africa Italia: due continenti si avvicinano, Fara Editor, 99; auth, africa e/e Italia: Lettera-introduzione di un figlio lontano," in Africa Italia, 99; auth, "Ossianism and Risorgimento," in Romanticism across the Disciplines, Univ Press of Am, 98; auth, "Preface," in Onofrio annibalini, Guernica,00; auth, "When Snow Was snowier and roads Were roadier and We all Loved Each Other so Much," in the flight of Ulysses: Studies in Memory of Emmanuel Hatzantonis, Chapel Hill, 97; auth, "Traduzione come contagio: Di come la traduzione ha diffuso l'epidemia ossianic," Testo a fronte, (98): 71-93 **CONTACT ADDRESS** Dept French & Italian, Miami Univ, 500 E High St, Oxford, OH 45056-1602. **EMAIL** matteos@muohio.edu

MATTHEWS, JOHN F.
PERSONAL Born 02/15/1940, Leicester, England, m, 1965, 2 children **DISCIPLINE** CLASSICS, ANCIENT HISTORY **EDUCATION** Oxford Univ, BA, 63; MA, 67; PhD, 70. **CAREER** Res Fel, Balliol Coll, Oxford, 65-69; Univ Lecturer, Univ of Oxford, 69-90; reader, 90-92: prof, 92-96. **HONORS AND AWARDS** Fel of Brit Acad; Fel of Royal Hist soc; Fel of Soc of Antiquaries of London. **MEMBERSHIPS** Soc for the Promotion of Roman Studies London; Am Philol Asn, Byantine Studies Asn. **RESEARCH** Late Roman History. **SELECTED PUBLICATIONS** Auth, Western Aristocracitsand Imperial Court, 75,90; Political Life and Culture in Late Roman Society, 85; The Roman Empire of America, 89; Laying down the Law: a Study of the Theodosian Code, 00; coauth, Atlas of Roman World, 82; The Goths in the Fourth Century, 91. **CONTACT ADDRESS** 160 McKinley Ave, New Haven, CT 06515. **EMAIL** john.matthews@yale.edu

MATTHEWS, VICTOR J.
PERSONAL Born 01/29/1941, Londonderry, Northern Ireland, m, 1967, 1 child **DISCIPLINE** CLASSICS **EDUCATION** Queen's Univ, Belfast, BA, 63; Queen's Univ, Belfast, Dip Educ, 64; McMaster Univ, Hamilton, Ontario, MA, 65; Queen's Univ, Belfast, PhD, 68. **CAREER** Lectr, 65-69, asst prof, 69-74, assoc prof, 74-94, prof, 94-, classics, Univ Guelph. **HONORS AND AWARDS** Nat Humanities Ctr fel, 86-87; SSHRC leave fel, 86-87. **MEMBERSHIPS** Ontario Class Asn; The Class Asn of Can; The Amer Philol Asn; The Israel Soc for the Promotion of Class Studies. **RESEARCH** Greek epic; Hellenistic literature; Greek athletics. **SELECTED PUBLICATIONS** Auth, Antimachus of Colophon: Text and Commentary, Leiden, 96; auth, Aphrodite's Hair: Colluthus and Hairstyles in the Epic Tradition, Eranos 94, 96; auth, The Greek Pentathlon Again, Zeitschrift fur Papyrologie und Epigraphik 100, 94; auth, In Defense of the Artemis of Antimachos, Liverpool Class Mth, 18.6, 93. **CONTACT ADDRESS** School of Languages & Lits, Univ of Guelph, Guelph, ON, Canada N1G2W1. **EMAIL** vjmatthe@uoguelph.ca

MATTHIAS, BETTINA ULRIKE
PERSONAL Born 05/13/1969, Germany **DISCIPLINE** GERMAN **EDUCATION** Univ Hamburg, MA, 93; Univ Wash, PhD, 98. **CAREER** Vis instr, Spokane Falls Community Col, 98-99; asst prof, Middlebury Col, 99-. **HONORS AND AWARDS** Fulbright Grant, 93; Boetzke Prize for Teaching Excellence, 97. **MEMBERSHIPS** AATG, MLA, GSA, MAL. **RESEARCH** Turn of the century Venice, music and literature. **SELECTED PUBLICATIONS** Auth, Masken des Lebens - Gesichter des Todes: Zum Verholthis von Darstellnng und Tod in Arthur Schnitzlers Lpohlerischen Werk, Konigshawenurd Newman, (Wurzburg), 99. **CONTACT ADDRESS** Dept Ger, Middlebury Col, Middlebury, VT 05753. **EMAIL** bmatthia@middlebury.edu

MATTINGLY, IGNATIUS G.
DISCIPLINE LINGUISTICS **EDUCATION** Yale Univ, PhD. **CAREER** Prof emer, Univ Conn. **RESEARCH** Experimental phonetics, writing systems. **SELECTED PUBLICATIONS** Auth, Speech Cues and Sign Stimuli, Amer Scientist 60, 72; Reading, the Linguistic Process, and Linguistic Awareness, In Lang by Ear and by Eye, MIT Press, 72; Synthesis by Rule of General American English, Haskins Laboratories Status Report on Speech Res, Supp, 68; coauth, The Motor Theory of Speech Perception Revised, Cognition 21, 85. **CONTACT ADDRESS** Dept of Linguistics, Univ of Connecticut, Storrs, 1266 Storrs Rd, Storrs, CT 06269-1085. **EMAIL** ignatius@uconnvm.uconn.edu

MAURER, WARREN R.
DISCIPLINE GERMAN LITERATURE **EDUCATION** Franklin and Marshall Col, BA; Univ Chicago, MA; Univ CA at Berkeley, PhD. **CAREER** Prof, 68-, Univ KS. **HONORS AND AWARDS** Dept ch. **SELECTED PUBLICATIONS** Auth, bk(s) on Gerhart Hauptmann; a bk on Ger Naturalism; co-ed, anthology of articles on Rilke; pub(s), articles on Ger lit, folklore and lit onomastics. **CONTACT ADDRESS** Dept of Ger Lit and Lang, Univ of Kansas, Lawrence, Admin Building, Lawrence, KS 66045.

MAXMIN, JODY
DISCIPLINE CLASSICS **EDUCATION** Oberlin Col, BA, 71; Oxford Univ, 73; Oxford Univ, 79. **CAREER** Acting asst prof, Stanford Univ, 79-80; asst prof, Stanford Univ, 80-88; assoc prof, Stanford Univ, 88-. **HONORS AND AWARDS** Phi Beta Kappa, Oberlin Col, 70; Danforth Found Fel, 71; Woodrow Wilson Found Fel, 71; Leonard and Katherin Woolley Fel, Oxford Univ, 73; Junior Res Fel, Oxford Univ, 75-79; Millard Meiss Found Award, 82; Dean's Award for Distinguished Teaching, Stanford Univ, 83; Hoagland Award for Undergraduate Teaching, Stanford Univ, 89; Associated Students of Stanford Univ Award for Teaching Excellence, 91; Phi Beta Kappa, Northern California Asn, Excellence in Teaching Award; Bing Teaching Initiative Grant, 92; Phi Beta Kappa, Undergraduate Teaching Prize; Associated Students of Stanford Univ Award for Teaching Excellence, 96-97. **RESEARCH** Greek and Roman art; Greek vase-painting and sculpture; Archaeological Institute of America; College Art Association; Society for the Promotion of Hellenic Studies (London). **SELECTED PUBLICATIONS** Auth, "The Anatomy Lesosn of Miss Richter," in Arion, (74): 740-44; auth, Meniskoi and the Birds," Journal of Hellenic Studies, (75): 175-80; auth, "Betes Noires from Amathus," Report of the Department of Antiquities of Cyprus, (82): 183-86; Articles on Exekias, The Amasis Painter, Lydos and Sophilos in The Encyclopedia of Visual Art, vol. II, A Biographical Dictionary, ed. Sir Lawrence Gowing, Englewood Cliffs, (83): 12-13, 208, 400, 647-48; auth, "A Hellenistic Echo in Daumier's Penelope?" Art International, 84; auth, "The Painter of Berlin 1686 Comes to Stanford," notice in The Committee for Art Calendar, 86; auth, "A New Amphora by the Painter of Berlin 1686," Studien zur Mythologie und Vasenmalerei, Festschrift for Knorad Schauenburg, Mainz, (86): 35-40; auth, Addendum to an article by Edward Courtney, "Two Catullian Questions," Prometheus, 89; auth, The Painter of Acropolis 606, the painters of Group E and the Swing Painter in The Dictionary of Art, vol. 32, ed. Jane Turner, Grovve's Dictionaries, Inc., New York, 96; coauth, "Euphronios: A Presbyope in Ancient Athens?" Marmor and Ravin, eds., The Eye of the Artist, Mosby-Year Book, Inc. St. Louis, (97): 48-57. **CONTACT ADDRESS** Dept of Art, Stanford Univ, Stanford, CA 94305-2018.

MAXWELL, DONALD R.
PERSONAL Born 03/30/1929, Paris, France, m, 1955, 8 children **DISCIPLINE** FRENCH LITERATURE **EDUCATION** Univ Cambridge, BA; MA; PhD; Univ Mich, MA, PhD. **CAREER** Res scholar, Univ of Cambridge, Attache de recherches, Institut Curie, Paris, Sr VP, Warner-Lambert, Parke-Davis; instr and vis asst prof, Univ of Mich. **HONORS AND AWARDS** Res Scholar, Univ of Cambridge; Med Res Counc Scholar, Univ of Cambridge. **MEMBERSHIPS** MLA, Am Soc for Pharmacology and Exp Therapeutics, Brit Pharmacological Soc, Physiological Soc, Biochemical Soc, Int Col of Neuro-Psychopharmacology, Brit Soc for Immunology, Europ Soc for the Study of Drug Toxicity. **RESEARCH** Marcel Proust, Henri Bergson, Science and Literature, Memory as depicted in literature and described by neuroscience. **SELECTED PUBLICATIONS** Auth, The Abacus and the Rainbow: Bergson, Proust and the digital analogic Oppostion, Lang, NY, 99; auth, Science or Literature? The Divergent Cultures of Discovery and Creation, Lang, NY, 00. **CONTACT ADDRESS** Univ of Michigan, Ann Arbor, 2940 Fuller Rd, Ann Arbor, MI 48105-2448. **EMAIL** maxwelld@umich.edu

MAY, GEORGES
PERSONAL Born 10/07/1920, Paris, France, m, 1949, 2 children **DISCIPLINE** FRENCH LITERATURE **EDUCATION** Univ Paris, Lic es Lett, 41; Univ Montpellier, dipl, 41; Univ Ill, PhD, 47. **CAREER** Instr, 45-46, 47-48, from asst prof to prof, 48-71, dean, Yale Col, 63-71, chmn dept, 78-80, provost, 79-81, Sterling Prof French, Yale Univ, 71-, Guggenheim fel, 50-51; secy, 4th Int Cong on Enlightenment, 71-75. **HONORS AND AWARDS** Chevalier, Legion d'honneur, France, 71. **MEMBERSHIPS** MLA; Am Asn Teachers Fr; Soc Hist Lit France; Am Soc 18th Century Studies (vpres, 72-74); Am Acad Arts & Sci. **RESEARCH** Various parts of French literature. **SELECTED PUBLICATIONS** Auth, J J Rousseau par Lui-Meme, Ed Seuil, France, 61; Le Dilemme du Roman au XVIIIe Siecle, Presses Univs, France & Yale Univ, 63; L'unite de sang chez Racine, Rev Hist Litteraire, France, 72; co-ed, Diderot's La Religieuse and Preface, In: Diderot's Oeuvres Completes, Hermann, Paris, 75; auth, Autobiography and the eighteenth century, In: The Author in His Work, Yale Univ, 78; L'Autobiographie, Presses Univs France, Paris, 79; Biography, autobiography and the novel in 18th century France, In: Bibliography in the 18th Century, Garland Publ Co, 80; co-ed, Diderot's Sur Terence, In: Diderot's Oeuvres Completes, Paris: Hermann, 80. **CONTACT ADDRESS** 77 Everit St, New Haven, CT 06511-1306. **EMAIL** georges.may@yale.edu

MAY, GITA
PERSONAL Born 09/16/1929, Brussels, Belgium, m, 1947 **DISCIPLINE** FRENCH **EDUCATION** Hunter Col, BA, 53, magna cum laude, phi beta kappa; Columbia Univ, MA, 54, PhD, 57. **CAREER** From lectr to instr, 53-58, from asst prof to assoc prof, 58-68, Prof French Lit & Dept Rep French, Columbia Univ, 68-; US Educ Comn lectr, Gt Brit, 65-83; prof and ch, French Lit, Columbia Univ, 83-92. **HONORS AND AWARDS** Coun Res Humanities grants, 60, 67 & 69; Am Coun Learned Soc grant, 61; Hunter Col Awd for Outstanding achievement, 63; Guggenheim fel & Fulbright grant, 64-65; Chevalier and Officier Palmes Academiques, 68, 81; Van Amringe Distinguished Bk Awd, 71; Nat Endowment for Humanities sr fel, 71-72; Fac Awd for Distinguished Teaching, Columbia Univ, 80; mem, Acad of Lit Studies, 86. **MEMBERSHIPS** Am Asn Teachers Fr; MLA (exec coun, 80-83); Soc Diderot; Rousseau Soc; Am Soc 18th Century Studies (vpres, 84-85, pres, 85-86); Fr Soc Studies 18th Century; Am Soc Fr Acad Palms. **RESEARCH** Aesthetics and history of ideas in the Age of Enlightenment; Diderot and Rousseau; Stendhal; women in history, literature and the arts. **SELECTED PUBLICATIONS** Auth, Diderot and Baudelaire, Art Critics, de Jean-Jacques Rousseau a Madame Roland; Diderot and Burke, PMLA, 12/60; Les pensees detachees sur la pointure de Diderot, Rev d'Hist Lit France, 1/70; Diderot et Roger de Piles, PMLA, 5/70; Madame Roland and the Age of Revolution, 70 & Stendhal and the Age of Revolution, 77, Columbia Univ Press; Les Confessions, Roman picaresque, Fritz Schalk Festschrift, 82; contrib, Oeuvres Complets de Diderot, 84,95; contrib, essay, Diderot nd George Sand in Europeoan Writers, 84,85 and on Rebecca West, Anita Brookener and Gsaham Srirft in British Writers, 96,97,99; ed, The Age of Revolution and Romanticism, Peter Lang, 90-; contrib, Encyclopedia of Asthetics, 98, Dictionnaire De Diderot, 99, French Women Writers, 91, The Feminist Enclopedia of French Literature,99; ed, 18th Century Studies , 75-78, French Review, 75-86, 98-, Romantic Review, 59-, Women in French Studies, 00. **CONTACT ADDRESS** Dept of French, Columbia Univ, mail code 4918, 516 Philos, New York, NY 10027-6900. **EMAIL** gm9@columbia.edu

MAYBERRY, NANCY KENNINGTON
PERSONAL Born St. Thomas, ON, Canada, m, 1967, 2 children **DISCIPLINE** SPANISH DRAMA AND LITERATURE **EDUCATION** Univ Western Ont, BA, 61; Univ NC Chapel Hill, MA, 63, PhD(Span), 66. **CAREER** Asst prof Span & French, Univ NC, Greensboro, 65-66; asst prof Span, Univ Western Ont, 66-67; assoc prof Span & French, 67-75, assoc prof, 75-82, Prof Span & French, East Carolina Univ, 82-. **RESEARCH** Spanish Golden Age drama; 19th century Spanish romanticism. **SELECTED PUBLICATIONS** Auth, 'Don Juan Tenorio' as the End Marker of Spanish Romanticism, Critica Hisp, vol 0018, 96. **CONTACT ADDRESS** Dept of Foreign Lang, East Carolina Univ, Greenville, NC 27834.

MAYER, BRUCE HILLIS
PERSONAL Born 09/09/1945, Cumberland, MD **DISCIPLINE** FRENCH LITERATURE **EDUCATION** Wesleyan Univ, BA (Liberal Arts), 68; Univ TX, Austin, MA (French Lit), 70, PhD (French Lit), 79. **CAREER** Teaching asst, Univ

TX, Austin, 72-74; Assistant de Langue vivante, Lycee Carnot, Paris, 70-71, Lycee Charlemagne, Paris, 74-75; Member of Foreign Lang Dept, Williston-Northhampton School, 76-82 (Director Intersession Prog in Paris, 76-82); asst prof of French and Italian, Tulane Univ, 82-84; asst prof French, 84-88, assoc prof French, 88-93, Chairperson Dept Foreign Langs and Lit, 92-97, Prof French, Lynchburg Col, 93-. **HONORS AND AWARDS** NDEA Title IV Fel, Univ TX, 68-72; Rotary Int Fel to France, 75-76; NEH Summer Seminar, Yale Univ, 89; Mednick Memorial Fel, VA Found for Independent Colleges, 92; CIBER Fel to CIEL de Strasbourg France, Ministry of Ed and French, San Diego State Univ, 94. **RESEARCH** French lit of the 18th century; French political hist; Ancien Regime; Italian lang. **SELECTED PUBLICATIONS** Auth, Machiavelli's Promise to the Citizen: Political Freedom?, in Machiavelli Studies, Vol 1, 87; The Strategy of Rehabilitation: Pierre Bayle on Machiavelli, in Studi Francesi, Anno 33, no 98, 89; bibliography prepared for Machiavelli Studies, Vols I, II, & III, 87-90; book review, Christopher Lasch, The True and Only Heaven: Progress and its Critics, in Utopian Studies, Vol 4, no 1, 93. **CONTACT ADDRESS** Dept of Foreign Langs and Lit, Lynchburg Col, Lynchburg, VA 24501. **EMAIL** mayer_b@mail.lynchburg.edu

MAYER, REINHARD
PERSONAL Born 08/01/1942, Germany **DISCIPLINE** GERMAN LITERATURE **EDUCATION** Tubingen Univ, MA, 67; Northwestern Univ, PhD, 77. **CAREER** Asst prof, Carthage Col, 69-70; asst prof, Kendall Col, 70-72; asst prof, Bennington Col, 73-94; assoc prof, Skidmore Col, 96-. **HONORS AND AWARDS** Fulbright Fel, 64-66. **MEMBERSHIPS** MLA, AARG, ACTFL, GSA. **RESEARCH** Classical and Romantic Periods, Translation Theory, Business German. **SELECTED PUBLICATIONS** Auth, Fremolinge im Eigener Haus, Peter Lang Berlag, 96. **CONTACT ADDRESS** 81 Locust Grove Rd, Saratoga Springs, NY 12866.

MAYER, SIGRID
DISCIPLINE GERMAN **EDUCATION** Univ UT, PhD, 73. **CAREER** Emer prof, Univ Wyo, 73. **RESEARCH** Contemp Ger lit. **SELECTED PUBLICATIONS** Publ, bk on the Golem legend, 2 vol(s) of graphic art and texts by Gunter Grass & an annotated bibliog on Ernst Cassirer. **CONTACT ADDRESS** Dept of Mod and Class Lang, Univ of Wyoming, PO Box 3964, Laramie, WY 82071-3964. **EMAIL** mayersig@uwyo.edu

MAYERS, MARVIN K.
PERSONAL Born 10/25/1927, Canton, OH, m, 1952, 2 children **DISCIPLINE** ANTHROPOLOGY, LINGUISTICS **EDUCATION** Wheaton Col, BA, 49; Fuller Theol Sem, Mdiv, 52; Univ Chicago, MA, 58; PhD, 60. **CAREER** Field Dir, Bd of Dir, SIL Calif, 60-61; Field Res in Ling and Soc Anthrop, SIL, Guatemala, Caif, 53-65; Prof, Wheaton Col, 65-74; Chair, Dept of Sociol and Anthrop, Wheaton Col, 68-74; Adj Prof, Univ of Tex Arlington, 74-82; Dir, Tex SIL Dallas, 76-82; Assoc Coordr for Res in Anthrop in the Inst of Ling Tex, 89-93; Prof/Prof Emeritus, Biola Univ, 82-89, 92-; Founding Dean, Dean Emeritus, Grad Sch of Intercultural Studies, Biola Univ, Calif, 83-89, 92-. **HONORS AND AWARDS** NSF Grant, 58; OAS Grant, 59-60; Teacher of the Year, Wheaton Col, 67; Christianity Confronts Culture named among 30 most significant books in Protestant Christian Mission, 96; Who's Who in Am Educ, 80-. **MEMBERSHIPS** Am Anthrop Asn. **RESEARCH** Latin America, Cross-Cultural Communication. **SELECTED PUBLICATIONS** Auth, Pocomchi Texts, The Univ of Okla and SIL (Norman, OK), 58; ed, Languages of Guatemala, Mouton (The Hague), 65; ed, Love Goes on Forever, Zondervan (Grand Rapids), 72; coauth, Reshaping Evangelical Higher Education, Zondervan (Grand Rapids), 72; auth, A Look At Filipino Lifestyles, Int Mus of Cultures (Dallas, Tex), 80, 84; coauth, Ministering Cross-Culturally, Baker Books (Grand Rapids), 86, in Korean, 89, in Ger, 91; coauth, Cultural Anthropology, Zondervan (Grand Rapids), 79, 87, Spanish Ed, 97; auth, Christianity Confronts Culture, 74, 88, in Korean, 88; co-ed, Nucleation in Papua New Guinea Cultures, Int Mus of Cultures, (Dallas, Tex), 88; auth, A Look at Latin American Lifestyles, 4th ed, Int Mus of Cultures (Dallas, Tex), 90. **CONTACT ADDRESS** Dept Arts and Sci, Fla Gulf Coast Univ, 19501 Treeline Ave S, Fort Myers, FL 33965-0001.

MAYR, FRANZ KARL
PERSONAL Born 03/12/1932, Linz, Austria, m, 1968, 2 children **DISCIPLINE** PHILOSOPHY OF RELIGION & LANGUAGE; METAPHYSICS; LEGAL PHILOSOPHY **EDUCATION** Univ Innsbruck, LPh, 56, PhD(philos), 57, MLaw, 62. **CAREER** Asst prof philos, Univ Innsbruck, 63-64 & 65-68; asst prof relig & philos, 64-65, assoc prof, 68-76, Prof Philos, Univ Portland, OR, 76- . **RESEARCH** Political philosophy; Philosophy of religion. **SELECTED PUBLICATIONS** auth, Lenguaje: Dicconario de Hermenentica, Univ de Deusto Bilbao, 77; auth, El Matriarcalismo Vasco, Bilbao, 80; auth, Simbolos, Mitos Y Archetypos, Antropologia Vasca: Gran Encyclopedia Vasco, Bilbao, 80; auth, Sprache, Sprachphilosophie, Herders Theologisches Taschenlexikon, 81; coauth, El Inconsciente Colectivo Vasco, San Sebastian, 82; auth, La mitologia Occidental, Barcelona, 89; auth, Wort grgen bild, Zur Friihgeschichte der Symbolik des Horens: Das Buch von Horen Freiburg, 91; coauth, Arquetipos y Simbolos Colectivos: Circulo Eranos I, Barcelona, 94; auth, Seeing and Hearing in Pheno-Menology, Analytic Philosophy and Hermeneutics, Frebourg, 00; auth, M Heidegger, Zollikon Seminars, Northwestern Univ Press, 00. **CONTACT ADDRESS** Dept of Philosophy, Univ of Portland, 5000 N Willamette, Portland, OR 97203-5798.

MAZZOCCO, ANGELO
PERSONAL Born 05/13/1936, Isernia, Italy, m, 2 children **DISCIPLINE** SPANISH, ITALIAN **EDUCATION** OH State Univ, BA & BSc, 59, MA, 63; Univ CA, Berkeley, PhD, 73. **CAREER** Instr Span, John Carroll Univ, 62-65; tchg asst Ital, Univ CA, Berkeley, 66-69; asst prof Ital, Northern IL Univ, 70-75; asst prof Ital & Span, 75-76, Assoc Prof Ital & Span, 76-83, Prof Ital & Span 83- Chmn Dept, 81-84, 93-96, 99; Chmn Romance Lang(s) and Lit(s) 89-93, 99-00; Assoc Columbia Univ Renaissance Seminar 81-90. **HONORS AND AWARDS** Univ CA Ital-Am Traveling fel, 69-70; Fel, Nat Endowment for Hum, 81; Grantee, Am Council of Learned Societies, 85; Res fel, Gladys Krieble Delmas Found, 93-94, 96-97; Grantee, Nat Endowment for the Hum/Nat Sci Found, 95-98; Fel in Residence, Inst for Advanced Studies, IN Univ, Bloomington, 98. **MEMBERSHIPS** MLA (Exec com Medieval and Ren Ital Lit, 81-85, assembly del 85-87); Am Asn Tchr(s) Ital; Dante Soc Am (coun assoc 85-90, coun 94-97); Renaissance Soc Am; Med Academy; Int Asn Neo-Latin Studies; N Am Asn His Lang Soc; Asn Int Studi di Lingua e Letteratura Italiana; Int Soc Classical Tradition, Am Boccaccio Asn (vp 82-83); Nat Asn Scholars. **RESEARCH** Latin humanism; hist linguistics of Ital and Span, Dante antiq, intellectual hist. **SELECTED PUBLICATIONS** Auth, Linguistic Theories in Dante and the Humantists, 93; contbr numerous chpts in bks and many articles and review to profl jours. **CONTACT ADDRESS** Dept of Span & Ital, Mount Holyoke Col, 50 College St, South Hadley, MA 01075-1461. **EMAIL** amazzocc@mtholyoke.edu

MAZZOCCO, ELIZABETH H.
DISCIPLINE FRENCH LITERATURE **EDUCATION** Bryn Mawr Univ, PhD. **CAREER** Prof, Univ MA Amherst. **RESEARCH** Italian epic; Italian theater; for lang tech. **SELECTED PUBLICATIONS** Auth, pubs on Boiardo's Orlando Innamorato; Renaissance chivalry. **CONTACT ADDRESS** Dept of French and Italian Studies, Univ of Massachusetts, Amherst, Mass Ave, Amherst, MA 01003. **EMAIL** mazzocco@frital.umass.edu

MAZZOLA, MICHAEL LEE
PERSONAL Born 01/19/1941, Frankfort, NY **DISCIPLINE** ROMANCE LINGUISTICS **EDUCATION** Le Moyne Col, NYork, AB, 62; Middlebury Col, MA, 64; Cornell Univ, PhD, 67. **CAREER** Lectr French, Cornell Univ, 65-66, asst prof ling, 66-68; asst prof French & Ital, Ind Univ, Bloomington, 68-74; vis fel, Cornell Univ, 74-75; asst prof, 75-79, assoc prof French & Ital, Northern Ill Univ, 79-, French/Italin Prof, North ILL Univ, 01-. **HONORS AND AWARDS** Grant, Summer Linguistics Inst at UCLA, Am Coun Learned Soc, 66; grant, NEH Summer Seminar, Harvard Univ, 82; grant, NEH, Folger Library, 84. **MEMBERSHIPS** Am Assoc of teach of French, Am Assoc of teachers of Italian, Ling Soc Am. **RESEARCH** The Hist of French, the hist of Itlian, Italian Phonology. **SELECTED PUBLICATIONS** Auth, Proto-Romance and Sicilian, Peter de Ridder, Lisse, Neth, 76; The Romance Stammbaum in the South, in Semasia, Vol V, 78; French Rhythm and French Segments, in Ling Perspectives on the Romance Lang: Selected Papers from the 21st LSRL, J. Benjamins, 93; Indirect Phonology & French Segments, in Generative French Phonology: Retrospective and Perspectives, Asn Fr Lang Studies & Europ Studies Res Inst, 94; Syntactic Constituency and Prosodic Phenomena, in Aspects of Romance Linguistics: Selected Papers from the LSRL XXIV, Georgetown Univ Press, 96; From Stress in Latin and Romance to Lexical Stress in Italian, in Certamen Phonologicum III, Turin, Rosenberg & Sellier, 97; Issues and Theory in Romance Linguistics: Selected Papers from the Linguistic Symposium on Romance Languages XXIII, Georgetown Univ Press, 94; auth, Suprasegmental Constutuency as the Domain for Sandhi Variation: Proceedings of the 16th Internationa Congressof Linguists,CDRom #0175, Oxford: Pergamon, 98; **CONTACT ADDRESS** Dept of Foreign Lang & Lit, No Illinois Univ, 1425 W Lincoln Hwy, De Kalb, IL 60115-2825. **EMAIL** mlmazzola@niu.edu

MAZZOTTA, GIUSEPPE F.
PERSONAL Born 01/01/1942, Curinga, Italy, m, 3 children **DISCIPLINE** ITALIAN LITERATURE **EDUCATION** Univ Toronto, BA, 65; Univ Toronto, MA, 66; Cornell Univ, PhD, 69. **CAREER** Asst Prof, Cornell Univ, 69-70; Asst Prof, Yale Univ, 70-72; Assoc Prof, Univ Toronto, 72-73; Assoc Prof, Cornell Univ, 73-78; Prof, Cornell Univ, 78-83; Prof, Yale Univ, 83-. **HONORS AND AWARDS** NEH Fel, 77; Fel, Cornell Univ, 80-81; Sen Fel, Yale Univ, 86-87; Guggenheim Fel, 86-87; Fel, Yale Univ, 92-95. **MEMBERSHIPS** ALSC, ACYBE, ALS, ACLS. **SELECTED PUBLICATIONS** Auth, The New Map of the World: The Poetic Philosophy of Giambattista Vico, Princeton UP (Princeton), 98; transl, La nuova mappa del mondo: La filosofia poetica de Giambattista Vico, Einaudi (Torin), 99; auth, "L'Albero enciclopedico e la poesia nella Scienza nuova," All'ombra de Vico, Edizione Sestante (99): 297-299; auth, "Theology and Exile," Dante, Addison Wesley Longman, Inc (99): 137-159; auth, "Croce on Vico," The Legacy of Benedetto Croce, Univ Toronto Pr (99): 163-173; auth, "Liminalita e utopia della letteratura," 3 Intersezioni Rivista de storia delle idee, il Mulino anno XIX (99). **CONTACT ADDRESS** Dept Lang, Yale Univ, PO Box 208311, New Haven, CT 05620-8311. **EMAIL** giuseppe.mazzotta@yale.edu

MC CULLOH, MARK R.
PERSONAL Born 09/10/1955, Birmingham, AL, m, 1985, 2 children **DISCIPLINE** GERMAN **EDUCATION** Univ Illinois, PhD, 82; Univ Illinois, MA, 79; Univ Ala, AB, 77. **CAREER** Davidson Col, 82-. **MEMBERSHIPS** MLA; AATG. **RESEARCH** Romantic Period. **SELECTED PUBLICATIONS** Auth, "Sarah Austin's Correspondence with K. A. Varnhagen von Ense (1833-1843)," with T.H. Pickett, Euphorion. Zeitschrift fur Literaturgeschichte, 82, 88: 63-88; auth, "The Letters of Mel 'gunov and Neverov to K. A. Varnhagen von Ense," with T. H. Pickett, Germano-Slavica 5, 86, 131-174; auth, "Bettina's 'englisches Wagnis' in Light of the Correspondence between Sarah Austin and Bettina von Arnim," with T.H. Pickett, Euphorion, 84, 90, 397-408; auth, "German Writers from the Enlgihtenment to Sturm und Drang," Johann Joachim Eschenburg, Dictionary of Literature Biography, vol. 97, 90. **CONTACT ADDRESS** Dept German, Davidson Col, PO Box 1719, Davidson, NC 28036-1719. **EMAIL** mamculloh@davidson.edu

MCALPIN, MARY
DISCIPLINE FRENCH LITERATURE **EDUCATION** Columbia Univ, PhD, 94. **CAREER** Asst prof, French, Univ Tenn. **RESEARCH** French enlightenment. **CONTACT ADDRESS** Dept of Mod For Langs & Lits, Univ of Tennessee, Knoxville, 701 McClung Tower & Plaza, Knoxville, TN 37996. **EMAIL** mmcalpin@utk.edu

MCBRIDE, ANGELA BARRON
PERSONAL Born 01/16/1941, Baltimore, MD, m, 1965, 2 children **DISCIPLINE** PSYCHIATRIC-MENTAL HEALTH NURSING **EDUCATION** Georgetown Univ, BSN, 62; Yale Univ, MSN, 64; Purdue Univ, PhD, 78. **CAREER** Adjunt Assoc Prof, 81-present, Dept of Psychiatry, Indiana Univ Sch of Medicine; Adjunct Prof, 81-present, Dept of Psychology, Purdue Univ Sch of Sci at Indianapolis; Adjunct Prof, 88-present, Indiana Univ Women's Studies; Execu Assoc Dean for Research, 90-91, Interim Dean, 91-92, University Dean, 92-, Distinguish Prof of Nursing, 92-,Indiana Univ Sch of Nursing; Adjunct Prof, 95-, Philanthropic Studies Sch of Liberal Arts IUPUI, Senior Vice Pres for Academic Affairs Nursing, 97-present, Nursing/Patient Services Clarian Health Partners, Inc. **HONORS AND AWARDS** Fel, Am Acad of Nursing, 80; Nat Kellogg Fel, 81-84; ANA Counc of Specialists in Psychiatric and Mental Health Nursing Awd, 83; Dist Res Awd of Midwest Nursing Res Soc, 85; Fel, Nat Academies of Practice as a Dist Practitioner, 86; MacDonald Hospital for Women Awd, 88; hon doctorate, Univ Cincinnati, 83, Eastern Kent Univ, 91, Georgetown Univ, 93, Med Col of Ohio, 95, Univ Akron, 97, Purdue Univ, 98; Fel, Am Psychol Asn, 91, 96; Univ Medallion, Univ of San Francisco, 93; Mentor Awd, Sigma Theta Tau Intl, 93; Outstanding Contribution to Nursing and Health Psychology Awd, Am Psychol Asn Div 38, 95; elected, Inst of Med, Nat Acad of Scis, 95; named "Who's Who in Health care" by Indianapolis Business Journal, 95, 96, 98; hon mem, Chi Eta Phi, 99; Hoosier Heritage Awd, 00; Dist Nurse Educator Awd, Col of Mount St Joseph, Cincinnati, 00. **MEMBERSHIPS** Am Asn for the Advancement of Sci; Am Nurses' Asn; Am Psychol Soc; Sigma Xi. **RESEARCH** Experience of parents, health concerns of women, and functional assessment of the seriously mentally ill. **SELECTED PUBLICATIONS** Ed, Psychiatric nursing and the demand for comprehensive health care, Yale Univ Printing Office, 72; auth, The growth and development of mothers, Harper & Row, 73; auth, Vart morsideal -- en myte for fall?, Dreyers Forlag, 74; auth, Das normal verruckte Dassein als Hausfrau and Mutter, Rowohlt Verlag, 74; auth, A married feminist, Harper & Row, 76; auth, The secret of a good life with your teenager, Time/Random House, 87; ed, Eighty-nine reasons to be a professional nurse, Sigma Theta Tau Int, 89; co-ed, Psychiatric-mental health nursing: Integrating the behavioral and biological sciences, Saunders, 96; ed, Nursing and philanthropy. An energizing metaphor for the 21st century, Ctr Nursing Pr, 00. **CONTACT ADDRESS** Sch of Nursing, Dept of Psychiatric/Mental Health , Indiana Univ-Purdue Univ, Indianapolis, Indianapolis, IN 46202-5107. **EMAIL** amcbride@iupui.edu

MCCAFFREY, DANIEL
PERSONAL Born Teaneck, NJ, m, 1971, 2 children **DISCIPLINE** CLASSICS **EDUCATION** Fordham Univ, AB, 68; Univ Mich, PhD, 74. **CAREER** Vis asst prof, Hope Col, 74-75; prof, Randolph-Macon Col, 75-. **HONORS AND AWARDS** NEH Summer Inst, Ohio State Univ, 83; NEH Summer Inst, Univ Southern Calif, 87; Dana fel, Carnegie Mellon Univ, 88-89; mem, va's lat textbk adoption comt, 90. **MEMBERSHIPS** Mem, Bd of Dir, Class Asn of Va 91-95; mem, APA Comt on Comput Activ, 91-94; mem, APA Subcomt on Assessment, 91-95; Comt mem, For Lang Asn of Va, 96-97. **SELECTED PUBLICATIONS** Auth, Some Dangers in the Uncritical Use of

CAI in the Classroom, in Computer-Aided Instruction in the Humanities, ed by Solveig Olsen, MLA, 85; Teaching Ancient Languages with the Computer, Prospects, Summer, 92; coauth, Building Collegiality through Co-operative Programs, CJ 83, 88. **CONTACT ADDRESS** Dept of Class, Randolph-Macon Col, Ashland, VA 23005-5505.

MCCALL, MARSH H., JR.

DISCIPLINE CLASSICS **EDUCATION** BA, 60; Harvard Univ, PhD, 65. **CAREER** Prof class and dean cont studies/ summer sess, Stanford Univ. **RESEARCH** Greek lit; Greek tragedy; rhetoric; lit and textual criticism. **SELECTED PUBLICATIONS** Auth, Ancient Rhetorical Theories of Simile and Comparison,69; The Chorus of Aeschylus' Choephori in Cabinet of Muses: Essays in Honor of Thomas G. Rosenmeyer, 90; ed, Aeschylus, A Collection of Critical Essays, 72. **CONTACT ADDRESS** Stanford Univ, Bldg 20, Main Quad, Stanford, CA 94305.

MCCANN, DAVID RICHARD

PERSONAL Born 07/01/1944, Lewiston, ME, m, 1968, 2 children **DISCIPLINE** KOREAN AND JAPANESE LITERATURE **EDUCATION** Amherst Col, BA, 66; Harvard Univ, MA, 71, PhD(Korean lit), 76. **CAREER** Asst prof, Cornell Univ, 76-77, asst prof Japanese lit, 78-79; staff writer, 79-80, Asst Dir Fedn Rels, Univ Develop, 80-. **HONORS AND AWARDS** Pushcart Prize, Pushcart Prize Anthology III, 78. **MEMBERSHIPS** Asn for Asian Studies; Asn Teachers of Japanese (secy, 78-); Poetry Soc of Am; Poets & Writers, Inc. **RESEARCH** Japanese and Korean verse literature; modern poetry. **SELECTED PUBLICATIONS** Auth, Fault Lines, Modern Korean Poetry, Chicago Rev, vol 0039, 93. **CONTACT ADDRESS** Cornell Univ, 726 University Ave Univ Develop, Ithaca, NY 14853.

MCCARREN, VINCENT PAUL

PERSONAL Born 03/22/1939, New York, NY, m, 1968 **DISCIPLINE** CLASSICAL STUDIES, MEDIEVAL LITERATURE, GLOSSOGRAPHY, TEXTUAL CRITICISM, PALAEOGRAPHY **EDUCATION** Fordham Univ, AB, 60; Columbia Univ, AM, 67; Univ Mich, PhD, 75. **CAREER** Lectr Greek & Latin, Brooklyn Col, 63-68; instr, Hunter Col, 68-69, class lang & lit, Herbert H Lehman Col, 69-70; Iectr Greek & Latin, 75-76, Univ Mich, acad coun gen acad areas, 77-78, researcher, Middle English Dict, Univ Mich, 79-01. **MEMBERSHIPS** Am Soc Papyrologists; Am Philol Soc; Medieval Acad of Am; Medieval Latin Asn of North Am. **RESEARCH** Documentary papyrology; Greek and Latin etymological studies; Medieval Glossology. **SELECTED PUBLICATIONS** Auth, A Critical Concordance to Catullus, E. J. Brill (Leiden), 77; auth, Michigan Papyri XIV, Scholars Press (Chico, CA), 80; coauth, "P.HAUN.14, P.MICH.679, and P.HAUN.15 - A Re-Edition," Zeitschrift Fur Papyrologie Und Epigraphik 58 (85): 71-79; auth, "Two Receipts for Payment of Poll Tax," Zeitschrift fur Papyrologie und Epigraphik 61 (85): 58-60; coauth, "The Abecedarium from B.M. Cotton MS.TITUS D18," Modern Philology 87 (90); auth, P.Michigan Koenen (P.MICH XVIII) - festschrift edition, V.McCarren #792 (P.MICH. Inventory 258): Receipt for Advamces Occassioned by the Lease of Vineyard Properties, 285-295, J.C. Geiben (Amsterdam), 96; coed and contributor, A Guide to Editing Middle English, Univ Mich Press, 98; auth, "Gloucester Fragement of the Medulla Grammatice: GDR/Z1/31: a critical edition," The Journal of Medieval Latin 10, BREPOLS, 01. **CONTACT ADDRESS** 302 Memory Lane, Brookings, OR 97415. **EMAIL** VPM@umich.edu

MCCARTHY, JOHN A.

PERSONAL Born 01/09/1942, St Clair, MI, m, 1965, 3 children **DISCIPLINE** GERMAN, COMPARATIVE LITERATURE **EDUCATION** Oakland Univ, BA, 64; SUNY Buffalo, MA, 67; PhD, 72. **CAREER** Instr, SUNY Buffalo, 68-69; instr, Oakland Univ, 69-72; assoc prof to prof, Univ Pa, 72-91; prof, Vanderbilt Univ, 91-; dir of Undergraduate Studies. **HONORS AND AWARDS** DAAD/GSA Biannual Book Prize; NDEA Fel, 64-66; Am Philos Asn Fel, 77, 83; Univ Pa Res Found Fel, 82, 84; Deutsche Forschungsgemeinschaft Fel, 91, 97, 00; Vanderbilt Res Coun Fel, 93, 97, 98; Fulbright Fel, 93; Spence and Rebecca Webb Wilson Fel, 94-95. **MEMBERSHIPS** MLA, Am Soc for 18th Century Studies, Am Asn of Teachers of Ger, AAUP, Ger Studies Asn, Lessing Soc, Int Herder Soc, Goethe Soc of N Am, Am Comp Lit Asn, Deutsche Schillergeschellschaft. **RESEARCH** The Enlightenment and its legacy, Sensibility, Sturn und Drang, Weimar Classicism, G E Lessing, Chr M Wieland, Fr Schiller, Goethe, Nietzsche's impact on literature, science and literature (chaos and complexity theory), philosophy and literature, the essay as an art form history of Germanics, the institutionalization of literature, rise of the professional writer, theory and practice of censorship, empirical readership studies, nature of creativity. **SELECTED PUBLICATIONS** Auth, "Lekture und Lesertypologie im 18. Jahrhundert (1730-1770). Ein Beitrag zur Lesergeschichete am Beispiel Wolfenbuttels," Int Archiv fur Sozialgeschichte der deutschen Literatur 8, (93): 35-82; auth, Crossing Boundaries: A Theory and History of Essayistic Writing in German (1680-1815), Univ of Pa Pr, (Philadelphia), 89; auth, "Verstandigung and Dialektik: The Origins of Consensus theory and the Dialectics of Enlightenment," Impure Reason: Dialectic of Enlightenment in Germany, ed W Daniel Wilson and Robert c Holub, (Detroit: Wayne State Univ Pr, 93): 13-33; auth, Christoph Martin Wieland: Epoch - Werk - Wirkung, Beck Verlag (Munchen), 94; auth and ed, "Einleitung. Zensur und Kultur: Autoren nicht Autoritaten," Zensur und Kultur zwischen Weimarer Klassik und Weimarer Republik, ed John A McCarthy and Werner von der Ohe, (Tubingen: Max Neimeyer, 95): 1-13; auth and ed, "Double Optics: The Americanization of Germanstik - The Germanization of Americans," The Future of Germanstik in the USA: Changing our Prospects, ed John A McCarthy and Katrin Schneider, (Nashville: Vanderbilt Univ Pr, 96): 1-13; auth, "Die Nietzsche-Rezeption in der Literatur 1890-1918," Hansers Sozialgeschichte der deutschen Literatur. Band 7, ed York-Gotart Mix, (Munchen: Hanser Verlag, 00): 192-206; auth and ed, "Beyond a Philosophy of Alternatives: Chaos, Cosmology, and the 18th Century," Disrupted Patterns: Chaos in the Long 18th Century, ed Theodore E D Braun and John A McCarthy, (Amsterdam and Atlanta: Rodopi, 00): 21-36; auth and ed, "Auf Lessing zuruckgehen heibt allerdings fortschreiten: Lessing Reception and Strategies of Communication," Lessing International: Lessing Reception Abroad, ed John A McCarthy, Herbert Rowland and Richard Schade, (Gottingen: Wallstein Verlag, 00): 15-27; auth, "Critique and Experience: Philosophy and Literature in the German Enlightenment," German Lit and Philos, ed Nicholas Saul, (Cambridge Univ Pr, 01). **CONTACT ADDRESS** Dept Ger and Slavic Lang, Vanderbilt Univ, Box 1567B, Station B, Nashville, TN 37235. **EMAIL** john.a.mccarthy@vanderbilt.edu

MCCARTHY, MARY THERESA

PERSONAL Born 08/13/1927, Plainfield, NJ **DISCIPLINE** FRENCH LANGUAGE & LITERATURE **EDUCATION** Georgian Court Col, BA, 57; Laval Univ, MA, 65; Inst Cath Paris, dip d'Etudes Francaises, 67; Sorbonne, dipl cult Francaise contemp, 67; Ruigers Univ, PhD(French), 73. **CAREER** Teacher Latin, Mt St Mary Acad, North Plainfield, NJ, 45-46; teacher social studies, St Mary Sch, South Amboy, NJ, 47-49; teacher prim grades, Cathedral Grammar Sch, Trenton, 49-56; teacher mid grades, St Matthew Sch, Edison, 56-57; teacher Latin & French, Holy Spirit High Sch, Atlantic City, 57-59; instr French, 59-75, PROF FRENCH, 75-, DIR, FOREIGN STUDY, GEORGIAN COURT COL, 86-; Fulbright Scholar French, Univ Paris, 66-67; Nat Endowment Humanities fel comp lit, Univ Chicago, 75; reader, advan placement tests French lang, Educ Testing Serv, 76-81; Exxon Educ Found grant lang model workshop, Dartmouth Col, 77, Univ PA, 80; assoc Danforth Found, 78-84; Nat Endowment for Humanities fel French lit, Princeton Univ, 79, 87, Columbia Univ, 83, Univ CA Santa Cruz, 89, Radcliffe Col, 91; sr lang consult, Rassias Found, 79-; writer, Col Bd French Achievement Test, 80; consult, NJ Comt for Humanities, 80-81; Quebec gov grant, 90. **MEMBERSHIPS** Sisters of Mercy; MLA; Am Asn Teachers French; Am Transit Asn; Alliance Francaise; Am Coun for Quebec Studies. **RESEARCH** Modern French literature, especially the modern French novel, most especially Henri Bosco's dream novels. **SELECTED PUBLICATIONS** Contribr, The Adventures of Pascalet, Oxford Univ, 76; Historic Houses of New Jersey, William H Wise & Co, 77; Culotte the Donkey, Oxford Univ, 78; auth, Winter Idyl (poem), Poet Lore, spring 78; Today Never Came (poem), Revue de Louisiane/La Rev, fall 78; Autumn Passion (poem), NJ Poetry Monthly, 10/78; Faith on Easter Morn (poem), 4/81 & Autumn Air (poem), 10/78, Villager; Georgian Court-An Estate of the Gilded Age, Philadelphia Art Alliance Press, 82; Quebec's Ursline Foundation, Sisters Today, Jan 91; Being Irish (poem), Irish Echo, 3/25/92; Blackeyed (poem), The Cord, Dec 92; Anti-Nuclear Exposition (poem), Sisters Today, May 93; Climat d'ecoute #1, Alternative Physiognomy and Climat d'ecoute #2: Alternative Metaphysics (poems), Rev for Religions, Dec 94; Gabriel Redican: Early Days of Mercy Higher Education, The MAST J, summer 95; Prayers for All People, Doubleday, 95; Americanization of Art: Mere Maufils (1671-1702), Sisters Today, Nov 96; Une Autre Abbeville, Le Bull des Antiquaires de Picardie, Nov 96; auth, Mercy Memoirs 1925-1975, American Press, 98; Contrib, Prayers for a Thousand Years, Harper, San Francisco, 99; contrib, The Flowering of the Soul, Ballantine Wellspring, 99. **CONTACT ADDRESS** Georgian Court Col, 900 Lakewood Ave, Lakewood, NJ 08701-2697. **EMAIL** mccarthy@georgian.edu

MCCASH, JUNE

PERSONAL Born 06/08/1938, Newberry, SC, m, 2 children **DISCIPLINE** FRENCH **EDUCATION** Agnes Scott Col, BA, 60; Emory Univ, MA, 63; PhD, 67. **CAREER** Instr, Emory Univ, 64-66; From Asst Prof to Prof, Mid Tenn St Univ, 67-. **HONORS AND AWARDS** NEH Fel, 75; Outstanding Hon Fac Awd, 81; Am Coun Educ Fel, 86-87; Career Achievement Awd, Agnes Scott Col, 97; Distinguished Res Awd, Mid Tenn St Univ, 97; Phi Kappa Phi, 97-99. **MEMBERSHIPS** SMA, ICLS, IMFS, MAA, IAS. **RESEARCH** Medieval French literature, Marie de france, cultural patronage, Jekyll Island. **SELECTED PUBLICATIONS** Auth, "Images of Women in the 'Lais' of Marie de France," Medieval Perspectives 11 (96): 96-112; auth, The Cultural Patronage of Medieval Women, Univ Ga Pr (Athens, GA), 96; auth, "Amor in Marie de France's 'Equitan' and 'Frene': The Failure of the Courtly Ideal," The Court and Cult Diversity, Boydell and Brewer Publ (97): 179-188; auth, The Jekyll Island Cottage Colony, Univ Ga Pr (Athens, GA), 98; auth, "The Lady in Marie de France's 'Chaitivel': Villainous or Vilified?" Medieval Perspectives 14 (99): 140-151; auth, "'Ensemble poent bien durer': Time and Timelessness in the Chevrefoil of Marie de France," Arthuriana 9:4 (99): 32-44; auth, "Eructavit cor meum: Sacred Love in a Spiritual Context at the Court of Marie de Champagne," in Earthly Love, Spiritual Love, Love of the Saints, Sewanee Mediaeval Studies, vol 8 (99), 159-178. **CONTACT ADDRESS** Dept Lang, Middle Tennessee State Univ, 1301 E Main St, Murfreesboro, TN 37132-0001. **EMAIL** jmccash@mtsu.edu

MCCAW, R. JOHN

PERSONAL Born Palo Alto, CA **DISCIPLINE** SPANISH LITERATURE, CULTURE **EDUCATION** Univ Cal, Berkeley, AB. 89; Princeton Univ, MA, 91; PhD, 94. **CAREER** Asst prof, Montevallo Univ, 99-. **RESEARCH** Spanish literature and culture; Spanish Golden Age and Colonial studies; poetry, poetics, pastoral; Baroque culture; Gongora. **SELECTED PUBLICATIONS** Auth, The Transforming Text: A Study of Luis De Gongora's Soledad's, Scripta Humanistica (Potomac, MD), 00. **CONTACT ADDRESS** Dept Foreign Language, Univ of Montevallo, PO Box 6000, Montevallo, AL 35115-6000.

MCCAWLEY, JAMES D.

PERSONAL Born 03/30/1938, Glasgow, Scotland **DISCIPLINE** LINGUISTICS **EDUCATION** Univ Chicago, MS, 58; Mass Inst Technol, PhD, 65. **CAREER** Asst prof ling, 64-70, Prof Ling, Univ Chicago, 70. **MEMBERSHIPS** Ling Soc Am; Soc Exact Philos; Asn Tchr(s) of Japan. **RESEARCH** Syntax; semantics; struct of Eng and Japan. **SELECTED PUBLICATIONS** Auth, The Phonological Component of a Grammar of Japanese, Mouton, The Hague, 68; Adverbs, Vowels, and Other Objects of Wonder, Univ Chicago Press, 79; Everything that Linguists have Always Wanted to Know About Logic, Univ Chicago Press, 82; Thirty Million Theories of Grammar, Croom Helm, 82; The Eater's Guide to Chinese Characters, Univ Chicago Press, 84; The Syntactic Phenomena of English, Univ Chicago Press, 88. **CONTACT ADDRESS** Dept of Ling, Univ of Chicago, 1010 E 59th St, Chicago, IL 60637-1512. **EMAIL** jmccawle@midway.uchicago.edu

MCCLAIN, T. VAN

PERSONAL Born 06/10/1952, Dallas, TX, m, 1977, 3 children **DISCIPLINE** OLD TESTAMENT AND HEBREW **EDUCATION** SW Baptist Theol Sem, MDiv, 77, PhD, 85. **CAREER** Assoc Prof, Dir library serv, 89-, Mid-Amer Baptist Theol Sem. **MEMBERSHIPS** ETS; SBL. **RESEARCH** Old Testament and New Testament; Semitic Languages; Cults; Hermeneutics. **SELECTED PUBLICATIONS** Auth, The Use of Amos in the New Testament, Mid-America Theol J, 95; Hosea's Marriage to Gomer, Mid-Amer Theol J, 93; Introduction to the Book Of Isaiah, Mid-Amer Theol J, 91. **CONTACT ADDRESS** Northeast Branch, Mid-America Baptist Theol Sem, Northeast, 2810 Curry Rd, Schenectady, NY 12303. **EMAIL** VMcClain@mabtsne.edu

MCCLOSKEY, JAMES

DISCIPLINE LINGUISTICS **EDUCATION** Univ Col, Dublin, BA; Univ Tex, Austin, PhD, 79. **CAREER** Prof, Ling, Univ Calif, Santa Cruz. **RESEARCH** Theory of syntax. **SELECTED PUBLICATIONS** Auth, Clause Structure, Ellipsis and Proper Government in Irish, Lingua, 91; Resumptive Pronouns, A-Binding, and Levels of Representation in Irish, The Syntax of the Modern Celtic Languages, Acad Press, 90; co-auth, Control and A-Chains in Modern Irish, Natural Lang and Ling Theory, 88; Government, Barriers and Small Clauses in Modern Irish, Ling Inquiry, 87; On the Syntax of Person-Number Inflection in Modern Irish, Natural Lang and Ling Theory, 84. **CONTACT ADDRESS** Dept of Ling, Univ of California, Santa Cruz, 1156 High St, Santa Cruz, CA 95064.

MCCLURE, LAURA KATHLEEN

PERSONAL Born 12/26/1959, Wichita Falls, TX, m, 1988, 3 children **DISCIPLINE** CLASSICS **EDUCATION** Bard Col, BA, 82; St. John's Col, MA, 84; Univ Chicago, MA, 86, PhD, 91. **CAREER** Univ Wisconsin, Madison, asst prof, classics, 91-99; Assoc Prof, 99-. **HONORS AND AWARDS** Univ of WI Distinguished Teaching Awd, 99; Associate Res Awd, 99-00. **MEMBERSHIPS** APA, CAMS, WCC **RESEARCH** Athenian drama; women in antiquity; classical tradition. **SELECTED PUBLICATIONS** Auth, Spoken Like a Woman: Speech and Gender in Athenian Drama, Princeton Univ Press, forthcoming/ 99; ed, Blackwell Reader on Sexuality and Gender in the Classical World; auth, "'The Worst Husband': Discourses of Praise an Blame in Euripides' Media," 99; co-edit, Making Silence Speak: Women's Voices in Ancient Greece, forthcoming, PUP, fc; He Is and Is Not: Euripides as a Comic Character, in: Approaches to Teaching World Literature; ed R. Mitchell-Boyask, fc; Gunaikos Logos: Speech, Gender and Spectatorship in Aeschylus' Agamemnon, Helios, 97; Teaching a Course on Gender in the Classical World, Class Jour, 97; Clytemnestra's Binding Song, Class Jour, 97; Female Speech and Characterization in Euripides, in: Lo spettacolo delle voci, ed A.H. Sommerstein and F. de Martino, Bari, 95; On Knowing Greek: George Eliot and the Classical Tradition, in: Clas & Mod Lit, 93. **CON-**

TACT ADDRESS Dept of Classics, Univ of Wisconsin, Madison, 1220 Linden Dr, Madison, WI 53706. **EMAIL** lmcclure@facstaff.wisc.edu

MCCONNELL, WINDER
PERSONAL Born 11/19/1945, Belfast, Ireland, m, 1973, 2 children **DISCIPLINE** GERMAN MEDIEVAL LITERATURE **EDUCATION** McGill Univ, BA, 67; Univ Kans, MA, 69, PhD(Ger), 73. **CAREER** Instr Ger, Univ Western Ont, 72-73; Ordinarius English, Hist & Gemeinschaftskunde, Gym Munden, West Ger, 73-74; res & teaching fel Ger, Stanford Univ, 74-76; asst prof, Johns Hopkins Univ, 76-78; asst prof, 78-82, from assoc prof to prof German, Univ Calif, Davis, 82-88; vis prof, sum 90, UC Santa Barbara; vis prof, Univ Stirling, Scotland, 90-91. **HONORS AND AWARDS** Medal of Honor, Heinrich-Heine Univ, Dusseldorf, Ger. **MEMBERSHIPS** Med Assoc of the Pacific; Assoc Lit Scholars and Critics. **RESEARCH** Medieval German heroic epic; Jungian approaches to lit. **SELECTED PUBLICATIONS** Auth, Wate and Wada, MLN, 77; The Wate Figure in Medieval Tradition, Peter Lang Verlag, 78; Ritual and literary tradition: The brobdingnagian element in Dukus Horant, Mediaevalia, 81; Hagen and the other-world in Kudrun, Res Publ Litterarum, 82; Kriemhild and Gerlind, Houston Ger Studies, 82; Marriage in the Nibelungenlied and Kudrun: A contrastive analysis, Festschrift for George F Jones, 83; The Nibelungenlied, Twayne's World Authors Series, 84; The Lament of the Nibelungen, Diu Chlage, 94; Companion to the Nibelungenlied, 98. **CONTACT ADDRESS** Dept of German, Univ of California, Davis, Davis, CA 95616. **EMAIL** wamcconnell@ucdavis.edu.

MCCORT, DENNIS
PERSONAL Born 09/25/1941, Hoboken, NJ, m, 1973, 2 children **DISCIPLINE** GERMAN **EDUCATION** St Peter's Col, BA, 63; Johns Hopkins Univ, MA, 64; PhD, 70. **CAREER** Grad teaching asst, Johns Hopkins Univ, 65-68; from asst prof to assoc prof, Syracuse Univ, 68-. **HONORS AND AWARDS** DAAD grant, Univ of Tubingen, 64-65. **MEMBERSHIPS** Am Asn of Teachers of Ger. **RESEARCH** German Romanticism, 19th-century German fiction, literature and religion, literature and psychology, comparative literature (especially German-American literary relations), Franz Kafka. **SELECTED PUBLICATIONS** Auth, States of Unconsciousness in Three Tales by C.F. Meyer, Bucknell Univ Press, 88; auth, "Kafka Koans," Relig and Lit 23 (91): 51-74; auth, "Romanticism, Zen and Deconstruction: A Synoptic View," European Studies J 9 (92): 1-17; auth, "Hyakujo's Geese, Amban's Doughnuts and Rilke's Carrousel: Sources East and West for Salinger's Catcher," comparative Lit Studies 34 (97): 260-278; auth, Going Beyond the Pairs: The Coincidence of Opposites in German Romanticism, Zen and Deconstruction, SUNY Press, forthcoming. **CONTACT ADDRESS** Dept Foreign Lang, Syracuse Univ, 37 H.B. Crouse Hall, Syracuse, NY 13244-1160. **EMAIL** dmccort@mailbox.syr.edu

MCCULLOH, WILLIAM EZRA
PERSONAL Born 09/08/1931, McPherson, KS, m, 1956, 2 children **DISCIPLINE** CLASSICAL LANGUAGES & LITERATURES **EDUCATION** Ohio Wesleyan Univ, AB, 53; Oxford Univ, BA, 56; Yale Univ, PhD, 62. **CAREER** Instr classics, Wesleyan Univ, 56-61; from instr to assoc prof, 61-68, prof classics, Kenyon Col, 68-99, prof emer, 99-. **HONORS AND AWARDS** Am Philological Assoc Awd for Excellence in Teaching, 85; Nat Endowment for the Humanitites Fel for Col Teachers, 84-85; Ohio Prof of the Year, Carnegie Fund for the Advancement of Teaching and Council for Advancement and Support of Educ, 95. **MEMBERSHIPS** Am Philol Asn; Class Asn Mid W & S; Soc Ancient Greek Philos; NAm Patristics Soc; Int Soc for Neoplatonic Studies. **RESEARCH** Greek poetry and philosophy; the ancient novel; Greek patristics. **SELECTED PUBLICATIONS** Auth, Introduction to Greek Lyric Poetry, Bantam, 62; Metaphysical solace in Greek tragedy, Class J, 12/63; Aristophanes seen whole, Sewanee Rev, fall 65; Longus, Twayne, 70. **CONTACT ADDRESS** Dept of Classics, Kenyon Col, Ascension Hall, Gambier, OH 43022-9623. **EMAIL** mcculloh@kenyon.edu

MCCUMBER, JOHN
DISCIPLINE GERMAN **EDUCATION** Pomona Col, BA; Univ Toronto, MA, PhD. **CAREER** Prof, Northwestern Univ. **HONORS AND AWARDS** Koldyke prof tchg excellence, 94-96; Jean Gimbal Lane Humanities prof, 96-97. **RESEARCH** Include two manuscripts: Metaphysics and Oppression; Heidegger's Challange and The Capture of Time: Situation and Logos in Post-Kantian Philosophy. **SELECTED PUBLICATIONS** Auth, Poetic Interaction and The Company of Words; essays and articles on, philos from Aristotle to Derrida; Metaphysics and Oppression: Heidegger's Challenge to Western Philosophy; auth, Philosophy and Freedom: Rorty, Derrida, Habermas, Foucalut; auth, Time in the Ditch" Am Philos and the McCarthy Era. **CONTACT ADDRESS** Dept of German, Northwestern Univ, 152 Kresge Hall, 1859 Sherican Rd, Evanston, IL 60208-2203. **EMAIL** jmcc@northwestern.edu

MCDANIEL, THOMAS F.
PERSONAL Born Baltimore, MD, m **DISCIPLINE** OLD TESTAMENT STUDIES AND HEBREW **EDUCATION** Univ Richmond, BA; E Baptist Theol Sem, BD; Univ Pa, MA, 56; Johns Hopkins Univ, PhD, 66. **CAREER** Prof, E Baptist Theol Sem. **SELECTED PUBLICATIONS** Auth, rev, Deborah Never Sang: A Philol Commentary on Judges 5, Makor Press, Jerusalem, 83. **CONTACT ADDRESS** Eastern Baptist Theol Sem, 6 Lancaster Ave, Wynnewood, PA 19096.

MCDONALD, CHRISTIE
PERSONAL Born 05/04/1942, New York, NY, m, 2 children **DISCIPLINE** FRENCH **EDUCATION** Mount Holyoke Col, AB, 64; Yale Univ, PhD, 69. **CAREER** Instructor, Yale Univ, 68-69; Asst Prof, Univ Montreal, 69-77; Assoc Prof to Prof, Emory Univ, 77-3; Prof, Harvard Univ, 94-. **HONORS AND AWARDS** Fel, Royal Soc of Canada; Clifford Prize, Am Soc for 18th Century Studies; Chevalier, l'ordre des Palues Academiques. **MEMBERSHIPS** MLA; ASECS; CSECS; FCECS. **RESEARCH** 18th Century and 20th Century French Literature; Literary Theory and Cultural Studies; Feminism; Questions of Change in Thought. **SELECTED PUBLICATIONS** Auth, The Extravagant Shepherd, 73; co-ed, L'Oreille de l'autre, 82; auth, The Dialogue of Writing, 84; auth, Dispositions, 86; auth, The Proushan Fabric, 91; ed, The Ear of the Other, 86. **CONTACT ADDRESS** Dept Romance Lang, Harvard Univ, Boylston Hall, Cambridge, MA 02138.

MCDONALD, WILLIAM CECIL
PERSONAL Born 01/26/1941, Mt Clemens, MI, m, 1968, 1 child **DISCIPLINE** MEDIEVAL GERMAN LITERATURE AND LANGUAGE **EDUCATION** Wayne State Univ, BE, 62, MA, 63; Ohio State Univ, PhD(Ger medieval studies), 72. **CAREER** Instr, Wayne State Univ, 62-64; teaching asst, Ohio State Univ, 65-68, instr, 68-71; asst prof, Va Polytech Inst, 71-75; asst prof, 75-80, Assoc Prof Ger, Univ VA, 80-, Assoc ed, Semasia, 74-76 St Ger Quart, 76-77; exec coun, Southeastern Medieval Asn, 77-; vis prof, Ger Acad Exchange Serv, 77; bd rev ed, Tristania, 82- **MEMBERSHIPS** Int Courtly Lit Soc (Am pres, 80-82); South Atlantic Mod Lang Asn; MLA; Medieval Acad; Southeastern Medieval Ago. **RESEARCH** Medieval rhetoric; development of literary motifs; late medieval studies. **SELECTED PUBLICATIONS** Coauth, German Medieval Literary Patronage from Charlemagne to Maximilian I: A Critical Commentary with Special Emphasis on Imperial Promotion of Literature, Amsterdam, Rodopi, 73; auth, Michel Beheim reconsidered: On imagery in his Erzraberbispel, Ger Quart, 75; ed, Semasia: Essays in Honor of Wolfgang Fleischhauer, Amsterdam, 75; Auth, Maximilian I of Habsburg and the veneration of Hercules: On the revival of myth and the German Renaissance, J Medieval & Renaissance Studies, 76; King Mark: Gottfried's version of the Ovidian husband-figure?, Forum Mod Lang Studies, 78; Concerning ambiguity as the poetic principle in Kurenberg's Falcon Song, Euphorion, 78; The maiden in Hartmann's Armen Heinrich: Enite redux?, Deut Vierteljahrs-schrift Lit-wiss u Geistesge, 79; Whose Bread I Eat: The Song-Poetry of Michel Beheim, Goppingen, 81. **CONTACT ADDRESS** Dept of Ger Lang, Univ of Virginia, 1 Cocke Hall, Charlottesville, VA 22903-3248.

MCDONOUGH, C. J.
PERSONAL Born 04/10/1942, United Kingdom, m, 1967, 2 children **DISCIPLINE** CLASSICS **EDUCATION** Univ Col London, BA, 63, MA, 65; Univ Toronto, PhD, 68. **CAREER** Prof, Univ Toronto, 67- **MEMBERSHIPS** APA, Medieval Acad Am. **RESEARCH** Latin satire; medieval latin lit; textual criticism and editing. **SELECTED PUBLICATIONS** ed, Warner of Rouen, Pims, 95. **CONTACT ADDRESS** Dept of Classics, Univ of Toronto, 97 St. George St., Toronto, ON, Canada M5S 2E8. **EMAIL** mcdonough@trinity.utoronto.ca

MCDONOUGH, CHRISTOPHER MICHAEL
PERSONAL Born 12/28/1963, Boston, MA, m, 1994, 1 child **DISCIPLINE** CLASSICAL PHILOLOGY **EDUCATION** Tufts Univ, BA, 86; Univ North Carolina, MA, 91, PhD, 96. **CAREER** Adj prof, Univ North Carolina, Greensboro, 92-96; vis asst prof, Princeton Univ, 96-97; asst prof, Boston Col, 97-. **MEMBERSHIPS** APA; CAMWS; Am Soc of Lit Critics; Am Acad in Rome. **RESEARCH** Roman religion; social history. **SELECTED PUBLICATIONS** "Soaking Your Head: Horace Epistles 1.15.8-9 and CIL 11,2097" Classical Wrold 90.6 (1997) 429; "Carna, Proca and the Strix on the Kalends of June" Transactions of the American Philogical Association 127 (1997) 315-44; "From Parnassus to Eden" American Journal of Philogogy 120.2 (1999) 297-301; "Forbidden to Enter the Ara Maxima: Dogs and Flies, or Dogflies?" Mnemosyne 52.4 (1999) 464-477. **CONTACT ADDRESS** Dept of Classical Studies, Boston Col, Chestnut Hill, 158 Carney, Chestnut Hill, MA 02467. **EMAIL** mcdonoch@bc.edu

MCENTYRE, MARILYN CHANDLER
DISCIPLINE COMPARATIVE LITERATURE **EDUCATION** Princeton Univ, Phd, 84. **CAREER** Assoc prof, Mills Col, 84-94; vis prof, Princeton theol Sem, 95; asst prof, Trenton State Col, 94-96; assoc prof, Westmont Col, 96-. **HONORS AND AWARDS** Whiting fel, Princeton Univ, 84; Arnold Graves award outstanding tchg award, ACLS, 88; outstanding tchg award, Northen Calif, 89; dean's nomination, national prof yr awards, 91. **RESEARCH** Literature and medicine. **SELECTED PUBLICATIONS** Auth, Mercy that Burns: Violence and Vision in Flannery O'Connor's Fiction, Theology Today, 96; Cripple Time, Academic Medicine, 96; rev, In the Beauty of the Lilies, by John Updike, Princeton Theol Bulletin, 96; Who Cares?: Stories of Healing in Community, Literature and Medicine, 96; A Virtuous Woman, Contemp Lit Criticism, Gale Press, 96; Fishing on the Arid Plain: Reflections on Teaching The Waste Land, The Waste Land, Univ Calcutta Press, 96; My Brother's Keeper: The Cain and Abel Motif in 'Of Mice and Men, Univ Tenn Press, 96; Natural Wisdom: Steinbeck's Men of Nature as Prophets and Peacemakers, Steinbeck and the Environment, Univ Ala Press, 96; Salt: The Spirit and Spunk of Flannery O'Connor, Theology Today, 96; Beyond Chicken Soup: Food Fads and Folk Medicine, Mid-Atlantic Almanack, 95. **CONTACT ADDRESS** Dept of Rel, Westmont Col, 955 La Paz Rd, Santa Barbara, CA 93108-1099.

MCGAHA, MICHAEL DENNIS
PERSONAL Born 12/31/1941, Dallas, TX, m, 1964, 2 children **DISCIPLINE** SPANISH LANGUAGE & PENINSULAR LITERATURE, JEWISH STUDIES **EDUCATION** Univ Dallas, BA, 65; Univ Tex, Austin, PhD, 70. **CAREER** Instr Span, Univ Tex, Austin, 69-70; Prof Romance Languages, Pomona Col, 70-. **HONORS AND AWARDS** Fulbright grant, 65-66; Woodrow Wilson fel, 66-67, NEH fel, 80-81. **MEMBERSHIPS** AATSP; Asociacion Internacional de Hispanistas; Asn Jewish Studies; Cervantes Soc Am; Middle East Studies Asn. **RESEARCH** Cervantes; Spanish theatre of Golden Age; history and literature of Sephardic Jews. **SELECTED PUBLICATIONS** Auth, The Theatre in Madrid during the Second Republic, Grant & Cutler, 79; Ed, Cervantes and the Reanissance, Juan de la Cuesta, 80; Approaches to the Theater of Calderon, UP of Am, 82; Lope de Vega's La fabula de Perseo, Reichenberger, 85; Editing the Comedia, Mish Romance Studies, 85; transl, Lope de Vega's Acting Is Believing, Trinity UP, 86; Antonio Mira de Amescua's The Devil's slave, Doehouse, 89; ed, Editing the Comedia II, Mich Romance Studies, 91; Antonio Enriquez Gomez's The Perfect King, Bilingual Rev/Press, 91; Calderon de la Barca's Suenos hay que verdad son, Reichenberger, 97; Auth, Coat of Many Cultures: The Story of Joseph in Spanish Literature, 1200-1492, Jewish Publ Soc, 97; The Story of Joseph in Spanish Golden Age Drama, Bucknell UP, 98; over 60 articles & book reviews. **CONTACT ADDRESS** Dept Romance Lang, Pomona Col, 550 N Harvard Ave, Claremont, CA 91711-6369. **EMAIL** mmcgaha@pomona.edu

MCGARRELL, HEDY M.
DISCIPLINE LINGUISTICS **EDUCATION** Univ Concordia, BA; Univ Ottawa, MA, PhD. **CAREER** Assoc prof. **RESEARCH** Development of metalinguistic ability in first and second language acquisition; Acquisition of temporality in second/subsequent languages; Writing skills in second/subsequent languages; Language teacher development; Self-directed learning. **SELECTED PUBLICATIONS** Auth, "Writing a Research Paper: Eight Steps to Keep on Track," Intl Jour for Tchrs Eng Wrtg Skills, Vol 1, No 1, 95; "Exchanging Superstitions for Writing Fluency," Virtual Connections: Online Act and Proj for Networking Lang Learners, Univ Hawaii, 95; "Pen Pals for Purpose, Practice and Product," Virtual Connections: Online Activities and Projects for Networking Language Learners, Honolulu, HI: Univ Hawaii, 95; "Self-Directed Learning Contracts to Individualize Language Learning in the Classroom," For Lang Annals 96, Vol 29, 96. **CONTACT ADDRESS** Humanities, Brock Univ, 500 Glenridge Ave, Saint Catharines, ON, Canada L2S 3A1. **EMAIL** hmcgarre@spartan.ac.BrockU.CA

MCGINNIS, SCOTT G.
PERSONAL Born 05/02/1955, Fostoria, OH, m, 1985, 1 child **DISCIPLINE** EAST ASIAN LANGUAGE, LITERATURE **EDUCATION** Univ of the State of NYork, BS, 80; Ohio State Univ, MA, 84; PhD, 90. **CAREER** Asst Prof, Univ of Md Col Park, 93-00; Exec Dir, Nat Coun of Orgn of Less Commonly Taught Lang, 99-; Sr Assoc for Projects, Nat For Lang Center, 99-. **HONORS AND AWARDS** Who's Who in Am (54th, 55th ed); Who's Who in the E (27th ed); Phi Kappa Phi. **MEMBERSHIPS** Chinese Lang Teachers Asn, Am Asn for Appl Ling, Asn for Asian Studies. **RESEARCH** Chinese language (language acquisition, pedagogy, testing, linguistics). **SELECTED PUBLICATIONS** Coauth, "Learning Less Commonly Taught Languages: An Agreement on the Bases for the Training of Teachers," Pathways Ser No FLP01 For Lang Publ (Columbus, OH), 95; auth, "Tonal distinction errors by beginning Chinese language students: A comparative study of American English and Japanese native speakers," in Chinese Pedagogy: An Emerging Field, ed. Scott McGinnis (Columbus, OH: For Lang Publ, 96), 81-91; auth, "Teaching Chinese to the Chinese: The Development of an Assessment and Instructional Model," in Patterns and Policies: The Changing Demographics of Foreign Language Instruction, ed. Judith E. Liskin-Gasparro (Boston: Heinle & Heinle, 96), 107-121; ed, Chinese Pedagogy: An Emerging Field, For Lang Publ (Columbus, OH) 96; auth, "Tonal Spelling versus Diacritics for Teaching Pronunciation of Mandarin Chinese," The Modern Lang J 81.2 (Summer 97): 228-236; coauth, "How to From a Partitive Construction in Chinese," J of the Chinese Lang Teachers Asn 33.1 (Feb 98): 31-50; auth, "Articulation," in Mapping the Course of the Chinese Language Filed: CLTA Monographt #3, ed. Madeline Chu (Kalamazoo, MI: Chinese Lang Teachers Asn, 99), 331-344; auth, "Reassessing Authentic Materials," n Mapping the Course

of the Chinese Language Filed: CLTA Monographt #3, ed. Madeline Chu (Kalamazoo, MI: Chinese Lang Teachers Asn, 99), 229-253; auth, "Student Goals and Approaches," n Mapping the Course of the Chinese Language Filed: CLTA Monographt #3, ed. Madeline Chu (Kalamazoo, MI: Chinese Lang Teachers Asn, 99), 151-188. **CONTACT ADDRESS** Nat For Lang Center, 1619 Massachusetts Ave, Washington, DC 20036. **EMAIL** smcginnis@nflc.org

MCGLATHERY, JAMES MELVILLE

PERSONAL Born 11/22/1936, New Orleans, LA, m, 1963, 4 children **DISCIPLINE** GERMANIC LANGUAGES **EDUCATION** Princeton Univ, AB, 58; Yale Univ, AM, 59, PhD(Ger), 64. **CAREER** Instr Ger, Phillips Andover Acad, 59-60; instr, Harvard Univ, 63-65; from Asst Prof to Assoc Prof, 65-84, Prof Ger, Univ Ill, Urbana-Champaign, 84-00, Dept Head, 85-95; Managing ed, J English & Ger Philol, 72-00; Vis Prof, Univ Gottingen, Ger, 93-94; Prof Emeritus, 00-. **RESEARCH** Romanticism and the 19th century literature. **SELECTED PUBLICATIONS** Auth, The Suicide Motif in E.T.A. Hoffmann's Der goldne Topf, Monatshefte, 6/66; Kleist's uber das Marionetten-Theater, Ger Life & Lett, 7/67; Fear of perdition in Droste-Hulshoff's Judenbuche, In: Lebendige Form: Festschrift fur Heinrich E K Henel, Wilhelm Fink, Munich, 70; Kleist's Version of Moliere's Amphitryon: olympian cuckolding and unio mystica, In: Moliere and the Commonwealth of Letters, Univ Miss, 75; Der Himmel hangt ihm voller Geigen: E T A Hoffmann's Rat Krespel, Die Fermate, and Der Baron von B, Ger Quart, 3/78; Bald dein Fall ins-Ehebett?: A new reading of E T A Hoffmann's Goldner Topf, Ger Rev, No 3, 78; Demon love: E T A Hoffmann's Elixiere des Teufels, Colloquia Germanica, Nos 1/2, 79; Mysticism and Sexuality: E T A Hoffmann Part One: Hoffmann and His Sources, Peter Lang, Berne, 81; Desire's Sway: The Plays and Stories of Heinrich von Kleist, Wayne State Univ Press, 83; Mysticism and Sexuality: E T A Hoffmann Part Two: Interpretations of the Tales, Peter Lang, Berne, 85; Fairy Tale Romance: The Grimms, Basile, Perrault, Univ Ill Press, 91; Grimms' Fairy Tales: A History of Criticism on a Popular Classic, Literary Criticism in Perspective, Camden House, 93; E.T.A. Hoffmann, Twayne's World Author's Series, 868, Twayne Publishers, 97; Wagner's Operas and Desire, North American Studies in Nineteenth-Century German Literature, 22, Peter Lang, 98; author of numerous journal articles and other book contributions. **CONTACT ADDRESS** Dept of Ger Lang & Lit, Univ of Illinois, Urbana-Champaign, 707 S Mathews Ave, Urbana, IL 61801-3675. **EMAIL** mcglath@uiuc.edu

MCGOWAN, JOHN P.

PERSONAL Born 07/12/1953, Rockville Centre, NY, m, 1984, 2 children **DISCIPLINE** ENGLISH, COMPARATIVE LITERATURE **EDUCATION** Georgetown Univ, AB, 74; SUNY at Buffalo, PhD, 78. **CAREER** Asst prof, Univ of Mich, 79-82; ed asst, Univ of Calif Pr, 83-84; asst prof to assoc prof, Univ of Rochester, 84-92; prof, Univ of NC, 92-. **HONORS AND AWARDS** NEH Fel, 89; NEH Seminar, 97; Chapman Family Teaching Awd, Univ NC, 99. **MEMBERSHIPS** MLA. **RESEARCH** Literary Theory, American Pragmatism, Victorian Literature, Political Philosophy. **SELECTED PUBLICATIONS** Auth, Representation and Revelation: Victorian Realism from Carlisle to Yeats, 86; auth, Postmodernism and its Critics; coed, Hannah Arendt and the Meaning of Politics, 91; coed, Hannah Arendt and the Meaning of Politics, 97; auth, Hannah Arendt: An Introduction, 98; coed, Norton Anthology of Theory and Criticism, (forthcoming). **CONTACT ADDRESS** Dept English, Univ of No Carolina, Chapel Hill, CB # 3520, Chapel Hill, NC 27599-3520. **EMAIL** jpm@email.unc.edu

MCGRATH, MICHAEL J.

PERSONAL Born 08/19/1966, Holland, PA, m, 1998, 1 child **DISCIPLINE** SPANISH **EDUCATION** Univ of KY, PhD, 98; Middlebury Col, MA, 89; GA S Univ, BA, 88 **CAREER** Asst Prof, 97-, Kings Col; asst prof, Georgia Southern Univ, 00-. **HONORS AND AWARDS** Sigma Delta Pi, 86 **MEMBERSHIPS** Am Classical League; Cervantes Soc of Am **RESEARCH** Modern Spanish lit; early modern Spanish lit. **SELECTED PUBLICATIONS** Bulletin of the Comediantes, vol 51, nos 1 & 2, 99. **CONTACT ADDRESS** Georgia So Univ, PO Box 8081, Statesboro, GA 30460. **EMAIL** mjmcgrat@kings.edu

MCGREGOR, JAMES H. S.

PERSONAL Born 10/01/1946, Frostburg, MD, m, 1985, 2 children **DISCIPLINE** COMPARATIVE LITERATURE **EDUCATION** Princeton Univ, BA, 68; PhD, 75. **CAREER** Asst prof, Univ Ga, 81-; asst prof, Ga Studies Abroad Prog, Cortona, Italy, summer 83; vis asst prof, Univ Calif, Berkeley, 84-85; assoc prof, Univ Ga, 88-. **HONORS AND AWARDS** Rome Prize Fel in Post-Classical Humanistic Studies, Am Acad in Rome, 81-82; Creative Res Medal, Univ Ga. **MEMBERSHIPS** Am Boccaccio Asn, Am Asn of Italian Studies, MLA, Asn Int per gli Studi di Lingua e Letteratura Italiana. **RESEARCH** Renaissance Italian literature, Boccaccio, Renaissance fictions about artists, Rome. **SELECTED PUBLICATIONS** Auth, The Shades of Aeneas: The Imitation of Vergil and the History of Paganism in Boccaccio's Filostrato, Filocolo and Teseida, Athens and London: Univ of Ga Press (91); auth, The Image of Antiquity in Boccaccio's Filocolo, Filostrato and Teseida, Studies in Italian Culture: Literature in History, Volume 1, Aldo Scaglione, gen ed, NY, Bern, Frankfurt am Main, Paris: Peter Lang (91); transl with intro and annotations, The Sack of Rome, Luigi Guicciardini, Il Sacco di Roma, NY: Italica Press (93); auth, Approaches to Teaching Boccaccio's Decameron, NY: Modern Lang Asn (2000); co-ed with Charlotte Nichols and John Monfasani, Renaissance Naples, 1400-1600, NY: Italica Press (forthcoming 2000); auth, Tricks of the Light Fantastic: Art and Artists in Renaissance Fiction (submitted). **CONTACT ADDRESS** Dept Comparative Lit, Univ of Georgia, 232 Joe Brown Hall, Athens, GA 30602-6204. **EMAIL** mcgregor@uga.edu

MCGUIRE, DONALD T., JR.

DISCIPLINE CLASSICS **EDUCATION** Brown Univ, BA; Cornell Univ, MA; PhD. **CAREER** Asst prof, Univ Southern CA, 84-92; to dir summer progr Greece, 86-88; asst prof, SUNY Buffalo, 92. **RESEARCH** Latin imperial poetry; epic poetry; Greek and Roman hist and historiography; hist of archit; and mod popular cult and the ancient world. **SELECTED PUBLICATIONS** Auth, Textual Strategies and Political Suicide in Flavian Epic in The Imperial Muse: Ramus Essays on Roman Literature of the Empire, vol 2; History Compressed: The Roman Names of Silius' Cannae Episode, Latomus, 95. **CONTACT ADDRESS** Dept Classics, SUNY, Buffalo, 712 Clemens Hall, Buffalo, NY 14260.

MCHUGH, MICHAEL P.

PERSONAL Born 06/07/1933, Lackawanna, NY, m, 1961, 4 children **DISCIPLINE** CLASSICAL PHILOLOGY, PATRISTIC STUDIES **EDUCATION** Cath Univ Am, AB, 55, MA, 56, PhD(classics), 65. **CAREER** From instr to asst prof classics & humanities, Howard Univ, 58-68; from asst prof to assoc prof, 68-77; Prof Classics, Univ Conn-Storrs, 77-97; Prof Emer, Univ Conn-Storrs, 97- . **MEMBERSHIPS** NAm Patristic Soc; Am Philol Asn; Vergilian Soc; Am Class League; Medieval Acad Am. **RESEARCH** St Ambrose; Prosper of Aquitaine; textual studies. **SELECTED PUBLICATIONS** Auth, The Carmen de Providentia Dei: A Revised Text with Introduction, Translation and Notes, Cath Univ Pr (Washington, DC), 64; auth, St. Ambrose: Seven Exegetical Works, Cath Univ Pr (Washington, DC), 72; assoc ed, The Encyclopedia of Early Christianity, Garland Pub (New York), 90, 97. **CONTACT ADDRESS** 274 Hanks Hill Rd, Storrs, CT 06268.

MCKAY, ALEXANDER G.

PERSONAL Born 12/24/1924, Toronto, ON, Canada **DISCIPLINE** CLASSICS **EDUCATION** Univ Toronto, BA, 46; Yale Univ, MA, 47; Princeton Univ, PhD, 50. **CAREER** Instr, Princeton Univ, 47-49; instr, Wells Col, 49-50; instr, Univ Pa, 50-51; instr, Univ Man, 51-52; asst prof, Mt Allison Univ, 52-53; asst prof, Waterloo Col, 53-55; Dir, Classical Sumer Sch Italy, Vergilian Soc Am, 55-97; asst prof, Univ Man, 55-57; asst prof, 57-59, assoc prof, 59-61, prof, 61-90, Prof Emer Classics, McMaster Univ, 90-, chmn, 62-68, 76-79, dean hum, 68-73; adj prof hum, York Univ, 90-96; vis lectr, Concordia Univ, 92-93. **HONORS AND AWARDS** Off, Order Can; Queen's Silver Jubilee Medal; Centenary Medal, Royal Soc Can; Canada 125 Medal; Woodrow Wilson fel; Killam sr res fel; LLD(hon), Univ Man, 86; LLD(hon), Brock Univ, 90; LLD(hon), Queen's Univ, 91; DLitt (hon), McMaster Univ, 92; DLitt(hon), Waterloo Univ, 93. **MEMBERSHIPS** Acad Hum Soc Sci; Class Asn Can; Vergilian Soc; Int Acad Union **RESEARCH** Ancient Roman architecture and literature. **SELECTED PUBLICATIONS** Auth, Naples and Campania, 62; auth, Victorian Architecture in Hamilton, 67; auth, Vergil's Italy, 70; auth, Ancient Campania, 72; auth, Houses, Villas and Palaces in the Roman World, 75; auth, Vitruvius, Architect and Engineer, 78, 85; auth, Romische Hauser, Villen und Palaste, 80; auth, Roma Antiqua, Latium & Erturia, 86; coauth, Roman Lyric Poetry: Catullus and Horace, 69, 74; coauth, Roman Satire: Horace, Juvenal, Persius et al, 76; coauth, Selections from Vergil's Aeneid, Books I, IV, VI (Dido and Aeneas), 88; coauth, The Two Worlds of the Poet: New Perspectives on Vergil, 92; coauth, Tragedy, Love and Change: Roman Poetic Themes and Variations, 94. **CONTACT ADDRESS** Classics Dept, McMaster Univ, 706 Togo Salmon Hall, Hamilton, ON, Canada L8S 4M2.

MCKAY, DOUGLAS R.

PERSONAL Born 11/12/1936, Salt Lake City, UT, m, 1989, 2 children **DISCIPLINE** SPANISH LANGUAGE & LITERATURE **EDUCATION** Univ Utah, BA, 62; Univ Oregon, MA, 64; Michigan State Univ, PhD, 68. **CAREER** From asst prof to prof, 68-99, chemn 68-75, 81, 97, Prof Emeritus, Dept of Lang and Cultures, 99- , Univ Colorado, Colorado Springs. **HONORS AND AWARDS** Hon Woodrow Wilson fel; NDEA fel; NEH Summer Sem grants; res and tchg awards; Civic Service Awd, UCCS. **RESEARCH** Twentieth century Spanish peninsular drama; local and regional history. **CONTACT ADDRESS** 1116 Westmoor Dr, Colorado Springs, CO 80904. **EMAIL** mckdoug36@hotmail.com

MCKENNA, ANDREW JOSEPH

PERSONAL Born 11/29/1942, Massapequa, NY, m, 1964, 2 children **DISCIPLINE** FRENCH LITERATURE **EDUCATION** Col Holy Cross, BA, 64; Johns Hopkins Univ, MA, 66, PhD, 70. **CAREER** Instr French, Northwestern Univ, 67-70; asst prof, 71-80, assoc prof French, Loyola Univ, Chicago, 80-86. **RESEARCH** Nineteenth century French literature; 20th century French literature; critical theory. **SELECTED PUBLICATIONS** Auth, Violence and Difference: Girard, Perrida and Deconstruction, University of Illinois Press, 92; ed in chief, Contagion: Journal of Violence, Milnesis, and Culture, 96; auth, "Religious Differance," Anthropoetics 4 (98); auth, "Aristotle's Theatre of Envy," in Philosophical Designs for a Socio-Cultural Transformation: Beyond Violence and the Modern Era, ed. T. Yamamoto (Tokyo: Roman and Littlefield, 99), 633-654. **CONTACT ADDRESS** Dept of Mod Lang and Lit, Loyola Univ, Chicago, 6525 N Sheridan Rd, Chicago, IL 60626-5385. **EMAIL** amckenn@luc.edu

MCKEOWN, JAMES C.

DISCIPLINE CLASSICAL STUDIES **EDUCATION** Cambridge Univ, PhD, 78. **CAREER** Dept Classics, Wisc Univ **RESEARCH** Latin literature. **SELECTED PUBLICATIONS** Auth, pubs on Latin poetry, and Ovid's Amores. **CONTACT ADDRESS** Dept of Classics, Univ of Wisconsin, Madison, 500 Lincoln Drive, Madison, WI 53706. **EMAIL** jmckeown@macc.wisc.edu

MCKINLEY, MARY B.

PERSONAL Born 05/15/1943, Pittsburgh, PA **DISCIPLINE** FRENCH RENAISSANCE LITERATURE **EDUCATION** Seton Hill Col, BA, 65; Univ Wis, MA, 66; Rutgers Univ, PhD(French), 74. **CAREER** Instr French, Albertus Magnus Col, 67-69; acad dir Ital, Exp Int Living, 72-73; asst prof, 74-80, Assoc Prof French, Univ Va, 80-, Mem Cent Exec Comt, Folger Inst Renaissance & 18th Century Studies, 76- **MEMBERSHIPS** MLA: Renaissance Soc Am; Am Asn Teachers Fr. **RESEARCH** Montaigne; history of rhetoric and language theory. **SELECTED PUBLICATIONS** **CONTACT ADDRESS** Dept of French, Univ of Virginia, 1 Cabell Hall, Charlottesville, VA 22903.

MCKINNEY, MARK

DISCIPLINE FRENCH **EDUCATION** Univ Tex at Austin, BA, MA; Cornell Univ, PhD. **CAREER** Asst prof to assoc prof, Miami Univ **RESEARCH** Fiction from the North African diaspora in France; nationalism and identity; racism and gendered identities; popular culture and imperialism; North African literature; 20th-century French and francophone literatures and cultures. **SELECTED PUBLICATIONS** Auth, Haunting Figures in Contemporary Discourse and Popular Culture in France in Sites: The Journal of Twentieth-Century/Contemporary French Studies Vol 1, 97; co-ed, Post-Colonial Cultures in France, Routledge, 97. **CONTACT ADDRESS** Dept of French and Italian, Miami Univ, Oxford, OH 45056. **EMAIL** mckinnm@muohio.edu

MCKNIGHT, EDGAR VERNON

PERSONAL Born 11/21/1931, Wilson, SC, m, 1955, 2 children **DISCIPLINE** RELIGION, CLASSICAL LANGUAGES **EDUCATION** Col Charleston, BS, 53; Southern Baptist Theol Sem, BD, 56, PhD, 60; Oxford Univ, MLitt, 78. **CAREER** Chaplain, Chowan Col, 60-63; from asst prof to assoc prof, 63-74, assoc dean acad affairs, 70-73, prof relig & classics, 74-82, chemn, dept classics, 78-80, chemn, dept relig, 91-95, William R Kenan Prof Relig, Furman Univ, 82-; vis prof, Southern Baptist Theol Sem, 66-67; Fulbright sr res prof, Univ Tubingen, 81-82, Univ Muenster, 95-96; NEH study grant, Yale Univ, summer, 80; Bye-fel Robinson Col, Univ Cambridge, 88-89. **HONORS AND AWARDS** Bk of Year Awd, MLA, 78. **MEMBERSHIPS** Soc Bibl Lit; Am Acad Relig; Am Schs Orient Res; Studiorum Novi Testamenti Soc. **RESEARCH** Biblical scholarship among American and Baptist scholars, espec A T Robertson; Biblical hermeneutics; structuralism and semiotics. **SELECTED PUBLICATIONS** Coauth, A History of Chowan College, Graphic Arts, 64; auth, Opening the Bible: A Guide to Understanding the Scriptures, Broadman, 67; coauth, Introd to the New Testament, Ronald 69; auth, What is Form Criticism?, In: Series on Introduction to Biblical Scholarship, Fortress, 69; coauth, Can the Griesbach Hypothesis be Falsified?, J Bibl Lit, 9/72; auth, Structure and Meaning in Biblical Narrative, Perspectives Relig Studies, spring 76; Meaning in Texts: The Historical Shaping of a Narrative Hermeneutics, Fortress, 78; The Bible and the Reader, Fortress, 85; Postmodern Use of the Bible, Abringdon, 88; ed, Reader Perspectives on the New Testament, Semeia 48, 89; NT ed, Mercer Dictionary of the Bible, 90; NT ed, Mercer Commentary on the Bible, Mercer, 94; co-ed, The New Literary Criticism and the New Testament, Sheffield and Trinity, 94. **CONTACT ADDRESS** Dept of Relig, Furman Univ, 3300 Poinsett Hwy, Greenville, SC 29613-1218. **EMAIL** edgar.mcknight@furman.edu

MCKNIGHT, PHILLIP S.

PERSONAL Born 08/29/1942, Seattle, WA, m, 1998, 1 child **DISCIPLINE** GERMAN **EDUCATION** Univ Colo, BA; MA, 69; Brown Univ, PhD, 78. **CAREER** Prof, Chair, Univ Ky, 82-01; prof, chair, Ga Inst of Tech, 01- **HONORS AND AWARDS** Phi Beta Kappa; DOE Title VI co-recipient; NDEA Fel, 67-70; Woodrow Wilson, 71-72; Lufbruckendank, 72-72; Mellon, 79-80; IRES, 83, 84; DAAD, 95, 96; Fulbright, 97-98.

MEMBERSHIPS MLA, AATG, Lessing Soc, Johann Karl Wezel Soc. **RESEARCH** 18th Century Literature, GDR Literature, History and Literature, Christoph Hein, Johann Karl Wezel, German Drama, Business German. **SELECTED PUBLICATIONS** Auth, Versuch einer Gesamtbibliographie uber Johann Karl Wezel, Wezels Kritische Schriften, Metzler, 71; AUTH, The Novels of Johann Karl Wezel. Satirc, Realism and Social Criticism in Late 18th Century Literature, NY Univ Ottendorfer Series, Lang, 81; auth, Ein Mosaik zu Christoph Heins Roman Horns Ende, Sinn und Form (87); auth, "Wezelforschung in der DDR: Miszellaneen, Material und Mutmabungen aus Sondershausen und Leipzig," Lessing Yearbook, (88); aith, "Lieber Autor, wie soll ich leben? Aufklarung und die Literatur der DDR," Aufklarung nach Lessing, Berlag der Lessing Gesellschaft, (92); auth, "Iphigenia, King Arthur, and the East German Stage after Unification," Contemp Theatre Rev, (95); auth, Understanding Christoph Hein, Univ SCar Pr, 95; auth and ed, Johann Karl Wezels Padagogische Schriften, Regensburger Beitrage zur deutschen Sprach-und Literaturwissenschaft, Lang, 96; auth, Wezel Jahrbuch. Schriften zur Europaischen Aufklarung, Wehrhahn Verlag, (97). **CONTACT ADDRESS** Sch of Mod Lang, Georgia Inst of Tech, Atlanta, GA 30332-0375.

MCKULIK, BEN

DISCIPLINE COMPARATIVE LITERATURE **EDUCATION** Princeton Univ, AB; Univ SC, PhD. **CAREER** Prof; **SELECTED PUBLICATIONS** Areas: Jungian archetypes and a variety of critical approaches to international literature. **CONTACT ADDRESS** York Col, Pennsylvania, 441 Country Club Road, York, PA 17403.

MCLEAN, HUGH

PERSONAL Born 02/05/1925, Denver, CO, m, 1957, 3 children **DISCIPLINE** SLAVIC LANGUAGES & LITERATURES **EDUCATION** Yale Univ, AB, 47; Columbia Univ, AM, 49; Harvard Univ, PhD(Slavic lang & lit), 56. **CAREER** From instr to asst prof Slavic Lang & Lit, Harvard Univ, 53-59; from assoc prof to prof Russ Lit, Univ Chicago, 59-68, chmn Dept Slavic Lang & Lit, 61-67; chmn Dept, 70-72, 74-76, dean Div Humanities, Col Lett & Sci, 76-81, actg provost & dean, 80-81, prof Slavic Lang & Lit, Univ Calif, Berkeley, 68-94; prof Emeritus, 94; Fulbright Award, UK, 58-59; Am Coun Learned Soc fel Humanities, 58-59; Guggenheim fel, 65-66; IREX fellowships to Russian Academy of Sciences, 83; 92. **HONORS AND AWARDS** Festschrift; O Rus! Studia litteraria in honorem Hugh McLean, 95. **MEMBERSHIPS** Am Asn Teachers Slavic & East Europ Lang; Am Asn Advan Slavic Studies. **RESEARCH** Russian literature of the 19th and 20th centuries. **SELECTED PUBLICATIONS** Auth, The development of modern Russian literature, Slavic Rev, 9/62; Nikolai Leskov: The Man and his Art, Harvard Univ, 77. **CONTACT ADDRESS** Dept of Slavic Lang & Lit, Univ of California, Berkeley, 6210 Dwinelle Hall, Berkeley, CA 94720-2979. **EMAIL** hmclean@uclink4.berkeley.edu

MCLENDON, WILL LOVING

PERSONAL Born 08/26/1925, Center, TX **DISCIPLINE** FRENCH **EDUCATION** Univ Tex, BS, 45; Middlebury Col, MA, 47; Univ Paris, DUniv, 52. **CAREER** Instr French, Tex Technol Col, 47-48; instr, Southern Methodist Univ, 50; from asst prof to assoc prof, 53-68, Prof French, Univ Houston, Chmn Dept, 77-. **HONORS AND AWARDS** Chevalier, Palmes Academiques, 65. **RESEARCH** The 20th century novel; the works of Jean Giraudoux; modern poetry. **SELECTED PUBLICATIONS** Co-transl, Charles Mauron, Introduction to the Psychoanalysis of Mallarme, Univ Calif, 63; auth, Giraudoux and the impossible couple, PMLA, 5/67; Themes wagneriens dans les romans de Julien Gracq, Fr Rev, 2/68; Lettre inedite de Marcel Proust a Leon Bailby, Soc Amis Marcel Proust, 71; Proust: la presentation differee, Revue Pacifique, 77; The Grotesque in Jean Lorrain's New Byzantium, in pre-text, text, context, Ohio State Univ, 80; Une Tenebreuse Carriere: Le Comte de Courchamps, Minard, Paris, 81. **CONTACT ADDRESS** Dept of French, Univ of Houston, Houston, TX 77004.

MCMANUS, JAMES

PERSONAL Born 03/22/1951, New York, NY, m, 1992, 4 children **DISCIPLINE** COMPARATIVE LITERATURE **EDUCATION** Univ Illinois, MA, 77; Univ Illinois, BA, 74. **CAREER** Prof, Chair, Dept of Liberal Arts, The School of the Art Institute of Chicago, 87-90; Chair, Faculty Senate, 92-94; Founding Dir, MFA in Writing, 96; Vis Prof, Univ of Illinois at Chicago; Loyola Univ; Kalamazoo Col; Warren Wilson MFA Program; Glasgow School of Art; SACI in Florence. **HONORS AND AWARDS** Di Castagnola Awd, Poetry Society of America, for Tunnel of Love, 98; Bellagio Residency, Rockefeller Foundation, for Going to the Sun/Tunnel of Love, 97; Society of Midland Authors for Going to the Sun, 97; Carl Sandburg Prize for Going to the Sun, 96; Guggenheim Fel, 94-95; Travel Awd from Arts International, 90; Shifting Foundation Fellowship for Chin Music, 88; NEA Fellowship in prose, 85; Illinois Arts Council Fellowship in prose, 85; NEA Fellowship in poetry, 79. **MEMBERSHIPS** PEN. **RESEARCH** Joyce; Beckett; Casanova; Literature; Science of Poker. **SELECTED PUBLICATIONS** Auth, Antonio Salazar is Dead, prose poems, Syncline Press, 79; auth, "Out of the Blue, a novel, Crown, 84, paper, Grove Press, 89; auth, "Curtains, stories, Another Chicago Press, 85; auth, "Chin Music, a novel, Crown, 1985; paper, Grove Press, 87; Ghost Waves, a novel, Grove Press, 88; Great America, poems, HarperCollins, 93; auth, Going to the Sun, a novel, HarperCollins, 96; paper, 97; auth, "Tunnel of Love," stories (in final stages of completion); auth, "Spike Logic," poems, Harper Collins, 01; auth, "Tunnel of Love, stories(in final stages of completion). **CONTACT ADDRESS** Dept Liberal Arts, Sch of the Art Inst of Chicago, 37 South Wabash Ave, Chicago, IL 60603-3002. **EMAIL** jarra@artic.edu

MCNAMEE, KATHLEEN

PERSONAL Born 11/27/1949, Cambridge, MA, m, 1986, 2 children **DISCIPLINE** CLASSICS **EDUCATION** Duke Univ, PhD, 77. **CAREER** From instr to prof to ch, Dept Classics, Greek, &Latin, Wayne State Univ, 76-; interim dean, Col Lib Arts, Wayne State Univ, 92-94, chair 94-99. **MEMBERSHIPS** Am Philol Asn. **RESEARCH** Papyrology; Greek literature; Latin poetry. **SELECTED PUBLICATIONS** Auth, Abbreviations in Greek Literary Papyri and Ostraca, 81; auth, Sigla and Select Marginalia in Greek Literary Papyri: Papyrologica Bruxellensia, Aug, 92; auth, Classical Studies Presented to William Hailey Willis, Bulletin of the Am Soc Papyrologists, 85; auth, Another Chapter in the History of Scholia, Class Quart, 98; auth, An Innovation in Annotated Codices on Papyrus, Akten des 21, Internationalen Papyrologenkongresses, Berlin, 1995, 97; auth, Missing Links in the Development of Scholia, Greek, Roman, & Byzantine Studies, July, 96. **CONTACT ADDRESS** Dept of Classics, Greek & Latin, Wayne State Univ, 431 Manoogian Hall, Detroit, MI 48202. **EMAIL** k.mcnamee@wayne.edu

MCNEILL, DAVID

PERSONAL Born 12/21/1933, Santa Rosa, CA, m, 1957, 2 children **DISCIPLINE** PSYCHOLINGUISTICS **EDUCATION** Univ Calif, Berkeley, AB, 53, PhD(psychol), 62. **CAREER** Res fel, Ctr Cognitive Studies, Harvard Univ, 63-65; from asst prof to assoc prof psychol, Univ Mich, 65-68; Prof Behav Sci & Ling, Univ Chicago, 69-, Guggenheim Found fel, 73-74; mem, Inst Advan Studies, 73-75. **MEMBERSHIPS** Ling Soc Am; Am Asn Advan Sci. **RESEARCH** Psychological processes involved in the use of language; comparison of gestures for language; development of gesture in children. **SELECTED PUBLICATIONS** Auth, Abstract Deixis, Semiotica, vol 0095, 93. **CONTACT ADDRESS** Dept of Behav Sci, Univ of Chicago, Chicago, IL 60637.

MCNERNEY, KATHLEEN

PERSONAL Born Albuquerque, NM **DISCIPLINE** HISPANIC LITERATURE **EDUCATION** Univ NMex, BA, 67; MA, 69; PhD, 77. **CAREER** Prof, W Va Univ, 80. **HONORS AND AWARDS** Benedum Distinguished Scholar Awd, 95; Singer Endowed Chair, 00. **MEMBERSHIPS** MLA; N Am Catalan Soc; Asoc Int de Hispanistas. **RESEARCH** Literature by women. **SELECTED PUBLICATIONS** Auth, The Influence of Ausias March on Early Golden Age Castilian Poetry, Rodopi (Amsterdam), 82; auth, Tirant lo Blanc Revised: A Critical Study, Fifteenth-Century Studies, Ann Arbor, 83; coed, Women Writers of Spain: An Annotated Bio-bibliographical Guide, Greenwood Pr, (Westport, CT), 86; auth, On Our Own Behalf: Women's Tales from Catalonia, Univ of Neb Pr, (Lincoln), 88; coed, Feminine Concerns in Contemporary Spanish Women Writers, Scripta Humanistica, (Potomac, MD), 88; auth, Understanding Garcia Marquez, Univ of SC Pr, (Columbia), 89; coauth, Espana y su civilacion, McGraw Hill, (NY), 92; coed, The Garden across the Border: Merce Rodereda's Fiction, Susquehanna Univ Pr, (Selinsgrove), 94; coed, Double Minorities of Spain: A Bio-Bibliographic Guide to Women Writers of the Catalan, Galician, and Basque Countries, MLA of Am, (NY), 94; auth, Voices and Visions: The Words and Works of Merce Rodoreda, Susquehanna Univ Pr, (Selinsgrove), 99. **CONTACT ADDRESS** Dept Foreign Lang, West Virginia Univ, Morgantown, PO Box 6298, Morgantown, WV 26506-6298. **EMAIL** kmcnerney@as.wvu.edu

MEAD, GERALD

DISCIPLINE FRENCH **EDUCATION** Yale Univ, PhD. **CAREER** Assoc prof, Northestern Univ; past dir, CIC Summer Prog Univ Laval, Quebec; asst dean, Col Arts Sci. **HONORS AND AWARDS** E. Leroy Hall Awd, 77; Excellence tchg, 97. **RESEARCH** Quebec literature; 19th century France; modernism; cultural studies. **SELECTED PUBLICATIONS** Auth, The Surrealist Image: A Stylistic Study and of articles on literary style and on writers Gabrielle Roy and Maupassant; The Representation of Solitude in Gabrielle Roy's Bonheur d'occasion, Quebec Studies, 88; The Representation of Fictional Character, Style, 90; Social Commentary and Sexuality in Maupassant's La Maison Tellier, 19th-Century Fr Studies, 96. **CONTACT ADDRESS** Dept of French, Northwestern Univ, 1801 Hinman, Evanston, IL 60208. **EMAIL** g-mead@northwestern.edu

MEADORS, GARY T.

PERSONAL Born 06/03/1945, Connersville, IN, m, 1967 **DISCIPLINE** GREEK, NEW TESTAMENT **EDUCATION** Grace Coll and Theol Sem. ThD, 83. **CAREER** Asst Prof, 79-83, Piedmont Baptist Coll; Prof of NT, 83-93, Grace Theol Sem; Prof of NT, 93-95, Baptist Sem of PA; Prof of NT, 95-, Grand Rapids Baptist Sem; Dean of the School of Theology, 00-. **HONORS AND AWARDS** Homer A. Kent Sr. Awd in Church History, 75; Summa cum laude Mdiv, 76; Alumni Educational Achievement Awd, 96. **MEMBERSHIPS** ETS, IBR, SBL. **RESEARCH** New Testament; Ethics. **SELECTED PUBLICATIONS** Auth, "John R.W. Stott on Social Action," GTJ 1:2 NS, 80; auth, "The Poor in the Beatituder of Matthew and Luke," GTJ 6:2 NS, 85; auth, Can a Believer Fall from Grace?, Spire 14:2, 86; auth, "New Testament Essays," Winona: BMH Books, 91; Discipleship-Another Nuance to Consider, Exposition 4:3, 93; Evangelical Dictionary of Biblical Theology, ed by Walter Elwell, Grand Rapids, Baker Book House, 96; Love is the Law of Spiritual Formation, Presidential address to the Midwest Region Meeting of the Evangelical Theological Society, 98; Why Are They Looking At Jesus?, The Jesus Seminar, Baptist Bulletin, 97. **CONTACT ADDRESS** Grand Rapids Baptist Sem, 1001 E Beltline NE, Grand Rapids, MI 49525. **EMAIL** gary_t_meadors@cornerstone.edu

MEADOWS, PATRICK

DISCIPLINE FRENCH LITERATURE **EDUCATION** Princeton Univ, PhD, 90. **CAREER** Asst prof. **SELECTED PUBLICATIONS** Auth, Le Thanh Khoi, Pham Van Ky et Pierre Do Dinh: Trois poetes vietnamiens face a la transition entre societe archaique et societe moderne, 97. **CONTACT ADDRESS** Dept of French and Italian, Indiana Univ, Bloomington, 300 N Jordan Ave, Bloomington, IN 47405.

MEANS, JAMES

PERSONAL Born 07/12/1932, Springfield, IL, m, 6 children **DISCIPLINE** PASTORAL MINISTRIES AND HOMILETICS **EDUCATION** Wheaton Col, BA; Denver Sem, BD; Univ Denver, MA; PhD. **CAREER** Prof, Denver Sem, 68-. **HONORS AND AWARDS** Gold Medallion Bk Awd winner; sr pastor, s gables evangel free church; pastor, evangel free churches in loomis and omaha, nebr. **MEMBERSHIPS** Soc for Pastoral Theol; Assn of Practical Theol. **SELECTED PUBLICATIONS** Auth, Leadership in Christian Ministry; auth, Effective Pastors for a New Century. **CONTACT ADDRESS** Denver Conservative Baptist Sem, PO Box 10000, Denver, CO 80250. **EMAIL** jimm@densem.edu

MEANS, JOHN B.

PERSONAL Born 01/02/1939, Cincinnati, OH, s **DISCIPLINE** LINGUISTICS **EDUCATION** Univ Ill, Urbana-Champaign, BA, 60; MA, 62; PhD, 68. **CAREER** Asst to prof, Temple Univ, 68-, co-chair, dept Spanish & Portuguese, 71-75, dir, Critical Lang Center, 75-, dir, Inst for Langs & Int Studies, 88-. **HONORS AND AWARDS** "Exec Dir Emeritus," Nat Asn of Self-Instructional Lang Progs, 99. **MEMBERSHIPS** Brazilian Studies Asn, Nat Coun Orgs of Less Commonly Taught Langs, Nat Asn of State Univs and Land Grant Cols, NASILP. **RESEARCH** Second-language acquisition in the less-commonly taught (non-Western) languages. **SELECTED PUBLICATIONS** Auth, Essays on Brazilian Literature, Simon & Schuster (71); coauth with others, Language in Education: Theory and Practice (88); numerous pubs in prof journals, 70-. **CONTACT ADDRESS** Dept Critical Lang, Temple Univ, 1114 W Berks St, Philadelphia, PA 19122-6007. **EMAIL** means@astro.temple.edu

MEDINA, CINDY

DISCIPLINE SPANISH **EDUCATION** Pa State Univ, BA, PhD. **CAREER** Coor, foreign lang. **SELECTED PUBLICATIONS** Auth, Nuevos Destinos. **CONTACT ADDRESS** York Col, Pennsylvania, 441 Country Club Road, York, PA 17403.

MEDINA, JEREMY TYLER

PERSONAL Born 08/01/1942, Orange, NJ, m, 1966, 3 children **DISCIPLINE** SPANISH, SPANISH LITERATURE, SPANISH CULTURE **EDUCATION** Princeton Univ, AB, 64; Middlebury Span Sch, Spain, MA, 66; Univ Pa, PhD(Span), 70. **CAREER** Instr Span, Phillips Acad, Andover, Mass, 64-65; from instr to asst prof, 68-75, founder and dir in residence, acad year in Spain, 74-75, 79-80, 84-85, 89-90, 93-94, 97-98, 01-02; assoc prof, 75-82, prof Span, Hamilton Col, 82-; gen dir acad year in Spain, 74-; founder and co-director Summer Instutite of Hispanic Studies (Leon), 92-. **HONORS AND AWARDS** Burgess Prof of Romance Languages and Literature, 97-. **MEMBERSHIPS** MLA; AAUP; Am Asn Teachers Span & Port. **RESEARCH** Nineteenth century Spanish realism; generations of 1898 and 1927 in Spain; Cervantes. **SELECTED PUBLICATIONS** Auth, Theme and Structure in Herrera's Cancion de Lepanto, 72 & Theme and Structure of Alarcon's El sombrero de tres picos, 73, Romance Notes; Introduction to Spanish Literature: An Analytical Approach, Harper 74, Krieger, 82; The Artistry of Blasco Ibanez' Canas y barro, Hispania, 77; Spanish Realism: The Theory and Practice of a Concept in the Nineteenth Century, Jose Porrua, 78; The Artistry of Blasco Ibanez' Flor de Mayo, Hispania, 82; Leopoldo Alas (Clarin), Vicente Blasco Ibanez, Benito Perez Galdos, and Emilia Pardo Bazan, in Critical Survey of Long Fiction, Salem Press, 84; Blasco Ibanez' Arroz y yartana, Hispanic J, 84; The Valencian Novels of Vicente Blasco Ibanez, Albatros, 84; The Psychological Novels of Vicente Blasco Ibanez, Albatross, 90; A Note on Narrative

Structure, Don Quijote, Part II, Critica Hispanica, 90; Gibraltar Interlude: the Artistry of Blasco Ibanez' Luna Benamor, Hispania, 90; From Sermon to Art: the Thesis Novels of Vicente Blasco Ibanez, Albatross, 98; Narrative Framing and the Structure of Don Quijote, Part I, Confluencia, 98. **CONTACT ADDRESS** Dept of Romance Lang, Hamilton Col, New York, 198 College Hill Rd, Clinton, NY 13323-1292. **EMAIL** jmedina@hamilton.edu

MEDINA, MANUEL F.
PERSONAL Born 10/30/1961, Ecuador, m, 1990 **DISCIPLINE** LATIN AMERICAN LITERATURE **EDUCATION** Brigham Young Univ, BA, 87; MA, 90; Univ Kans, PhD, 94. **CAREER** Teach asst, BYU, 89-90; teach asst, Univ Kans, 90-94; vis lectr, Univ Nat Autonoma de Mex, 95, 98, 99; asst prof, Univ Louisville, 94-98; assoc prof, 99-. **HONORS AND AWARDS** Laminate Scholar; Sigma Delta Pi; Intl Students Hon Roll, BYU, 85, 86, 87; Acad Scholar, 87, 89; Outstand Grad, BYU; Nat Hisp Scholar; Mod Lang Grant, 96, 97; Pres Initiative Grant, 95, 98; Coll Arts Sci Res Grant; US Dept St Grant. **MEMBERSHIPS** MLAA; AATSP; ACTFL; Asn Ecuadorianists; KCTFL; BSA. **RESEARCH** Twentieth Century Latin American Narrative; theater and film; contemporary literary theory and criticism; cultural studies; US Latino narrative; modern histiographical criticism. **SELECTED PUBLICATIONS** Auth, "La voz del subalterno y el inconsciente pólitico en la novela regiomontana de los noventa," Casa del Tiempo 2 (00): 76-77; auth, Inventando la nacion ecuatoriana en El ojo de la aguja de Alvaro San Felix," J Andinas de Lit Latinoamericana. Memorias 1, ed. Raul Vallejo (Quito: Univ Andina Simon Boliivar, 99); auth, Imaginando al otro: el deseo y la selva en El triestino James Joyce Francescoli de Guido Jalil," Todo esefuego, Serie el Prestidigitador 4, eds. Mara Garcia, Douglas Weatherford (Tlaxcala: Univ Autonoma de Tlaxcala, 99), 155-65; auth, "El objeto y el sujeto de deseo: Los nombres del aire de Alberto Ruy Sanchez," Lit Mexicana 9 (98): 155-66; auth, Heroes o antiheroes?: La escritura e invencion de la nacion ecuatoriana en La historia de Dios Alvaro San Felix," Ollantay Theater Mag 6 (98): 25-33; auth, "An/alfabetismo electronico: los desafios de la cultura hipertextual," Nuevas tecnologias para las humanidades, ed. Carmen Carrion Carranza (Mex: Facultad de Filosofia y Letras, Univ Nac Autonoma de Mex, 98), 61-78; auth, "La seduccion de los estudios culturales," Casa del Tiempo 14 (98): 39-43; co-ed, La seduccion de la escritura. Los discursos de la cultura hoy, Univ Autonoma de Mex Azcapotzalco (Mex), 97. **CONTACT ADDRESS** Dept Classical and Modern Lang, Univ of Louisville, 2301 S 3rd St, Louisville, KY 40292-0001.

MEGENNEY, WILLIAM WILBER
PERSONAL Born 04/13/1940, Langley AFB, VA, m, 1963, 3 children **DISCIPLINE** LATIN AMERICAN LINGUISTICS **EDUCATION** Rutgers Univ, BA, 62; Univ NMex, MA, 67, PhD, 69. **CAREER** Prof Span & Port, Univ Calif, Riverside, 69-. **HONORS AND AWARDS** NEH grants, 75, 81; Fulbright fel, 87. **MEMBERSHIPS** Am Asn Teachers Span & Port; Ling Soc Am; Caribbean Studies Asn; Asn Afro-Hisp & Cultural Studies. **RESEARCH** Latin American linguistics. **SELECTED PUBLICATIONS** Auth, A Bahian Heritage, Univ NC, 78; African en Venezuela: su herencia linguistica y su cultura literaria, In: Montalban series of Catholic University of Venezuela, 85; El palenquero: un lenguaje post-criollo de Colombia, Inst Caro y Cuervo, Bogota, Colombia, 86; Africa en Santo Domingo: su herencia linguistica, Museo del Hombre Dominicano and the Acad de Ciencias de la Republica Dominicana, 90; auth, Aspectos del lenguaje afronegroide en Venezuela, 99; ed, Cuba y Brasil: etnohistoria del empleo religioso del lenguaje afroamericano, Universal (Miami), 99; author of numerous articles. **CONTACT ADDRESS** Dept of Hispanic Studies, Univ of California, Riverside, 900 University Ave, Riverside, CA 92521-0001. **EMAIL** william.megenney@ucr.edu

MEIER, A. J.
PERSONAL Born 11/15/1952, IA **DISCIPLINE** LINGUISTICS **EDUCATION** Wartburg Coe, BA summa cum laude ; Univ Iowa, MA; Univ Vienna Austria, PhD. **CAREER** Univ Vienna, lectr, 81-92; Univ N Iowa, asst prof, assoc prof, 92 to 98-. **MEMBERSHIPS** TESOL; MIDTESOL; AAAL; IPra. **RESEARCH** Sociopragmatics, sociolinguistics; grammar in edu; politeness theory; apologies and conflict mgmt; intercultural communication. **SELECTED PUBLICATIONS** Auth, Apologies: What do we know?, Intl Jour of Applied Linguistics, forthcoming; Grammar in MA TESOL programs: Form function usage and application, Teacher Edu Interest Sec NL, forthcoming; Meeting the editors at Orlando, TESOL Matters, 97; What's the excuse: Image repair in Austrian German, The Mod Lang Jour, 97; Teaching the universals of politeness, Eng Lang Teach Jour, 97; Two cultures mirrored in repair work, Multilingua, 96; Hey-Lady, Dictionaries, 96; Passages of politeness, Jour of Pragmatics, 95. **CONTACT ADDRESS** Dept of English, Univ of No Iowa, Cedar Falls, IA 50613-0502. **EMAIL** aj.meier@uni.edu

MEIER, MARGA
PERSONAL Born 04/22/1922, Bad Kissingen, Germany **DISCIPLINE** GERMAN **EDUCATION** Univ Wurzburg, PhD, 44. **CAREER** Court interpreter, Nurnberg War Crimes Trials, 46-49 and US Court Appeals, Frankfurt, 49-52; Assoc Prof Ger, 55-76, Prof to prof emer, Lang,Univ of Indianapolis, 76- . **MEMBERSHIPS** Am Asn Teachers Ger; Foreign Lang Teachers Asn. **SELECTED PUBLICATIONS** Auth, Maimonides School and the Rav, Trad J Orthodox Jewish Thought, Vol 31, 97. **CONTACT ADDRESS** Dept of German, Univ of Indianapolis, Indianapolis, IN 46227.

MEINHARDT, WARREN LEE
PERSONAL Born 03/30/1931, Lennox, CA, m, 1953, 4 children **DISCIPLINE** LATIN AMERICAN LITERATURE **EDUCATION** Pomona Col, BA, 53; Stanford Univ, MA, 55: Univ Calif Berkeley, PhD(Romance lang and lit), 65. **CAREER** Asst instr Span, Univ Ill, Urbana, 60-64; from instr to asst prof, 64-69; asst prof foreign lang, 69-73, Assoc Prof Foreign Lang and Lit, Southern Ill Univ, Carbondale, 73-, Fac fel, Univ Ill, Urbana, 66; Univ Ill fac fel, 66 and 73; Nat Endowment for Humanities fels, summer 78 and 81. **MEMBERSHIPS** Am Asn Teachers Span and Port. **RESEARCH** Latin American prose fiction; the new Latin American novel; Chicano literature. **SELECTED PUBLICATIONS** Auth, Entrando a El tunel de Ernesto Sabato, Rev Iberoam, 72; coauth, Hacia una bibliografia de la novela contemporanea en Latinoamerica, Nueva Narativa Hispanoam, 72; auth, Cabrera Infante: Asi en el cuento como en la novela?, Chasqui, 72; Juan Zorrilla de San Martin, JAPOS, 4/81. **CONTACT ADDRESS** Dept of Foreign Lang and Lit, So Illinois Univ, Carbondale, Carbondale, IL 62901-4300.

MEININGER, ROBERT ALAN
PERSONAL Born 03/29/1938, Torrington, WY, m, 1962, 1 child **DISCIPLINE** FRENCH **EDUCATION** Univ Wyo, BA, 61; Univ Nebr, MA, 64, PhD(Romance lang), 70. **CAREER** Instr French, Univ Nebr, 68-70; asst prof, 70-72, assoc prof, 72-80, Prof French, Nebr Wesleyan Univ, 80-, Chm Dept, 72-, Chm, Humanities Div, 78-. **HONORS AND AWARDS** Phi Beta Kappa; Phi Beta Phi; Fulbright grants. **MEMBERSHIPS** Am Asn Teachers Fr; Am Asn Teachers Ger; Asn of Slavic Studies. **RESEARCH** French, Belgian cultural history; Russian history. **SELECTED PUBLICATIONS** Auth, Belgian culture, In: Encycl Am, Grolier, 68-98; translations from German and Russian for Am Hist Soc Ger/Rus. **CONTACT ADDRESS** Dept of Foreign Lang, Nebraska Wesleyan Univ, 5000 St Paul Ave, Lincoln, NE 68504-2760. **EMAIL** ram@NebrWesleyan.edu

MEISEL, MARTIN
PERSONAL Born 03/22/1931, New York, NY, m, 1957, 3 children **DISCIPLINE** ENGLISH, COMPARATIVE LITERATURE **EDUCATION** Queens Col, NYork, BA, 52; Princeton Univ, MA, 57, PhD(English), 60. **CAREER** Army, 54-56; instr English, Rutgers Univ, 57-58; from instr to assoc prof, Dartmouth Col, 59-65; prof, Univ WI, 65-68; vchm dept, 73-76, prof English, 68-86, chm dept English & comp lit, 80-83, vice pres arts and sciences, 86-87, 89-93, Brander Matthews prof of dramatic lit, Columbia Univ, 87-; Guggenheim fel, 63-64, 87-88; Am Coun Learned our Carribean Poets, Duluth: Poetry Harbor, 96; Lawrence Ferlinghetti, Gregory Corso and Gwendolyn Brooks, in Frank N Magill, ed, Cyclopedia of World Authors, Revised Edition, Pasadena, CA: Salem Press, 97; If Beale Street Could Talk, in Frank N Magill, ed, Masterplots II: Juvenile and Young Adult Literature Series, Supplement, 3 vols, Pasadena, CA: Salem Press, 97; The Wapshot Scandal, The Country Husband, and John Cheever, in David Peck, ed, Identities and Issues in Literature, 3 vols, Pasadena, CA: Salem Press, 97; The Beat Generation: A Bibliographical Teaching Guide, Lanham, MD: Scarecrow Press, 98. **CONTACT ADDRESS** Dept of English, Univ of Wisconsin, Stevens Point, 2100 Main St, Stevens Point, WI 54481-3897.

MELCHERT, H. CRAIG
PERSONAL Born 04/05/1945, Manhattan, KS **DISCIPLINE** LINGUISTICS **EDUCATION** Mich State Univ, BA, 67; Harvard Univ, PhD, 77. **CAREER** From asst prof to assoc prof to prof, 78-, distinguished prof, 93-96, Univ North Carolina, Chapel Hill; vis prof, Yale Univ, 90; vis prof, Harvard Univ, 96; vis prof, Cornell Univ, 97. **HONORS AND AWARDS** Nat Merit Scholar, 63-67; Woodrow Wilson Fel, 67-68; Whiting Fel, 76-77. **MEMBERSHIPS** Linguistic Soc Am; Indogermanische Gesellschaft; Am Oriental Soc. **RESEARCH** Indo-European linguistics; Hittite and Anatolian languages. **SELECTED PUBLICATIONS** Auth, Studies in Hittite Historical Phonology, 84; auth, Cuneiform Luvian Lexicon, 93; auth, Lycian Lexicon, 93; auth, Anatolian Historical Phonology, 94. **CONTACT ADDRESS** Dept of Linguistics, Univ of No Carolina, Chapel Hill, CB 3155, Chapel Hill, NC 27599-3155. **EMAIL** melchert@email.unc.edu

MELE, ALFRED R.
DISCIPLINE CLASSICS AND PHILOSOPHY **EDUCATION** Wayne State Univ, BA, 73; Univ MI, PhD, 79. **CAREER** Vail Prof Philos, Davidson Col; William H. and Lucyle T. Werkmeister Prof of Philos, Fla State Univ. **RESEARCH** Cognitive philos; hist of ancient philos. **SELECTED PUBLICATIONS** Auth, Irrationality, Oxford Univ Press, 87; auth, Springs of Action, Oxford Univ Press, 92; coed, Mental Causation, Clarendon, 93; auth, Autonomous Agents, Oxford Univ Press, 95; ed, The Philosophy of Action, Oxford Univ Press, 97; auth, Self-Deception Unmasked, Princeton Univ Press, 01. **CONTACT ADDRESS** Dept of Philos, Florida State Univ, 288 Dodd Hall, Tallahassee, FL 32306-1500. **EMAIL** almele@mailer.fsu.edu

MELLOR, ANNE KOSTELANETZ
PERSONAL Born 07/15/1941, m, 1969, 1 child **DISCIPLINE** ENGLISH AND COMPARATIVE LITERATURE **EDUCATION** Brown Univ, BA (summa cum laude, English & Philos), 63; Columbia Univ, MA (English & Comparative Lit), 64, PhD (English & Comparative Lit), 68; Courtauld Inst of Art, London, Fulbright-Hays Scholar, 64-65. **CAREER** Asst prof of English, Stanford Univ, 66-73, assoc prof, 73-80, founding dir of Feminist Studies Prog, 82-84, Howard H. and Jessie T. Watkins Univ Prof of English and Feminist Studies, 83-85; vis assoc prof of Humanities, 77, Prof of English, Univ CA, Los Angeles, 84-, Distinguished Prof of English, 96-, dir of Women's Studies Prog, 86-87. **HONORS AND AWARDS** Phi Beta Kappa, 63; Guggenheim fel, 72-73, 83-84; NEH fel for Younger Humanists (declined), 72-73; NEH Summer Stipend, 76; NEH/Huntington Library Fel, 77-78; dir, NEH Summer Seminar for College Teachers, 82, 89, 94; Stanford Univ Deans' Awd for Excellence in Teaching, 82; exec comm, 82-87, Romantics Div, MLA, chair of comm, 86; Howard H. and Jessie T. Watkins Univ Prof of English and Feminist Studies, 83-85; English Lit and Lang Selection Comm, Coun for Int Exchange of Scholars, 87-90, chair of comm, 89-90; Humanities Res Centre fel, Nat Univ of Austalia, Canberra, 90; Rockefeller Found Fel, Bellagio Study Centre (declined), 91; Clark Prof, Clark Library, UCLA, 92. **MEMBERSHIPS** Modern Lang Asn; North Am Soc for the Study of Romanticism; Int Asn of Univ Profs of English; Am Conference on Romanticism; Interdisciplinary Nineteenth Century Studies Asn. **RESEARCH** British Romantic Writing; Women's Studies; 19th Century Art and Lit. **SELECTED PUBLICATIONS** Auth, Blake's Human Form Divine, Univ Calif Pr, 74; auth, English Romantic Irony, Harvard Univ pr, 80; ed, Romanticisim and Feminism, Ind Univ Pr, 88; auth, Mary Shelley, Her Life, Her Fiction, Her Monsters, Routledge, 88; ed, with Audrey Fisch and Esther Schor, The Other Mary Shelley: Beyond Frankenstein, Oxford Univ Press, 93; auth, Romanticism and Gender, Routledge, Chapman & Hall, 93, paperback, 93; ed, with Richard Matlak, British Literature, 1780-1830, Harcourt Brace Pubs, 96; ed, with Maximillian Novak, The Age of Sensibility in a Time of Terror, Univ DE Press, 00; auth, Mothers of the Nation--Women's Political Writing in England, 1780-1830, Ind Univ Press, 00 **CONTACT ADDRESS** 2620 Mandeville Canyon Rd., Los Angeles, CA 90049. **EMAIL** mellor@ucla.edu

MELLOR, CHAUNCEY JEFFRIES
PERSONAL Born 11/10/1942, Pittsburgh, PA, m, 1977 **DISCIPLINE** GERMANIC PHILOLOGY **EDUCATION** Univ Chicago, BA, 65, MA, 67, PhD(Ger), 72. **CAREER** Instr, 70-72, Asst Prop Ger, Univ Tenn, Knoxville, 72-, Ed, Der Spottvogel, Am Asn Teachers Ger, 72- **MEMBERSHIPS** Am Asn Teachers Ger; Ling Soc Am; MLA. **RESEARCH** German lexicography. **SELECTED PUBLICATIONS** Auth, Jacob Grimm's use of the term Fremdwort, 72 & Theodor Mommsen, Daniel Sanders and the establishment of the term Lehnwort in German, 72, Mod Lang Notes; Contirbr, Selected Proceedings of MIFLC: Kriemhild and Hagen in MSS B and C of the Nibelungenlied, ETenn State Univ, 78; auth, Jacob Grimm's inclusion of loanwords and compounds in the Deutsches Worterbuch, J English & Ger Philos, (in press). **CONTACT ADDRESS** Dept of Ger and Slavic, Univ of Tennessee, Knoxville, Knoxville, TN 37916.

MELLOR, RONALD
PERSONAL Born 09/30/1940, New York, NY, m, 1969, 1 child **DISCIPLINE** CLASSICS **EDUCATION** Fordham Col, BA, 62; Princeton Univ, MA, 64, PhD, 68. **CAREER** Stanford Univ, asst prof, 65-75; UCLA, Assoc prof, prof, dept ch, 76-. **HONORS AND AWARDS** NEH fel, ACLS fel, Australian Nat Univ Fel. **MEMBERSHIPS** AHA, APA, AAH, SPRS. **RESEARCH** Roman studies; ancient religion; historiography. **SELECTED PUBLICATIONS** Auth, Thea Rhome: The Worship of the Goddess Roma in the Greek World, Gottingen, 75; auth, From Augustus to Nero: The First Dynasty of Imperial Rome, ed., MSU Pr, 90; auth, Tacitus, Routledge, 93; auth, Tacitus: The Classical Tradition, Garland Books, 95; auth, The Historians of Rome, ed., Routledge, 97; auth, The Roman Historians, Routledge, 99. **CONTACT ADDRESS** Dept of History, Univ of California, Los Angeles, Los Angeles, CA 90095-1473. **EMAIL** mellor@history.ucla.edu

MELZI, ROBERT C.
PERSONAL Born 03/12/1915, Milano, Italy, m, 1948, 3 children **DISCIPLINE** ITALIAN **EDUCATION** Univ Padua, D in L, 38; Univ Pa, MA, 53, PhD, 62. **CAREER** Asst instr Romance lang, Univ Pa, 50-53; interpreter French and Ital, US Dept Justice, 53-56; teacher French and Span, Plymouth Whitemarsh High Sch, 58-61; assoc prof, Millersville State Col, 62-63; assoc prof, 63-67, prof French and chmn dept mod lang, 67-80, prof romance lang, Widener Col, 67-90; Vis lectr, Univ Pa, 68-69. **MEMBERSHIPS** MLA; Dante Soc Am; Renaissance Soc Am; Am Asn Teachers Ital. **RESEARCH** Italian Renais-

sance; Lodovico Castelvetro; bilingual lexicography. **SELECTED PUBLICATIONS** Auth The Giuliano Dalmati in Canada--Considerations and Imagery, Forum Italicum, Vol 29, 95; Scripts and Scenarios, 16th Century Jour, Vol 25, 94; Jewish Life in Renaissance Italy, 16th Century Jour, Vol 26, 95; The Giuliano Dalmati in Canada--Considerations and Imagery, Forum Italicum, Vol 29, 95; Viaggio Di Francia, Costumi E Qualita Di Quei Paesi 1664-1665, Italica, Vol 69, 92; The Isole Fortunate,16th Century Jour, Vol 27, 96; Tommaseo, Niccolo Il Dizionario Dei Sinonimi, Italica, Vol 69, 92; Jews and Marranos in Italian Renaissance Comedies , Sefarad, Vol 55, 95. **CONTACT ADDRESS** Dept of Mod Lang, Widener Univ, Pennsylvania, Chester, PA 19013. **EMAIL** rcm5@bellatlantic.net

MENDEZ-CLARK, RONALD
DISCIPLINE SPANISH **EDUCATION** Univ de Puerto Rico, 73; Princeton Univ, MA, 76; PhD, 80. **CAREER** Instr, Fordham Univ, 78-80; asst prof, 80-92; assoc prof, 92-. **HONORS AND AWARDS** Fac Fel, 88, 98, Fordham Univ; Mellon Grants; Alpha Mu Gamma; Dist Grant; UPR, Europe Trv Grant. **MEMBERSHIPS** CLASP; MLA; LASA; LAWI; IPRP. **SELECTED PUBLICATIONS** Auth, Onetti y la (in fidelidad a las reglas del juego, Univ Press Am, (Lanham), 93; auth, Jose Gorostiza: lectura de Preludio," Texto critico 9 (78): 46-57; auth, "Dejemos hablar al viento, Juan Carlos Onetti," Sin nombre 3 (80): 58-62; auth, Lo femenino en Onetti: versiones?" Sin nombre 2 (83): 44-52; transl of Shadow Play/The Rats, by Jose Bianco LatinAmerica Bks 2 (84): 23-26; auth, "La pasion y la marginalidad en (de) Ia escritura: Rosarlo Ferre," in La sarten por el mango, eds. P Gonzalez, E Ortega (Rio Piedras: Ediciones Huracan, 84, 85), 119-13I; auth, "Dejemos hablar al veinto: suma y culminacioin da las tentativas anteriores de Juan Carlos Onetti?" Inti 21 (85): 37-49; auth, "Inventano (agotamiento?) de las escritura en Onetti," Hispamerica 46-47 (87): 25-40; auth, "Del second guessing a los calculos: rescritura y traduccion en Rosano Ferr," Nomada 4 (99): 62-72. **CONTACT ADDRESS** Dept Modern Languages, Fordham Univ, 441 East Fordham Rd, Bronx, NY 10458-5149.

MENN, LISE
PERSONAL Born 12/28/1941, Philadelphia, PA, 2 children **DISCIPLINE** LINGUISTICS **EDUCATION** Swarthmore Col, BA, 62; Brandeis Univ, MA, 64; Univ Ill, MA, 75, PhD, 76. **CAREER** Asst prof, Boston Univ, 77-86; assoc prof to prof, Univ of Colo, 86-. **HONORS AND AWARDS** Soc Sci Res Coun, 77; Nat Res Serv Awd, 83-84; Fulbright Fel, 91. **MEMBERSHIPS** Ling Soc of Am, Acad of Aphasia, AAAS, Int Assoc for the Study of Child Lang. **RESEARCH** Language acquisition, aphasia, psycholinguistics. **SELECTED PUBLICATIONS** Coed, Exceptional Language and Linguistic, Acad Pr, 82; coed, Agrammatic Aphasia: A Cross-Language Narrative Sourcebook, Benjamins, 90; coed, Phonological Development: Models, Research, Implication, York Pr, 92; coed, Nonfluent Aphasia in a Multi-Lingual World, Benjamins, 95; coed, Methods for Studying Language Production, Erlbaum, 00; auth, "Comparative aphasiology," Oxford Int Encycl of Ling, Oxford Univ Pr, in press. **CONTACT ADDRESS** Ling Dept, Univ of Colorado, Boulder, 295 UCB, Boulder, CO 80309-0295. **EMAIL** lise.menn@colorado.edu

MENTON, SEYMOUR
PERSONAL Born 03/06/1927, New York, NY **DISCIPLINE** SPANISH AMERICAN LITERATURE **EDUCATION** City Col NYork, BA, 48; Nat Univ Mex, MA, 49; NYork Univ, PhD(Span Am lit), 52. **CAREER** Teacher English and hist of Span lang, Inst Recapacitation, Mex, 48-49; teacher, Pub Schs, NY, 49-52; instr Span and Span Am lit, Dartmouth Col, 52-54; from asst prof to prof, Univ Kans, 54-65; chmn dept foreign lang, 65-70, Prof Span and Port, Univ Calif, Irvine, 65-, Ed, Hispania, 63-65. **HONORS AND AWARDS** Judge, Plaza y Jans Colombian Novel Compeetition, 81; judge, Guatemalan Novel Competition, (Concurso Rin), 83; Univ of Calif, Irvine, Ch of Academic Senate, 84-86; Vice-pres of the Asociaci-n Norteamerricana de Colombianistas, 87-89; Pres, 89-93; Pres of the Local Organizing comt for the Meeting at UCI of the Asociaci-n Internacional de Hispanistas, 92; Orden Andr-s Bello, cultural award given by the Venezuelan government, 91; judge, Juan Rulfo International Prize for Literature, Guadalajara, Mexico City, 92, 93; Medal from the Instituto Tecnol-gico y de Estudios Superiores de Monterrey (ITESM) in recognition for contributions to Spanish Am lit, 94; Orden Francisco de Miraanda, cultrual award given by the Venezuelan government, 96; Orden Miguel Angel Asturias, cultural award given by the Guatemalan government, 97. **MEMBERSHIPS** Int Inst Span Am Lit; Am Asn Teachers Span and Port; MLA. **RESEARCH** Cuban prose fiction; Mexican novel; Spanish American short story. **SELECTED PUBLICATIONS** Auth, Saga de Mexico, New York: Appleton-Century-Crofts, 55; auth, Historia cr'tica de la novela guatemalteca, Guatemala City: Universidad de San Carlos Press, 60; auth, El cuento hispanoamericano, Mexico City: Fondo de Cultura Econ-mica, 2 vols., 64; auth, La novela colombiana: planetas y sat-lites, Bogot: Plaza y Jan-s, (78): 394; auth, Magic Realism Rediscovered, 1918-1981, East Brunswick, NJ: Associated Univ Presses and Philadelphia Art Alliance Press, 83; transl, of Alvaro Cepeda Samudio, La casa grande, (Austin: Univ of Texas Press, 91); auth, La narrativa mexicana desde, "Los de abajo," hasta "Noticias del imperio," Tlaxcala: Universidad Aut-noma de Tlaxcala, 91; coord, Critical edition of Mariano Azuela's The Underdogs, Pittsburgh: Univ of Pittsburgh Press, 92; auth, Latin America's New Historical Novel, 1979-1992, Austin: Univ of Texas Press, 93; auth, Historia verdaderra del realismo m-gico, Mexico City: Fondo de Cultura Econ-mica, 98. **CONTACT ADDRESS** Dept of Spanish & Portuguese, Univ of California, Irvine, 2641 Basswood St, Irvine, CA 92697-5275. **EMAIL** smenton@uci.edu

MERCERON, JACQUES E.
DISCIPLINE FRENCH LITERATURE **EDUCATION** Univ Ca, PhD, 93. **CAREER** Asst prof. **SELECTED PUBLICATIONS** Auth, Le Message et sa fiction: la communication par messager dans la litterature francaise des XIIe et XIIIe siecles, 98; pubs on French and Celtic folklore, folklore and Old French prose Lancelot, communication and medieval messenger motifs in epic poetry. **CONTACT ADDRESS** Dept of French and Italian, Indiana Univ, Bloomington, 1020 E Kirkwood Ave, Ballantine Hall 642, Bloomington, IN 47405. **EMAIL** jmercero@indiana.edu

MEREDITH, HUGH EDWIN
PERSONAL Born 10/07/1930, Muskogee, OK, 4 children **DISCIPLINE** GERMANIC LANGUAGES & LITERATURE **EDUCATION** Okla Baptist Univ, BA, 52; Int Baptist Theol Sem Ruschlikon, Zurich, Switz, cert, 53; Southwestern Baptist Theol Sem, BD, 55; Univ Tex, MA, 60, PhD, 63. **CAREER** Prof Ger & vpres acad afairs, Angelo State Univ, 67-74; pres, Sul Ross State Univ, 74-76; Prof Mod Lang, Sam Houston State Univ, 76- **MEMBERSHIPS** MLA; Am Asn Teachers Ger; Ling Soc Am. **RESEARCH** Eighteenth and 19th century German literature; Karl Philipp Moritz; Jeremias Gotthelf; German immigration to Texas. **CONTACT ADDRESS** Dept of English and Foreign Langs, Sam Houston State Univ, PO Box 2147, Huntsville, TX 77341-2147. **EMAIL** fol_hem@shsu.edu

MERITHEW, CHARLENE L.
PERSONAL Born Worcester, MA **DISCIPLINE** SPANISH **EDUCATION** Assumption Col, BA, 93; Simmons Col, MA, 94; Univ Md, PhD, 99. **CAREER** Teaching asst to instr, Univ Md, 94-96; instr, Univ Alcala de Henares, 97; instr, Simmons Col, 97; teaching asst, Univ Md, 97-98; lectr, Clark Univ, 00; adj asst prof, Worcester Polytech Inst, 00-; instr to vis asst prof, 98-. **HONORS AND AWARDS** Acad Excellence in Spanish, Assumption Col, 93; Simmons Col Award, 94; Grant, Univ Md, 96; Fel, Univ de Alcala de Henares, 96-97; CIBER Grant, Tex AM Univ, 01. **MEMBERSHIPS** MLA; ACTFL; LASA; ACLA; ALFH; ISL/HH. **RESEARCH** Latin American Women Writers; Mexican Literature and Culture; Contemporary Latin American Literature and Culture; Contemporary Peninsular Women Writers; Business Spanish; Women's Studies. **SELECTED PUBLICATIONS** Auth, "La busqueda eterna de 'otro modo de ser humano y libre': los ensayos de Rosario Castellanos," Letras Femeninas, (98):95-110; rev, of "Yo solo soy memoria: biografia visual de Elena Garro," by Patricia Rosas Lopateui in Letras Femeninas, (01): 247-249; auth, "Silencios poderosos: el tema de la quietud en los ensayos de Soledad Puertolas," Monographic Rev, 01; auth, "Rompiendo las jaulas patriarcales de sexo y genero: Sabina Berman y Luisa Valenzuela," in Las desobedientes: mujeres de nuestra America, (forthcoming); auth, Re-Presenting the Nation: Contemporary Mexican Women Writers, Univ Press of the South, (forthcoming). **CONTACT ADDRESS** Dept Lang, Worcester Polytech Inst, 203 Stafford St, Worcester, MA 01603. **EMAIL** cmerithew@hotmail.com

MERITT, LUCY SHOE
PERSONAL Born 08/07/1906, Camden, NJ, w **DISCIPLINE** CLASSICS **EDUCATION** Bryn Mawr Col, AB, 27, MA, 28, PhD, 35; Brown Univ, LHD, 74; Hamilton Col, LHD, 94. **CAREER** Asst prof, 37-41, assoc prof, 41-50, counsellor to chief counsellor of students, Mount Holyoke Col; member of Institue for Advanced Study, 48-49, 50-73, Princeton; ed of publications, 50-72, Amer Sch of Classical Studies at Athens; vis prof, 58, 60, Washington Univ; vis lect, 59, Princeton Univ; prof, 73-74, 75-76, 90, Univ of Texas at Austin, vis scholar, 73- . **HONORS AND AWARDS** Gold Medal of the Archaeological Inst of Amer for Distinguished Archaeological Achievement, 76; Outstanding Woman of Texas Humanities AAUW, 80; Pro Bene Meritis Awd, Univ of Texas at Austin, 97; Centennial med of the Am Acad in Rome, 99. **MEMBERSHIPS** Member of the managing committee of the Amer Sch of Classical Studies at Athens; pres Pathfinders Club Austin, 76-77, 91-92; Thankful Hubbard Chapter DAR, vice-regent 84-86, regent 90-92, honorary regent 92-; Archaeol Inst of Am; Deutsches Archaeol Inst; Soc of Archit Hists. **RESEARCH** Greek, Roman & Etruscan archit. **SELECTED PUBLICATIONS** Auth, Profiles of Greek Mouldings, cambridge, 36; auth, Profiles of Western Greek Mouldings, AAR, 52; auth, Estruscan and Republican Roman Mouldings, AAR, 65; auth, "Geographical Distribution of Greek and Roman Ionic Bases," Hesperia (69); auth, History of the American School of Classical Studies at Athens, 1939-1980, 84; auth, The Athenian Ionic Capital, Eius Virtutis Studiosi, Classical and Post-Classical Studies in Memory of Frank Edward Brown, 1908-1988, Studies in the History of Art, 93; auth, Athenian Ionic Capitals from the Athenian Agora, Hesperia, 96. **CONTACT ADDRESS** Dept Class, Univ of Texas, Austin, Austin, TX 78712.

MERIVALE, PATRICIA
PERSONAL Born 07/19/1934, Derby, England **DISCIPLINE** ENGLISH, COMPARATIVE LITERATURE **EDUCATION** Univ Calif, Berkeley, BA, 55; Oxford Univ, BA, 58, MA, 62; Harvard Univ, PhD(comp lit), 63. **CAREER** From instr to assoc prof, 62-70, Prof English, Univ BC, 70-00, Can Coun fels, 69-70; Prof, emer, Univ BC, 00-. **MEMBERSHIPS** Can Comp Lit Asn (secy-treas, 77-79); MLA; Asn Can Univ Teachers English; Am Comp Lit Asn. **RESEARCH** Artifice and the artist parable; thematics; narrative structure in contemporary fiction. **SELECTED PUBLICATIONS** Auth, Pan the Goat God: His Myth in Modern Times, Patricia Merivale; co-ed, Detecting Texts: The Metaphysical Detective Story from Poe to Postmodernism, Patricia Merivale, Susan Elizabeth Sweeney, 99. **CONTACT ADDRESS** Dept of English, Univ of British Columbia, 397-1873 E Mall, Buchanan Tower, Vancouver, BC, Canada V6T 1Z1. **EMAIL** merivale@interchange.ubc.ca

MERLER, GRAZIA
PERSONAL Born 06/16/1938, Trento, Italy **DISCIPLINE** FRENCH AND FRENCH CANADIAN LITERATURE **EDUCATION** Univ BC, BA, 59; Laval Univ, MA, 61, PhD(-French), 67. **CAREER** Instr French and Ital, Univ Tex, 63-65; lectr Ital, Univ BC, 65-66; prof French, Col Ste-Foy, 67-69; asst prof, 69-76, cmm French, 75-77, Assoc Prof French, Dept Mod Lang, Simon Fraser Univ, 76-, Can Coun leave fel, 77-78. **MEMBERSHIPS** MLA; Can Semiotics Res Asn; Asn Can Studies; Asn Can Univ Teachers Fr. **RESEARCH** 19th Century French Lit, Contemporary lit, Individual Psychology and the literary text, narration and its sequencing, Lit and art. **SELECTED PUBLICATIONS** Auth, Mavis Gallant: Narrative Patterns and Devices, 78. **CONTACT ADDRESS** Dept of Fr, Simon Fraser Univ, 8888 Univ Dr, Burnaby, BC, Canada V5A 1S6. **EMAIL** merler@sfu.ca

MERMALL, THOMAS
PERSONAL Born 09/20/1937, Czechoslovakia, m, 1977 **DISCIPLINE** SPANISH **EDUCATION** Ill Wesleyan Univ, BA, 61; Univ Conn, MA, 65, PhD(Span), 68. **CAREER** Asst prof Span, State Univ NY, Stony Brook, 68-73; asst prof, 73-75, assoc prof, 75-80, Prof Span, Brooklyn Col, 80- ; vis prof, NYU, 88; vis prof, St Johns Col, 88; vis prof, Univ Penn, 90. **HONORS AND AWARDS** Fulbright; ACLS; Am Philos Soc. **MEMBERSHIPS** Asn Int de Hispanistas. **RESEARCH** Contemporary Spanish essay; history of ideas. **SELECTED PUBLICATIONS** Auth, The Rhetoric of Humanism: Spanish Culture After Ortega y Gasset, Bilingual Pr (NYork), 76; auth, La retorica del humanismo: La cultura espanyola despues de Ortega, Taurus (Madrid), 78; auth, Las alegorias del poder en Francisco Ayala, Fundamentos-Espiral (Madrid), 84; auth, "Tiempo, narracion y conciencia historica en Francisco Ayala," Anthropos (Barcelona) 139 (Dec 92): 32-37; auth, "En torno al casticismo and Unamuno's rhetorical evolution," Anales de la Literatura Espanola Contemporanea 18.1 & 2 (93): 281-294; auth, "How to do Things with Rhetoic: The Uses of Argument in Larra, Unamuno, and Ortega," Siglo XX/20th Cent 11 1& 2 (93): 155-79; auth, "Entre episteme y doxa: el trasfondo retorico de la razon vital," Revista Hispanica Moderna 47 (94): 72-85; auth, "Abstracto/Concreto: clave retorica para la comprension de Ortega," Revista Canadiense de Estudios Hispanicos 21 No 1 (96): 180-90; auth, "Un 'postmoderno' inteligible: en torno al estilo filosofico de Ortega y Gasset, Revista de Occidente 192 (May 97): 47-58; ed, Jose Ortega y Gasset, 'La rebelion de las masas' (edicion de Thomas Mermall), Castalia (Madrid), 98; **CONTACT ADDRESS** Dept of Mod Lang, Brooklyn Col, CUNY, 2901 Bedford Ave, Brooklyn, NY 11210-2813. **EMAIL** tmermall@msn.com

MERMIER, GUY R.
PERSONAL Born 10/20/1931, Grenoble, France, m, 1954, 2 children **DISCIPLINE** FRENCH **EDUCATION** Univ Grenoble, Lic es-let and DES, 53; Univ Pa, PhD, 61. **CAREER** Instr French, Amherst Col, 52-53; instr Romance lang, Univ Mass, 54-55; asst instr, Univ Pa, 55-56; instr foreign lang, Temple Univ, 56-61; from instr to asst prof Romance lang, 61-67, Rackham grant, 62, Assoc Prof Romance Lang, Univ Mich, Ann Arbor, 67-, Fulbright grant, Amherst Col, 52-53; Smith-Mundt fel, 52; NDEA consult, Temple Univ, 56; Prof, Laval Univ, 57-; dir, Mich-Wis Jr Year in France, 67-68; Pres, Alliance Francaise, Ann Arbor, 68- **MEMBERSHIPS** MLA; Am Asn Teachers French; Int Arthurian Soc; Mod Humanities Res Asn; Am Asn Teachers Ital. **RESEARCH** Medieval; Renaissance; 19th century literature and existentialist 20th century literature. **SELECTED PUBLICATIONS CONTACT ADDRESS** Dept of Romance Lang, Univ of Michigan, Ann Arbor, Ann Arbor, MI 48104.

MERRIFIELD, WILLIAM R.
PERSONAL Born 09/28/1932, Chicago, IL, m, 1952, 4 children **DISCIPLINE** LINGUISTICS, ANTHROPOLOGY **EDUCATION** Wheaton Col, Ill BA, 54; Cornell Univ, MA, 63, PhD(cult anthrop), 65. **CAREER** Ling consult in Mex, 62-74, coordr anthrop res in Mex, 65-69, coordr ling res in Mex, 65-59, 72-74, dir sch, Univ Okla, 74-77, Int Coordr Anthrop and Commun Develop, Summer Inst Ling, 72-, Dir, Mus Anthrop, Tex, 74-, Vis asst prof ling, Univ Wash, 65-72; vis prof anthrop, Wheaton Col, 71-72; Adj Prof Ling, Univ Tex, Arlington, 74-;

adj prof anthrop, Univ Okla, 75-77, adj prof ling, 77. **MEMBERSHIPS** Am Anthrop Asn; Ling Soc Am; Am Sci Affiliation; Am Asn Mus; Ling Asn Can and US. **RESEARCH** Cultural and applied anthropology; social organization; theory of grammar. **SELECTED PUBLICATIONS** Auth, Linguistic Theory and Grammatical Description Joseph, Je, Lan, Vol 70, 94. **CONTACT ADDRESS** Summer Inst of Ling, 7500 Camp Wisdom Rd, Dallas, TX 75236.

MERRILL, REED
PERSONAL Born 10/28/1929, Provo, UT, m, 1951 **DISCIPLINE** COMPARATIVE LITERATURE **EDUCATION** Univ Utah, BS, 61, MA, 65; Univ Colo, Boulder, PhD(comp lit), 70. **CAREER** Bus mgr, Univ Utah Comput Ctr, 64-65; asst ed, Rocky Mountain Mod Lang Asn Bull, Univ Colo, Boulder, 67-68; lectr, 69-70, asst prof, 70-74, Assoc Prof English, Western Wash Univ, 74- **MEMBERSHIPS** Fedn Int Lang Lit Mod; Int Comp Lit Asn; MLA; Am Comp Lit Asn. **RESEARCH** Modern novel; literary criticism and theory; history of ideas. **SELECTED PUBLICATIONS** Auth, The Tucker Review--A 1/2 Century After his Met Debut, Colleagues Voice Their Feelings About A Great American Tenor/, Opera News, Vol 59, 95 Faulknerian Tragedy, The Example of As I Lay Dying , Mississippi Quart, Vol 47, 94; Something and Nothingness--The Fiction of Updike, John and Fowles, John, Am Lit, Vol 64, 92; The American Roman Noir--Hammett, Cain, and Chandler, Am Lit, Vol 69, 97; Mailer Tough Guys Dont Dance and the Detective Traditions, Critique Stud Contemporary Fiction, Vol 34, 93; Writing the American Classics, Mod Philol, Vol 90, 93; Critical Edition , Opera News, Vol 59, 94; Writing the American Classics, Modern Philol, Vol 90, 93. **CONTACT ADDRESS** Dept of English, Western Washington Univ, Bellingham, WA 98225.

MERRILL, SAMMY RAY
PERSONAL Born 09/06/1941, Morehead City, NC, m, 1962, 2 children **DISCIPLINE** GERMAN, GERMAN LITERATURE **EDUCATION** Wake Forest Univ, BA, 63; Duke Univ, MA, 66; Cornell Univ, PhD, 72. **CAREER** Instr, Wake Forest Univ, 67-69; asst prof, Cornell Univ, 72-73; assoc prof to prof, Mary Washington Col, 73- . **HONORS AND AWARDS** NDEA Title IV Grad Fel, 69-72; Simpson Awd for Excellence in Undergrad Teaching, 93; german acad exchange svc fel, 66-67; neh grant, 76. **MEMBERSHIPS** Amer Assoc of Teachers of German; Foreign Lang Assoc of Va. **RESEARCH** Nineteenth & twentieth cent German lit; German lang. **CONTACT ADDRESS** Dept of Modern Foreign Lang, Mary Washington Col, Fredericksburg, VA 22401. **EMAIL** smerrill@mwc.edu

MESAVAGE, RUTH MATILDE
PERSONAL Born New York, NY **DISCIPLINE** FRENCH **EDUCATION** Julliard Sch, BS; Hunter Col, MA, 72; Yale Univ, MPhil, 75; PhD, 79. **CAREER** Asst Prof, SUNY, 77-79; Asst Prof, Wake Forest Univ, 79-81; From Asst Prof to Prof, Rollins Col, 81-. **HONORS AND AWARDS** Who's Who in Am; Jack B Crutchfield Res Grant, 92. **MEMBERSHIPS** AATF, ACQS, ACSUS, ASECS, MLA, SCCS. **RESEARCH** French and Canadian cultures, literature. **SELECTED PUBLICATIONS** Rev, "The Eighteenth Century: A Current Bibliography of Paradis de Moncrif, Francois-Augustin," Papers on Fr Seventeenth Century Lit, biblio 17, Paris, Seattle and Tubingen (94): 102; rev, "Quebec Studies: Brulotte, Gaetan," L'Univsers de Jean Paul Lemieux, vol 24 Fides Publ (97): 282; rev, "Le XVIIIe siecle: Une bibliographie actuelle," The Eighteenth Century: A Current Biog, VI (98): 441-442. auth, "Le Desert et la parole poetique dans l'oeuvre d'Abdelhak Serhane," Conseil Int d'Etudes Francophones, New-Brunswick (98). **CONTACT ADDRESS** Dept For Lang, Rollins Col, 1000 Hold Ave, Winter Park, FL 32789-4499.

MESTER, ARMIN
DISCIPLINE LINGUISTICS **EDUCATION** Univ Mass-Amherst, PhD, 86. **CAREER** Prof, Ling, Univ Calif, Santa Cruz. **RESEARCH** Theoretical phonology. **SELECTED PUBLICATIONS** Auth, Patterns of Truncation, Ling Inquiry, 90; Dependent Tier Ordering and the OCP, Features, Segmental Structure, and Harmony Processes, Foris, 88; The Quantitative Trochee in Latin, Natural Lang and Ling Theory, 94; co-auth, Japanese Phonology, Handbook of Phonological Theory, Blackwell, 94; Feature Predictability and Underspecification: Palatal Prosody in Japanese Mimetics, Language, 89. **CONTACT ADDRESS** Dept of Ling, Univ of California, Santa Cruz, 1156 High St, Santa Cruz, CA 95064. **EMAIL** mester@ling.ucsc.edu

METCALF, ALLAN ALBERT
PERSONAL Born 04/18/1940, Clayton, MO, m, 1994, 4 children **DISCIPLINE** ENGLISH, LINGUISTICS **EDUCATION** Cornell Univ, BA, 61; Univ Calif, Berkeley, MA, 64, PhD(English), 66. **CAREER** Asst prof English, Univ Calif, Riverside, 66-73; assoc prof, 73-81, prof English & chmn dept, MacMurray Col, IL, 81-, exec sec, Am Dialect Soc, 81-. **HONORS AND AWARDS** Phi Beta Kappa, Cornell, 61. **MEMBERSHIPS** MLA; Ling Soc Am; Mediaeval Acad Am; Am Dialect Soc; NCTE. **RESEARCH** American English dialects and Lexicography; California dialects; medieval English literature. **SELECTED PUBLICATIONS** Auth, Sir Gawain and you, Chaucer Rev, Winter 71; Riverside English; The Spoken Language of a Southern California Community, Univ Calif, Riverside, 71; Directions of change in Southern California English, J English Ling, 3/72; Poetic Diction in the Old English Meters of Boethius, Mouton, The Hague, 73; Silent Knight: Sum for Cortaysye? Archiv fur das Studium der neueren Sprchen und Literaturen, 76; Chicano English, Ctr Appl Ling, 79; A guide to the California-Nevada field records of the linguistic atlas of the Pacific Coast, Univ Calif, Berkeley, 79; Gawain's number, In: Essays in the Numerical Analysis of Medieval Literature, Bucknell Univ Press, 80; Typography of the Century Dictionary, Dictionaries, v 17, 96; The South in the Dictionary of American Regional English, in: Language Variety in the South Revisited, Univ of Alabama Press, 97; America in So Many Words: Words that Have Shaped America, with David K Barnhart, Houghton Mifflin, 97; The World in So Many Words, Houghton Mifflin, 99; How We Talk: American Regional English Today, Houghton Mifflin, 00. **CONTACT ADDRESS** Dept of English, MacMurray Col, 477 E College Ave, Jacksonville, IL 62650-2510. **EMAIL** aallan@aol.com

METCALF, WILLIAM E.
PERSONAL Born 12/16/1947, East Grand Rapids, MI, m, 1991, 2 children **DISCIPLINE** CLASSIC STUDIES **EDUCATION** Univ Michigan, BA 69, MA 70, PhD 73. **CAREER** The American Numismatic Society, chief curator, curator, assoc curator, asst curator, 73 to 79-00; teaching at Columbia Univ, Princeton Univ, NYU, Bryan Maur College, Universita' di Padova. **HONORS AND AWARDS** NEA Fel; Kraay and Robinson Fel; IAS mem. **MEMBERSHIPS** APA; AIA; RNS; ANS; SPRS. Soc of Antiguaries. **RESEARCH** Roman imperial history and coinage. **SELECTED PUBLICATIONS** Auth, The Silver Coinage of Caesarea in Cappadocia Vespasian to Commodus, NY, Numis Notes and Mono, 96; A Primer of Roman Numismatics, E. J. Brill, 99; Regionalism in the imperial coinage of Asia Minor, in: Region in Asia Minor in the Hellenistic and Roman Periods, Hartford 98; Coins as Primary Evidence, in: Togo Salmon Studies, Ann Arbor, 98; Aurelian's reform at Alexandria, in: studies in Greek Numismatics in memory of Martin Jessop Price, eds, R. H. Ashton, S Hurter, London, 98; Byzantine Imperial Coinage, in: The Glory of Byzantine, art and Cultur of the Middle Byzantine Era A.D. 843-1261, eds, Helen C. Evans, William D. Wixom, New York, 97. **CONTACT ADDRESS** American Numismatic Society, 17 Prescott Ave, Montclair, NJ 07042. **EMAIL** wemetcalf@aol.com

METZGER, ERIKA ALMA
PERSONAL Born 04/08/1933, Berlin, Germany, m, 1958 **DISCIPLINE** GERMAN LANGUAGE & LITERATURE **EDUCATION** Teachers' Training Col, Gottingen, dipl, 54; Free Univ Berlin, dipl, 58; Cornell Univ, MA, 61; State Univ NYork Buffalo, PhD(Ger), 67. **CAREER** Teaching asst Ger, Cornell Univ, 58-61; instr, Univ Ill, 61-63; instr, Millard Fillmore Col, 63-67; asst prof, 67-72, assoc prof, 72-79, Prof Ger, State Univ NY, Buffalo, 79. **MEMBERSHIPS** MLA; Am Asn Teachers Ger, Int Ver Ger Sprach-u Literaturwiss. **RESEARCH** Development of German lyric poetry; Baroque; 20th century. **SELECTED PUBLICATIONS** Coauth, Paul Klee, 67 & Clara and Robert Schumann, 67, Houghton; ed, H A von Abschatz, Werke, Herbert Lang, Bern, 70; co-ed, Neukirch-Anthologie, Vol III, IV, V, VII, Niemeyer, Tubingen, 70; coauth, Stefan George, Twayne, 72; ed, H A von Abschatz, Gedichte, Herbert Lang, Bern, 73; auth, Marc-Antoine e Saint-Amant und Hans ABmann von Abschatz, In: Europaische Tradition, Francke, Bern, 73; Diatonisch-Doppelt-Erfahrenes, Blaeschke, Darmstadt, 77; co-ed, A Albertinus: Hofschul, Lang, Bern, 78; auth, Reading Andreas Gryphius, Critical Trends 1664-1993, Camden, 94. **CONTACT ADDRESS** Dept of Mod Lang, SUNY, Buffalo, PO Box 604620, Buffalo, NY 14260-4620. **EMAIL** eam3@acsu.buffalo.edu

METZGER, LORE
PERSONAL Born 05/08/1925, Frankfurt, Germany **DISCIPLINE** ENGLISH AND COMPARATIVE LITERATURE **EDUCATION** Hunter Col, BA, 46; Columbia Univ, MA, 47, PhD, 56. **CAREER** Instr English, Mt Holyoke Col, 56-59; Am Asn Univ Women fel, 59-60; from instr to asst prof English, Univ Wash, 60-64; assoc prof English and comp lit, Mich State Univ, 64-68; Prof English, Emory Univ, 68-, Huntington Libr res grant, 63; fel consult, Nat Endowment for Humanities, 71-74. **MEMBERSHIPS** MLA; Am Comp Lit Asn; Southern Comp Lit Asn; Northeast Mod Lang Asn. **RESEARCH** Romanticism; literary theory; modern drama. **SELECTED PUBLICATIONS** Auth, Korinth, Studies in Eighteenth Century Culture, Vol 22, 92. **CONTACT ADDRESS** Dept of English, Emory Univ, Atlanta, GA 30322.

METZGER, MICHAEL MOSES
PERSONAL Born 06/02/1935, Frankfurt, Germany, m, 1958 **DISCIPLINE** GERMAN LANGUAGE & LITERATURE **EDUCATION** Columbia Univ, BA, 56; Cornell Univ, PhD(Ger lit), 62. **CAREER** Instr Ger, Univ Ill, Urbana, 61-63; from asst prof to assoc prof, 63-71, prof Ger, State Univ NY, Buffalo, 71-, guest prof Ger Lit, Univ Va, Charlottesville, 77. **MEMBERSHIPS** MLA; Am Asn Teachers Ger; Internationale Vereinigung fur Germanische; Sprach-und Literaturwissenschaft. **RESEARCH** German literature of the Enlightenment and 20th century; Lessing; the early 18th century. **SELECTED PUBLICATIONS** Auth, Lessing and the Language of Comedy, Mouton, The Hague, 66; coauth, Paul Klee, 67 & Clara und Robert Schumann, 67, Houghton; Der Hofmeister und die Gouvernante, de Gruyter, 69; Stefan George, Twayne, 72; co-ed, Aegidius Albertinus Hof-Schul, Lang, Bern, 78; Neukirch-Anthologie, Vol V-VII, Niemeyer, Tubingen, 81-91; Fairy Tales as Ways of Knowing, Lang, Bern, 81; co auth Reading Andreas Gryphius, Camden, Columbis, SC, 95. **CONTACT ADDRESS** Dept of Mod Lang & Lit, SUNY, Buffalo, PO Box 604620, Buffalo, NY 14260-4620. **EMAIL** mmetzger@acsu.buffalo.edu

METZIDAKIS, ANGELO
DISCIPLINE FRENCH LANGUAGE AND LITERATURE **EDUCATION** Yale Univ, BA; MA; MPhil; PhD. **CAREER** Prof, Sweet Briar Col. **RESEARCH** 19th-century French civilization; French romanticism; the 19th century French novel; Victor Hugo; stylistics; transl. **SELECTED PUBLICATIONS** Auth, publ(s) about Victor Hugo's Les Miserables. **CONTACT ADDRESS** Sweet Briar Col, Sweet Briar, VA 24595. **EMAIL** pr@sbc.edu

MEWS, SIEGFRIED
PERSONAL Born 09/28/1933, Berlin, Germany, 1 child **DISCIPLINE** GERMAN LITERATURE, COMPARATIVE LITERATURE **EDUCATION** Univ Hamburg, Staatsexamen, 61; Southern Ill Univ, MA, 63; Univ Ill, Urbanna, PhD(comp lit), 67. **CAREER** Instr Ger, Centre Col, 62-63; instr, Univ Ill, 66-67; from asst prof to assoc prof Ger, 67-77, ed, Studies Germanic Lang & Lit, 68-80, Prof Ger, Univ NC, Chapel Hill, 77-. **MEMBERSHIPS** MLA; Am Asn Teachers Ger; AAUP; Am Comp Lit Asn; Int Brecht Soc. **RESEARCH** German and comparative literature of the 19th and 20th centuries. **SELECTED PUBLICATIONS** Ed, Studies in German Literature of the Nineteenth and Twentieth Centuries, Univ NC, 70, 2nd ed, 72; Carl Zuckmayer: Der Hauptmann von Koepenick, 72, 3rd ed, 82 & Zuckmayer: Des Teufels General, 73, 2nd ed, 79, Diesterweg; co-ed, Essays on Brecht: Theater and Politics, Univ NC, 74 & 79; ed, Bertolt Brecht: Herr Puntila und sein Knecht Matti, 75 & Brecht: Der Kaukasische, Kreidedreis, 80, Diesterweg; auth, Carl Zuckmayer, 81, Twayne; ed, The Fisherman and His Wife: Gunter Grass's The Flounder in Critical Perspective, AMS Press, 82. **CONTACT ADDRESS** Dept of Ger Lang, Univ of No Carolina, Chapel Hill, Chapel Hill, NC 27514. **EMAIL** Mews@email.unc.edu

MEYER, DORIS
PERSONAL Born 01/02/1942, Summit, NJ, m **DISCIPLINE** SPANISH **EDUCATION** Harvard Univ, Radcliffe, BA, 63; Univ Va, MA, 64, PhD, 67. **CAREER** Asst prof, 67-69, Univ NC Wilmington; instr to assoc prof to prof, 69-86, Brooklyn Col; vis prof to Roman S & Tatiana Weller Prof Emeritus, 86-, Ct Col; vis scholar, 98-, Univ NM. **HONORS AND AWARDS** Phi Beta Kappa, 63; Spanish Embassy Fell, 61; Harvard Latin Amer Travel Fel, 62; Woodrow Wilson Fel, 63-64, 64-65; Fulbright Fel, 63-64; CUNY Faculty Res Awds, 73-74, 76-77, 77-78; Amer Philos Soc Grant, 76; NEH Fel, 77-78. **MEMBERSHIPS** PEN, Modern Lang Assoc; Amer Assoc of Teachers of Spanish & Portuguese; Latin Amer Stud Assoc; Feministas Unidas. **SELECTED PUBLICATIONS** Auth, Victoria Ocampo: Against the Wind and the Tide, Brazilles, 79, reprint Univ Tex Pr, 90; ed, Lives on the Line: The Testimony on Contemporary Latin Am Authors, Univ Calif Pr, 88; ed, Reinterpreting the Spanish American Essay: Women Writers of the 19th and 20th Centuries, Univ Tx Press, 95; ed, Rereading the Spanish American Essay: Translations of 19th and 20th Centuries Women's Essays, Univ Tx Press, 95; auth, Speaking for Themselves: Neomexicano Cultural Identity and the Spanish-Language Press, 1880-1920, Univ NM Press, 96; art, The Early (Feminist) Essays of Victoria Ocampo, Stud Twentieth Century Lit, 96; art, The Correspondence of Gabriela Mistral and Victoria Ocampo: Reflections on American Identity, J of Inst of Romance Stud, 96. **CONTACT ADDRESS** 68 Estates Dr, Santa Fe, NM 87501. **EMAIL** dmey22@aol.com

MEYER, PAUL HUGO
PERSONAL Born 12/05/1920, Berlin, Germany, m, 1946, 3 children **DISCIPLINE** FRENCH **EDUCATION** McGill Univ, BA, 43, MA, 45; Columbia Univ, PhD (French), 54. **CAREER** Lectr French, Columbia Univ, 51-52; instr, Bryn Mawr Col, 52-54; instr, 54-57, asst prof, 57-62, assoc prof, 62-66, Prof French, Univ Conn, 66-, Am Coun Learned Soc res grant-in-aid, 58; Fulbright res scholar in France, 61-62; mem nat selection comt, Inst Int Educ, 71-73. **MEMBERSHIPS** MLA; Am Asn Teachers Fr; Am Soc 18th Century Studies; Int Asn Fr Studies; Soc Fr Etud XVIIIe Siecle. **RESEARCH** French philosophers; 18th century French and comparative literature; history of ideas. **SELECTED PUBLICATIONS** Auth, Blueprint--A Study of Diderot and the Encyclopedie Plates, Fr Rev, Vol 68, 95. **CONTACT ADDRESS** Dept of Romance Lang, Univ of Connecticut, Storrs, Storrs, CT 06268.

MEYER, PRISCILLA
PERSONAL Born 08/26/1942, New York, NY, m, 1974, 1 child **DISCIPLINE** RUSSIAN **EDUCATION** Univ Calif, BA, 64; Princeton Univ MA, 66; PhD, 71. **CAREER** Lecturer to Full Prof, Wesleyan Univ, 68-.; Vis Fel, London Univ, 97; Vis

Asst Prof, Yale Univ, 74. **HONORS AND AWARDS** Fel, Ford Foundation, 64-68; Grant, Ford Foundation, 70; Sen Exchange Scholar, Moscow State Univ, 73; Fel, Ctr for the Humanities, 73. **MEMBERSHIPS** AAASS, ATSEEL, Tolstoy Soc, Dostoevsky Soc, Nabokov Soc. **SELECTED PUBLICATIONS** Auth, find What the Sailor Has Hidden: Vladimir Nabokov's Pale Fire, Wesleyan Univ Press, 88; ed, Dostoevsky and Gogol: Prose and Criticism, Ardis Pub, 79; ed, Andrey Bitov, Life in Windy Weather, Ardis, 86; ed, Essays on Nikolai Gogol: Logos and the Russian Word, Northwestern Univ Press, 92; auth, "Anna Karenina: Tolstoy's Polemic with Madame Bovary," Russian Review, (95): 243-259; auth, "Supernatural Doubles: Vii and The Nose," the Russian Gothic, forthcoming; auth, "Nabokov's Sebastian Knight and Despair: Thesis and Antithesis," Egzil Emigracija, (97): 105-105; auth, "Crime and Punishment and Jules Janin's La confession," Russian Review, 99; auth, "The Fantastic in the Everyday: Gogol and Hoffmann," Cold Fusion, forthcoming; auth, "The Real Mound, The Real Knight: Stoppard and Nabokov," Nabokov at the Crossroads, Macmillan, forthcoming. **CONTACT ADDRESS** Dept Russian, Wesleyan Univ, 300 High St, Middletown, CT 06459-3233. **EMAIL** pmeyer@wesleyan.edu

MEYER, RONALD
DISCIPLINE SLAVIC LANGUAGES **EDUCATION** Ind Univ, PhD, 86. **CAREER** Prof. **RESEARCH** 20th-century Russian prose and poetry; contemporary Russian literature; Russian women's literature. **SELECTED PUBLICATIONS** Ed, My Half Century. **CONTACT ADDRESS** Dept of Slavic Languages, Columbia Col, New York, 2960 Broadway, New York, NY 10027-6902. **EMAIL** rm56@columbia.edu

MEYERS, CAROL L.
PERSONAL Born 11/26/1942, Wilkes-Barre, PA, m, 1964, 2 children **DISCIPLINE** WOMEN STUDIES **EDUCATION** Wellesley Col, AB, 64; Brandeis Univ, MA, 66; PhD, 75. **CAREER** Prof Religion, Duke Univ, 90-; dir Women's Studies Program, Duke Univ, 92; assoc dir Women's Studies Program, Duke Univ, 86-90, 92-98; consultant, DreamWorks production of Prince of Egypt, 97-98; Ntl Endowment Humanities Inst on Image & Reality of Women in Near East Soc, 95; vis fac, Univ Conn, 94-; Consultant, Lilith Publications Network, 94-; Consultant, "Mysteries of the Bible," for Cable TV, 93; Consultant, New Dominion Pictures, 92-93; Consultant, "Religion, Culture, and Family," Univ Chi Divinity School, 91-97; assoc prof, Duke Univ, 84-90; Res Fac, Duke Univ, 83-; co-dir, Duke Univ Summer Prog in Israel, 80-. **HONORS AND AWARDS** Wellesley Wellesey Col Alumnae Achievement Awd, 99; Intl Correspondence Fel, Bar Ilan Univ, 98-; Frankfurt am Main Res Assoc, Johann Wolfgang Goethe Universitat, 95; Alumni Distinguished Undergraduate Tchg Awd Nominee, 94; Severinghaus Awd, Wellesley Col, 91; Princeton Univ Vis Fel, 90-91; Princeton Univ Res Member, 90-91; Ntl Endowment Humanities, 82-83, 90-91; Howard Found Fel, 85-86; Duke Univ Res Council, 83-84, 85-86, 87-88, 90-91, 92-93, 93-94, 99-00; Oxford Univ Vis Res Fel, 82-83; Oxford Centre for Postgraduate Hebrew Studies Vis Scholar, 82-83; Duke Univ Fac Summer Fel, 82; Cooperative Program in Judaic Studies Publications Grant, 81. **MEMBERSHIPS** Amer Acad Relig; Amer Schools of Oriental Res; Archaeol Inst Amer; Archaeol Soc Jordan; Assoc Jewish Studies; British School of Archaeol in Jerusalem; Cath Bibl Assoc; Center for Cross-Cult Res on Women; Harvard Semitic Museum; Israel Exploration Soc; Palestine Exploration Soc; Soc Bibl Lit; Soc Values in Higher Ed; Wellesley Col Center for Res on Women; Women's Assoc of Ancient Near East Studies; Women's Caucus, Assoc for Jewish Studies. **RESEARCH** Syro-Palestinian Archaelogy; Hebrew Bible; Gender in the Biblical World **SELECTED PUBLICATIONS** Ed, Women in Scripture, Houghton-Mifflen, 00; Coauth, Families in Ancient Israel, Westminister/John Knox Pr, 97; co-ed, Sepphoris in Galilee: Cross-Currents of Culture, N Carolina Museum Art, 96; coauth, Zippori (Sepphoris) 1994, Excavations & Surveys in Israel, 97; "New Faces of Eve," Humanistic Judaism, 97-98. **CONTACT ADDRESS** Dept of Religion, Duke Univ, Box 90964, Durham, NC 27708-0964. **EMAIL** carol@.duke.edu

MEYERS, WALTER EARL
PERSONAL Born 07/01/1939, Pittsburgh, PA, m, 1961, 3 children **DISCIPLINE** SCIENCE FICTION, ENGLISH LINGUISTICS **EDUCATION** Duquesne Univ, BA, 64; Univ Fla, PhD(English), 67. **CAREER** From asst prof to assoc prof, 67-78, Prof English, NC State Univ, 78- **HONORS AND AWARDS** SAtlantic Mod Lang Asn Studies Awd, 78. **MEMBERSHIPS** Am Dialect Soc; MLA; Sci Fiction Res Asn. **RESEARCH** Medieval drama; modern English usage. **SELECTED PUBLICATIONS** Auth, Linguistics in TextbooksA 40-Year Comparison, Am Speech, Vol 70, 95;The Work of Aldiss, Brian, W.--An Annotated Bibliography and Guide, Sci Fiction Stu, Vol 20, 93; The Grammarians Desk--Krankor, Sci Fiction Stud, Vol 24, 97. **CONTACT ADDRESS** Dept of English, No Carolina State Univ, Raleigh, NC 27650. **EMAIL** meyers@social.chass.ncsu.edu

MIANO, ALICE
PERSONAL Born 01/30/1960, Poughkeepsie, NY, m, 1994, 2 children **DISCIPLINE** LINGUISTICS **EDUCATION** Univ Calif at Los Angeles, BA, 82; MA, 90. **CAREER** Lectr, Stanford Univ, 91-; Spanish Lang Coord, Stanford Univ, 96-. **HONORS AND AWARDS** Gores Awd for Excellence in Teaching, Stanford Univ, 97; Flanders Fel, Univ Calif at Berkeley, 99-00. **MEMBERSHIPS** ACTFL, AAAL, AATSP. **RESEARCH** Cross-cultural Pragmatics, Language and Identity, Latinos and Literacy in the U.S. **CONTACT ADDRESS** Span & Port, Stanford Univ, Stanford, CA 94305. **EMAIL** alimiano@leland.stanford.edu

MICHAEL, COLETTE
PERSONAL Born, France, d **DISCIPLINE** FRENCH, PHILOSOPHY **CAREER** Prof, N Ill Univ. **HONORS AND AWARDS** Ford Fel. **RESEARCH** Phenomenology. **CONTACT ADDRESS** Dept For Lang, No Illinois Univ, 1425 W Lincoln Hwy, Dekalb, IL 60115-2828. **EMAIL** cmichael@niu.edu

MICHAEL, COLETTE VERGER
PERSONAL Born Marseille, France, 6 children **DISCIPLINE** FRENCH AND PHILOSOPHY **EDUCATION** Univ Wash Seattle, fr and philos, BA, 69; Univ Wash Seattle, romance lang, MA, 70; Univ Wisc Madison, hist of sci, MA, 75; Univ Wisc Madison, fr and minor philos, PhD, 73. **CAREER** Tchg asst, Fr and Ital Dept, Univ Wisc Madison, 9/73-12/73; lectr, extension dept, Univ Wisc Madison, 7/74-8/74; lectr, fr and ital dept, Univ Wisc Madison, 2/74-8/74; prof, humanities, Shimer Col, Mt Carroll, Ill, 75-77; asst prof, foreign lang and lit, Northern Ill Univ, 77-84; assoc prof, foreign lang and lit, Northern Ill Univ, 84-90; prof, foreign lang and lit, Northern Ill Univ, 90-. **HONORS AND AWARDS** Consulat General de France Svc Culturel, Subvention for Bulletin de la Soc Amer de Philos, Jan, 92; Facul Develop grant, Hist and Tech of Fr Cinema, Fall, 91; Deans fund for res in the humanities, Spring, 87; Deans' Fund for Res, Grad Sch, Northern Ill Univ, asst for res on Negritude, Fall, 85; Deans's Fund for Res, Grad Sch, Northern Ill Univ, asst for res on The Marquis de Sade: The Man, His Works and His Critics, Fall, 83; Res award from Dean of Grad Sch, Northern Ill Univ, Topic: Choderlos de Laclos, The Man, His Works, and His Critics, Jan 80-Jun 80; Grad Sch Summer grant, NIU Topic: The Marquis de Condorcet, His Work, His Ideology, His Influence, 78; Nat Endow for the Humanities Summer Fel for Col Tchrs, Univ Ill Univ, Champaign, Topic: The European Enlightenment in the Amer Revolution, Summer, 77; Ford Found Fel, Fr and Ital Dept, Univ Wisc Madison, 71, 72, 73; Nonresident scholar, The Grad Sch, Univ Wisc Madison, 71-72. **RESEARCH** Philosophy, 18th Century. **SELECTED PUBLICATIONS** Articles, Camus, Science and Metaphors, Bull de la Soc Amer de Philos de Lang Fr VIII, 2, 78-88, 96; A la recherche de l'absolu: le neant des ecrivains maudits, Actes du Congres Intl des Soc de Philos de lang Fr, Poitiers, Fr, 167-169, 96; L'audiovisuel et la litterature francophone, Rev Francophone, VIII, 2, 73-83, 95; Justine ou la vertu devant la violence, Actes de Ile Congres mondial sur la violence et la coexistence humaine, Montreal, Vol VII, 429-435, 95; Billy Budd: An Allegory on the Rights of Man, Allegory Old and New: Creativity and Continuity in Culture, Analecta Husserliana, XLII, 251-258, 94; Light and Darkness and the Phenomenon of Creation in Victor Hugo, Analecta Husserliana: The Elemental Dialectic of Light and Darkness, XXXVIII, 131-149; Les Lettres de Doleances: Un Genre de Cahiers, ou Cahiers d'un nouveau Genre? Lang de la Revolution 1770-1815, Inst Nat de la Lang Fr: Lexicometrie et textes polit, Paris, Klimcksieck, 251-264, 95. **CONTACT ADDRESS** 635 Joanne Ln., De Kalb, IL 60115. **EMAIL** tc0cvm1@corn.cso.niu.edu

MICHAEL, WOLFGANG FRIEDRICH
PERSONAL Born 02/23/1909, Freiburg, Germany, m, 1952, 3 children **DISCIPLINE** GERMAN **EDUCATION** Univ Munich, Phd, 34. **CAREER** Instr Ger, Bryn Mawr Col, 39; asst prof, Chestnut Hill Col, 39-46; from asst prof to assoc prof, 46-61, Prof Ger, Univ Tex, Austin, 61- **HONORS AND AWARDS** Verdienstkreuz der Bundesrepublik, Goethemedaille. **MEMBERSHIPS** MLA. **RESEARCH** Renaissance and Reformation; Thomas Mann. **SELECTED PUBLICATIONS** Auth, The staging of the Bozen Passion Play, Ger Rev; Das deutsche Drama und Theater vor der Reformation: ein Forschungsbericht, 57 & Stoff und Idee im Tod in Venedit, 59, Deut Viertel-jahrs-schrift fur Literaturwissenschaft und Geistesgeschichte; Die Anfaenge des Theaters zu Freiburg im Breisgau; Die Geistlichen Prozessionsspiele in Deutschland; Fruhformen der Deutschen Buhne, Selbstverlag der Ges fur Theatergeschichte, Berlin, 63 Das Deutsche Drama des Mittelalters, de Gruyter, Berlin, 71. **CONTACT ADDRESS** Dept of Ger, Univ of Texas, Austin, Austin, TX 78712.

MICHAELIS, LAURA A.
PERSONAL Born 06/18/1964, Fort Eustis, VA **DISCIPLINE** LINGUISTICS **EDUCATION** Univ Calif Berkeley, BA, 86; MA, 88; PhD, 93. **CAREER** Asst Prof, Univ Colo, 93-. **HONORS AND AWARDS** Fel, Nat Sci Found, 98; Dept Citation, Univ Calif Berkeley, 86. **MEMBERSHIPS** Intl Pragmatics Asn; Ling Soc of Am. **RESEARCH** The relationship between meaning and formal structure and between meaning and inference. **SELECTED PUBLICATIONS** Auth, "Expectation Contravention and Use Ambiguity: The Vietnamese Connective 'cung'," J of Pragmatics, 94; auth, "The Ambiguity of the English Perfect," J of Linguistics, 94; auth, "A Case of Constructional Polysemy in Latin," Studies in Lang, 94;co-auth, "Toward a Construction-based Account of Language Function: The Case of Nominal Extraposition," Lang, 96; auth, "The Use and Meaning of 'already'," Ling and Philos, 96; auth, Aspectual Grammar and Past-Time Reference, Routledge, 98; co-auth, Beyond alternations: A Construction-based Account of the German Applicative Pattern, CSLI Pub, 01; co-auth, "Topicalization and Left Dislocation: A Functional Opposition Revisited," J of Pragmatics, 01; co-auth, "Valence Creation and the German Applicative: The Inherent Semantics of Argument-Structure Constructions," J of Semantics, 01. **CONTACT ADDRESS** Dept Ling, Univ of Colorado, Boulder, 295UCB, Boulder, CO 80309. **EMAIL** laura.michaelis@colorado.edu

MICHAELS, DAVID
DISCIPLINE LINGUISTICS **EDUCATION** Univ Mich, PhD. **CAREER** Prof, Univ Conn. **RESEARCH** Phonological theory. **SELECTED PUBLICATIONS** Auth, Syllable structure, phonetics and phonology, Revue de Phonetique Appliquee 91-93, (89): 331-346; Prosegments and Syllable Structure, Revista di Grammatica Generativa 14, 89; Movement Rules in Phonology, In Certamen Phonologicum II, Rosenberg and Seiler, Torino, 91; auth, Adjunction in syllable structure, Proceedings of the XIIth International Congress of Phonetic Sciences 5, Universite de Provence, (91): 114-117; auth, Natural and Unnatural Phonology, Phonologica, 88, Cambridge Univ Press, 92. **CONTACT ADDRESS** Dept of Linguistics, Univ of Connecticut, Storrs, 1266 Storrs Rd, Storrs, CT 06269-1085. **EMAIL** david.michaels@uconn.edu

MICHAELS, JENNIFER
PERSONAL Born 05/19/1945, United Kingdom, m, 1972, 3 children **DISCIPLINE** GERMAN **EDUCATION** Edinburgh Univ, MA, 67; McGill Univ, MA, 71; PhD, 74. **CAREER** Teaching Asst, Wesleyan Univ, 67-68; Instr, Bucknell Univ, 68-69; From Assoc Prof to Prof, Grinnell Col, 75-. **HONORS AND AWARDS** Samuel R and Marie-Louise Rosenthal Fel, 94-96. **MEMBERSHIPS** Ger Studies Asn, Otto Gross Soc, Franz Werfel Soc, Soc for Exile Studies, MLA, RMMLA, AATG. **RESEARCH** Twentieth-Century German and Austrian literature and culture. **SELECTED PUBLICATIONS** Auth, D H Lawrence: The Polarity of North and South, 76; auth, Anarchy and Eros: Otto Gross, 83; auth, Franz Jung, 89; auth, Franz Werfel, 94, Numerous articles on Twentieth-Century German and Austrian authors. **CONTACT ADDRESS** Dept Lang, Grinnell Col, PO Box 805, Grinnell, IA 50112-0805. **EMAIL** michaels@grinnell.edu

MICHALCZYK, JOHN JOSEPH
PERSONAL Born 06/26/1941, Scranton, PA, m, 3 children **DISCIPLINE** FRENCH LITERATURE, CINEMA **EDUCATION** Boston Col, BA, 66, MA, 67; Harvard Univ, PhD (French lit & cinema), 72; Weston Col, MDiv, 74. **CAREER** Instr & chmn French & cinema, Loyola High Sch, Towson, Md, 67-69; instr, int French through film, Harvard Univ, 71-71; instr, graduate summer program in French, Rivier Col (Nashua, NH), 72-76; asst prof French & cinema, 74-80, assoc prof Fine Arts Dept, Boston Col, 80-, dir of film studies, Boston Col, 84-, prof & chmn Fine Arts Dept, 96-. **HONORS AND AWARDS** 2 New England Emmy Nominations for films: "Of Stars and Shamrocks: Boston's Jews & Irish" and "In the Shadow of the Reich: Nazi Medicine"; Distinguished documentary award from TASH (The Asn for the Severely Handicapped) for "Nazi Medicine"; "Palmes Academiques" from French Government for 25 years of contributions to French culture; Contemporary Authors; Fulbright (Italy); Mellon (Costa-Gavras). **MEMBERSHIPS** Malraux Soc. **RESEARCH** Issues of Social Justice in art, literature, and film; documentary film production. **SELECTED PUBLICATIONS** Auth, Malraux, le cinema, et La Condition humaine, 1/74 & Le cinema polonais en '73, 4/74, Cinema '74; Camus/Malraux: A staged version of Le Temps du mepris, 10/76 & Robbe-Grillet, Michelet and Barthes: From La Sorciere to Glissements progressifs du plaisir, 12/77, Fr Rev; Andre Malraux's Film Espoir: The Propaganda/Art Film and the Spanish Civil War, Romance Monogr, 77; Ingmar Bergman: La, Passion d'etre homme aujourd'hue, Beauchesne, Paris, 77; Recurrent Imagery of the Labyrinth in Robbe-Grillet's Films, Stanford Fr Rev, spring 78; The French Literary Filmmakers, Asn Univ Press, 80; Costa-Gavras: The Political Fiction Film, Arts Alliance Press, 84; Italian Political Filmmakers, Fairleigh Dickinson Univ Press, 86; Medicine, Ethics, and the Third Reich: Historical and Contemporary Issues, Sheed and Ward, 94; The Resisters, the Rescuers, and the Refugees, Sheed and Ward, 97; and articles on film and its relation to literature and the arts in: American Soc Legion of Honor; Annali d'Iliansistica; Cineaste; Cinema (Paris); Cinema and Soc (Paris); Contemporary French Civ; Current Research in Film; French Review; Lit/Film Quart; Magill's Cinema Annual; Melanges Malraux Miscellany; Stanford French Review; Twentieth Century Lit. **CONTACT ADDRESS** Fine Arts Dept, Boston Col, Chestnut Hill, 140 Commonwealth Ave, Chestnut Hill, MA 02167-3800. **EMAIL** john.michalczyk@bc.edu

MICHALSKI, JOHN
PERSONAL Born 10/13/1934, Czernowitz, Rumania **DISCIPLINE** COMPARATIVE LITERATURE & LINGUISTICS

EDUCATION Univ Toledo, BA, 53; Inst World Affairs, cert; Northwestern Univ, MA, 54. CAREER Asst Ger, Northwestern Univ, 53-55; lectr mod lang, Roosevelt Univ, 56-57; instr, Marquette Univ, 57-61; asst prof Europ lang, Univ Hawaii, 61-68; asst to dean educ serv, 70-71, chmn First Hawaiian Innovations Inst, 72-73, prof Ger, Speech -Commun, Ling & Chmn Div Lang Arts, Leeward Community Col, 68-, Consult export & import policies, 54-; co-dir int serv ctr, Chicago Machine Tool Expos, 55; ed, Hawaii Lang Teacher. MEMBERSHIPS MLA; Am Asn Teachers Ger; Am Anthrop Asn; Am Comp Lit Asn; Am Coun Teaching Foreign Lang. RESEARCH Language teaching; communications; creative writing. SELECTED PUBLICATIONS Contribr, Am Peoples Encycl, 56-57 & Encycl World Lit, 63-64; auth, Stefan Andres: Wir sind Utopia, Heath, 63; Deutsche Dichter und Denker, Blaisdall, 67; Ferdinant Raimund, Twayne, 68. CONTACT ADDRESS Div of Lang Arts, Leeward Comm Col, 96-045 Ala Ike, Pearl City, HI 96782-3393. EMAIL j-michalski@lccada.lcc.hawaii.edu

MICHELINI, ANN NORRIS
PERSONAL Born 03/14/1939, Baltimore, MD, m, 1958, 3 children **DISCIPLINE** CLASSICS **EDUCATION** Radcliff Col, AB, 60; Harvard Univ, PhD, 71. **CAREER** Asst prof, 71-73, Univ Mass Boston; asst prof, 73-78, Harvard Univ; asst, assoc, prof, 78-, Univ of Cincinnati. **MEMBERSHIPS** APA; AAUP; AAUW; Class Asn of Midwest & South. **RESEARCH** Greek tragedy; Plato **SELECTED PUBLICATIONS** Auth, Tradition and Dramatic Form in the Persians of Aeschylus, Cin Class Series 4, sec 1 & sec 2, Brill, 82; auth, Euripides and the Tragic Tradition, Part 1 & Part 2, Wisconsin Univ Press, 87; rev, Black Athena Journal of Womens History, 93; art, The Dance of the Elements Fragment B17 of Empedocles, Power and Spirit, Annalex Univ Turkuensis, 93; art, Political Themes in Euripides Suppliants, Amer Jour Of Phil, 94; rev, Euripides Conformist Deviant or Neoconservative, Arion, 97; art, Alcibiades and Theseus in Euripides Suppliants Colby Quart, 97; art, Rudeness and Irony in Platos Gorgias, Class Phil, 93. **CONTACT ADDRESS** Classics Dept, Univ of Cincinnati, ML 0226, Cincinnati, OH 45221-0226. **EMAIL** ann.michelini@uc.edu

MICKEL, EMANUEL J.
PERSONAL Born 10/11/1937, Lamont, IL, m, 1959, 3 children **DISCIPLINE** FRENCH LITERATURE **EDUCATION** La State Univ, BA, 59; Univ of NC, MA, 61; PhD, 65. **CAREER** Asst to assoc prof, Univ of Nebr, 65-68; assoc prof to prof, Ind Univ Bloomington, 68-. **HONORS AND AWARDS** Lilly Open Fel, 81-82; NEH Grant, 80-82; 82-83; 84-86; Chevalier dans l"ordre des Palmes Academiques, 97. **MEMBERSHIPS** ALSC, Medieval Acad of Am; Int Marie de France Soc. **RESEARCH** Medieval French Literature, Nineteenth-Century French Literature and Painting, Chanson de geste, romance, Drama, Poetry, Novel, Painting, Allegory. **SELECTED PUBLICATIONS** Auth, Marie de France, 74; auth, Naissance du Chevalier au Cygne, 77; auth, Eugene Fromentin, 82; auth, Genelon Treason and the Chanson de Roland, 89, auth, auth, Jules Verne's Complete Twenty Thousand Leagues Under the Sea, 92; auth, The Enfances Godefroc and the Retour de Cornumarant, 99. **CONTACT ADDRESS** Dept Fr and Ital, Indiana Univ, Bloomington, 1020 E Kirkwood Ave, Ballantine Hall 642, Bloomington, IN 47405-7103. **EMAIL** mickel@indiana.edu

MICKLESEN, LEW R.
PERSONAL Born 01/09/1921, Red Wing, MN, m, 1950, 3 children **DISCIPLINE** SLAVIC LINGUISTICS **EDUCATION** Univ Minn, BS, 42; Harvard Univ, PhD, 51. **CAREER** Instr Russ and Span, US Navel Acad, 45-46; sr instr Russ, Air Force Russ Prog, Syracuse Univ, 51-52; asst prof, Univ Ore, 52-53; asst prof Slavic ling, Univ Wash, 53-59; group mgr mech transl, Int Bus Machines Res Ctr, 59-63; assoc prof Slavic ling, Univ Colo, 63-64; prof, Univ Ill, 64-66; Prof Slavic Ling, Univ Wash, 66- **MEMBERSHIPS** Am Asn Teachers Slavic and EEurop Lang; Ling Soc Am; Int Ling Asn. **RESEARCH** Balto-Slavic accentology; Russian morphology; Russian syntax. **SELECTED PUBLICATIONS** Auth, The Accentual Patterns o te Slavic Languages, Elementa Jur Slavic Stud Comp Cult Semiotics, Vol 2, 95. **CONTACT ADDRESS** Dept of Slavic Lang and Lit, Univ of Washington, Seattle, WA 98195. **EMAIL** lrmickl@u.washington.edu

MIGIEL, MARILYN
DISCIPLINE ITALIAN LITERATURE **EDUCATION** Cornell Univ, AB, 75; Yale Univ, PhD, 81. **CAREER** Assoc prof **HONORS AND AWARDS** Stephen and Margery Russell awd for Distinguished tchg, 95; Amer Coun of Learned Societies, Grant-in-Aid, $3000, 92; Mellon Postdoc res and tchg fel, Cornell Univ, 86-87; Phi Beta Kappa, 75; Lane Cooper Scholarship, 74-75; scholarship, Cornell Branch Telluride Asn, 72-75. **RESEARCH** Italian literature. **SELECTED PUBLICATIONS** Auth, Gender and Genealogy in Tasso's, Gerusalemme Liberata, Lewiston, NY: Edwin Mellen Press, 93; Veronica Franco, In Italian Women Writers: A Bio-Bibliographical Sourcebook, Westport, CT: Greenwood Press, 94; Olimpia's Secret Weapon: Gender, War, and Hermeneutics in Ariosto's Orlando Furioso, Critical Matrix: The Princeton Journal of Women, Gender, and Culture 95; ed, Refiguring Woman: Perspectives on Gender and the Italian Renaissance, Ithaca: Cornell UP, 91. **CONTACT ADDRESS** Dept of Romance Studies, Cornell Univ, 293 Goldwin Smith Hall, Ithaca, NY 14853. **EMAIL** mm55@cornell.edu

MIGNOLO, WALTER
PERSONAL Born, Argentina, m, 2 children **DISCIPLINE** ROMANCE STUDIES **EDUCATION** Univ Nac Cordobe, Licenciatura,68; Ecole des Hautes Etudes, Doctorat de Troisieme Cycle, 74. **CAREER** Vis asst prof, Indiana Univ, 73-74; vis asst prof, Univ Mich, 74-75; from asst to assoc to prof, Univ Mich, 75-92; William H. Wannamaker Dist Prof, Duke Univ, 93-. **HONORS AND AWARDS** Fel study abroad, 69; Katherine Singer Kovacs Awd, MLA, 94. **MEMBERSHIPS** LASA, MLA, AAA, ASA. **RESEARCH** Globalization **CONTACT ADDRESS** Dept of Romance Studies, Duke Univ, 205 Language Bldg., Box 90257, Durham, NC 27708-0257. **EMAIL** wmignolo@acpub.duke.edu

MIGNONE, MARIO B.
PERSONAL Born 07/26/1940, Benevento, Italy, m, 1968, 3 children **DISCIPLINE** ITALIAN **EDUCATION** CUNY, BA, 67; Rutgers Univ, MA, 69; PhD, 72. **CAREER** Instr to Prof and Dept Chair, SUNY, 70-. **HONORS AND AWARDS** Who's Who in Am, Who's Who among Ital Am, Cavaliere el Menito della Republica Italiana. **MEMBERSHIPS** NE HLA, Am Asn of Teachers of Ital, Am Asn of Ital Studies, Asn of Ital Am Educators. **RESEARCH** contemporary Ital theater and fiction; The literature of emipration. **SELECTED PUBLICATIONS** Auth, Il teatro di Eduardo De Filippo: Critica sociale, Rome, 74; auth, Anormalita e angoscia nella narrativa di Dino Buzzati, Ravenna, 81; auth, Eduardo De Filippo, Boston, 84; ed, Pirandello in America, 88; ed, Columbus: Meeting of Cultures, Forum Italicum, 93; co-ed, Homage to Maravia, Forum Italicum, 93; auth, Italy Today: A Country in Transition, Peter Lang Pub, 95; auth, Italy Today: At the Crossroads of the New Millennium, Peter Lang Pub, 98. **CONTACT ADDRESS** Dept of European Lang, Lit and Culture, SUNY, Stony Brook, 100 Nicolls Rd, Stony Brook, NY 11794-3359. **EMAIL** mmignone@notes.cc.sunysb.edu

MIHAILESCU, CALIN ANDREI
DISCIPLINE FRENCH LITERATURE **EDUCATION** Univ Bucharest, BA; Univ Toronto, MA; PhD. **RESEARCH** Continental philosophy; postmodern trends; 17th century philosophy and theology; French thought. **SELECTED PUBLICATIONS** Auth, pub(s) on Pascal, St. John of the Cross, St. Teresa, Plato, Aristotle, Baltasar Gracian, Kant, Benjamin, Heidegger, Adorno, Huxley, T. Mann, utopian and dystopian discourses, semiotics of folklore and myth, and economic aspects of narrative. **CONTACT ADDRESS** Dept of Modern Languages, Univ of Western Ontario, London, ON, Canada N6A 5B8. **EMAIL** cmihails@julian.uwo.ca

MIHAILOVICH, VASA D.
PERSONAL Born 08/12/1926, Prokuplje, Yugoslavia, m, 1957, 2 children **DISCIPLINE** SLAVIC LANGUAGES AND LITERATURES **EDUCATION** Wayne State Univ, BA, 56, MA, 57; Univ Calif, Berkeley, PhD(Ger), 66. **CAREER** Teaching asst Ger, Univ Calif, Berkeley, 57-61; instr Russ, 61-63, from asst prof to assoc prof, 63-75, Prof Slavic Lang and Lit, Univ NC, Chapel Hill, 75-95. **MEMBERSHIPS** MLA; Am Asn Teachers Slavic and EEurop Lang; Am Asn Advan Slavic Studies; Am Asn SSlavic Studies; NAm Soc Serbian Studies. **RESEARCH** Russian literature; Yugoslav literatures; comparative study of Russian and Yugoslav literature and German. **SELECTED PUBLICATIONS** Auth, Introduction to Yugoslav Literature, 73, Auth, "White Stones and Fir Trees: An Anthology of Slavic Lit," 77, Auth, Contemporary Yugoslav Poetry, 77, Auth, "Songs of the Serbian People: From the Collections of Vuk St. Karadzic," 97, Auth, Modern Slavic Literature, 72, Auth, "Dictionary of Literary Biography: south Slavic Writers before World War II," 94, Auth, South Slavic Writers Since World War II, 97, Transl, Gorski vijenac--the Mountain Wreath. **CONTACT ADDRESS** Dept Slavic Lang and Lit, Univ of No Carolina, Chapel Hill, Chapel Hill, NC 27514. **EMAIL** vdmihail@email.unc.edu

MIKHAIL, MONA
PERSONAL Born, Egypt, s **DISCIPLINE** MODERN ARABIC LITERATURE, GENDER STUDIES **EDUCATION** Univ Mich, PhD, 73. **HONORS AND AWARDS** PEN Prize for Translation; Translation Prize, Columbia Univ. **MEMBERSHIPS** MESA; Am Res Cent in Egypt Ara Am Univ Grad; Middle E Studies Asn. **RESEARCH** Arabic comparative Literature; Gender/Women Studies. **SELECTED PUBLICATIONS** Auth, Images of Arab Women Fact and Fiction, Three Contintents Press, 79; auth, Studies in the Short Fiction of Idris and Mahfouz, NYU Press, 92. **CONTACT ADDRESS** Dept Near East Lang & Lit, New York Univ, 50 Washington Square S, New York, NY 10012-1018. **EMAIL** mnml@is.nyu.edu

MILEHAM, JAMES WARREN
PERSONAL Born 03/31/1943, Aruba, West Indies, m, 2 children **DISCIPLINE** FRENCH LITERATURE **EDUCATION** Lafayette Col, AB, 65; Univ Ala, MA, 69; Univ Wis- Madison, PhD(French), 75. **CAREER** Asst prof, 75-81, Assoc Prof French, Univ Wis-Milwaukee, 81-; ed, the U.S.A. bibliography in the Ann e Balzacienne, 95-. **RESEARCH** French novel. **SELECTED PUBLICATIONS** Auth, A web of conspiracy: Structure and metaphor in Balzac's novels, Ky Romance Quart, 79; Blazac's Seven of Probation, winter 80 & Numbers in the Comedic humaine, Vol XXII, No 1, Romance Notes; The Conspiracy Novel: Structure and Metaphor in Balzac's Comedic humaine, Fr Forum Publ, 82; Labyrinths in Balzac's Ferragus, Nineteenth Century Fr Studies, 23, 3 & 4, 95. **CONTACT ADDRESS** Dept of French, Ital, and Comp Lit, Univ of Wisconsin, Milwaukee, PO Box 413, Milwaukee, WI 53201-0413. **EMAIL** jmile@uwm.edu

MILES, DAVID HOLMES
PERSONAL Born 05/25/1940, Bangor, ME **DISCIPLINE** GERMAN **EDUCATION** Univ Maine, Orono, BA, 62; Princeton Univ, PhD, 68. **CAREER** Asst prof Ger, Univ Mass, Boston, 67-72; assoc prof, Ohio State Univ, 72-75; chmn dept, 78-80, Assoc Prof Ger, Univ VA, 75-, Alexander von Humboldt fel, Freiburg, Ger, 70-71; Guggenheim fel, 76-77; mem, Ctr Advan Study, Univ Va, 77-78. **HONORS AND AWARDS** PMLA Parker Prize, 79. **MEMBERSHIPS** MLA; Am Asn Teachers Ger. **RESEARCH** Modern German literature; comparative literature; literary theory and the visual arts. **SELECTED PUBLICATIONS** Auth, Up Close and In Motion, Volvo Invents Cubist TV, Jour Film Video, Vol 46, 95. **CONTACT ADDRESS** Dept of Ger, Univ of Virginia, Charlottesville, VA 22903.

MILES, GARY B.
PERSONAL Born 07/21/1940, St. John, NB, Canada, m, 1962, 2 children **DISCIPLINE** CLASSICS **EDUCATION** Colby Col, BA, 62; Harvard Univ, AM, 64; Yale Univ, PhD, 71. **CAREER** Philips Acad, Andover, 64-66; Wesleyan Univ, 68-69; Univ Texas, 70-71; Univ Cal, Santa Cruz, 71-. **HONORS AND AWARDS** Danforth fel, 62-68; NEH fel 86, Excellence Tchg, Univ Cal, 98. **MEMBERSHIPS** AIA/APA; Virgilian Soc; AHA **RESEARCH** Roman literature and cultural history, especially of the Late Republic; Early Empire; Historiography. **SELECTED PUBLICATIONS** Auth, The First Roman Marriage and the Theft of the Sabine Women, Innovations of Antiquity, Routledge, 92; Livy: Reconstructing Early Rome, Cornell Univ Press, 95; auth, The 'Aeneid' as Foundation Story, Reading Vergil's 'Aeneid,' 99. **CONTACT ADDRESS** Cowell Col, Univ of California, Santa Cruz, Santa Cruz, CA 95064. **EMAIL** miles@cats.ucsc.edu

MILHAM, MARY ELLA
PERSONAL Born 03/22/1922, Waukesha, WI **DISCIPLINE** CLASSICS **EDUCATION** Carroll Col, BA, 43; Univ Wis, MA, 44, PhD(classics, ling), 50. **CAREER** Instr classics and integrated lib studies, Univ Wis, 50-54; from asst prof to assoc prof, 54-68, Prof Classics, Univ NB, 68-, Can Coun sr res fel, 61-62, leave fel, 68-69; Soc Sci Human Res Coun leave fel, 81-82. **MEMBERSHIPS** Am Philol Asn; Ling Soc Am; Class Asn Can (vpres, 76-78); Humanities Asn Can (secy-treas, 66-68); Renaissance Soc Am. **RESEARCH** Late Latin; Renaissance Latin; textual criticism. **SELECTED PUBLICATIONS** Auth, Editions of Apicius, Feubner, 69, Apatina (MRTS, 98); Phoenix J Classical Assoc Can, Vol 45, 91. **CONTACT ADDRESS** 20900 W Cleveland Ave, New Berlin, WI 53151. **EMAIL** milham@nbnet.nb.ca

MILLER, ANDREW M.
PERSONAL Born 05/26/1947, CA **DISCIPLINE** CLASSICS **EDUCATION** Univ Calif, BA, anthrop, Greek, 69, MA, 71, PhD, 77, comparative lit. **CAREER** Asst prof classics, 77-83, assoc prof classics, 83-97, prof classics, 97-, Univ Pittsburgh. **HONORS AND AWARDS** NEH Fellowship for Study and Research, 81-82. **MEMBERSHIPS** Amer Philological Assn; Classical Assn Atlantic States. **RESEARCH** Greek and Roman poetry; translation studies. **SELECTED PUBLICATIONS** Auth, From Delos to Delphi: A Literary Study of the Homeric Hymn to Apollo, 86; auth, "Inventa Componere: Rhetorical Process and Poetic Composition in Pinder's Ninth Olympian Ode," Transactions of the American Philological Assn, vol 123, 93; auth, "Pindaric Mimesis: The Associative Mode," Classical Journ, vol 87, 93; auth, Greek Lyric: An Anthology in Translation, 96; auth, "Levels of Argument in Pinder's Second Nemean Ode," Hellas 7, 96. **CONTACT ADDRESS** Dept of Classics, Univ of Pittsburgh, Pittsburgh, PA 15260. **EMAIL** amm2@pitt.edu

MILLER, D. GARY
PERSONAL Born 12/12/1942, Allentown, PA, m, 1967, 2 children **DISCIPLINE** LINGUISTICS CLASSICS **EDUCATION** Moravian Col, AB, 64; Harvard Univ, PhD(ling), 69. **CAREER** Instr ling, Southern Ill Univ, 68-69; asst prof, Univ Ill, Urbana, 69-71 and McGill Univ, 71-72; asst prof ling and classics, 72-76, Assoc Prof Ling and Classics, Uiiv Fla, 76-, Pres, Academics Plus, Inc. **MEMBERSHIPS** Ling Soc Am; Philol Soc. **RESEARCH** Indo-European studies; linguistic theory. **SELECTED PUBLICATIONS** Auth, A Subharmonic Vibratory Pattern in Normal Vocal Folds, JSpeech Hearing Rsch, Vol 39, 96; The Birth of a Journal, Interpretation J Bible Theol, Vol 50, 96; A Structured Approach to Voice Range Pro-

file Phonetogram Analysis, JSpeech Hearing Rsch, Vol 37, 94. **CONTACT ADDRESS** Dept of Classics, Univ of Florida, 3c Arts and Sciences, Gainesville, FL 32611-9500.

MILLER, ERIC
DISCIPLINE GERMAN **CAREER** Assoc Prof of Literature, Pomona College, 98-; Active Faculty in Philosophy, Claremont Graduate Univ, 98-; Asst Prof of Modern Literature, Pomona College, 91-98; Lecturer in English, Univ of Pennsylvania, 89-90; Lecturer in Comp Lit, German, and Classics, Princeton Univ, 88-89; Research Assist for Dept of Comp Lit, Princeton Univ 84-86; Research Asst for Prof, Gunther Patzig, Philosophisches Seminar, Universitat Gottingen, 82-83; Research Assist for Prof, Albrecht Schone, Seminar fur deutsche Philologie, Universitat Gottingen, 80-82. **HONORS AND AWARDS** Wig Distinguished Teaching Awd, Pomona, 95; Jacob Javits Fellowship, 86-88; Fulbright-IIE Research Grant, 86-87; Bernhard Blume Prize for best senior thesis, 79; Phi Beta Kappa, elected in junior year, 78. **MEMBERSHIPS** Amer Assoc of Univ Professors; Amer Philosophical Assoc; Modern Language Assoc; Pacific Ancient and Modern Language Assoc; Amer Assoc of Teachers of German; Far West Popular Culture Assoc; Phi Beta Kappa. **SELECTED PUBLICATIONS** Auth, "Without a Key," The Narrative Structure of Kafka's Das Schlob, The Germanic Review, 91: 132-140; auth, "Is Literature Self-Referential?" Philosophy and Literature, 20, 96: 475-486; auth, "Literary Fiction and As-If Fiction," Philosophy and Rhetoric, 30, 97, 428-442; auth, "Masks of Negation," Greek eironeia and Schlegel's Ironie, European Romantic Review 8, 97, 360-385; auth, "Romantic Irony and Virtual Reality," Popular Culture Review 9, 98: 115-124; auth, "Der Stechlinsee, Symbol und Struktur in Fontanes Altersroman," Journal of English and Germanic Philology, 97, 98, 352-370; auth, "Die roten Faden des roten Hahns," Zu einem Motivkomplex im Stechlin, Fontane-Blatter, 67, 99: 92-106.; auth, "On Teaching Homer," Humanities/Communitas, forthcoming 00; **CONTACT ADDRESS** Dept German & Slavic Languages, Pomona Col, 333 North College Way, Claremont, CA 91711-4429. **EMAIL** emiller@pomona.edu

MILLER, J. MAXWELL
PERSONAL Born 09/20/1937, Kosciusko, MS, m, 1962, 2 children **DISCIPLINE** HEBREW BIBLE **EDUCATION** Millsaps Col, AB, 59; Emory Univ, PhD, 64; post-doctoral, Biblisch-arcaologisches Institut, Tubingen Univ, W Ger, 74-75, 81-82; Millsaps Col, hon DD, 84. **CAREER** Instr, old testament, Interdenominational Theol Ctr, Atlanta, 62-63; grad asst instr, Hebrew, Emory Univ, 63-64; asst prof, old testament, Birmingham-Southern Col, 64-67; asst prof, 71-78, full prof, 78-, dir, grad div of relig, 83-92, Candler Sch of Theol, Emory Univ. **HONORS AND AWARDS** Nat Defense Educ Act grad fel, 60-64; Nat Found of the arts and Humanities, summer res stipend, 66; Emory Univ summer res grant, 67, 69, 72, 78, 79, 82; Alexander von Humbolt Stiftung stipend, 74-75, 81-82; Woodruff Res Support Grant, 80; Asn of Theol Sch res grant, 81-82; Nat Endow for the Humanities res grant, 87-88. **MEMBERSHIPS** Soc of Bibl Lit; Amer Sch of Oriental Res; Palestine Exploration Soc; Deutsche Verein fur Erforschung Palastinas. **RESEARCH** History and archaeology of biblical times. **SELECTED PUBLICATIONS** Auth, Separating the Solomon of History from the Solomon of Legend, The Age of Solomon: Scholarship at the Turn of the Millenium, Leiden, The Netherlands, Brill, 97; auth, Biblical Archaeologist, 60/4, Ancient Moab: Still Largely Unknown, 194-204, 97; auth, Central Moab and History of Moab, Encycl of Near Eastern Archaeol, Oxford Univ Press, 96; auth, The Ancient Near East an Archaeology, Old Testament Interpretation: Past, Present and Future, Abingdon Press, 245-260, 95; auth, Explorations in Ancient Moab, Qadmoniot, 28, 77-82, 95; auth, Introduction to the History of Ancient Israel, The New Interpreter's Bible, Abingdon Press, 244-271, 94; auth, Israel, History of, Judah, Oxford Companion to the Bible, Oxford Univ Press, 93; auth, Reading the Bible Historically: The Historian's Approach, chap I, 11-28, To Each Its Own Meaning: An Introduction to Biblical Criticisms and Their Application, Westminster/John Knox Press, 93; ed, Archaeological Survey of the Kerak Plateau, Amer Sch of Oriental Res Archaeol Reports, 1, Scholars Press, 91; co-auth, A History of Ancient Israel and Judah, Westminster Press/SCM Press, 86. **CONTACT ADDRESS** Candler School of Theology, Emory Univ, Atlanta, GA 30322. **EMAIL** theojmm@emory.edu

MILLER, JOHN F.
PERSONAL Born 02/04/1950, Washington, DC, m, 1972 **DISCIPLINE** CLASSICS **EDUCATION** Xavier Univ, HAB, 72; Univ North Carolina Chapel Hill, MA, 74, PhD, 79. **CAREER** Vis instr, N Carolina State Univ, 77-78; asst prof, Univ Minn, 78-84; asst to assoc prof, Univ Va, 84- . **HONORS AND AWARDS** Alexander von Humboldt-Stiftung fel, Heidelberg, 85-86; ed, Class J, 91-98; ovatio & pres, Class Assoc of Middle West and South, 99. **MEMBERSHIPS** APA; Class Assoc of Middle West and South; Class Assoc of Va; Roman Soc. **RESEARCH** Latin literature; Roman religion; Hellenistic poetry. **SELECTED PUBLICATIONS** Auth, Ovid's Elegiac Festivals: Studies in the Fasti, Studien zur klassischen Philologie 55, NY, 91; auth, Ovidian Allusion and the Vocabulary of Memory, Materiali e discussioni per l'analisi dei testi classici, 93; auth, Virgil, Apollo, and Augustus, in Solomon, ed, Apollo, Origins and Influences, Tucson & London, 94; auth, Apostrophe, Aside and the Didactic Addressee: Poetic Strategies in Ars Amatoria III, Materiali e discussioni per l'analisi dei testi classici, 94; auth, The Memories of Ovid's Pythagoras, Mnemosyne, 94; auth, Lucretian Moments in Ovidian Elegy, Class J, 97. **CONTACT ADDRESS** Dept of Classics, Univ of Virginia, Charlottesville, VA 22903. **EMAIL** JFM4J@virginia.edu

MILLER, MARGARET P.
PERSONAL Born 08/08/1950, Columbus, OH, m, 1976, 2 children **DISCIPLINE** FRENCH **EDUCATION** Ohio State Univ, BA, 72; George Washington Univ, MA, 77; Univ Del, MA, 96; Univ Md, PhD, 01. **CAREER** Asst prof, Chesapeake Col, 92-96; TA, Univ of Md, 99-01; vis instr, Hood Col, 01-. **HONORS AND AWARDS** Certificate of Merit, Univ of Md, 00. **MEMBERSHIPS** MLA, Women in French, Assoc for Res on Mothering, Conseil International d'Etudes Francophones. **RESEARCH** French and Francophone women writers, Psychology and Literature, the cognitive processes of reading space, images and transformation in texts. **SELECTED PUBLICATIONS** Auth, Introduction, Trading Secrets, Paule Constant, Univ of Neb Pr, (01); auth, "Reconstructing Reading: Resurrecting Cognitive Processes in the (Foreign) Language Classroom," CAUCE: Revista de Filologia y su Didactica: Seville, Spain, (01); auth, "Les Yeux d"Emma: Ensemble fendue ou indechiffrable enigme?" Monstres et le monstreux, L'instant meme, Quebec, forthcoming. **CONTACT ADDRESS** Hood Col, Frederick, MD 21701-8575. **EMAIL** mpmiller@themillers.org

MILLER, PAUL
PERSONAL Born 11/07/1959, Kansas City, MO, m, 1987, 1 child **DISCIPLINE** COMPARATIVE LITERATURE **EDUCATION** Univ Texas, PhD 89. **CAREER** Drary Col, asst prof, 89-91; Tex Tech Univ, asst prof, assoc prof, 91-98; Hamilton Col, vis prof, 96; Univ S Carolina, assoc prof, dir comp lit, 98-. **HONORS AND AWARDS** Who's Who in Amer Tchrs. **MEMBERSHIPS** MLA; APA; CAMWS; WCC; ACLA; Renaissance Soc. **RESEARCH** Lyric poetry; Classical tradition; Gender studies; Literary theory. **SELECTED PUBLICATIONS** Auth, Lyric Texts and Lyric Consciousness: The Birth of a Genre from Archaic Greece to Augustan Rome, London, Routledge, 94; auth, French Feminism Across the Disciplines, co-ed, spec issue, Intertexts, 98; auth, Rethinking Sexuality: Foucault and Classical Antiquity, co-ed, Princeton Univ Press, 98; auth, Sex and Gender in Medieval and Renaissance Texts: The Latin Tradition, co-ed, Albany, SUNY Press, 97; auth, Recapturing the Renaissance: Perspectives on Humanism Dialogue and Tradition, co-ed, Knoxville TN, New Paradigm Press, 96; Russian Literature and the Classics, co-ed, NY, Harwood Press, 96; auth, The Suppression of the Negative in Foucault's History of Sexuality, Arcadia, 98; auth, Floating Uteruses and Phallic Gazes: Hippocratic Medicine in the Encycl, Intertexts, 98; auth, Persius Ref Guide to World Literature, London, St James Press, 95; rev, Allen Cameron, Callimachus and Critics, Rel Stud Rev, 98; auth, Thomas Wiedemann, Emperors and Gladiators, Classical Outlook, 94. **CONTACT ADDRESS** Dept of French and Class, Univ of So Carolina, Columbia, Humanities 405, Columbia, SC 29208. **EMAIL** pamiller@sc.edu

MILLER, WILLIAM IRVIN
PERSONAL Born 11/14/1942, Cincinnati, OH, m, 1970, 1 child **DISCIPLINE** SPANISH LANGUAGE & LINGUISTICS **EDUCATION** Wittenberg Univ, BA, 65; Univ Fla, PhD(Romance Lang), 70. **CAREER** Assoc prof Span, Univ Akron, 70-. **MEMBERSHIPS** Am Asn Teachers Span & Port; Am Coun Teachers Foreign Lang. **RESEARCH** Hispanic and Romance Linguistics; foreign language pedagogy. **CONTACT ADDRESS** Dept of Mod Lang, Univ of Akron, 302 Buchtel Mall, Akron, OH 44325-1907. **EMAIL** wmiller@uakron.edu

MILLS, CARL RHETT
PERSONAL Born 05/05/1942, Hillsboro, OR, m, 1968, 2 children **DISCIPLINE** LINGUISTICS, ENGLISH LITERACY **EDUCATION** Cent Wash State Col, BA, 69; Univ Ore, DA, 72, PhD(English & ling), 75. **CAREER** Instr English, Ore State Correctional Inst, 71-73; teacher, Univ Ore, 74-75; instr ling, 75-76, chm English lang & ling comt, 75-82, asst prof ling, 76-81, assoc prof Ling, Univ Cincinnati, 81-, Vpres, Grad Student Coun, Univ Ore, 70-72; Fulbright lectr, Univ Tromso, Norway, 77-78 & Cairo Univ, Egypt, 82-83. **RESEARCH** Psycholinguistics; sociolinguistics; computer approaches to literacy research. **SELECTED PUBLICATIONS** Auth, Stylistic application of ethnosemantics, Lang & Style, 76; Perceptual economy and sound change, Lang Today, 76-77; contribr, Papers for the Fourth Scandinavian Conference of Linguistics, Odense Univ Press, 78; Language Use and the Uses of Language, Georgetown Univ Press, 80; auth, The sociolinguistics of the merger in Pacific Northwest English, Papers Ling, 80; Speech samples in analysis of language attitudes, J Psycholing Res, 81; American Grammar: Sound, Form and Meaning, Peter Lang, 90; author of numerous articles, reviews, and papers from 75-98. **CONTACT ADDRESS** Dept of English, Univ of Cincinnati, PO Box 210069, Cincinnati, OH 45221-0069. **EMAIL** carl.mills@uc.edu

MILLS, DAVID OTIS
PERSONAL Born 05/06/1936, Chicago, IL, m, 1963, 2 children **DISCIPLINE** JAPANESE LANGUAGE & LITERATURE, LINGUISTICS & LANGUAGE **EDUCATION** Univ Tex, Austin, BA, 58; Univ Mich, Ann Arbor, MA, 66, PhD, 74. **CAREER** Instr, assoc prof Japanese, 77-, chmn dept E Asian Lang & Lit, Univ Pittsburgh, 77-91; dir, Tech Japanese Lang Proj, MIT 87-97; Ling Ed, 77-91, Coord Ed, 91-94, Jour of Assoc of Teachers of Japanese; Nat Sci Grants, MIT: Tech Jap Lang Proj, 87-90, Univ of Pittsburgh: Intl Sem on Teaching Tech Japanese, 94. **MEMBERSHIPS** Assn Teachers Japanese; Soc Study Japanese Lang; Soc Teaching Japanese as Foreign Lang; Assn Asian Studies. **RESEARCH** History of the Japanese language; teaching Japanese as a second language; Japanese literature. **SELECTED PUBLICATIONS** Auth, Proceedings of 1994 US-Japan Seminar: State of Teaching Japanese to Scientists and Engineers, 95; auth, Giving Scientists the Japanese They Need, in Eleanor Jorden Festschrift, 97; auth, Models of Instruction for a Technical Japanese Course in Japanese Language for Scientists and Engineers, Tsukuba University, 96. **CONTACT ADDRESS** Dept of Foreign Lang & Lit, Univ of Pittsburgh, 1501 Cathedral/Learn, Pittsburgh, PA 15260-0001. **EMAIL** dom@pitt.edu

MILLS, SOPHIE J.
PERSONAL Born 06/20/1969, London, England **DISCIPLINE** CLASSICS **EDUCATION** Oxford Univ, BA, 87; MA, 91; DPhil, 92. **CAREER** Randall Maelver Junior Res Fel, Imerulle Col, 91-93; lectr, London Col, 93-94; asst prof, Univ NC at Asheville, 94-. **MEMBERSHIPS** Am Philos Asn, Classical Asn of the Middle W & S, Classical Asn, Hellenic Soc. **RESEARCH** Greek Tragedy, Mythology, History. **SELECTED PUBLICATIONS** Auth, Theseus, Tragedy, & the Athenian Empire, 97. **CONTACT ADDRESS** Dept Classics, Univ of No Carolina, Asheville, 1 University Heights, Asheville, NC 28804-3251. **EMAIL** smills@unca.edu

MINER, ELLIS D.
PERSONAL Born 04/16/1937, Los Angeles, CA, m, 1961, 7 children **DISCIPLINE** GERMAN & PHYSICS & ASTRONOMY **EDUCATION** Utah State Univ, BS, 61; Brigham Young Univ, PhD, 65. **CAREER** Space Sci, Jet Propulsion Lab (NASA & Calif Tech), 65-. **HONORS AND AWARDS** NASA Medal for Exceptional Scientific Achievement, 81, 86; NASA Medal for Outstanding Leadership, 90; sci manager for cassini mission to saturn. **MEMBERSHIPS** Am Astron Soc; AAS Div for Planetary Sci. **RESEARCH** Planetary exploration via robotic spacecraft. **SELECTED PUBLICATIONS** Auth, URANUS: the planet, rings, and satellites, 1s ed, 91, 2nd ed, 97; co-ed, URANUS, 92; auth, NEPTUNE: the planet, rings, and satellites, 01 (in prep); co-ed, URANUS, 92. **CONTACT ADDRESS** Jet Propulsion Lab, 4800 Oak Grove Dr, M/S 230-260, Pasadena, CA 91109. **EMAIL** ellis.d.miner@jpl.nasa.gov

MINKOFF, HARVEY
PERSONAL Born New York, NY **DISCIPLINE** LINGUISTICS, ENGLISH **EDUCATION** City Col New York, BA, 65, MA, 66, Grad Ctr, PhD, 70. **CAREER** Asst prof English, Iona Col, 67-71; assoc prof English & Ling, 71-90, prof Eng and Ling, Hunter Col, 90-. **MEMBERSHIPS** Ling Soc Am. **RESEARCH** Applications of linguistics to language teaching and learning; theory and practice of literary translation. **SELECTED PUBLICATIONS** Ed, Teaching English Linguistically: Five Experimental Curricula, 71 & auth, The English Verb System, 72; (N)ever write like(?) you talk: Teaching the syntax of reading & composition, English Record, 74; coauth, Mastering Prestige English, Villa Press, 75; auth, Teaching the Transition From Print to Script Analytically, Elementary English, 75; Some Stylistic Consequences of Aelfric's Theory of Translation, Studies in Philol, 76; coauth, Transitions: A key to mature reading and writing, In: Classroom Practices in Teaching English, NCTE, 77; coauth, Complete Course in College Writing, Kendall-Hunt, 84; coauth, Visions and Revisions, Prentice-Hall, 90; ed, Approaches to the Bible, 2 Vols, Bibl Arch Soc, 95; coauth, Exploring America, Harcourt, 95; auth, Mysteries of the Dead Sea Scrolls, Ottenhenmer, 98. **CONTACT ADDRESS** Dept of English, Hunter Col, CUNY, 695 Park Ave, New York, NY 10021-5085.

MINKOVA, DONKA
PERSONAL Born 01/13/1944, Sofia, Bulgaria, 2 children **DISCIPLINE** ENGLISH LINGUISTICS **EDUCATION** Univ Sofia, Bulgaria, BA, MA (English and German), 66, PhD (English Linguistics), 82. **CAREER** Lect, Univ Sofia, 68-79, senior lect, 79-83; vis lect, Univ Edinburgh, Scotland, 80-81; asst prof, 83-89, assoc prof, 89-92, Prof, UCLA, 92-. **HONORS AND AWARDS** British Coun Res fel, 77-78; Honorary fel, Inst for Advanced Studies in the Humanities, Edinburgh, 80-81; UC President's Research Fellowship in the Humanities, 94-95; Guggenheim Fellowship, 00-01; exec bd member, soc for germanic philol, 98-; ed bd member, diachronica, j of english lang and lings, am j of germanic lings, j of english lings, annotated bibliography of english studies, edinburgh univ press, peter lang verlag. **MEMBERSHIPS** Ling Soc Am; Am Dialect Soc; Int Soc for Hist Ling; New Chaucer Soc; Soc for Germanic Philol. **RESEARCH** Hist of the English lang; hist phonology and metrics. **SELECTED PUBLICATIONS** Auth, The History of

Final Vowels in English. The Sound of Muting, Topics in English Linguistics 4, Mouton de Gruyter, 91; with Robert Stockwell, Prosody, in A Beowulf Handbook, ed by Robert E. Bjork and John D. Niles, Univ NE Press and Exeter Univ Press, 97; The Credibility of Pseudo-Alfred: Prosodic Insights Into Post-Conquest Mongrel Meter, Modern Philol, Vol 94, no 4, May 97; Constraint Ranking in Middle English Stress-shifting, English Lang and Lings, CA Univ Press, Vol 1, no 1, 97; with Robert Stockwell, The Origins of Short-Long Allomorphy in English, in Advances in English Hist Lings, ed by Jacek Fisiak and Marcin Krygier, Mouton de Gruyter, 98; Velars and Palatals in Old English Alliteration, in Hist Lings 1997, ed by Monika Schmid, Jennifer Austin and Dieter Stein, John Benjamins, 98. **CONTACT ADDRESS** Dept of English, Univ of California, Los Angeles, Los Angeles, CA 90095. **EMAIL** minkova@humnet.UCLA.edu

MIRAGLIA, ANNE MARIE
DISCIPLINE FRENCH LITERATURE **EDUCATION** Univ Toronto, BA; MA, PhD. **RESEARCH** Contemporary Quebecois novel; literary theory; semiotics; Francophone literatures of Africa and the Caribbean. **SELECTED PUBLICATIONS** Auth, L'Ecriture de l'Autre chez Jacques Poulin, Quebec, 93; pub(s) on Claude Simon, Jacques Poulin, and Dany Laferriere. **CONTACT ADDRESS** Dept of French, Univ of Waterloo, 200 University Ave W, Waterloo, ON, Canada N2L 3G1. **EMAIL** ammiragl@watarts.uwaterloo.ca

MISTACCO, VICKI
PERSONAL Born 11/18/1942, Brooklyn, NY **DISCIPLINE** FRENCH LANGUAGE & LITERATURE **EDUCATION** NYork Univ, BA, 63; Middlebury Col, MA, 64; Yale Univ, M Phil, 68, PhD, 72. **CAREER** Instr, 68-72, asst prof, 72-78, chmn dept, 78-81, assoc prof, 78-84, Prof French, Wellesley Col, 84-. **HONORS AND AWARDS** Phi Beta Kappa, 62; Fulbright Fel, 63-64; Woodrow Wilson Fel, 64-65, 66-67; NEH Fel, 83-84, 94-95; Dir, NEH special project, 80-81. **MEMBERSHIPS** MLA; AATF; NE Mod Lang Asn. **RESEARCH** Twentieth century French fiction; theories of reading; narratology; French women writers, Middle Ages to present; Eighteenth Century French fiction. **SELECTED PUBLICATIONS** Auth, Narcissus and the image: symbol and meaning in L'Immoraliste, Ky Romance Quart, 76; co-auth, Interview: Alain Robbe-Grillet, Diacritics, winter 76; auth, Robbe-Grillet's Topologie d'une cite fantome: The theory and practice of reading Nouveaux Romans, In: The Reader in the Text, Princeton Univ, 80; Reading The Immoralist: The relevance of narrative roles, Bucknell Rev, 81; ed, Breaking the Sequence: Women, Literature, and the Future, and transl, To Break the Sequence Inscribe Oneself in the Memory of the Future, In: Breaking the Sequence, Wellesley Col Center Res Women, 82; Le Noeud de Viperes ou les limites de la lisibilite, Cahiers Francois Mauriac, 86; Marguerite Duras, ou les lectures illimitees, Roman, 6/88; Nomadic Meanings: The Woman Effect in La Femme adultere, In: Albert Camus L'Exil et le Royaume: The Third Decade, Les Editions Paratexte, 88; Mama's Boy: Reading Woman in L'Etranger, In: Camus's L'Etranger: Fifty Years On, Macmillan, 92; Plus ca change ..: The Critical Reception of Emily L, French Rev, 10/92; rev, Prevost, Antoine, Histoire d'une Grecque moderne, Flammarion, 90, The Eighteenth Century: A Current Bibliography, 98; Sample Course Outline: Women and the Literary Tradition, Teacher's Guide to Advanced Placement Course in French Literature, Col Entrance Exam Bd and Educ Testing Serv, 94. **CONTACT ADDRESS** Dept of French, Wellesley Col, 106 Central St, Wellesley, MA 02481-8204. **EMAIL** vmistacco@wellesley.edu

MITCHELL, CHRISTOPHER
PERSONAL Born 11/04/1957, Palo Alto, CA, m, 1977, 2 children **DISCIPLINE** HEBREW **EDUCATION** Univ of Wis, BS, 78, MA, 80, PhD, 83 **CAREER** Ed, 89-pres, Concordia Publ Hse; Pastor, 87-89 **HONORS AND AWARDS** Phi Kappi Phi **MEMBERSHIPS** Soc of Bibl Lit **RESEARCH** Hebrew; Old Testament; New Testament; Lutheran Theology **SELECTED PUBLICATIONS** Auth, The Meaning of BRK "to Bless" in the Old Testament, Scholars Press, 87 **CONTACT ADDRESS** 8921 Westhaven Ct, Saint Louis, MO 63126.

MITCHELL, DOUGLAS
DISCIPLINE LINGUISTICS, SANSKRIT **EDUCATION** Baylor, BA; Univ TX, PhD. **CAREER** Instr, Rice Univ. **SELECTED PUBLICATIONS** Auth, History of the Latin Language, Tex Educ Agency, 67; coed, Sprung from Some Common Source: Investigations into the Prehistory of Languages, Stanford UP, 91. **CONTACT ADDRESS** Rice Univ, PO Box 1892, Houston, TX 77251-1892. **EMAIL** douglas@ruf.rice.edu

MITCHELL-BOYASK, ROBIN N.
PERSONAL Born 05/20/1961, Cambridge, Britain, m, 1990, 2 children **DISCIPLINE** CLASSICS **EDUCATION** Univ Chicago BA, 82; Brown Univ, MA, 85; PhD, 88. **CAREER** Asst prof to assoc prof, Temple Univ, 88-. **HONORS AND AWARDS** Jr Fel, Center for Hellenic Studies, 93-94. **MEMBERSHIPS** Am Philol Asn; Pa Class Asn; Philadelphia Class Soc; Class Asn of the Atlantic States. **RESEARCH** Greek drama; Greek and Roman epic. **SELECTED PUBLICATIONS** Auth, Miasma, Mimesis and Scapegoating in Euripides' Hippolytus, CA, 91; auth, Sine Fine: The Aeneid and Freud's Masterplot, AJP, 96; auth, "Euripides Hippolytus and the Trials of Manhood," Bucknell Rev, 99; auth, Approaches to Teaching the Dramas of Euripides, MLA Press. **CONTACT ADDRESS** Dept Class, Temple Univ, 1114 W Berks St, 353 Anderson Hall, Philadelphia, PA 19122. **EMAIL** robin@astro.temple.edu

MITREVSKI, GEORGE G.
PERSONAL Born 04/01/1951, Macedonia, m, 1980, 2 children **DISCIPLINE** RUSSIAN **EDUCATION** SUNY, BA, 75; Ohio State Univ, MA; PhD, 84. **CAREER** Assoc Prof, Auburn Univ, 83-. **HONORS AND AWARDS** Fel, IREX Dissertation Res, 80-81; Fulbright Fel, 97 **MEMBERSHIPS** AATSEEL; AAASS; IALL; CALICO. **RESEARCH** Computer-assisted language instruction; Russian literature and culture; Macedonian language, literature and culture. **CONTACT ADDRESS** Dept of For Langs & Lits, Auburn Univ, 6030 Haley Center, Auburn, AL 36849. **EMAIL** mitrege@auburn.edu

MITTERAND, HENRI
PERSONAL Born 08/07/1928, France, m, 1955, 2 children **DISCIPLINE** FRENCH **EDUCATION** Ecole Normale Superieure, 48-51; Universite de Paris, MA, 50; PhD, 69. **CAREER** Asst/Assoc Prof, Universite Besancen Paris, 57-71; Prof, Univ of Paris, 71-90; Prof, Columbia Univ NY, 89-. **HONORS AND AWARDS** Chevalier de La Legion d'Honeur; Prix de l'Academie Fr. **MEMBERSHIPS** Societe literaire des amis d'Emile Zola, Societe D'Histoire del'affaire Dreyfus. **RESEARCH** French Novel, Emile Zola, Naturalism, Literary Semiotics. **SELECTED PUBLICATIONS** Auth, L'Illusion realesde, P.U.F.(Paris), 94; auth, La Literature Francaise du XXe siecle, Nathan (Paris), 96; auth, Le Roman a l'deudre, P.U.F.(Paris), 98; auth, Zola, I. Silces ke regard d'Olympia (niography), Fayard (Paris), 99; auth, Zola: Le Roman naturaliste (anthologie), Le Livre de leche (Paris), 99. **CONTACT ADDRESS** Dept French, Columbia Univ, 2960 Broadway, New York, NY 10027-6944. **EMAIL** hm12@columbia.edu

MOAYYAD, HESHMAT
PERSONAL Born 11/28/1927, Hamadan, Iran, m, 1958, 2 children **DISCIPLINE** ORIENTAL LANGUAGES **EDUCATION** Univ Teheran, LL, 49; Univ Frankfurt, PhD(Persian Lit, Ger), 58. **CAREER** Lectr Persian, Univ Frankfurt, 52-59; lectr, Univ Naples, 60-61, assoc prof, 64-65; lectr, Harvard Univ, 62-63; from asst prof to assoc prof, 65-74, prof Persian Lit, Univ Chicago, 74-. **MEMBERSHIPS** Am Orient Soc; MidE Studies Asn NAm. **RESEARCH** Persian literature and philology; German literature. **SELECTED PUBLICATIONS** Auth, Die Magamat des Gaznawi, Univ Frankfurt, 59; Zum Problemkreis und Stand der Perischen Lexikographie, 62, Nachtrag zum Deutsch-Persischen Worterbuch von Eilers, 62 & Eine Wiedergefundene Schrift uber Ahmad-E Gam und Seine Nachkommen, 64, Annali 1st Univ Napoli; Parvin's poems: A cry in wilderness, In: Festschrift for Prof F Meier, Wiesbaden, Steiner, 73; ed, Faraid-I Chianthi (Medieval text), Vol I & II, Bonyad-I Farhang-1, Iran, 77-78; Once a Dewdrop, Essays on the Poetry of Parvin E'tesami, Mazda Publishers, 94. **CONTACT ADDRESS** Dept of Near East Lang, Univ of Chicago, 1155 E 58th St, Chicago, IL 60637-1540.

MODER, CAROL LYNN
DISCIPLINE PSYCHOLINGUISTICS AND MORPHOLOGY **EDUCATION** SUNY, Buffalo, PhD, 86. **CAREER** Assoc head, dept Engl, Okla State Univ. **SELECTED PUBLICATIONS** Areas: discourse analysis and language testing. **CONTACT ADDRESS** Oklahoma State Univ, Stillwater, 101 Whitehurst Hall, Stillwater, OK 74078.

MOEDERSHEIM, SABINE
PERSONAL Born Freiburg, Germany **DISCIPLINE** GERMAN **EDUCATION** Univ Freiburg, PhD, 92. **CAREER** Univ Freiburg; McGill Univ; Univ Wisc. **HONORS AND AWARDS** Lynen Fel, Alexandes von Humboldt Foundation. **RESEARCH** 17th Century literature and culture; German literature, Philosophy **SELECTED PUBLICATIONS** Auth, Domini doctrina coronat. Die geistliche emblematik Daniel Cramers (1568-1637), Peter Lang Pub, 94; auth, Daniel Cramer: emblemata Sacra, Frankfurt, 94; auth, Hieronymus ammon: Imitatio crameriana., Brepols, 99; auth, "Duke Ferdinand albrecht's Self-Protrayal in the emblematic Programme of Castle Bevern," in The emblem and architecture, Studies in applied Emblematics from the Sixteenth Century to the Eighteenth Century, Brepols, 99; auth, "Christo et Rei publicae. Martin Marstaller's emblematum Liber Philippi II, in emblematica, (99): 41-73; auth, "Materiale und mediale Aspekte der emblmatik," in allegorie-Konfigurationen von Text, Bild und Lekture, Westdeutscher Verlag, 98; auth, "Igel oder amor? Zum Briefwechsel zwischen Anna Louisa Karsch und U.W.L. Gleim," in Gottfried August Burger und Johann Wilhelm Ludwig Sleim, Niemeyer, 96; auth, "Mater et matrix,. Michael Maiers alchemistische sinnbilder der Mutter," in Mutter und Mutterlichkeit. Festschrift fur Verena Ehrich-Haefeli, Konigshausen und Neumann, 96; auth, "Skin Deep, Mind Deep. Emblem and Tattoo," in Acta of the Fourth International Emblem Conference, vol III: emblems in Modern Culture, Tournhout, 99; auth, "Hennig Wedemann's emblem Panels for Georg Wilhelm Sacer's Tagliches Hertzens Opfer, (Wolfenuttel 1686)," in the German-Language emblem in its european context: Exchange and Transmission, Glasgow Univ Press, 00. **CONTACT ADDRESS** Dept German, Univ of Wisconsin, Madison, 1220 Linden Dr, Madison, WI 53706-1525. **EMAIL** smoedersheim@facstaff.wisc.edu

MOELLER, HANS-BERNHARD
PERSONAL Born 06/26/1935, Hannover, Germany, m, 1986, 1 child **DISCIPLINE** GERMAN LITERATURE, EUROPEAN STUDIES, GERMAN CINEMA **EDUCATION** Knox Col, Ill, BA 60; Univ Southern CA, MA, 62; PhD, 64. **CAREER** Instr, Northwestern Univ, 62-64; asst prof, Univ Md, College Park, 64-66; lectr, Inst Aleman Cult, Goethe Inst, Barcelona, Spain, 67-68; asst prof, Hofstra Univ, 69-70; asst prof, 70-72; Assoc Prof Ger, Univ Tex, Austin, 72-; vis prof, Univ Southern Calif, Los Angeles, 74-75; vis prof, Univ Marburg, FRG, 88; Andrew Mellon fel, Univ Pittsburgh, 68-69. **HONORS AND AWARDS** Thyssen res grant, 86; FRG, Ausw.Amt Grant f Sesquicentennial, 86; DFG & Thyssen grants for Symposium, 86; Goethe Ins grants, RMMLA, Ger Spec Session on German 20th Century Writers & the Idea of Europe, 90. **MEMBERSHIPS** Ger Studies Asn; Internationale Vereinigung fur germanische Sprach- und Literaturwissenschaft. **RESEARCH** 20th Century literature; exile literature including Spanish & Slavic exiles in Latin America; 20th Century novel; Literature in the new German cinema; Film history & genre; comparative media criticism. **SELECTED PUBLICATIONS** Auth, Introduction, Alexander Kluge, Case Histories, Holmes & Meier, 88; auth, Deutsche Literatur zur Zeit des Faschismus, in Geschichte der deutschen Literatur, ed. Ehrhard Bahr (Tuebingen: Francke Verlag, 88); auth, Schlondorff's Adult Children in the Context of the New German Cinema's Portrait of Youth, Germanistische Medienwissenschaft, 89; auth, Fassbinder's Use of Brechtian Aesthetics: The Marriage of Maria Braun, Veronika Voss, Lola, Jump Cut, 90; coauth, Frederic Morton, Die deutschsprachige Exilliteratur seit 1933 in New York, ed. John M Spalek and Joseph Strelka (Bern: Francke Verlag, 90); auth, Der deutsche Film in amerikanischer forschung und Lehre IV, FFFL, 91; auth, Frederic Morton, in Deutschsprachige Exilliteratur, ed. John M Spalek, Konrad Feilchenfeldt and Sandra Hawrylchack, (Bern: Saur, 94); auth, This Is to Be Seen Dialectically: Schlondorffs 1960er/70er Projekt des Brechtschen Films. Alte Welten - neue Welten, Akten des IX Internationalen Germanisten-Kongresses, Niemeyer (Vancouver), 96; auth, Literatur/filom-Beziehungen: Frischs Homo faber als Schlondorffs Film, in Desde la actualidad, ed. Oscar Caeiro and Beatriz Mayor, (Cordoba/Argentina: Comunic-Arte Editorial, 98); auth, Zur deutschen Filmkomodie der Generation nach 1968, Monatscheft Summer, 01. **CONTACT ADDRESS** Dept of Ger Studies, Univ of Texas, Austin, E P Schoch 3 102, Austin, TX 78712-1026. **EMAIL** h-b.moeller@mail.utexas.edu

MOEVS, CHRISTIAN
PERSONAL Born 09/21/1958, Boston, MA, s **DISCIPLINE** ITALIAN LITERATURE **EDUCATION** Harv Col, AB, 80; Colum Univ, MA, 89; PhD, 94. **CAREER** Precep. Columbia Univ, 91-92; asst prof, Univ Notre Dame, 94-. **HONORS AND AWARDS** NEH; ISLA, 7 Res/Int Awds; Pres Fel. **MEMBERSHIPS** MAA; MLA; DSA; SDI; AATI; AAIS. **RESEARCH** Dante; medieval Italian literature; philosophy; lyric poetry. **CONTACT ADDRESS** Dept Romance Languages, Univ of Notre Dame, 343 O'Shaugnessy Hall, Notre Dame, IN 46556-5639. **EMAIL** moevs.1@nd.edu

MOHLER, STEPHEN CHARLES
PERSONAL Born 11/28/1937, Washington, DC, m, 1959, 3 children **DISCIPLINE** SPANISH & PORTUGUESE LANGUAGES **EDUCATION** George Washington Univ, PhD(Romance lang & lit), 69. **CAREER** Teacher Span, George C Marshall High Sch, 62-70; asst prof Romance lang & lit, Univ NC, Greensboro, 70-76, chmn dept, 74-76; assoc prof, 76-81, Prof Mod Foreign Lang, Univ TN, Martin, 82-, Chmn dept, 77-92. **MEMBERSHIPS** SCent Mod Lang Asn; Am Asn Teachers Span & Port. **RESEARCH** Teaching Spanish and Portuguese; Spanish American literature; language teaching methods. **SELECTED PUBLICATIONS** Auth, El Estilo Poetico de Leon de Greiff, Tercer Mundo, 75; coauth, Descubrir y Crear, Harper & Row, 76, 2nd ed, 81, 3rd ed, 86. **CONTACT ADDRESS** Dept of Mod Foreign Lang, Univ of Tennessee, Martin, 554 University St, Martin, TN 38238-0002. **EMAIL** smohler@utm.edu

MOLINA-GAVILAN, YOLANDA
PERSONAL Born 07/07/1963, Madrid, Spain **DISCIPLINE** SPANISH **EDUCATION** Univ Wis Eau Claire, BA, 85; Univ Oreg, MA, 88; Ariz State Univ, PhD, 96. **CAREER** Asst prof, Eckerd Col, 96-. **MEMBERSHIPS** MLA, Sci Fiction Res Asn, Int Asn of the Fantastic in the Arts. **RESEARCH** Science fiction literature in the Spanish-speaking world, Contemporary Spanish cinema. **SELECTED PUBLICATIONS** Cotransl, La Funcion delta by Rosa Montero, (Univ Nebr Pr, 92); auth, "Poeticas regionales ante la postmodernidad: dos escritores andaluces," Lucero: Jour of Iberian and Latin Am Studies (94): 106-113; auth, "El viaje de Lucio: Naturalieza alegorica y subversiva de un cuento fantastico," Textos 6.1 (99): 39-44; auth, "Alternate Realities from Argentina: Angelica Gorodischer's

Los embriones del violeta," Sci Fiction Studies 79.26, (99): 401-411; coauth, "The Ill-fated Awakening of Sleeping Beauty. The Tairy Tale Demystified in Carlos Saura's Outrage," Quaderni Iberoamericani 87-88, (00): 73-87; coauth, "Cronologia de CF latinoamericana: 1775-1999," Chasqui: Revista de Literatura Latinoamericana (00); auth, Ciencia ficcion en espanol: Una mitologia moderna ante el cambioEdwin Mellon Pr, (forthcoming); coed, Science Fiction in Latin America and Spain: A Critical Anthology, Wesleyan Univ Pr, (forthcoming). **CONTACT ADDRESS** Eckerd Col, 4200 54th Ave S, Saint Petersburg, FL 33711. **EMAIL** molinay@eckerd.edu

MONAS, SIDNEY
PERSONAL Born 09/15/1924, New York, NY, m, 1986, 3 children **DISCIPLINE** RUSSIAN **EDUCATION** Princeton Univ, AB, 48; Harvard Univ, AM, 52; PhD, 55. **CAREER** Instr, Amherst Col, 55-57; asst prof, Smith Col, 57-62; prof and chair, Univ Rochester, 62-69; prof and chair, 69-97. **HONORS AND AWARDS** Fel, Russ Res Center Harvard, 51-54; Ford Fel, 54-55; Jr Fac Fel, Smith Col, 60-61; Fulbright vis prof, Hebrew Univ, 66-67; ACLS and IREX Fel, Acad of Sci Leningrad, 73-74; Lady Davis Fel, Hebrew Univ, 92; ACLS, Univ Chicago, 77-78; Fel, Humanities Res Center, Australia Nat Univ, 77. **MEMBERSHIPS** Am Hist Asn; MLA; Am Asn for Adv of Slavic Studies. **RESEARCH** 19th and 20th Century Russian History; Russian Literature; Comparative Literature; History of Russian Thought; Historiography; James Joyce. **SELECTED PUBLICATIONS** Auth, "Unreal City," in Russian Literature and American Critics; auth, "Censorship as a Way of Life," in Perspectives on Literature; auth, "Literature, Medicine and the Celebration of the Body in Rabelais, Tolstoy and Joyce," in The Body and the Text, 90. **CONTACT ADDRESS** Dept Slav Lang, Univ of Texas, Austin, Slav Langs, Austin, TX 78712. **EMAIL** smonas@mail.utexas.edu

MONGA, LUIGI
DISCIPLINE FRENCH **EDUCATION** Liceao Manzoni; SUNY Buffalo, MA, 70, PhD, 72. **CAREER** Asst prof, SUNY,Buffalo, 69-76; prof, Vanderbilt Univ, 76-. **CONTACT ADDRESS** 1903 Linden Ave, Nashville, TN 37212.

MONOSON, S. SARA
DISCIPLINE CLASSICS AND POLITICAL SCIENCE **EDUCATION** Brandeis, BA, 81; London Sch Econ and Polit Sci, MSc, 82; Princeton Univ, PhD, 93. **CAREER** Asst prof, Northwestern Univ, 93-. **RESEARCH** Plato and Athenian democracy. **SELECTED PUBLICATIONS** Auth, Citizen as Erastes: Erotic Imagery and the Idea of Reciprocity in the Periclean Funeral Oration, Polit Theory, 94; Frank Speech, Democracy and Philosophy: Plato's Debt to a Democratic Strategy of Civic Discourse, Athenian Polit Thought and the Reconstruction of Am Democracy, Cornell, 94; auth, Plato's Democratic Entanglements: Athenian Politics and the Practice of Philosophy, Princeton Univ Press, 00. **CONTACT ADDRESS** Dept of Classics, Northwestern Univ, 1801 Hinman, Evanston, IL 60208. **EMAIL** s-monoson@nwu.edu

MONTGOMERY, MICHAEL M.
DISCIPLINE LINGUISTICS **EDUCATION** Univ Florida, PhD, 79; Univ Tenn-Knoxville, MA, 75; Maryville Col, BA, 73. **CAREER** Univ Florida, asst prof, assoc prof, 86 to 91-; Memphis State Univ, asst prof, 79-81; Univ Arkansas LR, instr, 78-79. **HONORS AND AWARDS** TESOL Lifetime Achv Awd; Forum Res Lang Scot/Ulster Hon Pres. **MEMBERSHIPS** ADS; SCL; LSA; ASA; ACIS; USLS. **RESEARCH** American English Dialects; Appalachian English. **SELECTED PUBLICATIONS** Auth, The Dictionary of Smoky Mountain English, coauth, 98, forthcoming; auth, The Scots Language in Ulster, coauth, The History of Scots, ed, Charles Jones, Edinburgh, Edin U Press, 97; Language Variety in the South: A Retrospective and Assessment, Language Variety in the South Revisited, eds, Cynthia Bernstein, Thomas Nunnally, Robin Sabino, U of Alabama Press, 97; auth, The Rediscovery of Ulster Scots, Englishes Around the World: Festschrift for Manfred Gorlach, ed, Edgar W Schneider, Amsterdam, Benjamins, 97; auth, The Scotch-Irish Influence on Appalachian English: How Broad? How Deep?, Ulster and N Amer: Transatlantic Perspectives on the Scotch-Irish, ed, Curtis Wood, Tyler Blethen, Tuscaloosa, U of Alabama Press, 97; auth, How Scotch-Irish is Your English?, Jour of E Tenn Hist, 96; auth, The Linguistic Value of Ulster Emigrant Letters, Ulster Folklife, 95. **CONTACT ADDRESS** Dept of English, Univ of So Carolina, Columbia, Columbia, SC 29208. **EMAIL** n270053@univscvm.edu

MONYE, LAURENT
DISCIPLINE FRENCH LANGUAGE AND LITERATURE **EDUCATION** Universite de Nancy II, PhD. **CAREER** Assoc prof Fr; coord Fr prog. **MEMBERSHIPS** CLA; AATF. **SELECTED PUBLICATIONS** Auth, Les Oeuvres de SembFne Ousmane. **CONTACT ADDRESS** Clark Atlanta Univ, 223 James P Brawley Dr, SW, Atlanta, GA 30314.

MOONEY, SUSAN K.
DISCIPLINE ENGLISH, SPANISH **EDUCATION** Queen's Univ, BA, 88; McGill Univ, MA, 91; Univ of Toronto, PhD, 01. **CAREER** Lectr, Nipissing Univ, 99-01; asst prof, Concordia Univ, 01-02. **MEMBERSHIPS** Comp Lit Asn of Can, MLA, Int Comp Lit Asn. **RESEARCH** 19th and 20th Century English, Hispanic, French and Russian Literatures, Literary Theory, Psychoanalytic Approaches to Literature and Theory, Philosophy of Law and Ethics. **SELECTED PUBLICATIONS** Auth, "Bronze by Gold by Bloom: the Aurteur of 'Sirens,'" Bronze by Gold: The Music of Joyce, ed Sebastian DG Knowles, Garland, (NY), 99. **CONTACT ADDRESS** 288 Grosvenor Ave, Westmount, QC, Canada H3Z 2L9. **EMAIL** smooney@chass.utoronto.ca

MOORE, CHARLES B.
PERSONAL Born 07/18/1959, Bristol, IN, d **DISCIPLINE** SPANISH **EDUCATION** Univ Tenn, BS, 81; George Mason Univ, MA, 84; Univ NC, PhD, 97. **CAREER** Vis lectr, Univ of NC, 90-94; vis lectr, NC State Univ, 94-97; asst prof, Gardner-Webb Univ, 97-. **HONORS AND AWARDS** Gamma Beta Phi, 78-81; Fel, George Mason Univ, 83-84; Dana B Drake Doctoral Fel, 97; Grants, Gardner-Webb Univ, 98, 99. **MEMBERSHIPS** SAMLA; FLANC; AATSP, Sigma Delta Pi; MLA. **RESEARCH** Colonial Spanish Americas - chronicles of discovery, sacred oratory. **SELECTED PUBLICATIONS** Auth, "Estructura y tema retoricos en el Sermon de Neustra Senora del Carmen de Juan de Espinosa Medrano", Lexis 28.2 (94): 257-69; auth, "Retorica y personaje en tres dramas de Lope de Vega", Revista de Filogia 13, (94): 263-75; auth, "oratoria sagrada y retorica barroca en el Sermon de Neustra Senora del Carmen de Juan de Espinosa Medrano", Rev Interamerica 26.1-4; (96): 49-65; auth, "El papel del lector activo en La Immigrante de Armonia somers', Chasqui 26.1 (97): 45-55; auth, "El fracaso de ser ermitafto en el Quijote", Letras de Deusto 74. 27, (97): 183-88; auth, "La sacralizacion de la historia naturel en la novena maravilla de Juan de Espinosa Medrano", Lexis 22.2 (98): 147-75; auth, "La digresion y otros aspectos multimedios en La novena maravilla de Juan de Espinosa Medrano", rivista de literatura hispanoamericana 37, (98): 33-51; auth, "La estructura retorica de la Epistola a boscan de Garcilaso de la Vega", Boletin de la biblioteca de Menendez Pelayo, (forthcoming); auth, "La sacralizacion de las joyas preciosas y la mitologia grego-latina en La novena maravilla de Juan de Espinosa Medrano", Confluencia, (forthcoming). **CONTACT ADDRESS** Dept For Lang, Gardner-Webb Univ, Boiling Springs, NC 28017-9999. **EMAIL** cmoore@gardner-webb.edu

MOORE, T. J.
PERSONAL Born 12/11/1959, Bristol, PA **DISCIPLINE** CLASSICS **EDUCATION** Millerville Univ BA 81; Univ North Carolina PhD 86. **CAREER** Univ Texas, assoc and assist prof 91 to 98-; Texas A M Univ, asst prof 86 to 91. **HONORS AND AWARDS** Mellon Fel Harvard, 91; Rome Prize Fel 98; Humboldt Fel, 99. **MEMBERSHIPS** APA; AIA; ACL; TCA; Classical Assoc Middle West and South **RESEARCH** Roman comedy and historiography. **SELECTED PUBLICATIONS** Auth, Artistry and Ideology: Livy's Vocabulary of Virtue, Athenaeum Press, 89; Seats and Social Status in the Plautine Theater, Class Jour 94; Morality, History and Livy's Wronged Woman, Eranos 93; auth, The Theater of Plautus: Playing to the Audience, Univ TX 98; Music and Structure in Roman Comedy, Amer Jour of Philology 98; auth, Facing the Music: Character and Musical Accompaniment in Kemon Comedy, Syllecta Classica 99. **CONTACT ADDRESS** Dept of Classics, Univ of Texas, Austin, Austin, TX 78712-1181. **EMAIL** timmoore@utxvms.cc.utexas.edu

MORAN, F.
PERSONAL Born 04/29/1952, Havana, Cuba, s **DISCIPLINE** SPANISH **EDUCATION** Univ Havana, BA, 94; Univ New Orleans, MA, 98. **CAREER** Prof, Pre-Univ Inst, Havana, 71-91; Instructor, Univ New Orleans, 96-98; Instructor, Georgetown Univ, 98-. **HONORS AND AWARDS** "Razon de Ser" Awd, Havana, 94; Accesit Awd, Spain, 97; First place in "Il Premio nacional de poesia Luys Santamarina", Cieza City Spain, 97. **MEMBERSHIPS** MLA, LASA. **CONTACT ADDRESS** Dept Span & Port, Georgetown Univ, PO Box 571039, Washington, DC 20057-1039.

MORAN, THOMAS HILLCREST
DISCIPLINE CHINESE **EDUCATION** Syracuse Univ, BA, 80; Cornell Univ, MA, 88, PhD, 84. **CAREER** Asst prof, Middlebury Col **RESEARCH** Modern and contemporary Chinese literary. **SELECTED PUBLICATIONS** Transl, The Leader's Demise, In Chinese Lit: The Modern Tradition, Columbia UP, 95; First Person, In Chem Mao Would Not Be Amused: Fiction from Today's China, Grove Press, 95; rev, Modernism and the Nativist Resistance: Contemporary Chinese Fiction from Taiwan by Yvonne Sung-sheng Chang, Australian J Chinese Aff, 95 **CONTACT ADDRESS** Dept of Chinese, Middlebury Col, Middlebury, VT 05753. **EMAIL** moran@middlebury.edu

MORAVCSIK, EDITH ANDREA
PERSONAL Born 05/02/1939, Budapest, Hungary **DISCIPLINE** LINGUISTICS **EDUCATION** Univ Budapest, Hungary, DrDipl(classics), 63; Ind Univ, MA, 68, PhD(ling), 71. **CAREER** Instr classics, Univ Debrecen, Hungary, 63-64 & Vassar Col, 64-66; teaching asst & lectr Hungarian, Ind Univ, 66-68; coordr, Lang Universals Proj, Stanford Univ, 68-72; actg asst prof ling, Univ Calif Los Angeles, 72-74; coordr, Lang Universals Proj, Stanford Univ, 75-76; from asst prof toProf Ling, Univ Wis-Milwaukee, 76-, Ed, Working Papers Lang Universals, 68-76; vis prof ling, Univ Vienna, 74, 80 & 82; consult, Proj Lang Typology & Syntactic Fieldwork, NSF, 76-78; assoc ed, Lang, 81-84; Editorial board of Studies in Linguistics, 89-; Editorial board of Language Typology, 96-. **MEMBERSHIPS** Ling Soc of Am; Assoc for Ling Typology. **RESEARCH** Language universals; language typology; syntax. **SELECTED PUBLICATIONS** Auth, Agreement, Working Papers Lang Universals, 71; Borrowed verbs, Wiener Ling Gazette, 75; Necessary and possible universals about temporal constituent relations in language, Ind Ling Club, 77; Universals of language contact, Vol I & On the case-marking of objects, Vol IV, In: Universals of Human Language, Stanford Univ Press, 78; coed, Universals of Human Language, Vol I-IV, Stanford Univ Press, 78; auth, On the distribution of ergative and accusative patterns, Lingua, 78; co-ed, Current Approaches to Syntax, Acad Press, 80; coed, "Studies in syntactic typology," 88; coed, "Functionalism and formalism in Linguistics, 99; **CONTACT ADDRESS** Dept of Foreign Lang and Ling, Univ of Wisconsin, Milwaukee, PO Box 413, Milwaukee, WI 53201-0413. **EMAIL** edith@uwm.edu

MORFORD, JILL P.
DISCIPLINE LINGUISTICS **EDUCATION** Univ Chicago, PhD. **CAREER** Instr, Univ NMex. **RESEARCH** Understanding of lang acquistion by studying commun in the visual modality; aquisition and processing of Am Sign Lang. **SELECTED PUBLICATIONS** Auth, How to hunt an iguana: The gestured narratives of non-signing deaf children, in H Bos & T Schermer, eds, Sign Language Research 1994: Proc of the 4th Europ Cong on Sign Lang Res in Munich, Signum Press, 95; Insights to language from the study of gesture: A review of research on the gestural communication of non-signing deaf people, Lang and Commun, 16 (2), 96; coauth, The genesis of language: How much time is needed to generate arbitrary symbols in a sign system?, in K Emmorey & J Reilly, eds, Language, Gesture and Space, Lawrence Erlbaum Assoc, 95; From homesign to ASL: Identifying the influences of a self-generated childhood gesture system upon language proficiency in adulthood, in D MaCLaughlin & S McEwen, eds, Proc of the 19th Boston Univ Conf on Lang Develop, Cascadilla Press, 95; From here and now to there and then: The development of displaced reference in homesign and English, Child Develop, 68 (3), 97; coauth, Constituent order in picture pointing sequences produced by speaking children using AAC, Applied Psycholinguistic, 19, (98): 525-536; auth, Delayed phonological development in ASL: Two case studies of deaf isolates, Recherches linguistiques de Vinennes, (00): 121-142; auth, Language acquisition by eye, Mawtaw, NJ: Lawrence Erlbaum Associates, (00). **CONTACT ADDRESS** Univ of New Mexico, Albuquerque, Albuquerque, NM 87131. **EMAIL** morford@unm.edu

MORGAN, JERRY LEE
PERSONAL Born 06/04/1939, Mt Clemens, MI **DISCIPLINE** LINGUISTICS **EDUCATION** Ind Univ, AB, 66; Univ Chicago, PhD(ling), 73. **CAREER** From instr to asst prof, 70-76, Assoc Prof Ling, Univ Ill, 76-. **RESEARCH** Linguistic theory; pragmatics; computational linguistics. **SELECTED PUBLICATIONS** Co-ed, Speech Acts, In: Vol 3, Syntax and Semantics, Acad Press, 75; auth, Conversational postulate revisited, Language, 77; Two types of convention in indirect speech acts, In: Syntax and Semantics, Vol 9, Acad Press, 78. **CONTACT ADDRESS** Dept of Ling, Univ of Illinois, Urbana-Champaign, 707 S Mathews Ave, Urbana, IL 61801-3625.

MORGAN, KATHRYN A.
PERSONAL Born 04/15/1962, Montreal, PQ, Canada, m **DISCIPLINE** CLASSICS **EDUCATION** Univ Calif, Berkeley, PhD, 91. **CAREER** Asst prof classics, Ohio State Univ, 91-95; asst to assoc prof classics, Univ Calif, Los Angeles, 95- . **HONORS AND AWARDS** Jr fel, Ctr for Hellenic Stud, 95-96; Visiting Sr Res Fel, Jesus Col, Oxford, 99-00; George A. and Eliza Gardner Howard Found Fel, 99-00; Univ of Calif President's Res Fel in the Humanities, 99-00. **MEMBERSHIPS** APA. **RESEARCH** Archaic and classical Greek literature; intellectual history; archaeology. **SELECTED PUBLICATIONS** Coauth, A Trophy from the Battle of Chaironeia of 86 BC, Am J of Archaeol, 92; auth, "Pindar the Professional an dthe Rehtoric of the komos," Classical Philology 88, (93): 1-15; auth, Socrates and Gorgias at Delphi and Olympia, Phaedrus 235d6-236b4, Class Q, 94; auth, Apollo's Favorites, Greek, Roman, and Byzantine Stud, 94; coauth, An Athenian Dedication to Herakles at Panopeus, Hesperia, 97; auth, "Designer History: Plato's Atlantis Story and Fourth-Century Ideology," Journal for Hellenic Studies 118, (98): 101-118; auth, Myth and Philosophy form the Presocratics to Plato, Cambridge Univ Press, 00. **CONTACT ADDRESS** Classics Dept, Univ of California, Los Angeles, Dodd 100, 141702, PO Box 951417, Los Angeles, CA 90095-1417. **EMAIL** kmorgan@humnet.ucla.edu

MORGAN, LESLIE ZARKER
PERSONAL Born 02/03/1954, Norfolk, VA, m, 1978 **DISCIPLINE** ITALIAN & FRENCH **EDUCATION** Mt Holyoke Col, AB, 74; Middlebury Col, MA, 75; Yale Univ, MA, 77; MPhil, 79; PhD, 83. **CAREER** Lectr to asst prof, 82-89, St

Univ NY Stony Brook; asst prof to assoc prof, 89-, Loyola Col Md. **MEMBERSHIPS** AAIS; AATF; AATI; ACH; CALICO; Dante Soc of Amer; IAHS; ICLS; MLA; Societe Rencevals. **RESEARCH** Romance epic; computational philol; computer assisted language learning. **SELECTED PUBLICATIONS** Auth, "Evidence of Oral Interference in Franco-Italian: 'bragagner,' 'sberna,' 'seterer,' 'smenaventure,'" Canadian Journal of Linguistics 30.4 (85): 407-414; auth, "An Ariostan Note: 'bere alla francesca,'" Forum Italicum 20.1 (86): 100-106; auth, "Computer Assisted Instruction - How, When, and Why," Foreign Language Annals 19.6 (86): 515-519; coauth, "Personalities: A Conversational Review Technique Across Languages," Canadian Modern Language Jour 48 (92): 611-613; auth, "A Terminological Confusion in the Romance Languages: the Gerund," Canadian Modern Language 48 (92): 360-377; auth, "Meter and Rhyme in Franco-Italian Ms. 13 (the Geste francor)," Italian Culture XI (93): 13-29; coauth, "Making the Most of Scarse Resources: A Small College Language Department's Experience with Hypercard," Calico 11.4 (94): 41-59; coauth, "A Survey of Pedagogical Software Use in Italian, 1995," Italica 72.4 (95): 425-451; auth, Berta ai piedi grandi: Historical Figure and Literary Symbol, Olifant 19 (94-95): 37-56; auth, "Bovo d'Antona in the Geste Francor (V 13): Unity of Composition and Clan Destiny," Italian Culture 16.2 (99): 15-38. **CONTACT ADDRESS** Dept of Modern Lang & Lit, Loyola Col, 4501 N Charles St, Baltimore, MD 21210-2699. **EMAIL** lmorgan@loyola.edu

MORGAN, TERRELL A.
DISCIPLINE SPANISH **EDUCATION** Col Wm & Mary, BA, 79; Univ NC, Chapel Hill, MA, 83; Univ Tex, Austin, PhD. 84. **CAREER** Assoc prof, Ohio State Univ, 90-; vis assoc prof, Mich State Univ, 91; asst prof, Ohio State Univ, 84-90; asst instr, Univ Tex, 81-83; teach asst, Univ NC, 79-81; act dhair, dept Span, Port, Ohio State Univ, 91, 94; dir, Ohio State Univ summer sems abroad, 91-. **CONTACT ADDRESS** Dept of Span, Port, Ohio State Univ, Columbus, 1841 Millikin Rd, Columbus, OH 43210-1229. **EMAIL** morgan.3@osu.edu

MORISON, WILLIAM S.
PERSONAL Born 05/15/1965, Fresno, CA, m, 1997, 1 child **DISCIPLINE** CLASSICS, HISTORY **EDUCATION** Calif State Univ Fresno, BA, 87; MA, 90; BA, 91; Univ Calif Santa Barb, MA, 93; PhD, 98. **CAREER** Vis asst prof, Univ Calif, 98-99; vis asst prof, Utah State Univ, 99-00; vis asst prof, Temple Univ, 00-01; vis asst prof, Grand Val State Univ, 01. **HONORS AND AWARDS** Univ Calif Reg Fel, 91-92, 96-97; John Patrick Sullivan Trav Fel, 93-94; ASCS Fel, 93-94. **MEMBERSHIPS** APA; AAH. **RESEARCH** Classical Athens; critias; epigraphy; philosophy. **SELECTED PUBLICATIONS** Auth, "An Honorary Deme Decree and the Administration of a Palaistra in Kephissia," Zeits fur Papyr Epigr 131 (00); auth, "Attic Gymnasia and Palaistrai: Public or Private?," Ancient World 31 (00); co-auth, "An Encomium on the Life of Saint Theognius, Bishop of Bethelia by Paul of Elusa," Cist Stud Qtly 30 (95); rev, Plutarch: Greek Lives (Oxford, 98) and Plutarch: Roman Lives, trans by R. Waterfield (Oxford, 99) Ploutarchos 17 (00); auth, "Critias," Internet Encycl Philo (00); auth, "Lyceum," Internet Encycl Philo (00). **CONTACT ADDRESS** Dept Hist, Grand Valley State Univ, 1121 Au Sable Hall, Allendale, MI 49010. **EMAIL** wmorison@gvsu.edu

MORITA, JAMES R.
PERSONAL Born 06/13/1931, Salem, OR, 2 children **DISCIPLINE** JAPANESE LITERATURE **EDUCATION** Univ Mich, MA, 59, MA, 60; Univ Chicago, PhD(Far Eastern lang & civilizations), 68. **CAREER** Instr Japanese, Univ Chicago, 66-68, asst prof Japanese lit, 68-69, Japanese librn, Far Eastern libr, 67-69; asst prof Japanese lit, Univ Ore, 69-72; Assoc Prof E Asian Lang & Lit, Ohio State Univ, 72-, Am Coun Learned Soc & Soc Sci Res Coun fel, 70; Japan Found prof fel, 77-78. **MEMBERSHIPS** Asn Teachers Japanese; MLA; Asn Asian Studies. **RESEARCH** Modern Japanese literature, especially poetry. **SELECTED PUBLICATIONS CONTACT ADDRESS** Dept of Asian Lang & Lit, Ohio State Univ, Columbus, Columbus, OH 43210.

MORRIS, IAN
DISCIPLINE CLASSICS **EDUCATION** BA, 81; Cambridge Univ, PhD, 86. **CAREER** Ch dept class and prof class/hist, Stanford Univ. **RESEARCH** Greek hist; archaeol. **SELECTED PUBLICATIONS** Auth, Death-Ritual and Social Structure in Classical Antiquity, 92; Classical Greece: Ancient History and Modern Archaeologies, 94. **CONTACT ADDRESS** Stanford Univ, Bldg 20, Main Quad, Stanford, CA 94305.

MORRIS, MARCIA A.
PERSONAL Born 08/12/1952, Somerville, NJ **DISCIPLINE** RUSSIAN LITERATURE **EDUCATION** Georgetown Univ, BS, 74; MS, 77; MS, 78; Columbia Univ, PhD, 87. **CAREER** Asst prof, 87-93, assoc prof, 93-, Georgetown Univ. **RESEARCH** Medieval and early modern Russian literature and culture. **SELECTED PUBLICATIONS** Auth, Saints and Revolutionaries: The Ascetic Hero in Russian Literature; auth, the Literature of Roguery in Seventeenth and Eighteenth-century Russia. **CONTACT ADDRESS** Dept of Slavic Langs, Georgetown Univ, Washington, DC 20057-1050. **EMAIL** morrisma@georgetown.edu

MORRIS, MARGARET LINDSAY
PERSONAL Born 12/23/1950, Princess Anne Co, VA, m, 1984 **DISCIPLINE** SPANISH **EDUCATION** Norfolk State U, BA 1973; Iberian Am Univ Mexico City, 1975; Univ of IL Urbana-Champaign, MA 1974, PhD 1979; Univ of Madrid, summer 1982; Michigan State Univ, summer, 1991. **CAREER** Lincoln U, asst prof of Spanish 1980-; Central State Univ Wilberforce OH, language lab dir 1980; Livingstone Coll Salisbury NC, asst prof 1981-85; Portsmouth City Schools, teacher 1986-; Hampton University, asst prof of Spanish. **HONORS AND AWARDS** Fellowship Univ of IL 1973-74; Fellowship Grad Coll Univ of IL 1975; 1st Black to Receive PhD in Spanish Univ of IL 1979; wrote proposal entitled "Personalizing Instruction in Modern Foreign Langugages" 1982-84; Ford Foundation Fellowship, 1992. **MEMBERSHIPS** Mem Am Assn of Tchr of Spanish & Portuguese 1976-80; mem Am Assn of Univ Prof 1976-80; mem Coll Language Assn 1980; life mem Alpha Kappa Mu Honor Soc 1972-; life mem Sigma Delta Pi Spanish Hon Soc 1974-; life mem Alpha Gamma Mu Spanish Hon Soc 1972-; mem Alpha Kappa Alpha Sor 1983-. **CONTACT ADDRESS** Hampton Univ, Hampton, VA 23668.

MORRIS, WALTER D.
PERSONAL Born 06/24/1929, Austin, TX, m, 1956, 4 children **DISCIPLINE** GERMANIC LANGUAGES & LITERATURES **EDUCATION** Univ Calif, Los Angeles, BA, 49; Univ Tex, Austin, MA, 55, PhD, 59. **CAREER** Assoc prof Ger, Birmingham-Southern Col, 58-62; assoc prof, Bowling Green State Univ, 62-70; Prof to prof emer Ger, Iowa State Univ, 70-. **MEMBERSHIPS** MLA; Am Asn Teachers Ger. **RESEARCH** German literature of the 19th century, especially Conrad Ferdinand Meyer; Norwegian literature, especially Ibsen and post World War II. **SELECTED PUBLICATIONS** Auth, 'Fortaering' - Norwegian - Ulven,T, World Literature Today, 92; 'Eks Og Sett' - Herbjornsrud,H, World Literature Today, 93; 'Tiden' - Hofmo,G, World Literature Today, 93; A Circle Of Ice - Norwegian - Vold,Je, World Literature Today, 94; 'Han Som Kommer' - Johanssen,T, World Literature Today, 94; Collected Poems 1973-1994 - Norwegian - Aamodt,B, World Literature Today, 96; 'En Liten Kvast Med Tusenfryd Og Fire Rare Lok' - Unknown Poems And Prose, 1925-1993 - Norwegian - Jacobsen,R, World Literature Today, 97; 'Denne Gangen Horer Du Deg Selv', Vol 2, 'Pasjonene' 'Minnetapet' - Norwegian - Kiosterud,E, World Literature Today, 97. **CONTACT ADDRESS** Dept of Foreign Lang, Iowa State Univ of Science and Tech, Ames, IA 50010.

MORRISON, JAMES V.
PERSONAL Born 02/26/1956, New York, NY, m, 1982, 3 children **DISCIPLINE** CLASSICS **EDUCATION** Oberlin Col, BA; Univ Wash, MA; Univ Mich, PhD. **CAREER** Vis fac, Davidson Col; vis fac, Georgetown Univ; fac, Centre Col, 93-; assoc prof, current. **HONORS AND AWARDS** NEH Pres, 00-02. **MEMBERSHIPS** APA; CAMWS. **RESEARCH** Homer and ancient epic; Greek literature and philosophy; late republican and Augustan literature; history and classical tradition in 20th-century literature and culture; Derek Walcott's poetry and drama. **SELECTED PUBLICATIONS** Auth, Homeric Misdirection: False Predictions in the Iliad, Univ Mich Press, 92; contribur, Latomus, Jour Am Cult, Relig Studies Rev. **CONTACT ADDRESS** Centre Col, 600 W Walnut St, Danville, KY 40422. **EMAIL** morrison@centre.edu

MORRISON, MOLLY
PERSONAL Born 06/03/1966, Portland, OR, s **DISCIPLINE** ITALIAN **EDUCATION** Pepperdine Univ, BA, 88; Middlebury Col, MA, 90; Ind Univ, PhD, 96. **CAREER** Assoc Instr, Ind Univ, 91-96; Lecturer, Univ Mich, 96-97; Vis Asst Prof to Asst Prof, Ohio Univ, 97-99. **HONORS AND AWARDS** Mario Vangeli Awd, Ind Univ, 94; Camillo P Merlino Awd, Middlebury Col, 90; Scholarship, Intl Rotary Foundation Graduate Year Abroad, 88; Scholarship, Los Angeles Philanthropic Foundation, 86. **MEMBERSHIPS** Mod Lang Asn, Am Asn of Teachers of Italian, Dante Soc of Am, Am Asn for Italian Studies **SELECTED PUBLICATIONS** Auth, "Angela of Foligno," in Catholic Women Writers: A Bio-bibliographical Sourcebook, Greenwood Pub, forthcoming; auth, "Clare of Assisi," in Catholic Women Writers: A Bio-bibliographical Sourcebook, Greenwood Pub, forthcoming; auth, "Catherine of Genoa," in Catholic Women Writers: A Bio-bibliographical Sourcebook, Greenwood Pub, forthcoming; auth, "Catherine of Siena," in Catholic Women Writers: A Bio-bibliographical Sourcebook, Greenwood Pub, forthcoming; co-auth, "Divine Comedy: Moral structure," The Dante Encyclopedia, Garland Pub, forthcoming; auth, "Argia," The Dante Encyclopedia, Garland Pub, forthcoming; auth, "Crassus," The Dante Encyclopedia, Garland Pub, forthcoming; auth, "Franco of Bologna," The Dante Encyclopedia, Garland Pub, forthcoming; auth, "Guano Scornigiani," The Dante Encyclopedia, Garland Pub, forthcoming; auth, Giano della Bella," The Dante Encyclopedia, Garland Pub, forthcoming; auth, "Connecting with the God-Man: Angela of Foligno's Sensual Communion and Priestly Identity," Romance Languages Annual, X (99): 308-314; auth, "Dante and Dionysius: The articulation of the heavenly vision of Canto 28 of the Paradiso," Cincinnati Romance Review, (98): 86-92. **CONTACT ADDRESS** Dept Mod Lang, Ohio Univ, 1 Ohio Univ, Athens, OH 45701-2942. **EMAIL** morrisom@ohiou.edu

MORTIMER, ARMINE KOTIN
PERSONAL Born 05/13/1943, Detroit, MI, m, 1980, 2 children **DISCIPLINE** FRENCH LITERATURE & CRITICISM **EDUCATION** Radcliffe Col, BA, 64; UCLA, MA, 70; Yale Univ, MPhil, 73, & PhD, 74. **CAREER** From Asst Prof to Assoc Prof, 74-88, Prof French, Univ IL, Urbana-Champaign, 88-; Fel, 77, Assoc, Ctr Advan Study, Univ IL, 99. **MEMBERSHIPS** MLA. **RESEARCH** Analysis of narrative; interpretive theory; 19th & 20th century French lit. **SELECTED PUBLICATIONS** Auth, Pantagruel: language vs communication, Mod Lang Notes, 77; The Narrative Imagination: Comic Tales by Philippe de Vigneulles, Univ Ky, 77; La Maison Nucingen, ou le recit financier, Romanic Rev, 1/78; La lecture de la mort: Le Scarabee d'or d'Edgar Allan Poe, Litterature, 80; Problems of Closure in Balzac's Stories, Fr Forum, 85; La Clature narrative, Corti, 85; The Gentlest Law: Roland Barthes's The Pleasure of the Text, Lang, 89; Plotting to Kill, Lang, 91; auth, "The Death of Autobiography in Doubrovsky's Broken Novel, Genre," 93; The Devious Second Storyn Kleist's Die Marquise von O, The Ger Quart, 94; Le corset de La Vieille Fille de Balzac, In: L'oeuvre d'identite: Essais sur le romantisme de Nodier a Baudelaire, Paragraphes 13, Univ Montreal, 96; Dialogues of the Deaf: The Failure of Consolation in Les Liaisons dangereuses, MLN, 96; Naive and Devious: La religieuse, Romanic Rev, 97; auth, "Balzac's Ursule Mirouet: Genealogy and Inheritance," The Modern Language Review, 97; Romantic Fever: The Second Story as Illegitimate Daughter in Wharton's Roman Fever, Narrative, 98; auth of numerous other articles and publ; auth, "L'ecriture cure: Femmes de Sollers," Le topos du manuscrit trouve, 99; auth, "Loving Writing Fragments d'un discours amoureux," Symposium, 00; auth, "Philippe Sollers, Secret Agent," Journal of Modern Literature, 00; auth, "Myth and Mendacity: Balzac's Pierrette and Beatrice Cenci," Dalhousie French Studies, 00; auth, "Paradise on TV: Philippe Sollers's Video Art, The Visual-Narrative Matrix: Interdisciplinary Collisions and Collusious," Southampton, 00, auth, Writing Realism: Representation in French Literature, Johns Hopkins, 00. **CONTACT ADDRESS** Dept of French, Univ of Illinois, Urbana-Champaign, 707 S Mathews Ave, Urbana, IL 61801-3625. **EMAIL** armine@uiuc.edu

MORTON, JACQUELINE
PERSONAL Born 10/21/1934, Paris, France, 3 children **DISCIPLINE** TWENTIETH CENTURY FRENCH LITERATURE **EDUCATION** Hunter Col, BA, 54; Columbia Univ, MA, 65, PhD(French), 69. **CAREER** Instr, Smith Col, 66-67; asst prof, 75-79, Prof French, Wayne State Univ, 80-. **MEMBERSHIPS** Asn des Amis d'Andre Gide; Am Asn Teachers French; MLA. **RESEARCH** Andre Gide; Francois Mauriac; Andre Gide translator. **SELECTED PUBLICATIONS** Ed, La Correspondance d'Andre Gide et de Francois Mauriac, Gallimard, Paris, 71; coauth, La Presse Contemporary Issues in French Newspapers, Heath, 72; auth, Andre Gide and his American translator Justin O'Brien, Mich Aca, 77; coauth, La Presse II, Heath, 77; Mosaique, Van Nostrand, 77; English Grammar for Students of French, 79 & ed, English Grammar Series, 79, Olivia & Hill Press. **CONTACT ADDRESS** 905 Olivia, Ann Arbor, MI 48104.

MOSHI, LIOBA
DISCIPLINE LINGUISTICS **EDUCATION** Univ Dar Es Salaam, Tanzania, BA, 73, MS, 77; Univ York, England, MPhil, 81; Univ Calif, Los Angeles, PhD, 85. **CAREER** Instr, Marangu Teachers Col, Tanzania, 73-74; instr, dept head, Kigoma Sec Sch, Tanzania, 74-75; Instr, Tanzania Civil Svc, Secretarial Col, 75-78; asst res, Univ Dar Es Salaam, Tanzania, 78-79; Instr, Univ York, England, 79-81; teach assoc, Univ Calif, 81-85; res assoc, Ctr Stud Lang, Info, Standord Univ, 86-92; vis lectr, Univ Calif, Berkeley, 85-87; lectr, Stanford Univ, 85-88; asst prof anthropol, 88-91, asst prof, comp lit, 91-94; assoc prof, comp lit, 94-, Univ Ga. **RESEARCH** Discourse Analysis, Sociolinguistics, African Lang Pedagogy. **SELECTED PUBLICATIONS** Auth, "The Category Adjectives," In Africa und Ubersee, Band 5, 92; coauth, "Time Stability," In Studies on African Languages, eds. Salikoko Mufwene and Lioba Moshi, (Philadelphia: John Benjamins Publishing Company, 93): 163-184; auth, "Locatives in Kivunjo Chaga," Studies on African Languages, John Benjamins, 95; ed, The Manifestation of Gender in African Languages," A Journal of Womenist, Theory and Research, Univ of Ga, 97; auth, Swahili, Language and Culture, a companion to a 23 lesson video series for the teaching of the Swahili language and culture, Hyattsville MD: Dunwoody Press, 98; auth, "Word Order in Multiple Object Construction in Kivunjo-Chaga, In Journal of African Languages & Linguistics, 19, Leiden Univ, The Netherlands, (98): 137-153; co-ed, Instructional Manual for Teachers of Kiswhili, Global Publications, Binghamton Univ, 99; ed, "The implementation of the Language Learning Framework: the case of Materials Development in Less Commonly Taught Languages," To appear in Special Papers on African Language Instruction, Antonia Schleiher & John Hutchson eds., Global Publications, Binghamton Univ, 99. **CONTACT ADDRESS** African Studies Prog, Univ of Georgia, 141 Joe Brown Hall, Athens, GA 30602-6204. **EMAIL** moshi@uga.edu

MOSKOS, GEORGE
PERSONAL Born 10/16/1948, Charleston, SC, d **DISCIPLINE** FRENCH LITERATURE **EDUCATION** Davidson

Col, BA, 70; Univ Wis-Madison, MA, 73, PhD(French), 75. **CAREER** Teaching asst, Univ Wis, 73-75; Asst Prof French, Swarthmore Col, 75- **RESEARCH** Flaubert; Stendhal; romanticism. **SELECTED PUBLICATIONS** Auth, Mythe, ecriture et revolution, In: Espagne erivains: Guerre civile, Pantheon Press, Paris, France, 75; coauth, Saint Oedipus: Psychocritical Approaches to Flaubert's Art, Cornell Univ Press, 82; Engendering Power In Hugo,Victor 'Hernani', Neophilologus, Vol 0078, 1994. **CONTACT ADDRESS** Dept Mod Lang & Lit, Swarthmore Col, 500 College Ave, Swarthmore, PA 19081-1306.

MOSKOWITZ, ANDRE J.
PERSONAL Born 02/05/1962, Berkeley, CA, m, 1990, 1 child **DISCIPLINE** LINGUISTICS **EDUCATION** CUNY, MA, 88; Univ Fla, MA, 95. **CAREER** Teach, Colegio Panam, 84-85; interp, NY Un Court, 85-88; interp, Dept of St, 88-89; ling, GlobaLink, 90; instr, Am Lang Sch, 90-92; instr, Univ Fla, 92-95; interp, Atand T Lang Line, 96-97; lang spec, Exec Off Imm Rev, 97-. **MEMBERSHIPS** ATA; NCTA; MLA; NCLR; Trans and Interp Guild. **RESEARCH** Spanish lexical dialectology. **SELECTED PUBLICATIONS** Auth, "A box of office supplies: dialectological fun," Georgetown J of Lang Ling 1(90): 315-344; auth, "Contribucidn al estudio del espanol ecuatoriano," Univ Fla, Dept Roman (95); auth, "Car terminology in the Spanish-speaking world," in Proceedings of the 36th Annual Conference of the American Translators Association, ed. Peter W. Krawutschke (Nashville, TN: Am Trans Asn, 95): 331-340; auth, "Clothing terminology in the Spanish-speaking world: regional variation," in Proceedings of the 37th Annual Conference of the American Translators Association, eds. Ed. Muriel M. Jerome-O'Keefe (CO: Am Trans Asn, 96): 287-308; auth, "Fruit and vegetable terminology in the Spanish-speaking world: regional variation," in Proceedings of the 38th Annual Conference of the American Translators Association, ed. Muriel M. Jer6me-O'Keeffe (CA: Am Trans Asn, 97): 233-261; auth, "Topics in Spanish lexical dialectology: the home," in Proceedings of the 39th Annual Conference of the American Translators Association, ed. Ann G. McFarlane (SC: Am Trans Asn, 98): 221-253; co-auth, "Talking with Andre Moskowitz," ATA Chron 10 (99): 61-63; auth, "Topics in Spanish lexical dialectology: food and drink," in Proceedings of the 40th Annual Conference of the American Translators Association, ed. Ann G. McFarlane (MO: Am Trans Asn, 99); auth, "Topics in Spanish lexical dialectology: kids' stuff," in Proceedings of the 41st Annual Conference of the American Translators Association, ed. Thomas L. West (FL: Am Trans Asn, 00): 328-366; auth, "Topics in Spanish lexical dialectology: folks," in Proceedings of the 42nd Annual Conference of the American Translators Association, ed. Thomas L. West (CA: Am Trans Asn, forthcoming). **CONTACT ADDRESS** 550 Kearney St, Ste 800, Exec Off Immigration Rev, San Francisco, CA 94108. **EMAIL** amoskow@aol.com

MOSS, JANE
PERSONAL Born 05/08/1947, Boston, MA, m, 1979, 1 child **DISCIPLINE** FRENCH **EDUCATION** Wellesley Col, AB, 69; Yale Univ, MPhil, 72; PhD, 76. **CAREER** Asst Prof, Carthage Col, 74-79; Asst Prof to Prof, Colby Col, 79-. **HONORS AND AWARDS** Phi Beta Kappa, 68; Woodrow Wilson Fel, 69; Can Govt Sen Res Awd, 98. **MEMBERSHIPS** MLA; ACSUS; ACQS; AATF; CIEF. **RESEARCH** Quebec and Francophone Canadian theater. **SELECTED PUBLICATIONS** Auth, "Hysterical Pregnancies and Post-Partum Blues: Staging the Maternal Body in Quebec Plays," in Essays on Modern Quebec Theater, (MI State Univ Press, 95), 47-60; auth, "Multiculturalism and Postmodern Theater: Staging Quebec's Otherness," Mosaic, (96): 75-96; auth, "Dramatizing the Discourse of Female Desire," in Women by Women, (Fairleigh Dickinson Press, 97), 17-33; auth, "Daniel Danis et le drame de la Parole," Nouveaux Regards sur le theatre quebecois, Dalhousie French Studies, (97): 117-128; auth, "Staging the Act of Writing: Post modern Theater in Quebec," French Review, (98): 940-948; auth, "Yvan Bienvenue and the conte urbain," Theatre Research in Canada, (99): 16-34; auth, "Passionate Post-Mortems: Couples Plays by Quebec Women Dramatists," in Doing Gender: Franco-Canadian Women Writers of the 1990s, (Fairleigh Dickinson UP, 00), 114-140. **CONTACT ADDRESS** Dept French, Colby Col, 150 Mayflower Hill Dr, Waterville, ME 04901-4799. **EMAIL** jmmoss@colby.edu

MOSSER, KURT
DISCIPLINE PHILOSOPHY OF LOGIC AND LANGUAGE **EDUCATION** Univ Chicago, PhD, 90. **CAREER** Dept Philos, Univ Dayton **RESEARCH** Kant, epistemology and metaphysics. **SELECTED PUBLICATIONS** Auth, Stoff and Nonsense in Kant's First Critique, Hist Philos Quart, 93; Was Wittgenstein a neo-Kantian? A Response to Prof Haller, Grazer Philos Stud, 93; Kant's Critical Model of the Experiencing Subject, Idealistic Stud, 95. **CONTACT ADDRESS** Dept of Philos, Univ of Dayton, 300 Col Park, Dayton, OH 75062. **EMAIL** mosser@checkov.hm.udayton.edu

MOSSHAMMER, ALDEN ADAMS
PERSONAL Born 03/22/1941, Greenwich, CT, m, 1971 **DISCIPLINE** ANCIENT HISTORY, CLASSICS **EDUCATION** Amherst Col, BA, 62; Brown Univ, PhD(classics), 71. **CAREER** Instr Latin, Laconia High Sch, NH, 62-63; instr classics, Mercersburg Acad, Pa, 63-67, registr, 65-67; instr, Kenyon Col, 70-71; asst prof, Swarthmore Col, 71-72; asst prof, 72-77, Assoc Prof Hist, Univ Calif, San Diego, 77-83; Prof Hist, 83-. **MEMBERSHIPS** Am Philol Asn, North Am Patristic Soc. **RESEARCH** Greek chronography; archaic Greek history; church history. **SELECTED PUBLICATIONS** Auth, The epoch of the seven sages, 76 & Phainias of eresos and chronology, 77, Calif Studies Class Antiq; The Chronicle of Eusebius and Greek Chronographic Tradition, Assoc Univ, 79; The Barberini manuscript of George Syncellus, Greek, Roman, Byzantine Studies, 80; Two fragments of Jerome's chronicle, Rheinisches Mus, 81; Thales' Eclipse, Am Philol Asn, 81; The date of the first pythiad-again, Greek, Roman, Byzantine Studies, 82; auth, "Non-Being and Evil in Gregory of Nyssa," Vigiliae Christianae 44 (90):136-67; ed, Ecolga Chronographiae Georgii Syncelli, Teubner ; Agatharchides Of Cnidos 'On The Erythraean Sea' - Burstein,Sm, J Of The American Oriental Society, Vol 0112, 1992; auth, "Gregory of Nyssa and Christian Hellenism," Studia Patristica 32 (97): 170-195; auth, "Gregory of Nyssa as Homilist," Studia Patristica, 01. **CONTACT ADDRESS** Dept of Hist B-007, Univ of California, San Diego, 9500 Gilman Dr, La Jolla, CA 92093-5003. **EMAIL** amosshammer@ucsd.edu

MOST, GLENN WARREN
PERSONAL Born 06/12/1952, Miami, FL **DISCIPLINE** COMPARATIVE LITERATURE, CLASSICAL LANGUAGES **EDUCATION** Harvard Univ, AB, 72; Yale Univ, MPhil, 78; PhD(comp lit), 80; Tubingen, WGer, DPhil, 80. **CAREER** Teaching asst philos, Yale Univ, 75, teaching asst lit, 76; teaching asst Latin, Univ Tubingen, 77-78; vis lectr lit theory, Yale Univ, 78-79; teaching asst classics, Univ Heidelberg, 79-80; Mellon Asst Prof Classics, Princeton Univ, 80-85; Mellon fel, Am Acad Rome, 82-83; Universita degli di Siena: Prof a Contratto, 85-86; Vis Assoc Prof of Classics, Univ of Mich, 86-87; Universitat Innsbruck: Ordentlicher Universitats, Prof fur Klassische Philologie, 87-91; Universitat Heidelberg, Universitats Prof fur Grazistik, 91-97; Vis prof, Univ of Mich, 93; Vis Prof, Committee on Social Thought, Univ of Chicago 93, prof committee on Social Thought, 97-. **HONORS AND AWARDS** Andrew W. Mellon Fel, American Academy, 82-83; John Witherspoon Bicentennial Preceptorship, 84-86; Fel, Wissenschaftliches Mitglied, Wissenschaftskolleg zu Berlin, 88-89; Visiting fel, Institute for the Humanities, Univ of Mich, 93; Gottfried Wilhelm Leibniz Preis, Deutsche Forschungsgemeinschaft, 94-99. **RESEARCH** Literature; literary theory; philosophy. **SELECTED PUBLICATIONS** Auth, "Polvemo" pathvr. Die Vorsokratiker in der Forschung der Zwainger Jahre," Altertumswissenschaft in der 20er Jahren, Franz Steiner Verlag, (Stuttgart) (95): 87-114; auth, "Horatian and Pindaric Lyric in England," Zeitgenosse Horaz, Der Dichter und seine Leser seit zwei Jahrtausenden, Gunter Narr Verlag, (Tubingen) (96):117-52; auth, "Classical Scholarship and literary criticism," in The Cambridge History of Literary Criticism 4 (Cambridge Univ Pr, 97), 742-757; auth, "Philogie- und Bildungsgeschichte seit der Renaissance 3.2: Die Geschichte seit dem 19. Jahrhundert," Einleitung in die lateinische Philogie, B.G. Teubner (Stuttgart-Leipzig, 97): 43-48; auth, Texte edieren, Appremata 2, Vandenhoeck und Ruprecht (Gottingen), 98; auth, "Karl Otfried Muller's Edition of Aeschylus Eumenides," Zwischen Rationalismus und Romantik. Karl Otfried Muller und die antike Kultur, Weidmann (Hildesheim, 98): 349-373; auth, The Routledge Encyclopedia of Philosophy, Epicharmus 4:336-37, Hesoid 4:412-13, Homer 4:501-02, Katharsis 5:218-20, Mimeis 6:381-82, Routledge (London), 98; auth, The Poetics of Early Greek Philosophy," The Cambridge Companion to Early Greek Philosophy (Cambridge Univ Pr, 99), 332-62; auth, "From Logos to Mythos," From Myth to Reason? Studies in the Development of Greek Thought, Oxford Univ Pr (Oxford, 99), 25-47; auth, "Le Combat. Picasso und die Antike," Pablo Picasso. Les Femmes de Picasso, Galerie Michael Vlaszczyk (Bad Hamburg, 00), 25-27. **CONTACT ADDRESS** Committee on Social Thought, Univ of Chicago, 1130 E. 59th St., Chicago, IL 60637. **EMAIL** gmost@midway.uchicago.edu

MOTTO, ANNA LYDIA
PERSONAL Born New York, NY, m, 1959, 2 children **DISCIPLINE** CLASSICS **EDUCATION** Queen's Col, NYork, BA, 46; NYork Univ, MA, 48; Univ NC, PhD, 53. **CAREER** Asst, Univ NC, 49-50, part-time instr, 51-52; asst prof Latin, Greek & Span, Washington Col, 53-57; teacher Latin & French, Northport High Sch, NY, 57-58; asst prof Latin & Greek & chmn dept classics, Alfred Univ, 58-65; assoc prof Latin & Greek & chmn dept, Muhlenberg Col, 65-66; assoc prof, St John's Univ, NY, 66-68; from assoc prof to prof, Drew Univ, 68-73; chmn dept for lang, 74-78, Prof Classics, Univ South Fla, 73-, Fulbright grant, Am Acad Rome & Vergilian Soc, Cumae, 56; vis prof, Univ Mich, 69. **MEMBERSHIPS** Classic Asn Atlantic States (vp, 72-73); Am Philol Asn; Am Classic League; MLA; S Atlantic Mod Lang Asn. **RESEARCH** Seneca the philosopher; Roman Stoicism; Roman satire. **SELECTED PUBLICATIONS CONTACT ADDRESS** Dept of Classics, Univ of So Florida, 4202 Fowler Ave, Tampa, FL 33620-9951.

MOUKHLIS, SALAH M.
PERSONAL m, 1998 **DISCIPLINE** ENGLISH AND COMPARATIVE LITERATURE **EDUCATION** Mohamed V Univ, BA, 86; Keele Univ, MA, 88; SUNY Stony Brook, PhD, 94. **CAREER** Asst prof, Moulay Ismail Univ, 88-00; asst prof, Holyoke Comm Col, 00-. **MEMBERSHIPS** MLA, NEMLA, ALA, Morocco Min Ed. **RESEARCH** Post colonial theory, cultural studies, emerging literatures. **SELECTED PUBLICATIONS** Trans, "In Defense of the Author," by David Hirsch (Maknasat, Univ Moulay Ismail Press, 93), auth, "Spring Cleaning: A Novel by Miloudi Chaghmoum," Offshoot (98); auth, History and Representation in Assia Djebar, Univ Moulay Ismail Press, 99; auth, "Driss Chraibi," ed. John Hawley, Encycl Postcol Stud (forthcoming). **CONTACT ADDRESS** Dept of Eng, Holyoke Comm Col, 303 Homestead Ave, Holyoke, MA 01040. **EMAIL** moukhlis@hotmail.com

MOURELATOS, ALEXANDER PHOEBUS DIONYSIOU
PERSONAL Born 07/19/1936, Athens, Greece, d **DISCIPLINE** PHILOSOPHY, CLASSICAL PHILOLOGY **EDUCATION** Yale Univ, BA, 58, MA, 61, PhD(philos), 64. **CAREER** Instr, Yale Univ, 62-64; from asst prof to assoc prof, 65-71, Prof Philos, Univ Tex Austin, 71-, Jr fel, Inst Res Humanities, Univ Wis, 64-65; mem, Inst Advan Study, Princeton, NJ, 67-68; Nat Endowment for Humanities fel, 68 & 82-83; jr fel, Ctr Hellenic Studies, Washington, DC, 73-74; Am Coun Learned Soc fel, 73-74; vis fel, Humanities Res Ctr, Australian Nat Univ, Canberra, 78 and 91; Guggenheim Fellow, 88-89. **HONORS AND AWARDS** Dr phil. hon, Univ of Athens (Greece), 94. **MEMBERSHIPS** Am Philos Asn; Am Philol Asn; Can Philos Asn; Correspdg member of the Academy of Athens, 99. **RESEARCH** Pre-Socratic philosophy; Plato; Aristotle; philosophical linguistics. **SELECTED PUBLICATIONS** Auth, Aristotle's Powers and Modern Empiricism, Ratio, 67; The Route of Parmenides, Yale Univ, 70; co-ed, Exegesis and Argument: Studies Presented to Gregory Vlastos, Van Gorcum, Assen, Neth, 73; ed, The Pre-Socratics: A Collection of Critical Essays, Doubleday, 2nd ed., Princeton Univ Press, 93; 74; Events, processes, and states, Ling & Philos, 78; Astronomy and kinematics in Plato's project of rationalist explanation, Study Hist & Philos of Sci, 80; auth, Quality, Structure, and Emergence in Later Pre-Socratic Philosophy, Proceedings of the Boston Area Colloquium in Ancient Philosophy, 87. **CONTACT ADDRESS** Dept of Philos, Univ of Texas, Austin, Austin, TX 78712-1180. **EMAIL** apdm@mail.utexas.edu

MOUTSOS, DEMETRIUS GEORGE
PERSONAL Born 11/06/1934 **DISCIPLINE** LINGUISTICS **EDUCATION** Univ Athens, dipl classics, 56; Univ Chicago, AM, 60, PhD(ling), 63. **CAREER** From instr to assoc prof, 63-77, Prof Ling, Univ Rochester, 77-. **MEMBERSHIPS** Ling Soc Am; Am Name Soc. **SELECTED PUBLICATIONS** Auth, The origin of a Balkanism, Z Balkanologie, 69; Romanisn stapin and OChCl stopans, Z Vergleichende Sprachforsch, 70; The origin of a Balkan pastoral term, Sprache, 72; Byzantion, Zietschrift fur Balkanologie, Z Vergleichende Sprachforschung Akten des internationalen Kolloquicuims, Innsbruck, 72; Gothic Puggs And Middle-Greek Poungion, Indogermanische Forschungen, Vol 0098, 1993. **CONTACT ADDRESS** Dept of Foreign Lang Lit & Ling, Univ of Rochester, Rochester, NY 14627.

MOWRY, HUA-YUAN LI
DISCIPLINE ASIAN AND MIDDLE EASTERN LANGUAGES AND LITERATURES **EDUCATION** Tunghai Univ, BA; Univ Calif Berkeley, MA, PhD. **CAREER** Assoc prof, Dartmouth Col. **HONORS AND AWARDS** EDUCOM Software Awd, 91; proj dir, byrne dictionary; res dir, dartmouth-at-bnu prog, 82, 84, 87, 90, 92, and 94. **SELECTED PUBLICATIONS** Auth, Chinese Love Stories from Ch'ing-shih; Yan-pan Hsi--New Theater in China; Hanzi Assistant; auth, A Multimedia Chinese Reader for Advanced Students. **CONTACT ADDRESS** Dartmouth Col, 3529 N Main St, #207, Hanover, NH 03755. **EMAIL** hua-yuan.l.mowry@dartmouth.edu

MOYSEY, ROBERT ALLEN
PERSONAL Born 06/27/1949, Richmond, IN **DISCIPLINE** CLASSICAL LANGUAGES, ANCIENT HISTORY **EDUCATION** Univ Cincinnati, BA, 71; Princeton Univ, MA, 73, PhD(class), 75. **CAREER** Teaching asst class, Princeton Univ, 73-75; vis asst prof, Hamilton Col, 77-78; vis asst prof hist, Univ Del, 79-80; asst prof class, 80-85, assoc prof class, 85-90, prof class, 90-, chair and prof class, Univ Miss, 93-. **HONORS AND AWARDS** Phi Beta Kappa; Charles McMicken Honors Prize. **MEMBERSHIPS** Archaeol Inst Am; Am Philol Asn; Asn Ancient Historians; Am Numis Soc. **RESEARCH** Greek & Persian history, 4th century BC; Greek epigraphy; Greek numismatics. **SELECTED PUBLICATIONS** Auth, The Date of the Strato of Sidon Decree, Am J of Ancient Hist, 76; The Thirty and the Pnyx, Am J of Archaeol, 81; Greek Funerary Monuments in Mississippi, Zeitschrift fur Papyrologie und Epigraphik, 88; Three Fragmentary Attic Inscriptions, Zeitschrift fur Papyrologie und Epigraphik, 89; Observations on the Numismatic Evidence relating to the Great Satrapal Refolt of 362/1 BC, Revue des Etudes Anciennes, 89; Thucydides, Kimon and the Peace of Kallias, Ancient His Bulletin, 91; Diodoros, the Satraps and the Decline of the Persian Empire: A Book Review of Michael Weiskopf's The So-Called Great

Satrapal Revolt 366-360 BC, Ancient Hist Bulletin, 91; A Brief History of Olynthus, Olynthus: An Overview, Univ Miss, 92; Plutarch, Nepos and the Satrapal Revolt of 362/1 BC, Historia, 92. **CONTACT ADDRESS** Dept of Classics, Univ of Mississippi, University, MS 38677-9999. **EMAIL** clmoysey@olemiss.edu

MOZEJKO, EDWARD
PERSONAL Born 07/15/1932, Czemierniki, Poland, m, 1968, 1 child **DISCIPLINE** COMPARATIVE LITERATURE **EDUCATION** Jagiellonian Univ, MA, 56, PhD(Slavic lit), 64. **CAREER** Asst prof Slavic lit, Jagiellonian Univ, 57-65; lectr, Polish lang & lit, 69-71, assoc prof Russ & comp lit, 71-76, Prof Slavic Lang, Univ Alta, 76-, Alexander von Humboldt fel, Univ Munich, 71-72. **HONORS AND AWARDS** Poland Nat Professorship, J. Gordin Kaplan Awd, Royal Soc of Canada Fel. **MEMBERSHIPS** Can Asn Slavists; Int Comp Lit Asn. **RESEARCH** Avant-garde trends; theory of literature; eastern-western literary relations in Europe. **SELECTED PUBLICATIONS** Coauth, Romantic Irony in Polish Literature and Criticism; auth, Yordan YovKov, 84; ed, Vasiliy Pavlovich Aksenov: A Writer in Quest of Himself, 86. **CONTACT ADDRESS** Dept of Comp Lit, Relig, & Film/Media Studs, Univ of Alberta, 347 Arts, Edmonton, AB, Canada T6G 2G6. **EMAIL** emozeiko@gpu.srv.ualberta.ca

MUDIMBE, VALENTINE
DISCIPLINE FRENCH AND COMPARATIVE LITERATURE AND LANGUAGE **EDUCATION** BA, 66; Louvain Univ, DPhil, 70. **CAREER** Prof, Stanford Univ. **RESEARCH** Indo-European langs and lits. **SELECTED PUBLICATIONS** Auth, Fables and Parables, 91; Shaba Deux, Paris Presence Africaine, 89; The Invention of Africa, 88. **CONTACT ADDRESS** Stanford Univ, Bldg 20, Main Quad, Stanford, CA 94305.

MUELLER, AGNES C.
PERSONAL Born 04/03/1968, Germany **DISCIPLINE** GERMANIC STUDIES, COMPARATIVE LITERATURE **EDUCATION** Munich Univ, MA, 93; Vanderbilt Univ, PhD, 97. **CAREER** Teaching asst, Vanderbilt Univ, 94-97; instr to lectr to vis asst prof to asst prof, Univ SCar, 97-. **HONORS AND AWARDS** Univ SCar Fel; DAAD Fel; Max Kade Fel; Goethe Inst Fel; Vanderbilt Univ Grant, 96. **MEMBERSHIPS** MLA; GSA; SAMLA; AATG; ACLA; WIG; IVG. **RESEARCH** German studies; post-WWII and contemporary literature and culture; cultural studies; critical theory; international studies; German American studies; popular culture. **SELECTED PUBLICATIONS** Transl, Chevalier, Tracy: Das Dunkelste Blau (Munchen: DTV, 1999); auth, Lyrik 'Made in USA:' Vermittlung and Rezeption in der Bundesrepublik, Rodopi Pr (Amsterdam/Atlanta), 99; auth, "Poesie, Pop, Postmoderne: Ver¤nderungen der Westdeutschen Lyrik Durch Brinkmann's U.S.-Poetik," in Amerikanischer Speck, Englischer Honig, Italienische N¤sse: Rolf Dieter Brinkmann zum 60 (Eiswasser Sonderband, 00): 90-98; auth, "Brinkmanns US-Poetik im Postkolonialen Diskurs," Compass (01). **CONTACT ADDRESS** Dept Ger Slav E Asian, Univ of So Carolina, Columbia, Columbia, SC 29208. **EMAIL** agnes.mueller@sc.edu

MUELLER, ROSEANNA M.
PERSONAL Born 12/24/1948, Italy, m, 1971, 2 children **DISCIPLINE** SPANISH, ITALIAN **EDUCATION** Hunter Col, BA, 71; City Col NYork, MA, 77; CUNY Grad Sch, PhD, 77. **CAREER** Instr/dir, Morton Col, 82-91; prof, Columbia Col Chicago, 91-. **HONORS AND AWARDS** NEH Fel, 90, 92, 95; Ill Dev Award, 95; MLA, ILA, 89. **MEMBERSHIPS** MLA; MMLA; RSA; ICTFL; AATSP. **RESEARCH** 16th-century Italy and Spain; conquest chronicles; contemporary Latin American women writers. **SELECTED PUBLICATIONS** Transl, The Diana, by Jorge de Montemayor (Edwin Mellen Pr, 1989); co-auth, LaGrange and LaGrange Park, Acadia Pub, 99; articles in A Twice Told Tale, The Encycl of Mexico, Chicago Tribune. **CONTACT ADDRESS** 106 N Madison Ave, La Grange, IL 60525-2033. **EMAIL** roseannamueller@compuserve.com

MULLEN, KAREN A.
PERSONAL Born 07/05/1941 **DISCIPLINE** ENGLISH, LINGUISTICS **EDUCATION** Grinnell Col, BA, 63; Univ Iowa, MA, 66, PhD(English), 73. **CAREER** Asst rhet, 66-70, asst ling, 70-73, from instr to asst prof ling, 74-75, coord English as foreign lang prog, 75-77, assoc dir, Intensive English Prog, Univ Iowa, 76-78; Assoc Prof & Dir Intensive English, Univ Louisville, 78-, Ed, News lett for spec interest group lang anal & studies humanities, Asn Comput Mach, 71-75; consult ed, Comput & Humanities, 72-75. **MEMBERSHIPS** Asn Teachers English to Speakers Other Lang; Ling Soc Am; MLA; Nat Asn Foreign Student Affairs; Asn Comput Mach. **RESEARCH** Cloze-passage test; relationship between second-language proficiency and intelligence. **SELECTED PUBLICATIONS** Auth, In-core PLI sort and search procedures for lexical data, Siglash Newslett, 73; The Wanderer: Considered again, Neophilologus, 74; Rater reliability and oral proficiency evaluations, Occas Papers Ling, 77; Using rater judgments in the evaluation of writing proficiency for non-native speakers of English, Teaching & Learning English as 2nd Lang: Trends Res & Pract, 77; Direct evaluation of second language proficiency, Lang Learning, 79; More on Cloze tests, Concepts Lang Testing 79; An alternative to the Cloze test, TESOL, 79; Evaluating writing in ESL, chap 15 & Rater reliability and oral proficiency evaluations, chap 8, In: Research in Language Testing, Newbury House, 80; Making Progress In English - Furey,Pr, Menasche,L, Modern Language J, Vol 0077, 1993. **CONTACT ADDRESS** Dept of English, Univ of Louisville, Louisville, KY 40208.

MULLER, MARCEL
PERSONAL Born 06/02/1926, Forty Fort, PA **DISCIPLINE** FRENCH **EDUCATION** Athenee Royal de Charleroi, Belgium, BA, 44; Univ Liege, MA, 51; Univ Wis, MA, 54, PhD(French), 65. **CAREER** Instr French & Latin, Ill Col, 54-56; teaching asst, Univ Wis, 57-58; instr French & Ger, Lawrence Univ, 58-59; from instr to asst prof French, 61-66; assoc prof, 66-76, Prof French, Univ Mich, Ann Arbor, 76-, mem fac, French School, Middlebury, 72; Nat Endowment for Humanities summer grant, 79; mem, Inst Res in Humanities, Wis, 79-80. **MEMBERSHIPS** Am Asn Teachers French; MLA; Soc Amis Marcel Proust; Int Asn Fr Studies. **RESEARCH** Proust; Valery; structuralism. **SELECTED PUBLICATIONS** Auth, Paul Valery lecteur de Leon Bloy, Romanic Rev, 10/59; Romananfang und Romanschluss bei Marcel Proust, In: Romananfange: Versuch zu einer Poetik des Romans, Literarisches Colloquium, Berlin, 65; Les voix narratives dans La Recherche du temps perdu, Droz, 65; La naturalisation de Charlus, Poetique, fall 71; Charlus dans le metro, Etudes proustiennes, 78; Ancien Testament et Noveau Testament dans 'A la Recherche du Temps Perdu, French Forum Monogr, 79; La Dialectique De L'ouvert Et Du Ferme Chez Paul Valery, Mich Romance Studies, 80. **CONTACT ADDRESS** Dept of Romance Lang, Univ of Michigan, Ann Arbor, Ann Arbor, MI 48109.

MULLER-SIEVERS, HELMUT
DISCIPLINE GERMAN **EDUCATION** Stanford Univ, PhD. **CAREER** Assoc prof, Northwestern Univ. **RESEARCH** Monograph on Georg B chner's physiological writings and an investigation into the aporia of orientation. **SELECTED PUBLICATIONS** Auth, Epigenesis: Naturphilosophie im Sprachdenken Wilhelm von Humboldts; Self-Generation: Biology, Philosophy, and Literature Around 1800; essays on, the history of hermeneutics; Latin and German poetry and poetics; the relation of the natural sciences to philosophy and literature; the hermeneutics of American football. **CONTACT ADDRESS** Dept of German, Northwestern Univ, 1801 Hinman, Evanston, IL 60208. **EMAIL** hms@nwu.edu

MUMBY, DENNIS K.
DISCIPLINE ORGANIZATIONAL COMMUNICATION, PHILOSOPHY OF COMMUNICATION **EDUCATION** Southern Ill Univ, PhD, 84. **CAREER** Assoc prof, Purdue Univ. **SELECTED PUBLICATIONS** Auth, The Political Function of Narrative in Organizations, Commun Monogr, 87; Communication & Power in Organizations, Ablex, 88; ed, Narrative & Social Control, Sage, 93. **CONTACT ADDRESS** Dept of Commun, Purdue Univ, West Lafayette, 1080 Schleman Hall, West Lafayette, IN 47907-1080. **EMAIL** dmumby@purdue.edu

MUNDT, HANNELORE
DISCIPLINE GERMAN **EDUCATION** Univ CA, Irvine, PhD, 84. **CAREER** Assoc prof; Univ WY, 96-. **RESEARCH** Contemp Ger lit. **SELECTED PUBLICATIONS** Publ on, questions of intertextuality in lit. **CONTACT ADDRESS** Dept of Mod and Class Lang(s), Univ of Wyoming, PO Box 3964, Laramie, WY 82071-3964. **EMAIL** HMUNDT@UWYO.EDU

MUNIZ, OLGA
PERSONAL Born 09/28/1954, Isabela, Puerto Rico, m, 1984, 1 child **DISCIPLINE** SPANISH LITERATURE **EDUCATION** Recinto Univ Mayaguez, Puerto Rico, BA, 78; Ind Univ Bloomington, MA, 84; MA, 86; PhD, 94. **CAREER** Assoc instr, Ind Univ, 82-91; lectr to asst prof, Hillsdale Col, 91-. **HONORS AND AWARDS** Fel, Govt of Puerto Rico, 73-78; Agapito Rey Schol, 82; Nat Hispanic Fund, 84; Gamma Kappa Alpha, Sigma Delta Pi. **MEMBERSHIPS** MLA; AATSP; Int Poetry Soc. **RESEARCH** Spanish poetry, Italian poetry, Renaissance Literature, Translation. **SELECTED PUBLICATIONS** Auth, La mujer en el contexto epistolar poetico del Siglo de Ono, Peter Lang, 96; auth, The Sparrow's Song;El canto del govrion, Verbum, 00. **CONTACT ADDRESS** Dept Mod Lang, Hillsdale Col, 33 E College St, Hillsdale, MI 49242-1205.

MUNOZ, WILLY O.
PERSONAL Born 04/06/1949, Cochabamba, Bolivia, m, 1999, 1 child **DISCIPLINE** SPANISH **EDUCATION** Loras Col, BA, 72; Univ Iowa, MA, 74; PhD, 79. **CAREER** Instructor, St Ambrose Col, 76-77; Instructor, Clarke Col, 78-79; Asst Prof, Center Col, 81-84; Asst Prof to Prof, Kent State Univ, 84-. **HONORS AND AWARDS** First Prize, XIV Franz Tamayo annual Literary Contest, Bolivia, 80. **MEMBERSHIPS** Am Asn of Teachers of Spanish and Portug, Asn de Hispanistas, Inst Intl de Teoria y Practica del Teatro Latinoamericano. **RESEARCH** Latin American Literature; Latin American Women Writers; Bolivian Theatre. **SELECTED PUBLICATIONS** Auth, Polifonia de la marginalidad: La narrativa de escritoras latinoamericanas, 99; auth, El personaje femenino en la narrativa de escritoras hispanoamericanas, 92; auth, Teatro boliviano contemporaneo, 81. **CONTACT ADDRESS** Dept Mod & Classical Lang, Kent State Univ, PO Box 5190, Kent, OH 44242-0001. **EMAIL** wmunoz@kent.edu

MURATORE, MARY JO
PERSONAL Born 08/16/1950, OH **DISCIPLINE** FRENCH **EDUCATION** Kent St Univ, 72, MA, 74, Univ Calif David, PhD, 80. **CAREER** Vis asst prof, 79-80, Va Polytechnic Inst, Va St Univ; vis asst prof, 80-83, Purdue Univ; asst prof to assoc prof to prof, 83-, Univ Mo Columbia. **HONORS AND AWARDS** Univ Mo, Kemper Fellow for excellence in teaching & res, 91, Purple Chalk Teaching Awd, 84, Prof Develop Awd for Discipline Assessment, 90; ba, ma, phd with honors; univ calif davis outstanding doctoral student award, 79, regent's fel, 79, 80, patton res award, 76. **MEMBERSHIPS** MLA. **RESEARCH** Seventeenth century French literature. **SELECTED PUBLICATIONS** Auth, The Evolution of the Cornelian Heroine, Studia Humanitatis, 82; auth, Corenelian Theater: The Metadramatic Dimension, Summa, 90; auth, Mimesis and Metatextuality in the Neo-Classical Text, Droz, 94; auth, " Loveless Letters: Narrative Deceits in Guilleragues's Lettres portugaises," Symposium,94; auth, Narrative Unbound: Dyrcona's Quest for Textual Liberation in L' Autre Monde," Seventeenth Century French Studies, 94; auth, Deceived by Truth: The Maxim as a Discourse of Deception in La Princess De Cleves, " Zeitschrift fur Franzosische Sprache und Literatur, 94; auth, The Gender of Truth: Rhetorical Privilege in Tristan's Mariane, Papers on French Seventeenth Century Literature, 97; auth, Strategies of Containement: Repetition as Ideology in Horace, Ramanische Forschungen, 97; auth, " Strategies of Containment: Repetition as Ideology in Horace, " Romanische Forschungen, 97; auth, " Racine's Athalie of The Power of Precedent," Dalhousie French Studies,99. **CONTACT ADDRESS** Dept of Romance Languages, Univ of Missouri, Columbia, 143 Arts & Science Bldg, Columbia, MO 65211. **EMAIL** muratoreM@missouri.edu

MURDICK, WILLIAM
DISCIPLINE RHETORIC AND LINGUISTICS **EDUCATION** SUNY, Albany, BA; Univ IA, MFA; IN Univ PA, PhD. **CAREER** Instr, CA State Univ PA. **SELECTED PUBLICATIONS** Auth, What English Teachers Need to Know about Grammar, Eng J, Nov 96; coauth, Evolution of a Writing Center, Writing Ctr J, 91; Placing Whole Language in a Workshop Setting, Eng Leadership Quart, Dec 91; Art, Writing, and Politics, Art Educ, Sept 92; Journal Writing and Active Learning, Eng Leadership Quart, Oct 93. **CONTACT ADDRESS** California Univ of Pennsylvania, California, PA 15419s. **EMAIL** murdick@cup.edu

MURDOCH, H. ADLAI
PERSONAL Born, Antigua **DISCIPLINE** FRENCH LITERATURE **EDUCATION** Univ W Indies, BA; Howard Univ, MA; Cornell Univ, PhD. **CAREER** Asst prof, Univ Ill Urbana Champaign. **RESEARCH** French Literature; postcolonial studies; with a special interest in the narratives of the Francophone Caribbean and Francophone West Africa **SELECTED PUBLICATIONS** Auth, "Displacing Marginality: Cultural Identity and Creole Resiestance in Glissant and Maximin," Res in Africa Lit, (94), 81-101; auth, "The Novels of Jamaica Kincaid: figures of Exile, Narratives of Dreams," Clockwatch Rev 9, (94) 141-154; auth, "Divdided Desire: biculturality and the Representation of Identity in En attendant le bonheur," Callaloo 18, (95), 579-592; auth, "James' Literary dialectic: the Literary and Cultural space of Minty Alley," CLR James: His Intellectual Legacies, Boston: Univ of Mass Press, (95), 61-71; auth, "dedoublement Creolise et Performance Natttative: Le Discours Postcolonial des Antilles Francophones," Regards sur la francophonie, Rennes: Presses Univ de Rennes, (96), 211-216; auth, "Exploring the Margin: Models of Cultrual Identity in the Postcolonial French Caribbean," Journal of Commonwealth and Postcolonial Studies, (99); auth, "Re-siting Resistance: Chamoiseau's Articulation of Creole Identity," The Journal of 20th Century, Contemporary French Studies, (99); auth, "Narrating Creole Culture: strategies of Selfhood in the French Caribbean Novel," Migrating Words and Worlds: Pan-Africanism (Updated), Trenton, N.J.: African World Press, (99); auth, "Inscribing caribbean Oraliture: The Polysemic Discourse of Patrick Chamoiseau," Multiculturalism and Hybridity in African Lit, Trenton, N.J.: Africa world Press, (00); auth, "Postcolonial Peripheries Revisted: Chamoiseau's Rewriting of Francophone Culture," French Prose in 1999, (00). **CONTACT ADDRESS** French Dept, Univ of Illinois, Urbana-Champaign, 52 E Gregory Dr, Champaign, IL 61820. **EMAIL** hmurdoch@uiuc.edu

MURGIA, CHARLES EDWARD
PERSONAL Born 02/18/1935, Boston, MA, s **DISCIPLINE** CLASSICS **EDUCATION** Boston Col, AB, 56; Harvard Univ, MA, 60, PhD(Class Philol), 66. **CAREER** Instr Classics, Franklin & Marshall Col, 60-61; vis instr, Dartmouth Col, 64-65; asst prof, 66-72, assoc prof, 72-78, prof Classics, Univ Calif, Berkeley, 78-94, chmn, 80-83, Am Coun Learned Soc grant-in-aid, 68; appointed to edit Vol V of Editio Harvardiana

of Servius; Univ Calif Humanities Res Comt res fels, Fall 70; Am Coun Learned Soc fel, 74-75; Nat Endowment for Humanities fel, 78-79; prof Emeritus, 94-; prof grad school, Univ Calif, Berkeley, 95-01. **MEMBERSHIPS** Am Philol Asn; Philol Asn Pac Coast. **RESEARCH** Latin textual criticism; Latin paleography; classical literature. **SELECTED PUBLICATIONS** Auth, Critical notes on the text of Servius' commentary on Aeneid III-V, Harvard Studies Class Philol, 67; Avienus' supposed iambic version of Livy, 70 & More on the Helen episode, 71, The Donatian life of Virgil, DS, and D, 74, Calif Studies Class Antiq; Prolegomena to Servius V--the manuscripts, Vol 11, Class Studies Ser, Univ Calif, 75; The minor works of Tacitus--a study in textual criticism, Class Philol, 77; The length of the lacuna in Tacitus' Dialogus, Calif Studies Class Antiq, 79; The date of Tacitus' Dialogus, Harvard Studies Class Philol, 80. **CONTACT ADDRESS** Dept of Classics, Univ of California, Berkeley, 7303 Dwinelle Hall, Berkeley, CA 94720-2520. **EMAIL** cem@socrates.berkeley.edu

MURPHY, JOSEPH ANTHONY
PERSONAL Born 03/27/1937, Philadelphia, PA **DISCIPLINE** FRENCH **EDUCATION** LaSalle Col, BA, 58; Ohio State Univ, PhD(foreign lang educ), 68. **CAREER** Asst prof French, Mich State Univ, 68-70; assoc prof, Lycoming Col, 70-72; Assoc Prof French & Lang Educ, W VA Univ, 72-. **MEMBERSHIPS** Am Asn Teachers Fr; Am Coun Teaching Foreign Lang; Teachers English to Speakers Other Lang. **RESEARCH** Foreign culture and English as second language library reference materials; language teaching methodology; French and English as second language culture reader production. **SELECTED PUBLICATIONS** Coauth, The use of the language laboratory to teach the reading lesson, Mod Lang J, 68; auth, MLA cooperative FL proficiency tests, 7th Mental Measurements Yearbk, 72; A mini- course in problem solving, Foreign Lang Annals, 73; contribr, How to do library research on a foreign culture, Eric Doc, 75; auth, Advanced placement in French literature St national teacher examinations: French, 8th Mental Measurements Yearbk, 78; French Review index of non-literary articles: 1960-79, Fr Rev, 380; ed, Proc Conf Southern Grad Schs, 80-82; auth, Cadres Culturels, Heinle & Heinle (in prep); Quebec Literary Bibliography - A Library Acquisitions Approach, French Review, Vol 0067, 1994; Kaleidoscope - Grammar In Context - French - Hadley,A, Chamberlain,J, Coulonthenderson,F, Chevillot,F, Harbour,L, Modern Language J, Vol 0079, 1995. **CONTACT ADDRESS** Dept of Foreign Lang, West Virginia Univ, Morgantown, Morgantown, WV 26506.

MURPHY, LAURENCE LYONS
PERSONAL Born 08/23/1948, New York, NY **DISCIPLINE** COMPARATIVE LITERATURE, PHILOSOPHY **EDUCATION** Rugers Univ, PhD, 90 **CAREER** Asst prof Intellectual Heritage, Philos, Temple Univ, Tyler Sch Art, 91- . **HONORS AND AWARDS** Merit Hons; Violet Keters awd for disting Srv and tchg. **MEMBERSHIPS** Amer Philos Asn **RESEARCH** Phenomenology, Hermeneutics. **SELECTED PUBLICATIONS** Exec ed, Ellipses, Jour Arts and Ideas. **CONTACT ADDRESS** Intellectual Heritage Prog, Col of Liberal Arts, Temple Univ, 214 Anderson Hall, 1114 W-Berks St, Philadelphia, PA 19122-6090. **EMAIL** laurence_murphy@hotmail.com

MURSTEIN, NELLY KASHY
PERSONAL Born 04/13/1932, Bagdad, Iraq, m, 1954, 2 children **DISCIPLINE** FRENCH **EDUCATION** Univ Paris, BA, 49; Univ Tex, BA, 53; Rice Univ, MA, 53; PhD, 60. **CAREER** Lectr French, Univ Portland, 59-60; instr, Reed Col, 61-62; from instr to assoc prof, 62-76, chmn dept French & Ital, 70-74 & 80-82, Prof French, Conn Col, 76-99. **HONORS AND AWARDS** Hanna Hafkesbrink Prof of Fr. **MEMBERSHIPS** Am Asn Teachers French; Am Asn Dept Foreign Lang. **RESEARCH** Contemporary theatre and poetry. **SELECTED PUBLICATIONS** Auth, Jean Giraudoux: A Passing Fad?, New Theater Mag, summer 69; auth, Une entrevue avec Eugene Ionesco, French Rev, 2/72; auth, L'Etrange Electra de J Giraudoux, Rice Univ Studies, summer 73; coauth, "Women as Faculty Leaders," in Arming Athena. Career Strategies for Women in Academe, ed. L. Collins, J. Chrisler, and K. Quina (Sage Publication, 98). **CONTACT ADDRESS** Dept of French & Ital, Connecticut Col, 270 Mohegan Ave, Box 1503, New London, CT 06320-4125. **EMAIL** nkmur@conncoll.edu

MUSA, MARK
DISCIPLINE ITALIAN LITERATURE **EDUCATION** Johns Hopkins Univ, PhD, 61. **CAREER** Prof. **HONORS AND AWARDS** Distinguished Tchg Mentoring Awd. **RESEARCH** Dante and Medieval literature. **SELECTED PUBLICATIONS** Ed, The Divine Comedy, Petrarch's Canzoniere, Pirandello's Six Characters in Search of an Author. **CONTACT ADDRESS** Dept of French and Italian, Indiana Univ, Bloomington, 1020 E Kirkwood Ave, Ballantine Hall 642, Bloomington, IN 47405. **EMAIL** musa@indiana.edu

MUST, GUSTAV
PERSONAL Born 02/02/1908, Estonia, m, 1939 **DISCIPLINE** GERMANIC PHILOLOGY, COMPARATIVE LINGUISTICS **EDUCATION** Tartu State Univ, PhM, 38; Univ Gottingen, PhD, 49. **CAREER** Teacher Ger & Estonia, col, Estonia, 34-44; asst prof Ger philol, Baltic Univ, Ger, 46-49; res assoc mod lang, Cornell Univ, 52; asst prof Ger, Baldwin-Wallace Col, 56-57; from asst prof to assoc prof, Augustana Col, Ill, 57-60, head dept, 57-60; assoc prof, Univ Conn, 60-62; assoc Prof, 62-68, res, prof, 67- 70, prof, 68-78, Emer Prof Ger, Valparaiso Univ, 78-, Am Coun Learned Soc fel, 50-51. **MEMBERSHIPS** MLA; Ling Soc Am. **RESEARCH** Germanic and other Indo-European languages; West Finnic languages; comparative philology. **SELECTED PUBLICATIONS** Auth, The origin of the Germanic dental preterit, Language, 51, 52; The problem of the inscription on helmet B of Negau, Harvard Studies Class Philol, 57; The origin of the German word Ehre, PMLA, 6 1; The spelling or Proto-Germanic f in Old High German, Language, Vol 43; Das St Galler Paternoster, Akten des V Int Germanisten-Kongresses Cambridge 1975, 76; Das ST Galler Credo, Fruhmittelalterliche Studien 15, 81; The Origins of The Word Deutsch, German, Indogermanische Forschungen, Vol 0097, 1992. **CONTACT ADDRESS** 1953 Lawndale Dr, Valparaiso, IN 46383.

MUYSKENS, JUDITH A.
PERSONAL Born 06/05/1948, Holland, MI, m, 1981, 2 children **DISCIPLINE** FRENCH **EDUCATION** Sorbonne, diplome, 70; Central Col, BA, 70; Ohio State Univ, MA, 73; PhD, 77. **CAREER** Instr, Va Tech, 76-78; asst prof to prof, chair, Univ of Cincinnati, 78-94, 96-98; Fel, Univ Ky, 94-95; director, Colby-Sawyer Col, 98-. **HONORS AND AWARDS** Award for Excellence in Teaching, Va Tech, 77; Dean's Awd, Univ Cincinnati, 92; ACE Fel, Univ Ky, 94-95; Awd for Excellence, Ohio Mod Lang Teachers Assoc, 97. **MEMBERSHIPS** MLA, AATF, Am Counc on Teaching For Lang, Am Coun on Educ, Am Assoc of Higher Educ. **RESEARCH** Mentoring Faculty, Leading in a liberal arts setting, Intermediate-Level Curriculum in French, Technology and second language learning, Teaching beginning French, Teaching Literature in a second language. **SELECTED PUBLICATIONS** Auth, "Preservice and Inservice Teaching Training: Focus on Proficiency," ACTFL For Lang Educ Series, (83); auth, "Teaching Second-Language Literatures: Past, Present, and Future," Mod Lang Jour, (83); auth, "Teaching Foreign Language Literatures: A Comparative Study, ACTFL For Lang Educ Series, (92); coauth, "Priorities for Intermediate-Level Language Instruction," Mod Lang Jour, (94); coauth, Technology and Learning in the Foreign Language Classroom, Heinle and Heinle, 97; coauth, Bravo!, Heinle and Heinle, 98; coauth, Rendez-vous: An Invitation to French, McGraw-Hill, 98; coauth, Vis- a- Vis: Beginning French, McGraw-Hill, 00; coauth, "Whole System Change Methodologies for Campus-Wide Planning," ACE Counc of Fel Newsletter, (00); coauth, "Leading a College as a Liberal Arts Practice," Jour of the Nat Col Honors Coun, (00). **CONTACT ADDRESS** Colby-Sawyer Col, 100 Main St, New London, NH 03257. **EMAIL** jmuyskens@colby-sawyer.edu

MYERS, EUNICE DOMAN
PERSONAL Born 12/01/1948, Lexington, NC, m, 1969, 1 child **DISCIPLINE** SPANISH LITERATURE & LANGUAGE **EDUCATION** Univ NC, Chapel Hill, BA, 71; MA, 73; PhD, 77. **CAREER** Teaching asst Span, Univ NC, Chapel Hill, 71-76; vis instr, NC State Univ, 76-77, asst prof, 77-81; Asst Prof Span, Wichita State Univ, 81-, Consult & reviewer, Eirik Borve Inc, 77- & Scott Foresman, 78- **MEMBERSHIPS** Am Asn Teachers Span & Port; MLA; Asoc Pensamiento Hisp. **RESEARCH** Modern Spanish novel; modern women authors from Spain especially Rosa Chacel; Ramon Perez de Ayala's essays. **SELECTED PUBLICATIONS** Auth, Tradition and modernity in Perez de Ayalas literary theories, Critica Hisp, Vol II, No 1; contribr, Sentimental Club: Un cuento filos ofico de Ramon Perez de Ayala, In: Simposio Int Ramon Perez de Ayala, Imprenta Flores, Gijon, 81; La 'Perla Del Oriente', J Devoted to The Teaching of Spanish And Portuguese, 95; El 'Corazon Inmovil' - Spanish - J Devoted to The Teaching of Spanish And Portuguese, 97; The 'Maravillas District' - Spanish - J Devoted to The Teaching of Spanish And Portuguese, 95; The Canon - Meditations on Its Literary And Theatrical Reception Perezdeayala With Regard to Benavente - Spanish - J Devoted to The Teaching of Spanish And Portuguese, 95; The Canon - Meditations on Its Literary And Theatrical Reception Perezdeayala With Regard to Benavente - Spanish - J Devoted to The Teaching of Spanish And Portuguese, 95; El 'Corazon Inmovil' - Spanish - J Devoted to The Teaching of Spanish And Portuguese, 97. **CONTACT ADDRESS** Dept of Modern and Classical Lang and Lit, Wichita State Univ, Wichita, KS 67208. **EMAIL** emeyers@twsuvm.us.twsu.edu

N

NABARRA, ALAIN
DISCIPLINE FRENCH LANGUAGE **EDUCATION** Univ Sorbonne, Paris, MLit, DES, LL. **CAREER** Assoc prof, Lakehead Univ, 68-. **HONORS AND AWARDS** Contribution to Teaching Awd. **SELECTED PUBLICATIONS** Contrib, Dictionnaire de la presse de langue francaise 1600-1784, Oxford and Paris, 91; Women Intellectuals of the French Eighteenth Century, NY, 94; La lettre au XVIIIe siecle, Toronto, 96. **CONTACT ADDRESS** Dept of Lang, Lakehead Univ, 955 Oliver Rd, Thunder Bay, ON, Canada P7B 5E1. **EMAIL** ANABARRA@Mist.Lakeheadu.Ca

NADAR, THOMAS R.
PERSONAL Born 01/26/1946, Chicago, IL **DISCIPLINE** GERMAN **EDUCATION** Univ Notre Dame, BA, 67; Univ Mich, MA, 68; PhD, 74. **CAREER** Asst prof, SUNY Albayn, 74-79; vis asst prof, Univ Ore, 80-84; vis asst prof, Ore State Univ, 84-87; assoc prof, Auburn Univ, 87-. **HONORS AND AWARDS** Panhellenic Coun, Auburn Univ; Outstanding Prof Award, 96; German Prof of the Year Award, 94; Excellence in the Humanities Teaching Award, 91; Festival Award of Excellence, Am Col Theatre, 85; Fulbright Scholar, 68. **MEMBERSHIPS** MLA; S Atlantic MLA; Am Asn of the Teachers of German. **RESEARCH** Bertolt Brecht; German Drama; German Film; Literature and Music. **SELECTED PUBLICATIONS** Auth, "Brecht and Musical Aesthetics: Brecht's Impact on Film Music," in Brecht Unbound, Univ De, 95; auth, "The German-German Relationship in Popular Culture: Recent Literary, Musical and Cinematic Views," in The Berlin Wall: Representations and Perspectives, Peter Lang, 96; auth, "Brecht and Music: The Playwright's Career in America and His Influence of North American Music," in A Bertolt Brecht Reference Companion, Greenwood Press, 97; auth, "The Director and the Diva: The Film Musicals of Zarah Leander and Detlev Sierck," in Cultural History Through a National Socialist Lens: Essays on the Cinema of the Third Reich," Camden House, 00; auth, "The Question of Cultural Identity: The Figure of the Outsider in Michael Haneke's Adaptation of Joseph Roth's Die Rebellion," in After Postmodernism: Austrian Literature and Film in Transition, Ariadne Press, 00. **CONTACT ADDRESS** Dept For Lang and Lit, Auburn Univ, 6030 Haley Center, Auburn, AL 36849. **EMAIL** nadartr@mail.auburn.edu

NAFF, WILLIAM E.
PERSONAL Born 02/14/1929, Wenatchee, WA, m, 1957 **DISCIPLINE** JAPANESE **EDUCATION** Univ Wash, MA, PhD(Japanese lang), 66. **CAREER** Asst Japanese, Univ Calif, Los Angeles, 58-59; lectr, Stanford Univ, 59-60; from asst prof to assoc prof, Univ Ore, 62-69; assoc prof, 69-80, Prof Asian Studies & Chmn Prog, Univ Mass, Amherst, 80-, Dir ctr Japanese studies, Univ Ore, 65-66 & 67-68. **MEMBERSHIPS** Asn Asian Studies; Asn Teachers Japanese. **RESEARCH** Japanese language; history of Japanese literature; modern Japanese literature. **SELECTED PUBLICATIONS** Auth, Shimazaki Toson, an introduction, Univ Wash; Toson The 'Three' + Translating Shimazaki,toson 'Sannin', Literary Review, Vol 0039, 1996. **CONTACT ADDRESS** Asian Studies Prog, Univ of Massachusetts, Amherst, Amherst, MA 01002.

NAGASE, TAKAKO
PERSONAL Born 04/05/1936, Tokyo, Japan, m, 1964, 2 children **DISCIPLINE** JAPANESE **EDUCATION** Tohoku Nat Univ, BS, 59; MS, 61; Morgan State Univ, MS, 93. **CAREER** Instructor, Lincoln Univ, 87. **HONORS AND AWARDS** E W Ctr Scholarship, Harvard Univ, 61-63. **SELECTED PUBLICATIONS** Trans, "The study of Biological Water Pollution," by Charles wilbur; trans, "Selection of Scott Joplin Piano Music," by Ritto Music. **CONTACT ADDRESS** Dept Lang & Linguistics, Lincoln Univ, Pennsylvania, PO Box 179, Lincoln University, PA 19352-0999. **EMAIL** tnagase1@aol.com

NAGEL, ALAN FREDERICK
PERSONAL Born 03/09/1941, Beverly, MA, m, 1973 **DISCIPLINE** COMPARATIVE LITERATURE, ENGLISH **EDUCATION** Harvard Col, BA, 63; Cornell Univ, MA, 65, PhD(comp lit), 69. **CAREER** Asst prof, 69-72, chmn, Grad Prog, 71-75, assoc prof, 72- 80, Prof English & Comp Lit, Univ Iowa, 80-, Chmn, BA Lett, Univ Iowa, 71-81, chmn, Interdiscipline Prog Lit, Sci & Arts; vis prof, Univ Paul Valery, Montpelier, France, fall, 82. **MEMBERSHIPS** MLA; Am Comp Lit Asn; Midwest Mod Lang Asn. **RESEARCH** Poetics; Renaissance literature, literary theory. **SELECTED PUBLICATIONS** Co-ed, The Three Crowns of Florence: Humanist Assessments of Dante, Petrarca, Boccaccio, Harper, 72; auth, Lies and the limitable inane Contradiction in More's Utopia, Renaissance Quart, 73; Literary and historical context in Ronsard's Sonnets pour Helene, Pub Mod Lang Asn, 79; Rhetoric, value and action in Alberti, Mod Lang Notes, 80; 'Mastro Don Gesualdo', Gender, Dialect, And The Body, Stanford Italian Review, Vol 0011, 1992; Countercurrents - on The Primacy of Texts in Literary-criticism - Prier,ra, Comparative Literature Studies, Vol 0031, 1994. **CONTACT ADDRESS** Dept of Comp Lit, Univ of Iowa, 308 English Phil Bld, Iowa City, IA 52242-1492.

NAGELE, RAINER
PERSONAL Born 08/02/1943, Triesen, Liechtenstein, m, 1971 **DISCIPLINE** GERMAN LITERATURE, LITERARY THEORY **EDUCATION** Univ Calif, Santa Barbara, PhD, 71. **CAREER** Asst prof Ger, Univ Iowa, 71-74; assoc prof Ger lit, Ohio State Univ, 75-77; assoc prof, 77-79; prof, 79-, Johns Hopkins Univ, **MEMBERSHIPS** MLA; Am Asn Teachers Ger. **RESEARCH** German literature of the 20th century; German literature from 1700 to present; literary theory and aesthetics. **SELECTED PUBLICATIONS** Auth, Text, Geschichte und Subjekivitat in Holderlins Dichtung Unebarer Schrift gleich, Metzler (Stuttgart), 85; auth, Reading After Freud. Essays on Goethe, Holderlin, Habermas, Nietzsche, Brecht, Celan, and Freud, Columbia Univ Press (NYork), 87; auth, Theater, Theory, Speculation: Walter Benjamin and the Scenes of Mo-

dernity, Johns Hopkins Univ Press (Baltimore), 91; auth, Echoes of Translation. Reading Between Texts, John Hopkins Univ Press (Baltimore), 97; auth, Lesarten der Moderne, Edition Isele (Eggingen), 98. **CONTACT ADDRESS** Dept of Ger, Johns Hopkins Univ, Baltimore, 3400 N Charles St, Baltimore, MD 21218-2680. **EMAIL** nagele@jhn.edu

NAGEM, MONIQUE F.
PERSONAL Born 05/24/1941, Paris, France, m, 1964 **DISCIPLINE** COMPARATIVE LITERATURE **EDUCATION** Univ Tex at Austin, PhD, 86. **CAREER** Prof, McNeese State Univ, 81-. **MEMBERSHIPS** Am Translators Asn; Am Lit Translators Asn; Women in French; Am Asn of Tchrs of French. **RESEARCH** Translation. **SELECTED PUBLICATIONS** Transl, Mother love/Mother earth, by Chantal Chawaf (Garland Press, 92); transl, Redemption, by Chantal Chawaf (Dalkey Arch Press, 92); auth, Chantal Chawaf: en quete des origines, d'un lieu mythique, Mythes dans litterature contemporaine d'expression francaise, Univ Ottawa, 94; auth, Chantal Chawaf's Redemptive Literature, Continental, Latin American and Francophone Women Writers, Vol IV, Wichita State Univ, 97; transl, The Garden of Delights, by Dominique Robin (Peter Lang, 98). **CONTACT ADDRESS** Dept of Languages, McNeese State Univ, Lake Charles, LA 70609-2655. **EMAIL** mnagem@mail.mcneese.edu

NAGLE, BETTY ROSE
DISCIPLINE CLASSICAL STUDIES **EDUCATION** Univ Pa, BA, 70; Univ Ind, PhD, 75. **CAREER** Prof, Ind Univ, Bloomington. **SELECTED PUBLICATIONS** Auth, Ovid's Fasti: Roman Holidays, Ind Univ, 95; Ovid: Fasti V, Bryn Mawr, 96. **CONTACT ADDRESS** Dept of Classical Studies, Indiana Univ, Bloomington, 1020 E Kirkwood Ave, 547 Ballantine Hall, Bloomington, IN 47405. **EMAIL** nagle@indiana.edu

NAGY, EDWARD
PERSONAL Born 09/27/1921, Yugoslavia, m **DISCIPLINE** SPANISH **EDUCATION** Univ Zagreb, Can Zwv, 45; Univ Madrid, Lic, 50, PhD, 52. **CAREER** Instr Span & Ital, 56-60, from asst prof to assoc prof Span, 60-67, dir Span grad prog, 67-81, Prof Span, Rutgers Univ, New Brunswick, 67-. **MEMBERSHIPS** MLA; Am Asn Teachers Span & Port; Cervantes Soc Am. **RESEARCH** Picaresque novel and drama of the Spanish Golden Age. **SELECTED PUBLICATIONS** Auth, Rodrigo Fernandez de Ribera, El meson de mundo, 63, Miguel de Cervantes, Pedro de Urdemalas, 65, Las Americas; Lope de Vega y la Celestina, Univ Veracruzana, Mex, 68; El anhelo del Guzman de Aleman de conocer su sangre, Ky Romance Quart, 69; La parodia y la satira en El alcaide de si mismo de Pedro Calderon de la Barea, Romanische Forschungen, 71; El Prodigo ye el Picaro, Ed Sever-Cuesta, Valladolid, 74; El galeote de Lepanto de Luis Velez de Guevara: la diversion en vez del escarmiento, Bull of Comediantes, 77; ed, Miguel de Cervantes, El Rufian Dichoso, Ediciones Catedra, Madrid, 77; La picardia castrense en Flandes y su utilizacion por Lope de Vega, Lope de Vega y los origenes del Teatro Espanol, Actas del I Congreso Internacional sobre Lope de Vega, Patronato Archipreste de Hita, Madrid, 81; The Relationship Between Royalty And Craftiness in El 'Principe Don Carlos' of Jimenezdeenciso,diego + The Picaresque Philosophy of Tejoletas And Its Influence on Don-carlos, Bulletin of The Comediantes, Vol 0046, 1994. **CONTACT ADDRESS** Dept of Span & Port, Rutgers, The State Univ of New Jersey, New Brunswick, New Brunswick, NJ 08903.

NAGY, GREGORY JOHN
PERSONAL Born 10/22/1942, Budapest, Hungary **DISCIPLINE** CLASSICS, LINGUISTICS **EDUCATION** Ind Univ, AB, 62; Harvard Univ, PhD(classics), 66. **CAREER** Instr classics & ling, Harvard Univ, 66-69, asst prof classics, 69-73; from assoc prof to prof, Johns Hopkins Univ, 73-75; Prof Classics, Harvard Univ, 75- **MEMBERSHIPS** Am Philol Asn; Ling Soc Am. **RESEARCH** Greek literature; Indo-European linguistics; poetics. **SELECTED PUBLICATIONS** Auth, Observations on the sign-grouping and vocabulary of linear A, Am J Archaeol, 65; On dialectal anomalies in Pylian texts, Atti Memorie 1st Cong Int Micenologia, 68; Greek Dialects and the Transformation of an Indo-European Process, Harvard Univ, 70; coauth, Greek: A Survey of Recent Work, Mouton, The Hague: 73; auth, Phaethon, Sappho's Phaon, and the White Rock of Leukas, Harvard Studies Class Philol, 73; Comparative Studies in Greek and Indic Meter, Harvard Univ, 74. **CONTACT ADDRESS** Dept of Classics, Harvard Univ, 204 Boylston Hall, Cambridge, MA 02138-3800. **EMAIL** gnagy@fas.harvard.edu

NAGY, MOSES MELCHIOR
PERSONAL Born 01/05/1927, Hadikfalva, Romania **DISCIPLINE** FRENCH **EDUCATION** Marquette Univ, MA, 56; Laval Univ, PhD(French), 60; Sorbonne, dipl French lang & lit, 66. **CAREER** Chmn dept, 65-76, Prof French, Univ Dallas, 65-, Pres, Cercle Francais, Dallas, 70; vp, Alliance Francaise, Dallas, 72; ed-in-chief, Claudel Studies, 72- **MEMBERSHIPS** MLA; Am Asn Teachers French; SCent Mod Lang Asn; Paul Claudel Soc Am. **RESEARCH** French Catholicism and literature; surrealism; La Joie dans l'oeuvre de Claudel. **SELECTED PUBLICATIONS** Auth, Claudel's Immortal Heroes, Am Benedictine Rev, 672; Report on rencontres internationales Claudeliennes de Branques, Claudel Studies, spring 73; Claudel: From the Absurd of Death to the Joy of Life, Rev Nat Lit, fall 73; International-colloquium on Claudel,paul Les 'Odes' + Toronto, October 22-23, 1993, Claudel Studies, Vol 0020, 1993; The Marvels of Tragic Life - Zaza-mabille %Lacoin And Claudel, Claudel Studies, Vol 0022, 1995; The Franco-german Conflict Seen by Lacoin,zaza Elizabeth 1928-1929, Claudel Studies, Vol 0023, 1996; La 'Crise' - Diplomatic Correspondence - America, 1927-1932 - French - Claudel,p, Claudel Studies, Vol 0021, 1994; 2 Experiences of Spiritual Pilgrimage, 'Israel' And The 'Apocalypse', Claudel Studies, Vol 0021, 1994; Claudel,paul 'Partage De Midi' - French - Antoine,g, Claudel Studies, Vol 0021, 1994; Understanding French Poetry, Essays For a New Millennium - Metzidakis,s, Claudel Studies, Vol 0023, 1996; Claudel,paul Silent Dialog With The 3rd-repubic of France, Claudel Studies, Vol 0024, 1997; Great Readers And Readings of Claudel - Introduction, Claudel Studies, Vol 0024, 1997. **CONTACT ADDRESS** Dept of Languages, Univ of Dallas, PO Box 1330, Irving, TX 75060.

NAGY-ZEKMI, SILVIA
PERSONAL Born 05/15/1953, Budapest, Hungary, m, 1995 **DISCIPLINE** HISPANIC STUDIES, LATIN AMERICAN LITERATURE **EDUCATION** Rakoczi Ferenc Gimnasium, Budapest, BA, 71; Eotvos Lorand Univ, Budapest, 80, MA, PhD, 81. **CAREER** Asst prof, Loyola Univ, 87-90; asst prof, Catholic Univ, Washington, DC, 90-97; assoc prof, SUNY Albany, 98-. **HONORS AND AWARDS** PhD, Cum Laude, 81; Fac grants, Catholic Univ, 93, 95, SUNY, 98. **MEMBERSHIPS** MLA, LASA, CIEF. **RESEARCH** Post-colonial theory, literary theory, 20th century Latin American literature, women's writing, indigenous literature, cultural studies. **SELECTED PUBLICATIONS** Auth, Paralelismos transatlanticos: postcolonalismo y narrativa femenina en America Latina y Africa del Norte (Providence, RI: Ediciones INTI, 96); rev, of "Christine Achour," Anthologie de la lineature algerienne, Paris: Bordas, 90, Middle East Studies Asn Bulletin 30 (96): 233-234; auth, "Textualidad femenina en America Latina, " Letras Femeninas XXIII, 1-2: 41-58 (97); ed, Identidades en transformacion: El discurso neoindigenista de los paises andinos (Quito: Abya Yala, 97); auth, "Aquel Senor Muteczuma: Construccion literia del Otro en las cronicas mesoamericansas," Labertino II, 1-2 (98), http://www.utsa.edu/academics/cofah/laberinto/frameset1997.htm; auth, "Entierro en el Este: Orientalismo en la poesia de Neruda," MACLAS XI, 121-132 (98); ed, De texto a contexto: Practicas discurs vas en la literatura espanola e hispanoamericana (Barcelona: Puvill, 98); auth, "Ficcion y testimonio en la obra de Manlio Argueta," De texto a contaxto: practicas discursives en la literatura espanola e hispoamericana (Barcelona: Puvill, 55-62, 1998); auth, "La novela rosa como disfraz: ironia en Angeles Mastretta," in Reflecciones: esayos sobre escritoras hispanoamericanas, ed Priscilla Gac-Artigas, http://www.monmouth.edu/~pgacarti/M-Mastretto-Ensayo.htm, 99; auth, "Silencio y ambiguedad en Blanca Sol de Mercedes Cabello de Carbonera," in La voz de la majer en la literatura hispanoamericana, ed Luis A. Jimenez, 51-60 (San Jose: Univ de Costa Rica, 99). **CONTACT ADDRESS** Dept Hispanic Studies, SUNY Albany, 1400 Washington Ave, HV 215, Albany, NY 12222-0100. **EMAIL** sng@csc.albany.edu

NAHSON, DANIEL L.
DISCIPLINE SPANISH **EDUCATION** Hebrew Univ Jerusalem, BA, 85, Columbia Univ, MA, 90; Mphil, 92; PhD, 95. **CAREER** Vis asst prof, Williams Col, 98; vis asst prof, Allegheny Col, 99-00; asst prof Spanish, Emory Univ, 00-. **HONORS AND AWARDS** Span Embassy Dissertation res grant, 94; Jewish Theol Sem Am Res Asst Scholar, 90; San Martin fel, 99. **MEMBERSHIPS** MLA; North Eastern Modern Languages Asn; Am Asn of Oriental Res; Asociatcion Internacional de Hispanistas; Asociacion Internacional del Siglo de Oro; Instituto Internacional de Literatura Iberoamericana; Centre d'etudes des litteratures et des civilisations du Rio de la Plata. **RESEARCH** Golden Age Literature; Spanish Mysticism; The Realist Novel; Literary Theory; Second Language Acquisition; The Short Story in Spanish America; Spanish and Latin-American Film. **SELECTED PUBLICATIONS** Auth, "Borges por Borges: Su literatura como palimpsesto de un sueno autobiografico," in Teoria y critica de la cultura y literatura," Editorial Universidad de Puerto Rico (Arecibo, 00); auth, "La polivalencia semantica y el lenguaje de los afectos: Las traducciones biblicas de Fray Luis de Leon y el estilo de Santa Teresa de Jesus," in Criticon, (Presses Universitaires du Mirail, Toulouse, 00); auth, Fray de Luis de Leon's translation and interpretation of the Song of Sons: Subversive didacticism in the vernacular, Universidad de Alcala, Servicio de Publicaciones, Alcala, 98. **CONTACT ADDRESS** Division of the Huamanities, Emory Univ, 106 Language Hall, Oxford, GA 30054. **EMAIL** dnahson@emory.edu

NAIDITCH, P. G.
PERSONAL Born Los Angeles, CA, s **DISCIPLINE** CLASSICS **EDUCATION** SMCC, AA 69; Univ Southern Calif, BA, 71; Univ London, MA, 76; Ind Univ, MLS, 80. **CAREER** Publ ed, Dept Spec Collections, 87-; classics bibliogr 91-; Curator of Medieval and Renaissance Manuscripts, 00-; Charles E. Young Res Libr, UCLA. **MEMBERSHIPS** Am Philo Asn; Bibliog Soc. **RESEARCH** A.E. Housman; history of classical scholarship; history of the book. **SELECTED PUBLICATIONS** Auth, A.E. Housman at University College, London, 88; coauth, Philodemus and Greek Papyri, 94; auth, Problems in the Life and Writings of A.E. Housman, 95. **CONTACT ADDRESS** Special Collections, Charles E. Young Research Lib, Univ of California, Los Angeles, Box 951575, Los Angeles, CA 90095-1575. **EMAIL** naiditch@library.ucla.edu

NAIM, CHOUDHRI MOHAMMED
PERSONAL Born 06/03/1936, Bara Banki, India, 2 children **DISCIPLINE** URDU LANGUAGE & LITERATURE **EDUCATION** Univ Lucknow, BA, 53, MA, 55; Univ CA, Berkeley, MA, 61. **CAREER** From instr to asst prof, 63-71, Assoc Prof Urdu, Univ Chicago, 71-98; Co-ed, J South Asian Lit, 63-78; reader Urdu, Aligarh Muslim Univ, India, 71-72; Prof 98-01; Prof Emeritus 98-. **RESEARCH** Cultl hist of Muslim South Asia; Muslim society in India, Pakistan and Bangladesh. **SELECTED PUBLICATIONS** Ed, Readings in Urdu: Prose and Poetry, East-West, Honolulu, 65; auth, The consequences of Indo-Pakistani war for Urdu language and literature, J Asian Studies, 69; Introductory Urdu (2 vols), Cosas, 75; auth, ZIKR-I MIR, THE AUTOBIOGRAPHY OF THE 18TH CENTURY MUGHAL POET, MIR TAQI MIR, Oxford Univ. Press, 99; AMBIGUITIES OF HERITAGE: FICTIONS AND POLEMICS, City Press, 99; transl, A SEASON OF BETRAYALS, two novellas by Q. Hyder Kali for Women Press, 99; articles: "The Outrage of Bernard Lewis," in Social Text, #30, 92; auth, "Popular Jokes and Political History: The Case of Akbar, Birbal and Mulla Do-Piyaza," in Economic & Political Weekly, June 17, 1995; auth, Introductory Urdu (2 vols), Third revised edition, Center for South Asian Studies, Univ of Chicago, 99. **CONTACT ADDRESS** Dept of S Asian Lang, Univ of Chicago, 1130 E 59th St, Chicago, IL 60637-1539. **EMAIL** naim@midway.uchicago.edu

NAKAYAMA, MINEHARU
PERSONAL Born 12/11/1958, Nagano, Japan, m, 1992, 1 child **DISCIPLINE** LINGUISTICS **EDUCATION** Waseda Univ, Tokyo, Japan, BA, 83; Univ Ct, MA, 86, PhD, 88. **CAREER** Lectr, Univ Ct, 84-86; vis instr, Ct Col, 85-88; asst prof to assoc prof, Oh St Univ, 94- . **HONORS AND AWARDS** Waseda Univ Centennial Celebration Awds for Study Papers, 82; Rotary Found Awd, 83; Extraordinary Expenses Awd, Res Found, Univ Ct, 87; Off of Int Educ Outstanding Int Faculty Awd, Oh St Univ, 98. **MEMBERSHIPS** Asn for Asian Stud; Asn of Teachers of Japanese; Ling Soc of Amer; Central Asn of Teachers of Japanese. **RESEARCH** Psycholinguistics; syntax; learnability; lang teaching. **SELECTED PUBLICATIONS** Auth, Acquisition of Japanese Empty Categories, Kuroshio Publ, 96; Empty categories and argument structures, in Formal Approaches to Japanese Ling, MIT Working Papers in Ling, 96; Numeral Classifier Systems: The Case of Japanese by Pamela Downing, Modern Lang J, 97; An Introduction to Japanese Ling by Natsuko Tsujimura, Modern Lang J, 98; Sentence processing, in A Handbook of Japanese Linguistics, Blackwell, 99. **CONTACT ADDRESS** Dept of East Asian Lang & Lit, Ohio State Univ, Columbus, 204 Cunz Hall, 1841 Millikin Rd, Columbus, OH 43210. **EMAIL** nakayama.1@osu.edu

NAKHIMOVSKY, ALICE
PERSONAL m **DISCIPLINE** MODERN RUSSIAN LITERATURE **EDUCATION** Cornell Univ, Ab, PhD, 75. **CAREER** Prof, Colgate Univ, dept ch. **RESEARCH** Russ 20th century fiction, mod Jewish fiction and Western Traditions. **SELECTED PUBLICATIONS** Auth, Russian-Jewish Literature and Identity, Johns Hopkins, 92); Witness to History: The photographs of Yevgeny Khaldei, Aperture, 97. **CONTACT ADDRESS** Dept of Russ Stud, Colgate Univ, 13 Oak Drive, Hamilton, NY 13346.

NAKUMA, CONSTANCIO
DISCIPLINE FRENCH LITERATURE **EDUCATION** Univ Ghana, BA, 82; Univ de Paris, MA, 84; DEA, 85; La Sorbonne Nouvelle, PhD, 90; St Mary's Univ, MBA, 91. **CAREER** Lectr, St Mary's Univ, 89-92; asst prof, 92-98, assoc prof, French, Univ Tenn, 98- ; assoc hd, Dept of Mod For Langs & Lits, Univ Tenn, 98-99; Dir, Lang & World Bus Prog, Univ Tenn, 99- . **HONORS AND AWARDS** Prof Develop Awd, Univ Tenn, 93; CIBER Awd, French Cult Svcs/San Diego State Univ, 95; Awd for Excel in Tchg & Advising, Lang & World Bus Students Asn, Univ Tenn, 97. **MEMBERSHIPS** MLA; Col Lang Asn; Tenn For Lang Tchrs Asn. **RESEARCH** Foreign language acquisition, attrition, & loss studies; linguistic & cultural interference in the learning of languages beyond the second; African & Romance linguistics; exploring the develop of a letter-based tone; language orthorgraphy; languagess for the professions; application of linguistic & visual semiotic techniques to analyzing social & cultural phenomena; proper name morphology across cultures **SELECTED PUBLICATIONS** Auth, "'Sir is There a Rule for That?'" A Report on Differences in SL Learning Approach Styles, " Lang Q 33.1-2 (95): 45-65; auth, "Cleaning up Spontaneous Speech for Use in L2 Attrition Research: A Proposal," J of Multilingual & Multicult Develop 18 (97): 135-44; auth, "A Method for Measuring Attrition of Communicative Competence: A Pilot Study with Spanish L3 Subjects," Appl Psycholing 18 (97): 219-35; auth, "Associative

Discourse in Scientific Onomastics: Abuse of the Prefix 'Africanized'," CLA J 40 (97): 479-96; auth, "Use of Visual Semiotics in LSP Content Learning: A Business French Example," Semiotica 115.3-4 (97): 381-90; auth, "Loss of Communicative Competence: Measurability and Description of a Method," IRAL 35.3 (97): 199-209; auth, Phonie et Graphie Tonale du Dagaare (Langue Voltaique du Ghana), L'Harmattan (Paris), 98; auth, "A New Theoretical Account of 'Fossilization': Implications for L2 Attrition Research," IRAL 36.3 (98): 247-56; auth, "Proper Name Morphology and Significance among the Dagaaba of Ghana," J of Dagaare Studies 1 (01): 1-14. **CONTACT ADDRESS** Dept of Mod For Langs & Lits, Univ of Tennessee, Knoxville, 701 McClung Tower & Plaza, Knoxville, TN 37996. **EMAIL** cnakuma@utk.edu

NALBANTIAN, SUZANNE
DISCIPLINE COMPARATIVE LITERATURE, CRITICAL THEORY **EDUCATION** Columbia Univ, PhD. **CAREER** Prof, Long Island Univ, C.W. Post Campus. **SELECTED PUBLICATIONS** Auth, Aesthetic Autobiography; The Symbol of the Soul from Holderlin to Yeats: A Study in Metonymy; Seeds of Decadence in the Late Nineteenth-Century Novel. **CONTACT ADDRESS** Long Island Univ, C.W. Post, Brookville, NY 11548-1300.

NANFITO, JACQUELINE C.
DISCIPLINE SPANISH AND COMPARATIVE LITERATURE **EDUCATION** Saint Mary's Col Notre Dame, BA, 79; Univ Mich, MA, 82; UCLA, PhD, 87. **CAREER** English, Case Western Reserve Univ. **HONORS AND AWARDS** Nancy Wing Awd Outstanding Performance Doctoral Qualifying Exams; Alpha Chi Nat Honor Soc Outstanding Prof Awd; Fac Appreciation Awd Student Senate; Phi Gamma Outstanding Fac Mem Awd; Tex Educ Agency Grant; Prof Develop Grant; Flora Stone Mather Alumnae Asn Grant. **SELECTED PUBLICATIONS** Articles, Latin American and Spanish Peninsular literature. **CONTACT ADDRESS** Case Western Reserve Univ, 10900 Euclid Ave, Cleveland, OH 44106. **EMAIL** jcn@po.cwru.edu

NANJI, AZIM A.
PERSONAL Born Nairobi, Kenya **DISCIPLINE** ISLAMIC, AFRICAN STUDIES **EDUCATION** Makerere Univ, Uganda, BA, 68; McGill Univ, MA, 70, PhD(Islamic studies), 72. **CAREER** Res fel Islamic studies, Inst Islamic Studies, McGill Univ, 72-73; Chmn Dept Humanities, Okla State Univ 73-, Killam fel relig, Dalhousie Univ, 74-76. **HONORS AND AWARDS** Can Coun Pub Awd, 77. **MEMBERSHIPS** Mid E Studies Asn; Am Orient Soc. **RESEARCH** Ismaili studies; Medieval Muslim history; modernization and change in religion. **SELECTED PUBLICATIONS** Auth, Modernization and change in the Nizari Ismaili community in East Africa, J Relig Africa, 74; The Ginan tradition among the Nizari Ismailis, Actes du XIX Congr Int des Orientalistes, 75; A theory of learning in the Rasail Ikhwan Al Safa, Muslim World, 76; contribr, An Ismaili theory of Walayah, In: Essays on Islamic Civilization Presented to N Berkes, E JBrill, 76; The Ismailis in history, In: Ismaili Contributions to Islamic Culture, Imperial Iranian Acad Philos, 77; auth, The Nizari Ismaili Tradition in the Indo-Pakistan Subcontinent, Caravan Bks, 78; The Just Ruler Al-sultan Al-adil in Shiite Islam - The Comprehensive Authority of The Jurist in Imami Jurisprudence - Sachedina,AA, J of The American Academy of Religion, Vol 0062, 1994; The 'Bujh Niranjan' - an Ismaili Mystical Poem - Asani,as, J of The American Oriental Society, Vol 0117, 1997. **CONTACT ADDRESS** Dept of Relig, Univ of Florida, PO Box 117410, Gainesville, FL 32611-7410.

NAPOLI, DONNA JO
PERSONAL Born 02/28/1948, Miami, FL, m, 1968, 5 children **DISCIPLINE** LINGUISTICS **EDUCATION** Harvard Univ, BA, 70; PhD, 73. **CAREER** Asst Prof, Georgetown Univ, 75-80; Asst Prof to Prof, Univ MI, 80-87; Prof, Swarthmore Col, 87-. **HONORS AND AWARDS** Fel, NSF; Fel, NEH; Fel, AAUW. **MEMBERSHIPS** Ling Soc of Am. **RESEARCH** Syntax; Structure of Holian; Structure of American sign language. **SELECTED PUBLICATIONS** Co-auth, "Evaluative affixes in Italian," in Yearbook of Morphology 1994, (Kluwer Acad Pub, 95), 151-178; co-auth, "The Verbal component in Italian Compounds," in Contemporary Research in Romance Linguistics: Papers from the LSRL XXII, (John Benjamins, 95), 367-381; co-auth, "On root structure and the destiny of the Latin second conjugation," Folia Linguistica Historica, (96): 97-113; co-auth, "An OT Account of Italian codas," in Proceedings of EXCOL 1995, (Cornell Univ Press, 96), 212-223; co-auth, "Hand en Mond; tong en Nagel: Eeen Vergelijking van de Morfologische Mogelijkheden van ASL en Gesproken Talen," Taalkundig bulleting, (96): 213-231; auth, Lnguistics: Theory and Problems, Oxford Univ Press, 96. **CONTACT ADDRESS** Dept Ling, Swarthmore Col, 500 College Ave, Swarthmore, PA 19081-1306. **EMAIL** dnapoli1@swarthmore.edu

NAPPA, CHRISTOPHER
DISCIPLINE CLASSICAL STUDIES **EDUCATION** Univ Tex, BA, 90; Univ Va, MA, 92, PhD, 96. **CAREER** Instr. **SELECTED PUBLICATIONS** Auth, Agamemnon 717-36: The Parable of the Lion Cub, 94; Catullan Provocations (rev), Univ Ca, 93; Virgil, New Haven, 91. **CONTACT ADDRESS** Dept of Classics, Knoxville, TN 37996.

NARO, ANTHONY JULIUS
PERSONAL Born 11/12/1942, Nashville, TN, m, 1966, 2 children **DISCIPLINE** LINGUISTICS **EDUCATION** Polytech Inst NYork, BSc, 63; Mass Inst Technol, PhD(ling), 68. **CAREER** Asst prof ling & philol, Univ Chicago, 68-74; prof ling, Fed Univ & prof lett, Pontif Cath Univ, Rio de Janeiro, 74-79; Res Prof Ling, Nat Coun Res & Sci Develop, Brazil, 79-, Researcher, Univ Coimbra, 68; Angola Sci Res Inst, 70-72; vis prof, Fed Univ Rio de Janeiro, 72; researcher, Ctr Philol Res, Lisbon, 73; res dir, Brazilian Literacy Found & Brazilian Found Res. **MEMBERSHIPS** Ling Soc Am; Asn Brasileira Ling; Asn Lit & Ling Comput; Asn Comput Ling. **RESEARCH** Historical linguistics; Pidgins and Creoles; romance linguistics. **SELECTED PUBLICATIONS** Auth, Da metrica medieval galaico-portuguesa, Ocidente, Lisbon, 402: 227-236; On f h in Castilian and western Romance, Z romanische Philol, 88: 435-447; ed, Tendencias Atuais da Linguistics e da Filologia no Brasil, Livraria Francisco Alves, Rio de Janeiro, 76; auth, The Genesis of the Reflexive Impersonal in Portuguese, 76 & A Study on the Origins of Pidginiation, 78, Language, coauth, Competencias Basicas do Portugues, Fundacao Mobral, 78; Portuguese in Brazil, In: Trends in Romance Linguistics and Philology, Mouton Pub, 82; The social and structural dimensions of a syntactic change, Language, 63- 98; Arguing About Arguin + a Reply to Clements,j.clancy on The Origins of Pidgin Portuguese, J of Pidgin And Creole Languages, Vol 0008, 1993. **CONTACT ADDRESS** 191 Waverly Pl, New York, NY 10014.

NASH, JERRY
PERSONAL Born 05/05/1946, Longview, TX **DISCIPLINE** FRENCH **EDUCATION** Tex Tech Univ, BA, 68; Univ Kans, MPhil; PhD. **CAREER** Res prof, Univ of New Orleans, 72-97; prof and chemn, Univ of N Tex, 97-. **MEMBERSHIPS** MLA, RSA, AATF. **RESEARCH** French Renaissance Literature (Francois Rabelais, Maurice Sceve, Pleiade Poets, Helisenne de Crenne). **SELECTED PUBLICATIONS** Ed, Maurice Sceve: Concodance de la "Delie" (2 vols), NC Studies in the Romance Lang and Lit, 76; ed, Pre-Pleiade Poetry, French Forum Monographs, 85; auth, The Love Aesthetics of Maurice Sceve: poetry and Struggle, Cambridge Univ Press, 91; co-ed, Lapidary Inscriptions: Renaissance Essays for Donald A. Stone, French Forum Monographs, 91; ed, A Sceve Celectration: "Delie" 1544-1994, Stanford French and Ital Studies, 94; co-ed, A French Forum: Melanges de litterature offerts a Raymond et Virginia La Charite, Klincksieck, 00. **CONTACT ADDRESS** Dept For Lang, Univ of No Texas, PO Box 311127, Denton, TX 76203-1127. **EMAIL** jnash@unt.edu

NASH, STANLEY
DISCIPLINE HEBREW LITERATURE **EDUCATION** Columbia Univ, PhD, 72. **CAREER** Prof, HUC-JIR/NY; ordained, Jewish Theol Sem, 67. **SELECTED PUBLICATIONS** Auth, Migvan: Studies related to Hebrew Literature in America dedicated to Jacab Kabakoff Lod, Israel: The Katz Institute, 86; auth, Between History and Literature: Studies in Honor of Isaac Barzilay Israel: Hakibbutz Hameuchad, 97. **CONTACT ADDRESS** Hebrew Union College-Jewish Institute of Religion, Univ of So California, University Park Campus, Los Angeles, CA 90089. **EMAIL** snash@huc.edu

NATALICIO, DIANA
PERSONAL Born 08/25/1939, St Louis, MO **DISCIPLINE** LINGUISTICS, ENGLISH AS SECOND LANGUAGE **EDUCATION** St, Louis Univ, BS, 61; Univ Tex, Austin, MA, 64; PhD, 69. **CAREER** Res assoc eval res, Ctr Commun Res, 70-71; asst prof ling & mod lang, 71-73, chmn mod lang & assoc prof, 73-77, assoc dean lib arts, 77-79, Prof Ling & Mod Lang, Univ Tex, El Paso, 77- & Dean Lib Arts, 80-84, vp, acad aff, 84-88, pres, 88-. **HONORS AND AWARDS** Harold W. McGraw Jr. Prize in Educ; Torch of Liberty Awd; Conquistador Awd for Outstand Svc to Citizens of El Paso; El Paso Women's Hall of Fame; Humanitarian Awd; Fulbright scholar, Rio de Janeiro, Brazil; Gulbenkian fel, Lisbon, Portugal. **MEMBERSHIPS** Nat Sci Bd; NASA Adv Cnl; US-Mexico Comm for Educ and Cultural Exchange; Nat Act Cnl for Minorities in Engineering; Coun for Aid to Education; Nature Conservancy of Tex. **RESEARCH** Language acquisition; bilingualism; language testing. **SELECTED PUBLICATIONS** Coauth, A comparative study of English pluralization by native and nonnative English speakers, Child Develop, 71; auth, Sentence repetition as a language assessment technique: Some issues and applications, Bilingual Rev/La Rev Bilingue, 77; coauth, The Sounds of Children, Prentice-Hall, 77 & 81; contribr, Theory & Practice or Early Reading, Lawrence Earlbaum Assoc, 79; auth, Repetition and dictation as language testing techniques, Mod Lang J, 79; contribr, Festschrift in Honor of Jacob Ornstein: Studies in General and Sociolinguistics, Newbury House, 80; coauth, Some characteristics of word classification in a second language, Mod Lang J, 82. **CONTACT ADDRESS** Off of President, Univ of Texas, El Paso, El Paso, TX 79968-0500. **EMAIL** dnatlicio@utep.edu

NATHAN, GEOFFREY STEVEN
PERSONAL Born 10/18/1949, Hove, England **DISCIPLINE** LINGUISTICS **EDUCATION** Univ Toronto, BA, 71; Univ Hawaii, MA, 72, PhD(ling), 78. **CAREER** Vis asst prof, Univ Mont, 77-78 & Univ Hawaii, 78-80; vis asst prof, 80-82, asst prof, 82-88, assoc prof, 89-, Southern Ill Univ. **MEMBERSHIPS** Ling Soc Am; Acoustic Soc Am. **RESEARCH** English as a second language; phonology; syntax. **SELECTED PUBLICATIONS** Auth, Nauruan in the Austronesian language family, Oceanic Ling, Vol XII, No 1-2; Towards a literate level of language, Elements: Chicago Ling Soc Parasession, 78; What's these facts about?, Ling Inquiry, Vol 12, No 1; Nauruan: A small language with an uncertain future, Lang Policy & Planning (in press); coauth, Negative polarity and romance syntax, Ling Symp Romance Lang, Vol XII, Benjamin (in press). **CONTACT ADDRESS** Dept of Ling, So Illinois Univ, Carbondale, Carbondale, IL 62901-4300. **EMAIL** geoffn@siu.edu

NATUNEWICZ, MARY ANN T.
PERSONAL Born 12/16/1937, NJ, m, 1966, 2 children **DISCIPLINE** CLASSICS **EDUCATION** Wellesley Col, BA, 58; Univ Wis, MA, 61; Univ Wis, PhD, 70. **CAREER** Wells Col, 64-67; Houston Independent School District, 86-. **MEMBERSHIPS** Am Philol Assoc; J Classical League **RESEARCH** Cicero; Homer **SELECTED PUBLICATIONS** Auth, Thucydides and Euripides: Changing Civic and Moral Values, Houston Teachers Inst, 99; auth, Foundation Myths of Rome, Univ at Houston Teachers Inst, 00. **CONTACT ADDRESS** 2107 Teague Rd, Houston, TX 77088. **EMAIL** cmanatun@gateway.net

NAUDIN, MARIE
PERSONAL Born 06/18/1926, Auxerre, France, 1 child **DISCIPLINE** FRENCH **EDUCATION** Sorbonne, BA, 46; Univ Pittsburgh, MA, 62, PhD, 66. **CAREER** From instr to asst prof French, Univ Mich, 64-67; asst prof, 67-71, Assoc Prof French, Univ Conn, 71-. **MEMBERSHIPS** Am Asn Teachers Fr; MLA; Soc Fr Prof Am. **RESEARCH** Relation between music and French poetry; 19th century French literature. **SELECTED PUBLICATIONS** Auth, La chanson francaise contemporaine, Fr Rev, 67; Evolution Parallele de la Poesie et de la Musique en France, Nizet, Paris, 68; Les 'Jours Ne Sen Vont Pas Lomgtemps' - French - Rinaldi,a, French Review, Vol 0068, 1995; Djaout,tahar + Assassinated Algerian Writer - The Metaphorical Landscape of Algeria, French Review, Vol 0070, 1996; L'incendie De La Sainte- victoire' - French - Fauconnier,b, French Review, Vol 0070, 1996. **CONTACT ADDRESS** Dept of Romance & Class Lang, Univ of Connecticut, Storrs, Storrs, CT 06268. **EMAIL** naudin@uconnvm.uconn.edu

NAUGHTON, JOHN
DISCIPLINE 19TH AND 20TH CENTURY FRENCH POETRY, THE CONTEMPORARY FRENCH NOVEL **EDUCATION** Stanford Univ, BA, MA; Univ CA, Santa Cruz, MA, PhD. **CAREER** Former instr, Univ Tours, France; Univ CA; consult, Univ Chicago Press, 87; dir, Dijon Study Group, 95; prof. **HONORS AND AWARDS** Picker sr fac grant, Colgate Univ, 87; medal, Col de France, Paris, 91; hon(s), Phi Eta Sigma; nominee, colgate prof yr, 91, 97. **SELECTED PUBLICATIONS** Transl, In the Shadows Light, Univ Chicago Press, 91; auth, Louis-Rene des Forets, Rodopi, 93; Yves Bonnefoy: New and Selected Poems, Univ Chicago Press and Carcanet Press, London, 95; articles, L'Esprit Createur; Sud; Temenos; Studies in 20th Century Literature; Dalhousie Fr Studies; transl(s), New Lit Hist; Critical Inquiry; Yale Fr Studies; Fr-Brit Studies; Poetry Rev; Tel-Aviv Rev; Graham House Rev; Mod Poetry in Translation; rev(s), World Lit Today; S Hum Rev; L'Esprit Createur; Fr Forum. **CONTACT ADDRESS** Dept of Romance Lang, Colgate Univ, 13 Oak Drive, Hamilton, NY 13346. **EMAIL** jnaughton@center.colgate.edu

NAYLOR, ERIC WOODFIN
PERSONAL Born 12/06/1936, Union City, TN **DISCIPLINE** SPANISH **EDUCATION** Univ of the South, BA, 58; Univ Wis, MA, 59, PhD(Span), 63. **CAREER** From instr to assoc prof, 62-76, Prof Span, Univ of the South, 76-, Fulbright res grant, 64-65; lectr, Escuela de Investigacion Linguistica, Madrid, 70. **MEMBERSHIPS** Mediaeval Acad Am; Am Asn Teachers Span & Port; MLA; S Am Mod Lang Asn. **RESEARCH** Medieval Spanish literature; Golden Age literature. **SELECTED PUBLICATIONS** Coauth, Libro de Buen Amor, Consejo Super Invest Cientificas, 65; auth, La encomienda del Capitan Conreras, Rev Span Philol, 70; coauth, Glosario del Libro de Buen Amor, Soc Espanola de Reimpresiones y Edicones, SA ,Barcelona, 73; Libro de buen amor: Edicion critica y artistica, Ed Aguilar, 76; Libro de Buen Amor, Facsimil, Introduccion y Transcripcion del Codice de Toledo (2 vols), Espasa Calpe, Madrid, 77. **CONTACT ADDRESS** Dept of Span, Univ of the South, Sewanee, TN 37375.

NDIAYE, CHEIKH
PERSONAL Born 10/04/1963, Senegal, s **DISCIPLINE** FRENCH **EDUCATION** Univ Cheikh Anta Diop, MA, 93; Univ Conn, PhD, 00. **CAREER** Teacher, Lycee John Kennedy, 93; grad asst, Univ of Conn, 94-97; grad fel, Trinity Col, 97-00; vis asst prof, Union Col, 00-02. **HONORS AND AWARDS** Grant for Field Res on African Oral Lit, Univ Cheikh Anta Diop; Fel. **MEMBERSHIPS** MLA; NEMLA; CIEF; SIEF. **RESEARCH** Francophone Studies. **SELECTED PUBLICATIONS** Auth, "La zombification vue par Jean Stephen Alexis dans Chronique d'un faux-amour et par Rene Depestre dans Ha-

driana dans tous mes reves", Francographies, (98):107-114; ed, "La metaphore de l'exil dans l'ecriture romanesque de Calixthe Beyala" in Lucy McNeece, Actes du Seminaire Int d"Etudes Francophones. **CONTACT ADDRESS** Dept Mod Lang, Trinity Col, Connecticut, 300 Summit St, Hartford, CT 06106-3100. **EMAIL** cheikh.ndiaye@mail.trincoll.edu

NEDASHKIVSKA, ALLA

PERSONAL Born 05/11/1969, L'viv, Ukraine, s **DISCIPLINE** SLAVIC LANGUAGES **EDUCATION** Ivan Franko Univ, BA, 90; Univ Pittsburgh, MA, 94; PhD, 98. **CAREER** Vis lectr, Univ Toronto, 96-99; asst prof, Univ Alta, 99-. **HONORS AND AWARDS** SSRHC Grant, Univ Alta, 00-01; Winspear Res Grant, Univ Alta, 99-01; Grant, Univ Alta, 99-01; Teaching Fel, Univ Pittsburgh, 96; Eugene Manasterski Memorial Award, 96; Helen Sherban Lapica Educ Fund Scholar Award, 95; Study Abroad Scholar, Univ L'viv, 88-89. **MEMBERSHIPS** AATSEEL; AAASS; ASN; ACTFL; CAS. **RESEARCH** Slavic linguistics: Ukrainian, Russian; Gender linguistics; Discourse analysis; Pragmatics. **SELECTED PUBLICATIONS** Auth, "-No/-To and Voice: Statality and Actionality in Contemporary Ukrainian," in Canadian Slavonic Papers, Vol 40, 98; ref, of "The Dawn of Slavic," by Alexander Schenker, J of Ukrainian Studies, 98; rev, of "Slavic Gender Linguistics," by Margaret Mills, in Slavic and East Europ J, 00; auth, "The Language of Women's Magazines and Two Polarized Femininities in Contemporary Ukraine," J of Ukrainian Studies, (01): 1-2; co-ed, Dictionary of Selected Synonyms in the Principal Indo-European Language, Intercontinental Dictionary Series, (forthcoming). **CONTACT ADDRESS** Dept Mod Lang and Cultural Studies, Univ of Alberta, 200 Arts Bldg, Edmonton, AB, Canada T6G 2E6. **EMAIL** alla.nedashkivska@ualberta.ca

NEEDLER, HOWARD

PERSONAL Born 07/22/1937, Manchester, England, m, 1963, 3 children **DISCIPLINE** ITALIAN LITERATURE **EDUCATION** Yale Univ, BS, 58; Oxford Univ, BA, 60, MA, 65; Columbia Univ, PhD, 65. **CAREER** Instr Ital, Barnard Col, Columbia Univ, 63-64; lectr, Yale Univ, 64-65; lectr, Hebrew Univ, 65-66; asst prof, Univ Colo, 67-69; asst prof, 69-72, assoc prof, 73-80, Prof, 81-, Wesleyan Univ. **HONORS AND AWARDS** Phi Beta Kappa; Rhodes scholarship; ACLS fel. **RESEARCH** Medieval literature, especially Dante; modern poetry; Jewish history, especially in medieval Italy. **CONTACT ADDRESS** Col of Lett, Wesleyan Univ, Middletown, CT 06457. **EMAIL** hneedler@wesleyan.edu

NEGUS, KENNETH GEORGE

PERSONAL Born 12/23/1927, Council Bluffs, IA, w, 1952, 3 children **DISCIPLINE** GERMAN **EDUCATION** Princeton Univ, BA, 52, MA, 54, PhD, 57. **CAREER** Asst instr Ger, Princeton Univ, 53-54; instr, Northwestern Univ, 55-57; instr, Harvard Univ, 57-59; asst prof, Princeton Univ, 59-61; from asst prof to assoc prof, 61-66, Prof Ger, Rutgers Univ, 66- **MEMBERSHIPS** MLA; Am Asn Teachers Ger; ETA Hoffmann Ges; Am Soc Ger Lit of 16th & 17th Cent. **RESEARCH** Symbolism of the occult; German Romanticism; German Baroque literature. **SELECTED PUBLICATIONS** Auth, ETA Hoffmann's Other World, Univ Pa, 65; Paul Heyse's Novellentheorie: A Revaluation, Ger Rev, 65; Grimmelshausen, World Authors Series, Twayne, 74. **CONTACT ADDRESS** 175 S Harrison St, Princeton, NJ 08540. **EMAIL** kennegus@aol.com

NEHRING, WOLFGANG

PERSONAL Born 11/15/1938, Oppeln, Germany, m, 1964, 1 child **DISCIPLINE** GERMAN LITERATURE **EDUCATION** Univ Bonn, PhD, 65. **CAREER** Sci asst Ger Lit, Univ Bonn, 65-66; asst prof, Boston Col, 66-67; from asst prof to assoc prof, 67-78, Prof Ger Lit, Univ Calif, Los Angeles, 78-, Co-ed, Kritische Hofmannsthal-Ausgabe, Arbeitsstelle Basel, 71-73; adv bd, Hugo von Hofmannsthal Ges, 76-. **MEMBERSHIPS** Am Asn Teachers Ger; Int Arthur Schnitzler Res Asn; Hugo von Hofmannsthal Ges (secy, 71-74); Int Asn Ger Studies; Schiller Ges; Kleist Ges, Erchendorff ges, ETA Hoffmann Ges. **RESEARCH** German Romanticism; JahrhundertwendeModerne; Austrian literature, especially Hofmannsthal and Schnitzler. **SELECTED PUBLICATIONS** Die Tatbeiltofmannsthal , 67; Ed, E T A Hoffmann, Prinzessin Brambilla, 71 & WackenroderTieck, Phantasien uber die Kunst, 73, Reclam, Stuttgart; auth, Hofmannsthal und der Wiener Impressionismus, 75 & E T A Hoffmanns Erzahlwerk, Ein Modell und seine Variationen, 76, Z Deut Philol; Eichendorff und der Leser, Aurora, 77; Die Buhne als Tribunal Der zweite Weltkrieg im dokumentarischen Theater, In: GegenwartslitDrittes Reich, Reclam, Stuttgart, 77; Der Beginn der Moderne, In: Handbuch der deutschen Erzahlung Bagel, Duusseldorf, 81; E T A Hoffmann: Die Elixiere des Teufels, In: Romane und Erzahlungen der deutschen Romantik, Reclam, Stuttgart, 81; Schnitzler,Arthur And The French- revolution, Modern Austrian Literature, Vol 0025, 1992; Dorothea Schiegel: Florentine, 1993; The Rediscovered Poet - Schreyvogl,friedrich Novel About Grillparzer And The Present- day Reception of Grillparzer Works, Modern Austrian Literature, Vol 0028, 1995; Spatromantika, Eichenmdorff und E.T.A., Hoffman 1997. **CONTACT ADDRESS** Dept of Ger Lang, Univ of California, Los Angeles, Los Angeles, CA 90024. **EMAIL** nehring@humnet.ucla.net

NELSON, ARDIS L.

PERSONAL Born 08/14/1942, Auburn, NY **DISCIPLINE** HISPANIC CINEMA, CUBAN AND CENTRAL AMERICAN LITERATURE **EDUCATION** Oberlin Col, Ba, 65; Middlebury Col, Madrid, MA, 72; IN Univ, Bloomington, PhD, 80 **CAREER** Prof, 94-99, E TN St Univ; Assoc Prof, 85-94, Asst prof, 81-85, FL St Univ; Inst, 79-81, Dickinson Col; Lect, 77-78, Gettysburg Col; Assoc Inst, 72-77, IN Univ; Second Sch Tchr, 65-71, Rochester, NY **MEMBERSHIPS** Modern Language Assoc, Instituto Internacional de Literatura Iberoamericana, Am Asn of Tchrs of Spanish and portugese. **RESEARCH** Juan felyre Toruino, Carmen Naranjo. **SELECTED PUBLICATIONS** Auth, Cabrera Infante in the Menippean Tradition, Newark, Delaware: Juan de la Cuesta Hispanic monographs, 83; ed, Guillermo Cabrera Infante: Assays, Essays, and other Arts, Twayne Publishers, 99. **CONTACT ADDRESS** Dept of Foreign Lang, East Tennessee State Univ, Johnson City, TN 37614-0312. **EMAIL** nelsona@etsu.edu

NELSON, ROBERT J. AMES

PERSONAL Born 03/29/1925, Woodside, NY, m, 1947, 2 children **DISCIPLINE** FRENCH **EDUCATION** Columbia Univ, BA, 49, MA, 50, PhD, 55. **CAREER** Instr French, Columbia CoL, 53-55; instr, Yale Univ, 55-58; asst prof, Univ Mich, 58-59; from assoc prof to prof Romance lang, Univ Pa, 59-69; Prof French & Comp Lit, Univ Ill, Urbana, 69, Head Dept, 73-, Morse fel, Yale Univ, 57-58; grant-in-aid fels, Am Coun Learned Soc, 60 & 65; Am Philos Soc, 63; dir Northeast Conf Teaching Foreign Lang, 64-68; Guggenheim fel, 66- 67; assoc, Ctr for Adv Study, Univ Ill, 76. **HONORS AND AWARDS** Chevalier, Palmes Academiques, 72. **MEMBERSHIPS** MLA; Am Asn Teachers Fr. **RESEARCH** Pascal; world theater; French civilization. **SELECTED PUBLICATIONS** Auth, Play Within a Play: The Dramatist's Conception of His Art--Shakespeare to Anouilh, Yale Univ, 58; Corneille: His Heroes and Their Worlds, Univ Pa, 63; Immanence and Transcendence: The Theater of Jean Rotrou (1609-1650), Ohio Univ, 69; Bipolarity of French classicism, Essays Fr Lit, 71; Classicism: The Crises of the Baroque, Esprit Createur, 71; The fiction of John Williams, Denver Quart, 73; France, Impressed And Suppressed Voices in French Literature From The 'Song of Roland' to 'Waiting For Godot', J of Aesthetic Education, Vol 0030, 1996; The Tragedy of Origins - Corneille,pierre And Historical-perspective - Lyons,jd, French Forum, Vol 0022, 1997. **CONTACT ADDRESS** Dept of French, Univ of Illinois, Urbana-Champaign, Urbana, IL 61822. **EMAIL** rjnelson@staff.uiuc.edu

NELSON, ROY RAY

PERSONAL Born 07/27/1929, Pittsburgh, PA, m, 1954, 2 children **DISCIPLINE** LITERATURE, FRENCH **EDUCATION** Univ Pitts, AB; 51; Middlebury Col, MA, 52; Univ Ill, PhD, 58. **CAREER** Instr to asst prof to assoc prof to emer, Univ Mich, 57-. **HONORS AND AWARDS** Emeritus Fr Lit. **MEMBERSHIPS** AATF; MLA. **RESEARCH** Modern French prose fiction. **SELECTED PUBLICATIONS** Auth, Peguy, Poete du Sacre, L'Amitie Charles Peguy (Paris), 60; auth, "Reflections in a Broken Mirror: Varda's Cleo de 5 a 7," Fr Rev 5 (83): 735-743; auth, Causality and Narrative in French Fiction from Zola to Robber Grilet, Ohio State UP, 89; auth, "Joris-Karl Huysmans," Dict Lit Biog 123 (93): 138-157. **CONTACT ADDRESS** 8730 Midnight Pass Rd, Apt 304A, Sarasota, FL 34242-2894. **EMAIL** rnelson01@home.com

NELSON, WILLIAM B.

DISCIPLINE NEAR EASTERN LANGUAGES AND CIVILIZATIONS **EDUCATION** Harvard Univ, PhD, 91. **CAREER** Assoc prof, 86-; chaplain, US Air Force Reserves, 93-; asst pastor, First Baptist Church, 92. **HONORS AND AWARDS** Tchr yr, 90. **RESEARCH** Biblical lang; Old Testament hist; Old Testament theol. **SELECTED PUBLICATIONS** Auth, Revelation; Eschatology; Jebusites; Melchizedek; Promised Land; Rechabites, in Oxford Companion to the Bible, 93. **CONTACT ADDRESS** Dept of Rel, Westmont Col, 955 La Paz Rd, Santa Barbara, CA 93108-1099.

NEMCOVA, MARIA

PERSONAL Born 11/22/1937, Prague, Czechoslovakia, m, 1961 **DISCIPLINE** RUSSIAN & COMPARATIVE LITERATURE **EDUCATION** Univ Paris, Baccalaureat, 55; Univ Montreal, MA, 57; Harvard Univ, PhD(Slavic), 62. **CAREER** Tutor Russ lit, Harvard Univ, 61-62; asst prof, Brown Univ, 62-64; from vis lectr to asst prof, 64-72, assoc prof, 72-79, Prof Russ Lit, Smith Col, 79-, Vis lectr, Wellesley Col, 63-64; Int Res & Exchanges Bd sr scholar, Int Russ Lit, Leningrad, 73-74. **MEMBERSHIPS** Am Asn Advan Slavic Studies; Czech Soc Arts & Sci Am. **RESEARCH** Nineteenth and 20th century Russian and European literatures, especially Dostoevsky and symbolism; Pushkin; Russian and European realism in the novel. **SELECTED PUBLICATIONS** Auth, Rozanov on Dostoevsky, Slavic East Europ J, winter 71; The Metamorphosis of an Icon, Female Studies, Vol IX, 75; Pushkin's The Bronze Horseman: An Agonistic Vision, Mod Lang Studies, 78; The Narrator and His Masks in Viacheslew Ivanov's Povest' o Suetomire Tsareviche, Can-Am Slavic Studies, 78; Vitezslov Nezval's Progue with Fingers of Rain: A Surrealistic Image, Slavic and East Europ J, 79; The American Revolver: An Essay on Dostoevsky's The Devils, Mod Fiction Studies, 81; Pavel Yavor and the Pathos of Exile, In: From Far You, Toronto, 81; auth, Terminal Paradox: The Novels of Mulan Kundera, Grove Weidenfeld, 90, expanded paperback of same, Grove Evergreen, 92; auth, Paradoxes Terminaux, Gallinard, Paris, 93; Metapoesis-The Russian Tradition from Pushkin to Chekhov, with M. C. Finke, Russian Rev, Vol 55, 96; auth, A Lime Tree in Progue, Pegaro, Pisa, 97. **CONTACT ADDRESS** Dept of Russ, Smith Col, Northampton, MA 01061. **EMAIL** mbanerje@smith.edu

NEMEC-IGNASHEV, DIANE M.

PERSONAL Born 09/15/1951, Chicago, IL, w, 1974 **DISCIPLINE** SLAVIC LANGUAGES AND LITERATURE **EDUCATION** Univ Chicago, Dept of Slavic Langs and Lit, PhD, 84. **CAREER** Prof, Dept of Russian, Carleton Col, Northfield, MN. **MEMBERSHIPS** AAASS; AATSEEL. **RESEARCH** Russian theater; women's studies; Russian film/visual art. **CONTACT ADDRESS** Dept of Russian, Carleton Col, 100 S College St, Northfield, MN 55057. **EMAIL** dignasche@carleton.edu

NEMES, GRACIELA PALAU

PERSONAL Born 03/24/1919, Cuba, m, 1943, 1 child **DISCIPLINE** HISPANIC LITERATURE **EDUCATION** Trinity Col, BA, 42, Univ Md, MA, 49, PhD, 52. **CAREER** Instr to prof emerita, Univ Md, 46-93; vis prof emerita, 99-; vis assoc prof, Johns Hopkins Univ, 64-65; vis lectr, Latin Am Sem Foreign Serv Inst, Dept of State, 66-79. **HONORS AND AWARDS** Mem, Ateneo Americano de Washington, 58; Official Lectr, Foreign Serv Inst, Dept of State, 69; Order of Merit, Span Govt, 73; Outstanding Alumna, Trinity Col, 81; Hon Juan Ramon Jimenez Scholar, JRJ Found, 81; President's Medal, Univ of Md, 89; Silver Sprig of Parsley, JRJ Found, 00. **MEMBERSHIPS** Am Assoc Teachers Span & Port, Hispanic Soc Am, Int Assoc Hispanists, MLA. **RESEARCH** Juan Ramon Jimenez, Modernismo, 20th century Spanish American Poets. **SELECTED PUBLICATIONS** Auth, "Tres momentos del neo-misticismo del siglo modernista," Estudios sobre Ruben Dario, Fondo Cult, Mex (68); auth, "Octavio Paz: Invention and tradition," The poetry and prose of O Paz, Univ Okla, (73); auth, Vida y obra de Juan Ramon Jimenez 57 & Ibid: La poesia desnuda 1 & 2, Gredos, (Madrid), 74; auth, Inicios de Zenovia y JRJ en America, Fund Univ, (Madrid), 82; auth, Zenobia Camprubi. Diario 1 Cuba (1937 - 39 & 2 EEUU (1939-50), Alianza Ed and Univ Pr, 91, 95; auth, "J.R.J.," Premio Nobel: 11 grandes escritories, Georgetown Univ, (97); auth, "Marti, J.R.J. y el Modernismo", Unidad III, JRJ Found, Spain, (00). **CONTACT ADDRESS** Dept Port and Span, Univ of Maryland, Col Park, J R Jimenez Hall, College Park, MD 20742. **EMAIL** mh117@umail.umd.edu

NEPAULSINGH, COLBERT IVOR

PERSONAL Born 05/10/1943, Sangre Grande, Trinidad, m, 1966, 3 children **DISCIPLINE** SPANISH LANGUAGE AND LITERATURE **EDUCATION** Univ BC, BA, 66, MA, 67; Univ Toronto, PhD(Span lang & lit), 73. **CAREER** Assoc VP Acad Aff, Univ Albany, 88-91; Prof Span, State Univ NY Albany, 86- **HONORS AND AWARDS** Guggenheim fel, 81; Excel in Teaching; Excel in Acad Serv. **MEMBERSHIPS** MLA; Medieval Acad Am; Int Asn Hispanists. **RESEARCH** Medieval Spanish literature; Spanish literature of the Golden Age. **SELECTED PUBLICATIONS** Auth, La poesia de Micer Francisco Imperial, Clasicos Castellanos; Towards a History of Literary Composition in Medieval Spain, Univ Toronto; auth, Apples of Gold in Filigrees of Silver, Holmes and Meier. Peno Tafur and Cyprus (Greece & Cyprus Research Center). **CONTACT ADDRESS** Dept of Latin Am and Carib Stu, SS250C, SUNY, Albany, 1400 Washington Ave, Albany, NY 12222-1000. **EMAIL** bertnepo@cs.com

NEPOMNYASHCHY, CATHARINE THEIMER

PERSONAL Born 01/05/1951, East Orange, NJ, m, 1977, 1 child **DISCIPLINE** RUSSIAN LITERATURE **EDUCATION** Brown Univ, BA, 73; MA, 73; Columbia Univ, PhD, 87. **CAREER** Asst to prof, Barnard Col, 87-; assoc dir to dir, Harriman Inst, Columbia Univ, 99-. **HONORS AND AWARDS** Pushkin Prize, Columbia Univ, 74, 78; Merit Awd, Columbia Univ Transl Ctr, 92; AATSEEL Translation Awd, 94. **MEMBERSHIPS** MLA, AATSEEL, AAASS, AWSS, BASEES. **RESEARCH** Post-Stalin Russian Literature, Pushkin, Soviet Culture, Post-Soviet Popular Culture. **SELECTED PUBLICATIONS** Cotransl, Strolls With Pushkin, Abram Tertz (Andrei Sinyavsky), (Yale Univ Pr, 93); auth, Abram Tertz and the Poetics of Crime, Yale Univ Pr, 95. **CONTACT ADDRESS** 219 W 80 St, Apt 1D, New York, NY 10024-7061. **EMAIL** cn29@columbia.edu

NESBITT, JOHN D.

PERSONAL Born 12/14/1948, Lompoc, CA, m, 1 child **DISCIPLINE** ENGLISH, SPANISH **EDUCATION** Univ Calif, Los Angeles, BA, 71; Univ Calif, Davis, MA, 74; PhD, 80. **CAREER** Instr, Eastern Wyo Col, 81-. **HONORS AND AWARDS** Phi Beta Kappa, 71; Fel, Wyo Counc for the Humanities, 88; Fel, Wyo Counc on the Arts, 1988, NISOD Excellence in Tea;ching Awd, 94; Arizola Magnenat Awd, 99; Fiction Awd, Wyo Hist Soc. 99. **MEMBERSHIPS** Western Lit

Assoc; Western Writers of Am; Wyo Poets. **RESEARCH** History of prose fiction, Western American literature, popular fiction, Wyoming in general, Mexican fiction. **SELECTED PUBLICATIONS** Auth, "Lesser Known Works of Wyoming Fiction", Eastern Wyo col, 90; auth, One Foot in the Stirrup: Western Stories, Thorndike Pr, (Thorndike, Maine), 95; auth, Blue Book of Basic Writing, Endeavor Books, (Casper), 96; auth, Adventures of the Ramrod Rider: Gripping Tales, Augmented and Revised by the Author, Endeavor books, (Casper), 99; auth, A Good Man to Have in Camp, Endeavor Books (Casper), 99; auth, Coyote Trail, Leisure Books (NY), 00; auth, Writing for Real, Endeavor Books, (forthcoming); auth, North of Cheyenne Leisure Books, (forthcoming), auth, Man from Wolf River, Leisure Books (forthcoming). **CONTACT ADDRESS** Dept Humanities and Soc Sci, Eastern Wyoming Col, 3200 West C St, Torrington, WY 82240-1603.

NETHERCUT, WILLIAM ROBERT
PERSONAL Born 01/11/1936, Rockford, IL **DISCIPLINE** CLASSICS **EDUCATION** Harvard Univ, AB, 58; Columbia Univ, MA, 60, PhD(Classics), 63. **CAREER** From instr to asst prof Greek & Latin, Columbia Univ, 61-67; from assoc prof to prof Classics, Univ Ga, 67-75; prof Classics, Univ Tex, Austin, 75-, Lawrence Chamberlain fel, Columbia Univ, 67; lectr, First Int Conf on Ovid, Constanta, Romania, 72, Int Soc Homeric Studies, Athens, 73, 74, Int Congr Cypriot Studies, 74 & Int Congr SE Europ Studies, 74. **MEMBERSHIPS** Am Philol Asn; Class Asn Mid W & S; Archaeol Inst Am; Vergilian Soc Am; Petronian Soc. **RESEARCH** Propertius; Vergil; Greek poetry. **SELECTED PUBLICATIONS** Auth, The conclusion of Lucretius' fifth book, Class J, 12/67; Notes on the structure of Propertius, book IV, Am J Philol, 10/68; Apuleius' literary art, Class J, 69; The ironic priest: Propertius' Roman elegies, Am J Philol, 10/70; Propertius, 3/11, Trans Am Philol Asn, 71; The imagery of the Aeneid, Class J, 71-72; Vergil's De Return Natura, 73 & The epic journey of Achilles, 76, Ramus; Recent Scholarship on Propertius, Aufstieg und Noedergang cler Romischer Welt, 83. **CONTACT ADDRESS** Dept of Classics, Univ of Texas, Austin, 123 Waggener Hall, Austin, TX 78712-1026. **EMAIL** nethercut@mail.utexas.edu

NEUSE, ERNA KRITSCH
PERSONAL Born 08/07/1923, Austria, w, 1965 **DISCIPLINE** GERMAN LANGUAGE & LITERATURE **EDUCATION** Univ Vienna, Austria, PhD, 47. **CAREER** Prof German, Rutgers Univ, New Brunswick, 54-97; dir, Grad Prog, Rutgers Univ, New Brunswick, 81-92. **HONORS AND AWARDS** Warren L. Susman Awd for Excellence in Teaching. **MEMBERSHIPS** MLA; Am Asn Teachers Ger. **RESEARCH** Modern German literature; methods of teaching German. **SELECTED PUBLICATIONS** Auth, Modernes Deutsch, 60, Moderne Erzahlungen, 64, Neue deutsche Prosa, 68 & Modern German, 70, Prenticc-Hall; Buchners Lenz-zur Struktur der Novelle, Ger Quart, 3/70; Deutsch fur Anfanger, Prentice-Hall, 71; Die Funktion von Motiven und Stereotypen Wendungen in Schnitzlers Reigen, Monatshefte, winter 72; Das Rhetorische in Durrenmatts Der Besuch der alten Dame, Zur Funktion des Dialogs im Drama, Seminar, 2/75; Die deutsche Kurzgeschichte, Bouvier, Bonn, 80;Der Erzahler in der deutschen Kurzgeschichte, Camden House, 91. **CONTACT ADDRESS** 7 Cobb Rd, New Brunswick, NJ 08901.

NEVIN, THOMAS R.
PERSONAL Born 10/27/1944, m, 1977, 4 children **DISCIPLINE** CLASSICAL STUDIES **EDUCATION** Univ of Colo, BA, 66; Univ of Wisc, MA, 68; PhD, 73 **CAREER** Asst Prof, 80-88, Assoc Prof, 88-95, Prof, 95-, John Carroll Univ **HONORS AND AWARDS** Phi Beta Kappa; Woodrow Wilson Fel **MEMBERSHIPS** Am Philol Asn; Dante Soc of Am **RESEARCH** Dante; Catholicism. **SELECTED PUBLICATIONS** Auth, Ernst Junger and Germany: Into the Abyss, 1914-1945, Duke Univ Press, 96, London: Constable, 97; Simone Weil: Portrait of a Self-Exiled Jew, Chapel Hill, Univ of NC Press, 91 **CONTACT ADDRESS** Class & Mod Langs & Cultures Dept, John Carroll Univ, 20700 N Park Blvd, University Heights, OH 44118. **EMAIL** tnevin@jcu.edu

NEWMAN, GAIL M.
DISCIPLINE GERMAN **EDUCATION** Northwestern Univ, BA, 76; Univ Minn, PhD, 84. **CAREER** Assoc prof, Williams Col, 83-; fac coordr for Williams Writing Prog with Theodore Roosevelt High Sch Bronx, NY,95-. **RESEARCH** German romanticism; psychoanalytic theory; turn of the century and 20th-century Austria. **SELECTED PUBLICATIONS** Auth, Du bist nicht anders als ich:' Kleist's Correspondence with Wilhelmine von Zenge, Ger Life and Letters, 89; The Status of the Subject in Novalis's Heinrich von Ofterdingen and Kleist's Die Marquise von O., Ger Quart, 90; Family Violence in Kleist's Der Findling, Colloquia Germanica, 96; Locating the Romantic Subject: Novalis with Winnicott, Wayne State Univ Press, 97; Narrating the Asymbolic Subject in Hoffman's Der Sandmann, Sem, 97. **CONTACT ADDRESS** Center for Foreign Languages, Literatures and Cult, Williams Col, Williamstown, MA 01267. **EMAIL** Gail.M.Newman@williams.edu

NEWMAN, JOHN KEVIN
PERSONAL Born 08/17/1928, Bradford, Yorkshire, England, m, 1970, 3 children **DISCIPLINE** CLASSICAL PHILOLOGY, COMPARATIVE LITERATURE **EDUCATION** Oxford Univ, BA (Lit Humaniores), 50, BA(Russ), 52, MA, 53; Bristol Univ, PhD (Classics), 67. **CAREER** Master classics, Downside Sch, Bath, England, 55-69; assoc prof, 70-80, prof Classics, Univ Ill, Urbana, 80-00, chmn dept, 81-85, Ed, Ill Class Studies, 81-87, emeritus, 00-. **HONORS AND AWARDS** Vatican Int Latin Poetry Competition, Silver Medals, 60, 63, 66, 97; Certamen Capitolinum, 68 & 80; assoc mem, center for Adv Study, 73-74, 91-92, Univ Ill; mem, senior common room, 85-86, Corpus Christi Col, Oxford; vis fel, 86. Institute for Adv Studies in the Humanities, Univ Edinburgh. **RESEARCH** Greek and Latin poetic traditions. **SELECTED PUBLICATIONS** Auth, Augustus and the new poetry, 67, Univ Ill; auth, The concept of Vates in Augustan poetry, 67, Collection Latomus; co-ed, Serta Turyniana, 74, Univ Ill; auth, Latin Compositions, Urbana, Ill, 76; auth, Golden Violence, Urbana, Ill, 76; auth, Dislocated: An American Carnival, Urbana, Ill, 77; Ex Aedibus, Urbana, Ill; auth Pindar's Art: Its Tradition and Aims, Weidmann, 84; auth, The Classical Epic Tradition, Univ Wisconsin Press, 86; Roman Catullus: the Modification of the Alexandrian Sensibility, Weidmann, 90; Lelio Guidiccioni, Latin Poems: Rome 1633, Weidmann, 92; co-auth, Horace-Benedict de Saussure: Forerunner in Glaciology, 95, Memoires de la Societe de Physique et d'Histoire Naturelle de Geneve, vol. 48, Editions Passe Present; auth, Augustan Propertius. The Recapitulation of a Genre, Olms, 97; contbr, The New Princeton Encyclopedia of Poetry and Poetics, Princetone Univ Press, 93. **CONTACT ADDRESS** 707 S Matthews Ave, Urbana, IL 61801-3625. **EMAIL** j-newman@uiuc.edu

NEWMAN, JUDITH H.
PERSONAL Born 02/01/1961, Alexandria, VA, m, 1987, 2 children **DISCIPLINE** NEAR EASTERN LANGUAGES AND CIVILIZATIONS **EDUCATION** Princeton, AB, 83; Yale Divinity School, MAR, 88; Harvard Univ, 96. **CAREER** Asst prof, General Theol Sem, 98-; Assoc Prof, 00. **HONORS AND AWARDS** Episcopal church Found fel, 92-95. **MEMBERSHIPS** SBL; CBA; AJS. **RESEARCH** History of Biblical interpretation; Second Temple Judaism; history of Jewish and Christian Liturgy. **SELECTED PUBLICATIONS** Auth, Praying By the Book: the Scripturalization of Prayer in Second Temple Judaism, EJL Series, Atlanta: Scholars, 99. **CONTACT ADDRESS** General Theol Sem, 175 Ninth Ave, New York, NY 10011-4977. **EMAIL** newman@gts.edu

NEWMAN, PAUL
PERSONAL Born 03/07/1937, Jacksonville, FL **DISCIPLINE** LINGUISTICS **EDUCATION** Univ Pa, BA, 58; MA, 61, Univ Calif, PhD, 67. **CAREER** Asst prof, Yale Univ, 66-73; prof, dir, Bayero Univ, 72-75, prof, Univ of Leiden, 75-82; prof, Ind Univ, 83-; chair, 92-98. **HONORS AND AWARDS** Fel, Ctr for Advan Study in the Behav Sciences, Stanford, Univ, 88; Teaching Excellence Recognition Awd, Ind Univ 98. **MEMBERSHIPS** Linguistic Soc of Am. **RESEARCH** African linguistics, Hausa language. **SELECTED PUBLICATIONS** Coauth, West African Travels and Adventures: Two Autobiographical Narratives from Northern Nigeria, Yale Univ Pr, (New Haven) 71; coauth, Modern Hausa-English Dictionary, Oxford Univ Pr, (Nigeria), 77; auth, The Classification of Chadic within Afroasiatic, Universitaire Pers, (Leiden) 80; auth, Nominal and Verbal Plurality in Chadic, Foris Publ, (Dordrecht), 90; auth, The Hausa Language: An Encyclopedic Reference Grammar, Yale Univ Pr, (New Haven) 00. **CONTACT ADDRESS** Dept Linguistics, Indiana Univ, Bloomington, 1021 E 3rd St, Bloomington, IN 47405-7005. **EMAIL** pnxxpn@indiana.edu

NEWMARK, LEONARD
PERSONAL Born 04/08/1929, Attica, IN, m, 1951, 2 children **DISCIPLINE** LINGUISTICS **EDUCATION** Univ Chicago, AB, 47; Ind Univ, MA, 51, PhD, 55. **CAREER** Instr to assoc prof, OH State Univ, 54-61; vis asst prof, Univ MI, 61; assoc prof, IN Univ, 62; prof, Univ CA, San Diego, 63-92, prof Emeritus, 93-. **HONORS AND AWARDS** ACLS; NEH; Office of Education; NSF. **MEMBERSHIPS** Linguistics Soc of Am; Dictionary Soc of North Am. **RESEARCH** Albanian language. **SELECTED PUBLICATIONS** Auth, Introduction to the Linguistic History of English, 63; Using American English, 64; Standard Albanian: A Reference Grammar, 82; Spoken Albanian, 97; Oxford Albanian-English Dictionary, 98. **CONTACT ADDRESS** 2643 St Tropez Place, La Jolla, CA 92037. **EMAIL** ldnewmark@ucsd.edu

NEWMYER, STEPHEN THOMAS
PERSONAL Born 07/10/1948, Pittsburgh, PA, w, 1978 **DISCIPLINE** CLASSICS **EDUCATION** Duquesne Univ, BA, 70; Univ NC, Chapel Hill, PhD(classics), 76. **CAREER** Asst prof, 76-80, Assoc Prof Classics, 80-84, Prof Classics, 84-, Duquesne Univ, Fel, Inst Teaching Post-Bibl Found Western Civilization, Jewish Theol Sem Am, 78. **MEMBERSHIPS** Am Philol Asn; Vergilian Soc; Class Asn Middle West & South; Class Asn Atlantic States. **RESEARCH** Roman epic poetry; classical influence on later literature; medicine. **SELECTED PUBLICATIONS** Auth, Pessimistic Prometheus: A Comparison of Aeschylus and Robert Lowell, Helios, fall-winter 78-79, The Silvae of Statius: Structure and Theme, Brill, Leiden, 79; Ancient and Talmudic Medicine: A Course Description, Helios, winter-spring 79-80; Talmudic medicine: A Classicist's perspective, Judaism, 29: 360- 367; Robert Lowell and the weeping philosopher, Class and Mod Lit, winter 80; Talmudic medicine, Jewish Digest, 81; Charles Anthon: Knickerbocker scholar, Class Outlook, 12-181-82; Statius, 'Thebaid Ix' - English And Latin - Dewar,m, Editor- translator, American J of Philology, Vol 0113, 1992. **CONTACT ADDRESS** 119 S 21st St, Pittsburgh, PA 15203. **EMAIL** newmyer@duq.edu

NEWTON, ROBERT PARR
PERSONAL Born 07/31/1929, San Antonio, TX, m, 1959, 2 children **DISCIPLINE** MODERN GERMAN LITERATURE, STYLISTICS **EDUCATION** Rice Univ, BA, 50, MA, 58; Johns Hopkins Univ, PhD(Ger), 64. **CAREER** From instr to asst prof Ger, Univ Pa, 62-70; assoc prof, 70-76, prof Ger, 76-94, prof emer, 94- , Univ NC, Greensboro; vis lectr Ger, Swarthmore Col, 65-70. **MEMBERSHIPS** MLA; SAtlantic Mod Lang Asn; Am Asn Teachers Ger; AAUP. **RESEARCH** Linguistic metrics, German poetry, modern German drama. **SELECTED PUBLICATIONS** Auth, Dada, Expressionism and Some Modern Modes, Rice Univ Studies, summer 69; The First Voice: Vowel Configuration in the German lyric, J English & Ger Philol, 10/69; Vokallange und Vokalgleichklang als Rhythmische Antriebs-und Gestaltungsmomente, LiLi: Z Ling und Lit, 9/71; Form in the Menschheitsdammerung, The Hague, 71; Ditonic Rhythmemes: Formal Elements of Rhythmic Patterning, Poetics: Int Rev Theory Lit, 74; Trochaic and Iambic, Lang & Style, Int J, spring 75; Vowel Undersong: Studies of Vocalic Timbre and Chroneme Patterning in German Lyric Poetry, The Hague, 81; Eye Imagery in Else Lasker-Schuer, Mod Lang Notes, 3/82. **CONTACT ADDRESS** 114 E Brentwood, Greensboro, NC 27403. **EMAIL** Robert_Newton@compuserve.com

NEY, JAMES WALTER
PERSONAL Born 07/28/1932, Nakuru, Kenya, m, 1954, 3 children **DISCIPLINE** ENGLISH, LINGUISTICS **EDUCATION** Wheaton Col, Ill, AB, 55, AM, 58; Univ Mich, EdD(English), 63. **CAREER** English specialist, Dade County Pub Schs, Fla, 61-62 & Univ Ryukyus, 62-64; asst prof, Mich State Univ, 65-69; assoc prof, 69-75, Prof English, Ariz State Univ, 75-98, Res grant, NCTE, 76, chmn comt to evaluate ling, 77-80; Prof Emer, 98. **MEMBERSHIPS** Can Ling Soc; Nat Asn Foreign Student Affairs; Teaching English to Speakers Other Lang; Ling Soc Am; MLA. **RESEARCH** Teaching English as a second language; teaching of written composition to native speakers of English. Coauth, Readings on American Society, 69, Readings from Samuel Clemens, 69, Blaisdell; Adventures in English, Laidlaw Bros, 72; Marckwardt, 72; Two apparent fallacies in current grammatical thought, Gen Ling, 74; Linguistics, Language Teaching and Composition in the Grades, Mouton, The Hague, 75; The modals in English: A floating Semantic feature analysis, JEnglish Ling, 76; Sexism in the English language: A biased view in a biased society, ETC, 76; Semantic Structures, Mouton, The Hague, 81; Generativity, The History of a Notion That Never Was, Historiographia Linguistica, Vol 0020, 1993; Letters - Resource Books For Teachers - Burbidge,n, Gray,p, Levy,s, Rinvolucri,m, Modern Language J, Vol 0081, 1997. **CONTACT ADDRESS** Dept of English, Arizona State Univ, Tempe, AZ 85281. **EMAIL** james.ney@asu.edu

NGUYEN, DINH-HOA
PERSONAL Born 01/17/1924, Hanoi, Vietnam, m, 1952, 4 children **DISCIPLINE** LINGUISTICS, LITERATURE **EDUCATION** Union Col, BA, 50; NYork Univ, MA, 52, PhD(English educ), 56. **CAREER** Lectr Vietnamese, Columbia Univ, 53-57; from asst prof to prof English & ling, Univ Saigon, 57-65, dean fac lett, 57-58, chmn dept, 57-65; Prof Ling & Foreign Lang to Prof emer, Southern Ill Univ, Carbondale & Dir Ctr Vietnamese Studies, 69-, Dir cult affairs, Ministry of Educ, Saigon, Vietnam, 62-65; secy-gen, Vietnam Nat Comm, Unesco, 62-65; vis prof, Univ Wash, 65-66; cult counr, Embassy of Vietnam, Washington, DC, 66-69. **HONORS AND AWARDS** Fulbright prof ling & English, Rabat, Morocco, 81-82; two res grants, Nat Endowment for Humanities, 77-82; Fulbright grant ling, Morocco, 81-82. **MEMBERSHIPS** Ling Soc Am; Am Orient Soc; Asn Asian Studies; Dict Soc NAm; Am Coun Teachers Uncommonly-Taught Asian Lang (pres, 76-77 & 77-78). **RESEARCH** Students' review grammar of Vietnamese; English-Vietnamese dictionary; outline of Vietnamese culture. **SELECTED PUBLICATIONS** Auth, Read Vietnamese, 66 & Hoa's Vietnamese-English Dictionary, 66 Tuttle; Vietnamese-English Student Dictionary, 71 & Colloquial Vietnamese, 74, Southern Ill Univ; Beginning English for Vietnamese Speakers & Intermediate English for Vietnamese Speakers, Tuttle, 76; 201 Vietnamese Verbs, Barron's 79; Language in Vietnamese Society, 80 & Essential English- Vietnamese Dictionary, 80, Asia Bks; 'Nuoc Chay Qua Cau' - Tran,tbg, World Literature Today, Vol 0067, 1993; Ca Lon' - Dao- khanh, World Literature Today, Vol 0067, 1993; 'Dam Khuya' - Hoang,tdt, World Literature Today, Vol 0067, 1993; Les 'Enfants De Thai Binh,' Vol 1, 'Nostalgies Provinciales' - Duyen-anh, World Literature Today, Vol 0068, 1994; Tuyen-tap Van-tho Van But Nam Hoa-ky' - Nguyen,vs, World Literature Today, Vol 0069, 1995; Bao-

ninh The 'Sorrow of War' - a Novel of North-vietnam - Palmos,f, Hao,pt, World Literature Today, Vol 0069, 1995; 'Two Shores Deux Rives' - English, French - Vuongriddick,t, World Literature Today, Vol 0070, 1996; The 'Stone Boy' And Other Stories - Thich,nh, World Literature Today, Vol 0071, 1997; The 'Other Side of Heaven' - Postwar Fiction by Vietnamese And American Writers - Karlin,w, World Literature Today, Vol 0071, 1997; 'Hoa Dia-nguc' - The 'Flowers of Hell' - English, Vietnamese - Nguyen,ct, Nguyen,nb, World Literature Today, Vol 0071, 1997; an Anthology of Vietnamese Poems - From The 11th Through The 20th Centuries - Huynh,st, World Literature Today, Vol 0071, 1997; b Vietnam - a Travelers Literary Companion - Balaban,j, Nguyen,qd, World Literature Today, Vol 0071, 1997. **CONTACT ADDRESS** Dept of Ling, So Illinois Univ, Carbondale, Carbondale, IL 62901.

NI, W. J.
PERSONAL Born 10/21/1954, China, m, 1985, 1 child **DISCIPLINE** LINGUISTICS **EDUCATION** Univ Conn, PhD, 91. **CAREER** Res assoc, Univ Conn, 91-93; res scientist, Haskins Lab, New Haven, Conn; res assoc, Yale Univ Sch of Med, 96-98; Res Scientist, Yale Univ School of Med, 99 . Res scientist, Yale Univ Sch of Med, 99-. **MEMBERSHIPS** Ling Soc Am; Acad of Aphasia. **RESEARCH** Language comprehension and production in normal and abnormal populations. **SELECTED PUBLICATIONS** Coauth, Learning, Parsing and Modularity, in Frazier, ed, Perspectives on Sentence Processing, Lawrence Erlbaum, 94; coauth, Syntactic Complexity and Working Memory in Explaining Comprehension Difficulties, Brain and Lang, 95; coauth, Production in Broca's Aphasia: A Case of Syntactic and Phonetic Aspects, Brain and Lang, 96; coauth, Tasks and Timing in the Perception of Linguistic Anomaly, J of Psycholinguistic Res, 96; coauth, Meaning, Memory and Modularity, MIT Occas Papers in Ling, 96; coauth, Individual Differences in Working Memory and Eye-Movement Patterns in Reading Relative Clauses, Univ Conn Working Papers in Ling, 96; coauth, Sidestepping Garden Paths: Assessing the Contributions of Syntax, Semantics and Plausibility in Resolving Ambiguities, Lang and Cognitive Proc, 96; coauth, Production and Comprehension of Relative Clause Syntax in Nonfluent Aphasia: A Coordinated Study, Brain and Lang, 97; coauth, "Anomaly Detection: Eye-Movement Patterns," J of Psycholinguistic Res, 98; coauth, "An event-related neuroimaging study distinguishing form and content in sentence processing," J of Cognitive Neuroscience, 00. **CONTACT ADDRESS** 831 Rail Fence Rd, Orange, CT 06477. **EMAIL** weijia.ni@yale.edu

NICASTRO, ANTHONY J.
DISCIPLINE SPANISH **EDUCATION** NYork Univ, BA, 64; Columbia Univ, PhD, 71. **CAREER** Vis prof, Williams Col, 83-; prof, N Adams State Col. **HONORS AND AWARDS** NEH, Wayne State Univ, 82; NEH, Yale Univ, 85; NEH, Univ Miss Ctr for the Stud of Southern Cult, 95. **RESEARCH** Foreign-language acquisition and pedagogy with emphasis on teaching strictly in the target language at all levels; history of the romance languages; Flamenco history; Flamenco guitar technique; Flamenco as literature; Flamenco as compared with Blues. **SELECTED PUBLICATIONS** Auth, Modernidad y reminiscencias de la literatura francesa en Concierto barroco de Alejo Carpentier, Confluencia, Univ Northern Colorado. **CONTACT ADDRESS** Center for Foreign Languages, Literatures and Cult, Williams Col, Williamstown, MA 01267. **EMAIL** anicastro@nasc.mass.edu

NICCOLI, GABRIEL
DISCIPLINE ITALIAN; FRENCH STUDIES **EDUCATION** Univ British Columbia, BA, 70; MA, 73; PhD, 83. **CAREER** Assoc prof, St Jerome's Univ; vis asst prof, Univ of Victoria B.C.; chair, dept of Ital and Fr Studies, St Jerome's Univ; asst prof, Univ of Wash. **RESEARCH** 16th century pastoral drama in Italy and France; literate women of the Italian renaissance. **SELECTED PUBLICATIONS** Auth, Autobiography and Fiction in Veronica Franco's Epistolary Narrative; Eros and the Art of Self-Promotion in Veronica Franco's Terze rime; Teoria e prassi: note sulla questione della tragicommedia pastorale: in Italia e in Francia; The God of Love in Pastor Fido: Blindness in Arcadia; Cupid Satyr and the Golden Age: Pastoral Dramatic Scenes of the Late Renaissance; "A Post World War II Settlement: The Italian Community of Kitchener-Waterloo"; "Re(de)fining the Genre, Probing the Canon: The Representation of the Immaterial: in the Pastoral Plays of Luigi Groto and Antoine de Montchrestien"; "Shaping Fantasies: Writing as Revision in Caterina Vannini's Correspondence"; "Wild Boar as Satiro: Transgressing the Rules of the Pastoral Game". **CONTACT ADDRESS** Dept of Italian and French Studies, St. Jerome's Univ, Waterloo, ON, Canada N2L 3G3. **EMAIL** ganiccol@watarts.uwaterloo.ca

NICHOLAS, ROBERT LEON
PERSONAL Born 12/10/1937, Lebanon, OR, m, 1967, 2 children **DISCIPLINE** MODERN SPANISH LITERATURE **EDUCATION** Univ Ore, BA, 59, MA, 63, PhD(romance lang), 67. **CAREER** From instr to assoc prof, 65-76, chmn dept Span & Port, 79- 82, Prof Span, Univ Wis-Madison, 76-, Dir study prog, Madrid, 72-73. **MEMBERSHIPS** Am Asn Teachers Span & Port; MLA. **RESEARCH** Modern Spanish Theater; modern Spanish novel; generation of 1898. **SELECTED PUBLICATIONS** Contribr, The history plays: Buero Vallejo's experiment in dramatic expression, Rev Estud Hispanicos, 11/69; auth, El Mundo de Hoy, Scott, 71; The Tragic Stages of Antonio Buero Vallejo, Estud Hispanofila, Univ NC, 72; coauth, En Camino!, Adelante! & Churros y Chocolate!, Scott, 77; La historia de historia de una escalera, Estreno, spring 79; En Camino! Adelante! Scott, 2nd ed, 81; El proceso de creacion en Abel Sanchez, Homenaje a Antonio Sanchez-Barbudo: Ensayos de literature espanola moderna, Univ Wis-Madison, 81; La camisa, entre el sainete y el melodrama, Primer Acto, 82; coauth, En camino: motivos de conversacion, Scott (in prep). **CONTACT ADDRESS** Dept of Span & Port, Univ of Wisconsin, Madison, Room 1038 Van Hise Hall, Madison, WI 53706.

NICHOLLS, JAMES C.
DISCIPLINE INTERMEDIATE FRENCH, INTRODUCTION TO FRENCH LITERATURE **EDUCATION** BA, Univ Wis, 51, MA, 52, PhD, 62. **CAREER** Assoc dean, Colgate Univ, 80-82; ch, Fr Achievement Test Comm, 87-90; prof. **HONORS AND AWARDS** Fulbright scholar, Univ Dijon, 57-58. **RESEARCH** Eighteenth-century french lit, Diderot. **SELECTED PUBLICATIONS** Auth, Grading the Advanced Placement Examination in French Literature, 81; Grading the Advanced Placement Examination in French Language, 81; Toward a Chronology of Jacques le Fataliste, Studies on Voltaire and the Eighteenth Century, 93. **CONTACT ADDRESS** Dept of Romance Lang, Colgate Univ, 13 Oak Drive, Hamilton, NY 13346.

NICHOLLS, MARIA
DISCIPLINE FRENCH LITERATURE **EDUCATION** SUNY-Morrisville, BA, 81; SUNY-Binghamton, MA, 84, PhD, 91. **CAREER** Soc dir, NDEA Summer Inst, 64, 65; dir, Lang Lab, 72-87; spec instr, Neglected Language Prog, Portugese; lectr, 87-91; asst prof-. **SELECTED PUBLICATIONS** Auth, Lady Dedlock's Sin, The Dickensian, 93. **CONTACT ADDRESS** Dept of Romance Lang, Colgate Univ, 13 Oak Drive, Hamilton, NY 13346. **EMAIL** mnicholls@center.colgate.edu

NICHOLLS, ROGER ARCHIBALD
PERSONAL Born 05/24/1922, London, England, m, 1955 **DISCIPLINE** GERMAN **EDUCATION** Oxford Univ, BA, 49; Univ Calif, PhD, 53. **CAREER** Instr Ger, Univ Toronto, 52-54; asst prof, Univ Chicago, 54-61; assoc prof, Reed Col, 61-63; asst prof, 63-65, Prof Ger, Univ ORE, 65-. **MEMBERSHIPS** MLA; Am Asn Teachers Ger; Philol Asn Pac Coast (pres, 67- 68). **RESEARCH** Nineteenth century drama; literary movements at the end of the nineteenth century; Thomas Mann. **SELECTED PUBLICATIONS** Auth, Nietzsche in the Early Work of Thomas Mann, Univ Calif, 55; The Dramas of CD Grabbe, Mouton, 68. **CONTACT ADDRESS** 2840 Elinor St, Eugene, OR 97403.

NICHOLS, ANN
DISCIPLINE LINGUISTICS **EDUCATION** St. Mary's Col , BA; Univ Wash, MA, 58, PhD, 64. **CAREER** Prof; **HONORS AND AWARDS** NEH grant, 95. **RESEARCH** Text and image in late medieval culture; indexing all illustrations in English manuscripts 1377-1508. **SELECTED PUBLICATIONS** Auth, Seeable Signs: The Iconography of the Seven Sacraments 1350-1544 **CONTACT ADDRESS** Winona State Univ, PO Box 5838, Winona, MN 55987-5838.

NICHOLS, FRED JOSEPH
PERSONAL Born 03/24/1939, Staten Island, NY, 1 child **DISCIPLINE** COMPARATIVE LITERATURE **EDUCATION** Georgetown Univ, AB, 61; NYork Univ, MA, 66, PhD, 67. **CAREER** From instr to asst prof English, Yale Univ, 67-76; from assoc prof to PROF COMP LIT, GRAD CTR, CITY UNIV NEW YORK, 76-. **MEMBERSHIPS** MLA; Renaissance Soc Am; Am Comp Lit Asn; Am Asn Neth Studies. **RESEARCH** Renaissance literature; Netherlandic literature; Latin literature. **SELECTED PUBLICATIONS** An Anthology of Neo-Latin Poetry, Yale Univ Press, 79. **CONTACT ADDRESS** Dept of Comp Lit, Graduate Sch and Univ Ctr, CUNY, New York, NY 10016-4309.

NICHOLS, PATRICIA CAUSEY
PERSONAL Born 12/29/1938, Conway, SC, m, 1959, 2 children **DISCIPLINE** ENGLISH, LINGUISTICS **EDUCATION** Winthrop Col, BA, 58; Univ Minn, MA, 66; San Jose State Univ, MA, 72; Stanford Univ, PhD(ling), 76. **CAREER** Teacher, Hampton Pub Schs, Va, 58-60; Lectr English, Ling & Educ, San Jose State Univ, 76-, Co-ed, Women & Lang News, 76; vis asst prof English, Univ SC, 80-81; vis instr, Univ Calif, Santa Barbara, 82. **MEMBERSHIPS** MLA; Ling Soc Am; Am Dialect Soc. **RESEARCH** Gullah; gender and sex differences in speech; American dialects. **SELECTED PUBLICATIONS** Auth, A sociolinguistic perspective on reading and black children, Lang Arts, 54: 150-157; Ethnic consciousness in the British Isles, Lang Problems & Lang Planning, 1: 10-31; Black women in the rural south: Conservative and innovative, Int J Sociol Lang, Vol 17, 78; Planning for language change, San Jose Studies, 6: 18-25; Variation among Gullah speakers in rural South Carolina, In: Language Use and the Uses of Language, Georgetown Univ Press, 80; Women in their speech communities, In: Women and Language In Literature and Society, Praeger Publ, 80; Creoles in the USA, In: Language in the USA, Cambridge Univ Press, 81; Linguistic options and choices for black women in the rural South, In: Language, Gender and Society, Newbury House Publ (in press). **CONTACT ADDRESS** 1430 Westmont Ave, Campbell, CA 95008.

NICHOLSON, JOHN H.
PERSONAL Born 01/11/1958, Atlanta, GA **DISCIPLINE** CLASSICS **EDUCATION** Univ South, BA, 80; Univ Ga, MA, 86; Univ NC, PhD, 91. **CAREER** Asst prof, Univ Del, 91-98; instr, Univ Ga, 98-. **HONORS AND AWARDS** Fourmy Classical Scholar, 86-89. **MEMBERSHIPS** Am Philol Asn **RESEARCH** Latin literature **SELECTED PUBLICATIONS** Auth, Cicero's Return from Exile, 92; auth, The Delivery and Confidentiality of Cicero's Letters, 94; auth, Goats and Gout in Catullus 71, 97; auth, The Survival of Cicero's Letters, 98; auth, Catullus 84: In vino veritas?, 99; auth, Chiasmus in Catullus 85, 00. **CONTACT ADDRESS** Dept of Classics, Univ of Georgia, Park Hall, Athens, GA 30602. **EMAIL** jhn@arches.uga.edu

NICHOLSON, NIGEL
PERSONAL Born 10/30/1968, Aldershot, United Kingdom, m, 1996, 1 child **DISCIPLINE** CLASSICS **EDUCATION** Oxford Univ, BA, 90; Univ Penn, MA, PhD, 94. **CAREER** Asst prof, Wellesley Col, 94-95; asst prof, Reed Col, 95- . **HONORS AND AWARDS** Sunderland Prize, 90; first class honors, 90; William Penn Fel, 90-93; Dean's Scholar, 91; Andrew W. Mellon Diss Fel, 93-94. **MEMBERSHIPS** Am Philol Asn; Class Asn of the Pacific Northwest. **RESEARCH** Archaic Greek lyric poetry. **SELECTED PUBLICATIONS** Auth, The Truth of Pederasty: A Supplement to Foucault's Genealogy of the Relation between Truth and Desire in Ancient Greece, Intertexts, 98; auth, Bodies Without Names, Names Without Bodies: Propertius 1.21-22, Class J, 98/99; auth, Pederastic Poets and Adult Patrons, Class W, 00; auth, Victory without Defeat? Carnival Laughter and its Appropriation in Pindar's Victory Odes, in Barta; ed, Carnivalizing Difference: Bakhtin and the Other, Harwood, forthcoming; auth, Pindar NE, 4.57-58, Arethusa, forthcoming; auth, Polysemy and Ideology in Pindar, Pythian T, Phoenix, Az, forthcoming. **CONTACT ADDRESS** Classics Dept, Reed Col, 3203 SE Woodstock Blvd, Portland, OR 97202. **EMAIL** nigel.nicholson@reed.edu

NICOLAI, ELKE
DISCIPLINE GERMAN **EDUCATION** Univ-Gh- Siegen, Ger, PhD. **CAREER** Asst prof. **MEMBERSHIPS** MLA; Amer Coun Teaching For Languages; Ger Stud Asn & Women in Ger Asn. **RESEARCH** Literature of the 19th and 20th centuries. **SELECTED PUBLICATIONS** Auth, bk on Klaus Mann and his literary contemporaries in the mid-twenties and early thirties; bibliog of the int lit of the Spanish Civil War 36-39. **CONTACT ADDRESS** Dept of German, Hunter Col, CUNY, 695 Park Ave, New York, NY 10021.

NIEBYLSKI, DIANNA
DISCIPLINE LATIN AMERICAN & COMPARATIVE LITERATURE **EDUCATION** Brandeis Univ, PhD, 88. **CONTACT ADDRESS** Dept of Spanish & Italian, Univ of Kentucky, Lexington, KY 40506. **EMAIL** dcniebz@pop.uky.edu

NIEMAN, NANCY DALE
PERSONAL Born 05/10/1939, St. Paul, MN **DISCIPLINE** SPANISH **EDUCATION** Beloit Col, BA, 61; Middlebury Col, Vt, MA, 62; Inst Phonetique, Univ Paris, dipl, 65; Univ Madrid, Dr Philos & Lett(Span), 66; Inst Brasil-Estados Unidos, cert, 74. **CAREER** Instr Span, Wayne State Col, 62-64; from instr to asst prof, Beloit Col, 64-71, assoc prof Mod Lang, 71-79; sr lectr, Univ Southern Calif, 79-81; prof Mod Lang, Santa Monica Col, 81-; Univ So Calif Madrid Cen, res dir, 89; Int Inst Foundation of Spain, res dir, 90-91; chmn, Dept Modern Languages, Santa Monica Coll, 94-98; coord, Overseas Progs, SMC, 95-97. **MEMBERSHIPS** Am Asn Teachers Span & Port; MLA; AAUP; Am Asn Advan Humanities. **RESEARCH** Contemporary Spanish literature, especially theater and novel. **SELECTED PUBLICATIONS** Auth, El mundo poetico de Alejandro Casona, Rev Univ Madrid, 10/66; The festival of the dove, Beloit Daily News, 3/23/73; Feast of the Holy Name, The Garden of Your Delights, translations of two poems by Ana Rossetti, RE:AL, 97. **CONTACT ADDRESS** Dept Spanish, Santa Monica Col, 1900 Pico Blvd, Santa Monica, CA 90405-1644. **EMAIL** nieman_nancy@smc.edu

NIERS, WERNER GERT
PERSONAL Born 10/10/1943, Dresden, Germany, m, 1971, 2 children **DISCIPLINE** GERMAN, FRENCH **EDUCATION** Univ Cologne, Staatsexamen, 71; Rutgers Univ, PhD, 87. **CAREER** Prof, Ocean County Col, 99-. **MEMBERSHIPS** PEN; AATF; AATG; MLA. **RESEARCH** German Americana. **SELECTED PUBLICATIONS** Auth, Frauen Schreiber in Exile, 88. **CONTACT ADDRESS** 1201 Sleepy Hollow Rd, Point Pleasant, NJ 08742-3526. **EMAIL** tniers@aol.com

NIGHTINGALE, ANDREA WILSON
DISCIPLINE CLASSICS **EDUCATION** BA, 81; Oxford Univ, MA, 84; Univ CA Berkeley, MA, 85; PhD, 89. **CAREER** Assoc prof, Stanford Univ. **RESEARCH** Ancient philos, Greek and Latin lit, lit and philos of ecology. **SELECTED PUBLICATIONS** Auth, Writing/Reading a Sacred Text: A Literary Interpretation of Plato's Laws, Class Philol, 93; Towards an Ecological Eschatology: Plato and Bakhtin on Other Worlds and Times in Bakhtin and the Classics, Northwestern UP, 97; Aristotle on the 'Liberal' and 'Illiberal' Arts, Proceedings Boston Area Colloq Ancient Philos, 97; Genres in Dialogue: Plato and the Construct of Philosophy, Cambridge, 95; auth, "Plato on the Origins of Evil: The Statesman Myth Reconsidered," Ancient Philosophy 88 (96): 65-91; auth, "Historiography and Cosmology in Plato's Laws," Ancietn Philosophy 19 (99): 1-28; auth, "Sages, Sophists, and Philosophers: Greek Wisdom Literature," in Literature in the Greek and Roman Worlds: A New Perspective, ed. Oliver Taplin (Oxford Univ Press, 00), 156-191; auth, "Distant Views: Realistic and Fantastic Mimesis in Plato," in New Approaches to Plato and Socrates, ed. J. Annas and C. Rowe (Harvard Univ Press, 01). **CONTACT ADDRESS** Dept of Classics, Stanford Univ, Bldg 20, Main Quad, Stanford, CA 94305. **EMAIL** andrean@leland.stanford.edu

NILSEN, ALLEEN PACE
PERSONAL Born 10/10/1936, Phoenix, AZ, m, 1958, 3 children **DISCIPLINE** ENGLISH EDUCATION AND LINGUISTICS **EDUCATION** Brigham Young Univ, BA, 58; Am Univ, MEd, 61; Univ Iowa, PhD(English, ling), 73. **CAREER** Instr English, Eastern Mich Univ, 66-67; teacher, Am Int Sch Kabul, Afghanistan, 67-69: instr English, Eastern Mich Univ, 69-71; asst prof educ, Univ Northern Iowa, 71-73; assoc prof, 73-80, Prof English, Ariz State Univ, 80- **HONORS AND AWARDS** Rewey Belle Inglis Awd, Natl Coun of Tchrs of English, 90; Nicholas J. Silvaroli Awd, 94 for Outstanding Contribution to Literacy in Arizona. **MEMBERSHIPS** Nat Coun Teachers English; Membership in International Soc of Humor Studies (ISHS), Pres, 01; MLA. **RESEARCH** Sexism as shown in language; children's and adolescent literature; humor scholarship. **SELECTED PUBLICATIONS** Coauth, Pronunciation Contrasts in English, Simon & Schuster, 71; auth, Sexism in English: A feminist view, In: Female Studies VI: Closer to the Ground, Feminist Press, 72; coauth, Semantic Theory: A Linguistic Perspective, Newbury House, 75; ed & coauth, Sexism and Language, Nat Coun Teachers English, 77; Five factors contributing to the unequal treatment of females in picture books, Top News, spring 78; coauth, Language Play: An Introduction to Linguistics, Newbury House, 78; auth, Living Language, Allyn & Bacon, 99; co-auth, Encyclopedia of 20th Century American Humor, Oryx 00; ; coauth, Literature for Today's Young Adults, 6th ed, Longman, 01. **CONTACT ADDRESS** Dept of English, Arizona State Univ, PO Box 870302, Tempe, AZ 85287-0302. **EMAIL** Alleen.Nilsen@asu.edu

NILSEN, DON LEE FRED
PERSONAL Born 10/19/1934, Spanish Fork, UT, m, 1958, 3 children **DISCIPLINE** ENGLISH LINGUISTICS **EDUCATION** Brigham Young Univ, BA, 58; Am Univ, MA, 61; Univ Mich, Ann Arbor, PhD(ling), 71. **CAREER** Asst prof English ling, State Univ NY Oswego, 64-66; specialist compos, Teachers Col, Columbia Univ, 67-69; dir sect ling & teaching English as foreign lang, Univ Northern Iowa, 71- 73; assoc prof, 73-77, Prof English Ling, Ariz State Univ, 78- **MEMBERSHIPS** Ling Soc Am; MLA; NCTE; Am Dialect Soc; International Society of Humor Studies; Workshop Libr World Humour. **RESEARCH** Componential analysis; language deviation; linguistic humor. **SELECTED PUBLICATIONS** Coauth, English Conversational Practices, Univ Mich, 68; auth, Toward a Semantic Specification of Deep Case, 72, English Adverbials, 72 & The Instrumental Case in English, 73, Mouton, The Hague; Pronunciation Contrasts in English, Regents, 2nd ed, 73; coauth, Semantic Theory: A Linguistic Perspective, 75 & Language Play: A Intro to Linguistics, 78, Newbury House; Humor in 18th and 19th Century British Lieterature, Greenwood, 98; Humor in British Literature from the Middle Ages to the Restoration, Greenwood, 97; Humor in Irish Literature, Greenwood, 96; Humor in 20th Century British Literature, Greenwood, 00; co-auth, Encyclopedia of 20th Century Am Humor, Oryx, 00. **CONTACT ADDRESS** 1884 E Alameda Dr, Tempe, AZ 85282. **EMAIL** don.nilsen@asu.edu

NISETICH, FRANK
PERSONAL Born 05/29/1942, Sacramento, CA, 2 children **DISCIPLINE** CLASSICAL PHILOLOGY **EDUCATION** Univ Calif, Berkeley, BA, 65, MA, 67; Harvard Univ, PhD(-class philol), 73. **CAREER** From instr to asst prof, 71-78, fac growth grant, 77, assoc to prof and chmn Classics, Univ Mass, Boston, 78-, vis asst classics, Yale Univ, 73-74. **HONORS AND AWARDS** Translation Awd, 78; Chancellor's Distinguished Scholar Awd, 81. **MEMBERSHIPS** Am Philol Asn. **RESEARCH** Classical philology; ancient Greek lyric poetry; tragedy; Callimachus. **SELECTED PUBLICATIONS** Auth, Olympian 1.8-11: An Epinician Metaphor, Harvard Studies Class Philol, 75; The Leaves of Triumph and Mortality, Trans Am Philol Asn, 77; Convention and Occasion in Isthm.2, Calif Studies in Class Antiquity, 77; Pindar's Victory Songs, Johns Hopkins Univ, 80; Immortality in Heragas, Class Philol, 88; Euripides, Orestes, Oxford Univ, 95. **CONTACT ADDRESS** Dept of Classics, Univ of Massachusetts, Boston, 100 Morrissey Blvd, Boston, MA 02125-3300. **EMAIL** Nisetich@umbsky.cc.umb.edu

NISHIMURA-JENSEN, JULIE M.
PERSONAL Born 07/26/1965, Berkeley, CA, m, 1993, 1 child **DISCIPLINE** CLASSICS **EDUCATION** Univ Wis, Madison, PhD, 96. **CAREER** Asst prof of Classical Languages, AZ State Univ, 97-. **HONORS AND AWARDS** Col of Liberal Arts and Sciences Undergraduate Teaching Development Grant, ASU, 97-98; fac grant-in-aid of res, ASU, 97. **MEMBERSHIPS** Am Philol Asn; Classical Asn of the Middle West and South; Women's Classical Caucus. **RESEARCH** Hellenistic poetry; genre studies. **SELECTED PUBLICATIONS** Auth, The Poetics of Aethalides: Silence and Poikilia in Apollonius' Argonautica, Classical Quart, 98. **CONTACT ADDRESS** Dept of Classics, Univ of Pennsylvania, 3451 Walnut, Philadelphia, PA 19104. **EMAIL** julienj@sas.upenn.edu

NITSCHE, RICHARD
PERSONAL Born 09/28/1939, Cleveland, OH, d, 1 child **DISCIPLINE** ENGLISH, ENGLISH AS A SECOND LANGUAGE, CHINESE **EDUCATION** Oh State Univ, BA, 66; PhD, 77; Nat Taiwan Univ, MA. **CAREER** Instr, Youngstown State Univ, 69-75; asst prof, prog dir, Monterey Inst Intl Stud, 77-80; lectr, Tianjin Univ, China, 80-81; instr, Monterey Peninsula Univ, 81-. **HONORS AND AWARDS** Rockefeller Gnt; Geraldine R Dodge Found Gnt; Fulbright Gnt. **MEMBERSHIPS** CLTA; CFLP. **SELECTED PUBLICATIONS** Auth, Situational Exercises in Cross-Cultural Awareness, Chas Merrill Pub (77); auth, Becoming Fluent in English, Kendall/Hunt pub, (73). **CONTACT ADDRESS** Dept Humanities, Monterey Peninsula Col, 980 Fremont St, Monterey, CA 93940. **EMAIL** rnitsche@hotmail.com

NNAEMEKA, OBIOMA G.
PERSONAL Born Agulu, Nigeria, d, 2 children **DISCIPLINE** FRENCH **EDUCATION** Univ Dakar, Diplome d'etudes francaises, 71; Univ Nigeria, BA, 72; Univ Minn, MA, 77, PhD, 89. **CAREER** Jr. Res Fel, 72-74, Lectr, Univ Nigeria, 82-88; Asst Prof, Concordia Col, 88-89; Asst Prof, Univ Minn, 90-91; Asst Prof, Metro State Univ, 91; Asst Prof, Col Wooster, 89-91; Assoc Prof, Ind Univ, 91-. **HONORS AND AWARDS** Queen's Merit Awd, Queen's Sch, 65; Bus & Professional Women's Asn Schol, 63-65; East Central State (Nigeria) Govt Schol, 66-67, 70-72; Fr Govt Schol, 70-72; Jr. Res Fel, Univ Nigeria, 72-78; Fed Govt Nigeria Schol, 74-80; Colonial Dames Fel, 79-80, 80-81; Altrusa Found Fel, 80-81; Business and Professional Women's Asn Merit Awd, 86; Edith Kreeger Wolf Distinguished Vis Prof, Northwestern Univ, 92; Rockefeller Humanist-in-Residence, Ctr Advanced Feminist Studies, Univ Minn, 91-92; Nigerian Achiever of the Year in Leadership Awd, Network Africa, 94; Teaching Excellence Recognition Awd, Ind Univ, 97; Fac Achievement Awd, Ind Univ, 97; Black Schol in Residence, Col Wooster, 98; Outstanding Fac Awd, Ind Univ, 98; recipient of numerous grants. **MEMBERSHIPS** African Lit Asn; African Studies Asn; Am Asn Teachers Fr; Am Asn Univ Women; Ind For Lang Teachers Asn; Asn of African Women's Studies. **SELECTED PUBLICATIONS** Auth, Black Women Writers, Women's Studies Quart, 97; Development, Cultural Forces, and Women's Achievement in Africa, Law & Pol, 97; Fighting on All Fronts: Gendered Spaces, Ethnic Boundaries, and the Nigerian Civil War, Dialectical Anthropol 22, 97; ed, The Politics of (M)Othering: Womanhood, Identity, and Resistance in African Literature, Routledge, 97; Sisterhood, Feminisms, and Power: From Africa to the Diaspora, African World Press, 98; author of numerous other publications. **CONTACT ADDRESS** Indiana Univ-Purdue Univ, Indianapolis, Indianapolis, IN 46202. **EMAIL** nnaemeka@iupui.edu

NOAKES, SUSAN
DISCIPLINE THE MEDIEVAL AND RENAISSANCE PERIODS IN FRENCH AND ITALIAN **EDUCATION** Yale Univ, PhD. **CAREER** Instr, Univ Minn, Twin Cities. **RESEARCH** Economics and gender in the Decameron. **SELECTED PUBLICATIONS** Auth, Timely Reading: Between Exegesis and Interpretaion, Cornell, 88; coed, Tommaseo Schifaldo, De indagationibus grammaticis, Humanistica Lovaniensia, 82; The Comparative Perspective on Literature, Cornell, 88. **CONTACT ADDRESS** Univ of Minnesota, Twin Cities, 9 Pleasant St. SE, 260 Folwell Hall, Minneapolis, MN 55455.

NOEGEL, SCOTT B.
PERSONAL Born 05/29/1962, Richfield, WI, m, 1995 **DISCIPLINE** NEAR EASTERN LANGUAGES, RELIGION **EDUCATION** Univ of Wisc, BA, 89; Cornell Univ, MA, 93; PhD, 95. **CAREER** Lectr, Cornell Univ, 93-94; lectr, Ithaca Col, 94; consult, Discovery Channel-CD ROM, 94-95; vis summer lectr, Univ Wash, 96; vis asst prof, Rice Univ, 96-97; High Sch Instr, Jewish Fed of Greater Seattle, 97-98; act asst prof, Univ Wash, 97-98; consult, Hist Channel, 99; consult, SMiles Productions, 00; asst prof, Univ Wash, 98- . **HONORS AND AWARDS** NY State Council on the Arts Technical Asst Grant, 95; Electronic Media and Film Program Grant, 95-96; Hazel Cole Fel in Jewish Studies at the Univ WA, 95-96; NY State Council on the Arts Technical Asst Grant, 96-97; Rockefeller Found Natl Fil/Video/Multimedia Fel Nominee for Interactive/Digital Work, 97-98; Natl Endowment for the Arts, 98-99. **MEMBERSHIPS** Am Acad of Religion; Amr Oriental Soc; Am Schs of Oriental Research; Asn for Jewish Studies; Phi Beta Kappa; Phi Kappa Phi; Soc of Biblical Lit. **RESEARCH** Hebrew Bible; Assyriology, Egyptology languages, literatures, history, culture, archaeology and linguistics. **SELECTED PUBLICATIONS** Auth, "The Aegean Ogygos of Boeotia and the Biblical Og of Bashan: Reflections of the Same Myth," Zeitschrift fur die alttestamentlich Wissenschaft 110 (98), 411-426; auth, "A Crux and a Taunt: Night-Time Then Sunset in Genesis 15," The World of Genesis: Persons, Places, Perspectives, ed, Philip R. Davies and David J. A. Clines (Sheffield: Sheffield Acad Pr, 98): 128-135; auth, "The Book of Genesis," in Reader's Guide of Judaism (Fitzroy Dearborn Pub), in press; auth, "Babylonia," in Reader's Guide of Judaism (Fitzroy Dearborn Pub), in press; auth, "Ancient Near East," in Reader's Guide of Judaism (Fitzroy Dearborn Pub), in press; auth, Hermeneutics," in Reader's Guide of Judaism (Fitzroy Dearborn Pub), in press; auth, "Canaanites," in Reader's Guide of Judaism (Fitzroy Dearborn Pub), in press; auth, "Song of Songs," in Reader's Guide of Judaism (Fitzroy Dearborn Pub), in press; auth, Drinking Feasts and Deceptive Feats: Jacob and Laban's Double Talk," in Puns and Pundits: Wordplay in the Hebrew Bible and Ancient Near Eastern Literature, ed Scott B. Noegel (Bethesda, MD: CDL Pr, 00), 163-179; auth, "New Observations on Scribal Activity in the Ancient Near East," in Voice, Text and Hypertext at the Millennium, ed, Rona Modiano (Seattle, WA: Univ Wash Pr), in press. **CONTACT ADDRESS** Dept of Near East Langs & Civilizations, Univ of Washington, Box 353120, Seattle, WA 98195-3120. **EMAIL** snoegel@u.washington.edu

NOEL, ROGER A.
PERSONAL Born 11/22/1942, Belgium, m, 1969, 2 children **DISCIPLINE** FRENCH **EDUCATION** Liege, Belgium License, 65; Univ of Mo, MA, 66; Wash Univ, PhD, 84. **CAREER** Lectr, UMSL, 70-86; Monmouth col, 86-92; Ga Col and State Unv, 92-. **HONORS AND AWARDS** Palmes Academiques, 94. **MEMBERSHIPS** AAUP; MLA; AATF; AATG; AATSP; Arthurian Soc; Alliance Francaise. **RESEARCH** Medieval Literature (French), Translation. **SELECTED PUBLICATIONS** Auth, Joufroi de Poitiers: Traduction critique, Peter Lang (NY), 87; coauth, An Introduction to An Academic Vocabulary, UPA (Lanham), 89; coauth, A Thesaurus of Word Roots of the English Language, UPA (Lanham), 92; coauth, A Thesaurus of Medical Word Roots, Imprimis (Occoquan, VA), 96; coauth, Discover It!, Imprimis, (Occoquan, VA), 96; coed, The Independence of the Baltic States: Origins, Causes, and Consequences, Lithuanian Res and Studies Center, (Chicago), 96. **CONTACT ADDRESS** Dept Foreign Lang, Ga Col and State Univ, PO Box 46, Milledgeville, GA 31061-0490. **EMAIL** moel@mail.gcsu.edu

NOGUEIRA, CLAUDIA B.
PERSONAL Born 11/18/1972, Sao Paulo, Brazil **DISCIPLINE** COMPARATIVE LITERATURE **EDUCATION** Univ Calif Berkeley, BA, 94; Ariz State Univ, MFA, 98. **CAREER** TA, res asst, Ariz State Univ, 95-98, TA, Univ Md College Park, 98-. **HONORS AND AWARDS** Ina Coolbrith Mem Prize for Poetry, 2nd Place, 93; Elizabeth Mills Crothers Prize for Short Fiction 4th Prize, 94; Award of Merit in Am Poets Competition, 94; Frederick County Rep, ARTSCAPE, 95; Fel, Ariz State Univ, 95-98; Fel, Univ Md College Park, 98-00. **MEMBERSHIPS** MLA, Caribbean Studies Asn, Int Womens Writing Guild. **RESEARCH** Literature and film of the Americas, particularly road films and travel narratives, Creative Writing - Fiction and Poetry. **SELECTED PUBLICATIONS** Auth, "The Mule Without a Head," Berkeley Fiction Rev, (93); auth, "The Family Dinner," Berkeley Poetry Rev, (93); auth, "Frederick, Maryland," Poetic Voices of Am, (95); auth, Iole," Maverick Pr, (97); auth, "Marcia," Spout, (97); auth, "Maria de Jesus," Colo Rev, (00), The Year's Best Fantasy and Horror: 14th Annual Collection (St Martins Pr, 01); auth, "Vanishing Points: Roads and National Identitites in Modern Brazilian Film," Southern Quarterly, (01); auth, "Sonia Sanchez Headnote" and "Sapphire Headnote," New Bones: Contemporary Black Writers in America (Prentice Hall, 01). **CONTACT ADDRESS** Comp Lit Prog, Univ of Maryland, Col Park, 2107 Susquehanna Hall, College Park, MD 20742-8825. **EMAIL** cbnoguei@wam.umd.edu

NOLAND, CARRIE J.
DISCIPLINE FRENCH LANGUAGE **EDUCATION** Harvard Univ, PhD. **CAREER** Assoc Prof, Fr, Univ Calif, Irvine. **MEMBERSHIPS** MLA. **RESEARCH** Experimental poetry. **SELECTED PUBLICATIONS** Auth, The Poetics of Motherhood: Yves Bonnefoy and Julia Kristeva; "What's in a Name? Yves Bonnefoy and the Creation of Douve"; "Allegories of Temporality: Philippe Jaccottet, Francis Ponge and the Poetics of the Notebook;" auth, Poetry at Stake: Lyric Aesthetics and the Challenge of Technology, Princeton UP, 99; auth, "The Metaphysics of Coffee," Modernism/Modernity; auth, "Seule vue d'aurore: Andreno et Rimbaud," in Live Rimbaud: Appoaches critiques; auth, "High Decoration: Blaise Cendrars, Sonia Delanay, and the Poem as Fashion Design," Journal X; auth, "The Performance of Solitude: Bandelaire, Rimbaud, and the Resistance Poetry of Rene Char," (The French Review); auth, "Poetry at Stake: Blaise Cendrars, Cultural Studies, and the Fu-

ture of Poetry in the Literature Classroom," (PMLA); AUTH, "Rimbaudand Patti Smith: Syle as Social Deviance," (Critical Inquiry). **CONTACT ADDRESS** Dept of Fr and Ital, Univ of California, Irvine, Irvine, CA 92697. **EMAIL** cjnoland@uci.edu

NOLLENDORFS, VALTERS
PERSONAL Born 03/22/1931, Riga, Latvia, m, 1955, 6 children **DISCIPLINE** GERMAN & LATVIAN LITERATURE **EDUCATION** Univ Nebr, BSc in Ed, 54, MA, 55; Univ Mich, PhD, 62. **CAREER** Teaching asst, Univ Nebr, 54-55; instr Ger, Univ Mich 59- 61; from instr to assoc prof, 61-74, Prof Ger, Univ Wis, Madison, 74-, Chmn Dept, 75-, Ed, Monatshefte, 72-; mem exec bd, Asn Advan Baltic Studies, 74, pres, 76-78; mem exec comt, div 18th & early 19th century Ger Lit, MLA. **MEMBERSHIPS** MLA; Am Asn Teachers Ger; Asn Advan Baltic Studies. **RESEARCH** Age of Goethe; Goethe's Faust; contemporary Latvian literature. **SELECTED PUBLICATIONS** Auth, Der Steit um den Urfaust, Mouton, The Hague, 67; The rite of life: A theme and its variations in the poetry of Soviet Latvia, Mosaic, 73; Time and experience in Goethe's Trilogie der Leidenschaft, In: Husbanding the Golden Grain, Studies in Honor of Henry Nordmeyer, Ann Arbor, 73; The demythologization of Latvian literature, Books Abroad, 73; Partial rhyme in contemporary Latvian poetry, Baltic Lit & Ling, 73; The voices of one calling: The mastering of the Latvian legacy in Bels and Rungis, J Baltic Studies, 75; co-ed, Ger Studies in the United States: Assessment and Outlook, Univ Wis, 76; auth, Latvian literature, In: Reader's Adviser, Bowker, 77; for Poems Are Forever Spirals Without End - a Meditative Letter to Ivask,ivar 1927-1992 on His Baltic-elegies, J of Baltic Studies, Vol 0026, 1995. **CONTACT ADDRESS** Dept of Ger, Univ of Wisconsin, Madison, Madison, WI 53706.

NORAT, GISELA
PERSONAL Born Havana, Cuba, m, 1994, 1 child **DISCIPLINE** SPANISH **EDUCATION** St Peter's Col, BS, 80; Montclair State Univ, BA, 84; NY Univ, MA, 86; Washington Univ, PhD, 91. **CAREER** Asst prof, Hobart and William Smith Col, 91-93; assoc prof, Agnes Scott Col, 930. **HONORS AND AWARDS** Fel, Washington Univ, 91. **MEMBERSHIPS** MLA, Asociacion de Literatura Femenina Hispanica. **RESEARCH** Latin American Women Writers, US Latina/o Writers. **SELECTED PUBLICATIONS** Auth, ""Dialogo fraternal: El cuarto mundo de Diamela Eltit y Cristobal Nonato de Carlos Fuentes," Chasqui, (91); auth, "Writing the Female body in Marta Traba's Conversacion al sur," Romance Lang Annual VIII, (94); auth, Marginalities: Diamela Eltit and the Subversion of Mainstream Literature in Chile, Del Univ Pr, 95; auth, Violence, Silence and Anger: Women's Writing as Transgression, Univ Va Pr, 95; auth, "Textual/Sexual Inscription of Lesbian Identity in Sylvia Molloy's en breve carcel," Monographic Rev, (97); auth, Proyecciones sobre la novela: Latinoamerica y Espana, Ediciones del Norte, 97. **CONTACT ADDRESS** Agnes Scott Col, 141 E College Ave, Decatur, GA 30030. **EMAIL** gnorat@agnesscott.edu

NORDLING, JOHN G.
PERSONAL Born 03/17/1957, Portland, OR, m, 1985 **DISCIPLINE** CLASSICS AND LATIN LITERATURE **EDUCATION** Concordia Col, AA, 77; Valparaiso, BA, 80; Concordia Sem, M.Div, 85; Washington Univ, MA, 85; Univ of Wis-Madison, Ph.D, 91. **CAREER** Asst prof, dept foreign lang & lit, Valparaiso Univ, 94-. **MEMBERSHIPS** Amer Philol Asn; Soc of Bibl Lit; Archaeol Inst of Amer. **RESEARCH** Ancient epistelography; Paul - life and theology; Ancient slavery. **SELECTED PUBLICATIONS** Auth, "Onesimus Fugitivus: a Defense of the Runaway Slave Hypothesis in Philemon" Journal for the Study of the New Testament 41 (91): 97-119; auth, "The Ph.D. in the Parish", Logia 4 (950: 88-91; auth, "The Pastoral Office is Not an Option", Journal of English District Pastors 8 (96): 4-7; auth, New Testament Backgrounds, ed, C.E. Evans and S.E. Porter, Sheffield (97): 263-283; "Valparaiso Goes to Rome," Cresset 61 (97): 15-19; auth, "Christ Leavens Culture: St. Paul on Slavery," Concordia Journal 24 (98): 43-52; auth, "The Prayer that Jesus Gave," For the Life of the World 3 (99): 6-7; auth, "Christians in Context: The Four 'House Church' Passages," Spade and Stole: Festschrift in Honor of Professor Horace Hummel (forthcoming). **CONTACT ADDRESS** Dept of Classics, Baylor Univ, Waco, 303 Old Main, PO Box 97352, Waco, TX 76798. **EMAIL** john_nordling@baylor.edu

NORMAN, G. BUFORD
PERSONAL Born 07/26/1945, Columbus, MS, m, 1996, 1 child **DISCIPLINE** FRENCH LITERATURE & LANGUAGE **EDUCATION** Davidson Col, AB, 67; Yale Univ, PhD, 71. **CAREER** Fac, Iowa State Univ, 71-80; from asst prof to prof, Univ SC, 80-; chemn, Univ SC, 90-93. **HONORS AND AWARDS** NEH Fel for Univ Teachers, 94; Chevalier dams l'Ordre des Palmes Academiques. **MEMBERSHIPS** MLA, Am Asn of Teachers of French, Ctr Int de Recontres sur le XVIIe Siecle. **RESEARCH** Seventeenth-century French Literature & Opera, Quinault, Racine. **SELECTED PUBLICATIONS** Coauth, Quinault, Phillipe. Alceste, suivi de La Querelle d'Alceste: anciens et modernes avant 1680, Droz (Geneva), 94; auth, "Les Folles conventions: le langage musical dans les dernieres comedies-ballets de Moliere," Litteratures Classiques 21 (94): 91-101; auth, "The Best Way to Skin a Cat: Thought and Expression, Words and Music in Quinault and Lully," L'esprit en France au XVIIe siecle," Biblio 17.101 (97): 239-247; auth, "Remaking a Cultural Icon: Phedre and the Operatic Stage," Cambridge Opera J 10.3 (98): 225-245; auth, Quinault, Phillipe. Livrets d'opera. Edition critique, Litteratures Classiques (Toulouse), 99. **CONTACT ADDRESS** Dpet French & Classics, Univ of So Carolina, Columbia, Columbia, SC 29208. **EMAIL** norman-buford@sc.edu

NORMAND, GUESSLER
PERSONAL Born 02/24/1937, 2 children **DISCIPLINE** FRENCH LITERATURE **EDUCATION** Univ Aix-Marseille, dipl Fr, 63; Univ Ky, MA, 67, PhD(French), 70. **CAREER** Instr French, Southern Univ, 61-62 & 63-64, Univ Akron, 68-70; Asst Prof French, Univ Toledo, 70-, Fac res fel, Univ Toldeo, summer, 79. **MEMBERSHIPS** Am Asn Teachers Fr; AAUP; Am Coun Teaching Foreign Lang. **RESEARCH** Twentieth century French literature; the literature of commitment. **SELECTED PUBLICATIONS** Henri Barbusse and his Monde (1928-1935): Progeny of the Clarte Movement and the Rev Clarte, J Contemp Hist, 7/76; Henri Barbusse and his Monde (1928-1935): Precursors to the Litterature Engagee Movement, Ky Romance Quart, Vol XXIV, No 4, 449-460; Meeting individual needs in the college foreign language classroom, Foreign Lang Ann, 2/79; Toward better articulation between high school and college foreign language teachers, ADFL Bull, 3/80; Motivating with media: The use of video in the foreign language classroom, Can Mod Lang Rev, 10/80. **CONTACT ADDRESS** 2801 W Bancroft St, Toledo, OH 43606-3390.

NORTON, GLYN P.
DISCIPLINE FRENCH, ITALIAN **EDUCATION** Univ Mich, AB, 63; AM, 65; PhD, 68. **CAREER** Willcox B. & Harriet M. Adsit prof, Williams Col, 88-; asst prof, Dartmouth Col, 68-71; prof, Pa State Univ, 71-88; dir, Ctr For Lang(s), Lit(s) & Cult(s), Williams Col, 90-92. **HONORS AND AWARDS** Sr fel, NEH, 73-74; La Medaille de Melun, Fr, 85; The Pa State Univ Scholar Medal for Outstanding Achievement in the Arts and Humanities, 86; Guggenheim fel, Paris, 86-87; Distinguished PhD Recipient, Hon by Rackham Sch of Grad Stud, Univ Mich, 88. **RESEARCH** French and Italian literature and criticism of the renaissance; the theory and practice of translation. **SELECTED PUBLICATIONS** Auth, Montaigne and the Introspective Mind, 75; The Ideology and Language of Translation in Renaissance France and their Humanist Antecedents, 84; Literary Translation in the Continuum of Renaissance Thought: A Conceptual Overview, Die literarische ubersetzung: Stand u Perspektiven ihrer Erforschung, 88; Du Bellay and the Emblematics of Regret, Writing the Renaissance: Essays on Fr Renaissance Lit Presented to Floyd Gray, 92; Image and Introspective Imagination in Montaigne's Essais, Collections of Criticism on Montaigne, 95; auth, The Cambridge History of Literary, Criticism, Volume III, The Renaissance, 99. **CONTACT ADDRESS** Center for Foreign Languages, Literatures and Cult, Williams Col, Williamstown, MA 01267. **EMAIL** glyn.p.norton@williams.edu

NORTON, ROBERT E.
DISCIPLINE GERMAN, RUSSIAN **EDUCATION** Univ Calif, Santa Barbara, BA, 82; Princeton Univ, MA, 85, PhD, 88. **CAREER** Vis asst prof, Mount Holyoke Col, 88-89; asst prof, 89-93, assoc prof, 93-97, prof, 97-98, Vassar Col; PROF, UNIV NOTRE DAME, 98. **CONTACT ADDRESS** Dept of German & Russian, Univ of Notre Dame, Notre Dame, IN 46556. **EMAIL** norton.15@nd.edu

NOSTRAND, HOWARD LEE
PERSONAL Born 11/16/1910, New York, NY, m, 1987, 3 children **DISCIPLINE** FRENCH CULTURE **EDUCATION** Amherst Col, AB, 32; Harvard Univ, AM, 33; Univ Paris, D Univ, 34. **CAREER** Instr, Univ Buffalo, 34-36 & US Naval Acad, 36-38; asst prof French, Brown Univ, 38-39; chmn dept, 39-64, prof, 39-80, Emer Prof Romance Lang, Univ Wash, 80-, Romance ed, Mod Lang Quart, 40-45; cult relat attache, US Embassy, Peru, 44-47; El sol del Peru, 47; Guggenheim fel, 53-54; mem adv comt, New Media Prog, US Off Educ, 58-61; dir NDEA Inst Lang Teachers, Univ Wash, 59-60, proj, dir, res in culturography, 62-63; mem Nat Comn Teacher Educ & Prof Standards, Nat Educ Asn, 63-67, chmn, 66-67; mem ERIC adv Bd, MLA, 66-71; Nat comn Ethnography, Am Asn Teachers French, 74-; vis prof Col France, 75; Stepladder prog, Am Coun Teaching Foreign Lang, 81-; vis prof, Simon Fraser Univ, 82. **HONORS AND AWARDS** Palmes Academiques, 50; Chevalier, Legion d'honneur, 62; Officier, 94, Leadership Award, Northeast Conf Teaching Foreign Lang, 78; Northeast Conf Award, 78; Officier dans l'Ordre des Arts et des Letters, 79. **MEMBERSHIPS** Am Asn Teachers Fr(vp, 56-58, pres, 60-62); MLA. **RESEARCH** Modern French literature; history of ideas; description of literate cultures; development of cross-cultural competence. **SELECTED PUBLICATIONS** Auth, Ortega y Gasset's Mission of the University, Princeton Univ; The Cultural Attache, The Hazen Found; coauth, Research on Language Teaching: An Annotated International Bibliography for 1945-64, 65; Background Data for Teaching French, 67; Honored by Festschrift, Essays on the Teaching of Culture, Advancement Press, Am, 74; coauth, Arguing Cross-Cultural Competence, 86. **CONTACT ADDRESS** Dept of Romance Lang, Univ of Washington, GN-60, Seattle, WA 98195. **EMAIL** nostrand@u.washington.edu

NUESSEL, FRANK
PERSONAL Born 01/22/1943, Evergreen Park, IL, d, 1968 **DISCIPLINE** HISPANIC LINGUISTICS **EDUCATION** Ind Univ at Bloomington, BA, 65; Mich State Univ, MA, 67; Univ of Ill at Urbana-Champaign, PhD, 73. **CAREER** Instr, N Ill Univ, 67-70; asst prof, Ind State Univ at Terre haute, 73-75; prof, Univ of Louisville, 75-. **HONORS AND AWARDS** Oppenheimer Fel, 85-86; Awd for Distinguished Res, Univ of Louisville, 97. **MEMBERSHIPS** Am Asn of Teachers of Span & Port, Am Asn of Teachers of Ital, Gerontological Soc of Am. **RESEARCH** Hispanic Linguistics, Italian Studies, Gerontology, Esperantic Studies, Semiotics, Applied Linguistics. **SELECTED PUBLICATIONS** Coauth, The Imaginative Basis of Thought and Culture: Contemporary Perspectives on Giambattista Vico, Canadian Scholars' Press, (Toronto Canada), 94; auth, The Esperanto Language, LEGAS Press (Ottawa), 00. **CONTACT ADDRESS** Dept Modern & Classical Lang, Univ of Louisville, 2301 S 3rd St, Louisville, KY 40292-0001. **EMAIL** fhnues01@athena.louisville.edu

NUNEZ-BETELU, MAITE
PERSONAL Born 11/08/1967, Donostia **DISCIPLINE** PENINSULAR LITERATURE **EDUCATION** Univ del Pais Vasco, BA, 91; W Va Univ, MA, 95; Univ Mo Columbia, PhD, 01. **CAREER** TA, W Va Univ, 93-95; TA, Univ Mo, 95-01. **MEMBERSHIPS** MLA. **RESEARCH** Basque Women Writers, Basque Literature, Women Studies, Children's Literature, Peninsular Cultural Studies. **SELECTED PUBLICATIONS** Coauth, "Catalan Speaking Regions," The Current State of Research in fifteenth-Century Literature: Germania-Romania, II, ed, DuBruck and McDonald, (96); auth, "In honor of Basque Women," ed Linda White, Univ Nev Pr, (forthcoming). **CONTACT ADDRESS** Dept For Lang, Univ of Missouri, St. Louis, 8801 Natural Bridge Rd, Clark Hall 554, Saint Louis, MO 63121. **EMAIL** pilarrika@yahoo.com

NUNNALLY, THOMAS E.
PERSONAL Born 06/10/1950, Tuscaloosa, AL, m, 1972, 2 children **DISCIPLINE** ENGLISH, LINGUISTICS **EDUCATION** Univ Ala, BA, 72; Univ Georgia, MA, 74; PhD, 85. **CAREER** Instr, asst prof, assoc prof, Auburn Univ, 84-. **HONORS AND AWARDS** Fulbright Lectr, Res, 88, 01-02; NEH, 95; Phi Kappa Phi, Nat Hon Soc. **MEMBERSHIPS** ADS; DSNA; LSA; LSN; SAMLA; SCL. **RESEARCH** Linguistics change in English grammar and lexis; development of world Englishes; language uses attitudes; linguistic studies of literature. **SELECTED PUBLICATIONS** Co-ed, From the Gulf States and Beyond: The Legacy of Lee Pedersen and LAGS, Univ Ala Press, 98; auth, co-ed, Language Variety in the South Revisited, Univ Ala Press, 97; auth, "Glossing the Folk: A Review of Selected Lexical Research into American Slang and Americanisms," Am Speech 66 (01); auth, "Word Up, Word Down: The Social Vicissitudes of 'Blop' and 'Bleeper,''' Nat Forum 75 (95): 36-39; auth, "Man's Son/Son of Man: Translation, Textual Conditioning, and the History of the English Genitive," in History of Englishes: New Methods and Interpretations in Historical Linguistics, ed. Matti Rissanen, Ossi Ihalainen, Terttu Nevalainen, Irma Taavitsainen (Berlin and NY: de Gruyter, 92): 359-72; auth, "The Possessive with Gerunds: What the Handbooks Say and What They Should Say," Am Speech 66 (91): 359-370; auth, "Morphology and Word Order Within the Old English Noun-Phrase: Grammatical Efficiency," Neuphilol Mitteil 92 (91): 421-431; auth, "An Evaluative Taxonomy of Diachronic Corpora," SECOL Rev 15 (91): 21-36. **CONTACT ADDRESS** Eng Dept, Auburn Univ, Auburn, AL 36849-0002. **EMAIL** nunnath@auburn.edu

NUSSBAUM, ALAN
PERSONAL Born 12/17/1947, New York, NY, m, 1987, 3 children **DISCIPLINE** LINGUISTICS **EDUCATION** Wash Sq Col of NYork Univ, BA, 69; Oxford Univ, diploma, 74; Harvard Univ, PhD, 76. **CAREER** Instr, 75-85, asst prof, 76, assoc prof, 81, Yale Univ; prof/assoc prof, Cornell Univ, 85-. **MEMBERSHIPS** Amer Philological Assoc (APA) **RESEARCH** Indo-European linguistics, Greek and Latin historical grammar **SELECTED PUBLICATIONS** Auth, Head and Horn in Indo-European, 86; coauth, Black Athena Revisited, Word Games: The linguistic evidence in Black Athena, Chapel Hill, 96; auth, Sound Law and Analogy: Papers in honor of R.S.P. Beekes, The Saussure Effect in Latin and Italic, Amsterdam-Atlanta, 97; Mir Curad: Studies in honor of Calvert Watkins, Severe Problems, Innsbruck, 98. **CONTACT ADDRESS** Classics Dept, Cornell Univ, 120 Goldwin Smith Hall, Ithaca, NY 14853-3201. **EMAIL** ajn8@cornell.edu

NYE, JEAN C.
PERSONAL Born 03/16/1932, New Sewickley Twp, PA, m, 1955 **DISCIPLINE** SPANISH **EDUCATION** Geneva Col, BA, 53; Univ Pittsburgh, MLitt, 57; Univ Toledo, PhD, 72. **CAREER** Teacher English & French, Zelienople High Sch, 53-59; from asst prof to assoc prof, 59-72, prof Span & French, Findlay Col, 72-, Spanish transl, Centrex Corp; mem bd dirs, Cent

States Conf Teaching Foreign Lang; asst vpres Instit Advancement. **MEMBERSHIPS** Teachers English to Speakers Other Lang; MLA; Am Asn Teachers Span & Port; founder Int Cen for Lang & Resource Development. **RESEARCH** Teaching of English in the junior high schools in Puerto Rico; billingual, bicultural education. **SELECTED PUBLICATIONS** Auth, Christmas as portrayed in Spanish art, 12/66 & Easter as protrayed in Spanish art, 3/70, Church Advocate. **CONTACT ADDRESS** Dept of Mod Lang, Univ of Findlay, 1000 N Main St, Findlay, OH 45840-3695. **EMAIL** nye@lucy.findlay.edu

O

O'CONELL, ROBERT J.
DISCIPLINE CLASSICS **EDUCATION** Sorbonne, PhD. **CAREER** Prof emer, Fordham Univ. **SELECTED PUBLICATIONS** Auth, Augustine's Early Theory of Man, 68; St Augustine's Confessions: The Odyssey of Soul, 69; Soundings in St Augustine's Imagination, 94. **CONTACT ADDRESS** Dept of Class Lang and Lit, Fordham Univ, 113 W 60th St, New York, NY 10023.

O'CONNELL, JOANNA
DISCIPLINE SPANISH AND PORTUGUESE LITERATURE **EDUCATION** Univ Calif Berkeley, BA, 79; MA, 82; PhD, 88. **RESEARCH** Latin American literature and culture; feminism and feminist theory; issues of colonialism, race, and nationalism; indigenous revitalization movements and writing; African and Caribbean writing in French and English. **SELECTED PUBLICATIONS** Auth, Prospero's Daughter: The Prose of Rosario Castellanos, Univ Tex, 95; Pre-Columbian Literatures in Mexico, Manual Mex Lit, 94; co-ed, Post-Colonial, Emergent, and Indigenous Feministms, J Women Cult Soc, 95. **CONTACT ADDRESS** Spanish and Portuguese Dept, Univ of Minnesota, Twin Cities, 34 Folwell Hall, 9 Pleasant St SE, Minneapolis, MN 55455. **EMAIL** oconn001@maroon.tc.umn.edu

O'CONNOR, EUGENE
PERSONAL Born 09/03/1948, Buffalo, NY **DISCIPLINE** CLASSICS **EDUCATION** Univ Cal Santa Barbara, PhD 84. **CAREER** Prometheus Book, editor 89-; Univ Montana, vis asst prof 88-89; The Col of Wooster, vis asst prof 87-88; Univ Cal Irvine, vis lect 85-87; Univ Cal Santa Barbara, vis lectr 84-85. **HONORS AND AWARDS** BA Cum Laude **MEMBERSHIPS** APA **RESEARCH** Greek and Roman satire and epigram; neo latin; gay studies. **SELECTED PUBLICATIONS** Auth, Martial the Moral Jester: Priapic Motifs and the Restoration of Order in the Epigrams, in: Martial, ed, F. Grewing, N. Holzberg, Stuttgart: Franz Syeiner Verlag, 98; Panormita's Reply to His Critics: The Hermaphroditus and the Literary Defense, Renaissance Quart, 97; Hell's Pit and Heaven's Rose: The Typology of Female Sights and Smells in Panormita's Hermaphroditus, Medievalia et Humanistica, 96; The Essential Epicurus: Letters, Principal Doctrines, Vatican Sayings and Fragments, translated with an introduction by Eugene O'Connor, Amherst NY, Prometheus Books, 93. **CONTACT ADDRESS** Prometheus Books, Apt B30, Buffalo, NY 14201. **EMAIL** pontano@aol.com

O'CONNOR, PATRICIA W.
PERSONAL Born 04/26/1931, Memphis, TN, m, 1953, 2 children **DISCIPLINE** SPANISH **EDUCATION** Univ Fla, BAE, 53; MA, 54; PhD, 62. **CAREER** From Instr to Prof Span, 62-96, Charles Phelps Taft Prof Span Lang & Lit, Univ Cincinnati, 96-. **HONORS AND AWARDS** Taft res grant, Spain, 65, 72, 75, 79 & 81; Rieveschl Awd for creative & scholarly works, 82; Correspondiente of the Royal Span Acad of Lang, 90; Distinguished Res Prof of the Year, 90; Alumna of Achievement, Univ Fla, 97. **MEMBERSHIPS** Am Asn Teachers Span & Port; MLA; Midwest Mod Lang Asn; AAUP. **RESEARCH** Contemporary Spanish theater; post-war Spanish novel; sexism in literature. **SELECTED PUBLICATIONS** Auth, Women in the Theater of Gregorio Martinez Sierra, American, 67; Gregorio and Maria Martinez Sierra, Twayne, 77; Contemporary Spanish Theater, Scribner's, 80; transl & ed, Plays of Protest from the Franco Era, Madrid, 81; auth, Contemporary Spanish Theater: The Social Comedies, Madrid, SGEL, 83; Dramturgas espanolas de hoy: una introducci-n, Madrid, Fundamentos, 89; Plays of the New Dramatic Spain (1975-1990), Univ Press Am, 92; Julia Maura: Lark in a Hostile Garden, In: Studies in Honor at Geogina Sabat-Rivers, Madrid, Castalia, 92; Julia Maura, In: Spanish Women Writers, Greenwood Press, 93; Antonio Buero Vallejo en sus espejos, Fundamentos, 96; Piezas Breves de mujeres sobre mujeres/Short Spanish Plays By Women About Women (Bilingual ed), Madrid, Fundamentos, 98; author of numerous journal articles. **CONTACT ADDRESS** Dept of Romance Lang & Lit, Univ of Cincinnati, PO Box 210377, Cincinnati, OH 45221-0377. **EMAIL** pat.oconnor@uc.edu

O'CONNOR, THOMAS
PERSONAL Born 08/19/1943, New York, NY, m, 1969, 2 children **DISCIPLINE** SPANISH LANGUAGE AND LITERATURE **EDUCATION** SUNY Albany, PhD. **CAREER** Prof, SUNY Binghamton. **MEMBERSHIPS** AIH, AATSP, Comediates, Cervantes Soc, of Amer, AITENSO **RESEARCH** Span lit of the Golden Age, particularly Calderonian theater; myth studies; and the relationship of theatrical discourse to soc practice. **SELECTED PUBLICATIONS** Auth, Myth and Mythology in the Theater of Calderon, 88; auth/ed, El encanto es la hermosura/La segunda Celestina, 94; ed, Spanish Classical Texts, Pegasus; co-ed, Spanish Golden Age Theater, Bilingual, auth, Love in the Corral: Conjugal Spirituality & Anti-Theatrical Polemic in Early Modern Spain, 00; ed, Studies in Spanish Classical Literature. **CONTACT ADDRESS** SUNY, Binghamton, PO Box 6000, Binghamton, NY 13902-6000. **EMAIL** toconnor@binghamton.edu

O'DONNELL, JAMES J.
PERSONAL Born 02/26/1950, Germany **DISCIPLINE** CLASSICAL STUDIES **EDUCATION** Princeton Univ, AB, 72; Yale Univ, PhD, 75. **CAREER** Lectr to prof, classics, Bryn Mawr, 75-76; Catholic Univ, 76-77; Cornell Univ, 77-81; Univ Pa, 81-; vice prov, 96-. **HONORS AND AWARDS** Guggenheim Fel; NEH Fel. **RESEARCH** Late antiquity, esp, Augustine. **SELECTED PUBLICATIONS** Auth, Cassiodorus, Univ Cal Press (Berkeley and LA), 79; auth, Boethius, Consolatio Philosophiae: Text and Commentary, Bryn Mawr Commentaries, 84; auth, Augustine, Twayne Pub (Boston), 85; auth, Augustine, Confessions: Text and Commentary, Clarendon Press (Oxford), 92; co-ed, Scholarly Journals at the Crossroads: A Subversive Proposal for Electronic Publishing, Asn Res Libraries (Washington), 95; auth, Avatars of the Word, Harvard Univ Press (Cambridge, MA), 98. **CONTACT ADDRESS** Dept Classical Studies, Univ of Pennsylvania, 255 S 36th St, Philadelphia, PA 19104-3805. **EMAIL** jod@sas.upenn.edu

O'DONNELL, MABRY MILLER
PERSONAL Born 07/18/1945, Huntsville, AL, m, 1972, 3 children **DISCIPLINE** SPEECH COMMUNICATION, GENDER STUDIES **EDUCATION** La State Univ, BA, 67; Univ Ala, MA, 69; Bowling Green State Univ, PhD(interpersonal and public commun), 77. **CAREER** Instr to assoc prof, 69-88, Prof Speech, Mairetta Col, 88-, Forensics Coach, 69-; dir of forensics, 95-. **HONORS AND AWARDS** Outstanding Fac Awd, 88, 97; Alpha Lambda Delta Fac Awd, 89, 90; Outstanding Fac Mem in Continuing Educ, 91; Harness Fel, 92-95, 99-02; McCoy Prof, 94-98; Speech Commun Asn of Ohio's 1994 Col Teacher of the Year; William R. and Marie Adamson Flescher Prof of Humanities, 95-99; Pi Kappa Delta Coaches Hon Roll, 95, 97; E.R. Nichols Awd, Outstanding Forensics Instr in the Nation, presented by Pi Kappa Delta, 96. **MEMBERSHIPS** Nat Commun Asn; Ohio Acad of Hist; Ohio Forensic Asn; Alpha Epsilon Rho; Alpha Lambda Delta; Delta Gamma; Omicron Delta Kappa; Order of Omega; Phi Alpha Theta; Pi Kappa Delta. **RESEARCH** Frances Wright; forensics; public address. **SELECTED PUBLICATIONS** Auth, Effective Interviewing or How to Get Your Client to Tell You What You Need to Know, Proc of Small Bus Inst Dir Asn, 2/94; Interpersonal Communication, In: Ready for the Real World. **CONTACT ADDRESS** 215 5th St., Marietta, OH 45750-4025. **EMAIL** odonnelm@marietta.edu

O'FLAHERTY, JAMES CARNEAL
PERSONAL Born 04/28/1914, Henrico Co, VA, m, 1936, 1 child **DISCIPLINE** GERMAN **EDUCATION** Georgetown Col, BA, 39; Univ Ky, MA, 41; Univ Chicago, PhD, 50. **CAREER** Instr hist & relig, Georgetown Col, 39-41; from instr to assoc prof, 47-58, chmn dept, 61-69, Prof Ger, Wake Forest Univ, 58-, Am Philos Soc res grant, Ger, 58; Beecher lectr, Amherst Col, 58; Fulbright res fel, Ger, 60-61; lectr Kulterelles Wort Ser, Sudwestfunk, Baden-Baden, Ger, 61; mem adv comt, Fulbright Awards, 62, chmn, 63; lectr, 4th Int Cong Germanists, Princeton Univ, 70; lectr, 1st Int Hamann-Colloquium, Luneburg, Ger, 76. **HONORS AND AWARDS** Friendship Awd, Fed Rep Germany, 83 **MEMBERSHIPS** S Atlantic Mod Lang Asn; Am Asn Teachers Ger; NAm Nietzsche Soc. **RESEARCH** Johann Georg Hamann; Nietzsche; philosophy of language. **SELECTED PUBLICATIONS** Auth, Unity and Language: A Study in the philosophy of Johann Georg Hamann, Univ NC, Chapel Hill, 52, Ams Press, 66; Max Planck and Adolf Hitler, AAUP Bull, 56; Hamann's Socratic Memorabilia, Johns Hopkins Univ, 67; co-auth, Raabe's Else von der Tanne, Univ Ala Press, 72; auth, The Quiarrel of Reason with Itself: Essays on Hamann, Michaelis, Lessing, Camden House, 88; East and West in the thought of Hamann, Ger Rev, 68; Eros and creativity in Nietzsche's Birth of Tragedy, In: Studies in German Literature of the Nineteenth and Twentieth Centuries, Univ NC, 70; The Concept of knowledge in Hamann's Sokratische Denkwurdigkeiten and Nietzsche's Geburt der Gragodie, Monatshefte, 4/72; co-ed & contribr, Studies in Nietzsche and the Classical Tradition, Univ NC, Chapel Hill, 76; auth, Johann Georg Hamann, G K Hall, 79; auth, Werner Heisenberg on the Nazi Revolution: Three Hitherto Unpublished Letters, J Hist Ideas, Oct 92; Johann Georg Hamann, Dictionary of Literary Biography, 90; Encyclopedia of German Literature, 00. **CONTACT ADDRESS** 2164 Faculty Dr, Winston-Salem, NC 27106. **EMAIL** jjcof@netunlimited.net

O'HEARN, CAROLYN
DISCIPLINE ENGLISH LINGUISTICS AND LITERATURE **EDUCATION** Univ Mo, BS; Ariz State Univ, MA, PhD; **CAREER** Assoc prof. **RESEARCH** Medieval literature, technical writing. **SELECTED PUBLICATIONS** Auth, Writing, Grammar and Usage, 89; articles on ling and lit. **CONTACT ADDRESS** Dept of Eng, Pittsburg State Univ, 1701 S Broadway St, Pittsburg, KS 66762. **EMAIL** cohearn@pittstate.edu

O'NEAL, JOHN COFFEE
PERSONAL Born Birmingham, AL, m, 1976, 2 children **DISCIPLINE** FRENCH, LANGUAGE, LITERATURE, CLASSICS **EDUCATION** Wash/Lee Univ, BA, 72; Middlebury Col, MA, 75; Univ Calif Los Angeles, PhD, 80. **CAREER** Saint Mary's Col, 80-84; Hamilton Col, 84-. **HONORS AND AWARDS** Chevalier dans L'Ordre de Palmes Acad, 98; NEH Fel, 89-90. **MEMBERSHIPS** MLA; ASECS; Rousseau Soc; Voltaire Soc. **RESEARCH** Sensibility and sensationalism; literature and philosophy; Rousseau; Condillac. **SELECTED PUBLICATIONS** Auth, Seeing and Observing: Rousseau's Rhetoric of Perception, 85; auth, The Authority of Experience: Sensations and Theory in the French Enlightenment, 96; auth, Changing Minds: The Shifting Perception of Culture in 18th-Century France (forthcoming). **CONTACT ADDRESS** Dept Romance Lang Lit, Hamilton Col, New York, Clinton, NY 13323.

O'NEILL, KERILL
PERSONAL Born 06/30/1965, Dublin, Ireland **DISCIPLINE** CLASSICS **EDUCATION** Trinity Col, BA, 87; Cornell Univ, PhD, 95. **CAREER** Vis asst prof, 94-99; Colby Col. **MEMBERSHIPS** APA; CAMWS. **RESEARCH** Latin love elegy; Greek tragedy, intertextuality. **SELECTED PUBLICATIONS** Auth, "Neolithic Chipped Stone," "Excavations at Halai, 1990-1991," Hesperia 61, 92, 265-289; auth, "Propertius 4.4: Tarpeia and the Burden of Aetiology," Hermathena 158, 95, 53-60; auth, "Propertius 4.5 The Classical Journal 94.1, 98, 49-80; auth, "Aeschylus, Homer, and the Serpent at the Breast;" Phoenix 52, 98, 216-229; auth, "The Shadow of Clytemnestra in Louisa Siefert's Jalousie: Maternity, Sexuality, and a Woman's Poetic Voice," Classical and Modern Literature, 99, 257-277; auth, "Ovid and Propertius: Reflexive Annotation in Amores 1.8," Mnemosyne 99, 286-307; auth, "Second Preliminary Report on Neolithic Chipped Stone Artifacts from Halai," an appendix to John E. Coleman, "Halai, 92-94" Hesperia 68.3, 99; auth, "Slumming with Vertumnus," American Journal of Philology, 00 **CONTACT ADDRESS** Dept of Classics, Colby Col, 4161 Mayflower Hill, Waterville, ME 04901. **EMAIL** knoneill@colby.edu

OATES, MICHAEL DAVID
PERSONAL Born 09/23/1939, Derby, CT, m, 1963, 2 children **DISCIPLINE** FRENCH LINGUISTICS & METHODOLOGY **EDUCATION** Fairfield Univ, AB, 61; Assumption Col, MAT, 63; Georgetown Univ, PhD(French ling), 70. **CAREER** Intern French, Framingham High Sch, Mass, 61-62; teacher, Malden High Sch, 62-65; assoc prof, 67-75, Prof French, Univ Northern Iowa, 75-, Pres, Study Ed Asn Conn, 60-61; honors intern, Assumption Col, 61-62; Univ Northern Iowa study grant, Univ Besancon, 72. **MEMBERSHIPS** Am Coun Teachers Foreign Lang; Am Asn Teachers Fr. **RESEARCH** French linguistics; language teaching research. **SELECTED PUBLICATIONS** Auth, A Syntactic Classification of French Verbs as a Basis for a Monostructural Presentation at the Beginning Level, Current Issues in Teaching French, 4/72; Principles and Techniques for Stimulating Foreign-Language Conversation, Foreign Lang Annals, 1/-72; Grass Roots Efforts to Encourage the Study of French, 4/76 & Commentetre francais, 11/78, AATF Nat Bull; A Non-Intensive FLES Program in French, Fr Rev, 3/80; Oral Translation: An Old Horse for the New Frontier, In: The Report of the 1980 Central States Conference on the Teaching of Foreign Languages, New Frontiers in Foreign Lang Educ, 80; Cooperative Grouping in French Conversation and Composition, In: Proceedings of the Second National Conference on Individualized Instruction in Foreign Languages, Ohio State Univ, 81; Keys to Study Abroad Programs, Alberta Mod Lang J, spring 81. **CONTACT ADDRESS** Dept of Foreign Lang, Univ of No Iowa, Cedar Falls, IA 50613.

OBERHELMAN, HARLEY DEAN
PERSONAL Born 06/30/1928, Clay Center, KS, m, 1954, 2 children **DISCIPLINE** SPANISH LANGUAGE & LITERATURE **EDUCATION** Univ Kans, BSEd, 50, MA, 52, PhD(romance lang), 58. **CAREER** Teaching asst Span, Univ Kans, 50-56; dir foreign lang, Lawrence Pub Schs, Kans, 56-58; from asst prof to assoc prof foreign lang, 58-64, chmn dept, 63-70, prof Class & Romance Lang, Tex Tech Univ, 64-92, lectr Span methodology, Univ Wis, 55, Univ NMex, 56, Eastern Mont Col, 59 & Univ Kans, 60; Fulbright lectr, Nat Univ Tucuman, 61; State of Tex res study grant, Uruguay, 61 & Colombia, 77; assoc ed, Hispania, 62-66; chmn Latin Am area studies, Tex Tech Univ, 69-77; Paul Whitfield Horn Prof of Romance Langs, 92-99. **MEMBERSHIPS** Am Asn Teachers Span & Port. **RESEARCH** Spanish American literature; methodology of second language teaching; River Plate literature. **SELECTED PUBLICATIONS** Auth, Sobre la vida y las ficciones de Ernesto Sabato, In: Obras de Ficcion, Losada, Buenos Aires, 67; Ernesto Sabato, Twayne, 70; coauth, Espanol Moderno, Merrill, 70; auth, Jose Donoso and the Nueva Narrativa, Revista de Estudios Hi-

spanicos, 1/75; Garcia Marquez and the American South, Chasqui, 11/75; Education and History of Knowledge, In: Cien Anos de Soledad, Studies by SCMLA, 4/75; Myth and Structure in Sabato's Abaddon, Am Hispanist, 3/76; The Presence of Faulkner in the Writings of Garcia Marquez, Tex Tech Press, 80; auth, Gabriel Garcia Marquez, A Study of the Short Fiction, Twayne, 80; The Presence of Hemingway in the Short Fiction of Gabriel Garcia Marquez, York, 94; Garcia Marquez and Cuba, York, 95; ed, Alone Against the Sea, Poetry from Cuba, York, 98. **CONTACT ADDRESS** Dept of Class & Modern Lang, Texas Tech Univ, Lubbock, TX 79409-2071. **EMAIL** harley.oberhelman@ttu.edu

OCAMPO, FRANCISCO
DISCIPLINE SPANISH AND PORTUGUESE LITERATURE **EDUCATION** State Univ NYork Buffalo, MA, 82; Univ SC, PhD, 89. **RESEARCH** Relationship between syntax, cognition and discourse; word order in spoken Spanish; language variation; conversation analysis; language and ideology. **SELECTED PUBLICATIONS** Auth, Pragmatic factors on word order: constructions with a verb and an adverb in spoken Spanish, Probus, 95; The word order of two-constituent constructions in Spoken Spanish, John Benjamins, 95; The word order of constructions with a verb, a subject, and a direct object in spoken Spanish, John Benjamins, 94; co-auth, Spanish OV/VO word order variationin Spanish/Quechua bilingual speakers, Georgetown Univ, 95. **CONTACT ADDRESS** Spanish and Portuguese Dept, Univ of Minnesota, Twin Cities, 34 Folwell Hall, 9 Pleasant St SE, Minneapolis, MN 55455. **EMAIL** Francisco.A.Ocampo-1@tc.umn.edu

OCASIO, RAFAEL
PERSONAL Born 08/22/1960, Puerto Rico, s **DISCIPLINE** SPANISH, LITERATURE, LANGUAGE **EDUCATION** Univ PR, BA, 81; E Mex Univ, MA, 82; Univ Ky, PhD, 87. **CAREER** Teaching asst, Univ Ky, 82-87; asst prof, Univ S Ala, 87-89; assoc prof, Agnes Scott Col, 89-. **HONORS AND AWARDS** Teaching Excellence Awd; 92-93. **MEMBERSHIPS** MLA; SAMLA; AATSP. **RESEARCH** Contemporary Latin American literatures; Cuban literatures; Reinaldi Arenos; Judith Oritz Cofer. **SELECTED PUBLICATIONS** Auth, "Africa, the Caribbean, and Modern Folklore: A Study in the Development of National Identities," Quart J African, Asian, Lat Am Study 3 (90): 266-276; auth, "Babalu Aye: Santeria and Contemporary Cuban Literature," J Caribbean Study 9 (92): 29-40; auth, "Puerto Rican Literature in Georgia?: An Interview with Judith Ortiz Cofer," Kenyon Rev (92): 43-50; auth, "Speaking in Puerto Rican: An Interview with Judith Ortiz Cofer," Bilingual Rev (92): 143-146; auth, "In Search of a Socialist Identity in Revolutionary Cuban Children's Literature," in Imagination, Emblems and ExPrions: Essays on Latin American, Caribbean, and Continental Culture and Identity, ed. Helen Ryan-Ranson (Bowling Green: Bowling Green State Univ Pr Pop Pr, 93): 89-98; auth, "The Infinite Variety of the Puerto Rican Reality: An Interview with Judith Ortiz Cofer," Callaloo 17 (94): 730-742; co-auth, "Literary Offspring: The Figure of the Child in Marcel Proust and Reinaldo Arenas," Romance Quart 41 (94): 110-118; auth, "From Nuyorican Barrio Literature to Issues on Puerto Rican Literature Outside New York City," in Literature and Ethnic Discrimination, ed. Michael J. Meyer (Atlanta/Amsterdam: Rodopi, 97): 187-203; auth, "Autobiographical Writing and the 'Out of the Closet' Literature by Gay Latino Writers," Rev Estude Hisp (00): 273-282; co-auth, "Dinamica racial en la Talia del Siglo de Oro," in El Texto Puesto en Escena: Estudios Sobre la Comedia del Sigo de Oro en honor a Everett W. Hesse, eds. Anita Stoll, Barbara Mujics (London: Tamesis, 00): 128-138. **CONTACT ADDRESS** Span Dept, Agnes Scott Col, 141 E College Ave, Decatur, GA 30030. **EMAIL** rocasio@agnesscott.edu

OCHNER, NOBUKO M.
PERSONAL Born, Japan, m, 1945 **DISCIPLINE** JAPANESE LITERATURE **EDUCATION** Tokyo Univ, BA, 69; Univ Haw, MA, 71, 77; PhD, 84. **CAREER** Asst prof to assoc prof, Univ of Haw Manoa, 84-. **HONORS AND AWARDS** East-West Centre Fel, 69-71, 77-79; Mary McEwen Schimke Scholar, Wellesley Col, 82-83; NEH Awd, 86. **MEMBERSHIPS** Assoc for Asian Studies; Assoc of Teachers of Japanese; MLA; Am Comp Lit Assoc. **RESEARCH** Modern Japanese literature, comparative literature of Japan and the West, research methods. **SELECTED PUBLICATIONS** Auth, " A Japanese Writer in Micronesia: Nakajima Atsushi's Experiences of 1941-42", J of the Assoc of Teachers of Japanese, 21.1 (87): 37-58; auth, "Robert louis Stevenson through a Japanese Eye: The Silkworm Image in 'Light, Wind, and Dreams'", Comp Lit East and West: Traditions and Trends, eds, Cornelia Moore and Raymond Moody, Col of Lang, Ling and Lit, UHM, and E-W Center, (89): 58-64; auth, "Secrets in My Heart: The Poetry of Sato Haruo", Monumenta Nipponica, 44.3 (89): 261-282; auth, "History and Fiction: Portrayals of Confucius by Tanizaka Jun'ichiro and Nakajima Atsushi", Lit Relations East and West: Selected Essays, eds Jean Yamasaki Toyama and Nobuko Ochner, Col for Lang, Ling and Lit, UHM, East-West Center, (90): 68-79; coed, Literary Relations East and West: Selected Essays, Col of Lang, Ling and Lit, UHM, East-West Center, 90; auth, "Contact of Cultures in Akutagawa Ryunosuke's Short Story 'Hankechi" (The Handkerchief), Contacts Between Cultures, Vol 3: Eastern Asia: Lit and Human, eds, Bernard Hung-Kay Luk and Barry D. Steban, Edwin Mellen Pr, (NY,92): 246-251; auth, "Two Snow Countries: Transforming Kawabata's Novel into Film", Translations/Transformations: Gender and Culture in Film and Lit East and West, Eds, Valerie Wayne and Cornelia Moore, Col of Lang, Ling and Lit, UHM, East-West Center, (93): 45-52; auth, "Yukiguni to Kawabata Yasunari no biishiki" (Snow Country and Kawabata Yasunari's Sense of Beauty), Sekai ga yomu Nihon no kindai bungaku (World Reads Modern Japanese Literature), ed Fukuoka, Maruzen, (Tokyo, 96): 106-119; auth, "Beyond Stereotype: Teaching Japanese Culture Through Literature", New Trends and Issues in Teaching Japanese Lang and Culture, eds Haruko M. Cook, Kyoko Hijirida and Mildred Tahara, SLTCC Tech Rep 15, (97): 1-14; auth, "Perception of Self in Modern Japanese Literature: Two Adaptations of Classical Chinese Historiography", Self as Image in Asian Theory and Practice, eds Roger T. Ames, Thomas P. Kasulis and Wimal Dissanayake, SUNY Pr, (Albany, 98): 372-391; transl, "The Disciple" of Deshi by Nakajima Atsushi, S Humanities Rev 32.2 (98): 137-172. **CONTACT ADDRESS** Dept E Asian Lang and Lit, Univ of Hawaii, Manoa, 1890 E W Road, Honolulu, HI 96822-2318.

ODEN, ROBERT A., JR.
PERSONAL Born 09/11/1946, SD, m, 1967, 2 children **DISCIPLINE** NEAR EASTERN LANGUAGES **EDUCATION** Harvard Col, AB, 69; Cambridge Univ, BA, MA, 71; Harvard Univ, PhD, 75. **CAREER** Asst, assoc, full prof Relig, Dartmouth Col, 75-89; headmaster, Hotchkiss sch, 89-95; Pres, Kenyon Col, 95- . **HONORS AND AWARDS** Dartmouth Col disting tchg awd, first recipient, 79. **MEMBERSHIPS** Soc Biblical Lit **RESEARCH** Ancient Near Eastern languages and literatures. **SELECTED PUBLICATIONS** Auth, The Bible Without Theology, Harper, 87; The Phoenician History, 83. **CONTACT ADDRESS** Office of the President, Kenyon Col, Ransom Hall, Gambier, OH 43022. **EMAIL** odenr@kenyon.edu

ODHOJI, BENJAMIN M. M.
PERSONAL Born 05/02/1960, Siaya, Kenya **DISCIPLINE** COMPARATIVE LITERATURE **EDUCATION** Univ Nairobi, BA, 84-86; MA, 87-89; Emory Univ, PhD, 00. **CAREER** Lectr, Egerton Univ, 90-00. **HONORS AND AWARDS** Fulbright Scholar, 95-99; Ford Res Assoc, 00. **MEMBERSHIPS** ALA; ASA; KOL; MLA; Cen Woman Studies/Gender Anal. **RESEARCH** Cross-cultural comparative and literacy studies; theories of the self and autobiography; African and African Diaspora literature. **SELECTED PUBLICATIONS** Auth, "Social Death: Essays in Gender and Culture," KOLA (97). **CONTACT ADDRESS** 1520 Farnell Ct, Apt 357, Decatur, GA 30033. **EMAIL** odhoji@excite.com

OGDEN, ESTRELLA V.
PERSONAL Born Havana, Cuba, m, 1 child **DISCIPLINE** SPANISH, LATIN AMERICAN STUDIES **EDUCATION** Univ Havana, Universidad de la Habana, Doctor in law, 61; Temple Univ, Philadelphia, PA, PhD, 80. **CAREER** Prof of Spanish, Latin American Studies. **HONORS AND AWARDS** Pennsylvania Humanities Council; Phi Kappa Phi National Honor Society 89-; International Honor Society; Latin Am Guild for Arts. **MEMBERSHIPS** Modern Language Assoc (MLA); Association International de Hispanistas (ILCH); Instituto Literario y cultural Hispanics (ILCH); Northeast modern Language (NEMLA). **RESEARCH** Latin Amer Poetry; Relationship between Literature & Art. **SELECTED PUBLICATIONS** Auth, "El creacionismo de Vicente Huidobro en sus relaciones con la estetica cubista, Madrid, Playor, 83; auth, "El juego en el teatro de Carlos Fuentes," Literatura Mexicana/ Mexican Literature, ed. Jose Miguel Oviedo, Philadelphia, University of Pennsylvania Press, 94; auth, "La Ruta del Tajo en El rio que nos lleva," Camineria Hispanica, Madrid, Ediciones AACHE, 96; auth, "Borges en la poesia de Gonzalo Rojas: Aleph, Aleph," Alba de America, 00; auth, "An interview with Gonzalo Rojas," Hispanic Literary Criticism Supplement, ed. Susan Sales, The Gale Group, 99. **CONTACT ADDRESS** Dept Modern Languages, Villanova Univ, 800 East Lancaster Ave, Villanova, PA 19085-1603. **EMAIL** estrella.ogden@villanova.edu

OHALA, JOHN JEROME
PERSONAL Born 07/19/1941, Chicago, IL, m, 1969 **DISCIPLINE** LINGUISTICS **EDUCATION** Univ Notre Dame, BA, 63; Univ Calif, Los Angeles, MA, 66, PhD(ling), 69. **CAREER** Nat Sci Found fel, Res Inst Logopedics & Phoniatrics, Fac Med, Univ Tokyo, 69-70; asst prof, 70-72, assoc prof, 72-77, Prof Ling, Univ Calif, Berkeley, 77-, Vis lector, Inst Fonetik, Copenhagen Univ, 73. **MEMBERSHIPS** Ling Soc Am; AAAS; Acoust Soc Am. **RESEARCH** Physiology of speech; sound change; phonology. **SELECTED PUBLICATIONS** Auth, Aspects of the Control and Production of Speech, Univ Calif, 70; Physical Models in Phonology, Proc Cong Phonetic Sci, 72; contribr, Experimental historical phonology, In: Historical Linguistics II, North Holland, 74; Production of tone, In: Tone: A Linguistic Survey, Acad Press, 78; Coarticulation And Phonology, Language And Speech, Vol 0036, 1993; Listeners Normalization of Vowel Quality Is Influenced by Restored Consonantal Context, Phonetica, Vol 0051, 1994; A Probable Case of Clicks Influencing The Sound Patterns of Some European Languages, Phonetica, Vol 0052, 1995. **CONTACT ADDRESS** Dept of Ling, Univ of California, Berkeley, 2337 Dwinelle Hall, Berkeley, CA 94720-2651.

OINAS, FELIX JOHANNES
PERSONAL Born 03/06/1911, Estonia, m, 1937, 2 children **DISCIPLINE** SLAVIC & FINNO-UGRIC LINGUISTICS **EDUCATION** Tartu Univ, MA, 37; Ind Univ, PhD(ling), 52. **CAREER** Lectr Finno-Ugric, Pazmany Peter Univ, Budapest, 38-40; vis lectr Estonian, Baltic Univ, Ger, 46-48; lectr Slavic lang & lit, 51-52, from instr to assoc prof, 52-65, actg chmn Uralic & Altaic prog, 60-61, Prof Slavic Lang & Lit & Uralic & Altaic Studies, Ind Univ, Bloomington, 65-, Fulbright scholar, Finland, 61-62; Guggenheim scholar, Finland, 61-62 & 66-67; Fulbright- Hays grant, Yugoslavia, 64-65; Nat Endowment for Humanities grant, 74; fel, Folklore Inst, Ind Univ Commemorative Medal, Finnish Govt, 68; vis prof folklore, Univ Calif, Berkeley, 76. **HONORS AND AWARDS** Cultural Awd, Found Estonian Arts & Lett, 78; First Prize, Arthur Puksow Found, 80; Honorary Doctorate of Tartu Univ, Estonic. **MEMBERSHIPS** MLA; corresp mem Finnish Lit Soc; Asn Advan Baltic Studies (vp, 72-73); fel Am Folklore Soc; Finnish Acad Sci. **RESEARCH** Slavic and Finno-Ugric linguistics and folklore. **SELECTED PUBLICATIONS** Estonian General Reader, 63 & Basic Course in Estonian, 66, Mouton; Studies in Finnic-Slavic Folklore Relations, Finnish Acad Sci, 69; co-ed, The Study of Russian Folklore, Mouton, 75; ed, Folklore, Nationalism, and Politics, Slavica, 78; Heroic Epic and Saga: An Introduction to the World's Great Folk Epics, Ind Univ, 78; Kalevipoeg kutkeis, Mans, 79; ed, European Folklore, Trickster Press, 81; Shamanism - Soviet Studies of Traditional Religion in Siberia And Central-asia - Balzer,mm, J of Folklore Research, Vol 0029, 1992; Couvade in Estonia + Transferring The Mothers Birth Pangs to Her Husband, Slavic And East European J, Vol 0037, 1993; The Great Bear, a Thematic Anthology of Oral Poetry in Finno-ugrian Languages - Honko,l, Timonen,s, Branch,m, J of Folklore Research, Vol 0032, 1995. **CONTACT ADDRESS** 2513 E 8th St, Bloomington, IN 47401.

OJO-ADE, FEMI
PERSONAL Born 07/23/1941, La Gos, Nigeria, m, 1969, 5 children **DISCIPLINE** FRENCH, AFRICAN LITERATURE, CULTURE **EDUCATION** McMaster Univ BA, 67; Queen's Univ, MA, 68; Univ Toronto, PhD, 75. **CAREER** Prof Univ Nigeria, 80-90; Prof, St Mary's Col, 90-. **HONORS AND AWARDS** Rockefeller Found Fel; Blk Consc Awd. **MEMBERSHIPS** ASA; ALA; MLA. **RESEARCH** Black literatures and cultures; creative writing; fiction and poetry. **SELECTED PUBLICATIONS** Auth, Being Black, Being Human, Obafemi Awolowo Univ Press (Ile-Ife), 96; ed, Of Dreams Deferred, Dead or Alive, African Perspectives on African- American Writers, Greenwood Press (Westport, CT), 96; auth, Exile at Home, Intl Pub (Ibadan), 98; auth, One Little Girl's Dreams, College Press (Thadan), 98; auth, Ken Saro-Wiwa: A Bio-Critical Study, Afric Leg Press (NY), 99. **CONTACT ADDRESS** Dept Arts, St. Mary's Col of Maryland, Saint Mary's City, MD 20686. **EMAIL** fojoade@oprey.smcm.edu

OLCOTT, ANTHONY
PERSONAL m **DISCIPLINE** MODERN RUSSIAN-LANGUAGE AND LITERATURE **EDUCATION** Stanford Univ, PhD, 76. **CAREER** Instr, Univ VA, Hamilton Col, SUNY Oswego, Phillips Acad; instr, 86-. **HONORS AND AWARDS** Asst dir, Colgate Univ, Moscow Study Group, 97. **RESEARCH** Crime genre in Russ. **SELECTED PUBLICATIONS** Auth, Murder at the Red October; May Day in Magadan. **CONTACT ADDRESS** Dept of Russ Stud, Colgate Univ, 13 Oak Drive, Hamilton, NY 13346.

OLDCORN, ANTHONY
PERSONAL Born 06/20/1935, Longridge, England, m, 1960, 2 children **DISCIPLINE** ITALIAN LANGUAGE AND LITERATURE **EDUCATION** Oxford Univ, BA, 58; Univ Virginia, MA, 61; Harvard Univ, PhD, 70. **CAREER** Instr French & Ital, Boston Col, 60-62; teaching fel, Harvard Univ, 62-65; from instr to asst prof Ital, Wellesley Col, 66-71, acting chmn dept, 69-70; asst prof, 71-76; assoc prof, 76-80, Prof Ital Studies, Brown Univ, 80-, Nat Endowment for Humanities fel, 78-79; vis prof Ital, Vassar Col, 80-81, Dante Antolini chair, 81-; Ital field ed, Twayne World Authors Series, 81; Chair, Italian Studios, 81- . **HONORS AND AWARDS** MA, Brown Unvi, 77. **MEMBERSHIPS** Am Asn Tchr(s) Ital; Am Comt Hist 2nd World War; Dante Soc Am; MLA. **RESEARCH** Medieval, Renaissance, baroque and mod Italian lit; textual criticism; rhetoric and lit stylistics. **SELECTED PUBLICATIONS** Auth, A Recensio of the Sources of the Gerusalemme Conquistata: Notes for a New Edition, Forum Italicum, 75; Virgilio Giotti (poems) (Transl), Copper Beech Press, 75; Pirandello o del candore?, Mod Lang Notes, 76; The Textual Problems of Tasso's Gerusalemme Conquistata, Longo, 76; Tasso's Epic Theory, Italica, 77. **CONTACT ADDRESS** Italian Stu Dept, Brown Univ, PO Box 1942, Providence, RI 02912-9127. **EMAIL** anthony_oldcorn@brown.edu

OLENIK, JOHN KENNETH
PERSONAL Born 05/07/1941, Cleveland, OH, m **DISCIPLINE** MODERN CHINESE HISTORY AND LITERATURE **EDUCATION** John Carroll Univ, BSS, 63; Seton Hall Univ, MA, 66; Cornell Univ, MA, 70, PhD(hist China), 73. **CAREER** Asst prof, 71-78, Assoc Prof Hist E Asia, Montclair State Col, 78-, Am Coun Learned SocNat Endowment for Humanities lang & res fel, Japan, 76-77; vis scholar, Fac Law, Keio Univ, Japan, 76-77. **MEMBERSHIPS** AHA; Asn Asian Studies. **RESEARCH** China, Repubican Period; China, political parties and movements; China, poetry of the Six Dynasties Period. **SELECTED PUBLICATIONS CONTACT ADDRESS** 1 Normal Ave, Montclair, NJ 07043-1699.

OLESZKIEWICZ, MALGORZATA
DISCIPLINE LATIN AMERICAN LITERATURE AND CULTURE **EDUCATION** Queens Col, BA, 79, MA, 81; Warsaw Univ, Magister, 81; New York Univ, MPhil, 85, PhD, 91. **CAREER** Grad teaching asst, Queens Col, CUNY, 79-81; teacher of Spanish, United Nations, NY, 82; lang instr, Brooklyn Col, CUNY, 83-84; instr, Rutgers Univ, 87; lang instr, SUNY, New Palz, 88; lang instr, NYU Sch of Continuing Educ, 83-84, 90-91; grad teaching asst, NYU, 81-83, adjunct instr, 84-87, 90-91; asst prof, Bard Col, Annandale-on-Hudson, New York, 91-95; asst prof, Univ Tex at San Antonio, 95-. **HONORS AND AWARDS** Dean's Scholarship Awd for Outstanding Academic Achievement, Warsaw Univ, 73-77; Penfield Fel, NYU, 87-88; Consejo Nacional de Ciencia y Tecnologia Grant, 88-89; Dean's Diss Fel, NYU, 88-89; Univ Fel, NYU, 89-90, 86-87; Asther Edelman Released Time Fel, Bard Col, 92; Fac Res Awd, Univ Tex San Antonio, 95-96; NEH Summer Stipend recommendation, Univ Tex San Antonio, 96-97; Dean's Circle Res Grant, 98, 99; Office of Int Progs Travel Awd, Univ Tex San Antonio, summer and fall 98, fall 99; Int Res and Exchanges Bd Grant, 98; Polish Ministry of Educ under the aegis of the Kosciuszko Found Res grant, 99; Fac Res Awd, Univ Tex at San Antonio, 99. **MEMBERSHIPS** Latin Am Studies Asn, Modern Lang Asn, Brazilian Studies Asn, Afro-Latin Am Res Asn, Intstituto Internacional de Literatura Iberoamericana. **RESEARCH** Comparative cultural studies dealing with popular religiosity; identity at the borderlands in Latin America, the Southwestern U. S. and Eastern Europe. **SELECTED PUBLICATIONS** Auth, Teatro popular peruano: del precolombiasno al siglo XX, co-pub by the Center for Latin Am Studies, Warsaw Univ, and the Austrian Inst of Latin Am (95); auth, "Postmodernidad y teatro en America Latina," Alba de America, 26/27 (96): 221-227; auth, "La danza de la pluma y el sincretismo cultural en Mexico," Revista de Critica Literaria Latinoamericana, 46 (97): 105-114; auth, "Los cultos marianos nacionales en America Latina: Guadalupe/Tonantzin y Aparecida/Iemanja," Revista Iberoamericana, 182-183 (98): 241-252; auth, "Teatro popular peruano," Documentos de trabajo, Warsaw Univ, tomo 29 (98): 15-17; auth, "Ile Ase Orisania J'Omin: Syncretism or Orthodoxy?" Proceedings of the Brazilian Studies Asn Fourth Conf #30 (98); auth, "El papel de la mujer en el Candomble," Religion and Latin America in the Twenty-First Century: Libraries Reacting to Social Change, Austin: Benson Latin Am Collection, The Univ Tex at Austin (99): 193-200. **CONTACT ADDRESS** Dept Foreign Langs, Univ of Texas, San Antonio, 6900 N Loop 1604 W, San Antonio, TX 78249-1130. **EMAIL** moleszkiewicz@utsa.edu

OLIVERA, OTTO H.
PERSONAL Born 04/20/1919, Cuba, m, 1950, 3 children **DISCIPLINE** LITERATURE, SPANISH **EDUCATION** Univ de la Habana, Doc Filo, 45; La State Univ, MA, 47; Tulane Univ, PhD, 53. **CAREER** Asst prof to assoc prof to prof, Syracuse Univ, 54-65; prof to dept chmn to emer, Tulane Univ, 65-. **MEMBERSHIPS** MLA; AAUL; AATSP; IILI. **RESEARCH** Spanish American literature; Colonial 19th-century; modernismo; literature of Spanish Antilles. **SELECTED PUBLICATIONS** Auth, Breve Historia de la Literatura Antillana, 57; auth, Cuba en su Poesia, 65; co-auth, La Prosa Mondernista en Hispano-American, 71; auth, La Literatura en Publicaciones Periodicas de Guatemala, 74; auth, La Literatura en Periodicos y Revista de Puerto Rico, 86. **CONTACT ADDRESS** 3801 St Charles Ave, Apt 203, New Orleans, LA 70115-7107.

OLIVIA, LEONORA
DISCIPLINE GREEK AND LATIN LANGUAGES AND LITERATURES **EDUCATION** Brown Univ, PhD. **CAREER** Dept Classics, Millsaps Col **SELECTED PUBLICATIONS** Publ on, comp lit. **CONTACT ADDRESS** Dept of Classics, Millsaps Col, 1701 N State St, Jackson, MS 39210. **EMAIL** olivil@okra.millsaps.edu

OLLER, JOHN WILLIAM
PERSONAL Born 10/22/1943, Las Vegas, NV, m, 1976, 4 children **DISCIPLINE** LINGUISTICS **EDUCATION** Fresno State Col, BA, 65; Univ Rochester, NYork, MA, 68, PhD, 69. **CAREER** Assoc prof, Dept of English, UCLA, 69-72; prof, Dept of Linguistics, Univ NM, 72-96; prof and head, Dept of Communicative Disorders, Univ Louisiana at Lafayette, LA, 97-. **HONORS AND AWARDS** MLA Middleberger Medal, 83 (best book on foreign language teaching); NDEA Fel, Univ Rochester, 66-69. **MEMBERSHIPS** Linguistic Soc Am; Am Speech Language Hearing Asn. **RESEARCH** Language and intelligence, autism. **SELECTED PUBLICATIONS** Auth, Coding Information in Natural Languages, Mouton, 71; ed with Jack C Richards, Focus on the Learner: Pragmatic Perspectives for the Language Teacher, Newbury House, 73; ed with Kyle Perkins, Language in Health Education: Testing the Tests, Newbury House, 78; auth, Language Tests at School: A Pragmatic Approach, Longman, 79, Japanese trans, Longman, 94; ed with Kyle Perkins, Research in Language Testing, Newbury House, 80; ed, Issues in Language Testing Research, Newbury House, 83; ed with Patricia Richard-Amato, Methods That Work: A Smorgasbord of Ideas for Language Teachers, Newbury House, 83; ed, Language and Experience: Classic Pragmatism, Univ Press Am, 89; auth with J. Robert Scott and S Chesarek, Language and Bilingualism: More Tests of Tests, Bucknell Univ Press, 91; auth with Saowalak Rattanavich and R F Walker, Teaching All the Children to Read, Open Univ Press, 92; ed, Methods That Work: Ideas for Literacy and Language Teachers, Heinle and Heinle Pubs, 93; auth with Jon Jonz, Cloze and Coherence, Bucknell Univ Press, 94; coauth, Images That Work, Greenwood, 99. **CONTACT ADDRESS** Dept of Communicative Disorders, Univ of Louisiana, Lafayette, PO Box 43170, Lafayette, LA 70504-3170. **EMAIL** joller@louisiana.edu

OLLIVIER, LOUIS L.
DISCIPLINE SPANISH **EDUCATION** St Mary's Col Calif, BA, 64; Middlebury Col, MA, 66; Univ NMex, PhD, 73. **CAREER** Asst prof, 96-; **HONORS AND AWARDS** NDEA Title VI fel, Univ NMex, 70; Org Am States res fel, Porto Alegre, Brazil, 71. **SELECTED PUBLICATIONS** Auth, Cien anos de soledad: Existence is the Word, Latin Am Lit Rev, 75; O Tempo e o Vento: Universality of Yesterday, Chasqui, revista de lit latinoamericana, 74; rev, Graciliano Ramos by Richard Mazarra,Twayne Publ(s) Inc, 74. **CONTACT ADDRESS** Dept of For Lang, Western New Mexico Univ, 1000 West College Ave., Silver City, NM 88061. **EMAIL** cowlingl@cs.wnmu.edu

OLSEN, SOLVEIG
PERSONAL Born 08/23/1940, Hamburg, Germany **DISCIPLINE** GERMAN LANGUAGE & LITERATURE **EDUCATION** Univ Oslo, Cand Mag, 63, Cand Phil, 64; Pedag Sem, Oslo, Norway, teaching cert, 65; Rice Univ, Phd(Ger), 68. **CAREER** AdJGer, English & Norweg, Manglerud Komb Sk, Oslo, Norway, 60-64, lector, 64-65; asst prof, 68-74, Assoc Prof Ger & Chairperson Dept Foreign Lang & Lit, NTex State Univ, 74-, Res grant NTex State Univ, 76; Danforth fel, Danforth Found, 77-. **MEMBERSHIPS** MLA; AAUP; Am Asn Teachers Ger; Int Arbeitskreis fur Barockliteratur; Am Coun Teaching Foreign Lang. **SELECTED PUBLICATIONS** Auth, Der Anfang der Weltlichen Kantate in Deutschland, Lang Quart, Univ SFla, 72; Chr Hch Postels Beitrag zur Deutschen Literatur: Versuch einer Darstellung, Rodopi, Amsterdam, 73. **CONTACT ADDRESS** Dept of Foreign Lang & Lit, Univ of No Texas, PO Box 311127, Denton, TX 76203-1127.

OLSON, PAUL RICHARD
PERSONAL Born 11/02/1925, Rockford, IL, m, 1953, 4 children **DISCIPLINE** SPANISH LANGUAGE & LITERATURE **EDUCATION** Univ Ill, AB, 48, AM, 50; Harvard Univ, PhD, 59. **CAREER** From instr to asst prof Span, Dartmouth Col, 56-61; from asst prof to assoc prof, 61-68, Prof Span, Johns Hopkins Univ, 68-90, Emer, 91-. **HONORS AND AWARDS** Guggenheim fel, 64-65; Fulbright Awd, Spain, 64-65. **MEMBERSHIPS** MLA; Asoc Int Hispanistas. **RESEARCH** Spanish literature. **SELECTED PUBLICATIONS** Auth, Circle of Paradox: Time and Essence in the Poetry of Juan Ramon Jimenez, Johns Hopkins Press, 67; Galdos and history, MLN, 70; Unamuno's lacquered boxes, RHM, 74; Unamuno's Niebla, Ga Rev, 75; ed, Miguel de Unamuno: Como se hace una novela, Ediciones Guadarrama, Madrid, 77; contribr, Dos metafisicas del texto poetico, Asn Int Hisp, Toronto, 78. **CONTACT ADDRESS** 100 W University Pkwy, #4F, Baltimore, MD 21210. **EMAIL** poison5772@aol.com

OLSON, STUART DOUGLAS
PERSONAL 2 children **DISCIPLINE** GREEK **EDUCATION** Bryn Mawr Col, PhD, 87. **CAREER** Lectr, 87-90, Howard Univ; Assoc Prof to Prof, Univ of Minn, 97-. **HONORS AND AWARDS** Whiting Fellowship in Hum, 86-87; James Rignall Wheeler Fellow; ASCSA; Outstanding Faculty Member; LAS Coll Award for Excellence; Alpha Epsilon Delta Outstanding Tchr Award; Outstanding Fac Member, Illlini Dads Asn; 93; Jr Fel, Center for Hellenic Studies, 94-95; Fel, Center for Advanced Study, UIUC, 95; Helen Corley Petit Prof, UIUC, 96-97; Univ Scholar, UIUC, 96-99; NEH Res Fel, 00-01. **MEMBERSHIPS** APA, Classical Asn of the Middle West of South. **RESEARCH** Greek Poetry. **SELECTED PUBLICATIONS** Auth, Blood and Iron: Stories and Storytelling in Homer's Odyssey, Mnemosyne Supplement 148, Leiden, 95; auth, Politics and Poetry in Aristophanes Wasp, 96; auth, Aristophanes: Peace, Oxford University Press, 98; auth, Studies in the Later Manuscript Tradition of Aristophanes Peace, 98; auth, Was Carcinus I a Tragic Playwright?, A Response, CP97; coauth, ¿Matro of Pitane and the Tradition of Epic Parody in the Fourth Century BCE¤, Am Classical Studies 44 (Atlanta, 99): 172; coauth, Archestratos of Gela, Text, Translation and Commentary, Oxford University Press, 00; auth, Aristophanes: Acharnians, Oxford Univ Press, forthcoming. **CONTACT ADDRESS** Dept of Classical & Near Eastern Studies, Univ of Minnesota, Twin Cities, 9 Pleasant St SE, Minneapolis, MN 55455-0125. **EMAIL** sdolson@tc.umn.edu

OMAGGIO HADLEY, ALICE
DISCIPLINE FRENCH LITERATURE **EDUCATION** Pa State Univ, BS, 69; Ohio State Univ, MA, 72; PhD, 77. **CAREER** Prof, Univ Ill Urbana Champaign. **HONORS AND AWARDS** Stephen A. Freeman Awd, 70; Paul Pimsleur Awd, 80; Kenneth W. Mildenberger Awd, 87; Anthony Papalia Awd, 89. **RESEARCH** Foreign language education; teacher education; second language learning. **SELECTED PUBLICATIONS** Auth, "The Proficiency-Oriented Classroom," chapter 2 in Proficiency: The Organizing Principle, ed. T.V. Higgs, (Lincolnwood, IL: Nat Textbook Co, 84); auth, "Making Reading Comprehensible,' Foreign Language Annals, 17, (84): 305-308; auth, "Proficiency-Based Instruction: Implications for Methodology," IDEAL, 3, (88): 25-37; auth, "Profiency: Le concept de competence fonctionelle et son impact sur les programmes et l'enseignement des langues etrangeres," Etudes de Linguistiqque Appliquee, 77, (90): 85-95; coauth, Bonjour ca va?, New York: McGraw Hill, 91; coauth, Kaleidoscope: Grammaire en contexte, 3rd ed, New York: Random House, 93; ed, Research in Language Learning: Principles, Processes nad Prospects, Lincolnwood, IL: Nat Textbook Co, 93; auth, Teaching Language in Context: Proficiency-Oriented Instruction, Boston, MA: Heinle & Heinle Publishers, 2nd ed, 93; coauth, Rendezvous: An Invititation to French, New York: McGraw-Hill, 4th ed., 94; coauth, Vis a vis: Beginning French, San Francisco: McGraw Hill, 96. **CONTACT ADDRESS** French Dept, Univ of Illinois, Urbana-Champaign, 52 E Gregory Dr, Champaign, IL 61820. **EMAIL** acoh@uiuc.edu

OPERE, FERNANDO
PERSONAL Born 10/13/1946, Madrid, Spain, m, 1978, 4 children **DISCIPLINE** SPANISH LANGUAGE & LITERATURE **EDUCATION** Univ Va, PhD, 85. **CAREER** Prof, Univ of Va. **HONORS AND AWARDS** Harrison Ford Awd for Excellence in Teaching. **MEMBERSHIPS** MLA; LASA; AATSP; ALDEEV; SCOLAS; CEPI. **RESEARCH** Hispanic American (colonial and 19th century) literature and history. **SELECTED PUBLICATIONS** Auth, Vamos, Workbook/Laboratory Manual, Heinle and Heinle, (Boston), 85; auth, Despedidas, Ardeas (Sagunto, Valencia), 87; auth, Civilizacion y barbarie en la literatura argentina del siglo XIX, Conorg, (Madrid), 87; auth, Acrobata de ternuras, Ediciones Endymion, (Madrid), 94; auth, Amor a los cuerpos, Editorial Isla Negra (Puerto Rico), 97; auth, Cautivos, Ediciones Instituto Movilizador de Fondos Cooperativos, (Buenos Aires), 97; auth, "Espanoles cautivos en Norteamerica", De la catedral al rascacielos, eds Corbalan, Pina and Toscano, Peconic co, (NY, 98): 235-44; auth, "Cumanda: la novela ecuatoriana entre la cruz y la espads", Critica Hispanica 1&2, XX (98): 77-87; auth, Salmos de la materia, Editorial verbum, (Madrid), 00; auth, Historias de la frontera. El cautiverio en la America hispanica, (forthcoming), auth, "Senas de identidad en la poesia de Cesar Simons", Quaderns de Filogia, Estudis Literaris, (forthcoming); auth, Voces ignoradas de la frontera patagonica", Explicacion de textos literarios (forthcoming). **CONTACT ADDRESS** Span, Ital and Port, Univ of Virginia, 115 Wilson Hall, Charlottesville, VA 22903-3238. **EMAIL** fo@virginia.edu

OPPENHEIM, LOIS B.
PERSONAL Born 10/14/1945, New York, NY, m, 1970, 2 children **DISCIPLINE** FRENCH **EDUCATION** New York Univ, BA, 67; MA, 70; PhD, 76. **CAREER** Asst prof to prof, Montclair State Univ, 88-. **HONORS AND AWARDS** Distinguished Scholar, Montclair State Univ, 96. **MEMBERSHIPS** MLA, Samuel Becault Soc, Jean-Paul Sarte Soc. **RESEARCH** Psychoanalysis and aesthetics, Philosophical approaches to literature and the visual arts, Contemporary French Studies. **SELECTED PUBLICATIONS** Auth, Three Decades of the French in New World, Univ of Ill Pr, 86; coed, Beckett in the 1990s, Rodopi, (Amsterdam, Atlanta), 93; auth, Directing Beckett, Univ of Mich Pr, 94, 97; coed, Beckett On and On©, Assoc Univ Pr, (NY, London), 96; ed, Improvisations on Brown: Transformation of Writing, Univ Pr of Fla, 96; auth, Samuel Beckett and the Arts: Music, Visual Arts and Non-Print Media, Garland Publ, (NY, London), 99; auth, The Painted Word: Samuel Beckett's Dialogue with Art, Univ of Mich Pr, 00. **CONTACT ADDRESS** Dept Fr, Ger, Russ, Montclair State Univ, Upper Montclair, NJ 07043. **EMAIL** oppenheiml@mail.montclair.edu

OPPENHEIMER, FRED E.
PERSONAL Born 02/22/1929, Berlin, Germany, d, 2 children **DISCIPLINE** GERMAN LANGUAGE & LITERATURE **EDUCATION** Cent MI Col, BA, 51; Univ Wis, MA, 57, PhD, 61. **CAREER** From instr to asst prof Ger, Purdue Univ, 61-65; asst prof, Colo Col, 65-71; assoc prof Ger, 71-88, Prof German, Millersville State Col, 88-98, Chmn, Dept of Foreign Lang, 79-98, Retired 8/21/98; Dir Jr Year Abroad, 72-. **MEMBERSHIPS** Am Asn Teachers Ger; MLA. **RESEARCH** Literature of German Classicism; the German novelle; literary allusion in the novels of Theodor Fontane. **CONTACT ADDRESS** Dept of Foreign Lang, Millersville Univ of Pennsylvania, PO Box 1002, Millersville, PA 17551-0302.

ORBAN, CLARA E.
DISCIPLINE ITALIAN **EDUCATION** Univ Chicago, BA, 81; PhD, 90; Univ de Geneve, BA, 83; MA, 84; MA, 85. **CAREER** From Asst Prof to Prof, Univ Chicago, 90-. **HONORS AND AWARDS** Angela and Anne V Marinelli Fel, 88; Gilbert Chinard Pedagogy Prize, 90; Grant, Ill Humanities Coun, 93; Excellence in Teaching Awd, 97; Six Grants, 90-00. **MEMBERSHIPS** AATF, IAWIS, AATI, AAIS, MLA. **RESEARCH** Avant-garde (early 20th Century), word and image studies, literature and medicine studies. **SELECTED PUBLICATIONS** Auth, Au travail, Workbook for Business French, McGraw-Hill (San Francisco, CA), 95; auth, "Women, Futurism and Fascism," in Mothers of Invention: Critical Studies on Women in Ital Cult and Soc During Fascism (Minneapolis, MN: Univ Minn Pr, 95), 52-75; auth, "Real Talk: Interviews, Radio Broadcasts and Videotaping as Context in Advanced Italian Conversation Courses," Italica (97): 466-484; auth, The Culture of Fragments: Words and Images in Futurism and Surrealism, Editions Rodopi (Amsterdam), 97; auth, "Writing, Time and AIDS in the Works of Herve Guibert," Lit and Med (99): 132-150; auth, "Bruised Words, Wounded Images, in Frida Kahlo," Text and Visuality: Word and Image Interactions 3, Rodopi (99): 163-171; auth, "Powerlines: The Discourse of Power in the Medical Chart," in Making the Case (forthcoming); auth, "Antonioni's Women, Lost in the City," in Ital Women and the City: Essays (forthcoming). **CONTACT ADDRESS** Dept Lang, DePaul Univ, 2320 N Kenmore Ave, Chicago, IL 60614-3210.

ORDONEZ, ELIZABETH JANE
PERSONAL Born 07/27/1945, Los Angeles, CA **DISCIPLINE** SPANISH LITERATURE **EDUCATION** Univ Calif, Los Angeles, BA, 66, MA, 69; Univ Calif, Irvine, PhD(Span lit), 76. **CAREER** Asst prof Span, Ripon Col, 74-79; Assoc Prof Span, Univ Tex, Arlington, 79-, Span Govt grant, Ministerio de Asuntos Exteriores, 77. **MEMBERSHIPS** MLA; Am Asn Teachers Span & Port; Asoc Lit Femenina Hisp; Sch Latin Am; Am Asoc Advan Humanities. **RESEARCH** Spanish feminist literary theory and practice; film; Chicana literature. **SELECTED PUBLICATIONS** Auth, Forms of alienation in Matute's La Trampa, J Span Studies: 20th Century, winter 76; Symbolic vision in Clarice Lispector's The Applie in the Dark, Letras Femeninas, spring 76; Nada: initiation into bourgeois patriarchy, In: The Analysis of Hispanic Texts: Current Trends in Methodology, Bilingual Press, 77; Mitificacion e imagen de la mujer en La Enferma de Elena Quiroga, Letras Femeninas, fall 77; The decoding and encoding of sex roles in Carmen Martin Gaite's Retahilas, Ky Romance Quart, 80; The female quest pattern in Concha Alos, Os habla Electra, Revista de estudios hispanicos, 1/80. **CONTACT ADDRESS** Dept Foreign Lang & Ling, Univ of Texas, Arlington, Arlington, TX 76019.

ORDONEZ, FRANCISCO
DISCIPLINE SPANISH LITERATURE **EDUCATION** City Univ NYork, M.Phil, PhD, 97. **CAREER** Asst prof, Univ Ill Urbana Champaign. **RESEARCH** Syntax; comparative syntax; dialectology. **SELECTED PUBLICATIONS** Auth, The inversion construction in interrogatives in Spanish and Catalan, John Benjamins, 98; Post-verbal asymmetries in Spanish, Natural Lang Ling Theory, 98. **CONTACT ADDRESS** Spanish, Italian, and Portuguese Dept, Univ of Illinois, Urbana-Champaign, 52 E Gregory Dr, Champaign, IL 61820. **EMAIL** fordonez@uiuc.edu

ORENSTEIN, GLORIA FEMAN
PERSONAL Born New York City, NY, d, 2 children **DISCIPLINE** GENDER STUDIES AND COMPARATIVE LITERATURE **EDUCATION** NYork Univ, PhD. **CAREER** Assoc prof, Univ Southern Calif. **RESEARCH** Feminist Scholar on a Spiritual Quest. **SELECTED PUBLICATIONS** Auth, The Theater of the Marvelous: Surrealism and The Contemporary Stage; The Reflowering of the Goddess; Multi-Cultural Celebrations: Betty La Duke Paintings 1972-1992; co-ed, Reweaving The World: The Emergence of Ecofeminism; coauth, The Women's Salon for Literature in New York, 75-85; auth, The Women of Surrealism. **CONTACT ADDRESS** Col Letters, Arts & Sciences, Univ of So California, University Park Campus, Los Angeles, CA 90089. **EMAIL** orenstei@usc.edu

ORLANDO, VALERIE
DISCIPLINE FRENCH LANGUAGE **EDUCATION** Brown Univ, PhD. **CAREER** Vis asst prof Fr, Purdue Univ. **RESEARCH** 19th century French Literature; Francophone Literature of North Africa; 20th century French Literature and Philosophy. **SELECTED PUBLICATIONS** Auth, Assia Djebar's Vaste est la prison: Platform for a New Space of Agency and Feminine Enunciation in Algeria, Paroles GelSes, Vol 16. 97; Who's Covering Who in the Postmodern 90s: Subverting the Orientalist Image, Contemporary North African Francophone Text, Romance Lang Annual, Vol.8, 97; The Algerian Family Code: A Product of Falsified History and the Subversion of Political Literalism, Women, Politics and Law: A Code of Shame, Leeds Univ Press, 97; Women, War, Autobiography and the Historical Metafictional Text: Unveiling the Veiled Feminine Identity in Assia Djebar's L'Amour, la fantasia, in Spoils of War: Women, Cultures and Revolutions, Rowman & Littlefield, 97; Beyond Postcolonial Discourse: The Problematic of Feminine Identity in Contemporary Francophone Literature of the Maghred, Ohio Univ Press, 98. **CONTACT ADDRESS** Dept of For Lang and Lit, Purdue Univ, West Lafayette, 1080 Schleman Hall, West Lafayette, IN 47907-1080. **EMAIL** orlandov@omni.cc.purdue.edu

ORMAND, KIRK
PERSONAL Born 11/05/1962, Traverse City, MI, m, 1989, 2 children **DISCIPLINE** CLASSICAL STUDIES **EDUCATION** Stanford Univ, PhD, 92. **CAREER** Vis Asst Prof, Oberlin Col, 92-93; Asst Prof, Loyola Univ Chicago, 93-97. **HONORS AND AWARDS** John J. Winkler Memorial Prize, 91; Gildersleeve Prize, Am J Philol, 96; Solmsen Fel, Inst Res Humanities, 98-99. **MEMBERSHIPS** Am Philol Asn; Women's Classical Caucus; Lesbian Gay and Bisexual Classical Caucus. **RESEARCH** Ancient Greek literature and culture; modern critical theory. **SELECTED PUBLICATIONS** Auth, Trachiniae 1055ff: More Wedding Imagery, Mnemosyne 67, 93; Lucan's auctor vix fidelis, Classical Antiquity, 94; Silent by Convention? Sophocles' Tekmessa, AJP, 96; Exchange and the Maiden: Marriage in Sophoclean Tragedy, Univ Tex Press (forthcoming 99). **CONTACT ADDRESS** 2 Haverhill Circle, Madison, WI 53717. **EMAIL** kormand@facstaff.wisc.edu

ORO, CESAR
PERSONAL Born 03/15/1928, Lahn, Spain, s **DISCIPLINE** SPANISH LITERATURE **EDUCATION** Univ Santiago Spain, BA; Univ Boca Raton, BA; MA; Univ MD, PhD. **CAREER** Asst to full prof, Howard Univ, 85-. **HONORS AND AWARDS** Three Max Cum Laude, Univ Havana. **MEMBERSHIPS** Sigma Delta Pi, Am Asn of Teachers of Spanish and Portuguese. **RESEARCH** Spanish Topics: Research in Gellego-Portuguese, The Regularization of Spanish Irregular Verbs. **CONTACT ADDRESS** Dept Mod Lang, Howard Univ, 2400 6th St NE, Washington, DC 20059-0001.

ORRINGER, NELSON R.
PERSONAL Born 11/09/1940, Pittsburgh, PA, m, 1965, 3 children **DISCIPLINE** SPANISH **EDUCATION** Dartmouth Col, AB, 62; Brown Univ, MA, 65; PhD, 69. **CAREER** Asst prof, Williams Col, 68-74; from assoc prof to prof, Univ of Conn, 74-. **HONORS AND AWARDS** Distinguished Vis Scholar, Brown Univ, 81; Fulbright Postdoctoral Res Grant to Spain, 81 & 89; Distinguished Grad Sch Alumnus, Brown Univ, 99. **MEMBERSHIPS** Xavier Zubiri Found of N Am, Am Asn of Univ Professors, Sem of Hist of Span Philos. **RESEARCH** Nineteenth- and Twentieth-Century Hispanic Literature and Philosophy, German Philosophy. **SELECTED PUBLICATIONS** Auth, Nuevas fuentes germanicas de "Que ed filosofia?" De Ortega, Inst de , Filosofia "Luis Vives," 84; authUnamuno y los protestantes liberales (1912). Sobre las fuentes de "Del sentimiento tragico de la vida," Gredos, 85; auth, La aventura de curar: La antropologia medica de Pedro Lain Entrago, Galaxia Gutemberg/Circulo de Lectores, 97; auth, Agnel Ganivet (1865-1898). La inteligencia escindida, Ediciones del Orto, Biblioteca Filosofica, 98; auth, Herman Cohen (1842-1918). Filosofar como fundamentar, Ediciones del Orto, Biblioteca Filosofica, 00. **CONTACT ADDRESS** Dept Modern & Classical Lang, Univ of Connecticut, Storrs, Arjona Bldg, Unit 1057, Storrs, CT 06269-1057. **EMAIL** nelson.orringer@uconn.edu

ORTH, GEOFFREY C.
PERSONAL Born 02/12/1947, Philadelphia, PA, m, 1973, 2 children **DISCIPLINE** GERMAN **EDUCATION** Washington and Lee Univ, BA, 69; Univ Va, MA, 73; PhD, 76. **CAREER** Instr, Univ Va, 75-77; instr to prof, chair, Longwood Col, 77-. **HONORS AND AWARDS** Maria Bristow Starke Awd for Fac Excellence. **MEMBERSHIPS** MLA, SAMLA, AATG, AAUP. **RESEARCH** German-American literary connections, 19th Century German Literature. **SELECTED PUBLICATIONS** Auth, "The Critical Reception of Goethe in the Ante-Bellum South," Southern Lit Jour, (86); ed, Literary and Musical Notes: A Festschrift for Wm A Little, Peter Lang, 95; auth, "Mary E Lee, Martha Fenton Hunter, and the German Connection to Domestic Fiction in the Southern Literary Messenger," Southern Quart, (96); auth, "Charles Follen Adams," Am Nat Biog, (Oxford Univ Pr, 99); auth, "The Great War, Literary Tastes, and Political Correctness: The Strange Case of Charles Follen Adams, German Dialect Poet," Yearbook of Ger-Am Studies, (01). **CONTACT ADDRESS** Eng, Philos and Mod Lang, Longwood Col, Farmville, VA 23909. **EMAIL** gorth@luna.moonstar.com

ORTIZ, MARIO A.
PERSONAL Born 07/15/1964, Costa Rica, M, 1988, 1 child **DISCIPLINE** SPANISH LITERATURE **EDUCATION** Grinnell Col, BA, 87; Univ of Houston, MM, 90; Ind Univ, PhD, 00. **CAREER** Assoc instr to vis lectr, Ind Univ, 92-00; vis instr to asst prof, Miami Univ, 00-. **HONORS AND AWARDS** Sigma Delta Pi; Pi Kappa Lambda; Ind Univ Fel, 94; JM Hill Prize, Ind Univ, 97; Miami Univ Grant, 01, 02. **MEMBERSHIPS** MLA, Soc for Renaissance and Baroque Hispanic Poetry, Asn of Hispanic Class Theater, Ohio For Lang Asn, Midwest MLA. **RESEARCH** Golden Age and Colonial Hispanic Literature, Hispanic Poetry, Music and Literature in Relationships. **SELECTED PUBLICATIONS** Coauth, "The Transcendent Harmony: Celestial Music in the Paradiso of Dante," Sophia, (96); auth, "El discurso especulativo musical de Sor Juana Ines de la Cruz," sor Juana y su Mundo, (98); auth, "San Manuel bueno, martir: Divina novela de Miguel de Unamundo, archimensajero," Letras Peninsulares, (01). **CONTACT ADDRESS** Miami Univ, 260 Irwin Hall, Oxford, OH 45056. **EMAIL** ortizma@muohio.edu

OSSAR, MICHAEL LEE
PERSONAL Born 03/31/1938, Bryn Mawr, PA, m, 1963, 2 children **DISCIPLINE** GERMAN LITERATURE **EDUCATION** Cornell Univ, AB, 61; Univ Pa, MS, 63, MA, 67, PhD(Ger lit), 73. **CAREER** Res fel physics, Univ Pa, 61-61, teaching fel Ger, 63-67; lektor English, Univ Freiburg, Ger, 67-68; instr Ger, Sweet Briar Col, 68-71; from Asst Prof to Assoc Prof, 71-88, Prof Ger, Kans State Univ, 88-, Dept Head, 95-; Vis lectr, Swarthmore Col, 66; ed, Studies in Twentieth Century Lit, 78-; vis prof, Giessen Univ, 88. **HONORS AND AWARDS** Nat Endowment for Humanities grant, 76, 77 & 81. **MEMBERSHIPS** MLA; Am Asn Teachers Ger. **RESEARCH** Expressionism; post-war German literature; politics and literature; Adolf Muschg; Celan. **SELECTED PUBLICATIONS** Auth, Das Erdbeben in Chili und Die Marquise von O--, Revue des Langues Vivantes, 68; Die Kunstlergestalt in Goethes Tasso und Grillparzers Sappho, Ger Quart, 72; Note on relativity theory in Der Zauberberg, PMLA, 73; Ernst Toller's Masse-Mensch, Germanic Rev, 76; Anarchism in the Dramas of Ernst Toller, Suny Press, 80; Der eigebildet Kranke bei Adolf Muschg, Neophilogus, 82; Muschg's Ein Glockenspiel, Transl Rev; Individual & Type in Schnitzler's Liebelei, Mod Austrian Lit; Toller: Life and Works, In: Dictionary of Literary Biography; Malevolent God in Celan's Tenebrae, Deutsche Vierteljahrsschrift; Kafa's Forschuugen eines Hundes, Colloquia Germanica; Frischmuth's Amy oder die Metamorphose, In: The Writer as I; The Ludic Principle in Christoph Hein, German Quarterly; Robert Schindels Gebuertig, Aesthetische und religioese Erfahrungen. **CONTACT ADDRESS** Dept of Mod Lang, Kansas State Univ, 104 Eisenhower Hall, Manhattan, KS 66506-1003. **EMAIL** mlo@ksu.edu

OSTERLE, HEINZ D.
PERSONAL Born 08/29/1932, Ulm, Germany, m, 1960, 3 children **DISCIPLINE** GERMAN LITERATURE **EDUCATION** Univ Freiburg, MA, 57; Brown Univ, PhD(Ger), 64. **CAREER** From asst prof to assoc prof Ger, George Washington Univ, 60-65; asst prof, NY Univ, 65-67 & Yale Univ, 67-72; dir div Ger & classics, 73-74, assoc prof, 72-82, Prof Ger to Prof Emer, Northern Ill Univ, 82-, Mem screening comt Ger lit, Int Educ & Cult Exchange Prog, 69-72, chmn comt, 71-72. **HONORS AND AWARDS** Am Asn Teachers Ger Awd for Best Article in Unterrichts praxis, 81. **MEMBERSHIPS** MLA; Am Asn Teachers Ger. **RESEARCH** Twentieth-Century German literature; German literature in exile 1933-45; American-German literary relations. **SELECTED PUBLICATIONS** Auth, The other Germany: Resistance to the Third Reich in German literature, Ger Quart, 68; Alfred Doblin's Revolutionstrilogie November 1918, Monatshefte, spring 70; Hermann Broch, Die Schlafwandler: Kritik der Zentralen Metapher, Deutsche Vierteljahrsschrift Literaturwissenschaft und Geistesgeschichte, summer 70; Hermann Broch, Die Schlafwandler: Revolution and Apocalypse, PMLA, 71; Uwe Johnson, Jahrestage: Das Bild der USA, Ger Quart, 75; Denkbilder uber die USA: Gunter Kunerts Reisebuch Der andere Plante, In: Basis: Jahrbuch fur deutsche Literatur der Gegenwart, Frankfurt Suhrkamp, 77; Alfred Doblins Revolutionsroman, postscript to Alfred Doblin, November 1918, (4 vols), Munich, 78; coauth, German studies in America, In: German Studies Notes Ser, Inst Ger Studies, Ind Univ, Bloomington, 78; The lost utopia: New images of America in German literature, Ger Quart, 81. **CONTACT ADDRESS** Dept of For Lang and Lit, No Illinois Univ, Watson Hall 111, Dekalb, IL 60115-2825. **EMAIL** hosterle@niu.edu

OSTWALD, MARTIN
PERSONAL Born 01/15/1922, Dortmund, Germany, m, 1948, 2 children **DISCIPLINE** CLASSICAL PHILOLOGY **EDUCATION** Univ Toronto, BA 46; Univ Chicago, AM, 48; Columbia Univ, PhD, 52. **CAREER** Instr class philol, 50-51, Wesleyan Univ; lectr & assoc Greek & Latin, 51-54, Columbia Univ; asst prof, 54-58, assoc prof, 58-66, prof classics, 66-92, Swarthmore Col; prof class studies, 68-92, prof emeritus, 92- Univ Pa; Fulbright res fel, Greece, 61-62; Am Coun Learned Soc res fel, 65-66; NEH sr fel, 70-71; vis fel, 70-71, Balliol Col Oxford Univ; mem, Inst Adv Study, 74-75 & 81-82, Princeton Univ; dir, NEH fel-in-residence in classics, 76-77; Guggenheim fel, 77-78. **HONORS AND AWARDS** Goodwin award of Merit of Amer Philol Assn, 90; fel, Amer acad of Arts & Sci, 91; Amer Philos Soc, 93; hon mem, Soc for Promotion of Hellenic Stud, 95; Dr Honoris Causa, Fribourg, Suisse, 95. **MEMBERSHIPS** Soc Prom Hellenic Studies; Am Philol Assn; Class Assn Can; Archaeol Inst Am. **RESEARCH** Greek social and political thought and institutions; Greek history, philosophy and literature. **SELECTED PUBLICATIONS** Auth, Autonomia: Its Genesis and Early History, Scholars, 82; auth, From Popular Sovereignty to the Sovereignty of Law, Univ Calif Press, 86. **CONTACT ADDRESS** 408 Walnut Ln, Swarthmore, PA 19081. **EMAIL** mostwal1@swarthmore.edu

OTERO, JOSE
PERSONAL Born 07/18/1932, Ecuador, m, 1957, 2 children **DISCIPLINE** HISPANIC AMERICAN LITERATURE **EDUCATION** Univ NM, BA, 62, MA; 64, PhD(Span), 69. **CAREER** Teaching asst Span, Univ NM, 64-68; asst prof, 68-73, Assoc Prof Span, Colo State Univ, 73- **MEMBERSHIPS** Rocky Mountain Mod Lang Asn; Am Asn Teachers Span & Port; Casa Cult Am, Filial de Guayaquil. **RESEARCH** Hispanish American poetry and novel. **SELECTED PUBLICATIONS** Auth, Los Pajaros en la Poesia de Jorge Carrera Andrade, El Comercio, Quito, 67; El tiempo en la poesia de Jose Asuncion Silva, Bull Rocky Mountain Mod Lang Asn, 70; Nuevas voces del reino de Strossner, Nueva Narrativa Hispanoam, 71; La estetica del doble en Aura de Carlos Fuentes, Explicacion de Textos Lit, 76; Hispanic Colorado, Centenial, 76; H G Wells y E Anderson Imbert: The Truth About Pyecraft y El leve Pedro, Hispanofila, 79; El misticismo poetico de Pablo, Explicacion de Textos Literarios, 80-81; Delmira Agustini: Erotismo poetico o misticismo erotico?, In: In Honor of Boyd G Carter, Univ Wyo, 81; Contemporary Spanish-american Poets - a Bibliography of Primary And Secondary Sources - Sefami,j, Chasqui-revista De Literatura Latinoamericana, Vol 0021, 1992; 'Querido Diego, The Abraza Quiela', Destruction And Reconstruction of The Personality - Language, Structure And Symbols, Confluencia- revista Hispanica De Cultura Y Literatura, Vol 0007, 1992; Writing in Cuba, Interviews With Cuban Writers 1979-1989 - Spanish - Bejel,e, Chasqui-revista De Literatura Latinoamericana, Vol 0022, 1993. **CONTACT ADDRESS** Dept of Foreign Lang, Colorado State Univ, Fort Collins, CO 80523.

OTERO-KRAUTHAMMER, ELIZABETH
PERSONAL Born Buenos Aires, Argentina, d, 2 children **DISCIPLINE** LINGUISTICS **EDUCATION** Univ Pittsburg, BA; MA; Rutgers Univ, PhD. **CAREER** Lectr, Rutgers Univ, 86-87; instr, SW Tex State Univ, 87-89; vis asst prof, Tulane Univ, 89-91; assoc prof, SUNY-Oneonta, 91. **HONORS AND AWARDS** Phi Sigma Iota, Int For Lang Asn; Merit increase for Excellence in Acad Performance, SW Tex Univ, Magna Cum Laude, Rutgers Univ. **MEMBERSHIPS** La Chispa, NEMLA, Hispamerica, Int Conf on Caribbean Lit, MLA **RESEARCH** Latin American women writers, Spanish Caribbean writers, Latin American Jewish Writers. **SELECTED PUBLICATIONS** Auth, "Manuel Puig," Latin Am Writers (NY: Charles Scribners Sons, 89): 1405-1413; auth, "La orilla inmenente de Saul Sosnowski: Un manifiesto revisionista y renovador," Revista Lit NOAJ 6 (Isreal, 91): 66-67; auth, "Las moradas interiores en Cartas apocrifas de Gloria Guardia," in Cambios esteticos y nuevos proyectos culturales en Centroamerica, ed. Amelia Mondragon (MD: Literal Books, 94): 123-133; auth, "Sicologia y literatura en la narrativa de Lucia Guerra," Textos: Works and Criticism 5.1 (97): 34-37; auth, "The Psychosexual Unity in 'Kiss of the Spider Woman'," Textos: Works and Criticism (99); auth, Represion y libertad de la condicion humana en la narrativa de Manuel Puig: Un analisis sicosocial (forthcoming). **CONTACT ADDRESS** Dept For Lang, SUNY, Col at Oneonta, PO Box 4015, Oneonta, NY 13820-4015. **EMAIL** oteroke@snyoneva.cc.oneonta.edu

OTTENHOFF, JOHN
DISCIPLINE RHETORIC, LINGUISTICS AND BRITISH LITERATURE **EDUCATION** Univ Chicago, PhD. **CAREER** Prof, adv, Sigma Tau Delta, Alma Col. **HONORS AND AWARDS** Outstanding Fac Mem in Hum Awd. **RESEARCH** Shakespeare; Shakespeare on film. **SELECTED PUBLICATIONS** Publications in his specialty, Renaissance devotional poetry. **CONTACT ADDRESS** Alma Col, Alma, MI 48801.

OTTO, KARL F.
PERSONAL Born 09/03/1940, MI, d, 2 children **DISCIPLINE** GERMAN LITERATURE **EDUCATION** Aquinas Col, BA, 62; Northwestern Univ, MA, 63; PhD, 67. **CAREER** From Asst Prof to Prof, Univ Ill, 67-85; Prof, Univ Pa, 85-. **HONORS AND AWARDS** Alexander vo Humbolt Found Fel; IREX Grant; NEH Grants; Goethe Inst Grants, DAAD Grants. **MEMBERSHIPS** MLA, AATG, ACTFL, AAUSC. **RESEARCH** Seventeenth-Century German literature. **SELECTED PUBLICATIONS** Auth, "Die zehnte Muse im Pegnesischen Blumenorden: Anna Maria Nutzel," in der Franken Rom: Nurnbergs Blutezeit in der zweiten Halfte des 17. Jahrhunderts, Harrassowitz (95): 331-341; auth, "Daniel Klesch und die Deutschgesinnten," in Bruckenschlage: Eine baroke Festgabe fur Ferdinand van Ingen, Rodopi (95): 233-243; auth, "Daniel Georg Morhof," in Ger Baroque Writers, Gale Res, Inc (96): 224-229; auth, "Philipp von Zesen," in Ger Baroque Writers 1580-1660, Gale Res, Inc (96): 370-378; coauth, Bibliographia Kleschiana: The Writings of a Baroque Family, Camden House (Columbia, SC), 96. **CONTACT ADDRESS** Dept Lang, Univ of Pennsylvania, 255 S 36th St, PO Box 42813, Philadelphia, PA 19101-2813. **EMAIL** otto@pobox.upenn.edu

OUIMETTE, VICTOR
PERSONAL Born 04/21/1944, Calgary, AB, Canada, m, 1967 **DISCIPLINE** SPANISH LITERATURE **EDUCATION** McGill Univ, BA, 65; Yale Univ, PhD(Span), 68. **CAREER** Asst prof, 68-73, Assoc Prof Span, McGill Univ, 73-. **MEMBERSHIPS** MLA; Am Asn Teachers Span & Port; Can Asn Hispanists; Northeast Mod Lang Asn; Asoc Pensamiento Hisp. **RESEARCH** The generation of 1898; the realist novel in Spain and France; modern Spanish currents of ideas. **SELECTED PUBLICATIONS** Auth, Reason aflame: Unamuno and the Heroic Will, Yale Univ, 74; Unamuno, Blasco Ibanez and Espana con Honra, Bull Hisp Studies, 1076; The liberalism of Baroja and the second RePubic, Hispia, 377; Unamuno and Le Quotidien, Rev Can Estudios Hispan, 1077; Jose Ortega y Gasset, G K Hall, 82; Marias,julian, The 1st 80-years, Hispania-a J Devoted to The Teaching of Spanish And Portuguese, Vol 0077, 1994; Crossfire - Philosophy And The Novel in Spain, 1900-1934 - Johnson,r, Hispanic Review, Vol 0064, 1996. **CONTACT ADDRESS** Dept of Hisp Studies, McGill Univ, Montreal, QC, Canada H3A 1G5.

OVERBECK, JOHN CLARENCE
PERSONAL Born 11/04/1933, Tulsa, OK, m, 1972, 1 child **DISCIPLINE** CLASSICAL ARCHEOLOGY, ANCIENT GREEK **EDUCATION** Univ Okla, AB, 55; Univ Cincinnati, PhD(classics), 63. **CAREER** Asst prof, 63-66, Assoc Prof Classics, State Univ NY Albany, 66-, Mem managing comt, Am Sch Class Studies, Athens, 66-75; dir archaeol surv, Dept of Antiquities, Repub of Cyprus, 70. **MEMBERSHIPS** Archaeol Inst Am; Soc Prom Hellenic Studies; Asn Field Archaeol; Mod Greek Studies Asn. **RESEARCH** Cycladic Bronze Age; early Greek literature. **SELECTED PUBLICATIONS** Auth, Tacitus and Dio on Boudicca's rebellion, Am J Philol, 4/69; Greek towns of the Early Bronze Age, Class J, 10/69; Some notes on the interior of the Erechtheum, Athens Ann Archaeol, 4/72; coauth, Two Cypriot Bronze Age Sites at Kafkallia, Paul Astrom, Goteborg, Sweden, 72; The date of the last palace at Knossos, Am J Archaeol, spring 76; auth, Pioneers of Attic Vase Painting, In: The Greek Vase, Hudson-Mohawk Asn Cols & Univs, 81; The hub of commerce: Keos and Middle Helladic Greece, In: Temple University Aegean Symposium, Betancourt, 82; coauth, Consistency and diversity in the Middle Cycladic Era, In: Papers in Cycladic Prehistory, Univ Calif, Los Angeles, 79. **CONTACT ADDRESS** Dept of Classics, SUNY, Albany, 1400 Washington Ave, Albany, NY 12222-1000.

OVERFIELD, DENISE
DISCIPLINE LINGUISTICS **EDUCATION** Univ Pittsburgh, MA, PhD. **RESEARCH** Community based language learning. **SELECTED PUBLICATIONS** Auth, pubs on community-based language learning. **CONTACT ADDRESS** Dept Foreign Languages and Literature, State Univ of West Georgia, Carrollton, GA 30118.

OWENS, WILLIAM M.
DISCIPLINE CLASSICS **EDUCATION** Cornell Univ, BA, 76; Yale Univ, PhD, 86. **RESEARCH** Social hist; anc slavery; Roman comedy; the Greek novel. **CONTACT ADDRESS** Dept of Classics, Ohio Univ, Athens, OH 45701. **EMAIL** owensb@ohio.edu

OXENHANDLER, NEAL
PERSONAL Born 02/03/1926, St. Louis, MO, 3 children **DISCIPLINE** FRENCH **EDUCATION** Univ Chicago, AB, 48; Columbia Univ, MA, 50; Yale Univ, PhD, 55. **CAREER** Instr French, Yale Univ, 53-57; from asst prof to assoc prof, Univ CA, Los Angeles, 57-66; prof French lit, Cowell Col, Univ CA, Santa Cruz, 66-69; Prof French Lit, 69-87, Edward Tuck Prof French, Dartmouth Col, 87-94, Prof Emeritus, 94-, Ch, Dept Fr & Ital, 87-91, Fac, Semester at Sea, 95. **HONORS AND AWARDS** Fulbright fel, 53; Guggenheim fel, 61-62; cross disciplinary fel, 66 & 67; dir, Nat Endowment for Hum sem, 81. **MEMBERSHIPS** MLA. **RESEARCH** French lit of the 19th and 20th centuries; psychoanalysis and lit; French cinema. **SELECTED PUBLICATIONS** Auth, Scandal and Parade, Rutgers Univ, 57; coauth, Aspects of French Literature, Appleton, 61; auth, A Change of Gods, Harcourt, 62; Max Jacob and Les Feux de Paris, Univ Calif, 64; French Literary Criticism, Prentice-Hall, 66; Quest for pure consciousness in Husserl and Mallarme, In: Quest for Imagination, Case-Western Reserve, 71; Literature as perception in the work of Merleau-Ponty, In: Modern French Criticism, Univ Chicago Press, 72; Intimacy and Distance in the Cinema of Jean-Luc Godard, Symp, 73; The Man with Shoes of Wind, In: The Gadamer-Derrida Encounter, SUNY Press, 89; Listening to Burroughs' Voice, In: Burroughs at the Front: Critical Reception 1959-1989, 91; coauth, Looking for Heroes in Postwar France, Univ Press New England, 96; auth, Cocteau on Video, Bucknell Rev, 97. **CONTACT ADDRESS** Dept of French & Ital, Dartmouth Col, 6087 Dartmouth Hall, Hanover, NH 03755-3511. **EMAIL** neal.oxenhandler@dartmouth.edu

OXFORD, JEFFERY
PERSONAL Born 06/25/1966, Nashville, TN, m, 1991 **DISCIPLINE** SPANISH LITERATURE **EDUCATION** Austin Peay State Univ, BA, 87; Tex Tech Univ, MA, 89; PhD, 92. **CAREER** Asst prof, McNee Univ, 92-95; asst prof, Univ N Tex, 95-; asst dept ch, 99-. **HONORS AND AWARDS** Who's Who, AM, World, SSW; Gold Rule Awd; Outstand Yng Men Am. **MEMBERSHIPS** Alpha Lambda Delta; Omnicron Delta Kappa; Sigma Delta Pi; SCMLA; TFLA; AATSP; AERA; AIH; MLA. **SELECTED PUBLICATIONS** Coed, The Languages of Addiction, St Martin's Press (NY), 99; auth, Conversarpara aprender, Stipes Pub, 99; auth, Vicente Blasco Ibanez: Color Symbolism in Selected Novels, Peter Lang (NY), 97; auth, "Alcoholic Implications: A Catalyst of Valencian Culture," in The Languages of Addiction, eds. Jane Lilienfield, Jeffery Oxford (NY: St. Martin's Press, 99), 161-173; auth, "Pardo Bazan and Blasco Ibanez: A Comparative Overview of Selected Criticism," in Estudios en honor de Janet Perez: El sujetofemenino en escritoras hispanicas, eds. Susana Cavallo, Luis Jimenez, Oralia Preble-Niemi (Potomac, Maryland: Scripta Humanistica, 98), 233-44; auth, "Huevos estrellados.. y catados: Pichula Cuellar," in Mario Vargas Llosa: Opera omnia, ed. Ana Maria Hernandez de Lopez (Madrid: Editorial Pliegos, 94), 327-330; auth, "Giants of Spanish Literature: Archetypes and Nobel Winners," in Proceedings of the Philological Asn of Louisiana, ed. Scott Goins (Lake Charles, LA: McNeese State Univ, 96), 41-44; auth, "Ekphrasis and Nineteenth-Century Spanish Naturalism," in Proceedings of the Philological Asn of Louisiana, ed. Scott Goins (Lake Charles, LA: McNeese State Univ, 95), 89-94; auth, "Revelations of Language: Mimetic, Artistic and Coincidental Parallels of Women's Voices," CLA J (97): 44-54; auth, "Asociaciones cromaticas a la falacia patetica dentro de las obras valencianas y naturalistas de Blasco Ibanez," Explic lit (97): 23-29. **CONTACT ADDRESS** Dept Foreign Languages, Literatures, Univ of No Texas, PO Box 311127, Denton, TX 76203-1127. **EMAIL** oxford@unt.edu

P

PAAS, JOHN ROGER
PERSONAL Born 03/14/1945, Chicago, IL, m, 1968, 2 children **DISCIPLINE** GERMAN **EDUCATION** Hamilton Col, BA, 67; Bryn Mawr Col, PhD, 73. **CAREER** Asst prof, Bryn Mawr Col, 73-74; prof, Carleton Col, 74; Chair, 85-88, 99. **HONORS AND AWARDS** IREX Fel, 78; Bush Found Grant, 78; Fulbright Fel, 88-89; NEH Travel to Collections, 90; Fel, Yale Univ, 91; NEH, 92-93; Humboldt Res Fel, 00-01. **MEMBERSHIPS** MLA; Wolfenbutteler Arbeitskreis fur Barockforschung; Fruhe Neuzeit Interdisziplinar; Gutenberg Soc; Soc of Ger Renaissance and Baroque Lit. **RESEARCH** 17th Century German literature, political prints. **SELECTED PUBLICATIONS** Auth, The German Political Broadsheet, 1600-1700, Wiesbaden: Harrassowitz, 85; auth, Effigies et Poesis: An Illustrated Catalogue of Printed Portraits with Laudatory Verses by German Baroque Poets, Wiesbaden: Harrassowitz, 88; auth, "Unbekannte Gedichte und Lieder des Sigmund von Birken", Chloe 11, 90; auth, Hollstein's German Engravings, Etchings and Woodcuts 1400-1700, Vols 38-41, Sound and Vision Interactive, 94-95; auth, "der Franken rom: Nurnbergs Blutezeit in der zweiten Halfte des 17. Jahrhunderts, Wiesbaden: Harrassowitz, 95. **CONTACT ADDRESS** Dept German, Carleton Col, Northfield, MN 55057-4044. **EMAIL** rpaas@carleton.edu

PACHECO-RANSANZ, ARSENIO
PERSONAL Born 02/08/1932, Barcelona, Spain, m, 1956, 2 children **DISCIPLINE** SPANISH **EDUCATION** Univ Barcelona, MA, 54; PhD, 58. **CAREER** Instr, Univ Barcelona, 54-56; lectr, Nurnberg, 56; asst lectr, Univ Glasgow, 57-59; asst lectr to lectr, Univ St Andrews, 59-70; vis prof, Univ Pitt, 66; vis asst prof to assoc prof to prof to emer, Univ Brit Colum, 68-. **HONORS AND AWARDS** RSC Fel, 81; Izaak Walton Killam Fel, 83; Hon Pres NACS, 93. **MEMBERSHIPS** MLA; AIH; AILLC; CAH; NACS; Anglo-Catalan Soc; AHGBI. **RESEARCH** Catalan and Castilian narrative from the Middle Ages to the 17th century. **SELECTED PUBLICATIONS** Auth, Historia de Xacob Xalabin, Ed Barcino (Barcelona), 64; auth, Viatges a L'Altre Mon, Edicons (Barcelona), 71; auth, Cespedes y Meneses, Fortuna Varia del Soldado Pindaro, Espasa Calpe (Madrid), 75; auth, Testament d'En Serradell de Vic, Ed Barcino (Barcelona), 80; auth, Les Amoroses I Morals, Ed Barcino (Barcelona), 82; auth, Blandin de Cornualla i Altres Narracions en Vers Dels Segles XIV I XV, Edicons (Barcelona), 83; auth, Francesco de la Via, Obres, Quaderns Crema (Barcelona), 97; auth, "St. Patrick's Purgatory: The Waning of a Legend," Catalan Rev 13 (99). **CONTACT ADDRESS** Dept Fr Hisp Ital Studies, Univ of British Columbia, Vancouver, BC, Canada V6T 1Z1. **EMAIL** arp@interchange.ubc.ca

PACHMUSS, TEMIRA
PERSONAL Born Vask, Estonia, d **DISCIPLINE** RUSSIAN LITERATURE & LANGUAGE; COMPARATIVE LITERATURE **EDUCATION** Univ Melbourne, BA, 54, MA, 55; Univ Wash, PhD, 59. **CAREER** Court interpreter, US Mil Govt Court, Ger, 45-49; instr Russ, Univ Melbourne, 52-54, teacher, Univ High Sch, 54-55; teaching assoc Russ, Univ Wash, 55-58; instr, Russ lang, Univ Mich, 58-59; instr Russ lang & lit, Univ Colo, 59-60; from instr to assoc prof, 60-68, Prof Russ Lit, Univ Ill, Urbana, 68-. **HONORS AND AWARDS** Phi Kappa Phi; Nat Slavic Honor Soc "Dobro Slovo"; Estonian Learned Soc Am; Medal of the Order of the White Star, 01. **MEMBERSHIPS** Estonian Learned Soc Am; Asn of the Russian and Am Scholars. **RESEARCH** Works of Dostoevsky and Zinaida Hippius; women writers in Russian modernism; Russian literature in exile 1921-1939. **SELECTED PUBLICATIONS** Auth, Zinaids Hippins: An Intellectual Profile, Southern Ill Univ, 72; auth, D.S. Merezhkovsky in Exile: The Master of the Genre of

Biographie Romancee, Peter Lang, 90; co-ed, Vadim Gardner: At the Bay of Finland, Granite, 90; ed, D.S. Merezhkovsky, Reformatory: Luther, Calvin, Pascal, Foyer Oriental Chretiens and La Presse Libre, 90; ed, D.S. Merezhkovsky/Z.N. Hippius, Dante. Boris Godunov, Gnosis Press, 90; auth, A Moving River of Tears: Russia's Experience in Finland, Peter Lang, 91. **CONTACT ADDRESS** Dept of Slavic Lang & Lit, Univ of Illinois, Urbana-Champaign, 707 S Mathews Ave, Urbana, IL 61801-3625. **EMAIL** tpachmus@uiuc.edu

PACHOW, WANG
PERSONAL Born 06/01/1918, Chungking, China, m, 1956, 1 child **DISCIPLINE** ASIAN CIVILIZATION, BUDDHIST STUDIES **EDUCATION** Mengtsang Col, BA, 36; Visva-Bharati Univ, MA, 42; Univ Bombay, PhD, 48. **CAREER** Lectr, Visva-Bharati Univ, 41-47; lect & head dept, Univ Allahabad, 47-53; sr lectr, Univ Ceylon, 54-65, reader, 66-68; assoc prof, 68-75, Prof, prof emer, Sch Relig, Univ Iowa, 75-. **HONORS AND AWARDS** Res fel, Yale Univ, 61; Acad Hospitality Awd, Univ London, 61-62; vis prof, Visva-Bharati Univ, 62; hon consult for the Humanities, Washington, 77; external examr, Univ Delhi, India, 78-. **MEMBERSHIPS** Am Acad Relig; Am Orient Soc; Asn Asian Studies; Maha-Bodhi Soc; Soc Study Chinese Relig. **RESEARCH** Chinese thought and literature; Sino-India culture. **SELECTED PUBLICATIONS** Auth, A Comparative Study of Pratimoksa, On the Basis of Its Chinese, Tibetan, Sanskrit and Pali Versions, Comp Sino- Indian Cult Soc, 55; A study of the Dotted Record, J Am Orient Soc, 7-965; Tripitaka, Encycl Britannica, 68; Gautama Buddha: Man or superman?, In: Malalasekera Commemoration Volume, Colombo, Ceylon, 76; The controversy over the immortality of the soul in Chinese Buddhism, J Orient Studies, Univ Hong Kong, 1278; A Study of the Twenty-Two Dialogues on Mahayana Buddhism, The Chinese Culture, 79; Chinese Buddhism: Aspects of Interaction and Reinterpretation, Univ Am Press, 80; Arahant, Bhavacakra, Paticcasamuppada, In: Abingdon Dict of Living Religions, 81; Tan,yun-shan And Cultural-relations Between China And India, Indian Horizons, Vol 0043, 1994; Tan,yun-shan And Cultural-relations Between China And India, Indian Horizons, Vol 0043, 1994. **CONTACT ADDRESS** 3600 Wonderland Park Ct, Kissimmee, FL 34746. **EMAIL** wang-pacho@uiowa.edu

PACKER, JAMES
DISCIPLINE CLASSICS **EDUCATION** UC Berkeley, BA, 59, MA, 60, PhD, 64. **CAREER** Prof, Northwestern Univ, 66-. **RESEARCH** The Temple of the Divine Trajan, Rome; The Theatre of Pompey, Rome. **SELECTED PUBLICATIONS** Auth, The West Library of the Forum of Trajan: the Problems and Some Solutions, Nat Gallery Art, 92; The Forum of Trajan: A Study of the Monuments, Calif, 97. **CONTACT ADDRESS** Dept of Classics, Northwestern Univ, 1859 Sheridan Rd, Kresge 12, Evanston, IL 60208-2200. **EMAIL** j.packer@nwu.edu

PADEN, WILLIAM D.
PERSONAL Born 06/20/1941, Lawrence, KS, m, 1973, 2 children **DISCIPLINE** FRENCH **EDUCATION** Yale Univ, BA, 63, PhD, 71; Univ IL, MA, 66. **CAREER** Instr to prof, Northwestern Univ, 68-. **HONORS AND AWARDS** NEH Fel, 76, 87; Director NEH Inst, 95. **MEMBERSHIPS** MLA; Medieval Acad; Am Assoc Teacher of French; Societe Greilhem IX; Assoc Int d"Etudes Orcitanes, Int. Courtly Lit Soc. **RESEARCH** Troubadours, Medieval Poetry. **SELECTED PUBLICATIONS** Auth, Voice of the Trobairitz, 89; ed, Introduction to Old Occitan, 98; ed, Medieval Lyric: Genres in Historial Context, 00. **CONTACT ADDRESS** Dept Fr and Ital, Northwestern Univ, 150 Kresge Hall, Evanston, IL 60208-2204. **EMAIL** wpaden@nwu.edu

PADGETT, JAYE
DISCIPLINE LINGUISTICS **EDUCATION** Univ Md, BA; Univ Mass-Amherst, PhD, 91. **CAREER** Asst Prof, Ling, Univ Calif, Santa Cruz. **RESEARCH** Slavic phonology. **SELECTED PUBLICATIONS** Auth, "OCP Subsidiary Features," Proc of the Northeast Ling Soc 22, 92. **CONTACT ADDRESS** Univ of California, Santa Cruz, 1156 High St, Santa Cruz, CA 95064.

PADILLA, MARK
DISCIPLINE CLASSICS **EDUCATION** Princeton, PhD, 87. **CAREER** Asst prof, 85-92, assoc prof, 93-present, Assoc Prof, 93-99; Prof, Bucknell Univ, 99-. **HONORS AND AWARDS** Summer NEH Fel **MEMBERSHIPS** Amer Philogical Assn **RESEARCH** Greek drama; Greek myth. **CONTACT ADDRESS** Classics Dept, Bucknell Univ, Lewisburg, PA 17837.

PAGANINI, MARIA
DISCIPLINE 19TH- AND 20TH-CENTURY NARRATIVE IN FRENCH LITERATURE **EDUCATION** Zurich Univ, PhD. **CAREER** Instr, Univ Minn, Twin Cities. **RESEARCH** The relation of literature to the law. **SELECTED PUBLICATIONS** Auth, Flaubert: La Presence de l'ecrivain dans l'oeuvre, Juris Verlag, 74; Reading Proust: In Search of the Wolffish, Univ Minn Press. **CONTACT ADDRESS** Univ of Minnesota, Twin Cities, 72 Pleasant St. SE, 104 Scott Hall, Minneapolis, MN 55455.

PALACIOS, CONNY
PERSONAL Born 12/08/1953, Nicaragua, m, 1971, 3 children **DISCIPLINE** SPANISH **EDUCATION** St Thomas Univ, BA, 84; Univ Miami, Coral Gables, Fla, PhD, 95. **CAREER** Lang instr, Johnson & Waks Univ, North Miami, Fla, 96; asst prof, Whitworth Col, 97-00; Southeast Mo State Univ, Aug 00-. **HONORS AND AWARDS** Dean's List, 82-83; Sigma Delt Pi, Spanish Nat Honor Soc, 91; Who's Who in the South and Southwest, Silver (25th) Ed, 97-98; Diccionario de Autores Nicaraguenses. **MEMBERSHIPS** Am Asn of Teachers of Spanish and Portuguese; mem, Instituto Cultural Ruben Dario, sponsored by the Nicaraguan consulate. **RESEARCH** Central American poetry. **SELECTED PUBLICATIONS** En carne viva (novel), Miami: La Torre de Papel, (94); Auth, Pluralidad de mascaras en la lirica de Pablo Antonio Cuadra, Nicaragua: Editorial ciencias speciales INIES, Academia Nicaraguense de la lengua (96); Exorcisno del absurdo (poetry), Nicaragua: PAVSA, (99); Percepcion Fractal (poetry), Nicaragua: PAVSA (99). **CONTACT ADDRESS** Dpet Modern Langs, Whitworth Col, 300 W Hawthorne Rd, Spokane, WA 99251-2515.

PALENCIA-ROTH, MICHAEL
PERSONAL Born 06/26/1946, Girardot, Colombia, m, 1968, 2 children **DISCIPLINE** COMPARATIVE LITERATURE **EDUCATION** Vanderbilt Univ, BA, 68; Harvard Univ, MA, 71, PhD(comp lit), 76. **CAREER** Tutor comp lit, Harvard Univ, 71-73; from instr to asst prof, Univ Mich, Dearborn, 74-77; from Asst Prof to Assoc Prof, 77-87, Prof Comp Lit, Univ Ill, 87-, Dir Undergrad Studies Comp Lit, 78-80, 81-87, Dir, Program Comp Lit, 88-94; Assoc ed, Philos & Lit, 75-77; asst ed, Comp Lit Studies, 77-86; Dir, Univ of Michigan-Dearborn, at the Universitat Wien, Vienna, Summer 77; permanent academic consultant and distinguished extra-mural professor for the Escuela de Estudios Literarios and the Facultad de Humanidades, Universidad del Valle, Colombia; coed, Revista de Estudios Colombianos, 00-. **HONORS AND AWARDS** Univ Schol, 64-68; Merrill Moore Awd, Vanderbilt, 67; Phi Beta Kappa, Magna Cum Laude, Honors in English & Philos, 68; Woodrow Wilson Fel, 68; DAAD Fel to Harvard, 69-73; Grad Prize Fel to Harvard, 69-73; Grad Prize Dissertation Fel, 73-74; Res Assistance Grants, Univ Ill, 78-79, 81-82, 83-84, 88-89; Nat Endowment for Humanities fel, 80-81; Exploratory Grant, Ill, for research in Mexico City, 83; Newberry Libr Fel in Paleography, 84; Herman Dunlap Smith Fel in the Hist of Cartog, Newberry Libr, 85; Order of Merit in Art and Cult Pedro Morale Pino, Colombia, 98; Int Adv Bd of UNEDA, 99. **MEMBERSHIPS** MLA; Am Comp Lit Asn; Int Soc Comp Study Civilizations; Inst Int de Lit Iberoamericana. **RESEARCH** The Faustiansensibility; philosophical and psychoanalytic approaches to literature; the literature and thought of cross-cultural encounters; 20th-century Latin American narrative. **SELECTED PUBLICATIONS** Auth, Thomas Mann's non relationship to James Joyce, Mod Lang Notes, 76; The anti-faustian ethos of Die Blechtrommel, J Europ Studies, 79; Faust and the cultural stages of Wagner's Ring, The Opera J, 79; The Contexts of Busoni's Doktor Faust, Science/Technology and the Humanities, 79; Mothers, fathers and the life of reason in Mill's Autobiography, Comp Civilizations Rev, 80; Albrecht Durer's Melencolia I and Thomas Mann's Doktor Faustus, Ger Studies Rev, 80; La imagen del Urboros: el incesto en Cien anos de soledad, Cuadernos Americanos, 81; ed, Perspectives on Faust, Alpha Academic, 83; auth, Gabriel Garcia Marquez: La linea, el circulo y las metamorfosis del mito, Editorial Gredos, 84; ed, The New World, the New Man, and Latin America, special Latin American Issue of Comp Civilizations Rev, no 12, 85; auth, Myth and the Modern Novel, Garland Publ Co, 87; co-ed, Comparative Literature in the Nineties, Am Comp Lit Asn, special double issue of the ACLA Bulletin, 24, no 2, 93; coauth, The Narrow Bridge: Beyond the Holocaust, Univ of Ill Press, 00. **CONTACT ADDRESS** Prog in Comp Lit, Univ of Illinois, Urbana-Champaign, 707 S Mathews Ave, Urbana, IL 61801-3625. **EMAIL** palencia@uiuc.edu

PALEY, SAMUEL M.
PERSONAL Born 10/15/1941, Manchester, NH, M, 3 children **DISCIPLINE** CLASSICS **EDUCATION** Columbia Univ, PhD, 74. **CAREER** Fac, 77; prof, present, The Univ at Buffalo, SUNY; Asst dir Alishar Hoyuk Res Proj, Sorgun, Turkey; dir Emeq Hefer Proj, Israel. **HONORS AND AWARDS** Asst dir Alishar Hoyuk Res Proj, Sorgun, Turkey; dir Emeq Hefer Proj, Univ Buffalo. **MEMBERSHIPS** AIA, ASOR, BSAI, IES, AOS. **RESEARCH** The ancient Near East and Egypt, Judaism, Semitic Languages. **SELECTED PUBLICATIONS** Auth, King of the World: Ashurnasirpal II of Assyria (833-859 B.C.), Brooklyn Mus, 76; coauth, The Reconstruction of the Relief Representations and Their Positions in the Northwest Palace of Kalhu (Nimrud), vols II/III, Philipp von Zabern, 87 and 92. **CONTACT ADDRESS** Dept Classics, SUNY, Buffalo, 338 Millard Fillmore Acad Core, Buffalo, NY 14261. **EMAIL** clapaley@acsu.buffalo.edu

PALIYENKO, ADRIANNA M.
PERSONAL Born 02/28/1956, Kingston, ON, Canada, m, 1986, 3 children **DISCIPLINE** FRENCH, LANGUAGE, LITERATURE **EDUCATION** Univ NC Chapel Hill, MA, 77, PhD, 88; Boston Univ, MA, 82. **CAREER** Assoc prof, 89-, Colby Col. **HONORS AND AWARDS** Fulbright-Hays Scholar, 82-83; Phi Beta Kappa, Phi Eta Sigma, French Gov Awd, 75-76. **MEMBERSHIPS** MLA; NE Modern Lang Assoc; S Atlantic Modern Lang Assoc; Amer Assoc of Teachers of French; Women in French. **RESEARCH** French and Francophone women poets; 19th cent French poetry; Surrealism: 20th cent French theatre; feminist & psychoanalytic approaches to creativity; gender & poetry; reception theory. **SELECTED PUBLICATIONS** Auth, " the Dialogic je in Rimbauds Illuminaions: The Subject of Self and Other," French Forum 19, (94): 261-277; auth , " Margins of Madness and Creativity: Nineteenth Century French Psychiatric and Literary Discourses on he Dream" Dreams in French Literature: The Persistent Voice, Amesterdam-Atlanta, Georgia: Editons Rodipi, (95): 173-198; auth, Rereading Breton's Debt to Apollinaire: Surrealism and Aesthetics of Creative Imaging, " Romance Quarterly 42:1, (95): 18-27; auth, " Dream-work in Rimbauds Illuminations: The Scend of the Other in Bottom," Romanic Review 86:4, (95): 697-706; auth, " Rereading la femme poete: Rimbaud and Louisa Siefert," Nineteenth-Century French Studies, 26,1-2, (97-98): 146-160; auth, Mis-Reading the Creative Impulse: The Poetic Subject in Rimbaud and Claudel, Restaged, S Il Univ Press, 97; contr, A Feminist Companion to French Literature, 98; art, Postmodern Turns Against the Cartesian Subject: Descartes' "I", Lacan's Other, Feminist Interpretations of Descartes, Pa St Univ Press, 99; art, Is a Woman Poet Born or Made?: Discourse of Maternity in Louise Ackermann and Louisa Siefert, Esprit Createur, 99; auth, " Replacing Women in French Poetic History: The Romantic Legacy," Symposium 53.4. (00): 261-282. **CONTACT ADDRESS** Dept of French, Colby Col, 4670 Mayflower Hill, Waterville, ME 04901-8846. **EMAIL** ampaliye@colby.edu

PALLEY, JULIAN
PERSONAL Born 09/16/1925, Atlantic City, NJ, m, 1950, 4 children **DISCIPLINE** SPANISH LANGUAGE & LITERATURE **EDUCATION** Mexico City Col, BA, 50; Univ Ariz, MA, 52; Univ NM, PhD, 58. **CAREER** Asst Romance lang, Univ NM, 52-55; instr, Rutgers Univ, 56- 59; asst prof Span, Ariz State Univ, 59-62; assoc prof, Univ Ore, 62-66; assoc prof Span, 66-73, chmn dept Span & Port, 70- 73, Prof Span & Port, Univ Calif, Irvine, 73-. **MEMBERSHIPS** MLA; Am Asn Teachers Span & Port. **RESEARCH** Contemporary Spanish literature; Pedro Salinas; modern Spanish novel. **SELECTED PUBLICATIONS** Auth, La Luz no Usada: La Poesia de Pedro Salinas, Studium, Mex, 66; ed, Jorge Guillen: Affirmation, A Bilingual Anthology, 1919-1966, Univ Okla, 68; auth, Spinoza's Stone and Other Poems, JNR Publ, 76; El Laberinto y la Esfera: Cien Anos de la novela Espanola, Insula, Madrid, 78. **CONTACT ADDRESS** Dept of Span & Port, Univ of California, Irvine, Irvine, CA 92717.

PALLISTER, JANIS LOUISE
PERSONAL Born 01/12/1926, Rochester, MN **DISCIPLINE** FRENCH LANGUAGE & LITERATURE **EDUCATION** Univ Minn, BA, 46, MA, 48, PhD(French), 64. **CAREER** Instr French, Span & English, Black Hills Teachers Col, 48- 50; teaching asst French, Univ Wis, 51-52; teaching asst, Univ Minn, 54-59; instr, Colby Col, 59-61; from instr to assoc prof, 61-71, prof French, 71-79, Distinguished Univ Prof, Bowling Green State Univ, 79-. **HONORS AND AWARDS** OEA Human Rels Comn Award, 79. **MEMBERSHIPS** Am Asn Teachers Fr; MLA; AAUP; Renaissance Soc Am; Mediaeval Acad Am. **RESEARCH** French medieval language and literature; French Renaissance and baroque literature; lyric poetry. **SELECTED PUBLICATIONS** Auth, Beroalde de Verville's Stances de la Mort and Soupirs Amoureux, Nottingham French Studies, 70; Presentation motifs in the prologue of Claudel's L'Annonce Faite a Marie, Romance Notes, 72; coauth, En attendant Godot, tragedy or comedy?, Esprit Createur, fall 71; auth, The World View of Beroalde de Verville, Vrin, Paris, 71; translr, Bolamba's Esanzo, 77; coauth, Waiting for Death: The Philosophical Significance of Beckett's En Attendant Godot, Univ Ala, 79; The Bruised Reed, Naaman, 78; On Monsters and Marvels, Univ Chicago, 82; b Duras,marguerite - Fascinating Vision And Narrative Cure - Glassman,dn, J of Popular Film And Television, Vol 0020, 1992; Review of 'Aime Cesaire' - Authors Reply, French Review, Vol 0068, 1994; auth, The Cinema of Quebec, Fairleigh Dickinson ,95; Sampling The Book - Renaissance Prologues And The French Conteurs - Losse,dn, French Review, Vol 0070, 1996; The Apotheosis of Orpheus - Aesthetics of The Ode in France in The 16th-century From Sebillet to Scaliger 1548-1561- French - Rouget,f, French Review, Vol 0070, 1996; Social And Political- change in Literature And Film - Chapple,rl, J of Popular Film And Television, Vol 0024, 1996; Gold, Currency, And Exchange in Renaissance Culture - French - Tournon,a, Perouse,ga, French Review, Vol 0070, 1997; auth, French Speaking Women Film Directors, Fairleigh Dickinson, 98. **CONTACT ADDRESS** Dept of Romance Lang, Bowling Green State Univ, Bowling Green, OH 43403. **EMAIL** jpallis@bgnet.bgsu.edu

PALMA, RONALD B.
PERSONAL Born 11/18/1946, Suffern, NY **DISCIPLINE** CLASSICS **EDUCATION** Cornell Univ, BA, 68; Univ Cincinnati, MA, 72, and work completed to PhD. **CAREER** Tchr, classics, Dept of Lang, Holland Hall Sch, Tulsa, Okla, 73- . **HONORS AND AWARDS** Merit Scholar, Cornell Univ, 64-68; Semple fel, Univ Cincinnati, 68-73; Fulbright fel, 81; Rockefeller Found fel, 87; tchr of the year, 82; citation, Comt

on Pres Scholars, 83; Col Bd Advanced Placement Special Recognition Awd, 91; APA/ACL Excellence in PreCollegiate Teaching Awd, 99. **MEMBERSHIPS** Am Philol Asn; Am Class League; Vergilian Soc. **RESEARCH** The connection between high school and college teaching in Classics and establishing national standards in teaching Latin and Greek. **SELECTED PUBLICATIONS** Coauth, Ecce Romani: A Latin Reading Program, Addison-Wesley, 84, 95; ed, Review and Test Preparation Guide for the Beginning Student, Addison-Wesley, 95; ed, Review and Test Preparation Guide for the Intermediate Student, Addison-Wesley, 95; articles in The Class Outlook, The New England Class Newsl, The Longman Latin Newsl; ACL Newsl. **CONTACT ADDRESS** Holland Hall School, 5666 E 81st St., Tulsa, OK 74137. **EMAIL** ronpalma@iamerica.net

PAN, DA'AN
DISCIPLINE COMPARATIVE LITERATURE **EDUCATION** Rohester Univ, PhD, 91. **CAREER** Asst prof, Univ IL Urbana Champaign. **RESEARCH** Class Chinese poetry and painting; comp poetics; interartistic semiotics. **SELECTED PUBLICATIONS** Auth, Decoding the Textual Other-Deconstructive Subtext in Shitao's Landscape; Decoding Sharawadgi-Taoist Influence on the Chinese Landscape Garden; A Compendium of Basic Learning from the Collegiate Chinese Program. **CONTACT ADDRESS** Comp Lit Dept, Univ of Illinois, Urbana-Champaign, E Gregory Drive, PO Box 52, Champaign, IL 61820.

PANCRAZIO, JAMES
DISCIPLINE SPANISH AMERICAN LITERATURE **EDUCATION** Ill State Univ, BA, 87; Univ Ill, MA, 91, PhD, 95. **CAREER** Asst prof, The Univ of Ark at Little Rock, 95-97; asst prof, Ill State Univ, 97-. **HONORS AND AWARDS** Tinker Res Grant, 94; Univ Res Grant, 99; Univ Res Grant to travel, 00. **MEMBERSHIPS** Latin Am Studies Asn; AATSP; Midwest Modern Lang Asn. **RESEARCH** Cuban and Caribbean Culture; (Neo)Baroque and Post-Modern culture in Cuba and the Caribbean; Cuban Narrative; The Baroque in Colonial Latin America. **SELECTED PUBLICATIONS** Auth, "Etica y estetica: el cuerpo en Songoroo cosongo y otros poemas tempranos de Nicolas Guillen," Memorias de la conferencia international sobre la obra de Nicolas Guillen, Havana: La Fundacion Nicolas Guillen, 94; auth, "Rethinking Carpentier's Baroque," Monographic Rev/Revista monografica, X, (94): 82-91; auth, "El terreno corporal: las fronteras de identidad en Songoro cosongo de Nicolas Guillen," Marges 18, (97): 237-249; auth, "Bodily Terrain and the Borders of Identity in Latin America," Diaspora 6.6, (97): 48-65; auth, "We're all Guilty: Lo Cubano in the Confession," Imagination Beyond Nation: Latin American Popular Culture, Pittsburgh: Univ of Pittsburgh Press, (98): 129-41; auth, La lepra creadora: El barroco como discurso poscolonial, Hojas universitarias 48, (99): 132-40; auth, Maceo's Corps(e): The Paradox of Black and Cuban, Caribe 2.2, (99): 83-99. **CONTACT ADDRESS** Dept of Foreign Languages, Illinois State Univ, 243 Stevenson Hall, Normal, IL 61790-4300. **EMAIL** jjpancr@ilstu.edu

PAOLINI, GILBERTO
PERSONAL Born 12/22/1928, L'Aquila, Italy, m, 1960, 2 children **DISCIPLINE** SPANISH LANGUAGE & LITERATURE **EDUCATION** Univ Buffalo, BA, 57; MA, 59; Univ Minn, PhD, 65. **CAREER** Instr Ital & Latin lit, Univ Mass, 58-60; from instr to asst prof Span & Ital, Syracuse Univ, 62-67; assoc prof, 67-76, Prof Span Lit, 76-93, prof emer, 93-, Tulane Univ; dir, Tulane Scholars & Honors Prof, 81-83; chmn, Colloquia Dept, 81-83; editorial bd, Forum Italicum, 67-71; editorial bd, Critica Hispanica, 79-89; editorial bd, Discurso Literario, 85-90; editorial bd, Letras Peninsulares, 87-; assoc ed, South Central MLA Bul, 78-80; cons ed, South Central Review, 88-92; chmn advisory comm, Jambalya Prog, Nat Endowment Humanities, New Orleans, 75-80; originator, Spanish Culture Week, New Orleans, 77, 79; founder, Theta of Louisiana Chapter of Sigma Delta Pi, 77; founder, Louisiana Chapter AATSP, 79; reader, Educ Testing Serv, Princeton, 79-85; exec bd, Southeastern Am Soc 18th Cent Studies, 79-82; exec comm, Louisiana Collegiate Honors Council, 82; chmn, Nat Comm on Public Relations of AATSP, 82-86; founder and dir, Louisiana Conference on Hispanic Langs and Lit (LA CHISPA), 81, 83, 85, 87, 89, 91, 93, 95, 97, 99. **HONORS AND AWARDS** Distinguished Service Awd, Soc Espanola, 79; Knighted by King of Spain in the Order of Isabel la Catolica, 84; subject of Festscrift Studies in Honor of Gilberto Paolini, Juan de la Cuesta, 96; listed in Who's Who in America, Marquis, 81-; listed in Contemporary Authors, 74, 80, 95. **MEMBERSHIPS** MLA; Am Asn Teachers Span & Port; Asn Int Hispanistas; Am Soc 18th Century Study; AAUP; AATI; SCMLA; SAMLA; Am Asn Advancement Humanities; Soc for Lit and Sci; Asn Internat Galdosistas; Soc Literatura Espanola del Siglo XIX. **RESEARCH** Nineteenth century Spanish and Italian novel; naturalism; literature and psychopathology; criminal anthropology. **SELECTED PUBLICATIONS** Auth, Bartolome Soler, novelista: Procedimientos estilisticos, Ed Juventud, 63; auth, An Aspect of Spiritualistic Naturalism in the Novels of B P Galdos: Charity, Las Americas, 69; auth, "Alejandro Sawa, Crimen legal y la antropologia criminal," Critica Hispanica (84); auth, "Polivalente rebeldia en La desheredada de B Perez Galdos," Lingua e Letteratura (Milan, 85); auth, "Ambicion y muerte en una novela de A. Sawa: Analisis de patologia femenil," Actas Selectas (Brown Univ, 86); auth, "Interaccion del mundo artistico y psicologico en Dona Luz de Juan Valera, Juan Valera," Taurus (90); auth, "La conciencia de Palacio Valdes: El capitan Ribot," Boletin Biblioteca Menendez Pelayo (94); auth, "Un acercamiento a la obra de Echegaray," in Studi in onore di Giovanni Allegra (Univ Perugia, Italy, 95); auth, "Spanish Perspectives on Nineteenth-Century Naturalism," Letras Peninsulares (97); auth, 'Inquietudes eticas de los escritores de fin del siglo diecinueve," in Del romanticismo al realismo (Univ Barcelona, 98). **CONTACT ADDRESS** 3 Gregory Farm Road, Easton, CT 06612. **EMAIL** gpaolini@mailhost.tcs.tulane.edu

PAPACHRISTOS, KATHERINE
PERSONAL Born 06/27/1961, Montreal, PQ, Canada, 1 child **DISCIPLINE** FRENCH LITERATURE **EDUCATION** Laval Univ, BA, 84; MA, 87; McGill Univ, PhD, 96. **CAREER** Lectr, Univ de Montreal, 90; lectr, McGill Univ, 89-01. **HONORS AND AWARDS** Fel, Univ Laval, 87, Fel, McGill Univ, 89, 91, 92; Bourse de doctorat du fonds FCAR, 90-91; Dean's Hon List, McGill, 96. **RESEARCH** Litterature francaise du XXe siecle, avant-garde, dada, surrealisme, Nouveau Roman philosophie du langage, pragmatique, esthetique de la reception ethnolinguistique. **SELECTED PUBLICATIONS** Auth, "L'inscription de l'oral dans La Premiere Aventure Celeste de Monsieur Antipyrine de Tristan Tzara, Etudes Litteraires, (98); auth, L'inscription de l'oral et de l'ecrit dans le theatre de Tristan Tzara, Peter Lang, 99. **EMAIL** kpapac@videotron.ca

PAPER, HERBERT HARRY
PERSONAL Born 01/11/1925, Baltimore, MD, m, 1949, 2 children **DISCIPLINE** LINGUISTICS **EDUCATION** Univ Colo, BA, 43; Univ Chicago, MA, 48, PhD (Assyriology), 51. **CAREER** Res asst, Orient Inst, Univ Chicago, 49-51; res assoc, Div Mod Lang, Cornell Univ, 52-53; from asst prof to assoc prof Near Eastern lang & ling, Univ Mich, Ann Arbor, 53-62, prof ling, 62- 76, chmn Dept, 63-68; Prof Ling & Dean Grad Studies, Hebrew Union Col, 77-, Fulbright fel, Iran, 51-52; Am Coun Learned Soc fel, Cambridge, 59-60; mem comt lang prog, Am Coun Learned Soc, 59-, chmn, 61-63; mem comt, Near & Mid East Studies, Am Coun Learned Soc-Social Sci Res Coun, 62-63; Nat Sci Found res grant, 68-70; res prof, Ben-Zvi Inst, Hebrew Univ, Jerusalem, 68-69; trustee, Ctr Appl Ling, 73-75; NEH fel, 75-76; vis prof Hebrew Univ, Jerusalem, 75-76. **MEMBERSHIPS** Ling Soc Am; Am Orient Soc; Am Asn Jewish Studies. **RESEARCH** Indo-Iranian linguistics; modern Persian including Judeo- Persian; Elamite. **SELECTED PUBLICATIONS** Coauth, English for Iranians, 55 & The Writing System of Modern Persian, 55, Am Coun Learned Soc; auth, The Phonology and Morphology of Royal Achaemenid Elamite, Univ Mich, 55; ed, Jewish Languages: Theme & Variations, Am Asn Jewish Studies, 70; auth, A Judeo-Persian Pentateuch, Ben-Zvi Inst, Hebrew Univ Jerusalem, 72; Biblia Judaeo-Persica: Editio Variorum, Univ Microfilms, 73; ed, Language and Texts, Univ Mich, 75; coauth, The Song of Songs in Judeo-Persian, Royal Danish Acad, 77; Elamite Dictionary, Vol 1, A-h, Vol 2, I-z - German - Hinz,w, Koch,h, J of The American Oriental Society, Vol 0112, 1992; The Judeo-persian Poet Emrani And His 'Book of Treasure' - Emrani 'Ganjname', a Versified Commentary on The Mishnaic Tractate 'Abot' - Yeroushalmi,d, J of The American Oriental Society, Vol 0117, 1997. **CONTACT ADDRESS** Sch of Grad Studies, Hebrew Union Col-Jewish Inst of Religion, Ohio, Cincinnati, OH 45220.

PARATI, GRAZIELLA
PERSONAL Born 05/26/1960, Milan, Italy, s **DISCIPLINE** ITALIAN LANGUAGE **EDUCATION** Univ Milan, BA, 87; Univ Wash, MA, 88; Northwestern Univ, PhD, 92. **CAREER** Asst/Assoc Prof, Dartmouth Col, 92-. **MEMBERSHIPS** MLA, AATI, AAUP, ACLA, AAIS. **RESEARCH** Women's Studies, Autobiography, Migration Studies, Cultural Studies. **SELECTED PUBLICATIONS** Auth, Margins at the Center: African Italian Voices, Special Issue of Ital Studies in Southern Africa 8-2 (95); auth, "Italophone voices," Ital Studies in Southern Africa 2 (95); auth, "Testu Migranti," in Via Dogana: Rivista di politica, ed. Luisa Muraro (Dec 96); auth, "Living in Translation, Thinking with and Accent," Romance Lang Annual (96); auth, Public History, Private Stories: Italian Women's Autobiographies, Minn Univ Press (Minneapolis and London), 96; auth, "Lo sguardo dell'altro," in Destini sospesi di volti in cammino (Santarcangelo di Romagna: Fara Editore, 98); auth, "Literature and Immigration" and 3 biog entries in Encyclopedia of Contemporary Italian Culture, ed. Gino Moliterno (NY and London: Routledge, 99); auth, "Mediterranean Crossroads," in Mediterranean Crossroads: Migration Literature in Italy (Farleigh Dickinson Univ Press, 99); auth, "Un altro premio letterario?," in Prole oltre i confini (Santarcangelo do Romagna: Fara Editore, 99); auth, "Cinema e immigrazione nell'Italia contemporanea," in Africa Italia: Due continenti si avvicianano, ed. Sante Matteo and Stefano Bellucci (Santarcangelo do Romagna: Fara Editore, 99); ed, Mediterranean Crossroads: Migration Literature in Italy, Farleigh Dickinson Univ Press (Madison, NJ), 99. **CONTACT ADDRESS** Dept French and Italian, Dartmouth Col, 6087 Dartmouth Hall, Hanover, NH 03755-3511. **EMAIL** graziella.parati@dartmouth.edu

PAREDES, LILIANA
DISCIPLINE SPANISH, LINGUISTICS **EDUCATION** Univ S Calif, PhD, 96. **CAREER** Asst prof, Univ NC-Greensboro, 97-; instr, coodr, Span Lang Prog, Duke Univ. **HONORS AND AWARDS** New Fac Grant/Res, UNC; Summer Excellency Awd, UNC. **MEMBERSHIPS** LSA, MLA, ALFAL. **RESEARCH** Bilingualism; languages in contact; sociolinguistics. **SELECTED PUBLICATIONS** Coauth, art, Null Objects In Bilingual Andean Spanish, 97; coauth, art, The genitive clitic and the genitive construction in Andean Spanish, 97. **CONTACT ADDRESS** Dept of Romance Studies, Duke Univ, 214 Languages Bldg, Box 90257, Durham, NC 27708. **EMAIL** lparedes@duke.edu

PARENT, DAVID J.
PERSONAL Born 05/31/1931, Hamlin, ME, m, 1971, 2 children **DISCIPLINE** GERMAN LANGUAGE & LITERATURE **EDUCATION** Marist Col, BA, 53; Univ Heidelberg, cert, 57; Univ Cincinnati, MA, 65, PhD (Ger), 67. **CAREER** Instr Ger & Russ, Col Mt St Joseph, 63-66; from instr to asst prof Ger, Boston Col, 66-68; Assoc Prof Ger, Ill State Univ, 68-, Ed, Appl Lit Press, 76-; ed assoc, Telos, 78-. **MEMBERSHIPS** MLA; Am Asn Teachers Ger **RESEARCH** Modern German literature. **SELECTED PUBLICATIONS** Transl, Michael Landmann's Reform of the Hebrew Alphabet, 76; Juan Garcia Ponce's Modern Literature and Reality, 76; Jorge Millas' The Intellectual and Moral Challenge of Mass Society, 77; Michael Landmann's Philosophy: Its Mission and its Disciplines, 77; Alienatory Reason, 78; Gustav Landauer's For Socialism, 78; Michael Landmann's De Homine: Man in the Mirror of his Thought, 79; auth, Franz Kafka, and ETA Hoffmann, In: Critical Survey of Short Fiction, 81; Hebbel Dramatic Fantasy - a Categorial Analysis - German - Nolle,v, German Quarterly, Vol 0067, 1994. **CONTACT ADDRESS** Dept of Foreign Lang, Illinois State Univ, Normal, IL 61761.

PARENTE, JAMES A., JR.
DISCIPLINE MEDIEVAL AND EARLY MODERN GERMAN, SCANDINAVIAN, AND NETHERLANDIC LITERATURE **EDUCATION** Yale Univ, PhD. **CAREER** Prof, Univ Minn, Twin Cities. **SELECTED PUBLICATIONS** Auth, Religious Drama and the Humanist Tradition: Christian Theatre in Germany and the Netherlands, 87; ed, Socio-Historical Apporaches to Early Modern German Literature, 93; coed, Literary Culture in the Holy Roman Empire, 1580-1720, 93; Studies in German and Scandinavian Literature after 1500, 93. **CONTACT ADDRESS** Dept of Ger, Scand & Dutch, Univ of Minnesota, Twin Cities, 216 Folwel, Minneapolis, MN 55455. **EMAIL** paren001@tc.umn.edu

PARISH, CHARLES
PERSONAL Born 05/11/1927, Shreveport, LA, m, 1965, 3 children **DISCIPLINE** ENGLISH, LINGUISTICS **EDUCATION** Brooklyn Col, BA, 52; Univ NM, MA, 55, PhD (English ling), 58. **CAREER** Instr English, Univ Wichita, 56-57, asst prof, 58-59; asst prof English & ling, Southern Ill Univ, Alton, 59-63; assoc prof, 65-71, Prof Ling to Prof Emer, Southern Ill Univ, Carbondale, 71-. **HONORS AND AWARDS** Fulbright lectr, Univ Mandalay, 61-62 & Univ Rome, 62-64, 68-69; Coun Am Study Rome, 63-65; consult, Univ Rome, 79. **MEMBERSHIPS** Ling Soc Am; MLA; Teachers English to Speakers Other Lang. **RESEARCH** English as a foreign language teacher-training; second- language acquisition. **SELECTED PUBLICATIONS** Ed, Corso d'Inglese Parlato, Vol 3, 65 & coauth, Vol 4, 68, Harcourt; auth, Some phonetic problems for Burmese speakers of English, Lang Learning, 64; Tristram Shandy Notes, Cliff's Notes, 68; Agenbite of Agendath Netaim, James Joyce Quart, spring 69; The Shandy Bull vindicated, Mod Lang Quart, 370; ESL practice-teaching utilizing videotape, 76 & A practical philosophy of pronunciation, 77, TESOL Quart. **CONTACT ADDRESS** Dept of Ling, So Illinois Univ, Carbondale, Carbondale, IL 62901. **EMAIL** cparish@siu.edu

PARKER, HENRY H.
PERSONAL Born 09/11/1933, Memphis, TN, M, 1987, 2 children **DISCIPLINE** CLASSICAL PHILOLOGY **EDUCATION** St Thomas Coll, BA 1956; Univ of MN, MA 1959; Univ of IL, PhD 1975. **CAREER** Inst, Univ of MN, 61-65; asst prof to full prof, Univ of N Iowa, 65-90, Cunningham Dist Prof of Philos, Univ of Tenn at Martin, 90-. **HONORS AND AWARDS** NDEA Lecturer in Rhetoric 1965; Danforth Assoc Danforth Found; Iowa's Most Outstanding Prof Awd 1972; Geo Wash Carver Disting Lecturer Awd 1975; Ford Foundation Fellow, 1969; Co-Dir, People to People Citizen Ambassador Delegation to South Africa and Zimbabwe, 95. **MEMBERSHIPS** Pres the Off-Campus Univ consulting firm; founder & principal Waterloo-Pre-Sch Acad; pres The Parker Reading Co; pub The Parker Reader Elem Sch Newspaper; producer & star the Hank Parker Show Ch 7; co-dir with Marilyn Crist of CP Collegians Gifted Children's Prog; National Director of Curriculum, Jesse Jackson's PUSH-Excel. **RESEARCH** College Retention, Ebonics, Financial Planning. **SELECTED PUBLICATIONS** Auth, Linnaeus on Drugs, Lund Univ, (Lund Sweden), 94; auth, Teaching Minorities to Play the Corporate Language Game, Univ of SC, 95; auth, Apollo vs. Dionysus: A Philosophy to Increase College Success by 85%, Thomson Co, 01. **CONTACT ADDRESS** Dept of Psych, Philos & Rel, Univ of Tennessee, Martin, Martin, TN 38237. **EMAIL** hparker@utm.edu

PARKER, HOLT
DISCIPLINE CLASSICS **EDUCATION** Tulane Univ, BA, 78; Yale Univ, MA, 80, MPhil, 82, PhD, 86. **CAREER** Assoc prof, Univ Cincinnati. **HONORS AND AWARDS** 5-Star Teaching Awd, 86; Provost's Teaching Improvement Awd, 87; Res Grant, 88; NEH Summer Stipend, Univ of Ariz, 89; Phi Beta Kappa, Judah Touro Medal in Classics, Phi Delta Kappa (German), German Dept Book Prize, Univ Col London: Platt Prize in Greek; NEH Fel, 90-91; Women's Classical Caucus Prize, 92; Rome Prize, Fel of Am Academy in Rome, NEH Fel, 96; Nomination: A B Cohen Teaching Awd, Univ of Cinnati, 96. **MEMBERSHIPS** Am Philol Asn; Soc Ancient Med; Women's Classical Caucus; Screen Actor's Guild. **RESEARCH** Gender studies; Augustan poetry; Greek lyric poetry; Roman comedy; linguistics; literary theory; ancient medicine. **SELECTED PUBLICATIONS** Auth, Crucially Funny or Tranio on the Couch, TAPA, 89; auth, Another Go at the Text of Philaenis, ZPE, 89; auth, The Bones: Propertius 1.21.9-10, Clas Philol, 91; auth, In the Mood: Prop. 2. 26. 1-3, Mnemosyne, 92; auth, The Fertile Fields of Umbria: Propertius 1. 22. 10, Mnemosyne, 92; auth, Love 's Body Anatomized: The Ancient Erotic Manuals and the Rhetoric of Sexuality, Oxford Univ Press, 92; auth, Fish in Trees and Tie-Dyed Sheep: A Function of the Surreal in Roman Poetry, Arethusa, 92; auth, Other Remarks on the Other Sulpicia, CW, 92; auth, Sappho Schoolmistress, TAPA, 93; auth, Sulpicia, the Auctor de Sulpicia and the Authorship of 3.9 and 3.11 of the Corpus Tibullianum, Helios, 94; auth, Innocent on the Face of it: An Overlooked Obscenity in Martial, Mnemosyne, 94; auth, A Curiously Persistent Error: Satyricon 43.4, Clas Philol, 94; auth, Heterosexuality, Oxford Univ Press, 96; auth, Women Physicians in Greece, Rome, and the Byzantine Empire, Univ Press Ky, 97; auth, Latin and Greek Poetry by Five Renaissance Italian Women Humanists, SUNY Press, 97; auth, Plautus vs. Terence: Audience and Popularity Re-examined, AJP, 96; auth, The Teratogenic Grid, Princeton Univ Press, 97. **CONTACT ADDRESS** Dept of Classics, Univ of Cincinnati, PO Box 210226, Cincinnati, OH 45210-0226. **EMAIL** parkerhn@email.us.edu

PARKER, MARGARET
PERSONAL Born 11/10/1941, Lubbock, TX, 1 child **DISCIPLINE** SPANISH **EDUCATION** Tex Tech Univ, BA, 63, MA, 64; Ind Univ, PhD, 69. **CAREER** Instr Span, Odessa Col, 64-65; instr, 68-69, asst prof, 69-78; assoc prof, prof Spanish, La State Univ, Baton Rouge, 79-. **MEMBERSHIPS** MLA; Am Asn Teachers Span & Port; SCent Mod Lang Asn. **RESEARCH** Spanish medieval literature; Women in Hispanic literature. **SELECTED PUBLICATIONS** Auth, The Didactic Structure and Content of El libro de Calila e Digna, Ed Universal, 78; auth The Story of a Story: The Case of the Concella Teodor. Tamesis, 96. **CONTACT ADDRESS** Dept Foreign Lang, Louisiana State Univ and A&M Col, Baton Rouge, LA 70803-5306. **EMAIL** mparker@lsu.edu

PARKER, RICHARD W.
DISCIPLINE CLASSICS **EDUCATION** Univ of Calif at Santa Barbara, BA, 74; MA, 78; Univ of British Columbia, PhD, 86. **CAREER** Lect, Univ of Saskatchewan, 84-85, 86-87; lect, Brock Univ, 85-86; asst prof, Univ Western Ontario, 87-88; asst prof, 88-96, Assoc Prof, 96-, Dept Chair, Brock Univ, 93-98. **HONORS AND AWARDS** Am School of Classical Studies in Athens, 80-81. **MEMBERSHIPS** Archaeological Inst of Am, brd of governors (AIA-Canada); Can Archaeological Inst in Athens; Am Philol Asn; Classical Asn Can; Asn Internationale d'Epigraphie Grec et Latine. **RESEARCH** Greek hist; Greek epigraphy; Greek lit. **SELECTED PUBLICATIONS** Auth, A Greek Inscription from Honoring a Julio-Claudian, Zeitschrift fur Papyrologie und Epigraphik 75, 88; Potamon of Mytilene and His Family, Zeitschrift fur Papyrologie und Epigraphik 85, 91; with E. H. Williams, A Fragment of a Diocletianic Tax Assessment from Mytilene, Echos du Monde Classique XXXIX, New Series 14, 95. **CONTACT ADDRESS** Dept of Classics, Brock Univ, 500 Glenridge Ave, Saint Catherines, ON, Canada L2S 3A1. **EMAIL** rparker@spartan.ac.brocku.ca

PARKER, SIMON B.
PERSONAL Born 02/23/1940, Manchester, England, m, 1961, 2 children **DISCIPLINE** ANCIENT NEAR EASTERN STUDIES, SEMITIC LANGUAGES, HEBREW BIBLE **EDUCATION** Univ Manchester, BA, 60; Asbury Theol Sem, BD, 63; Johns Hopkins Univ, PhD, 67. **CAREER** Asst prof of Humanities and Relig, Reed Col, 67-75; asst to the Pres, Boston Univ, 77-78; asst provost, 78-81, assoc dean and assoc prof, Boston Univ School of Theol, 81-88, assoc prof of Hebrew Bible, 88-97, prof of Hebrew Bible, Boston Univ School of Theol, 97-. **HONORS AND AWARDS** Graves Awd, 72; Named First Harrell F Beck Scholar of Hebrew Scripture, Boston Univ. **MEMBERSHIPS** Am Oriental Soc; Am Schools of Oriental Res; Soc of Biblical Lit; Soc for Old Testament Study, UK. **RESEARCH** Continuities and discontinuities in the lit and relig of ancient Israel, Canaanite, Israelite culture and social hist. **SELECTED PUBLICATIONS** Auth, The Pre-Biblical Narrative Tradition: Essays on the Ugaritic Poems Keret and Aqhat, Resources for Biblical Study 24, Scholars Press, 89; Officials Attitudes Toward Prophecy at Mari and in Israel, Vetus Testamentum 45, 93; The Beginning of the Reign of God--Psalm 82 as Myth and Liturgy, Revue Biblique 102, 95; Stories in Scripture and Inscriptions, Oxford Univ Press, 97; ed and trans, Ugaritic Narrative Poetry, Writings From the Ancient World, Scholars Press, 97; gen ed since 1994 of Writings From the Ancient World, Scholars Press; numerous scholarly articles in books and journals. **CONTACT ADDRESS** School of Theology, Boston Univ, 745 Commonwealth Ave, Boston, MA 02215. **EMAIL** sbparker@bu.edu

PARKER, STEPHEN JAN
PERSONAL Born 08/05/1939, Brooklyn, NY, m, 1965, 2 children **DISCIPLINE** RUSSIAN & COMPARATIVE LITERATURE **EDUCATION** Cornell Univ, BA, 60, MA, 62, PhD (Russ & comp lit), 69. **CAREER** Asst prof Russ, Univ Okla, 66-67; from asst prof to prof Russ, Univ Kans, 67-; mem nat selection comt, Coun Int Educ Exchange, Russ Lang Prof, 77; assoc chmn & dir grad studies to chair, Univ Kansas, 78-; ed, The Nabokovian, 78-. **HONORS AND AWARDS** Nat Endowment for Humanities younger humanist fel, 70-71. **MEMBERSHIPS** MLA; Am Asn Advan Slavic Lang; Am Asn Teachers Slavic & East Europ Lang; Vladimir Nabokov Soc. **RESEARCH** Russian prose fiction of the 19th and 20th centuries; Europan and American modern novel; writings of Vladimir Nabokov. **SELECTED PUBLICATIONS** Coauth, Russia on Canvas: Ily a Repin, Pa State Univ Press, 81; co-ed, The Achievements of Vladimir Nabokov, Cornell Univ, 85; auth, Understanding Vladimir Nabokov, 89; author of numerous articles and reviews. **CONTACT ADDRESS** Dept of Slavic Lang & Lit, Univ of Kansas, Lawrence, Lawrence, KS 66045-0001. **EMAIL** sjparker@ukans.edu

PARR, JAMES A.
PERSONAL Born 10/07/1936, Ritchie Co, WV, m, 1985, 1 child **DISCIPLINE** HISPANIC STUDIES **EDUCATION** Ohio Univ, BA, 59, MA, 61; Univ Pitts, PhD, 67. **CAREER** Instr, Univ Toledo, 63-64; prof, Murray State Univ, 64-70; assoc prof to prof, 70-90, Univ S Calif; prof, Univ Calif-Riverside, 90- . **HONORS AND AWARDS** Del-Amo, 85; Mellon, 61-63; Fulbright, 91. **MEMBERSHIPS** MAL; AATSP; AIH; ALSC; PAMLA; CSA. **RESEARCH** Cervantes, Golden Age literature. **SELECTED PUBLICATIONS** Auth, Don Quixote: An Anatomy of Subversive Discourse, 88; auth, After its Kind: Approaches to the Comedia, 93; auth, Confrontaciones calladas: el critico frente al clasico, 90; co-auth, El infenioso hidalgo don Quijote de la Mancha, 98. **CONTACT ADDRESS** Dept Hisp Stud, Univ of California, Riverside, 900 University Ave, Riverside, CA 92501-0001. **EMAIL** PATXIYYO@AOL.COM/JAMES.PARR@UCR.EDU

PARRY, HUGH
PERSONAL Born 07/11/1934, Liverpool, England, m, 1931, 2 children **DISCIPLINE** CLASSICS **EDUCATION** Cambridge Univ, BA, 56; Univ Calif Berkeley, 63. **CAREER** Lectr to prof and div chair, York Univ, 63-. **HONORS AND AWARDS** Scholar, Cambridge Univ, 53-56; Fulbright Travel Grant, 59-64; Can Coun Leave Fel, 78; Outstanding Teaching Awd, York Univ, 91. **MEMBERSHIPS** APA; CAMWS; Class Asn of Ont. **RESEARCH** Greek drama and religion; Magic in ancient and modern fiction. **SELECTED PUBLICATIONS** Auth, Thelxis: Magic and Imagination in Greek Myth and Poetry, Lanham, 92; auth, "The Apologos of Odysseus: Lies, All Lies?," Phoenix (94): 1-20; auth, Visions of Enchantment: Essays on Magic in Fiction, Lanham, 01. **CONTACT ADDRESS** Div Humanities, York Univ, 4700 Keele St, 262 Vanier Col,, Toronto, ON, Canada M3J 1P3. **EMAIL** hparryhm@yorku.ca

PARSELL, DAVID BEATTY
PERSONAL Born 12/04/1941, Charleston, SC, m, 1967, 2 children **DISCIPLINE** FRENCH **EDUCATION** Hamilton Col, AB, 63; Vanderbilt Univ, MA, 68, PhD(French), 70. **CAREER** Instr French, Grinnell Col, 67-69; from instr to assoc prof, 69-86, Prof Mod Foreign Lang, Furman Univ, 86-. **MEMBERSHIPS** Am Asn Teachers Fr; Southern Comp Lit Asn. **RESEARCH** Georges Neveux; French theatre 1930-1960; surrealism. **SELECTED PUBLICATIONS** Auth, Le Voyageur Sans Bagage and the case against tragedy, Fr Rev, 3/77; Sign and Image in Peret and Magritte, Univ SC Fr Lit Set, Vol 5, 78; Aspects of Comedy in Camus' Le Malentendu, Symposium, Winter 83-84; Louis Auchincloss, Twayne, 86; Michel de Ghelderode, Twayne, 94. **CONTACT ADDRESS** Dept of Mod Foreign Lang, Furman Univ, 3300 Poinsett Hwy, Greenville, SC 29613-0002. **EMAIL** david.parsell@furman.edu

PARSONS, JEDEDIAH DAVID
PERSONAL Born 02/02/1971, New York, NY, m, 1997 **DISCIPLINE** CLASSICS **EDUCATION** Harvard Univ, BA, 93; Univ Calif Berk, MA, 95, PhD, 00. **RESEARCH** Roman comedy; Latin literature. **SELECTED PUBLICATIONS** Auth, A New Approach to the Saturnian Verse, Trans of the APA, forthcoming. **CONTACT ADDRESS** Dept of Classics, Univ of California, Berkeley, 7233 Dwinelle Hall No 2520, Berkeley, CA 94720-2520. **EMAIL** jed@socrates.berkeley.edu

PARSONS, ROBERT A.
PERSONAL Born 04/08/1948, Ft. Benning, GA, m, 1970, 2 children **DISCIPLINE** SPANISH **EDUCATION** WV Univ, BA, 70, MA, 72; OH Univ, MA, 76; Penn St Univ, PhD, 82 **CAREER** Asst prof, 79-83, Assoc prof, 84-91; Prof, 91-, Univ of Scranton **HONORS AND AWARDS** NEH, 84 **MEMBERSHIPS** AATSP, LASA **RESEARCH** Latin Am lit, satire **SELECTED PUBLICATIONS** Coauth, "An Interdisciplinary Approach to Politics and Lit: the Latin Am Case," Teaching Political Science: Politics in Perspective 13.4 (spring 86): 148-153; auth, "The Vision of Horror or Opposing Self: The Double in Three Novels by Carlos Fuentes," J of Evolutionary Psychology 8.1-2 (March 87): 105-114; auth, "Mirror Symbolismin Carlos Fuentes' 'Terra nostra,'" Col Language Asn J 31.1 (Sept 87): 77-86; auth, "Carols Rangel's 'Del buen salvaje al buen revolucionario:' A Maverick's View of US Imperialism," Inter-Am Rev of Bibliography 38.3 (Nov 88): 354-362; auth, "Parody and Self-Parody in 'Lo demas es silencio: (La vida y la obra de Eduardo Torres)' by Augusto Monterroso," Hispania 72.4 (Dec 89): 938-945; auth, "Mempo Giardinelli's 'que solos se quedan los muertos:' An Investigation of Argentina in Mexico," selected Proceedings of the Philological Asn of Louisiana (90): 21-32; auth, "Watches without Owners: Variations on a Spanish Am Satirical Theme," Confluencia: Revista Hispanica de Cultura y Literatura 7.1 (fall 91): 55-61; auth, "Progress in Reverse: Some Spanish Am Satirical Views of Development," Abstracts and Selected Papes from the Second Biennial Conference on Culture, Society and Change in the Americas, Univ South Florida and VENUSA (Tampa, FL), (93): 295-303; auth, "Satira anticlerical en algunos cuentos de Jorge Kattan Zablah," Alba de America, 16 (June 98): 269-285. **CONTACT ADDRESS** Dept of Foreign Lang, Univ of Scranton, Scranton, PA 18510. **EMAIL** parsonsr1@uofs.edu

PARTEE, BARBARA H.
PERSONAL Born 06/23/1940, Englewood, NJ, m, 1997, 3 children **DISCIPLINE** LINGUISTICS **EDUCATION** Univ Swarthmore, BA, 61; Univ Mass, PhD, 65. **CAREER** Prof, Univ Mass. **HONORS AND AWARDS** Am Acad of Arts & Scis Fel, 84; mem, Nat Acad of Scis, 89; Hon Dr of Sci degree, Swarthmore Co, 89; Hon Dr of Math & Physics degree, Charles Univ, Prague, 92; Max Planck Res Awd, 92; Am Asn for the Advancement of Sci, 96; IREX Fel; Fulbright Fel; NEH Fel; NSF Res Gr; Nat Res Council Res Gr; System Devel Found Res Gr; Sloan Found Res Gr. **MEMBERSHIPS** Ling Soc Am; Am Philos Asn; Asn for Comp Ling; Soc for Exact Philos. **RESEARCH** Semantics; semantics relation to syntax, pragmatics, logic, philosophy of language, and cognitive and representational theories of language. **SELECTED PUBLICATIONS** Co-auth, The Major Syntactic Structures of English, Holt, Rinehart, & Winston, 72; auth, "Montague grammar and transformational grammar," Ling Inq 6.2 (75): 203-300; ed, Montague Grammar, Acad Pr, 76; auth, Subject and Object in Modern English, Garland Pub, Inc, 79; auth, Fundamentals of Mathematics for Linguists, Greylock Pub, 79; auth, "Nominal and temporal anaphora," Ling & Philos 7 (84): 243-86; auth, "Noun Phrase Interpretation and Type-shifting Principles," in Studies in Discourse Representation Theory and the Theory of Genrealized Quantifiers, ed J Groenendijk, D. de Jongh, and M Stokhof (Dordrecht, 87), 115-143; co-auth, Mathematical Methods in Linguistics, Kluwer, 90; co-ed, Possible Worlds in Model-Theoretic Semantics: A Linguistic Perspective, de Gruyter, 89; auth, Nominal and Temporal Anaphora, Ling Philos, 84; co-auth, Mathematical Methods in Linguistics, Kluwer, 90; co-ed, Quantification in Natural Languages, Luwer Acad Pub, 95; co-auth, Topic-focus Articulation, Tripartite Structures, and Semantic Content, Kluwer, 98. **CONTACT ADDRESS** Linguistics Dept, Univ of Massachusetts, Amherst, S College 222, Amherst, MA 01003. **EMAIL** partee@linguist.umass.edu

PARTSCH, CORNELIUS
DISCIPLINE GERMAN **EDUCATION** Oberlin Col, BA; Brown Univ, Ma, PhD. **CAREER** Instr, Hamilton Col; vis asst prof-, Colby Col. **SELECTED PUBLICATIONS** Publ, pop cult, lit, music, second lang acquisition. **CONTACT ADDRESS** Dept of Ger, Colby Col, 4000 Mayflower Hill, Waterville, ME 04901-8840.

PASCAL, CECIL BENNETT
PERSONAL Born 05/04/1926, Chicago, IL, m, 1959, 1 child **DISCIPLINE** CLASSICAL PHILOLOGY **EDUCATION** Univ Calif, Los Angeles, AB, 48, MA, 50; Harvard Univ, MA, 53, PhD, 56. **CAREER** Instr classics, Univ Ill, 55-56; instr, Cornell Univ, 57- 60; asst prof classic lang, 60-65; head dept classics, Chinese & Japanese, 65-67 & 72-73, assoc prof, 65-76, Prof Classics, Univ Ore, 76-, Head Dept Classics, 78-, William Amory Gardner traveling fel, Harvard Univ, 56-57; Fulbright-Hays res fel, Univ Rome, 67-68; prof, emer, 96. **MEMBERSHIPS** Am Philol Asn; Philol Asn Pac Coast; Classic Asn Pac Northwest; Archaeol Inst Am; AAUP. **RESEARCH** Latin and Greek literature; Roman religion. **SELECTED PUBLICATIONS** Auth, The Cults of Cisalpine Gaul, Brussels, 64; auth, Horatian Chiaroscuro, In: Hommages a Marcel Renard, Latomus, 69; Rex Nemorensis, Numen, 76; October Horse, Harvard State Col Philol, 81. **CONTACT ADDRESS** Dept of Classics, Univ of Oregon, Eugene, OR 97403. **EMAIL** cbpasc@darkwing.uoregon.edu

PASCAL, PAUL
PERSONAL Born 03/26/1925, New York, NY, m, 1948, 2 children **DISCIPLINE** CLASSICS, MEDIEVAL LATIN **ED-**

UCATION Univ VT, BA, 48; Univ NC, PHD(classics), 53. **CAREER** Prof Classics, Univ Wash, 53-. **MEMBERSHIPS** Am Philol Asn. **RESEARCH** Mediaeval Latin literature. **SELECTED PUBLICATIONS** Coauth, The Institutionum Disciplinae of Isidore of Seville, Traditio, 57; Notes on Missus Sum in Vineam of Walter of Chatillon, Studies in Honor of B L Ullman, Rome, 64; The Conclusion of the Pervigilium Veneris, Neophilologus, 65; The Julius Exclusus of Erasmus, Ind Univ, 68. **CONTACT ADDRESS** Dept of Classics, Univ of Washington, Seattle, WA 98105.

PASCO, ALLAN
PERSONAL Born 08/29/1937, Nashville, TN, m, 1960, 4 children **DISCIPLINE** FRENCH & ITALIAN **EDUCATION** Whitman Col, BA, 60; Northwestern Univ, MA, 61; Univ Mich, PhD, 68. **CAREER** Asst Prof, Univ Chicago, 67-73; Assoc Prof, Purdue Univ, 73-79; Vis Prof, Univ Calif, 79; Prof, Purdue Univ, 79-89; Prof, Univ Kan, 89-. **HONORS AND AWARDS** Fel, Purdue Univ, 85; Distinguished Alumnus, Univ Mich, 88; Fel, Univ Kans, 96; Cramer Fr Teaching and Res Awd, 96, 99. **MEMBERSHIPS** AATF, MSA, Asn of Literary Scholars & Critics, Am Soc of Eighteenth-Century Studies. **RESEARCH** France of the 18th, 19th and 20th-Centuries, the novel, the short story and their cultural and aesthetic context, period 1750-1850, comparative literature. **SELECTED PUBLICATIONS** Auth, The Color-Keys to A La Recherche du temps perdu, Droz (Geneva), 76; auth, Novel Configurations: A Study of French Fiction, Summa (Birmingham),87; auth, Allusion: A Literary Graft, Univ Toronto Pr (Toronto, CAN), 94; co-ed, The Play of Terror in Nineteenth-Century France, Univ Del Pr (Newark), 96; auth, Sick Heroes: French Society and Literature in the Romantic Age 1750-1850, Univ Exeter Pr (Exeter), 97. **CONTACT ADDRESS** Dept Lang, Univ of Kansas, Lawrence, 1 University of Kansas, Lawrence, KS 66045-0001. **EMAIL** apasco@ukans.edu

PASLICK, ROBERT H.
PERSONAL Born 02/11/1930, Denver, CO, m, 1958, 3 children **DISCIPLINE** GERMAN LITERATURE **EDUCATION** Univ Louisville, AB, 52; Ind Univ, MA, 58, PhD(Ger), 62. **CAREER** From instr to asst prof, 61-74, Assoc Prof Ger, Univ Mich, Ann Arbor, 74-. **HONORS AND AWARDS** Sinclair Counseling Awd, 68. **RESEARCH** European 20th century prose. **SELECTED PUBLICATIONS** Auth, Dialectic and non-attachment: The structure of Hermann Hesse's Siddhartha, Symp, 73; The tempter: Bergengruen's Grande Prince and the Hermetic tradition, Neophilologus, 73; Narrowing the distance: Siegfried Lenz's Deutschstunde, Ger Quart, 73; From Nothingness to Nothingness - The Nature And Destiny of The Self in Boehme And Nishitani, Eastern Buddhist, Vol 0030, 1997. **CONTACT ADDRESS** Dept of Ger Lang & Lit, Univ of Michigan, Ann Arbor, Ann Arbor, MI 48104.

PASSARO, MARIA C. PASTORE
DISCIPLINE ITALIAN LANGUAGE AND LITERATURE **EDUCATION** CUNY Univ Ctr, PhD, 87. **CAREER** Assoc prof. **HONORS AND AWARDS** Acad Honors,NEH, Agnelli Found, NIAF, Fulbright; Excel Tchg Awd, Central Conn State Univ, 94; grant, Yale/Mellon, 96-97. **RESEARCH** Middle Ages and Renaissance. **SELECTED PUBLICATIONS** Auth, several short plays; trans, Longfellow's Michael Angelo, Tusiani's Gente Mia and Other Poems, Rind and All, The Fifth Season; trans, Tasso's King Torrismondo, Fordham Univ Press, 97. **CONTACT ADDRESS** Central Connecticut State Univ, 1615 Stanley St, New Britain, CT 06050.

PASSARO, MARIA P.
PERSONAL Born 10/02/1948, Brienza, Italy, w, 2 children **DISCIPLINE** MODERN LANGUAGES **EDUCATION** CUNY, BA, 74; MA, 80; PhD, 87. **CAREER** Adj prof, CUNY, Fordham Univ, 81-88; Instr, Yonkers Pub School, 88-89; asst prof to prof, Cen Conn State Univ, 89-. **HONORS AND AWARDS** Fulbright Scholar, Italy, 81; NEH, Yale, 91; Excellence in Teaching Awd, CCSU, 94-95; CCSU Res Grant, 95; Fel, Yale/Mellon, 96-97; Scholar, Centro Nazionale Studi Leopardiana, Recanati, Italy, 97. **MEMBERSHIPS** MLA; AAIS; AATI; AAHI. **RESEARCH** Renaissance Literature. **SELECTED PUBLICATIONS** Auth, "L'autobiografia di Joseph Tusiana" in A Century of Italian Immigration, Tex Woman's Univ (94):145-152; auth, "Tasso's Rime d'Amore" in Forum Italicum 28.2 (94):414-424; auth, "Gente Mia, An Indispensable Reading, Joseph Tusiana Poet Translator Humanist, (IN:Bordighera, 94), 100-112; auth, "Some Examples of 'Wisdom' and 'Folly' in the Decameron", Forum Italicum 31.1 (97): 145-152; auth, "Joseph Tusiani's Cain: the Better Giver", Gradiva (98):59-63; transl, King Torrismondo by Tasso (Fordham Univ Pr), 97; auth, "From Theory to History and Poetry: Dante's Hunt in the Forest of Dialects", Rivista di Studi Italiani (98):104-115; auth, "Leonardo Sinisgalli's Luciana", Gradiva 18 (00):132-135. **CONTACT ADDRESS** Dept Mod Lang, Central Connecticut State Univ, 1615 Stanley St, New Britain, CT 06053-2439.

PASTOR, BEATRIZ
PERSONAL Born 07/25/1948, Seo de Urgel, Spain, m, 1978, 2 children **DISCIPLINE** LATIN AMERICAN & SPANISH LITERATURE **EDUCATION** Univ Barcelona, BA, 68; Univ Minn, Minneapolis, MA, 71, PhD(Latin Am lit), 77. **CAREER** Asst Prof Latin Am, Span & Comp Lit, Dartmouth Col, 76-. **MEMBERSHIPS** Latin Am Studies Asn; MLA. **RESEARCH** Contemporary Latin American literature; colonial Latin American literature. **SELECTED PUBLICATIONS** Auth, Rupture y Limiles and la narrative de Roberto Arlt, Revista de Critica Lit Latinam, 80; Los 7 Locos y Los Lanfallamas: De le rebelion al Jascismo, Hisp Rev, spring 81; Roberto Arlt y la Rebelion Alienada, Hispamerica, 81; El Mib en la Historie: Camino de Santiago de A Carpenter, Cuadernos Hispanoam, 82; Utopia And Conquest - Utopian Dynamics And Colonial Identity, Revista De Critica Literaria Latinoamericana, Vol 0019, 1993. **CONTACT ADDRESS** Dept of Span & Port, Dartmouth Col, 6072 Dartmouth Hall, Hanover, NH 03755-3511.

PASTOR, LESLIE P.
PERSONAL Born 05/08/1925, 2 children **DISCIPLINE** EUROPEAN HISTORY, GERMAN **EDUCATION** Educ: Seton Hall Univ, AB, 56; Columbia Univ, MA, 59, PhD, 67; Inst E Cent Europe, cert, 60. **CAREER** Instr Seton Hall Prep Sch, 56-60; from instr to asst prof, 60-68, Assoc Prof Ger, Seton Hall Univ, 68-. **MEMBERSHIPS** Am Asn Advan Slavic Studies; Am Asn Tchr(s) Ger; Am Asn for Study Hungarian Hist. **RESEARCH** Ger lang and lit; 18th and 19th century Hungarian hist; hist of East Central Europe; mod East Europ hist. **SELECTED PUBLICATIONS** Auth, Young Szechenyi; The Shaping of a Conservative Reformer, 1791-1832 (Ann Abor, MI), 70. **CONTACT ADDRESS** Dept of Mod Lang, Seton Hall Univ, So Orange, 400 S Orange Ave, South Orange, NJ 07079-2697. **EMAIL** pastorle@shu.edu

PATERNOST, JOSEPH
PERSONAL Born 03/17/1931, Slovenia, m, 1960 **DISCIPLINE** RUSSIAN **EDUCATION** Ohio Univ, BA, 55; Ind Univ, MA, 56, PhD(Slavic ling), 63. **CAREER** From instr to asst prof Russ, 60-68, assoc prof Slavic lang, 68-77 Prof Slavic Lang, PA State Univ, University Park, 77-96, Prof Emeritus of Slavic Languages, 96; Nat Defense Foreign Lang fel, 59-60. **MEMBERSHIPS** Am Asn Teachers Slavic & E Europ Lang; Am Asn Advan Slavic Studies; MLA; Am Asn Southeast Europ Studies; Soc Slovene Studies. **RESEARCH** Slovenian; Russian; theory and practice of translation. **SELECTED PUBLICATIONS** Auth, Russian-English Glossary of Linguistic Terms, 65 & Slovenian-English Glossary of Linguistic Terms, 66, PA State Univ; From English to Slovenian: Problems in Translation Equivalence, PA State Univ, 70; The Adequacy of Translations from English into Slovenian from the Point of View of Formal and Dynamic Equivalence & Three-Level Theory of Translation (both written in Slovenian), Prostor in cas, Ljubljana, Yugoslavia, 72; Slovenian lanugage on Minnesota's iron range: Some sociolinguistic aspects of language maintenance and language shift, Gen Ling, 76; a Basic Reference Grammar of Slovene - Derbyshire,ww, Slavic Review, Vol 0054, 1995. **CONTACT ADDRESS** Pennsylvania State Univ, Univ Park, 100 Colonial Ct, State College, PA 16801-7677.

PATERSON, JANET M.
PERSONAL Born Berne, Switzerland **DISCIPLINE** FRENCH LITERATURE **EDUCATION** Univ Toronto, BA, 64, MA, 75, PhD, 81. **CAREER** Lang tchr, Reform Sch for Girls, 65-70; lectr, 70-74; prof French, Univ Toronto, 81-; ch, grad stud, 91-95. **HONORS AND AWARDS** Gabrielle Roy Prize, 90. **MEMBERSHIPS** Asn Can Que Lit; Asn Can Stud. **SELECTED PUBLICATIONS** Auth, Anne Hebert: architexture romanesque, Ottawa, Les Editions de l'Universite d'Ottawa, 85; auth, Moments postmodernes dans le roman quebecois, Ottawa, Les Presses de l'Universite d'Ottawa, 90; auth, Defis, projets et tetes dans l'edition critique au Canada, New York, AMS Press Inc, (93): 117; transl, Postmodernism and the Quebec Novel, Toronto, Univ of Toronto Press, (94): 167; auth, La Didactique a l'oeuvre; perspectives theoriques et pratiques, Toronto, canadian Scholars Press, (95): 132; auth, Voix et images, "Dossier: Madeleine Ouelleette-Michaalska", no. 1, (97): 9-116; auth, "Alterite dans Kamouraska d'Anne Hebert", Hommages a Anne Hebert, Paris/Quebec, L'Hexagone, (97): 243-250; auth, "Fast so fast: derives identitaires dans Le Desert mauve de Nicole Brossard" dans Roman contemporain et identite culturelle en Amerique du Nord, Quebec, Nota Bene, (98): 45-57. **CONTACT ADDRESS** Dept of French, Univ of Toronto, 50 St. George St, 2nd Fl, Toronto, ON, Canada M5S 1J4. **EMAIL** jpaters@chass.utoronto.ca

PATTY, JAMES SINGLETON
PERSONAL Born 07/17/1925, Florence, AL **DISCIPLINE** FRENCH **EDUCATION** Univ NC, AB, 45, MA, 47, PhD, 53. **CAREER** Instr French, Univ NC, 46-53; instr French St Span, Univ Colo, 53-54; from asst prof to assoc prof French, Univ Tenn, 54-60; assoc prof, Washington & Lee Univ, 60-64; assoc prof, 64-69, Prof French, PROF FRENCH EMER, 88- , Co-ed, Bull Baudelairien; ed bd, Romance Quart; Phi Beta Kappa, 45. **HONORS AND AWARDS** Outstanding Chap Treas Am Asn Tchrs Fr, 81 **MEMBERSHIPS** Am Asn Teachers Fr; MLA; Am Comp Lit Asn; Soc Etudes Romantiques. **RESEARCH** Nineteenth century French literature; Baudelaire; Romanticism. **SELECTED PUBLICATIONS** Auth, Baudelaire's knowledge and use of Dante, Studies Philol, 10/56; Baudelaire and Bossuet on laughter, Publ Mod Lang Asn Am, 9/65; ed, Jean Giraudoux's Electre, Appleton, 65; auth, Baudelaire et Hippolyte Babou, Rev Hist Lit France, 4-6/67; co-ed, Hommage a W T Bandy, La Baconniere, 73; coed Hommage a Claude Pichois, La Baconniere, 85; Durer in French Letters, Honore Champion-Slatkine, 89. **CONTACT ADDRESS** Vanderbilt Univ, Station B, Box 1630, Nashville, TN 37235.

PAUL, GEORGE MACKAY
PERSONAL Born 07/16/1927, Glasgow, Scotland, m, 1956, 3 children **DISCIPLINE** CLASSICS, ANCIENT HISTORY **EDUCATION** Oxford Univ, BA & MA, 54; Univ London, PH-D(classics), 63. **CAREER** From asst lectr to lectr classics, Univ W Indies, 55-64; from asst prof to assoc prof, 64-70, chmn dept, 73-76, Prof Classics, McMaster Univ, 70, Mem, Comt Coord Acad Libr Serv Ont Univs, 66-67; Can Coun leave fel, 71-72. **MEMBERSHIPS** Class Asn Can (treas, 67-69); Am Philol Asn; Soc Prom Roman Studies; Asn Ancient Historians; Soc Prom Hellenic Studies. **RESEARCH** Greek and Roman historiography; Roman history. **SELECTED PUBLICATIONS** Ed, Roman Coins and Public Life under the Empire: E. Togo Salmon Papers II, Univ Mich Press, (Ann Arbor, Mi), 99. **CONTACT ADDRESS** Dept of Classics, McMaster Univ, 1280 Main St W, Hamilton, ON, Canada L8S 4M2. **EMAIL** gepaul@mcmaster.ca

PAULSEN, WOLFGANG
PERSONAL Born 09/21/1910, Dusseldorf, Germany, m, 1938, 1 child **DISCIPLINE** GERMAN LITERATURE **EDUCATION** Univ Berne, PhD, 34. **CAREER** Asst lectr Ger, Univ Durham, 35-37; asst lectr, Univ Reading & asst, Westfield Col, London, 37-38; asst prof mod lang, Southwestern Col, 38-43; asst prof Ger, State Univ IA, 43-47; assoc prof, Smith Col, 47-53; assoc prof, NY State Col for Teachers, Albany, 53-54; asst prof, Univ CT, 54-61, prof, 61-66; chmn dept, 66-71, Prof Ger, Univ MA, Amherst, 66-. **MEMBERSHIPS** MLA; Schiller Ges. **RESEARCH** Eighteenth to twentieth century German literature; modern German drama. **SELECTED PUBLICATIONS** Auth, Georg Kaiser, Die Perspektiven seines Werkes, 60 & Die Ahnfrau, Zu Grillparzers fruher Dramatik, 62, Niemeyer, Tubingen; Versuch uber Rolf Bongs, Blaschke, Darmstadt, 74; Chr M Wieland, Der Mensch und sein Werk, 75, Eichendorff und sein Taugenichts, 76 & Johann Elias Schlegel und die Komodie, 77, Francke, Bern; Der Expressionismus in der deutschen Literatur, Peter Lang, Bern, 82. **CONTACT ADDRESS** Dept of Ger Lang & Lit, Univ of Massachusetts, Amherst, Amherst, MA 01002.

PAULSON, MICHAEL G.
PERSONAL Born 09/27/1945, Pittsburgh, PA, m, 1972 **DISCIPLINE** FRENCH, SPANISH **EDUCATION** Kutztown Univ, BS, 67; Fla State Univ, MA, 68, PhD, 73; Univ Central Ark, MA, 83. **CAREER** Asst prof of Foreign Langs, South Dakota State Univ, 73-76; lectr of Foreign Langs & English, Univ Central Ark, 76-85; adjunct prof of Foreign Langs, Northampton Community Col, 85-86; asst prof of Foreign Langs, Muhlenburg Col, 86-87; assoc prof, 87-89, Prof of Foreign Langs, Kutztown Univ, 93-. **HONORS AND AWARDS** Roubey Romance Lang Awd, 67; AAUP Grad Student Awd, 67; NDEA Fel, 68-69 & 71-72. **MEMBERSHIPS** South Central MLA; Mountain Interstate Foreign Lang Conf. **RESEARCH** 17th Century French literature; Golden Age Spanish literature; urban literature. **SELECTED PUBLICATIONS** Auth, Kings, Queens, and Splendor: A Critical Analysis of La Princesse de Cleves as a Royal Exemplary Novel, The Edwin Mellen Press, 91; The Youth and the Beach: A Comparative Study of Thomas Mann's A Death in Venice and Reinaldo Arenas' Otra vez el mar, Ediciones Universal, 93; Madame de La Fayette's The Princess of Cleves: A New Translation, Univ Press of Am, 95; Facets of a Princess: Multiple Readings of Madame de La Fayette's La Princesse de Cleves, Peter Lang, 98. **CONTACT ADDRESS** Dept of Foreign Langs, Kutztown Univ of Pennsylvania, Kutztown, PA 19530.

PAULSTON, CHRISTINA BRATT
PERSONAL Born Stockholm, Sweden, m, 1963, 2 children **DISCIPLINE** LINGUISTICS, LANGUAGE TEACHING **EDUCATION** Carleton Col, BA, 53; Univ Minn, Minneapolis, MA, 55; Columbia Univ, EdD(ling), 66. **CAREER** Teacher English, Pub High Schs, Clara City & Pine Island, Minn, 55-60; teacher English & French, Am Sch Tangier, 60-62; teacher, Katrineholm Hogre Allmanna Laroverk, Sweden, 62-63; instr, Teachers Col, Columbia Univ, 64-66; AID spec, Punjab Univ, India, 66 & Cath Univ Peru, 66-67; consult lang teaching, Inst Ling Verano, Peru, 67-68; from asst prof to assoc prof, 69- 76, asst dir English Lang Inst, 69-70, Prof Ling, Univ Pittsburgh, 76-, Dir, English Lang Inst, 70, NDEA & Nat Endowment for Humanities grant & prog dir, Quechua-Aymara Inst, 72. **MEMBERSHIPS** Teachers English to Speakers Other Lang (2nd vp, 71-72, pres, 75-76); Ling Soc Am; Int Asn Teachers English as Foreign Lang; Am Coun Teaching Foreign Lang; MLA. **RESEARCH** Sociolinguistics; language policy. **SELECTED PUBLICATIONS CONTACT ADDRESS** Dept of Gen Ling, Univ of Pittsburgh, Pittsburgh, PA 15213.

PAUTROT, JEAN-LOUIS
DISCIPLINE FRENCH **EDUCATION** Washington Univ, PhD, 92 **CAREER** Asst prof, St. Louis Univ, 91-95; assoc prof,

St. Louis Univ, 95- **HONORS AND AWARDS** Egilrud Fel Humanities, Washington Univ, 88-89 **MEMBERSHIPS** Mod Lang Assoc; Consei Int des Etudes Francophones; Missouri Philoi Soc; 20-Century Fr Studies; Amer Assoc Teachers Fr; Int Assoc Word Music Studies **RESEARCH** Interrelations between Music and Literature; French Literature and Cinema 1945 to Present; Cultural Stereotypes **SELECTED PUBLICATIONS** Auth, La Musique Oubliee, Droz (Geneva), 94; auth, "Pacal Quignard, le structuralisme et le postmoderne," French Forum 22 (97); auth, "La Voix narrative chez Pascal Quignard," 00; auth, "Musical Dimensions of Prose Narratives: 'Musikant' by Andre Hodeir," Mosaic, June 00; auth, "Music and Memory," Dalhousie French Studies, 01. **CONTACT ADDRESS** Dept Modern & Classical Lang, Saint Louis Univ, 221 N Grand Blvd., Saint Louis, MO 63103. **EMAIL** pautropj@slu.edu

PAZ, FRANCIS XAVIER
PERSONAL Born 11/05/1931, Chicago, IL, m, 1973, 1 child **DISCIPLINE** COMPARATIVE LITERATURE, ORIENTAL STUDIES **EDUCATION** Univ Chicago, BA, 52, MA, 57; Columbia Univ, PhD(Orient studies), 72. **CAREER** Lectr humanities, Bishop Col, 56-57; lectr Orient humanities, Columbia Univ, 63-65; Prof English & Comp Lit, State Univ NY, New Paltz, 66, Univ fel Arabic lit, Columbia Univ, 77-. **HONORS AND AWARDS** Fulbright Fels to Pakistan, 79 and Syna, 01. **MEMBERSHIPS** MLA; Am Orient Soc; Mideast Studies Asn. **RESEARCH** Modern American and Arabic fiction. **SELECTED PUBLICATIONS** Translr, The Assemblies of Al-Hamadhani, State Univ NY, (in press); The Monument - Art, Vulgarity And Responsibility in Iraq - Alkhalil,s, J of The American Oriental Society, Vol 0113, 1993. **CONTACT ADDRESS** Dept Lit, SUNY, New Paltz, New Paltz, NY 12562.

PAZ-SOLDAN, JOSE EDMUNDO
PERSONAL Born 03/29/1967, Cochabamba, Bolivia, m, 1998, 1 child **DISCIPLINE** LATIN AMERICAN LITERATURE **EDUCATION** Univ Ala Huntsville, BA, 91; Univ Calif Berkeley, MA, 93; PhD, 97. **CAREER** Vis asst prof to asst prof, Cornell Univ, 97-. **HONORS AND AWARDS** Juan Rulfo Short Story Awd, 97. **MEMBERSHIPS** MLA; LASA; LASP. **RESEARCH** Latin American literature; mass media; Andean literature. **SELECTED PUBLICATIONS** Co-auth, Latin American Literature and Mass Media, Garland (NYork), 00; co-ed, Se Hasla Espanol, Alfaquara (Miami), 00; auth, Suenos Digitales, Alfaquara (La Paz), 00. **CONTACT ADDRESS** 103 Second St, Ithaca, NY 14850. **EMAIL** jep29@cornell.edu

PAZDERNIK, CHARLES
PERSONAL Born 07/03/1968, Breckenridge, MN, m, 1996 **DISCIPLINE** CLASSICS **EDUCATION** Cornell Univ, BA summa cum laude 90; Oxford Univ, Mphil 92; Princeton Univ, MA 95, PhD 97. **CAREER** NY Univ Law Sch, Samuel I. Golieb Fel, 97-98; Brooklyn College, adj asst prof, 98; Emory Univ Law Sch, Mellon post doc fel, 98-. **HONORS AND AWARDS** Phi Beta Kappa; Telluride Sch; Stanley Seeger Fel; Princeton Grad Fel. **MEMBERSHIPS** APA. **RESEARCH** Ancient law; classical historiography; late antiquity; epic poetry; Greco-Roman legal and political history. **SELECTED PUBLICATIONS** Auth, Justinian's Novels and the law of succession, in: The Transformation in Law and Society in Late Antiquity Proceedings of Shifting Frontiers II, ed, R. Mathisen, forthcoming; Odysseus and his audience: Odyssey 9.30-40 and its formulatic resonance's, The Amer Jour of Philology, 95; Our most pious consort given us by God: Dissident reactions to the partnership of Justinian and Theodora AD 525-48, Classical Antiquity, 94; auth, "Procopius and Thucydides on the Labors of War: Belisarius and Brasdas in the Field," Transactions of the Am Philol Asn 130 (00). **CONTACT ADDRESS** Dept of Classics, Emory Univ, N404G Callaway Ct, Atlanta, GA 30322. **EMAIL** cpazder@emory.edu

PEALE, C. GEORGE
PERSONAL Born 09/17/1944, Whittier, CA, d, 2 children **DISCIPLINE** SPANISH LITERATURE **EDUCATION** Univ Southern Calif, BA, 66; Univ Iowa, MA, 68; Univ Calif at Irvine, PhD, 73; Pepperdine Univ, MS, 89. **CAREER** From asst to assoc prof, Univ of Kans, 71-82; vis assoc prof, Univ of Calif at Riverside, 79-81; teacher, Santa Ana High Sch, 81-89; from assoc prof to prof, Calif State Univ, 89-. **HONORS AND AWARDS** NEH Fel, 78-81 & 94-97. **MEMBERSHIPS** Hispanic Soc of Am, AATSP, MLA, PAMLA, PEN, AIH, ITENSO. **RESEARCH** Sixteenth- and Seventeenth-Century Spanish Literature, Satire Theory & Practice, The Theoretical Works of Luis Velez de Suevara, Editing Theory & Practice. **SELECTED PUBLICATIONS** Auth, Hernan Perez de Oliva, Teatro estudio critico y edicion, 76; auth, La anatomia de El Diablo Cojuelo: Desliudes del genero anatomistico, 77; ed, Antiguedad y actualidad de Luis Velez de Guevava, 83; ed, Razonamiento sobre la navegacion del Guadalquivir, 87; co-ed, El espejo del mundo, 97; co-ed, Don Pedro Miago, 97; co-ed, La Serrana de la Vera, 97. **CONTACT ADDRESS** Dept For Lang & Lit, California State Univ, Fullerton, 800 N State Col Blvd, Fullerton, CA 92831-3547. **EMAIL** gpeale@fullerton.edu

PEARCE, JAMES
DISCIPLINE GREEK AND LATIN LANGUAGE AND LITERATURE **EDUCATION** Baylor Univ, BA; Univ TX-Austin, MA, PhD. **CAREER** Prof,68-, Trinity Univ. **RESEARCH** Pastoral poetry. **SELECTED PUBLICATIONS** Auth, The Eclogues of Calpurnius Siculus, 90; The Eclogues of Nemesian and the Einsiedeln Manuscript, 92. **CONTACT ADDRESS** Dept of Class, Trinity Univ, 715 Stadium Dr, San Antonio, TX 78212.

PEARSON, LON
PERSONAL Born 02/13/1939, Murray, Utah, m, 1961, 5 children **DISCIPLINE** SPANISH LANGUAGE AND LITERATURE **EDUCATION** Univ Utah, BA, magna cum laude, 65; UCLA, MA, 68, CPhil, 69, PhD, 73. **CAREER** Tchg fel, Univ Utah, 65-66; assoc, UCLA, 69-70; instr, Univ Mo, Rolla, 70-73; asst prof, 73-77, hd, Lang Sect, 74, 77, 79, 87-91, grad fac, 76-91, assoc prof, 77-87, doctoral fac, 77-91, prof, Univ Mo, Rolla, 87-91; vis prof, Brigham Young Univ, 82-83; grad fac, 91-, grad fel, 92-, prof, 91, ch, dept Mod Lang, Univ Nebr, Kearney, 91-96; ed, Mo For Lang J, 73-78; ed, 79-93, assoc ed/bk rev ed, Chasqui, J of Lat Am Lit, 93-; consult ed, Stud in Contemp Satire, 94-. **HONORS AND AWARDS** Phi Eta Sigma, 63; Phi Kappa Phi, 65; Phi Beta Kappa, 66; Sigma Delta Pi, 66; fac res fel Univ Mo, Rolla, 71, 73, 81, 85; NEH Yr Fel in Residence, Johns Hopkins Univ, 75-76; NEH-Exxon grant, 79; Scouting Awd of Merit, Ozark Coun of Boy Scouts of Am, 81; Weldon Springs grant, Chile, 81; NEH summer sem, Yeshiva Univ, 81. **MEMBERSHIPS** Am Asn of Tchr of Span & Port, 68-; Int Inst of Iberoamerican Lit, 69-; MLA, 69-85; exec bd, 73-80, exec secy, For Lang Asn Mo, 78-79; Rocky Mt Coun on Lat Am Stud, 83-90; Mo Philol Asn. **SELECTED PUBLICATIONS** Auth, Nicomedes Guzman: Proletarian Author in Chile's Literary Generation of 1938, Univ Mo Press, 76; auth, "La novela de la generacion de 1938 de Chile y su herencia poetica: Influencia de la novela espanola y el poema en prosa francesa," in La hora actual de la novela hispanica, ed, Eduardo Godoy Gallardo, Ediciones Universitarias de Valparaiso de la Universidad Catolica de Valparaiso, 94; auth, "An Overview of Computers and How They Can Aid Translations," in Platte Vly Rev, 23:2, 95. **CONTACT ADDRESS** Dept of Mod Langs, Univ of Nebraska, Kearney, Kearney, NE 68849. **EMAIL** PearsonLon@UNK.edu

PEARSON, LYNN E.
PERSONAL Born 06/02/1963, Urbana, IL **DISCIPLINE** SPANISH **EDUCATION** American Univ, BA, 85; La State Univ, MA, 92; Univ Tex Austin, PhD, 01. **CAREER** TA, La State Univ, 90-93; asst instr, Univ Tex Austin, 93-00; asst prof, Bowling Green State Univ, 00-. **HONORS AND AWARDS** Phi Kappa Phi; Phi Sigma Iota; Sigma Delta Pi; Mem Choice Award, Phi Sigma Iota, 93; Fel, 98; Prof Dev Award, 98. **MEMBERSHIPS** MLA, LASSO, S Central MLA. **RESEARCH** Second Language Acquisition, Pragmatics, Discourse Analysis, Foreign Language Teaching. **SELECTED PUBLICATIONS** Coauth, "Development of communication strategies among foreign language learners," Mountain Interstate For Lang Conf Rev, (99); coauth, "Pragmatics and Discourse Analysis in Spanish Second Language Acquisition," Spanish Second Language Acquisition (forthcoming). **CONTACT ADDRESS** Dept Romance Lang, Bowling Green State Univ, Bowling Green, OH 43403. **EMAIL** pearson@bgnet.bgsu.edu

PEAVLER, TERRY J.
PERSONAL Born 10/25/1942, Seminole, OK, 2 children **DISCIPLINE** SPANISH **EDUCATION** Univ Colo, Boulder, BA, 65, MA, 67; Univ Calif, Berkeley, PhD(comp lit), 73. **CAREER** Asst prof, 71-79, Assoc Prof, 79-88, Prof Span & Comp Lit, PA State Univ, Univ Park, 88- . **HONORS AND AWARDS** Nat Sci Found Inst grant, 73-74. **MEMBERSHIPS** MLA; Am Asn Teachers Span & Port. **RESEARCH** Latin American novel; Cuban, Mexican, Argentine literature; narrative theory. **SELECTED PUBLICATIONS** Auth, The source for the archetype in Los Pasos Perdidos, Romance Notes, 74; A new novel by Alejo Carpentier, Latin Am Lit Rev, 76; Prose fiction criticism and theory in Cuban journals, Cuban Studies, 77; Edmundo Desnoes and Cuba's lost generation, Latin Am Res Rev, 77; Guillermo Cabrera Infante's Debt to Ernest Hemingway, Hispania, 79; Blow-Up: A reconsideration of Antonioni's Infidelity to Cortazar, PLMA, 79; Teaching film and literature: A few principles, J Gen Educ, 80; Alejo Carpentier and the humanization of Spanish American fiction, Hispanofila, 82; auth, Individuations: The Novel as Dissent, Univ Press Am, 87; auth, El texto en llamas: al arte narrativo de Juan Rulfo, Lang, 88; auth, Julio Cortazar, Twayne, 90; auth, Structures of Power: Essays on Spanish American Fiction, State Univ NY, 96. **CONTACT ADDRESS** Dept of Span Ital & Port, Pennsylvania State Univ, Univ Park, 352 N Burrowes Bldg, University Park, PA 16802. **EMAIL** tjp@psu.edu

PECK, JEFFREY MARC
PERSONAL Born 01/05/1950, Pittsburgh, PA **DISCIPLINE** GERMAN & COMPARATIVE LITERATURE **EDUCATION** Mich State Univ, BA, 72; Univ Chicago, MA, 74; Univ Calif, Berkeley, PhD(comp lit & Ger), 79. **CAREER** Actg instr world lit & comp, Univ Calif, Berkeley, 78; Asst Prof Germanics & Comp Lit, Univ Washington, 79- **MEMBERSHIPS** MLA; Am Comp Lit Asn; Int Verein Germanistik; Am Asn Teachers Ger; Philol Asn Pac Coast. **RESEARCH** Literary criticism and theory, especially hermeneutics; 19th and 20th century German literature; academic institutionalization of literature and criticism. **SELECTED PUBLICATIONS** Auth, Comparative historiography: Canonization and perrodization in German, French and English literary histories, Proc Int Ger Studies Conf, Peter Lang, 80; The policies of reading and the poetics of reading: The Hermeneutic Text--Heinrich von Kleist's Die Marquise von O, Cahiers roumains etudes litteraires, 82; Hermes Disguised: Literary Hermeneutics and the Interpretation of Literature, Kleist, Grillparzer, Fontane, Peter Lang (in press). **CONTACT ADDRESS** Dept of Germanics, Univ of Washington, Denny Hall DH-30, Seattle, WA 98195.

PECORARO, ROSILIE HERNANDEZ
DISCIPLINE SPANISH LITERATURE **EDUCATION** Boston Univ, BA, 90; Univ Calif Irvine, MA, 94; PhD, 98. **CAREER** Asst prof, Univ Ill Urbana Champaign. **HONORS AND AWARDS** Recipient of 00-01 Newberry Library Monticello Fel. **RESEARCH** Peninsular literature; Golden Age narrative, poetry, and theatre; literary and critical theory. **SELECTED PUBLICATIONS** Auth, The Absence of the Absence of Women: Cervantes's Don Quixote and the Explosion of the Pastoral Tradition, 98; auth, "Cervantes's La Galatea: Feminine Spaces, subjects, and Communities," Pacific Coast Philology, 98. **CONTACT ADDRESS** Spanish, Italian, and Portuguese Dept, Univ of Illinois, Urbana-Champaign, 52 E Gregory Dr, Champaign, IL 61820. **EMAIL** rhernan@uiuc.edu

PEDRONI, PETER
DISCIPLINE ITALIAN **EDUCATION** Yale Univ, BA; Middlebury, MA; Rutgers, PhD. **CAREER** Prof; Int Stud Assoc, Miami Univ **SELECTED PUBLICATIONS** Auth, Existence as Theme in Carlo Cassola's Fiction, NY: Peter Lang, 85; The Anti-Naturalist Experience: Federigo Tozzi, Tallahassee: De Soto, 89; transl and introd, Last Act in Urbino, NY: Italica, 95; articles on, Cassola, Tozzi, Volponi, Moravia & Verga in Italica, Forum Italica, Italian Cult, Can J Italian Stud, Italian Criticism: Lit and Cult. **CONTACT ADDRESS** Dept of French and Italian, Miami Univ, Oxford, OH 45056. **EMAIL** pedronpn@muohio.edu

PEER, LARRY HOWARD
PERSONAL Born 01/02/1942, Ogden, UT, m, 1967, 9 children **DISCIPLINE** COMPARATIVE LITERATURE **EDUCATION** Brigham Young Univ, BA, 63, MA, 65; Univ Md, PhD, 69. **CAREER** Instr Ger, Univ Md, 67-68; from asst prof to assoc prof comp lit, Univ Ga, 68-75, acting head dept, 73-74; assoc prof, 75-78, dir hon prog, 77-78, chmn dept 78-81, Prof Comp Lit, Brigham Young Univ, 78-, Pres, Western Regional Hon Coun, 78-80; Exec Dir, Am Conf on Romanticism; Ed, Prism(s): Essays in Romanticism. **HONORS AND AWARDS** Alcuin Prof of General Educ, Brigham Young Univ. **MEMBERSHIPS** Int Comp Lit Asn; Am Comp Lit Asn; MLA; Am Soc Aesthet; Am Conf Romanticism; Int Byron Soc. **RESEARCH** Literary theory; Romanticism. **SELECTED PUBLICATIONS** Auth, Pushkin and Goethe again: Lensky's character, Papers on Lang & Lit, summer 69; Schlegel, Christianity and history: Manzoni's theory of the novel, Comp Lit Studies, fall 62; Friedrich Schelgel's Theory of the Novel, Colloquia Germanica, 76. **CONTACT ADDRESS** Dept of Comp Lit, Brigham Young Univ, 3010 JHKB, Provo, UT 84602-6047. **EMAIL** lhp@email.byu.edu

PEISCHL, MARGARET THERESA
PERSONAL Born 02/05/1933, Pottsville, PA **DISCIPLINE** GERMAN LANGUAGE AND LITERATURE **EDUCATION** PA State Univ, BA, 55; Univ Southern Calif, MA, 74, PhD(Ger), 81. **CAREER** Head, English Dept, John Burroughs Jr High Sch, 67-71; instr Ger, El Camino Col, 72-80; asst prof, Old Dominion Univ, 80-81; Asst Prof Ger, VA Commonwealth Univ, 81-. **MEMBERSHIPS** MLA; Am Asn Teacher Ger; Theodor-Storm Soc. **RESEARCH** Theodor Storm; 19th century Novella German literature. **SELECTED PUBLICATIONS** Auth, Das Damonische im Werk Theodor Storms, Peter Lang, Verlag, Ger, 82; Buchner 'Lenz' - a Study of Madness, Germanic Notes And Reviews, Vol 0027, 1996. **CONTACT ADDRESS** 666 Elgin Terrace, Richmond, VA 23225. **EMAIL** mpeisch1@atlas.vcu.edu

PELAEZ-BENITZ, LOLA
PERSONAL Born 12/04/1958, Madrid, Spain, m, 1990, 2 children **DISCIPLINE** SPANISH **EDUCATION** Universidad Complutense, PhD. **CAREER** Lectr, Boston Univ, 86-90; Preceptor, Boston Univ, 90-92; Asst Prof, Simmons Col, 92-. **RESEARCH** Medieval Spanish literature. **SELECTED PUBLICATIONS** Auth, "Fernando Diaz-Plaja and William W Cressey 'La Espana que sobrevive,'' Mod Lang J, vol 58 (97): forthcoming; auth, El Libro de la Historia troyana de Pedro de Chinchilla: estudio y edicion, Editorial Complutense (Madrid, Spain), 99; auth, "La Historia troyana en prosa y verso: otro intento de nueva epica dentro de la epica culta," Olifant, vol 20 (forthcoming). **CONTACT ADDRESS** Dept Lang, Simmons Col, 300 Fenway, Boston, MA 02115-5820. **EMAIL** dpelaez@simmons.edu

PELLICER, JAMES O.
PERSONAL Born 11/13/1927, m, 2 children **DISCIPLINE** SPANISH **EDUCATION** Inst S Jose Argentina, BA, 47; Licentiate, 50; Adams State Col, MA, 67; NYork Univ, PhD, 73. **CAREER** Instructor, Adams State Col, 67-68; Asst Prof, Kings Col, 68-70; Asst Prof, Upsala Col, 70-71; Visiting Asst Prof, NY Univ, 71-72; Asst Prof to Prof, Hunter Col of CUNY, 72-. **HONORS AND AWARDS** Phi Delta Kappa; Kappa Delta Pi; Founders Day Awd, NY Univ, 73; Sigma Delta Pi,; Essay Awd, New York, 84; Fel Awd, Hunter Col, 90; George N. Shuster Fac Fel Fund Awd, 92. **MEMBERSHIPS** Am Asn of Teachers of Spanish and Portuguese; Inst Intl de Lit Iberoamericana; Latin Am Writers Inst; Intituto Literario y Cultural Hispanico; Centro de Escritores y Poetas Iberoamericanos. **SELECTED PUBLICATIONS** Auth, "Ficcion sobre forma cientifica," in Encuentro de la literatura con la ciencia,, Alba de America, 90; auth, "Vicente Fidel Lopez en el Facundo," Bulletin of Hispanic Studies, 91; auth, "Los Estados Unidos en Sarmiento?," Introduction to the Edicion critica Sarmiento's Viajes, Argentin, 96; auth, "El contexto del Facundo," Ambas Americas, 95; auth, Twentieth Century Themes in the Poetry of Hispanic American Women: A Selected Anthology, forthcoming. **CONTACT ADDRESS** Dept Romance Lang, Hunter Col, CUNY, 695 Park Ave, New York, NY 10021-5024.

PELOSI, OLIMPIA
PERSONAL Born 08/27/1957, Italy, m, 1994, 1 child **DISCIPLINE** ITALIAN **EDUCATION** Univ Salerno, Laurea, 78; Laurea, 81; Univ NC, PhD, 90. **CAREER** Asst Prof to Assoc Prof, SUNY, 90-. **HONORS AND AWARDS** Who's Who of Women in the World, 95; Two Thousand Notable Women, 94; Fel, am Biographical Inst, 94; Who's Who in the East, 94. **MEMBERSHIPS** Mod Lang Asn of Am, The renaissance Soc of Am, Am Asn of Italian Studies, Am Asn of Teachers of Italian, Associazione Internazionale per gli Studi di Lingua e Letteratura Italiana, Asn of Literary Scholars and Critics. **RESEARCH** Italian renaissance; Modern comparative literature. **SELECTED PUBLICATIONS** Auth, Teseo e l'anima errante, Una rilettura della "Nadja" di Breton, Napoli, 96; auth, Satira barocca e teoriche sul genere dal cinque all'Ottocento, Napoli, 91; auth, Il "Sogno di Polifilo": una quete dell'Umanesimo, Salerno, 88; auth, Cinque saggi sul "Polifilo" Forum Italicum (88): 291-294; auth, "Nadja" (frammenti di un ritorno). Andre Breton e la femminilita trasparente, Salerno, 81. **CONTACT ADDRESS** Dept of Lang, Lit and Cultures, SUNY, 1400 Washington Ave, Albany, NY 12222-0100.

PENCE, ELLSWORTH DEAN
PERSONAL Born 03/18/1938, Carbon Hill, OH, 4 children **DISCIPLINE** FRENCH LANGUAGE & LITERATURE, LATIN **EDUCATION** Ohio Univ, BA, 59; Univ Wis, MA, 64, PhD, 71. **CAREER** Teacher French & English, Bettsville High Sch, Ohio, 59-60; instr French, Univ Wis, Ctr-Manitowoc, 67-68; asst prof, Univ Wis, Manitowoc & Green Bay, 68-73; prof French, Humboldt State Univ, 73-, resident dir, int prog, Aix-en-Provence, France, 82-83. **MEMBERSHIPS** Am Asn Teachers French; CLTH; Am Names Soc. **RESEARCH** French romantic fiction; French prose poem; 19th century French novel; French place names. **SELECTED PUBLICATIONS** French Place Names in California. **CONTACT ADDRESS** Dept of Modern Lang, Humboldt State Univ, 1 Harpst St, Arcata, CA 95519-8299. **EMAIL** edp1@axe.humboldt.edu

PENCHANSKY, DAVID
PERSONAL Born 12/03/1951, Brooklyn, NY, d, 2 children **DISCIPLINE** HEBREW BIBLE **EDUCATION** Vanderbilt Univ, PhD, 88. **CAREER** Instr, Evangel Col, 79-84; instr, Western Ky Univ, 85-89; assoc prof, Univ of St. Thomas, 89-. **MEMBERSHIPS** Soc of Bibl Lit; Cath Bibl Asn; Amer Asn of Univ Prof. **RESEARCH** Wisdom literature; Hermeneutics; Literary criticism. **SELECTED PUBLICATIONS** Auth, The Betrayal of God, Westminster/John Knox, 90; auth, Storyteller's Companion, vol III, Abingdon Press, 92; auth, Up for Grabs: A Tentative Proposal for Ideological Criticism, Semeia, 59, 92; auth, Staying the Night, Reading Between Texts, Westminster/John Knox, 92; auth, Proverbs, The Mercer Bible Commentary, Mercer Press, 94; auth, The Politics of Biblical Theology, Studies in American Biblical Hermeneutics Series, Mercer Press, 95; auth, God the Monster, The Monstrous and the Unspeakable, Sheffield Acad Press, 97; auth, What Rough Beast, Westminster/John Knox, 99; co-ed, Shall Not the Judge of All the Earth Do What is Right?, Eisenbraun, 00. **CONTACT ADDRESS** Mail #4328, 2115 Summi, Saint Paul, MN 55105. **EMAIL** d9penchansky@stthomas.edu

PENDERGRAFT, MARY L.
PERSONAL Born 02/14/1953, Charlotte, NC, m, 1975, 3 children **DISCIPLINE** CLASSICS **EDUCATION** Univ NC at Chapel Hill, AB, 75; PhD, 82. **CAREER** Vis asst prof, Univ of NC at Greensboro, 84, 86; vis asst prof, Duke Univ, 87-88; from vis asst prof to assoc prof, Wake Forest Univ, 83-. **HONORS AND AWARDS** Nat Merit Scholar; Phi Beta Kappa; Eben Alexander Prize in Greek; Albert Suskin Prize in Latin; Univ Fel, 76-77. **MEMBERSHIPS** Am Philol Asn, Classical Asn of the Middle W and S, Archaeol Inst of Am, NC Classical Asn, Am Asn of Univ Professors, Vergilian Soc, Am Classical League, For Lang Asn of NC. **RESEARCH** Greek and Latin Literature. **SELECTED PUBLICATIONS** Auth, "Aratean Echoes in Theocritus," Quaderni Urbinati di Cultura classica, 24.3 (86): 47-54; auth, "On the Nature of the constellations: Aratus, Ph. 367-85," Eranos 88 (90): 99-106; auth, "Eros at Play: Arg. 3.132-41," Materiali e discussioni per l'analisi dei testi classici 26 (91): 95-102; auth, "Thou Shalt Not Eat the Hyena: A Note on "Barnabas' Epistle 10.7," Vigiliae Christianae 46 (92): 75-79; coauth, "Naming the Figures: A Controversial Stele in the Sparta Museum," Maia 46 (94): 283-289; auth, "Euphony and Etymology: Aratus' Phaenomena," Syllecta Classica 6 (95): 43-57. **CONTACT ADDRESS** Dept Classical Lang, Wake Forest Univ, PO Box 7343, Winston-Salem, NC 27109-7343. **EMAIL** pender@wfu.edu

PENELLA, ROBERT J.
PERSONAL Born 02/16/1947, Boston, MA, m, 1968, 1 child **DISCIPLINE** CLASSICS **EDUCATION** Boston Col, AB, 67; Harvard Univ, MA, 69, PhD, 71. **CAREER** Asst prof, Fordham Univ, 71-78, assoc prof, 78-91, prof, 91-, chemn, Classics, 77-83. **HONORS AND AWARDS** Boston Col, AB, summa cum laude, 67; Woodrow Wilson Fel, 67-68; Am Coun of Learned Socs grant-in-aid, 84; NEH Fel for Univ Teachers, 93. **MEMBERSHIPS** Am Philol Asn, Classical Asn of Atlantic States. **RESEARCH** Late Antiquity, Imperial Greek prose, Roman historiography. **SELECTED PUBLICATIONS** Auth, The Letters of Apollonius of Tyana: A Critical Text with Prolegomena, Translation and Commentary, Leiden: E. J. Brill (79); auth, Greek Philosophers and Sophists in the Fourth Century A.D.: Studies in Eunapius of Sardis, Leeds: Francis Cairns (90); auth, The Private Orations of Themistius, Berkeley: Univ of Calif Press (90). **CONTACT ADDRESS** Dept Classics, Fordham Univ, 441 E Fordham Rd, Bronx, NY 10458-5149. **EMAIL** rpenella@fordham.edu

PENNISTON, JOYCE K.
PERSONAL Born 12/22/1939, Buffalo, NY, m, 1960, 2 children **DISCIPLINE** CLASSICS **EDUCATION** Radcliffe, BA, 61; Harvard Grad Sch of Educ, MAT, 62; Univ NC Chapel Hill, MA, 76; Univ Mn, PhD, 83. **CAREER** Instr, St. Olaf Col, 79-81; instr, Mn Bible Col, 81- ; instr, St. Mary's Univ Mn, 93-. **HONORS AND AWARDS** Summer stud, Amer Sch for Classical Stud, Athens, Greece, 81, Rome, Italy, 78; NEH Summer Sem, Harvard with Gregory Nagy, 84. **MEMBERSHIPS** Amer Philol Assoc; Classical Assoc of the Midwest & South; Vergilian Soc; Classical Assoc of Mn. **RESEARCH** Ancient comedy. **SELECTED PUBLICATIONS** Auth, Quot Homines Tot Sententiae: Off-Stage Acquaintances in Ancient Comedy, Classical J, 91; Pragma and process in Greek and Roman Comedy, Syllecta Classica, 96; Commentary on the Acts of the Apostles in Study Bible for Women, Baker books, Grand Rapids, Mich, 96; Translation of Cicero's De Finibus, Hackett, 00-01; Translation of Latin passages in Anatomy of Radical Prostatectomy as defined by Magnetic Resonance Imaging, The J of Urology, 98. **CONTACT ADDRESS** 835 10 1/2 St SW, Rochester, MN 55902. **EMAIL** joyce.penniston@prodigy.net

PENROD, LYNN K.
PERSONAL Born Piqua, OH **DISCIPLINE** FRENCH LITERATURE **EDUCATION** Ohio State Univ, BA, 67, PhD, 75; Yale Univ, MAT, 68; Univ Alberta, LLB, 80, LLM, 86; BAR: Alta, 84. **CAREER** Tchr, Paul Dunbar High Sch, 68-69; tchr, Oakwood St. High, 70-72; adj asst prof, Fr, Wright State Univ, 70-72; grad tchg asst, Ohio State Univ, 72-75; asst prof, Univ South Carolina, 75-77; lectr, Romance langs, 77-79, asst prof, 79-83, assoc prof, 83-89, Lectr, Fac Law, Univ Alberta, 86-, Prof Romance Langs 89-. **HONORS AND AWARDS** Fullbright Fel; Outstanding Grad, Tchr Assoc Awd; Novice G. Fawcett President's Gold Medal; Col Arts & Scis Coun Gold Medal; Women's Panhellenic Scholar Gold Medal, Ohio State Univ. **MEMBERSHIPS** Law Soc Alta; MLA; Am Asn Tchrs Fr; Can Comp Lit Asn; The Friends of George Sand; Nat Asn Women Educ; Can Asn Law Soc; Can Asn Law Tchrs; Nat Asn Women & Inst Law Res & Reform Law. **RESEARCH** Women's Writing in French, Children's Lit in French, Translation. **SELECTED PUBLICATIONS** Auth, Divorce Mediation: Helping to Ease the Pain, in Network of Sask Women, 86; auth, Canadian Children's Literature in French: an Annotated Bibliography; auth, Experiences Litteraires, 89; auth, Helene Cixous: The Future Feminine, 94. **CONTACT ADDRESS** Dept of Modern Lang & Cultural Studies, Univ of Alberta, 200 Arts Bldg, Edmonton, ON, Canada T6G 2E6. **EMAIL** lpenrod@gpu.srv.ualberta.ca

PENROSE, MEHL A.
PERSONAL Born 10/30/1967, Independence, MO **DISCIPLINE** SPANISH **EDUCATION** Univ Mo Columbia, BA, 90; Univ Kans, MA, 93; UCLA, PhD, 00. **CAREER** Asst prof, Maimi Univ Ohio, 00-01; asst prof, Prairie View A&M Univ, 01-. **HONORS AND AWARDS** William Kemp Literature Award, 90; UCLA Fel, 95-96, 99-00; Outstanding Teacher Award, UCLA, 98; Del Amo Fel, 00. **MEMBERSHIPS** MLA. **RESEARCH** 18th, 19th and 20th century Spanish literature, 20th century American literature, 20th century Latin American literature, queer theory, reception theory. **SELECTED PUBLICATIONS** Auth, "La historia en dos obras de Rodolfo Usigli, o el juego entre la fantasia y la realidad," Mester, 98; transl and auth, "The Old Castilian," by Larra, World Lit and Its Times, 01. **CONTACT ADDRESS** Dept Lang and Commun, Prairie View A&M Univ, Prairie View, TX 77446. **EMAIL** mehl_penrose@yahood.com

PENTLIN, SUSAN LEE
PERSONAL Born 02/09/1947, Warrensburg, MO, m, 1971 **DISCIPLINE** GERMAN **EDUCATION** Central Mo State Col, BA, 68; Univ Mo, MA, 70; Univ Kansas, PhD, 77. **CAREER** TA, Univ of Mo, 68-69; prof, Central Mo State Univ, 70-; Comnr, Mo Comn on Human Rights, 96-. **HONORS AND AWARDS** Fulbright Techer, 73-74; Fulbright Sem, Ger, 77; NEH Sem, 78; Grant, Am Counc of Learned Soc, 85. **MEMBERSHIPS** Fulbright Alumni Assoc; Hist of Educ Soc; Ger Studies Assoc; Soc for Ger-Am Studies; Assoc of Holocaust Org; Mo Folklore Soc. **RESEARCH** The history of teaching German in the United States, Holocaust memoirs, Missouri Folklore, the academic response to Holocaust denial. **SELECTED PUBLICATIONS** Auth, "German Teachers' Reaction to the Third Reich", Teaching German in America: Prolegomena to a History, ed David P. Benseler et al, Univ of Wisc (Madison, 88): 228-253; auth, "Maude Williams Martin, Early Ballad Collector in Missouri", Mo Folklore Soc J, XIII-IX (88-89): 45-70; auth, "Mary Berg's Warsaw Ghetto: A Diary", Bearing Witness to the Holocaust 1939-1989, ed Alan L. Berger, Edwin Mellen, (Lewiston, NY) (91): 255-271; auth, "Ist dies mein Land?: The Memoirs of German Women", Burning Memory: Times of Testing and Reckoning, ed Alice Eckardt, Pergamon, (Oxford, 93): 203-217; auth, "Holocaust Victims of Privilege", Problems Unique to the Holocaust, ed Harry James Cargas, Univ of Ky, (Lexington, 99): 25-41; coauth, "Dealing with Holocaust Denial: An Academic Dilemma", Hearing the Voices: Teaching the Holocaust to Future Generations, eds Michael Hayse, Didier Pollefeyt, G. Jan Colijn and Marcia S. Littell, Merion Westfield (Philadelphia, 99): 299-321. **CONTACT ADDRESS** Dept Mod Lang, Central Missouri State Univ, Warrensburg, MO 64093.

PERADOTTO, JOHN JOSEPH
PERSONAL Born 05/11/1933, Ottawa, IL, m, 1959, 4 children **DISCIPLINE** GREEK & LATIN LANGUAGES & LITERATURE **EDUCATION** St Louis Univ, AB, 57, MA, 58; Northwestern Univ, PhD(Greek & Latin), 63. **CAREER** Instr Greek, Latin & English, Western Wash State Col, 60-61; from instr to asst prof Greek & Latin, Georgetown Univ, 61-66; from asst prof to assoc prof classics, State Univ NY Buffalo, 66-73; prof & chmn dept, Univ Tex, Austin, 73-74; chmn dept, 74-77, Prof Classics, State Univ NY Buffalo, 74-, Dean, 78-, Nat Endowment for Humanities fel, Ctr Hellenic Studies, 72-73; ed-in-chief, Arethusa, 75-; distinguished teaching prof emer. **HONORS AND AWARDS** Chancellor's Awd for Excellence in Teaching, State Univ NY, 75. **MEMBERSHIPS** Am Philol Asn; Class Asn Atlantic States. **RESEARCH** Greek literature; Greek mythology and religion; narrative analysis. **SELECTED PUBLICATIONS** Auth, The omen of the eagles and the ethos of Agamemnon, Phoenix, 69; Classical Mythology, Am Philol Asn, 73; Odyssey 8 564-671: Verisimilitude, narrative analysis, and bricolarge, Tex Studies Lit & Lang, 74; co-ed, Population Policy in Plato and Aristotle, 75; ed, Classical Literature and Contemporary Literary Theory, 77, Women in the Ancient World, 78, co-ed, Virgil 2000 Years, 81 & Semiotics and Classical Studies, 83, Arethusa; Rethinking the Classical Canon, 94; ed, Horace: 2000 Years, 95; co-ed, The NewSimonides, 96; The Iliad and its Contexts, 97, Arethusa; co-ed, Modern Theoretical Approaches to Homer," in Barry Powell and Ian Morris eds., A New Companion to Homer, (Leiden 97): 380-95. **CONTACT ADDRESS** Dept of Classics, SUNY, Buffalo, 346 Milard Fillmore Academic Ctr, Buffalo, NY 14260-4650. **EMAIL** peradott@acsu.buffalo.edu

PERCIVAL, WALTER KEITH
PERSONAL Born 02/24/1930, Leeds, England, m, 1968 **DISCIPLINE** LINGUISTICS **EDUCATION** Leeds Univ, BA, 51; Yale Univ, MA, 59, PhD(ling), 64. **CAREER** Lectr ling, Brandeis Univ, 62-63; from asst prof to assoc prof, Univ Wis-Milwaukee, 64-69, chmn dept, 64-69; assoc prof, 69-74, Prof Ling, Univ Kans, 74-95, Am Philos Soc res grant, 72-; Prof, Univ Kans, 74-95; Prof Emer, Univ Kans, 95-. **HONORS AND AWARDS** Am Acad of Arts and Scis, Fel, 91. **MEMBERSHIPS** Ling Soc Am; Renaissance Soc Am; Mediaeval Acad Am; Soc Ling Europaea; Int Soc Hist Rhetoric. **RESEARCH** History of linguistics; Austronesian languages; Medieval and Renaissance grammar, rhetoric and logic. **SELECTED PUBLICATIONS** Auth, On the Non-Existence of Cartesian Linguistics, In: Cartesian Studies, 72; contribr, The Grammatical Tradition and the Rise of the Vernaculars, In: Current Trends in Linguistics, 75; Deep and Surface Structure Concepts in Syntactic Theory, In: History of Linguistic Thought and Contemporary Linguistics, 76; auth, The Applicability of Kuhn's Paradigms to the History of Linguistics, Language, 76; The Artis Grammaticae Opusculum of Bartolomeo Sulmonese, Renaissance Quart, 78; Ferdinand de Saussure and the History of Semiotics, In: Semiotic Themes, 81; A Grammar of the Urbanised Toba-Batak of Medan, Canberra, The Australian Nat Univ, 81; The Saussurean Paradigm: Fact or Fantasy? Semiotica, 81; Nebrija Syntactic Theory in Its Historical Setting, Historiographia Linguistica, Vol 0024, 1997. **CONTACT ADDRESS** 3815 N E 89th St, Seattle, WA 98115-3742. **EMAIL** percival@u.washington.edu

PERDICOYIANUI-PALEOLOGOU, HELENE
PERSONAL Born 02/12/1959, Greece **DISCIPLINE** CLASSICS **EDUCATION** Sorbonne Univ, PhD, 92. **CAREER** From vis prof to lectr, Hellenic Col, 96-; vis scholar, Harvard Univ, 98; guest vis scholar, Harvard Divinity Sch, 97-01, vis scholar, Brown Univ, 97-01. **MEMBERSHIPS** Can Asn Univ Tchrs; Int Asn Papyrology; Int Asn Greek & Latin Epigraphy; Asn Linguistics Paris; Grammatical Info; Asn Guillaume Bude; Am Philol Asn; Chronicle High Educ; VITA LATINA; Int Soc Class Tradition; Am Soc Papyrologists; Ling Soc Am. **RESEARCH** Greek and Latin Philology and Linguistics. **SELECTED PUBLICATIONS** Auth, Etude Lexicologique des Familles de Daenai, de Didaskein et de Paideuein d'Homere a Hippocrate, 94; auth, L'enonciation dans l'Hecube d'Euripide, Miscellanea Linguistica Graeco-latina, 93; auth, Le vocabulaire de l'education d'Homere a Euripide. Etude lexicologique: les familles de daenai de didaskein et de paideuein d'Homere a Euripide, IG, 93; auth, Le Vocabulaire de la douleur dans l'Hecube et les Troyennes d'Euripide, LEC, 93; auth, Le vocabulaire de l'habitation chez Euripide, LEC, 96; auth, Philos chez Euripide, RB Ph. H, 96. **CONTACT ADDRESS** Dept of Classics, Hellenic Col, 50 Goddard Ave., Brookline, MA 02146. **EMAIL** hperpal@hotmail.com

PEREZ, GENARO J.
PERSONAL Born 01/26/1943, Columbia, m, 1981, 1 child **DISCIPLINE** SPANISH, PORTUGESE LITERATURE **EDUCATION** La State Univ, BA, 67; Tulane Univ, MA, 73; PhD, 76. **CAREER** Instr, Univ of New Orleans, 75-78; asst prof to prof, Univ of Tex of the Permian Basic, 78-95; prof, Tex Tech Univ, 95-. **HONORS AND AWARDS** NEH, 77; ACLS Grant, 86; Am Philos Soc, 86; Who's Who in the SW, 86-87. **MEMBERSHIPS** MLA, Am Assoc of Teachers of Span and Port, SCMLA, SW Coun of Lat Am Studies, Asociacion Internacional de Hispanistas. **RESEARCH** The contemporary nove. **SELECTED PUBLICATIONS** Auth, Formalist Elements in the Novels of Juan Goytisolo, Porrua Turanzas, Madrid, 79; auth, La novelistica de J Leyva, Porrua, Madrid, 87; auth, La novela como burla/juego: siete experimentos novelescos de Gonzalo Torrente Ballester, Albatros, Valencia, 89; auth, La narrativa de Concha Alos, Tamesis, London, 93; auth, The Memoirs of John Conde, iunverse.cpm, 00. **CONTACT ADDRESS** Dept Class and Mod Lang, Texas Tech Univ, Lubbock, TX 79409. **EMAIL** wlgjp@ttu.edu

PEREZ, MIREYA
PERSONAL Born, Columbia, d, 2 children **DISCIPLINE** SPANISH **EDUCATION** Hunter Col, BA, 65; Boston Univ, MA, 70; Rutgers Univ, PhD, 77 **CAREER** Assoc Prof, Col of New Rochelle, 75-. **HONORS AND AWARDS** Fulbright Fel, Mexico; Sigma Delta Pi; Phi Sigma Iota; NEH Summer Awd, Col New Rochelle. **MEMBERSHIPS** Am Poets Soc, Poetry Soc of Am. **RESEARCH** Latina Writers and artista; self-Narratives; Latino poetry. **SELECTED PUBLICATIONS** Auth, the female body: Latina Perspectives from Frida Kahlo to Isabel Allende, forthcoming; auth, Carreras: Casos en la comunidad, Houghton Mifflin, 85; auth, La picara y la dama, ediciones Universal, 70; auth, "Madame Rashel," revista del had, 96; auth, "Inventario," Diosas en Bronce, Anthology of Colombian Women Poets, 95; auth, "Dulce," Revista del had, 94; auth, "Cross rites, The American Experience, 91; auth, "Fragile," forthcoming; auth, "Gato encerrardo," Ollantay center for the arts,' auth, "Paz en la tierra," Teatro Repertorio Espanol. **CONTACT ADDRESS** Dept For Lang, Col of New Rochelle, 29 Castle Place, New Rochelle, NY 10805-2338. **EMAIL** poema99@aol.com

PEREZ-FIRMAT, GUSTAVO
PERSONAL Born 03/07/1949, Havana, Cuba, m, 1981, 2 children **DISCIPLINE** LINGUISTICS **EDUCATION** Miami-Dade Comm Col, AA, 70; Univ Miami, BA, 72; MA, 73; Univ Mich, PhD, 79. **CAREER** Teach asst, Univ Miami, 72-73; teach asst, Univ Mich, 73-79; asst prof, assoc prof, prof, Duke Univ, 79-99; David Feinson prof, Columbia Univ, 99-. **HONORS AND AWARDS** ACLS, 81; Mellon PostDoc Fel, 81-82; NEH, 85-86: Guggenheim, 86-87; Phi Beta Kappa; Eugene M. Kayden Univ P Nat Bk Awd for 'Life on the Hyphen,' 95; Duke Univ Teac of Yr, 95; Excel Awd for Facts About Cuban Exiles, 96; Palma Espinada Prize, CCACI, 00. **MEMBERSHIPS** AATSP; ALSC. **RESEARCH** Spanish and Spanish American literature; Latino literature and culture. **SELECTED PUBLICATIONS** Auth, Idle Fictions, Duke UP, 82; rev 93; auth, Literature and Liminality, DUP, 86; auth, The Cuban Condition, Cambridge UP, 89; auth, Do the Americas Have a Common Literature?, Duke UP, 90; auth, Life on the Hyphen, TX UP, 94; auth, Bilingual Blues, BiLing Rev Press, 95; auth, Next Year in Cuba, Doubleday, 95; auth, My Own Private Cuba, Colorado UP, 99; auth, Cincuenta lecciones de exilio y desexilio, Universal, 00; auth, Anything But Love, Arte Pub, 00. **CONTACT ADDRESS** Dept of Spanish, Columbia Univ, New York, NY 10025. **EMAIL** gpf@columbia.edu

PEREZ-PISONERO, ARTURO
DISCIPLINE SPANISH **EDUCATION** Our Lady Lake Col, BA, 66; Univ Okla, PhD, 70. **CAREER** From asst prof, 70-76 to assoc prof , 76-, Univ Tex at El Paso. **HONORS AND AWARDS** Symposium of the Asociacion Internacional de Teatro Espanol y Novohispano en los Siglos de Oro, 92; grants for the Golden Age Spanish Drama Symp, 81-; grants from, Univ Tex at El paso, Univ Tex at Austin, Tex Endowment for the Humanities and URI. **MEMBERSHIPS** Dir and founder of TEXTO Y ESPECTACULO. Golden Age Drama Symposium, 80-91; VP Asn Int de Teatro Espanol y Novohispano, 92; Comt for Premio Nacional de Literatura Jose Fuentes Mares, 91; bd dir, Centro de Estudios Alarconianos, 89; Siglo de Oro Drama Festival. **RESEARCH** Latin American literature. **SELECTED PUBLICATIONS** Auth, El texto literario y sus multiples lecturas, 8 estrategias de cretica literaria, Cuestionario y temas de composicion; Nicolas Guillen y la intrahistoria cubana, Afro-Hisp Rev; Norte y Frontera: Dicotomea y simbiosis en la novela de Ricardo Elizondo Setenta veces 7. Actas del IV Encuentro Nacional de Escritores en la Frontera Norte; Las luces del mundo, Entorno; Jesusa Palancares, esperpento femenino, Mujer y Literatura, Mexicana y Chicana; La novela Chicana: Un pueblo en busca de su historia, Romanische Forschungen. **CONTACT ADDRESS** Dept of Languages and Linguistics, Univ of Texas, El Paso, 500 W University Ave, El Paso, TX 79968. **EMAIL** aperez@utep.edu

PERISSINOTTO, GIORGIO
PERSONAL Born 06/13/1942, Trieste, Italy, m, 1968 **DISCIPLINE** HISPANIC LINGUISTICS **EDUCATION** Syracuse Univ, BA, 65; Columbia Univ, MA, 66, PhD(Span), 71. **CAREER** Instr Span, State Univ NY Stony Brook, 68-72, asst prof, 72-75; asst prof, Univ Tex, San Antonio, 75-76; Assoc Prof Span, Univ Calif, Santa Barbara, 76-, Vis prof ling, Inst Invest Integracion Social Estado Oaxaca, 72-73. **RESEARCH** Hispanic linguistics. **SELECTED PUBLICATIONS** Auth, Education reform and government intervention in Mexico, Current Hist, Vol 66, 74; Fonologia del espanol hablado en la ciudad de Mexico, Colegio Mex, 75; La Reconquista en el Poema del Cid: Una nueva lectura, Hispanofila, Vol 65, 79; A proposito de Ins versos 793 y 794 de las Mocedades de Rodrigo, Cult Neolatina, Vol 39, 79. **CONTACT ADDRESS** Dept of Spanish, Univ of California, Santa Barbara, Santa Barbara, CA 93106. **EMAIL** giorgio@humanitas.ucsb.edu

PERKINS, ALLAN KYLE
PERSONAL Born 11/14/1947, Corbin, KY, m, 1978, 2 children **DISCIPLINE** APPLIED & THEORETICAL LINGUISTICS **EDUCATION** Union Col, Ky, BA, 69; Southern Ill Univ, MA, 71; Univ Mich, PhD(ling), 76. **CAREER** Instr, 75-76, asst prof, 76-80, Assoc Prof Ling, Southern Ill Univ, 80-, Vis assoc prof, English Lang Inst, Am Univ Cairo, 82-83; prof, Ling, SIU, 85. **MEMBERSHIPS** Teachers English Speakers Other Lang; Midwest Mod Lang Asn. **RESEARCH** Language testing; second language testing methodology; theoretical syntax. **SELECTED PUBLICATIONS** Coauth, Language in Education: Testing the Tests, 78 & Research in Language Testing, 80, Newbury House Publ Inc; co-ed, On Tesol 79: The Learner in Focus, Teachers English Other Langs, 79; auth, Using objective methods of attained writing proficiency, Teacher English Speaker Other Langs Quart, 80; Determining coreferentiality by sight and sound, Regional English Lang Ctr J, 81; On predicate complements, Int Rev Appl Ling, 81; coauth, Discourse analysis and the art of coherence, Col English, 82; Test of ability to subordinate: Predictive and concurrent validity, Proc Fourth Int Lang Testing Symp, 82. **CONTACT ADDRESS** Acad Affairs, So Illinois Univ, Carbondale, Carbondale, IL 62901-4305. **EMAIL** kperkins@siu.edu

PERKINS, GEORGE W.
PERSONAL Born 07/11/1937, m, 1961, 6 children **DISCIPLINE** JAPANESE LITERATURE & LANGUAGE **EDUCATION** Brigham Young Univ, BA, 62; Stanford Univ, MA, 67, PhD, 77. **CAREER** Lectr Japanese, Stanford Univ, 69-70; lectr, Auckland Univ, 71-74; asst prof Japanese, Brigham Young Univ, 75-99, assoc prof Japanese, BYU, 99-. **MEMBERSHIPS** Asn Asian Studies; Asn Teachers Japanese. **RESEARCH** Premodern Japanese literature; the modern Japanese novel. **SELECTED PUBLICATIONS** Auth, The Clear Mirror: A Chronicle of the Japanese Court During the Kamakura Period (1185-1333), Stanford Univ Press, 98. **CONTACT ADDRESS** Dept of Asian & Slavic Lang, Brigham Young Univ, 4052 Jkhb, Provo, UT 84602-0002. **EMAIL** george_perkins@byu.edu

PERKINS, JEAN A.
PERSONAL Born 03/18/1928, Bombay, India, m, 1949, 2 children **DISCIPLINE** FRENCH **EDUCATION** Swarthmore Col, BA, 49; Columbia Univ, MA, 51; PhD, 57. **CAREER** Instr, Bryn Mawr Col, 54-56; instr to prof, Swarthmore Col, 57-90. **HONORS AND AWARDS** ADFL Award for Distinguished Serv, 98; ACLS grant, 78. **MEMBERSHIPS** MLA; ADFL; ASECS; ISECS. **RESEARCH** 18th Century French literature; 18th Century French family history. **SELECTED PUBLICATIONS** Auth, The Concept of the Self in the French Enlightenment, 69. **CONTACT ADDRESS** Dept Mod Lang, Swarthmore Col, 44 Crosslands Dr, Kennett Square, PA 19348-2010.

PERKOWSKI, JAN LOUIS
PERSONAL Born 12/29/1936, Perth Amboy, NJ, m, 1989, 3 children **DISCIPLINE** SLAVIC LANGUAGES **EDUCATION** Harvard Univ, AB, 59, AM, 60, PhD(Slavic lang & lit), 65. **CAREER** Asst prof Russ, Univ CA, Santa Barbara, 64-65; from asst prof to assoc prof slavic lang, Univ TX, Austin, 65-74, chm dept, 66-68 & 73-74; prof Slavic lang, univ VA, 74-, chm dept Slavic lang & lit, 76-83, 96-98. **HONORS AND AWARDS** Over 30 fellowships and grants. **MEMBERSHIPS** Am Asn Advan Slavic Studies; Am Asn Southeast European Studies; Am Asn of Teachers of Slavic and E Europ Lang. **RESEARCH** Balkan religious syncretism and South Slavic demonology. **SELECTED PUBLICATIONS** Auth, A Kashubian Idiolect in the United States, Lang Sci Monogr, IN Univ, 69; Vampires, Dwarves and Witches Among the Ontario Kashubs, Mercury Set 1, Nat Mus of Man, Ottwa, 72; Vampires of the Slavs, Slavica, 76; Linguistic Change in Texas Czech, Studies in Czechoslovak Hist, 76; Gusle and Ganga among the Hercegovinians of Toronto, Ann Arbor, 78; The Darkling: A Treatise on Slavic Vampirism, Slavica, 89; Slavic Soothsayers in Numinous Settings, Zeitschrift fur Balkanologie, Wiesbaden, 95; Ethnic and Religious Identity in Balkan Oral Tradition: The Case of Hercegovinia's Croats and Serbs, The South Slav J, London, 98; author of a total of five books and 60 articles. **CONTACT ADDRESS** Dept Slavic Lang & Lit, Univ of Virginia, 109 Cabell Hall, Charlottesville, VA 22903-3125. **EMAIL** slavic@virginia.edu

PERL, JEFFERY MICHAEL
PERSONAL Born 05/30/1952, Minneapolis, MN **DISCIPLINE** COMPARATIVE LITERATURE **EDUCATION** Stanford Univ, AB, 74; Oxford Univ, BA philos, 76; Princeton Univ, MA, 79, PhD, 80. **CAREER** Asst Prof, eng comp, Columbia Univ, 80-87; Assoc Prof, Columbia Univ, 87-89; Prog of Humanities, Univ Texas at Dallas, 89-98; Fulbright, vis, Hebrew Univ, Jerusalem, 98-99; Founding Editor, Common Knowledge, 92-. **HONORS AND AWARDS** NEH, 83; vis fel, Mansfield Col, Oxford, 83; Rockefeller fel, 84-85; Guggenheim fel, 88-89; Fulbright Sr Scholar, 98-99. **MEMBERSHIPS** MLA, Am Comp Lit Asn. **RESEARCH** Modernizing History of Aesthetics **SELECTED PUBLICATIONS** Auth, Skepticism and Modern Enmity, Johns Hopkins Univ, 89; The Tradition of Return: The Implicit History of Modern Literature, Princeton, 84; pubs in TLS, Partisan Rev, Sewanee Rev, S Rev, Philos East and West. **CONTACT ADDRESS** Dept of English, Univ of Texas, Dallas, Dallas, TX 95105. **EMAIL** perl@utdallas.edu

PERNA, MICHAEL
PERSONAL Born Hampton, VA **DISCIPLINE** LINGUISTICS **EDUCATION** Washington Col, 63; Duke Univ, MA, 72, PhD, 77. **CAREER** Acting asst, Univ Va, 73-76; Tandem School, Charlottesville, Va, 77-78; asst prof, Univ Maine at Orono, 78-79; asst prof to assoc prof, Hunter Col, CUNY, 79-. **MEMBERSHIPS** Renaissance Soc of Am, AATSP, NEMLA, Lyrica Soc for Word-Music Relations. **RESEARCH** Spanish poetry. **SELECTED PUBLICATIONS** Rev, Discurso retorico y Mundo Pastoral, by Ine's Azar, in MLN, 98 (83): 289-91; auth, "Pacifism," in J. C. Seignevret, Dictionary of Literary Themes and Motifs, 2, Westport, Ct: Greenwood (88); ed, Twentieth-Century Spanish Poets, First Series, Detroit, Mich (91); auth, "Antonio Jose Saraiva," (necrology), Hispania, 76 (93): 517-18. **CONTACT ADDRESS** Dept Romance Langs, Hunter Col, CUNY, 695 Park Ave, New York, NY 10021-5024. **EMAIL** mperna@shiva.hunter.cuny.edu

PEROZO, JAIME J.
DISCIPLINE SPANISH **EDUCATION** Univ Central de Venezuela, BA, 71; Tex A&I Univ, BA, 75; WA State Univ, MA Sociol, 79, MA Span & Span Am Lit, 86; Univ OR, PhD Sociol, 84; Univ WA, PhD Span & Span Am Lit, 94. **CAREER** Res asst, Univ OR & WA State Univ. **MEMBERSHIPS** Am Sociol Asn; MLA. **SELECTED PUBLICATIONS** Auth, The Sociopolitical Cosmovision in the Work of Miguel Otero Silva, Univ WA, 94; The role of Oil in Shaping Mexico and Venezuela as Semi peripheral Countries, Univ OR, 84; The Impact of Petroleum on the Human Carrying Capacity of Venezuela, WA State Univ, 79; Mahor Educ Community Res Proj, Dominican Repub Proj, Seattle, WA, 93; rev, Entre amigos, Houghton & Mifflin Co, 93. **CONTACT ADDRESS** Dept of For Lang, Seattle Univ, 900 Broadway, Seattle, WA 98122-4460. **EMAIL** jperozo@seattleu.edu

PERRY, CATHERINE
DISCIPLINE FRENCH LITERATURE **EDUCATION** Indiana Univ, BA, 87, MA, 91; Princeton Univ, PhD, 95. **CAREER** Asst prof. **HONORS AND AWARDS** NEH Fellowship, 97. **MEMBERSHIPS** MLA, WIF, ALSC, CIEF, AATF, AAUW. **RESEARCH** French literature of the 19th and early 20th centuries; intellectual history; literary theory; gender studies; artistic relations between France and the Maghreb. **SELECTED PUBLICATIONS** Auth, pubs on Anna de Noailles, Ronsard, Stendhal, Balzac, Barres and Wagner, Gerard d'Houville, Valery, Nicole Brossard and Malika Oufkir. **CONTACT ADDRESS** Romance Languages and Literatures Dept, Univ of Notre Dame, Notre Dame, IN 46556. **EMAIL** cperry@nd.edu

PESCA-CUPOLO, CARMELA
DISCIPLINE ITALIAN LANGUAGE AND LITERATURE **EDUCATION** Univ Salerno, Laurea; Univ Conn, PhD. **CAREER** Fac, Univ Conn, Trinity Col Hartford; Central Conn

State Univ, 95-. **RESEARCH** Medieval and Renaissance Italian literature; interdisciplinicary pedagogy and collaboration. **SELECTED PUBLICATIONS** Auth, articles of literary criticism on Medieval and Renaissance authors. **CONTACT ADDRESS** Central Connecticut State Univ, 1615 Stanley St, New Britain, CT 06050.

PETERS, ANN MARIE
PERSONAL Born 07/31/1938, Pasadena, CA **DISCIPLINE** LINGUISTICS **EDUCATION** Bryn Mawr Col, BA, 59; Univ Wis-Madison, MA, 61, PhD(ling), 66. **CAREER** Assoc Researcher Ling, Univ Hawaii, Manoa, 71-. **MEMBERSHIPS** Ling Soc Am. **RESEARCH** Child language acquisition; phonological rule testing; African tone languages. **SELECTED PUBLICATIONS** Auth, Algorithms for processing phonological rule schemata, Prof Fourth Int Conf Syst Sci, 71; A new formalization of downdrift, Studies African Ling, 73; Language learning strategies, Lang, 77; False Starts And Filler Syllables - Ways to Learn Grammatical Morphemes, Language, Vol 0069, 1993. **CONTACT ADDRESS** Dept of Ling, Univ of Hawaii, Manoa, 1890 E West Rd, Honolulu, HI 96822-2318.

PETERSON, DALE E.
PERSONAL Born 11/10/1966, Bridgewater, MA, m, 1966, 2 children **DISCIPLINE** ENGLISH, RUSSIAN **EDUCATION** Harvard Col, BA, 63; Yale Univ, MA, 65; PhD, 70. **CAREER** Instr to prof, Amherst Col, 68-. **HONORS AND AWARDS** Trustee Fac Fel, Amherst, 74-75; Fac Res Fel, Amherst, 97-00. **MEMBERSHIPS** MLA, Assoc of Teachers of Slavic and E Europ Lang, Am Assoc for the Advan of Slavic Studies, Nabokov Soc. **RESEARCH** Comparative American and Russian Literature and intellectual history. **SELECTED PUBLICATIONS** Auth, The Clement Vision: Poetic Realism in Turgenev and James, Kennikat Pr,/Nat Univ Pr, 75; auth, "Solzhenitsyn's Image of America: The Survival of a Slavophile Idea," Mass Rev, (78); auth, "Nabokov's Invitation: Literature as Execution," PMLA, (81); auth, "Maiakovskii's Lenin: The Fabrication of a Bolshevik bylina," Slavic Rev, (82); auth, "Russian Gothic: The Deathless Paradoxes of Bunin's Dry Valley," Slavic and E Europ Jour, (87); auth, "Nabokov and the Poe-etics of Composition," Slavic and E Europ Jour, (89); auth, "Response and Call: The African American Dialogue with Bakhtin," Am Lit, (93); auth, "Richard Wright's Long Journey from Gorky to Dostoevsky," African Am Lit, (94); auth, Up From Bondage: The Literatures of Russian and African American Soul, Duke Univ Pr, 00. **CONTACT ADDRESS** Amherst Col, Campus Box 2234, Amherst, MA 01002-5000. **EMAIL** depeterson@amherst.edu

PETERSON, PHILIP LESLIE
PERSONAL Born 03/12/1937, San Francisco, CA, m, 1967, 2 children **DISCIPLINE** PHILOSOPHY, LINGUISTICS **EDUCATION** Col William & Mary, AB, 59; Duke Univ, PhD (philos), 63. **CAREER** From asst prof to assoc prof, 63-76, Prof Philos, Syracuse Univ, 76-, Res assoc, Century Res Corp, 59-63, consult, 63-; Woodrow Wilson fel, 60-63; proj leader ling, Info Processing Systs Res, US Air Force Contracts, 66-71; partic, Early Mod Philos Inst, R Williams Col, 74. **MEMBERSHIPS** Am Philos Asn; AAAS; AAUP; Ling Soc Am. **RESEARCH** Philosophy of language; semantics; epistemology. **SELECTED PUBLICATIONS** Auth, Concepts and Language, Mouton, The Hague, 73; An abuse of terminology, Found Lang, 76; On specific reference, Semantikos, 76; How to infer belief from knowledge, Philos Studies, 77; On representing event reference, In: Presupposition, Acad Press, 79; On the logic of few, many, and most, Notre Dame J Formal Logic, 79; What causes effects?, Philos Studies, 81; Philosophy of Language, Social Res, 81. **CONTACT ADDRESS** 222 Buckingham Ave, Syracuse, NY 13210.

PETERSON, TARLA RAI
DISCIPLINE ENVIRONMENTAL COMMUNICATION **EDUCATION** Wash State Univ, PhD. **CAREER** Assoc prof, Texas A&M Univ. **SELECTED PUBLICATIONS** Auth, Sharing the Earth: The Rhetoric of Sustainable Development; co-ed, Communication and the Culture of Technology; Contribur, Transforming Visions:Feminist Critiques in Speech Communication & A Voice of Their Own: The Woman Suffrage Press, 1840-1910; assoc ed, Quart J Speech; bk rev ed, Quart J Speech. **CONTACT ADDRESS** Dept of Speech Communication, Texas A&M Univ, Col Station, College Station, TX 77843-4234. **EMAIL** tarla@unix.tamu.edu

PETIT, SUSAN
PERSONAL Born 08/25/1945, OH, m, 1984 **DISCIPLINE** FRENCH, ENGLISH **EDUCATION** Knox Col, BA, 66; Purdue Univ, MA, 68; Notre Dame Col, MA, 83. **CAREER** Prof, Col San Mateo, 68-. **HONORS AND AWARDS** Phi Beta Kappa. **MEMBERSHIPS** AATF; ALSC; CCCFLC; CLTA; Christianity and Literature; CCHA; CIEF; FSFS; FLANC; FLASC; MLA; PAMLA; Simone de Beauvoir Soc; Women in Fr. **RESEARCH** 20th-century French novel. **SELECTED PUBLICATIONS** Auth, "Joachim de Fiore, the Holy Spirit, and Michel Tournier's Les Maeores," Modern Lang Studies 16 (86): 88-100; auth, "Fugal Structure, Nestonanism, and St. Christopher in Michel Tournier's Le Roi des Aulnes," Novel 19 (86): 232-45; auth, "Psychological, Sensual, and Religious Initiation in Tournier's Pierrot ou les Secrets de la Nuit," Children's Lit 18 (90): 87-100; auth, "Michel Tournier's Metaphysical Fictions," in Monographs in Romance Languages 37 (91); auth, "Michel Tournier and Victor Hugo: A Case of Literary Parricide," Fr Rev 68 (94): 251-60; auth, "Michel Tournier," in The Contemporary Novel in France, ed. William Thompson (FL: UP of Florida, 95): 248-63; auth, "The Meaning of Food and the Body in Mallet-Jons's Divine," Lit Interpretations Theory 8 (97): 105-22; auth, "La Critique Religieuse de L'oeuvre de Tournier," Euvres et Critiques 23 (98): 40-51; auth, Francoise Mallet-Joris, Rodopi (Amsterdam/Atlanta) 01; auth, "Mallet-Joris's Divine: A Twentieth-Century Mystic," in Divine Aporia: Postmodern Conversations about the Other, ed. John C. Hawley (PA: Bucknell UP, 01): 190-207. **CONTACT ADDRESS** Fr Dept, Col of San Mateo, San Mateo, CA 94402. **EMAIL** petits@pacbell.net

PETRAGLIA-BAHRI, JOSEPH
DISCIPLINE RHETORIC AND COGNITIVE SCIENCE **EDUCATION** Carnegie Mellon Univ, PhD, 91. **CAREER** Asst prof, Ga Inst of Technol. **RESEARCH** The rhetoric of inquiry. **SELECTED PUBLICATIONS** Ed, Reconceiving Writing, Rethinking Writing Instruction, Lawrence Erlbaum, 95. **CONTACT ADDRESS** Sch of Lit, Commun, & Cult, Georgia Inst of Tech, Skiles Cla, Atlanta, GA 30332. **EMAIL** joseph.petraglia@lcc.gatech.edu

PETREMAN, DAVID A.
PERSONAL Born 11/25/1948, Kenosha, WI, m, 4 children **DISCIPLINE** SPANISH **EDUCATION** Ill Wesleyan Univ, BA, 70; Univ Iowa, MA, 76; PhD, 84. **CAREER** Asst Prof, Wake Forest Univ, 81-86; Assoc Prof, Wright State Univ, 86-. **HONORS AND AWARDS** President's Awd for Excellence in Teaching, Wright State Univ, 93; President's Awd for Excellence for Collaborative Effort, Wright State Univ, 95; Fel, Va Ctr for Creative Art, 89, 91. **RESEARCH** 20th Century and Contemporary Latin American Literature, Latin American Culture, Latin Americans in Professional Baseball. **SELECTED PUBLICATIONS** Auth, La obra narratie de Francisco Coloane, Santiago, 87; auth, Cape Horn and Other Stories from the End of the World, Pittsburgh, 91. **CONTACT ADDRESS** Dept Mod Lang, Wright State Univ, Dayton, 3540 Colonel Glenn Highway, Dayton, OH 45435-0001. **EMAIL** david.petreman@wright.edu

PETREY, SANDY
PERSONAL Born 08/29/1941 **DISCIPLINE** FRENCH LITERATURE **EDUCATION** Emory Univ, BA, 62; Yale Univ, PhD, 66. **CAREER** Prof, 82-. **SELECTED PUBLICATIONS** Auth, History in the Text: Quatrevingt-Treize and the French Revolution, Purdue, 80; Realism and Revolution: Balzac, Stendhal, Zola, and the Performances of History, Cornell, 88; Speech Acts and Literary Theory, Routledge, 90; ed, French Studies/Cultural Studies: Reciprocal Invigoration or Mutual Destruction?, 95; Anna-Nana-Nana: Identite sexuelle, ecriture naturaliste, lectures lesbiennes, 95; Men in Love, Saint-Simonism, Indiana, 95; Identite et alterite sous la Monarchie de juillet, 96. **CONTACT ADDRESS** English Dept, SUNY, Stony Brook, Stony Brook, NY 11794.

PETROVIC, NJEGOS M.
PERSONAL Born 05/20/1933, Vucitrn, Yugoslavia, m, 1960, 3 children **DISCIPLINE** SERB, FRENCH, AND RUSSIAN LANGUAGE & LITERATURE **EDUCATION** Univ Belgrade, BA, 53, super dipl, 57; Univ Montreal, MA, 62, PhD, 67. **CAREER** Instr mod lang, Class Col, Belgrade, 56-57; instr, Univ Paris, 58-61; asst prof French, Class Col St Jean, 61-64; asst prof, Royal Mil Col, Que, 64-65; asst prof Nebr Wesleyan Univ, 65-67; assoc prof, 67-74, Prof French and comp lit, Univ Scranton, 74-; chmn, Concert & Theater Scr, 69-92. **MEMBERSHIPS** Humanities Assn Can; MLA; AAUP. **RESEARCH** French, Serb, Greek (classical and modern), and Russian language and literature. **SELECTED PUBLICATIONS** Auth, Tisina Kamenja (poems), Prosveta, Belgrade, 54; art, Reve de bonheur, Provinces, Paris, 12/59; Carillon, 5/65 & Les Faubourgs, 6/65; auth, Ivo Andric, l'homme et l'oeuvre, Les Ed Lemeac, Montreal, 69; ed, Everhart Museum Catalog, Art Print Co, Scranton, Pa, 74. **CONTACT ADDRESS** 800 Linden St, Scranton, PA 18510-4501. **EMAIL** petrovicn1@hotmail.com

PETTEY, JOHN CARSON
DISCIPLINE GERMAN LANGUAGE, LITERATURE, AND CULTURE **EDUCATION** Wash Univ, PhD. **CAREER** Instr, Wash Univ; assoc prof Ger, Univ Nev, Reno. **SELECTED PUBLICATIONS** Published on the the female aphorism, as well as one on Nietzsche and Garcea Marquez. **CONTACT ADDRESS** Univ of Nevada, Reno, Reno, NV 89557.

PFANNER, HELMUT F.
PERSONAL Born 11/08/1933, Hohenweiler, Austria, m, 1995, 6 children **DISCIPLINE** GERMAN **EDUCATION** Teachers Training Col, 52, 57; Stanford Univ, MA, 61; PhD, 65. **CAREER** Teacher, Vorarlberg Austria, 52-57, 58-59; Instructor, Univ WA, 64-67; Asst Prof, Univ Va, 67-69; Assoc Prof, Univ NHamp, 69-79; Visiting Prof, Purdue Univ, 79-82; Prof, Univ NHamp, 82-86; Prof, Univ Neb, 86-90; Prof, Vanderbilt Univ, 90-. **HONORS AND AWARDS** o **MEMBERSHIPS** Alexander Von Humboldt Asn of Am; AATG; Am Coun for the Study of Austr Lit; Austr Asn of Germanists; Ger Studies Asn; Intl Asn for Germ Studies; MLA. **RESEARCH** German language literature of the 19th and 20th Century; American-European cross-cultural relations; Exile literature. **SELECTED PUBLICATIONS** Co-ed, Karl Jakob Hirsch: Quintessenz meines Lebens, Mainz, 90; ed, Der zweit Weltkrieg und die Exilanten: eine literarische Antwort. World War II and the Exiles: A Literary Response, Bonn, 91; ed, Alfred Doblin. Briefe II, Dusseldorf, in press; ed, Karl Jakob Hirsch. Heute und morgen, Peter Lang Pub, in press. **CONTACT ADDRESS** Dept German & Slavic Lang, Vanderbilt Univ, 2201 W End Ave, Nashville, TN 37235-0001. **EMAIL** h.pfanner@vanderbilt.edu

PFOHL, RUSSELL
DISCIPLINE FRENCH LITERATURE **EDUCATION** Johns Hopkins Univ, PhD, 67. **CAREER** Assoc prof. **SELECTED PUBLICATIONS** Auth, Racine's "Iphigenie": Literary Rehearsal and Tragic Recognition, 74; articles on Italo Svevo, Proust, French and Italian literature. **CONTACT ADDRESS** Dept of French and Italian, Indiana Univ, Bloomington, Indiana University, Bloomington, IN 47405.

PHILIPPIDES, DIA M.
DISCIPLINE CLASSICS **EDUCATION** Radcliffe Col, BA, 70; Boston Col, MA, 72; MA, 74; Princeton Univ, MA, 76; PhD, 78. **CAREER** Lecturer, Harvard Univ, 78-84; Asst to Full Prof, Boston Col, 84-. **HONORS AND AWARDS** Fulbright Program, Greece, 85, 90, 98; Literary Awd, Acad of Athens Greece, 88; Res grant, Jasper and Marion Whiting foundation, 91; Summer stipend, NEH, 94; Visiting Bye-Fel, Univ Cambridge, 94; Awd for res, Alexander S Onassis Public Benefit foundation, 96. **MEMBERSHIPS** Am Philol Asn, Mod Greek Studies Asn, Asn for Literary and Linguistic Computing. **RESEARCH** Modern Greek literature (Cretan Renaissance); Literary and linguistic analysis by computer; ancient Greek tragedy (especially meter). **SELECTED PUBLICATIONS** Auth, The Iambic Trimiter of Euripides: Selected Plays, Arno Press, 81; auth, The Sacrifice of Abraham on the Computer, Hermes Press, 86; auth, Census of Modern Greek Literature: Check-list of English-Language Sources useful in the Study of Modern Greek Literature (1824-1987), Modern Greek Studies Association, 90; auth, As the Wheel Turns: Electronic Analysis of the Erotokritos, Hermes Pub, 96. **CONTACT ADDRESS** Dept classical Studies, Boston Col, Chestnut Hill, 140 Commonwealth Ave, Chestnut Hill, MA 02467-3800. **EMAIL** dia.philippides@bc.edu

PHILIPPIDES, MARIOS
PERSONAL Born 08/05/1950, Athens, Greece, m, 1973 **DISCIPLINE** GREEK, LATIN **EDUCATION** Queens Col, BA, 73; State Univ NYork Buffalo, MA, 76, PhD(classics), 78. **CAREER** Asst prof, Union Col, 77-78; Asst Prof Classics, Univ Mass, Amherst, 78- **MEMBERSHIPS** Am Philol Asn; Class Asn New England; Modern Greek Studies Asn; Am Inst Archaeol; Am Class League. **RESEARCH** Palaeologan period of the Byzantine empire; ancient Greek religion and Mediterranean ritual and myth; the ancient novel. **SELECTED PUBLICATIONS** Auth, A note on Longus' Lesbiaka, The Class World, 78; The foundation of Taras and the Spartan partheniai, The Ancient World, 79; The Fall of the Byzantine Empire, Univ Mass Press, 80; The digressive aitia in Longus, The Class World, 80; The characters in Freedom or Death, The Charioteer, 80; The pronunciation of Greek, Phone, 81; The fall of Constantinople 1453, Greek, Roman & Byzantine Studies, 81; the prooemium in Lorgus, The Class Bull, 82. **CONTACT ADDRESS** Dept of Classics, Univ of Massachusetts, Amherst, Amherst, MA 01003-0002.

PHILLIPS, JANE ELLEN
PERSONAL Born 09/27/1943, Philadelphia, PA **DISCIPLINE** CLASSICS **EDUCATION** Millersville State Col, BA, 65; Univ NC, Chapel Hill, PhD(classics), 69. **CAREER** Asst prof classics, Univ NC, Chapel Hill, 69-71; adj instr, Dickinson Col, 71-72; adj instr, Franklin & Marshall Col, 71-72, vis asst prof, 72-73; asst prof, 73-80, Assoc Prof Classics, Univ KY, 80-91, ; Visiting Assoc Prof, Univ of Toronto, 90-91; Full Prof, 91-. **HONORS AND AWARDS** Fel in residence for col teachers, Nat Endowment for Humanities, 75-76. **MEMBERSHIPS** Am Philol Asn; Class Asn Midwest & South, Archaeol Inst Am, Am Class League, Vergilian Soc, Renaissance Soc of Am, Erasmus of Rotterdam Soc. **RESEARCH** Latin historiography and Latin poetry, Erasmus' biblical scholarship. **SELECTED PUBLICATIONS** Auth, Verbs compounded with trans in Livy's triumph reports, 74 & Form and language in Livy's triumph notices, 74, Class Philol; The pattern of images in Catullus, Am J Philol, 76; Juno in Aeneid, Vergilius, 77; Roman mothers and the lives of their adult daughters, Helios, 78; Livy and the beginning of a new society, Class Bull, 79; Lucretian echoes in Shelley's Mont Blanc, Class & Mod Lit, 82; auth, "The Gospel, the Clergy, and the Laity in Erasmus' Paraphrase on the Gospel of John, " Erasmus of Rotterdam Society Yearbook 10 (90): 85-100; transl and annot, "Collected Works of Erasmus, Vol 46 Paraphrase on the Gospel of John, Toronto, 91; auth, "Food and Drink in Erasmus' Gospel Paraphrase,"

Erasmus of Rotterdam Society Yearbook 14 (94): 24-25; Roman Marriage - Iusti-coniuges from the Time of Cicero to the Time of Ulpian - Treggiari,s/, Classical World, Vol 0087, 94 **CONTACT ADDRESS** Dept of Classics, Univ of Kentucky, 500 S Limestone St, Lexington, KY 40506-0027. **EMAIL** claphil@pop.uky.edu

PHILLIPS, JOANNE HIGGINS
PERSONAL Born 08/26/1946, Boston, MA **DISCIPLINE** CLASSICAL PHILOLOGY **EDUCATION** Boston Univ, AB, 68; Harvard Univ, MA, 71, PhD(class philol), 77. **CAREER** Assoc Prof Classics, Tufts Univ, 77-. **MEMBERSHIPS** Am Philol Asn; Am Asn Hist Med. **RESEARCH** History of Greek and Roman medicine. **SELECTED PUBLICATIONS** Auth, The boneless one in Hesiod, Philogus, 80; Early Greek medicine and poetry of Solon, Clio Medica, 80; The emergence of the Greek medical profession in the Roman Republic, Trans and Studies of Col of Physicians Philadelphia, 80; Juxtaposed medical traditions: Pliny NH 27 106 131, 81 & Lucretius on the inefficacy of the medical art: 6 1179 and 6 1226-1238, 82, Class Philol; The Hippocratic physician and astronomy, Proc of the IVth Int Colloquium on Hippocratic Med, Lausanne, Switz, 81, 82. **CONTACT ADDRESS** Dept of Classics, Tufts Univ, Medford, 318 Eaton Hall, Medford, MA 02155-0000. **EMAIL** jphillip@emerald.tufts.edu

PHILLIPS, KLAUS
DISCIPLINE NEW GERMAN CINEMA **EDUCATION** Univ AR, BA, MA; Univ TX, Austin, PhD, 84. **CAREER** Instr, Univ IL, VA Mil Inst; vis prof, Sweet Briar Col; prof Ger and Film, ch, dept Ger & Russ, dir, grad program in screenwriting & film studies, Hollins Univ. **HONORS AND AWARDS** NEH; DAAD. **MEMBERSHIPS** AATG; GSA. **SELECTED PUBLICATIONS** Auth, Rainer Maria Rilke: Nine Plays; Women in Recent German Films; New German Filmmakers: From Oberhausen Through the 1970's. **CONTACT ADDRESS** PO Box 9596, Roanoke, VA 24020. **EMAIL** kphillips@hollins.edu

PHILLIPS, LOUIS
PERSONAL Born 06/15/1942, Lowell, MA, m, 1973, 2 children **DISCIPLINE** ENGLISH, COMPARATIVE LITERATURE **EDUCATION** Stetson Univ, BA, 64; Univ NC, MA, 65; City Univ New York, MA, 67. **CAREER** Sch of Visual Arts, New York City, 75-. **HONORS AND AWARDS** NEA in Playwriting; Regents Fel in Playwriting at the Univ of Calif at San Diego. **MEMBERSHIPS** Dramatists Guild, Soc of Am Magicians. **RESEARCH** Theater history, the films of Alfred Hitchcock, American humor. **SELECTED PUBLICATIONS** Auth, Alligator Wrestling and You (juvenile), New York: Avon Books (92); auth, A Dream of Countries Where No One Dare Live (short stories), SMU Press (94); auth, Savage Steps to the House of Meaning (poetry), New York: Prologue Press (95); ed, The Random House Treasury of Humorous Verse, Random House (95); auth, Plays (comic one-acts), Broadway Play Pubs (95); auth, Hot Corner: Baseball Stories, Livingston Press (96); auth, The Ballroom in St Patrick's Cathedral (full length play), Louisville: Aran Press (96); auth, Ask Me Anything About Monsters (nonfiction), New York: Avon Books (97); auth, 16 Points on a Hurricane's Compass (full length play), Louisville: Aran Press (97); auth, The Krazy Kat Rag (poetry), Chicago: Light Reprints 999). **CONTACT ADDRESS** Dept Humanities and Scis, Sch of Visual Arts, New York, 209 E 23rd St, New York, NY 10010-3901.

PICARD, ANNE MARIE
DISCIPLINE FRENCH LITERATURE **EDUCATION** Univ Haute Normandie, BA; Rollen, MA; Univ Toronto, PhD. **RESEARCH** Lacanian psychoanalysis; theories of the body; theories of reading; 19th and 20th century French literature; history of criticism; existentialism; narratology; Saussurian linguistics; semantics. **SELECTED PUBLICATIONS** Auth, Le Corps et la lettre: psychanalyse et metacritique, Nuit Blanche, 95; ed, Mises-en-scenes du regard, Dalhousie, 95. **CONTACT ADDRESS** Dept of French, Univ of Western Ontario, London, ON, Canada N6A 5B8. **EMAIL** picard@julian.uwo.ca

PICERNO, RICHARD A.
DISCIPLINE SPANISH LANGUAGE AND LITERATURE **EDUCATION** Providence Col, BA, 61; Boston Col, MA, 64; Univ Conn, PhD, 69. **CAREER** Fac, Univ Conn, Storrs, Suffolk Univ and Boston Univ; prof mod langs, 66-. **HONORS AND AWARDS** Fulbright Scholar, Universidad de Madrid, 61-62. **SELECTED PUBLICATIONS** Auth, Lope de Vega's: Lo que pasa en une tarde, Univ NC Press, 71; La Estrella de Sevilla, Ediciones Universal, 83; Medieval Spanish Ejempla, A Study of Selected Tales from Calila y Dimna, El libro de los engaos, Libro de los exemplos por ABC, Ediciones Universal, 88. **CONTACT ADDRESS** Central Connecticut State Univ, 1615 Stanley St, New Britain, CT 06050.

PICHERIT, JEAN-LOUIS
DISCIPLINE FRENCH **EDUCATION** Univ NC at Chapel Hill, PhD, 71. **CAREER** Prof; Univ WY, 76-; coord exchange progr, UW & Univ Tours and Strasbourg. **HONORS AND AWARDS** Arts & Sci Seibold Professorship. **RESEARCH** French medieval epic; study of med metaphors in French medieval lit; Middle-French lit. **SELECTED PUBLICATIONS** Ed & transl, medieval epic. **CONTACT ADDRESS** Dept of Mod and Class Lang(s), Univ of Wyoming, PO Box 3964, Laramie, WY 82071-3964. **EMAIL** PICHERIT@UWYO.EDU

PICHOIS, CLAUDE
PERSONAL Born 07/21/1925, Paris, France, m, 1961 **DISCIPLINE** FRENCH LITERATURE, COMPARATIVE LITERATURE **EDUCATION** Hautes Etudes Commerciales, Paris, Dipl, 48; Sorbonne, Doctorat d'Etat, 63. **CAREER** Assoc prof French lit, Faculte des Lettres d'Aix-en- Provence, France, 56, assoc prof comp lit, 58-61; prof French lit, Faculte d'Hist et de Philos, Basel, Switz, 61-70; prof, 70- 73, Distinguished Prof French Lit, Vanderbilt Univ, 73-, CO-ed, Revue d'Hist litteraire de la France, Armand Colin, Paris, 50-, Etudes baudelairiennes, La Baconniere, Switz, 69- & Bull baudelairien, Vanderbilt Univ, 70-; gen ed, Litterature francaise, Arthaud, Paris, 68-80; vis res prof, Inst Res Humanities, Madison, Wis, 68; John Simon Guggenheim Mem Found fel, 78. **MEMBERSHIPS** MLA; Soc d'Hist litteraire France. **SELECTED PUBLICATIONS** AUth, L'Image de Jean-Paul Richter dans les lettres francasies, 63 & Philarete Chasles et la vie litteraire au temps du romantisme, 65, Jose Corti, Paris; Litterature et Progres: Vitesse et vision du monde, La Baconniere, 73; ed, Baudelaire's Correspondence, 2 vols, 73 & Baudelaire's Complete Works, 2 vols, 75-76, Bibliot de la Pleiade, Paris. **CONTACT ADDRESS** Vanderbilt Univ, Box 6203 Sta B, Nashville, TN 37235.

PICHUGIN, VALENTINA
PERSONAL Born 02/26/1960, Russia, m, 1991, 1 child **DISCIPLINE** RUSSIAN SLAVIC LANGUAGES, LITERATURE, CULTURE, FOLKLORE **EDUCATION** Omsk State Univ, Rus, MA, 85; Inst Acad Sci, Rus, PhD, 90. **CAREER** Asst prof, Fla State Univ, 93-. **HONORS AND AWARDS** FSU Res Gnt; FSU Teach Awd; FSU Res Gnt. **MEMBERSHIPS** AATSEEL; AAASS; MLA; SCSS; BASEEL. **RESEARCH** Russian linguistics (synchrony and diachrony); pre-19th century literature; folklore; culture; film. **SELECTED PUBLICATIONS** Auth, Deverbatives with Suffix -k(a), in Russian Language (from 11th to 17th century), Hermitage Pub (Tenafly) 98; auth "Russian Surnames in the Seventeenth Century: Sociolinguistics Aspect," Palaeoslavic 5 (97): 347-357; auth, "Neumatic Designations in Old Russian Chant," Palaeoslavic 6 (98): 314-330. **CONTACT ADDRESS** Dept Modern Languages, Florida State Univ, PO Box 3061540, Tallahassee, FL 32306-1540.

PICKERING-IAZZI, ROBIN
PERSONAL Born 07/06/1953, Seattle, WA, m, 1978, 1 child **DISCIPLINE** ITALIAN, COMPARATIVE LITERATURE **EDUCATION** Univ Wash, BA, 75; MA, 79; PhD, 85. **CAREER** Lectr to prof, Univ of Wis-Milwaukee, 85-. **HONORS AND AWARDS** Co-Recipient of Res Awd, Consiglio Nazionale Delle ricerche of Italy, 95; Uwm Res Awds. **MEMBERSHIPS** Am Assoc of Teachers of Ital; Am Assoc for Ital Studies; MLA. **RESEARCH** 19th and 20th Century Italian culture; feminist studies; film. **SELECTED PUBLICATIONS** Coauth, "In terza Pagina", Italian cultural reader, 89; trans, "Unspeakable Women: Selected Short Stories Written by Italian Women During Fascism", City Univ of NY, 93; ed, Mothers of Invention: Women, Italian Fascism, and Culture, Univ of Minn Pr, 95; auth, Politics of the Visible: Writing Women, Culture and Fascism, Univ of Minn Pr, 97. **CONTACT ADDRESS** Dept Fr Ital Comp Lit, Univ of Wisconsin, Milwaukee, PO Box 413, Milwaukee, WI 53201-0413. **EMAIL** rpi2@uwm.edu

PICKETT, TERRY H.
PERSONAL Born 04/14/1941, Washington, GA, m, 1962, 2 children **DISCIPLINE** GERMAN STUDIES **EDUCATION** Univ of Ga, AB, 66; Univ of Ala, MA, 68; Vanderbilt Univ, PhD, 70. **CAREER** Prof Emeritus, Univ of Ala, 69-97; vis prof, N Ga Col and State Univ, 98-00. **HONORS AND AWARDS** Fulbright Scholar, 72-73, 80-81, & 89-90; IREX; NEH; DAAD; Univ Res Grants. **MEMBERSHIPS** SAMLA. **RESEARCH** 18th-19th Century. **SELECTED PUBLICATIONS** Auth, "The Unseasonable Democrat: K. A. Varnhagen von Ense 1785-1858," Modern Ger Studies vol 14, Bouvier Verlag Herbert Grundmann (Bonn), 85; coauth, The Letters of the American Socialist Albert Brisbane To K. A. Varnhagen von Ense, Carl Winter Univ Publ, 86; auth, "Bettina's englisches Wagnis in Light of the Correspondence between Sarah Austin and Bettina von Arnim," Euphorion. Zeitschrift fuer Literaturgeschichte 84 (90): 397-407; auth, "Harriet Grote's Correspondence with K. A. Varnhagen von Ense 1845-1854," Cahiers Victoriens & Edouardiens 37 (93): 13-53; auth, "The Bruderkrieg and the Crisis of Constitutional Government: The Treatment of the American Civil War by Georg von Cotta's German War Correspondents 1861-65," Schatzkammer der deutschen Literatur und Geschichte XX (94): 13-15; auth, "Inventing Nations: Justifications of Authority in the Modern World," Contributions in Philos 56, Westport (London, Eng), 96. **CONTACT ADDRESS** Dept Lang and Lit, No Georgia Col, 100 College Cr, Dahlonega, GA 30597-0001. **EMAIL** tpic940967@aol.com

PICKMAN-GERTZ, CHARLOTTE
PERSONAL w, 3 children **DISCIPLINE** FRENCH, ITALIAN **EDUCATION** C.U. Post Col, BA, 66; MA, 68; City Univ NY, PhD, present. **CAREER** Adj Assoc Prof, Molloy Col, 83-. **HONORS AND AWARDS** Excellence in Italian, C.U. Post Col; Grants to write Book II - French and Italian, Molloy Col. **SELECTED PUBLICATIONS** Auth, Practical Spoken French; auth, Practical Spoken French - Book II; auth, Practical Spoken Italian; auth, Practical Spoken Italian - Book II. **CONTACT ADDRESS** Dept Mod Lang, Molloy Col, PO Box 5002, Rockville Centre, NY 11571-5002.

PICONE, MICHAEL D.
DISCIPLINE LINGUISTICS, FRENCH **EDUCATION** Univ Ore, BA, 74; MA, 78; Faculte libre de theol reformee, Licence en Theol, 83; Univ de Paris-Sorbonne, Doctorat de III eme cycle, 87. **CAREER** Univ Ala, 88-. **RESEARCH** Languages in Contact, Dialectology, Romance Linguistics, Phonology, Lexicology, Native American Languages, Morphosyntax. **SELECTED PUBLICATIONS** Auth, "Lexicogenesis and Language Vitality," Word 45 (94): 261-285; auth, Anglicisms, Neologisms and Dynamic French, John Benjamins (Amsterdam & Philadelphia), 96; auth, "Strategies lexicogeniques franco-louisianaises," Plurilinguismes 11 (96): 63-99; auth, "Code-switching and loss of Inflection in Louisiana French," Language Variety in the South Revisited, eds. Cynthia Bernstein, Tom Nunnally, & Robin Sabino (AL: Univ Ala Press, 97), 152-162; auth, "Enclave Dialect Contraction: An External Overview of Louisiana French," Am Speech 72 (97): 117-153. **CONTACT ADDRESS** Modern Lang & Classics, Univ of Alabama, Tuscaloosa, PO Box 870246, Tuscaloosa, AL 35487-0246. **EMAIL** mpicone@bama.ua.edu

PIEDMONT, FERDINAND
PERSONAL Born 11/19/1926, Trier, Germany, m, 1966, 2 children **DISCIPLINE** GERMAN **EDUCATION** Univ Bonn, MA, 53, PhD, 54. **CAREER** Studienrat Ger & English, Schiller Gym, Cologne, 58-63; from asst to assoc prof, 63-76, Prof Ger, Ind Univ, Bloominton, 76-, Fulbright vis lectr, 60-61. **HONORS AND AWARDS** ACLS, NEH, Iulbright **MEMBERSHIPS** MLA; Am Asn Teachers Ger; Am Lessing Soc. **RESEARCH** Late 18th and early 19th century literature; drama and Theater; teaching methodology. **SELECTED PUBLICATIONS** Auth, Textsammlung Moderner Kurzgeschichten, Diesterweg, Ger, 59; Coauth, Kurz belichtet (German Literature Reader), Rinehart, 73; auth, Zur Rolle des Erzahlers in der Kurzgeschichte, Z Deut Philol, 11/73; Tendenzen moderner Schiller-Auffuehrungen 1965-1975, Jb Deut Schillerges, 77; Wittkowski,w. Review of Piedmont Book on Staging Schiller Dramas 1946-1985 - a Reply/, German Quarterly, Vol 0065, 1992; Ed, Schiller Spielen. Stimmen der Theater-Kritik 1946-1985, Wiss. Buchgesellschaft, Darmstadt, 1990; Reisst- diemauern-ein - Schiller 'Wilhelm Tell' on the Stage in the Year of the German Revolution, 1989/, German Studies Review, Vol 0018, 1995; Schiller Dramas - Idealism and Skepticism - German - Guthke,ks/, Colloquia Germanica, Vol 0029, 1996; Ed., Schiller Spielen. Stimmen der Teaterkritik, 1946-1985, Wiss. Buchgesellschaft, Darmstadt, 1990. **CONTACT ADDRESS** Dept of Ger, Indiana Univ, Bloomington, Bloomington, IN 47401. **EMAIL** piedmont@Indiana.edu

PIEDRA, JOSE
DISCIPLINE SPANISH LITERATURE **EDUCATION** Yale Univ, PhD. **CAREER** Assoc prof and co-founder and first dir, Prog of Hisp-Amer Stud, Cornell Univ; art curator. **RESEARCH** Early modern images and contributions of blacks in Spanish and Spanish American cultures. **SELECTED PUBLICATIONS** Auth, In Search of the Black Stud, in Pre-Modern Sexualities, Routledge, 97; Nationalizing Sissies, in Entiendes, Queer Readings, Hisp Writings, Duke, 97. **CONTACT ADDRESS** Dept of Romance Studies, Cornell Univ, 283 Goldwin Smith Hall, Ithaca, NY 14853.

PIEPKE, SUSAN L.
PERSONAL Born 03/05/1949, Kerrville, TX, m **DISCIPLINE** GERMAN, SPANISH **EDUCATION** SUNY Albany, BA, 71; Univ Rochester, MA, 75; Middlebury Col, DML, 86. **CAREER** Teach, Brockport HS, 71-83; asst prof, Elon Col, 84-88; assoc prof, 88-98, prof, 98-, Bridgewater Coll. **HONORS AND AWARDS** Who's Who - Am Women, Am Teach; NEH Gnt; VFIC Mednick Fel. **MEMBERSHIPS** AATG; ACTFL; FLAVA; MLA; AATSP; AAUW. **RESEARCH** 19th century German women writers; woman's literature; 19th century literature. **SELECTED PUBLICATIONS** Auth, "A Sor Juana Anthology," in Masterplots II: Woman's Lit, Salem Press, 95; auth, "A Sor Juana Ines de la Cruz," in Magill's Survey of Women's Literature, Salem Press, 95; Auth, Women and Their Vocation: A Nineteenth Century View by Luise Buchner, Peter Lang Pub (NY), 99. **CONTACT ADDRESS** Dept Foreign Language, Bridgewater Col, 402 East College St, Bridgewater, VA 22812-1511. **EMAIL** spiepke@bridgewater.edu

PIERCE, GLENN
PERSONAL Born San Diego, CA **DISCIPLINE** ITALIAN **EDUCATION** UCLA, PhD, 77 **CAREER** Asst prof, UVA, 78-84; prof, Italian, UMC, 98; prof of Italian, MU, 99-. **HONORS AND AWARDS** Golden Key Honor Soc, Georgetown

Univ; Scholar, Johns Hopkins Bologna Ctr. **MEMBERSHIPS** MLA; AAIS; AATI. **RESEARCH** Italian Baroque. **SELECTED PUBLICATIONS** Auth, art, What is Tragic About Torrismondo, 91; auth, art, Tecniche teatrali ne I promessi sposi, 95; auth, art, A bacchic dithyramb in the Ottocento?, 95; auth, Alessandro Manzoni and the Aesthetics of the Lombard Seicento: Finding the arts in the narra; auth, Manzoni and the Aesthetics of the Lombard Seicento, Bucknell Univ Press, 98. **CONTACT ADDRESS** Dept of Romance Lang, Univ of Missouri, Columbia, A/S 123, Columbia, MO 65211. **EMAIL** pierceg@missouri.edu

PIERREHUMBERT, JANET
DISCIPLINE LINGUISTICS **EDUCATION** MIT, PhD. **CAREER** Prof, Northwestern Univ. **RESEARCH** Phonetics; phonology; prosody and intonation. **SELECTED PUBLICATIONS** Auth, Syllable Structure and Word Structure, Papers in Lab Phonology, Cambridge Univ Press, 94; Lenition of /h/ and glottal stop, Papers in Lab Phonology, Cambridge Univ Press, 91; On ichlaut, achlaut, and structure preservation, Phonol, 91; On Attributing Grammars to Dynamical Systems, J. Phonetics, 90; Categories of Tonal Alignment in English, Phonetica, 90; The Timing of Prenuclear High Accents in English, Papers in Lab Phonology I, Cambridge UP, 90; Japanese Tone Structure, Linguistic Inquiry Monograph 15, MIT Press, Cambridge, 88; Prosodic Effects on Glottal Allophones in Vocal Fold Physiology 8, Singular Press, 94; rev, Autosegmental and Metrical Phonology, J Phonetics, 94. **CONTACT ADDRESS** Dept of Linguistics, Northwestern Univ, 2016 Sheridan Rd, Evanston, IL 60208.

PIFER, ELLEN
PERSONAL Born 06/26/1942, New York, NY, m, 1962, 1 child **DISCIPLINE** ENGLISH AND COMPARATIVE LITERATURE **EDUCATION** Mills Col, Oakland, CA; Univ CA, Berkeley, BA (English, with Distinction), MA, PhD (Comparative Lit, English, Russian, French), 76. **CAREER** Asst prof, dept of English, Univ DE, 77-81; asoc prof, English and Comparative Lit, dept of English, Univ DE, 81-89; vis prof, Comparative Lit, Univ CA, Berkeley, spring 90; Distinguished Vis Prof of Am Lit, Universite Jean Moulin, Lyon III, France, spring 92; prof of English and Comparative Lit, Dept of English, Univ DE, 89-. **HONORS AND AWARDS** Nominated for Excellence in Teaching Awd, Univ DE, 86, 88, 97; General Univ Res grant, Univ DE, 78, 81, 86, 90; DE Humanities Forum Res fel, 87-88; DE Arts Coun Individual Artists fel (Non-Fiction Prose), 89-90; Nat Endowment for the Humanities summer stipend for res, 91; Outstanding Academic Book Awd (for Saul Bellow Against the Grain), Choice Magazine, 90-91; Distinguished Vis Prof of Am Lit, Univ Lyon III, France, 92; Fulbright Scholar, France, 92; Rector's Distinguished Vis Prof in Am Lit, Univ Helsinki, Finland, March 28-April 8, 93; Center for Advanced Studies fel, Univ DE, 93-94; listed in Who's Who in the World, Who's Who in Ed, The International Authors and Writers Who's Who, Dictionary of Am Scholars, etc. **MEMBERSHIPS** Modern Language Asn; Am Lit Asn; Int Vladimir Nabokov Soc (pres, 98-2000, vice-pres, 96-98, member, bd of dirs). **RESEARCH** Modern and contemporary lit; the novel; the image of childhood in contemporary writing and culture. **SELECTED PUBLICATIONS** Auth, Nabokov and the Novel, Harvard Univ Press, 80, 81; ed and intro, Critical Essays on John Fowles, G K Hall, 86; auth, Saul Bellow Against the Grain, Univ PA Press, 90; Lolita, The Garland Companion to Vladimir Nabokov, ed Vladimir E Alexandrov, Garland, 95; Birds of a Different Feather: Nabakov's Lolita and Kosinski's Boy, Cycnos 12, 2, 95; Nabokov's Discovery of America: From Russia to Lolita, in The American Columbiad: Discovering America, Inventing the United States, eds Mario Materassi and Maria I Ramalho de Sousa Santos, VU Univ Press, 96; Winners and Losers: Bellow's Dim View of Success, in Saul Bellow and the Struggle at the Center, ed Eugene Hollahan, AMS Press, 96; The River and Its Current: Literary and Collective Memory in Toni Morrison's Beloved, Sounding the Depths: Water as Metaphor in North American Literatures, eds Gayle Wurst and Christine Raguet-Bouvart, Univ of Liege Press, 98; The Children: Wharton's Creative Ambivalence to Self, Society and the New World, in Edith Wharton: A Forward Glance, eds Clare Colquitt, Susan Goodman and Candace Waid, Univ DE Press, 99; Her Monster, His Nymphet: Nabakov and Mary Shelley, in Nabokov and His Fiction: New Perspectives, ed Julian W Connolly, Cambridge Univ Press, 99; auth, Demon or Doll: Images of the Child in Contemporary Writing and Culture, Univ Pr Va, 00; 'Did she have a precursor?': 'Lolita' and Wharton's 'The Children,' ed. Jane Grayson, Arnold McMillin & Priscilla Meyer, MacMillan/St. Martin's Pr, forthcoming. **CONTACT ADDRESS** English Dept, Univ of Delaware, Memorial Hall, Newark, DE 19716. **EMAIL** epifer@udel.edu

PILUSO, ROBERT VINCENT
PERSONAL Born 04/05/1937, Yonkers, NY, m, 1967, 3 children **DISCIPLINE** SPANISH **EDUCATION** Fordham Univ, AB, 58, AM, 60; NYork Univ, PhD, 65. **CAREER** Instr Span & French, St Peter's Col, 59-60; tchr Span & Latin, Tuckahoe High Sch, 60-63; instr Span & French, Manhattan Col, 63-65; instr Span, Hunter Col, 65-67; assoc prof, 67-72, Prof Romance Lang, State Univ NY Col New Paltz, 72. **HONORS AND AWARDS** Who's Who Among Italian Am, 93; Directory of Ital Am Scholars, 92; Lectured at the Congresses of the Intl Hispanists, Salamanca Spain, 71, Bordeaux France, 74, Toronto Ontario, 77, Venice Italy, 80, Brown Univ Rhode Island, 83; Fulbright Grant to Burgos Spain, 65; Founders Day Awd, NY Univ, 65; Span tchg Fel, Fordham Univ, 58. **MEMBERSHIPS** Am Assoc Tchrs Span & Port, Tchrs of Italian, Tchrs of French; MLA; Assoc Int Hispanists; Nat Italian Am Federation; Am Classical League; Classical Assoc of the Atlantic States; Alliance Francaise de Westchester. **RESEARCH** Cervantes and Golden Age prose; Golden Age drama; contemp theater, espec Span; Garcia-Loca. **SELECTED PUBLICATIONS** Auth, La fuerza de la sangre: Un analisis estructural, Hispania, 64; Amor, matrimonio y honra en Cervantes, Las Americas, 67; Analisis de El infamador, Duquesne Hisp Rev, 68; Honor in Valdivielso and Cervantes, Ky Romance Quart, 70; Co ed, Jose de Valdivielso: Teatro completo, volumen I and II, Madrid: editorial Isla, 75 and 81; Italian Fundamentals, Barron's Edu series, 92; Italian on Location, eng ver, Barron's Edu series, 92. **CONTACT ADDRESS** Dept Span State, SUNY, New Paltz, 75 S Manheim Blvd, New Paltz, NY 12561-2400. **EMAIL** rpiluso@worldnet.att.net

PINET, CHRISTOPHER
PERSONAL Born 05/06/1944, Chelsea, MA, m, 1969, 2 children **DISCIPLINE** FRENCH **EDUCATION** Univ Kans, BA, 66; Brown Univ, MA, 68; PhD, 71. **CAREER** Asst prof, Ind State Univ, 71-73; asst to assoc prof, Marquette univ, 73-81; asst to assoc prof, Mont State Univ, 81-. **HONORS AND AWARDS** Woodrow Wilson Fel, 69-70; NDEA Fel, 66-69; Burlington Northern Outstanding Teacher Awd, 92; Mont State Univ, Teaching Awd, 86, 89, 91, 93, 96; Chevalier in Palmes Academiques, 95. **MEMBERSHIPS** MLA; AATF. **RESEARCH** Renaissance history and society, contemporary French popular culture, contemporary French society and politics, urban studies. **SELECTED PUBLICATIONS** Auth, "The Cobbler in French Farce of the Renaissance", Fr Rev 48.2 (74): 308-20; auth, "Myths and Stereotypes in Asterix le Gaulois" Can Mod Lang Rev 1.3 (78): 317-36; auth, "Some Reflections on French Farce and the Genre Approach", Res Publica Litterarum 2.1 (79): 243-51; auth, "French Farce: Printing, Dissemination and Readership from 1500-1560", Renaissance and Reformation 15.2 (79): 111-32; auth, "Monks, Priests, and Cuckholds: French Farce and Criticism of the Church from 1500-1560", Stanford Fr Rev, (80): 453-74; auth, "The Image of the French in the Songs of Georges Brassens", Contemp Fr Civ 6.3 (82): 271-94; auth, "From Fabliau to Farce: A Case Study", Essays in Early French Literature, eds Norris J Lacy and Jerry C Nash, Fr Lit Pub, (York, SC), (82): 93-108; auth, "Teaching Civilization with Le Petit Nicolas", Fr Rev 56.4 (83): 599-607; auth, "Asterix, Brassens and Cabu: The ABC's of Popular Culture", Popular Traditions Learned Culture in France, ed Marc Bertrand, Stanford Fr and Ital Studies 35, Anma Libri, (85): 275-87. **CONTACT ADDRESS** Dept Mod Lang, Montana State Univ, Bozeman, W Kagy Ave, Bozeman, MT 59717-0001. **EMAIL** umlcp@montana.edu

PINET, SIMONE
PERSONAL Born 07/20/1971, Mexico, m, 2000 **DISCIPLINE** SPANISH LITERATURE **EDUCATION** Universidad Nacional autonoma de Mexico, Lengua y Literaturas Hispanicas, 96; Harvard Univ, AM, 98; PhD, 02. **CAREER** Instr, Harvard Univ, 00; lectr to asst prof, Yale Univ, 01-. **HONORS AND AWARDS** Jens Aubrey Westergard Scholar; Dumbarton Oaks Exchange Fel, Grad Soc Diss Completion Grant, Grad Soc Summer Fel, Real Glegio Complutense, Harvard Grant, Lucy Allen Paton Fund Grnat, Medalla Gabiro Bavreda. **MEMBERSHIPS** MLA, IAPL. **RESEARCH** Spanish Literature of the Middle Ages, Prose fiction of the Golden Age, Critical Theory, Theories of Fiction, Theories of Space. **SELECTED PUBLICATIONS** Auth, El baladro del sabio Merlin: Notas para la historia y caracterizacion del personaje en Espana, JGH, (Mexico), 97; auth, "De Babel y los gigantes: in episodio del Libro de Alexandre," Actas de las VIII Jordnadeas Medievales, forthcoming; auth, "La Insola No Fallada del Amadis: in itinecio," Medievalia, forthcoming. **CONTACT ADDRESS** 423 at 120 St, Apt 27, New York, NY 10027-6028. **EMAIL** pinet@fas.harvard.edu

PINKUS, KAREN
DISCIPLINE FRENCH AND ITALIAN AND COMPARATIVE LITERATURE **EDUCATION** City Univ NYork, PhD. **CAREER** Prof, Univ Southern Calif. **RESEARCH** Cultural history of Italy in the 1950s. **SELECTED PUBLICATIONS** Auth, Bodily Regimes: Italian Advertising under Fascism, Univ Minn Press, 95; Picturing Silence: Emblem, Language, Counter-Reformation Materiality, Univ Mich Press; The Body, in Theory ser, 96. **CONTACT ADDRESS** Col Letters, Arts & Sciences, Univ of So California, University Park Campus, Los Angeles, CA 90089.

PINNINGTON, NOEL J.
PERSONAL Born 11/23/1950, Slough, England, m, 1992, 1 child **DISCIPLINE** JAPANESE LITERATURE **EDUCATION** London Univ, BSc, 74; Rolle Coll, PGCE, 76; London Univ, MA, 89; Univ Cambridge, PhD, 94. **CAREER** Fel, Univ Cambridge, 94-99; Asst Prof, Univ Ariz, 99-. **HONORS AND AWARDS** Yasuda Res Fel, 94-97; Brit Acad Awd, 90-93. **MEMBERSHIPS** Asn of Asian Studies; Brit Asn of Japanese Studies; PMJS. **RESEARCH** Performance and Art theory in Medieval Japan; Pre-modern Japanese literature; Pre-modern Japanese Mathematics; Pre-modern Japanese Intellectual History. **SELECTED PUBLICATIONS** Auth, "Crossed Paths: Zeami's transmission to Zenchiku," Monumenta Nipponica, 97; auth, "Invented Origins: Muromachi interpretations of okina sarugaku," Bulletin of the Sch of Oriental and African Studies, 98; ed, Essays in Idleness, Wordsworth Classic Books, 98; co-ed, Teaching about Japan in Japan, Univ of Kyushu Press, 01. **CONTACT ADDRESS** Dept E Asian Studies, Univ of Arizona, Tucson, AZ 85721. **EMAIL** noelp@u.arizona.edu

PINTADO-CASAS, PABLO
PERSONAL Born 07/09/1966, Madrid, Spain, m, 1996, 1 child **DISCIPLINE** SPANISH **EDUCATION** Univ of Madrid, BA, 89; Certificate in Education, 90; PhD, 96. **CAREER** Teaching asst, 92-93, Skidmore Col; teaching asst, 95, Univ of Maryland; adjunct asst prof, 97-98, adjunct asst prof, 97-present, Long Island Univ; prof, 97-present, Cervantes Institute; lectr, 98-present, Columbia Univ; The Cooper Union; adjunct asst prof, 98, Wagner Col; asst prof, Spanish, Drew Univ. **HONORS AND AWARDS** Academic Scholarship, Ministry of Public Administration, 88-89; research fel, 90-92, dept of logic and linguistics, Univ of Madrid; research fel, 92-93, dept of language and literatures, Skidmore Col; research fel, 95, dept of linguistics, Univ of Maryland. **MEMBERSHIPS** APA. **RESEARCH** Philosophy of language; logic; linguistics; Spanish language. **SELECTED PUBLICATIONS** Auth, Book Review: Wittgenstein on Mind and Language (David Stern), Teorema, 97; auth, Book Review: Wittegensteinian Themes (Norman Malcom), Teorema, 97; auth, Libros al aire libre: La Feria del Libro en el Parque del Retiro de Madrid, Hispania, March 98; auth, The Antecedents of Situation Semantics: Boguslaw Wolniewicz's Interpretation of the Notion of Situation in Wittgenstein, Teorema, forthcoming; Differences and Similarities Between Situation Semantics and Possile Worlds, Teorema, forthcoming. **CONTACT ADDRESS** Spanish Dept, Drew Univ, Madison, NJ 07940. **EMAIL** ppintado@drew.edu

PIPER, ANSON CONANT
PERSONAL Born 08/14/1918, Newton, MA, m, 1945, 3 children **DISCIPLINE** SPANISH LANGUAGE & LITERATURE **EDUCATION** Williams Col, Mass, BA, 40; Univ Wis, MA, 47, PhD(Span), 53, U.S. Navy, 42-46. **CAREER** From instr to prof Romanic lang, 49-68, chmn dept, 61-71, William Dwight Whitney Prof Romanic Lang, Williams Col, 68-86. **MEMBERSHIPS** Am Asn Teachers Span & Port; Phi Beta Kappa. **RESEARCH** Portuguese literature; Spanish literature, especially 19th century novel; Romance linguisitics. **SELECTED PUBLICATIONS** Auth, Asi es la vida, Norton, 58; coauth, Fundamental Portuguese Vocabulary, Univ Louvain, 68. **CONTACT ADDRESS** 70 Baxter Rd, Williamstown, MA 01267.

PIREDDU, NICOLETTA
DISCIPLINE COMPARATIVE LITERATURE, ITALIAN LITERATURE AND LANGUAGE **EDUCATION** Universita' degli Studi di Venezia, Ca' Foscari, 89; Univ Calif Los Angeles, MA, 91, PhD, 96; Universita degli Studi de Venezia, Ci' Foscari, Italy, Dottorato, 97. **CAREER** Vis asst prof, Duke Univ, 96-97; asst prof, Univ Houston, 97-98; asst prof, Georgetown Univ, 98- . **HONORS AND AWARDS** Doctoral res fel, Universita degli Studi di Venezia, Calif' Foscari; Dissertation Year Fel, Univ Calif Los Angeles; Paris Prog in Critical Theory & Borchard Found Fel; Laurea in Lingue e Letterature Straniere, summa cum laude; Jr Fac Res Fel, Georgetown Univ. **MEMBERSHIPS** Modern Lang Assoc of Amer; Soc for Critical Exchange; Am Comp Lit Asn; Int Comp Lit Asn; Am Asn of Ital Studies; Am Asn of Univ Prof; Int VA Wolf Soc. **RESEARCH** Nineteenth-& twentieth-century Italian, English, French lit & culture; decadence, modernism, postmodernism in lit & the visual arts; literary theory; European studies; anthropological approaches to lit; relations between lit & sci. **SELECTED PUBLICATIONS** Auth, Antropologi alla corte della bellezza; Decadenza ed economia simbolica nell ' Europa fin-desiecle, 01; auth, "Paolo Mantegazza: ritratto dell ' antropologo come esteta", Archivio per l 'antropologia e l 'etnologia, 00; auth, "Vernon Lee: aesthetic expenditure, noblesse oblige", Athena's shuttle, 00; auth, The Importance of Being Earnest Loffredo Editore, 99; auth, 'Il divino pregio del dono': Andrea Sperelli's economy of pleasures, Annali d 'italianistica, 97; auth, Carterbury Tales: Romances of Disenchantment in Geoffrey Chaucer and Angela Carter, Comp, 97; auth, "The Terrible pleasure of a double life': Dorian Gray tra estetica ed etica", L 'ombra, il doppio, il riflesso, 97; auth, "bussola e cornucopia: la caccia al tesoro di Gadda e Beckett", La linea longobarda, ed L Ballerini, 96; auth, "The Mark and the mask: psychosis in Artaud's alphabet of cruelty", Arachne, 96; auth, "Saints and aesthetes in J-K Huysman's artificial paradises", Orbis Litterarum, 95. **CONTACT ADDRESS** Dept of Italian, Georgetown Univ, ICC 307, 37th and O Sts, Washington, DC 20057. **EMAIL** pireddun@georgetown.edu

PIROG, GERALD
PERSONAL Born 01/12/1948, NJ **DISCIPLINE** SLAVIC LANGUAGES AND LITERATURES **EDUCATION** Rutgers Univ, AB, 69; Yale Univ, MPhil, 72, PhD(Slavic), 75. **CAREER** Instr Russ, William Patterson Col NJ, 73-75; asst prof,

75- 80, Prof Russ & Polish, Rutgers Univ, 80-. **MEMBERSHIPS** Am Asn Advan Slavic Studies; Am Asn Teachers Slavic & E Europ Lang & Lit; MLA. **RESEARCH** Russian symbolist poetry, particularly Aleksandr Blok; early period of Soviet Cinema; Slavic literary theory. **SELECTED PUBLICATIONS** Auth, The city, the woman, the Madonna: Metaphorical inference in Blok's Ital janskie stixi, Forum Iowa Russ Lit, 12/77; Blok's Blagovescenie: A study in iconological transformation, Vol VII, 79 & Blok's Ravenna: The city as sign, Vol VII, 80, Russ Lit; Iconicity & narrative: The Eisenstein-Vertor controversy, Semiotica (in press); Aleksandr Blok's Italjanski Stikhi: Confrontations and disillusionment, Slavica Publ (in press). **CONTACT ADDRESS** Dept of Slavic, Rutgers, The State Univ of New Jersey, New Brunswick, P O Box 5062, New Brunswick, NJ 08903-5062.

PITT, DAVID
DISCIPLINE PHILOSOPHY OF LANGUAGE, FORMAL SEMANTICS, AND THE PHILOSOPHY OF MIND **EDUCATION** CUNY, PhD, 94. **CAREER** Vis asst prof, Univ Nebr, Lincoln. **SELECTED PUBLICATIONS** Published in music and the philosophy of mind. **CONTACT ADDRESS** Univ of Nebraska, Lincoln, Lincoln, NE 68588-0417.

PIZER, JOHN
PERSONAL 1 child **DISCIPLINE** 18TH-20TH CENTURY GERMAN LITERATURE, GERMAN LANGUAGE, COMP LIT **EDUCATION** Univ Wash, PhD, 85. **CAREER** Prof Ger and Comp Lit, sect hd, Ger, recycling comt, Rally Day coordr for Ger prog, univ fac senate, Col Arts & Sci fac senate, La State Univ. **RESEARCH** 18th-20th Century German Literature; Hermeneutics; Critical Theory. **SELECTED PUBLICATIONS** Auth, The Historical Perspective in German Genre Theory: Its Development from Gottsched to Hegel, 85; Toward a Theory of Radical Origin: Essays on Modern German Thought, 95. **CONTACT ADDRESS** Dept of For Lang and Lit, Louisiana State Univ and A&M Col, 145 B Prescott Hall, Baton Rouge, LA 70803. **EMAIL** pizer@lsu.edu

PLANT, HELMUT R.
PERSONAL Born 01/15/1932, Munich, Germany, m, 1957, 1 child **DISCIPLINE** GERMAN **EDUCATION** Fairmont State Col, AB, 57; Univ Cincinnati, MA, 61, PhD(Ger), 64. **CAREER** Instr Ger, Cornell Univ, 63-65, asst prof, 65-66; wiss asst, Aachen Tech, Ger, 66-67; asst prof, 67-71, assoc prof Ger, Univ Ore, 71-. **MEMBERSHIPS** Am Asn Teachers Ger; Ling Soc Europe. **RESEARCH** German grammar; audiovisual instruction. **SELECTED PUBLICATIONS** Auth Syntaktische Studien zu den Monseer Fragmenten, Mouton, The Hague, 69; Syntactic devices in the teaching of manuscript Middle High German, Folia Ling, Vol II, Nos 1-2; coauth, Guten Tag at Oregon: an audiovisual experiment, Unterrichtspraxis, Vol VI, No 1; coed Die sogenannte Mainauer Naturlehre der Basler Hs B VIII 27, Abbildung, Transkription, Kommentar Herausgegeben von Helmut R Plant, Marie Rowlands und Rolf Burkhart, Verlag Alfred Kummerle, Goppingen, 72. **CONTACT ADDRESS** Dept of German, Univ of Oregon, Eugene, OR 97403-1250. **EMAIL** hplant@oregon.uoregon.edu

PLATA, FERNANDO
DISCIPLINE RENAISSANCE AND BAROQUE SPANISH LITERATURE **EDUCATION** Univ de Navarra, Pamplona, Spain, licenciado, 87; Univ MI, MA, 89, PhD, 94. **CAREER** Assoc prof, Colgate Univ. **HONORS AND AWARDS** Rackham predoctoral fel, Univ MI, 92-93; dissertation scholar, prog for cult coop, Spain Ministry of Cult and US Univ(s), 92; Tercer Premio Nacional de Terminacion de Estudios de Filologia, 87; scholar, Universidad Internacional Menendez Pelayo, Santander, 86. **SELECTED PUBLICATIONS** Ed, Calderon de la Barca, Pedro, La primer flor del camelo, Reichenberger, 98; auth, "Los codices del emigma, 'Las dos somos hermanas producitas' y el problema de su autoria" Siglo de Oro, 98; auth, "Contrijucion al estudio de las fuentes de la poesia satirica de Queuedo: Ateneo, Berni y Owen", La Perinola, 99; auth, Ocho poemas satiricos de Quevedo, EUNSA, 97; Inquisicion y censura en el siglo XVIII: El Parnaso espanol de Quevedo, La Perinola. Revista de investigacion quevediana, 97; rev, Robert L. Hathaway, Not Necessarily Cervantes: Readings of the 'Quixote', Juan de la Cuesta, 95; Una nota sobre Lope de Vega y las 'lineas del amor' de Terencio, Romance Notes 32, 92; Hacia una edicion critica de la comedia La inclinacion espanola de Bances Candamo, RILCE, Revista de Filologia Hispanica 8, 92. **CONTACT ADDRESS** Dept of Romance Lang, Colgate Univ, 13 Oak Drive, Hamilton, NY 13346. **EMAIL** fplata@mail.colgate.edu

PLATER, EDWARD M. V.
PERSONAL Born Saginaw, MI **DISCIPLINE** GERMAN **EDUCATION** Univ Mich, AB, 60, MA, 62, PhD(Ger), 68. **CAREER** Instr Ger, Univ Mich, 66-67; instr, 67-68, asst prof, 68- 80, Assoc Prof Ger, Miami Univ, 68-, Nat Endowment for Humanities summer sem, 78. **MEMBERSHIPS** Am Asn Teachers Ger. **RESEARCH** Conrad Ferdinand Meyer; 19th century German literature. **SELECTED PUBLICATIONS** Auth, The Banquet of Life: Conrad Ferdinand Meyer's Die Versuchung des Pescara, Seminar, 6/72; The figure of Dante in Die Hochzeit des Momchs, Mod Lang Notes, 75; Der schone Leib in the prose of C F Meyer, Seminar, spring 79; The symbolism in Ferdinand von Saar's Norelle, Marianne, Sem, spring 82; Kautner,helmut Film Adaptation of Des Taufels General Literature-film Quarterly, Vol 0022, 1994. **CONTACT ADDRESS** Dept of Foreign Lang, Miami Univ, 500 E High St, Oxford, OH 45056-1602.

PLOTTEL, JEANINE PARISIER
PERSONAL Born 09/21/1934, Paris, France, m, 1956, 3 children **DISCIPLINE** FRENCH LANGUAGE & LITERATURE **EDUCATION** Columbia Univ, BA, 54, MA, 55, PhD, 59. **CAREER** Lectr French, Columbia Univ, 55-59; res assoc, MLA, 59-60; asst prof French, Juilliard Sch Music, 60-65; from asst prof to assoc prof Romance lang, 65-81, Prof French, Hunter Col, 82-, Lectr, City Col New York, 59-60, French Embassy, 59- & Ecole Libre des Hautes Etudes, 59; City Univ New York res grant, 72- 73; ed, New York Lit Forum, 77-; Nat Endowment for Humanities fel, 79-80; fac res fel, City Univ New York, 81. **MEMBERSHIPS** Asn Int Etudes Fr; Soc Paul Valery; MLA; Am Asn Teachers Fr; Am Comp Lit Asn. **RESEARCH** Nineteenth and twentieth century French literature; comparative literature. **SELECTED PUBLICATIONS** Auth, Les Dialogues de Paul Valery, Presses Univ France, 60; Structures and counter-structures in Raymond Roussel's Impressions of Africa, Dada/Surrealism, 75; Anamorphose d'un coute, Sub-Stance, 76; Rhetoric of chance, Dada/Surrealism, 77; Anamorphosis in painting & literature, Yearbk Gen & Comp Lit, 79; The mathematics of Surrealism, Romantic Rev, 80; The poetics of autobiography in Paul Valery, L'Eprit Createur, Prevost, Laclos & Constant, Scribner's (in press); Colette Love Triangles/, Esprit Createur, Vol 0034, 1994. **CONTACT ADDRESS** Hunter Col, CUNY, New York, NY 10036.

POAG, JAMES F.
PERSONAL Born 08/07/1934, IL, m, 1960, 2 children **DISCIPLINE** GERMAN PHILOLOGY **EDUCATION** Univ Ill, BA, 56, MA, 58, PhD, 61. **CAREER** From instr to assoc prof Ger, Ind Univ, Bloomington, 61-76; Prof Ger & Chmn Dept, Wash Univ, 76-, Fulbright & Humbold res grants, Univ Gottingen, 63-64. **MEMBERSHIPS** MLA; Am Asn Teachers Ger. **RESEARCH** Mediaeval German literature. **SELECTED PUBLICATIONS CONTACT ADDRESS** Dept of Ger, Washington Univ, 1 Brookings Dr, Saint Louis, MO 63130-4899.

PODUSKA, DONALD MILES
PERSONAL Born 12/02/1934, Chicago, IL, m, 1958, 3 children **DISCIPLINE** CLASSICAL LANGUAGES **EDUCATION** Loyola Univ, Ill, AB, 56; Univ Ky, MA, 57; Ohio State Univ, PhD, 63. **CAREER** From instr to assoc prof, 60-73, prof class lang, John Carroll Univ, 73-; vis assoc prof class lang, 70-71, vis prof class lang, 85-86, Rome Ctr, Loyola Univ, Ill. **MEMBERSHIPS** Am Philol Assn; Am Class League; Vergilian Soc; Class Assn Mid W & S. **RESEARCH** Roman comedy; Roman historians; Vergil. **SELECTED PUBLICATIONS** Auth, "Classical Myth in Music: A Selective List," Classical World 92.3 (99): 195-276. **CONTACT ADDRESS** Dept of Class Lang, John Carroll Univ, 20700 N Park Blvd, Cleveland, OH 44118-4581. **EMAIL** poduska@jcu.edu

POE, JOE PARK
DISCIPLINE GREEK AND LATIN LITERATURE **CAREER** Instr, NY Univ, 60-62; lectr, Brooklyn Col, 62; instr, Univ TX, 62-64; act asst prof, Univ CA-Barkeley, 64-65; asst prof, 65-70, assoc prof, 70-89, prof, 89-, dept ch, 71-74, 77-88, Tulane Univ. **RESEARCH** Greek and Latin Literature, especially Greek tragedy, Senecan tragedy, Aristophanic comedy; theatrical antiquities; Roman topography. **SELECTED PUBLICATIONS** Auth, Caesure in the Hexameter Line of Latin Elegaic Verse, Hermes Einzelschriften, Wiesbaden, 74; auth, Heroism and Divine Justice in Sophocles' Philoctetes, Mnemosyne Supplement, Leiden, 74; auth, Genre and Meaning in Sophocles' Ajax, Beitrage zur klaissischen Philogie, Frankfurt, 87; auth, Pollux and the Klision, Philologus 138, 94; auth, The Supposed Conventional Meanings of Dramatic Masks: A Reexamination of Pollux 4. 133-54, Philologus 140, 96; auth, "Entrances, Exits, and the Structure of Aristophanic Comedy," Hermes 127 (99): 189-207; auth, "Multiplicity, Disconinuity, and Visual Meaning in Aristophanic Comedy," Rheinisches Museum (00); auth, "Pollux and the Aulaia," Hermes 128 (00): 247-250; auth, "Phoenissae 88D201 and Pollux' Distegia," Classical Philology (01). **CONTACT ADDRESS** Dept of Class Stud, Tulane Univ, 200 Gibson Hall, New Orleans, LA 70118. **EMAIL** jpoe@tulane.edu

POHLSANDER, HANS ACHIM
PERSONAL Born 10/10/1927, Celle, Germany, m, 1956, 3 children **DISCIPLINE** CLASSICS **EDUCATION** Univ Utah, BA, 54; Univ Calif, Berkeley, MA, 55; Univ Mich, PhD, 61. **CAREER** Teacher Latin & Ger, Carmel High Sch, Calif, 56-58; asst prof Classics, Wash Univ, 61-62; asst prof to prof Classics, 62-95, prof Relig Studies, 91-95, emeritus 95-, State Univ NY Albany; vis assoc prof classics & cult studies, Am Univ Beirut, 68-69; vis prof Classics, Ohio State Univ, Columbus, 83-83. **HONORS AND AWARDS** Am Coun Learned Soc grant-in-aid, 62; Ger Acad Exchange Serv study grant, 82; Am Philos Soc res grants, 83, 88; NEH res grant, 86. **MEMBERSHIPS** Am Philol Asn; Archaeol Inst Am; Hagiographic soc. **RESEARCH** Later Roman Empire; early Christianity; Trier. **SELECTED PUBLICATIONS** Auth, Metrical Studies in the Lyrics of Sophocles, Brill, Leiden, 64; Helena: Empress and Saint, Ares, Chicago, 95; The Emperor Constantine, Routledge, London, 96; Maximinus und Paulinus: Two Bishops of Trier in the Fourth Century, Trierer Zeitschrift, 96; Die Anfunge des Christentums in der Stadt Trier, Trierer Zeitschrift, 97. **CONTACT ADDRESS** Dept of Classics, SUNY, Albany, 1400 Washington Ave., Albany, NY 12222-1000. **EMAIL** pohlsander@global2000.net

POLACHEK, DORA
DISCIPLINE FRENCH LANGUAGE AND LITERATURE **EDUCATION** Barnard Col, BA; NYork Univ, MA; Univ NC Chapel Hill, PhD. **CAREER** Fac. SUNY Binghamton. **RESEARCH** French Renaissance lit. **SELECTED PUBLICATIONS** Auth, publ about Marguerite de Navarre and Montaigne, French Renaissance theater, and issues relating to gender and power in the early mod period. **CONTACT ADDRESS** SUNY, Binghamton, PO Box 6000, Binghamton, NY 13902-6000. **EMAIL** dpolachk@binghamton.edu

POLAKIEWICZ, LEONARD A.
PERSONAL Born 03/30/1938, Kiev, Ukraine, m, 1963, 3 children **DISCIPLINE** SLAVIC LANGUAGES & LITERATURE **EDUCATION** Univ Minn, BS, BA, 64; Univ Wis, Madison, MA, 68; PhD, 78; Maria Curie-Sklodowska Univ, Poland, Diploma, 81. **CAREER** Teac asst, Univ Minn, 64, 69-70; Univ Minn; asst prof, 70-90, assoc prof, Slavic langs, lits, Univ Minn, 90-; Horace T. Morse Distinguished teaching Assoc prof, Univ Minn, 92-; Acad of Distinguished Teachers mem, Univ Minn, 99-; vis prof, Sch Slavonic, E European Stud, Univ London, 84; assoc chair, dept Russian, E European Stud, 83-85; dir, Polish stud, 85-, Univ Minn; dir, instr, Lublin Prog, Maria Curie-Sklodowsha Univ, Poland, 84-89(summers); dir, Inst of Languages and Literatures, Univ Minn, 91-93; chair, Slavic & Central Asian Languages and Literatures, Univ Minn, 93-97, 99-00; dir, Univ Minn - Maria Curies-Sklodowska Univ Fac Exchange, 86-; dir, Univ Minn - Herzen Pedagogical Univ (St. Petersburg, Russia) fac exchange, 93-. **HONORS AND AWARDS** Polanie Club Merit Award, 82; IREX Collaborative Activities & New Exchanges grant for Poland, 84; Bush Found Res grant, 86-87; Dept of Education Title VI grant for Poland, 88-91; Fulbright-Hays Group projects Abroad grant for Poland, 89; Distinguished Service Medal, Maria Curie-Sklodowska Univ, 92; U.S. Information Agency grants for Poland, 89-93, 95-00; Horace T. Morse Award for Outstanding Contributions to Undergraduate Education, Univ Minn, 92; Nat Teacher of the Year Award, Am Asn of Teachers of Slavic and East European Languages, 94; Nat Council of Organizations of Less Commonly Taught Languages Res grant, 95; Cavalier's Cross of the Order of Merit of the Republic of Poland, 99. **MEMBERSHIPS** Am Asn of Teachers of Slavic and East European Languages; Polish Teachers Asn of Am; Am Asn for the Advancement of Slavic Studies; assoc ed, Slavic and East European Jour; Polish Studies Asn; Selection Comm, Fulbright Teacher Excahnge prof, 89; reviewer, Nat Endowment for the Humanities Translation prog, 93, 94; Biannual Polish Studies Asn Nat Prize Jury, 98; North Am Anton Chekhov Soc; Am Council of Teachers of Russian; Russian Language Prog Academic Policy Comm, CIEE; Polish Inst of Arts and Sciences of Am; ed board, The Learning and Teaching of Slavic Langauges and Culture: Toward the 21st Century; Bristol Group, Int Asn of Teachers of Polish; reviewer, CHOICE, Modern Language Jour, Canadian Slavonic Studies, Slavic and East European Jour. **RESEARCH** Anton Chekhov; 19th and 20th century Polish and Russian literature; Polish and Russian pedagogy. **SELECTED PUBLICATIONS** Auth, Nauczanie jezyka polskiego w Stanach Zjednoczonych obecnie I w przeszlosci, Naucznie jezyka polskiego jako obcego (Krzkow, Uniwersytet Jagiellonski, 97); auth, "The Theme of Protest and The Protesting Hero in Chekhov's Writing," Annales Universitatis Mariae Curie-Skolodowska (Lublin, Poland, 97); auth, PIASA Directory of US Institutions of Higher Education and Faculty Offering Instruction in Polish Language, Literature, and Culture, 96-97, The Polish Inst of Arts and Sciences Inc. (New York), 97; auth, "Nikolai Ivanovich Nadezhdin, Russian Literature in the Age of Pushkin and Gogol," Dictionary of Literary Biography (Bruccoli Clark Layman, Inc., 98); auth, "Ocena czestotliwosci uzywania I poziomu merytorycznego podrecznikow I wypisow do nauki jezyka polsjiego wykorzystywanych obecnie w Stanach Zjednoczonych," Pamietnik Literacki (London, 99). **CONTACT ADDRESS** Inst of Ling, English as a Second Language, and Slavic Languages and Literatures, Univ of Minnesota, Twin Cities, 215 Nolte Center, Minneapolis, MN 55455. **EMAIL** polak001@tc.umn.edu

POLANSKY, SUSAN
DISCIPLINE SPANISH **EDUCATION** Boston Col, PhD. **CAREER** Languages, Carnegie Mellon Univ. **SELECTED PUBLICATIONS** Auth, Narrators and Fragmentation in Cela's Mrs. Caldwell habla con su hijo, Revista de Estudios Hispanicos, 88; Provocation to Audience Response: Narrators in the Plays of Antonio Buero Vallejo, Letras Peninsulares, 88; Textual Coherence in the Duke of Rivas's El desenga-o en un sue-o: The Dramaturgy of Destiny, Mod Lang Studies, 89; Irony, Allusion, and the Nature of Tyranny in Pedro Salinas's Judit y el tirano, Revista de Estudios Hispanicos, R'o Piedras, 90; Puntos de vista Lectura. Heinle and Heinle, 94. **CONTACT**

ADDRESS Carnegie Mellon Univ, 5000 Forbes Ave, Pittsburgh, PA 15213.

POLLACK, GLORIA W.
DISCIPLINE HEBREW LITERATURE **EDUCATION** Yeshiva Univ, Stern Col, BA, 67; NYork Univ, MA, 68; Columbia Univ, MPhil, 78, PhD, 81. **CAREER** ASST PROF HEBREW, COORD HEBREW PROG, KINGSBOROUGH COMMUNITY COL, CUNY, 94-. **CONTACT ADDRESS** 333 Meehan Ave, Far Rockaway, NY 11691. **EMAIL** glorpol@earthling

POLLITT, JEROME J.
PERSONAL Born 11/26/1934, Fair Lawn, NJ **DISCIPLINE** HISTORY OF ART, CLASSICAL PHILOLOGY **EDUCATION** Yale Univ, BA, 57; Columbia Univ, PhD(hist of art), 63. **CAREER** Instr classics, 62-65, from asst prof to assoc prof class art & archaeol, 65-73, chmn, Dept Classics, 75-77, Prof Class Archaeol & Hist of Art, Yale Univ, 73-98, prof emer, 98-, Chmn, Dept Hist of Art, 81-, Dean, 86-91; Morse fel, 67-68; ed, Am J Archaeol, 73-77. **MEMBERSHIPS** Archaeol Inst Am **RESEARCH** Greek art and archaeology; art criticism. **SELECTED PUBLICATIONS** Auth, The Art of Greece: 1400-31 BC, 65 & The Art of Rome: c 753 BC-337 AD, 66, Prentice-Hall; Art and Experience in Classical Greece, Cambridge Univ, 72; The Ancient View of Greek Art, Yale Univ, 74; The impact of Greek art on Rome, Trans Am Philol Asn, 78; Kernoi from the Athenian Agora, Hesperia, 79; Art in the Hellenistic Age, Cambridge Univ, 86; The Art of Greece, Sources and Documents, Cambridge Univ, 90; Personal Styles in Greek Sculpture, Cambridge Univ, 96. **CONTACT ADDRESS** Dept of Classics, Yale Univ, PO Box 208272, New Haven, CT 06520-8272. **EMAIL** jerome.pollitt@yale.edu

POLLY, LYLE R.
PERSONAL Born 02/13/1940, Cornwall, NY, m, 1962, 3 children **DISCIPLINE** FRENCH LANGUAGE AND LITERATURE **EDUCATION** Geneva Col, BA, 61; Univ Wis, MA, 62; State Univ NYork Buffalo, PhD(French), 72. **CAREER** Teacher French, Span & Latin, Ardsley High Sch, 62-64; asst prof French & Span, Geneva Col, 64-67; asst prof French, State Univ NY Geneseo, 70-72; Assoc Prof French & Span, Southwest MO State Univ, 72-. **MEMBERSHIPS** Am Asn Teachers French; Soc Amis Romania; Am Coun Teaching Foreign Lang; Soc Rencesvals; Nat Fedn Mod Lang Teachers Asn. **RESEARCH** Medieval literature; pedagogy. **SELECTED PUBLICATIONS** Coauth, Meusault on trial: multi-skills activities for teaching L'Etranger, Can Mod Lang Rev, 1078; auth, A note on the rhyme Henrilit and the dating of the Chanson de Toile Bele Siglentine, Orbis, 27: 31-32; Three Fifteen-Minute Activities for Beginning Foreign Language Students: Reading, Writing, and Arithmetic, NALLD J, 79; Two Visuals to Accompany Albert Valdman's Langue et Culture, 80 & coauth, Communicative Competence and Ancillary Cources in French, 281, Foreign Lang Annals; The Chanson de Toile an the Chanson de Geste: Reconsidering some Considerations, Romance Notes, 81; Aw-3.0 to French Conversion Program - Lurot,d, French Review, Vol 0066, 1993. **CONTACT ADDRESS** Dept of Foreign Lang, Southwest Missouri State Univ, Springfield, 901 S National, Springfield, MO 65802.

POLT, JOHN H. R.
PERSONAL Born 08/20/1929, Usti nad Labem, Czechoslovakia, m, 1953, 3 children **DISCIPLINE** SPANISH LITERATURE **EDUCATION** Princeton Univ, AB, 49; Univ Calif, MA, 50, PhD (Romance lang & lit), 56. **CAREER** From instr to assoc prof, 56-70, Prof Span, Univ Calif, Berkeley, 70-92; Am Philos Soc grant, 59-60; assoc dir, Univ Calif Studies Ctr, Madrid, 64-65, dir, 68-70; vis assoc prof, Univ Calif, Santa Barbara, 65-66; Am Coun Learned Soc fel, 73; Guggenheim Mem Found fel, 74. **MEMBERSHIPS** Instituto Fei/00 de Estudios del Siglo XVIII; Centro di Studi sul Settecento Spaguolo; Foro Jovellanos del Principado de Asturias. **RESEARCH** Spanish literature, 18th to 20th century. **SELECTED PUBLICATIONS** Auth, The Writings of Eduardo Mallea, Univ Calif, 59; Jovellanos and His English Sources, Am Philos Soc, 64; ed, Forner, Los Gramaticos, Univ Calif & Ed Castalia, 70; auth, Gaspar Melchor de Jovellanos, Twayne, 71; ed, Poesia del siglo XVIII, Ed Castalia, 75; co-ed, Juan Melendez Valdes, Poesias Selectas: La Lira de marfil, Ed Castalia, 81; Melendez Valdes, Obras en verso, Catedra Feijoo, 81; auth, Batilo: Estudios Sobre la evolucion estilistica de Melendez Valdes Univ Calif & Instituo Fei/00, 87. **CONTACT ADDRESS** Dept of Span & Port, Univ of California, Berkeley, Berkeley, CA 94720. **EMAIL** jpolt@uclink4.berkeley.edu

POMEROY, SARAH B.
PERSONAL Born 03/13/1938, New York, NY, m, 3 children **DISCIPLINE** CLASSICAL PHILOLOGY AND ANCIENT HISTORY **EDUCATION** Barnard Col, BA, 57; Columbia Univ, MA, 59, PhD, 61. **CAREER** Instr class lang, Univ Tex, 61-62; lectr classics, 63-68, asst prof, 68-75, Assoc Prof Classics, 75-97, distinguished prof, 97- , Hunter Col; Coordr, Women's Studies Prog, 75-, Lectr classics, Brooklyn Col, 66-67; Am Coun Learned Soc grant-in-aid, 73-74; Nat Endowment for Humanities summer stipend, 73; fel, 81-82; Ford Found fel, 74-75; res grant, Fac Res Award Prog, City Univ New York, 75-79 & 82-83; Danforth assoc, 76-. **HONORS AND AWARDS** ACLS grant, 73, 74; NEH summer stipend, 73; Hunter Col grant, 73-74; Ford Found fel, 74-75; fac res award CUNY 75-77, 82-83, 85-86; NEH fel 76; Danforth Assoc, 76-82; NEH grant, 79-81; NEH fel, 81-82; NEH, dir, Hum Inst on Women in Classical Antiquity, 83; fel, Hum Res Ctr, Australian Natl Univ, 86; NEH, dir, Summer Sem, 87, 89; NEH sr fel, 87-88; Scholars Incentive Awd, CUNY, 87; Pres Awd for Excellence in Scholarship, 95; Guggenheim fel, 99. **MEMBERSHIPS** Am Philol Asn; Archaeol Inst Am; Am Soc Papyrologists; Friends Ancient Hist; Asn Ancient Historians; American Historical Assoc. **RESEARCH** Greek literature; women in classical antiquity; social history. **SELECTED PUBLICATIONS** Auth, Women in hellenistic Egypt from Alexander to Cleopatra, Wayne State Univ, reissue, 90; ed, Women's History and Ancient History, Univ North Carolina, 91; auth, Goddesses, Whores, Wives, and Slaves: Women in Classical Antiquity, Schocken, reissue 94; coauth, Women in the Classical World: Image and Text, Oxford, 94; auth, Xenophon Oeconomicus: A Social and Historical Commentary, Oxford, 94; coauth, Women's Realities, Women's Choices: An Introduction to Women's Studies, 2d ed, Oxford, 95; auth, Families in Classical and Hellenistic Greece: Representations and Realities, Oxford, 97; coauth, Ancient Greece, Oxford, 98; auth, Plutarch Advice to the Bride and Groom, Oxford, 99. **CONTACT ADDRESS** Dept of Classics, Hunter Col, CUNY, 695 Park Ave, New York, NY 10021-5085.

PONCE DE LEON, GINA
PERSONAL Born Bogota, Colombia, s **DISCIPLINE** SPANISH **EDUCATION** Universidad Pedagogico Nacionol, BA, 83; Pontificio Universidad Jareriana, BA, 89; Univ Colo Boulder, MA, 92; PhD, 97. **CAREER** Asst prof, Niagara Univ, 98-. **HONORS AND AWARDS** MISA Recognition Awd; Dean's Grant, Univ Colo, 92; Grant, Niagara Univ, 98-99. **MEMBERSHIPS** MLA. **RESEARCH** Latin American Literature, Chicano Literature. **SELECTED PUBLICATIONS** Auth, CoCuyo o el espacio de lo residual, Universitas Humanistica; auth, El traspaso de la frontera como busqueda en la obra de Alvaro Mutis, expedicion Cientifica y cultural. **CONTACT ADDRESS** 4895 W Eddy Dr, Apt 336, Lewiston, NY 14092-2322. **EMAIL** gmp@niagara.edu

POPESCU, NICOLAE
DISCIPLINE FRENCH LITERATURE **EDUCATION** McGill Univ, BA, 87; MA, 89; Yale Univ, MA, 91; PhD, 93. **CAREER** Prof, Univ Ill Urbana Champaign. **SELECTED PUBLICATIONS** Auth, Le sentier de la tanisre, Libert¤ 92; Le catafalque de Cioran, Libert¤ 92; L'exil permanent, Liberte, 91; La mortelle condition de M. Kundera, Libert¤ 90; La quitude de Carver, Libert, 90; La trs orthodoxe demeure d'A. Tarkovski, Libert¤, 89; Les yeux de Buster Keaton, Libert, 89. **CONTACT ADDRESS** French Dept, Univ of Illinois, Urbana-Champaign, 52 E Gregory Dr, Champaign, IL 61820. **EMAIL** npopescu@uiuc.edu

POPLACK, SHANA
PERSONAL Born Detroit, MI **DISCIPLINE** LINGUISTICS **EDUCATION** Queens Col, BA, 68; NY Univ, MA, 71; Univ Pa, PhD(ling), 79. **CAREER** Res assoc ling, Ctr Puetro Rican Studies, CUNY, 77-81; asst prof, 81-82, Assoc Prof Ling, Univ Ottawa, 82-, Vis asst prof, NY Univ, 78-79. **MEMBERSHIPS** Ling Soc Am; Can Ling Asn. **RESEARCH** Sociolinguistics; bilingualism; Hispanic and French dialectology. **SELECTED PUBLICATIONS** Auth, Dialect acquisition among Puerto Rican bilinguals, Lang & Soc, 7: 89-103; Deletion and disambiguation in Puerto Rican Spanish, Language, 56.2: 371-385; Sometimes I'll start a sentence in Spanish y termino in Espanol: Toward a typology of code-switching, Linguistics, 18: 7-8; coauth (with D Sankoff), A formal grammar for code-switching, Papers in Ling, 14:2:3-46; auth, Syntactic structure and social function of code-switching, In: Latino Discourse and Communicative Behavior, Ablex Pub Corp, 81; Bilingualism and the vernacular, In: Issues in International Bilingual Education: The role of the Vernacular, Plenum Pub Corp, 82; coauth, Competing influences on gender assignment: Variable process, stable outcome, Lingua, 56: 139-166; -S or Nothing, Marking the Plural in the African-American Diaspora, American Speech, Vol 0069, 1994; Plural Marking Patterns in Nigerian Pidgin English, J of Pidgin and Creole Languages, Vol 0012, 1997. **CONTACT ADDRESS** Dept of Ling, Univ of Ottawa, 70 Laurier, Arts Building, Ottawa, ON, Canada K1N 6N5. **EMAIL** spoplack@aix1.uottawa.ca

PORTER, ABIOSEH MICHAEL
DISCIPLINE COMPARATIVE LITERATURE **EDUCATION** Univ Alberta, PhD, 84. **CAREER** Assoc prof, 86-91, asst prof, 91-, Drexel Univ. **SELECTED PUBLICATIONS** Auth, They Were There Too: Women and the Civil War(s) in Emecheta's Destination Biafra, Africa World, 96; An Afrocentric View of Religion in Baldwin's Go Tell it on the Mountain and Jumbam's The White Man of God (rev), 93. **CONTACT ADDRESS** Dept of Hum and Commun, Drexel Univ, MacAlister Hall 9-5042, Philadelphia, PA 19104. **EMAIL** abiosehp@drexel.edu

PORTER, CHARLES ALLEN
PERSONAL Born 05/31/1932, Chicago, IL, m, 1956 **DISCIPLINE** FRENCH LANGUAGE & LITERATURE **EDUCATION** Northwestern Univ, BS, 53, MA, 54; Yale Univ, PhD, 62. **CAREER** From instr to assoc prof, 60-75, Dir Summer Lang Inst, Yale Univ, 71-, Prof French, 75-, Chmn Dept, 80-, Lect, Univ Lyons, 55-56. **MEMBERSHIPS** MLA; Am Asn Teachers Fr. **RESEARCH** Restif de la Bretonne; Chateaubriand; French roman personnel. **SELECTED PUBLICATIONS** Auth, Restif's Novels, or an Autobiography in Search of an Author, Yale Univ, 67; Chateaubriand: Composition, Imagination, and Poetry, ANMA Libri, 78. **CONTACT ADDRESS** Yale Univ, P O Box 208251, New Haven, CT 06520-8251.

PORTER, DAVID H.
PERSONAL Born 10/29/1935, New York, NY, m, 1987, 4 children **DISCIPLINE** CLASSICS; MUSIC. **EDUCATION** Swarthmore College, BA, 58; Princeton Univ, PhD, 62; Philadelphia Conserv Music, 55-62. **CAREER** Instr, Carleton Col 62-63; from asst prof to prof, Skidmore Col, 63-; pres, Skidmore Col, 74-99; vis prof, Williams Col, 99-. **HONORS AND AWARDS** NEH fel, 69-70, 83-84; ACLS fel, 76-77; hon doctor of letters, Skidmore Col, 98. **MEMBERSHIPS** Am Philol Asoc; Classical Asoc of the Atalantic States. **RESEARCH** Greek tragedy; Latin poetry, especially Horace; contemporary music. **SELECTED PUBLICATIONS** Auth, Horace's Poetic Journey: A Reading of Odes 1-3, 87; auth, Only Connect: Three Studies in Greek Tragedy, 87; auth, A Note on Aeschylus, Agamemnon 332, Classical Philol, 88; auth, The Structure of Beethoven's Diabellil Variations, op. 120-Again, Music Rev, 93; auth, Quo, quo scelesti ruitis: The Downward Momentum of Horace's Epodes, Ill Classical Studies, 95. **CONTACT ADDRESS** Skidmore Col, 5 Birch Run Drive, Saratoga Springs, NY 12866. **EMAIL** ddodger@skidmore.edu

PORTER, DENNIS
DISCIPLINE FRENCH AND COMPARATIVE LITERATURE **EDUCATION** Univ CA, PhD. **CAREER** Prof, Univ MA Amherst; asst prof, Univ of Cal, Berkeley. **HONORS AND AWARDS** NEH Fel, 77-78; ACLS Fel, 85-86; Vis Fel, Nat Humanities Ctr, Canberra, Australia, 94. **RESEARCH** French lit and cult hist from the late 18th century to the present, French intellectuals, contemp literary theory, mass cult genres, French film, French and Comparative Literature from late 18th century, European travel writing, crime and detective fiction. **SELECTED PUBLICATIONS** Auth, Rousseau's Legacy: Emergence and Eclipse of the Writer in France; Haunted Journeys; The Pursuit of Crime. **CONTACT ADDRESS** Dept of French and Italian Studies, Univ of Massachusetts, Amherst, Mass Ave, Amherst, MA 01003. **EMAIL** dporter@fritał.umass.edu

PORTER, J. I.
DISCIPLINE CLASSICAL STUDIES AND COMPARATIVE LITERATURE **EDUCATION** Univ CA, Berkeley, PhD, 86. **CAREER** Asst and assoc prof, Dept of Classical Studies and Prog in Comparative Lit, Univ MI, 86-. **HONORS AND AWARDS** NEH, 89; fel, Stanford Humanities Center, 95, 96; Humboldt fel, 97, 98. **MEMBERSHIPS** APA. **RESEARCH** Cultural and literary history. **SELECTED PUBLICATIONS** Auth, Nietzsche and the Philosophy of the Future, Stanford, 00; The Invention of Dionysus, Stanford, forthcoming; ed, Construction of the Classical Body, Univ MI press, 99; articles on Greek philos and poetics. **CONTACT ADDRESS** Dept of Classical Studies, Univ of Michigan, Ann Arbor, Ann Arbor, MI 48109. **EMAIL** jport@umich.edu

PORTER, LAURENCE M.
PERSONAL Born 01/17/1936, Ossining, NY, m, 1993, 3 children **DISCIPLINE** FRENCH & COMPARATIVE LITERATURE **EDUCATION** Harvard Univ, AB, 57, AM, 59, PhD(French lit), 65. **CAREER** Instr French, 63-65, from asst prof to assoc prof, 65-73, Prof French & Comp Lit, Mich State Univ, 73-, Interim Chair, Dept of Romance & Classical Languages, 99-00; Co-dir, Nat Colloquium 19th Century Fr Studies, 78; vis Andrew W Mellon disting prof comp lit, Univ Pittsburgh, 80. **HONORS AND AWARDS** Ford Foundation Grant, NEH Senior Fellowship 98; USIA Grant 91; The Distinguished Faculty Awd of Michigan Nate U., 95. **MEMBERSHIPS** MLA; AAUP; Am Comp Lit Asn; Int Comp Lit Asn. **RESEARCH** Romanticism; French poetry; literature and psychology; Women's Studies. **SELECTED PUBLICATIONS** The Renaisance of the Lyric in French Romanticism, French Forum, 78; Te Literary Dream in French Romanticism, Wayne State UP, 79; ed., Critical Essays on Gustave Flaubert, Hall, 86; Co-ed, Aging in Literature, Internation Book Publisher, 84; The Interpretation of Dreams; Freud's Theories Revisited, Twayne, 87; The Crisis of French Symbolism, Cornell, 90; co-ed, Approaches to teaching Flaubert's Madame Bovary, MLA, 95; Vitor Hugo, Twayne, 99; ed, Approaches to teaching Baudelaire's Fleurs du Mal, MLA, 99; Ed., A Gustave Flaubert Encyclopedia, 01. **CONTACT ADDRESS** Dept of Romance & Class Lang, Michigan State Univ, 341 Old Horticulture, East Lansing, MI 48824-1112. **EMAIL** porter@pilot.msu.edu

PORTER, MICHAEL
PERSONAL Born 02/26/1942, New Haven, CT **DISCIPLINE** COMPARATIVE & GERMAN LITERATURE **EDUCATION** Yale Univ, BA, 65; Cornell Univ, PhD(comp lit), 70. **CAREER** Lectr Ger, Rutgers Univ, 69-70, asst prof, 70-73; asst prof, Tulane Univ, 73-80. **MEMBERSHIPS** MLA; Am Comp Lit Asn; Hugo von Hofmannsthal Ges; Int Arthur Schnitzler Res Asn. **RESEARCH** Post-Romantic Lyric Poetry; Theory Of Literature; Modern German Literature. **SELECTED PUBLICATIONS** Auth Hugo von Hofmannsthal's Der Tor und der Tod: The poet as fool, Mod Austrian Lit, 72; Leitchsan-Leicht and schwer in the poetry of Hugo von Hofmannsthal, Monatshefte, 73. **CONTACT ADDRESS** 2035 Jenn, New Orleans, LA 70115.

PORTUGES, CATHERINE
DISCIPLINE FRENCH LITERATURE **EDUCATION** UCLA Univ, PhD. **CAREER** Prof, Univ MA Amherst. **RESEARCH** French women writers; autobiog lit. **SELECTED PUBLICATIONS** Auth, Screen Memories: The Hungarian Cinema of Marta Meszaros. **CONTACT ADDRESS** Dept of French and Italian Studies, Univ of Massachusetts, Amherst, Mass Ave, Amherst, MA 01003. **EMAIL** portuges@complit.umass.edu

POSTHOFEN, RENATE
DISCIPLINE GERMAN **EDUCATION** Staufen im Breisgau, AB,79; Univ Pittsburgh, MA, 85; Freiburg, Staatsexamen, 87; SUNY, PhD, 93. **CAREER** Instructor, Valley Community Col, 90-91; Asst Prof, Old Dominion Univ, 92-95; Asst Prof to Assoc Prof, Ut State Univ, 95-. **HONORS AND AWARDS** Taft Fel, SUNY, 89; Nominee, HASS Res of the Year Awd, 00; Teaching Asst, Univ Pittsburgh, 82; Grant, UT For Lang Asn, 99-00; Grant, UT State Univ, 98; Subsidy, Austrian State Res Council, 94; Subsidy, Austrian State Ministry, 94; Benevolent Asn Grant Awd, SUNY, 91. **MEMBERSHIPS** AATG; WIG; GSA; IVG; MLA; NEMLA; RMMLA; SAMLA; Intl Arthur Schnitzler Res Org, Soc for Exile Studies. **RESEARCH** 20th Century German and Austrian Literature/Culture and Film; Minority and Multicultural Discourse; Pedagogical approaches to Computer Assisted Instruction/Language Learning; Integration of audio-visual media in academic language curricula. **SELECTED PUBLICATIONS** Auth, Treibgut-Das vergessene Werk George Saikos, Vienna, 95; co-ed, Transforming the Center, Eroding the Margins: Essays on Ethnic and Cultural Boundaries in German-Speaking Countries, Camden House, SC, 98; auth, "Claire Goll (1891-1977): Visionary Power and Creative Symbiosis-Fictionalized Identity as Survival Strategy," in Transforming the Center, Eroding the Margins: Essays on Ethnic and Cultural Boundaries in German-Speaking Countries, Camden House, SC, 98; auth, "Of Inclusions and Exclusions: Austrian Identity Reconsidered," in Transforming the Center, Eroding the Margins: Essays on Ethnic and Cultural Boundaries in German-Speaking Countries, (Camden House, SC, 98), pp 199-204; auth, "Introduction," in Barbara Frischmuth in Contemporary Context, Ariadne Press, 99, 1-20; auth, "Robert Schubumkehr im Spiegel zeitgenossischer Kritik," in Towards the Millennium: Interpreting the Austrian Novel 1971-1996, (Stauffenburg Verlag, 99), 241-260; ed, Barbara Frischmuth in contemporary Context, Ariadne Press, 99; auth, "Mapping the Point of No Return: Robert Menasse's Novel Schubumkehr," in Modern Austrian Literature: Interpretations and Insights, Ariadne Press, 00; auth, "Gemeinsam (einsam) das Schicksal entratseln: George Saiko und Gyorgy Sebestyen," in Gyorgy Sebestyen: Aufsatze Zu Seinem Werk Und Leben, Wien, 00. **CONTACT ADDRESS** Dept Lang & Philos, Utah State Univ, 720 Univ Blvd, Logan, UT 84322-0720. **EMAIL** posthofr@cc.usu.edu

POTHECARY, SARAH
PERSONAL Born 05/10/1958, Trinidad and Tobago, m, 1986, 1 child **DISCIPLINE** CLASSICS **EDUCATION** St Anne's Col, Oxford Univ, BA, 81; Univ Toronto, MA, 89, PhD, 95. **CAREER** Author **RESEARCH** Shrabo; ancient geography. **CONTACT ADDRESS** 117 Lytton Blvd, Toronto, ON, Canada M4R 1L5. **EMAIL** spothecary@aol.com

POUWELS, JOEL
DISCIPLINE HISPANIC LITERATURE AND CULTURE **EDUCATION** Mich State Univ, PhD, 72. **CAREER** Prof, Univ Central Ark. **HONORS AND AWARDS** NEH grant. **MEMBERSHIPS** UCA's Latin Am Studies Comt. **RESEARCH** Contemporary Spanish American novel. **SELECTED PUBLICATIONS** Auth, Luis Spota Revisited, Revista de Estudio Hispanicos, 94; Mexican Presidential Futurology, Studies Latin Am Popul Cult, 97. **CONTACT ADDRESS** Univ of Central Arkansas, 201 Donaghey Ave, Conway, AR 72035-0001.

POWELL, AMANDA W.
DISCIPLINE SPANISH **EDUCATION** Yale Col, BA, 77; Boston Univ, MA, 83. **CAREER** Copy ed, Houghton Mifflin Co, 84-86; pub off, Harvard Univ, 85-90; sen instr, Univ Ore, 91-. **HONORS AND AWARDS** NEH Res Fel, 92-93; Fel, Ore Humanities Center, 93; Fel, Center for the Study of Women in Soc, 98. **MEMBERSHIPS** MLA; Asn do Escritoras de Espana y Am; Soc for Renaissance and Baroque Hispanic Poetry. **RESEARCH** Sixteenth and Seventeenth Century Spanish and Colonial Latin American women writers; Snr Juan Ines de la Cruz. **SELECTED PUBLICATIONS** Auth, The Answer/La Respnesta. Snr Juan Inse de la Cruz, Feminist Press, 94; co-auth, A Wild Country Out in the Garden: The Spiritual Journals of a Colonial Mexican Nun, Ind Univ Press, 99. **CONTACT ADDRESS** Dept Romance Lang, Univ of Oregon, 3520 Glen Oak Dr, Eugene, OR 97405-4735. **EMAIL** apowell@darkwing.uoregon.edu

POWELL, BARRY
PERSONAL Born 04/30/1942, Sacramento, CA, m, 1967, 2 children **DISCIPLINE** CLASSICS **EDUCATION** Berkeley Univ, BA, 63, PhD, 70; Harvard, MA, 65. **CAREER** Asst Prof, 69-73, Northern Arizona Univ; Asst, Assoc to Full Prof, 73-. **HONORS AND AWARDS** Woodrow Wilson Nat Fel. **MEMBERSHIPS** Am Philos Asn, Archaeological Institute of Am, Phi Beta Kappa. **RESEARCH** Homer; Mythology; Writing; Egyptology. **SELECTED PUBLICATIONS** Auth, Classical Myth, 2nd ed, 97; A New Companion to Homer, 97; Homer and the Origin of the Greek Alphabet; auth, Classical Myth, 3rd ed, 00. **CONTACT ADDRESS** Dept Classics, Univ of Wisconsin, Madison, 1220 Linden Dr, Madison, WI 53706. **EMAIL** BBPowell@facstaff.wisc.edu

POWER, MARGARET
PERSONAL Born 08/15/1953, Nashville, TN, s **DISCIPLINE** PHILOSOPHY, FRENCH, HISTORY **EDUCATION** Georgetown Univ, BA, 75; San Francisco State Univ, MA, 79; Univ Ill Chicago, PhD, 97. **CAREER** Vis Asst Prof/Asst Prof, Ill Inst of Technology, 98-. **HONORS AND AWARDS** Orgn of Am States, Res, 93-94; Woodrow Wilson Women Studies, 95; Guggenheim, 96-97. **MEMBERSHIPS** AHA, Latin Am Studies Asn, Congress on Latin Am Hist. **RESEARCH** Women, gender, the Armed Forces, technology, the right in Chile and Latin America. **SELECTED PUBLICATIONS** Auth, Right-using Women in Chilean Politico, 1964-1973, Penn State Press, forthcoming; auth, Right-using Women Across the Ilahe, Routledge Press, forthcoming. **CONTACT ADDRESS** Dept Humanities, Illinois Inst of Tech, 3300 S Federal St, Chicago, IL 60616-3795. **EMAIL** Power@iit.edu

POWNALL, FRANCES SKOCZYLAS
PERSONAL Born 10/17/1963, Sarnia, ON, Canada, m, 1994, 1 child **DISCIPLINE** CLASSICS **EDUCATION** McGill, BA, 85; Univ British Columbia, MA, 87; Univ Toronto, PhD, 93. **CAREER** Lectr, Memorial Univ, Newfoundland, 92-93; asst prof, Univ Alberta, 93- . **HONORS AND AWARDS** Summer scholar, Center for Hellenic Stud, 94. **MEMBERSHIPS** APA; Class Asn of Can; Class Asn of the Can West; Class Asn of the Middle West and South; Vergilian Soc. **RESEARCH** Greek history and historiography; Greek religion; Greek oratory. **SELECTED PUBLICATIONS** Auth, Presbeis Autokratores: Andocides' De Pace, Phoenix, 95; auth, Condemnation of the Impious in Xenophon's Hellenica, Harvard Theol Rev, 98; auth, What Makes A War A Sacred War, Class Views, 98; auth, Shifting Viewpoints in Xenophon's Helenica: The Arginusae Episode, Athenaeum, forthcoming. **CONTACT ADDRESS** Dept of History and Classics, Univ of Alberta, 2-28 Tory, Edmonton, AB, Canada T6G 2H4. **EMAIL** fskoczl@gpu.srv.ualberta.ca

PRATS, JORGE
PERSONAL Born 08/01/1932, Barcelona, Spain, m, 1961, 3 children **DISCIPLINE** SPANISH **EDUCATION** Univ Ill, BA, 60; MA, 62; Univ of Barcelona, PhD, 68. **CAREER** Instr, 62-64, from asst prof to prof emer, Knox Col, Ill, 68-; Dir, Jr Year Abroad, Barcelona, Spain, 71-72, 77-79, 82-84, 87, 91-94, 96-99. **HONORS AND AWARDS** Philip Green Wright Lombard Col Prize for Dist Teaching, Knox Col, 68. **MEMBERSHIPS** MLA; Am Asn Teachers Span & Port; Am Coun Teaching Foreign Lang. **SELECTED PUBLICATIONS** Coauth, Contribucion a una bibliografia de dialectologia espanola y americana, 67; auth, America poetica--JMG, 68, Real Acad Espanola. **CONTACT ADDRESS** Dept of Lang, Knox Col, Illinois, 2 E South St, Galesburg, IL 61401-4999. **EMAIL** 106101.573@compuserve.com

PRATT, DALE J.
PERSONAL Born 03/09/1965, Washington, DC, 5 children **DISCIPLINE** COMPARATIVE LITERATURE, SPANISH **EDUCATION** Brig Young Univ, BA, 90; Cornell Univ, PhD, 94. **CAREER** Asst prof to assoc prof, Brig Young Univ, 94-. **HONORS AND AWARDS** Mellon Fel, 90-94. **MEMBERSHIPS** MLA; AATSP; SLS; ACLA. **RESEARCH** Literature and science; Spanish realism; and generation of 1898; Santiago Ramony Cajal. **SELECTED PUBLICATIONS** Auth, Suenos, Recuerdos, Memoria: La Metaficcion en las Novelas de Joaquin-Armando Chacon, UNAM, 95; auth, Signs of Science: Literature, Science, and Spanish Modernity Since 1868, Purdue Univ Pr, 01. **CONTACT ADDRESS** Dept Romance Lang, Brigham Young Univ, Provost, UT 84604-4705. **EMAIL** dale-pratt@byu,edu

PRATT, L.
PERSONAL Born 11/24/1960, New York, NY, m, 1988, 2 children **DISCIPLINE** CLASSICAL STUDIES **EDUCATION** Williams Col, BA 82; Univ Michigan, AM 84, PhD 88. **CAREER** Bowdoin Col, vis asst prof, 88-89; Emory Univ, asst prof, assoc prof, 89 to 95-. **HONORS AND AWARDS** BK **MEMBERSHIPS** APA; CA of Midwest and S; WCC; GCA; ACL. **RESEARCH** Ancient Greek and Roman Lang; Literature and Culture. **SELECTED PUBLICATIONS** Auth, Lying and Poetry for Homer to Pindar: Falsehood and Deception in Archaic Greek Poetics, Univ Mich Press, 93; auth, Odyssey: On the Interpretations of Dreams and Signs in Homer, Classical Philos, 94; auth, The Seal of Theognis Writing and the Oral Poetry, Amer Jour of Philo, 95. **CONTACT ADDRESS** Dept of Classics, Emory Univ, 404 D Callaway Cen North, Atlanta, GA 30322. **EMAIL** lpratt@emory.edu

PRATT, MARY LOUISE
PERSONAL Born Listowel, Ontario, Canada **DISCIPLINE** COMPARATIVE LITERATURE, LATIN AMERICAN LITERATURE **EDUCATION** Univ Toronto, BA; Univ IL, MA; Stanford Univ, PhD. **CAREER** Dept Comp Lit, Univ Mass; Dept Spanish & Portuguese, Dept Comp Lit, Stanford Univ. **RESEARCH** Latin American literature; cultural theory; post-colonial theory. **SELECTED PUBLICATIONS** Auth, Toward a Speech Act Theory of Literary Discourse; Imperial Eyes: Travel Writing and Transculturation; coauth, Linguistics for Students of Literature and Women, Culture and Politics in Latin America. **CONTACT ADDRESS** Dept Comp Lit, Stanford Univ, Pigott Hall, Stanford, CA 94305-2031. **EMAIL** mpratt@leland.stanford.edu

PRECKSHOT, JUDITH
DISCIPLINE 20TH-CENTURY FRENCH POETRY, FEMINISM, AND FRANCOPHONE LITERATURE **EDUCATION** Univ Calif, Irvine, PhD. **CAREER** Instr, Univ Minn, Twin Cities. **RESEARCH** African women's autobiographies and novels. **SELECTED PUBLICATIONS** Published on the use of prose poetry (Ponge Michaux), the relation of the text to image (Breton, Apollinaire), and the role of the woman writer in Surrealism (Mansour). **CONTACT ADDRESS** Univ of Minnesota, Twin Cities, 9 Pleasant St. SE, 260 Folwell Hall, Minneapolis, MN 55455.

PREDMORE, MICHAEL P.
PERSONAL Born 02/05/1938, New Brunswick, NJ **DISCIPLINE** SPANISH LANGUAGE & LITERATURE **EDUCATION** Swarthmore Col, BA, 59; Univ Wis, MA, 61, PhD(Span), 65. **CAREER** From asst prof to assoc prof, 65-74, Prof Span, Univ Wash, 74-, Jr fel, Inst Res Humanities, Univ Wis, 68-69; Guggenheim Mem Found fel, 75-76; Coun Int Exchange Scholars grant, Spain, 82. **MEMBERSHIPS** Am Asn Teachers Span & Port; MLA. **RESEARCH** Nineteenth and 20th century Spanish peninsular literature; aesthetics. **SELECTED PUBLICATIONS CONTACT ADDRESS** Dept of Romance Lang, Univ of Washington, Seattle, WA 98195.

PRESBERG, CHARLES D.
PERSONAL Born 05/03/1956, Evanston, IL, m, 1992, 3 children **DISCIPLINE** SPANISH LITERATURE **EDUCATION** Harvard Univ, PhD, 94. **CAREER** Asst prof, Univ S Calif, 92-95; asst prof, Univ Mo Columbia, 95-. **MEMBERSHIPS** Cervantes Soc of Am. **RESEARCH** Cervantes Spanish literature of renaissance & baroque periods. **SELECTED PUBLICATIONS** Auth, " Yo se qien soy: Don Quixote, Don Diego de Miranda and the Paradox of Self-knowledge," Cervantes, 94; auth, "El condenado por presumido: The Rhetoric of Death and Damnaiton in Tirso de Molina's El burlador de Sevilla," Bulletin of the Comediantes, 95; auth, Deliverance in the Prison-House: Paradoxes of Self, Culture and Language in the Writings of Quevedo, Hispania, 95; auth, This is Not a Prologue: Paradoxes of Historical and Poetic Discourse in the Prologue to Don Quixote, 95; auth, Precious Exchanges: The Poetics of Desire, Power and Reciprocity in Cervantes' La gitanilla, Cervantes, 98; auth, Transfiguring Form: The Poetics of Self, Contradiction and Silence in San Juan de la Cruz, Laberinto, 98; auth, "Anatomy of Contemporary Cervantes Studies: A Romance of 'Two Cities,'" Cervantes and His Postmodern Constituencies, Garland, 98; auth, Making a Liar of Truth: The 'Play' of Society, Fiction and Deceit in Cervantes, El viejo celoso, Revista de Estudios Hispanicos, 99; auth, " Dreams of Reason Create Monsters of Culture: La vida es sueno," Bulletin of the Comediantes, 00; auth, Adventures in Paradox: " Don Quixote" and the Western Tradition, Pennsylvania State Univ Press, 00. **CONTACT ADDRESS** Dept of Romance Languages, Univ of Missouri, Columbia, 143 Arts & Science, Columbia, MO 65211. **EMAIL** cpresberg@bigfoot.com

PRESTEL, DAVID K.
PERSONAL Born 07/16/1948, Detroit, MI, m, 1971, 2 children **DISCIPLINE** SLAVIC LITERATURE AND LANGUAGE **EDUCATION** Wayne State Univ, BA, 70, Mich State Univ, AM, 75; Univ Mich, PhD, 83. **CAREER** Vis prof to prof, Chair, Mich State Univ, 83-. **HONORS AND AWARDS** IREX Exchange Scholar, 80-81; State of Mich Teaching Excellence Awd, 91. **MEMBERSHIPS** Am Assoc of Teachers of Slavic and E Europ Lang; Am Assoc for the Advan of Slavic Studies;

Early Slavic Studies Assoc. **RESEARCH** Early Slavic Studies, F.M. Dostoevsky, Russian language teaching and methodology. **SELECTED PUBLICATIONS** Auth, "Creating an Effective Cultural Component in Business Russian Programs", SE Europ Monitor II.2 (95): 45-56; auth, "Situational Role-Play as a Basis for a Business Russian Program", Jof Lang for Int Bus, VI.2 (95): 26-37; auth, "Integrating Business-Related Materials into First-Year Russian Courses", in Metodika prepodavaniia russkogo iazyka I literatuy v Amerike, ed D. Phillips , Sintaksis (Moscow, 96), 161-174; auth, "They Seeing See Not; and Hearing they Hear Not, Neither do they Understand: Controversy Dialogues in Kievan Texts", Russ Lit XXXIX.II (96): 223-234; auth, "Dormition, Cathedral of (Kiev)", Modern Encycl of Relig in Russ and the Sovier Union, 97; auth, "The Tale of Moses the Hungarian: From Egypt to the Land of Promise", Slavic and E Europ J42.2 (98): 201-215; auth, "The Search for the Word: Echoes of the Apophthegma in the Kievan Caves Patericon", Russ Rev 57.4, (98): 568-582; auth, "Father Zosima and the Eastern Orthodox Hesychast Tradition", Dostoevsky Studies, II.1 (98): 41-59; auth, "Ascent to the Cave: Cyril ofTurov and Kievan Monasticism" Slavica Bergensia 2, ed Ingunn Lunde, Univ of Bergen, (Bergen, Norway) (forthcoming). **CONTACT ADDRESS** Dept Ling, Michigan State Univ, A615 Wells Hall, East Lansing, MI 48824. **EMAIL** prestel@pilot.mus.edu

PREUSS, MARY
PERSONAL Born, PA, m **DISCIPLINE** MAYAN LITERATURE **EDUCATION** Univ Pittsburgh, PhD, MED, BA **CAREER** Assoc Prof, 89-, PA St Univ at mcKeesport; Assoc Prof, 81-89, Geneva Col; Lect, 79-81, Carlow Col; Lect, 78-80 Chatham Col **HONORS AND AWARDS** Acad Exc Awd; Scholar of the yr awd; pres, laila/alila **MEMBERSHIPS** AATSP; LAILA/ALILA; MLA **RESEARCH** Mayan lit **SELECTED PUBLICATIONS** Ed, Beyond Indigenous voices, Lancaster, CA: Labyrinthos, 96; Messages and Meanings, Lancaster, CA: Labyrinthos, 97 **CONTACT ADDRESS** Dept of Liberal Arts, Penn State Univ, McKeesport, PA 15229-1058. **EMAIL** mhp1@psu.edu

PREVOST, MAXIME
PERSONAL Born 04/29/1968, Montreal, QC, Canada **DISCIPLINE** FRENCH LITERATURE **EDUCATION** McGill Univ, BA, 93; MA, 96; PhD, 00. **HONORS AND AWARDS** James McGill Award, 92; Noah M Lenoir Prize, Norman Prentice Award, McGill Univ; Prix du Consulat general de France a Montreal, Solvay Fel, McGill, 93; Masters Fel, FCAR, 93-95; Dr Fel, FCAR, 96-99; Grant Fondation Desjardins, 98-99; Grant, FCAR, 98-99; Fel, SSHRC, 96-00, 02; Alma Mater Grant, McGill Univ, 00; Deans Honor List, McGill, 01. **MEMBERSHIPS** PMLA. **RESEARCH** Romanticism, Victor Hugo, Alexandre Dumas, Popular and Gothic literature, Literature, politics and society. **SELECTED PUBLICATIONS** Auth, "Acte de parole, acte d'ecriture. Celine, le mot ecrit et l'imputabilite dans la trilogie allemande," Studi francesi 122, (97); auth, "Le Christ qui rit: la 'blague' du messianisme pictural dans Manette Salomon des freres Goncourt," Litteratures 19, (99); auth, "Portrait de la femme auteur en cantatrice. George Sand et Marceline Desbordes-Valmore," Masculin/Feminin, Le XIXe siecle a l'epreuve du genre (Centres d'etudes du XIXe siecle Joseph Sable, 99); auth, Victor Hugo, L'Homme qui rit et l'orateur maudit," Les Rates de la Litterature (Editions du Lerot, 99); auth, "Le Cadavre de Schopenhauer dans le cercueil d'Edgar Poe. Notes sur Aupres d'un mort de Guy de Maupassant," Neophilogues LXXXIV.3 (00); ed, Melanges a la memoire de Jean-Claude Morisot, Litteratures nos 21-22, (Montreal, 00); auth, "Penombre historique (Ann Radcliffe) et noirceur social (Eugene Sue, Paul Feval). Le mystere des Mysteres," Discours social/Social Discourse III, (Montreal, 01). **CONTACT ADDRESS** 3463 Ste-Famille, Apt 1412, Montreal, QC, Canada H2X 2K7. **EMAIL** maximeprevost@hotmail.com

PRIBIC, RADO
PERSONAL Born 02/04/1947, Dorfen, Germany **DISCIPLINE** INTERNATIONAL AFFAIRS, GERMAN & RUSSIAN LITERATURES & SOCIETIES **EDUCATION** Fla State Univ, BA, 68; Vanderbilt Univ, MA, 70, PhD(Ger), 72. **CAREER** Teacher Ger, Russ, Latin & World Lit, Webb Sch, Bell Buckle, Tenn, 69-71; prof Foreign Lang & Lit; chmn Int Affairs Prog, Lafayette Col, 71-. **HONORS AND AWARDS** Linback, Jones, Marquis Teaching Awds; Fulbright; NEH. **MEMBERSHIPS** Am Asn Teachers Ger; SAtlantic Mod Lang Asn; MLA; Int Dostoevsky Soc; Southern Comp Lit Asn. **RESEARCH** Germano-Slavic literary relations; South German regional literature; 19th century European literature. **SELECTED PUBLICATIONS** Auth, Bonaventura's Nachtwachen and Dostoevsky's Notes From the Underground: A Comparison in Nihilism, Otto Sagner, Munich, 74; Alienation in Nachtwachen by Bonaventura and Dostoevskij's Notes From the Underground, Germano-Slavica, 75; America's image in Mayakovski and Essenin, Sci Technol & Humanities, 78; Keyserling's Schwule Tage and Turgenev's First Love, In: Festschrift for Andre von Gronicka, 78; The Importance of German for the Science Student, Die Unterrisfts Praxis, 80; Young people's literature in the Federal Republic of Germany Today, J Reading, 81; The German Public and the Persecution of Jews, 1933-1945, No One Participated, No One Knew It, ed Jorg Wollenber, ed, trans Rado Pribic, Atlantic Highlands, NJ, Humanities Press, 96; Die Carpetbaggers in den Neuen Bundeslandern, In Schreiben im heutigen Deutschland, Die literarische Szene nach der Wende, ed Ursula E Beitter, New York, Peter Lang Publishing, 97. **CONTACT ADDRESS** Dept of Foreign Languages and Lit, Lafayette Col, Easton, PA 18042-1798. **EMAIL** pribicr@lafayette.edu

PRIDEAUX, GARY DEAN
PERSONAL Born 04/21/1939, Muskogee, OK, m, 1989 **DISCIPLINE** LINGUISTICS **EDUCATION** Rice Univ, BA, 61; Univ Tex, PhD(ling), 66. **CAREER** Asst prof, 66-71, Assoc Prof Ling, Univ Alta, 71-78, Chmn Dept, 75-, Fulbright-Hays exchange grant, Japan, 67-68; co-ed, Can J Ling; Experimental Ling, 76; Prof, Univ Alta, 78-96; McCalla Res Prof, 91-92; Prof Emer, 92-. **HONORS AND AWARDS** Sigma Xi, The Scientific Res Soc, 94; Fac of Arts Undergraduate Teaching Awd, 97. **MEMBERSHIPS** Ling Soc Am; Can Ling Asn; Cognitive Science Soc; International Progmatics Asn; Ling Asn of Canada and the US. **RESEARCH** Psycholinguistics, Forensic linguistics, Discourse Analysis, Japanese syntax and semantics. **SELECTED PUBLICATIONS** Auth, Perspectives in experimental linguistics, Prideaux, G.D., Amsterdam: John Benjamins B.V., 79; auth, Experimental linguistics; Intergration of theories and applications, Prideaux, G.D., Derwing, B.L., & Baker, W.J., Ghent: E. Story-Scientia, 80; auth, Psycholinguistics: The experimental study of language, Prideaux, G.D., London: Croom Helm: New York: Guilford, 85; auth, Strategies and structures: The processing of relative clauses, Prideaux, G.D., & Baker, W.J., Amsterdam: John Benjamins, 86; auth, Changes in the representation on mental events over time, Prideaux, G.D., S. Embleton, Lacus Forum, 24, (98): 316-325; auth, 'God's truth' and structuralism: A new look at an old controversy, Pridauex, G.D., The emergence of the modern language sciences: Studies on the transition from comparative-historical to structural linguistics, vol 2, Amsterdam & Philadelphia: John Benjamins, (99): 68-79; auth, Forensic aspects of discourse analysis, Pirdeaux, G.D., LACUS Forum, 25, (99): 287-296; auth, Prototype lexical effects in planned versus unplanned discourse, Festschrift for Bruce Derwing, Prideaux, G.D., (in press); auth, How much lexical in formation if accessed in parsing? Prideaux, G.D., Festchrift for Takashi Yoshida, Fukushima, Japan: Fukushima Univ Seikyo, S. Inoi, N. Itagaki, & Y. Tomita, eds, (in press); auth, Discourse analysis and psycholinguistics: Breaking down barriers, Presidental Address, Annual meeting, Linguistic Asn of Canada and the United States, A. Lommel & A. Melby, LACUS Forum, 26, 1-16, (in press). **CONTACT ADDRESS** Dept of Ling, Univ of Alberta, 4-32 Assiniboia Hall, Edmonton, AB, Canada T6G 2E7. **EMAIL** gary.prideaux@ualberta.ca

PRIESTLY, TOM M. S.
PERSONAL Born 05/16/1937, Kampala, Uganda, m, 1966, 2 children **DISCIPLINE** LINGUSITICS **EDUCATION** Downing Col, BA, 60; MA, 65; Simon Fraser Univ, PhD, 72. **CAREER** Teacher, Withywood Comprehensive Sch, 61-66; grad assoc, Simon Fraser Univ, 66-70; asst prof to prof, Univ Alta, 70-. **HONORS AND AWARDS** Henry Kreisel Teaching Awd, 00; McCalla Res Prof, 00; Freedom medal of Honour, Republic of Slovenia, 00; Prize for Translation, Austria, 01. **MEMBERSHIPS** Soc for Slovene Studies; Can Asn of Slavists. **RESEARCH** Sociolinguistics of Slovene minority in Carinthia, Austria; Minority Languages; Sociolinguistics; Translation, especially Slovene poetry into English. **SELECTED PUBLICATIONS** Auth, "Slovene," in The Slavonic Languages, (London, 93), 388-451; auth, "Effects of educational and social mobility on language maintenance, language attitudes and language structure: The case of Sele in Carinthia," J of Multilingual and Multicultural Develop, (94): 199-217; auth, "On levels of analysis of sound symbolism in poetry, with an application to Russian poetry," in Sound Symbolism, (Cambridge Univ, 94); auth, "Denial of ethnic identity: The political manipulation of beliefs about language in Slovene minority areas of Austria and Hungary," Slavic Rev, (96): 364-398; auth, "On the etymology of the ethnic slur Tschusch," J of Slavic Ling, (96): 109-132; coauth, Pronunciation Rules for Russian. A Systematic Approach for Converting Russian Spelling to Sound, Bloomington, 01. **CONTACT ADDRESS** Dept Mod Lang & Cultural Studies, Univ of Alberta, 200 Arts Bldg, Edmonton, AB, Canada T6G 2E6. **EMAIL** tom.priestly@ualberta.ca

PRIETO, CHAR
PERSONAL Born 10/17/1954, Spain, m, 1980, 2 children **DISCIPLINE** SPANISH **EDUCATION** Ind Univ, BS, 89; Purdue Univ, ME, 93. **CAREER** Guest lectr, Purdue Univ Calumet, 90-94; TA, Purdue Univ, 94-96; professional specialisit, Univ of Notre Dame, 96-. **HONORS AND AWARDS** First place, ESL Div of Ind Adult Lit Coalition, 96. **RESEARCH** 20th Century Spanish Literature. **SELECTED PUBLICATIONS** Auth, "Sevilla y la Expo' 98", El Puente 1.6, (92); auth, "Homage to Fellini", Chronicle 12.11 (93); auth, "El complejo de Edipo: Elemento transgresor en Reinvindicacion del conde Don Julian", Romance Lang Annual, Purdue Univ, 96; auth, "A turning point", News-Dispatch 9.8, (96); auth, "Journey to Georgia", Beacher 2.2 (96): auth, "Las Sonatas como sable de doble filo: Esteticismo e ironia de la glorificacion de Espana", Romance Lang Annual, Purdue Univ, 97; auth, "Integracion de sueno y realidad como evasion en la lirica becqueriana", Romance Lang Annual, 99. **CONTACT ADDRESS** Dept Romance Lang, Univ of Notre Dame, 343 O Shaugnessy Hall, Notre Dame, IN 46556-5639. **EMAIL** char.prieto.3@nd.edu

PRINCE, GERALD
PERSONAL Born 11/07/1942, Alexandria, Egypt, m, 1967 **DISCIPLINE** FRENCH LITERATURE **EDUCATION** Brooklyn Col, BA (magna cum laude), 63; Univ of Fla, MA, 63; Brown Univ, PhD, 68. **CAREER** Vis prof, Trent Univ, 95; vist prof, Emory Univ, 90; vis prof, Johns Hopkins Univ, 86, vis prof, Univ of Alberta at Edmonton, 86, vis prof Univ of Queensland, 83; Instr, 67-68, Prof of Romance Lang, 81-, Lois & Jerry Magnin Family Term Prof, Univ of PA, 93-98. **HONORS AND AWARDS** Phi Beta Kappa, 63; Lindback Awd for Excellence in Tchg, 74; Awd of Honor, Brooklyn Col, 78. **MEMBERSHIPS** AATF; ACLA; AAUP; MLA. **RESEARCH** Narrative theory; modern French Lit; Twentieth-Century French fiction. **SELECTED PUBLICATIONS** Auth, Metaphysique et technique dans l'oeuvre romaneque de Sartre, 68; A Grammer of Stories, 73; Narratology: The Form and Functioning of Narrative, 82; A Dictionary of Narratology, 87; Narrative as Theme: Studies in French Fiction, 92. **CONTACT ADDRESS** Univ of Pennsylvania, 521 Williams Hall, Philadelphia, PA 19104-6305. **EMAIL** gerry@babel.ling.upen.edu

PRINCE, SUSAN
PERSONAL Born 06/26/1964, Wilmington, DE, m, 1999 **DISCIPLINE** CLASSICS **EDUCATION** Yale Univ, BA, 86; Oxford Univ, BA, 89; Univ of Mich, PhD, 97. **CAREER** Vis asst prof, Mich State Univ, 97-98; asst prof, Univ of Colo, 98. **HONORS AND AWARDS** Distinguished Diss Awd, Univ of Mich, 97. **MEMBERSHIPS** Am Philolol Assoc; Class Assoc of the Middle West and South; Women Class Caucas; Soc of Ancient Greek Philos. **RESEARCH** Intellectual history, philosophy, rhetoric, fiction. **SELECTED PUBLICATIONS** Auth, "Ajax, Odysseus, and the Act of Self-Representation", Ancient Philos 19, (99): 55-64. **CONTACT ADDRESS** Dept Classics, Univ of Colorado, Boulder, Boulder, CO 80309. **EMAIL** susan.prince@colorado.edu

PRINCIPE, D. DEL
PERSONAL Born 12/26/1960, m, 1989 **DISCIPLINE** SPANISH, ITALIAN **EDUCATION** PhD, 93. **CAREER** Asst Prof, Montclair State Univ, 93-. **RESEARCH** Italian literature. **SELECTED PUBLICATIONS** Auth, Rebellion, Death and Aesthetics in Italy, Fairleigh Dickinson Univ Pr, 96. **CONTACT ADDRESS** Dept Span and Ital, Montclair State Univ, 1 Normal Ave, Montclair, NJ 07043-1624. **EMAIL** delprinciped@mail.montclair.edu

PRITCHETT, KAY
PERSONAL Born 09/10/1946, Greenville, MS, m, 1988 **DISCIPLINE** SPANISH **EDUCATION** Univ NC, PhD, 79. **CAREER** Prof of Spanish, Univ Arkansas, 82-; Fulbright-Hays fel. **RESEARCH** Contemporary poetry and fiction; Psychoanalytic theory; Feminism; Spanish literature of 20th Century. **SELECTED PUBLICATIONS** Auth Four Postmodern Poets of Spain: A Critical Study with Translations of the Poems, 91; transl Jonah and the Pink Whale, 91; In the Land of Silence, 94; Pureza Canelo's Celda verde/Green Cell: A Critical Introduction with Translations of the Poems, Nuestra Voz (New York), Peter Lang Publishing, 00. **CONTACT ADDRESS** 523 N Willow Ave, Fayetteville, AR 72701. **EMAIL** pritche@comp.uark.edu

PROFIT, VERA BARBARA
PERSONAL Born Vienna, Austria **DISCIPLINE** FRENCH & GERMAN LITERATURE **EDUCATION** Alverno Col, BA, 67; Univ Rochester, MA, 69, PhD(comp lit), 74. **CAREER** Instr Ger, St Olaf Col, 74-75; asst prof, 75-81, assoc prof, German & comp lit, 81-96, prof Ger & comp lit, Univ Notre Dame, 96-; vis scholar, Harvard Univ, 79-80; vis scholar, Northwestern Univ, 84. **HONORS AND AWARDS** NDEA Title IV Fel. **MEMBERSHIPS** MLA; Am Asn Teachers Ger. **RESEARCH** Poetry and novel of the German-speaking countries, written after 1945; 20th century French and German prose and poetry. **SELECTED PUBLICATIONS** Auth, Interpretations of Iwan Goll's Late Poetry with a Comprehensive and Annotated Bibliography of the Writings by and about Iwan Goll, Peter Lang, Bern, Switz, 77; Ein Portrat meiner Selbst: Karl Krolow's Autobiographical Poems (1945-1958) and Their French Sources, Peter Lang, Bern, Switz, 91; Menschlich: Gesprache mit Karl Krolow, Peter Lang, Bern Switz, 96. **CONTACT ADDRESS** Dept Ger, Russian Lang & Lit, Univ of Notre Dame, 318 O'Shaughnessy Hall, Notre Dame, IN 46556. **EMAIL** vera.b.profit.1@nd.edu

PUCCI, JOSEPH M.
PERSONAL Born 09/25/1957, Cleveland, OH, m, 1982, 1 child **DISCIPLINE** COMPARATIVE LITERATURE **EDUCATION** John Carroll Univ, BA, 79; Univ Chicago, MA, 82, PhD, 87. **CAREER** Asst Prof, Assoc Prof, 89 to 97-, Brown Univ; Asst Prof 87-89, Univ Kentucky. **HONORS AND AWARDS** Dist Teach Awd; Dist Adv Awd. **MEMBERSHIPS** APA; MLA; MLANA. **RESEARCH** Later and Medieval Latin, language and literature. **SELECTED PUBLICATIONS** Auth, Medieval Latin, 2nd edition, U of Chicago Press, 97; Full Knowing Reader: Allusion and the Power of the Reader in the Western Lit Tradition, Yale, 98. **CONTACT ADDRESS** Dept Classics, Brown Univ, Box 1856, Providence, RI 02912. **EMAIL** joseph_pucci@brown.edu

PUCCI, PIETRO
PERSONAL Born 11/27/1927, Modena, Italy, m, 1984, 2 children **DISCIPLINE** CLASSICS **EDUCATION** Liceo Muratori, BA (Classics), 45; Univ Pisa, PhD (Classics), 49; Univ Florence, Libera Docenza (Classics), 60. **CAREER** Asst prof, Classics, Univ Florence, 51-52; asst prof, Classics, Univ Ottawa; asst prof, Classics, Univ KS, 61-62; vis prof, Classics, Santa Cruz Univ, 69; vis prof, Classics, Univ Florence, 70; Directeur d'Etudes, Ecole des Hautes Etudes Paris, 84, 89; asst prof, 62-67, assoc prof, 67-72, prof, dept of Classics, 72-91, chmn, 83-87, 90-91, 92-93, Golwin Smith prof of Classics, Cornell Univ, 91-. **HONORS AND AWARDS** Fel of the French govt, 55-57; fel of the German govt, 57-58; Jr fel at the Center for Hellenic Studies, Washington, 70; fel of the ACLS, 72; fel of the Guggenheim Memorial Found, 80-81; fel of the NEH, 89; resident of the Am Academy in Rome, 96. **SELECTED PUBLICATIONS** Auth, "Hesiod and the Language of Poetry," Baltimore: Johns Hopkins Univ Press, 77; auth, "The Violence of Pity in Euripides," Media, Ithaca: Cornell University Press, 80; auth, Oedipus and the Fabrication of the Father, Johns Hopkins Univ Press, 92; Human Sacrifice in the Oresteia, in Innovations in Antiquity, Ralph Hexter and Daniel Seldon, eds, Routledge, 92; Io e l'altro nel racconto di Odisseo sui Ciclopi, SIFC XI, 93; Antiphonal Lament between Achilles and Briseis in Colby Quart, XXXIX, 93; God's Intervention and Epiphany in Sophocles, AJP 115, 94; Persuasione nell' Orestea di Eschilo, Museum Criticum, XXXIX, 94; Ulysse Polytropos, French trans of Odysseus Polytropos, Septentrion, Presses Univ, Lille, 95; Enigma Segreto Oracolo, Instituto Editoriale: Roma, 96; L'Apologie d'Apollon, METIS, 96; Auteur et Destinataires dans le Travaux d'Hesiode, in Le Metier du Mythe, Lectures d'Hesiode, Septentrion, Presses Univ, Lille, 96; The Song of the Sirens and Other Essays, a book of old and new Homeric essays, Rowman & Littlefield, 97; numerous other publications. **CONTACT ADDRESS** Dept of Classics, Cornell Univ, 125 Goldwin Smith Hall, Ithaca, NY 14853. **EMAIL** pp26@cornell.edu

PUGH, ANTHONY ROY
PERSONAL Born 08/16/1931, Liverpool, England, m, 1962, 3 children **DISCIPLINE** FRENCH LITERATURE **EDUCATION** Cambridge Univ, BA, 53, MA, 56, PhD(French), 59. **CAREER** Asst lectr French, King's Col, Univ London, 56-59; lectr, Queen's Univ Belfast, 59-69; chmn dept Romance lang, 73-75, Prof French, Univ NB, Fredericton, 69-, Vis prof, Univ NB, 68. **MEMBERSHIPS** MLA. **RESEARCH** European lit since 1600, Proust's manuscripts. **SELECTED PUBLICATIONS** Auth, Beaumarchais: Le Mariage de Figaro, an interpretation, Macmillan, 68; coed, of Balzac and the nineteenth century, studies in French literature presented to H.J. Hunt, Leicester Univ Press, 72; auth, Balzac's recurring characters, Univ of Toronto Press, 74; auth, The Composition of Pascal's Apologia, Univ of Toronto Press, 84; auth, The Birth of 'A la recherche du temps perdu', French Forum Publishers: Kentucky, Lexington, 87; coauth, with Allan J. Pasco, Chapter on BALZAC in A Critical Bilbiography of French Literature, The Nineteenth Century, ed, D. Baguley, Syracuse Univ Press, (94): 323-405; auth, The Growth of 'A la recherche du temps perdu', Proust's manuscripts from 1909 to 1913, (forthcoming). **CONTACT ADDRESS** Dept of Fr, Univ of New Brunswick, Fredericton, PO Box 4400, Fredericton, NB, Canada E3B 5A3. **EMAIL** pugh@unb.ca

PUGLIESE, OLGA
PERSONAL Born 11/04/1941, Toronto, ON, Canada, m, 1969 **DISCIPLINE** ITALIAN, LITERATURE, LANGUAGE, CLASSICS **EDUCATION** Univ Toronto, BA, 63; MA, 64; PhD, 69. **CAREER** Fac mbr, dept chmn, Univ Toronto, 67-. **HONORS AND AWARDS** Victoria Col Fel; Vis Distinguished Scholar, Queen's Univ, 98. **MEMBERSHIPS** MLA; CSRS; AAIS; AATI. **RESEARCH** Renaissance literature and manuscript research. **SELECTED PUBLICATIONS** Ed, transl, Lorenzo Valla, The Profession of the Religious and Selections from The Donation of Constantine (1985, 3rd ed, 1998); co-ed, Ficino and Renaissance Neoplatonism, 86; ed, transl, La Falsa Donazione di Constantino, by Lorenzo Valla (1994); auth, Il Discorso Labirintico del Dialogo Rinascimentale (95); auth, "Humour in Il Libro del Cortegiano," Quaderni d'Ital 14 (93); co-auth, Rekindling Faded Memories: The Founding of the Famee Furlane of Toronto and Its First Years, 96; auth of 38 articles on Ital Lit, Cult, Renaissance; auth, 26 Bk Reviews. **CONTACT ADDRESS** Dept Ital Studies, Univ of Toronto, 100 Joseph St 2nd Fl, Carr Hall, Toronto, ON, Canada M5S 1J4. **EMAIL** pugliese@chass.utoronto.ca

PULLEYBLANK, EDWIN GEORGE
PERSONAL Born 08/07/1922, Calgary, AB, Canada, m, 3 children **DISCIPLINE** CHINESE LANGUAGE & HISTORY **EDUCATION** Univ Alta, BA, 42; Univ London, PhD(Chinese), 51; Cambridge Univ, MA, 53. **CAREER** Lectr, Univ of London, 48-53; Prof, Univ of Cambridge, 53-66; Prof, Univ of BC, 66-87; Prof Emer, Univ of BC, 88-. **HONORS AND AWARDS** Fel, Royal Soc of Canada, 80; Corresponding Fel, Istituto Italiana per il Medio ed Estramo Oriente, 93. **MEMBERSHIPS** Asn Asian Studies; Am Orient Soc; Ling Soc Am; Can Soc Asian Studies (pres, 71-74); fel Royal Soc Can. **RESEARCH** Chinese history; historical phonology and grammar of classical Chinese. **SELECTED PUBLICATIONS** Auth, The Background of the Rebellion of An Lu-shan, London: Oxford Univ Press, 55; auth, Chinese History and World History: An inaugural lecture, Cambridge, Cabridge Univ Press, 55; auth, Historians of China and Japan, ed with W.G. Beasley, London: Oxford Univ Press, 61; auth, Middle Chinese: A Study in Historical Phonology, Vancouver: UBC Press, 84; auth, Studies in Language Origins, Vol I, ed by Jan Wind, Edwin G. Pulleyblank, Eric de Grolier and Bernard H. Bichakjian, Amsterdam and Philadelphia: Benjamins, 89; auth, A Lexicon of Reconstructed Pronunciation in Early Middle Chinese, Late Middle Chinese and Early Madarin, Vancouver: UBC Press, 91; auth, A Chinese text in Central Asian Brahmi script: New evidence for the pronunciation of Late Middle Chinese and Khotanese, With R.E. Emmerick, Rome: Istituto Italiano per il Medio ed Estremo Oriente, 94; auth, Outline of Classical Chinese Grammar, Vancouver: UBC Press, 95; auth, 'Morphology in Old Chinese,' Journal of Chinese Linguistics 28, (00): 26-51. **CONTACT ADDRESS** Dept of Asian Studies, Univ of British Columbia, 2708 W 3rd Ave, Vancouver, BC, Canada V6K 1M5. **EMAIL** edwin@interchange.ubc.ca

PULLUM, GEOFFREY K.
PERSONAL Born 03/08/1945, Irvine, Scotland, m **DISCIPLINE** GENERAL LINGUISTIC THEORY AND THE SYNTAX OF ENGLISH **EDUCATION** Univ York, BA; Univ London, PhD, 76. **CAREER** Prof, Ling, Univ Calif, Santa Cruz. **RESEARCH** Interface between syntax and phonology, phonetics, and philosophy of linguistics. **SELECTED PUBLICATIONS** Coed, Handbook of Amazonian Languages, Mouton de Gruyter, 86-93; auth, The Great Eskimo Vocabulary Hoax, Univ of Chicago Press, 91; coauth, Phonetic Symbol Guide, Univ of Chicago Press, 96. **CONTACT ADDRESS** Dept of Ling, Univ of California, Santa Cruz, 1156 High St, Santa Cruz, CA 95064.

PURCELL, JOHN MARSHALL
PERSONAL Born 11/25/1932, Pittsburgh, PA **DISCIPLINE** SPANISH **EDUCATION** Univ Cincinnati, BA, 54, BEd, 55; Middlebury Col, MA, 62; Ohio State Univ, PhD(foreign lang educ), 69. **CAREER** Teacher Span & chmn dept, Hughes High Sch, Cincinnati, Ohio, 59-62 & Aiken Sr High Sch, Cincinnati, Ohio, 62-70; asst prof, 70-73, Assoc Prof Span & Foreign Lang Educ, Cleveland State Univ, 73-, Consult, NDEA title III workships, Ohio, 68-70 & Cleveland Pub Schs Biling-Bicult Prog, 75-79. **MEMBERSHIPS** Am Asn Teachers Span & Port; Am Coun Teaching Foreign Lang; Cent States Conf Foreign Lang Teaching. **RESEARCH** Foreign language methodology. **SELECTED PUBLICATIONS** Auth, A Liberal Education In The United States, J Gen Educ, 71; How To Help Your Student Teacher, 10/72 & Teaching The Short Story, Winter 74, Am Foreign Lang Teacher; Simulation And Success In Business Spanish, Accent Am Coun Teaching Foreign Lang, 1/75; Co-Ed, Personalizing Foreign Language Instruction, Nat Txtbk Co, 77; Auth, Teaching Novels And Plays, In: Filling And Fulfilling The Advanced Foreign Language Class & Co-Ed, Filling And Fulfilling The Advanced Foreign Language Class, 81, Heinle & Heinle; Auth, The Preparation Of Modern Language Teachers In Latin America, The Modern Lang J, 81; Livelier Fles-Asterisk Lessons Through Role-Play + In The Primary And Middle School Spanish-Language Classroom, Hispania-A J Devoted To The Teaching Of Spanish And Portuguese, Vol 76, 93. **CONTACT ADDRESS** Dept of Mod Lang, Cleveland State Univ, Euclid Ave at 24th st, Cleveland, OH 44115.

PURCZINSKY, JULIUS O.
PERSONAL Born 01/06/1925, Levi, TX **DISCIPLINE** MEDIEVAL PHILOLOGY, STRUCTURAL LINGUISTICS **EDUCATION** Baylor Univ, BA, 49; Univ Tex, Austin, MA, 53, PhD, 57. **CAREER** Asst prof Span, Baylor Univ, 57-58; Fulbright lectr English, Nat Univ Athens, 58-59; assoc prof Ger, French & Span, Univ Southwestern La, 59-61; asst prof Span, Kans State Univ, 61-63; assoc prof Span & French, Univ Nev, 63-65; asst prof, 65-72, Assoc Prof Romance Ling, Hunter Col, 72- **MEMBERSHIPS** Int Ling Asn; Mediaeval Acad Am. **SELECTED PUBLICATIONS** Auth, Additional Frankish superstratum in Old French, 64 & Germanic influence in the Sainte Eulalie, 65, Romance Philol; auth, A Neo-Schushardtian Theory of General Romance Diphthongization, 70. **CONTACT ADDRESS** Dept of Romance Lang, Hunter Col, CUNY, 695 Park Ave, New York, NY 10021-5085.

PURDY, ANTHONY
DISCIPLINE FRENCH LITERATURE **EDUCATION** Cambridge Univ, BA, MA; Queen's Univ, PhD, MA. **RESEARCH** Collecting; cultural memory; literature and modernity; narrative theory; interarts; migration of concepts across disciplines. **SELECTED PUBLICATIONS** Auth, A Certain Difficulty of Being: Essays on the Quebec Novel, McGill-Queen's, 90; coauth, Peter Greenaway: Architecture and Allegory, Acad, 97; ed, Writing Quebec, Alberta, 88; Problems of Literary Reception, Alberta, 88; Prefaces and Literary Manifestoes, Alberta, 90; Literature and the Body, Rodopi, 92; Literature and Money, Rodopi, 93; Literature and Science, Rodopi, 94. **CONTACT ADDRESS** Dept of French, Univ of Western Ontario, London, ON, Canada N6A 5B8. **EMAIL** apurdy@julian.uwo.ca

PURINTON, JEFFREY S.
PERSONAL Born 05/08/1960, Wilmington, DE **DISCIPLINE** CLASSICS **EDUCATION** Princeton Univ, PhD, 92. **CAREER** Vis asst prof philos, Univ Okla, 93- . **MEMBERSHIPS** APA. **RESEARCH** Epicureanism. **SELECTED PUBLICATIONS** Auth, Epicurus on the Telos, Phronesis, 93; auth, Magnifying Epicurean Minima, Ancient Philos, 94; auth, Aristotle's Definition of Happiness, Oxford Stud in Ancient Philos, 98. **CONTACT ADDRESS** Dept of Philosophy, Univ of Oklahoma, Dale Hall Tower 622, Norman, OK 73019. **EMAIL** Jeffrey.S.Purinton_1@ou.edu

PUTNAM, MICHAEL C. J.
PERSONAL Born 09/20/1933, Sprinfield, MA **DISCIPLINE** CLASSICS **EDUCATION** Harvard Univ, AB, 54; MA, 56; PhD, 59; Lawrence Univ, LlD (hon), 85. **CAREER** Instructor, Smith Col, 59-60; Instructor to Prof, Brown Univ, 60-. **HONORS AND AWARDS** Goodwin Awd of Merit, Am Philol Asn, 71; Fel, Guggenheim Memorial Foundation, 66-67; Sen Fel, NEH, 73-74; Fel, Am Coun of Learned Soc, 83-84. **MEMBERSHIPS** Am Acad in Rome; Am Philol Asn; Am Acad of Arts and Sci; Am Philos Soc; Classical Asn of N Eng; Medieval Acad of Am; Asn of Literary Scholars and Critics. **RESEARCH** Greek and Latin Literature, expecially the poetry of the Roman Republic and Empire. **SELECTED PUBLICATIONS** Ed, Virgil: 2000 Years, Arethusa, 81; auth, Essays on Latin Lyric, Elegy, and Epic, Princeton Univ Press, 82; auth, Artifices of Eternity: Horace's Fourth book of Odes, Cornell Univ Press, 86; auth, Virgil's Epic Designs: Ekphrasis in the Aeneid, Yale Univ Press, 98. **CONTACT ADDRESS** Dept Classics, Brown Univ, Providence, RI 02912-1856. **EMAIL** michael_putnam@brown.edu

Q

QIAN, NANXIU
DISCIPLINE LINGUISTICS, CHINESE LITERATURE **EDUCATION** Nanjing Univ, China, MA, 82; Yale Univ, PhD, 94. **CAREER** Instr, Nanjing Univ, China; instr, Univ MN, 92-93; asst prof, Rice Univ, 93-. **MEMBERSHIPS** Asn for Asian Stud; Am Orient Soc. **RESEARCH** The Shih-shuo hsin-yu in the Chinese literary tradition. **SELECTED PUBLICATIONS** Ed, A Guide to Chinese Culture; transl, A Selected Translation of the Shih-shuo hsin-yu, with Annotations and An Introduction. **CONTACT ADDRESS** Rice Univ, PO Box 1892, Houston, TX 77251-1892. **EMAIL** nanxiuq@owlnet.rice.edu

QIAN, ZHAOMING
PERSONAL Born 07/25/1944, Shanghai, China, m, 1969, 2 children **DISCIPLINE** ENGLISH, COMPARATIVE LITERATURE **EDUCATION** Beijing For Studies Univ, BA, 67; MA, 80; Tulane Univ, PhD, 91. **CAREER** Instr, Tulane Univ, 88-91; from asst prof to assoc prof, Univ of New Orleans, 91-. **HONORS AND AWARDS** Beinecke Fel, Yale Univ, 92-93; NEH Fel, 98-99. **MEMBERSHIPS** MLA, Ezra Pound Soc, William Carlos Williams Soc, Wallace Stevens Soc. **RESEARCH** Chinese influence in modern American poetry. **SELECTED PUBLICATIONS** Ed & contribur, Annotated Shakespeare: The Sonnets, Commecid Press, 91; auth, Orientalism and Modernism: The Legacy of China in Pound and Williams, Duke Univ Press, 95. **CONTACT ADDRESS** Dept English, Univ of New Orleans, 2000 Lakeshore Dr, New Orleans, LA 70148-0001.

QUACKENBUSH, LOUIS HOWARD
PERSONAL Born 11/28/1939, Bellingham, WA, m, 1963, 7 children **DISCIPLINE** LATIN AMERICAN LITERATURE **EDUCATION** Brigham Young Univ, BA, 65, MA, 67; Univ Ill, Urbana, PhD(Span), 70. **CAREER** Teacher, teacher suprv & counr Span lang training, Lang Training Mission, 63-67, Assoc Prof Span, Brigham Young Univ, 70 **MEMBERSHIPS** MLA; Rocky Mountain Mod Lang Asn; Am Asn Teachers Span & Port. **RESEARCH** Spanish American drama; Brazilian drama; Spanish American poetry. **SELECTED PUBLICATIONS** Auth, The Other Pastorelas Of Spanish American Drama, Latin Am Theatre Rev, Spring 73; The Auto In Contemporary Mexican Drama, Ky Romance Quart, 74; Theatre Of The Absurd, Reality And Carlos Maggi, J Span Studies: 20th Century, Spring 75; La Desavenencia Religiosa: Una Clave A El Tuerto Es Rey De Carlos Fuentes, Explicacion De Textos Literarios, 75/76; The Contemporary Latin American Short Story, 79; The Legacy Of Albee's Who's Afraid Of Virginia Woolf? In The Spanish American Absurdist Theatre, Spring 79 & Pablo Nervda: Sus Versos Finales Y Ultimos Comienzos, Summer 80, Revista/Rev Interamericana; Pugilism As Mirror And Metafiction In Life And In Contemporary Spanish-American Drama, Latin American Theatre Rev, Vol 26, 92; Reality Behind Reality, The Numinous In Gonzalo Rojas, Chasqui-Revista De Literatura Latinoamericana, Vol 22, 93. **CONTACT ADDRESS** Dept of Span, Brigham Young Univ, Provo, UT 84601.

QUINTANA, HILDA E.
PERSONAL Born 09/20/1950, Santurce, Puerto Rico, d, 1 child **DISCIPLINE** SPANISH **EDUCATION** Univ PR, BA, 71; SUNY Binghamton, MA, 75; PhD, 83. **CAREER** Prof to

assoc vp and center dir, Inter Am Univ of PR, 75-. **HONORS AND AWARDS** Outstanding Acad Work, Inter Am Univ, 89, 93, 94; Blue Book of PR, 87. **MEMBERSHIPS** AATSP; IRA; ALFAL **RESEARCH** Puerto Rican narrative; The teaching of writing and reading. **SELECTED PUBLICATIONS** Auth, "Francisco Gonzalo Marin: Sintesis del poeta y del hombre revolucionario," Talleres, (91): 61-73; auth, "Mito y realidad en La pasion segun Antigona Perez," Prisma, (92): 56-66; AUTH, "El portafolio como estrategia para la evaluacion de la redaccion," Lectura y Vida, (96): 39-43; auth, "El portafolio como estrategia para la evaluacion de la redaccion," Textos, (96): 89-96; auth, Personalidad y Literatura Puertorriquenas, Rio Piedras, 96; auth, "Puntos de Partida/Points of Departure, Rio Piedras, 97; auth, Hablemos de Escribir: Didactica de la expresion oral y escrita, Rio Piedras, 97; auth, "El Centro de Redaccion Multidisciplinario: Un model per imitar," Articles de Didactica de la Lengua y la Literatura, (98): 87-96. **CONTACT ADDRESS** Dept Spanish, Inter American Univ of Puerto Rico, Metropolitan, 115 Ave Arterial Hostos, Apt 73, San Juan, PR 00918-3034. **EMAIL** hquintan@inter.edu

QUIRK, RONALD JOSEPH
PERSONAL Born 03/22/1942, Bristol, CT, m, 1967, 4 children **DISCIPLINE** SPANISH LANGUAGE & LITERATURE **EDUCATION** Trinity Col, BA, 64; Brown Univ, MA, 66, PhD(Span), 71. **CAREER** Instr Span, RI Col, 68-69; from instr to asst prof, Trinity Col, 69-72; asst prof, 72-74, assoc prof, 74-80, prof Span, Quinnipiac Col, 80-. **MEMBERSHIPS** Am Asn Teachers Span & Port; Northeast Mod Lang Asn. **RESEARCH** Nineteenth century Spanish literature; linguistics and literature of Puerto Rico. **SELECTED PUBLICATIONS** Auth, Glosario Borinqueno, Trinity Col, 70; On the extent and origin of questions in the formque tu tienes?, Hispania, 5/72; The authorship of La gruta azul: Juan Valera or Serafin Estebanez Calderon, Romance Notes, spring 74; El problema del habla regional en Los Pazos de Ulloa, Inti, 10/75; Nueve cartas de Estebanez Calderon, Rev de Archivos, Bibliot y Museos, 1-3/76; Temporal adverbs in Puerto Rican Spanish, Hispania, 5/76; The Cebre Cycle: Emilia Pardo Bazan and Galician reform, Am Hispanist, 5/77; Basic Spanish for Legal Personnel, Collegium Bks, 79; Serafin Estebanez Calderon: Bajo la Corteza de su Obra, Peter Lang Pub, 92; Literature as Introspection: Spain Confronts Trafalgar, Peter Lang Pub, 98. **CONTACT ADDRESS** Dept of Mod Foreign Lang, Quinnipiac Col, 275 Mt Carmel Ave, Hamden, CT 06518-1908. **EMAIL** quirk@quinnipiac.edu

R

RAAFLAUB, KURT A.
PERSONAL Born 02/15/1941, Buea, Cameroon, m, 1978 **DISCIPLINE** CLASSICS **EDUCATION** Univ of Bard, PhD, 70. **CAREER** Asst prof, 72-78, Freic Univ, Berlin; asst, assoc, prof, 78-, Brown Univ; joint dir, 92-00, Ctrs for Hellenic Stud, Wash, DC. **RESEARCH** Social political and intellectual hist of archaic and classical Greece and of the Roman Rep **CONTACT ADDRESS** Dept of Classics, Brown Univ, Providence, RI 02912-1856. **EMAIL** kurt_raaflaub@brown.edu

RABASSA, CLEMENTINE CHRISTOS
PERSONAL Born 07/31/1932, New York, NY, m, 1966, 1 child **DISCIPLINE** LITERATURE, TRANSLATION **EDUCATION** Hunter Col, BA, 53; MA, 58; Columbia Univ, PhD, 71. **CAREER** Precept/instr, Columbia Univ, 63-66; asst prof to prof emer, CUNY Medgar Evers Col, 73-. **HONORS AND AWARDS** NEH Fel, 71-72; CUNY Fac Res Award, 74-75, 85-86; Rockefeller Found Fel, 79-80; Mellon Fel, 85; Gulbenkian Res Award, 89. **MEMBERSHIPS** MLA; ALTA; PEN; AAP. **RESEARCH** Epic; cameos; Spanish American literature; Luso-Brazilian literature; translation. **SELECTED PUBLICATIONS** Auth, Demetrio Aguilera-Malta and Social Justice, Fairleigh Dickinson Univ Pr, 80; auth, En Tornoa Aguilera-Malta: Temas Epicos y Negros, Casa Cult Ecuatoriana, 81; transl, Canticle for a Memory, by Francisco Arrivi (Cross-Cult Commun, 1993); auth, Summer II, Cross-Cult Commun, 99; transl, Emotions, by Julio Ortega (Cross-Cult Commun, 1999). **CONTACT ADDRESS** 140 E 72nd St, Apt 10B, New York, NY 10021-4243.

RABASSA, GREGORY
PERSONAL Born 03/09/1922, Yonkers, NY, m, 1966, 2 children **DISCIPLINE** SPANISH; PORTUGUESE **EDUCATION** Dartmouth Col, AB, 45; Columbia Univ, MA, 47; PhD, 54. **CAREER** Instructor to Assoc Prof, Columbia Univ, 48-69; Prof, Queens Col, 69-. **HONORS AND AWARDS** Fulbright Hays Fel; Nat Book Awd; PEN Translation Prize; Alexander Gode Medal; PEN Medal for Translation; Governor's Arts Awd; Order of San Carlos; Wheatland Prize for Translation; Guggenheim Fel; Ivan Sandrof Awd; Gabriela Mistral Medal; Literary Lion. **MEMBERSHIPS** Mod Lang Asn; Am Trans Asn; Am Literary Translation Asn. **RESEARCH** Luso-Brazilian literature; Spanish American literature; Translation. **SELECTED PUBLICATIONS** Auth, A Cloudy Day in Gray Minor: Early Poems, Merrick, 92; trans, The War of the Saints, by Jorge Amado, Bantam, 93. **CONTACT ADDRESS** Dept Hispanic Lang & Lit, Queens Col, CUNY, 6530 Kissena Blvd, Flushing, NY 11367-1575.

RABBITT, KARA
PERSONAL 2 children **DISCIPLINE** FRENCH LITERATURE AND LINGUISTICS **EDUCATION** Cornell Univ, PhD, 96. **CAREER** Asst prof. **RESEARCH** 19th-century French literature and contemporary Francophone literature. **SELECTED PUBLICATIONS** Publ on the works of, Charles Baudelaire, Aime Cesaire, CLR. James, Arthur Rimbaud, Stendhal & Quebecois and Caribbean artistic movements. **CONTACT ADDRESS** Dept of Language and Cultures, William Paterson Col of New Jersey, 300 Pompton Rd., Wayne, NJ 07470. **EMAIL** rabbittk@wpunj.edu

RABINE, LESLIE W.
DISCIPLINE FRENCH LANGUAGE **EDUCATION** Stanford Univ, PhD. **CAREER** Prof, Fr, Univ Calif, Irvine. **SELECTED PUBLICATIONS** Auth, Reading the Romantic Heroine: Text, History, Ideology; Rebel Daughters: Women and the French Revolution; Dominion, Socialism, and French Romanticism. **CONTACT ADDRESS** Dept of Fr and Ital, Univ of California, Irvine, Irvine, CA 92697.

RABINOWITZ, PETER JACOB
PERSONAL Born 02/18/1944, Brooklyn, NY, m, 2 children **DISCIPLINE** COMPARATIVE LITERATURE **EDUCATION** Univ Chicago, BA, 65, MA, 67, PhD(comp lit), 72. **CAREER** Asst prof humanities, City Col Chicago, 68-74; asst prof lit, Kirkland Col, 74-78; asst prof comp lit, 78-81, assoc prof Comp Lit, Hamilton Col, 81-87, prof Comp Lit, 87-; Chm, 79-84, 86-87, 94-98, 00-, Panelist, Music Prog, NY State Coun on Arts, 82-85; Fanfare, contrib ed, 89-; co-ed, Series on Theory and Interpretation of Narrative, Ohio State Univ Press, 91-; Narrative, Advisory Editor, 92-; ACLA Advisory Board, 93-97; PMLA Editorial Board, 93-95. **MEMBERSHIPS** MLA; Am Comp Lit Asn; Asn Recorded Sound Collections. **RESEARCH** Literary theory; literature and music. **SELECTED PUBLICATIONS** Auth, Before Reading: Narrative Conventions and the Politics of Interpretation, Cornell Univ Press, 87, reprint, Ohio State Univ Press, 98; co-ed, Understanding Narrative, Ohio State Univ Press, 94; coauth, Authorizing Readers: Resistance and Respect in the Teaching of Literature, Teachers Col Press, 98; author of numerous articles in PMLA, Critical Inquiry, 19th Century Music, Modern Philology, and other journals. **CONTACT ADDRESS** Dept of Comp Lit, Hamilton Col, New York, 198 College Hill Rd., Clinton, NY 13323-1292. **EMAIL** prabinow@hamilton.edu

RABY, MICHEL J.
PERSONAL Born 02/05/1945, Paris, France **DISCIPLINE** FRENCH **EDUCATION** Univ Paris, Licence d'anglais, 88; Univ Iowa, MA, 83; PhD, 88. **CAREER** Asst Prof, N Mo State Univ, 88-89; Asst Prof to Assoc Prof, Auburn Univ, 89-. **RESEARCH** Prose reworkings of Old French epics. **SELECTED PUBLICATIONS** Auth, "L'Origine du Huon de Bordeaux en prose du XVeme siecle," Romania III, (90): 236-253; auth, "Huon de Bordeaux: Les ecarts entre la version epique (1216?) et la version en prose du XVeme siecle," Olifant 18, (93): 21'83; auth, "Les Huons de Bordeaux (1216? Et 1454): ironie et parodie a travers l'aventure geographique," Fifteenth Century Studies, (93): 259-274; auth, "La metalite utopique et la transgression a travers l'aventure geographique," Wodan 45, (94): 87-99; auth, "I lost it at the movies: Teaching Culture through Cinematic Douyblets," French Rev 68, (95): 837-845; auth, "Le peche contre nature dans la litterature medievale: deux cas," Romance Quart, (97): 215-223; auth, Le Huon de Bordeaux en prose du XVeme siecle, Peter Lang Pub Inc, 98; auth, "Parodie, Ironie et humour a travers le merveilleux chretien et paien dans les Esclarmondes des 13eme et 15eme siecles," Etudes Medievales 2, (00): 151-164; auth, "Marie de France's 'fables de folie': Fables or Fabliaux?" Etudes Medievales 2, (00): 33-56. **CONTACT ADDRESS** Dept For Lang & Lit, Auburn Univ, 6030 Haley Center, Auburn, AL 36839. **EMAIL** rabymic@auburn.edu

RACE, WILLIAM H.
PERSONAL Born 03/24/1943, Wooster, OH, m, 1969, 2 children **DISCIPLINE** CLASSICS **EDUCATION** Univ Mich, BA, 65; Stanford Univ, MA, 72, PhD, 73. **CAREER** Tchr Latin & English, Detroit Country Day Sch, 68-69; asst prof Classics, Univ Calif Berkeley, 73-76; from asst prof to assoc prof to prof Classics, Vanderbilt Univ, 76-96; George L. Paddison prof Classics, Univ NC Chapel Hill, 96-. **HONORS AND AWARDS** Nat Endowment Hum grant, 85, 91; Outstanding Grad Tchr Awd, Vanderbilt Univ, 92. **MEMBERSHIPS** Phi Beta Kappa; Am Philological Asn; Class Asn Mid W & S; Am Inst Archeol; Am Class League; Vergilian Soc; Int Soc Class Trad; Int Plutarch Soc; ed bd, Am Jour Philol. **RESEARCH** Classical Greek poetry; Augustan Poetry; rhetoric; classical tradition. **SELECTED PUBLICATIONS** Auth, The Classical Priamel from Homer to Boethius, 82; auth, Pindar, Twayne World Auth Ser, 86; auth, Classical Genres and English Poetry, 88; auth, Style and Rhetoric in Pindar's Odes, 90; auth, Pindar, Loeb Class Libr, 97. **CONTACT ADDRESS** Dept of Classics, Univ of No Carolina, Chapel Hill, CB 3145, Chapel Hill, NC 27599-3145. **EMAIL** whrace@email.unc.edu

RADCHIK, LAURA
PERSONAL Born 05/13/1957, Mexico, s **DISCIPLINE** SPANISH **EDUCATION** Universidad La Salle, BA, 86; UCLA, MA, 91; PhD, 93. **CAREER** Instr, UCLA, 92-; Med Historian, Roback Med Corp, 00-. **HONORS AND AWARDS** Distinguished Teaching Awd, 86; Acad Meric, 93. **MEMBERSHIPS** AATSP, MLA, Am Transl Assoc. **RESEARCH** Spanish American Literature, Spanish as a Second Language. **SELECTED PUBLICATIONS** Auth, "Les memoria de cronos en les maneillas de Dios," Plural, (88): 82-85; auth, "Tempo, soledad y muejte: La encuajada del porta," Logos: Mexico: ULSA 55, (91): 109-117. **CONTACT ADDRESS** 969 Hilgard Ave, Apt 307, Los Angeles, CA 90024-3018. **EMAIL** lradchik@ucla.edu

RAHIMICH, NASRIN
PERSONAL Born 12/30/1958, Iran, m, 1986 **DISCIPLINE** COMPARATIVE LITERATURE **EDUCATION** Dalhousie Univ, BA, 81; MA, 83; Univ Albta, PhD, 88. **CAREER** Asst prof to assoc prof to assoc dean to prof, Univ Albta, 89-. **HONORS AND AWARDS** Canada Res Fel, 89-92; Teaching Awd, Fac Arts, Univ Albta, 00. **MEMBERSHIPS** MLA; MESA; STS. **RESEARCH** Modern Persian literature; post-revolutionary Iranian cinema; comparative European and Eastern literatures; women's literature. **SELECTED PUBLICATIONS** Auth, Oriental Reponses to the West: Comparative Essays in Muslim Writers from the Middle East, E. J. Brill (Leiden), 90; auth, Missing Persian: Discovering Voices in Iranian Cultural Heritage, Syracuse UP (Syracuse), 01. **CONTACT ADDRESS** English Dept, Univ of Alberta, 347 Arts Bldg, Edmonton, AB, Canada T6G 2E6. **EMAIL** nasrin.rahimich@ualberta.edu

RAINER, ULRIKE
DISCIPLINE GERMAN LANGUAGE **EDUCATION** Harvard Univ, PhD, 85. **CAREER** Chair, women's studies prog, 96-98; Assoc prof, Darmouth Col. **RESEARCH** Age of Goethe to the 20th century, centering on poetry and narrative fiction and the interrelation of lit and film. **SELECTED PUBLICATIONS** Auth, publ studies on Fontane, Elfriede Jelinek, Christine Lavant, Schiller, and Trakl. **CONTACT ADDRESS** Dept of German Studies, Dartmouth Col, 6084 Dartmouth Hall, Hanover, NH 03755-3511. **EMAIL** ulrike.rainer@dartmouth.edu

RAINEY, PENELOPE
PERSONAL Born 12/06/1940, New York, NY, m, 1986, 2 children **DISCIPLINE** CLASSICS **EDUCATION** Harvard, BA, 62; Columbia, MA, PhD, 72 **CAREER** Germantown Friends Sch, 74-present. **HONORS AND AWARDS** Phi Beta Kappa, NEH Research grant **MEMBERSHIPS** APA, ALA, Vergehan Soc **RESEARCH** Medieval Latin poetry; classical Latin poetry; Plato **SELECTED PUBLICATIONS** Plato Laches Bryan Manor Commentaries, Medieval Latin Verse **CONTACT ADDRESS** 20 W. Willow Grove Ave., Philadelphia, PA 19118. **EMAIL** pennyr@gfsnet.org

RAKOVA, ALFIA A.
PERSONAL Born 02/03/1958, Russia, m, 2 children **DISCIPLINE** RUSSIAN **EDUCATION** Kazan State Univ, PhD, 84. **CAREER** Sen Instructor, Rostov Russia, 84-91; Visiting Instructor & Translator, Univ IA, 91-99; Preceptor, Harvard Univ, 99-. **HONORS AND AWARDS** Dobro Slovo, Nat Slavic Honor Soc, 93; Awd, Univ IA, 95. **MEMBERSHIPS** AATSEEL **RESEARCH** Russian Language. **SELECTED PUBLICATIONS** Auth, Historical Word-Formation in the Russian Language. Collective monograph, Kazan State Univ Press, 84; auth, Russian Vocabulary, McGraw-Hill, 99. **CONTACT ADDRESS** Dept Slavic Lang, Harvard Univ, 12 Quincy St, Barker Center, Cambridge, MA 02138. **EMAIL** rakova@fas.harvard.edu

RAMBALDO, ANA M.
PERSONAL Born Galvez, Argentina **DISCIPLINE** SPANISH, SPANISH COMMUNITY RELATIONS **EDUCATION** Southern Methodist Univ, BA, 50; NYork Univ, MA, 67, PhD(Span), 71. **CAREER** Asst prof, 67-80, prof Span, Montclair State Col, 80-; retired, 98. **MEMBERSHIPS** MLA. **RESEARCH** Spanish medieval theater; Renaissance. **SELECTED PUBLICATIONS** Auth, El Cancionero de Juan del Encina Dentro de so Ambito Historico y Literario, Castellvi, Arg, 72; Obras Completas de Juan del Encina, Clasicos Castellanos (4 vols), Espasa-Calpe, Madrid, 78-82. **CONTACT ADDRESS** Dept of Span, Montclair State Univ, 1 Normal Ave, Montclair, NJ 07043-1699.

RAMBUSS, RICHARD
PERSONAL Born Buffalo, NY **DISCIPLINE** RENAISSANCE LITERATURE, CULTURAL STUDIES **EDUCATION** Amherst Col, BA, 83; Johns Hopkins Univ, MA, 86, PhD, 90. **CAREER** Asst prof, Kenyon Col, 90-92; asst prof, Tulane Univ, 92-96; assoc prof, Emory Univ, 96-2000, prof, 2000-. **HONORS AND AWARDS** Amherst Col, BA, summa cum laude, 83; Isabel MacCaffrey Prize, 93. **MEMBERSHIPS** MLA, SAA, RSA. **RESEARCH** Renaissance literature and culture; the metaphysical poets; Milton; Spenser; Shakespeare; film. **SELECTED PUBLICATIONS** Auth, Closet Devotions,

Duke UP, 98; Spenser's Secret Career, Cambrigge UP, 93; Spenser's Lives, Spenser's Careers in Spenser and the Subject of Biography, U Mass P, 97; Devotion and Defilement: The Haigiographics of Chaucer's 'Prioress' Tale' in Textual Bodies, SUNY P, 97; Homodevotion in Cruising the Performative, Indiana UP, 95; and Christ's Ganymede, Yale Jour Law Hum, 95. **CONTACT ADDRESS** Dept English, Emory Univ, Atlanta, GA 30322-1061'. **EMAIL** rrambus@emory.edu

RAMEH, CLEA ABDON
PERSONAL Born 01/09/1927, Recife, Brazil **DISCIPLINE** LINGUISTICS; PORTUGUESE LANGUAGE **EDUCATION** Univ Sao Paulo, BA, 47, Lic Anglo-Ger lang, 48, Especialization Anglo-Ger lang, 55; Georgetown Univ, MS, 62, PhD, 70. **CAREER** Teacher English State Schs Sao Paulo, Brazil, 51-63 & Regional Ctr Educ Res, Univ Sao Paulo, 63-65; linguist, Res Proj Port, US Naval Acad, 68-69; from instr to asst prof, 69-75, Assoc Prof Port, Georgetown Univ, 75- ; Chmn Dept, 79-87; Consult, Port Res Proj, US Naval Inst, 69-72; chmn, Georgetown Univ Round Table Lang & Ling, 76. **HONORS AND AWARDS** Gulbenkian Found grant, 80, 81; Fulbright, 59; Phi Beta Kappa, 69; GWATFL Distinguished Educ Awd, 85. **MEMBERSHIPS** Ling Soc Am; MLA; Am Coun Teaching Foreign Lang; Am Asn Teachers Span & Port; Asoc Ling y Filol Am Latina. **RESEARCH** Sociolinguistic implications of Portuguese linguistics; use of computer for language research applied to Portuguese; teaching of foreign languages. **SELECTED PUBLICATIONS** Coauth Portugues Contemporaneo, Vol I, 66, 67, 69, 71, 72 & 75 & Vol II, 67, 69, 71, 73 & 77; auth Toward a computerized syntactic analysis of Portuguese, Comput & Humanities, 9/71; auth, O preparo de material para analise do Portugues em computador, Construtura, 74; ed, Gurt 1976 Semantics: Theory and Application, Georgetown Univ, 76; auth, The Portuguese-English language contact in US, In: The Third Lacus Forum, Hornbeam, 76; Cecilia Meireles: Viagem e Solombra--uma analise linguistics, Rev Brasileira Ling, 77; O Vocabulo Portugues e o Computador, In: SENARA-Revista de filoloxia, Vol II, Colexio Univ, Spain, 80; Aspectos da Lingua Portuguesa nos Estados Unidos da America do Norte, In: From Linguistics to Literature: Romance Studies offered to Francis M Rogers, John Benjamins B V, Holland, 81. **CONTACT ADDRESS** Dept of Spanish & Port, Georgetown Univ, Washington, DC 20057. **EMAIL** ramehc@georgetown.edu

RAMIREZ, ARNULFO G.
DISCIPLINE APPLIED PSYCHOLINGUISTICS, SOCIOLINGUISTICS, SECOND LANGUAGE ACQUISITION **EDUCATION** Stanford Univ, PhD, 74. **CAREER** Prof Hisp Ling, hd, Span sect, dept ch, 89-95; core fac mem, Ling prog, 89-; adj fac mem, Comp Lit prog, 90; mem, the Int Bus Ctr Adv Coun, 93-, La State Univ. **RESEARCH** Bilingualism, language attrition, linguistic approaches to literature. **SELECTED PUBLICATIONS** Auth, El Espantildeol De Los Estados Unidos, Mapfre, 92; Creating Contexts For Second Language Acquisition, Longman, 95. **CONTACT ADDRESS** Dept of For Lang and Lit, Louisiana State Univ, 217 A Prescott Hall, Baton Rouge, LA 70803. **EMAIL** ramirez@lsu.edu

RAMIREZ, MARIA-ESTHER D.
DISCIPLINE SPANISH CIVILIZATION AND CULTURE, SPANISH GRAMMAR, SPANISH COMPOSITION AND **EDUCATION** Univ Madrid, Spain, PhD, 87. **CAREER** Instr Span, mem, undergrad curric comt, 90-; Span textbk sel comt, 93-, La State Univ. **RESEARCH** Social history of the Hispanic groups in different historical periods; acquisition of grammatical and discourse competence. **SELECTED PUBLICATIONS** Auth, San Antonio, Texas, En La Epoca Colonial (1718-1821), Eds de Cult Hispacutenica, 89. **CONTACT ADDRESS** Dept of For Lang and Lit, Louisiana State Univ, 241A Prescott Hall, Baton Rouge, LA 70803. **EMAIL** mdramirez@lsu.edu

RAMOS-GARCIA, LUIS A.
DISCIPLINE SPANISH AND PORTUGUESE LITERATURE **EDUCATION** Univ Tex Austin, BA, 72; MA, 75; PhD, 85. **SELECTED PUBLICATIONS** Auth, A Corrected and Annotated Edition of Pedro Montengon's Frioleras Eruditas, Edwin Mellen, 97; Bilingual Anthology of Contemporary Spanish Poetry: Circa 1970-1990, Edwin Mellen, 97; From the Threshold: Contemporary Peruvian Fiction in Translation, Hisp Studies, 87; ed, Sociolinguistics of the Spanish Speaking World: Iberia, Latin America, and United States, Bilingual Rev, 91. **CONTACT ADDRESS** Spanish and Portuguese Dept, Univ of Minnesota, Twin Cities, 34 Folwell Hall, 9 Pleasant St SE, Minneapolis, MN 55455. **EMAIL** laramosg@maroon.tc.umn.edu

RAMSEY, JOHN T.
PERSONAL Born 07/13/1946, Auburn, NY, m, 1976, 1 child **DISCIPLINE** CLASSICS **EDUCATION** Harvard Col, AB, 68; Balliol Col, BA, 70, MA, 80; Harvard Univ, PhD, 75. **CAREER** Vis assoc prof, Univ Chicago, 82; from asst prof to assoc prof to prof, UIC, 75-. **HONORS AND AWARDS** Phi Beta Kappa, 68; Phi Kappa Phi, 93; NEH Fel, 93-94; AB, summa cum laude; chemn, uic, 97-2000. **MEMBERSHIPS** Am Philological Asn; Asn Ancient Historians; Classical Asn Canada. **RESEARCH** Roman republican history; Roman prose authors; ancient astronomy. **SELECTED PUBLICATIONS** Auth, Studies in Asconius, 76; auth, The Prosecution of C. Manilius in 66 B.C. and Cicero's pro Manilio, 80; auth, Sallusts BELLUM CATILINAE, 84; auth, Cicero & Sallust on the Conspiracy of Catiline, 88; coauth, The Comet of 44 B.C. and Caesar's Funeral Games, 97. **CONTACT ADDRESS** Dept of Classics, Univ of Illinois, Chicago, 601 S Morgan, Chicago, IL 60607-7112. **EMAIL** j-ramsey@uic.edu

RANEY, GEORGE WILLIAM
PERSONAL Born 05/05/1938, Haverhill, MA, m, 1968, 4 children **DISCIPLINE** APPLIED LINGUISTICS, ENGLISH AS A SECOND LANGUAGE, WORLD ENGLISHES **EDUCATION** Loyola Univ Los Angeles, BA, 61; Univ Southern Calif, MA, 66, PhD, 72. **CAREER** Lang coordr, Tagalog, Peace Corps, Philippines, 66 & Univ Hawaii, Hilo, 66; Fulbright lectr teaching English as foreign lang, Adam Mickiewicz Univ, Poznan, 67-68; lectr English as second lang, Univ Southern Calif, 68-69; Consult, Bur Indian Affairs, 67; ed, Calif Ling Newslett, 73-76; asst prof, 69-74, dir Am English Inst, 72-77, fac develop fel, 76, Assoc Prof Ling, Calif State Univ, Fresno, 74-84, Prof, 84-; Dept Chair, 96-2000. **MEMBERSHIPS** Teachers English to Speakers Other Lang; NAS; AAUP. **RESEARCH** TESOL; English grammar; applied linguistics; world Englishes. **SELECTED PUBLICATIONS** Auth, Using the National Observer in the ESOL classroom, Teachers English to Speakers Other Lang Newslett, 4/76; On using the National Observer as an ESOL teaching device, Calif Asn of Teachers English to Speakers Other Lang, fall, 76. **CONTACT ADDRESS** Dept of Ling, California State Univ, Fresno, 5245 N Backer Ave, M/S 92, Fresno, CA 93740-8001. **EMAIL** geor@csufresno.edu

RANWEZ, ALAIN DANIEL
PERSONAL Born 06/25/1944, Paris, France, m, 1968, 2 children **DISCIPLINE** FRENCH LITERATURE **EDUCATION** Montclair State Col, BA, 67; Univ MO, Columbia, PHD, 73. **CAREER** Asst prof French, Northern State Col, 71-72; asst prof, 72-80, Assoc Prof French, Metrop State Col, 80-, Nat Endowment for Humanities fel comp lit, Univ Chicago, 75; mem bibliog staff foreign lang, Am Coun Teachers Foreign Lang, 78-; Nat Endowment for Humanities fel, Wash Univ, 80. **HONORS AND AWARDS** NEH grants. **MEMBERSHIPS** MLA; Am Coun Teachers Foreign Lang; Rocky Mountain Mod Lang Asn; Am Asn Teachers Fr; Colo Cong of Foreign Lang Teachers. **RESEARCH** Post World War II French novel; French feminine writing. **SELECTED PUBLICATIONS** Auth, Baudelaire's Une Charogne, Explicator, Summer 77; Sartre's Les Temps Modernes, Whitston, 79; L Homme-Au-Baton, French Rev, Vol 67, 94; L Ami Du Genre Humain, French Rev, Vol 68, 95; Chemin Decole, French Rev, Vol 70, 96. **CONTACT ADDRESS** Dept of Fr, Metropolitan State Col of Denver, PO Box 173362, Campus Box 026, Denver, CO 80217. **EMAIL** ranweza@mscd.edu

RAO, RAMESH N.
PERSONAL Born 11/18/1956, Ramanagara, m, 2000 **DISCIPLINE** INTERPERSONAL, INTERCULTURAL, AND MASS COMMUNICATION **EDUCATION** Bangalore Univ, India, BA, 77; Univ S MS, MS, 87; MI State Univ, PhD, 92. **CAREER** Assoc prof, 91-, Truman State Univ. **HONORS AND AWARDS** Kulapati award, Bharatiya Vidya Bhavan, India, 85; grad stud award for tchg excellence, Intl Commun Assn, 91. **MEMBERSHIPS** Mem, Nat Commun Assn; Consult Comm on Indic Traditions and Conflict Mgt, Columbia Univ. **RESEARCH** Asian Indians in the US, and hostage negotiations. **SELECTED PUBLICATIONS** Pub(s), Commun Res; Intl Jourf Gp Tensions; Media Devel; Jour Intl Commun. **CONTACT ADDRESS** Dept of Commun, Truman State Univ, 100 E Normal St, Kirksville, MO 63501-4221. **EMAIL** LL88@Truman.edu

RAOUL, VALERIE
PERSONAL Born Shrewsbury, England **DISCIPLINE** FRENCH AND WOMEN'S STUDIES **EDUCATION** Girton Col, Univ Cambridge, BA, 63, MA, 68; London Sch Econ, Dip Social Admin, 64; McMaster Univ, MA, 71, PhD, 78. **CAREER** Tchr, McMaster Univ, Univ Toronto, Ryerson Polytechnic Univ, 70-79; dept Fr, 79-, head dept, 91-96, Prof Univ British Columbia, 92-, dir, Ctr Res Women's Studs & Gender Rels 96-. **MEMBERSHIPS** Asn Prof Fr Can Univs; Asn Can Que Lits; CFH; Asn Chs Fr Depts Can Univs; **SELECTED PUBLICATIONS** Auth, The French Fictional Journal: Fictional Narcissism/Narcissistic Fiction, 79; auth, Distinctly Narcissistic: Diary Fiction in Quebec, 94; co-ed, The Anatomy of Gender: Women's Struggle for the Body, 88. **CONTACT ADDRESS** Dept of French, Univ of British Columbia, 1896 E Mall, Vancouver, BC, Canada V6T 1Z1. **EMAIL** valraoul@interchange.ubc.ca

RAQUIDEL, DANIELLE
DISCIPLINE FRENCH **EDUCATION** Univ Lyon, licence es lettres, 68; Univ Cincinnati, MA, 87; PhD, 92. **CAREER** Res asst, BBC, 74-76; prof, Instituto Universitario Pedagogics, 76-81; assoc prof, Univ Sc, 89-. **HONORS AND AWARDS** Taft grad Fel, 88-89, 89-90. **MEMBERSHIPS** AATS, ALDEEU, SCFLTA. **RESEARCH** 20th century female writers; France, Central America and other countries; Alima Reyes, Caribbean literature. **SELECTED PUBLICATIONS** Auth, Ensemble vol 1, London, 75; auth, Ensemble Vol 2, London, 76; auth, "De la sumision a la subversion: El desafio de la ley del padre en Aqualuma di Christian Santos," Suplemento cultural del nuevo diario, 99: auth, "Labyrinthe obsessif du Iudibrique dans Derriere la porte d'Alina Reyes," Neophiloloques, (99): 51-58; auth, "Opresion, descriminacion y conciencia en la experiencia de Rigoberta Menchu," La literatura centroamericana: Visiones y revisiones, New York, (94): 203-211. **CONTACT ADDRESS** Dept Lang & Fine Arts, Univ of So Carolina, Spartanburg, 800 Univ Way, Spartanburg, SC 29303-4932. **EMAIL** draquidel@uscs.edu

RASCH, WILLIAM
PERSONAL Born 10/25/1949, Waterbury, CT, m, 1977, 1 child **DISCIPLINE** GERMAN STUDIES **EDUCATION** Univ Wash, PhD. **CAREER** Lect, 87-90, Univ Mo; vis asst prof, 90-94, asst prof, Ind Univ, 00-. **MEMBERSHIPS** MLA; AATG; GSA; Int Brecht Soc. **RESEARCH** German philos tradition; social and political theory; Brecht and theater. **SELECTED PUBLICATIONS** Co-ed, Niklas Luhmann's Modernity: The Paradoxes of Differentation edited volume: Observing Complexity: Systems Theory and Postmodernity; ed, Niklas Luhmann: Theories of Sistinction: Re-Describing the Descriptions of Modernity, (forthcoming); Plus numerous articles on Carl Schmitt, Brecht, and the 18th century. **CONTACT ADDRESS** Dept of Germanic Studies, Indiana Univ, Bloomington, Ballantine Hall 644, 1020 E Kirkwood Ave, Bloomington, IN 47405-7103. **EMAIL** wrasch@indiana.edu

RASHKOW, ILONA N.
PERSONAL Born 04/26/1947, New York, NY, m, 1975, 0 child **DISCIPLINE** COMPARATIVE LITERATURE **EDUCATION** Cath Univ Am, BM, 71; Univ Md, MA, 84; PhD, 88. **CAREER** Assoc prof, dir of Graduate Studies, SUNY at Stony Brook, 95-. **HONORS AND AWARDS** Teaching Fel, Univ of MD, 84-85; Univ Fel, Univ of MD, 85-88; NY State/United Univ Professions New Faculty Development Awd, 90; State Univ of NY at Stony Brook Fac Development Grant, 90; American Council of Learned Societies Travel Grant, 90; Vis Chairholder, Aaron Aronov Chair of Judaic Studies, Univ of Ala at Tuscaloosa, 00. **MEMBERSHIPS** Soc Bibl Lit; Am Acad Relig; MLA; Am Comp Lit Asn; World Union Jewish Studies; Asn Jewish Studies; Asn for the Psychoanalysis of Culture and Society. **RESEARCH** Hebrew Bible; Feminist literary criticism; Psychoanalytic literary theory; Women's Studies; Literary theory. **SELECTED PUBLICATIONS** Auth, Upon the Dark Places: Sexism and Anti-Semitism in English Renaissance Biblical Translation, Sheffield, 90; auth, "Intertextuality, Transference, and the Reader in/of the Biblical Text," in Reading Between Texts, ed. Danna Nolan Fewell (Louisville: Westminster/John Knox Press, 92), 57-73; auth, The Phallacy of Genesis: A Feminist-Psychoanalytic Approach, Westminster/John Knox, 93; auth, "Oedipus Wrecks: Moses and God's Rod," in Reading Bibles, Writing Bodies, ed. David Gunn and Timothy Beal (London: Routledge Press, 96) 71-83; auth, "Daddy-Dearest and the 'Invisible Spirit of Wine,'" in Feminist Readings of the Book of Genesis, ed. Athalya Brenner (Sheffield, UK: Sheffield Academic Press, 98) 82-97; auth "Psychoanalytic Literary Theory," in Dictionary of Biblical Interpretation" (Nashville: Abingdon Press, 99) 335-338; auth, "Isis and Osiris/Moses and God: The Power of the Rod," in Feminist Companion to Exodus Through Deuteronomy, ed. Athalya Brenner (Sheffield, UK: Sheffield Academic Press, 00), 64-80; auth, "Lacan," in A Handbook for Postmodern Biblical Interpretation" (St. Louis: Chalice Press, 00) 151-155; auth, Taboo or Not Taboo: The Hebrew Bible and Human Sexuality, Fortress Press, 00; auth, "Esther," in Eerdman's Dictionary of the Bible (Grand Rapids: Erdman's Publishing Company), in press. **CONTACT ADDRESS** Dept of Comparative Studies, SUNY, Stony Brook, Stony Brook, NY 11794-3355. **EMAIL** Ilona.Rashkow@sunysb.edu

RASTALSKY, HARTMUT
DISCIPLINE COMPARATIVE LITERATURE **EDUCATION** Princeton Univ, BA (Mathematics), 86; Univ Mich, MA (Mathematics), 88, MA (Comp Lit), 90, PhD (Comp Lit), 97. **CAREER** LANG PROG DIR, ASST PROF, GER, UNIV MICH, 97-. **CONTACT ADDRESS** Dept of Germanic Lang & Lit, Univ of Michigan, Ann Arbor, 812 E Washington, Ann Arbor, MI 48109-1275. **EMAIL** hmr@umich.edu

RAUCH, IRMENGARD
PERSONAL Born 04/17/1933, Dayton, OH, m, 1965, 2 children **DISCIPLINE** GERMAN **EDUCATION** Univ Dayton, BS, 55; Ohio State Univ, MA, 57; Univ Munich, MA, 58; Univ Mich, PhD, 62. **CAREER** Asst Prof, Univ Wis, 62-66; Assoc Prof, Univ Pittsburgh, 66-68; From Assoc Prof to Prof, Univ Ill, 68-82; Prof, Univ Calif, 82-. **HONORS AND AWARDS** Fulbright Fel, 57-58; Guggenheim Fel, 82-83; Distinguished Alumnus Awd, Univ Dayton, 82. **MEMBERSHIPS** Am Asn of Teachers of Ger, Soc for Ger Philol, Semiotic Soc of Am, Int Asn for Semiotic Studies, Semiotic Circle of Calif, Int Soc of Phonetic Sci, Int Phonetics Asn. **RESEARCH** General Linguistics, German, Gothic, Old Icelandic, Old English, Old Frisian, Old Saxon, Old/Middle/Early New High German, Modern German, Phonology, morphology, syntax, semantics, pragmat-

ics, fieldwork, semiotics. **SELECTED PUBLICATIONS** Auth, The Old High German Diphthongization, 67; auth, Approaches in Linguistic Methodology, 67; auth, Der Heliand, 73; auth, Linguistic Method: Essays in Honor of Herbert Penzl, 79; auth, The Signifying Animal, 80; auth, Language Change, 83; auth, The Semiotic Bridge, 89; auth, The Old Saxon Language, 92; auth, On Germanic Linguistics, 92; auth, Semiotics Around the World, 96; auth, New Insights in Germanic Linguistics I, 99; auth, Semiotic Insights: The Data Do the Talking, 99; auth, New Insights in Germanic Linguistics II, 00. **CONTACT ADDRESS** Dept Lang, Univ of California, Berkeley, 5315 Dwinelle Hall, Berkeley, CA 94720-2521. **EMAIL** irauch@socrates.berkeley.edu

READ, CHARLES
PERSONAL Born 07/10/1940, Clinton, IA, m, 1967, 2 children **DISCIPLINE** LINGUISTICS, PSYCHOLINGUISTICS **EDUCATION** Haverford, Col, AB, 61; Harvard Univ, MAT, 63, PhD, 71. **CAREER** Prof Eng and Ling, Univ WI-Madison, 80-, Ed, Harvard Educ Rev, 65-67; vis sci ling, MA Inst Technol, 73-74; vis scholar ling, Univ Nijmegen, Netherlands, 78-79; chmn dept ling, Univ WI-Madison, 79-82; vis scholar ling, Beijing Normal Univ, 82-83; assoc dean, Grad Sch, 89-95; dean, Sch of Edu, 95-. **MEMBERSHIPS** Ling Soc Am; Acoustical Soc of Am. **RESEARCH** Ling Found of reading and writing. **SELECTED PUBLICATIONS** Auth, Pre-school children's knowledge of English phonology, Harvard Educ Rev, 71; Children's Categorization of Speech Sounds in English, Nat Coun Teachers English, 75; Children's awareness of language, with emphasis on sound systems, In: The Child's Conception of Language, Springer, 78; Creative spelling by young children, In: Standards and dialects in English, Winthrop, 80; Why short subjects are harder to find than long ones, In: Language Acquisition: The State of the Art, Cambridge, 82; Childrens Creative Spelling, Rutledge, 86; The Acoustic Analysis of Speech, Singular, 91. **CONTACT ADDRESS** Deans Office, Univ of Wisconsin, Madison, 1000 Bascom Mall, Madison, WI 53706.

REBAY, LUCIANO
PERSONAL Born 04/23/1928, Milan, Italy **DISCIPLINE** ITALIAN LITERATURE **EDUCATION** Univ Aix Marseille, Lic es Let, 51; Columbia Univ, PhD(Ital), 60. **CAREER** Lectr Ital, Ecole Norm, Ajaccio, France, 48-49, Ecole Norm, Nice, 49-50; prof, Lycee Francais, London, England, 52-55, Lycee Francais, New York, 55-56; from instr to assoc prof, Columbia Univ, 57-63, prof Ital, 65-72; GIUSEPPE UNGARETTI PROF ITAL LIT, 73-; Chamberlain fel, 62-63; Guggenheim fel, 66-67; Am Coun Learned Soc fel, 70-71; fel, Ctr Humanities, Wesleyan Univ, 71; vis prof Ital lit, Univ Calif, Berkeley, spring, 74; vis Mellon prof mod lang, Univ Pittsburgh, fall, 74; Nat Endowment for Humanities fel, 80-81. **MEMBERSHIPS** Am Asn Teachers Ital; MLA. **RESEARCH** Contemporary Italian literature; Italian lyric poetry; Franco-Italian comparative literature. **SELECTED PUBLICATIONS** Auth, Le origini della poesia di Giuseppe Ungaretti, Ed Storia e Lett, 62; I diaspori di Montale, Italica, 69; Invitation to Italian Poetry, Dover, 69; Alberto Moravia, Columbia Univ, 70; La rete a strascico di Montale, Forum Italicum, 71; co-ed, Giuseppe Ungaretti, Saggi e interventi, Mondadori, Milan, 74; Sull autobiografismo di Montale, Olschki, Florence 76; Ungaretti: Gli Scritti Egiziani 1909-1912, Forum Italicum, 80. **CONTACT ADDRESS** Columbia Univ, 513 Hamilton Hall, New York, NY 10027.

RECK, RIMA DRELL
PERSONAL Born 09/29/1933, New York, NY, m, 1956 **DISCIPLINE** COMPARATIVE LITERATURE **EDUCATION** Brandeis Univ, BA, 54; Yale Univ, PhD(Romance lang), 60. **CAREER** Instr French, Tulane Univ, 58-61; from asst prof to assoc prof French & comp lit, 61-68, res coun grant, 64, Prof Comp Lit, Univ New Orleans, 68-, Am Philos Soc res grants, 62, 64; assoc ed, Southern Rev, 63-; Am Coun Learned Soc res grant, 68; Guggenheim fel, 72-73. **MEMBERSHIPS** MLA; Am Asn Teachers Fr; SCent Mod Lang Asn; Am Comp Lit Asn; Soc Amis Marcel Proust. **RESEARCH** French novel of the 20th century; the novel and its relation to other arts; 19th century Russian literature. **SELECTED PUBLICATIONS** Coauth, Studies in Comparative Literature, 62, ed, Explorations of Literatue, 66 & auth, Literature and Responsibility: The French Novelist in the Twentieth Century, 69, La State Univ; Old and new in the French new novel, Southern Rev, 10/65; Celine and the Aural Novel, Bks Abroad, 65; coauth, Bernanos, Confrontations, Minard, Paris, 66 & The New Orleans Cookbook, 74; auth, The crises of French nationalism in the twentieth century, In: The Cry of Home, Univ Tenn, 72. **CONTACT ADDRESS** Dept of Foreign Lang, Univ of New Orleans, New Orleans, LA 70122.

RECTOR, MONICA PAULA
PERSONAL Born 08/03/1940, Sao Paulo, Brazil, 2 children **DISCIPLINE** PORTUGUESE AND BRAZILIAN LITERATURE PORTUGUESE AND BRAZILIAN LITERATURE **EDUCATION** Univ Sao Paulo, Brazil, BA, 62; MA, 70; PhD, 70; Universidade Federal do Rio de Janeiro, PhD, 75. **CAREER** Assoc prof, Univ Sao Paula, 67-70; prof, Pontificia Univ Catholica of Rio de Janeiro, 71-89; prof, Universidade Federal do Rio de Janeiro, 73-89; prof, Universidade Federal Fluminense, 78-89; vis prof, Univ North Carolina, 87, assoc prof, 89-97, full prof, 97-. **HONORS AND AWARDS** Ctr for European Studies, UNC, Travel Grant to Portugal, 95; W. R. Kenan Grant, UNC, spring 96; Mellon Fac Res Travel Awd, May-June 97; Biblioteca Nacional de Lisboa and Fundacao Luso-Americana re grant, 98. **MEMBERSHIPS** AATSP, ADS, APSA, ABS, Associacao Int de Lusitanistas, BRASA, IASS, MLA, NAB, SSA, SBPC, SBPL, SAMLA, Toronto Semiotic Circle. **RESEARCH** Portuguese and Brazilian Contemporary Literature, Women Writing, Semiotics. **SELECTED PUBLICATIONS** Auth, Bimba pensa na fazenda, Belo Horizonte: Ed. Comunicacao, Brasilia, (97, 80, 81); auth, Duas Selvas. Belo Horizonte: Ed. Comunicacao (81); auth, "The Code and Message of Carnival: Escolas-de-Samba," in Carnival!, Thomas A. Sebeok, ed, Berlin, NY, Amsterdam: Mouton (84, also pub in Japan and Mexico); coauth with Aluizio R. Trinta, Comunicacao do corpo, Sao Paulo: Atica (90); auth, A fala dos jovens, Petropolis: Vozes (94); co-ed with Eduardo Neiva, Comunicacao na era pos-moderna, Petropolis: Vozes (97, 98); auth, Muhler, sujeito e objeto da literatura portuguesa, Oporto: Fernando Pessoa Univ Press (99). **CONTACT ADDRESS** Dept Romance Langs, Univ of No Carolina, Chapel Hill, 440 W Franklin St, Chapel Hill, NC 27599-3170. **EMAIL** rector@email.unc.edu

REDFIELD, JAMES M.
PERSONAL Born Chicago, IL, m, 4 children **DISCIPLINE** CLASSICAL LANGUAGE AND LITERATURE **EDUCATION** Univ Chicago, BA, 54, PhD, 61. **CAREER** Instr, Comt Soc Thought, 60-62; Asst prof, 62-65; Assoc prof, 65-75; Prof, Univ Chicago, 76-. **HONORS AND AWARDS** Woodrow Wilson Fel; NEH Younger Sch; Am Coun Learned Socs; Martha Sutton Weeks Fel; NEH Grant. **MEMBERSHIPS** APA. **SELECTED PUBLICATIONS** Auth, Anthropology and the Classics, Arion, 91; auth, The Politics of Immortality, Recherches et Rencontres, 91; auth, The Sexes in Hesiod, Reinterpreting the Classics, 93; auth, Homo Domesticus, the Greeks, Univ Chicago Press, 94; auth, "Nature and Culture in the Iliad: The Tragedy of Hector," 2nd ed, Duke Univ Press, 94. **CONTACT ADDRESS** Univ of Chicago, 1126 E 59th St, SS Box 94, Chicago, IL 60637. **EMAIL** jmredfie@midway.uchicago.edu

REED, GERVAIS EYER
PERSONAL Born 08/06/1931, Greeley, CO, m, 1960, 2 children **DISCIPLINE** FRENCH **EDUCATION** Princeton Univ, AB, 54; Brown Univ, MA, 62, PhD(French), 64. **CAREER** Asst prof, 64-70, assoc prof, 70-81, Prof French, Lawrence Univ, 81- **MEMBERSHIPS** MLA; Am Asn Teachers French. **RESEARCH** French 17th century literature and bibliography. **SELECTED PUBLICATIONS** Auth, Claude Barbin, libraire de Paris sous le regne de Louis XIV, Droz, Geneva; Moliere's Privilege of 18 March 1671, The Library, 65; Stylistic and thematic parallels in Corneille's Theatre and his imitation de Jesus Christ, Symposium, XXXIII: 263-87. **CONTACT ADDRESS** Dept of French, Lawrence Univ, Appleton, WI 54911.

REED, WALTER
PERSONAL Born 02/09/1943, New York, NY, m, 1964, 3 children **DISCIPLINE** ENGLISH AND COMPARATIVE LITERATURE **EDUCATION** Yale, BA, 65; Yale, PhD, 69; Univ of Texas a Austin; Emery Univ, English and Comparative Literature. **CAREER** Fac, Yale Univ; fac, Univ Tex Austin; prof/chemn dept, Emery Univ, 87-. **HONORS AND AWARDS** Guggenheim Fel, 77-78; NEH, 95; Univ Scholar/Teacher Awd, Emery, 00; co-dir, neh summer sem col tchrs, 95. **MEMBERSHIPS** MLA, SAMLA, IATS. **RESEARCH** Romanticism, History and Theory of the Novel, Bible as literature. **SELECTED PUBLICATIONS** auth, Meditations on the Hero, 74; auth, An Exemplary History of the Novel, 81; auth, Dialogues of the Word, 93. **CONTACT ADDRESS** English Dept, Emory Univ, 1380 Oxford Rd NE, Atlanta, GA 30322-1950. **EMAIL** wlreed@emory.edu

REEDER, HEIDI M.
DISCIPLINE INTERPERSONAL COMMUNICATION, RELATIONAL COMMUNICATION **EDUCATION** Univ OR, BS, summa cum laude, 91; Stanford Univ, MA, 93; AZ State Univ, PhD, 96. **CAREER** Dept Comm, Univ NC **RESEARCH** Interpersonal commun; male-female relationships. **SELECTED PUBLICATIONS** Auth, The subjective experience of love through adult life, Int J of Aging and Human Develop, 43, 96; coauth, Unwanted escalation of sexual intimacy: Male and female perceptions of connotations and relational consequences of resistance messages, Commun Monogr, 62, 95; Disclosure of sexual abuse by children and adolescents, J of Appl Commun, 24, 96. **CONTACT ADDRESS** Dept of Commun Stud, Univ of No Carolina, Greensboro, 102 Fergus, Greensboro, NC 27412-5001. **EMAIL** hmreeder@hamlet.uncg.edu

REEVES-MARQUARDT, DONA
PERSONAL Born 03/09/1932, Kansas City, MO, w, 1985, 5 children **DISCIPLINE** GERMAN **EDUCATION** Univ Tex, BA, 53, MA, 55, PhD, 63. **CAREER** From istr to prof, Ger, 61-98; chemn, Dept of Mod Lang, 67-71; dir, Multicultural and Gender Studies, 84-86; prof emer, Ger, SW Tex State Univ, 98-; vis prof, Univ Wisc-Eau Claire, 91-92. **HONORS AND AWARDS** Fed Repub Ger for office study tour, 72; Danforth Asn, 77-86; Fulbright Summer Sem, 80; Cert of Merit, AATG & Goethe House NY, 78; For Lang Teacher Awd, TFLA, 81. **MEMBERSHIPS** Am Asn Teachers Ger; MLA; Am Coun Teaching Foreign Lang; S Cent Mod Lang Asn; Soc of Ger-Am Studies. **RESEARCH** Medieval and Renaissance Ger lit and philol; language teaching and linguistics; Ger-Am; Ger-Russ studies **SELECTED PUBLICATIONS** Auth, "Public Awareness, Am Coun Tchg For Lang Rev For Lang Educ (11/74); coauth, "Germans along the Guadalupe, Die Unterrichtspraxis (77); co-ed, Texas Country. The Changing Rural Scene, Tex A&M Univ, 86; co-trans, David Weigum: "My Home on the Crimean Steepe," Am Hist Soc Ger from Russ, 877; transl, Peter Sinner: "Germans in the Land of the Volga,: Am Hist Soc Ger from Russ, 89; co-trans, Gottieb Beratz: "German Colonies on the Lower Volga," Am Hist Soc Ger from Russ, 91; auth, "German Galveston: A Personal Narrative," Schatzkammer der deutschen Sprache, Dichtung und Geschichte, 91; auth, "A German Russian Artist from Kansas: E. Hubert Deines," J, Am Hist Soc Ger from Russ, 98. **CONTACT ADDRESS** 7116 Foxtree Cv, Austin, TX 78750-7918. **EMAIL** dr03@swt.edu

REGALADO, NANCY FREEMAN
PERSONAL Born 06/08/1935, Boston, MA, m, 1983, 2 children **DISCIPLINE** FRENCH LITERATURE **EDUCATION** Wellesley Col, BA, 57; Yale Univ, PhD, 66. **CAREER** Asst instr French, Yale Univ, 58-62, actg instr, 62-65; from instr to asst prof, Wesleyan Univ, 65-67; from asst prof to assoc prof, 68-77, prof French, 77-, NY Univ; NEH fel, 79-80; Am Coun Learned Soc grant, 79. **HONORS AND AWARDS** ACLS fel, 88; NEH fel, 79-80, 92; Officier de l'Ordre des Palmes Academiques, 92; Guggenheim fel, 93-94. **MEMBERSHIPS** MLA; Mediaeval Acad Am; International Courtly Lit Soc; Early Book Soc; International Center of Medieval Art. **RESEARCH** Medieval French literature; performance. **SELECTED PUBLICATIONS** Coauth, Feste: The Account of the 1313 Celebration of the Knighting of the Three Sons of Philip the Fair in the Chronique Metrique of in BN Ms Fr. 146, City and Spectacle in Medieval Europe, Minnesota, 94; contribur, Garland Encyclopedia of Medieval Literature, Garland, 95; auth, Speaking in Script: The Construction of Voice, Presence, and Perspective in Villon's TestamentOral Tradition in the Middle Ages, CEMERS, 95; auth, Staging the Roman de Renart: Medieval Theater and the Diffusion of Political Concerns into Popular Culture, Mediaevalia, 95; auth, Le Porcher au palais; Kalila et Dimna, Le Roman de Fauvel, Machaut, et Boccace, Etudes Litteraires, 98; auth, The Chronique Metrique and the Moral Design of Paris; Feasts of Good and Evil, Fauvel Studies, Oxford, 98. **CONTACT ADDRESS** Dept of French, New York Univ, 100 Bleecker St, Apt 7D, New York, NY 10012. **EMAIL** nancy.regalado@nyu.edu

REGINALD, ALLEN
DISCIPLINE CLASSICS **EDUCATION** Haverford, AB, 53; Yale Univ, MA, 55; St Andrews, BPhil, 57; Yale Univ, PhD, 58. **CAREER** Prof, Northwestern Univ, 78-. **RESEARCH** Socratic Ethics; Plato's Ion; Hippias Minor; Laches; Protagoras; Lysias. **SELECTED PUBLICATIONS** Auth, Collected Dialogues of Plato, v.II, Yale, 91; ed, R. E. Allen, Plato's Parmineds, trans and analysis, Univ Minn. **CONTACT ADDRESS** Dept of Classics, Northwestern Univ, Kresge 15, Evanston, IL 60201-2200. **EMAIL** r-allen2@nwu.edu

REGOSIN, RICHARD L.
DISCIPLINE FRENCH LANGUAGE **EDUCATION** Johns Hopkins Univ, PhD. **CAREER** Prof, Fr, Univ Calif, Irvine. **SELECTED PUBLICATIONS** Auth, Agrippa d'Aubigne's 'Les Tragiques'; The Poetry of Inspiration; The Matter of My Book: Montaigne's 'Essais' as the Book of the Self; Montaigne's Unruly Brood: Textual Engendering & the Challenge to Paternal Authority; pub(s), articles on sixteenth-century Fr lit. **CONTACT ADDRESS** Dept of Fr and Ital, Univ of California, Irvine, Irvine, CA 92697. **EMAIL** uci-cwis-support@uci.edu

REGUEIRO, JOSE MIGUEL
PERSONAL Born 12/20/1930, Cordoba, Argentina **DISCIPLINE** SPANISH LITERATURE **EDUCATION** Univ Pa, PhD(Span), 72. **CAREER** From instr to asst prof, 70-78, Assoc Prof Span, Univ PA, 78- **MEMBERSHIPS** Renaissance Soc Am; MLA; Am Asn Teachers Span & Port; AAUP. **RESEARCH** Spanish medieval and Renaissance theater; Spanish Golden Age literature. **SELECTED PUBLICATIONS** Auth, A catalogue of the Comedia collection at the University of Pennsylvania Libraries, 71; coauth, Dramatic Manuscripts in the Hispanic Society of America, 78; contrib reviews and articles to literary publications. **CONTACT ADDRESS** Dept of Romance Lang, Univ of Pennsylvania, 34th and Spruce St, Philadelphia, PA 19104.

REHM, RUSH
DISCIPLINE CLASSICS; DRAMA **EDUCATION** BA, 73; MA, 75; Stanford Univ, PhD, 85. **CAREER** Assoc prof, Stanford Univ. **RESEARCH** Greek tragedy. **SELECTED PUBLICATIONS** Auth, The Oresteia: A Theatre Version, 78; auth, Greek Tragic Theatre, 92; Marriage to Death: The Conflation of Marriage and Funeral Rituals in Greek Tragedy, 94; auth, The Play of Space: Spatial Transformations in Greek Tragedy, 01. **CONTACT ADDRESS** Stanford Univ, 551 Serra Mall, Stanford, CA 94305-5010. **EMAIL** mrehm@stanford.edu

REID, CONSTANCE L.
PERSONAL Born Neptune, NJ **DISCIPLINE** GERMAN **EDUCATION** S Methodist Univ, BA, 62; Ind Univ, MA, 64; PhD, 80. **CAREER** Assoc Instructor, Ind Univ, 78-79; Instructor, Gettysburg Col, 64-69; Asst Prof, Univ Colo, 80-82; Lecturer, Vanderbilt Univ, 82-83; Asst Prof to Prof, Truman State Univ, 83-. **HONORS AND AWARDS** Goethe-Inst, 96; Fac Res Grant, Truman State Univ, 88-89; Grant, 87-88; Awd, Goethe-Institus, 90; Pi Lambda Theta, 72; Fulbright-Hays Awd, 68; Ford Foundation Fac Fel, 68; Awd, US Office of Educ, 67. **MEMBERSHIPS** Am Asn of Applied Ling; Am Asn of Teachers of German; Am Asn of Univ Supervisors and Coordinators of For Lang Prog; Am Coun for the Study of Austrian Lit; Am Coun on the Teaching of For Lang; Cent States Conf; For Lang Ans of MO; German Studies Asn. **RESEARCH** German civilization and culture; Teaching English as a second language; Foreign language testing and assessment. **SELECTED PUBLICATIONS** Auth, "A Linguistic Coordinator," Journal of the National Association of Language Laboratory Directors, (68): 9-11; auth, "Discovery of Latent Structure as the Major Process in Language Acquisition: Implications for the Second Language Program," Foreign Language Annals, (73): 481-486; auth, "Problems in Writing the Spanish Business Letter: An Analysis of Interferences between Spanish and English," International Review of Applied Linguistics, (74): 252-258; auth, "The Acquisition of the Verb-Subject Structure-Rule by Gastarbeiterkinder: Implications for the Teaching of German," Die Unterrichtspraxis, (81): 195-207; auth, "Informationsseminare Berlin: A Description and a Classroom Application," Schatzkammer der deutschen Sprache, Dichtung und Geschichte, (85): 41-48. **CONTACT ADDRESS** Dept Lang & Lit, Truman State Univ, 100 E Normal St, Kirksville, MO 63501-4200.

REID, LAWRENCE ANDREW
PERSONAL Born 06/02/1934, New Zealand, 4 children **DISCIPLINE** LINGUISTICS **EDUCATION** Univ Hawaii, MA, 64, PhD, 66. **CAREER** Instr phonetics & grammar, Summer Inst Ling, Australia, 58-59; field researcher Bontok, Summer Inst Ling, Philippines, 59-63; field researcher Ivatan & Austronesian lang, Philippines & Taiwan, 65; instr ling, Univ Hawaii, 66; asst dir, Summer Inst Ling, Univ Auckland, 67; field researcher, Philippines, 68; chief ling consult, Summer Inst Ling, Philippines, 69; from asst linguist to assoc linguist, Pac & Asian Ling Inst, Univ Hawaii, Manoa, 70-77; Researcher Ling, Soc Sci Res Inst & Dept Ling, Univ Hawaii, 77-; Vis prof, Univ Auckland, 78; ed, Filipinas, 82-85; vis res prof, Institute for the Study of the Languages and Cultures of Asia and Africa, Tokyo Univ of Foreign Studies, 91-92, 98-99. **HONORS AND AWARDS** E-W Center Fel, 64; E-W Center Excellence in Scholarship Awd, 66; Nat Science Found Grant, 70, 93; UH Intramural Research Awd, 72, 73; UH Summer Research Initiation Awd, 72; UH Research Travel Awd, 72; Ford Found Asia Prog Res Fel, 74; NEH Grant, 74; Uh Res Travel Grant, 76, 80, 82, 85, 87, 88, 95; Pacific Area Lang Materials devel Center Office of Bilingual Ed Title VII Grant, 79; Am Coun of Learned Soc Travel Grant, 85; Computers for Pacific Lang Res Database--UH Vice-Pres for Res Grant, 86; Optical Character Scanner for the Pacific Lang Res Database--UH Res Relations Fund Grant, 87; UH Res Initiation Grant, 87; Wenner-Gren Found Res Grant, 90; Res Grant--Tokyo Univ Foreign Studies, 91; UH CSEAS Conference Travel Grant, 94, 95, 98; Anonymous Grant--Tasaday Res, 94-97; UH Res Relations Travel Grant, 97. **MEMBERSHIPS** Ling Soc NZ; Ling Soc Philippines; Ling Soc Am; Polynesian Soc; Asn Asian Studies. **RESEARCH** Philippine and aboriginal Formosan descriptive and comparative linguistics; ethnography of Northern Luzon; discourse analysis; the Austric hypothesis. **SELECTED PUBLICATIONS** Auth, A Guinaang Wedding Ceremony, Philippine Sociol Rev, 61; An Ivatan Syntax, Univ Hawaii, 66; ed, Philippine Minor Languages: Word Lists and Phonologies, Univ Hawaii, 72; auth, Central Bontoc: Discourse, Paragraph and Sentence Structures, Summer Inst Ling, 72; Diachronic Typology of Philippine Vowel Systems, In: Current Trends in Linguistics, Vol XI, Mouton, The Hague, 73; Bontoc-English Dictionary and Finder List, Pac Ling Ser C, 74; The Problem *R and *1 Reflexes in Kankanay, In: Festschrift in Honor of Cecilio Lopez, Ling Soc Philippines, 74; The State of the Art of Philippine Linguistics, 1970-1980, In: Philippine Studies: Political Science, Economics, and Linguistics, Occas Papers Ctr for Southeast Asian Studies, No 8, Northern IL Univ, 81; auth, Benedict's Austro-Tai Hypothesis, Asian Perspectives, 26, 84-85; The Early Switch Hypothesis: Linguistic Evidence for Contact Between Negritos and Austronesians, Man and Culture in Oceania 3, 87; Guinaang Bontok Texts, Institute for the Study of the Languages and Cultures of Asia and Africa, Monograph Series, Tokyo Univ Foreign Studies, 92; Unraveling the Linguistic Histories of Philippine Negritos, in T. E. Dutton and D. T. Tryon, eds, Language Contact and Change in the Austronesian World, Berlin: Mouton de Gruyter, 94; The Current State of Linguistic Research on the Relatedness of the Language Families of East and Southeast Asia, in Ian C. Glover and Peter Bellwood, ed coordinators, Indo-Pacific Prehistory: The Chiang Mai Papers, vol 2, Bulletin of the Indo-Pacific Prehistory Asn 15, Canberra: Australian Nat Univ, 96; Archaelogical Linguistics: Tracking Down the Tasaday Language, in Robert Blench, ed, Proceedings of the 3rd World Congress of Archaeologists, New Delhi, India, 97; and numerous other articles, papers, and research projects. **CONTACT ADDRESS** Dept of Ling, Univ of Hawaii, Manoa, 1890 E West Rd, Honolulu, HI 96822-2318. **EMAIL** reid@hawaii.edu

REID, PETER L. D.
PERSONAL Born 01/30/1937, Edinburgh, Scotland, m, 1995, 2 children **DISCIPLINE** CLASSICS **EDUCATION** Cambridge Univ, BA, 60, MA, 64; UCLA, PhD, 74. **CAREER** Tchr, 60-70; Sec Sch in Scotland, NZ, USA; Asst Prof, Assoc Prof, Prof, 73-, Class, Tufts Univ. **HONORS AND AWARDS** NEH Inst for Tchr. **MEMBERSHIPS** APA. **RESEARCH** Medieval Latin **SELECTED PUBLICATIONS** Auth, Ratherii Veronensis: Opera Minora, Brepols, Corpus Christianorum, Cont Mediaevalis XLVI, 76; Tenth Century Latinity, Undena, 81; Ratherii Veronensis: Opera Maiora, Brepols, Corpus Christianorum, Cont Med XLVIA, 84; Rather of Verona: Complete Works in Translation, CEMERS, Binghamton, 91; Reviewed in; Church History, 95; Speculum, 94; Manuscripta, 92; Ecclesiastical History, 93. **CONTACT ADDRESS** Dept of the Classics, Tufts Univ, Medford, Medford, MA 02155. **EMAIL** preid@infonet.tufts.edu

REIDEL-SCHREWE, URSULA
PERSONAL Born Hamburg, Germany **DISCIPLINE** GERMAN LANGUAGE, LITERATURE AND CULTURE **EDUCATION** Harvard Univ, MA, PhD. **CAREER** Assoc prof, Colby Col. **SELECTED PUBLICATIONS** Publ, Bk, articles, narrative theory and early 20th-century Ger lit. **CONTACT ADDRESS** Dept of Ger, Colby Col, 4450 Mayflower Hill, Waterville, ME 04901-8840. **EMAIL** u_reidel@colby.edu

REILLY, LINDA
DISCIPLINE CLASSICAL STUDIES **EDUCATION** Vassar Col, AB, 65; Johns Hopkins Univ, MA, 66, PhD, 69. **CAREER** Assoc prof, 74-; ch, 92-95; asst prof, 69-74; assoc provest, 81-86 & dean Undergrad Progr and asst VP for Acad Aff, Col William and Mary; Abby Leach fel, low, Amer Sch Class Stud, Athens, Greece, 66-67; Ctr Hellenistic Stud, Wash, 74-75; sr res assoc, Amer Sch Class Stud, Athens, Greece, 86-87 & 95-96. **RESEARCH** Ancient dogs; Ancient city; Neoclassical traditions in North America. **SELECTED PUBLICATIONS** Auth, Slaves in Ancient Greece, Ares Publishers, 78, repr, 84; The Dogs from the Hunting Frieze at Vergina, J Hellenic Stud, Vol 113, 93; A Greek Inscription at Williamsburg, Amer J Archaeol, 74; New Inscriptions from Echinos, Amer J Philol, 71; Who Stole the Sphinx's Nose, Mediter Soc Am, Richmond, 96; participant and guest lecturer, La State Semr for High Sch Humanities Teachers, Northwestern State Univ, Natchidoches, 93; A Protogemometric Naiskos From Crete CAMWS, Boulder, 97; Neo-Classical Achitecture in Williamsburg, VA, CAMWS-SS, Richmond, 92; Kerberos and Orthos: Two Monstrous Brothers, given at CAMWS in Austin, 92; Rumpus: One of A Kind, Dog World, 86 & Rumpus: A Full Life for a Deaf Corgi, Dog World, 90. **CONTACT ADDRESS** Dept of Classical Studies, Col of William and Mary, Morton Hall, Williamsburg, VA 23187-8795. **EMAIL** lcreil@morton.wm.edu

REINKING, VICTOR
DISCIPLINE FRENCH **EDUCATION** Univ CO, BA, 70; Univ WA, MA, 86, PhD, 93. **CAREER** Languages, Seattle Univ. **SELECTED PUBLICATIONS** Auth, Riddle on the Way to the Bottom: Moroccan Summer, poetry, Greensboro, NC: Int Poetry Rev, 90; Rousseau's Bliss: Jouissance, Oxford Univ, Voltaire Found: Stud on Voltair and the 18th Century, 95; Associate editor's Perspective on Critical Approaches, Seattle and Nantes, France: Para*doxa, 95; rev(s), in A Vietnam War Filmography, NY: MacFarlan, 93, contrib 7 rev(s) & commentaries on films depict/facultying US involvement in Vietnam War; transl, Suns Under Arrest & other poems by Abdellatif Laabi: Greensboro, NC: Int Poetry Rev, 91; Phenomenology and Ontology: Hannah Arrendt and Maurice Merleau-Ponty, article included Contemp Perspectives on Merleau-Ponty, Brussels, Kluver, 93; For a Poetics of Paraliterature, Part I: Paraliterature and the Oral Tradition, Seattle and Nantes, France: Para*doxa, 95; For a poetics of Paraliterature, Part II: Paraliterature and Rhetoric, Seattle and Nantes, France: Para*doxa, 95. **CONTACT ADDRESS** Dept of For Lang, Seattle Univ, 900 Broadway, Seattle, WA 98122-4460. **EMAIL** vicr@seattleu.edu

REINSHAGEN-JOHO, LIANE
DISCIPLINE LATIN-AMERICAN AND SPANISH LITERATURES AND SPANISH LANGUAGE **EDUCATION** Univ Wash, Seattle, PhD. **CAREER** Vis prof Span, Univ Nev, Reno. **RESEARCH** The phenomenology of the non-monolingual speaker; 19th Century Mexican and German literatures. **SELECTED PUBLICATIONS** Published translations of Graham Greene and Edna St. Vincent Millay. **CONTACT ADDRESS** Univ of Nevada, Reno, Reno, NV 89557. **EMAIL** reinshag@scs.unr.edu

REISS, CHARLES
DISCIPLINE PHONOLOGY **EDUCATION** Swarthmore Col, BA, 85; Harvard Univ, MA, 90, PhD, 95. **CAREER** Asst prof, dir, 95-; adj res prof, Carleton Univ, 98-; tchr, 5th Cent Europ Summer Sch in Generative Ling, Debrecen, Hungary, 98; vis res, Umea Univ, 97; adj asst prof, McGill Univ, 96; lectr, Harvard Univ Summer Sch, 95; res assoc, Harvard Univ, 95; preceptor, Harvard Univ, 95; lectr, Boston Univ, 94-95; asst Hd Tutor, Harvard Univ, 89-94; tchg fel, Harvard Univ, 89-94; lectr, Brandeis Univ, 93. **HONORS AND AWARDS** Res coun grants, Can Soc Sci and Hum, 95-96, 96-97; summer research travel grant, Concordia Univ, 97; Affinity MasterCard award, Concordia Univ, 96-97; Eva and Einar Haugen award, Scandinavian Forum, 94; Hoopes prize, Harvard Univ, 94; wrtg fel, Harvard Univ, 93; Howard Osborn scholar, Swarthmore Col, 84; Concordia Univ Fac Res Dev Program Grant, 99-01; manuscript ref, ling inquiry, can jour ling; abstract rev, e states conf ling, 97, yale univ, 97. **MEMBERSHIPS** Mem, Ling Soc Am, SIGPHON. **RESEARCH** Phonological Theory, Phonetics, Cognitive Science, Learnability and Acquisition of Phonology, Morphology, Historical Linguistics, Germanic, Old Icelandic, Cree. **SELECTED PUBLICATIONS** Coauth, Evidence in Phonological Acquisition: Implications for the Initial Ranking of Faithfulness Constraints, Proceedings of the 28th Annual Child Language Res Forum, Cambridge Univ Press, (97): 143-152; auth, The origin of the nn/ alternation in Old Icelandic, North West European Language Evolution 30, (97): 135-158; coauth, How To Parse and How Not To, Proceeding of the Northeast Linguistics Soc 27, (97): 159-170; coauth, What is Output? Output-Output Correspondence in OT Phonology, Proceedings of West Coast Conference on Formal Linguistics XVI, CSLI Publications, Cambridge Univ Press, 97; coauth, On the Empirical Basis of Output-Output Correspondence, Univ of Toronto Working Papers in Linguistics, (97): 61-75; coauth, Formal and Empirical Argumentsss concerning Phonological Acquisition, Linguistic Inquiry 29, (98): 656-683; co-ed, Working Papers from the Department of Classics, Modern Languages and Linguistics, Vol II, Concordia Univ, 99; coauth, Substance abuse and dysfunctionalism: Current trends in phonology, Linguistic Inquiry 313, (00): 157-169. **CONTACT ADDRESS** Dept of Classics, Mod Lang and Ling, Concordia Univ, Montreal, 1455 de Maisonneuve W, Montreal, QC, Canada H3G 1M8. **EMAIL** reiss@alcor.concordia.ca

REITZ, RICHARD ALLEN
PERSONAL Born 09/14/1937, Clay Center, KS, m, 1966, 1 child **DISCIPLINE** SPANISH **EDUCATION** Univ KS, BA, 59, MA, 61; Univ KY, PhD, 70. **CAREER** Instr Span, VA Mil Inst, 59-60; asst prof, Univ Kans, 60-61; asst prof, Univ Ky, 67-68; assoc prof, 63-74, prof, 74, Dept of Span Ch, Catawba Col, 97-00. **HONORS AND AWARDS** Nat Endowment for the Hum Sem fel, Univ Pittsburgh, 75. **MEMBERSHIPS** Am Asn Tchr(s) Span & Port. **RESEARCH** Span Am lit; Brazilian lit; Faulkerian influences on Gabriel Garcia Marquez. **SELECTED PUBLICATIONS** Translr, Noticias Secretas, R & D Bks, Salisbury, NC, 78. **CONTACT ADDRESS** Catawba Col, 227 Windsor Dr., Salisbury, NC 28144-7722. **EMAIL** rreitz@salisbury.net

REJHON, ANNALEE C.
PERSONAL Born 07/23/1949, Bathurst, Australia, m, 1981, 1 child **DISCIPLINE** MEDIEVAL MODERN WELSH, FRENCH LANGUAGE AND LITERATURE **EDUCATION** Univ Calif, Berkeley, AB, 71; MA, 73; PhD, 79. **CAREER** Lectr, ACLS, Cal State Univ, 80-81; lectr, Univ Cal, Berkeley, 79-. **HONORS AND AWARDS** Theresa F Colin Fel; ACLS Fel; APS Grant, 85, 91; ACLS Trv Grant; Fulbright Trv Grant; Univ Wales Vernam Hull Prize; NEH Grant. **MEMBERSHIPS** MAA; IAS; MAP; CSANA. **RESEARCH** Medieval French epic and romance; medieval French epics preserved in Middle Welsh; the interface between medieval French and Welsh cultures as seen in medieval French and Welsh romances; Indo-European mythology. **SELECTED PUBLICATIONS** Auth, The Song of Roland: Text of the Paris Version, Univ Calif Press, forthcoming; auth, C%on Rolant: The Medieval Welsh Version of the Song of Roland, in Modern Philology 113, Univ Calif Press (Berkeley and Los Angeles), 84; auth, "The Effects of Oral and Written Transmission in the Exchange of Materials between Medieval Celtic and French Literatures: A Physiological View," Oral Tradition 5 (90): 131-48; auth, "The French Reception of a Celtic Motif: The P leringe de Charlemagne, " J rusalem et " Constantinople," Zeitschrift fYr Celtische Philologie 42 (87): 344-61; auth, "The 'Mute Knight' and the 'Knight of the Lion': Implications of the Hidden Name Motif in the Welsh Historia Peredur vab Efrawc and Chr tien de Troyes' Yvain ou le Chevalier au Lion," Studia Celtica 20-21 (85-86): 110-122; auth, "Hu Gadarn: Folklore and Fabrication," in Celtic Folklore and Christianity: Studies in Memory of William W Heist, ed. Patrick K Ford, Cen for the Study of Comparative Folklore and Mythology (Univ Calif, Los Angeles and Santa Barbara: McNally and Loftin, 83): 201-12; auth, "The Roland-Oliver Relationship in the Welsh Version of the Chanson de Roland," Romance Philology 35 (81): 234-42. **CONTACT ADDRESS** Dept Scandinavian, Univ of California, Berkeley, 1056 Cragmont Ave, Berkeley, CA 94708. **EMAIL** cymraeg@socrates.berkeley.edu

RELIHAN, JOEL C.
DISCIPLINE CLASSICS **EDUCATION** Univ Ill, BA, 76; Univ Wis, MA, PhD,85. **CAREER** Class, Wheaton Col. **RESEARCH** Augustine; Boethius; myth; Egyptian lang & cult; ancient ecology; **SELECTED PUBLICATIONS** Auth, Ancient Menippean Satire, Johns Hopkins UP, 93. **CONTACT ADDRESS** Dept of Class, Wheaton Col, Massachusetts, 26

East Main St, Norton, MA 02766. **EMAIL** Joel_Relihan@wheatonma.edu

REMAK, HENRY HEYMANN HERMAN
PERSONAL Born 07/27/1916, Berlin, Germany, m, 1946, 4 children **DISCIPLINE** GERMAN, COMPARATIVE LITERATURE, WEST EUROPEAN STUDIES **EDUCATION** Univ Montpellier, lic es let, 36; Ind Univ, AM, 37; Univ Chicago, PhD, 47. **CAREER** Instr Ger & Span, Indianapolis Exten Ctr, Ind Univ, 39-43; from instr to prof Ger, 46-64, chmn W Europ studies, 66-69, vchancellor & dean fac, 69-74, Prof Ger & Comp Lit, Ind Univ, 64-, Dir Ger summer sch Middlebury College, Vermong, 67-71; assoc ed, Ger Quart, 58-62; ed, assoc ed, ed comm, 61-99, assoc ed, Yearbk Comp Lit, 61-66, ed, 66-78; Fulbright lectr comp & Ger lit, Univ Hamburg, 67; Guggenheim fel, 67-68; Nat Endowment for Humanities fel, 77-78; dir summer & yr-long seminars, Nat Endowmen for Humanities, 77 & 78-79; pres, Coordr Comt Comp Hist Lit in Europ Langs, Int Comp Lit Asn, 77-83 ; prof emer, 67-00. **HONORS AND AWARDS** Litt , Univ Lille, 73; Hon Prof, U of Sichuan, 99; litt d, univ lille, 73. **MEMBERSHIPS** Corresp mem Acad Sci, Arts & Lett, Marseilles. **RESEARCH** Franco-German literary relations; modern German literature; general comparative literature. **SELECTED PUBLICATIONS** Contribr, Comparative Literature: Method and Perspective, Southern Ill Univ, 71; auth, Der Rahmen in der deutschen Novelle, Delp, Munich, 72; Exoticism in Romanticism, Comp Lit Studies, 3/78; Der Weg zur Weltliteratur: Fontanes Bret Harteentwurf, 80; The Users of Comparative Literature, Value Judgment, 81; Die novelle in der Klassik uhd, Romanttik, 82; auth, Novellistische Struktur: Bassompierre, Goethe, Hofmannsthal, 83; Literary-History And Comparative Literary-History--The Odds For And Against It In Scholarship, Neohelicon, Vol 20, 93; auth, Structural Elements of the German Novelle from Goethe to Thomas Mann, 96. **CONTACT ADDRESS** Dept of Lit, Indiana Univ, Bloomington, Bloomington, IN 47401. **EMAIL** complit@indiana.edu

RENEHAN, ROBERT
PERSONAL Born 04/25/1935, M, 1965, 5 children **DISCIPLINE** GREEK AND LATIN LITERATURE **EDUCATION** Boston College, 56; Harvard Univ, MA, 58, PhD, 63; Greek & Latin literature. **CAREER** Prof, Univ Calif, Santa Barbara. **HONORS AND AWARDS** Seminar Fellow, NEH, 72-73; Academic Senate Distinguished Teaching Awd, UCSB, 81; Alumni Assoc Awd of Excellence in Arts & Humanities; Boston College, 90. **MEMBERSHIPS** Amer Philological Assoc, Soc Ancient Medicine, Platarch Soc. **RESEARCH** Ancient medicine; philos; hist of class scholar; textual criticism; lexicography. **SELECTED PUBLICATIONS** Auth, Greek Textual Criticism, Harvard Univ Press, 69; Leo Medicus, De Natura Hominis, Akademie Verlag, Berlin, 69; Greek Lexicographical Notes I and II, Gottingen, 75, 82; Studies in Greek Texts, Gottingen, 76; The Staunching of Odysseus' Blood: The Healing Power of Magic, AJP 92; "Some Special Problems in the Editing of Aristotle," SIFC, 3rd series, 92; "Plato, Apology 27A-B," CP 88, 93; "Of Mice and Men in Aristotle," CP 89, 94; "Polus, Plato, and Aristotle," CQ 45, 95; "On Some Genitives and a Few Accusatives in Aristotle: A Study in Style," Hermes 125, 97; rev(s), The New Oxford Sophocles, CP 87, 92; "Avotins, On the Greek of the Novels of Justinian," Phoenix 49, 95; numerous other articles and. **CONTACT ADDRESS** Dept of Classics, Univ of California, Santa Barbara, Santa Barbara, CA 93106-7150. **EMAIL** renehan@humanitas.ucsb.edu

RENNERT, HELLMUT HAL
PERSONAL Born 11/29/1939, Weimar, Germany, m, 1963, 1 child **DISCIPLINE** GERMAN & COMPARATIVE LITERATURE **EDUCATION** Wichita State Univ, BA, 66, MA, 69; Univ Wash, PhD(comp lit), 75. **CAREER** Instr, Wichita State Univ 73-74; asst prof, Carnegie-Mellon Univ, 76-79; Asst Prof German, Univ Fla, 79-; Pres, Asn Prof Transl, 78-79. **MEMBERSHIPS** MLA; Am Asn Teachers German; Deutsche Schillergesellschaft; Am Comp Lit Asn; Am Transl Asn **RESEARCH** Contemporary German literature; German area studies; early 19th century German literature. **SELECTED PUBLICATIONS** Auth, A comparison of two translations of Eduard Morikes poem auf eine Lampe, Univ South Fla Lang Quat, 72; Transformations: Thoughts regarding film title translations, Post Scripts, 81; Affinities in Romanticism: Kleist and Keats, Heinrich von Kleist Studies, AMS press and E Schmidt Verlag, 82; The threat of the invisible: The portrait of the physicist in modern German drama, Comp Drama Papers, 82; Deutsche Firmen, Deutsche Sprache in Florida, Unterrichtspraxis, 82. **CONTACT ADDRESS** Dept Germanic & Slavic Lang & Lit, Univ of Florida, PO Box 117430, Gainesville, FL 32611-7430. **EMAIL** rennert@nervm.nerdc.ufl.edu

RESINSKI, REBECCA
PERSONAL Born 11/19/1968, Johnstown, PA **DISCIPLINE** CLASSICS **EDUCATION** Bucknell Univ, BA, 90; Univ CA, Los Angeles, MA, 93, PhD, 98. **CAREER** Asst prof Classics, Dept of Relig and Classics, Univ Rochester, 98-. **HONORS AND AWARDS** William Bucknell Prize, 90; A D White fel at Cornell Univ, 90-92; Chancellor's fel at UCLA, 92-93; Luckman Awd for Distinguished Teaching, UCLA, 97. **MEMBERSHIPS** Am Philol Asn; Women's Classical Caucus. **RESEARCH** Ancient poetry; ancient social thought; representations of women in antiquity; the classical tradition in 20th century lit. **SELECTED PUBLICATIONS** Auth, Cosmos and Cosmetics: Constituting an Adorned Female Body in Ancient Greek Literature, UCLA dissertation, 98. **CONTACT ADDRESS** Hendrix Col, Department of Foreign Languages, Conway, AR 72032. **EMAIL** beci@troi.cc.rochester.edu

RESLER, MICHAEL
PERSONAL Born 07/07/1948, s **DISCIPLINE** GERMAN STUDIES **EDUCATION** William & Mary Col, AB, 70; Harvard Univ, AM, 73; Harvard Univ, PhD, 76. **CAREER** Teaching Fel, Harvard Univ, 72-76; Lectr, New England Conserv of Music, 74; From Asst Prof to Prof, Boston Col, 76-. **HONORS AND AWARDS** Phi Beta Kappa, William & Mary Col, 69; Woodrow Wilson Fel, 70; DAAD/Fulbright Fel, 70-71; Bernhard Blume Awd for Acad Excellence, Harvard Univ, 72-76; Grad Soc Prize, Harvard Univ, 75; Nat Endowment Humanities Fel, 80-81; Outstanding Acad Book Awd, Choice Mag, 88-89; Phi Beta Kappa Teaching Awd, Boston Col, 97. **MEMBERSHIPS** Goethe Soc of New England, MAA, AATG, Gesellschaft fur deutsche Sprache. **RESEARCH** Arthurian romance, Germanic philology, language pedagogy. **SELECTED PUBLICATIONS** Auth, "The Endings of the Definite Article as Primary Determinants in the Adjectival Phrase," Die Unterrichtspraxis 22 (89): 46-51; auth, "Daniel of the Blossoming Valley by der Stricker: Translation with Introduction and Notes," Garland Libr of Medieval Lit, vl 58 (94); auth, "Der Stricker," in Ger Writers and Works of the High Middle Ages: 1170-1280, Dict of Lit Biog, vol 138 (Detroit: Bruccoli Clark Layman, 94), 117-132; auth, "Thomasin von Zerclaere," in Ger Writers and Works of the High Middle Ages: 1170-1280, Dict of Lit Biog, vol 138 (Detroit: Bruccoli Clark Layman, 94), 133-140; auth, "Der Stricker, Daniel con dem Bluhenden Tal," Altdeutsche Textbibliothek, vol 92, 2nd rev Ed (95). **CONTACT ADDRESS** Dept Ger Studies, Boston Col, Chestnut Hill, 140 Commonwealth Ave, Lyons Hall 201c, Chestnut Hill, MA 02467-3800. **EMAIL** resler@bc.edu

RESTREPO, LUIS F.
PERSONAL Born 07/02/1962, Washington, DC, m, 1991, 1 child **DISCIPLINE** LATIN AMERICAN LITERATURE **EDUCATION** Univ Pontificia Bolivariana, BA, 88; Univ Md, College Park, MA, 92; PhD, 96. **CAREER** Grad asst, Univ Md, 89-95; asst prof, Univ Ark, 95-01; assoc prof, 01-. **HONORS AND AWARDS** Fulbright Scholar, 2000, Nat Hist Awd, 97. **MEMBERSHIPS** LASA, MLA, Asn of Colombianistas, Instituto Internacional de Literatura Iberoamericana, AAUP, Soc Renaissance and Baroque Hispanic Poetry **RESEARCH** Colonial Latin America, Post colonialism. **SELECTED PUBLICATIONS** Auth, Un nuevo reino imaginado, Inst Colombiano de Cultura Hispanica, 99. **CONTACT ADDRESS** Foreign Lang Dept, Univ of Arkansas, Fayetteville, Fayetteville, AR 72701. **EMAIL** lrestr@mail.uark.edu

REUSHER, JAY
DISCIPLINE CLASSICS **EDUCATION** Fordham Univ, PhD, 69. **CAREER** Assoc prof, 69-, Georgetown Univ. **RESEARCH** Kant. **CONTACT ADDRESS** 900 10th St NE, Washington, DC 20002-3718. **EMAIL** reushej@garnet.georgetown.edu

REY, WILLIAM HENRY
PERSONAL Born 04/07/1911, Frankfurt-am-Main, Germany, m, 1965, 4 children **DISCIPLINE** GERMAN LITERATURE **EDUCATION** Univ Frankfurt, PhD, 37. **CAREER** Instr, Ohio State Univ, 47-48; asst prof, Grinnell Col, 48-50; from asst prof to assoc prof, 50-59, exec off dept, 60-73, Prof Ger, Univ Wash, 59-81. **MEMBERSHIPS** MLA. **RESEARCH** Modern German and Austrian literature; contemporary poetry. **SELECTED PUBLICATIONS** Auth, Weltentzweiung und Weltversohnung in Hofmannsthals Griechischen Dramen, Univ Pa, 62; Arthur Schnitzler: Die spate Prosa als Gipfelseines Schaffens, Schmidt, Berlin, 68; Arthur Schnitzler: Professor Bernhardi, Fink, Munchen, 71; Poesie der Antipoesie, Moderne Lyrik: Genesis, Theorie, Struktur, Stiehm, Heidelberg, 78; auth, Deutschland und die Revolution: der Zerfall der humanistischen Utopie in Theorie und Drama, Lang, Bern, 83. **CONTACT ADDRESS** Dept of Ger Lang & Lit, Univ of Washington, Seattle, WA 98195.

REYDAMS-SCHILS, GRETCHEN
PERSONAL m, 3 children **DISCIPLINE** CLASSICS; ANCIENT PHILOSOPHY **EDUCATION** Katholieke Universiteit Leuven, Belgium, AB (classics, magna cum laude), 87; Univ Cincinnati, MA, 89; KU Leuven, Belgium, Inst of Philos, res, 91-92; Univ CA, Berkeley, Candidate Philos, 91, PhD, 94. **CAREER** Prog dir, Int House, Berkeley, 89-91; teaching asst, Univ Cincinnati, 88-89; press & info office, European Parliament, Brussels, summer 90; post-graduate sem moderator, KU Leuven, Inst for Philos, 91-92; grad student instr, Univ CA, Berkeley, 92-93; press office Brussels, Council of the European Communities, spring 94; asst prof, Prog Liberal Studies, Univ Notre Dame, 94-; vis prof, Spiritan Missionary Sem, Arusha, Tanzania, spring 98 (sabbatical); assoc prof, Univ of Notre Dame, 00-. **HONORS AND AWARDS** Fulbright fel, 87-92; Louise Semple-Taft fel, Univ Cincinnati, 87-89; Sather Assist, Univ CA, Berkeley, 89-91; Louise McKay Prize in Latin Prose Composition, Univ CA, Berkeley, 91; Mellon Dissertation Res grant, 91; fel, Center of Western European Studies, spring 93; Chancellor's Dissertation Year fel, Univ CA, Berkeley, 93-94; Scientific Council of the Found Hardt, Geneva, 96; Belgian Univ Found pub grant, 96; Fac Res Grant, Univ of Notre Dame, 99; Erasmus Institute Fac Workshop, Theol and Fiction, 99; Paul M. and Barbara Henkels Vis Scholars Series, Univ of Notre Dame, 99-00; Jr Fel at the Center for Hellenci Studies, Washington D.C., 00-01. **SELECTED PUBLICATIONS** Auth, Solon and the Hektemoroi, Ancient Soc 22, Leuven, 91; Plato's Myth of Er: the Light and the Spindle, l'Antiquite Classique 62, 93; Stoicized Readings of Plato's Timaeus in Philo of Alexandria, Soc Bib Lit, sem papers 94, Studia Philonica Annual 7, 95; The European Union and Cultural Policy, European Intergration and American Federalism: A Comparative Perspective, Richard Herr and Steven Weber, eds, Berkeley, 96; Plato's World Soul: Grasping Sensibles without Sense-Perception, Interpreting the Timaeus-Critias: Proceedings of the IV Symposium Platonicum, selected papers, Int Plato Studies 9, ed L. Brisson and T. Calvo, Sankt Augustin, 97; Posidonius and Plato's Timaeus: Off to Rhodes and Back to Plato?, Classical Quart 47, 97; Romand and Stoic, the Self as a Mediator, Dionysius, New Series 16, (98): 35-62; Demiurge and Providence, Stoic and Platonist Readings of Plato's Timaeus, Monotheismes et Philosophie, (Brepols Publishers: Turnhout, Belgium, 99); contrib, Socrates Request: Tim, 19B-20C in the Tradition of Platonism, forthcoming in The Ancient World, Conference Papers, 98; An Anthology of Snakebites, (Philosophy/Gender Studies, Seven Bridges Press, 01); ed, Plato's Timeus as Cultrual Icon. **CONTACT ADDRESS** Prog Liberal Studies, Univ of Notre Dame, Notre Dame, IN 46556. **EMAIL** gretchen.j.reydams-schils.1@nd.edu

REYFMAN, IRINA
DISCIPLINE SLAVIC LANGUAGES **EDUCATION** Stanford Univ, PhD, 86. **CAREER** Assoc prof. **RESEARCH** Eighteenth and early nineteenth-century Russian literature; cultural history; semiotics of culture. **SELECTED PUBLICATIONS** Auth, Imagery of Time and Eternity in Eighteenth Century Russian Poetry: Mikhail Murav'ev and Semen Bobrov, Ind Slavic Papers, 96; The Emergence of the Duel of Honor in Russia: Corporal Punishment and the Honor Code, Russian Rev, 95; Poetic Justice and Injustice: Autobiographical Echoes in Pushkin's The Captain Daughter, Slavic E Europ Jour, 94. **CONTACT ADDRESS** Dept of Slavic Languages, Columbia Col, New York, 2960 Broadway, New York, NY 10027-6902. **EMAIL** IR2@columbia.edu

REYNOLDS, AUDREY L.
PERSONAL Born 06/16/1943, Cape Girardeau, MO, s **DISCIPLINE** LINGUISTICS **EDUCATION** Southeastern Mo State Univ, BA, 65; Northwestern Univ, MA, 66; PhD, 69. **CAREER** Prof, Northeastern Ill Univ, 69-; Coordr of English Lang Prog, Northeastern Ill Univ, 83-89; Chair of Anthrop, Ling and Philos, Northeastern Ill Univ, 92-99. **HONORS AND AWARDS** Woodrow Wilson Fel, 65-66; Northwestern Univ Fel, 66-68; NDEA Fel, 68-69; Outstanding Serv to the Nat Asn of Remedial Develop Studies in Postsecondary Educ, 83. **MEMBERSHIPS** LSA, TESOL, NCTE. **RESEARCH** English Linguistics, Linguistics and Literacy (Reading and Writing). **SELECTED PUBLICATIONS** Auth, Exploring Written English, Little-Brown, 83; auth, Explorations in Basic Writing, St Martin's Press, 93. **CONTACT ADDRESS** Dept Ling, Northeastern Illinois Univ, 5500 N Saint Louis Ave, Chicago, IL 60625.

RHOADES, DUANE
DISCIPLINE SPANISH **EDUCATION** Univ IL, PhD, 76. **CAREER** Assoc prof; Univ WY, 82; past exec dir, Partners of the Am exchange-state Goias in Brazil & state coordr, Nat Span Exam. **HONORS AND AWARDS** UW's John P Ellbogen awd, 86. **RESEARCH** Dramatic lit in Span, Portuguese and related lang(s). **SELECTED PUBLICATIONS** Auth, bk on monotheatre in Lat Am, 86; publ on, Lat Am poetry, prose fiction,theater & Peninsular drama. **CONTACT ADDRESS** Dept of Mod and Class Lang(s), Univ of Wyoming, PO Box 3964, Laramie, WY 82071-3964. **EMAIL** DRHOADES@UWYO.EDU

RICAPITO, JOSEPH V.
PERSONAL Born 10/30/1933, Giovinazzo, Italy, m, 1958, 2 children **DISCIPLINE** SPANISH, COMPARATIVE LITERATURE **EDUCATION** Brooklyn Col, BA, 55; State Univ IA, MA, 56; Univ CA, Los Angeles, PhD(Romance lang), 66. **CAREER** Assoc Span, Univ CA, Los Angeles, 61-62; from instr to asst prof Span & Ital, Pomona Col, 62-70; assoc prof Span, 70-78, prof Span & comp lit, IN Univ, 78-80; prof Span & chemn dept, LA State Univ, Baton Rouge, 80-85, dir, program in comp lit, LSU, 94-; Ford Found & Pomona Col fel, 68-69. **MEMBERSHIPS** MLA; Am Comp Lit Asn; Renaissance Soc Am. **RESEARCH** Italian Renaissance; Spanish Golden Age; comparative literature. **SELECTED PUBLICATIONS** Auth, Lazarillo de Tormes y Machiavelli & El contorno picaresco del Conde Lucanor, 72, Romanische Forsch; Americo Castro y la novela picaresca, Insula, 73; La vida de Lazarillo de Tormes, Madrid, Catedra, 10th ed, 76; Bibliografia razonada y anotada .. Madrid, Castalia, 80. **CONTACT ADDRESS** Dept Span & Port, Louisiana State Univ and A&M Col, Baton Rouge, LA 70803-0001. **EMAIL** ricapito@homer.forlang.lsu.edu

RICARD, FRANCOIS
PERSONAL Born 06/04/1947, Shawinigan, PQ, Canada **DISCIPLINE** FRENCH AND QUEBEC LITERATURE **EDUCATION** Univ Laval, BA, 66; McGill Univ, MA, 68; Univ-d'Aix-Marseille (France), PhD, 71. **CAREER** Prof French & Quebec literature, McGill Univ, 71-. **HONORS AND AWARDS** Gov Gen Award Non-fiction (Fr lang), 86; Killam Res Fel, 88-90. **MEMBERSHIPS** Royal Soc Can **SELECTED PUBLICATIONS** Auth, Inventaire des archives personnelles de gabriell Roy conservees a la Bibliotheque nationale du Canada, 92; auth, La generation lyrique, essai, 92; auth, Gabrielle Roy, une vie, 96; auth, Ma chere petite soeur: lettres a Bernadette 1943-1970, de Gabrielle Roy, 99; auth, Gabrielle Roy: A Life , Gabrielle Roy, une vie, 99; auth, Le roman contre le monde, Liberte, 99; auth, Scandale du roman: Les Particules elementaires de Michel Houellebecq, L'Atelier du roman, 99; auth, Comedie de la fin, postface de Milan Kundera, La Valse aux adieux, 99; auth, A la une 5, Effets postmodernes 2: une nouvelle espece sociale, L'Atelier du roman, 99; auth, Le regard des amants, La Nouvelle Revue francise 1998, repris comme postface de Milan Kundera, L'identite, 00. **CONTACT ADDRESS** French Dept, McGill Univ, 3460 McTavish St, Montreal, QC, Canada H3A 1X9. **EMAIL** fricard@leacock.lan.mcgill.ca

RICE, LAURA
DISCIPLINE COMPARATIVE LITERATURE **EDUCATION** Ohio State Univ, BA, 68; Kent State Univ, MA, 71; Univ Wash, PhD, 76. **CAREER** Engl, Oregon St Univ. **SELECTED PUBLICATIONS** Auth, The Camera Always Lies, Review Essay of Trinh T. Minh-ha, The Framer Framed in The Women's Review of Books X, 93; Departures: Translations of and Essays on Isabelle Eberhardt, City Lights Press, 94. **CONTACT ADDRESS** Oregon State Univ, Corvallis, OR 97331-4501. **EMAIL** lrice@orst.edu

RICH, JOHN STANLEY
PERSONAL Born 03/05/1943, Birmingham, AL, s **DISCIPLINE** DIALECTOLOGY **EDUCATION** Univ Ala, BA, 66, PhD(English), 79; Univ Pa, MS, 68. **CAREER** Instr English, Stillman Col, 68-73; teaching asst, Univ Ala, 73-79; from Asst Prof to Prof English, Univ SC, Aiken, 79- **HONORS AND AWARDS** Fulbright Lect Awd to Poland, 93-94. **MEMBERSHIPS** MLA; Nat Coun Teachers English; Am Dialect Soc; Am Name Soc. **RESEARCH** American place names; English composition and rhetoric. **SELECTED PUBLICATIONS** Auth, Some South Carolina names transferred to West Alabama, Names in SC, 10/82; numerous articles in: Secol Rev, SAtl Rev, Folklore Quart, Names. **CONTACT ADDRESS** 171 University Pky, PO Box 2582, Aiken, SC 29801-6309. **EMAIL** stanr@aiken.sc.edu

RICH, LAWRENCE
PERSONAL Born 08/06/1951, Hong Kong, Hong Kong, m, 1989, 1 child **DISCIPLINE** SPANISH **EDUCATION** Johns Hopkins Univ, BM, 78; MM, 81; NY Univ, MA, 88; Univ Md, PhD, 95. **CAREER** Instr, Pa State Univ, 80-81; TA, Univ of Md, 89-94; asst prof, St Mary's Col of Md, 95-01. **HONORS AND AWARDS** Diss Grant, 94; Fac Develop Grants, 96-00; NEH Grant, 99. **MEMBERSHIPS** MLA, AATSP, Instituto Cervantes, Twentieth Century Spanish Assoc of Am. **RESEARCH** Twentieth Century Spanish peninsular narrative, Women's Literature. **SELECTED PUBLICATIONS** Auth, "Antonio Muroz Molina's Beatus ille and Beltenebros. Conventions of Reading in the Postmodern Anti-Detective Novel," Romance Lang Annual, (94), auth, "Kings and Counts: Pragmatics and the Poema de Feman Gonzalez in the Primena Cronica General," La Coronica, (97); auth, The Narrative of Antonio Munoz Molina: Self-conscious Realism and El Desencanto, Peter Lang, NY, 99; auth, "Fear and Loathing in Betusta: Coding Class and Gender in La Regenta," Revists canadiense de estudios hispanicos, (01). **CONTACT ADDRESS** 1502 Ogden St NW, Washington, DC 20010-1235. **EMAIL** lrich@smcin.edu

RICHARDSON, DONALD
DISCIPLINE GREEK AND ROMAN CLASSICS, WORLD CLASSICS **EDUCATION** Univ Minn, PhD; post-doc work, Stanford Univ; Univ Oslo. **CAREER** Ex dept ch; prof. **SELECTED PUBLICATIONS** Transl, Euripides' Iphigenia At Aulis; auth, Great Zeus And All His Children; Eyewitnesses; Stories of the Greeks and Romans. **CONTACT ADDRESS** Dept of Eng, Univ of Evansville, 1800 Lincoln Ave, Evansville, IN 47714. **EMAIL** dr26@evansville.edu.

RICHARDSON, HORST FUCHS
PERSONAL Born 06/11/1941, Nuremberg, Germany, m, 1967, 2 children **DISCIPLINE** GERMAN LANGUAGE & LITERATURE **EDUCATION** Univ CA, Riverside, BA, 63, MA, 66; Univ CT, PhD, 76. **CAREER** From instr to asst prof Ger, 65-77, Assoc Prof Ger, CO Col, 77. **MEMBERSHIPS** Am Asn Tchr() Ger; MLA; Asn Depts For Lang. **RESEARCH** Ger drama and theatre. **SELECTED PUBLICATIONS** Auth, The teaching of college German under a modular system, Mod Lang J, 73; A playwrite's experiment in third-yeard German, 73 & German play productions in US and Canadian colleges and universities since 1959, 74, Unterrichtspraxis; Sieg Heil: War letters of tank gunner Karl Fuchs, 1937-1941, Archon Books, 87. **CONTACT ADDRESS** Dept of Ger & Russ, Colorado Col, 14 E Cache La Poudre, Colorado Springs, CO 80903-3294. **EMAIL** hrichardson@cc.colorado.edu

RICHARDSON, SCOTT D.
PERSONAL Born 11/27/1956, St. Paul, MN, m, 1976, 2 children **DISCIPLINE** COMPARATIVE LITERATURE **EDUCATION** Harvard, BA, 78; Stanford, MA, 80, PhD, 84. **CAREER** Asst Prof, Assoc Prof, Prof, 84-, St John's Univ, Collegeville, MN. **HONORS AND AWARDS** Teacher of the Yr, 89; Advisor of the Yr, 93; NEH Summer Stipend, 89. **MEMBERSHIPS** APA, Class Assoc of MN. **RESEARCH** Homer; James Joyce; Thomas Pynchon. **SELECTED PUBLICATIONS** Auth, Truth in the Tales of the Odyssey, Mnemosyne, 96; The Homeric Narrator, Nashville, Vanderbilt Univ Press, 90; co-auth, Euriides Iphiegenia at Aulis, adaptation for the stage, Lanham, Maryland, Univ Press of Amer, 88. **CONTACT ADDRESS** Dept Modern & Class Languages, St. John's Univ, Collegeville, MN 56321. **EMAIL** SRichardson@csbsju.edu

RICHLIN, AMY
DISCIPLINE CLASSICS AND THE STUDY OF WOMEN AND MEN IN SOCIETY **EDUCATION** Yale Univ, PhD. **CAREER** Prof, Univ Southern Calif. **RESEARCH** Construction of masculinity in the Roman rhetorical schools. **SELECTED PUBLICATIONS** Auth, The Garden of Priapus: Sexuality and Aggression in Roman Humor, 83, rev 92; ed, Pornography & Representation in Greece & Rome, 92 & Feminist Theory & the Classics, co-edited with Nancy Sorkin Rabinowitz, 93. **CONTACT ADDRESS** Col Letters, Arts & Sciences, Univ of So California, University Park Campus, Los Angeles, CA 90089. **EMAIL** richlin@.usc.edu

RICHMAN, STEPHEN
PERSONAL Born Philadelphia, PA, m, 1962, 1 child **DISCIPLINE** LINGUISTICS **EDUCATION** Univ Pa, BA, 57, MS, 59, PhD, 65. **CAREER** PROF SPAN, (TRENTON JR COL)MERCER COUNTY COL, 65-; Asst. COORD, FOR LANGS, MERCER COUNTY COL, 85-; asst. chair hum, Mmercer, 10 yrs. **RESEARCH** Romance Linguistics; Hispanic Influence in the USA; Foreign Language Pedagogy. **SELECTED PUBLICATIONS** Auth, Conversational Spanish For Everyday Use, Mercer County College, 99. **CONTACT ADDRESS** Lib Arts Div, Mercer County Comm Col, 1200 Old Trenton Rd., Trenton, NJ 08690.

RICHTER, GERHARD
PERSONAL Born 10/04/1967, Cologne, Germany, m **DISCIPLINE** GERMAN LITERATURE **EDUCATION** Univ Calif, San Diego, BA, 89; MA, 91; Princeton Univ, MA, 93; PhD, 96. **CAREER** Lectr, Princeton Univ, 95-96; asst prof, Univ of Wisc, Madison, 96-. **HONORS AND AWARDS** Whiting Found Fel in the Humanities, 94-95; Fac Res Grants, Univ of Wisc, 97-00; Lilly Endowment Teaching Awd, 98-99; Hilldale Fac Res Awd, 00. **MEMBERSHIPS** MLA; Int Assoc for Philos and Lit; Am Assoc of Teachers of Ger; Ger Studies Assoc; Int Walter Benjamin Assoc. **RESEARCH** 20th Century German Literature and Culture, Critical Theory, Philosophy, Aesthetics and Politics, Comparative Literature, Ethics of Reading, Frankfurt School, Cultural Studies. **SELECTED PUBLICATIONS** Auth, "Siegfried Kracauer and the Folds of Friendship", Ger Quarterly 70.3 (97): 233-46; auth, "Face-Off", Monatshefte 90.4, (98): 411-44; auth, "Ethics and the Rhetoric of Culture", Concepts of Culture, eds Hans Adler and Jost Hermand, Lang, (NY, 99): 163-92; auth, "Holocaust und Katzenjammer. Lektureprotokolle zu Art Spiegelmans Comic Maus", Ger Studies Rev 23.1 (00): 85-114; auth, Walter Benjamin and the Corpus of Autobiography, Ger Lit Theory and Cult Studies, Wayne State Univ Pr, 00; auth, "Walter Benjamin, 1892-1940", Dict of Literary Biography: Twentieth Century European Cultural Theorists, Gale Res Co, (Detroit), (forthcoming); auth, "Introduction: Benjamin's Ghosts", Benjamin's Ghosts: Interventions in Contemporary Literary and Cultural Theory, ed Gerhard Richter, Stanford Univ Pr, (Stanford), (forthcoming); auth, "Introduction: Literary Friendship, Literary Paternity", Literary Friendship, Literary Paternity: Essays in Honor of Stanley Corngold, ed Gerhard Richter, (Forthcoming); auth, "Adorno's Scars, Bloch's Anacoluthon", Ger Politics and Soc, (forthcoming). **CONTACT ADDRESS** Dept German, Univ of Wisconsin, Madison, 1220 Linden Dr, 818 Van Hise Hall, Madison, WI 53706-1525. **EMAIL** grichter@facstaff.wisc.edu

RICHTER, GREGORY
PERSONAL Born 07/02/1955, Lynwood, CA, m, 1988, 1 child **DISCIPLINE** LINGUISTICS **EDUCATION** Univ Calif, BA, 77; MA, 79; PhD, 82. **CAREER** Prof, Truman State Univ, 83-. **MEMBERSHIPS** Ling Asn of the Southwest, For Lang Asn of Mo, Am Asn of Teachers of Ger. **RESEARCH** Theoretical and historical linguistics, Translation and translation theory. **SELECTED PUBLICATIONS** Auth, The Gate of All Marvelous Things: A Guide to Reading the Tao Te Ching (San Francisco: Red Mansions Press), 98; auth, Psychology and the Soul (Baltimore: Johns Hopkins Univ Press), 98; auth, "Psychology and the Soul: Self-Knowledge and Human Nature", Journal of Religion and Health, 96; auth, The Incest Theme in Literature and Legend, (Baltimore: Johns Hopkins Univ Press), 92; trans, Poems by He Dong, 91; trans, Poems by Einar Bragi and Mattias Johannessen, Chariton Review, 90; auth, "The Capon Theory of the Cuckold's Horns: Confirmation or Conjecture?", Journal of American Folklore, 87. **CONTACT ADDRESS** Dept Lang & Lit, Truman State Univ, 100 East Normal St, Kirksville, MO 63501-4200. **EMAIL** grichter@truman.edu

RICKER-ABDERHALDEN, JUDITH
DISCIPLINE CONTEMPORARY GERMAN **EDUCATION** Univ Nebr, BA, 72, MA, 74, PhD, 80. **CAREER** Prof German, Univ Ark. **HONORS AND AWARDS** Fulbright Col Master Tchr Awd; Certificate Merit Outstanding Achievements. **MEMBERSHIPS** Am Asn Tchrs German; German Studies Asn. **SELECTED PUBLICATIONS** Areas: contemporary German, Austrian, and Swiss literature and civilization, foreign language pedagogy, and dialects. **CONTACT ADDRESS** Univ of Arkansas, Fayetteville, Fayetteville, AR 72701.

RIEBER, STEVEN
DISCIPLINE PHILOSOPHY OF LANGUAGE, PHILOSOPHY OF MIND, METAPHYSICS, EPISTEMOLOGY, ETHI **EDUCATION** Princeton Univ, PhD, 91. **CAREER** Assoc prof, Ga State Univ. **SELECTED PUBLICATIONS** Author of eight recent articles in journals such as Analysis, Nous and Philos Stud. **CONTACT ADDRESS** Georgia State Univ, Atlanta, GA 30303. **EMAIL** phlsdr@panther.gsu.edu

RIEDEL, WALTER ERWIN
PERSONAL Born 08/03/1936, Germany, m, 1963 **DISCIPLINE** GERMAN **EDUCATION** Univ Alta, BEd, 60, MA, 63; McGill Univ, PhD(Ger), 66. **CAREER** Teacher high sch, Edmonton, 60-61; instr French & Ger, 62-64, asst prof, 66-70, Assoc Prof Ger, Univ Victoria, BC, 70- **MEMBERSHIPS** Can Asn Univ Teachers Ger; Can Comp Lit Asn. **RESEARCH** Expressionism; translation; German and Canadian literary relations. **SELECTED PUBLICATIONS** Ed, The Old and the New World: Literary Perspectives of German-Speaking Canadians, Univ Toronto Press, Toronto, ON, 84; coed, Der Wanderer, Peter Lang, 94. **CONTACT ADDRESS** Dept Germanic Stud, Univ of Victoria, PO Box 3045, Victoria, BC, Canada V8W 3P4. **EMAIL** weriedel@uvic.ca

RIGSBY, KENT JEFFERSON
PERSONAL Born 02/25/1945, Tulsa, OK, m, 1969, 2 children **DISCIPLINE** CLASSICAL LANGUAGES, ANCIENT HISTORY **EDUCATION** Yale Univ, BA, 66; Univ Toronto, MA, 68. **CAREER** Asst prof, 71-77, Assoc Prof Classics, Duke Univ, 77-, Asst ed, Greek, Roman & Byzantine Studies, 72-77, assoc ed, 77-79, Roman ed, 79 & sr ed, 80- **MEMBERSHIPS** Am Philol Asn. **RESEARCH** Greek epigraphy; Hellenistic history; ancient religion. **SELECTED PUBLICATIONS** Auth, Cnossus and Capua, Trans Am Philol Asn, 76; Sacred Ephebie games at Oxyrhynchus, Chronique D'Egypte, 77; The era of the Province of Asia, Phoenix, 79; Seleucid Notes, Trans Am Philol Asn, 80. **CONTACT ADDRESS** Dept Class Studies, Duke Univ, Durham, NC 27706.

RILEY, HELENE M.
PERSONAL Born 03/11/1939, Vienna, Austria, m, 1983, 4 children **DISCIPLINE** GERMANICS **EDUCATION** Univ N Tex, BA, 70; Rice Univ, MA, 73; PhD, 75. **CAREER** Asst prof, Yale Univ, 75-78; assoc prof, Yale Univ, WSU, 79-85; prof, Clemson Univ, 85-. **HONORS AND AWARDS** NEH Grants, 86, 91, 95; FRG Friendship Awd, 89; Provost's Grant, 89; MESDA Res Grant, 93, 96; SC Humanities Counc Grant, 96, 97. **MEMBERSHIPS** MLA; SAMLA; SCHFLT; SGAS; MIFLC; AATG; Verwertungsgesell-schaft WORT. **RESEARCH** German romanticism, Age of Goethe, Linguistics, Culture. **SELECTED PUBLICATIONS** Auth, Max Weber, Colloquium, (Berlin), 91; trans, Register of St. Johannes Lutheran Church, Charleston, S.C. 1878-1920, 92; auth, Achim von Arnim in Selbstzeugnissen und Bilddokumentum, Rowohlt, (Reinbek, Hamburg), 94; auth, Michael Kalteisen: Ein Deutscher in South Carolina, M. Fink Gmbh, (Merklingen), 95; auth, Hildegard von Bingen, Rowohlt, (Reinbek), 97; auth, "Voyage to Paradise. The Josephinian Expedition from the Crownlands to the Carolinas", Austrian Studies Newsletter, 9.3 (97): 18-19; auth, "Christian Friedrich Mayr", Antiques, (Nov 98): 688-695; auth, "A Silver Token of Remembrance: Abraham Remshard's Schraubtaler and the Salzburger settlement at Ebenezer, Georgia", Austrian Studies Newsletter 10.3 (98): 10-11; auth, "Michael Kalteisen and the Founding of the German Friendly Society in Charleston" SC Hist Mag, 100.1 (99): 29-48; auth, "Gottes Brunnelin hat Wassers die Fulle: Ein Geschichtsabrib der nach Ebenezer in amerikanisdhen Georgia ausgewanderten Salzburger", Salzburg Archiev, (Dec 99). **CONTACT ADDRESS** Dept Mod Lang, Clemson Univ, 1 Clemson Univ, Clemson, SC 29634-0001. **EMAIL** rhelene@clemson.edu

RINDISBACHER, HANS J.
PERSONAL Born 04/14/1955, m, 2 children **DISCIPLINE** GERMAN LANGUAGE AND LITERATURE **EDUCATION** Univ Bern, Switz, Lisc Phil 83; Stanford Univ, PhD, 89. **CAREER** Assoc Prof, Pomona College 00-; Asst Prof, Pomona College, 95-00; Asst prof, 93-; asst prof, 93-95, Swarthmore Col; instr, 92, Univ La Verne, 92; visiting asst, 89-91, Reed Col; tchg asst, 84-88, Stanford Univ; asst, 83-84, Univ Bern, Switzerland. . **HONORS AND AWARDS** Third Prize DAAD Ger Studies Syllabus Contest, 94; MLA Awd, 93; NEH Summer Seminar, Univ Wash, 92; fel(s), Stanford Univ, 85-89. **MEMBERSHIPS** GSA; AATG; MLA. **RESEARCH** Cultural Studies; Perception. **SELECTED PUBLICATIONS** Auth, bk The Smell of Books, Michigan UP, 92; publ, numerous articles.

CONTACT ADDRESS Dept of Ger, Pomona Col, 550 N. Harvard Ave., Claremont, CA 91711. EMAIL hjr047472@powoma.edu

RINGEN, CATHERINE OLESON
PERSONAL Born 06/03/1943, Brooklyn, NY, m, 1969, 2 children **DISCIPLINE** LINGUISTICS **EDUCATION** Ind Univ, BA, 70, MA, 72, PhD(Ling), 75. **CAREER** Vis lectr Ling, Univ Minn, 73-74; asst prof, 75-79, from assoc prof Ling, 80-88; prof, 88-; chmn, 87-93; act chmn, Fall, 96; Univ Iowa, 79-, Fulbright prof, Univ Trondheim, Norway, 80; Adam Nickiewicz Univ, Poznan, Poland, 94-95; co-ed Nordic Journal of Linguistics, 01-. **MEMBERSHIPS** Ling Soc Am; AAAS; Nordic Asn of Linguistics. **RESEARCH** Phonological theory; philosophy of linguistics; phonetics. **SELECTED PUBLICATIONS** Auth, Another view of the theoretical implications of Hungarian vowel harmony, Ling Inquiry, 78; Uralic and Altaic vowel harmony: A problem for Natural Generative Phonology, J Ling, 80; contribr, A concrete analysis of Hungarian vowel harmony, Issues in Vowel Harmony, 80; auth, Vowel Harmony: Theoretical Implications, Garland, 88; Catherine O Ringen and Robert Vago, A Constraints based analysis of Hungarian vowel harmony, in Approaches to Hungarian, Vol 5: Levels and Structures, Istvan Kenesei, ed, 95; Catherine O Ringen and Robert Vago, Hungarian roundness harmony in Optimality Theory, Approaches to Hungarian, Vol 6, Casper de Groot, ed, 98; auth, Hungarian Vowel Harmony in Optunality Theory, Phonology, 98; co-auth, Variation in Finnish Vowel Harmoney: An OT account, Natural Language and Linguistic Theory, 99; auth, Aspiration, Preaspiration, Deaspiration, Sonorant Devoicing and Spirantization in Icelandic, Nordic Journal of Linguistics, 99; Icelandic Umlaut in Optimality Theory, Nordic Journal of Linguistics, 00. **CONTACT ADDRESS** Dept of Linguistics, Univ of Iowa, 570 English Phil Bldg, Iowa City, IA 52242-1408. **EMAIL** catherine-ringen@uiowa.edu

RINI, JOEL
PERSONAL Born 12/04/1957, Cleveland, OH, m, 1985, 2 children **DISCIPLINE** SPANISH, ITALIAN, PORTUGUESE **EDUCATION** Univ Mich, PhD, 87. **CAREER** Prof, Univ Va, 87-. **RESEARCH** Spanish historical grammar **SELECTED PUBLICATIONS** Auth, "The Evolution of the Nature and Position of the Spanish Clitic Pronoun," La Coronica 24 (95): 173-195; auth, "The Origin of Spanish ser: A Phonosyntactic Analysis," Romance Philology 50 (97): 295-307; auth, "The Death of Old Spanish beuir," Studia Neophilologica 69 (97): 95-107; auth, "The 'Clinching Factor' in the Addition of -y in Spanish doy, estoy, soy, voy," J of Hispanic Res 4 (99): 1-12; auth, Exploring the Rose of Morphology in the Evolution of Spanish, Current Issues in Linguistic Theory, 179, 99. **CONTACT ADDRESS** Dept Lang, Univ of Virginia, 115 Wilson Hall, Charlottesville, VA 22903-3238.

RINKEVICH, THOMAS E.
DISCIPLINE CLASSICS **EDUCATION** Xavier Univ, BA, 64; Ohio State Univ, MA, 66, PhD, 73. **CAREER** Instr, 67-73, asst prof, 73-96, assoc prof, 96-, actg ch, Classics, Univ Nebr, Lincoln. **MEMBERSHIPS** APA, (CAMWS, ACL, CML); MAM. **RESEARCH** Greek & Latin languages; Greek poetry; Latin poetry; Egyptian language; ancient near-eastern literature. **SELECTED PUBLICATIONS** Auth, A KWIC Concordance to Lucretius, De Rerum Natura. **CONTACT ADDRESS** Dept of Classics, Univ of Nebraska, Lincoln, 234 Andrews, Lincoln, NE 68588-0337. **EMAIL** trinkevich1@unl.edu

RINKUS, JEROME JOSEPH
PERSONAL Born 09/11/1938, Baltimore, MD **DISCIPLINE** RUSSIAN LITERATURE **EDUCATION** Middlebury Col, AB, 60; Brown Univ, AM, 62, PhD, 71. **CAREER** Teaching asst Russ lang, Brown Univ, 62-64 & 67-68; asst linguist, Intensive Lang Training Ctr, Ind Univ, 65-66; asst prof Russ lang & lit, Bucknell Univ, 68-73; asst prof, 73-79, assoc prof Russ lang & lit & coordr Russ prog, Pomona Col, 79-. **HONORS AND AWARDS** NEH fel, 75 & grant, 78; consult, Nat Endowment for Humanities, 77-78; NEH grant, 87, Irex grant,88; ACTFL grant, 90; MLA grant, 90. **MEMBERSHIPS** Am Assn Advan Slavic Studies; Am Assn Teachers Slavic & East Europ Lang; MLA; Am Coun Teaching Foreign Lang; ACTR Amer Coun of Tchrs of Russi. **RESEARCH** Nineteenth century Russian literature; the novel; methodology of Russian language teaching. **SELECTED PUBLICATIONS** Auth, Pushkin's The Queen of Sages, Encyclopedia of Literary Characters II, Salem Press, 90, art, Sergei Timofeevich Alsakov, The Modern Encyclopedia of Russia and The Soviet Union, MERSU, Academic International Press, 90. **CONTACT ADDRESS** Dept of Mod Lang & Lit, Pomona Col, 333 N College Way, Claremont, CA 91711-6319. **EMAIL** jrinkus@pomona.edu

RIPPLEY, LA VERN J.
PERSONAL Born 03/02/1935, Waumandee, WI, m, 1960, 2 children **DISCIPLINE** GERMAN ROMANTICISM & IMMIGRATION HISTORY **EDUCATION** Col Holy Cross, BA, 56; Univ Wis, BS, 58; Kent State Univ, MA, 61; Ohio State Univ, PhD(Ger), 65. **CAREER** Teacher, River Falls Sr High Sch, 58-60; teaching asst, Ohio State Univ, 61-63; asst prof Ger, Ohio Wesleyan Univ, 64-67; assoc prof, 67-71, chmn dept, 67-74, Prof Ger, St Olaf Col, 71-, Ed, Newsletter Soc Ger-Am Studies; Fulbright fel, 63-64 & Deutscher Akademischer Austauschdienst Fulbright, 82. **MEMBERSHIPS** Cent States Mod Lang Asn; MLA; Am Asn Teachers Ger; Am Hist Soc Ger from Russia; Norweg Am Hist Asn. **RESEARCH** German-Americana; German Romanticism; German immigration hist. **SELECTED PUBLICATIONS** Transit, Excursion through America, R.R. Donnelley, 73; auth, The German-Americans, Twayne, 74; Germans from Russia, In: Harvard Encycl of American Ethnic Groups, Harvard Univ Press, 80; Immigrant Wisconsin, Twayne, 85; German Place Names in Minnesota / Deutsche Ortsnamen in Minnesota, St. Olaf Col / Rainer Schmeissner, 89; co-transl, The German Colonies on the Lower Volga, Their Origin and Early Development, Am Hist Soc of Germans from Russia, 91; auth, The Whoopee John Wilfahrt Dance Band. His Bohemian-German Roots, Northfield, 92; coauth, The German-American Experience, Ind-Purdue Univ at Indianapolis, 93; auth, German-Bohemians: The Quiet Immigrants, Northfield, 93; co-ed, Emigration and Settlement Patterns of German Communities in North America, Ind-Purdue Univ at Indianapolis, 95; Noble Women, Restless Men. The Rippley (Rieple, Ripley, Ripli, Rippli) Family in Wisconsin, North Dakota, Minnesota and Montana, St. Olaf Col Press, 96; author of numerous articles. **CONTACT ADDRESS** 1520 St Olaf Ave, Northfield, MN 55057-1098. **EMAIL** rippleyl@stolaf.edu

RITTERSON, MICHAEL
PERSONAL Born 12/04/1940, m, 2 children **DISCIPLINE** GERMAN LANGUAGE AND LITERATURE **EDUCATION** Franklin and Marshall Col, AB, 62; Harvard Univ, PhD, 73. **CAREER** Instr Ger, Northeastern Univ, 66-67; instr, Gettysburg Col, 68-74; Asst Prof Ger, Gettysburg Col, 74-84; Assoc Prof Ger, Gettysburg Col, 84-. **MEMBERSHIPS** Am Asn Tchrs Ger; Am Lit Trans Asn; Ger Studies Asn; Goethe Soc NAm; MLA; Raabe-Gesellschaft. **RESEARCH** Ger Lit 18th -20th centuries; Ger novel; Literary translation; Wilhelm Raabe. **SELECTED PUBLICATIONS** Auth, Ruckwendung, Vorausdeutung und Erzahlablauf in Wilhelm Raabes Das Odfeld und Hastenbeck, Jahrbuch Raabe-Gesellschaft, 76; Waiting for Synthesis: Kurt Tucholsky Views America, 1925-1935, Occasional Papers Soc Ger-Am Studies, 81; Irony in Enlightenment Novel and 19th Century German Realism, Oeuvres et Critiques, 85. **CONTACT ADDRESS** Dept of Ger, Gettysburg Col, 300 N Washington St, Gettysburg, PA 17325-1486. **EMAIL** mritters@gettysberg.edu

RIVERA, MARGARITA TAVERA
DISCIPLINE LATIN AMERICAN AND CHICANO LITERATURE **EDUCATION** Univ Ore, BA; Stanford Univ, MA, PhD; Univ Calif, MA; Humboldt State Univ, MA. **CAREER** English, Carthage Col. **SELECTED PUBLICATIONS** Articles: New Chicano Writing; Maize, El Tecolote Literary Magazine; El Chicano. **CONTACT ADDRESS** Carthage Col, 2001 Alford Dr., Kenosha, WI 53140.

RIVERA-RODAS, OSCAR
DISCIPLINE SPANISH LITERATURE **EDUCATION** Univ Ca, PhD, 80. **CAREER** Prof, Span, Univ Tenn. **SELECTED PUBLICATIONS** Auth, El pensar de la modernidad po¤etica; auth, Metateatro y la Dramatica de Vargas Llosa, John Benjamin's Pub Co, 92. **CONTACT ADDRESS** Dept of Mod For Langs & Lits, Univ of Tennessee, Knoxville, 701 McClung Tower & Plaza, Knoxville, TN 37996. **EMAIL** oriverar@utk.edu

RIVERO, ELIANA SUAREZ
PERSONAL Born 11/07/1942, Artemisa, Cuba, 1 child **DISCIPLINE** SPANISH, LATIN AMERICAN & U S LATINO LITERATURES **EDUCATION** Univ Miami, BA, 64, PhD(Span), 68. **CAREER** From asst prof to assoc prof, 67-78, Prof Span & Port Dept, Univ Ariz, 78-. **HONORS AND AWARDS** NEH res grant, 84; Rockefeller grant, 96. **MEMBERSHIPS** MLA; Am Asn Teachers Span & Port; Inst Int Lit Iberoam; Latin Am Studies Asn **RESEARCH** Poetry of Pablo Neruda; poetry of the 20th century; Latin American women writers; U S Latino writers **SELECTED PUBLICATIONS** Auth, El Gran Amor de Pablo Neruda, Plaza Mayor Ed, 71; Simbolismo tematico y titular de Las manos del dia, Mester, spring 74; La estetica esencial en una oda nerudiana, In: Simposio Pablo Neruda, Las Americas, 75; Analisis de perspectivas y significacion en La Rosa Separada, Rev Iberoam, 76; Dialectica de la Persona poetica en la obra de Julia de Burgos, Rev Critics Lit Latinoam, fall 76; Vision social y feminista en la obra lirica de Rosario Castellanos, In: Estudios de Hispanofila, Univ NC, 79; Reflexiones para una Nueva Poetica, Actas Asoc int de Hispanistas, Toronto, 80; Hacia una Lectura Feminista de Tres Tristes Tigres, Feminist Literary Criticism: Theory and Practice, Bilingual Press, 82; Relectura de Ismaelillo, Estudios Martianos, 84; Hispanic literature in the U S, Revista Chicano-Riquena, 85; From immigrants to ethnics: Cuban women writers in the U S, In: Breaking Boundaries, UMass Press, 89; Eva Luna and women storytellers, Splintering Darkness, Latin Am Lit Rev Press, 90; Testimonial literature as literary discourse, latin American Perspectives, 91; (Re)writing sugarcane memories: Cuban Americans and literature, Am Rev, 91; co-ed, Infinite Divisions: An Anthology of Chicana Literature, Univ Ariz Press, 93; Border islander, In: Bridges to Cuba, Univ Mich Press, 95; Flores ocultas de poesia cubana, Homenaje a Luis Monguio, Juan de la Cuesta, 98; Creative writing (poetry) in: Siete poetas, 77; Woman of her work, 83; Nosotras, 86; Veinte anos de literatura cubanoameriana, 88, Daughters of the fifth sun, 95; Floricanto si, An Anthology of Latina Poetry, Penguin 98. **CONTACT ADDRESS** Spanish and Portuguese Dept, Univ of Arizona, PO Box 210067, Tucson, AZ 85721-0067. **EMAIL** eliana@u.arizona.edu

RIVERO, MARIA LUISA
PERSONAL Born 02/01/1943, Madrid, Spain, m, 1964, 2 children **DISCIPLINE** LINGUISTICS **EDUCATION** Univ Rochester, MA, 64, PhD(ling), 70. **CAREER** Asst prof, 70-75, assoc prof, 75-82, Prof Ling, Univ Ottawa, 82-, Res grant, Can Coun, 71-82. **MEMBERSHIPS** Ling Soc Am; Can Ling Asn; Soc Espanola de Ling; Asn Can de Hispanistas. **RESEARCH** Romance syntax and semantics; generative grammar; history of logic and linguistics. **SELECTED PUBLICATIONS** Auth, On left dislocation and topicalization in Spanish, Linguistic Inquiry, 80; Theoretical implications of the syntax of left-branch modifiers in Spanish, Ling Analysis, 80; coauth, Catalan restrictive relatives: Core and periphery, Lang, 81; Bulgarian And Serbo-Croatian Yes-No Questions--V0-Raising To -Li Versus -Li Hopping, Linguistic Inquiry, Vol 24, 93; Long Head Movement Vs V2, And Null Subjects In Old Romance, Lingua, Vol 89, 93; Imperatives, V-Movement And Logical Mood, J Of Linguistics, Vol 31, 95; Clitic Auxiliaries And Incorporation In Polish, Natural Language & Linguistic Theory, Vol 12, 94; On Indirect Questions, Commands, And Spanish Quotative Que, Linguistic Inquiry, Vol 25, 94. **CONTACT ADDRESS** Dept of Ling, Univ of Ottawa, 70 Laurier, Ottawa, ON, Canada K1N 6N5. **EMAIL** mrivero@aix1.uottawa.ca

RIVERS, ELIAS LYNCH
PERSONAL Born 09/19/1924, Charleston, SC, m, 1945, 3 children **DISCIPLINE** SPANISH **EDUCATION** Yale Univ, AB, 48, MA, 50, PhD(Span), 52. **CAREER** Instr Span, Yale Univ, 51-52; from instr to asst prof, Dartmouth Uol, 52-62; prof, Ohio State Univ, 62-64; prof, Johns Hopkins Univ, 64-78; Prof Span & Comp Lit, State Univ NY, 78-, Howard fel, 56-57; Guggenheim fel, 59-60; Fulbright res grant, Madrid, 64-65; Nat Endowment for Humanities res grant, 67-68, 70-71 & 81-82, sem dir, 75-76. **HONORS AND AWARDS** MA, Dartmouth Col, 62. **MEMBERSHIPS** MLA; Am Asn Teachers Span & Port; Asoc Int Hispanistas (secy-gen, 62-80). **RESEARCH** Renaissance poetry in Spain; oral and written styles of composition. **SELECTED PUBLICATIONS** Auth, Francisco de Aldana, Poesias, Espasa-Calpe, 57; Thirty-Six Spanish Poems, Houghton, 57; Garcilaso de la Vega, Obras Completas, Ohio State Univ, 64; Nature, art and science in Spanish poetry of the Renaissance, Bull Hisp Studies, 67; ed, Hijos de la Ira, Labor Barcelona, 70 & English translr, Children of Wrath, Johns Hopkins Univ, 70; Spanish Renaissance & Baroque Poetry, Scribners, 72; auth, Talking and writing in Don Quixote, Thought, 76. **CONTACT ADDRESS** Dept of Hisp Studies, SUNY, Stony Brook, Stony Brook, NY 11794.

RIVERS, KENNETH T.
PERSONAL Born 07/18/1956, Oakland, CA, m, 1991 **DISCIPLINE** FRENCH **EDUCATION** Univ Calif Berkeley, BA, 71; MA, 73; PhD, 78. **CAREER** TA, Univ Calif Berkeley,75-81, 84-86; vis asst prof, Kans State Univ, 81-82; vis asst prof, Univ NCar Charlotte, 82-84; vis asst prof, Rollins Col, 86-88; instr, Col San Mateo, 88-89; prof, Lamar Univ, 89-. **HONORS AND AWARDS** Grand Prize Winner, KEST Radio Playwriting Competition, 74; NEH Fel, 82, 87; Excellence in Teaching Award, 97. **MEMBERSHIPS** MLA, SCMLA, Nat Soc Sci Asn, AATF, Tex For Lang Asn, Am Soc for Lit in Environ. **RESEARCH** French language, literature, and culture, 19th century literature and art, Balzac, Caricature, Film studies, Radio drama Studies, Video-based instruction, Climate and culture, Environmental literature, Internet and language. **SELECTED PUBLICATIONS** Auth, "Balzac and Visual Caricature," Revue du Pacifique, (77); auth, "A or De? A Rule for the Infinitif complement," NCar For Lang Jour, (84); auth, "Cor-norama: Exclusion, Fathers, and Language in the Society of Le Pere Foriot," Stanford Fr Rev, (85); auth, Transmutations: Understanding Literary and Pictorial Caricature, Univ Pr of Am, 91; auth, "Ways of Knowing: Omar S Castaneda's Cunuman," Lamar Jour of the Humanities, (92); auth, "Literature on Ice: Climatic Changes and European Cultural Dynamics," Europ Studies Jour, (95); coauth, "Historical Patterns of French and Other European Healthcare Initiatives and their Social Implications Today," Nat Soc Sci Perspectives Jour, (97); auth, "Infinite Identities, Endless Environments: Jack London's The Star Rover," Lamar Jour of the Humanities, (98); auth, "Alfred Hitchcock's WWII French Films and the Limits of Propaganda," Images Jour, (99); auth, "Black Cats, Urban Renewal, and Magic Windows: Paris in Recent French Cinema," Bright Lights Film Jour, (00). **CONTACT ADDRESS** Lamar Univ, Beaumont, PO Box 10023, Beaumont, TX 77710. **EMAIL** riverskt@hal.lamar.edu

RIVERS, WILGA MARIE
PERSONAL Born Melbourne, Australia **DISCIPLINE** FRENCH, ENGLISH **EDUCATION** Univ Melbourne, dipl educ, BA, 40, MA, 48; Univ Lille, dipl French studies, 50; Univs Lille & Montpellier, Lic es Lett, 52; Univ Ill, Urbana-

Champaign, PhD(educ & French), 62. **CAREER** Sr teacher French & English, Australian high & prep schs, 40-59; asst prof French, Northern Ill Univ, 62-64; from lectr to assoc prof, Monash Univ, Australia, 64-69; vis prof, Teachers Col, Columbia Univ, 70-71; prof, Univ Ill, Urbana-Champaign, 71-74; Prof Romance Lang & Lang Coordr, Harvard Univ, 74-, Teacher English Lycee Jeune Filles, Douai, & Norm Sch, Montpellier, 49-52; participant, Can UNESCO sem biling, 67; vis scholar, French govt, 68; consult, Rockefeller Found English teaching proj, Bangkok, 71; prof ling, Mid East Ling Inst, Cairo, 74 & Ling Soc Am, Ling Inst, Oswego, NY, 76; consult, Nat Endowment for Humanities, 75-76; JACET sem, Tokyo, 79. **HONORS AND AWARDS** Florence Steiner Awd, Am Coun Teachers Foreign Lang, 77. **MEMBERSHIPS** Am Asn Appl Ling (pres, 77-78); Ling Soc Am; Am Coun Teaching Foreign Lang; Am Asn Teachers Fr; Teachers English to Speakers Other Lang. **RESEARCH** Language teaching; psycholinguistics; college curriculum. **SELECTED PUBLICATIONS** Auth, The Psychologist and the Foreign Language Teacher, 64 & Teaching Foreign Language Skills, 68 & 81, Univ Chicago; Speaking in Many Tongues, 72, 76 & co-ed, Changing Patterns in Foreign Language Programs, 72, Newbury House; auth, Practical Guide to the Teaching of French, 75, coauth, Practical Guide to the Teaching of German, 75, Practical Guide to the Teaching of Spanish, 76 & Practical Guide to the Teaching of English SL, 78, Oxford Univ; Cultures, Languages And The International Smorgasbord--Musings For A New Millennium, Canadian Modern Language Review-Revue Canadienne Des Langues Vivantes, Vol 50, 93. **CONTACT ADDRESS** Dept of Romance Lang & Lit, Harvard Univ, 206 Boylston Hall, Cambridge, MA 02138.

RIZZUTO, ANTHONY
PERSONAL Born 03/25/1937, Brooklyn, NY, m, 1966, 2 children **DISCIPLINE** FRENCH LANGUAGE; LITERATURE **EDUCATION** Columbia Univ, PhD 66, MA 60; Columbia Col, BA 58. **CAREER** SUNY Stony Brook, assoc prof, 68-; Tufts Univ, asst prof, 66-68; Columbia Col, inst, 61-66. **HONORS AND AWARDS** Fulbright fel; NEH. **MEMBERSHIPS** MLA; ALSC; AATF; SEC. **RESEARCH** 19th and 20th Century French lit. **SELECTED PUBLICATIONS** Auth, Camus: Love and Sexuality, U of FL Press, 98. **CONTACT ADDRESS** Dept of French, SUNY, Stony Brook, PO Box 48, Miller Place, NY 11764.

ROBB, JAMES WILLIS
PERSONAL Born 06/27/1918, Jamaica, NY, m, 1972 **DISCIPLINE** SPANISH LANGUAGE & LITERATURE **EDUCATION** Studies at Sorbonne Institute De Touraine, France, 37-38; Univ Nacidnal De Mexico, 48; Colgate Univ, AB, 39; Middlebury Col, AM, 50; Cath Univ Am, PhD, 58. **CAREER** Instr, 46-50, Norwich Univ; from asst prof to assoc prof, 50-66, prof romance lang, 66-88, prof emeritus, 88-, George Washington Univ; Studies at Sorbonne, Institute de Touraine, France, 37-38; Universidad Nacional De Mexico, 48. **HONORS AND AWARDS** Alfonso Reyes Int Lit Prize, Mexico, 78; Diploma of Merit, State of Nuevo Leon and City of Monterrey, Mexico, 79; Corresponding Member, Academia Mexicana De La Lengua, 98. **MEMBERSHIPS** MLA; Am Asn Teachers Span & Port; Inst Int Lit Iberoam; Phi Beta Kappa; Asn De Colombianistas. **RESEARCH** The works of Alfonso Reyes and German Arciniegas; modern Spanish American literature; Mexican, Colombian & Brazilian literatures. **SELECTED PUBLICATIONS** Auth, Repertorio Biblioffico De Alfonso Reyes, 74; auth,El Estilo De Alfonso Reyes 1965, 78; auth, Por Loscaminos de Alfonso Reyes, INBA/Univ Valle Mex, 81; auth, Variedades de ensayismo en A Reyes y German Arciniegas, 81; auth, La cena de A Reyes, cuento onirico: Surrealismo o realismo magico?, 81; auth, Caminos cruzados en el epistolario de M Toussaint y A Reyes, A Reyes: Homenaje de la Facultad de Filosofia y Letras, Univ Nac Autonoma Mex, Mex, 81; auth, Prosa y Poesta De Alfonso Reyes 1975, 84; auth, Imfgenes De America en Alfonso Reyes y German Arciniegas, Mas Paginas sobre Alfonso Reyes, 96-97. **CONTACT ADDRESS** Dept of Romance Lang, The George Washington Univ, Washington, DC 20052.

ROBBINS, JILL
DISCIPLINE COMPARATIVE LITERATURE **EDUCATION** Cornell Univ, BA; Yale Univ, PhD. **CAREER** Assoc prof, SUNY Buffalo. **RESEARCH** Bibl and philosophical hermeneutics; the Bible as lit; lit theory; ethical thought of Emmanuel Levinas; Levinas' philos in its rel to lit. **SELECTED PUBLICATIONS** Auth, Prodigal Son/Elder Brother: Interpretation and Alterity in Augustine, Petrarch, Kafka, Levinas, Univ Chicago P, 91; The Writing of the Holocaust: Claude Lanzmann's Shoah; Visage, Figure: Reading Levinas' Totality and Infinity; An Inscribed Responsibility: Levinas' Difficult Freedom. **CONTACT ADDRESS** Dept Comp Lit, SUNY, Buffalo, 639 Clemens Hall, Buffalo, NY 14260.

ROBERTS, ANNA
DISCIPLINE FRENCH **EDUCATION** Brown, MA, PhD. **CAREER** Asst Prof, Miami Univ. **HONORS AND AWARDS** Co-organized, Brown University's Grad Conf in Fr Stud. **RESEARCH** Medieval and women's studies and on the history of art and technology. **SELECTED PUBLICATIONS** Ed, Violence against Women in Medieval Texts, UP Fla, 98. **CONTACT ADDRESS** Dept of French and Italian, Miami Univ, Oxford, OH 45056.

ROBERTS, HELEN FREEAR
DISCIPLINE SPANISH LITERATURE **EDUCATION** Univ New Hampshire, BS; Univ Conn, MA, PhD. **CAREER** Vis asst prof. **RESEARCH** Contemporary Spanish drama. **SELECTED PUBLICATIONS** Auth, Deconstruction and Enigma in 'Numa una leyenda' (rev), 96. **CONTACT ADDRESS** Spanish Dept, Col of the Holy Cross, Worcester, MA 01610-2395.

ROBERTS, MICHAEL
PERSONAL Born 09/16/1947, Eccles, United Kingdom, m, 1970, 1 child **DISCIPLINE** CLASSICS **EDUCATION** Cambridge Univ BA, 69, MA, 73; Univ IL Urbana-Champaign, MA, 74, PhD, 78. **CAREER** Vis lectr, Univ WI-Milwaukee, 78-80; asst prof, 80-86, assoc prof, 86-91, prof, 91-, Robert Rich Prof of Lat, 92-, Wesleyan Univ. **HONORS AND AWARDS** NEH summer sem fel, 82 & 86; ACLS fel, 87; NEH fel, Jan-June, 92. **MEMBERSHIPS** Am Philol Asn; Am Inst Archaeol; Medieval Acad of Am; N Am Patristic Societe; Medieval Lat Asn N Am. **RESEARCH** Late antiquity; Latin literature; rhetoric. **SELECTED PUBLICATIONS** Auth, Poetry and the Cult of the Martyrs, Michigan, 93; St. Martin and the Leper, Jour of Medieval Lat, 94; The Description of Landscape in the Poetry of Venantius Fortunatus, Traditio, 94; Martin Meets Maximus, Rev des etudes augustiniennes, 95. **CONTACT ADDRESS** Dept of Classical Studies, Wesleyan Univ, Middletown, CT 06459-0146. **EMAIL** mroberts@wesleyan.edu

ROBINSON, DANIEL N.
PERSONAL Born 03/09/1937, New York, NY, m, 1967, 2 children **DISCIPLINE** PHILOSOPHY OF SCIENCE; PHILOSOPHY OF MIND; NEUROPSYCHOLOGY **EDUCATION** Colgate Univ, BA, 58; Hofstra Univ, MA, 60; CUNY, PhD, 65. **CAREER** Res psychologist, Columbia Univ Sch Engineer & Applied Sci, 60-68; asst prof, Amherst Coll, 68-70; assoc prof, Psych, Amherst Coll, 70-71; vis lectr, Philos, Univ Oxford, 91-; prof, Psych, Georgetown Univ, 74-98; distinguished Res prof, Georgetown Univ, 98-; ed, Journl of Theor & Phil, Psychology, 98-. **HONORS AND AWARDS** Past Pres, Division of Hist of Psychol; Past Pres, Division of Theoritical & Philos Psychol. **MEMBERSHIPS** Am Psychol Asn; Am Philos Asn. **RESEARCH** Hist & Philosophical Psychology; Intellect hist; Philos of mind; Mind/Brain relations. **SELECTED PUBLICATIONS** "Wild Beasts and Idle Humours: Legal Insanity and the Finding of Fault," Philosophy, Psychiatry, and Psychology, Cambridge Univ Press, 95; "On the Laws of History," Psychological Inquiry, 95; "The Logic of Reductionistic Models," New Ideas in Psychology, 95; "On the Primacy of Duties," Philosophy, 95; "Radical Ontologies," Int Jour for the Philos of Sci, 95; "Therapy as Theory and Civics," Theory & Psychol, 97; "Studies of Hysteria a Century Later," Amer Jour of Clinical Hypnosis, 96; An Intellectual History of Psychology, Univ Wis, 95; Wild Beasts and Idle Humours: The Insanity Defense from Antiquity to the Present," Harvard Univ Press, 96; The Mind: An Oxford Reader, Oxford Univ Press, 98. **CONTACT ADDRESS** Dept Psychol, Georgetown Univ, Washington, DC 20007. **EMAIL** robinsdn@gunet.georgetown.edu

ROBINSON, FRED C.
PERSONAL Born 09/23/1930, Birmingham, AL, m, 1959, 2 children **DISCIPLINE** ENGLISH, PHILOLOGY **EDUCATION** Birmingham Southern Col, BA, 53; MA, 54, PhD, 61, Univ N Carolina; Williams Col, DLit (honorary), 85; Yale Univ, MA (honorary), 89. **CAREER** Instr and Asst Prof, 60-65, Assoc Prof/Prof, 67-72, Stanford Univ; Asst and Assoc Prof, Cornell Univ, 65-67; Visiting Prof, Harvard Univ, 82; Prof, 72-83, Douglas Tracy Smith Prof, 83-, Yale Univ. **HONORS AND AWARDS** Rector's Medal, Univ of helsinki, 84; Haskins Medal of the Medieval Acad of Am, 84; Sir Israel Gollancz Prize of the British Acad, 97; Wlliam Clyde DeVane Medal of Phi Beta Kappa at Yale, 99; fel, Am Acad of Arts and Sci, 76-; Fel, Medieval Acad of Am, 79-; Corresponding fel, British Acad, 94-; Corresponding fel, Meddeleuse Verenigung van Suidelike Afrika, 75-; Foreign mem, Finnish Acad of Sci and letters, 99-; Res fel, Japan Soc for the Promotion of Sci, 89; Ireland Distinguished Vis Scholar Awd, Univ of Alabama, 99; Professore solo per ricerca, La Sapienza, Univ of Rome, 00; Hon mem of Int Soc of Anglo-Saxonists, 99; Hon d.Littt., Williams col, 85; hon M.A., Yale Univ, 89. **MEMBERSHIPS** Early English Text Soc; Henry Bradshaw Soc; Medieval Acad of Am (pres 83-84); New England Medieval Confernece (pres 82-83). **RESEARCH** Old English language and literature; English philology of all periods. **SELECTED PUBLICATIONS** Auth, Old English Literature: A Select Bibliography (Toronto), 70; coauth, A Bibliography of Publications on Old English Literature (Toronto), 80; auth, Beowulf and the Appositive Style (Knoxville), 85; coauth, Old English Verse Texts from Many Sources: A Comprehensive Collection (Copenhagen), 91; auth, The Tomb of Beowulf (Oxford), 93; auth, The Editing of Old English (Oxford), 94; coauth, Beowulf: An Edition with Relevant Shorter Texts (Oxford), 98; coauth, A Guide to Old English, 6th ed. (Oxford), 00. **CONTACT ADDRESS** Dept of English, Yale Univ, PO Box 208302, New Haven, CT 06520-8302.

ROBINSON, IRA
PERSONAL Born 05/02/1951, Boston, MA, m, 1976, 2 children **DISCIPLINE** NEAR EASTERN LANGUAGES AND CIVILIZATIONS **EDUCATION** Johns Hopkins Univ, BA, 73; Columbia Univ, MA, 75; Harvard Univ, PhD, 80. **CAREER** Lectr, Concordia Univ, 79-80; asst prof, Concordia Univ, 80-84; assoc prof, Concordia Univ, 84-93; prof, relig, Concordia Univ, 93-. **HONORS AND AWARDS** Toronto Jewish Book award, 97; Kenneth B. Smilen book prize, Jewish Mus, 86. **MEMBERSHIPS** Asn for Can Jewish Studies; Asn for Jewish Studies; Soc Quebecois pour lietude de la religion; Am Jewish Hist Soc; Am Academy of Relig; Israel Hist Soc; Canadian Ethnic Studies Asn. **RESEARCH** Canadian Jewry; Orthodox Judaism in North America. **SELECTED PUBLICATIONS** Ed, The Thought of Moses Maimonides: Philosophical and Legal Studies, (Lewiston, Queenston and Lampeter, Edwin Mellen Press, 90; transl, Menahem Kaufman, An Ambiguous Partnership: Non-Zionist and Zionist in America, 1939-1948, (Jerusalem, Magnes Press, 91); auth, Moses Cordovero's Introduction to Kabbala: An Annotated Traslation of His or Ne'Erav, (Ktav/Yeshiva Univ Press, 94); co-ed, The Interaction of Scientific and Jewish Cultures In Modern Times, (Lewiston, Queenston and Lampeter, Edwin Mellen Press, 94); ed, Renewing Our Days: Montreal Jews in the Twentieth Century, (Montreal, Vehicule Press, 95); auth, "The Zaddik as Hero in Hasidic Hagiography," in Crisis and Reaction: the Hero in Jewish History, ed. Menachem Mor, (Omaha, Nebraska, Creighton Univ Press, (95): 93-103; auth, "Foreword," in A Selected Bibliography of Research on Canadian Jewry, 1900-1980, ed. Susan Vadnay, 95; auth, "An Identification and a Correction," Am Jewish Archives 47, (95): 331-332; auth, "The Foundation Documents of the Jewish Community Council of Montreal," New York, Jewish Theological Sem of Am, vol. 1, (97): 103-159; auth, "Virtual Reality Comes to Canadian Jewry," Jerusalem Letter/ Viewpoints no. 389, (98): 1-5. **CONTACT ADDRESS** Dept. of Religion, Concordia Univ, Montreal, 1455 Maisonneuve Blvd. W, Montreal, QC, Canada H3G 1M8. **EMAIL** robinso@vax2.concordia.ca

ROBISON, R. E.
PERSONAL Born 10/21/1950, Kansas City, MO, m, 1971, 10 children **DISCIPLINE** APPLIED LINGUISTICS **EDUCATION** Univ Cal LA, PhD 93, MA 85; Gordon-Conwell Theological Sem, Mdiv 76; Massachusetts Inst of Technology, SB 72. **CAREER** Azusa Pacific Univ, prof 97-, assoc prof 91-97; Univ Cal LA, tchg fel 87-92; Glendale Community Col, inst 86-91; Univ Cal LA, tchg assoc 82-86. **HONORS AND AWARDS** Phi Beta Kappa; Eugene Nida Awd. **MEMBERSHIPS** Teachers of Eng to Speakers of Other Lang; Cal Tchrs of Eng to Speaks of Other Lang **RESEARCH** Verb morphology in interlanguage; interlanguage analysis. **SELECTED PUBLICATIONS** Auth, Verb inflections in native speaker speech: Do the mean what we think?, in: The development of morphological systematicity: A cross-linguistic perspective, eds H. Pishwa and K. Maroldt, Tubingen, Gunter Narr, 95; The aspect hypothesis revisited: A cross sectional study of tense and aspect marking in interlanguage, Applied Ling, 95; Aspectual marking in English interlanguage, Stud in Sec Lang Acquis, 90. **CONTACT ADDRESS** Dept of Global Studies, Azusa Pacific Univ, 901 East Alosta Av, Azusa, CA 91702-7000. **EMAIL** rrobison@apu.edu

ROCHE, MARK W.
PERSONAL Born 08/29/1956, Weymouth, MA, m, 1981 **DISCIPLINE** GERMAN LITERATURE, PHILOSOPHY **EDUCATION** Williams Col, BA, 78; Ederhard Karls Univ, MA, 80; Princeton Univ, MA, 82, PhD, 84. **CAREER** Teaching asst, Williams Col, 77-78; teaching asst, Phillips Andover Acad, 78; asst instr, Princeton Univ, 82-83; asst prof to assoc prof to dept chmn, Ohio State Univ, 84-96; dept chmn to prof to dean, Univ Notre Dame, 96-. **HONORS AND AWARDS** Alexander von Humboldt Fel, 97; Distinguished Vis Lectr, Wake For Univ, 95; DAAD Res Grant, 91; NEH, 91; ACLS Fel, 85; Fac Development Grant, 85; Whiting Fel, 83-84; Max Kade Fel, 81-82; Fulbright Fel, 78-80; Benedict Prize, 78; Phi Beta Kappa. **MEMBERSHIPS** AATG; AAUP; APA; GSA; HAS; MLA; SPSCVA; Lessing Soc. **RESEARCH** German literature; philosophy; film; higher education. **SELECTED PUBLICATIONS** Auth, "Laughter and Truth in Doktor Faustus: Nietzschean Structures in Mann's Novel of Self-cancellations," Deut Vierte Lit Geistes 60 (86): 309-32; auth, "Holiness and Justice: Lessing's Nathan der Weise in the Context of Plato's Euthyphro," Antike Abend 34 (88): 42-62; auth, "Schnitzler's Anatol as a Philosophical Comedy," Modern Austrian Lit 22 (89): 51-63; auth, Gottfried Benn's Static Poetry: Aesthetic and Intellectual-Historical Interpretations, Univ NCar Pr, 91; uth, Dynamic Stillness: Philosophical Conceptions of Ruhe in Schiller Holderlin Michner and Heine, Studies Deuts Lit, 92; auth, "Apel and Lessing--or: The Ethics of Communication and the Strategies of Comedy," Lessing Yearbk 25 (93): 41-54; co-auth, "Vico's Age of Heroes and the Age of Men in John Ford's Film The Man Who Shot Liberty Valance," CLIO 23 (94): 131-47; auth, Tragedy and Comedy: A Systematic Study and a Critique of Hegl, Univ NYork Pr, 98; auth, "Justice and the Withdrawal of God in Woody Allen's Crimes and Misdemeanors," Film Philol (00): 68-83. **CONTACT ADDRESS** 12418 Range Line Rd, Berrien Springs, MI 49103-9632. **EMAIL** mroche@nd.edu

ROCKLAND, MICHAEL AARON
PERSONAL Born 07/14/1935, New York, NY, m, 1978, 5 children **DISCIPLINE** AMERICAN & LATIN AMERICAN STUDIES **EDUCATION** Hunter Col, BA, 55; Univ Minn, MA, 60, PhD(Am studies), 68. **CAREER** Teaching asst Am studies, Univ Minn, 57-59, instr, 60-61, counsel, Col Arts & Sci, 59-61; asst cult attache, Am Embassy, Buenos Aires, 62-63, asst cult attache & dir, Casa Am Cult Ctr, Am Embassy, Madrid, 63-67; exec asst to chancellor, NJ State Dept Higher Educ, 68-69; asst prof, 69-71, asst dean col, 69-72, assoc prof, 72-81, Prof Am Studies, Douglass Col, Rutgers Univ, 81-, Chm Dept, 69-; Lectr, Univ Santa Fe, Arg, 63; guest lectr, Span Univ Syst, 64-67; publ subventions, Rutgers Univ & Arg Embassy, 70; fac chm contemporary Am sem returning foreign serv officers, US Info Agency, 72-73, mem bd, Int Inst Women Studies, 72-; contrib ed, NJ Monthly, 77-; contrib reporter, NJ Nightly News, 78-. **HONORS AND AWARDS** Alumni Hall of Fame, Hunter Col, 73; NJ Pres Assoc Award, 80; Pulitzer Prize nominee, 80; Fulbright Lectureships in Uruguay, 82, and Peru, 85; First Prize for Feature Journalism, Am Soc of Jour, 92; The Nat Am Studies Prize for Distinguished Teaching, 97; The Warren Susman Award for Distinguished Teaching, 97; Teacher of the Year Award, Rutgers Col, 98; Served as distinguished lectr in India, Pakistan, Israel, Canada, Italy, Norway, Spain, Argentina, Colombia, El Salvador, Peru, Portugal, Korea, and Japan. **MEMBERSHIPS** Am Studies Asn (pres, 71-72); Orgn Am Historians; hon mem Inst Sarmiento, Arg; member, Spanish Asn for Am Studies. **RESEARCH** Foreign commentators on the United States; ethnic affairs in the United States, especially the relationship between Jews and the other ethnic groups; mobility in America; Am Aesthetics. **SELECTED PUBLICATIONS** Auth, Sarmiento's Travels in the United States in 1847, Princeton Univ, 70; ed, America in the Fifties and Sixties: Julian Marias on the United States, Pa State Univ, 72; coauth, Three Days on Big City Waters (film), Nat Educ TV, 74; auth, The American Jewish Experience in Literature, Haifa Univ, 75; Homes on Wheels, Rutgers Univ Pres, 80; A Bliss Case, Coffee House Press, 89; coauth, Looking for America on the New Jersey Turnpike, Rutgers Univ Press, 80; auth, Snowshoeing Through Sewers, Rutgers Univ Press, 94; auth, "what's American About American things?, Univ of Salamanca, 96; coauth, "The Jews of New Jersey: A Pictorial History, Rutgers Univ Press, 01. **CONTACT ADDRESS** Dept of Am Studies, Rutgers, The State Univ of New Jersey, New Brunswick, PO Box 270, New Brunswick, NJ 08903-0270. **EMAIL** rockland@rci.rutgers.edu

ROCKMORE, SYLVIE
PERSONAL Born 11/13/1945, Nice, France France, M, 2 children **DISCIPLINE** FRENCH AND FRANCOPHONE CULTURES **EDUCATION** Vanderbilt Univ, PhD. **CAREER** Languages, Carnegie Mellon Univ. **MEMBERSHIPS** Alliance francaise; Am Asn Tchrs French; MLA; WIF. **RESEARCH** Francophone and French Studies. **SELECTED PUBLICATIONS** Auth, De Leuk-le lievre a Brer Rabbit : transformations d'un conte. Presentation, 88; Organized the Conference on Simone de Beauvoir: Beauvoir at 90: A Reevaluation, Carnegie Mellon Univ, 98; Quelques idees pour celebrer la negritude. AATF Nat Bull, 96. **CONTACT ADDRESS** Dept Modern Languages, Carnegie Mellon Univ, 5000 Forbes Ave, Pittsburgh, PA 15213. **EMAIL** rockmore@andrew.cmu.edu

ROCKWELL, PAUL
PERSONAL m **DISCIPLINE** FRENCH **EDUCATION** Univ Wisc Madison, BA, 80; MA, 82; PhD, 88. **CAREER** Asst prof to prof, Amherst Col, 88-. **RESEARCH** Medieval French Romance, 12th and 13th Centuries. **SELECTED PUBLICATIONS** Auth, "Writing the Fountain: the Specificity of Resemblance in Arthurian Romance," Bulletin bibliographique de la societe internationale arturienne, (90): 267-282; auth, "The Falsification of Resemblance: Reading the False Guenievre," in The Arthurian Yearbook, (91): 27-42; auth, "Twin Mysteries: Ceci n'est pas un Fresne," in conjunctures: Medieval Studies in Honor of Douglas Kelly, Keith Busby and Norris Lacy, (Amsterdam, 94), 487-504; auth, Rewriting Resemblance in Medieval French Romance: Ceci n'est pas un graal, Garland, 95; auth, "Je ne sui mie soffisanz: Insufficiency and Cyclicity in the Lancelot-Grail cycle," in Transtextualities: Of Cycles and Cyclicity, Don Maddox and Sara Sturm-Maddox, (Binghamton, 96), 71-91; auth, "Remembering Troie: The Implications of Images in the Roman de Troie and the Prose Lancelot," Arthuriana, 97; auth, "Appelation controlee: Motif Transfer and the Adaptation of Names in the Chevalier as deus espees," in Por le soie amiste: Essays in Honor of Norris J. Lacy, Keith Busby and Catherine M. Jones, (Amsterdam, 00), 435-452. **CONTACT ADDRESS** Dept French, Amherst Col, PO Box 5000, Amherst, MA 01002-5000. **EMAIL** pvrockwell@yahoo.com

RODGER, VALENTINE WATSON
PERSONAL Born 02/14/1939, London, England, m, 1988 **DISCIPLINE** LANGUAGE, FRENCH, TRANSLATION **EDUCATION** St Anne's Col, Oxford, BA, 60; MA, 64; PhD, 67. **CAREER** Instr, Univ Western Ont, 65-67; lectr to asst prof to assoc prof, Huron Univ Col, 67-. **HONORS AND AWARDS** Gamble Open Exhib, Mod Lang, St Anne's Col, 57-60; Irene Jamison Scholar, 60-62; Res Miss, SSHRCC, CNRS, Paris, 78; Res Miss, France, 79. **MEMBERSHIPS** MLA; CATS. **RESEARCH** Translation techniques and theories from the sixteenth century to present day. **SELECTED PUBLICATIONS** Co-trans, Principles of Philosophy, by Rene Descartes (Dordrecht, Holland/Boston, D. Reidel Pub, 1983); auth, Apprendre a traduire, Can Scholar's Pr (Toronto, Ont), 90, 2nd ed. 93; auth, Mieux Traduire, Mieux S'exprimer: Cahier D'exercises pour L'appretissage du Francais Ecrit et Parle, Can Scholar's Pr (Toronto, Ont), 97. **CONTACT ADDRESS** Fr Lang Dept, Huron Univ Col, 1349 Western Rd, London, ON, Canada N6G 1H3. **EMAIL** vwrodger@uwo.ca

RODGERS, JOSEPH JAMES, JR.
PERSONAL Born 11/22/1939, Hopewell, VA **DISCIPLINE** LINGUISTICS **EDUCATION** Morehouse Coll, BA 1962; Univ de Grenoble France, Cert d'etudes 1960; Univ of Wis, MA 1965; Univ of So CA, PhD 1969. **CAREER** Los Angeles City Coll, lecturer 1966-67; Univ of So CA, instr 1968-69; Occidental Coll, asst prof 1968-73; VA State Coll, prof & chmn 1970-71; Intl Curriculum Devel Program Phelps-Stokes Fund, reg coord 1975-; Carib-Amer School to Dominican Republic, 75; Lincoln Univ, Chmn, Prof, 73-; Center for Critical Care Languages, Dir, 90-; American Univ of Uzes, France, Pres, 90-. **HONORS AND AWARDS** Merrill Travel Study Group to Europe 1959-60; W Wilson Fellowship to Harvard 1962-63; NDEA & Oakley Fellow Univ of So CA 1965-69; numerous articles in Maghreb Digest 1966-67; Distinguished Teaching 1974; Lindback Awd Pi Delta Phi Frat Honor Soc; Alpha Mu Gamma Natl Foreign Language Honor Soc; Honored Nominee, CASE Professor of the Year 1989; Distinguished Faculty Awd for Scholarship Lincoln Univ, 1989. **MEMBERSHIPS** Pr tutor Stanley Kramer's son 1966-67; mem African Ethnic Herit Sem 1974, 1975. **SELECTED PUBLICATIONS** "African Leadership Ideology" (w/Ukandi Damachi) Praeger 1976; "Sacrificing Qual Lang Learn for Pol Exped" 1977. **CONTACT ADDRESS** Dept of Languages/Linguistics, Lincoln University, PA 19352.

RODINI, ROBERT JOSEPH
PERSONAL Born 08/02/1936, Albany, CA, m, 1962, 2 children **DISCIPLINE** FRENCH **EDUCATION** Univ Calif, Berkeley, MA, 60, PhD, 67. **CAREER** Instr to Assoc Prof, 65-76, Prof Ital, 76-97, Prof emeritus, Univ WI-Madison, 97-, Dir, Univ MI, Dir, Univ WI, Academic Year in Florence, Italy, 00. **HONORS AND AWARDS** Am Coun Learned Soc, Fel, 76. **MEMBERSHIPS** MLA; Am Asn Teachers Ital; Renaissance Soc Am. **RESEARCH** Renaissance lyric poetry and drama, especially Italian, 16th century. **SELECTED PUBLICATIONS** Auth, Antonfrancesco Grazzini: Poet, Dramatist, Novelliere, Univ WI, 70; contribr, A Renaissance Alphabet, Univ Wis, 71; ed, Opere di Dio, Houghton, 76; Medieval and renaissance spectacle and theatre, Vol XIV, No 3, Forum Italium, 80; coauth, Ludovico Ariosto: An Annotated Bibliography of Criticism 1956-1980, Univ Missouri, 84; auth, "Dispersion and Reintergration: Ariosto"s I suppositi and Archetypal Mides of early sexteenth-Century italian Comedy," Journal of Medieval and renassiance Studies, (86), 197-212; auth, "Dispersion and Reintergration: Ariosto"s I Suppositi and Archetypal Modes of Early Sixteenth-Century Italian Comedy," Journal of Medieval and Renassiance Studies, (86), 197-212; auth, "The Weight of Words: Leonardo Da Vinci and The Anxiety of Language," Philological Quarterly, (91), 17-27; auth, "Michelangelos's RIME ant The Problematics of the Gaze," In Essays in Honor of Nicolas J. Perella, (94), 65-81); auth, "Avaro Seme Di Donna: Patrizia Cavalli's Transgressive Discourse," Romanic Rev, 98 **CONTACT ADDRESS** Dept of French and Italian, Univ of Wisconsin, Madison, 1220 Linden Dr, Madison, WI 53706-1557. **EMAIL** rjrodini@facstaff.wisc.edu

RODRIGO, VICTORIA
DISCIPLINE SECOND LANGUAGE ACQUISITION, METHODOLOGY, PEDAGOGY **EDUCATION** Univ Southern Calif, PhD, 95. **CAREER** Asst prof Span, undergrad comt, La State Univ. **RESEARCH** Reading and listening as ways to promote language acquisition. **SELECTED PUBLICATIONS** Coauth, La aplicacion del Argumento de la Audicion Enfocada en el Aula de Clase, Granada Eng Tchg Asn, Univ Granada, Spain; A Reading Din in the Head: Evidence of Involuntary Mental Rehearsal in Second Language Readers, in For Lang Ann, 95; Free Voluntary Reading and Vocabulary Knowledge in Native Speakers of Spanish, Perceptual and Motor Skills, 96. **CONTACT ADDRESS** Dept of For Lang and Lit, Louisiana State Univ, 245 Prescott Hall, Baton Rouge, LA 70803. **EMAIL** rodrigo@lsu.edu

RODRIGUEZ, ALVARO
PERSONAL Born 10/07/1953, Cuba, m, 1975, 2 children **DISCIPLINE** SPANISH LITERATURE **EDUCATION** Univ de La Habana, PhD, 78. **CAREER** MB Lamar High Sch International Baccalaureate Coord, Houston Independent Sch District, 80-; asst prof, Univ St Thomas, 93-. **HONORS AND AWARDS** Excellence in Teaching Awd, Brazo Chapter Houston Metropolitan Area--Local Chapter of AATSP, 96. **MEMBERSHIPS** AATSP, MLA, TAGT. **RESEARCH** Methodology, Foreign Languages & Gifted Education, Post-Civil War Peninsular Literature, Cervantes. **SELECTED PUBLICATIONS** Auth, curriculum guides for Spanish/French, Houston Independent Sch District; auth, teaching units for gifted & talented students in Spanish classes, Houston Independent Sch District. **CONTACT ADDRESS** Dept Modern & Classical Lang, Univ of St. Thomas, Texas, 3800 Montrose Blvd, Houston, TX 77006-4626. **EMAIL** rod@wt.net

RODRIGUEZ, LYDIA H.
PERSONAL Born 03/13/1967, Eureka, CA, s **DISCIPLINE** CLASSICS, LANGUAGE, LITERATURE **EDUCATION** Col Redwoods, AA, 91; Humboldt State Univ, BA, 92; Calif State Univ, MA, 94; Univ Cinci, PhD, 99. **CAREER** Instr, Pizer Col, Cinci State Col, 96-98; teaching asst to adj instr, Univ Cinci, 94-00; asst prof, Ind State Univ, 00-. **HONORS AND AWARDS** Grad Min Scholar; Cert Achievement Awd; Tuition Grant; Hon Soc Sigma Delta Pi. **MEMBERSHIPS** MLA; Sigma Delta Pi; CRR. **RESEARCH** Latin American female authors and literature; Chicana literature. **SELECTED PUBLICATIONS** Auth, "Teenagers of Peru," article (forthcoming); auth, The Mestizuje of the Canon represented in the Works of Helena Maria Vitamontes, bk, (forthcoming). **CONTACT ADDRESS** 131 Dolores Cir, Apt 4, Indiana, PA 15701-3323. **EMAIL** rodriglh@grove.iup.edu

RODRIGUEZ, RODNEY T.
PERSONAL Born 12/11/1946, Tampa, FL, m, 1968, 2 children **DISCIPLINE** SPANISH **EDUCATION** Northwestern Univ, PhD, 73. **CAREER** Chair Romance Lang, Kalamazoo Col, 91-95; Chair, Mod Lang, Manhattan Col and Col of Mount St. Vincent, 95-. **HONORS AND AWARDS** Fel Woodrow Wilson Found, 71-72; Fel, NEH, 77; Sr Fulbright Lectr, Guatemala, 86. **MEMBERSHIPS** MLA, AATSP. **RESEARCH** Spanish History, Literature, Civilization. **SELECTED PUBLICATIONS** Auth, Revista de Guatemala: Indice Literario, Univ Rafael Landivar (Guatemala), 87, condensed version in Inter-Am rev of Bibliog 38 (88): 29-56; auth, "Yo voy sonando caminos' de Machado a la luz de un intertexto de Rosalia de Castro," Explication de Textos Literarios 18 (89-90): 35-41; auth, "The Reader's Role in 'Tormento': A Reconstruction of the Amparo-Pedro Polo Affair," Anales Goldosianos 24 (89): 69-78; auth, "Icarus Reborn: Mythical Patterns in 'Pepita Jimenez," Revista de Estudios Hispanicos 19 (95): 75-85; auth, "El discurso narativo moral y su recepcion en la Espana de Fernando VII," Actas del X Congreso de la Asoc de Hispanistas II, Barcelona (92): 1475-1483. **CONTACT ADDRESS** Dept For Lang, Manhattan Col, 4513 Manhattan College Pkwy, Bronx, NY 10471-4004. **EMAIL** rrodrigu@manhattan.edu

RODRIGUEZ-FLORIDO, JORGE J.
PERSONAL Born 03/15/1943, Manzanillo, Cuba, s **DISCIPLINE** SPANISH AMERICAN LITERATURE, MATHEMATICS, AFRO-HISPANIC AND LATIN LITERATURE **EDUCATION** Univ Miami, BA, 66; Univ Wisc-Madison, MA, 67, PhD, 75; Univ Ill-Chicago, MS, 79. **CAREER** Cuba literature, Cuban-American literature, Afro-Hispanic literature, poetry, language education. **HONORS AND AWARDS** Chicago State Univ Fac Excellence Awd, 87, 91, 92, 96, 97, 98; Professional Advancement Increase, 93, 99; Instituto Cervantes Superior level diplomate, 96; CSU Fac Enrichment grants, 92, 93, 96, 97, 98. **MEMBERSHIPS** Am Asn of Teachers of Spanish and Portuguese, Ill Foreign Lang Teachers Asn. **RESEARCH** Cuban literature, Cuban-American literature, Afro-American literature, poetry, language education. **SELECTED PUBLICATIONS** Auth, El language en la literaria, Explicacion de tertos literarios, Sacramento (77); auth, Visions de ventana (86) and Por dentro (91); articles on Lydia Cabrera, Miguel Angel Asturias, Ciro Alegria, Matias Mostes Huidobro, Josi Angel Buera, Manuel Navano Luna, Salvador Novo, Enrique Laguerre, Leopol do Hernandez, Enrique Jaramillo Levi and Carloz Guillermo Wilson. **CONTACT ADDRESS** Dept English & Langs, Chicago State Univ, 9501 S King Dr, Chicago, IL 60628-1501. **EMAIL** J-Florido@csu.edu

RODRIGUEZ-LUIS, JULIO
PERSONAL Born 10/09/1937, Cuba, m, 1968, 1 child **DISCIPLINE** SPANISH **EDUCATION** Univ Puerto Rico, BA, 59; Brown Univ, MA, 60; Princeton Univ, PhD, 66. **CAREER** Asst Prof, SUNY, 65-67; Asst Prof, Wesleyan Univ, 67-70; Assoc Prof to Prof, SUNY, 70-93; Prof, Univ Wisc, 93-. **HONORS AND AWARDS** NEH Summer Stipend, 73; SUNY Fac Res Fel, 81; NEH Summer Inst for Teachers, 99. **MEMBERSHIPS** Latin Am Studies Asn, Cervantes Soc of Am, Asn de Cervantestas. **RESEARCH** 20th Century Spanish American narrative; Indigenismo; Poesia negra; Cervantes; The Picaresque novel; Latino Literature; Sociology of Literature; Development of realism in European fiction; 19th Century Spanish novel. **SELECTED PUBLICATIONS** Auth, Re-Reading Jose Marti (1853-1895) One Hundred Years Later, SUNY Press, 99; auth, "Una picara cervantina," Actas del tercer congreso internacional de la Asociacion de Cervantistas (III-Cindac) Cala Galdana, Menorca, 20-25 de octubre de 1997, Universitat de les Illes Balears, 98; auth, "Autorrepresentacion en Cervantes y el sentido del Coloquio de los perros," Cervantes, (97): 25-58; co-auth, A History of Literature in the Caribbean, I. Hispanic and Francophone Regions, John Benjamins, 94; auth, el enfoque documental en la narrativa hispanoamericana. Estudio taxonomico, Fondo de Cultura Economica, 97; auth, the contemporary Praxis of the Fantastic. Borges and Cortazar, Garland Pub, 91. **CONTACT ADDRESS** Dept Spanish & Port, Univ of Wisconsin, Milwaukee, PO Box 413, Milwaukee, WI 53201-0413. **EMAIL** jrluis@uwm.edu

RODRIQUEZ-HERNANDEZ, RAUL
PERSONAL Born 10/11/1944, Xalapa, Veracruz, Mexico, m, 1976 **DISCIPLINE** COMPARATIVE LITERATURE **EDUCATION** Univ Veracruzana, MA, 70; Univ Minn, MA, 76; Cornell Univ, MA, 92; PhD, 97. **CAREER** Instr, Ithaca Col, 86-89; Teaching Asst to Instr, Cornell Univ, 90-95; Vis Instr to Vis Asst Prof, Hamilton Col, 95-97; Asst Prof, Univ Houston, 97-98; Vis Asst Prof to Asst Prof, Univ Rochester, 98-. **HONORS AND AWARDS** Mellon Fel, 92; Nominated for Teacher of the Year, Univ Rochester, 99-00. **MEMBERSHIPS** MLA; IAPL. **RESEARCH** Comparative Literature and Literary theory; Continental Philosophy; Spanish-American Culture and Literature; Hispanic film. **SELECTED PUBLICATIONS** Auth, "Maria Luisa Puga: una nueva sensibilidad de narrar," La escritora hispanica, 90; auth, "Posmodernismo de resistencia y alteridad en La nave de los locos de Cristina Peri Rossi," Revista Canadiense de Estudios Hispanicos, 94; co-auth, "Cronos and the Man of Science: Madness, Monstrosity, Mexico," Revista de Estudios Hispanicos, 98; auth, "Eros in excelsis: Inmaculada o los placeres de la inocencia de Juan Garcia Ponce," Texto Critico, 99; auth, "Viajes con Charley: Despalazamiento cultural e identidad," Texto Critico, 00. **CONTACT ADDRESS** Dept Mod Lang and Cult, Univ of Rochester, 199 Farmington Rd, Rochester, NY 14609. **EMAIL** raul@mail.rochester.edu

ROEPER, THOMAS
DISCIPLINE LINGUISTICS **EDUCATION** Reed Univ, BA, 65; Harvard Univ, PhD, 73. **CAREER** Prof. **RESEARCH** Theoretical approaches to language acquisition and morphology. **SELECTED PUBLICATIONS** Auth, Compound Syntax and Head Movement, Foris, 88; co-auth, On the Ergative and Middle Constructions in English, Ling Inquiry, 84; Implicit Arguments and the Head-Complement Relation, Ling Inquiry, 87; Deductive Parameters and the Growth of Language, Reidel, 87. **CONTACT ADDRESS** Linguistics Dept, Univ of Massachusetts, Amherst, S College 218, Amherst, MA 01003. **EMAIL** roeper@linguist.umass.edu

ROETHKE, GISELA
PERSONAL Born 02/21/1946, Wittingen, Germany, m, 1990, 1 child **DISCIPLINE** 19TH AND 20TH CENTURY GERMAN LITERATURE **EDUCATION** Wash State Univ, MA; Harvard Univ, PhD, 88. **CAREER** Instr, 85-; coord, women's studies, Assoc Prof of German, 95; 95-96; chp-. **RESEARCH** Modern women authors, Women's Literature/Myth **SELECTED PUBLICATIONS** Publications on Christa Wolf, Barbara Frischmuth, Lilian Faschinger, and Hermann Broch. **CONTACT ADDRESS** Dept of Ger, Dickinson Col, Carlisle, PA 17013-2896. **EMAIL** roethke@dickinson.edu

ROGACHEVSKY, JORGE R.
PERSONAL Born 04/28/1954, Buenos Aires, Argentina, s, 2 children **DISCIPLINE** SPANISH **EDUCATION** SUNY, BA, 75; PhD, 87. **CAREER** Vis Instr, Temple Univ, 81-83; Instr, Germantown Friends School, 84-87; Asst Prof to Assoc prof, St Mary's Col, 87-. **HONORS AND AWARDS** Fulbright Scholar, 93-94. **MEMBERSHIPS** As of Acad Prog in Latin Am and the Caribbean, Fulbright Asn, Latin Am Studies Asn, Mod Lang Asn. **RESEARCH** Central American and Caribbean Literature; Latin American Cultural and Social History; Multicultural Studies; United States-Latin American Relations. **SELECTED PUBLICATIONS** Rev, of "Lockdown America" by Christian Parenti, Resist, (00): 5-7; rev, of "Rigoberta Menchu and the Story of all Poor Guatemalans" by David Stoll, Zmagazine, (99): 96-99; rev, of "At the Edge of the World: Caves and Late classic Maya World View" by Karen Bassie-Sweet, Philosophy East and West, (99): 388-391; auth, "Los anos sucios de la modernidad en la obra de Luis Aceituno," La Ermita, (98): 38-46; auth, "Maya Spirituality in the World Today," Resist, (97): 1-3; auth, "Once Again elections in Nicaragua: Can Democracy Triumph?," Resist, (96): 4-5; rev, of "En el filo: La crisis de la utopia revolucionaria," La Ermita, (96): 44-46; auth, "Civilizacion y barbarie en la obra de Flavio Herrera," Letras de Guatemala, (95): 9-29. **CONTACT ADDRESS** Dept For Lang, St. Mary's Col of Maryland, Saint Mary's City, MD 20686. **EMAIL** jrrogachevsky@osprey.smcm.edu

ROGERS, KENNETH HALL
PERSONAL Born 06/01/1939, Needham, MA, m, 1963, 2 children **DISCIPLINE** ROMANCE LINGUISTICS, FRENCH **EDUCATION** Boston Univ, BA, 61; Columbia Univ, MA, 63, PhD, 70. **CAREER** Instr French, 68-70, Asst Prof to Prof French & Romance Ling, Univ RI, 70-. **MEMBERSHIPS** MLA; Ling Soc Am; Int Ling Asn; Am Asn Teachers Fr; Am Soc Geoling. **RESEARCH** Romance linguistics-phonology and morphology; sociolinguistics and linguistic nationlism. **SELECTED PUBLICATIONS** Auth, Vocalic Alternation in the Surselvan Romansh Verb, In: Studies in Honor of Mario A Pei, 72; Romance Philology and the Sociology of Language: A Pedagogical Perspective, Yearbk 1975 Pedagog Sem Romance Philol, MLA, 75; La Situation Diglossique dan les Grisons, Cahier Groupe Recherches Diglossie, Univ Montpellier, 76; Rheto-Romance: Dialect and Geography in Southeastern Switzerland, Geoling Ill, 77; Studies on linguistic nationalism in the Romance languages, In: Trends in Romance Philology and Linguistics, Vol 2, Mouton, The Hague, 81; Selected recent studies in linguistic nationalism in the Romance languages, Rev Can Etudes sur Nationalisme VIII, Fall 81; Languages and language policies in the USSR, Geolinguistics, VII, 81. **CONTACT ADDRESS** Dept of Lang, Univ of Rhode Island, 60 Upper Col Rd, Kingston, RI 02881. **EMAIL** rqg101@uriacc.uri.edu

ROGERS, LAWRENCE WILLIAM
PERSONAL Born Oakland, CA, 2 children **DISCIPLINE** JAPANESE LITERATURE AND LANGUAGE **EDUCATION** Univ CA, Berkeley, BA, 61, MA, 66, PhD (oriental lang), 75. **CAREER** Actg instr Japanese, Univ CA, Berkeley, 72-74; actg asst prof, Univ CA, Los Angeles, 74-75; asst prof, 76- 82, assoc prof, 82-89, prof Japanese, Univ Hawaii, Hilo, 89-; vis fac, Univ BC, summer 78 & Int Christian Univ, Tokyo, summers 81 & 82. **HONORS AND AWARDS** Various travel grants. **MEMBERSHIPS** Asn for Asian Studies; Asn Teachers Japanese; Soc Writers, Ed & Transl. **RESEARCH** Modern Japanese poetry and fiction; the haibun essay. **SELECTED PUBLICATIONS** Auth, Rags and Tatters: The Uzuragoromo of Yokoi Yayu, Monumenta Nipponica, autumn 79; She Loves Me, She Loves Me Not, Shinju and Shikido okagami, Monumenta Nipponica, spring 94; transl, Citadel in Spring (novel), Kodansha Int, 90; various short story translations. **CONTACT ADDRESS** Dept Lang, Univ of Hawaii, Hilo, 200 W Kawili St, Hilo, HI 96720-4091. **EMAIL** rogers@hawaii.edu

ROGERS, NELS JEFFREY
PERSONAL Born 03/25/1970, Tuscon, AZ, m, 1995, 2 children **DISCIPLINE** GERMAN **EDUCATION** Univ Ore, BA, 93; Univ Pa, MA, 98; PhD, 01. **CAREER** Lectr, Univ Pa, 97-98; instr to asst prof, Univ Tenn Martin, 99-. **HONORS AND AWARDS** Univ Pa Dean's Scholar, 96; Phi Beta Kappa; Delta Phi Alpha. **MEMBERSHIPS** AATG; MLA; Intl Brecht Soc. **RESEARCH** 19th and 20th Century intellectual history; Aesthetics; Critical theory; Theado W. Adovno. **SELECTED PUBLICATIONS** Auth, The Brecht Industry: Politics and the Avant-garde in a divided Germany. **CONTACT ADDRESS** Dept Mod Lang, Univ of Tennessee, Martin, Dept German, Martin, TN 38238-0001. **EMAIL** nrogers@utm.edu

ROGERS, THOMAS FRANKLYN
PERSONAL Born 04/12/1933, Salt Lake City, UT, m, 1958, 7 children **DISCIPLINE** RUSSIAN LITERATURE **EDUCATION** Univ UT, BA, 55; Yale Univ, MA, 62; Georgetown Univ, PhD, 68. **CAREER** Instr Ger, Russ & humanities, Howard Univ, 62-66; asst prof Russ, Univ UT, 66-69; assoc prof, 69-76, Prof Russ, Brigham Young Univ, 76-, Dir hon prog, Brigham Young Univ, 74-77; ed, Encyclia, J of the UT Academy, 91-93; Russian Enterprises Development, Inc (REDI), member, bd of dirs, 96-. **HONORS AND AWARDS** Emeritus Member, Playwrights' Circle; Distinguished Service Awd, BYU Honors Prog, 77; Drama Prize, Asn of Mormon Letters, 83; Col of Humanities Awd for Academic Distinction, BYU, 84; Distinguished Teacher Awd, FORSCOM, 91; 2nd place Short Story Prize, Dialogue Magazine, 91; Lifetime Service Awd, Mormon Festival of the Arts, St George, UT, 98. **MEMBERSHIPS** Am Asn Teachers Slavic & East Europ Lang; Rocky Mountain Mod Lang Asn; Am Coun Teachers of Russian, member, bd of dirs, 97-. **RESEARCH** Soviet literature; drama; playwrighting. **SELECTED PUBLICATIONS** Auth, Trends in Soviet Prose of the Thaw Period, Rocky Mountain Mod Lang Asn J, winter 69; The Ironic Mode in Soviet Russian Prose, 69 & The Implications of Christ's Passion in Doctor Zhivago, Vol XVIII, No 4, 384-391, Slavic & East Europ J; transl, S Panchev, Turbulence and Random Functions, Pergamon Press, 71; Superflous Men and the Post-Stalin Thaw, The Hague: Mouton, 72; Ethical Idealism in Post-Stalin Fiction, Rocky Mountain Soc Sci J, 4/75; Hedonism and humanitas: The Pushkin Perplex, The Need Beyond Research, and Other Essays, Brigham Young Univ Press, 76; The Sacred in Literature, Lit & Belief, 81; The Suffering Christ in Grotowski's Apokalypsis cum Figuris, Relig & Theatre; God's Fools: Four Plays by Thomas F. Rogers, Midvale, UT: Edan Hill, 83; Myth and Symbol in Soviet Fiction, San Francisco: Mellon Research Univ Press, 92; Huebner and Other Plays, Provo, UT: Poor Robert's Pubs, 92; Twentieth Century Pioneers: Mormons in Russia, Provo, UT: BYU Studies, forthcoming; numerous articles and reviews. **CONTACT ADDRESS** Dept of Germanic & Slavic Lang, Brigham Young Univ, 4094 Jkhb, Provo, UT 84602-0002. **EMAIL** thomas_rogers@byu.edu

ROGLIERI, MARIA ANN
PERSONAL Born 01/16/1967, NY, m, 1992, 2 children **DISCIPLINE** ITALIAN **EDUCATION** Columbia Univ, BA, 88; Harvard Univ, MA, 89; PhD, 94. **CAREER** Assoc Prof, St Thomas Aquinas Col, 95-. **MEMBERSHIPS** AATI; Dante Soc. **RESEARCH** Dante; Ovid; Dante in music; Medieval European literature; Literature in music; Computers in the classroom. **SELECTED PUBLICATIONS** Auth, "I Can Talk to my computer: voice Recognition Systems for the disabled," connections: A Magazine for the disabled, 94; auth, "Ovid's Heavenly art of Love in Dante's 'Paradiso'," in Festschrift, Harvard Univ Press, 95; auth, "From le rime aspre e chiocche to la dolce sinfonia di Paradiso: Musical Adaptations of Dante's commedia from the sixteenth century to the present," Dante Studies, 97; auth, Dante and Music, Ashgate Pub, forthcoming. **CONTACT ADDRESS** Dept Humanities, St. Thomas Aquinas Col, 125 Rte 340, Sparkill, NY 10976-1041.

ROHINSKY, MARIE-CLAIRE
PERSONAL Born 05/05/1935, Boulogne-Billancourt, France, 2 children **DISCIPLINE** FRENCH **EDUCATION** Univ Caen, PhD. **CAREER** Assoc prof, Fr. **HONORS AND AWARDS** Coord, Lang Across Curr proj, Central Conn State Univ; organizer/co-dir French Summer Study Abroad Prog, Central Conn State Univ; Palmes Academiques. **MEMBERSHIPS** AATF; SPFFA; COLT. **RESEARCH** 19th and 20th century French poetry and music; French Women Writers and World War II. **SELECTED PUBLICATIONS** Auth, The Singer's Debussy, Rosen, 87. **CONTACT ADDRESS** Central Connecticut State Univ, 1615 Stanley St, New Britain, CT 06050. **EMAIL** rohinsky@ccsu.edu

ROHRBACHER, BERNHARD
DISCIPLINE LINGUISTICS **EDUCATION** Univ Mass Amherst, PhD. **CAREER** Prof, Northwestern Univ. **RESEARCH** What is the source for crosslinguistic variation, and how do young children acquire a first language. **SELECTED PUBLICATIONS** Auth, Explaining the Syntactic Consequences of Rich Agreement Morphology, On the Licensing of V-to-AgrS Raising and pro, Proceedings of the 13th West Coast Conf on Formal Ling, 95; Notes on the Antisymmetry of Syntax, Univ Pa Working Papers in Ling 1, 94; English Main Verbs Move Never, The Penn Rev Ling 18, 94; coauth, Features and Projections: Arguments for the Full Competence Hypothesis, Talk given at the 21th Annual Boston Univ Conf on Lang Develop, 96; Functional Projections, Markedness, and Root Infinitives in Early Child Greek, Talk given at the Workshop on Current Trends in Modern Greek Syntax at the 17th GLOW Conf, 96; Null Subjects in Russian Inverted Constructions, Proceedings of the 4th Annual Workshop on Formal Approaches to Slavic Ling, 96; On German Verb Syntax under Age 2, Proceedings of the 19th Annual Boston Univ Conf on Lang Develop 95; Null Subjects in Early Child English and the Theory of Economy of Projection, Univ Pa Working Papers in Ling 2, 95. **CONTACT ADDRESS** Dept of Linguistics, Northwestern Univ, 1801 Hinman, Evanston, IL 60208.

ROISMAN, HANNA M.
PERSONAL Born Wroclaw, Poland, m, 1971, 2 children **DISCIPLINE** CLASSICS **EDUCATION** Tel Aviv Univ, BA, 72, MA, 76; Univ Wash, PhD, 81. **CAREER** Lect, Tel Aviv Univ, 81-89; Assoc prof, Colby Col, 90-94, full prof, 94-. **HONORS AND AWARDS** Fel, Center Hellenic Studies **MEMBERSHIPS** APA **RESEARCH** Early Greek epic and tragedy; Classics and Film. **SELECTED PUBLICATIONS** Auth, Nothing Is As It Seems: The Tragedy of the Implicit in Euripedes, 98; co-auth, The Odyssey Re-Formed, 96; auth, Loyalty in Early Greek Epic and Tragedy, 84. **CONTACT ADDRESS** Dept of Classics, Colby Col, Waterville, ME 04901. **EMAIL** h_roisma@colby.edu

ROJAS, CARLOS
PERSONAL Born 08/12/1928, Barcelona, Spain, m, 1966, 2 children **DISCIPLINE** SPANISH LITERATURE, HISTORY **EDUCATION** Barcelona Univ, MA, 51; Univ Cent, Madrid, PhD(Span lit), 55. **CAREER** Asst prof Romance lang, Rollins Col, 57-60; from asst prof to assoc prof, 60-68, prof, 68-80, Charles Howard Candler Prof Romance Lang, 80-, emeritus, Emory Univ. **HONORS AND AWARDS** Nat Prize for Lit, Govt Spain, 68; Planeta Prize, Ed Planeta, 73; Ateneo de Sevilla Prize, 77; Nadal Prize, 80. **MEMBERSHIPS** MLA; SAtlantic Mod Lang Asn. **RESEARCH** Contemporary Spanish; art history. **SELECTED PUBLICATIONS** Auth, Dialogos Para Otra Espana, Ariel, 66; Auto de Fe, Guadarrama, 68; Diez Figuras Ante la Guerra Civil, Nauta, 73; Azana, 73, La Guerra Civil Vista por los Exiliados, 75, Retratos Antifranquistas, 77 & Memorias Ineditas, 78, Planeta; El Ingenioso Hidalgo y Poeta Federico Garcia Lorca Asciende a los Infiernos, 80, La Barcelonade Picasso, 81. **CONTACT ADDRESS** Dept of Romance Lang, Emory Univ, Atlanta, GA 30322.

ROJAS, J. NELSON
PERSONAL Born, Chile **DISCIPLINE** ROMANCE AND SPANISH LINGUISTICS, CONTEMPORARY LATIN AMERICAN POETRY, SPANIS **EDUCATION** Univ Wash, PhD. **CAREER** Prof Span, Univ Nev, Reno. **RESEARCH** Linguistic approaches to the poetry of Gabriela Mistral. **SELECTED PUBLICATIONS** Published widely in the areas of linguistics and Latin American poetry. **CONTACT ADDRESS** Univ of Nevada, Reno, Reno, NV 89557. **EMAIL** rojas@unr.edu

ROJAS-AUDA, ELIZABETH
PERSONAL Born, Chile, m, 1995, 1 child **DISCIPLINE** SPANISH **EDUCATION** Univ Wisc Milwaukee, MA, 84; Univ Wisc Madison, PhD, 98. **CAREER** Teaching asst, Univ Wisc Madison, 87-94; lectr, Univ N Tex, 94-96; adj asst prof, Brookhaven Col, 97-98; vis asst prof, Univ Tex Arlington, 99-. **HONORS AND AWARDS** Sigma Delta Pi; Spanish Honor Soc, 84; Nominee, Provost Teaching Award, Univ Tex, 00-01. **RESEARCH** Contemporary Spanish Peninsular Literature; Spanish and Hispanic Women Literature; Twentieth Century Spanish Literature; Cultural Anthropology; History of Women in the U.S., Europe and the Spanish-speaking countries; Nineteenth-Century Spanish Literature; Eighteenth-Century Spanish

Literature. **SELECTED PUBLICATIONS** Auth, "Gabriela Mistral," Univ Wisc Milwaukee, El Univ, 83; auth, Vision y Ceguera de Concha Espina: su obra comprometida, Madrid, 98. **CONTACT ADDRESS** Dept For Lang, Univ of Texas, Arlington, 10721 Marsh Ln, Dallas, TX 75229-5146. **EMAIL** erojas@uta.edu

ROLATER, FREDERICK STRICKLAND
PERSONAL Born 07/22/1938, McKinney, TX, m, 1960 **DISCIPLINE** AMERICAN HISTORY, CHURCH HISTORY **EDUCATION** Wake Forest Univ, BA, 60; Univ Southern Calif, MA, 63, PhD, 70 **CAREER** Assoc prof soc sci, Blue Mountain Col, 63-64; assoc prof hist & soc sci & chmn dept, Grand Canyon Col, 64-67; asst prof, 67-70, assoc prof, 70-80, dir grad studies, Dept Hist, 72-80, Prof Church Hist, Korea Bapt Theol Univ and Seminary, 00-. **HONORS AND AWARDS** Fulbright lectr, Japan, 87; Comnr, Southern Baptist Hist Comn, 84-92. **MEMBERSHIPS** Tenn Hist Soc; West Tenn Hist Soc; Southern Baptist Hist Soc; Tenn Baptist Hist Comt (chmn). **RESEARCH** History of the American Indian; Tennessee history; Public administration during the American Revolution. **SELECTED PUBLICATIONS** Auth, Charles Thomson, Prime Minister of the United States, Penn Mag Hist & Biogr, 7/77; The Doctor of Arts Degree and its Development at MTSU, in Proceedings of the Fifth Intl Conf on Improving Univ Teaching, 79; The Time They Cried (in Japanese), J Am Studies (Japan), 88; Japanese Americans, Rourke Press, 91; The American Indian and the Origin of the Second American Party System, Wis Mag Hist, spring 93; auth, Padlocking the Building; auth, Releasing the Spirit: Concord Baptist Association, 1930-50, Ten Bapt Hist, fall, 99. **CONTACT ADDRESS** 740-7 O Jung Dong, Daeduk-Gu, Taejon, Korea 306-817. **EMAIL** frolater@mtsu.edu

ROLFE, OLIVER WILLIS
PERSONAL Born 01/20/1938, Alamosa, CO, d, 2 children **DISCIPLINE** FRENCH LANGUAGE, LINGUISTICS **EDUCATION** Washburn Univ, Topeka, AB, 60; Stanford Univ, AM, 64, PhD, 67. **CAREER** Tchr & tutor, Menninger Found, Topeka, KS, 58-60; tchg asst French, Stanford Univ, 61-63, actg instr ling, 63-65, instr tchg Eng as a second lang, 65-66; asst prof Romance ling, Univ WA, 66-70; assoc prof, 70-76, Prof Foreign Lang, Univ MT, 76-, Res asst, Stanford Comput Ctr, 61-63; instr French, San Jose State Col, spring 64. **MEMBERSHIPS** Am Asn Tchr(s) Fr; Am Coun Tchg For Lang; AAUP. **RESEARCH** French and Romance linguistics; lang tchg methodology. **SELECTED PUBLICATIONS** Co-ed, Linguistic Studies Present to Andre Martinet on the Occassion of His 60th Birthday, Ling Circle of NY, 72; autb, Grammatical frequency and language teaching: Verbal categories in French and Spanish, In: Linguistic Studies Presented to Andre Martinet, 72; Morphological Frequency: French & Spanish Verbal Themes, In: Papers on Linguistics & Child Language, Hague, Mouton, 78. **CONTACT ADDRESS** Dept of For Lang, Univ of Montana, Missoula, MT 59812-1015. **EMAIL** olivier@selway.umt.edu

ROLLER, MATTHEW B.
PERSONAL Born 07/27/1966, Denver, CO **DISCIPLINE** CLASSICS, ROMAN STUDIES **EDUCATION** Stanford Univ, BA, 88; Univ Cal-Berkeley, MA, 90; PhD, 94. **CAREER** Asst prof of Classics, Johns Hopkins Univ, 94-00, assoc prof Classics, Johns Hopkins Univ, 00-; Mellon fel Hum, 88-90 and 93; Mellon Diss fel, 92 & 94. **HONORS AND AWARDS** Am Coun of Learned Societies Jun Fel, 00-01; Solmsen Fel, Inst for Res in the Humanities, Univ of Wisc-Madison, 00-01. **MEMBERSHIPS** Am Philol Asn; Archaeol Inst Am; Class Asn Atlantic Stud. **RESEARCH** Latin literature; Roman social and cultural history; Graeco-Roman philosophy. **SELECTED PUBLICATIONS** Auth Ethical Contradiction and the Fractured Community in Lucan's Bellum Civile, Class Antiquity, 96; Color-blindness: Cicero's death, declamation, and the production of history, Class Philol, 97; Pliny's Catullus: the politics of literary appropriation, Transactions of the Am Philol Asn; 98; auth, Constructing Autocracy: Aristocrats and Emperors in Julio-Claudian Rome, Princeton Univ Press, 01. **CONTACT ADDRESS** Dept of Classics, Johns Hopkins Univ, Baltimore, 3400 N Charles St, Baltimore, MD 21218-2690. **EMAIL** mroller@jhu.edu

ROMAN-MENDOZA, ESPERANZA
PERSONAL Born 06/20/1965, Madrid, Spain, m, 1996 **DISCIPLINE** CLASSICS **EDUCATION** Univ Complutense, Spain, lic, 89; transl dip, 92; Univ Nat de Edu a Dist, Spain, PhD, 97. **CAREER** Res assoc, Univ Nat de Edu a Dist, Spain, 92-96; instr, Univ Pont Com, Spain, 95-96; vis asst prof, George Mason Univ, 96-97; asst prof, 97-. **HONORS AND AWARDS** Extr Doct Awd, Spain, 97; Fel, Nat Plan Res, Spain, 92-95. **MEMBERSHIPS** MLA; AATSP; CALICO; FLAVA. **RESEARCH** Computer-assisted language learning; computer-assisted translation; Spanish sociolinguistics. **SELECTED PUBLICATIONS** Auth, "Eurodicautom: La base de datos terminol6gica de la Comunidad Europea" in Traducci6ny ensenanza de lenguas con ordenadores, ed. G. Ruiperez (Madrid: Ediciones Pedag6gicas, 95); auth, "Pasado, presente y flituro de la aplicaci6n de Ia informatica en Ia ensenanza de lenguas extranjeras." Puertas a Ia lectura 6/7 (99): 69-73; auth, "Adaptation of Video-based Language Learning Materials for the WWW" in Theory and Practice of Multimedia CALL, ed. K. Cameron (Exeter: Elm Bank Publications, 98); auth, "La World Wide Web y Ia enseiLanza del espanol como lengua extranjera: el ejemplo de Estados Unidos." Actas del VIII Congreso Internacional de la ASELE (Alcala' de Henares, Uuiversidad de Mcala, 97); auth, "Aplicaciones practicas de los recursos telematicos a la traducci6n de acro'nios y abreviaturas" in La Palabra Vertida. investigaciones en torno a la Traducci6n, eds.MA Vega, R Martin-Gaitero (Madrid, Univ Complutense, 97); coauth, "Aplicaci6n de Intemet en la difusi6n de la infonnaci6n sobre Terminologia" in La Palabra Vertida, eds. MA Vega, R Martin-Gaitero, Investigaciones en torno a Ia Traduccion (Madrid, Universidad Cornplutense, 97); coauth, "Erfahnmgen rnit Multirnedia-Software fur den DaFUnterricht mit Sprachausgabe und -eingabe" in Thesenband der X, Internationalen Deutschlehrertagung (Leipzig), 93. **CONTACT ADDRESS** Dept Modern and Classical Lang, George Mason Univ, Fairfax, 4400 University Dr, Fairfax, VA 22030-4422.

ROMAN-MORALES, BELEN
PERSONAL Born 01/17/1953, Puerto Rico, d, 3 children **DISCIPLINE** SPANISH AMERICAN LITERATURE **EDUCATION** Univ Puerto Rico, BA; MA, 85; Fla State Univ, PhD, 91. **CAREER** Teacher, Puerto Rico; prof, St Cloud State Univ, 1991-. **HONORS AND AWARDS** Teaching Asst Awd, Fla State Univ. **MEMBERSHIPS** ALFAL; AATSP. **RESEARCH** Spanish Linguistic, Poetry written by women. **SELECTED PUBLICATIONS** Auth, La Poetia de Julia de Burgess. **CONTACT ADDRESS** Dept Foreign Lang, St. Cloud State Univ, PO Box 64, Saint Cloud, MN 56302. **EMAIL** belen@stcloudstate.edu

ROMANOWSKI, SYLVIE
PERSONAL Born Paris, France, s **DISCIPLINE** FRENCH LITERATURE **EDUCATION** Carleton Univ, BA, 62, Harvard Univ, MA, 63; Yale Univ, PhD, 69. **CAREER** Lectr, York Univ, 68-69; asst prof, Univ of Wis Milwaukee, 69-71; asst prof to prof, Northwestern Univ, 71-. **HONORS AND AWARDS** Woodrow Wilson Fel, 62; DAAD, 63. **MEMBERSHIPS** MLA; ESECS; MWASECS; MMLA; IAPL. **RESEARCH** French literature of the 17th and 18th centuries, Modern literature, Women's writing. **SELECTED PUBLICATIONS** Auth, "La quete du savoir dans les Lettres persanes," in Eighteenth-Century Fiction, 91; auth, "Language and Space in Tartuffe," and Other Plays, MLA Publication, 95; auth, "Moliere's Misanthrope; A critique and Reluctant Defense of Courtly Life," in Contemporary Theater Review, 97; auth, "Cyrano de Bergerac's Epistemological Bodies," Science Fiction Stud, 98. **CONTACT ADDRESS** Dept Fr and Ital, Northwestern Univ, 1859 Sheridan Rd, Evanston, IL 60208-2204. **EMAIL** s-romanowski@northwestern.edu

ROMEISER, JOHN B.
DISCIPLINE FRENCH **EDUCATION** Vanderbilt Univ, PhD, 75. **CAREER** Prof, French, Univ Tenn. **RESEARCH** Twentieth-century French lit. **CONTACT ADDRESS** Dept of Mod For Langs & Lits, Univ of Tennessee, Knoxville, 701 McClung Tower & Plaza, Knoxville, TN 37996. **EMAIL** jromeise@utk.edu

ROMER, F. E.
PERSONAL Born 02/24/1946, Brooklyn, NY, s **DISCIPLINE** CLASSICS **EDUCATION** NYork Univ, BA, 68; Stanford Univ, MA, 71, PhD, 74. **CAREER** Asst prof, Univ Vt, Sept 74-jun 75; asst prof, Oh State Univ, Sept 77-jun 78; asst prof, Johns Hopkins Univ, Jul 78-jun 86; book rev ed, The Amer Jour of Philol, Jan 82-dec 86; assoc prof, Hobart and William Smith Col, Jul 86-jun 91; assoc prof, Univ Ariz, Aug 91-. **HONORS AND AWARDS** Sch of Hist Studies, Inst for Adv Study, Princeton, Aug 86-jun 87; jr fel, Ctr for Hellenic Studies, Sept 84-jun 85; Stanford Univ dissertation prize in humanities, Jun 74; NY Univ Maitland prize in classics, may 68. **MEMBERSHIPS** Amer Philol Asn; Archaeol Inst of Amer; Asn of Ancient Hist; Class Asn of the Midwest and South. **RESEARCH** Ancient geography; Greek and Roman intellectual history, literature, and religion; Historical analysis for archaeological excavations at Chianciano Terme and Lugnano, Italy. **SELECTED PUBLICATIONS** Auth, Pomponius Mela's Description of the World, Univ Mich Press, 98; article, Good Intentions and the .., The City As Comedy: Society and Representation in Athenian Comedy, Univ NC Press, 51-74, 97; article, Diagoras the Melian, CW, 89, 393-401, 95/96; article, Atheism, Impiety, and the Limos Melios at Aristoph, Birds, 186, AJP, 115, 351-365, 94; article, Pliny, Vesuvius, and the Troublesome Wind, CW, 78, 587-591, 85; article, A Case of Client-Kingship, AJP, 106, 75-100, 85; article, When is a Bird Not a Bird?, TAPA, 113, 135-142, 83; article, The Aesymneteia: A Problem in Aristotle's Historical Method, AJP, 103, 25-46, 82; article, Gaius Caesar's Military Diplomacy in the East, TAPA, 109, 199-214, 79; article, A Numismatic Date for the Departure of C. Caesar?, TAPA, 108, 187-202, 78; auth, "Explaining Suetonius (Tib. 16.1): Tiberius' Tribunicia Potestas in A.D.4, Eranos 95 (97): 89-98; auth, "Famine, Pestilence, and Brigandage in Italy in the Fifth Century A.D.," in D. and N. Soren, eds, A Roman Villa and Late Roman Infant Cemetery (Bretschneider, 99), 465-475; auth, "Okheia and Mules in a Prometheus Play: Amending LSJ and Unemending Aesch. 189a R," TAPA 130 (00): 67-87. **CONTACT ADDRESS** Dept. of Classics - ML 371, Univ of Arizona, Tucson, AZ 85721-0067. **EMAIL** feromer@u.arizona.edu

RONNICK, MICHELE VALERIE
DISCIPLINE CLASSICS, GREEK, LATIN **EDUCATION** Boston Univ, PhD, 90. **CAREER** Assoc Prof, Dept of Classics, Wayne State Univ; Classical Asn of the Middle West and South Award for Outstanding Projects for the Comm for the Promotion of Latin, 99 and 00. **HONORS AND AWARDS** Awd For Teaching Excellence, APA, 97; Awd for Outstanding State VP, Classical Asn of the Middle West and South, 96; Awd for the Most Significant Project, 96; Incentive Awd for Younger Scholars, Classical and Modern Literature, 94. **MEMBERSHIPS** Int Soc for the Classical Tradition; APA; Classical Asn of the Middle West and South; Classical Asn of the Atlantic States; Am Asn for Neo-Latin Studies; National Committee for Latin and Greek. **RESEARCH** Latin literature; Classical tradition; Classical studies & people of African descent. **SELECTED PUBLICATIONS** Auth, Substructural Elements of Architectonic Rhetoric and Philosophical Thought in Fronto's Epistles, Roman Persuasion, 97; Aratus, Dictionary of Literary Biography: Ancient Greek Authors, Gale Research Co, 97; Cicero's Paradoxa Stoicorum: A Commentary, an Interpretation, and a Study of Its Influence, 91; Frankfurt Bos, Fur, Sus, atque Sacerdotes: Additional Light on Kaiser's Solution of a Minor Mystery, Proceedings of the Mass Hist Sco, 95; Concerning the Dramatic Elements in Milton's Defensiones: Theater Without a Stage, Classical and Modern Lit, 95; Seneca's Medea and Ultima Thule in Poe's Dream-land, Poe Studies/Dark Romanticism, 94; David Paul Brown's Sertorius or The Roman Patriot (1830): Another Influence on John Wilkes Booth, J of Am Culture, 96; Seneca's Epistle 12 and Emerson's Circles, Emerson Soc Papers, 96; Further Evidence Concerning the Origin of Cromwell's Title Lord Protector: Milton's Pro Se Defensio, Cromwelliana, 97; After Lefkowitz and Bernal: Research Opportunities in Classica Africana, The Negro Hist Bull, 97; auth, "Horace's Ep. 1.24 and Hannibal's Escape from one Ager Falernus," Scholia (00). **CONTACT ADDRESS** Dept of Classics, Wayne State Univ, 431 Manoogian Hall, Detroit, MI 48202. **EMAIL** mronnic@wayne.edu

ROOD, DAVID STANLEY
PERSONAL Born 09/14/1940, Albany, NY, m, 1969, 3 children **DISCIPLINE** LINGUISTICS **EDUCATION** Cornell Univ, BA, 63; Univ Calif, Berkeley, MA, 65, PhD, 69. **CAREER** Instr Ger & ling, 67-69, asst prof ling, 69-77, assoc prof, 77-82, Prof Ling, Univ Colo, Boulder, 82-; NSF grants, 77-96; Nat Endowment for Humanities grants, 77-96; ed, Int J Am Ling, 81-. **MEMBERSHIPS** Ling Soc Am; Am Anthrop Asn; Teachers of English to Speakers of Other Lang. **RESEARCH** Applied linguistics in second language teaching; American Indian languages; linguistic theory and semantic-based grammar. **SELECTED PUBLICATIONS** Auth, Agent and Object in Wichita, Lingua, 71; Aspects of subordination in Lakhota and Wichita, In: You Take the High Node and I'll Take the Low Node, Chicago Ling Asn, 73; Implications of Wichita phonology, Language, 75; Wichita Grammar, Garland, 76; coauth, Beginning Lakhota, Univ Colo, Ling Dept, 76; contribr, Siouan, In: The Languages of Native America, Univ Tex, 79; auth, Locative Expressions in Siouan and Caddoan, Colo Res Ling, 79; User's Handbook for the Siouan Languages Archive, Univ Colo, Dept Ling, 81. **CONTACT ADDRESS** Dept of Ling, Univ of Colorado, Boulder, Box 295, Boulder, CO 80309-0295.

ROOT, REGINA A.
PERSONAL Born 05/24/1967, Lansing, MI, m, 1999 **DISCIPLINE** MODERN LATIN AMERICA **EDUCATION** Univ Iowa, BA, 87; MA, 89; Univ Cal, Berkeley, PhD, 97. **CAREER** Vis asst prof, Gustavus Adolphus Col, 97-98; asst prof, Old Dominion Univ, 98-. **HONORS AND AWARDS** Hum Grad Res Grant; Univ Cal Regents Fel; Lesley Byrd Simpson Fel; USIA Trv Grant; Fulbright Fel; Rachel Kersten Res Awd; CAL Res Grant. **SELECTED PUBLICATIONS** Auth, "La representacion fotografica en la literatura: El caso de Cien anos de soledad y Rayuela." Lucero: J Iberian Latin Am Stud 2 (91): 59-72; auth, "En la concha de Venus amarrado: The Female Body in Garcilaso de la Vega's Oda ad fiorem Gnidi." Lucero: J Iberian Latin Am Stud 4 (93): 16-21; auth, "La moda como metonimia," Folios 35 (99); auth, "Tailoring the Nation: Fashion Writing in Nineteenth-Century Argentina," Fashion Theory (Berg Pub, 00); co-transl of, "Marcar diferencias. Cruzar fronteras," by Jean Franco, Las culturas de fin de siglo de America Latina, ed. Josefina Ludmer (Rosario, Argentina: Beatriz Viterbo Editora, 94), 34-43. **CONTACT ADDRESS** Dept Foreign Languages, Literatures, Old Dominion Univ, Norfolk, VA 23529. **EMAIL** rroot@odu.edu

ROSA, WILLIAM
DISCIPLINE LATIN AMERICAN LITERATURE **EDUCATION** PhD **CAREER** Assoc prof & dept chp. **RESEARCH** 19th century novel and short story of the Caribbean basin. **SELECTED PUBLICATIONS** Auth bk on, Alfredo Collado Martell, Inst de Culturea Puertorriquena. **CONTACT ADDRESS** Dept of Language and Cultures, William Paterson Col of New Jersey, 300 Pompton Rd., Wayne, NJ 07470.

ROSE, GILBERT PAUL
PERSONAL Born 08/06/1939, New York, NY, m, 1961, 2 children **DISCIPLINE** GREEK & LATIN LITERATURE **EDUCATION** Univ CA, Berkeley, Ab, 63, PhD, 69. **CAREER** From instr to assoc prof, 67-81, Prof Classics, Swarthmore Col, 81-; Vis asst prof, OH State Univ, 69; vis assoc prof, Univ CA, Berkeley, 79. **HONORS AND AWARDS** Old Dominion Found fel, 70-71; Mellon Found fel, 74-75; Am Philol Asn Awd for Excellence in the Tchg of the Classics, 83. **MEMBERSHIPS** Am Philol Asn. **RESEARCH** Homer; Greek tragedy; Latin epic poetry. **SELECTED PUBLICATIONS** Auth, The Quest of Telemachus, 67, The Unfriendly Phaeacians, 69 & Odyssey 15 143-82: A Narrative Inconsistency?, 71 & Odysseus' Barking Heart, 79, Trans Am Philol Asn; The Swineherd and the Beggar, Phoenix, 80; ed, Plato's Crito, Bryn Mawr Commentaries, 80; Plato's Symposium, Bryn Mawr Commentaries, 81; auth, Plato's Republic, Book I, Bryn Mawr Commentaries, 83; Sophocle's Oedipus at Colonus, Bryn Mawr Commentaries, 88; Plato's Apology, Bryn Mawr Commentaries, 89. **CONTACT ADDRESS** Dept of Class, Swarthmore Col, 500 College Ave, Swarthmore, PA 19081-1306. **EMAIL** grose1@swarthmore.edu

ROSE, MARILYN GADDIS
PERSONAL Born 04/02/1930, Fayette, MO, m, 1968, 1 child **DISCIPLINE** COMPARATIVE LITERATURE **EDUCATION** Cent Methodist Col, BA, 52; Univ SC, MA, 55; Univ Mo, PhD, 58. **CAREER** Asst French, Univ SC, 54-55; instr, Univ Mo, 55-58; assoc prof comp lit, Stephens Col, 58-68; assoc prof French & comp lit, 68-73, chmn dept, 71-78, prof comp lit, 73-90, Distinguished Service Prof, comp lit, 91-, dir, Transl Prog, 73-, SUNY, Binghamton. **HONORS AND AWARDS** Alexander Gode Medal, Am Transl Asn, 88; ATA Special Service Awd, 95. **MEMBERSHIPS** MLA; Northeast Mod Lang Asn; Am Transl Asn; Am Lit Transl Asn. **RESEARCH** Anglo-Irish literature; French-American literary relations; translating; tanslation theory and pedagogy. **SELECTED PUBLICATIONS** Transl, Villiers de l'Isle-Adam, Eve of the Future Eden, Coronado; transl, Louise Colet, Lui, 87; transl, Sainte-Beuve, Volupte, 96; auth, Translation and Literary Criticism, 97. **CONTACT ADDRESS** CRIT/TRIP, SUNY, Binghamton, PO Box 6000, Binghamton, NY 13902-6000. **EMAIL** mgrose@binghamton.edu

ROSE, PETER WIRES
PERSONAL Born 05/13/1936, Paterson, NJ, m, 1997, 2 children **DISCIPLINE** CLASSICS **EDUCATION** Williams Col, BA, 57; Harvard Univ, MA, 58; PhD, 67. **CAREER** Lectr, 63-66, Yale Univ; asst prof, 71-74, Univ Texas Austin; vis assoc prof, 74, Haverford Col; fac mem, 77-80, prof and chmn, classics dept, 75-83, prof, 75-, Miami Univ. **HONORS AND AWARDS** Phi Beta Kappa, 56; Woodrow Wilson Fel, 57-58; Frank Knox fel, Harvard, 61; Fulbright Fel, Rome, 61-62; Billings fel, Wale, Summer, 67; Morse fel, Yale, 68-69; appointed fel at the Ctr for Hellenic Studies in Washington D.C., 75-76; Nat Endowment for the Humanities fel, 79-80. **RESEARCH** Homer Greek tragedy; Pindar and Greek lyric poetry. **SELECTED PUBLICATIONS** Auth, "Teaching Greek Myth and Confronting Contemporary Myths," in Classics and Cinema, ed. Martin M. Winkler (Bucknell Univ Press, London and Toronto, 91), 17-39; auth, Sons of the Gods, Children of Earth: Ideology and Literary Form in Ancient Greece, Cornell Univ Press (Ithaca, NY), 92; auth, "The Case for Not Ignoring Marx in the Study of Women in Antiquity," in Feminist Theory and Classics, ed. Nancy Rabinowitz and Amy Richlin (Routledge, 93); auth, "Historicizing Sophocles' Ajax," in History, Tragedy, Theory, ed. Barbara Goff (Univ of Tex Press, 94); auth, "Cicero and the Rhetoric of Imperialism: Putting Politics Back into Political Rhetoric," Rhetorica 13.4 (95): 359-399; auth, "The Politics of the Trilogy Form: Lucia, the Oresteia, and the Godfather," Film-Historia 5.2-3 (95): 93-116; auth, "Ideology in the Illiad: Polis, Basileus, Theoi" Arethusa 30 (97): 151-199; auth, "Theorizing Athenian Imperialism and the Athenian State," in Contextualizing Classics: Ideology, Performance, Dialogue. Essays in Honor of John J. Peradotto, ed. Thomas M. Falkner, Nancy Felson, and David Konstan (Rowman and Littlefield, 99). **CONTACT ADDRESS** Dept of Classics, Miami Univ, Oxford, OH 45056. **EMAIL** rosepw@muohio.edu

ROSE, SHARON
DISCIPLINE PHONOLOGY **EDUCATION** Univ Toronto, BA; Univ du Quebec a Montreal, MA; McGill Univ, PhD. **CAREER** Asst Prof, Ling, Univ Calif, San Diego. **RESEARCH** Ethiopian Semitic languages. **SELECTED PUBLICATIONS** Auth, Ethio-Semitic Inflectional Affix Order: A Phonological Solution, Langues Orientales Anciennes, Philol et Ling, 95; Allomorphy and Morphological Categories in Muher, Essays in Gurage Language and Culture, Wiesbaden: Harrassowitz Verlag, 96; Variable Laryngeals and Vowel Lowering, Phonology 13, 96; Inflectional Affix Order, Ethio-Semitic, Stud in AfroAsiatic Grammar, The Hague: Holland Academic Graphics, 96; Book Notice of Wolf Leslau: Reference Grammar of Amharic, Lang 72, 96; Featural Morphology and Dialect Variation: the Contribution of Historical Change, Variation, Change and Phonological Theory, Current Issues, Ling Theory 146, Amsterdam: John Benjamins, 97; Theoretical Issues, Comparative Ethio-Semitic Phonology and Morphology, 97. **CONTACT ADDRESS** Dept of Ling, Univ of California, San Diego, 9500 Gilman Dr, La Jolla, CA 92093. **EMAIL** rose@ling.ucsd.edu

ROSE, STANLEY LUDWIG
PERSONAL Born 02/03/1936, Richmond, IN **DISCIPLINE** LUSO--BRAZILIAN & SPANISH LANGUAGE & LITERATURES **EDUCATION** Univ AZ, BA, 58; Univ Wis-Madison, MA, 60, PhD, 69. **CAREER** Actg asst Span & Port, Univ OR, 65-69, asst prof, 69-72; asst prof Port, NDEA Inst Port, Vanderbilt Univ, 68; asst prof, 72-75, Assoc Prof Span & Port, Univ MT, 75; Prof Span, Port, 83-. **MEMBERSHIPS** Am Asn Tchr(s) Span & Port. **RESEARCH** Medieval Portuguese lang and lit; mod Brazilian lit. **SELECTED PUBLICATIONS** Auth, Alberto de Oliveira, In: Encycl World Lit 20th Century, Ungar, 70; translr, Carta de Doacoa and Foral of Duarte Coelho, In: A Documentary History of Brazil, Knopf, 71; auth, Ancedotal narrative in Fernao Lopes' Cronica de D Pedro I, Luso-Brazilian Rev, 71; The land and the peasant in the novel of the Brazilian Northeast, J Rocky Mt Coun Latin Am Studies, 12/75. **CONTACT ADDRESS** Dept of For Lang & Lit, Univ of Montana, Missoula, MT 59812-0001. **EMAIL** slrose@selway.umt.edu

ROSELLO, MICHELLE M.
DISCIPLINE FRENCH, COMPARATIVE LITERATURE **EDUCATION** Univ de Provence, Miatrise d'anglais, 78; Saint Cloud Paris, Agregation d'anglais, 81; Univ Mich, PhD, 86. **CAREER** Asst prof, Univ of Ill, 86-91; asst prof, Univ of Mich, 91-95; prof, Northwestern Univ, 98- **RESEARCH** Francophone literatures and cultures, Postcolonial and Diasporic discourses, Gender studies, Media and Film studies. **SELECTED PUBLICATIONS** Auth, L'Humour noir selon Andre Breton: Apres avoir assassine mon pauvre pere, Corti, Paris, France, 87; auth, L'in-difference chez Michel Tournier: L'un de ces types est le frere jumeau de l'autre, lequel?, Corti, Paris, France, 90; auth, Litterature et identite creole aux Antilles, Karthala, Paris, France, 92; auth, Infiltrating Culture: Power and Identity in Contemporary Women's Writing, Manchester UP, 96; auth, Declining the Stereotype: Representation and Ethnicity in French Cultures, UP New England, 99; auth, Postcolonial Hospitality: The Immigrant as Guest, Stanford UP, forthcoming. **CONTACT ADDRESS** Dept Fr & Ital, Northwestern Univ, 1859 Sheridan, Evanston, IL 60208. **EMAIL** m-rosello@northwestern.edu

ROSENBERG, JOEL WILLIAM
PERSONAL Born 04/13/1943, Los Angeles, CA **DISCIPLINE** HEBREW & COMPARATIVE LITERATURE **EDUCATION** Univ CA, Berkeley, BA, 65; Hebrew Union Col, BHL, 68; Univ CA, Santa Cruz, PhD, 78. **CAREER** Vis lectr relig, Univ CA, Davis, 73-74; vis lectr, Wesleyan Univ, 76-78, vis asst prof, 78-79; Asst prof, 80-84, assoc prof, Judaic Studies & World lit, Tufts Univ, 84, Lee S McCollester Assoc Prof, Bibl Lit, 92. **HONORS AND AWARDS** Phi Beta Kappa, 64; H W Hill Scholarship, Univ Calif Berkeley, 64; Fac Awd in Scholarship, Hebrew Unon Col-Jewish Inst of Relig, Regents's fel, Univ Calif, Santa Cruz, 71-72; Nat Defense Educ Act fel, Columbia Univ and Univ Calif, Berkeley, 66, 71; Poet-in-Residence, Del State Arts Counc/NEA, 4/79; Mellon Found Grant-in-Aid, Fac Develop, Tufts Univ, summer 82; NEH fel, 96. **MEMBERSHIPS** MLA; Asn Jewish Studies; Soc Bibl Lit; Am Acad Relig. **RESEARCH** Bibl lit; hist of bibl interpretation; comp lit; film hist and theory. **SELECTED PUBLICATIONS** Transl, Midrash on the Ten Commandments (transl), In: Rabbinic Fantasies (David Stern and Mark Mirsky, ed), JPS, 90, and Yale Univ Press, 98; Grammer with a Small g, Review of Lewis Glinert A Grammar of Modern Hebrew, Prooftexts: Jour of Jewish Lit Hist, 5/91; Genesis: A Commentary, In: The Harper Collins Study Bible (Wayne A Meeks, ed), Harper Collins, 93; Kol Haneshamah: The Reconstructionist Sabbath and Festival Prayer Book (transl), vol 1 (David A Teutsch, ed), Reconstructionist Press, 90, and vol 2, 93; Alternate Roads to Integrity: On Old Age in the Hebrew Bible, Melton Jour, 5/94; Jewish Experience on Film: An American Overview, Am Jewish Yearbk, 96; Shylock's Revenge: The Doubly Vanished Jew in Ernst Lubitsch's To Be or Not to Be, Prooftexts, 96; What the Bible and Old Movies Have in Common, Biblical Interpretation, 98; Kol Haneshamah: The Reconstructionist Daily Prayer Book ; Kol Haneshamah: The Reconstructionist High Holiday Prayer Book; Incarnation and Disguise: Jewish Experience on Film, 1920-1947. **CONTACT ADDRESS** Dept of Ger & Russ, Tufts Univ, Medford, 520 Boston Ave, Medford, MA 02155-5555. **EMAIL** jrosenb1@tufts.edu

ROSENBERG, JUSTUS
PERSONAL Born 01/23/1931, Danzig, Poland, m **DISCIPLINE** COMPARATIVE LITERATURE AND LINGUISTICS **EDUCATION** Sorbonne, BA, 46; Univ Calif, Los Angeles, MA, 48; Univ Cincinnati, PhD(comp lit), 50. **CAREER** Assoc prof foreign lang, Univ Dayton, 46-56 & Swarthmore Col, 56-62; Prof Foreign Language and Literature, Bard Col, 62-, vis prof, Univ Cincinnati, 51-56 & New Sch Social Res, 60-; fel, Columbia Univ, 65-66; vis prof, Nanyang Univ, 66-68; fel lit, Univ Belgrade, 72. **HONORS AND AWARDS** Lecturer, N. Y. S. Coun for the Humanities. **MEMBERSHIPS** AAUP; MLA; Am Acad Polit & Soc Sci. **RESEARCH** Ideology and Political Commitment in 20th Century Literature; methodology for teaching of English as a second language. **SELECTED PUBLICATIONS** Auth, Constant Factors in Translation, Princeton Univ, 56; Sound and Structure, D Moore, 68. **CONTACT ADDRESS** Dept of Lang and Lit, Bard Col, PO Box 508, Annandale, NY 12504-5000. **EMAIL** rosenber@bard.edu

ROSENBERG, SAMUEL N.
PERSONAL Born 01/19/1936, New York, NY, d **DISCIPLINE** FRENCH LANGUAGE, LITERATURE **EDUCATION** Columbia Col, AB, 57; Johns Hopkins Univ, PhD, 65. **CAREER** Lectr, 62-65; asst prof, 65-69; assoc prof, 69-81; ch, 77-84; prof, 81-99; Ind Univ, prof emer, 00-. **HONORS AND AWARDS** Phi Beta Kappa; Woodrow Wilson Fel; Fulbright Gnt; Lilly Fond Fel; NEH Res Gnt. **MEMBERSHIPS** AAUP; MLA; AATF; MAA; ICLS; ALTA. **RESEARCH** French lyric poetry; narrative of the Middle Ages. **SELECTED PUBLICATIONS** Auth, Harper's Grammar of French, 83; auth, The Monophonic Songs in The Roman De Fauvel, 91; auth, Chansons des trouveres, 95; auth, Ami Amile, 96; auth, Songs of the Troubadours and Trouveres, 97. **CONTACT ADDRESS** Dept French and Italian, Indiana Univ, Bloomington, 1020 E Kirkwood Ave, Ballantine Hall 642, Bloomington, IN 47405-7103. **EMAIL** srosenbe@indiana.edu

ROSENFELD, SIDNEY
PERSONAL Born 01/15/1931, Philadelphia, PA, m, 1959, 1 child **DISCIPLINE** GERMAN **EDUCATION** Temple Univ, BA, 53; Univ IL, MA, 58; PhD, 64. **CAREER** Prof, Oberlin Col, 63-99. **HONORS AND AWARDS** Fulbright Fel, Austria, 59-60. **RESEARCH** Modern Austrian Literature, German-Jewish writers and culture. **SELECTED PUBLICATIONS** Cotransl, At the Mind's Limits by Jean Amery; cotransl, Radical Humanism: Selected Essays by Jean Amery; ed, Jews in Germany: Memoirs; auth, Understanding Joseph Roth (forthcoming). **CONTACT ADDRESS** Dept Ger & Slavic Lang, Oberlin Col, 19 Elm St, Oberlin, OH 44074. **EMAIL** sidney.rosenfeld@oberlin.edu

ROSENTHAL, MARGARET F.
DISCIPLINE ITALIAN RENAISSANCE ITALIAN LITERATURE **EDUCATION** Yale Univ, PhD. **CAREER** Asso prof, Univ Southern Calif. **RESEARCH** Women writers in early-modern Venice; social, cultural, political forces in Venice in the 16th century. **SELECTED PUBLICATIONS** Auth, The Honest Courtesan, Veronica Franco, Citizen and Writer in Sixteenth-Century Venice, 92. **CONTACT ADDRESS** Col Letters, Arts & Sciences, Univ of So California, University Park Campus, Los Angeles, CA 90089.

ROSES, LORRAINE ELENA
PERSONAL Born New York, NY, m, 1981, 5 children **DISCIPLINE** SPANISH **EDUCATION** Mt Holyoke Col, BA, 65; Harvard Univ, MA, 66, PhD, 74. **CAREER** Lectr English & Span, Tel Aviv Univ, 69-71; instr Span, Mt Holyoke Col, 71-74, asst prof, 74-75; asst prof, Boston Univ, 75-77; asst prof, 77-81, assoc prof, 81-87, Prof Span, Wellesley Col 87-, co-dir, Latin Am Studies, 92-, visting res scholar, Center for Res Women. **HONORS AND AWARDS** Woodrow Wilson Nat fel, 65; Radcliffe Inst travel fel, 68; Mount Holyoke Col fac grant, 71; Boston Univ fac grant, 87; Summer fac res grants, Wellesley, 81-; Ford Commitment Fund Grant, summer 82; Mellon grant, 85; Phelps Fund, Center for Res Women, Wellesley, 85 & 86; NEH summer stipend, 87; Ford Found training stipend, 88; Pew grant, Wellesley, 89; NEH Summer Inst, 89; Pew grant, Wellesley Col, summer 91; NEH summer inst, lead scholar, Middlesex Comm Col, 92; Am Coun Learned Soc fel, 98-99; Fel, Bunting Inst, Radcliffe Col, 98-99. **MEMBERSHIPS** MLA; Am Asn Teacher Span & Port. **RESEARCH** Spanish American and African American literature. **SELECTED PUBLICATIONS** Auth, "National Literature, Hyemonic Discourse, Oral Traditin: Re-Reading Carpenter's Kingdom of This World," Anales del Caribe 16-19 (96-98): 65-73; auth, Lino Novas Calvo: A sense of the preternatural, Symp, 75; Myth montage in a contemporary Puerto Rican tragedy, Latin Am Lit Rev, 75; El realismo magico en la critica hispanoamericana, J Span Studies: 20th Century, Vol 4, No 3; La epoca espanola de Lino Novas Calvo: 1936-1939, Chasqui, 5, 77; Affirmation of black heritage in Arrivi's Mascara puertorriquena, Studies Afro-Hisp Lit, Vol I, 77; co-auth, Harlem Renaissance and Beyond: Literary Biographies of 100 Black Women Writers, 1900-1945, G K Hall, 90; Las esperanzas de Pandora: prototipos femeninos en la obra de Rosario Ferre, Revista Iberoamericana, 1-6, 93; Introduction and Selection, Selected Works of Edythe Mae Gordon, in African American Women Writers, 1910-1940, G K Hall, 96; ed, Harlem's Glory: Black Women Writing, 1900-1945, Harvard Univ Press, 96. **CONTACT ADDRESS** Span Dept, Wellesley Col, 106 Central St, Wellesley, MA 02481-8204. **EMAIL** lroses@wellesley.edu

ROSIVACH, VINCENT JOHN
PERSONAL Born 05/08/1940, Jersey City, NJ **DISCIPLINE** CLASSICAL STUDIES **EDUCATION** Fordham Univ, AB, 61, MA, 64, PhD(classics), 66. **CAREER** Adj instr Latin, Sch Educ, Fordham Univ, 63-64; from instr to assoc prof, 65-76, Prof Classics, Fairfield Univ, 76-. **MEMBERSHIPS** Am Philol Asn; Class Asn New Eng; Asn of Ancient Hist. **RESEARCH** Greek and Roman drama; Greek history. **SELECTED PUBLICATIONS** Auth, Plautine stage settings, Trans & Proc Am Philol Soc, 70; Manuscripts of Matthias Corvinus in the Barberini Collection, Manuscripta, 71; Terence, Adelphoe 155-9, Class Quart, 73; Terence, Adelphoe 60-63, Class Philol, 75; The first stasimon of the Hecuba, Am J Philol, 75; Sophocles' Ajax, Class J, 76; Hector in the Rhesus, Hermes, 77; Earthborns

and Olympians: The parodos of the Ion, Class Quart, 77; The System of Public Sacrifice in Fourth Century Athens, Scholars Press, 94; When a Young Man Falls in Love: The Sexual Exploitation of Women in New Comedy, Routledge, 98. **CONTACT ADDRESS** Greek and Roman Studies, Fairfield Univ, 1073 N Benson Rd, Fairfield, CT 06430-5195. **EMAIL** Rosivach@fair1.fairfield.edu

ROSS, CLAUDIA
DISCIPLINE LINGUISTICS, CHINESE **EDUCATION** Barnard Col, Columbia Univ, BA, 71; Univ Mich, MA, 73; PhD, 78. **CAREER** Prof, Col of Holy Cross. **HONORS AND AWARDS** Vpres and Pres-elect, Chinese Language Teachers Asn, 00-01. **MEMBERSHIPS** CLTA; AAS; LSA; ACTFL. **RESEARCH** Linguistics: Lexical and semantic structure; Chinese language teaching; Teacher training. **SELECTED PUBLICATIONS** Auth, Temporal and Aspectual Reference in Mandarin Chinese, J Chinese Ling 23 1, 95; auth, Traditional Chinese Tales: A Course in Intermediate Chinese, Far Eastern Publications (New Haven); auth, "Aspectual Category Shift in Mandarin Chinese," Journal of Chinese Linguistics; auth, "Evaluating Chinese Textbooks," Journal of Chinese Linguistics. **CONTACT ADDRESS** Dept of Modern Languages and Literatures, Col of the Holy Cross, 1 College St, PO Box 11A, Worcester, MA 01610-2395. **EMAIL** cross@holycross.edu

ROSS, MARILYN A.
PERSONAL Born 09/06/1946, New York, NY, s **DISCIPLINE** CLASSICAL PHILOLOGY **EDUCATION** Cornell Univ, PhD, 73. **CAREER** Assoc prof and assoc dean of the col, Wells Col; assoc prof and asst to the pres, Sweet Briar Col; pres, Ross Associates. **HONORS AND AWARDS** Phi Beta Kappa. **MEMBERSHIPS** Am Philol Asoc. **CONTACT ADDRESS** 6324 Burning Tree Terrace, Fayetteville, PA 17222. **EMAIL** maross@cvn.net

ROSS, MARY ELLEN
DISCIPLINE EIGHTEENTH CENTURY FRENCH LITERATURE **EDUCATION** Univ Toronto, PhD. **RESEARCH** Contemporary literature of Quebec. **SELECTED PUBLICATIONS** Realisme merveilleux et autorepresentation dans L'Amelanchier de Jacques Ferron, Voix et images 49, 91; Le Deuil et le probleme du paraitre chez la veuve comique de debut du dix-huitieme siecle, Nophilologus 76, 92; Que le diable l'emporte: realisme merveilleux et religion dans La Chaise du marechal ferrant, Can Lit 142/143, 94; Auth, Amazones et sauvagesses: roles feminins et societes exotiques dans le theatre de la Foire, Studies on Voltaire and the Eighteenth Century 319, 94. **CONTACT ADDRESS** Dept of French, Univ of Victoria, PO Box 3045 STN CSC, Victoria, BC, Canada V8W 3P4. **EMAIL** meross@uvic.ca

ROSSABI, MORRIS
PERSONAL Born 12/05/1941, Alexandria, Egypt, m, 1965, 2 children **DISCIPLINE** LINGUISTICS **EDUCATION** Columbia, PhD, 70. **CAREER** Prof, Case Western Reserve Univ, 70-85; adjunct prof, Columbia Univ, 87-; prof, City Univ New York, 87-. **HONORS AND AWARDS** Award from Nat Endowment for the Humanities, Coun of Learned Socs, ..Fel, 97-98; Smith-Richardson .., 1998-99. **MEMBERSHIPS** Asn for Asian Studies, .. Soc. **SELECTED PUBLICATIONS** Auth, Khubilai Khan, Calif Univ Press, 88; auth, Voyage for Xanadu, 92. **CONTACT ADDRESS** Dept Asian Lang & Lit, Columbia Univ, 420 W 118th St, MC 3333, New York, NY 10027. **EMAIL** MR63@Columbia.edu

ROTHENBERG, MOLLY
DISCIPLINE COMPARATIVE LITERATURE, LITERARY THEORY **EDUCATION** Yale Univ, BA, 74; Univ CA at Irvine, PhD, 85. **CAREER** Assoc Prof, Tulane Univ. **RESEARCH** Lit Theory, psychoanalysis; Romanticism. **SELECTED PUBLICATIONS** Auth, Para-Siting America: The Radical Function of Heterogeneity in Paine's Early Writing, Eighteenth Century Stud, 93; co-auth, Fashionable Theory and Fashionable Women, Critical Inquiry, 95. **CONTACT ADDRESS** Dept of Eng, Tulane Univ, 6823 St Charles Ave, New Orleans, LA 70118. **EMAIL** mollyr@tulane.edu

ROTHSTEIN, MARIAN
DISCIPLINE FRENCH LANGUAGE, LITERATURE **EDUCATION** Univ Wisc, BA, MA PhD. **CAREER** Vis asst prof, Grinnell Col; vis asst prof, Univ Wisc; prof, Carthage Col. **HONORS AND AWARDS** Newberry Library Resident fel, Nat Endowment Humanities grant. **RESEARCH** Fr Renaissance. **SELECTED PUBLICATIONS** Auth, Reading in the Renaissance, Newark, DE, 99; articles: Bibliotheque d'Humanisme et Renaissance; Renaissance Quart; Studies Philol. **CONTACT ADDRESS** Carthage Col, 2001 Alford Dr., Kenosha, WI 53140. **EMAIL** rothst1@carthage.edu

ROTHWELL, KENNETH S.
PERSONAL Born 03/27/1955, Rochester, NY, m, 1989, 2 children **DISCIPLINE** CLASSICS **EDUCATION** Univ Vt, BA, 77; Columbia Univ, PhD, 85. **CAREER** Asst prof, Holy Cross Coll, 84-91; asst prof, Wellesley Coll, 91-92; asst prof, Boston Coll, 92-94; asst prof, Univ Mass Boston, 95-; Assoc Prof, 99-. **MEMBERSHIPS** APA; CANE. **RESEARCH** Greek Comedy. **SELECTED PUBLICATIONS** Auth, Politics and Persuasion in Aristophanes' Ecclesiazusae, 90. **CONTACT ADDRESS** Univ of Massachusetts, Boston, 100 Morrissey Blvd, Boston, MA 02125. **EMAIL** kenneth.rothwell@umb.edu

ROULIN, JEAN-MARIE
PERSONAL Born 12/13/1960, Alexandria, Egypt, s **DISCIPLINE** FRENCH LITERATURE **EDUCATION** Univ Lausanne, Licence es Lettres, 83, Doctorat es Lettres, 92. **CAREER** Charge de cours, 83-84, Maitre-asst, 94-97, Univ Lausanne; asst & charge de cours, 84-89, res asst, 86-89, Univ Zurich; vis prof, Univ Neuchatel, 96-97; Asst Prof, Univ Penn, 97-; vis prof, Ecole Normale Superieure, (Rue d'Ulm, Paris), 98. **HONORS AND AWARDS** Fel Fonds Nat Suisse de la Recherche Sci Paris, 89-91 & 91-94; Award of Res Found, Univ Penn, 98. **MEMBERSHIPS** Soc Chateaubriand. **RESEARCH** French literature XIX Century; Romanticism epic in XVIII Century; Swiss literature. **SELECTED PUBLICATIONS** Auth, L'Exil et la Gloire. Du roman familial a l'identite litteraire dans l'oeuvre de Chateaubriand, Champion, 94; Ma Vie de Benjamin Constant: malaise dans la communication, Annales Benjamin Constant, 95; Le Grand Siecle au futur: Voltaire, de la prophetie epique a l'ecriture de l'histoire, Revue d'Histoire litteraire de la France, 96; Alexandre Vinet Histoire de la litterature en Suisse romande, Payot, 97; co-auth, Entre Humanisme et reverie. Etudes sur les litteratures francaise et italienne de la Renaissance au Romantisme, Champion, 98; La Reflexion sur l'epopee en Suisse au dix-huitieme siecle, Reconceptualizing Nature, Science and Aesthetics, UCLA, 98; La Grandeur chex Ramuz: une notion'passerelle', Revue des Lettres modernes, Ramuz, 98; Les travail de la negation dans les Memoires d'Outre-Tombe, Chateaubriand e i 'Memoires d'Outre-Tombe, ETS/Slatkine, 98. **CONTACT ADDRESS** Dept Romance Lang, Univ of Pennsylvania, 521 Williams Hall, Philadelphia, PA 19104-6305. **EMAIL** jmroulin@sas.upenn.edu

ROULSTON, CHRISTINE
DISCIPLINE FRENCH LITERATURE **EDUCATION** Univ Southampton, MA; Univ Toronto, PhD. **RESEARCH** Feminist theory; post-structuralist theory; subjectivity and the 18th century novel. **SELECTED PUBLICATIONS** Auth, Virtue, Gender and the Authentic Self in Eighteenth Century Fiction, Fla Univ, 98. **CONTACT ADDRESS** Dept of French, Univ of Western Ontario, London, ON, Canada N6A 5B8. **EMAIL** croulsto@julian.uwo.ca

ROUMAN, JOHN CHRIST
PERSONAL Born 05/01/1916, Tomahawk, WI **DISCIPLINE** CLASSICS, LINGUISTICS **EDUCATION** Carleton Col, BA, 50; Columbia Univ, MA, 51; Univ Wis-Madison, PhD, 65. **CAREER** Tchr, Seton Hall Prep Sch, NJ, 54-56 & Malverne High Sch, NY, 57-59; res asst Greek epigraphy, Inst Advan Study, Princeton Univ, 62-63; asst prof, 65-71, chmn dept Span & class, 72-76, assoc prof, 71-91, prof class, Univ NH, 91-, Chair classics, 87-98, Coord classics, 98-; Pres, Strafford Cty Greco-Roman Found, Bd mem, Phi Kappa Theta Nat Found. **HONORS AND AWARDS** Noyse Prize for Greek, Carleton Col, 50; Fulbright Scholar, Univ Kiel, WGer, 56-57; UNH Alumni Asn, Distinguished Tchg Awd, 85; Barlow-Beach Awd for Serv, Cause of Class, Class Asn of New Engl, 91; Am Philol Asn Nat Awd for Excellence in Tchg, Class, 91; AHEPA and Daughters of Penelope, Pericles Awd, 93. **MEMBERSHIPS** Am Philol Asn; Medieval Acad Am; Mod Greek Studies Asn; Class Asn New Engl. **RESEARCH** Class philol, espec Pindar and Homer; mod Greek studies; Byzantine hist. **SELECTED PUBLICATIONS** Auth, Nominal-Compound Epithets in Pindar: A Linguistic Analysis, Univ Microfilms, 67; coauth, More still on the Trojan Horse, Class J, 4-5/72. **CONTACT ADDRESS** Dept of Langs, Lit and Cult, Univ of New Hampshire, Durham, 209 Murkland Hall, PO Box 54, Durham, NH 03824-4724. **EMAIL** jcrouman@christa.unh.edu

ROY, G(EORGE) ROSS
PERSONAL Born 08/20/1924, Montreal, PQ, Canada, m, 1954, 1 child **DISCIPLINE** ENGLISH, COMPARATIVE LITERATURE **EDUCATION** Concordia Univ, BA, 50; Univ Montreal, MA, 51, PhD(English), 59; Univ Strasbourg, dipl, 54; Univ Paris, DUniv(comp lit), 58. **CAREER** Lectr English, Royal Mil Col, St Jean, 54-56; asst prof, Univ Ala, 58-61; from asst prof to assoc prof, Univ Montreal, 61-63; prof, Tex Technol Univ, 63-65; prof English & Comp Lit, Univ SC, 65-90; Huntington Libr grant, 62; Can Coun & Am Philos Soc grant, 63; founding mem bd gov & chmn libr comt, Am-Scottish Found, NY, 66-; founding ed, Studies in Scottish Lit, 63- ; gen ed, Scottish Poetry Reprints, Quarto Press, London & Dept English Bibliog Ser, Univ SC. **HONORS AND AWARDS** Founding vice-pres, Asn for Scottish Lit Stud; fel, Soc of Antiq of Scotland; hon life pres, Robert Burns Federation; Robert Bruce Award, Old Dominion Univ; distinguished prof Univ S Carolina, 89. **MEMBERSHIPS** Int Comp Lit Asn; Am Comp Lit Asn; MLA; S Atlantic MLA; Edinburgh Bibl Soc; Thomas Carlyle Soc; James Boswell Soc. **RESEARCH** Comparative literature; Scottish literature; Robert Burns. **SELECTED PUBLICATIONS** ed & trans, Twelve Modern French-Canadian Poets, Toronto, 58; auth, Le sentiment de la nature dans la poesie canadienne anglaise 1867-1918, Paris, 61; auth, French Translations/Critics of Robert Burns to 1893, Revue de Litterature Comparee, 63-4; auth, French Stage Adaptations of Tom Jones, Revue de Litterature Comparee, 70; ed, Scottish section, New Cambridge Bibliography of English Literature, 1660-1800, Cambridge, 71; auth, The French Reputation of Thomas Carlyle in the Nineteenth Century, in Drescher, ed, Thomas Carlyle 1981, Frankfurt am Main, 83; ed, The Letters of Robert Burns, 2 vols, Oxford, 85; auth, Scottish Poets and the French Revolution, Etudes Ecossaises, 92; auth, Editing Burns' Letters in the Twentieth Century, in Carnie, ed, Robert Burns: Some Twentieth Century Perspectives, Calgary, 93; auth, Editing Robert Burns in the Nineteenth Century, in Simpson, Burns Now, Edinburgh, 94. **CONTACT ADDRESS** Dept of English, Univ of So Carolina, Columbia, Columbia, SC 29208.

ROZIER, LOUISE
PERSONAL Born 02/15/1952, Sedilo, Italy, d, 1 child **DISCIPLINE** ITALIAN LITERATURE & TRANSLATION **CAREER** Instr Italian. **HONORS AND AWARDS** PEN Poggioli Awd, 96. **RESEARCH** Italian literature and translation. **SELECTED PUBLICATIONS** Transl, Fortunato Pasqualino, The Little Jesus of Sicily, Univ Ark Press, (99). **CONTACT ADDRESS** Dept For Lang, Univ of Arkansas, Fayetteville, 425 Kimpel, Fayetteville, AR 72701-1201. **EMAIL** Rozier@comp.uark.edu

RUBIN, DAVID LEE
PERSONAL Born 09/30/1939, Indianapolis, IN, m, 1965, 1 child **DISCIPLINE** FRENCH **EDUCATION** Univ Tenn, BA, 62; Univ Ill, MA, 64; Univ Ill, PhD, 67. **CAREER** Asst Prof, Univ Chicago, 67-69; From Asst Prof to Prof, Univ Va, 69-. **HONORS AND AWARDS** Fulbright Fel, 62; Woodrow Wilson Fel, 63-65; Guggenheim FEl, 80; Phi Beta Kappa, 84. **MEMBERSHIPS** MLA. **RESEARCH** Early modern French literature, poetics and modal semantics of literary translation. **SELECTED PUBLICATIONS** Auth, Higher, Hidden Order, 72; auth, The Knot of Artifice, 81; auth, A Pact of Silence, 91; auth, EMF: Studies in Early Modern France, EMF Critiques, EMF Texts, 94-00. **CONTACT ADDRESS** Dept French, Univ of Virginia, Box 400770, Charlottesville, VA 22904-4770. **EMAIL** dlr7r@virginia.edu

RUBIN, MORDECAI
PERSONAL Born 06/20/1930, Brooklyn, NY, m, 1977, 1 child **DISCIPLINE** SPANISH **EDUCATION** Rutgers Univ, AB, 52; Univ Md, PhD, 61. **CAREER** Instr Span, French & Ital, Gannon Col, 56-59: asst prof Spanish & French, Wash Col, 59-62; asst prof Romance lang, Clark Univ, 62-65; assoc prof, 65-69, Prof Span, Teachers Col, Columbia Univ, 69-, Lang educ consult, UN, Peace Corps & Teacher Corps. **HONORS AND AWARDS** Elected Spanish Royal Academy, Madrid, 95; Elected Iberian American Academy of Poetry, 96. **MEMBERSHIPS** Am Asn Teachers Span & Port; MLA. **RESEARCH** Bilingual education, Spanish poetry, Distance learning. **SELECTED PUBLICATIONS** Translr, Cargo loss prevention, Int Insurance Monitor, 63; auth, Una poetica moderns, Univ Ala & Nat Univ Mex, 66; The image of the language teacher, J English As Second Lang, 68; Toward a modern methodology for teaching Chinese, J Am Asn Teachers Chinese, 68; Considerations home dialect and English teaching Spanish bilinguals, In: Anthology, Louisville Linguistics Conference 1977, Georgetown Univ, 3/78; auth, A Sotto Voce, Iberoamerican Academy of Poetry, New York, 01; Original Spanish poems with poet's critical commentary. **CONTACT ADDRESS** Dept Span Teachers Col, Columbia Univ, 525 W 120th St, New York, NY 10027-6670. **EMAIL** MRubin@aol.com

RUCK, CARL ANTON PAUL
PERSONAL Born 12/08/1935, Bridgeport, CT **DISCIPLINE** GREEK LANGUAGE & LITERATURE **EDUCATION** Yale Univ, BA, 58; Univ Mich, Ann Arbor, MA, 59; Harvard Univ, PhD(classics), 65. **CAREER** From instr to assoc prof, 64-76, PROF CLASSICS, BOSTON UNIV, 76-. **MEMBERSHIPS** Am Philol Asn. **RESEARCH** Greek tragedy and comedy; Greek mythology; teaching methods for Greek and Latin; ethnobotany; ethnopharmacology; clinical mythologist. **SELECTED PUBLICATIONS** Coauth, The Sacred Mushroom Seeker (Mr Wasson and the Greeks), Dioscorides, 90; coauth, The World of Classical Myth: Gods and Godesses, Heroines and Heros, Carolina Academic Press, 94; coauth, Ethnobotany: Evolution of a Discipline (Gods and Plants in the Classical World), Dioscorides, 95; auth, Intensive Latin: First Year and Review (with computer tutorial Vade Mecum), Carolina Academic Press, 97; coauth, Mistletoe, Centaurs, and Datura, Eleusis n s 1.2, 98; auth, entry on Myth in the Blackwell Dictionary of Anthropology; coauth, Mistletoe, Centaurs , and Datura, (99), 25-55; coauth, Jason, the Drug Man, Eleusis n.s. 1.3, (99), 27-68; coauth, The Apples of Apollo: Pagan and Christiona Mystries of the Eucharist, Durham, NC, Carolina Acad Press, 00. **CONTACT ADDRESS** Dept of Classics, Boston Univ, 745 Commonwealth Ave, Boston, MA 02215-1401. **EMAIL** bacchus@bu.edu

RUDD, JILL
DISCIPLINE INTERPERSONAL COMMUNICATION, GROUP COMMUNICATION **EDUCATION** Kent State Univ, BA, MA, PhD. **CAREER** Comm, Cleveland St Univ. **SELECTED PUBLICATIONS** Auth, Divorce Mediation: One Step Forward Two Steps Back?, Communication and the Disenfranchised,L. Erlbaum Assoc, 96. **CONTACT ADDRESS** Commun Dept, Cleveland State Univ, 83 E 24th St, Cleveland, OH 44115. **EMAIL** j.rudd@csuohio.edu

RUDDER, ROBERT S.
DISCIPLINE SPANISH LITERATURE **EDUCATION** Univ Redlands, VA, 59; Univ Minn, MA, 64, PhD, 68. **CAREER** Instr, Univ of Minn, 63-68; asst prof, UCLA, 68-76; instr, Calif State Univ Pomona, 76-69; Instr, Calif State Univ, Los Angeles, 95-. **RESEARCH** Medieval Renaissance and Golden Age Spanish Literature, Literary Translations. **SELECTED PUBLICATIONS** Auth, Life of Lazarillo of Tormes, 73; auth, Literature of Spain in English Translation, 75; auth, City of Kings, 92; auth, Nazarin, 97; auth, Medicine Man, 00, auth, Solitaire of Love, 00. **CONTACT ADDRESS** Dept For Lang, California State Univ, Los Angeles, 5151 State Univ Dr, Los Angeles, CA 90032-4226. **EMAIL** rsrudder@aol.com

RUDNYTZKY, LEONID
PERSONAL Born 09/08/1935, Lviv, Ukraine, m, 1964, 3 children **DISCIPLINE** GERMAN & SLAVIC LITERATURE **EDUCATION** La Salle Col, BA, 58; Univ Pa, MA, 60; Ukrainian Free Univ, Munich, PhD, 65. **CAREER** Prof foreign lang, 63-75, prof Slavic & Ger Lit, La Salle Col, 75-; consult, Cath Renascence Soc, 65-68,; prof, Ukrainian Free Univ, 75; ethic heritage studies grants, 80, 81; NEH grant, 82; rector, Ukranian Ferr univ, Munich, 98-. **HONORS AND AWARDS** Lindback Awd for Distinguished Teaching, La Salle College, Philadelphia, 66; Doctor Habil; St. Clement Pope Ukrainian Catholic Univ, Rome, 76; Hon Dr, Holy Family Col, Philadelphia, 91; Ivan Franko Prize for Ukrainian Lit, The Writers' Union of Ukraine, Kiev, 92; Elected Pres of the World Council of The Shevchenko Scientific Soc, Lviv, Ukraine, 92; Honorary Doctorates, Univ of Lviv, Ukraine, 99 and Ukrainian State Univ of Forestry and Wood Tech, Lviv, Ukraine, 00. **MEMBERSHIPS** Shevchenko Sci Soc; MLA; Am Assn Teachers Ger; Am Assn Teachers Slavic & E Europ Lang; St. Sophia Rel Soc Assoc of Ukrainian Catholics-Exec Sec; Intl PEN Club. **RESEARCH** Comparative literature; history of Easten churches and Eastern spirituality; the Ukrainian Catholic Church. **SELECTED PUBLICATIONS** Auth, Research Guide to European Historial Biography 1450 - Present, Beachan Publishing, Washington, DC, 93; ed, Faith and Hope, The Ukrainian Church in Communion with Rome: 1596-1996, Philadelphia, Washington, Toronto, 97. **CONTACT ADDRESS** Ukranian Free Univ, Pienzenaverstr A5, 81679 Munchen.

RUEBEL, JAMES
PERSONAL Born 08/18/1945, Cincinnati, OH, m, 1966, 2 children **DISCIPLINE** ANCIENT ROMAN HISTORY, CLASSICAL LANGUAGES **EDUCATION** Yale Univ, BA, 67; Univ Cincinnati, MA, 70, PhD, 72. **CAREER** Instr Greek & Latin, Classics Dept, Univ Cincinnati, 72-73; asst prof, Classics Dept, Univ MN, 73-78; asst prof, 78-81, Assoc Prof, 81-93, Prof Classics, for Lang & Lit, IA State Univ, 93-00; dean, honors dol, Ball State Univ, 00-. **MEMBERSHIPS** Am Philol Asn; Asn Ancient Historians; Class Asn Midwest & South; Am Class League; Archaeol Inst Am. **RESEARCH** Roman republican history; Roman culture from Hannibal to Horace. **CONTACT ADDRESS** Honors College, Ball State Univ, 104 Carmichael, Muncie, IN 47306. **EMAIL** jruebel@bsu.edu

RUEDA, ANA
DISCIPLINE ROMANCE LANGS & LITS **EDUCATION** Vanderbilt Univ, PhD, 85. **CAREER** ASSOC PROF, SPAN, UNIV MO, 92-. **CONTACT ADDRESS** Dept of Romance Langs, Lit, Univ of Missouri, Columbia, 143 Arts & Scis, Columbus, MO 65211. **EMAIL** RuedaA@missouri.edu

RUESCHMANN, EVA
DISCIPLINE COMPARATIVE LITERATURE AND CULTURAL STUDIES **EDUCATION** Univ Heidelberg, Ger, BA; Univ MA, Amherst, PhD. **CAREER** Vis asst prof, Hampshire Col. **SELECTED PUBLICATIONS** Publ articles on Senegalese novelist Mariama Ba, African American writers Jessie Fauset and Dorothy West, filmmakers Alan Rudolph and Margarethe von Trotta, and psychoanalytic and cultural readings of sister relationships in contemp world cinema. **CONTACT ADDRESS** Hampshire Col, Amherst, MA 01002.

RUGG, LINDA HAVERTY
PERSONAL Born 11/17/1957, Meried, CA, m, 1991, 1 child **DISCIPLINE** COMPARATIVE LITERATURE **EDUCATION** Barnard Col, BA, 80; Harvard Univ, MA, 82; PhD, 89. **CAREER** Assoc prof, Ohio State Univ, 89-99; vis asst prof, BYU, 93-94; assoc prof, Univ Cal, Berkeley, 99-. **HONORS AND AWARDS** Aldo and Jean Scuglione Bk Prize. **MEMBERSHIPS** MLA; SASS; ASA. **RESEARCH** Scandinavian, German and American culture of the 19th and 20th centuries; literature and visual arts, esp photography; ecocriticsm; autobiography. **SELECTED PUBLICATIONS** Auth, Picturing Ourselves: Photography and Autobiography, Univ Chicago Press, 97. **CONTACT ADDRESS** Dept Scandinavian, Univ of California, Berkeley, 6406 Dwinelle Hall, Berkeley, CA 94720. **EMAIL** rugg@socrates.berkeley.edu

RUGG, MARILYN D.
DISCIPLINE SPANISH LITERATURE **EDUCATION** Cornell Univ, BA, 75, MA, 78; The Johns Hopkins Univ, PhD, 85; Marawood Col, MSW, 89. **CAREER** Assoc prof-, Colgate Univ. **HONORS AND AWARDS** Hon(s), Phi Eta Sigma; nominee, colgate univ prof yr, 90, 91, 95. **RESEARCH** 19th and early 20th-century Span lit. **SELECTED PUBLICATIONS** Auth, Self and Text in Unamuno's Amor y pedagogea, ALEC, 17, 92; The Figure of the Author in Gomez de la Serna's El novelista, ALEC, 14, 89; Dona Berta: Claren's Allegory of Signification, MLN, 103, 88. **CONTACT ADDRESS** Dept of Romance Lang, Colgate Univ, 13 Oak Drive, Hamilton, NY 13346. **EMAIL** MRugg@center.colgate.edu

RUIZ, MIGUEL
PERSONAL Born 10/07/1954, Puerto Rico, m, 1 child **DISCIPLINE** SPANISH LITERATURE **EDUCATION** Univ PR, BA, 76; Univ Kansas, MA, 82; Univ Nebr, PhD, 87. **CAREER** Asst prof, Univ of Tex, 93-96, asst prof, Austin Peay State Univ, 96-. **HONORS AND AWARDS** Cert of Teaching Excellence, Va Tech, 92; Outstanding Prof in Foreign Lang, Austin Peay State Univ, 99. **MEMBERSHIPS** MLA; AAUP; AATSP; Soc of Spanish and Spanish-Am Studies; Sigma Delta Pi. **RESEARCH** Nineteenth and twentieth Century Spanish literature. **SELECTED PUBLICATIONS** Auth, La Narrativa de Ramon Hernandez, Editorial Pliegos, 00. **CONTACT ADDRESS** Dept Lang Lit, Austin Peay State Univ, 601 College St, Clarksville, TN 37044-0001. **EMAIL** ruizavilesm@apsu.edu

RUIZ, ROBERTO
PERSONAL Born 12/20/1925, Madrid, Spain, m, 1956, 1 child **DISCIPLINE** LANGUAGE, LITERATURE, SPANISH **EDUCATION** Univ Nac Auto de Mex, Maestro en Filos, 52; Princeton Univ, MA, 56. **CAREER** Instr, Mt Holyoke Col, 53-55; lectr, Hunter Col, 56-58; lectr, Mex City Col, 58-59; lectr, Middlebury Col, 59-61; asst prof, Dickenson Col, 61-63; asst prof, Wheaton Col, 63-91; vis prof, Harvard Univ, 91-92, 95. **HONORS AND AWARDS** Silver Medal, Best Grad, Univ Nac Auto Mex, 52; Princeton Univ Span Lit Fel, 56; Commander's Cross, Order of Isabel la Catolica, 98. **MEMBERSHIPS** MLA; AATSP; AC; AIG. **RESEARCH** Contemporary Spanish fiction; Cervantes. **SELECTED PUBLICATIONS** Auth, La Etica de Saint-Exupery (Mex), 52; auth, Esquemas (Mex), 54; auth, Plazas Sin Muros (Mex), 60; auth, El Ultimo Oasis (Mex), 64; auth, Los Jueces Implacables (Mex), 70; auth, Paraiso Cerrado, Cielo Abierto (Mex), 77; auth, Contra la Luz Que Muere (NYork), 82. **CONTACT ADDRESS** 140 N Main St, PO Box 34-8D, Attleboro, MA 02703-2242.

RUNDELL, RICHARD JASON
PERSONAL Born 12/15/1939, Chicago, IL, m, 1969, 2 children **DISCIPLINE** GERMAN LITERATURE & LINGUISTICS **EDUCATION** Colo Col, BA, 61; Middlebury Col, MA, 62; Univ Colo, PhD, 72. **CAREER** Instr Ger, St Lawrence Univ, 62-65 & Univ Colo, 69-71; asst prof, Emporia Kans State Col, 71-72; lectr English, Univ Regensburg, W Ger, 72-75; asst prof, 75-80, assoc prof, 80-86, Prof Ger, NMex State Univ, 86-. **MEMBERSHIPS** Am Asn Teachers Ger; Int Brecht Soc; MLA; Ger Studies Asn. **RESEARCH** Twentieth century German literature; Brecht; East German literature; German film; German theater. **SELECTED PUBLICATIONS** Auth, Duerer year 1971, Ger Postal Spec, 71; The Brechtian influence and German Dem Repub poetry of political, criticism, Weber & Heinen: Bertolt Brecht, Polit Theory & Lit Pract, 78; Ragtime, bicentennial: Nostalgia, Gulliver, Deutschenglische Jahrbk, 78; Keller's Kleider machen leute as novelle and film, Unterrichtspraxis 13, 80; guest ed, Liedermacher issue of Dimension, vol 19, 1, 91; Liedermacher im Zeichen der Wende, in Literatur fur leser, 3/96. **CONTACT ADDRESS** Dept of Langs & Lings, New Mexico State Univ, MSC 3L, Las Cruces, NM 88003-8001. **EMAIL** rrundell@nmsu.edu

RUNNING, LEONA GLIDDEN
PERSONAL Born 08/24/1916, Mt Morris, MI, w **DISCIPLINE** SEMITIC LANGUAGES **EDUCATION** Emmanuel Missionary Col, BA, 37; Seventh-Day Adventist Theol Sem, MA, 55; Johns Hopkins Univ, PhD, 64. **CAREER** Teacher Lang, Laurelwood Acad, Ore, 37-41; lang secy, Voice of Prophecy Radio Broadcast, 44-48; ed secy, Gen Conf Seventh-Day Adventists, 50-54; from instr to assoc prof, 55-69, prof, 69-81, Emer Prof Bibl Lang, Andrews Univ, 81- **HONORS AND AWARDS** Weniger and Andrews medals; Medallion of Distinction, Gen Conf Dept Educ. **MEMBERSHIPS** Soc Bibl Lit; Chi Soc Bibl Res. **RESEARCH** The Syriac manuscripts of Isaiah. **SELECTED PUBLICATIONS** Auth, An investigation of the Syriac version of Isaiah, 7/65, 1/66 & 7/66 & Syriac variants in Isaiah 26, 1/67, Andrews Univ Sem Studies; coauth, William Foxwell Albright, A Twentieth-Century Genius, Andrews Univ Press, 91. **CONTACT ADDRESS** Theol Sem, Andrews Univ, Berrien Springs, MI 49104-0001.

RUNYON, RANDOLPH PAUL
PERSONAL Born 02/13/1947, Maysville, KY, m, 1983, 2 children **DISCIPLINE** FRENCH LITERATURE, AMERICAN STUDIES **EDUCATION** Johns Hopkins Univ, PhD(-French), 73. **CAREER** Asst prof, Case Western Reserve Univ, 74-76; asst prof to assoc prof, 77-84, Prof French, Miami Univ, 84-. **MEMBERSHIPS** MLA; Soc des Amis de Montaigne; Am Studies Asn; SAtlantic Mod Lang Asn; Robert Penn Warren Circle. **RESEARCH** Sixteenth century French literature; 20th century French literature; literary criticism; 20th century American literature. **SELECTED PUBLICATIONS** Auth, Fowles, Irving, Barthes: Canonical Variations on an Apocryphal Theme, Ohio State Univ Press, 81; The Braided Dream: Robert Penn Warren's Late Poetry, Univ Press of Ky, 90; The Taciturn Text: The Fiction of Robert Penn Warren, Ohio State Univ Press, 90; Reading Raymond Carver, Syracuse Univ Press, 92; Delia Webster and the Underground Railroad, Univ Press of Ky, 96; auth, In La Fontaine's Labyrinth: A Thread through the Fables, Charlottesville, Va, Rookwood Press, 00. **CONTACT ADDRESS** Dept of French & Ital, Miami Univ, Oxford, OH 45056-1602. **EMAIL** runyonr@muohio.edu

RUSH, PATRICIA
PERSONAL Born 10/29/1948, CA, m, 1969, 1 child **DISCIPLINE** SPANISH **EDUCATION** Calif State Univ, BA, 69; MA, 72. **CAREER** Teacher, asst principal dir of migrant educ, 70-80; prof, Ventura Col, 89-. **HONORS AND AWARDS** Grant, Lang Learning & Multimedia Applications; Teacher of the Year. **MEMBERSHIPS** Am Coun on Teaching of For Lang, Calif Lang Teachers Asn. **RESEARCH** Language instruction for occupational areas. **SELECTED PUBLICATIONS** Auth, Mosaicos, Spanish as a World Language, 98; auth, Trato Hecho, Spanish for Real Life, 00. **CONTACT ADDRESS** Dept Liberal Arts, Ventura Col, 4667 Telegraph Rd, Ventura, CA 93003-3872. **EMAIL** rush@west.net

RUSSELL, CHARLES
PERSONAL Born 12/16/1944, New York, NY, m, 1990 **DISCIPLINE** COMPARATIVE LITERATURE **EDUCATION** Wesleyan Univ, AB, 66; Cornell Univ, PhD, 72. **CAREER** Asst prof, Univ Va, 72-76; asst prof, 77-83, assoc dean arts scis, 85-87, assoc provost, 88-94, Assoc Prof English, 83-, Rutgers Univ, Newark. **HONORS AND AWARDS** Fulbright lect Univ Augsburg, 80 **MEMBERSHIPS** MLA; CAA. **RESEARCH** Contemporary lit and art **SELECTED PUBLICATIONS** Auth, Poets, Prophets and Revolutionaires: The Literary Avantgarde from Rimbaud through Postmodernism, Oxford Univ Press, 85; auth, The Avant-garde Today, Univ Ill Press, 81. **CONTACT ADDRESS** English Dept, Rutgers, The State Univ of New Jersey, Newark, Newark, NJ 07102. **EMAIL** crr@andromeda.rutgers.edu

RUSSELL, DELBERT
DISCIPLINE FRENCH LITERATURE **EDUCATION** Univ Toronto, BA; MA; PhD. **RESEARCH** French-Canadian literature; medieval French language and literature; bibliography. **SELECTED PUBLICATIONS** Auth, An Annotated Bibliography (rev), 87; Le Legendier apostolique anglo-normand, Montreal, 89; La Vie S. Richard, Bishop Chichester, 95. **CONTACT ADDRESS** Univ of Waterloo, 200 University Ave W, Waterloo, ON, Canada N2L 3G1. **EMAIL** drussell@watarts.uwaterloo.ca

RUSSELL, RINALDINA
PERSONAL Born Ancona, Italy **DISCIPLINE** ITALIAN LITERATURE **EDUCATION** Columbia Univ, PhD, 71. **CAREER** Instr Ital lang & lit, Barnard Col, Columbia Univ, 69-71; asst prof romance lang, 71-76, assoc prof romance lang, 76-85, Prof, Romance Lang, 76-85; Prof, European lang & lit, 85-. **MEMBERSHIPS** MLA; Dante Soc Am; Renaissance Soc Am; Am Asn Teachers Ital; Am Asn Ital Studies. **SELECTED PUBLICATIONS** Auth, Tre versanti delta poesia stilnovistica: Guinizzelli, Cavalcanti e Dante, Adriatica Editrice, Bari, 73; Generi poetici medievali, Modelli c funzioni letterarie, Societa Editrice Napoletana, Naples, 82; ed, Italian Women Writers, Greenwood, 94; The Feminist Encyclopedia of Italian Literature, Greenwood, 97; co-ed Tullia d' Aragona, Dialogue on the Infinity of Love, Univ Chicago, 97. **CONTACT ADDRESS** Dept of European Lang & Lit, Queens Col, CUNY, 6530 Kissena Blvd, Flushing, NY 11367-1597. **EMAIL** rinaldina.russell@worldnet.att.net

RUSSO, ADELAIDE
DISCIPLINE FRENCH **EDUCATION** Columbia Univ, PhD, 80. **CAREER** Instr, Columbia, 76-79, 81; asst prof, La State Univ, 81-87; Fac Fel, Harvard Univ, 84-85; assoc prof, La State Univ, 87-; vis prof, Vanderbilt Univ, 94. **MEMBERSHIPS** Modern Lang Asn; Northeast Lang Asn; Am Asn of Teachers of French; Semiotic Soc of Am; Asn for the Study of Dada and Surrealism; Societe des Professeurs Francais en Amerique; Soc for Critical Exchange; SAMLA; The Am Soc for Aesthetics; Asn des Amis de Robert Desnos. **RESEARCH** 19th and 20th Century Poetry and Prose (especially Surrealism); Contemporary French Criticism and Literary Theory including Semiotics and Feminist Theory; The Relationship between Literature, Aesghetics and the Plastic Arts; 16th Century French Poetry; Contemporary French Theatre; iterary Translation; Compara-

tive Literature. **SELECTED PUBLICATIONS** Auth, French in Action: The Capretz Method, New Haven: Yale Univ Press, 87; auth, French in Action, Part I, Washington DC: The Annenberg/CPB Project; auth, "Muthos et prophetie: L'elaboration d'une mythologoie moderne--poete, peintre, oracle," in Mythe et Pensee surrealiste, eds. Yves Vade and Jacqueline Chenieux-Gendron, (Paris: Lachenal & Ritter, 96): 209-228; auth, "Les Questionnements du Penseur-Voyageur," in Michel Deguy: Le Poete que je cherche a etre, ed. Yves Charnet, (Paris: Belin, 96): 260-273; auth, "Pour tout ce que les yeux voient: Pour Bona Tibertelli de Pissis de Mandiargues," in La Part du Feminin dans le Surrealisme, eds. Georgiana Colvile and Katharine Conley, (Paris: Lachenal & Rittner, 98): 153-173; auth, "La main de Jean Follain: Lecture d'un detail," in Le Monde de Jean Follain, ed. Arlette Albert-Birot, (Paris: Editions Jean-Michel Place, 98): 155-171; auth, "Texte qui de soi-meme s'ecrit: Les Collaborations de Benoit Peeters," Ecritures contemporaines, eds. Dominique Viart and Jan Baetens, Vol. II, (Paris: Minard-Les Lettres Modernes, 99): 203-220; auth, "Philippe Soupault: Cartographe et Architecte," in Patiences et Silences de Philippe Soupault, ed. Jacqueline Chenieux-Gendron, (Paris: L'Harmattan,00): 88-108; auth, "L'Hommage du Mage au Sage: Edmond Jabes et Jacques Derrida," in Hommage a Edmond Jaabes, ed. Didier Cahen, (Bordeau: Opales, 00): 94-107; auth, "Divagations sur un plan cadastral," Cahiers RITM, (Centre de Recherches Interdisciplinaires sur les Textes Modernes, Universite de Paris X-Nanterre), No. 21, (00): 177-198. **CONTACT ADDRESS** Dept of Fr & Italian, Louisiana State Univ and A&M Col, 7640 Lasalle Ave, Apt 203, Baton Rouge, LA 70806-8316. **EMAIL** frruss@lsu.edu

RUSSO, JOSEPH ANTHONY
PERSONAL Born 04/14/1937, Brooklyn, NY, m, 1960, 2 children **DISCIPLINE** CLASSICS **EDUCATION** Brooklyn Col, BA, 58; Yale Univ, MA, 60, PhD, 62. **CAREER** From instr to assoc prof classics, Yale Univ, 62-70; assoc prof, 70-76, prof classics, Haverford Col, 76-, chmn dept, 80-, fel, Ctr Hellenic Studies, Wash, DC, 65-66; Nat Endowment for Humanities younger humanist fel, 73-74; Am Coun Learned Soc grant-in-aid, 74; Nat Endowment Hum Summer Stipend, 82 & 90; vis prof class studies, Univ Mich, 77-78; Univ Ca Berkley, 83. **HONORS AND AWARDS** Distinguished Alumni Awd, Brooklyn Col, 82. **MEMBERSHIPS** Class Asn Atlantic States; Am Philol Asn. **RESEARCH** Greek literature and metrics; Homeric poetry; oral literature and folklore. **SELECTED PUBLICATIONS** Auth, A Closer Look at Homeric Formulas, Trans Am Philol Asn, 64; The Structural Formula of Homeric Verse, Yale Class Studies, 66; coauth, Homeric Psychology and the Oral Epic Tradition, J Hist Ideas, 68; Homer Against his Tradition, Arion, 68; The Inner Man in Archilochus and the Odyssey, Greek, Roman & Byzantine Studies, 74; Reading the Greek Lyric Poets, Arion, 75; How, and what, does Homer communicate, Class J, 76; contribr, Is Aural or oral composition the cause of Homer's formulaic style?, Oral Literature and the Formula, Univ Mich, 76; co-auth, A Commentary on Homer's Odyssey, Oxford Univ, 92; auth, Omero, Odissea V, Libri XVII-XX, Mondadori, Roma, 92. **CONTACT ADDRESS** Dept of Classics, Haverford Col, 370 Lancaster Ave, Haverford, PA 19041-1392. **EMAIL** jrusso@haverford.edu

RUTHERFORD, WILLIAM E.
PERSONAL Born 04/04/1929, Paterson, NJ **DISCIPLINE** LINGUISTICS **EDUCATION** UCLA, PhD. **CAREER** Prof, Univ Southern Calif. **MEMBERSHIPS** Linguistic Soc of Am; Am Asn of Applied Linguistics **RESEARCH** Second language acquisiton and grammatical theory. **SELECTED PUBLICATIONS** Co-gen ed ser, Language Acquisition and Language Disorders; auth, Workbook in the Structure of English: Linguistic Principles and Language Acquisition, Blackwell, 98; Second Language Grammar: Learning and Teaching, Longman 87; ed, Language Universals and Second Language Acquisition, Benjamins, 84; Sentence Sense, Harcourt Brace Jovanovich, 73. **CONTACT ADDRESS** Dept of Linguistics, Univ of So California, University Park Campus, Los Angeles, CA 90089-1693. **EMAIL** rutherfo@usc.edu

RUTLEDGE, HARRY CARRACI
PERSONAL Born 01/23/1932, Chillicothe, OH **DISCIPLINE** CLASSICS **EDUCATION** OH State Univ, BScEd, 54, MA, 57, PhD, 60. **CAREER** From asst prof to assoc prof classics, Univ GA, 60-68; assoc prof, head Romance lang, 72-79, Prof Class, Univ TN, Knoxville, 69-96, Prof Emer, 96-, Head Dept, 68-91, Secy adv coun, Am Acad Rome, 71-75. **MEMBERSHIPS** Am Philol Asn; Archaeol Inst Am; Vergilian Soc(pres, 77-79); Southern Comp Lit Asn (pres, 78-79); Class Asn Mid West & South (pres, 79-80); Am Class League (pres, 90-94). **RESEARCH** Lit of the Augustan Age; Vergil; class tradition in the 20th century. **SELECTED PUBLICATIONS** Auth, Propertius' Tarpeia: The poem itself, Class J, 11/64; Eliot and Vergil: Parallels in the Sixth Aeneid and Four Quartets, Vergilius, 66; Classical Latin poetry: An art for our time, In: The Endless Fountain, Ohio State Univ, 72; Contest and possession: Classical imagery in Henry James' The Golden Bowl, Comparatist, 5/77; Vergil's Dido in modern literature, Class & Mod Lit, summer 81; The Guernica Bull: Studies in the Classical Tradition in the Twentieth Century, Univ Ga Press, 89. **CONTACT ADDRESS** Dept of Class, Univ of Tennessee, Knoxville, 1101 McClung Tower, Knoxville, TN 37996-0471.

RUTLEDGE, STEVEN H.
PERSONAL Born 06/28/1963, Fresno, CA, m, 1985 **DISCIPLINE** CLASSICS **EDUCATION** Univ Mass - Boston, BA, 89; Brown Univ, PhD, 96. **CAREER** Asst Prof, Univ Md - College Park, 96-. **HONORS AND AWARDS** Grad Res Bd Fel, Univ Md, 97; Grad Res Board, Fel, 99. **MEMBERSHIPS** APA; CAAS; CAMWS. **RESEARCH** Roman social history; Roman literature of the Early Empire. **SELECTED PUBLICATIONS** Auth, Trajan and Tacitus Audience: reader Reception of Annales 1-2, Ramus vol 27, (98), 141-159; auth, Delatores and the Tradition of Violence in Roman Oratory," Am J of Philology 120, (99), 555-573; auth, "Plato, tacitus, and the dialogus de oratoribus," Latomus 254, (00), 345-357; auth, Tacitus in Tartan: Textual colonization and Expansionist Discourse in tacitus Agricol," gelios 27, (00), 75-95; auth, Imperial Inquisitions: Prosecutors and Informants from Tiberius to Domittian, 01. **CONTACT ADDRESS** Classics Dept, Univ of Maryland, Col Park, 2407 Marie Mount Hall, College Park, MD 20742. **EMAIL** srutled@deans.umd.edu

RUTTER, JEREMY B.
PERSONAL Born 06/23/1946, Boston, MA, m, 1970, 2 children **DISCIPLINE** CLASSICS **EDUCATION** Haverford Col, BA, 67; Univ Pa, PhD, 74. **CAREER** Vis asst prof, Univ Calif, Los Angeles, 75-76; from asst prof to assoc prof to prof to chairmn, 76-, Dartmouth Col. **HONORS AND AWARDS** Phi Beta Kappa, 67; Woodrow Wilson Fel, 67; Olivia James Travelling Fel, 75; NEH Res Grant, 79-81; ACLS Travel Grant, 82. **MEMBERSHIPS** Archaeol Inst Am; Am Sch Classical Stud, Athens; British Sch Archaeol, Athens; Classical Asn, New England. **RESEARCH** Aegean Prehistory; Ceramic Production and Exchange; Greco-Roman Athletics. **SELECTED PUBLICATIONS** Auth, The Transition to Mycenaean, 76; auth, Ceramic Change in the Aegean Early Bronze Age, 79; auth, Review of Aegean Prehistory II: The Pre-Palatial Bronze Age of the Southern and Central Greek Mainland, 93; auth, Lerna III: The Pottery of Lerna IV, 95; **CONTACT ADDRESS** Dept of Classics, Dartmouth Col, Hanover, NH 03755. **EMAIL** jeremy.rutter@dartmouth.edu

RYAN, JUDITH
PERSONAL Born 04/06/1943, m, 2 children **DISCIPLINE** GERMAN AND COMPARATIVE LITERATURE **EDUCATION** Sydney Univ, Australia, BA; Univ Mnnster, Ger, PhD. **CAREER** Harvard Col prof & Robert K. and Dale J. Weary prof; dir, Grad Stud; taught at, Smith Col. **HONORS AND AWARDS** NEH Fel, 78; Walter Channing Cabot Fel, 94; Basilius Awd in Germanics, 83; Best article of the year in German Quarterly, 82 and 90; Harvard Col Professorship (a teaching award), 98 **RESEARCH** 19th and 20th century literature, especially poetry and the novel. **SELECTED PUBLICATIONS** Auth, Umschlag und Verwandlung; The Uncompleted Past, 83; The Vanishing Subject, 91; articles on, Franz Kafka, Paul Celan, Christa Wolf & Gnnter Grass; auth, "Rilke, Modernism and Poetic Tradition," 99. **CONTACT ADDRESS** Dept of Germanic Languages and Literature, Harvard Univ, Barker Center 352, Cambridge, MA 02138. **EMAIL** jryan@fas.harvard.edu

RYAN, ROBERT
DISCIPLINE FRENCH LITERATURE **EDUCATION** Dalhousie Univ, BA; MA; Aix en Provence Univ, PhD. **RESEARCH** Acadian speech of Atlantic Canada. **SELECTED PUBLICATIONS** Auth, pub(s) on phonology and verb morphology of a Nova Scotian Acadian dialect. **CONTACT ADDRESS** Dept of French, Univ of Waterloo, 200 University Ave W, Waterloo, ON, Canada N2L 3G1. **EMAIL** rwryan@watarts.uwaterloo.ca

RYFA, JURAS
DISCIPLINE RUSSIAN **EDUCATION** Purdue Univ, MA, 93; Ind Univ, PhD, 97. **CAREER** Asst Prof, George Wash Univ, 96-. **HONORS AND AWARDS** Pedagogical Res and Innovative Develop in Educ Awd, 00. **MEMBERSHIPS** AATSEEL, AAASS **RESEARCH** Russian and east Europe. **SELECTED PUBLICATIONS** Auth, The Problem of Genre and the Quest for Justice in Chekov's "The Island of Sakhalin", The Edwin Mellen Pr (Lewiston, Queenston, Lampeter), 99; ed, Collected Essays in Honor of the Bicentennial of Alexander S Pushkin's Birth, The Edwin Mellen Pr (Lewiston, Queenston, Lampeter), 00; auth, "The Portrait of a Hero and the Problem of Romantic Artistry in Adam Mickiewicz's 'Pan Tadeusz'," Russian Lit, Croatian and Serbian, Czech and Slovak, Polish (forthcoming). **CONTACT ADDRESS** Dept Lang, The George Washington Univ, 2035 H St NW, Washington, DC 20052-0001. **EMAIL** jryfa@gwu.edu

RZHEVSKY, NICHOLAS
PERSONAL Born 11/08/1943, Linz, Austria, m, 1966, 2 children **DISCIPLINE** SLAVIC LANGUAGES **EDUCATION** Rutgers Univ, BA, 64; Princeton Univ, MA, 68; PhD, 72. **CAREER** Lect, Oberlin Col, 68-69; asst prof, Rutgers Univ, 70-76; asst prof, Univ Ill, Urbana, 76-82; assoc prof, SUNY, Stony Brook, 83-. **HONORS AND AWARDS** Phi Beta Kappa, 64; NEH res grant, 82; Am Philos Soc grant, 84-85; Fulbright-Hays Fels, 69-70, 77-78, 82-83, 90; IREX grants, 82-83, 92, 93-94; Dept of Ed Int Res and Studies grant, 98-99. **RESEARCH** Russian literature, culture, theater, ideology. **SELECTED PUBLICATIONS** Ed, Dramaturgs & Dramaturgy; ed, Anthology of Russian Literature From Earliest Writings to Modern Fiction. Introduction to a Culture; auth, Russian Literature and Ideology: Herzen, Dostoevsky, Tolstoy, Leontiev, Fadeyev; numerous articles and essays in Russian Rev, Slavic Rev, Encounter, Slavic and East European Js, Lit in Performance, Slavic and East European Arts, Russian Lang J, Modern Drama, Nation, New Lit Hist, Balagan, Comparative Lit, J of Int Doetoevsky Soc, Novyi zhurnal, The Handbook of Russian Lit, Shakespeare: Notable Int Revivals. **CONTACT ADDRESS** Dept Ger & Slavic Langs, SUNY, Stony Brook, 100 Nicolls Rd, Stony Brook, NY 11794-0001. **EMAIL** nicholas.rzhevsky@sunysb.edu

S

SAA, ORLANDO
PERSONAL Born 05/08/1925, Havana, Cuba, m, 1980 **DISCIPLINE** SPANISH LANGUAGE AND LITERATURE AND LATIN LANGUAGE **EDUCATION** Tulane Univ, PhD, 73. **CAREER** Prof, William Paterson Univ, 74-; VP, Circulo de Cult Panamericano, Chap NJ. **MEMBERSHIPS** Hispania, Circulo de Cultura Panamericano. **RESEARCH** Latin america essay and poetry. **SELECTED PUBLICATIONS** Auth, La serenidad en las obras de Eugenio Florit, 73; De una anguistia por destino, 86; El teatro escolar de los jesuitas en Espana; 90; auth, De tiempo, espacio y armonia, 99. **CONTACT ADDRESS** Dept of Lang and Cultures, William Paterson Col of New Jersey, 300 Pompton Rd., Wayne, NJ 07470. **EMAIL** saao@wpunj.edu

SABAT-RIVERS, GEORGINA
PERSONAL Born 06/20/1924, Santiago de Cuba, Cuba, m, 1969, 4 children **DISCIPLINE** LATIN AMERICAN LITERATURE **EDUCATION** Johns Hopkins Univ, MA, 67; PhD, 69. **CAREER** Asst prof to prof, W Md Col, 64-78; assoc prof to prof, SUNY Stony Brook, 78-91. **HONORS AND AWARDS** NEH. **MEMBERSHIPS** MLA; AIH. **RESEARCH** Juana Ines de la Cruz. **SELECTED PUBLICATIONS** Auth, Estudios de literature hispanoamericana, Sor Juana Ines de la Cruz y otros poetas barrocos de la Colonia, Barcelona, 92; auth, Bibliografia y otras cuestiunculas sorjuaninas, BTU, 95; ed, Sor Juana Ines de la Cruz and Her World, Colonial Latin Am Rev, 95; ed, Esta de nuestra America Pupila: Estudios de poesia colonial, SRBHS, 98; auth, En busca de Sor Juana, UNAM, 98. **CONTACT ADDRESS** Dept Hispanic Lang and Lit, SUNY, Stony Brook, 4206 Alhambra Cir, Coral Gables, FL 33146-1010. **EMAIL** elias-n-georgina@worldnet.att.net

SABINO, ROBIN
PERSONAL Born 07/01/1948 **DISCIPLINE** LINGUISTICS **EDUCATION** Adelphi Univ, AB, 69; Col of the Virgin Islands, MA, 77; Univ Pa, PhD, 90. **CAREER** Instr , Univ of Pa, 85 & 88-91; lectr, Univ of Pa, 86-91; from lectr to adj asst prof, Drexel Univ, 86-91; from asst prof to assoc prof, Auburn Univ, 91-. **HONORS AND AWARDS** Humanities Endowment Fund, Matching Fund, and the Res Grant-in-Aid Competitive Grants Prog, Auburn Univ, 91; Daniel F. Breeden Teaching Grant, Auburn Univ, 97; Small Equipment Grant, Auburn Univ, 99; Libr Travel Grant, Univ of Gainsville, 99. **MEMBERSHIPS** Southeastern Confr of Ling, Ling Soc of Am, Soc of Caribbean Ling. **RESEARCH** Language contact, variation, & change. **SELECTED PUBLICATIONS** Coauth, "Distinguishing Questions from Statements by Prosodic Cues Alone: You Didn't Hear What I Meant," SECOL Rev 19.2 (95): 151-170; auth, "A Peak at Death: Assessing Continuity and Change in an Underdocumented Language," Lang, Variation and Change 8 (96): 41-61; coauth, "The Implications of Lectal Variation for the Reassessment of Eric Pontoppidan's 19th Century Creole Material," SECOL Rev 21.1 (97): 126-140; coauth, Language Variation in the South, Univ of Ala Press (Tuscaloosa, AL), 97; coauth, "The Path Not Taken: Cultural Identity in the Interesting Life of Olaudah Equiano," Melus 24.1 (99): 5-19. **CONTACT ADDRESS** Dept English, Auburn Univ, 9030 Haley Center, Auburn, AL 36349-5203. **EMAIL** sabinro@auburn.edu

SACHS, MURRAY
PERSONAL Born 04/10/1924, Toronto, ON, Cananda, m, 1961, 2 children **DISCIPLINE** FRENCH LITERATURE **EDUCATION** Univ Toronto, BA, 46; Columbia Univ, AM, 47; PhD, 52. **CAREER** Lectr, Columbia Univ, 46-48; instr, Univ Calif Berkeley, 48-50; instr, Univ Detroit, 51-52; instr to asst prof, Williams Col, 54-60; asst prof to prof emeritus, Brandeis Univ, 60-96. **HONORS AND AWARDS** Governor Gen Silver Medal, 46; henry Alfred Todd Fel, Columbia Univ, 46-48; Palmes Acad, French Govt, 71; Phi Beta Kappa. **MEMBERSHIPS** MLA; Mod Humanities Res Asn; Am Asn of Univ Prof; Am Asn of Teachers of French; Am Comparative Lit Asn; Asn of Literary Scholars and Critics. **RESEARCH** Nineteenth and twentieth Century French literature; Francophone literature; The Modern Novel; The Modern Short Story; French cultural history. **SELECTED PUBLICATIONS** Auth, "Emile Zola and the Dreyfus Affairs. The Writer in the Public Arena," in Kaleidoscope, Toronto, 96. **CONTACT ADDRESS** Dept Lang, Brandeis Univ, 415 S St. Mailstop 024, PO Box 9110, Waltham, MA 02454-9110. **EMAIL** sachs@brandeis.edu

SACKETT, THEODORE ALAN
DISCIPLINE SPANISH **EDUCATION** Univ Ariz, PhD. **CAREER** Prof Span, ch, dept For Lang and Lit, Univ Nev, Reno; ed, J Hispania, 84-92; instr, Williams Col; asst, assoc prof, U of New Mexico; assoc prof to prof, U Southern Calif. **RESEARCH** Spanish literature of the 19th and 20th centures. **SELECTED PUBLICATIONS** Published extensively on the narratives and theatre of Perez Galdos, as well as on Pereda, Blasco Ibanez, Ortega y Gasset, Sastre, Delibes, and the Ecuadorian novelist Jorge Icaza. **CONTACT ADDRESS** Univ of Nevada, Reno, Reno, NV 89557. **EMAIL** sackett@unr.edu

SAENZ DE TEJADA, CRISTINA
PERSONAL Born London, England, m, 1993, 2 children **DISCIPLINE** LINGUISTICS, LATIN, SPANISH, LITERATURE **EDUCATION** Univ Barcelona, BA, 85; Penn State Univ, MA, 90; PhD, 94. **CAREER** Prof, Colegio La Salle Bonanova, 85-88; teach asst, Penn State Univ, 88-92; vis asst prof, Bucknell Univ, 92-93; asst prof, Goucher Col, 94-. **HONORS AND AWARDS** Phi Sigma Iota; Beatrice Atchison Sum Res Grnt; Who's Who Among Am Teach, 00. **MEMBERSHIPS** LASA; BRASA; MLA; ACTFL; APSA; AATSP; IFLHS. **RESEARCH** Brazilian historical narratives; Brazilian women writers; Cuban writers of the exile. **SELECTED PUBLICATIONS** Auth, Aprendizaje o el libro de los placeres, Siruela (90); auth, "Autobiografia, identidad y ficcion en Mulher no Espelho," travessia (95); auth, "The Eternal Non-Difference: Clarice Lispector's Concept of Androgyny," Luso Braz Rev (94); auth, "Ecologist and Ecofeminist Awareness in Agua Viva: A Brazilian Woman Rereading Nature," Brazil (97); auth, "Raza y Genero en la narrativa femenina afrobrasilena," Rev de Crit Latin Am (97); auth, La (re)construccion de la identidad femenina en la narrativa autobiografica Latino Americana, Peter Lang, 98; auth, "Yo tambien soy brasilena: Historia y sociedad en la obra de Carolina Maria de Jesus," Confluencia(98); auth, "O Sumiro da Santa: A Postmodern Reconstruction of Racial Dynamics in Contemporary Bahian Society," in Jorge Amado: Critical essays, eds. Keith Brower, Earl Fitz and Enrique Martinez-Vidal, Routledge, 01. **CONTACT ADDRESS** Eng Dept., Goucher Col, 1021 Dulaney Valley Rd, Towson, MD 21204. **EMAIL** ctejada@goucher.edu

SAEZ, RICHARD
PERSONAL Born 07/18/1936, New York, NY, p, 1980 **DISCIPLINE** LINGUISTICS **EDUCATION** Dartmouth Col, AB, 58; Yale Univ, PhD, 67. **CAREER** Instr, Queens Col CUNY, 64-67; asst prof, Richmond Col, 67-75; assoc prof, prof, CSI CUNY, 76-. **HONORS AND AWARDS** Dartmouth Fel, 54-58; Yale Fel, 59-63; Reynolds Fel, Univ Madrid, 58-59; Fulbright Fel, Univ Rome; NEH Fel, 76; Mellon Fel, CUNY, 87; Theron Rockwell Field prize Yale, 67. **MEMBERSHIPS** LTA, Am Intl Shakespeare Asn, MLA. **RESEARCH** Translation of Golden Age Spanish drama. **SELECTED PUBLICATIONS** Auth, Theodicy in Baroque Literature, Garland, 85; auth, "Memory & Forgetting in Augustine & Shakespeare," Shake Newsltr (85); auth, "James Merrill's Oedipal Fire," ed. Harold Bloom (Chelsea House, 86); auth, "Ray Ciarochi's Paintings," Arts Mag (85); co-ed, "Merrill's Apocalyptic Epic," (Cornell, 83); auth, "Elliot Carters Songs," Parnassus (82); auth, Lorca "Lorca's Poeta en Nueva York," ed. Manuel Duran (Garland, 77); co-ed, Garland Publications in Comparative Literature, Garland, 83. **CONTACT ADDRESS** Eng Dept, Col of Staten Island, CUNY, 130 Stuyvesant Place, Staten Island, NY 10314. **EMAIL** saez@nyc.rr.com

SAFFIRE, PAULA REINER
PERSONAL Born 09/05/1943, NJ, s, 2 children **DISCIPLINE** CLASSICS AND PHILOSOPHY **EDUCATION** Mount Holyoke Col, BA, 65; Harvard, PhD, 76. **CAREER** Assoc Prof, Butler Univ, 89-. **HONORS AND AWARDS** Writing Across the Curriculum Awd, Butler Univ; Creative Tchr Awd; Indiana Classical Conference. **MEMBERSHIPS** APA, ICC **RESEARCH** Sappho; tragedy; mythology; pedagogy; performance. **SELECTED PUBLICATIONS** Auth, Aristotle on Personality and Some Implications for Friendship, in: Ancient Phil, 91; auth, Ancient Greek Alive, Aldine Press, 92; Coauth, Deduke men a Selanna: The Pleiades Mid-Sky, Mnemosyne, 93; coauth, Ancient Greek Alive, Univ of North Carolina Press, Performer of Songs of Sappho, 93-; auth, Whip, Whipped and Doctors: Homers Iliad and Camus the Plague, Interpretations, 94. **CONTACT ADDRESS** Dept of Classics, Butler Univ, 4600 Sunset Ave, Indianapolis, IN 46208. **EMAIL** psaffire@butler.edu

SAG, IVAN ANDREW
PERSONAL Born 11/09/1949, Alliance, OH **DISCIPLINE** THEORETICAL & COMPUTATIONAL LINGUISTICS **EDUCATION** Univ Rochester, BA, 71; Univ Pa, MA, 73; Mass Inst Technol, PhD(ling), 76. **CAREER** Asst prof ling, Univ Pa, 76-79; Asst Prof Ling, Stanfrod Univ, 79-, A Mellon fel, Stanford Univ, 78-79; vist asst prof, Univ Tex, Austin, 79, Univ Calif, Berkeley, 80 & Ling Inst, Univ Md, 82; consult, Hewlett-Packard Labs, 81- **MEMBERSHIPS** Ling Soc Am; Asn Comput Ling. **RESEARCH** Natural language syntax and semantics; natural language processing. **SELECTED PUBLICATIONS** Auth, Pseudosolutions to the Pseudoparadox: Sanskrit Diaspirates Revisited, 76 & Deep and surface anaphora, 76, Ling Inquiry; Deletion and Logical Form, Garland, 80; co-ed, Elements of Discourse Understanding, Cambridge Univ Press, 80; auth, Coordination, extraction and generalized phase structure grammar, 82 & Coordination and transformational grammar (in press), Ling Inquiry; coauth, Auxiliaries and related phenomena in a restrictive theory of grammar, Language, 82; Referential and quantificational indefinites, Ling & Philos, 82. **CONTACT ADDRESS** Dept of Ling, Stanford Univ, Stanford, CA 97305.

SAGE, MICHAEL
PERSONAL Born 12/04/1944, New York, NY, m, 2 children **DISCIPLINE** ROMAN HISTORY & CLASSICS **EDUCATION** Univ Mich, BA, MA (hist); Univ Toronto, MA (classics), PhD. **CAREER** Univ Waterloo, asst prof (hist), 74-75; Univ Cincinnati, asst prof (classics), 75-81, assoc prof, 81-90, prof, 90-. **HONORS AND AWARDS** Canada Coun, Province of Ontario, Semple Fel. **MEMBERSHIPS** Am Philological Asn; Soc Promotion Roman Studies. **RESEARCH** Late Roman hist; Christianity; ancient mil hist. **SELECTED PUBLICATIONS** Ancient Greek Warfare, London, 96. **CONTACT ADDRESS** Univ of Cincinnati, 407 Blegen Libr, Cincinnati, OH 45221. **EMAIL** Michael.Sage@uc.edu

SAHA, PROSANTA KUMAR
PERSONAL Born 12/04/1932, Calcutta, India, m, 1958, 2 children **DISCIPLINE** ENGLISH, LINGUISTICS **EDUCATION** Univ Calcutta, BA, 56; Oberlin Col, MA 57; Western Reserve Univ, PhD(English), 66. **CAREER** Teacher, Hawken Sch, 57-62; instr English, 62-64, asst prof English & ling, 66-72, Assoc Prof English & Ling & Chmn Ling & Undergrad Humanities Prog, Case Western Reserve Univ, 72- **HONORS AND AWARDS** Carl F Wittke Awd, Case Western Reserve Univ, 71. **MEMBERSHIPS** Ling Soc Am. **RESEARCH** English literature and linguistics; computer analysis of literature, especially stylistics; Bengali literature and linguistics. **SELECTED PUBLICATIONS** Auth, Reflexive Revisited + English Pronouns/, Am Speech, Vol 0068, 1993. **CONTACT ADDRESS** Dept of English, Case Western Reserve Univ, Clark Hall Rm 103 Case, Cleveland, OH 44106.

SAIGAL, M.
PERSONAL Born 10/26/1938, Paris, France, m, 1972, 2 children **DISCIPLINE** FRENCH; SPANISH **EDUCATION** Lycee Laude Debussy, Paris; BA, MA, PhD, UCLA. **CAREER** Teaching asst, 62-65, Univ CA; instr, 65-70, asst prof, 70-75, assoc prof 76-84, Prof, 84-, Pomona Coll. **HONORS AND AWARDS** Wig award for Exceellent Teaching. **MEMBERSHIPS** MLA; Assn of French Teachers, Women in French. **RESEARCH** 20th century writings. **SELECTED PUBLICATIONS** Auth, Chantal Chawaf, Thirty Voices in the Feminine, 96;Recyclage urbain chez Annie Ernaux, Foreign Literature Series, 97; book reviews, Jeanne Hyvrard: Theorist of the Modern World by Jennifer Waelti-Walters, in The French Review, Feb 98; au presage de la mienne de Jeanne Hyvrard, in The French Review, May 98; rev, Issa by Chantal Chawaf in The French Review, 72, No. 4, 99; ed, The Feminist Encyclopedia of French Literature, Eva Martin Sartori, Greewood Press, 99; auth, L'ecriture:lien de mere a fille chez Jeanne Hyvrard, Chantal Chawaf et Annie Ernaux, Amsterdam: Rodopi, 00. **CONTACT ADDRESS** Dept of Romance Lang & Lit, Pomona Col, 550 Harvard Ave, Claremont, CA 91711. **EMAIL** msaigal@pomona.edu

SAINE, THOMAS PRICE
PERSONAL Born 03/08/1941, Brooklyn, NY, 2 children **DISCIPLINE** GERMAN LITERATURE **EDUCATION** Yale Univ, BA, 62, MPh, 67, PhD(Ger), 68. **CAREER** From instr to assoc prof Ger, Yale Univ, 68-75; assoc prof, 75-76, Prof Ger, Univ Calif, Irvine, 76-, Vis prof Ger, Univ Cincinnati, 74; assoc ed, Ger Quart, 78-81; ed, Goethe Yearbk, 82-. **HONORS AND AWARDS** Am Coun Learned Soc fel, 82-83; Guggenheim fel, 83. **MEMBERSHIPS** MLA; Lessing Soc; Am Asn Teachers Ger; Am Soc 18th Century Studies; Goethe Soc NAm. **RESEARCH** German 18th century literature; 18th century European intellectual history; Goethe and German classicism. **SELECTED PUBLICATIONS** Auth, Revolution And Reform In Goethe's Political-Historical Thought And In His Activities As A Government Official 1790-1800/, Goethe Jahrbuch, Vol 0110, 1993; auth, Black Bread-White Bread: German Intellectuals and the French Revolution, Columbia, SC 88; auth, The Problem of Being Modern, or The Pursuit of Enlightenment from Leibniz to the French Revolution, Wayne State UP (Detroit), 97. **CONTACT ADDRESS** Dept of Ger, Univ of California, Irvine, Irvine, CA 92697-3150. **EMAIL** tspaine@uci.edu

SAINT-AMAND, PIERRE N.
PERSONAL Born 02/22/1952, Port-au-Prince, Haiti, s **DISCIPLINE** FRENCH **EDUCATION** Univ ML, BA, 78; Johns Hopkins Univ, MA, 80; PhD, 81. **CAREER** Asst prof, Yale Univ, 81-82; asst prof, Stanford Univ, 82-86; assoc prof to prof, Brown Univ, 86-. **HONORS AND AWARDS** Stanford Humanities Center, 85-86; Guggenheim Fel, 89; Fel, E-W Sem Berlin, 97. **MEMBERSHIPS** MLA; ASECS. **RESEARCH** Eighteenth Century culture; Seventeenth Century Literature and culture. **SELECTED PUBLICATIONS** Auth, Les Lois de L'Histilite: La Politique a L'Age des Lumieres, 92; auth, The Laws of Hostility; auth, The Libertine's Progress, 94. **CONTACT ADDRESS** Dept French, Brown Univ, PO Box 1961, Providence, RI 02912-0001.

SAINT-JACQUES, BERNARD
PERSONAL Born 04/26/1928, Montreal, PQ, Canada **DISCIPLINE** LINGUISTICS **EDUCATION** Univ Montreal, BA, 49, Licence, 54; Sophia Univ (Tokyo), MA, 62; Georgetown Univ, MS, 64; Univ Paris, PhD, 66, DL, 75. **CAREER** Asst prof, Sophia Univ, 66-67; instr to assoc prof, 66-78, prof ling, 78-89, Prof Emer, Univ BC, 89-; Prof & Dir, Inst Language & Culture, Intercultural Communication Graduate Program, Aichi Shukytoku Univ (Japan), 90-. **HONORS AND AWARDS** Mem, Royal Soc Can. **MEMBERSHIPS** Ling Soc Am; Asn Tchrs Japanese; Can Soc Asian Stud; BC Asn Transl Interp (founding mem); Ibunkakan Kyoikukai (Int Soc Japan). **SELECTED PUBLICATIONS** Auth, Analyse structurale de la syntaxe du japonais moderne, 66; auth, Structural analysis of Modern Japanese, 71; auth, Aspects sociolinguistiques du bilinguisme canadien, 76; auth, Studies in Language and Culture, 95; coauth, Aspects of Bilingualism, 78; coauth, The Languages of Immigrants, 79; coauth, Atipa revisite, 89; coauth, Langue et Identite, 90; ed, Language and Ethnic Relations, 79; ed, Japanese Studies in Canada, 85. **CONTACT ADDRESS** Dept of Linguistics, Univ of British Columbia, Vancouver, BC, Canada V6T 1Z1. **EMAIL** saintj@asu.aasa.ac.jp

SAITZ, ROBERT LEONARD
PERSONAL Born 07/09/1928, Boston, MA, m, 1962, 1 child **DISCIPLINE** ENGLISH AS SECOND LANGUAGE, LINGUISTICS **EDUCATION** Boston Univ, BA, 49; Univ Iowa, MA, 50; Univ Wis, PhD(English ling), 55. **CAREER** Instr English, Univ Wis, 57-59; asst prof, Southern Ill Univ, 59-60; coord, English as second lang, Fulbright grant, Colombia, 60-62; from asst prof to assoc prof, 62-72, Prof Ling & English As Second Lang, Boston Univ, 72-, Consult English as second lang, Boston & New Bedford schs, 67; Fulbright lectr, Univ Seville, 69-70. **MEMBERSHIPS** Ling Soc Am; Nat Asn Foreign Student Affairs; Teachers English to Speakers Other Langs. **RESEARCH** Old English syntax; second language learning; kinesics. **SELECTED PUBLICATIONS** Coauth, Selected Readings in English, Winthrop, 72; Handbook of Gestures, Mouton, The Hague, 72; Ideas in English, Winthrop, 74; Advanced Reading & Writing, Holt, 78; Challenge, Winthrop, 78; Stimulus, Little Brown, 83; Contemporary Perspectives, Little Brown, 84; Points Wkbks, Addison-Wesley, 86; Milestones, Little Brown, 87; Short Takes, Addison-Wesley, 93, Workout in English, Prentic-Halle, 98. **CONTACT ADDRESS** Dept of English, Boston Univ, 236 Bay State Rd, Boston, MA 02215-1403. **EMAIL** bsaitz@bu.edu

SALE, MARY
PERSONAL Born 11/27/1929, New Haven, CT, m, 1991, 3 children **DISCIPLINE** PHILOSOPHY; CLASSICS **EDUCATION** BA, 51, MA, 54, PhD, 58, Cornell Univ. **CAREER** Instr, Yale Univ, 57-58; Instr, 58-59, Asst Prof, 59-64, Assoc Prof, 64-75, Prof, 75-, Washington Univ. **MEMBERSHIPS** London Inst of Classical Studies; Honorary Fel, Univ Wales, Univ College Cardiff. **RESEARCH** Philosophy; Classics **SELECTED PUBLICATIONS** Auth, Homer, Iliad, Odyssey, Reader's Guide to World Literature, 93; Homer and the Roland: the Shared Formulary Technique, Oral Tradition, 93; The Government of Troy: Politics in the Illiad, Greek, Roman and Byzantine Studies, 94; Homer and Avdo: Investigating Orality through External Consistency, Voice into Text, 96; In Defense of Milman Parry, Oral Tradition, 96; Virgil's Formularity and Pius Aeneas, Epos and Logos, 98. **CONTACT ADDRESS** 2342 Albion Pl, Saint Louis, MO 63104. **EMAIL** Aperkins@midwest.net

SALGADO, MARIA A.
PERSONAL Born 01/15/1933, Canary Islands, Spain, m, 1954, 2 children **DISCIPLINE** SPANISH LITERATURE **EDUCATION** Fla State Univ, BA, 58; Univ NC, Chapel Hill, MA, 60; Univ of Md, PhD, 66. **CAREER** Asst prof to prof, Univ NC at Chapel Hill, 67-. **HONORS AND AWARDS** Juan Ramon Jimenez Prize, 69; Favorite Faculty Awd, 97. **MEMBERSHIPS** MLA; AATSP; IILI; ASECS; SECOLAS; SAMLA; ANAC; AIA; AIH; ILCH; ALFH. **RESEARCH** Contemporary Hispanic Poetry, Literary Portraits and Self-Portraits, Women Writers. **SELECTED PUBLICATIONS** Auth, "Juana Manuela Gorriti: Una escritora decimononica ante el discurso de la enfermedad", Hispanic Journal (96):55-67; auth, "Ruben Dario's Short Stories: Autobiography, Fantasy and the Fantastic" The Dark Fantastic, Greenwood Publishing, 97; auth, "Convergencias y divergencias de la autorrepresentacion femenina en el contexto patriarcal", Estudios en honor de Janet Perez. El Sujeto femenino en escritoras hispanicas (98):91-103; auth, "De lo jocoso a lo joco-serio: el autorrentrato literario en los siglos de Oro y la Illustracion", Actas del XII Congreso Internacional de Hispanistas (98):212-20; auth, "Autorrepresentacion literaria y estetica fin-de-siglo", Canoes & Contextos (97):539-44; auth "Desenmarcando el cuardo: El Autorrentrato de Luisa Perez de Zambrana", Mujeres latinoamericanas: Siglos XVI al XIX (97): 295-305; auth "Maneiro's De vitis aliquot mexicanorum or Biography as Political Agenda, Dieciocho. Hispanic Enlightenment (98):209-18; auth, "El Diario de Italia de Ruben Dario:

Entre el Modernismo y la Modernidad", Hispanofila 126 (99): 41-52; auth, "Ruben Dario y la Generacion del 98: Personas, personajes y mascaras del fin de signo espanol", Hispania (99): 725-32; auth, "Erotismo, cuerpo y revolucion en Linea de fuego de Gionconda Belli", Afrodita en el tropicao: Erotismo y construccion del sujeto en obas de autoras centroamericans, Scripta Humanistica (99):3-23. **CONTACT ADDRESS** Dept Romance Lang, Univ of No Carolina, Chapel Hill, CB 3170, Chapel Hill, NC 27599-3170. **EMAIL** masal@email.umc.edu

SALIEN, JEAN
DISCIPLINE LINGUISTICS, LITERATURE **EDUCATION** Univ de Montreal, BA, 67; Columbia Univ, MA, 71; Univ de Strasbourg, MA, 75; Univ Kans, PhD, 77. **CAREER** Prof, Fort Hays State Univ, 77-. **HONORS AND AWARDS** NEH Summer Scholar for Col Teachers, 82 & 85. **MEMBERSHIPS** Am Asn of Teachers of French **RESEARCH** Eighteenth century French literature, pre-romantic era, Pere Dumas, francophone literatures. **SELECTED PUBLICATIONS** Auth, "Passions et raison dans la pensee de Jean-Jacques Rousseau," Int Studies in Philos (81); auth, "Negritude et lutte des classes..," Presence Francophone (82); auth, "Francophonie et sous-developpement.., Contemporary French Civilization (81); auth, "Syncretisme religieux et theatre aux Antilles francophones," Etudes Francophones de Louisiane (87); auth, "Quebec french: Attitudes and pedagogical Perspectives," Modern Lang J (98); auth, "Appropriation et publics du discours antillais," Mots Pluriels (98). **CONTACT ADDRESS** Dept Modern Lang, Fort Hays State Univ, 600 Park St, Hays, KS 67601-4009. **EMAIL** jsalien@fhsu.edu

SALLUSTIO, ANTHONY THOMAS
PERSONAL Born 06/26/1936, Flushing, NY, m, 1960 **DISCIPLINE** FRENCH **EDUCATION** Iona Col, AB, 58; St John's Univ, MA, 60; Fordham Univ, PhD, 73. **CAREER** Instr Mod lang, Iona Col, 60-63; from asst prof to assoc prof, 63-78, Prof Foreign Lang, Pace Univ, NY, 78-, Chmn Dept, 68-79, 85-93. **HONORS AND AWARDS** Kenan Awd for Teaching Excellence, Pace, 87; NEH Summer Seminars, Columbia, 83, Princeton, 867, Duke, 94. **MEMBERSHIPS** MLA; Am Asn Teachers of French; Am Asn Teachers Span & Port; Sixteenth Century Studies Conference. **RESEARCH** The works of Jean-Pierre Camus; early 17th century fictional prose in France; Hispanic and Italian literary influences on 17th century French letters. **CONTACT ADDRESS** Dept of Foreign Lang, Pace Univ, New York, 1 Pace Plaza, New York, NY 10038-1598. **EMAIL** asallustio@fsmail.pace.edu

SALMON, JOHN HEARSEY MCMILLAN
PERSONAL Born 12/02/1925, Thames, New Zealand **DISCIPLINE** EARLY MODERN HISTORY, FRENCH LITERATURE **EDUCATION** Victoria Univ Wellington, BA, 50, MA, 52, LittD(hist), 70; MLitt, Cambridge Univ, 57. **CAREER** Approved lectr hist, Cambridge Univ, 55-57; lectr, Victoria Univ Wellington, 57-60; prof, Univ NSW, 60-65 & Univ Waikato, NZ, 65-69; prof, 69-71, Marjorie Walter Goodhart Prof Hist, Bryn Mawr Col, 71-, Ed bds, Fr Hist Studies, Sixteenth Century J & J Mod Hist. **MEMBERSHIPS** AHA; fel Royal Hist Soc; Soc Fr Hist Studies. **RESEARCH** Early modern French history; French literature in the early modern period; French political theory. **SELECTED PUBLICATIONS** Auth, The French Religious Wars in English Political Thought, Clarendon, 59 & Greenwood Press, 81; A History of Goldmining in New Zealand, NZ Govt Printer, 63; ed, The French Wars of Religion: How Important Were Religious Factors, Heath, 67; auth, Cardinal de Retz, Weidenfeld & Nicholson, 69; co-ed, Francogallia by Francois Hotman, Cambridge Univ, 72; Society in Crisis: France in the Sixteenth Century, St Martin's, 75 & Methuen, 2nd ed, 79; French satire in the late sixteenth century, Sixteenth Century J, 75; Cicero and Tacitus in sixteenth-century France, Am Hist Res, 80. **CONTACT ADDRESS** Dept of Hist, Bryn Mawr Col, Bryn Mawr, PA 19010.

SALOMON, RICHARD
PERSONAL Born 08/12/1948, New York, NY, m, 1970, 1 child **DISCIPLINE** SANSKRIT **EDUCATION** Univ Pa, PhD, 75. **CAREER** From Asst Prof to Prof, Univ Wash, 81-. **HONORS AND AWARDS** Guggenheim Feel; Saionji For Area Studies Feel; 3 NEH Fels. **MEMBERSHIPS** Am Orient Soc, Int Assoc. of Buddhist Studies, Am Acad of Relig, Royal Asiatic Soc. **RESEARCH** Sanskrit language and literature, Indian epigraphy, Gandharon studies. **SELECTED PUBLICATIONS** Auth, "Five Kharosthi Inscriptions," Bull of the Asia Inst 10 (96): 233-246; auth, "South Asia Writing Systems: Introduction," in The World's Writing Systems (NY: Oxford Univ Pr, 96), 371-372; auth, "An Inscribed Silver Buddhist Reliquary of the Time of King Kharaosta and Prince Indravarman," J of the Am Orient Soc 116 (96): 418-452; auth, "A Preliminary Survey of Some Early Buddhist Manuscripts Recently Acquired by the British Library," J of the Am Orient Soc 117 (97): 353-358; auth, Indian Epigraphy: A Guide to the Study of Inscriptions in the Indo-Aryan Languages, Oxford Univ Pr (New York, NY), 98; auth, Ancient Buddhist Scrolls from Gandhara: The British Library Kharosthi Fragments, Univ Wash Pr/British Libr (Seattle, WA/London, UK), 99. **CONTACT ADDRESS** Dept Lang, Univ of Washington, PO Box 353521, Seattle, WA 98195. **EMAIL** rsalomon@u.washington.edu

SALTARELLI, MARIO
DISCIPLINE HISPANIC LINGUISTIC **EDUCATION** Univ Ill, PhD. **CAREER** Prof, Univ Southern Calif. **RESEARCH** Romance languages and its dialects, with particular attention to Spanish and Italian, Latin and Basque. **SELECTED PUBLICATIONS** Publ on, Phonology of Italian in a Generative Grammar; La Grammatica Generativa Trasformazionale, and Most Recently Basque; Romance and Latin Phonology; Morphology; and Syntax; Italian; Spanish; Southern Italian Dialects; Chicano Spanish; Catalan; Development and Maintenance of Spanish and Italian as Emigrant Languages; co-ed, Diachronic Studies in Romance Linguistics; ed, vol(s) on applied ling. **CONTACT ADDRESS** Dept of Spanish and Portuguese, Univ of So California, University Park Campus, Los Angeles, CA 90089. **EMAIL** saltarel@usc.edu

SAMMONS, JEFFREY LEONARD
PERSONAL Born 11/09/1936, Cleveland, OH, m, 1967, 4 children **DISCIPLINE** GERMAN LITERATURE **EDUCATION** Yale Univ, BA, 58; PhD, 62. **CAREER** From instr to asst prof of German, Brown Univ, 61-64; asst prof to assoc prof, Yale Univ, 64-01; prof German, 69-79, Leavenworth prof of German, Yale Univ, 79-; Guggenheim fel, 72-73: Am Coun Learned Socs fel, 77-78. **MEMBERSHIPS** MLA; Am Asn Teachers Ger; N Am Heine Soc; N Am Goethe Soc. **RESEARCH** Nineteenth-Century German Literature. **SELECTED PUBLICATIONS** Coed, Lebendige Form: Festschrift fur Heinrich E K Henel, Fink, Munich, 70; auth, Six Essays on the Young German Novel, Univ NC, 72; Literary Sociology and Practical Criticism: An Inquiry, IN Univ, 77; Heinrich Heine: A Modern Biography, Princeton Univ, 79; A Selected Critical Bibliography 1956-1980, Garland, 82; Wilhelm Raabe: The Fiction of the Alternative Community, Princeton Univ, 87; Heinrich Heine, Metzler, Stuttgart, 91; The Shifting Fortunes of Wilhelm Raabe: A History of Criticism as a Cautionary Tale, Camden House, Columbia, SC, 91; Ideology, Mimesis, Fantasy: Charles Sealsfield, Friedrich Gerst¤cker, Karl May, and Other German Novelists of America, Univ NC, 98; ed, Die Protokolle der Weisen von Zion, Die Grundlage des modernen Antisemitismus--eine Falschung, Text und Kommentary, Wallstein, G¤ttingen, 98. **CONTACT ADDRESS** Dept German, Yale Univ, 211 Highland St., New Haven, CT 06511-2001. **EMAIL** jeffrey.sammons@yale.edu

SAMPEDRO, BENITA
PERSONAL Born 11/27/1965, Spain, m, 1994, 1 child **DISCIPLINE** SPANISH **EDUCATION** NYork Univ, PhD, 97. **CAREER** Asst Prof, Hofstra Univ. **MEMBERSHIPS** MLA. **RESEARCH** Colonial Spanish American Literature. **CONTACT ADDRESS** Dept of Romance Lang & Lit, Hofstra Univ, Calkins 317, Hempstead, NY 11549. **EMAIL** rllb25@hofstra.edu

SAMPON-NICOLAS, ANNETTE
DISCIPLINE TWENTIETH-CENTURY FRENCH LITERATURE AND CONTEMPORARY POETRY **EDUCATION** Univ Wis, Madison, PhD. **CAREER** Instr, 85, ch, dept Fr, Hollins Col. **RESEARCH** The relationship between lit and the visual arts. **SELECTED PUBLICATIONS** Auth, Francis Ponge: La Poetique du figural. **CONTACT ADDRESS** Hollins Col, Roanoke, VA 24020.

SAN PEDRO, TERESA ANTA
PERSONAL Born 10/10/1948, Spain, m, 1972, 2 children **DISCIPLINE** LATIN AMERICAN LITERATURE, SPANISH **EDUCATION** Montclair State Univ, BA, 72; MA, 82; Rutgers Univ, PhD, 87. **CAREER** Dept head to teacher, Vail Dean Sch, 85-91; teacher, Newark Acad, 91-97; Col NJers, 97-. **HONORS AND AWARDS** IPA, Ariel Awd, 00; SOSA Awd, 00-01; Distinguished Guest Awd, Gov Nicaragua and Honduras, 93, 94; Teaching Recognition Awd, 93. **MEMBERSHIPS** MLA; CILA; Asn Americanists; CILA; ASPUS; ALDEEU; AATSP; Inst Ibero-Americano. **RESEARCH** Hispanic women's literature; Central American literature; Caribbean literature. **SELECTED PUBLICATIONS** Auth, "La Caida de loss 'Dioses en el Cuento de Elena Garro' el Dia Que Fuimos Prose," Mono Rev 6 (88): 116-126; auth, "La Esperpentica del Cuento Tradicional en el Poema 'Cuento sin Hardas' de Luz Maria Umpierre-Herrera," Am Rev (91): 92-100; auth, "El collage Narrativo y la Verosimilitud en La Importancia de Iamarse Daniel Santos," J Council For Lang 13 (92): 93-97; auth, "La Importancia de Lamarse Daniel Santos y la Metaficcion," in Tradicion de la Literatura Ibero-Americana, Actas del XXX Congreso del Instituto Internacional de Literatura Iberoamericana, ed. Pamela Bacarise (Penn: Univ Pitt, 94): 243-251; auth, "Intertextuality, Text and Metatext in Concha Romero's Unolor a Ambar: The Eternal Gender Struggle," E NMex Univ, 95; auth, "La desmitificaci6n de to Sagrado en La Importancia de Lamarse Daniel Santos," in Proyecciones Sobre 1a Novela: Actas del XVI Congreso de Literatura Latino Americana, eds. Linda Levine, Ellen Engelson (Montclair: Edic Norte and Montclair State Univ, 97): 173-186; auth, La Palabra Directa de Ana Maria Rodas o la Negacion de la Estetica Poetica Tradicional," ISTMICA-Rev (98): 196-206; auth, "El 'collage' Vital en la Obra de la Escritora Costarricense Carmen Naranjo," De la Catedral al Rascacielos: Actas de 1a XVII Asamblea General de ALDEEU (NYork: ALDEEU, Span Profess Am, 98): 125-132; auth, "'El Amor Carnal': La Maquina que Mueve el Universo de Christian Santos," in Aphrodite en el Tropico: Erotismo y la Construccion del Sujeto Femenino en Obras de Autoras Centro-Americanas, ed. Oralia Preble-Niemi (Univ Tenn: Script Human, 99): 209-223. **CONTACT ADDRESS** For Lang Dept, The Col of New Jersey, PO Box 7718, Ewing, NJ 08628-0718. **EMAIL** sanpedra@tcnj.edu

SANCHEZ, ELIZABETH DOREMUS
DISCIPLINE COMPARITIVE LITERATURE: SPANISH, ENGLISH AND FRENCH **EDUCATION** Univ Tex, BA, 66; Plan II Honors, UT Austin; Smith Col Jr Year Abroad, MA, 64-65; MA, UT, PhD, 69; Cornell Univ, 83. **CAREER** Assoc prof Span. **HONORS AND AWARDS** Sears Teaching Excellence and Campus Leadership Award, 90; King/Haggar scholar award, Univ of Dallas, 90; Kirby Prize, SCMLA, 97. **MEMBERSHIPS** Mem, Mod Lang Assn; S Cent Mod Lang Assn. **RESEARCH** Nineteenth-century realism and naturalism; chaos theory and the novel. **SELECTED PUBLICATIONS** Auth, "Hispanic review" Hispanic Rev, 78; auth, From World to World: Realism and Reflexivity in Don Quijote and La Regenta," Hispanic Review, 87; auth, The Missing Mother: Locating the Feminine Other in La Regenta," Romance Languages Annual, 1989; auth, Beyond the Realist Paradigm: Subversive Strategems in la Regenta and Madame Bovary, " Malevolent Insemination, 90; auth, La Regenta as Fractal, Revista de Estudios Hispanicos, 92; auth, Spatial Forms and Fractals: A Reconsideration of Azorins's Dona Ines, " J of Interdisciplinary Lt studies, 93; auth, Oreder/Disoreder and Complexity in La Regenta: A Case for Spiraling Outward and Upward," S Central Rev, 96. **CONTACT ADDRESS** Dept of Mod Lang and Lit, Univ of Dallas, 1845 E Northgate Dr, Irving, TX 75062. **EMAIL** sanchez@acad.udallas.edu

SANCHEZ, MONICA E.
DISCIPLINE LINGUISTICS **EDUCATION** Univ Toronto, BA, 88, MA, 89; Univ Brit Columbia, PhD, 96. **CAREER** Asst prof. **RESEARCH** Syntactic theory; Acquired language disorders; Clinical applications of linguistic theory; Dialect variation in Romance languages, focusing on Iberian Spanish dialects. **SELECTED PUBLICATIONS** Auth, Language Breakdown: Implications for the Theory of Functional Categories, Working Papers of the Ling Circle of the Univ Victoria, 95; Nominal and Verbal Extended Projections in Agrammatism, Proc of the 95 Can Ling Assn Annual Conf, 95; Categorial, Agreement and Case Features in Agrammatism, Proc 96 Northwestern Ling Conf, Univ Wash, 96; Categorial and Agreement/Case Features are Different: Evidence from Language Disorders, Proc 96 Can Ling Assn Annual Conf, 96. **CONTACT ADDRESS** Dept of Applied Lang Stud, Brock Univ, 500 Glenridge Ave, Saint Catharines, ON, Canada L2S 3A1. **EMAIL** msanchez@spartan.ac.BrockU.CA

SANDERS, IVAN
PERSONAL Born 01/24/1944, Budapest, Hungary, m, 1968, 2 children **DISCIPLINE** COMPARATIVE LITERATURE, EAST EUROPEAN FICTION **EDUCATION** Brooklyn Col, BA, 65, MA, 67; NYork Univ, PhD(comp lit), 72. **CAREER** Prof English, Suffolk County Community Col, 68-, vis assoc prof, Sch Continuing Educ, Columbia Univ, 78-79. **HONORS AND AWARDS** Irex fel, Hungarian Acad Sci, Inst Lit Res, Budapest, 79; sr fel, Inst ECent Europe, Columbia Univ, 82; Fulbright fel, 89. **MEMBERSHIPS** MLA; Am Hungarian Educ Asn; Am Fed Teachers. **RESEARCH** Contemporary American fiction; contemporary East European fiction and film; Hungarian literature. **SELECTED PUBLICATIONS** Auth, Engaol'd tongue?: Notes on the Language of Hungarian Americans, Valosag, Budapest, Vol XVI, No 5; The Gifts of Strangeness: Alienation and Creation in Jerzy Kosinski's Fiction, Polish Rev, Vol XIX, No 3-4; Human Dialogues are Born, Nation, 4/23/77; trans, George Konrad's The City Builder, Harcourt Brace Jovanavich, 77; auth, Simple Elements and Violent Combinations: Reflections on the Fiction of Amos Oz, Judaism, Vol XXVII, No 1; The Possibilities of Fiction: On Recent American Novels, Valosag, Vol XXI, No 1, 78; trans, George Konrad's The Loser, Harcourt Brace Jovanavich, 82; co-ed, Essays on World War I: Total War and Peacemaking, A Case Study on Trianon, Columbia Univ Press, 82; auth, The Other Europeans, The Nation, 87; trans, Milan Fust, The Story of My Wife, PAJ, 87; auth, Budapest Letter: New Themes, New Writers, NY Times Book Rev, 88; co-trans, Peter Nadas, A Book of Memories, Farrar STraus & Giroux, 97. **CONTACT ADDRESS** 4 Coed Ln, Stony Brook, NY 11790. **EMAIL** sanderi@sunysuffolk.edu

SANDLER, SAMUEL
PERSONAL Born 10/25/1925, Lodz, Poland, m, 1948, 1 child **DISCIPLINE** POLISH LITERATURE **EDUCATION** Wroclaw Univ, MA, 50, PhD(Polish philol), 51 **CAREER** Instr Polish lit, Wroclaw Univ, 50-51; asst prof, Inst Lit Res, Polish Acad Sci, 51-57, 62-69; asst prof, Univ Warsaw, 54-57 & Univ Lodz, 55-62; assoc prof, Tel-Aviv Univ, 69-72; Prof Polish Lit, Univ Chicago, 72-, Co-ed & co-dir, Ed Polish & For Lit Classics Ser, Nat Libr, Ossolineum, 51-69; mem comt lit, Polish Acad Sci, 60-69; vis prof Polish lit, Univ Lodz, 64-69; vis assoc prof, Univ Ill, Chicago Circle, 70-72. **MEMBERSHIPS** Polish Inst Arts & Sci Am; MLA; Am Asn Teachers Slavic & E Europ

Lang. **RESEARCH** Polish literature of the 19th and 20th century; literary criticism; sociology of literature. **SELECTED PUBLICATIONS** Auth, A Laboratory Of Impure Forms - The Plays Of Rozewicz,Tadeusz - Filipowicz,H/, Slavic Rev, Vol 0053, 1994. **CONTACT ADDRESS** 1465 E 55th Place, Chicago, IL 60637.

SANDRO, PAUL DENNEY
PERSONAL Born 11/10/1944, Marshfield, WI, m, 1967, 1 child **DISCIPLINE** FRENCH LANGUAGE & LITERATURE **EDUCATION** Comparative Literature, Beloit College, 66; French Literature, University of Wisconsin--Madison, 67, MA; Romance Studies, Cornell University, Ph.D. 74. **CAREER** Prof of French, Miami Univ, Dept of French & Italian, 74; Chair, Film Studies Minor Program, 84-90; vis prof, Department of French & Italian, Univ of Iowa, 79. **RESEARCH** Film theory and criticism; Photography and Culture; 20th century French literature. **SELECTED PUBLICATIONS** Rev, Alain et Odette Virmaux, Les Surrealistes et le cinema, Paris: Seghers, 76, in French Review, Vol. 51, No. 6, May 78; rev, Keith Cohen, Film and Fiction: The Dynamics of Exchange, New Haven and London: Yale University Press, 79, in Sub-stance, Vol. 9, No. 1, 80; auth, Signification in the Cinema, Diacritics, Vol. 4, No. 3, Fall, 74; auth, Parodic Narration in Entr'acte, Film Criticism, Vol 4, No. 1, Fall, 79; auth, The Space of Desire in An Andalusian Dog, Purdue Film Studies Annual, Purdue University: West Lafayette, Ind., 79; auth, Textuality of the Subject in Belle de Jour, Sub-stance, No. 26, 80; rev, Annette Insdorf, Francois Truffaut, Boston: Twayne, 78, in French Review, Vol. 54, No. 3, Spring, 81; auth, The Management of Destiny in Narrative Form, Cine-tracts, Vol. 4, No. 1, Spring 81; auth, Signification in the Cinema, Diacritics, Vol. 4, No. 3 Fall, 74, reprinted in Bill Nichols, Movies and Methods, Vol. 2, University of Calif Press, 85; auth, Singled Out by History: La Jetee and the Aesthetics of Memory, French Cultural Studies, Vol. 10, No 28, February 99. **CONTACT ADDRESS** Dept of French & Ital, Miami Univ, 500 E High St, Oxford, OH 45056-1602. **EMAIL** sandrop@muohio.edu

SANKO, HELENE N.
PERSONAL Born 03/26/1938, France, m, 1961, 3 children **DISCIPLINE** FRENCH **EDUCATION** Acad de Paris, Baccalaureat, 56; Ecole Nat des Lang Orientales, Diplome del Lang Orientales, 59; Licence-es-lettres & certificats d'etudes supeveures, lettezature fransaise, 60; letties etrangeres, Univ de Paris, 61; Case Western Univ, MA, 65; PhD, 72. **CAREER** From instr to prof, John Caroll Univ, 62-; coord of French Section, John Carroll Univ, 90-. **HONORS AND AWARDS** NEH seminar, 79 & 83. **MEMBERSHIPS** Am Asn of Teachers of French, Am Asn for the Advancement of Slavic Studies. **RESEARCH** Diderot, Diderot's Encyclopedia, Eighteenth-Century Literature, France and Other Countries, Francophone Literatures, Ukrainian Literature and Culture, Folklore. **SELECTED PUBLICATIONS** Auth, "Our Life," monthly publication of the Ukrainian Women's League of Am, 95-; ed & transl, Treasury of Ukrainian Love poems, Quotations, and Proverbs, 97. **CONTACT ADDRESS** Dept Modern & Classical Lang, John Carroll Univ, 20700 N Park Blvd, Cleveland, OH 44118-4520. **EMAIL** helenesanko@ameritech.net

SANKOVITCH, TILDE
DISCIPLINE FRENCH **EDUCATION** Northwestern Univ, PhD. **CAREER** Prof emer, Northwestern Univ; ed bd, Simone de Beauvoir Studies; Exec Comt, Newberry Library Center for Renaissance Studies; Harold H and Virginia Anderson Ch Col Arts Sci, Northwestern Univ; dir, Women's Studies; plenary address, 7th Annual Meeting of the Illinois Medieval Asn; lect, Renaissance Soc Am Int Renaissance Colloquium, Amherst; Newberry Library, Chicago; Nat Mus Women in the Arts, Wash, DC. **HONORS AND AWARDS** Alumnae distinguished tchg awd, Col Arts Sci distinguished tchg awd; chevalier, Ordre des palmes Acad miques. **RESEARCH** Theater and women's writing; early women authors and Montaigne. **SELECTED PUBLICATIONS** Auth, The Body and its Figures: Textual Strategies in the Writings of the Dames des Roches, Women Writers in Pre-Revolutionary France, Garland Press, 97; Un travail fort n cessaire: the 1724 Edition of Montaigne's Essais, Montaigne Studies, 95; Catherine des Roches and Claudian's 'Le ravissement de Proserpine: A Humanist, Feminist Translation, Fr/Am Perspectives on Fr Renaissance Women Writers: Texts and Context, Wayne State Univ Press, 93; Jodelle et la cr ation du masque: Etude structurale et normative de l'Eug ne; French Women Writers; Myths of Access and Desire; co-ed, The Poems of the Troubadour Bertran de Born. **CONTACT ADDRESS** Dept of French and Italian, Northwestern Univ, 1859 Sheridan Rd, Evanston, IL 60208-2204.

SANSONE, DAVID
PERSONAL Born 09/23/1946, New York, NY, m, 1969, 2 children **DISCIPLINE** CLASSICS **EDUCATION** Hamilton Col, AB, 68; Univ Wis, MA, 69, PhD, 72. **CAREER** Asst prof, Univ HI, 72-74; from asst prof to prof, Univ Ill, 74-; chair, classics dept, 96-. **MEMBERSHIPS** Am Philol Asn; Soc for the Promotion of Hellenic Studies; Cambridge Philol Soc; Int Plutarch Soc. **RESEARCH** Greek tragedy; ancient biography; Greek and Roman sport. **SELECTED PUBLICATIONS** Auth, Aeschylean Metaphors for Intellectual Activity (Hermes Einzelschriften 35), F. Steiner Verlag, Wiesbaden, 75; Euripides, Iphigenia in Tauris, B. G. Teubner Verlag, Leipzig, 81; Greek Athletics and the Genesis of Sport, Univ CA Press, Berkeley, 88; Plutarch: Lives of Aristeides and Cato, Aris & Phillips, Warminster, 89; Towards a New Doctrine of the Article in Greek: Some Observations on the Definite Article in Plato, Classical Philol 88, 93; Plato and Euripides, IL Classical Studies 21, 96. **CONTACT ADDRESS** Dept of Classics 4090 For Lang, Univ of Illinois, Urbana-Champaign, 707 S Mathews Ave., Urbana, IL 61801. **EMAIL** dsansone@uiuc.edu

SANTANA, JORGE ARMANDO
PERSONAL Born 11/21/1944, Rosarito, Mexico, m, 1999, 2 children **DISCIPLINE** LATIN AMERICAN LITERATURE, CHICANO STUDIES **EDUCATION** San Diego Univ, AB, 67, MA 70; Univ Madrid, PhD(Span), 72. **CAREER** Instr Span, San Diego State Univ, 69-70; chmn dept Span & Port, 76-79, Assoc Prof, Calif State Univ, Sacramento, 72-, Ed, Explicacion Textos Literarios. **RESEARCH** The Mexican revolution novel; Chicano literature and culture. **SELECTED PUBLICATIONS** Auth, The Riddle Throughout 500-Years of Hisp Cult + Spain And Latin-America/, Explicacion de Textos Literarios, Vol 0021, 1992. **CONTACT ADDRESS** Dept of Span & Port, California State Univ, Sacramento, 6000 J St, Sacramento, CA 95819-2694. **EMAIL** santana@csus.edu

SANTOS, JOSE ANDRE
PERSONAL Born 09/12/1956, Provins, France, s **DISCIPLINE** CLASSICS, LINGUISTICS **EDUCATION** Univ Paris, Lic de Let, 79; Univ Vir, MA, 85; CUNY Grad Sch, PhD, 91. **CAREER** Vis asst prof, Bard Col, 91-92; asst prof, Russell Sage Col, 92-99; asst prof, Tex Tech Univ, 99-. **MEMBERSHIPS** MLA; AATF. **RESEARCH** 19th C French literature; Francophone literature. **SELECTED PUBLICATIONS** Auth, L'Art du Recit Court Chez Jean Lorrain, Nizet (Paris), 95; auth, "Actualite de Jean Lorrain," Asn Jean Lorr (00); auth, "Les Revers de la Fraternite: Le Cas de Jean et Taos Amrouche," La Mag Let (forthcoming); auth, entry on 'Fadhma Amrouche,' in Who's Who in Contemporary Women Writers (NY: Routledge, 00). **CONTACT ADDRESS** Classics Dept, Texas Tech Univ, Lubbock, TX 79409. **EMAIL** jose.santos@ttu.edu

SANZ, CRISTINA
PERSONAL Born 10/14/1962, Barcelona, Spain, m, 1989, 2 children **DISCIPLINE** SPANISH **EDUCATION** Univ Barcelona, Licenciatura, 85; Univ Ill, MA, 90; PhD, 94; SLATE, 93. **CAREER** Res asst, Univ of Ill, 88-93; vis lectr, Penn State Univ, 93-94; assoc prof, Georgetown Univ, 00-. **HONORS AND AWARDS** Tinker Found Fel; List of Excellent Teachers, Univ of Ill, 90-93. **MEMBERSHIPS** Am Assoc for Appl Ling, MLA, North Am Catalan Studies. **RESEARCH** Bilingualism and Cognition, Classroom Second Language Acquisition. **SELECTED PUBLICATIONS** Auth, "Diglossia a Catalunya? Teoria I realitat als 60 I present," Sintagma 3, (91): 49-61; coauth, "Non-native processing of verbal morphology in Spanish," MIT Working Papers in Ling 16 (92): 155-69; coauth, "Ser and estar in Tortosi Catalan: Language Use, Language Variation, and Language Change," Sintagma 7, (95): 5-25; coauth, "From Input to Output: Processing Instruction in Communicative Tasks," in Second Language Acquisition Theory and Pedagogy, eds R.F. Eckman, D. Highland, P.W. Lee, J. Mileham and R.R. Weber, (NY: Lawrence Erlbaum, 95): 169-86; coauth, "On Input Processing, Processing Instruction, and the nature of replication tasks: A response to M. Rafael Salaberry," Can Mod Lang Rev 54, (98): 263-73; coauth, "A conceptual replication study of VanPatten 1991," Span Appl Ling 3 (99): 65-90; auth, "Implementing LIBRA for the design of experimental research in SLA," Lang Learning and Tech 13, (00): 27-31; auth, "Bilingual education enhances third language acquisition: Evidence from Catalonia," Appl Psycholinguistics 21, (00): 23-44; coed, Spanish Applied Linguistics at the Turn of the Millennium, Cascadilla Press, (Somverville, MA), 00. **CONTACT ADDRESS** Georgetown Univ, 5410 Nevada Ave NW, Washington, DC 20015-1728. **EMAIL** sanzc@georgetown.edu

SAPORTA, SOL
PERSONAL Born 03/12/1925, New York, NY, m, 1952, 3 children **DISCIPLINE** SPANISH, LINGUISTICS **EDUCATION** Brooklyn Col, BA, 44; Univ Ill, MA, 52, PhD, 55. **CAREER** Asst prof Span & ling, end Univ, 55-60; chmn dept ling, 62-77, assoc prof, 60-79, Prof Romance Lang & Ling, Univ Wash, 80-. **MEMBERSHIPS** Am Asn Teachers Span & Port; Ling Soc Am. **RESEARCH** Structural linguistics; psycholinguistics; Spanish linguistics. **SELECTED PUBLICATIONS** Auth, Expressions For Sexual Harassment - A Semantic Hole/, Verbatim, Vol 0021, 1995. **CONTACT ADDRESS** Dept of Ling, Univ of Washington, Seattle, WA 98105.

SARA, SOLOMON ISHU
PERSONAL Born 05/01/1930 **DISCIPLINE** THEORETICAL LINGUISTICS & PHONOLOGY **EDUCATION** Boston Col, BA, 56, MA, 57; Weston Col, STB, 64; Georgetown Univ, PhD(ling), 69; Cleveland Inst Electronics, dipl, 76. **CAREER** Asst prof, 69-80, Assoc Prof Ling, Georgetown Univ, 80-. **MEMBERSHIPS** Ling Soc Am; Int Ling Asn; Int Phonetic Asn; Am Asn Adv Sci. **RESEARCH** Instrumental phonetics; linguistic theory; comparative semitics. **SELECTED PUBLICATIONS** Auth, Modern Standard Arabic (19 vols), 71 & Spoken Iraqi Arabic (4 vols), 71, Monterey Lang Sch; A Grammar of Modern Chaldean, Mouton, 74; Vocalic Variability in Palatographic Impressions, Benjamins B V, 79. **CONTACT ADDRESS** Sch of Lang & Ling, Georgetown Univ, 1421 37th St N W, Washington, DC 20057-0001.

SARGENT, STUART H.
PERSONAL Born Portland, OR **DISCIPLINE** CHINESE LITERATURE **EDUCATION** Stanford Univ, PhD. **CAREER** Assoc prof. **RESEARCH** Chinese poetry of the late 11th century. **SELECTED PUBLICATIONS** Auth, pubs on literary theory and poetry. **CONTACT ADDRESS** Foreign Languages and Literature Dept, Colorado State Univ, Fort Collins, CO 80523. **EMAIL** stuart.sargent@colostate.edu

SARLES, HARVEY BURTON
PERSONAL Born 07/12/1933, Buffalo, NY, m, 1956, 2 children **DISCIPLINE** CULTURAL STUDIES, COMPARATIVE LITERATURE **EDUCATION** Univ Buffalo, BA, 54; MA, 59; Univ Chicago, PhD, 66. **CAREER** Mathematician, Cornell Aeronaut Lab, 55-56; res asst Ling, Univ Chicago, 60-61; asst prof Anthrop & Ling, Sch Med, Univ Pittsburgh, 62-66; from assoc prof to prof Anthrop, Univ Minn, Minneapolis, 66-88; Leverhulme vis fel ethnoling, Univ Sussex, 70-71; consult, Allegheny County Ment Health/Ment Retardation, 73-74; vis prof Ling, State Univ NYork, Buffalo, 74; vis prof Sci, Tech & Soc, Cornell Univ, 79; prof Cult Studies & Comp Lit, Univ Minn, 92-. **HONORS AND AWARDS** Invited Speaker, Univ Chicago Anthrop Dept 50th Anniversary, 79. **MEMBERSHIPS** MLA. **RESEARCH** Pragmatism; cultural critique; teaching as dialogue; language and human nature. **SELECTED PUBLICATIONS** Auth, Language and Human Nature, Univ Minn, 85; auth, Teaching As Dialogue, Univ Press of Am, 93; auth, "Ethology and the Philosophy of Language," in Handbuch Sprachphilosophie, ed. M. Dascal et al (Berlin: De Gruyter, 95); auth, "Essentialism and Evolutionism in the Nature of Language: The Biology of Language," in The Biology of Language, ed. Stanislaw Puppel (Amsterdam: John Benamins, 95); Toward an Anthropology of the Ordinary: Seeing with New Lenses, In Ethics and Cultural Diversity, ed, L Olive, Univ Nacional Autonoma de Mexico, publishing in Spanish, 95; Is Life But a Dream? The World as Text or Text as the World, Religious Humanism: vol XXX, nos 1-2, 96; The Emergent University, Humanism Today, vol 11, 97; auth, Nietzscheçs Prophecy: The Crisis in Meaning, Humanity Press, 01. **CONTACT ADDRESS** Univ of Minnesota, Twin Cities, 9 Pleasant St. SE, 350 Folwell Hall, Minneapolis, MN 55455. **EMAIL** sarle001@tc.umn.edu

SASKOVA-PIERCE, MILA
PERSONAL Born 06/29/1968, CZ, m, 1977, 2 children **DISCIPLINE** SLAVIC LANGUAGES AND LINGUISTICS **EDUCATION** Univ Kans, MA, 80, PhD, 86. **CAREER** Assoc prof Czech and Russ, Univ Nebr, Lincoln, 89. **HONORS AND AWARDS** 1988 Awd for Outstanding Contribution to Czech and Slovak cultures in greater CIFIJ Kansas City ethnic counl and the; 91, 92, 95, 96, Univ of Nebraska, Recognition Awd for contribution to students. **RESEARCH** Teaching methodology; Slavic linguistics. **CONTACT ADDRESS** Univ of Nebraska, Lincoln, Lincoln, NE 68588-0417. **EMAIL** msaskova-pierce1@unl.edu

SAURET, MARTINE
DISCIPLINE FRENCH **EDUCATION** Univ Langues Orientales Paris, Univ Diploma, 80; Univ Sorbonne, Licence, 80; Certificat, 82; Univ Minn, MA, 84; PhD, 91. **CAREER** Asst Prof to Assoc Prof, Western Mich Univ, 92-. **HONORS AND AWARDS** NEH Grant, 98; Fel, Newberry Library Short Term Fel, 98; Grant, Western Mich Univ, 00; Fac Res Fel, FRACASF, 95; Appreciation Awd, Col of Arts and Sci, 96. **MEMBERSHIPS** French Women in the Renaissance Newsletter, L'Esprit Createur, Mod Lang Asn, Renaissance Quarterly, Societe Francaise des Etudes du Seizieme siecle. **SELECTED PUBLICATIONS** Auth, Gargantua et les delits du corps, peter Lang Pub, 97; trans, The Graphic Unconscious in Early Modern french Writing, by Tom Conley, Cambridge Univ Press, 92; auth, "Ecrits cartographiques: mouvances et distorsions chez Montaigne et Rabelais," Romance Languages annual, forthcoming. **CONTACT ADDRESS** Dept Lang & Linguistics, Western Michigan Univ, 1201 Oliver St, Kalamazoo, MI 49008-3804. **EMAIL** martine.sauret@wmich.edu

SAUTERMAISTER, GERT
PERSONAL Born Ulm, Germany **DISCIPLINE** GERMAN **EDUCATION** Univ Munich, PhD, 71. **CAREER** Prof Ger, Univ Bremen; vis prof, Univ Munich, Ger; Univ Aarhus, Denmark; Univ Nizza, Fr; Univ Zix-Marseille, Fr; Max Kade distinguished vis prof-. **RESEARCH** Gottfried Keller and exile lit. **SELECTED PUBLICATIONS** Auth, monographs on Friedrich Schiller, Georg Christoph Lichtenberg, and Thomas Mann; articles on Ger lit from the period of the Enlightenment until the present. **CONTACT ADDRESS** Dept of Ger Lang and Lit, Univ of Kansas, Lawrence, Admin Building, Lawrence, KS 66045.

SAVVAS, MINAS
PERSONAL Born 04/02/1939, Athens, Greece, M, 2 children **DISCIPLINE** COMPARATIVE LITERATURE, CREATIVE WRITING **EDUCATION** Univ Ill, BA, 64, MA, 65; Univ Calif, Santa Barbara, PhD(English), 71. **CAREER** Asst prof English, Univ Calif, Santa Barbara, 65-68; assoc prof, 68-74, Prof English, San Diego State Univ, 74- **HONORS AND AWARDS** Best Review Awd, Books Abroad, 71; NEH Fellowship, 87; Golden Poet Awd, 89; MPPP Professional Merit Awd, 89; Alexandrian Awd, Hellenic Cultural Society, 93. **MEMBERSHIPS** MLA; Mod Greek Studies Asn; Hellenic Cult Soc. **RESEARCH** Modern Greek literature; continental novel; translation. **SELECTED PUBLICATIONS** Auth, Scars and Smiles, Diegenes Press, Athens, 75; auth, Chronicle of Exile, verse translations of Y. Ritsos, WirePress, San Francisco, 77; auth, The Subterranean Herses, Ohio Univ Press, 81; Auth, Remembering Ritsos,Yannis + Poet/, Literary Review, Vol 0036, 93; The 'Fourth Dimension' - Ritsos,Y, Green,P, Translator, Bardsley,B, Translator/, World Lit Today, Vol 0068, 94; The Oldest Dead White Europ Males And Other Reflections On The Classics - Knox,B/, J Of Modern Greek Studies, Vol 0012, 94; 'Vreghmeno Rouho' - Bramos,G/, World Lit Today, Vol 0068, 94; 'Mavra Litharia' - Ganas,M/, World Lit Today, Vol 0068, 94; I 'Mihani Ton Mistikon' - Siotis,D/, World Lit Today, Vol 0068, 94; The Poetry And Poetics Of Cavafy,Constantine,P - Aesthetic Visions Of Sensual Reality - Anton,Jp/, World Lit Today, Vol 0070, 96; 'Oudheteri Zoni' - Greek - Kariotis,M/, World Lit Today, Vol 0070, 96; To 'Taxidi 1963-1992' - Greek - Tsaloumas,D/, World Lit Today, Vol 0070, 96. **CONTACT ADDRESS** Dept of English & Comparative Lit, San Diego State Univ, San Diego, CA 92115.

SAYLOR, CHARLES F.
DISCIPLINE LATIN LITERATURE **EDUCATION** Univ Wash, BA, MA; Univ Calif Berkeley, PhD. **CAREER** Prof & supv Grad tchg asstants; past dir, Undergrad Study & Grad Study & 3 terms, ch; Univ Mo, 68-; thaught at, St Mary's Col, Calif, UC Davis & San Diego State Univ. **RESEARCH** Roman Comedy; silver Latin literature. **SELECTED PUBLICATIONS** Publ on, Propertius, Plautus, Terence, Vergil, Lucan, Pliny, Horace, Lucretius & Petronius. **CONTACT ADDRESS** Dept of Classical Studies, Univ of Missouri, Columbia, 309 University Hall, Columbia, MO 65211. **EMAIL** saylorc@missouri.edu

SAYWARD, CHARLES
DISCIPLINE PHILOSOPHY OF LOGIC, PHILOSOPHY OF LANGUAGE, AND POLITICAL PHILOSOPHY **EDUCATION** Cornell Univ, PhD, 64. **CAREER** Prof, Univ Nebr, Lincoln. **RESEARCH** The philosophy of mathematics. **SELECTED PUBLICATIONS** Auth, Definite Descriptions, Negation and Necessitation, Russell 13, 93; coauth, Two Concepts of Truth, Philos Stud 70, 93; The Internal/External Question, Grazer Philosophische Studien 47, 94; Intentionality and truth: an essay on the philosophy of Arthur Prior. **CONTACT ADDRESS** Univ of Nebraska, Lincoln, Lincoln, NE 68588-0417.

SAZ, SARA M.
DISCIPLINE SPANISH LITERATURE **EDUCATION** Univ Southampton, PhD. **CAREER** Prof. **SELECTED PUBLICATIONS** Auth, pubs on English as a Second Language, Argentinian poetry and prose, Spanish and Latin American literature and film. **CONTACT ADDRESS** Foreign Languages and Literature Dept, Colorado State Univ, Fort Collins, CO 80523. **EMAIL** ssaz@vines.colostate.edu

SAZAKI, KRISTINA R.
DISCIPLINE GERMAN **EDUCATION** Calif State Univ, Sacramento,BA, 80, MA, 82; Univ Calif, Los Angeles, PhD, 88. **CAREER** Asst Prof. **RESEARCH** Berthold Auerbach; Annette von Droste-Hulshoff; Amerikabild; German-Jewish literary history 1800-1945; technology in the classroom. **SELECTED PUBLICATIONS** Auth, Mimicking Theater: Charlotte Birch-Pfeiffer's Dorf und Stadt in Relation to Berthold Auerbach's Die Frau Professorin, Thalia's Daughters: German Women Dramatists from the Eighteenth Century to the Present, Tubingen: Franke, 96 & Franz Grillparzer's and Lion Feuchtwanger's Die Judin von Toledo, Was nutzt der Glaube ohne Werke Studien zu Franz Grillparzer anlasslich seines 200. Geburtstages, Otago Ger Stud 7, Dunedin: Univ Otago, 92. **CONTACT ADDRESS** Dept of Modern Languages and Literatures, Col of the Holy Cross, 1 College St, PO Box 189A, Worcester, MA 01610-2395. **EMAIL** ksazaki@holycross.edu

SBAIT, DIRGHAM H.
PERSONAL Born 02/03/1945, Iqrith, Palestine/Israel, m, 1972, 3 children **DISCIPLINE** ARABIC, SEMETIC LANGUAGES AND LITERATURES **EDUCATION** Hebrew Univ, Univ Haifa, BA, 71; Univ Wash, MA, 78; PhD, 82. **CAREER** Teach asst, Univ Wash, 75-81; asst prof, Univ Calif, Los Angeles and PSU, 82-93; asst prof, to assoc prof, Portland State Univ, 85-95; prof, 95. **HONORS AND AWARDS** ACTFL Grant; Res Pub Awd; Univ Calif, Los Angeles, Res Grants. **MEMBERSHIPS** AATA; AAUP; AOF. **RESEARCH** Folk literature of the Palestine's; folk poetry, songs, tales, and proverbs; wedding traditions; Arab culture; classical and modern Arab poetry. **SELECTED PUBLICATIONS** Auth, "Palestinian Wedding Songs," Garland Encyclopedia of World Music 6: "The Middle East," supervised by The Archive of World Music, Harvard Univ, forthcoming; auth, "The Literary, Musical, & Socio-Cultural Aspects of the Palestinian Arab Wedding: Critical Presentation," Foreign Films & Literature Abstracts, Villanova Univ (96); auth, "Debate In The Improvised-Sung Poetry of The Palestinians," Asian Folklore Studies (Nanzan Univ, Nagoya, Japan, 93): 93-117; rev of Diwan a-Dalcona al-Pilastini," The Palestinian Dalcona, cAbd al-Latif al-Barghuthi, al-Birih (The West Bank) and Middle East/ South Asia Folklore Bulletin, Ohio State Univ (92): 2-3; auth, "Palestinian Folk Poetry: The Genres of Hida and Oarradi, Performance, and Transmission," Oral Tradition 4 (89): 213-235; auth, "Poetic and Musical Structure in the Improvised Sung Colloquial Oasidih of the Palestinian Poet Singers," Am Asn Teachers of Arabic 19 (86): 75-108. **CONTACT ADDRESS** Dept Foreign Lang, Portland State Univ, Box 571, Portland, OR 97207-0751.

SBROCCHI, LEONARD G.
DISCIPLINE ITALIAN LANGUAGE AND LITERATURE **EDUCATION** Univ Toronto, BA, PhD; Univ Wash, MA. **CAREER** Prof, Univ Ottawa. **HONORS AND AWARDS** Ed, monogr series Biblioteca di Quaderni d'Italianistica, Ottawa: CSIS, 84-; assoc ed, Il Forneri; ed, Legas. **RESEARCH** Renaissance, 18th and 20th century Italian literature. **SELECTED PUBLICATIONS** Auth, Stilistica nella narrativa Pavesiana, Casamari, 67; Renato Fucini, L'uomo e l'opera, D'Anna, 77; I verbi italiani, et leurs equivalents francais-and their English Equivalents, LEGAS, 89; co-ed, transl, The Comedies of Ariosto, Univ, Chicago Press, 75; Aretino's Marescalco, Dovehouse Editions, 86; Pirandello's Tonight We Improvise, Can Soc Ital Stud, 87; Leonora addio! Can Soc Ital Stud, 87; ed, Renato Fucini, Napoli a occhio nudo, Einaudi, 76; co-ed, L'enigma Pirandello, Can Soc Ital Stud, 88; L2 and Beyond, Legas, 93; Moral and Political Philosophies in the Middle Ages, Legas, 95. **CONTACT ADDRESS** Dept of Modern Languages and Literature, Univ of Ottawa, 70 Laurier Ave, PO Box 450, Ottawa, ON, Canada K1N 6N5. **EMAIL** lsbrocch@aix1.uottawa.ca

SCALABRINI, MASSIMO
PERSONAL Born 05/20/1964, Toano, Italy **DISCIPLINE** ENGLISH, LITERATURE, SPANISH, FRENCH **EDUCATION** Univ di Balogna, Laur Let, 90; Yale Univ, PhD, 98. **CAREER** Teach asst, Yale Univ, 92-95; lectr, Princeton Univ, 95-98; asst prof, Univ Wash Seattle, 98-00; asst prof, Ind Univ, 00-. **HONORS AND AWARDS** Baltz-Seronde Fel, 92-94; Sterling Prize Fel, 92-94; Grad Student Exchange Award, 91-92; Erasmus Scholar, 89. **MEMBERSHIPS** AATI; AAIS; MLA; RSA. **RESEARCH** Renaissance and early modern literature and culture; lyric poetry; heroic and mock-heroic poetry; comic literature; humanism. **SELECTED PUBLICATIONS** Auth, "Il Cigno Senz'ali" L'idea di Dante Nell 'Orlando Furioso," Schede Umanistiche (94); auth, "La Schiatta di Mastro Iachelino: Una Proposta per Il Negromante," Lingua e Stile (96); auth, "Cingar 'Salsa Diabli' e La Strategia del Comico Folenghiano," Quaderni Folenghiani (97); auth, "Umanesimo e Anti-Umanesimo in Giovanni Della Casa," Schede Umanistiche (99); auth, "Un Edito Travestimento Secentesco del Baldus," Rivista di Let Ital (01); auth, "Nascita e Infanzia Dell'eroe Macaronia, " Quaderni Folenghiani (01). **CONTACT ADDRESS** For Lang Dept, Indiana Univ, Bloomington, Bloomington, IN 47405. **EMAIL** mscalabr@indiana.edu

SCALES, MANDERLINE ELIZABETH
PERSONAL Born 03/14/1927, Winston-Salem, NC, m, 1955 **DISCIPLINE** SPANISH **EDUCATION** Spelman Coll, AB 1949; Univ Pittsburgh, MEd; Univ of Valencia, Spain; Univ of NC at Greensboro, doctorate. **CAREER** Winston-Salem State U, prof Soc Sci Spanish; The Winston-Salem Forsyth Co Schs Forsyth Tech Inst, tchr; Assn of Classroom Tchrs, past Pres; Dist & State Levels of Foreign Lang Tchrs In NCTA, chmn; Forsyth PTA Enrich Proj, chmn; Forsyth Co YWCA, dir on bd; Winston-Salem Natl Council of Negro Women. **HONORS AND AWARDS** Recip Outstanding Woman in Civic & Comm Winston-Salem 1974; hon by 1972 class of Winston-Salem State U; Commandress of Yr Nat Organ of Daughters of Isis; Com on the Forsyth County Hall of Justice in Winston-Salem; Relationships of Members and Non-Members of Fraternities & Sororities, 1982. **MEMBERSHIPS** Past Loyal Lady Ruler Golden Circ, past Commandress Daughters of Isis; mem OES; Delta Sigma Theta Sor; The Delta Fine Arts Proj bd of dirs; trust Shiloh Bapt Ch; pres Union RJ Reynolds Flwshp to study in Spain; dir, Shilohian St Peter's Corp Family Center 1984-98; pres, Top Ladies of Distinction, Inc, 1986-89; natl pres, Nation Women of Achievement Inc. **CONTACT ADDRESS** Past Assistant Vice-Chancellor for Student Affairs/Devt, Winston-Salem State Univ, 601 Martin Luther King Jr Dr, Winston-Salem, NC 27101.

SCANLAN, MARGARET C.
PERSONAL Born 10/15/1944, Battle Creek, IA, m, 1968, 3 children **DISCIPLINE** COMPARATIVE LITERATURE **EDUCATION** Univ Mich, MA, 66; Univ Iowa, PhD, 72. **CAREER** From instr to prof, Ind Univ South Bend, 76-. **HONORS AND AWARDS** NEH Summer Sem, Princeton, 88; NEH Summer Sem, Yale, 94; FACET; Margaret Church Prize, 94. **MEMBERSHIPS** MLA, ACLA, IASIL, ACIS. **RESEARCH** Politics and Fiction, Contemporary British Fiction, Irish Literature and Culture. **SELECTED PUBLICATIONS** Auth, Traces of Another Time, Princeton, 90; auth, Plotting Terror: Terrorists and Novelists in Contemporary Fiction, Univ Press of Va, forthcoming. **CONTACT ADDRESS** Dept English, Indiana Univ, South Bend, PO Box 7111, South Bend, IN 46634-7111. **EMAIL** mscanlan@iusb.edu

SCANLAN, RICHARD T.
PERSONAL Born 05/30/1928, St. Paul, MN, m, 1951, 5 children **DISCIPLINE** CLASSICS **EDUCATION** Univ Minn, BS, 51, MA, 52. **CAREER** Teacher Latin, Edina High Sch, Minn, 55-67; assoc prof, 67-80, prof Classics, Univ Ill, Urbana, 80-, mem Latin Achievement Test Comt, Col Entrance Exam Bd, 60-65, chmn Latin Advan Placement Exam Comt, 67-72, chief examr, Classics Prog, 73-77. **MEMBERSHIPS** Am Philol Asn; Am Class League; Class Asn midwest & S; Am Coun Teaching Foreign Lang; Archives Asn Am. **RESEARCH** The teaching of Latin; computer applications to the teaching of Latin; teaching of classical humanities. **SELECTED PUBLICATIONS** Auth, A survey of Latin textbooks, Class J, 76; A computer-assisted instruction course in vocabulary building, Foreign Lang Ann, 76; Suggestions for a course in ancient and modern tragedy, Class Outlook, 77; Beginning Latin, 77, Word Power, 77 & Latin Composition, 77, Control Data Co; Some criteria for the evaluation of Latin textbooks, 78 & The grading of the 1977 advanced placement examination, 78, Class J. **CONTACT ADDRESS** Dept of Classic, Univ of Illinois, Urbana-Champaign, 707 S Mathews Ave, Urbana, IL 61801-3625. **EMAIL** rscanlon@uiuc.edu

SCANLAN, TIMOTHY MICHAEL
PERSONAL Born 08/31/1946, Akron, OH, m, 1969, 1 child **DISCIPLINE** FRENCH LITERATURE **EDUCATION** Univ Akron, BA, 66; Case Western Reserve Univ, MA, 68, PhD(-French), 71. **CAREER** From instr to asst prof, 70-75, assoc prof, 75-80, Prof French, Univ Toledo, 80- **MEMBERSHIPS** MLA; Am Asn Teachers Fr; Am Soc 18th Century Studies; Am Coun Teaching Foreign Lang; NAm Soc 17th Century Fr Lit. **RESEARCH** Foreign language pedagogy; 17th and 18th century French literature. **SELECTED PUBLICATIONS** Auth, The Portrayal Of Columbus,Christopher And The Natives Of San-Salvador In Rousseau La 'Decouverte Du Nouveau Monde'/, Orbis Litterarum, Vol 0051, 1996. **CONTACT ADDRESS** Dept of Foreign Lang, Univ of Toledo, 2801 W Bancroft St, Toledo, OH 43606-3390.

SCANLON, THOMAS FRANCIS
PERSONAL Born 09/26/1951, Pittsburgh, PA **DISCIPLINE** CLASSICAL LANGUAGES **EDUCATION** Duquesne Univ, BA, 72; Ohio State Univ, MA, 75, PhD(classics), 78. **CAREER** Asst prof classics, Univ Md, College Park, 79-80 & Univ Calif, Los Angeles, 80-81; Asst Prof Classics, Univ Calif, Riverside, 81-, Scholar, Univ Vienna, Austria, 78-79; Fulbright fel, Austrian Fulbright-Hays Prog, 78-79. **MEMBERSHIPS** Am Philol Asn. **RESEARCH** Greek and Roman historical writing, athletics and linguistics. **SELECTED PUBLICATIONS** Auth, Echoes Of Herodotus In Thucydides - Self-Sufficiency, Admiration, And Law/, Historia-Zeitschrift Fur Alte Geschichte, Vol 0043, 1994; Games For Girls/, Archaeol, Vol 0049, 1996. **CONTACT ADDRESS** Dept of Lit & Lang, Univ of California, Riverside, 900 University Ave, Riverside, CA 92521-0001.

SCARLETT, ELIZABETH
PERSONAL Born Brooklyn, NY, m, 1995, 1 child **DISCIPLINE** SPANISH **EDUCATION** WA Univ, AB, 83; Harvard Univ, MA, 86; PhD, 91. **CAREER** Visiting Asst Prof, Univ de Sevilla, 88-89; Teaching Fel, Harvard Univ, 85-88, 89-91; Asst Prof, Univ Va, 91-97; Asst Prof, SUNY, 97-. **HONORS AND AWARDS** Nat Merit Scholar, WA Univ, 79-83; Harvard Danforth Commendation for Excellence in Teaching, 89; Choice Selection, Outstanding Acad Books, 95; Sesquicentennial Fel, Univ VA, 95. **MEMBERSHIPS** MLA; NEMLA; AATSP, 20th Century Spanish Asn; Asociacion Internacional de Galdosistas; Instituto Cervantes; Feministas Unidas. **RESEARCH** Spanish Literature and Culture, 1750 to present; Feminism; Film Studies. **SELECTED PUBLICATIONS** Auth, "Rosa Chacel's Reception of Silent Film in Estacion. Ida y vulta," Letras peninsulares, (94); 209-219; auth, "Conversacion con Antonio Munoz Molina," Espana contemporanea, (94); 69-82; auth, Under Construction: The Body in Spanish Novels, Univ Press of VA, 95; auth, "Bunuel y Galdos: la amistad subversiva en Nazarin," La Nueva Literatura Hispanica, (97): 85-94; auth, "Antonio Machado's Fountains: Archeology of an Image," MLN, (98): 305-323; auth, "Mapping out the Cartas marruecas: Geographical, Cultural, and Gender Coordinates," Revista de Estudios Hispanicos, (99): 65-83. **CONTACT ADDRESS** Dept Mod Lang, SUNY, Buffalo, 910 Clemens Hall, PO Box 604620, Buffalo, NY 14260-0001. **EMAIL** scarlett@acsu.buffalo.edu

SCATTON, ERNEST ALDEN
PERSONAL Born 09/04/1942, Hazleton, PA, m, 1964, 2 children **DISCIPLINE** SLAVIC LINGUISTICS **EDUCATION** Univ PA, BA, 64; Harvard Univ, MA, 67, PhD(Slavic lang & lit), 70. **CAREER** From lectr to asst prof Slavic lang, IN Univ, 70-72; asst prof, Univ VA, 72-76; assoc dean, Humanities &

Fine Arts, 77-79, assoc prof Slavic lang, to dist service prof, SUNY, Albany, 76-97, chemn Slavic lang & lit, 80-, assoc dir, Slavic Workshop, IN Univ, 71. **HONORS AND AWARDS** Dir, Philol Sciences (honoris causae), Sofia Univ, 96. **MEMBERSHIPS** Bulgarian Studies Asn; Am Asn Teachers Slavic & East Europ Lang. **RESEARCH** Phonology of Slavic languages, especially Russian, Bulgarian & Serbo-Croatian; Balkan linguistics; general phonology. **SELECTED PUBLICATIONS** Auth, Bulgarian Phonology, Slavica, 75; co-ed, A Festschrift for Horace G Lunt, Slavica, 78; Reference Grammar of Modern Bulgarian, Slavica, 83. **CONTACT ADDRESS** Languages, Literatures, Cultures, SUNY, Albany, 1400 Washington Ave, Albany, NY 12222-1000.

SCHADE, GEORGE D.
PERSONAL Born 07/16/1923, Portland, OR, m, 2 children **DISCIPLINE** SPANISH **EDUCATION** Univ Ore, BA, 45, MA, 47; Univ Calif, Berkeley, PhD, 53. **CAREER** Instr Romance lang, Univ Ore, 46-47; lectr Span, Univ Calif, 53-54; instr, Univ NMex, 54-55; from instr to assoc prof, 55-66, Prof Span, Univ Tex, Austin, 66-98, Prof Emer, Univ Tex, Austin, 98-; Fulbright-Hays Advan Res grant, 67-68 & 79-80. **MEMBERSHIPS** MLA; Am Asn Teachers Span & Port Chile, Mexico, and Argentina. **SELECTED PUBLICATIONS** Auth, Augury in Al filo del agua, Tex Studies in Lit & Lang, spring 60; Juan Jose Arreola, Confabulario and Other Inventions, translated with critical introd, 64, Juan Rulfo, The Burning Plain and Other Stories, transl with critical introd, 67, co-ed, Ruben Dario Centennial Studies, 70 & contrib, Introduction to The Decapitated Chicken and Other Stories by Horacio Quiroga, 76, Univ Tex, Austin; co-ed, Literatura espanola contemporanea, Antologia, Introduccion, notas, Charles Scribner's Sons, 65; El arte narrativo de Garcia Marquez en su novels corta La increible y triste historia de la candida Erendira y de su abuela desalmada, Thesaurus, Mayoagosto, 77; Costumbrismo y novela sentimental, Literatura en imagenes, 79; Le segunda generacion modernista, Literatura en imagenes, 79; Sight, Sense and Sound: Seaweed, Onions and Oranges: Notes on Translating Neruda, Symposium, spring 84; Encyclopedia of Latin American Writers (articles on Alberto Blest Gana, Eugenio Cambaceres, Horacio Quiroga, and Pablo Neruda); El llano en llamas: mundo poetico y monstruoso, Homenaje a Ricard Gullon, 95; tranls with introduction, Pablo Neruda, Fify Odes, 96. **CONTACT ADDRESS** Dept of Span & Port, Univ of Texas, Austin, Campus Mail code B3700, Austin, TX 78712. **EMAIL** schade@mail.utexas.edu

SCHADE, RICHARD E.
PERSONAL Born 03/12/1944, Concord, NH, m, 1972, 2 children **DISCIPLINE** GERMANIC LANGUAGES **EDUCATION** Univ New Hampshire, BA, 66; MA, 68; Yale Univ, PhD, 76. **CAREER** Prof, Univ of Cincinnati, 75-; Editor, Lessing Yearbook, 75-; Honorary Consul of Germany, 96-. **HONORS AND AWARDS** Univ Best Teaching Awd, 94; Numerous research fellowships; Secretary/Treasurer, Lessing Society. **RESEARCH** Germany Literary Culture Luther-Lessing, 1500-1750. **SELECTED PUBLICATIONS** Auth, Studies in Early German Comedy, 88. **CONTACT ADDRESS** Dept Germanic Languages, Univ of Cincinnati, PO Box 210372, Cincinnati, OH 45221-0372. **EMAIL** richard.schade@uc.edu

SCHAEFFER, PETER MORITZ-FRIEDRICH
PERSONAL Born 05/14/1930, Breslau, Germany, m, 1968 **DISCIPLINE** GERMANIC STUDIES, CLASSICS, RELIGIOUS STUDIES. **EDUCATION** Univ Ottawa, Lic Theol, 59; Princeton Univ, PhD(Germanic studies), 71. **CAREER** From lectr to asst prof Germanic studies, Princeton Univ, 70-74; vis lectr Ger & comp lit, Univ CA, Berkeley, 74-76; Assoc Prof to Prof Ger, Univ CA, Davis, 76-. **HONORS AND AWARDS** Outstanding Advisor, 86; Outstanding Mentor of the Year, 93. **MEMBERSHIPS** ALSC; Renaissance Soc Am; Erasmus Soc; Tyndale Soc. **RESEARCH** Renaissance; Neo-Latin literature; Classical tradition. **SELECTED PUBLICATIONS** Auth, Joachim Vadianus, De poetica, Text, Translation & Commentary, Wilhelm Fink, Munich, 73; Hoffmannswaldau, De curriculo studiorum, Peter Lang, Bern, 91; Sapidus Consolator, Annuaire de Selestat, 96. **CONTACT ADDRESS** German Dept, Univ of California, Davis, One Shields Ave, Davis, CA 95616-5200. **EMAIL** pmschaeffer@ucdavis.edu

SCHAFFER, DEBORAH
PERSONAL Born 05/12/1955, Syracuse, NY **DISCIPLINE** LINGUISTICS **EDUCATION** Univ Rochester, BA, 76; Ohio State Univ, MA, 78; PhD, 82. **CAREER** Res assoc, 77-82, lectr, 83, Ohio State Univ; asst prof to prof, MSU-Billings, 83-. **HONORS AND AWARDS** Phi Beta Kappa, 76; Phi Kappa Phi, 79; MSU Studententententent Sen Outstanding Fac Awd, 95; MSU-Billings Found Fac Achievement Awd, 98. **MEMBERSHIPS** Ling Soc Am; Nat Coun Teachers English; Popular Cult Asn; Am Asn Univ Women; Am Asn Applied Ling; Mont Asn Teachers English & Lang Arts. **RESEARCH** Topics in popular linguistics, sociolinguistics, writing attitudes. **SELECTED PUBLICATIONS** Co-ed, Language Files, (79); co-ed, Feats and Faces, (94); auth, The Jnal of Popular Culture, (91); auth, ETC>: A Review of General Semantics, (98). **CONTACT ADDRESS** Dept English & Philos, Montana State Univ, Billings, 1500 N 30 St, Billings, MO 59101-0245.

SCHAMSCHULA, WALTER
PERSONAL Born 12/23/1929, Prague, Czechoslovakia, m, 1958, 1 child **DISCIPLINE** SLAVIC LANGUAGES & LITERATURES **EDUCATION** Univ Frankfurt, PhD(Slavic lang & lit), 60, Habil, 70. **CAREER** Asst Slavic lang & lit, Univ Frankfurt, 58-60, lectr Czech, 60-70, privatdocent Slavic lang & lit, 70-72; Prof Slavic Lang & Lit, Univ Calif, Berkeley, 72-, Vis lectr, Univ Calif, Berkeley, 70-71; Univ Calif humanities res fel, 76. **HONORS AND AWARDS** Moritz-von-Bethmann-Preis Frankfurt, 70. **MEMBERSHIPS** Asn Slavicists Fed Repub Ger. **RESEARCH** Czech literature and language, Polish literature, Russian literature, translation. **SELECTED PUBLICATIONS** Auth, The Igor' Tale From Its Czech To Its Gaelic Connection/ American Contr to the 11th Int Congr of Slavists, Columbus /Ohio, 93, R A Maguire & A Timberlake eds. 130-153; auth, A History of Czech Literature, vol 1, 90 , vol 2, 96/ Bausteine zur slav Phil u Kulturgeschiche, Cologne; auth, An Anthology of Czech Lit, 1st Period/ West Slavic Contributions, vol 2, Frankfurt; ed, Westslavic Contributions; Coed, Bohemia, biannual, Munich. **CONTACT ADDRESS** Dept of Slavic Lang & Lit, Univ of California, Berkeley, Berkeley, CA 94720.

SCHARF, PETER M.
PERSONAL Born 06/14/1958, New Haven, CT, s **DISCIPLINE** SANSKRIT LANGUAGE & LITERATURE, INDIAN PHILOSOPHY, LINGUISTICS **EDUCATION** Weslyan Univ, BA, 81; Brown Univ, 82-83; Univ Penn, PhD, 90. **CAREER** Comp prog, Microtex,81; comp prog, Real Dec Corp, 81-82; comp prog, Lang Sys, 82-83; teach asst, Univ Pa, 85-86; vis lectr, Univ Vir, 92; vis lectr, 92-94; SAF comm, 92-; chair, 95-96; FAC comp, 94-97; lectr, 94-, Brown Univ. **HONORS AND AWARDS** Outstand HS Sr Sems Schl; Foreign Lang Area Stud Fel; AIIS, Res Fel; Mellon Grad Fel; UP Dean Fel; NEH Fel; Post Doc Fel; APS Gnt. **MEMBERSHIPS** BORI; AOS; AAS; APA; BLS; Dharam Hinduja Indic Res Cen. **RESEARCH** Indian philosophy of language and linguistics; Indian philosophy; concepts of the self; Vedic interpretation in Indian literature; text encoding and computational analysis of Sanskrit. **SELECTED PUBLICATIONS** Auth, The Denotation of Generic Terms in Ancient Indian Philosophy: Grammar, Nyaya, and Mimamsa, Trans Am Philo Soc 86 APS (Philadelphia), 96; auth, "Pan mi, vivaksa, and karaka-rule-ordering," in Madhav Deshpande, ed. George Cardona, in press; auth "The term 'akrti' and the Concept of a Class Property in the Mahabhasya," Wiener Zeitschrijtfur die Kunde Sudasiens 36 (92): 31-48; auth, "Assessing Sabara's Arguments for the Conclusion that a Generic Term Denotes Just a Class Property, " J Indian Philo 21 (93): 1-10; auth, "Does Panini prohibit prohibitive compounds? An analysis of negation in the term anupasarge," Wiener Zeitschrififtir die Kunde Sudasiens 39 (95): 15-24; auth, "Early Indian Grammarians on a speaker's intention," J Am Oriental Soc 115 (95): 66-76; auth, "Clause-initial dvayam: One less case of an extra posed adverb," Indo-Iranian J 40 (97): 327-338; rev of, "Panini Re-Interpreted," by Charu Deva Shastri, Hist Ling 18 (91): 399-402; rev of, "Sanskrit Syntax: A Volume in Honor of the Centennial of Speijer's Sanskrit Syntax," ed, Hans Henrich Hock, J Am Oriental Soc 114 (94): 485-487; rev of, "Ideology and Status of Sanskrit: Contributions to the History of Sanskrit Language," ed. Jan E M Houben, Anthro Ling 40 (98): 167-174. **CONTACT ADDRESS** Dept Classics, Brown Univ, 1 Prospect St, Providence, RI 02912-9100. **EMAIL** Peter_Scharf@Brown.edu

SCHAUMANN, CAROLINE
PERSONAL Born 09/07/1969, Berlin, Germany, d **DISCIPLINE** GERMAN **EDUCATION** Justus Liebig Univ Giessen, 88-89; Freie Univ Berlin, 89-92; San Francisco State Univ, 92-93; Univ Calif, Davis, MA, 94, PhD, 99. **CAREER** Asst prof Ger, Middlebury Col, 99-. **HONORS AND AWARDS** KAPLAN Awd, 97; UC Davis Humanities Grad Res Awd, 97; UC Davis Outstanding Grad Student Teaching Campus Awd, 97; Robert Stroller Found Diss Res Prize, 98; UC Davis Fel, 97-98; Max Hayman Endowment Fel for Psychanalytically Informed Dissertation Res, 98; Project 2001 Materials Production Grant, 2000; Grant for the Ctr for Advan Holocaust Studies, Holocaust Mem Museum, 2000. **MEMBERSHIPS** Modern Lang Asn, Ger Studies Asn, Am Asn of Teachers of Ger, Foreign Lang Asn of Northern Calif, Women in Ger. **RESEARCH** Postwar German Literature, Holocaust studies, psychoanalysis, autobiographical studies, gender studies, language pedagogy and technology. **SELECTED PUBLICATIONS** Rev, of ""My Years in Theresienstadt: How One Woman Survived the Holocaust," by Gerty Spies, Women in Ger Newsletter (fall 97); rev, of "Harrys Kopf," by Tankred Dorst, Focu on Lit (spring 99); auth, "Women Revisit the Third Reich: Autobiographical Writings by Melita Maschmann, Christa Wolf, and Eva Zeller," Glossen Heft 6 (Jan 99), http://www.dickinson.edu/glossen; rev, "Austrian Women in the Nineteenth and Twentieth Centuries," by David Good and Margarete Grandner, eds, Women in Ger Newsletter (spring 99); re, of "Der Erzahler Heinrich Boll, by Inga Lenick, Ger Studies Rev (forthcoming); coauth with Christina Frei and Sabine von Mering, Deutsch Na Klar! CD-ROM,McGraw-Hill (forthcoming); coauth with Christina Frei, Fokus Deutsch Testing Program," McGraw-Hill (forthcoming). **CONTACT ADDRESS** Ger Dept, Middlebury Col, FIC Cook, TL 15, Middlebury, VT 05753.

SCHEIN, BARRY
DISCIPLINE LINGUISTICS **EDUCATION** MIT, PhD. **CAREER** Assoc prof & ch, Univ Southern Calif. **RESEARCH** Semantics; syntax of logical form. **SELECTED PUBLICATIONS** Auth, Plurals and Events, MIT Press, 94; coauth, Plurals, NELS, 89. **CONTACT ADDRESS** Dept of Linguistics, Univ of So California, University Park Campus, Los Angeles, CA 90089. **EMAIL** schein@usc.edu

SCHEINDLIN, RAYMOND PAUL
PERSONAL Born 05/13/1940, Philadelphia, PA, m, 1986, 2 children **DISCIPLINE** HEBREW LITERATURE & ARABIC **EDUCATION** Gratz Col, Cert, 59; Univ Pa, BA, 61; Jewish Theol Sem Am, MHL, 63, Rabbi, 65; Columbia Univ, PhD, 71. **CAREER** Asst prof Hebrew, McGill Univ, 69-72; asst prof Hebrew & Arabic, Cornell Univ, 72-74; Assoc Prof, 74-85, Prof Medieval Hebrew Lit, Jewish Theol Sem Am, 85-, Provost, 84-89; Dir, Shalom Spiegel Inst Medieval Hebrew Poetry, 96-. **HONORS AND AWARDS** Guggenheim Fel, 98. **MEMBERSHIPS** Asn Jewish Studies; Rabbinical Assembly Am; Am Acad Jewish Res; Soc Judeo-Arabic Studies; World Union Jewish Studies; PEN American Center. **RESEARCH** Medieval Hebrew and Arabic poetry; Judeo-Arabic lit and civilization. **SELECTED PUBLICATIONS** Transl, Of Bygone Days, In: A Stetl and Other Yiddish Novellas, 73; auth, Form and Structure in the Poetry of al-Mu'Tamid Ibn 'Abbad, De Goeje Fund, 74; 201 Arabic Verbs, Barrons Educ Series, 78; Wine, Women, and Death: Medieval Hebrew Poems on the Good Life, Jewish Publ Soc, 86; The Gazelle: Medieval Hebrew Poetry on God, Israel, and the Soul, Jewish Publ Soc, 86; transl, Jewish Liturgy in Its Historical Development, Jewish Publ Soc, 93; Chapter from Voyage to the End of the Millenium, Mod Hebrew Lit NS 19, 97; auth, The Book of Job translated, introduced, and annotated, W.W. Norton, 98; auth, A Short History of the Jewish People, 98. **CONTACT ADDRESS** Jewish Theol Sem of America, 3080 Broadway, New York, NY 10027-4650. **EMAIL** ibngabiroll@aol.com

SCHENKER, DAVID J.
DISCIPLINE GREEK PROSE AND POETRY **EDUCATION** Vanderbilt, BA; Univ Calif Berkeley, MA, PhD. **CAREER** Taught 2 yrs at Allegheny Col, Pa, Assoc prof & dir Undergrad Stud, Univ Mo, 91-; dept chair **RESEARCH** Greek drama. **SELECTED PUBLICATIONS** Publ in, Rheinisches Mus, 95; Mnemosyne, 95; Phoenix, 94 & TAPA, 91; co-ed, Classical and Modern Literature. **CONTACT ADDRESS** Dept of Classical Studies, Univ of Missouri, Columbia, 420 General Classroom Bldg, Columbia, MO 65211. **EMAIL** SchenkerD@missouri.edu

SCHER, STEVEN PAUL
PERSONAL Born 03/02/1936, Budapest, Hungary **DISCIPLINE** GERMAN STUDIES & COMPARATIVE LITERATURE **EDUCATION** Yale Univ BA, 60, MA, 63, PhD, 65. **CAREER** Instr, 65-67, Columbia Univ; asst to assoc prof, 67-74, Yale Univ; chmn, German dept, 74-80, 93-96, prof, 74-, Dartmouth Col. **HONORS AND AWARDS** DAAD Grant, 64-65; Morse fel, 69-70; Humboldt fel, 72-73; Geisel Third Century Prof, Humanities, 84-89; dir, NEH Sum Sem, 86, 89, 94; Daniel Webster prof, Ger & Comp Lit, 00. **MEMBERSHIPS** MLA; Am Comp Lit Assn; Am Assn Tchrs Ger; Intl Assn of Work & Music Stud. **RESEARCH** Romanticism; 19th & 20th century lit, lit & music. **SELECTED PUBLICATIONS** Auth, Verbal Music in German Literature, Yale Univ, 68; co-ed, Postwar German Culture: An Anthology, Dutton, 74, Ind Univ, 80; ed, Interpretationen zu ETA Hoffmann, Klett, 81; co-ed, Literature and the Other Arts, Univ Innsbruck, 81; ed, Literature und Musik, Ein Handbuch zur Theorie und Praxis eines Komparatistischen Grenzgebietes, E Schmidt, Berlin, 84; Music and Text: Critical Inquiries, Cambridge Univ, 92; ed. Word and Music Studies: Defining the Field, Rodopi (Amsterdam), 00. **CONTACT ADDRESS** Dept of German Stud, Dartmouth Col, 6084 Dartmouth Hall, Hanover, NH 03755-3511. **EMAIL** Steven.P.Scher@Dartmouth.edu

SCHERER, WILLIAM F.
PERSONAL Born 08/05/1939, Eureka, IL, m, 1968 **DISCIPLINE** GERMAN LITERATURE **EDUCATION** Univ Colo, AB, 61; Univ Southern Calif, MA, 62, PhD(Ger), 67. **CAREER** Asst prof Ger, Univ Calif, Berkeley, 65-68; asst prof, 68-72, curric develop grant, 69-70, chmn Ger div, 75-77, Assoc Prof Ger & Europ Lit, Univ Hawaii, Manoa, 72-, Grad Chmn Ger Studies, 75-, Consult, Am Coun Educ, 69; Univ Hawaii Found grant, Wash, 70; guest lectr, Mich State Univ, 72; 15th Congr Australasian Univs Lang & Lit Asn, Univ New South Wales, 73; Am Philos Soc res fel, Stuttgart, Ger, 74-75. **MEMBERSHIPS** Am Asn Teachers Ger; Philol Asn Pac Coast; Rocky Mtn Mod Lang Asn; Pac Northwest Conf Foreign Lang; Australasian Univs Lang & Lit Asn. **RESEARCH** Sixteenth and 17th century German literature; medieval European lyric; history of Western consciousness and European civilization. **SELECTED PUBLICATIONS CONTACT ADDRESS** Dept Europ Lang & Lit, Univ of Hawaii, Manoa, 1890 E West Rd, Honolulu, HI 96822-2362.

SCHERR, BARRY
PERSONAL Born 05/20/1945, Hartfort, CT, m, 1974, 2 children **DISCIPLINE** RUSSIAN **EDUCATION** Harvard Univ, AB; Univ of Chicago, AM, 67; PhD, 73. **CAREER** Asst prof to prof, Univ of Wash, 70-74; asst prof to prof, Dartmouth Col,

74-; chair, 81-90, 96-97; assoc Dean, 97-. **HONORS AND AWARDS** IREX Grant; NEH Grant, 87, 89; Phi Beta Kappa, 96. **MEMBERSHIPS** MLA; Am Assoc of Teachers of Slavic and E Europ Lang; Am Assoc for the Advan of slavic Studies. **RESEARCH** 20th Century Russian Literature, Russian verse theory, Russian film. **SELECTED PUBLICATIONS** Auth, Russian Poetry: Meter, Rhythm, and Rhyme, Univ of Calif Pr, (Berkeley), 86; coed, O RUS!: Studia litteraria slavica in honorem Hugh McLean, Berkeley: Berkeley Slavic Specialties, 95; coed, cotransl, "Maksim Gorky: Selected Letters" Clarendon Pr, (Oxford), 97; coauth, "Russian Verse Theory, 1982-1988: A Commentary and Bibliography", Int Jof Slav Ling and Poetics XLI (97): 143-91; auth, "To and from Autumn: Pasternak's Translations of Keats", in Essays in the Art and Theory of Translation, ed Lenore Grenoble and John Kopper, (NY: Edwin Mellen Pr, 97), 322-47; coauth, "Searching for the Ur-Text; Gorky's English Mother", Russ Lang J168-170, (97): 125-48; auth, "Synagogues, Synchrony and the Sea: Babel's Odessa", in And Meaning for a Life Entire: Festschrift for Charles A. Moser on the Occasion of His Sixtieth Birthday, ed Peter Rollberg, Slavica (Columbus, OH, 97), 337-50; corev, of "Westward Flows the Don: The Translation and the Text", Slavic and E Europ J42.1, (98): 119-25; auth, "To Urania", in Joseph Brodsky: The Art of Poem, ed Lev Loseff and Valentina Polukhina, Macmillan (London, 99), 92-106; auth, "Cherubina de Gabiak", in Russ Women Writers, ed Christine D. Tomei, Garland (NY, 99), I: 481-503. **CONTACT ADDRESS** Dept Russ, Dartmouth Col, 44 N College St, Hanover, NH 03755-1801. **EMAIL** barry.scherr@dartmouth.edu

SCHIERLING, STEPHEN P.
DISCIPLINE ANCIENT GREEK AND LATIN LANGUAGE, GREEK AND ROMAN COMEDY **EDUCATION** St Louis Univ, PhD, 80. **CAREER** Assoc prof Lat and Ancient Greek, coordr, undergrad Lat instr, 80-88; sec hd, Class, 86-89; Arts and Sci fac senate, 87-91, 95-97; pres, Arts and Sci fac senate, 90-91; Prescott Hall comp network admin, 92-, La State Univ. **RESEARCH** Greek and Latin paleography; textual criticism; computer applications to textual criticism. **SELECTED PUBLICATIONS** Auth, Vaticanus Graecus 2203 in the Manuscript Tradition of Thucydides, in Rev d'Hist des Texts, 11, 81; Rossi 508 and the Text of Sallust, in Manuscripts, XXIX, 85; New Evidence for Diomedes in Two Passages of Sallust, in Hermes, 113, 2, 85; Bellum Jugurthinum 113.3: A Restoration of the Text, in Manuscripta, XXXI. 87; SPSS/PC As a Useful Tool in Determining the Text of Sallust's Jugurtha: A Text Critic's Point of View, in The Class Bull, 65, nos 1 & 2, 89; The Jugurtha Epitaphs: The Texts and Tradition, in Manuscripta, 93. **CONTACT ADDRESS** Dept of For Lang, La State Univ, Baton Rouge, Baton Rouge, LA 70803-0001. **EMAIL** sschierl@homer.forlang.lsu.edu

SCHIFFMAN, LAWRENCE H.
PERSONAL Born 05/04/1948, New York, NY, m, 1970, 3 children **DISCIPLINE** HEBREW & JUDAIC STUDIES **EDUCATION** Brandeis Univ, BA & MA, 70, PhD(Near Eastern & Judaic studies), 74. **CAREER** Instr in Hebrew, Univ Minn, 71-72; from instr to Hebrew to asst prof Hebrew, 72-77, Assoc Prof Hebrew & Judaic Studies, New York Univ, 77-, Lectr, Hebrew Union Col, 75-; ed consult, KTAV Publ House, 76-; grants, Am Coun Learned Socs & Am Philos Soc. **MEMBERSHIPS** Asn Jewish Studies; Soc Bibl Lit; Am Orient Soc; World Union Jewish Studies; Israel Explor Soc. **RESEARCH** Dead Sea Scrolls; Judaism in late antiquity; Jewish law. **SELECTED PUBLICATIONS** Auth, Eschatology In The Theodicies Of 2-Baruch And 4-Ezra - Wilett,Tw/, Jewish Quart Rev, Vol 0083, 1992; The Greek Minor-Prophets-Scroll From Nahal-Hever - The Seiyal-Collection - Tov,E, Kraft,Ra, Parsons,Pj/, J Of Bibl Lit, Vol 0111, 1992; Origin And Early Hist Of The Qumran Sect/, Biblical Archaeol, Vol 0058, 1995. **CONTACT ADDRESS** Kevorkian Ctr Near Eastern Studies, New York Univ, New York, NY 10003.

SCHLAM, CARL C.
PERSONAL Born 10/23/1936, New York, NY, m, 1967 **DISCIPLINE** CLASSICS **EDUCATION** Columbia Univ, BA, 56, MA, 58, PhD(Greek & Latin), 68. **CAREER** Instr classics, Rutgers Univ, 64-66; preceptor Greek & Latin, Columbia Col, 66-67; asst prof, 67-73, Assoc Prof Classics, Ohio State Univ, 73-. **MEMBERSHIPS** Am Philol Asn. **RESEARCH** Ancient literature; neo-Latin; paleography. **SELECTED PUBLICATIONS CONTACT ADDRESS** Dept of Classics, Ohio State Univ, Columbus, Columbus, OH 43210.

SCHLANT, ERNESTINE
PERSONAL Born 08/14/1935, Passau, Germany, m, 2 children **DISCIPLINE** GERMAN, COMPARATIVE LITERATURE **EDUCATION** Emory Univ, PhD(compt lit), 65. **CAREER** Instr French, Spelman Col, 63-65; asst prof Ger, State Univ NY Stony Brook, 65-69; asst producer films, Cinema Arts Inc, 69-71; assoc prof, 71-80, Prof Ger, Montclair State Col, 81-. **HONORS AND AWARDS** Phi Beta Kappa; fel, Woodrow Wilson Int center.. for scholars. **MEMBERSHIPS** AAUP; MLA; AATG. **SELECTED PUBLICATIONS** Coauth, various Ger textbks for Holt, 69,71 & 73; auth, Die Philosophie Hermann Brochs, Francke, Bern, 71; Hermann Broch, Twayne, 78; co-ed, Legacies and Ambiguities: Postwar Fiction and Culture in West Germany and Japan, Washington, DC: Woodrow Wilson center.. Press and Baltimore: Johns Hopkins Univ Press, 91; auth, The Language of Silence West German literature and the Holocaust, (NY: Routledge, 99). **CONTACT ADDRESS** Dept of Ger, Montclair State Univ, Upper Montclair, NJ 07043.

SCHLATTER, FREDRIC WILLIAM
PERSONAL Born 06/16/1926, Tacoma, WA **DISCIPLINE** CLASSICAL LANGUAGES, HISTORY **EDUCATION** Gonzaga Univ, AB, 49, MA, 50; Alma Col, Calif, STL, 57; Princeton Univ, PhD(classics), 60. **CAREER** Instr classics, Gonzaga Prep, 50-52; instr, St Francis Xavier Div, 52-53, from asst prof to assoc prof, 61-74, dean, 62-65, Prof Classics, Gonzaga Univ, 74-, Chmn Dept Class Lang, 68-, Prof Hist, 76- **HONORS AND AWARDS** Prof Emeritus, 98; Festschrift: Nova Doctrina Veturque, 99. **MEMBERSHIPS** Am Philol Asn; Archaeol Inst Am; Asn Ancient Historians. **RESEARCH** Justin's Epitome of Pompeius Trogus. **SELECTED PUBLICATIONS** Auth, A Mosaic Interpretation Of Jerome, 'In Hiezechielem'/, Vigiliae Christianae, Vol 0049, 95; The 2 Women In The Mosaic Of Santa-Pudenziana, J Of Early Christian Studies, Vol 0003, 95; The Clash Of Gods - A Reinterpretation Of Early-Christian Art - Mathews,Tf/, Heythrop J-A Quart Rev Of Philos And Theol, Vol 0037, 96; auth, G.M. Hopkins: The Dublin Notes of Homer; The Hopkins Quart, Vol 0024, 97. **CONTACT ADDRESS** Dept of Class Lang, Gonzaga Univ, 502 E Boone Ave, Spokane, WA 99258-0001.

SCHLEINER, WINFRIED H.
PERSONAL Born 10/19/1938, Mannheim, Germany, w, 1968, 3 children **DISCIPLINE** ENGLISH & COMPARITIVE LITERATURE **EDUCATION** Univ Kiel, Staatsexamen, 64; Brown Univ, MA, 65, PhD, 68. **CAREER** Asst master & schoolmaster Eng & French, Max-Planck-Schule, Kiel, Ger, 68-70; asst prof Eng, RI Col, 70-73; asst prof, 73-75, assoc prof, prof eng, Univ CA, Davis; Full Prof, 85-. **HONORS AND AWARDS** UC Pres Fel Hum; NEH; Foreign Lib; Wolfenbuttel Biblothek fel. **MEMBERSHIPS** MLA; 16th Century Conf; Renaissance Soc Am; Am soc Hist of Med. **RESEARCH** Renaissance lit; comp lit; linguistics; hist med; gender studies. **SELECTED PUBLICATIONS** Auth, The Imagery of John Donne's Sermons, Brown Univ, 70; Aeneas' flight from Troy, Comp Lit, 75; Franklin and the infant Hercules, 18th Century Studies, 76-77; coauth, New material from the Grimm-Emerson correspondence, Harvard Libr Bull, 77; The Imagery of John Donnes Sermons, Brown Univ Press, 70; Melancholy Genius and Utopia in the Renaissance, Harrassowitz, 91; Medical Ethics in the Renaissance, Georgetown Univ Press, 95; A plot to his mose and cares cutt of: Schoppe as seen by the Archbishop of Canterbury, Renaissance and Reformation, 95; Cross-Dressing, Gender Errors and Sexual Taboos in Renaissance Literature in: Gender Reversals and Gender Cultures, London, 96; auth, John Selden's Letter to Ben Jonson on Cross-Dressing and Bisexual Gods, English Literary Renaissance, 99; auth, Early Modern Controversies about the One-Sex Model, Renaissance, 00. **CONTACT ADDRESS** Dept of Eng, Univ of California, Davis, Davis, CA 95616-5200. **EMAIL** whschleiner@ucdavis.edu

SCHLENOFF, ZEINA TAMER
PERSONAL Born 10/04/1956, Zahle, Lebanon, m, 1988, 2 children **DISCIPLINE** LINGUISTICS, LANGUAGE, ARABIC **EDUCATION** Lebanese Univ, BA, 81; MA, 81; Univ Mass, PhD, 95. **CAREER** Adj prof, Fla State Univ, 96-; vis asst prof, Am Univ Beirut, 98-01; dir summer prog, Am Univ Beirut, 01. **HONORS AND AWARDS** Fabriano Prize, 74; Who's Who Am. **MEMBERSHIPS** MLA; MEWSA. **RESEARCH** Middle Eastern women writers; women writers of the Belle Epoque; travel to the Middle East in 19th-century. **SELECTED PUBLICATIONS** Auth, Le Bonheur Chez la Femme Colettienne, Peter Lang Pub, 97. **CONTACT ADDRESS** 6274 Hines Hill Cres, Tallahassee, FL 32312-1557. **EMAIL** zschleno@mailer.fsu.edu

SCHLOSSMAN, BERYL
DISCIPLINE FRENCH **EDUCATION** John Hopkins Univ, PhD. **CAREER** Languages, Carnegie Mellon Univ. **SELECTED PUBLICATIONS** Auth, Joyce's Catholic Comedy of Language, Univ Wisc Press, 85; The Orient of Style: Modernist Allegories of Conversion, Duke Univ Press, 91; Baudelaire: Liberte, Libertinage, and Modernite. Sub-Stance, 93. **CONTACT ADDRESS** Carnegie Mellon Univ, 5000 Forbes Ave, Pittsburgh, PA 15213.

SCHLUNK, JUERGEN ECKART
PERSONAL Born 05/26/1944, Marburg, Germany, 1 child **DISCIPLINE** GERMAN LANGUAGE & LITERATURE **EDUCATION** Univ NH, MA, 68; Philipps-Univ Marburg, PhD(Am drama), 70. **CAREER** Dir & resident adv Ger, Jr Year Abroad Prog, Davidson Col, 72-73; asst prof, Franklin & Marshall Col, 73-74; asst prof, 74-80, assoc prof Ger, WVa Univ, 80-, Dramatist, Theater tri-buehne, Stuttgart, Ger, 76-77 & 80-81. **HONORS AND AWARDS** Salzburg Seminar for Am. Studies, Fel, 81; Outstanding Teacher Awd, W VA Univ, 91. **MEMBERSHIPS** Am Asn Teachers Ger; MLA. **RESEARCH** Theater; film. **SELECTED PUBLICATIONS** Auth, Foreign language exposure beyond the classroom: How to import theater, Die Unterrichtspraxis, 78; The image of America in German literature and in the new German cinema: Wim Wenders' The American Friend, Lit/Film Quart, Vol 7, No 3; ed, Martin Walser: International Perspitves, 87; ed, Doctor Faustus: Archetypal Subtext at the Millennium, 99. **CONTACT ADDRESS** Dept of Foreign Lang, West Virginia Univ, Morgantown, PO Box 6298, Morgantown, WV 26506-6298. **EMAIL** jschlunk@wvu.edu

SCHMALSTIEG, WILLIAM RIEGEL
PERSONAL Born 10/03/1929, Sayre, PA, m, 1952, 2 children **DISCIPLINE** SLAVIC LINGUISTICS **EDUCATION** Univ Minn, BA, 50; Univ Pa, MA, 51, PhD, 56. **CAREER** Asst prof Russ, Univ Ky, 56-59; asst prof Russ & French, Lafayette Col, 59-63; assoc prof Slavic ling, Univ Minn, 63-64; assoc prof, 64-67, Prof Slavic Lang, PA State Univ, University Park, 67-, Head Dept, 69-91, Ed, Gen Ling, 71-82; consult, ling div, MLA Bibliog, 72-73; Nat Endowment for Humanities fel, 78. **HONORS AND AWARDS** Fulbright Schol on exchange with Lithuanian Acad Sci, 86; Distinguished Alumnus, Breck Sch, 90; Friend of Lithuania Awd, 90; PhD (honoris causa), Univ Vilnius, 94. **MEMBERSHIPS** Am Asn Teachers Slavic & EEurop Lang; Ling Soc Am. **RESEARCH** Historical linguistics; comparative Balto-Slavic linguistics. **SELECTED PUBLICATIONS** Coauth, Introduction to Modern Lithuanian, Franciscan Fathers Press, 66, 5th ed, 93; Lithuanian Reader for Self-Instruction, Franciscan Fathers Press, 67; Janis Endzelins' Comparative Phonology and Morphology of the Baltic Languages, Mouton, The Hague, 71; auth, Die Entwicklung der a-Deklination im Slavischen, Z Slavische Philol, 72; An Old Prussian Grammar, 74 & Studies in Old Prussian, 76, Pa State Univ; An Introduction to Old Church Slavic, Slavica, 76, 2nd ed, 83; Indo-European Linguistics, Penn State Univ Press, 80; Lithuanian Historical Syntax, Slavica Press, 88; coauth, Beginning Hittite, Slavica Press, 88; auth, An Introduction to Old Russian, J Indo-Europ Studies, Monograph Fifteen, 95; A Student Guide to the Genitive of Agent in the Indo-European Languages, J Indo-Europ Studies, Monograph 14, 95. **CONTACT ADDRESS** Sch of Lang, Pennsylvania State Univ, Univ Park, 302A Burrowes Bldg, University Park, PA 16802-6204. **EMAIL** wxs1@psu.edu

SCHMELING, GARETH LON
PERSONAL Born 05/28/1940, Algoma, WI, m, 1963 **DISCIPLINE** GREEK & LATIN LITERATURE **EDUCATION** Northwestern Col, Wis, BA, 63; Univ Wis, MA, 64, PhD(Greek & Latin), 68. **CAREER** Asst prof Greek & Latin, Univ Va, 68-70; assoc prof, 70-75, Prof & Chmn Dept Classics, Univ Fla, 75-93, Dir, Humanities Ctr, 78-90, prof, Classics, 93-98, Disting prof, 98-, Am Philos Soc fel, 70-78; Univ Fla fel, 71-74; Nat Endowment for Humanities fel, 73-74; Am Coun Learned Soc grant-in-aid, 74; Rome prize, Am Acad, Rome, 77-78. **MEMBERSHIPS** Am Philos Asn; Am Class League; Class Asn Mid W & S; Vergilian Soc; Soc Studies Classics, France. **RESEARCH** Ancient prose fiction; Petronius; Apuleius, Chariton, Xenophon. **SELECTED PUBLICATIONS** Contribr, Exclusus Amator Motif in Petronius, Baccola & Gili, Turin, 71; ed, Cornelius Nepos: Lives of Famous Mem, Coronado, 71; auth, Chariton, Twayne, 74; coauth, TS Eliot and Petronius, Comp Lit Ser, 75; coauth, Bibliography of Petronius, Brill, Leiden, 77; auth, The satyricon: Forms in search of a genre, Class Bull, 71; Humanities perspectives on the professions, Lib Educ, 77; Xenophon of Ephesus, Twayne, 80; Authority of the Author: From Muse to Aesthetics, MCSN, 81; auth, Manners and Morality in the Historia Apollonii, Picolo Moando Antico, Univ Perugin, 89; auth, The Satyricon: Sense of an Ending, Rheisches Museum, 91; auth, Notes to the Text of the Historian Apollonii, Ramuz, 94; auth, Notes to the Text of the Historian Apollonii, Latomus, 94; auth, Quid attinet veritaten per interpretem quaerere, Ramus, 94; auth, The Novel in the Ancient World, Brill, Leinden, 96; Ed, A History of Roman Literature, Brill, Leiden, 97; auth, Qui Miscuit Utile Dulci, Bolchozy, 98. **CONTACT ADDRESS** Dept of Classics, Univ of Florida, 3c Arts and Sciences, Gainesville, FL 32611-9500. **EMAIL** schemlin@classics.ufl.edu

SCHMIDT, JOANNE (JOSEPHINE A.)
PERSONAL Born 06/07/1950, New York, NY, s **DISCIPLINE** FRENCH **EDUCATION** Chestnut Hill Col, AB, 72; Univ Va, MA, 74; PhD, 80. **CAREER** Teaching Asst, Univ Va, 73-76; Teaching Asst Lycee Marie Curie, 76-77; Lecturer, Univ VA, 77079, asst Prof, Cedar Crest Col, 81-84; Asst Prof to Prof and Dept Chair, 84-. **HONORS AND AWARDS** Fulbright-Hays Grant, Paris, 76-77; Grant, Wellesley Col Ctr, 82-84; Performance and Professional Promise Awd, 86-87, 90-91. **MEMBERSHIPS** MLA, AATF, Calif Lang Teachers Asn, Delta Kappa Gamma Intl, NOW, Poets and Writers. **RESEARCH** 19th Century and 20th Century French Literature; Cross-cultural business education, French women writers, Translation; Poetry-writing. **SELECTED PUBLICATIONS** Auth, If There are No More Heroes, There Are Heroines: A feminist Critique of Caravelle's Heroines, 1632-1643, Univ Press of am, 87; auth, Portraits, 91. **CONTACT ADDRESS** Dept Mod Lang & Lit, California State Univ, Bakersfield, 9001 Stockdale Hwy, Bakersfield, CA 93311-1022. **EMAIL** jschmidt@csub.edu

SCHMIDT, SABINE I.
PERSONAL Born Wiesbaden, Germany **DISCIPLINE** GERMAN **EDUCATION** Univ Hamburg, MA, 86; Univ Ark Fayetteville, MFA, 93. **CAREER** Ed, Downtown News, Hamburg, 94-95; vis instr to instr, Rhodes Col, 95-. **HONORS AND AWARDS** Lily Peter Fel, 92-93; Hamburger Forderpresi fur literarische, 00. **MEMBERSHIPS** MLA, Women in German, Am Asn of Teachers of Ger. **RESEARCH** Literary Translation Theory and Practice, Film, Popular Music, 20th Century German Literature and Culture. **SELECTED PUBLICATIONS** Cotransl, of Tobermory und noch ein paar Geschichten by Saki, Deutscher Taschenbuch Verlag, 92; trans, Weight by Henry Rollins, auth, "Heimatworter," 40 Jahre Gastarbeiter, ed K H Meier Braun, auth, Encyclopedia of Contemporary German Culture, ed John Sandford, Encycl of Contemp Ger Cult, 99. **CONTACT ADDRESS** Dept For Lang and Lit, Rhodes Col, 2000 N Parkway, Memphis, TN 38112. **EMAIL** schmidt@rhodes.edu

SCHMIEDEL, DONALD EMERSON
PERSONAL Born 11/21/1939, Kent, OH, m, 1965 **DISCIPLINE** SPANISH **EDUCATION** Kent State Univ, AB, 61; Univ Southern CA, AM, 63, PhD, 66. **CAREER** From lectr to asst prof, 65-73, Assoc Prof Span, Univ Nev, Las Vegas, 73. **MEMBERSHIPS** Am Assoc of Teachers of Span and Port; Assoc for Hispanic Classical Theater; MLA. **RESEARCH** Span Golden Age drama. **SELECTED PUBLICATIONS** Auth, El Conde de Sex (Antonio Coello), a critical edition and study, Plaza Mayor, 72; Coello's debt to Gongora, Bull Comediantes, fall 73. **CONTACT ADDRESS** Dept of Span, Univ of Nevada, Las Vegas, PO Box 455047, Las Vegas, NV 89154-5047.

SCHMIESING, ANN
PERSONAL Born 10/14/1969, Minneapolis, MN, m, 1997 **DISCIPLINE** GERMANIC LANGUAGES & LITERATURE, SLAVIC LANGUAGES **EDUCATION** Willamette Univ, BA, 89; Univ of WA, MA, 91; Cambridge Univ, PhD, 96 **CAREER** Inst, 95-96, Asst Prof, 96-, Univ of Co **HONORS AND AWARDS** Jr Facul Develop Awd, 98; Tiarks Res Grant, 93 **MEMBERSHIPS** Am Asn of Tchrs of German **RESEARCH** Lessing and the Enlightenment; German drama; Scandinavian lit **SELECTED PUBLICATIONS** Auth, Remembering and Forgetting in Miss Sara Sampson, Lessing Yearbook, 95; Showing versus Telling: Johan Falkberget and the Interpretation of Scripture in Den fjerde nattevakt, Scandinavica, 37:1, 98 **CONTACT ADDRESS** Dept of Germanic and Slavic Langs, Univ of Colorado, Boulder, Boulder, CO 80309-0276.

SCHNAPP, JEFFREY
PERSONAL Born 09/22/1954, New York, NY, s **DISCIPLINE** FRENCH, ITALIAN **EDUCATION** Vassar Col, BA, 75; Stanford Univ, PhD, 83. **CAREER** Lecturer, Univ Nice, 76-78; Asst prof, Dartmouth Col, 83-85; Assoc Prof to Prof and chair, 85-. **HONORS AND AWARDS** Ailsa Mellon Bruce Sen Fel, CASVA, 96; Travel Grant, Hewlett Foundation, 95; Fel, Stanford Univ, 93-95; Travel Grant, Hewlett Foundation, 93; Res Grant, Andrew W Mellon Foundation, 92; Fel, Nat Humanities Ctr, 91; Fel, Guggenheim foundation, 91; NEH Fel, 87; Fel, Mabelle McLeod Lewis Foundation, 82; Fulbright Res Fel, 82; Spanish consulate Prize, Vassar Col, 75; Phi Beta Kappa. **MEMBERSHIPS** Am Asn of Italian Studies, Am Asn of Teachers of Italian, Am Boccaccio Asn, am Comparative Literature Asn, Associazione Internazionale di Studi di Lingua e Letteratura Italiana, Dante Soc of Am, Medieval Acad of Am, Mod Lang Asn, Renaissance Soc of Am. **SELECTED PUBLICATIONS** Auth, Staging Fascism: 18BL and The Theater of Masses for Masses, Stanford Univ Press, 96; ed, A Primer of Italian Fascism, Univ Neb Press, 00; ed, Novantiqua (Dign Margins Masks Maneuvers, Late antique to Early Modern), Rio de Janeiro, forthcoming; ed Verso la chiara scienza. Gaetano Ciocca ingegnere-architetto tra fascismo e democrazia, Skira Pub, forthcoming; auth, Un crocerossina americana a Fiume, Venice, forthcoming; auth, cultural and Technological Incubations of fascism," Stanford Humanities Review, 96; co-ed, "Disciplining Literature," Stanford Humanities Review, 98; co-ed, "The athlete's Body," Stanford Humanities Review, 98; auth, "The rebirth of Tragedy," Medieval Theatricality, forthcoming; auth, "1354 - Charles IV meets petrarch in Mantua on the way to his coronation in Rome," in The New History of German Literature, Harvard Univ Press, forthcoming. **CONTACT ADDRESS** Dept French & Italian, Stanford Univ, Stanford, CA 94305. **EMAIL** schnapp@stanford.edu

SCHNAUBER, CORNELIUS
PERSONAL Born 04/18/1939, Freital, Germany, m, 1966, 2 children **DISCIPLINE** GERMAN **EDUCATION** Univ of Hamburg, PhD, 65 **CAREER** Asst Prof, 66-67, Univ ND; Asst Prof, 68-72, Univ So CA; Chmn, 75-84, USC; Dir, 84-, Max Kade Inst; Diction Coach, 92-, Los Angeles Opera **HONORS AND AWARDS** Cross of the Order of Merit of the Fed Rep of Ger, 86 **MEMBERSHIPS** PEN Center London; Soc of Phonetic Sci **RESEARCH** Music theory; opera **SELECTED PUBLICATIONS** Auth, Placido Domingo. Boston: Northeastern Univ Press, 97; Placido Domingo. London: jerome Robson, 97; Die Hausmanns. Eine Hollywood-Chronik, Munchen: ECON, 98 **CONTACT ADDRESS** Max Kade Inst, Univ of So California, Los Angeles, CA 90089-0351.

SCHNEIDER, GERD K.
PERSONAL Born 04/01/1931, Berlin, Germany, m, 1967, 1 child **DISCIPLINE** GERMAN, LINGUISTICS **EDUCATION** Univ BC, BA, 62; Univ Washington, Seattle, MA, 63; PhD, 68. **CAREER** Asst prof to prof, Syracuse Univ, 66-. **HONORS AND AWARDS** New York State of Foreign Language Teachers' Ruth E. Wasley Distinguished Teacher Awd, 82; Teacher of the Year, Col of Arts and Sciences, Syracuse Univ, 84; Certificate of Merit, Oethe Inst, 92; proficiency tester for AATG/Goethe Insts; field reader, US Dept Education; MLA, executive committee, division on the teaching of language; AATG Executive Coun; Board of Dirs, NY State Asn of Foreign Language Teachers. **MEMBERSHIPS** AATG; MLA; Northeast Modern Lang Asn; Am Coun on the Teaching of Foreign Languages; Arthur Schnitzler Res Asn Inst zur Erforschung und Forderungosterreichischer und internationaler Literaturprozesse. **SELECTED PUBLICATIONS** Auth, "Ton- und Schriftsprache in Schnitzlers Fraulein Else und Schumanns Carnaval, Modern Austrian Lit, 2.iii: 17-20 (69); auth, Topical Bibliography in Theoretical and Applied German Linguistics, MLA/ERIC publications Office (72); auth, "Arthur Schnitzler," Dictionary of Literary Biography, Vol 81, Austrian Fiction Writers 1875-1913, eds Donald Daviau/Wolfgang Elfe, pp 272-292, Detroit, MI: Gale Research Co. (89); auth, Die Rezeption von Arthur Schnitzlers reigen 1897-1994, Pressespiegel und andere zeitgenossische Kommentare, Riverside, CA: Aridane Press (95); auth, "Sexual Freedon and Political Repression, An Early Parody of Arthur Schnitzler's Reigen," ed Beate Muller, Amsterdam-Atlanta, GA: Rodopi, pp 223-235 (97); auth, "Anna Mitgutsch's Portrayal of Women: Not only a Feminist Issue," in Out from the Shadows, Essays on Contemporary Austrian Women, ed Margerate Lamb-Faffelberger, Riverside, CA: Aridane Press, pp 111-127 (97). **CONTACT ADDRESS** Dept Languages, Literature, Linguistics, Syracuse Univ, Syracuse, NY 13244-1160. **EMAIL** gkschnei@mailbox.syr.edu

SCHNEIDER, JEFFREY A.
PERSONAL Born 07/07/1963, Erie, PA **DISCIPLINE** GERMAN STUDIES **EDUCATION** Bates Col, BA, 85; Cornell Univ, MA, 92; PhD, 97. **CAREER** Asst prof, Vassar Col, 97-. **HONORS AND AWARDS** DAAD Fel, 92-94. **MEMBERSHIPS** MLA, GSA, WiG, AHA. **RESEARCH** German militarism, gender, sexuality, popular culture, foreign language pedagogy, media studies. **CONTACT ADDRESS** Vassar Col, 124 Raymond Ave, PO Box 501, Poughkeepsie, NY 12604. **EMAIL** jeschneider@vassar.edu

SCHNEIDER, MARSHALL JERROLD
PERSONAL Born 09/21/1942, Bronx, NY **DISCIPLINE** SPANISH LITERATURE **EDUCATION** City Col New York, BA, 62; Univ Conn, MA, 67, PhD, 69. **CAREER** From Asst Prof to Assoc Prof, 67-91, Prof Span, Baruch Col, 91-, Chair, Dept Mod Lang & Comp Lit, 96-; Consult, Holt, Rinehart & Winston & Harper & Row, 70-75, Encycl World Lit 20th Century, 79- & Al-Anon, 81-. **MEMBERSHIPS** Am Asn Teachers Span & Port; AAUP; MLA. **RESEARCH** Novels of Ramon J Sender; studies in literary structure and theory. **SELECTED PUBLICATIONS** Auth, articles on Blasco Ibanez, Buero Vallejo, Casona, Garcia Lorca, Jimenez, In: Encycl of World Literature in the 20th Century, Vols I & II, 81-82; co-ed, Modern Spanish and Portuguese Literature (Libr of Criticism Series), Continum, 88; auth, "Mary S. Vasquez: Ramon J. Sender and His Contemporaries: Essays in Honor of Charles L. King," Altoaragonese, Huesca, Spain and Davidson College, NC; auth of several chapters in: Contexts and Comparisons: A Student Guide to the Great Works Courses, Kendall/Hunt, 91; author of numerous other articles. **CONTACT ADDRESS** Dept of Mod Lang & Comp Lit, Baruch Col, CUNY, 17 Lexington Ave, New York, NY 10010-5518. **EMAIL** marshall_schneider@baruch.cuny.edu

SCHNEIDER, MATTHEW T.
DISCIPLINE ENGLISH AND COMPARATIVE LITERATURE **EDUCATION** Univ CA, Berkeley, BA, 80; Univ Chicago, MA, 82; UCLA, PhD, 91. **CAREER** Lect, Conspiracy Cult Conf, King Alfred's Col, Engl, Jl 98; Interdisciplinary 19th-century Stud Ann Conf, New Orleans, La, Apr 98; UCLA Ctr Stud Rel, Los Angeles, CA, Apr 97; Int Conf on Representations Despair and Desire, Atlanta, GA, Oct 96; Chapman Univy Fac Develop Workshop, Mar 96; Northeast Mod Lang Asn Ann Conv, Boston, MA, Apr 95; Chapman Univ Engl Grad Colloquium, Mar 95; referee, PMLA, Mosaic; ed bd, Anthropoetics. **HONORS AND AWARDS** Fac excellence, Chapman Univ Awd, 97; fac Summer res grant, Chapman Univ, 94; Valerie Scudder Awd, Chapman Univ, 94; fac Summer res grant, Chapman Univ; 93; best essay awd, UCLA grad stud asn, 91; HT Swedenberg dissertation fel, UCLA, 90; grad high Hon & distinction, Univ CA, Berkeley, 80. **MEMBERSHIPS** Colloquium on Violence and Rel; MLA; NAm Soc for the Stud Romanticism; Pac Ancient & Mod Lang Asn; Wordsworth-Coleridge Asn. **SELECTED PUBLICATIONS** Auth, The Sign, The Thing, and Titanic, Chronicles of Love and Resentment 132, Apr, 98; Violent Delights and Violent Ends: Abjection in Oliver Twist, J Asn Interdisciplinary Stud of the Arts 3:1, 97; Writing in the Dust: Irony and Lynch-Law in the Gospel of John, Anthropoetics III,97; Wrung by sweet enforcement: Druid Stones and the Problem of Sacrifice in British Romanticism, Anthropoetics II, 97; Mimetic Polemicism: Rene Girard and Harold Bloom contra the School of Resentment, Anthropoetics II, 96; Romantic Bards and English Composers: The Case of Keats and Holst, Europ Romantic Rev 6, 95; Original Ambivalence: Violence and Autobiography in Thomas De Quincey, Peter Lang Publ, Inc, 95; Sacred Ambivalence: Mimetology in Aristotle, Horace, and Longinus, Anthropoetics I, 95. **CONTACT ADDRESS** Dept of Eng and Comp Lit, Chapman Univ, Orange, CA 92866. **EMAIL** schneide@chapman.edu

SCHNEIDER, ROBERT J.
PERSONAL Born 02/28/1939, Saginaw, MI, m, 1997 **DISCIPLINE** MEDIEVAL STUDIES, RELIGIOUS STUDIES **EDUCATION** Univ of the South, BA, 61; Univ of Notre Dame, MSM, 63, DSM, 65. **CAREER** Asst prof, 65-68, Univ of Southern CA; asst prof, 68, assoc 72, prof, 81, distinguished prof of general studies, 98, Berea Col. **HONORS AND AWARDS** Seabury Awd for Excellence in Teaching, 89; Acorn Awd for excellence in teaching and scholarship, 93; Templeton Found Sci and Relig Course Prize, 97. **MEMBERSHIPS** Medieval Acad of Amer; Soc for Values in Higher Education; Episcopal Church Working Group on Science, Technology, and Faith. **RESEARCH** Issues in science and religion. **SELECTED PUBLICATIONS** Auth, Vincent of Beauvais' Opus universale de statu principis: A Reconstruction of Its History and Contents, in Vincent de Beauvais: intentions et receptions d'une oeuvre encyclopedique au moyen-age, 91; coauth, The Medieval Circulation of the De morali principis institutione of Vincent of Beauvais, Viator, 91; auth, Vincentii belvacensis De morali principis institutione, 95; auth, Vincent of Beauvais, Dominican Author: From Compilatio to Tractatus, in Lector et compilator, Vincent de Beauvais, Frere Precheur: un intellectuel et son milieu au XIIIe siecle, 97. **CONTACT ADDRESS** Dept of Foreign Lang, Berea Col, 113 Tremont Dr, Berea, KY 40403. **EMAIL** robert_schneider@berea.edu

SCHNEIDER, VALERIE LOIS
PERSONAL Born 02/12/1941, Chicago, IL **DISCIPLINE** SPEECH & COMMUNICATION **EDUCATION** Carrol l Col, BA, 63; Univ Wis, Madison, MA, 66; Univ FL, PhD(speech), 69; Appalachian State Univ, cert, 81. **CAREER** Interim asst prof speech, Univ FL, 69-70; asst prof, Edinboro State Col, 70-71; assoc prof, 71-75, prof speech, 75-97, prof emeritus, speech & commun, E TN State Univ, 98-; Danforth assoc, 77. **HONORS AND AWARDS** Best Article Awd, Relig Speech Commun Asn, 76; Finalist, Money Magazine Best Personal Finance Manager in America contest, 94. **MEMBERSHIPS** Speech Commun Asn; Southern Speech Commun Asn; Relig Speech Commun Asn. **RESEARCH** Persuasion; rhetorical criticism; study skills. **SELECTED PUBLICATIONS** Auth, Informal Persuasion Analysis, Speech Teacher, 1/71; Hugh Blair's Theories of Style and Taste, NC J Speech, 12/71; Role-playing and your Local Newspaper, Speech Teacher, 9/71; Parker's Assessment of Webster: Argumentative Synthesis through the Tragic Metaphor, Quart J Speech, 10/78; Mainlining the Handicapped: An Analysis of Butterflies are Free, J Humanics, 12/78; A Process for Self-mastery for Study Habits, J Develop & Remedial Educ, winter 79; Experimental Course Formats, Nat Asn Pub Continuing & Adult Educ Exchange, winter 80; Two Courses for the Price of One: A Study Skills Component for a Speech Communications Course, J Develop & Remedial Educ, spring 82; and various other articles in Speech Communication Teacher, 88-94; writer of Video Visions column, Kingsport Times-News, 84-86; ed, ETSU Evening and Off-Campus newsletter, 86-93. **CONTACT ADDRESS** East Tennessee State Univ, PO Box 23098, Johnson City, TN 37614-0001.

SCHOEPS, KARL H.
PERSONAL Born 12/08/1935, Dinslaken, West Germany, m, 1965 **DISCIPLINE** GERMAN COMPARATIVE LITERATURE **EDUCATION** Bonn Univ, Staatsexam, 62; Univ Wis-Madison, PhD(Ger), 71. **CAREER** Teacher English, Gymnasium Wipperfurth & Wuppertal, Ger, 64-67; teaching asst Ger, Univ Kans, 63-64 & Univ Wis, 67-71; asst prof, Univ Il, 71-76 & Mt Holyoke Col, 77; Assoc Prof Ger, Univ Ill, 77-89; Full Prof Ger, Univ IL, 89-00. **HONORS AND AWARDS** Col of Liberal Arts and Sciences Teaching Award, 99. **MEMBERSHIPS** Am Asn Teachers Ger; Int Brecht Soc. **RESEARCH** Modern German drama; East German literature; Anglo-American and German literary relations, German Studies Association, Literature of the Third Reich. **SELECTED PUBLICATIONS** Co-ed, DDR: Literatur im Tanwetter, Lang, 85; auth, Bertolt Brecht: Life, Work, and Criticism, York, 89; co-ed, Neue Interpretationen von der Aufularung zur Moderne, Lang, 91; auth, Literatur im Dritten Reich, Lang, 92; auth, Intellectuals, unification and Political Change 1990: The Case of Christa Wolf, 1870-71 - 1989-90, German Unifications, 93; auth, Der Lohndrucker Revisited, Miller, 95; auth, Brecht and the Weimar Republic, Brecht Unbound, 95; auth, Brecht's Lehrstudie, in Bertolt Brecht Reference Companion, 97; auth, Erlost von der DDR?: Erlich Loest und die Wende, 97; auth, Zur Kontinuitatder Volkisch-national-konservativen Literatur vov, wahvend un nach 1945: Der Fall Gerhard Schumann, 99; auth, Literatur im Dritten Reich, Weidler, 00. **CONTACT ADDRESS** Dept of Ger Lang & Lit, Univ of Illinois, Urbana-Champaign, 707 S Mathews Ave, Urbana, IL 61801-3625. **EMAIL** schoeps@uiuc.edu

SCHOLES, ROBERT
PERSONAL Born 05/19/1929, Brooklyn, NY **DISCIPLINE** ENGLISH, COMPARATIVE LITERATURE **EDUCATION** Yale Univ, AB, 50; Cornell Univ, MA, 56, PhD, 59. **CAREER** From instr to asst prof English, Univ Va, 59-63; from assoc prof to prof, Univ Iowa, 64-70; Prof English, Brown Univ, 70-; Jr fel, Inst Res Humanities, Univ Wis, 63-64; Guggenheim Found fel, 77-78. **HONORS AND AWARDS** Am Acad Arts & Sci, 98. **MEMBERSHIPS** MLA; NCTE; PEN; Acad Lit Studies; Science Fiction Res Asn. **RESEARCH** Semiotics; composition; modern literature. **SELECTED PUBLICATIONS** Coauth, The Nature of Narrative, 66 & auth, The Fabulators, 67, Oxford Univ; auth, Structuralism in Literature, Yale Univ, 74; coauth, Science Fiction: History, Science, Vision, 77 & Elements of Literature, 78, Oxford Univ; auth, Fabulation and Metafiction, Univ Ill, 79; coauth, The Practice of Writing, St Martin's, 81; auth, Semiotics and Interpretation, Yale Univ, 82; auth, Textual Power, Yale Univ, 85; auth, Protocols of Reading, Yale Univ, 89; co-auth, Hemingway's Genders, Yale Univ, 94; auth, The Rise and Fall of English, Yale Univ, 98. **CONTACT ADDRESS** ENGLISH, Brown Univ, MCM Box 1957, Providence, RI 02912-9127. **EMAIL** Robert_Scholes@brown.edu

SCHOLES, ROBERT JAMES
PERSONAL Born 08/15/1932, Ft Wayne, IN, m, 1962, 2 children **DISCIPLINE** LINGUISTICS **EDUCATION** Ind Univ, AB, 57, PhD(ling), 64. **CAREER** Teacher high sch, Ind, 57-59; from instr to asst prof ling, Ind Univ, 61-66; from asst prof speech to assoc prof speech & ling, 67-76, Prof Speech & Ling, Univ Fla, 76-, Mem res staff speech synthesis, Int Bus Machines Res Lab, Calif, 63-65. **MEMBERSHIPS** Ling Soc Am; Ling Circle NY; Asn Machine Transl & Computational Ling. **RESEARCH** Language production and perception in children and adults; psycholinguistics. **SELECTED PUBLICATIONS** Coauth, Spoken Tunisian Arabic, Peace Corps, 66; auth, Phonotactic Grammaticality, Mouton, 67; The categorization of synthetic speech sounds as a predictive device in language teaching, J Eng Second Lang, 2/67; Categorial responses to synthetic vocalic stimuli by speakers of various languages, Lang & Speech, 10/67; Syllable segmentation and identification, Linguistics. **CONTACT ADDRESS** Dept of Speech & Ling, Univ of Florida, 335 J Manning Dauer, Gainesville, FL 32611-9500.

SCHONBERGER, VINCENT L.
DISCIPLINE FRENCH LANGUAGE AND LITERATURE **EDUCATION** Univ Ottawa, PhD. **CAREER** Assoc prof, Lakehead Univ, 86-. **HONORS AND AWARDS** Legal interpreter, Min of the Atty Gen of On. **MEMBERSHIPS** Mem, Aesthetics Soc of Can. **RESEARCH** French-Canadian novel, literary works of Gabrielle Roy. **SELECTED PUBLICATIONS** Auth, "The Problem of Language and the Difficulty of Writing in the Literary Works of Gabrielle Roy," Stud in Can Lit, 89; "Tentatives d'evasion dans Huis clos," Proc of the Sartre Soc of Can, 90; Alexandre Chenevert: Un recit pluricodique, Portes de communication, Etudes discursives et stylistiques de l'oeuvre de Gabrielle Roy, Pres de l'Univ Laval, 95; Strategies de demythification du discours ideologique dans Alexandre Chenevert, Actes du Colloque Intl Gabrielle Roy, Pres Univ de Saint-Boniface, 96. **CONTACT ADDRESS** Dept of Lang, Lakehead Univ, 955 Oliver Rd, Thunder Bay, ON, Canada P7B 5E1. **EMAIL** VLSCHONB@Mist.Lakeheadu.Ca

SCHOOLFIELD, GEORGE C.
PERSONAL Born 08/14/1925, Charleston, WV, m, 1949 **DISCIPLINE** GERMANIC LANGUAGES & LITERATURES **EDUCATION** Univ Cincinnati, BA, 46, MA, 47; Princeton Univ, PhD(Ger), 49. **CAREER** Instr Ger, 49-52, tutor hist & lit, Harvard Univ, 50-52; from asst prof to assoc prof Ger lang, Univ Buffalo, 52-59; assoc prof Ger, Duke Univ, 59-61; prof Ger & Scand & head dept, Univ Cincinnati, 61-64; prof Ger lang & lit, Univ Pa, 64-69; Prof Ger & Scand Lit, Yale Univ, 69-, Fulbright res fel, Austria, 52-53, Finland, 67-68, US Educ Found, Finland, 72; Guggenheim fcl, Sweden, 55-56; managing ed, Scand Studies, 69-73, rev ed, 73-; vis prof Ger lit, Univ Fla, 71; grad ctr, City Univ New York, 71-72. **MEMBERSHIPS** Rilke Soc; Acad Lit Studies; Am Coun Studies Austrian Lit; MLA; Am Asn Teachers Ger. **RESEARCH** German Scandinavian literary relations; recent German and Scandinavian literature. **SELECTED PUBLICATIONS** Auth, 'Ditt Hjarta Fargar Din Ros' - A Novel About Almqvist,Carl,Jonas,Love And His Times - Swedish - Stigsjoo,S/, World Lit Today, Vol 0066, 1992; 'Hid' - Agren,G/, World Lit Today, Vol 0067, 1993; 'Berattelser Om Mig Och Andra' - Hulden,L/, World Lit Today, Vol 0067, 1993; 'Sormenjalkia Tyhjassa' - Holappa,P/, World Lite Today, Vol 0067, 1993; 'Psalmer For Trolosa Kristna' - Hulden,L/, World Lit Today, Vol 0067, 1993; 'Arnaia Kastad I Havet' - Tikkanen,M/, World Lit Today, Vol 0067, 1993; A Lexicon Of Rhetoric - Norwegian - Eide,T/, Ger Notes And Rev, Vol 0025, 1994; 'I Det Sedda' - Swedish - Carpelan,B/, World Lit Today, Vol 0070, 1996; 'Tanten Och Krokodilen' - Swedish - Mazzarella,M/, World Lit Today, Vol 0070, 1996; Rilke,Rainer,Maria Correspondence With Key,Ellen - Ger - Fiedler,T, Rilke,Rm/, Scandinavian Studies, Vol 0068, 1996; Collected Poems, Vols 1 And 2 - Swedish - Columbus,S/, Scandinavian Studies, Vol 0069, 1997; Olsson,Hagar And Growing Melancholia - Her Life And Writings 1945-1978 - Swedish - Holmstrom,R/, Ger Notes And Revs, Vol 0028, 1997. **CONTACT ADDRESS** Dept of Ger Lang & Lit, Yale Univ, New Haven, CT 06520.

SCHOVILLE, KEITH NORMAN
PERSONAL Born 03/03/1928, Soldiers Grove, WI, 5 children **DISCIPLINE** HEBREW, BIBLICAL STUDIES **EDUCATION** Milligan Col, BA, 56; Univ Wis-Madison, MA, 66, PhD(Hebrew & Semitic studies), 69. **CAREER** From instr to asst prof, 68-74, assoc prof, 74-81, chmn dept, 77-82, Prof Hebrew & Semitic Studies, Univ Wis-Madison, 81-95, Emer, 95. **MEMBERSHIPS** Am Orient Soc, Soc Biblical Lit, Am Schs Orient Res, Nat Asn Prof Hebrew (secy); Archaeol Inst Am, Near East Archaeol Soc. **RESEARCH** The human factor in archaeology; literary and historical illumination of biblical literature; the Intertestamental Period. **SELECTED PUBLICATIONS** Auth, Bab-Edh-Dhra - Excavations In The Cemetery Directed By Lapp,Paul,W 1965-67 - Schaub,Rt, Rast,Pw/, J Of The Am Oriental Soc, Vol 0112, 1992; auth, The Canaanites Peoples of the Old Testament World, 94. **CONTACT ADDRESS** 5689 County Hwy D, Oregon, WI 53575. **EMAIL** knschovi@facstaff.wisc.edu

SCHOW, WAYNE
DISCIPLINE COMPARATIVE LITERATURE **EDUCATION** Univ Iowa, PhD, 70. **CAREER** Prof. **RESEARCH** Scandinavian literature; literature and religion. **SELECTED PUBLICATIONS** Auth, Remembering Brad: On the Loss of a Son to AIDS; co-ed, Peculiar People: Mormons and Same Sex Orientation. **CONTACT ADDRESS** Dept of English and Philosophy, Idaho State Univ, Pocatello, ID 83209. **EMAIL** schowayn@isu.edu

SCHRADER, DOROTHY LYNNE
PERSONAL Born 08/13/1947, Pensacola, FL, 1 child **DISCIPLINE** FRENCH **EDUCATION** Agnes Scott Col, BA, 69; Middlebury Col, MA, 71; Univ Paris III, lic es lett, 74; Fla State Univ, PhD(Fr), 76. **CAREER** Asst prof French, Southern Ill Univ, Edwardsville, 76-77; asst prof, 77-82, assoc Prof French, Okla State Univ, 82-, lectr English, Ecole Nat Admin, Paris & Inst Nat Agronomique, Paris, 72-74. **MEMBERSHIPS** MLA; Societe Rencesvals; Mid-America Medieval Asn; Southeastern Medieval Asn. **RESEARCH** Women protagonists in the French Medieval epics; Parise la Duchesse, critical edition; Le Dit de l'Unicorne, critical edition. **SELECTED PUBLICATIONS** Coauth, Teaching the Basics in the Foreign Language Classroom: Options and Strategies, Nat Textbk Co, 79. **CONTACT ADDRESS** Dept of Foreign Lang, Oklahoma State Univ, Stillwater, Stillwater, OK 74078-0002. **EMAIL** schrade@okstate.edu

SCHRADER, RICHARD J.
PERSONAL Born Paris, France, m, 1972, 2 children **DISCIPLINE** FRENCH LITERATURE **EDUCATION** Univ Calif, Los Angeles BA, MA, PhD, 70. **CAREER** Teaching asst, Univ Calif, Los Angeles; instr, asst prof, assoc prof, prof of French, Pomona Coll. **HONORS AND AWARDS** Regents Fel, Univ Calif, Los Angeles; Wig Awd for Best Teacher, Pomona Coll. **MEMBERSHIPS** Am Assoc of Teacher of France; Modern Language Assoc. **RESEARCH** 20th Century Women Writers; 20th Century Poetry. **SELECTED PUBLICATIONS** Auth, "L'ecriture: lien de mere a fille chez Jeanne Hyvrard, Chantal Chawaf et Annie Ernaux," Amsterdam: Rodopi, (00); auth, "The Feminist Encyclopedia of French Literature," Greenwood Press (99); auth "The Discovery of Light in Chawaf's Black Coat," Chantal Chawaf's Newsletter (98); auth, Recyclage urbain chez Annie Ernaux," Foreign Literature Series, Vol. XXIV (97): 141-151; auth, "Chantal Chawaf. Comment peut-on creer un nouveau langage feminin aujourd'hui," Thirty Voices in the Feminine, Michael Bishop, contirbutor, Rodopi (96): 65-76; auth, "L'Oppresson maternelle et salut par l'ecriture dans La jeune Morte en robe de dentelle" de Jeanne Hyvrard, in Collana di letterature moderne et contemporanee, Edizoni Scientifiche Italiane, Uniersita degli Studi Perugia, mai-juin(95): 633-649. Rev, "Issa" de Chantal Chawaf in The French Review, Vol 74 (00); rev, "Le manteau noir" de Chantal Chawaf in The French Review, Vol. 72. No. 4. (Mar 99); rev, "Jeanne Hyvrard: Theorist of the Modern World" by Jennifer Waelti-Walters, in The French Review, Vol 71. No. 3. (Feb 98); rev, "Vers la Lumiere by Chantal Chawaf" in The French Review, Vol. 69, No. 1. (Oct 95). **CONTACT ADDRESS** Dept Romance Lang, Pomona Col, 550 Harvard Ave, Mason Hall, Claremont, CA 91711-4429.

SCHRAIBMAN, JOSEPH
PERSONAL Born 09/29/1935, Havana, Cuba, m, 1963 **DISCIPLINE** SPANISH, COMPARATIVE LITERATURE **EDUCATION** Brooklyn Col, BA, 55; Univ Ill, MA, 56, PhD, 59. **CAREER** From instr to asst prof Romance lang, Princeton Univ, 59-65, bicentennial preceptor, 63-65; assoc prof Span & Port, Ind Univ, Bloomington, 65-69; chmn dept, 72-78, Prof Romance Lang, Wash Univ, 69-, Am Coun Learned Soc grant-in-aid, 62-63; Fulbright res grant, Spain 62-63; consult, Educ Testing Serv Advan Placement Exam; chmn, Comt Advan Placement & consult cd, Xerox Publ Co, 65-; Danforth teaching assoc, 68; mem exec comt, Bks Abroad, 71-74; Mellon fel, Univ Pittsburgh-, 75-; Fulbright travel, 80, Spanish Gov't Grant, 91; Kemper Teaching Awaros, 91, 01. **HONORS AND AWARDS** Fulbright Travel, 80; Spanish Gov't Grant, 91; Kemper Teaching Awds, 91, 01. **MEMBERSHIPS** MLA; Am Asn Teachers Span & Port; Am Asn Teachers Fr. **RESEARCH** Stylistics; Galdos; Clarin; literature and history: the inquisition spanish civil war Norrt. **SELECTED PUBLICATIONS** Auth, Dreams in the Novels of Galdos, Hisp Inst, 60; coauth, Cartas del archivo de Galdos, 67 & Cartas a Galdos, 68, Taurus, Madrid; ed & contrib, Homenaje a Sherman H Eoff, Castalia, 70; auth, Las Citas biblicas en Misericordia de Galdos, Cuadernos Hipanoam, 10/70-1/71; coauth, Estructura simbolica de El jarama, Homenaje a Edumundo de Chasca, Philol Quart, 72; auth, Espacio histoco literario en Espacio Gerona, Am Hisp, 11/76; Tiempo de silencio y la cura siquiatrica de un pueblo, Insula, 3/77; Tiempo de destruccion, Revista lbero en Espacio Gerona, Am Hisp, 11/76; Tiempo de silencio y la cura siquiatrica de un pueblo, Insula, 3/77; Tiempo de sdestruccion, ReVista lbero Americana, 7-12/81; Benito Perez Galdos, Los articulos politicos en la revista de Espana, 1871-1872, 82; auth, "Galas del canon euteuodo," Univ of Borselons Aetas, 01. **CONTACT ADDRESS** 10 Pricewoods Lane, Saint Louis, MO 63132. **EMAIL** jschraib@artsci.wusti.edu

SCHRIBER, MARY SUZANNE
PERSONAL Born 09/22/1938, Muskegon, MI **DISCIPLINE** COMPARATIVE LITERATURE **EDUCATION** Mich State Univ, BS, 60, MA, 63, PhD, 67. **CAREER** From Asst Prof to Prof, 67-96, Distinguished Teaching Prof English, Nothern Ill Univ, 96-. **MEMBERSHIPS** MLA; Midwest Mod Lang Asn; Edith Wharton Soc; ALA. **RESEARCH** Edith Wharton; 19th century American literature; feminist criticism; travel writing by women. **SELECTED PUBLICATIONS** Auth, Isabel Archer and Victorian manners, Studies Novel, winter 76; Anderson in France: 1919-1939, Twentieth Century Lit, 2/77; Bringing chaos to order: The novel tradition and Kurt Vonnegut, Genre, summer 77; Darwin, Wharton, and the descent of man: Blueprints of American society, Studies in Short Fiction, winter 80; Edith Wharton and the French critics, 1906-1937, Am Lit Realism, spring 80; Toward Daisy Miller: Cooper's idea of the American girl, Studies in the Novel, fall 81; Justice to Zenobia, New England Quart, 3/82; Gender and the Writer's Imagination, 87; Telling Travels, 95; Writing Home: American Women Abroad, 1830-1920, 97. **CONTACT ADDRESS** Dept of English, No Illinois Univ, De Kalb, IL 60115-2825. **EMAIL** mschriber@niu.edu

SCHROEDER, FREDERIC M.
PERSONAL Born 12/19/1937, Ottawa, ON, Canada, m, 1984 **DISCIPLINE** CLASSICS **EDUCATION** Univ Toronto, BA, 61; MA, 64; PhD, 70. **CAREER** Lectr to prof, Queen's Univ, 66-. **HONORS AND AWARDS** Res Grant, German Acad Exchange Serv, 82; Can Coun Leave Fel, 74-75. **MEMBERSHIPS** Class Asn of Can; Ont Class Asn; Can Soc for Neoplatonic Studies; Am Soc for Neoplatonic Studies; Soc Aristotelica Jannone. **RESEARCH** Ancient Philosophy; Neoplatonism; Late Aristotelianism. **SELECTED PUBLICATIONS** Coauth, Two Greek Aristotelian Commentators on the Intellect, Toronto, 90; auth, Form and Transformation. A Study in the Philosophy of Plotinus, Queen's Press, 92; auth, "Plotinus and Language", in Cambridge Companion to Plotinus, (Cambridge Univ Press, 96), 336-355; auth, "Prophecy and Remembrance in Plotinus," Colloquium, (96): 1-22; auth, "Plotinus and Aristotle on the good Life," in The Perennial Tradition of Neoplatonism, (Leuven Univ Press, 97), 207-220; **CONTACT ADDRESS** Dept Class, Queen's Univ at Kingston, 99 University Ave, Kingston, ON, Canada K7L 3N6. **EMAIL** schroedr@post.queensu.ca

SCHUBERT, VIRGINIA ANN
PERSONAL Born 10/15/1935, St. Paul, MN, s **DISCIPLINE** FRENCH LANGUAGE & LITERATURE **EDUCATION** Col St Catherine, St Paul, Minn, BA, 57; Univ Minn, Minneapolis, MA, 63, PhD(French), 74. **CAREER** Instr French, Col St Catherine, 58-60; teacher, Alexander Ramsey High Sch, Roseville, 61-65; Prof French, Ch, Macalester Col, 65- **HONORS AND AWARDS** Chevalier Ordre des Palmes Academiques, French govt, 75; Officer Ordre des Palmes Academiques, Fr Govt, 94. **MEMBERSHIPS** MLA; Am Asn Teachers French; Am Coun Teachers Foreign Lang. **RESEARCH** Nineteenth century French literature; humanities, especially nineteenth century France. **SELECTED PUBLICATIONS** Coauth, Le Nouveau Passe-Muraille, Prentice-Hall, 70. **CONTACT ADDRESS** Dept of French, Macalester Col, 1600 Grand Ave, Saint Paul, MN 55105-1899. **EMAIL** schubert@macalester.edu

SCHUHL, MARK
PERSONAL Born 12/05/1967, Camden, NJ **DISCIPLINE** SPANISH **EDUCATION** BA, 90, MA, 93, PhD, 99, Univ Penn **CAREER** Visting Asst Prof, 96-97, Asst Prof, Fort Hays State Univ, 97-99; asst prof, Wingate Univ, 99- . **HONORS AND AWARDS** Andrew W. Mellon Dissertation Fel, Univ Penn, 95-96; Univ Fel, Univ Penn, 94-95; Andre W. Mellon Summer Award, Univ Penn, 99. **MEMBERSHIPS** MLA; AATSP **RESEARCH** 19th and 20th Century Latin American Literature **CONTACT ADDRESS** Dept of For Langs, Wingate Univ, PO Box 3059, Wingate, NC 28174. **EMAIL** mschuhl@wingate.edu

SCHULTZ, JOSEPH P.
PERSONAL Born 12/02/1928, Chicago, IL, m, 1955, 3 children **DISCIPLINE** JEWISH STUDIES, RELIGION **EDUCA-**

TION Yeshiva Univ, BA, 51; Jewish Theol Sem, MHL, 55; Brandeis Univ, PhD, 62. **CAREER** Lectr foreign lang, Boston Univ, 63-64, instr foreign lang, 64-68, asst prof relig, 68-73; assoc prof hist, 73-78, Oppenstein Bros Distinguished Prof Judaic Studies, Univ MO-Kansas City, 78-, Dir Judiac Studies Prog, 73-, dir Center for Relig Studies, 95; Res grant, Grad Sch Arts & Sci, Boston Univ, 71-72. **HONORS AND AWARDS** Hyman G Enelow Awd, Jewish Theol Sem, 76. **MEMBERSHIPS** Asn Jewish Studies; Am Acad Relig. **RESEARCH** Comparative religion; Jewish studies. **SELECTED PUBLICATIONS** Auth, Angelic opposition to the ascension of Moses and the revelation of the law, Jewish Quart Rev, 71; The religious psychology of Jonathan Edwards and the Hasidic Masters of Habad, J Ecumenical Studies, 73; The Lurianic strand in Jonathan Edwards' Concept of Progress, Judaica, 74; Reciprocity in confucian and Rabbinic ethics, J Relig Ethics, 74; contribr, Studies and Texts in Honor of Nahum Glatzer, Brill, 75; auth, From My Father's Vineyard, Vile-Goller, 78; co-ed, From Destruction to Rebirth: The Holocaust and the State of Israel, Univ Am, 78; auth, Judaism and The Gentile Faiths; Comparative Studies in Religion, Fairleigh Dickinson Univ, 78; Mid-America's Promise: A Profile of Kansas City Jewry, Am Jewish Hist Soc, 82; ed, Ze'enah U-Re'enah: Book of Genesis, Dropsie Col, 85; Sinai and Olympus: A Comarative Study with Lois S. Spatz, Univ Press of Am, 95. **CONTACT ADDRESS** Naropa Inst, 2130 Arapahoe Ave., Boulder, CO 80302.

SCHULTZE, SYDNEY
PERSONAL Born 01/20/1943, Louisville, KY, m, 1974, 2 children **DISCIPLINE** RUSSIAN STUDIES **EDUCATION** Univ Louisville, BA, 65; Indiana Univ, MA, 68, PhD, 74. **CAREER** Prof, Univ of Louisville, 70-; vis asst prof, Indiana Univ, 74-75. **HONORS AND AWARDS** Arts and Sciences Teaching Awd; Metroversity Teaching Awd; Distinguished Teaching Prof. **MEMBERSHIPS** AATSEEL; AAASS; AWSS; ACTR; SCSS; MRI. **RESEARCH** Russian literature and culture, detective fiction. **SELECTED PUBLICATIONS** Auth, Structure of Anna Karina; ed, Meyerhold the Director, auth, Culture and Customs of Russia. **CONTACT ADDRESS** Dept Mod Class Lang, Univ of Louisville, 3601 Sudbury Ln, Louisville, KY 40220. **EMAIL** sydney.schultze@louisville.edu

SCHULZ, RENATE A.
PERSONAL Born 02/24/1940, Lohr/Main, Germany, d, 1 child **DISCIPLINE** GERMAN STUDIES, SECOND LANGUAGE ACQUISITION **EDUCATION** Mankato State Coll, BS, 62; Univ Co, MA, 67; Oh State Univ, PhD, 74. **CAREER** Asst prof, Otterbein Col, 74-76; asst prof, SUNY, Buffalo, 76-77; asst, assoc prof, Univ AR, 77-81; prof Univ AZ, 81-. **HONORS AND AWARDS** Creative Tchg Awd, 84 Univ Az; ACTFL's Florence Steiner Awd, 93; Verdienstkreuz erster Klasse, 90, Federal Republic Germany; J. William Fulbright Fel, 97. **MEMBERSHIPS** AAAL; AATG; ACTFL; MLA; ATTF; AATSP; TESOL; Az Foreign Lang Asn. **RESEARCH** Second language acquisition; foreign language learning and teaching; testing and evaluation; foreign language teacher development. **SELECTED PUBLICATIONS** Co-auth, Im Kontext: Lesebuch zur Landdskunde, Holt, Rinehart, and Winston, 90; auth, "Second Language Acquistion Theories and Teaching Practice: How Do They Fit?," Modern Lang Jour, 91; "Profile of the Profession: Results of the 1992 AATG Membership Survey," Unterrichtspraxis, 93; co-auth, "Beer, Fast Cars, and . . .: Stereotypes Held by US College-Level Students of German," Unterrichtspraxis, 95; auth, "Focus on Form in the Foreign Language Classroom: Students and Teachers Views on Error Correction and the Role of Grammar," For Lang Annals, 96. **CONTACT ADDRESS** Dept of German Studies, Univ of Arizona, Tucson, AZ 85721-0067. **EMAIL** schulzr@u.arizona.edu

SCHURLKNIGHT, DONALD E.
DISCIPLINE SPANISH LANGUAGE & LITERATURE **EDUCATION** Duke Univ, BA, 69; Univ Pa, MA, 71, PhD, 75. **CAREER** Lectr, Rosemont Col, 72-76; prof, Wayne St Univ, 76- . **HONORS AND AWARDS** Fulbright Fel, Coun for Int Exchange of Scholars; Amer Philos Soc Grant. **MEMBERSHIPS** AATSP; MLA. **RESEARCH** Spanish romanticism; Spanish eighteenth & nineteenth centuries lit. **SELECTED PUBLICATIONS** Auth, Some Forgotten Poetry by Larra, Romance Notes, 89; Romantic Literary Theory as Seen Through Post-Fernandine Periodicals: El Correo de las Damas, Rivista de Estudios Hispanicos, 91; Spanish Romanticism and Mannerism: Pedro de Madrazo, Critica Hispanica, 92; La conjuracion de Venecia , Revista de Estudios Hispanicos, 98; Spanish romanticism in Context: Of Subversion, Contradiction and Politics, Univ Press Amer, 98. **CONTACT ADDRESS** Dept of Romance Lang & Lit, Wayne State Univ, 487 Manoogian Hall, Detroit, MI 48202. **EMAIL** D.Schurlknight@wayne.edu

SCHUSTER, MARILYN R.
PERSONAL Born 09/23/1943, Washington, DC **DISCIPLINE** FRENCH, WOMEN'S STUDIES **EDUCATION** Mills Coll, BA, Fr, 65; Yale Univ, PhD, Fr Lang & Lit, 73. **CAREER** Instr, Sonoma Sate Col, 67; tchg assoc, Yale Univ, 67068; instr, Yale Summer Lang Inst, 70; instr, Fordham Univ-Lincoln Center, 70-71; from isntr to prof Fr & women's stud, Smith Col, 71-; dean, Smith Col, 81-83; dir, Women's Stud Prog, Smith Coll, 86-87; assoc dean of faculty, Smith Col, 87-90; ch, Fr dept, Smith Col, 92-95. **MEMBERSHIPS** MLA; NWSA. **RESEARCH** 20th century women's fiction in France & England; gay/lesbian/queer studies **SELECTED PUBLICATIONS** Co-ed, Women's Place in the Academy: Transforming the Liberal Arts Curriculum, Rowman & Allanheld, 85; Marguerite Duras Revisited, MacMillan publ, 93; "The Gendered Politics of Knowledge: Lessons from the US," Asian Women, 96; "Inscribing a Lesbian Reader, Projecting a Lesbian Subject: A Jane Rule Diptych," The Jour of Homosexuality, Gay & Lesbian Lit Since World War II: His & Memory, 98; Passionate Communities: Reading Lesbian Resistance in Jene Rule's Fiction, NYork Univ Pr, 99. **CONTACT ADDRESS** Neilson Libr, Smith Col, Northampton, MA 01063. **EMAIL** mschuste@smith.edu

SCHUTZ, ALBERT J.
PERSONAL Born 08/09/1936, Mishawaka, IN **DISCIPLINE** LINGUISTICS **EDUCATION** Purdue Univ, BS, 58; Cornell Univ, PhD, 62. **CAREER** From asst prof to assoc prof, 62-72, prof Ling, Univ Hawaii, Manoa, 72-, prin investr, NSF Grant, Nguna, New Hebrides Lexicography, 69-70; dir, Fijian Dictionary Proj, 71-79; prin investr, Prof, Emer, 99-. **HONORS AND AWARDS** Nat Endowment for Humanities res grant, 78-80; **MEMBERSHIPS** Ling Soc Am; Polynesian Soc. **RESEARCH** Malayo-Polynesian linguistics; lexicography. **SELECTED PUBLICATIONS** Coauth, Spoken Fijian, Univ Hawaii, 71; auth, The Languages of Fiji, Clarendon, Oxford, 72; Say it in Fijian, Pac Publ, Sydney, 72; ed, The Diaries and Correspondence of David Cargill, 1832-1843, Australian Nat Univ, 77; auth, Suva: A History and Guide, Pac Publ, 78; ed, Fijian Language Studies: Borrowing and Pidginization, Fiji Mus, 78; auth, Fijian Grammar for Teachers of Fijian, Univ SPac, Suva, 79; co-ed, David Cargill's Fijian Grammar, Fiji Mus, 80; The Fijian Language, Univ Hawaii, 85; The Voices of Eden: A History of Hawaiian Language Studies, Univ Hawaii, 94; All about Hawaiian, Univ Hawaii, 95; Things Hawaiian: A Pocket Guide to the Hawaiian Language, Island Heritage, 97; Hawaiianisch, Abera, 98. **CONTACT ADDRESS** Dept of Linguistics, Univ of Hawaii, Manoa, 1890 E West Rd, Honolulu, HI 96822-2318. **EMAIL** schultz@hawaii.edu

SCHWALLER, JOHN
PERSONAL Born 07/02/1948, Aays, KS, m, 1970, 2 children **DISCIPLINE** COLONIAL LATIN AMERICAN HISTORY AND LITERATURE **EDUCATION** Grinnell Col, BA, 69; Univ Kans, MA, 71; Ind Univ, PhD, 78. **CAREER** Assoc instr, Univ of Kans, 69-71; teaching asst, Ind Univ, 73-74; instr, Ind Univ, 74 & 77; asst prof, Hays State Univ, 78-79; asst prof to assoc prof, Fla Atlantic Univ, 79-86; coord of Curriculum in Latin Am Studies, Fla Atlantic Univ, 79-93; acting chemn dept of hist, Fla Atlantic Univ, 84 & 88; vis prof, Inst Nac de Antropologia e Hist, 85-86; prof, Fla Atlantic Univ, 86-93; asst dean of col of humanities, Fla Atlantic Univ, 89-90; assoc dean of The Schmidt Col of Arts and Humanities, Fla Atlantic Univ, 90-93; acting chemn dept of lang and ling, Fla Atlantic Univ, 90, 92, & 93; adj prof, Regional Sem of St Vincent de Paul, 90-93; vis scholar, Franciscan Sch of Theol, 93-95; dir of Acad of Am Franciscan Hist, Franciscan Sch of Theol, 93-; assoc provost and assoc vpres for Academic Affairs, Univ of Mont, 95-; prof of hist, Univ of Montana, 95-. **HONORS AND AWARDS** Benito Juarez-Abraham Lincoln Fel, Mexican Secretaria de Relaciones Exteriores, 75-76; res fel, Org of Am States, 76-77; James A. Woodburn Fel, Ind Univ, 77; Am Philos Soc Res Grant, 82; Newberry Libr Associates' Fel, 82; Fla Atlantic Univ Seed Grant, 80-81 & 82; NEH summer sem, 80 & 84; Fac Equipment Grant, Fla Atlantic Univ, 83; Andrew W. Mellon Fel, Tulane Univ Libr, 83; Fulbright-Hays Fel, U.S. Dept of Educ, 82-83; Libr Development Awd for Res, Univ of Fla, 84; Distinguished Teacher of the Year, Fla Atlantic Univ, 83-84; Tinker Postdoctoral Fel, Tinker Found, 84-86; res grants, NEH, 89-90 & 93-95; listed in Who's Who in the South and Southwest; listed in Who's Who in the West; distinguished adminr, Univ of Mont, 99-00. **MEMBERSHIPS** AHA, CLAH, RMCLAS, ACHA. **RESEARCH** 16th Century Latin America. **SELECTED PUBLICATIONS** Auth, Partidos y parrocos bajo la real corona en la Nueva Espana siglo XVI, Inst Nac de Antropologia e Hist (Mexico), 81; auth, Origins of Church Wealth in Mexico: Ecclesiastical Finances and Church Revenues 1523-1600, Univ of NMex Press (Albuquerque, NM) 85; auth, The Church and Clergy in Sixteenth-Century Mexico, Univ of NMex Press (Albuquerque, NM), 87; co-ed, A Guide to Confession Large and Small in the Mexican Language (1634), Univ of Okla Press, 99; auth, "Encoded Behaviors: Society, the Church, and Cultural History in Early Colonial Latin America," Latin Am Res Rev (99): 246-270; auth, The Church in Colonial Hispanic America: A Reader, forthcoming; auth, "Don Luis de Velasco," Guide to Documentary Sources for Andean Art and Archeology, Nat Gallery of Art (Washington, DC), forthcoming; auth, "Don Luis de Velasco" and "Archives and Libraries," Oxford Encycl of Mesoamerican Cultures, Oxford Univ Press (New York), forthcoming; auth, "Juan de Zumarraga" and "Inquisition: New World," Encycl of the Renaissance, Charles Scribner's Sons (New York), forthcoming. **CONTACT ADDRESS** Office of the Provost, Univ of Montana, Missoula, MT 59812. **EMAIL** schwallr@selway.umt.edu

SCHWARTZ, JEROME
PERSONAL Born 02/10/1935, New York, NY, m, 1959, 2 children **DISCIPLINE** FRENCH LITERATURE **EDUCATION** Columbia Univ, BA, 56, MA, 60, PhD(French), 65. **CAREER** Asst English, Lycee Henri IV, Paris, 56-57; instr French, Columbia Col, Columbia Univ, 60-65; Prof French, Univ Pittsburgh, 89-97; Prof Emer, 97-. **MEMBERSHIPS** MLA; RSA. **RESEARCH** Sixteenth and 18th century French literature. **SELECTED PUBLICATIONS** Auth, Diderot and Montaigne: The Essais and the shaping of Diderot's humanism, Librairie Droz, 66; auth, Irony and Ideology in Rabelais: Structures of Subversion, Cambridge Univ Press, 90. **CONTACT ADDRESS** 2031 Locust St, Apt 1901, Philadelphia, PA 19103. **EMAIL** schw@pitt.edu

SCHWARTZWALD, ROBERT
DISCIPLINE FRENCH LITERATURE **EDUCATION** Laval Univ, PhD. **CAREER** Prof, Univ MA Amherst. **RESEARCH** Lit and cult of Quebec; cult studies, espec issues of nationalism, gender, and identity in France; francophone world. **SELECTED PUBLICATIONS** Auth, Fictions de l'identitaire au Quebec; The Brown Plague, Travels in Late Weimar and Early Nazi Germany (rev); ed, Quebec Studies. **CONTACT ADDRESS** Dept of French and Italian Studies, Univ of Massachusetts, Amherst, Mass Ave, Amherst, MA 01003. **EMAIL** rss@frital.umass.edu

SCHWARZ, E.
PERSONAL Born 08/08/1922, Vienna, Austria, m, 1950, 3 children **DISCIPLINE** GERMAN LITERATURE **EDUCATION** Univ Wash, Seattle. **CAREER** Harvard Univ, 54-61; Wash Univ, 61-93; prof emer, Rosa May Distinguished Univ. **HONORS AND AWARDS** Joseph von Eichendorff medal; Austrian medal of art und science; honorary dr of philos, Univ Vienna; Humboldt Scholar prize. **MEMBERSHIPS** Modern Lang Asn; Amer Asn of Tchrs of Ger; Austrian Asn of Ger. **RESEARCH** European literature; History of Jews in modern times. **SELECTED PUBLICATIONS** Literatur aus vier Kulturer: Essays und Bespreslusyer, Vandenhoech & Ruprecht Gotinger, 87; Veine Jeit fur Eichlendorff: Chronik unfreiusliger Wanderjerher, Buchergilde Gutenberg Frankfurt, 92; Dratung, Kulik, Geschilte, Essays aur Literatur 1900-1950, Vandenhoech & Ruprecht Gotinger, 83; Poetry and Politics in the Works of Rainer Maria Rolke, Unger, NY, 81; Das Verschluchte Schluchtan: Poesic und Politik bir Rainer Maria Rilke, 72; Joseph von Eichendorff, Twayne, 72; Hofrueniusthal und Calderon, Harvard Univ Press, 62. **CONTACT ADDRESS** 1036 Oakland Av., Saint Louis, MO 63122.

SCHWEITZER, CHRISTOPH EUGEN
PERSONAL Born 07/11/1922, Berlin, Germany, m, 1949, 2 children **DISCIPLINE** GERMAN **EDUCATION** Univ Wis, MA(Span), 49, MA(Ger), 50; Yale Univ, PhD(Ger), 54. **CAREER** From instr to asst prof Ger, Yale Univ, 53-59; from assoc prof to prof, Bryn Mawr Col, 59-70; chmn dept, 70-75, Prof Ger Lang, Univ NC, Chapel Hill, 70-, Vis prof, Yale Univ, spring 80. **HONORS AND AWARDS** Cert of Merit, Am Asn of Tchrs of Germ. **MEMBERSHIPS** MLA, Am Asn Teachers Ger, Lessing Soc, Soc for Ger-Am Studies. **RESEARCH** German baroque and classical literature; early German-American literature. **SELECTED PUBLICATIONS** Auth, Men Viewing Women as Art Objects: Studies in German Litertature; ed, Das Loffelchen, Lessing: Nathan der Weise Pastorius: Deliciae Hortenses, Albertinus: Verachtung dess Hoflebens, Dictionary of Literary Biography, vols 90, 94, 97, Early and Miscellaneous Letters of J.W. Goethe; Carove: Kinderleben/Austin: Story Without an End. **CONTACT ADDRESS** Dept of Ger Lang, Univ of No Carolina, Chapel Hill, Chapel Hill, NC 27514.

SCHWEIZER, NIKLAUS R.
PERSONAL Born 08/24/1939, Zurich, Switzerland **DISCIPLINE** GERMAN **EDUCATION** Univ Calif, Davis, MA, 66, PhD, 68. **CAREER** Teacher Ger, Punahou Sch, Honolulu, 68-70; Prof Ger, Univ Hawaii, 70-. **HONORS AND AWARDS** First Annual Awd of the Ger Hawaiian Friendship Club for having Fostered good relations between Hawaii and Ger. **MEMBERSHIPS** AAUP; Am Asn Teachers Ger. **RESEARCH** Eighteenth century German literature; Germans in the Pacific. **SELECTED PUBLICATIONS** Auth, The Ut Pictura Poesis Controversy in Eighteenth-Century England and Germany, Lang, 72; The Germans in old Hawaii, Ethnologische Zeitschrift Zurich, 72; A Poet among Explorers: Chamisso in the South Seas, Lang, 73; Introduction to Hildebrand Jacob of the sister arts: An essay, London, 1734, Augustan Reprint Soc, 74; The Swiss in Hawaii, Newslett Swiss Am Hist Soc, 76; Hawaii two centuries later, Swiss Rev World Affairs, 78; Hawai'i und die deutschsprachigen Volker, Lang, 82; Hawai'i and the German Speaking Peoples, Topgallant, 82; His Hawaiian Excellency, Lang 87/94; ed, By Royal Command, Hui Hanai, 88; auth, Turning Tide: The Ebb and Flow of Hawaiian Nationality, Lang, 99; ed, Journal des Malers Ludwig York Choris, Lang, 99. **CONTACT ADDRESS** Dept Lang & Lit of Europe & the Americas, Univ of Hawaii, Manoa, 1890 E West Rd, Moore 483, Honolulu, HI 96822. **EMAIL** niklans@hawaii.edu

SCLIPPA, NORBERT
PERSONAL Born 03/29/1944, Belesta, France, m, 1978, 2 children **DISCIPLINE** FRENCH **EDUCATION** PhD. **CAREER** Prof of French, Col of Charleston. **MEMBERSHIPS** ASECS. **RESEARCH** 18th century philosophy. **SELECTED**

PUBLICATIONS Auth, Le Jeu de la Sphinge: Sade, et la philosophie des Lumieres, New York: Lang (2000). **CONTACT ADDRESS** Dept French, Col of Charleston, 66 George St, Charleston, SC 29424-1407. **EMAIL** sclippan@cofc.edu

SCOTT, CHARLES THOMAS
PERSONAL Born 10/21/1932, New York, NY, m, 1957, 4 children **DISCIPLINE** LINGUISTICS **EDUCATION** St John's Univ, NYork, BA, 54; NYork Univ, MA, 58; Univ Tex, PhD(ling), 63. **CAREER** Specialist comp lit, Teachers Col, Columbia Univ-Int Coop Admin, Afghanistan Proj, 58-60; from asst prof to assoc prof English, 63-68, chmn dept, 70-74, Prof English, Univ Wis-Madison, 68-; Consult for Japan Soc, Inc to English lang Educ Coun, Tokyo, 65-66; mem, US Info Agency English Teaching Adv Panel, 67-73; Nat Adv Coun on Teaching English as Foreign Lang, 67-70; chmn, Comt on Inst Coop Panel in English Lang Teaching, 68-70; Comt Int Exchange Persons Screening Panel, Ling & Teaching English as Foreign Lang, 73-76. **MEMBERSHIPS** Ling Soc Am; aal; MLA; AAUP. **RESEARCH** Formal criteria for definition of literary folkloristic genres; contemporary English linguistics; application of linguistics to literary theory. **SELECTED PUBLICATIONS** Auth, Persian and Arabic Riddles: A Language-Centered Approach to Genre Definition, Ind Univ, 65; Preliminaries to English Teaching, English Lang Educ Coun, Tokyo, 66; Linguistics basis for development of reading skill, Mod Lang J, 66; co-ed, Approaches in Linguistic Methodology, Univ Wis, 67; Readings for the History of the English Language, Allyn & Bacon, 68; auth, Transformational grammar and English as a second language /dialect, Georgetown Monogr Ser, 68; Literary history at Wisconsin, New Lit Hist, 73; co-ed w/T W Machan, English in its Social Contexts, Oxford Univ Press, 92. **CONTACT ADDRESS** Dept of English, Univ of Wisconsin, Madison, 600 North Park St, Madison, WI 53706-1403. **EMAIL** ctscott@facstaff.wisc.edu

SCOTT, DANIEL MARCELLUS
PERSONAL Born 10/13/1960, Gardena, CA, s **DISCIPLINE** COMPARATIVE LITERATURE **EDUCATION** Univ IL Urbana, PhD 72. **CAREER** Univ N Carolina Chapel Hill, postdoc fel, 92-94; Rhode Island Col, asst prof, 94-. **MEMBERSHIPS** MLA; MELUS; NCTE. **RESEARCH** Colonial and Post Colonial; African American Studies. **SELECTED PUBLICATIONS** Auth, Fossil and Psyche, Issues and Identities in Lit, Pasadena CA, Salem Press, forthcoming; Womb of Space, Issues and Identities in Lit, Pasadena CA, Salem Press, forthcoming; Theodore Wilson Harris, Issues and Identities In Lit, Pasadena CA, Salem Press, forthcoming; John Francisco Rechy, Issues and Identities In Lit, Pasadena CA, Salem Press, forthcoming; Marlon Riggs, The African American Encycl Supplement, Marshall Cavendish NY, 96; auth, Walter Mosley, The African American Encycl, Supplement, Marshall Cavendish NY, 93; auth, From Myth to Ritual: Jung Soyinka and the Modern World, World Lit Written In English, 96; auth, Interrogating Identity: Appropriation and Transformation in Middle Passage, Afri Amer Rev, 95; Dreaming the Other: Breton Cesaire and the Problematics of Influence, Romance Quart, 95; auth, Cahier d'un retour au pays natal: la poetique de la vilonce, Romance Notes, 93. **CONTACT ADDRESS** Dept of English, Rhode Island Col, 600 Mt Pleasant Ave, Providence, RI 02908. **EMAIL** dscott@grog.ric.edu

SCOTT, LINDY
PERSONAL Born 12/26/1951, Columbus, OH, m, 1978, 3 children **DISCIPLINE** SPANISH **EDUCATION** Ohio Univ, BA, 73; Trinity Evang Div Sch, MA, 75, Mdiv, 76; Northwestern Univ, PhD, 91 **CAREER** Assoc Prof, 95-, Wheaton Col; Dean, Prof, 90-95, Comunidad Teologica de mexico; Prof, 82-84, 88-92, Centro de Estudios Superiores de Integracion Cristiana; Prof, 80-82, Universidad nacional Autonoma de Mexico **HONORS AND AWARDS** Christian Writer of the Year Awd, 95; cum laude or with honors in all graduate work **MEMBERSHIPS** FTL **RESEARCH** Christianity in Latin Am, CEHILA, NACFLA, Hispanics in US; Mexico. **SELECTED PUBLICATIONS** Co-ed, Mujer: Primera Consulta de Reflexion Biblica. La Participacion de la Mujer en la Iglesia y en la Sociedad. Mexico City: Editorial Kyrios, 90; auth, Los Evangelicos Mexicanos en el Siglo Veinte. Mexico City: Editorial Kyrios, 91; auth, Las Mujeres, La Iglesia yla Timoteo 2:9-15, Mexico City: Editorial Kyrios, 91; auth, Salt of the Earth: A Scoio-Political History of Mexico City Evangelical Protestants (1964-1991), Mexico City: Editorial Kyrios and Casa Unida de Publicacciones, 91; ed, La Educacion en Mexico: Tercera Consulta de Reflexion Biblica, Mexico City: Editorial Kyrios, 92; auth, La Sal de la Tierra: Una Historia Socio-Politica de los Evangelicos en la Ciudad de Mexico (1964-1991), Mexico City: Editorial Kyrios, 94; auth, Bibliografia de los Evangelicos en Mexico, vol 6 of the Series Mexico Hoy y Manana, Mexico City: VELA, 97; auth, Siguiendo las Pisadas del Senor: Los Evangelicos en Tabasco. Mexico City: Editorial Kyrios, 98. **CONTACT ADDRESS** Foreign Lang Dept, Wheaton Col, Illinois, Wheaton, IL 60187. **EMAIL** Lindy.scott@wheaton.edu

SCOTT, NINA MARGARET
PERSONAL Born 09/04/1937, Hamburg, Germany, m, 1961, 3 children **DISCIPLINE** MODERN SPANISH LITERATURE, SPANISH CIVILIZATION **EDUCATION** Wellesley Col, BÀ, 59; Stanford Univ, MA, 61, PhD(Span), 68. **CAREER** Teachers Ger, Am Sch in Switz, 63-64; asst prof, 68-74, Assoc Prof Span & Port, Univ Mass, Amherst, 74-, Fac Growth grant for teaching, Univ Mass, Amherst, 75; Mary Elvira Stevens Travelling fel, Wellesley Col, 76-77. **MEMBERSHIPS** Am Asn Univ Women; Am Asn Teachers Span & Port; MLA; Northeast Mod Lang Asn; Int Inst, Spain. **RESEARCH** Contemporary Spanish literature; comparative North/South American literature; art and literature. **SELECTED PUBLICATIONS** Auth, Sight and insight in La casa de Bernarda Alba, Rev Estud Hisp, 10/75; Unamuno y el Cristo de Velazquez, Rev de lit, 70; Unamuno and Painting, Hispanofila, 75; Honors and the Family in La fuerza de la sangre, Studies in Honor of Ruth Lee Kennedy, 77; James Fenimore Cooper y Juan Leon Mera: Progenitoreo del mito del indio, El Tiempo, 77; The Tenth Muse, America, 78. **CONTACT ADDRESS** Dept of Span & Port, Univ of Massachusetts, Amherst, Amherst, MA 01003-0002.

SCOTT, WILLIAM CLYDE
PERSONAL Born 09/14/1937, Oklahoma City, OK, m, 1964, 3 children **DISCIPLINE** CLASSICS **EDUCATION** Princeton Univ, AB, 59, MA, 62, PhD(classics), 64. **CAREER** Instr classics, Phillips Acad, Andover, 59-60; asst prof, Haverford Col, 64-66; asst prof classics, 66-70, assoc prof classics & drama, 70-75, assoc dean fac, 70-72, chemn dept, 70-76, prof classics & drama, 75-, humanities res prof, 88-, Dartmouth prof of classics, Dartmouth Col, 94-, Dartmouth fac fel, 67-68; mem managing comt, Am Sch Class Studies Athens. **HONORS AND AWARDS** Goodwin Awd of Merit, Am Philol Asn, 86. **MEMBERSHIPS** Am Philol Asn; Am Inst Archaeol. **RESEARCH** Greek epic; Greek drama; Roman lyric. **SELECTED PUBLICATIONS** Auth, The confused chorus (Agamemnon 975-1034), Phoenix, 69; Catullus and Caesar (c 29), Class Philol, 71; A repeated episode at Odyssey 1 125-48, TAPha, 71; The Oral Nature of the Homeric Simile, Leiden, 74; Lines for Clytemnestra (Ag 489-502), 78 & Non-Strophic Elements in the Oresteia, 82, TAPhA; Musical Design in Aeschylean Theater, 84; Plato's The Republic, 85; Musical Design in Sophoclean Theater, 96. **CONTACT ADDRESS** Dept of Classics, Dartmouth Col, 6086 Reed Hall, Hanover, NH 03755-3506. **EMAIL** william.c.scott@dartmouth.edu

SCROGGINS, DANIEL COY
PERSONAL Born 06/19/1937, Compton, AR, m, 1961, 1 child **DISCIPLINE** HISPANIC LITERATURE **EDUCATION** Univ Ark, BA, 58, MA, 61; Univ Mich, PhD, 67. **CAREER** Asst prof Span, Univ Miami, 63-65, Ind Univ, Bloomington, 66-69; asst prof, 69-71, Assoc Prof Span, Univ Mo-Columbia, 71- **MEMBERSHIPS** MLA; Am Asn Teachers Span & Port; Latin Am Studies Asn. **RESEARCH** Argentine literature; colonial Latin American literature; the essay. **SELECTED PUBLICATIONS** Auth, A Concordance of Jose Hernandez Martin Fierro, University of Missouri Press, 71; auth, "The Crisis of 1930 in the Aguafuertes portenas of Roberto Arlt," Kentucky Romance Quarterly 26 (79): 469-478; auth, Las Aguafuertes portenus de Roberto Arlt, Ediciones Culturales Argentinas, 81; auth, "Brotherhood and Fratricide in the Early Fiction of Augusto Roa Bastos," Hispanic Journal 6 (85): 137-147; auth, "Three Points in the Trajectory of the Gaucho," Gaucho Literature, ed. Russell O. Salmon (Bloomington, IN: Indiana Univertity, 90), 3-15; auth, 20,000 Spanish American Pseudonyms, Scarecrow Press, 97. **CONTACT ADDRESS** Dept of Romance Lang, Univ of Missouri, Columbia, Columbia, MO 65201.

SCULLION, SCOTT
DISCIPLINE CLASSICS **EDUCATION** Univ Toronto, BA, 82; Harvard Univ, PhD, 90. **MEMBERSHIPS** Am Philol Asn. **RESEARCH** Greek religion; Greek literature, especially drama. **SELECTED PUBLICATIONS** Auth, Three Studies in Athenian Dramaturgy, Teubner, 94; auth, Olympian and Chthonian, Class Antiquity, 94; auth, Dionysos and Katharsis in Antigone, Class Antiquity, forthcoming; auth, Three Notes on Attic Sacrificial Calendars, Zeitschrift fur Papyrologie und Epigraphik, forthcoming; auth, Saviours of the Father's Hearth: Olympian and Chthonian in the Oresteia, in Hagg, ed, Greek Sacrificial Ritual, Olympian and Chthonian, Stockholm, Paul Astroms Forlag, forthcoming. **CONTACT ADDRESS** Dept of Classics, Union Col, New York, Schenectady, NY 12308.

SCULLY, STEPHEN P.
PERSONAL Born 06/04/1947, m, 3 children **DISCIPLINE** CLASSICAL STUDIES **EDUCATION** NYork Univ, BA, 71; U NC Chapel Hill, MA, 75; Brown Univ, PhD, 78. **CAREER** Mellen Fellow, 78-80, John Hopkins Univ; Assoc Prof, 80-, Boston Univ. **HONORS AND AWARDS** NEH Summer Stipend; Jasper Whiting Fellowship; Honor and the Sacred City; Best Acad Books, Choice. **MEMBERSHIPS** Amer Philos Assoc; New England Class Assoc. **RESEARCH** Epic; Tragedy; Near Eastern Lit; Renaissance Stud. **SELECTED PUBLICATIONS** Coauth, Arion, 3rd Series, 3.1 and 4.1, Special Issue, The Chorus in Greek Tragedy and Culture, 96 & 96; auth, Homer and The Sacred City, Ithaca, NY, Cornell Univ, 90; coauth, Euripides Suppliant Women, Oxford, Oxford Univ Press, 95. **CONTACT ADDRESS** Dept Classics, Boston Univ, 745 Commonwealth Ave, Boston, MA 02215. **EMAIL** sscully@bu.edu

SEARS, DIANNE
DISCIPLINE FRENCH LITERATURE **EDUCATION** Yale Univ, PhD. **CAREER** Prof, Univ MA Amherst. **RESEARCH** Poetry; 20th-century lit; contemp lit of Quebec; literary theory. **SELECTED PUBLICATIONS** Auth, pubs on art criticism and metatextuality in Ponge's work; female leads in the works of Queneau and Vian; transgression in Blais' work; language in Lalonde's work. **CONTACT ADDRESS** Dept of French and Italian Studies, Univ of Massachusetts, Amherst, Mass Ave, Amherst, MA 01003. **EMAIL** dsears@frital.umass.edu

SEATON, JEROME P.
PERSONAL Born 03/23/1941, Lafayette, IN, m, 1961, 3 children **DISCIPLINE** CHINESE LANGUAGE AND LITERATURE **EDUCATION** Ind Univ, BA, 63; PhD, 68. **CAREER** From asst prof to prof, Univ NC, 68-. **HONORS AND AWARDS** Tanner Awd for Inspirational Teaching of Undergraduates, 76. **RESEARCH** Translation of Classical Chinese Poetry, Chinese Buddhism. **SELECTED PUBLICATIONS** Auth, Love and Time: Poems of Ou-yang Hsiu, Copper Canyon Press, 89; co-ed, A Drifting Boat: An Anthology of Chinese Zen Poetry, White Pine Press, 94; ed & contribur, I Don't Bow to Buddhas: Selected Poems of Yuan Mei, Copper Canyon Press, 97; coauth, The Tao Te Ching of Lao Tzu, Shambhala, 97; ed and contribur, The Essential Chuang Tzu, Shambhala, 98. **CONTACT ADDRESS** Dept Asian Studies, Univ of No Carolina, Chapel Hill, 440 W Franklin St, Chapel Hill, NC 27599-2319. **EMAIL** jpseaton@email.unc.edu

SEAVEY, WILLIAM
DISCIPLINE CLASSICS **EDUCATION** Univ NC, PhD, 93. **CAREER** Vis asst prof, E Carolina Univ, 94-00. **HONORS AND AWARDS** Outstanding hist prof, E Carolina Univ, 97. **MEMBERSHIPS** APA, CAMWS, Ploutarchos. **RESEARCH** Roman War law; Greek and Roman intellectual history. **CONTACT ADDRESS** Dept of History, East Carolina Univ, Brewster A-305, Greenville, NC 27858-4353. **EMAIL** seaveyw@mail.ecu.edu

SEBESTA, JUDITH LYNN
PERSONAL Born Chicago, IL **DISCIPLINE** CLASSICAL LANGUAGES AND LITERATURE, ANCIENT HISTORY, WOMEN IN ANTIQUITY **EDUCATION** Univ Chicago, AB, 68; Stanford Univ, PhD, 72. **CAREER** From instr to asst prof, 72-77, Assoc Prof Classics, Univ S Dak, 77-, Dir, Integrated Humanities Prof, Univ SDak, 81, Dir Classics, 81, Chair, Dept Hist, 97-. **HONORS AND AWARDS** Phi Beta Kappa, 67; Harrington Lectr, Col Arts & Sci, 94. **MEMBERSHIPS** Am Philol Asn; Class Asn Midwest & South; Am Classical League. **RESEARCH** The Roman army; provinces of the Roman empire; classical philology. **SELECTED PUBLICATIONS** Auth, Carl Orff Carmina Burana, Bolchazy-Carducci Publ, 84, 96; Mantles of the Gods and Catullus 64, Syllectu Classica 5, 93; coauth, The World of Roman Costume, Univ Wis Press, 94; auth, Women's Costume and Feminine Civic Morality in Augustan Rome, Gender & Hist 9, 97; Aliquid Sem per Novi: New Challenges & New Approaches, in Latin for the 21st Century, Addison-Wesley, 97. **CONTACT ADDRESS** Dept of Hist, Univ of So Dakota, Vermillion, 414 E Clark St, Vermillion, SD 57069-2390. **EMAIL** jsebesta@sunbird.usd.edu

SEBOLD, RUSSELL PERRY
PERSONAL Born 08/20/1928, Dayton, OH, m, 1955, 2 children **DISCIPLINE** SPANISH **EDUCATION** Ind Univ, BA, 49; Princeton Univ, MA, 51, PhD, 53. **CAREER** Instr Span, Duke Univ, 55-56; from instr to assoc prof, Univ Wis, Madison, 56-66; prof foreign lang & chmn dept, Univ Md, 66-68; chmn dept, 68-78, Prof Romance Lang, Univ Pa, 68-, Guggenheim fel, 62-63; co-ed, Hisp Rev, 68-73, gen ed, 73-; Am Philos Soc grant-in-aid, 71, 76 & 82; Am Coun Learned Soc fel, 79-80. **MEMBERSHIPS** MLA; Am Asn Teachers Span & Port; Hisp Soc Am; Centro de Estudios del Siglo XVIII (Oviedo, Spain). **RESEARCH** Eighteenth century Spanish literature; Spanish Romanticism; aesthetics and poetics. **SELECTED PUBLICATIONS** Auth, El Rapto de la Mente, Poetica y Poesia Diechiochescas, Prensa Espanola, Madrid, 70; Colonel Don Jose Cadalso, Twayne, 71; ed, Ignacio Lopez de Ayala, Numancia Destruida, Ed Anaya, Salamanca-Madrid, 71; Cadalso: El Primer Romantico Europeo de Espana, Ed Gredos, Madrid, 74; Novela Y Autobiografia en la Vida de Torres Villarroel, Ed Ariel, Barcelona, 75; ed, Ignacio de Luzan, La Poetica, Ed Labor, Barcelona, 77; Tomas de iriarte, El Senorito Mimado (y) La Senorita Malcriada, Ed Castalia, Madrid, 78; auth, Becquer y la lima de Horacio, Insula, 1/82. **CONTACT ADDRESS** Dept of Romance Lang, Univ of Pennsylvania, 34th and Spruce St, Philadelphia, PA 19104.

SEEBA, HINRICH CLAASSEN
PERSONAL Born 02/05/1940, Hannover, Germany **DISCIPLINE** GERMAN LITERATURE **EDUCATION** Univ Tubingen, DPhil(Ger & Greek), 67. **CAREER** From asst prof to assoc prof, 68-76, chmn dept, 77-81, 89-91, Prof Ger, Univ Calif, Berkeley, 76-, Studienstiftung des deutschen Volkes fel, 63-68. **HONORS AND AWARDS** Guggenheim Found fel, 70-71; visting prof, IU Berlin, 92, Stanford, 94, Sao Paulo, 99. **MEMBERSHIPS** MLA; Am Asn Teachers Ger; Philol Asn Pac Coast; Am Lessing Soc; Am Asn Advan Humanities; Ger-

man Studies Assoc. **RESEARCH** Eighteenth to 20th century German literature; hermeneutics; methods of literary criticism; Lessing; Kleist. **SELECTED PUBLICATIONS** Auth, "New Historicism und Kulturanthropologie: Ansatze eines deutsch-amerikanischen Dialogs," in: Historismus am Ende des 20. Jahrhunderts, Eine internationale Diskussion, Herausgegeben von Gunter Scholtz, Berlin: Akademie-Verlag (97): 40-54; auth, "Zwischen den Kulturen: Wissenschaftsemigration und German Studies," in Der Exodus aus Nazideutschland und die Folgen, Judische Wissenschaftler im Exil, Herausgegeben von Marianne Hassler und Jurgen Wertheimer, Tubingen: attempto verlag (97): 304-324; auth, "Interdisziplinare Praxis der German Studies: Zum Beispiel Berlin," in Uber Grenzen: Neue Wege in Wissenschaft und Politik, Beitrage fur Evelies Mayer, Herausgegeben von Bettina Schmitt, Karin Hartmann, Beate Krais, Frankfurt am Main: Campus Verlag (98): 59-71; auth, "Inventing the Nation: Literary Study as Discipline of Identity," in Klaus J. Milich and Jeffrey M. Peck, eds, Multiculturalism in Transit, Providence/Oxford: Berghahn Books (98): 183-189; auth, "Deutschtum, Zur Rhetorik des nationalen Narzissmus beim sogenannten Rembrandt-Deutschen," in Henk de Berg, Matthias Prangel, Hrsg, Interpretation 2000: Positionen und Kontroversen Festschrift zum 65 Geburtstag von Horst Steinmetz, Heidelberg: Universitatsverlag C. Winter, (99): 215-222; auth, "German Studies in the U.S.: History, Theory and Practice," in Pandaemonium Germanicum Revista de Estudos Germanicos 3/1 (99): 151-181; auth, "Keine Systematie: Heine in Berlin and the Origin of the Urban Gaze," in Heinrich Heine's Contested Identities: Politics, Religion and Nationalism in Nineteenth-Century Germany, ed. Jost Hermand & Robert C. Holub, New York et al: Peter Lang (99): 89-108; auth, "Soweit die deutsche Zunge klingt: The Role of Language in German Identity Formation," in Nicholas Vazsonyi, ed., Searching for Common Ground: Diskirse zir deutschen Identitat 1750-1871, Koln, Weimer, Wien: Bohlau (00): 45-57; auth, "Cultural Exchange: The Historical Context of German Kulturpolitik and German Studies in the U.S.," in Peter Uwe Hohendahl und Cora Lee Nollendorfs, eds, History of German in the US, forthcoming 01; auth, "The Eye of the Beholder: Kleist's Visual Poetics of Knowledge," in Bernd Fischer, ed, A Companion to the Works of Heinrich von Kleist, Camden House, forthcoming 01. **CONTACT ADDRESS** Dept of Ger, Univ of California, Berkeley, 5315 Dwinelle Hall, Berkeley, CA 94720-3244. **EMAIL** hcseeba@socrates.berkeley.edu

SEELIG, HARRY E.
PERSONAL Born 03/13/1937, New York, NY, m, 1967, 2 children **DISCIPLINE** GERMAN LITERATURE, MUSIC **EDUCATION** Oberlin Col, AB, 59, Conserv, BM, 61; Univ Kans, MA, 64, PhD(German), 69. **CAREER** Instr, Univ Kans, 66-67; instr, 67-69, asst prof, 69-80, assoc prof German, Univ Mass, 80-, vis lectr, Univ Kent, 78-79; res dir, UMass Baden-Wuerttemberg Exchange Prog, 85-86m 86-97. **HONORS AND AWARDS** NDEA Fell, 961-65; German Govt Grant, Dankstipendium, 63-64; Newberry Library Grant in Aid, 67; Pi Kappa Lambola; Delta Phi Alpha. **MEMBERSHIPS** MLA; Am Asn Teachers German. **RESEARCH** German literature since Goethe; poetry and music; translation of contemporary German poetry. **SELECTED PUBLICATIONS** Transl, Rolf Bongs, Insel-Ile-Island, Guido Hildebrandt Verlag Duisburg, WGermany, 73; Rolf Bongs, Aufstieg zum Kilimandscharo, The Literary Rev, 74; auth, Schuberts Beitrag zu besserem Verstadnis' von Goethes Suleika-Gestalt: Eine literarischmusikalische studie der Suleika-Lieder, Beitrage zur Musikwissenschaft, 75; transl, Rolf Bongs, Oberwelt, 76 & Ralph Glockler's, Ich Sehe Dichnoch und andere lyrik, 76, Dimension; The Literary Context: Goethe as Source and Catalyst, in: German Lieder of the Nineteenth Century, New York: Macmillan, G Schirmer Books, 96. **CONTACT ADDRESS** German Dept, Univ of Massachusetts, Amherst, Herter Hall, Amherst, MA 01003-0002. **EMAIL** seelig@german.umass.edu

SEGAL, CHARLES P.
PERSONAL Born 03/19/1936, Boston, MA, m, 1988, 3 children **DISCIPLINE** CLASSICS **EDUCATION** Harvard Col, AB, 57; Harvard Univ, PhD, 61. **CAREER** Teaching Fel to Instructor, Harvard Univ, 59-64; Asst Prof to Assoc Prof, Univ Pa, 64-67; Assoc Prof to Prof, Brown Univ, 68-86; Prof, Princeton Univ, 87-90; Prof, Harvard Univ, 90-. **HONORS AND AWARDS** Detur Prize, Harvard Col, 54-55; Bowdoin Prize, Harvard Col, 55-57; Richardson Prize, Harvard, 57; Fulbright Fel, Athens, 57-58; Fel, Guggenheim, 81-82; Fel, NEH, 85-86; Fel, Ctr for Adv Study in the Beh Sci, 89-90; Fel, Am Acad of Arts and Sci, 92-. **MEMBERSHIPS** Am Philol Asn; classical Asn of N Eng; Virgilian Soc; Alumni Asn of the Am Sch of Classical Studies in Athens; Alumni Asn of Am Acad in Rome; Women's Classical Caucus. **SELECTED PUBLICATIONS** Auth, Lucretius on Death and Anxiety: Poetry and Philosophy in De Rerum Natura, Princeton Univ Press, 90; auth, Singers, Heroes, and Gods in the Odyssey, Cornell Univ Press, 94; auth, Sophocles' Tragic World: Divinity, Nature, and Society, Harvard Univ Press, 95; auth, Aglaia: The Poetry of Alcman, Sappho, Pindar, Bacchylides, and Corinna, Rowman and Littlefield, 98; auth, Sophocles' Oedipus Tyrannus: Tragic Heroism and the Limits of Knowledge, Oxford Univ Press, 00; auth, Euripides' Bakkhai, Oxford Univ Press, 00. **CONTACT ADDRESS** Dept Classics, Harvard Univ, 319 Boylston Hall, Cambridge, MA 02138. **EMAIL** cpsegal@fas.harvard.edu

SEGEL, HAROLD BERNARD
PERSONAL Born 09/13/1930, Boston, MA **DISCIPLINE** SLAVIC LANGUAGES AND LITERATURES **EDUCATION** Boston Col, BS, 51; Harvard Univ, PhD, 55. **CAREER** Asst prof Slavic lang & lit, Univ Fla, 55-59; from asst prof to prof emer Slavic Lit, Columbia Univ, 59-. **HONORS AND AWARDS** Polish Ministry of Cult Awd, 75. **MEMBERSHIPS** Am Asn Advan Slavic Studies; Am Soc 18th Century Studies. **RESEARCH** Slavic literatures; drama and theatre; Polish literature. **SELECTED PUBLICATIONS** Auth, The Literature of 18th Century Russia (2 vols), 67 & The Trilogy of Alexander Sukhovo-Kobylin, 69, Dutton; The Major Comedies of Alexander Fredro, Princeton Univ, 69; contribr, The Eighteenth Century in Russia, Oxford Univ, 73; The Baroque Poem, Dutton, 74; ed, Polish Romantic Drama, Cornell Univ, 77. **CONTACT ADDRESS** Dept of Slavic Lang and Lit, Columbia Univ, 1130 Amsterdam Ave, Mailcode 2839, New York, NY 10027. **EMAIL** hs11@columbia.edu

SEIDEN, MORTON IRVING
PERSONAL Born 07/29/1921, New York, NY **DISCIPLINE** ENGLISH, COMPARATIVE LITERATURE **EDUCATION** NYork Univ, BS, 43; Columbia Univ, MA, 44, PhD, 52. **CAREER** Instr English, City Col New York, 45-46, NY Univ, 46-49, Smith Col, 49-52 & Queens Col, NY, 52-53; from instr to assoc prof, 53-70, Prof English, Brooklyn Col, 70-; Lectr, Columbia Univ Grad Sch, 48-49. **HONORS AND AWARDS** Brooklyn Col Excellence in Teaching Awd, 67. **MEMBERSHIPS** MLA; Mod Humanities Res Asn; English Inst. **RESEARCH** Nineteenth and Twentieth Century English literature; English, Irish Renaissance; Comparative Literature. **SELECTED PUBLICATIONS** Auth, A psychoanalytical essay on William Butler Yeats, Accent, spring 46; Myth in the Poetry of William Butler Yeats, Am Imago, 12/48; W B Yeats as a playwright, Western Humanities Rev, winter 49; William Butler Yeats: The Poet as a Mythmaker-- 1865-19339, Mich State Univ, 62; The Paradox of Hate: A Study in Ritual Murder, Yoseloff, 68; coauth, Ivan Goncharov's Oblomov: A study of the anti-Faust as a Christian saint, Can Slavic Studies, spring 69. **CONTACT ADDRESS** Dept of English, Brooklyn Col, CUNY, 2901 Bedford Ave, Brooklyn, NY 11210-2813.

SEIDENBERG, MARK
DISCIPLINE PSYCHOLOGY, LINGUISTICS, COMPUTER SCIENCE **EDUCATION** Columbia Univ, PhD, 80. **CAREER** Prof, Univ Southern Calif. **RESEARCH** Psycholinguistics, Neurolinguistics. **SELECTED PUBLICATIONS** Auth, Language Acquisition and Use: Learning and Applying Probabilistic Constraints, Sci, 275, 97; coauth, Evaluating Behavioral and Neuroimaging Data on Past Tense Processing, Language, 74, 98; Category Specific Semantic Deficits in Focal and Widespread Brain Damage: A Computational Account, J Cognitive Neuroscience 10, 98; Learning to Segment Speech Using Multiple Cues: A Connectionist Model, Language and Cognitive Processes 13, 98; On the Nature and Scope of Featural Representations of Word Meaning, J Experimental Psychology: Gen 126, 97; On the basis of Two Subtypes of Developmental Dyslexia, Cognition 58, 96. **CONTACT ADDRESS** Dept of Linguistics, Univ of So California, University Park Campus, Los Angeles, CA 90089. **EMAIL** marks@gizmo.usc.edu

SEIDLER, INGO
PERSONAL Born 10/08/1928, Graz, Austria, m, 1958, 3 children **DISCIPLINE** GERMAN & COMPARATIVE LITERATURE **EDUCATION** Cornell Univ, BA 51; Univ Vienna, Dr Phil, 53. **CAREER** From instr to assoc prof, 57-68, Prof Ger, Univ Mich, Ann Arbor, 68-, H Rackham res fel, 60, 66 & 77; Am Coun Learned Soc travel grant, 65; vis prof, Washington Univ, 69, Univ Freidburg & res dir, jr year, 71-72 & Northwestern Univ, 82; res grant, Deutscher Akademisher Austauschdienst, 77; reader, Adv Placement Prog, 78; mem, Nat Endowment for Humanities transl proj, 79. **MEMBERSHIPS** Brecht Soc; Int Ver Germanisten; Am Nietzsche Soc; MLA. **RESEARCH** Nineteenth and 20th century literature, especially poetry and drama; criticism; theory of literature. **SELECTED PUBLICATIONS** Auth, Kafkas Urteil, Psychol in Lit Wiss, Stiehm, 71; Peter Huchel, Uber P H Suhrkamp, 73; co-ed, W A Reichart Festschrift, 75, auth, Amerikaperspektive Nietzsches, Am in Deutsch Lit, Reclam, 75; Art and Power: G Benn, Mich Ger Studies, 76 ?; Rilke in English, Can Rev of Comp Lit, 79; Theater in West Germany, Col Germmanica, 81; Who is E Canetti?, Cross Currents, 82. **CONTACT ADDRESS** Dept of Ger, Univ of Michigan, Ann Arbor, Ann Arbor, MI 48109.

SELIMOV, ALEXANDER R.
DISCIPLINE SPANISH LITERATURE **EDUCATION** Univ Pa, PhD, 96. **CAREER** Asst prof, Univ of Del. **HONORS AND AWARDS** Mellon Fel; GUR, 98. **MEMBERSHIPS** AATSP; MLA; SSPHS. **RESEARCH** 18th and 19th Century Spanish and Cuban Literature. **SELECTED PUBLICATIONS** Auth, "La historia de dos Adanes: la estructuria integral de El diablo mundo", Hispania, 78.4 (95): 773-779; auth, "La sensibilidad y la verosimilitud en la prosa romantica: un acercamiento al arte narrativo de la Avellaneda", Salina: Revista de lletres, 11 (97): 100-107; auth, "La ensenanza, el deleite y la sensibilidad en Eusebio de Montengon", Diechiocho 21.1 (98): 107-118; auth, "La verdad vence apariencias: hacia la etica de Gerturdis Gomez de Avellaneda a traves de su prosa" Hispanic Rev 67 (99): 215-241; auth, "La poetica de Luzan y la prosa romantica de Avellaneda", Ideas en sus pasages, ed Guillermo Carnero, Universidad de alicante, 99; ed, Gertrudis gomez de Avellaneda, Juan de la Cuesta, (Newark), 99; auth, "El honor, el amor y la inmortal hazana del inclito Pelayo en tres tragedias neoclasicas", Dieciocho, Univ of Va, 00. **CONTACT ADDRESS** Dept Foreign Lang, Univ of Delaware, 18 Amstel Ave Rm 325, Newark, DE 19716-2599.

SELKIRK, ELISABETH
DISCIPLINE LINGUISTICS **EDUCATION** Univ Calif Berkeley, BA, MAss Inst Tech, PhD, 72. **CAREER** Prof. **RESEARCH** Phonological theory; interfaces of phonology with other components of grammar; prosodic phrasing in English. **SELECTED PUBLICATIONS** Auth, The Syntax of Words, MIT, 82; The Role of Prosodic Categories in English Word Stress, Ling Inquiry, 80; Phonology and Syntax: The Relation between Sound and Structure, MIT, 84; The Major Class Features and Syllable Theory, MIT, 85; Derived Domains in Sentence Phonology, 86; co-auth, Government and Tonal Phrasing in Papago, 87. **CONTACT ADDRESS** Linguistics Dept, Univ of Massachusetts, Amherst, S College 231, Amherst, MA 01003. **EMAIL** selkirk@linguist.umass.edu

SENN, HARRY
PERSONAL 2 children **DISCIPLINE** FRENCH LANGUAGE AND LITERATURE **EDUCATION** Univ Minn, BA, MA; Univ Calif, Berkeley, PhD. **CAREER** Prof, 70-. **MEMBERSHIPS** Mem, S Calif Mediation Assn. **RESEARCH** Folklore, folk mythology, personal mythology in literature and psychology. **SELECTED PUBLICATIONS** Auth, The Shamanic Narrative in the Post-Modern Era, The Humanistic Psychologist, 95; Jungian Shamanism, Jour of Psychoactive Drugs, 91; Marcel Proust and Melusine: From Fairy Magic to Personal Mythology, Southern Folklore Quart, 84. **CONTACT ADDRESS** Dept of Lang, Pitzer Col, 1050 N. Mills Ave., Claremont, CA 91711-6101. **EMAIL** harry-senn@pitzer.edu

SENNER, WAYNE
PERSONAL Born 05/09/1939, Portland, OR, m, 1991, 2 children **DISCIPLINE** LANGUAGE, LITERATURE, SCANDINAVIAN STUDIES, GERMAN **EDUCATION** Univ Wash, MA, 63; Univ Ill, PhD, 72. **CAREER** Prof, Ariz State Univ, 73-. **HONORS AND AWARDS** DAAD; Fulbright; Iceland Govt Stud Grnt; DAAD Res Grnt; ASU State Press Out Teach Awd; NEH, Scan Stud; NEH, Beethoven Inst. **MEMBERSHIPS** SASS; GSA. **RESEARCH** German Scandinavian cultural relations; Icelandic literary criticism; critical reception of Beethoven; history of world writing systems. **SELECTED PUBLICATIONS** Auth, The Critical Reception of Beethoven's Compositions by his Contemporaries, Univ Neb Press; auth, The Origins of Writing, Univ Neb Press (also translated into Spanish); auth, The Reception of German Literature in Iceland, Univ Amsterdam Press. Numerous articles on German-Scandinavian cultural relations, Icelandic literature, Icelandic criticism and theory and textbooks. **CONTACT ADDRESS** Dept of Lang and Lit, Arizona State Univ, MC 0202, Tempe, AZ 85287. **EMAIL** wayne.senner@asu.edu

SEPULVEDA-PULVENTINI, EMMA
PERSONAL Born, Chile **DISCIPLINE** SPANISH **EDUCATION** Univ Calif, Davis, PhD. **CAREER** Assoc prof Span, Univ Nev, Reno. **RESEARCH** Contemporary Latin American and Spanish poetry and testimonial literature. **SELECTED PUBLICATIONS** Ed, two collections--personal testimonies of the Chilean arpilleristas and essays on female testimonial writings. **CONTACT ADDRESS** Dept of For Lang and Lit, Univ of Nevada, Reno, Reno, NV 89557. **EMAIL** sepulveda@unr.edu

SERRANO, RICHARD
DISCIPLINE COMPARATIVE LITERATURE, FRENCH **EDUCATION** Stanford Univ, BA, 88; Univ of Calif, MA, 91, PhD, 96. **CAREER** Asst Prof of French and Comparative Lit, Rutgers Univ, 98-. **HONORS AND AWARDS** Mellon Tchg fel, Columbia Univ Soc of Fels in the Humanities, 96-98. **MEMBERSHIPS** Rutgers Univ Prog in Middle Eastern Studies; Rutgers Univ African Studies Coord Comt; Middle Eastern Studies Asn; African Lit Asn; Modern Lang Asn. **RESEARCH** Lyric poetry; Francophone lit; Classical Arabic lit; Classical Chinese lit. **SELECTED PUBLICATIONS** Auth, Translation and the Interlingual Text in the Novels of Rachid Boudjedra, Critical Perspectives on Maghrebian Lit, Lynn Rienner, 99; Fans, Silks, and Ptyx: Mallarme and Classical Chinese Poetry, Comparative Lit, 98; Lacan's Oriental Language of the Unconscious, SubStance, 97; Al-Buhturi's Poetics of Persian Abodes, J of Arabic Lit, 97; Al-Sharif Al-Taliq, Jacques Lacan, and the Poetics of Abbreviation, Homoeroticism in Classical Arabic Writing, Columbia Univ Press, 97; No Place for a Lady in the Chanson de Roland, pacific Coast Philology, 92. **CONTACT ADDRESS** Dept of French, Rutgers, The State Univ of New Jersey, New Brunswick, 131 George St, New Brunswick, NJ 08903-0270. **EMAIL** rserrano@rci.rutgers.edu

SEVERINO, ROBERTO
PERSONAL Born 07/19/1940, Catania, Italy, d, 1 child **DISCIPLINE** ITALIAN LITERATURE **EDUCATION** Columbia Union Col, BA, 67; Univ Il Urbana, MA, 69, PhD, 73. **CAREER** Prof, chair, Georgetown Univ. **HONORS AND AWARDS** Who's Who; Gold Medal & Diploma First-Class, by decree of Pres of Italy; Marranzano d'argento, Acireale, 89; Commendatore dell'Ordine al Merito della Repubblica Italiana, by decree of Pres of Italy, 90; Georgetown Univ Vicennial Medal, 94; Premio Telamone, Agrigento, 95. **SELECTED PUBLICATIONS** Auth, A Carte Scoperte: Manzoniana e Altri Saggi Filologici e Critici sulla Cultura Italiana in America, Roma, 90; auth, The Battle for Humanism, Washington DC, 94; auth, Alessandro Dumas: Mariano Stabile, Sindaco di Palermo, Valverde, 94; coauth, coed, Preserving and Promoting Italian Language and Culture in North America, Toronto, 97; auth, Italian Verbs At a Glance, Falls Church Va, 98. **CONTACT ADDRESS** Georgetown Univ, 307 ICC, Washington, DC 20007. **EMAIL** severiro@gunet.georgetown.edu

SEVIN, DIETER H.
PERSONAL Born 11/05/1938, Muchlanger, Germany, m, 1963, 2 children **DISCIPLINE** GERMAN **EDUCATION** San Jose State Univ, BA, 63; Univ Washington, MA, 64; PhD, 67. **CAREER** Teaching Asst, Univ Washington, 63-67; Asst Prof, Pacific Lutheran Univ, 67-68; Asst Prof to Prof, Vanderbilt Univ, 68-. **HONORS AND AWARDS** Grant, Am Coun of Learned Soc, 81-82; Grant, German Acad Exchange, 80, 97; Res Grant, Am Philos Asn, 91. **MEMBERSHIPS** Am Asn of Teachers of German, Am Asn of Univ Prof, Am Goethe Soc, Am Nietzsche Soc, Bertolt Brecht Soc, Georg Buchner Gesellschaft, German Studies Asn, Intl Asn for Germanic Studies, Intl Grillparzer Gesellschaft, Mod Lang Asn, Philol Asn of the Pacific coast, Soc for Exile Studies, Soc for German Am Studies, S Atlantic Mod Lang Asn, Tenn Asn of German Teachers, Tenn For Lang Teaching Asn. **RESEARCH** German Exile Literature; East German Literature; 19th Century German Prose. **SELECTED PUBLICATIONS** Auth, Christa Wolf: Der geteilte Himmel/Nachdenken uber Christa T Interpretationen 4th ed, Munich, 00; auth, Textstrategien im DDR-Roman zwischen Bau und Durchbruch der Berliner Mauer, Heidelberg, 94; ed, Die Resonanz des Exils. Gelungene und miblungene Rezeption deutschsprachiger Exilanten, Rodopi, 92; co-auth, Wie gehts? An Introductory German Course, New York, 80. **CONTACT ADDRESS** Dept German & Slavic Lang, Vanderbilt Univ, Box 1699, Stn B, Nashville, TN 37235-0001. **EMAIL** dieter.h.sevin@vanderbilt.edu

SEYMOUR, HARRY N.
DISCIPLINE LINGUISTICS **EDUCATION** Ohio State Univ, PhD, 71. **CAREER** Adj prof. **RESEARCH** Child language disorders. **SELECTED PUBLICATIONS** Auth, Clinical intervention strategies for language disorders among nonstandard English speaking children, Hil, 86; co-auth, Black English and Standard American English Contrasts in Consonantal Development of Four and Five year old Children, J Speech Hearing Disorders, 81; A minority perspective in diagnosis of child language disorders, 91; Speech and language assessment of preschool children, 92. **CONTACT ADDRESS** Linguistics Dept, Univ of Massachusetts, Amherst, 720 Massachusetts Ave, Amherst, MA 01003. **EMAIL** hseymour@comdis.umass.edu

SEYMOUR, RICHARD KELLOGG
PERSONAL Born 06/21/1930, Hinsdale, IL, m, 1951, 2 children **DISCIPLINE** GERMAN **EDUCATION** Univ Mich, BA, 51, MA, 52; Univ Pa, PhD(Ger philol), 56. **CAREER** Asst instr Ger, Univ Pa, 52-54; instr Ger & ling, Princeton Univ, 54-58; asst prof, Duke Univ, 58-63, assoc prof, 63-67; prof Ger & chmn dept Europ lang, Univ Hawaii, Manoa, 67-75; vis prof English, Univ Cologne, Ger, 75; prof Ger, Pennsylvania State Univ, 75-77; Prof Ger, Univ Hawaii, 77-, Actg Dean, Lang, Ling & Lit, Arts & Sci 81-, Assoc ed, Unterrichtspraxis, 69-80; Fulbright travel grant, 81. **MEMBERSHIPS** Am Asn Teachers Ger; Ling Soc Am; Int Ling Asn; SAtlantic Mod Lang Asn (secy-treas, 62-67); Nat Ger Hon Soc (secy-treas, 68-). **RESEARCH** German dialectology; German word formation; collegiate slang. **SELECTED PUBLICATIONS** Auth, Glossary Of Middle High Ger Lexicographic Word Origins - Ger - Gartner,K, Ed/, Speculum-A J Of Medieval Studies, Vol 0069, 1994; Glossary Of Middle High Ger Lexicographic Word Origins - Ger - Gartner,K, Ed/, Speculum-A J Of Medieval Studies, Vol 0069, 1994; Which-Way-Is-East Revisited + Honolulu Compass Directions/, Am Speech, Vol 0070, 1995. **CONTACT ADDRESS** Dept of German, Univ of Hawaii, Manoa, Honolulu, HI 96822.

SHANE, ALEX MICHAEL
PERSONAL Born 07/16/1933, San Francisco, CA, m, 1957, 2 children **DISCIPLINE** SLAVIC LANGUAGES & LITERATURES **EDUCATION** Univ Chicago, BA, 53; MA, 55; Univ CA, Berkeley, PhD, 65. **CAREER** Instr Russ, Princeton Univ, 58-60; from asst prof to assoc prof, Univ CA, Davis, 63-71; chmn dept, 71-80, Prof & Dir, Slavic Lang & Lit, State Univ NY Albany, 71-99, prof emer, 99-; Dir Off Int Prog, 81-, Am Coun Learned Soc grant-in-aid, 66; Humanities inst grant, Univ CA, 67; vis assoc prof Russ lit, Stanford Univ, 69-70; fel, NEH Independent Study & Res, 77-78; State Univ NY-Moscow State Univ exchange scholar, 82, 84. **MEMBERSHIPS** Am Asn Teachers Slavic & East Europ Lang (pres, 77, 78); Am Asn Advan Slavic Studies. **RESEARCH** Nineteenth and 20th century Russian prose fiction. **SELECTED PUBLICATIONS** Auth, The Life and Works of Evgenij Zamjatin, Univ Calif, 68; The slavic workforce in the United States and Canada: Survey and commentary, Slavic & EEurop J, fall 78; contrib, Columbia Dictionary of Modern European Literature, ed by Jean-Albert Bede and William B. Edgerton, 2nd ed, NY: Columbia Univ Press, 80; auth, Individualized, self-paced instruction: Alternative to the traditional classroom? ADFL Bull, 4/81; contrib, Encyclopedia of World Literature of the 20th Century, vol 4, ed by Leonard S. Klein, rev ed, NY: Frederic Ungar Pub Co, 84; contrib, Handbook of Russian Literature, ed by Victor Terras, New Haven, CT: Yale Univ Press, 85; auth, Rhythm Without Rhyme: The Poetry of Aleksej Remizov, Aleksej Reminov: Approaches to a Protean Writer, ed by Greta Slobin, Columbus: Slavica Pubs, 87; contrib, European Writers: The Twentieth Century, vol 10, ed by George Stade, NY: Charles Scribner's Sons, 90. **CONTACT ADDRESS** Int Programs, LI-66, SUNY, Albany, 1400 Washington Ave, Albany, NY 12222. **EMAIL** ams71@cnsibm.albany.edu

SHANNON, THOMAS F.
PERSONAL Born 03/16/1948, Cambridge, MS, m, 1 child **DISCIPLINE** GERMAN **EDUCATION** Boston Col, BA, 69; SUNY Albany, MA, 73; Ind Univ, MA, 75; PhD, 82. **CAREER** Asst prof to prof, Univ of Calif Berkeley, 80-. **HONORS AND AWARDS** Alpha Sigma Nu; NDEA Fel, 69; Fulbright Grant, 69, 76-78; 92-93; Woodrow Wilson Fel, 69; Regents Jr Fac Fel, 83; ACLS Travel Grant, 87; UCB Grants; Ger Acad Exchange Serv, 96; Res Grant, Inst fur deutsche Sprache, Ger, 97. **MEMBERSHIPS** AANS; AATG; AVT; IVN; IVG; ICLA; LSA; LASSO; MLA; NAUL; PAMLA; SGP. **SELECTED PUBLICATIONS** Auth, Aspects of complementation and control in modern German, Kummerle (Goppingen), 87; coed, Vantage points: Festschrift for Johan Snapper, Univ Pr of Am, (Lanham, MD), 96; coed, Berkeley Conference on Dutch Literature 1995. Dutch poetry in a modern context, Univ Pr of Am, (Lanham, MD), 97; auth, "Word order change in Dutch as reflect in the Ulenspieghel", NW Europ Lang Evolution 31.32, (97): 361-388; coauth, "Shakespeare's stage pronunciation: part of Proto-American English?", Int J of Ger Ling and Semiotics 3.1 (98): 141-162; auth, Berkeley Conference on Dutch Linguistics 1997: Dutch linguistics at the Millenium, Univ Pr of Am, (Lanham, MD), 00; auth, "Rule loss: The case of final devoicing in Yiddish reconsidered", Glossa 19, (forthcoming); auth, Word order and word order change in Dutch and German: A functionalist empirical study, (forthcoming). **CONTACT ADDRESS** Dept German, Univ of California, Berkeley, 5319 Dwinelle Hall, Berkeley, CA 94720-3243. **EMAIL** tshannon@socrates.berkeley.edu

SHAPIRO, GAVRIEL
PERSONAL Born 08/24/1945, Moscow, Russia, d **DISCIPLINE** RUSSIAN, COMPARATIVE LITERATURE **EDUCATION** Moscow Univ, MSc, 68; Hebrew Univ, BA, 73; Univ Ill, MA, 80; PhD, 84. **CAREER** Asst Prof, Northern Ill Univ, 84-87; Asst Prof, Cornell Univ, 87-93; Assoc Prof, Cornell Univ, 93-. **HONORS AND AWARDS** Outstanding Academic Book of the Year, J of the Am Libr Assoc, 95; Berlin Prize Fel, Am Acad in Berlin, 99. **MEMBERSHIPS** MLA, AAASS, AATSEEL, The Gogol Soc, The Nabokov Soc. **RESEARCH** Russian and comparative literature, visual art. **SELECTED PUBLICATIONS** Auth, Nikolai Gogol and the Baroque Cultural Heritage, Pa State Pr, 93; auth, "'Lolita' Class List," Cahiers du monde russe 37 (96): 317-335; auth, The Salome Motif in Vladimir Nabokov's 'Invitation to a Beheading'," Nabokov Studies 3 (96): 101-122; auth, "Nabokov's Allusions: Dividedness and Polysemy," Russ Lit 43 (98): 329-338; auth, Delicate Markers: Subtexts in Vladimir Nabokov's "Invitation to a Beheading," Peter Lang, 98; auth, "Nabokov and Comic Art," in Nabokov at the Limits: Redrawing Critical Boundaries, (Garland, 99), 213-234; auth, "Setting His Myriad Faces in His Text: Nabokov's Authorial Presence Revisited," in Nabokov and His Fiction: New Perspectives, (Cambridge Univ Pr, 99), 15-35; ed, Nabokov at Cornell, Cornell Univ Pr, forthcoming. **CONTACT ADDRESS** Dept Mod Lang, Cornell Univ, 236 Goldwin Smith Hall, Ithaca, NY 14853-3201. **EMAIL** gs33@cornell.edu

SHAPIRO, LEWIS P.
DISCIPLINE PSYCHOLINGUISTICS **EDUCATION** Brandeis Univ, PhD, 87. **CAREER** Dir, Lang Processes Lab; ERP Lab Doctoral Program Executive Comt. **RESEARCH** Adult lang disorders. **SELECTED PUBLICATIONS** Auth, An introduction to syntax, Jour of Speech, Lang, and Hearing Res 40, 97; co-auth, Context effects re-visited, Sentence Processing: A Cross-Linguistic Perspective, Acad Press; How to milk a coat: The effects of semantic and acoustic information on phoneme categorization, Jour Acoustical Soc Am 103, 98; On-line examination of language performance in normal and neurologically-impaired adults, Amer Jour Speech-Lang Pathol, 98; Training wh-question productions in agrammatic aphasia: An analysis of lexical and syntactic properties, Brain and Lang, 98. **CONTACT ADDRESS** Dept of Commun Disorders, San Diego State Univ, 5500 Campanile Dr, San Diego, CA 92182. **EMAIL** shapiro@mail.sdsu.edu

SHAPIRO, MARIANNE
PERSONAL Born 04/14/1940, Budapest, Hungary, m, 1967, 1 child **DISCIPLINE** ITALIAN **EDUCATION** Barnard Col, BA, 60; Harvard Univ, AM, 62; Columbia Univ, PhD, 68. **CAREER** Asst Prof, Univ Calif, Los Angeles, 68-70; Prof, Sarah Lawrence Col, 71-72; Asst Prof to Assoc Prof, Yale Univ, 72-78; Assoc Prof, New York Univ, 80-83; Adj Prof to Vis Scholar, Brown Univ, 95-. **HONORS AND AWARDS** Am Council of Learned Soc Travel Grant, 87; NEH Translation Grant, 80; Whitney A. Griswold Grant, Yale, 75-78; Nat Endowment for the Humanities Younger Humanists Fel, 74-75; Morse Fel, Yale, 74-75; Fulbright Scholar, Univ Rome, 64-65; Garibaldi Memorial Scholarship, columbia Univ, 63-64. **MEMBERSHIPS** Asn of Literary Scholars and Critics. **RESEARCH** Medieval and renaissance romance literature, Comparative literature. **SELECTED PUBLICATIONS** auth, Dante and the Knot of Body and Soul, New York, 98; auth, Higher Learning: A Novel; auth, "Tenson et partimen: la tenson fictive," The Fictive Tenso; auth, De vulgari eloquentia, Dante's book of Exile, Univ Neb, 90; auth, Figuration in Verbal Art, Princeton Univ Press, 88; auth, The Poetics of Ariosto, Wayne State Univ Press, 88; auth, Hieroglyph of Time: The Petrarchan Sestina, Univ Minn, 80; auth, "Structure and Content: Essays in Applied Semiotics," Monographs, Working Papers and Prepublications, 79; auth, "Hierarchy and the Structure of Tropes," Studies in Semiotics, (76): 37. **CONTACT ADDRESS** Dept Ital Studies, Brown Univ, 1 Prospect St, Providence, RI 02912-9100.

SHAPIRO, MICHAEL
PERSONAL Born 11/29/1939, Japan, m, 1967, 1 child **DISCIPLINE** RUSSIAN **EDUCATION** Univ Calif, AB, 61; Harvard Univ, AM, 62; PhD, 65. **CAREER** Acting Instructor to Prof, UCLA, 63-83; Visiting Lecturer, Princeton, 83-86; Visiting Prof, Univ Calif, 86; Prof, Brown Univ, 89-. **HONORS AND AWARDS** NY State Regents Scholarship, Barnard, 57-60; Italian Prize, Barnard, 60; Radcliffe Fel, Harvard Univ, 61-62; Am Coun of Learned Soc Grant, 68, 72; Univ CA Humanities Inst Awd, 68; NSF Project Grant, UCLA, 68-72; Grant, Am Philos Soc, 71; Fel, Univ CA Regents, 74; NEH Summer Sem, 79; NEH Fel, 81; Visiting Scholar, Columbia Univ, 80-82; Visiting Sen Fel, Princeton Univ, 82-83; Salomon Fac Res Awd, Brown Univ, 99-00. **SELECTED PUBLICATIONS** Ed, Constantine Shapiro, Selected Writings, Continental Graphics, 77; co-auth, "Structure and Content: Essays in Applied Semiotics," in Monographs, Working Papers and Prepublications of the Toronto Semiotic Circle, (Toronto, 79), 69; auth, "The Sense of Grammar: Language As Semeiotic," Advances in Semiotics, (83): xv, 286; co-auth, Figuration in Verbal Art, Princeton Univ Press,88; auth, "The Sense of Change: Language As History," Advances in Semiotics, (91): xiv, 146; ed, The Peirce Seminar papers: An Annual of Semiotic Analysis, Vol I, Berg Pub, 93; ed, The Peirce Seminar papers: An Annual of Semiotic Analysis, Vol II, Berg Pub, 94; ed, The Peirce Seminar papers: An Annual of Semiotic Analysis, Vol III, Berg Pub, 98; auth, The Sense of form in Literature and Language, St Martin's Press, 98; ed, The Peirce Seminar papers: An Annual of Semiotic Analysis, Vol IV, Berg Pub, 99. **CONTACT ADDRESS** Dept Slavic Lang, Brown Univ, 1 Prospect St, Providence, RI 02912-9100.

SHAPIRO, MICHAEL C.
DISCIPLINE ASIAN LANGUAGE; LITERATURE **EDUCATION** Queens Col, BA, 67; Univ Chicago, MA, 70, PhD, 74. **CAREER** Prof. **RESEARCH** Hindi language; linguistics and literature; Indo-Aryan linguistics; historical and comparative linguistics. **SELECTED PUBLICATIONS** Auth, A Primer of Modern Standard Hindi; Current Trends in Hindi Syntax: A Bibliographic Survey; coauth, Language and Society in South Asia. **CONTACT ADDRESS** Univ of Washington, Mail Box 353521, Seattle, WA 98195-3521. **EMAIL** hindimcs@u.washington.edu

SHARP, FRANCIS MICHAEL
PERSONAL Born 02/10/1941, Troy, KS, m, 1968, 1 child **DISCIPLINE** GERMAN LITEARTURE **EDUCATION** Univ Mo, BA, 64; Univ Calif, Berkeley, MA, 69, PhD(German lang & lit), 74. **CAREER** Asst prof German lang & lit, Princeton Univ, 73-79; Asst Prof German Lang & Lit, Univ of the Pac, 79- **MEMBERSHIPS** MLA; Am Asn Teachers German. **RESEARCH** Modern German poetry; contemporary German prose; literature and psychology. **SELECTED PUBLICATIONS** Auth, Georg Heym and the aesthetics of traumatization, Rev of Nat Lit, 78; Expressionism and psychoanalysis, Pac Coast Philol, 10/78; Georg Buchner's Lenz: A futile madness, Wissenschaftliche Buchgeselschaft, 81; The Poet's Madness: A Reading of Georg Trakl, Cornell Univ Press, 81; Literature as self-reflection: Thomas Bernhard and Peter Handke, World Lit Today, autumn 81; Georg Trakl: Poetry and psychopathology, Bouvier Verlag (in prep). **CONTACT ADDRESS** Dept of Mod Lang & Lit, Univ of the Pacific, Stockton, Stockton, CA 95211.

SHARPE, PEGGY
DISCIPLINE PORTUGUESE LITERATURE **EDUCATION** Iowa State Univ, BS, 70; NYork Univ, MA, 72; Univ of NMex, PhD, 81. **CAREER** Assoc prof, Universidade Federal do Maranhao, 79-82; visiting assoc prof, Universidade Federal de Pernambuco, 89-90; assoc prof, Univ of Illinois, 86-99; assoc dean,

Col of Liberal Arts and Sciences, 95-99; prof and ch, Univ of Miss, 99-. **MEMBERSHIPS** Modern Lang Asn, Latin Am Studies Asn, Brazilian Studies Asn, Am Portuguese Studies Asn, 96-; Am Asn of Teachers of Spanish and Portuguese, Executive Council, 98-00. **RESEARCH** Gender and literary studies, specifically the study of Brazilian women novelists and essayists from the mid-nineteenth century to the present and the contribution these writers have made to Brazilian intellectual hist. **SELECTED PUBLICATIONS** Auth, Opusculo humanitario, Floresta, Nisia, Sao Paulo: Editora Cortez, 89; auth, Espelho na rua: A cidade na ficcao de Eca de Queiros, Rio de Janeiro: Presenca Editores, 92; auth, Visoes do passado, Previsoes do futuro: Duas modemistas esquecidas, Introduction and notes by Susan C. Quinlan and Peggy Sharpe, Rio de Janeiro: Tempo Brasileiro e Goiania: Universidade Federal de Goias, 96; auth, Entre resistir e identificar-se: Para uma teoria da pratica da narrativa brasileira de autoria feminina, Forging a Theory: Resistance and Identity in Brazilian Women's Narrative, ed, Peggy Sharpe, Florianopolis, SC, Editora Mulheres, e Goiania, GO, UFG, 97; transl, In Praise of Difference: The Emergence of a Global Feminism, Trans. and Intro, Peggy Sharpe, New Brunswick, NJ: Rutgers Univ Press, 98; auth, A viuva Simoes, Almeida, Julia Lopes de, 2 ed, Intro and notes, Peggy Sharpe, Florianopolis, SC: Editora das Mulheres, 99; auth, "Imagens e poder: construindo a obra de Marina Colasanti," in Entre resistir e identificar-se: Para uma teoria da pratica da narrativa brasileira de autoria feminina, ed, Peggy Sharpe, Florianopolis, SC: Editora das Mulheres e Goiania, GO: UFG, 97; auth, "A Tropical Utopia: The Brazilian Fairy Tales of Marina Colasanti," Daughters of Restlessness: Women's Literature at the End of the Millenium, ed, Sabine Coelsch-Foisner, Gerhild Reisner, Hanna Wallinger, Heidelberg: Universitatsverlag C. Winter, 98; auth, Construindo o caminho da nacao atrves da obra de Julia Lopes de Almeida e Adalzira Bittencourt," Letras de Hoje, Porto Alegre, Rio Grande do Sul (PUC), 98; auth, "Last Tango in Jacobina," in Urban Voices/Urban Tales: Contemporary Brazilian Short Stories, Trans. Peggy Sharp, Denser, Marcia, ed, Cristina Ferreira-Pinto, Lanham, MD: Univ Press of Am, (99). **CONTACT ADDRESS** Dept Modern Lang, Univ of Mississippi, 312a Bishop, University, MS 38677. **EMAIL** psharpe@uiuc.edu

SHAW, BRADLEY ALAN
PERSONAL Born 12/23/1945, Tremonton, UT, m, 1969, 2 children **DISCIPLINE** SPANISH LANGUAGE, HISPANIC LITERATURE, TRANSLATION **EDUCATION** Lewis & Clark Col, BA, 68; Northwestern Univ, Evanston, MA, 69; Univ NM, PhD, 74. **CAREER** From instr to asst prof Span, Va Commonwealth Univ, 72-74; asst prof, 74-80, Assoc Prof Span & Dir, Secondary Maj Prog Latin Am Studies, Kans State Univ, 80-, Assoc Dir, Tri-Univ Ctr Latin Am Studies, 76-; assoc ed, Studies in Twentieth Century Lit; head, dept modern lang, 88-95; dir intl and area studies, coll of atrs and sci, 95. **MEMBERSHIPS** MLA; ACTFL; Am Transl(s) Assoc. **RESEARCH** Contemp Peruvian lit; Latin Am novel; Latin Am theater. **SELECTED PUBLICATIONS** Auth, Latin American Literature in English Translation: An Annotated Bibliography, New York Univ, 76; coauth, Hispanic Writers in French Journals: An Annotated Bibliography, Soc of Span & Span-Am Studies, 78; The new Spanish American narrative, Pac Quart, 78; auth, Latin American Literature in English: 1975-1978, suppl to Rev, 4/79; coauth, Luis Romero, Twayne, 79; translr, Mogollon (transl, Augusto Higa Oshiro, El equipito de Mogollon, In: Between Fire and Love: Contemporary Peruvian Writing, Miss Mud Press, 80; The Indigenista Novel in Peru After Arguedas: The Case of Mauel Scorza, Selecta, 82; The Overt Narrator in Scorzas Redoble Por Rancas, Discurso Literario, 86; Narrative Distance in Arguedas, La Agonia de Rasu-Niti, 86, Manue Scorza: Su Vision de la Realidad Mitica del Peru, 91. **CONTACT ADDRESS** Dept of Mod Lang, Kansas State Univ, 104 Eisenhower Hall, Manhattan, KS 66506-1003. **EMAIL** bradshaw@ksu.edu

SHAW, MICHAEL
DISCIPLINE CLASSICS **EDUCATION** Univ TX, PhD, 71. **CAREER** Assoc prof, Univ KS. **HONORS AND AWARDS** Mem, Ad hoc Comm for Women's Stud, 72-77. **RESEARCH** Greek and Roman lit. **SELECTED PUBLICATIONS** Auth, The Female Intruder: Women in Fifth-century Drama, Class Philol 70, 75; The ethos of Theseus in The Suppliant Women, Hermes ll0, 82. **CONTACT ADDRESS** Dept of Class, Univ of Kansas, Lawrence, Admin Building, Lawrence, KS 66045. **EMAIL** gorgo@kuhub.cc.ukans.edu

SHEA, GEORGE W.
PERSONAL Born 10/07/1934, Paterson, NJ, m, 1956, 3 children **DISCIPLINE** CLASSICAL LANGUAGES **EDUCATION** Fordham Univ, BA, 56; Columbia Univ, MA, 60, PhD(classics), 66. **CAREER** Asst prof Latin & Greek, St John's Univ, NY, 61-65; asst prof classics, asst dean, Fordham Col & dir jr year abroad prog, 67-70, assoc prof classics & dean Col at Lincoln Ctr, Fordham Univ, 70-85.; Prof Classics, 98-. **MEMBERSHIPS** Am Philol Asn **RESEARCH** Latin epic poetry and Roman history; Johannis of Flavius Cresconius Corippus. **SELECTED PUBLICATIONS** Auth, The Poems of Alcimus Avitus, MRTS, 97; The Iohannis of Flavius Crescorius Corippus, Mellon, 98; Delia and Nemesis, UPA, 98. **CONTACT ADDRESS** Classics Dept, Fordham Univ, 113 W 60th St, New York, NY 10023-7484. **EMAIL** gshea@fordham.edu

SHEA, KERRY
DISCIPLINE MIDDLE HIGH GERMAN AND OLD NORSE LITERATURE **EDUCATION** Cornell Univ, PhD. **CAREER** Eng, St. Michaels Col. **SELECTED PUBLICATIONS** Auth, Engendering Romance: Women and European Medieval Romance. **CONTACT ADDRESS** Saint Michael's Col, Winooski Park, Colchester, VT 05439. **EMAIL** kshea@smcvt.edu

SHEETS, GEORGE ARCHIBALD
PERSONAL Born 08/18/1947, Buenos Aires, Argentina, m, 1969, 2 children **DISCIPLINE** CLASSICAL LANGUAGES, HISTORICAL LINGUISTICS **EDUCATION** Univ NC, BA, 70; Duke Univ, PhD(class studies), 74; JD W. Mitchell Col of Law, 90. **CAREER** Instr classics, Univ TX, Austin, 74-75; Mellon fel classics, Bryn Mawr Col, 76-77; asst prof, 77-82, ASSOC PROF CLASSICS, UNIV MN, MINNEAPOLIS, 82-. **HONORS AND AWARDS** Rome Prize, Am Academy, 85. **MEMBERSHIPS** Am Philol Asn; Class Asn Mid West & South; Minnesota State Bar. **RESEARCH** Historical linguistics; Roman literature; legal history. **SELECTED PUBLICATIONS** Auth, Palatalization in Greek, Indoger Forsch, 75; Secondary midvowels in Greek, Am J Philol, 79; The dialect gloss, Hellenistic poetics and Livius Andronicus, 81, Am J Philol; Grammatical commentary to Book I of the Histories of Herodotus, Bryn Mawr Commentaries, 81; Ennius Lyricus, 8 IL Class Studies; Plautus and early Roman Tragedy, 8 Ill Class Studies, Conceptualizing International Law in Thucydides, 115, Am J Philol. **CONTACT ADDRESS** Classical and NE Studies, Univ of Minnesota, Twin Cities, 9 Pleasant St S E, 330 Folwel, Minneapolis, MN 55455-0194. **EMAIL** gasheets@umn.edu

SHELDON, RICHARD
PERSONAL Born 07/12/1932, Kansas City, KS, m, 1964, 4 children **DISCIPLINE** SLAVIC LANGUAGE & LITERATURE **EDUCATION** Univ Ks, BA, 54; Univ Mich, JD, 60, MA, 62, PhD, 66. **CAREER** Asst prof, 65-66, Grinnell Col; vis prof, 68, Univ Calif Berkeley; vis prof, 74, Stanford Univ; asst prof to prof, 66-, chair, 70-81, 90-00, dept of Russian lang & lit, assoc dean, 84-89, Dartmouth Col. **HONORS AND AWARDS** Phi Beta Kappa, 54; Nat Defense Act Fel, 61-64; Center for Adv Stud Fel, 69-70; Amer Coun of Learned Soc Grant, 70; Sr Assoc Member, St Antony's Col, Oxford, 83-84. **MEMBERSHIPS** AAASS; AATSEEL. **RESEARCH** Twentieth-century Russian lit **SELECTED PUBLICATIONS** Coed Soviet Society and Culture, Westview Press, 88; auth, The Transformations of Babi Yar, Soviet Society and Culture, Westview Press, 88; art, Problems in the English Translation of Anna Karenina, Essays in the Art and Theory of Translation, Edwin Mellen Press, 97; coauth, Westward Flows the Don: The Translation and the Text, Slavic & E Europ J, 98. **CONTACT ADDRESS** 86 S Main, Hanover, NM 03755-2029. **EMAIL** Richard.Sheldon@Dartmouth.edu

SHELMERDINE, CYNTHIA WRIGHT
PERSONAL Born 01/07/1949, Boston, MA **DISCIPLINE** CLASSICS; CLASSICAL ARCHAEOLOGY **EDUCATION** Bryn Mawr Col, AB, 70; Cambridge Univ, BA, 72, MA, 80; Harvard Univ, AM, 76, PhD, 77. **CAREER** Asst prof Classics, Univ Tex, Austin, 77-84; assoc prof, 84-97; prof, 97-; chair, 98-. **HONORS AND AWARDS** Marshall scholar, 70-72; Ctr. for Hellenic Studies, jr fel, 81-82; Pres assocs tchg award, Univ of Texas, 88. **MEMBERSHIPS** Archaeol Inst Am; Am Philol Asn; Am Sch Class Studies Athens Alumni Asn; Class Asn Middle West & South. **RESEARCH** Mycenaean Greek; Bronze Age Archaeology. **SELECTED PUBLICATIONS** Auth, The Pylos Ma tables reconsidered, Am Jour Archaeol, 73; contribur, Excavations at Nichoria (vol II), Univ Minn, (in press); Nichoria in context, Am Jour Archeol, 81; coauth, The Pylos Regional Archaeological Project. Part1: Overview and the Archaeological Survey, Hesperia 66, 97; auth, Review of Aegean Prehistory VI: The Palatial Bronze Age of the Central and Southern Greek Mainland, Am Jour of Archeol 101, 97; contribur, Sandy Pylos. From Nestor to Navarino, Univ Texas, 98. **CONTACT ADDRESS** Dept of Classics, Univ of Texas, Austin, Austin, TX 78712-1181. **EMAIL** cwshelm@mail.utexas.edu

SHELMERDINE, SUSAN C.
PERSONAL Born 04/21/1954, Boston, MA, s **DISCIPLINE** CLASSICAL STUDIES **EDUCATION** Smith Col, BA, 76; Univ Mich, MA, 77, PhD, 81. **CAREER** Lect, Univ N Carolina, 81-82, ast prof, 82-88; vis asoc prof, Univ Mich, 88-89; asoc prof, Univ N Carolina, 88-, dept head, 89-92, asoc dean, 92-95. **HONORS AND AWARDS** Jr fel, Ctr Hellenic Stud, Washington DC, 95-86; NEH Fel, 96-97. **MEMBERSHIPS** APA; Class Asn Middle West & South. **RESEARCH** Greek poetry; language pedagogy. **SELECTED PUBLICATIONS** Co-auth, Greek for Reading, Univ Mich, 94; auth, The Homeric Hymns, Focus Information Grp, 95; contribur, HarperCollins Dictionary of Religion, HarperCollins, 95; auth, "Greek Studies Today," Class Jrnl, 96 **CONTACT ADDRESS** Dept of Classical Studies, Univ of No Carolina, Greensboro, PO Box 26170, Greensboro, NC 27402-6170. **EMAIL** shelmerd@uncg.edu

SHERAK, CONSTANCE E.
PERSONAL Born 10/14/1958, Santa Rosa, CA **DISCIPLINE** LINGUISTICS, FRENCH **EDUCATION** Univ Calif Davis, BA, 80; Stanford Univ, MA, 84; PhD, 94. **HONORS AND AWARDS** Am Coun Learn Soc Trav Grnt, 96; Chateaubriand Fel Postdoc Res, 94-95; Whiting Found Fel, 87-88; Fr Govt Grnt Dis Res, 85-86; Fr Dept Fel, Stan Univ, 82-86. **MEMBERSHIPS** MLA; NMLA; AATF; AAUW; TCFS; INCS; ISSEI. **RESEARCH** Nineteenth-Century French studies; twentieth-century French studies; interrelations of art and literature; memory and literature cultural studies. **SELECTED PUBLICATIONS** Auth, Investing in the Past: Victor Hugo's ODE A LA BANDE NOIRE, Romance Lang Ann (99); auth, "Didactic Literature," in A Feminist Companion to French Literature, ed. Eva Sartori (Greenwood Press, 99); auth, "Exhibition at the Pictures: The Museological Text," in Hiroshima Mon Amor by Marguerite Duras, Memory, History, and Critique: European Identity (98); auth, "Wrapping Presence and Bridging the Cultural Gap: The Case of the Pont Neuf," in So Rich at Tapestry: The Sister Art and Cultural Theory, eds. Anne Hurley, Kate Greenspan (Bucknell UP, 95); auth, Die verhullte Gegenwart and die "Uberbruckung der kulturellen Kluft: Der Fall Pont-Neuf, Christo: The Pont Neuf Wrapped: Paris, 1975-85 (Kunstmuseum: Bonn, 93); auth, "Ouvert au public: The Musee Napoleon and the Politics of Appropriation," Stanford Lit Rev (89); auth, "Roland Barthes: Critique ou verite?," Constructions (85); auth, David Carrier: High Art: Charles Baudelaire and the Origins of Modernist Painting, Art Bull (97). **CONTACT ADDRESS** Dept of French, Connecticut Col, 270 Mohegan Ave, New London, CT 06320. **EMAIL** ceshe@conncoll.edu

SHERIDAN, JENNIFER A.
PERSONAL Born 04/01/1962, Englewood, NJ **DISCIPLINE** CLASSICS **EDUCATION** Montclair State Col, BA, 84; Columbia Univ, MA, 85, PhD, 90. **CAREER** Asst prof, St Joseph's Univ, 90-95; Asst prof, Wayne State Univ, 95-. **MEMBERSHIPS** APA, ANS, ASP, AIP, DCA, MCC, CAMWS **RESEARCH** Papyrology; Women in the ancient world. **SELECTED PUBLICATIONS** co-auth, Greek and Latin Documents from 'Abu Sha'ar, 1990-1991, Jour Amer Res Ctr In Egypt 31, 94; Greek and Latin Documents from 'Abu Sha'ar, 1992-1993, Bull Amer Soc Papyrologists 31, 94; auth, Women without Guardians: An Updated List, Bull Amer Soc Papyrologists 33, 96; Papyri numbers 257, 259, 286, Columbia Papyri X, 96; Not at a Loss for Words: The Economic Power of Literate Women in Late Antique Egypt, Transactions of Amer Philol Asn, 98; Columbia Papyri IX: The Vestis Militaris Codex, 98. **CONTACT ADDRESS** Dept of Classics, Wayne State Univ, 431 Manoogian Hall, Detroit, MI 48202. **EMAIL** aa2191@wayne.edu

SHERK, ROBERT K.
DISCIPLINE CLASSICS **EDUCATION** Johns Hopkins Univ, PhD, 50. **CAREER** Fac, 62; to prof emer, present, SUNY Buffalo. **RESEARCH** Hellenistic and Roman hist; epigraphy; ancient biog; Roman empire from Augustus to Hadrian. **SELECTED PUBLICATIONS** Auth, Roman Documents from the Greek East, Johns Hopkins, 69; Municipal Decrees of the Roman West, Buffalo, 70; The Roman Empire from Augustus to Hadrian, Cambridge, 88; articles on Hellenistic and Roman history; co-ed, Translated Documents of Greece and Rome, Cambridge, 177-85. **CONTACT ADDRESS** Dept Classics, SUNY, Buffalo, 712 Clemens Hall, Buffalo, NY 14260.

SHERMAN, CAROL LYNN
PERSONAL Born Fairfield, IA **DISCIPLINE** EIGHTEENTH-CCENTURY FRENCH LITERATURE **EDUCATION** Parsons Col, BS, 61; Northwestern Univ, Evanston, MA, 68; Univ Chicago, PhD(French), 72. **CAREER** Asst prof, 72-77, Assoc Prof French Lit, Univ NC, Chapel Hill, 77-83, Full Prof 83-, Ed, NCSRLL. **MEMBERSHIPS** Am Soc 18th Century Studies; SEASEÇS; MLA. **RESEARCH** Family-structures in 18th century French fictions. **SELECTED PUBLICATIONS** Auth, Diderot and the Art of Dialogue Genera: Droz, 76; auth, Reading Voltaire's "Contes" Chapel Hill: NCSRLL, 85; auth, Sample article "C'est l'insuffisance de 'etre qui fait naitre L'amihe": Women's Friendships in 18th-Century France: Women in French, 99. **CONTACT ADDRESS** Dept of Romance Lang, Univ of No Carolina, Chapel Hill, Chapel Hill, NC 27599-3170. **EMAIL** clsherman@email.unc.edu

SHERRY, LEE F.
PERSONAL Born 08/22/1954, Marietta, OH, m, 1992 **DISCIPLINE** CLASSICS **EDUCATION** Univ Texas, Austin, BA, 79; Columbia Univ, MA, 82, MPhil, 84; PhD, 91. **CAREER** Instr, Columbia Univ, 82-89; instr, NY Univ, 86-87; lectr, Queens Col, 88; tchr Latin, Trinity School, 87-91; lectr, Catholic Univ, 92-96; res assoc, Dumbarton Oaks, 91-96; tchr Latin, Kent Place School, Summit NJ, 96- . **HONORS AND AWARDS** Phi Kappa Phi, 78; Phi Beta Kappa, 79; Summa Cum Laude, 79; ETS approved scorer of AP Latin examination essays, 98-03; Cum Laude Soc, Kent Place Sch Chapter, 99; fac consultant to the AP 2000 Latin Reading, 00. **MEMBERSHIPS** APA; Am Class League; Class Asn of the Atlantic States; NJ Class Asn. **RESEARCH** Greek language and literature; Latin language and literature; Medieval and Byzantine studies; patristics; computers and the humanities. **SELECTED PUBLICATIONS** Coauth, Dumbarton Oaks Hagiography Database of the Ninth Century, 95; cotrans, The Poem of Maria Komnene Palaiologina to the Virgin and Mother of God, the

Chorine, Cahiers Archeologiques, 95; coauth, Thesaurus Pseudo-Nonni quondam Panopolitani, Paraphrasis Evangelii S. Ioannis, Corpus Christianorum, 95; coauth, The Dumbarton Oaks Byzantine Hagiography Database Project, Medieval Prosopography, 96; trans, Vita of Athanasia of Aegina, in Talbot, ed, Byzantine Saints' Lives in Translation Series, Dumbarton Oaks, 96; auth, The Paraphrase of St. John Attributed to Nonnus, Byzantion, 96; coauth, The Tale of a Happy Fool: The Vita of St. Philaretos the Merciful, Byzantion, 96; coauth, "Anonymous Miracles of St. Artemios," in AETOE: Studies in honour of Cyril Mango, ed. I. Sevcenko & I. Hutter (Teubner, 98), 200-209; coauth, History of Byzantine Lit, Vol I, Lit from 650 to 850, Inst for Byzantine Res/The Nat Hellenic Res Foundations (Athens), 99; transl, "Sappho 1," in The Classical Outlook, 77 (00): 2. **CONTACT ADDRESS** Kent Place Sch, 42 Norwood, Summit, NJ 07902-0308. **EMAIL** sherryl@kentplace.summit.nj.edu

SHERWIN, BYRON LEE
PERSONAL Born 02/18/1946, New York, NY, m, 1972, 1 child **DISCIPLINE** JEWISH STUDIES, CULTURAL HISTORY **EDUCATION** Columbia Univ, BS, 66; Jewish Theol Sem Am, BHL, 66, MHL, 68; New York Univ, MA, 69; Univ Chicago, PhD, 78. **CAREER** Res Asst, 66-70; Instr, Jewish theol Sem, 69; Vis Prof Chicago theol Sem, 72-74; Vis Prof, Mundelein Col, 74-82, Asst Prof, 70-74, Assoc Prof, 74-78, Prof, 78-, V Pres for Academic Affairs, 84-, Spertus Inst of Jewish Stud. **HONORS AND AWARDS** Presidential Medal, Poland, 95; Man of Dialogue Awd, Warsaw, 92; Life Tenure, Spertus Inst of Jewish Studies, 72; Cytron Prize, 70; Jacob Minkin Prize, 69; Cyrus Adler Scholar, 69; Friedenwald Prize, 67; Doctor of Hebrew Letters, Honoris Causa, 96. **MEMBERSHIPS** Rabbinical Assembly Am; Authors Guild; Am Philos Soc. **RESEARCH** Mysticism; ethics. **SELECTED PUBLICATIONS** Auth, Duchowe Dziedzictwo Zydow Polskich (The Spiritual Heritage of Polish Jews), Vocatio Pub, 95; art, The Tower of Babel, in: Bible Today, 95; art, Toward a Just and Compassionate Society: A Jewish View, in: Cross Currents, 95; art, The Golem, Zevi Ashkenazi and Reproductive Biotechnology, in: Judaism, 95; art, Euthanasia: A Jewish View, in: Reader in Jewish Ethics, 95; art, Jewish View of Abortion, in: New Theol Rev, 96; Inward Journeys: Life as Art Form, Comm in the Midst of Pluralism, 96; auth, Sparks Amidst the Ashes: The Spiritual Legacy of Polish Jewry, Oxford Press, 97; art, Yehudah Liva Ben Betsalel, in: Oxford Dict of the Jewish Rel, Oxford Univ Press, 97; art, Jewish Views on Euthanasia, Last Rights? Assisted Suicide and Euthanasia Debated, Eerdmans, 98; art, Memories and Meanings of Being Heschels Disciple, in: Consr Judaism, 98; auth, Crafting the Soul: Creating Your Life as a Work of Art, Inner Trad, 98; auth, Why Be Good?, Rodale, 98; auth, John Paul II and Intereligious Dialogue, Orbis, 99; auth, Jewish Ethics for the 21st Century, Syracuse Univ Pr, 00. **CONTACT ADDRESS** Spertus Inst of Jewish Studies, 618 S Michigan Ave, Chicago, IL 60605-1901. **EMAIL** bsherwin@spertus.edu

SHETTER, WILLIAM ZEIDERS
PERSONAL Born 08/17/1927, Allentown, PA **DISCIPLINE** GERMANIC LANGUAGES & LINGUISTICS **EDUCATION** Univ Pa, AB, 51; Univ Calif, MA, 53, PhD(Ger), 55. **CAREER** Teaching asst, Univ Calif, 51-55; instr Ger, Univ Wis, 56-59, asst prof, 59-61; from asst prof to assoc prof Ger, Bryn Mawr Col, 62-65, assoc prof Ger lang, 65-71, Prof Ger Lang, Ind Univ, 71-, Fulbright fel, State Univ Leiden, 55-56; res grant ling, State Univ Groningen, 61-62. **HONORS AND AWARDS** Officer in the Order of Oranje-Nassau (Netherlands). **MEMBERSHIPS** Ling Soc Am; MLA; Maatschappij der Nederlandse Taal - en Letterkunde; Amer Assoc for Netherlandic Studies. **RESEARCH** Linguistics; civilization of the Netherlands. **SELECTED PUBLICATIONS** Auth, The Netherlands in Perspective: The Dutch way of Organizing a Soc and its settings, Utrecht: NCB, 97. **CONTACT ADDRESS** Dept Ger Studies, Indiana Univ, Bloomington, Bloomington, IN 47401. **EMAIL** shetter@indiana.edu

SHEY, HOWARD JAMES
PERSONAL Born 07/21/1935, m, 1962, 2 children **DISCIPLINE** CLASSICS **EDUCATION** Creighton Univ, BA, 62; Ind Univ, Bloomington, MA, 63, Univ Iowa, PhD(classics), 68. **CAREER** From instr to asst prof classics, 66-72, Assoc Prof Classics, Univ Wis-Milwaukee, 72-, Bk rev ed, Class J, 68-73. **MEMBERSHIPS** Am Philol Asn; Class Asn Mid W & S. **RESEARCH** Latin and Greek lyric poetry; Latin epic. **SELECTED PUBLICATIONS** Auth, Petronius and Plato's Gorgias, Class Bull, 5/71; The poet's progress: Horace Ode 1 1,9/71 & Tyrtaeus and the art of propaganda, 5/76, Arethusa; Petrarch's Secretum, 89. **CONTACT ADDRESS** Dept of Classics, Univ of Wisconsin, Milwaukee, PO Box 413, Milwaukee, WI 53201-0413.

SHIELDS, JOHN CHARLES
PERSONAL Born 10/29/1944, Phoenix, AZ, s **DISCIPLINE** AMERICAN & CLASSICAL LITERATURES, COMPARATIVE LITERATURE **EDUCATION** Univ Tenn, Knoxville, BA, 67, MACT, 79, PhD(English), 78; George Peabody Col Teachers, EdS, 75. **CAREER** Teacher English & art hist, Sevier County High Sch, Sevierville, Tenn, 67-68; head dept English & teacher Latin, Battle Ground Acad, Franklin, Tenn, 67-68; dir acad, Brentwood Acad, Tenn, 71-73; Instr English, Columbia State Community Col, 75-76; assoc prof english, Ill State Univ, 86-93; prof, 93-; Instr English & dir writing lab, Univ Tenn, Nashville, 71-74; fac res grant, Ill State Univ, summers 80 & 81. **HONORS AND AWARDS** Nat Endowment for the Humanities Summer Seminar, 89, 93; Principal Project director of "Phillis Wheatley: An Aesthetic Appreciation on the Bicentennial of Her Death," funded by Nat Endowment for the Humanities, 84; Fel of the Soc for the Humanities at Cornell Univ, 84-85; Nat Endowment for the Humanties Summer Stipend, 83; The John C. Hodges Awd for teaching Excellence at the Univ of Tenn; Ford Found Fel. **MEMBERSHIPS** MLA; Medieval Acad Am; Soc Cinema Studies; Melville Soc; Am Studies Asn; Int Soc for Eighteenth-century Studies. **SELECTED PUBLICATIONS** Ed, The Collected Works of Phillis Wheatley, Oxford Up, 88; guest ed, African American Poetics: Style 26(3), 93; auth, Wheatley,Phillis Subversive Pastoral/, Eighteenth-Century Studies, Vol 0027, 1994; advisory ed and contrib, Oxford Companion to African American Literature, 97; advisory ed and contrib, American Naional Biography, 99; auth, The American Aeneas: Classical Origins of the American Self (forthcoming). **CONTACT ADDRESS** English Dept, Illinois State Univ, Normal, IL 61761.

SHIPLEY, GEORGE A.
DISCIPLINE SPANISH **EDUCATION** Dartmouth Col, AB, 59; Harvard Univ, AM, 62; PhD, 68. **CAREER** Teaching Fel, Harvard Univ, 61-64; Asst Prof and Lectr, Univ Calif, 64-67; From Asst Prof to Assoc Prof, Univ Wash, 67-. **MEMBERSHIPS** CSA. **RESEARCH** Experimental and innovative literary forms in Spain between 1490 and 1620, Cervantes, socio-historical approaches to literary study. **SELECTED PUBLICATIONS** Auth, "Fray Luis de Leon," Dict of the Lit of the Iberian Peninsula (Westport, CT: Greenwood Pr, 93), 930-936; auth, "Sancho's Jokework," Quixotic Desire: Psychoanalytic Perspectives on Cervantes, Greenwood Pr (93): 135-154; auth, "'Otras cosillas que no digo': Lazarillo's Dirty Sex," Renaissance Displacements: The Enduring Marginality of the Picaresque, Prisma Inst (96): 40-65; auth, "Some Novel Forms of Tension and Release," Hispanic Essays in Hon of Frank P Casa, Peter Lang Publ (97): 41-48; auth, "Longinus, Two Burkes, Tom Paine and Don Quixote: On the Sublime . . . and the Ridiculous," Yearbk of Comparative and Gen Lit, Ind UP (99): 53-70. **CONTACT ADDRESS** Dept Lang, Univ of Washington, PO Box 354360, Seattle, WA 98195-4360. **EMAIL** gshipley@u.washington.edu

SHIPLEY, WILLIAM F.
DISCIPLINE LINGUISTICS **EDUCATION** Univ Calif, Berkeley, PhD, 59. **CAREER** Prpf Emer, Univ Calif, Santa Cruz. **RESEARCH** Language and culture of the Maidu Indians; Linguistic hisotry of the languages of Western North America. **SELECTED PUBLICATIONS** Auth, Maidu Texts and Dictionary, Univ Calif Publ in Ling, vol 33, 63; Maidu Grammar, Univ Calif Publ in Ling, vol 41, 64; The Maidu Indian Myths and Stories of Hancibyjin, Heyday Press, 91; co-auth, Nisenan Texts and Dictionary, Univ Calif Publ in Ling, vol 46, 66; Proto-Maidun Stress and Vowel Length: Reconstruction of One, Two, Three, and Four, Intl Jour of Amer Ling, 79; auth, "Spanish loanwords in the National Languages of California," Romance Philology. **CONTACT ADDRESS** Dept of Ling, Univ of California, Santa Cruz, 1156 High St, Santa Cruz, CA 95064. **EMAIL** whipley@cruzio.com

SHIRINIAN, LORNE
DISCIPLINE ARMENIAN-NORTH AMERICAN LITERATURE **EDUCATION** Univ of Montreal, PhD. **CAREER** Prof and head of the Dept, Royal Military Col of Canada. **RESEARCH** Armenian-North American Lit; multiculturism; film noir, hard-boiled fiction, cinema and the cinematic adaptation of literary works. **SELECTED PUBLICATIONS** Auth, In a Dark Light: David Goodis and Film Noir; auth, Writing Memory: The Search for Home in Armenian Diaspora Literature and Film; auth, Survivor Memoirs and Photographs of the Armenian's Genocide; auth, History of Armenia and Other Fiction, auth, Forced Departures, auth, Rough Landing, auth, Ripe for Shaking. **CONTACT ADDRESS** Dept of English, Royal Military Col, 323 Massey Bldg., PO Box 17000, Kingston, ON, Canada K7K 7B4. **EMAIL** shirinian-l@rmc.ca

SHIRLEY, PAULA
PERSONAL Born 11/27/1945, Charleston, NC, m, 1969 **DISCIPLINE** COMPARATIVE LITERATURE **EDUCATION** Univ SC, Ba, 67, MA, 69, PhD, 76. **CAREER** Prof, 78. **HONORS AND AWARDS** NEH Summer Sem Fel, 83; Fulbright Hays Sem in India, 90. **RESEARCH** US Hispanic Literature. **SELECTED PUBLICATIONS** Co-auth, Understanding Chicano Literature, Univ SC Press, 88; auth, "Estela Portillo Trambley" in Chicago Writers: Third series, vol 212-221, DLB (Detroit: Gale Press, 99); "Reading Desi Arnaz in The Mambo Kings Play Songs of Love," in MELUS, vol 20, no 3 (Fall, 95). **CONTACT ADDRESS** Dept of Mod Lang and Lit, Columbia Col, So Carolina, 1301 Columbia Col Dr, Columbia, SC 29203. **EMAIL** pshirley@colacoll.edu

SHIVERS, GEORGE ROBERT
PERSONAL Born 09/09/1943, Salisbury, MD, m, 1988, 1 child **DISCIPLINE** SPANISH LAGUAGE & LITERATURE **EDUCATION** Am Univ, BA, 65; Univ Md, MA, 69, PhD(Span), 72. **CAREER** From Asst Prof to Assoc Prof, 69-86, Prof Span, Washington Col, 86-. **HONORS AND AWARDS** NEH Summer Inst 86; Fulbright Summer Study in Brazil, 87; NEH Summer Fel, 92. **MEMBERSHIPS** Am Asn Teachers Span & Port; Brazilian Studies Asn; Am Lit Transl Asn. **RESEARCH** Contemporary Spanish American literature and culture; literary translation; Brazilian literature and culture. **SELECTED PUBLICATIONS** Auth, La historicidad de El Cerco de Numancia de Milguel de Cervantes Saavedra, Hispanofila, 70; La vision magico-mesianica en tres relatos de Garcia Marquez, 6/75, El tema del hombre y su destino en Borges y Cortazar, 12/76 & La dualidad y unidad en La Casa Verde de Vargas Llosa, 6/77, Arbor; contribr, La unidad dramatica en la Cisma de Inglaterra de Calderon de la Barca, In: Perspectivas de la Comedia, Estudios de Hispanofila, 78; auth, The Other Without and the Other Within in Works by Julio Cortzar and Gabriel Garcia¤Marquez, In: In Retrospect: Essays on Latin American Literature, Span Lit Asn Publ, 87; transl, The Last Song of Manuel Sendero, Viking Press, 87; Trademark Territory, Index on Censorship, 5/88; My House is on Fire, Viking Press, 90; Hard Rain, Readers Int, 90; Some Write to the Future, Duke Univ Press, 91; auth, "God's Handwriting," English translation of "A caligrafia de Deus" by Marcio Souza, In Amazonian Literary Rev, 2, (99): 92-132. **CONTACT ADDRESS** Dept of For Lang, Lit, and Cult, Washington Col, 300 Washington Ave, Chestertown, MD 21620-1197. **EMAIL** george.shivers@washcoll.edu

SHOOKMAN, ELLIS
DISCIPLINE GERMAN LANGUAGE **EDUCATION** Yale Univ, PhD, 87. **CAREER** Assoc prof, Dartmouth Col. **HONORS AND AWARDS** Fulbright, Whiting, and Dartmouth Fels. **RESEARCH** 18th and 20th-century narratives and in subj such as fictionality and physiognomy **SELECTED PUBLICATIONS** Auth, Eighteenth Century German Prose, 92; auth, The Faces of Physiognomy: Interdisciplinary Approaches to Johann Caspar Lavater, 93; auth, Noble Lies, Slant Truths, Necessary Angels: Aspects of Fictionality in the Novels of Christoph Martin Wieland, 97. **CONTACT ADDRESS** Dept of German Studies, Dartmouth Col, 6084 Dartmouth Hall, Hanover, NH 03755-3511. **EMAIL** ellis.shookman@dartmouth.edu

SHORES, DAVID LEE
PERSONAL Born 01/28/1933, Tangier, VA, m, 1956, 2 children **DISCIPLINE** ENGLISH, LINGUISTICS **EDUCATION** Randolph-Macon Col, BA, 55; George Peabody Col, MA, 56, EdS, 64, PhD(English), 66. **CAREER** Instr English & Ger, Richard Bland Col, Col William & Mary, 61-62; from asst prof to assoc prof, 66-70, dir freshman English, 70-73, grad prog dir English, 73-75, chmn dept, 75-80, PROF ENGLISH, OLD DOMINION UNIV, 70-, Instr & assoc dir, US Off Educ Inst Col English Instr Black Cols, 70-73; consult, Nat Teachers Exam, Educ Testing Serv, 72-73. **MEMBERSHIPS** MLA; SAtlantic Mod Lang Asn; NCTE; Am Dialect Soc; Southeast Conf Ling. **RESEARCH** Old and Middle English language and literature; Chaucer; English linguistics. **SELECTED PUBLICATIONS** Auth, More On Porchmouth + Va Tidewater Pronunciation/, Am Speech, Vol 0069, 1994. **CONTACT ADDRESS** Dept of English, Old Dominion Univ, Norfolk, VA 23508.

SHOWALTER, ENGLISH
PERSONAL Born 05/14/1935, Roanoke, VA, m, 1963, 2 children **DISCIPLINE** FRENCH LANGUAGE **EDUCATION** Yale Univ, BA, 57; MA, 59; PhD, 64. **CAREER** Instr, Haverford Col, 61-64; Asst Prof, Univ of Calif Davis, 65-66; Asst Prof, Princeton Univ, 66-74; Exec Dir, MLA, 83-85; from Assoc Prof to Emer Prof, Rutgers Univ Camden, 74-. **HONORS AND AWARDS** Nat Endowment for the Humanities Fel, 77-78; Guggenheim Found Fel, 82-83; Warren L. Suman Awd for Excellence in Teaching, Rutgers, 86; Vis Int Res Prof, Reohampton Inst, London Eng, 93-95; Nat Endowment for the Humanities Collaborative Projects Grant, 97-98. **MEMBERSHIPS** MLA, ASECS, AATF, Societe Francaise d'etude du dix-huitieme siecle, AAUP. **RESEARCH** Eighteenth-century French Literature, ecpecially fiction, correspondence, salon womwn, Albert Camus. **SELECTED PUBLICATIONS** Auth, The Evolution of the French Novel, 1641-1782, Princeton Univ Press (Princeton), 72; auth, "Voltaire et ses amis, d'apres la correspondance de Madame de Graffigny," Studies on Voltaire and the Eighteenth Century 139 (Banbury: The Voltaire Found, 75); auth, "Madame de Graffigny and Rousseau: Between the Two 'Discours'," Studies on Voltaire and the Eighteenth Century 175 (Banbury: The Voltaire Found, 78); auth, Exiles and Strangers: A Reading of Camus's 'Excile and the Kingdom', Ohio State Univ Press (Columbus), 84; co-ed, La Correspondance complete de Madame de Graffigny, The Voltaire Found (Oxford), Vol 1- 85, Vol 2-89, Vol 3 - 92, Vol 4 - 96; Vol 5 - 97, Vol 6 - 00; auth, A Career Guide for PhDs and PhD Candiadiates in English and Foreign Lanaguages, MLA (NY), 85, coauth of retitled version, The MLA Guide to the Job Search, 96; auth, The Stranger: Humanity and the Absurd, Twayne Masterwork Studies 24, Boston: Twayne Publ (Boston), 89; ed, transl, My Night at Maud's, Films in Print Series, Rutgers Univ Press (New Brunswick), 93; ed, "La Modernite du genre romanesque en France au XVIIIe siecle," Special Issue

of Eighteenth-Century Fiction 7-4 (July 95); auth, "'Madame a fait un livre': Madame de Graffigny, Palissot et le 'Philosophes'," Recherches sur Diderot et L'Encyclopedie 23 (Oct 97): 109-125. **CONTACT ADDRESS** Dept French, Rutgers, The State Univ of New Jersey, Camden, 311 N 5th St., Camden, NJ 08102-1405. **EMAIL** showalte@crab.rutgers.edu

SHRAYER, MAXIM D.
PERSONAL Born 06/05/1967; Moscow, Russia **DISCIPLINE** SLAVIC AND EASTERN LANGUAGES **EDUCATION** Brown Univ, BA, 89; Rutgers Univ, MA, 90; Yale Univ, PhD, 94. **CAREER** Asst prof, Conn Col, 95-96; asst prof, Boston Col, 96-. **HONORS AND AWARDS** Nat Endowment for the Humanities, Fel for Univ Teachers, 97. **MEMBERSHIPS** AAASS, MLA, AATSEEL, Vladimir Nabokov Soc. **RESEARCH** Russian literature and culture; Jewish studies; cinema; translation. **SELECTED PUBLICATIONS** Auth, "Fall on Nantucket Island," AGNI, 48 (98): 119-120; auth, "Refuge in Paradise," The Southwest Rev, 83.3 (July 98): 348-55; auth, "Nabokov's sexography," Russian lit (99); auth, "Nabokov's 'Vasiliy Shishkov': An Author-Text Interpretation, " in Torpid Smoke: The Stories of Vladimir Nabokov, ed. Stephen G, Kellma and Irving Malin (Amsterdam: Rodopi, 99); auth, The World of Nabokov's Stories, Austin: Univ Tex Press (99); auth, Russian Poet/Soviet Jew: The Legacy of Edward Bagritskii, Lantham: Rowman and Littlefield (2000); auth, "The Perfect Glory of Nabokov's Exploit," Russian Studies in Lit (forthcoming); auth, Nabokov: Temy I variatsii (Nabokov: Themes and Varitations), St Petersburg: Akademic Proj (forthcoming). **CONTACT ADDRESS** Dept Slavic & Eastern Lang, Boston Col, Chestnut Hill, 210 Lyons Hall, Chestnut Hill, MA 02467-3804. **EMAIL** shrayerm@bc.edu

SHUFORD, WILLIAM HARRIS
PERSONAL Born 10/28/1932, Lincolnton, NC **DISCIPLINE** SPANISH **EDUCATION** Lenoir-Rhyne Col, AB, 54; Univ Fla, MA, 56; Univ NC, PhD(Romance lang), 63. **CAREER** Asst prof Span, Lenoir-Rhyne Col, 61-64, assoc prof, 64-67; assoc prof, Furman Univ, 67-69; chm dept mod & class lang, 69-, prof Span, Lenoir-Rhyne Col, 69-99; Pro Emer, Lenoir-Rehyne Col, 99-. **MEMBERSHIPS** MLA; SAtlantic Mod Lang Asn; Am Asn Teachers Span & Port. **CONTACT ADDRESS** Dept of Mod & Class Lang, Lenoir-Rhyne Col, 743 6th St. NE, Hickory, NC 28601-3976. **EMAIL** shufordw@lrc.edu

SHUMWAY, ERIC BRANDON
PERSONAL Born 11/08/1939, Holbrook, AZ, m, 1963, 7 children **DISCIPLINE** ENGLISH LITERATURE & POLYNESIAN LANGUAGES **EDUCATION** Brigham Young Univ, BA, 64, MA, 66; Univ VA, PhD, 73. **CAREER** From instr to assoc prof, 66-78, prof eng, Brigham Young Univ, HI, 78. **RESEARCH** Browning's love poetry; love in 19th century lit; the Tongan oral tradition. **SELECTED PUBLICATIONS** Auth, Intensive Course in Tongan, Univ HI, 71, rev, Inst of Polynesian Studies, with tapes, 88; Coe Ta'ane: A Royal Marriage (video doc), fall 76 & The Punake of Tonga (video doc), fall 77, Brigham Young Univ-HI; The eulogistic function of the Tongan poet, Pac Studies, fall 77; Tonga Saints: Legacy of Fartl, Inst for Polynesian Studies, 91; Koe Fakapangai: In the Circle of the Sovereign, 93 (video doc). **CONTACT ADDRESS** 55-220 Kulanui St, Laie, HI 96762-1294. **EMAIL** shumwaye@byuh.edu

SHUMWAY, NICOLAS
PERSONAL Born 09/22/1945, AZ, s **DISCIPLINE** LITERATURE, SPANISH **EDUCATION** BYU, BA, 69; UCLA, MA, 71; PhD, 76. **CAREER** Prof, Yale Univ, 92; prof to dir, Univ Tex, 93-. **HONORS AND AWARDS** Fulbright Prof, 00; Tomas Rivera Regents Prof, 93. **MEMBERSHIPS** MLA; LASA. **RESEARCH** Nationalism issues through literature. **SELECTED PUBLICATIONS** Auth, Invention of Argentina, Univ Calif Pr, 91; auth, Espanol en Espanol, Holt, Rinehart and Winston, 96, 4th ed. **CONTACT ADDRESS** Inst Latin Am Studies, Univ of Texas, Austin, Austin, TX 78712. **EMAIL** shumway@mail.utexas.edu

SHUY, ROGER W.
PERSONAL Born 01/05/1931, Akron, OH, m, 1952, 3 children **DISCIPLINE** LINGUISTICS **EDUCATION** Wheaton Col, IL, AB, 52; Kent State Univ, MA, 54; Western Reserve Univ, PhD, 62. **CAREER** Tchr lang arts, Kenmore Jr & Sr High Sch, Akron, OH, 56-58; from instr to asst prof Eng & ling, Wheaton Col, Ill, 58-64; assoc prof, MI State Univ, 64-67; dir sociolinguistics prog, Ctr Appl Ling, 67-70; dir Nat Sci Found grant to estabish prog in socioling, 70-73, Prof Ling & Dir Socioling Prog, Georgetown Univ, 70-87, Am Coun Learned Soc grant, 57; Univ Chicago res grant, 62; dir, Detroit Dialect Studies, 66-67; Carnegie Corp NY & Nat Inst Ment Health grants, Ctr Appl Ling, 67-; ling adv, Xerox Intermediate Dictionary, 72; mem eval panel, early childhood educ, Nat educ, Nat Inst Educ, 72-; comt socioling, Soc Sci Res Coun, 72-; assoc dir, Ctr Appl Ling, 74-; res award on acquistion of children's use of lang functions, Carnegie Corp of NY, 75; ch liguistics, 87-90; distinguished res prof, 96-98; prof Emeritus, 98. **MEMBERSHIPS** Int Reading Asn; Ling Soc Am; AAAS; Am Asn Appl Ling (pres, 78); Int Assoc of Forensic Linguistics; NCTE. **RESEARCH** Ling and educ; sociolinguistics; forensic linguistics. **SELECTED PUBLICATIONS** Auth, Discovering American Dialects, NCTE, 67; Field Techniques in an Urban Language Study, Ctr Appl Ling, 68; co-auth, New Ways of Analyzing Variation in English, 73, Language Attitudes, 73 & ed, Sociolinguistics: Current Trends and Prospects, 73, Georgetown Univ; co-ed, Dialect Differences: Do They Interfere?, Int Reading Asn, 73; ed, Linguistic Theory: What Does it Have to Say About Reading, Int Reading Asn, 77; Studies in Language Variation, Georgetown Univ, 77; ed, The Relation of Theoretical and Applied Linguistics, Plenum, 87; co auth, Dialogue Journal Communication, Ablcx, 88; auth, Language Crimes, Blackwell, 96; auth, The Language of Confession, Interrogation and Deception, Sage, 98; auth, Bereaucratic Language, Geargetown Press, 98. **CONTACT ADDRESS** 629 Beverly Ave, Missoula, MT 59801. **EMAIL** shuyr@gusun.georgetown.edu

SICES, DAVID
PERSONAL Born 06/10/1933, New York, NY, m, 1964, 4 children **DISCIPLINE** FRENCH LANGUAGE & LITERATURE **EDUCATION** Dartmouth Col, BA, 54; Yale Univ, PhD, 62; Fulbright fel, Paris, 56-57; Fulbright Summer fel, Rome, 66. **CAREER** Fulbright Fel, Paris, 56-57; Fulbright Summer Fel, Rome, 66; From instr to asst prof French, 57-66, assoc prof French & Ital, 66-71, chmn dept Romance lang & lit, 70-79, Prof French & Ital, 71-95, Prof Emer French & Italiab, 95- , Dartmouth Col, 71- ; Am Coun Learned Soc fel, Paris, 69-70; asst ed, French Rev, 80-; Nat Screening Comt, Inst Int Educ, 80- . **HONORS AND AWARDS** MA, Dartmouth Col, 71. **MEMBERSHIPS** Am Asn Teachers Fr; Am Asn Teachers Ital; Am Asn Univ Professors Ital. **RESEARCH** Theater of Musset and the Romantics; 19th century French poetry and novel; translation of French and Italian drama. **SELECTED PUBLICATIONS** Auth, Music and the Musician in Jean-Christopher, Yale Univ, 68; Theater of Solitude: The Drama of Alfred de Musset, New England Univ, 74; transl, Machiavelli, Comedies, New England Univ, 85; auth, Musset, Comedies and Proverbs, Johns Hopkins Univ, 94; auth, Machiavelli, Personal Correspondence, Northern Illinois Univ, 96; auth, 2001 French and English Idioms, Barron's, 96; auth, Musset, Historical Dramas, Peter Lang, 97; auth, Zink, Invention of Literary Subjectivity, Johns Hopkins Univ, 99. **CONTACT ADDRESS** Dept of French & Italian, Dartmouth Col, Hanover, NH 03755. **EMAIL** David.Sices@Dartmouth.edu

SICK, DAVID
PERSONAL Born 01/24/1966, Lancaster, PA, s **DISCIPLINE** CLASSICS **EDUCATION** Univ MN, PhD, 96. **CAREER** Instr, Macalester Col, 96-97; Asst Prof, Rhodes Col, 97-. **MEMBERSHIPS** Amer Philol Assoc; Amer Academy Relig; Soc Biblical Lit. **RESEARCH** Graeco-Roman relig; comparative myth. **SELECTED PUBLICATIONS** Auth, Cattle-Theft and the Birth of Mithras, JIES 24, 96. **CONTACT ADDRESS** Greek and Roman Studies, Rhodes Col, 2000 North Parkway, Memphis, TN 38112-1690. **EMAIL** sick@rhodes.edu

SIDER, DAVID
DISCIPLINE GREEK POETRY AND PHILOSOPHY **EDUCATION** Columbia Univ, PhD. **CAREER** Prof, Fordham Univ. **SELECTED PUBLICATIONS** Ed, The Fragments of Anaxagoras, Introduction and Commentary, 81; auth, Parmenides, The Fragments, Bryn Mawr Commentaries, 86; co-ed, The New Simonides, Arethusa volume 26 2, 96. **CONTACT ADDRESS** Dept of Class Lang and Lit, Fordham Univ, 113 W 60th St, New York, NY 10023.

SIEBER, JOHN HAROLD
PERSONAL Born 09/19/1935, Janesville, WI, m, 1960, 2 children **DISCIPLINE** RELIGION, CLASSICS **EDUCATION** Luther Col, BA, 58; Luther Theol Sem, BD, 62; Claremont Grad Sch, PhD(relig), 66. **CAREER** Asst prof classics, 65-67, asst prof relig, 67-72, assoc prof, 72-78, Prof to Prof Emer Relig & Classics, Luther Col, 78-. **HONORS AND AWARDS** Am Philos Soc res grant, 72. **MEMBERSHIPS** Soc Bibl Lit. **RESEARCH** Theology of Rudolf Bultman; Gnostic library from Nag-Hammdi, Egypt. **SELECTED PUBLICATIONS** Auth, An introduction to the Tractate Zostrianos from Nag Hammadi, Novum Testamentum, 7/73. **CONTACT ADDRESS** Dept of Relig, Luther Col, 700 College Dr, Decorah, IA 52101-1045. **EMAIL** sieberjo@luther.edu

SIEBURTH, STEPHANIE
DISCIPLINE SPANISH **EDUCATION** Univ Toronto, BA, 80; Princeton Univ, PhD, 84. **CAREER** Lectr, Brandeis, Univ, 84-87; asst prof to assoc prof, Duke Univ, 87-; assoc dir, 98-. **HONORS AND AWARDS** NEH Inst, Duke Univ, 99. **MEMBERSHIPS** MLA; Int Assoc of Hispanists. **RESEARCH** Mass culture and psychology, gender and economics, 19th and 20th century Spanish culture and literature. **SELECTED PUBLICATIONS** Auth, Reading La Regenta: Duplicitous discourse and the Entrophy of Structure, Purdue Univ Monographs, no 29, 90; auth, "Kiss and Tell: The Toad in La regenta" in Malevolent Insemination and Other Essays on Clarin, ed Noel M. Valis, Mich Romance Studies Series Vol X (90):87-100; auth, "Enlightenment, Mass Culture and Madness: The Dialectic of Modernity in La desheredada" in A Sesquicentennial Tribute to Galdos, ed Linda Willem (DE: Juan de la Cuesta, 93), 27-40; auth, Inventing High and Low: Literature, Mass Culture, and Uneven Modernity in Spain, Duke Univ Pr, 94; coauth, Keeping a Crime Unsolved: Characters and Critics Responses to Incest in Garcia Marquez's Chronicle of a Death Foretold, Revista de estudios hispanicos 30 (96):433-59; auth, "What Does it Mean to Study Modern Spanish Culture?", in Cambridge Companion to Modern Spanish Culture, ed David Gies, Cambridge Univ Pr, (99):11-20. **CONTACT ADDRESS** Dept Romance Lang, Duke Univ, PO Box 90257, Durham, NC 27708.

SIEKHAUS, ELISABETH
DISCIPLINE GERMAN STUDIES **EDUCATION** Univ Calif, Berkeley, BA, 65, MA, 67, PhD, 72. **CAREER** Prof; Mills Col, 77. **RESEARCH** German culture and literature; German poetry and music; Age of Goethe and the 19th century; interdisciplinary studies. **SELECTED PUBLICATIONS** Auth, Die lyrischen Sonette der Catharina Regina von Greiffenberg, Berner Beitraege zur Barockgermanistik: Peter Lang, Bern/ Frankfurt, 82; Europaeische Hochschulschriften: Peter Lang, Bern/ Frankfurt, 82 double-publ; Six Hundred Years of German Women's Poetry; introduced and ed, articles by Mills Col Ger majors, 92-94, 95; Strategies to Enhance the Foreign Language Learning Experience of Adult Beginners, In: The Canberra Linguist, Vol XVIII, 89. **CONTACT ADDRESS** Dept of German Studies, Mills Col, 5000 MacArthur Blvd, Oakland, CA 94613-1301. **EMAIL** siekhaus@mills.edu

SIGALOV, PAVEL S.
DISCIPLINE RUSSIAN AND SLAVIC LINGUISTICS **EDUCATION** Leningrad Univ, PhD, 63. **CAREER** Prof, Univ WY, 83-; vis prof, Harvard Univ, 89-91. **SELECTED PUBLICATIONS** Coauth, comp grammar of the Slavic lang; publ over 60 academic articles on Slavic ling & Russ lit. **CONTACT ADDRESS** Dept of Mod and Class Lang(s), Univ of Wyoming, PO Box 3964, Laramie, WY 82071-3964. **EMAIL** PSIGALOV@UWYO.EDU

SIHLER, ANDREW L.
PERSONAL Born 02/25/1941, Seattle, WA **DISCIPLINE** LINGUISTICS **EDUCATION** Harvard Univ, BA, 62; Yale Univ, MA, 65, PhD, 67. **CAREER** From asst prof to assoc prof ling, 78-99, prof ling, Univ Wis-Madison, 78-; emer, 99-. **SELECTED PUBLICATIONS** Auth, New Comparative Grammar of Greek and Latin, Oxford, 95; auth, Language History, an Introduction, John Benjamins, 00. **CONTACT ADDRESS** Dept of Ling, Univ of Wisconsin, Madison, 1220 Linden Dr, Madison, WI 53706-1557. **EMAIL** alsihler@facstaff.wisc.edu

SILBAJORIS, RIMVYDAS
PERSONAL Born 01/06/1926, Kretinga, Lithuania, m, 1955, 2 children **DISCIPLINE** RUSSIAN AND LITHUANIAN LITERATURES **EDUCATION** Antioch Col, BA, 53; Columbia Univ, MA, 55, PhD, 62. **CAREER** Instr to Asst Prof, Oberlin Col, 57-63; Assoc Prof to Prof, 67-91, Prof Emeritus Slavic & East Europ Langs, Ohio State Univ, 91-; Special Instr in Scientific Russ, Case Inst Technol, 57-58; Vis Prof, The Vytautas Magnus Univ, Lithuania, 92, 94; Vis Prof, Vilnius Pedagogical Univ, Lithuania, 97; Vis Prof, Univ NC, 95; Vis Prof, Northwestern Univ, 96. **HONORS AND AWARDS** Antioch Col For Students Scholarship, 49-53; Inter-University Travel Grant, 63-64; Lithuanian Community Achievement Awd for Publications on Lithuanian Literature in English, 82; Lithuanian Med Asn Achievement Awd for contributions to Lithuanian cultural activities abroad, 85; The Vilis Vitols Prize for contribution to the J Baltic Studies in the 1989 publication year; recipient of numerous grants and fellowships. **MEMBERSHIPS** Am Asn Teachers Slavic & East Europ Langs; Am Asn Advancement Slavic Studies; Baltiska Inst, Stockholm Univ; Asn Advancement Baltic Studies; Am Asn Univ Prof; Inst Lithuanian Studies; Asn Russ-Am Schol USA. **RESEARCH** Russian poetry and prose, particularly Tolstoy; Lithuanian literature. **SELECTED PUBLICATIONS** Ed, Tolstoy and the Teachers. Essays on War and Peace, Ohio State Univ Slavic Papers, 85; auth, Tolstoy's Aesthetics and His Art, Slavica Publ, 91; Netekties zenklai (Signs of Dispossession), Vaga Publ house, 92; War and Peace. Tolstoy's Mirror of the World, Twayne Publ, 95; author of numerous journal articles and other publications. **CONTACT ADDRESS** Slavic Languages Dept, Ohio State Univ, Columbus, Columbus, OH 43210. **EMAIL** Silbajoris.1@osu.edu

SILBER, CATHY L.
DISCIPLINE CHINESE **EDUCATION** Univ Iowa, BA, 80, MA, 84; Univ Mich, Ann Arbor, PhD, 95. **CAREER** Asst prof & coordr, Chinese Lang and Lit Prog, Williams Col, 97-; asst prof, Iowa State Univ, Ames, 95-97. **HONORS AND AWARDS** Am Coun of Learned Soc, Fel, 00-01; Radcliffe Ins for Advan Study, Harvard Univ, Bunting Fel., 00-01. **RESEARCH** Chinese language, literature, and culture; gender studies. **SELECTED PUBLICATIONS** Trans, Wang Meng, A Winter's Topic, The Stubborn Porridge and Other Stories, NY: George Braziller, 94; cotransl & co-ed, Ding Xiaoqi, Maidenhome, Melbourne: Hyland House in assoc with Monash Asia Inst, 93; San Francisco: Aunt Lute Bk(s), 94; auth, From Daughter to Daughter-in-law, Women's Script of Southern Hunan, Engendering China: Women, Culture, and the State, Harvard Univ Press, 94; trans, Women Writers of Traditional China: An Anthology of Poetry and Criticism, 99; trans, Yan

Geling: The Lost Daughter of Hapiness, Hyperion, 01. **CONTACT ADDRESS** Dept of Asina Studies, Williams Col, Stetson Hall, Williamstown, MA 01267. **EMAIL** csilber@williams.edu

SILBERMAN, M.
PERSONAL Born 04/08/1948, Minneapolis, MN, m, 1981 **DISCIPLINE** GERMAN **EDUCATION** Univ Minn, BA cum laude 69; Indiana Univ, MA 72, PhD 75. **CAREER** Univ Texas SA, asst, assoc prof 75-88; Univ Wisconsin Madison, assoc prof, prof, 88 to 98-; UCLA, guest prof 89; Free Univ of Berlin, guest prof, 95 & 99. **MEMBERSHIPS** MLA; ATG; IBS; SCS; GSA. **RESEARCH** German lit, cult, theater and cinema in 20th century. **SELECTED PUBLICATIONS** Auth, German Cinema: Texts in Context, Detroit, WSU Press, 95; Contentious Memories: Looking Back at the GDR, co-ed, NY Peter Lang, 98; drive b: Brecht 100, Berlin, Theater der Zelt Intl Brecht Soc, 97. **CONTACT ADDRESS** German Dept, Univ of Wisconsin, Madison, 818 Van Hise Hall, Madison, WI 53706. **EMAIL** mdsilber@facstaff.wisc.edu

SILENIEKS, JURIS
PERSONAL Born 05/29/1925, Riga, Latvia, m, 1952, 2 children **DISCIPLINE** FRENCH LITERATURE **EDUCATION** Univ Nebr, BA, 55, MA, 57, PhD, 63. **CAREER** Instr French, Univ Nebr, 57-60; from instr to assoc prof, 61-71, head dept, 68-79, Prof Mod Lang, Carnegie-Mellon Univ, 71-, Dir Prog Mod Lang, 79- **MEMBERSHIPS** MLA; Am Asn Teachers Fr; Asn Advan Baltic Studies. **RESEARCH** Black writers of French expression; contemporary French theater; Latvian literature. **SELECTED PUBLICATIONS** Auth, Themes and Dramatic Forms in the Plays of Armand Salacrou, Univ Nebr, 67; The image of the United States in the writings of French-speaking Black authors, Africa Today, summer 72; Latvian literature in exile, Lituanus, 72; contribr, The middle passage in Francophone literature (festschrift), Soc Span Am Studies, 78; Glissant's prophetic vision of the past, African Lit, Today, 80; ed, Monsieur Toussaint (play by Glissant), Three Continents Press, 82. **CONTACT ADDRESS** Dept of Mod Lang, Carnegie Mellon Univ, Schenley Park, Pittsburgh, PA 15213.

SILVA, ARLYN SANCHEZ
DISCIPLINE CONTEMPORARY SPANISH-AMERICAN LITERATURE **EDUCATION** Univ Puerto Rico, BA; Harvard Univ, MA, PhD. **CAREER** Lit, Emmanuel Col. **MEMBERSHIPS** MLA; Am Asn Tchrs Span & Portuguese; Sine Nomine. **SELECTED PUBLICATIONS** Coauth, Davis Grant proposal for assessment of the tech needs in for lang pedag; auth, La Novelistica de Manuel Zeno Gandra, Instituto de Cutlura Puertorriquena, 96. **CONTACT ADDRESS** Emmanuel Col, Massachusetts, 400 The Fenway, Boston, MA 02115. **EMAIL** silva@emmanuel.eduv

SILVA, DAVID JAMES
DISCIPLINE LINGUISTICS **EDUCATION** Harvard Univ, AB, 86; Cornell Univ, MA, 89; PhD, 92. **CAREER** Asst Prof, Univ Tex, 93-99; Assoc Prof, Univ Tex, 99-. **HONORS AND AWARDS** John Harvard Scholar, Harvard Univ, 84-86; Clark Distinguished Teaching Awd, Cornell Univ, 89; Fulbright Fel, Korean-Am Educ Commn; Phi Kappa Phi, Cornell Univ, 91; Gertrude Golladay Mem Awd for Outstanding Teaching, Univ Tex, 95; **MEMBERSHIPS** Am Asn of Teachers of Span and Port, AAUP, ICKL, LASSA, LSA. **RESEARCH** Language variation, phonetics, phonology, Korean, Portuguese. **SELECTED PUBLICATIONS** Auth, "The Variable Deletion of Unstressed Vowels in Azorean Portuguese," Lang Variation and Change, 9.3 (97): 1-15; auth, "Vowel Elison in Sao Miguel Portuguese," Hispania, 81 (98): 166-178; auth, "Reevaluating Syntax-to-Phonology Mapping in Korean: An Optimality-Acoustic Account," Lang Res, 34 (98); auth, Japanese-Korean Linguistics, Vol 8, CLSI (Stanford, CA). **CONTACT ADDRESS** Dept Ling, Univ of Texas, Arlington, Hammond Hall 403, PO Box 19559, Arlington, TX 76019-0559. **EMAIL** david@uta.edu

SILVA-CORVALAN, CARMEN M.
PERSONAL Born, Chile **DISCIPLINE** LINGUISTICS **EDUCATION** Univ Chile, BA, 70; Univ London, MA, 73; Univ Calif, Los Angeles, MA, 77, PhD(Ling), 79. **CAREER** Assoc prof Appl Ling, Univ Chile, 73-78; prof Span Ling, Univ Southern Calif, 79-. **HONORS AND AWARDS** NSF grants 83, 88; Ford Found Fell, 75-79; Brit Council Scholarship, 71-73. **MEMBERSHIPS** Ling Soc Am; Am Asn Teachers Span & Port; Asn Ling y Filol America Latina; Soc. Espanola de Linguistica. **RESEARCH** Sociolinguistics; language change; Spanish syntax and semantics; bilingualism; discourse analysis. **SELECTED PUBLICATIONS** Auth, La funcion pragmatica de la duplicacion de pronombres cliticos, Boletin Filologia, Vol XXXI, 80; The diffusion of object verb agreement in Spanish, Papers in Romance, 12/81; contribr, Spanish in the United States: Sociolinguistics Aspects, Cambridge Univ Press, 82; On the interaction of word order and intonation, In: Discourse Perspectives on Syntax, Acad Press, 82; Sociolinguistica: Teoria y analisis, Alhambra, 89; Language Contact and Change: Spanish in Los Angeles, Clarendon, 94; Invariant meanings and contextbound functions of tense in Spanish, In: The Function of Tense in Texts, North-Holland, 91; The gradual Loss of Mood Distinctions in Los Angeles Spanish, Lang Variation and Change, 94; Contextual Conditions for the interpretation of poder and deber in Spanish, In: Modality in Grammar and Discourse, Benjamins, 95; auth, "Spanish in Four Continents," ed., Georgetown Univ Press, 95; On Borrowing as a Mechanism of Syntactic Change, in: Romance Linguistics: Theoretical Perspectives, J Benjamins, 98. **CONTACT ADDRESS** Dept of Spanish & Portuguese, Univ of So California, 3501 Trousdale Pky, Los Angeles, CA 90089-0008. **EMAIL** csilva@usc.edu

SILVA-FILHO, EURIDICE
DISCIPLINE PORTUGUESE LITERATURE **EDUCATION** Univ NC, PhD, 94. **CAREER** Asst prof, Port, Univ Tenn. **MEMBERSHIPS** Am Port Studies Asn. **RESEARCH** Post modernism in Brazil; literary theory; popular culture; foreign language acquisition. **CONTACT ADDRESS** Dept of Mod For Langs & Lits, Univ of Tennessee, Knoxville, 701 McClung Tower & Plaza, Knoxville, TN 37996. **EMAIL** esilva@utk.edu

SILVER, PHILIP WARNOCK
PERSONAL Born 11/12/1932, Bryn Mawr, PA, m, 1958, 3 children **DISCIPLINE** SPANISH **EDUCATION** Haverford Col, BA, 54; Middlebury Col, MA, 55; Princeton Univ, MA, 60, PhD, 63. **CAREER** Instr Span, Rutgers Univ, 61-63; asst prof, Oberlin Col, 63-66, assoc prof, 67-71; vis prof, 71-72, chmn dept, 73-76, Prof Span & Port, Columbia Univ, 72-, Guggenheim fel, 66; Nat Endowment for Humanities fel, 76. **MEMBERSHIPS** MLA; Am Transl Am. **RESEARCH** Modern Spanish poetry & novel; philosophy and esthetics of Oretga y Gasset. **SELECTED PUBLICATIONS** Auth, Towards A Revisionary Theory Of Spa Romanticism/, Revista De Estudios Hispanicos, Vol 0028, 1994; The Politics Of Spa Romanticism/, Critica Hispanica, Vol 0018, 1996. **CONTACT ADDRESS** Dept Span & Port, Columbia Univ, 2960 Broadway, New York, NY 10027-6900.

SILVERBERG, JOANN C.
PERSONAL Born 05/19/1940, New York, NY, 1 child **DISCIPLINE** CLASSICAL PHILOLOGY **EDUCATION** Barnard, AB, 60; Radcliffe, AM, 62; Harvard, PhD, 67. **CAREER** Sweet Briar Col, 64-65; from asst prof to assoc prof, 67-, Conn Col. **HONORS AND AWARDS** Phi Beta Kappa; Woodrow Wilson Fel; Mellon, Fulbright, Dartmouth-Dana, NYS Regents Grants. **MEMBERSHIPS** APA; CANE. **RESEARCH** Latin and Greek language and literature; historiography, comedy and love poetry; linguistics, gender and women's studies. **SELECTED PUBLICATIONS** Auth, for, A Feminist Classicist Reflects on Athena; auth, rev, The Chilly Classroom Climate: A Guide to Improve the Education of Women, 98; coauth, Semantic and pragmatic aspects of set-relational reference in modern Indo-European languages, with Camille Manlon, Pragmatics vol 8, no. 4, December 98; Culture Wars: Rome 56 B.C., Published in Language and Ideology Selected Papers from the 6th International Pragmatics Conference, jef Verschueren vol. 1, 99. **CONTACT ADDRESS** Connecticut Col, 270 Mohegan Ave, Box 5551, New London, CT 06320. **EMAIL** jcsil@conncoll.edu

SILVERMAN, DANIEL
PERSONAL Born 03/09/1963, s **DISCIPLINE** LINGUISTICS **EDUCATION** Univ of Pensylvania, BA, 85; UCLA, PhD, 95. **CAREER** Asst Prof, 97-, UIUC. **RESEARCH** Phonology. **SELECTED PUBLICATIONS** Auth, Reduplication in Kihehe The Asymmetrical Enforcement of Phonological and Morphological Principles, Ling Jour of Korea, 93; CoAuth, Aerodynamic Evidence for Articulatory Overlap in Korean, Phonetica, 94; CoAuth, Phonetic Structures in Jalapa Mazatec, Anthropological Ling, 95; Auth, Optional Conditional and Obligatory Prenasalization in Bafanji, Jour of W African Lang, 95; Phonology at the Interface of Morphology and Phonetics Root-Final Laryngeals in Chong Korean and Sanskrit, Jour of E Asian Ling, 96; Tone Sandhi in Comaltepec Chinantec, Language, 97; Laryngeal complexity in Otomanguean vowels, Phonology, 97. **CONTACT ADDRESS** 212 W Healey #203, Champaign, IL 81820. **EMAIL** daniel@cogsci.uiuc.edu

SILVERMAN, MALCOLM NOEL
PERSONAL Born 04/18/1946, New York, NY, m, 1974, 2 children **DISCIPLINE** PORTUGUESE & SPANISH LANGUAGES **EDUCATION** Queens Col, NYork, BA, 67: Univ Ill, MA, 68, PhD, 71. **CAREER** Asst prof Port & Span, Univ Kans, 70-73, dir jr year abroad, Costa Rica, 73; sr lectr Port, Univ Witwatersrand, 74-75; lectr, 75-77, asst prof, 77-79, assoc prof, 79-82, prof Port & Span, San Diego State Univ, 82-; vis prof Port, Univ Costa Rica, 73. **MEMBERSHIPS** Am Asn Teachers Span & Port. **RESEARCH** Contemporary Brazilian prose fiction; Luso-Brazilian literature; 20th Century Portuguese novel. **SELECTED PUBLICATIONS** Auth, Moderna Ficcao, Brasileira, Vol I, 78 & Vol II, 81, Civilizacao Brasileira/MEC; O Novo Conto Brasileiro, Nova Fronteira; A Satira na Prosa Brasileira Pos-1964, Codecri; Imagens Jornalisticas Brasileiras, McGraw-Hill; Protesto c o Novo Romance Brasileiro, Civilizacao Brasileira. **CONTACT ADDRESS** Dept Span & Port, San Diego State Univ, 5500 Campanile Dr, San Diego, CA 92182-7703. **EMAIL** silverma@mail.sdsu.edu

SILVESTRI, ELENA M.
PERSONAL Born 06/11/1961, Hamilton, ON, Canada **DISCIPLINE** FRENCH, ENGLISH AS SECOND LANGUAGE **EDUCATION** McMaster Univ, BA, 84; Universite Rene Descartes, DEA, 85; doctorat en linguistique, 96. **CAREER** Lectr, instr, McMaster Univ, 92-97, 00; prof, Univ Regina, 97; asst prof, Yamaguchi Univ, 98-00; asst prof, McMaster Univ, 01-02, director, Int Lang and Cult Center, 00-. **HONORS AND AWARDS** Dalley Scholarship; Yates Scholarship; French Govt Book Prize; Swiss Govt Book Prize; 1st Prize, McMaster Univ Classics Contest. **MEMBERSHIPS** MLA, Can Ling Assoc. **RESEARCH** Bilingualism, Code-Switching, Conversational Analysis of bilingual interactions. **SELECTED PUBLICATIONS** Auth, "Choix de langues et roles discursifs dans une conversation familiale italo-canadienne," Plurilinguismes, no 1, (90): auth, "Personalized Profiles of Code-Switching," Europ Sci Found - Network on Code Switching and Lang Contact, (95); auth, "L'Alternance des langues dans une conversation familiale bilingue italo-canadienne," Presses Universitaires du Septentrion, (97); auth, "this is regular conversation©": Auto-commentaires dans une conversation familiale bilingue," Plurilinguismes, no 14, (98). **CONTACT ADDRESS** Int Lang and Cult Centre, McMaster Univ, 65 Christopher Dr, Hamilton, ON, Canada L9B 1G6. **EMAIL** ilcc@canada.com

SIMON, ECKEHARD
PERSONAL Born 01/05/1939, Schneidemuhl, Germany, m, 1959, 4 children **DISCIPLINE** MEDIEVAL GERMAN LITERATURE, PHILOLOGY, CULTURAL HISTORY **EDUCATION** Columbia Col, AB, 60; Harvard Univ, AM, 61, PhD, 64. **CAREER** From Instr to Prof Ger, 64-96, Victor S. Thomas Prof Ger Lang, Harvard Univ, 96-, Chmn Dept Ger Lang & Lit, 76-82, 85-86, 96-99; asst ed, Speculum, J Medieval Studies; 76-00. **HONORS AND AWARDS** Nat Endowment for Hum younger scholar fel, 69; Guggenheim Mem Found fel, 69; Nat Endowment for Hum fel for Independent study and res, 77; Fulbright sr res grant, Cologne, 83. **MEMBERSHIPS** Medieval Acad Am; MLA; Am Asn Tchr(s). **RESEARCH** Middle High German song poetry; Medieval German drama; Editing; codicology. **SELECTED PUBLICATIONS** Auth, Neidhart von Reuental: Geschichte der Forschung und Bibliographie, Harvard Germanic Studies 4, Harvard Univ Press, 68; Neidhart von Reuental, Twayne's World Authors ser, 364, Twayne, G K Hall, 75; The Turkenkalender (1454) Attributed to Gutenberg and the Strasbourg Lunation Tracts, Speculum Anniversary Monographs 16, The Medieval Acad Am, 88; ed, The Theatre of Medieval Europe. New Research in Early Drama, Cambridge Studies in Medieval Lit 9, Cambridge Univ Press, 91; Die Anfange des weltlichen deutschen Schauspiels, 1370-1530, Press; The Carnival of Nuremberg (in progress); author of numerous articles and rev. **CONTACT ADDRESS** Harvard Univ, Barker Ctr 345, Cambridge, MA 02138-3879. **EMAIL** simon2@fas.harvard.edu

SIMON, ROLAND HENRI
PERSONAL Born 10/07/1940, Haiphong, North Vietnam **DISCIPLINE** LITERARY SEMIOTICS, FRENCH CIVILIZATION **EDUCATION** Univ Wis, MA, 67 Stanford Univ, Ph-D(French & humanities), 76. **CAREER** Instr French, Middlebury Col, 72-75, dean French sch, 73-76, asst prof, 75-76; Asst Prof French, Univ VA, 76-. **MEMBERSHIPS** MLA; Am Asn Teachers French; NEastern Mod Lang Asn; SAtlantic Mod Lang Asn. **RESEARCH** Theory of literature; autobiography; French civilization. **SELECTED PUBLICATIONS** Auth, Le role de l'ecriture dans La Chute de Camus et Quelqu'un de Pinget, 74 & Les Prologues du Quart Livre de Rabelais, 74, French Rev; Langage et authenticate dans Biffures de Michel Leiris, Stanford French Rev, 78; Pour une nouvelle pedagogie du theatre classique, Australian J French Studies, 78. **CONTACT ADDRESS** Dept of French & Gen Ling, Univ of Virginia, 1 Cabell Hall, Charlottesville, VA 22903-3125.

SIMONS, JOHN DONALD
PERSONAL Born 10/05/1935, Lone Oak, TX, m, 1962 **DISCIPLINE** GERMAN & COMPARATIVE LITERATURE **EDUCATION** Univ TX, BA, 59, MA, 6 1; Rice Univ PhD, 66. **CAREER** Instr English, Berlitz Sch Lang, Paris, 59-61; instr Ger, TX Southern Univ, 62-66; asst prof, Univ IA, 66-70; Assoc Prof Ger & Comp Lit, FL State Univ, 70-. **HONORS AND AWARDS** Fulbright Teacher Exchange, Bremen, GER, 87-88. **MEMBERSHIPS** MLA; Am Asn Teachers Ger; AAUP; Int Dostoevsky Soc. **RESEARCH** Eighteenth and 20th century German literature. **SELECTED PUBLICATIONS** Auth, The Nature of Oppression in Don Carlos, Mod Lang Notes, 4/69; Myth of Progress in Schiller and Dostoevsky, Comp lit, 4/72; Hermann Hesse's Steppenwolf. A Critical Commentary, 72, Gunter Grass' The Tin Drum, 73, Thomas Mann's Death in Venice, 74, Dostoevsky's Crime and Punishment, 76 & The Brothers Karamazov, 76, Simon & Schuster; Friedrich Schiller, Twayne, 81; Literature and Film in the Historical Dimension, Univ Press FL, 94; and numerous articles on German literature. **CONTACT ADDRESS** Dept of Mod Lang, Florida State Univ, 600 W College Ave, Tallahassee, FL 32306-1096. **EMAIL** jsimons@mailer.fsu.edu

SIMPSON, ETHEL C.
PERSONAL Born 07/22/1937, Opelousas, LA, w, 1959, 2 children **DISCIPLINE** COMPARATIVE LIT **EDUCATION** Univ Arkansas PhD, 77. **CAREER** Univ MD, Instr eng stud, 60-64; Southeastern LA Univ, asst prof eng, 65-69; Univ Arkansas, various, 74-, prof, librarian, hd of arch and manuscripts, special col, 87-. **MEMBERSHIPS** Phi Beta Kappa; Phi Kappa Phi. **RESEARCH** Arkansas and regional stud **SELECTED PUBLICATIONS** Simkinsville and Vicinity: Arkansas Stories of Ruth McEnery Stuart, Fayetteville, Univ AR Press, 83; Tulip Evermore: Emma Butler and William Paisley, Their Lives in Letters, 1857-1887, with Eliz Paisley Huckaby, Fayet, Univ AR Press, 85; Arkansas in Short Fiction, with William M Baker, Little Rock, August House, 86; Image and Reflection: Pictorial Hist of Univ AR, Fayet, Univ AR Press, 90; The Selected Letters of John Gould Fletcher, with Leighton Rudolph, Fayet, Univ AR Press, 96. **CONTACT ADDRESS** Univ of Arkansas, Fayetteville, Special Collections, Mullins Library, Fayetteville, AR 72701. **EMAIL** esimpson@comp.uark.edu

SIMPSON, MICHAEL
DISCIPLINE CLASSICAL STUDIES **EDUCATION** Yale Univ, PhD, 64. **CAREER** Prof. **SELECTED PUBLICATIONS** Auth, Gods and Heroes of the Greeks: The Library of Apollodorus, Univ Mass, 95; Manners as Morals: Hospitality in the Odyssey, Art Inst, 92; Artistry in Mood: Iliad 3.204-224, Class Jour, 88; Cosmologies and Myths, Charles Scribner's Sons, 88. **CONTACT ADDRESS** Dept of Classics, Univ of Texas, Dallas, Richardson, TX 75083-0688. **EMAIL** msimpson@utdallas.edu

SIMPSON, PETER P.
PERSONAL Born, England **DISCIPLINE** CLASSICS, PHILOSOPHY **EDUCATION** Victoria Univ Manchester, UK, PhD **CAREER** Asst prof, Univ Col Dublin, Ireland, 82-84; asst prof, Catholic Univ Am, DC, 84-88; Full prof, City Univ NY, 88- . **HONORS AND AWARDS** Earhart found fel, 95; Jr fel, Ctr Hellenic stud, 92. **MEMBERSHIPS** APA; ACPA; APSA; SAGP; APPA. **RESEARCH** Ancient and medieval philosophy; moral and political philosophy. **SELECTED PUBLICATIONS** Auth, The Politics of Aristotle, U of North Carolina P, 97; A Philosophical Commentary on the Politics of Aristotle, U of North Carolina P, 98. **CONTACT ADDRESS** Dept of Philosophy, Col of Staten Island, CUNY, 2800 Victory Blvd, 2N, Staten Island, NY 10314. **EMAIL** simpson@postbox.csi.cuny.edu

SIMS, EDNA N.
PERSONAL Born Joliet, IL **DISCIPLINE** SPANISH LANGUAGE & LITERATURE **EDUCATION** Univ Ill, Urbana, BAT, 62; MA, 63; Cath Univ Am, PhD, 70. **CAREER** Instr Span & French, Howard Univ, 63-69; Prof Span & French, DC Teachers Col, 70-, Vis prof Span, Inter-Am Univ PR, San German, 70; mem foreign lang comt, US Dept Agr Grad Sch, 70-; vis prof Span, Univ Panama, 71. **MEMBERSHIPS** Am Coun Teachers Foreign Lang; Am Asn Teachers Span & Port; Hisp Rev Suc; Col Lang Asn. **RESEARCH** Spanish language; Spanish literature. **SELECTED PUBLICATIONS** Auth, Poet, Mystic, Modern-Hero, Revista De Estudios Hispanicos, 92; Ideas + The Use Of Electronic Equipment In Learning A Foreign-Lang - A Cult Excursion With A Tape-Recorder Devoted To The Teaching Of Spa And Port, 95. **CONTACT ADDRESS** Dept of Foreign Lang, Univ of the District of Columbia, Washington, DC 20009.

SIMS, ROBERT LEWIS
PERSONAL Born 10/26/1943, Petoskey, MI **DISCIPLINE** FRENCH & SPANISH **EDUCATION** Univ Mich, BA, 66; Univ Wis, MA, 68, PhD(French), 73. **CAREER** Asst prof French & Span, Colby Col, 73-74; asst prof, Pa State Univ, 74-76; Asst Prof French & Span, VA Commonwealth Univ, 76-. **HONORS AND AWARDS** Best Article Awd, Am Asn Teachers Span & Port, 77. **MEMBERSHIPS** Am Asn Teachers Fr; Am Asn Teachers Span & Port. **RESEARCH** Twentieth century French literature; myth and novel; modern Latin American novel. **SELECTED PUBLICATIONS** Auth, L'influence du cinema et ses techniques Sur quelques romans de Claude Simon, fall 75 & Memory, structure and time in La Route des Flandres, spring 76, Bonnes Feuilles; Garcia Marquez' La hojarasca: Paradigm of time and search for myth, 12/76 & The creation of myth in Garcia Marquez' Los funerales de la Mama Grande, 3/78, Hispania; The myths of war and the hero in Drieu LaRochelle's La Comedie de Charleroi, Bonnes Feuilles, fall 78; Myth and historico-primordial memory in Claude Simon's La Route des Flandres, Nottingham Fr Studies, 10/78; The banana massacre in Cien anos de soledad: A micro structural example of myth, history and bricolage, Chasque, VIII: 3-23; The Evolution of Myth in Gabriel Garcia Marquez from La hojarasca to Cien anos de soledad, Ediciones Universal, 82. **CONTACT ADDRESS** Dept of Foreign Lang, Virginia Commonwealth Univ, B0x 2021, Richmond, VA 23284-9004.

SINGERMAN, ALAN J.
DISCIPLINE FRENCH LANGUAGE AND LITERATURE **EDUCATION** OH Univ, BA, 64; IN Univ, MA, 66; PhD, 70. **CAREER** French, Davidson Col. **HONORS AND AWARDS** Dir, study abroad progs in Pau, Rennes, Montpellier; dir, study abroad progs Paris, Tour 95-96. **RESEARCH** 18th-century French novel and film adaptations. **SELECTED PUBLICATIONS** Auth, articles on French lit and film; monograph on the novels of the Abbe Prevost, L'Abbe Prevost: l'amour et la morale. Droz, 87; ed, crit ed Prevost's Histoire d'une Grecque moderne, Flammarion, 90; Toward A New Integration of Language and Culture, NE Conf Rpts, 88; Acquiring Cross-Cultural Competence: Four Stages For Students of French, Nat Textbook, 96. **CONTACT ADDRESS** Davidson Col, 102 N Main St, PO Box 1719, Davidson, NC 28036.

SINKA, MARGIT M.
PERSONAL Born Debrecen, Hungary **DISCIPLINE** GERMAN LITERATURE & LANGUAGE **EDUCATION** Baldwin-Wallace Col, BA, 64; Middlebury Col, MA, 65; Univ NC, PhD, 74. **CAREER** Jr instr German, Univ Va, 65-66 St Univ NC, 67-71; instr, Ill State Univ, 66-67; asst prof German & Span, Mars Hill Col, 71-74; asst prof, 74-79, Assoc Prof to prof German & Span, Clemson Univ, 79-. **HONORS AND AWARDS** Nat Endowment for Humanities grant, Ind Univ, summer 77 & Fordham Univ, summer 81; Fulbright grant modern cult, Germany, summer 78; Clemson Univ grant medieval lit, summer 79. **MEMBERSHIPS** Am Asn Ger Teachers; SAtlantic Mod Lang Asn; MLA. **RESEARCH** German medieval literature, epics and mysticism; 19th and 20th century German prose, genre studies and symbolism; pedagogy. **SELECTED PUBLICATIONS** Auth, Happiness, Death, And The Moment - Realism And Utopia In The Works Of Wellershoff,Dieter - Ger - Tschierske,U/, Colloquia Germanica, Vol 0025, 1992. **CONTACT ADDRESS** Lang Dept, Clemson Univ, Clemson, SC 29631. **EMAIL** smargit@clemson.edu

SINOS, REBECCA H.
PERSONAL Born 12/13/1954, Baltimore, MD, m, 1991 **DISCIPLINE** CLASSICS **EDUCATION** Col William and Mary, AB, 76; Johns Hopkins Univ, MA; PhD, 80. **CAREER** Asst Prof to Prof, Amherst Col, 80-. **HONORS AND AWARDS** Fel, Am Coun of Learned Soc, 82; Fel, NEH, 86; Phi Beta Kappa. **MEMBERSHIPS** Am Philol Asn; Archaeol Inst of Am; Am Sch of Class Studies at Athens. **RESEARCH** Ancient Greek literature; Archaeology; Religion. **SELECTED PUBLICATIONS** Co-auth, The Wedding in Ancient Athens, Univ Wis Press, 93. **CONTACT ADDRESS** Dept Class, Amherst Col, Amherst, MA 01002. **EMAIL** rhsinos@amherst.edu

SIRACUSA, JOSEPH
PERSONAL Born 07/30/1929, Siculiana, Italy **DISCIPLINE** ROMANCE LINGUISTICS **EDUCATION** Univ Rochester, AB, 58; Univ Ill, MA, 59, PhD, 62. **CAREER** Asst prof Span & Ital, Rice Univ, 62-65; assoc prof, Del Mar Col, 65-67; Prof Span & Ital, State Univ NY Col, Brockport, 67-, NDEA lang inst, vis prof Ital ling, Cent Conn State Col, 60 & Span ling, Knox Col, 61, 62; prof, Univ NC, 63; assoc dir & prof Span ling, Rice Univ, 64, 65, vis prof, San Lorenzo de El Escorial, Spain, 67; mem test develop comt, Am Asn Teachers Span & Port Nat Span Exam, 66-76. **RESEARCH** Spanish and Italian historical linguistics; literary relations between Italy and the Hispanic world; Italian dialectology. **SELECTED PUBLICATIONS** Coauth, Relaciones literarias entre Espana e Italia (ensayo de una bibliografia de literature comparada), G K Hall, 72; Federico Garcia Lorca y su mundo (Ensayo de una bibliografia, general), Scarecrow Press, Inc, 74. **CONTACT ADDRESS** Dept of Foreign Lang, SUNY, Col at Brockport, 350 New Campus Dr, Brockport, NY 14420-2914.

SIVERT, EILEEN
DISCIPLINE FRENCH LITERATURE **EDUCATION** Univ Calif, Riverside, PhD. **CAREER** Instr, Univ Minn, Twin Cities. **RESEARCH** Narrative theory and feminist criticism. **SELECTED PUBLICATIONS** Published on various aspects of 19th-century French writing, on political and labor writings in the 19th century, and on 19th- and 20th century autobiographical writing by women. **CONTACT ADDRESS** Univ of Minnesota, Twin Cities, 9 Pleasant St. SE, 260 Folwell Hall, Minneapolis, MN 55455.

SJOBERG, ANDREE FRANCES
PERSONAL Born 01/19/1924, Jamaica, NY, m, 1947 **DISCIPLINE** LINGUISTICS **EDUCATION** Univ NMex, BS, 47; Univ Tex, MA, 51, PhD, 57. **CAREER** Spec insts, 60-63, asst prof ling, 63-76, Assoc Prof Orient & African Lang & Lit, Ctr Asian Studies, Univ Tex, Austin, 76-, Grants, US Off Educ & Am Coun Learned Soc, 60-62; Ctr Appl Ling, Washington, DC, fall 62; assoc, Current Anthrop; NDEA-Fulbright-Hays res award, SIndia, 65-66; US Off Educ, 68-69. **MEMBERSHIPS** Ling Soc Am; Am Anthrop Asn; Am Orient Soc; Ling Soc India; Asn Asian Studies. **RESEARCH** Structure of Dravidian languages, especially Telugu; structure of Turkic languages, especially Uzbek; writing systems and literacy. **SELECTED PUBLICATIONS** Coauth, Culture as a significant variable in lexical change, Am Anthrop, 4/56; auth, Coexistent phonemic systems in Telugu: A socio-cultural perspective, Word, 12/62; Uzbek Structural Grammar, Uralic & Altaic Series, Ind Univ, 63; Sociocultural and linguistic factors in the development of writing systems for preliterate peoples, In: Sociolinguistics, Mouton, The Hague, 66. **CONTACT ADDRESS** Ctr for Asian Studies, Univ of Texas, Austin, 0 Univ of Texas, Austin, TX 78712-1026.

SKALITZKY, RACHEL IRENE
PERSONAL Born 02/07/1937, Waterloo, WI **DISCIPLINE** COMPARATIVE LITERATURE, MEDIEVAL STUDIES **EDUCATION** Mt Mary Col, BA, 62; Fordham Univ, MA, 66, PhD(class lang & lit), 68. **CAREER** Teacher 6th grade, St Boniface Sch, Milwaukee, 58-62; teacher Latin & music, St Anthony High Sch, Detroit, 62-63; instr classics, Mt Mary Col, 68-69, asst prof & chmn, 69-72; lectr classics, 72-73, asst prof, 73-76, Assoc Prof Comp Lit, Univ WI-Milwaukee, 76-, Coordr Women's Studies, 75-82. **MEMBERSHIPS** Am Comp Lit Asn; Am Philol Asn; Nat Women's Studies Asn; MLA; Am Asn Univ Women. **RESEARCH** Classical philology; literary criticism; patristic lit. **SELECTED PUBLICATIONS** Auth, Good wine in a new vase, Horace, Epistles 1.2, Trans & Proc Am Philol Asn, 68; Annianus of Celeda: His Text of Chrysostom's Homilies on Matthew, Aevum, 71; Horace on travel, Epistles 1.11, Class J, 73; Plotinian Echoes in Peri Hypsous 7.2 and 9.7-10, Class Bull, 2/77. **CONTACT ADDRESS** Dept of Comp Lit, Univ of Wisconsin, Milwaukee, Po Box 413, Milwaukee, WI 53201-0413. **EMAIL** rachelsk@uwm.edu

SKELNAR, ROBERT JOHN
PERSONAL Born 04/20/1963, Detroit, MI **DISCIPLINE** CLASSICS **EDUCATION** Univ Mich, BA, 85; Princeton Univ, MA, 88; Univ Mich, JD, 91, PhD, 96. **CAREER** Asst Inst, Princeton Univ, 87-88; tchg asst, 91-95; lect Class Studs, 96-97, Univ Mich; inst, Latin, The Emerson Sch, 96-97; Mellon postdoc fel, vis asst prof Classics, Swarthmore Col. **HONORS AND AWARDS** Phi Beta Kappa; Mellon Fellow Humanities; Mellon Diss Grant. **MEMBERSHIPS** Amer Philol Asn; Class Asn Middle West and South. **RESEARCH** Greek and Roman civilization, Greek Mythology. **SELECTED PUBLICATIONS** Auth, The Death of Priam: Aeneid 2.506-558, Hermes 118, 90, 67-75; Horace, Odes 1, 3, AC 60, 91, 266-269; Multiple Structural Divisions in Horace, Odes 1.38, pp 46, 91, 444-448; Rullus' Colonies: Cicero, De Lege Agraria 1.16-17 and 2. 73-75, Eos 80, 92, 81-82; Recusatio and Praeteritio in American Judicial Rhetoric, Acta Univ Carolinae, 38, 92, 97-114; Charles Baudelaire: Meditation, The Formalist, 3,1,92; SEG XXXII 1243, 13-15, RhM 136, 93, 93-94; Rainer Maria Rilke: Autumn Day, The Formalist, 4,1, 93; Papinian on the Interdict unde vi, RiDA 41, 94, 379-389; Catullus 36: Beyond Literary Polemics, RBPh 74, 96, 57-59; The Centrality of the Civic Image in Droste's Mondesaufgang, Droste-Jahrbuch 3, 97, 127-134. **CONTACT ADDRESS** Dept of Classics, Swarthmore Col, Swarthmore, PA 19081. **EMAIL** rsklenal@swarthmore.edu

SKILLMAN, JUDITH
PERSONAL Born 05/04/1954, Syracuse, NY, m, 1976, 3 children **DISCIPLINE** ENGLISH LITERATURE, COMPARATIVE LITERATURE **EDUCATION** Univ Md, BA, 76, MA, 83. **CAREER** TA, Univ of Md, 76-77; instr, Bellevue Community Col, 87-90; tutor, Educ Tutoring and Consulting Inc, 89-92; adj fac mem, City Univ, 90-. **HONORS AND AWARDS** William Stafford Awd, 83; King County Arts Comm Publ Prize, 87; Wash State Arts Comm Writer's Fel, 91; King County Pub Arts Project, 94-97; Centrum Found, 96, 98; Eric Mathieu King Awd, 98. **MEMBERSHIPS** ALTA, MLA, AWP. **SELECTED PUBLICATIONS** Auth, Worship of the Visible Spectrum, Breitenbush Books, 88; auth, Beethoven and the Birds, Blue Begonia Pr, 96; auth, Storm, Blue Begonia Pr, 98; auth, Red Town, Silverfish Rev Pr, 01; Sweetbrier, Blue Begonia Pr, 01. **CONTACT ADDRESS** 14206 SE 45th Pl, Bellevue, WA 98006. **EMAIL** jskillman@halcyon.com

SKITTER, HANS GUNTER
PERSONAL Born 07/26/1936, Bad Kreuznach, Germany, m, 1970, 2 children **DISCIPLINE** GERMAN & AMERICAN LITERATURE **EDUCATION** Univ Freiburg, PhD, 68. **CAREER** Asst teacher Ger, Queen Elizabeth's Sch Girls, London, 59-60; asst English, Univ Freiburg, 64-67; asst prof Ger, Shippensburg State Col, 68-69; asst prof, 69-71, dir jr yr abroad, 70-72, assoc prof Ger, 71-97, Prof, Dept of Foreign Lang, Millersville Univ, 98-; Dir Jr Yr Abroad, Marburg, 73-. **MEMBERSHIPS** Am Asn Teachers Ger; Deut Shakespeare Ges. **RESEARCH** Twentieth century German and American literature; language teaching. **SELECTED PUBLICATIONS** Auth, Die drei Letzten Romane F Scott Fitzgeralds, Bouvier, Bonn, 68. **CONTACT ADDRESS** Dept of Foreign Lang, Millersville Univ of Pennsylvania, PO Box 1002, Millersville, PA 17551-0302. **EMAIL** hans.skitter@millersville.edu

SKLAR, ROBERT ANTHONY
PERSONAL Born 12/03/1936, New Brunswick, NJ, m, 1958, 2 children **DISCIPLINE** CINEMA STUDIES, CULTURAL HISTORY **EDUCATION** Princeton Univ, AB, 58; Harvard Univ, PhD, 65. **CAREER** From asst prof to prof hist, Univ Mich, Ann Arbor, 65-76; PROF CINEMA STUDIES & CHMN DEPT, NY UNIV, 77-, Rackham fel, 67; Fulbright lectr, USEC, Japan, 71; distinguished vis prof, Bard Col, 75-76; Rockefeller Found humanities fel, 76-77; contribr ed, Am Film Mag, 77-. **HONORS AND AWARDS** Theatre Libr Asn Awd, 75. **MEMBERSHIPS** Am Studies Asn (vpres, 71); Soc Cinema Studies; Nat Film Preserv Bd; New York Film Fest Selec Cmt; Mich Am Stu Asn; ed bd, Am Qrt. **RESEARCH** American movies and television; twentieth century American culture and society. **SELECTED PUBLICATIONS** Auth, F Scott Fitzgerald, Oxford

Univ, 67; ed, The Plastic Age: 1917-1930, Braziller, 70; auth, Movie-Made America: A Cultural History of American Movies, Random House, 75; auth, Prime Time America: Life On and Behind the Television Screen, Random House, 82; co-ed, Resisting Images: Essays on Cinema and History, Temple Univ, 90; auth, City Boys: Cagney, Bogart, Garfield, Princeton Univ, 92; auth, Film: An International History of the Medium, Prentice Hall, 93; auth, Movie-Made AmericaL A Cultural History of American Movies, Vintage Bks, 94; co-ed, Frank Capra: Authorship and the Studio System, Temple Univ, 98. **CONTACT ADDRESS** Dept of Cinema Studies, New York Univ, 721 Broadway, Rm 600, New York, NY 10003-6807. **EMAIL** rs9@is2.nyu.edu

SKOUSEN, ROYAL
PERSONAL Born 08/05/1945, Cleveland, OH, m, 1968, 7 children **DISCIPLINE** LINGUISTICS **EDUCATION** Brigham Young Univ, BA, 69; Univ Ill, MA, 71; PhD, 72. **CAREER** Asst Prof, Univ Tex, 72-79; Prof, Brigham Young Univ, 79-. **HONORS AND AWARDS** Fulbright Fel, 82; Karl G. Maeser Res and Creative Arts Awd, Brigham Young Univ, 99. **MEMBERSHIPS** Int Soc of Quantitative Ling, Nat Asn of Scholars, Asn of Lit Scholars and Critics. **RESEARCH** Analogical modeling of language, quantum computing, natural statistics, textual criticism. **SELECTED PUBLICATIONS** Auth, Substantive Evidence in Phonology, The Hague, 75; auth, Analogical Modeling of Language, Dordrecht, 89; auth, "Towards a Critical Edition of the Book of Mormon," BYU Studies (90); auth, Analogy and Structure, Dordrecht, 92. **CONTACT ADDRESS** Dept Ling, Brigham Young Univ, 3187 JKHB, Provo, UT 84602. **EMAIL** royal_skousen@byu.edu

SKRUPSKELIS, VIKTORIA
PERSONAL Born 12/01/1935, Kaunas, Lithuania **DISCIPLINE** FRENCH **EDUCATION** St Joseph Col, Conn, BA, 55; Fordham Univ, MA, 59; Univ Ill, PhD(French), 66. **CAREER** Instr French, Univ Ill, 62-63; asst prof, Univ Chicago, 63-67; asst prof, 67-76, Assoc Prof French, Oberlin Col, 76- **SELECTED PUBLICATIONS CONTACT ADDRESS** Dept of Romance Lang, Oberlin Col, Oberlin, OH 44074.

SLADE, CAROLE
PERSONAL Born, CA **DISCIPLINE** COMPARATIVE LITERATURE, ENGLISH **EDUCATION** Pomona Col, BA, 65; Univ Wis, MA, 66; New York Univ, PhD(comp lit), 73. **CAREER** Lectr English, Bronx Community Col, City Univ New York, 71-74, asst prof, 74-78; asst prof, Baylor Univ, 78-80; Asst Prof English & Comp Lit, Columbia Univ, 80- **MEMBERSHIPS** MLA; Northeast Mod Lang Asn; Am Comp Lit Asn; Dante Soc Am; NCTE. **SELECTED PUBLICATIONS CONTACT ADDRESS** Dept of English, Columbia Univ, New York, NY 10027.

SLATKIN, LAURA M.
DISCIPLINE CLASSICAL PHILOLOGY **EDUCATION** Radcliffe Col, BA, 68; Cambridge Univ, MA, 70; Harvard Univ, PhD, 79. **CAREER** Asst prof, Univ Calif, 76-80; Vis Asst Prof, Yale Univ, 80-81; Lectr, Columbia Univ, 81-83; Asst prof to Assoc prof, Columbia Univ, Colubia Univ, 83-90; Assoc prof, Univ Chicago, 93- . **HONORS AND AWARDS** NEH Fel; Columbia Univ Coun Res Hum Fel; Mellon Fel; ACLS Fel; Am Asn Univ Women Fel. **SELECTED PUBLICATIONS** Auth, Oedipus at Colonus: Exile and Integration, Univ Calif Press, 86; The Wrath of Thetis, TAPA, 86; Genre and Generation in the Odyssey, METIS, 87; Univ Calif Press, 92; auth, The Power of Thetis: Allusion and Interpretation in the Iliad, Univ Calif Press, 92; auth, Myth in Homer, Leiden, 95; Composition by Theme and the Metis of the Odyssey, Princeton Univ Press, 96; auth, the Poetics of Exchange in the Iliad, The Iliad and Its Contexts, 97; auth, Measure and mortality in Hesiod's Works and Days, Metis, 97. **CONTACT ADDRESS** Dept of Classics, Univ of Chicago, 1050 E 59th St, Chicago, IL 60637.

SLAVUTYCH, YAR
PERSONAL Born 01/11/1918, Blahodatne, Ukraine **DISCIPLINE** UKRAINIAN LANGUAGE & LITERATURE **EDUCATION** Pedagogic Inst Zaporizhia, dipl 40; Univ Pa, MA, 54, PhD, 55. **CAREER** Sr instr, US Army Lang Sch, 55-60; asst prof to prof, 60-83, Prof Emer, Univ Alta, 83-; mgr, Slavuta Publs, 60-. **HONORS AND AWARDS** Ukrainian Poet Laureate Abroad; Shevchenko Gold Medal; Can Coun res award; Ukrainian Can Centennial Medal. **MEMBERSHIPS** Can Soc Stud Names; Ukrainian Shakespeare Soc; W Can br, Shevchenko Sci Soc. **SELECTED PUBLICATIONS** Auth, Conversational Ukrainian, 59, 5th ed, 87; auth, Ukrainian for Beginners, 62, 8th ed, 93; auth, Zhyvi smoloskypy, 83, 2nd ed, 92; auth, Standard Ukrainian Grammar, 87, 2nd ed, 90; auth, Ukrains'ka literatura v Kanadi, 92; auth, Rozstriliana muza, 92; auth, Shabli topol, 92; auth, Tvory v dvokh tomakh, 94; auth, Tvory v piaty tomakh, 98; comp & ed, Collected Papers on Ukrainian Settlers in Western Canada, 2 vols, 73, 75; comp & ed, An Annotated Bibliography of Ukrainian Literature in Canada, 84, 86, 87; comp & ed, Ukrainian Shakespeariana in the West, 2 vols, 87, 90; bibliogr, MLA Int Bibliog, 68-. **CONTACT ADDRESS** 72 Westbrook Dr, Edmonton, AB, Canada T6J 2E1.

SLOANE, DAVID
PERSONAL Born 01/29/1946, New York, NY, m, 1968, 1 child **DISCIPLINE** RUSSIAN **EDUCATION** Williams Col, BA, 68; Harvard Univ, MA, 73; PhD, 79. **CAREER** Asst/ Assoc Prof, Tufts Univ, 79-. **MEMBERSHIPS** AAASS, AATSEEL. **RESEARCH** Tolstoy, Bakhtin. **SELECTED PUBLICATIONS** Coauth, Making Progress in Russian: Required Vocabulary and Workbook, John Wiley & Sons (NY), 88; auth, Aleksandr Blok and the Dynamics of the Lyric Cycle, Slavica Publ (Columbus, OH), 88; auth, "The Poetry in 'War and Peace'," Slavic and E Europ J 40-1 (96): 63-84; auth, "Aleksandr Blok," in The Encyclopedia of the Essay (London: Fitzroy Dearborn Publ, 97), 92-94; auth, "Katherine Fauer's 'The Genesis of War and Peace'," Tolstoy Studies J 9 (97): 59-62; auth, "Aleksandr Blok and the First World War: A Search for Poetic Meaning," (forthcoming). **CONTACT ADDRESS** Dept Ger and Slavic Lang, Tufts Univ, Medford, 520 Boston Ave, Medford, MA 02155-5500. **EMAIL** dsloane@tufts.edu

SLOBIN, DAN ISAAC
PERSONAL Born 05/07/1939, Detroit, MI, d, 2 children **DISCIPLINE** PSYCHOLINGUISTICS **EDUCATION** Univ Mich, Ann Arbor, BA, 60; Harvard Univ, MA, 62, PhD(social psychol), 64. **CAREER** From asst prof to assoc prof, 64-72, Prof Psychol, Univ Calif, Berkeley, 72- ; res psychologist, Inst of Cognitive Stud and Inst of Human Develop; mem, 90- , chemn, 94- , Sci Council Max-Planck-Inst for Psycholinguistics. **HONORS AND AWARDS** Guggenheim fel, 84-85; NY Acad Sci award in behavioral sci, 86. **MEMBERSHIPS** Asn for Ling Typology; Int Asn of Cross-Cultural Psychol; Int Asn for Study of Child Lang; Int Cognitive Ling Asn; Ling Soc of Am; Int Pragmatics Asn; Soc for Study of Child Development; Turkish Stud Asn. **RESEARCH** Language and cognitive development in the child; linguistics; sign language. **SELECTED PUBLICATIONS** Auth, Psycholinguistics, Scott, Foresman, 71, 2nd ed, 79; auth, Cognitive Prerequisites for the Development of Grammar, in, Ferguson & Slobin, ed, Studies of Child Language Development, Holt, Rinehart & Winston, 73; auth, Crosslinguistic Evidence for the Language-Making Capacity, in Slobin, ed, The Crosslinguistic Study of Language Acquisition, vol, 2, Lawrence Erlbaum, 85; coauth, Relating Events in narrative: A Crosslinguistic Developmental Study, Lawrence Erlbaum, 94; coauth, Reference to Movement in Spoken and Signed Languages: Typological Considerations, Proc of Twentieth Annual Meeting of the Berkeley Ling Soc, 94; auth, From Thought and Language to Thinking for Speaking, in Gumperz, ed, Rethinking Linguistic Relativity, Cambridge, 96. **CONTACT ADDRESS** Dept of Psychology, Univ of California, Berkeley, 3210 Tolman Hall, #1650, Berkeley, CA 94720-1650. **EMAIL** slobin@cogsci.berkeley.edu

SMARR, JANET LEVARIE
DISCIPLINE COMPARATIVE LITERATURE **EDUCATION** Princeton Univ, PhD, 75. **CAREER** Prof, Univ IL Urbana Champaign . **RESEARCH** Early Renaissance in rel to the Class and the Middle Ages; Vergil and Petrarch; Ovid, Dante and Boccaccio; women writers in the Renaissance. **SELECTED PUBLICATIONS** Auth, Italian Renaissance Tales; Boccaccio and Fiammetta: The Narrator as Lover; Boccaccio's Eclogues; ed, Historical Criticism and the Challenge of Theory; publ(s) on Renaissance poetry, plot theory, Chaucer, Spenser, Anacreontics, and Renaissance women writers. **CONTACT ADDRESS** Comp Lit Dept, Univ of Illinois, Urbana-Champaign, E Gregory Drive, PO Box 52, Champaign, IL 61820. **EMAIL** j-smarr@staff.uiuc.edu

SMETHURST, MAE J.
PERSONAL Born 05/28/1935, Houghton, MI, m, 1956 **DISCIPLINE** CLASSICS **EDUCATION** Dickinson Col, BA, 57; Univ Mich, MA, 60, PhD(classics), 68. **CAREER** Instr classics, Univ Mich, 66-67; from instr to asst prof, 67-76, Assoc Prof Classics, Univ Pittsburgh, 76- **MEMBERSHIPS** Am Philol Asn. **RESEARCH** Aeschylus; tragedy; Oresteia. **SELECTED PUBLICATIONS** Auth, The Appeal Of A Plotless Tragedy + Aeschylus And Zeami, A Comparative-Study Of Greek Tragedy And No/, Coll Lit, Vol 0023, 1996. **CONTACT ADDRESS** Dept of Classic, Univ of Pittsburgh, 207 Hillman Libr, Pittsburgh, PA 15260-0001.

SMITH, BARDWELL L.
PERSONAL Born 07/28/1925, Springfield, MA, m, 1961, 5 children **DISCIPLINE** RELIGIOUS TRADITIONS OF ASIA **EDUCATION** Yale Univ, BA, BD, PhD. **CAREER** Religion, Carleton Univ. **HONORS AND AWARDS** Phi Beta Kappa; magna cum laude (Yale, BA; Yale, BD); fel, Am Coun of Learned Societies, 72-73; Fulbright fel, 86-87; collaborative res grant, Nat Endowment for the Humanities, 91-94. **MEMBERSHIPS** Am Academy of Religion; Asn of Asian Studies; Am Soc for the Study of Religion. **RESEARCH** Buddhism and soc in Sri Lanka and Japan; Buddhist pilgrimages; Japanese gardens; Japanese women and child loss. **SELECTED PUBLICATIONS** Auth, The Two Wheels of Dhamma, 72; auth, Unsui: A diary of Zen Monastic Life, 73; auth, The Tenure Sabare, 73; auth, Essays on T'ang Soc: The Interpaly of Social, Political and Economic Forces, 76; auth, Religion and the Legitimation of Power in Sri Lanka, 78; auth, Essays on Qupta Culture, 83; auth, ed, The City as a Sacred Complex, 87; auth, Warlords, Artists, Commoners: Japan in the Sixteenth Century, 81. **CONTACT ADDRESS** Carleton Col, 100 N College St., Northfield, MN 55057. **EMAIL** bsmith@carleton.edu

SMITH, CARLOTA S.
PERSONAL Born 05/21/1934, New York, NY, d, 2 children **DISCIPLINE** LINGUISTICS, PSYCHOLINGUISTICS **EDUCATION** Radcliffe Col, BA, 55; Univ Pa, MA, 62; PhD(ling), 67. **CAREER** Res asst ling, Univ Pa, 59-60 & 61-63 & Mass Inst Technol, 60-61; asst prof English, Univ Pa, 67-69; fac assoc ling, 69-71, asst prof, 71-72, assoc prof, 73-80, Prof & Chmn Ling, Univ Tex, Austin, 80- **MEMBERSHIPS** Ling Soc Am; Int Ling Asn. **RESEARCH** Syntax and semantics; language acquisition; text structure. **SELECTED PUBLICATIONS** Auth, Aspectual Viewpoint And Situation Type In Mandarian Chinese/, J Of E Asian Linguistics, Vol 0003, 1994. **CONTACT ADDRESS** Dept Ling, Univ of Texas, Austin, 0 Univ of Texas, Austin, TX 78712-1026.

SMITH, DANIEL L.
DISCIPLINE LAW, LIBRARY SCIENCE, COMPARATIVE LITERATURE **EDUCATION** Univ Iowa, BS (biochemistry), 80, BA (Russian), 89, MFA (Comp lit), 93, JD, 93, MA (Libr, Info Sci), 94. **CAREER** Publisher, Canonymous Pr, 92-; ref librn, curator, Cornell Law Libr, 97-00; asst ed, Exchanges: A J of Translations, Univ Iowa, 89-93. **SELECTED PUBLICATIONS** Auth, "Postmodern [Sic]ness: Ecritique of Anesthetic Judgement," Ecritique 1 (92); auth, Minims, 93; auth, "Self-Determination in Tibet: The Politics of Remedies," Ecritique, 2 (96); auth, "The Legacy of Nuremberg: Sustaining Human Rights," Cornell Law Forum, 25 (99). **CONTACT ADDRESS** Canonymous Pr, P. O. Box 6613, Ithaca, NY 14851-6613. **EMAIL** smith@canonymous.com

SMITH, DAVID RICHARD
PERSONAL Born 04/24/1942, Jersey City, NJ, m, 1989, 5 children **DISCIPLINE** CLASSICAL STUDIES **EDUCATION** David Lipscomb Col, BA, 64; Vanderbilt Univ, MA, 66; Univ PA, PhD(class studies), 68. **CAREER** Asst prof classics, Univ CA, Riverside, 68-70; asst prof, 70-75, assoc prof, 75-80, prof hist, CA State Polytech Univ Pomona, 80-; assoc ed, Helios J Class Asn Southwest, 75-77. **MEMBERSHIPS** Class Asn Southwest; Am Philol Asn; AHA; WHA. **RESEARCH** Greek history; religion and philosophy of history; world history and teaching methodologies. **SELECTED PUBLICATIONS** Auth, Hieropoioi and Hierothytai on Rhodes, L'Antiquite Classique, 72; The Hieropoioi on Kos, Numen, 73; The Coan Festival of Zeus Polieus, Class J, 10/73; Review of G S Kirk, Myth: Its Meaning and Function in Ancient and Other Cultures, Helios, 5/76; The Poetic Focus in Horace, Odes 3.13, Latomus, 76; Teaching Religion in the Medieval Period, World Hist Bull, 90-91; Teaching and Assessing the Doing World History Method in the World History Survey, Aspen World Hist Handbook, vol 2, 97; Technology in the World History Survey, Aspen World Hist Handbook, vol 2, 97. **CONTACT ADDRESS** Dept Hist, California State Polytech Univ, Pomona, 3801 W Temple Ave, Pomona, CA 91768-4001. **EMAIL** drsmith2@csupomona.edu

SMITH, DIANE E.
PERSONAL Born 02/27/1959, Grand Rapids, MI, m, 1981, 4 children **DISCIPLINE** CLASSICS, LATIN **EDUCATION** Villanova Univ, MA 86; Univ of Michigan, BA, 80; Richmond Col, 76-77; Intercollegiate Center for Classical Stud, Rome, 79-80; Amer School of Classical Stud, Athens, 82. **CAREER** Tchr, 86-88, School of the Holy Child, Rye NY; Scholar and Typesetter, in Greek, Latin, Linguistics and Modern Lang, 88-, Teacher, 87-, Waco Christian Sem, Waco, TX. **HONORS AND AWARDS** Graduate Fellowship, Villanova Univ. **MEMBERSHIPS** Classical Assoc of Midwest and South; Amer Classical League. **SELECTED PUBLICATIONS** Typesetting in the following; Bolchazy-Carducci, Schemling, Gareth and Jøn D. Mikalson, eds, Qui Miscuit Utile Dulci, Festschrift Essays for Paul Lachlan MacKendrick, 98; L & L Enterprises/Bolchazy-Carducci, DuBose, Gaylan, Farrago, 97; Franz Steiner Verlag, Linderski, J., Ed, Imperium Sine Fine, Festschrift for T.R.S. Broughton, Historia-Einzelschrift, 105, 96; Rowmand and Littlefield, Edmunds, Lowell, Oedipus at Colonus, 96; Oxford University Press, Battye, Adriand and Ian Roberts, eds, Clause Structure and Language Change, 95; Longman Publishing Group, Davis, Sally, Review and Test Preparation Guide for the beginning Latin Student, 94. **CONTACT ADDRESS** 5801 Fairview Dr, Waco, TX 76710.

SMITH, EVANS L.
PERSONAL Born 08/23/1950, Baltimore, MD, m, 1984, 3 children **DISCIPLINE** ENGLISH, COMPARATIVE LITERATURE **EDUCATION** Williams Col, BA, 73; Antioch Int, MA, 76; Claremont Graduate Univ, MA; PhD, 86. **CAREER** Adj instr, Harvey Mudd Col, 80-86; adj instr, Mt San Antonio Community Col, 83-86; adj instr, Pitzer Col, 84-86; instr, Franklin Col, 86-88; instr, Anne Arundel Community Col, 88-90; prof, Midwestern State Univ, 90-. **MEMBERSHIPS** MLA. **RESEARCH** Modernist Literature, Painting, and Film, Manhattan and London in the 18th and 19th Centuries. **SELECTED PUBLICATIONS** Auth, The Descent to the Underworld: Jung and His Brothers, Princeton Univ Pr, 90; auth, "Perinatal Imagery in Hamlet," Explicatory, (94); auth, Ricorso and Revelation;

An Archetypal Poetics of Modernism, Camden House, 95; auth, "The Golem and the Garland of Letters," Jour of the Fantastic in the Arts, (96); auth, Figuring Poesis: A Muthical Geometry of Postmodernism, Peter Lang, 97; auth, The Hero Journey in Literature: Parables of Poesis, Univ Pr of Am, 97; auth, "The Lyrical Nekyia: Metaphors of Poesis in Wallace Stevens," Jour of Mod Lit, (98); auth, "Amazing Underworlds: Yourcenar and Nabokov," Yearbook of Comp and Gen Lit, (98); auth, "Postmodernist Revisionings of the Grail," Mythosphere, (99); auth, The Descent to the Underworld in Modernist Literature, Film, and Painting, 01. **CONTACT ADDRESS** Midwestern State univ, 3410 Taft Blvd, Wichita Falls, TX 76308. **EMAIL** lansing.smith@nexus.mesu.edu

SMITH, NIGEL
DISCIPLINE FRENCH LITERATURE **EDUCATION** Univ NC Chapel Hill, MA, PhD. **RESEARCH** Romanticism; fantastic literature; gender studies. **SELECTED PUBLICATIONS** Auth, pubs on nineteenth and seventeenth century French literature. **CONTACT ADDRESS** Dept Foreign Languages and Literature, State Univ of West Georgia, Carrollton, GA 30118.

SMITH, REBEKAH M.
DISCIPLINE CLASSICS **EDUCATION** Univ S, BA, 82; Univ NC, Chapel Hill, PhD, 91. **CAREER** Lectr, Univ NC, Chapel Hill. **HONORS AND AWARDS** Phi Beta Kappa, 80-82; tchg fel, Univ S, 80-82; Wilkins scholar, 80-81; Salutatorian, Class of 82; Green Latin Medal, 82. **SELECTED PUBLICATIONS** Auth, Photius on the Ten Attic Orators, Greek, Roman and Byzantine Stud 33, 92; Two Fragments of 'Longinus' in Photius, Class Quart 44, 94; A Hitherto Unrecognized Fragment of Caecilius, Am J of Philol 115, 4, 94; A New Look at the Canon of the Ten Attic Orators, Mnemosyne 48, 95. **CONTACT ADDRESS** Univ of No Carolina, Chapel Hill, Chapel Hill, NC 27599.

SMITH, RILEY BLAKE
PERSONAL Born 07/07/1930, Mexico, MO **DISCIPLINE** ENGLISH, LINGUISTICS **EDUCATION** Univ Tex, Austin, BA, 58, PhD, 73. **CAREER** Asst prof English, Tex A&M Univ, 68-70; actg asst prof, Univ Calif, Los Angeles, 70-72; lectr Anglistics, Univ Duisburg, Ger, 74-76 & Univ Wuppertal, Ger, 76-77; asst prof, 77-81, Assoc Prof English, Bloomsburg Univ, 81-; Fulbright lectr, Leningrad Polytech Inst, USSR, 81. **HONORS AND AWARDS** Nat Endowment for Humanities fel, summer sem, Univ Pa, 80; Fulbright Grantee, USSR, 81. **MEMBERSHIPS** Ling Soc Am; Am Dialect Soc; Teachers English to Speakers Other Lang; Ling Asn Can & US; Int Sociol Asn. **RESEARCH** American dialects; language attitudes; language policy. **SELECTED PUBLICATIONS** Auth, Interrelatedness of certain deviant grammatical structures of Negro nonstandard dialects, 3/69 & Hyperformation and basilect reconstruction, 3/74, J English Ling; Black English: Books for English education, English educ, 4-5/75; Research perspectives on American Black English: A brief historical sketch, Am Speech, 76; Interference in phonological research in nonstandard dialects: its implication for teaching, In: Soziolinguistik, Hochschulverlag, Stuttgart, 78; coauth, Standard and disparate varieties of English in the United States: Educational and sociopolitical implications, Int J Sociol Lang, 79. **CONTACT ADDRESS** Dept of English, Bloomsburg Univ of Pennsylvania, 400 E 2nd St, Bloomsburg, PA 17815-1399.

SMITH, ROCH CHARLES
PERSONAL Born 04/01/1941, Sturgeon Falls, ON, Canada, m, 1962, 3 children **DISCIPLINE** FRENCH LITERATURE, SPANISH **EDUCATION** Univ Fla, AB, 62, MAT, 65; Emory Univ, MA, 70, PhD, 71. **CAREER** Instr French & Span, Palm Beach Com Col, 65-67, teaching assoc French, Emory Univ, 69-70; from lectr to assoc prof Romance lang, 70-82, prof Romance Lang, Univ NC, Greensboro, 82-, head, Dept Romance Lang, Univ NC, Greensboro, 81-85, assoc Dean, Col of Arts and Sciences, 85-87, assoc Vice-Chancellor, Academic Affairs, 88-90. **HONORS AND AWARDS** Phi Eta Sigma; Alpha Lambda Delta; Phi Kappa Phi; Kappa Delta Pi; Dean's Merit Awd for Research, 93, 97; Dean's Merit Awd for Contributions to College and University Programs, 94; NEH Summer Stipend, 91; NDEA Fellowship, 67-70. **MEMBERSHIPS** MLA; Am Asn Teachers Fr; Malraux Soc; New Novel Assoc. **RESEARCH** Andre Malraux; Gaston Bachelard; Alain Robbe-Grillet. **SELECTED PUBLICATIONS** Auth, Le Meurtrier et la vision tragique: Essai sur les romans d'Andre Malraux, Didier, 75; Orphic Motifs in Malraux's last novels, 76 & Gaston Bachelard and the Power of Poetic Being, 77, Fr Lit Ser; Malraux's Miroir des Limbes and the Orphic Temptation, Symp, 78; French Canadian Literature: A Not-So-Anonymous Impertinence, Sci, Technol & Humanities, 79; Gaston Bachelard, Critical Bibliog Fr Lit, 80; Gaston Bachelard and Critical Discourse: The Philosopher of Science as Reader, Stanford Fr Rev, 81; Gaston Bachelard, Twayne, 82; Tchen's Sacred Isolation: Prelude to Malraux's Fraternal Humanism, Twentieth Century Lit, 82; Naming the M/inotaur: Beckett's Trilogy and the Clown of Illusion in the Trilogy, Philological Papers, 83; Bachelard's Logosphere and Derrida's Logocentrism: Is There a Difference?, French Forum, 85; Generating the Erotic Dream Machine: Robbe-Grillet's L'Eden et Apres and La Belle Captive, French Review, 90; Open Narrative in Robbe-Grillet's Glissements progressifs du plaisir and Wim Wenders' Paris, Texas, Lit/Film Quart, 95; The Erotic Dream Machine: Interviews with Alain Robbe-Grillet on his Films, Southern Ill Univ Press, 92, 95; The Image as Generative Narrator in L'Annee derniere a Marienbad and L'Immortelle, New Novel Review, 96; Gaston Bachelard, The Encyclopedia of Aesthetics, 98; auth, Homomensura: Beckett's Clown of Illusion in the Trilogy, Philological Paper, 83; auth, Voices of Quebec Poetry--At Home in a Diverse World, International Poetry Review, 94; Le Meurtrier exalte, Malraux, La Condition humaine, 95; auth, Understanding Alain Robbe-Grillet, Univ of South Carolina Press, 00. **CONTACT ADDRESS** Dept of Romance Lang, Univ of No Carolina, Greensboro, Greensboro, NC 27402-6170. **EMAIL** rochsr@earthlink.net

SMITH, VONCILE MARSHALL
PERSONAL Born 03/17/1931, Ft Myers, FL, m, 1951, 5 children **DISCIPLINE** SPEECH COMMUNICATION, COMMUNICATION THEORY **EDUCATION** Univ Fla, BAEd, 60, MA, 64, PhD(speech), 66. **CAREER** Asst prof speech, 60-70, assoc prof, 70-78, prof Commun, Fla Atlantic Univ, 78-, Chm Dept Commun, 73-82, 94-98, ed, Fla Speech Commun J, 78-81; ed, J Int Listening Asn, 86-88. **HONORS AND AWARDS** Phi Kappa Phi. **MEMBERSHIPS** Nat Commun Asn; Southern States Commun Asn; Asn for Commun Admin; Fla Commun Asn. **RESEARCH** Studies in listening; interpersonal communication; communication theory. **SELECTED PUBLICATIONS** Coauth, Communication for Health Professionals, Lippincott, 79. **CONTACT ADDRESS** Dept of Commun, Col of Arts and Letters, Florida Atlantic Univ, PO Box 3091, Boca Raton, FL 33431-0991. **EMAIL** vsmith@acc.fau.edu

SMITH-SOTO, MARK
PERSONAL Born 05/29/1948, Washington, DC, m **DISCIPLINE** SPANISH STUDIES **EDUCATION** Univ Md, BA, 70; Univ Calif at Berkeley, MA, 72, PhD, 75. **CAREER** Teach asst, Univ Calif, Berkeley, 74; instr of Spanish to asst prof to assoc prof to Prof, Spanish, 75-, head, dept of Romance Languages, 86-94, Univ NC, Greensboro. **HONORS AND AWARDS** Danforth fel, 70-74; Woodrow Wilson fel, 70; Acad Am Poets Prize, Univ Calif at Berkeley, Hon Men, 72; Nimrod Pablo Neruda Poetry Competition, Finalist, 86; Plum Review Int Poetry Contest, Finalist, 95; Salmon Run Press Nat Poetry Bk Awd, Finalist and Hon Men, 96; Randall Jarrell Poetry Contest, finalist, 97; Univ NC, Greensboro's Sen Alumni Teach Excellence Awd, 97; Persephone Publication Awd, NC Writers Network, 00. **MEMBERSHIPS** NC Writers' Network; NC Poetry Soc; Mod Lang Asn; Asoc Int de Hispanistas. **RESEARCH** Spanish-American modernismo; 19th and 20th -century Spanish- American poetry. **SELECTED PUBLICATIONS** Auth, Jose Asuncion Silva: contexto y estructura de su obra, Editorial Tercer Mundo, 81; auth, "See It on Video," The Sun 232, 95; "Latino," The Plum Review 9, 96; "My Tongue Finds Itself," The Sun, 96; "The Parting," Poetry East 42, 96; "Why I am Afraid of Physical Harm," and "Frieze," The Chattahoocheee Rev XVI, 4, 96; "Caf of Mirrors," Q West, 97; "How It Happened," The Sun, 98; "Jose Asuncion Silva y el 'sadismo intelectual," Thesaurus, XLIX, 98; auth "Yesterday, Tomorrow," Kenyon Rev (00); auth, Green Mango Collage, Birch Book Press. **CONTACT ADDRESS** Dept of Romance Languages, Univ of No Carolina, Greensboro, Greensboro, NC 27402-6170. **EMAIL** smithsom@uncg.edu

SNAPPER, JOHAN PIETER
PERSONAL Born 06/04/1935, Naaldwijk, Netherlands, m, 1959, 3 children **DISCIPLINE** GERMANIC LANGUAGES **EDUCATION** Calvin Col, BA, 58; Univ Chicago, MA, 62; Univ Calif, Los Angeles, PhD(Ger), 67. **CAREER** Instr Ger, Univ Calif, Los Angeles, 64-66; asst prof Ger & Dutch, 66-73, Princess Beatrix prof Dutch lang, lit & cult, 71, assoc prof, 73-82, Queen Beatrix Prof Ger & Dutch, Univ Calif, Berkeley, 82-, Dir Dutch Studies, 73- **MEMBERSHIPS** MLA; Philol Asn Pac Coast; Am Asn Teachers Ger; Int Asn Netherlandists. **RESEARCH** German literature, Aufklarung, Sturm und Drang, classicism; 20th century Dutch literature. **SELECTED PUBLICATIONS** Auth, Evenbeeld en tegenbeeld: de fata morgana in Heeresma's Dagje naar het strand, Raster, spring 70; The solitary player in Klinger's dramas, Ger Rev, 3/70; Post War Dutch Literature: A Harp Full of Nails, Delta, 71; G K van het Reve en de re vistische heterokliet, Raster, fall 72; Nederlands in het buitenland: heeft het nog zin?, Ons Erfdeel, 1/77; Teeth on edge: The child in the modern Dutch short story, Rev Nat Lit, 77; From Cronus to Janus: The problem of time in the works of G K Reve, Dutch Studies, 77. **CONTACT ADDRESS** Dept of Ger, Univ of California, Berkeley, 5315 Dwinelle Hall, Berkeley, CA 94720-3244.

SNELL, ANA MARIA
PERSONAL Born 02/19/1933, Santandeo, Spain, m, 1961, 1 child **DISCIPLINE** SPANISH **EDUCATION** John Hopkins Univ, MA, 72; PhD, 76. **CAREER** Instr, Towson Univ, 77-80; asst prof, Goudier Col, 75-79; asst prof, Loyola Col, 80-84; lecturer to director of Span lang prog, 84-. **HONORS AND AWARDS** Gilman Fel, John Hopkins Univ, 72. **MEMBERSHIPS** AAUP, MLA, AATSP, Editorial Bd of CONFLUENCIA. **RESEARCH** Peninsular and Latin American Literature especially Medieval and Golden Age peninsular authors. **SELECTED PUBLICATIONS** Auth, Hacia el Verbo: Signos y transignificacion en la poesia de Quevedo, Tamesis Books, 81; auth, "el lenguaje de los 'Bailes' en Quevedo," in Seminario Edad de Oro: Quevedo y su tiempo, Madrid, 94; auth, "Acercamiento a los 'Bailes' de Quevedo," Confluencia, (94); auth, "The Wound and the Flame: Desire and Transcendence in Quevedo and St. John of the Cross," Studies in Honor of Elis Rivers, 89; auth, "Poesia satirica de Quevedo," Historia y Critica de la Literatura Espanola, 83; auth, "Quevedo ante el barroco," Historia y Critica de la Literatura Espanola, 83. **CONTACT ADDRESS** Dept Span & Ital, Johns Hopkins Univ, Baltimore, 3400 N Charles St, Baltimore, MD 21218-2608. **EMAIL** anamaria@jhunix.hcf.jhu.edu

SNELL, DANIEL C.
PERSONAL Born 10/01/1947, Jackson, MI, m, 1986, 2 children **DISCIPLINE** NEAR EASTERN LANGUAGES & CIVILIZATIONS **EDUCATION** Stanford, MA, 71; Yale Univ, PhD, 75. **CAREER** Instr, Near Eastern Languages, 75-76, Univ Wash; Mellon fel, CUNY, 76-77; vis asst prof, Near Eastern Studies, Univ Mich, 77; asst prof, Religious Studies, Conn Col, 77-78; asst prof, Religious Studies, Barnard Col, 78-80; NEH fel, 80-81; asst prof Religion, Gustavus Adolphus Col, 81-82; Fulbright res Syria, 82-83; from asst prof, 83-87, to assoc prof, 87-92, to prof of history, 92-, Univ of Okla, 83-. **HONORS AND AWARDS** Edinburgh Ctr Advan Studies Hum, 97; Oregon Hum Ctr Summer fel, 96; Hum Res Ctr fel, 90; Nat Hum Ctr fel, 89-90. **MEMBERSHIPS** Amer Orient Soc; Amer Hist Asn; Soc Bibl Lit **RESEARCH** Ancient Near Eastern social and economic history; Money and prices; Slavery; Biblical Book of Proverbs **SELECTED PUBLICATIONS** Auth, Taxes and Taxation. Tax Office. Trade and Commerce in the Ancient Near East, Anchor Bible Dictionary, Doubleday, 92; Ancient Israelite and Neo-Assyrian Societies and Economics, The Tablet and The Scroll, Near Eastern Studies in Honor of William W Hallo, CDL Press, 93; Twice-Told Proverbs and the Composition of the Book of Proverbs, Eisenbrauns, 93; A Neo-Babylonian Colophon, Revue d Assyriologie, 94; Methods of Exchange and Coinage, Civilizations of the Ancient Near East, Scribners, 95; Life in the Ancient Near East 3100-332 BC, Yale Univ Press, 97. **CONTACT ADDRESS** Dept of History, Univ of Oklahoma, 455 W Lindsey, Norman, OK 73019. **EMAIL** dcsnell@ou.edu

SNYDER, EMERY
PERSONAL Born 08/04/1960, Bethlehem, PA **DISCIPLINE** LINGUISTICS & LITERATURE **EDUCATION** Princeton Univ, AB, 82; Harvard Univ, AM, 86; PhD, 92. **CAREER** Asst prof, Princeton Univ, 92-99; asst prof, Rutgers Univ, 99-00; info archit, igicom inc, 00-. **HONORS AND AWARDS** Harvard GSAS, 88; Whiting Found, 91-92; DAAD, 93; Harv Teach Awd. **MEMBERSHIPS** Asn Comput Mach. **RESEARCH** Early modern European literature; pragmatics; rhetoric; linguistics and literature; letters as a literary form. **SELECTED PUBLICATIONS** Auth, "Sketches of Johnson and Johnson's 'Skizze,'" in Barock: Neue Sichtweisen (Wien: Bohlau, 94); auth, "Is Freud's model of the mind autopoietic?," Germ Rev 74 (99); auth, "Eine Problemstellung der Barocken Semiotik," Uwe-Johnson Jahrbuch (01). **CONTACT ADDRESS** igicom, 580 Broadway, Ste. 601, New York, NY 10012.

SNYDER, WILLIAM
DISCIPLINE LINGUISTICS **EDUCATION** Mass Institute of Technology, SB, 89; Mass Institute of Technology, PhD, 95. **CAREER** Co-Dir, Dept of Linguistics Laboratory for Child Lang Res, ch, of Departmental Committee on Commun; asst prof, Univ Conn. **MEMBERSHIPS** Am Asn for the Advan of Science; International Asn for the Study of Child Lang; Linguistic Soc of Am; Sigma Xi Scientific Res Soc. **RESEARCH** Child Language Aquisition (Syntax, Morphology, Semantics), Comparative Syntax and Morphology, Syntax-Semantics Interface. **SELECTED PUBLICATIONS** Auth, The Acquisitional Role of the Syntax-Morphology Interface: Morphological Compounds and Syntactic Complex Predicates, In Proceedings of the 20th Annual Boston Univ Conf on Lang Develop. Somerville, MA: Cascadilla Press, 96; A Neo-Davidsonian Approach to Resultatives, Particles, and Datives, Proceedings of the North East Linguistics Society 25, Amherst: GLSA, 95; coauth, Romance Auxiliary Selection with Reflexive Clitics: Evidence for Early Knowledge of Unaccusativity, In Proceedings of the Twenty-sixth Annual Child Language Research Forum, Stanford, CA: CSLI, 95; The Syntactic Representation of Degree and Quantity: Perspectives from Japanese and Child English, In Proceedings of the West Coast Conference on Formal Linguistics XIII, CSLI, 95. **CONTACT ADDRESS** Dept of Linguistics, Univ of Connecticut, Storrs, 1266 Storrs Rd, Monteith Hall, Unit 1154, Storrs, CT 06269-1085. **EMAIL** william.snyder@uconn.edu

SO, SUFUMI
DISCIPLINE JAPANESE **EDUCATION** Univ Toronto, PhD. **CAREER** Languages, Carnegie Mellon Univ. **SELECTED PUBLICATIONS** Coauth, Comparing writing process and product across two languages: A study of 6 Singaporean university student writers, Jour Sec Lang Writing, 93;Tutoring second language text revision: Does the approach to instruction or the language of communication make a difference, Jour Sec Lang

Writing, 96; Learning to do research on language teaching and learning: Graduate apprenticeships, 97; The teaching of English-as-a-second-language writing in the Asia-Pacific region: a cross-coutry comparison, RELC Jour, 97; To be a reflective teacher, The Canadian Mod Lang Rev, 97. **CONTACT ADDRESS** Carnegie Mellon Univ, 5000 Forbes Ave, Pittsburgh, PA 15213.

SOBEJANO-MORGAN, ANTONIO
PERSONAL Born 12/18/1955, Zamora, Spain, m, 1998, 1 child **DISCIPLINE** CONTEMPORARY SPANISH NARRATIVE **EDUCATION** Mich State Univ, PhD, 87. **CAREER** Assoc prof, Binghampton Univ, 14 years. **MEMBERSHIPS** Hispania. **RESEARCH** Contemporary Spanish Narrative. **SELECTED PUBLICATIONS** Auth, La Metaficcion Creadora en Antagonia de Luis Goytisolo; ed, Feminism in Multicultural Literature; auth, Metaficcion Espanola en la Postmodernidad. **CONTACT ADDRESS** Dept Romance Languages, SUNY, Binghamton, PO Box 6000, Binghamton, NY 13902-6000.

SOBIN, NICHOLAS
DISCIPLINE LINGUISTICS **EDUCATION** Univ Tex, PhD. **CAREER** English and Lit, Univ Ark **SELECTED PUBLICATIONS** Auth, Agreement, Default Rules, and Grammatical Viruses, Linguistic Inquiry; Case Assignment in Ukrainian Morphological Passive Constructions, Linguistic Inquiry; The Variable Status of COMP-trace Phenomena, Natural Language & Linguistic Theory; An Acceptable Ungrammatical Construction, The Reality of Linguistic Rules; On the Syntax of English Echo Questions; Lingua; Agreement in CP; Gapping as Evidence of Distinct L2 Acquisition, Spanish in the U.S. Setting. **CONTACT ADDRESS** Univ of Arkansas, Little Rock, 2801 S University Ave., Little Rock, AR 72204-1099. **EMAIL** njsobin@ualr.edu

SOBRER, JOSEP MIQUEL
PERSONAL Born 09/01/1944, Barcelona, Spain, m, 1994, 3 children **DISCIPLINE** LITERATURE, LINGUISTICS **EDUCATION** Univ Barcelona, Lic, 66; Univ Ore, MA, 69; PhD, 72. **CAREER** Asst prof, Univ Puget Sound, 74-75; asst prof, Univ Mich, 75-81; asst prof to assoc prof to chmn to dir grad studies to prof, Univ Ind, 85-. **HONORS AND AWARDS** ACLS Fel, 79-80; NEH, 89; NACS Pres, 95-98. **MEMBERSHIPS** MLA; NACS. **RESEARCH** Current projects: A study of machismo in modern Spanish literature. A translation into English of Merce Rodoreda's Mirall trencat. **SELECTED PUBLICATIONS** Auth, La Doble Soledat d'Ausias March, Edicions dels Quadrens Crema (87); auth, Catalonia, a Self-Portrait, Ind UP, 92; auth, "Ironic Allegory in Terenci Moix's El Sexe dels Angels," Bulletin Hisp Studies 75 (98): 339-356; auth, "Man and Beast: the Nietzschean Heroics of Angel Guimera's Terra Baixa," Romance Quart 46 (99): 196-203. **CONTACT ADDRESS** Dept Foreign Lang, Indiana Univ, Bloomington, Bloomington, IN 47405. **EMAIL** sobrer@indiana.edu

SOCHA, DONALD
DISCIPLINE SPANISH LITERATURE **EDUCATION** Univ Va, PhD. **CAREER** Dept For Lang, Wisc Univ **MEMBERSHIPS** Spanish Nat Honor Soc. **RESEARCH** Foreign language teaching. **SELECTED PUBLICATIONS** Auth, pubs on Garcia Lorca, Calderon de la Barca and Miguel de Cervantes. **CONTACT ADDRESS** Dept of Foreign Languages, Univ of Wisconsin, La Crosse, 1725 State St, La Crosse, WI 54601. **EMAIL** socha@mail.uwlax.edu

SOCKEN, PAUL
DISCIPLINE FRENCH LITERATURE **EDUCATION** Univ Toronto, BA; Univ Iowa, MA; Univ Toronto, PhD. **CAREER** Prof **RESEARCH** Thematic and stylistic aspects of Gabrielle Roy. **SELECTED PUBLICATIONS** Auth, Gabrielle Roy's Bonheur d'Occasion; Myth and Morality in Alexandre Chenevert; The Myth of the Lost Paradise in the Novels of Jacques Poulin, Fairleigh Dickinson, 93; pub(s) in area of mythology and French-Canadian literature. **CONTACT ADDRESS** Dept of French, Univ of Waterloo, 200 University Ave W, Waterloo, ON, Canada N2L 3G1. **EMAIL** psocken@watarts.uwaterloo.ca

SOKEL, WALTER H.
PERSONAL Born 12/17/1917, Vienna, Austria, m, 1961, 1 child **DISCIPLINE** GERMAN LANGUAGE & LITERATURE **EDUCATION** Rutgers Univ, AB, 41, MA, 44; Columbia Univ, PhD(Ger), 53. **CAREER** Instr Ger, OH State Univ, 46-47; instr, Temple Univ, 47-53; from instr to assoc prof Ger & hum, Columbia Univ, 53-64; prof Ger, Stanford Univ, 64-73; Commonwealth Prof Ger & Eng Lit, Ctr Advan Studies, 73-94, Commonwealth Prof Emeritus, Ger and Eng Lit, 94- , Univ VA; Am Coun Learned Soc grant-in-aid, 62; exchange prof, Univ Hamburg, 65; Nat Endowment for Hum sr fel, 71-72; vis prof Ger, Harvard Univ, 78-79; exch prof, Univ Freiburg, Ger, 85; guest prof, Univ Graz, Austria, 88, 90, 92. **HONORS AND AWARDS** Alex von Humboldt Res Prize, Fed Repub Ger, 82; Cross of Honor First Class for Sci and Art, Rep of Austria, 97; hon doc, Univ Graz, Austria, 98. **MEMBERSHIPS** Int Brecht Soc (vpres, 74-); MLA; Am Asn Tchrs Ger; Am Comp Lit Asn; Am Kafka Soc, hon pres; Leo Baeck Inst, mem bd; Int Robert-Musil-Soc; Int Pen Club. **RESEARCH** Mod Ger lit; the existentialist tradition; intellectual hist and lit. **SELECTED PUBLICATIONS** Auth, The Writer in Extremis, Stanford Univ, 59; ed, An Anthology of German Expressionist Drama, Anchor Bks, 63; auth, Franz Kafka: Tragik und Ironie, Langen-Muller, Munich, 64; Franz Kafka, Columbia Univ, 66; Brecht's concept of character, Comp Drama, 71; Demaskierung und Untergang wilh Repraesentaz, In: Herkomen und Erneuerung, Max Niemeyer Verlag, 76; Perspectives and truth in The Judgment, In: The Problem of The Judgment, 77 & The three endings of Josef K, In: The Kafka Debate, 77, Gordian; auth, The Myth of Power and the Self, Wayne State Univ, 99. **CONTACT ADDRESS** 5764 E Camino del Celador, Tucson, AZ 85750-1825.

SOKOL, ELENA
PERSONAL Born 07/17/1943, Chicago, IL, m, 1 child **DISCIPLINE** RUSSIAN LITERATURE **EDUCATION** Colo Univ, BA, 65; Univ Calif-Berkeley, MA, 67, PhD, 74. **CAREER** Prof. **HONORS AND AWARDS** Phi Beta Kappa, 64; Woodrow Wilson Fel, 65-66; IREX Sr Facul Exchange, 88; Henry Luce III Research Awd, 94. **MEMBERSHIPS** AAASS, AATSEEL, MLA, ACTR, NAATC, SUV. **RESEARCH** Contemporary Czech fiction. **SELECTED PUBLICATIONS** Auth, Russian Poetry for Children, U Tenn Press, 84; transl story by Prochazkova, Artful Dodge, a lit mag published at Wooster; auth, " From Prague to New York City: The Feminist Poetics of Iva Pekarkova," Brown Slavic Contributions, XI, 99. **CONTACT ADDRESS** Dept of Russ, The Col of Wooster, Wooster, OH 44691. **EMAIL** esokol@acs.wooster.edu

SOLAN, LAWRENCE
PERSONAL Born 05/07/1952, New York, NY, m, 1982, 2 children **DISCIPLINE** LAW, LINGUISTICS **EDUCATION** Brandeis Univ, BA, 74; Univ Massachusetts, PhD Linguistics, 78; Harvard Law School, JD, 82. **CAREER** Law Clerk, Supreme Ct of NJ, 83-86; assoc, Orans, Elsen & Lupert, 83-86; partner, Orans, Elsen & Lupert, 89-96; Assoc Prof, Brooklyn Law School ol, 96-. **HONORS AND AWARDS** Bd Dir, Int Acad of Law and Mental health, 98-. **MEMBERSHIPS** Ling Soc of Am; Asn of the Bar of the City of New York; Law and Soc Asn; Int Asn of Forensic Ling; Int Acad of Law and Mental Health. **RESEARCH** Law; Language; Cognition. **SELECTED PUBLICATIONS** Auth, The Language of Judges, 993; When Judges Use the Dictionary, Am Speech, 93; Chomsku and Cardozo: Linguistics and the Law, 94; When All is Lost: Why it is Difficult for Judges to Write About Concepts, Graven Images, 94; Judicial Decision and Linguistic Analysis: Is There a Linguist in the Court?, Wash Univ, 95; Learning Our Limits: The Decline of Textualism in Statutory Cases, Wisconsin L Rev, 97; rev, Making Sense in Law, Forensic Ling, 97; Law, Language, and Lenity, William & Mary Rev, forthcoming; coauth, Linguists on the Witness Stand: law, Language and Cognition, forthcoming. **CONTACT ADDRESS** Brooklyn Law Sch, 250 Joralemon St, Brooklyn, NY 11201. **EMAIL** lsolan@brooklaw.edu

SOLE, CARLOS A.
PERSONAL Born 09/09/1938, Panama, RP, m, 1964, 1 child **DISCIPLINE** HISPANIC LINGUISTICS **EDUCATION** Georgetown Univ, BSL, 60; PhD, 66. **CAREER** Asst prof, Harvard Univ, 66-70; assoc prof, Univ Tex, Austin, 70-84; prof, 84-. **HONORS AND AWARDS** Acad de Numero; Acad Nortez de la Lengua Espanola; Acad Corr; Res Acad de la Lengua Espanola. **MEMBERSHIPS** AATSP; MLA; ALFAL. **RESEARCH** Spanish of the Americas; Spanish sociolicjustice; Spanish syntax. **SELECTED PUBLICATIONS** Auth, Bibliograhasobre d espanol en America: 1920-1985, ICC (Bogot'), 91; auth, El espanol en America: Perspectives y materiales, Arco Libros (Madrid) 96; auth, Latin American Writers, Scribner and Sons (NY), 89. **CONTACT ADDRESS** Dept Spanish Portuguese, Univ of Texas, Austin, Austin, TX 78712-1013. **EMAIL** carolus@mail.utexas.edu

SOLODOW, JOSEPH B.
PERSONAL Born 11/13/1946, Brooklyn, NY, m, 1967 **DISCIPLINE** CLASSICS **EDUCATION** Columbia Univ, AB, 67; Harvard Univ, MA, 69; PhD, 71. **CAREER** Instr, Univ Mass, 70-71; asst prof, Columbia Univ, 71-77; assoc prof, Bard col, 77-83; adj assoc prof, Boston col, 83-84; vis assoc prof, Columbia Univ, 84-85; vis res scholar, Yale Univ, 85-88; vis assoc prof, Univ Calif, 88-89; vis assoc prof, Stanford Univ, 88; vis assoc prof, Univ Calif, 89-90; vis assoc prof, State Univ New York, 90-92; asst to full prof, Southern Conn State Univ, 92-99; vis prof, Yale Univ, 00-. **HONORS AND AWARDS** Phi Beta Kappa, 67; Rome Prize, Am Acad in Rome, 80-81; Scaglione Translation Prize, Mod Lang Asn, 95. **MEMBERSHIPS** AAUR, Am Philol Asn. **RESEARCH** Latin literature and philology, Spanish-American literature. **SELECTED PUBLICATIONS** Auth, " Ars Poetica," New England Classical Newsletter, (91): 42-45; auth, "Persistence of Virgilian Memories," Liverpool Classical Monthly (89): 119-121; auth, "Forms of Literary Criticism in Catullus: Polymetric vs. Epigram," Classical Philology, (89): 312-319; auth, "The Canon of Texts for a Latin Data Bank," Favoniu, (87): 21-24; auth, "On Catullus 95," Classical Philology, (87): 141-145; auth, "Ravcae, Tva Cvra, Palvmbes: Study of a Poetic Word Order," Studies in Classical Philology, (86): 129-153; auth, "Livy and the Story of Horatius, 1.24-26," Transactions of the Philological Associations, (79): 251-268; auth, The Latin Particle Quidem, American Classical Studies, American Philological Asn: Boulder, 78; auth, The World of Ovid's Metamorphoses, Univ NC: Chapel Hill, 88; auth, "Poeta Impotens: the Last Three Eclogues," Latomus 36 (77): 757-771. **CONTACT ADDRESS** Dept For Lang, So Connecticut State Univ, 501 Crescent St, New Haven, CT 06515-1330. **EMAIL** solodow@southernet.edu

SOLOMON, JANIS VIRGINIA LITTLE
PERSONAL Born 06/09/1938, Ranger, TX, m, 1978, 1 child **DISCIPLINE** GERMAN LITERATURE **EDUCATION** Univ Tex, Austin, BA, 60; Yale Univ, MA, 64, PhD(Ger lit), 65. **CAREER** From instr to assoc prof, 65-78, Prof Ger, Conn Col, 81-, actg chmn dept, 67-71, chmn dept Ger, 71-79, 81-82, & 92-, dir mod Europ studies, 74- 79, dir film studies, 84-. **HONORS AND AWARDS** Alexander von Humboldt-Stiftung fel, 72-73; Yale fac fel, 75. **MEMBERSHIPS** MLA; Am Asn Teachers Ger. **RESEARCH** Baroque lyric; modern drama; expressionism; film studies. **SELECTED PUBLICATIONS** Auth, Liebesgedichte & Lebensgeschichte bei Martin Opitz, Deut Vierteljahrsschrift fur Literaturgeschichte, Vol 42, 161-181; contribr, Lebendige Form (Henelfestschrift), Fink, Munich, 70; Europaische Tradition & deutsche Barockliteratur, Francke, Bern, 73; auth, Die weltliche Lyrik des Martin Opitz, Francke, Bern & Munich, 73; Buchner's Dantons Tod: History as theatre, Ger Rev, Vol 54, 9-19; Further Dutch Sources Used by Martin Opitz, Neophilologus, Vol 53, 157-175; contribr, Arbeit als Thema in der deutschen Literatur vom Mittelalter bis zur Gegenwart, Athenaum, Konigstein, 79; auth, Die Kriegsdramen Reinhard Goerings, Francke, Bern & Munich, 85; Martin Opitz: Ihr Himmel trieffetdoch, Daphnis 11, 55-63; contribr, German Baroque Literature: The European Perspective, Ungar, 83. **CONTACT ADDRESS** Dept of Ger, Connecticut Col, 270 Mohegan Ave, New London, CT 06320-4196. **EMAIL** jlsol@conncoll.edu

SONKOWSKY, ROBERT PAUL
PERSONAL Born 09/16/1931, Appleton, WI, m, 1956, 3 children **DISCIPLINE** CLASSICS **EDUCATION** Lawrence Col, AB, 54; Univ NC, PhD, 58. **CAREER** Teaching asst, Univ NC, 55-56, teaching fel, 57-58; from instr to asst prof classics, Univ Tex, 58-61; assoc prof, Univ Mo, 62-63; chmn dept, 64-78, assoc prof Classics, Speech & Theatre Arts, Univ Minn, Minneapolis, 63-, Johnson fel, Inst Res Humanities, 61-62; vis prof, Univ of Colo, 68; selection juror, Am Acad Rome Fels, 70; distinguished Marbook vis prof, Macalester Col, 89. **HONORS AND AWARDS** U of Minn Distance Education Awd: Interactive TV. **MEMBERSHIPS** Am Philol Asn: Class Asn Mid W & S; Int Soc Chronobiol; Classical Asn of Atlantic States; Soc for the Oral Reading of Greek and Latin Lit. **RESEARCH** Ancient rhetoric and drama; Latin lit; oral performance. **SELECTED PUBLICATIONS** Auth, An Aspect of Delivery in Ancient Rhetorical Theory, Trans & Proc Am Philol Asn, 59; Scholarship and Showmanship, 61 & Greek Euphony and Oral Performance, 67, Arion; A Fifteenth Century Rhetorical Opusculum, Class Medieval & Renaissance Studies for B L Ullman, 69; Euphantastik Memory and Delivery in the Classical Rhetorical Tradition, Rhetoric, Brown & Steinmann, 79; Recordings: selections from Cicero, Vergil, Cattullus, Horace, Ovid, Jeffrey Norton, In: Oedipus in Oedipus Rex, Digital Excellence, Inc. **CONTACT ADDRESS** Dept of Classical and near Eastern Studies, Univ of Minnesota, Twin Cities, 9 Pleasant St S E, Minneapolis, MN 55455-0194. **EMAIL** sonko001@tc.umn.edu

SONNENFELD, ALBERT
PERSONAL Born 07/22/1934, Berlin, Germany, m, 1987, 2 children **DISCIPLINE** COMPARATIVE LITERATURE FRENCH **EDUCATION** Oberlin Col, BA, 55; Princeton Univ, MA, 57, PhD, 58. **CAREER** Asst prof, 60-64, assoc prof, French, 64-68, prof French and Comp Lit, 68-86, chamn 78-84, Princeton Univ; M.F. Chevalier Prof of French and Comp Lit, 87- , chamn 86-98, Univ So Calif; Nat Bd of Dir, Am Inst of Wine and Food, 88- . **HONORS AND AWARDS** Officer des Palmes academiques & Officer des Arts et lettres, French Republic; Bicentennial preceptorship, Princeton Univ, 62-64; Raubenheimer Prize, Univ S Cal, 92; Fulbright lectr; Fulbright fel, NEH St Fel; ACLS grants; Am Philos Soc grants; Princeton Hum Res grants. **MEMBERSHIPS** The Athenieum (London), Princeton Club. **RESEARCH** Culinary history; modern European literature; Proust; Joyce. **SELECTED PUBLICATIONS** Ed, Thirty-Six French Poems, 60; auth, LJ'Oeuvre poetique de Tristan Corbiere, 61; coauth, Temoins de l'Homme, 65; auth, Crossroads: Essays on the Catholic Novelists, 82; ed, Food: a Culinary History from Antiquity to the Present, 2000. **CONTACT ADDRESS** Univ of So California, University Park, Los Angeles, CA 90089-0359. **EMAIL** Albertsonn@aol.com

SONNENFELD, MARION WILMA
PERSONAL Born 02/13/1928, Berlin, Germany **DISCIPLINE** GERMAN **EDUCATION** Swarthmore Col, BA, 50; Yale Univ, MA, 51, PhD, 56. **CAREER** From instr to asst prof Ger, Smith Col, 54-62; assoc prof, Wells Col, 62-67, chmn dept, 65-67; from assoc prof to prof, 67-77, Distinguished Teaching Prof Ger, 77-93, Distinguished Teaching Prof Emer, State Univ NY Col Fredonia, 93-; Mem fac, Middlebury Col Ger Sch, 61-63; asst dir, Wells Col Summer Sch Ger, 64, dir, 65-67; actg

dean arts & humanities, 80-81; actg dir, Int Educ, 80-81; coordr, Stefan Zweig Symp, Fredonia, 81; mem Nat Screening Comt,Fulbright grants, 89-91. **HONORS AND AWARDS** State Univ NY Summer Awd, 80; Fund for the Improvement of Post Secondary Educ grant, mem comt assessment, 88-90. **MEMBERSHIPS** MLA; Int Germanisten Ver; Am Asn Teachers Ger. **RESEARCH** Novelle; Kafka; the German drama. **SELECTED PUBLICATIONS** Auth, An etymological interpretation of the Hagen figure, Neophilologus, 57; Paralleles in Novelle und Verwandlung, Symp, 59; Amerika und Prozess als Bildungsromanfragmente, Ger Quart, 62; transl, Kleist's Amphitryon, Ungar, 62; ed, Wert und Wort, Wells Col, 65; ed, Gepragte Form, Fredonia, 75; transl, Three Plays by Hebbel, 74 & co-transl, The Narrative Prose of C F Meyer, 76, Bucknell Univ. **CONTACT ADDRESS** Dept of Foreign Lang & Lit, SUNY, Col at Fredonia, Fredonia, NY 14063-1143. **EMAIL** marionw@netsync.net

SOONS, C. ALAN

PERSONAL Born 02/09/1925, Grantham, England, m, 3 children **DISCIPLINE** SPANISH LITERATURE **EDUCATION** Univ Sheffield, BA, 51, MA, 53; Harvard Univ, PhD(Romance lang & lit), 71. **CAREER** Asst lectr Span, Univ St Andrews, 55-57; from lectr to sr lectr, Univ W Indies, Jamaica, Barbados & Trinidad, 57-68; vis assoc prof Romance lang, Univ Mass, Amherst, 68-70; vis assoc prof Span, Rice Univ, 71-72; assoc prof, 72-81, Prof Span to Prof Emer, SUNY Buffalo, 81-. **HONORS AND AWARDS** Vis fel, St Catherine's Col, Oxford, 80. **MEMBERSHIPS** Asoc Int Hispanistas; Soc Saint-Simon. **RESEARCH** Late medieval and Renaissance literature; Spanish-American literature of the colonial period; folk-narrative. **SELECTED PUBLICATIONS** Auth, Ficcion y comedia en el Siglo de Oro, Madrid, 67; The patterning of La gitanilla, Romanistisches Jahrbuch, 75; Alonso Ramirez in an enchanted and a disenchanted world, Bull Hisp Studies, 76; Haz y enves del cuento risible en el Siglo de Oro, Tamesis, London, 76; contribr, Enxyklopadie des Marchens, Gottingen, 76; ed, Esteban Terralla Landa Lima por dentro y fuera, Exeter: Exeter Hisp Texts, 78; auth, Alonso de Castillo Solorzano, Twayne, 78; Juan de Mariana, Twayne, 82; Theaters And Theater Life In Tudela, 1563-1750--Studies And Documents, Bulletin Of The Comediantes, Vol 45, 93. **CONTACT ADDRESS** Dept of Mod Lang and Lit, SUNY, Buffalo, 910 Clemens Hall, N Campus, Buffalo, NY 14260.

SORIA, REGINA

PERSONAL Born 05/17/1911, Rome, Italy, m, 1936 **DISCIPLINE** ITALIAN, ART **EDUCATION** Univ Rome, LittD, 33. **CAREER** From instr to assoc prof foreign lang, 42-61, prof Ital, 61-76, Emer Prof Mod Lang, Col Notre Dame, MD, 76. Instr Span, McCoy Col, 50-52; field researcher, Arch Am Art, 60-63, archivist, Rome Off, 63-64. **MEMBERSHIPS** MLA; Am Studies Asn; Am Asn Teachers Ital; AAUP. **RESEARCH** Biography and catalogue of the works of Elihu Vedder-American painter; American artists in Italy, 1760-1914; Italian participation in the visual arts of 18th and 19th century America. **SELECTED PUBLICATIONS** Auth, Washington Allston's lectures on art, the first American art treatise, J Aesthet & Art Criticism, 3/60; Some background for Elihu Vedder's Cumean Sibyl and Young Marysays, spring 60 & Elihu Vedder's mythical creatures, summer 63; Art Quart; Mark Twain and Vedder's Medusa, Am Quart, winter 64; Life of Elihu Vedder & spring, 76; Elihu Vedder, American Old Master, Ga Mus Art Bull, spring 76; Hendrik Andersen: American Sculptor, Ny Rev Of Books, Vol 40, 93. **CONTACT ADDRESS** 1609 Ramblewood Rd, Baltimore, MD 21239.

SORKIN, ADAM J.

PERSONAL Born 08/09/1943, New York, NY, m, 1964, 2 children **DISCIPLINE** AMERICAN LITERATURE PROSE FICTION, TRANSLATION OF CONTEMPORARY ROMANIAN LITERATURE **EDUCATION** Cornell Univ, AB, 64, MA, 65; Univ NC, PhD, 72. **CAREER** Instr Eng, Univ IL, Chicago Circle, 65-66; instr Eng & Am lit, Univ NC, Chapel Hill, 70-71; instr, Stockton State Col, 71-73; instr, Drexel Univ & Community Col Philadelphia, 73; asst prof Eng & Am lit, Bluefield State Col, 74-78; from Asst Prof to Prof Eng, PA State Univ, 78-; Fulbright lectr, Univ Bucharest, Romania, 80-81. **HONORS AND AWARDS** NEH Summer Seminar, 75; IREX Fel, 91; Rockefeller Found Residency, Study and Conf Ctr, Italy, 95; Recommended Transl, Poetry Bk Soc, for The Sky Behind the Forest, 97; The Sky Behind the Forest shortlisted for Weidenfeld Prize for Translation, 97; Crossing Boundaries Translation Awd, Int Quart, for The Europ Mechanism, Fall 97; Story Short Short Competition winner, 14th place, for The Telephone, 97; Kenneth Rexroth Memorial Translation Prize, for Marta Petrey translations, 99. **MEMBERSHIPS** Am Lit Translr(s) Asn. **RESEARCH** Am lit; Romanian lit; mod lit. **SELECTED PUBLICATIONS** Ed, Politics and the Muse: Studies in the Politics of Recent American Literature, Bowling Green State Univ Popular Press, 89; Conversations with Joseph Heller, Literary Conversations Series, Univ Press MS, 93; auth, Marin Sorescu: Comedian of Antiheroic Resistance, Romanian Civilization, Summer 92; Half in Flight Half in Chains: The Paradoxical Vision of Iona Ieronim's Poetry, Conn Rev, Fall 95; Petre Stoica's Tiananmen Square II: Anger, Protest, and an Angel with a Crow's Wings, Romanian Civilization, Winter 95-96; Liliana Ursu's Poetry, Delos: A J Transl & World Lit 18, 96; The Forbidden World and Hidden Words: Steadfast Illumination in Marin Sorescu's Poems Selected by Censorship, Romanian Civilization, Fall 96; Postmodernism in Romanian Poetry: The Abnormally Normal, Romania & Western Civilization / Romania si civilizatia occidentala, Iasi: The Ctr for Romanian Studies, 97; On The Circle by Martin Sorescu, Two Lines: A J of Transl, Spring 97; I Was of Three Minds: Some Notes on Translating, Metamorphoses, April 98; author of numerous other articles, translator of short stories and hundreds of poems in 13 books and in 200 literary magazines. **CONTACT ADDRESS** Eng Dept, Pennsylvania State Univ, Delaware County, 25 Yearsley Mill Rd, Media, PA 19063-5596. **EMAIL** ajs2@psu.edu

SORUM, CHRISTINA ELLIOTT

DISCIPLINE CLASSICS **EDUCATION** Wellesley Col, BA, 67; Brown Univ, PhD, 75. **CAREER** Asst prof, for lang and lit, North Carolina State Univ, 75-82; chemn, 82-91, assoc prof, 82-86, Frank Bailey Assoc Prof, 86-92, Frank Bailey Prof, Classics, 92- , Dean of Arts and Sci, Union Col,94-99; Dean of Faculty and VP for Acad Affairs, 99-. **HONORS AND AWARDS** Outstanding Teacher Award, 82; Fac Merit Service Award, 94. **MEMBERSHIPS** Am Philol Asn; Class Asn of the Atlantic States; Class Asn of the Middle W and S; Class Asn of the Empire State; Asn of Am Col and Univ; Asn of General and Liberal Studies; AAUW. **RESEARCH** Greek and Latin language and literature; Greek and Latin drama and epic in translation; classical mythology. **SELECTED PUBLICATIONS** Auth, Monsters and the Family: The Exodos of Sophocles' Trachiniae, Greek, Roman and Byzantine Stud, 78; auth, The Family in Sophocles' Antigone and Electra, the Classical World, 82; auth, The Authorship of the Agesilaus, La Parola del Passato, 84; auth, Sophocles' Ajax in Context, The Classical World, 86; auth, Myth, Choice, and Meaning in Euripides: Iphigenia at Aulis, Am J of Philology, 92; auth, Euripides' Judgment: Literary Creation in Andromache, Am J of Philology, 95; auth, "Vortex, Clouds, and Tongue: New Problems in the Humanities?," J of the Acad of Arts and Sciences, (99). **CONTACT ADDRESS** Dept of Classics, Union Col, New York, Feigenbaum Hall, Schenectady, NY 12308. **EMAIL** sorumc@union.edu

SOSOWER, MARK L.

PERSONAL Born 04/26/1949, Teaneck, NJ, m, 2000, 2 children **DISCIPLINE** CLASSICS **EDUCATION** Univ Rochester, BA, 71; MA, 72; MA, 75; NYU, PhD, 81. **CAREER** Asst prof, assoc prof, prof, NYU, 92-. **HONORS AND AWARDS** NEH, 91, 98; Andrew W. Mellon Trav Grnt, 91; A. Bartlett Giamatti Fel, Ren Stud, 90; APS Trav Grnt, 90; NEH Sum Sem, 89; NCar State Alumni Outs Ext Awd, 91. **MEMBERSHIPS** APA; USNCB; AFVL; CAMWS; NCCA; Richard Stanhope Pullen Soc; Sigma Iota Rho Hon Soc. **RESEARCH** Greek Paleography and codicology; history of early humanistic libraries. **SELECTED PUBLICATIONS** Auth, Palatinus Graecus 88 and the Manuscript Tradition of Lysias, Adolf Hakkert, 87; co-auth, Learning from the Greeks: An Exhibition commemorating the 500th Anniversary of the Founding of the Aldine Press, Yale UP, 94; co-auth, Librorum graecorum Bibliothecae Vaticanae index a Nicolao de Maioranis compositus a Fausto Saboeo collatus anno 1533, Vatican Lib, 98; auth, "Palla Strozzi's Greek Manuscripts," Stud Itali de fiolo Class 3 (86): 140-51; auth, "Marcus Musurus and a Codex of Lysias," Greek Roman Byz Stud 23 (82): 377-92; auth, "Seven Manuscripts Palla Strozzi Gave to the S. Giustina Library," J Warburg Court Inst 47 (84): 190-91; auth, "A Greek Codex of Sir Thomas Phillips Once in the Clermont Library," Syllecta Class 2 (90): 95-102; auth, "Antonio's Eparchos and a Codex of Archimedes in the Bodmer Library," Museum Helvet 50 (93): 144-57; auth, "A Forger Revisited: Andreas Darmarios and Beinecke," Jahrb der Oster Byzan 43 (93): 289-306; auth, "A Manuscript of Guillaume Pellicier," (d. 1567) in the Beinecke Library, Scriptorium 52 (98): 372-80. **CONTACT ADDRESS** Dept of Classics, No Carolina State Univ, PO Box 8106, Raleigh, NC 27695. **EMAIL** mlsfll@unity.ncsu.edu

SOUSA, RONALD W.

PERSONAL Born 08/14/1943, Santa Cruz, CA, m, 1968, 2 children **DISCIPLINE** PORTUGUESE LANGUAGE & LITERATURE **EDUCATION** Univ Calif Berkeley, BA, 66, MA, 68, PhD, 73. **CAREER** Asst prof, 71-74, Univ Tx Austin; asst prof to assoc prof to prof, 74-93, Univ Mn Minneapolis; vis prof, 77, Univ Calif Berkeley; prof, 94-, Univ Il Champaign-Urbana. **HONORS AND AWARDS** Nat Endow for the Humanities Summer Stipend, 76, 86; Grant-in-Aid Amer Philos Soc, 76-77; Putnam Dana MacMillan Fel, 79; Bolsa de Estudos, Fundacao Calouste Gulbenkian, 80; **RESEARCH** Portuguese lit; lit & hist; theory of hist; lit theory. **SELECTED PUBLICATIONS** Auth, The Rediscoverers: Major Figures in the Portuguese Literature of National Regeneration, Pa St Univ Press, 81; art, Vos outros tambem cantai por vosso uso acostumado.., Literature Among Discourses: The Spanish Golden Age, Univ Mn Press, 87; coauth, Reading the Harper: On A Portuguese Immigrant Poem, California, 1901, Gavea-Brown, 96; art, Pessoa Criticism and the Antagonistic Literary Institutionality of the Estado Novo, J of Hispanic Lit, 96; art, Cannibal, Cartographer, Soldier, Spy: The Peirai of Mendes Pinto's Peregrinacao, The Project of Prose in Early Modern Europe and the New World, Cambridge Univ Press, 97; coauth, The Humanities in Dispute, Purdue, U. Press, 98. **CONTACT ADDRESS** 1807 Bentbrook Dr, Champaign, IL 61822. **EMAIL** r-sousa@uiuc.edu

SOUTHERN, MARK R. V.

PERSONAL Born 03/03/1961, Cambridge, England, m, 1995, 2 children **DISCIPLINE** GERMANIC LINGUISTICS **EDUCATION** Oxford Univ, BA, 83; MA, 92; Princeton Univ, MA, 86; PhD, 97. **CAREER** TA, Princeton Univ, 91-92; asst prof, Carthage Col, 92-95; asst prof, Univ of Tex, 95-. **HONORS AND AWARDS** Newcastle Medal, 78; Urquhart Fel, 80, 82; Fel, Princeton, 84-88, 90-92; Seeger Fel, 85, 86; President's Associates Teaching Excellence Awd, 98; Fel, Univ Tex Austin, 98-01; 99. **MEMBERSHIPS** MLA, Ling Soc of Am, Soc for Ger Philol, Tex Ling Soc, Am Transl Assoc, Celtic Studies Assoc of NA. **SELECTED PUBLICATIONS** Transl, Italy: Seasons of Light, by Michael Ruetz (Boston: Little, Brown, 88); transl, Gustav Klimt: Masterpieces, by Gabriella Belli (Boston: Bullfinch Pr, 89); auth, "The Problem of the s-mobile in Indo-European," Pa Review of Ling 16, Univ of Pa, (92); coauth, "Where have all the nasals gone?: nC > in North Semitic," Jour of Semitic Studies 42.2, (97); auth, Sub-grammatical Survival: Indo-European s-mobile and its Regeneration in Germanic, Inst for the Study of Man, Washington, DC, 99; auth, "The Road to Dzernowitz and the Yiddish Golden Age: A sociolinguistic exploration," Yiddish 12.1, Queen's Col, NY, (00); auth, "Tabula Rasa: the tablet word in italic, and its Indo-European relatives," Munchener Studien zur Sprachwissenschaft 60, (00); auth, "caribbean creoles as a convergence conduit: English boss and overseer, Ndjuka basia, Sranan basja, jamaican Busha, Dutch Bas (-je)," Folia Ling Hist 21, (00); auth, "Formulaic binomials, morphosymbolism and Behaghel's Law: The Grammatical status of expressive iconicity," Am Jour of Ger Ling and Lit 12.2, (00); auth, "Identity and contact in three Jewish languages," Archaeol, Lang and Hist, (01). **CONTACT ADDRESS** Dept Germanic Studies, Univ of Texas, Austin, EPS 3.102, Austin, TX 78712. **EMAIL** m.southern@mail.utexas.edu

SOUZA, RAYMOND D.

PERSONAL Born 03/11/1936, Attleboro, MA, m, 1966, 2 children **DISCIPLINE** SPANISH **EDUCATION** Drury Col, BA, 58; Univ Mo, MA, 60, PhD(Span), 64. **CAREER** Teacher high sch, Mo, 58-59; instr Span, Kent State Univ, 61-62; from asst prof to assoc prof, 63-73, chmn dept Span & Port, 68-74, prof Span, Univ Kans, 73-, Am Philos Soc Johnson Fund fel, 68; Exxon inter-univ vis prof ling & philos, 81-82; Tinker Found fel, Costa Rica, 82. **MEMBERSHIPS** Am Asn Teachers Span & Port; Inst Int Lit Iberoam; MLA; Assoc of North American Colombianists, Pres, 87-89. **RESEARCH** Spanish American prose fiction and poetry; Cuban literature; Colombian literature, film. **SELECTED PUBLICATIONS** Auth, Language vs Structure in the contemporary Spanish American Novel, Hispania, 12/69;Time and Terror in the Stories of Lino Novas Calvo, Symposium, winter 75; Time and Space Configurations in Two Poems of Octavio Paz, J Span Studies: Twentieth Century, fall 76; Major Cuban Novelists: Innovation & Tradition, Univ Mo, Columbia 76, London 76; ; Lino Novas Calvo, G K Hall, 81; The Poetic Fiction of Jose Lezama Lima, Univ Mo, Columbia, 83; Novel and Context in Costa Rica and Nicaragua, Romance Quart, April 86; Yes, We Have No Havana(s): Requiem for a Lost City, World Lit Today, April 87; La Historia en la novela hispanoamericana moderna, Tercer Mundo, Bogota, 88; Columbus in the Novel of the Americas: Alejo Carpentier, Abel Posse, & Stephen Marlowe, in Raymond Williams ed, Reading the Americas, Univ Colorado, Boulder, 92; Guillermo Cabrera Infante: Two Islands, Many Worlds, Univ Tx, Austin, 96. **CONTACT ADDRESS** Dept of Span & Port, Univ of Kansas, Lawrence, Lawrence, KS 66045-0001. **EMAIL** rdsouza@ukans.edu

SPACCARELLI, THOMAS DEAN

PERSONAL Born 09/25/1947, Chicago, IL, m, 1970 **DISCIPLINE** SPANISH LINGUISTIC, MEDIEVAL SPANISH LITERATURE **EDUCATION** Univ Ill, Chicago Circle, AB, 69; Univ Wis-Madison, MA, 71, PhD(Span), 75. **CAREER** Lectr Span, Univ Ill Chicago Circle, 73-74; instr, 74-75, Asst Prof Span, Univ Of The South, 75-, Mem, Span Joint Comt, Educ & Cult Affairs, 80-81. **MEMBERSHIPS** Am Asn Teachers of Span & Port; MLA; Mediaeval Acad Am. **RESEARCH** Spanish lexicography; medieval romance. **SELECTED PUBLICATIONS** Ed, Complete Concordances and Texts of the Fourteenth-Century Aragonese Manuscripts of Jaun Fernandez de heredia, Hisp Sem of Medieval Studies, Ltd, 82; The Emergence Of The Erotic In Don Juan Tenorio, Romance Notes, Vol 34, 93. **CONTACT ADDRESS** Dept of Span, Univ of the South, Sewanee, TN 37375.

SPAETHLING, ROBERT H.

PERSONAL Born 07/30/1927, Weissenstadt, Germany, m, 1953, 3 children **DISCIPLINE** GERMAN, LITERATURE, MUSIC **EDUCATION** Univ Regensburg, 50; Univ Wurzburg; Univ Calif Berkeley, MA, 57; PhD, 59. **CAREER** Asst to assoc prof, Harvard Univ, 59-68; assoc prof, Williams Col, 65-66; prof, dean, vice chancellor, Univ of Mass Boston, 68-. **HONORS AND AWARDS** Danforth Teaching Awd, 74; NEH Feel, 82; NEH Grant, 91; Distinguished Serve Medal, Univ of Mass, 91. **MEMBERSHIPS** MLA; AATG, ASCS. **RESEARCH**

18th and 20th Century German Literature, Mozart's Letters. **SELECTED PUBLICATIONS** Coauth, A Reader in German Literature, Oxford Univ Pr, 69; coauth, Literature Ins, Revised 2nd Ed, WW Norton, 75; auth, "Folklore and Enlightenment in the Libretto of "The Magic Flute,'" 18th Century Studies, (75); auth, "Christian Furchtegott Gellert," Dict of Lit Biog 97, (90): auth, "Christian Thomasius", Dict of Lit Biog 168, (96); auth, Mozart's Letters, Mozart's Life, WW Norton/Faber & Faber, 00. **CONTACT ADDRESS** 101 Washington Ave, Cambridge, MA 02140-2716. **EMAIL** elrobspaeth@earthling.net

SPAHR, BLAKE LEE
PERSONAL Born 07/11/1924, Carlisle, PA, m, 1957, 1 child **DISCIPLINE** GERMAN & COMPARATIVE LITERATURE **EDUCATION** Dickinson Col, BA, 47; Yale Univ, MA, 48, PhD, 51. **CAREER** Instr Ger and Comparative Lit, Dickinson Col, 46-47; instr, Yale Univ, 52-55; from asst prof to assoc prof, 55-58; assoc prof to prof, 58-64, chmn dept Ger and Comp Lit, 64-69; chmn dept comp lit, 71-74, Prof Ger & Comp Lit, Univ Calif, Berkeley, 64-92; prof emer, 92-; guest prof, L'Universite de Geneve (Geneva, Switzerland), 61; Northwestern Univ (Evanston, IL, 71); Univ of Colorado (Boulder, Col, Summer, 59); Univ of Hawaii (Honolulu, HI, 85); Morse res fel, Yale Univ, 52-53; Guggenheim fel, 62; ed, Nachdrucke deutscher Literatur des 17. Jhs, 83-92; ed, Berner Beitrage zur deutschen Barocklit, 83-92, rev ed, Daphnis; ed, staff, Comp Lit Rev. **HONORS AND AWARDS** Bundesverdienstkreuz 1. KL, 1985; Berkeley Citation for Distinguished Achievement, 92; Barocker Lust-Spiegel, Festschrift fur Blake Lee Spahr; Doctor of Human Letters (h.C.), Dickinson Col, 00. **MEMBERSHIPS** Int Arthurian Soc; Pegnesischer Blumenorden; Oakland Commun Orch. **RESEARCH** German lit of the Middle Ages and the 17th century; Comparative Arthurian literature. **SELECTED PUBLICATIONS** Auth, Archives of the Pegnesischer Blumenorden, 60; auth, Anton Ulrich and Aramena, 66; auth, Problems and Perspectives: A Col of Essays on German Barock lit, 81; Andreas Gryphius, A Modern Perspective, 93; numerous articles on German, and Dutch lit. of the Mid Ages & of the 17th cent. **CONTACT ADDRESS** Dept of Ger & Comp Lit, Univ of California, Berkeley, Berkeley, CA 94720. **EMAIL** blspahr@socrates.berkeley.edu

SPANGLER, MAY
PERSONAL Born 04/24/1956, Boulogne Billahcourt, France, m, 1980, 3 children **DISCIPLINE** FRENCH LITERATURE, ARCHITECTURE, ART **EDUCATION** Ecole des Beaux-Arts, MA, 82; Emory Univ, MA, 92; PhD, 96. **CAREER** Intern architect, Ateliers Remondet and Taieb, 79; intern architect, Helfrich and Briles Architects, 80-83; intern architect, Rabun and Hatch Architects, Inc., 85-89; free-lance architect, 85-89; instr, Agnes Scott Col; instr, Emory Univ. **HONORS AND AWARDS** Scholar, Ga Inst of Technol Col of Archit, 78; Traveling Scholar, Ga Inst of Technol Col of Archit, 78; Traveling Grant, Ecole des Beaux-Arts, 79; Grad Sch Fel, Emory Univ, 91-96; Anne Amari Perry Awd, 95. **MEMBERSHIPS** MLA. **RESEARCH** Cultural Studies: Literature, Architecture and Art (with an emphasis on Paris), Eighteenth-Century French Literature and History of Ideas (with an emphasis on Diderot and Natural Science). **SELECTED PUBLICATIONS** Auth, "Science, philosophie et litterature: le polype de Diderot," Recherches sur Diderot et sur l'Encyclopedie 23 (97); auth, "L'accident du moderne dans l'ubanisme parisien," Orage 11 (97); rev, of "Denis Diderot: Extravagance et genialite," by Marie-Helene Chabut, Symposium (forthcoming). **CONTACT ADDRESS** Dept Fr & Ital, Emory Univ, 1364 Clifton Rd NE, Atlanta, GA 30322-1061. **EMAIL** mspangl@emory.edu

SPARKS, KIMBERLY
PERSONAL Born 10/02/1930, Baltimore, MD, m, 1952, 3 children **DISCIPLINE** GERMANIC LANGUAGES **EDUCATION** Princeton Univ, AB, 56, MA, 59, PhD(Ger), 63. **CAREER** From instr to foreign lang, 66-71, chmn comt, 73-76, Charles A Dana Prof Ger, Middlebury Col, 71-, Chmn exam comt, Ger Achievement Test, 66-68; dir, Northeast Conf Teaching Foreign Lang, 68-72; mem nat bd consults, Nat Endowment for Humanities, 77- **MEMBERSHIPS** MLA. **RESEARCH** Novels of Hermann Broch; language teaching. **SELECTED PUBLICATIONS** Auth, Korfs Uhr, In: Perspective der Forschung; Drei Schwarze Kaninchen Z Deut Philol, 65; coauth, Der Web zum Lesen, 67, German in Review, 67, Modern German, 71, S ist es, 71 & Thomas Manns Tonio Kroger als Weg zur Literatur, 74, Harcout; auth, The radicalization of space in Kafka, In: On Kafka, Elek, London, 77; Schnitzler The 'Dead Are Silent--Introduction, New England Review-Middlebury Series, Vol 18, 1997. **CONTACT ADDRESS** Dept of Ger, Middlebury Col, Middlebury, VT 05753.

SPEAS, MARGARET
DISCIPLINE LINGUISTICS **EDUCATION** Wash Univ, BA, 73; Univ Ariz, MA, 81; Univ Mass, PhD, 86. **CAREER** Assoc prof. **SELECTED PUBLICATIONS** Auth, Optimality in Syntax: Control and Null Arguments, Blackwell, 97; Null Arguments in a Theory of Economy of Projection, 94; Functional Heads and Inflectional Morphemes, ling rev, 91; Phrase Structure in Natural Language, Kluwer, 90. **CONTACT ADDRESS** Linguistics Dept, Univ of Massachusetts, Amherst, S College 220, Amherst, MA 01003. **EMAIL** pspeas@linguist.umass.edu

SPECK, OLIVER C.
DISCIPLINE GERMAN **EDUCATION** Univ Waterloo, MA, 90; Univ Mannheim, PhD, 96. **CAREER** Adj lectr, Northwestern Univ. **RESEARCH** German, English and French Literature; Film; Film and media theory; literary theory; cultural studies. **SELECTED PUBLICATIONS** Auth, Lemmy Caution als Bildner der Ich-Funktion: Intermedialit t in Godards Alphaville, in: Volker Roloff und Scarlett Winter, Hrsg Godard Intermedial; Tubingen: Stauffenberg Verlag, 97. **CONTACT ADDRESS** Dept of German, Northwestern Univ, 1801 Hinman, Evanston, IL 60208. **EMAIL** ocspeck@northwestern.edu

SPEER, MARY B.
PERSONAL Born Bennettsville, SC, m, 1970 **DISCIPLINE** FRENCH LITERATURE, MEDIEVAL, LANGUAGE **EDUCATION** Duke Univ, BA, 64; Princeton Univ, MA, 67; PhD, 71. **CAREER** Instr to asst prof, Boston Univ, 69-72; lectr, Princeton Univ, 73-75; lectr to assoc prof to prof, Rutgers Univ, 77-. **HONORS AND AWARDS** Fulbright Fel; Woodrow Wilson Fel; Distinguished Fel; NEH Grant, 79-80; Rutgers Awd for Excellence, 99. **MEMBERSHIPS** MLA; MA; ICLS; SR; SSS; STS; IAS; Soc Guilhem. **RESEARCH** Medieval French literature; 12th and 13th-century romance and lyric; codicology and textual criticism. **SELECTED PUBLICATIONS** Co-auth, On Editing Old French Texts; auth, Le Roman des Sept Sages de Rome; auth, "Editing Old French Literary Texts," in Scholarly Editing, ed. D. C. Greetham; auth, "Gaston Paris: Philologist and Mythographer," in Translation Studii Essays; auth, "Abbreviation as Rewriting in LaMort Leroi Artu," in Text and Intertext in Medieval Arthurian Lit, ed. Norris Lacey; auth, "L'Espirit Createur," "Medievalia et Humanistica," "Romania," Romance Philol; auth, "Exhuming the First Guide to Editing Old French Texts: Prompsault's Discourse," (98). **CONTACT ADDRESS** Fr Dept, Rutgers, The State Univ of New Jersey, New Brunswick, 131 George St, 103 Ruth Adams Bldg., New Brunswick, NJ 08901-1414. **EMAIL** mspeer@rci.rutgers.edu

SPENCER, JANINE
DISCIPLINE FRENCH **EDUCATION** Northwestern Univ, PhD. **CAREER** Sr lectr; coordr, second-yr Fr, Northwestern Univ; trained, ACTFL oral proficiency tester; dir,Multi-Media Learning Center. **RESEARCH** Material development for oral and written communication, instructional technology in foreign language instruction and alternate models of instruction. **SELECTED PUBLICATIONS** Coauth, Et votre avis, Holt, Rinehart and Winston, 90. **CONTACT ADDRESS** Dept of French, Northwestern Univ, Kresge 150, 1859 Sheridan, Evanston, IL 60208. **EMAIL** j-spencer@northwestern.edu

SPENCER, SAMIA I.
PERSONAL Born 07/04/1943, Alexandria, Egypt, m, 1969, 2 children **DISCIPLINE** FRENCH **EDUCATION** Alexandria Univ, Egypt, BA, 64; Univ Ill, Urbana, MA, 69, PhD(French), 75. **CAREER** Secy & gen asst, US Info Serv, Egypt 65-67; secy, World Health Orgn, Egypt, 67 & UN Develop Prog, NY, 68; teaching asst French, Univ Ill, Urbana, 68-72; instr, 72-75, asst prof, 75-80, Assoc Prof French, Auburn Univ, 80-85, prof, 85-. **HONORS AND AWARDS** Outstanding Fac Mem Awd in Humanities, Student Government Asn, Auburn Univ, 85; Best Secretary-Treasurer (small chapters), Am Asn of Teachers of Fr, 89; Chevalier dan l'Ordre des Palmes Academiques, Government of France, 90; Fac Achievement Awd in the Humanities, Col of Liberal Arts, Auburn Univ, 91; Prix d'Excellence, Alabama Chapter, Am Asn of Teachers of Fr, 96; Outstanding Teacher Awd (Postsecondary), Alabama Asn of Foreign Lang Teachers, 98; Who's Who Among America's Teachers, 00 **MEMBERSHIPS** Am Asn Teachers of Fr ; Asn for Canadian Studies in the United States; Am Asn for Eighteenth-Century Studies; Southeastern Am Asn for Eighteenth-Century Studies; Am Coun for Quebec Studies; MLA; South Atlantic Mod Lang Asn; Alabama Asn of Foreign Lang Teachers; Southern Coun on Lang Teaching. **RESEARCH** The eighteenth century French novel; women in eighteenth century French literature; the teaching of foreign languages. **SELECTED PUBLICATIONS** Ed and contrib, French Women and the Age of Enlightenment, Bloomington: Indiana Univ Press, 84, 92; ed and contrib, Foreign Languages and International Trade: A Global Perspective, The University of Georgia Press (Athens), 87; ed and contri, The Feminist Encyclopedia of French Literature, Greenwood Press (Wesport, CT), 99; auth, The French Enlightenment, Columbia SC: Bruccoli, Clark, Layman (in progress). **CONTACT ADDRESS** Dept of Foreign Lang and Literatures, Auburn Univ, Auburn, AL 36849. **EMAIL** spencsi@auburn.edu

SPILKA, MARK
PERSONAL Born 08/06/1925, Cleveland, OH, m, 7 children **DISCIPLINE** ENGLISH, COMPARATIVE LITERATURE **EDUCATION** Brown Univ, BA, 49; Ind Univ, MA, 53, PhD(-comp lit), 56. **CAREER** Ed asst, Am Mercury, 49-51; instr English lit, Univ Mich, 54-58, asst prof, English, 58-63; assoc prof, 63-67, chmn, Dept English, 68-73, PROF ENGLISH LIT, BROWN UNIV, 67-, Fel, Ind Sch Lett, 61; managing ed, Novel: A Forum on Fiction, Brown Univ, 67-77, ed, 78-; Guggenheim fel, 67-68; Nat Endowment for Humanitites fel independent study & res, 78-79; vis prof, Ind Univ, summer, 76. **MEMBERSHIPS** MLA **RESEARCH** English and American novel, especially 19th and 20th centuries; comparative literature; modern literary criticism. **SELECTED PUBLICATIONS** Auth, Love Ethic of D H Lawrence, 55 & Dickens and Kafka: A Mutual Interpretation, 63, Ind Univ; ed, D H Lawrence: A Collection of Critical Essays, Prentice-Hall, 63; Towards a Poetics of Fiction, Ind Univ, 77; auth, Virginia Woolf's Quarrel with Grieving, Univ Nebr Press, 80; auth, Renewing the Normative D. H. Lawrence: A Personal Progress, Missouri, 92; auth, Eight Lessons in Love: A Domestic Violence Reader, Missouri, 97. **CONTACT ADDRESS** 294 Doyle Ave, Providence, RI 02906. **EMAIL** mark.spilka@brown.edu

SPIRES, ROBERT CECIL
PERSONAL Born 12/01/1936, Missouri Valley, IA, m, 1963, 2 children **DISCIPLINE** CONTEMPORARY SPANISH LITERATURE **EDUCATION** Univ Iowa, BA, 59, MA, 63, PhD(-Span), 68. **CAREER** From instr to asst prof Span, Ohio Univ, 67-69; asst prof, 69-74, assoc prof, 74-78, Prof Span, Univ Kans, 78-. **HONORS AND AWARDS** Univ Kans Mortar Bd Awd, 77; NEH Fel for Independent Study and Res, 81-82; U.S.-Spanish Joint Comm Fel for Res in Spain, 85-86; Chancellor's Teaching Awd, Univ of Kans, 88-89; Spain's Ministry of Culture and United States' Universities Fel for Res in Spain, Spring 92. **MEMBERSHIPS** MLA; Am Asn Teachers Span & Port. **RESEARCH** Contemporary Hispanic novel; contemporary Spanish drama; contemporary Spanish poetry. **SELECTED PUBLICATIONS** Auth, Tecnica y tema en La familia de Pascual Duarte, Insula, 9/71; Systematic doubt: The moral art of La familia de Pascual Duarte, Hisp Rev, summer 72; Cela's La colmena: The creative process as message, Hispania, 12/72; contribr, Novelistas Epanoles de Postguerra, Taurus, Madrid, 76; auth, Linguistic codes and dramatic action in La casa de Bernarda Alba, Am Hispanist, 1/78; La Novela Espanola de Postguerra: Creacion Artistica y Experiencia Personal, Editorial Planeta/Universidad, Madrid, 78; Latrines, whirlpools and voids: The metafictional mode of Juan sin Tierra, Hisp Rev, spring 80; La colera de Aguiles: Un texto producto del lector, Revista Iberoamericana, Julio-Dic, 81; Beyond the Metafictional Mode: Direction in the Modern Spanish Novel, Univ Press of Ky, 84; Transparent Simulacra: Spanish Fiction 1902-1926, Univ of Mo Press, 88; Post-Totalitarian Spanish Fiction, Univ of Mo Press, 96. **CONTACT ADDRESS** Dept of Span & Port, Univ of Kansas, Lawrence, Lawrence, KS 66045-0001. **EMAIL** rspires@kuhub.cc.ukans.edu

SPIVAK, GAYATRI CHAKRAVORTY
PERSONAL Born 02/24/1942, Calcutta, India **DISCIPLINE** COMPARATIVE LITERATURE **EDUCATION** Univ Calcutta, BA, 59; Univ Calcutta, MA, 62; Cornell Univ, PhD, 67 **CAREER** Avalon prof Humanities, Cornell Univ, 91- **HONORS AND AWARDS** Fel, Nat Humanities Inst; Fel, Center for the Humanities Wesleyan; Fel, Humanities Res Center at Australian National Univ; Kent Fel; Guggenheim Fel; Tagore Fel Maharaja Sayajirao Univ Baroda, India; Translation Prize Sahitya Akademi, 1997; Dr of Letters, honoris causa, Univ of Toronto, 00. **RESEARCH** Nineteenth Century Literature; Marxism; Feminism; Deconstruction; Poststructuralism **SELECTED PUBLICATIONS** Auth, Murti, Seagull, 98; auth, A Critique of Postcolonial Reason, Harvard Univ, 99; auth, The Breast Stories, Seagull, 97; auth, The Spivak Reader, Routledge, 95; Grammatology, 76. **CONTACT ADDRESS** Dept English, Columbia Univ, 602 Philosophy Hall, New York, NY 10027.

SPRINGER, CARL P. E.
PERSONAL Born 11/28/1954, San Diego, CA, m, 1980, 4 children **DISCIPLINE** CLASSICS **EDUCATION** Univ of Wis Madison, PhD, 84. **CAREER** Asst prof, Ill State Univ, 84-90; assoc prof, Ill State Univ, 91-96; prof and chair dept of Foreign Lang, Ill State Univ, 96- ; assoc dean, Southern Illinois Univ Edwardsville. **HONORS AND AWARDS** Fulbright res Grant, 90; Alexander von Humboldt Fel, 93-94. **MEMBERSHIPS** Am Philos Asn; N Am Patristic Soc. **RESEARCH** Late Antiquity; Latin Epic; Biblical Poetry. **SELECTED PUBLICATIONS** Auth, Fannius and Scaevola in Cicero's De Amicitia, Studies in Latin Lit and Roman Hist VII, 94; The Concinnity of Ambrose's Illuminans Altissimus, Panchaia, Festschrift fur Professor Klaus Thraede, 95; The Manuscripts of Sedulius, A Provisional Handlist, 95; rev, early Christian Poetry, J of Early Christian Studies, 96. **CONTACT ADDRESS** College of Arts and Sciences, Campus Box 1608, Illinois State Univ, Peck Hall 3432 Southern Illinois University Edwardsville, Edwardsville, IL 62026. **EMAIL** cpsproner@stu.edu

SPRINKER, MICHAEL
PERSONAL Born 02/08/1950, m **DISCIPLINE** ENGLISH AND COMPARATIVE LITERATURE **EDUCATION** Northwestern Univ, BA, 72; Princeton Univ, MA, 74; PhD, 75. **CAREER** Prof, 88-. **SELECTED PUBLICATIONS** Auth, Counterpoint of Dissonance: The Aesthetics and Poetry of Gerard Manley Hopkins, Johns Hopkins Univ, 80; Imaginary Relations: Aesthetics and Ideology in the Theory of Historical Materialism, 87; History and Ideology in Proust: 'A la recherche du temps perdu' and the Third French Republic, Cambridge, 94; The Mughal Empire (rev), Radical History Rev, 94; co-ed, Late Imperial Culture, 95. **CONTACT ADDRESS** English Dept, SUNY, Stony Brook, Stony Brook, NY 11794.

SPURLOCK, JOHN HOWARD
PERSONAL Born 10/22/1939, Huntington, WV, m, 1962, 1 child **DISCIPLINE** LINGUISTICS, AMERICAN LITERATURE **EDUCATION** WVa Univ, BA, 62; Univ Louisville, MA, 64, PhD, 86. **CAREER** Instr English, Western Ky Univ, 64-69 & Louisville Country Day Sch, 69-70; assoc prof, 71-86, prof English, Western Ky Univ, 86-. **HONORS AND AWARDS** Awd for Editorial Excellence, Jesse Stuart Found, 96. **MEMBERSHIPS** Appalachian Writers Asn; Jesse Stuart Found (ed and mem bd dir); Ky Speakers' Bureau. **RESEARCH** Sociolinguistics; Appalachian literature; Kentucky literature. **SELECTED PUBLICATIONS** Auth, He Sings For Us--A Sociolinguistic Analysis of the Appalachian Subculture and of Jesse Stuart as a Major American Author, Univ Press of Am, 80 & 82; Appalachian--Appalachia/strange man--strange land, In: Speechways of American Subcultures, Univ Press of Ky, 82; ed, Jesse Stuart's Daughter of the Legend, Jesse Stuart Found, 94; Jesse Stuart's Beyond Dark Hills, Jesse Stuart Found, 96. **CONTACT ADDRESS** 1 Big Red Way St, Box 495, Bowling Green, KY 42101-3576. **EMAIL** john.spurlock@wku.edu

SRIDHAR, S. N.
PERSONAL Born 05/26/1950, Shimoga, India, m, 1974 **DISCIPLINE** LINGUISTICS, COMPARATIVE LITERATURE **EDUCATION** Bangalore Univ, India, BA Hons, 69, MA, 71; Univ Ill, MA, 75, PhD(ling), 80. **CAREER** Res assoc, Teachers English to Speakers Other Lang, Cent Inst English & Lang, Hyderabad, India, 71-72, lectr ling, 72-73; res asst ling, Univ, Ill, Urbana,, 73-79; Asst Prof Ling, State Univ NY, Stony Brook, 80-,Consult, Dict Int Varieties of English, 78- & Univ Wash, Seattle, 79; secy, NY State Coun Ling, 81-82. **MEMBERSHIPS** Ling Soc Am; Teachers English to Speakers Other Lang; Ling Soc India; Dravidian Ling Asn; Am Asn Applied Ling. **RESEARCH** Dravidian linguistics; psycholinguistic aspects of sentence production, bilingualism and second language acquisition; teaching English as a second language. **SELECTED PUBLICATIONS** Co-ed, Language Through Literature, Vol II, Oxford Univ Press, 75; coauth, Clause-union and relational grammar, Ling Inquiry, 77; co-ed, Aspects of sociolinguistics in South Asia, Int J Sociol Lang, 78; auth, Dative subjects and the notion of subjective, Lingua, 79; Contrastive analysis, error analysis and interlanguage, In: Readings in English as a Second Language, Winthrop, 2nd ed, 80; coauth, Syntax & psycholinguistics of bilingual code mixing, Can J Psychol, 80; auth, Kannada: A Descriptive Grammar, North Holland Publ Co, 82; Language teaching and litercy in South Asia, In: Annual Review of Applied Linguistics, Newbury House, 82; A Reality Check For Sla Theories, Tesol Quart, Vol 28, 94. **CONTACT ADDRESS** Prog in Ling State, SUNY, Stony Brook, 100 Nicolls Rd, Stony Brook, NY 11794-0002.

ST CLAIR, ROBERT
PERSONAL Born 04/24/1934, Honolulu, HI, d, 1 child **DISCIPLINE** LINGUISTICS **EDUCATION** Univ Haw, BA, 63; Univ Wash, MA, 67; Univ Calif, MA, 70; Univ Kans, PhD, 74. **CAREER** Lectr to prof, Univ of Louisville, 73-. **HONORS AND AWARDS** Outstanding Educator Awd, NEA, 75; Distinguished Vis Prof, Univ of Waikato, New Zealand, 92; Distinguished Prof Res Awd, Univ of Louisville, 93-94; Int Vis Prof, Josai Int Univ, Japan, 96, 97; Int Vis Lectr Series, Long Island Univ, 98. **MEMBERSHIPS** AAUP; Ling Soc of Am; Soc for Teachers of Japanese; NCTE; MLA; ACTE; Int Assoc of Cross-Cultural Commun; Int Reading Assoc; Int Ling Assoc; Adult Educ Assoc. **SELECTED PUBLICATIONS** Coauth, Languages Across Cultures, Simm Pub, (Seoul, Korea), 89; coauth, The Business of Advertising in America, Soc Sys Pr, 95; coauth, Understanding American Culture Through Advertising: Volume One, Tohikaku Pr, (Tokyo); 96; coauth, The Expression of Public Self in Korea", Korean J, (96); auth, Plot Structure and Character Development in the Category Novel, Commonwealth Pub, (Edmonton, Can), 97; auth, Social Metaphors: A Cultural Profile of Western Epistemology, Social Systems Pr, 98; auth, "The Reigning Social Metaphors of European Culture", Europ Studies J, (98); coed, Metaphorical Domains, IAICS Monograph Series, (San Antonio, TX), 00; auth, Language and the Sociology of Knowledge, (forthcoming); coauth, Writing on Social Issues, (forthcoming). **CONTACT ADDRESS** Dept English, Univ of Louisville, 2301 S 3rd St, Louisville, KY 40292-0001. **EMAIL** rnstclr@msn.com

ST. CLAIR LESMAN, ANN
DISCIPLINE SPANISH LANGUAGE **EDUCATION** Rollins Col, BA; Duke Univ, MEd; Univ MD, MA, PhD. **CAREER** Prof, Shenandoah Univ. **HONORS AND AWARDS** Awd for Excellence in For Lang Educ, For Lang Asn VA, 80; outstanding fac mem, Alumni Fedn Fac of the Yr Awd, Shenandoah Univ, 96; Fulbright-Hayes fel, 96. **MEMBERSHIPS** Pres, For Lang Asn VA, 89-90 **SELECTED PUBLICATIONS** Wrote articles on the tchg of conversational skills. **CONTACT ADDRESS** Shenandoah Univ, Winchester, VA 22601.

ST. OMER, GARTH
DISCIPLINE AMERICAN AND CARIBBEAN LITERATURE **EDUCATION** Princeton Univ, PhD, 75. **CAREER** Prpf, Eng, Univ Calif, Santa Barbara. **RESEARCH** Fiction; creat writing. **SELECTED PUBLICATIONS** Auth, A Room on the Hill, Faber and Faber, 68; Shades of Grey, Faber and Faber, 68; Nor Any Country, Faber and Faber, 69; Black Bam and the Masqueraders, Faber and Faber, 72. **CONTACT ADDRESS** Dept of Eng, Univ of California, Santa Barbara, Santa Barbara, CA 93106-7150.

STADLER, EVA MARIA
PERSONAL Born 03/28/1931, Prague, Czechoslovakia, m, 1957 **DISCIPLINE** COMPARATIVE LITERATURE, FILM STUDIES **EDUCATION** Barnard Col, AB, 52; Columbia Univ, PhD(French), 67. **CAREER** Lectr French, Columbia Univ, 53-57; instr French & Ger, Wash Col, 57-58; instr French, Douglass Col, Rutgers Univ, 58-64; asst prof French & Ger, 65-67, assoc prof, Manhattan Community Col, 67-68; assoc prof Comp Lit, French & Film Studies, 68-95, chair Humanities div, 73-79, dir Media Studies, 88-95, Assoc Prof English Commun & Media Studies, Fordham Univ, Lincoln Center, 95-. **MEMBERSHIPS** MLA; ACLA; Soc 18th Century Studies; ACLA Nat Cmt on Undergraduate prog, 71-75 & 78-82; Colloquium fel in Comp Lit, NYU, 72-92; Juror, Am Film Festival 80 & 81 **RESEARCH** History and theory of the novel; fiction and film; French film and film theory; 18th Century literature. **SELECTED PUBLICATIONS** Coauth, Premiers textes litteraires, Blaisdell, 66, Wiley, 75; auth, Rameau's Nephew by Diderot: Un film de Michael Snow, In: Interpeter Diderot Au-jourd'hui, Le Sycomore, 84; Espace acoustique et cinema moderne: l'exemple de Rovert Bresson, In: Bulletin de la SPFFA, 86-87; The Red Dress of Oriane de Guermantes, In: Reading Proust Now, Lang, 90; Diderot et le cinema: Les paradoxes de l'adaptation, Francographies, 92; Defining the Female Body within Social Space; The Function of Clothes in Some 18th Century Novels, Proceedings of the XIIth Congress of the ICLA, 90; Francophonie et cinema: l'exemple de deux cineastes senegalais, Francographies, 93; Addressing Social Boundaries: Dressing the Female Body in Early Realist Fiction, In: Reconfigured Spheres: Feminist Explorations of Literary Space, Univ Mass Press, 94; Une femme douce de Robert Bresson: Le cinema et ses pre-textes, Francographies, 95 **CONTACT ADDRESS** Dept of English, Fordham Univ, 441 E Fordham Rd, Bronx, NY 10458. **EMAIL** evastadler@aol.com

STAHULJAK, ZRINKA
PERSONAL Born 02/27/1969, Zagreb, Croatia **DISCIPLINE** FRENCH LITERATURE **EDUCATION** Univ Zagreb, BA, 93; Univ Kans, MA, 95; Emory Univ, PhD, 00. **CAREER** Instr, Agnes Scott Col, 00-01; asst prof, Boston Univ, 01-. **HONORS AND AWARDS** Award, Univ of Pittsburgh, 97; Anne Amary Perry Scholarship, Emory Univ, 98-99. **MEMBERSHIPS** MLA. **RESEARCH** Medieval French literature, history, art history, translation theory, linguistics, anthropology, psychoanalysis, contemporary French philosophy. **SELECTED PUBLICATIONS** Auth, "The Violence of Neutrality: Translators in and of the War (Croatia, 1991-92)," Col Lit (99): auth, "Future's Phantoms, or Reincarnations of the Parricidal Past in the Roman d'Eneas," L'Esprit Createur, (00); auth, "Violent Distortions: Bearing Witness to the Task of Wartime Translators," Traduction Terminologie Redaction, forthcoming; auth, "Jean Froissart's Chroniques: Translation and the Impossible Apprenticeship of Neutrality," Politics of Translation in the Middle Ages and the Renaissance, ed Renate Blumenfeld-Kosinski, Luise von Glotow, Daniel Russell, Univ of Ottawa Pr, forthcoming. **CONTACT ADDRESS** Dept Mod For Lang and Lit, Boston Univ, 718 Commonwealth Ave, Boston, MA 02215.

STALEY, GREGORY A.
PERSONAL Born 08/12/1948, Hagerstown, MD, m, 1979, 1 child **DISCIPLINE** CLASSICS **EDUCATION** Dickinson Col, AB, 70; Princeton Univ, MA, 73, PhD, 75. **CAREER** Instr, Dickinson Col, 74-75; Asst Prof, Fordham Univ at Lincoln Center, 75-76; Sessional Lectr, Univ Alberta, 76-78; Asst Prof, Dickinson Col, 78-79; Asst Prof to Assoc Prof Classics, Univ Md, 79-. **HONORS AND AWARDS** NEH Grants, Div Educ, 80, 89; Rome Prize Fel, Am Acad Rome, 83-84. **MEMBERSHIPS** Am Philol Asn; Am Classical League; Int Soc Classical Tradition. **RESEARCH** Classical tradition in America; Latin literature; mythology. **SELECTED PUBLICATIONS** Auth, But Ancient Violence Longs to Breed: Robinson Jeffers' The Bloody Sire and Aeschylus' Orestia, Classical & Mod Lit, 83; The Literary Ancestry of Sophocles' Ode to Man, The Classical World, 85; Aeneas' First Act, The Classical World, 90. **CONTACT ADDRESS** Classics Dept, Univ of Maryland, Col Park, 2407 Marie Mount Hall, College Park, MD 20742-4811. **EMAIL** gs32@umail.umd.edu

STALKER, JAMES CURTIS
PERSONAL Born 06/23/1940, Louisville, KY, m, 1964, 2 children **DISCIPLINE** APPLIED ENGLISH LINGUISTICS **EDUCATION** Univ NC, Chapel Hill, BA, 62; Univ Louisville, MA, 64; Univ Wis-Madison, PhD, 70. **CAREER** Instr English ling, Univ Wis-Exten, 67-69; asst prof, 69-74, assoc prof, 74-82, prof English, Mi State Univ, 82-, dir English Lang Ctr, 80-90; dir MA TESOL Prog, Mi State Univ, 78-90; dir MA TESOL Prog, Billent Univ, Ankara, Turkey, 90-92. **HONORS AND AWARDS** Phi Beta Kappa, Phi Eta Sigma, Fulbright Scholar, Ankara, Turkey, 90-92. **MEMBERSHIPS** NCTE; TESOL; Am Asn Appl Ling. **RESEARCH** Slang, Language variation, International English, Pedogical linguistics, Stylistics. **SELECTED PUBLICATIONS** Auth, The poetic dialect: Syntactic ambiquity, Mich English Teacher, 5/77; A linguist's view of the composing process, CEA Critic, 5/78; Introduction to American dialects, Bridging the Gap, Mich State Univ, 79; Reader expectations and the poetic line, Resources Educ, 3/79; Reading is non-linear, Reading, Mich Coun Teachers English, 80; Propriety and dogma, Linguistics and the University Education, Mich State Univ, 80; Usage: Or back to basics: An old saw resharpened, ERIC, 8/81; Review: Crowley, Robert, ed, Proper English: Readings in Language, History and Cultural Identity, World Englishes, 94; Review of Trudgill, Peter and Chambers, J K, 91; Dialects of English: Studies in Grammatical Variation, London:Longman, World Englishes, 95; Idioma, Cognicion y cultura: Conexiones culturales y politicas, Las Lenguas Extanjeras en la Ensenanza: Lengua y Cultura, Montevideo, Uruguay: Alianza Cultural Uruguay-Estados Unidos, 96; Slang is Not Novel, ERIC Document Repro Serv, 96; Language Variation and Cultural Identity: Reader and Writer Conflicts in Language Use, Approaches to Teaching Non-Native English Speakers Across the Curriculum, New Directions for Teaching and Learning, No 70, San Francisco: Jossey-Bass Publ, 97; Some comments on dude, Comments on Etymology, 27, 16-18, 97. **CONTACT ADDRESS** Dept of English, Michigan State Univ, 201 Morrill Hall, East Lansing, MI 48824-1036. **EMAIL** stalker@pilot.msu.edu

STAMELMAN, RICHARD
PERSONAL Born 03/07/1942, m **DISCIPLINE** FRENCH **EDUCATION** Hamilton Col, BA, 63; Duke Univ, PhD, 68. **CAREER** Dir, Center for the Humanities, Wesleyan Univ, 77-82; Prof, Williams Col, 93-; -William R Kenan, Jr, prof, Humanities, Wesleyan Univ, 83-92; dean, Humanities, Wesleyan Univ, 86-89; ch, Dept Fr & Italian, Univ Colorado, 91-92. **HONORS AND AWARDS** La medaille du College de Fr, 93; Chevalier dans l'Ordre des Palmes Academiques, 93; Suggenheim Foundation Fellowship, 99. **RESEARCH** 19th and 20th-century French poetry; relationship of art and literature; French cultural studies: fashion and perfume; literary theory. **SELECTED PUBLICATIONS** Auth, The Drama of Self in Guillaume Apollinaire's Alcools, 76; Lost beyond Telling: Representations of Death and Absence in Modern French Poetry, 90; ed, Ecrire, le livre: d'Edmond Jabes. Colloque de Cerisy la Salle, 89; guest ed, French Poetry Since the War: The Poetics of Presence and Passage, L'Esprit createur, 92; transl & ed, The Lure and the Truth of Painting. Selected Essays of Yves Bonnefoy on Art, 95. **CONTACT ADDRESS** Center for Foreign Languages, Literatures and Cult, Williams Col, 995 Main St, Williamstown, MA 01267. **EMAIL** rstamelm@williams.edu

STAMPINO, MARIA GALLI
PERSONAL Born 12/18/1964, Gallarate, Italy, m, 1993 **DISCIPLINE** ITALIAN, FRENCH **EDUCATION** Universita Cattolica, Milan, Italy, laurea, For Lang & Lit, 88; Univ Kansas, MA, Am Stud, 90; Stanford Univ, Ital & Compar Lit, MA, 92, PhD, 96. **CAREER** Tchg asst, Univ Kansas, Ital, 88-90; tchg asst, Stanford Univ, Ital, 90-93; lectr, Wash Univ, Ital, 96; asst prof, Univ Miami, Ital & French, 96-98; VIS ASST PROF, ST LOUIS UNIV, ITAL & FRENCH, 98-99. **MEMBERSHIPS** MLA; Am Asn Tchrs of Ital; Nat Commun Asn; Renaissance Soc Am; Am Soc Theater Res; Asn Theater in High Educ; Am Ass Italian Studies. **RESEARCH** European Renaissance; Lyric poetry; Theater; Baroque. **SELECTED PUBLICATIONS** "Bodily Boundaries Represented: The Petrarchan, the Burlesque, and the Arcimboldo's Example," Quaderni d'Italianistica, 95; "The Space of the Performance: Aminta, the Court, and the Theater," Romance Review, 96; "Epideictic Pastoral: Rhetorical Tensions in the Staging of Torquato Tasso's Aminta," Theater Symposium: Drama as Rhetoric/Rhetoric as Drama, 97; "Performance, text, and Canon: The Case of Aminta," RLA, 98; auth, "Publish or Perish: An Early-Seventeenth-Century Paradox," RLA 99. **CONTACT ADDRESS** Dept of Foreign Lang & Lit, Univ of Miami, PO Box 248093, Coral Gables, FL 33124-4650. **EMAIL** mgstampino@miami.edu

STANLEY, PATRICIA H.
PERSONAL Born New Bedford, MA **DISCIPLINE** GERMAN, LITERATURE **EDUCATION** Univ Louisville, AB, 64, MA, 69; Univ Va, PhD(Ger), 75. **CAREER** Asst prof Ger, Univ Va, 76-77; asst prof, 77-80, Prof Ger, Fla State Univ, 94-. **MEMBERSHIPS** Am Asn Teachers Ger; MLA; S Atlantic Mod Lang Asn; Am Lit Translators Asn; Kafka Soc Am. **RESEARCH** Literature of the absurd; women's issues; literary theory. **SELECTED PUBLICATIONS** Auth, Wolfgang Hildesheimer's Das Opfer Helena: Another Triumph of the "They", In: University of Florida Drama Conference Papers, II, 83; Hoffman's Phantasiestcke in Callots Manier in Light of Friedrich Schlegel's Theory of the Arabesque, Ger Studies Rev, VIII, October 85; Wolfgang Hildesheimer, biographical entry in Dictionary of Literary Biography, 69, Contemp Ger Fiction Writers, 88; Walter Kempowski, biographical entry in Dictionary of Literary Biography, 75, Contemp Ger Fiction Writers, 88; The Realm of Possibilities. Wolfgang Hildesheimer's Non-Traditional Non-Fictional Prose, Univ Press of Am, 88; More than a Misspelling: (Con)Textual Differences in Woyzeck/Wozzeck, In: Theoretically Speaking, 7, 92; Gunter Herberger, Wolfgang Hildesheimer, biographical entries in Dictionary of Literary Biography, 124, Twentieth-Century German Dramatists, 1919-1992, 92; Wolfgang Hildesheimer and His Critics,

Camden House, 93; Sum, ergo spero?, Wolfgang Hildesheimer's Tentative Absurd Hope, Seminar, 2/95; auth of several other books and articles. **CONTACT ADDRESS** Dept of Mod Lang, Florida State Univ, Tallahassee, FL 32306-1540. **EMAIL** pstanley@mailer.fsu.edu

STANSFIELD, MARIA PILAR PEREZ
DISCIPLINE SPANISH LITERATURE **EDUCATION** Univ Colo, PhD. **CAREER** Assoc prof. **SELECTED PUBLICATIONS** Auth, pubs on avant-garde theatre, and feminist and minorities literature. **CONTACT ADDRESS** Foreign Languages and Literature Dept, Colorado State Univ, Fort Collins, CO 80523. **EMAIL** pperez-stansfield@vines.colostate.edu

STANTON, EDWARD F.
PERSONAL Born 10/29/1942, Colorado Springs, CO, m, 1996, 2 children **DISCIPLINE** HISPANIC STUDIES **EDUCATION** UCLA, BA, 64; MA, 69; PhD, 72. **CAREER** Asst prof, 72-78; assoc prof, 79-89; prof, 89-; Bingham prof, 98-; Univ Ken; vis prof, Univ Comp, Spn, 96; vis prof, Univ, Intl Mend, Spain, 99. **HONORS AND AWARDS** Sr Fulbright Lectr; SMC Res Gnt; Phi Eta Sigma; Phi Beta Kappa; NEH Gnt; Innov Teach Awd; Nat Def Res Fel; Del Amo Found Res Fel; Dict Am Schl, Contemp Auth, Intl Biog. **MEMBERSHIPS** Hemingway Soc; FGL. **RESEARCH** Modern Spanish literature film and culture; comparative literature. **SELECTED PUBLICATIONS** Auth, The Tragic Myth: Lorca and Cante Jondo, Univ Press Kentucky (Lexington, KY), 78; auth, Hemingway and Spain: A Pursuit, Univ Wash Press, 89; auth, Road of Stars to Santiago, Univ Press Kentucky (Lexington, KY), 94; auth, Hemingway y el Pais Vasco, Centro Vasco de las Artes y las Letras (Bilbao, Spain), 97; auth, Handbook of Popular Spanish Culture, Greenwood Press (Westport, CT), 99; auth, Culture and Customs of Spain, Greenwood Press (Westport, CT), forthcoming; auth, Notable Hispanic Quotations, Greenwood Press (Westport, CT), forthcoming. **CONTACT ADDRESS** Dept Spanish, Italian, Univ of Kentucky, 500 S Limestone St, Lexington, KY 40506-0001. **EMAIL** stanton@pop.uky.edu

STANTON, LEONARD J.
DISCIPLINE RUSSIAN LANGUAGE, 19TH AND 20TH CENTURY LITERATURE, CULTURE AND INTERDISCIP **EDUCATION** Univ Kans, PhD, 84. **CAREER** Assoc prof Russ, comt on acad plan and prog eval, La State Univ. **RESEARCH** Religious literature; iconography; hypertext. **SELECTED PUBLICATIONS** Auth, Three Levels of Authorship in the Way of a Pilgrim, in St Vladimir's Theol Quart, 33, 89; The Optina Pustyn Monastery in the Russian Literary Imagination, Peter Lang, 95. **CONTACT ADDRESS** Dept of For Lang and Lit, Louisiana State Univ and A&M Col, 153 B Prescott Hall, Baton Rouge, LA 70803. **EMAIL** stanton@homer.forlang.lsu.edu

STANTON, MARGARET
DISCIPLINE SPANISH LANGUAGE AND LITERATURE **EDUCATION** Mt Mercy Col, BA; Univ Wis Madison, PhD. **CAREER** Assoc prof; coord, Latin Am Studies Prog. **RESEARCH** Latin Am lit. **SELECTED PUBLICATIONS** Auth, transl of Latin Am short stories. **CONTACT ADDRESS** Sweet Briar Col, Sweet Briar, VA 24595.

STARK, JAMES
DISCIPLINE GERMAN **EDUCATION** Portland Univ, BA, 64; Univ WA, BA, 64, PhD, 72. **CAREER** Languages, Seattle Univ. **MEMBERSHIPS** AATG, Europ Stud Asn; Asn for Interdisciplinary Stud of Arts; NEMLA; MLA; ISSEI. **SELECTED PUBLICATIONS** Auth, Wolfgang Burchert's Germany: Reflections of the Third Reich, UP Amer, Baltimore, 96; cotransl, Outside in Front of the Door; Crossing Subtle Borders in the Works of German Immigrant Writers; E Pluribus Unum: Literary Reflections of a New German Identity; Wolfgang Borchert's 'Die Kuechenluhr' and 'Das Brot' Love Among the Ruins; Der Staendebaum' and 'Das Schaukelbrett: Two Symbols of Oppression; Symbolic Gender Transformation: A Comparison of Brecht and Grimmelshausen; **CONTACT ADDRESS** Dept of For Lang, Seattle Univ, 900 Broadway, Seattle, WA 98122-4460. **EMAIL** jstark@seattleu.edu

STARKEY, KATHRYN
PERSONAL Born 12/12/1966, London, ON, Canada, s **DISCIPLINE** GERMAN **EDUCATION** Queens Univ, Kingston, Can, BA, 90; Univ Calif Berkeley, MA, 93; PhD, 98. **CAREER** Asst Prof, Univ of NC Chapel Hill, 98-. **HONORS AND AWARDS** Willaimson Bequest for Gay and Lesbian Studies Course Develop Grant, Univ NC Chapel Hill; Univ Res Coun Grant, Univ NC Chapel Hill. **MEMBERSHIPS** Medieval Asn of Am, MLA, Am Asn of Teachers of Ger, Ger Soc of Am, Soc for the Advan of Scand Study. **RESEARCH** Visual Culture, Medieval Literature and Culture, Early Modern Literature and Culture, Linguistics and Textual Criticism, General Theory. **SELECTED PUBLICATIONS** Coauth, "English Phonetic Contrasts in San Francisco Bay Area German," in Across the Oceans: Studies from East to West in Honor of Richard K. Seymour, ed. C. Moore and I. Rauch (Honolulu: Univ of Haw Press, 95); coauth, "Bay Area German V: PC German," in Insights in Germanic Linguistics II, ed. G.F. Carr and I. Rauch (Berlin: Mouton de Gruyter, 96), 2-7-226; auth, "Imagining an Early Odin: Gold Bracteates as Visual Evidence," Soc for the Advan of Scand Studies 71 (99). **CONTACT ADDRESS** Dept Ger Lang, Univ of No Carolina, Chapel Hill, 440 W Franklin ST, Chapel Hill, NC 27599-2319. **EMAIL** kstarkey@email.unc.edu

STARR, PETER
DISCIPLINE FRENCH AND COMPARATIVE LITERATURE **EDUCATION** Johns Hopkins Univ, PhD. **CAREER** Assoc prof, Univ Southern Calif. **RESEARCH** Vicissitudes of paranoia in modern and postmodern literature, film, and theory **SELECTED PUBLICATIONS** Auth, Logics of Failed Revolt: French Theory After May '68, 95; **CONTACT ADDRESS** Col Letters, Arts & Sciences, Univ of So California, University Park Campus, Los Angeles, CA 90089. **EMAIL** pstarr@usc.edu

STARR, RAYMOND JAMES
PERSONAL Born 05/17/1952, Grand Rapids, MI, m, 1975 **DISCIPLINE** CLASSICAL LANGUAGES **EDUCATION** Univ Mich, BA, 74; Princeton Univ, MA, 76, PhD(class), 78. **CAREER** Lectr class, Princeton Univ, 78-79; asst prof to prof, Greek & Latin, Wellesley Col, 79-, Theodora Stone Sutton Prof of Classics, Wellesley Col, 97-; Fel, Am Coun Learned Soc, 82-83, 96-97. **MEMBERSHIPS** Am Philol Asn; Class Asn Can; Class Asn New England. **RESEARCH** Social context of ancient literature; Roman historiography; comedy. **SELECTED PUBLICATIONS** VERGIL 'SEVENTH ECLOGUE' AND ITS READERS - BIOGRAPHICAL ALLEGORY AS AN INTERPRETATIVE STRATEGY IN ANTIQUITY AND LATE-ANTIQUITY/, CLASSICAL PHILOLOGY, Vol 0090, 1995 **CONTACT ADDRESS** Dept of Classical Studies, Wellesley Col, 106 Central St, Wellesley, MA 02181-8203. **EMAIL** rstarr@wellesley.edu

STATHATOS, CONSTANTINE CHRISTOPHER
PERSONAL Born 04/12/1939, Athens, Greece **DISCIPLINE** SPANISH **EDUCATION** Eastern Ore Col, BA, 63; Univ Ore, MA, 66, PhD(Span), 70. **CAREER** Asst prof, 70-75, assoc prof Span, Univ Wis-Parkside,75-, prof, 86-; Prof Emeritus, 00-. **RESEARCH** Spanish drama of the Siglo de Oro; Gil Vicente; translation. **SELECTED PUBLICATIONS** Ed, A Critical Edition with Introduction and Notes of Gil Vicente's Floresta de Enganos, Univ NC, 72; auth, Antecendents of Gil Vicente's Floresta de Enganos, Luso-Brazilian Rev, 72; co-ed, En onda, Norton, 75; A bibliography of translations of Gil Vicente's works since 1940, Vortice, 75; French contributions to the study of Gil Vicente (1942-1975), Luso-Brazilian Rev, 78; Another Look at Mira de Amescua's Don Alvaro de Luna, Segismundo, 78-80; A Gil Vicente Bibliography (1940-1975), Grant & Cutler, 80; Lazarillo de Tormes in Current English: Two Notes, Hispanofila, 82, Ed, A Critical Edition of Gil Vicente's Auto da India, Puvill, 97, A Gil Vicente Bibliography, 75-95, Leigh UP, 97; ed, Lucas Fernandex: A Bibliography (1514-1995), Reichenberger, 99. **CONTACT ADDRESS** Mod Lang Dept, Univ of Wisconsin, Parkside, Box 2000, Kenosha, WI 53141-2000. **EMAIL** constantin.stathatos@uwp.edu

STAVAN, HENRY-ANTHONY
PERSONAL Born 06/13/1925, Ostrava, Czechoslovakia **DISCIPLINE** FRENCH **EDUCATION** San Francisco State Col, BA, 56; Univ Calif, Berkeley, MA, 60, PhD(Romance lit), 63. **CAREER** Instr Span, Sacramento State Col, 61-62; asst prof French, Univ Wyo, 63-64; asst prof, Univ Minn, 64-66; assoc prof, 66-75, Prof French, Univ Colo, Boulder, 75-, Foe fel, Colo Univ, 69-70 & 74-75; vis prof, Univ of Tubingen, Ger, 78-79. **MEMBERSHIPS** Fr Soc 18th Century Studies. **RESEARCH** Eighteenth century French literature. **SELECTED PUBLICATIONS** Auth, Un roman sentimental entre Rousseau et Bernardin de Saint-Pierrc, Rev Univ Ottawa, 72; Quelques aspects de lyrisme dans la poesie du XVIIIe siecle, Rev Sci Huamaines, 73; coauth, Editing The Complete Works of Voltaire, Voltaire Found, Banbury, Oxfordshire, UK, 73-75; auth, Le lyrisme dans la poesie francaise de 1760 a 1820, Mouton, The Hague, 76; The Ugly Americans of 1780, Stanford Fr Studies, 78; Voltaire und Kurfurst Karl Theodor von der Pfalz, Gesellschaft der Freunde Mannheims, 78; Voltaire et la Duchesse de Gotha, Studies Voltaire, 80; Herzogin Louise Dorothee von Sachsen-Gotha und Voltaire, Jahrbuch Coburger Landesstiftung, 80; French Adaptation Of L Alcade De Zalamea At The End Of The 18th-Century, Revue D Histoire Du Theatre, Vol 44, 92; French Adaptation Of Calderondelabarca,Pedro, Revue D Histoire Du Theatre, Vol 44, 92. **CONTACT ADDRESS** Dept of French, Univ of Colorado, Boulder, Boulder, CO 80302.

STAVANS, ILAN
PERSONAL Born 04/07/1961, Mexico City, Mexico, m, 1988, 2 children **DISCIPLINE** SPANISH **EDUCATION** Univ Autonoma Metropolitana, BA, 84; Jewish Theol Sem, MA, 87; Columbia Univ, MA, 88; MPhil, 89; PhD, 90 **CAREER** Prof, Amherst Col, 93-; res fel, Univ London, 98-99; assoc fac, Bennington Col, 00. **HONORS AND AWARDS** Pushcart Prize nomination, 00; Littauer Found, 00; Andrew W Mellon Found, 00; Book-of-the-Month Club, 99; Nat Found for Jewish Culture, 99; Nona Balakian Excellence in Reviewing Awd, 94; Bernard M Baruch Excellence in Scholar Awd, 93; Latino Lit Prize, 92; Translation Fel, NY State Coun on the Arts, 89. **RESEARCH** Literature; Translation; Jewish Latin America; U.S. Latinos. **SELECTED PUBLICATIONS** Co-ed, Growing up Latino: Memoirs and Stories, Houghton Mifflin, 93; ed, Tropical Synagogues, short Stories by Jewish-Latin American Writers, Holmes and Meier, 94; auth, The Hispanic Condition. Reflections on Culture and Identity in America, HarperCollins, 95; auth, Bandido. Oscar 'Zeta' Acosta and the Chicano Experience, HarperCollins, 95; auth, The One-Handed Pianist and Other Stories, Univ N Mex Press, 96; auth, Art and Anger: Essays on Politics and the Imagination, Univ N Mex Press, 96; auth, Riddle of Cantinflas: Essays on Popular Hispanic Culture, Univ N Mex Press, 98; ed, Calvert Casey: The Collected Stories, Duke Univ Press, 98; auth, The Oxford Book of Jewish Stories, Oxford Univ, 98; auth, Mutual Impressions: Writers of the Americas Reading One Another, Duke Univ Press, 99; auth, Latino U.S.A.: A Cartoon History, Basic Books, 00; auth, The Essential Ilan Stavans, Routledge, 00; auth, The Inveterate Dreamer: Essays and Conversations on Jewish Literature, Univ Nebr Press, 01; auth, On Borrowed Words: A Memoir of Language, Viking, 01; auth, Octavio Paz: Intellectual in Motion, Univ Ariz Press, 01. **CONTACT ADDRESS** Dept Spanish, Amherst Col, PO Box 5000, Amherst, MA 01002-5000. **EMAIL** istavans@amherst.edu

STECKLINE, C. TURNER
PERSONAL Born 12/28/1954, Sanborn, NY **DISCIPLINE** SPEECH COMMUNICATION, DRAMTIC ARTS, PERFORMANCE STUDIES **EDUCATION** Univ of Northern Colo, BA, 75; Univ of Iowa, MA, 78; Southern Ill Univ at Carbondale, PhD, 97. **CAREER** Chair, dept of speech commun, Univ of Dubuque, 79-82; asst prof of speech commun, Loras Col, 82-87; instr/asst dir of forensics, Iowa State Univ, 88-89; dir of forensics, 89-91, asst prof, 91-95, Univ of Wis-Platteville; ASST PROF OF SPEECH COMMUN AND THEATRE ARTS, NORTHEAST LA UNIV, 97-. **HONORS AND AWARDS** Marion Kleinau Theatre Awd, Southern Ill Univ, 95; Kleinau Theatre Production Assistantship, 95 & 96; Graduate Teaching Assistantship, Southern Ill Unive, 92-95, 97; initiating honors sequence: Vision, Language & Reality, Univ of Wis-Platteville, 91-92; adjunct fac appointment, 80-82, teaching Excellence, Loras Col, 86; grad teaching asst, The Rhetoric Prog, Univ of Iowa, 76-79. **MEMBERSHIPS** Nat Commun Asn; Southern States Commun Asn; La Commun Asn; Nat Coun for Teachers of English; Nat Women's Studies Asn; Nat Storytelling Asn. **RESEARCH** Whistleblowing/ethical resistances; diffusion; response theory & bearing witness; disability and family communication; performance of ethnography/ethnography of performance. **SELECTED PUBLICATIONS** Auth, Ideas and Images of Performed Witnessing: A Cross-Genre Analysis, Southern Ill Univ at Carbondale, 97; auth, Books in Review: Ecological Feminism, Ecological Literary Criticism: Romantic Imagining and the Biology of the Mind, Text and Performance Quarterly, 96. **CONTACT ADDRESS** Dept of Speech Commun & Theatre, Univ of Louisiana, Monroe, Monroe, LA 71203. **EMAIL** coyote@hc3.com

STEELE, MARTA N.
PERSONAL Born 05/20/1949, Trenton, NJ, d, 1 child **DISCIPLINE** CLASSICAL PHILOLOGY **EDUCATION** Wellesley Col, BA, 71; Univ CA, Los Angelos, MA, 73; Boston Univ, PhD candidate, 80-. **CAREER** Full-time and freelance newspaper reporter, 83-85; adjunct instr, English composition, res and exposition, business writing, Rider Col Dept of English, 84-85; copy chief, NJ Network, Trenton, NJ, 85; freelance manuscript ed, indexer, and proofreader, 87-91; freelance trans/author, 95-97; manuscript ed, series ed, Princeton Univ Press, 91-. **HONORS AND AWARDS** Listed in Who's Who in the East and Int Who's Who of Professionals; honored at Royal Danish Embassy, Washington, DC, and Princeton Univ Press, 5/98, for completeion of the 25 text volumes of the Kierkegaard's Writings series. **MEMBERSHIPS** Am Philol Asn; Am Classical League. **RESEARCH** Homeric philology (PhD thesis topic); poetics, epic in general; computer programs to facilitate various aspects of Classics editing and indexing. **SELECTED PUBLICATIONS** Editor, R Rehm, Marriage to Death: The Conflagation of Wedding and Funeral Rituals in Greek Tragedy, 94; P C Miller, Dreams in Late Antiquity: Studies in the Imagination of a Culture, 94; D J Furley and A Nehamas, eds, Aristotle's Rhetoric: Philosophical Essays, 94; G Vlastos, ed by D Graham, Studies in Greek Philosophy: Volume 1: The Presocratics; Volume II, Socrates, Plato, and Their Tradition, 95; M W Gleason, Making Men: Sophists and Self-Presentation in Ancient Rome, 95; N Loraux, trans Paula Wissing, The Experiences of Tiresias: The Feminine and the Greek Man, 95; E Stehle, Performance and Gender in Ancient Greece, 96; S Schein, Reading the Odyssey: Selected Interpretive Essays, 96; J Ober and C Hendrick, eds, Demokratia: A Conversation on Democracies, Ancient and Modern, 96; D Lyons, Gender and Immortality: Heroines in Ancient Greek Myth and Cult, 97; Patricia Curd, The Legacy of Parmenides: Eleatic Monism and Later Presocratic Thought, 98; Johanna Prins (Yopi), Victorian Sappho, forthcoming 99; Sidney Alexander, trans and commentator, The Complete Odes and Satires of Horace, forthcoming 99; editor of numerous other publications. **CONTACT ADDRESS** Univ Press, Princeton Univ, 41 William St, Princeton, NJ 08540. **EMAIL** marta_steele@pupress.princeton.edu

STEFANOVSKA, MALINA
PERSONAL Born 12/30/1952, Yugoslavia, m, 1997, 1 child **DISCIPLINE** FRENCH LITERATURE **EDUCATION** Univ Grenoble, BA, 73; Univ Oregon, MA, 84; Johns Hopkins Univ, PhD, 90. **CAREER** Assoc prof, Univ Calif Los Angeles, 90-. **HONORS AND AWARDS** UCLA Career Develop Awd, 93, 95; Acad Senate Res Grant, 90-97; Gilman fel, 84-90; selected to teach at Ecole Normale Superieure, Fontenay/Saint-Cloud, 97-98, through the Education Abroad Program. **RESEARCH** Memoirs and historiography; seventeenth century studies; cultural studies. **SELECTED PUBLICATIONS** Auth, Histoire ou historiette: le portrait du prince par Tellemant des Reaux et Saint-Simon, Papers on French Seventeenth-Century Lit, 93; auth, Saint-Simon: un moraliste dans le reel, Dalhousie French Stud, 94; auth, Strolling through the Galleries, Hiding in A Cabinet: Clio at the French Absolutist Court, Eighteenth Century: Theory and Interpretation, 94; auth, Un solipe absolu: le portrait de Louis XIV par Saint-Simon, Actes de Lexington, Papers on Seventeenth-Century French Lit, 95; auth, Le corps de la nation selon l'opposition novilaire a Louis XIV, Biblio 17, Papers on French Seventeenth-Century Lit, 95; auth, A Well-staged Coup de theatre: The Royal Lit de Justice in 1718, Sub/Stance, 96; auth, A Monumental Triptych: The Parallel of the First Three Bourbon Kings by Saint-Simon, Fr Hist Stud, 96; auth, Saint-Simon, Un Historien Dans Les Marges, Paris, Honore Champion, 98. **CONTACT ADDRESS** Univ of California, Los Angeles, Los Angeles, CA 90024. **EMAIL** stefanov@humnet.ucla.edu

STEINBRUCKNER, BRUNO
PERSONAL Born 08/22/1941, Linz, Austria, m, 1973 **DISCIPLINE** GERMAN **EDUCATION** Univ Innsbruck, PhD, 65. **CAREER** Asst Prof, Univ Innsbruck, 65; Instructor to Prof and Dept Chair, Am Univ, 65-. **MEMBERSHIPS** Am Goethe Soc, 71-73; Am Asn of Teachers of German. **RESEARCH** German Literature of the 19th and 20th Centuries; German History since WWII. **CONTACT ADDRESS** Dept For Lang, American Univ, 4400 Mass Ave NW, Washington, DC 20016. **EMAIL** bfst@american.edu

STEINER, CARL
PERSONAL Born 08/05/1927, Vienna, Austria, m, 1954, 3 children **DISCIPLINE** GERMAN LANGUAGE & LITERATURE **EDUCATION** George Washington Univ, BA, 58; MA, 62; PhD, 66. **CAREER** From instr to asst prof, 64-68, assoc prof, 68-78, chmn dept Ger lang & lit, 70-82, Prof Ger, George Washington Univ, 78-95, Recording secy, Am Goethe Soc, 67; consult, Can Coun, 76-77. **MEMBERSHIPS** SAtlantic Mod Lang Asn; Am Asn Teachers Ger; Am Goethe Soc. **RESEARCH** German emigre literature; 19th century German realism; 20th century German literature; German socio-critical literature. **SELECTED PUBLICATIONS** Auth, Uber Gottfried Kellers Verhaltnis zur Demokratie, Vol LX, No 4 & Die Goethe- Geselschaft von Washington, Vol LX, No 4, Monatsh, Univ Wis; Frankreichbild und Katholizismus bei Joseph Roth, Ger Quart, 1/73; Moliere und die Kleistische Komodie Versuch einer Deutung, In: Moliere and the Commonwealth of Letters, Univ Miss, 75; Kafkas Amerika Illusion oder Wirklichkeit?, In: Franz Kafka-Symposium, Agora Verlag, Berlin, 78; Georg Kaiser, Ein Moderner Mythenmacher, In: Georg Kaiser, Agora Verlag, Berlin, 80; Franz Werfel Novel Jeremias Horet Die Stimme, A Confession Of Jewish Faith, Modern Austrian Literature, Vol 27, 94; Storm,Theodor, German Studies Rev, Vol 16, 93. **CONTACT ADDRESS** Dept of Ger, The George Washington Univ, 801 22nd St NW, Washington, DC 20052.

STEINER, RICHARD C.
PERSONAL Born 11/07/1945, New York, NY, m, 1969, 3 children **DISCIPLINE** SEMITIC LANGUAGES AND LITERATURE **EDUCATION** Yeshiva and Isaac Breuer Col, BA, BHL, 63, 66; Univ Pa, PhD, 74. **CAREER** Asst prof, Dropsie Univ, 72-73; asst prof, Touro Col, 73-75; asst prof, Yeshiva Univ, 75-78; vis assoc prof, Univ Chicago, spring 81; assoc prof, Yeshiva, 78-84; Gerard Weinstock Vis Prof of Jewish Studies, Harvard Univ, spring 99; prof of Semitic Langs and Lit, Yeshiva Univ, Bernard Revel Grad Sch, 84-. **HONORS AND AWARDS** NDEA Title IV grant, 67-70; Am Coun of Learned Socs grant, 76; Memorial Found for Jewish Culture, 76-77, 78-79, 80-81; NEH, General Res Prog, 78-81; Inst for Advanced Studies, Jerusalem, 83-84; Biblical Archaeology Soc, co-winner, Publication Awd, 84; NEH Texts Prog, 84-88; Littauer Found, 85-86, 86-87; Humphrey Inst for Soc Ecology (Beersheba), 89; Dutch Org for Sci Res, 90; Inst for Advanced Studies (Jerusalem), 94-95; Fel, Am Acad for Jewish Res, 95-; President, Am Friends of the Acad of the Hebrew Lang, 98-. **MEMBERSHIPS** North Am Conf on Afrosiatic (Hamito-Semitic) Linguistics, Nat Found for Jewish Culture, Am Acad for Jewish Res, Am Friends of the Acad of the Hebrew Lang. **SELECTED PUBLICATIONS** Auth, "Incomplete Circumcision in Egypt and Edom: Jeremiah (9:24-25) in the Light of Josephus and Jonckheere," J of Biblical Lit 118 (99): 497-505; auth, "Philology as the Handmaiden of Philosophy in R. Saadia Gaon's Interpretation of Gen 1:1," Israel Oriental Studies, 19 (99): 379-389; auth, "Vowel Length in Hebrew: Descriptions and Theories from Jerome to Judah Halevy in the Light of Religious Polemics," Mehqarim Belason 8 (forthcoming, in Hebrew); auth, "Does the BH Conjunction waw Have Many Meanings, One Meaning, or No Meaning At All?," J of Biblical Lit, 119 (2000): 249-267; auth, "Semitic Names for Utensils in the Demotic Word-List from Tebtunis," J of Near Eastern Studies, 59 (2000, forthcoming); auth, Sycamores from South Arabia for Cattle from Tekoa: A Study of Amos' Occupations (CBQ Monograph Series) (forthcoming); auth, The Aramaic Text in Demotic Script (forthcoming). **CONTACT ADDRESS** Bernard Revel Grad Sch, Yeshiva Univ, 500 W 185th St, New York, NY 10033-3201. **EMAIL** rsteiner@ymail.yu.edu

STEINER, THOMAS ROBERT
PERSONAL Born 08/18/1934, Budapest, Hungary, m, 1991, 2 children **DISCIPLINE** ENGLISH, COMPARATIVE LITERATURE **EDUCATION** Cornell Univ, BA, 55; Columbia Univ, MA, 60 PhD, 67. **CAREER** Lectr, Hunter Col, City Univ NYork, 61-64; lectr, Brooklyn Col, City Univ NYork, 64-66; vis assoc prof, Univ Ill, Urbana-Champaign, 74-74; from asst prof to full prof, Univ Calif, Santa Barbara, 66-94; prof emeritus, Univ Calif, Santa Barbara, 94-; adj prof, Univ S Calif, 96, 98-99. **HONORS AND AWARDS** Calif Humanities Inst Fel, 69; Nathanael West Essay Contest Prize, Southern Rev, 70; Univ Calif, Santa Barbara, Instruct Dev Awd, 83-84. **RESEARCH** Eighteenth century English literature; detective fiction; literary theory. **SELECTED PUBLICATIONS** Auth, "Precursors to Dryden: Seventeenth-Century French and English Theories of Translation," CLS 7 (70): 50-81; auth, "West's Lemuel and the American Dream," S Rev 7 (71): 994-1006; auth, English Translation Theory, 1650-1800, Van Gorcum, 75; auth, "Homer's Ape: Teaching Pope," ECL 5 (79): 46-53; auth, "Stanislaw Lem's Detective Stories," MFS 29 (83): 451-462; auth, "The Mind of the Hard-boiled: Ross Macdonald and the Roles of Criticism," SDak Rev 24 (86): 29-53; auth, "The Origin of Raymond Chandler's 'Mean Streets,'" ANQ 7 (94): 225-227; auth, "Richard Gwinnett and His 'Virtuous Lover,' Elizabeth Thomas: A Literary Romance of Eighteenth-Century Gloucestershire," Ga Hist Quart 78 (94): 794-809. **CONTACT ADDRESS** Dept of English, Univ of California, Santa Barbara, Santa Barbara, CA 93106. **EMAIL** tsteiner@humanities.ucsb.edu

STENSON, NANCY JEAN
PERSONAL Born 08/07/1945, San Mateo, CA, m, 1976, 1 child **DISCIPLINE** LINGUISTICS **EDUCATION** Pomona Col, BA, 67; Univ Calif, San Diego, MA, 70, PhD(ling), 76. **CAREER** English as second lang specialist, Lang Res Found, 71-72; Assoc Prof Ling, Univ Minn, Minneapolis, 78-, Dublin Inst for Advan Studies scholar, 76-77; consult, Havasupai & Hualapai Bilingual Ed Prog, 75-76. **MEMBERSHIPS** Ling Soc Am; Am Asn Applied Ling; N Am ASN Celtic Lang Teachers. **RESEARCH** Syntax; Irish language; language contact; code switching. **SELECTED PUBLICATIONS** Auth, Overlapping systems in the Irish comparative construction, Word, 77: Plural formation in Rath Cairn Eigse: J Irish Studies, 78; Questions on the accessibility hierarchy, Elements, Chicago Ling Soc, 79; Studies in Irish syntax, Gunter Narr Verlag, 81; On short term language change: Developments in Irish Morphology, Proc 5th Int Cong Hist Ling, 82; Irish Autonomous Impersonals, Natural Lang & Ling Theory, 7, 89; Prepositional pronouns in a transitional dialect, Celtica, 21, 90; Patterns of initial mutation in Irish loanwords, Eigse, 24, 90; Phrase structure congruence, government & Irish-English code switching, Syntax and Semantics, 23, 90; Code Switching vs. Borrowing in Modern Irish, In: Language Contact in the British Isles, 91; coauth, Learner-controlled listening materials using a commercial videodisk, CAELL J, 2, 91; The effectiveness of computer-assisted pronunciation training, Calico J, 9, 92; auth, English Influence on Irish: the last 100 Years, J Celtic Ling, 2, 93; Patterns of variation in Irish loan phonology, Principles & Predictions: the Analysis of Natural Language, 93; Language Contact & the development of Irish directional phrase idioms, Dan do Oide, 97; Video in the Irish language classroom, Teanga, 16, 96; auth, "Use of Irish Among Immigrants to the U.S.," New Hibernia Review, 2 (98). **CONTACT ADDRESS** Dept of Ling, Univ of Minnesota, Twin Cities, 315 Pillsbury Dr SE, Minneapolis, MN 55455-0143. **EMAIL** stenson@tc.unm.edu

STEPHAN, ALEXANDER
PERSONAL Born 08/16/1946, Germany, m, 1969, 1 child **DISCIPLINE** GERMAN **EDUCATION** Freie Univ Berlin, BA, 68; Univ Mich, MA, 69; Princeton Univ, PhD, 73. **CAREER** Instructor, Princeton Univ, 72-73; Asst Prof to Prof, Univ Calif, 73-85; Prof, Univ Fla, 85-00; Prof, Oh State Univ, 00-. **HONORS AND AWARDS** Guggenheim Fel, 89-90; Humboldt, 88, 94, 98-99; NEH, 75, 84, 97; ACLS, 76, 77, 84; DAAD, 93, 97; APS, 79, 81, 92; Weichmann Stiftung, 98; Feuchtwanger Mem Library, 98; VG Wort, 91; IREX, 85, 93; Sch of Theory and Criticism, 78. **MEMBERSHIPS** Anna-Seghers-Gesellschaft; Intl Brecht Soc; Soc for Exile Studies. **RESEARCH** German literature, culture studies, film; German-American relations. **SELECTED PUBLICATIONS** Auth, Im Visier des FBI. Deutsche Exilschriftsteller in den Akten amerikanischer Geheimdienste, 95; ed, Christa Wolf: The Author's Dimension, 95; auth, Anna Seghers. Das siebte Kreuz, Welt und Wirkung eines Romans, 97; co-ed, The New Sufferings of Young W. and Other Stories, 97; ed, Themes and Structures. Studies in German Literature from Goethe to the Present A Festschrift for Theodore Ziolkowski, 97; ed, Uwe Johnson, Speculations About Jakob and Other Writings, 00; ed, Rot Braun? Bredit Dialog 2000, Nat Sozialiswus, 00. **CONTACT ADDRESS** Dept German & Slavic Lang, Univ of Florida, PO Box 117430, Gainesville, FL 32611-7430. **EMAIL** stephan.30@osu.edu

STEPHENS, SUSAN A.
DISCIPLINE CLASSICS **EDUCATION** BA, 65; Columbia Univ, MA, 67; Stanford Univ, PhD, 72. **CAREER** Prof, Stanford Univ. **RESEARCH** Ancient novel; attic prose; Greek prose compos; papyrology. **SELECTED PUBLICATIONS** Auth, Yale Papyri in the Beinecke Library II, 85; Who Reads Ancient Novels? in Search for the Ancient Novel, 94; coauth, Ancient Greek Novels--the Fragments, 95. **CONTACT ADDRESS** Stanford Univ, Bldg 20, Main Quad, Stanford, CA 94305.

STERN, GUY
PERSONAL Born 01/14/1922, Hildesheim, Ger, m, 1979, 1 child **DISCIPLINE** GERMAN, COMPARATIVE LITERATURE **EDUCATION** Hofstra Univ, BA, 48; Columbia Univ, MA, 50; PhD, 54. **CAREER** Lecturer, Columbia Univ, 48-55; asst prof, Denison Univ, 55-63; prof, Univ of Cincinnati, 63-76; dept chair, Univ MD, 76-78; sen VP, Wayne State Univ, 78-81; distinguished prof, Wayne State Univ, 81-. **HONORS AND AWARDS** Distinguished Grad Sch Award, Wayne State Univ, 98; Hon Doctorate, Hofstra Univ, 98; Pres Award for Exc in Teachin, Wayne State Univ, 92. **MEMBERSHIPS** AATG, MLA, Lessing Soc, Soc for Exile Studies, Leo Baeck Inst. **RESEARCH** Age of Enlightenment, Exile Studies, 20th Century German novel. **SELECTED PUBLICATIONS** Literarische Kultur im Exil, Dresden Univ Press (Dresden, Ger) 97; auth, Nazi Book Burning and the American Response, Wayne State Univ (Detroit, MI) 91; auth, Literatur im Exil, Max Hueber (Munich, Ger) 89; auth, Alfred Neumann, Steiner (Wiesbaden, Ger) 79. **CONTACT ADDRESS** Dept German/Slavic Lang, Wayne State Univ, 409 Manoogian, Detroit, MI 48202-3919. **EMAIL** ad5422@wayne.edu

STERN, IRWIN
PERSONAL Born 07/28/1946, Brooklyn, NY **DISCIPLINE** LUSO-BRAZILIAN LANGUAGE & LITERATURE **EDUCATION** Queens Col, NYork, BA, 67, MA, 69; City Univ New York, PhD, 72. **CAREER** Instr Romance lang, Univ Nebr-Lincoln, 69-71; adj lectr, City Col New York, 71-72, asst prof Port & Span, 72-76. Grad fac comp lit, City Univ New York, 75-76; adj asst prof Span & Port, New York Univ, 77-; lectr Port, Columbia Univ, 79-; vis asst prof, Adelphi Univ, spring, 76; vis prof, Univ Pittsburgh, 78; vis asst prof, Queens Col, 79; prof, North Carolina State Univ. **HONORS AND AWARDS** PEN Club Transl Prize, 81. **MEMBERSHIPS** Am Asn Teachers Span & Port; MLA; Am-Port Soc; Int Conf Group Mod Port. **RESEARCH** Nineteenth century Portuguese literature; 19th and 20th centuries Luso-Brazilian fiction; Spanish fiction. **SELECTED PUBLICATIONS** Auth, Julio Dinis e o romance portugues, Porto: Lello & Irmao, Editores, 72; Suppressed Portuguese Fiction: 1926-1974, Bks Abroad, winter 76; Jane Austen e Julio Dinis, 3/76 & Ecade Queiroz e Pinhero Chagas, 5/80, Coloquio/Letras; Luandino Vieira's Short Fiction: Decolonization in the Third Register, When the Drumbeat Changes, Three Continents, 81; Continuing the Marvelous Journes, Review, 1-4/81; Violeta E A Noite--Portuguese, World Lit Today, Vol 66, 92. **CONTACT ADDRESS** Dept of Foreign Languages and Literatures, No Carolina State Univ, Box 8106, Raleigh, NC 27695-8106. **EMAIL** istern@social.chass.ncsu.edu

STERNBACH, NANCY SAPORTA
PERSONAL Born 04/05/1945, New York, NY, 2 children **DISCIPLINE** SPANISH **EDUCATION** Univ Wi, BA, 71, Middlebury Col, MA, 73; Univ Az, PhD, 84. **CAREER** Assoc prof, Chair, Smith Col **HONORS AND AWARDS** Nat Endow for the Humanities, 97 **MEMBERSHIPS** MLA **RESEARCH** Latina writers. **SELECTED PUBLICATIONS** Auth, Engendering the Future: Cenizas de Izalco and the Making of a Writer, in Claribel Alegria and Central American Literature: Critical Essays, Oh Univ Center for Latin Amer Stud, 94; coauth, Latin American Women Essayists: Intruders and Usurpers, in The Politics of the Essay: A Feminist Perspective, Univ Ind Press, 94; auth, Mejorar la condicion de mi secso: The Essays of Rosa Guerra, in Reinterpreting the Spanish-American Essay, Univ Tx Press, 95; coauth, Rehearsing in front of the Mirror: Marga Gomez' Lesbian Subjectivity as a Work-in-progress, in women and Performance, 96; coed, Puro Teatro: An Anthology of Latina Theatre, Performance and Testimonio, Univ Az Press, 99; auth, Puro Teatro: A Latina Anthology, Univ of Ariz Press, 00. **CONTACT ADDRESS** Dept of Spanish & Portuguese, Smith Col, Hatfield Hall, Northampton, MA 01063. **EMAIL** nsternba@email.smith.edu

STEUSSY, MARTI J.
PERSONAL Born 09/07/1955, Dayton, OH, m, 1978, 2 children **DISCIPLINE** HEBREW BIBLE **EDUCATION** St Olaf Col, BA, 77; Earlham Sch of Relig, 82; Vanderbilt Univ, 92. **CAREER** Vis instr, Christian Theol Sem, 88-89, asst prof of O. T., 89-95, assoc prof of Biblical Interpretation, 96-. **HONORS AND AWARDS** Presidential Scholar, 73; Nat Sci Found Grad Fel, 79; Phi Beta Kappa; ATS Women's Fac Develop Grant, 93; Nat Relig Leadership Prog participant, 97-99. **MEM-**

BERSHIPS SBL, Network of Biblical Storytellers, Asn of Disciples for Theol Discussion, Forrest-Moss Inst. **RESEARCH** Psalms, biblical narrative, religion and science, Bible and ecology. **SELECTED PUBLICATIONS** Auth, Gardens in Babylon: Narrative Faith in the Greek Legends of Daniel, SBLDS, Atlanta: Scholar's Press (93); auth, David: Biblical Portraits of Power Studies on Personalities of the O. T., Columbia, SC: Univ of SC Press (99). **CONTACT ADDRESS** Dept Biblical Studies, Christian Theol Sem, PO Box 88267, Indianapolis, IN 46208-0267. **EMAIL** Mstreussy@cts.edu

STEVENS, JOHN A.
PERSONAL Born 09/11/1963, Elmhurst, IL, m, 1988, 2 children **DISCIPLINE** CLASSICS **EDUCATION** Univ Iowa, BA, 86, MA, 88; Duke Univ, PhD, 92. **CAREER** Vis asst prof, NY Univ, 92-93; vis asst prof, E Carolina Univ, 93-94; from asst prof to assoc prof, E Carolina Univ, 94-. **MEMBERSHIPS** Soc Ancient Greek Philos; Am Philol Asn; Classical Asn Middle W & S; Vergilian Soc. **RESEARCH** Latin literature; ancient philosophy; lyric poetry. **SELECTED PUBLICATIONS** Auth, Posidonian Polemic and Academic Dialectic: The Impact of Carneades Upon Posidonius, GRBS, 95; Friendship and Profit in Xenophon's Oeconomicus in The Socratic Movement, 94. **CONTACT ADDRESS** Classical Studies Dept FLL, East Carolina Univ, General Classroom Bldg., Greenville, NC 27858-4353. **EMAIL** stevensj@mail.ecu.edu

STEVENSON, WALT
PERSONAL Born 08/03/1961, Philadelphia, PA, m, 1989, 2 children **DISCIPLINE** CLASSICAL PHILOLOGY **EDUCATION** Carleton Col, BA (classical philol), 83; Brown Univ, PhD (classical philol), 90. **CAREER** Lect, Univ RI, 88-89; instr, Dickinson Col, 89-90; vis prof, L'rivskaj Derzhavni Universitet/L'rivska Bohoslorska Akademia, 97-98; assoc prof, Univ Richmond, 90-. **HONORS AND AWARDS** Fulbright fel, 97-98. **MEMBERSHIPS** Am Philol Asn; Classical Asn of the Midwest and South. **RESEARCH** Greek and Latin lit; Roman Imperial Social History. **SELECTED PUBLICATIONS** Auth, Plato's Symposium 190d7, Phoenix 47, 93; The Rise of Eunuchs in Greco-Roman Antiquity, J of the Hist of Sexuality 5, 95; De Italia: Italy Goes Multimedia, New England Classical Newsletter & J 23, 95; Professional Poets and Poetic Heroes in Homeric Greece, Usna Epika: Etnichni Tradytsii ta Vykonavstvo II, Kiev, 97. **CONTACT ADDRESS** Dept of Classics, Univ of Richmond, Richmond, VA 23173. **EMAIL** wstevens@richmond.edu

STEWART, JOAN HINDE
PERSONAL Born New York, NY, m, 1970, 2 children **DISCIPLINE** FRENCH LITERATURE **EDUCATION** St Joseph's Col, BA, 65; Yale Univ, PhD(romance lang), 70. **CAREER** From instr to asst prof French, Wellesley Col, 70-72; asst prof, 73-77, assoc prof, 77-81, Prof French, NC State Univ, 81-99; Prof French and Dean of Liberal Arts, Univ of South Carolina, 99-. **HONORS AND AWARDS** NC State Univ Outstanding Teacher Awd, 77; Fel Nat Humanities Ctr, 82-83. **MEMBERSHIPS** MLA; SAtlantic Mod Lang Asn; Southeast Am Soc for 18th Century Studies; Southern Comp Lit Asn; Am Asn Teachers of Fr. **RESEARCH** Eighteenth-century fiction; women wirters; Colette. **SELECTED PUBLICATIONS** Auth, The Novels of Madame Riccoboni, NC Studies Romance Lang & Lit, 76; Some aspects of verb use in Aucassin et Nicolette, Fr Rev, 77; Sensibility with irony: Mme de Montolieu at the end of an era, Ky Romance Quart, 78; Colette: The Mirror Image, Fr Forum, 78; Colette and the hallowing of age, Romance Notes, 79-80; Colette's Gynaeceum: Regression and Renewal, Fr Rev, 80; The School and the Home, Women's Studies, 81; auth, Gynographs, UP of Nebraska, 93; auth, MME De Charriee, Letters De Mistriss Henley, ed Philip Stewart, 93; Colette, G K Hall; auth, MME Riccoboni, Ernestine, ed and transl Philip Stewart, 98; MME De Charriee, Lettres De Mistriss Henley (ed w/Philip Stewart), 93. **CONTACT ADDRESS** College of Liberal Arts, Univ of So Carolina, Columbia, Dean's Office, Columbia, SC 29208. **EMAIL** jhs@sc.edu

STEWART, PHILIP R.
PERSONAL Born 05/21/1940, Kansas City, MO, m, 1970, 2 children **DISCIPLINE** FRENCH, COMPARATIVE LITERATURE **EDUCATION** Yale Univ, BA, 62; PhD, 67. **CAREER** Instr, Yale Univ, 66-68; asst prof, Harvard Univ, 68-72; assoc prof to prof, Duke Univ, 72-. **HONORS AND AWARDS** Phi Beta Kappa; Ordre des Palmes Academiques; Recueil biographique de la Francophonie; Woodrow Wilson, 62; Carnegie Teaching Fel, 62-63; Fulbright, 65-66; NEH, 78-79, 94-95. **MEMBERSHIPS** MLA, ASECS, Societe d'Histoire Litteraire de la France, AATF, Societe Diderot, Societe Francaise d'etude du XVIIIe siecle. **RESEARCH** French literature, 18th Century, History of the Novel, Literature and Art. **SELECTED PUBLICATIONS** Auth, Imitation and Illusion in the French Memoir-Novel, 1700-1750, Yale Univ Pr, 69; auth, Le Masque et la parole: le langage de l'amour au XVIIIe siecle, Jose Corti, 73; ed, Prevost: Le Philosphie anglais, Univ Pr of Grenoble, 77; auth, Rereadings: eight early French novels, Summa, 84; auth, Half-Told Tales, Univ NCar, 87; auth, Engraven Desire, Duke Univ Pr, 92; cotransl, Rousseau: Julie, or the New Heloise, Univ Pr of New England, 97; cotransl, Les Smith: Oral History, Climats, 00; ed, Crebillon: Les Heureux Orphelins, Classiques Garnier, 01. **CONTACT ADDRESS** Dept Romance Studies, Duke Univ, Durham, NC 27708-0257. **EMAIL** pstewart@duke.edu

STEWART, WALTER K.
PERSONAL Born Los Angeles, CA **DISCIPLINE** GERMAN LITERATURE **EDUCATION** Calif State Univ, Northridge, BA, 68; Univ Calif, Los Angeles, MA, 70, PhD(Ger lit), 75. **CAREER** Scholar Ger, Univ Calif, Los Angeles, 78-79; Asst Prof Ger & Chmn Dept, Calif Lutheran Col, 79- **MEMBERSHIPS** MLA; Am Asn Teachers Ger; Philol Asn Pac Coast. **RESEARCH** Goethe period literature; dramatic theory; Thomas Mann. **SELECTED PUBLICATIONS CONTACT ADDRESS** Dept of German, California Lutheran Univ, 60 Olsen Rd, Thousand Oaks, CA 91360-2700.

STICCA, SANDRO
DISCIPLINE FRENCH LANGUAGE AND LITERATURE **EDUCATION** Columbia Univ, PhD. **CAREER** Prof/Dir grad studies, SUNY Binghamton. **HONORS AND AWARDS** Ed-in-chief, Mediaevalia. **RESEARCH** Romance Philology; medieval lit (Latin, French and Italian); medieval drama and lyric; the Renaissance; mod French and Italian lit and comp lit. **SELECTED PUBLICATIONS** Auth, The Latin Passion Play, 70; The Planctus Mariae in the Dramatic Tradition of the Middle Ages, 89; Il Convento di S Maria del Paradiso, 89; Studio Iconografico-Storico, 86; La poetica del tempo sacramentale, 66; ed, Medieval Drama, 72; Arte ed esistenza in Gennaro Manna, 93; Studies in Hagiography, 96. **CONTACT ADDRESS** SUNY, Binghamton, PO Box 6000, Binghamton, NY 13902-6000. **EMAIL** cstiner@binghamton.edu

STIGLITZ, BEATRICE
PERSONAL Born 04/24/1945, Russia, s **DISCIPLINE** LANGUAGE, LITERATURE, FRENCH, RUMANIAN **EDUCATION** Sorbonne Univ, MA, 71; CUNY, MPh, 78; PhD, 81. **CAREER** Instr, Univ Vt, 78; asst prof to assoc prof to prof, Col Univ Charleston, 79-. **HONORS AND AWARDS** Distinguished Teaching Awd, 92; Pi Delta Phi Fr Hon Soc; Sigma Iota Rhu Intl Studies Soc; Phi Kappa Phi Hon Soc; Golden Key Nat Hon Soc. **MEMBERSHIPS** MLA; AFC; PWAB. **RESEARCH** French literature history; popular culture; French and Italian cinema; intellectual history; women's studies. **SELECTED PUBLICATIONS** Contrb, "Erasmus," in Encycl of Multicultural Writers (Greenwood Pr); other publications of Fr lit, history, and politics. **CONTACT ADDRESS** 186 Queen St, Charleston, SC 29401-1946. **EMAIL** stiglitzb@cofc.edu

STIMILLI, DAVIDE
DISCIPLINE ITALIAN LITERATURE **EDUCATION** Yale Univ, PhD. **CAREER** Asst prof; Northwestern Univ, 97-; lect, Brit Soc for 18th-Century Studies, Conf Int Soc Study Europ Ideas, Johns Hopkins Humanities Center, Univ Chicago, MLA. **HONORS AND AWARDS** Searle Jr Fel, 99-00. **RESEARCH** History and theory of physiognomy, Italian literature, intellectual history. **SELECTED PUBLICATIONS** Auth, "Italics vs. Black-Letter: The Triestine Typography," Atenea 17, (97): 93-99; auth, "Kaftka e la musics," Il Bianco e il nero 1, (97): 189-198; auth, "Findlinge: Franz Kafka und Jakob Wassermann," Deutsche Vierteljahrsschrift fur Literaturwissenschaft und Giestesgeschichte 3, (99): 478-500; auth, "Identity of a Jewish Community in a Provincial Town: Ancona," The Italian Jewish Experience, ed. Thomas P. DiNapoli, Stony Brook, NY: Forum Italicum, (00): 97-107. **CONTACT ADDRESS** Dept of French, Northwestern Univ, 1801 Hinman, Evanston, IL 60208. **EMAIL** d-stimilli@atsnorthwestern.edu

STIMSON, HUGH MCBIRNEY
PERSONAL Born 12/05/1931, Port Chester, NY **DISCIPLINE** LINGUISTICS, PHILOLOGY **EDUCATION** Yale Univ, BA, 53, MA, 57, PhD, 59. **CAREER** Sci linguist, Foreign Serv Inst, US Dept State, 59; suprvy instr Chinese, Chinese Lang Sch, China, 59-60; from asst prof to assoc prof, 60-69, assoc prof Chinese lang & ling, 69-74, Prof Chinese Ling, Yale Univ, 74. **MEMBERSHIPS** MLA; Ling Soc Am; Am Orient Soc(secy-treas, 69-76); Asn Asian Studies. **RESEARCH** Chinese historical phonology; Chinese grammar espec class and mod; Chinese poetics. **SELECTED PUBLICATIONS** Auth, The Jong-yuan in yunn: A Study of Early Mandarin Phonology, Far Eastern Publ, 66; The sound of a Tarng poem: Grieving about Green Slope by Duh-Fuu,' 69 & Sheir, Shwu 'who? whom?' and moh 'none' in old Chinese, 71, J Am Orient Soc; More on Peking archaisms, T'oung Pao, 72; T'ang Poetic Vocabulary, 76, Fifty-Five T'ang Poems, 76 & coauth, Spoken Standard Chinese Vols 1 & 2, 76 & 78 & Written Standard Chinese, Vol I, 80, Far Eastern Publ. **CONTACT ADDRESS** Dept of East Asian Lang & Lit, Yale Univ, PO Box 208308, New Haven, CT 06520-8308.

STINE, PHILIP C.
PERSONAL Born 08/30/1943, Harrisburg, IL, m, 1976, 2 children **DISCIPLINE** LINGUISTICS **EDUCATION** Univ Mich, PhD 68, MA 65; Asbury Col, BA 64. **CAREER** United Bible Societies, Dir trans, prod dist, 68-98; Executive and Management Consultancy, 98-. **MEMBERSHIPS** LSA; SBL; AAA. **RESEARCH** Translation **SELECTED PUBLICATIONS** Auth, A Handbook on Jeremiah, coauth, NY, United Bible Soc, forthcoming; Facing the Third Millennium: Bible Societies and the Long View, Reading UK, UBS Bull, 97; Doke, Clement Martyn, Smith, Edwin Williams, van Bulck, Gaaston, Westerman, Diedrich Hermann, Articles in: Biographical Dictionary of Christian Missions, ed, Gerald H. Anderson, Simon and Schuster, 97; auth, The Training of Missiologists to Develop Local Bible Translators, Missiological Edu for the 21st Century: The Book the Circle and the Sandals, eds, J. Dudley Woodberry, Charles van Engen, Edgar J. Elliston, NY, Orbis Books, 96; auth, Trends in Translation, in: The Bible Translator, 95; auth, Relating to Others: Facing the Facts, The Bible Distributor, 95; Managing the Publishing Process, The Bible Distributor, 95. **CONTACT ADDRESS** USIS/USEU Brussels, PSC 82, PO Box 002, APO, AE 09710. **EMAIL** pcstine@compuserve.com

STIVALE, CHARLES J.
PERSONAL Born 12/13/1949, Glen Ridge, NJ, m, 1981 **DISCIPLINE** FRENCH LANGUAGE & LITERATURE **EDUCATION** Knox Col, BA, 71; Sorbonne Paris-IV, MA, 73, Maitrise, 74; Univ IL Urbana-Champaign, PhD, 81. **CAREER** Inst, W Mich Univ, 80-81; res dir, Univ of Haute Bretagne, Rennes, France, 81-82; asst prof, Franklin & Marshall Col, 82-86; asst prof, Tulane Univ, 86-90; assoc prof to prof & chair, Wayne St Univ, 90- . **HONORS AND AWARDS** Choice Outstanding Acad Book Awd from ALA; 99; Wayne St Univ Brd of Governors' Fac Recognition Awd, 99;l Wayne St Univ Brd of Governors' Distinguished Fac Fellow, 00; election to Wayne St Univ Acad of Scholars (lifetime term). **MEMBERSHIPS** Modern Lang Assoc; Midwest Modern Lang Assoc, Amer Assoc of Teachers of French; Alliance Francaise. **RESEARCH** Nineteenth-century French lit; twentieth-century critical theory; French cultural stud; cybercriticism; ableuze & Guattari. **SELECTED PUBLICATIONS** Auth, The Art of Rupture, Narrative Desire and Duplicity in the Tales of Guy de Maupassant, Univ Mich Press, 94; 'help manners', Cyber-democracy and Its Vicissitudes, Enculturation, 97; On Cultural Lessons, French and Other, Contemporary French Stud, 97; auth, On hecceites and ritournelles: Movement and Affect in the Cajun Dance Arena, in Articulating the Global and the Local (Boulder, CO), Westview Press, 97; auth, Spam: Heteroglossia and Harassement in Cyberspace, In Internet Culture (NY) Routledge, 97; The Two-Fold Thought of Deleuze and Guattari: Intersections and Animations. Guilford Publ, 98; auth, Comment peut-on-etre deluzien?, Pursuing a Two-fold Thought, In A Deleuzean Century (Durham, NC), Duke Univ Press, 99; auth (Se) Rendre Compte: Orienting Graduate Students to Market (Un)Realities, The French Review, 99; The MLA Moment, Profession, 1999 (NY) MLA, 99; auth, Becoming Cajun, Cultural Studies, 00. **CONTACT ADDRESS** Dept of Romance Lang & Lit, Wayne State Univ, 487 Manoogian Hall, Detroit, MI 48202. **EMAIL** C_Stivale@wayne.edu

STOCKWELL, ROBERT PAUL
PERSONAL Born 06/12/1925, OK, m, 1946, 1 child **DISCIPLINE** ENGLISH LANGUAGE & LINGUISTICS **EDUCATION** Univ VA, BA, 46, MA, 49, PhD(English philol & ling), 52. **CAREER** Instr English, Univ Okla City, 46-48; dir English for foreigners proj Nashville Auto-Diesel Col, 52; from instr to assoc prof ling, Foreign Serv Inst, US Dept State, 52-56, chmn Latin-Am lang & area prog, 53-56; asst prof English, 56-58, from assoc prof to prof, 58-62, chmn dept, 66-73, Prof Ling, Univ Calif, Los Angeles, 66-, Chmn Dept, 80-85, Vis prof, Philippines, 59 & 60, vis prof, Univ Tex, 61; Am Coun Learned Soc fel, 63-64; vis prof, Univ Mich, 65; Dir Lim Inst, UCLA, 83. **HONORS AND AWARDS** Distinguished Teaching Awd, Univ Calif, Los Angeles, 68; Fel of the ACLS, 63-64. **MEMBERSHIPS** MLA; Ling Soc Am; Philol Soc, England. **RESEARCH** English and Spanish language; history of English phonology and syntax; general linguistic theory. **SELECTED PUBLICATIONS** Coauth, Patterns of Spanish Pronunciation, 60, Sounds of English and Spanish, 65 & Grammatical Structure of English and Spanish, 65, Univ Chicago; co-ed, Linguistic Change and Generative Theory, Ind Univ 72; coauth, Major Syntactic Structures of English, Holt, 73; auth, Foundations of Syntactic Theory, Prentice-Hall, 77; A History of Old-English Meter, Language, Vol 71, 95; Dwight,L Bolinger, Language, Vol 69, 93; The Cambridge Hist of the English-Language, Vol 2 1066-1476, J Of Linguistics, Vol 30, 94; coauth, Structure and History of English Words, Cambridge Univ Press, 01. **CONTACT ADDRESS** Dept of Ling, Univ of California, Los Angeles, Los Angeles, CA 90024. **EMAIL** stockwel@ucla.edu

STOHL, CYNTHIA B.
DISCIPLINE ORGANIZATIONAL COMMUNICATION, SOCIAL NETWORKS **EDUCATION** Univ Purdue, PhD, 82. **CAREER** Prof, Purdue Univ. **RESEARCH** Participatory processes in multicultural/international organizations. **SELECTED PUBLICATIONS** Auth, European Managers Interpretations of Participation: a semantic network analysis, Human Commun Res, 93; Participating and Participation, Commun Monogr, 93; Organizational Communication: Connectedness in Action, Sage, 95; Paradoxes of Participation, Orgn and Commun, 95. **CONTACT ADDRESS** Dept of Commun, Purdue Univ, West Lafayette, 1080 Schleman Hall, West Lafayette, IN 47907-1080. **EMAIL** cstohl@purdue.edu

STOKKER, KATHLEEN MARIE
PERSONAL Born 10/10/1946, St. Paul, MN **DISCIPLINE** NORWEGIAN LANGUAGE & LITERATURE **EDUCATION** St Olaf Col, Minn, BA, 68; Univ Wis-Madison, MA, 71,

PhD(Scand), 78. **CAREER** Instr Norweg, Moorhead State Univ, 73-77 & St Olaf Col, 77-78; asst prof, 78-82, assoc prof Norweg, 82-87, prof, 87-, Luther Col, Iowa, 82-, res fel, Am Scand Found, 72-73 & Nat Endowment for Humanities, 81-82; trustee Norweg-Am Cult Inst, 78-. **HONORS AND AWARDS** Phi Beta Kappa. **MEMBERSHIPS** Soc Advan Scand Study; Norweg Am Hist Asn; Am Scand Found; Norweg Am Cult Inst; Ibsen Soc Am. **RESEARCH** Norwegian folklore, folkbelief and legends, study of cultural historical background and function of folktales; Norwegian literary and cultural periodicals pre-1900; foreign language pedagogy; humor, World War II. **SELECTED PUBLICATIONS** Auth, J E Sars and Nyt Norsk Tidsskrift: Their Influence on the Modern Breakthrough in Norway, Norweg Scholarly Res Asn, 78; coauth, Norsk, nordmenn og Norge, Univ Wis Press, 81; Norsk, nordmenn og Norge: Antologi, Univ Wis Press, 93; Folklore Fights the Nazis: Humor in Occupied Norway 1940-45, Univ Wis Press, 96; auth, Keeping Christmas: Yuletide Traditions in Norway and the New Land, Minnesota Historical Soc Press, 00. **CONTACT ADDRESS** Dept of Norweg, Luther Col, 700 College Dr, Decorah, IA 52101-1045. **EMAIL** Stokkeka@Luther.edu

STOLL, ANITA K.
DISCIPLINE SPANISH AND LATIN AMERICAN LITERATURE **EDUCATION** Case Western Reserve Univ, PhD. **CAREER** Prof, Cleveland State Univ, chp. **SELECTED PUBLICATIONS** Publ, Spanish Golden Age Drama, Twentieth-century Mexican literature. **CONTACT ADDRESS** Dept of For Lang, Cleveland State Univ, 83 E 24th St, Cleveland, OH 44115.

STOLTZFUS, BEN F.
PERSONAL Born 09/15/1927, Sofia, Bulgaria, m, 1975, 3 children **DISCIPLINE** FRENCH, COMPARATIVE LITERATURE **EDUCATION** Amherst Col, BA, 49; Middlebury Col, MA, 54; Univ Wisc, PhD, 59. **CAREER** Instructor, Smith Col, 58-60; Prof to Prof Emeritus, Univ Calif, 60-93. **HONORS AND AWARDS** Fulbright Res Grant, Paris, 55-56, 63-64; Awd, Univ CA Creative Arts, 68-69; Awd, Univ CA, Humanities, 71-72; Camargo Foundation, Cassis France, 83, 85; NAAP Gradiva Awd, 97. **MEMBERSHIPS** Mod Lang Asn; New Novel Asn; Albert Camus Soc; Ernest Hemingway Asn; Am Lit Asn; Am Comp Lit Asn; S Comp Lit Asn; Assoc Writers; Poets and Writers. **RESEARCH** French/American literary relationships; Art and literature; Alain Robbe-Grllet and postmodern French fiction; Ernest Hemingway; Postmodern American fiction. **SELECTED PUBLICATIONS** Auth, The Eye of the Needle, Viking Press, 67; auth, Black Lazarus, Winter House, 72; auth, Gide and Hemingway: Rebels Against God, Kennikat, 78; auth, Alain Robbe-Grillet: The Body of the Text, Fairleigh Dickinson UP, 85; auth, Alain Robbe-Grillet: Life, Work ad Criticism, York, 87; auth, "Postmodern Poetics: Nouveau Roman and Innovative Fiction," in Occasional Papers in Language, Literature and Linguistics, 87; auth, Red White and Blue, York, 89; trans, "La Belle Captive" by Alain Robbe-Grillet and Rene Magritte, Univ CA Press, 95; auth, Lacan and Literature: Purloined Pretexts, SUNY Press, 96; co-auth, Romoland, forthcoming. **CONTACT ADDRESS** Dept Comp Lit & For Lang, Univ of California, Riverside, 900 Univ Ave, Riverside, CA 92521-0001.

STOLZ, BENJAMIN ARMOND
PERSONAL Born 03/28/1934, Lansing, MI, m, 1962, 2 children **DISCIPLINE** SLAVIC LANGUAGES **EDUCATION** Univ Mich, AB, 55; Univ Brussels, cert Polish, 56; Harvard Univ, AM, 57, PhD(Slavic), 65. **CAREER** Lectr, 63, from asst prof to assoc prof, 64-73, Prof Slavic Lang & Lit, Univ Mich, Ann Arbor, 73-, Chmn Dept, 71-, Fulbright-Hays fel, Eng & Yugoslavia, 70-71. **MEMBERSHIPS** Am Asn Advan Slavic Studies; Am Asn Teachers Slavic & EEurop Lang; Ling Soc Am; MLA; Midwest Mod Lang Asn (pres, 76-77). **RESEARCH** Slavic linguistics and folklore. **SELECTED PUBLICATIONS** Auth, Nikac and Hamza: multiformity in the Serbo-Croatian heroic epic, J Folklore Inst, 69; On the history of the Serbo-Croatian diplomatic language and its role in the formation of the contemporary standard, In: American Contributions to the Seventh International Congress of Slavists, Vol I, 73 & Serbo-Croatian in the works of Bartholomaeus Georgievits (Bartol Durdevic): a reappraisal, In: Konstantin Mihailovic, Memoirs of a Janissary, 75 & ed, Papers in Slavic Philology, Vol I & IV, 77, Mich Slavic Publ; co-ed, Oral Literature and the Formula, Ctr Coord Ancient & Mod Studies, 77; On the language of Kanstantin Mihailovic's Kronilca turecka, Am Contribr 8th Int Congr Slavists, Vol I, 78; Kopitar and Vuk: An assessment of their roles in the rise of the new Serbian literary language, Vol II, 82. **CONTACT ADDRESS** Dept of Slavic Lang & Lit, Univ of Michigan, Ann Arbor, 812 E Washington St, Ann Arbor, MI 48109-1275.

STONE, CYNTHIA
DISCIPLINE SPANISH **EDUCATION** Williams Col, BA, 83; Columbia Univ, MA, 86; Univ Mich, PhD, 92. **CAREER** Asst prof. **RESEARCH** Compilations of indigenous traditions; films set in Colonial Spanish America. **SELECTED PUBLICATIONS** Auth, The Filming of Colonial Spanish America, Colonial Latin Amer Rev 5 2, 96; Multiple Authorship in the Relacion de Michoacan, Hacia un nuevo canon literario, New Hampshire: Ediciones del Norte, 95; Rewriting Indigenous Traditions: The Burial Ceremony of the Cazonci, Colonial Latin Amer Rev 3 1-2, 94 & El lector implecito de Rayuela y los blancos de la narracion, Los ochenta mundos de Cortazar: ensayos, Madrid: Edi-6, 87. **CONTACT ADDRESS** Dept of Modern Languages and Literatures, Col of the Holy Cross, 1 College St, PO Box 10A, Worcester, MA 01610-2395. **EMAIL** cstone@holycross.edu

STONE, JENNIFER
DISCIPLINE FRENCH & ITALIAN LITERATURE & CULTURE, COMPARATIVE LITERATURE **EDUCATION** Univ Witwatersrand, BA, 71; London Univ, PhD, 82. **CAREER** Asst prof, 82-88, assoc prof, Univ Mass Amherst, 88- . **MEMBERSHIPS** Soc Pirandello Studies. **RESEARCH** Freudian psychoanalytic theory in relation to lit, film, art & culture; new digital media & globalization **SELECTED PUBLICATIONS** Auth, Pirandello's Naked Prompt: The Structure of Repetition in Modernism, Ravenna, 82; auth, Italian Freud: A History of Resistance; auth, American Freud: Multimedia Moses and Monotheism et al. **CONTACT ADDRESS** Dept of French and Italian Studies, Univ of Massachusetts, Amherst, 161 Presidents Dr, 312 Herter Hall, Amherst, MA 01003-9312. **EMAIL** Jastonephd@aol.com

STRATER, HENRY A.
PERSONAL Born 10/28/1934, Cleveland, OH, m, 3 children **DISCIPLINE** ENGLISH, CLASSICAL LANGUAGES **EDUCATION** John Carroll Univ, AB, 56, MA; Case Western Univ, MA, 59; Ohio State Univ, PhD, 71. **CAREER** Tchr, Shaker Heights Sch, Ohio, 56-84; holder of Waldron ch in Classics, Univ Sch, 84- . **HONORS AND AWARDS** Good tchr awd, Class Asn Mid W and S; Seelbach awd for excel in tchg. **MEMBERSHIPS** Amer Class League; Ohio Class Conf; Amer Philol Asn; Class Asn Mid W and S. **RESEARCH** Vergil; Methods of teaching Classical Languages. **SELECTED PUBLICATIONS** Auth, Greek to Me: An Introduction to Classical Greek. **CONTACT ADDRESS** Univ Sch, 1131 Blanchester Rd, Lyndhurst, OH 44124. **EMAIL** hastrater@aol.com

STRAUSE, GLYNIS
PERSONAL Born 09/11/1952, McAllen, TX, m, 1978, 2 children **DISCIPLINE** LINGUISTICS **EDUCATION** Howard Payne Univ, BSc, 75; Univ Tenn Knoxville, MA, 77. **CAREER** Vis instr, Tex A & M Univ, 77-78; instr, Coastal Bend Col, 78-; dir of cont ed, Coastal Bend Col, 98-. **HONORS AND AWARDS** Educ of the Year for Commun Cols, TSCA, 97; Trained Leader in Commun, TSCA, 97; Outstanding Serv Awd, TSCA, 98. **MEMBERSHIPS** TSCA, Tex Asn Cont Ed. **RESEARCH** Interpersonal communication, small group interaction. **SELECTED PUBLICATIONS** Auth, Interpersonal Communication, 80; auth, A Rhetoric of Interpersonal Communication, 84; auth, A Rhetoric of Interpersonal Communication and Relationships, 97. **CONTACT ADDRESS** Dept Lang Arts, Coastal Bend Col, 3800 Charco Rd, Beeville, TX 78102-2110. **EMAIL** ghstraus@cbc.cc.tx.us

STRAUSS, JONATHAN
DISCIPLINE FRENCH **EDUCATION** Yale Univ, PhD, 93. **CAREER** Assoc prof & ch, Miami Univ. **RESEARCH** 19th- and 20th-century French literature; Romanticism; philosophy and literature; poetry; theory; visual arts. **SELECTED PUBLICATIONS** Auth, Nerval's 'Le Christ aux oliviers': The Subject Writes After His Own Death, in Romanic Rev, 97; Death-Based Subjectivity in the Creation of Nerval's Lyric Self, in Death in French Literature and Film, L'Esprit Createur, 95; The Inverted Icarus, in Yale Fr Stud, 78; transl, Helmut Federle, The line which I have chosen, Painting: Current Territories, Valence: Editions de l'Ecole de Beaux Arts de Valence, 97; Gilles Deleuze, Material Coils, in Yale Fr Stud, 80 & Georges Bataille, Hegel, Death, and Sacrifice, in Yale Fr Stud, 78; auth, Subjects of Terror: Nerval, Hegel, and the Modern Self, Stanford Univ Press, 98; auth, "Subject and Image in Eluard's Early Poetry," Mosaic 33:2 (00). **CONTACT ADDRESS** Dept of French and Italian, Miami Univ, Oxford, OH 45056. **EMAIL** strausja@muohio.edu

STRAUSS, WALTER ADOLF
PERSONAL Born 05/14/1923, Mannheim, Germany, m, 5 children **DISCIPLINE** FRENCH LANGUAGE & LITERATURE **EDUCATION** Emory Univ, BA, 44; Harvard Univ, MA, 48, PhD, 51. **CAREER** Instr Romance lang & gen educ, Harvard Univ, 51-54; from asst prof to prof Romance lang, Emory Univ, 54-70, dir dlv humanities prog, 65-70; Treuhaft Prof Humanities, Case Western Reserve Univ, 70-, Chmn Dept Mod Lang, 79-, Guggenheim & Bollingen fels, 62-63; NDEA summer fel, 77. **MEMBERSHIPS** MLA; Dante Soc; Midwest Mod Lang Asn; Kafka Soc; Beckett Soc. **RESEARCH** Contemporary French literature; comparative literature, 19th and 20th centuries. **SELECTED PUBLICATIONS** Auth, Proust and literature: The novelist as a critic; Twelve unpublished letters of Marcel Proust, Harvard Libr Bull; Dante's Belacqua and Beckett's tramps, Comp Lit, 59; Descent and Return: The Orphic Theme in Modern Literature, Harvard Univ, 71. **CONTACT ADDRESS** Dept of Mod Lang & Lit, Case Western Reserve Univ, Cleveland, OH 44106.

STREET, JACK DAVID
PERSONAL Born 04/17/1929, Lafayette, AL, m, 1955, 2 children **DISCIPLINE** FRENCH, ENGLISH **EDUCATION** Jacksonville State Col, AB & BS, 50; Univ Ala, MA, 52; State Univ Iowa, PhD(French), 64 Univ of Florence, dipl(Ital lang, lit & cult), 75; Scuola Dante Alighieri, dipl(Ital lang, lit & cult), 77. **CAREER** Teacher French & English, Tuscaloosa High Sch, 51-52; asst prof mod lang, NCent Col, 58-61; from asst prof to assoc prof, 61-72, prof mod lang, 72-97, chmn dept of mod lang & lit, 75-97, Harry C Moore Prof Mod Lang, Beloit Col, 97-. **MEMBERSHIPS** Am Asn Teachers Fr; Am Coun Teaching Foreign Lang; AAUP **RESEARCH** Marcel Proust; Chateaubriand; Montherlant; French in the Valley d'Aosta, Italy. **SELECTED PUBLICATIONS** Auth, Seminar in France, 1959: An appraisal, 2/60 & A statistical study of the vocabulary of Les aventures du dernier Abencerage by Chateaubriand, 10/68, Fr Rev; 8 articles on French in the Valley d'Aosta, Italy, in: Contemporary French Civilization and French Rev. **CONTACT ADDRESS** Dept of Mod Lang, Beloit Col, 700 College St, Beloit, WI 53511-5595. **EMAIL** streetj@beloit.edu

STRELKA, JOSEPH PETER
PERSONAL Born 05/03/1927, Wiener Neustadt, Austria, m, 1963, 1 child **DISCIPLINE** GERMAN LITERATURE, THEORY OF LITERATURE **EDUCATION** Univ Vienna, PhD(Ger lit), 50. **CAREER** Assoc prof Ger lit, Univ Southern Calif, 64, dir Vienna prog, Univ Vienna, 65; prof Ger, Pa State Univ, University Park, 66-71; Prof Ger & Comp Lit, State Univ NY Albany, 71-, Theodor Koerner Found award, 55-57; City of Vienna award, 58; Austrian Govt res fel, Austrian Inst Cult Affairs Paris, 58-59; ed, Yearbook of Comparative Criticism Ser, 68 & Penn State Series in German literature, 71-; exchange scholar, State Univ NY, 75; Inst Humanistic Studies fel, 77; New Yorker Beitrage zur Vergleichenden Literaturwissenschaft, 82-; New Yorker Studien zur Neueren Deutschen Literaturgeschichte, 82-. **HONORS AND AWARDS** Austrian Cross of Honor for the Arts and Sci First Class, Republic of Austria, 78. **MEMBERSHIPS** Pen Club; Int Asn Ger Studies, Int Comp Lit Asn; MLA; Humboldt-Gesellschaft. **RESEARCH** LIterary theory; literature of the Renaissance; German literature of the 20th century. **SELECTED PUBLICATIONS** Brucke u vielen Ufern, Europa, Vienna, Frankfurt, Zurich, 66; Vergleichende Literaturkritik, Francke, Bern, 70; Die gelenkten Musen, Europa, Vienna, Frankfurt, Zurich, 71; Auf der Suche nach dem verlorenen Selbst, Francke, Bern, 77; Werk, Werkverstandnin, Wertung, Francke, Bern, 78; Methodologie der Literaturwissenschaft, Nimeyer, Tubingen, 78; Esoterik bei Goethe, Niemeyer Tubingen, 80; Stefan Zweig, Osterreichischer Bundesverlag, Vienna, 81. **CONTACT ADDRESS** Dept of Ger, SUNY, Albany, Albany, NY 12222.

STROLLE, JON M.
PERSONAL Born 04/21/1940, Gaylord, MI, m, 2000, 2 children **DISCIPLINE** SPANISH **EDUCATION** Oberlin Col, Ba, 62; Univ Wisc, Madison, MA, 64, PhD, 68. **CAREER** Asst prof, 67-74, Ind Univ; asst prof, 74-76, SUNY Brockport; dean, Spanish Schl, 76-80, Middlebury Col; fel, US dept of Ed, 80-81, Wash, DC; 81-85, dean, 85-, SAGE Jr Col, Albany; dean, grad schl of lang & ed ling, assoc provost, Monterey Inst of Intl Stud, 96-00; prof Hispanic Studies, Monterey Inst of Intl Stud, 00-. **RESEARCH** Language policy, Spanish in the US. **CONTACT ADDRESS** Monterey Inst of Intl Studies, Van Buren St, Monterey, CA 93940. **EMAIL** jstrolle@miis.edu

STROUD, MATTHEW DAVID
PERSONAL Born 10/04/1950, Hillsboro, TX **DISCIPLINE** SPANISH **EDUCATION** Univ Tex, Austin, BA, 71; Univ Southern Calif, MA, 74, PhD(Span), 77. **CAREER** Asst Prof Span, Trinity Univ, 77-83; Assoc Prof, Trinity Univ, 83-89; Prof 89-; Chair, 84-87. **HONORS AND AWARDS** Phi Beta Kappa; Sigma Delta Pi; Pi Delta Phi; Computer Science Creativity Awd, Univ Tex, 71; Mrs Z. T. Scott Faculty Fellowship for Outstanding Teaching and Advising, Trinity Univ, 99; Lifetime Memberships, Board of Directors, Assoc for Hisp Class Theater; Corresponding Member, Hispanic Soc of America. **MEMBERSHIPS** MLA; SCent Mod Lang Asn; Am Asn Teachers Span & Port; AAUP; Asoc Int Hisp; Cervantes Soc Am; Assoc for Hisp Classical Theater. **RESEARCH** Seventeenth century Spanish literatures; literary theory. **SELECTED PUBLICATIONS** Aut"The Demand for Love and the Mediation of Desire in La traicion en la Amistad," Maria de Zayas: Dynamics of Discourse, Fairleigh Dickinson Univ Pr, 95; auth, "Sainthood and Psychoanalysis." Tirso de Molina: His Theatre Then and Now, Dovehouse, 96; auth, The Play in the Mirror: Lacanian Perspectives on Spanish Baroque Theater, Bucknell Univ Pr, 96; auth, "The Lessons of Calderon's La cisma de Inglaterra," Hispanic Essays in Honor of Frank P. Casa, Peter Lang, 97; auth, The Comedia in Amsterdam, 1609-1621: Rodenburgh's Translation of Aguilar's La venganza honrosa, Labertino, Vol 1, online; auth, Pedro Calderon de la Barca, Spanish Dramatists of the Golden Age: A Bio-Bibliographical Sourcebook, Greenwood, 98; Performativity and Sexual Identity in Calderon's Las manos blancas no ofenden, Gender Identity, and Representation in Spain's Golden Age, Bucknell Univ Pr, 00; auth, "Comedy Foppery, Camp: Moreto's El lindo don Diego," Lesbianism and Homosexuality in Early Modern Spain, Univ Pr of the South, 00; Trans, The Phatom Lady, By Pedro Calderon de la Barca, online, 00; auth,"Homo/Hetro/Social/

Sexual: Gila in Velez's La serrana de la Vera," Caliope, 00. **CONTACT ADDRESS** Dept of Modern Language, Trinity Univ, San Antonio, TX 78212. **EMAIL** mstroud@trinity.edu

STROUD, RONALD SIDNEY
PERSONAL Born 07/08/1933, Toronto, ON, Canada, m, 1963, 2 children **DISCIPLINE** CLASSICS **EDUCATION** Univ Toronto, BA, 57; Univ Calif, Berkeley, PhD(classics), 65. **CAREER** Secy, Am Sch Class Studies Athens, 60-63; from asst prof to assoc prof, 65-72, Prof Classics, Univ Calif, Berkeley, 72-, Am Philos Soc, Am Coun Learned Socs & Guggenheim fels, 77-78; Mellon Prof, Classical Studies, Am Sch Class Studies Athens, 96-99. **RESEARCH** Greek history; Greek epigraphy; classical archaeology. **SELECTED PUBLICATIONS** Auth, Drakon's Law on Homicide, Univ Calif, 68; An Ancient Fort on Mt Oneion, 71 & Inscriptions from the North Slope of the Acropolis, 71 & 72, Hesperia; Thucydides and the Battle of Solygeia, Calif Studies Class Antiq, 71; An Athenian Law on Silver Coinage, Hesperia, 74; The Axones and Kyrbeis of Drakon and Solon, Univ Calif, 79; Athenian Economy And Society--A Banking Perspective, Mnemosyne, Vol 49, 96; auth, The Athenian Grain-Tax Law of 374/3 B.C., Hesperia, Suppl, 29 (98); co-ed, Supplementum Epigraphieum Graecum, Vol 26, 79, 47 (00). **CONTACT ADDRESS** Dept Classics, Univ of California, Berkeley, Berkeley, CA 94720. **EMAIL** rsstroud@socrates.berkeley.edu

STROUP, SARAH CULPEPPER
PERSONAL Born 11/10/1967, Honolulu, HI **DISCIPLINE** CLASSICS **EDUCATION** Univ Wash, BA, 92; Univ Calif Berkeley, MA, 95; PhD, 00. **CAREER** Acting asst prof to prof, Univ Wash, 00-. **HONORS AND AWARDS** Lulu J. Blumberg Fel, 93-94; Chancellor's Humanities Fel, 95; Outstanding Grad Student Instr Award, 98; Mellon Dissertation Fel, 98; Women's Class Caucus Paper Award, 99. **MEMBERSHIPS** Am Philol Asn; Archaeol Inst of Am; Women's Class Caucus. **RESEARCH** Roman Prose, especially rhetoric, philosophy, and epistolography; Greek and Roman Drama; Greek and Roman Art and Archaeology; Literary and Cultural Criticisms. **SELECTED PUBLICATIONS** Rev, of "Changing Bodies, Changing Meanings," by Dominic Montserrat, Bryn Mawr Class Rev, (98): 7-20; co-auth, "Phthonos d'Apesto: The Translation of Transgression in Aiskhylos' Agamemnon," Class Antiquity, (99): 153-182; auth, Political Muse: Cicero, Catullus, and Textual Culture in the Late Republic, (forthcoming); auth, By Fire of By Sword: The Catilinarian Conspiracy through the Eyes of Cicero, Sallust, Appian and Dio, Focus Pub, (forthcoming); auth, "Designing Women: Aristophanes' Lysistrata and the 'Hetairization' of the Greek Wife," (forthcoming). **CONTACT ADDRESS** Dept Class, Univ of Washington, PO Box 353110, Seattle, WA 98195-3110. **EMAIL** scstroup@u.washington.edu

STUART, DOUGLAS KEITH
PERSONAL Born 02/08/1943, Concord, MA, m, 1971, 8 children **DISCIPLINE** OLD TESTAMENT, NEAR EASTERN LANGUAGES **EDUCATION** Harvard Univ, BA, 64, PhD, 71. **CAREER** Instr Near East hist, 68-69, Gordon Col; asst prof, 71-77, assoc prof, 78-81, prof Old Testament, 81-, Gordon-Conwell Theol Sem; pres, 74-, Boston area chap, Huxley Inst Biosocial Res; co-chmn, 75-, Boston Theol Inst; trustee, 80-, Mass Bible Soc; trustee, Boxford Acad, 96-. **MEMBERSHIPS** Am Schs Orient Res; Inst Bibl Res; Evangel Theol Soc; Soc Bibl Lit; Bibl Archeol Soc. **RESEARCH** Hebrew meter; minor prophets; exegesis techniques. **SELECTED PUBLICATIONS** Coauth, How to Read the Bible for All Its Worth, Zondervan Publ House, 82; auth, Hosea-Jonah, Word Biblical Comm, 87; auth, Hosea-Jonah, Word Biblical Themes, 88; auth, Favorite Old Testament Passages, Westminster Press, 89; auth, Malachi, Baker Bk House, 98. **CONTACT ADDRESS** Gordon-Conwell Theol Sem, 130 Essex St, South Hamilton, MA 01982-2395.

STURM-MADDOX, SARA
PERSONAL Born 12/22/1938, Nashville, TN, m, 2 children **DISCIPLINE** FRENCH & ITALIAN LITERATURE **EDUCATION** Univ MN, BA, 63, MA, 65; Univ NC, PhD(Romance philol), 67. **CAREER** Asst prof French, Queens Col, NC, 66-67; asst prof Ital, Univ KY, 67-69; Prof French & Ital, Univ MA, Amherst, 75-, Am Coun Learned Soc. **HONORS AND AWARDS** Foundation Camargo, NEH **MEMBERSHIPS** MLA, Dante Soc Am; Int Arthurian Soc; Soc Rencesvals; Am Asn Tchrs; Int Courtly Lit Soc. **RESEARCH** Medieval French romance, epic and lyric; Dante; Renaissance Italian. **SELECTED PUBLICATIONS** Auth, The Lay of Guingamor: A Study, Univ NC, 68; Lorenzo de'Medici, Twayne, 74; Petrarch's Metamorphoses, Univ MO, 85; Petrarch's Laurels, Penn State Univ, 92; co-ed, Literary Aspects of Courtly Culture, Boydell & Brewer, 94; Transtextualities, MRTS, 96; Melusine of Lusignan, Univ of GA, 96; Froissart Across the Genres, Univ of FL, 98. **CONTACT ADDRESS** Dept of French & Ital, Univ of Massachusetts, Amherst, 316 Herter Hall, Amherst, MA 01003. **EMAIL** ssmaddox@frital.umass.edu

STYCOS, MARIA NOWAKOWSKA
PERSONAL Born 06/04/1937, Lwow, Poland, m, 1964, 1 child **DISCIPLINE** SPANISH **EDUCATION** King's Col, Univ London, BA, 58; Cornell Univ, MA, 67; PhD, 77. **CAREER** Dir, Handwerker Gallery of Art, Ithaca Col, New York, 81-82; asst prof (part-time), SUC at Courtland, New York, 82-86; sr lectr, Cornell Univ, 86-. **HONORS AND AWARDS** State Scholarship, UK, 55-58; NEH Summer grant for Col Teachers, 78; grant from the Consortium for Language Teaching, 90. **MEMBERSHIPS** MLA, Asn Int De Hispanistas, Asn de Literatura Femenica Hispanica. **RESEARCH** Women's writing, 20th century Hispanic and Polish poetry. **SELECTED PUBLICATIONS** Auth, "Spanish Poetry of the Post-War Period: The Changing Poetrics of the 70's Generation?," in Mountain Interstate Conference on Foreign Languages: Selected Proceedings, ed R. Fernandez-Rubio (86); auth, "La nueva mujer en los poemas de Mia Gallegos y Gioconda Belli," in Mairena, Ano XI, No 28 (89): 103-112; auth of biographical entry on "Susana March" in Dictionary of the Literature of the Iberian Peninsula, eds, German Beliberg & Maureen Ihrie, Greenwood Press (93); auth, "El 'espejo' en La mujer habitada de Gioconda Belli," AIH, Madrid, Spain (99). **CONTACT ADDRESS** Dept Modern Langs, Cornell Univ, 283 Goldwin Smith, Ithaca, NY 14853-4701. **EMAIL** mns2@cornell.edu

SUAREZ-GALBAN, EUGENIO
DISCIPLINE LATIN AMERICAN NARRATIVE, COMPARATIVE LITERATURE, SPANISH GOLDEN AGE, ANGLO **EDUCATION** BA, Boston Col, 61; NYork Univ, MA, 65, PhD, 67. **CAREER** Vis prof, Colgate Univ. **HONORS AND AWARDS** PhD with hon(s), NYU, 67; Sesamo prize, 82 ;tchg award, Hamilton Col, 91; medal, Inst De Cult Puertorriquena, 97; selected for anthol poesia espanola e hispanoamericana, madrid, 96. **CONTACT ADDRESS** Dept of Romance Lang, Colgate Univ, 13 Oak Drive, Hamilton, NY 13346.

SUITS, THOMAS ALLAN
PERSONAL Born 04/05/1933, Milwaukee, WI, m, 1955, 2 children **DISCIPLINE** CLASSICAL PHILOLOGY **EDUCATION** Yale Univ, AB, 55, MA, 56, PhD(classics), 58. **CAREER** From instr to asst prof Greek & Latin, Columbia Univ, 58-66; from assoc prof classics to prof emeritus classis, Univ Conn, 66-97; mem class jury, Am Acad in Rome, 77-79. **HONORS AND AWARDS** Hon Citizen, Greece, 97. **MEMBERSHIPS** Am Philol Asn; Class Asn New England (pres, 80-81). **RESEARCH** Latin literature, especially elegy; Propertius. **SELECTED PUBLICATIONS** Coauth, Latin Selections, Bantam, 61, 2nd ed, 92; auth, Mythology, address, and structure in Propertius 2.8, 65 & The Vertumnus elegy of Propertis, 69, Trans & Proc Am Philol Asn; ed, Macrobius: The Saturnalia, Columbia Univ, 69; auth, The structure of Livy's 32nd book, Philologus, 74; The knee and the shin: Seneca, Apocolocyntosis 10.3, Class Philol, 75; The iambic character of Propertius 1.4, Philologus, 76; Tibullus, Elegies --With Introduction and Commentary, Am J Of Philology, Vol 117, 96. **CONTACT ADDRESS** 12 Hillyndale Rd, Storrs, CT 06268. **EMAIL** suits147@cs.com

SULEIMAN, SUSAN RUBIN
PERSONAL Born 07/18/1939, Budapest, Hungary, d, 2 children **DISCIPLINE** FRENCH & COMPARATIVE LITERATURE **EDUCATION** Columbia Univ, BA, 60; Harvard Univ, MA, 64, PhD(Romance lang & lit), 69. **CAREER** Asst prof French, Columbia Univ, 69-76; vis asst prof, Univ Calif, Los Angeles, 76; from asst prof to assoc prof, Occidental Col, 76-81; from assoc prof Romance Lang & Lit, Harvard Univ, 81-84; assoc Prof Humanities, Harvard Univ, 83-84; prof Romance Languages and Literature, Harvard Univ, 84-85; prof, Romance and Comparative Literatures, Harvard Univ, 86-97; C. Douglas Dillon Prof Civilization of France, Harvard Univ, 97-; prof, cmparative lit, Harvard Univ, 97-. **HONORS AND AWARDS** Phi Beta Kappa, 60; Fel, Woodrow Wilson, 61-62; Best Teaching Fel Awd, Harvard Univ, Fel, Harvard Univ, 62-65; Am Assoc of Univ Women, 65-66; Fel, Columbia Univ Chamberlain, 73; Coun, Research in Humanities Summer Research, Columbia 72,73,74; Nat Endowment for the Humanities, stipend in 77 and fellowship 80; Fulbright Senior Research Grant, 83; Fel, Rockefeller Foun Humanities, 84; Fel, Guggenheim 88-89; Radcliffe Grad Medal for Distinguished Achievement, 90; Officer of the Order of Academic Palms (by French Govt), 92; Fel, Collegium Budapest Inst for Advan Study, 93; Vpres, Am Comp Lit Assoc (by Nat election), 95-97; Pres, Am Comp Lit Assoc (by Nat election), 97-99; summer seminar dir, Nat Endowment for Humanities, 95, 98, 00. **MEMBERSHIPS** MLA; Am Asn Teachers French; Am Comp Lit Asn. **RESEARCH** Twentieth century French fiction; theory of narrative; feminist theory; the Holocaust. **SELECTED PUBLICATIONS** Co-ed & contribr, The Reader in the Text: Essays on Audience and Interpretation, Princeton Univ Press, 80; contribr, What is Criticism?, Ind Univ Press, 81; The question of readability in Avant-Garde fiction, Studies in Twentieth Century Lit, 82; auth, Authoritarian Fictions: The Ideological Novel as a Literary Genre, 83; auth, Subversive Interit: Gender, Politics, and the Avant-Garde, 90; auth, Risking Who One Is: Encounters with Contemporary Art and Lit, 94; Comparative Literature And The Amn-University and Introduction--Three Papers From the 97 Acla Annual-Meeting, Comparative Lit, Vol 49, 97; Introduction--On Signposts, Travelers, Outsiders, And Backward Glances, Poetics Today, Vol 17, 96; Ed & Contribur, Creativity and Exile: European/American Perspectives, Poetics Today Vol 17: 3-4, 96; Contribur, Criticism and the Autobiographical Voice, Franklin and Walkowitz, Field Work: Sites in Literary and Cultural Studies, 96; Contribur, Diary as Narrative: Theory and Practice, Hendrix, The Search for a New Alphabet: Literary Studies in a Changing World, 96; auth, Budapest Diary: In Search of the Motherbook, 96; contribur, Susan Suleiman (interview), Corredor, Lukacs After Communism: Interviews with Contemporary Intellectuals, 97; auth, Monuments in a Foreign Tongue: On Reading Holocaust Memoirs be Emigrants, Poetics Today Vol 17:4, 97; contribur, The Intellectual Sublime: Zola as Archetype of Cultural Myth, Goux and Wood, Terror and Consensus: Vicissitudes of French Thought, 98; Contribur, Dialogue and Double Allegiance: Some Contemporary Women Artists and the Historical Avante-Garde, Chadwick, Mirror Images: Women, Surrealism, and Self-Representation, 98; auth, Undoing Amnesia: An Interview with Susan Rubin Suleiman, Women: A Cultural Review Vol 9:2, 98; auth, What's in a Noun? Gender and Power en Francais, Radcliffe Quarterly 98; Rereading Rereading, Further Reflections on Sartre's Reflexions, October 87, 99; Contribur, Interview with Marjorie Agosin, in Uncertain Travelers: Conversations with Jewish Women Immigrants to America, 99; auth, "The End of an Affair," Radcliffe Quarterly, 99; auth, Big Bad Wolf? A Short Chapter in the Long Story of Franco-American Relations, Sites, 00. **CONTACT ADDRESS** Dept of Romance Lang & Lit, Harvard Univ, Boylston Hall, Cambridge, MA 02138-3800. **EMAIL** suleiman@fas.harvard.edu

SULLIVAN, CONSTANCE
DISCIPLINE SPANISH AND PORTUGUESE LITERATURE **EDUCATION** Univ Rochester, BA, 60; Univ Ill, MA, 62; PhD, 68. **RESEARCH** Spanish literature and culture of the 18th, 19th, and 20th centuries; women writers of Spain; feminist theories. **SELECTED PUBLICATIONS** Auth, Gender, Text, and Cross-Dressing: The Case of 'Beatriz Cienfuegos' and La Pensadora Gaditana, Dieciocho, 95; The Quiet Feminism of Josefa Amar y Borbon's Book on the Education of Women, Ind J Hisp Lit, 93; The Boundary-Crossing Essays of Carmen Martin Gaite, Univ Ind, 93; Josefa Amar y Borbon (1749-1833), Greenwood, 93; 'Dinos, dinos quien eres': The Poetic Identity of Maria Gertrudis Hore (1742-1801), Mich Romance Studies, 92; Josefa Amar y Borbon and the Royal Aragonese Economic Society, Dieciocho, 92. **CONTACT ADDRESS** Spanish and Portuguese Dept, Univ of Minnesota, Twin Cities, 34 Folwell Hall, 9 Pleasant St SE, Minneapolis, MN 55455. **EMAIL** sulli002@maroon.tc.umn.edu

SULLIVAN, DENIS
DISCIPLINE GREEK, LATIN, CLASSICAL PHILOLOGY AND ANCIENT HISTORY **EDUCATION** Tufts Univ, AB, 66; Univ NC Chapel Hill, PhD, 72; Cath Univ, MS, 75. **CAREER** Libr staff, Univ Md, 75-78; asst dean, Univ Md, Univ Col, 78-82; asst prof, Univ Md Col Pk, 82-88; assoc prof, Univ Md Col Pk, 88-. **HONORS AND AWARDS** Phi Beta Kappa; NDEA Title IV Fel; Woodrow Wilson Dissertation Fel; Dumbarton Oaks Byzantine Fel, 91-92 and 98-99. **MEMBERSHIPS** Amer Philol Asn; US Nat Comt on Byzantine Studies. **RESEARCH** Byzantine studies; Textual criticism. **SELECTED PUBLICATIONS** Auth, The Life of St. Ioannikios in Byzantine Defenders of Images, ed A. M. Talbot, Dumbarton Oaks, Wash, DC, 243-351, 98; Tenth Century Byzantine Offensive Siege Warfare: Instructional Prescriptions and Historical Practice, Byzantium at War, Athens, Nat Hellenic Res Foun, 179-200, 97; Was Constantine VI Lassoed at Markellai?, Greek, Roman and Byzantine Studies, 35, 3, 287-291, 94; Legal Opinion of Eustathios (Romaios) the Magistros, A. Laiou, Consent and Coercion to Sex and Marriage in Ancient and Medieval Societies, Wash, 175-175, 93; The Life of Saint Nikon: Text, Translation and Commentary, Brookline, Ma, Hellenic Col Press, 87; The Versions of the Vita Niconis, Dumbarton Oaks Papers, 32, 157-173, 78; auth, Siegecraft: Two Tenth-Century Instructional Manuals by "Heron of Byzantium," Dumbarton Oaks (Wash, DC), 00. **CONTACT ADDRESS** EDCI, Univ of Maryland, Col Park, Benjamin Bldg, College Park, MD 20742. **EMAIL** ds77@umail.umd.edu

SULLIVAN, JOHN P.
PERSONAL Born 07/13/1930, Liverpool, England **DISCIPLINE** CLASSICAL LANGUAGES AND LITERATURE **EDUCATION** Cambridge Univ, BA, 53, MA, 57; Ozford Univ, MA, 57. **CAREER** Teacher classics, Clare & Magdalene Cols, Cambridge Univ, 52-53; teacher philos & classics, Hertford & Lincoln Cols, Oxford Univ & Queens' Col, Cambridge Univ, 53-55; fel & tutor classics, Lincoln Col, Oxford Univ, 55-62, dean, 60-61; vis prof class lang, Univ Tex, Austin, 61-62, assoc prof, 62-63, prof class lang, 63-69, actg chmn dept classics, 62-63, chmn dept, 63-65, Univ Res Inst grants, 61, 62, Bromberg award, 62; provost, State Univ NY, Buffalo, 72-75, fac profarts & lett, 69-78; Prof Classics, Univ Calif, Santa Barbara, 78-, Lectr, Oxford Univ, 56-60; co-ed, Arion, 61-69; Am Coun Learned Soc grant, 63; Nat Endowment Humanities sr fel, 67-68; ed, Arethusa, 71-; vis fel classics, Clare Hall, Cambridge Univ, 75-76; Martin lectr Neronian lit, Oberlin Col, 76; vis prof classics, Univ Hawaii, Manoa, 77; Gray lectr Martial, Cambridge Univ, 78; vis fel, Wolfson Col, Oxford Univ, 81; vis Hill prof, Univ Minn, 82. **MEMBERSHIPS** Am Philol Asn; Hellenic Soc. **RESEARCH** Latin literature; comparative literature. **SELECTED PUBLICATIONS CONTACT ADDRESS**

Classics Dept, Univ of California, Santa Barbara, Santa Barbara, CA 93010.

SUMNER, GORDON H.

PERSONAL Born 05/21/1945, Ancon, Panama **DISCIPLINE** LINGUISTICS **EDUCATION** Fla State Univ, BA, 66; MA, 76; PhD, 79. **CAREER** Grad TA, FSU, 77-79; vis asst prof, Ball State Univ, 79-80; vis asst prof, SD State Univ, 80-83; from asst prof to assoc prof, Ala State Univ, 83-. **HONORS AND AWARDS** NDEA Fel, 66-67; Pi Delta Phi; Sigma Delta Pi; Phi Kappa Phi, 66; AATSP Scholar, 77; Fulbright, Spain, 78. **MEMBERSHIPS** MLA, Am Asn of Teachers of Spanish. **SELECTED PUBLICATIONS** Auth, "Artistic Creativity and Order in Ruiz de Alarcon's "La verdad sospechosa" and Corneille's "Le menteur,"" in Nat Symp on Hispanic Theatre, 1982, ed. Adolfo M. Franco (Univ of N Iowa, 85); auth, "Lope de Vega's Barlan y Josafa: The Old World Reborn," in Looking at the Comedia in the Year of the Quincentennial, eds. Barbara Mujica and Sharon Voros (Univ Press of Am, 93); auth, "Canonicity and the comedias de santos: Was Cervantes Correct?" in TEXTO ESPECTACULO: Selected Proceedings of the Thirteenth International Golden Age Spanish Theatre Symposium, ed. Jose Luis Suarez Garcia (Spanish Lit Publ Co, 95); auth, "Glimpses of Spanish Golden Age Drama in Unamuno's "San Manuel Bueno, martir,"" in TEXTO ESPECTACULO: Selected Proceedings of the Fourteenth International Golden Age Spanish Theatre Symposium, ed. Jose Luis Suarez Garcia (Spanish Lit Publ Co, 95); auth, "Astraea, the Pax Christiana, and Lope de Vega's Santa Casilda," in A Star-Crossed Golden Age: Myth and the Spanish Comedia, ed. Frederick A. de Armas (Bucknell UP, 98). **CONTACT ADDRESS** Dept English & Lang, Alabama State Univ, PO Box 271, Montgomery, AL 36101-0271. **EMAIL** gregor63@earthlink.net

SUNER, MARGARITA

PERSONAL Born Buenos Aires, Argentina, 2 children **DISCIPLINE** THEORETICAL SYNTAX, HISPANIC LINGUISTICS **EDUCATION** Univ del Salvador, EFL, 65; Univ Kans, MA, 68; Ind Univ, MA, 70, PhD(Span ling), 73. **CAREER** Asst prof, 73-79, Assoc Prof, 79-86, prof ling, 86- , Cornell Univ. **HONORS AND AWARDS** Humanities fac res grants, Cornell Univ; Fulbright-Hays Fac Res Grant, 93; ACLS Travel Grant, 93. **MEMBERSHIPS** Ling Soc Am; Am Asn Teachers Span & Port; Asn Ling y Filologia de America Latina; Glow. **RESEARCH** General and Spanish syntax; clause structure; indirect questions; relative clauses; clitics; agreement. **SELECTED PUBLICATIONS** Auth, Subject Clitics in the Northern Italian Vernaculars and the Matching Hypothesis, in Natural Language and Linguistic Theory, 92; auth, About Indirect Questions and Semi-Questions, Linguistics and Philosophy, 93; auth, Verb-movement and the Licensing of Argumental Wh-phrases in Spanish, Natural Language and Linguistic Theory, 94; auth, The Syntax of Direct Quotes with special reference to Spanish and English, Natural Language an Linguistic Theory, 00; auth, Object-Shift: Comparing a Romance Language to Germanic, probus, 00; auth, Neg-elements, island Effects, and Resumptive No, The Ling Rev, 95; auth, Resumptive Restrictive Relative Clauses: A Crosslinguistic Perspective, Language, 98; coauth, Gramatica Espanola: Analisis Linguistico y Practica, McGraw-Hill, 98. **CONTACT ADDRESS** Dept of Linguistics, Cornell Univ, Morrill Hall, Ithaca, NY 14853-4701. **EMAIL** ms24@cornell.edu

SUNGDAI, CHO

PERSONAL Born 01/25/1958, Seoul, Korea, m, 1989, 2 children **DISCIPLINE** LINGUISTICS **EDUCATION** Univ Hawaii, PhD, 95. **CAREER** Korean Prog Coordr, Univ Michigan, Ann Arbor, 93-96; Korean Prog Coordr, Stanford Univ, 96-. **MEMBERSHIPS** LSA; AAS; AATK; TESOL; ACFEL. **RESEARCH** Syntax and morphology; language pedagogy. **SELECTED PUBLICATIONS** Auth, On The Potential Middle Constructions in Korean, Lang Res, 93; auth, Review for Korean Textbooks for English Speakers: Grammar, Culture and Task/Function, Jour Am Asn of Tchrs of Korean, 98; auth, Passive and Middle Constructions in Korean, Jour of the Int Circle of Korean Ling, 98; auth, An Optimality-Theoretic Account of Korean Nominal Inflection: Selected Papers from the 11th International Conference on Korean Linguistics, Univ Hawaii, 98. **CONTACT ADDRESS** Dept of Asian Languages, Stanford Univ, Stanford, CA 94305. **EMAIL** sundy@leland.stanford.edu

SUNGOLOWSKY, JOSEPH

PERSONAL Born 12/21/1931, BEL, m, 1967, 2 children **DISCIPLINE** FRENCH LITERATURE **EDUCATION** Yeshiva Univ, BA, 55; NY Univ, MA, 58; Yale Univ, PhD, 63. **CAREER** Instr, Yale Univ; Asst Prof, Vassar Col; Assoc Prof, Queens Col, NY, 72-84, Prof, 84- **HONORS AND AWARDS** Chevalier dans l'Ordre des Palmes Adademiques, Fr Gov. **MEMBERSHIPS** Societe des Professeurs Francais, francophones en Amerique Assoc Internationale des Etudes sur Zola & le Naturalisme; Assn Int on Zola and Naturalism. **RESEARCH** Emile Zola, Stendhal, Edmond Fleg (1874-1963), French Jewish literature and thought. **SELECTED PUBLICATIONS** Auth, "Emile Zola et la condition juive," Excavatio 00; auth, "The Centennial of J'Accuse," Midstream 44.2 (98): 39-40; Auth, "Flaubert a-t-il prevu l'univers concentrationnaire?" Guerres Mondiales et Conflits Contemporains, 186 (97): 73-79; auth, Romain Gary and the Holocaust," European Judaism 28.54 (95): 48-52. **CONTACT ADDRESS** Dept of Europ Lang & Lit, Queens Col, CUNY, 6530 Kissena Blvd, Flushing, NY 11367-1575. **EMAIL** sungolowsky@aol.com

SURRIDGE, MARIE

PERSONAL Born London, England **DISCIPLINE** FRENCH STUDIES **EDUCATION** Oxford Univ, BA, 53, MA, 57, PhD, 62. **CAREER** Tchr, part-time, Oxford Univ, 55-67; asst prof, 70-77, assoc prof, 77-87, head Fr dept, 83-93, Prof, Queen's Univ, 87-. **SELECTED PUBLICATIONS** Auth, Le ou la? The Gender of French Nouns, 95. **CONTACT ADDRESS** Dept of French Studies, Queen's Univ at Kingston, Kingston, ON, Canada K7L 3N6.

SUSSMAN, HENRY

PERSONAL Born 02/10/1947, m, 2 children **DISCIPLINE** COMPARATIVE LITERATURE **EDUCATION** Brandeis Univ, BA; Johns Hopkins Univ, PhD. **CAREER** Fac hum ctr, Johns Hopkins Univ; Julian Park Prof Comp Lit, SUNY Buffalo, present. **HONORS AND AWARDS** Johns Hopkins Society of Scholars, 88 **MEMBERSHIPS** MLA, ACLA **RESEARCH** Critical Theory: Modernism & Postmodernism; Psychoanalysis; Frankfurt School. **SELECTED PUBLICATIONS** Auth, Afterimages of Modernity 90; High Resolution: Critical Theory and the Problem of Literacy, 89; The Hegelian Aftermath, 82; Franz Kafka: Geometrician of Metaphor, 79; The Aesthetic Contract: Statutes of Art and Intellectual Work in Modernity, Stanford, 97, Psyche and Text: The Sublime and the Grandiose in Literature, Psychopathology, and Culture, 93; The Trial: Kafka's Unholy Trinity, 93; co-ed, Psychoanalysis And©; auth, Engagement and Indifference: Beckett and the Political, 01; auth, The Aesthetic Contract, 97; auth, Kaflia's Unholy Trinity, 93; Psyche and Text, 93. **CONTACT ADDRESS** Dept Comp Lit, SUNY, Buffalo, 638 Clemens Hall, Buffalo, NY 14260. **EMAIL** hsussman@acsu.buffalo.edu

SUSSMAN, LEWIS ARTHUR

PERSONAL Born 06/26/1941, New York, NY, m, 1965 **DISCIPLINE** CLASSICS **EDUCATION** Princeton Univ, AB, 64; Univ NC, Chapel Hill, PhD(classics), 69. **CAREER** Asst prof classics, Univ CA, Irvine, 69-76, chm dept, 72-75; assoc prof classics, 76-94, prof, Univ FL, 94-,chm dept, 93-00; Univ FL Humanities Coun grant, 77; Nat Endowment for Humanities summer sem, Rome, 79. **MEMBERSHIPS** Am Philol Asn; Class Asn Mid West & South (secy-treas, 77-78). **RESEARCH** Ancient rhetoric; Ovid; Roman literature of the Augustan Age. **SELECTED PUBLICATIONS** Auth, Early imperial declamation: A Translation of the Elder Seneca's Prefaces, Speech Monogr, 6/70; The Artistic Unity of the Elder Seneca's First Preface & Controversiae as a Whole, Am J Philol, 4/71; The Elder Seneca's Discussion of the Decline of Roman Eloquence, CA Studies Class Antiq, 72; The Elder Seneca, E J Brill, 78; Latin and Basic Skills, Class J, 78; Arellius Fuscus and the Unity of Seneca's Suasoriae, Rheinisches Mus, 78; The Major Declamations Ascribed to Quintilian, Peter Lang, 87; The Declamations of Calpurnius Flaccus, E J Brill, 94. **CONTACT ADDRESS** Dept Classics, Univ of Florida, 3c Daver Hall, Gainesville, FL 32611-7435. **EMAIL** sussman@ufl.edu

SUTHERLAND, ELIZABETH H.

PERSONAL Born 07/05/1963, Princeton, NJ, m, 2000 **DISCIPLINE** CLASSICS **EDUCATION** Univ of Calif Berk, PhD, 94. **CAREER** Univ Calif Santa Cruz, lectr, 95; Univ Calif Irvine, lectr, 95-96; Univ Tenn Knoxville, asst prof, 96-. **MEMBERSHIPS** APA; CAMWS; TFLTA; TCA. **RESEARCH** Augustan poetry; feminist theory **SELECTED PUBLICATIONS** Auth, Visions and Desire in Horace's Carm 2.5, Helios, 97; auth, Audience Manipulation and Emotional Experience in Horace's Pyrrha Ode, AJP, 95; auth, Literary Women in Horace's Odes 2.11 and 2.12, forthcoming in Festschrift for WS Anderson. **CONTACT ADDRESS** Dept of Classics, Univ of Tennessee, Knoxville, 1101 McClung Tower, Knoxville, TN 37996. **EMAIL** ehsuther@utk.edu

SUTTON, DANA FERRIN

DISCIPLINE CLASSICS **EDUCATION** The New Sch for Soc Res, BA, 65; The Univ Wis, MA, 66, PhD, 70; postdoc, sr mem, Darwin Col, The Univ Cambridge, Eng, 72-74; postdoc res fel, The Univ Auckland, New Zealand, 74-75. **CAREER** Instr, Univ Minn, 67-68; tchg asst, Univ Wis, 68-69; lectr, Herbert Lehman Col, City Univ NY, 69-72; asst prof, Univ Ill, 75-79; asst prof, 79-81; assoc prof, 81-88; Prof, Univ Calif, Irvine, 88-. **HONORS AND AWARDS** Fel, John Simon Guggenheim Memorial Found, 75-76; Adele Mellen prize, Edwin Mellen Press, 96; grad prog dir, 80-83, 85-86, 94-96; ch, sch hum grants and travel comm, 84-85; act ch, dept classics, 85; dept ch, 86-94; sr admin off, s calif classics res sharing consortium, 90-92; ch, acad sen, 94. **MEMBERSHIPS** Am Philological Assn; Am Neo-Latin Assn; Calif Renaissance Soc; Calif Classics Assn. **RESEARCH** Greek and Latin poetry and drama; Anglo-Latin literature. **SELECTED PUBLICATIONS** Auth, Self and Society in ARitsophanes, Univ Press Am, 80; auth, The Dramaturgy of the Octavia, in Beitrage zur klassischen Philologie, Verlag Anton Hain, Konigstein/Taunus, 83; auth, The Lost Sophocles, Univ Press Am, 84; auth, The Satyr Play, in Cambridge History of Classical Literature I, 85; auth, Seneca on the Stage, in Mnemosyne, E. J. Brill, 86; auth, The Greek Dithyrambographers, Georg Olms Verlag, 89; auth, Thomas Legge: The Complete Plays, Peter Lang Verlag, 93; auth, Ancient Comedy: The Conflict of the Generations, in Twaynes' Literary Genres and Themes Series, Macmillan, 93; auth, The Catharsis of Comedy, in Greek Studies: Interdisciplinary Approaches, Rowman and Littlefield, 94; auth, William Gager: The Complete Works, Garland Press, 94; auth, Oxford Poetry by Richard Eedes and George Peele, Garland Press, 95; auth, The Complete Works of Thomas Watson (1556-1592), Edwin Mellen Press, 96; auth, The Complete Latin Poetry of William Savage Landor, Edwin Mellen Press, forthcoming. **CONTACT ADDRESS** Dept of Classics, Univ of California, Irvine, 120 HOB II, Irvine, CA 92697. **EMAIL** danas64562@aol.com

SUTTON, HOMER B.

PERSONAL Born 01/18/1949, Dalton, GA, m, 1973, 2 children **DISCIPLINE** FRENCH LANGUAGE AND LITERATURE **EDUCATION** Davidson Col, BA, 71; IN Univ, MA and PhD, 79. **CAREER** Fac, Sorbonne Nouvelle, 77-79; fac, Davidson Col, 81-; coord study abroad progs, 83-94; interim dean admissions, 91-92; Prof, 95. **HONORS AND AWARDS** NEH, 89, 99. **RESEARCH** French lang, lit, and civilization; hist of France and French soc since 1945. **SELECTED PUBLICATIONS** Auth, publ articles on French univ reform, changes in the FM band in France in the early 80's when Mitterrand liberalized the airwaves, and "harkis" allied with French during the Algerian struggle for independence. **CONTACT ADDRESS** Davidson Col, 102 N Main St, PO Box 1719, Davidson, NC 28036. **EMAIL** hosutton@davidson.edu

SUWARNO, PETER

DISCIPLINE LINGUISTICS, LANGUAGES, COMMUNICATION **EDUCATION** Satya Wacana Christian univ, BA, 85; Ohio Univ, MA, 87; PhD, 91. **CAREER** From asst prof to assoc prof, Ariz State Univ, 94-. **MEMBERSHIPS** Nat Commun Asn, Asn of Asian Studies, Coun of Teachers of Southeast Asian Lang, Consortium for the Teaching of Indonesian. **RESEARCH** Javanese and Komering in South Sumatra (Interethnic Communication in Ind.), Langage Teaching, Pedagogy and Rhetorical Analysis. **SELECTED PUBLICATIONS** Auth, Dictionary of Javanese Proverbs, Gajah Mada Univ Press; auth, "An Analysis of Habibie's Speeches," Asian J of Commun (96). **CONTACT ADDRESS** Dept Lang & Lit, Arizona State Univ, PO Box 870202, Tempe, AZ 85287-0202. **EMAIL** peter.suwarno@asu.edu

SWAFFAR, JANET KING

PERSONAL Born 04/28/1935, Minneapolis, MN, m, 1964, 2 children **DISCIPLINE** GERMAN, GERMAN LITERATURE **EDUCATION** Mankato State Teachers Col, BA, 56; Univ Wis, MA, 59, PbD, 65. **CAREER** From instr to asst prof, 65-71, assoc prof, 71-82, prof German, Univ Tex, Austin, 82-, dir, Nat Endowment for Humanities Prog grant, Univ Tex, 77-80. **HONORS AND AWARDS** Paul Pimsleur Awd, Am Coun Teaching Foreign Lang, 80; Guest FRG, 85; Univ Tex Centennial Teaching Awd, 87; Secy Navy Fel, 90; Pres Assoc Teaching Excellence Awd Univ Tx, 94. **MEMBERSHIPS** MLA; Am Asn Teachers Ger; Am Coun Teaching Foreign Lang. **RESEARCH** Modern Germany (east-west), foreign language acquistion, reading history. **SELECTED PUBLICATIONS** Coauth, Imitation and correction in foreign language learning, Mod Lang J, 12/71 & Educ Digest, 72; Literarische Zeitschriften 1945-70, Sammlung, Stuttgart, 74; Lenz viewed sane, Ger Rev, 74; The Ethics of Exploitation: Brecht's Der gute Mensch von Sezuan, University of Dayton Review, spring 79; Foreign Languages in the University: The Case for a Content Orientation for the Discipline, Monatshefte, Vol 73, 271-288; Reading in the Foreign Language Classroom: Focus on Process, Unterrichtspraxis, Vol 14, 176-194; (with Arens & Morgan), Teacher classroom practices: Redefining method as task hierarchy, Mod Lang J, Vol 66, 24-33; Using Foreign Languages to Learn: Rethinking the College Foreign Language Curriculum, Reflecting on Proficiency for the Classroom Perspective, Nat Textbook Co, 93; Reading and Listening Comprehension: Perspectives on Research and Implications for the Classroom, Research in Language Learning Principles, Processes, and Prospects, Nat Textbook Co, 93; Aesthetics and Gender: Anna Seghers as a Case Study, Monatshefte 87, 95; Institutional Mission and Academic Disciplines: Rethinking Accountability, J Gen Educ, 95; Instructor's Resource Manual for Treffpunkt Deutsch, 2 ed, Prentice Hall, 96; A Sequential Model for Video Viewing in the Foreign Language Curriculum, Mod Lang J, 97; Language on Line: Research and Pedagogy in ESL and L2, Daedalus Grp, 98. **CONTACT ADDRESS** Dept of German Lang, Univ of Texas, Austin, Austin, TX 78712-1026. **EMAIL** jswaffar@mail.utexas.edu

SWANSON, ROY ARTHUR

PERSONAL Born 04/07/1925, St. Paul, MN, m, 1946, 4 children **DISCIPLINE** PHILOLOGY, COMPARATIVE LITERATURE **EDUCATION** Univ of Minn, BA, 48; BS, 49; MA, 51; Univ of IL, PhD, 54. **CAREER** Instr, Ind Univ, 54-57, asst prof to prof, Univ of Minn, 57-65; prof, Macalester Col, 65-67; prof, Univ of Wis Milwaukee, 67-. **HONORS AND AWARDS** Alumni Distinguished Teaching Awd, Univ of Minn, 62;

Steiger Distinguished Teaching Awd, Univ of Wis Milwaukee, 74; Distinguished Teaching Awd, Univ of Wis Milwaukee, 74; Alumni Awd for Teaching Excellence, Univ of Wis Milwaukee, 99. **MEMBERSHIPS** Am Philol Assoc; MLA; Am Comp Lit Assoc; Soc for the Advan of Scandinavian Study; Int Com Lit Assoc. **RESEARCH** Green and Latin lyric poetry, Existentialism, Par Lagerkvist. **SELECTED PUBLICATIONS** Auth, Odi et Amo: The Complete Poetry of Catullus, 59; auth, Heart of Reason, 63; auth, Pindar's Odes, 74; auth, Par Lagerkvist: Five Early Works, 89. **CONTACT ADDRESS** Dept Fr Ital and Comp Lit, Univ of Wisconsin, Milwaukee, PO Box 413, Milwaukee, WI 53201-0413. **EMAIL** rexcy@uwm.edu

SWEETSER, MARIE-ODILE
PERSONAL Born 12/28/1925, Verdun, France, m, 1955, 1 child **DISCIPLINE** FRENCH LANGUAGE & LITERATURE **EDUCATION** Univ Nancy, Lic es Let, 44, dipl, 45; Bryn Mawr Col, MA, 50; Univ Pa, PhD, 56. **CAREER** Lectr French, McGill Univ, 50-52; asst instr, Univ Pa, 52-56; instr, Cedar Crest Col, 56-57 & Mills Col, 57-60; from instr to asst prof, City Coll New York, 60-69; assoc prof, 69-79, Prof French, Univ Ill, Chicago Circle, 79-, Chmn, Fourth Conf 17th Century French Lit, Corneille Symp, 72; exec comt MLA div French 17th century lit, 71-78; Nat Endowment for Humanities panelist, 80 & 81; consult, La Bd of Regents, 82. **MEMBERSHIPS** MLA; Am Asn Teachers Fr; Soc Prof Fr Am; Int Asn Fr Studies. **RESEARCH** French literature of the 17th century; theater, novel, literary criticism poetry; classical tradition in French literature. **SELECTED PUBLICATIONS** Auth, A Pact With Silence--Art and Thought In the Fables of Jean De Lafontaine, French Rev, Vol 66, 93; Moliere, Proceedings Of The Nottingham Moliere Confr, December-17-18, 93, Esprit Createur, Vol 36, 96; Jean De Lafontaine: Fables, French Rev, Vol 69, 96; Literature And Anthropology--Human-Nature And Character In The Classical-Age--French-, French Rev, Vol 69, 96; Madame De Sevigne and the Love Letter, French Rev, Vol 67, 94; The Commedia-Dellarte In Paris 1644-1697, French Rev, Vol 66, 93; Henriette-Dangleterre, Duchess Of Orleans, French Rev, Vol 70, 96; The Pastoral Masquerade--Disguise And Identity In L Astree, French Rev, Vol 68, 95. **CONTACT ADDRESS** Dept French, Univ of Illinois, Chicago, Chicago, IL 60680.

SWIFT, LOUIS JOSEPH
PERSONAL Born 08/01/1932, Scranton, PA, m, 1964, 3 children **DISCIPLINE** LATIN LITERATURE AND PATRISTICS **EDUCATION** St Mary's Univ, Md, AB, 54; Pontif Gregorian Univ, STB, 56; Johns Hopkins Univ, MAT, 58, PhD(classics), 63. **CAREER** Chmn, Univ of Kentucky, 70-76; assoc prof, Univ of Kentucky, 70-82; prof, Univ of Kentucky, 82-; dir, Univ Studies Program, 86-; dean, Undergraduate Studies, 90-. **MEMBERSHIPS** Am Philol Asn; Arch Archaeol Inst Am; Class Asn Mid West & South; NAm Patristic Soc; AAUP. **RESEARCH** Latin literature; pastristics; ancient rhetoric. **CONTACT ADDRESS** Dept of Classics and Lit, Univ of Kentucky, 1077 Patterson Office Tower 0027, Lexington, KY 40506-0003. **EMAIL** lswift@pop.uky.edu

SWIRSKI, PETER
DISCIPLINE COMPARATIVE LITERATURE **EDUCATION** McGill Univ, BA, 89; MA, 90; PhD, 96. **CAREER** Lectr, McGill Univ, 93-96; lectr, Concordia Univ, 96-97; lectr, McGill Univ, 98-99; lectr, Univ Toronto, 99-00; asst prof, Univ Albta, 00-. **HONORS AND AWARDS** SSFC, 98-01, 96-98; FCAR, 93-94; Humanities SSFC, Dean's Honor List, 96. **RESEARCH** 20th-century literature and culture; American literature and culture; popular fiction and genre theory; interdisciplinary studies in philosophy, science, cognitive sciences, analytic aesthetics and game theory; Stanislaw Lem; Arkady and Boris Strugatsky. **SELECTED PUBLICATIONS** Auth, "Game Theory In the Third Pentagon: A Study in Strategy and Rationality," Criticism 38 (96): 303-330; auth, A Stanislaw Reader, Northwestern Univ Pr, 97; auth, "Genres in Action: the Pragmatics of Literary Interpretation," Int Rev Lit Studies 52 (97): 141-156; auth, "Literature and Literary Knowledge," MLA 31 (98): 6-23; auth, "Stanislaw Lem," in Science Fiction Writers, ed. Richard Bleiler (Charles Scribner's and Sons, 99): 453-466; auth, "The Pleasures of Comparative Aesthetics," Can Rev Comp Lit 26 (99): 187-198; auth, "The Nature of Literary Fiction: From Carter to Spiegelman," MLA 33 (00): 58-73; auth, "In the Blink of an Eye: Games of Power in Y2K," auth, Dialogue/Universalism (00): 17-38; auth, Between Literature and Science: Poe, Lem and Explorations in Aesthetics, Cognitive Science and Literary Knowledge, McGill/Queen's Univ Pr and Liverpool Univ Pr, 00; auth, "Interpreting Art, Interpreting Literature," Int Rev Lit Studies 56 (01): 17-36. **CONTACT ADDRESS** English Dept, Univ of Alberta, 347 Arts Bldg, Edmonton, AB, Canada T6G 2E6. **EMAIL** pete.swirski@ualberta.ca

SWITTEN, MARGARET L.
PERSONAL m, 1950 **DISCIPLINE** FRENCH & PROVENCIAL LANGUAGE & LITERATURE **EDUCATION** Westminster Choir Col, BMus, 47; Barnard Col, BA, 48; Bryn Mawr Col, MA, 49, PhD(Fr), 52. **CAREER** From asst prof to assoc prof Music & French, Hampton Inst, 52-62, prof French, 62-63; Class of 1926 prof French, 63-; from asst prof to assoc prof, chmn dept, 69-76 & 82-83, prof French, Mt Holyoke Col, 63-, chmn dept, 82-, lectr, Smith Col, 66 & 68. **HONORS AND AWARDS** Fulbright Post-Doctoral Research Awd to Paris, 56-7; American Council of Learned Societies Fellowship, 69-70; Officier dans l'Ordre des Palmes Academiques. **MEMBERSHIPS** Am Asn Teachers Fr; Medieval Acad Am; MLA; Mod Humanities Res Am; Int Courtly Lit Asn. **RESEARCH** The poetry and the music of the Old Provencal troubadours; literature and society in 12th century France; medieval music. **SELECTED PUBLICATIONS** Auth, Diderot's theory of language as the medium of literature, 44: 185-196, L'Histoire and La Poesie in Diderot's writings on the novel, 47: 259-269 & Metrical and musical structure in the Songs of Peirol, 51: 241-255, Romanic Rev; Text and melody in Peirol's Cansos, Publ Mod Lang Asn, 86: 320-325; Raimon de Miraval's Be m'agrada and the unrhymed refrain in troubadour poetry, Romance Philol, 11: 432-448; The CanSos of Raimon de Miraval: A Study of Poems and Melodies, Med Acad Am; 85; Of the Comtessa and the Vilana: Women in Troubadour Song, forthcoming in Women and Music: A Journal of Gender and Culture, Fall, 98; Music and Versification: Fetz Marcabrus los mots e i so, in The Troubadours: An Introduction, forthcoming, Spring, 99. **CONTACT ADDRESS** 50 College St, South Hadley, MA 01075-1461. **EMAIL** mswitten@mtholyoke.edu

SYED, JASMIN
DISCIPLINE CLASSICS **EDUCATION** Staatsexamen, PhD, 91. **CAREER** Asst prof, Stanford Univ. **RESEARCH** Latin lit; Roman cult hist; lit theory; gender in the ancient world. **SELECTED PUBLICATIONS** Auth, The Construction of Roman Identity in Vergil's Aeneid; Creating Roman Identity: Subjectivity and Self-Fashioning in Latin Literature, 97. **CONTACT ADDRESS** Stanford Univ, Bldg 20, Main Quad, Stanford, CA 94305.

SYPHER, FRANCIS JACQUES
PERSONAL Born 11/04/1941, Hackensack, NJ, d, 1 child **DISCIPLINE** ENGLISH, COMPARATIVE LITERATURE **EDUCATION** Columbia Univ, AB, 63, MA, 64, PhD, 68. **CAREER** Precep, Eng, 65-68, Columbia Univ; asst prof, Eng, 68-75, SUNY, Albany; ed consul, 75-81, R.R. Bowker, NYU Press, & other publ; Fulbright Sr lectr, Amer lit, 81-83, Univ du Benin, Lome Togo, W Africa; asst to pres, 83-85, NY Schl of Inter Design, concurrent, adj prof, Eng, NY Univ; dir, 85-86, Amer Eng Lang Prog, Amer Cult Ctr, US Info Svc, Dakar Senegal, W Africa; Fulbright Sr Lectr, 86-88, Amer Lit, Univ Omar Bongo, Libreville Gabon, C Africa; writer, ed consul, 88-, NY. **HONORS AND AWARDS** NY St Regents Fel, 63-65; SUNY Res Found Awd, 74; Fulbright Sr Lectr, 81-83, 86-88; Pres Bronze Medal, 93, St Nicholas Soc NY. **MEMBERSHIPS** Art Stud League of NY; NY Genealogical and Biographical Soc; Friends of the Columbia Univ Lib. **RESEARCH** English & comparative lit; life and works of Letitia Elizabeth Landon, 1802-1838; NY history & biography. **SELECTED PUBLICATIONS** Auth, Stories of Africa, 89; ed, Works by Letitia Elizabeth Landon, 90-00; auth, The Yorkville Civic Council, 91; ed, The St. Nicholas Society, A 150 Year Record, 93; transl and ed, The Iskenius Letters, 94; ed, The Image of Irelande, Derricke, 98; ed, The Chronicle of the Society of Colonial Wars in the State of NY, 99; **CONTACT ADDRESS** FDR Station, PO Box 1125, New York, NY 10150-1125.

SZARYCZ, IRENEUSZ
DISCIPLINE RUSSIAN LITERATURE **EDUCATION** Kazan State Univ, BA; Adam Mickiewicz, Univ Poznan, MA; Univ Ottawa, PhD. **CAREER** Asst prof, Univ Wroclaw; Assoc prof, Univ of Waterloo. **HONORS AND AWARDS** Grant, Soc Scis and Humanities Res Coun of Canada. **MEMBERSHIPS** Waterloo Fac Assn; Can Asn of Slavists. **RESEARCH** Contemporary Russian literature; Russian folklore. **SELECTED PUBLICATIONS** Auth, Obraz nochi i vselennoi v tvorchestve Rainera Marii Rilke i Borisa L. Pasternaka, 95; Zatovarennaja bochkotara Vasiliia Aksenova: Stilisticheskii analiz odnogo abzatsa, Poznan, 95; Symbols of the National Past: Nibelungenlied and Slovo o polku Igoreve, 97. **CONTACT ADDRESS** Dept of German and Slavic, Univ of Waterloo, 200 University Ave W, Waterloo, ON, Canada N2L 3G1. **EMAIL** iszarycz@watarts.uwaterloo.ca

SZPEK, HEIDI M.
PERSONAL Born 09/27/1958, Milwaukee, WI, m, 1984, 2 children **DISCIPLINE** HEBREW STUDIES **EDUCATION** Univ of Wis, BA, 80, MA, 83, MA, 88, PhD, 91. **CAREER** Lectr, 80-84, 87-93, Concordia Univ Wis; lect, Univ Wis, Milwaukee, 93-97, Guest Lectr, Madison, Univ of Wis; adj fac, Pima Community Col W, Tucson, 98-00; guest lectr, Central Wash Univ, 00; assoc prof, Shoreline Community Col, 00-. **HONORS AND AWARDS** Grad Fel Univ Wis; Honor Soc Phi Beta Kappa; Liakon Awd. **MEMBERSHIPS** SBL, AAR, Phi Beta Kappa. **RESEARCH** Women in the bible, Peshitta studies, Ancient Language, Literature and Culture. **SELECTED PUBLICATIONS** Auth, "Translation Technique in the Peshitta to Job, A Model for Evaluating a Text with Documentation from the Peshitta to Job," in J of Biblical Lit Dissertation Series, Scholars Press, 92; co-ed & contribur, Women in the Hebrew Bible, A Literary Approach, Andrews Univ Press, forthcoming; "The Peshitta on Job 7:6, My days are swifter than an arg," JBL, 94; On the Influence of the Targum on the Peshittato Job, USF Stud in the Hist of Judaism, Atlanta GA, Scholars Press 98; An Observation of the Peshitta's Translation of Shaddai in Job, VT, 97; On the Influence of the Septuagint on the Peshitta to Job, CBQ, 99. **CONTACT ADDRESS** 1912 214th St SW, Lynnwood, WA 98036. **EMAIL** hszpek@aol.com

T

TABOADA, MARIA
PERSONAL Born 02/24/1970, Madrid, Spain **DISCIPLINE** LINGUISTICS **EDUCATION** Univ Complutense, MA, 93, PhD, 01; Carnegie Mellon Univ, MSc, 97. **CAREER** Vis asst prof, Univ Complutense, 97-98; lectr, Univ Albta, 99-00; chief scientiest, MindfulEye Systems, 00-01; vis asst prof, Simon Fraser Univ, 01-. **MEMBERSHIPS** MLA, LACUS, Ling Soc of Am, Int Systemic Functional Ling Asn, Can Asn of Hispanists, Can Asn of Ling, Can Asn of Applied Ling, Asn for Computational Ling. **SELECTED PUBLICATIONS** Coauth, "Dialogue Processing in a Conversational Speech Translation Program," Proceedings of the 1996 Int Symp on Spoken Dialogue, (96): 177-182; auth, Improving Translation through Contextual Information," Proceedings of the 35th Annual Meeting of the Asn for Computational Ling, (97): 510-512; coauth, "Expanding the Domain of a Multilingual Speech-to-Speech Translation System," Proceedings of the Spoken Lang Transl Workshop(97): 67-72; auth, "Corpus-Based Methods in Language and Speech Processing," Corpus-Based Methods in Language and Speech Processing, eds S Young and G Bloothooft, (98: auth, "Cohesion as a Measure in Generic Analysis, LACUS Forum XXVI, eds A Melby and A Lommel, (00):35-49; auth, "A General Description for the Structure of Conversation: A Hopeless Task," Panorama Actual de la Linguistica Aplicada: Conocimiento, (01); auth, "Rhetorical Relations in Dialogue: A Contrastive Study,"; auth, "Rhetorical Relations in Dialogue: A Contrastive Study," Discourse Across Languages and Cultures, eds CL Moder and A Martinovic-Zic, (01). **CONTACT ADDRESS** Dept Ling, Simon Fraser Univ, Burnaby, BC, Canada V5A 1S6. **EMAIL** maite.taboada@primus.ca

TAGGE, ANNE
PERSONAL Born Naples, Italy, m, 1953, 2 children **DISCIPLINE** ARTS, SCIENCES **EDUCATION** Wellesley Col, BA, 53; Baylor Univ, MA, 64. **CAREER** Prof, Lasell Col, 65-. **HONORS AND AWARDS** Phi Beta Kappa; Durant Schl, 52, 53. **MEMBERSHIPS** Jane Austen Soc NA. **RESEARCH** Conrad's Malay fiction. **SELECTED PUBLICATIONS** Auth, " Jane Austen and the Raja of Sarawak," Persuasions (93); auth, "The Butterfly Hunters," Conradiana (96); auth, "A Glimpse of Paradise: Feminine Impulse and Ego," in Conrad's Malay Fiction, Conradiana (97); auth, "Hatton's Folly: Assaulting 'This Eden of the Eastern Wave'," J Malaysian Br RAS (97). **CONTACT ADDRESS** Dept Arts Sci, Lasell Col, 1844 Commonwealth Ave, Auburndale, MA 02466-2709.

TAHARA, MILDRED MACHIKO
PERSONAL Born 05/15/1941, Hilo, HI **DISCIPLINE** CLASSICAL & MODERN JAPANESE LITERATURE **EDUCATION** Univ Hawaii, Manoa, BA, 63, MA, 65; Columbia Univ, PhD(Japanese Lit), 69. **CAREER** Asst prof, 69-76, Assoc Prof Japanese Lit, Univ Hawaii, Manoa, 76-. **MEMBERSHIPS** Asn Asian Studies; Asn Teachers Japanese; Mod Lang Assoc. **RESEARCH** Heian literature; modern and contemporary novels and short stories; classical poetry; image and text. **SELECTED PUBLICATIONS** Auth, Heichu, As Seen in Yamato Monogatari, 71 & Yamato Monogatari: A Poem-tale of Heian Japan, 72, Monumenta Nopponica; Genji monogatari: Heian loves, Orientations, 12/72; The ink stick (short story), Japan Quart, Vol 22, No 4; Fujiwara Michinaga, In: Great Historical Figures of Japan, Japan Cult Inst, 78; auth & transl, Tales of Yamato, Univ Hawaii Press, 80; transl, Ariyoshi Sawako, The River Ki, Kodansha Int, 80, trans, Ariyoshi Sawako, The Twilight Years, Kodansha Int, 84. **CONTACT ADDRESS** Dept of East Asian Lit, Univ of Hawaii, Manoa, 1890 E West Rd, Honolulu, HI 96822-2318. **EMAIL** tahara@hawaii.edu

TALBOT, EMILE
PERSONAL Born 04/12/1941, Brunswick, ME, m, 1966, 2 children **DISCIPLINE** FRENCH **EDUCATION** St Francis Col, BA, 63; Brown Univ, MA, 65, PhD(French), 68. **CAREER** From instr to asst prof, 67-73, assoc prof French, Univ Ill, Urbana, 73-86; prof French and Comparative Literature, 86-; head dept French, 88-94. **HONORS AND AWARDS** Fel, Ctr Advan Studies, Univ Ill, 73; Nat Endowment for Humanities younger humanist fel, 73-74; Camargo Found fel, 77; distinguished vis prof, Eastern Ill Univ, Summer, 81; recipient, Palmes academiques from French government, 98. **MEMBERSHIPS** MLA; Am Asn Teachers Fr; Asn for Can Studies US; American Council for Quebec Studies, vp 95-97, pres, 97-99. **RESEARCH** 19th Century French; criticism; French Canadian literature. **SELECTED PUBLICATIONS** Auth, La Critique stendhalienne de Balzac a Zola, York, SC: French Literature Publications, (79): 273; auth, Stendhal and Romantic Esthetics, Lexington: French Forum Monographs, (85): 181; auth, Stendhal Revisited, Twayne World Authors Series, 839, New York:

Twayne, (93): 171; auth, "Nelligan et la poetique des tombeaux," in Emile Nellilgan: Cinquante ans apres sa mort, ed. Yolande Grise et al, (Montreal: Fides, 93): 327-37; auth, Anne Hebert's la file maigre: Gendering Poetics," Studies in Canadian Literature/Etudes en litterature canadienne 20.1, (95): 80-92; auth, "Proletarian Poetics in the 1930s: Clement Marchand's Les Soirs rouges," Am Review of Canadian Studies 26, (96): 101-14; auth, "Reading Ambiguity: Violence, Character, and Change in Jacques Godbout's Une histoire americaine," Dalhousie French Studies 36, (96): 135-43; auth, "Stendhal [Henri Beyle]," Encyclopedia of the Novel, Chicago: Fitzroy Deaborn, 98; auth, "Literature and Ideology in the Thirties: Fictional representations of Communism in Quebec," International Journal of Canadian Studies 20, (99): 53-66; auth, "Serge Patrice Thibodeau: Conjugating the Sensual and the Spritual," World Literature Today 73, (99): 261-68. **CONTACT ADDRESS** Dept of French, Univ of Illinois, Urbana-Champaign, 707 S Mathews Ave, Urbana, IL 61801-3625. **EMAIL** ejtalbot@uiuc.edu

TALL, EMILY
PERSONAL Born 05/22/1940, New York, NY **DISCIPLINE** RUSSIAN **EDUCATION** Cornell Univ, BA, 61; Middlebury Col, MA, 67; Brown Univ, PhD(Slavic lang & lit), 74. **CAREER** Asst prof, 73-80, Assoc Prof Russ, State Univ NY Buffalo, 80-. **MEMBERSHIPS** Am Asn Teachers Slavic & EEurop Lang; Am Asn Advan Slavic Studies; Am Coun Teachers Russ. **RESEARCH** Russian language teaching; Soviet literary criticism; Soviet literature. **SELECTED PUBLICATIONS** Auth, Selected Songs of Vladimir Vysotsky, 92; auth, James Joyce and the Russians, Slavic E Europ J, Vol 37, 93; auth, auth, Let's Talk About Life: An Integrated Approach to Russian Conversation, 96. **CONTACT ADDRESS** SUNY, Buffalo, Buffalo, NY 14260. **EMAIL** mllemily@acsu.buffalo.edu

TAMBURRI, ANTHONY J.
PERSONAL Born 07/24/1949, Stamford, CT, m, 2000 **DISCIPLINE** ITALIAN, COMPARATIVE LITERATURE **EDUCATION** Southern Conn State Col, BS, 71; Middlebury Col, MA, 72; Univ Calif Berkeley, PhD, 81. **CAREER** Instr, Smith Col, 81-83; asst prof, Middlebury Col, 84-86; asst prof, Auburn Univ, 86-87; prof, Purdue Univ, 87-00. **HONORS AND AWARDS** Ital-Am Fel, 78-79; NEH 89; Fondazione Giovanni Agnelli Found, 89; Nat Ital Found Fel, 90, 92-96; Purdue Res Found Grant, 95-00; Sonia Raiziss-Giop Found Fel, 96-; Distinguished Alumnus, Southern Conn State Univ, 00. **MEMBERSHIPS** MLA, Semiotics Soc of Am, Am Assoc of Teachers of Ital, Am Ital Hist Assoc, Am Assoc of Ital Studies, Ital/Am Writers Assoc, SAMLA, Multi-Ethnic Lit of the US. **RESEARCH** 19th and 20th Century Italian Literature, Italian/America studies (literature and cinema), Modernism/Postmodernism/the Avant-Gardes, Comparative Literature, Semiotics. **SELECTED PUBLICATIONS** Auth, Of 'Saltimbanchi' and 'Incendiari': Aldo Palazzeschi and Avant-Gardism in Italy, Fairleith Dickinson Univ Pr, (90); auth, "To Hyphenate or not to Hyphenate: the Italian/American Writier: Or, An Other American?" Guernica Editions, (91); auth, Per una lettura retrospettiva. Prose giovanili di aldo Palazzeschi, Gradiva Publ, 94; auth, A Reconsideration of Aldo Palazzeschi's Poetry, Edwin Mellen Pr, 98; coed, Beyond the Margin: Readings in Italian Americana, Fairleigh Dickinson Univ Pr, 98; auth, A Semiotic of Ethnicity: In (Re)cognition of the Italian/American Writer, SUNY Pr, 98; auth, A Semiotic of Re-reading: Italo Calvino's 'Snow Job', Chancery Pr, 99; coed, From the Margin: Writings in Italian Americana, Purdue Univ Pr, 00; coed, L'etnia celluloide: la rappresentizione cinematografica degli italoamericana negli Stati Uniti, Luca Sossella Editore, 01; auth, Italian/American Short Films and Video: A Semiotic Reading, Purdue Univ Pr, 01. **CONTACT ADDRESS** Dept Lang and Ling, Florida Atlantic Univ, Boca Raton, FL 33431. **EMAIL** atamburri@fau.edu

TAMINIAUX, PIERRE S.
PERSONAL Born 03/19/1958, Brussels, Belgium, m, 1999 **DISCIPLINE** FRENCH STUDIES **EDUCATION** Univ Libre Bruxelles, BA, 81; Univ Calif Santa Barb, MA, 86; Univ Calif Berkeley, PhD, 90. **CAREER** Asst prof, Miami Univ, 90-91; asst to assoc prof, Georgetown Univ, 91-. **HONORS AND AWARDS** FLL Res Grant, 95, 99; Belgian Am Educ Found. **MEMBERSHIPS** MLA; SCS. **RESEARCH** 20th century French literature and culture; literature and the visual arts; cultural and national identities film. **SELECTED PUBLICATIONS** Auth, Robert Pinget, Le Seuil, 94; auth, Spectres de Nations, 96; auth, Sacred Text/Scared Nation, Camden House, 96; auth, The Show Must Not Go On, Lignes, 97; auth, "Nation et Insurrection," Les Temps Mod (97; auth, Poetique de la Negation, L'Harmattan, 98; auth, Faire Ou Ne Pas Faire: Telle N'est Pas la Question, Jean-Michel Place, 00; auth, Pour une Poetique Cinematographique de la Lecture, L'Harmattan, 01. **CONTACT ADDRESS** Fr Dept, Georgetown Univ, Washington, DC 20057. **EMAIL** taminiap@gunet.georgetown.edu

TANDY, DAVID
PERSONAL Born 04/19/1950, New York, NY, 2 children **DISCIPLINE** CLASSICAL PHILOLOGY **EDUCATION** Yale, PhD, 79 **CAREER** Distinguished Prof in Humanities, Univ TN, 98-; Asst Prof, 80-pres, Univ of TN **MEMBERSHIPS** Am Philol Assoc; Econ Hist Assoc; Karl Polanyi Inst of Polit Econ **RESEARCH** Forms of Domination & Resistance in the Classical World; Social & Economic History of Ancient Greece & Rome **SELECTED PUBLICATIONS** Auth, Warriors into Traders, Univ of CA, 97 **CONTACT ADDRESS** Dept of Classics, Univ of Tennessee, Knoxville, Knoxville, TN 37996-0413. **EMAIL** dtandy@utk.edu

TANG, CHENXI
PERSONAL Born 01/20/1968, Henan, China, m, 1998 **DISCIPLINE** LITERATURE, LINGUISTICS, GERMAN STUDIES **EDUCATION** Fudan Univ, BA, 87; Ludwig Max Univ, MA, 93; Columbia Univ, PhD, 00. **CAREER** Asst prof, Univ Chicago. **HONORS AND AWARDS** Whiting Found Fel; DAAD Fel; Dan Res Acad Fel. **MEMBERSHIPS** MLA; ACLA; Herdes-Ges. **RESEARCH** European enlightenment; German literature; Kierkegaard. **CONTACT ADDRESS** Ger Studies Dept, Univ of Chicago, 1050 E 59th St, Chicago, IL 60637-1559. **EMAIL** tang@midway.uchicago.edu

TANNEN, DEBORAH F.
PERSONAL Born Brooklyn, NY **DISCIPLINE** LINGUISTICS, MODERN GREEK LITERATURE **EDUCATION** State Univ NYork, Binghamton, BA, 66; Wayne State Univ, MA, 70; Univ Calif, Berkeley, MA, 76, PhD, 79. **CAREER** Instr English, Mercer County Community Col, 70-71; lectr acad skills, Lehman Col, City Univ New York, 71-74; asst prof Ling, 79-85, univ prof, 91-, Georgetown Univ, Rockefeller Humanities fel, Rockefeller Foundation, 82-83. **MEMBERSHIPS** Ling Soc Am; Mod Greek Studies Asn; Am Anthrop Asn; MLA; Am Asn App Ling; Intl Pragmatics Asn. **RESEARCH** Discourse analysis; cross-cultural communication. **SELECTED PUBLICATIONS** Auth, The Argument Culture: Moving from Debate to Dialogue, Random House, 98; Talking from 9 to 5: Women and Men in the Workplace: Language, Sex, and Power, Avon, 95; Gender & Discourse, Oxford, 94; You Just Don't Understand: Women and Men in Conversation, Ballantine, 90; ed, Framing in Discourse, Oxford, 93; Gender and Conversational Interaction, Oxford, 93; Linguistics in Context: Connecting Observation and Understanding, Ablex, 88. **CONTACT ADDRESS** Linguistics Dept, Georgetown Univ, Box 571051, Washington, DC 20057-1051. **EMAIL** robinsda@gunet.georgetown.edu

TAPPY, RON E.
DISCIPLINE NEAR EASTERN LANGUAGES AND CIVILIZATIONS **EDUCATION** Harvard Univ, PhD, 90. **CAREER** Res assoc, Harvard Univ, 90-91; vis asst prof, Univ Mich, 90-92; assoc prof, Westmont Col, 92-. **RESEARCH** Archaeology of Ancient Syria-Palestine; Biblical Archaeology **SELECTED PUBLICATIONS** Auth, Samaria, Encycl Near Eastern Archaeol, Oxford UP, 96; Review of Ancient Jerusalem Revealed, Jour of Near Eastern Stud, 96; Did the Dead Ever Die in Biblical Judah, Bulletin of the Amer Sch of Oriental Res, 95; Psalm 23: Symbolism and Structure, The Cath Bibl Quart, 95; Ahab, Hazor, Megiddo, The Oxford Companion to the Bible, Oxford UP, 93. **CONTACT ADDRESS** Dept of Rel, Westmont Col, 955 La Paz Rd, Santa Barbara, CA 93108-1099. **EMAIL** tappy@westmont.edu

TARAN, LEONARDO
PERSONAL Born 02/22/1933, Galarza, Argentina, m, 1971, 1 child **DISCIPLINE** CLASSICS, ANCIENT PHILOSOPHY **EDUCATION** Princeton Univ, PhD, 62. **CAREER** Fel res, Inst Res Humanities, Univ Wis, 62-63; jr fel res, Ctr Hellenic Studies, 63-64; asst prof classics, Univ Calif, Los Angeles, 64-67; assoc prof, 67-71, chmn dept, 76-79, Prof, 71-87, Jay Prof Greek & Latin Langs, Columbia Univ, 87-; Am Philos Soc grant, 63, 71 & 75; fel Am Coun Learned Soc, 66-67, 71-72; Guggenheim Found fel, 75; mem Inst Advan Study, Princeton, 66-67 & 78-79; NEH fee. 1986-87. **MEMBERSHIPS** Am Philol Asn; Soc Ancient Greek Philos. **RESEARCH** Ancient philosophy; Greek literature. **SELECTED PUBLICATIONS** Auth, Parmenides, Princeton Univ, 65; Asclepius of Tralles: Commentary to Nicomachus' introduction to arithmetic, Am Philos Soc, 69; The creation myth in Plato's Timaeus, in Essays in Greek Philosophy, State Univ NY, 71; coauth, Eraclito, testimonianze e imitazioni, La Nuova Italia Editrice, 72; auth, Academica: Plato, Philip of Opus and the Pseudo-Platonic Epinomis, Am Philos Soc Memoirs, 75; Anonymous Commentary on Aristotle's de Interpretatione, Anton Hain, 78; Speusippus and Aristotle on homonymy and synonymy, Hermes, 106: 73-99; Speusippus of Athens, Leiden, Brill, 81. **CONTACT ADDRESS** Dept of Classics, Columbia Univ, 2960 Broadway, New York, NY 10027-6900. **EMAIL** lt1@columbia.edu

TARICA, RALPH
PERSONAL Born 09/09/1932, Atlanta, GA, m, 1964, 2 children **DISCIPLINE** FRENCH LITERATURE **EDUCATION** Emory Univ, BA, 54, MA, 58; Harvard Univ, PhD, 66. **CAREER** Instr mod lang, Ga Inst Technol, 58-60; from instr to asst prof French, Brandeis Univ, 63-69; from assoc prof to prof French, Univ MD, College Park, 69-. **HONORS AND AWARDS** French Academic Palmes, 94. **MEMBERSHIPS** MLA; S Atlantic Mod Lang Asn. **RESEARCH** Modern French literature; the novel; stylistics. **SELECTED PUBLICATIONS** Contrib, Image and Theme in Modern French Fiction, Harvard Univ, 69; auth, The Child Motif in Malraux's fiction, Malraux Miscellany, 78; Imagery in the Novels of Andr¤ Malraux, Fairleigh Dickinson, 80; Les signes de l'anxiete dans les romans de Malraux, Berenice, 83; contribr, Witnessing Andr¤ Malraux: Visions and Re-Visions, Wesleyan Univ, 84; Antoine de Saint-Exupery, Scribner's, 90. **CONTACT ADDRESS** Dept of French and Ital, Univ of Maryland, Col Park, College Park, MD 20742-4821. **EMAIL** 102535.2017@compuserve.com

TARKOW, THEODORE A.
DISCIPLINE CLASSICAL STUDIES **EDUCATION** Oberlin Col, AB, 66; Univ Mich, MA, 67; Univ Mich, PhD, 71. **CAREER** Asst prof to prof, class studies, Univ Mo Columbia, 70-; assoc dean, col of arts and sci; Univ Mo Columbia, 82-. **HONORS AND AWARDS** Woodrow Wilson fel, 67; Amer Philos Asn award for excellence in teaching of the classics, 81; pres, Class Asn of Middlewest & South, 87. **MEMBERSHIPS** Amer Philol Asn; Archaeol Inst of Amer; Class Asn of Middlewest & South. **RESEARCH** Greek comedy & tragedy; Greek lyric poetry. **SELECTED PUBLICATIONS** Auth, Scan of Orestes, Rheinisches Mus fur Philol, 124; auth, Ainthes & the ghost of Aeschylus in Aristophanes Frogs, Traditio, 38; auth, Tyrtaeus 9D, L'antiquite Classique, 52; auth, Sight & Seeing in the Prometheus Board, Eranus, 89. **CONTACT ADDRESS** Univ of Missouri, Columbia, 317 Lowry Hall, Columbia, MO 65211. **EMAIL** tarkowt@missouri.edu

TARRANT, RICHARD JOHN
PERSONAL Born 04/04/1945, New York, NY, m, 1968 **DISCIPLINE** CLASSICS **EDUCATION** Fordham Univ, BA, 66; Oxford Univ, DPhil, 72. **CAREER** From lectr to prof classics, Univ Toronto, 70-82; Prof Greek & Latin, Harvard Univ, 82-, Rev ed, Phoenix, Class Asn Can, 75-78, ed, 78-82. **MEMBERSHIPS** Am Philol Asn; Class Asn; Class Asn Can. **RESEARCH** Greek and Latin drama; Latin poetry; textual criticism. **SELECTED PUBLICATIONS** Auth, Greek and Latin Lyric Poetry in Translation, Am Philol Asn, 72; ed & auth, Seneca, Agamemnon, Cambridge Univ, 76; auth, Senecan drama and its antecedents, 78, The addressee of Virgil's eighth eclogue, 78 & Aeneas and the gates of sleep, 82, Harvard Studies Class Philol. **CONTACT ADDRESS** Dept of Greek & Latin, Harvard Univ, 319 Boylston Hall, Cambridge, MA 02138-3800.

TATAR, MARIA
PERSONAL Born 05/13/1945, Germany, d, 2 children **DISCIPLINE** GERMAN **EDUCATION** Denison Univ, BA, 67; Princeton Univ, MA, 69; PhD, 71. **CAREER** Asst prof to prof, Harvard Univ, 71-. **HONORS AND AWARDS** NEH Fac Fel, 74-75; Carnegie Fel, 78-80; Alexander von Humboldt Fel, 85-86; NEH Grant, 88; Ger Studies Book Awd, 92; Ger Studies Syllabus Awd, 95; Guggenheim Found Fel, 99. **MEMBERSHIPS** MLA; Ger Studies Assoc; Am Assoc of Teachers of Ger. **SELECTED PUBLICATIONS** Auth, Spellbound: Studies on Mesmerism and Literature, Princeton Univ Pr, 78; auth, The Hard Facts of the Grimms' Fairy Tales, Princeton Univ Pr, 87; auth, Off with Their Heads! Fairy Tales and the Culture of Childhood, Princeton Univ Pr, 92; ed, Neverending Stories: Toward a Critical Narratology, Princeton Univ Pr, 92; auth, Lustmord: Sexual Violence in Weimar Germany, Princeton Univ Pr, 95; ed, Grimms' Grimmest, Continuum, NY, 95; auth, The Classic Fairy Tales, WW Norton, (NY), 99. **CONTACT ADDRESS** Dept Ger Lang and Lit, Harvard Univ, Boylston Hall, Cambridge, MA 02138. **EMAIL** tatar@fax.harvard.edu

TATE, PAUL DEAN
PERSONAL Born 11/22/1945, Fort Worth, TX, m, 1976 **DISCIPLINE** PHILOSOPHY, SANSKRIT **EDUCATION** Univ Tex, Austin, BA, 67; Yale Univ, MPhil, 74, PhD, 76. **CAREER** Dean of Grad Studies, Idaho State Univ **MEMBERSHIPS** Am Philos Assn. **RESEARCH** The philosophy of Martin Heidegger; the nature of language; Indian philosophy. **SELECTED PUBLICATIONS** Auth, His Holiness Gives an Example, Kite Bks, 73; auth, The Agivtic Hotel, Latitude Press, 87. **CONTACT ADDRESS** Idaho State Univ, 921 S 8th Ave, Box 8399, Pocatello, ID 83209-0001. **EMAIL** tatepaul@isu.edu

TATLOCK, LYNNE
PERSONAL Born 10/24/1950, Clinton, IN, m, 1988 **DISCIPLINE** GERMAN LITERATURE **EDUCATION** Ind Univ, BA, 71, MA, 75, PhD, 81. **CAREER** Asst prof, 81-87, assoc prof, 87-94, PROF, 94-, dept chair, 92-97, 00-, Wash Univ. **HONORS AND AWARDS** Distinguish Fac Awd, Wash Univ, 99; StADad grants 98-01; Translation Subvention, InterNationes; GAANN; NE Fel 90-91; Am Philo Sic Summer grant 86; ACLS, summer grant 86; DAAD, summer grant, 84; Teaching Awd, Coun of Students of Arts and Sci at Wash Univ, 84. **MEMBERSHIPS** MLA, Midwest MLA, Women in German, SGRABL, North Am Heine Soc, Am Asn of Teachers of German, German Studies Asn,, Grimmeshausen Geselleschaft, Schnabel Gesellschaft, Fr he Neuzeit Interdisziplin,,r, Am Friends of the Herzog-August-Bibliothek, Forum Vorm,,rz Forschung. **RESEARCH** German literature and culture, especially 1650-1730 and 1800-1914, the novel, gender, literature and medicine, translation. **SELECTED PUBLICATIONS** The Graph of Sex and the German Text: Gendered Culture in Early

Modern Germany 1500-1700, Chole, Beihefte zum Daphnis 19, Amsterda: Ridopi, 94; auth, From a Good Family, Columbia, SC: Camden House, 99; Their Pavel (Das Gemeindekind), Columbia, SC: Camden House, 96; auth, Regional History as National History: Gustac Freytag's Bilder aus der deutschen Vergangenheit, Searching for Common Ground: Diskurse zur deutschen Identit,,t 1750-1871, K''ln: B''halu: 00, 161-78; auth, Our Correspondent in Weimar: Gabriele Reuter and The New York Times, German Studies Rev 22-3, 99, 369-84; auth, Disease and Communion in Wilhelm Raabe's Unruhigh G,,ste, Monatshefte 91.3, 99, 323-41; auth, Scientia divinorum: Anatomy, Transmutation, and Incorporation in Catharina Regina von Greiffenberg's Meditations on Incarnation the Gestation of Christ, German Hist 17.1, 99, 9-24; auth, Carnal Knowledge and the Populating of Paradise: J B Schnabel's 'Insel Felsenburg, Knowledge, Science, and Literature, Chapel Hill: Univ of NC Pr, 96, 262-285; auth, The Marshall Plan at the Movies: Marlene Dietrich and her Incarnations, German Quarterly 65. 3-4, 92, 429-42; auth, Speculum feminarum: Gendered Perspectives on Gynecology and Obstetrics in Early Modern Germany, Signs: Journal fo Women in Culture and Society, 17.4, 92, 725-60. **CONTACT ADDRESS** Washington Univ, 1 Brookings Dr, Box 1104, Saint Louis, MO 63130. **EMAIL** ltatlock@artsci.wustl.edu

TAYLOR, ALLAN ROSS
PERSONAL Born 12/24/1931, Palisade, CO, m, 1958, 5 children **DISCIPLINE** LINGUISTICS **EDUCATION** Univ Colo, Boulder, BA, 53; Univ Calif, Berkeley, PhD(ling), 69. **CAREER** Teaching assoc Russ, Univ Calif, Berkeley, 58-61, lectr, 61-62; from instr to assoc profling, 64-77, Prof Ling, Univ Colo, Boulder, 77-, Consult, MLA, 65-66; mem Russ listening comprehension comt, Col Entrance Exam Bd, Educ Testing Serv, Princeton, NJ, 66-71; dir Lakhota proj, Nat Endowment for Humanities grant, 72-75; asst dir, Siouan Lang Archives, Nat Endowment for the Humanities, 78; dir, Gros Ventre Dict, Nat Endowment for Humanities grants, 80. **MEMBERSHIPS** Ling Soc Am; Am Anthrop Asn. **RESEARCH** American Indian languages; applied linguistics. **SELECTED PUBLICATIONS** Auth, The Classification of the Caddoan Languages, Proc Am Philos Soc, 63; Comparative Caddoan, 63 & On verbs of motion in Siouan languages, 76, Int J Am Ling; Nonverbal Communications Systems in Native North America, Semiotica, 74; Nonverbal Communication in Aboriginal North America: The Plains Sign Language, Plenum, 78; co-auth, Languages of the plains & A grammar of Lakhota, In: Handbook of North American Indians, Smithsonian Inst, (in press). **CONTACT ADDRESS** Dept of Ling, Univ of Colorado, Boulder, Boulder, CO 80309.

TAYLOR, DANIEL JENNINGS
PERSONAL Born 09/01/1941, Covington, KY, m, 1966, 2 children **DISCIPLINE** CLASSICS, LINGUISTICS **EDUCATION** Lawrence Col, BA, 63; Univ Wash, MA, 65, PhD(classics), 70. **CAREER** From instr to asst prof classics, Univ Ill, Urbana, 68-74; asst prof, 74-78, Assoc Prof Classics, Lawrence Univ, 78-, Chmn Dept, 75-, Actg vpres & dean for Campus life, Lawrence Univ, 77-78, 79-80; Nat Endowment for Humanities fel, 80-81. **MEMBERSHIPS** Am Philol Asn; Am Class League; Archaeological Inst Am. **RESEARCH** Syntax of Greek and Latin; history of linguistics; Varro. **SELECTED PUBLICATIONS** Auth, Rationalism in language learning, Asn Dept Foreign Lang Bull,.72; Aspects of negation in classical Greek, Studies Ling Sci, 72; Declinatio: A Study of the Linguistic Theory of MT Varro, Amsterdam: John Benjamins, 74; Varro, De Lingua Latina, 76 & Two notes on Varro, 77, Am J of Philol; Varro's mathematical models of inflection, Trans & Proc Am Philol Asn, 77; Ordo in book ten of Varro's De Lingua Latina, Melanges Collart, 78; Palaemon's Pig, Historiographia Linguistica, 81. **CONTACT ADDRESS** 115 S Drew St, Appleton, WI 54911-5798.

TAYLOR, JON
PERSONAL Born 06/30/1938, Gays Mills, WI, 1938 children **DISCIPLINE** HEBREW SCRIPTURES **EDUCATION** Pontifical Bibl Inst, SSL, 70. **CAREER** Prof Relig, Univ Great Falls, 85-. **MEMBERSHIPS** CBA; AAR; SBL; ASOR; HIART. **RESEARCH** Science and religion. **CONTACT ADDRESS** 1301 20th St S, Great Falls, MT 59405. **EMAIL** jtaylor01@ugf.edu

TAYLOR, RICHARD A.
PERSONAL Born 03/25/1944, Sikeston, MO, m, 1969, 2 children **DISCIPLINE** SEMITIC LANGUAGES **EDUCATION** Cath Univ Am, PhD, 90. **CAREER** Prof of Old Testament Studies, Dallas Theol Sem, 89-. **MEMBERSHIPS** Am Orient Soc; Soc Bibl Lit; Int Orgn Septuagint & Cognate Studies; Int Asn Coptic Studies; Evangelical Theol Soc; Inst Bibl Res; Nat Asn Prof Hebrew. **RESEARCH** Text criticism of Hebrew Bible; Ancient versions of the Bible; Syriac patristics; Semitic philology. **SELECTED PUBLICATIONS** Auth, The Peshitta of Daniel, Monographs of the Peshitta Institute, 94. **CONTACT ADDRESS** Dept of Old Testament Studies, Dallas Theol Sem, 3909 Swiss Ave., Dallas, TX 75204. **EMAIL** rick_taylor@dts.edu

TAYLOR, STEVEN MILLEN
PERSONAL Born 06/13/1941, Detroit, MI, m, 1973, 3 children **DISCIPLINE** FRENCH MEDIEVAL LITERATURE **EDUCATION** Wayne State Univ, PhD(French), 76. **CAREER** Asst prof 78-85; Assoc Prof Medieval French, Coordinator Med. Studies, Marquette Univ 85-. **HONORS AND AWARDS** Phi Betta Kappa; Palmes Academiques. **MEMBERSHIPS** Medieval Academy; AATF; MLA; SPFFA; Societe Rencevals. **RESEARCH** French medieval literature; African francophone cinema. **SELECTED PUBLICATIONS** 21 articles in refereed journals. **CONTACT ADDRESS** Dept For Lang & Lit, Marquette Univ, P O Box 1881, Milwaukee, WI 53201-1881. **EMAIL** Steven.Taylor@marquette.edu

TAYLOR, TALBOT J.
PERSONAL Born 07/23/1952, New York, NY, m, 1975, 3 children **DISCIPLINE** LINGUISTICS **EDUCATION** Tufts Univ, BA (French), 74, MA, 75; Oxford Univ, M Litt, 79, D Phil (linguistics), 82. **CAREER** Asst prof, 82-88, assoc prof, 89-95, L G T Cooley prof of English and Linguistics, Col of William and Mary, 96-. **HONORS AND AWARDS** Guggenheim fel, 94-95; Outstanding Faculty award, Virginia. **MEMBERSHIPS** North Am Asn for Hist of Lang Sciences; Am Anthropological Asn. **RESEARCH** Linguistic theory; philos of lang; hist of linguistics. **SELECTED PUBLICATIONS** Auth, Mutual Understanding, Duke Univ Press, 92; Theorizing Language, Pergamm Press, 97; Apes, Language & Human Mind, with S Savage-Rumbaugh & S Shanuer, Oxford Univ Press, 98. **CONTACT ADDRESS** Col of William and Mary, P O Box 8795, Williamsburg, VA 23187. **EMAIL** txtayl@wm.edu

TEBBEN, JOSEPH RICHARD
PERSONAL Born 11/26/1943, Columbus, OH, m, 1968, 6 children **DISCIPLINE** CLASSICS **EDUCATION** Duquesne Univ, BA, 65; Univ Pittsburgh, MA, 66; OH State Univ, PhD, 71. **CAREER** From instr to asst prof, 70-77, Assoc Prof Classics, OH State Univ, 77; Prof, Greek and Latin, OH State University, 99. **RESEARCH** Ancient Greek epic; Computing and class. **SELECTED PUBLICATIONS** Auth, A Course in Medical and Technical Terminology, Burgess, 79; Verba: A computer-assisted course in terminology, Class World, 75; Hesiod Konkordanz, 77 & Homer Konkordanz, 77, Georg Olms; Computer restoration of Greek diacritical symbols, Relo Rev, 77; Alkinoos and Phaiakian Security, Symbolae Osloenses, 91; Concordantia Homerica: Odyssea, Georg Olms, 94; Concordantia Homerica: Ilias, Georg Olms, 98. **CONTACT ADDRESS** Dept of Class, Ohio State Univ, Newark, 1179 University Dr, Newark, OH 43055-1797. **EMAIL** tebben.1@osu.edu

TEISER, STEPHEN F.
DISCIPLINE RELIGIOUS STUDIES; EAST ASIAN STUDIES **EDUCATION** Oberlin Col, AB, 78; Princeton Univ, MA, 83; PhD, 86. **CAREER** Vis asst prof, Middlebury Col, 86-87; asst prof, Univ S Ccalif, 87-88; prof dept of religion, Princrton Univ, 88- ; **HONORS AND AWARDS** ACLS Awd Best Book Hist Relig, 88; AAS Joseph Levenson Awd Best Book Chinese Studies, 94. **MEMBERSHIPS** Asn Asian Studies; Am Acad Relig; Soc Study Chinese Relig; Am Asn Study Relig. **RESEARCH** Chinese Buddhism; manuscripts from Dunhuang. **SELECTED PUBLICATIONS** Auth, The Growth in Purgatory, Religion and Society in T'ang and Sung China, Univ Hawaii Press, 93; The Scripture on the Ten Kings and the Making of Purgatory in Medieval Chinese Buddhism, Univ Hawaii, 94; Popular Religion, Chinese Religion: The State of the Field, Jour Asian Studies, 95; Introduction: The Spirits of Chinese Religion, Religions of China in Practice, Princeton Univ Press, 96; The Ghost Festival in Medieval China, Princeton Univ Press 88. **CONTACT ADDRESS** Dept of Religion, Princeton Univ, Seventy-Nine Hall, Princeton, NJ 08544-1006. **EMAIL** sfteiser@princeton.edu

TERAOKA, ARLENE
DISCIPLINE GERMAN STUDIES **EDUCATION** Yale Univ, BA, 76; Stanford, MA, 77; PhD, 83. **CAREER** Asst Prof, Univ of Wash, 83-85; Asst Prof, Princeton Univ, 85-89; Assoc Prof/Prof, Univ of Minn, 89-. **HONORS AND AWARDS** ACLS/SSRC E Europ Studies, 86-87; DDAD Prize for Distinguished Scholar in Ger Studies, 99. **MEMBERSHIPS** MLA, GSA, AATG, Int Brecht Soc, Women in Ger. **RESEARCH** 20th-century German Literature, culture, politics. **SELECTED PUBLICATIONS** Auth, The Silence of Entropy or Universal Discourse: The Postmodernist Poetics of Heiner Mueller, 85; auth, East, West, and Others: The Third World in Postwar German Literature, 96. **CONTACT ADDRESS** Dept German, Univ of Minnesota, Twin Cities, 9 Pleasant St SE, 205 Folwell Hall, Minneapolis, MN 55455-0194. **EMAIL** terao001@tc.umn.edu

TERNES, HANS
PERSONAL Born 09/10/1937, Kogolniceanu, Romania, m, 1962, 2 children **DISCIPLINE** GERMAN LITERATURE, AESTHETICS, ROMANCE PHILOSOPHY **EDUCATION** Univ Il, BA, 61, MA, 63; Univ Pa, PhD, 68. **CAREER** Lectr English, Univ Freiburg, Ger, 65-66; instr Ger, Univ Pa, 66-68; asst prof, 68-75, from assoc prof to prof Ger, Lawrence Univ, 76-. **MEMBERSHIPS** Am Asn Teachers Ger; MLA. **RESEARCH** Twentieth century German literature, primarily Thomas Mann, Friedrich Durrenmatt, Franz Kafka; problems in aesthetics, the grotesque; genre studies, nature poetry. **SELECTED PUBLICATIONS** Auth, Das Problem der Gerechtigkeit in Durrenmatts Die Panne, Germanic Notes, 75; Das Groteske in den Werken Thomas Manns, Stuttgarter Arbeiten zur Germanistik, 75; Anmerkungen zur Zeitblomgestalt, Germanic Notes, 76; co-ed, Probleme der Komparatistik & Interpretation, Festschrift for Prof Andre von Gronicka, Bouvier Vlg, Bonn, 78; contribr, Franz Kafka's Hunter Gracchus: an interpretation, Festschrift for Prof Andre von Gronicka, 78; Das Bild des Helden in DDR Roman, Rocky Mtn Rev, 83; The fantastic in the works of Franz Kafha, The Scope of the Fantastic, Greenwood, Inc, 85; Wolfgang Ammon Ein Deutsch-Brasilianischer Schriftsteller, Hans Staden-Jahrbuch, Sao Paulo, 86; Franz Xaver Kroetz, Magill's Critical Survey of Drama: Foreign Languages, Salem Press Ca, 86. **CONTACT ADDRESS** Dept of German, Lawrence Univ, 115 S Drew St, Appleton, WI 54911-5798. **EMAIL** Hans.Ternes@Lawrence.edu

TERRAS, RITA
PERSONAL Born, Germany, m, 1951, 1 child **DISCIPLINE** GERMAN LANGUAGE & LITERATURE **EDUCATION** Univ Ill, Urbana, BA, 61, MA, 66; Univ Wis-Madison, PhD, 69. **CAREER** Lectr Ger, Univ Wis, 69-70; asst prof, Univ RI, 71-72; asst prof, 72-76, Assoc Prof Ger, Conn Col; prof, Conn Col; prof emeritus, Conn Col; vis assoc prof Ger, Brown Univ, 81-82. **HONORS AND AWARDS** Vis fac fel, Yale Univ, 78-79 **MEMBERSHIPS** MLA; Am Asn Teachers Ger; Lessing Soc; Am Soc 18th Century Studies. **RESEARCH** German Classicism & Romanticism; the contemporary German novel; contemporary poetry. **SELECTED PUBLICATIONS** Auth, Ein 'Stein Aus Davids Hirtentasche', World Lit Today, Vol 67, 93; 'Landlaufiges Wunder', World Lit Today, Vol 70, 96; 'Epikurs Garten', World Lit Today, Vol 70, 96; 'Veritas'--Lyric Poetry and Prose 1950-1992, World Lit Today, Vol 68, 94; 'Staub Von Stadten'--Selected Poems, World Lit Today, Vol 70, 96; 'Von Der Grammatik Des Heutigen Tages', World Lit Today, Vol 67, 93; 'Erlkonigs Tochter', World Lit Today, Vol 67, 93; 'Wiese Und Macht', World Lit Today, Vol 68, 94. **CONTACT ADDRESS** Dept of Ger, Connecticut Col, 270 Mohegan Ave, Box 1586, New London, CT 06320.

TERRAS, VICTOR
PERSONAL Born 01/21/1921, Estonia, m, 1951, 1 child **DISCIPLINE** SLAVIC LANGUAGES & LITERATURE **EDUCATION** Univ Estonia, Cand Phil, 41, Mag Phil, 42; Univ Chicago, PhD(Russ lit), 63. **CAREER** From instr to assoc prof Russ, Univ IL, 59-65, prof Slavic lang & lit, 65-66; prof Slavic lang, Univ WI-Madison, 66-70; chmn dept, 72-76, Prof Slavic Lang, Brown Univ, 70-89, Prof emer, Brown Univ, 89-. **RESEARCH** Comp Slavic linguistics; Russ lit. **SELECTED PUBLICATIONS** Auth, The Young Dostoevsky, 1846-1849: A Critical Study, Mouton, The Hague & Paris, 69; Belinskij and Russian Literary Criticism, Univ WI-Madison, 73; A Karamazov Companion: Commentary on the Genesis, Language, and Style of Dostoevsky's Novel, Univ Wis-Madison, 81; Aleksis Rannit: Luhimonograafia, Lund, 75, Vladimir Maiakovsky, Twayne Publishers, 83; A Handbook of Russian Literature, Yale Univ Press, 85; The Idiot: An Interpretation, Twayne Publishers, 90; A History of Russian Literature, Yale Univ Press, 91; Poetry of the Silver Age: The Various Voice of Russian Modernism, Dresden Univ Press, 98; auth, Reading Dostoevsky, Univ Wis-Madison, 98. **CONTACT ADDRESS** Dept of Slavic Lang, Brown Univ, Providence, RI 02912.

TERRERO, IRENE
PERSONAL Born 03/12/1938, Venezuela, D, 2 children **DISCIPLINE** NEUROPSYCHOLOGY, NEUROLINGUISTICS **EDUCATION** Kendall Col, AA, 70; George Washington Univ, BA, 72; Northwestern Univ, MA, 74; Univ Paris, Doctorate, 83. **CAREER** Clinical Dir, Clinica de Lenguaje IT, Clinica de Idiomas IT, 74-00; res assoc, Gallandet Univ, 84-94; res assoc, Int Cendie Universidad Metropolitana, 89-98. **HONORS AND AWARDS** Phi Beta Kappa; Gallandet Univ, Res Awd Nomination; Ministry of Educ, Special Educ Honors, 90, 00. **MEMBERSHIPS** ASHA, AAUW, George Sand Lit Assoc. **RESEARCH** Linguistics, Languages, Neurlinguistics, Hearing Impaired, Special Education, Bilingual Education and Development. **CONTACT ADDRESS** 13895 Folkstone Cir, Wellington, FL 33414-7738. **EMAIL** ireneterrero@hotmail.com

TERRY, ROBERT MEREDITH
PERSONAL Born 12/16/1939, Danville, VA, m, 1965, 3 children **DISCIPLINE** FRENCH **EDUCATION** Randolph-Macon Col, BA, 62; Duke Univ, PhD(Romance lang), 66. **CAREER** Instr French, Duke Univ, 63-64, 65-66; asst prof, Univ Fla, 66-68; Assoc Prof French, Univ Richmond, 68-, Ed, Les Nouvelles. **MEMBERSHIPS** Am Asn Teachers Fr; Am Coun Teaching For Lang. **RESEARCH** Contemporary French language; foreign language methodology. **SELECTED PUBLICATIONS** Auth, The frequency of use of the interrogative formula est-ce que, 5/67 & Faut-il or Est-ce qu'il faut: Inversion vs est-ce que, 2/70, Fr Rev; Contemporary French Interrogative Structures, Ed Cosmos, 70; Students work with Monique and learn French, Foreign Lang Ann, 4/77; En Bref . . . Enfin, Univ Richmond, 77; Let Cinderella & Luke Skywalker help you

teach the passe compose & imperfect, Am Coun Teaching Foreign Lang, 78; Open syllabification and diphthongization of e and o in preliterary Spanish, Word, 7/80; Concepts of pastness: The passe compose and the imperfect, For Lang Annual, 4/81. **CONTACT ADDRESS** Dept of Mod Foreign Lang, Univ of Richmond, 28 Westhampton Way, Richmond, VA 23173-0002.

TESCHNER, RICHARD VINCENT
PERSONAL Born 07/19/1942, Madison, WI **DISCIPLINE** SPANISH, LINGUISTICS **EDUCATION** Stanford Univ, AB, 65; Middlebury Col, MA, 66; Univ Wis-Madison, PhD(Span), 72. **CAREER** From instr to asst prof Span, Univ Wis-Parkside, 70-74; asst prof, Univ Iowa, 74-76; from asst prof to prof Span Ling, Univ Tex, El Paso, 76-; Dir, Nat Endowment for the Humanities sponsored Surv of Res Tool Needs in the Hisp Lang and Lit, 77-78. **MEMBERSHIPS** Ling Soc Am; MLA; Am Asn Teachers Span & Port; Ling Asn Southwest. **RESEARCH** Spanish morphosyntaxis, Spanish phonetics/phonology. **SELECTED PUBLICATIONS** coauth, Spanish and English of United States Hispanos: A Critical, Annotated, Linguistic Bibliography, Ctr Appl Ling, 75; Espanol escrito: curso para hispano-hablantes bilingues, Charles Scribner's Sons, 78, 4th ed, Prentice Hall, 98; Festschrift for Jacob Ornstein, Newbury House, 80; coauth, El triple diccionario de la lengua espanola (TRIDIC), CD-ROM, Star-Byte, Inc., 96; auth, La ortografia sincronica del espanol a base de estadisticas comparativas, Lincom Europa, 99; coauth, Analyzing the Grammar of Eng: A Brief Undergraduate Textbook, Georgetown Univ Pr, 2nd ed, 00; auth, Camino oral: Fonetica, fonologia y practica de los sonidos del espanol, McGraw-Hill, 2nd ed, 00; auth, Cubre: Curso breve de gramatica espanola, 3rd ed, McGraw-Hill Primis, 00; auth, El libro completo del acento ortografico espanol, Para que se usa y en que palabras exactamente se encuentra, Manual con ejercicios, Lincom Europa, 00. **CONTACT ADDRESS** Dept of Lang & Linguistics, Univ of Texas, El Paso, 500 W University Ave, El Paso, TX 79968-0531. **EMAIL** teschner@utep.edu

TETEL, MARCEL
PERSONAL Born 10/11/1932, Paris, France, m, 1957, 1 child **DISCIPLINE** FRENCH **EDUCATION** Univ Chattanooga, BA, 54; Emory Univ, MA, 56; Univ Wis, PhD, 62. **CAREER** From asst prof to assoc prof, 60-68, Prof to Prof Emer Romance Lang, Duke Univ, 68-, Am Coun Learned Soc grant-in-aid, 63; Fulbright res grant, Florence, 66-67; Guggenheim fel, 70; Am Philos Soc grant, 73. **MEMBERSHIPS** Int Asn Fr Studies; Am Asn Teachers Fr; Am Asn Teachers Ital; MLA; SAtlantic Mod Lang Asn. **RESEARCH** French and Italian Renaissance. **SELECTED PUBLICATIONS** Auth, Rabelais et L'Italie, 69, Olschki, Florence; Rabelais, 67 & Montaigne, 74, Twayne; ed, Pirandello: Enrico IV, Appleton, 71; auth, Marguerite de Navarre's Heptameron: Themes, Language and Structure, 73 & ed, Symbolism and Modern Literature, 78, Duke Univ; auth, Lectures sceviennes: L'embleme et les mots, Klincksieck, Paris; ed, Colloque Montaigne: Duke-UNC, Nizet, Paris. **CONTACT ADDRESS** Dept of Romance Lang, Duke Univ, 213 Languages Bldg, Box 90257, Durham, NC 27708. **EMAIL** mtetel@acpub.duke.edu

TETZLAFF, OTTO W.
PERSONAL Born 08/26/1930, Noerenberg, Germany, m, 1958, 3 children **DISCIPLINE** MEDIEVAL LATIN DRAMA, LITERATURE **EDUCATION** N Ill Univ, BA, 62; Univ Ill, MA, 63; Univ Tex, PhD, 68. **CAREER** Instr, N Ill Univ, 63-65; asst prof, Va Polytechnical Univ, 68-69; from assoc prof to prof, 69-, Angelo State Univ. **HONORS AND AWARDS** NDEA Fel Title VI, 66-68; Nat Endowment Humanities, 72; Fulbright Post-doctoral Fel, 89; Minnie Stevens Piper Professorship, 91. **MEMBERSHIPS** AATG; MLA; TFLA; Schoperhauer Gesellshaft. **RESEARCH** Medieval Latin drama; 19th century literature. **SELECTED PUBLICATIONS** Auth, art, Johannes Urzidil, 80; auth, art, A Glimpse at the Stonemasons, 87; auth, art, The Best Kept Secret in the West, 92; auth, art, Public Education, The Brethren of the Common Life, and Their Theatrical Endeavor, 92; auth, The Handbook of Texas, 96. **CONTACT ADDRESS** Dept of Modern Languages, Angelo State Univ, San Angelo, TX 76909. **EMAIL** otto.tetzlaff@angelo.edu

THIBAULT, BRUNO
PERSONAL Born 05/22/1956, Neuilly sur Seinne, France, m, 1984, 1 child **DISCIPLINE** FRENCH LITERATURE **EDUCATION** Univ Paris, Maitrise de Lettres Modernes, 80; Doctorat de Lettres Modernes, 84; Univ Md, PhD, 86. **CAREER** Instr, Col Cevenol, 81; instr, Middlebury Col, 82; instr, Univ of Md, 82-87; asst prof to prof, Univ of Del, 87-. **MEMBERSHIPS** MLA, AATF. **RESEARCH** Contemporary French Literature and Film, J.M.G. Le Clezio, Daniele Sallenave. **SELECTED PUBLICATIONS** Auth, L'Allure de Morand: Du modernisme au petainisme, Summa Publ, 92; auth, "Depaysement: une nouvelle manquee de Jean-Paul Sartre," Fr Forum 16, (93): 81-90; auth, "Du stereotype au mythe: l'ecriture du fait divers dans La Ronde de J.M.G. Le Clezio," Fre Rev 68 (95): 964-975; auth, "Daniel Sallenave et le theme de la vie separee dans les nouvelles d'un Printemps froid," Fr Forum 22, (96): 75-91; auth, "Awaite Pawana: Le Clezio's Vision of the Sacred," World Lit Today 17, (97): 723-30; auth, "Le Chant e l'abime et la voix chamanique dans Le Proces verbal et dans Voyages de l'autre cote," Symposium 46 (99): 37-50; auth, "La Metaphore exotique: l'ecriture du processus d'individuation dans Le Chercheur d'or et dans La Quarantaine," Fr Rev 73, (00): 845-861; auth, "La Chute du communisme et l'acceleration de l'histoire dans Les Trois Minutes du diable," Symposium 54 (00): 113-25; auth, "Errance et initiation a travers la ville postmoderne: de La Guerre a Poisson d'or de J.M.G. Le Clezio," Nottingham Fr Rev 39, (00): 96-108; auth, "A l'ecoute de ceux qui sont a la traine: le recit dialogue dans Adieu et Viol de Daniele Sallenave," French Prose in 2000, Rodopi, 01. **CONTACT ADDRESS** Dept For Lang, Univ of Delaware, Smith Hall 326, Newark, DE 19716. **EMAIL** thibault@udel.edu

THIEL, ANNE
PERSONAL Born 11/17/1967, Germany, s **DISCIPLINE** GERMAN **EDUCATION** Univ MO, MA, 97. **CAREER** Teachers asst, Univ MO, 95-97; teachers asst, Georgetown Univ, 97-. **HONORS AND AWARDS** Grad Scholarship for training, 99; Ruth Fel, 98; Georgetown Fel, 97-; Superior Grad Achievement Awd, 96. **MEMBERSHIPS** GSA, MLA, Women in German, AATG. **RESEARCH** Women's literature - 18th and 19th century, Contemporary women's issues, Foreign language teaching and curriculum. **SELECTED PUBLICATIONS** Auth, "From Woman to Woman: Benedikte Naubert's 'Der kurze Mantel'," Collected Papers of German Day School of Women Writers in the 18th and 19th Centuries, (forthcoming); auth, Bohler, Liette: Der Mythos der Weiblichkeit im Werke Max Frischs, New York, 98; auth, Marie von Ebner-Eschenbach: Beyond Atonement, Columbia SC, 97. **CONTACT ADDRESS** Dept German, Georgetown Univ, PO Box 571048, Washington, DC 20057-1048. **EMAIL** thiela1@georgetown.edu

THIEM, JON
PERSONAL Born 10/09/1946, Cincinnati, OH, m, 2000, 2 children **DISCIPLINE** COMPARATIVE LITERATURE **EDUCATION** Dickinson Col, BA, 68; Ind Univ, MA, 74; PhD, 75. **CAREER** Peace Corps Teacher, 68-70; asst prof, Univ of Tex at Dallas, 75-79; from asst prof to prof, Colo State Univ, 79-00. **MEMBERSHIPS** Asn for the Study of Lit and the Environment. **RESEARCH** Comparative Literature, Translation, Poetry, Creative Non-fiction and Local History Writing, Literature and the Environment. **SELECTED PUBLICATIONS** Auth, Lorenzo de Medici: Selected Poems and Prose, Pa State Univ Press, 91; auth, "The Translator as Hero in Postmodern Fiction, " Trans and Lit 4 (95); auth, "Myths of the Universal Library from Alexandria to the Cyberage," Cyberspace Textuality, IU Press, 99; auth, "Intertextual Lives: the Novel of Biographical Quest as a Postmodern Genre," Sincronie 3.5 (99). **CONTACT ADDRESS** Dept English, Colorado State Univ, Fort Collins, CO 80523-0001.

THIHER, OTTAH ALLEN
PERSONAL Born 04/04/1941, Fort Worth, TX, m, 1997 **DISCIPLINE** FRENCH **EDUCATION** Univ Tex, BA, 63; Univ Wisc, PhD, 68. **CAREER** Asst prof, Duke Univ, 67-69; asst prof, Middlebury Col, 69-75; assoc prof to prof and dept chair, 76-. **HONORS AND AWARDS** Fel, Univ Wisc, 63-66; Fulbright Scholar, 66-67; Guggenheim Fel, Berlin, 76-77; Chancellor's Award, Univ Mo, 81; Fel, Weldon Springs Humanities, 86; Fel, Camargo Found, 88; Res Fel, Clare Hall, 99-00. **MEMBERSHIPS** Am Asn of Teachers of French; Les Amis de Valentin Bru; Soc for Lit and Sci; MLA: Asn of Literary Scholars and Critics. **RESEARCH** Modern fiction and its relation to science; Proust; Musil; Kafka; Borges; Woolf; Nineteenth-Century French fiction and its relations to science. **SELECTED PUBLICATIONS** Auth, The Power of Tautology: The Roots of Literary Theory, Assoc Univ Press, 97; auth, "The Tautological Thinking of Historicism," Tex Studies in Lit and Lang, (97): 193-224; auth, "The Legacy of Kafka's Short Fiction: Knowledge of the Impossibility of Knowledge," in The Legacy of Kafka in Austrian Literature, (Ariadne Press, 97), 1-26; auth, Revels in Madness: Insanity in Medicine and Literature, Univ Mich Press, 99; auth, fiction Rivals Science: The French Novel from Balzac to Proust, Univ Mo Press, (forthcoming). **CONTACT ADDRESS** Dept Romance Lang, Univ of Missouri, Columbia, 143 Arts and Sci Bldg, Columbia, MO 65211. **EMAIL** thihero@missouri.edu

THOMAS, DOMINIC R.
PERSONAL Born 06/23/1966, Berlin, Germany **DISCIPLINE** FRENCH **EDUCATION** Univ Col Lo, BA, 89; Yale Univ, MA, 92; MPhil, 94; PhD, 96. **CAREER** Asst Prof, Univ Notre Dame, 96-00; Mellon Fel, Cornell Univ, 99-00; Asst Prof, UCLA, 00-. **HONORS AND AWARDS** Mellon Postdoc Fel, 99-00; Vis Scholar, Northwestern Univ, 99. **MEMBERSHIPS** MLA; ALA; CIEF. **RESEARCH** Francophone African literatures and cultures; South African literature; Immigration; Racism; Nationalism; Postcoloniality. **SELECTED PUBLICATIONS** Auth, "Constructing national and cultural identities in francophone Africa," in Not on Any Map: Postcolonialism and Cultural Nationalism, (Exeter Univ Press, 97), 115-134; auth, "Silence et Violence chez Sony Labou Tansi," in Francophonie litteraire Africaine en proces. Le destin unique de Sony Labou Tansi, (Ed Nouvelles du Sud, 99), 99-128; auth, "Official Writers: The Engineers of the Congolese Soul," S Cent Rev, (00): 77-102; auth, "Committed Performances: Oppositionality and Sony Labou Tansi," in Francophone Theater, Spring 01; auth, "Daniel Biyaoula: Exile, Immigration and Transnational Cultural Productions," in Immigrant Narratives in contemporary France, Greenwood Press, 01; auth, "Nationalism and Masculinity in francophone sub-Saharan Literature," in Gender and Francophonie, Spring 01. **CONTACT ADDRESS** Dept French, Univ of California, Los Angeles, 212 Royce Hall, Los Angeles, CA 90095. **EMAIL** dominict@humnet.ucla.edu

THOMAS, GARY CRAIG
PERSONAL Born 11/20/1944, Long Beach, CA **DISCIPLINE** GERMAN LITERATURE, MUSICOLOGY **EDUCATION** Univ Calif, Los Angeles, AB, 66; Harvard Univ, MA, 70, PhD, 73. **CAREER** Asst prof, Humanities & Ger, 71-91, Assoc Prof Cultural Studies & Ger, Univ Minn, Minneapolis, 91-. **MEMBERSHIPS** MLA; Am Soc Study 16th & 17th Century Ger Lit; Renaissance Soc Am; Am Guild Organists. **RESEARCH** Cultural Studies; musical-literary relations; queer theory. **SELECTED PUBLICATIONS** Auth, Philipp von Zesen's German Madrigals, Argenis, 78; Zesen, Rinckart and the Musical Origins of the Dactyl, Argenis, 78; Dance Music and the Origins of the Dactylic Meter, in Daphnis, Zeitschrift fur Mittlere Deutsche Literatur, 87; Die Aelbianische Musen-Lust, Peter Lang, 91; Musical Rhetoric and Politics in the Early German Lied, in Music and German Literature: Their Relationship since the Middle Ages, Camden House, 92; Philipp von Zesen's German Madrigals, in Daphnis: Zeitschrift fur Mittlere Deutsche Literatur, 92; co-ed, Queering the Pitch: The New Gay and Lesbian Musicology, Routledge, 93; Was George Frideric Handel Gay? - On Closet Questions and Cultural Politics, in Queering the Pitch: The New Gay and Lesbian Musicology, Routledge, 94. **CONTACT ADDRESS** Univ of Minnesota, Twin Cities, 9 Pleasant St. SE, 350 Folwell Hall, Minneapolis, MN 55455. **EMAIL** thoma002@tc.umn.edu

THOMAS, JOHN WESLEY
PERSONAL Born 05/24/1916, Thomas, OK, m, 1948, 3 children **DISCIPLINE** GERMAN **EDUCATION** Houghton Col, AB, 37; Pa State Col, AM, 39, PhD, 42. **CAREER** Instr, Cent Jr Col, 37-38, Roberts Col, 41-42, Washington & Jefferson Coll, 42-44 & Univ Mich, 46-47; from assoc prof to prof Ger, Univ Ark, 47-69; Prof Ger, Univ KY, 69-, Fulbright res scholar, Luxembourg, 49-50; guest prof, Univ Hamburg, 55-56 & Univ Tubingen, 59-60. **MEMBERSHIPS** MLA; SAtlantic Mod Lang Asn. **RESEARCH** German. **SELECTED PUBLICATIONS** Auth, Domestic Tragedy in Works of the German High-Middle-Ages, Germanic Notes Rev, vol 0028, 97; The Other Kingdom in the Arthurian Romances of Medieval Germany and the Motif of Departure and Return, Germanic Notes Rev, Vol 25, 94; The Other Kingdom in the Arthurian Romances of Medieval Germany and the Motif of Departure and Return, Germanic Notes Rev, Vol 25, 94; Hartmann-Von-Aue Humor, Neuphilologische Mitteilungen, Vol 94, 93; Invisibility in the Narratives of the German High-Middle-Ages, Germanic Notes Rev, Vol 27, 96. **CONTACT ADDRESS** Dept of Ger, Univ of Kentucky, Lexington, KY 40506.

THOMAS, KATHERINE
PERSONAL Born 07/15/1940, Nashville, TN, m, 1961, 6 children **DISCIPLINE** HIGHER EDUCATION, COMPARATIVE LITERATURE **EDUCATION** St Louis Univ, AB, 61; Fordham univ, MA, 63; Pa State Univ, DEd, 81. **CAREER** Instr & grant writer, Ga Col, 87-92; assoc prof, Southeast Community Col, 94-. **HONORS AND AWARDS** Woodrow Wilson Fel, Fordham Univ, 61-63; NEH Fel, Univ of Ariz, 96; Univ of Ky Community Col Leadership Acad, 96-97. **MEMBERSHIPS** Ky Philol Asn, Int Asn of Caribbean Studies, Two Year Col English Asn. **RESEARCH** Caribbean Women's Literature, Classical Studies. **SELECTED PUBLICATIONS** Auth, "Mythic Archetypes in Casona's Le dama del alba," Text & Presentation 14 (93); auth, "Jocasta and Pertho: The Persuasive Voice in Oedipus Tyramos," Ky Philol Rev (99); auth, "Caribbean Women's Voices Speak to Two-Year College Students," Teaching English in the Two Year Col (99). **CONTACT ADDRESS** Dept Humanities, Southeast Community Col, 700 College Rd, Cumberland, KY 40823-1046.

THOMAS, MARGARET
PERSONAL Born 04/05/1952, Woodbury, NJ, m, 1990, 3 children **DISCIPLINE** LINGUISTICS **EDUCATION** Yale Univ, BA, 74; Boston Univ, Med, 83; Harvard Univ, AM, 85; PhD, 91. **CAREER** Teaching Fel, Harvard Univ, 86-90; Vis Asst Prof, Boston Col, 91-92; Asst Prof, Boston Col, 92-96; Assoc Prof, Boston Col, 96-. **HONORS AND AWARDS** Sumitomo Travel-Study Fel, Yale Univ, 74-75; For Lang and Area Studies Fel, Harvard Univ, 87; Am Asn of Applied Ling Grad Student Prize, 89; Dokkyo Int Coop Res Fel, Dokkyo Univ, 89; Harvard-Radcliffe Certification of Distinction in Teaching, 90; Spencer Postdoctoral Fel, Stanford Univ, 95-96. **MEMBERSHIPS** Ling Soc of Am, Am Assoc of Applied Ling, Mod Lang Assoc, N Am Soc for the Hist of the Lang Sci. **RESEARCH** Second language acquisition and linguistic theory, history of linguistics. **SELECTED PUBLICATIONS** auth, "The Interpretation of English Reflexive Pronouns by Non-Native Speakers," Studies in Second Lang Acquisition 11: 281-303; auth, "The Acquisition of English Articles by First and Second Lan-

guage Learners," Applied Psycholinguistics 10 (89): 335-355; auth, "Universal Grammar and the Interpretation of Reflexives in a Second Language," Lang 67 (91): 211-239; auth, Knowledge of Reflexives in a Second Language, John Benjamins Pr (Amsterdam, Holland), 93; auth, "Assessment of Proficiency in Second Language Acquisition Research," Lang Learning 44 (95): 307-336; auth, "Linguistic Variation in Spike Lee's School Daze," Col English 56 (94): 911-927; auth, "Acquisition of the Japanese Reflexive Zibun and Movement of Anaphors in Logical Form," Second Lang Res 11 (95): 206-234; auth, "Medieval and Modern Views of Universal Grammar and the Nature of Second Language Learning," The Mod Lang J 79 (95): 345-355; auth, "Programmatic Historicity in Second Language Acquisition Theory," Studies in Second Lang Acquisition 20 (98): 387-405. **CONTACT ADDRESS** Dept Ling, Boston Col, Chestnut Hill, 140 Commonwealth Ave, Chestnut Hill, MA 02467. **EMAIL** thomasm@bc.edu

THOMAS, ROGER K.
PERSONAL Born 12/18/1953, Spanish Ford, UT, m, 1984, 1 child **DISCIPLINE** JAPANESE LITERATURE **EDUCATION** Ind Univ, PhD, 91 **CAREER** ASSOC PROF, ILL STATE UNIV, 90-. **MEMBERSHIPS** Asn Asian Studies, Asn Teachers of Japanese, Asn Japanese Lit Studies. **RESEARCH** Waka poetry and poetics of Tokugawa period, Tokugawa aesthetics. **SELECTED PUBLICATIONS** Auth, "Macroscopic vs. Microscopic: Spatial Sensibilities in Waka of the Bakumatsu Period," Harvard Jour of Asiatic Studies, Winter 98; auth, "Okuma Kotomichi and the Re-Visioning of Kokinshu Elegance," PMAJLS, Summer 97; auth, "Akera Kanko no 'tenko' to kaikaku-go no kyoka," in Uta no hibiki, monogatari no yokubo, 96, Shinwasha; auth, "Kawatake Mokuami as Lyricist," PMAJLS, Summer 95; auth, "High vs. Low: The Fude no Saga Controversy and Bakumatsu Poetics," Monumenta Nipponica, Winter 94. **CONTACT ADDRESS** Dept For Lang, Illinois State Univ, Box 4300, Normal, IL 61790. **EMAIL** rkthoma@ilstu.edu

THOMAS, RUTH PAULA
PERSONAL Born 11/09/1935, New York, NY, m, 1974, 2 children **DISCIPLINE** FRENCH **EDUCATION** Bryn Mawr Col, BA, 57; Yale Univ, MA, 58, PhD(French), 64. **CAREER** Instr French, Simmons Col, 61-63; asst prof, 64-73, Assoc Prof French, Temple Univ, 73- **MEMBERSHIPS** Am Asn Teachers Fr; MLA; Am Soc Eighteenth Century Studies. **RESEARCH** Eighteenth and 17th century French novel. **SELECTED PUBLICATIONS** Auth, Essays on the 'Neveu De Rameau' of Diderot, French Rev, Vol 66, 93; Eroticism and the Body-Politic, French Rev, Vol 67, 94. **CONTACT ADDRESS** 1530 Locust St Apt 5F, Philadelphia, PA 19012.

THOMASON, PHIL
PERSONAL Born 12/12/1949, Shawmut, AL, m, 1975, 1 child **DISCIPLINE** LINGUISTICS **EDUCATION** Univ Ky, PhD. **CAREER** Teacher, Kendrick High Sch, 72-74; instr, Marion Mil Sch, 76-81; instr, Auburn Univ, 82; grad teaching asst, Univ of Ky, 82-86; instr, Asbury Col, 86; from assoc prof to prof, Pepperdine Univ, 87-. **HONORS AND AWARDS** Fel, Ministry of Culture of Spain. **MEMBERSHIPS** AATSP, ACTFL **RESEARCH** Teatro de la Cruz (Madrid), municipal archives (Madrid). **SELECTED PUBLICATIONS** Auth, "The Quest of Rita Geada," Ariel 1.1 (83): 33-37; auth, "Visceral Imagery in Miguel Hernandez Poetic Works of the [Spanish Civil] War Period," Ky Philol Asn Bull (86): 78; trans, "The Gnosis of Princeton: Wise Men in Search of God," by Juan Antonio Monroy, The European Challenge 1, (88); trans, "The Meaning of Love in the "Song of Solomon,"" by Juan Antonio Monroy, The European Challenge 1.4 (88); 6-7; trans, "Listen Europe," by Juan Antonio Monroy, The European Challenge 2.3 (89): 6-7; auth, "El Coliseo de la Cruz: Illustrations from the Archivo Municipal de Madrid," Bull of Hispanic Studies, Univ of Liverpool. **CONTACT ADDRESS** Pepperdine Univ, 24255 Pacific Coast Hwy, Malibu, CA 90263-4212. **EMAIL** thomason@pepperdine.edu

THOMPSON, BRIAN
PERSONAL Born 04/01/1941, Boston, MA, m, 1963, 2 children **DISCIPLINE** FRENCH **EDUCATION** Harvard, AB, 63; AM, 65; PhD, 70. **CAREER** Instr, Northeastern Univ, 67-68; From Instr to Prof, Univ of Mass Boston, 68-. **HONORS AND AWARDS** General Motors Nat Scholar, 59-63; Harvard Nat Scholar, 59-63; Fulbright Fel Paris, 63-64; Woodrow Wilson Fel, 63-65; Chevalier des Arts et des Lettres, Fr Govt; Distinguished Serv Awd, Mass For Lang Asn; Distinguished Serv Awd, Col of Arts and Sci, Univ Mass Boston. **MEMBERSHIPS** Am Asn of Teachers of Fr, Mass For Lang Asn, Ancties Int Andre Malraux, Comite Int Andre Malraux, Asn Int des Amis de Francois Mauriac. **RESEARCH** French novel, French song, Andre Malraux, Francois Mauriac. **SELECTED PUBLICATIONS** Transl, co-transl, Christliches Bewubstein: Versuche uber Pascal, by Romano Guardini, Herder & Herder (NY); transl, co-transl, L'Homme problematique, by Gabriel Marcel, Herder & Herder (NY); co-ed, Witnessing Andre Malraux: Vision and Re-visions, Wesleyan Univ Press (Middletown, CT), 84, 88; auth, La Clef des Chants: La Chanson dans la classe de francais," Polyglot (Cambridge, MA), 86. **CONTACT ADDRESS** Dept Mod Lang, Univ of Massachusetts, Boston, 100 Morrissey Blvd, Dorchester, MA 02125-3300. **EMAIL** brian.thompson@umb.edu

THOMPSON, EWA MAJEWSKA
PERSONAL Born Kaunas, Lithuania, m **DISCIPLINE** COMPARATIVE LITERATURE **EDUCATION** Vanderbilt Univ, PhD, Comp Lit, 67. **CAREER** Tchr, Vanderbilt Univ; Ind State Univ; Ind Univ; Univ Va, PROF, RICE UNIV, 79-. **MEMBERSHIPS** Am Asn Advancement Slavic Stud; Am Asn Tchrs of Slavic and East Europ Lang **RESEARCH** Colonialism in Russian literature; Russian & Polish culture & politics **SELECTED PUBLICATIONS** Understanding Russia: The Holy Fool in Russian Culture, Oxford Univ Press, 95; "Why the Conservative Tradition Is an Important Philosophical Option in Polish Intellectual Life," Periphery, 97; "Thomas Venclovas Aleksander Wat," The Chesterton Rev, 97; "Aleksandr Solzhenitsyn's Cancer Ward and the Russian Colonialist Experience," Slavia Orientalis, 97; "Nationalism, Imperialism, Identity: Second Thoughts, Modern Age, 98; auth, The Holy Fool in Russian Culture, Beijing, 98; auth, Imperial Knowledge: Russian Literature and Colonialism (Westport, CT: Greenwood Pr, 00). **CONTACT ADDRESS** Dept German & Slavic Stud, Rice Univ, 6100 S Main St, Houston, TX 77005-1892. **EMAIL** ethomp@atsrice.edu

THOMPSON, ROGER MARK
PERSONAL Born 07/15/1942, Oakland, CA, m, 1967, 10 children **DISCIPLINE** LINGUISTIC, SOCIOLINGUISTICS, TESL **EDUCATION** Brigham Young Univ, BA, 66, MA, 68; Univ Tex, Austin, PhD(Ling), 71. **CAREER** Prog specialist teaching English as Foreign Lang, Int Off, Univ Tex, Austin, 68-71; asst prof, 71-76, assoc prof English & Ling, Univ Fla, 76-, ed, Southern Folklore Quart, 72-75; vis prof Universidad de las Americas, Cholula, Puebla, Mexico, 82-83. **HONORS AND AWARDS** Fulbright Travel Grant/Hungary, 90; Fulbright Scholar, Philippine Depart of Ed, Culture and Sports, 96-97. **MEMBERSHIPS** Ling Soc Am; Am Dialect Soc; Teachers of English to Speakers of Other Lang; Am Asn Applied Ling. **RESEARCH** Bilingualism; second language acquisition; English as a second language. **SELECTED PUBLICATIONS** Coauth, Cakchiquel Basic Course, Brigham Young Univ, Vol I, 69; auth, Mexican American language loyalty and the validity of the 1970 census, Int J Sociol Lang, 74; The decline of Cedar Key: Mormon stories in North Florida and their social function, Southern Folklore Quart, 75; Mexican-American English: Social correlates of regional pronunciation, Am Speech, 75; Language planning in frontier America, Lang Problems & Lang Planning, 82; Linguistics Studies in Honor of Bohdan Saciuk, West Lafayett IN: Learning Systems, 97; Why can't they take a hint? The negative in spoken English, ACELT Journal, 97. **CONTACT ADDRESS** Dept of English, Univ of Florida, 4008 Turlington Hall, PO Box 117310, Gainesville, FL 32611-7310. **EMAIL** rthompso@english.ufl.edu

THOMSON, CLIVE
DISCIPLINE FRENCH LITERATURE **EDUCATION** Univ Toronto, BA; MA; PhD. **RESEARCH** Late 19th century French literature; women writers; interdisciplinary discourses on homosexuality in France between 1880-1900; literary and cultural theories of Mikhail Bakhtin; critical reception of work by the Bakhtin Circle. **SELECTED PUBLICATIONS** Co-ed, Le singe a la porte, Peter Lang, 84; Dire la parodie: colloque de Cerisy, Peter Lang, 89; Dialogism and Cultural Criticism, Mestengo, 95; Scientific Discourse as Prejudice Carrier, Mestengo, 98. **CONTACT ADDRESS** Dept of French, Univ of Western Ontario, London, ON, Canada N6A 5B8. **EMAIL** cthomson@julian.uwo.ca

THORBURN, CAROLYN COLES
PERSONAL Born 12/20/1941, Newark, NJ **DISCIPLINE** SPANISH **EDUCATION** Douglass Coll, BA Spanish 1962; Rutgers Univ, MA Spanish 1964, PhD Spanish 1972; PhD, nutrition, 1987. **CAREER** Barringer HS, Spanish teacher 1964-66; Rutgers Univ, teaching asst Spanish 1966-67; Upsala Coll, prof of Spanish/coord of black studies 1967-95; Union County College, adjunct prof of Spanish, 92-; Seton Hall Univ and E. Orange School District, educational consultant, 95-. **HONORS AND AWARDS** Romance Language Honor Soc Phi Sigma Iota 1972. **MEMBERSHIPS** Mem Modern Language Assoc, Natl Council of Black Studies, Amer Assoc of Univ Profs, Amer Assoc of the Teachers of Spanish & Portuguese. **SELECTED PUBLICATIONS** Author, Mastery of Conversational Spanish, 92; author, Complete Mastery of Spanish, 93; author, Complete Mastery of Spanish Workbook, 94. **CONTACT ADDRESS** Prof of Spanish, Educational Research Center Language School, 75 Central Avenue, East Orange, NJ 07018. **EMAIL** healing222@aol.com

THORN, ARLINE ROUSH
PERSONAL Born 11/22/1946, New Haven, WV, d, 1 child **DISCIPLINE** COMPARATIVE & ENGLISH LITERATURE **EDUCATION** Marshall Univ, AB, 67; Univ IL, Urbana, MA, 68, PhD, 71. **CAREER** From Instr to Assoc Prof, 71-79, prof eng, WVA State Col, 79-, Ch, Dept Eng, 86-94; Adj prof Eng, Marshall Univ Grad Col, 75-; mem, State Col System Bd Dir, 94-97. **HONORS AND AWARDS** Woodrow Wilson Inst on Interpreting Hum, 86; Citation as Outstanding Fac Mem, WVA Legislature, 89; Fulbright Seminar in Brazil, 93; First Prize, WVA Writers statewide competition, poetry, 96, 98. **MEMBERSHIPS** Am Comp Lit Asn; MLA; Asn for Integrative Studies. **RESEARCH** Women's studies; hist and theory of the novel; Holocaust Studies. **SELECTED PUBLICATIONS** Coauth, The veluminous word: McLuhan-D H Lawrence, Midwest Monogr, 71; The pivotal character in Dickens' novels, Papers WV a Asn Col Eng Tchr(s), spring 72; Shelley's Cenci as Tragedy, Costerus: Essays Eng Lit & Lang, 12/73; Harriette Arnow's mountain women, Bull WVA Asn Col Eng Tchr(s), 77; Feminine time in Dorothy Richardson's Pilgrimage, Int J Women's Studies, 78; How I became a historian, Kanawha Rev, 80; A mighty maze: Ulysses, Perspectives Contemp Lit, 80; co-ed, Origins: Texts for an Inquiry, Tapestry Press, 91; author of poems in Pikeville Rev, Southern Humanities Rev, and various anthologies. **CONTACT ADDRESS** Dept of Eng, West Virginia State Col, PO Box 1000, Institute, WV 25112-1000. **EMAIL** athorn@wvsvax.wvnet.edu

THORSEN, KRISTINE
DISCIPLINE GERMAN **EDUCATION** Cornell Univ, AB; Univ Chicago, AM; Northwestern Univ, MA, PhD. **CAREER** Dir, first yr German, Northwestern Univ. **RESEARCH** German literature; contemprary poetry and novels by women, pedagogy and methodology. **SELECTED PUBLICATIONS** Auth, Poetry by American Women: A Bibliography; Gertrud v. le Fort's Recollections of an Era in Imperial Germany. **CONTACT ADDRESS** Dept of German, Northwestern Univ, 1801 Hinman, Evanston, IL 60208. **EMAIL** kat162@nwu.edu

THORSON, HELGA
DISCIPLINE GERMAN **EDUCATION** Earlham Col, BA, 87; Univ Minn, MA, 90, PhD, 96. **CAREER** German, Univ Ark **SELECTED PUBLICATIONS** Coauth, Schriftbilder, Independence Press, 89; Writing Theory and Practice in the Second Language Classroom: A Selected Annotated Bibliography, Univ Minn, 95; Using Intensive Writing-to-Learn Activities in the Foreign Language Classroom, Univ Minn, 96; coauth, "Writing and Foreign Language Pedagogy: Theories and Implications," 3-14, "Quality vs. Quality? Using Extensive and Intensive writing in the FL classroom", 141-152. In: Writing Across Languages, ed. Gerd Brauer, Stanford Ct, Ablex, 00; auth, Helga Thorson, "Using the Computer to Compare Foreign and Native Language Writing Processes: A Statistical and Case Study Approach," The Modern Language Journal, 84.2 (00): 155-170. **CONTACT ADDRESS** Univ of Arkansas, Little Rock, 2801 S University Ave., Little Rock, AR 72204-1099. **EMAIL** hmthorson@ualr.edu

THREATTE, LESLIE L.
PERSONAL Born 02/01/1943, Miami, FL **DISCIPLINE** CLASSICS **EDUCATION** Oberlin Col, BM and BA, 64; Harvard Univ, PhD, 69. **CAREER** Asst prof, Cornell Univ, 68-70; asst prof to prof, Univ of Calif at Berkeley, 70-. **HONORS AND AWARDS** NEH Summer Fel, 74; Guggenheim, 81; Inst for Advanced Study, 95. **MEMBERSHIPS** Am Philol Asn. **RESEARCH** Greek Epigraphy and Linguistics. **SELECTED PUBLICATIONS** Auth, Grammar of Attic Inscriptions Vol 1: Phonology, 80; auth, Grammar of Attic Inscriptions Vol 2: Morphology, 96. **CONTACT ADDRESS** Dept Classics, Univ of California, Berkeley, 7211 Dwinelle Hall, Berkeley, CA 94720-2520. **EMAIL** poovanna@earthlink.net

THUENTE, MARY HELEN
PERSONAL Born 03/21/1946, Chicago, IL, m, 1967, 2 children **DISCIPLINE** ENGLISH, IRISH LIT **EDUCATION** Clarke Col, BA, 67; Univ Kans, MA, 69, PhD, 73. **CAREER** Asst prof, 75-80, assoc prof, 80-94, prof, 94-, Ind Univ/Purdue Univ. **MEMBERSHIPS** MLA; Am Comt Irish Studies; Can Assn Irish Studies; Int Assn Study Irish Lit. **RESEARCH** Irish literature, hist. **SELECTED PUBLICATIONS** Auth, The Harp Re-Strung, 94. **CONTACT ADDRESS** Dept of English, Indiana Univ-Purdue Univ, Fort Wayne, 2101 Coliseum Blvd E, Fort Wayne, IN 46805-1445. **EMAIL** thuentem@ipfw.edu

THUNDY, ZACHARIAS P.
PERSONAL Born 09/28/1936, Changanacherry, India, m, 1983, 2 children **DISCIPLINE** ENGLISH, LINGUISTICS, MEDIEVAL STUDIES, INDOLOGY **EDUCATION** Pontif Athenaeum, India, BPh, 58; LPh, 59; BTh, 61; STL, 63; DePaul Univ, MA, 66; Univ Notre Dame, PhD(English), 69. **CAREER** Instr philos, Dharmaram Col, Bangalore, India, 63-64; from asst prof to assoc prof, 68-77, prof English, Northern Mich Univ, 77-, Am Inst Indian Studies sr fel, 74-75; Fulbright fel, 78-79; Joseph J. Malone fel, 93. **HONORS AND AWARDS** Citation & Medal, Mich Acad Sci, Arts & Lett, 77; Distinguised Fac Awd, 88; Killeen Lectr at St. Norbert Col, 00. **MEMBERSHIPS** MLA; Midwest Mod Lang Asn; Mich Acad; Medieval Asn of the Midwest; AAUP. **RESEARCH** Anthropological linguistics; American dialect survey; feminism in the Middle Ages; east-west relationship in literature and culture. **SELECTED PUBLICATIONS** Auth, Circumstance, Circumference, and Center, Hartford Studies Lit, 71; auth, Oaths in Germanic folklore, Folklore, 71; auth, Covenant in Anglo-Saxon Thought, Macmillan, 72; coed, Language and Culture, Northern Mich Univ, 73; auth, Beowulf and Jus diaboli, Christian Scholar's Rev, 73; coed, Chaucerian Problems and Perspectives, Univ Notre Dame, 78; auth, South Indian Folktales of Kadar, Meerut, & Berkeley, 83; auth, Buddha and Christ: Nativity Stories and Indian Traditions, Brill, 93; auth, Millennium: Apocalypse and

Antichrist, Crosscultural Pub., 98. **CONTACT ADDRESS** 1414 North Ivy Rd. B4, South Bend, IN 46637-5690. **EMAIL** zthundy@nmu.edu

TIKKU, GIRDHARI
DISCIPLINE COMPARATIVE LITERATURE **EDUCATION** Tehran Univ, PhD, 61. **CAREER** Prof, Univ IL Urbana Champaign. **HONORS AND AWARDS** Jammu and Kashmir Cult Acad Awd. **RESEARCH** Indo Iranian cult; Persian lit; East West encounters; Inter Asian rel(s); comp mystical poetry; Asian responses to the West; transl theory. **SELECTED PUBLICATIONS** Auth, Persian Poetry in Kashmir; Islam and its Cultural Divergence; Mysticism in Kashmir; pubs on Persian poetry, Indian and Iranian Islam, Tagore, fiction, and poetry from Persian. **CONTACT ADDRESS** Comp Lit Dept, Univ of Illinois, Urbana-Champaign, E Gregory Drive, PO Box 52, Champaign, IL 61820.

TIMPE, EUGENE FRANK
PERSONAL Born 09/24/1926, Tacoma, WA, w, 1950, 3 children **DISCIPLINE** COMPARATIVE LITERATURE **EDUCATION** Occidental Col, BA, 48; Univ Southern Calif, MA, 52, PhD(comp lit), 60. **CAREER** Instr English, El Camino Col, 53-66; assoc prof Ger & comp lit, PA State Univ, University Park, 66-72; chmn dept foreign lang & lit, 72-81, dir, Foreign Lang and International Trade Prog, 86; prof Ger & Comp Lit, Southern Ill Univ, Carbondale, 72-; lectr, Univ Md, Munich, 63-64; vis prof, Univ Neuchatel, Switz, 70-71. **HONORS AND AWARDS** Fulbright grants, Vienna, 58-59, Rome 60-61, Ger, 85; Am Philos Soc grant, 70; NEH grant, 83; US Dept Educ Title VI A grant, 87-90, 92-94, 99-01; US Dept Educ Title VI B grant, 89-91. **MEMBERSHIPS** Grillparzer Gesellschaft, Asn Dept Foreign Lang (pres, 77). **RESEARCH** 18th century; literary theory. **SELECTED PUBLICATIONS** Auth, American Literature in Germany, 1861-1872, Chapel Hill, 64; Hesse's Siddhartha and the Bhagavad Gita, Comp lit, 70; The Spatial Dimension: A Stylistic Typology, In: Yearbook of Comparative Criticism, Vol III, 71; ed & contribr, Thoreau Abroad, Archon Bks, 71; auth, Infernal space: Structure and Context, Ital Quart, 72; Wieland's Singspiele and the Rebirth of German Opera, Seminar, 77; Memory and Literary Structures, J Mind & Behav, 81; Metastasio and Austrian Rococo Literature, Ital Quart, 118, 92. **CONTACT ADDRESS** Dept of Foreign Lang & Lit, So Illinois Univ, Carbondale, Carbondale, IL 62901-4521. **EMAIL** etimpe@siu.edu

TINSLEY, JAMES R.
PERSONAL Born 02/15/1944, Shreveport, LA, w, 1944 **DISCIPLINE** HISTORY; FRENCH **EDUCATION** Centenary Col, BA, 66; E Tex State Univ, MA, 67; Univ Ala, MLS, 75; Univ St Anne, Dipl Fr. **CAREER** Instr, Wm Carey Col, 67; asst prof, Morehead State Univ, 68-74; arch, St Mary Parish, 76-79; Acad Sacred Heart, 80-81; prefect, Trinity Heights Acad, 82-86; asst headmaster, Grawood School, 88-90; teacher, Glenbrook School, 90-94; Caddo Parish School, 94- . **HONORS AND AWARDS** Gorgas Fel, Univ Ala; Conofil Fel, Univ Ste Anne. **MEMBERSHIPS** S Hist. **RESEARCH** Edward Irving, Catholic Apostolic Church, GOA. **SELECTED PUBLICATIONS** Auth, The Church in the War-A History of St. Marks Cathedral in WW II. **CONTACT ADDRESS** Dept Behav Sci, Bossier Parish Comm Col, 2719 Airline Dr, Bossier City, LA 71111-5801.

TITCHE, LEON L.
PERSONAL Born 01/14/1939, Monroe, LA, m, 1985, 4 children **DISCIPLINE** COMPARATIVE LITERATURE **EDUCATION** Tulane Univ, BA, 61; PhD, 64. **CAREER** Prof, Purdue Univ. **MEMBERSHIPS** ALCS; Friedrich Nietzsche Soc. **RESEARCH** Comparative literature, Jung, Nietzsche. **SELECTED PUBLICATIONS** Auth, Reflections From a Desert Pond, Century Press, (98); auth, Abishag's Lament, Mellen Press, (00); auth, A Pavilion for the Sun, Mellen Press, (00). **CONTACT ADDRESS** Dept For Lang, Purdue Univ, West Lafayette, 510 Renard Rd, West Lafayette, IN 47906. **EMAIL** ljtitche@concentric.net

TOBIN, RONALD WILLIAM FRANCIS
PERSONAL Born 06/19/1936, New York, NY, m, 1960, 1 child **DISCIPLINE** FRENCH LANGUAGE & LITERATURE **EDUCATION** St Peter's Col, AB, 57; Princeton Univ, MA, 59, PhD(Romance lang), 62. **CAREER** Instr French Lang & Lit, Williams Col, 61-63; from asst prof to assoc prof French, Univ Kans, 63-69, chmn Dept French & Ital, 67-69; chmn Dept French & Ital, 69-71, chmn Dept French & Ital, 75-80, prof French, Univ Calif, Santa Barbara, 69-, asst, Princeton Univ, 60-61; Am Philos Soc res grant, 63; mem univ adv coun, Am Coun Life Insurance, 70-; mem bd trustees, Baudry Franco-Am Found, 77-; Am Coun Learned Soc grant, 78 & 80; sr fel Monterey Inst of Inter Studies, 78-84; mem Higher Ed Adv Council for Apple Computer, Inc, 90-91. **HONORS AND AWARDS** Chevalier, Palmes Academiques, 72; Order of Merit, 84; Orders of Arts and letters, 98. **MEMBERSHIPS** Mod Humanities Res Asn; MLA; Am Asn Teachers Fr; Soc Etude XVIIe Siecle. **RESEARCH** Seventeenth century French tragedy; Racine; Moliere. **SELECTED PUBLICATIONS** Auth, Racine and Seneca, Univ NC, 71; coauth, Paths to Freedom: Studies in French Classicism in Honor of E B O Borgerhoff, L'Esprit Createur, 71; auth, Trends in Racinian Criticism, Fr Rev, 72; ed, Myth and Mythology in 17th Century French Literature, L'Esprit Createur, 76; Esthetique et Societe au 17e Siecle, Papers on French 17th Century Literature, No 6, 76; Theme et Thematique de la Tragedia, Papers French 17th Century Lit, 79; auth, Litterature it gast ronomie, paperson 17th-Century, French Lit, ed, 85; auth, Tarte a la Creme: Comedy and Gastronomy in Motiere's Theater, Ohio State, ed, 90; auth, Le Corpsau 17 siecle, Paperson 17th-Century, French Lit, 95; Papers on 17th-Century Fr Lit, 1995; Moliere a tavola, Bulzoni, 98; Jean Racine Revisited, Simon & Schuster, 99. **CONTACT ADDRESS** Dept of French, Univ of California, Santa Barbara, 552 University Rd, Santa Barbara, CA 93106-0001. **EMAIL** rwtobin@humanitas.ucsb.edu

TOHER, MARK
DISCIPLINE CLASSICS **EDUCATION** Brown Univ, BA, 74, PhD, 85; Univ Oxford, BA, 76. **CAREER** Chemn, Dept of Classics, St George's Sch, 77-80; asst prof, 83-89, assoc prof, Classics, 89- , chemn dept, 91-94, Union College. **HONORS AND AWARDS** Phi Beta Kappa; Brown Univ Sr Scholarship, 74-76; dir of sem for NEH summer inst, 87; NEH summer inst, 88; NEH travel grant, 92; mem Managing Comm of Am School of Class Stud, Athens, 84- . **SELECTED PUBLICATIONS** Auth, The Tenth Table and the Conflict of the Orders, in Raaflaug, ed, Social Struggles in Archaic Rome: New Perspectives on the Roman Conflict of the Orders, Los Angeles, 86; auth, On the Terminal Date of Nicolaus' Universal History, Ancient Hist Bull, 87; auth, On the Use of Nicolaus' Historical Fragments, Class Antiquity, 89; auth, Augustus and the Evolution of Roman Historiography, in Raaflaub, ed, Between Republic and Empire: Interpretations of Augustus and His Principate, Los Angeles, 90; auth, Greek Funerary Legislation and the Two Spartan Funerals, in Flower, ed, Georgica: Studies in Honor of George Cawkwell, London, 91. **CONTACT ADDRESS** Dept of Classics, Union Col, New York, Schenectady, NY 12308.

TOLEDANO, JAUN CARLOS
PERSONAL Born 03/18/1971, Adra, Spain, m **DISCIPLINE** LINGUISTICS, SPANISH, LANGUAGE, LITERATURE **EDUCATION** Univ Granada, BA, 96; Univ Miami, PhD, 01. **CAREER** Teaching asst, Univ Miami, 96-01; asst prof, Lewis Clark Col, 01-. **HONORS AND AWARDS** CCLAS, Res Grant, 01; Marta S. Weeks Teaching Excellence Awd, 00; Outstanding Grad Awd, Univ Miami, 99. **MEMBERSHIPS** MLA; LASA; IAFA. **RESEARCH** 20th-century Spanish American literature; the Hispanic Caribbean; 19 and 20th peninsular literatures; cultural studies and critical theory; the fantastic in literature, art and the media. **SELECTED PUBLICATIONS** Auth, "Ciencia-ficcion en la Revolution Caba¤a," Romance Lang Annual 10 (99): 848-852; auth, "The Caribbean: A Non-Defined Place," Modern Post 5 (99):14-16; auth, "Ciencia-Ficcion Habana '99," Locus (99): 42-43; co-auth, "Cronologia de la Ciencia-ficcion Latino Americana: 1775-1999," Chasaui (01); transl, "The Annunciation" by Diana Chaviano, Anthology of Latin American Science Fiction, ed. Andrea Bell (Wesleyan up, forthcoming); auth, "Felix Lizarraga," "F. Mond," "Agustin de Rojas," in Latin American Science Fiction Writers: A Bio-Bibliographical Source Book, ed. Darrell Lockhart (Greenwood Pr, forthcoming). **CONTACT ADDRESS** Dept For Lang, Lewis and Clark Col, Portland, OR 97219-7899. **EMAIL** toledano@lclark.edu

TOLLEFSON, JAMES WILLIAM
PERSONAL Born 02/19/1950, WA, m, 1990, 2 children **DISCIPLINE** LINGUISTICS **EDUCATION** Stanford Univ, PhD, 78. **CAREER** Lect, 79-80, San Jose St Univ; asst prof, 80-84, assoc prof, 84-90, prof, 90-, Univ Wash. **HONORS AND AWARDS** Fulbright-Hays Lect, 76-77; Fulbright-Hays Sr Researcher, 80. **MEMBERSHIPS** Am Asn for Applied Linguistics; Mod Lang Asn; Nat Coun of Tchrs of Eng; Soc for Slovene Stud; Tchrs of Eng to Speakers of Other Lang. **RESEARCH** Language policy; language aquisition; language ed; pacifism and war resistance. **SELECTED PUBLICATIONS** Auth, Planning Language, Planning Inequality: Language Policy in the Community, Longman, 91; auth, Language Policy and Migration in the United States, Lit, Cult & Ethnic, Ljubljana: Filozofska fakulteta, 92; auth, The Strength Not to Fight: An Oral History of the Conscientious Objectors of the Vietnam War, Little, Brown, 93; auth, Conscientous Objection to Military Service, in Peace and Conflict Resolution, Ohio St Univ Mershon Ctr, 94; auth, Conscientious Objection to the Vietnam War, Mag of Hist, vol 8, no 3, 94; auth, Power and Inequality in Language Education, Cambridge Univ Press, 95; auth, Language Policy and Changing Patterns of Migration, Ethnic Lit & Cult in the USA, Canada, & Australia, Peter Lang, 96; auth, Language Policy in Independent Slovenia, Int J of the Sociology of Lang, no 126, 97; auth, Draft Resistance and Evasion, Oxford Comp to Am Mil Hist, Oxford Univ Press. **CONTACT ADDRESS** Dept of English, Univ of Washington, Seattle, WA 98195. **EMAIL** tollefso@u.washington.edu

TOLLIVER, JOYCE
DISCIPLINE SPANISH LITERATURE **EDUCATION** Univ Southern Calif, PhD, 87. **CAREER** Assoc prof, Univ Ill Urbana Champaign. **RESEARCH** 19th Century Peninsular spanish literature, womens's studies, linguistic approaches to literature. **SELECTED PUBLICATIONS** Auth, "Discourse Analysis and the Interpreation of Lieterary Narrative," Style, (90), 266-283; auth, "Otro mode de ver: the Gaze in La ultima niebla," Revista Canadiense de Estudios Hispanicos, (92), 105-121; auth, "La que entrega la mirada, lo entrega todo: The Sexual economy of the Gaze in Pardo Bazan's La mirada," Romance Lang Annual 1992, vol 4, (93), 620-626; auth, "Script Theory, Perspective and Message in Narrative: The case of Mi Suicidio," The Text and Beyond: Essays in Literary Linguistics, (Tuscloosa: Univ of Ala Press, 94), 97-119; auth, "Sor Aparicion and the Gaze: Pardo Bazan's Gendered Reply to the romantic Don Juan," Hispania, (94), 185-196; ed, "Torn Lace" and other stories by Emilia Pardo Bazan, New York: Modern Lang Assoc texts and Translations series, 96; auth, El encaje roto: y otros cuentos de Emilia Pardo Bazan, New York: Modern Lang Assoc Texts and Translations series, 96; auth, "From Labov and Waletsky: contextualist narratology 1967-1997," Journal of Narrative and life Hist, (97), 53-60; auth, Cigar Smoke and Violet-Water: Gendered Discourse in th Stories of Emilia Pardo Bazan, Lewisburg, PA: Bucknell Univ Press, 98. **CONTACT ADDRESS** Spanish, Italian, and Portuguese Dept, Univ of Illinois, Urbana-Champaign, 707 S Mathews, 4080 FLB, MC 176, Urbanan, IL 61801. **EMAIL** joycet@uiuc.edu

TOLO, KHAMA-BASILLI
DISCIPLINE FRENCH **EDUCATION** Vanderbilt Univ, PhD, 90. **CAREER** Assoc prof; Univ WY, 90-. **RESEARCH** 19th-century French; 19th- and 20th- century Francophone lit(s). **SELECTED PUBLICATIONS** Publ, short stories and poems, articles on lit criticism. **CONTACT ADDRESS** Dept of Mod and Class Lang(s), Univ of Wyoming, PO Box 3964, Laramie, WY 82071-3964. **EMAIL** KBTOLO@UWYO.EDU

TOMAYKO, JAMES EDWARD
PERSONAL Born 07/08/1949, Charleroi, PA, m, 1972 **DISCIPLINE** CHINESE LANGUAGE, HISTORY OF TECHNOLOGY **EDUCATION** Carnegie-Mellon Univ, BA, 71, DA, 80; Univ Pittsburgh, MA, 72. **CAREER** Headmaster, Self-Directed Learning Ctr, 75-80; instr hist, Garden City Community Col, 80-81; tech pub specialist, NCR Corp, 81; ASST PROF COMP SCI, HIST AND CHINESE, WICHITA STATE UNIV, 82- **MEMBERSHIPS** Soc for the Hist of Technol; Asn Comput Mach; Chinese Lang Teachers Asn; Am Asn Artificial Intelligence; Asn Comput Ling. **RESEARCH** History of computing; Chinese natural language processing. **SELECTED PUBLICATIONS** Auth, The Ditch Irrigation Boom in Southwest Kansas, J West, fall 82; A Simple, Comprehensive Input/Output System for Chinese Natural Language Processing, Comp Sci Dept, Wichita State Univ, 5/82; The Relationship Between the N-BU-N and V-BU-V Constructions in Chinese, Proc of the Mid-Am Ling Conf, 82; Memories of Turing, Alan in Annals of the History of Computing, Vol 0015, 93. **CONTACT ADDRESS** 828 S Holyoke, Wichita, KS 67218. **EMAIL** jet=@ux6.sp.cs.cmu.edu

TONG, DIANE
PERSONAL Born 06/19/1943, New York, NY **DISCIPLINE** LINGUISTICS **EDUCATION** Queens Col, BA 69; NYork Univ, MA 82. **CAREER** Author **MEMBERSHIPS** Authors Guild **RESEARCH** Gypsy Studies; Photography. **SELECTED PUBLICATIONS** Auth, Gypsies: An Interdisciplinary reader, NY, Garland Pub, 98; Jour of Mediterranean Studies, ed, Gypsies and Gypsy Cultures in the Mediterranean, 97; Gypsies: A Multidisciplinary Annotated Bibliography, NY, Garland Pub, 95; Gypsy Folktales, San Diego, Harcourt Brace Jovanovich, 89; Milano, 90 and Madrid, 97. **CONTACT ADDRESS** 67 Park Av Apt 5D, New York, NY 10016. **EMAIL** dianetong@delphi.com

TONKIN, HUMPHREY R.
PERSONAL Born 12/02/1939, Truro, United Kingdom, m, 1983, 2 children **DISCIPLINE** ENGLISH, LINGUISTICS **EDUCATION** Cambridge Univ, BA, 62; Harvard Univ, MA, PhD, 62-66. **CAREER** Asst prof, assoc prof, v prov, co-od intl prog, mst Stouffer Col House, Univ Penn, 66-83; vis prof, Columbia Univ, 80-81; pres, SUNT Potsdam, 83-88; pres, Univ Hartford, 89-98; vis scholar, Yale Univ, 98-99; prof, Univ Hartford, 98-. **HONORS AND AWARDS** Knox Fel, 62-66; Guggenheim Fel, 74; Linback Awd, Dis Teach, 71; DLit, Univ Hart, 99. **MEMBERSHIPS** MLA; RSA; ACTFL; Spenser Soc; Milton Soc; CAAS; IASSM. **RESEARCH** Shakespeare and early modern English literature; English romantic poets; sociolinguistics and language policy and planning. **SELECTED PUBLICATIONS** Spenser's Courteous Pastoral, Oxford UP, 72; auth, The Faerie Queene, Unwin Hyman: Unwin Critical Library (London, 89); compiler, Sir Walter Raleigh: Elizabethan Bibliographies Supplements (London: Nether Press, 71); coauth, The World in the Curriculum, Change Magazine Press (New Rochelle, NY), 82; co-ed, Language in Religion (Lanham, MD: UP of Am, 89); ed and trans, Esperanto: Language, Literature and Community by Pierre Janton (Albany: SUNY Press, 93); ed, Esperanto, Interlinguistics and Planned Language (Lanham: UP of Am, 97); ed and trans, Maskerado: Dancing Around Death in Nazi Hungary by Tivadar Soros, Canongate (Edinburgh), 00; auth, "Esperanto and International Language Problems," Esperantic Stud (77). **CONTACT ADDRESS** Mortensen Lib, Univ of Hartford, West Hartford, CT 06117. **EMAIL** tonkin@mail.hartford.edu

TORGOVNICK, MARIANNA DE MARCO
PERSONAL Born 08/31/1949, Brooklyn, NY, m, 1968, 2 children **DISCIPLINE** ENGLISH, COMPARATIVE LITERATURE **EDUCATION** NYork Univ, BA, 70; Columbia Univ, MA, 71; PhD, 75. **CAREER** Asst prof, Williams Col, 75-81; vis prof, Princeton Univ, 93; asst prof to prof, Duke Univ, 81-, assoc chair, 86-92, chair, 96-99, Dir, Duke in New York Arts Prog, 99. **HONORS AND AWARDS** John Simon Guggenheim Fel, 81; Cohen-Porter Vis Scholar, Tel Aviv Univ, 93; Winner, Am Book Awd for Crossing Ocean Parkway, 94; ed bd, Twentieth Century Literature, Religion, and the Arts; NEH Summer Seminar Grant, 97; numerous radio and television interviews, including in-depth Nat Public Radio Shows in New York, Washington, San Francisco, etc. **MEMBERSHIPS** Modern Lang Asn, Int Soc for the Study of Time. **RESEARCH** Twentieth-century literature and culture, contemporary America (U.S.), contemporary fiction, cultural criticism. **SELECTED PUBLICATIONS** Auth, Closure in the Novel, Princeton: Princeton Univ Press (81); auth, The Visual Arts, Pictorialism, and the Novel: James, Lawrence and Woolf, Princeton: Princeton Univ Press (85); auth, "Experimental Critical Writing," ADE Bull, 9, 6 (fall 90): 8-11; auth, "On Being White, Female, and Born in Bensonhurst," Partisan Rev, 57:3 (summer 90): 456-66; auth, Gone Primitive: Savage Intellects, Modern Lives, Chicago: Univ of Chicago Press (90, 91); auth, Eloquent Obsessions: Writing Cultural Criticism, Durham: Duke Univ Press (93); auth, Crossing Ocean Parkway: Readings by an Italian American Daughter, Chicago: Univ of Chicago Press (94); auth, Primitive Passions: Men, Women, and the Quest for Ecstasy, New York: Knopf (97). **CONTACT ADDRESS** Dept English, Duke Univ, PO Box 90015, Durham, NC 27708-0015. **EMAIL** Tor@Duke.edu

TORRANCE, ROBERT M.
PERSONAL Born 05/09/1939, Washington, DC, m **DISCIPLINE** COMPARATIVE LITERATURE **EDUCATION** Harvard, BA, 1961; Univ California, MA, 63; Harvard, PhD, 70. **CAREER** Asst Prof, Harvard, 71-75; assoc Prof, Brooklyn Col, 75-76; assoc, Prof, Univ of California, 76-00. **RESEARCH** Ancient and Modern European and American Literature; philosophy, religion, anthropology, nature and history, translation and poetry. **SELECTED PUBLICATIONS** Transl, Sophocles, The Women of Trachis and Philoctetes (Boston: Houghton Mifflin, 66); auth, The Comic Hero, (Cambridge, Mass: Harvard U.F., 78); auth, Idral and Spleen:The Crisis of Transcendent Vision in Romantic, Symbolist, and Modern Poetry, (N.Y. to London: Garland, 1987); auth, The Spritual Quest: Transcendence in Myth, Religion, and Science, (Berkeley: UC Press, 1994); ed, "Emcompassing Nature: A Sourcebook, (Washington, D.C.: Counterpoint, 98). **CONTACT ADDRESS** Dept Comparative Literature, Univ of California, Davis, 1 Shields Ave, Davis, CA 95616-5270. **EMAIL** rmtorrance@ucdavis.edu

TORRES-RECINOS, JULIO
PERSONAL Born 06/15/1962, Chalatenango, El Salvador **DISCIPLINE** SPANISH, LATIN AMERICAN LITERATURE **EDUCATION** York Univ, BA; Univ Toronto, MA; PhD. **CAREER** TA, Univ of Toronto, 89-94; lectr, Univ of Guelph, 94-99; asst prof, Univ Sask, 99-01. **HONORS AND AWARDS** Univ of Toronto Open Fel; Milton A Buchanan Fel. **MEMBERSHIPS** MLA, Can Assoc of Hispanics, Can Assoc of Latin Am and Caribbean Studies. **RESEARCH** Central American literature, Testimonial Literature, Latin American Poetry, Modern Spanish Literature, Latin American Nove. **SELECTED PUBLICATIONS** Rev, of "La estacion de fiebre y otros amaneceres" by Ana Istaru, Tinta y sombra (93); auth, "Voz narrativa, audiencia y autoridad testual en 'Diario de una multitud' de Carmen Naranjo," ISTMICA, (99-00); auth, "Valores viejos y cambio social en 'Dos senoras conversan' de Bryce Echenique," Revista Tinta y sombra, (99); auth, Nosotros, Ediciones Amaranta, 00; auth, Crisol del tiempo, Ediciones Amaranta, 00. **CONTACT ADDRESS** Dept Lang and Ling, Univ of Saskatchewan, 9 Campus Dr, Saskatoon, SK, Canada S7N 5A5. **EMAIL** julio.torres@usask.ca

TORUNO, RHINA
PERSONAL Born San Salvador, El Salvador, w, 3 children **DISCIPLINE** SPANISH **EDUCATION** Nat Univ El Salvador, BA, 71; Cath Univ Louvain Belgium, MA, 73; Nat Univ Paris-Sorbonne, MA, 76; Cath Univ Louvain Belgium, PhD, 78; IN Univ, Bloomington, PhD, 94. **CAREER** Asst prof, Univ TX Permian Basin, Odessa, 95-; vis asst prof, FL State Univ, Tallahassee, 94-95; part timr lectr, IN Univ,Bloomington, 90-93; vis prof, Collegium Pro Am Lat, Louvain, Belgium, 89; assoc instr, IN Univ, Bloomington, 83-89; tchg asst, Univ CA, Irvine, 82-83; vis scholar, Stanford Univ, 81-82; prof, Nat Univ El Salvador, 76-81. **HONORS AND AWARDS** Elected chp, session Mex lit for, Nat Conf 98, 78 Nat Conf Am Asn Tchrs Span & Port, Inc, Orlando, 96; key-note speaker, Hisp Grad Ceremony, Univ TX of Permain Basin, 96; Awd for Educ Res & publ, Pan Amer Round Table Odessa, 96; key-note speaker, 3rd Coloquio Bi-Annual Span & Span-Am Lit, AZ State Univ, 96; nominated, Honor Mem Ecologic Mex Club, Monterrey, 96; inducted as 1st female mem, Salvadoran Acad Span Lang, 95. **MEMBERSHIPS** Asoc de Ling y Filologia de la America Latina; Amer Asn Tchr(s) Span & Port, Inc; Asociacion de Lit Femenina Hispanica; Asn des Amis d'Emmanuel Mounier, Fr; Asociacion de Mujeres Univ de El Salvador; Club Ecologico Novaterra, Monterrey, Mex; Feministas Unidas, USA; Inst Int de Literatura Iberoamericana; Lat Amer Stud Asn; Midland Hisp Chamber Commerce; MLA; Southwest Coun Lat Am Stud; S Atl Mod Lang Asn; S Ctr Mod Lang Asn; Royal Acad Span Lang Spain; Salvadoran Acad Lang; Salvadoran Acad Arts & Sci. **RESEARCH** 20th century Spain and Latin Am narrative; poetry; drama and literary theory; educ exchange with Mexico. **SELECTED PUBLICATIONS** Auth, Tiempo, Destino Y Opresion El La Obra De Elena Garro, Time, Destiny and Oppression in the Work of Elena Garro, NY, Mellen UP, 96; Del realismo magico de Los recuerdos del porvenir al realismo social de Y Matarazo no llamo, From the Magical Realism of Recollection of Things to Come to the Social Realism of And Matarazo didn't call, Deslinde Nuevo Leon, Mexico, UP, 95; Y Matarazo no llamo Novela poletica y la ltima escrita por Elena Garro, And Matarazo didn't call, Analysis of the Political Novel and the Most Recent Work by Elena Garro, Letras Informa, Ano II, U, San Carlos, Guatemala, 94; Distintos referentes y afines significantes en La muerte de Artemio Cruz y El siglo de las luces, Distinct References and Related Significance in the Death of Artemio Cruz, and The Century of Light, Arts 3, San Salvador, 93; Protesta contra la opresion: categoreas medulares en la obra narrativa y dramatica de Elena Garro, Protest Against Oppression: Central Categories in the Narrative and Drama Work of Elena Garro, Deslinde Nuevo Leon, Mex UP, 92; Sobre la vida desgarradora de Elena Garro, Concerning the Shattered Life of Elena Garro, El Diario, Las Prensa, New York Times, NY, 96; Dialogo con Elena Garro sobre sus tecnicas literarias, Dialog with Elena Garro about her literary style, Diario Latino, Lit Supplement, 96; coauth, La cenicienta en una fiesta de medianoche en el paes de la sonrisa, Despues de Medianoche, Cinderella in the Midnight Ball in the Country of Smile in After Midnight by David Escobar Galindo, Drama in Obras teatrales de un solo acto de dramaturgos latinoamericanos, Drama Works of One Act by Latin-American Dramatists, Univ de Antioquia, Colombia, 96. **CONTACT ADDRESS** Dept of Mod Lang, Univ of Texas of the Permian Basin, Odessa, TX 79762. **EMAIL** toruno_r@utpb.edu

TOUMAYAN, ALAIN P.
DISCIPLINE FRENCH LITERATURE **EDUCATION** Univ of Penn, BA, 76; Yale Univ, MA, 78, Mphil, 80, PhD, 82. **CAREER** Assoc prof. **RESEARCH** 19th and 20th century French literature. **SELECTED PUBLICATIONS** Auth, pubs on the problem of evil in 19th century texts, 19th and 20th century subjects, and Festschrift on literary generations. **CONTACT ADDRESS** Romance Languages and Literatures Dept, Univ of Notre Dame, Notre Dame, IN 46556.

TOUMAZOU, MICHAEL K.
PERSONAL Born 12/11/1952, Famagusta, Cyprus, m, 1978, 3 children **DISCIPLINE** CLASSICS **EDUCATION** Marshall Col, BA, 77; Loyola Univ Chicago, MA, 80; Bryn Mawr Col, MA, 83, PhD, 87. **CAREER** Asst prof, classics, 87-93, Assoc Prof Classics, 93-, Dept Chair, 95-, Davidson Col. **HONORS AND AWARDS** Whiting Fnd fel, 86-87; NEH senior fel, 1994-95; Trustee of Cyprus Am Archeol Res Inst, 96-. **MEMBERSHIPS** Archeol Inst Am; Am Schs Oriental Res; Soc Promotion Hellenic Stud; Classical Asn Midwest & South; NC Class Asn. **RESEARCH** Classl & Cypriote Archeol **SELECTED PUBLICATIONS** Articles in Zeitsmrift fur Papyrologie und Epigraphic, 41, 81, Am J Archeol, 91-99, Bulletin de Correspondence Hellenique, J Field Archeol 25, 98; auth, Aspects of Burial Practices in Prehistoric Cypriote Site, c.7,000-25,000 B.C., Univ Mich, 87. **CONTACT ADDRESS** Dept of Classics, Davidson Col, Davidson, NC 28036. **EMAIL** mitoumazou@davidson.edu

TOURNIER, CLAUDE
DISCIPLINE FRENCH **EDUCATION** Northwestern Univ, PhD. **CAREER** Sr lectr; prog coordr, first-yr Fr and tchg asst supvr Northwestern Univ; lect, ACTFL, Central States, IFLTA; trained as, ACTFL oral proficiency tester. **RESEARCH** Cooperative learning, curriculum design, development of materials for a communicative approach to teaching, and the use of technology in the classroom. **SELECTED PUBLICATIONS** Coauth, Voil, Heinle & Heinle. **CONTACT ADDRESS** Dept of French, Northwestern Univ, 1801 Hinman, Evanston, IL 60208.

TOURNISSAC, ANNICK-FRANCE
PERSONAL Born Montpellier, France, m, 1998 **DISCIPLINE** FRENCH, FRANCOPHONE STUDIES **EDUCATION** Univ Montpellier, BS, 86; Univ Paris Pantheon-Sorbonne, BA, 88; MA, 90; PhD, 97. **CAREER** Lectr, Univ Montpellier, 96-97; lectr, Univ Santa Barbara, 99; lectr, Univ Calif Los Angeles, 00-. **MEMBERSHIPS** MLA; SCS. **SELECTED PUBLICATIONS** Auth, Le Docudrame Americain, Septentrion Univ Pr (France), 99; auth, The Role of French Women in Television: Policewomen (forthcoming). **CONTACT ADDRESS** Fr Dept, Univ of California, Los Angeles, 212 Royce Hall, PO Box 951550, Los Angeles, CA 90095-1550. **EMAIL** annick@humnet.ucla.edu

TOWNER, WAYNE SIBLEY
PERSONAL Born 01/10/1933, Scottsbluff, NE, m, 1956, 2 children **DISCIPLINE** RELIGION, PHILOLOGY **EDUCATION** Yale Univ, BA, 54, BD, 60, MA, 61, PhD, 65. **CAREER** Eng tchr, Gerard Inst, Sidon, Lebanon, 54-57; instr Old Testament, Princeton Theol Sem, 63-64; lectr, divinity sch, Yale Univ, 64-65, asst prof 65-69, assoc prof Old Testament, 69-71; prof & dean Theol Sem, Univ Dubuque, 71-75; Prof Old Testament, Union Theol Sem, Richmond, Va, 75-, Dean, 85-88. **HONORS AND AWARDS** First Prize, Theology Category, Harper Collins Annual Best Sermons Awd, 87; Second Prize, Christian Ministry, Alfred P Klausner Sermon Awd, 97; Doctor of Div, Coe College, 00. **MEMBERSHIPS** Soc Bibl Lit. **RESEARCH** Old Testament; rabbinic lit. **SELECTED PUBLICATIONS** Auth, The Rabbinic Enumeration of Scriptural Examples, Brill, Leiden, 73; How God Deals with Evil, Westminster, 76; Daniel, Westminster John Knox, 84; Genesis, Westminster Bible Companion, 01. **CONTACT ADDRESS** 3401 Brook Rd, Richmond, VA 23227-4514. **EMAIL** stowner@union-psc.edu

TOWNSEL, SYLVIANE
PERSONAL Born 12/03/1943, Moule, Guadeloupe, m, 1978, 1 child **DISCIPLINE** LITERATURE, SPANISH **EDUCATION** Emory Univ, BA; MA; PhD, 87. **CAREER** Asst prof, SUNY Oswego, 88-93; asst prof, Murray State, 93-94; asst prof Ball State Univ, 95-97; assoc prof, Albany State Univ, 97-. **HONORS AND AWARDS** Grant, Univ of Ga, 98; Grant, Univ of Haw, 00. **RESEARCH** Francophone Literature, Negritude, Colonization and Decolonization in French Antillean Literature, 20th Century French and Francophone Literature, 19th and 20th Century Spanish and Spanish American Literature. **SELECTED PUBLICATIONS** Auth, Negritude in French Caribbean Literature, 92; auth, "La Mujer en Secdun", 96. **CONTACT ADDRESS** Dept English and Lang, Albany State Univ, 504 College Dr, Albany, GA 31705-2717. **EMAIL** atownsel@asurams.edu

TRAHAN, ELIZABETH WELT
PERSONAL Born 11/19/1924, Berlin, Germany, d, 1957, 1 child **DISCIPLINE** COMPARATIVE LITERATURE **EDUCATION** Sarah Lawrence Col, BA, 51; Cornell Univ, MA, 53; Yale Univ, PhD, 57. **CAREER** Instr, German and Russian, Univ Mass, 56-60; asst prof, Univ Pitt, 60-64; assoc prof, 64-66; assoc prof Humanities,Monterey Inst of For and Internatl Stud, 68-75, ch, Dept of Translation & Interpretation, 68-74, prof Humanities, 75-88, act dean, 76-77; vis prof Amherst Col, 85-92. **MEMBERSHIPS** MLA; Nat Coalition of Independent Scholars. **RESEARCH** Comparative literature of the nineteenth and twentieth centuries; literary translation; Holocaust studies. **SELECTED PUBLICATIONS** Auth, Crime and Punishment: A Basic Approach, Univ Mass, 59; ed, Gogol's Overcoat: Critical Essays, Ardis, 82; trans, Leo Tolstoy: The Divine and the Human, Delos, 90; auth, The Door is Always Open: The Ironic Subtexts of Kafka's Before the Law and Dygat's Usher of the Helios Movie Theatre, in Comparatist, 93; auth, George Bendemann's Path to the Judgment, in Approaches to Teaching: Kafka's Short Fiction, MLA, 95; auth, The Possessed as Dostoevskij's Homage to Gogol: An Essay in Traditional Criticism, in Russian Lit, 96; auth, Geisterbeschworung: Eine Judische Jugend im Wien der Kriegsjahre, Picus Verlag, 96; auth, Walking with Ghosts: A Jewish Childhood in Wartime Vienna, Peter Lang, 98. **CONTACT ADDRESS** 222 North East St, Apt. 1, Amherst, MA 01002.

TRAILL, DAVID ANGUS
PERSONAL Born 01/28/1942, Helensburgh, Scotland **DISCIPLINE** LATIN, GREEK **EDUCATION** Univ St Andrews, MA, 64; Univ Calif, Berkeley, PhD(classics), 71. **CAREER** Asst prof, 70-78; assoc prof, 78-85; prof, 85-, Univ Calif, Davis, **MEMBERSHIPS** Am Philol Asn; Medieval Asn Pac; Am Inst Archaeol; Medieval Acad of Am. **RESEARCH** Classical Latin and Greek and medieval Latin poetry, Schliemann. **SELECTED PUBLICATIONS** Auth, Walafrid Strabo's Visio Wettini: Text, Translation, and Commentary, Lateinische Sprache und Literature des Mittelalters, Peter Lang, 74; auth, "Catullus 63: Rings Around the Sun," Class Philol 76 (81): 211-214; coed, Myth, Scandal, and History: The Heinrich Schliemann Controversy and a First Edition of the Mycenaean Diary, Wayne State Univ (Detroit), 86; auth, "Parce Coninuis: A New Text and Interpretative Notes," Mittellateinisches Jahrbuch 21 (88): 114-124; auth, "Unfair to Hector?," Classical Philology 85 (90): 299-303; auth, "Excavating Schliemann: Collected Papers on Schliemann," Illinois Classical Studies 4, Scholars Press (Atlanta), 93; auth, "Parody and Original: The Structure and Interretation of CB 197 and CB 62," Medievalia et Humanistica 20 (93): 137-146; auth, "Propertius 1.21: The Sister, the Bones, and the Wayfarer," Am Jour of Philology 115 (94): 89-96; auth, Schliemann of Troy: Treasure and Deceit, St. Martins Press (NYork), 95; auth, "Callimachus' Singing Sea (Hymn 2.106)," Classical Philology 93 (98): 215-222. **CONTACT ADDRESS** Dept Classics, Univ of California, Davis, Davis, CA 95616. **EMAIL** datraill@ucdavis.edu

TRAPNELL, WILLIAM HOLMES
PERSONAL Born 09/16/1931, Richmond, VA, m, 1958 **DISCIPLINE** FRENCH LITERATURE **EDUCATION** Hamp-

den-Sydney Col, BA, 54; Middlebury Col, MA, 62; Univ Pittsburgh, PhD (French lit), 67. **CAREER** Instr French, Hampden-Sydney Col, 59-60; instr, Rollins Col, 60-63; asst instr, Univ Pittsburgh, 66-67; asst prof, Brown Univ, 67-69; asst prof, 69-73, ASSOC PROF FRENCH, IND UNIV, BLOOMINGTON, 73-83; prof, 83-96; prof emer. **HONORS AND AWARDS** Eli Litty Fel 87-88. **MEMBERSHIPS** Societe Challe, ADIREL. **RESEARCH** Eigteenth century literature; Challe, Woolston, the Arabian Nights **SELECTED PUBLICATIONS** Auth, Voltaire and his Portable Dictionary, Analecta Romanica 32, Frankfurt am Main: Klostermann, 72; auth, Voltaire and the Eucharist, Studies on Voltaire and the Eighteenth Century 198, Oxford, 81; auth, Eavesdropping in Marivaux, Geneva: Droz, 87; auth, The Treatment of Christian Doctrine by Philosophers of the Natural Light from Descartes to Berkeley, Studies on Voltaire and the Eighteenth Century, 252, Oxford, 88; auth, Thomas Woolston, Madman and Deist? Bristol: Thoemmes, 94. **CONTACT ADDRESS** 123 Bastille Court, Williamsburg, VA 23185. **EMAIL** whtrapnell@aol.com

TRAUGOTT, ELIZABETH CLOSS
PERSONAL Born 04/09/1939, Bristol, England, m, 1967, 1 child **DISCIPLINE** LINGUISTICS **EDUCATION** Oxford Univ, BA, 60,Univ Calif, Berkeley, PhD(English lang), 64. **CAREER** Asst prof English, Univ Calif, Berkeley, 64-70; assoc prof, 71-77, PROF LING AND ENGLISH, STANFORD UNIV, 77-, Mem, Joint Inst/Ministry Educ Lang and Lit Panel, Dar es Salaam, Tanzania, 65-66; vis lectr ling, Univ EAfrica, 65-66 and Univ York, England, 66-67. **HONORS AND AWARDS** Am Coun Learned Soc fel, 75-76; Guggenhein fel, 83-84; CASBS fel, 83-84. **MEMBERSHIPS** Ling Soc Am; Int Ling Asn; Ling Asn Gt Brit; Am Asn Univ Women. **RESEARCH** Language change; stucture and history of the English language; linguistics and literature. **SELECTED PUBLICATIONS** Auth, A History of English Syntax, New York, Holt, Rinehart and Winston, 72; auth, Elizabeth Closs Traugott and Mary L Pratt, Linguistics for Students of Literature, New York, Harcourt, Brace, Jovanovich, Inc, 80; coed, On Conditionals, Cambridge, Cambridge Univ Press, 86; coed, Approaches to Grammaticalization, 2 vols, Amsterdam, Benjamins, 91; coauth, Grammaticalization, Cambridge, Cambridge Univ Press, 93.auth, " Diachronic Syntax and Generative Grammer," Language 41:402-14, 65; auth, On the Expression of Spaito-Temporal Relations in Language" Joseph H Greenberg, Universals of Human Language III, Stanford Univ Press, (78), 369-400; auth, " From Propostional to Textual and Expressive Meanings: Some Semantic-Pragmatic Aspects of Grammaticalizaiton," Perspectives on Historical Linguistics, Amsterdam, Benjamins, (82), 245-271; auth, On the Rise of Epistmeic Meanings in English: an Example of Subjectificaition in Semantic Change," Language 57:33-65, 89; auth, " The role of pragmatics in a theory of semantic change," Pragmatics in1998: Selected Papers from the 6th International Pragmatics Conference, vol 2, Antwerp: International Pragmatic Association, (99), 93-102. **CONTACT ADDRESS** Dept of Ling, Stanford Univ, Stanford, CA 94305-1926.

TRAUPMAN, JOHN CHARLES
PERSONAL Born 01/02/1923, Nazareth, PA, m, 1949, 1 child **DISCIPLINE** CLASSICAL LANGUAGES **EDUCATION** Moravian Col, BA, 48; Princeton Univ, MA, 51, PhD(classics), 56. **CAREER** From instr to assoc prof, 51-61, Prof Classics, 61-89, chemn 57-89, St Joseph's Univ; Assoc ed, Scribner Bantam English Dictionary, 77. **HONORS AND AWARDS** Magna cum laude, 48; Schulze Greek Awd, 48; Robbins Scholar, Princeton Univ, 50-51; Faculty Merit Awd for Research, 82; St Joseph's Univ Col Tchg Awd, 86; Awd of the Class Asn of the Atlantic States, 90; Special Awd of the Class Asn of the Atlantic States, 96. **MEMBERSHIPS** Am Philol Asn; Archaeol Inst Am; Am Class League. **RESEARCH** Archaeology; Latin lexicography. **SELECTED PUBLICATIONS** Auth, New Collegiate Latin and English Dictionary, Bantam, 66, rev ed, 95; The New College Latin and English Dictionary, Amsco 68; ed, German-English Dictionary, Bantam, 82; auth, latin is Fun,, book I, Amsco, 88, book II, Amsco, 94; assoc ed, Scribner English Dictionary, Scribner, 77; auth, German Fundamentals, Barron's, 92; auth, Conversational latin for Oral Proficiency, 2d ed, Bolchazy-Carducci, 97; auth, Lingua Latina, book I, Amsco, 98. **CONTACT ADDRESS** Dept of Classics, Saint Joseph's Univ, Philadelphia, PA 19131. **EMAIL** traupman@sju.edu

TRAVERSA, VINCENZO
PERSONAL Born 04/08/1923, Venice, Italy, m, 1984 **DISCIPLINE** ITALIAN **EDUCATION** Univ Orientale, Lingue Dottore, 49; Univ Calif at Los Angeles, MA, 59; PhD, 63. **CAREER** Instr, Univ Calif, Los Angeles, 57-60; asst prof, Stanford Univ, 60-67; assoc prof, Univ Kans, 67-70; dept ch, Cal State Univ, Hayward, 70-83; prof, 70-. **HONORS AND AWARDS** Awd Title, Knight in the Order of Merit, by Pres of Italian Republic, 86. **MEMBERSHIPS** AATI; MLA; AAUP; FLANC; Leonardo da Vinci Soc; Friends of Photography. **RESEARCH** Italian and European Medieval and Renaissance literature; modern and contemporary Italian literature; Italian language and linguistics. **SELECTED PUBLICATIONS** Auth, The Laude in the Middle Ages, Peter Lang Pub, 94; auth, Parola e Pensiero: Introduzione Alla Lingua Italiana Moderna, Harper and Row, 81, 75, 67; auth, Racconti di Alberto Moravia, Irvington, 80; auth, Idioma in Prospecttia: Profili da il Gattopardo, Harper and Row, 69. **CONTACT ADDRESS** Dept Modern Lang, Lit, California State Univ, Hayward, 25800 Carlos Bee Blvd, Hayward, CA 94542-3001. **EMAIL** vtravers@csuhayward.edu

TREADGOLD, WARREN
PERSONAL Born 04/30/1949, Oxford, United Kingdom, m, 1982 **DISCIPLINE** HISTORY, CLASSICS **EDUCATION** Harvard Univ, AB, 70; PhD, 77. **CAREER** Lectr, UCLA, 77-78; Univ Munich, Free Univ Berlin, 78-80; 82-83; Lectr, Standford Univ, 80-82; asst prof, Hillsdale Col, 83-88; vis prof, Univ Calif at Berkeley, 86; asst prof, Fla Int Univ, 88-97; prof, St Louis Univ, 97- **HONORS AND AWARDS** Woodrow Wilson Int Center for Scholars Fel; NEH Fel (2); Visiting Fel, All Souls Col, Oxford; Alexander von Humboldt Fel; Outstanding Achievements and Performance awards, Fla Int Univ. **MEMBERSHIPS** AHA; Am Philos Assoc; Medieval Acad of Am; AAUP. **RESEARCH** Byzantine history and literature. **SELECTED PUBLICATIONS** Auth, The Nature of the Bibliotheas of Photrus, 80; auth, The Byzantine State Finances in the Eighth and Ninth Centures, 82; ed, Renaissances Before the Renaissance, 84; auth, The Byzantine Revivial, 88; auth, Byzantium and It's Army, 95; auth, A History of the Byzantine State and Society, 97; auth, A Concise History of Byzantium, 00. **CONTACT ADDRESS** Dept Hist, St. Louis Univ, 221 N Grand Boulevard, Saint Louis, MO 63103-2006. **EMAIL** treadgw@slu.edu

TREGGIARI, SUSAN M.
DISCIPLINE CLASSICS **EDUCATION** BA, 62; MA, 65; BLitt, 67; Oxford Univ, DLitt, 93. **CAREER** Anne T. and Robert M. Bass Prof Schl Hum and Sci; prof class/hist. **RESEARCH** Roman hist; Roman soc in the late Republic and Principate; lit, epigraphic and juristic sources. **SELECTED PUBLICATIONS** Auth, Roman Freedmen During the Late Republic, 69; Roman Marriage: Iusti Coniuges from the Time of Cicero to the Time of Ulpian, 91; Social Status And Social Legislation in the Cambridge Ancient History X, 96. **CONTACT ADDRESS** Stanford Univ, Bldg 20, Main Quad, Stanford, CA 94305.

TREGOUET, ANNIE D.
DISCIPLINE FRENCH STUDIES **EDUCATION** Univ Montpellier, BA, 86; MA, 87; Univ Colo Boulder, PhD, 00. **CAREER** Vis asst prof, Case Western Reserve Univ, 00-01; vis asst prof, Oberlin Col, 01-. **MEMBERSHIPS** MLA; LFA. **RESEARCH** Film and literary theory; modern and contemporary French and Francophone literature; French and Francophone cinema; European cinema. **SELECTED PUBLICATIONS** Auth, "Une Adaptation d'Auteur: Les Miserables de Claude Lelouch," Etudes Romances (98); auth, "The Male Gaze Subverted: Germaine Dulac's Le Belle Dame sans Merci," WVa Univ Philol (01). **CONTACT ADDRESS** Dept Romance Lang, Oberlin Col, 173 West Lorain St, Oberlin, OH 44074. **EMAIL** adrmtregouet@yahoo.com

TROIANO, JAMES J.
PERSONAL Born 12/17/1944, Elizabeth, NJ, m, 1972 **DISCIPLINE** SPANISH **EDUCATION** Rutgers Univ, AB, 66; State Univ NYork, Buffalo, AM, 68; PhD, 73. **CAREER** Instr, SUNY-Buffalo, 70; from instr to asst prof, Canisius Col, 70-75; from instr to prof, Univ Maine, 75-. **MEMBERSHIPS** MLA; Am Asn Teachers Span and Port; Nat Educ Asn. **RESEARCH** Contemporary Latin American theater and short story. **SELECTED PUBLICATIONS** Auth, "Social Criticism and the Fantastic in Roberto Arlt's 'La fiesta del hierro,'" Latin Am Theater Rev (Fall, 79): 39-45; auth, "The Relativity of Madness in Roberto Arlt's 'Escenas de un grotesco,'" Latin Am Theater Rev (Fall, 85): 49-56; auth, "Literary Traditions in 'El Fabricante de fantasmas' by Roberto Arlt," Inti: Rev de lit hisp (Spring, 88): 163-172; auth, "Illusory Worlds in Three Short Stories by Emilio Carballido," Hisp J (Spring, 89): 63-79; auth, "Love and Madness in Arlt's 'La juerga de los Polichinelas,'" Confluencia (Fall, 90): 135-140; auth, "Life as Theater in Aloisi's 'Nada de Pirandello, por favor,'" Inti: Rev de lit hisp 34 & 35 (91 & 92): 159-168; auth, "The Theater of Roberto Arlt," in International Dictionary of Theater (London: St James Press, 94); auth, "The Theater of Life in Aurelio Ferretti's 'La cama y el sof','" Hisp J 1 (Spring, 94): 147-164; auth, "Interplay of Life and Theater in 'Ide y vuelta' by Mario Benedetti," Confluencia 2 (96): 20-26; auth, "The Influence of Pirandello in Latin America," PSA, forthcoming. **CONTACT ADDRESS** Dept of Mod Lang and Classics, Univ of Maine, Orono, ME 04469. **EMAIL** James.Troiano@umit.maine.edu

TROMMLER, FRANK ALFRED
PERSONAL Born 05/11/1939, Zwickau, Germany, m, 2 children **DISCIPLINE** GERMAN AND COMPARATIVE LITERATURE **EDUCATION** Univ Munich, Dr phil (Ger lit), 64. **CAREER** Vis lectr Ger Lit, Harvard Univ, 67-69; prof Ger Lit, Univ Pa, 70-, vis prof, Princeton Univ, 78, Johns Hopkins Univ, 80, chmn Ger Dept, 80-86, 95-97; acting chair Slavic dept, 96-00, dir Humanities Prog, Am Inst for Contemp Ger Studies, 95-. **HONORS AND AWARDS** Dir NEH Summer Sem, 83; Guggenheim Fellow 84-85; Dir DAAD Summer Sem 88, 90; Certificate of Merit AATG/Goethe Inst, 91. **MEMBERSHIPS** MLA Exec Council 95-98; AATG chp Philadephia Pres 86-90, German Studies Assoc Vice Pres, 88-90; Pres 90-92; PMLA Editorial Bd, 99-01. **RESEARCH** German literature of the 19th and 20th centuries; modernism and Technology, Ger-Am cultural relations. **SELECTED PUBLICATIONS** Auth, Roman und Wirklichkeit, Kohihammer, 66; Der zogernde Nachwuchs: Entwicklungsprobleme der Nachkriegsliteratur, Tendenzen der deutschen Literatur seit 1945, Kroner, 71; Sozialistische Literatur in Deutschland, Kroner, 76; coauth, die Kultur der Weimarer Republik, Nymphenburger, 78; co-ed, Jahrhundertwende Deutsche Literatur VIII, Rowohlt, 82; co ed, American and the Germans, Univ of Pa Press, 85; Der Mythos Jugend, Suhrkamp, 85; ed, Germanistik in den USA, Westdeutscher, 89; auth, "Normality and Resistance," J of Mod History (92); ed Thematics Reconsidered Rodopi, 95; co ed Revisiting Zero Hour, 1945, AICGS Washington, 96; ed, Berlin: The New Capital, AICGS Washington, 00; coed, The German-American Encounter, Berghahn, 01; ed, Deutsch-amerikanische Begegnungen, Deutsche Verlagsanstalt, 01. **CONTACT ADDRESS** Dept of German, Univ of Pennsylvania, 255 S 36th St, Philadelphia, PA 19104-6305. **EMAIL** trommler@ccat.sas.upenn.edu

TROUILLE, MARY S.
PERSONAL Born 02/23/1951, Chicago, IL, m, 1978, 3 children **DISCIPLINE** FRENCH LITERATURE **EDUCATION** Northwestern Univ, PhD, 88. **CAREER** TA to lectr, Northwestern Univ, 83-90; lectr, Univ of Chicago, 90-93; asst prof to assoc prof, IL State Univ, 93-. **HONORS AND AWARDS** Fel, School of Criticism and Theory, 85; Fel, Int Summer Inst for Semiotic and Structural Studies, 86; Res Awd, IL State Univ, 93; ACLS Grant, 95; Outstanding Col Res in the Humanities, IL State Univ, 98. **MEMBERSHIPS** ASECS; Int Soc for Eighteenth Century Studies; Midwest Am Soc for Eighteenth Century Studies; MLA; Am Assoc of Teachers of French. **SELECTED PUBLICATIONS** Auth, "The Failings of Rousseau's Ideals of Domesticity and Sensibility", Eighteenth Century Studies 24.4 (98): 451-83; auth, "A Bold New Vision of Women: Stael and Wollstonecraft Respond to Rousseau", Studies on Voltaire and the Eighteenth Century 292, (91): 277-319; transl, The Writing of Melancholy: Modes of Opposition in Early French Modernism, by Ross Chambers, Univ of Chicago Pr, 93; auth, "Sexual/Textual Politics in the Enlightenment: Diderot and d'Espinay Respond to Thomas's Essay on Women", Romanic Rev 84.2 (94): 98-116; auth, "Eighteenth-Century Amazons of the Pen: Stephanie de Genlis and Olyympe de Gouges", Eighteenth Century French Women Writers and Intellectuals, ed Roland Bonnel and Catherine Rubinger, Peter Lang, (NY, 94): 341-70; auth, "The Circe of the Republic: Mme Roland, Rousseau, and Revolutionary Politics", Literate Women and the 1789 Revolution, ed Catherine Montfort, SUMMA Pr, (Birmingham, 95): 81-109; auth, "Women's Autobiography in Eighteen-Century France: the Emergence of a Feminine Voice in d'Epinay's Histoire de Madame de Montbrillant", Autobiographik von Frauen, ed Michaela Holdenried, Eric Schmidt Verlag, (Berlin, 95): 109-18; auth, Sexual Politics in the Enlightenment: Women Writers Read Rousseau, SUNY Pr, (Albany), 97; auth, "Toward a New Appreciation of Madame de Genlis: The Influence of Les Battuecas on George Sand's Political and Social Thought", Fr Rev 71.4 (98): 565-76; auth, "Battered Wife or Clever Opportunist? - The Separation Case of Jeanne F (Toulouse, 1782)", Eighteenth-Century Studies, (forthcoming). **CONTACT ADDRESS** Dept For Lang, Illinois State Univ, Box 4300, Normal, IL 61790-0001.

TRUCKENBRODT, HUBERT
PERSONAL Born 07/10/1962, Erlangen, Germany, s **DISCIPLINE** LINGUISTICS **EDUCATION** Universitat Tubingen, MA, 89; Mass Inst Technol (MIT), PhD, 96. **CAREER** Asst Prof, Universitat Tubingen, 95-96; Asst Prof, Rutgers Univ, 96-. **MEMBERSHIPS** Ling Soc of Am. **RESEARCH** Phonology, optimality theory, prosodic structure, syntax-phonology interface, intonation, tone and register. **SELECTED PUBLICATIONS** Auth, "The OCP, Underspecification and Articulatory Faithfulness," MIT Working Papers In Ling, vol 21 (94): 227-274; auth, "Position Neutralization and OCP-Subsidiary Features," Toronto Working Papers in Ling, vol 13.1 (94): 172-187; auth, "Wolfgang Sternefeld, Syntaktische Grenzen, Chomskys barrierentheorie und ihre Weiterentwicklungen, Linguistische Berichte, 155 (95): 65-75; auth, "Extraposition from NP and Prosodic Structure," Proceedings of NELS 25 (95): 503-517; auth, "Phonological Phrases: Their Relation to Syntax, Focus and Prominence," MIT Working Papers in Ling (Cambridge), 95; auth, "On the Relation Between Syntactic Phrases and Phonological Phrases," Ling Inquiry, vol 30.2 (99): 219-255. **CONTACT ADDRESS** Dept Ling, Rutgers, The State Univ of New Jersey, New Brunswick, 18 Seminary Pl, New Brunswick, NJ 08901-1184. **EMAIL** hubert@ruccs.rutgers.edu

TSIAPERA, MARIA
PERSONAL Born 07/26/1932, Cyprus **DISCIPLINE** LINGUISTICS, ARABIC **EDUCATION** Univ Tex, BA, 57, MA, 58, PhD(ling), 63. **CAREER** Asst prof ling, Fresno State Col, 64-66; from asst prof to assoc prof, 66-68, from actg chmn dept to chmn dept, 67-73, PROF LING, UNIV NC, CHAPEL HILL, 72-, Fel, Univ Tex, 63-64; NSF travel grant, 77; res grant, Univ NC, 77. **MEMBERSHIPS** Ling Soc Am; Southeastern Conf Ling (vpres, 70-71, pres, 71-72); SAlantic Mod Lang Asn; Am Orient Soc; Am Asn Teachers Arabic. **RESEARCH** History and philosophy of linguistics; Greek historical dialectology; Ar-

abic dialectology. **SELECTED PUBLICATIONS** Auth, Aristotle and the Grammaire Generale et Raisonee, Folia Ling Hist, Vol 0011, 92. **CONTACT ADDRESS** Dept of Linguistics, Univ of No Carolina, Chapel Hill, Chapel Hill, NC 27514.

TU, CHING-I
PERSONAL Born 05/13/1935, Nanking, China, m, 1970, 2 children **DISCIPLINE** CHINESE LITERATURE, CHINESE HISTORY **EDUCATION** Nat Taiwan Univ, BA, 58; Univ Wash, PhD, 67. **CAREER** Asst prof to assoc prof to prof to chemn, 66-, Rutgers Univ; vis assoc prof, Univ Hawaii, 71-72; vis prof, Nat Taiwan Univ, 74-75. **HONORS AND AWARDS** Res grant, US Dept Educ; res grant, Chiang Ching-Kuo Found; grants, Korean Found; found dir, chinese prog, found chair, dept e asian lang and cultures, rutgers univ. **MEMBERSHIPS** Asn Asian Stud; Am Asn Chinese Stud; MLA. **RESEARCH** Chinese literary criticism; Chinese intellectual history; cultural changes in Asia. **SELECTED PUBLICATIONS** Auth, Anthology of Chinese Literature, 72-; auth, Readings in Classical Chinese Literature, 81; auth, Tradition and Creativity: Essays on East Asian Civilization, 88; auth, Essays on East Asian Humanities; 91; auth, Classics and Interpretations: The Hermeneutic Traditions in Chinese Culture, 00. **CONTACT ADDRESS** Dept of Asian Lang and Cultures, Rutgers, The State Univ of New Jersey, New Brunswick, New Brunswick, NJ 08903. **EMAIL** citu@rci.rutgers.edu

TUCKER, CYNTHIA GRANT
PERSONAL Born 06/17/1941, New York, NY, m, 1966, 2 children **DISCIPLINE** COMPARATIVE LITERATURE, ENGLISH **EDUCATION** Denison Univ, BA, 63; Univ Iowa, PhD(comp lit), 67. **CAREER** Prof English, Univ Memphis; vstg fac, IA Summer Writing Festival, 99, 00; GTU in Berkeley, Summer 97, 99. **HONORS AND AWARDS** NEH prog gtants, 78-81; NEH fel for col teachers, 82; Schlesinger Lib res grants, 85, 94, 00; HW Durham Found grants, 95-98, 00. **MEMBERSHIPS** Unitarian Universalitst Hist Soc. **RESEARCH** Biography, Humor, Women's Studies, Women in Religion, Journals Diary Lit. **SELECTED PUBLICATIONS** Auth, Meredith's broken laurel: Modern Love and the Renaissance sonnet tradition, Victorian Poetry, 72; The Rilkean poet-lover and his laurel, Philol Quart, 74; Translation as resurrection: Rilke and Louise Labe, Mod Lang Notes, 74; Petrarchizing into the horrible: Baudelaire's Grotesque, Fr Rev, 75; Kate Freeman Clark: A Painter Rediscovered, Univ Press Miss, 81; Spirited Threads: The Writing and Art of Patricia Roberts Cline, Portland, OR, Sibyl Publications, Fall, 97; Prophetic Sisterhood: Liberal Women Ministers©1880-1930, 90, 95, 00; Healers in Harm's Way: Mary Collison, A Clergywoman in Christian Science, 85, 95. **CONTACT ADDRESS** Univ of Memphis, Patterson Hall, Memphis, TN 38152. **EMAIL** cgtucker@cc.memphis.edu

TUCKER, JANET
PERSONAL m, 1 child **DISCIPLINE** NINETEENTH AND TWENTIETH-CENTURY RUSSIAN WRITERS **EDUCATION** Indiana Univ, BA, 63, MA, 65, PhD, 73. **CAREER** English and Lit, Univ Ark. **HONORS AND AWARDS** Fulbright Col Res Incentive Grant, 91. **MEMBERSHIPS** AAASS, AATSEEL **SELECTED PUBLICATIONS** Areas: the Russian poet Innokentij Annenskij, Anatolij Gladilin; auth, Revolution Betrayed: Jurij Olesha's Envy, Slavica Publishers, 96; auth, Against the Grain: Parody & Satire in Russian Literature, Slavica Publishers; auth, The Religious Significance of Clothing in Dostoevsky's Crime & Punishment, Slavica East European Journal; auth, Skaz & Oral Usage as Satirical Devices in Isaak Babel's Red Cavalry, Canadian-Am Slavic Review; auth, Plot Rhyme in Aleksandr Pushkin's Eugene Omegin, New Zealand Slavonic Journal, 99. **CONTACT ADDRESS** Univ of Arkansas, Fayetteville, Fayetteville, AR 72701. **EMAIL** jtucker@comp.uark.edu

TUCKER, JOHN J.
DISCIPLINE OLD ICELANDI; OLD ENGLISH LITERATURE **EDUCATION** Univ Toronto, BA, MA, PhD; Univ Oxford, BLitt. **CAREER** Prof; dept ch, Univ of Victoria. **RESEARCH** History of the language; the historical film; hagiography. **SELECTED PUBLICATIONS** Ed, Sagas of the Icelanders: A Book of Essays, Garland, 89; coauth, Islensk-ensk ordabok, Idunn, 89; Glossary to the Poetic Edda, 92; transl, Saga and Society, Odense, 94; auth, Placitus Saga Editiones Arnamagnaeanae, Series B, Vol. II, Copenhagen: Reitzels, 98. **CONTACT ADDRESS** Dept of English, Univ of Victoria, PO Box 3070, Victoria, BC, Canada V8W 3W1. **EMAIL** jtucker@uvic.ca

TUCKER, RICHARD
DISCIPLINE APPLIED LINGUISTICS **EDUCATION** McGill Univ, PhD. **CAREER** Languages, Carnegie Mellon Univ. **HONORS AND AWARDS** Dept head. **MEMBERSHIPS** Eng Lang Progs Advisory Panel; Discipline Advisory Comt; TEFL/Applied Linguistics Fulbright prog, Board Dirs Consortium Soc Sci Asns; Exec Comt Nat Ctr Res Cult Diversity & Sec Lang Learning. **SELECTED PUBLICATIONS** Auth, Language learning for the 21st century: Challenges of the North American Free Trade Agreement, Canadian Mod Lang Rev; 93; Policy and practice in the education of culturally and linguistically diverse students. Alexandria, VA: TESOL, 94; Concluding thoughts: Language planning issues for the coming decade, Annual Rev Applied Linguistics, Cambridge Univ Press, 94; Coauth, A multiple perspectives analysis of a Japanese FLES program. For Lang Annals, 95. **CONTACT ADDRESS** Carnegie Mellon Univ, 5000 Forbes Ave, Pittsburgh, PA 15213.

TUCKER, ROBERT ASKEW
PERSONAL Born 03/23/1930, Atlanta, GA **DISCIPLINE** LATIN, GREEK **EDUCATION** Emory Univ, BBA, 51, MAT, 62; Johns Hopkins Univ, PhD(classics), 67. **CAREER** Teacher Latin, Cross Keys High Sch, DeKalb County, Ga, 62-65; asst prof classics, 67-72, ASSOC PROF CLASSICS, UNIV GA, 72-. **MEMBERSHIPS** Class Asn Mid W and S (secy-treas, 71-73); Am Philol Asn; Vergilian Soc Am; Am Archaeol Inst; Am Class League. **RESEARCH** Roman epic, especially Lucan. **SELECTED PUBLICATIONS** Auth, Vergil, Class Bulletin, Vol 0070, 94. **CONTACT ADDRESS** Dept of Classics, Univ of Georgia, Athens, GA 30602.

TUNINETTI, ANGEL T.
PERSONAL Born 12/03/1960, Argentina, m, 1985, 3 children **DISCIPLINE** SPANISH LANGUAGE **EDUCATION** Universidad Nacional de Cordoba, Argentina, Licenciado en letras, 86; Wash Univ St Louis, MA, 92; PhD, 99. **CAREER** Asst prof, Lebanon Valley Col, 96-. **MEMBERSHIPS** MLA, LASA. **RESEARCH** Travel literature, Colonial and 19th Century Latin American Literature. **SELECTED PUBLICATIONS** Auth, Nuevas tierras con biegjos ojos: Viajeros espanoles y latinomericanos en Sudamerica, Ediciones Correjidor, (Buenos Aires), 01. **CONTACT ADDRESS** 988 Reber St, Lebanon, PA 17042-6934. **EMAIL** tuninett@lvc.edu

TURGEON, GABRIELLE S.
PERSONAL Born 01/30/1938, France, m, 1969, 3 children **DISCIPLINE** FRENCH **EDUCATION** Bethune-Cookman Col, BA, 69; Calif State Univ, MA, 72; Fla State univ, PhD, 75. **CAREER** Lectr, Mary Washington Col, 85-86; asst prof to assoc prof, Northern Va Community Col, 86-90; prof, Univ of Charleston, 90-. **HONORS AND AWARDS** Pi Delta Phi; NEH Grant. **MEMBERSHIPS** Mensa Soc. **RESEARCH** Literary theory, Presently tracing "The French Among Us", In the Gallia Region seeking traces of Louis XVII. **SELECTED PUBLICATIONS** Auth, Dictionnaire biographique des personages dans les oeuvres de Gustave Flaubert, Ann Arbor, MI, 76; auth, "Barbey d'Aurevilly", XIXth Century Fr Studies VII.1, 79; auth, Foundation French, Vol I, Editions Naaman, (Sherbrooke, QC), (forthcoming). **CONTACT ADDRESS** Dept Humanities, Univ of Charleston, 2300 Maccorkle Ave SE, Charleston, WV 25304-1045. **EMAIL** gturgeon@uchaswv.edu

TURNER, JAMES HILTON
PERSONAL Born 04/19/1918, Woodville, ON, Canada, m, 1945, 3 children **DISCIPLINE** CLASSICAL LANGUAGES **EDUCATION** Univ Toronto, BA, 40; Univ Cincinnati, PhD, 44. **CAREER** Mem fac, Bishop's Col Sch, 44-45 McCallie Sch, 45-47; from instr to asst prof class lang, Univ Vt, 47-51; asst prof, Heidelberg Col, 51-52; from asst prof to assoc prof, 52-57, chmn dept lang, 53-62, PROF CLASS LANG, WESTMINSTER COL, 57-, Assoc ed, Class World, 57-60. **MEMBERSHIPS** Class Asn Atlantic States; Am Class League (vpres, 58-59); AAUP. **RESEARCH** Aristophanes. **SELECTED PUBLICATIONS** Auth, Epicurus and friendship & Roman elementary mathematics: The operations, Class J; Audiovisual materials for the teaching of the classics, Class World; ed, Aristophanes, Lysistrata, Bryn Mawr Col, 82. **CONTACT ADDRESS** Dept of Foreign Languages, Westminster Col, Pennsylvania, New Wilmington, PA 16142.

TURNER, JOAN
DISCIPLINE NINETEENTH AND TWENTIETH-CENTURY RUSSIAN WRITERS **EDUCATION** Brown Univ, BA, 67, MAT, 69; Ohio State Univ, PhD, 88. **CAREER** English and Lit, Univ Ark. **SELECTED PUBLICATIONS** Areas: TA training/supervision and language learning disabilities. **CONTACT ADDRESS** Univ of Arkansas, Fayetteville, Fayetteville, AR 72701.

TUSIANI, JOSEPH
PERSONAL Born 01/14/1924, San Marco in Lamis, Italy **DISCIPLINE** ITALIAN LANGUAGE AND LITERATURE **EDUCATION** Univ Naples, Dott in Lettere, 47. **CAREER** Instr Ital, Col New Rochelle, 48-51; asst prof Ital, 51-60; from assoc prof to prof, Col Mt St Vincent, 60-71; PROF, LEHMAN COL CITY UNIV, NEW YORK, 71-, Vis prof, New York Univ, 58-63, Cent Conn State Col, 64, Fairleigh Dickinson Univ, 68, Rutgers Univ, 70 and Fordham Univ, 80. **HONORS AND AWARDS** Greenwood Prize, Poetry Soc England, 56; Di Castagnola Awd, Poetry Soc Am, 68; Spirit Gold Medal, Cath Poetry Soc Am, 69; littd, col mt st vincent, 71. **MEMBERSHIPS** Dante Soc Am; Am Asn Teachers Ital; Poetry Soc Am (vpres, 57-69); Am Pen. **RESEARCH** Verse translation of Pulci's Morgante. **SELECTED PUBLICATIONS** Auth, The Contingent Word--Avant-Garde and Experimentalism in 20th-Century Italian--Italian, World Lit Today, Vol 0067, 93. **CONTACT ADDRESS** 2140 Tomlinson Ave, Bronx, NY 10461.

TUTTLE, EDWARD FOWLER
PERSONAL Born 03/08/1942, Los Angeles, CA, m, 1983, 4 children **DISCIPLINE** ROMANCE LINGUISTICS **EDUCATION** Univ Calif, Los Angeles, BA, 65, MA, 67; Univ Calif, Berkeley, PhD(Romance philol), 72. **CAREER** PROF ITAL AND ROMANCE LING, UNIV CALIF, LOS ANGELES, 71-. **MEMBERSHIPS** Ling Soc Am; Mediaeval Acad Am, Accademia della Crusca. **RESEARCH** Comparative Romance linguistics; Italian dialectology and philology. **SELECTED PUBLICATIONS** Auth, On Placing Northern Italian Noun Singulars from Plurals of the Type Amis-Friend Within a Theory of Optimality and Markedness, Romance Philol, Vol 0048, 95. **CONTACT ADDRESS** 662 Loring Ave, Los Angeles, CA 90024-2551. **EMAIL** tuttle@ucla.edu

TWERASER, FELIX W.
PERSONAL Born 04/03/1961, Vienna, Austria, m, 1990, 1 child **DISCIPLINE** LINGUISTICS, GERMAN, LITERATURE **EDUCATION** Grinnell Col, BA, 83; Ind Univ, MA, 87; PhD, 95. **CAREER** Asst prof, Idaho State Univ, asst prof, Utah State Univ, 00-. **HONORS AND AWARDS** Fulbright Res Fel, Vienna, 88-89; Oskar Seidlin Fel, Ind Univ, 90-91; NEH Fel, Vienna, 01. **MEMBERSHIPS** MLA; AATG; GSA. **RESEARCH** Turn-of-the-century Vienna; modern Austrian literature. **SELECTED PUBLICATIONS** Auth, Political Dimensions of Arthur Schnitzler's Late Fiction, Camden House, 98; auth, "Imagining the Holocaust: The Problems and Promise of Representation," Rendezvous 34 (00); auth, "Arthur Schnitzler's Reigen and the Freedom of the Artist: The First Austrian Republic in Constitutional Crisis," in Arthur Schnitzler: Contemporaneities (Bern: Peter Lang, 01). **CONTACT ADDRESS** Lang Philol Dept, Utah State Univ, 0720 Old Main Hall, Logan, UT 84322-0720. **EMAIL** twerfeli@cc.usu.edu

U

UDWIN, VICTOR
PERSONAL Born 01/19/1953, Bedford, England, m, 1973, 4 children **DISCIPLINE** GERMAN, COMPARATIVE LITERATURE **EDUCATION** Univ Calif, Berkeley, BA, 76, MA, 80, PhD, 85. **CAREER** Vis lectr, rhet, UC Berkeley, 85-86; vis prof, inst for Geistes-and Sozialwissenschaften, univ-Gesamthochschule-Siegen, Ger, 86-87; vis prof, Graduierten Kolleg, Siegen, Ger, 87; dir, Fifth Col writing prog, UC San Diego, 88-89; lectr, Ger, UC San Diego, 89-90; asst prof, 90-98, assoc prof, Ger and comp lit, Univ Tulsa, 98-. **HONORS AND AWARDS** Univ Tulsa fac develop fel, 91, 93, 95, 96, 97; UC Berkeley Comp Lit dept citation, 76; Phi Beta Kappa, 76; UC Berkeley BA with high hon, 76; Regents fel, UC Berkeley 83-84; women's studs course develop grant, 92; Okla Arts and human counc grant, 93; Okla State Senate citation for outstanding svc, 95. **MEMBERSHIPS** ACLA; APA; AATG; AAH; OFLTA; MMSA. **RESEARCH** Epic (German and Greek); Medieval studies; literary and cultural theory; Languages and literature: German, Classic Greek, Old English. **SELECTED PUBLICATIONS** Auth, Reading and Writing--the Rhetoric of Reversal, Reader 17, 87, 5-16; Reading the Red Ball--A Phenomenology of Narrative Processes, in Papers in Comp Lit 5, 88, 115-126; Der materiale Signifikant, in Materialitat der Kommunikation, Frankfurt, Suhrkamp, 88; Autopoiesis and Poetry, in Textuality and Subjectivity, Columbia, S.C., Camden House, 91; Between Two Armies, Leiden, Brill, 98. **CONTACT ADDRESS** Dept of Languages, Univ of Tulsa, 600 S College Ave, Tulsa, OK 74104. **EMAIL** victor-udwin@utlsa.edu

UGARTE, MICHAEL
PERSONAL Born 02/16/1949, Hanover, MA, m, 2 children **DISCIPLINE** SPANISH LITERATURE **EDUCATION** Cornell Univ, PhD, 78. **CAREER** Full Prof-writer, Univ of Missouri, 79-present. **HONORS AND AWARDS** Gugganheim Fellowship, Catherine P. Middlehash Prof, Univ of MO, Columbia, 95-99. **MEMBERSHIPS** MLA; AATSP. **RESEARCH** Modern Pennsular Lit, Cultural Studies. **SELECTED PUBLICATIONS** Auth, "Tiempo de silencio and the Language of Displacement," MLN 96 (1981): 340-357; auth, "Trilogy of Treason: An Intertexual Study of Juan Goytisolo," Columbia: University of Missouri Press," 82; auth, "Max Aub's Labyrinth of Exile," Hispania 68, 4 (1984): 733-739; auth, "Luis Ceruda's Poetics of Exile," MLN, 101 (1986): 325-341; auth, "Shifting Ground: Spanish Civil War Exile Literature," Durham: Duke UP, 89; auth, "Cela Vie," The Nation (1989): 646-650; auth, "Tetual Limits: Jose Caldalso's Noches lugubres," Dieciocho 12 (1989): 3-19; auth, "New Historicism and Galdo's Fortunata," Romance Languages Annual, 11, (1990): 569-574; auth, "Testimonios de exilio: desde el campo de concentracion a America," El exilio de las Espanas de 1939, Jose Maria Navarro, ed. Barcelona: Anthropos, 91, 43-62; auth, "Espana y su civilizacion, 4th ed., McGraw Hill, 92; "Madrid 1900: The Capital as Cradle of Culture," Penn State UP, 96. **CONTACT ADDRESS** Dept of Romance Languages, Univ of Missouri, Columbia, Columbia, MO 65201. **EMAIL** ugartem@missouri.edu

UITTI, KARL D.
PERSONAL Born 12/10/1933, Calumet, MI, m, 1974, 2 children **DISCIPLINE** ROMANCE LANUSGES AND LITERAURES **EDUCATION** Univ Calif, Berkeley, BA, 52; MA, 52; PhD, 59. **CAREER** Instr to prof of Romance Langs & Lits, Princeton Univ, 59-, The John N. Woodhull Prof of Modern Langs, 76-. **HONORS AND AWARDS** Phi Beta Kappa, 52; Guggenheim Fel, 63; NEH Fel, 74; vis fel, All Souls Col, Oxford, 75; Officier, Palmes Academiques, 76. **MEMBERSHIPS** Codrington Club, Oxford; Societe de Linguistique Romane. **RESEARCH** Romance philology, Medieval Romance literatures. **SELECTED PUBLICATIONS** Auth, Story, Myth and Celebration in Old French Narrative: 1050-1200, Princeton: Princeton Univ Press (73); coauth with Alfred Foulet, Chretien de Troyes, Le Chevalier de la Charrette (Lancelot), Paris: Bordas-Classiques Garnier (89); auth, Letteratura enropea: epica e romanzo cavalleresco in Europa: dalle origini alla Commedia di Dante, Un'Eciclopedia d'Orientamento, Milan: Jaca Book (93); auth, Chretien de Troyes, Le Chevalier au Lion (Yvain), Critical edition, Notes, Varients, in Daniel Poirion, gen ed, Chretien de Troyes, Euvres completes, Bibliotheque de la Pleiade, Paris: Gallimard (94); auth, "A le Recherche du texte perdu: reflexions sur la textualite en ancient francais," in L'Hostellerie de pensee, Etudes sur l'art litteraire au Moyen Age offertes a Daniel Poirion par ses anciens eleves, Michel Zink, Eric Hicks, et al, eds, Cultures et Civilisations Medievales, XII, Paris: Presses Universitaires de la Sorbeonne (95): 468-86; coauth with Michelle A. Freedman, Chretien de Troyes Revisited, Twayne's World Author Series Revisited, NY: Twayne Pubs/Maxwell Macmillan Int (95), auth, "Alexis, Roland, and French 'Poesie Nationale," Ninth Annual Dartmouth Colloquium in Medieval and Early Romance Modern Romance Literatures, ed by David Rollo, Comparative Lit Studies, 32:2 (95): 131-50; auth, "Remarks on Old French Textuality and Language," Romance Philology 52 (fall 98): 95-117; auth, "Thinking in Verse Lines: Some Medieval French Examples," to be published in Melanges R. et V. La Charite, Paris: Klincksieck (2000); auth, "The Spanish Santiago and Latin Europe," to be published in P. F. Dembowski Festschrift, Lexington, Ky: French Forum (2000). **CONTACT ADDRESS** Dept Romance Langs & Lits, Princeton Univ, 201 E Pyne Hall, Princeton, NJ 08544-0001. **EMAIL** kduitti@princeton.edu

ULATOWSKA, HANNA K.
PERSONAL Born 03/14/1933, Krynica-Zdroj, Poland **DISCIPLINE** LINGUISTICS **EDUCATION** Univ Warsaw, MA, 55; Univ Edinburgh, dipl, 59, PhD(ling), 6 1. **CAREER** Lectr English, Univ Warsaw, 55-58; res scientist ling, Georgetown Univ, 62-63; lectr, Witwatersrand Univ, 63-65; res scientist, Ling Res Ctr, Univ Tex, Austin, 65-67; comput syst analyst, Div Comput Res and Technol, NIH, 67-70, sr staff fel, 70-71; assoc prof, Univ Tex, Arlington, 71; via prof, Southern Methodist Univ, 71-72; ASSOC PROF OF LING, UNIV TEX, DALLAS, 73-, Assoc prof dept neurol, Univ Tex Health Sci Ctr, Dallas, 71. **MEMBERSHIPS** Acad Aphasia; Soc Neurosci; Ling Soc Am; MLA. **RESEARCH** Neurolinguistics. **SELECTED PUBLICATIONS** Auth, Narrative Discourse in Aphasia on the Example of Aesop Fables, Pamietnik Literacki, Vol 0085, 94. **CONTACT ADDRESS** 4422 Wildwood Rd, Dallas, TX 75208.

ULERY, ROBERT W.
PERSONAL Born 04/02/1944, Goshen, IN, s **DISCIPLINE** CLASSICS, ITALIAN, GREEK **EDUCATION** Yale Univ, BA, 66; MA, 68; PhD, 71. **CAREER** Asst prof, Wake Forest Univ, 71-78; assoc prof, 78-89; prof, 89-. **HONORS AND AWARDS** Beinecke Rar Bk, vis Fel. **MEMBERSHIPS** APA; RSA; ACL; CAMWS; AANLS; IANLS; NAS. **RESEARCH** C Sallustius Crispus and Cornelius Tacitus; manuscript tradition; Nachleben. **SELECTED PUBLICATIONS** Auth, "Sallust," in Dictionary of Literary Biography, ed. Ward W Briggs (Detroit, 99); auth, "Cornelius Tacitus," in Catalogus Translationum et Commentariorum, eds. F Edward Cranz et al (Wash, DC, 86): 87-174. **CONTACT ADDRESS** Dept Classical Languages, Wake Forest Univ, PO Box 7343, Winston-Salem, NC 27109-7343. **EMAIL** ulery@wfu.edu

ULLMAN, PIERRE LIONI
PERSONAL Born 10/31/1929, Nice, France, m, 1956, 2 children **DISCIPLINE** SPANISH **EDUCATION** Yale Univ, BA, 52; Columbia Univ, MA, 56; Princeton Univ, PhD, 62. **CAREER** Master French and Span, Choate Sch, Wallingford, Conn, 56-57; master French, Latin and Span, St Bernard's Sch, Gladstone, NJ, 57-58; asst French and Span, Princeton Univ, 58-61; instr Rutgers Univ, 61-63; asst prof Span, Univ Calif, Davis, 63-65; assoc prof, 65-48, chmn dept, 66-67, PROF Emer SPAN, UNIV WIS-MILWAUKEE, 68- Adv ed, Papers on Lang and Lit, 66-80; vis prof Span, Univ Minn, Minneapolis, 70-71; adv ed, Estudos Ibero-Americanos, Brazil, 75-; vis prof, Univ Mich, summer 75; adv ed, Los Ensayistas, 77-85. **MEMBERSHIPS** Am Asn Teachers Span and Port; MLA; Am Asn Teachers Esperanto; Midwest Mod Lang Asn; Universal Esperanto Asn; Esperanto League NAm. **RESEARCH** Spanish literature; contemporary Esperanto poetry. **SELECTED PUBLICATIONS** Auth, "A Hypothesis Regarding the Religious and Mathematical Bases of Western Civilization," Logos 3.1 (00): 146-176. **CONTACT ADDRESS** Dept of Spanish and Portuguese, Univ of Wisconsin, Milwaukee, Milwaukee, WI 53201.

UMANZOR, MARTA A.
PERSONAL Born 10/26/1943, El Salvador, m, 1977, 3 children **DISCIPLINE** SPANISH **EDUCATION** Univ Ariz, PhD, 90. **CAREER** TA, Univ of Ariz, 82-90; asst prof to prof, St Michaels Col, 90-. **HONORS AND AWARDS** Outstanding Teacher Awd, 86; Centennial Achievement Awd, 88; Class Appreciation Awd, 96; ALIANZA Awd, 96; School of Int Studies Awd, 97. **MEMBERSHIPS** AATSP. **RESEARCH** Women and Hispanic Literature, Changing Images of Women. **SELECTED PUBLICATIONS** Auth, "Take care of the Earth before It's too Late", Defender, (Dec 5, 90) ; auth, "Thankful for Peace in El Salvador", Burlington Free Pr, (March 8, 92); auth, "La lectura y relectura del poema Los ojos de Eleggua de Nancy Morejon", ed Elba D Birmingham-Pokorny, Diaspora 4, (95): 110-119; auth, La vision de la mujer en la obra de Elena Garro: El arbol, Los perros, Los recuerdos del porvenir, Testimonios sobre Mariana y La casa junto al rio, Ediciones Universal, (Miami), 96; auth, "el mundo artistico de Clorina Matto de turner en Aves sin nido", Diaspora, (99); auth, Introduccion a Entrevistas a Enrique Jaramillo-Levi", Referencias Cruzadas: Entrevistas al escritor panameno Enrique Jaramillo Levi, eds E. Birmingham-Pokorny and C. Adams, Ediciones Peero Azul (Puerto Rico, 99): 13-22; auth, "La busqueda de la salida laberintica en la vida de Renata en la relectura de Mundo Demonio y mujer", Protestas, Interrogantes y Agonias en la obra de Rima de Valbaona, ed Juana Alcira Arancibia y Luis Jiminez, Ediciones Perro Azul (Costa Rica, 99); 321-34. **CONTACT ADDRESS** Dept Mod Lang, Saint Michael's Col, 1 Winooski Pk, Colchester, VT 05439-0002. **EMAIL** mumanzor@smcvt.edu

UNGAR, STEVEN
PERSONAL Born 09/08/1945, Chicago, IL, m, 1968, 2 children **DISCIPLINE** FRENCH, COMPARATIVE LITERATURE **EDUCATION** Univ Wis-Madison, BA, 66, MA, 68; Cornell Univ, PhD, 73. **CAREER** Asst prof French, Case Western Reserve Univ, 72-76; asst prof to assoc prof, 76-85, Prof French & Comp Lit, Univ Iowa, 85-; Lectr English, Lycee Technique d'Etat, Rennes, France, 68-69; res fel, Camargo Found, Cassis, France, 81. **HONORS AND AWARDS** NEH Interp Proj Awd, 87-90. **MEMBERSHIPS** Mod Lang Asn; Soc Cinema Student. **RESEARCH** 20th Century French fiction, poetry & thought, France between the wars, Post-new wave French film. **SELECTED PUBLICATIONS** Auth, Roland Barthes: The Professor of Desire, (83); co-ed, Signs in Culture: Roland Barthes Today, (89); auth, Scandal & Aftereffect: Blanchot & France since 1930; co-ed, Identity Papers: Contested Nationhood in 20th Century France. **CONTACT ADDRESS** Dept Com Lit, Univ Iowa, 425 Engl Phil Bldg, Iowa City, IA 52242. **EMAIL** steven-ungar@uiowa.edu

UNGER, JAMES MARSHALL
PERSONAL Born 05/28/1947, Cleveland, OH, m, 1976 **DISCIPLINE** JAPANESE LANGUAGE, LINGUISTICS **EDUCATION** Univ Chicago, BA, 69, MA, 71; Yale Univ, MA, 72, PhD(ling), 75. **CAREER** Sr lectr Japanese, Univ Canterbury, NZ, 75-76; PROF JAPANESE, UNIV HAWAII, MANOA, 77-92, Univ Maryland Col Park, 92-96, Ohio State, 96-. **MEMBERSHIPS** Ling Soc Am; Asn Asian Studies; Asn Teachers Japanese; Am Oriental Soc. **RESEARCH** Historical linguistics. **SELECTED PUBLICATIONS** Auth, The Fifth Generation Fallacy, New York: Oxford Univ Press, 87; auth, Literacy and Script Reform in Occupation Japan, New York: Oxford University Press, 96; auth, Studies in Early Japanese Morphophonemics, Bloomington: Indiana Linguistics Club, 97. **CONTACT ADDRESS** Dept of East Asian Languages and Literatures, Ohio State Univ, Columbus, 204 Dieter Cunz Hall, 1841 Millikin Rd, Columbus, OH 43210-1229. **EMAIL** unger.26@osu.edu

URBAIN, HENRI
PERSONAL Born 05/24/1927, Hanoi, Indochina, m, 1962, 3 children **DISCIPLINE** FRENCH LITERATURE **EDUCATION** Univ Calif, Berkeley, AB, 56, MA, 57, PhD(Romance lang & lit), 70. **CAREER** Teaching asst, Univ Calif, Berkeley, 57-61; assoc, Univ Calif, Santa Barbara, 61-63; asst prof French, San Diego State Col, 63-64 & Mills Col, 65-66; prof French, Salem State Col, 68-. **MEMBERSHIPS** MLA; Soc d'Etudes du XVIIeme siecle. **RESEARCH** Seventeenth century French literature; Franco-Spanish literary relations in the 17th century. **CONTACT ADDRESS** Dept of Foreign Lang, Salem State Col, 352 Lafayette St, Salem, MA 01970-5353.

URBANC, KATICA
PERSONAL Born 10/11/1964, Montreal, QC, Canada, m, 1996, 1 child **DISCIPLINE** SPANISH LITERATURE **EDUCATION** Concordia Univ, BA, 86; Georgetown Univ, MS, 89; PhD. **CAREER** Lectr, Skidmore Col, 92-95; asst prof, Wagner Col, 95-. **HONORS AND AWARDS** Excell Teach Awd, 89. **MEMBERSHIPS** MLA; AATSP; AHLF. **RESEARCH** Modern peninsular narrative. **SELECTED PUBLICATIONS** Auth, "Entrevista con Soledad Puertolas," Especulo 8 (98); rev, Una vida inesperada, Soledad Puertolas, Hispania, forthcoming; rev, La senora Berg, Hispania (99); auth, "Libros al aire libre: La Feria del Libro en el Parque del Retiro de Madrid," Hispania (98); rev, Madres e ijas (96); ed, Laura Freixas, Hispania (97). **CONTACT ADDRESS** Dept Humanities, Wagner Col, 1 Campus Rd, Staten Island, NY 10301-4479. **EMAIL** kurbanc@wagner.edu

UZGALIS, WILLIAM
DISCIPLINE PHILOSOPHIES OF CHINA **EDUCATION** Univ Calif, Irving, BA; Calif State Univ, Long Beach, MA; Stanford Univ, PhD. **CAREER** Philos, Oregon St Univ. **SELECTED PUBLICATIONS** Auth, The Anti-Essential Locke and Natural Kinds; The Same Tyrannical Principle: The Lockean Legacy on Slavery. **CONTACT ADDRESS** Dept Philos, Oregon State Univ, Corvallis, OR 97331-4501. **EMAIL** wuzgalis@orst.edu

V

VAHLKAMP, CHARLES G.
PERSONAL m **DISCIPLINE** FRENCH LANGUAGE AND LITERATURE **EDUCATION** Vanderbilt Univ, BA; MA; Phd. **CAREER** Fac, 67; Hazelrigg Prof Hum. **HONORS AND AWARDS** Exec Comm Fac Athletics Reps Asn, NCAA. **RESEARCH** Voltaire and the 18th century; film history and criticism. **SELECTED PUBLICATIONS** Auth, scholarly studies on Voltaire and the 18th century published in Romance Notes. **CONTACT ADDRESS** Centre Col, 600 W Walnut St, Danville, KY 40422. **EMAIL** vahlkamp@centre.edu

VAILAKIS, IVAN GORDON
PERSONAL Born Quito, Ecuador **DISCIPLINE** LATIN AMERICA LITERATURE **EDUCATION** Univ Calf Irvine, PhD, **CAREER** Prof, Univ Redlands. **RESEARCH** Contemporary Latin American Poetry. **SELECTED PUBLICATIONS** Auth, Colibries en el exilio, 97; Nuestrario, 87; pubs on Gabriela Mistral, Alicia Y¤nez Cossio, Sandra Cisneros, and Helen Maria Viramontes. **CONTACT ADDRESS** History Dept, Univ of Redlands, 1200 E Colton Ave, Box 3090, Redlands, CA 92373-0999.

VAILLANCOURT, DANIEL
DISCIPLINE FRENCH LITERATURE **EDUCATION** Univ Quebec, BA; PhD. **RESEARCH** Semiotics; narrative theory; mystical discourse; theories of reading; travel narratives; Quebec literature. **SELECTED PUBLICATIONS** Auth, Figures and Seriation: A Semiotic Theory of Reading. **CONTACT ADDRESS** Dept of French, Univ of Western Ontario, London, ON, Canada N6A 5B8. **EMAIL** vaillan@julian.uwo.ca

VAJDA, EDWARD J.
PERSONAL Born 09/10/1958, Camp LeJuene, NC, m, 1991, 3 children **DISCIPLINE** RUSSIAN, LINGUISTICS **EDUCATION** Ind Univ, BA, 80; Univ Wash, MA, 83; PhD, 87. **CAREER** Asst Teacher, Univ Wash, 80-86; From Asst Prof to Prof, Western Wash Univ, 87-. **HONORS AND AWARDS** Fulbright Res Grant, Siberia, Moscow, 98. **MEMBERSHIPS** LSA, ELA, ASLIP, SSILA, ILA, CLA. **RESEARCH** Aboriginal languages, linguistic isolates, Asia and native America. **SELECTED PUBLICATIONS** Auth, "Kitchenmaids or Stateswomen: A Political History of Women in Russia," Festschrift for Vladimir Milicic, WWU Pr (95); rev, The Literature of Naturalism: Essays on East European Identity, Choice, 96; auth, "Duranty, Walter," Encycl USA, vol 24, Acad Int Pr (97): 111-113; auth, "Dialects of American English," Vestnik TGPU. Humanities Ser, 6 (98): 36-37; auth, "The Kets and Their Language," Mother Tongue IV (98): 4-16; coauth, Russian Punctuation and Related Symbols, Slavica Publ, 99; auth, "Actant Conjugations in the Ket Verb," Voprosy iazykoznaniia [Linguistic Inquiry], vol 67, issue 3 (00); auth, Yeniseian Peoples and Languages, Curzon Pr (Surrey, UK), forthcoming. **CONTACT ADDRESS** Dept For Lang, Western Washington Univ, M/S 9057, Bellingham, VA 98225. **EMAIL** vajda@cc.wwu.edu

VALBUENA-BRIONES, ANGEL JULIAN
PERSONAL Born 01/11/1928, Madrid, Spain, m, 1957, 2 children **DISCIPLINE** HISPANIC LITERATURE **EDUCATION** Univ Murcia, MA, 49; Univ Madrid, PhD, 52. **CAREER** Lectr Span & Span-Am lit, Oxford Univ, 53-55; asst prof Span lit, Univ Madrid, 55-56; vis lectr Span-Am lit, Univ Wis, 56-58; asst prof Span lit, Yale Univ, 58-60; Elias Ahuja Prof Span Lit, 60-99, Prof Emeritus, Univ Del 99-; post-doctoral fel; Consejo Super Invest Ciient , Madrid, 70-71; vis prof, Univ Madrid, 70-71; vis prof, Inst Caro y Cuervo, Columbia, summer 80; Nat Screening bd, Fulbright-Hays Comt, Spain & Port, 80-84 & 89-91; chmn, div 16th & 17th century Span Lit, MLA, 77; Sigma Delta Pi, 56; Phi Kappa Phi, 75; UD Excellence Tchg Award, 88; Col Arts & Sci Outstanding Scholar Award, 96; Prof Emeritus, 99. **MEMBERSHIPS** Asn Teachers Span & Port; MLA; Renaissance Soc Am; Am Asn Univ Prof, Int Asn Hispanist; Asn Lit Scholars & Critics; Inst Int de Lit Iberoamericana; Anglo-Ger Asn Calderonists. **RESEARCH** Spanish Golden Age literature; Latin American literary currents; history of the Spanish language; Contemporary Spanish Literature. **SELECTED PUBLICATIONS** Auth, Obras completas de Calderon, Aguilar, Madrid, Vols I & II, 56, 59; Literatura Hispanoamericana, Gustavo Gili, Barcelona, 62, 4th ed, 69; Perspectiva critica de Ios dramas de Calderon, Rialp, Madrid, 65; Ideas y palabras, Eliseo Torres, 68; ed, Calderon's El alcalde de Zalamea, Anaya, Madrid, 71; Primera parte de las com-

edias de Calderon, Vol I, 74, Vol II, 81, Consejo Superior de Investigaciones Cientificas, Madrid; La dama duende de Calderon, 76 & El alcalde de Zalamea, Calderon, 77 Catedra, 77; auth, Calderon y la comedia nueva, Espasa-Calpe, 77; El mayor monstruo del mundo de Calderon, Juan de la Cuesta, 95; Teatro Espanol del Siglo de Oro, CD-ROM, 98. **CONTACT ADDRESS** 203 Nottingham Rd, Newark, DE 19711. **EMAIL** 18402@udel.edu

VALDMAN, ALBERT
PERSONAL Born 02/15/1931, Paris, France, m, 1960, 1 child **DISCIPLINE** FRENCH, LINGUISTICS **EDUCATION** Univ Penn, AB, 53; Cornell Univ, MA, 55; PhD, 60. **CAREER** Linguistic scientist, US Dept of State, 57-59; asst prof, Penn State Univ, 59-60; NDEA Summer FL Inst, Univ Oregon, 60-62; asst prof to prof, 60, dept chair, Ind Univ, 63-68; fulbright lecturer to visiting prof, Univ of Nic, 75-76, 83-87, 89; prof, Ind Univ, 86-. **HONORS AND AWARDS** Guggenheim Fel; NATO-NSF Summer Fel, 74; Fulbright Senior Res Fel, 85; Doctorate Honouis causa, Univ Neuchatel Switzerland, 91; Order des Palmes Academiques France; Chavalier, 86; Officier, 93; Commandeur, 98; John Ryan Awd, Ind Univ, 98; Florence Steiner Prize, 98 **MEMBERSHIPS** Am Asn for Applied Linguistics; Am Asn of Teachers of French; Am Council on the Teaching of Foreign Languages; Comite International des Etudes Creoles; Linguistic Soc of Am; MLA; Nat Asn for Bilingual Education; Soc for Caribbean Linguistics; Soc ofor Pidgin and Creole Linguistics; Teachers of English to Speakers of Other Languages. **RESEARCH** French linguistics, Creole studies, Second language learning and teaching, Sociolinguistics. **SELECTED PUBLICATIONS** Auth, Bien Entendu! Introduction a la prononciation francaise, NJ: Prentice Hall, 93; coauth, Chez Nous, Introduction au monde francophone, Prentice Hall, 96; Learner's Dictionary of Haitian Creole, 96; ed, French and Creole in Louisiana, Plenum: New York, 97; coed, Meaning and form: Multiple perspectives, Boston: Heinle and Heinle, 99; auth, Dictionary of Louisiana Creole, 98. **CONTACT ADDRESS** Dept French and Ital, Indiana Univ, Bloomington, Ballantine Hall 604, 1020 E Kirkwood Ave, Bloomington, IN 47405-7103. **EMAIL** valdman@indiana.edu

VALENTE, LUIZ FERNANDO
PERSONAL Born 03/16/1950, Rio de Janeiro, Brazil **DISCIPLINE** COMPARITIVE LITERATURE, BRAZILIAN LITERATURE **EDUCATION** Bowdoin Col, AB, 71; Brown Univ, PhD, 83. **CAREER** Asst prof, Providence Col, 76-82; assoc prof, Brown Univ, 83-. **HONORS AND AWARDS** Phi Beta Kappa. **MEMBERSHIPS** MLA; ICLA; ACLA; AATSP; LASA; SCLA; BSA; APSA. **RESEARCH** Nineteenth and twentieth century Brazilian literature and intellectual history; contemporary historical novel; fiction and history; comparative literature; literary theory. **SELECTED PUBLICATIONS** Auth, "Affective Response in Grande Sertao: Veredas," Luso Brazilian Rev (86); auth, "Against Silence: Fabulation and Mediation in Joao Guimaraes Rosa and Italo Calvino," MLA 19 (89); auth, "Beyond Narcissism: Ralfo's Parodic Confessions," Port Studies 5 (89); auth, "Variations on the Kenotic Hero: Tolstoy's Ivan Ilych and Guimaraes Rosa's Augusto Matraga," Symposium 45 (91); auth, "Fiction as History: The Case of Joao Ubaldo Ribeiro," Latin Am Res Rev 28 (93); auth, "Alencar's Flawed Blueprints," Host (93); auth, "Marriages of Speaking and Hearing: Mediation and Response in Absalom, Absalom and Grande Sertao: Veredas," Faulkner J 9 (96); auth, "Entre Clio a Caliope: A Construgao da Narrativa Historica em Os Sertoes," Historia Ciencias Saude (98); auth, Historia a Ficcao: Convergencias a Contrastes, Univ Federal do Rio de Janeiro (00); auth, "Machado's Wounded Males," Hisp 84 (01). **CONTACT ADDRESS** Lat Am Studies Dept, Brown Univ, PO Box O, Providence, RI 02912. **EMAIL** luiz_valente@brown.edu

VALENTINE, TAMARA M.
PERSONAL Born 03/03/1954, Chicago, IL, m **DISCIPLINE** LINGUISTICS **EDUCATION** Univ Ill, Urbana-Champaign, BA, 77, MA, 79, PhD, 86. **CAREER** Mich State Univ, East Lansing, 86-87; prof, Univ SC, Spartanburg, 87-; vis prof, Univ of Ill, Urbana-Champaign, fall 98; LSA Linguistic Inst, Univ Ill, Urbana-Champaign, summer 99. **HONORS AND AWARDS** Am Prof Partnership for Lithuanian Educ, 93, 94, 95; Am Inst of Indian Studies, 75-76, 89-90; Linguistic Soc of Am, Linguistic Inst, 99. **MEMBERSHIPS** Int Asn for World Englishes, Am Prof Partnership for Lithuanian Educ, South Asian Lang Analysis, Am Asn for Applied Linguistics, Pragmatics & Language Learning, TESOL. **RESEARCH** Sociolinguistics, language and gender, South Asian studies, women's studies, teaching English as a second language. **SELECTED PUBLICATIONS** Auth, "Getting the Message Across: Discourse Markers in Spoken Indian English," World Englishes, 10.3 (91): 325-334; auth, "The Nativizing of Gender: Speech Acts in the New Englishes Literatures," The English Family: English in Global Bilingualism, ed by L. Smith and S. N. Sridhar, special issue of World Englishes, 11.2/3 (92): 259-270; auth, "Linguistic Imperialism: The Feminist Perspective," World Englishes, 12.3 (93): 361-365; auth, "Asian American Women," The Encyclopedia of Multiculturalism, (94): 207-211; auth, "What's the Point? Storytelling by Women of India," Language, Gender and Power, ed by Yamuna Kachru and Lawrence F. Bouton, Studies in the Linguistic Scis, 25.2 (95): 77-102; auth, "Agreeing and Disagreeing in Indian English Discourse: Implications for Language Teaching," Issues and Attitudes: An Anthology of Invited Papers, ed by Makhan L. Tickoo, SEAMEO Regional Lang Centre: Singapore (95): 227-250; auth, "Politeness Models in Indian English," Revista de Lenguas para Fines Especificos, 3, ed by Santiago Henriquez, Univ Las Palmas de Gran Canaria, Canary Islands (96): 279-300; auth, "Women and the Other Tongue. The Three Circles of English. Papers in Honour of Professor Braj B. Kachru, ed by E. Thumboo, Nat Univ of Singapore (99); auth, "Cross-Cultural Communication in World Englishes," South Asian Lang Analysis Proceedings, ed by Anvita Abbi, New Delhi (forthcoming); auth, "Reconstructing Identities and Gender in Discourse: English Transplanted," Language, Creativity and Identity in Diaspora Communities," ed by Braj B. Kachru (forthcoming). **CONTACT ADDRESS** Dept Fine Arts, Langs, & Lit, Univ of So Carolina, Spartanburg, 800 Univ Way, Spartanburg, SC 29303-4932. **EMAIL** tvalentine@uscs.edu

VALETTE, REBECCA MARIANNE
PERSONAL Born 12/21/1938, New York, NY, m, 1959, 3 children **DISCIPLINE** FRENCH **EDUCATION** Mt Holyoke Col, BA, 59; Univ Colo, PhD(French), 63. **CAREER** Instr and examr French and Ger, Univ SFla, 61-63; res assoc phonetics, Supreme Hq Allied Powers Europe Educ Off, Paris, 63-64; instr French, Wellesley Col, 64-65; from asst prof to assoc prof French, 65-73, PROF FRENCH, BOSTON COL, 73-, Fulbright Comn sr lectr, Ger, 73-74; fel acad admin, Am Coun Educ, 76-77; mem, MLA Task Force on Commonly Taught Languages. **HONORS AND AWARDS** Phi Beta Kappa; lhd, mt holyoke col, 74. **MEMBERSHIPS** Am Council Teaching Foreign Lang; MLA; Am Asn Teachers Fr (vpres, 80-82, pres. 90-92); Am Asn Teachers Ger; Am Asn Teachers Span and Port. **RESEARCH** Modern language testing and methodology. **SELECTED PUBLICATIONS** Auth, Modern Language Testing, 67, 77; auth, Contacts, 97; auth, Weaving the Dance: Navajo Yeibichai Textitles, 00; auth, with Jean-Paul Valette, Discovering French, 1994, 01. **CONTACT ADDRESS** Dept of Romance Languages, Boston Col, Chestnut Hill, 140 Commonwealth Ave, Chestnut Hill, MA 02167-3800. **EMAIL** valette@bc.edu

VALIS, NOEL M.
PERSONAL Born 12/24/1945, Lakewood, NJ, d, 1 child **DISCIPLINE** SPANISH AND FRENCH STUDIES **EDUCATION** Douglas College, BA, summa cum laude, 68; Bryn Mawr, MA, 75, PhD, 75. **CAREER** Prof, Ch, 91-, John Hopkins Univ; vis Prof, 95, NY Univ; vis Prof, 93, Bryn Mawr College; Prof, 86-91, Univ Michigan; vis Prof, 85-86, Univ Penn; Asst Prof, Assoc Prof, 77-85, Univ Georgia; Lectr, 71-72,76-77, Rosemont College. **HONORS AND AWARDS** Phi Beta Kappa; Woodrow Wilson Fel; NDEA Grad Fel; NEH Fel; US Spain Friend/Treaty Res Fel. **MEMBERSHIPS** MLA; AIH; AIG; FUCL. **RESEARCH** 19th & 20th Century Literature and Culture; Gender Studies; Translation. **SELECTED PUBLICATIONS** Auth, Poetry of Julia Uceda, intro, trans, NY, Peter Lang, 95; Prelude to Pleasure, by Pedro, trans, intro, Lewisburg, Bucknell UP, 93; Confesion y cuerpo en Insolacion, de Emilia Pardo Bazan, Estudios sobre Emilia Pardo Bazan, ed, JMG Herran, Santiago de Compostela, Santiago Univ, 97; Aspects of an Improper Birth: Clarin's La Rengenta, New Hispanisms Li Culture Theory, ed PJ Smith, Mark Millington, Ottawa, Dovehouse, 94; La autoridad en Galdos, Insuls, 93; auth, Fabricating Culture in Galdos's Canovas, MLN, 92; books in progress: Metaphor and Identity in Modern Spain; Body Sacraments; Hispanic Narratives of Authority and Revelation. **CONTACT ADDRESS** Dept of Hispanic and Italian Studies, Johns Hopkins Univ, Baltimore, 3400 N Charles St, Baltimore, MD 21218. **EMAIL** noel.valis@yale.edu

VAN, THOMAS A.
PERSONAL Born 05/22/1938, New York, NY, m, 1963 **DISCIPLINE** ENGLISH, LINGUISTICS **EDUCATION** City Col New York, BA, 60; Duke Univ, MA, 63, PhD(English), 66. **CAREER** Instr English, Univ NC, Chapel Hill, 65-66; asst prof, Univ Ky, 66-70; Assoc Prof English, Univ Louisville, 70-, Chmn Dept, 80-. **MEMBERSHIPS** MLA; NCTE; Mediaeval Acad Am; fel NDEA. **RESEARCH** Dante; Chaucer; Shakespeare. **SELECTED PUBLICATIONS** Auth, False Texts and Disappearing Women in the Wife of Baths Prologue and Tale--An Analysis of the Thematic Development of Contradiction and Anomaly Between Teller and Tale in the Canterbury Tales of Chaucer, Geoffrey, Chaucer Rev, Vol 0029, 94. **CONTACT ADDRESS** Dept of English, Univ of Louisville, Louisville, KY 40208.

VAN BAELEN, JACQUELINE
DISCIPLINE FRENCH LANGUAGE AND LITERATURE **EDUCATION** Vassar Univ, BA; MA; UCLA, PhD. **CAREER** Prof emer, SUNY Binghamton. **RESEARCH** 17th Century French lit; feminist lit and criticism. **SELECTED PUBLICATIONS** Auth, publ in 17th xentury French lit. **CONTACT ADDRESS** SUNY, Binghamton, PO Box 6000, Binghamton, NY 13902-6000.

VAN DEN HOVEN, ADRIAN
DISCIPLINE FRENCH **CAREER** Prof & dir, 3rd Yr Nice prog, Univ of Windsor; co-ed, Sartre Stud Int. **MEMBERSHIPS** Conseil d'Administration of the Groupe d'etudes sartriennes. **RESEARCH** Existentialism; Sartre Studies; Netherlandic Studies. **SELECTED PUBLICATIONS** Pub (s), Sartre, de Beauvoir and Camus; transl, Truth and Existence and of Hope Now, The Sartre-Benny Levy Interviews, 80; co-ed, Sartre Alive. **CONTACT ADDRESS** Dept of French Language and Literature, Univ of Windsor, 401 Sunset Ave, Windsor, ON, Canada N9B 3P4. **EMAIL** vdhoven@uwindsor.ca

VAN SETERS, JOHN
PERSONAL Born 05/02/1935, Hamilton, ON, Canada, m, 1960, 2 children **DISCIPLINE** OLD TESTAMENT, NEAR EASTERN STUDIES **EDUCATION** Univ Toronto, BA, 58; Yale Univ, MA, 59, PhD(Near Eastern studies), 65; Princeton Theol Sem, BD, 62. **CAREER** Asst prof Near Eastern studies, Waterloo Lutheran Univ, 65-67; assoc prof Old Testament, Andover Newton Theol Sch, 67-70; assoc prof Near Eastern studies, Univ Toronto, 70-76, prof Near Eastern studies, 76-77; James A Gray Prof Bibl Lit, Dept Of Relig, Univ NC, Chapel Hill, 77- & Chmn Dept, 80-88, 93-95; emer distinguished Univ prof, 00-. **HONORS AND AWARDS** Woodrow Wilson fel, 58; Princeton fel Old Testament, 62; Obermann fel Yale, 62, 63; Agusta-Hazard Fel, 64; Canada Council res grant, 73; Guggenheim Mem Awd; 79-80; NEH sem, 84, 89; NEH res fel, 85-86; ACLS res fel, 91-92; sen res fel, Katholiek Univ Leuven, 97; AHA Breasted Prize, 85; Am Acad Rel bok award, 86; Canadian Hist Asn Ferguson Prize, hon men, 86; Th.D (honoris causa), The Univ of Lausanne, Switzerland, 99; assoc dir wadi tumilat archaeol expedition to tell el maskhuta, egypt, 78,81. **MEMBERSHIPS** Am Schs Orient Res; Soc Bibl Lit; Soc Study Egyptian Antiq; Am Orient Soc; Catholic Biblical Asn; Canadian Soc of Biblical Studies, 00. **RESEARCH** Book of Genesis; Pentateuch; historical books: Joshua to II Kings; Hebrew Law; Near Eastern Historiography. **SELECTED PUBLICATIONS** Auth, The Hyksos: A New Investigation, Yale Univ, 66; auth, Abraham in History and Tradition, Yale Univ, 75; Histories and historians of the Ancient Near East: The Israelite, Orientalia, 81; auth, In Search of History, Historiography in the Ancient World and the Origins of Biblical History, Yale Press, 83; auth, Prologue to History: The Yahwist as Historian in Genesis, Westminster/John Knox Press and Theologischer Verlag (Zurich), 92; auth, The Life of Moses: The Yawhist as Historian in Exodus-Numbers, Westminster/John Knox Press and Kok-Pharos:Lampen, Netherlands, 94; auth, From Faithful Prophet to Villain: Observations on the Tradition History of the Balaam Story, in a Biblical Itinerary: In Search of Method, Form and Content. Essays in Honor of George W. Coats, 97; auth, "Solomon's Temple: Fact and Ideology in Biblical and Near Eastern Historiography," Catholic Bibl Quart 59 (97); auth, "The Deuteronomistic Reaction to the Pentateuch: The Case Against it," in Deuteronomy and Deuteronomic Literature: Festscrift for C Brekelmans, Leuven Univ Press, 97; auth, The Pentateuch: A Social-Science Commentary, Sheffield Acad Press, 99. **CONTACT ADDRESS** Dept of Relig, Univ of No Carolina, Chapel Hill, 600 Maple Forest Place, Waterloo, ON, Canada N2T 2S8. **EMAIL** jvansete@wlu.ca

VAN SLYKE, GRETCHEN J.
PERSONAL Born 10/08/1951, Hibbing, MN **DISCIPLINE** FRENCH **EDUCATION** Univ Minn, BA, 74; MA, 76; Univ Pa, PhD, 84. **CAREER** Asst prof to prof, Univ Vt, 83-. **MEMBERSHIPS** MLA. **SELECTED PUBLICATIONS** Auth, "Militancy in the Making: The Example of Le Bachelier," Stanford Fr Rev 11.3, (87); auth, "Reinventing Matrimony: Rosa Bonheur, Her Mother and Her Friends," Women's Studies Quart 19, (91); auth, "Ad-dressing the Self: Costume, Gender and Autobiographical Discourse in l'Abbe de Choisy and Rosa Bonheur," Autobiography. Historiography. Rhetoric. A Festschrift in Honor of Frank Paul Bowman, eds Mary Donaldson-Evans, Lucienne Frappier-Mazur and Gerald Prince, (Amsterdam, Atlanta: Editions Rodopi, 94); auth, "L'Auto/biographie de Rosa Bonheur: un testament matrimonial," Romantisme 85; (94); auth, "Rebuilding the Bastille: Women's Dress-Code Legislation in the Nineteenth Century," Repression and Expression: Literary and Social Cody in Nineteenth-Century France, ed Carrol F Coates, (NY: Peter Lang, 96); transl, Rosa Bonheur: The Artist's (Auto)Biography, Univ Mich Pr, 97; auth, "Portrait de l'artiste en femme," Rosa Bonheur (1822-1899), ed Francis Ribemont, (Bordeaux: William Blake & Co, 97); auth, "The Sexual and Textual Politics of Dress: Rosa Bonheur and Her Cross-Dressing Permits," Nineteenth-Century French Studies 26.3/4, (98); auth, "Autobiographical matrices and Mothers' Tongues in Nathalie Sarraute's ENFANCE," Corps/decors: Femmes, orgies, pardody. Homage a Lucienne Frappier-Mazur, ed Catherine Nesci (Editions rodopi, 99). **CONTACT ADDRESS** Dept Romance Lang, Univ of Vermont, 517 Waterman Bldg, Burlington, VT 05404. **EMAIL** vanslyke@polyglot.uvm.edu

VAN STEEN, GONDA ALINE HECTOR
PERSONAL Born 04/08/1964, Aalst, Belgium, m, 1996 **DISCIPLINE** CLASSICS **EDUCATION** Princeton Univ, MA, 93, PhD, 95. **CAREER** Asst Prof, 95-97, Cornell Univ; Asst Prof, Classic & Modern Greek, 97-, Univ of Ariz. **HONORS AND AWARDS** Undergrad full tuition fel Govt Belgium, Undergrad Dissertation Awd, J D & C T MacArthur Found Grant, Alexander Papamarkou Awd, Gennadeion Fel, AGTE Awd, Stanley J Seeger Fel, Mary Isabel Sibley Fel, MGSA PhD Dissertation Prize. **MEMBERSHIPS** APA, MGSA, MLA. **RESEARCH**

Ancient & modern Greek drama, film & performance criticism, gender studies, language instruction, foreign studies program. **SELECTED PUBLICATIONS** Auth, Venom in Verse, Aristophanes in Modern Greece, Princeton Univ Press, 00; Destined to Be? - Tyche in Chariton's Chaereas and Callirhoe and in the Byzantine Romance of Kallimachos and Chrysorroi, in: L'Antiquite Classique, 88; Aristophanes Revival on the Modern Greek Stage, in: Dialogos, Hellenic Studies Review, Kings Coll London, 95; Aspects of Public Performance in Aristophanes' Acharnians, AC, 94. **CONTACT ADDRESS** Dept of Classics, Univ of Arizona, Mod Lang Bldg, Box 210067, Tucson, AZ 85721-0067. **EMAIL** gonda@u.arizona.edu

VAN VLIET, EDWARD RICHIE
DISCIPLINE LATIN, FRENCH, ITALIAN **EDUCATION** Bowdoin Col, AB, 65; Brown Univ, AM, 67, PhD, 73. **CAREER** Adj, Brown Univ, Univ RI, 65-77; asst prof, Salve Regina Univ, 69-71; asst prof, 71-74, chair, dept mod lang, 72-78, assoc prof, 74-80, Elizabethtown Col; instr, Interlangues, Paris, vic lectr, Univ Paris, 77-78; headmaster, Cellucam Int Sch, Cameroon, 78-79; assoc, SUNY, 80-92; postgrad stud, Syracuse Univ, 91-92; prof, Kansai Gaidai Univ, Osaka, 94-97; ASSOC PROF, SUNY, GENESEO, 80-. **CONTACT ADDRESS** Dept of For Langs & Lits, SUNY, Col at Geneseo, Welles Hall 211, Geneseo, NY 14454. **EMAIL** vanvliet@.geneseo.edu

VANCE, BARBARA
DISCIPLINE FRENCH LITERATURE **EDUCATION** Cornell Univ, PhD, 89. **CAREER** Assoc prof. **SELECTED PUBLICATIONS** Auth, Syntactic Change in Medieval French, 97; articles on the syntax of Old, Middle, and Modern French. **CONTACT ADDRESS** Dept of French and Italian, Indiana Univ, Bloomington, 1020 E Kirkwood Ave, Ballantine Hall 642, Bloomington, IN 47405. **EMAIL** bvance@indiana.edu

VANCE, SYLVIA P.
PERSONAL Born 12/24/1925, New Britain, CT, m, 1948, 3 children **DISCIPLINE** FRENCH, LITERATURE **EDUCATION** Otterbein Col, BA, 47; Ohio State Univ, MA, 48; PhD, 80. **CAREER** Instr, asst prof to assoc prof to prof to dept chmn to prog dir to emer, Otterbein Col, 61-. **HONORS AND AWARDS** OSU Fel, 47-48; Sch Critical Theory, 84; NEH Chall Grant, Otterbein Col; AAC Project Team Leader, 91. **MEMBERSHIPS** AATF; SFHS; MLA; SES; NASSCFl; CIRS. **RESEARCH** 17th-century France; memoirs, esp. Cardinal de Retz; book on memoirs. **SELECTED PUBLICATIONS** Auth, "History as Dramatic Reinforcement: Voltaire's Use of History in Four Tragedies Set in the Middle Ages," Voltaire Studies 18th-Century (76); auth, "Retz's Narration of the Monstrous Body of History," in Actes de Columbus: Paper on French Seventeenth-Century Literature, ed. Charles G. S. Williams (Bibliog 17, 89); auth, "Retz and His Memoirs: The Question of Orthodoxy and Subversion," Seventeenth-Century Fr Studies 21 (99). **CONTACT ADDRESS** 223 S Knox St, Westerville, OH 43018-2224. **EMAIL** waid2@juno.com

VANCE, TIMOTHY
PERSONAL Born 08/25/1951, Minneapolis, MN **DISCIPLINE** JAPANESE LANGUAGE **EDUCATION** WA Univ, BA, 73; Univ Chicago, MA, 76, PhD, 79. **CAREER** Lectr, Univ IL, 79-80; asst prof, Univ FL, 81-86; asst prof, 86-88; assoc prof, Univ HI, 88-93; assoc prof, 93-94; prof, CT Col, 94-99; prof and dept head, Univ Arizona, 99-. **HONORS AND AWARDS** Am Oriental Soc; Asn Asian Studies: Asn Tchr Japanese; Int Phonetic Asn; Ling Soc Am. **RESEARCH** Phonology; Japanese linguistics. **SELECTED PUBLICATIONS** Auth, An Introduction to Japanese Phonology, Univ NY, 87; Instant Vocabulary through Prefixes and Suffixes, Kodansha Int, 90; Final Accent vs. No Accent: Utterance Final Neutralization in Tokyo Japanese, Jour Phonetics, 95; Sequential Voicing in Sino-Japanese, Jour Asn Tchr Japanese, 96. **CONTACT ADDRESS** Dept of E Asian Studies, Univ of Arizona, Franklin Bldg 404, Tucson, AZ 85721. **EMAIL** vancet@u.arizona.edu

VANDELOISE, CLAUDE
DISCIPLINE FRENCH LINGUISTICS, COGNITIVE LINGUISTICS **EDUCATION** Univ of Paris, BA; MA; Univ Calif, PhD, 84. **CAREER** Prof, Univ Instelling Antwerpen, 86-87; asst prof, 87-88, Penn State Univ; prof, 89-, La State Univ. **MEMBERSHIPS** Linguistic Soc of Am; Int Cognitive Linguistics Asn; Int Scientific Board of VISIO. **RESEARCH** French linguistics; cognitive linguistics; semantics of space and time; conceptual and linguistic categorization; history of linguistics; philosophy of language. **SELECTED PUBLICATIONS** Auth, L'espace en francais: semantique des prepositions spatiales, Les Editions du Seuil (Paris), 86; auth, "L'expression du mouvement," Langue Francaise 76 (Larousse, Paris, 87); auth, "Semantique Cognitive," Commun 53 (91); auth, Spatial Prepositions, A Case Study in French, Univ of Chicago, 91; auth, "La couleur des prepositions," Langages 110 (93); auth, "La categorisation en semantique cognitive," Le Francais Moderne LXII (94): 224-233; auth, "De la matiere a l'espace," Cahiers de Grammaire 20 (95): 123-145; auth, "La Meronomie, l'inclusion topologique et la preposition dans," in La relation d'appartenance: Faits de Langues 7 (Ophrys, Paris, 96), 81-91; auth, "Touching and the Minimal Transmission of Energy," in Linguistic in the Redhood, ed. Eugene Casad (Mouton-de Gruyter, Berlin, 96), 541-569. **CONTACT ADDRESS** Dept of Fr Grad Stud, Louisiana State Univ and A&M Col, Baton Rouge, LA 70803. **EMAIL** cvande@lsu.edu

VANDIVER, ELIZABETH
DISCIPLINE CLASSICS **EDUCATION** Univ Tex, Austin, PhD, 90. **CAREER** Vis asst prof, 96-98; Univ of Maryland in January 00 from Northwestern Univ, 96-; assoce head, Willard Residential Col; co-organizer, 3-yr Colloquium on Translation in Context; **HONORS AND AWARDS** Am Philological Assoc "Excellence in Teaching Awd," 98 **RESEARCH** A Reader's Guide to Shakespeare's Mythology; 19th and 20th century British and American literature **SELECTED PUBLICATIONS** Auth, Heroes in Herodotus: The Interaction of Myth and History, Studien zur klassische philol, 91; Fireflies in a Jar, Sappho in Translation, Poetry in Rev, 96; Ex hoc ingrato gaudia amore tibi: Catullus' Unhappy Love and the Modern Reader, The New Engl Class Newsletter and J, 92; Greek Heroic Mythology and the Ritual Theory of Tragedy's Origin, Text and Presentation, 91; Sound Patterns in Catullus 84, Class J, 90. **CONTACT ADDRESS** Dept. of Classics, Univ of Maryland, Col Park, 2407 Marie Mount Hall, College Park, MD 20742. **EMAIL** ev23@umail.umd.edu

VANPATTEN, BILL
DISCIPLINE SPANISH LITERATURE **EDUCATION** Univ of Santa Clara, BA, 76; Univ Tex, MA, 81; PhD, 83. **CAREER** Asst prof, Michigan State Univ, 83-85; Univ of Ill Urbana-Champaign, 85-89; assoc prof, Univ of Ill Urbana-Champaign, 89-95; prof, Univ Ill Urbana-Champaign, 95-. **HONORS AND AWARDS** Phi Kappa Phi Honorary Soc; Lilly Endowment Teaching Fel, 87-88; Nelson Brooks Awd for Excellence in the Teaching, 92; UIUC Humanities Awd for Excellence in Teaching, 97. **MEMBERSHIPS** Am Coun on the Teaching of Foreign Languages; Am Asn of teachers of Spanish and Portugeuse; Am Asn for Applied Ling; Teachers of Eng to Speakers of Other Languages. **RESEARCH** Second language acquisition theory and research; input processing; psycholinguistics of focus on form. **SELECTED PUBLICATIONS** Co-ed, Second Language Acquisition and Foreign Language Learning: Perspectives on Research and Practice, Clevedon, UK: Multilingual Matters, (90): 276; coauth, Making Communicative Language Teaching Happen, New York: McGraw-Hill, 95; coauth, "From Input to Output: Processing Instruction and Communicative Tasks," in Second Language Acquisition Theory and Pedagogy, (Earlbaum, 95): 169-185; auth, Input Processing and Grammar Instruction: Theory and Research, Norwood, NJ: Ablex, 96; auth, "The Case for Psycholinguistics," in Beyond Methods: Components of Teacher Education, eds. Kathleen Bardovi-Harlig & Beverly T. Hartford, (97): 1-17; coauth, "Acoustic Salience: Testing Location, Stress and the Boundedness of Grammatical Form in Second Language Acquisition Input Perception," in Contemporary Perspectives on The Acquisition of Spanish: Vol. 2 Production, Processing, and Comprehension, (Cascadilla Press, 97): 109-121; auth, "On the Relevnace of Input Processing to Second Langauge Acquisition Theory and Second Language Instruction," in Contemporary Perspectives on The Acquisition of Spanish: Vol 2 Production, Processing, and Compehension, (Cascadilla Press, 97): 93-108; auth, "Cognitive Characteristics of Adult Second Language Acquisition," in Learning Foreign and Second Languages: Perspectives in Research and Scholarship, ed. Heidi Byrnes, (New York: The Modern Language Asn, 98): 105-127; coauth, "Anxiety and Grammar Acquisition," in Anxiety in Second Language Acquisition: Theory to Practice, (New York: MacGraw-Hill, 99): 89-105; auth, "Processing Instruction as Form-Meaning Connections: Issues in Theory and Research," in Form and Meaning in Language Teaching, eds. J.F. Lee and A. Valdman, (Boston: Heinle & Heinle, 99). **CONTACT ADDRESS** Spanish, Italian, and Portuguese Dept, Univ of Illinois, Urbana-Champaign, 52 E Gregory Dr, Champaign, IL 61820. **EMAIL** bvp@staff.uiuc.edu

VARALLO, SHARON
DISCIPLINE INTERPERSONAL COM, FAMILY AND GENDER COMMUNICATION **EDUCATION** PhD, OH State Univ, MA, Univ of NC, Chapel Hill, BA, Col of William and Mary. **CAREER** Comm, Cleveland St Univ. **SELECTED PUBLICATIONS** Co-auth, Dialectic of Difference: A Thematic Analysis of Intimates' Meanings for Differences, Interpretive Approaches to Interpersonal Communication, 94; auth, Family Photos: A Generic Critique, Rhetorical Criticism: Exploration and Practice, 96. **CONTACT ADDRESS** Commun Dept, Cleveland State Univ, 83 E 24th St, Cleveland, OH 44115.

VARDERI, ALEJANDRO
PERSONAL Born 01/17/1960, Caracas, Venezuela, d **DISCIPLINE** SPANISH, GENDER STUDIES **EDUCATION** Univ Central de Venezuela, BA, 84; Univ Ill, MA, 88; NY Univ, PhD, 95. **CAREER** Teaching Asst, Univ Ill, 85-88; From Instr to Assoc Prof, Bor of Manhattan Community Col, 93-. **HONORS AND AWARDS** Latino Recognition Awd, 88; Pennfield Fel, NY Univ, 93; BMCC Fac Develop Grant, 97; Res Awd, CUNY, 96, 98. **MEMBERSHIPS** AIH, LCI, ILI, MLA, NACH. **RESEARCH** Spanish and Latin American literature and film, gender studies. **SELECTED PUBLICATIONS** Auth, "Marco Antonio Ettedgui: A Profile," Latin Am Writers on Gay and Lesbian Themes, Greenwood Pr (94): 151-153; auth, Severo Sarduy y Pedro Almodovar: del barroco al kitsch en la narrativa y el cine postmodernos, Pliegos (Madrid, Spain), 96; auth, Anatomia de una seduccion: Reescrituras de lo femenino, Acad Nat de la Hist (Caracas, Venezuela), 96; auth, "Luis Lopez Alvarez: Literatura e identidad en Venezuela," Alba de Am, vol 16, no 30-31 (98): 365-369; auth, "Nueva York en Lorca," Verbigracia: El Universal (98): 2-3; auth, "Pasion y resurreccion del cuerpo de Marco Antonio Ettedgui," Verbigracia: El Universal (99); auth, "A La Recherche d'Isabel I Maria," in Voices and Visions: The Words and Works of Merce Rodoreda (Selinsgrove: Susquehanna UP, 99), 208-223; auth, Amantes y reverentes, Red Int del libro (Santiago de Chile), 99. **CONTACT ADDRESS** Dept Lang, Borough of Manhattan Comm Col, CUNY, 119 Chambers St, New York, NY 10007-1044. **EMAIL** avarderi@bmcc.cuny.edu

VARGAS, MARGARITA
PERSONAL Born 05/20/1956, El Paso, TX, m, 1984, 3 children **DISCIPLINE** SPANISH LITERATURE **EDUCATION** Univ Kansas, PhD 85, MA 82; Yale Univ BA 79. **CAREER** SUNY Buffalo, vis prof, asst prof, assoc prof, 85 to 98-. **HONORS AND AWARDS** Elected to MLA Del Assem Org Comm; Chancellor's Awd; Sigma Delta Pi; Yale Cum laude; Bildner Prize; DeForest Prize. **MEMBERSHIPS** MLA; AATSP; FU **RESEARCH** Questions of Identity in Span/Amer Theater; Post modernism and feminism; Translation. **SELECTED PUBLICATIONS** Auth, Power and Resistance in De noche vienes, by Elena Poniatowska, Hispanic Jour, 95; Mexican Romanticism, Mexican Literature: A History, ed, David William Foster, trans, David E Johnson, Austin, U of TX Press, 94; Bio-bibliographic entries in: Dictionary of Mexican Literature, ed, Eladio Cortes, 13 entries, Westport CT and London, Greenwood, 92; Women Writing Women: An Anthology of Spanish-American Theater og the 1980's, co-trans, Albany, SUNY Press, 97; The House on the Beach, by Juan Garcia Ponce, co-trans, Austin, U of TX Press, 94. **CONTACT ADDRESS** Dept of Modern Languages and Literature, SUNY, Buffalo, 910 Clemens Hall, Buffalo, NY 14260. **EMAIL** mvargas@acsu.buffalo.edu

VASVARI, LOUISE O.
PERSONAL Born 05/13/1943, Budapest, Hungary **DISCIPLINE** COMPARATIVE LITERATURE **EDUCATION** Montclair State Univ, BA, 63; Univ Ca, MA, 66, PhD, 69. **CAREER** Prof, Central European Univ, Budapest, 01; Visiting Prof, NY Univ, 01; Prof, SU.N.Y., Stony Brook, 84; Visiting Prof, U.C., Berkeley, 96; Prof, Oetvos Lorand Univ, Budapest, 95; Assoc Provost, S.U.N.Y., Stony Brook, 82-84; Visiting Assoc Prof, U.C., Davis, 81; Chair, S.U.N.Y., Stony Brook, 79-83; Assoc Prof, S.U.N.Y., S.B., 77-84; Assistant Prof, S.U.N.Y., S.B., 73-77; Teacher, 63-64. **HONORS AND AWARDS** Fulbright Senior Sch Awd, 95; John K. Walsh Prize for Best Article, 94; N.E.H. Senior Fel, 88-89; N.E.H. Summer Grant, 85; Chancellor's Statewide Awd for Excellence in Teaching, S.U.N.Y., 76; Fac Res Fel, S.U.N.Y., 76; National Defense Education Act Fel, 66-67. **MEMBERSHIPS** Am Comp Lit Asn; MLA; Ling Soc Am; Boccaccio Soc; Int Lings Asn; Asn Int de Hispanistas; Asn Hispanica de Literatura Medieval; Medieval Acad; Hungarian-Am Educr Asn. **SELECTED PUBLICATIONS** Auth, "Tratado sobre el titulo de duque," Tamesis, (76); auth, "El laberinto de Fortuna: edicion critica," Alhambra (76), second edi., (82); auth, "Nouns and Countability: Towards A Contrastive Teaching Grammar of English and Spanish," (95); auth, "Peregrinaciones por Topografias Pornograficas en el LBA," In Actas del VI Congreso de la Asociacion Hispanica de Literatura Medieval," (97); auth, "Las Trescientas prenadas' de Juan de Mena: la politica de la traduccion y pedanteria latinizantes," In Lectures d'une oeuvre: 'Laberinto de Fortuna' de Juan de Mena, (98); auth, "Fowl Play in My Lady's Chamber: Textual Harassment of a Middle English Pornithological Riddle and Visual Pun," Obscenity: Social Control & Artistic Creation in the European Middle Ages, (98); auth, "La morilla d'un bel catar:" The Body of the Text, Papers of the Medieval Hispanic Research Seminar, (99); auth, "The Semiotics of Phallic Aggression & Anal Penetration as Male Agonistic Ritual in the Libro de Buen Amor," Queer Iberia: Sexualities, Cultures, and Crossings from the Middle Ages to the Renaissance, (99); auth, "Pornografia, politica sexual y performance anxiety: el enxiemplo de la fierecilla domada (Conce Lucanor XXXV), (99); auth, "Hit the Cat and Tame the Bride': Shrew-Taming as Wedding Ritual, East to West," American and British Interactions, Perceptions & Images of North Africa, (00). **CONTACT ADDRESS** English Dept, SUNY, Stony Brook, Stony Brook, NY 11794. **EMAIL** lvasvari@notes.cc.sunysb.edu

VAUTIER, MARIE
DISCIPLINE COMPARATIVE CANADIAN LITERATURE, FRENCH LANGUAGE **EDUCATION** Univ Toronto, PhD. **CAREER** Prof, Univ of Victoria, 00-. **RESEARCH** Literary theory; Quebecois literature; stylistics and translation. **SELECTED PUBLICATIONS** Auth, "Le desours feminin et le mythe postmodern: Commu une enfant de la tere de Jovette Marchessault et Obasan de Joy Kogawa," in les Desours feminins dans la litterature postmoderne au Quebec, San Francisco: Mellen Res UP, (93), 291-305; auth, "Postmodern Myth, Post-Europen History, and the Figure of the Amerindian: Fran-

cois Barcelo, George Bowering , and Jacques Poulin," Candian Lit 141, (94), 15-33; auth, "Les metarecits, le postmodernisme et le mythe postcolonial au Quebec," etudes litteraires 27.1, (94), 43-61; auth, "Comparative Postcolonialism and the Amerindian in english-speaking Canada and Quebec," Cnaadian Ethnic Studies 28.3, (96), 4-15; auth, "Naugrage ou navire,: la memeoire de lecriture migrante des annees quatre-vingt et quatre-vingt-dix au Quebec," Avec Karyn Marzak, LitteRealite 92, (97), 65-78; auth, "Canadian Fiction Meets History and Historiography," Colby Quarterly 3.1, (99),18-34; auth, New World Nyth: Postmodernism and Postcolonialism in Canadian Fiction, Montreal/Kingston: McGill-Queen's Univ Press, 98. **CONTACT ADDRESS** Dept of French, Univ of Victoria, PO Box 3045 STN CSC, Victoria, BC, Canada V8W 3P4. **EMAIL** mvautier@uvic.ca

VAZSONYI, NICHOLAS
PERSONAL Born 05/31/1963, m, 1996 **DISCIPLINE** GERMAN **EDUCATION** Ind Univ, BA, 82; Univ Calif at Los Angeles, MA, 88; PhD, 93. **CAREER** Asst prof, Vanderbilt Univ, 94-97; asst prof, Univ SC, 97-. **HONORS AND AWARDS** DAAD Stp; CLASS Awd. **MEMBERSHIPS** MLA; Phi Beta Kappa; GSA; AATG; ASECS. **RESEARCH** 18th-20th century literature; national identity; music. **SELECTED PUBLICATIONS** Auth, Lukacs Reads Goethe: From Aestheticism to Stalinism, Camden House (Columbia, SC), 97; ed, Searching for Common Ground: Diskurse zur deutschen Identitat 1750-1877, Koln and Weimar, forthcoming; auth, "Goethe's Wilhelm Meisters Lehrjahre: A Question of Talent," Ger Quart 62 (89): 39-47; auth, "Deflated Hybris -- Uncertain Telos: The Humbling of Faust and the Revival of Merlin," in Merlin versus Faust: Contending Archetypes in Western Culture, ed. Charlotte Spivack (Lewiston: Edwin Mellen Press, 92), 41-64; auth, "Searching for 'The Order of Things': Does Goethe's Faust, Part II Suffer from the 'Fatal Conceit'?," Monatsheffe 88 (96): 83-94; auth, "A Wall of Silence?: The Case of Christa Wolf," in The Berlin Wall: Representations and Perspectives, eds. Ernst Schurer, Manfred Keune, Philip Jenkins (New York: Peter Lang, 96), 81-90; auth, "Liszt, Goethe and the Faust Symphony," J Am Liszt Soc 40 (96): 1-23; auth, "Of Genius and Epiphany: Schlafes Bruder, Das Parfum, and Babette's Feast," Stud 20th Cent Lit 23 (99): 331-51; auth, "Montesquieu, Friedrich Carl von Moser and the 'National Spirit Debate' in Germany (1765-1767)," Ger Stud Rev 22 (99): 225-46. **CONTACT ADDRESS** Dept German, Slavic Languages, Univ of So Carolina, Columbia, Columbia, SC 29225. **EMAIL** vazsonyi@sc.edu

VEGA, CARLOS
PERSONAL Born 08/20/1953, McKinney, TX, s **DISCIPLINE** SPANISH **EDUCATION** Columbia Col & Columbia Univ, BA, 74; Univ Va, MA, 76; Harvard Univ, PhD, 84. **CAREER** Teaching asst, Univ Va, 74-77; teaching asst, Harvard Col, 78-81; lectr, Brandeis Univ, 81-84; part-time lectr, Tufts Univ, 84-85; asst prof, Princeton Univ, 85-87; prof, Wellesley Col, 87-. **HONORS AND AWARDS** Ford Found Fel, 77-80; grant, Princeton Univ Comt for Res in the Humanities, 86; NEH Summer Stipend, 88; grant in aid, Am Philos Soc, 89; NEH Fel, 89-90 & 97-98. **MEMBERSHIPS** Philos Soc; Hagiography Soc; Asn of N Am Univ Prog in Spain. **RESEARCH** Spanish Literature, Medieval Studies, Hagiography. **SELECTED PUBLICATIONS** Auth, "Erotismo y ascetismo: Imagen y texto en un incunable hagiografico," in Erotismo en las letras hispanicas, ed. Luce Lopez-Baralt and Francisco Marquez Villanueva (Mex: El Col de Mex Centro de Estudios Linguisticos y Literarios, 95), 479-499; auth, "La literatura religiosa," Antropos: Revista de documentacion cientifica de la cultura (95): 111-113; auth, "Spain," in The Current State of Research in Fifteenth-Century Literature. Studies in Medieval Literature Volume 16, eds. Edelgard E. Dubruck and William C. McDonald (The Edwin Mellen Press, 96), 187-209; rev, of "La tercera cronica de Alfonso X: 'La gran conquista de Ultramar," by Cristina Gonzalez, Speculum 72 (97): 474-476; auth, "Libros de milagros," "Misales," "Novenarios," and "Vidas de santos," in Diccionario de literatura popular espanola, eds. Joaquin Alvarez Barrientos and Ma. Jose Rodriquez Sanchez de Leon (Madrid: Ediciones Colegio de Espana, 97), 169-172, 199-200, 225-226, & 354-356. **CONTACT ADDRESS** Dept Span, Wellesley Col, 106 Central St, Wellesley Hills, MA 02481-8268. **EMAIL** cvega@wellesley.edu

VELEZ, JOSEPH FRANCISCO
PERSONAL Born 01/29/1928, Puebla, Mexico, m, 1969, 6 children **DISCIPLINE** SPANISH LANGUAGE & LITERATURE **EDUCATION** Howard Payne Univ, BA, 62; Univ Okla, MA, 68, PhD(romance lang), 69. **CAREER** Instr Span, Univ Okla, 65-68; from asst prof to assoc prof Span and French, Western Ky Univ, 68-71; co-chmn dept Span, 76-77, ASSOC PROF SPAN, BAYLOR UNIV, 71-, DIR LATIN AM STUDIES, 77-, Interim pastor for Span speaking congregation, First Baptist Church, Marlin, Tex, 81. **MEMBERSHIPS** MLA; SCent Mod Lang Asn; Nat Asn Chicano Studies; Am Asn Teachers Span and Port; AAUP. **RESEARCH** Latin American literature. **SELECTED PUBLICATIONS** Auth, Paradise-Lost or Gained, the Literature of Hispanic Exile, Hispania-Jour Devoted Tchg Span and Port, Vol 0076, 93. **CONTACT ADDRESS** Dept of Spanish, Baylor Univ, Waco, Waco, TX 76798.

VENA, MICHAEL
PERSONAL Born 07/04/1941, Jelsi, Italy **DISCIPLINE** ITALIAN **EDUCATION** Univ Bridgeport, BA, 65; Yale Univ, MA, 67, PhD(Ital), 72; Univ Rome, dipl Ital, 72. **CAREER** Lectr Ital, Yale Univ, 69-70; assoc prof, 70-80, PROF ITAL, SOUTHERN CONN STATE COL, 80-, CHMN DEPT FOREIGN LANG, 76-. **MEMBERSHIPS** MLA; Am Asn Teachers Ital. **RESEARCH** Renaissance literature and language; modern theatre. **SELECTED PUBLICATIONS** Auth, The Grotteschi Revisited--20th-Century Grotesque Theater, Forum Italicum, Vol 0031, 97. **CONTACT ADDRESS** Dept of Ital, So Connecticut State Univ, 501 Crescent St, New Haven, CT 06515-1330.

VENCLOVA, TOMAS ANDRIUS
PERSONAL Born 09/11/1937, Klaipeda, Lithuania, m, 1990, 2 children **DISCIPLINE** SLAVIC & LITHUANIAN LITERATURES **EDUCATION** Univ Vilnius, dipl, 60; Yale Univ, PhD, 85. **CAREER** Lectr lit, Univ Vilnius, 66-73; jr fel philosophy, Acad Sci, Lithuania, 74-76; Regents prof semiotics art, Univ Calif, Berkeley, 77; lectr semiotics art, Univ Calif, Los Angeles, 77-80; Lectr Russ Lit, 80-85, Asst prof Slavic Lit, 85-90, Assoc prof Slavic Lit, 90-93, PROF SLAVIC LIT, 93- ,YALE UNIV, 80- ; Lit consult, Siauliai Drama Theater, Lithuania, 74-76. **HONORS AND AWARDS** Int Lit Prize Vilenica, 90; Dr Hon Causa, Univ Lublin, 91. **MEMBERSHIPS** PEN Club; Am Asn Advan Slavic Studies; Am Asn Tchr Slavic E Europ Lang; Asn Advan Baltic Stud (pres, 89-91). **RESEARCH** Slavic literatures; Lithuanian literature; semiotics of art. **SELECTED PUBLICATIONS** Auth, Unstable Equilibrium: Eight Russian Poetic Texts, Yale Ctr Int & Area Stud, 86; Aleksander Wat: Life and Art of an Iconoclast, Yale Univ Press, 96; Participants in the Feast, Baltos Lankos, 97. **CONTACT ADDRESS** Dept of Slavic Lang & Lit, Yale Univ, PO Box 208236, New Haven, CT 06520-8236. **EMAIL** tomas.venclova@yale.edu

VERANI, HUGO JUAN
PERSONAL Born 04/04/1941, Montevideo, Uruguay, m, 1964, 2 children **DISCIPLINE** LATIN AMERICAN LITERATURE **EDUCATION** Phillips Univ, AB, 66; Univ Wis-Madison, MA, 67, PhD(Span), 73. **CAREER** From instr to asst prof, Mt Holyoke Col, 70-74; asst prof, 74-78, assoc prof, 78-82, PROF SPAN, UNIV CALIF, DAVIS, 82-. **MEMBERSHIPS** MLA; Am Asn Teachers Span and Port; Inst Int Lit Iberam; Asn Int Hispanistas; Philol Asn Pac Coast. **RESEARCH** Contemporary Spanish American literature; 20th century fiction; literary theory. **SELECTED PUBLICATIONS** Narrativa contemporanea, La Muralla, Madrid, 80; Onetti: el ritual de la impostura, Monte Avila, Caracas, 81; Las vanguardias literarias en America Latina, Mexico, Centroamerica, Caribe, 82 & auth intro & ed, Maria Eugenia Vaz Ferreira, In: Poesias completes, 82, Arca, Montevideo; auth, Octavio Paz: Bibliografia critical UNAM, Mexico, 82. **CONTACT ADDRESS** Dept of Spanish, Univ of California, Davis, Davis, CA 95616.

VERDESIO, GUSTAVO
DISCIPLINE LATIN AMERICAN COLONIAL LITERATURE **EDUCATION** Northwestern Univ, PhD, 92. **CAREER** Asst prof, La State Univ; asst prof, Univ of Mich. **RESEARCH** Latin American colonial literature; literary theory. **SELECTED PUBLICATIONS** Auth, Escritura e identidad cultural en el Uruguay colonial, in Letterature d' America: Revista Trimestrale, Univ Roma, 13, 49, 93; Una ausencia en el canon: Los discursos coloniales sobre el Uruguay en el marco de la historiografia literaria uruguaya y los estudios coloniales latinoamericanos, Revista Iberoamericana, 60, 95; auth, La invencion del Uruguay: la entrada del territorio y sus habitantes a la cultura occidental, Trazas, 96; auth, Forgotten Conquests: Re-reading New World History from the Margins, Temple Univ Press, 00. **CONTACT ADDRESS** Dept of Romance Lang and Lit, Univ of Michigan, Ann Arbor, Ann Arbor, MI 48109. **EMAIL** verdesio@umich.edu

VERGNAUD, JEAN-ROGER
DISCIPLINE LINGUISTICS **EDUCATION** MIT, PhD. **CAREER** Prof, Univ Southern Calif. **RESEARCH** Syntax; Phonology; Morphology. **SELECTED PUBLICATIONS** Auth, Dependances et niveaux de representation en syntaxe, John Benjamins BV, 85; coauth, An Essay on Stress, MIT Press, 87. **CONTACT ADDRESS** Dept of Linguistics, Univ of So California, University Park Campus, Los Angeles, CA 90089. **EMAIL** vergnaud@usc.edu

VERMETTE, ROSALIE ANN
PERSONAL Born 05/10/1946, Lewiston, ME, m, 1982 **DISCIPLINE** FRENCH LANGUAGE & LITERATURE **EDUCATION** Univ Lyon, France, diplome, 67; Univ Maine, Orono, AB, 68; Univ Iowa, MA, 70, PhD, 75. **CAREER** Lectr English, Univ Poitiers, France, 72-73; from instr to asst prof French, Univ Iowa, 74-76; from asst prof to prof French, Ind Univ/ Purdue Univ, Indianapolis, 76-. **HONORS AND AWARDS** Phi Beta Kappa, 68. **MEMBERSHIPS** Mediaeval Acad Am; Int Arthurian Soc; MLA; Am Asn Teachers Fr; Midwest Mod Lang Asn. **RESEARCH** Medieval French hagiographic textual studies; medieval French romance studies; cultural studies; foreign language pedagogy. **SELECTED PUBLICATIONS** Auth, The Huit Beatitudes in old French prose, Manuscripta, 74; coauth, Un manuscit inconnu de Bartolomeo Visconti: les Dialogi de Gregoire le grand, Scriptorium, 78; auth, An Unrecorded Fragment of Richart d'Irlande's Propheties de Merlin, Romance Philol, 81; Some Dim Notion, the World Viewed Through Old French Saints' Lives, Romance Lanugages Annual, 94; coauth, "Teaching cultural competence," in Acquiring Cultural Competence, ed. A. S. Singerman, 96. **CONTACT ADDRESS** Dept of Foreign Languages & Cultures, Indiana Univ-Purdue Univ, Indianapolis, 425 University Blvd, Indianapolis, IN 46202-5148. **EMAIL** rvermett@iupui.edu

VERNIER, RICHARD
PERSONAL Born 02/01/1929, Clermont-Ferrand, France, m, 1962, 3 children **DISCIPLINE** FRENCH LITERATURE **EDUCATION** Univ Calif, Berkeley, AB, 58, PhD(Romance lang), 65. **CAREER** Lectr French, City Col New York, 62-63; asst prof, San Diego State Col, 63-66 and Univ Wash, 66-72; assoc prof, State Univ NY Fredonia, 72-73; ASSOC PROF FRENCH, WAYNE STATE UNIV, DETROIT, 73-, Vis assoc prof, Scripps Col, 75-76. **HONORS AND AWARDS** Palmes Academiques, Fr Govt, 81. **MEMBERSHIPS** MLA; Am Asn Teachers Fr. **RESEARCH** Modern poetry and poetics; French culture and civilization; Swiss-French literature. **SELECTED PUBLICATIONS** Auth, Poesie ininterrompue et la poetique de Paul Eluard, Mouton & Co, 71; Lettres de l'interieur, poemes, Subervie, 71; Prosodie et silence dans on recueil d'Yves Bonnefoy, Studia Neophilol, 73; Poeta ludens: Le rire de Saint-John Perse, Pac Coast Philol, 76; Locus patriae, L'Arc, 76; Words like the sky: The accomplishment of Yves Bonnefoy, World Lit Today, 79; La Voix de Gustave Roud, Swiss-French Studies, 80; Le Feu parmi les arbres, poemes, Solaire, 81. **CONTACT ADDRESS** 1706 Oxford, Berkley, MI 48072.

VESSELY, THOMAS RICHARD
PERSONAL Born 11/06/1944, San Marcos, TX, m, 1978, 1 child **DISCIPLINE** FRENCH LITERATURE **EDUCATION** Ind Univ, PhD, 79. **CAREER** Asst Prof French, Univ Tex, Austin, 79-. **MEMBERSHIPS** MLA; Am Asn Teachers Fr; Soc 18th Century Studies. **RESEARCH** The French fairy tale; short prose fiction. **SELECTED PUBLICATIONS** Auth, Innocence and impotence: The scenario of initiation in L'Ecumoire and in the literary fairy tale, 18th Century Life, 82. **CONTACT ADDRESS** Dept Fr & Ital, Univ of Texas, Austin, Austin, TX 78712-1026. **EMAIL** trv@mail.utexas.edu

VETRANO, ANTHONY JOSEPH
PERSONAL Born 02/03/1931, Endicott, NY, m, 1964, 2 children **DISCIPLINE** SPANISH **EDUCATION** State Univ NYork Binghamton, BA, 55; Univ Rochester, MA, 56; Syracuse Univ, PhD(Romance lang), 66. **CAREER** From instr to assoc prof, 59-74, prof mod lang, Le Moyne Col, 74-, chemn dept, 62-86; fac res grants, Le Moyne Col, 67-68 & 73-74. **HONORS AND AWARDS** Recipient of Loyola Awd (40 years service to the College), September 99. **MEMBERSHIPS** AAUP; MLA; Am Asn Teachers Span & Port. **RESEARCH** Twentieth century Spanish American novel, especially the Ecuadorian novel of social protest; modern Spanish Peninsular literature; Italian Trecento. **SELECTED PUBLICATIONS** Auth, Imagery in Two of Jorge Icaza's Novels: Huasipungo and Huairapamushcas, Rev Estudios Hisp, 5/72; La problematica Psico-social y su correlacion linguistica en las novelas de Jorge Icaza, Ed Universal, 74; Jorge Icaza and the Spanish-American Indianist Novel: Some Observations on Huasipungo, In: Studies in Romance Languages and Literature, State Univ NY Binghamton, 79. **CONTACT ADDRESS** Dept of For Lang & Lit, Le Moyne Col, 1419 Salt Springs Rd, Syracuse, NY 13214-1300. **EMAIL** vetrano@maple.lemoyne.edu

VICKERS, NANCY J.
DISCIPLINE COMPARATIVE LITERATURE, FRENCH, ITALIAN **EDUCATION** Mt Holyoke Col, BA, 67; Yale Univ, MA, 71; PhD, 76. **CAREER** Teaching asst to actg instr, Yale Univ, 69-72; instr, Dartmouth Col, 73-76, asst prof, 76-82, assoc prof, 82-87, summer 90; vis prof, Harvard Univ, spring 89; vis prof, Univ Pa, fall 91; vis prof, Univ Calif, Los Angeles, fall 92; dean and prof, Univ Southern Calif, 87-97, Dean of Curriculum and Instruction, Col of Letters, Arts and Scis, 94-97; prof, Bryn Mawr Col, 97-, Pres, 97-. **HONORS AND AWARDS** Sarah Williston Scholar, Mt Holyoke Col, 65; Yale Univ Fels, 67-71; Bardwell Memorial Fel, 71-72; Dartmouth Fac Fel, 80; Vis Fel, Princeton Univ, 80; Huntington Distinguished Teaching Award, Dartmouth Col, 82; MLA's James Russell Lowell Prize, 90; Presidential Medal for Outstanding Leadership and Achievement, Dartmouth Col, 91; Mortar Bd Sr Honor Soc Outstanding Teacher Award, USC, 92; Phi Beta Delta Honor Soc for Int Scholars, 93; Univ Southern Calif Assocs Award for Excellence in Teaching, 94; The Honor Soc of Phi Kappa Phi, 94; Doctor of Humane Letters, Honorary, Mt Holyoke Col, 99. **MEMBERSHIPS** Dante Soc of Am, USC Bd of Councilors, Modern Lang Asn, Col of Letters, Arts & Scis. **RESEARCH** Literatures and cultures of 16th century England, France, and Italy; lyric; technologies of cultural production; feminist criticism; renaissance poetry; the transformation of the lyric genre as a result of changing technologies. **SELECTED PUBLICATIONS** Auth, A New History of French Literature, with D. Hollier, gen ed, and R. H. Block, P. Brooks, J. DeJean, B. Johnson, P. E. Lewis, N. K. Miller, and F. Rigolot, Cam-

bridge, MA and London, Eng: Harvard Univ Press (89), French transl, De la litterature francaise, Paris: Bordas (93), awarded the James Russell Lowell Prize of the Modern Lang Asn, 90; auth, "Maternalism and the Material Girl," in Embodied Voices: Representing Female Vocality in Western Culture, eds Leslie C. Dunn and Nancy A. Jones, Cambridge, Eng: Cambridge Univ Press (94); auth, "Lyric in the Video Decade," Discourse, 16.1 (93): 6-27; auth, "Courting the Female Subject," in The French Renaissance in Prints from the Collection of the Bibliotheque Nationale de France, ed Cynthia Burlingham, Marianne Grivel, and Henri Zerner, Los Angeles: Grunwald Center for the Graphic Arts, Univ Calif (94): 94-107, French transl, (95); auth, "Dante in the Video Decade," in Dante Now: Current Trends in Dante Studies, ed Theodore J. Cachey, Notre Dame and London: Univ Notre Dame Press (95): 263-276; auth, "The Unauthored 1539 Volume in Which is Printed the 'Hecatomphile,' 'The Flowers of French Poetry,' and 'Other Soothing Things,' " in Subject and Object in Renaissance Culture, eds M. de Grazia, M. Quilligan, and P. Stallybrass, Cambridge, Eng: Cambridge Univ Press (96): 166-188; auth, "The Status of Evidence: A Roundtable," PMLA 111 (96): 21-31; auth, "Members Only: Marot's Anatomical Blazons," in The Body in Parts: Fantasies of Corporeality in Early Modern Europe, eds D. Hillman and C. Mazzio, New York and London: Routledge (97): 2-21; co-ed, A New History of French Literature; auth, "Blazing Beauties: Marot's Poetic Anatomies," in The Body in Parts, (97)co-ed with J. Mastern and P. Stallybrass, Language Machines: Technologies of Literary and Cultural Production, New York and London: Routledge (97); co-ed with M. Garber, Don't Look Now! The Medusa Reader, New York and London: Routledge (forthcoming 2000). **CONTACT ADDRESS** President's Office, Bryn Mawr Col, 101 N Merion Ave, Bryn Mawr, PA 19010-2899.

VICKERY, WALTER
PERSONAL Born 09/14/1921, London, England, m, 6 children **DISCIPLINE** SLAVIC LANGUAGE AND LITERATURE **EDUCATION** Oxford Univ, BA, 48, MA, 52; Harvard Univ, PhD, 58. **CAREER** Lectr Russ, Oxford Univ, 48-53; from asst prof to assoc prof Slavic lang and lit, Ind Univ, Bloomington, 58-64; prof, Univ Colo, 64-69; PROF SLAVIC LANG AND LIT, UNIV NC, CHAPEL HILL, 69-, Ind Univ fac fel, Oxford Univ, 63; Fulbright-Hays fel, Italy, 65; Am Coun Learned Soc fel, Leningrad, 67-68; Univ Colo fac fel, Italy, 68; mem screening comt, Int Asn Exchange of Persons, 72-; vis prof Yale Univ, 75; exchange scholar, Am Coun Learned Soc, Soviet Acad, 1-6/76. **MEMBERSHIPS** Am Asn Advan Slavic Studies. **RESEARCH** Soviet literary problems; Pushkin; Russian versification. **SELECTED PUBLICATIONS** Auth, A History of Russian Poetry, Russ Rev, Vol 0053, 94. **CONTACT ADDRESS** Dept of Slavic Lang, Univ of No Carolina, Chapel Hill, Chapel Hill, NC 27514.

VICKREY, JOHN FREDERICK
PERSONAL Born 08/24/1924, Chicago, IL, m, 1966 **DISCIPLINE** ENGLISH LINGUISTICS AND PHILOLOGY **EDUCATION** Univ Chicago, PhB, 49, MA, 52; Ind Univ, PhD(English), 60. **CAREER** Instr English, Rutgers Univ, 57-61; from asst prof to assoc prof, 61-74, Prof English Lit, Lehigh Univ, 74-. **MEMBERSHIPS** MLA; Mediaeval Acad Am. **RESEARCH** Old English, Old Saxon and Middle English language and literature. **SELECTED PUBLICATIONS** Auth, The Seafarer 111-15--Old-English Poem by Gordon,II, Papers on Lang and Lit, Vol 0028, 92; On the Earth Compounds in the Old-English Finn-Stories--The Finn Episode in Beowulf, Stud Neophilol, Vol 0065, 93; Inferno VII--Dante-Alighieri Divina Commedia--Deathstyles of the Rich and Famous, Neophilologus, Vol 0079, 95; The Seafarer 97-102--Dives and the Burial of Treasure, Jour Eng and Ger Philol, Vol 0094, 95. **CONTACT ADDRESS** Dept of English, Lehigh Univ, Bethlehem, PA 18015.

VIDAL, HERNAN
PERSONAL Born 04/18/1937, Villa Alemana, Chile, m, 1962, 3 children **DISCIPLINE** SPANISH AMERICAN LITERATURE **EDUCATION** Univ Iowa, PhD(Span), 67. **CAREER** Instr English, Univ Chile, Temuco, 62-64; instr Span, Univ Iowa, 66-67; asst prof, Univ Va, 67-72; assoc prof, 72-80, PROF SPAN AND PORT AND DIR GRAD STUDIES, UNIV MINN, MINNEAPOLIS, 80-. **MEMBERSHIPS** Am Asn Teachers Span and Port; MLA. **RESEARCH** Spanish American novel and drama. **SELECTED PUBLICATIONS** Auth, Postmodernism, Postleftism, Neo-Avant-Gardism, the Case of Chiles Revista-De-Critica-Cultural, Boundary 2-Intl Jour Lit and Cult, Vol 0020, 93. **CONTACT ADDRESS** Univ of Minnesota, Twin Cities, 9 Pleasant St. SE, 34 Folwell Hall, Minneapolis, MN 55455.

VIEHMEYER, L. ALLEN
PERSONAL Born 07/30/1942, Peoria, IL, w, 1967, 2 children **DISCIPLINE** GERMAN LITERATURE & LINGUISTICS **EDUCATION** Western Ill Univ, BSEd, 64; Univ Ill, Urbana-Champaign, AM, 67, PhD, 71. **CAREER** Instr Ger, Wartburg Col, 69-71; asst prof, 71-78, assoc prof Ger, 78-85; prof Ger, 85-, Youngstown State Univ. **MEMBERSHIPS** Am Assn Teachers Ger, Society for German-American Studies, Communal Societies Assoc. **RESEARCH** Pennsylvania German literature 1683-1830; German-American hymnology 1683-1830. **SELECTED PUBLICATIONS** Auth, An Index to Hymns and Hymn Tunes of the Ephrata Cloister 1730-1766, Ephrata Cloister Associates, Ephrata, PA, 95. **CONTACT ADDRESS** Dept of Foreign Lang & Lit, Youngstown State Univ, One University Plz., Youngstown, OH 44555-0002. **EMAIL** laviehme@cc.ysu.edu

VIERA, DAVID JOHN
PERSONAL Born 06/09/1943, Providence, RI, d, 2 children **DISCIPLINE** MEDIEVAL HISPANIC LITERATURE **EDUCATION** Providence Col, BA, 65; Cath Univ of Am, MA, 69, PhD(Iberian studies), 72. **CAREER** Asst prof Spanish, Tenn Tech Univ, 72-74; asst prof, State Univ Col Geneseo, NY, 75-77; Prof Spanish, Tenn Tech Univ, 80-. **HONORS AND AWARDS** Ferran Soldevila Awd, Fundacio Salvador Vives Casajuana, 79. **MEMBERSHIPS** Southeastern medieval Assoc; South Atlantic Mod Lang Asn; Am Asn Teachers Spanish and Portuguese; NAm Catalan Soc. **RESEARCH** Francesc Eiximenis; Antero de Quental; Vincent Ferrer. **SELECTED PUBLICATIONS** Auth, Eiximenis, Francesc Dissension with the Royal House of Aragon, Jour Medieval Hist, Vol 0022, 96. **CONTACT ADDRESS** Dept of Foreign Lang, Tennessee Tech Univ, Cookeville, TN 38505. **EMAIL** dviera@tntech.edu

VILLENA-ALVAREZ, JUANITA
PERSONAL Born 04/27/1965, Philippines, m, 1992, 1 child **DISCIPLINE** LINGUISTICS **EDUCATION** Instituo de Cooperacion Iberoamericana de Madrid, MA, 87; Univ Paris-Sorbonne, Magistere, 88; Univ Cincinnati, MA, 89; PhD, 94. **CAREER** Dir Study Abroad Prog, Univ SC Beaufort, 94-99. **HONORS AND AWARDS** Proof of the Year, Univ SC, 98. **MEMBERSHIPS** MLA, AATF, ADFL. **RESEARCH** International business and foreign languages, theater. **SELECTED PUBLICATIONS** Auth, The Allegory of Literary Representation as Hybrid, Peter Lang (New York, NY), 97. **CONTACT ADDRESS** Dept Ling, Univ of So Carolina, Beaufort, 801 Carteret St, Beaufort, SC 29902. **EMAIL** alvarezbabet@yahoo.com

VINE, BRENT
DISCIPLINE CLASSICS **EDUCATION** Phillips Exeter Acad, Class Dipl, 69; Harvard Col, AB, 73; Harvard Univ, AM, 75, PhD, 82. **CAREER** Tchg fel, Harvard Univ, 74-80; vis instr, Tex Tech Univ, 81-82; sec, Mass Inst Tech, 82-83; instr, Phillips Acad, 83-86; asst prof, Yale Univ, 86-91; asst prof, Princeton Univ, 91-94; assoc prof, Princeton Univ, 91-94; Assoc Prof, UCLA, 95-. **SELECTED PUBLICATIONS** Auth, "On the 'Missing' Fourth Stanza of Catullus 51," Harvard Stud Class Philol 92; "On Phonetic Repetition in Moby-Dick," Lang and Style 22, 89; Gk. -isko: and Indo-European *-iske/o-, Hist Sprachforschung 106, 93; "Catullus 76.21: ut torpor in artus," Rheinisches Museum fur Philol 136, 94; "Greek opeas/opear 'awl'," Glotta 72, 94/95; rev(s), J. Gager, "Curse Tablets and Binding Spells from the Ancient World," Bryn Mawr Class Rev 4, 91-94; comment on P. Keyser, review of J. Riddle, "Contraception and Abortion from the Ancient World to the Renaissance," Bryn Mawr Classl Rev 5, 95. **CONTACT ADDRESS** Dept of Classics, Univ of California, Los Angeles, PO Box 951436, Los Angeles, CA 90095-1436.

VISCARRI, DIONISIO
PERSONAL Born Barcelona, Spain **DISCIPLINE** SPANISH LITERATURE **EDUCATION** Univ Houston, BA, 88; MA, 90; Ohio State Univ, PhD, 96. **CAREER** Vis prof, Benson Univ, 94-96; asst prof, Univ NH, 96-98; asst prof, Ohio State Univ, 98-. **RESEARCH** Franco-Falangist litrature, Film studies, Catalan literature. **SELECTED PUBLICATIONS** Auth, "Raza, JaimedeAndrade," in Espana Contemporanea: Revista de Literatura y Cultura, (forthcoming); auth, "Diario de una Bandera," in Censorship: An International Encyclopedia, (forthcoming); auth, "Pre-Fascist Spanish Literature: Morocco 1920's," in Censorship: An International Encyclopedia (forthcoming): auth, "Catalan Literature After 1975," in Encyclopedia of Literature in the 20th Century, St James Press, (98): 195-198; auth, "Luys Santa Marina: En busca de los origenes del fascismo literario espanol," in Letras Peninsulares, (98): 103-119; auth, "Cartas a Victor Balaguer, Enrique Miralles," in Espana Contemporanea: Revistade Literatura y Cultura, (98): 108-110; auth, "Madrid, Jose Martinez Ruiz 'Azorin'," in Espana Contemporanea: Revista de Literatura y Cultura, (97): 103-104; auth, "Cosas que fueron: sociedad e ideologia en el costumbrismo alarconiano," in Boletin de la Biblioteca Menendez y Pelayo, (96): 127-142. **CONTACT ADDRESS** Dept Humanities, Ohio State Univ, Newark, 1179 Univ Dr, Newark, OH 43055-1766. **EMAIL** viscarri.1@osu.edu

VISSON, LYNN
PERSONAL Born 04/26/1945, New York, NY **DISCIPLINE** RUSSIAN LANGUAGE AND LITERATURE **EDUCATION** Radcliffe Col, BA, 66; Columbia Univ, MA, 67; Harvard Univ, PhD (Slavic lang and lit), 72. **CAREER** Instr and assoc Russ, Barnard Col, Columbia Univ, 69-70, from instr to asst prof, 71-76; Mem fac exchange with Soviet Union, Moscow State Univ, 70-71; asst prof, Bryn Mawr Col, 76-78; Am Coun Learned Soc grant in Soviet Studies, 76; asst prof Russ, Hunter Col, 78-79; Interpreter, UN, 81-. **MEMBERSHIPS** Am Asn Teachers Slavic and East Europ Lang; Am Coun Teachers Russ. **RESEARCH** Soviet poetry; Esenin; Russian language. **SELECTED PUBLICATIONS** Auth, Classic Russian Cooking in Molokhovets, Elena, A Gift to Young Housewives, Slavic Rev, Vol 54, 95; auth, Wedded Strangers; auth, From Russian into English. **CONTACT ADDRESS** 60 Riverside Dr Apt 7H, New York, NY 10024.

VITELLO, RALPH MICHAEL
PERSONAL Born 12/26/1949, Buffalo, NY **DISCIPLINE** FRENCH RENAISSANCE LITERATURE **EDUCATION** State Univ NYork Buffalo, BA, 71; Yale Univ, MPhil, 77, PhD (French), 78. **CAREER** Actg instr French, Yale Univ, 75-77; lectr, Univ Calif, Los Angeles, 77-78; ASST PROF FRENCH, YALE UNIV, 78-; Assoc prof, East Stroudsburg Univ. **MEMBERSHIPS** Soc Amis Montaigne; MLA; Am Asn Teachers Fr. **RESEARCH** Literature of ideas in the Renaissance; French and American modern poetry. **SELECTED PUBLICATIONS** Auth, Montaigne Unruly Brood in Textual Engendering and the Challenge to Paternal Authority, Sixteenth Century J, Vol 28, 97. **CONTACT ADDRESS** Dept of Foreign Languages, East Stroudsburg Univ of Pennsylvania, 200 Prospect St., East Stroudsburg, PA 18301-2999.

VITIELLO, JUSTIN
PERSONAL Born 02/14/1941, New York, NY, s, 1 child **DISCIPLINE** COMPARATIVE LITERATURE **EDUCATION** Cuidad Univ, Mex City, 60; Brown Univ, BA, 63; Univ Madrid, Fulbright Scholar, 63-64; Columbia Univ, 65; Univ Mich, MA, 66; Middlebury Col, 68; Univ Mich, PhD, 70. **CAREER** Teaching fel, Univ Mich, 64-69, lectr, 69-70, asst prof, 70-73, head of residential Col's Comparative Lit Prog and coordr of the intensive lang prog in Ital and Spanish, 69-73; asst prof, Temple Univ, 74-80, assoc prof, 80-91, full prof, 91-. **HONORS AND AWARDS** Phi Beta Kappa, 62-63; Fulbright Scholar to Spain, 63-64; Distinguished Teaching Fel, Univ Mich, 67; Nominated for Jr Fac Service, Univ Mich, 71, 72; nominee, Temple's ATTIC Distinguished Teaching Awd, 88, finalist for ATTIC, 89, winner, ATTIC Awd, 90; Arba Sicula, ed bd; consult ed, Almanacco, 91-92; MLA, Exec comt of the div on Twentieth-century Ital Lit, 99-2003; numerous nat and int Who's Who. **MEMBERSHIPS** Modern Lang Asn, Am Ital Hist Asn, Arba Sicula, Am Asn for Ital Studies, Almanacco, MELUS Life member. **RESEARCH** Naples as City from Neapolis to the Present: A Multidisciplinary Study; the History of Anarchism in Italy, Spain and America; consolidation of research on Gandhian constructive work, done in India in 89; a fourth book of poetry: Suicide of an Ethnic Poet. **SELECTED PUBLICATIONS** Auth, Il Carro del pesce di Vanzetti, poems, Milan: Corpo 10 (89); auth, Vanzetti's Fish Cart, poems, San Francisco: Mellen Poetry Press (91); auth, Sicily Within, essay, New York: Arba Sicula (92); auth, Italy's Ultramodern, Experimental Lyrics: Corpo 10, New York: Peter Lang (92); auth, Poetics and Literature of the Sicilian Diaspora: Studies in Oral History and Story Telling, San Francisco: Mellen Res Univ Press (93, 98); auth, subway home, poems, Lincoln Springs Press (94), in Italian, Martina di Minturno: Caramanica (98); auth, Labyrinths and Volcanoes: Windings Through Sicily, Brooklyn: Legas (99); transl and ed with Luigi Bonaffini and Achille Serrao, Via Terra: Anthology of Neodialect Poetry, Brooklyn: Legas (99). **CONTACT ADDRESS** Dept French & Italian-Anderson, Temple Univ, 1114 W Berks St, Philadelphia, PA 19122-6007. **EMAIL** jvitielli@nimbus.temple.edu

VITZ, EVELYN BIRGE
PERSONAL Born 10/16/1941, Indianapolis, IN, m, 1969, 3 children **DISCIPLINE** FRENCH MEDIEVAL AND FRENCH RENAISSANCE LITERATURE **EDUCATION** Smith Col, BA, 63; Yale Univ, PhD (French), 68. **CAREER** From instr to asst prof, 68-74, ASSOC PROF FRENCH, DEPT FRENCH AND ITAL, NEW YORK UNIV, 74-; Nat Endowment for Humanities younger humanist fel, 74-75. **MEMBERSHIPS** MLA; Medieval Acad Am. **RESEARCH** Medieval narrative; modern narrative theory; medieval and Renaissance lyric poetry. **SELECTED PUBLICATIONS** Auth, Symbolic contamination in the Testament of Francois Villon, Mod Lan Notes, 71; The I of the Roman de la Rose, Genre, 3/73; Type et individu dans l'autobiographie medievale, Poetique, 75; Ronsard's Sonnets pour Helene: Narrative structures and poetic language, Romanic Rev, 11/76; Narrative analysis of medieval texts: La Fille du Comte de Pontieu, Mod Lang Notes, 77; La Vie de Saint Alexis: Narrative analysis and the quest for the sacred subject, PMLA, 78. **CONTACT ADDRESS** Dept of French, New York Univ, University Pl, New York, NY 10003-4556.

VOGELEY, NANCY JEANNE
PERSONAL Born 06/19/1937, San Pedro, CA **DISCIPLINE** LATIN AMERICAN AND SPANISH LITERATURE **EDUCATION** Pa State Univ, BA, 58, MA, 62; Univ Madrid, dipl de Estudios Hispanicos, 60; Stanford Univ, PhD, (Span), 80. **CAREER** Instr Span, Allegheny Col, 62-63, instr, Ithaca Col, 63-64 & instr, Col San Mateo, 65-66; instr, 66-70, asst prof, 70-81, Assoc Prof Span, 81-86, prof Span, Univ San Francisco, 86-00; vis assoc prof, Duke Univ, 89; prof emerita, 00-. **HONORS AND AWARDS** Scholarship, Instituto de Cultura Hispanica Madrid for study at the Universidad de Madrid, 59-60; Ful-

bright grant to Colombia, summer 63; NEH Summer Seminar grant, Univ of Pennsylvania, 80; NEH Summer Seminar grant, Cornell Univ, 83. **MEMBERSHIPS** Am Asn Teachers Span & Port; MLA; Latin Am Studies Asn. **RESEARCH** Jose Joaquin Fernandez de Lizardi and the period of Mexican Independence; Alfonso Sastre and contemporary Spanish theater. **SELECTED PUBLICATIONS** Auth, "China and the American Indies: A Sixteenth-Century History," Colonial Latin American Review 6, (97): 165-84; auth, "Mexican Readings of Hugh Blair's Rhetoric," Dieciocho 21 (98): 153-165; auth, Death and its Challenge to Decolonization: Jose Joaquin Fernandez de Lizardi's Last Will and Testament, eds. Victor Pereira Da Rosa e Susan Castillo, Pos-Colonialismo e Identidade, Porto: Edicoes Universidade Fernando Pessoa, 98; auth, "Mexican Attitudes toward the Inquisition: Two Views, 1814, 1824," Dieciocho 23.1 (00): 91-96; auth, "How Chivalry Formed the Myth of California," Modern Language Quarterly; auth, Alfonso Sastre, Mary Parker, ed. Modern Spanish Theater, Greenwood P, to appear. **CONTACT ADDRESS** Dept of Modern Lang, Univ of San Francisco, San Francisco, CA 94117-1050. **EMAIL** vogeleyn@usfca.edu

VOGLER, FREDERICK WRIGHT

PERSONAL Born 05/27/1931, Burlington, VT, m, 1965, 1 child **DISCIPLINE** FRENCH LIT AND CIV **EDUCATION** Univ NC, Chapel Hill, AB, 53, MA, 55, PhD (Romance lang), 61. **CAREER** Instr French, Univ NC, Chapel Hill, 61-62; asst prof, Univ Iowa, 62-63; From asst prof to assoc prof, 63-78, PROF FRENCH, UNIV NC, CHAPEL HILL, 78-; ASSOC DEAN COL ARTS AND SCI, 76-; Mem French achievement comt, Col Entrance Exam Bd, 67-70. **HONORS AND AWARDS** Fulbright Scholar, 53-54, Phi Beta Kappa, 52. **MEMBERSHIPS** SAtlantic Mod Lang Asn; Am Asn Teachers French; Swiss-American Hist Soc. **RESEARCH** Early 17th century French novel; French classical doctrine and practice. **SELECTED PUBLICATIONS** Auth, Moliere Mocked, 75; "D'Audiguier, Vital, and Lennox, Charlotte: A Lit Resurrection," Romance Notes, Vol 36, 96. **CONTACT ADDRESS** Dept of Romance Lang, Univ of No Carolina, Chapel Hill, Chapel Hill, NC 27599-3170. **EMAIL** fwvogler@email.unc.edu

VOIGTS, LINDA EHRSAM

PERSONAL Born 05/09/1942, Abilene, KS, m, 1963, 1 child **DISCIPLINE** OLD AND MIDDLE ENGLISH, HISTORY OF MEDICINE **EDUCATION** William Jewell Col, BA, 63; Univ Mo-Kansas City, MA, 66; Univ Mo-Columbia, PhD (English), 73. **CAREER** Teacher Ger and English, North Kansas City High Sch, 63-65; instr English, William Jewell Col, 65-69; instr compos, Univ Mo-Columbia, 72; vis asst prof English, William Jewell Col, 73-74 and Univ Mo-Columbia, 74-75; asst prof, 75-79, Assoc Prof English, Univ MO-Kansas City, 79-; Am Coun Learned Soc grant-in-aid, 75; Andrew W Mellon fac fel humanities, Harvard Univ, 78-79; vis instr, Harvard Univ, summer, 80. **HONORS AND AWARDS** Zeitlin-VerBrugge Prize, Hist of Sci Soc, 81. **MEMBERSHIPS** Mediaeval Acad Am; MLA; Hist of Sci Soc; Am Asn Hist Med; New Chaucer Soc. **RESEARCH** Old English; Middle English. **SELECTED PUBLICATIONS** Auth, A new look at a manuscript containing the Old English translation of the Herbarium Apulei, Manuscripta, 76; One Anglo-Saxon view of the classical Gods, Studies in Iconography, 78; The significance of the name Apuleius to the Herbarium Apulei, Bull Hist of Med, 78; Anglo-Saxon Plant Remedies and the Anglo-Saxons, Isis, 79; A Boece fragment, Studies in the Age of Chancer, 79; coauth, A missing leaf from Douce 250, Bodleian Libr Record, 81; A Letter from a Middle English Dictaminal Formulary in Harvard Law Library MS.43, Speculum, 81; Editing Middle English medical texts, In: Editing Texts in the History of Science and Medicine, Garland, 82. **CONTACT ADDRESS** Dept of English, Univ of Missouri, Kansas City, 5100 Rockhill Rd, Kansas City, MO 64110-2499.

VOLEK, EMIL

PERSONAL Born 03/22/1944, Czechoslovakia **DISCIPLINE** SPANISH **EDUCATION** Charles Univ, PhD, 70. **CAREER** Res fel, Inst of Lang Czechoslovakia, 69-74; vis prof, Charles Univ, 72-73; vis prof, Cologne Univ, 74-76; asst prof to prof, Ariz State Univ, 76-. **HONORS AND AWARDS** NEH Fel, 78; Fulbright Fel, 85, 87; Outstanding Mentor Award, Assoc Students of Ariz State Univ, 93. **MEMBERSHIPS** LASA; IILL; AIH. **RESEARCH** Latin American literature, theater, comparative literature, avant-garde through postmodern culture, theory of literature, narratology, versology, history of modern criticism. **SELECTED PUBLICATIONS** Auth, Antologia del formalismo ruso y el grupo de Bajtin. I. Polemica, historia y teoria literaria. II. Semiotica del discurso y postformalismo bajtiniano, Madrid, 92; auth, Literatura hispanoamericana entre la modernidad y la postmodernidad, Bogota, 94; auth, Signo, funcion y valor: Estetica y semiotica del arte de Jan Mukarovsky, Bogota, 00; auth, Postmodernity in the Periphery: Latin America Writes Back: An Interdisciplinary Cultural Perspective, Garland, 01. **CONTACT ADDRESS** Dept Lang and Lit, Arizona State Univ, MC 0202, Tempe, AZ 85287. **EMAIL** emil.volek@asu.edu

VOLKOVA, BRONISLAVA

PERSONAL Born 05/15/1946, Decin, Czechoslovakia, w **DISCIPLINE** CZECHOSLOVAKIAN LANGUAGE AND LITERATURE **EDUCATION** Charles Univ, PhD, 70. **CAREER** Prof, Ind Univ, 95-; Res Dir, CIEE Charles Univ, Prague, 99-. **HONORS AND AWARDS** Harvard Mellon; ACLS; Fulbright. **MEMBERSHIPS** PEN; Intl Semiotic Soc. **RESEARCH** Semantics; Textology; Literature. **SELECTED PUBLICATIONS** Auth, Roztristene svety (The Shattered Worlds), Votobia, Czech Rep, 95; rev of Cross Currents 11: A Yearbook of Central European Culture, ed L. Matejka, Fall, 95; auth, "Knedliky a smysl zivota," (Dumplings and the Meaning of Life), Listopad, 95; auth, "Hodina zeme/The Hour of the Earth," Metamorphoses, Amherst, 96; auth, "Exil, drive a dnes," Literature in Prison and Exile/Exile and Prison in Literature, Prague, 96; auth, A Feminist's Semiotic Odyssey through Czech Literature, Edwin Mellen Press, 97; auth, "Pet basni," Aluze, Olomouc, 97; auth, "My body is a Vessel.", Massage Magazine, 97. **CONTACT ADDRESS** Dept Slavic Lang, Indiana Univ, Bloomington, 1020 E Kirkwood Ave, Bloomington, IN 47405-7103. **EMAIL** volkova@indiana.edu

VOLPE, GERALD CARMINE

PERSONAL Born 05/27/1931, Fitchburg, MA **DISCIPLINE** FRENCH **EDUCATION** Holy Cross Col, BA, 54; Fordham Univ, MA, 56; Princeton Univ, PhD (Romance lang), 63. **CAREER** From instr to asst prof French and Ital, Brandeis Univ, 60-66; asst prof, 66-72, acting chmn dept Ital, 73-74, chmn dept, 74-75, ASSOC PROF FRENCH AND ITAL, UNIV MASS, BOSTON, 72-. **MEMBERSHIPS** MLA; AAUP; Am Asn Teachers Fr; Am Asn Teachers Ital; Dante Soc. **RESEARCH** French Renaissance; Dante; Ethnic studies. **SELECTED PUBLICATIONS** Auth, Le Gout De La Catastrophe, Fr Rev, Vol 66, 93; Charles, Fr Rev, Vol 68, 95; La Folie Du Moment, Fr Rev, Vol 70, 97. **CONTACT ADDRESS** Dept of French and Ital, Univ of Massachusetts, Boston, Boston, MA 02116.

VON DASSANOWSKY, ROBERT

PERSONAL Born 01/28/1960, New York, NY, s **DISCIPLINE** GERMAN AND AUSTRIAN LITERATURE AND CULTURE, FILM **EDUCATION** Am Acad of Dramatic Arts, Pasadena, 77-78; Am Film Inst Conservatory Prof, Los Angeles, 79-81; Univ of Calif, Los Angeles, BA, 85, MA, 88, PhD, 92. **CAREER** Teaching assoc and fel, Dept of Germanic Langs, Univ Calif, Los Angeles, 89-92, vis asst prof of German, 92-93; asst prof of German, Univ Colo, Colorado Springs, 93-99, Head of German Prog, 93-, Dir, Film Studies, 97-, assoc prof of German and Film, 99-, interim chair, Dept of Visual and Performing Arts, 200-2001. **HONORS AND AWARDS** City of Los Angeles Cultural Affairs Grant Awd, 90, 91, 92; Univ of Colo, Colorado Springs Fac Res and Creative Proj Grant Awd, 94, 95, 97, 99; Univ Colo President's Fund for the Humanities Grant, 96; Univ of Colo, Colo Springs Letters, Arts and Sciences outstanding Fac Awd, 98. **MEMBERSHIPS** Austrian Am Film Asn, Int Alexander Lernet-Holenia Soc, PEN/USA West, Austrian PEN, MLA, IFP/West: Independent Features Proj, EPA: European Features Proj, Soc for Cinema Studies, AATG, Poets and Writers. **RESEARCH** 18th and 19th century German and Austrian Literature; Impressionism and Symbolism; First Republic Austrian and Weimar German Culture; Austrofascism; Third Reich and Exile culture; Second Republic Austrian, West German and GDR literature; Women's literature and Feminism; Postmodernism; Austrian, German, Italian, British and American film. **SELECTED PUBLICATIONS** Auth, Phantom Empires: The Novels of Alexander Lerner-Holenia and the Question of Postimperial Austrian Identity, Riverside: Ariadne (96); transl, Verses of a Marriage: Translation of Strophen einer Ehe by Hans Raimund, Los Angeles: Event Horizon (96); co-ed, Filmkunst No 154, Special Issue: Austria's Hollywood/Hollywood's Austria, Vienna: Osterreichische Gesellschaft fur Filmwissenschraft (97); auth, Telegrams from the Metropole: Selected Poetry 1980-1998, Salzburg: Poetry Salzburg/University of Salzburg Press (99); contribur ed, Gale Encyclopedia of Multicultural America, 2nd Ed, 3 vols, Farmington Hills: Gale Res (99); commentary to Leni Riefenstahl's Tag der Freiheit (1935), Short Vision DVD Series, Los Angeles (2000); auth, " 'A Mountain of a Ship': Locating the Bergfilm in James Cameron's 'Titanic', " Cinema J (fall 2000); contribur and ed adv, International Dictionary of Films and Filmmakers, 4th ed, St James Press (2000); co-exec producer, Semmelweis, Swinging Tree Productions/Belvedere Film (2001); transl, Mars in Aries: Translation of Mars im Widder by Alexander Lerner-Holenia, Los Angeles: Green Integer Series/Sun and Moon (2001). **CONTACT ADDRESS** Langs and Cultures, Univ of Colorado, Colorado Springs, 1420 Austin Bluffs Pkwy, Colorado Springs, CO 80918-3733. **EMAIL** Rvondass@mail.uccs.edu

VON DER EMDE, SILKE

DISCIPLINE GERMAN **EDUCATION** Ind Univ, Bloomington, PhD, 94. **CAREER** Asst prof; prof, Dartmouth Col. **RESEARCH** Contemporary German literature, especially East German women writers; women in German film; women studies; literary theory. **SELECTED PUBLICATIONS** Publ on research interest. **CONTACT ADDRESS** Classics Dept, Vassar Col, 124 Raymond Ave., Poughkeepsie, NY 12604. **EMAIL** vonderemde@vassar.edu

VON DIRKE, SABINE B.

PERSONAL Born, Germany **DISCIPLINE** GERMAN LANGUAGE **EDUCATION** Stanford Univ, PhD, 91. **CAREER** Assoc Prof of German, Univ of Pittsburgh, 98-; Asst Prof, Univ of Pittsburgh, 91-98. **MEMBERSHIPS** MLA; GSA; AATG. **RESEARCH** Contemporary German Culture; Cultural Studies. **SELECTED PUBLICATIONS** Auth, "All Power to the Imagination," The West German Counterculture From the Student Movement to the Greens. **CONTACT ADDRESS** Dept German Languages, Univ of Pittsburgh, 1409 Cathedral Of Learning, Pittsburgh, PA 15260-6299. **EMAIL** vondirke@pitt.edu

VON SCHNEIDEMESSER, LUANNE

PERSONAL Born 02/28/1945, San Diego, CA, m, 1972, 2 children **DISCIPLINE** GERMAN LINGUISTICS AND PHILOLOGY **EDUCATION** Kansas State Univ, BA, 68; MA, 70, PhD, 79, Univ Wisconsin, Madison. **CAREER** Ed, 78-88, sr ed, 88- , Dictionary of American Regional English, lector, Dept of German, 91, Univ of Wisc, Madison. **HONORS AND AWARDS** Seaton Awd, Kansas Q, 91; prof dev grant, 86-87, 99-00; featured paper, Methods VIII: Int Conf on Dialectology, 93, DSNA-Urdang Awd in Lexicography, 99-00. **MEMBERSHIPS** Dictionary Soc N Am; Am Dialect Soc; Soc of German-American Stud; Am Coun of Learned Soc Conf of Admin Off. **RESEARCH** Lexicography; sociolinguistics; dialect geography; American English; German. **SELECTED PUBLICATIONS** Auth, Introduction, to An Index by Region, Usage, and Etymology to the Dictionary of American Regional English, PADS, 93; auth, DARE's Completion A Beginning?, in Zeitschrift fur Dialektologenkongresses, 93; auth, More German Loanwords from the Dictionary of American Regional English, in The German Lang in Am, 93; auth, Gesundheit!, in Soc for German Am Stud Newsl, 95; auth, Terms Used for Children's Games: Comparing DARE's Findings with Usage of Today's Youth, in Varieties of English around the World: Focus on the USA, 96; auth, Soda or Pop?, in J of Eng Ling, 96; auth, Expletives and Euphemisms in DARE: An Initial Look, in Language Variety in the South Revisited, 97; auth, Regional Labels in DARE, in Dictionaries, 97; auth, An Index by Region, Usage and Etymology to the Dictionary of American Regional English, v 3, PADS, 99. **CONTACT ADDRESS** Dictionary of American Regional English, Univ of Wisconsin, Madison, 600 N Park St, 6121 H. C. White, Madison, WI 53706. **EMAIL** lvonschn@facstaff.wisc.edu

VOS, MORRIS

PERSONAL Born 12/10/1944, Mahaska Co, IA, m, 1966, 2 children **DISCIPLINE** GERMAN LITERATURE & LANGUAGE **EDUCATION** Calvin Col, BA, 66; Ind Univ, Bloomington, MA, 67, PhD(Ger), 75. **CAREER** Assoc instr Ger, Ind Univ, Bloomington, 70-71; asst prof, 71-79, Assoc Prof Ger, 79-91, prof, Western Ill Univ, 91- . **HONORS AND AWARDS** Am Asn of Teachers of German Chapter Service Awd, 90; Western Illinois Univ Faculty Development Travel Grant, 92; State of Illinois Lieutenant Governor's Awd for Enhancement of the Profession, 93; German Academic Exchange Service Research Grant, 94; Am Asn of Teachers of German Certificate of Merit, 96; WIU College of Arts and Science Awd for Outstanding Service, 98. **MEMBERSHIPS** Mod Lang Asn; Am Asn Teachers Ger; Am Coun Teaching Foreign Lang; Conf Christianity & Lit. **RESEARCH** German narration theory of the 18th century; religion and literature; foreign language pedagogy. **SELECTED PUBLICATIONS** Auth, The concept of dramatic narration, In: Jahrbuch fur Internationale Germanistik, Band 4, 79; co-ed, Shaping the Future of Foreign Language Education, 88; auth, Dramatic Narration: The Speech Criterion in Seventeenth-Century German Narration Theory, Neophilologus, 91; transl, U. Wesche, "Peter Handke, Walker Percy, and the End of Modernity, " Essays in Literature 19 (92): 291-97. **CONTACT ADDRESS** Foreign Lang & Lit, Western Illinois Univ, 1 University Cir, Macomb, IL 61455-1390. **EMAIL** m-vos@wiu.edu

VOSTEEN, THOMAS

PERSONAL Born 02/07/1944, Buffalo, NY, m, 1990 **DISCIPLINE** FRENCH **EDUCATION** Dartmouth Col, BA, 66; Middlebury Col, MA, 67, Univ Iowa, MAT, 81; PhD, 90. **CAREER** Instr, Cornel Col, 80-90; asst prof to prof, Eastern Mich Univ, 91-. **MEMBERSHIPS** MLA, AATF, Amer Lit Trans Soc. **RESEARCH** French literature 1850 - 1950. **SELECTED PUBLICATIONS** Trans, You've Always Been Wrong, by Rene Daumal, (Lincoln: Univ of Nebr Pr, 1995). **CONTACT ADDRESS** Univ of Michigan, Ann Arbor, 2906 Brandywine Dr, Ann Arbor, MI 48104-5308. **EMAIL** vosteen@online.emich.edu

W

WAAGE, FREDERICK O.

PERSONAL Born 12/01/1943, Ithaca, NY, m, 1977, 2 children **DISCIPLINE** ENGLISH, FRENCH **EDUCATION** Princeton Univ, BA, 65; PhD, 71. **CAREER** Instr, Northwestern Univ, 68-71; Adj Asst Prof, Calif State Univ, 71-73; Asst Prof, Douglass Col, 74-77; Asst Prof, Col Misevicordia, 77-78; From Asst Prof to Prof, E Tenn State Univ, 78-. **MEMBERSHIPS** Popular Cult Asn, Mod Lang Asn, Asn for the Study of Lit and the Environ. **RESEARCH** Renaissance literature, popular culture, literature of the U S 1950's-1960's, authobiographies and memoirs, environmental writing. **SELECTED PUBLICATIONS** Auth, The White Devil Discover'd, Peter Lang Publ, 85; auth, Teaching Environmental Literature, Mod Lang Asn, 85; auth, "Warren's New Dawn," Souchen Quart, 31.4 (93); auth, "Traumatic Conformity: Robert Linduei's Narratives of Rebellion, JAC, 22.2 (99). **CONTACT ADDRESS** Dept English, East Tennessee State Univ, PO Box 23081, Johnson City, TN 37614-0001. **EMAIL** waage@etsu.edu

WACHAL, ROBERT STANLEY
PERSONAL Born 03/13/1929, Omaha, NE, m, 1968 **DISCIPLINE** LEXICOGRAPHY, APPLIED LINGUISTICS **EDUCATION** Univ Minn, Minneapolis, BA, 52; Univ Wis-Madison, MS, 59, PhD (English, ling), 66. **CAREER** From asst prof to assoc prof, 70-75, PROF LING, UNIV IOWA, 75-; Coordr English lang prog, US Educ Found, Greece, 66-67. **MEMBERSHIPS** Ling Soc Am; Acad Aphasia; Am Dialect Soc. **RESEARCH** Lexicography; style and statistics; sociolinguistics. **SELECTED PUBLICATIONS** Auth, Social Stylistics in Syntactic Variation in British Newspapers, Am Speech, Vol 69, 94; Heartland English, Variation and Tradition in the American Midwest, Am Speech, Vol 70, 95. **CONTACT ADDRESS** Dept of Ling, Univ of Iowa, Iowa City, IA 52242. **EMAIL** robert-wachal@uiowa.edu

WAELTI-WALTERS, JENNIFER
PERSONAL Born, England **DISCIPLINE** FRENCH AND WOMEN'S STUDIES **EDUCATION** Univ London, BA, 64, PhD, 68. **CAREER** Instr, Univ de Paris, 67-68; Prof French to Prof Emer, Univ Victoria, 68-, ch Fr dept, 79-84, instr, 79-, dir women's studs, 88-95. **HONORS AND AWARDS** Prize Best Work Pub French, Asn Profs de Francais des Univs Can, 89; Community Awd, Univ Victoria, 93. **MEMBERSHIPS** Can Fedn Hum; Hum Asn Can; Can Res Inst Advan Women; Can Asn Women's Studs; Sr Women Acad Admins Can. **SELECTED PUBLICATIONS** Auth, Fairytales and the Female Imagination, 82; auth, Jeanne Hyrvrard: Theorist of the Modern World, 96; coauth, Feminisms of the Belle Epoque, 94. **CONTACT ADDRESS** Women's Studies Dept, Univ of Victoria, PO Box 3045 Stn CSC, Victoria, BC, Canada V8W 3P4.

WAGENER, GUY
DISCIPLINE FRENCH LANGUAGE, LITERATURE, AND CULTURE **EDUCATION** Univ Calif, Irvine, PhD, **CAREER** Assoc prof Fr, Univ Nev, Reno. **RESEARCH** Epicurus, Diderot, and Michel Serres; women's access to culture as reflected in Moliere's theatre. **SELECTED PUBLICATIONS** Published on Diderot. **CONTACT ADDRESS** Univ of Nevada, Reno, Reno, NV 89557.

WAGENER, HANS
PERSONAL Born 07/27/1940, Lage, West Germany, m, 1999, 3 children **DISCIPLINE** GERMAN LITERATURE **EDUCATION** Univ Freiburg, BA, 63; Univ Calif, Los Angeles, MA, 65, PhD, 67. **CAREER** Asst prof Ger, Univ Southern Calif, 67-68; From asst prof to assoc prof, 68-75, chmn dept, 77-81, 84-93, Prof Ger, Univ Calif, Los Angeles, 75-. **HONORS AND AWARDS** Cross of Merit, FRG, 99. **MEMBERSHIPS** Am Asn Teachers Ger. **RESEARCH** Modern German literature; 17th century German literature. **SELECTED PUBLICATIONS** Auth, Sarah Kirsch, Colloquium (Berlin), 89; auth, Understanding Erich Maria Remarque, Univ SC Press (Columbia, SC), 91; auth, "The Novels of Erich Maria Remarque in American Reviews," in The Fortune of German Writers in America: Studies in Literary Reception, ed. Wolfgang Elfe, James Hardin, and Gunther Holst (SC: Univ SC Press, 92), 211-230; auth, "Heinrich Mann," in Twentieth Century German Dramatists, 1889-1918, ed. Wolfgang D. Elfe and James Hardin (MI: Gale Res Inc., 92), 162-171; auth, Understanding Franz Werfel, Univ SC Press (Columbia, SC), 93; auth, "Siegfried Lenz' Novelle 'Ein Kriegsende - moralischer Modellfall und Historiographie,'" Lit in Wissenschaft und Unterricht 17 (94): 3-11; auth, Carl Zuckmayer Criticism: Tracing Endangered Fame, Camden House (Columbia, SC), 95; auth, Lion Feuchtwanger, Morgenbuch Verlag, 96; auth, "Zwischen Huldigung und Polemik: Die Rezeption Karl Heinrich Waggerls in Wissenschaft und Literaturkritik," in Nichts Komplizierteres heutzutage als ein einfacher Mensch, ed. Karl M¤ller (Otto M¤ller, 98), 245-281; coed, Zuckmayer-Jahrbuch, R¤hrig, 99. **CONTACT ADDRESS** Dept of Germanic Lang, Univ of California, Los Angeles, 212 Royce Hall, PO Box 951539, Los Angeles, CA 90095-1539. **EMAIL** wagener@humnet.ucla.edu

WAILES, STEPHEN L.
PERSONAL Born 05/28/1937, Summit, NJ, m, 1964 **DISCIPLINE** GERMANIC LANGUAGES **EDUCATION** Harvard Univ, AB, 60, PhD, 68. **CAREER** Asst prof, 68-72, assoc prof, 72-80, Prof Ger, Ind Univ, Bloomington, 80-; Assoc Dean Fac, 78-. **HONORS AND AWARDS** Soc for Values in Higher Educ fel, 72; Alexander von Humboldt-Stiftung fel, 76. **RESEARCH** Medieval and 16th century German literature. **SELECTED PUBLICATIONS** Auth, Early German Novella Art, J Eng Ger Phil, Vol 92, 93; The Envy of Angels in Cathedral Schools and Social Ideals in Medieval Europe, 950-1200, J Eng Ger Phil, Vol 95, 96. **CONTACT ADDRESS** Dept of German, Indiana Univ, Bloomington, 107 S Indiana Ave, Bloomington, IN 47405-7000. **EMAIL** wailes@indiana.edu

WAKEFIELD, RAY MILAN
PERSONAL Born 01/30/1942, Fremont, MI, m, 1964, 2 children **DISCIPLINE** PHILOLOGY, NETHERLANDIC LITERATURE **EDUCATION** Dartmouth Col, BA, 64; Ind Univ, Bloomington, MA, 66, PhD(Ger, dutch & Scand), 72. **CAREER** From Instr to Asst Prof, 69-87, Assoc Prof Ger & Dutch, Univ Minn, Minneapolis, 87-. **HONORS AND AWARDS** Officer in the Order of Oranje-Nassau, by Her Majesty Queen Beatrix of the Netherlands, 91. **MEMBERSHIPS** MLA; Am Asn Teachers Ger; Int Ver Ned. **RESEARCH** Comparative Germanic prosody; courtly Romance; second language acquisition; medieval Dutch literature. **SELECTED PUBLICATIONS** Auth, Nibelungen Prosody, Mouton, 76; Hadewijch: A Formalist's Dream, Dutch Crossings, 79; The Early Dutch-German Poetic Tradition, Amsterdammer, Bertragezur Alteren Germanistik, 79; coauth, Kreise, Heinle & Heinle, 92; auth, Heinsiusund Opitz: Germanic Prosody Revisited, PAANS, 94; Excalibur: Film Reception vs Political Distance, Politics in Ger Lit, 98. **CONTACT ADDRESS** Dept of Ger, Scandinavian, & Dutch, Univ of Minnesota, Twin Cities, 205 Folwell Hall, Minneapolis, MN 55455-0194. **EMAIL** wakef001@tc.umn.edu

WALBANK, MICHAEL BURKE
PERSONAL Born 04/14/1933, Bristol, England, m, 1978 **DISCIPLINE** CLASSICS, ARCHEOLOGY **EDUCATION** Univ Bristol, BA, 54; Univ BC, MA, 65, PhD (classics), 70. **CAREER** Asst prof, 70-76, Assoc Prof Classics, Univ Calgary, 76-; Can Coun fels, 71-72 and 76-77; consult, BBCOpen Univ Prod, 78. **MEMBERSHIPS** Am Sch Class Studies Athens; Class Asn of Can; Archaeol Inst of Am; Soc Prom Hellenic Studies; Soc Prom of Roman Studies. **RESEARCH** Greek epigraphy; Greek archaeology; ancient science and technology. **SELECTED PUBLICATIONS** Auth, A Lex Sacra of the State and of the Deme of Kollytos, Hesperia, Vol 63, 94; Greek Inscriptions from the Athenian Agora in Lists of Names, Hesperia, Vol 63, 94; Greek Inscriptions from The Athenian-Agora in Building Records, Hesperia, Vol 64, 95; An Inscription from the Athenian Agora in Thasian Exiles at Athens, Hesperia, Vol 64, 95; Greek Inscriptions from the Athenian Agora Financial Documents, Hesperia, Vol 65, 96; Greek Inscriptions from the Athenian Agora, Hesperia, Vol 66, 97. **CONTACT ADDRESS** 14 Harcourt Rd SW, Calgary, AB, Canada T2V 5J1.

WALCHAK, KAROL L.
PERSONAL Born 06/16/1958, Alpena, MI, d, 2 children **DISCIPLINE** LITERATURE, LINGUISTICS **EDUCATION** Calif State Univ, Bakersfield, BA, 81; Calif State Univ, Sacramento, MA, 85; Univ Nev Reno, PhD, 95. **CAREER** Instr, Univ Nev Reno, 87-96; asst prof, Central Mich Univ, 96-. **HONORS AND AWARDS** Who's Who inAm Col and Univ, 90. **MEMBERSHIPS** TESOL; MITESOL; Medieval Soc of the Pacific; Phi Kappa Phi; Phi Beta Delta. **RESEARCH** Chaucer, John Lydate, sound and meaning, TESOL methodology, theory. **SELECTED PUBLICATIONS** auth, TESOL Methods and Approaches, Prentice-Hall. **CONTACT ADDRESS** Dept English, Central Michigan Univ, 100 W Preston Rd, Mount Pleasant, MI 48859-0001. **EMAIL** karol.walchak@cmich.edu

WALDINGER, RENEE
PERSONAL Born 08/26/1927, m, 1948, 2 children **DISCIPLINE** FRENCH LANGUAGE AND LITERATURE **EDUCATION** Hunter Col, BA, 48; Columbia Univ, MA, PhD, 53. **CAREER** Lectr French, Queens Col, NY, 54-55; From instr to assoc prof, 57-70, chmn dept Romance lang, 70-76, Prof emer, PROF FRENCH, GRAD SCH AND UNIV CTR, CITY UNIV OF NEW YORK, 72-; EXEC OFF, 81-. **HONORS AND AWARDS** Chevalier, Ordre Palmes Acad, 80; Nat Endowment for Humanities grant, Inst Contemp Cult, 82. **MEMBERSHIPS** MLA; Am Asn Teachers Fr; Am Asn 18th Century Studies; AAUP. **RESEARCH** French literature of the 18th century; pedagogy; French contemporary culture. **SELECTED PUBLICATIONS** Auth, Writings on the Body from Descartes to Laclos, Fr Rev, Vol 67, 93; Histoire Dune Grecque Moderne, Fr Rev, Vol 66, 93; Between Melting Pot and Mosaic in african Americans and Puerto Ricans in the New York Political Economy, J Am Ethnic Hist, Vol 15, 96; Newcomers in the Workplace in Immigrants and the Restructuring of The Us Economy - Lamphere,L, Stepick,A, Grenier,G, J American Ethnic History, Vol 15, 96. **CONTACT ADDRESS** Romance Lang Dept, Graduate Sch and Univ Ctr, CUNY, New York, NY 10016-4309.

WALDMAN, GLENYS A.
PERSONAL Born 03/24/1945, Philadelphia, PA **DISCIPLINE** GERMAN LANGUAGES **EDUCATION** Oberlin Col, BA, 67; Univ Pa, MA, 70, PhD, 75; Drexel Univ, MSLS, 78. **CAREER** Assoc/actg librn, Hist Soc Pa, 84-87; asst librn, Grand Lodge F & AM of Pa Libr, 87-89; asst libr, cur, Masonic Libr & Mus Pa, 90-95; LIBR, CUR, MASONIC LIBR, MUS PA, 96-. **MEMBERSHIPS** Modern Lang. Asn, Am Library Asn, Special Library Asn, Pennsylvania German Society, Society for Germanic Philogy, Society for German Am Studies. **RESEARCH** Germanic Philology esp, Pennsylvania German. **CONTACT ADDRESS** Masonic Libr/Mus of Pa, 1 N Broad St, Philadelphia, PA 19107-2520. **EMAIL** gawaldman@pagrandlodge.org

WALKER, ANDREW DAVID
DISCIPLINE CLASSICS **EDUCATION** Univ Wash, BA, 82; Univ NC, Chapel Hill, BA, 84, PhD, 93. **CAREER** Lectr, class, 91-92, Univ Va; lectr, class, Univ S Calif, 93-94. **MEMBERSHIPS** APA. **RESEARCH** Cultural stud; gender & comparative lit. **SELECTED PUBLICATIONS** Art, Eros and the Eye in the Love Letters of Philostratus, PCPS, 92; art, Enargeia and the Spectator in Greek Historiography, TPAP, 93; art, Lucan's Legends of the Fall, Ramus, 96; art, Oedipal Narratives and the Exilic Ovid, Ramus, 97. **CONTACT ADDRESS** 3444 Glenhurst Ave, Los Angeles, CA 90039. **EMAIL** adwalker@usc.edu

WALKER, HALLAM
PERSONAL Born 05/23/1921, Newark, NJ, m, 1949, 2 children **DISCIPLINE** FRENCH **EDUCATION** Princeton Univ, AB, 43, MA, 50, PhD (Romance lang), 52. **CAREER** Instr French, Pa State Univ, 49-51; instr, Washington and Lee Univ, 53-54; asst prof, Duke Univ, 54-65; assoc prof, 65-72, PROF FRENCH AND CHMN DEPT, DAVIDSON COL, 72-. **MEMBERSHIPS** MLA; Am Asn Teachers Fr; SAtlantic Mod Lang Asn. **RESEARCH** Classical French theater; nineteenth and twentieth centuries French novel and poetry. **SELECTED PUBLICATIONS** Auth, JAPANESE VENTURE AND THE NEWLY FORMED BALLET-DEPARTMENT AT THE SHOWA-ACADEMIA-MUSICAE IN TOKYO, DANCING TIMES, Vol 87, 97. **CONTACT ADDRESS** Dept of French, Davidson Col, Davidson, NC 28036.

WALKER, JANET ANDERSON
PERSONAL Born Milwaukee, WI, m, 1967 **DISCIPLINE** COMPARATIVE AND ASIAN LITERATURE **EDUCATION** Univ Wis, Madison, BA, 65; Harvard Univ, AM, 68, PhD (comp lit), 74. **CAREER** Asst prof, 71-77, ASSOC PROF COMP LIT, RUTGERS UNIV, 77-; Japan Found Short-term fel, 82-83. **MEMBERSHIPS** Am Comp Lit Asn; Int Comp Lit Asn; Int Courtly Lit Soc; Asn Asian Studies; Asn Teachers Japanese. **RESEARCH** Japanese-Western literary relations; narrative East and West; courtly literature in Japan and Western Europe. **SELECTED PUBLICATIONS CONTACT ADDRESS** Dept of Com Lit, Rutgers, The State Univ of New Jersey, New Brunswick, Ac Hlth Sc Ctr-Cn, New Brunswick, NJ 08903.

WALKER, JANET L.
DISCIPLINE FRENCH **EDUCATION** Chatham Col, BA, 67; Bryn Mann Col, MA, 69; PhD, 74. **CAREER** Prof, Chatham Col, 70-. **HONORS AND AWARDS** NDEA Fel, Bryn Mann Col. **CONTACT ADDRESS** Dept Mod Lang, Chatham Col, Woodland Rd, Pittsburgh, PA 15232. **EMAIL** walker@chatham.edu

WALKER, RACHEL
DISCIPLINE LINGUISTICS **EDUCATION** Univ Toronto, BA, 92; Univ Toronto, MA, 93; Univ Calif, Santa Cruz, PhD, 98. **CAREER** Asst Prof, Linguistics, Univ of Southern California, 98-. **MEMBERSHIPS** Linguistics Society of America; Canadian Linguistics Association. **RESEARCH** Phonology; Phonetics; Morphology; Amazonian Languages; Artaic Languages. **SELECTED PUBLICATIONS** Auth, "Nasalization, Neutral Segments and Opacity Effects," New York: Gartland; auth, "Nasal reduplication in Mbe affixation, Phonology;" "Guarani voiceless stops in oral versus nasal contexts: An acoustical study, Journal of the International Phonetic Association;" "Reinterpreting transparency in nasal harmony, Proceedings of the Fourth HIL Phonology Conference (HILP 4)," Leiden University, The Netherlands, January 28-30, 99; auth, "Possible and impossible segments," with Walker, Rachel, and Geoffrey K. Pullum, Language 75.4, 764-780. **CONTACT ADDRESS** Dept Linguistics, Univ of So California, 3601 Watts Way, GFS 301, Los Angeles, CA 90089-0046. **EMAIL** rwalker@usc.edu

WALKER, RICHARD E.
PERSONAL Born 01/31/1941, Cedar Grove, WV, m, 1970, 2 children **DISCIPLINE** GERMAN, RUSSIAN **EDUCATION** WVa Univ, BA, 66; MA, 68; Univ Chicago, PhD, 73. **CAREER** Assoc prof, Howard Univ, 87-92; chair Dept Ger & Russian, Howard Univ, 88-92; assoc prof, Univ Md Col Park, 92-; chair Dept Ger Studies, Univ Md Col Park, 93-97; assoc dean for undergrad studies, Univ Md Col Park, 00-. **HONORS AND AWARDS** German Acad Exchange Grant, DAAD, 68-69; NEH Summer Sem, Duke Univ, 92; Herzog August Bibliothek Wolfenbuttel Res Grant, 94 & 97; Fulbright Summer Sem Grant, 95. **MEMBERSHIPS** Medieval Acad of Am, Sixteenth-Century Studies Asn. **RESEARCH** Medieval German Literature & Culture, Mythology & Folklore, Narrative Theory, Literature/Culture of Early Modern Germany, Sociology of Literature. **SELECTED PUBLICATIONS** Auth, Peter von Staufenberg It's Origins, Development, and Later Adaptation, Goppinger Arbeiten zur Germanistik, Kummerle Verlag, 80; auth, The Corpus Christi Sermons of Johannes Nas. An Edition

with Commentary, Goppinger Arbeiten zur Germanistik, Kummerle Verlag, 88; auth, The Uses of Polemic: The Centuriae of Johnnes Nas, Goppinger Arbeiten zur Germanistik, Kummerle Verlag, 00. **CONTACT ADDRESS** Office Undergrad Studies, Univ of Maryland, Col Park, 2130 Mitchell Bldg, College Park, MD 20742-5152. **EMAIL** walkerre@deans.umd.edu

WALKER, STEVEN FRIEMEL
PERSONAL Born 03/28/1944, Washington, DC, m, 1966 **DISCIPLINE** COMPARATIVE LITERATURE **EDUCATION** Univ Wis-Madison, BA, 65; Harvard Univ, MA, 66, PhD (comp lit), 73. **CAREER** Asst prof, 71-79, ASSOC PROF COMP LIT, RUTGERS UNIV, 79-; Prof, Comp Lit, 98-. **MEMBERSHIPS** Am Comp Lit Asn; MLA; Asn Asian Studies. **RESEARCH** Renaissance love poetry; th century literature; pastoral poetry. **SELECTED PUBLICATIONS** Auth, the Possible Role of Asymmetric Laryngeal Innervation in Language Lateralization in Points For and Against, Brain Lang, Vol 46, 94; Integrity In Depth, Zygon, Vol 30, 95; auth, Jung and the Jungians on Myth, Garland, 95, Routledge, 01. **CONTACT ADDRESS** 77 Lincoln Ave, Highland Park, NJ 08904. **EMAIL** sfw@rci.rutgers.edu

WALKER, WILLARD
PERSONAL Born 07/29/1926, Boston, MA, m, 1952, 2 children **DISCIPLINE** ANTHROPOLOGY, LINGUISTICS **EDUCATION** Harvard Univ, AB, 50; Univ Ariz, MA, 53; Cornell Univ, PhD (gen ling), 64. **CAREER** Res assoc, Univ Chicago Carnegie Cross-Cult Educ Proj, Tahlequah, Okla, 64-66; From asst prof to assoc prof anthrop, 66-77, prof Anthrop, 77-89; prof emeritus, 89-, Wesleyan Univ. **MEMBERSHIPS** Southern Anthropological Soc; SSILA. **RESEARCH** North American Indian languages; ethnology of North America; native writing systems. **SELECTED PUBLICATIONS** Auth, The Proto-Algonquians, Peter Ridder (Lisse), 75; auth, "Cherokee" in Studies in Southeastern Indian Languages (Univ Ga, 75); auth, "Zuni Semantic Categories," in Handbook of North American Indians, Vol 9 (Smithsonian Inst, 79); auth, "Cherokee Curing and Conjuring, Identity and the Southeastern Co-Tradition," in Persistent Peoples (Univ Az, 81); auth, "Wabanaki Wampum Protocol," Papers of the Fifteenth Algonquian Conference, Carelton Univ (Ottowa, 84); auth, "Literacy, Wampums, the Gud Buk and How Indians in the Far Northeast Read," Anthropological Linguistics (84); auth, "Creek Curing in Academe," in General and Amerindian Ehtnolinguistics in Rememberance of Stanley Newman, Moutou de Guryter, 89; coauth, The Early History of the Cherokee Syllabary, Ethnohistory, 93; auth, "Native Writing Systems," in Handbook of North American Indians, Vol 17 (Smithsonian Inst, 96); auth, "The Wabauaki Confederacy," in Special Issue in Honor of D. Frank T. Siebert, Maine Historical Quarterly (98). **CONTACT ADDRESS** Dept of Anthrop, Wesleyan Univ, Middletown, CT 06457. **EMAIL** wbwalker@kyud,com

WALLACE, JOHN R.
PERSONAL Born 07/29/1955, Kansas City, KS, m, 1988, 1 child **DISCIPLINE** CLASSICAL JAPANESE LITERATURE **EDUCATION** Univ Okla, BA, 77; Stanford Univ, MA, 81; MA, 86; PhD, 91. **CAREER** Asst prof, Univ Wis, 91-98; vis asst prof, Univ Calif Berkeley, 98-99; acting asst prof, Stanford Univ, 99-. **HONORS AND AWARDS** Fulbright-Hayes Fac Grant. **MEMBERSHIPS** MLA, Assoc of Asian Studies. **RESEARCH** Western critical theory, Psychoanalysis, Classical Japanese literature, Classical Japanese poetry, Japanese aesthetics, Buddhism. **SELECTED PUBLICATIONS** Auth, "Fitful Slumbers," Monumenta Nipponica, (81); auth, "Tarrying with the Negative," Monumenta Nipponica, (97); auth, "Reading the Rhetoric of Seduction in Izumi Shikibu Nikki," Harvard Jour of Asiatic Studies, (98). **CONTACT ADDRESS** Asian Lang Dept, Stanford Univ, Bldg 50, Stanford, CA 94305. **EMAIL** jwallace@dnai.com

WALLACE, KAREN SMYLEY
PERSONAL Born 12/11/1943, New Orleans, LA, m **DISCIPLINE** FRENCH **EDUCATION** Hunter Coll NYork, BA 1965; Middlebury Grad Sch, MA 1967; City Univ of NYork, PhD 1977. **CAREER** SUNY Stony Brook, instructor 1967-71; Univ of MD, instructor 1972-75; Howard Univ Washington, assoc prof 1975-. **HONORS AND AWARDS** Fulbright Hayes Study Abroad 1965-67; Ford Found Dissertation Grant 1971; Phelps Stokes Teacher Exchange 1979; AW Mellon Rsch Grant 1984. **MEMBERSHIPS** Chair of educ comm Mayor's Intl Advisory Council 1980-. **CONTACT ADDRESS** Dept of Romance Languages, Howard Univ, Room 350, Locke Hall, Washington, VT 20059.

WALLACE, ROBERT
PERSONAL Born 03/20/1950, Baltimore, MD, d, 1982, 1 child **DISCIPLINE** CLASSICS **EDUCATION** Columbia Col, BA, 72; Oxford Univ, MA, 77; Harvard Univ, PhD, 84. **CAREER** Asso prof, Class dpt ch, Northwestern Univ,91-; master, Chapin Humanities Residential Col. **HONORS AND AWARDS** NEH Univ fel, 91-92; Keeley vis fel, Oxford, 01. **RESEARCH** Music, Philosophy, and Politics in 5th-Century Athens. **SELECTED PUBLICATIONS** Auth, The Areopagos Council, to 307 BC, Hopkins, 89; co-ed, Poet, Public and Performance in Ancient Greece, Hopkins, 97; Studies in Greco-Roman History 360-146 BC in Honor of Ernst Badian, Okla, 96; coauth, Harmonia Mundi: Music and Philosophy in the Ancient World, Quaderni Urbinati di Cultura Classica, 91. **CONTACT ADDRESS** Dept of Classics, Northwestern Univ, 1801 Hinman, Kresge 11, Evanston, IL 60208. **EMAIL** rwallace@nwu.edu

WALLACE, VESNA ACIMOVIC
PERSONAL Born 11/02/1952, Croatia, m, 1989, 1 child **DISCIPLINE** SOUTH ASIAN STUDIES, SANSKRIT-BUDDHISM **EDUCATION** Univ Calif, Berkeley, PhD, 95. **CAREER** Lectr, Stanford Univ, 93-95; vis scholar, Stanford Univ, 96-97; lectr, Univ Calif Santa Barbara, 97-. **MEMBERSHIPS** Am Acad of Rel; Am Oriental Soc; Mongolia Soc; Asn for Asian Studies. **RESEARCH** South Asian and Inner Asian Buddhism. **SELECTED PUBLICATIONS** Auth, "The Buddhist Tantric Medicine in the Kalacakratantra," The Pacific World: J of the Inst of Buddhist Studies (95); auth, Santideva, A Guide to the Bodhisattva Way of Life (Bodhicaryvatara), 97. **CONTACT ADDRESS** Dept of Religious Studies, Univ of California, Santa Barbara, Santa Barbara, CA 93106-3130. **EMAIL** vwallace@humanitas.ucsb.edu

WALLACH, LUITPOLD
PERSONAL Born 02/06/1910, Munich, Germany, m, 1970 **DISCIPLINE** CLASSICS, MEDIEVAL LATIN **EDUCATION** Univ Tuebingen, DPhil(hist), 32; Cornell Univ, PhD (classics), 47. **CAREER** Asst prof classics, Hamilton Col, 51-52; asst prof hist, Univ Ore, 53; asst prof classics, Cornell Univ, 53-55; asst prof, Univ Okla, 55-57; asst prof, Harpur Col, 57-62; prof, Marquette Univ, 62-67; prof, 67-78, EMER PROF CLASSICS, UNIV ILL, URBANA, 78-; Fund Advan Educ fel, 52; Am Coun Learned Soc grant, 60; mem bd, Grad Sch, Marquette Univ, 63-67, fac fel, 67; Leo Baeck Inst fel, 67; assoc, Ctr Advan Studies, Univ Ill, 69-70. **HONORS AND AWARDS** Festschrift: Beitraege Luitpold Wallach Gewidmet, Hiersemann, Stuttgart, 75. **MEMBERSHIPS** Am Philol Asn; AHA; Mediaeval Acad Am. **RESEARCH** Philology; mediaeval Latin and history. **SELECTED PUBLICATIONS** Auth, Coercive Uses of Mandatory Reporting in Therapeutic Relationships, Behavioral Scis Law, Vol 11, 93. **CONTACT ADDRESS** Dept of Classics, Univ of Illinois, Chicago, Urbana, IL 61801.

WALLACH, MARTHA K.
PERSONAL w, 3 children **DISCIPLINE** GERMAN LANGUAGE AND LITERATURE **EDUCATION** Univ Wash, PhD, 72. **CAREER** Fac, Univ Wisc Green Bay; fac, Central Conn State Univ, 88; prof Ger and chr Mod Lang Dept, 97-00; CSU Prof, 99. **HONORS AND AWARDS** Bd dirs, N Am Heine Soc; CSU Prof, 99. **MEMBERSHIPS** N Am Heine Soc; Women in Ger. **RESEARCH** German literature; Heirich Heine; Therese Albertine Luise von Jakob Robinson; Barbara Frischmuth. **SELECTED PUBLICATIONS** Auth, pubs about Heinrich Heine and Therese Albertine Luise von Jakob Robinson, on mother-daughter relationships in German literature, and the image of Poles in German literature; trans, works of Barbara Frischmuth. **CONTACT ADDRESS** Central Connecticut State Univ, 1615 Stanley St, New Britain, CT 06050. **EMAIL** wallachma@ccsu.edu

WALLACKER, BENJAMIN E.
PERSONAL Born 11/27/1926, San Francisco, CA **DISCIPLINE** EAST ASIAN PHILOLOGY **EDUCATION** Univ Calif, Berkeley, AB, 50, MA, 54, PhD (Orient lang), 60. **CAREER** Instr Chinese, Univ Kans, 59-60, from asst prof to assoc prof Orient lang, 60-64; assoc prof, 64-69; PROF ORIENT LANG, UNIV CALIF, DAVIS, 70-. **MEMBERSHIPS** Am Orient Soc; Asn Asian Studies. **RESEARCH** The art of war in traditional China; the growth of imperial institutions in Former Han; the development of law in early China. **SELECTED PUBLICATIONS** Auth, Fairbank Remembered, J Asian Hist, Vol 27, 93; The Common-Law System in Chinese Context in Hong Kong in Transition, J Asian Hist, Vol 27, 93; Law and Legality in China in The Testament of a China Watcher, J Asian Hist, Vol 28, 94; The Textual History of the Huai Nan Tzu, J Asian Hist, Vol 28, 94; Law and Morality in ancient China in The Silk Manuscripts of Huang Lao, J Asian Hist, Vol 28, 94; Policing and Punishment in China in from Patriarchy to the People, J Asian Hist, Vol 28, 94; Chinese Loan Agreements from Discoveries at Turfan in a Study of the History of Chinese Civil Law, J Asian Hist, Vol 28, 94; Law and Order in Sung China, J Asian Hist, Vol 28, 94; Law and Morality in ancient China in The Silk Manuscripts of Huang Lao, J Asian Hist, Vol 28, 94; Policing and Punishment in China in from Patriarchy to the People, J Asian Hist, Vol 28, 94; The Textual History of The Huai Nan Tzu, J Asian Hist, Vol 28, 94; Heaven and Earth in Early Han Thought in Chapters 3, 4 and 5 of Huainanzi, J Asian Hist, Vol 28, 94; Law and Order in Sung China, J Asian Hist, Vol 28, 94; Autocratic Tradition and Chinese Politics, J Asian Hist, Vol 29, 95; Civil Law in Qing and Republican China, J Asian Hist, Vol 29, 95; To Steal a Book is an Elegant offense in Intellectual Property Law in Chinese Civilization, J Asian Hist, Vol 30, 96; Law and Local Society in Late Imperial China in Northern Taiwan in The 19Th Century, J Asian Hist, Vol 30, 96; Negotiating Daily Life in Traditional China in How Ordinary People Used Contracts, 600-1400, J Asian Hist, Vol 31, 97; Scarlet Memorial in Tales of Cannibalism in Modern China, J Asian Hist, Vol 31, 97. **CONTACT ADDRESS** Dept of Anthrop, Univ of California, Davis, Davis, CA 95616.

WALLER, MARGUERITE R.
PERSONAL Born 03/16/1948, Nyack, NY, 1 child **DISCIPLINE** COMPARATIVE LITERATURE **EDUCATION** Cornell Univ, BA, 69; Yale Univ, M Phil, 72, PhD, 78. **CAREER** Asst, assoc, full prof English, Amherst Col, 74-90; prof English and Women's Studies, Univ CA, Riverside, 90-. **HONORS AND AWARDS** Phi Beta Kappa; Fulbrights: Italy, France, Hungary; Woodrow Wilson Fac Development grant; NEH Summer fel. **MEMBERSHIPS** MLA; Am Asn of Italian Studies; Am Studies Asn; Nat Women's Studies Asn. **RESEARCH** Film and visual culture; global feminism; new media; cultural studies. **SELECTED PUBLICATIONS** Auth, Petrarch's Poetics and Literary History, U Mass Press, 80; auth, The Voice of Woman in Contemporary Society: Hillary Rodham Clinton, Reden: The J of the North Am Studies Center, Alcala, Spain, spring 94; The Art of Miscegenation in an Age of Electronic Communication, Romance Languages Annual, Purdue Res Found, 94; Hungarian Film Week, 1994, The Am Historical Rev, vol 99, no 4, Oct 94; Border Boda or Divorce Fronterizo, Negotiating Performance in Latin(o) America, ed Diana Taylor and Juan Villegas, Duke Univ Press, 94; Signifying the Holocaust: Liliana Cavani's Portiere di notte, Feminisms in the Cinema, ed Laura Pietropaolo and Ada Testaferri, IN Univ Press, 95; If 'Reality is the Best Metaphor,' It Must be Virtual?, Diacritics, 97; New Media in Old Film Cans: Maurizio Nichetti's Multi-Media Cinema, in Romance Languages Annual, Purdue Res Found, 98; Declonizing the Screen: From Ladri di biciclette to Ladri di saponette, in Designing Italy: Italy in Asia, Africa, the Americas, and Europe, ed Beverly Allen and Mary Russo, Univ MN Press, 98; Pocha or Porkchop?: Introduction to and Interview with Laura Esparza, in Latinas on Stage: Practice and Theory, ed Alicia Arrizon and Lilian Manzor Coats, Berkeley: Third Woman Press, forthcoming; nunmerous other publications, videos and exhibitions; ed, Frontline Feminisms: Women, War, and Resistance, Garland Press, 00. **CONTACT ADDRESS** Dept of English, Univ of California, Riverside, Riverside, CA 92521. **EMAIL** marguerite.waller@ucr.edu

WALSH, CAREY ELLEN
PERSONAL Born 04/03/1960, Troy, NY **DISCIPLINE** HEBREW BIBLE **EDUCATION** Allegeury Col, BA, 82; Yale Divinity Sch, M Div, 85; Univ Chicago, AM, 89; Harvard, ThD, 96. **CAREER** Asst prof, Hebrew Bible, Rhodes Col. **MEMBERSHIPS** CBA; SBL. **RESEARCH** Archaelogy, Social hist of ancient Israel; Ancient Agriculture. **SELECTED PUBLICATIONS** Auth, Fruit of the Vine: Viticulture in Ancient Israel and the Hebrew Bible, HSM, in press; auth, Gods's Vineyard, BR, 98. **CONTACT ADDRESS** Rhodes Col, 2000 N Parkway, Memphis, TN 38104. **EMAIL** walsh@rhodes.edu

WALSH, JEROME T.
PERSONAL Born 06/14/1942, Detroit, MI **DISCIPLINE** HEBREW BIBLE **EDUCATION** Pontifical Bible Inst, SSL, 75; Univ Mich, PhD, 82. **CAREER** Assoc prof, 89-95, St John's Univ, NY; prof, 96-, dept head, theol & relig stud, 97-, Univ Botswana. **MEMBERSHIPS** Soc of Biblical Lit; Catholic Biblical Assn Amer. **RESEARCH** Literary analysis of Hebrew Bible. **SELECTED PUBLICATIONS** Auth, 1 Kings, Collegeville, Litur, 96. **CONTACT ADDRESS** 32-23 88th St, Apt 404, Jackson Heights, NY 11369. **EMAIL** jwalsh3000@cs.com

WALSH, JONATHAN D.
DISCIPLINE 17TH AND 18TH CENTURY FRENCH THEATER AND PROSE **EDUCATION** Univ Calif, Santa Barbara, PhD. **CAREER** Fr, Wheaton Col. **RESEARCH** Psychoanalysis and literature; jealousy and symbolic exchange in the French novel; French moralists and philosophes. **SELECTED PUBLICATIONS** Publ, on Abbe Prevost, Marcel Proust and Enlightenment authors appear in Romance Quart and Esprit Createur. **CONTACT ADDRESS** Dept of Fr, Wheaton Col, Massachusetts, 26 East Main St, Norton, MA 02766. **EMAIL** jwalsh@wheatonma.edu

WANG, BAN
PERSONAL Born 06/23/1957, Amoy, China, m, 1985, 1 child **DISCIPLINE** COMPARATIVE & CHINESE LITERATURE **EDUCATION** Beijing Foreign Studies Univ, BA, 82, MA, 85; Univ Iowa, PhD, 90; Univ Calif, PhD, 93. **CAREER** Asst prof, SUNY-Stony Brook, 93-98; assoc prof, Rutgers Univ, 98- . **HONORS AND AWARDS** NEH Fel; Ctr for the Crit Analysis of Contemp Culture Fel, Rutgers Univ; Presiden'ts Fel for the Humanities, UCLA. **MEMBERSHIPS** MLA; Asn of Asian Studies; Socs for Cinema Studies. **RESEARCH** Chinese lit, culture & film; aesthetics; intellectual hist. **SELECTED PUBLICATIONS** Auth, "The Sublime Subject of History and Desublimaion in Contemporary Chinese Narrative," Comp Lit 47.4 (95): 330-353; auth, The Sublime Figure of History: Aesthetics and Politics in Twentieth-Century China, Stanford, 97; auth, "Memory as History: Making Sense of the Past in Contemporary Chinese Fiction," Am J of Chinese Studies 5 (Spring 98): 301-319; co-transl, Illuminations, by Walter Benjamin (Oxford Univ Pr, 98); auth, "Trauma and History in Chinese

Film: Reading 'The Blue Kite' against Melodrama," Mod Chinese Lit & Culture (Spring 99): 125-155; auth, "Memory, Narcissism, and Sublimation: Reading Lou Andreas-Salome's 'Freud Journal'," The Am Imago 57.2 (Summer 00): 215-234. **CONTACT ADDRESS** East Asian Langs & Cultures, Rutgers, The State Univ of New Jersey, New Brunswick, 330 Scott Hall, New Brunswick, NJ 08901. **EMAIL** banwang@rci.rutgers.edu

WANG, JOAN PARSONS
PERSONAL Born 10/21/1925, Cincinnati, OH, w, 1947, 2 children **DISCIPLINE** ENGLISH, COMPARATIVE LITERATURE **EDUCATION** Radcliffe Col, AB, 47; Brown Univ, MA, 49; Ind Univ, PhD (comp lit), 64. **CAREER** Asst prof, 66-80, Assoc Prof English, Independent Studies Div, Sch Continuing Studies, Ind Univ, Bloomington, 80-. **HONORS AND AWARDS** Cert Merit, Nat Univ Exten Asn, 71 and 81. **MEMBERSHIPS** Nat Univ Exten Asn. **RESEARCH** Writing syllabi for independent study courses in English and world literature; modern European drama; women's studies. **CONTACT ADDRESS** Dept of English, Indiana Univ, Bloomington, 1 Ind Univ, Bloomington, IN 47405. **EMAIL** wang@indiana.edu

WANG, JOHN C. Y.
DISCIPLINE CHINESE LANGUAGE, LITERATURE **EDUCATION** Nat Taiwan Univ, BA, 57; Univ Minn, MA, 62; Cornell Univ, PhD, 68. **CAREER** Asst Prof, Univ of Mich, 68-69; Asst to Full Prof, Stanford Univ, 69-; Chair of Dept of Asian Lang, Stanford Univ, 79-90; Bd Dir, Asn for Asian Studies, 78-81. **HONORS AND AWARDS** Distinguished Chair Professorship, Acad Simica, Taipei; ACLS Fel; Fulbright-Hayes Fac Res Abroad Fel. **MEMBERSHIPS** Asn for Asian Studies, Chinese Lang Teachers Asn. **RESEARCH** Early Chinese Narrative, Chinese Literary Criticism, Narrative Theory. **SELECTED PUBLICATIONS** Auth, Chin Shang-T'an (a 17th century Chinese literary critic), Twayne Publ (NY), 72; auth, Essays on the Zuozhkan and the Traditional Chinese Novel, Peking Univ Press (Beijing), 89; auth, Chinese Literary Criticism of the Ch'ing Period (1644-1911), Hong Kong Univ Press (Hong Kong), 94; auth, Studies in Early Chinese Narrative, Academic Sinica (Taipei), 99. **CONTACT ADDRESS** Dept Asian Lang, Stanford Univ, Bldg 50, Stanford, CA 94305-2034. **EMAIL** jcywang@leland.stanford.edu

WANG, MASON YU-HENG
PERSONAL Born 05/07/1936, China, m, 1963, 3 children **DISCIPLINE** SHAKESPEARE, COMPARATIVE LITERATURE **EDUCATION** Nat Taiwan Univ, BA, 59; IN Univ, MA, 65, PhD(English), 72. **CAREER** Instr English, Cent MO State Col, 65-68; from instr to asst prof, 69-76, chmn dept, 74-78, assoc prof, 76-83, Prof English Saginaw Valley State Univ, 83-. **HONORS AND AWARDS** Fel, Li Foundation, 61-63; fel, Indiana Univ Foreign Student, 64-65; Natl Endowment for the Humanities Grant, Stanford Univ, 76; Natl Endowment for the Humanities Grant, Univ of Calif, Santa Cruz, 87; Correspondent, Intl Committee, World Shakespeare Bibliography, 92-. **MEMBERSHIPS** Shakespeare Asn Am. **RESEARCH** Shakespeare; comparative literature; Chinese literature. **SELECTED PUBLICATIONS** Auth, Burlesque and Irony in The Two Gentlemen of Verona, Shakespeare Newslett, 9/72; Review of Ten Poems and Lyrics by Mao Tse-tung, Green River Rev, 76; ed, Perspectives in Contemporary Chinese Literature, Green River Press, 83; tr & ed, Zhang Siyang, Hamlet's Melancholy, and Zhang Xiaoyang, Shakespeare and the Idea of Nature in the Renaissance, Shakespeare and the Triple Play, ed Sidney Homan, Bucknell Univ Press, 88; contrib & ed, Meng Xianqiang. A Historical .Survey of Shakespeare in China, Shakespeare Res Center of NE Normal Univ, 96; co-tr & ed, Meng Xianqiang. A Historical Survey of Shakespeare. **CONTACT ADDRESS** Dept of English, Saginaw Valley State Univ, 7400 Bay Rd, University Center, MI 48710-0001. **EMAIL** mywang@svsu.edu

WANG, SHUNZHU
PERSONAL Born 06/21/1957, Yancheng, Jiangsu, China, M, 1981, 1 child **DISCIPLINE** CHINESE **EDUCATION** Jiangsu Teachers Col, BA, 80; Jiangsu Col of Educ, Diploma, 83; Wayne State Col, MA, 94; Purdue Univ, PhD, 01. **CAREER** Teacher, Yangcheng High School, 83-84; lectr, Yangcheng Educ Inst, 84-89; lectr, Nanjing Col of Commun, 89-92; TA, Wayne State Col, 92-94; TA, Purdue Univ, 94-99; master teacher, Bennington Col, 99-. **HONORS AND AWARDS** Excellent Educ Award, Yancheng Educ Inst, 86; Excellent Teacher Award, Nanjing Col of Commun, 90; Int Club Scholar, WSC, 93; Purdue Res Found Fel, 98, 99. **MEMBERSHIPS** MLA, Am Coun of Teaching of For Lang, Chinese Lang Teachers Asn, Vt For Lang Asn. **RESEARCH** Comparative Studies/ Theory, Critical Theory, Chinese Literature, American Literature, Language Teaching. **SELECTED PUBLICATIONS** Coed, Middle School English Companion Vol 6, Jinagsu Educ Pr, 85; transl, Yu shizi wei su, Huayue Publ House, China, 86; auth, "The Double-Voiced Feminist Discourse in Ding Ling's 'Miss Sophie's Diary' and Zora Neale Hurston's their Eyes Were Watching God," Tamkang Rev, (97); coed and cotransl, Contemporary Rhetoric: Speech and Discourse Criticism, China Soc Sci Publ House, 98; coed and cotransl, Contemporary Western Rhetoric: Critical methods and Paradigms, China Publ House, 98; auth, "Of What/Whom Was Tao Yuanming Thinking," Negotiating Space and Crossing Borders, (FLL, Purdue Univ, 99); auth, "Min Anchee," and "Louis Hing chu," Asian Am Novelists, ed Emmanuel S Nelson, (Greenwood Pr, 00). **CONTACT ADDRESS** Bennington Col, Rte 67A, Bennington, VT 05201. **EMAIL** shunzhu@bennington.edu

WANG, WILLIAM S. Y.
PERSONAL Born 08/14/1933, Shanghai, China, m, 1973, 4 children **DISCIPLINE** LINGUISTICS **EDUCATION** Columbia Col, AB, 55; Univ Mich, MA, 56, PhD (ling), 60. **CAREER** Mem staff, Res Lab Electronics, Mass Inst Technol, 60; instr commun sci and res assoc, Commun Sci Lab, Univ Mich, 60-61; mem staff, Int Bus Machines Res Ctr, 61; asst prof ling and chmn dept Eastern Asian lang and lit, Ohio State Univ, 61-63, assoc prof ling, 62-65, chmn div, 62-65; PROF LING, UNIV CALIF, BERKELEY, 65-; Nat Sci Found rea grant, 61; Ohio State Univ grant to establish ling res lab, 62; fel ling, Ctr Advan Studies Behav Sci, 69-70; Fulbright prof ling, Sweden, 71-72; ED, J CHINESE LING, 73-; Guggenheim fel, 78. **MEMBERSHIPS** Charter mem Am Asn Phonetic Sci; Ling Soc Am; MLA; Acoust Soc Am. **RESEARCH** Languages; speech. **SELECTED PUBLICATIONS** Auth, Lexical Diffusion in Semantic Change with Special Reference to Universal Changes, Folia Ling Hist, Vol 16, 95; Bai Ma Si, A Case of Folk Etymology and The Name of the Temple Comes from the Sanskrit Word Padma, Which Means Lotus, J Chinese Ling, Vol 24, 96. **CONTACT ADDRESS** Dept of Ling, Univ of California, Berkeley, Berkeley, CA 94720.

WANNER, ADRIAN J.
PERSONAL Born 01/26/1960, Bern, Switzerland, m, 1989, 2 children **DISCIPLINE** RUSSIAN LITERATURE **EDUCATION** Columbia Univ, PhD, 92. **CAREER** Asst prof, 92-96, Univ Evansville; asst prof to assoc prof, 96-, Penn St. **HONORS AND AWARDS** Poetry Prize, Columbia Univ, 90; AAASS Nat Awd for best Slavic Paper, 92. **MEMBERSHIPS** MLA; AAASS; AATSEEL; ALTA. **RESEARCH** Russian symbolism; comparative literature. **SELECTED PUBLICATIONS** Auth, Alexander Blok: Gedichte, Suhrkamp Verlag, 90; auth, Baudelaire in Russia, Univ Press Fl, 96; art, From Subversion to Affirmation: The Prose Poem as a Russian Genre, Slavic Review, 97; auth, Innokentij Annenskij: Die Schwarze Silhouette, Pano Verlag, 98; art, Aleksei Remizov's Dreams: Surrealism Avant la Lettre?, Russian Review, 99. **CONTACT ADDRESS** Dept of Germanic & Slavic Lang, 315 Burrowes Bldg, University Park, PA 16802. **EMAIL** ajw3@psu.edu

WARD, DOROTHY COX
PERSONAL Born 07/14/1925, Birmingham, AL, m, 1949, 4 children **DISCIPLINE** GERMANIC STUDIES **EDUCATION** Birmingham-Southern Col, AB, 45, BM, 50; Columbia Univ, MA, 54, PhD, 76. **CAREER** Instr Ger and French, Birmingham-Southern Col, 46-49; instr Ger, Univ Ala, 49-50; instr Ger and French, Birmingham-Southern Col, 50-52; instr Ger, Sch Gen Studies, Columbia Univ, 52-54; asst prof Ger and French, Birmingham-Southern Col, 54-56; instr English and French, Walddorfer Schule, Hamburg, Ger, 56-57; From asst prof to assoc prof Ger and French, 57-76, PROF GER AND FRENCH AND CHMN DEPT MOD FOREIGN LANG, BIRMINGHAM-SOUTHERN COL, 76-; CHAIRPERSON DIV HUMANITIES, 80-. **MEMBERSHIPS** Am Asn Teachers Ger; SAtlantic Mod Lang Asn, Southern Conf on Foreign Lang Teaching. **RESEARCH** Modern German literature; Hermann Hesse. **SELECTED PUBLICATIONS CONTACT ADDRESS** Dept of Mod Foreign Lang, Birmingham-So Col, Birmingham, AL 35204.

WARD, GREGORY
PERSONAL Born 10/08/1955, Northridge, CA, m, 1992 **DISCIPLINE** LINGUISTICS **EDUCATION** Univ CA, Berkeley, BA (Linguistics, with honors, and Comparative lit), 78; Univ PA, PhD (Linguistics), 85. **CAREER** Lect, Dept of Linguistics, Univ PA, 83-84; lect, Dept of Linguistics, San Diego State Univ, 85-86; asst prof, 86-91, assoc prof, 91-97, prof/chmn, Dept of Linguistics, Northwestern Univ, 97-; consult, AT & T Labs-Res, 86-97; vis prof, LSA Linguistic Inst, OH State Univ, 93; vis prof, UFR Angellier, Universite Charles de Gaulle-Lille 3, 96; vis prof, LSA Linguistic Inst, Cornell Univ, 97. **HONORS AND AWARDS** Phi Beta Kappa; graduated with Great Distinction in General Scholarship from the College of Letters and Sciences, Univ CA, Berkeley, 78; Meritorious Performance and Professional Promise Awd, Col of Arts and Letters, San Diego State Univ, 86; Northwestern Univ grant for Ed Excellence, 91; Northwestern Univ Res grant, 91-93; Co-PI, Nat Inst on Deafness and Other Communication Disorders, Dept of Health and Human Services, 91-96; fel, Center for Advanced Study in the Behavioral Sciences, to be arranged. **MEMBERSHIPS** Linguistic Soc of Am; ed bd, Computational Linguistics, 95-97; adv ed, Current Res in the Semantics/Pragmatics Interface, 97-. **SELECTED PUBLICATIONS** Auth, Ward, Gregory and Julia Hirschberg. "Implicating Uncertainty: The Pragmatics of Fall-Rise Intonation," in Language 61:747-776, 85; auth, Ward, Gregory, "The Discourse Functions of VP Preposing," in Language 66:742-763, 90; auth, Hirschberg, Julia and Gregory Ward. "Accent and Bound Anaphora," in Cognitive Linguistics 2:101-121, 91; Ward, Gregory and Ellen F. Prince. "On the Topicalization of Indefinite NPs," in Journal of Pragmatics 16:167-177, 91; auth, Ward, Gregory, Richard Sproat, and Gail McKoon. "A Pragmatic Analysis of So-Called Anaphoric Islands," in Language 67:439-474, 91; auth, McKoon Gail, Gregory Ward, Roger Ratcliff, and Richard Sproat. "Morphosyntactic and Pragmatic Factors Affecting the Accessibility of Discourse Entities," in Journal of Memory and Language 32:56-75, 93; auth, Ward, Gregory and Betty J. Birner. "Definiteness and the English Existential," in Language 71:722-742, 93; auth, Birner, Betty and Gregory Ward. Information Status J. and Noncanonical Word Order in English. Amsterdam/ Philadelphia: John Benjamins. 314 pp., 98; auth, Kehler, Andrew and Gregory Ward. "On the Semantics and Pragmatics of 'Identifier' So"," in The Semantics/Pragmatics Interface from Different Pointts of View (Current Research in the Semantics/ Pragmatics Interface Series, Volume I), edited by Ken Turner, 99; auth, Horn, Laurence R. and Gregory Ward, co-editors. Handbook of Pragmatics. Oxford: Basil Blackwell. In prep. **CONTACT ADDRESS** Dept of Linguistics, Northwestern Univ, 2016 Sheridan Rd, Evanston, IL 60208-4090. **EMAIL** gw@northwestern.edu

WARD, MARGARET CHARLOTTE
PERSONAL Born 04/10/1946, Miami Beach, FL, m, 1975, 2 children **DISCIPLINE** TRANSLATION **EDUCATION** Wellesley Col, BA, 68; Harvard Univ, MA, 71; PhD, 81. **CAREER** Teaching fel to tutor, Harvard Univ, 69-72, 76-78; instr, Univ Conn, 78-82; asst prof, Ohio Univ, 82-83; asst prof, Univ Minn, 83-89; assoc prof to prof, Univ PR, 89-. **HONORS AND AWARDS** NEH, 88, 89; Andrew Mellon Fac Development, 89; Exxon Res Fel, 82; MAA Grant, 77; Sir John Williams Res Fel, 75-76; Wellesley Col Workman Fel, 74-75; Rotary Intl Fel, 73-74; NDEA Fel, 70-71; Radcliffe Inst Fel, 69; Phi Beta Kappa Sibley Fel, 72-73. **MEMBERSHIPS** MLA; MAA; CSANA; IAS; APTIPR. **RESEARCH** Literary translation; medieval lyric and romance; modernism. **SELECTED PUBLICATIONS** Auth, "French Ovidian Beasts in 'Sir Gawain and the Green Knight,'" Neuphilol Mitt 89 (78): 152-61; auth, Pound's Translations of Arnaut Daniel, Garland, 91; auth, Ezra Pound, Forked Branches: Translations of Medieval Poems, Windhover Pr, 85; auth, "A Formulaic Consideration of 'The Mabinogion, Branch I," Etud Celt 29 (92): 423-39; auth, "Arthur in the Welsh Bruts," in Celtic Languages and Celtic Peoples, eds. Cyril J. Byrne, Margaret Harry, Padraig O. Siadhail (Halifax: St Mary's Univ, 92): 383-90; auth, "Aldington and Pound: Partners in Translation," in Richard Aldington: Essays in Honor of the Centenary of his Birth, eds. A. Blayac, C. Zilboorg (Montpellier: Univ Paul Valery, 94): 85-98; auth, "The Sleep of King Arthur in Avalon by Edward Burne-Jones in the Ponce Museum," in Romantics/Victorians: Studies in Nineteenth-Century British Poetry and Art, ed. Elisabeth Sanders Arbuckle (Rio Piedras: Univ PR, 97): 147-64; auth, "The Fourteenth-Century Welsh Treatise of Einion Offeiriad as a Renaissance Phenomenon," in De Consolatione Philological: Studies in Honor of Evelyn S. Firchow, eds. Anna Grotans, Heinrich Beck, Anton Schwob (Goppingen: Kummerle, 00): 433-42; auth, "Synge's 'Riders to the Sea' Translated by Juan Ramon, Zenobia Jimenez," Rev de Estudies Hisp 27 (01). **CONTACT ADDRESS** Trans Humanities Dept, Univ of Puerto Rico, San Juan, PO Box 22613, San Juan, PR 00931-2613.

WARD, PATRICIA A.
PERSONAL Born 08/26/1940, Warren, PA, s **DISCIPLINE** FRENCH, LITERATURE **EDUCATION** Eastern Nazarene Col, BA, 62; Univ of Wis, MA, 64; PhD, 68. **CAREER** Asst Prof, State Univ NY at Albany, 68-72; asst prof, 72-75, actg head, dept French, 80-81, assoc prof, 75-82, prof fr and comp lit, PA State Univ, 82-; assoc ed, Christian Scholar's rev, 81-; vis prof comp lit, Baylor Univ, 82. **HONORS AND AWARDS** Fulbright Fel, Paris, 66-67; Class of 1934 Awd in the Humanities, Penn State Univ, 82; Alumni Achievement Awd, Eastern Nazarene Col, 79; Coolidge Res Fel, 94; State Univ NY Res Found grant-in-aid, 71; res initiation grant, Pa State Univ, 73-74; fel Inst of Arts and Humanistics Studies, Pa State Univ, 79. **MEMBERSHIPS** MLA; Am Comp Lit Asn; Conf Christianity and Lit; Am Asn Teachers Fr; Alliance Fr. **RESEARCH** Literary Criticism; French Literature; European Romanticism. **SELECTED PUBLICATIONS** Auth, "Getting it Right in Language, Literature, and Ethics," Relig Lit, Vol 25 (93); auth, "The Sublime and Revolutionary Oratory in Themes and Myths of the Restoration and the July Monarchy," Nineteenth Century Fr Stud, Vol 22 (93); auth, "Contemporary Literary Theory in a Chrisian Appraisal," Religion Lit, Vol 25 (93); auth, "The Culture of Redemption," Phil Lit, Vol 17 (93); auth, "The Ethics of Criticism," Religion Lit, Vol 25 (93); auth, "The Thought and Art of Joubert, Joseph 1754-1824," Rev D Hist Lit de la France, Vol 94 (94); auth," A Southern Story," New Orleans Rev, Vol 23 (97); auth, "Dictionary for Les Miserables in an Encylopedia Dictionary of Hugo, Victor Novel Created Using the Latest Technologies," Nineteenth-Century Fr Stud, Vol 25 (97). **CONTACT ADDRESS** Dept of Fr, Pennsylvania State Univ, Univ Park, University Park, PA 16802. **EMAIL** pward@psu.edu

WARD, SETH
PERSONAL Born 12/15/1952, New York, NY, m, 1978, 4 children **DISCIPLINE** NEAR EASTERN LANGUAGES **EDUCATION** Yale Univ, BA, 74, MA, 78, PhD, 84. **CAREER** Instr, 84-85, Yale Univ; lectr, 85-88, Univ Haifa; guest lectr, 89, Ben Gurion Univ, Negev; lectr, 89-91, Israel Inst Techn; asst prof, 91-, Univ Denver. **RESEARCH** Jewish-Muslim relation-

ship; Jews of Islamic lands; Egypt; land of Israel; crypto-Jews. **SELECTED PUBLICATIONS** Art, Taqi al-Din al-Subki on Construction, Continuance and Repair of Churches and Synagogues in Islamic Law, Stud in Islamic & Judaic Traditions II, Scholars Press, 89; art, Expel the Jews and Christians from the Arabian Peninsula, Bull of Schl of African & Oriental Stud, 53, 90; art, Dhimmi Women and Mourning, Islamic Legal Interpretation: Muftis and the Fatwas, Harvard Univ Press, 96; art, Sepphoris in the Arab Period, Sepphoris in Gallilee: Crosscurrents of Culture, NC Museum of Art, 96; art, Sepphoris in Sacred Geography, Galilee, Confluence of Cultures, Winona Lake Ind, 99; art, Tsippori be-tekufah ha-aravit (Sepphoris in the Arabic Period) Yerushalayim ve-Eretz Yisrael I, Bar-Ilan Univ Press, 99; art, Ibn Rifa on the Churches and Synagogues of Cairo, Avoda & Ibada, Lit & Rit in Islamic and Judaic Soc, Mediaeval Encounters: Jewish Christian and Muslim Culture in Confluence and Dialogue, 99; ed, Avoda and Ibada, Liturgy and Ritual in Islamic and Judaic Societies, Mediaeval Encounters: Jewish Christian and Muslim Culture in Confluence and Dialogue, 99. **CONTACT ADDRESS** Center for Judaic Studies, Univ of Denver, Denver, CO 80208. **EMAIL** sward@du.edu

WARG, ILSE-ROSE
PERSONAL Born 06/30/1936, Gera, Germany, m, 1962, 2 children **DISCIPLINE** GERMAN **EDUCATION** Pa State Univ, BA, 69; MA, 70; PhD, 91. **CAREER** Res asst to TA, Pa State Univ, 67-92; asst prof, Central Mich Univ, 93; lectr, Franciscan Univ, 00; lectr, Pa State Univ, 00-01. **HONORS AND AWARDS** Inst for the Arts and Humanistic Studies Fel, 67, 68, 69, Phi Kappa Phi, 68; Delta Phi Alpha, 68; Outstanding Woman Fac Member Awd, 91; Achieving Women of PSU, 92. **MEMBERSHIPS** MLA, AATG. **RESEARCH** German Post War Authors. **SELECTED PUBLICATIONS** Auth,"Ein verstummelter, aber unsterblicher Till," Eulenspiegel Jahrbuch, (92); auth, "Doch ich krumm mich um alles, was lebt," Wolfdietrich Schnurres lyrisches Schaffen, Peter Lang Verlag, (NY, 93); ed, Er Bleibt dabei, Igel Verlag, Paderborn, 95; auth, "Raging Against the Berlin Wall: the Case of Wolfdietrich Schnurre," Berlin Wall, ed Ernst Schurer, Manfred Keune, Philip Jenkins, (96). **CONTACT ADDRESS** Pennsylvania State Univ, Altoona, 202 D Adler Bldg, 3000 Ivyside Pk, Altoona, PA 16601. **EMAIL** jirwarg@penn.com

WARGA, RICHARD G., JR.
DISCIPLINE GREEK, LATIN, MYTHOLOGY, SCIENTIFIC TERMINOLOGY **EDUCATION** Univ Ill, Urbana-Champaign, PhD, 88. **CAREER** Instr Classics, coordr, elem Lat crse, La State Univ. **RESEARCH** Epigraphy; papyrology; Coptic studies. **SELECTED PUBLICATIONS** Auth, A Coptic-Greek Stele from Memphis, Tennessee, in Chronique d'Egypte LXVI, 91; A Repayment of a Loan, in Zeitschrift f(r Papyrologie und Epigraphik 100, 94. **CONTACT ADDRESS** Dept of For Lang and Lit, Louisiana State Univ, 122 A Prescott Hall, Baton Rouge, LA 70803. **EMAIL** warga@lsu.edu

WARNER, NICHOLAS OLIVER
PERSONAL Born 02/11/1950, San Francisco, CA, m, 3 children **DISCIPLINE** COMPARATIVE ; ENGLISH & AMERICAN LITERATURE **EDUCATION** Stanford Univ, BA, 72; Univ Calif, Berkeley, PhD, 77. **CAREER** Vis asst prof Eng, Oberlin Col, 78-80; asst prof Lit, Claremont McKenna Col, 80-86; assoc prof, Claremont McKenna Col, 86-94; full prof, Claremont McKenna Col, 94-. **HONORS AND AWARDS** Huntton Awd for Superior Tchg, 83, 84, 88, 90, 99; Graves fel in the Humanities. **MEMBERSHIPS** MLA; Am Asn Advan Slavic Studies; Am Studies Assoc. **RESEARCH** Literature and visual arts; 19th century British, Am & Russ lit. **SELECTED PUBLICATIONS** Auth, Blakes Moon-Ark symbolism, Blake Quart, fall 80; Spirits of America: Intoxication in 19th Century American Literature, Univ Oklahoma, 97; auth, "The Texture of Time in War & Peace," Slavic & East European Journal, 86. **CONTACT ADDRESS** Dept of Literature, Claremont McKenna Col, 850 Columbia Ave, Claremont, CA 91711-6420. **EMAIL** nwarner@mckenna.edu

WARNKE, NINA
PERSONAL Born 08/22/1959, Dusseldorf, Germany, s **DISCIPLINE** YIDDISH STUDIES, LITERATURE **EDUCATION** Mount Holyoke Col, BA, 83; Columbia Univ, MA, 88; MPil, 90; PhD, 01. **CAREER** Lectr, Columbia Univ, 94-97; vis lectr, Ind Univ, 97-00; asst prof, Univ Tex Austin, 01-. **HONORS AND AWARDS** Cen Advanced Judicial Studies Fel, 00-01; Mem Found Distinguished Fel; Max Weinreich Cen Advanced Jewish Studies Fel; Fulbright Travel Grant. **MEMBERSHIPS** MLA; AJS. **RESEARCH** Yiddish theater and film; Jewish popular culture; immigrant culture; Yiddish theater and drama. **SELECTED PUBLICATIONS** Auth, "The Politics of Yiddish Theater: Sholem Aleichem's First Visit to America," YIVO Ann 20: 239-276; auth, "The Child that Wouldn't Grow Up: Yiddish Theatre and Its Critics," in Yiddish Theater: New Approaches, ed. Joel Berkowiz (London: Littman Lib Jewish Civil Press); auth, "Immigrant Popular Culture as Contested Sphere: Yiddish Music Halls, the Yiddish Press, and the Processes of Americanization, 1900-1910," Thea J 48 (96): 321-335. **CONTACT ADDRESS** Dept Ger Studies, Univ of Texas, Austin, PO Box C 3300, Austin, TX 78712-1190. **EMAIL** ninawarnke@hotmail.com

WARREN, EDWARD W.
PERSONAL Born 01/20/1929, San Francisco, CA, m, 1955, 3 children **DISCIPLINE** PHILOSOPHY, GREEK **EDUCATION** Stanford Univ, BA, 50; Johns Hopkins Univ, PhD (philos), 61. **CAREER** Asst prof philos, Syracuse Univ, 59-63; From asst prof to prof, 63-70, PROF CLASSICS AND PHILOS, SAN DIEGO STATE UNIV, 70-. **MEMBERSHIPS** Am Philol Asn; Soc Greek Philos; AAUP; Int Soc Neo-Platonic Studies. **RESEARCH** Greek philosophy; Plotinus; metaphysics. **SELECTED PUBLICATIONS CONTACT ADDRESS** Dept of Class and Orient Lang and Lit, San Diego State Univ, San Diego, CA 92182.

WARREN, M.
DISCIPLINE FRENCH, COMPARATIVE LITERATURE **EDUCATION** Univ Calif, Berkeley, BA, 88; Stanford Univ, MA, 91; PhD, 93. **CAREER** Vis asst prof, Bennington Col, 93-94; asst prof to assoc prof, Univ of Miami, 94-. **HONORS AND AWARDS** Excellence in Teaching Awd, Univ of Miami, 97. **MEMBERSHIPS** MLA; AAUW; AATF; AAUP; Arthurian Soc. **RESEARCH** Medieval Studies, Post-colonial Studies. **SELECTED PUBLICATIONS** Auth, History on the Edge: Excaliber and the Borders of Britain, 1100-1300, Univ of Minn Pr, 00. **CONTACT ADDRESS** Dept Foreign Lang, Univ of Miami, PO Box 248093, Miami, FL 33124-8093. **EMAIL** mrw@miami.edu

WARRIN, DONALD OGDEN
PERSONAL Born 04/17/1933, Montclair, NJ, m, 1986, 4 children **DISCIPLINE** PORTUGUESE **EDUCATION** Univ Southern Calif, BA, 60; NYork Univ, MA, 66, PhD(Port), 73. **CAREER** Prof Port, Calif State Univ, Hayward, 69-; Prof Emer, Calif State Univ, Hayward. **HONORS AND AWARDS** Causa Portuguesa, Portuguese Union of the State of Calif (UPEC), 87. **MEMBERSHIPS** Immigration Hist Soc; Hist Inst of Terceira, Azores; California Hist. Soc.; Nev Hist Soc; Western Hist Asn **RESEARCH** Portuguese immigrant history and literature **SELECTED PUBLICATIONS** Auth, Aguarelas Florentinas e Outras Poesias, Angra do Heroismo, Portugal, 86; Portuguese Pioneers in Early Nevada, Nev Hist Soc Quart, spring 92; co-auth, Portuguese Women on the American Frontier, O Rosto Feminino da Expansao Portuguesa, Lisbon, 95; auth, An Immigrant Path to Social Mobility: Portuguese Atlantic Islanders in the California Sheep Industry, Calif Hist, 97/98; The Portuguese in Nevada: A Visual History, hist photograph exhibit, Nev State Libr and Archives, 95; Cowboys, Miners, and Sheepherders: Portuguese in the Old West, hist photograph exhibit, Univ Mass, Dartmouth, 96; auth, Os Acorianos nas Terras dos Indios: Enconters na Fonteira Oitocentista Norte-American, O Faialea Periferia Acoriana nos Seculos 15 or 20, Horta, Portugal, 98; auth, Nevada's Pioneer Portuguese Communities: A Pictorial History, Community in the American West, Reno, Nev., 99; auth, O Lendario John Portuguese Phillips do Estado de Wyoming Revisto, Arquipalago-historia, Ponta Delgada, Portugal, 00; coauth, Land As Far As the Eye Can See: Portuguese in the Old West, Arthur H. Clar, Co. Spokane, 01. **CONTACT ADDRESS** Dept of Modern Languages and Literatures, California State Univ, Hayward, 25800 Carlos Bee Bvd, Hayward, CA 94542-3038. **EMAIL** dwarrin@csuhayward.edu

WASHBURN, DENNIS
DISCIPLINE ASIAN AND MIDDLE EASTERN LANGUAGES AND LITERATURES **EDUCATION** Harvard Univ, BA, 76; Oxford Univ, MA, 79; Yale Univ, MPhil, PhD, 91. **CAREER** Asst prof, Dartmouth Col; Asst Prof, Conn Col, 87-91; Vis Instructor, Yale Univ, 89-90; Asst Prof, Harvard Univ, 91-92; Chair and Assoc Prof, Dartmouth, 92-; Dir of Japanese School, 00-. **HONORS AND AWARDS** Monbusho Scholar, Japanese Min Educ. **RESEARCH** Transition from Edo to Meiji lit; transl of moral categories in Meiji fiction. **SELECTED PUBLICATIONS** Auth, The Dilemma of the Modern in Japanese Fiction, Yale UP, 95; auth, "Toward A View from Nowhere: Perspective and Ethical Judgment in Fires on the Plain," Journal of Japanese Studies, 97; auth, "Structures of Emptiness: Kitsch, Nihilism and the Inauthentic in Mishima's Aesthetics, " in Studies in Modern Japanese Literature, 97; coed, Studies in Modern Japanese Literature, Univ of Mich, 97; coed, Between Word and Image: Essays on the Japanese Cineam, Cambridge Univ Pr, 00; auth, "The Arrest of Time: Sacred Trangressions of Vengeance Is Mine," in Between Word and Image: Essays on the Japanese Cinema, Cambridge Univ Pr, forthcoming. **CONTACT ADDRESS** Dartmouth Col, 3529 N Main St, #207, Hanover, NH 03755. **EMAIL** dennis.washburn@dartmouth.edu

WASHBURN, YULAN M.
DISCIPLINE PORTUGUESE LITERATURE **EDUCATION** Univ NC, PhD, 67. **CAREER** Prof emer, Univ Tenn. **CONTACT ADDRESS** Dept of Mod For Langs & Lits, Univ of Tennessee, Knoxville, 701 McClung Tower & Plaza, Knoxville, TN 37996. **EMAIL** yulan@utk.edu

WASHINGTON, IDA HARRISON
PERSONAL Born Port Washington, NY, m, 1948, 6 children **DISCIPLINE** GERMAN LITERATURE **EDUCATION** Wellesley Col, AB, 46; Middlebury Col, AM, 50; Columbia Univ, PhD, 62. **CAREER** Instr Ger, Univ Minn, 61-62; instr, Drew Univ, 64; instr, NY Univ, 64-65; lectr, Seton Hall Univ, 65-66; asst prof, 66-72, assoc prof mod lang, 72-77, Prof Mod Lang, Southeastern Mass Univ, 77-; Exec Secy, Northeast Mod Lang Asn, 80-. **MEMBERSHIPS** Am Asn Teachers Ger; MLA; Northeast Mod Lang Asn; Soc Ger-Am Studies. **RESEARCH** Poetic realism. **SELECTED PUBLICATIONS CONTACT ADDRESS** Dept of Mod Lang, Southeastern Massachusetts Univ, North Dartmouth, MA 02747.

WASIOLEK, EDWARD
PERSONAL Born 04/27/1924, Camden, NJ, m, 1948, 3 children **DISCIPLINE** COMPARATIVE LITERATURE **EDUCATION** Rutgers Univ, BA, 49; Harvard Univ, MA, 50, PhD, 55. **CAREER** Res assoc, Russ Res Ctr, Harvard Univ, 51-53, teaching fel English, 53-54; instr English & humanities, Ohio Wesleyan Univ, 54-55; asst prof English, 55-59, assoc prof English, Slavic lang & lit, 59-64, chmn dept, 70-76, prof Comp Lit, English & Slavic Lang & Lit, Univ Chicago, 64-, chmn Dept Comp Lit, 65-, mem adv bd, Encycl Brittanica, 73. **RESEARCH** Modern novel; especially technique and comparative aspects; theory of criticism. **SELECTED PUBLICATIONS** Soviet Portraits, Mass Inst Technol, 55; Croce and contextualist criticism, Mod Philol, 8-59; Tolstoy's The Death of Ivan Ilych, and James' fictional imperatives, Mod Fiction Studies, winter 61; ed, Crime and Punishment and the Critics, Wadsworth, 61; Aut Caesar, aut Nihil, a study of Dostoevsky's moral dialectic, PMLA, 3/63; auth, Dostoevsky: The Major Fiction, Mass Inst Technol, 64; The Brothers Karamazov and the Critics, Wadsworth, 67; The Notebooks for Crime and Punishment, 67, The Notebooks for the Idiot, 68, The Notebooks for the Possessed, 68, ed & transl, The Notebooks for the Brothers Karamazov, 71 & ed, The Gambler and Paulina Suslova's diary, 72, Univ Chicago; auth, Tolstoy's Major Fiction, Univ Chicago, 78; Fathers and Sons: Russia at the Crossroads, Twayne, 93. **CONTACT ADDRESS** Dept of Slavic Language & Literature, Univ of Chicago, 1130 E 59th St, Chicago, IL 60637-1539. **EMAIL** e-wasiolek@uchicago.edu

WASOW, THOMAS ALEXANDER
PERSONAL Born 12/14/1945, New Rochelle, NY, m, 1971, 2 children **DISCIPLINE** THEORETICAL LINGUISTICS **EDUCATION** Reed Col, BA, 67; Mass Inst Technol, PhD (ling), 72. **CAREER** Asst prof ling, Hampshire Col, 72-73; asst prof, 74-78, Assoc Prof Ling and Philos, Stanford Univ, 78-95; prof ling and philos, Stanford Univ, 85-; Dean of undergraduate studies, Stanford Univ 87-91; dir, symbolic systems program, Stanford Univ 92-; assoc Dean of grad policy, Stanford univ 96-00. **MEMBERSHIPS** Ling Soc Am; Asn Comput Ling. **RESEARCH** Syntactic theory; psycholinguistics. **SELECTED PUBLICATIONS** Coauth, Syntactic Theory: A Formal Introduction, CSLI Publications, 99. **CONTACT ADDRESS** Dept of Ling, Stanford Univ, Stanford, CA 94305. **EMAIL** wasow@csl.stanford.edu

WATERS, HAROLD A.
PERSONAL Born 11/08/1926, Wilmington, NC, m, 1989, 3 children **DISCIPLINE** POET, FRENCH **EDUCATION** Harvard Univ, AB, 49; Univ Paris, dipl & cert, 51; Univ WA, MA, 54, PhD(Romance lang), 56. **CAREER** From instr to asst prof mod lang, Col William & Mary, 55-60; asst prof Romance lang, Carleton Col, 60-62; from asst prof to assoc prof French, 62-69, Prof French, 69- , prof emeritus, Univ RI; Founder & coordr, Claudel Newslett, 68-72; assoc ed, Claudel Studies, 72-. **HONORS AND AWARDS** Betsy Colquitt Awd for Poetry, 98; BBC Contest for peoms on Africa, 80; Community Writers Asn Poetry Contest, 96; elected to Asn des Ecrivains de Langue Francaise, 98; Phi Beta Kappa, Rhode Island Beta Chapter--elected: Honorary Mem, 89; VP, 93-93; Pres, 93-94; Hist 96-98. **MEMBERSHIPS** Am Asn Tchrs Fr; AAUP; Northeast Mod Lang Asn; African Lit Asn; Acad of Am Poets; Asn Pour l' dtude des Litteratures Africainesdes. **RESEARCH** Black French lit; French soc theater; Claudel. **SELECTED PUBLICATIONS** Auth, Philosophic progression in Anouilh's plays, Symposium, summer 62; A propos de la seconde version de l'Echange, Rev Lett Mod annual Paul Claudel issue, 65; Paul Claudel, Twayne, 70; The heroic years of French Social Theater, Mod Lang Studies, spring 75; Black Theater in French: A Guide, Editions Naaman, 78; coauth, Today's English, Hatier-Nouvelles Editions Africaines, 79; auth, Theatre Noir, Three Continents, 88; Sengal, Poems on Africa, March St Pr, 00; 180 poems in various books, anthologies, magazines. **CONTACT ADDRESS** Box 233, Saunderstown, RI 02874. **EMAIL** hwa8559u@postoffice.uri.edu

WATKINS, CALVERT WARD
PERSONAL Born 03/13/1933, Pittsburgh, PA, m, 1980, 4 children **DISCIPLINE** LINGUISTICS **EDUCATION** Harvard Univ, BA, 54, PhD(ling), 59. **CAREER** From instr to assoc prof, 59-66, chmn dept ling, 63-66, 69-70, 71-72 & 85-91, Prof Ling & Classics, 66-89, Victor S. Thomas Prof Linguistics & Classics, 89- ,Harvard Univ; Vis prof, Sch Celtic Studies, Dublin Inst Advan Studies, 61-62 & 81; Ctr Advan Study Behav Sci fel, 66-67; overseas fel, Churchill Col, Cambridge, 70-71; Ling Soc Am Collita Prof, Salzburg, 79; vis prof Ecole Normale, Univ Sorbonne, 83; NEH fel, 84-85; Guggenheim fel, 91-92. **HONORS AND AWARDS** Hon mem Royal Irish Acad, 68;

fel, Am Acad Arts & Sci, 73; mem, Am Philos Soc, 75; corresp fel, British Acad, 87; member associe, Acad des Inscriptions et Belles-Lettres, 99; (corresp. Stranger 90) festschrift, 98; Goodwin Award, Am Philol Asn, 98; gaisford lecture, Classics, Oxford, 00. **MEMBERSHIPS** Ling Soc Am (Pres, 89); Am Orient Soc; Philol Soc; hon mem Royal Irish Acad; Am Philol Soc; Soc Ling Paris. **RESEARCH** Indo-European; linguistics and poetics; Hittite and Anatolian. **SELECTED PUBLICATIONS** Auth, American Heritage Dictionary of Indo-European Roots, Houghton Mifflin, 85; ed, Studies in memory of Warner Cowgill, 1929-1985, de Gruyter, 87; ed, C. Watkins, Selected Writings, 2 v, Innsbrucker Beitrage zur Sprachwissenschaft, 94; auth, How to Kill a Dragon: Aspects of Indo-European Poetics, Oxford, 95. **CONTACT ADDRESS** Dept of Ling Sci, Harvard Univ, Boylston 314, Cambridge, MA 02138. **EMAIL** watkins@fas.harvard.edu

WATSON, JOHN A.
PERSONAL Born 07/08/1920, Greenville, SC, d, 2 children **DISCIPLINE** SPANISH **EDUCATION** Howard Univ, AB, 42; Univ Paris, cert French, 46; Columbia Univ, MA, 50; Cath Univ Am, PhD, 76. **CAREER** Instr Span & French, Va Union Univ, 48-50; instr, Howard Univ, 53; asst prof, 54-57, assoc prof, 59-76, prof Span & French, VA Union Univ, 76-, Danforth spec award, 57-58; assoc prof Span & French, Va State Col, 59-61. **MEMBERSHIPS** NEA; MLA; Am Asn Teachers Span & Port; Nat Asn Lang Lab Dir. **RESEARCH** Gongorism: Luis de Gongora, sixteenth century Spanish poet; metaphorical procedure of Gongora and Calderon. **CONTACT ADDRESS** Dept of Mod Lang, Virginia Union Univ, 1500 N Lombardy St, Richmond, VA 23220-1711.

WATSON, JOHN W.
PERSONAL Born 11/09/1917, Blacksburg, VA, m, 1941, 3 children **DISCIPLINE** LINGUISTICS, STATISTICS **EDUCATION** Va Polytech Inst, BS, 37; Univ Va, MA, 39, PhD (English philol), 41. **CAREER** Asst prof English, Tulane Univ, 45-46; analyst, US Dept Navy, 46-49; analyst, Armed Forces Security Agency, Nat Security Agency, 49-6 1; staff engr and scientist, Radio Corp Am, 61-64; Mem Tech Staff, Mitre Corp, 64-; Lectr, George Washington Univ, 46-58; consult, Govt Employees Ins Co, 52-54; mem, Architectural Bd Rev, Alexandria, Va, 54-57; lectr, Univ Vs Ext, 54-60. **MEMBERSHIPS** Old English phonology; statistical inference; computer simulation. **SELECTED PUBLICATIONS** Auth, Leadership Secrets of Attila the Hun, Mil Law Rev, Vol 145, 94; Unabsorbed Overhead Costs and the Eichleay Formula, Mil Law Rev, Vol 147, 95. **CONTACT ADDRESS** 8131 Saxony Dr, Annandale, VA 22003.

WATT, JONATHAN M.
PERSONAL Born 05/16/1957, Sydney, Australia, m, 1977, 4 children **DISCIPLINE** LINGUSTICS **EDUCATION** Univ Pittsburgh, PhD. **CAREER** Instr, Geneva Col; instr, Reformed Presby Theol Sem; pastor, Reformed Presby Church of North Am. **MEMBERSHIPS** Soc of Bibl Lit; Evangelical Theol Soc. **RESEARCH** Sociolingistics of Biblical literature. **SELECTED PUBLICATIONS** Auth, Code-Switching in Luke and Acts, 97. **CONTACT ADDRESS** 510 32nd St., Beaver Falls, PA 15010. **EMAIL** jwatt@geneva.edu

WATT, WILLIAM CARNELL
PERSONAL Born 04/23/1932, Philadelphia, PA, s, 4 children **DISCIPLINE** SEMIOTICS, LINGUISTICS **EDUCATION** Univ NC, AB, 54; Georgetown Univ, MSL, 59; Univ Pa, PhD(ling), 67. **CAREER** Systems analysis, Nat Bureau of Standards, 63-66; asst prof comput sci, Carnegie-Mellon Univ, 67-70; assoc prof, 70-80, Prof Ling & Semiotics, Univ Calif, Irvine, 80-, Consult, Bunker-Ramo Corp, 69-70, Nat Bureau of Standards, 69- & Tech Operations Res, 70-72. **MEMBERSHIPS** Semiotic Soc Am; AAAS; Soc Archit Historians. **RESEARCH** Cognitive semiotics; cognitive linguistics. **SELECTED PUBLICATIONS** Auth, Competing economy critera, Prob actuels en psycholinguistique, CNRS, Paris, 74; The indiscreteness with which impenetrables are penetrated, Lingua, 75; What is the proper characterization of the alphabet?, I: Desiderata, Visible Lang, 75 Iconic perspectives on linguistic explanation, Perspectives on Experimental Ling, John Benjamins BV, 79; Against evolution, Ling & Philos, 79; Iconic equilibrium, Semiotica, 79; What is the proper characterization of the alphabet?, II: Composition, 80 & What is the proper characterization of the alphabet?, III: Appearance, 81, Ars Semiotica; Signification And Its Discontents, Semiotica, Vol 0097, 1993; Critique Of Evolutionary Accounts Of Writing - Pettersson,Js, Semiotica, Vol 0098, 1994; Before Writing, Vol 1, From Counting To Cuneiform - Schmandtbesserat,D/, Semiotica, Vol 0099, 1994. **CONTACT ADDRESS** Sch Social Sci, Univ of California, Irvine, Irvine, CA 92717. **EMAIL** wcwatt@uci.edu

WAUGH, LINDA RUTH
PERSONAL Born 11/02/1942, Boston, MA **DISCIPLINE** LINGUISTICS, FRENCH **EDUCATION** Tufts Univ, BA, 64; Stanford Univ, MA, 65; Ind Univ, PhD(ling), 70. **CAREER** Asst prof, 71-76, assoc prof, 76-82, Prof Ling, Cornell Univ, 82-, Ford Found fel, 77; vis assoc prof ling, Yale Univ, 78; Nat Endowment for Humanities fel, 79-80. **MEMBERSHIPS** Ling Soc Am; Am Asn Teachers French; Semiotic Soc Am; Int Ling Asn. **RESEARCH** Semantics; structure of French; semiotics. **SELECTED PUBLICATIONS** Auth, Lexical meaning: The prepositions en and dans in French, Lingua, 76; Roman Jakobson's Science of Language, Peter de Ridder, 76; A Semantic Analysis of Word Order: Adjective Position in French, Brill, Leiden, Holland, 77; coauth, Basic Course in Susu/Susu: Cours de base, Ind Univ (in press); The context-sensitive meaning of the French subjunctive, In: Cornell Linguistic Contributions, Grammatical Studies, 79; coauth, The Sound Shape of Language, Ind Univ, 79; co-ed, The Melody of Language, Univ Pk Press, 80; Contributions to Historical Linguistics, Brill, 80; Marks Sign's Poems: Semiotics, Linguistics, Poetics, Toronto Semiotic Circle, 82; Degrees Of Iconicity In The Lexicon/, Journal Of Pragmatics, Vol 0022, 1994. **CONTACT ADDRESS** Dept of Mod Lang & Lit, Cornell Univ, 203 Morrill Hall, Ithaca, NY 14853-4701.

WAYMAN, ALEX
PERSONAL Born 01/11/1921, Chicago, IL, m, 1956 **DISCIPLINE** SANSKRIT & TIBETAN LANGUAGES **EDUCATION** Univ Calif, Los Angeles, BA, 48, MA, 49; Univ Calif, Berkeley, PhD, 59. **CAREER** Vis lectr Buddhism & Sanskrit, Univ Mich, 60-6 1; from asst prof to assoc prof Buddhism, Univ Wis-Madison, 61-66; vis assoc prof, 66-67, Prof Sanskrit, Columbia Univ, 67-. **HONORS AND AWARDS** Am Inst Indian Studies res grant, India, 63-64 & 76-77; Soc Sci Res Coun res grant, Japan, 76, Switz, 77. **MEMBERSHIPS** Am Orient Soc; Asn Asian Studies; Am Soc Study Relig; Soc Asian & Comp Philos; Int Asn Buddhist Studies. **RESEARCH** Sanskrit and Tibetan Buddhism; Indian philosophy; Tantrism. **SELECTED PUBLICATIONS** Auth, Analysis of the Sravakabhumi manuscript, Vol 17, In: University of California Publications in Classical Philology, Univ Calif, 61; coauth, Mkhas grub rje's Fundamentals of the Buddhist Tantras, Vol VIII, In: Indo-Iranian Monographs, Mouton, The Hague, 68; auth, Buddhism, In: Historia Religionum, Vol II, E J Brill, Leiden, 71; The Buddhist Tantras: Light on Indo-Tibctan Esotericism, Weiser, 73; coauth, The Lion's Roar of Queen Srimala: A Buddhist Scripture on the Tathagatagarbha Theory, Columbia Univ, 74; auth, Yoga of the Guhyasamajatantra: The Arcane Lore of Forty Verses, Motilal Banarsidass, Delhi, 77; Who Understands the four alternatives of the Buddhist texts?, Philos E & W, 1/77; Mind Only - A Philosophical And Doctrinal Analysis Of The 'Vijnanavada' - Wood,Te/, Journal Of The American Oriental Society, Vol 0112, 1992; Response To Tatz,Mark Review Of 'Ethics Of Tibet' - Bodhisattva-Section Of Tsong-Kha-Pa 'Lam Rim Chen Mo'/, Philosophy East & West, Vol 0044, 1994; Calming the Mind and Discerning the Real: Buddhist Meditation and the Middle View, from the Tibetan of Tson-kha-pa's Lam rim Chen mo, Columbia Univ, 78; The Realm Of Awakening - Chapter-10 Of Asanga 'Mahayanasangraha' - Griffiths,Pj, Hakamaya,N, Keenan,Jp, Swanson,Pl, Journal Of The American Oriental Society, Vol 0112, 1992; A Defense Of Yogacara Buddhism/, Philosophy East & West, Vol 0046, 1996. **CONTACT ADDRESS** Dept of Mid E Lang, Columbia Univ, Kent Hall, New York, NY 10027. **EMAIL** aw10@columbia.edu

WEAVER, ELISSA B.
PERSONAL Born 04/11/1940, Springfield, IL **DISCIPLINE** ITALIAN **EDUCATION** Univ Ill, Urbana, BS, 61; UCLA, MA, 65, PhD, 75. **CAREER** Instr, 68-72, Rutgers Univ; asst prof, 72-77, assoc prof, 77-89, prof, 89-, chmn, dept romance lang & lit, 94- Univ Chicago. **RESEARCH** Italian lit & lang in early modern period, women's lit. **CONTACT ADDRESS** Romance Langs and Lit, Univ of Chicago, 1050 E 59th St, Chicago, IL 60637. **EMAIL** e-weaver@uchicago.edu

WEBB, EUGENE
PERSONAL Born 11/10/1938, Santa Monica, CA, m, 1964 **DISCIPLINE** COMPARATIVE LITERATURE, RELIGION **EDUCATION** Univ Calif, Los Angeles, BA, 60; Columbia Univ, MA, 26, PhD(comp lit), 65. **CAREER** Asst prof English, Simon Fraser Univ, 65-66; asst prof, 66-76, Prof Comp Relig & Comp Lit, Univ Wash, 76-. **MEMBERSHIPS** Am Acad Relig. **RESEARCH** Twentieth century English, German and French literature; 18th century English; philosophy of history. **SELECTED PUBLICATIONS** Auth, Samuel Beckett: A Study of His Novels, 70 & The Plays of Samuel Beckett, 72 Univ Wash; Peter Owen, London; The Dark Dove: The Sacred and Secular in Modern Lit, 75 & Eric Voegelin: Philosopher of History, 81, Univ Wash. **CONTACT ADDRESS** Dept of English, Univ of Washington, Seattle, WA 98195.

WEBB, GISELA
PERSONAL Born 07/15/1949, San Juan, Puerto Rico, m, 2 children **DISCIPLINE** ISLAMIC STUDIES, COMPARATIVE RELIGION STUDIES, PHILOSOPHY OF MYSTICISM **EDUCATION** Temple Univ, PhD, 89. **CAREER** Assoc prof Dept Relig Stud, Seton Hall Univ, 89-; Phi Beta Kappa; NEH award. **MEMBERSHIPS** AAR; MESA; ACSIS. **RESEARCH** Medieval and contemporary developments of mysticism, esp Sufism womens studies. **SELECTED PUBLICATIONS** Tradition and Innovation in Contemporary American Islamic Spirituality, Muslim Communities in North America, SUNY Press, 94; Islam, Sufism, & Subud, Am Alternative Relig, SUNY Press, 95. **CONTACT ADDRESS** 125 Union Ave, Bala-Cynwyd, PA 19004. **EMAIL** webbgise@shu.edu

WEBBER, PHILIP ELLSWORTH
PERSONAL Born 12/02/1944, Akron, OH, m, 1966, 4 children **DISCIPLINE** GERMANIC PHILOLOGY **EDUCATION** Earlham Col, AB, 67; Univ Chicago, MA, 68; Bryn Mawr Col, PhD(Ger philol), 72. **CAREER** Instr English community col, Reutlingen, Ger, 70-71; asst prof Ger, ling & educ, Widener Col, 72-76; prof Ger, Ling & Dutch, Central Col, IA, 76-; Res counr, Shipley Sch, Bryn Mawr, 71-72; prog coordr Ger, Alternative Schs Proj, 71-72; instr Ger, Bryn Mawr Col, 72. **HONORS AND AWARDS** Mellon, 80, 81; Exxon, 85; NEH Fellowship, 77, 87; Outstanding Faculty Awd, 84, 89, 99; numerous IA Humanities Board grants. **MEMBERSHIPS** Int Ver Ned; Am Asn Teachers Ger; Maatschappij der Nederlandse Letterkunde. **RESEARCH** Mediaeval Netherlandic manuscripts; ethnic sociolinguistics. **SELECTED PUBLICATIONS** Auth, Pella Dutch: The Portrait of a Language and its Use in one of Iowa's Ethnic Communities, Ames, IA: IA State Univ Press, 88; A Late Medieval Devotional Anthology from Salzburg, Nonnberg Passion: Huntington Library HM 195, Commentary and Edition, Goppingen, GER: Kummerle, 90; chief coauth, Medieval Netherlandic Manuscripts in the Piermont Morgan Library, New York, Brussels: Archief-en Bibliotheekwezen in Belgie, 91; Kolonie-Deutsch: Life and Language in Amana, Ames, IA: IA State Univ Press, 93. **CONTACT ADDRESS** Dept of Mod Lang, Central Col, Iowa, 812 University St, Pella, IA 50219-1999. **EMAIL** webberp@central.edu

WEBER, CLIFFORD WHITBECK
PERSONAL Born 04/22/1943, Scranton, PA, m, 1967 **DISCIPLINE** CLASSICS **EDUCATION** Harvard Univ, AB, 65; Univ Calif, Berkeley, PhD, 75. **CAREER** Asst prof, 69-78, assoc prof classics, Kenyon Col, 78-89. **HONORS AND AWARDS** Harvard Col, Detur Prize for acad distinc, Louis Curtis Prize, Phi Beta Kappa; Kenyon Col Fac Develop Grants, 71, 72; NEH Sum Sem Grant at the Univ of Tex, 76. **MEMBERSHIPS** Am Philol Assn. **RESEARCH** Latin poetry. **SELECTED PUBLICATIONS** Art, Dodona Reneges: A Neglected Oxymoron in Georgics 1, Classical Philology, 91; auth, The Allegory of Virgil's Golden Bough, 95; art, Roscius and the Roscida Dea, Classical Quarterly, 96. **CONTACT ADDRESS** Kenyon Col, Ascension Hall, Gambier, OH 43022-9623. **EMAIL** weberc@kenyon.edu

WEDBERG, LLOYD W.
PERSONAL Born 02/29/1924, Fremont, NE, m, 1945, 2 children **DISCIPLINE** MODERN GERMAN AND ENGLISH WRITING **EDUCATION** Univ Mich, BA, MA, PhD. **CAREER** Prof, 61-, Dean, Continuing Prof Educ, 82-91-. **HONORS AND AWARDS** Grant, Exxon Edu Found. **MEMBERSHIPS** AATG, MLA. **RESEARCH** 19th Century German Prose. **SELECTED PUBLICATIONS** Pub(s), 19th Century German Novelle; connections between the German Narrenschiff and Katherine Anne Porter's Ship of Fools; auth, The Theme of Loneliness in Theodor Storms Novellen, Mouton, 64. **CONTACT ADDRESS** Dept of Eng, Univ of Detroit Mercy, 4001 W McNichols Rd, PO BOX 19900, Detroit, MI 48219-0900. **EMAIL** wedbergsyl@aol.com

WEDEL, ALFRED R.
PERSONAL Born 10/31/1934, Sevilla, Spain, d, 2 children **DISCIPLINE** GERMAN, SPANISH **EDUCATION** Univ Madrid, BA, 60; Univ Pa, MA, 65; PhD, 70. **CAREER** Instr, Marple Newtown High School, 61-65; Instr to Full Prof, Univ Del, 70-. **HONORS AND AWARDS** Excellence in Teaching Awd, Univ Del, 75; Res grant, Spanish Ministry of Educ, 88; Excellence in Teaching Awd, Univ Del, 95. **MEMBERSHIPS** AATG, AATSP, MLA, MACLAS, NETYLA, DCTFL, Medieval Soc. **RESEARCH** Germanic philology, Romance philology, Medieval society. **SELECTED PUBLICATIONS** Auth, "The 'Constative' and the 'Complexive' Aspects in Gothic and in the Old Bulgarian of the Zograph Codes," Germano-Slavica, (89): 195-208; auth, "El prejuicio y la tradicion literaria: el autor aleman Moscherosch y los 'Walsche' del siglo XVII," Revista de Filolologia y Linguistica de la Universidad de Costa Rica, (92): 33-37; auth, "Bulgarian Evidential, German subjunctive and the Category of Person," Germano-Slavica, (910: 25-41; auth, "Verbal Prefixation and the 'Complexive Aspect' in Germanic," Neuphilologische Mitteilungen, (97): 321-332; auth, "El estilo indirecto: categorias gramaticales y pragmatica," Revista Espanola de Linguistica Aplicada, 11 (97): 245-254; auth, "Alliteraton and the Prefix Ge- in Cynewulfs Elene." In: Journal of Englihs and Germanic Philology, 100 (01): 200-210, **CONTACT ADDRESS** Dept For Lang, Univ of Delaware, 18 Amstel Ave, Newark, DE 19716-2599. **EMAIL** fredy@udel.edu

WEIGEL, RICHARD DAVID
PERSONAL Born 02/01/1945, Teaneck, NJ, m, 1968, 1 child **DISCIPLINE** HISTORY, CLASSICS **EDUCATION** Dickinson Col, BA, 66; Univ Del, MA, 68, PhD, 73. **CAREER** From instr to asst prof hist, Univ Del, 72-76; asst prof, Univ RI, 75; from Asst Prof to Assoc Prof, 76-84, Prof Hist, Western Ky Univ, 84-, Dept Head Hist, 98-. **HONORS AND AWARDS** Nat Endowment for Humanities summer sem grants, 77 & 80; Vis Schol, Wolfson Col, Oxford Univ, 93-; Am Acad in rome Advisory Coun, 94-. **MEMBERSHIPS** Am Philol Asn; Am Numismatic Soc; Assn Ancient Historians; Soc Prom Roman Studies; Royal Numismatic Soc. **RESEARCH** Roman Repub-

lic; ancient numismatics; Roman religion. **SELECTED PUBLICATIONS** Coauth, Peace in the Ancient World, McFarland, 81; auth, Lepidus: The Tarnished Triumvir, Routledge, 92; Roman History in the Age of Enlightenment: The Dassier Medals, Revue Numismatique 36, 95; Roman Coins: An Iconographical Approach, Annali dell Istituto di Numismatica 42, 95; auth, "Roman Republican Generals and the Vowing of Temples," Classica et Medievalia 49 (98); auth, "The Anonymous Quadrantes Reconsidered," Annotazioni Numismatich Suppl 11 (98); author of numerous other articles. **CONTACT ADDRESS** Dept of Hist, Western Kentucky Univ, 1 Big Red Way, Bowling Green, KY 42101-3576. **EMAIL** Richard.Weigel@wku.edu

WEIGER, JOHN GEORGE
PERSONAL Born 02/06/1933, Dresden, Germany, m, 1955, 3 children **DISCIPLINE** SPANISH, LINGUISTICS **EDUCATION** Middlebury Col, BA, 55; Univ Colo, MA, 57; Ind Univ, PhD(Span), 66. **CAREER** Instr Span, Univ Colo, 55-57 & Lawrence Col, 57-58; from instr to assoc prof, 58-73, from asst dean to dean, Col Arts & Sci, 68-76, Prof Span, Univ VT, 73-, Consult, Eirikk Borue, Inc; vis lectr, Univ Bologna, Italy, 78. **MEMBERSHIPS** Renaissance Soc Am; MLA; Am Asn Teachers Span & Port; Comediantes; Asoc Int Hisp. **RESEARCH** Spanish comedia; Cervantes; linguistics. **SELECTED PUBLICATIONS** Auth, The Valencian Dramatists of Spain's Golden Age, 76 & Cristobal de Virues, 78, Twayne; Initial and extended speech in the theater of Guillen de Castro, In: Studies in Honor of Gerald E Wade, 78; La supercheria esta descubierta: Don Quijote and Gines de Pasamonte, Philol Quart, spring 78; The Individuated Self: Cervantes and the Emergence of the Individual, Univ Ohio, 79; Hacia la comedia: De los valencianos a lope, Cupsa, Madrid, 78; Las Hazanas del cid, Puvill, Barcelona, 80; The curious pertinence of Eugenio's tale in Don Quixote, Mod Lang Notes, 81; **CONTACT ADDRESS** Dept of Romance Lang, Univ of Vermont, Waterman Bldg, Burlington, VT 05405-0001.

WEINER, JACK
PERSONAL Born 01/13/1934, Baltimore, MD, m, 1968, 1 child **DISCIPLINE** SPANISH **EDUCATION** Univ Md, BA, 56; Middlebury Col, MA, 59, 63; Ind Univ, PhD, 68. **CAREER** Asst prof Span, Univ Kans, 66-70; assoc prof, 70-77, Prof Span, Northern Ill Univ, 77-00; vis prof, The Univ of Ill at Chicago, 01. **HONORS AND AWARDS** Ind Univ Fel, 64-65, 65-66; Inter-Univ Res Fel, IREX, 64-65; Univ Kans Summer Res Assistance, 67; N Ill Univ Summer Res, 72; Fulbright and IREX Grants, 75; Direccion General de Relaciones culturales Grant, Madrid, 75; Grant, N Ill Univ, 78; Res Grant, am Philos soc, 80, 83; Summer Grad School Grant, N Ill Univ Summer, 84, 86, 88. **MEMBERSHIPS** Am Asn Teachers Span & Port; Int Asn Hispanists; Ill Medieval Asn. **RESEARCH** Spanish Golden Age literature, especially the comedia and prose; Hispano-Russian literary and cultural relations, Medieval Spanish Literature. **SELECTED PUBLICATIONS** Auth, Mantillas in Moscovy: The Spanish Golden Age Theater in Tsarist Russia: 1672-1917, Humanities Ser, Univ Kans, 70; El Diario Espanol de Alexander Veselovskii, Cuadernos Hispanoamericanos, 70; Cancionero de Sebastian de Horozco, Utah Studies in Lit & Ling, 75; El escudeero y las prostitutas: Lazaro y el escuder o en el rio, Rev Signos, Vol IV, No 2 & Romance Notes, Vol XIII, No 2; coauth, Turgenev's Fathers and Sons and Galdos' Dona Perfecta, PMLA, LXXXVI: 19-23; Cervantes La Numancia And The Convenant Between God and Israel, Neophilologus, Vol 0081, 97; Los Ninos Y Los Locos Dizen Las Verdades', An Anti-Clerical Folktale By Horozco, Sebastian, De 1510-1580, Revista De Filologia Espanola, Vol 0076, 96; auth, "Espana como el Nuevo Pueblo Escogido enlapoesia epica medieval espanola," Cuadernos para investigacion de la literatura hispanica 25 (00): 177-209. **CONTACT ADDRESS** Dept For Lang, Northeastern Illinois Univ, 1560 N Clark St, No. 4203, Chicago, IL 60610. **EMAIL** amalia@aol.com

WEINER, NEAL O.
PERSONAL Born 07/24/1942, Baltimore, MD, 2 children **DISCIPLINE** PHILOSOPHY, CLASSICS **EDUCATION** St John's Col, Md, BA, 64; Univ Tex, PhD, 68. **CAREER** Asst prof philos, State Univ NY Col Old Westbury, 68-70; Assoc Prof Philos, Marlboro Col, 70-, Vis assoc prof philos, St Mary's Col, Notre Dame, IN, 77-78; tutor, Grad Inst St John's Col, NM, 78. **HONORS AND AWARDS** Wilson Fellow; Danforth Fellow. **MEMBERSHIPS** Am Philos Asn; Northern New Eng Philos Asn. **RESEARCH** Class philos; psychiatry and ethics. **SELECTED PUBLICATIONS** Auth, The Articulation of Thought, Marlboro Col, 86; The Harmony of the Soul, SUNY, 93 **CONTACT ADDRESS** Dept of Philos, Marlboro Col, General Delivery, Marlboro, VT 05344-9999.

WEING, SIEGFRIED
DISCIPLINE GERMAN **EDUCATION** Vanderbilt Univ, PhD. **CAREER** Dept head, Mod lang. **SELECTED PUBLICATIONS** Author 2 bk(s) & articles on, Ger novella; German Review Grammar, second-yr Ger textbk. **CONTACT ADDRESS** Dept of Modern Languages, Virginia Military Inst, Lexington, VA 24450.

WEIS, CAROL M.
PERSONAL Born 12/11/1949, Philadelphia, PA, m, 1 child **DISCIPLINE** FRENCH, ITALIAN **EDUCATION** Penn State, BA, 69; Villanova MA, 73; Univ Penn, MA, PhD. **CAREER** Lectrice, Universite de Dijon, 74-75; Asst Prof, La State Univ, 78-80; Instr, Univ Md, 80-84; Asst Prof to Prof, Southern Univ, 84-. **HONORS AND AWARDS** Res Grant, La State Univ, 79; Res Grant, Coun of southern Univ, 86-87; SCMLA Travel Grant, 89; ACLS Res Grant, 90-91; Fulbright Sen Res Grant, Univ Rome, 90-91; Elton c Harrison Scholar of the Year, 92; NEH Summer Seminar, 94; Bogliasco Foundation Fel, 99. **MEMBERSHIPS** Mod Lang Asn, Col Lang Asn, South Central Mod Lang Asn, Am soc of eighteenth Century Studies, Am Asn of Teachers of French, Am an of Teachers of Italian, Am Asn of Italian studies. **RESEARCH** Eighteenth-Century French Literature, Modern Italian Literature 1750-Present, women's Studies, Francophone Literature. **SELECTED PUBLICATIONS** Auth, Confused Epiphanies: L'abbe Prevost and the romance Tradition, Peter Lang Pub, 91; auth, From Margins to Mainstream: Feminism and fictional Modes in Italian Women's Writings (1969-1992), Univ Penn Press, 93; auth, Uncertain vocations and Other Stories by Anna Banti, forthcoming; auth, "Stranger than Life? Autobiography and Historical Fiction," in Gendering Italian fiction: feminist Revisions of Italian History, Fairleigh Dickenson Press, 99; auth, "Genre," "Tradition," "Bonding (Female)," "Friendship (Female)," "Activism (Twentieth Century)." "Novel, Feminist of the 1980s," "Dacia Maraini," in Feminist Encyclopedia of Italian Literature, Greenwood Pub Group, 97; auth, "Walcott's don Juans: comparing the Trickster in a Postmodern, Postcolonial World," Connotations, (96): 130-134; auth, "History, fiction and the Female autobiographical Voice," Romance Languages annual, (96): 273-278; auth, "Dacia Maraini," encyclopedia of Italian women Writers, Greenwood Pub Group, 95. **CONTACT ADDRESS** Dept For Lang, So Univ and A&M Col, 500 Jess Stone, Baton Rouge, LA 70813-5000. **EMAIL** cmarieweis@yahoo.com

WEISS, BENO
PERSONAL Born 08/07/1933, Fiume, Italy, m, 2 children **DISCIPLINE** ITALIAN LITERATURE **EDUCATION** NYork Univ, BA, 63, MA, 65, PhD, 71. **CAREER** Instr Ital, NY Univ, 66-69; asst prof Ital, Pa State Univ, 69-76; assoc prof Ital, Pa State Univ, 76-88; prof Ital, Pa State, 88 -; Inst Arts & Humanistic Studies res fel, Italy, 72, 74, 81, 91; Am Philos Soc fel, 78, 85, 91. **HONORS AND AWARDS** Tchg Awd, Col Lib Arts, Pa State Univ, 77; Kagey Awd; Cervantes Medal, NY Univ. **MEMBERSHIPS** MLA; Am Asn Tchrs Ital; Am Ital Hist Asn; Am Soc of Sephardic Studies; Am Asn Tchrs Spanish; Am Asn Italian Studies, Sons of Italy. **RESEARCH** 19th and 20th Century Italian lit., espec Italo Svevo, Pirandello and Calvino. **SELECTED PUBLICATIONS** Auth, Svevo's Inferiorita, Mod Fiction Studies, spring 72; Translation of a husband: a play in three acts by Italo Svevo, Mod Int Drama, fall 72; An Annotated Bibliography on the Theater of Italo Svevo, Pa State Univ, 74; Federico Garcia Lorca in Italy, Garcia Lorca Rev, spring-fall, 75; Italo Svevo, Boston:Twayne World, 87; Maria de Zayas y Sotomayor: El castigo de la miseria y La inocencia castigada, Valencia: Albatros ediciones, 90; Understanding Italo Calvino, Univ of South Carolina, 93; coauth, Beginnings and Discoveries. Polydore Vergil's De Inventoribus rerum. An Unabridged Translation and Edition with Introduction, Notes and Glossary, Nieuwkoop: De Graaf, 97; Drama Across the Centuries: A Style Guide, Penn State Univ, 81. **CONTACT ADDRESS** Dept of Span, Ital, and Port, Pennsylvania State Univ, Univ Park, 352 N Burrowes Bldg, University Park, PA 16802-6203. **EMAIL** bxw@psu.edu

WEISS, HERMANN FRIEDRICH
PERSONAL Born 06/17/1937, Beuel, Germany, m, 1997 **DISCIPLINE** GERMAN LANGUAGE & LITERATURE **EDUCATION** Univ Bonn, Staatsexamen, 63; Princeton Univ, MA, 67, PhD(Ger lit), 68. **CAREER** Lektor Ger, Univ St Andrews, 63-64; instr, Univ Ore, 64-65; from asst prof to assoc prof, 68-82, Prof Ger, Univ Mich, Ann Arbor, 82-; Book Review Ed, Mich Germanic Studies, 92-. **MEMBERSHIPS** MLA; Am Asn Teachers Ger; AAUP. **RESEARCH** Achim von Arnim; fiction from the 18th to the 19th century; 18th and 19th century drama; Heinrich von Kleist; Novalis. **SELECTED PUBLICATIONS** Auth, Vorspiel zur Revolution. Die Bewertung der Demut in den vierziger Jahren des 19 Jahrhunderts, Zeitschrift fur Deut Philol, 78; Ein unbekannter brief Heinrichs von Kleist an Marie von Kleist, Jahrbuch der Deutachen Schillergesellschaft, 78; Funde und Studien zu Heinrich von Kleist, Tingen: Niemeyer, 84; ed, Unbekannte B riefe von und an Achim von Arnim aus der Sammlung Varnhagen und anderen Bestanden, Berlin: Duncker & Humblot, 86; co-ed, Achim von Arnim, Werke, vol 6, Deutscher Klassiker Verlag, 92; author of other journal articles; auth, "Unbeachtete Zeugnisse zu Novalis' Wittenberger Studienzeit, Literaturwissenschafliches Jahrbuchder Gooresgesellschaft 38 (97): 27-61, auth, "Der Mittwochs- und der Professoreklub. Zur geselligkeit in Jena am Ausgang des achtzehnten Jahrhunderts," (99): 94-120; auth, "Ein unbekannter Brief Friedric Holderlins n Johann Gottfried Ebel vom Jahre 1799," Textkritische Beitrage 5 (99): 109-135. **CONTACT ADDRESS** Dept of Ger, Univ of Michigan, Ann Arbor, 812 E Washington St, Ann Arbor, MI 48109-1275. **EMAIL** hfweiss@umich.edu

WEISS, MICHAEL L.
DISCIPLINE CLASSICS **EDUCATION** Univ PA, BA, 87; Univ Vienna, extra-mural stud, 91-92; Cornell Univ, PhD, 93. **CAREER** Asst prof, Univ NC, Chapel Hill. **RESEARCH** Class linguistics; Greek and Latin linguistics; Indo-Europ linguistics. **SELECTED PUBLICATIONS** Auth, Old Church Slavonic spodu and Avestan spada-, Die Sprache 35,1, 93; On the Non-Verbal Origin of the Greek Verb naefein," Historische Sprachforschung, 94; Life Everlasting: Latin iugis 'everflowing', Greek Igiaew 'healthy', Gothic ajukduKs 'eternity' and Avestan yauuaeji- 'living forever', Munchener Studien zur Sprachwissenschaft 55 (94), 96; An Oscanism in Catullus 53, Class Philol, 96; Greek muriow'countless,' Hittite muri- 'bunch (of fruit),' Historische Sprachforschung 96. **CONTACT ADDRESS** Univ of No Carolina, Chapel Hill, Chapel Hill, NC 27599. **EMAIL** mweiss@email.unc.edu

WEISSENBERGER, KLAUS
PERSONAL Born 11/15/1939, Sydney, Australia, m, 1974 **DISCIPLINE** GERMAN LITERATURE **EDUCATION** Univ Hamburg, Staatsexamen, 65; Univ Southern Calif, PhD(Ger), 67. **CAREER** From asst prof to assoc prof, 67-77, chmn dept, 72-79, Prof Ger, Rice Univ, 77- **MEMBERSHIPS** Am Asn Teachers Ger; MLA; Int Asn Ger Studies; SCent Mod Lang Asn. **RESEARCH** Lyric poetry as a genre; German exile literature; development of lyric poetry from Rilke to Celan. **SELECTED PUBLICATIONS** Auth, Formen der Elegie von Goethe bis Celan, 69, Die Elegie bei Paul Celan, 69 & Zwischen Stein und Stern, Mystische Formgebung in der Dichtung von Else Lasker-Schuler, Nelly Sachs und Paul Celan, 74, Franke, Bern; Dissonanzen und neugestimmte Saiten--eine Typologie der Exillyrik, Literaturwissenschaftliches Jahrbuch, Vol 17, 76; Mythopoesis in German literary criticism, Lit & Myth, Vol 9, 79; Eine systematische Stiltypologie als Antwort auf einen dichtungsfrmeden Systemzwang, Jahrbuch fur Int Germanistik, Vol 12, 80; ed, Die deutsche Lyrik von 1945 bis 1975, Zwischen Botschaft und Spiel, 81. **CONTACT ADDRESS** Dept of Ger, Rice Univ, Houston, TX 77001.

WEISSTEIN, ULRICH
PERSONAL Born 11/14/1925, Breslau, Germany, m, 1952, 4 children **DISCIPLINE** COMPARATIVE LITERATURE, GERMAN **EDUCATION** Ind Univ, MA, 53, PhD(comp lit), 54. **CAREER** From instr to asst prof Ger & fine arts, Lehigh Univ, 54-58; from asst prof to assoc prof English & comp lit, 59-66, Prof Ger & Comp Lit, Ind Univ, Bloomington, 66-, Vis prof comp lit, Univ Wis-Madison, 66, Univ Vienna, 76 & Stanford Univ, 78, vis prof Ger, Deut Sommerschule, Middlebury Col, 70, Univ Hamburg, 71 & 82; Guggenheim Found fel, 73; dir, Ind Purdue Studienprogramm, Hamburg, 81-82. **MEMBERSHIPS** Am Asn Teachers Ger; MLA; Am Comp Lit Asn; Int Comp Lit Asn. **RESEARCH** Anglo-German and Franco-German relations; literature and the arts; German literature, especially since 1870. **SELECTED PUBLICATIONS** Auth, The Essence of Opera, Free Press, 64; Max Frisch, Twayne, 67; Einfuhrung in die vergleichende Literaturwissenschaft, Kohlhammer, Stuttgart, 68; ed, Expressionism as an International Literary Phenomenon, Akad Kiado, Budapest & Didier, Paris, 73; co-ed, Texte and Kontexte: Festschrift fur Norbert fuerst zum 65 Geburstag, Francke, Bern, 73; auth, Comparative Literature and Literary Theory: Survey and Introduction, Ind Univ, Bloomington, 73; ed, Literature and the other arts, Vol III, Proc IXth ICLA Cong, Innsbruck, 81; Vergleichende Literaturwissenschaft: Ein Forschungsbericht 1968-1977, Lang, Berne, 82. **CONTACT ADDRESS** 2204 Queens Way, Bloomington, IN 47401.

WEITZMAN, RAYMOND STANLEY
PERSONAL Born 06/23/1938, Los Angeles, CA, 1 child **DISCIPLINE** LINGUISTICS, JAPANESE LANGUAGE **EDUCATION** Univ Calif, Los Angeles, AB, 64; Univ Southern Calif, MA, 66, PhD(ling), 69. **CAREER** From asst prof to assoc prof, 71-76, chmn dept, 79-82, prof ling, Calif State Univ, Fresno, 77-, Proj dir grant, Nat Sci Found Instr Sci Equip Prog, 70-72. **MEMBERSHIPS** Ling Soc Am; Asn of Behavior Analysis; Phonetic Soc Japan; Acoust Soc Am. **RESEARCH** Acoustic phonetic properties of speech; the structure of the Japanese language; language acquisition. **SELECTED PUBLICATIONS** Auth, Lacuna in Generative Phonology: Contrast and Free Variation, Papers Ling, 72; coauth, Devoiced and Whispered Vowels in Japanese, Ann Bull Res Inst Logopedics & Phoniatrics, 76; Rehabilitation of a Patient with Complete Mandibulectomy and Partial Glossectomy, Am J of Otolaryngology, 80; Vowel Categorization and the Critical Band, Language and Speech, Vol 35 (1,2), pp 115-126; The Relative Perceptual Salience of Spectral and Durational Differences, in Proceedings of the 2nd International Conference on Spoken Language Processing, Banff, Alberta, Can, pp 1095-1098; How to Get the Horse to Open Its Mouth: Using the Concept Formation Paradigm in Speech Perception Research, in Honor of Frederick Brengelman on the Occasion of the 25th Anniversary of the Linguistics Department at California State University, Fresno, pp 141-149. **CONTACT ADDRESS** Dept of Ling, California State Univ, Fresno, 5245 N Baker, Fresno, CA 93740-8001. **EMAIL** raymondw@csufresno.edu

WELDON, JAMES
DISCIPLINE OLD; MIDDLE ENGLISH LITERATURE **EDUCATION** New Brunswick, BA, MA; Queen's, PhD. **CAREER** Assoc Prof **RESEARCH** Old and Middle English lit, medieval dream vision narrative and romance, genre theory. **SELECTED PUBLICATIONS** Auth, Decorative Reading: Some Implications of Ordinatio in Piers Plowman; Ordinatio and Genre in MS CCC 201: Piers Plowman; Gesture of Perception: The Pattern of Kneeling in Piers Plowman B.18-19; The Structure of Dream Visions in Piers Plowman; The Infernal Present: Auden's Use of Inferno III in The Chimeras. **CONTACT ADDRESS** Dept of English, Wilfrid Laurier Univ, 75 University Ave W, Waterloo, ON, Canada N2L 3C5. **EMAIL** jweldon@wlu.ca

WELLBERY, DAVID E.
PERSONAL Born 01/01/1947, Cooperstown, NY, m, 2 children **DISCIPLINE** GERMAN **EDUCATION** State Univ NY at Binghamton, BA, 69; Johannes Gutenberg Univ Mainz, 70; Yale Univ, PhD, 77. **CAREER** From Acting Asst Prof to Prof, Stanford Univ, 75-90; Prof/William Kurrelmeyer Prof, The Johns Hopkins Univ, 90-; Guest Prof, Rheinische Friedrich-Wilhelms Universitat Bonn, 80-81; Vis Assoc Prof, Princeton Univ, 84-85. **HONORS AND AWARDS** Woodrow Wilson Fel, declined, 69; Fulbright Fel, 69-70. **RESEARCH** Enlightenment, Romanticism, History of aesthetics, semiotics, lyric poetry, narrative theory, Lessing, Goethe, Kleist, Nietzsche. **SELECTED PUBLICATIONS** Auth, Lessing's "Laocoon": Semiotics and Aesthetics in the Age of Reason, Cambridge, 84; coauth, Goethe's "Harzreise im Winter": Eine Deutungs-Kontroverse, Paderborn, 84; auth, The Specular Moment. Goethe's Lyric and the Beginnings of Romanticism, Stanford, 96; auth, Schopenhauers Bedeutung fur die moderne Literatur, Munich, 99. **CONTACT ADDRESS** Dept Ger, Johns Hopkins Univ, Baltimore, 3400 N Charles St, Baltimore, MD 21218-2608. **EMAIL** wellbery@jhu.edu

WELLE, JOHN PATRICK
DISCIPLINE LITERATURE, ITALIAN **EDUCATION** St John's Univ, BA, 74; Ind Univ, MA, 81; PhD, 83. **CAREER** Asst prof to assoc prof, Univ Notre Dame, 83-89; vis assoc prof, Univ Mich, 92; vis assoc prof, Northwestern Univ, 93. **HONORS AND AWARDS** Raizis de Palchi Bk Awd, Acad Am Poets; NEH, 95, 01. **MEMBERSHIPS** MLA; SCS; AAIS. **RESEARCH** Modern poetry; film; film and literary interactions. **SELECTED PUBLICATIONS** Auth, The Poetry of Andrea Zanzotto: A critical Study of Il Galateo in Bosco, Bulzoni (Rome), 87; co-ed, transl, Peasants Wake for Fellini's Casanova, by Andrea Zanzotto (Univ Ill Pr, 1997). **CONTACT ADDRESS** 18820 Cherokee Ln, South Bend, IN 46637-4507. **EMAIL** welle.1@nd.edu

WELLES, MARCIA LOUISE
PERSONAL Born 06/17/1943, Bridgeport, CT, m, 1967, 2 children **DISCIPLINE** SPANISH LITERATURE **EDUCATION** Columbia Univ, AB, 65, PhD(Span), 71; Middlebury Col, MA, 66. **CAREER** Asst Prof Span, Barnard Col, Columbia Univ, 70-. **MEMBERSHIPS** MLA; Am Asn Teachers Span & Port. **RESEARCH** Seventeenth century Spanish prose; feminist studies in Spain and Latin America; relationship between literature and the visual arts. **SELECTED PUBLICATIONS** Auth, Style and Structure in Gracian's "El Criticon,"; auth, "Arachnes Tapestry: The Transformation of Myth in Seventeenth-Century Spain,"; ed, From Fiction to Metafiction: Essays in Honor of Carmen Martin Gaite. **CONTACT ADDRESS** Dept of Span Barnard Col, Columbia Univ, New York, NY 10028. **EMAIL** mlwll@columbia.edu

WELLINGTON, MARIE ANNETTE
PERSONAL Born 12/04/1953, Chicago, IL, s **DISCIPLINE** FRENCH LANGUAGE AND LITERATURE **EDUCATION** Wellesley Col, BA, 76; Harvard Univ, AM, 77; PhD, 81. **CAREER** Teaching Fel, Harvard Univ, 77-81; asst prof, Mich State Univ, 81-83; asst prof, Loyola Univ Chicago, 86-87; asst prof, Univ Notre Dame, 87-91; asst prof to prof, Mary Washington Col, 91-. **HONORS AND AWARDS** Durant Scholar, 76; Phi Beta Kappa, 76; Best Teaching Fel, 80, 81; Fel, Harvard Univ, 77-81; Fel, Univ of Notre Dame, 88. **MEMBERSHIPS** MLA, SAMLA, Am Soc for 18th Century Studies, Midwestern Am Soc for 18th Century Studies, Northeastern Am Soc For 18th Century Studies. **RESEARCH** French philosophical writings and prose fiction of the eighteenth century. **SELECTED PUBLICATIONS** Auth, The Art of Voltaire's Theater: An Exploration of Possibility, Peter Lang Publ, (NY, Bern), 87; auth, "Crossovers from Theater to Narrative in a Voltairian conte," Studies on Voltaire and the Eighteenth Century, vol 278, ed Haydn Mason, Voltaire Found, (90): 187-196; auth, "Unity and Symmetry of the Character of Tiberge," Romance Quart 38.1, (91): 27-37; auth, "Hercule, Mlle de St Yves and the Unity of 'L'Ingenu,'" Australian Jour of Fr Studies 28.1 (91): 5-16; auth, "Des Grieux: Person, Impersonation and Self-discovery," Studies on Voltaire and the Eighteenth Century, vol 296, ed Haydn Mason, Voltaire Found, (92): 43-52; auth, "L'Imagination, la raison et l'esthetique personnelle de Rousseau dans 'La Reine Fantasque,'" Moderna Sprak 87.2, (93): 173-179; auth, "Montesquieu's Troglodytes and Voltaire's Quakers: A Case of Ideological Kinship," Dalhousie Fr Studies 28, (94): 29-41; auth, "Mademoiselle de Saint-Yves: The Constant Catalyst," Studies on Voltaire and the Eighteenth Century, vol 332, ed Haydn Mason, Voltaire Found, (95): 121-132; auth, "Textual Elaboration in Two Versions of the Story of the Comte de Comminge," Altered Narratives: Female Eighteenth-Century French Authors Reinterpreted, ed Servanne Woodward, Mestengo Pr, (London, Can: 97): 41-63; auth, "Dying for Love? Three Case Studies: Prevost, Voltaire, Laclos," Dalhousie Fr Studies 45, (98): 3-17. **CONTACT ADDRESS** 904 Marye St, Fredericksburg, VA 22401-5629. **EMAIL** mwelling@mwc.edu

WELLS, COLIN
PERSONAL Born 11/15/1933, West Bridgeford, England, m, 1960, 2 children **DISCIPLINE** CLASSICAL STUDIES **EDUCATION** Univ Oxford, BA, MA, PhD. **CAREER** Prof and Chair, Univ Ottawa, 60; T Frank Murchison distinguished prof, 87-; dept ch. **HONORS AND AWARDS** Fellow of the Society of Antiquaries of London, Corresponding Member of the German Archaeological Institute; dir, sec can team excavations, carthage, tunisia, 76-86; dir, trinity univ excavations, 90-. **MEMBERSHIPS** Archaeological Institute of Am. **RESEARCH** Roman frontier studies, Roman, Africa. **SELECTED PUBLICATIONS** Auth, The German Policy of Augustus, 72; The Roman Empire, Harvard UP, 95. **CONTACT ADDRESS** Dept of Class, Trinity Univ, 715 Stadium Dr, San Antonio, TX 78212. **EMAIL** cwells@trinity.edu

WELLS, MARIA XENIA ZEVELECHI
DISCIPLINE FRENCH; ITALIAN **EDUCATION** Univ of Pisa, Italy, PhD, 59. **CAREER** Teacher, Am High Sch, Pisa, Italy and asst prof, Univ of Pisa, Italy, 57-62; lectr, Univ of Tex, 62-72; cur of Ital Collections, H. Ransom Hums Res Ctr, Univ or Tex, 73-97; adj prof, French & Italian; consultant, HRHRC, 97-. **HONORS AND AWARDS** Fulbright Scholar, 54-55; Inst of Am Studies in Rome Scholar, 56; App to the Libr Servs and Construct Act Adv Coun, 86, 89; App to attend the Conv of Ital Lang and Cult in Rome, Italy, Ital Ministry of Foreign Affairs, 87; J.R. Dougherty Jr. Found Grant, 87; Ital Private Found Grant, 89; Fulbright Res Grant, 91; App to the Fulbright Campus Screening Comt, 92; App mem fo the Am Comt for the Medici Arch Proj Inc. Florence and NY, 96 TIL Coun, the Soerette Diehl Fraser Transl Awd Adv Coun, 97; received title of Cavalier fo th Order of Merit of the Italian Republic, 92. **MEMBERSHIPS** Am Asn for Ital Studies; Associazione Internazionale di Studi di Lingua e Letteratura Italiana; Am Translators Asn; Fulbright Asn; Minerva Hist Asn; Nat Fulbright Alumni Asn; Soc for Ital Hist Studies; Nat Ital Am Found; Fulbright screening comit, 00. **RESEARCH** Carlo Levi; Bernard Simiot, gentic criticism of mss. "Le Maroc dans les livres de B.S." **SELECTED PUBLICATIONS** Auth, The Ranuzzi Manuscripts, in exhibit catalog, H. Ransom Hums Res Ctr Publs, 80; Annibale Ranuzzi e La Repubblica del Texas, 1842, in Il Carrobbio 10, 84; Una Biblioteca Italiana nel Texas, in Biblioteche Oggi, vol VII-n.1, 89; Libraries and Cultures, issue on the history of Italian libraries, twelve essays, vol 25/no. 3, 90; Italian Post-1600 Manuscripts and Family Archives in North American Libraries, 92; The Italian Collections Across the Centuries: Literature, Art, and Theatre, exhibit catalog as double issue of The Libr Chronicle, vol 21, nos. 2/3, 93; Fuochi d'Artificio: manoscritto del 1500, in FMR aprile, 95; I Paladini di Sicilia, in FMR dicembre, 95; auth, "Carlo Levi, la parola e l'immagine," Edizioni dell Orso, 98; auth, Carlo Levi, scrittura e pittura, atti del convegno, Roma 1996 Ed. Fahrenheit 451, Roma, 99. **CONTACT ADDRESS** Harry Ransom Humanities Research Center, Univ of Texas, Austin, Austin, TX 78713-7219. **EMAIL** mxwells@mail.utexas.edu

WENDLAND, ERNST R.
PERSONAL Born 10/14/1944, Washington, IA, m, 1971, 4 children **DISCIPLINE** AFRICAN LANGUAGES AND LITERATURE **EDUCATION** NW Col, BA, 68; Univ Wisc, MA, 75, PhD, 79; MST, 00. **CAREER** Instr, Lutheran Sem (Lusaka, Zambia), 68-; Lang coordr publ, Lutheran Church Cent Africa, 71-; transl adv, 75-96, transl consult, united bible soc, 96-; Vis Prof, U of Stellenbosch, South Africa **MEMBERSHIPS** New Testament Soc S Africa; Old Testament Soc S Africa **RESEARCH** Discourse, stylistic, and rhetorical analysis of Biblical and Bantu language texts, especially poetry, prophecy, and preaching. **SELECTED PUBLICATIONS** Ed, Discourse Perspectives on Hebrew Poetry in the Scriptures, United Bible Soc, 94; auth, The Discourse Analysis of Hebrew Prophetic Literature, Mellen Bibl Press, 95; Buku Loyera: An Introduction to the New Chichewa Bible Translation, Kachere Books, 98; Analyzing the Psalms, Summer Inst Ling, 98; auth, Preaching That Grabs the Heart, Kachere Books, 00. **CONTACT ADDRESS** Dept of State, 2310 Lusaka Place, Washington, DC 20521-2310. **EMAIL** wendland@zamnet.zm

WENSINGER, ARTHUR STEVENS
PERSONAL Born 03/09/1926, Grosse Pointe, MI **DISCIPLINE** GERMAN LITERATURE & LANGUAGE **EDUCATION** Dartmouth Col, BA, 48; Univ Mich, MA, 50, PhD, 58. **CAREER** From instr to prof, 55-77, Marcus Taff Prof Ger & Humanities, Wesleyan Univ, 77-, Sr Tutor, Col Lett, 63-, emer, 94. **HONORS AND AWARDS** Reynolds Fel, 50-52; Fulbright, 53-54, 54-55; Danforth, 59; Ford Found Grant, 70-71; Int Nationes Grants, 78, 84; Fel Ctr for the Humanities (Wesleyan), 74; Kenan Grants, 76, 78, 79. **MEMBERSHIPS** MLA; Am Asn Teachers Ger; Heinrich von Kleist Ges; Am translr Asn; Kafka Soc Am; Int Brecht Soc; Am Literary Translators Asn; Connecticut Acad of Arts and Sciences; Phi Beta Kappa; Phi Kappa Phi; The W.H. Auden Soc. **RESEARCH** Heinrich von Kleist; translations from German; Thomas Mann & Franz Kafka. **SELECTED PUBLICATIONS** Trans and co-ed, The Theater of the Bauhaus, Wesleyan Univ Press, 62, 2nd, 71; transl, Gunter Grass, Two States--One Nation? Harcourt Brace Jovanovich, 90; transl, Niklas Frank, In the Shadow of the Reich, Alfred A. Knopf, 91; contrib, The Anarchy of the Imagination, Johns Hopkins, 92; contrib, to Jewish Voices, German Words, Catbird Press, 94; auth, Paul Hogan and His Table, A memorial pamphlet, Wesleyan Univ, 00; auth, "The Letters of Norman Douglas, A Progress Report," in Norman Douglas, Schriftsteller, Vorarlberger Landesmuseum und Landesbibliothek (00). **CONTACT ADDRESS** Dept Ger Studies, Wesleyan Univ, Middletown, CT 06459. **EMAIL** awensinger@wesleyan.edu

WERTZ, CHRISTOPHER ALLEN
PERSONAL Born 06/13/1941, Lakewood, OH **DISCIPLINE** SLAVIC & GENERAL LINGUISTICS **EDUCATION** Columbia Univ, BA, 63; Univ Michigan, Ann Arbor, PhD(Slavic), 71. **CAREER** Asst prof Russ & ling, Washington Univ, St louis, 71-75 & Univ Wyo, Laramie, 75-77; asst prof, 77- 80, Assoc Prof Russian, Univ Iowa, Iowa City, 81-. **RESEARCH** Russian morphology; Polish morphology; interlinguistics. **SELECTED PUBLICATIONS** Auth, The number of genders in Polish, Can Slavonic Papers, Vol 19, No 1; entry on Baudouin de Courtenay, Mod Encycl Russ & Soviet Lit, Vol 2, 78; An alternate way of teaching verbs of motion in Russian, Russ Lang J, Vol 32, No 116; coauth, entry on Ferdinand de Saussure, Mod Encycl Russ & Soviet Lit, Vol 5, 81; auth, Some proposals regarding the creation of an international auxiliary language, Brit J Lang Teaching, Vol 19, No 3; The Pedagogical Case For Predicatives In Russian, Slavic And East European Journal, Vol 0038, 1994. **CONTACT ADDRESS** Dept of Russ, Univ of Iowa, 230 Jessup Hall, Iowa City, IA 52242-1316.

WESCOTT, ROGER WILLIAMS
PERSONAL Born 04/28/1925, Philadelphia, PA, m, 2 children **DISCIPLINE** LINGUISTIC ANTHROPOLOGY **EDUCATION** Princeton Univ, AB, 44 & 45, MA, 47, PhD(ling sci), 48; Oxford Univ, BLitt, 52. **CAREER** Ed & interviewer, Gallup Poll, 52; asst prof hist & human rels, Mass Inst Technol & Boston Univ, 53-57; assoc prof English & soc sci, Mich State Univ, 57-62, dir African lang prog, 59-62; prof anthrop & hist & chmn, Div Soc Sci, Southern Conn State Univ, 62-63; lectr sociol & anthrop, Wilson Col, 64-66; co-dir behav studies prog, 73-76, Prof Anthrop & Ling & Chmn Dept Anthrop, Drew Univ, 66-93, prof emer, 93-; Ford fel, Univ Ibadan, Nigeria, 55-56; foreign lang consult, US Off Educ, 61; West African Ling Surv grant, Ibadan, 61-62; consult ed, J African Lang, 62-; poetry ed, The Interpreter, 62-; ling fieldworker, Sierra Leone, 63; linguist, Bur Appl Social Res, Columbia Univ, 63-64; rev ed, Int Soc Comp Study Civilizations, 73-; pres prof humanities & soc sci, Colo Sch Mines, 80-81. **MEMBERSHIPS** Fel African Studies Asn; fel Am Anthrop Asn; fel AAAS; Int Ling Asn; Int Soc Comp Study of Civilizations. **SELECTED PUBLICATIONS** Auth, The Divine Animal: An Exploration of Human Potentiality, Funk, 69; coauth, A Pre-Conference Volume on Cultural Futurology, Am Anthrop Asn, 70; Human Futuristics, Univ Hawaii, 71; The Experimental Symposium on Comparative Futurology, Univ Minn, 71; auth, Traditional Greek conceptions of the future, In: The Experimental Symposium on Comparative Futurology, Univ Minn, 71; coauth, The Highest State of Consciousness, Anchor Bks, 72; auth, Seven Bini charms, Folklore Forum, 10/72; Metaphones in Bini and English, In: Studies in Linguistics in Honor of George L Trager, Mouton, The Hague, 73; Sound and Sense, Jupiter Press, 80. **CONTACT ADDRESS** 16-A Heritage Crest, Southbury, CT 06488-1370. **EMAIL** whilro@aol.com

WESSELSCHMIDT, QUENTIN F.
PERSONAL Born 02/03/1937, Washington, MD, m, 1963 **DISCIPLINE** THEOLOGY, CLASSICS (GREEK AND LATIN) **EDUCATION** St Paul's Jr Coll, Concordia, MO, 57; Concordia Sr Coll, BA, 59; Concordia Sem, BD, 63; Marquette Univ, MA, 69, Univ Iowa, PhD, 79. **CAREER** Pastor, Our Savior Lutheran Church, IL, 63-65; prof, Concordia Coll, WI, 65-73; instr, Milwaukee Lutheran High Schhol, WI, 74-77; prof, Concordia Sem, Mo, 77-. **MEMBERSHIPS** North Am Patristic Soc; Am Philol Asn; Class Asn of the Mid w and s. **RESEARCH** Patristics. **SELECTED PUBLICATIONS** Auth, chapter, Heritage, Motion; Chapter, Light from Above; articles, Concordia J. **CONTACT ADDRESS** 801 De Mun Ave, Saint Louis, MO 63105.

WEST, CORNEL
PERSONAL Born 06/02/1953, Tulsa, OK, d **DISCIPLINE** NEAR EASTERN LANGUAGES **EDUCATION** Harvard University, bachelor's degree (magna cum laude), Near Eastern languages and literature; Princeton Univeristy, PhD work. **CAREER** Yale University Divinty School, professor, 84; Le Monde Diplomatique, American correspondent; University of

Paris, educator, one semester; Princeton University, Dept of Religion, professor, Dept of Afro-American Studies, director; Harvard University, African American studies, currently. **HONORS AND AWARDS** Harvard University, Du Bois Fellow. **SELECTED PUBLICATIONS** Author: Race Matters, Beacon Press, 1993; co-author with bell hooks, Breaking Bread: Insurgent Black Intellectual Life, South End Press, 1992; Prophesy Deliverance! An Afro-American Revolutionary Christianity, Westminster/John Knox Press; The American Evasion of Philosophy: A Genealogy of Pragamatism, University of Wisconsin Press. **CONTACT ADDRESS** African American Studies, Harvard Univ, 12 Quincy St., Cambridge, MA 02138.

WEST, GRACE STARRY
PERSONAL Born 10/05/1946, Oklahoma City, OK, m, 1974, 4 children **DISCIPLINE** CLASSICS **EDUCATION** Scripps Col, BA, 68; Univ Calif, Los Angeles, CPhil, 72, PhD, 75. **CAREER** Univ of Dallas, 75- . **HONORS AND AWARDS** Fulbright full grant, 72-74, Univ Heidelberg. **MEMBERSHIPS** APA; Vergilian Soc; CAMWS; TCA; ACL; Nat Asn of Scholars. **RESEARCH** Greek and Roman literature and its survival to present times; teaching of Latin; myth; women in antiquity. **SELECTED PUBLICATIONS** Commentary, Cornelius Nepos, Dion, Bryn Mawr Commentaries, 85; commentary, Cicero, Pro Archia, Bryn Mawr Commentaries, 87; coauth, Four Texts on Socrates, rev ed, Cornell, 98. **CONTACT ADDRESS** Dept of Classics, Univ of Dallas, 1845 E Northgate Dr, Irving, TX 75062. **EMAIL** gwest@acad.udallas.edu

WEST, LARRY E.
PERSONAL Born 05/09/1942, Canada, KY, m, 1963, 2 children **DISCIPLINE** LANGUAGE; LITERATURE **EDUCATION** Berea Col, BA 64; Vanderbilt Univ, PhD, 69. **CAREER** Asst Prof, West Georgia Col, 67-69; Asst Prof, Assoc Prof, Prof, 69-, Wake Forest Univ. **HONORS AND AWARDS** Fullbright Grant for Study at Goethe Inst, 70; Amer Phil Soc Grant for Research, 80; Lower Division Advising Award, Wake Forest Univ, 95. **RESEARCH** Medieval German literature; The German Passion Play of Late Middle Ages **SELECTED PUBLICATIONS** Auth, The Saint Gall Passion Play, transl with an Introduction, 76; auth, The Alsfeld Passion Play transl with an Introduction, 97. **CONTACT ADDRESS** Dept of German and Russian, Wake Forest Univ, Winston-Salem, NC 27109. **EMAIL** westle@wfu.edu

WEST, WILLIAM C., III
DISCIPLINE CLASSICS **EDUCATION** Univ NC, Chapel Hill, PhD. **CAREER** Prof, Univ NC, Chapel Hill. **RESEARCH** Greek prose; Greek historians. **SELECTED PUBLICATIONS** Auth, "Socrates as a Model of Civil Disobediece in the Writings of Martin Luther King, Jr." Classical Bulletin 76, 191; auth, The Public Archives in Fourth Century Athens, Greek, Roman, and Byzantine Stud 30, 89; M. Ulpius Domesticus and the Athletic Synod at Ephesus, Ancient Hist Bull 4.4, 90; The Decrees in Demosthenes' Against Leptines, Zeitschrift fur Papyrologie und Epigraphik 107, 95; New Light on an Opisthographic Lead Tablet in Chapel Hill, XI Int Cong of Greek and Latin Epigraphy, Ed Quasar, 99 **CONTACT ADDRESS** Univ of No Carolina, Chapel Hill, Chapel Hill, NC 27599. **EMAIL** wwest@email.unc.edu

WEST-DURAN, ALAN
PERSONAL Born 01/31/1953, Havana, Cuba, m, 1993 **DISCIPLINE** SPANISH, LANGUAGE LITERATURE **EDUCATION** Univ Columbia, BA, 75; New York Univ, PhD, 94. **CAREER** Lectr, Babson Col, 93-96; vis prof, Brown Univ, 96-98; asst prof, Northern Ill Univ, 98-99; asst prof, Northeastern Univ, 99-. **HONORS AND AWARDS** Vasyl Stuo Trans Awd; NEF Arts; Latino Lit Poetry Prize; MAF Poetry Finalist. **MEMBERSHIPS** MLA; LASA; Advis Bd Cuban Studies. **RESEARCH** Caribbean; Latin America; US Latino/A Diaspora Studies; Spanish language. **SELECTED PUBLICATIONS** Auth, Dar nombres a la lluvia/Finding Voices in the Rain, Ediciones Verbum (Madrid), 95; auth, tropics of History: Cuba Imagined, Greenwood Pub (CT), 97; auth, El tejido de Asterion o las mascaras del logos, Ediciones Vigia (Matanzas, Cuba), 00; auth, Blacks in the Caribbean, Greenwood Pub (CT), forthcoming; auth, "Breathing Signs," Mich Quart Rev (96); auth, "The Stone and It's Images: The Poetry of Nancy Morejon," Stud 20th Cent Lit (96); auth, "El travestismo tranculturacion en tres novels de Severo Sarduy," Union (98); trans of, "Las hermanas Aguero," by Cristina Garcia, Knopf (97). **CONTACT ADDRESS** Dept Modern Language, Northeastern Univ, 447 Meserve Hall, Boston, MA 02115-5005.

WESTFALL, R.
PERSONAL Born 06/22/1960, Albion, NE, m, 1989, 2 children **DISCIPLINE** LINGUISTICS **EDUCATION** Univ Iowa, BA; Ind Univ, MA; Univ Tex at Austin, PhD. **CAREER** Lectr, Univ of Tex at Austin, 95-98; asst prof, Luther Col, 98-. **HONORS AND AWARDS** Phi Beta Kappa. **MEMBERSHIPS** ACTFL. **RESEARCH** Semantics, applied linguistics. **SELECTED PUBLICATIONS** Coauth, "Beyond Aspect: New Strategies for Teaching the Preterite & Imperfect," Hispania 79 (96): 55-61. **CONTACT ADDRESS** Dept Modern Lang, Luther Col, 700 College Dr, Decorah, IA 52101-1039. **EMAIL** westfaru@luther.edu

WETSEL, WILLIAM DAVID
PERSONAL Born Sweetwater, TX, s **DISCIPLINE** FRENCH **EDUCATION** Univ Texas, BA, 71; Brandeis Univ, MA, 74, PhD, 78; The Divinity School, Univ Chicago, MA, 88. **CAREER** Vis asst prof, Dept Fr & Ital, Univ Mass-Amherst, 78-79; Andrew Mellon fel, Dept Fr & Ital, Univ Pitts, 80-81; vis asst prof, Dept Fr & Ital, Univ Texas-Austin, 81-85; asst prof, Dept For Lang, Centenary Col Louisiana, 85-86; asst prof, Univ Hon Prog, Dept For Lang, Portland State Univ, 88-89; asst prof, 89-92, assoc prof, 92-95, Prof, Dept Lang & Lit, Arizon State Univ, 95- . **HONORS AND AWARDS** Fulbright Tchg Asst, 71-72; Woodrow Wilson Fel, 72-73; Gilbert Chinard Scholar, 80; res grant, Am Coun Learned Soc, 80; Fulbright Scholar Univ Paris, 82; Phi Beta Kappa. **MEMBERSHIPS** N Am Soc Fr 17th Century Lit. **RESEARCH** 17th Century French literature: Pascal/Port-Royal. **SELECTED PUBLICATIONS** Auth, L'Ecriture et le hasta The Persies of Pascal in the Exegetical Tradition of Poet-Royal, Ohio State Univ Pr, 81; auth, "Meaning, Structure and History in the Persies of Pascal," Biblio 17 (90); auth, Pascal's Pensees and Recent Critical Theory: Illumination or Deformation of the Text?, Papers on French Seventeenth-Century Literature, 93; La religion de Mahomet: Pascal and the Tradition of Anti-Islamic Polemics, Papers on French Seventeenth-Century Lit, 93; Pascal and Mitton: Theological Objections to l'honnetete in the Pensees in French Studies, 93; Pascal's Attack on Deism: the Pensees and the Quatrains du Deiste, Papers on French Seventeenth-Century Literature, 94; Copi: His Theater and Novels, Latin American Gay Literature: A Biographical and Critical Sourcebook, Greenwood Press, 94; Pascal and the Polemics of Christian Orthodoxy, Papers on French Seventeenth Century Literature, 95; auth, Pascal and Disbelief: Catechesis and Conversion in the Pensees, Cath Univ Am Press, 95; Pascal: Moralist or Theologian in De la morale a l'economie politique: dialogue franco-americain sur les moralistes francais, Publ de l'Univ de Pau, 96; Pascal on Death, Papers on French Seventeenth Century Literature, 99; La Mothe le Vayer and the Subversion of Christian Belief, Seventeenth-Century French Studies, 99; auth, L'Ecriture et le reste: The Persies of Pascal in the Exegetical Tradition of Port-Royal, Ohio State Univ Press,81; auth, Meaning, Structure and History in the Pensies of Pascal, Biblio 17,90 . **CONTACT ADDRESS** Dept of Lang & Lit, Arizona State Univ, PO Box 870202, Tempe, AZ 85287-0202. **EMAIL** David.Wetsel@asu.edu

WETZELL, RICHARD
PERSONAL Born 08/05/1961, Hannover, Germany, s **DISCIPLINE** GERMAN STUDIES **EDUCATION** Swarthmore Col, BA, 84; Columbia Univ, MA, 85; Fordham Univ, PhD, 91. **CAREER** Asst prof, Univ Maryland, 91-93; postdoc fel, Harvard Univ, 93-95; asst prof, Univ Maryland, 95-00; res fel, Ger Hist Inst, 00-. **HONORS AND AWARDS** James Bryant Conant Postdoc Fel; Guggenheim Res Gnt. **MEMBERSHIPS** AHA; GSA; HSS. **RESEARCH** Modern German, intellectual, political; legal history; history of science. **SELECTED PUBLICATIONS** Auth, Inventing the Criminal: A History of German Criminology, 1880-1945, Univ NC Press (Chapel Hill), 00; auth, "The Medicalization of Criminal Law Reform in Imperial Germany," in Institutions of Confinement: Hospitals, Asylums and Prisons in Western Europe and North America, 1500-1950, ed. Norbert Finzsch, Robert Jutte (Cambridge Univ Press, 96). **CONTACT ADDRESS** Dept Research, German Historical Institute, 1607 New Hampshire Ave, Washington, DC 20009.

WHALEY, LINDSAY
DISCIPLINE LINGUISTICS AND CLASSICS **EDUCATION** SUNY Buffalo, PhD, 93. **CAREER** From asst prof to assoc prof, Dartmouth Col. **MEMBERSHIPS** Linguistic Soc of Am, Assoc of Linguistic Typology. **RESEARCH** Lang typology; syntactic theory; word order variability; Bantu linguistics; Tungus linguistics. **SELECTED PUBLICATIONS** Auth, An Introduction to Language Typology: The Unity and Diversity of Language, Sage, 97; coed, Endangered Languages: Current Issues and Future Prospects, Cambridge Univ Press, 98; coauth, "Language Policy and the Loss of Tungusic Languages," Lang and Commun 19 (99): 373-386; coauth, "Revisiting Tungusic Classification for the Bottom Up: A Comparison of Evenki and Orogen," Lang 75 (99): 286-321; coauth, "Oroqen Dialects," Central Asiatic J 44 (00): 1-26; coauth, "Emphatic Reduplication in Oroqen and Its Altaic Context," Linguistics 38 (00): 1-18; auth "Language Loss and Culture Change among Manchu-Tungusic Peoples," in Archaeology, Language and History: Essays on Culture and Ethnicity, ed. J.E. Terrell (Westport, CT: Bergin & Garvey, 01), 103-124; auth, "The Case for Dialect Continua in Tungusic: Plural Morphology," in Non-Slavic Languages of the Former USSR, ed. D.A. Holisky and K. Tuite (forthcoming); coauth, "Evaluating the Impact of Literacy: The Tungusic Languages," in Languages in Conflict, ed. Johanna Destefano et al (Columbus, OH: OSU Press, forthcoming). **CONTACT ADDRESS** Dept of Linguistics, Dartmouth Col, 6086 Reed, Hanover, NH 03755. **EMAIL** lindsay.j.whaley@dartmouth.edu

WHELAN, ROBERT
PERSONAL Born 02/23/1932, Waltham, MA, m, 5 children **DISCIPLINE** GERMAN **EDUCATION** Boston Col, BS, 53; Cath Univ Am, MA, 59. **CAREER** Instr, Boston Col, 60-63; instr, Kings Col, 65-66; asst to assoc prof, Univ of Mass Lowell, 66-. **MEMBERSHIPS** MLA. **RESEARCH** Niederdeutsch, Medieval Manuscripts, Translations, Currently investigating Sallust as translated into early new high German, especially the prefaces to the German historians Von Pleningen, Schrayer and Von Lohausen. **SELECTED PUBLICATIONS** Auth, Karl Jaspers on Max Weber, Paragon House, (NY), 89. **CONTACT ADDRESS** Dept Foreign Lang, Univ of Massachusetts, Lowell, 1 University Ave, Lowell, MD 01854-2827.

WHIDDEN, SETH A.
DISCIPLINE LINGUISTICS, LANGUAGE, LITERATURE, FRENCH **EDUCATION** Union Col, BA; 91; Ohio St, MA, 94; Brown Univ, AM, 97; PhD, 00. **CAREER** Lectr, Univ de Rennes, 91-92; lectr, Univ RI, 00-01; asst prof, Univ Mo Columbia, 01-. **HONORS AND AWARDS** Manning Fel, Brown Univ, 00; Joukowsky Res Trav Grnt, Brown Univ, 99; Sum Grnt, Northeast MLA, 97, 99; Jeanne Marandon Res Grnt, 99; Phi Kappa Phi. **MEMBERSHIPS** Asn des Amis de Rimbaud; Soc des etudes romant et dix-neuviem; MLA. **RESEARCH** Nineteenth-century French literature and culture; poetry; gender issues; comparative studies. **SELECTED PUBLICATIONS** Auth, "Comment aller de Trouver une langue? A Plus de mots? Parcours d'une langue en devenir chez Rimbaud," eds. Graham Falconer, Andrew Oliver, Dorothy Speirs, Lang du XIXe siecle (99); auth, "Rimbaud Writing on the Body: Anti-Parnassian Movement and Esthetics in Venus Anadyomene?," Nineteenth Cen Fr Stud (99); auth, "Lire H?: Une question de temps," Lire Rimbaud App Crit (00); auth, "Marie Krysinska's Prefaces and Letters: Not du Voyant but d'une Defiante?," in Women Seeking Expression: France 1789-1914, eds. Rosemary Lloyd, Brian Nelson (00); auth, "Le corps feminin comme objet en mouvement: Arthur Rimbaud et Marie Krysinska," Poetiques de l'object en Fr (01); auth, "'A la Marie-Antoinette': Llerotisme bisexuel dans 'Reddition,'" Rev Verlaine (01); auth, "'Nous les prendrons, nous les comprendrons': une mini-querelle du Chat Noir," Hist Litt (01); ed, "Rythmes pittoresques," by Marie Krysinska (Univ Exeter Press, 01). **CONTACT ADDRESS** Dept Romance Lang and Lit, Univ of Missouri, Columbia, Columbia, MO 65211.

WHITE, CYNTHIA
PERSONAL Born Philadelphia, PA, m, 1992, 1 child **DISCIPLINE** CLASSICS **EDUCATION** Chestnut Hill Col, BA, 76; Villanova Univ, MA, 78; Cath Univ Am, PhD, 91. **CAREER** Asst prof, Cath Univ Am, 86-91; asst prof, assoc prof, Univ Ariz, 91-. **HONORS AND AWARDS** NEH, Medieval Pilg, 99; AM Acad Rome, Cen Hellen Stud Fel, 97; Wakonse Teach Awd, 96; CAMWS Awd. Comm Promo Latin, 95; Rome Prize, 88-89; Fulbright Res Grnt, Italy, 88-89; ACL McKinlay Scholar, 88. **MEMBERSHIPS** APA; ACL; CAMWS; NAPS; APS, Vergillian Soc. **RESEARCH** Greek and Latin Epithalamia; patristic and medieval Latin; medieval pilgrimage; Latin pedagogy; iopography of Rome. **SELECTED PUBLICATIONS** Auth, "De Raptu Proserpinae in the Church Fathers: The Sacrum Mysterium of Marriage," in Kaina; kai; Palaiav: Festschrift for Thomas P. Halton (Wash: DC, Cath Univ Am Press, 98): 244-269; auth, "Agnes," "Catherine of Alexandria," "Cecilia" "Eustochium," "Gervasius and Protasius," in Encycl of Early Christ, ed. E. Ferguson (Garland Pub Inc, 97); auth, "Music in the Latin Classroom," Teach Guide Adv Place Cour in Latin (01); auth, "Docere Docentes: Training New Teachers in an Ancient Discipline," in Latin for the 21st Century: From Concept to Classroom, ed. Richard A. LaFleur (Glenview, IL: Scott Foresman, Addison Wesley, 97). **CONTACT ADDRESS** Dept Classics, Univ of Arizona, ML371, Tucson, AZ 85712. **EMAIL** ckwhite@u.arizona.edu

WHITE, HUGH
PERSONAL Born 12/02/1936, Columbus, GA, m, 1960, 2 children **DISCIPLINE** HEBREW BIBLE **EDUCATION** Asbury Col, AB, 58; Candl Sch of Theol, BD, 61; Drew Univ, Phd, 67 **CAREER** Assoc Prof, 65-70 TN Wesleyan Col; asst prof to prof, 70-99, Rutgers Univ; emeritus prof, 99-, Rutgers Univ. **HONORS AND AWARDS** Outst Tch Awd, 70; RJ Dept of Higher Educ Awd, 85 **MEMBERSHIPS** Am Acad of Relig; Soc of Bibl Lit; Soc for Study of Narrative; Walker Percy Soc **RESEARCH** Ancient Narrative **SELECTED PUBLICATIONS** Auth, Narration & Discourse in the Book of Genesis, Cambridge, 91 **CONTACT ADDRESS** 47 Truman Ave, Haddonfield, NJ 08033. **EMAIL** hwhite@crab.rutgers.edu

WHITE, MARSHA
PERSONAL Born 04/02/1950, Boston, MA **DISCIPLINE** HEBREW BIBLE **EDUCATION** Harvard Univ, PhD, 94. **CAREER** Instr, Phillips Exeter Academy, 84-85; teaching fel, Harvard Col, 88, 90, 91; instr, Harvard Divinity School, fall 91; lect, Col of the Holy Cross, 93-94; instr, Hebrew Col, Brookline, MA, 94-95; lect, Univ MA, spring 95; instr, Classical Asn of New England Summer Inst, 94-98; instr, Temple Bethel, 95-96; vis asst prof, Wesleyan Univ, fall 96; lect, Andover Newton Theol School, 95-97; vis lect in Judaic Studies, Brown Univ, fall 97; instr, Havurat Shalom, Sommerville, MA, 97-98. **HONORS AND AWARDS** Listed in Who's Who in Biblical Studies and Archaeology, 2nd ed (1992-93), Washington, DC: Biblical Archaeology Soc, 93; Soc Biblical Literature Regional Scholar. **MEMBERSHIPS** Soc Biblical Lit; Asn for Jewish Studies. **RESEARCH** Ancient Israelite historiography. **SELECTED PUBLICATIONS** Auth, The Elohistic Depiction of Aaron: A

Study in the Levite-Zadokite Controversy, in Studies in the Pentateuch, ed, J. A. Emerton, supplemental to Vetus Testamentum 41, Leiden: Brill, 90; Jonah, in The Women's Bible Commentary, eds Carol Newsom and Sharon Ringe, Louisville: Westminster/John Knox, 92; Naboth's Vineyard and Jehu's Coup: The Legitimation, of a Dynastic Extermination, Vetus Testamentum 44, 94; The Elijah Legends and Jehu's Coup, Brown Judaic Studies 311, Atlanta: Scholars, 97; Review of Diversity in Pre-Exilic Hebrew by Ian Young, JBL 116, 97; Bathsheba, Elisha, Nathan, Uriah, in Eerdmans Dictionary of the Bible, eds, David Noel Freedman, Allen C. Myers, Astrid B. Beck, Grand Rapids: Eerdmans, forthcoming. **CONTACT ADDRESS** 16 Mountain Ave., Somerville, MA 02143-1309. **EMAIL** mesh33@aol.com

WHITE, PETER
PERSONAL Born 09/24/1941, Washington, DC, m, 1968, 2 children **DISCIPLINE** CLASSICAL PHILOLOGY **EDUCATION** Boston Col, BA, 63; Harvard Univ, PhD, 72. **CAREER** From asst prof to prof, Univ Chicago, 68-; chmn dept classics, Univ Chicago, 80-83, 97-98; ed, Classical Philology, 74-78; chmn comt publ, 82-84, vice pres publ, 85-87, Am Philol Asn. **HONORS AND AWARDS** Am Coun Learned Soc fel, 78-79; natl endow human fel, 94-95; Goodwin award merit, Am Philol Asn, 95. **MEMBERSHIPS** Am Philol Asn. **RESEARCH** Latin lit of the early Empire; Greek and Roman historiography. **SELECTED PUBLICATIONS** Auth, The authorship of the Historia Augusta, J Roman Studies, 67; Vibius Maximus the friend of Statius, Historia, 73; The presentation and dedication of the Silvae and the Epigrams, J Roman Studies, 74; The friends of Martial, Statius and Pliny, Harvard Studies in Class Philol, 75; Amicitia and the profession of poetry in early Imperial Rome, J Roman Studies, 78; Julius Caesar in Rome, Phoenix, 88; Maecenas Retirement, class philos, 91; Promised Verse: Poets in the Society of Augustan Rome, harvard univ press, 93; Julius Caesar and the Publication of Acta in Late Republican rome, chiron, 97. **CONTACT ADDRESS** Dept of Class, Univ of Chicago, 1010 E 59th St, Chicago, IL 60637-1512. **EMAIL** p-white@uchicago.edu

WHITENACK, JUDITH A.
PERSONAL Born 10/29/1944, Milwaukee, WI **DISCIPLINE** SPANISH LITERATURE **EDUCATION** Univ Wis, BS, 66, MA, 70, PhD(Span), 80. **CAREER** Lectr, Univ Wis, 78-79; Asst Prof Span, Univ Nev, Reno, 79-. **MEMBERSHIPS** MLA; Medieval Asn Pac; Philol Asn Pac Coast; Rocky Mountain Mod Lang Asn; Am Asn Teachers of Span & Port. **RESEARCH** Goldn age Spanish prose and poetry; Medieval Spanish poetry; Judaeo-Spanish poetry. **SELECTED PUBLICATIONS CONTACT ADDRESS** 1530 Hillside Dr, Reno, NV 89503.

WHITLARK, JAMES S.
DISCIPLINE WORLD LITERATURE **EDUCATION** Univ Chicago, PhD, 76. **CAREER** Prof, TX Tech Univ. **RESEARCH** Relig in lit. **SELECTED PUBLICATIONS** Auth, Illuminated Fantasy: From Blake's Visions to Recent Graphic Fiction, Assoc UP, 88; Behind the Great Wall: A Post-Jungian Approach to Kafkaesque Literature, Assoc UP, 91; coed, The Literature of Emigration and Exile, TX Tech, 92. **CONTACT ADDRESS** Texas Tech Univ, Lubbock, TX 79409-5015. **EMAIL** ditjw@ttacs.ttu.edu

WICKER, KATHLEEN O'BRIEN
PERSONAL Born 05/24/1937, Buffalo, NY **DISCIPLINE** NEW TESTAMENT, CLASSICAL LANGUAGES **EDUCATION** Mundelein Col, BA, 59; Loyola Univ, Chicago, PhD(hist western origins), 66. **CAREER** From instr to asst prof hist & classics, Mundelein Col, 65-71; asst prof, 71-77, assoc prof, 76-84, prof, 84- , New Testament, Mary W Johnson and J Stanley Johnson prof in Hum, 96- , Scripps Col. **HONORS AND AWARDS** Lectr classics, Loyola Univ Chicago, 70-71; partic, Corpus Hellenisticum Novi Testamenti Proj, 71-77; actg dean fac, Scripps Col, 79-81. **MEMBERSHIPS** Am Acad of Relig. **RESEARCH** NT and ECL; African Christianity. **SELECTED PUBLICATIONS** Auth, Plutarch: Mulierum Virtutes, In: Plutarch's Ethical Writings and the Early Christian Literature, E J Brill, Leiden, 78; auth, Porphyry, Letter to Marcella, Scholars, 87; auth, "Conversion and Culture: A Comparative Study of the Conversions of Paul and Christians," In: Ancient and Modern Perspectives on the Bible and Culture, Scholars (98); auth, "Mami Water in African Religion and Spirituality, In: African Spirituality forms, Meanings and Expressions, Crossroad (00). **CONTACT ADDRESS** Dept of Religion, Scripps Col, 1030 Columbia Ave, Claremont, CA 91711-3948. **EMAIL** kwicker@scripps@ol.edu

WICKERSHAM, ERLIS
PERSONAL Born 12/24/1941, Philadelphia, PA, m, 1985, 2 children **DISCIPLINE** GERMAN LANGUAGE & LITERATURE **EDUCATION** Harvard Unv, BA, 63; MA, 64; Bryn Mawr Col, PhD, 73. **CAREER** Asst prof to prof, rosemont col, 66-. **HONORS AND AWARDS** NEH Summer Inst, 83, 87, 93; Lindback Awd for Excellence in Teaching, 00. **MEMBERSHIPS** MLA, AATG, ASECS, ECIASECS, Goethe Soc of NA, Lessing Soc, Ger Soc of Pa, Ger Studies Assoc, Phi Beta Kappa. **RESEARCH** Goethe, German Romanticism, German Expressimism, Nelly Sachs, Monika Maron. **SELECTED PUBLICATIONS** Trans, of "Protestant Revolution," for Occasional Papers on Relig in Eatern Europe, (90); auth, "Ludwig Tieck's Der blonde Eckbert: Romantic Medievalism in Germany," Medievalism: The Year's Work 1991, (96); auth, "Entrepreneurial Empowerment of Women in Brecht's Dreigroschenoper: Film versus Theaterstuck," Annals of film and Lit, (97); auth, "The Aftermath of East-West Separation: Metaphorical Realities in Monika Maron's Animal triste," Schreiben imn heutigen Deutschland, Lang Publ Co, (98); auth, "Women as Agents of Suffering and Redemption in the Poetry of Nelly Sachs," Women and the Holocaust: Narrative and Representation, Studies in the Shoah XXII, (99): 63-87, auth, "Death and Transfiguration: Eduard and Ottilie in Goethe's Electrive Affinities in 1650-1850," Aesthetics and Inquiries in the Early Modern Era, forthcoming. **CONTACT ADDRESS** 770 Holly Rd, Wayne, PA 19087-2749. **EMAIL** eglass@rosemont.edu

WICKHAM, CHRISTOPHER
PERSONAL Born 05/26/1950, Reading, United Kingdom **DISCIPLINE** GERMAN **EDUCATION** Univ Reading, BA, 72; MPhil, 74; Univ Wis, PhD, 82. **CAREER** Lectr, Univ Regensburg, 74-76; ASST Prof, Allegheny Col, 82-85; Asst Prof, Univ Ill, 85-91; From Asst Prof to Assoc Prof, Univ Tex, 91-. **HONORS AND AWARDS** DAAD Fel, 72-73; King Edward VII Brit-Ger Found Fel, 73-74; Wis Alumni Res Found Fel, 76-77; DAAD Study Grant, 90, 95. **MEMBERSHIPS** MLA, AATG, SLS, NEMLA. **RESEARCH** Eighteenth, Nineteenth and Twentieth-Century German language, literature and culture, regional culture, German and Austrian cinema, German explorers, German dialect literature, Bavaria. **SELECTED PUBLICATIONS** Co-ed, Framing the Past: The Historiography of German Cinema and Television, Southern Ill UP (Carbondale, IL: 92); coauth, "The Attraction and Retention of Undergraduate Students," in Monatshefte 72 (80), 311-337; auth, "The Business of Survival: Aspects of Economy in Pevny/Turrini's 'Alpensaga'," Mod Lang Studies 24:3 (94): 55-61; auth, "Oil and Water: The Development of the Portrayal of Native Americans by 19th-Century German Painters," Yearbook of Ger-Am Studies 13 (96): 63-106; auth, Constructing Heimat in Postwar Germany: Longing and Belonging, Edwin Mellen, 99; auth, "Wohin und zuruck: Perspectives on Axel Corti's Jewish Trilogy," Crossing Cult Bounds in Contemp Austrian Lit and Cinema (forthcoming). **CONTACT ADDRESS** Dept Lang, Univ of Texas, San Antonio, 6900 N Loop 1604 W, San Antonio, TX 78249-1130. **EMAIL** cwickham@lonestar.utsa.edu

WIGODSKY, MICHAEL M.
PERSONAL Born 05/23/1935, Houston, TX **DISCIPLINE** CLASSICS **EDUCATION** Univ of Texas, BA, 57; Princeton Univ, MA, 59; PhD, 64. **CAREER** Prof Emer, Stanford Univ. **RESEARCH** Latin poetry; Hellenistic and Roman philos. **SELECTED PUBLICATIONS** Auth, Vergil and Early Latin Poetry, 72; Horace's Miser (Sat. 1.1.108) and Aristotelian Self-love, 80; The Alleged Impossibility of Philosophical Poetry, in Philodemus and Poetry, 94. **CONTACT ADDRESS** Stanford Univ, Bldg 20, Main Quad, Stanford, CA 94305. **EMAIL** wigodsky@leland.stanford.edu

WILCOX, JOHN CHAPMAN
PERSONAL Born 04/20/1943, Liverpool, England, m, 1967 **DISCIPLINE** SPANISH LITERATURE, POETRY **EDUCATION** Univ Bristol, BA, 65; Univ Tx Austin, PhD, 76. **CAREER** Teaching asst, Univ Tex Austin, 66-70; lects, Queens Col, 70-75; fel, Univ Cincinnati, 77-78, asst prof, 78-79; Univ Illinois, asst prof Span, 79-85, assoc prof Spanish, 85-96, prof Spanish, 96-, Dir Grad Studies dept Spanish, Italian and Portugues, 88-92, Int head: Dept of Spanish, Italian and Portuguese, 92-94, Univ Ill-Urbana, 79; Resident Dir-Educ Abroad Prog Univ Ca and Il, 86-88 and 94-96, Head of Dept of spanish, Italian and Portuguese, 00-. **HONORS AND AWARDS** Charles Phelps Taft Postdoctoral Fel, Univ Cincinnati, 77-78; Fel Ctr Advan Study, Univ Il-Urbana, 84; LAS Coun Awd, 87-88; LAS Dean's Awd for Excellence in Undergraduate Teaching 99-00. **MEMBERSHIPS** MLA; Am Asn Teachers Span & Port; Asoc Int de Hispanistas; Twentieth Century Span Assoc Am; Asoc de Literatura Femenina Hispanica; Sigma Delta Pi Span Hon Soc. **RESEARCH** The poetry of Juan Ramon Jimenez; Spanish poetry of the 20th Century: Women poets of Spain. **SELECTED PUBLICATIONS** Auth, Juan Ramon Jimenez: transformacion y evolucion poetica de cuatro temas fundamentales de su obra, Cuadernos Hispanoamericas CXXV, 81; Arbol arraigado y pleamar: respuesta a la transformacion de la decadencia y la estetica en Juan Ramon y Nietzsche, La Torre, 81; Naked versus Pure Poetry in Juan Ramon Jimenez, with Remarks on the Impact of W B Yeats, Hispania, 83; At Home and Beyond: New Essays on Spanish Poets of the Twenties, Soc Span and Span-Am Studies, 83; Self and Image in Juan Ramon Jimenez (Modern and Post-Modern Readings, Univ Ill, 87; After the War: Essays on Recent Spanish Poetry, Soc Span and Span-Am Studies, 88; Anales de la literatura espanola contemporanea, 91; Anales de la literatura espanola contemporanea, 93; Women Poets of Spain, 1860-1990: Toward a Gynocentric Vision, Univ Ill, 97. **CONTACT ADDRESS** Dept of Spanish, Italian and Portoguese, Univ of Illinois, Urbana-Champaign, 707 S Mathews Ave, 4080 FLB, MC-176, Urbana, IL 61801-3625. **EMAIL** j-wilcox@uiuc.edu

WILCOX, PHYLLIS PERRIN
DISCIPLINE LINGUISTICS **EDUCATION** Univ NMex, PhD. **CAREER** Asst prof, Univ NMex. **RESEARCH** Signed lang ling in both theoretical and pplied framworks; Metonymy and metaphorical mapping in Am Sign Lang. **SELECTED PUBLICATIONS** Coauth, The Use of Court Interpreters in New Mexico: A Handbook For Judges, Attorneys, and Interpreters, New Mexico Administrative Office of the Courts, (86): 65; coauth, "Acceptance of American Sign Language at the University of New Mexico: The History of a Process," Sign Lang Studies 59, 88; coauth, "A Commitment to Professionalism: Educational Interpreting Standards Within A Large Public School System," Sign Lang Studies, 68, 90; auth, "Dual Interpretation and Discourse Effectiveness in Legal Settings," Journal of Interpretation, 7, 95; coauth, "Gestural Expression of Modals in American Sign Language," eds. J. Bbybee & S. Fleischman, (Amsterdam: John Benjamins, 95): 135-162; auth, " Deontic and Epistemic Modals in ASL: A Discourse Analysis," ed. A. Goldberg, Conceptual Sturcture, Discourse and Language, (Stanford, CA, 96): 471-492; coauth, Learning to See: American Sign Language as a Second Language, Galludet Univ Press. **CONTACT ADDRESS** Univ of New Mexico, Albuquerque, Albuquerque, NM 87131. **EMAIL** pwilcox@unm.edu

WILCOX, SHERMAN E.
DISCIPLINE LINGUISTICS **EDUCATION** Univ NMex, PhD. **CAREER** Assoc Prof, Univ NMex. **RESEARCH** Deaf education, interpreter education, ASL literacy, signed language linguistics, signed language dictionaries and lexicography, the evolution of language, educational linguistics **SELECTED PUBLICATIONS** Auth, The Multimedia Dictionary of American Sign Language, Proc of Assets Conf, Asn Comput Machinists, 94; Struggling for a Voice: An Interactionist Approach to Literacy in Deaf Education, in V John-Steiner, C Panofsky, & L Smith, eds, Interactionist Approaches to Language and Literacy, Cambridge UP, 94; coauth, Signs of the Origins of Syntax, Current Anthrop, 94; Representation of the Dynamic Elements of Signs: Issues in the Development of the Multimedia Dictionary of American Sign Language, J of Contemp Legal Issues, Vol 6, 95; The Gestural Expression of Modals in American Sign Language, in S Fleischman & J Bybee, eds, Modality in Grammar and Discourse, John Benjamins, 95;The Gestural Expression of Modality in ASL, in J Bybee & S Fleischman, eds, Modality in Grammar and Discourse, John Benjamins, 95; Gesture and the Nature of Language, Cambridge UP, 95; Learning to See: American Sign Language as a Second Language, 2nd ed, Gallaudet UP, 96. **CONTACT ADDRESS** Univ of New Mexico, Albuquerque, Albuquerque, NM 87131. **EMAIL** wilcox@unm.edu

WILDBERG, CHRISTIAN
PERSONAL Born 02/12/1957, Flensburg, Germany, m, 1997, 1 child **DISCIPLINE** CLASSICS, ANCIENT PHILOSOPHY **EDUCATION** Cambridge Univ, PhD, 84; Marburg Univ, MTh, 85. **CAREER** Res Fellow, 84-87, Caius Coll Cambridge; Vis Lectr, 87-88, Univ of TX at Austin; Asst Prof, 88-94, Freie Univ Berlin; Res Fellow, 95-96, Center for Hellenic Studies, Washington; Assoc Prof of Classics 96-, Princeton Univ. **HONORS AND AWARDS** Res Grant-DFG; Res grant, Howard Found. **MEMBERSHIPS** Amer Philos Assoc; Amer Philo Assoc; **RESEARCH** Aristotle, Neoplatonism, Tragedy. **SELECTED PUBLICATIONS** Auth, Philoponus against Aristotle on the Eternity of the World, London, Duckworth, 87; John Philoponus Criticism of Aristotle's Theory of Aether, Peripatio vol 6, pp 274, Berlin, NY, 88; Simplicius against Philpopnus on the Eternity of the World, London, Duckworth, pp 95-135, 91; Hyperesie und Epiphanie, Zur Bedeutung und Funkiton der Gotter in den Dramen des Euripdes, in prog; Aristoteles, DeCaelo, Translation, into German and Commentary, in prog. **CONTACT ADDRESS** Dept of Classics, Princeton Univ, 108 East Pyne, Princeton, NJ 08544. **EMAIL** wildberg@princeton.edu

WILDNER-BASSETT, MARY E.
PERSONAL Born 10/26/1952, Billings, MT, m, 1978, 3 children **DISCIPLINE** GERMAN STUDIES, SECOND LANGUAGE ACQUISITION **EDUCATION** E IL Univ, BA, 74; Univ Wis, Madison, MA, 78; Ruhr Univ, Bochum, Germany, PhD, 83. **CAREER** Asst prof, Univ Hamburg, 83-86; asst prof, 86-93, assoc prof, 93-, fac, 91-, Univ AZ. **HONORS AND AWARDS** Small Grant, 90-91, Diversity Action Coun Awd, 94-95, Hum Tchg Initiative Awd, 96-97, Univ AZ; Fulbright Sen Res full maintenance Awd, 93-94; Burlington Fac Excellence Tchg Awd, 93; Instructional Computing Grant, 94-95; Awd to attend Wakonse Tchg Conference, 95. **MEMBERSHIPS** AATG; ACTFL; AAUSC. **RESEARCH** Second language acquistion and teaching; interlanguage pragmatics; pragmatics of multiple literacies. **SELECTED PUBLICATIONS** Auth, Improving Pragmatic Aspects of Learners' Interlanguage, Gunter Narr Verlag, 84; Gesprachsroutinen und -strategien fur Deutsch als Alltags- und Wirtschaftssprache, Goethe Institut, 85; "Intercultural Pragmatics and Proficiency: Polite Noises for Cultural Appropriateness," Int Rev of Applied Ling, 94; "The Language Discovery Environment in the German Classroom of the 21st Century," Die Unterrichtspraxis, 94; "Intercultural Pragmatics and Metapragmatic Knowledge: Tapping the Source Using the Pragmatic Differential," Jour of Intensive Eng Studies, 97; auth, "Positionality, Cognition, and Complexity as

Research Ideologies for Explorations in Interlanguage Pragmatics," in Cognitive Aspects of Foreign Language Learning and Teaching, ed. C. Riemer, Tubingen: Narr Verlag, 00. **CONTACT ADDRESS** Dept of German Studies, Univ of Arizona, ML 571, Tucson, AZ 85721. **EMAIL** wildnerb@u.arizona.edu

WILEY, RAYMOND A.
PERSONAL Born 10/30/1923, New York, NY, m, 1948, 8 children **DISCIPLINE** GERMAN, MYTHOLOGY & CLASSICAL LITERATURE **EDUCATION** Fordham Univ, AB, 46, MA, 48; Goethe Inst, Munich, cert, 56; Syracuse Univ, PhD(humanities), 66. **CAREER** Instr Ger & English, Boston Col, 47-48; from instr to assoc prof Ger, 48-71, dir lang lab, 70-77, actg chm dept mod lang, 76, actg chm dept classics, 76-78, Prof, 71-89, Adjunct Prof Emeritus Foreign Lang & Lit, Le Moyne Col, 89-, chm, Dept For Lang & Lit, 86-89. **HONORS AND AWARDS** Fordham Univ Encaenia award, 56; Fulbright Summer Teachers Awd to Germany, 56; NEH Summer Seminar, Stanford Univ, 80. **MEMBERSHIPS** Am Asn Teachers Ger. **RESEARCH** The Correspondence between John Mitchell Kemble and Jakob Grimm, 1832-52; 19th century German-English literary relations; Teutonic mythology; Biography of Alford J. Williams (1896-1958), Aircraft Pilot. **SELECTED PUBLICATIONS** Auth, Four unpublished letters of Jacob Grimm to John Mitchell Kemble, 1832-40, J English & Ger Philol, 7/68; ed, John Mitchell Kemble and Jacob Grimm, a Correspondence: 1832-1852, Brill, Leiden, 71; auth, From letters to life, Heights Mag, Le Moyne Col, fall 71; The German-American verse of Dr Franz Lahmeyer, Ger-Am Studies, spring 74; ed, Austausch, Cent NY Chap Am Asn Teachers Ger Newslett, Vols 1-5, 70-74; auth, Dear Harriet: Fanny Kemble's View of Centennial America, Pa Gazette, 7/76; Anglo-Saxon Kemble, The Life and Works of John Mitchell Kemble 1807-57: Philologist, Historian, Archaeologist, Brit Archaeol Rec, No 72: Anglo-Saxon Studies Archaeol & Hist, I: 165-273; ed, John Mitchell Kemble's Review of Jacob Grimm's Deutsche Grammatik, State Univ NY Ctr Medieval & Early Renaissance Studies, 81; transl, On the Origin of Language, Leiden, Brill, 84; auth, Tints and Texts, A Comparison of the Nibelungenlied's MS Illustrations with Its Narrative, Acta, X, 86; Grimm's Grammar Gains Ground in England, In: The Grimm Brothers & The Germanic Past, J. Benjamins, 90; auth, Science in Fiction: Aviation in Nevil Shute's Works, pub on web at http://web.lemoyne.edu/~wileyra/shutelif.htm. **CONTACT ADDRESS** Dept of Foreign Lang, Le Moyne Col, 1419 Salt Springs Rd., Syracuse, NY 13214-1300. **EMAIL** oparay@juno.com

WILHELM, JAMES JEROME
PERSONAL Born 02/02/1932, Youngstown, OH **DISCIPLINE** COMPARATIVE LITERATURE **EDUCATION** Yale Univ, BA, 54, PhD(comp lit), 61; Columbia Univ, MA, 58. **CAREER** From instr to asst prof English, Queens Col, 61-65; PROF COMP LIT, RUTGERS UNIV, NEW BRUNSWICK, 65-, Gen Ed, Garland Libr of Medieval Lit. **MEMBERSHIPS** MLA; Dante Soc; Mediaeval Acad Am; Am Comp Lit Asn. **SELECTED PUBLICATIONS** Auth, The Cruelest Month: Spring, Nature & Love in Classical & Medieval Lyrics, Yale Univ, 65; Seven Troubadours, Pa State Univ, 70; Medieval Song, Dutton, 71 & Allen & Unwin, 72; Dante and Pound: The Epic of Judgement, Univ Maine, 74; Arnaut Daniel's Legacy to Dante and to Pound, Italian Lit: Roots & Branches, Yale Univ, 76; The Later Cantos of Ezra Pound, Walker, 77; The Poetry of Arnaut Daniel, Garland, 81; IE Miglior Fabbro: The Cult of the Difficult in Daniel, Dante, and Pound, Maine, 82; In The Haunt Of The Priestess Of The Hidden Nest - A Tribute To Rudge,Olga, Paideuma-A Journal Devoted To Ezra Pound Scholarship, Vol 0026, 1997. **CONTACT ADDRESS** 165 E 35 St 3 E, New York, NY 10016.

WILKENS, ANN
PERSONAL Born 01/23/1944, Portsmouth, NH, m, 1966, 2 children **DISCIPLINE** CLASSICS **EDUCATION** Wellesley Col, BA, 66; Univ Pittsburgh, MA, 75; PhD, 90. **CAREER** Instr, Vasser col, 78-79; lecturer, Univ Pittsburgh, 86-94; lecturer, Winchester Thurston, 80-87; asst prof to assoc prof, Duquesne Univ, 94-. **HONORS AND AWARDS** Teach of the Year Awd; AAUW; Apple for the Tchr Awd; Mellon Fel; Tchg Asstshps and Felshps; Thomas Lawrence Fel; Presidential Sch awd; Noble K Dick Gnt; NEH. **MEMBERSHIPS** Am Philol Inst, Am Inst of Archaeol, Classical Asn of Midwest & S, Classical Asn of Atl States. **RESEARCH** Classical tradition. **SELECTED PUBLICATIONS** Auth, Villain or Hero: Sallust's Portrayne of Catiline; auth, "Sallust's Tullianum: Reality, Description and Beyond," in Rome and Her Monuments, Carducci Press, 00; auth, "Bernini and Ovid: Expanding the concept of Metamorphosis," in International Journal of the Classical Tradition, Vol 29. **CONTACT ADDRESS** Dept Classics, Duquesne Univ, 600 Forbes Ave, Pittsburgh, PA 15282-0001. **EMAIL** wilkins@duq2.cc.duq.edu

WILKIE, NANCY C.
PERSONAL Born 12/27/1942, Milwaukee, WI, m **DISCIPLINE** GREEK ARCHEOLOGY, CLASSICS **EDUCATION** Stanford Univ, AB, 64; Univ Minn, MA, 67, PhD(Greek), 75. **CAREER** Instr classics, Macalester Col, 72-75; adj instr, 74-75, adj asst prof classics, 75-79, Prof Classics & Socioanthrop, Carleton Col, 79-, Field dir, Phocis-Doris Exped, Loyola Univ, Chicago, 77-80; Dir, Grevena Project, 88-. **MEMBERSHIPS** Archaeol Inst Am, Pres, 98-; Am Philol Asn; Soc Prof Archaeologists; Soc Am Archaeol; Register of Professional Archaeologists. **RESEARCH** Prehistoric Greek archaeology; archeological sampling. **SELECTED PUBLICATIONS** Auth, The Nichoria Tholos & Area-IV-6, Hesperia, 75; Area I, Evacuations at Nichoria in Southwest Greece, Vol I, Minn, 78; Early Helladic Pottery from Phokis and Doris, Teiresias, 79; Shaft Graves at Nichoria, Temple Univ Aegean Symp, 81; ed. With W.D.E. Coulson Contributions to Aegean Archaeology, CAS, U of MN, 85; auth, Excavations at N. Choria. Vol 2 (U of MN Press) editor with W.A. McDonald, 92; The Earliest Farmers In Macedonia, Antiquity, Vol 0071, 1997; **CONTACT ADDRESS** Carleton Col, 1 N College St, Northfield, MN 55057-4044. **EMAIL** nwilkie@carleton.edu

WILLARD, CHARITY CANNON
PERSONAL Born 08/09/1914, Eureka, IL, w, 1944 **DISCIPLINE** FRENCH LITERATURE **EDUCATION** Hiram Col, AB, 34; Smith Col, MA, 36; Radcliffe Col, PhD, 40. **CAREER** Instr, Lake Erie Col, 40-41; head, Westbrook Sr Col, 42-45; vis lectr, Bennington Col, 49-50; vis prof, St Lawrence Univ, 50-51; lectr to prof, Lady Cliff Col, 61-80. **HONORS AND AWARDS** Ann Radcliffe Fel, 53-54; Bunting Inst, 62-64; Phi Beta Kappa; Ordre des Palmes Academiques, 84; Hiram Col Alumni Awd, 88; Smith Col Medal, 98. **MEMBERSHIPS** MLA, Medieval Acad, Renaissance, Soc, AAUP, Int Courtly Lit Soc. **RESEARCH** 15th Century French Literature, Christine de Pizan, The Court of Burgundy. **SELECTED PUBLICATIONS** Auth, Le Livre de la Paix of Christine de Pizan. Critical Edition, Mouton, (The Hague), 58; auth, Christine de Pizan: Her Life and Works, Persea Books, 85; auth, Le Livre de Trois Vertus de Christine de Pizan, Champion (Paris), 89; auth, The Writings of Christine de Pizan, Persea Books, (NY), 93; auth, Christine de Pizan, The Book of Feats of Arms and of Chivalty, Pa State Pr, (University Port), 99. **CONTACT ADDRESS** 11 Prospect St, Cornwall on Hudson, NY 12520-1114. **EMAIL** ccw@warwick.net

WILLEM, LINDA M.
PERSONAL Born 06/06/1949, Chicago, IL, m, 1991, 1 child **DISCIPLINE** SPANISH LITERATURE **EDUCATION** Univ Wi Milwaukee, BS, 71, MA, 77; Univ Calif Los Angeles, PhD, 88. **CAREER** Teaching asst, Univ Wi Milwaukee, 75-76; instr, 77-80, Alverno Col; teaching fel to teaching assoc, 80-86, Univ of Calif Los Angeles; instr to asst prof to assoc prof to dept head, 87-, Butler Univ. **HONORS AND AWARDS** Butler Academic Grants for archival res, Filmoteca Nacional, Madrid, 97-98; Nat Endowment, Humanities Summer Seminar for Col Teachers: Rhetorical Theory of Narrative, 95; Butler Academic Grants, archival res, Casa-Museo Perez Galdos, Las Palmas, Biblioteca Nacional, Madrid, 93-94; Del Amo Endowment Dissertation Fel, 86-87; Nancy N Wing Awd, Outstanding Performance, Doctoral Qualifying Exams, 85; James A Phillips Awd, Outstanding Article Published by a UCLA Student, 85; Nat Endowment, Humanities Summer Seminar, College Teachers: Case History & Fiction, 79. **MEMBERSHIPS** Int Assoc of Galdosian Scholars; Int Assoc of Hispanists, Amer Assoc of Teachers of Spanish & Portuguese; Soc for Study of Narrative Lit; Modern Lang Assoc; Soc for Cinema Stud; Sigma Delta Pi; Phi Sigma Iota; Phi Kappa Phi. **RESEARCH** 19th century Spanish lit & Spanish cinema **SELECTED PUBLICATIONS** Ed, A Sesquicentennial Tribute to Galdos 1843/1993, Newark, De, 93; auth, Test and Intertext: James Whale's Frankenstein in El espiritu de la colmena, Romance Lang Annual, 98; art, Almodovar on the Verge of Cocteau's La Voix humaine, Kterature/Film Quart, 98; art, Linearity and Circularity in Carlos Saura's Peppermint Frappe, Romance Lang Annual, 99; auth, Galdos's Segunda Manera: Thetorical Strategies and Affective Response, Univ of N Calif, 99. **CONTACT ADDRESS** Dept of Modern Foreign Lang, Butler Univ, 4600 Sunset Ave, Indianapolis, IN 46208. **EMAIL** lwillem@thomas.butler.edu

WILLIAMS, BRUCE
DISCIPLINE FILM THEORY, HISTORY, HISPANIC LANGUAGES & LITERATURES **EDUCATION** Univ Calif-Los Angeles, PhD, 86. **CAREER** Assoc prof. **RESEARCH** Film theory and cinema history and aesthetics. **SELECTED PUBLICATIONS** Publ on res interest. **CONTACT ADDRESS** Dept of Language and Cultures, William Paterson Col of New Jersey, 300 Pompton Rd., Wayne, NJ 07470. **EMAIL** williamsb@wpunj.edu

WILLIAMS, CHARLES GARFIELD SINGER
PERSONAL Born 05/17/1939, Mt Vernon, OH **DISCIPLINE** FRENCH LITERATURE, COMPARATIVE LITERATURE **EDUCATION** Kenyon Col, AB, 63; Oxford Univ, BA, 65; Yale Univ, MPhil, 69; Oxford Univ, MA, 70; Yale Univ, PhD(-Fr), 70. **CAREER** From instr to asst prof, 68-74, assoc prof French, 74-88, Prof, OH State Univ, 89-, chair, 89-95; Contrib ed, French 17, 79-. **HONORS AND AWARDS** Phi Beta Kappa; Fulbright Scholar, Hon Woodrow Wilson Scholar; Lounsbury Cross Scholar (Yale); G.R. Havens Prize (French, OSU). **MEMBERSHIPS** MLA; Mod Humanities Res Asn; Am Asn Teacher Fr; Am Soc 18th Century Studies; Fr Hist Soc. **RESEARCH** Sevigne; Valincour; 17th century French prose and academic eloquence. **SELECTED PUBLICATIONS** Auth, Valincour's life of guise, In: Literature and History in the Age of Ideas, OH State Univ, 75; ed, Literature and History in the Age of Ideas, OH State Univ, 75; Madame de Sevigne, G K Hall, 81; Memorialists, Historiography & History of Science and Medicine, In: Cabeen Bibliography, Suppl III, 82; Valincour, 91. **CONTACT ADDRESS** Dept of French, Ohio State Univ, Columbus, 1841 Millikin Rd, Columbus, OH 43210-1229.

WILLIAMS, DANIEL ANTHONY
PERSONAL Born 05/08/1942, Frederick, MD, m, 1963, 2 children **DISCIPLINE** SPANISH LANGUAGE & LITERATURE **EDUCATION** Univ Md, College Park, AB, 64; Johns Hopkins Univ, MA, 67, PhD, 72. **CAREER** Instr Span, Villa Julie Col, 66-67 & Sweet Briar Col, 67-71; asst prof, Va Wesleyan Col, 69; asst prof, 72-79, Assoc Prof & Chmn, Western MD Col, 79-. **RESEARCH** Contemporary Latin American narrative; comparative studies; 20th century Spanish poetry. **SELECTED PUBLICATIONS** Auth, Phantoms of the Afternoon (poem), Delta, 5/60; translr, War (poem), Brambler, 5/68 & Numbers (poem), Inlet, 5/72. **CONTACT ADDRESS** Dept of Foreign Langs, Western Maryland Col, 2 College Hill, Westminster, MD 21157-4390. **EMAIL** dwilliam@wmdc.edu

WILLIAMS, ERIC
PERSONAL Born 01/12/1950, Renton, WA, d, 1 child **DISCIPLINE** GERMAN **EDUCATION** Ariz State Univ, BA, 74; State Univ NYork, Albany, MA, 76; Univ Calif, Berkeley, PhD, 85. **CAREER** Asst prof, Lehigh Univ, 86-87; asst prof, Lafayette Col, 87-88; vis asst prof, Univ Haw, 88-91; asst prof, Tex A & M Univ, 91-93, assoc prof, 93-. **HONORS AND AWARDS** Ariz State Univ, BA with Distinction, 74; Fulbright-Hays travel grant to Germany, 76-77; German Academic Exchange (DAAD) Fel, Tubingen, 80-81; 10 Univ grants (internal), 85-2000; Distinguished Teaching Awd, Tex A & M Univ, 98. **MEMBERSHIPS** MLA, South Central MLA, Goethe Soc of North Am, Am Asn of Teachers of German, German Studies Asn. **RESEARCH** European modernism, expressionism, Goethe, Kafka, Trakl, Max Frisch, psychological approaches to literature film and film theory, critical theory, Holocaust studies/postwar American fiction. **SELECTED PUBLICATIONS** Ed and contribur, The Dark Flutes of Fall: Critical Essays on Georg Trakl, Studies in German Literature, Linguistics, and Culture, Columbia, SC: Camden House (91); auth, "Georg Trakl's Dark Mirrors," Modern Austrian Lit, 25 (92): 15-35; auth, The Mirror and the Word: Modernism, Literary Theory, and Georg Trakl, Lincoln & London: Nebr Univ Press (93); auth, "Incest and Ponytales: Max Frisch's Montauk," in Mimetic Desire: Narcissism in German Literature from Romanticism to Post-Modernism, Studies in German Literature, Linguistics, and Culture, Columbia, SC: Camden House (95):167-186; co-ed and contribur, Mimetic Desire: Narcissism in German Literature from Romanticism to Post-Modernism, Studies in German Literature, Linguistics, and Culture, Columbia, SC: Camden House (95): auth, "Schweigendes Tonen: Zur Wiederkehr der Floten," in Zyklische Kompositionsformen in Georg Trakls Dichtung, ed Karoly Csuri, Tubingen: Niemeyer (96): 149-167; auth, :Untergang der Spiegelbildwelt," in Interpretationen: Gedichte von Georg Trakl, ed Hans-Georg Reclam (99): 154-168; auth, Georg Trakl: The Shaping of an Image, Literary Criticism in Perspective, Columbia, SC: Camden House (forthcoming). **CONTACT ADDRESS** Dept Modern & Classical Lang, Texas A&M Univ, Col Station, 1 Tex A & M Univ, College Station, TX 77843-4238.

WILLIAMS, FREDERICK
PERSONAL Born Denver, CO **DISCIPLINE** CLASSICAL GREEK, LATIN LANGUAGE, LITERATURE **EDUCATION** Univ Tex, BA, 65; Univ Col, MA, 72; Cornell Univ, PhD, 76. **CAREER** Instr, Converse Col, 68-71; asst prof, Cornell Univ, 76-77; asst prof, assoc prof, dir, SIU Carbondale,77-. **HONORS AND AWARDS** SIUC Teach of Yr Awd, 84. **MEMBERSHIPS** APA **RESEARCH** Performance translations of Greek and Roman drama; elementary language instruction; Greek and Latin poetry. **SELECTED PUBLICATIONS** Auth, Elementary Classical Greek, SIU Press, 83, rev ed 91; auth, A Cry of Kings: Six Greek Dramas in Modern English, Stipes, 99; auth, "Neapolitanus II.C.32: a New Source for the Text of Pausanias," Scrip 36 (82): 190-218; auth, "Odysseus' Homecoming as a Parody of Homeric Formal Welcomes," Classic World 79 (86): 395-97; co-auth, "Lewes at Colonus: an Early Victorian View of Translation from the Greek," Mod Lang Rev 82 (87): 293-312. **CONTACT ADDRESS** Dept For Lang and Lit, So Illinois Univ, Carbondale, Carbondale, IL 62901-4521. **EMAIL** rickw@siu.edu

WILLIAMS, GARETH D.
PERSONAL Born 05/29/1965, Wales, s **DISCIPLINE** CLASSICS **EDUCATION** Cambridge Univ England, BA 86. **CAREER** Columbia Univ, asst prof, 95-98. **MEMBERSHIPS** APA **RESEARCH** Silven Latin; Pros and Poetry. **SELECTED PUBLICATIONS** Auth, Banished Voices: Readings in Ovid's Exile Poetry, Cambridge, 94. **CONTACT ADDRESS** Dept of Classics, Columbia Univ, 614 Hamilton Hall, MC 2861, New York, NY 10027. **EMAIL** gdw5@columbia.edu

WILLIAMS, JOHN HOWARD
PERSONAL Born 11/19/1946, Louisville, KY, m, 1969, 2 children **DISCIPLINE** FRENCH LANGUAGES & LITERATURE, CLASSICS **EDUCATION** David Lipscomb Col, BA, 67; Univ Wis-Madison, MA, 68, PhD(French), 72. **CAREER** Instr French, Tenn Technol Univ, 68-69; Fulbright advan teaching fel Am lit, Univ Besancon, 71-72; asst prof French, Eastern Ky Univ, 72-74; asst prof, 74-76, assoc prof, 76-82, Prof French & Chmn Dept, Abilene Christian Univ, 82-. **MEMBERSHIPS** MLA; Am Asn Teachers Fr. **RESEARCH** Contemporary French culture; 16th century French Poetry. **CONTACT ADDRESS** Abilene Christian Univ, Station Box 824, Abilene, TX 79601.

WILLIAMS, JOSEPH M.
PERSONAL Born 08/18/1933, Cleveland, OH, m, 1960, 2 children **DISCIPLINE** ENGLISH, LINGUISTICS **EDUCATION** Miami Univ, BA, 55, MA, 60; Univ Wis, PhD(English), 66. **CAREER** Instr English, Miami Univ, 59-60; from instr to assoc prof, 65-76, Prof English, Univ Chicago, 76-, Consult med writing, Am Med Asn, 66. **MEMBERSHIPS** MLA; Lang Soc Am; Col English Asn. **RESEARCH** Stylistics; rhetoric; generative grammars. **SELECTED PUBLICATIONS CONTACT ADDRESS** Dept of English, Univ of Chicago, 5845 Ellis Av, Chicago, IL 60637-1476.

WILLIAMS, LYNN BARSTIS
PERSONAL Born 07/10/1946, Detroit, MI; United States, D **DISCIPLINE** COMPARATIVE LITERATURE, ART HISTORY **EDUCATION** Univ of IL, PhD, 74; SUNY-Albany, MLS, 76 **CAREER** Librn III, 89-, Auburn Univ; Assoc Prof, 76-89, Volun St Comnty col **HONORS AND AWARDS** AL Libr Asn Col and Univ Div awd for outstand contrib to prof lit **MEMBERSHIPS** Am Libr Asn; AL Hist Asn; AL Libr Asn **RESEARCH** AL art colonies, Southern Prints. **SELECTED PUBLICATIONS** Auth, Printmaking as a Bozart of the South, 1914-1947, Southern Quarterly, 98; American Printmakers, 1880-1945: An Index to Reproductions and Biocritical Information, Scarecrow, 93; Images of Scottsboro Souther Cultures 6:1 (Spring 00), 50-65 Another Provincetown? Alabama's Gulf Coast Art Colonies at Bayou La Batre and Coden Gulf South Historical Review 15:2 (00) 41-58. **CONTACT ADDRESS** Reference Dept, Auburn Univ, Auburn, AL 36849-5606. **EMAIL** willily@auburn.edu

WILLIAMS, MARIA ROSA OLIVERA
DISCIPLINE SPANISH LITERATURE **EDUCATION** Univ Toledo, BAS, 76; Ohio State Univ, MA, 78; PhD, 83. **CAREER** Assoc prof. **HONORS AND AWARDS** Fac fel of the Helen Kellogg Inst for Int Studies; Teachers as Scholars; The Kaneb Award in the Col of Arts and Letters for Excellence in Undergraduate Education; The Helen Kellogg Inst Residential fel; The Nat Endowment for the Humanities fel; The American Philos Soc fel; The Presidential fel. **RESEARCH** Spanish American literature of the 19th and 20th centuries; feminist criticism; contemporary women authors. **SELECTED PUBLICATIONS** Auth, La poesia gauchesca de Hidalgo a Hernandez; pubs on Uruguayan literature in exile, Mario Benedetti, Armonia Somers, Cristina Peri-Ross, Juan Gelman, Jose Emilio Pacheco, modernization in turn of the century Uruguay, Delmira Agustini, Alfonsina Storni, Gabriela Mistral, Teresa Porzecanski, Andrea Blanque, and Juan Carlos Onetti. **CONTACT ADDRESS** Romance Languages and Literatures Dept, Univ of Notre Dame, Notre Dame, IN 46556. **EMAIL** Olivera-Williams.1@nd.edu

WILLIAMS, PHILIP F. C.
PERSONAL Born, AR, m, 1990, 1 child **DISCIPLINE** CHINESE LITERATURE **EDUCATION** UCLA, MA, 81, PhD, 85. **CAREER** Vis asst prof, Chinese, 86, UCLA; contract escort, Chinese interpreter, 86-96, US Dept of St, Office of Language Svcs; asst prof, Chinese, 86-92, Ariz St Univ; post doc res fel, 90-91, Fairbank Center for East Asian Research, Harvard Univ; asst prof, 91-92 Univ of Vermont; assoc prof, Chinese Literature and Interdisciplinary Humanities, 93-99, Ariz St Univ; prof, Chinese Literature and Interdisciplinary Humanities, Ariz St Univ, 00-. **HONORS AND AWARDS** Phi Beta Kappa, 78; UCLA Alumni Asn Awd for Academic Achievement, 81; Humanities Res Awd, AZ St Univ, 89; Svc Awd, AZ St Univ, 97; Pres Southwest Conf on Asian Stud, 96-97. **MEMBERSHIPS** Council of Conf Member of the Asn for Asian Stud; Exec Bd Mem of the Southwest Conf on Asian Stud; Exec Comm of the Am Asn for Chinese Comparative Lit; AZ Beta Chapter of the Phi Beta Kappa Honorary Soc. **RESEARCH** Chinese literature and society, esp in 20th century; Chinese language and cultural history. **SELECTED PUBLICATIONS** Auth, Village Echoes: The Fiction of Wu Zuxiang, Westview Press, 93; auth, Chinese the Easy Way, Hauppauge, NY Barron's Ed Series, 99; auth, Selected Papers of the 1997 Southwest Conference on Asian Studies, Tempe: Southwest Conf on Asian Stud, 98. **CONTACT ADDRESS** Dept of Languages and Lit, Arizona State Univ, PO Box 870202, Tempe, AZ 85287-0202. **EMAIL** pfwms@juno.com

WILLIAMSON, KEITH
DISCIPLINE INTERPERSONAL COMMUNICATION, COMMUNICATION THEORY **EDUCATION** Temple Univ, PhD. **CAREER** Asst prof, Director of the Basic Course. Chair Depart Speech Commun,Wichita State Univ. **SELECTED PUBLICATIONS** Publ, Communication Education; co-auth, Leading Interpersonal Communication Textbook. **CONTACT ADDRESS** Wichita State Univ, 1845 Fairmont, Wichita, KS 67260-0062. **EMAIL** williamson@elliott.es.twsu.edu

WILLIS, WILLIAM HAILEY
PERSONAL Born 04/29/1916, Meridian, MS, m, 1943, 4 children **DISCIPLINE** CLASSICAL PHILOLOGY **EDUCATION** Miss Col, AB, 36; Columbia Univ, AM, 37; Yale Univ, PhD(Greck), 40. **CAREER** Instr classics, Yale Univ, 40-42; assoc prof Greek & Latin, Univ Miss, 46-47; prof Greek & Latin & chmn dept classics, 47-63; Prof to Prof Emer Greek, Duke Univ, 63-; Fund Advan Educ fac fel, Harvard Univ, 52-53; mem managing comt, Am Sch Class Studies Athens, 53-, vchmn, 79-81; vis prof class lang, Univ Tex, 57-58; vis prof classics, Univ NC, 59, 63-64, 66; fac fel theol, Church Divinity Sch Pac, 59; sr ed, Greek, Roman & Byzantine Studies, 59-79; vis scholar, Fac of Relig, Oxford Univ, 61-62, vis mem, Brasenose & Queen's Cols, 61-62; Am Philos Soc Penrose Fund res grant, 62; Am Coun Learned Soc fac res grant, 62; corresp mem, Inst Antiquity & Christianity, 68-; Guggenheim fel, 80-81. **MEMBERSHIPS** Archaeol Inst Am; Am Philol Asn (pres, 72-73); Southern Class Asn (pres, 58-60); Southern Humanities Conf (secy, 56-58); Class Asn Mid W & S (pres, 66-67). **RESEARCH** Greek philology; papyrology; Coptic studies. **SELECTED PUBLICATIONS** Auth, A Parchment Palimpsest of Plato, Archiv fur Papyrusforschung, 74; Cession of Catoecic Land, Collectanea Papyrologica I, Bonn, 76; Recent Papyrological Work in North America, Studia Papyrologica, 76; Two Literary Papyri in an Archive from Panopolis, Ill Class Studies, 78; The Letter of Ammon of Panopolis to his Mother, Papyrologica Bruxellensia, 79; Three Robinson Papyri, Bull Am Soc Papyrologists, 79. **CONTACT ADDRESS** Dept of Class Studies, Duke Univ, 236 Allen Bldg, PO Box 90103, Durham, NC 27708-0103. **EMAIL** whwillis@acpub.duke.edu

WILLS, JEFFREY
DISCIPLINE CLASSICS **EDUCATION** Harvard Univ, PhD, 88 **CAREER** Assoc Prof, 88-99, Univ of WI. **HONORS AND AWARDS** Fulbright Scholar, Ukraine, 97-98 **RESEARCH** Latin Literature **CONTACT ADDRESS** Dept of Classics, 212 N Broom St, Madison, WI 53703. **EMAIL** wills@ucef.org

WILSON, DON
DISCIPLINE FRENCH LITERATURE **EDUCATION** Trinity Col, MA; PhD. **RESEARCH** Twentieth century literature; contemporary novel. **SELECTED PUBLICATIONS** Auth, pub(s) on Andre Gide, critical theory and contemporary criticism. **CONTACT ADDRESS** Dept of French, Univ of Waterloo, 200 University Ave W, Waterloo, ON, Canada N2L 3G1. **EMAIL** wdwilson@watarts.uwaterloo.ca

WILSON, DONNA M.
PERSONAL Born 02/25/1947, Columbus, OH, m, 1968 **DISCIPLINE** SPANISH **EDUCATION** Ohio State Univ, BA, 73, MA, 76; Univ Salamanca, Spain, Univ Wash, doctoral studies. **CAREER** Prof, 86-98, chair for lang, 90-94, chair arts & hum, 94-98, Highline Col; assoc dean acad aff, Greenfield Community Col, 98-. **HONORS AND AWARDS** Phi Theata Kappa Teaching Excellence, 90; Phi Beta Kappa; Pathfinder Awd, 95; Who's Who, 95-00. **MEMBERSHIPS** ACTFL; MLA; NAWE; AAHE; Coun of Academic Deans, Mass. **SELECTED PUBLICATIONS** Rev, Modern Language Journal, 87-; rev, Hispania, 87-; auth, "The Microcomputer vs. the Language Laboratory: New Technology or Deja Vu?", FACTC Focus, 92; auth, "A Journal Entry from Spain," Crosscurrents, Nov 93; auth, "Building Bridges: Community Col and High School Articulation," Managing the High School Foreign Language Dept: A Handbook for Teachers and Administrators, 96; auth, "An Alternative Lesson Plan: Preparing to Teach in a Two-Year Community Col," ADFL Bulletin, 96; auth, "I Speak Spanish to God, Italian to Women, French to Men and German to My Horse," ADFL Bulletin, 97. **CONTACT ADDRESS** Greenfield Comm Col, 1 College Dr, Greenfield, MA 01301. **EMAIL** wilsond@gcc.mass.edu

WILSON, JOE BRANSFORD, JR.
DISCIPLINE SOUTH ASIAN STUDIES, RELIGIOUS STUDIES **EDUCATION** Univ Wis, Madison, BA, MA; Univ Va, PhD. **CAREER** Assoc prof Philos and Relig, asst ch and chair-elect, dept Philos and Relig, Univ NC, Wilmington. **RESEARCH** Yogacara School of Buddhism. **SELECTED PUBLICATIONS** Auth, Translating Buddhism from Tibetan: An Introduction to the Language of Literary Tibetan and the Study of Philosophy in Tibetan, Snow Lion, 92; Problems and Methods in the Translation of Buddhist Texts from Tibetan, in Buddhist Translations: Problems and Perspectives, Tibet House, 95; Tibetan Commentaries on Indian Shastras, in Jose Cabezon and Roger Jackson, eds, Tibetan Literature: Studies in Genre, Snow Lion, 96; Persons, Minds, and Actions: Indo-Tibetan Analyses of the Person in Anglo-American Perspective, in Ninian Smart and B Srinivasa Murthy, eds, East-West Encounters in Philosophy and Religion, Popular Prakashan, 96; The Monk as Bodhisattva: a Tibetan Integration of Buddhist Moral Points of View, J of Relig Ethics 24.2, 96. **CONTACT ADDRESS** Univ of No Carolina, Wilmington, Bear Hall, Wilmington, NC 28403-3297. **EMAIL** wilsonj@uncwil.edu

WILSON, JOSEPH BENJAMIN
PERSONAL Born 10/11/1928, Houston, TX, m, 1947, 4 children **DISCIPLINE** GERMANIC LANGUAGES AND LITERATURE **EDUCATION** Rice Univ, BA, 50, MA, 53; Stanford Univ, PhD, 60. **CAREER** From instr to asst prof, 54-63, Assoc Prof Ger, Rice Univ, 63-86, prof, 86-98, prof emer, 98-; Humboldt Found fel, Univ Kiel, 65-66 & Univ Marburg, 79. **HONORS AND AWARDS** Disting Serv Awd, Concordia Hist Inst, St. Louis, 86. **MEMBERSHIPS** Am Asn Teachers Ger; Soc Advan Scand Studies. **RESEARCH** Germanic philology; Texas Wendish-Germans; computerized lexicography; Paleo-Indian archaeology. **SELECTED PUBLICATIONS** Auth, A conjecture on the second Merseburg charm, Rice Univ Studies, 69; Unusual German lexical items from Lee-Fayette County, In: Texas Studies in Bilingualism, de Gruyter, Berlin, 70; Probleme der Wortindexarbeit, In: Literatur und Datenverarbeitung, Niemeyer, Tubingen, 72; Extended Rime in Otfrid, Rice Univ Studies, 76; ed, Texas and Germany: Crosscurrents, Rice Univ, 77; English of German Americans in Texas, In: Languages in Conflict, Univ Nebr Press, 81; A prelim report on a Clovis-Plainview site, Bull Tex Archeol Soc, 80; Earliest Anglicisms in Texas German, Yearbk Ger-Am Studies, 81; ed, Baptismal Records of Serbin, TX, 1854-83, 85. **CONTACT ADDRESS** Dept of German, Rice Univ, Houston, TX 77001. **EMAIL** jwilson@rice.edu

WILSON, JOSEPH P.
DISCIPLINE CLASSICS **EDUCATION** Univ Toledo, BA; Univ IA, PhD. **CAREER** Assoc prof, Univ of Scranton. **RESEARCH** Greek and Latin poetry; Greek tragedy; 20th-century Italian Women's Writing; Roman hist; Roman law. **SELECTED PUBLICATIONS** Auth, Defending an Unwed Stepmother: Catullus 64.402, The Death of Lucan: Suicide and Execution in Tacitus, The Hero and the City: An Interpretation of Sophocles' Oedipus at Colonus. **CONTACT ADDRESS** Dept of For Lang(s) and Lit(s), Univ of Scranton, Scranton, PA 18510.

WILTROUT, ANN ELIZABETH
PERSONAL Born 08/03/1939, Elkhart, IN **DISCIPLINE** SPANISH **EDUCATION** Hanover Col, BA, 61; Ind Univ, MA, 64, PhD, 68. **CAREER** Vis asst prof Span, Ind Univ, Bloomington, 68-69; asst prof foreign lang, 69-71, Assoc Prof Foreign Lang, Miss State Univ, 71-87; prof of For Lng, 87-; Nat Endowment for Humanities fel-in-residence for col teachers, 77-78. **HONORS AND AWARDS** Distinguished Alumni, Hanover College, 74. **MEMBERSHIPS** MLA; Am Asn Teachers Span & Port; SCent Mod Lang Asn; SAtlantic Mod Lang Asn; AAUP. **RESEARCH** Spanish Renaissance and Golden Age literature. **SELECTED PUBLICATIONS** Auth, A Patron and a Playwright in Renaissance Spain: The House of Feria and Diego Sanchez de Badajoz, LindonL Tameses, 87; auth, The Lazarillo de Tormes and Erasmus Opulentia Sordida, Romanische Forschungen, Vol 69; Hacia algunas interpretaciones dramaticas de la leyenda de Santa Barbara, Filologia, Vol 15; Women in the Works of Antonio de Gueriara, Neophilologus, Vol 60; Quien espere desespera: El suicidio en el teatro de Juan del Encina, Hispanofila, Vol 72; Gines de Pasamonte: The Picaro and his Art, Anales Cervantinos, Vol 17; Gomez Suarez de Figueroa, Patron od Diego Sanchez de Badajoz's Recopilacion en metro, Bull Comediantes, Vol 31; auth, Role Playing and Rites of Passage: La ilustre fregona and La gitanilla, Hispania, Vol 64; auth, El Villano del Danubio: Foreign Policy and Literary Structure, Critica Hispanica, Vol 3. **CONTACT ADDRESS** Dept of Foreign Languages Drawer FL, Mississippi State Univ, Box Fl, Mississippi State, MS 39762-5720. **EMAIL** wiltrout@ra.msstate.edu

WILTSHIRE, SUSAN FORD
PERSONAL Born 10/13/1941, Amarillo, TX, m, 1969, 2 children **DISCIPLINE** CLASSICS **EDUCATION** Univ Texas, Austin, BA, 63; Columbia Univ, MA, 64, PhD, 67. **CAREER** Asst prof classics, Univ Ill, Champaign-Urbana, 67-69; asst prof English & dir Honors Program, Fisk Univ, 69-71; asst prof to prof classics, 71- , chair Dept of Class Stud, Vanderbilt Univ. **HONORS AND AWARDS** Phi Beta Kappa; Woodrow Wilson Fel, Dissertation Fel, 63-64, 66-67; Madison Sarratt Prize for Excellence in Undergrad Tchg, 79; Phi Beta Kappa Assoc Lctr Panel, 91-92, 92-93; listed in Contemp Auth; Alex Haley Mem Awd, 93; Overall Awd of Excellence, So Books Competition, 98. **MEMBERSHIPS** Nat Coun on Hum; Am Philol Asn; Class Asn of the Middle West and South; Overseers' Comm to Visit the Dept of Classics, Harvard Univ, 96-99; Int Bonhoeffer Soc. **RESEARCH** Latin poetry; Greek epic and drama; the classical tradition in America. **SELECTED PUBLICATIONS** Auth, Public and Private in Vergil's Aeneid, (Massachusetts), 89; auth, Greece, Rome, and the Bill of Rights, (Oklahoma), 92; auth, Seasons of Grief and Grace: A Sister's Story of AIDS, Vanderbilt, 94; coauth, Classical Nashville: Athens of the South, Vanderbilt, 96; auth, Athena's Disguises: Mentors in Everyday Life, John Knox, 98; ed, Prairie Laureate: The Collected Poems of Robert Lee Brothers, Eakin, 98. **CONTACT ADDRESS** Vanderbilt Univ, PO Box 18 Station B, Nashville, TN 37235. **EMAIL** Susan.F.Wiltshire@vanderbilt.edu

WIMMER, ALBERT K.
PERSONAL Born 08/20/1939, Ger, m, 1986, 4 children **DISCIPLINE** GERMAN LITERATURE **EDUCATION** Univ

Notre Dame, BA, 64; MA, 67; IN Univ, PhD, 75. **CAREER** Assoc Prof, Univ Notre Dame, 97-. **MEMBERSHIPS** AATS, MLA. **RESEARCH** Medieval German Literature, Business German, Language pedagogy. **SELECTED PUBLICATIONS** Auth, Anthology of Medieval German Literature; auth, Life in the Middle Ages. **CONTACT ADDRESS** Dept Ger & Rus Lang, Univ of Notre Dame, 318 O'Shaugnessy Hall, Notre Dame, IN 46556-5639. **EMAIL** albertkwimmer1@nc.edu

WINDFUHR, GERNOT LUDWIG
PERSONAL Born 08/02/1938, Essen, Germany, m, 1965, 2 children **DISCIPLINE** IRANISTICS **EDUCATION** Univ Hamburg, Dr Phil, 65. **CAREER** Acad asst ling, Univ Kiel, 65-66; from asst prof to assoc prof, 66-73, Prof Iranian Lang & Ling, Univ Mich, Ann Arbor, 73-, Chmn Dept Near Eastern Studies, 77-. **MEMBERSHIPS** Ling Soc Am; Ling Soc Europe; MidE Studies Asn NAm; Am Orient Soc. **RESEARCH** Linguistics; literary theory; Zoroastrianism. **SELECTED PUBLICATIONS** Auth, Verbalmorpheme in Sangesari, privately publ, 65; Diacritic and Distinctive Features in Avestan: Some Avestan Rules and Their Signs, J Am Orient Soc, 71 & 72; coauth, A Dictionary of Sangesari with a Grammatical Outline, Franklin BK, Tehran, 72; A Linguist's Criticism of Persian Literature, In: Neue Methodologia in der Iranistik, Harrassowitz, Wiesbaden, 74; Isoglosses: A Sketch on Persians and Parthians, Kurds and Medes, Acts Iranica, V, 75; Vohu Manah: A Key to the Zoroastrain World Formula, Studies in Honor of GG Cameron, Ann Arbor, 76; Linguistics: The Study of the Middle East: Research and Scholarship in the Humanities and Social Sciences, John Wiley, NY, 76; Auth, Persian Grammar: History and State of Research, In: Jauna Linguarum Series Critica, Mouton, The Hague, 79. **CONTACT ADDRESS** Dept of Near Eastern Studies, Univ of Michigan, Ann Arbor, 2068 Frieze Bldg, Ann Arbor, MI 48109-1285.

WINKLER, MARTIN M.
PERSONAL Born 05/24/1952, Germany **DISCIPLINE** CLASSICS **EDUCATION** Univ of Southern CA, PhD, 82 **CAREER** Lectr, Univ CA-Riverside, 81-82; asst prof, Univ Utah, 82-83; asst prof, Univ Wisconsin-Madison, 83-87; asst prof, Bucknell Univ, 87-89; assoc prof, prof, 89-, George Mason Univ **HONORS AND AWARDS** Mellon Found post doctoral research fel, 89-90 **MEMBERSHIPS** Amer Assoc of Univ Profs; Amer Philological Assoc; Classical Assoc of the Middle West and South; Vergician Soc of Amer **RESEARCH** Roman satire; classical tradion; classics and cinema **SELECTED PUBLICATIONS** Ed, Classics and Cinema, 91; auth, Der lateinische Eulenspiegel des Ioannes Nemius: Text und Ubersetzung, Kommentar und Untersuchungen, 95; Alogia and emphasis in Juvenal's Fourth Satire, Ramus: Critical Studies in Greek and Roman Literature, 95; Cinema and the Fall of Rome, Transactions of the American Philological Association, 95; Homeric Kleos and the Western Film, Syllecta Classica, 96; The Roman Empire in American Cinema After 1945, The Classical Journal, 98. **CONTACT ADDRESS** Dept of Modern and Classical Languages, George Mason Univ, Fairfax, 4400 Univ Dr., Fairfax, VA 22030. **EMAIL** mwinkler@gmu.edu

WINN, COLETTE HENRIETTE
PERSONAL Born 12/10/1951, La Grand-Combe, France, m, 1974 **DISCIPLINE** FRENCH LITERATURE AND LANGUAGE **EDUCATION** Universite Paul Valery Montpellier, Fr, Lic D'Anglais, 73; Univ Mo, MA, 76, PhD(Fr lang & lit), 80. **CAREER** Teaching asst Fr, Winslow Pub Sch, England, 71-72 & Univ Mo-Columbia, 75-79; Asst Prof French, Washington Univ, St Louis, 80-, Instr Fr, Univ Mo-Columbia, 78-79. **MEMBERSHIPS** MLA; Am Asn Teachers Fr. **RESEARCH** French poetry, particularly sixteenth and twentieth centuries; women poets and writers of the sixteenth century; Marguerite de Navarre. **SELECTED PUBLICATIONS** Auth, Sponde's Sonnet de la Mort II: A Semantic analysis, Lang & Style (in press); Le symbolisme des mains dans la poesi de Paul Eluard, Romanische Forschungen (in press). **CONTACT ADDRESS** 15975 Deer Trail, Chesterfield, MO 63017.

WINNER, ANTHONY
PERSONAL Born 08/17/1931, New York, NY, m, 1964, 1 child **DISCIPLINE** ENGLISH, COMPARATIVE LITERATURE **EDUCATION** Harvard Univ, AB, 53, PhD, 62; Columbia Univ, MA, 54. **CAREER** Instr English, Univ Pa, 61-63 & Hunter Col, 63-65; asst prof, 65-68, ASSOC PROF ENGLISH, UNIV. VA, 68-. **MEMBERSHIPS** MLA **RESEARCH** The novel; realism; character in fictio **SELECTED PUBLICATIONS** Auth, Adjustment, tragic humanism, and Italy, Studi Americani, 61; co-transl, Ugo Foscolo, Last letters of Jacopo Ortis, In: Great European Short Novels, 68 & ed, Great European Short Novels, 68, Perennial Libr, Harper; Characters in the Twilight: Hardy, Zola, and Chekhov, Univ Va, 81. **CONTACT ADDRESS** Dept of English, Univ of Virginia, 219 Bryan Hall, Charlottesville, VA 22903.

WINSTON, JANE
DISCIPLINE FRENCH **EDUCATION** Duke Univ, PhD. **CAREER** Asst prof, Alice Berline Kaplan Center fel, Northwestern Univ fel; lectr, Twentieth-Century Colloquium, Fr; Francophone Studies, Stanford and Amherst; Fr Feminist Theory Conf; Dalhousie Univ, Nova Scotia; Univ Va. **HONORS AND AWARDS** Gerald Kahane Scholar's Prize, 96; fel, from the Alice Berline Kaplan Center for the Humanities at Northwestern Univ. **RESEARCH** Postcolonial theory and literature (especially Southeast Asia), cross-cultural feminist and gender studies (especially postcolonial and psychoanalytic), literary and cultural studies; women's, feminist and autobiographical writings across cultures, the 1950's, theories of social change, cultural rpoduction nad censorship, and the social theory of Pierre Bourdieu. **SELECTED PUBLICATIONS** Auth, Gender and Sexual Identity in the Modern French Novel, Cambridge Companion to the Modern Fr Novel, 97; Marguerite Duras: Marxism, Feminism, Writing, Theatre J, 95; Autour de la rue Saint-Benoit: An interview with Dionys Mascolo, Contemp Fr Civilization, 94; Forever Feminine: Marguerite Duras and Her Critics, New Lit Hist, 93. **CONTACT ADDRESS** Dept of French & Italian, Northwestern Univ, 1859 Sheridan Rd, Kresge 152, Evanston, IL 60208-2204. **EMAIL** j-winston@northwestern.edu

WINSTON, KRISHNA
PERSONAL Born 06/07/1944, Greenfield, MA, d, 1 child **DISCIPLINE** GERMAN LANGUAGE; LITERATURE **EDUCATION** Smith Col, BA, 61; Yale Univ, MPhil, 69, PhD, 74. **CAREER** Instr to asst prof to assoc prof to prof, acting dean, 70-, Wesleyan Univ. **HONORS AND AWARDS** Schlegel-Tieck Translation Prize; DAAD Fel, 73-74; summa cum laude, phi beta kappa, smith col. **MEMBERSHIPS** MLA; AATG; ALTA. **RESEARCH** Literary translation; exile literature **SELECTED PUBLICATIONS** Auth, Peter Handke, Essay on the Jukebox, Farrar Straus Giroux, 94; auth, Robert Menasse, excerpt from Happy Times, Brittle World, Fiction, 94; auth, Peter Handke, My Year in the No-Man's-Bay, Farrar Straus Giroux, 98; auth, Gunter Grass, Too Far Afield, Harcourt Brace, 2000. **CONTACT ADDRESS** Dept of German Stud, Wesleyan Univ, 262 High St, Middletown, CT 06459-0040. **EMAIL** kwinston@wesleyan.edu

WINTER, IAN JAMES
PERSONAL Born 05/21/1927, Penang, Malaya, m, 1958 **DISCIPLINE** FRENCH LANGUAGE AND LITERATURE **EDUCATION** Univ Lyon, dipl, 50; Univ Edinburgh, MA, 51, dipl educ, 54; Wash Univ, PhD(French), 70. **CAREER** Instr French, Moray House Teachers Col, Edinburgh, 56-58; instr French & Span, Fettes Col, Edinburgh, 58-63 & Principia Col, 63-66; asst prof French, Millikin Univ, 67-70; asst prof, 70-76, Assoc Prof French, Univ Wis-Milwaukee, 76-, Chmn Dept French & Ital, 77-. **MEMBERSHIPS** Am Asn Teachers French; Mod Humanities Res Asn; La Societe des amis de Montaigne; Bibliog Soc, Renaissance Soc Am. **RESEARCH** Montaigne; 16th century French literature. **SELECTED PUBLICATIONS** Auth, Mon livre et moi: Montaigne's deepening evaluation of his own work, Renaissance Quart, 3/72; From self-concept to self-knowledge: Death and nature in Montaigne's de la phisionomie, In: French Renaissance Studies in Honor of Isidore Silver & Ky Romance Quart, Vol 21, 74; Montaigne's self-portrait and its influences in France, 1580-1630, French Forum, Lexington, 76; Montaigne's self-portraiture: Contemporary and societal reaction, Ky Romance Quart, Vol 23, 76; Concordances to Montaigne's J De Voyage, Lettres and Ephemerides, Hist Sem Medieval Studies, 81. **CONTACT ADDRESS** Dept of French and Italian, Univ of Wisconsin, Milwaukee, Milwaukee, WI 53201.

WINTER, THOMAS NELSON
PERSONAL Born 01/27/1944, Lansing, MI, m, 1964, 2 children **DISCIPLINE** CLASSICS **EDUCATION** Mich State Univ, BA, 64; Northwestern Univ, MA, 65, PhD, 68. **CAREER** Guest lectr, Adler Planetarium, 66; asst prof, 68-70, actg hd, Classics Div, Univ Hawaii, 69; asst prof, 70-75, assoc prof, Univ Nebr, Lincoln, 76-. **HONORS AND AWARDS** Merit Increment for Excellence in Tchg and Res, Univ Hawaii, 69; NEH summer sem, Am Acad Rome, 78; Parents Assn Award for Serv to Stud, Univ Nebr, Lincoln, 95, 96. **MEMBERSHIPS** APA, CAMWS, ACL, EAA, AOPA. **RESEARCH** Circumstantial case-assignment in the Latin of Caesar. **SELECTED PUBLICATIONS** Auth, When Quod is 'Which' and When Quod is 'Because', Class Outlook 72, 95. **CONTACT ADDRESS** Univ of Nebraska, Lincoln, 233 Andrews Hall, Lincoln, NE 68855-0337. **EMAIL** twinter1@unl.edu

WINTERGERST, ANN C.
PERSONAL Born 03/11/1950, Memmingen, Germany, s **DISCIPLINE** LINGUISTICS **EDUCATION** St. John's Univ NY, BA, 72; Teachers Col, Columbia Univ, MA, 78; MEd, 81; EdD, 89. **CAREER** Teaching Fel, Univ of Pa, 72; Teacher, Our Lady Miraculous Medal Sch, Diocese of Brooklyn, 73-81; ESL Assoc, Columbia Univ, summers 78-82; Asst Prof to Tenured Assoc Prof, St. John's Univ, 81-; Dir of ESL, St. John's Univ, 86-91. **HONORS AND AWARDS** NY State TESOL's James A. Lydon Distinguished Serv Awd, 98; Who's Who in Am; Who's Who in the World; The World's Who's Who of Women; Who's Who in E; Who's Who of Am Women; St. John's Univ Fac Merit Awd; Who's Who in Am Educ: Classroom Educators; Int Who's Who in Educ; Phi Delta Kappa Prof Fraternity in Educ; Kappa Delta Pi Nat Hon Soc in Educ; Pi Lambda Theta Nat Hon and Prof Asn in Educ; Prof Develop Incentive Awd for Grad Studies in TESOL, Teachers Col, Columbia Univ; Phi Delta Phi French Hon Soc; Delta Phi Alpha Ger Hon Soc; Teaching Fel to the Univ of Pa; Who's Who in Am Col and Univ; Who's Who Among Greek Fraternities and Sororities in Am; Skull and Circle Hon Soc. **MEMBERSHIPS** TESOL-Teachers of English to Speakers of Other Lang, NY State TESOL, Nat Coun of Teachers of English, Am Asn for Appl Ling, Am Asn of Univ Prof, NY State Coun on Lang, NY State Coun of Educ Asn, Asn of Int Educators, NY State Asn for Bilingual Educ, Nat Asn for Bilingual Educ, MLA. **RESEARCH** Second language acquisition, English as a second language learning styles research, writing assessment and evaluation of ESL students, interaction analysis in the second language classroom, pragmatics. **SELECTED PUBLICATIONS** Coauth, "TESOL Self-Study Workshop," in How Are We Doing? Evaluating Ourselves, Our Students, And Our Programs, ed. S. Price, V. Cummings, and S. Mettler (NY: CUNY ESL Coun, 90), 12-14; co-ed, "State Council on Languages Monograph," Lang Asn Bul 43-2 (90); auth, "Classroom Interaction: Solicits and Responses," in Issues and Innovations in ESL Teaching and Learning, ed. J. Gantzer and E. Brooks (NY: NY TESOL, 91), 45-58; auth, "Why-Questions in Classroom Discourse," Col ESL 3-1 (93): 70-79; auth, "Adapting 'TWE' Scoring Guidelines to ESL Writing Assessment," in Student-Centered Perspectives and Practices, ed. J. Macero and V. Chesser (NY: NY TESOL, 94), 63-74; auth, Second-Language Classroom Interaction, Univ of Toronto Press (Toronto, Can), 94; auth, Preface and Introd, in Focus on Self-Study: Evaluating Postsecondary ESOL Programs, ed. A. Wintergerst (Alexandria, VA: TESOL, 95), 1-3; coauth, "The TESOL Study Program," in Focus on Self-Study: Evaluating Postsecondary ESOL Programs, ed. A. Wintergerst (Alexandria, VA: TESOL, 95), 7-19; ed, Focus on Self-Study: Evaluating Postsecondary ESOL Programs, TESOL (Alexandria, VA), 95; coauth, "Employment Conditions in Higher Education ESL Programs," Col ESL 7-2 (97): 47-52. **CONTACT ADDRESS** Dept of Mod For Lang, St. John's Univ, 8000 Utopia Pky, Jamaica, NY 11439. **EMAIL** winterga@stjohns.edu

WISHARD, ARMIN
DISCIPLINE GERMAN LITERATURE **EDUCATION** Univ Ca, BA, 65, MA, 66; Univ Oregon, PhD, 70. **CAREER** Prof. **RESEARCH** Medieval literature; Romantic German literature. **SELECTED PUBLICATIONS** Auth, Salman und Morolf; pubs on German literature and teaching methodology. **CONTACT ADDRESS** German Dept, Columbia Col, New York, 14 E Cache La Poudre St, Colorado Springs, CO 80903. **EMAIL** awishard@cc.colorado.edu

WISSE, RUTH R.
PERSONAL Born 05/13/1936, Cernauti, Rumania, m, 1957, 3 children **DISCIPLINE** COMPARATIVE LITERATURE **EDUCATION** Columbia Univ, MA, 61; McGill Univ, PhD, 69. **CAREER** Prof, McGill Univ, 67-93; prof, Harvard Univ, 93-. **HONORS AND AWARDS** Fieldhouse Awd, McGill, 85; Manger Prize, Tel Aviv, 88; J.I. Segal Awd, 71, 89; Maurice Stiller Prize, Baltimore Hebrew Univ, 98. **MEMBERSHIPS** Am Acad for Jewish Res; Assoc for Jewish Studies. **RESEARCH** Yiddish Literature, Jewish Literature, Political Culture. **SELECTED PUBLICATIONS** Auth, The Schlemiel as Modern Hero, 71; coed, The Best of Sholem Aleichem, 79; ed, A Shtetl and Other Yiddish Novellas, 86; coed, The Penguin Book of Modern Verse, 87; auth, A Little Love in Big Manhattan, 88; ed, The I.L. Peretz Reader, 90; auth, I.L. Peretz and the Making of Modern Jewish Culture, 91; auth, If I Am Not for Myself: The Liberal Betrayal of the Jews, 92; auth, The Modern Jewish Canon (forthcoming). **CONTACT ADDRESS** Dept Near East Lang, Harvard Univ, Semetic Museum, Cambridge, MA 02138. **EMAIL** wisse@fas.harvard.edu

WITT, MARY ANN FRESE
PERSONAL Born 11/30/1937, Urbana, IL, m, 1965, 3 children **DISCIPLINE** COMPARATIVE LITERATURE **EDUCATION** Harvard Univ, PhD, 68 **CAREER** Asst prof, Wellesley Col, 69-70; asst prof, NC Central Univ, 72-76; from asst prof to prof, NC State Univ, 77-. **HONORS AND AWARDS** Fulbright Scholar, 85-86; Outstanding Book Awd, NCSU Hums and Soc Scis, 87; Hums Ctr Fel, Univ of Utah, 96-97. **MEMBERSHIPS** ACLA; SCLA; MLA **RESEARCH** Modern French and Italian literature; drama theory. **SELECTED PUBLICATIONS** Auth, The Humanities: Cultural Roots and Continuities with Instructor's Guide, 80, 85, 89, 93, 97, 01; Existential Prisons: Confinement in Mid-Twentieth Century French Literature, 85; Murder as Sign and Cycle in Les Negres, in Proceedings of the Am Semiotic Soc, 90; Towards a Theater of Immobility: Henry IV, The Condemned of Altona, and The Balcony, in Comparative Drama, 24, 90; Pirandello's Sicilian Comedies and the Comic Tradition, in Pirandello and the Commedia dell'Arte, vol. VI, 90; Mothers or Women? Feminine Conditions in Pirandello, in A Companion to Pirandello Studies, 91; Pirandellian Theater and Fascist Discourse, in South Atlantic Quart, 92; Pirandello's 'La Patente': mode, genre, narrative, in Aesthetics and the Text, 92; Reading Modern Drama: Voice in the Didascaliae, in Studies in the Literary Imagination, vol.25, no.1, 92; Fascist Aesthetics and Theatre under the Occupation: The Case of Anouilh, in J of European Studies xxiii, 93; Il linguaggio femminile nel teatro di Pirandello, in Pirandello e la lingua, 94; Authority and Constructions of Actress in the Drama of Pirandello and Genet, in Comparative Literature Studies, vol.32, no.1, 95; Pirandellian dislocation or

the dying dramatic author, in Ars dramatica, 97; ed, "Mimesi e diegesi nella 'Patente'" in Enzo Lauretta, Pirandello e la sua opera, Milan: Mursia, 98; ed, AestheticFascism and the Search for Modern Tragedy, 01. **CONTACT ADDRESS** Dept of Foreign Languages & Literature, No Carolina State Univ, Raleigh, NC 27695-8106. **EMAIL** witt@social.chass.ncsu.edu

WITTKOWSKI, WOLFGANG
PERSONAL Born 08/15/1925, Halle, Germany, m, 1954, 4 children **DISCIPLINE** GERMAN LITERATURE **EDUCATION** Univ Frankfurt, PhD(Ger), 54. **CAREER** Asst Ger, Univ Frankfurt, 50-53; studienrat, gymnasium, Bad Nauheim, Ger, 56-63; from assoc prof to prof, Ohio State Univ, 63-77; Prof Ger, State Univ NY, Albany 78-, Vis prof Ger, State Univ NY, Albany, 77-78. **MEMBERSHIPS** MLA; Am Asn Teachers Ger. **RESEARCH** Classical and 19th century German literature; Kleist; ETA Hoffmann. **SELECTED PUBLICATIONS** Auth, Fathers and Daughters in a Middle Class Drama, or, Did Really Nothing Happen in 'Miss Sara Sampson's + Lessing, G.E., J Engl and Ger Philol, Vol 0092, 93; The Motif and Structural Principle of a Threshold in Grillparzer Is Die 'Judin Von Toledo', Mod Austrian Lit, Vol 0028, 95; Heimat is Not Enough, Mod Austrian Lit, Vol 0029, 96; ed, Friedrich Schiller, 82; Goethe in Context, 84; Classical Literature Lost?, 86; Utopism and Responsibility, 88; Friedrich Schiller, 'Maria Stuart', 94; Goethe, Schopenhauer and Faust's Last Vision, Goethe Yearbook V, 95. **CONTACT ADDRESS** 1370 Rosehill Blvd, Schenectady, NY 12309. **EMAIL** wittkoed@taconic.net

WOLFE, ETHYLE RENEE
PERSONAL Born 03/14/1919, Burlington, VT, m, 1954 **DISCIPLINE** CLASSICAL LANGUAGES AND LITERATURE **EDUCATION** Univ Vt, BA, 40, MA, 42; NYork Univ, PhD, 50. **CAREER** Lectr classics, eve session, 47-49, from instr to assoc prof, 49-67, acting chmn dept classics & comp lit, 62-63, chmn, 67-72, Prof Classics, Brooklyn Col, 68-, Dean Sch Humanities, 71-, Assoc ed, Class World, 65-70; co-ed, Am Class Rev, 70-. **MEMBERSHIPS** Am Philol Asn; Archaeol Inst Am; Am Soc Papyrologists. **RESEARCH** Latin poetry; Greek tragedy; papyrology. **SELECTED PUBLICATIONS** Auth, The Brooklyn College Core Curriculum, Arethusa, Vol 0027, 94; Cicero 'De Oratore' and the Liberal Arts Tradition in America, Class World, Vol 0088, 95. **CONTACT ADDRESS** Brooklyn Col, CUNY, Brooklyn, NY 11210.

WOLFF, JOHN ULRICH
PERSONAL Born 11/01/1932, Berlin, Germany, m, 1963, 4 children **DISCIPLINE** GENERAL AND MALAYO-POLYNESIAN LINGUISTICS **EDUCATION** Cornell Univ, BA, 54, MA, 55; Yale Univ, PhD(ling), 64. **CAREER** Prof 80, Prof Mod Lang & Ling, Cornell Univ, 80-. **MEMBERSHIPS** Ling Soc Am; Asn Asian Studies. **SELECTED PUBLICATIONS** Auth, The Polynesians, J Amer Oriental Soc, Vol 0112, 92; Everyday Malay, Mod Lang J, Vol 0079, 95; Comparative Austronesian Dictionary, Language, Vol 0073, 97. **CONTACT ADDRESS** Cornell Univ, 203 Morrill Hall, Ithaca, NY 14853-4701. **EMAIL** juw1@cornell.edu

WOLFF, ROLAND A.
DISCIPLINE GERMAN LITERATURE **EDUCATION** Univ Wisc, PhD. **CAREER** Assoc prof, German Lang, Univ Wisc. **RESEARCH** German pedagogy; contemporary German sociolinguistics. **CONTACT ADDRESS** Foreign Languages and Literature Dept, Colorado State Univ, Fort Collins, CO 80523. **EMAIL** roland.wolff@colostate.edu

WOLFGANG, LENORA D.
PERSONAL Born 09/25/1934, Philadelphia, PA, w, 1957, 2 children **DISCIPLINE** FRENCH, LITERATURE **EDUCATION** Univ Pa, BA, 56; MA, 65; PhD, 73. **CAREER** Prof, Lehigh Univ, 80-. **HONORS AND AWARDS** Fulbright Fel, 56-57; Woodrow Wilson Fel, 56-57; NEH Fel, 84-85, 95-96; Phi Beta Kappa, Univ Pa, 96. **MEMBERSHIPS** IAS, MLA, ICLS, Societe Rencesvals. **RESEARCH** Medieval and Renaissance literature, French literature. **SELECTED PUBLICATIONS** Auth, Le Lai de l'Oiselet, An Old French Poem of the Thirteenth Century, Edition and Critical Study, Am Philos Soc (Philadelphia, PA), 90; auth, "Versification," in Medieval Fr: An Encycl (New York: Garland Publ Co, 95), 955; auth, "Jean de Vignay," in Medieval Fr: An Encycl (New York: Garland Publ Co, 95), 948-949; auth, "'Out of the French': Lydgate's Source of the 'Churl and the Bird'," English Lang Notes 32 (95): 10-22; auth, "William J Roach (1907-1993) A Biographical Memoir," Proceedings of the Am Philos Soc 139 (95): 185-189. **CONTACT ADDRESS** Dept Lang & Lit, Lehigh Univ, 9 W Packer Ave, Bethlehem, PA 18015-3082. **EMAIL** ldw0@lehigh.edu

WOLOCH, GEORGE MICHAEL
PERSONAL Born 06/01/1934, Akron, OH **DISCIPLINE** CLASSICS **EDUCATION** Yale Univ, BA, 56; Oxford Univ, BA, 60, MA, 63; Johns Hopkins Univ, PhD(classics), 66. **CAREER** Instr Latin, Pomfret Sch, 56-57; lectr sch gen studies, Brooklyn Col, 61; instr classics, McGill Univ, 61-63; jr instr, Johns Hopkins Univ, 63-64; asst prof, 66-70, Assoc Prof Classics, McGill Univ, 70-, Res assoc, Ctr Medieval Studies, Univ Calif, Los Angeles, 70; Can Coun leave fel, 70-71; hon cur, McGill Univ Coin Collection. **MEMBERSHIPS** Am Philol Asn; Class Asn Can; fel Royal Numis Soc. **RESEARCH** Roman cities; Ostrogothic Italy, AD 489-552; Ammianus Marcellinus. **SELECTED PUBLICATIONS** Auth, Mediterranean Cities, Phoenix-J Class Asn Can, Vol 0046, 92; Emperors and Gladiators, Amer Hist Rev, Vol 0099, 94. **CONTACT ADDRESS** Dept of Classics, McGill Univ, 855 Sherbrooke St W, Montreal, QC, Canada H3A 2T5.

WOLSEY, MARY LOU MORRIS
PERSONAL Born 02/21/1936, Baltimore, MD, m, 1965, 2 children **DISCIPLINE** MEDIEVAL FRENCH LANGUAGE & LITERATURE **EDUCATION** Mary Washington Col, BA, 58; Univ Kans, MA, 61; Univ Besancon, cert etudes super, 64; Univ Minn, PhD(French), 72. **CAREER** Asst instr French, Univ Kans, 58-61; instr, Mary Washington Col, 61-63; asst English, Teachers Col, Besancon, France, 63-64; teaching assoc French, Univ Pa, 64-65 & Univ Minn, 65-67; instr, Macalester Col, 67-68, adj prof, 72-78; part-time asst prof, 76-81, Asst Prof to Assoc prof French, Univ of St Thomas, 76-, Vis prof, Univ Bristol, England, 78-79. **MEMBERSHIPS** Am Asn Teachers French; Am Coun Teaching Foreign Lang; Mediaeval Acad Am; Alliance Francaise; Midwest Mod Lang Asn Am. **RESEARCH** Medieval French romance; the French novel; computer research in French. **SELECTED PUBLICATIONS** Auth, The Eracle of Gautier d'Arras: A critical study, Diss Abstr Int, 10/72. **CONTACT ADDRESS** 2115 Summit Ave, Mail 4196, Saint Paul, MN 55105-1096. **EMAIL** mlwolsey@stthomas.edu

WOLVERTON, ROBERT E.
PERSONAL Born 08/04/1925, Indianapolis, IN, m, 1952, 4 children **DISCIPLINE** CLASSICS **EDUCATION** Hanover Col, AB, 48; Univ MI, MA, 49; Univ NC, PhD(Latin, Greek & ancient hist), 54. **CAREER** Asst prof classics, Univ GA, 54-59; from asst to assoc prof classics & hist, Tufts Univ, 59-62; assoc prof classics & dir hon prog, FL State Univ, 62-67; assoc dean grad col, Univ Ill, 67-69; dean grad sch, Miami Univ, OH, 69-72; prof classics & pres, Col of Mt St Josephs on the OH, 72-77; Prof Classics & Educ Leadership & Vpres Acad Affairs, MS State Univ, 77-86, Title IV consult-reader of langs, NDEA, 67-72; consult-reviewer admin, NCent Asn Cols & Schs, 67-77; instr personnel mgt, Main Event Mgt Inc, 76-; mem exec comt, Nat Coun Chief Acad Officers, 81-; Head dept. For Lang, Miss State Univ, 91-96. **HONORS AND AWARDS** Alumni Achievement Awd, Hanover Col, 71; hon life pres, Am Class League, 77, Outstanding Tchr Awd, 91; John Grisham Master Tchr, 91; littd, col of mt st joseph on the oh, 77. **MEMBERSHIPS** Am Class League (pres, 72-76); Am Philol Asn; Class Asn Mid West & South; Am Asn Higher Educ. **RESEARCH** Administration in higher educ; class mythology; etymology. **SELECTED PUBLICATIONS** Auth, Classical Elements in English Words, 66 & An Outline of Classical Mythology, 67, Littlefield; contribr, Graduate Programs and Admission Manual, 4 vols, Grad Record & Exam Bd & Coun Grad Schs USA, 71 & 72; auth, The future of classics, Class Outlook, 76; contrib auth & translr, A Life of George Washington, in Latin Prose, George Washington Univ, 76; The future of graduate studies in the humanities, Nat Forum, 79; contribr, Mythological References, Arete Publ, 80. **CONTACT ADDRESS** Dept of Foreign Langs, Mississippi State Univ, PO Drawer FL, Mississippi State, MS 39762. **EMAIL** REW1@RA.MSSTATE.EDU

WOLVIN, ANDREW D.
PERSONAL Born Columbus, NE, m, 2 children **DISCIPLINE** ORGANIZATIONAL COMMUNICATION AND COMMUNICATION EDUCATION **EDUCATION** Purdue Univ, PhD, 68. **CAREER** Prof, Univ MD. **HONORS AND AWARDS** Lilly Teaching Fel; Eastern Commun; Assoc Distinguished Teaching Fel. **MEMBERSHIPS** International Listening Assoc; Nat Commun Assoc; Assoc of Business Commun. **RESEARCH** The study of listening behavior. **SELECTED PUBLICATIONS** Co-auth, Listening, 5th edn, Brown, 96; auth, Business Communication in a Changing World, St. Martins, 97; Communicating: A Social and Career Focus, 8th edn, Houghton-Mifflin, 01. **CONTACT ADDRESS** Dept of Commun, Univ of Maryland, Col Park, 211 Skinner Building, College Park, MD 20742-1335. **EMAIL** awolvin@deans.umd.edu

WONG, JEAN
PERSONAL Born 05/05/1951, Boston, MA, m, 1978, 2 children **DISCIPLINE** APPLIED LINGUISTICS **EDUCATION** Connecticut Col, BA (summa cum laude and with honors), 73; UCLA, MA, 85, PhD, 94. **CAREER** Asst prof, The Col of New Jersey, 97-. **HONORS AND AWARDS** Phi Beta Kappa; recipient of a Thomas Watson Found fel; UCLA, Faculty Woman's Club fel. **MEMBERSHIPS** TESOL; AAAL; IRA; NCA; ICA. **RESEARCH** Discourse and conversation analysis; sociolinguistics. **SELECTED PUBLICATIONS** Auth, The Token 'Year' in Nonnative Speaker English Comminication, Research on Languages and Social Interaction. **CONTACT ADDRESS** Dept of Lang and Commun Sciences, The Col of New Jersey, PO Box 7718, Ewing, NJ 08628. **EMAIL** jwong@tcnj.edu

WONG, TIMOTHY C.
PERSONAL Born 01/24/1941, Hong Kong, China, m, 1970, 3 children **DISCIPLINE** CHINESE LITERATURE **EDUCATION** St Mary's Col, BA, 63; Univ Hawaii, MA, 68; Stanford Univ, PhD, 75. **CAREER** Asst prof, 74-79, assoc prof, 79-85, prof, 95-, Arizona St Univ; assoc prof, 85-95, Ohio St Univ. **HONORS AND AWARDS** ACLS grants, 77, 81-82. **MEMBERSHIPS** Asn for Asian Studies; Am Oriental Soc; Chinese Lang Teachers Asn. **RESEARCH** Traditional Chinese fiction and narratology **SELECTED PUBLICATIONS** Wu Chingtzu, Boston, 78. **CONTACT ADDRESS** Center for Asian Studies, Arizona State Univ, PO Box 871702, Tempe, AZ 85287-1702. **EMAIL** twong@asu.edu

WOOD, BRYANT G.
PERSONAL Born 10/07/1936, Endicott, NY, m, 1958, 4 children **DISCIPLINE** NEAR EASTERN STUDIES, BIBLICAL HISTORY, AND SYRO-PALESTINIAN ARCHAEOLOGY **EDUCATION** Univ Mich, MA, 74; Univ Toronto, PhD, 85. **CAREER** Visitng Prof, Dept of Near Eastern Studies, Univ Toronto, 89-90; Res Analysit, 90-94, Dir, Assoc for Biblical Res, 95-. **HONORS AND AWARDS** Endowment for Biblical Res Grant, 81; Travel Grant, 81, Summer Stipend, Nat Endowment for the Humanities, 92. **MEMBERSHIPS** Near East Archaeol Soc; Inst for Biblical Res. **RESEARCH** Archaeology of the Bronze Age and Iron Age Periods in Palestine. **SELECTED PUBLICATIONS** Auth, Pottery Making in Bible Times, By the Sweat of Thy Brow: Labor and Laborers in the Biblical World, Sheffield Academic Press, forthcoming; Cisterns and Reservoirs, Encyclo of the Dead Sea Scrolls, Oxford Univ Press, forthcoming; Water Systems, Encyclo of the Dead Sea Scrolls, Oxford Univ Press, forthcoming; The Role of Shechem in the Conquest of Canaan, To Understand the Scriptures: Essays in Honor of William H. Shea, Inst of Archeaol/Siegfried H. Horn Archaeol Museum, Andrews Univ, 97; Kh. Nisya, 94, Israel Exploration J, 95; Biblical Archaeology's Greatest Achievement, Failure and Challenge, Biblical Archaeol Rev, 95; Rev of Excavations at Tell Deir Alla, Bullet of the Am Schools of Oriental Res, 94; coauth, Kh. Nisya, 93, Israel Exploration J, 94. **CONTACT ADDRESS** Associates for Biblical Res, 4328 Crestview Rd., Harrisburg, PA 17112-2005. **EMAIL** bryantwood@email.msn.com

WOOD, CAROL L.
PERSONAL Born 07/18/1949, Fayetteville, AR, m, 1972, 1 child **DISCIPLINE** LINGUISTICS, LITERATURE **EDUCATION** Univ Ark, BA; MA; PhD. **CAREER** From assoc prof to prof, McNeese State Univ, 87-. **HONORS AND AWARDS** Shearman Prof of Liberal Arts, 98-99; project assistance grants, Calcasieu Arts & Humanities Coun, 98-99; Humanist of the Year, Calcasieu Arts & Humanities Coun, 99-00; artist's minigrants, La Div of the Arts, 99-00. **MEMBERSHIPS** Hist Harp Soc. **RESEARCH** Literature and Music (especially harp) of the Medieval Period. **SELECTED PUBLICATIONS** Auth, An Overview of Welsh Poetry Before the Norman conquest, Edwin Mellen Press, 96; auth, The Chaucer Songbook, Mel Bay, 00. **CONTACT ADDRESS** Dept Lang Arts, McNeese State Univ, PO Box 92655, Lake Charles, LA 70605. **EMAIL** woodharp@hotmail.com

WOOD, PAUL WILLIAM
PERSONAL Born 03/24/1933, Cincinnati, OH, m, 1960, 4 children **DISCIPLINE** FRENCH LANGUAGE & LITERATURE **EDUCATION** Athenaeum of Ohio, BA, 54; Univ of Cincinnati, MA, 60; Northwestern Univ, Evanston, PhD(-French), 70. **CAREER** High sch teacher French & Latin, Forest Hills Sch Dist, Ohio, 60-62; instr French, Loyola Univ Chicago, 62-67; asst prof, Univ Akron, 67-71; asst prof, 71-76, assoc prof French, St Bonaventure Univ, 76-88, chmn dept mod lang & lit, 77-83, prof, St. Bonaventure Univ, 88-. **HONORS AND AWARDS** Ferdinand Di Bartholo NY State Distinguished Leadership Awd, 86. **MEMBERSHIPS** MLA; Am Asn Teachers Fr; Am Coun Teaching Foreign Lang; AAUP. **RESEARCH** Modern French theatre; Moliere. **SELECTED PUBLICATIONS** Auth, How to Conduct a Language Fair (Filmstrip), NY State Asn Foreign Lang Teachers, 77; coauth, Student Motivation: Try a Foreign Language Day, Foreign Lang Annals/ Accent on Am Coun Teachers For Lang, 2/78; Creating an Environment for Second Language Aquisition, ed, NY State Asn of Foreign Lang Teachers, 88. **CONTACT ADDRESS** Dept of Modern Lang & Lit, St. Bonaventure Univ, Saint Bonas, NY 14778-9999. **EMAIL** pswood@sbu.edu

WOOD, PHILIP R.
DISCIPLINE FRENCH **EDUCATION** English Univ Cape Town, BA, 70-74; Univ York, MA, 78-80; Yale Univ, PhD, 82-88. **CAREER** Assoc prof, Rice Univ, 92-; asst prof, Rice Univ, 90-92; asst prof, Purdue Univ, 88-90; vis asst prof Univ Wash Seattle, 86-88; asst prof, Universidade de Coimbra Portugal, 80-82. **HONORS AND AWARDS** Amer Council Learned Soc Fel, 91; XL Summer Res Grant, Purdue Univ, 90; Yale Univ Lurcy Fel, 84-85; Yale Univ Fel, 82-86; FR Leavis Awd, Univ York, 79. **SELECTED PUBLICATIONS** Co-ed, Terror and Consensus: Vicissitudes of French Thought, Stanford Univ Pr, 98; Introduction, in Terror and Consensus: a French Debate, Stanford Univ Pr, 98;"Apotheosis and Demise of the Philosophy of the Subject: Hegel, Sartre, Heidegger, Structuralism and

Poststructuralism, Sartre Revisited, St Martin's Pr, 97; Heidegger Debates, Ethics in Poststructuralism, the 'Death' of the Subject and the Future of the Earth," Contemporary French Civilization, 95. **CONTACT ADDRESS** Dept of French Studies, Rice Univ, Box 1892, Houston, TX 77251. **EMAIL** prw@ruf.rice.edu

WOODARD, ROGER
DISCIPLINE LINGUISTICS **EDUCATION** Univ NC, PhD. **CAREER** Assoc prof, joint app with Classics, Univ Southern Calif. **RESEARCH** Language change. **SELECTED PUBLICATIONS** Auth, In On Interpreting Morphological Change, 90. **CONTACT ADDRESS** Dept of Linguistics, Univ of So California, University Park Campus, Los Angeles, CA 90089. **EMAIL** woodard@usc.edu

WOODBRIDGE, HENSLEY CHARLES
PERSONAL Born 02/06/1923, Champaign, IL, m, 1953, 1 child **DISCIPLINE** SPANISH **EDUCATION** Col William & Mary, AB, 43; Harvard Univ, MA, 46; Univ Ill, PhD(Span), 50, MSLS, 51; Lincoln Mem Univ, Tenn, DA, 76. **CAREER** Instr French & Span, Univ Richmond, 46-47; teaching asst Span, Univ Ill, 48-50; ref librn, Ala Polytech Inst, 51-53; head librn, Murray State Col, 53-63; assoc prof foreign lang, 65-71, bibliogr Latin Am, 65-74, Prof Foreign Lang, Southern Ill Univ, Carbondale, 71-, Assoc ed, Hispania, 67-81; contrib ed, Am Bk Collector; ed, Jack London Newslett. **MEMBERSHIPS** Am Asn Teachers Span & Port; MLA; Medieval Acad Am. **RESEARCH** Spanish nautical terms; Jack London; Ruben Dario. **SELECTED PUBLICATIONS** Auth, Contemporary Spanish American Poets, Hispania-J Devoted Tchg Spanand Port, Vol 0076, 93; Mistral, Gabriela and the Critics, Chasqui-Revista de Lit Latinoamericana, Vol 0024, 95. **CONTACT ADDRESS** Dept of Foreign Lang, So Illinois Univ, Carbondale, Carbondale, IL 62901.

WOOLDRIDGE, JOHN B.
DISCIPLINE SPANISH **EDUCATION** Univ Richmond, BA; Univ MD, MA, PhD. **CAREER** Adj prof, Shenandoah Univ; pres, Potomac Chap, Am Asn Tchr(s) Span & Port, 82-86 & pres, For Lang Asn of VA, 83-84. **HONORS AND AWARDS** Awd Excellence in For Lang Educ, 83 & campus's Alumni Fedn Fac of the Yr Awd, 97. **SELECTED PUBLICATIONS** Auth, critical edition of Lope de Vega's El amor enamorado, Spain, 78, subsequent res on Span Golden Age drama, has produced some 20 articles and rev(s) in scholarly jour both in this country and abroad. **CONTACT ADDRESS** Dept of Span, Shenandoah Univ, 1460 University Dr., Winchester, VA 22601.

WOOLEY, ALLAN D.
PERSONAL Born 01/01/1936, Rumford, ME, m, 1 child **DISCIPLINE** CLASSICAL PHILOLOGY **EDUCATION** Bowdoin Col, BA, 58; Princeton Univ, PhD, 62. **CAREER** Asst prof, Duke Univ, 62-67; dept chair, Gould Acad, 67-68; instr, Greek and Latin, Phillips Exeter Acad, 68-84; instr and coord, acad computing, Phillips Exeter Acad, 84-89; dept chair, Phillips Exeter Acad, 91-96; Bradbury Longfellow Cilley prof, Greek, Phillips Exeter Acad, 96-. **HONORS AND AWARDS** Barlow Beach Dist Serv Awd, CANE. **MEMBERSHIPS** Class Asn of New England; Am Class League; Am Philol Asn. **RESEARCH** Ancient Philosophy, Vergil. **SELECTED PUBLICATIONS** Article, Ideographic Imagery in Aeneid and Vergil's Philosophizing, New Eng Class Jour, may, 98. **CONTACT ADDRESS** Phillips Exeter Acad, 20 Main St., MSC 81420, Exeter, NH 03833. **EMAIL** awooley@exeter.edu

WOOLFORD, ELLEN
DISCIPLINE LINGUISTICS **EDUCATION** Rice Univ, BA, 71; Duke Univ, PhD, 77. **CAREER** Prof. **SELECTED PUBLICATIONS** Auth, VP Internal Subjects in VSO and Non-Configurational Languages, Ling Inquiry, 93; Symmetric and Asymmetric Passives, Natural Lang Ling Theory, 94; Why Passive Can Block Object Marking, 95; Object Agreement in Palauan: Specificity, Humanness, Economy, and Optimality, Univ Mass, 97; Four-Way Case Systems: Ergative, Nominative, Objective and Accusative, Natural Lang Ling Theory, 97; More on the Anaphor-Agreement Effect, Linguistic Inquiry, 99; Case Patterns in G. Legendre S Vikner, and J Grimshaw eds, OT Syntax, MIT, 01 **CONTACT ADDRESS** Linguistics Dept, Univ of Massachusetts, Amherst, S College 131, Amherst, MA 01003. **EMAIL** woolford@linguist.umass.edu

WOOTEN, CECIL W.
DISCIPLINE CLASSICS **EDUCATION** Davidson Col, AB, 67; Univ NC, Chapel Hill, MA, 68; Middlebury Col and Univ Paris, AM, 73; Univ NC, Chapel Hill, PhD, 72. **CAREER** Prof, Univ NC, Chapel Hill. **RESEARCH** Greek and Latin rhetoric and oratory; the ancient novel. **SELECTED PUBLICATIONS** Auth, The Elusive 'Gay' Teenagers of Classical Antiquity, The High Schl J 77, 93/94; The Peripatetic Tradition in the Literary Essays of Dionysius of Halicarnassus, in Peripatetic Rhetoric after Aristotle, eds, W. Fortenbaugh and D. Mirhady, New Brunswick, 94. **CONTACT ADDRESS** Univ of No Carolina, Chapel Hill, Chapel Hill, NC 27599. **EMAIL** cwwooten@email.unc.edu

WORTH, DEAN STODDARD
PERSONAL Born 09/30/1927, Brooklyn, NY, m, 1953, 1 child **DISCIPLINE** SLAVIC LINGUISTICS **EDUCATION** Dartmouth Col, AB, 49; Ecole Langues Orient, Paris, dipl, 52; Sorbonne, cert, 52; Harvard Univ, AM, 53, PhD, 56. **CAREER** Res fel, Russ Res Ctr, Harvard Univ, 56-57; from asst prof to assoc prof Slavic lang, 57-65, Prof Slavic Lang, Univ Calif, Los Angeles, 65-, Secy, Am Cont Slavists, 60-, CHMN, 78-; Guggenheim fel, 63-64; fel, Konnan Inst Advan Ress Studies (Wilson Ctr), 78-79. **MEMBERSHIPS** Am Asn Advan Slavic Studies; Ling Soc Am; Medieval Acad Am; Am Asn Teachers Slavic & East Europ Lang; Ling Soc Europe. **RESEARCH** Paleosiberian languages; Old Russian literature. **SELECTED PUBLICATIONS** Ed, Kamchadal Texts Collected by W Jochelson, 61, coauth, Sofonija's Tale of the Russian-Tatar Battle on the Kulikovo Field, 63 & Selected Bibliography of Slavic Linguistics, Vol I, 66, Vol II, 68, Mouton, The Hague; Russian Derivational Dictionary, Am Elsevier, 72; auth, Dictionary of Western Kamchadal, Univ Calif, 72; A Bibliography of Russian Word-Formation, Slavica, 77; On the Structure and History of Russian, Selected Essays, Sagner, 77. **CONTACT ADDRESS** Univ of California, Los Angeles, Los Angeles, CA 90024.

WORTH, FABIENNE ANDRE
PERSONAL Born 05/24/1944, Lyon, France, m, 1967, 2 children **DISCIPLINE** FRENCH LITERATURE, CINEMA **EDUCATION** Univ NC, Chapel Hill, BA, 70, MA, 73, PhD(comp lit), 79. **CAREER** Vis lectr, 78-79, Vis Lectr French Lit, Duke Univ, 80-, Instr, French Cinema Arts Sch, Carrboro, NC, 80. **MEMBERSHIPS** MLA; Am Asn Teachers Fr; Am Comp Lit Asn. **RESEARCH** History and the novel; authorship in the cinema. **SELECTED PUBLICATIONS** Auth, Le Sacre Et Le Sida--Representations of Sexuality and Their Contradictions in France, 1971-1996, a Perspective from Across the Atlantic, Temps Modernes, Vol 0052, 97. **CONTACT ADDRESS** 209 Pritchard Ave, Chapel Hill, NC 27514.

WORTHEN, THOMAS
PERSONAL Born 08/18/1937, Salt Lake City, UT, 4 children **DISCIPLINE** CLASSICS **EDUCATION** Univ Utah, BA, 59; Univ Wash, MA, 63, PhD, 68. **CAREER** Lectr, 65-68, asst prof, 68-72, Assoc Prof to Assoc Prof Emer Greek, Univ Ariz, 72-. **MEMBERSHIPS** AAS (HAD div); AAAS. **RESEARCH** Greek science and proto science. **SELECTED PUBLICATIONS** Auth, Pneumatic Action in the Klepsydra and Empedocles' Account of Breathing, Isis, 70; Note on Ajax 494-5, Class Philol, 72; co-auth, The Thucydides Syndrome: A New Hypothesis for the Cause of Plague of Athens, NEJM, 86; rev, English Words from latin and Greek Elements by Donald Ayers, Univ Ariz Press, 86; Ideas of Sky in Archaic Greek Poetry, Glotta, 88; The Myth of Replacement: Stars, Gods and Order in the Univers, Univ Ariz Press, 91; contribr, Stalking the Second Tier, An Occasional Paper on Neglected Problems in Science Education, Res Corp, 91; Eclipses by the Semester, Griffith Observer, 93; Pleiades and Hesperides, Vistas in Astronomy, 95; Herodotos's Report on Thales' Eclipes, Electronic Antiquity, 97. **CONTACT ADDRESS** Dept of Classics, Univ of Arizona, 371 Modern Languages Bldg, PO Box 210067, Tucson, AZ 85721-0067. **EMAIL** tdw@u.arizona.edu

WORTHINGTON, IAN
PERSONAL Born 03/19/1958, Lytham Lanes, United Kingdom, m, 1996, 1 child **DISCIPLINE** CLASSICS, ANCIENT HISTORY **EDUCATION** Univ Hull, BA, 79; Univ Durham, MA, 81; Monash Univ, PhD, 87. **CAREER** Lectr, Univ New England, 88-92; sr lectr, Univ Tasmania, 93-97; prof, Univ Mo Columbia, 98-. **RESEARCH** Greek History, Alexander the Great, Greek Oratory. **SELECTED PUBLICATIONS** Auth, "[Plutarch], X.Or. 848e: A Loeb Mistranslation and Its Effect on Hyperides' Entry Into Athenian Political Life," Electronic Antiquity 3.2 (95); ed, Voice Into Text. Orality and Literacy in Ancient Greece, Brill, 96; rev, of "Theopompus of Chios, History and Rhetoric in the Fourth Century BC," by M. Flower, Classical Rev 46 (96): 179; rev, of "Faces of Power. Alexander's Image and Hellenistic Politics," by A. Stewart, Classical J 91 (96): 210-211; auth, "Alexander the Great and the 'Interests of Historical Accuracy': A Reply," Ancient Hist Bull 13.4 (99): 121-127; auth, "How 'Great' was Alexander?," Ancient Hist Bull 13.2 (99): 39-55; auth, Greek Orators Volume 2: Dinarchus and Hyperides, Aris & Phillips, 99; rev, of "Thucydides and Ancient Simplicity," by G. Crane, Classical Rev 49 (99): 368-369; **CONTACT ADDRESS** Dept Hist, Univ of Missouri, Columbia, 101 Read Hall, Columbia, MO 65211-7500. **EMAIL** worthingtoni@missouri.edu

WOSHINSKY, BARBARA
PERSONAL m, 1 child **DISCIPLINE** FRENCH LANGUAGE & LITERATURE **EDUCATION** Oberlin Col, BA, 63; Yale Univ, PhD, 68. **CAREER** Vis asst prof, Kenyon Col, 69-70; asst prof, Edinboro State Col, 70-71; asst prof, Boston Univ, 75-79; vis asst prof, Clark Univ, 80-81; from asst prof to prof, Univ of Miami, 81-; Dir of Women's Studies, Univ of Miami, 95-98. **SELECTED PUBLICATIONS** Auth, La Princesse de Cleves: The Tension of Elegance, The Hague, 73; coauth, La France et la francophonie, Random House, 91; auth, Signs of Certainty: The Linguistic Imperative in French Classical Literature, Anma Libri (Saratoga, CA), 91; auth, "Words and Music in Esther," Cahiers du dix-septieme: an Interdisciplinary J (95): 81-90; auth, "Allegorie et corporalite feminine: les deux muses de Poussin," Le Corps au dix-septieme siecle, Biblio 17 (95): 151-160; auth, "Esther aux portes de Versailles," Esthetique baroque et imagination creatrice, Biblio 17, 98. **CONTACT ADDRESS** Dept For Lang, Univ of Miami, PO 248093, Miami, FL 33124. **EMAIL** bwoshins@miami.edu

WRAGE, WILLIAM
PERSONAL Born 01/10/1936, Lincoln, IL, m, 1959, 2 children **DISCIPLINE** FRENCH **EDUCATION** Wash Univ, BA, 57; Univ Wis-Madison, MA, 60, PhD, 64. **CAREER** From instr to asst prof French, Miami Univ, 63-69, adv studies abroad, 66-69; assoc prof, 69-73, grad chmn mod lang, 70-72 & 77-80, chmn dept mod lang, 72-77, grad chmn mod lang, 77-80, Prof French, Ohio Univ, 73-. **MEMBERSHIPS** Am Asn Teachers Fr. **RESEARCH** French civilization; 18th century French literature. **CONTACT ADDRESS** Dept of Mod Lang, Ohio Univ, Athens, OH 45701-2979. **EMAIL** wmwrage@frognet.net

WRAY, DAVID L.
PERSONAL Born 05/25/1959, Atlanta, GA, m, 1997 **DISCIPLINE** CLASSICAL PHILOLOGY **EDUCATION** Emory Univ, BA, 80; Harvard Univ, PhD, 96. **CAREER** Asst prof, class lang and lit, Univ Chicago, 97-. **MEMBERSHIPS** Am Philol Asn; Am Class League. **RESEARCH** Latin poetry; Hellenistic poetry; literary criticism. **SELECTED PUBLICATIONS** Auth, Catullus and the Poetics of Roman Manhood, Cambridge, forthcoming; auth, Lucretius, in Briggs, ed, Roman Authors vol of Dictionary of Literary Biography, Bruccoli Clark Layman, forthcoming; auth, Apollonius Masterplot: A Reading of Argonautical in Harder, ed, Apollonius Rhodius: Hellenistica Groningana IV, Groningen, forthcoming. **CONTACT ADDRESS** Dept of Classics, Univ of Chicago, 1010 E 59th St, Chicago, IL 60637. **EMAIL** d_wray@uchicago.edu

WRIGHT, JOHN
DISCIPLINE LATIN LANGUAGE AND LITERATURE **EDUCATION** Swarthmore, BA, 62; Ind Univ, MA, 64; Am Acad Rome, FAAR, 68; Ind Univ, PhD, 71. **SELECTED PUBLICATIONS** Auth, Dancing in Chains, Rome, 74; The Life of Cola di Rienzo, Toronto, 75; rev, Homeric Greek: A Book for Beginners, Okla, 85; rev, ed, Plautus' Curculio, Okla, 93. **CONTACT ADDRESS** Dept of Classics, Northwestern Univ, 1801 Hinma, Evanston, IL 60208. **EMAIL** jhwright@northwestern.edu

WROBEL, JANUSZ
PERSONAL Born 07/05/1953, Cieszyn, Poland, m, 1998, 5 children **DISCIPLINE** LINGUISTICS **EDUCATION** Jagiellonian Univ, BA; MA, 78; PhD, 84. **CAREER** Instructor to Asst Prof, Jagiellonian Univ, 78-84; visiting Prof, Wayne State Univ, 84-86; Lecturer, Oakland Univ, 90-; Asst Prof to Prof and Dept Chair, St Mary's Col, 86-. **HONORS AND AWARDS** Gold Cross, Govt Poland, 99; Otto Bremer Foundation, 96; Hoover Inst, Stanford Univ, 94; Excellence Awd, Ministry of Educ Poland, 91; Woodrow Wilson Intl Ctr for Scholars in Washington, 87. **MEMBERSHIPS** Mich Soc for Psychoanalytic Psychol, The Florian Znaniecki Sci Foundation, Polish Studies Asn, Am Asn for the Advancement of Slavic Studies, Polish Inst of Arts and Sci of Am, Mich Acad of Sci. **RESEARCH** Post communist Europe; East-Central Europe after 1945. **SELECTED PUBLICATIONS** Auth, "A Struggle for Academic Freedom: the contribution of solidarity to Reform in Higher Education," Solidarity, Martial Law and Aftermath, in press; auth, "Young, Westernized, Moderate: The Polish Left after communism," Beyond the return of the Left in Post-Communist states, in press; auth, People's Poland Through the Eyes of the Younger Generation, forthcoming; auth, "Philosophy of Schizophrenia," Michigan society for Psychoanalytic Psychology News, (97): 5-9; auth, "Trybuna Ludu, Ronald Reagan and the Pope," Samaritan Review, (94): 270-278; auth, "Capitalist Aspirations and the communist Legacy in Poland," Journal of Interdisciplinary Studies, (92): 139-162; auth, Language and Schizophrenia, John Benjamins Pub co, 90; auth, Polska po poisku (Poland in Polish): A Polish Language Handbook for Beginners, Interpress, 86; auth, Papers from the Second Congress of the Scholars of Polish Origin, Ossolineum, 84. **CONTACT ADDRESS** Dept Humanities, Saint Mary's Col, Michigan, 3535 Indian Trail, Orchard Lake, MI 48324-1623. **EMAIL** wrobel@oakland.edu

WU, JOSEPH SEN
PERSONAL Born 09/10/1934, Canton, China, m, 1982, 3 children **DISCIPLINE** PHILOSOPHY, CHINESE CLASSICS **EDUCATION** Taiwan Norm Univ, BA, 59; Wash Univ, MA, 62; Southern Ill Univ, PhD(philos), 67. **CAREER** From instr to asst prof philos Univ Mo-St Louis, 63-67; asst prof, Northern Ill Univ, 67-70; assoc prof, 70-73, prof, philos, Calif State Univ Sacramento 73-, vis prof, Loyola Univ, Ill, 69-70 & Nat Taiwan Univ, 76-77. **MEMBERSHIPS** Am Philos Asn; Soc Comp & Asian Philos. **RESEARCH** American philosophy; Far Eastern philosophy; philosophy of culture. **SELECTED PUBLICATIONS** Auth, Contemporary Western Philosophy from an Eastern viewpoint, Int Philos Quart, 68; The Paradoxical Situation of Western Philosophy and the Search for Chinese Wisdom, Inquiry, 71; Understanding Maoism, Studies Soviet Thought, 74;

Comparative Philosophy and Culture (in Chinese), Tung Ta, Taiwan, 78; Clarification and Enlightenment: Essays in Comparative Philosophy, Univ Am, 78; many articles in contemporary philosophy and comparative philosophy in 1980's and 1990's. **CONTACT ADDRESS** Dept of Philos, California State Univ, Sacramento, 6000 J St, Sacramento, CA 95819-6033.

WU, PEI-YI
PERSONAL Born 12/03/1927, Nanking, China **DISCIPLINE** CHINESE LITERATURE, INTELLECTUAL HISTORY **EDUCATION** Nat Cent Univ, Nanking, AB, 50; Boston Univ, MA, 52; Columbia Univ, PhD(Chinese lit), 69. **CAREER** Ibstr Chinese, Army Lang Sch, 53-58; res linguist, Univ Calif, Berkeley, 58-59; preceptor, Columbia Univ, 62-63; instr, 63-66, lectr, 66-67; vis assoc prof, 67-69, Assoc Prof Chinese, Queens Col, 69-, Mem univ fac senate, City Univ New York, 71-74; VIS Assoc Prof, Columbia Univ, 72-; Nat Endowment for Humanities fel, 74. **MEMBERSHIPS** Am Orient Soc; Asn Asian Studies. **RESEARCH** Chinese autobiography and myth. **SELECTED PUBLICATIONS** Auth, Memories of Kai-Feng--Meng,Yuan-Lao Description of the City in Tung-Ching Meng Hua Lu, New Lit Hist, Vol 0025, 94. **CONTACT ADDRESS** Dept of Class & Orient Lang, Queens Col, CUNY, 6530 Kissena Blvd, Flushing, NY 11367.

WYATT, WILLIAM F.
PERSONAL Born 07/14/1932, Medford, MA, m, 1989, 3 children **DISCIPLINE** CLASSICS **EDUCATION** Bowdoin Col, AB; Harvard Univ, PhD 62. **CAREER** Univ Washington, asst prof, assoc prof, 60-67; Brown Univ, assoc prof, prof, 67 to 98. **RESEARCH** Homer; Linguistics. **SELECTED PUBLICATIONS** Auth, Several books, many articles and reviews. **CONTACT ADDRESS** Dept of Classics, Brown Univ, Providence, RI 02912. **EMAIL** william_wyatt_jr@brown.edu

WYATT-BROWN, ANNE M.
PERSONAL Born 04/18/1939, Baltimore, MD, m, 1962, 1 child **DISCIPLINE** LINGUISTICS **EDUCATION** Radcliffe Col, AB, 61; Johns Hopkins Univ, MA, 62; Case Western Reserve Univ, PhD, 72. **CAREER** Instructor, Cleveland Inst of Art, 74-83; Adj Asst Prof, Case Western Reserve Univ, 82-83; Lecturer to Assoc Prof and Prog Dir, Univ Fla, 83-. **HONORS AND AWARDS** Fel, Gerontol Soc of Am, 99; Teaching Improvement Prog Awd, Univ FL, 94. **RESEARCH** Creativity; Aging and writing; Holocaust literature. **SELECTED PUBLICATIONS** Auth, "The Coming of Age of Literary Gerontology," Journal of Aging Studies, (90): 299-315; auth, Barbara Pym: A Critical biography, Columbia, 92; auth, "Creativity as a Defense against Death: Maintaining One's Professional Identity," Journal of Aging Studies, (95): 349-354; auth, "Literary Legacies: Continuity and Change," Generations, (96): 65-68; auth, "Creative change: The Life and Work of Four Novelists: Jane Austen, E.M. Forster, Barbara Pym, and Henry Roth," Journal of Aging and Identity, (98): 67-75; auth, "Holocaust Survival Stories: change over Time," Journal of Aging and Identity, in press. **CONTACT ADDRESS** Dept Ling, Univ of Florida, PO Box 115454, Gainesville, FL 32611-5454. **EMAIL** amwbolin@ufl.edu

WYLIE, HAL
PERSONAL Born 09/16/1935, New York, NY, m, 1971, 5 children **DISCIPLINE** FRENCH AND AFRICAN LITERATURE **EDUCATION** Univ Ariz, BA, 57; Stanford Univ, MA, 61, PhD(French & humanities), 65. **CAREER** Asst ed, Agr Experiment Station, Univ Ariz, 57-59; Asst Prof French, Univ Tex, Austin, 64-; Assoc Prof, French, Univ Texas, 80-. **MEMBERSHIPS** African Lit Asn; Am Asn Teachers Fr. **RESEARCH** Caribbean and African literature. **SELECTED PUBLICATIONS** Auth, World Literature Today; auth, The Gar, Literary Review, 71-80; auth, Contemporary African Literature, Three Continents Press, 83; auth, African Literature 1988: New Masks, Three Continents, 91; auth, Cosmopolitan Conde, or Unscrambling the Worlds, World Lit Today, Vol 0067, 93; auth, Multicultralism and Hybridit in African Literature, Africa World Press, 00. **CONTACT ADDRESS** Dept of French, Univ of Texas, Austin, Austin, TX 78712. **EMAIL** hwylie@mail.utexas.edu

WYNGAARD, AMY S.
PERSONAL Born 09/22/1970, Cambridge, MA **DISCIPLINE** FRENCH LITERATURE **EDUCATION** Univ Colo, BA, 92; Univ Penn, MA, 94; PhD, 98. **CAREER** Asst prof, Syracuse Univ, 98-. **HONORS AND AWARDS** Phi Beta Kappa, 90; Crisp Fel, Phi Beta Kappa, 92; Benjamin Franklin Fel, 93-97; Mellon Fel, 97-98; Meredith Teaching Awd, 01. **MEMBERSHIPS** MLA, Am Soc for 18th Century Studies. **RESEARCH** Eighteenth-Century French literature and cultural history, interdisciplinary studies. **SELECTED PUBLICATIONS** Auth, "Libertine Spaces: Anonymous Crowds, Secret Chambers, and Urban Corruption in Retif de la Bretonne," Eighteen-Century Life, (98); auth, "Switching Codes: Class, Clothing and Cultural Change in the Works of Marivaux and Watteau," Eighteen-Century Studies, (00). **CONTACT ADDRESS** Syracuse Univ, 340 H B Crouse Hall, Syracuse, NY 13244. **EMAIL** asyngaa@syr.edu

WYRICK, STEPHEN VON
PERSONAL Born Dallas, TX, 2 children **DISCIPLINE** HEBREW BIBLE **EDUCATION** SW Baptist Theol Sem, M Div, 76, PhD, 81. **CAREER** Prof & Religion Dept Chr, Calif Baptist Col, 86-94; PRof& Relig Dept Chr, Univ Mary Hardin-Baylor, 94- **HONORS AND AWARDS** NEH; Sr Res fel Wm F Albright Inst. **MEMBERSHIPS** SBL; ASOR; NABPR; NAPH; IES **RESEARCH** Iron I & Late Bronze Age **CONTACT ADDRESS** Univ of Mary Hardin-Baylor, 900 College St., UMHB Station Box 8356, Belton, TX 76513. **EMAIL** swyrick@umhb.edu

X

XU, PING
PERSONAL Born 06/13/1957, Jilin, China **DISCIPLINE** COMPARATIVE LITERATURE **EDUCATION** Jingzhou Teachers Col, China, Diploma, 81; Nanjing Univ, China, MA, 87; State Univ NYork at Binghamton, MA, 96; PhD, 97. **CAREER** Substitute asst prof, Baruch Col, CUNY, 97-98, asst prof of Chinese & Comparative Lit, Dept of Modern Langs & Comparative Lit, Coordr of CUNY Lower Manhattan/Downtown Brooklyn Consortium of Foreign Langs, New York, NY, Baruch Col, CUNY, 98-. **HONORS AND AWARDS** Grad Student Awd for Excellence in Res, SUNY, Binghamton, 96-97; Proj dir, the City Univ of New York, 99; proj assoc, the U. S. Dept of Educ, 98-2000; principle investigator, PSC-CUNY Res Awds, 99-2000. **MEMBERSHIPS** Asn for Asian Studies, Chinese Lang Teachers Asn, Modern Lang Asn of Am, Am Coun on the Teaching of Foreign Langs. **SELECTED PUBLICATIONS** Auth, Art as the First Light of Knowledge: An Introduction to Benedetto Croce's Aesthetics, Nanjing: Jiangsu Educ Press (90); transl, "Four Classical Chinese Poems," Concourse, no 9 (94): 20-23; transl, "Flag," in Debbie Folaron, ed, Folio, Center for Res in Transl, SUNY, Binghamton, (95): 56; auth, "Irigaray's Mimicry and the Problem of Essentialism," Hypatia, A J of Feminist Philos, vol 10, no 4 (95): 76-89; rev of "Taiwan Today: An Intermediate Course," coauth with Prof Theresa Jen, CLASS J (fall 96): 52-53; auth, "Croce's Notion of Externalization and the Alleged 'Unpainted painting'," Italian Quart, Nos 137-138 (summer/fall 98): 13-22; auth, " 'Rose-Cherry-Sunset-Iron Rust-Flamingo' Diagram and the Genesis of Ezra Pound's Ideogrammic Method," Paideuma, A J Devoted to Ezra Pound Scholarship, vol 27, nos 2 & 3 (fall and winter 98): 53-68; auth, "Chinese Characters in the Computer Age," Geolinguistics: The J of the Am Soc of Geolinguistics, Vol 25 (99): 103-112. **CONTACT ADDRESS** Dept Modern Langs, Baruch Col, CUNY, 17 Lexington Ave, New York, NY 10010-5518. **EMAIL** ping_xu@baruch.cuny.edu

Y

YALDEN, JANICE
PERSONAL Born Kingston, Jamaica **DISCIPLINE** LINGUISTICS **EDUCATION** Univ Toronto, BA, 52; Univ Michigan, MA, 56. **CAREER** Lectr, 69-83, founding dir, Ctr Applied Lang Studs, 81-84, Prof Linguistics to Prof Emer, Carlton Univ 83-, dean arts, 87-92, ch, dept Ling & Applied Lang Studs, 94-. **MEMBERSHIPS** Ont Mod Lang Tchr Asn; Can Asn Applied Ling; Maurice Price Found; Soc Educ Visits & Exchanges Can. **SELECTED PUBLICATIONS** Auth, Communicative Language Teaching: Principles and Practice, 81; auth, The Communicative Syllabus: Evolution, Design and Implementation, 83; auth, Principles of Course Design for Language Teaching, 87; auth, Second Language Teaching at the Post-Secondary Level, in Bull Can Asn Applied Ling, 84. **CONTACT ADDRESS** Dept Ling & Applied Lang Studies, Carleton Univ, 1125 Colonel By Dr, 215 Paterson Hall, Ottawa, ON, Canada K1S 5B6. **EMAIL** jyalden@ccs.carleton.ca

YAMADA, REIKO
DISCIPLINE JAPANESE **EDUCATION** Portland State Univ, BA, 78; Cornell Univ, MA, 82; PhD, 88. **CAREER** Assoc prof & coordr, Japanese Lang Prog, Williams Col, 86; assoc prof, Hokkaido Tokai Univ; vis asst prof, , Meiji Gakuin Univ. **HONORS AND AWARDS** Tokai Univ env res grants; Heiwa Nakajima Found grant; Clark Awd, excellence in tchg, Cornell Univ. **RESEARCH** Japanese language pedagogy; linguistics; intercultural communication. **SELECTED PUBLICATIONS** Auth, Pragmatics and Sociolinguistics of -tara and -(r)eba in Japanese Conversational Discourse, Univ Microfilms Int, 88. **CONTACT ADDRESS** Center for Foreign Languages, Literatures and Cult, Williams Col, Williamstown, MA 01267. **EMAIL** Reiko.Yamada@williams.edu

YAMAUCHI, EDWIN MASAO
PERSONAL Born 02/01/1937, Hilo, HI, m, 1962, 2 children **DISCIPLINE** ANCIENT HISTORY, SEMITIC LANGUAGES **EDUCATION** Shelton Col, BA, 60; Brandeis Univ, MA, 62, PhD(Mediter studies), 64. **CAREER** Asst prof ancient hist, Rutgers Univ, New Brunswick, 64-69; assoc prof, 69-73, dir grad studies, Hist Dept, 78-82, prof Hist, Miami Univ, 73-, Nat Endowment for Humanities fel, 68; Am Philos Soc grant, 70; consult ed hist, J Am Sci Affiliation, 70-; sr ed, Christianity Today, 92-94. **MEMBERSHIPS** Am Sci Affil (pres, 83); Archaeol Inst Am; Conf Faith & Hist (pres, 74-76); Near E Archaeol Soc (vpres, 78); Inst Bibl Res (pres, 87-89). **RESEARCH** Gnosticism; ancient magic; Old and New Testaments. **SELECTED PUBLICATIONS** Pre-Christian Gnosticism, Tyndale Press, London & Eerdmans, 73; The Archaeology of New Testament Cities in Western Asia Minor, Baker Bk, 80; The Scriptures and Archaeology, Western Conserv Baptist Sem, 80; World of the New Testament, Harper & Row, 81; Foes from the Northern Frontier, Baker Bk, 82; coeditor, Chronos, Kairos, Christos, Eisenbrauns, 89; Persia and the Bible, Baker Bk, 90; coauth, The Two Kingdoms, Moody, 93; coed, Peoples of the Old Testament World, Baker, 94; ed, Africa and Africans in Antiquity, Mich State Univ Pr, 00. **CONTACT ADDRESS** Dept of History, Miami Univ, 500 E High St, Oxford, OH 45056-1602. **EMAIL** Yamauce@muohio.edu

YAN, MARGARET M.
PERSONAL Born 09/11/1938, Amoy, Fujian, China, m, 1964, 1 child **DISCIPLINE** ANTHROPOLOGY, LINGUISTICS **EDUCATION** Nat Taiwan Univ, BA, 62; Cornell Univ, MA, 79. **CAREER** Asst prof, Univ of San Francisco, 73-74; lectr, Calif State Univ, 73-75; asst prof to prof, Ind Univ, 75-. **HONORS AND AWARDS** Fulbright-Hays Res Fel, 81-82; Pres, Chinese Teachers Assoc, 86-88; Grants, Ind Univ, 87, 88, 92, 95; grant, Academia Sinica, 93, 94. **MEMBERSHIPS** Ling Soc of Am; Chinese Lang Teachers Assoc; Chinese Lang Computer Soc; Int Assoc of Chinese Ling; Int Assoc for the Teaching Chinese as a Second Lang. **RESEARCH** Phonology, Chinese historical phonology, Chinese Dialectoloty, Anthropological/socio-linguistics, Taiwan Aboriginal Languages. **SELECTED PUBLICATIONS** Auth, "Historical Sound Changes as Criteria for the Classification of Fujian Dialects", A collected Volume on Sociocultural Studies on Taiwan and Fujian, eds Ying-chang chunag and Ying-hai Pan, Academica Sinica (Taiwan, 94): 257-283; coauth, Interactions I: A Cognitive Approach to Beginning Chinese, Ind Univ Pr, (Bloomington), 97; coauth, Workbook for Interactions I: A Cognitive Approach to Beginning Chinese, Ind Univ Pr, (Bloomington), 97; coauth, Interactions II: A Cognitive Approach to Beginning Chinese, Ind Univ Pr, (Bloomington), 97; coauth, Workbook for Interactions II: A Cognitive Approach to Beginning Chinese, Ind Univ Pr, (Bloomington), 97; coauth, Teacher's Manual for Interactions I-II, Ind Univ Pr, (Bloomington), 97; auth, "The Evolutionary Deverlopment of the MC *ri initial in the Dialects of Fujian and Taiwan", Proceedings of the 10th N Am Conf on Chinese Ling, Vol I, ed Chaofen Sun, Stanford Univ, (99): 74-89. **CONTACT ADDRESS** Dept E Asian Lang, Indiana Univ, Bloomington, 1011 E 3rd St, Bloomington, IN 47405-7005. **EMAIL** yan@indiana.edu

YANG, INSUN
DISCIPLINE LINGUISTICS, KOREAN LANGUAGE **EDUCATION** Ehwa Woman's Univ, Korea, BA; PA State Univ, MA; Rice Univ, PhD. **CAREER** Instr, 93-, dir, Korean Stud, Rice Univ. **RESEARCH** Korean and other Ural-Altaic dative markers. **SELECTED PUBLICATIONS** Publ articles in the J of Korean-Am Educ and the J of the Ling Asn of Can and the US. **CONTACT ADDRESS** Rice Univ, PO Box 1892, Houston, TX 77251-1892. **EMAIL** iyang@rice.edu

YANG, MIMI
DISCIPLINE SPANISH LANGUAGE AND LITERATURE **EDUCATION** Beijing, BA; Univ Ariz, MA PhD. **CAREER** Spanish, Carthage Col; Asst Prof, Carthage Col. **SELECTED PUBLICATIONS** Auth, To be Human: Is the Rassias Method the Rassias Madness?, Ram's Horn, 95; Una mirada oriental a las letras perunas, Lundero, 89; Pain and Painting: Frida Kahlo's Visual Autobiography, Autobiographic Studies, 1997. **CONTACT ADDRESS** Carthage Col, 2001 Alford Dr., Kenosha, WI 53140. **EMAIL** yang@carthage.edu

YANG, PETER JIANHUA
PERSONAL Born Jiangsu, m, 1981, 1 child **DISCIPLINE** GERMAN, CHINESE, COMPARATIVE LIT **EDUCATION** Univ Utah, PhD, 96. **CAREER** Translator, Central Trnslating & Editing Ctr, Beijing, 75- 79; res, interpreter, Ministry For Econ Relations, Trade, Beijing, 82-89; instr, 90-94, LANG LAB DIR, 94-, JESSE HAWK SHERA ASST PROF GERMAN, CHINESE, COMP LIT, 96-. **HONORS AND AWARDS** Nord Grant for Innovative Teaching with Technology: W.P. Jones Presidential Grant; Language Learning Technology **MEMBERSHIPS** MLA, IALL (Int Asn of Am Asn of Modern Language. **RESEARCH** Modern German Literature and Theater, Instructional Technology. **SELECTED PUBLICATIONS** Auth, Theater is Theater, Peter Lang Publishing, 98; auth, Play is Play, Univ Press of Am, 00. **CONTACT ADDRESS** 10900 Euclid Ave, Bldg 7118, Cleveland, OH 44106-7118. **EMAIL** pjyz@po.cwra.edu

YANG, XIAOBIN
PERSONAL Born Shanghai, China **DISCIPLINE** CHINESE LITERATURE **EDUCATION** Yale Univ, PhD, 96. **CAREER** Adj prof, Fairfield Univ, 97-98; Croft Asst Prof, Univ Miss, 98-. **RESEARCH** Chinese Literature and Culture, Poetry, Compar-

ative Literature, Literary Theory. **SELECTED PUBLICATIONS** Auth, Across the Sunlight Zone, Modern Poetry Soc, 94; auth, Negative Aesthetics: Literary Theory and Cultural Criticism of the Frankfurt School, 95 & 99; auth, History and Rhetoric: On Contemporary Chinese Literature, 99. **CONTACT ADDRESS** Dept Modern Lang, Univ of Mississippi, University, MS 38667-9999.

YARDLEY, J. C.
DISCIPLINE CLASSICS **EDUCATION** St Andrews, MA, 66, PhD, 76; Oxford, BA, 70. **CAREER** Asst, Assoc to Prof, 69-88, Univ of Calgary; Prof, Chr, 88-, Univ of Ottawa. **HONORS AND AWARDS** Pres, Class Assoc of Can, 94-96. **MEMBERSHIPS** CAC; Amer Philos Assoc. **RESEARCH** Roman Poetry; The Alexander Hist; Justin. **SELECTED PUBLICATIONS** Auth, Quintus Curtis Rufus, Penguin Classics, 84; Justin, Scholars Press, 94; Justin 11-12, Oxford Univ Press, 97. **CONTACT ADDRESS** Dept Classic Studies, Univ of Ottawa, Ottawa, ON, Canada K1N 6N5. **EMAIL** JCYard@AIX1.UOTTAWA.ca

YARRISON, BETSY
DISCIPLINE COMPARATIVE LITERATURE **EDUCATION** Univ Wisc, PhD. **CAREER** Asst prof, Univ Baltimore. **RESEARCH** Dramatic theory; language behavior; professional writing. **CONTACT ADDRESS** Commun Dept, Univ of Baltimore, 1420 N. Charles Street, Baltimore, MD 21201.

YATES, DONALD ALFRED
PERSONAL Born 04/11/1930, Ayer, MA, m, 1951, 3 children **DISCIPLINE** SPANISH **EDUCATION** Univ Mich, BA, 51, MA, 54, PhD(Span), 61. **CAREER** Teaching asst Span, Univ Mich, 53-57; all-univ res grant to Mex, 58 & 61, Prof Span, Mich State Univ, 57-, Fulbright res award, Arg 62-63; gen ed, Macmillan Mod Span Am Lit Ser, 62-; Fulbright lectr, Arg, 67-68 & 70; lectr Am lit, Univ Buenos Aires & Univ La Plata; vis prof, Ctr 20th Century Studies, Univ Wis-Milwaukee, 74; vis prof, San Francisco State Univ, 81. **HONORS AND AWARDS** Silver Medallion for Contrib to Field of Latin Am Lit, Instituto de Cultura Hisp, Madrid, Spain, 75. **MEMBERSHIPS** Am Asn Teachers Span & Port; MLA; Inst Int Lit Iberoam; Latin Am Studies Asn; Asoc Int Hispanistas. **RESEARCH** Spanish American literature of fantasy and imagination; Argentine literature; writings of Jorge Luis Borges. **SELECTED PUBLICATIONS** Auth, Borges Craft of Fiction--Selected Essays on His Writing, World Lit Today, Vol 0067, 93; A Tribute to Earle, Peter,G., Hisp Rev, Vol 0061, 93. **CONTACT ADDRESS** Michigan State Univ, 537 Wells Hall, East Lansing, MI 48824.

YEH, MICHELLE
DISCIPLINE COMPARATIVE LITERATURE **EDUCATION** Univ S Calif, PhD, 82. **CAREER** Prof, Univ Calif Davis, 94-. **HONORS AND AWARDS** ACLS Fel; CCK Found Res Grant. **MEMBERSHIPS** Assoc for Asian Studies; Assoc of Lit Critics and Scholars. **RESEARCH** Poetry, Chinese Literature, Translation. **SELECTED PUBLICATIONS** Auth, No Trace of the Gardener: Poems of Yang Mu, 98. **CONTACT ADDRESS** Dept E Asian Lang and Cult, Univ of California, Davis, 1 Shields Ave, Davis, CA 95616-8601. **EMAIL** mmyew@ucdavis.edu

YEHUDA, SIMONE N.
PERSONAL Born 12/04/1943, Cambridge, MA, m, 1999, 2 children **DISCIPLINE** COMPARATIVE LITERATURE, CREATIVE WRITING **EDUCATION** Bennington Col, BA, 65; Columbia Univ, MA, 67; Union Inst, PhD, 99. **CAREER** Playwt res, Attic Th, 82-86; dir, Ann Arbor Rep Th, 86-90; prof, Siena Hts Univ, 93-. **HONORS AND AWARDS** Cir Schls, Un Inst, 99; NEH Sem, 97; MCA Creat Ach Awd, 83; Who's Who in US Writ, Eds, Poets. **MEMBERSHIPS** MLA; AAUW; Dram Guild; SWGW; DAPFW; DCW; **RESEARCH** Women's studies; film studies; theater studies; multiculturalism; Judaic studies; playwriting; screenwriting; poetry; memoir; creative non-fiction. **SELECTED PUBLICATIONS** Auth, Lifting Water, Crowfoot Press (79); auth, Thaw, Horizon Press (74). **CONTACT ADDRESS** Dept Humanities, Siena Heights Univ, 1247 East Siena Hts Dr, Adrian, MI 49221-1755. **EMAIL** syehuda@sienahts.edu

YERKES, DAVID
DISCIPLINE ANGLO-SAXON LANGUAGE AND LITERATURE **EDUCATION** Yale Univ, 71; Oxford Univ, BA, 73 Dphil, 76. **CAREER** Prof, 77-. **MEMBERSHIPS** Mem, London Medieval Soc; Medieval Acad; Soc Text Scholar. **SELECTED PUBLICATIONS** Auth, An Old English Thesaurus; Syntax and Style in Old English; The Old English Life of Machutus. **CONTACT ADDRESS** Dept of Eng, Columbia Col, New York, 2960 Broadway, New York, NY 10027-6902.

YETIV, ISAAC
PERSONAL Born 03/13/1929, Nabeul, Tunisia, m, 1953, 3 children **DISCIPLINE** FRENCH AND HEBREW LANGUAGE AND LITERATURE **EDUCATION** Hebrew Univ Jerusalem, BA, 67; Univ Wis- Madison, PhD, 70. **CAREER** Teacher math, physics & lang, Safed High Sch, Israel, 50-54; teacher math & physics, Reali Lyceum, Haifa, 54-67; teaching asst Hebrew, Univ Wis-Madison, 67-69; from asst prof to assoc prof French & Hebrew, Univ Hartford, 69-75; prof French & Hebrew & head dept mod lang, Univ Akron, 75-93, Dir English Lang Inst, 76-93, Lectr Hebrew, Univ Conn, 70-71. **MEMBERSHIPS** MLA; Nat Asn Prof Hebrew. **RESEARCH** Twentieth century French and Hebrew literature; Black African and North African literature in French; alienation of the marginal man in world literature. **SELECTED PUBLICATIONS** Auth, Judeo-Maghrebian Literature Written in French--French, Res African Lit, 92. **CONTACT ADDRESS** Dept of Modern Languages, Univ of Akron, Olin Hall 304, Akron, OH 44325-1907.

YODER, LAUREN WAYNE
PERSONAL Born 03/09/1943, Newport News, VA, m, 1964, 2 children **DISCIPLINE** FRENCH LANGUAGE AND LITERATURE **EDUCATION** Eastern Mennonite Col, BA, 64; Univ Iowa, MA, 69, PhD(French), 73. **CAREER** Teacher physics, Ecole Pedag Protestante, Kikwit, Zaire, 66-68; vis asst prof English, Univ Paris, 71-72; asst prof, 73-80, Assoc Prof French, Davidson Col, 80- **MEMBERSHIPS** MLA; Am Asn Teachers Fr; African Lit Asn; Southern Asn Africanists. **RESEARCH** Medieval French tale; African novel. **SELECTED PUBLICATIONS** Auth, L'aventure ambigue, Bull Southern Asn Africanists, 9/74; Les quatre elements dans L'Enfant Noir, Fer de Lance, 9/77 & spring 78. **CONTACT ADDRESS** Davidson Col, Po Box 1719, Davidson, NC 28036-1719.

YOKEN, MEL B.
PERSONAL Born 06/25/1939, Fall River, MA, m, 1976, 3 children **DISCIPLINE** FRENCH LANGUAGE & LITERATURE **EDUCATION** Univ Mass, Amherst, BA, 60; Brown Univ, MAT, 61; Five-Col Prog, Univ Mass, Amherst Col, Smith Col, Mt Holyoke Col & Hampshire Col, PhD(French), 72. **CAREER** From instr to asst prof, 66-76, assoc prof, 76-81, Prof French, Univ of Mass Dartmouth, 82-, Res fel, Quebec Studies, 81-, Univ of Montreal, 81-88. **HONORS AND AWARDS** Distinguished Service Award, City of Fall River, 74, 80; Excellence in Teaching French Award, 84, 85; Governor's Citation, 86; Nat Distinguished Leadership Award, 90; Distinguished Service Award from Mass Foreign Lang Asn, 92; Medaille de Vermeil from the French Acad, 93; Outstanding Service Award, Fall River Chamber of Commerce, 97, Outstanding Teaching award, Univ of Mass, 97; Distinguished Alumni Award, Durfee High Sch, 98; Golden Apple Award for exellence in teaching, 98. **MEMBERSHIPS** MLA; Am Asn Teachers Fr; Am Com Teaching Foreign Lang; New England Foreign Lang Asn; Middlebury Amicale, Francophone Asn; Richeliew Int, Brown Univ Alumni Asn. **RESEARCH** The French novel; French literature of the 19th century; French literature of the 20th century; Quebec literature. **SELECTED PUBLICATIONS** Auth, Paleneo, Mass Foreign Lang Bull, fall 73; Wise guy Solomon, Outlook 3/74; Claude Tillier, Twayne, 76; Speech is Plurality, Univ Press of Am, 78; Claude Tillier: Fame and fortune in his novelistic work, Fairleigh Dickinson Univ, 77; France's Shakespeare: Moliere, Cambridge Univ Press, 78; Speech is Plurality, 78; auth, Entretians Quebecois II, 89; auth, Stowell Goding and France, 93; auth, Entretians Quebecois III, 99. **CONTACT ADDRESS** Dept of Modern Lang, Univ of Massachusetts, Dartmouth, 285 Old Westport Rd, North Dartmouth, MA 02747-2300.

YOUNG, DAVID CHARLES
PERSONAL Born 12/09/1937, Lincoln, NE, m, 1958, 3 children **DISCIPLINE** CLASSICS **EDUCATION** Univ Nebr, BA, 59; Univ Iowa, MA, 60 , PhD(classics), 63. **CAREER** From asst prof to assoc prof, 63-72, chmn dept, 68-72, Prof Classics, Univ Calif, Santa Barbara, 72- **MEMBERSHIPS** Am Philol Asn. **RESEARCH** Greek poetry, especially choral lyric. **SELECTED PUBLICATIONS** Auth, Myths About the Ancient Games, Archaeol, Vol 0049, 96. **CONTACT ADDRESS** Dept of Classics, Univ of California, Santa Barbara, Santa Barbara, CA 93106.

YOUNG, DOLLY J.
DISCIPLINE SPANISH APPLIED LINGUISTICS **EDUCATION** Univ Tex, PhD, 85. **CAREER** Assoc prof, Univ Tenn. **RESEARCH** Language acquisition; psycholinguistics; foreign language education. **SELECTED PUBLICATIONS** Co-ed, Language Anxiety: From Theory & Research to Classroom Implications, Prentice-Hall (Englewood Cliffs: NJ), 91; auth, "New Directions in Language Anxiety Research," in Faces in a Crowd: The Individual Learner in Multisection Courses, ed Carol A. Klee, (Boston: Heinle & Heinle, 94), 3-46. **CONTACT ADDRESS** Dept of Romance Languages, Univ of Tennessee, Knoxville, Knoxville, TN 37996. **EMAIL** djyoung@utk.edu

YOUNG, DWIGHT WAYNE
PERSONAL Born 12/15/1925, Lambert, OK, m, 1946, 2 children **DISCIPLINE** SEMITIC PHILOLOGY **EDUCATION** Hardin Simmons Univ, BA, 49, ThM(Semitics), 56; Dropsie Col, PhD(Egyptol), 55. **CAREER** Asst prof Semitic lang, Dallas Theol Sem, 54-58; asst prof, Brandeis Univ, 58-63, assoc prof Mediterranean studies, 63-67; vis prof Coptic, Hebrew Univ, Israel, 65; vis prof Semitic lang, Cornell Univ, 67-69; assoc prof Semitic lang, 69-72, Prof Ancient Near East Civilization, Brandies Univ, 72-, NDEA fel, 60; mem, Am Res Ctr Egypt. **HONORS AND AWARDS** Solomon Awd, Dallas Theol Sem, 51. **MEMBERSHIPS** Am Orient Soc; Soc Bibl Lit; Am Res Ctr Egypt. **RESEARCH** Comparative Semitic grammar; ancient history; Egyptology. **SELECTED PUBLICATIONS** Auth, On Shenoute's use of present I, 4/61 & Esope and the conditional conjugation, 7/62, J Near Eastern Studies; Unfulfilled conditions in Shenoute's dialect, J Am Orient Soc, 4/69; The milieu of Nag Hammadi: Some historical considerations, Vigiliae Christianae, 70; With snakes and dates: A sacred marriage drama at Ugarit, 77 & The Ugaritic Myth of the god Horan and the mare, 79, Ugarit Forschungen; A ghost word in the Testament of Jacob (Gen 49:5)?, J Bibl Lit, 81; ed, Studies presented to Hans Jakob Polotsky, 81. **CONTACT ADDRESS** Dept of Near East Studies, Brandeis Univ, Waltham, MA 02154.

YOUNG, HOWARD THOMAS
PERSONAL Born 03/24/1926, Cumberland, MD **DISCIPLINE** SPANISH, FRENCH **EDUCATION** Columbia Univ, BS, 50, MA, 52, PhD(Span), 56. **CAREER** Lectr, Columbia Col, Columbia Univ, 53-54; prof Romance Lang, Pomona Col, 54-, chmn Dept Mod Lang, 77-, Fulbright lectr, Spain, 67-68; independent study & res, Nat Endowment for Humanities, 75-76; chmn Span Lang Develop Comt, Educ Testing Serv, Princeton, NJ, 77-81. **MEMBERSHIPS** MLA; Am Asn Teachers Span & Port; Am Comp Lit Asn; Asn Dept For Lang. **RESEARCH** Contemporary Spanish poetry; comparative study of modern Spanish and English poetry. **SELECTED PUBLICATIONS** Auth, Mexico-a revolution gone bankrupt, New Repub, 4/60; Pedro Salinas y los Estados Unidos, Cuadernos Hispanoam, 62; The Victorious Expression, Univ Wis, 64; Juan Ramon Jimenez, Columbia Univ, 67; Anglo-American poetry in the correspondence of Luisa and Juan Ramon Jimenez, Hispanic Rev, 76; On using foreign service institute tests and standards on campuses, In: Measuring Spoken Language Proficiency, Georgetown Univ, 80; The Line in the Margin: Juan Ramon Jimenez and His Readings in Blake, Shelley, and Yeats, Univ Wis, 80; The exact names, Modern Lang Notes, 81; Rereading and Rewriting the Poem: Juan Ramon Jimenez and Jorge Guillen, Guillen at McGill, Essays for a Centenary, ed, K M Sibbald, Ottowa: Dovehouse Editions, 96; In Loving Translation: Zenobia and Juan Ramon, Revista Hispanica Moderna, 96. **CONTACT ADDRESS** Pomona Col, 333 N College Way, Claremont, CA 91711-6319. **EMAIL** htyoung@pomona.edu

YOUNG, MARY
DISCIPLINE AFRICAN-AMERICAN AND ASIAN-AMERICAN LITERATURE **EDUCATION** St Louis Univ, BA, 63, MA, 71; Univ Tex, MA; St Louis Univ, PhD, 90. **CAREER** Asst prof. **SELECTED PUBLICATIONS** Auth, Mules and Dragons: Popular Culture Images, Selected Writings of African-American and Chinese-American Women Writers. **CONTACT ADDRESS** Dept of Eng, The Col of Wooster, Wooster, OH 44691.

YOUNG, RICHARD F.
PERSONAL Born 10/15/1948, London, England, m, 1983, 2 children **DISCIPLINE** APPLIED LINGUISTICS **EDUCATION** Univ Pa, PhD, 89. **CAREER** Asst prof, Southern Ill Univ at Carbondale 90-93; from asst prof to prof, Univ Wis-Madison, 93-. **MEMBERSHIPS** Am Asn for Applied Ling; Ling Soc of Am; Teachers of English to Speakers of Other Lang. **RESEARCH** Applied linguistics; second language acquisition; English as a second language; interactional competence. **SELECTED PUBLICATIONS** Auth, Form-function Relations in Articles in English Interlanguage, Second Language Acquisition and Linguistic Variation, 96; auth with M.D. Shermis, K. Perkins, and S.R. Brutten, From Conventional to Computer-Adaptive Testing of ESL Reading Comprehension, System, 96; auth with G.B. Hallek, Let Them Eat Cake! Or How to Avoid Losing your Head in Cross-Cultural Conversations, Talking and Testing: Discourse Approaches to the Assessment of Oral Proficiency, 98; Auth with A.W. He, Language Proficiency Interviews: A Discourse Approach, Talking and Testing: Discourse Approaches to the Assessment of Oral Proficiency, 98; co-ed with A.W. He, Talking and Testing: Discourse Approaches to the Assessment of Oral Proficiency, 98; auth, "Sociolinguistic Approaches to SLA," Annual Rev of Appl Ling, 99. **CONTACT ADDRESS** Dept of Eng, Univ of Wisconsin, Madison, 600 N Park St, 5129 Helen C. White Hall, Madison, WI 53706-1403. **EMAIL** rfyoung@facstaff.wisc.edu

YOUNG, ROBERT VAUGHAN
PERSONAL Born 06/20/1947, Marianna, FL, m, 1968, 5 children **DISCIPLINE** RENAISSANCE ENGLISH, COMPARATIVE LITERATURE **EDUCATION** Rollins Col, BA, 68; Yale Univ, 71, PhD(English), 72. **CAREER** Asst prof, 72-79; Visiting prof & Acting Chair English, Chistendom Coll, 79-80; Assoc Prof, 80-86 Prof English NC State, 87-; Visiting Prof & Acting Dept Chair, Franciscan Univ of Steubenville, 91-93; Dir Grad Prog, English NC State, 98-. **HONORS AND AWARDS** Southeastern Inst Medieval and Ren Studies Fellow, 79; Fulbright Fellow Belguim. 83; ACLS Fellow 86-87; Fulbright Fellow Belgium, 00. **MEMBERSHIPS** NAS, ALSC, Ren Soc of Am, Shakespeare Assoc of Am, John Donne Society, Fellow-

ship of Am School, Conf on Christianity and Literature. **RESEARCH** Comparative literature of Baroque Age, especially English, Latin and Spanish; neo-Latin rhetorical studies, especially Justus Lipsius; contemporary moral & social issues. **SELECTED PUBLICATIONS** Auth, Richard Crashaw and the Spanish Golden Age, Yale, 82; auth, At War with The Word, ISI, 99; auth, Doctrine and Devotion in 17th -Century Literature, Boydell & Brewer, 00; auth, A Student's Guide to Literature, ISI, 00; ed and transl, Justus Lipsius Principles of Letter-Writing, with M.T. Hester, Southern Ill, 96; ed, John Donne Journal, with M.T. Hester, 82. **CONTACT ADDRESS** Dept of English, No Carolina State Univ, English NC State U Raleigh, 8105, Raleigh, NC 27695-8105. **EMAIL** vyoung@social.chass.ncsu.edu

YOUNG, THEODORE ROBERT
DISCIPLINE SPANISH AND PORTUGUESE LITERATURE **EDUCATION** Harvard Univ, PhD, 93. **CAREER** Asst prof, Florida State Univ; assoc prof and dir acad progs, Latin Am and Caribbean Ctr, Florida Int Univ. **SELECTED PUBLICATIONS** Auth, O Questionamento da Historia em O Tempo e o Vento de Erico Verissimo, 97; Um Realismo M gico no Brasil?: Um Levantamento, 95; A Fabricat o de um Sonho: A Recriat o do Processo Sonhador em Sinais de Fogo de Jorge de Sena, 95; Subvers o da Imagem do Estado Paternalista em O Tempo e o Vento, 95; auth, "A apresentacao narrativa em O Delfim de Jose Cardoso Pires," SIGNOS 28 (97): 101-110; auth, "Three Views of the Amazon in International Commercial Film," Luso-Brazilian Review 36.2 (99); co-ed, A Twice-Told Tale: Reinventing the Old World-New World Encounter in Latin American Literature and Film, Univ of Delaware Press, 00; auth, "Antropofagia, Tropicalismo, e Como era gostoso meu frances," Revista Letras 21 (00); co-auth, "Brazil's Political and Economic Policies, 1995-1999: The Impact on Capital Flight," eds Thomas P. Chen, Nejdet Delener, Edward B. Flowers, New York: St. John's Univ (00): 265-268; auth, "Como era gostoso meu frances: Tropicalismo in the Cinema," Studies in Latin American Popular Culture 19 (00): 93-102. **CONTACT ADDRESS** Dept of Modern Languages, Florida Intl Univ, University Park Campus, Miami, FL 33199. **EMAIL** youngtr@fiu.edu

YOUNG-FERRELL, BRENDA
PERSONAL Born 06/20/1955, Fort Worth, TX, m, 1992, 1 child **DISCIPLINE** FRENCH **EDUCATION** Carson-Newman Col, BA, 77; Univ Tenn, MA, 81; Tex Wesleyan Univ, MSE, 89; Univ Tenn, PhD, 97. **CAREER** Missionary Journeyman, Internal Missions Board, SBC, 78-80; Instructor, Tex Wesleyan Univ, 81-85; Instructor, Tarrant Co Jr Col, 85-89; Asst Prof, Carson-Newman Col, 89-. **HONORS AND AWARDS** Mellon Appalachian Fel, 92-93, 95-96; UTK Alumni Fel, 92-93. **MEMBERSHIPS** AATF, TFLTA, TESOL. **RESEARCH** 20th Century Feminine Writers **CONTACT ADDRESS** Dept For Lang, Carson-Newman Col, 1634 Russell Ave, Jefferson City, TN 37760-2204. **EMAIL** ferrell@cncacc.cn.edu

YU, ANTHONY C.
PERSONAL Born 10/06/1938, Hong Kong, m, 1963, 1 child **DISCIPLINE** RELIGION, WESTERN & CHINESE LITERATURE **EDUCATION** Houghton Col, BA, 60; Fuller Theol Sem, STB, 63; Univ Chicago, PhD(relig & lit), 69. **CAREER** Instr English, Univ Ill Chicago Circle, 67-68; from instr to asst prof relig & lit, 68-74, assoc prof, 74-78, Prof Relig & Lit, Divinity Sch & Prof Dept Far Eastern Lang & Civilizations, Comt Social Thought, English & Comp Lit, Univ Chicago, 78-90, Asst ed, J Asian Studies, 75-77, co-ed, Monogr Ser, 77-; Guggenheim Mem Found fel Chinese Lit, 76-77; Nat Endowment for Humanities special grant, 77-80 & 81-82; co-ed, J Relig, 80-90; Carl Darling Buck Distinguished Service Prof Humanities, 90; Sr Fel, Am Coun of Learned Soc, 86-87; Master Texts Study Grant, Seminar for Public Sch Teachers, NEH, 92; Phi Beta Kappa vis scholar, 01-02. **HONORS AND AWARDS** Gordon J Laing Prize, Univ of Chicago Press, 83. **MEMBERSHIPS** Asn Asian Studies, Elec Mem, China & Inner Asia Coun, 79-82; Am Acad Relig; Milton Soc of Am, Life Mem; MLA, Elec Mem, Exec Council, 98-01; Mem, Board of Dir, Illinois Hum Coun, 95-98; Elec Academician, Academia Sinica, 98; Elc Fel, Am academy of Arts and Sciences, 00. **RESEARCH** Religious approaches to classical literatures, western and non-western; comparative literature; translation. **SELECTED PUBLICATIONS** Auth, New Gods and old order: Tragic theology in the Prometheus Bound, J Am Acad Relig, 71; ed, Parnasus Revisited: Modern Criticism and The Epic Tradition, Am Libr Asn, 73; auth, Problems and prospects in Chinese-Western literary relations, In: Yearbook of General and Comparative Literature, 74; Chapter nine and the problem of narrative structure, J Asian Studies, 75; On translating the Hsi-yu chi, In: The Art and Profession of Translation, Hong Kong Transl Soc, 76; translr & ed, The Journey to the West, Vol I-IV, Univ Chicago, 77-83; Self and family in the Hung-lou meng, Chinese Lit: Essays, Articles, Rev, 80; Life in the garden: Freedom and the image of God in Paradise Lost, J Relig, 80; Order of Temptations in Paradis Regained, in Perspectives on Christology, ed, Marguerite Shuster & Richard Muller, Zondervan, 91; Rereading the Stone: Desire and the Making of Fiction in Honglou-meng, Princeton, 97. **CONTACT ADDRESS** Divinity Sch, Univ of Chicago, 1025-35 E 58th St, Chicago, IL 60637-1577. **EMAIL** acyu@midway.uchicago.edu

YU, CLARA
DISCIPLINE CHINESE **EDUCATION** Nat Taiwan Univ, Taipei, BA, 71; Univ Ill, Urbana, MA, 73, PhD, 78. **CAREER** Cornelius V. Starr prof Ling and Lang & dir, Proj 2001, opp 97; asst, assoc & prof, Middlebury Col, 87-; asst prof, Univ Md, Col Park, 79-83; exec VP, Middlebury Col, 96; VP, Lang & dir, Lang Sch(s), Middlebury College, 93-96; dir, Mellon Initiative in Teaching Languages with Technol, 94-00. **RESEARCH** Second Language Acquisition; Artificial Intelligence; Comparative literature; Chinese literature; Chinese Culture. **CONTACT ADDRESS** Middlebury Col, Center for Educational Technology, Middlebury, VT 05753. **EMAIL** yu@middlebury.edu

YU, NING
PERSONAL Born 09/09/1954, Shangai, China, m, 1985, 1 child **DISCIPLINE** LINGUISTICS **EDUCATION** Univ Arizona, PhD, 96; Central China Normal Univ, MA, 1987. **CAREER** Asst Prof, Univ of Oklahoma, 97-. **MEMBERSHIPS** International Cognitive Linguistics Assoc; International Assoc of Chinese Linguistics. **RESEARCH** Cognitive Semantics; Language, Culture and Cognition. **SELECTED PUBLICATIONS** Auth, "The Contemporary Theory of Metaphor: A Perspective from Chinese," Amsterdam: John Benjamins. **CONTACT ADDRESS** Dept Modern Languages, Univ of Oklahoma, 780 Van Vleet Oval, Rm 202, Norman, OK 73019. **EMAIL** ningyu@ou.edu

YU, SHIAO-LING
PERSONAL Born 12/16/1936, Nanking, China, m, 1960, 4 children **DISCIPLINE** CHINESE **EDUCATION** Caldwell Col, BA, 58; Boston Col, MS, 61; Univ Kans, MA, 77; Univ Wis Madison, PhD, 83. **CAREER** Lectr, Qinghua Univ Beijing, 80-81; Vis Asst Prof, Ohio State Univ, 83-84; Vis Asst Prof, Univ of Kans, 84-86; Asst/Assoc Prof, Ore State Univ, 87-. **HONORS AND AWARDS** Regents Fel, Univ Calif, Los Angeles, 77; Advan Opportunity Fel, Univ of Wis, 78-81; Newcombe Dissertation Fel, 82; Nat Endowment for Arts Transl Fel, 94; Fac Develop Awd, Ore State Univ, 88, 90, 93, 98. **MEMBERSHIPS** Asn for Asian Studies, Asn for Theater in Higher Educ, MLA, Asoc for Asian Performance. **RESEARCH** Chinese drama, modern and classical, post-Mao Chinese Literature. **SELECTED PUBLICATIONS** Auth, "The Taoist Themes in Yuan Drama," J of Chinese Philos (88); auth, "Pan Jinlian: A New Sichuan Opera," Asian Theatre J (93); auth, "The Themes of Exile and Identity Crisis in Nieh Hualing's Fiction," Nativism Overseas, Contemporary Chinese Women Writers (93); auth, Chinese Drama After the Cultural Revolution, 1979-1989: An Anthology, 96. **CONTACT ADDRESS** Dept For Lang, Oregon State Univ, 210 Kidder Hall, Corvallis, OR 97331-8553. **EMAIL** syu@orst.edu

YUDIN, FLORENCE L.
PERSONAL Born 01/26/1937, Brooklyn, NY **DISCIPLINE** SPANISH, LITERATURE **EDUCATION** Brooklyn Col, BA, 58; Univ IL, Urbana, MA, 60, PhD, 64. **CAREER** From instr to asst prof Span, Univ MI, Ann Arbor, 64-69; asst prof, Dartmouth Col, 69-71; assoc prof, 71-74, chmn dept mod lang, 71-76, Prof Span, FL Int Univ, 74-98, Publ subsidy, FL Int Univ Found, 74. **HONORS AND AWARDS** Fla Int Univ Found, Publ Subvention, 74; Excellence in Tchg Awd, FL Int Univ, 87; Acad Affairs Res Competition, Summer A, 90; Latin Am and Caribbean Affairs Center, Res Support, fall 90, spring 91; Excellence in Res Awd, FL Int Univ, 95; Latin Am and Caribbean Center: Publ Subvention, 97. **MEMBERSHIPS** MLA; Midwest Mod Lang Asn. **RESEARCH** Contemp Span poetry; contemp Eng poetry; 17th & 20th century Span lit. **SELECTED PUBLICATIONS** Auth, The novela corta as comedia: Lope's Las Fortunas de Diana, Bull Hisp Studies, 68; Theory and practice of the novela comdiesca, Romanishche Forsch, 69; Earth words, 74 & Whose House of books, 74, Caribbean Rev; The Vibrant Silence in Jorge Guillen's Aire Nuestro, Univ NC, 74; The dark silence in Lorca's poetry, Garcia Lorca Rev, 78; The Yes and the No of Lorca's Ocean, The World of Nature in the Works of Federico Garcia Lorca, 80; Lawrence Durrell's Songs to Syntax, Lang and Style, 83; The Dialectical Failiure in Neruda's Las furias y las penas, Hispania, 3/85; The Poetry of Jorge Guillen, In: Contemporary World Writers, St James Press, 86; The Dark Canticles in Jorge Guillen's Y otros poemas, Hispania, 12/87; From Synthesis to Continuity: Jorge Guillen's Y otros poemas, In: Jorge Guillen Aire nuestro, Anthropos, 10/91; Rozando el paraiso (Poety in Spanish), Thesaurus, Brazil, 95; Nightglow: Borges' Poetics of Blindness, Catedra de Poetica Fray Luis de Leon, Salamanca, Spain, 97. **CONTACT ADDRESS** Dept of Mod Lang, Florida Intl Univ, 1 F I U Univ Park Campus, Miami, FL 33199.

Z

ZACHAU, REINHARD KONRAD
PERSONAL Born 05/04/1948, Lubeck, Germany, m, 1975, 1 child **DISCIPLINE** GERMAN LANGUAGE AND LITERATURE **EDUCATION** Univ Hamburg, Staatsexamen, 74; Univ Pittsburgh, PhD, 78. **CAREER** Instr, Christian-Albrechts-Universitat, 76-77; from asst prof to prof Ger, Univ of the S, 78-; instr, Lessing-Kolleg, 86. **HONORS AND AWARDS** Teaching Fel, Univ Pittsburgh, 75-76; Fulbright Grant, Univ Pittsburgh, 75-76; Andrew Mellon Predoctoral Fel, Univ Pittsburgh, 77-78; Andrew Mellon Res Scholar, Univ of the S, 81; Fac Dev Grant, Univ of the S, 88; Fac Res Grants, Univ of the S, 91-99. **MEMBERSHIPS** MLA; Am Asn Teachers German; S Atlantic Mod Lang Asn; S Cent Mod Lang Asn; Tenn For Lang Teaching Asn; Int Soc for Exile Students. **RESEARCH** 20th century German literature, exile literature, Nazi literature, Holocaust literature, GDR literature, post World War II literature. **SELECTED PUBLICATIONS** Auth, Stefan Heym, 82; auth, Hans Fallada als politischer Schriftsteller, Lang (Berne, NY), 90; auth, Forty Years of Boll Scholarship, Camden House (Columbia, SC), 94; auth, Hans Fallada 1893-1947: Bibliographie zur Sekundarliteratur, Literaturzentrum Neubrandenburg, 98; auth, Hans Fallada: Eine kritische Untersuchung zur Rezeption seines Werks in den Jahren 1930-1997, Akademischer Verlag Georg Heinz, 99. **CONTACT ADDRESS** Dept Ger, Univ of the South, 735 University Ave, Sewanee, TN 37383-0001. **EMAIL** rzachau@sewanee.edu

ZADERENKO, IRENE
PERSONAL Born 04/01/1956, Topeka, KS, s **DISCIPLINE** SPANISH **EDUCATION** Univ de Buenos Aires, MA, 84; City Univ NY Grad Sch, MPhil, 92; PhD, 94. **CAREER** Adj lectr, Fordham Univ, 89-94; adj instr, Medgar Evers Col, 91-94; asst prof, Borough of Manhattan Community Col, 94-95; asst prof, Boston Univ, 95-. **HONORS AND AWARDS** Helena Rubinstein Found, 89; Res Found of the City Univ of NY, 90; Univ Tuition Scholar & Univ Fel, City Univ of NY Grad Sch, 94; Found, Boston Univ, 95-00; Res Awd, Humanities Found of Boston Univ, 98. **MEMBERSHIPS** MLA, Soc Rencesvals American-Canadian Branch. **SELECTED PUBLICATIONS** Rev, of "The 'Cantar de Mio Cid.' Poetic Creation in its Economic and Social Contexts," by J. J. Duggan, Filologia XXIX (96): 191-193; auth, "Acerca de la fecha de composicion del *Cantar de los siete infantes de Lara," La Coronica XXVI (97): 247-255; auth, Problemas de autoria, de estructura y de fuentes en el 'Poema de mio Cid,' Univ de Alcala, 98; auth, "Dante en la ficcion sentimental," Dicenda (forthcoming); auth, "El tema de la tradicion en Los siete infantes de Lara y su tradicion en la epica romanica," Bull of Hispanic Studies (forthcoming); auth, Cantar de mio Cid, Filologia (forthcoming). **CONTACT ADDRESS** Dept For Lang, Boston Univ, 718 Commonwealth Ave, Boston, MA 02215-2423. **EMAIL** izaderen@bu.edu

ZAFERSON, WILLIAM S.
PERSONAL Born 02/10/1925, Greece, m, 1955 **DISCIPLINE** PHILOSOPHY; CLASSICAL LANGUAGES & LITTERATURE **EDUCATION** Univ Athens, BA, 52, PhD, 76; Univ Chicago, MA, 65. **CAREER** Asst prof, philos, Univ Upper Iowa, Fayette, 66-68; prof philos, marymount Col, 68-70; prof philos, St Mary's Univ, 70-72. **HONORS AND AWARDS** Magna Cum Laude, 76; A. Daniel Shorey fel, Univ Chicago. **MEMBERSHIPS** Am Asn Learned Soc; APA; AAUP; NRTA; Univ of Chicago Alumni Asn; National Asn of Scholars Who's Who in Am; Who Who in the World 18th Edition, 01; Goethe-Institut Chicago; The Swedish Cultural Society in Am-Chicago Chapter; Center for Scandinavian Studies. **RESEARCH** Ancient Greek mythology; original Greek texts of Hesiod, Homer, Pindar; the Greek tragedians; Plato; Aristotle; Plotimes; he Bible; Epictetus; Heraclitus. **SELECTED PUBLICATIONS** Auth, The Meaning of Metempsychosis, 65; auth, The Universe, Its Elements and Justice, 74; auth, A Hymn to Health, 75; auth, The Platonic View of Moral Law and the Influence of the Tragedians on Plato's Thoughts, 76; auth, The Songs of the Muses for Gods and Men, 97; Auth, Poem & Music Hephaetus, 99, 00. **CONTACT ADDRESS** PO Box 1551, Chicago, IL 60690.

ZAHAREAS, ANTHONY
DISCIPLINE SPANISH AND PORTUGUESE LITERATURE **EDUCATION** Ohio State Univ, BA, 56; MA, 58; PhD, 62. **SELECTED PUBLICATIONS** Auth, Le Funcion Historica delHumor en Don Quiiote, Tulane Univ, 93; Cervantes, Shakespeare and Calderon: Theater and Society, Baton Rouge, 95; Primera Memoria como Realidad y Metafora, Compas de Letras, 94; Modernidad y Experimentalismo Revista de Filologia y Linguistica, Univ Costa Rica, 96. **CONTACT ADDRESS** Spanish and Portuguese Dept, Univ of Minnesota, Twin Cities, 34 Folwell Hall, 9 Pleasant St SE, Minneapolis, MN 55455. **EMAIL** zahar001@maroon.tc.umn.edu

ZALACAIN, DANIEL
PERSONAL Born 12/15/1948, Havana, Cuba, m, 1976, 1 child **DISCIPLINE** LATIN AMERICAN LITERATURE & THEATRE **EDUCATION** Wake Forrest Univ, BA, 71; Univ NC, Chapel Hill, MA, 72, PhD, 76. **CAREER** Asst prof Span lang & lit & bus Span, Northern IL Univ, 77-80; Asst Prof Span Lang & Lit & Bus Span, Seton Hall Univ, 80. **MEMBERSHIPS** Am Asn Tchr(s) Span & Port; MLA. **RESEARCH** Latin Am theatre of the absurd; Span for business careers; Latin Am myths. **SELECTED PUBLICATIONS** Auth, Rene Marques, del absurdo a la realidad, Latin Am Theatre Rev, fall 78; El arte dramatico en Cuculcan, Explicacion textos lit, 78; Calabar: O elogio da traicao, Chasqui: Rev Lit Latinoam, 2/79; Falsa alarma: Vanguardia del absurdo, Romance Notes, 80; El tiem-

po, tema fundamental en la obra de Rene Marques, Ky Romance Quart, 80; El personae fuera del juego en el teatro de Griselda Gambaro, Rev Estudios Hispanicos, 5/80; Los recursos dramaticos en Soluna, Latin Am Theatre Rev, spring 81; La Antigona de Sanchez: Recreacion puertorriquena del mito, Explicacion Textos Lit, 81. **CONTACT ADDRESS** Dept of Mod Lang, Seton Hall Univ, So Orange, 400 S Orange Ave, South Orange, NJ 07079-2697.

ZAMORA, JUAN C.
PERSONAL Born 05/14/1930, New York, NY, m, 1953, 2 children **DISCIPLINE** HISPANIC LINGUISTICS & HISTORY OF LINGUISTICS **EDUCATION** Univ Havana, JD, 52, Lic Soc Sc, 60; State Univ NYork Buffalo, MA, 66, PhD(Span), 71. **CAREER** Prof law, Univ Popular, Havana, 47-57; adv, Ministry Educ & chief of chancellery, Ministry Foreign Affairs, Cuba, 59-60; teacher English, Dade County pub schs, 62-63; from instr to lectr Span, State Univ NY Buffalo, 63-70; asst prof, Cent Conn State Col, 70-71; asst prof to assoc prof ,Span, Univ Mass, Amherst, 71-83, prof Span, Univ Mass, Amherst, 83-, grad prog dir,80-82, dept chair, 87-93, Dept Span & Port, Univ Mass, Amherst. **MEMBERSHIPS** MLA; Am Asn Teachers Span & Port; Ling Soc Am; Int Ling Asn; Caribbean Stds Asn, Soc Espanola Hist Ling. **RESEARCH** Spanish American Dialectology: Bilingualism and Language Contact; Language Aquisition; History of Linguistics. **SELECTED PUBLICATIONS** Auth, Indigenismos en la lengua de los conquistadores, Univ of PR, 76; coauth, Dialectologia hispanoamericana, 2nd ed, Col de Esp, Spain, 88; coauth, Fundamentos de Linguistica hispanica, Playor, Spain, 88; Historiografia linguistica: Edad Media y Renacimiento, Col de Esp, Spain, 93; articles in prof journals and books pub in Mexico, PR, Spain, U.K., and U.S. **CONTACT ADDRESS** Dept of Span & Port, Univ of Massachusetts, Amherst, Amherst, MA 01003-0002. **EMAIL** zamora@spanport.umass.edu

ZAMPARELLI, THOMAS
PERSONAL Born 04/16/1944, New York, NY, s **DISCIPLINE** FRENCH LITERATURE **EDUCATION** Queens Col, CUNY, BA, 65, MA, 67; Yale Univ MPhil, 70; PhD, 72. **CAREER** Asst prof, Tulane Univ, 72-80; assoc prof, Loyola Univ, 87- . **HONORS AND AWARDS** Phi Beta Kappa; NY State Col Teaching fel. **RESEARCH** Frence Renaissance poetry and theater, Discourse analysis. **SELECTED PUBLICATIONS** Auth, The Theater of Claude Billard: A Study in Post-Renaissance Dramatic Esthetics, TSRLL, (78). **CONTACT ADDRESS** Dept Mod Lang, Loyola Univ, New Orleans, 6363 Saint Charles Ave, New Orleans, LA 70118-6143. **EMAIL** tlzampar@loyno.edu

ZANTS, EMILY
PERSONAL Born 08/03/1937, Tulsa, OK **DISCIPLINE** FRENCH LITERATURE; FILM **EDUCATION** Stanford Univ, BA, 58; Columbia Univ, MA, 61, PhD(French), 65; Barch, U of HI, 85. **CAREER** Instr French, Brooklyn Col, 65-67; asst prof, Univ Calif, Davis, 67-72; assoc prof, 72-80, Prof French Lang & Lit, Univ Hawaii, Manoa, 80-96. **HONORS AND AWARDS** Mabelle McLeod Lewis Awd, Stanford Univ, 72. **MEMBERSHIPS** Santa Fe Cir. **RESEARCH** The novel; Flaubert; Proust, film. **SELECTED PUBLICATIONS** Auth, The Aesthetics of the New Novel in France, Univ Colo, 68; Dialogue, Diderot and the new novel in France, 18th Century Studies, winter 68; The relation of Epiphany to description in the modern French novel, Comp Lit Studies, winter 69; Proust and the new novel in France, PMLA, 1/73; auth, Chaos Theory, Complexity, Cinema, and the Evolution of the French Novel, Vthe Edwin Mellen Press (Lewiston), 96; auth, Bertrand Tavernier: Fractured Narrative and Bourgeois Values, Scarecrow Press (Lanham, Md), 99; auth, Creative Encounters with French Film, 2nd edition Edwin Mellen Press (Lewiston), 00. **CONTACT ADDRESS** 7 Camdel Prado, Santa Fe, NM 87501. **EMAIL** emily@ezdigitaldesign.com

ZATLIN, PHYLLIS
PERSONAL Born 12/31/1938, Green Bay, WI, m, 1962, 2 children **DISCIPLINE** SPANISH **EDUCATION** Rollins Col, BA, 60; Univ Fla, MA, 62; PhD, 65. **CAREER** Instr to assoc prof, Rutgers Univ, 63-79, prof of Spanish, 79-, Assoc Dean, 74-80, Dept Chair and Grad Dir, 80-87, coordr of translator training, 87-. **HONORS AND AWARDS** Woodrow Wilson Fel, 60; Fulbright Fel, 60-61; Prof Awd for Outstanding Contribution to Foreign Language Educ, Foreign Lang Educs of NJ, 89; Awd from the Sociedad General de Autores y Editores, Madrid, 97. **MEMBERSHIPS** Am Asn of Teachers of Spanish & Portuguese, Am Soc for Theatre Res, 20th Century Spanish Asn of Am, Am Translators Asn, Am Asn of Univ Profs. **RESEARCH** Contemporary Spanish theatre, film, narrative (with emphasis on women writers). **SELECTED PUBLICATIONS** Transl, play ed, Eduardo Manet's Lady Strass (92, 97); transl, play ed, Paloma Pedrero's Parting Gestures with A Night in the Subway (94, 99); transl, play ed, J. L. Alonso de Santo's Hostages in the Barrio (97); co-ed, book, Un escenario propio/A Stage of Their Own (98); co-ed, book, Entre Actos: Dialogos sobre teatro espanol entre siglos (99); auth, The Novels and Plays of Eduardo Manet. An Adventure in Multiculturalism (2000). **CONTACT ADDRESS** Dept Spanish & Portuguese, Rutgers, The State Univ of New Jersey, New Brunswick, 105 George St, New Brunswick, NJ 08901-1414.

ZAWAWI, SHARIFA
PERSONAL Born 03/26/1934, Muscat, Oman, s **DISCIPLINE** LINGUISTICS **EDUCATION** State Univ N.Y., BA, 64; Columbia Univ, MA, 68; MPhil, 74; PhD, 74. **CAREER** Assoc prof, Columbia Univ, 64-68; prof to prof emeritus, CUNY City Col, 68-. **HONORS AND AWARDS** Lang Survery Res grant; Fac Res Awd; Soc Sci Res Coun Fel. **MEMBERSHIPS** Ling Soc of Am, Middle East Studies Asn, African Stud Asn, Am Coun on the Teaching of For Lang. **RESEARCH** The interrelationship of language, literature and culture, Language contact and change,; The role of language in education. **SELECTED PUBLICATIONS** Auth, Fast Track Swahili, Jeffre Norton, 99; auth, African Muslim Names: Images and Identities, Africa World Press, 98; auth, What's In a Name? Unaitwaje?, Africa World Press, Treton, 93; auth, Converse Kiswahili-Ongea, Africa World Press, Trenton, 90; Kiswahili Kwa Kitendo, Africa World Press, Trenton, 88; auth, Loan Words and their effect on the Classification of Swahili Nominals, Leiden Brill, 79; auth, Kiswahili Kwa Kitendo, Harper & Row, New York, 71. **CONTACT ADDRESS** Dept For Lang & Lit, City Col, CUNY, 138 Convent Ave, New York, NY 10031-9101.

ZAYAS-BAZAN, EDUARDO
PERSONAL Born 11/17/1935, Camaguay, Cuba, m, 1959, 2 children **DISCIPLINE** HISPANIC CULTURE AND LITERATURE **EDUCATION** Nat Univ Jose Marti, Havana, JD, 58; Kans State Teachers Col, MA, 66. **CAREER** Teacher Span, Plattsmouth High Sch, Nebr, 64-65 & Topeka West High Sch, Kans, 65-66; instr, Appalachian State Univ, 66-68; asst prof, 68-73, assoc prof, 73-79, Prof Span Foreign Lang Dept, East Tenn State Univ, 79-, Chmn Dept, 73-93. **HONORS AND AWARDS** Distinguished Faculty award, 78. **MEMBERSHIPS** Am Asn Teachers Span & Port; MLA; Am Coun on the Tchg of For Lang; Tenn Foreign Lang Tchg Asn; Nat Asn Cuban-Am Educ; Sigma Delta Phi. **RESEARCH** Bilingual education. **SELECTED PUBLICATIONS** Co-ed, Del amor a la revolucion, Norton,'75; auth, "Hemingway: His Cuban Friends Remember," Fitzgerald/Hemingway Annual, 75; co-ed, MIFC Selected Proceedings; coauth, De aqui y de alla, D C Heath & Co, 80; Secret Report on the Cuban Revolution, Trans, 81; coauth, Como dominar la redaccion, 89; coauth, Como aumentar su vocabulario 3, Como escribir cartas eficaces, 89; coauth, Nuestro mundo, 90; coauth, Arriba!, 93; coauth, No se equivoque con el ingles, 93; auth, El ingles que usted no sabe que sabe, 93. **CONTACT ADDRESS** Dept of Foreign Lang, East Tennessee State Univ, PO Box 10001, Johnson City, TN 37614-0001. **EMAIL** Zayasbae@etsu.edu

ZEGURA, ELIZABETH CHESNEY
PERSONAL Born 09/07/1949, Knoxville, TN, m, 1983, 1 child **DISCIPLINE** RENAISSANCE LITERATURE, FRENCH, ITALIAN **EDUCATION** Bryn Mawr Col, AB, 71; Duke Univ, MA, 74, PhD, 76. **CAREER** Instr, Davidson Col, 75-76; asst prof, DePauw Univ, 81-82; vis asst prof, 78-80, lectr, 85, 87-88, sr lectr, 89-, Univ of Ariz. **HONORS AND AWARDS** AB (magna cum laude), Bryn Mawr, 71; NDEA Fel, Duke Univ. **MEMBERSHIPS** Renaissance Soc of Am. **RESEARCH** Renaissance Literature: Rabelais, Ariosto, Marguerite de Navarre. **SELECTED PUBLICATIONS** Auth, The Countervoyage of Rabelais and Ariosto: A Comparative Reading of Two Renaissance Mock Epics, Duke Univ Press, 82; coauth, Rabelais Revisited, MacMillan/Twayne, 93. **CONTACT ADDRESS** Dept of French and Italian, Univ of Arizona, 556 Modern Lang Bldg, Tucson, AZ 85721. **EMAIL** zegurae@u.arizona.edu

ZEITLIN, FROMA I.
PERSONAL Born 05/09/1933, New York, NY, m, 1953, 3 children **DISCIPLINE** GREEK LANGUAGE AND LITERATURE **EDUCATION** Radcliffe Col, AB, 54; Cath Univ, Mass, 65; Columbia Univ, PhD, 70. **CAREER** Prof, Princeton Univ; dir, Prog in Jewish Studies. **HONORS AND AWARDS** Phi Beta Kappa; Fac Fel, Columbia, 67-68; F.J.E. Woodbridge Fel, Columbia, 68-69; Fac res grant, Rutgers, 73; Nat Endowment for the Humanities fel, 75-76; Directeur d'Etudes Associe, College de France, 81-82; Guggenheim Fel, 84-85; Nat Endownment for the Humanities Fel, 88-89; Mem, High Table, Kings Col, Cambridge; Hon Fel, Newnham Col, Cambridge Univ, 88-; Behrmann Awd in the Humanities, Princeton, 95; Sather Prof, Univ of Calif, Berkeley, 95-96; Fel, Humanities inst, Univ of Mich, 96-97; Directeur d'Etudes Associe, Ecole Pratique des Hautes Etudes, May-June 98; Nat Endowment for the Humanities Fel, 99-00; Am Coun of Learned Soc Fel, 99-00. **MEMBERSHIPS** Am Philol Asn. **RESEARCH** Mythology; Greek tragedy and lyric poetry; poetics; religion; gender studies. **SELECTED PUBLICATIONS** Auth, Under the Sign of the Shield: Semiotics and Aeschylus' Seven Against Thebes; auth, Nothing to Do with Dionysos?; auth, Playing the Other: Gender and Society in Classicl Greek Literature. **CONTACT ADDRESS** Dept of Classics, Princeton Univ, 1 Nassau Hall, Princeton, NJ 08544. **EMAIL** fiz@princeton.edu

ZEITZ, EILEEN
PERSONAL Born 05/26/1948, Chicago, IL, m, 2 children **DISCIPLINE** SPANISH AMERICAN LITERATURE **EDUCATION** Univ Ill, Urbana-Champaign, PhD. **CAREER** Instr to prof, Univ Minn, Duluth. **HONORS AND AWARDS** NEA Creative Writing Fel, 80-81; Horace T. Morse, Minn Alumni Assoc Awd (Excellence in Teaching), 97. **MEMBERSHIPS** MLA, MMLA, LASA, Asoc Int de Hsipanistas, ASCD, AATSP. **RESEARCH** Spanish American prose fiction. **SELECTED PUBLICATIONS** Published critical articles on a variety of Spanish American prose fiction writers, and a critical book on the novels of the Uruguayan writer Mario Benedetti; she also has published two books of creative fiction--short stories and poetry--in Spanish. **CONTACT ADDRESS** Univ of Minnesota, Duluth, Duluth, MN 55812-2496. **EMAIL** ezeitz@d.umn.edu

ZEKULIN, NICHOLAS GLEB
PERSONAL Born 01/23/1946, Prague, Czechoslovakia, m, 1968, 3 children **DISCIPLINE** RUSSIAN LITERATURE **EDUCATION** McGill Univ, BA, 66; Yale Univ, MPhil, 69, PhD-(Slavic), 74. **CAREER** Asst prof, 71-79, Assoc Prof Russ Lang & Lit, Univ Calgary, 79- **MEMBERSHIPS** Can Asn Slavists (secy-treas, 79-82, vpres, 82-83); Am Asn Advan Slavic Studies; Asn des Amis d'Ivan Tourgueniev, Pauline Viardot, Maria Malibran. **RESEARCH** Nineteenth Century Russian Lit, Comparative Arts. **SELECTED PUBLICATIONS** Auth, "Turgenev I Richard Pohl," In Ivan S. Turgenev, Leben, Werk und Wirkung, Ed, P. Thiergen, Munich, (95), 243-271; auth, "Turgenev's 'Croquet at Windssor," In Ivan Turgenev and Britain, Ed, P. Waddington, London-Providence, R.I, (95), 194-207; auth, "Vospriiatie Khudozhnikom Proiizvedeniia Iskusstva, Sonet Viach, Ivanova I Chast' Simfonicheskoi poemy O, Repighi Rimskie Fontany, Posviashchennye Fonatnu Trevi," Litteraaria Humanitas, IV (Sbornik prac Folosofike Fakulty Brnenske University), (96), 291-306; auth, P.V. Annenkov I Ottsy I Denti," Russkaia literatura, (98), No 1, 3-15. **CONTACT ADDRESS** Dept of Ger & Slavic Stud & E Asian Stud, Univ of Calgary, Calgary, AB, Canada T2N 1N4. **EMAIL** zekulin@ucalgary.ca

ZENTENO, GLORIA ESTELA GONZALEZ
PERSONAL Born 03/03/1963, Guadalajara, Mexico, m, 1995, 1 child **DISCIPLINE** LATIN AMERICAN LITERATURE **EDUCATION** Universidad Autonoma de Guadalajara, Licenciatura, 88; SUNY Stony Brook, MA, 90; PhD, 96. **CAREER** Lectr, Universidad Autonoma de Guadalajara, 85-88; instr, Volkshochschule, Ger, 90-92; TA, SUNY Stony Brook, 88-90, 94-95; vis lectr, Skidmore Col, 95-96; asst prof, Middlebury Col, 96-. **HONORS AND AWARDS** Andrew Mellon Found Fel, 97; Davis Fel, 98; Ada Howe Kent Fac Fel, 99. **MEMBERSHIPS** MLA. **RESEARCH** The fantastic in Hispanic literature, Women in the Mexican cultural 'Renaissance', The cinema of Pedro Almodovar, Gender in film and popular culture, Music in literature and film. **SELECTED PUBLICATIONS** Auth, "El escritor: Sujeto escrito por la tropologia animal," Romance Lang Annual, (98); auth, "Augusto Monterroso. El animal y la recreacion paradocis de la tradicion," Chasqui, Revista de literatura latinoamericana, (99); auth, "El lector, complice y adversario en Augusto Monterroso," Romance Lang Annual, (99); auth, "Augusto Monterroso: De la America maravillosa a la ironia de la historia," Romance Lang Annual, (00). **CONTACT ADDRESS** Dept Span, Middlebury Col, Middlebury, VT 05753. **EMAIL** ggonzale@middlebury.edu

ZEVIT, ZIONY
PERSONAL Born 02/13/1942, Winnipeg, MB, Canada, m, 1966, 3 children **DISCIPLINE** NEAR EASTERN LANGUAGES **EDUCATION** Univ Calif, PhD, 73. **CAREER** Prof, Univ Judaism, 74-; vis prof, Univ Calif, 98; vis prof, Univ Penn Ctr Judaic Studies, 97; vis prof, W.F. Albright Inst, 94; vis prof, Hebrew Univ, 94-00; vis prof, Univ Calif LA, 91-92; vis prof, Claremont Grad Sch, 92. **HONORS AND AWARDS** Univ Penn Ctr Judaic Studies Fel, 97; John Simon Guggenheim Mem Found, 94; Abraham Biran Fel Bibl Archeol, 87. **MEMBERSHIPS** ASOR; AOS; AJS; CBA; NAPH; NACAAL; SBL. **RESEARCH** Near Eastern languages; semitic philology; Bible; ancient Near Eastern history and archeology. **SELECTED PUBLICATIONS** Auth, Solving Riddles and Untying Knots: Biblical, Epigraphic and Semitic Studies Presented to Jonas C. Greenfield, 95; auth, Philology, Archeology, and a Terminus a Quo for P's Hatta't Legislation, Pomegranates and Golden Bells: Studies in Bibl, Jewish, and Near Eastern Ritual, Law, and Lit in Honor of Jacob Milgrom, 95; auth, The Earthen Altar Laws of Exod 20:24-26 and Related Sacrificial Restrictions in their Cultural Context, Texts, Temples, and Traditions: A Tribute to Menahem Haran, 96; auth, The Israelite Ethos in which Deuteronomy Developed, Shnaton: An Annual for Bibl and Ancient Near Eastern Studies, 97; auth, The Gerizim-Samarian Community In and Between Texts and Times: An Experimental Study, The Quest for Context and Meaning: Studies in Bibl Intertextuality in Honor of James A. Sanders, 97; auth, Proclamations to the Fruitful Tree and the Spiritualization of Androgyny, The Echoes of Many Texts: Reflections on Jewish and Christian Traditions, Essays in Honor of Lou H. Silberman, 97; auth, The Anterior Construction in Ancient Hebrew, 98. **CONTACT ADDRESS** Dept of Near Eastern Languages, Univ of Judaism, 15600 Mulholland Dr., Los Angeles, CA 90077. **EMAIL** zzevit@uj.edu

ZGUSTA, LADISLAV
PERSONAL Born 03/20/1924, Libochovice, Czech Republic, m, 2 children **DISCIPLINE** PHILOLOGY **EDUCATION** Prague Univ, PhD, 49, DSc, 64. **CAREER** Hd, lexicographic teams, Czech Acad Sci, 58-70; prof, linguistics and classics, 71-95, dir, Ctr for Advan Stud, 87-95, prof emer, 95- , Univ of Ill. **HONORS AND AWARDS** Res grant, Am Coun Learned Soc, 73; Guggenheim Found fel, 77, 84; mem, Austrian Acad Sci, 83; NEH res grant, 89. **MEMBERSHIPS** Am Acad Sci; Ling Soc Am; Dict Soc N Am; European Lixicographic Asn; Am Name Soc; Indogermanische Ges. **RESEARCH** Theory and practice of lexicography; Indo-European linguistics; name studies. **SELECTED PUBLICATIONS** Auth, Kleinasiatische Ortsnamen, Carl Winter, 84; auth, The Old Ossetic Inscription from the River Zelencuk, Verlag der Osterreichischen Akademie der Wissenschaften, 87; auth, Lexicography Today: An Annotated bibliography of the Theory of Lexicography, Max Niemeyer, 88; ed, International Encyclopedia of Lexicography, de Gruyter, 89; auth, Name Studies: An International Handbook of Onomastics, de Gruyter, 95; auth of numerous articles and book reviews. **CONTACT ADDRESS** Ctr for Advanced Study, Univ of Illinois, Urbana-Champaign, 912 W Illinois Ave, Urbana, IL 61801. **EMAIL** l-zgusta@uiuc.edu

ZHOLKOVSKY, ALEXANDER
DISCIPLINE SLAVIC LANGUAGES AND LITERATURES **EDUCATION** Moscow Univ, MGU, USSR, PhD. **CAREER** Prof, Univ Southern Calif. **RESEARCH** Aesopian language; dystopian writing; avantgardist debasement of classical hypograms; 20th-century appropriation of the earlier tradition. **SELECTED PUBLICATIONS** Auth, Themes and Texts, 84; Bluzhdaiushchie sny, Wandering Dreams, 92, 94; Text Counter Text: Rereadings in Russian Literary History, 94; Inventsii, Inventions, 95; NRZB, UNRDBL, 91; coauth, Poetics of Expressiveness, 87; Isaak, Babel, 94. **CONTACT ADDRESS** Col Letters, Arts & Sciences, Univ of So California, University Park Campus, Los Angeles, CA 90089. **EMAIL** alik@usc.edu

ZHOU, PETER XINPING
PERSONAL Born 09/01/1956, Wuhan, China, m, 1983, 1 child **DISCIPLINE** LINGUISTICS **EDUCATION** Wuhan Univ China, MA, 81; Univ Ill at Urbana-Champaign, MS, 91; PhD, 90. **CAREER** Chinese Studies Librn, Adj Prof, Univ of Iowa, 91-95; Head of Dept E Asian Studies, Adj Assoc Prof, Univ of Pittsburgh, 95-. **HONORS AND AWARDS** Phi Kappa Phi, Univ of Ill at Urbana-Champaign, 87; US Inst Museum and Libr Serv, Nat Leadership Grant Awd, 98-00. **MEMBERSHIPS** Asn for Asian Studies, Am Libr Asn. **RESEARCH** Library and information science, Linguistics, History of Chinese printing. **SELECTED PUBLICATIONS** Auth, "Electronic Resources for Chinese Studies: An Overview," Committee on E Asian Libr Bull (July 95); auth, "East Asian collections in the global information network," J of E Asian Libr 111 (Feb 97): 23-32; auth, "Acquisitions of hard-to-find backfiles of Chinese periodicals from the People's Republic of China," in Libr Resources and Tech Serv 40-1(Chicago: Am Libr Asn, 96); auth, "Electronic Resources for Chinese studies in a global context," in The Electronic Library 14-1 (Oxford, Gr Brit: Learned Infor, 96); auth, "Global Information Network and the Development of East Asian Collections," Libr and Infor Serv (Beijing: Chinese Acad of Sci, 97), 4; auth, "Document delivery service of Chinese academic journals publication," Libr Hi Tech News 161 (99): 25-27; auth, "Global information services and resource sharing; a shared vision for the 21st century," in IT and Global Digital Library Development, ed. Ching-chih Chen (Boston: MicroUse Infor, 99); coauth, "Global resource sharing: a gateway model," J of the Acad Librarianship 25-4 (99): 281-287; **CONTACT ADDRESS** Dept E Asian Languages, Univ of Pittsburgh, 234 Hillman Library, Pittsburgh, PA 15260-6299. **EMAIL** pxzhou@pitt.edu

ZIADEH, FARHAT JACOB
PERSONAL Born 04/08/1917, Palestine, m, 1949, 5 children **DISCIPLINE** ARABIC, ISLAMICS **EDUCATION** Am Univ Beirut, BA, 37; Univ London, LLB, 40. **CAREER** Magistrate, Govt of Palestine, 47-48; from lectr to assoc prof Orient studies, Princeton Univ, 48-66; Prof Near Eastern Studies, Univ Wash, 66-, Gov Am Res Ctr, Egypt, 70-78, fel, 71-72 & 77. **MEMBERSHIPS** Am Orient Soc; Mid East Studies Asn NAm (pres, 80). **RESEARCH** Arabic language and literature; Islamic law; Islamic institutions. **SELECTED PUBLICATIONS** Auth, The Reliance of the Traveler--A Classical Manual of Islamic Sacred Law by Ibnnaqibalmisri, Ahmad D. 769/1368--In Arabic with Facing English Text, Commentary and Appendixes, Jour Amer Oriental Soc, Vol 0115, 95. **CONTACT ADDRESS** Dept of Near Eastern Lang & Lit, Univ of Washington, Seattle, WA 98195.

ZIEFLE, HELMUT W.
PERSONAL Born 04/02/1939, Heilbronn, Germany, m, 1965, 2 children **DISCIPLINE** GERMAN LITERATURE, MODERN GERMAN HISTORY **EDUCATION** SUNY, BA, 64, MA, 66; Univ ILL, PhD, 73. **CAREER** Tchr, German, 65-67, Bethlehem Cent High Schl; instr, 67-72, asst prof, 72-77, assoc prof, 77-82, prof, 82-, Wheaton Col. **MEMBERSHIPS** Am Asn of Teachers of German; Illinois Foreign Lang Teachers Asn; Illinois Council on the Teaching of Foreign Langs, 88-89; Modern Lang Asn, 97-98; North Am Asn of Christian Foreign Lang & Lit Fac; Delta Phi Alpha. **RESEARCH** Hermann Hesse, German theology, German hist. **SELECTED PUBLICATIONS** Auth, Sibylle Schwarz: Leben und Werk (Life and Work), Studien zur Anglistik und Komparatistik, Vol 35, Bonn: Bovier, 75; auth, Edited, Sibylle Schwarz Deutsche Poetische Gedichte, Sibylle Schwarz German Poetic Poems, Mittlere Deutsche Literatur, vol 25, Bern: Lang, 80; auth, Una Mujer Contra el Reich, Mexico: ediciones las americas, 89; auth, Glenn Ellyn: Advanced Memory Res, Beginning German Language Course, 83; auth, Glenn Ellyn: Advanced Memory Res, Advanced German Language Course, 83; auth, Theological German: A Reader, Grand Rapids, Baker Book House, 86; auth, Dictionary of Modern Theological German, Grand Rapids, Baker Book House, 92; auth, Theological German: A Reader, Grand Rapids, Baker Book House, 93; auth, edited and commentated, Hermann Hesse und das Christentum, Wuppertal and Zurich: Brockhaus, 94; auth, Modern Theological German: A Reader and Dictionary, Grand Rapids: Baker Book House, 97. **CONTACT ADDRESS** Wheaton Col, Illinois, 501 College Ave, Wheaton, IL 60187. **EMAIL** helmut.w.ziefle@wheaton.edu

ZIEGLER, VICKIE LYNNE
PERSONAL Born Rock Island, IL **DISCIPLINE** GERMAN **EDUCATION** MacMurray Col, BA, 64; Yale Univ, PhD(Ger), 70. **CAREER** Asst prof, 70-76, Assoc Prof Ger, Pa State Univ, University Park, 76-, dir, Ctr for Medieval Stu, 93-. **MEMBERSHIPS** Mediaeval Acad Am; Int Vereinigung fu germanische Sprachen und Literaturwissenschaft. **RESEARCH** Medieval German lyric; Medieval German romance; romantic Rahmennovelle. **SELECTED PUBLICATIONS** Auth, The Leitword in Minnesang, Ger ser, Pa State Univ, 74; Justice in Brentano's 'Die Schactel mit der Friedenspuppe', Ger Rev, fall 78; auth, Goethe and the French ActressL How Clarion became Antonelli, Monatshefte 76, 84; auth, Bending the Frame in the German Cyclical Narrative: Achim von Arnim's Der Wintergarten and E.T.A. Hoffman's Die Serapionsbruder, Catholic Univ of Am, 91; auth, Arnims Amazonen, Grenzgange: Studien zu L. Achim von Arnim, Bonn, 94; auth, A Burning Issue: Isolde's Ordeal by Fire, The Germanic MosaicL Cultural and Linguistic Diversity in Society, Westport, 94. **CONTACT ADDRESS** Dept of German, Pennsylvania State Univ, Univ Park, University Park, PA 16802-1014. **EMAIL** vlz1@psu.edu

ZILCOSKY, JOHN
DISCIPLINE GERMAN **EDUCATION** Harvard Univ, AB, 87; Temple Univ, MA, 92; Univ Pa, PhD, 98. **CAREER** Vis asst prof, Williams Col, 98-99. **HONORS AND AWARDS** Sch of Arts and Sci Dissertation fel, Univ Pa, 97-98; Fulbright Scholar, 96-97; DAAD res grant, 95. **RESEARCH** 19th and 20th century German, Austrian, and American literature; literary theory and philosophy; psychoanalysis and the history of psychoanalysis; German film; modern central European history; creative writing and translation. **SELECTED PUBLICATIONS** Auth, Of Sugar Barons and Banana Kings: Franz Kafka, Imperialism, and Schaffsteins Grune Bandchen, J of the Kafka Soc of Amer, 90. **CONTACT ADDRESS** Center for Foreign Languages, Literatures and Cult, Williams Col, Williamstown, MA 01267. **EMAIL** John.Zilcosky@williams.edu

ZIMMERMAN, ZORA DEVRNJA
PERSONAL Born 05/12/1945, Marienbad, Czechoslovakia, m, 1976, 2 children **DISCIPLINE** COMPARATIVE LITERATURE, FOLKLORE **EDUCATION** State Univ of NY (Buffalo), BA, 67, PhD, 74. **CAREER** Asst prof, 74-79, assoc prof, 80-84, Prof English, Iowa State Univ, 85-90; assoc dean, Col of Liberal Arts and Sci, IA State Univ, 90-. **HONORS AND AWARDS** NEH summer fel. **MEMBERSHIPS** AAASS; Am Folklore Soc; CCAS; Nat Asn Ethnic Studies; NAASS. **RESEARCH** Serbian traditional narrative and lyric, dynamics of change and persistence in folklore, English and European Romanticism, Orality theory, folk belief, contemporary literature in Eastern Europe. **SELECTED PUBLICATIONS** Co-ed, The Arc from Now (poems), Iowa State Univ, 78; auth, Moral vision in the Serbian folk epic: The foundation sacrifice of Skadar, Slavic & East Europ J, Vol 23, 79; The changing roles of the Vila in Serbian traditional literature, J of Folklore Inst, Vol 26, 79; Metrics of passion: The poetry of Carl Dennis, Poet & Critic, Vol 12, 80; Teaching folklore in Iowa, in Teaching Folklore, Am Folklore Soc Inc, 84, rev ed, 89; Tradition and change in a ritual feast: The Serbian Krsna Slava in America, Great Lakes Rev, fall 85; auth & trans & ed, Serbian Folk Poetry: Ancient Legends, Romantic Songs, Kosovo Publ Co, 86; On the hermeneutics of oral poetry: The Kosovo Mythos, Serbian Studies, fall 90; The building of Skadar, in The Walled-Up Wife Casebook, Univ Wisc Press, 96; auth Revisiting the Muse: Oral Tradition and the Legacy of Vuk Stefanovic Karadzic in a Foreign Harbor: Essays in hone of Vasa D Mihailovich, Slavica, 00. **CONTACT ADDRESS** Col of Lib Arts & Sci, Iowa State Univ of Science and Tech, Ames, IA 50011-0002. **EMAIL** zdzimme@iastate.edu

ZINNI, HANNAH CASE
PERSONAL Born 10/01/1944, Cincinnati, OH, m, 1977, 3 children **DISCIPLINE** FRENCH LANGUAGE & LITERATURE **EDUCATION** Oberlin Col, BA, 66; Northwestern Univ, MA, 67, PhD, 71. **CAREER** Asst prof, 70-75, assoc prof, 75-81, prof French, 81-, Slippery Rock Univ. **HONORS AND AWARDS** Phi Beta Kappa, Oberlin College, 66. **MEMBERSHIPS** Am Assn Teachers French; MLA; PSMLA. **RESEARCH** Art and the artist in the works of Samuel Beckett; the couple in Samuel Beckett's works; the Louisiana French; Franco-American history; the French in America. **SELECTED PUBLICATIONS** Auth, Art and the Artist in the Works of Samuel Beckett, Mouton, 75; art, The couples in Comment C'est, Samuel Beckett: The Art of Rhetoric, Univ NC, 76; art, Bibliog for Andre DuBouchet, Andre Frenaud & Philippe Soupault, Critical Bibliography of French Literature of the Twentieth Century, 80. **CONTACT ADDRESS** Dept of Mod Lang & Cult, Slippery Rock Univ of Pennsylvania, 14 Maltby Dr, Slippery Rock, PA 16057-1326. **EMAIL** hannah.zinni@sru.edu

ZIOLKOWSKI, JOHN EDMUND
PERSONAL Born 06/19/1938, Montevallo, AL **DISCIPLINE** CLASSICAL LANGUAGES **EDUCATION** Duke Univ, AB, 58; Univ NC, PhD(classics), 63. **CAREER** Instr Latin, Univ NC, 62-64; asst prof classics, Randolph-Macon Woman's Col, 64-67; asst prof, 67-72, Assoc Prof Classics, George Washington Univ, 72-, Chmn Dept, 71-88; Prof, 88. **MEMBERSHIPS** Am Philol Asn; Am Inst Archeol. **RESEARCH** Greek and Roman literature; Renaissance Latin; Classical influence on Washington DC. **SELECTED PUBLICATIONS** Auth, The Parthenon Stone in the Washington Monument, Prologue-Quart Nat Archv, Vol 0025, 93; A Commentary on Thucydides, Vol 1, Books-1-3, Class World, Vol 0086, 93; City-States in Classical Antiquity and Medieval Italy, Class World, Vol 0087,,94; The Classics in American Theater of the 1960s and Early 1970s, Class World, Vol 0088, 95; Shakespeare and Classical Comedy--The Influence of Plautus and Terence, Class World, Vol 0090, 97; Sacred Geography of the Ancient Greeks--Astrological Symbolism in Art, Architecture, Class World, Vol 0090, 97. **CONTACT ADDRESS** Dept of Classics, The George Washington Univ, Washington, DC 20052-0001. **EMAIL** ccojez@gwu.edu

ZIOLKOWSKI, MARGARET C.
PERSONAL Born 09/14/1952, Birmingham, AL, m, 1979, 2 children **DISCIPLINE** RUSSIAN LANGUAGE, LITERATURE, & FOLKLORE **EDUCATION** Princeton Univ, AB, 73; Yale Univ, PhD, 78. **CAREER** Lectr, Univ Tex at El Paso, 84-87; from asst prof to prof, Miami Univ, 87-. **HONORS AND AWARDS** Postdoctoral Fel, Int Res & Exchanges Board, 78-79; Mellon Postdoctoral Fel, Emory Univ, 79-80; NEH Summer Stipend, 90. **MEMBERSHIPS** Am Asn for the Advancement of Slavic Studies, Am Asn of Teachers of Slavic and E European Lang. **RESEARCH** Russian Literature. **SELECTED PUBLICATIONS** Auth, Hagiography and Modern Russian Literature, Princeton Univ Pr (Princeton, NJ), 88; auth, Literary Exorcisms of Stalinism: Russian Writers and the Soviet Past, Camden House (Columbia, SC), 98; auth, The Tale of Boiarynia Morozova: A Seventeeth-Century Religious Life, Lexington Books (Lanham, Md), forthcoming. **CONTACT ADDRESS** Dept For Lang, Miami Univ, 211 North Ridge Dr, Oxford, OH 45056. **EMAIL** ziolkom@muohio.edu

ZIOLKOWSKI, THEODORE J.
PERSONAL Born 09/30/1932, Birmingham, AL, m, 1951, 3 children **DISCIPLINE** GERMAN LITERATURE, COMPARATIVE LITERATURE **EDUCATION** Duke Univ, AB, 51; AM, 52; Yale Univ, PhD, 57. **CAREER** Instr to asst prof, Yale Univ, 56-62; assoc prof, Columbia Univ, 62-64; prof, Princeton Univ, 64-69; Class of 1900, prof mod lang, 69-; dept ch, 73-79; dean grad sch, 79-92. **HONORS AND AWARDS** Phi Beta Kappa, 51; Fulbright Fel; Guggenheim Fel; James Russell Lowell Prize; Behrman Awd; Wilbur Lucius Cross Medal; Gold Medal, Goethe Inst; Henry Allen Moe Prize; Jacob and Wilhelm Grimm Prize; Humboldt Found Prize; Christian Gauss Awd. **MEMBERSHIPS** MLA; AATG; AAAS; APS; AWG; AW; ASD. **RESEARCH** Literature and law; religion; reception of classical tradition; German romanticism. **SELECTED PUBLICATIONS** Auth, German Romanticism and Its Institutions, 90; auth, Virgil and the Moderns, 93; auth, The Mirror of Justice, 97; auth, Das Wunderjahr in Jena, 98; auth, The View from the Tower, 98; auth, The Sin of Knowledge, 00. **CONTACT ADDRESS** 36 Bainbridge St, Princeton, NJ 08540. **EMAIL** tjziol@aol.com

ZIRIN, RONALD A.
DISCIPLINE CLASSICS **EDUCATION** Princeton Univ, PhD, 67; Univ Buffalo, PhD, 85. **CAREER** Assoc prof emer, Fac, 66; prof, present, SUNY Buffalo. **RESEARCH** Linguistics; mythology; Sanskrit; applications of psychoanalysis to Classical traditions. **SELECTED PUBLICATIONS** Auth, The Phonological Basis of Latin Prosody, Mouton, 70; articles on Greek and Latin linguistics. **CONTACT ADDRESS** Dept Classics, SUNY, Buffalo, 705 Clemens Hall, Buffalo, NY 14260.

ZLOTCHEW, CLARK M.
PERSONAL Born 10/14/1932, Jersey City, NJ, m, 1965, 3 children **DISCIPLINE** SPANISH **EDUCATION** NYork Univ, BS, 57; Middlebury Col, MA, 66; SUNY, PhD, 74. **CAREER** Asst Prof, Norwich Univ, 66-68; Teaching Asst to In-

structor, SUNY, 68-74; Asst Prof to Prof, SUNY 75-. **HONORS AND AWARDS** president's Awd; Fac Exchange Sch; Fac Grant, SUNY, 89; NEH Grant, Univ CA, 87; NEH Grant, Princeton Univ, 78. **MEMBERSHIPS** MLA; AATSP; NEMLA; ALTA; Academia Portena del Lunfardo; Intl Asn of Torch Clubs; State Coun on Ling; Instituto Literario y Cultural Hispanico; Circulo de Cultura Panamericano. **RESEARCH** Galdos and 19th Century Spanish Literature; Borges and 20th Century Latin American Literature. **SELECTED PUBLICATIONS** Auth, Libido into Literature: The 'Primera Epoca' of Benito Perez Galdos, Borgo Press, 93; auth, Estilo literario; Analisis y creacion, Borgo Press, 93; auth, Voices of the River Plate: Interviews with Writers of Argentina and Uruguay, Borgo Press, 95; auth, Teach Yourself Spanish in One Day, Alpha books, 00. **CONTACT ADDRESS** Dept For Lang, SUNY, Col at Fredonia, Fredonia, NY 14063-1143. **EMAIL** zlotchew@fredonia.edu

ZLOTSKY, ANDRES
PERSONAL Born 07/25/1958, Buenos Aires **DISCIPLINE** COMPARATIVE LITERATURE, ENGLISH **EDUCATION** Univ Amsterdam, Propedeutic, 88; Doctorandus, 92; SUNY, MA, 97; PhD, 01. **CAREER** TA to lectr, SUNY, 93-01. **HONORS AND AWARDS** Univ of Amsterdam, 87-92; Excellence in Teaching Awd, 98; SUNY, 93-99; Univ Honors Lectr, 99, 00. **MEMBERSHIPS** MLA. **RESEARCH** UFO Phenomenon, Popular Culture, Media Studies, Psychoanalysis, Semiotics, Science Fiction. **SELECTED PUBLICATIONS** Ed, Psychoanalysis and the Debate on Abortion: Dossier on Contempt, Umbr(a), 95; transl, The Flirtatious Remark, Umbr(a, 96); auth, Antigone and the Real: Two Reflections on the Notion of Coherence, Umbr (a), 96; auth, Supposed Science, Alleged fiction; Patterns of Distortion in the Transmission of Cultural paradigms in the Twenty Century, SUNY, 01. **CONTACT ADDRESS** Dept Comp Lit, SUNY, Buffalo, 638 Clemens Hall, Buffalo, NY 14214-3001. **EMAIL** zlotsky@acsu.buffalo.edu

ZOHN, HARRY
PERSONAL Born 11/21/1923, Vienna, Austria, m, 1962, 2 children **DISCIPLINE** GERMAN **EDUCATION** Suffolk Univ, BA, 46; Clark Univ, MA Ed, 47; Harvard Univ, AM, 49, PhD(Ger lang & lit), 52. **CAREER** From instr to assoc prof, 51-67, Prof Ger, Brandeis Univ, 67-96, Trustee, Suffolk Univ, 78-81, 83-; chmn grad prog lit studies, 81- **HONORS AND AWARDS** LittD, Suffolk Univ, 76. **MEMBERSHIPS** Am Transl Asn; Am Asn Teachers Ger; MLA; PEN Club; Int Arthur Schnitzler Res Asn (vpres, 77-00). **RESEARCH** Problems of translation; Austrian literature; German-Jewish writers. **SELECTED PUBLICATIONS** Auth, Benjamin,Walter, Colloquia Ger, Vol 0025, 92; Heine,Heinrich, Ger Stud Rev, Vol 0016, 93; Die Fliegenpein, World Lit Today, Vol 0067, 93; -Essays on Humor, Satire, and the Comic, Ger Quart, Vol 0066, 93; Wir Heimatlosen, 1989-1992, World Lit Today, Vol 0067, 93; Reception of Heine, Heinrich, Jour Eng and Ger Philol, Vol 0093, 94; Plague in Siena, World Lit Today, Vol 0068, 94; The Jewish Reception of Heine,Heinrich, Jour Eng and Ger Philol, Vol 0093, 94; Professor Bernhardi and Other Plays, World Lit Today, Vol 0068, 94; Inventory of the Zweig, Stefan Collection in Reed Library, Mod Austrian Lit, Vol 0028, 95; BeerHofmann,Richard--Self-Awareness of Viennese Jews at the Turn-of-the-20th-Century--German, Mod Austrian Lit, Vol 0028, 95; Hier Kocht der Wirt, World Lit Today, Vol 0070, 96; Criminal-Law and Satire in Kraus, Karl Work--German, Mod Austrian Lit, Vol 0029, 96; Kraus Contra George--Commentaries on the Translation of Shakespeare Sonnets--German, Mod Austrian Lit, Vol 0029, 96; Absterbende Gemutlichkeit--12 Stories from the Center of the World--German, World Lit Today, Vol 0071, 97; The Good Life-German, World Lit Today, Vol 0071, 97. **CONTACT ADDRESS** 48 Davis Ave, West Newton, MA 02465. **EMAIL** wienbos@att.net

ZOLBROD, PAUL GEYER
PERSONAL Born 12/10/1932, Pittsburgh, PA, m, 1967, 2 children **DISCIPLINE** LITERARY CRITICISM, LINGUISTICS **EDUCATION** Univ Pittsburgh, BA, 58, MA, 62, PhD(English), 67. **CAREER** Instr English, Univ Pittsburgh, Titusville, 63-64; from instr to assoc prof 64-77, Prof English, Allegheny Col, Meadville, 77-, Fel, Univ NMex, 71-72; consult, Public Broadcasting Northwest Pa, 76-78; Res fel, Nat Endowment Humanities, 78-79. **MEMBERSHIPS** MLA; AAUP; NCTE; Northwest Mod Lang Asn; Soc Am Indian Studies. **RESEARCH** Renaissance literature; ethnopoetics; linguistics. **SELECTED PUBLICATIONS** Auth, The Wind in a Jar, Amer Indian Cult and Res Jour, Vol 0018, 94; Saanii-Dahataal--The Women Are Singing, Amer Indian Cult and Res Jour, Vol 0018, 94. **CONTACT ADDRESS** Dept of English, Allegheny Col, Park Ave, Meadville, PA 16335.

ZORITA, C. ANGEL
DISCIPLINE SPANISH LANGUAGE, LITERATURE, AND CIVILIZATION **EDUCATION** Gregorian Univ, Rome, AD; Univ Madrid, MA; Univ Seville, PhD. **CAREER** Former instr, Univ Madrid; W VA Univ; prof. **RESEARCH** Old Span song books. **SELECTED PUBLICATIONS** Publ, Spanish Literature. **CONTACT ADDRESS** Dept of For Lang, Cleveland State Univ, 83 E 24th St, Cleveland, OH 44115.

ZOU, KE
PERSONAL Born 10/30/1956, Nanchang, China, m, 1985 **DISCIPLINE** LINGUISTICS **EDUCATION** Jiangxi Normal Univ, Nanchang, BA, 82; Guangzhou For Lang Inst, MA, 85; Ohio State Univ, MA, 89; Univ So Calif, Los Angeles, MA, 91, PhD, 95. **CAREER** Instr, Eng Dept, 82-83, instr, ling, 85-86, Jiangxi Normal Univ; instr ling, Ohio State Univ, 88-89; lectr, Eng Dept, Calif State Univ, Dominguez Hills, 90-97; lectr, Eng Dept, El Camino Col, 96-97; lectr, Eng Dept, Chapman Univ, 98; asst prof, Eng Dept, Calif State Univ, Hayward, 98-. **HONORS AND AWARDS** Hum Dean's Fel, 89-90, 94-95, Outstanding Academic Achievement Awd, 91; Hum Grad Fel, 90-94, Univ So Calif; res grant award, 92-94, travel award, 94-97, internationalization award, 97, Affirmative Action Fac Dev Awd, 97, Calif State Univ, Dominguez Hills; **MEMBERSHIPS** Ling Soc Am; Int Asn of Chinese Ling. **RESEARCH** Syntax; morphology; Chinese linguistics. **SELECTED PUBLICATIONS** Auth, Preverbal and Postverbal Objects in the Chinese BA-construction, Proc of the 23rd W Conf on Ling, 93; auth, The Syntax of the Chinese BA-construction, Linguistics, 93; auth, Resultative V-V Compounds, Proc of MIT Morphology-Syntax Connection Workshop, 94; auth, Directional Verb-compounds, Proc of 30th Conf of Chicago Ling Soc, 94; auth, The Negation of the Chinese BA-Construction, Proc of the 4th Int Conf on Chinese, 95; auth, The Syntax of the Chinese BA-Construction: A Minimalist Approach, Proc of the 25th W Conf on Ling, 95; auth, Resultative Verb Compounds and Non-Personal Subjects, Proc of the 8th N Am Conf on Chinese Ling, 96; auth, Unergative and Unaccusative Verb Compounds, Proc of the 31st Mid-Am Ling Conf, 96; auth, Alienable and Inalienable Objects in the Passive Construction, Proc of the 9th N Am Conf on Chinese Ling, 97; auth, The Chinese BA-construction: A Morpho-syntactic Analysis, Symp Ser of the Inst of Hist and Philol: Morphology and Lexicon, 97; auth, Directional Verb Movement in Chinese; Proc of the 10th N Am Conf on Chinese Ling, 98; auth, "The Hybrid of the Chinese Passive and Causative Constructions," Proceedings of the 11th North Am Conference on Chinese Linguistics, 99; auth, "Verb Reduplication and Indefiniteness Effect," Proceedings of the 12th North Am Conference on Chinese Linguistics, 00. **CONTACT ADDRESS** English Dept, California State Univ, Hayward, Hayward, CA 94542-3037. **EMAIL** kzou@csuhayward.edu

ZUBIZARRETA, ARMANDO F.
DISCIPLINE 20TH CENTURY SPANISH LITERATURE **EDUCATION** Pontificia Universidad Catolica del Peru, MA, 59; Universidad de Salamanca, PhD, 59. **CAREER** English, Case Western Reserve Univ. **HONORS AND AWARDS** Premio Extraordinario, 59; Premio Nacional de Critica Literaria Manuel Gonzalez Prada, 68. **SELECTED PUBLICATIONS** Auth, Perfil Y Entrana De "El Caballero Carmelo", 68; Cuando Mas Ardea El Fuego. **CONTACT ADDRESS** Case Western Reserve Univ, 10900 Euclid Ave, Cleveland, OH 44106. **EMAIL** afz@po.cwru.edu

ZUBIZARRETA, MARIA LUISA
PERSONAL Born Asuncion, Paraguay, m, 2 children **DISCIPLINE** LINGUISTICS **EDUCATION** MIT, PhD. **CAREER** Assoc prof, Univ Southern Calif; full prof, Univ of Southern Calif. **RESEARCH** Syntax; representation of the Lexicon. **SELECTED PUBLICATIONS** Auth, The Relation Between Morphophonology and Morphosyntax: The Case of Romance Causatives, Ling Inquiry, MIT Press, 85; Levels of Representation in the Lexicon and in the Syntax, Foris Publ, 87; coauth, The Definite Determiner and the Inalienable Constructions in French and in English, in Ling Inquiry, MIT Press, 92; auth, Prosody, Focus, and Word Order, MIT Press, 98. **CONTACT ADDRESS** Dept of Linguistics, Univ of So California, University Park Campus, Los Angeles, CA 90089. **EMAIL** zubizarr@usc.edu

ZUCKER, GEORGE K.
PERSONAL Born 10/05/1939, New York, NY, m, 1960, 4 children **DISCIPLINE** SPANISH **EDUCATION** Queens Col, BA, 60; Univ Iowa, MA, 61; PhD, 64. **CAREER** Asst prof, Ind Univ, 64-68; assoc prof to prof, Univ of N Iowa, 68-. **MEMBERSHIPS** AATSP; MMLA; MJSA; LAJSA; Casa Shalom. **RESEARCH** Sephardic Studies, Teaching of Writing, Translation. **SELECTED PUBLICATIONS** Trans, Sephardim: Jews from Spain by Paloma Diaz-Mas, Univ of Chicago Pr, 92. **CONTACT ADDRESS** Dept Modern Lang, Univ of No Iowa, Cedar Falls, IA 50614-0027. **EMAIL** george.zucker@uni.edu

ZUPANCIC, METKA
PERSONAL Born 06/18/1950, Celje, Slovenia **DISCIPLINE** FRENCH **EDUCATION** Univ Ljubljana, Slovenia, 2nd cycle degree, 74; 75; Doctorat de 3e cycle, 77; Univ Zagreb, Croatia, PhD, 88. **CAREER** Asst, Univ of Ljubljana, 79-89; vis assoc prof, Univ of the South, 89-90; vis asst prof, Wash Col, 90; lectr, McGill Univ, 91-92; asst prof, Univ of Ottawa, 92-97; asst prof, Univ of Guelph, 97-98; vis asst prof, Bowdoin Col, 99; lectr, Univ of Minn, 99-00; asst prof, Univ of Ala, 00-. **MEMBERSHIPS** CIEF, WIF, IAPL, SUS. **RESEARCH** French New Novel, Claude Simon, Helene Cixous, French and Quebecois feminist literature, mythical criticism, history of ideas. **SELECTED PUBLICATIONS** Ed, Mythes dans la litterature contempoiraine d'espression francaise, Editions du Nordir (Ottawa), 94; ed, Orphee et Eurydice: mythes en mutation, Religiologiques 15 (Montreal), 97; coed, Reecriture des mythes: l'utopie au feminin, Rodopi, (Amsterdam/Atlanta, GA), 97; auth, "L'orphisme comme systeme mythologique chez Claude Simon," Les systemes mythologiques, ed Jacques Boulogne, Pr Univ du Septentrion, (Villeneuve d'Ascq, 97): 197-205; auth, "Erotisme et mythisation dans Triptyque et Les Georgiques," Recit et connaissance, eds Francois Laplantine, Joseph Levy, Jean-Baptiste Martin, Alexis Nouss, Pr Univ de Lyon, (Lyon, 98): 109-120; coed, Le Mal dans l'imaginaire litteraire francais (1850-1950), Editions David, L'Harmattan, (Ottawa/Paris, 98); auth, "Le rire redempteur: Annie Lecler, vingt-cinq ans apres," Tessera, feminist Utopias/Utopies feministes, Vol 26, (99): 41-52; auth, Lectures de Claude Simon, Editions du GREF (Toronto), forthcoming. **CONTACT ADDRESS** Dept Mod Lang & Classics, Univ of Alabama, Tuscaloosa, Box 870246, Tuscaloosa, AL 35401. **EMAIL** mzupanci@bama.ua.edu

ZWEERS, ALEXANDER FREDERIK
PERSONAL Born 06/11/1931, Amsterdam, Netherlands, m, 1963, 2 children **DISCIPLINE** RUSSIAN LITERATURE **EDUCATION** Univ Amsterdam, Drs, 59; Univ Groningen, Holland, PhD(Russ lit), 71. **CAREER** Instr, Univ BC, 62-67; asst prof, 67-73, Assoc Prof Russ & Church Slavonic, Univ Waterloo, 73-, Can Coun Res Grants, 71, 72, 74 & 77; Partic, Exchange Prog Can & Soviet Scholars, 74. **MEMBERSHIPS** Can Asn Slavists, Can Asn Advan Netherlandic Studies. **RESEARCH** L N Tolstoy, I A Bunin, Russian-Dutch literary relations. **CONTACT ADDRESS** 116 Keats Way Pl, Waterloo, ON, Canada N2L 5H3.

ZYLA, WOLODYMYR T.
PERSONAL Born 06/25/1919, Zbaraz, Ukraine, m, 1945, 3 children **DISCIPLINE** SLAVIC PHILOLOGY **EDUCATION** Univ Man, BS, 59, MA, 62; Ukrainian Free Univ, Munich, PhD(Slavic philol), 67. **CAREER** Assoc prof Russ & Ger lang & Russ lit, 63-74, Prof Slavic Lang & Lit, Tex Tech Univ, 74-, Ed, Proc Comp Lit Symp, Vol I-IV, 68-71, coed, Vol V-X, 72-77; chmn, Interdept Comt Comp Lit, Tex Tech Univ, 69-76; Nat Endowment for Humanities grant, 75. **HONORS AND AWARDS** Lett & Cert, Am Revolution Bicentennial Admin, 76. **MEMBERSHIPS** Multi-Ethnic Lit US; Am Asn Teachers Slavic & East Europ Lang; Am Name Soc; Shevcheko Sci Soc; Am Comp Lit Asn. **RESEARCH** Ukrainian literature, 16th and 17th centuries; literary criticism of modern literature; comparative literature. **SELECTED PUBLICATIONS CONTACT ADDRESS** 5220 29th St, Lubbock, TX 79407.

Geographic Index

Long Beach
Domingo-Foraste, Douglas

Los Angeles
Andersen, Elaine
Ando, Clifford
Aoun, Joseph
Babcock, Arthur Edward
Bahr, Ehrhard
Barber, Elizabeth J. Wayland
Barnouw, Dagmar
Bauml, Franz H.
Bergren, Ann L. T.
Birge, Bettine
Birnbaum, Henrik
Blank, David L.
Blumberg, Sherry H.
Bonebakker, Seeger A.
Borer, Hagit
Bruneau, Marie Florine
Carnicke, Sharon Marie
Carron, Jean-Claude
Chambers, Mortimer Hardin
Cheung, Dominic C. N.
Chrzanowski, Joseph
Clausing, Gerhard
Coleman, Patrick J.
Crowe, P. S.
Cuenca, Jose Ramon Araluce
Diaz, Roberto Ignacio
Diaz-Jimeno, Felipe
Dyck, Andrew R.
Eekman, Thomas
Ehret, Christopher
Finegan, Edward J.
Frakes, Jerold C.
Frischer, Bernard D.
Fromkin, Victoria A.
Fulco, William J.
Gans, Eric L.
Georges, Robert A.
Goldberg, Sander M.
Gonzalez, Alfonso
Gurval, Robert Alan
Haidu, Peter
Han, Mieko
Hawkins, John A.
Hayden, George A.
Heidsieck, Arnold
Hoji, Hajime
Hsu, Kylie
Ilie, Paul
Ivanov, Vyacheslav V.
Johnson, Carroll B.
Jun, Sun-Ah
Kamuf, Peggy
Kim, Nam-Kil
King, Katherine Callen
Komar, Kathleen Lenore
Koropeckyj, Roman
Ladefoged, Peter
Lanham, Carol D.
Lattimore, Steven
Lazar, Moshe
Li, Audrey
Lionnet, Francoise
Lofstedt, Bengt
Lopez-Calvo, Ignacio
MacDonald, Maryellen
Maniquis, Robert Manuel
Mellor, Anne Kostelanetz
Mellor, Ronald
Minkova, Donka
Morgan, Kathryn A.
Naiditch, P. G.
Nash, Stanley
Nehring, Wolfgang
Orenstein, Gloria Feman
Pinkus, Karen
Radchik, Laura
Richlin, Amy
Rosenthal, Margaret F.
Rudder, Robert S.
Rutherford, William E.
Saltarelli, Mario
Schein, Barry
Schnauber, Cornelius
Seidenberg, Mark
Silva-Corvalan, Carmen M.
Sonnenfeld, Albert
Starr, Peter
Stefanovska, Malina
Stockwell, Robert Paul
Thomas, Dominic R.
Tournissac, Annick-France
Tuttle, Edward Fowler
Vergnaud, Jean-Roger
Vine, Brent
Wagener, Hans
Walker, Andrew David
Walker, Rachel
Woodard, Roger
Worth, Dean Stoddard
Zevit, Ziony
Zholkovsky, Alexander
Zubizarreta, Maria Luisa

Malibu
Casmir, Fred L.
Durham, Ken R.
Lorenzi, Paola G.
Thomason, Phil

Monterey
Cooper, Danielle Chavy
Glon, Daniel
Nitsche, Richard
Strolle, Jon M.

Mount View
Brennan, Mary Alethea

Mountain View
Jobim, Jose Luis
Mariani, Bethania S. C.

Northridge
Ford, Alvin Earle
Gariano, Carmelo

Oakland
Caufield, Carlota
Cavallari, Hector Mario
Siekhaus, Elisabeth

Orange
Axelrod, Mark R.
Deck, Allan F.
Schneider, Matthew T.

Pacific Palisades
Grimstad, Kirsten J.

Palm Desert
Kreuter, Katherine

Pasadena
Allocati, Iris F.
Barber, Paul Thomas
Bogen, Joseph E.
Miner, Ellis D.

Playa del Rey
Mahoney, John Francis

Pomona
Smith, David Richard

Redlands
Vailakis, Ivan Gordon

Riverside
Chen, Jingsong
Daviau, Donald G.
Fagundo, Ana Maria
Ganim, John Michael
Gericke, Philip Otto
Grimm, Reinhold
King, Ben L.
Levin, Jules Fred
Megenney, William Wilber
Parr, James A.
Scanlon, Thomas Francis
Stoltzfus, Ben F.
Waller, Marguerite R.

Rohnert Park
Haslam, Gerald William
Martinez, Elizabeth Coonrod

Sacramento
Dennis, Harry Joe
Giles, Mary E.
Santana, Jorge Armando
Wu, Joseph Sen

San Bernardino
Golden, Bruce

San Diego
Case, Thomas Edward
Donadey, Anne
Dukas, Vytas
Farber, Gerald Howard
Genovese, Edgar Nicholas
Jackson, Elizabeth R.
Lawson, Richard H.
Lyman-Hager, Mary Ann
Mapa, Marina Vargas
Savvas, Minas
Shapiro, Lewis P.
Silverman, Malcolm Noel
Warren, Edward W.

San Francisco
Bodkin, Robin O.
Chinosole
Gries, Frauke
Leitao, David
Moskowitz, Andre J.
Vogeley, Nancy Jeanne

San Jose
Leung, Kai-Cheong

San Luis Obispo
Frantz, Barbara
Hellenbrand, Harold

San Mateo
Petit, Susan

Santa Barbara
Ashby, William James
Athanassakis, Apostolos N.
Avalle-Arce, Juan Bautista
Blackwood-Collier, Mary
Cook, Elizabeth Heckendorn
Cortijo, Antonio
Docter, Mary K.
Drake, Harold A.
Exner, Richard
Garr, W. Randall
Hahn, Francis V. Hickson
Helgerson, Richard
Hernadi, Paul
Hoffmeister, Gerhart
Jackman, Jarrell C.
Johnson, Donald Barton
Jordan, Borimir
Leal, Luis
Li, Charles N.
Lindheim, Sara H.
Lundell, Torborg Lovisa
Mahlendorf, Ursula R.
Martinez-Lopez, Enrique
Mcentyre, Marilyn Chandler
Nelson, William B.
Perissinotto, Giorgio
Renehan, Robert
St. Omer, Garth
Steiner, Thomas Robert
Sullivan, John P.
Tappy, Ron E.
Tobin, Ronald William Francis
Wallace, Vesna Acimovic
Young, David Charles

Santa Clara
Jimenez, Francisco

Santa Cruz
Aissen, Judith
Chung, Sandra
Farkas, Donka F.
Hankamer, Jorge
Ito, Junko
Ladusaw, William A.
Mccloskey, James
Mester, Armin
Miles, Gary B.
Padgett, Jaye
Pullum, Geoffrey K.
Shipley, William F.

Santa Monica
Nieman, Nancy Dale

Stanford
Bloomer, W. Martin
Clark, Eve Vivienne
Cohn, Robert G.
Connolly, Joy P. T.
Felstiner, John
Fleishman, Lazar
Gleason, Maude
Goetschel, Willi
Gregg, Robert C.
Hester, Ralph M.
Huang, Alexander C. Y.
Hunt, Patrick
Jameson, Michael H.
Lindenburger, Herbert S.
Manning, Joseph G.
Martin, Richard Peter
Maxmin, Jody
McCall, Marsh H., Jr.
Miano, Alice
Morris, Ian
Mudimbe, Valentine
Nightingale, Andrea Wilson
Pratt, Mary Louise
Rehm, Rush
Sag, Ivan Andrew
Schnapp, Jeffrey
Stephens, Susan A.
Sungdai, Cho
Syed, Jasmin
Traugott, Elizabeth Closs
Treggiari, Susan M.
Wallace, John R.
Wang, John C. Y.
Wasow, Thomas Alexander
Wigodsky, Michael M.

Stockton
Giraldez, Susan C.
Sharp, Francis Michael

Thousand Oaks
Stewart, Walter K.

Turlock
Andres, Carlos M.

Ventura
Rush, Patricia

Whittier
Charbran, H. Rafael

COLORADO

Boulder
Barchilon, Jacques
Bejel, Emilio
Einbeck, Kandace
Engel, Barbara
Frajzyngier, Zygmunt
Fredricksmeyer, Ernst A.
Geary, John Steven
Gonzalez-del-Valle, Luis T.
Jensen, Frede
Junod, Samuel A.
Kopff, Edward Christian
Lee, Charles Nicholas
Lipovetsky, Mark
Long, Mary
Menn, Lise
Michaelis, Laura A.
Prince, Susan
Rood, David Stanley
Schmiesing, Ann
Schultz, Joseph P.
Stavan, Henry-Anthony
Taylor, Allan Ross

Colorado Springs
Bizzarro, Salvatore
Cramer, Owen C.
Davis, William
Koc, Richard
McKay, Douglas R.
Richardson, Horst Fuchs
Von Dassanowsky, Robert
Wishard, Armin

Denver
Castellani, Victor
DeForest, Mary Margolies
Furness, Edna Lue
Gilroy, James Paul
Glatz, Lawrence F.
Ishimatsu, Ginette
Means, James
Ranwez, Alain Daniel
Ward, Seth

Evergreen
Gibson, Todd

Fort Collins
Bodine, Jay F.
Castro, Amanda
Fowler, Carolyn A.
Garcia, Jose Luis Suarez
Gilmore, Roger H.
Hoffmann, Klaus D.
Hunt, Irmgard
Jones, Tobin H.
Jordan, Sabine D.
Kennedy, George A.
Malpezzi Price, Paola
Otero, Jose
Sargent, Stuart H.
Saz, Sara M.
Stansfield, Maria Pilar Perez
Thiem, Jon
Wolff, Roland A.

Greeley
George, Hermon, Jr.
Marecaux, Marie-Laure

Gunnison
Hansen, Helynne

Littleton
Bennett, Janice L.

Louisville
Del Caro, Adrian

CONNECTICUT

Bethel
Dobsevage, Alvin P.

Easton
Paolini, Gilberto

Fairfield
Campos, Javier F.
Klee, Ildora
Leeber, Victor F.
Levitt, Jesse
Rosivach, Vincent John

Hamden
Magnarelli, Sharon
Quirk, Ronald Joseph

Hartford
Kaimowitz, Jeffrey H.
Lahti, Katherine
Lee, Sonia M.
Macro, Anthony David
Ndiaye, Cheikh

Middletown
Dunn, Peter Norman
Gonzalez, Bernardo Antonio
Katz, Marilyn A.
Lowrie, Joyce Oliver
Meyer, Priscilla
Needler, Howard
Roberts, Michael
Walker, Willard
Wensinger, Arthur Stevens
Winston, Krishna

New Britain
Auld, Louis
Passaro, Maria C. Pastore
Passaro, Maria P.
Pesca-Cupolo, Carmela
Picerno, Richard A.
Rohinsky, Marie-Claire
Wallach, Martha K.

New Haven
Anderson, Michael John
Babcock, Robert
Bers, Victor
Brooks, Peter Preston
Chang, Kang-I S.
Erlich, Victor
Fink, Hilary L.
Gaylin, Ann E. E.
Hubert, Marie Louise
Insler, Stanley
Jackson, K. David
Jackson, Robert Louis
Martin, Samuel Elmo
Matthews, John F.
May, Georges
Mazzotta, Giuseppe F.
Pollitt, Jerome J.
Porter, Charles Allen
Robinson, Fred C.
Sammons, Jeffrey Leonard
Schoolfield, George C.
Solodow, Joseph B.
Stimson, Hugh McBirney
Vena, Michael

De Kalb
Barbe, Katharina
Mazzola, Michael Lee
Michael, Colette Verger
Schriber, Mary Suzanne

Dekalb
Michael, Colette
Osterle, Heinz D.

Edwardsville
Griffen, Toby David
Mann, Joan Debbie
Springer, Carl P. E.

Evanston
Birner, Betty
Cummins, Fred
Durham, Scot
Durr, Volker
Eldred, Katherine O.
Fenves, Peter
Fox, Edward Inman
Garrison, Daniel H.
Ginsburg, Michal P.
Kennedy, Chris
Kerr, Lucille
Levi, Judith N.
Levin, Beth
Lys, Franziska
McCumber, John
Mead, Gerald
Monoson, S. Sara
Muller-Sievers, Helmut
Packer, James
Paden, William D.
Pierrehumbert, Janet
Reginald, Allen
Rohrbacher, Bernhard
Romanowski, Sylvie
Rosello, Michelle M.
Sankovitch, Tilde
Speck, Oliver C.
Spencer, Janine
Stimilli, Davide
Thorsen, Kristine
Tournier, Claude
Wallace, Robert
Ward, Gregory
Winston, Jane
Wright, John

Galesburg
Prats, Jorge

Jacksonville
Metcalf, Allan Albert

La Grange
Mueller, Roseanna M.

Macomb
Conger, Syndy Mcmillen
Frazer, Timothy C.
Kurman, George
Vos, Morris

Normal
Alstrum, James
Bohn, Willard
Laurenti, Joseph L.
Pancrazio, James
Parent, David J.
Shields, John Charles
Thomas, Roger K.
Trouille, Mary S.

Peoria
Maier, Carol Smith

River Forest
Froehlich, Charles Donald
Kreiss, Paul Theodore

Techny
Luzbetak, Louis Joseph

Urbana
Borgeson, Paul A.
Bristol, Evelyn C.
Calder, William M., III
Cassell, Anthony K.
Chow, Kai-Wing
De Ley, Herbert C.
Fresco, Karen
Friedberg, Maurice
Gerlach, U. Henry
Gladney, Frank Y.
Goodman, David G.
Green, Georgia Marks
Hill, Steven Phillips
Jenkins, Frederic Magill
Kachru, Braj Behari
Kachru, Yamuna
Lasersohn, Peter
Lott, Robert Eugene
Mall, Laurence
Marchand, James Woodrow
McGlathery, James Melville
Morgan, Jerry Lee
Mortimer, Armine Kotin
Nelson, Robert J. Ames
Newman, John Kevin
Pachmuss, Temira
Palencia-Roth, Michael
Sansone, David
Scanlan, Richard T.
Schoeps, Karl H.
Talbot, Emile
Wallach, Luitpold
Wilcox, John Chapman
Zgusta, Ladislav

Urbanan
Tolliver, Joyce

Wauconda
Bolchazy, Ladislaus J.

Wheaton
Hawthorne, Gerald F.
Scott, Lindy
Ziefle, Helmut W.

INDIANA

Bloomington
Ankrom, Jeffrey
Ansart, Guillaume
Auger, Julie
Bannon, Cynthia J.
Banta, Frank Graham
Barnstone, Willis
Beltran, Luis
Berkvam, Michael
Bieder, Maryellen
Boerner, Peter
Bondanella, Julia Conaway
Bondanella, Peter
Carr, Richard Alan
Chaitin, Gilbert D.
Christ, Matthew R.
Ciccarelli, Andrea
Cooper, Henry Ronald, Jr.
Davis, Stuart
Dekydtspotter, Laurent
Feldstein, Ronald Fred
Franklin, James L.
Franks, Steven
Friedman, Edward Herbert
Gerrard, Charlotte
Glowacki, Kevin T.
Gray, Margaret
Hansen, William F.
Hertz, David M.
Hinds, Leonard
Holschuh, Albrecht
Houston, Mona T.
Impey, Olga Tudorica
Isbell, John
Iwamoto, Yoshio
Kenshur, Oscar S.
Leach, Eleanor W.
Lebano, Edoardo A.
Lloyd, Rosemary
Long, Timothy
Lopez-Morillas, Consuelo
MacPhail, Eric
Meadows, Patrick
Merceron, Jacques E.
Mickel, Emanuel J.
Musa, Mark
Nagle, Betty Rose
Newman, Paul
Oinas, Felix Johannes
Pfohl, Russell
Piedmont, Ferdinand
Rasch, William
Remak, Henry Heymann Herman
Rosenberg, Samuel N.
Scalabrini, Massimo
Shetter, William Zeiders
Sobrer, Josep Miquel
Valdman, Albert
Vance, Barbara
Volkova, Bronislava
Wailes, Stephen L.
Wang, Joan Parsons
Weisstein, Ulrich
Yan, Margaret M.

Crawfordsville
Gomez, Gilberto
Kubiak, David Payne

Evansville
Caldwell, Larry
Richardson, Donald

Fort Wayne
Craig, Virginia Robertson
Fox, Linda Chodosh
Galoppe, Raul A.
Gerig, Wesley Lee
Thuente, Mary Helen

Greencastle
Evans, Arthur Bruce
Huffman, Carl A.

Indianapolis
Barlow, John Denison
Black, Margaretta
Detwiler, Louise A.
Hoyt, Giles Reid
Kooreman, Thomas Edward
McBride, Angela Barron
Meier, Marga
Nnaemeka, Obioma G.
Saffire, Paula Reiner
Steussy, Marti J.
Vermette, Rosalie Ann
Willem, Linda M.

Kokomo
Kelz, Rochelle Kanter

La Porte
Jones, Larry Bert

Muncie
Gauggel, Karl H.
Gilman, Donald
Guntsche, Marina
King, Adele C.
Ruebel, James

North Manchester
Glade, Henry

Notre Dame
Amar, Joseph P.
Anadon, Jose
Boulton, Maureen
DellaNeva, JoAnn
Douthwaite, Julia V.
Gasperetti, David
Hagens, Jan Luber
Ibsen, Kristine L.
Jerez-Farran, Carlos
Kusmer, Robert L.
Lanzinger, Klaus
MacKenzie, Louis A.
Marullo, Thomas Gaiton
Moevs, Christian
Norton, Robert E.
Perry, Catherine
Prieto, Char
Profit, Vera Barbara
Reydams-Schils, Gretchen
Toumayan, Alain P.
Williams, Maria Rosa Olivera
Wimmer, Albert K.

Plainfield
Beaudry, Agnes Porter

Richmond
Atkinson, James Blakely

Saint Meinrad
Davis, Kenneth G.

South Bend
Juarez, Encarnacion
Scanlan, Margaret C.
Thundy, Zacharias P.
Welle, John Patrick

Terre Haute
Blackshire-Belay, C. Aisha
Diaz, Lomberto
Jennermann, Donald L.
Krause, Maureen Therese

Valparaiso
Herrera, Enrique
Kumpf, Michael
Leeb, Carolyn
Must, Gustav

West Lafayette
Beer, Jeanette Mary Ayres
Broden, Thomas F.
Garfinkel, Alan
Hart, Patricia
Hatasa, Kazumi
Hislope, Kristi A.
Hong, Wei
Jaen-Portillo, Isabel
Keck, Christiane Elisabeth
Kirby, John T.
Martinez, Jacqueline M.
Mumby, Dennis K.
Orlando, Valerie
Stohl, Cynthia B.
Titche, Leon L.

Winona Lake
Lovelady, Edgar John

IOWA

Ames
Bowles, B.
Courteau, Joanna
Dow, James Raymond
Gasta, Chad M.
Morris, Walter D.
Zimmerman, Zora Devrnja

Cedar Falls
Meier, A. J.
Oates, Michael David
Zucker, George K.

Cedar Rapids
Inman, Beverly J.

Davenport
Hansen, Elena S.

Decorah
Bunge, Wilfred F.
Gibbs, Virginia
Iudin-Nelson, Laurie
Kath, Ruth R.
Kemp, Henrietta J.
Kurth, William Charles
Sieber, John Harold
Stokker, Kathleen Marie
Westfall, R.

Des Moines
Abel, Richard Owen
Beynen, Gijsbertus (Bert) Koolemans

Dubuque
Drummond, Richard Henry

Grinnell
Cummins, W. Joseph
Lalonde, Gerald Vincent
Michaels, Jennifer

Indianola
Gieber, Robert L.

Iowa City
Aikin, Judith Popovich
Altman, Rick (Charles Frederick)
Balderston, Daniel
Coblin, Weldon South
Detmer, Hellena R.
Douglass, R. Thomas
Ertl, Wolfgang
Garlinger, Patrick P.
Green, Peter
Hahn, Oscar
Hornsby, Roger Allen
Ke, C. R.
Kuenzli, Rudolf Ernst
Maierhofer, Walter
Nagel, Alan Frederick
Ringen, Catherine Oleson
Ungar, Steven
Wachal, Robert Stanley
Wertz, Christopher Allen

Mount Vernon
Crowder, Diane Griffin
Gruber-Miller, John C.

Orange City
Druliner, Marcia M.

Pella
Krogstad, Allison D.
Webber, Philip Ellsworth

KANSAS

Emporia
Clamurro, William

Hays
Firestone, Ruth H.
Hintz, Ernst Ralf
Salien, Jean

Lawrence
Anderson, Danny L.
Baron, Frank
Blue, William Robert
Boon, Jean-Pierre
Brushwood, John Stubbs
Chamberlin, V. A.
Conrad, Joseph Lawrence
Corbeill, Anthony
Debicki, Andrew Peter
Dick, Ernst S.
Dinneen, David A.
Doudoroff, Michael John
Fourny, Diane
Freeman, Bryant C.
Galton, Herbert
Greenberg, Marc L.
Hartman, James Walter
Herzfeld, Anita
Ingemann, Frances
Jewers, Caroline
Keel, William D.
Kelly, Van
Kozma, Janice M.
Lombardo, Stanley
Marx, Leonie
Maurer, Warren R.
Parker, Stephen Jan
Pasco, Allan
Sautermaister, Gert
Shaw, Michael
Souza, Raymond D.
Spires, Robert Cecil

Manhattan
Benson, Douglas Keith
Corum, Robert T., Jr.
Dehon, Claire L.
Kolonosky, Walter F.
Ossar, Michael Lee
Shaw, Bradley Alan

Pittsburg
Drew, Shirley K.
O'Hearn, Carolyn

Wichita
Bennett, Tina L.
Myers, Eunice Doman
Tomayko, James Edward
Williamson, Keith

KENTUCKY

Berea
Schneider, Robert J.

Bowling Green
Baldwin, Thomas Pratt
Spurlock, John Howard
Weigel, Richard David

Cumberland
Thomas, Katherine

Danville
Allen, John
Ciholas, Karin Nordenhaug
Finch, Patricia S.

Waltham
Engelberg, Edward
Fox, Dian
Harth, Erica
Jackendoff, Ray Saul
Johnston, Patricia A.
Kaplan, Edward Kivie
Lansing, Richard H.
Sachs, Murray
Young, Dwight Wayne

Wellesley
Galand, Rene
Lefkowitz, Mary Rosenthal
Mistacco, Vicki
Roses, Lorraine Elena
Starr, Raymond James

Wellesley Hills
Vega, Carlos

Wenham
Lutes, Leasa

West Newton
Zohn, Harry

Westfield
Fellbaum, Christiane
Kane, Leslie

Williamstown
Bell-Villada, Gene Harold
Cassiday, Julie A.
Chang, Cecilia
Christensen, Kerry A.
Desrosiers-Scholt, Nicole
Druxes, Helga
Dunn, Susan
Fuqua, Charles
Gagliardi, Frank M.
Gimenez, Antonio
Goldstein, Darra
Helfant, Ian M.
Ishikawa, Minako
Johnson, Emily
Katarzyna, Olga B.
Kieffer, Bruce
Knopp, Sherron Elizabeth
Kraus, Matthew A.
Newman, Gail M.
Nicastro, Anthony J.
Norton, Glyn P.
Piper, Anson Conant
Silber, Cathy L.
Stamelman, Richard
Yamada, Reiko
Zilcosky, John

Worcester
Aoki, Michikoy
Arend, Jutta
Bernstein, Eckhard Richard
Borland, Isabel Alvarez
Cababas, Miguel Angel
Catto, Bonnie A.
Cull, John T.
Dollenmayer, David Bristol
Ferguson, William Rotch
Fraser, Theodore
Hamilton, John Daniel Burgoyne
Kom, Ambroise
Kuzniewski, Anthony Joseph
Lamoureux, Normand J.
Lavery, Gerard B.
Merithew, Charlene L.
Roberts, Helen Freear
Ross, Claudia
Sazaki, Kristina R.
Stone, Cynthia

MICHIGAN

Adrian
Elardo, Ronald Joseph
Yehuda, Simone N.

Albion
Baumgartner, Ingeborg Hogh

Allendale
Franklin, Ursula
Hong, Ran-e
Morison, William S.

Alma
Ottenhoff, John

Ann Arbor
Arroyo, Jossiana
Becker, Alton Lewis
Bellamy, James Andrew
Billick, David Joseph
Burling, Robbins
Carpenter, Bogdana
Casa, Frank Paul
Chang, Chun-Shu
Collins, Derek B.
Cowen, Roy C.
Fabian, Hans Joachim
Freedman, David Noel
Frier, Bruce W.
George, Emery Edward
Goic, Cedomil
Gray, Floyd Francis
Hafter, Monroe Z.
Johnson, Mayumi Yuki
Koenen, Ludwig
Kyes, Robert L.
Maxwell, Donald R.
Mermier, Guy R.
Morton, Jacqueline
Muller, Marcel
Paslick, Robert H.
Porter, J. I.
Rastalsky, Hartmut
Seidler, Ingo
Stolz, Benjamin Armond
Verdesio, Gustavo
Vosteen, Thomas
Weiss, Hermann Friedrich
Windfuhr, Gernot Ludwig

Berkley
Vernier, Richard

Berrien Springs
Roche, Mark W.
Running, Leona Glidden

Detroit
Chauderlot, Fabienne Sophie
Cobbs, Alfred Leon
DuBruck, Edelgard E.
Duggan, Anne E.
Farrow, J. G.
Gutierrez, Jesus
Haase, Donald P.
Kibler, Louis Wayne
Koontz, Christian
Latta, Susan M.
Lauer, Janice M.
McNamee, Kathleen
Ronnick, Michele Valerie
Schurlknight, Donald E.
Sheridan, Jennifer A.
Stern, Guy
Stivale, Charles J.
Wedberg, Lloyd W.

East Lansing
Abbott, B.
Byron, Kristine Ann
Compitello, Malcolm Alan
Dulai, Surjit Singh
Fiore, Robert L.
Fogel, Jerise
Francese, Joseph
Goodson, Alfred Clement
Gray, Eugene Francis
Hughes, William Nolin
Imamura, Shigeo
Josephs, Herbert
Juntune, Thomas William
Koppisch, Michael Seibert
Kronegger, Maria Elisabeth
Mansour, George Phillip
Porter, Laurence M.
Prestel, David K.
Stalker, James Curtis
Yates, Donald Alfred

Grand Rapids
Ellis, Bradford
Fetzer, Glenn W.
Meadors, Gary T.

Hillsdale
Muniz, Olga

Holland
Andre, Maria Claudia
Larson, Ann R.

Kalamazoo
Blickle, Peter
Haenicke, Diether H.
Heller, Janet
Sauret, Martine

Lansing
Harrison, Ann Tukey

Marquette
Kupper, Nelly J.

Mount Pleasant
Labrie, Gilles R.
Walchak, Karol L.

Orchard Lake
Wrobel, Janusz

Rochester
Coppola, Carlo
Horning, Alice S.

University Center
Wang, Mason Yu-Heng

West Bloomfield
Bertman, Stephen

Ypsilanti
Cere, Ronald
Holoka, James P.
Kauffman, Janet
Keller, Gary D.
Kirby, Steven D.

MINNESOTA

Collegeville
Haile, Getatchew
Richardson, Scott D.

Duluth
Cole, Eve Browning
Conant, Jonathan Brendan
Jankofsky, Klaus P.
Linn, Michael D.
Zeitz, Eileen

Gorham
Cowart, Wayne
Fouchereaux, Jean

Mankato
Janc, John J.

Minneapolis
Akehurst, F. R. P.
Arenas, Fernando
Barnes, Betsy
Bashiri, Iraj
Belifiore, Elizabeth S.
Brewer, Maria Minich
Erickson, Gerald M.
Ferran, Ofelia
Firchow, Evelyn Scherabon
Firchow, Peter Edgerly
Fullerton, Gerald Lee
Grimstad, Kaaren
Gumpel, Liselotte
Gundel, Jeannette K.
Hirschbach, Frank Donald
Jahn, Gary Robert
Jara, Rene
Klee, Carol A.
Kraabel, Alf Thomas
Krevans, Nita
Lardinois, Andre P. M. H.
Liberman, Anatoly
Liu, Catherine
MacLeish, Andrew
Malandra, William
Martinez, Ronald L.
Noakes, Susan
O'Connell, Joanna
Ocampo, Francisco
Olson, Stuart Douglas
Paganini, Maria
Parente, James A., Jr.
Polakiewicz, Leonard A.
Preckshot, Judith
Ramos-Garcia, Luis A.
Sarles, Harvey Burton
Sheets, George Archibald
Sivert, Eileen
Sonkowsky, Robert Paul
Stenson, Nancy Jean
Sullivan, Constance
Teraoka, Arlene
Thomas, Gary Craig
Vidal, Hernan
Wakefield, Ray Milan
Zahareas, Anthony

Moorhead
Iverson, Stanley
Kaplan, James Maurice

Northfield
Achberger, Karen Ripp
Allen, Wendy
Cisar, Mary
Dust, Patrick
Fink, Karl J.
Groton, Anne H.
Kaga, Mariko
Nemec-Ignashev, Diane M.
Paas, John Roger
Rippley, La Vern J.
Smith, Bardwell L.
Wilkie, Nancy C.

Rochester
Penniston, Joyce K.

Saint Cloud
Roman-Morales, Belen

Saint Paul
Chew, Kristina
Cooey, Paula M.
Dye, Robert Ellis
Fritz, Annick
Penchansky, David
Schubert, Virginia Ann
Wolsey, Mary Lou Morris

Saint Peter
Alzate, Gaston A.
Flory, Marleen Boudreau
Flory, Stewart Gilman
Freiert, William K.

Winona
Nichols, Ann

MISSISSIPPI

Clinton
Martin, Charles Edward

Hattiesburg
Clark, Mark E.

Jackson
Beckers, Astrid M.
Freis, Catherine Ruggiero
Freis, Richard
Gleason, Michael
Harvey, Maria-Luisa Alvarez
Krabbe, Judith
Olivia, Leonora

Mississippi State
Blaney, Benjamin
Chatham, James Ray
Emplaincourt, Edmond Arthur
Wiltrout, Ann Elizabeth
Wolverton, Robert E.

Oxford
Gutierrez, John R.

University
Arrington, Melvin
Moysey, Robert Allen
Sharpe, Peggy
Yang, Xiaobin

MISSOURI

Billings
Schaffer, Deborah

Chesterfield
Winn, Colette Henriette

Columbia
Barabtarlo, Gene
Braun, Ernst
Cavigioli, Rita C.
Comfort, Kathleen
Curtis, James Malcolm
Foley, John Miles
Hooley, Daniel M.
Kuizenga, Donna
Lago, Mary Mcclelland
Lance, Donald M.
Lewis, Marvin A.
Muratore, Mary Jo
Pierce, Glenn
Presberg, Charles D.
Saylor, Charles F.
Schenker, David J.
Scroggins, Daniel Coy
Tarkow, Theodore A.
Thiher, Ottah Allen
Ugarte, Michael
Whidden, Seth A.
Worthington, Ian

Columbus
Rueda, Ana

Fayette
Burres, Kenneth Lee

Hannibal
Bergen, Robert D.

Kansas City
Andrews, Stephen J.
Brodsky, Patricia Pollock
Levy, Gayle A.
Lewis, Martha Hoffman
Voigts, Linda Ehrsam

Kirksville
Barnes, Jim Weaver
Rao, Ramesh N.
Reid, Constance L.
Richter, Gregory

Liberty
Kauffmann, Ruth A.

Rolla
Ivliyeva, Irina

Saint Louis
Beatty, Michael
Champagne, Roland A.
Danker, Frederick W.
Herron, Robert Deupree
Ifri, Pascal A.
Lopez, Oscar R.
Lutzeler, Paul M.
Marcus, Marvin H.
Mitchell, Christopher
Nunez-Betelu, Maite
Pautrot, Jean-Louis
Poag, James F.
Sale, Mary
Schraibman, Joseph
Schwarz, E.
Tatlock, Lynne
Treadgold, Warren
Wesselschmidt, Quentin F.

Springfield
Polly, Lyle R.

Warrensburg
Doyle, Ruth Lestha
Pentlin, Susan Lee

MONTANA

Billings
Jensen, Theodore Wayne

Bozeman
Coffey, Jerome Edward
Jelinski, Jack Bernard
Pinet, Christopher

Great Falls
Taylor, Jon

Missoula
Acker, Robert
Arens, Hiltrud

Gallucci, John
Hathaway, Robert L.
Johnson, Anita L.
Julien, Helene
Lintz, Bernadette C.
Luciani, Frederick
Nakhimovsky, Alice
Naughton, John
Nicholls, James C.
Nicholls, Maria
Olcott, Anthony
Plata, Fernando
Rugg, Marilyn D.
Suarez-Galban, Eugenio

Hempstead
Keener, Frederick M.
Sampedro, Benita

Ithaca
Arroyo, Ciriaco Moron
Babby, Leonard Harvey
Bereaud, Jacques
Browne, E. Wayles
Clinton, Kevin
Cohen, Walter Isaac
Colby-Hall, Alice Mary
Coleman, John E.
Deinert, Herbert
Gair, James Wells
Groos, Arthur
Grossvogel, David I.
Hohendahl, Peter U.
John, James J.
Kaplan, Jane Payne
Kaske, Carol Vonckx
Kennedy, William John
Kirkwood, Gordon Macdonald
Kronik, John W.
Lewis, Philip Eugene
McCann, David Richard
Migiel, Marilyn
Nussbaum, Alan
Paz-Soldan, Jose Edmundo
Piedra, Jose
Pucci, Pietro
Shapiro, Gavriel
Smith, Daniel L.
Stycos, Maria Nowakowska
Suner, Margarita
Waugh, Linda Ruth
Wolff, John Ulrich

Jackson Heights
Walsh, Jerome T.

Jamaica
Jones, Michele
Kramer-Hellinx, Nechama
Wintergerst, Ann C.

Lake Peekskill
Csaki, Luciana Cuppo

Lewiston
Ponce de Leon, Gina

Miller Place
Rizzuto, Anthony

New Paltz
Brown, Peter D. G.
Gillon, Adam
Paz, Francis Xavier
Piluso, Robert Vincent

New Rochelle
Colaneri, John Nunzio
Perez, Mireya

New York
Affron, Charles M.
Anderson, Helene M.
Andriopoulos, Stefan
Bacon, Helen Hazard
Bagnall, Roger Shaler
Barolini, Teodolinda
Beardsley, Theodore S., Jr.
Belknap, Robert Lamont
Benardete, Seth Gabriel
Bentley, Eric
Bishop, Thomas
Brush, Craig Balcombe
Cachia, Pierre J. E.
Cameron, Alan
Carrera, Alessandro
Carrubba, Robert W.
Carson, Katharine Whitman
Castronovo, David
Cavallo, JoAnn
Caws, Mary Ann
Chelkowski, Peter Jan
Chernetsky, Vitaly
Cohen, Robert
Compagnon, Antoine M.
Connor, Peter T.
Consenstein, Peter
Costello, John Robert
Cribiore, Raffaela
D'Arms, John H.
Damrosch, David N.
Dellepiane, Angela B.
DeSmidt, Ben
Dilts, Mervin R.
Dorenlot, Francoise
Doubrovsky, Serge
Dougherty, Ray Cordell
Evans, Harry B.
Felder, Mira B.
Feldman, Louis H.
Ferrante, Joan M.
Fine, Ellen Sydney
Fishman, Joshua Aaron
Fleischer, Georgette
Fletcher, Robert E.
Force, Pierre
Frankel, Margherita
Frydman, Anne
Fukuyama, Francis
Gavronsky, Serge
Gibaldi, Joseph
Goldin, Frederick
Gorbatov, Inna
Gorup, Radmila J.
Gross, Irena Grudzinska
Gura, Timothy
Gustafson, Richard Folke
Gutierrez-Vega, Zenaida
Hamalian, Leo
Haynes, Holly
Heinrich, Amy Vladeck
Hoover, David Lowell
Huppauf, Bernd
Huyssen, Andreas
Jacobs, Carol F.
James, Dorothy
Jofen, Jean
Jurkevich, Gayana
Kande, Sylvie
Karsen, Sonja Petra
Kastan, David Scott
Kennedy-Day, Kiki
King, Peter
Klibbe, Lawrence H.
Knapp, Bettina
Kneller, John William
Koch, Kenneth
Kra, Pauline
Krabbenhoft, Kenneth
Kuhn-Osius, Eckhard
Kussi, Peter
Kym, Annette
Lerner, Isaias
Lowrie, Michele
Mac Adam, Alfred J.
Macchiarulo, Louis
Malone, Joseph Lawrence
Marcus, David
Marincola, John
Martinez, H. Salvador
Martinez-Bonati, Felix
May, Gita
Meyer, Ronald
Mikhail, Mona
Minkoff, Harvey
Mitterand, Henri
Naro, Anthony Julius
Nepomnyashchy, Catharine Theimer
Newman, Judith H.
Nichols, Fred Joseph
Nicolai, Elke
O'Conell, Robert J.
Pellicer, James O.
Perez-Firmat, Gustavo
Perna, Michael
Phillips, Louis
Pinet, Simone
Plottel, Jeanine Parisier
Pomeroy, Sarah B.
Purczinsky, Julius O.
Rabassa, Clementine Christos
Rebay, Luciano
Regalado, Nancy Freeman
Reyfman, Irina
Rossabi, Morris
Rubin, Mordecai
Sallustio, Anthony Thomas
Scheindlin, Raymond Paul
Schiffman, Lawrence H.
Schneider, Marshall Jerrold
Segel, Harold Bernard
Shea, George W.
Sider, David
Silver, Philip Warnock
Sklar, Robert Anthony
Slade, Carole
Snyder, Emery
Spivak, Gayatri Chakravorty
Steiner, Richard C.
Sypher, Francis Jacques
Taran, Leonardo
Tong, Diane
Varderi, Alejandro
Visson, Lynn
Vitz, Evelyn Birge
Waldinger, Renee
Wayman, Alex
Welles, Marcia Louise
Wilhelm, James Jerome
Williams, Gareth D.
Xu, Ping
Yerkes, David
Zawawi, Sharifa

Old Westbury
Assa, Sonia

Oneonta
Macris, Peter John
Otero-Krauthammer, Elizabeth

Oswego
Fisher, John C.

Plattsburgh
Arredondo, Isabel

Port Jefferson
Dunham, Vera S.

Poughkeepsie
Arlyck, Elisabeth C.
Berkley, Constance E. Gresham
Grunfeld, Mihai
Hiner, Susan
Lipschutz, Ilse Hempel
Schneider, Jeffrey A.
von der Emde, Silke

Rochester
Bond, Gerald Albert
Braun, Wilhelm
Doolittle, James
Herminghouse, Patricia A.
Hollis, Susan T.
Jorgensen, Beth E.
Moutsos, Demetrius George
Rodriquez-Hernandez, Raul

Rockville Centre
Pickman-Gertz, Charlotte

Rushford
Biggs, Henry N.

Saint Bonas
Wood, Paul William

Saint Bonaventure
Etzkorn, Girard J.

Saratoga Springs
Gelber, Lynne Levick
Mayer, Reinhard
Porter, David H.

Schenectady
Mace, Sarah
McClain, T. Van
Scullion, Scott
Sorum, Christina Elliott
Toher, Mark
Wittkowski, Wolfgang

Sparkill
Roglieri, Maria Ann

Staten Island
Jochnowitz, George
Saez, Richard
Simpson, Peter P.
Urbanc, Katica

Stony Brook
Bethin, Christina Y.
Brown, Frederick
Charnon-Deutsch, Lou
Czerwinski, Edward J.
Franco, Charles
Gabbard, Krin
Godfrey, Aaron W.
Harvey, Robert
Kaplan, Elizabeth Ann
Mignone, Mario B.
Petrey, Sandy
Rashkow, Ilona N.
Rivers, Elias Lynch
Rzhevsky, Nicholas
Sanders, Ivan
Sprinker, Michael
Sridhar, S. N.
Vasvari, Louise O.

Syracuse
Archambault, Paul Joseph
Bulman, Gail A.
Frieden, Ken
Lichtblau, Myron Ivor
McCort, Dennis
Peterson, Philip Leslie
Schneider, Gerd K.
Vetrano, Anthony Joseph
Wiley, Raymond A.
Wyngaard, Amy S.

Utica
Bergmann, Frank

Yonkers
Fowkes, Robert Allen

NORTH CAROLINA

Asheville
Aaron, N. Grace
Mills, Sophie J.

Boiling Springs
Moore, Charles B.

Boone
Chen, Zhiyuan

Chapel Hill
Amer, Sahar
Bandera, Cesareo
Broughton, Thomas Robert Shannon
Casado, Pablo Gil
Connor, Carolyn
Cortes, Julio
Crowhurst, Megan J.
Debreczeny, Paul
Eble, Connie C.
Feinberg, Lawrence E.
Furst, Lillian R.
Haig, I. R. Stirling
Henry, Eric Putnam
Houston, George W.
Illiano, Antonio
Immerwahr, Henry R.
Koelb, Clayton L.
Kuzniar, A. A.
Linderski, Jerzy
Lore, Anthony George
Mack, Sara
Masters, George Mallary
McGowan, John P.
Melchert, H. Craig
Mews, Siegfried
Mihailovich, Vasa D.
Race, William H.
Rector, Monica Paula
Salgado, Maria A.
Schweitzer, Christoph Eugen
Seaton, Jerome P.
Sherman, Carol Lynn
Smith, Rebekah M.
Starkey, Kathryn
Tsiapera, Maria
Vickery, Walter
Vogler, Frederick Wright
Weiss, Michael L.
West, William C., III
Wooten, Cecil W.
Worth, Fabienne Andre

Charlotte
Gleaves, Robert Milnor
Hopper, Edward W.

Davidson
Ahrensdorf, Peter J.
Denham, Scott
Dockery, Charles D.
Kruger, Carole A.
Mc Culloh, Mark R.
Singerman, Alan J.
Sutton, Homer B.
Toumazou, Michael K.
Walker, Hallam
Yoder, Lauren Wayne

Durham
Boatwright, Mary T.
Borchardt, Frank L.
Caserta, Ernesto
Cooke, Miriam
Davis, Gregson
Hull, Alexander
Jonassaint, Jean
Meyers, Carol L.
Mignolo, Walter
Paredes, Liliana
Rigsby, Kent Jefferson
Sieburth, Stephanie
Stewart, Philip R.
Tetel, Marcel
Torgovnick, Marianna De Marco
Willis, William Hailey

Greensboro
Almeida, Jose Agusin
Deagon, Ann Fleming
Fein, David
Goode, William Osborne
Grossi, Veronica
Koenig, Jean-Paul Francois Xavier
Newton, Robert Parr
Reeder, Heidi M.
Shelmerdine, Susan C.
Smith, Roch Charles
Smith-Soto, Mark

Greenville
Buckley, Christina A.
Jensen, Birgit A.
Malby, Maria Bozicevic
Mayberry, Nancy Kennington
Seavey, William
Stevens, John A.

Hickory
Shuford, William Harris

Hillsborough
Connor, W. Robert

Mars Hill
Knapp, Richard Gilbert

Raleigh
Maldonado-Deoliveira, Debora
Marchi, Dudley M.
Meyers, Walter Earl
Sosower, Mark L.
Stern, Irwin
Witt, Mary Ann Frese
Young, Robert Vaughan

Salisbury
Reitz, Richard Allen

Wilmington
Kamenish, Paula K.
LaPaire, Pierre J.
Wilson, Joe Bransford, Jr.

Wingate
Schuhl, Mark

Winston-Salem
Andronica, John Louis
Barbour, Sarah E.
Bree, Germaine
Glenn, Kathleen Mary
Mathews, Gary
O'Flaherty, James Carneal
Pendergraft, Mary L.
Scales, Manderline Elizabeth
Ulery, Robert W.
West, Larry E.

Pittsburgh
Al-Kasey, Tamara
Ashliman, D. L.
Avery, Harry Costas
Bart, Benjamin Franklin
Castellano, Charlene
Citton, Yves
Clack, Jerry
Colecchia, Francesca
Dana, Marie Immaculee
Dekeyser, R. M.
Dworkin y Mendez, Kenya C.
Floyd, Edwin Douglas
Freed, Barbara
Frey, Herschel J.
Gaichas, Lawrence Edward
Green, Anne
Groch, John R.
Hallstein, Christian W.
Harris, Jane Gary
Hopper, Paul
Jonas, Klaus Werner
Jones, Christopher M.
Jones, Nicholas Francis
Juffs, Alan
Kaufman, Terrence Scott
Koch, Philip
Koda, Keiko
Looney, Dennis
Miller, Andrew M.
Mills, David Otis
Newmyer, Stephen Thomas
Paulston, Christina Bratt
Polansky, Susan
Rockmore, Sylvie
Schlossman, Beryl
Silenieks, Juris
Smethurst, Mae J.
So, Sufumi
Tucker, Richard
Von Dirke, Sabine B.
Walker, Janet L.
Wilkens, Ann
Zhou, Peter Xinping

Pottstown
Bender, Henry V.

Radnor
Halpern, Cynthia L.

Saint Davids
Boehne, Patricia Jeanne

Scranton
Kamla, Thomas A.
Ledford-Miller, Linda
Parsons, Robert A.
Petrovic, Njegos M.
Wilson, Joseph P.

Secane
Hoffer, Peter T.

Slippery Rock
Zinni, Hannah Case

Springfield
Malsbary, Gerald Henry

State College
Betlyon, John Wilson
Paternost, Joseph

Swarthmore
Avery, George Costas
Moskos, George
Napoli, Donna Jo
Ostwald, Martin
Rose, Gilbert Paul
Skelnar, Robert John

University Park
Begnal, Michael Henry
Brault, Gerard Joseph
Browning, Barton W.
De Armas, Frederick A.
Eckhardt, Caroline Davis
Engel, David M.
Fitz, Earl Eugene
Fleming, Raymond Richard
Frautschi, Richard Lane
Gentry, Francis G.
Greenberg, Wendy
Grossman, Kathryn Marie
Hale, Thomas Albert
Halsey, Martha T.
Knight, Alan Edgar
Lacy, Norris J.
Lima, Robert F.
Makward, Christiane Perrin
Peavler, Terry J.
Schmalstieg, William Riegel
Wanner, Adrian J.
Ward, Patricia A.
Weiss, Beno
Ziegler, Vickie Lynne

Villanova
Duran, Jaime
Helmetag, Charles Hugh
Hunt, John M., Jr.
Ogden, Estrella V.

Wallingford
De Cruz-Saenz, Michele S.

Wayne
Wickersham, Erlis

West Chester
Braidotti, Erminio
Gutwirth, Madelyn

Wilkes-Barre
Corgan, Margaret M.
Krawczeniuk, Joseph V.

Williamsport
Kingery, Sandra L.
Maples, Robert John Barrie

Wynnewood
McDaniel, Thomas F.

York
McKulik, Ben
Medina, Cindy

PUERTO RICO

Bayamon
Guzman-Merced, Rosa Maria

Humacao
Darhower, Martin L.

Mayaguez
Anderlini-D'Onofrio, Serena

San Juan
Diaz, Luis Felipe
Quintana, Hilda E.
Ward, Margaret Charlotte

RHODE ISLAND

Bristol
Hollingsworth, Anthony L.

Kingston
Durand, Alain-Philippe
Hutton, Lewis J.
Manteiga, Robert Charles
Rogers, Kenneth Hall

Providence
Ahearn, Edward J.
Blumstein, Sheila Ellen
Boegehold, Alan
Cappelletti, Salvatore
Carreno, Antonio
Chaika, Elaine Ostrach
Coons, Dix Scott
Crossgrove, William C.
deBoo, Edward L.
Durand, Frank
Fido, Franco
Fornara, Charles William
Francis, Winthrop Nelson
Haviland, Beverly
Honig, Edwin
Konstan, David
Kucera, Henry
Levi, Joseph Abraham
Levitsky, Alexander
Oldcorn, Anthony
Pucci, Joseph M.
Putnam, Michael C. J.
Raaflaub, Kurt A.
Saint-Amand, Pierre N.
Scharf, Peter M.
Scholes, Robert
Scott, Daniel Marcellus
Shapiro, Marianne
Shapiro, Michael
Spilka, Mark
Terras, Victor
Valente, Luiz Fernando
Wyatt, William F.

Saunderstown
Waters, Harold A.

SOUTH CAROLINA

Aiken
Rich, John Stanley

Beaufort
Villena-Alvarez, Juanita

Charleston
Sclippa, Norbert
Stiglitz, Beatrice

Clemson
Cranston, Mechthild
King, Samuel C.
Riley, Helene M.
Sinka, Margit M.

Columbia
Briggs, Ward W.
Charlebois, Lucile C.
Day, James T.
Disterheft, Dorothy
French, Harold Wendell
Fryer, T. Bruce
Hardin, James Neal
Hatch, Mary G.
Henry, Freeman George
Little, Greta D.
Mathisen, Ralph Whitney
Miller, Paul
Montgomery, Michael M.
Mueller, Agnes C.
Norman, G. Buford
Roy, G(eorge) Ross
Shirley, Paula
Stewart, Joan Hinde
Vazsonyi, Nicholas

Florence
Harding, George E.

Greenville
Cherry, Charles Maurice
Cox, Jerry Lynn
McKnight, Edgar Vernon
Parsell, David Beatty

Hartsville
Doubles, Malcolm Carroll

Rock Hill
Friedman, Donald F.

Spartanburg
Raquidel, Danielle
Valentine, Tamara M.

SOUTH DAKOTA

Vermillion
Klein, Dennis Allan
Sebesta, Judith Lynn

TENNESSEE

Bristol
Jordan, Gregory D.

Clarksville
Ruiz, Miguel

Cleveland
Kailing, Joel

Cookeville
Campana, Phillip Joseph
Viera, David John

Jefferson City
Young-Ferrell, Brenda

Johnson City
Harrington, Karen A.
Nelson, Ardis L.
Schneider, Valerie Lois
Waage, Frederick O.
Zayas-Bazan, Eduardo

Knoxville
Beauvois, Margaret H.
Brady, Patrick S.
Brizio-Skov, Flavia
Campion, Edmund J.
Cazenave, Odile
Craig, Christopher P.
Creel, Bryant L.
DiMaria, Salvatore
Dumas, Bethany K.
Essif, Les
Gesell, Geraldine C.
Hodges, Carolyn Richardson
Hoeng, Peter
Holmlund, Christine
Kaplan, Gregory
Kratz, Henry
Lacure, Jon W.
Leki, Ilona
Levy, Karen D.
Martin, Susan D.
McAlpin, Mary
Mellor, Chauncey Jeffries
Nakuma, Constancio
Nappa, Christopher
Rivera-Rodas, Oscar
Romeiser, John B.
Rutledge, Harry Carraci
Silva-Filho, Euridice
Sutherland, Elizabeth H.
Tandy, David
Washburn, Yulan M.
Young, Dolly J.

Martin
Mohler, Stephen Charles
Parker, Henry H.
Rogers, Nels Jeffrey

Memphis
Albanese, Ralph
Irwin, Amanda Lee
Manopolous, Monique M.
Schmidt, Sabine I.
Sick, David
Tucker, Cynthia Grant
Walsh, Carey Ellen

Murfreesboro
Harper, A. Dianne
McCash, June

Nashville
Barrett, Tracy
Bingham, John L.
Brennan, Virginia M.
Clendenen, E. Ray
Crispin, John
Crist, Larry S.
Franke, William
Froment-Meurice, Marc
Harris, Alice C.
Jrade, Cathy L.
Kustanovich, Konstantin
McCarthy, John A.
Monga, Luigi
Patty, James Singleton
Pfanner, Helmut F.
Pichois, Claude
Sevin, Dieter H.
Wiltshire, Susan Ford

Sewanee
Bates, Scott
Davidheiser, James Charles
Lumpkins, David W.
Naylor, Eric Woodfin
Spaccarelli, Thomas Dean
Zachau, Reinhard Konrad

Signal Mountain
Conwell, David

TEXAS

Abilene
Ellis, Robert
Williams, John Howard

Arlington
Katz, Michael Ray
Ordonez, Elizabeth Jane
Silva, David James

Austin
Abboud, Peter Fouad
Arens, Katherine M.
Baker, Mary Jordan
Bump, Jerome Francis Anthony
Cable, Thomas Monroe
Carter, Joseph Coleman
Cauvin, Jean-Pierre Bernard
Cook, Erwin
Dassonville, Michel
Dawson, Robert Lewis
Dee, James H.
Fontanella, Lee
Forster, Merlin Henry
Gagarin, Michael
Galinsky, Karl
Goff, Barbara E.
Grant, Richard Babson
Green, Lisa
Harms, Robert Thomas
Heinen, Hubert
Hensey, Frederick Gerald
Higginbotham, Virginia
Karttunen, Frances
Kaulbach, Ernest Norman
Koike, Dale A.
Lehmann, Winfred Philipp
Lindstrom, Naomi
Mackey, Louis Henry
Meritt, Lucy Shoe
Michael, Wolfgang Friedrich
Moeller, Hans-Bernhard
Monas, Sidney
Moore, T. J.
Mourelatos, Alexander Phoebus Dionysiou
Nethercut, William Robert
Reeves-Marquardt, Dona
Schade, George D.
Shelmerdine, Cynthia Wright
Shumway, Nicolas
Sjoberg, Andree Frances
Smith, Carlota S.
Sole, Carlos A.
Southern, Mark R. V.
Swaffar, Janet King
Vessely, Thomas Richard
Warnke, Nina
Wells, Maria Xenia Zevelechi
Wylie, Hal

Beaumont
Ellis, Marion Leroy
Rivers, Kenneth T.

Beeville
Strause, Glynis

Belton
Wyrick, Stephen Von

Brownsville
Diaz, Lidia
Green, George

College Station
Conrad, Charles R.
Imhoff, Brian
Peterson, Tarla Rai
Williams, Eric

Dallas
Merrifield, William R.
Perl, Jeffery Michael
Rojas-Auda, Elizabeth
Taylor, Richard A.
Ulatowska, Hanna K.

Denton
Bogle, Edra Charlotte
Carle, Barbara
Koop, Marie-Christine W.
Nash, Jerry
Olsen, Solveig
Oxford, Jeffery

Beloit
Freeman, Thomas Parry
Street, Jack David

Green Bay
Fleurant, Ken

Kenosha
Christoph, Siegfried
Dean, Dennis Richard
Loewen, Lynn
Rivera, Margarita Tavera
Rothstein, Marian
Stathatos, Constantine Christopher
Yang, Mimi

La Crosse
Socha, Donald

Madison
Bender, Todd K.
Berg, Willaim J.
Berghahn, Klaus L.
Ciplijauskaite, Birute
Cohen, L. Keith
Cunliffe, William Gordon
Gross, Sabine
Hanrez, Marc
Hemand, Jost
Ingwersen, Niels
Kleinhenz, Christopher
Kornblatt, Judith Deutsch
Latousek, Rob
Livorni, Ernesto
Marks, Elaine
Marquess, Harlan Earl
McClure, Laura Kathleen
McKeown, James C.
Moedersheim, Sabine
Nicholas, Robert Leon
Nollendorfs, Valters
Ormand, Kirk
Powell, Barry
Read, Charles
Richter, Gerhard
Rodini, Robert Joseph
Scott, Charles Thomas
Sihler, Andrew L.
Silberman, M.
Von Schneidemesser, Luanne
Wills, Jeffrey
Young, Richard F.

Manitowoc
Bjerke, Robert Alan

Milwaukee
Benda, Gisela
Christensen, Peter G.
Cordova, Sarah Davies
Corre, Alan David
Downing, Pamela A.
Filips-Juswigg, Katherina P.
Friedman, Melvin Jack
Grossfeld, Bernard
Gutierrez, Manuel Hierro
Martin-Rodriguez, Manuel M.
Mileham, James Warren
Moravcsik, Edith Andrea
Pickering-Iazzi, Robin
Rodriguez-Luis, Julio
Shey, Howard James
Skalitzky, Rachel Irene
Swanson, Roy Arthur
Taylor, Steven Millen
Ullman, Pierre Lioni
Winter, Ian James

New Berlin
Milham, Mary Ella

Oregon
Grittner, Frank Merton
Schoville, Keith Norman

Ripon
Lowry, Eddie R., Jr.

River Falls
Mannetter, Terrance

Stevens Point
Meisel, Martin

Whitewater
Adams, George Roy

WYOMING

Laramie
Bagby, Lewis
Bangerter, Lowell A.
Durer, Christopher
Hanson, Klaus D.
Langlois, Walter G.
Larsen, Kevin
Mayer, Sigrid
Mundt, Hannelore
Picherit, Jean-Louis
Rhoades, Duane
Sigalov, Pavel S.
Tolo, Khama-Basilli

Torrington
Nesbitt, John D.

CANADA

ALBERTA

Calgary
Walbank, Michael Burke
Zekulin, Nicholas Gleb

Edmonton
Blodgett, Edward D.
Brown, Janice C. L.
Buck, Robert J.
Dimic, Milan Velimir
Dryer, Matthew S.
Egert, Eugene
Fishwick, Duncan
Forcadas, Alberto M.
Landy, Francis
Marahrens, Gerwin
Margolin, Uri
Mozejko, Edward
Nedashkivska, Alla
Pownall, Frances Skoczylas
Prideaux, Gary Dean
Priestly, Tom M. S.
Rahimich, Nasrin
Slavutych, Yar
Swirski, Peter

BRITISH COLUMBIA

Burnaby
Davison, Rosena
Gomez-Moriana, Antonio
Merler, Grazia
Taboada, Maria

Delta
Gamlin, Gordon S.

Vancouver
Batts, Michael S.
Bongie, Laurence L.
Brinton, Laurel J.
Evans, James A. S.
Goetz-Stankiewicz, Marketa
Grigorut, Constantin
Hamlin, Frank Rodway
Harvey, William D.
Knutson, Harold Christian
Merivale, Patricia
Pacheco-Ransanz, Arsenio
Pulleyblank, Edwin George
Raoul, Valerie
Saint-Jacques, Bernard

Victoria
Bradley, Keith Richard
Campbell, David A.
Carlin, Claire L.
Hadley, Michael Llewellyn
Herique, Emmanuel
Holmberg, I. E.
Howard, Lloyd H.
Hsieh, Yvonne Y.
Lapprand, Marc
Limbrick, Elaine
Riedel, Walter Erwin
Ross, Mary Ellen
Tucker, John J.
Vautier, Marie
Waelti-Walters, Jennifer

MANITOBA

Winnipeg
Cooper, Craig
Doerksen, Victor Gerard
Egan, Rory Bernard
Golden, Mark
Gordon, Alexander Lobban
Harvey, Carol
Heidenreich, Rosmarin
Joubert, Andre
Marantz, Enid Goldstine

NEW BRUNSWICK

Fredericton
Dalzell, Alexander
Lorey, Christoph R.
Pugh, Anthony Roy

Moncton
Gallant, Christel

NEWFOUNDLAND

Saint John's
Clark, Raymond John
Hewson, John

NOVA SCOTIA

Halifax
Bishop, Michael
Chavy, Paul
Gesner, B. Edward

Wolfville
Best, Janice
Delpeche, Bernard

ONTARIO

Downsview
Corbett, Noel L.

Edmonton
Penrod, Lynn K.

Guelph
Benson, Renate
Matthews, Victor J.

Hamilton
Cro, Stelio
McKay, Alexander G.
Paul, George Mackay
Silvestri, Elena M.

Kingston
Bessette, Gerard
Kilpatrick, Ross S.
Schroeder, Frederic M.
Shirinian, Lorne
Surridge, Marie

London
Avotins, Ivars
Baguley, David
Cozea, Angela
de Looze, Laurence
Gerber, Douglas E.
Mihailescu, Calin Andrei
Picard, Anne Marie
Purdy, Anthony
Rodger, Valentine Watson
Roulston, Christine
Thomson, Clive
Vaillancourt, Daniel

Montreal
Bircher, Martin

North York
Brown, Michael G.
Cotnam, Jacques

Ottawa
Clayton, John Douglas
Delisle, Jean
Dionne, Rene
Elbaz, Andre Elie
Eldredge, Laurence Milton
Goheen, Jutta
Grise, Yolande
Imbert, Patrick L.
Jensen, John T.
Jurado, Jose
Kelly, Louis G.
Koerner, E. F. K.
Lapierre, Andre
Le Moine, Roger
Major, Jean-Louis
Poplack, Shana
Rivero, Maria Luisa
Sbrocchi, Leonard G.
Yalden, Janice
Yardley, J. C.

Rockwood
Eichner, Hans

Saint Catharines
McGarrell, Hedy M.
Sanchez, Monica E.

Saint Catherines
Parker, Richard W.

Scarborough
Irwin, Eleanor

Sudbury
Colilli, Paul
Lewis, Gertrud Jaron

Thunder Bay
Mamoojee, Abdool-Hack
Nabarra, Alain
Schonberger, Vincent L.

Toronto
Barnes, Timothy David
Beck, Roger L.
Blackmore, Joshiah
Bouissac, Paul A.
Burgess, Jonathan
Burke, James F.
Case, Fredrick I.
Chambers, J. K.
Clivio, Gianrenzo Pietro
Cloutier, Cecile
Conacher, Desmond J.
Curtis, Alexander Ross
Dainard, James A.
Danesi, Marcel
Dolezel, Lubomir
Dolezvelova-Velingerova, Milena
Ehrlich, Carl S.
Eisenbichler, Konrad
Elliott, Thomas G.
Ellis, Keith A. A.
Embleton, Sheila
Fitch, Brian T.
Genno, Charles N.
Grant, John Neilson
Gulsoy, J.
Hayne, David Mackness
Heinemann, Edward Arthur
Hutcheon, Linda
Iannucci, Amilcare Alfredo
Irvine, Margot Elisabeth
Joyce, Douglas A.
Kushner, Eva
Latta, Alan Dennis
Lee, M. Owen
Lehouck, Emile
Leon, Pierre R. A.
Levy, Kurt Leopold
Marmura, Michael Elias
Martin, Philippe Jean
Mason, H. J.
McDonough, C. J.
Parry, Hugh
Paterson, Janet M.
Pothecary, Sarah
Pugliese, Olga

Waterloo
Abbott, Carmeta
Ages, Arnold
Chamberlin, John
Dube, Pierre
Forsyth, Phyllis
Fournier, Hannah
Grubisic, Vinko
Hoefert, Sigfrid
John, David Gethin
Kuxdorf, Manfred
Liesbscher, Grit
Marteinson, Peter
Miraglia, Anne Marie
Niccoli, Gabriel
Russell, Delbert
Ryan, Robert
Socken, Paul
Szarycz, Ireneusz
Van Seters, John
Weldon, James
Wilson, Don
Zweers, Alexander Frederik

West Hill
Franceschetti, Antonio

Windsor
Halford, Peter W.
Kingstone, Basil D.
van den Hoven, Adrian

QUEBEC

Hull
L'Allier, Louis

Lennoxville
Kuepper, Karl Josef

Montreal
Austin, Paul Murray
Bauer, Karin
Benalil, Mounia
Bertrand de Munoz, Maryse
Clas, Andre
D'Andrea, Antonio
Dorsinville, Max
Duquette, Jean-Pierre
Gallati, Ernst
Germain, Claude
Godin, Jean Cleo
Gopnik, Myrna
Haberl, Franz P.
Hale, Mark
Hanna, Blake Thompson
Mangan, Jacqueline J. Samperi
Ouimette, Victor
Prevost, Maxime
Reiss, Charles
Ricard, Francois
Robinson, Ira
Woloch, George Michael

Quebec
Hirtle, Walter Heal
Mackey, William Francis
Manning, Alan

Sherbrooke
Forest, Jean

Westmount
Mooney, Susan K.

SASKATCHEWAN

Saskatoon
Corrigan, Kevin
Torres-Recinos, Julio

OTHER COUNTRIES

AUSTRALIA
Rothenberg, Gunther Eric

ENGLAND
Heilbron, John L.
Betz, Mark W.
Martines, Lauro
Pagel, Ulrich